McGRAW-HILL
ENCYCLOPEDIA OF RUSSIA
AND THE SOVIET UNION

McGraw-Hill

ENCYCLOPEDIA OF RUSSIA AND THE SOVIET UNION

EDITOR

Michael T. Florinsky, M.A., PH.D.

Professor of Economics, Columbia University

CONSULTANTS

HARRY SCHWARTZ, PH.D.
Editorial Council
The New York Times

JOHN TURKEVICH, M.A., PH.D.
Eugene Higgins Professor of
Physical Chemistry, Princeton University

THEODORE SHABAD, B.S.
Foreign News Staff
The New York Times
Editor, *Soviet Geography*

EARL UBELL, B.S.
Science Editor
New York Herald Tribune

A Donat **dp** *Publication*

McGRAW-HILL BOOK COMPANY, INC.
NEW YORK   TORONTO   LONDON

McGRAW-HILL ENCYCLOPEDIA OF RUSSIA AND THE SOVIET UNION

Library of Congress Catalog Card Number: 61–18169

First Edition

21380

Maps pp. 74, 197, 215, 217, 218, 219, 221, 222, 433 from *The Course of Russian History* by Melvin C. Wren, © 1958, The Macmillan Company, and used with their permission.

Map p. 97 appeared in *Geographical Review*, July 1958. Reprinted by permission of The American Geographical Society.

McGRAW-HILL ENCYCLOPEDIA OF RUSSIA AND THE SOVIET UNION

EDITOR

MICHAEL T. FLORINSKY, M.A., PH.D.
Professor of Economics
Columbia University

MANAGING EDITORS

DAVID S. ANIN, M.A.   ALEXANDER DONAT, B.S.

CONSULTANTS

HARRY SCHWARTZ, PH.D.
Editorial Council
The New York Times

JOHN TURKEVICH, M.A., PH.D.
Eugene Higgins Professor of Physical Chemistry
Princeton University

THEODORE SHABAD, B.S.
Foreign News Staff
The New York Times
Editor, *Soviet Geography*

EARL UBELL, B.S.
Science Editor
New York Herald Tribune

ASSISTANT TO THE EDITOR

GRACE B. GERBERICH, A.B.

CONTRIBUTORS

GREGOR ARONSON, Writer on Soviet Affairs

FREDERICK C. BARGHOORN, Ph.D. (Harvard), Professor of Political Science, Yale University; Author *Soviet Russian Nationalism*

EDWARD J. BROWN, A.M. (Chicago), Ph.D. (Columbia), Professor of Russian, Brown University; Author *The Proletarian Episode in Russian Literature*

JOEL CARMICHAEL, B.A., M.A. (Oxon), Editor and Translator; Author *An Illustrated History of Russia*

ITZHOK CHARLASH, Lecturer on Yiddish and General Literature, Jewish Teachers Seminary, New York

ANATOLE CHUJOY, Graduate, University of Petrograd; Founder and Editor-Publisher, *Dance News*; Author *The New York City Ballet*

RICHARD CORNELL, M.I.A. (Columbia)

JOHN S. CURTISS, M.A., Ph.D. (Columbia), Professor of History, Duke University; Author *Church and State in Russia 1900–1917, The Russian Church and the Soviet State 1917–1950*

ALEXANDER DALLIN, M.A., Ph.D. (Columbia), Associate Professor of International Relations, Russian Institute, Columbia University; Author *German Rule in Russia*; Editor, *Soviet Conduct in World Affairs*

ROBERT V. DANIELS, Ph.D. (Harvard), Associate Professor of History, University of Vermont; Author *The Nature of Communism*

JANE DEGRAS, B.A. (University of London); Research Specialist (USSR), Royal Institute of International Affairs; Editor, *Soviet Documents on Foreign Policy 1917–1941; The Communist International 1919–1943*

GEORGE P. DENIKE, American Committee for Liberation

GEORGE DENNIS, Ph.D. (University of London)

GEORGE DERUGIN, Dr. Rer. Pol. (University of Berlin), Assistant Professor of Business Economics and International Trade, University of Southern California

TANYA DERUGINE, Graduate, Technische Hochschule, Berlin; Author *Dictionary of Russian Geographical Names*

THOROLD DICKINSON, B.A. (Oxon), Senior Lecturer (Film), Slade School of Fine Art, University College, London; President, International Federation of Film Societies; Film Writer and Director, *Gaslight, Hill 24 Doesn't Answer;* Co-author *Soviet Cinema*

LUBOV DRASHEVSKY, M.A. (Columbia)

LEONARD B. DREYER, Graduate, University of Riga, U.S. Joint Publications Research Service

LESLIE CLARENCE DUNN, M.A., Sc.D. (Harvard), Professor of Zoology, Columbia University; Co-author *Heredity, Race and Society; Principles of Genetics*

NICHOLAS EFREMOV, Doctor of Science (University of Rostov); Institute of Soviet Studies, Middlebury College

ALEXIS VICTOR FEDOROV, M.A. (University of California)

LILY (Mrs. ALFRED W.) FEILER, Diplomée École des Sciences Politiques, M.A. (Columbia)

ROBERT A. FELDMESSER, M.A., Ph.D. (Harvard), Assistant Professor of Sociology, Brandeis University; Co-author *The Transformation of Russian Society*

MARK G. FIELD, M.A., Ph.D. (Harvard), Research Associate, Russian Research Center, Harvard University; Author *Doctor and Patient in Soviet Russia*

MICHAEL T. FLORINSKY, M.A., Ph.D. (Columbia), Professor of Economics, Columbia University; Author *The End of the Russian Empire; Towards an Understanding of the USSR; Russia: A History and An Interpretation*

CYRIL J. FOX, M.A. (Columbia), Lecturer, Department of History, Queens College

TATIANA D. GIDASPOW, B.S. (Institute of Zoology and Phytopatology, Leningrad); Entomologist

ERICH GOLDHAGEN, M.A. (McGill), Lecturer in Political Science, Hunter College

ALLEN GREENSTEIN, B.A. (Hunter College)

RICHARD C. HARMSTONE, M.A. (Harvard), Business Economist; Economic Officer, U.S. Embassy in Moscow (1957–1959)

HOLLAND HUNTER, M.A., Ph.D. (Harvard), Professor of Economics, Haverford College; Author *Soviet Transportation Policy*

PETER H. JUVILER, Ph.D. (Columbia), Assistant Professor of Political Science and Chairman of the Committee on Russian Area Studies, Graduate Division, Arts and Sciences, Hunter College

ADAM KAUFMAN, Graduate, University of Warsaw; M.A. (New School of Social Research, New York); Economist

GEORGE L. KLINE, Ph.D. (Columbia), Associate Professor of Philosophy and Russian, Bryn Mawr College; Author *Soviet Philosophy;* Editor *Soviet Education*

HANS KOHN, Dr. Juris (University of Prague), D.H.L. (Colby College), Professor of History, City College of New York; Author *The Idea of Nationalism; Pan-Slavism, Its History and Ideology*

VERA KOVARSKY, Graduate, University of Paris

ARNOLD KRAMISH, M.A. (Harvard), Senior Staff Member, RAND Corporation; Professor Institut de la communauté européenne pour les études universitaires, Paris; Author *Atomic Energy in the Soviet Union*

SAUL KRAVETZ, A.M., Ph.D. (Harvard), Assistant Professor of Mathematics, Hartford Graduate Division, Renssaeler Polytechnic Institute

CHRISTINA P. KROTKOVA, Translator and Russian Language Instructor, United Nations

WARREN LERNER, M.A. (Columbia), Assistant Professor of History, Roosevelt University

DAVID P. LERRY, B.S. (University of Pennsylvania), Economist, International Business Machines Corporation

CAROL (MRS. HOWARD) LEVINE, M.A. (Columbia), Formerly Translator-Editor, *Current Digest of the Soviet Press*

IVAN D. LONDON, M.A. (Northwestern), Ph.D. (Tulane), Associate Professor of Psychology and Director of the Institute of Political Psychology in Communist Societies, Brooklyn College

RICHARD LOWENTHAL, Dr. Phil. (University of Heidelberg); Foreign Affairs Commentator, *The Observer,* London; Professor of International Relations, Free University of West Berlin

J. MALCOLM MACKINTOSH, Graduate, Glasgow University; Adviser on Soviet Affairs, Institute for Strategic Studies, London; Co-author (with Captain Liddell Hart) *The Soviet Army*

ELIZABETH MARBURY, M.A. (Radcliffe); Senior Economic Analyst, Free Europe Committee, Inc.

CHARLES P. MARSDEN, B.S. Chemical Sciences (Carnegie Institute of Technology); Chief, Electron Devices Section, National Bureau of Standards

INNA MEDOW, B.S. (McGill)

PAUL I. MEDOW, Ph.D. (Columbia), Assistant Professor of Economics, Rutgers University

LEON MERKIN, M.D. (University of Berlin); Associate Fellow, American College of Cardiology; Fellow, American Geriatrics Society

ALFRED G. MEYER, M.A., Ph.D. (Harvard), Professor of Political Science, Michigan State University; Author *The Incompatible Allies; Communism*

HENRY W. MORTON, Ph.D. (Columbia), Instructor, Department of Political Science, Queens College

LYDIA NIKOLENKO, Graduate, Institute of Foreign Languages and Institute of Art History, Leningrad

EMANUEL NODEL, Ph.D. (University of Indiana); Assistant Professor of History, Western Michigan University

NICOLAI I. OULIANOFF, Candidate of Historical Science; Lecturer, Russian Department, Yale University

KARL RUDOLF PAKALNS, Latvian Journalist

ALBERT PARRY, Ph.D. (Chicago), Professor of Russian Civilization and Language, Chairman of the Department of Russian Studies, Colgate University; Author *Russia's Rockets and Missiles*

RICHARD PIPES, M.A. (Harvard), Associate Professor of History and Fellow, Russian Research Center, Harvard University; Author *The Formation of the Soviet Union;* Editor, *The Russian Intelligentsia*

HELEN PUSHCHIN, Research, Soviet Affairs

FRANCIS B. RANDALL, Ph.D. (Columbia), Instructor in History, Columbia University

MICHAEL RYWKIN, Ph.D. (Columbia), Assistant Professor of Romance and Slavic Languages and Literature, New York University

HARRISON E. SALISBURY, A.B. (University of Minnesota), Correspondent, *The New York Times*; Author *American in Russia; To Moscow—and Beyond*

HARRY SCHWARTZ, Ph.D. (Columbia), Member of Editorial Council, *The New York Times*; Author *Russia's Soviet Economy*

MORTON SCHWARTZ, M.I.A. (Columbia), Lecturer in Government, Columbia College

SOLOMON SCHWARZ, Doctor of Law (University of Heidelberg), Formerly Professor, New York University; Co-author *Management in Russian Industry and Agriculture;* Author *Labor in the Soviet Union*

DEREK J. R. SCOTT, M.A. (Cambridge), Ph.D. (Manchester), Lecturer in Government, University of Manchester; Author *Russian Political Institutions*

ANDREI SEDYCH, Graduate, École des Sciences Politiques, Paris; City Editor, *Novoye Russkoye Slovo,* New York

VICTOR SEEMANN, M.A. (Massachusetts Institute of Technology); Editor, McGraw-Hill Book Company

GERALD SEGAL, Technical Consultant, Writer on Soviet Affairs

FRANCIS SETON, M.A., D. Phil. (Oxon), Official Fellow of Nuffield College, Oxford

LEON SHAPIRO, Licencié en Droit, University of Toulouse; Writer on Russian Affairs

VSEVOLOD N. SHMELEV, M.A. (Columbia); Formerly Graduate Research Psychologist, University of California, Los Angeles

LEON SMOLINSKI, M.A. (University of Cincinnati), Ph.D. (Columbia), Assistant Professor of Economics, Boston College

STEFAN STASKEVICH, Senior Research Specialist (Mechanical Engineering), Library of Congress, Washington, D.C.

VICTOR SUKIENNICKI, Doctor of Political Science (University of Paris); Formerly Professor of Government, Vilna University

GERSHON SWET, Graduate, University of Kiev; Musicologist and Journalist

ILYA L. TARTAK, B.A. (McGill), Research, Russian Literature

ALEXIS B. TATISHCHEFF, Doctor of Economic and Political Sciences, University of Paris; Engineer and Economist

JOHN M. THOMPSON, M.A., Ph.D. (Columbia), Assistant Professor of Russian History, Indiana University; Co-author *American Teaching About Russia*

LEON TRILLING, M.A., Ph.D. (California Institute of Technology), Associate Professor of Aeronautics and Astronautics and Senior Staff Member of the Center for International Studies, Massachusetts Institute of Technology; Editor, *Applied Mathematics and Mechanics*

LYNN TURGEON, M.A. (University of California), Ph.D. (Columbia), Assistant Professor of Economics, Hofstra College; Formerly Economic Consultant, The RAND Corporation

JOHN TURKEVICH, M.S. (Dartmouth), M.A., Ph.D. (Princeton), Eugene Higgins Professor of Physical Chemistry, Princeton University; Consultant, U.S. Atomic Energy Commission; Science Attaché, U.S. Embassy, Moscow

EARL UBELL, B.S. (College of the City of New York), Science Editor, *New York Herald Tribune*

VLADIMIR M. VASSILIEV, Graduate, Alexander Lycée, Tsarskoye Selo, B.A. (Polytechnic School, Stockholm); Formerly Assistant Editor, McGraw-Hill Book Company, Inc.

MARK VISHNIAK, Graduate, University of Moscow, Formerly Professor in Institut des Etudes Slaves, Paris; Consultant on Russia, TIME Magazine

JAN Z. WILCZYNSKI, Sc.M., Ph.D.; Formerly Professor in Polish Universities and Lebanese State University, Beirut

SIMON WOLIN, Graduate, University of Tashkent; Author *Communism's Postwar Decade;* Co-editor, *The Soviet Secret Police*

PETER E. YERSHOV, Graduate, University of Odessa; Adjunct Professor of Russian Literature, Columbia University; Author *Comedy in the Soviet Theater*

ZOYA I. YURIEFF, A.M., Ph.D. (Radcliffe), Instructor in Russian Literature, Graduate School of Arts and Sciences, New York University

ALFRED ZAUBERMAN, LL.D. (University of Cracow), Lecturer, London School of Economics and Political Science; Author *Economic Imperialism*

V. K. ZAVALISHIN, Graduate, University of Leningrad; Author *Early Soviet Writers*

INITIALS OF CONTRIBUTORS' NAMES

A. B. T.	Alexis B. Tatishcheff		J. M. T.	John M. Thompson
A. C.	Anatole Chujoy		J. S. C.	John S. Curtiss
A. D.	Alexander Dallin		J. T.	John Turkevich
A. G. M.	Alfred G. Meyer		J. W.	Jan Z. Wilczynski
A. K.	Adam Kaufman		K. R. P.	Karl Rudolf Pakalns
A. Kr.	Arnold Kramish		L. C. D.	Leslie Clarence Dunn
A. P.	Albert Parry		L. D.	Lubov Drashevsky
A. S.	Andrei Sedych		L. M.	Leon Merkin
A. Z.	Alfred Zauberman		L. N.	Lydia Nikolenko
C. J. F.	Cyril J. Fox		L. S.	Leon Smolinski
C. L.	Carol Levine		L. Sh.	Leon Shapiro
C. P. K.	Christina P. Krotkova		L. T.	Leon Trilling
C. P. M.	Charles P. Marsden		L. Tu.	Lynn Turgeon
D. J. R. S.	Derek J. R. Scott		M. G. F.	Mark G. Field
D. L.	David P. Lerry		M. R.	Michael Rywkin
E. G.	Erich Goldhagen		M. S.	Morton Schwartz
E. J. B.	Edward J. Brown		M. T. F.	Michael T. Florinsky
E. M.	Elizabeth Marbury		M. V.	Mark Vishniak
E. N.	Emanuel Nodel		N. E.	Nicholas Efremov
E. U.	Earl Ubell		N. I. Ou.	Nicolai I. Oulianoff
F. B. R.	Francis B. Randall		P. E. Ye.	Peter E. Yershov
F. C. B.	Frederick C. Barghoorn		P. H. J.	Peter H. Juviler
F. S.	Francis Seton		P. I. M.	Paul I. Medow
G. A.	Gregor Aronson		R. A. F.	Robert A. Feldmesser
G. D.	George Derugin		R. C.	Richard Cornell
G. Den.	George Dennis		R. C. H.	Richard C. Harmstone
G. L. K.	George L. Kline		R. L.	Richard Lowenthal
G. P. D.	George P. Denike		R. P.	Richard Pipes
G. S.	Gerald Segal		R. V. D.	Robert V. Daniels
G. Sw.	Gershon Swet		S. K.	Saul Kravetz
H. E. S.	Harrison E. Salisbury		S. S.	Stefan Staskevich
H. H.	Holland Hunter		S. Sch.	Solomon Schwarz
H. K.	Hans Kohn		S. W.	Simon Wolin
H. P.	Helen Pushchin		T. D.	Tanya Derugine
H. S.	Harry Schwartz		T. D. G.	Tatiana D. Gidaspow
H. W. M.	Henry W. Morton		Th. D.	Thorold Dickinson
I. D. L.	Ivan D. London		V. K.	Vera Kovarsky
I. L. T.	Ilya L. Tartak		V. N. S.	Vsevolod N. Shmelev
I. M.	Inna Medow		V. S.	Victor Seemann
J. C.	Joel Carmichael		V. Su.	Victor Sukiennicki
J. D.	Jane Degras		V. Z.	V. K. Zavalishin
J. M. M.	J. Malcolm Mackintosh		Z. Yu.	Zoya I. Yurieff

Principal Entries

Insert between pp. 48 and 49 contains:

P. 1 — Full-color Physical Map of the USSR;

P. 2–3 — Full-color two-page Political Map of the USSR, including six Regional Maps (Leningrad Region, Moscow Region, Donets Basin, Kuznetsk Basin, the Urals, Central Asiatic Republics);

P. 4 — Index of Geographical Names to the Political Map.

TRANSLITERATION

The transliteration system adopted in this book is that of the American Geological Institute Translation Center (adoption of the essential features of Cyrillic Transliteration recommended by the U.S. Department of the Interior, Board of Geographical Names, Washington, D.C.), with certain modifications.

The principal departure from the accepted pattern is the use of Anglicized names of Russian rulers; thus, we write "Peter I," not "Pyotr I"; "Catherine II," not "Yekaterina II." We have also retained the generally accepted spelling of familiar Russian names and terms, even when it differs from our system of transliteration. Thus, we write Tchaikovsky (not Chaykovsky); Rachmaninoff (not Rakhmaninov); Diaghilev (not Dyagilev); Soviet (not Sovet); *Izvestia* (not *Izvestiya*); Byelorussia (not Belorussia). For other most important modifications see footnotes.[4]

Alphabet		Transliteration
А	а	a
Б	б	b
В	в	v
Г	г	g
Д	д	d
Е	е	e, ye[1]
Ё	ё	yo
Ж	ж	zh
З	з	z
И	и	i[2]
Й	й	y
К	к	k
Л	л	l
М	м	m
Н	н	n
О	о	o
П	п	p
Р	р	r
С	с	s
Т	т	t
У	у	u
Ф	ф	f
Х	х	kh
Ц	ц	ts
Ч	ч	ch
Ш	ш	sh
Щ	щ	shch
Ъ	ъ	—[3]
Ы	ы	y
Ь	ь	—[3]
Э	э	e
Ю	ю	yu
Я	я	ya

[1] "Ye" initially, after vowels, and after ъ, ь. "E" with dieresis in Russian (ё) is transliterated as "yo."

[2] Omitted if preceding a "y," e.g. Vasily (not "iy"; not "ii"). Combinations ый and ий are transliterated as "y."

[3] Generally omitted. Before vowels transliterated as "y."

[4] For technical reasons it has not always been possible to maintain the uniformity of transliteration in the geographical maps.

ABBREVIATIONS USED IN THE TEXT

The key word (or words) of each entry is represented in the text of that entry by the first letter (or letters), capitalized: e.g., Transportation, by T.; Criminal Law, by CL.

Ac.	academy	Lith.	Lithuanian
Ac. of S.	Academy of Sciences	m.	meter
adm.	administrative	mfg.	manufacturing
agr.	agriculture, agricultural	mi.	mile
A.O.	Autonomous Oblast	mill.	million
ASSR	Autonomous Soviet Socialist Republic	N.	North, -ern
		N.O.	National Okrug
bill.	billion	N.S.	New Style
cm.	centimeter	O.S.	Old Style
corr.	corresponding	pedag.	pedagogical
CP	Communist Party	Pol.	Polish
CPSU	Communist Party of the Soviet Union	pop.	population
		pseud.	pseudonym
cub.	cubic	prof.	professor
dept.	department	pron.	pronounced
E.	East, -ern	r.	river
f.	formerly	R.	Russia, Russian
ft.	foot, feet	R.R.	railroad
Ger.	German	Rum.	Rumanian
ha	hectare	S.	South, -ern
ind.	industry, industrial	sq.	square
inst.	institute	SSR	Soviet Socialist Republic
kg.	kilogram	Ukr.	Ukrainian
km.	kilometer	W.	West, -ern
lb.	pound		

Editor's Preface

THE object of the ENCYCLOPEDIA is to present, within the relatively brief space of a single volume, a mass of useful information on Russia before and after the revolution of 1917. While the ENCYCLOPEDIA endeavors to avoid a partisan approach, its scope is not limited to the mere listing of facts and figures — important as they are — but offers interpretations of the principal developments discussed. It strives to maintain a high level of scholarship without being too technical and to present the material in a clear and readable style. The amount of information that can be encompassed between the covers of one volume is necessarily limited, yet the coverage is broad and comprehensive and it is hoped that the ENCYCLOPEDIA will prove of real use to those who are interested in Russian affairs — and today who is not interested in the land of the Soviets and its predecessors? It is the expectation of those responsible for the ENCYCLOPEDIA that it will meet a real need of both the general public and the students of Russia and the Soviet Union. The importance of the USSR in world affairs has enormously increased since the end of World War II, but misconceptions about things Russian are still innumerable. It is believed that the ENCYCLOPEDIA will help to remove at least some of them. The articles and the shorter entries are written by qualified experts and are entirely up to date.

The preparation of a comprehensive volume on Russia, such as the ENCYCLOPEDIA, raises special problems of which the two most thorny ones are those of the calendar and transliteration. Prior to February 14, 1918, Russia used a calendar which differed from that adhered to in the West (*see* Calendar). As a rule, all dates in this book are given in accordance with the calendar in force in Russia at the time the event occurred; if, however, there is a possibility of confusion the date is followed by "O.S." (Old Style, the Russian calendar), or "N.S." (New Style, the Western calendar). Since February 14, 1918, the Soviet Union has used the Western calendar and the possibility of confusion has been eliminated.

The second major difficulty is that of transliteration. Systems of transliteration are many but none possesses real intrinsic value. The transliteration adopted in this book is that of the American Geological Institute Translation Center (adoption of the transliteration recommended by the U.S. Department of the Interior, Board of Geo-

xiii

graphical Names) which, however, has not been slavishly followed. The principal departure from the accepted pattern is the use of Anglicized names of Russian rulers; for instance, we write "Peter I," not "Pyotr I"; "Catherine II," not "Yekaterina II." To retain a measure of continuity, the Anglicized form of the name is followed, in parentheses, by the full Russian name spelled out according to our official transliteration; for instance, "Catherine II (Yekaterina Alekseyevna)." We have also retained the accepted Western spelling of familiar Russian names and terms, even when it is not in accord with our system of transliteration. Thus we have written Tchaikovsky (not Chaykovsky); Rachmaninoff (not Rakhmaninov); Diaghilev (not Dyagilev); Soviet (not Sovet); *Izvestia* (not *Izvestiya*); Byelorussia (not Belorussia). Accent marks on Russian names when they appear in the titles of entries should assist the reader in pronouncing them correctly.

It is the general rule of the ENCYCLOPEDIA that the key word (or words) of an entry is represented in the text of that entry by the first letter (or letters), capitalized; for instance, Agriculture, by A; Sugar, by S; Planned Economy, by PE. This rule, as well as the use of other abbreviations, is not applied if it is likely to obscure the meaning.

Weights and measures are generally expressed in terms of their United States equivalents, but in some cases Russian measures have been retained. Temperature is given according to Fahrenheit (*see* Weights and Measures).

The above examples indicate that uniformity and rigid consistency—meritorious as they are—were not our primary concern. Our principal objective was to prepare a text usable and easy to follow, even at the price of sacrificing uniformity.

The ruble is quoted at its value prior to the monetary reform of January 1, 1961 (*see* Monetary System).

In closing these introductory remarks it is my pleasant duty to express our sincere appreciation of the good work done by those associated with the preparation of the ENCYCLOPEDIA. Special mention must be made of our Consultants—Dr. Harry Schwartz, Mr. Theodore Shabad, Professor John Turkevich, and Mr. Earl Ubell—and Miss Grace H. Gerberich. The contributors are too numerous to be listed here individually but our gratitude to them is real and great.

MICHAEL T. FLORINSKY

McGRAW-HILL
ENCYCLOPEDIA OF RUSSIA
AND THE SOVIET UNION

A

AA: *see* GAUYA.

AAASS (American Association for the Advancement of Slavic Studies): *see* RUSSIAN STUDIES.

AATSEEL (American Association of Teachers of Slavic and East European Languages): *see* RUSSIAN STUDIES.

ABAKÁN, city, adm. center of Khakass Autonomous Oblast, Krasnoyarsk Kray, RSFSR; pop. 56,000 (1959). R.R. station, airport; meat-packing ind.

ABAKÁN RIVER, left tributary of the Yenisey; 315 mi. long; timber floating.

ABASTUMÁNI, village in Georgian SSR; pop. 3,100 (1956). Mountain resort (altitude 4,260 ft.) for treatment of tuberculosis; hot sulfur springs.

ABAZA: *see* POPULATION.

ABDÚLINO, city in Orenburg Oblast, RSFSR; pop. 27,500 (1956). R.R. station; flour mills, butter-casein plant.

ABKHÁZ ASSR (ABKHAZIA) in N.W. Georgian SSR, on the W. slopes of the Caucasus along the Black Sea coast; area 3,300 sq. mi.; pop. 405,000 (1959): Abkhaz, Georgians, Russians, Armenians. Cities: Sukhumi (capital), Tkvarcheli, Gagra, Gali, Ochamchire. Rivers: Bzyb, Kodori, Gumista, Galidzga. Agr.: orchards, citrus fruit, tea, tobacco plantations, cattle breeding. Ind.: essential oils, footwear, tobacco, fish canning, sawmills, coal mining; power plants on Gumista River. Known 500 B.C. as part of the Georgian Colchis kingdom; part of Russia since 1810; from 1931, an autonomous republic within the Georgian SSR.

ABORTIONS: *see* FAMILY LAW.

ABRAMÓVICH (Rein), **Rafaíl Abrámovich** (1880–), leader of the Bund and the Mensheviks; born in Dvinsk. Active in the 1905 revolution; in World War I Menshevik-internationalist. After the October revolution, member of the Executive Committee of the Soviets. In 1918 arrested. In 1920 opposed the fusion of the Bund with the CP; emigrated the same year. Together with Martov he founded *Sotsialistichesky Vestnik* (Socialist Courier). Was leader of the Menshevik groups in exile in Berlin, Paris, and New York; member of the executive committee of the Second International between the two world wars.

ABSOLUTISM: *see* MONARCHY.

ACADEMY, GULF OF (R. *Zalív Akadémii*), in S.W. part of Okhotsk Sea; length 70 mi., depth up to 160 ft.

ACADEMY OF FINE ARTS, association of masters of representational art, center of art and art school. The first Russian AFA was founded in St. Petersburg in 1757. It had an impact on the development of R. art and was the center of artistic life and professional education. In the 19th century in the St. Petersburg AFA there arose a conflict between conservative officials who adhered to the academic tradition and painters aspiring to realism. The conflict became particularly acute when a group of students withdrew in 1863 from the AFA as a protest against academism. Nevertheless the AFA maintained its importance as a school for training artists. In 1918 the AFA was abolished and its work was carried on by other schools. The All-Russian Academy of Fine Arts was formed in Leningrad in 1933. In 1948 it was reorganized as the Academy of Fine Arts of the USSR and transferred to Moscow. There is also an Academy of Fine Arts in Riga and in Tbilisi. There were in 1960 45 active members and 65 corresponding members in the AFA of the USSR. B. V. Ioganson is President.

ACADEMY OF SCIENCES, USSR (Ac. of S., USSR), highest Soviet institute of learning which counts among its members the most outstanding Soviet scientists. Founded in St. Petersburg (1724) by Peter the Great. Originally known as the Russian Academy of Sciences, the St. Petersburg Academy of Sciences, and until 1917 the Imperial Academy of Sciences. In 1917, the original name was resumed until it was finally renamed (1925) as the Academy of Sciences, USSR. In 1934, the Ac. of S. was moved to Moscow. Presently, it is composed of 167 active members (fellows), 361 corresponding members, and over 60 foreign members. The Academy is headed by a presidium and a president. Its tasks comprise the coordination of the work of various scientific institutes and institutes of higher learning and the establishment and maintenance of contacts with scientific institutes abroad. The Ac. of S. is a member of 42 international organizations. It organizes sessions, conferences, meetings, and discussions on current scientific problems. It is divided into the following departments: (1) Physics and mathematics; (2) Chemistry; (3) Geology and geography; (4) Biology; (5) Technology; (6) History; (7) Economy, philosophy, and law; (8) Literature and linguistics. It disposes over laboratories, observatories, museums, learned societies, commissions, committees in Leningrad, Moscow, and other regions of the USSR. Branches: Karelian ASSR, Kola Peninsula, Komi ASSR, Kazan, the Urals, Dagestan ASSR, Moldavian SSR, Bashkir ASSR, Ukrainian SSR, and the Siberian branch which was formed in 1957 and comprises E. and W. Siberia, the Far East. In addition, there is a Scientific Research Institute on Sakhalin Island, and an Institute of Physics in Krasnoyarsk. The branches study natural resources and the economy and culture of the various areas in the Soviet Union. Publications: 70 learned journals, numerous scientific papers in every field of knowledge. Since 1917 there were four presidents of the Ac. of S.: A. P. Karpinsky (1917), V. L. Komarov (1936), S. I. Vavilov

(1945), A. N. Nesmeyanov (1951), and M. V. Keldysh (1961).

In addition to the All-Union Ac. of S., the constituent republics have their own academies; there are also numerous academies in specialized fields (Medical, Military, Agricultural, Pedagogical, Construction and Architecture, Fine Arts, etc.). (*See also* SCIENCE)

BIBLIOGRAPHY: Alexander Vucinich, *The Soviet Academy of Sciences*, Stanford, 1956.

ACADEMY OF SCIENCES RANGE, in W. Pamir, Tadzhik SSR; year-round snow and glaciers. Highest point is Stalin Peak (24,584 ft.).

ÁCHINSK, city in Krasnoyarsk Kray, RSFSR; pop. 42,400 (1956). Ind.: flour mills, leather plants. Alumina plant based on nephelite deposits.

ACMEISTS were a group of R. poets in the second decade of the 20th century, who emphasized the cult of "art for art's sake." It included N. Gumilyov, O. Mandelshtam, M. Kuzmin, A. Akhmatova, S. Gorodetsky, B. Sadovsky, and others. Its journal, *Apollon* (1909–1917), was edited by the critic S. Makovsky. The name of the group stems from the Greek word "acme," which refers to the blossoming of something, or the attaining of its highest stage. In their poetry the A emphasized a sensual perception of the world, as well as such Nietzschean concepts as that of the strong personality and of the vitalism of the animal propensities in man (the image of "the new barbarian"). Their poems also reflected a sentimental attitude toward things past, such as "the vanishing manor," "the decline of culture," rococo, and antique Alexandrian verse. In spite of a generally positive attitude toward W. European culture, the poems of some of the A reflect nationalistic emotions. Their style was generally characterized by extreme individualism and by a strong emphasis on both esthetics and form. Although the A regarded their art as vitalistic, and hence as life-enhancing in that sense, their poems frequently contained strains of pessimism and of decadence, as well as images of death. The A ceased to exist as a group immediately after the Communist Revolution of 1917. Some of them, such as A. Akhmatova, have continued to adhere to their original views.

BIBLIOGRAPHY: Leonid I. Strakhovsky, *Craftsmen of the Word*, Cambridge, 1949.   C. P. K.

ADAMÓVICH, Geórgy Víktorovich (1894–), poet and literary critic. Graduated from St. Petersburg University. His initial books of poetry appeared in 1914–22. Left Russia in 1922 to settle in Paris. Since 1948 associated with the University of Manchester. Developed into a foremost Russian emigré literary critic. Author of *Solitude and Freedom*, New York, 1955.

ADÁSHEV, Alekséy Fyódorovich (died 1561), favorite of Ivan IV who had considerable influence during the beginning of his reign. Sided with boyars during the later 1550's. Died in prison.

ADMINISTRATIVE AND TERRITORIAL DIVISIONS. The USSR today is administratively divided on the basis of both nationality and economic efficiency. Formally, each nationality or ethnic group is granted

NATIONAL-TERRITORIAL STRUCTURE OF THE USSR

USSR

RSFSR

Union Republics (SSR): LITHUANIAN SSR, AZERBAIJAN SSR, MOLDAVIAN SSR, LATVIAN SSR, GEORGIAN SSR, KIRGHIZ SSR, KAZAKH SSR, TADZHIK SSR, UZBEK SSR, ARMENIAN SSR, BYELORUSSIAN SSR, TURKMEN SSR, UKRAINIAN SSR, ESTONIAN SSR

AUTONOMOUS OBLASTS (left): NAGORNO-KARABAKH A.O., SOUTH OSSETIAN A.O., ADYGEY A.O., JEWISH A.O., GORNO-ALTAY A.O.

AUTONOMOUS OBLASTS (right): GORNO-BADAKHSHAN A.O., KARACHAI-CHERKESS A.O., KHAKASS A.O., TUVA A.O.

ASSR: NAKHICHEVAN ASSR, ABKHAZ ASSR, ADZHAR ASSR, KARA-KALPAK ASSR, CHECHEN-INGUSH ASSR, TATAR ASSR, BASHKIR ASSR, DAGESTAN ASSR, BURYAT ASSR, KABARDINIAN-BALKARIAN ASSR, KOMI ASSR, MARI ASSR, MORDIVINIAN ASSR, NORTH-OSSETIAN ASSR, UDMURT ASSR, CHUVASH ASSR, YAKUT ASSR, KARELIAN ASSR, KALMYK ASSR

NATIONAL OKRUGS: KORYAK N.O., CHUKCHI N.O., TAYMYR N.O., EVENKI N.O., KHANTY-MANSI N.O., AGA BURYAT N.O., YAMAL-NENETS N.O., KOMI-PERMYAK N.O., NENETS N.O., UST-ORDA BURYAT N.O.

a degree of self-government and cultural autonomy. Within each major national area, further subdivision is made primarily on economic considerations. At the top of the administrative hierarchy are the fifteen constituent republics (also called union republics), which in theory form a voluntary union of nations reserving the right of free secession. All except the R. republic are known as Soviet Socialist Republics (SSR).

The Russian republic is a formal federation of a number of nationalities and is therefore known as the Russian Soviet Federated Socialist Republic (RSFSR). The governments of the constituent republics exercise a high degree of control over the institutions and officials of the smaller territorial subdivisions under their respective jurisdictions. Each constituent republic is divided further into *oblasts* (regions), which are the most important administrative subdivisions and which are further divided into *rayons* (districts). Within the RSFSR there are several *krays* (territories) which are virtually equivalent to *oblasts*. The *oblasts* are usually formed so as to create a distinctive economic region. As the economy of the USSR changes, the number and size of the *oblasts* change. The *rayon* is a unit of local government, and can be compared with the county. Within the constituent republics, the lesser nationalities form separate autonomous areas depending upon their size and/or importance. These range from autonomous republics down through autonomous *oblasts,* national *okrugs* (areas), and national *rayons*. Like the *oblasts,* the autonomous republics and the autonomous *oblasts* are divided directly into *rayons* and are under the immediate jurisdiction of the constituent republics. The national *okrugs* are found only in the RSFSR and are subordinate to the *oblast* or *kray* in which they are located. They are populated largely by minor Siberian ethnic groups. The national *rayons* are of minor importance and are formed locally from small ethnic groups living within the territory of a more important nationality. Unlike the other national areas, these send no representatives to the Soviet of Nationalities.

Prior to 1917, Russia was hierarchically divided into administrative units called *gubernia* (province), which were further divided into *uyezds* (counties) and *volosts* (rural districts). This arbitrary system was created by Peter the Great in 1708 with the formation of the first eight *gubernias* of Moscow, St. Petersburg, Archangel, Kiev, Smolensk, Kazan, Azov, and Siberia. The number of units steadily increased until by 1917 the R. Empire was divided into 101 *gubernias,* 777 *uyezds,* and 16,760 *volosts*.

The first administrative units to be set up after the revolution were the major national autonomous units. The RSFSR and the Ukrainian SSR were proclaimed in 1917; in 1919 the Byelorussian SSR and the German Volga and Bashkir autonomous republics were organized. In Dec. 1922 the RSFSR, the Ukrainian SSR, the Byelorussian SSR, and the Transcaucasian SFSR joined to form the Union of Soviet Socialist Republics (USSR). By that time about twenty autonomous republics and autonomous *oblasts* had been created. The number of national units has varied over the years. The present system was approved in March 1921, and

was introduced gradually until by 1930 a complete transformation had taken place.

ADMINISTRATIVE CONTROL. Administrative action in the Soviet governmental system is theoretically subject to check at each level of government by the elected Soviet at that level. In fact, however, the Soviet leaders exercise more significant control over the administrative apparatus through: the party, the security police, the plan, financial controls, the Ministry of State Control, legal controls, and personnel controls. The primary body for control over the government apparatus is the Ministry of State Control, which grew out of the Commissariat of Workers' and Peasants' Inspection formed in 1920. This latter body was an attempt to control the bureaucracy from below in that its local organs were supposed to contain a prescribed number of workers and peasants. At that time there were many bourgeois and other non-Bolshevik officials occupying important positions in the government. Control from below was abolished by Stalin in 1934 and replaced by control from above, or control by qualified officials appointed by the higher authorities. The Ministry of State Control has a broad mandate to check on the fulfillment of all governmental decisions.

ADMINISTRATIVE LAW regulates the structure, staffing, and activities of state administrative organs and the relations of these organs with private citizens and non-state organizations. Because of permeating state activities, AL affects vast, centralized bureaucracies in many fields of Soviet life, from health, education, and the court system (q.v.) to the economy and national defense. And because of the totalitarian nature of the Soviet political system, many non-state organizations such as collective farms, sports councils, bar associations (q.v.) and trade unions are under tight state control, and the boundaries of AL become the subject of controversy among Soviet jurists. At present internal relations and functions of non-state organizations are governed by other branches of Soviet law (q.v.).

Lenin could never achieve his original program of smashing the prerevolutionary state machinery and turning public administration over to the masses. Many ministries and "bourgeois" bureaucrats were retained by the Soviet government after the revolution, although they had been inherited from the tsars by the defunct Provisional Government. Selected parts of the state machinery were dismantled, however, including the court system (q.v.) while the old officials were watched by commissars until gradually replaced by "Red" cadres, who themselves were not free from political surveillance and purges.

The present system of centralized administration and planning requires a vast state bureaucracy topped by the USSR and republic councils of ministers, which operates under the following general principles: (a) *The CPSU must approve* all major administrative decisions which it does not itself originate. (b) *Checking on fulfillment* is vital to the success of centralized planning. This job is shared by the CPSU with various agencies of administrative control (q.v.). (c) *"Demo-*

cratic centralism" is supposed to combine centralization with maximum local initiative. Administration is in fact more centralized than it is democratic. Reforms since Stalin's death have increased local operative initiative, e.g., in the new economic regions set up in 1957, while placing political controls and planning more firmly in party organs. Democratic centralism involves also "dual subordination" of each administrative agency, horizontally to the people through elected organs, vertically to its superior agency. The vertical, bureaucratic controls are decisive, however. (d) *Participation of the masses in administration* takes the form of community work in commissions of the Soviet as deputies, complaints to the press, petitions of grievances against local officials, agitation and propaganda in the rigged election campaigns. (e) *"Socialist legality"* is the more stable and respectable version of the harsh and capricious "revolutionary legality" of the early years, and Stalin's terror-ridden "legality" when arbitrary purge countered the desired "stability of laws." Socialist legality is basically defined as strict observance of laws and administrative acts by all state and public organizations, officials, and citizens. It implies only limited rule of law in the Western sense because the CPSU is above law, initiating and approving law from a position of continuous political monopoly, and because procedural guarantees are relatively limited even after recent reforms in Soviet law. (f) *One-man management* replaced collective management in 1934. One manager or administrative chief is responsible for his enterprise or agency, but discusses major problems with a "collegium" of his assistants, reporting to his superior in the hierarchy any disagreements with the collegium. (g) *Planning and accounting* means that every administrative unit has an obligatory plan, and must account for its funds. Many enterprises operate under "economic accountability," responsible for the fulfillment of contracts (see LIABILITY LAW), planned profits, planned production or services. (h) *Training and recruitment* of professional administrators entails structuring higher and secondary education so as to fill the planned needs for specialists. The Civil Service Commission, founded in 1935, blueprints wage and organizational structures and personnel policy. There are no entrance examinations, since estimates of ability are based on educational and personal records compiled by the schools from which the specialists are assigned to jobs. Discrimination in hiring on the basis of nationality or sex is supposed to be banned, but Jews, at least, are virtually barred from certain administrative posts such as in the USSR Ministry of Foreign Affairs. (i) *Stratification of rank and pay* and other privileges has long since reversed the "leveling" tendencies of the early years when public officials were not supposed to be paid more than were skilled workers. (*See also* PROPERTY)

BIBLIOGRAPHY: A. Denisov and M. Kirichenko, *Soviet State Law*, Moscow, 1960; John N. Hazard, *The Soviet System of Government*, Chicago, 1960; Herbert McClosky and John E. Turner, *The Soviet Dictatorship*, New York, 1960.   P. H. J.

ADRIANOPLE, TREATY OF, 1829, between Russia and Turkey concluded the war of 1828–29. Russia obtained the right of unlimited transit of commercial ships through the Straits, and of free trade over the whole territory of the Turkish empire. The European border with Turkey was established along the Prut and Danube rivers. Turkey handed over to Russia the E. coast of the Black Sea from the mouth of the Kuban River to the port of St. Nicholas and acknowledged the transfer to Russia of Georgia and other Transcaucasian lands. Turkey obligated herself to give autonomy to Serbia, recognized the independence of Greece and the autonomy of Moldavia and Wallachia, and paid to Russia a considerable contribution.

ADYGÉY AUTONOMOUS OBLAST, part of Krasnodar Kray, RSFSR; area 1,740 sq. mi.; pop. 286,000 (1959). Adm. center Maykop; main river Kuban, navigable. Winter wheat, corn, technical crops, sunflowers, tobacco, soybeans, hemp; ind.: food, tobacco, vegetable oil. Pedag. inst., theater. Est. 1920.

ADZHÁR ASSR (ADZHARIA), in the S.W. Georgian SSR on the Black Sea coast; area 1,160 sq. mi.; pop. 245,000 (1959). Cities: Batumi (capital) and Kobuleti. Has a subtropical climate, grows tea, citrus fruits, produces essential oils and silk. Ind.: petroleum refining, lumber mills, power stations, shipping. A is famous for its Black Sea resorts. Became part of Russia in 1878 (Berlin Treaty). Est. 1921.

AFFORESTATION. In order to improve the climatic conditions in the forestless steppe areas of the USSR, to diminish the menace of drought which periodically plagues agriculture, and to prevent land erosion, considerable efforts are made by Soviet authorities to convert large areas into forest. In the years 1933–37, 525,000 hectares were afforested, eight times as much as the area converted into forest during the total prerevolutionary period. In Oct. 1948 the Soviet government promulgated a long-term plan of afforestation which called for the planting of over 6 mill. hectares of forest. Although this plan was later abandoned, about 2.6 mill. hectares were actually planted under forest in 1949–52. In 1951 afforestation by organizations under the jurisdiction of the Ministry of Forestry alone extended on an area of 870,000 hectares, 65 per cent of which were located in forest-deficient, steppe regions. In recent years on an average approximately one mill. hectares are converted into forest by agro-technical means.

AFINOGÉNOV, Aleksándr Nikoláyevich (1904–1941), playwright, art director of the "Proletkult" theater, 1926–29. He was a member of the state commission of control of theatrical productions. His best-known plays are *The Strange Fellow* (1928) and *Fear* (1930). The first depicts the conflict between the critically-minded youth of the 1920's and party machine politics; the second treats the popular fear of Stalinist repressions. These were followed by more politically palatable plays, *The Distant, Greetings Spain, Mashenka* and *On the Eve.* He perished in the bombing of Moscow at the start of World War II.

AGA (AGINSKY) BURYÁT NATIONAL OKRUG, in S.W. Chita Oblast, RSFSR; area 7,950 sq. mi.; pop. 49,000 (1959), mostly Buryats. Adm. center, village of Aginskoye. Sharply continental climate. Animal breeding, wheat, barley, oats; beginnings of mining ind. (non-ferrous metals). Est. 1937.

AGITPROP: *see* PROPAGANDA.

AGÓSHKOV, Mikhaíl Ivánovich (1905–), mining engineer. Corresponding member, Ac. of S., USSR (1953). Graduated from the Far Eastern Polytechnic Institute in Vladivostok (1931). Worked at the North Caucasian Mining and Metallurgical Institute (1933–41); deputy director, Mining Institute, Ac. of S. (1952).

AGRAKHÁN PENINSULA, on the W. shore of Caspian Sea in Dagestan ASSR; area 82 sq. mi.

AGRARIAN REFORMS, 1906–11. A series of agrarian reform laws was initiated by P. A. Stolypin shortly after he became premier, July 1906. A preliminary measure (Oct. 5, 1906) abolished certain legal disabilities such as restrictions on movement with which the peasantry had traditionally been burdened. The main body of reform consisted of three categories: 1. Abolition of peasant common tenure. A decree of Nov. 9, 1906 permitted householders to own shares of the arable land in all communes having repartitional tenure. In communes with hereditary household tenure, members were forced to take over individual ownership. A law of June 14, 1910 extended the system of individual ownership to those communes where land had not been redistributed since 1861. On May 9, 1911, pastures and grazing lands not thus far decommunized were ordered placed in the hands of individual owners. 2. Enclosure of scattered land strips. Provision for such enclosure was made in the acts of 1906, 1910, and 1911. It was hoped in this way to encourage establishment of independent farms working a concentration of land. The farmhouse was to be either adjacent to the fields (a type of farm known as *khutor*) or in the village (under the *otrub* arrangement). 3. Abolition of joint family ownership was attempted for the purpose of clarifying the obscurities of peasant ownership. After Nov. 1906, ownership of a land allotment was to reside in the household elder.

Stolypin's reform was implemented with utmost zeal. By 1916, more than half the households which were allotted lands in European Russia were estimated to hold them in hereditary tenure. Some 2.4 mill. enclosures were said to have been carried out, 1.2 mill. of which were of the *khutor* or *otrub* variety. But these enclosures affected only one-sixth of the total area decommunized. Moreover, some of the old paternalism and inequalities survived the abolition of peasant disabilities. The reform came to a standstill during World War I and was abandoned after the Bolshevik revolution. (*See also* AGRICULTURE, PEASANTS, STOLYPIN).

AGRICULTURAL MACHINERY: see TRACTOR.

AGRICULTURE. Prerevolutionary land tenure. Emancipation of serfs (1861) failed to put Russian farming upon a sound economic basis. The three main obstacles were the inadequate size of land holdings allotted to the liberated peasants, the crushing burden of redemption payments set at rates exceeding the market value of the land, and the institution of the village commune. The average allotment size, 14.4 hectares (35.6 acres) per household as of 1877, fell short of that of pre-reform peasant holdings. With adequate investment

and modern cultivation methods it might provide full employment and fair income. These were hampered though by the institution of village commune, membership in which was obligatory for all peasants. Land had been allotted to communes which, in turn, assigned it to member households in hereditary or, more common, repartitional tenure. Under this system, a peasant household owned individually only its home with the adjoining small garden plot. Pastures and woodland were used in common. Cropland was divided into three fields, one of which lay fallow each year. Each family received its land allotment in numerous scattered strips. Land was periodically repartitioned among commune members, in an attempt to equalize holdings per capita. Repartitional tenure deprived the individual farmer of any incentive to improve his land. Strip farming with compulsory rotation minimized the scope for initiative and innovation and involved enormous waste of land and labor. The communal system of land tenure was nevertheless sturdily protected by the government. It facilitated administration and guaranteed payment of taxes and redemption debt by the peasants, the commune being jointly responsible for each member's obligations.

Following peasant unrest before and during the 1905 revolution, the government withdrew its support from the commune and "placed its wager . . . on the sturdy individual proprietor" (Stolypin). Redemption payments were abolished and a land reform was decreed Nov. 9, 1906. Peasants were encouraged to consolidate their scattered strips and enclose them, forming individually owned farms. Government credit was provided to finance purchase of estate and state land by peasants. Within a short span of time, the reform had profound effects upon R. agriculture. By 1916, more than half of peasant households held their land in individual, hereditary tenure. Consolidation and enclosure of strips were carried out in some 2.4 mill. farms and were pending in as many. Peasants purchased over 10.5 mill. hectares additional land in European Russia alone and some 2.5 mill. colonists were settled in Siberia in 1905–14. Gross agricultural output rose by about one-third from 1900 to 1913; methods of production were improving.

On the eve of the 1917 revolution, the peasantry was well launched upon the road of individual farming. Peasants held some three-fourths of all privately owned land in European Russia; nobility about one-sixth; churches and monasteries, over 1%, townsmen the remainder. The huge holdings of the state and imperial family (157 mill. hectares) consisted overwhelmingly of forests and uncultivable land. Repartitional tenure communes still embraced some 40% of peasant households but were on the decline. Landed estates, while still accounting for 12% of grain output and 5–6% of livestock herds, had lost some 40% of their land since 1877, a process accelerated by the Stolypin reforms. The peasantry's living standards were still extremely low, illiteracy and ill health were widespread, and the peasants' "land hunger" was far from satisfied.

Soviet pre-collectivization policies. In a series of sweeping decrees the Bolshevik government expropriated landed estates (Nov. 8, 1917), nationalized all

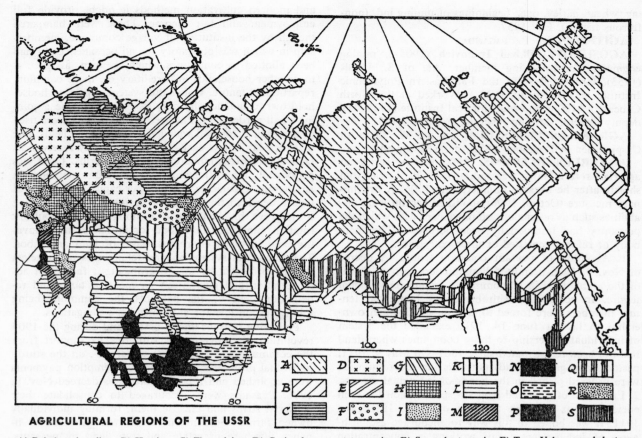

AGRICULTURAL REGIONS OF THE USSR

A) Reindeer breeding. B) Hunting. C) Flax, dairy. D) Grain, hemp, potatoes, pigs. E) Sugar beet, grain. F) Trans-Volga, wooded steppe grain region. G) Dairy, grain, flax. H) Grain, sunflower, stock raising. I) Grain, cotton. K) Grain, animal husbandry. L) Pastoral areas. M) Horticulture, viticulture, tobacco. N) Black Sea subtropics. O) Technical crops, grain, animal husbandry. P) Cotton. Q) Grain, animal farming. R) Suburban truck gardening. S) Rice, soya, sugar beet (Far East).

land (Feb. 19, 1918), and ordered creation of large state and cooperative farms (Feb. 14, 1919). These embodied the long-run, ultimate Soviet objectives. During the disorderly partition of landed estates that actually took place, however, only 5–6% of the expropriated land remained in the hands of state and cooperative farms. During War Communism (1918–21, q.v.), larger peasant farms were discriminated against and frequently subdivided. The gains of the Stolypin reforms were largely wiped out and the peasants affected by it were made to rejoin the village communes. These regressive processes affected adversely output, productivity, and especially marketings. Faced with forcible food requisitions, peasants shifted increasingly to subsistence farming. Under the NEP, 1921–29, a food tax at fixed rates replaced requisitions of "surplus" produce, market relationships were legalized, and recovery of output and livestock holdings was promptly achieved. Marketings continued however at a much lower level than in tsarist Russia, mainly as the result of the structural changes described above and of the terms of trade which shifted against the farmer. Compared to 1913, the 1928 grain marketings declined from 26 to 11% of gross output, and grain exports from some 12 to .5% of gross output. A drastic increase in the marketed share of agricultural output was a prerequisite for the success of the vast industrialization program (see NEP). The question how

to induce the peasants to part with the required share of their produce became the subject of the great party debate. The leftists, notably Trotsky, advocated at first a return to such methods of War Communism as forcible "grain loans," high taxes, and so on. A more sophisticated version was then presented by Ye. Preobrazhensky who proposed to take advantage of the state's monopolistic position as producer of industrial goods, to charge high prices for such goods while paying relatively low prices for agricultural produce. Profits thus realized were to finance capital formation. The leftists' proposals were attacked as aggravating the "scissors crisis" (see NEP) and as endangering the *smychka*, the workers-peasants alliance which provided the justification for the party's power. These policies were also held to be self-defeating since the farmers could react by reducing both their purchases of industrial goods and their output as well as marketings. The rightists, notably Bukharin and Rykov, sought to continue and further expand the NEP policies, to provide the farmers with incentives and rely on their voluntary savings as the source of capital formation. Prosperous farming was to be built up as the sound basis for industrialization policies. The rightists' proposals were criticized, however, on the grounds that they would shift the burden of industrialization upon the urban workers and would favor primarily the kulaks—richer peasants utilizing hired labor. It appeared thus that as long as the basic production decisions and control over marketings remained with the farmers, the solutions proposed by both the leftists and the rightists conflicted with the government's economic and political objectives.

The solution actually adopted was Stalin's policy of all-out collectivization of Soviet farming, an institutional "revolution from above," initiated in the winter of 1929. Collectivized farms lost control over agricultural marketings, extracted from them at extremely low prices. Their own consumption became a shock-absorber, and forced saving thus generated provided the main source of Soviet industrial growth.

All-out collectivization. Cooperative farms of three different types (artel, toz and commune) sprang into existence under War Communism. Virtually unmechanized (only 6 Machine Tractor Stations existed in 1928) and inefficient they failed to attract peasants. Their number declined from 22,000 to 14,000 between 1925 and 1927 when they comprised only .8% of peasant households. The First Five Year Plan anticipated that another 10% would join by 1933. Late in 1929, however, an all-out collectivization drive, "The Second Communist Revolution," began. The percentage of collectivized peasant households rose to 7.6 in Oct. 1929, to 21 by Jan. 20, 1930, and to 58 by March 10, 1930. Measures of compulsion were widely used. The official policy of "liquidating kulaks as a class" legalized con-

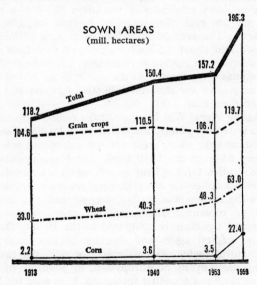

SOWN AREAS
(mill. hectares)

195.3
157.2
150.4
118.2
Total
104.6
Grain crops 110.5 106.7 119.7
33.0
63.0
48.3
Wheat 40.3
2.2 Corn 3.6 3.5 22.4
1913 1940 1953 1959

fiscation of land and all belongings of the kulaks and their wholesale deportation. The definition of a kulak was elastic and ambiguous enough to permit repressions against virtually any peasant who opposed collectivization. Large-scale destruction of property, especially livestock (*see* HORSES, HOGS, CATTLE), and the spreading unrest led to Stalin's pronouncement in March 1930. The blame for excesses was put on the "dizzy with success" local party and government workers, and further compulsion was officially discouraged. The proportion of collectivized households promptly declined to 21% by Sept. 1930. Administrative pressures and increasing fiscal discrimination against individual peasants

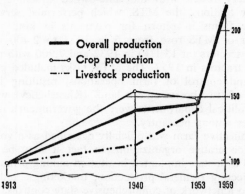

AGRICULTURAL PRODUCTION OF THE USSR
(1913 = 100)

— Overall production
—○— Crop production
--·-- Livestock production

200
150
100
1913 1940 1953 1959

brought it back to 52.7% by mid-1931 and then gradually to 93.0% by 1937, when collective farms accounted for over 99% of peasant sown area. The trends in collective farming are shown below.

End of year	Collective Farms in Operation (thous.)	Sown Area per Farm, Hectares	Households per Farm
1928	33.3	41	18
1932	211.7	434	71
1940	236.9	492	81
1949	252.0	453	80
1953	93.3	1,407	220
1959	54.8	2,316	342

State farms. Early experience with state farms created in some of the expropriated landed estates had been highly unsatisfactory. Nevertheless, creation of huge, highly specialized state farms on a large scale was decided in April 1928. These giant "grain factories," "meat factories" and such were to provide the state with "commanding heights" in the agricultural sector and enable it to control directly a sizable part of agricultural output and marketings. They were to be "completely mechanized" and serve as model farms: their superior productivity was to show the peasants the advantages of mechanized, large-scale production and thus facilitate the collectivization drive. The performance of these mammoth farms, created mainly at a considerable expense on previously unplowed lands, turned out to be highly unsatisfactory. Their split-up and despecialization were ordered by Stalin in 1934 and they played a relatively minor role until the mid-1950's (see below).

Year	Number of State Farms	Sown Area, Mill. hectares	% of All Sown Area	Grain Procurements % of Total
1928	1,407	1.73	1.5	4
1940	4,159	11.56	7.7	10
1953	4,857	15.16	9.7	12
1959	6,500	53.89	27.5	38

Collective farming prior to 1953. Meanwhile, by 1935, the system of collective farming evolved from the initially chaotic conditions into the forms in which it functioned until Stalin's death. All previously peasant farm land was cultivated in common with the exception of small household plots, of .25–.5 hectare each, left for farmers' personal use. These accounted in 1956 for only 3.7% of total Soviet sown area but produced 67% of potato output, 55% of milk, 57% of meat, 87% of eggs, accounting for a major portion of collective farmers' income and consumption in kind.

Field operations such as seeding and plowing were

highly mechanized but the monopoly for operating farm machinery rested with the state-owned Machine and Tractor Stations, the MTS, which performed services for the farms in return for payments in kind. The number of MTS rose from 6 in 1928 to 2,400 with 72,000 tractors (at 15 HP) in 1932 and 7,900 with over 1 mill. tractors in 1957. The MTS' tasks included guidance and control of farm operations, resulting in a system of "two bosses on one land" (Khrushchev), while their political departments were the government's main agencies among peasantry.

A collective farm was officially described as a voluntary, cooperative organization. In fact it may be described as a state-implanted institution aiming primarily at subjecting farmers' production, marketings, and income to a network of comprehensive state controls. The farm's production is regulated by a centralized plan imposed from above which until 1955 embraced 242 indicators, specifying, *inter alia*, the area of each crop, numbers of livestock, methods and timing of production, and so on. The farm's "First Commandment," to use an official term, is to meet its obligations to the state which until the mid-1950's embraced compulsory deliveries of farm products at fixed quotas per hectare of planned sown area, payments to MTS, contractual and above-quota sales to the state, taxes. Next, the prescribed amounts of cash and produce were to be allocated to seed and feed, reserve funds and other production needs. The remainder is distributed among households on the basis of their contribution to collective work, calculated in so-called workdays (*trudoden*). Farmers are thus residual claimants to the farm's income, bearing the entire risk of harvest fluctuations and

planning errors, while the basic production decisions are made by the state organs.

The main component of marketings was compulsory deliveries at extremely low prices which, as a rule, changed little between 1928 and 1953, while prices of manufactured goods were increasing. Compulsory deliveries were described by Stalin as "something in the nature of a tribute" imposed upon peasantry in order to finance industrialization. Additional sales to the state were made at somewhat higher "above-quota prices." After planned sales quotas were met, the farmers were allowed to sell the remainder at urban and rural bazaars directly to the population, at prices which were considerably in excess of those paid by the state and which were determined by the supply and demand (see below).

Product	Prices Received by Farmers for Various Types of Marketing (rubles per ton)					
	1937			1950		
	C.D.	A.Q.	F.M.	C.D.	A.Q.	F.M.
Grain	80	155	1,000	90	125	2,700
Potatoes	40	110	600	40	—	1,000
Meat	400	1,750	4,200	400	4,000	11,200
Milk	165	465	1,200	270	800	2,600

(C.D. = compulsory deliveries, A.Q. = above quota, F.M. = free market.)

Each farmer had a strong incentive to reduce to a minimum his inadequately compensated work for the *kolkhoz* and to concentrate on a very intensive cultivation of his private plot and cattle. To counteract these tendencies, restrictive legislation was enacted in 1939. A compulsory minimum of workdays (60–100 a year) was set for each farmer to be worked on collective property. The area of household plots was further restricted and about 2.5 mill. hectares of such land were transferred into collective ownership; compulsory delivery quotas were raised. At the outbreak of World War II, the grip of the state on collective farming was thus firmer than ever.

During World War II, some of the richest agricultural areas were occupied by the Germans and suffered severe devastation. In 1945, gross agricultural output was still at only 61% of the 1940 level. The Nazis maintained the collective farm system largely intact, as an efficient device for collection of agricultural produce. In postwar years the system was further strengthened and the degree of economic discrimination against the peasant increased significantly compared to the 1930's. Despite loss of capital assets and shortage of manpower, the agricultural sector was assigned not only the task of lifting itself by its bootstraps but, in addition, of providing surplus for capital formation. Fees paid for MTS services as well as compulsory delivery quotas were raised. The work at household plots was discouraged by various measures; their area was reduced by some 4 mill. hectares; and the farmers were pressured into selling their livestock to collective farms. Terms of trade shifted further against the farmers, and the 1947 currency reform hit them more severely than the urban dwellers and wiped out peasant savings.

In 1950, agglomeration of collective farms was ordered: from 2 to 15 neighboring units were merged into one big farm. The number of collective farms declined by about two-thirds (see p. 7). The action was to be combined with resettlement of peasants into large spe-

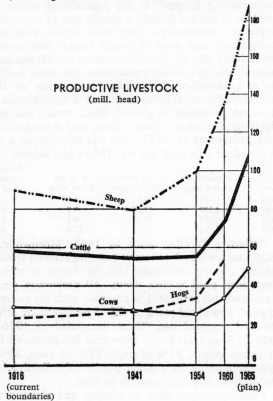

PRODUCTIVE LIVESTOCK
(mill. head)

Sheep

Cattle

Cows   Hogs

1916   1941   1954   1960   1965
(current   (plan)
boundaries)

cially constructed "agro-cities," with apartment buildings instead of farmsteads, and with a further reduction of household plots. These far-reaching plans were, however, shelved, possibly in face of peasant opposition and of enormous construction costs involved. The main motivation behind the merger decree seems to have been shortage of trusted managerial personnel and weakness of rural party organizations under the old system. In this the merger was successful: by 1953, 80% of collective farms had a party cell, against only 15% in 1949.

To sum up, agricultural policies were primarily concerned with strengthening the government's controls and with transferring income from the rural into the urban sector, rather than with raising output and productivity. The initial postwar upsurge of gross agricultural output which, according to official estimates, rose by 63% between 1945 and 1949, was thus effectively checked, and it remained largely stagnant in the years 1949–53. In 1952, it was only .7% above the 1940 level while industrial production was almost doubled over the same period.

Powerful barriers to improvement in productivity developed at all levels of the Soviet agricultural system. Under the *trudoden* system, collective farm managers lacked incentive to treat labor as a scarce resource. Cost accounting was held inapplicable to collective farming and, lacking it, the choice of alternative production methods, crops, and so forth was largely based on guesswork. Moreover, such choice was effectively discouraged, on the farm level, by numerous production and performance indicators imposed from above, often with disregard of local conditions. Costly mistakes were thus made. Crops were reported in terms of the so-called "biological yields," i.e. yields on the root including, *inter alia*, harvesting and threshing losses. Barn crop statistics were a closely guarded state secret. Thus, actual performance, its cost and the available alternatives were largely unknown, making productivity planning a difficult task.

Nor had the MTS an incentive to raise output. Their earnings depended on the volume of operations performed, regardless of the quality of work and of the yields and output achieved. Operations tended to be delayed and performed inefficiently.

As regards a collective farmer, his productivity was but weakly related to his share in the collective farm's disposable income. He tended to shirk his obligations toward the collective and to cultivate intensely his household plot, where the relationship between effort and award was far more direct. In this he was increasingly harassed by the state. Nine million rural dwellers migrated to cities during 1950–54, thus increasing demand for foodstuffs and reducing manpower available to produce them.

From 1947 on, the principle was introduced that all collective farms in a region were jointly responsible for fulfillment of compulsory delivery quotas by the region. The more efficient farms that met their obligations saw now their quotas raised so as to compensate for inadequate deliveries by the less successful farms. Efficiency was thus penalized and compulsory deliveries lost the

incentive functions they might have had. It may be finally noted that the collective farm system generated a huge bureaucratic apparatus, as administrative pressures were being increasingly substituted for incentives. Administrative personnel on the farm level alone typically absorbed 10 to 30% of the farm's disposable income. In the 1947 checkup as many as 747,000 administrative jobs were abolished, without ending the proliferation of desk jobs. Meanwhile, there developed an acute shortage of agricultural specialists in production work: in 1953, only 68,000 out of 350,000 held production jobs. Out of 94,000 collective farm chairmen, only 2,400 had higher and 14,200 specialized secondary education.

Agricultural policies since 1953. Agricultural reforms enacted since Stalin's death stemmed from the recognition that agriculture had become a major bottleneck for further economic growth. Agricultural output had to be drastically raised so as to improve living standards and productivity of labor everywhere. This goal presupposed intensification of Soviet farming and improvement of its efficiency. This was to be achieved by providing farmers with incentives, improving their terms of trade, raising their incomes, and shifting into the agricultural sector resources it had long been denied. The collective farm system was retained but some of its most characteristic institutions such as MTS, compulsory deliveries, multiple prices were abandoned or revamped. On the other hand, the importance of state farms increased a good deal raising a possibility that this type of agricultural organization, rather than the collective farm, may hold the key to the future of Soviet A. The main post-Stalin reforms were concerned with: household plots, procurement prices, compulsory deliveries, planning methods, shift of resources into farming, crash programs for the cultivation of virgin lands and for the expansion of corn acreage, and the MTS reorganization. They will be discussed in that order.

The first emergency measures taken by Stalin's suc-

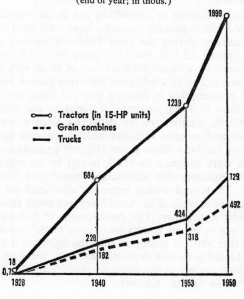

MECHANIZATION OF SOVIET AGRICULTURE
(end of year; in thous.)

o—o Tractors (in 15-HP units)
- - - Grain combines
— Trucks

1899
1239
684
729
492
424
318
228
182
18
0,7
1928   1940   1953   1959

cessors sought to increase production from the sector where least state investment was required: the collective farmers' household plots and privately owned livestock. The harassment of this sector was suspended and private ownership of livestock was now encouraged, tax relief and reduction of delivery quotas being granted as incentives thereto. The policy was effective and privately owned livestock was expanding faster than all livestock in the country, until 1957 when some checks were applied.

Prices paid by the state for procurements were significantly raised in 1953 and then again in 1956. Thus, according to calculations made by N. Nimitz, average procurement prices (in rubles per ton) paid to collective farms rose between 1950 and 1956: grain, from 91 to 530; milk, from 300 to 970; potatoes, from 40 to 410. How low were the originally paid prices may be gathered from the fact that even the new higher prices often failed to cover average production costs which amounted, e.g., over the period 1953–56, to 690 rubles per ton of grain, 350 of potatoes, 1,570 of milk. As the result of price increases and larger physical volume of procurements, sales by collective farms to procurement agencies rose (in bill. rubles) from 24.5 in 1952 to 108.0 in 1958 and their share in collective farms' total money income rose from 57% to 82%. According to official claims real farm income per capita (cash and in kind) increased by 85% between 1950 and 1958 while wage and salary earnings per capita rose by only 55%. Even so an average *kolkhoznik*'s income still lies substantially below the average wage.

Compulsory delivery quotas were reduced in 1954, with an increased reliance on above-quota purchases. In 1958, the whole system of multiple procurement prices was abandoned. All state purchases of a given product are now paid at a single price, differentiated according to region and adjusted periodically in accordance with supply fluctuations. Compulsory deliveries were simultaneously abolished but survive in fact, each farm being still assigned procurement quotas per 1 hectare of land.

State investment in agriculture ran at an annual rate of only 5 bill. rubles (or some 7.3% of total state investment outlays) during the years 1946–50 but was raised to an annual 22 bill. over the years 1956–58. Annual investment by collective farms out of their own funds rose from 6.2 to 18.1 bill. over the same period. Electric power consumption in farming was 2.5 times greater in 1958 than in 1953, against 1.7 times in the economy as a whole. Annual tractor deliveries were more than doubled and mineral fertilizer production rose by over 60%. In 1953–54 alone some 104,000 agricultural specialists were assigned to MTS, joined by an additional 32,000 engineers and technicians transferred from industry. These and similar measures alleviated the acute shortage of capital, skills, machinery and other resources in Soviet agriculture. The resettlement of hundreds of thousands of urban youths on "virgin lands" amounted to another shift of resources into the agicultural sector. The planted area was expanded by 23% between 1953 and 1959, mainly as the result of plowing up the "virgin lands" (*see* GRAIN CROPS).

POPULATION IN AGRICULTURE ($\uparrow$ = 1 MILLION)		
U.S.	$\uparrow\uparrow\uparrow\uparrow\uparrow\uparrow$	6
USSR	$\uparrow$ $\uparrow$	45

Planning methods were streamlined. Since 1955, responsibility for detailed production planning rests with the collective farm. Centralized planning is now mainly confined to fixing state purchase quotas. No longer is every collective farm required to raise sheep, to grow perennial grass, and so on, regardless of soil, climate, and local conditions. The old methods still survive, however, in such special campaigns as Khrushchev's plan, announced in Jan. 1955, to expand area planted to corn from 4 mill. hectares in 1954 to 28 mill. in 1960. Corn, "the sausage on the stalk," was to provide the main source of concentrated and succulent fodder and thus the basis for expansion of livestock and the eventual "overtaking the United States in meat and milk production per capita." Area under corn was actually expanded to 23.9 mill. hectares by 1956 but declined since much of the new area was found unsuitable for that crop.

Perhaps the most significant of post-Stalin reforms has been the liquidation of MTS decreed in Feb. 1958, with the sale of their equipment to collective farms and their reorganization into RTS, repair and technical stations. These were put in charge of technical services for the collective farms and have the monopoly for selling them new equipment, fuel and spare parts; they play a relatively minor part, however, compared to their predecessors and may be eventually incorporated into collective farms. The latter purchased, by July 1959, 512,000 tractors, 211,000 combines and other machinery valued at 21.7 bill. rubles and formerly owned by the MTS. The new setup streamlined the operation of collective farms by eliminating dual management. It did away with the wasteful hauls (often up to 60 mi.) between the MTS and the farms they served, thus saving on fuel and repairs. Political and control functions formerly performed by the MTS can now be adequately carried out by the party cells within the collective farms. These had been strengthened by the amalgamation movement in 1950, and even more by the recent influx of over 1 mill. tractor drivers and other workers formerly employed by the MTS.

While the MTS vanished, the state's other agricultural outpost, the state farms, expanded considerably (see table above, p. 7), following the creation of new state farms in "virgin lands," where they became the prevailing form of land tenure. Conversion of some suburban collective farms into state farms specializing in vegetable production was also encouraged. In 1959, state farms accounted for 27.5% of sown area, 14.2% of cattle, 38% of state grain procurements, 23% of meat and 25% of milk procurements. The question arises whether collective farms will continue to coexist with state farms, or be gradually swallowed by them, or whether the differences between the two forms of farming will gradually become obliterated. The latter possibility appears most likely, as indicated by some recent developments. A collective farm has differed from a state farm mainly by the cooperative character of property relationships, the mode of income distribution (collective farmers being residual sharers in the farm's income rather than wage-earners paid at a fixed rate as in state farms), and the smaller size. Since 1954, however, the *kolkhozy* have increasingly adopted a system of paying cash advances to their members and of guaranteeing them a minimum income per workday. Official encouragement is offered to collective farmers to relinquish or cede their household plots and, occasionally, to cede the farm's capital assets to the state. Finally, as the result of the repeated mergers, the size of an average collective farm (5,500 hectares in 1959, or almost 4 times more than in 1940) now approaches that of a state farm. If these trends continue, the position of a collective farmer will increasingly resemble that of a wage-earner and the farm's cooperative property will assume the character of state property, a development which would conform to the party's ideological long-term goals. An opposite trend, toward a strengthening of the collective farm system, is also discernible, however. Proposals to create inter-collective farm organizations, advanced at the Dec. 1959 meetings of the party's central committee, might work in that direction. As shown by the vacillating course of discussions at that session, the final decision on the future organizational forms of Soviet farming has not yet been reached.

Appraisal. Soviet agricultural policies have been dominated by three main themes: the need for agricultural marketings, the preference for large-scale mechanized production methods, the belief that peasant farming was a bulwark of capitalism. These three themes were intimately related to each other and to the goal of rapid industrialization, of which the farmers had to bear the main burden in a country where, at the outset of Five Year Plans, rural population made up 82% of the total.

The agricultural sector was to finance capital formation, to provide food and raw materials for urban dwellers and for exports, to release manpower for the expanding industry. This was to be achieved by subjecting it to a comprehensive network of administrative controls (rather than to rely on market forces) and by transforming peasant farming into large-scale enterprise, mechanized, electrified, and expected to be highly efficient. The Soviet planners have not been equally successful in achieving all these objectives.

The institution of collective farming, coupled with compulsory deliveries and administrative compulsion, proved to be a highly efficient machine for depressing peasant consumption and for financing industrial capital formation. Central planning of sown areas, combined with relatively high procurement prices paid for technical crops such as cotton, was successful in expanding production of such crops (q.v.). While this shift contributed toward intensification of Soviet farming, post-collectivization losses of livestock (*see* CATTLE, HORSES,

Hogs) worked in the opposite direction. Also, costly planning mistakes were made, such as an excessive emphasis on perennial grasses, which could be avoided with a less centralized system. Agriculture (where rural overpopulation was estimated at some 23.4 mill. in 1927) provided most recruits for the new industrial projects: 22.8 mill. rural dwellers moved into cities during the decade 1929–38 alone, and the number of peasant households dropped by 5.7 mill. between 1929 and 1935. Rather than being displaced by machinery, peasants were, however, fleeing depressed rural living

LABOR REQUIRED TO PRODUCE SAME AMOUNT OF PRODUCTS		
PRODUCT	IN U.S.	IN USSR
GRAIN	↟	↟↟↟↟↟↟↟
POTATOES	↟	↟↟↟↟↟
SUGAR BEETS	↟	↟↟↟↟↟↟↟
COTTON	↟	↟↟↟
MILK	↟	↟↟↟↟
BEEF	↟	↟↟↟↟↟↟↟↟↟↟↟↟↟↟↟
PORK	↟	↟↟↟↟↟↟↟↟↟↟↟↟↟↟↟↟↟↟↟

standards, or were moved by force as kulaks. Thus, agriculture lost some of the most skillful and efficient producers rather than submarginal farmers.

The objective of converting small-scale peasant farming into large-scale enterprise was met. The average size of a peasant farm in 1926 was 4.9 hectares; that of a collective farm in 1959, 2,400 hectares; of a state farm, 8,200. Methods of production were, in many instances, revolutionized. The number of tractors (in standard 15 HP units) rose from 18,000 to 1,790,000 between 1928 and 1959; consumption of electric power in agriculture, from .035 to 6.9 bill. kw-hr; output of commercial fertilizers, from .14 to 12.9 mill. tons. Nevertheless, the expected improvement in productivity was slow to materialize. Thus, according to A. Kahan's estimates, labor input per unit of land was 18% higher in 1950 than in 1926–29 and did not reach the pre-collectivization level until the mid-1950's. Trends in yields of major crops are shown below (five-year averages, in quintals per hectare):

	1925–29	1950–54	1955–58
Grain	7.91	7.85	9.49
Cotton	8.82	16.50	20.24
Sugar beet	132.0	150.8	185.6
Potatoes	79.3	86.2	90.9
Flax fiber	2.08	1.32	2.53

Labor productivity is still extremely low, as shown below (see comparisons with the United States).

The performance of Soviet farmers did not come up to expectations owing to a variety of causes. Impressive progress in the use of tractors and commerical fertilizers has to be set against post-collectivization losses of animal draft power and manure. Thus, *total* amount of draft power available in Soviet farming per acre (animal and mechanical) was in 1950 lower than in 1928, and by 1958 rose to some 105% of the 1928 level. Applica-

U.S. FARMER VS. SOVIET KOLKHOZNIK

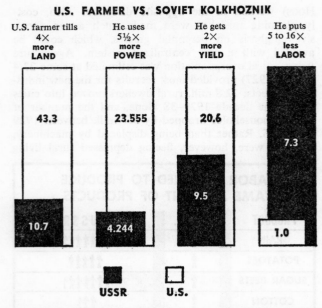

U.S. farmer tills	He uses	He gets	He puts
4× more LAND	5½× more POWER	2× more YIELD	5 to 16× less LABOR

43.3 — 10.7 — USSR / U.S.
23.555 — 4.244
20.6 — 9.5
7.3 — 1.0

■ USSR   □ U.S.

tion of fertilizers is limited by and large to high priority technical crops. Electric power is applied in only a narrow range of operations, and only 39% of collective farms had access to it as of 1957. Over-all labor productivity was adversely affected by a bureaucratization of farming, a corollary of reliance on administrative controls and, until recently, by a widespread neglect of incentives. Nevertheless, the very neglect in which the agricultural sector had been held for decades opens vast possibilities for improvement. Incentive policies and increased investment in agriculture initiated in 1953 were followed by a significant improvement in productivity, which still remains inordinately low, however, as suggested by the comparisons with the United States farming made below. Further rise in productivity is imperative if the Soviet planners are to approach their ambitious goals of improvement in living standards, especially of per capita milk and meat consumption. It is also a necessary prerequisite for release of agricultural manpower to industry, especially in view of the labor shortage owing to wartime losses. It is to be expected therefore that the current emphasis on "the carrot" rather than on "the stick" in dealing with farmers will continue.

In order to put the performance of Soviet farming into a better perspective some comparisons with the United States are made below.

	USSR	U.S.	USSR as % of U.S.	Year
Population active in agriculture, mill.	45	6	750	
Land, mill. acres	480	260	185	
Land/man ratio (acres per man)	10.7	43.3	25	
Livestock herds (mill.)				1959
— Cattle	70.8	96.9	72	
— Hogs	48.5	57.2	85	
— Sheep and goats	138.6	35.6	389	
Some agric. machinery (thous.)				
— tractors	996	4,975	20	1958
— combines	500	1,040	48	1958
— trucks	631	2,850	22	1956
Area sown per tractor, ha.	194	28	700	
Fertilizer input, mill. tons	2.7	6.7	40	
Electric power consumed on farms (bill. kw-hr)	4.244	23.555	18	1957

	USSR	U.S.	USSR as % of U.S.	Year
Crop yields (q. per ha.)				1958
Grain	9.5	20.6		
Potatoes	90.9	193.2		
Sugar beets	185.6	378.0		
Labor requirements (man-hours per 100 kg. produced)	1956–57	1956 (U.S.) (Soviet coll. farms)		
Grain	7.3	1.0	730	
Potatoes	5.1	1.0	510	
Sugar beets	3.1	.5	620	
Cotton	42.8	18.8	228	
Milk	14.7	4.7	313	
Beef	112.0	7.9	1,418	
Pork	103.0	6.3	1,635	

(*See also* PEASANTS, MTS, KOLKHOZ, SOVKHOZ, ECONOMIC DEVELOPMENT, EMANCIPATION OF SERFS, WAR COMMUNISM.)

BIBLIOGRAPHY: G. T. Robinson, *Rural Russia under the Old Regime*, New York, 1932; N. Jasny, *The Collectivized Agriculture of the USSR*, Stanford, 1949; L. Volin, *A Survey of Soviet Russian Agriculture*, Washington, 1951; Papers by Nancy Nimitz, Lasar Volin, D. Gale Johnson and Arcadius Kahan, in: Joint Economic Committee, Congress of the U.S., 86th Congress, *Comparisons of the United States and Soviet Economies*, Part I, Washington, 1959.

L. S.

AGULS: *see* POPULATION.

AIRCRAFT INDUSTRY. Unofficial estimates indicate that operational military aircraft in the USSR in 1959 included approximately 4,000 modern interceptor fighters, 1,000–1,500 long-range bombers, 10,000 tactical ground support aircraft, and 3,500–7,500 military transport aircraft and helicopters.

The construction of aircraft was initiated shortly before the First World War, and there were ten small aircraft plants operating during the war years that followed. The construction of aircraft on a large scale, however, was initiated during the 1930's in the course of the First and Second Five Year Plans. It has been associated, since that time, with the names of a relatively small number of designers, an abbreviation of whose names is usually employed to identify the models that they have produced. They include S. V. Ilyushin, S. A. Lavochkin, A. I. Mikoyan, M. I. Gurevich, V. M. Petlyakov, N. N. Polikarpov, A. N. Tupolev, and A. S. Yakovlev.

According to official data an annual production of about 40,000 aircraft of all types was achieved toward the end of the Second World War. Since that time, however, there has been a far-reaching modernization of both the production facilities themselves and the models. The new models produced on a large scale include jet aircraft of various types, equipped with modern instruments and radar, as well as large helicopters. The innovations introduced include the use of conveyor belts in assembly shops and in storage centers, the use of automatic and of semi-automatic machines for cutting and shaping, the use of precision molding methods to reduce the need for mechanical shaping, the use of a variety of types of welding, and the standardization of both parts and equipment to permit rapid adjustments to the production of new models.

The passenger aircraft produced in recent years include the pure jet models TU–104, TU–104A, and TU–110 (designed by Tupolev), and the jet-prop models IL–18 (designed by Ilyushin), AN–10 (designed by O. K. Antonov), and TU–114.

The military aircraft include the all-weather interceptor YAK–25, the supersonic jet fighters MIG–19 and MIG–25, the ground support types MIG–15, MIG–17, MIG–19, and IL–28, and the long-range bombers TU–16 (twin jet) and TU–20 (four turbo-jets).

Among the helicopters produced on a serial basis are the large YAK–24, and the smaller types MI–1 and MI–4 (designed by M. L. Mil) and KA–15 (designed by N. I. Kamenev). (*See also* AIR FORCE AND NAVY)

P. I. M.

AIR FORCE: *see* ARMED FORCES.

AISSORS: *see* POPULATION.

AKHMÁTOVA (Gorenko), **Ánna Andréyevna,** (1888–), poet, associated with the acmeists (q.v.). Her poems consist largely of lyrics on love, and combine, in a peculiar way, realism with mysticism. Her first poems, which were published in the journals of St. Petersburg, brought her immediate fame. Subsequently several collections of her verse appeared: *Evening* (1912); *The White Flock* (1917); *The Plantain* (1921); and *Anno Domini MCMXXI* (1921). A prolonged interruption ensued that was caused by the execution of her husband, the poet N. Gumilyov, in 1921, for supposed participation in an anti-Soviet conspiracy. Shortly before World War II, however, new poems by A were published in the journal *Zvezda* (Leningrad), and also in a one-volume collection of her earlier poems (the group entitled *The Willow Tree*, which was written between 1922 and 1938). In 1946 her poetry was harshly condemned for its "lack of ideological content" by critics representing the official position. In 1950 several new poems from her series "Glory to the World" appeared, and in 1958 an anthology, *Poems of Various Years,* was published.

ÁKHTUBA RIVER, the left arm of lower Volga, near Stalingrad; length about 320 mi.; navigable during flood time.

AKKERMÁN: *see* BELGOROD-DNESTROVSKY.

AKKERMÁN, TREATY OF, between Russia and Turkey on Sept. 25, 1826. It affirmed Russia's right to exercise the protectorate over the autonomous principalities of Moldavia, Wallachia, and Serbia and the right of free passage of R. ships on the Danube and Black Sea. Black Sea straits were declared free for commercial shipping.

AK-MECHÉT: *see* KZYL-ORDA.

AKMÓLINSK: *see* TSELINOGRAD.

AKMÓLINSK OBLAST, in Kazakh SSR; abolished in 1961 and incorporated into Virgin Lands Kray.

AKSÁKOV, Iván Sergéyevich (1823–1886), Slavophile poet, essayist, critic, and journalist, brother of K. S. Aksákov. Born into a literary Moscow family, A spent his life in literary and philosophical circles. As a publicist, he came to write striking poetry on radical and political themes. His best critical work was the life of his father-in-law, the poet Tyutchev. In later life, A was an influential Slavophile journalist, frequently in trouble with the censors, but sometimes the mouthpiece of the R. nationalistic groups, as during his campaign for the liberation of the Balkan Slavs, 1876–78.

AKSÁKOV, Konstantín Sergeyevich (1817–1860), Slavophile essayist and critic, brother of I. S. Aksákov. At first a Hegelian, he became an ardent champion of Slavophile ideas, even wearing peasant costume and beard until the police interfered during the reaction of 1848. A writer of historical and philological essays, and a literary critic, A distinguished between the R. people whose life he saw as organic, collective, and moral, and the R. state which he criticized as European-imposed, impersonal, and often tyrannical.

AKSÁKOV, Sergéy Timoféyevich (1791–1859), prose writer, born in Ufa in a family of country gentry.

Graduated from the University of Kazan (1807) and entered civil service. He settled in Moscow (1826) where he served as a censor and later as a school director. A translator in his youth, he became known in later years as the leading prose writer of his time. He met Gogol (1832) whose close friend he became; Pushkin also belonged to the circle of his friends. His greatest merits are the precision and simplicity of style, the objectivity and sensitivity of his recollections, and his feeling for nature and the landscape of the open steppe country of the Volga where he had lived as a child. A's *Family Chronicle* (1856) is more fictional than most of his work, describing the life of his grandparents and parents. *The Childhood of Bagrov the Grandson* (1858) is a continuation of A's youthful reminiscences in semifictional form. The book evokes a contented, nostalgic atmosphere. He also left a collection of *Literary and Theatrical Reminiscences* (1810–30) and *Recollections of Gogol,* the latter being of great value for an understanding of Gogol's complex psychology.

AKSELRÓD, Pável Borísovich (1850–1928), Menshevik leader. Joined the populist movement in 1872. In 1880 was one of the founders of "Black Repartition" (q.v.). He lived abroad from 1881. In 1883, jointly with Plekhanov, A founded the first Marxist group "Liberation of Labor." Contributed to many Socialist publications, including *Iskra.* At the 2nd Congress of the Russian Social-Democratic party (1903) A became a Menshevik. After 1905 he was one of the ideologists of "liquidationism"—a trend among Social Democrats to abandon the illegal activities of the party and to concentrate instead on legal work among trade unions and other labor organizations tolerated by the tsarist regime. After the October revolution, A was a right-wing Menshevik and represented his party in the Second International.

AKTÁU (or AK-TAU), group of mountains in Central Asia. **(1)** N. and S. range on Mangyshlak Peninsula; elevations 800–950 ft. **(2)** Branch of Nuratau mountain range in Samarkand Oblast, Uzbek SSR; elevations over 4,900 ft. **(3)** Mountains in Kyzylkum range in Uzbek SSR; elevations over 3,000 ft.

AKTYÚBINSK, city, oblast adm. center, Kazakh SSR; pop. 97,000 (1959). Ferrous alloys, X-ray equipment, mechanical workshops, food ind. Pedag. inst. Founded 1869.

AKTYÚBINSK OBLAST, in N.W. Kazakh SSR; area 115,500 sq. mi.; pop. 401,000 (1959): Kazakhs, Russians, Ukrainians. Cities: Aktyubinsk, Temir, Chelkar. Irrigated by upper Emba and Ural tributaries; has many salt lakes, few forests. The N. part is in S. Urals, the S. part on the Aral-Caspian plain; sharply continental climate. Cattle raising, wheat. Ind.: mining (coal, gold, nickel, chromium, bauxite, copper) and oil extraction, chemical, metallurgical, farm machinery, food.

ALAKÓL (ALAKUL), a shallow salt lake in E. Kazakh SSR, area 890 sq. mi.

ALAPÁYEVSK, city in Sverdlovsk Oblast, RSFSR; pop. 41,100 (1956). Ferrous metallurgy, woodworking, ore dressing, iron-ore mining. Two technical schools.

ALATÁU (ALA-TAU) ("mottled mountain"), six mountain ranges in Central Asia (Kungey-A., Terskey-A., Trans-Ili-A., and others).

ALÁTYR, city in Chuvash ASSR, landing on Sura River; pop. 34,700 (1956). Flour mills, distilleries, woodworking, locomotive-repair shops.

ALAVÉRDI, town in Armenian SSR; pop. 14,100 (1956); old copper center; superphosphate and refractory brick plants.

ALÁY RANGE, in S. Kirghiz SSR, elevations over 19,700 ft. Covered with snow and glaciers.

ALÁY VALLEY, in Kirghiz SSR and Tadzhik SSR; steppes used as pastures. Altitude 9,850 ft., area about 650 sq. mi.

ALAZÁN RIVER, in Georgian and Azerbaijan SSR's, left tributary of the Kura; length 220 mi.; not navigable.

ALAZÉYA RIVER, in Yakut ASSR; length 930 mi.; flows into E. Siberian Sea.

ALCHÉVSK: *see* VOROSHILOVSK.

ALCHÉVSKY, Iván Alekséyevich (1876–1917), dramatic tenor of international reputation, member of the company of the Mariinsky Imperial Opera House in St. Petersburg from 1901 to 1917.

ALCOHOLISM. Official Soviet ideology views alcoholism as a social problem caused by the inhuman conditions of capitalism. This view, originally expounded by Engels, holds that under conditions of capitalistic exploitation, the overworked, underpaid, underfed, ill-housed, and ill-clad worker seeks temporary solace and release from his misery in alcoholic fumes. Commercial interests supported by the state encourage the consumption of alcohol by workers for both economic and political reasons: It brings huge profits and revenues, and it dulls the edge of the workers' revolutionary ardor.

In Soviet society, on the other hand, "where class exploitation has been ended forever, where the welfare of the population increases all the time, the social roots of alcoholism have been extirpated." Soviet sources indicate that the consumption of alcohol in Russia (1948–1950) has declined by 38 per cent compared with 1891 (European Russia) and stands at 1.85 liters of pure alcohol per capita (2.8 liters of vodka, 1.3 of wine and 7.2 of beer), as against a much higher consumption in leading capitalistic countries for these years (21.5 liters in France, 6.1 in the United States, 6.0 in Great Britain).

Statistical data on alcoholism in the Soviet Union are not made public. A qualitative survey of the Soviet press shows, however, that the amount of attention paid to alcoholism and drunkenness by the party and other organizations is indicative of the continued existence and importance of this social problem. Material gathered by the Supreme Court of the Soviet Union indicates, for example, that 70 per cent of persons sentenced for premeditated murder were in a state of intoxication when they commited their crime, and so were 90 per cent of cases of hooliganism that went to court. Inordinate drinking is apparently found at all levels of the society: among collective farmers (who often make their home brew or *samogonka*), industrial workers (who consider drinking a sign of manliness), intellectuals and particularly writers (who in their productions often picture drinking in a favorable light), and youths even though it is illegal to sell drinks to them.

The continued existence of alcoholism baffles Soviet authorities. The official explanation is that drinking and intoxication are a legacy from the capitalistic past still lurking in the consciousness of some people, and that these remnants must actively be combated by all healthy elements and social organizations in the Soviet Union. A more likely explanation is that the universal availability of alcoholic products (a state monopoly), the presence of extra purchasing power that cannot be soaked up by consumers' goods, the general dreariness and drabness of Soviet life and housing, the erosion of family functions accompanying industrialization and urbanization and the lack of adequate parental supervision, the rigidity of class lines and the decrease of opportunities for meritorious upward social mobility, as well as the heavy cultural heritage of the past, may all contribute to the persistence of alcoholism under Soviet conditions.

Prohibition (actually in effect between 1914 and 1925) has been discarded in favor of other steps. These include: a reduction in the production of vodka, increasing the severity of measures against home-brewing, encouraging the drinking of wines and beer, limiting the sale of alcohol to certain days and hours, educational campaigns, and punishment for alcoholics. In addition to measures of social action, the treatment of alcoholics is also a medical function. Alcoholics may receive therapy, supervision, and help from either specialized psychiatric clinics or general neighborhood clinics. Hospitalization in mental hospitals for short periods of time is available when medically indicated, and chronic alcoholics may be sent to psychiatric colonies. In 1950–55, 2 per cent of the beds in psychiatric hospitals and colonies were occupied by alcoholics. Therapeutic methods include: pharmaceuticals, occupational and physical therapy, and psychotherapy (individual and group hypnosis, rational psychotherapy, and the development of conditioned negative reflexes toward alcohol).

BIBLIOGRAPHY: Vera Efron, "The Soviet Approach to Alcoholism," *Social Problems*, Spring 1960; Mark G. Field, "Alcoholism, Crime and Delinquency in Soviet Society," *Social Problems*, October, 1955. M. G. F.

ALDÁN (f. Nezametny), town in Yakut ASSR, center of Aldan gold and mica mining district; pop. 10,600 (1956). Machine-repair shops. Mining and pedag. inst.

ALDÁN PLATEAU, in Yakut ASSR, between upper Aldan and Uchur rivers; elevations reach 3,300 ft.

ALDÁN RIVER, in Yakut ASSR, largest tributary of the Lena; 1,300 mi. long; navigable; rich in fish.

ALDÁNOV (Landau), **Mark Aleksándrovich** (1886–1957), émigré novelist. He left Russia in 1916 for  political reasons and after 1919 he lived in Paris. He wrote primarily philosophical novels on historical themes. Among his best-known works are four novels from the series entitled "The Thinker," which are concerned with problems of revolution and emigration in France at the time of Napoleon. They are *The Ninth Thermidor* (1923), *The Devil's Bridge* (1925), *The Conspiracy* (1927), and *St. Helena, Little Island* (1928). *The Tenth Symphony*, which was published in 1931 and which is concerned with the life of Beethoven, is one of his most successful works. It was followed in 1939 by *The Beginning of the End*, subsequently published in English under the title *The Fifth Seal*—a novel about the civil war in Spain that conveys the general sense of helplessness in the face of catastrophe that preceded the outbreak of World War II. A's historical novels are marked by intellectual refinement, as well as by erudition, rather than by an originality of either style or contents. Their value, however, carries beyond the sphere of literature proper, for they are, in part, observations and reflections concerning the course of history, expressed through the medium of literature. In 1953 A's *A Novel about Death* appeared, which contains an analysis of the psychology of dying—a subject with which some of his other works are also concerned. In *Night at Ulm*, A returns once more to his earlier theme regarding the helplessness of man before the course of historical development. A number of A's works have been translated into French and English.

ALÉKHIN, Aleksándr Aleksándrovich (1892–1946), chess player; world champion from 1927 to 1935 and 1937 to 1946. Left Russia in 1921.

ALÉKHIN, Vasíly Vasílyevich (1882–1946), geobotanist. Graduate (1907) and professor (1918) of Moscow University. Research concerned the theory of plant communities (phytocenology), morphology, and the dynamics of phytocenosa as well as methods of their investigation. A studied the steppes, meadows, and flora of the Moscow and Gorky regions.

ALEKSANDR RANGE: *see* KIRGHIZ RANGE.

ALEKSANDRÍYA, city in Kirovograd Oblast, Ukrainian SSR; pop. 30,700 (1956). Lignite mining, flour mills, metalworking.

ALEKSANDRÓPOL: *see* LENINAKAN.

ALEKSÁNDROV, city in Vladimir Oblast, RSFSR; pop. 33,500 (1956). Ind.: radio, leather substitutes, weaving plant. On the site of Aleksandrovskaya Sloboda, a residence of Ivan IV during his feud with Moscow boyars. Buildings of 16th-17th centuries; museum.

ALEKSÁNDROV, Aleksándr Danílovich (1912–), mathematician. Corresponding member, Ac. of S., USSR (1946). Dean of Leningrad University. Founder of the Soviet geometrical school of thought. Investigated dif-

ferential geometry of general elements of surfaces and internal geometry of convex surfaces. Stalin prize (1942).

ALEKSÁNDROV, Anatóly Petróvich (1903–), physicist. Fellow, Ac. of S., USSR (1953). Graduated from Kiev University (1930). Associated with the Institute of Physical Technology, Ac. of S. (1930–46). Director, Institute of Physical Problems, Ac. of S. (1946–55). Research concerns the physics of dielectrics, mechanical and electrical properties of high polymers and amorphous substances, properties of polystyrene and the development of high-quality polystyrene capacitors. Introduced the statistical strength theory of solids. In collaboration with his associates he developed the relaxation theory of elasticity, clarified the nature of polymer solidification, and phase transformation. Stalin prize (1942).

ALEKSÁNDROV, Borís Kapitónovich (1889–), hydraulic engineer. Corresponding member, Ac. of S., USSR (1953). Graduated from Petrograd Polytechnic Institute (1917). Head and senior engineer of the "Greater Volga" Hydroelectric Power Plant Project. Professor of the Moscow Power Engineering Institute (1948). Research concerns the utilization of water power of large rivers (Volga, Oka). Participated in the design of hydroelectric power plants and navigable canals (Moscow Canal). Designed the Kama Hydrostation.

ALEKSÁNDROV, Iván Gavrílovich (1875–1936), power and hydraulic engineer. Fellow, Ac. of S., USSR (1932). Graduated from the Moscow School of Engineering (1901). Designed the Dnieper hydroelectric power plant (1921). Worked out the project of electrification of Central Asia. Participated in the State Commission for the Electrification of Russia (GOELRO). Member, State Planning Committee (1921).

ALEKSÁNDROV, Pável Sergéyevich (1896–), mathematician. Fellow, Ac. of S., USSR (1953). Member (1921), president (1932), and honorary member (1946) of the Moscow Mathematical Society. Graduate (1917) and professor (1929) of Moscow University. Member of foreign scientific societies including the American Philosophical Society in Philadelphia, the National Ac. of S. in Washington, D. C. Investigated the theory of functions of real variables and became a leading authority in topology. Editor of the journal *Uspekhi Matematicheskikh Nauk* (Progress of Mathematical Sciences). Published over 300 papers. Stalin prize (1943).

ALEKSANDRÓVICH (Dmitrievsky), **Pyotr Aleksándrovich,** Left Social Revolutionary, one of the organizers of the Cheka. Participated in the assassination of the German ambassador Mirbach in 1918; was arrested in July 1918 and shot by the Bolsheviks.

ALEKSÁNDROVSK, town in Perm Oblast, RSFSR, near R.R. station Kopi; pop. 16,700 (1956); mining-equipment plant.

ALEKSÁNDROVSK: *see* ZAPOROZHYE.

ALEKSANDROVSK-GRUSHEVSKY: *see* SHAKHTY.

ALEKSÁNDROVSK-SAKHALÍNSKY, town in Sakhalin Oblast, RSFSR, port in Tatar Strait of Sea of Okhotsk; pop. 23,100 (1956). Brick plant, coal mining; fisheries; technical schools. Founded 1881; was center of Sakhalin forced labor under tsarist regime.

ALEKSÉYEV, Aleksándr Yemelyánovich (1891–), electrical engineer. Corresponding member, Ac. of S., USSR (1953). Graduated from the Institute of Electrical Engineering in Leningrad (1925). Professor at the Institute of Railway Engineering (1936). Joined the Institute of Electrical Engineering (1952). Research concerns the theory and design of electrical machinery. Supervised the design and building of the first Soviet turbo- and hydrogenerators. Author of *The Building of Electric Machinery* (1949). Stalin prizes (1949, 1951).

ALEKSÉYEV, Mikhaíl Vasílyevich (1857–1918), general. Of peasant origin, he emerged from the Russo-Japanese War a general. Became commander of the armies of the N.W. in March 1915 and chief of the general staff five months later. Supreme military commander under the Provisional Government, March-May 1917. Recalled in Sept., he attempted unsuccessfully to effect a reconciliation between Kerensky and General Kornilov. Upon Kornilov's death (March 1918), he became leader of the White government in the S., but succumbed to a heart attack, Sept. 1918.

ALEKSÉYEV RAVELÍN, a fort of Petropavlovsk Fortress in St. Petersburg, solitary confinement prison with particularly severe regime, built in the 18th century. Decembrists K. F. Ryleyev and P. I. Pestel, N. G. Chernyshevsky (1862), and other prominent revolutionaries were jailed there.

ALEKSÉYEVSK: *see* SVOBODNY.

ALÉKSINSKY, Grigóry Alekséyevich (1879–), Bolshevik spokesman in the second State Duma. In 1909 he parted with Lenin and formed with Bogdanov and Lunacharsky the *Vpered* (Forward) group. During World War I was defensist; after the February revolution participated in the *Yedinstvo* (Unity) group headed by Plekhanov; after the revolution emigrated to France.

ALEUTS: *see* POPULATION.

ALEXANDER I (Aleksándr Pávlovich) (1777–1825), emperor of Russia (1801–1825). His grandmother Catherine II had chosen the Swiss revolutionary César La Harpe as A's tutor; through him, A developed a sincere emotional attachment to the philosophy of the Enlightenment. A preference for autocratic behavior, fostered in A by his father Paul I, coexisted and usually prevailed over his liberalism. A came to the throne in 1801 after having been indirectly involved in the palace conspiracy which led to the murder of Paul I. The abolition of torture and a law (1803) facilitating the voluntary emancipation of serfs by their owners were among his early reforms. But the discussions of constitutional reforms which A encouraged throughout his reign were almost fruitless, although the institutions of central government (ministries) were reorganized and there was established an advisory State Council (1810). From 1805 A devoted himself to the war of the third coalition which failed to stop Napoleonic expansion. The Treaty of Tilsit (1807) inaugurated an uneasy peace shattered by Napoleon's invasion of Russia (June 1812). After the battle of Borodino, the French occupation of Moscow and its destruction by fire, Napoleon's armies retreated from Russia. Then A played a leading role in the final defeat of Napoleon, in the formation of the Quadruple Alliance to maintain the status quo in Eu-

rope after the Congress of Vienna (1814–15), and in the signing of the ineffectual Holy Alliance—an agreement among European monarchs to apply the principles of Christian morality to foreign relations. Michael Speransky, a liberal, was A's trusted adviser till 1812; then Baroness von Krüdener strengthened his ill-defined mysticism while the reactionary Arakcheyev was his trusted agent, especially in the later part of the reign. A's death in Dec. 1825 was followed by a brief and ineffective revolt of the Decembrists (q.v.). The assertion which is sometimes made that A did not die in 1825 but lived on as a hermit, Fedor Kuzmich, is highly improbable. Under his reign Georgia (1801), Finland (1809), Bessarabia (1812), and Azerbaijan (1813) were incorporated into Russia.

BIBLIOGRAPHY: L. I. Strakhovsky, *Alexander I of Russia,* New York, 1947.

ALEXANDER II (Aleksándr Nikoláyevich) (1818–1881), emperor of Russia (1855–1881). Having been an indolent student, A imbibed little humanitarianism from his chief tutor, the poet Zhukovsky. He traveled extensively in Russia and abroad. His marriage (1841) to a German princess strengthened his ties with Germany but was an unhappy union. A's reign ("the era of great reforms") began in Feb. 1855 during the Crimean War which, after the fall of Sevastopol, ended ingloriously for Russia at the Congress of Paris (1856). The defeat was followed by several years of government and public discussions. Then the tsar-liberator issued the emancipation edict (Feb. 19, 1861) which gave freedom and land (too little, some said) to the peasants but retained many of the peasant disabilities. Four important reforms followed. An 1864 law on self-government established the zemstvo—county and provincial assemblies, elected by all social groups. The same year the judiciary was reorganized (trial by jury, elected justices of the peace). From 1870, the towns also enjoyed a measure of self-government, tempered, as elsewhere in Europe, by property qualifications. The army was reformed in 1874; all social groups were now liable to military service. A Polish insurrection had been suppressed in 1863–64 and Alaska was sold to the United States in 1867. Meanwhile the Russian Empire expanded in the Far East (Vladivostok founded in 1860), and in Central Asia; Bessarabia, lost in 1856, was recovered in 1878 at the Congress of Berlin which terminated a successful Russo-Turkish war, so much desired by the R. Panslavists. The radicals, dissatisfied by the moderate reforms, formed revolutionary societies (Land and Freedom, 1862), but their movement, "to the people," failed (1874) to enlist the support of the peasants. Then the terrorist group, the People's Will, became active (1879). Count Loris-Melikov, minister of the interior, fought the menace with arrests and with concessions to the liberals. A project (sometimes called erroneously a constitution), empowering the zemstvo to participate indirectly in legislation, was approved by A just before he was assassinated (March 1, 1881). His son and successor Alexander III rejected this proposal.

BIBLIOGRAPHY: S. Graham, *Tsar of Freedom,* New Haven, 1935.

ALEXANDER III (Aleksándr Aleksándrovich) (1845–1894), emperor of Russia (1881–1894), was the second  son of Alexander II. Partly because A became heir apparent only on the death of his elder brother (1865), his education was somewhat limited and he remained a man of simple ideas and tastes. In 1866, he contracted a happy marriage with a Danish princess (Maria Fyodorovna, 1847–1928). A devoted churchman, a firm believer in autocracy, an admirer of the editor Katkov (q.v.), A was influenced by his former tutor Pobedonostsev (q.v.). In 1881, the assassination of his father brought him to the throne, and "the era of counterreforms" began. Advised by Pobedonostsev, A rejected a liberal plan of Loris-Melikov, minister of Alexander II. The press was muzzled (1881) and the universities lost their autonomy (1884). In 1887, obstacles for students from the lower social classes and 3 to 10 per cent quotas for Jews were introduced for the first time in R. school admission policies. The preeminence of the nobility was strengthened: the State Nobility Bank was founded in 1885 and the appointed land captains (1889) took over the functions of the previously elected justices of the peace. Discriminatory laws were passed against religious minorities (Old Believers, Jews) and attempts at Russification were made in the border provinces (school instruction to be conducted in Russian). The revolutionaries became less active. The industrialization of Russia began in this period: higher tariffs, expansion of railroads under Witte's (q.v.) direction, emergence of an industrial proletariat and adoption of the first factory laws (e.g., eight-hour day for juveniles). The Three Emperors League (1881, renewed in 1884) had tied A to Germany and Austria but in 1892, France became Russia's main ally. However, Russia's social stability and strength of international position were illusory, as the reign of Nicholas II was to show.

ALEXANDER I LAND (R. *Zemlyá Aleksándra I*), hilly, ice covered area of Antarctic continent (possibly an island). Discovered by R. expedition of Bellingshausen and Lazarev in 1821.

ALEXANDER (Aleksándr Yaroslávovich) NÉVSKY (1220–1263), prince of Novgorod, Kiev, and from 1252 Grand Duke of Vladimir, statesman and strategist. In 1240 he destroyed the Swedish army at the Neva River (hence his surname); in 1242 gained a victory over German knights (Livonian Order) on the ice of Chudskoye Lake. Prevented new Tatar invasion. Forced Swedes and Germans to retreat from western Russia.

ALEXANDRA FYÓDOROVNA (1872–1918), the last Russian Empress, was born in Germany as Princess Alix of Hesse-Darmstadt and was educated in England, her mother being a daughter of Queen Victoria. Her marriage (1894) to Nicholas II in whose life she was the dominating influence, proved to be an exceptionally happy union. Her only son Alexis was born in 1904, after the successive births of four daughters. He had tragically inherited through her the incurable disease hemophilia, characterized by a tendency to bleed excessively from the smallest cut. The next year, the faith healer Rasputin (q.v.), allegedly endowed with hypnotic power, was introduced to the distraught parents. It is believed that his incredible success in stopping the bleedings at times may have been caused by his cunning ability to delay his appearance at the bedside of the ailing boy until the end of the bleeding period. AF's feelings of gratitude, as well as her mysticism and her religiosity, fostered Rasputin's influence at the court until even some ministers owed their appointments to him. During World War I, AF was very active in war relief organizations. In 1915, Nicholas II assumed the post of commander in chief, a decision of which AF entirely approved. Then, one incompetent minister after another was appointed or dismissed in accordance with the letters received by Nicholas from his wife who consulted Rasputin on matters of state. The neurotic and superstitious aspects of her personality and her blind acceptance of Rasputin's guidance can be clearly seen from her published letters which were written in English (*Letters from the Tsarina to the Tsar, 1914–1916*, London, 1923). The wartime rumors that she was favoring the Germans were baseless. Sincerely devoted to her ideals, she strongly opposed any limitations of autocracy. She died tragically in the slaughter of the Imperial family (night of July 16–17, 1918).

ALEXIS, son of Nicholas II: *see* ALEXANDRA FYODOROVNA.

ALEXIS (Alekséy Mikháylovich) (1629–1676), tsar, son of Mikhail Romanov, ascended the throne at the age of 16. His reign was marked by much internal unrest (revolt in Moscow in 1642, peasant revolt of Stepan Razin, 1670–71), a new code of law, involving the official sanction of peasant serfdom (1649), revision of the church ritual undertaken by Patriarch Nikon, resulting in the secession of the so-called Old-Believers who were condemned as schismatics. The war with Poland for the possession of the Ukraine ended by the Treaty of Andrusovo (1667) which gave Russia the E. Ukraine, Kiev, and the Smolensk region. By the end of his reign, the government established an effective control. The tsar felt strong enough to discontinue calling the *Zemsky sobor*, an advisory assembly. There was a rapid infiltration of western influences which foreshadowed the reign of Peter I and of his reforms.

ALEXIS (Alekséy Petróvich) (1690–1718), tsarévich, son of Peter I by his first wife (Lopukhina), lived with his exiled mother in Suzdal in an environment hostile to his father. Was sent abroad in 1709 for education, and married in 1711 to the German Princess Charlotte Wolfenbüttel. A was of delicate health and a heavy drinker. While not averse to western influence he could never gain his father's confidence and was made to renounce his rights to the throne in 1716. He fled to Vienna with his mistress Euphrosine Fedorov seeking the protection of Emperor Charles VI; was lured back to Russia by promises of forgiveness and "best love," but these were not kept. Upon his return, he, as well as his friends, were put to torture. On June 24, 1718 he was sentenced to death for conspiracy against his father and died after a session in the torture chamber.

ALÉYSK, town in Altay Kray, RSFSR; pop. 24,300 (1956); sugar factory and meat-packing plant.

ALIGÉR, Margaríta Iósifovna (1915–), poet, born in Odessa in a Jewish family. Graduate of a chemical technicum, she worked as a librarian and as editor of factory newspapers. In 1934–37 she studied at the Gorky Literary Institute in Moscow. Her works were published first in 1933. During World War II her poems enjoyed considerable popularity. They include: *Year of Birth* (1938), *The Railway* (1939), *Stones and Grass* (1940), *In Memory of the Brave,* narrative poem *Zoya* (1942), *Lyrics* (1943), *Poems* (1945), *A Tale of Truth* (play) (1945), *Selected Works* (1947), *The First Signs* (1948), *From My Notebook* (1955). She received the Stalin prize for *Zoya* (1943). Is a member of the CP. She wrote a sharply critical poem, *The Most Important Thing* (1956), depicting the tragic split in the character and life of the Soviet man: "hero and villain," "giant and scoundrel," "builder-creator and coward." Khrushchev has frequently criticized A's writings and her demand for greater freedom in creative work. She was induced to "repent."

ALIKHÁNOV, Abrám Isáakovich (1904–), physicist. Fellow, Ac. of S., USSR and Armenian SSR (1943). Graduated from Leningrad Polytechnic Institute (1931). Joined the Institute of Physical Technology (1927); director of the Power Engineering Laboratory at the Institute of Theoretical and Experimental Physics. Initial research on X-ray analysis and physics was followed by investigations of radioactivity and radiation. In collaboration with his brother A. I. Alikhanyan, A established the law governing the interrelation of β spectra and the atomic number of an element (1935), investigated cosmic rays (1939) which led to the discovery of unstable mesons, and has been working on nuclear reactors in recent years. Codesigner of the first Soviet reactor with a heavy-water inhibitor. Author of *Investigation of Artificial Radioactivity* (1936); *Cosmic Rays* (1939); *Modern Problems of Science and Technology* (1949). Stalin prizes (1941, 1948).

ALIMONY: *see* FAMILY LAW.

ALLIED INTERVENTION: *see* CIVIL WAR, HISTORY.

ALLILÚYEVA, Nadézhda Sergéyevna (1901–1932), Stalin's second wife. Born in Baku, A was the daughter of an old Bolshevik whose St. Petersburg apartment was Lenin's hiding place in 1917. She married Stalin in 1919 and bore him two children, Vasily and Svetlana. During the 1930's, she allegedly intervened with her husband in favor of those of her friends involved in opposition activities. A's sudden death in Nov. 1932 is attributed to either suicide or perhaps to murder.

ALMÁ-ATÁ (f. Verny), capital of Kazakh SSR, at the foot of Trans-Ili Alatau ridge; 2,300–2,900 ft. above sea level; pop. 45,000 (1926), 222,000 (1939), 456,000 (1959). Machine building, food processing, apple orchards. Seat of the Kazakh Ac. of S.; numerous schools of higher education, conservatoire, theaters. Founded 1854. In 1887 and 1910 there were serious earthquakes. Was the place of Trotsky's exile in 1925. Many sanatoriums in the picturesque environs.

ALMÁ-ATÁ OBLAST, in S.E. Kazakh SSR; area 87,850 sq. mi.; pop. 1,403,000 (1960): Kazakhs, Russians, Uygurs, and others. Cities: Alma-Ata (adm. center), Taldy-Kurgan. Rivers: Ili and its tributaries; Karatal. Severe continental climate in the N., milder in the S. Agr.: wheat, barley, millet, oats, corn, sugar beet, tobacco; orchards and vineyards, also cattle, sheep and horse raising. Ind.: machine building, food processing, woodworking. Est. 1932. In 1959 absorbed Taldy-Kurgan Oblast.

ALMÉTYEVSK, city in Tatar ASSR, RSFSR; pop. 37,500 (1956). Center of important new oil fields with oil and natural gas pipelines to Perm and Gorky.

ALPHABET. The Russian A is derived from the Cyrillic A, supposedly invented by St. Cyril in the ninth century. In 1708, Peter I decreed the separation of church and secular script and gave the latter (the so-called "civic" or "lay" A) a new, less-ornate graphic design based on the contemporary Latin "Antiqua"

RUSSIAN ALPHABET

Printed	Written	Pronounced approximately as	Names of the letters
А а	*Аа*	a in father	a
Б б	*Бб*	b in book	be
В в	*Вв*	v in vote	ve
Г г	*Гг*	g in good	ge
Д д	*Дд*	d in day	de
Е е	*Ее*	ye in yes	ye
Ё ё	*Ёё*	yo in yonder	yo
Ж ж	*Жж*	zh in pleasure	zhe
З з	*Зз*	z in zone	ze
И и	*Ии*	ee in meet	ee
Й й	*Йй*	y in boy	short ee
К к	*Кк*	k in kind	ka
Л л	*Лл*	l in lamp	el
М м	*Мм*	m in man	em
Н н	*Нн*	n in note	en
О о	*Оо*	o in shawl	o
П п	*Пп*	p in pen	pe
Р р	*Рр*	r in red	er
С с	*Сс*	s in speak	es
Т т	*Тт*	t in too	te
У у	*Уу*	oo in book	oo
Ф ф	*Фф*	f in fire	ef
Х х	*Хх*	kh in "loch"	kha
Ц ц	*Цц*	ts in cats	tse
Ч ч	*Чч*	ch in chair	che
Ш ш	*Шш*	sh in short	sha
Щ щ	*Щщ*	shch	shcha
Ъ ъ	*ъ*	—	"hard" sign
Ы ы	*ы*	y in story	yerý
Ь ь	*ь*	—	"soft" sign
Э э	*Ээ*	e in men	reversed "e"
Ю ю	*Юю*	u in university	yoo
Я я	*Яя*	ya in yard	ya

Additional Ukrainian letters: є, і, ї, ґ.
Additional Byelorussian letters: і, ў.

typeface. After undergoing several reforms, the Russian A now consists of 33 letters (10 vowels, 20 consonants, 1 semivowel, and 2 special signs). It serves as a basis for the languages of the USSR, except Estonian, Karelian (Finnish), Latvian, and Lithuanian, which use the Latin A with some special diacritical marks. Also the Georgian and Armenian languages have their own traditional alphabets. For languages that had previously used the Arabic A (Azerbaijan, Tadzhik, Tatar, Turkmen, Uzbek, and others) the latter was replaced in the late 1930's or early 1940's by an A based on Latin and, then, on Russian script. The Russian A is also used in Bulgaria, Serbia, and Outer Mongolia.

ALTÁY, mountain system in S.W. Siberia and Mongolia. Highest peak Belukha (14,780 ft.). Source of Irtysh and Ob rivers, traversed by Ob tributaries: Katun, Biya, Chulyshman, Bukhtarma. Large lakes: Teletskoye, Markakol. Rich nonferrous metals deposits.

ALTÁY KRAY of RSFSR, includes Gorno-Altay Autonomous Oblast; area 101,000 sq. mi.; pop. 2,685,000 (1959). Cities: Barnaul (center), Biysk, Gorno-Altaysk, Rubtsovsk, Slavgorod. Encompasses most of Altay covered with forests in the S., and fertile forest-steppe in the N.; drains into the upper Ob and its tributaries; sharply continental climate. Minerals are: salt in steppes, nonferrous metals and gold in the mountains. Wheat, barley, animal breeding, hunting; tractor and machine building, foodstuffs, flour mills, dairy products. Several institutions of higher education, museums; resorts.

ALUMINUM INDUSTRY. Production of aluminum in 1955 is estimated at about 520,000 tons, (as compared with 1,725,000 tons in the United States in the same year, 556,000 tons in Canada, and 230,000 tons in W. Germany). The first aluminum plants in the USSR —the Volkhov plant near Leningrad (1932) and that at Zaporozhye (1933)—employed bauxite from the Tikhvin deposits and produced 57,000 tons of aluminum in 1938. Additional facilities were subsequently built at Kamensk-Uralsk (Chelyabinsk Oblast), at Kemerovo (Siberia), and at Krasnoturyinsk (Urals). The growth of aluminum production was particularly rapid after 1945.

PRODUCTION OF ALUMINUM
IN THE USSR
(tons)

1933	7,000
1938	57,000
1939	50,000
1950	200,000
1958	520,000

P. I. M.

ALÚPKA, resort on S. Crimean coast, Ukrainian SSR; 10.5 mi. from Yalta; pop. 8,200 (1956). Sanatoriums, beaches, grape cures.

ALÚSHTA, city in Crimean Oblast, Ukrainian SSR; resort, 27 mi. from Yalta; pop. 9,300 (1956). Sanatoriums, beaches, grape cures.

ALYÁBYEV, Aleksándr Aleksándrovich (1787–1851), composer, author of more than 150 songs, operas, symphonies, and other works. Typical subjects of his lyrics are: elegy, homesickness, compassion. Well known is the romance *Nightingale* (lyrics by A. A. Delvig). A had great influence on the development of R. chamber music (his quartets and trios).

AMBARTSUMYÁN, Víktor Amazáspovich (1908–), astrophysicist. Fellow, Ac. of S., USSR (1953); vice president (1943–47), president (1947), Armenian Ac. of S. Fellow and honorary member of several foreign Ac. of S. and scientific societies. Graduate (1928) and professor (1934–46) of Leningrad University. Professor and head of the Astrophysical Department, Yerevan University (1947). Director, Byurakan Astronomical Observatory (1946). Vice president, International Union of Astronomers (1948–55). Research concerns the interstallar absorption of light, the luminance of interstallar substance, methods of calculating the mass ejected by newly formed stars. Author of *Dispersion and Absorption of Light in the Atmospheres of Planets* (1941); *Evolution of Stars and Astrophysics* (1947); *Star System* (1949). Stalin prizes (1946, 1950), numerous orders and medals.

AMBÓDIK-MAKSIMÓVICH, Néstor Maksímovich (1744–1812), scientist; one of the founders of obstetrics, botanics, and phytotherapy in Russia. As professor in the St. Petersburg School of Obstetrics A-M modified and improved the teaching of obstetrics. Introduced the application of forceps. Author of a manual of obstetrics, *The Art of Midwifery* (1784–86), which is considered the foremost 18th-century book on the subject; and *Principles of Botany*.

AMFITEÁTROV, Aleksándr Valentínovich (1862–1938), journalist and popular columnist in prerevolutionary newspapers. In 1902 was exiled for publishing in the newspaper *Rossiya* a piece entitled "The Obmanovs" (from *obman*, deceit), a satire on the tsar and his entourage. In 1905 A went abroad where he published the revolutionary magazine *Krasny Flag* (Red Flag). On his return to Russia he was the editor of the newspaper *Russkaya Svoboda* (Russian Freedom). After the revolution A emigrated, and wrote anti-communist articles. His principal books are *Maria Luseva* (1904), *Those of the Eighties* (1907–08), *Those of the Nineties* (1910), and the play *Poisoned Conscience*.

AMGÁ RIVER, in Yakut ASSR, left tributary of Aldan; 1,000 mi. long; navigable in its lower course.

AMGÚN RIVER, in Khabarovsk Kray, RSFSR, left tributary of the Amur; length 450 mi.; partly navigable.

AMTÓRG (Amtorg Trading Corporation), founded in 1924 in New York to conduct trade with the U.S., with an initial capital of $1,000,000, subsequently raised to $3,000,000. Its shareholders were Soviet import- and export-trade organizations, and its headquarters were in Moscow. Was very active before and during World War II; later its activities declined. The company performs the same functions as trade delegations in other countries but does not enjoy their official or diplomatic status.

AMÚ DARYÁ (ancient *Oxus*), river in Central Asia, source in Hindu Kush, flows into Aral Sea. Length 1,577 mi.; tributaries: Gunt, Bartang, Murgab, Vakhsh, Kunduz. Its basin is important as a source of irrigation for Uzbekistan, Turkmenistan, and Tadzhikistan. Navigable between city of Chardzhou and the sea; main landings: Chardzhou, Farab, Turtkul, Khodzheyli. Rich in fish and minerals.

AMÚR, GULF OF, N.W. part of the Gulf of Peter the Great (Sea of Japan). On its E. shore is the port of Vladivostok.

AMÚR OBLAST, in RSFSR; area 140,400 sq. mi.; pop. 717,000 (1959). Cities: Blagoveshchensk (adm. center), Belogorsk, Raychikhinsk, Svobodny, Zeya, Skovorodino, Shimanovsk. Main rivers: Amur, Zeya, Bureya, Selemdzha. A considerable part of the territory is in Zeya-Bureya lowlands, but is mountainous in N.E. and S.E., with 50 per cent of the area covered with forests; summer is hot and humid, winter cold. It is the granary of Far East, with its wheat, oats, potatoes, soybeans. Ind.: metalworking, food, building materials; coal, gold, iron ore.

AMÚR REGION (R. *Priamúrye*), large area in Khabarovsk Kray and in Amur Oblast. It is transected by two systems of ranges: in the W. by Tukuringra and Dzhagdy; and in the E. by the Bureya ranges. Between these two systems lies the Zeya-Bureya plain where the so-called Amur steppes are located. There are many rare animals and birds. The population consists mainly of Russians, Ukrainians, Evenki (Tungus). The mineral resources include gold and lignite. There is some agr. in the S. and hunting and fishing in the N.

AMÚR RIVER (Chinese *Hei-lung-kiang*), in E. Asia, formed by confluence of the Shilka and Argun rivers, flows into Tatar Strait; borders on China; length 2,700 mi.; in a fertile valley. Its chief tributaries are: Sungari, Ussuri, Zeya, Bureya, Amgun; is navigable, with main landings at Blagoveshchensk, Khabarovsk, Komsomolsk, Nikolayevsk. Has important fisheries (salmon, humpback).

AMVRÓSIEVKA, town in Stalino Oblast, Ukrainian SSR; pop. 20,200 (1956); major center of cement industry; industrial technical school.

ANABÁR RIVER, in Yakut ASSR, length 574 mi. Its valley is in the tundra area; has considerable fisheries.

ANADÝR, GULF OF, in N.W. part of Bering Sea, up to 250 mi. wide; incorporates the Bay of Holy Cross (Svyatoy Krest) and the Anadyr estuary.

ANADÝR RANGE, mountains in N.E. Asia, in the Chukchi National Okrug; altitudes up to 5,750 ft.; highest peak 7,600 ft.

ANADÝR RIVER, in Chukchi National Okrug of Magadan Oblast, RSFSR; falls into Bering Sea; length 693 mi., 300 mi. navigable.

ANÁPA, city in Krasnodar Kray, RSFSR; health resort on the Black Sea; pop. 16,700 (1956).

ANARCHISTS. The anarchist movement in Russia was inspired by the doctrines of M. A. Bakunin (1814–76), P. A. Kropotkin (1842–1921), and L. N. Tolstoy (1828–1910). The Bakuninists opposed parliamentarianism and the concept of a republic. They sought to bring about a socialist revolution and to establish a federation of free workers in agriculture, the crafts, and factories. P. A. Kropotkin advocated a federation of communes representing associations of small producers. The religious anarchism of L. N. Tolstoy not only opposed the concept of government but advocated the Christian idea of nonresistance to evil through force.

A variety of anarchist groupings existed during the period of the first and second revolutions (1905 and 1917). They included Syndicalists, "Black-banner Bearers," "Makhayevists," "Makhnovists," and "Anarchists of the Underground." With the exception of the followers of Kropotkin, of the "Makhayevists," and, of course, of the followers of Tolstoy, all other groupings made use of terroristic methods in their activities. The principal centers of anarchist activity in Russia were Belostok (1903–04), Odessa, Warsaw, and Yekaterinoslav. After 1905, groups of A were also formed in St. Petersburg, Moscow, Kiev, and Riga, as well as in the Caucasus and in the Urals. In 1906 and 1907, a wave of anarchistic "expropriations" (armed robberies) swept over Russia. In 1907 a "Militant International Group of Anarchist-Communists" was active in the south of the country.

The anarchist publications included the journal *Khleb i Volya* (Bread and Freedom) (Geneva, 1903–04) and *Listki Khleba i Voli* (Sheets on Bread and Freedom) (1906–07) which reflected the Kropotkin position, and the journal *Buntar* (The Rebel) (1908) which was published in the Crimea. The leaders of the various branches of the anarchist movement at the time of the revolution of 1905 included I. Vetrov, Novomirsky, Grossman-Roshchin, Borovoy, and Rogdayev. A prominent position among its ideological leaders was held by Makhaysky, who was the author, under the pseudonym of "Volsky," of a book directed against the intelligentsia entitled *The Intellectual Worker*. Among the outstanding anarchist speakers of this period one should mention Bleikhman, who was particularly known in Kronstadt. Closely related to the A was a grouping of the Maximalists that had been associated, at first, with the Socialist Revolutionary party. The leaders of this group, which committed acts of terror, among them the "expropriation" of the Moscow Mutual Credit Society (1905) and an attempt on the life of Stolypin (Aug. 1906), were M. N. Sokolov ("The Bear") and V. Mazurin. The ideological leaders of the Maximalists were E. Ma-gin, and Engelhart.

After the October revolution a split occurred among the A, some of whom joined the Bolsheviks. A number of prominent A came to Moscow from abroad. They included A. Berkman and Emma Goldman from the United States, but they were disappointed in the Bolsheviks. Although some A were pro-Soviet, as early as during the civil war the "All-Russian Organization of Underground Anarchists" was established, which in 1919 was responsible for the explosion of a bomb at a communist meeting in Moscow in the Leontyevsky Passage. Subsequently (in 1921) this organization was routed by the Soviet security police and its leaders were shot.

A special place in the R. anarchist movement is held by Nestor Makhno (q.v.). In 1918–21 he organized military units in the Ukraine whose operations extended from the town of Gulyay-Pole to various parts of the Yekaterinoslav, Poltava, and Kharkov provinces. They published two newspapers, *Put k Svobode* (Path to Freedom) and *Nabat* (The Tocsin). The aim of Makhno's movement was the establishment of free communes in the form of soviets. During their occupation of cities, however (e.g., Yekaterinoslav), pogroms against Jews took place, and Makhno's detachments came to be regarded as bandits rather than as units of a political movement. Although they fought behind the lines of the White armies during the civil war, their guerrilla units fought the Bolsheviks as well.

BIBLIOGRAPHY: V. M. Eichenbaum (Voline), *Nineteen Seventeen* (The Russian Revolution Betrayed), New York, 1954.

G. A.

ANASTASIA (Grand Duchess Anastasia Nikolayevna), youngest daughter of the last emperor of Russia, Nicholas II, was born in 1901 and was, it is believed, murdered together with the other members of the Imperial family in 1918. From 1920, a Mrs. Chaykovsky, whose name in 1928 was changed to Anna Anderson, claimed to be A and described a fantastic escape; her story, believed by some, was rejected by a court in Hamburg, Germany, in May 1961.

ANDI RANGE, N. part of the main Caucasus Mountain Range in Georgian SSR and Dagestan ASSR. Watershed of Terek and Andi Koysu rivers; its peak, Tebulos-Mta, is 14,760 ft. high.

ANDIZHÁN, city in Uzbek SSR; pop. 129,000 (1959). Cotton processing, butter, fruit canneries, silk; tractor parts, road-building machinery, mechanical repair shops. Pedag. inst.; agricultural technical school. Settled in 9th century.

ANDIZHÁN OBLAST, in Uzbek SSR; lies in Fergana valley; area 2,470 sq. mi.; pop. 1,163,000 (1960). Cities: Andizhan (adm. center), Leninsk. Fertile soil, hot, dry summer, mild winter, is main cotton-growing area; also important in oil production. Agr. depends on irrigation, with crops of cotton (70%), rice, vineyards; cotton processing, butter, foods, oil refining and natural gas. Increased in 1960 by parts of Namangan Oblast.

ANDRÉY BOGOLYÚBSKY, the prince of Suzdal (1111–1174), grand duke of Vladimir (capital of Suzdal). He fought against feudal separatism of local nobility, strengthened his power with the help of the cities, and subordinated Kiev in 1169. Was killed by boyar plotters.

ANDRÉYEV, Andréy Andréyevich (1895–), party and government official, and a trade-union leader in

the 1920's. He was a party member since 1914 and active participant in the October revolution. Member of the Politburo since 1932, he was active in the fight against the Trotsky and Zinoviev opposition. From 1939 to 1952 he was chairman of the Central Committee's Control Commission; from 1943 to 1946 commissar of agriculture, from 1946 to 1953, deputy chairman, USSR Council of Ministers and chairman of the Kolkhoz Affairs Council. He was removed from the Politburo in 1952, being blamed for the failures of agriculture and attacked for permitting decentralization of work brigades on the kolkhoz. In the post-Stalin reorganization, however, he was elected to the Supreme Soviet Presidium and Central Committee. In March 1953 he was elected head of the Presidium Commission to Review Cases of Those Sentenced during the Stalinist

purges. Since 1957, he has been chairman of the Society for Soviet-Chinese friendship.

ANDRÉYEV, Leoníd Nikoláyevich (1871–1919), short story writer, novelist, and playwright. Born in

Orel, he studied law in St. Petersburg and Moscow; painted portraits in order to support himself; graduated as a lawyer. Having lost his first case in the court, he gave up law and worked as newspaper reporter. He published short stories in Orel papers; supported by Gorky he rapidly gained fame. Author of realistic stories (*In the Fog*, 1902, *The Governor*, 1906, *Seven That Were Hanged*, 1908), he turned to symbolism and allegory (*Red Laugh*, 1904, and *King Hunger*, 1907). An atheist and pessimist, he laid stress on death and sex in his stories and depicted everything else as delusion, thus reflecting the state of mind that prevailed in Russia after the failure of the Revolution of 1905. Other known stories and plays of his are: *Thought* (1902); *Lazarus* (1906); *Judas Iscariot* (1907); *The Life of Man* (1906); *Sashka Zhigulyov* (1910); *He Who Gets Slapped* (1914). During World War I he waged a vigorous anti-German campaign; later he bitterly opposed the Bolshevik revolution. He died in exile in a small village in Finland.

ANDRÉYEV, Nikoláy Nikoláyevich (1880–), physicist. Fellow, Ac. of S., USSR (1953). Graduated from Basel University (1909). Head of Acoustic Laboratory, Leningrad Electrophysical Institute (1926); professor and head of Chair of Acoustics, Leningrad Polytechnic Institute (1940), and Acoustic Institute (1953). Honorary degree from Dresden Polytechnic Institute. Member of the executive board of the International Acoustic Commission. Founder of the school of Soviet acousticians. Extensive research in acoustics, thermodynamics, electrodynamics, and wave mechanics. Author of *Airplane Noise and Its Suppression* (1942); *Hearing Organs of Insects* (1955). Three Lenin orders, Order of the Red Banner of Labor, and other medals.

ANDRIÁNOV, Kuzmá Andriánovich (1904–), chemist. Corresponding member, Ac. of S., USSR (1953). Graduated from Moscow University (1930). Joined the All-Union Institute of Electrical Engineering (1930) and the Institute of Organic Compounds (1954). Professor at the Institute of Power Engineering in Moscow (1946). Research concerns compounds of high-molecular weight, especially silicoorganic compounds. Developed new polymers (1947) and heat-resistant insulating material. Author of *Heat-Resistant Silicoorganic Dielectrics* (1957). Stalin prizes (1943, 1946, 1950).

ANDRIÁNOV, Vasíly Mikháylovich (1902–), party and government official; linked to Malenkov's rise and fall. He was first secretary of the Leningrad Party Committee, and elected to the Central Committee Presidium at the 19th Party Congress in 1952, but was dropped in the post-Stalin reorganization. He was publicly disgraced by Khrushchev and not re-elected to the Central Committee in 1956.

ANDRÓNOV, Aleksándr Aleksándrovich (1901–1952), physicist. Fellow, Ac. of S., USSR (1946). Deputy to the Supreme Soviet (1946, 1950). Graduated from Moscow University and taught at Gorky University (1931). Mathematically substantiated the theory of self-induced vibrations and solved important non-linear problems of theoretical radio engineering, automatic control. *Collected Works,* 1956.

ANDRÚSOV, Nikolay Ivánovich (1861–1924). Geologist, paleontologist. Fellow, Ac. of S. (1914). Graduated from Novorossiysk University in Odessa (1884). Professor of Kiev University (1905). His studies were concerned with the stratigraphy and paleontology of the Neogene system of the Pontocaspian basin. Participated in expeditions to the Black Sea and Sea of Marmara. His discovery of Post-Tertial fauna and hydrogen sulfide on the sea bottom is described in a monograph which earned him the M. V. Lomonosov prize (1897).

ANDRÚSOVO, ARMISTICE OF, between Russia and Poland concluding the war for the domination of the Ukraine (1654–1667). The Ukraine on the left bank of the Dnieper, Kiev, Smolensk and Seversk lands became Russian. The armistice was ratified by the 1686 treaty.

ANGARÁ, two rivers in Siberia: **(1)** Angara proper (in lower course Upper Tunguska) flows from Lake Baykal into Yenisey River; length 1,140 mi.; navigable only from source to Bratsk and from rapids to Yenisey; main landings: Irkutsk, Makaryevo, Zayarsk. Hydroelectric power station. **(2)** Upper Angara flows into Baykal; length 397 mi.

ANGÁRSK, city in Irkutsk Oblast, RSFSR; pop. 134,000 (1959); founded after World War II; important petroleum-refining and chemical center.

ANGLO-RUSSIAN ENTENTE, signed on Aug. 31, 1907 in St. Petersburg by both powers uneasy about German expansionist policy in the Near East. In a compromise of interests in Persia, England and Russia divided spheres of interest (Persian Gulf and the N., respectively). The agreement was a link in the *Entente Cordiale* between England, France, and Russia.

ANGRÉN, city in Tashkent Oblast, Uzbek SSR; pop. 55,000 (1959). The largest center of coal mining developed after World War II in Central Asia.

ANIMAL LIFE of the USSR is varied and abundant. There are about 300 species of mammals, 703 of birds, 128 of reptiles, about 1,500 fishes, of which 528 are fresh-water or transitory species. There are: 9 forms of Cyclostomata, 127 of Urochorda, 410 of Echinoderms, 465 of Bryozoa among which 27 are fresh-water forms, 2,000 mollusks of which 600 are terrestrial, 470 fresh-water, and 1,100 salt-water species; 80–90 thousand insects among which there are 20 thousand Diptera, 6,480 Hymenoptera, 8,500 Lepidoptera, about 600 Trichoptera, 2,000 Coleoptera, about 2,000 Hemiptera, 500–600 Coccidae, 800 Orthoptera, about 200 Ephemeridae, 200 Odonata; 5,000 Arachnida of which there are 2,500 mites, 2,000 spiders, 3,500 Pantopoda, 70 Tardigrada, 72 Phalangida, 15 Solpugida, and 12 scorpions; about 300 Crustaceae; 1,100 Annelida of which there are about 750 Polychaeta, 300 Oligochaeta, 100 earthworms, 60 leeches; more than 80 species of ribbon worms, of which about 115 forms are Acanthocephala, 550 Rotifera, 100 hairworms, and 1,000 Nematoda; 2,000 species of Plathelminthes; 500 Coelenterata; 400 sponges, a large number of Protozoa, and more than 100 species which belong to the smaller groups of animals. Altogether the number of known animal species found on the territory of the USSR amounts to 100,000–110,000.

There is a definite relation between the distribution of the animals and the natural regions of the country.

THE ANIMAL WORLD OF THE NATURAL REGIONS

The Northern Islands, the N. part of European Russia, and the N. part of Siberia and of the Pacific Ocean are inhabited by the shore birds and by mammals which stay on the land only during the breeding season. Common seals, arctic ringed seals, and bearded seals are common in this region. Among the birds guillemots and eiders are the best known.

There are two N. regions with more or less different faunas: the W. which comprises the N. Atlantic and the Barents Sea; and the E., which comprises the N. of the Pacific Ocean, the Bering Sea, and part of the Okhotsk Sea and is known for its rich bird fauna. Greenland seals, gray seals, razorbills, and dovekies are usual in the W. region. White bears, walruses, and gulls (rosa's gull, ivory gull, and sabine gull) are common on the coasts of Siberia. Striped seals, Steller's sea lions, sea bears, Kamchatka beavers are abundant in the E. region. Some birds, such as horned puffins, Rhinoceros auklets, tufted puffins, ancient murrelets, and auklets (*Aethia pygmaea, Ae. cristatella,* and *Ae. pusilla*), form large communities on the cliffs during the breeding season.

FAUNA OF NORTHERN ISLANDS: 1. Kittiwake (Rissa tridactyla). 2. Glaucous gull (Larus hyperboreus). 3. Brünnich's murre (Uria lomvia). 4. Dovekie. 5. Guillemot. 6. Ancient murrelet. 7. Puffin (Fratercula corniculata). 8. Tufted puffin. 9. Puffin (Cyclorrhynchus psittacula). 10. Small auklet. 11. Large auklet. 12. Short-tailed gull (Stercorarius parasiticus). 13. Fulmar (Fulmarus glacialis). 14. Bering cormorant. 15. Eiders. 16. Beaver. 17. Common seal. 18. Auklet (Aethia pusilla). 19. Steller's sea lion. 20. Walrus. 21. Greenland seal. 22. Striped seal. 23. Sea bear.

In the **Tundra** the fauna is limited in species. Wolves, arctic foxes, ermines, arctic hares, lemmings (Norwegian, *L. obensis,* and *Dicrostonyx torquatus*), gray field mice (*Microtus*), two species of northern deer, and toward the E. long-tailed marmots are the common mammals. Among the birds the most typical are: partridges (*Lagopus mutus* and *L. lagopus*), snow buntings, horned larks, Lapland longspurs, rough-legged hawks, arctic owls, and also fresh-water fowl, such as geese (different barnacle geese: white-fronted, small one, black, Canadian, and red-breasted; white goose, white-fronted goose, *Anser erythropus,* brant, *Chen caerulescens,* and bean goose), swans, and a few ducks. Reptiles and amphibians are absent except in the southernmost part of the tundra, where common vipers, viviparous lizards, and frogs (*Rana temporaria* and *R. terrestris*) are found. Invertebrates are limited in species. There are a few hundred species of moths. Sawflies and bumblebees predominate among the Hymenoptera. The most common beetles belong to the families of rove beetles, ground beetles, and water beetles. Gnats, mosquitoes, deer flies, and other suckers are extremely numerous.

In the **Forested Tundra** the fauna is not specific and consists of animals which penetrate from the neighboring tundra and the tayga.

The Forested Zone occupies a vast territory which may be divided into three regions: tayga, western broadleaf forests, and far eastern broadleaf forests (the Amur, the Ussuri, and Manchuria).

FAUNA OF THE TAYGA: 1. Great, gray owl. 2. Bohemian waxwing. 3. Cross bill (Loxia curvirostra). 4. Cross bill. 5. Squirrel. 6. Sable. 7. Chipmunk. 8. Woodpecker (Picoides tridactylus). 9. Black woodpecker (Dryocopus martius). 10. Long-tailed owl (Strix uralensis). 11. Siberian jay. 12. Common capercaillie. 13. Wood hen. 14. Nutcracker. 15. Flying squirrel. 16. Red deer. 17. Red meadow mouse. 18. Elk. 19. Musk deer. 20. Siberian roe deer. 21. Lynx. 22. Siberian weasel. 23. Brown bear. 24. Glutton. 25. Hare. 26. Boreal owl. 27. Hawk owl. 28. Sparrow owl (Glaucidium passerinum).

The fauna of the tayga is spread over the territory of Siberia, some areas in the Far E., and in the N. of European Russia. The mammals are quite numerous: brown bears, lynxes, sables, gluttons, arctic hares, flying squirrels, chipmunks, a few species of field mice (Siberian red-backed mouse—*Clethrionomys rutilus,* and *C. rufocanus*), forest lemmings, elks, northern reindeer; to the E. of the Yenisey and on the Altay musk deer are well known. Red deer, Siberian roe deer, and weasels (*Mustela sibirica*) are limited to the S. edge of the tayga. Among the birds the common capercaillies, wood hens, crossbills, Clark's nutcrackers, Bohemian waxwings, Siberian jays, Boreal owls, *Glaucidium passerinum,* great gray owls, Uralian owls, hawk owls, black woodpeckers, and three-toed woodpeckers are the most abundant. Reptiles and amphibians are

scarce, only viviparous lizards, common vipers, Siberian four-toed salamanders, Siberian grass frogs (*Rana chensinensis* and *R. terrestris*) occur in the tayga. This region is richer in insects than the tundra. Flies are quite numerous, among them the crane flies, fungus gnats, and different suckers which annoy men and animals. Geometridae and Notodontidae prevail among the moths. Hymenoptera, especially sawflies, and also plant lice, beetles (usually timber destroyers—Ipidae) are very abundant. There are only a few species of true bugs and grasshoppers, but more spiders than in any other zone. The fauna in Kamchatka and on Sakhalin is poorer; many species that are common in the tayga are absent here.

FAUNA OF THE WESTERN BROADLEAF FORESTS: 1. Squirrel. 2. Dormouse (Muscardinus avellanarius). 3. Garden dormouse. 4. Reindeer. 5. Oriole. 6. Green woodpecker. 7. Western nightingale. 8. Forest cat. 9. Forest dormouse (Dyromys nitedula). 10. Dormouse "polchock". 11. Forest marten. 12. Grosbeak. 13. European roe deer. 14. Chloris chloris. 15. Gray owl. 16. Tree frog. 17. Wild boar. 18. Green lizard. 19. Mink. 20. Slow worm. 21. Smooth snake. 22. Bison. 23. Blue titmouse. 24. Black polecat (Mustela putorius). 25. Black thrush (Turdus merula).

The western broadleaf forests occupy the territory between the Gulf of Finland, S. Urals, and Moldavia. Wild boars, bison, European roe deer, small otters, common martens, forest cats, yellow field mice (*Clethrionomys glareolus*), yellow-breasted mice (*Apodemus flavicollis*), and dormice (*Glis glis, Dyromys nitedula, Eliomys quercinus,* and *Muscardinus avellanarius*) are common mammals of this region. Green finches, green woodpeckers, middle spotted woodpeckers, orioles, blue titmice, and gray owls predominate among the birds. Slowworms, green lizards, smooth snakes, *Elaphe longissima* (snake), and swamp turtles (*Emys orbicularis*) are the best known reptiles. Tree frogs, pond frogs, grass frogs, *Rana terrestris,* and red-bellied frogs prevail among the amphibians; in the Caspian region yellow-bellied frogs, toads (*Bombina bombina* and *B. variegata*), and newts, and in the W. Carpathian Mountains spotted salamanders. The insect fauna is richer than in the tayga, but with similar species.

The fauna of the far eastern broadleaf forests occupies the basin of the Ussuri, the lower Amur, S. Sakhalin, and the S. islands of the Kuril archipelago. Northern species, such as elk, musks, sables, brown bears, white hares, chipmunks, flying squirrels, and southern species: yellow-throated martens, black bears, far eastern forest cats (*Felis euptilura*), some Manchurian and Manchurian-Chinese species are found there. Spotted deer, gorals, red wolves, raccoons, tigers, panthers, Manchurian hares, and Ussurian moles are also common. The bird fauna consists mostly of pheasants, Chinese orioles, minivets, mandarin ducks, mergansers, broad-billed rollers, and blue magpies. Chinese soft-shelled turtles, long-tailed lizards, tiger adders, Japanese adders, and Amurian boas are common reptiles; the far eastern tree frogs and Ussurian clawed newts are common amphibians. Insects are numerous and colorful. The most characteristic of this region are, among the Lepidoptera: the Sericinus, Leuhdorfia, Notodontidae, tropical Uraniidae, Epicopidae, the blue Indian swallowtail butterflies, and the Luna moths. Some of them are strictly limited to this region. Mosquitoes, usually Megarrhinus, are very abundant. Plautia and Lelia represent the Hemiptera, and among the beetles the beautiful Cerambicidae, *Callipogon relictus* is really remarkable. Some Arachnids, as Pedipalpi are typical only of S. Asia.

FAUNA OF THE FAR EASTERN BROADLEAF FORESTS: 1. Leopard (Panthera pardus). 2. Minivet. 3. Chipmunk. 4. Sable. 5. Far-Eastern frog. 6. Ussurian mole. 7. Raccoon. 8. Owl (Ketupa ceylonensis). 9. Black headed jay. 10. Broad billed roller. 11. Spotted deer. 12. European whip snake. 13. Manchurian hare. 14. Hawk (Butastur indicus). 15. Mandarin duck. 16. Amurian badger. 17. Far-Eastern forest cat. 18. Long tailed lizard (Tachydromus amurensis). 19. Ussurian tiger. 20. Weasel. 21. Yellow-throated marten. 22. Ussurian pheasant. 23. Clawed newt. 24. Goral. 25. Merganser. 26. Hamster (Cricetulus triton). 27. Red wolf. 28. Soft-shelled turtle. 29. Black bear.

The Amur-Ussurian fauna of the forests consists of relic species, which lived before the glacial period, and of newcomers, which sought shelter in the S. from the advancing ice. The influence of the glacial period was much stronger in Europe and in W. Siberia; and as a result, quite a few species which lived during the preglacial period, and managed to survive, are now living in widely separated areas.

Some species, as the Japanese field mice, far eastern skinks, and three species of boa (*Elaphe*), penetrated to S. Sakhalin and the Kuril islands from Japan.

In the **Forested Steppe** the fauna is not specific, the animals here being from the forests and steppes.

The Steppes have not many species, yet there are more animals in Asia, where they originated and from which they spread over the territory of Europe. Because of the cultivation of the land the fauna has been completely changed. Hares, partridges, quails, and marsh harriers are moving to the N. into the forest zone, and even into the tayga.

Saigas, hares, mouse hares, bobacs, hamsters, Siberian marmots (*Citellus pygmeus, C. erythrogenys, C. major, C. fulvus*), jerboas (large jerboa, and three-toed sand jerboa), mole rats, and short-tailed steppe voles are characteristic animals of the European-Kazakhstan steppes. Bustards, kestrels, steppe eagles, imperial eagles, cranes, Calandra larks, short-toed larks, white-winged and black larks, black-winged pratincoles, social plovers, also some water fowl, such as ducks (ruddy duck and red-crested pochard), a few herons (glossy ibis and *N. nycticorax*), and sandpipers (avocet and stilt sandpiper) breed and live in the steppes. Steppe vipers, European whip snakes, and quick lizards are well-known reptiles. Amphibians, because of the dry climate, are not abundant; green toads and garlic toads (Pelobates) are more common. Locusts are extremely numerous and destructive to the crops. Hymenoptera are represented by wasps, two species of ants, and Tenthredinoidea. Weevils, ground beetles, Scarabaeidae, and especially darkling beetles are usually found in great numbers. Flies are also abundant. The fauna is much poorer in the steppes of Minusinsk. The Transbaykalia steppe has a much dryer climate and a different fauna, with the same species as in Mongolia. Mongolian serens, Mongolian marmots, hares (*Lepus tolai*), Daurian mouse hares, Mongolian field mice, and many birds, such as Mongolian larks, occur in this steppe. The Mongolian lizards are also common.

The steppe and desert species live together in the semidesert.

FAUNA OF THE STEPPE: 1. Hamster (Cricetus cricetus). 2. Blind mole-rat (Spalax microphthalmus). 3. Hare. 4. Bustard. 5. Short-tailed steppe vole. 6. Birch mouse (Sicista subtilis). 7. Bobac. 8. Steppe viper. 9. Steppe mouse-hare. 10. Calandra lark. 11. Black lark. 12. Large jerboa. 13. Three-toed sand jerboa. 14. Saiga. 15. Small marmot. 16. Steppe polecat. 17. Crane. 18. Great bustard. 19. Flat-tailed jerboa (Pygerethmus platyurus). 20. Marmot (Citellus erythrogenys). 21. Vormela peregusna. 22. European whip snake. 23. Spotted marmot. 24. Steppe eagle. 25. Marmot (Citellus major). 26. Yellow marmot (Citellus fulvus). 27. Wolf. 28. Wild ass. 29. Shrew. 30. Blind mole-rat (Ellobius talpinus). 31. Corsac fox. 32. Common fox. 33. Wild horse.

The Desert Region occupies the plains of Central Asia, including S. Kazakhstan and the Caspian lowland. Here the fauna is well adapted to the severe conditions of the desert: high temperature in summer and low in winter, absence of water and poor vegetation.

Goitered gazelles, wild asses (now rare), wild cats (*Felis caracal*), velvet cats (*F. margarita*), spotted cats (*F. libyca*), *Vormela peregusna, Gerbillinae,* jerboas, and long-toed sand marmots are typical animals. Pander's chough thrushes, desert crows, Macqueen's bustards, haloxylon sparrows, desert sparrows, and desert warblers are characteristic birds. Among the many reptiles, the best-known are toadheads, R. house agamas, giant desert monitor lizards, sand geckos, arrow snakes, steppe pythons, carpet vipers, blunt-nosed vipers, and steppe turtles. Amphibians are rare and live only in the river valleys. Insects are quite numerous, especially the endemic genera: darkling beetles, Scarabaeidae, ground beetles, weevils, Oedimeridae and Elateridae. There are also many Hymenoptera, such as bees, wasps,

FAUNA OF THE DESERT: 1. Pander's chough thrush. 2. Pheasant. 3. Long-toed marmot (Spermophilopsis leptodactylus). 4. Caracal. 5. Mongolian goitered gazelle. 6. Arrow snake. 7. Shrew (Diplomesodon pulchellum). 8. Tiger. 9. Cobra. 10. Steppe turtle. 11. Giant desert monitor lizard. 12. Toad head. 13. Cheetah. 14. Macqueen's bustard. 15. Large jerboa (Rhombomys opimus). 16. Stripped hyena. 17. Asiatic wild cat. 18. Wild ass. 19. Steppe cat. 20. Paradise fly catcher. 21. Jerboa (Paradipus ctenodactylus). 22. Sand grouse (Pterocles alchuta). 23. Long-eared hedegehog. 24. Python (Erix jaculus). 25. Bukharian deer. 26. Sand hare (Lepus tibetanus). 27. Vormela peregusna. 28. Porcupine. 29. Mountain sheep (Ovis ammon).

ants, velvet ants, and even termites. Among the moths there are many tropical and subtropical forms. Scorpions and Solpugidas live in Central Asia, and do not penetrate to the north, as do some tarantulas.

Quite a few animals, as ground rats (*Nesokia indica*), pheasants, wild boars, tugay deer (*Cervus elaphus bactrianus*), *Ablepharus,* skinks, green toads, and lake frogs are adapted to the cultivated land and inundated forests.

The Mountain fauna is noted for its variety. The most typical animals are found in higher regions. Lower mountain belts are inhabited by the animals which live in the same areas where the mountain range lies. Some lower mountains, as the Urals, the mountains of Siberia and the Kola Peninsula, have no characteristic fauna of their own, and are inhabited by the ani-

mals of the tundra and the tayga. Neither do the Carpathian Mountains have many typical species, yet certain ones, especially the amphibians, live only there, and seldom or never occur in the other parts of Russia.

Alpine meadow mice, Alpine shrews, mountain wagtails, white-breasted thrushes, Alpine and Carpathian newts, spotted salamanders, and reed toads (*Bufo calamita*) are the best representatives of the Carpathian fauna.

The fauna of the C r i m e a is more limited in species. Crimean deer, roe deer, stone martens, yellow-throated mice, squirrels, and mountain sheep (*Ovis ammon musimon*), which were recently introduced to this region, are rather common in the Crimean Mountains. Among the birds some local subspecies of the blue jay are the most abundant. Reptiles, such as Balkan sand geckoes, mountain and Crimean lizards, leopard snakes, and amphibians (newts and frogs) live in the Crimean Mountains. Fresh-water crabs and insects (mantes, singing cicadas, and Crimean ground beetles) are widely spread in the S. Different kinds of mollusks are quite numerous, also polypods, scolopendra, flycatchers, and Crimean scorpions.

The fauna of the C a u c a s i a n M o u n t a i n s which is rich and varied originated partly in Asia and partly in the S. and S.E. of Europe. Typical animals of the Caucasus are: wild goats, two species of Caucasian ibex, chamois, Caucasian deer, European and Siberian roe deer, mountain sheep, wild boars, porcupines, burrowing voles, dormice, bush and snowy field mice, hamsters, Transcaucasian squirrels, a few Gerbillinae and jerboas, brown bears, leopards, forest cats, lynx, striped hyenas, jackals, common martens, and, until recently, tigers and bison. Characteristic mountain birds are: Caucasian and Caspian wild turkeys, Caucasian woodcocks, rock partridges, great rose finches, wall creepers, Güldenstädt's redstarts, sittas, jays, crossbills, finches, and black woodpeckers. Reptiles and amphibians are extremely numerous. Lizards, such as *Ophisaurus apodus, Mabuya aurata,* long-legged gold skinks, *Ophiops elegans,* green lizards, rock lizards, geckoes, Caucasian agamas, are very abundant, as are snakes, such as *Typhlops vermicularis,* steppe pythons, and vipers (Persian, Armenian, and blunt-nosed). Some turtles (Caspian, swamp, and Greek), Caucasian salamanders, three kinds of newts, Transcaucasian frogs, tree frogs, and toads (Syrian garlic toad and *Pelodytes caucasicus*) are also common. The insect fauna is one of the richest in the USSR. There are several forms of scorpions and solpugida, fresh water crabs, and Polipoda.

The fauna of C e n t r a l A s i a varies in different localities, the E. Tien Shan having the same animals as the N. forest zone. The same species live in Kopet Dagh and the Near E.: wild goats, rock martens, mouse hares, field mice, rock and desert partridges, Caucasian agamas, cobras, and fresh water crabs. The fauna in other regions of Central Asia is poorer, and is the same as in the mountains of central Tibet. There are also a few species which originated in India, such as laughing thrushes, Paradise flycatchers, and a reptile, *Lycodon striatus.* Mountain sheep and Asiatic ibexes are

FAUNA OF CENTRAL ASIA: 1. White winged grosbeak. 2. Ibis-bill. 3. Mountain sheep. 4. Gray marmot. 5. Güldenstädt's redstart. 6. Griffon vulture. 7. Rock partridge. 8. Caspian mountain turkey. 9. Mouse hare. 10. Asiatic ibex. 11. Blue whistling thrush. 12. Bar-headed goose. 13. Tibetan mountain turkey. 14. Red wolf. 15. Striped laughing thrush (Garrulax lineatus). 16. White-throated marten. 17. Large-eared mouse hare (Ochotona macrotis). 18. Red marmot. 19. Altay marten (Mustela altaica). 20. Little forktail. 21. Tibetan sand grouse (Syrrhaptes tibetanus). 22. White-clawed bear (Ursus arctos). 23. Ermine. 24. Snow leopard.

typical of the mountains. They are replaced by a goat (*Capra falconeri*) in the E. regions. *Uncia uncia*, red wolves, mouse hares, red bobacs, field mice, and, in the hills, porcupines are also found there. Among the mountain birds of Central Asia rock partridges, two kinds of wild turkey, ibis-bills, bar-headed geese, grosbeaks, and little forktails are the best known. There are a few reptiles (Turkestanian and Himalayan agamas) and amphibians (*Ranodon sibiricus*).

The S. Siberian Mountains are inhabited by the same kind of animals as the Siberian tayga, with a few mountain species, such as Asiatic ibexes, mountain sheep, two species of mouse hares, Altay-Tien Shanian bobacs, Kamchatka bobacs, mountain field mice, and finches.

ANIMAL LIFE OF THE FRESH WATERS

The Soviet Union may be divided into four subregions. The rivers which flow into the Arctic Ocean and to the N. Pacific belong to the polar region; those flowing to Lake Baykal, to the Baykal region; those of the Baltic, Black, Caspian, and Aral seas, including the Chu and the Sary-Su, to the Mediterranean region; the basin of Lake Balkhash, the upper Syr Darya and the Amu Darya, with its tributaries, and the Zeravshan, to the mountainous Asia region. The basin of the Amur is a separate region. Species are more or less limited in the N. rivers of the Arctic Ocean and the N. Pacific, salmon being the most common. There are also many transitory species and a few carps.

Sturgeons, sterleds, charrs, brown trout, white fishes, graylings, gudgeons, minnows, crucian carps, loaches, perches, common gremilles, oil fishes (Cottus), sticklebacks, and eel pouts are characteristic of the basin of the Arctic Ocean; far eastern salmon, *Onchorhynchus keta*, *O. gorbuscha*, *O. tschawytscha*, black fishes (*Dallia*), of the basin of the N. Pacific.

The fauna of the Baykal is known for its great number of endemic species. Baykal oil fishes are found only in this lake; a fish closely related to the Cottocomephoridae family, loaches, and a few kinds of white fish are common there. Baykal hair seals penetrated to the lake in ancient times from the Arctic Ocean. Among the invertebrates there are numerous beach fleas, mollusks, sponges, Polychaeta worms, and tricho worms. The fauna of the Baykal originated in the upper Tertiary period. The modern species of this lake are descendants of the ancient rich fauna which was formerly spread over the vast N. territory.

The basin of the Baltic, Black, Caspian, and Aral seas has a rich fauna; yet the Baltic Sea basin was affected by the cold during the glacial period. A few Mediterranean species which are now found there penetrated in the rivers only in recent times. Lakes Ladoga and Onega are inhabited by the same species as in the Baltic fresh-water basins. Numerous kinds of fishes live in the rivers of the Black, Caspian, and Aral seas. Shovel-nosed and other kinds of sturgeon, Clupeonella, Capoetobrama, a few Cottocomephoridae, *Percarina*, roaches, minnows, bony fishes (*Chondrostoma*), barbels, *Alburnus*, and loaches are the best known. There are about 61–74 different species in the Danube, Dniester, Dnieper, and Don rivers. Carps predominate everywhere.

The rivers of Lake Balkhash, the upper Syr Darya, the Amu Darya, and the Zeravshan rivers are inhabited by the fishes which like a swift current. Old-world minnows, *Schizopygopsis*, osman, *Diplophysa*, and mountain bullheads (*Glyptosternum*) live there. Trout are found in the upper Amu Darya, and a certain kind of perch in Lake Balkhash.

Chinese and northern species occupy the basin of the Ussuri, the Amur, and the rivers of Sakhalin and the Kuril Islands. The northern species are: far eastern salmon, graylings, eel pouts, minnows, and pikes. The southern species are: Donzellina, *Elopichthys bambusa*, *Hypophthalmichthys molitrix*, gudgeons, *Ctenopharyngodon idella*, *Pseudobagrus fulvidraco* and *Siniperca chua-tsi*.

FRESH WATER FISHES: 1. Shovelnosed sturgeon. 2. Sturgeon (Acipenser ruthenus). 3. Asiatic carp. 4. Stickle back. 5. Common mullet. 6. Eel. 7. Barbel. 8. Crucian carp. 9. Miller's thumb (Aspius aspius). 10. Bream. 11. Sandre. 12. Roach. 13. Black bullhead. 14. Blicca bjorkna. 15. "Bersh" (Lucioperca volgensis). 16. Minnow. 17. Bony fish. 18. Miller's thumb (Aspiolucius esocinus). 19. Rhodeus sericeus. 20. Gudgeon. 21. (Alburnoides bipunctatus). 22. Umbra. 23. "Chop" (Aspro zingel). 24. Oil fish. 25. (Varicorhinus capaeta). 26. Razor-fish.

Many common species live in the basin of the Black, Caspian, and Aral seas, species which are absent in the rivers of Siberia and Central Asia. Among these are *Rhodeus sericeus,* eels, and carps. Some of the fishes of the Amur River are common with the American species.

SEA ANIMALS

There are several regions of seas in the USSR: the White Sea, most of the Barents Sea, all Siberian seas, and the N. of the Bering Sea lie in the Arctic zone; the Baltic Sea, in the boreal Atlantic zone; the Black and Azov seas in the tropical Atlantic zone; most of the Bering Sea, the Okhotsk Sea, the N. part of the Sea of Japan, in the boreal Pacific zone; Peter the Great Bay and the S. of the Sea of Japan in the Indio-Western Pacific tropical zone.

Both marine and fresh-water species occur in the Baltic Sea. Sea herrings, northern pilchards, viviparous eel pouts, Rhombus maximus, cods, smelts, common seals, Baykal hair seals, and gray seals are salt-water species; perches and pikes are the fresh-water forms; eels, salmon, and river minnows are transitory. Some Crustacea are ancient species of the preglacial period.

There are two groups of animals in the Black Sea. The ancient group, of the upper Tertiary period, consists of four kinds of oil fish, herrings (Atlantic herring and northern pilchard), silversides, sea sanders and sturgeons, and of numerous invertebrates, such as mollusks (*Monodacna* and *Adacna*), a few Crustacea and Polychaeta, all of which live in brackish water and do not mix with the salt-water forms. The second group, the newcomers, which appeared after the glacial period and penetrated into the Black Sea from the Mediterranean, consists of numerous invertebrates, such as mollusks, crabs, shrimps, jellyfishes, hydroids, and also fishes: striped mullets, common mackerels, goatfishes, sea robins, *Grenilabrus tinca,* needlefishes, scorpion fishes, and Cottonomephoridae. Three kinds of porpoises (common porpoise, common dolphin, and bottle-nosed dolphin) also live there; and occasionally a seal (*Monachus monachus*) appears. Because of lower temperature and salinity of the water the fauna of the Black Sea is poorer than in the Mediterranean.

The fauna of the Sea of Azov is the same as in the Black Sea, but more limited in species, except for the relic invertebrate fauna in the estuaries. Because of the lower salinity of the water there are many fresh-water forms living in the Caspian Sea. The Sarmatian relic fauna is partly preserved there. A few northern species, such as Caspian salmon, Siberian white fishes, and sea roachers apparently penetrated to the Caspian Sea during the glacial period. Striped mullets, sand worms, and a mollusk (*Mytilaster lineatus*) appeared there quite recently. The Aral Sea has the same kind of animals as the Caspian Sea, with which it was connected in ancient times. Fresh-water forms, such as barbels, chamois, a rare species of Aral sturgeon, and one form of Mediterranean mollusk predominate there.

There are two types of animals in the Barents Sea: the arctic, and the boreal of the Atlantic Ocean. The arctic forms, which live in the E. and N.E. of the Barents Sea, are mostly arctic cods, *Boreogadus saida,*

dorses (*Eleginus navaga*), *Cottocomephoridae,* smooth flounders, many kinds of eel pout, walruses, and some invertebrates (Echinoderms, Crustacea, Polychaeta worms, and a mollusk Portlandia). The boreal forms which predominate in the W. are usually rosefishes, common wolf fishes, a few kinds of flounder, including the halibuts, sea herrings, cods, haddocks, occasionally a mackerel, two species of roachers, and a few Polychaeta worms. The plankton consists mostly of Copepods.

The White Sea, which is cooler than the Barents Sea, has a similar fauna, but more limited in species. Some of the forms are relics from the Yoldian Sea. Herrings, Arctic cods, Boreogadus saida, salmon, brown trout, smelts, lumpfishes, and seals (Arctic ringed seal and Greenland seal) are characteristic. The Kara, Laptev, the E. Siberian, and Chukchi seas have a definite Arctic fauna. The island Novaya Zemlya makes a barrier, and the boreal forms do not penetrate farther to the N. Arctic cods, Siberian cods, a few Cottocomephoridae, and dorses are typical of this region. There are also a few specific forms of sea roachers and Polychaeta worms. Different species of whales are occasionally found here.

The fauna of the Pacific Ocean is very rich. There are 400 different fishes, while from Nordcape to the Bering Strait there are only 100. Arctic species live in the N. of the Bering Sea, boreal species in the S. Sea snails are very common. The deep sea fauna is very rich. The fauna of the Okhotsk Sea is similar to the Bering Sea, but poorer. Real deep-sea fishes of some Pacific families are also found here.

The Sea of Japan lacks the deep-sea fauna. There are tropical forms in the Peter the Great Bay, like cutlass fishes, tunny, and one kind of flying fish. Whales (gray whale, *Rhachianectes glaucus,* and killer whale) and different porpoises are rather numerous.

Echinoderms, Holoturia, numerous mollusks, among which are the giant Cryptochiton, giant oysters, the beautiful Rapana, and many Crustacea, especially different kinds of crabs, are typical of the Pacific Ocean.

The N. Pacific has many forms common with the N. Atlantic, the Barents and Kara seas, while these forms are absent in the Siberian seas. Pacific minnows, halibuts, common wolf fishes, salmon, cods, and squirrel fishes are common in both regions. Apparently they moved to the S. in the Pliocene period, and after the glacial period.

USEFUL AND DESTRUCTIVE ANIMALS

Many animals of the Soviet Union are hunted for their furs and meat, squirrels, muskrats, and sables being very important in the fur industry. Greenland and Caspian seals are hunted in the White and Caspian seas. The whale industry uses mostly the striped and spermacet whales, porpoises, and common dolphins. The fishing industry is well developed in the Black, Azov, Caspian, and Aral seas, less in the N. European seas and Atlantic Ocean, and still less in the Pacific Ocean.

Many animals are of great importance because they feed on destructive insects and rodents: for example, foxes, steppe weasels, ermines, birds of prey, and owls;

also bats, shrews, hedgehogs, frogs, toads, lizards, snakes, and many parasitic insects. At the same time many animals are very dangerous. Human and animal parasites, especially Trematoda, Cestoda, Acanthocephala, Nematodes, and many mites are the first enemies; and some Protozoa cause malaria, dysentery, and other sicknesses. The birds usually suffer from Mallophaga, gadflies, lice, and fleas. Some insects, such as mosquitoes, lice, and flies are sickness carriers, typhus, malaria, dysentery, encephalitis, and different viruses being spread by them. Wolves and most of the rodents are destructive to the crops and to cattle.

Because of man's activities on land and sea, and of the annihilation of the forests, the fauna is constantly changing. Such animals as wild horses, bison, and Steller's sea cows have completely disappeared; Kamchatka beavers, sables, martens, elks, wild asses, and gorals have become extremely rare. Many animals have now been brought in from other countries, or to new areas: raccoons and spotted deer to European Russia from the Far E.; squirrels to the Crimea and Caucasus from Siberia; gray mullets and sand worms, from the Black Sea to the Caspian Sea; white fishes and carps from the Aral Sea to Lake Balkhash; sturgeons and barbels to the Pechora and Dvina rivers; ondatra and coypu from abroad.   T. D. G.

ANÍVA, gulf in Sea of Okhotsk at S. Sakhalin, fishing grounds; coastal towns: Aniva, Korsakov.

ÁNNA IVÁNOVNA (1693–1740), empress, daughter of Ivan V, niece of Peter I, married to Frederick Wilhelm, Duke of Courland. She became empress in 1730, after the death of Peter II. An uneducated and foolish woman, she was dominated by her favorite, Biron. The government was actually in the hands of the German party, many of them adventurers, but some were able. Foreign affairs were controlled by Ostermann; the army scored successes under Munnich. War with Poland (1733–35) prepared the way for her partition. War with Turkey (1736–1739) ended by the Treaty of Belgrade. Russia retained Azov but had to raze its fortifications.

ÁNNA LEOPÓLDOVNA (1718–1746), granddaughter of Tsar Ivan V, Regent (1740–41) during infancy of her son Ivan VI (born 1740). The actual rulers were the German party at the court. She was deposed 1741 by the Guards and died in exile.

ÁNNENSKY, Innokénty Fyódorovich (1856–1909), poet. He translated into Russian the works of Euripides, and first began to write poems in 1904. The sadness of existence, the awaiting of death, the unpleasantness of reality—such are the themes of A's poetry. In the view of critics he succeeded best in his descriptions of nightmares and sleepless nights. A also wrote several tragedies on themes taken from the works of Euripides. His works include: *Quiet Songs* (under the characteristic pseudonym "No one" [1904]); *The Cypress Casket* (1910); *Posthumous Poems* (1923); *Famira Kifared,* a "bacchanalian drama" (performed in Moscow in 1916–17); two *Books of Reflections,* a collection of articles.

ÁNNENSKY, Nikoláy Fyódorovich (1843–1912), statistician, journalist, politician. A government statistician, his liberal proclivities brought him exile to Siberia,

1880–83. On his return, he rose to head the St. Petersburg statistical office in 1895. He joined the staff of *Russkoye Bogatstvo* (Russian Wealth), the Populist monthly, and became editorial chief in 1904. In 1906 he was one of the founders of the People's Socialist party (formerly a Right-wing faction of the Socialist Revolutionaries) and its chairman until his death.

ANÓSOV, Pável Petróvich (1797–1851), metallurgist. Graduated from the Military Mining School in St. Petersburg (1817). Joined the Zlatoust plant where he remained for 30 years and of which he became director (1831). Director of Altay plants (1847). Developed all stages of high-grade steel production, direct processes of iron and steel production in crucibles, direct carburization of iron in melting crucibles, preheating and lubrication of ingot molds, air blowing prior to pouring, methods of macroetching, the use of the microscope for the study of steel structure. Established the effects of the crystalline structure on the properties of the metal. Designed a gold dredging machine. A's work in the field of physical metallurgy and heat treatment has greatly contributed to the modernization of metallurgical processes. Author of *Damask Steel* (1841), which was translated into German and French. In commemoration of his 150th birthday the Council of Ministers of the USSR resolved to publish his collected works and name a fellowship and a medal after him.

ANTI-COMINTERN PACT. On Nov. 25, 1936, Germany and Japan signed a five-year "Agreement against the Third International" calling for closest collaboration between the two nations in the defeat of Communist subversive activities. Generally known as the "Anti-Comintern Pact," it invited other states to take similar steps or to become signatories to the existing arrangement. Italy joined, Nov. 6, 1937, so that the Pact came to constitute an extension of the original Rome-Berlin Axis. When, in Nov. 1941, it was renewed for a further five years, the signatories included Hungary, Bulgaria, Rumania, Spain, Finland, Slovakia, and Manchukuo, in addition to the three major adherents.

ANTI-PARTY GROUP: *see* OPPOSITION.

ANTI-SEMITISM: *see* JEWS.

ANTOKÓLSKY, Mark Matvéyevich (1843–1902), sculptor, born in Vilna, in a Jewish family, died in  Homburg, Germany. From 1862 a nonmatriculated student at St. Petersburg Academy of Fine Arts. Received academic rank in 1871; later settled abroad. In his earliest haut-reliefs *Tailor,* 1864, *Miser,* 1865, *Inquisition,* 1863–69, he sought new methods, free from academic tradition for interpretation of genre and historical subjects. His important works on historical topics are distinguished by psychological insight and faithfulness to historical detail (*Ivan the Terrible,* in bronze, 1870–71, Russian Museum; in marble, 1875, Tretyakov Gallery; *Peter I,* in plaster of Paris, 1872, Russian Museum; in bronze, 1872, Tretyakov Gallery; *Nestor,* in marble, 1889, Russian Museum; in bronze, 1890, Tretyakov Gallery). A number of statues were dedicated to moral and philosophical themes (*Christ Being Judged by the People,* in bronze, 1874, Russian Museum, in marble, 1876, Tretyakov Gallery; *Mephistopheles,* in marble, 1883, Russian Museum; *Dying Socrates,* in marble, 1875, Russian Museum; *Spinoza,* in marble, 1882, Russian Museum). Author of sculptural portraits and projects for memorials.

ANTÓNOV-OVSÉYENKO, Vladímir Aleksándrovich (1884–1938), Bolshevik, born in Chernigov, educated in a military school. In 1905, as a R. officer in Warsaw, he tried to organize a military revolt. When it failed, he was sentenced to death, but managed to escape. In 1910 he went to Paris where he worked closely with Trotsky. In May 1917 he joined the Bolsheviks and in October was the secretary of the Petrograd Soviet's Military-Revolutionary Committee. He led a detachment against the Winter Palace and arrested the members of the Provisional Government. In the first Soviet government he was a member of the People's Commissariat of War. After 1924, he was in diplomatic service; was Soviet envoy in Prague, Kaunas, and Warsaw. Joined, for a short time, the Trotskyite opposition, but retracted in 1927. During the civil war in Spain, he was one of the chief Soviet political and military agents there. After Franco's victory, he returned to Russia and shortly thereafter was arrested and disappeared without trace. He was rehabilitated after the 20th Party Congress in 1956.

ANTONÓVICH, Nikoláy Bonifátievich (1843–1912). Historian. A graduate of Kiev University, he became prof. of history there in 1878. He published many records and articles on Ukrainian history, together with collections on witchcraft and songs of the Little Russians. A Populist and cultural nationalist, he organized the work of local historians and founded the magazine *Kievskaya Starina.*

ANTRÓPOV, Alekséy Petróvich (1716–1795), portrait painter, the teacher of Levitsky. Son of a soldier, he studied art under Matveyev, Caravaque and Count Rotari. In 1752–56 he decorated the Church of St. Andrew in Kiev, and in 1756, the ceiling at the Golovkin palace in Moscow. Among his portraits, those of Catherine II and Peter III are the best known.

ANZHÉRO-SÚDZHENSK, city in Kemerovo Oblast, RSFSR; pop. 116,000 (1959). One of principal centers of the Kuzbas coal ind.; mining machinery, railway-car repairing, glass ind.; mining schools.

ANZHÚ ISLANDS, N. group of New Siberian Islands in the N. Arctic Ocean; area 12,000 sq. mi.; explored in 1821–23 by R. admiral P. F. Anzhu. Main islands: Kotelny, Faddeyevsky, Novaya Sibir.

ANZHÚ, Pyótr Fyódorovich (1796–1869), arctic explorer, admiral of the Russian navy and a leader of an expedition of N. Siberia between the Olenek and Indigirka rivers. He studied ice conditions in Laptev Sea; prepared map of New Siberia Islands, a group of which is named after him.

APICULTURE is carried on mainly on collective farms, 70% of which have apiaries. In addition, collective farmers are allowed to keep up to 20 beehives on their household plots. The number of swarms amounted (in mill.) to 6.3 in 1910, 5.6 in 1930, and 10.0 in 1940, or ⅓ of the world's total, putting the USSR ahead of other countries in this field. The war damages were not repaired until 1958 when the number of swarms again reached its prewar level. Beekeepers were encouraged to shift toward frame hives; these accounted for 18% of all hives in 1913, 63% in 1930 and about 100% by 1940.

APOLLÓN, a journal of art and literature, published from 1909 to 1917 in St. Petersburg and edited by the art critic S. Makovsky. Many artists of *Mir Iskusstva* (q.v.) collaborated in this publication, and works of symbolists and acmeists were published in it.

APRÁKSIN, Count Fyódor Matvéyevich (1661–1728), collaborator of Peter I, general-admiral, creator of the R. navy. He was the successful defender of St. Petersburg in 1708; a member of Supreme Privy Council.

APRÁKSIN, Stepán Fyódorovich (1702–1758), general, field-marshal, commander in chief of R. army during the Seven Years' War. After a brilliant victory over Prussians in Gross Egersdorf battle (1757) he unexpectedly pulled out troops to winter quarters; he was then accused of inactivity.

APSHERÓN PENINSULA, on the W. shore of the Caspian Sea in Azerbaijan SSR; very important oil fields. The city of Baku is on it.

APSHERÓNSK, city in Krasnodar Kray, RSFSR; pop. 26,600 (1956). Fruit-packing, lumber ind.

APRIL THESES. Before Lenin's arrival in Petrograd on April 16, 1917 the Bolsheviks were divided in their attitude toward the Provisional Government. Only a minority favored outright opposition to it. Lenin and other leaders were abroad, and the party minority was without any contact with them. In his *Letters from Afar* Lenin stressed repeatedly his opposition to the Provisional Government but found little support even among the Bolsheviks. After his journey in a sealed train across Germany, Lenin reached Petrograd and immediately defined his position in a document later published and known as the AT. He denounced the continuation of the war, advocated all power to the Soviets, abolition of the existing police, army and bureaucracy, confiscation of all private lands, establishment of Soviet control of banks, production and distribution of goods, proposed to change the name of the party from Social Democratic to Communist and to rebuild the Socialist International. AT met with hostile response both outside and inside the party. Plekhanov wrote that the AT were "interesting deliriums." The Bolshevik Petrograd and Moscow committees voted against Lenin's AT. Kamenev stated in *Pravda* that the AT were only Lenin's personal opinions to which the Central Committee was opposed. But the situation changed within a few weeks. Events revealed the popularity of the AT, especially in its opposition to war. The Bolshevik party firmly adopted the AT.   K. R. P.

APÚKHTIN, Alekséy Nikoláyevich (1841–1893), poet. His conventional poems are filled with nostalgia for lost youth and its pleasures. Some of his poems were set to music by Tchaikovsky and Mussorgsky. He was extremely popular in his time but later forgotten.

ARAKCHÉYEV, Count Alexis Andréyevich (1769–1834), soldier and statesman, influential with Paul I and Alexander I. A started his career as an artillery drill master, was a major general at age of 27, made a baron by Paul in 1797 and a count in 1799. Alexander I appointed him chief inspector of artillery in 1803 and minister of war in 1808. A resigned the ministry in 1810 because of a conflict with Speransky, but remained a close companion of Alexander during the Napoleonic wars, acting as liaison to the Council of Ministers, tantamount to prime minister without portfolio. He was especially influential during the last years of Alexander's reign, although he was not always in complete agreement with the emperor. A was reactionary, ambitious, rude, vindictive, and cruel. He was an excellent administrator and devoted to the emperor. A convinced serf-owner, he nonetheless prepared the 1818 project for the peasants' emancipation out of obedience to the emperor. A's era is recorded in history as the *Arakchéyevshchina,* a symbol of military regimentation.

ARÁKS RIVER, in Transcaucasia, right tributary of the Kura, flows through Turkey, along the Soviet-Turkish and Iranian borders with Azerbaijan. Length, 567 mi. (according to some sources, about 665 mi.); nonnavigable; used for irrigation.

ARÁL SEA, salt lake in Kazakh SSR and Uzbek SSR; fourth largest lake in the world (Caspian Sea, L. Superior, Victoria Nyanza), with an area of 25,475 sq. mi., and a depth to 225 ft. Has many islands and the Amu Darya and Syr Darya rivers flow into it; its coastal town is Aralsk. Has fisheries (sazan, bream) and sodium sulfate deposits in vicinity.

ARÁLSK, city in Kzyl-Orda Oblast, Kazakh SSR. Port on Aral Sea; pop. 17,000 (1956). Fisheries; ship-repairing plant. Salt and sodium sulfate.

ARBITRATION by state or departmental tribunals takes the place of the courts in settling most unresolved disputes among state and other organizations, save when collective farms are involved, or in other exceptional cases heard by the courts. *State A* tribunals at the All-Union, republic, and local levels, established in 1931, hear mostly contractual and precontractual and property disputes between economic organizations subordinated to different agencies. Disputes between organizations subordinated to the same higher agency are heard by *departmental A* which works under the supervision of *state A.* If an arbitrator cannot promote voluntary agreement, he makes a binding decision on the basis of civil law (q.v.) and administrative law (q.v.) and dictates of the national economic plan. Decisions may not be appealed, but they may be reviewed by the chief arbitrator in the *state A* under the USSR Council of Ministers. Arbitrators report violations of law revealed in hearings to party and state organs.

The *Foreign Trade Arbitration Commission* (FTAC) and the *Maritime Arbitration Commission* (MAC) under the All-Union Chamber of Commerce, Moscow, differ from the *state* and *departmental A,* first, in that they are not organs of state administration with compulsory jurisdiction, but rather "public" organizations to which parties submit disputes by prior voluntary agreement; second, because they handle most disputes not under domestic but private international law, between Soviet and foreign organizations. FTAC, founded in 1932, handles disputes between the state firms in the Soviet foreign trade monopoly and foreign firms or states. Each party to a dispute names one arbitrator from a panel of 15 selected yearly by the All-Union Chamber of Commerce. The third, chief arbitrator in a case, is selected by FTAC or the All-Union Chamber of Commerce. Hearings are open, unless the parties wish them closed. Decisions of the three arbitrators may not be appealed. MAC, founded in 1930, hears shipping disputes arising out of salvage, freight and insurance payments and deliveries, collisions, damages to harbor facilities. Procedures are similar to those in FTAC, save that the panel is 25 arbitrators, and the arbitrators chosen by each side hear the case alone, unless they cannot agree, in which case a chief arbitrator is chosen. Decisions may be appealed by the parties to the USSR Supreme Court or protested there by the procurator, and the Supreme Court may either annul the decision or remand the case for a new hearing in MAC. (*See also* COURT SYSTEM, LIABILITY LAW, SOVIET LAW)

P. H. J.

ARBÚZOV, Aleksándr Yerminingéldovich (1877–), organic chemist. Fellow, Ac. of S., USSR (1942). Deputy, Supreme Soviet (1946, 1950, 1954). Hero of Socialist Labor (1957). Graduated (1900), Dean (1924), Department of Physics and Mathematics, Kazan University; professor, Kazan Institute of Chemical Technology, chairman of the executive board, Kazan Branch, Ac. of S. (1945). Applied A. M. Butlerov's theory of chemical structure to organic phosphorous compounds. Established the chemical structure of phosphorous acid and its ethers (1905). Discoverer of the "Arbuzov Rearrangement." Developed a method of collecting galipot from coniferous trees without loss of gaseous substances which contributed to the development of this industry in the USSR. Publications concern organic phosphorous compounds, industrial chemistry, history of chemistry. Stalin prizes (1943, 1947).

ARBÚZOV, Borís Aleksándrovich (1903–), organic chemist, son and student of A. Ye. Arbuzov. Fellow, Ac. of S., USSR (1953). Graduated from Kazan Institute of Agriculture and Forestry (1926). Professor, Kazan Institute of Chemical Technology (1935), Kazan University (1938). Joined the Kazan Branch, Ac. of S. (1945). Research mainly in terpenes, diene and other organic compounds, the application of physical methods to the study of organic compounds. Author of "Sur la rotation des groupes irréguliers dans les molécules," *Journal de chimie physique* (1953). Mendeleyev prize (1949), Stalin prize (1951), and other awards.

ARCHAEOLOGY. The territory of Russia, especially its southern part, was the scene of the rise and fall of many civilizations (Scythians, Greek colonists, Turks, Mongols, Slavs—to mention but a few). At all times the seeking and excavation of objects of archaeological significance (especially in *kurgans* or burial mounds) was done by the local inhabitants for profit.

The first scientific interest in archaeological finds and the first official instructions with regard to the archaeological excavations date back to 1684. Following the excavation of the remains of a mammoth by a Cossack captain, Tsar Fedor decreed: "To send someone suitable from Kursk in the spring to those places, and order his emissary to dig out the bones and measure them . . . write an inventory and draw up a sketch." Peter I ordered, in 1718, the collection of all objects "very old and rare" especially weapons.

In the 18th century the first scientific excavations of *kurgans* were attempted in the Black Sea region. In 1763 General Melgunov excavated the burial place of a Scythian king. Around 1800 the excavation of the ancient Greek city-colonies, (notably Olbia) in Crimea, was begun. The French *émigré*, the archaeologist Dubrux, who excavated the Kul-Oba *kurgan* has found the now famous *kul-oba* bowl depicting Scythian warriors after battle.

The region of Kerch (Crimea) was the site of a particularly lively archaeological activity since it had been the location of the ancient capital of the Graeco-Scythian Bosporus kingdom. The number of excavated objects increased so rapidly that in 1826 the first A museum in Russia was opened in Kerch. During the second half of the 19th century, the archaeological work progressed greatly. In St. Petersburg the Imperial Archaeological Commission was founded which, apart from coordination of archaeological work, published sumptuous annual reports (*Otchoty . . .*) from 1861 through 1918. In Moscow Count A. Uvarov and his wife organized an independent Imperial Russian Archaeological Society which published 30 volumes of Transactions (*Drevnosti . . .*). A. Uvarov organized the first archaeological congress in Moscow in 1869 and the Moscow Historical Museum in 1883.

While the St. Petersburg center was oriented toward the European concepts and methodology, the Moscow school had developed a unique Russian approach to A. This resulted in a rivalry between the two centers as well as lively polemics. By the end of the century, the contributions made by R. archaeologists included also works on the methodology of excavation, archaeological systematics, the scope and task of A, and so forth. I. Zabelin introduced the method of excavating *kurgans* by two cross-trenches. I. Polyakov developed the methodology for the location of paleolithic sites.

With the diversification of archaeological activity in Russia, the main areas of work began to be formalized: (1) classical A in Russia—excavation of the Greek city-colonies on the north coast of the Black Sea; (2) the Slavo-Russian prehistoric A and the Slavo-Russian Medieval A; (3) the A of southern Russian steppe (Scythian A—primarily); (4) the A of Central Asia and Transcaucasus barely begun by the turn of the century; (5) prehistoric A.

By the time of the revolution, the Russian A had been enriched by several significant discoveries: (1) the discovery of the Tripolye Culture (an agricultural, cattle-breeding society, 3rd–2nd millennium B.C.) near Kiev by V. Khvoyka; (2) the discovery of the Gothic cemeteries in the Crimea; (3) the Burial Fields (Polya, Pogrebeny) of the La Tene culture and the Gothic culture; (4) the Bronze Age culture in the middle Volga basin; and many others.

The theoretical foundations and the goals of Soviet A or the History of Material Culture—as it is often called—took shape in the 1920's and early 1930's. Contemporary Soviet A, as the Soviet authorities state, rests on Marxist premises. The goal of A is the investigation and understanding of the origins and development of the pre-capitalistic society from an economic standpoint. The archaeological remains are significant only as a source for reconstruction of the society that produced them, i.e. for the reconstruction of its economic basis, its productive forces, technology, social relations, and ideology. Thus the archaeological findings are used for the purpose of discovery and formulation of the general laws of social evolution. Soviet A maintains that the social evolution, no matter what specific society is dealt with, is determined by the same laws and, in general, proceeds along the same lines of development.

Five stages of socioeconomic evolution have been identified: (I) pre-class society (clan-matriarchal, clan-patriarchal, and so forth); (II) class society (slave-holding formations); (III) feudal system; (IV) capitalist society; (V) classless society (socialism, communism).

A deals with the first three (pre-capitalist) stages. One of the tasks for the historian of the material culture is to identify and locate in this scheme the socioeconomic formation and the stage of its development from the archaeological remains that represent it.

The direction and coordination of all the archaeological work in the Soviet Union are accomplished by the Institute of the History of the Material Culture of the USSR Ac. of S., which was initially organized in 1919 as the Academy of the History of the Material Culture and reorganized in 1937. Over 500 museums in all the republics have archaeological departments. Fifteen universities offer advanced training in A. The number of expeditions increases every year (25 were reported in 1945, immediately after the war).

The greater portion of work performed by Soviet A since 1919 continued to be in the same general areas as before the revolution. However, the archaeological activity in Central Asia and Transcaucasus has increased greatly and significant findings were made. Most intense work has been done in the field of Slavo-Russian A especially since World War II. Following the war, the Baltic regions and areas formerly belonging to Poland received the attention of archaeologists. There has been an increase in specific studies on various aspects of ancient economic activity: handicrafts (ceramics and others), industry (metallurgy), fishing, and so forth.

Questions of theoretical and methodological importance, as well as the role and relation of Soviet A to Marxian theory, have been paid considerable attention. A few of the more significant contributions and discoveries made by Soviet A are as follows: Numerous paleolithic sites were discovered in the Caucasus (Armenia), Ural Mountains, and Central Asia. P. P. Yefimenko, one of the leading experts on the paleolithic era created a new methodology of excavation of paleolithic sites. The remains of a child of the Neanderthal type were discovered at Teshik-Tash (Uzbekistan). Great progress has been made in the study of the economy of the early agricultural tribes in E. Europe, notably the Tripolye culture. The study of the Siberian area, continued for many years, culminated in a volume by S. V. Kiselev, *The Ancient History of Southern Siberia,* describing the four thousand years of the socioeconomic history of Siberia. Numerous expeditions have been conducted on the territories of ancient Khorezm, Bukhara, and the Parthian kingdom in Central Asia. S. P. Tolstov's (*The Ancient Khorezm*) expedition has worked in the Khorezm territory for 20 years. He has excavated two remarkable sites: the fortress Koy-Krylgan-Kala (4th century B.C.—1st century A.D.) and the fortified city Toprak-Kala. Ancient Trancaucasus was a part of the powerful kingdom of Urartu (between the 8th century and the 6th century B.C.). One of the most significant archaeological finds there is the excavation of Karmir-Blur—the palace of the Urartu viceroy in Transcaucasus.

Over the years and especially since World War II, there has been mounting interest in Slavo-Russian A and some very important contributions were made toward the study of the origins of the Russian Slavs, the development of and the economic conditions in the Russian towns, and the study of the ancient Russian handicrafts, industry, technology, agriculture, and trade. An important large-scale excavation continues in Novgorod; A. V. Artsikhovsky has been directing it. Similar large-scale excavations are done in Kiev, Old Ryazan, Vladimir, and Moscow. The high level of development of the handicrafts in the ancient Russian towns reflects the fact that the Russian towns like their medieval European counterparts were not primarily administrative or trade centers but the centers of handicrafts.

BIBLIOGRAPHY: M. O. Miller, *Archaeology in the USSR,* New York, 1956.

V. N. S.

ARCHANGEL (R. *Arkhángelsk*), city, oblast adm. center in RSFSR, major sea and river port in the mouth of N. Dvina River on the White Sea (ice-free July-Sept.); pop. 256,000 (1959). A center of timber sawmilling and export from USSR; numerous other industries (fish canning, tanning of sea-animal hides, pulp, turpentine, shipyards, cod-liver oil) are of importance. There are several institutions of higher learning and numerous technical schools. It was founded in 1584 as Novo-Kholmogory after R. Chancellor had landed here, and was Russia's only seaport before the foundation of St. Petersburg; played a very important role during two world wars as supply port; was occupied 1918–20 by Allies and White army.

ARCHÁNGEL OBLAST, in N.E. of European RSFSR at the White, Barents, Pechora and Kara seas; includes Nenets National Okrug and islands in the Arctic Ocean: Novaya Zemlya, Franz Josef Land, Kolguyev, Vaygach. Connected by a canal system with the Volga; area 226,700 sq. mi.; pop. 1,278,000 (1959). Cities: Archangel, Kotlas, Severodvinsk (f. Molotovsk), Naryan-Mar. Plain is irrigated by N. Dvina, Onega, Mezen, Pechora; cold climate; pine forests, tundra in the north. Is the greatest lumbering region of USSR, with wood-pulp, wood-chemicals, shipbuilding ind.; flax, grain farming, dairying, reindeer breeding, fishing, hunting. Several schools of higher education, scientific re-

search institutes, museums, theaters; birthplace of M. V. Lomonosov.

ARCHITECTURE. Russian architecture represents a blending of foreign influences and native traditions.

The native tradition is founded on a geographical fact: Russia is a country of forests. Wood has been the chief building material until quite recent times. Towns were built of wood except for a few important buildings; the Moscow of 1812, whose burning Tolstoy so vividly described in *War and Peace,* was such a wooden town. The vernacular tradition of building in wood has not only persisted but has also affected and assimilated foreign influences. A good example is the Kolomenskoye Church near Moscow, built in 1532, which is an almost literal translation of wood forms into a stone building.

The foreign influences were from three main sources:

(1) *Byzantine.* This influence, which reached Russia after her conversion to Christianity in 988, marked the start of her architectural history (earlier buildings, made of wood, have all perished) and was dominant until Peter the Great. It was revived, not too successfully, in the 19th century.

(2) *Western* architectural influences reached Russia quite early. Romanesque came soon after the Byzantine, though its influence was felt in details rather than in structure; Gothic missed Russia altogether, but Italian Renaissance architects left their mark in Moscow, and Baroque and Rococo builders in the Ukraine. W. influence, replacing the Byzantine with Peter the Great, has continued to be dominant, but has been subject to periodical nativist reactions. It is being increasingly realized of late that Russia has made some significant contributions to the W. architectural tradition, notably in the city of St. Petersburg (now Leningrad).

(3) *Eastern.* Architectural historians of the past used to call R. A "semi-barbaric" or "Asiatic." The great French architect Viollet-le-Duc who, although he never came to Russia, did much to acquaint Europe with R. A, wrote that R. churches reminded him of Chinese pagodas, Hindu temples, and Arabian mausoleums, as well as of Byzantine cathedrals. Actually, though Oriental influences have been active in Russia since the Kievan days—the St. Sophia Cathedral of Kiev has certain Syrian and Persian features—they have been, on the whole, subordinate.

Kiev and other early centers. A number of churches of Kiev, the earliest center of R. A, have survived, though they suffered damage in World War II. The oldest, the Desyatinnaya Church, which was begun in 991, is rectangular with 3 altar apses on a Byzantine plan. The most important survival is the St. Sophia Cathedral, dated 1017, but often remodeled. It is the largest R. building in the first two centuries after the conversion, and has 5 apses and 13 cupolas. Other 11th-century monuments of Kiev are the churches of Lavra and Saint Michael, and the Monastery of the Caves.

Byzantine influences merged with W. and the native as A moved northward. The latter influence was so strong that some historians speak of a national R. A making its appearance in the Novgorod-Pskov area in the 12th century. The church plan was changed to suit local conditions: the dominant form was the two-story cross-shaped church with one-story lateral additions and a single apse. The roof became sloped, to deal with the winter snow, and the cupola asssumed the characteristic R. onion shape. Decoration became less gorgeous and less Byzantine. The St. Sophia Cathedral of Novgorod (11th century) is the prime example, with its great austere walls and simple gilded domes. Other outstanding buildings include the churches of the Intercession on the Nerl, of the Savior at Nereditsa, and of St. Nicholas the Wonderworker at Novgorod, as well as the Mizhorsky Monastery at Pskov.

The churches of the Vladimir and Suzdal area are characterized by some Romanesque features like the arched gallery on the second story, and by a renewed burst of ornamentation. Native wooden carving was prominent in projecting beams and in decorated exteriors generally. These features can best be studied in the Pokrov Church of Vladimir (1163).

Moscow A has two main periods: (1) The early, when native masters, mainly from Novgorod and Pskov, worked there and the influence of A in wood made itself felt (14th and 15th centuries); (2) the late, beginning with the last decades of the 15th century, when foreign architects, especially Italians, began to come to Moscow. The Moscow A of the 16th and 17th centuries represents a blending of W. and R. styles.

The application of wooden A to stone found its most splendid expression in the tented church, in which the square plan of the stone church was transformed into an octagon by a system of peculiarly R. arches called *Kokoshniki*. The turret-shaped church was frequent in the 16th and 17th centuries; the tent shape was also applied to roofs of belfries and towers. An earlier austerity yielded, as time went on, to decoration and overdecoration, e.g., in the Church of St. Basil the Blessed, in Moscow's Red Square (1555).

The first important Italian architect to work in Russia was Aristotle Fioravanti from Bologna, who came to Moscow in 1477, to rebuild the Cathedral of the Dormition. Fioravanti decided to follow R. architectural styles while using Italian building methods, an example that was widely followed. Ivan III called in Italians to build the Moscow Kremlin, the chief monument of that period. Antonio Solario built its walls in 1490.

The A of the Kremlin incorporates, in addition to Italian and R. elements, the Oriental tradition of the fortified city. It is also important in another respect: it is the best example of one of the greatest achievements of R. A of the Moscow period, i.e., the grouping of buildings in ensembles which produced picturesque effects. The Kremlin includes both churches and palaces, like the Granovitaya Palace, designed by Italians. Its secular buildings are among the first to survive in Russia, except for some parts of Vladimir's palace in Kiev and some other early relics. Other R. cities also had their Kremlins (i.e., fortified enclosures) but none could compare with Moscow's.

St. Petersburg was the new capital founded by Peter I on the marshy banks of the Neva "to break through a window into Europe," in Pushkin's famous words. But this was not the only reason his town grew into one of Europe's notable artistic monuments; Peter continued the blending of W. and R. A inaugurated under Ivan III. He called in a number of foreign architects: the Frenchman Le Blond, who made the master plan of the city; the Italians, Trezzini and Michetti, and the German, Schaedel, and others. But among his prominent architects was a Russian builder Zemtsov. Peter assembled for his new capital the best masons, carpenters, and craftsmen of Russia, by persuasion—or by force. Moreover, he issued a decree that henceforth no stone building could be constructed anywhere else in the country.

This policy of hiring the best talent available, R. or foreign, for the embellishment of the new capital was continued by Peter's successors, up to and including Nicholas I (1825–1855), by which time the creative impetus weakened and all but died. St. Petersburg owes a good deal to the city planning by European Renaissance and Baroque architects; but it also owes a debt to the R. tradition of the architectural ensemble, applied on a grand scale by rulers with a sense of the grandiose. Catherine the Great, in particular, personally supervised many of the projects, examined plans and buildings, and offered original suggestions.

The Empresses Anna and Elizabeth, Peter's daughter, called in the Italian, Rastrelli, as builder of the Winter Palace (1732). Catherine's architects included the Italian, Quarenghi, and the Scotsman, Charles Cameron, whose best work can be seen in the country palaces of Tsarskoye Selo and Peterhof (now renamed Detskoye Selo and Petrodvorets), as well as the R. Starov (q.v.) who built for her the Tauride Palace (1783). Other St. Petersburg landmarks include the Admiralty by Sakharov (1806); the Kazan Cathedral (1801); the Mining Institute by Voronikhin (1806); the Cathedral of Saint Isaac (1819) by Montferrand; and the Hermitage Museum by Leo von Klenze (1839–52). The last two buildings represent the neoclassic revival that swept Russia at the beginning of the 19th century. The chief model was Palladio, whose style, originally conceived for elegant town and country houses in Italy, was applied with ever less and less discrimination to R. banks, hotels, railroad stations, and government offices.

Meanwhile, Moscow, though abandoned by the government, continued to grow as a trading center and as a residential town of the R. nobility. Baroque came to it in the 18th century—its most splendid example is just outside the city: the Church of Our Lady in the village of Fili, where Baroque is grafted on the R. tented church. With the 19th century came the neoclassic revival, which created in Moscow some excellent town houses such as the residence of Prince V. N. Gagarin (1817).

But perhaps the most successful application of neoclassicist principles was the R. country house. To be sure, it produced some extravaganzas like the stables on the estate of Prince Golitsin near Moscow (1823), a monumental structure that looks not unlike the entrance to Grand Central Station; but it is at its best in the innumerable country houses, often with characteristic triangular pediments resting on four columns, that were scattered throughout European Russia. These country houses were residences of nobility with less pretentious tastes than those of the old or new capital. They are the setting of Pushkin's *Eugene Onegin*, of the novels of Turgenev and Tolstoy, and of the plays of Anton Chekhov.

An increasingly sterile eclecticism became the rule in R. A, as in W. A generally, in the second half of the 19th century. The architectural renewal that was to give birth to modern A had barely time to hit Russia before the revolution of 1917. The great merchants and industrialists, whose town houses began to rise at the turn of the century, preferred the splendors of the "renaissance" style to the extravaganzas of the *art nouveau* and the bare façades of modernism.

Since the Revolution. Although Russia was in the throes of civil war and foreign intervention for five years, remarkably few of her great architectural monuments were destroyed or suffered serious damage. A great deal of the credit belongs to the first Soviet commissar for education, Lunacharsky, who inaugurated a policy of preserving the cultural heritage of the past, including the architectural, which has been maintained, with few exceptions, ever since. In the early days of the revolution, when the Communists fought for power in the streets of St. Petersburg, Lunacharsky personally persuaded Communist soldiers to spare the monuments of the capital. He ran great personal risks; e.g., when he successfully stopped Red Army men from blowing up the Winter Palace.

On the other hand, Russia's architectural heritage suffered great and sometimes irreparable damage in World War II, through military operations as well as through Nazi vandalism and a deliberate policy of destroying buildings of cultural and historical importance. Kiev, Novgorod, and Leningrad and its environs were the chief sufferers, and restoration work is, in some cases, still in progress.

The architectural history of Russia after the revolution falls into two main periods: (1) from 1917 to about 1932–35, when the dominant tendencies were experimentalism and the international modernist style; (2) from about 1932–35 on, when the two leading tendencies have been a return to the architectural traditions of the Russians and of the other peoples of the Soviet Union, and neoclassicism.

Experimentalism flourished in the early 1920's and produced a number of strange projects. Some were actually built, like a workers' club by Golosov, which had a roof in the form of a cogwheel, complete with gears; others, like Tatlin's Monument to the Communist International (1918) in the form of an ascending spiral, remained in the planning stage.

After the revolution cubist, futurist, and constructivist architects were able to put their theories into practice. They were animated by a hatred of the past, which to them was "rotten" and "bourgeois," and a

desire to be "modern" at all cost; practical considerations played an entirely secondary part. Ladovsky, a prof. of modern architecture at the Moscow Academy who tried to interpret Freud's theories of psychoanalysis through A, stated with more than usual candor: "The future belongs to those who have remarkably little talent for the fine arts."

Some of the architectural experiments were more sensible and determined by prevailing conditions. Capital and building materials were very scarce in the early years; consequently stone and wood were replaced by concrete, and unnecessary ornament was eliminated. But flat roofs and glass walls proved extremely unpopular with the inhabitants of houses exposed to the vagaries of the R. climate, with its heavy snowfalls and extremes of heat and cold.

The late twenties and early thirties were years of consolidation. The wild experimentalism of the early days of the revolution died down, but a more moderate version of the international modern style prevailed. It was favored by visits of such prominent foreign architects as May, Meyer, Schmidt, Lurcat, and Le Corbusier who is represented in Moscow by the building of the Commissariat of Light Industry (1932). Prominent R. modernists included Ginsberg who built apartment houses in Moscow, the Vesnin brothers who designed the community center of the Moscow "Proletarian" district (1934), and Golusov, responsible for the *Pravda* building (1936). Perhaps the best architectural monument of the modernist school is the great Dneprostroy dam, destroyed in World War II and since rebuilt.

Modernist A went the way of all modern art tendencies in Russia in the 1930's. Although there were no spectacular arrests, executions, or even official rebukes, as there were in literature or music, modernism gave way to more nativist tendencies and, in particular, to neoclassicism.

There were some attempts to revive R. A of the days before Peter the Great, but they could produce only museum pieces. The only viable prerevolutionary architectural tradition was neoclassicism. More successful were adaptations of native architectural styles of the non-Russian peoples of the Soviet Union, though even here there has been no lack of ugly hybrids. Some of the more successful examples include the Government House at Yerevan (1942) built by A. Tamanyan in the Armenian style, and the Uzbek pavilion at the Moscow Agricultural Fair, inspired by the architecture of Samarkand.

The two most successful Soviet neoclassicists are Karo Alabyan and Boris Iofan. Alabyan's best work is the star-shaped and porticoed Theater of the Red Army in Moscow (1938). Iofan, who tries to combine neoclassicism with some modernist elements, built the Palace of the Soviets in Moscow (1937) and the Soviet pavilions at the international exhibitions in Paris (1937) and New York (1939). But the bulk of neoclassical building in the Soviet Union seems remarkably tame and uninspired.

Some of the best building is utilitarian: factories, workers' flats and sanatoria, e.g. at Sochi on the Black

Sea. Another strong point is city planning: the master plan for Moscow, the rebuilding of Stalingrad, and the new towns in Siberia and Central Asia. None the less, it can hardly be said that revolutionary Russia has produced much in A that can match the great achievements of the past. The two main faults are: at the one extreme, an all-pervading shabbiness and shoddiness that make new apartment buildings show cracks even before they are completed; at the other, a heavy-footed splendor that is, quite mistakenly, viewed as grandeur. A reader of *Time Magazine* who sent in two photographs, one of the new Moscow University, and another of the Chicago Tribune Building, challenged his fellow-readers to tell the difference. It was, indeed, not easy to tell.

Recent contacts between Soviet and W. architects may have fruitful effects in the future, but the present remains rather bleak.

BIBLIOGRAPHY: Michael T. Florinsky, *Russia: A History and an Interpretation*, New York, 1953; A. Voyce, *Russian Architecture*, New York, 1947; Tamara Talbot Rice, *Russian Art*, London, 1949; George H. Hamilton, *The Art and Architecture of Russia*, Baltimore, 1954.   G. DEN.

ARCHIVES OF THE RUSSIAN REVOLUTION (*Arkhiv russkoy revolyutsii*), a valuable collection of documents and memoirs bearing on the revolution of 1917. Twenty-one volumes of ARR edited by I. V. Hessen were published in Berlin in the 1920's.

ARCOS, LTD., formerly the All-Russian Co-operative Society Ltd. which was established by L. B. Krasin in London in 1920 as a private company for promoting trade with Russia. It was reorganized as A in May 1922, and, after the recognition of the Soviet government in 1924, A was retained as a commercial agency of the Soviet Embassy, but was used allegedly for propaganda and subversive purposes. In May 1927 the British police made a raid on A's premises in London which led to the breaking off of Anglo-Soviet diplomatic relations. They were resumed in 1929 but A never regained its importance as a trading agency.

ARÉNSKY, Antón Stepánovich (1861–1906), composer of songs, miniatures for piano, instrumental ensembles (two trios, quartets, suites) as well as three operas (*A Volga Dream*, 1890; *Raphael*, 1894; and *Nal and Damayanti*), two symphonies, a concerto for piano and orchestra, and others. A's music is lyrical, melodic, and elegant.

ARGÚN RIVER, boundary between USSR and China, unites with Shilka R. to form the Amur R.; length 945 mi.; partly navigable.

ARGUNÓV, Iván Petróvich (1727–1802), portrait painter; serf. Author of several truthful and expressive portraits, he had considerable impact on further development of realistic portraiture in Russia. The first R. academicians of the St. Petersburg Academy of Fine Arts were his pupils.

ÁRISTOV, Avérky Borísovich (1903–), party and government official, born in Krasny Yar in Astrakhan Oblast. In 1919–21 he was active in Komsomol and has been a CP member since 1921. He served in the Red Army 1925–26; became an active party worker thereafter. He was first secretary of the Chelyabinsk Oblast party committee, 1950–52; secretary of the Central Committee, 1952–53; chairman of the Khabarovsk Kray executive committee, 1954–55. Temporarily demoted after Stalin's death, he rose with Khrushchev. In July 1955, he was elected secretary of the Central Committee and since June 1957 has been a member of the Presidium of the Central Committee. He is also a deputy to the USSR and RSFSR Supreme Soviets. After the 20th Party Congress, 1956, he was made a member of the newly organized RSFSR bureau of the Central Committee. In May 1960 he was relieved of the duties of secretary of the Central Committee. In 1961 nominated Ambassador to Poland. Two Lenin orders.

ARKÁDYEV, Vladímir Konstantínovich (1884–1953), physicist. Corresponding member, Ac. of S., USSR (1927). Professor, Moscow University (1930). Research concerned electromagnetic phenomena in metals. Developed methods of magnetic spectroscopy. Author of *Electromagnetic Processes in Metals* (1934–36).

ARKHÁNGELSK: *see* ARCHANGEL.

ARKHÁNGELSKY, Andréy Dmítrievich (1879–1940), geologist. Fellow, Ac. of S., USSR (1929). Graduate, Moscow University (1904). Professor of Moscow University (1920–32) and Mining Academy (1924–32). As the director of the Institute of Geology (1934–40) organized major expeditions to study the geological structure of Kazakhstan and the European part of the USSR. Lenin prize (1928).

ARKHÍPOV, Abrám Yefímovich (1862–1930), painter, academician (1898), People's Artist (1927). Studied intermittently in Moscow 1877–88 (pupil of Perov and Polenov) and St. Petersburg, 1884–86. Member of the Society of Circulating Exhibitions (*Peredvizhniki*) from 1891. In 1880's painted scenes from peasant life (*Visiting an Ill Woman*, about 1885; *Village Painter of Icons*, 1889). His reproduction of light and air is particularly fine (*Along the Oka-River*, 1890, Tretyakov Gallery; *The Ice Is Gone*, 1895, Ryazan Art Museum). Author of several realistic pictures (*Charwoman in Iron Foundry*, 1896, *Washer Women*, 1899, Russian Museum, and 1901, Tretyakov Gallery).

ARMÁND (née Stephen), **Inéssa Fyódorovna** (1875–1920), communist. Born in Paris of an English father and French mother, she was brought up by her aunt, a governess in Moscow, and, in 1893, she married there a son of a wealthy family. In 1904, she joined the Bolshevik party. From 1909 she was abroad; she met Lenin in Paris and became his personal friend. In July 1914, she represented the Bolsheviks at the International Socialist Bureau in Brussels and in 1915–16 at the Zimmerwald and Kienthal conferences. In 1917, she returned with Lenin to Russia and settled in Moscow. Was active in the Comintern. In the summer of 1920, she went for a cure to the Caucasus and died there of cholera.

ARMAVÍR, city in Krasnodar Kray, RSFSR, on Kuban River; pop. 111,000 (1959). Flour, butter, tobacco, agric. machinery. Pedag. inst., technical schools.

ARMED FORCES. Imperial Russia. In medieval times the R. army was formed from feudal levies of nobles, called out for each campaign. Ivan IV added the *Streltsy* (q.v.) (Musketeers), a permanent force, who by 1600 numbered 12,000. In peacetime they did police duty and other nonmilitary tasks. In 1632 several regiments of troops which were organized along W. lines were formed, and often officered by foreigners. By 1681 they had grown to 78,000 and formed the backbone of the army. The feudal levies were still used, however, and the systems of command and supply were extremely complicated, so that the army lacked effectiveness.

With Peter I the R. army took more modern form. His "play regiments," which he had formed for his childhood games of war, became the Preobrazhensky and Semyonovsky Guards. In 1698 Peter destroyed the unruly Streltsy and in the Northern War built a regular army of almost 200,000 men around the nucleus of W.-style regiments, formed out of volunteers and peasants conscripted for life and commanded largely by nobles, who had learned warfare in the ranks. Units of infantry, cavalry, and artillery used the tactics of W. armies to good effect against the Swedes, to win the Baltic coastline and to make Russia a great power. Irregular forces of Cossacks and Bashkir tribesmen were also used, but it was the regular army founded by Peter that made Russia powerful throughout the 18th century.

In the Seven Years' War (1756–63) the R. army numbered 331,000. Its troops fought against the Prussian armies of Frederick II with much success, in spite of incompetent generals. At Zorndorf the stubborn R. forces stood up to the best Prussian troops, and at Kunersdorf in 1759 R. and Austrian troops almost destroyed Frederick's army. In 1760 R. troops briefly occupied Berlin. They failed to follow up their advantage, however, and eventually a new R. ruler made peace with Prussia. Nevertheless, this war had produced talented R. young commanders. Pyotr Aleksandrovich Rumyantsev introduced new light infantry tactics and attack by columns rather than in line with great effect in the Turkish wars of Catherine II. He was followed by Aleksandr Vasilyevich Suvorov, probably Russia's greatest soldier.

Suvorov, an eccentric, knew military history and developed his troops into highly effective soldiers. He insisted on decent treatment of the enlisted men and he carefully explained his plans to them before leading them into battle. Long, rapid marches were one of the secrets of his success. In battle he emphasized musketry and artillery fire to disorganize the enemy, but in attack his troops charged in columns with bayonet without halting to fire. By stressing rapid movement, dashing attack, and close pursuit of a beaten foe, he overcame huge Turkish forces and defeated Polish insurgents. His greatest feats were in Italy in 1799 where, in command of R. and Austrian troops, he repeatedly defeated veteran French armies. From Italy he led his forces into Switzerland. Here, unsupported by Austria, he fought his way out of a trap and led his unvanquished army home in triumph. Suvorov's ideas on warfare have had a great influence on R. military thinking to the present day.

In 1805 Alexander I entered the war against Napoleon. The R. army marched to join the Austrians, only to be crushingly defeated at Austerlitz. Austria had to make peace, but the Russians continued the war, counting on Prussia, their new ally. Prussia was overwhelmed at Jena, leaving the Russians alone against the French. At Eylau R. stubbornness resulted in a drawn battle, but at Friedland, in June 1807, R. bravery could not redeem poor generalship, and Alexander made peace at Tilsit. In 1812 Napoleon invaded Russia with the enormous Grande Armée, and the outnumbered R. troops (less than 200,000) were forced into a fighting retreat. West of Moscow Mikhail Illarionovich Kutuzov made a stand at Borodino, where he fought an indecisive battle with losses on both sides. Although the R. army was still full of fight, Kutuzov felt it necessary to retreat through Moscow to a defensive position S.E. of the city. When the French retreated in Oct., Kutuzov harassed them, leaving hunger, cold, and peasant bands to complete their destruction. After Kutuzov died in April 1813, Alexander insisted on no peace with Napoleon. Aided by other powers, the R. army pursued Napoleon to his defeat at Leipzig and then into France. In March 1814, R. forces took part in the capture of Paris.

After the Napoleonic Wars Alexander came under the influence of Aleksey Andreyevich Arakcheyev, an able artillery officer, whose brutality became notorious. He intensified the tendency toward parade-ground training instead of the battle practice of the Suvorov school, enforcing this by discipline of the fist and stick. Arakcheyev also built up Alexander's "military colonies," where regiments were quartered on villages of peasants who, together with the soldiers, had to drill and farm under incessant, harsh supervision. When the exasperated men revolted, Arakcheyev flogged them with a cruelty remarkable even in that day. In 1820 the mutiny of the Semyonovsky Guards against a brutal commander merely convinced Alexander of the need for Arakcheyev's system of unthinking obedience.

During the wars, however, idealistic young officers had seen freer military systems. R. brutality aroused them to conspire and to rise in the Decembrist revolt of 1825 against the new tsar Nicholas. While the revolt was easily quelled, it convinced this ruler that his security required iron military discipline.

Under Nicholas I (1825–55) the R. army grew to almost one million men and was famed for the perfection of its vast parades. It was, however, poorly prepared for war. The infantry, which relied on the bayonet, had scanty training in musketry. The resplendent cavalry knew little about scouting and outpost duty and the pampered horses were not fit for hard campaigning. There were few capable generals. Nevertheless, this army won several wars, but this was owing to the weakness of the foe and the toughness of the R. soldier rather than to good military technique. In the Crimean War the Russians, 200,000 strong, fought well against the British and French, although weak in leadership and weapons. The siege of Sevastopol ended in Aug. 1855 in a humiliation for Russia.

After this defeat Dmitry Alekseyevich Milyutin, minister of war, dealt with the glaring weaknesses of the R. army. He humanized its discipline, greatly improved its technique and its supply system, and in 1874 introduced universal service, with a term of service of six years instead of fifteen years. In the R.-Turkish war of 1877–78 the new army of 724,000 did well, in spite of poor leadership, weak supply and medical services, and a lack of rifles equal to those of the Turks. After having starved the Turks at Plevna into surrender, the R. forces, with 300,000 men south of the Danube, crossed the Balkan Mountains in midwinter and compelled the Turks to ask peace. The Russians were also victorious in Transcaucasia.

The Japanese War of 1904–05 was fought at the end of a long, unfinished railroad against superior Japanese numbers. The R. army also was weak in machine guns and mountain artillery. After retreating from Korea into Manchuria it tried vainly to defeat one Japanese army while the other was besieging Port Arthur. Finally Port Arthur fell and the Japanese armies united to defeat the 300,000 Russians at Mukden in Feb. 1905, with heavy losses on both sides.

By Aug. 1914 the R. army was greatly improved, with a war strength of 5.5 million. It was, however, much inferior to the German army in artillery, machine guns, planes, and communications, although stronger than the Austrians. R. commanders mistakenly underestimated fire-power and copied Suvorov in stressing the bayonet. To relieve the hard-pressed French the army invaded E. Prussia, suffering grave defeats at Tannenberg and the Masurian Lakes. It also overran Galicia and roundly whipped the Austrians, although by early 1915 its ammunition was spent. In May the Germans attacked with overwhelming artillery and drove the Russians back with frightful losses to a line from Riga to Galicia. Under an incapable minister of war the Russians even lacked rifles as well as shells. When the Germans halted in Oct., the Russians rebuilt the army, which had lost 3,400,000 men since Aug. 1914, and by June 1916 it was stronger than ever. Under Gen. Aleksey Alekseyevich Brusilov the Russians overran the Austrians and by Sept. had taken 400,000 prisoners. But the R. losses of almost 2,500,000 men during 1916 demoralized the soldiers, who were already deserting in large numbers. On the Turkish front the Russians also achieved considerable but indecisive successes. Thus by early 1917 the R. army, which had several times given great aid to its allies, was itself close to collapse.

BIBLIOGRAPHY: Walter Lyon Blease, *Suvorov*, London, 1920; Rupert Furneaux, *The Siege of Plevna*, London, 1958; N. N. Golovine, *The Russian Army in the World War*, New Haven, 1931; Sir Alfred W. F. Knox, *With the Russian Army, 1914–17*, London, 1921; Eugene Tarle, *Napoleon's Invasion of Russia*, New York, 1942.   J. S. C.

THE RED ARMY, 1917–1941. On Jan. 15, 1918, the Council of People's Commissars of the new Soviet government decreed the formation, on a voluntary basis, of a "Workers' and Peasants' Red Army" to serve as defender of the Russian Revolution and military vanguard of the world proletarian movement. Leon Trotsky, as commissar of war after March 1918, undertook to organize the new army from a nucleus of former imperial officers and detachments of the Red Guards, the latter a scattered force of military formations, some 50,000 strong.

A coherent war effort was soon under way against the White and foreign "enemies of the Revolution." Trotsky became chairman of a supreme war council in June 1918 and, in this capacity as well as through his work at the War Commissariat, he became the leading spirit behind the military operations of the next two years. The army grew as the civil war proceeded. With the introduction of compulsory service for men between 18 and 40 (July 10, 1918), its numbers increased from 300,000 at the end of 1918 to 5,300,000 by 1920.

Lacking trained leadership, the Red Army was forced to rely on the services of thousands of former tsarist officers. Some of these were attracted by promises of good treatment and prospects of advancement; others were the victims of varying degrees of compulsion. Their presence led the government to appoint "political commissars" for all army units as a precaution against the possible subversive influence of such remnants of the Old Regime and to maintain political enthusiasm among the troops. Commanders were left free to plan military operations, but their orders had to be countersigned by the commissars attached to their respective units. The result was a duality of command, the source of considerable friction between civil and military authorities before such commissariats were downgraded in 1942.

The campaigns of 1918–20 saw the emergence of a new group of revolutionary officers. New commanders like M. V. Frunze, S. K. Timoshenko, S. M. Budyonny, A. I. Yegorov, K. Ye. Voroshilov now joined such former imperial officers as S. S. Kamenev, B. M. Shaposhnikov, and the youthful M. N. Tukhachevsky to form a new Soviet military elite, the high command of the future. Their ranks were bolstered by the arrival of fresh command material from the temporary officer-training schools established by the Commissariat of War.

Then came peace, which, for the Red Army, meant demobilization and the beginning of a long period of intensive reorganization and expansion. Between 1921 and 1924 there was much, and sometimes bitter, discussion as to the form and size of the permanent peace-time Red Army. With the resignation of Trotsky in 1925 and his replacement as war commissar by Mikhail V. Frunze, it was decided that the army should consist of 562,000 men, made up of 29 infantry and 12 cavalry divisions. A territorial militia was also to be organized, with 42 infantry and 4 cavalry divisions. The army was to remain an exclusively workers' force recruited on a compulsory service basis, while the "bourgeois" were left to do their service in unarmed labor battalions. Provision of training facilities and courses in the military arts was to be speeded up, with the continued presence of political commissars intended as a final guarantee of high morale and peak efficiency.

Implementation of these measures began under Frunze who also, before his death in 1925, took action to restore order and discipline at all levels of military life. Thus his successor, Kliment Voroshilov, a long-time associate of Stalin, was able to concentrate his ministerial attentions elsewhere, notably on the modernization of arms and equipment. This proceeded apace with the general economic and industrial development of the Soviet Union after 1925. By 1933, the Red Army's heavy and light artillery was said to be comparable with any in Europe and its air arm already superior to that of the French. Tanks increased in number from 10,000 in 1935 to upwards of 15,000 in 1937–38, and planes from roughly 5,000 to 10,000.

At the same time the quality of officer personnel improved steadily. The secret exchanges with the German military establishment before 1933 were of considerable use in this respect. Under the German influence, Tukhachevsky and others found the idea of airborne troop operations especially salutary and urged its adoption by the Red command.

Further measures of improvement and expansion followed Hitler's rise to power and the increased military activity of the Japanese. In March 1934, a Commissariat of Defense was formed with sweeping powers over the armed forces. This was followed four years later by the establishment of a Supreme Military Council headed by Stalin. The general character of the army also underwent changes at this time. Originally envisioned as the military vanguard of the world proletarian movement, the Red Army now became more self-consciously "Russian" in orientation. After Jan. 1939, the Soviet soldier swore to "fight for his homeland, the USSR," whereas under the soldier's oath decreed in 1918 he had taken the working classes not only of Russia but of all the world as the object of his protective ardors. This development was in line with Stalin's policy of "Socialism in One Country" and the Constitution of 1936. Another old revolutionary principle, that of the Red Army as an exclusively working-class force, was similarly abandoned with the military service law of 1939, which made all male citizens over nineteen, regardless of social origin, eligible for military duty. This same desire to rationalize military organization, regardless of ideological scruples, was also manifest in 1935 with the establishment of a system of officer ranks reminiscent of the old Imperial army and the institution of a new rank of Marshal of the Soviet Union.

Such reforms were accompanied, after 1934, by a steady rise in the number of men under arms, until by 1939 the Red Army reached an estimated 2 mill. To bolster the reserves of trained manpower, the work of the para-military organization *Osoaviakhim*, first established as a means of universal military training in 1927, was extended into every area of Soviet life. Some 12 mill. were involved in its activities by 1939.

Thus did the Red Army after 1924 develop into a very considerable fighting unit. Yet the achievement was somewhat vitiated by the great purge of the mid-thirties which took a heavy toll of top-ranking military men. In 1937 Stalin claimed to have discovered a number of Red Army officers in treasonous conspiracy with the German and Japanese general staffs and otherwise plotting against the life of party leaders, including himself. The chief political commissar of the army,

Ian Gamarnik, committed suicide in May. Within a month, Marshal M. N. Tukhachevsky and Generals I. E. Yakir, Kork, I. P. Uborevich, R. P. Eideman, Feldmann, V. M. Primakov, and V. K. Putna were all arrested, tried *in camera* and sentenced to death. Among the purged were also Marshal A. I. Yegorov and Gen. V. K. Blücher. Some 35,000 officers were in one way or another disposed of, including a great number of the Soviet high command. Numbered among them were most of the veterans of the civil war and the remnants of the old Imperial officer corps.

The victims were replaced by men whose greatest claim to military rank lay in their absolute loyalty to Joseph Stalin. Thus G. K. Zhukov, A. I. Antonov, A. M. Vasilevsky, I. S. Konev, R. Ya. Malinovsky, S. K. Timoshenko, and others of similar ilk now rose to prominence under one of the few remaining officers of tsarist days, B. M. Shaposhnikov, who became Chief of the General Staff. This massive shake-up is often held responsible for the poor showing of Soviet arms in the initial stages of both the Finnish war and World War II.

The Finnish campaign was the first major test faced by the Red Army after its years of development. Some important defects were quickly noticed, and there followed the dismissal of Voroshilov as war commissar together with a concerted effort, under the direction of Marshal Timoshenko, to achieve greater toughness and efficiency on the part of the troops. The German invasion brought a belated general mobilization, involving 170 army divisions, and the assumption by Stalin of supreme command over the country's defenses.

1941–1945. In June 1941 the Red Army was in many respects, numerically if not qualitatively, superior to the German invader. By 1945, this superiority was overwhelming, with 5.3 mill. Soviet troops on the European front alone. There were 527 rifle divisions, 302 armored and mechanized brigades, 43 artillery divisions, 13,400 tanks and 16,000 planes. Officer schools turned out more and better command personnel as the war proceeded; troops were tough and well trained for their task; organization became more efficient; and service and supply facilities improved steadily. The vast human reserves were a boon to the Soviet command which, despite great casualties, depended on mass infantry attacks supported by armored and mechanized forces both for initial break-throughs and advances in depth—forces which, in the latter case, were further augmented by heavy artillery fire and strong air support employed.

The exigencies of war forced continuation of the long-standing trend toward repudiation of the military legacy of the revolution and civil war. In Oct. 1942 the political commissars were made subordinate to the military commanders. The war became a "patriotic" war and nationalist propaganda among the troops was intensified accordingly. Guards regiments and divisions, reminiscent of tsarist times, were created; traditionalist decorations instituted; Cossack formations restored. Nov. 1942 saw epaulettes reintroduced, though once they had been regarded as symbols of a reactionary military caste system. Saluting again became obligatory, and officers were given their own social and dining facilities.

The officer corps received further recognition when Stalin entered it as a marshal in March 1943. Many of the officers who had been exiled or dismissed during the prewar purge were reinstated. Wholesale promotions became common and were duly celebrated in the Soviet press. New men, many of them young, all battle-tested, rose to top commands. They included Zhukov, Vasilevsky, Rokossovsky, and Malinovsky whose performances won them distinctions far surpassing those once enjoyed by such fading veterans as Budyonny and Shaposhnikov. By 1945 the prestige of the Red Army and its commanders was very high.

BIBLIOGRAPHY: E. M. Earle, "Soviet Concepts of War," in Earle, ed., *Makers of Modern Strategy*, Princeton, 1943; B. H. Liddell Hart, ed., *The Red Army*, New York, 1956; D. F. White, *The Growth of the Red Army*, Princeton, 1943; Erich Wollenberg, *The Red Army: A Study in the Growth of Soviet Imperialism*, London, 1940.
                                                               C. J. F.

SOVIET ARMY, 1945–1960. At the end of World War II in 1945, Soviet military power stood at its height in both Europe and the Far East. Soviet armies had driven the Germans out of Russia, and had occupied East and Central Europe, and in the Far East the Russians had occupied Manchuria and part of Korea. Some 19 mill. men were under arms; the land forces comprised 70 armies (11 of them elite "Guards Armies"), with a total of over 500 active divisions. The SA was, moreover, not only a victorious conqueror in war: from the moment of victory it was used to decide the political future of five European countries and one Asian country; for, wherever Soviet military power was firmly established, Soviet political power followed.

Within the SA itself, the end of the war brought a major release of manpower to civilian life. From 1945 to 1947, the forces were reduced from 19 mill. men to just under 4 mill., of which the A accounted for over 3 mill. Stalin handed over the Ministry of Defense to Marshal Bulganin, who, with Marshal Vasilevsky as his Chief of the General Staff, launched a program of reorganization and reequipment in accordance with the Soviet Union's economic and strategic position. The Soviet government's decision to resume the prewar policy of priority for heavy industry gave the forces the arms which they needed, but until the Soviet Union acquired its own atomic weapons (the first Soviet atomic bomb was tested in 1949), the A concentrated on those aspects of military policy which, in the Soviet view, would be most likely to deter the Americans from using their monopoly of the bomb against the Soviet Union. Soviet military planners, therefore, turned their attention to air defense, and the creation of a large and mobile land army capable of sweeping westward in the event of war and occupying the whole of continental Europe.

From 1947, when the A's reorganization was completed, to 1953, when the Soviet Union exploded its first hydrogen bomb, the military leaders concentrated on modernization of the land A. Armored forces were divided into tank and mechanized divisions, instead of the wartime corps and brigades; a tank division had 10,500 men, and a mechanized division 13,000 men. A new formation was introduced—the mechanized army, consisting of 3 mechanized divisions and 1 tank division—which was intended to exploit a strategic breakthrough by assault (or "shock" armies, to give their Soviet title), with close air support. Four of these mechanized armies were stationed in E. Germany, and were deployed immediately behind the assault armies along the zonal boundary, and this deployment of the SA's western spearhead was intended by the Soviet command as the most effective deterrent to American military power which the Russians could devise in the absence of their own nuclear weapons.

In 1949, Marshal Vasilevsky became minister of defense, and a year later, minister of war, when, as an experiment, the Navy was given its own ministry. By this time the number of A divisions had been fixed at 175, of which 65 were armored (tank or mechanized) and the remainder infantry (or rifle), with a few cavalry divisions stationed in remote areas. Of the 22 divisions deployed in E. Germany, 18 were armored and 4 were rifle. Small forces were also maintained in Austria (1 division); Hungary (2 divisions); Poland (2 divisions); and Rumania (2 divisions). The remainder of the Soviet land army was concentrated in three main areas: west of a line from Leningrad to Odessa, in the Caucasus, on the Turkish and Iranian frontiers, and in the Far East.

Internally at this time, the A was in the hands of senior officers of Stalin's choice, and some distinguished wartime commanders, like Marshal Zhukov, were in disgrace. After the war, the A's political organization was given the task of reviving the indoctrination of all ranks with communist beliefs, a program which had lapsed during the war. Much more sinister, however, was the influence of the secret police network in the A, which maintained agents with wide powers in all branches of the service, and was Stalin's particular instrument for keeping the forces under his control.

After Stalin's death in 1953, the subsequent fall of Beria, and the partial dismantling of the security apparatus in the forces, the High Command was reorganized under a Ministry of Defense, and Marshal Zhukov returned to become a deputy minister. Two years later he was appointed minister of defense. At the same time, a debate of considerable proportions developed within the SA on the need to reexamine military doctrine and the role of the A in the light of nuclear weapons and guided missiles. By 1955, military leaders were beginning to accept the implications of the destructiveness of the new weapons, and abandoned the concept of a land campaign after the pattern of World War II, using the vast spaces of Soviet territory for maneuver. The marshals and generals put through a second reorganization of the A, setting up an independent Air Defense Command, and cutting down the strength of the land A both in manpower and numbers of divisions ready for active service.

They withdrew their troops from Austria and from their bases in Finland and Port Arthur, and embarked on a tactical reorganization of the ground forces aimed at increasing mobility in conditions of nuclear warfare. In 1959 and 1960 further reductions in manpower were made, and at the end of the current program, in Dec.

1962, the SA is expected to number 2,430,000 men, organized in 110–120 divisions, all of which are likely to be either armored or motorized. There will, of course, be large trained reserves, and military service will, no doubt, be retained at its present period of two years for the A. But the trend in Soviet military organization appears to be toward mobile, hard-hitting formations, armed with nuclear weapons and rockets, and trained to operate on battlefields contaminated by atomic radiation. In the event of war, the A could be quickly expanded to meet the needs of the existing situation.

Nevertheless, it would be true to say that the mainstay of the Soviet forces is still the land A, relying on tactical air support. As far as organization is concerned, the armed forces in the Soviet Union are concentrated in the hands of the minister of defense, Marshal R. Ya. Malinovsky, who succeeded Marshal Zhukov in Nov. 1957. He governs mainly through a General Staff and five commanders in chief. The General Staff is headed by Marshal M. V. Zakharov, who was Soviet commander in chief in Germany from 1957 to 1960, and has held his present post since April 1960. The chain of command passes from the minister to the commander in chief of the land forces, Marshal V. I. Chuykov; of the air force, Air Marshal K. A. Vershinin; of the navy, Admiral S. G. Gorshkov; of the air defense forces, Marshal S. S. Biryuzov; and of the rocket forces command, Marshal Kiril S. Moskalenko. Also within the Ministry of Defense, but not subordinate to these headquarters—acting in a technical capacity—are the chief directorates for artillery, armored forces, the air-borne troops, the rear (or supply) services, and, of course, the influential chief political directorate, which is responsible for the political indoctrination of the officers and men of the Soviet forces.

The next link in the chain is the military district. For military purposes the Soviet Union is divided into 20 districts, each commanded by a marshal or a senior general, according to the geographical position and importance of the district. The commander of a military district is advised by a military council, on which the chief political officer of the district occupies a key position. Few reliable details are, naturally, available in the West about the distribution of Soviet or satellite ground or air forces. There are certainly 20 divisions, 8 AA divisions and two artillery divisions in E. Germany, two armored divisions in Poland, and three in Hungary; and it is not believed that there has been any major redeployment of Soviet land forces inside the USSR since the mid-1950's. Most estimates place the number of divisions in the A which can be regarded as operational in the region of 140, of which about half are armored. From 30 to 35 other divisions, mostly stationed in the interior of the country, are regarded primarily as training formations, and cannot be counted as mobilized or ready for military operations.

Soviet troops stationed in E. Germany and in the W. districts of the Soviet Union are organized in armies, but in the interior of the country, the division is the highest field formation. The tank division is now believed to have a strength of 13,500 men, and the mechanized divisions of 16,000. Ultimately, as more wheeled transport becomes available, the conception of a rifle division of 13,000 men may disappear altogether from the field armies. These armies appear to be flexible in composition, with no fixed establishment of divisions. Field armies are made up according to the needs of the situation, and the proportion of rifle and armored divisions varies considerably. It seems likely, however, that each will still have a strong component of field artillery —one or more artillery divisions—and an antiaircraft division as well.

We now come to the problem of the equipment maintained in Soviet operational formations. On the use of nuclear and atomic weapons we have the statement of the former minister of defense, Marshal Zhukov, made in March 1957, in which he said: "Atomic weapons at present . . . will be adopted more and more in the place of conventional arms. In the event of a major armed conflict, atomic weapons will inevitably be brought into action as the basic means of striking." But there has been some criticism in the Soviet military press of the atomic cannon on the grounds of its unwieldiness, and it seems likely that in the foreseeable future, the tactical air force will be the main arm of service entrusted with the delivery of the atomic weapon.

This does not mean that the Soviet military planners neglect conventional weapons. Conventional artillery and armored vehicles have a high priority, and the T-34, with which the A has been equipped for many years, is giving way in the best formations to the new T-54, with increased speed, firepower, and protection. There are also the heavier Joseph Stalin tanks and self-propelled guns of advanced pattern. No reliable information is available on the distribution or use of any kind of tactical guided weapon in A. Indeed, the Soviet press does not give either Soviet citizens or the outside world an accurate assessment of weapons and military equipment, but every military writer in the Soviet press is at pains to assure his readers that no expense is being spared to give the SA the best and latest in tanks, guns, automatic weapons, and innovations on the battlefield, such as television.

So much for a brief survey of the postwar development and organization of the SA today. But in order to understand the significance of the military machine at the disposal of the Soviet Union, it is essential to look in addition at Soviet military doctrine.

The forces of the Soviet bloc are organized, trained, equipped, and deployed according to a very precise military-political doctrine. Briefly, this doctrine holds that victory in war can be won only by military occupation of the enemy's territory, and the exploitation of all his natural and industrial resources in the interests of the Soviet bloc. This fits in with the Marxist-Leninist conception of the role of war in the communist revolution. Occupation of territory can come only after the destruction of the enemy's land forces in ground and air combat, and therefore it is the battlefield which still counts in warfare, not what happens to the civilian and industrial centers of the Soviet homeland. Soviet military doctrine does not believe that a war between the United

States and the Soviet Union could be won by either side through a nuclear strike against each other's country. They do not believe in the power of one weapon, however terrible, to win victory. In fact, Soviet military theory envisages a war in which the armed forces and the home defense organizations are waging two separate wars: the home defense, composed of guided missiles, fighter defense, and anti-aircraft artillery, warding off or limiting the effect of an American nuclear strike; and the ground and tactical air forces conducting a land battle far away against the enemy's field forces, aiming at the latter's destruction, and the final occupation of his territory. In the event of war, since the possibility that the land mass of North America could be occupied by Soviet ground forces is not considered feasible in the context of existing weapons systems, Soviet military thought is concerned with the destruction of enemy forces and other bases within reach of the Soviet bloc in a series of land campaigns waged in conditions of nuclear warfare.

Evidence for this outlook is to be found in the pages of the Soviet military publication *Military Herald* of June 1958, which contained an article called "Soviet Military Science on the Characteristics of Modern War." The article included the following passage:

"One of the most important tasks of military science is to foresee and correctly determine the nature of a future war, its basic characteristics and peculiarities. It it impossible to conduct a war successfully and to win it without adequately preparing the armed forces, and the whole country in peacetime. And the general theory of warfare must supply an answer to the question as to what sort of war we must prepare for.

"The armed forces peculiar to contemporary war, far exceeding in number those of earlier wars, and the technical weapons with a range unknown in history, can no longer be fitted into those limits which characterized past wars. The massive armies of today, consisting of many millions of men, require an immeasurably greater space than armies of the past. And the greater the numerical strength of armies, and the range of technical fighting equipment, the greater the territorial and strategic dimensions of a war.

"It can hardly be doubted that if a third world war is unleashed, it will exceed the First and Second World Wars in its territorial scope and may embrace the land and water surface of the whole globe.

"The armed forces of both sides and the territorial extent of armed struggles are so great under contemporary conditions that it is scarcely possible to conclude a war within a short period of time. Even the appearance of atomic and hydrogen weapons, of medium and long-range rockets, cannot ensure the swift destruction of such massive armed forces, and consequently a swift conclusion to the war. In fact, the use of these weapons by both sides leads rather to the prolonging of a war, than to its speeding up. Thus, if in the past big wars might just as well be short as long, in our epoch, all big wars are inevitably acquiring a more or less long-drawn-out character. . . .

"The appearance of atomic and hydrogen weapons on the scene alters the nature of war in many ways,

but of course a war cannot and will not be fought with these weapons alone. We must prepare not for a mild but for an extremely extensive war, which for its whole duration will require huge replacements for armed forces. The possibility of great losses likewise leads to a considerable increase in the number of reserves—strategic, operational and tactical—which in a future war will, to a much higher degree than in the past wars, be earmarked to replace troops that have been put out of action. Thus, as regards the advent of weapons of mass destruction, we must by no means expect armed forces to vanish or to be reduced in a future war but in fact to continue expanding."

This outlook is also apparent in Soviet training. Exercises are devised to practice the crossing of rivers and other natural obstacles at night in conditions which might be encountered after an atomic explosion has taken place. Great attention is being paid to the training of armored forces, which, in Soviet military literature, are envisaged not only as a method of speeding up the advance and increasing mobility, but also as a vehicle for protection. Much importance is being given to speed of maneuver, to dispersal, and to the need for operating in difficult country in order to avoid the more natural targets for the enemy's atomic strike in open ground or main lines of communication.

In conclusion, it seems clear that the SA is a large, well-trained and well-equipped weapon of war in the hands of the Soviet leaders, who attach great importance to its development and armament. One of the reasons for this is that armed force occupies a well-defined place in communist political thought. This in its turn has led to the development of a precise military doctrine involving the belief that whatever destruction is wrought inside the Soviet Union in nuclear war, the conventional A, equipped with the latest atomic weapons and guided missiles, must be preserved to fight the critical series of land battles which must precede final victory and the occupation of the enemy's land bases and, if possible, his complete territory.

BIBLIOGRAPHY: B. H. Liddell Hart, *The Soviet Army*, London, 1956; Raymond L. Garthoff, *Soviet Military Doctrine*, Glencoe, 1954; Raymond L. Garthoff, *Soviet Strategy in the Nuclear Age*, New York, 1958; H. S. Dinerstein, *War and the Soviet Union*, New York, 1959; G. I. Pokrovsky, *Science and Technology in Contemporary War* (edited and translated by Raymond L. Garthoff), New York, 1959.

                                             J. M. M.

SOVIET AIR FORCE AND NAVY. Because of the nature of Russia as a massive land power dependent for her defense mainly on the Army, the Air Force and the Navy originated as auxiliary services to the land army. The air arm of the Red Army after the revolution grew out of the small but efficient air force of the Imperial Army; the N, of course, had a much longer tradition dating back to the early 18th century, which included a number of naval actions in the Baltic, the Black Sea, the Mediterranean, and in the Far East.

The early years of the Soviet AF were dominated by the need to build up a corps of AF officers from the ranks of the land army, and to develop an aircraft industry capable of providing efficient Russian-built machines designed for the air support of the ground forces. Under the direction of Army Commander Alksnis, the AF became one of the most efficient branches of the service and, had its senior ranks not been decimated in the army purge of 1937–39, there is little doubt that it would have been more ready than it was to take the blows of the German invasion in 1941. As it was, the AF was very nearly destroyed on the ground in the early days of the war—as has been admitted by Soviet military historians—and the losses suffered in these first battles were so great that it was not until the summer of 1943 that the AF really returned to exercise a decisive influence on the land battle. By 1945, the Soviet field armies had air support from 18 air armies, which were subordinate administratively to the headquarters of the AF in the Commissariat of Defense, but tactically to the front commanders in the field. In addition, there was a small long-range AF, under Air Marshal Golovanov, built up toward the end of the war, which carried out a few small raids against German cities in the east. Its contribution to the war effort was small, for strategic bombing formed no part of Soviet military doctrine.

After the end of World War II the AF began to develop a long-range striking capabiilty, but the bulk of the AF remained a tactical arm designed for close support of land operations. No separate AF was established, however. The commander in chief of the Soviet air arm, Chief Marshal of Aviation K. A. Vershinin, today ranks as one of the deputy ministers of defense, and he has a combined air staff under Air Marshal S. I. Rudenko, and a number of headquarters, each dealing with one type of air operation. These are the headquarters of tactical, or front-line, aviation, the AF of the air defense command, and the AF of the air-borne troops. Marshal Vershinin also has a technical staff and a political deputy, responsible for the political loyalty and indoctrination of the personnel of the AF. The long-range AF is an independent headquarters directly subordinate to the Ministry of Defense, and comprises three independent long-range air armies, two of which are established in W. Russia and one in the Far East. What is not yet clear is the relationship between the long-range AF and the newly-formed command of the rocket troops, announced by Khrushchev in May 1960. The commander of the rocket troops, Marshal Kirill S. Moskalenko, is not an AF officer; his headquarters is directly subordinate to the Ministry of Defense. But in the sphere of long-range air operations, it seems only logical that some form of close association should exist between the firing of intercontinental ballistic missiles and strikes by long-range aircraft.

Perhaps because of the nature of air operations in modern warfare, the commander in chief of the AF, unlike his naval counterpart, does not have operational control of the formations which make up his command. The chain of administrative control, however, passes from Marshal Vershinin to the AF units stationed in the military districts into which the Soviet Union is divided. This control is effective for training, technical services, and exercises, but, in the event of war, it would pass to the commander of the district or front, that is, to the land forces.

The divisions of the tactical AF are organized in air armies in the frontier military districts and in the groups of forces stationed abroad in E. Germany and Poland; otherwise the highest formation is a division. An air army may contain any number of subordinate formations according to the operations to be undertaken, including close support, air cover, interdiction bombing, and all kinds of reconnaissance. The air force attached to the air-borne troops also comes under Marshal Vershinin for administrative purposes, but operationally is subordinate to the commander of the airborne forces, another independent command under the Ministry of Defense. The fighter element of the air defense command also comes under the air headquarters administratively, but operationally is subordinate to the commander of the air defense district concerned.

Among the aircraft prominent in different roles in the tactical AF and the fighter force of the air defense command is the daylight interceptor fighter MIG–21, which, with a combat range in the region of 180 miles, has been in service with fighter divisions since 1958. Other formations are equipped with MIG–19 and –17. In fighter-bomber divisions and ground-assault formations, the MIG–15, with a combat range of 300 miles, is in service. The most effective medium bomber now in service is the TU–16, known as the "Badger," which is regarded in the West as the most dangerous aircraft for targets within the European zone of NATO's defense system. It has a Mach number attainable in level flight of 0.85, and a range of 1,500 miles. The long-range AF's standard heavy bombers are the TU–20 (the Bear) with a range of 2,150 miles and a Myasishchev aircraft (the Bison) with a range of 1,500 miles. Both aircraft have a height ceiling of 40,000 feet, but the latest indications are that production of both these aircraft has been slowed down, and may even have been stopped.

The main theme of Soviet air doctrine is that the primary role of aviation in wartime is to provide an aerial artillery service for the land army, either in advance or retreat. Air planners believe that the importance of strategic bombing with nuclear weapons has increased since World War II, but Soviet military thought appears to be directed toward the ultimate removal of this task from the bomber to the rocket command. In the long run, therefore, air power in the Soviet forces is likely to be regarded as air cover for the land forces, and as a transport service to bring land power to bear over long distances at short notice. In the realm of air defense, fighter aviation will continue to operate alongside ground-to-air missiles, and for the time being forms the major element of the Air Defense Command of the Soviet Union.

The N is the smallest of the three services, and the one on which, as far as surface craft at least are concerned, the cuts announced in 1960 will fall most heavily. The Soviet government inherited a N with a long tradition, but which had seen relatively little action during World War I. In the period between the two wars the N suffered severely in the purge of the armed forces, losing its commander in chief, Admiral Orlov, and most of its senior officers. During the German invasion, the fleets in the Baltic and the Black seas were driven back to their most easterly ports, and not until 1944 was the N able to cooperate with the land forces in significant operations. In the Black Sea, the N took part in the capture of R., Rumanian, and Bulgarian ports, and in the Baltic Sea contributed to the reoccupation of the Estonian Islands. In the Arctic Ocean the northern fleet helped to keep open the northern sea route from Britain to Murmansk and Archangel, and Soviet submarines scored a number of victories in coastal operations. Probably the most ambitious operation carried out by the N was the capture of the Kuril chain of islands from the Japanese in Aug. 1945 against stiff resistance.

After the war, there is some evidence that the future of the N was the subject of dispute among Soviet defense chiefs. At one time, from 1950 to 1953, the N was separated from the Army, and had its own Ministry. This experiment was not, apparently, a success, and in 1953 the N was returned to a new Ministry of Defense, under a commander in chief, Admiral of the Fleet N. G. Kuznetsov. He was believed to favor the creation of a large surface N with ocean-going heavy cruisers, and perhaps even a few aircraft carriers. He is believed to have clashed with Khrushchev himself on this point, who opposed the expansion of a surface fleet in conditions of nuclear warfare. Kuznetsov was dismissed in 1955, and replaced by Admiral S. G. Gorshkov. As a result, the emphasis of naval construction swung decisively over to submarines and those surface vessels which could be adapted to carry a missile armament. According to the program of cuts in the armed forces announced in Jan. 1960, the remaining surface ships are to be cut to a minimum, cruiser building is not to be resumed, and the Black Sea surface fleet, in particular, is to be reduced to small coastal units. Military planners apparently believe that this sea can be covered by land-based rockets and the naval air force.

The current strength of the N is believed to be: 25 cruisers, 130 destroyers, about 450 submarines, 300 frigates and escort vessels, 1,000 mine sweepers, 125 patrol boats, 500 motor torpedo boats and coasters, 120 landing craft, and 160 auxiliary vessels. The N also possesses two nuclear-powered icebreakers, the first of which, the *Lenin*, was hailed at its launching in Dec. 1957 as the "first atom-powered surface ship in the world." There is no firm evidence that the N has built any nuclear-powered submarines, but this would be a logical consequence of Khrushchev's ideas on sea power, and should be expected. In support of the N the Soviet Union maintains a naval air force of 3,500 modern jet aircraft—fighters and light bombers based on shore stations.

The N is divided into four fleets, and a number of flotillas in the Caspian and Azov seas, the Danube, the Amur River, and Lake Ladoga. The fleets are under the operational command of Admiral Gorshkov, and are organized as follows:

BALTIC FLEET: .... 6 cruisers
                                          35 destroyers
                                          120 submarines
BLACK SEA FLEET: .... 5 cruisers
                                          30 destroyers
                                          70 submarines

NORTHERN FLEET: .... 8 cruisers
                                          30 destroyers
                                          130 submarines
PACIFIC FLEET: .... 6 cruisers
                                          30 destroyers
                                          100 submarines

Of these fleets, the Northern and the Pacific are the only formations which have easy access to the open seas. There was also a small force of submarines based in the Albanian port of Valona, withdrawn in mid-1961.

In general, Soviet naval thought has concentrated on two functions for the N: coastal defense, its traditional role, and a new concept of long-range striking power through submarines, and some cruisers armed with missiles. But there seems little likelihood that the N will reach a position in the hierarchy of the armed forces comparable with the AF or the Army, and in the eyes of Soviet political and defense planners will continue to be, in the nuclear age as well, an auxiliary service. (*See also* AIRCRAFT INDUSTRY, SHIPBUILDING INDUSTRY, ROCKETRY)

BIBLIOGRAPHY: Asher Lee, *The Soviet Air and Rocket Forces,* London, 1959; Asher Lee, *Air Power,* (second edition), London, 1957; M. G. Saunders, *The Soviet Navy,* London, 1959.

J. M. M.

ARMENIAN PLATEAU (R. *Armyánskoye Nagórye*), volcanic highlands in the USSR, Turkey and Iran, divided by mountain ranges. Average elevations over 5,000 ft; the highest volcano is Ararat (16,912 ft.). Has frequent earthquakes.

ARMENIAN SOVIET SOCIALIST REPUBLIC (ARMENIA, Arm. *Haiastan*). Located in S. Transcaucasia, in the E. part of "Greater Armenia," Soviet Armenia borders on Georgia and Azerbaijan as well as on Turkish Armenia and Iran. Area, 11,500 sq. mi. Capital, Yerevan (509,000); other cities, Leninakan (108,000), Kirovakan (41,000).

Population is 1,763,000 (1959 census). Armenians account for 88% of the total (1,552,000), Azeri Turks for 6.1% (108,000), Russians for 3.2% (56,000) as against 2% in 1939, Kurds 1.5% (26,000), and others 1.2% (21,000). The average population density is about 143 persons per sq. mi.; 45% of the population live in the cities. Over one million Armenians live in other parts of the USSR (443,000 in Georgia, 442,000 in Azerbaijan), and over 1.2 mill. outside the USSR, many in the United States.

Nature and Climate. A is a mountainous country with several mountain ridges, plateaus, and valleys. The Ararat plain is south of Yerevan, along the Araks River. East of Yerevan, near the Azerbaijan border is Lake Sevan with its mountain plateau. The climate is continental—dry with strong temperature variations. The average July temperature is 64.5° F to 77° F; average Jan. temperature, 34° F to 8° F. The average yearly precipitation is between 12 and 32 in. in the mountains; 8–12 in. in the plain. The rivers of A belong to the Caspian basin. Mountains spread over half the territory, forests occupy 10%.

National Economy. A has several large hydroelectric

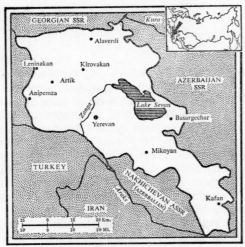

Armenian SSR

stations, nonferrous metallurgy (processing copper, molybdenum and other metals found in A), chemical factories (synthetic rubber, fertilizers), light industry (textiles and leather), canneries, and a wine industry.

Of the land 28.1 per cent is arable, 28 per cent is used as pasture, 5 per cent for hay; vineyards, fruit and vegetable gardens are numerous. Cattle breeding accounts for one third of the gross output. Sericulture exists in some areas.

History. Armenian history begins in the 9th century B.C. with the state of Urartu. The A people are said to have developed as a result of fusion of several ancient tribes after the fall of Urartu (6th century B.C.). By the end of that century A had been conquered by Persia and later, together with Persia, fell to Alexander the Great. By the end of the 4th century B.C. an independent A state emerged which managed to unite all A lands into a "Great Armenia." In the 1st century B.C., A was an important part of the Hellenistic world, having an active trade, a high degree of culture, and several urban centers (Artashat, Armavir, Tigranakert). Afterwards Rome and Persia fought over A and her position deteriorated. Christianity was introduced in the 4th century. In 387, A was divided between Persia and Byzantium, but A culture flourished and the A alphabet was invented in the year 393. In the second half of the 7th century A fell into Arab hands. By the end of the 9th century Armenians once again managed to establish their own kingdom, but subsequent Turkish (11th century) and Tataro-Mongol (13th century) invasions brought about the collapse of the A state and resulted in the first wave of A migration westward. From the middle of the 14th century the Khans of the Golden Horde fought the Turks for the possession of A. During the 16th and 17th centuries Iran (Persia) and Turkey fought for A and finally divided her in 1555 and again in 1639 (Iran got the E. and Turkey the W. part). Constant wars and religious persecution from their more powerful Moslem neighbors resulted in heavy population loss. In 1801 Russia, after annexing E. Georgia, appeared at the A borders. In 1828, as a result of the Russian-Iranian war, the main part of E. Armenia fell into R. hands. After the 1877–78 war against Turkey,

Russia annexed Kars and Ardagan, but Turkey managed to keep W. Armenia, where heavy massacres occurred in 1895–96 and 1915–16 taking a toll of hundreds of thousands Armenian lives.

In Russian Armenia a land reform took place in 1870 and industry and mining started to develop. However, national animosity among Georgians, Armenians, and Azeri Turks complicated the situation in Transcaucasia. Bolshevik groups became active in A on the eve of the 1905 revolution. Among their leaders were S. Shaumyan, S. Spandaryan, and B. Knunyants. The February revolution (1917) stimulated local nationalist movements. After the October revolution, the Transcaucasian Soviet headed by the Georgian Menshevik Zhordania refused to recognize the Bolshevik government and, faced with the Turkish menace, proclaimed the independence of Transcaucasia. In May 1919, owing to internal friction, the federation broke down and A became independent, with the Dashnak Nationalist party in power. Soon, however, Turkish troops entered A and stayed until the collapse of the Central Powers. British troops restored A independence, but left the area by the end of 1919. A Bolshevik revolt was easily suppressed, but A was soon invaded by Turkish armies of the new Turkish regime of Kemal Ataturk. Taking advantage of the situation, Soviet troops entered A, on Nov. 29, 1920 established the Armenian SSR, and concluded a peace with Turkey for the price of Kars and Ardagan.

In 1921 a nationalist revolt temporarily overthrew the Soviet regime, but was repressed a few months later by the Red Army. In March 1922 A was again included in a Transcaucasian Federation, this time a Soviet one. A became a union republic on Dec. 5, 1936. The great purge of 1936–37 did not spare A. Thousands of people were liquidated, including the secretary of the Armenian CP Khandzyan, the writer Bakunts, and many others. After World War II the USSR failed to recover Kars and Ardagan but succeeded in luring a large number of Armenians abroad into returning to Soviet A.

The best known Soviet statesman of A descent is A. Mikoyan.

Culture. Armenian literature goes back to the beginning of the 5th century. The epic *Sasuntsi David* (9th-10th centuries) describes A struggle against Arab invaders. In the 10th century Gregor Narekatsi wrote the first lay poetry. During the Middle Ages poetry prevailed in A secular literature. The masters of modern A literature (19th century) are Kh. Abovyan, the novelist Raffi, and the playwright G. Sundukyan. Twentieth-century writers of note are E. Charents, D. Demirchyan, and Marrietta Shaginyan in the USSR and especially William Saroyan in the United States.

The history of fine arts in A is older than the history of the country. Metal, wood and stone carving, ceramics, painting existed before the state of Urartu. Sculpture, miniature, jewelry, and embroidery have a millennial tradition. In the 17th and 18th centuries the Ovnatanyan family of painters was famous. The most prominent 19th-century artist of A origin was I. K. Ayvazovsky. Among those working in A were V. Surenyants and G. Bashindzhagyan. Of particular note in the 20th century are E. Tatevosyan, S. Agadzhanyan,

P. Terlemezyan, and M. Saryan in the USSR, Arshile Gorky in the U.S. and Carzou in France. Among sculptors: Ter-Haroutian in the U.S. and Sarksyan in the USSR.

Some architectural monuments in A date back to prehistoric times. Ruins of Unerhi forts (1st millennium B.C.), Hellenistic temples, and early Christian basilicas (4th-6th centuries A.D.), are found, together with the classical A architecture which developed in the 7th century and flourished in the 9th to 14th centuries. A number of medieval churches, palaces, houses, and other structures of stone employing a dome, arch, and vault construction are well represented.

Armenian music is very ancient; many of the songs existed before Christ and developed in the Middle Ages. The best-known Soviet A composer is Aram Khachaturyan, many of whose ballets and symphonies are known the world over. Alan Hovaness, an American-Armenian composer is known in the United States.

The A theater is almost 2,000 years old, but the modern theater began only in the 19th century. The playwright Sundukyan, the producer Chmskyan, and the actor Adamyan are among the pioneers of the modern A theater. The American movie actor Akim Tamirov is of A descent. M. R.

ARNÓLDI, Vladímir Mitrofánovich (1871–1924), botanist. Graduated from Moscow University (1893). Professor at Kharkov (1909), Kuban (1919), and Moscow (1922) universities. Research concerned the morphology of the gymnosperms and green algae.

ARTÉK, All-Union pioneer camp-sanitarium in Crimea on the Black Sea shore between Gurzuf and Ayu-Dag, founded in 1925. Accommodates 6,000 children a year.

ARTEL: *see* AGRICULTURE, KOLKHOZ.

ARTOBOLÉVSKY, Iván Ivánovich (1905–), machine and mechanical engineer. Fellow, Ac. of S., USSR (1946). Honored Scientist and Technologist, RSFSR (1945). Graduated from the K. A. Timiryazev Agricultural Academy in Moscow (1926). Professor, at the Moscow Institute of Chemical Technology (1932), Institute of Chemical Machinery (1932), the N. Ye. Zhukovsky Academy of Military Aircraft Engineering, Moscow University (1932–41), and Moscow Institute of Aviation (1941). Deputy academic secretary, Division of Technical Sciences, Ac. of S. (1942–54). Author of the first Soviet paper on three-dimensional mechanisms, *The Theory of Space Mechanisms* (1937), and of *Synthesis of Mechanisms* (1944) and *The Scientific Legacy of Chebyshov* (1945) for which he was awarded the P. L. Chebyshov medal by the Ac. of S. (1946). In collaboration with other scientists, developed methods of investigation of modern automatic machinery.

ARTSIMÓVICH, Lev Andréyevich (1909–), physicist. Fellow, Ac. of S., USSR (1953). Graduated from Byelorussian University (1928). Joined the Institute of Physical Technology, Ac. of S. (1930–48). Research in atomic and nuclear physics, particularly internal X-ray reflection, properties of fast electrons, and theoretical electron optics. Advanced a theory of chromatic aberration in electron optical systems (1943–46). In recent years, has been investigating powerful electric dis-

charges, control of thermonuclear reactions, and electromagnetic methods of isotope separation. Member of the editorial board of the journals *Doklady Akademii Nauk SSSR* (Reports of the Academy of Sciences, USSR) and *Vestnik Akademii Nauk SSSR* (Herald of the Academy of Sciences, USSR). Three orders of the Red Banner of Labor; Lenin prize (1958).

ARTSYBÁSHEV, Mikhaíl Petróvich (1878–1927), novelist, essayist, and playwright. His frank discussion of sex created a sensation. A's novel *Sanin* written in that vein enjoyed great popularity. His other better-known prewar books were *The Millions, Shevyrev, A Working Man* and *The Last Line.* World War I and the revolution added depth and earnestness to his work. His plays, *Jealousy* and *War* (1914–16), and his story, *The Wild Ones,* might have exerted an influence upon Sholokhov's *Quiet Flows the Don.* Expelled from the Soviet Union, A wrote anti-communist articles in the *émigré* press in Poland.

ARTYOM, city in Maritime Kray, RSFSR; pop. 56,000 (1959). R.R. station; coal-mining center; building materials.

ARTYÓM'S ISLAND, in Caspian Sea, near Baku; area about 4 sq. mi.; connected with the mainland by dam; crude oil.

ARTYÓMOVSK (f. Bakhmut), city in Stalino Oblast, Ukrainian SSR; pop. 61,000 (1959). Major center of salt mining, building materials. Pedag. inst., technical schools. Known since 1571.

ARTYÓMOVSKY, city in Sverdlovsk Oblast, RSFSR; pop. 31,900 (1956). Coal industry.

ARTYÓM VESYÓLY: *see* VESYOLY.

ARZAMÁS, a literary society at the beginning of the 19th century (1815–18). It included the so-called junior Karamzinists such as V. A. Zhukovsky, K. N. Batyushkov, Prince P. A. Vyazemsky, A. S. Pushkin, and others. The aim of the circle was the creation of a pure R. language similar in style to the conversational and colloquial language. In A there were no unified political and literary opinions.

ARZAMÁS, city in Gorky Oblast, RSFSR; pop. 39,000 (1939). Mfg. of felt, footwear, distilleries. R.R. junction. Pedag. inst.

ASÁFYEV, Borís Vladímirovich (pen name Igor Glébov) (1884–1949), music researcher, composer, academician, People's Artist, twice laureate of the Stalin prize. Author of many books on the history of music (*Symphonic Studies,* 1922; *Russian Music from the Beginning of the 19th Century,* 1930; *Glinka,* 1947), the theory of music (*Musical Form as a Process,* 2 vols. 1930–47). A composed 27 ballets (*The Flame of Paris,* 1932; *The Fountain of Bakhchisaray,* 1934) and 10 operas. In 1948 A was elected chairman of the Union of Soviet Composers.

ASBÉST, city in Sverdlovsk Oblast, RSFSR; pop. 60,000 (1959), Main asbestos mining and manufacturing center in USSR (Bazhenovskoye).

ASÉYEV, Nikoláy Nikoláyevich (1889–), futuristic poet. His early poetry—the collections *Night Flute* (1914), *Letorey* (1915), and *Oksana* (1916)—shows the influence of Igor Severyanin and the Ukrainian poet Pavlo Tylin. His artistry is manifested especially in

Queen of the Cinema (early 1920's), *Lyrical Interlude* (1924), and *Mayakovsky's Beginnings* (1936–39); it is less in evidence in his numerous poems with a political undertone, such as *Twenty Six* (1923), *The Sverdlov Storm* (1924), and *Semyon Proskakov* (1926). A is the author of a utopian novel *Tomorrow* (1923–24), only excerpts of which have been published, and of *The Beautiful Woman Without Makeup* (1928) which is a collection of impressions during his travels in European countries.

ASHÁ, city in W. Chelyabinsk Oblast, RSFSR; pop. 32,000 (1956). R.R. station; metallurgical plant and wood-chemical combine.

ASHKHABÁD, capital of Turkmen SSR; pop. 170,-000 (1959). Has cotton and silk mills, motion pictures, carpet mfg. Several schools of higher education (one university), museums, theaters. Seat of the Turkmen Ac. of S. Founded 1881; suffered considerable damage from 1948 earthquake.

ASHKHABÁD OBLAST, in Turkmen SSR, abolished May 1959.

ASPIRÁNT, a graduate student studying full-time or part-time in the *aspirantura* of a higher school and preparing for the degree of *kandidat nauk,* usually a prerequisite for advancement in teaching at higher schools or in research.

ASSR: *see* AUTONOMOUS SOVIET SOCIALIST REPUBLIC.

ASSÚR, Leoníd Vladímirovich (1878–1920), mechanical engineer. Graduated from Moscow University (1901) and the College of Technology in Moscow (1906). Professor, Petrograd Institute of Forestry (1918). Developed a rational classification of two-dimensional hinged mechanisms. Research concerned the theory of mechanisms and machinery.

ÁSTRAKHAN, city in RSFSR; pop. 296,000 (1959). Important Volga port for Baku oil, lumber, fish, salt, and grain shipments. It has fish-canning, lumber, ship-building ind. Fish-industry, medical, pedag. institutes and numerous technical schools. Was the capital of Astrakhan khans until 1556 when conquered by Ivan IV. Old kremlin, cathedral, and palace.

ÁSTRAKHAN, KHANATE OF, a Tatar state on the lower Volga, existing in the 15th and 16th centuries. It was annexed by Russia as a result of campaigns of Ivan IV (1556). This completed the R. control of the Volga waterway from central Russia to the Caspian Sea, Transcaucasia, Middle Asia, and Persia.

ÁSTRAKHAN OBLAST, RSFSR, on lower Volga, near Caspian Sea; area 17,000 sq. mi.; pop. 702,000 (1959); adm. center Astrakhan. Has sharply continental arid climate; fisheries and fish canning; salt ind.; very fertile flooded meadows, with cotton, truck farming, sheep breeding, karakul. Schools of higher education, theaters.

ASTRONOMY. The foundation of the following institutes and observatories greatly contributed to the development of Soviet astronomy: Leningrad Institute of Astronomy (now Institute of Theoretical Astronomy); P. K. Shternberg Institute of Astronomy at Moscow University; observatories at Abastuman, Stalinabad, and Byurakan (Yerevan area); Ashkhabad Astrophysical Laboratory; Astrophysical Institute of the Ac. of S., Kazakh SSR; mountain station at Kislovodsk of the Pulkovo Observatory; Division of Astronomy of the Physical Institute of the Latvian Ac. of S., and others. In postwar years the Pulkovo and Simeiz observatories which were destroyed during World War II have been restored and expanded. The Astrophysical Observatory of the Ac. of S., USSR, largest in the USSR, was built in the Crimea. Soviet observatories have worked extensively on the composition of various star catalogs. During 1932–38 observatories at Pulkovo, Moscow, Nikolayev, Tashkent and Kazan carried out work in compiling an over-all catalog for stars up to the sixth magnitude. Since 1938 the compilation work with participation of observatories of several foreign countries concerned the catalog of faint stars. This work is supervised by the astronomers (headed by M. S. Zverev) of Pulkovo Observatory. In 1940 A. N. Deych published his catalog of proper motion of 18,000 stars in selected areas of the sky according to the international plan, a result of studies which date back to 1906.

The development of stellar A is marked by such important accomplishments as the clarification of principal features of the structure and the development of our galaxy and other galaxies. V. A. Ambartsumyan, B. V. Kukarkin and others proved that our galaxy presents a complex system comprising a multitude of stars of various types and ages developing in different ways. It was shown that star formation in stellar systems is still in the process of development. During the past three decades the physical theory of nebulae was developed (V. A. Ambartsumyan, A. Ya. Kipper); P. P. Parenago and B. A. Vorontsov-Velyaminov made considerable corrections in the spectrum-luminosity diagram; light absorption in interstellar space was studied by P. P. Parenago who investigated the dependence of light absorption on the position of a star in space and compiled a light absorption map for the entire Milky Way. V. V. Sobolev developed a theory of mobile star atmospheres. O. A. Melnikov completed significant investigations on the spectroscopy of stars and V. A. Dombrovsky studied the polarization of star light. Soviet scientists are engaged in research work concerning variable stars, the designation of new variable stars, and the compilation of catalogs of these stars. A special bulletin *Variable Stars* has been published since 1928.

The new branch of the science of the universe, i.e. radio A, is also being developed in the USSR. Large radio-telescopes are installed at numerous observatories. The discovery of light polarization of crab nebula by V. A. Dombrovsky is of vital importance for the clarification of the nature of most recent stars. I. S. Shklovsky developed a theory of cosmic radiation and of the radio-astronomical origin of cosmic rays. Considerable accomplishments were made in the study of the sun and the relation between solar and geophysical phenomena. A bulletin entitled *Solar Data* is published regularly. Special techniques and instruments have been introduced for the observation of the sun, e.g. coronographs, photoheliographs, polarizing interferences filters, photoelectric spectrophotometry, radio observation. There is a large tower-type telescope for the observation of the sun at the Astrophysical Observatory of the Ac. of S., USSR, in the Crimea and a horizontal sun-telescope at the Main Astronomical Observatory of the Ac. of S., USSR. Modern ingenious instruments have been designed for the observation of eclipses of the sun.

Together with the general problems of the evolution of the universe, the study of the origin of the earth and planets of the solar system is being emphasized. V. G. Fesenkov advanced new hypotheses in this field.

s. s.

ATAMÁN, chief, commander of troops and Cossack combat units; in Ukraine initially an elected official but from 1723 the appointed head of the military and civil administration. The leaders of popular uprisings, for instance S. Razin, were also called A.

ATOMIC ENERGY. The late 1930's were a period of stimulating discovery in the world of nuclear physics. The excitement was shared and contributed to by a small group of highly competent Soviet physicists working in three or four research laboratories. On an official level the "Special Committee for the Problem of Uranium," which was established in the spring of 1940, represented state cognizance of the probable practical importance of the newly discovered fission of the uranium nucleus. World War II effectively terminated the work of the Special Committee but the AE program was revived in 1943 after the victory at Stalingrad. The Special Committee has since undergone a series of metamorphoses and may still actually exist as a high-level advisory group; administratively the atomic energy industry is directed by the State Committee of the Council of Ministers for the Utilization of AE. For many years the military phases of the program had been directed by the Ministry of Medium Machine Building, an organization which has been seldom mentioned. The key administrative individual for well over a decade since the program was revived had been General Boris Lvovich Vannikov, but from time to time others such as Vasily Semyonovich Yemelyanov, head of the State Committee, and Yefim Pavlovich Slavsky, Minister of Medium Machine Building, have been better known. Other ministries and state committees contribute their special talents and industrial resources.

On the basis of the first few laboratories, there has evolved a complex of scientific institutions with specialized tasks relating to the AE program; the signal for the proliferation of the AE installations was the successful operation of the first Soviet nuclear research reactor in the spring of 1947. Some of these laboratories are concerned with weapons production or other military operations and are unrecorded except for a large enterprise in Siberia which incorporates several nuclear reactors of comparatively low efficiency, each of which is projected to produce 100,000 kilowatts of electric power as well as large quantities of plutonium for military purposes. This plant represents the largest planned AE installation in the USSR and is one of three large-scale nuclear power plants scheduled for completion under the Plan which terminates in 1965. The other two are primarily for the production of atomic power and represent more advanced stages of that art.

The Novovoronezh plant under construction in the N.E. Ukraine, which has a rating of 210,000 kilowatts (perhaps to be doubled later), will be of the pressurized-water type. At Beloyarsk, 35 mi. E. of Sverdlovsk, an advanced type, of approximately the same rating incorporating a unique nuclear superheating principle, is also part of the Seven Year Plan.

The sum total of electric kilowatts to be installed by 1965 represents possibly half or less of the original goals at first prognosticated by 1963. Thus, as elsewhere in the world, the production of large amounts of nuclear power in the USSR has been delayed until such action is warranted by more advanced technical development which will give power rates competitive with conventional fuels.

Meanwhile several other concepts, none of them novel however, are being developed at an atomic test station near Ulyanovsk on the Volga. Generally it can be said that the present Soviet atomic power research program, although it has achieved very significant advanced results, has not been as extensive in scope of investigations as western programs and reflects a certain disenchantment with economic prospects.

Many aspects of the three large stations under construction were developed at the institute of the State Committee at Obninsk, 75 miles S.W. of Moscow, and at the Institute of Atomic Energy in Moscow. Obninsk is the site of the widely heralded "first atomic power plant" rated at 5,000 electric kilowatts, which began in 1954. Several interesting advanced reactor concepts, including a beryllium-moderated reactor and several plutonium-fueled fast reactors have also been investigated there. At the Institute of Atomic Energy emphasis has been placed on pressurized-water reactors. But the program of the Institute has a wider scope than atomic power and includes research and engineering into almost every aspect of AE such as isotope separation, thermonuclear power, and propulsion.

The icebreaker *Lenin*, which first journeyed under nuclear power in late 1959, represents the world's first use of atomic energy for *surface* propulsion. The problem of propulsion in all media from beneath the surface of the ocean and through outer space is one of high priority in the USSR, and it should be expected that AE is being investigated and applied where appropriate.

Among other organizations which have made significant contributions in the development of AE are the Institute of Theoretical and Experimental Physics (Moscow), the Moscow Engineering Physics Institute, the Radium Institute, the Ukrainian Physico-Technical Institute, the Institute of Chemical Physics, the Institute of Physical Problems. Large and competent cadres of nuclear physicists and engineers have been organized to staff these institutes. Igor Vasilyevich Kurchatov, until his death in early 1960, had been the primary force in the build-up of physical and personnel strength of the AE program, and no single individual seems qualified to inherit all of his responsibilities. His name now honors the Institute of Atomic Energy, of which he was the Director, and the Beloyarsk Atomic Energy

Station. Among other outstanding persons now well known in the world of science are A. I. Alikhanov, L. A. Artsimovich, I. K. Kikoin, A. P. Vinogradov, L. D. Landau, S. L. Sobolev, N. N. Semenov. They are men of senior responsibility, most of them heading their own laboratories or institutes.

Initially the centers of development were Moscow and Leningrad. However, as the AE programs proliferated and as advanced scientific techniques began to be appreciated in all other areas of scientific development, other centers such as the Ukrainian Physico-Technical Institute were expanded and new institutes established in remote areas. Presently under development is a scientific city being constructed south of Novosibirsk which will have a number of important institutes, some of them specializing in AE techniques.

AE demands employment of, and indeed can assist, a great number of arts other than that of nuclear physics, and accordingly institutes of widely different disciplines will be found associated with the utilization of nuclear forces. For example, at the Novosibirsk complex, the Institute of Inorganic Chemistry, which is a branch of the Kurnakov Institute of General and Inorganic Chemistry in Moscow, will expand many of the important investigations on implementing AE in the chemical industry. For the entire Novosibirsk complex the Institute of Mathematics and Computing Center, directed by S. L. Sobolev, will provide the computational assistance which becomes vital in the advanced stages of an AE program.

Another, the Nuclear Physics Institute, will be headed by G. I. Budker and will investigate the harnessing of thermonuclear power. Several others, including the Institute of Atomic Energy in Moscow, the Electro-Technical Institute in Leningrad, and laboratories in Sukhumi and Kharkov, are also attempting to solve this difficult problem. Large-scale experimental thermonuclear devices, some of them duplicating western machines, have been constructed but as of 1960 Soviet scientists seemed as distant as others from achieving the goal of thermonuclear power. This goal, however, is the first task listed for Soviet science under the Seven Year Plan.

Other advanced phases of Soviet nuclear research emphasize the use of accelerators, the most prominent center being at Dubna at the juncture of the Volga and the Moscow–Volga Canal where there are a 680-Mev phasotron and a 10-Bev synchrophasotron. A 50-Bev accelerator will be built at another site. The Joint Institute for Nuclear Research in Dubna is a somewhat unique research establishment for Russia since it represents the Soviet equivalent of the European Organization for Nuclear Research (CERN) at Geneva. Working at Dubna with Soviet personnel are scientists from the bloc nations. None of the problems at Dubna can be said to pertain directly to the harnessing of nuclear energy. The research relates primarily to defining the behavior and constitution of nuclear particles.

On the more applied level, despite the de-emphasis on atomic power, AE is being widely exploited by means of radioactive isotopes which have found wide application in Soviet industry. Yearly savings in industrial processes due to isotope uses amount to several billion rubles. A unique sales outlet is the isotope store and showroom in Moscow which, on presentation of proper licenses, disperses radioactive isotopes and special small-scale nuclear measurement equipment.

The raw materials for the Soviet AE program initially came from uranium deposits in East Germany and in Czechoslovakia and from well-known deposits in the Fergana Valley in Soviet Central Asia. However, these are now supplemented by materials from several other domestic discoveries. Heavy water, graphite, beryllium, and other necessary adjunct materials are in routine production.

One of the newer large uranium complexes is near the steel center of Krivoy Rog in the Ukraine. It is estimated that the production of this complex is 1,000 to 1,500 tons of ore containing about .2 per cent of uranium oxide. The ore from the Krivoy Rog and other plants is then processed through several routes into uranium-235 or plutonium to serve peaceful or military purposes.

For the military program, nuclear weapons have been overtly tested until the general world-wide cessation in 1958 at at least two sites, one near Semipalatinsk in Central Asia and the other in the vicinity of the northern island of Novaya Zemlya. The first Soviet atomic explosive device was tested on Aug. 29, 1949, and the first hydrogen device on Aug. 12, 1953; since then the art of nuclear weapons has advanced until they are now an integrated component of many sectors of Soviet armament.

Nuclear weapons are also an important constituent of Soviet political policy, a policy which encompasses as well attitudes toward peaceful sharing of AE. The Soviet Union participates in the International Atomic Energy Agency but has offered limited assistance through it. Soviet direct bilateral assistance to other nations has also not been extensive but is expanding. The first to receive atomic aid were the bloc nations, at least two of which—East Germany and Czechoslovakia—appear to have been given substantial assistance toward the construction of atomic power plants. The other bloc nations have been provided with research reactors, and there have been exchanges of data and personnel. Outside the bloc, Yugoslavia and the United Arab Republic and Indonesia have received small amounts of atomic research aid from the Soviet Union. In 1960 a major overture was made to India by an offer to participate in the designing and construction of a large power reactor; this may be a forerunner of overtures to other developing areas.

The advent of *Sputnik*, which was coincidental with a sudden world-wide realization of the vast amounts of conventional fuels available, has served to depress the subject of AE temporarily as a major economic and psychological force, except with respect to bomb testing. The re-emergence of other applications for power, for propulsion, or perhaps in some unique ways is, however, inevitable and the strong substructure of So-

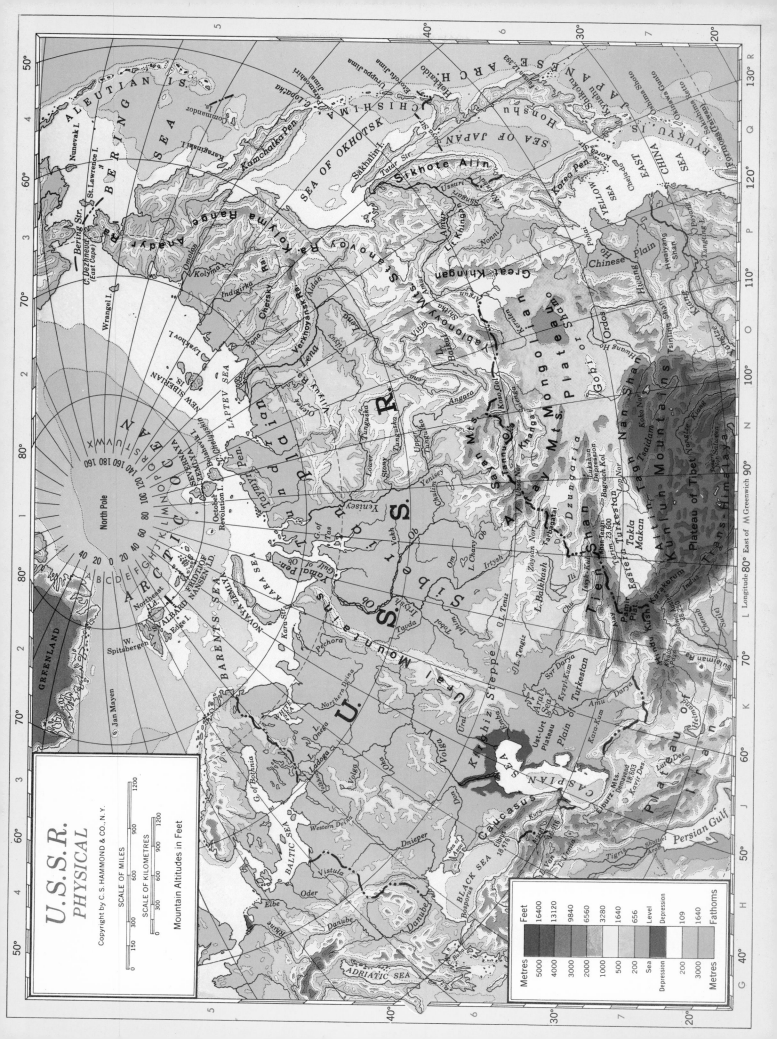

U.S.S.R.
PHYSICAL

Copyright by C.S. HAMMOND & CO., N.Y.

SCALE OF MILES
0   150   300   600   900   1200

SCALE OF KILOMETRES
0   300   600   900   1200

Mountain Altitudes in Feet

Feet
16400
13120
9840
6550
3280
1640
656
Sea Level
Depression

Metres
5000
4000
3000
2000
1000
500
200
Sea Level
Depression
109
1640
Fathoms

200
3000
Metres

INDEX OF GEOGRAPHICAL NAMES

viet nuclear research and industrial facilities should enable effective exploitation of that force.

BIBLIOGRAPHY: *Atomnaya Energia,* Moscow. (English translation published in L. and N.Y.); Arnold Kramish, *Atomic Energy in the Soviet Union,* Stanford, Cal., 1959; George A. Modelski, *Atomic Energy in the Communist Bloc,* Melbourne, 1959; Yemelyanov, Vasily Semyonovich, Editor. *Kratkaya entsiklopedia "Atomnaya Energia,"* Moscow, 1958.
A. Kr.

ATRÉK RIVER, in Central Asia along the Iran-Turkmenistan border; length about 310 mi.; used for irrigation.

ÁUER, Leopóld Semyónovich (1845–1930), violinist, teacher and conductor of Hungarian extraction. Worked in Russia until 1917. His class at the St. Petersburg Conservatoire was world famous. Among his pupils were Yasha Heifetz, E. Zimbalist, Mischa Elman. From 1918 he lived in New York.

AUGUST BLOC, an organization of R. socialist factions which met in Vienna in Aug. 1912. The mutual bond that held the diverse groups together was the desire to keep the Russian Socialist Democratic Labor party from being fragmented by Lenin and others. However, so many factions boycotted the AB that any chance of success was virtually precluded from the outset. The dominant figure of the AB was L. Trotsky who was supported by the Mensheviks and the Bundists. The AB failed in its ostensible goal of unity and succeeded only in establishing several short-lived periodicals. In 1914, even Trotsky disowned the group and it faded into oblivion.

AULIÉ-ATÁ: *see* Dzhambul.

"AURORA" CRUISER played a spectacular role in the revolution, especially in the Bolshevik seizure of power. In Aug. 1917 the sailors of A guarded the Winter Palace against Kornilov. Early in the morning of Nov. 7, A on the orders of the Military Revolutionary Committee entered Neva and anchored near the Nikolayevsky Bridge. In the evening A opened fire at the Winter Palace. The fire did very little damage and lasted only one hour because the Winter Palace soon surrendered.

AUTHORSHIP AND INVENTION are rewarded, so as to combine material incentives with preservation of the interests of the state. Authorship rights combine relatively high material incentives and copyright protection with relatively rigid restrictions on creative freedom. The right to create as one pleases has been circumscribed by censorship since the comparative freedom of the 1920's. Some creators find solace in the generous royalties included under standard contracts with state publishing houses. Copyright protection is provided automatically when the publishing contracts are signed, but does not extend to many translations, to excerpts in anthologies, to free-admission performances of works, and to original newspaper printings of speeches, nonfiction, sketches, and photographs. Authors have the right to prevent and receive compensation for plagiarism and unauthorized alteration of their works, going to court, if necessary, to assert this right. But no court will protect them against party pressure to alter their own works for political reasons. Copyrights last for life on literature, nonfiction writing, and works of art. Restricted copyrights on dance and pantomime arrangements, scenarios, films, collections of photographs last only 10 years, and on single photographs, five years. Heirs of lifetime copyrights enjoy the royalties for 15 years after the author's death; heirs of restricted copyrights, for the unexpired time of the copyrights. Works of foreign authors published in the USSR do not enjoy copyright protection; but fees are sometimes credited to them in the USSR. The USSR has not adhered to international copyright conventions.

The Soviet regime used to award patents to inventors, but by 1941 it was considered no longer expedient to allow inventors to have personal monopoly control over the use of their discoveries. Patents are now awarded only to foreigners. Soviet citizens must turn their inventions over to the state, for which they receive in return "certificates of invention," professional prestige, and fees whose size depends, first, on whether the discovery is an actual invention, a technological improvement, or a suggestion for rationalizing production; second, on the amount of yearly saving which the application of the invention brings to the state. (*See* Civil Law, Inheritance, Property)
P. H. J.

AUTOMATION. The over-all aim of Soviet A is the achievement of such an increase in the productivity of labor as will enable the USSR to lay the material-technical basis of communism and to overtake the U.S. in the per capita production of goods in the shortest possible time.

In March 1959, the State Committee for Automation and Machine Construction of the Council of Ministers of the USSR was constituted. This Committee, which is of equivalent status to a ministry, has accorded to its chairman, A. I. Kostousov, the following three tasks: (1) to work out the basic trends in all branches of the national economy; (2) to secure priority development of machine construction, instrument construction, electronics, and the other means of mass A at a high technological level; (3) to coordinate research work in the field of machine construction and A.

The first heading presumably includes the building of about 81 of what are called "trial demonstration enterprises" in various branches of the economy; apparently, the idea is to build highly automated control plants, to test their operation and performance, and to extend the experience derived therefrom to some 4,800 Soviet plants and factories. It is possible that what are called the automatic ball-bearing plant and the automatic piston factory are such trial demonstration enterprises. It is to be noted that these factories are not automatic according to the current western definition, as there is no over-all computer control; in effect, although worthy engineering achievements, they are extensions of the ideas embodied in the automatic production lines of most western motorcar plants.

The drive behind the second task is held to be necessary for the further expansion and development of the chemical and other industries, as its success will secure the necessary amount of machinery; latest figures do, however, indicate that all has not gone well with the plan, and as Mr. Kostousov pointed out at the July 1960 plenum, the failure to fulfill the plan for the delivery of machines, machine tools, instruments, and mechanisms has meant that the capital investment plan for machinery as a whole has been only 88 per cent fulfilled, with the result that it has proved impossible to introduce the required power capacities into the chemical, cement, machine-building, and other industries.

In regard to the third task, the published material reveals that the Committee stands at the head of some 58 research institutes and 25 design offices. The aims of the Committee under this head are first to eradicate duplication in the work of the research institutes. Thus, it was discovered that more than 100 organizations were working on the problem of the program control of machine tools, but that only five, each working in isolation, produced actual designs. A second aim is to reorganize them on what is called the technological principle. Thus, it is planned to replace existing research institutes attached to the automobile, agricultural, and electrical industries. A further aim is to secure standardization of the products of the various machine-building industries, so as to facilitate mass production on flow line principles, of the various components and machines required.

Bearing in mind Mr. Kostousov's recent statement that as of Aug. 1, 1959 more than 47 per cent of all industrial workers were in fact working by hand, and, he emphasized, without any machines or mechanisms, it would appear to be a fair summary that the purpose of the Committee is finally to complete the Industrial Revolution in the Soviet Union, and this at the most highly automated level possible.

The State Scientific Technical Committee is concerned with all branches of science and technology including A when necessary. This Committee is also of ministerial status, and its chairman is K. D. Petukhov, the former chairman of the Moscow Region Economic Council. This Committee, which has branches in the union republics and works closely with the Region Economic Councils, can organize research into any scientific or technological matter, and see to it that the results of such research are introduced into the national industry.

There are also state committees for radio electronics, and for the chemical industry, all of which must, at some point, be involved with the work done on A, not only by the committees already referred to, but also by the research institutes, which do not fall within the authority of the State Committee on Automation and Machine Construction.

Among the latter bodies, the Institutes of Automation and Telemechanics in Moscow and in Kiev are the most outstanding. The Moscow Institute is a branch of the USSR Ac. of S. and was set up in 1936. It was headed in 1960 by academician V. A. Trapeznikov. The staff consists of about 70 postgraduate students, all of whom must be candidates of the technical sciences (doctors in western terms), working in various departments of the Institute.

The Telemechanics Laboratory headed by Prof. Ilyin is engaged on the research into the remote control of the long-distance transmission of information signals,

and methods are being worked out for use in oil pipelines, irrigation systems, and natural gas supply systems.

Prof. Chelyuskin's department is concerned with the automatic control of industrial processes, particularly in steel, and the department on adaptive (optimum-seeking) control systems is engaged on working out methods in designing mechanisms for the optimum control of industrial processes. A device which, it was claimed, could maintain at optimum control a 12-variable industrial process was demonstrated in this laboratory during the International Automation Congress in Moscow in June 1960; the claim was doubted by most western scientists present.

The department headed by Prof. M. A. Ayzerman is engaged on building pneumatic controllers and computers which, it is asserted, are cheaper and more reliable, if less speedy, than electronic computers, but are as useful in the control of chemical processes.

The Institute of Automation and Telemechanics in Kiev is subject to the State Planning Commission of the Ukraine. It has branches in the most highly industrialized areas of the Ukraine, including Lugansk, Lisichansk, Zaporozhye, Kharkov. Its total staff in 1960 amounted to 2,000, but it is planned to increase this to 6,000 in the next five years.

Unlike its Moscow counterpart, the Kiev Institute is more concerned with the practical application of automatic control, and much of its work is concerned with introducing automatic control into the manufacturing processes of the chemical, coal-mining, metallurgical, power, machine-building, and gas industries of the Ukraine.

There are other research institutes, for example, the Central Laboratory for Automation in Moscow, and the Central Scientific Institute for Integrated Automation which is working on the centralized control of plants and processes, the Institute of Electromechanics, at Leningrad, and others, but little is known on their detailed operation.

Research into computers is being conducted at the Institute of Precision Mechanics and Computer Techniques (Director, S. A. Lebedev) in Moscow, and at the Computer Center of the Ac. of S. in Moscow. Four different Soviet electronic digital computers are known: the Ural, the Strela, the Besm I, and the Besm II, but it is thought by western experts that they are not up to western standards.

Training in the theory and practice of automatic control is generally thought to be of a high quality, as exemplified by the undergraduates teaching in the Automatic Control Department of the Moscow Power Institute.

A feature of Soviet A is the endeavor on the part of the government to encourage those working in industry to invent automatic devices or systems, and to reward such inventors with membership in the All-Union Society for Rationalizers and Inventors, and with a monetary prize usually amounting to 5 per cent of the saving to the enterprise concerned resulting from the introduction of the given invention.

To sum up, the position in 1961 is that in automatic control theory, the Soviets are on a level with the West and many of their theoreticians, for example, Pugachov and Tsypkin, in the fields of statistical theory and pulse systems, and Pontryagin, in the mathematics and nonlinear systems, are recognized as of world-wide eminence, but, earth satellites and guided missiles notwithstanding, the Soviets are behind the West in the general level of applications and components. **G. S.**

AUTOMOBILE INDUSTRY. The automobile industry in the USSR is classified as a subdivision of the machine-making industry. In 1960, 139,000 passenger automobiles and 385,000 trucks were produced (as compared with 5,591,000 passenger cars and 1,137,000 trucks in the United States, in 1959, and 1,190,000 passenger cars and 371,000 trucks in the United Kingdom). Although the making of automobiles was initiated early in the century (450 automobiles had been produced at the Russian-Baltic plant in Riga before its closing in 1915), and additional factories were established in Moscow and in Yaroslavl in the 1920's, a significant rate of production was not attained until 1935 (77,000 trucks and 19,000 passenger automobiles), following the introduction of mass-production techniques in the Moscow plant (renamed the Moscow Stalin Automobile Works) and at a newly constructed plant at Gorky (the Molotov Automobile Works). The original emphasis on the production of trucks was retained during World War II, when an additional plant was established at Miass (Chelyabinsk Oblast), and also in the postwar period, when new plants were constructed at Minsk, Kutaisi (Georgia), Lvov, Odessa, Pavlov (Gorky Oblast), and Ulyanovsk. Among the plants producing buses are those at Pavlov, Lvov, and the Likhachev Automobile Works in Moscow. Passenger automobiles are produced at Gorky and at the Moscow Light Automobile Works. Over sixty types of trucks, buses, and passenger automobiles were produced in 1956.

AUTOMOBILE PRODUCTION IN THE USSR

	Pass. cars	Trucks	Total
1928	50	791	841
1935	18,969	77,747	96,716
1939	19,647	182,040	201,687
1958	122,191	388,883	511,074
1959	124,519	370,464	494,983
1960	139,000	385,000	524,000	P. I. M.

Soviet Automobile Models

AUTONOMOUS SOVIET SOCIALIST REPUBLIC (ASSR), a national state within one of the constituent Soviet republics. Each ASSR is represented directly in the Soviet of Nationalities of the USSR by 11 deputies and in the Presidium of the Supreme Soviet of the respective SSR. There are 19 ASSRs (1961): 15 in the

RSFSR—Bashkir, Buryat, Chechen-Ingush, Chuvash, Dagestan, Kabardinian-Balkarian, Kalmyk, Karelian, Komi, Mari, Mordvinian, North Ossetian, Tatar, Udmurt, Yakut; in the Azerbaijan SSR—Nakhichevan ASSR; in the Georgian SSR—Abkhaz and Adzhar ASSRs; in the Uzbek SSR, Kara-Kalpak ASSR.

AVÁCHA GULF, a bay in S.E. Kamchatka; on it is the city of Petropavlovsk-Kamchatsky.

AVÁCHA PEAK, an active volcano in Kamchatka; height 9,000 ft.; perennial snow.

AVARS: *see* POPULATION.

ÁVERBAKH, Leopóld Leonídovich (1903–1939), literary critic. Editor of the newspapers *Uralsky Rabochy* (Worker of the Urals), in the early 1920's; *Smolenskaya Pravda* (Smolensk Truth), during the closing years of his life; also *Molodaya Gvardia* (The Young Guard) and *Na Literaturnom Postu* (On Literary Assignment). He was the principal ideologist of the RAPP (Russian Association of Proletarian Writers). As a critic, he defended the communization of R. literature. Nevertheless, he lost Stalin's confidence, was arrested, and died in prison.

AVÉRCHENKO, Arkády Timoféyevich (1881–1925), writer of the early 20th century, and editor of the humorous magazine *The Satiricon*. His stories are full of humor. This magazine which was widely read by the middle class poked fun at the banality of Philistine life. After the war he emigrated, and his literary activities were directed against the Soviet regime.

AVIATION: *see* CIVIL AVIATION, ARMED FORCES.

AVKSÉNTYEV, Nikoláy Dmítrievich (1878–1943), prominent leader of the Socialist Revolutionary party. Participated in the first Soviet in 1905. Minister of interior in the Kerensky government (Aug.-Sept. 1917). Chairman of All-Russian Soviet of Peasants' Deputies; chairman of Democratic Conference and of the Pre-Parliament in 1917. In 1918 A was active in the Ufa Directorate with Admiral Kolchak, who soon expelled him. After the civil war he settled in France, where he was one of the editors of the quarterly *Sovremennye Zapiski* (Contemporary Notes). In 1940 A came to the United States.

AVVAKÚM Petróvich (c. 1621–1682), priest, advocate of the Old-Believers, with numerous followers. He fought against Patriarch Nikon's reforms and was burned at the stake in 1682. His autobiography *Zhitie* is a valuable historic and literary document of the 17th century.

AY, river in Chelyabinsk Oblast, RSFSR, and in Bashkir ASSR, left tributary of the Ufa; length 336 mi.

ÁYKHENVALD, Yúly Isáyevich (1872–1928), literary critic. Published philosophical works, translated Schopenhauer. Became known as literary critic of *Russkie Vedomosti* (Russian News), and *Russkaya Mysl* (Russian Thought). His articles were later republished in two collections entitled *Silhouettes of Russian Writers* and *Studies of Western Writers*. A treated each writer as standing alone, rejecting division into "schools" and psychological and social analysis. Expelled from Russia after the revolution, he contributed articles to the *émigré* press.

AYÓN, island in the E. Siberian Sea at the entrance of Chaún bay, Chukchi National Okrug, Magadan Oblast, RSFSR; area 770 sq. mi. of arctic tundra.

AYVAZÓVSKY (Gayvazovsky), **Iván Konstantínovich** (1817–1900), seascape painter. Born in Feodosia, Crimea, to the family of an Armenian small merchant. From 1833 studied at the St. Petersburg Academy of Fine Arts. In 1839 he was an established painter, in 1845 an academician; a member of several European academies. Traveled extensively; from 1845 settled in Feodosia, Crimea. His works comprise about 6,000 paintings of unequal quality, a number of drawings and water colors. Peculiar to his art is romantic representation of the boundless grandeur and power of the sea, fiery sunsets, moonlight playing on the waves, bravery of the men fighting the sea (*The Ninth Breaker,* 1850, Russian Museum) and sea battles (*Battle of Chesmen, Battle of Navarin,* 1848, Feodosian Picture Gallery). In his best pictures of a later period (*The Black Sea,* 1881, Tretyakov Gallery) there is more restraint in the use of color and powerful realism in presentation of the expanse of sea, movement of water and light.

ÁZEF, Yevno-Méyer Físhelevich (Yevgény Filipovich) (1869–1918), socialist revolutionary and agent of the police. Graduated in engineering in Germany. In 1903 A became the head of the terrorist organization of the Socialist Revolutionary party; from 1905 on he was a member of the Central Committee of the party. Organized a number of terrorist assassinations (Plehve in 1904, Grand Duke Sergey Aleksandrovich in 1905). On the other hand he denounced the revolutionaries to the police. In 1908, after having been exposed by V. L. Burtsev, he was sentenced to death by the party but managed to escape to Germany.

BIBLIOGRAPHY: B. I. Nikolayevsky, *Azef, The Spy,* London and New York, 1934.

AZERBAIJAN SOVIET SOCIALIST REPUBLIC. The Azerbaijan SSR is located in the E. section of Transcaucasia and borders on Iran and Turkey on the S., Armenia and Georgia on the W., Dagestan on the N., and the Caspian Sea on the E. The Nakhichevan Autonomous Republic (separated from A by Armenian territory and bordering on Turkey for a few miles) and the Nagorno-Karabakh Autonomous Oblast are part of A. Its total territory is 33,425 sq. mi. The capital city is Baku.

Population is 3,698,000 (1959). This includes 2,481,000 Azeri Turks (67.1% of the pop., as against 82.5% in 1920); 515,000 Russians (13.9% as against 2.5% in 1920); 442,000 Armenians (12%), 98,000 Lezghins (2.7%), and 162,000 other nationalities (4.3%). The main cities are: Baku (971,000) and

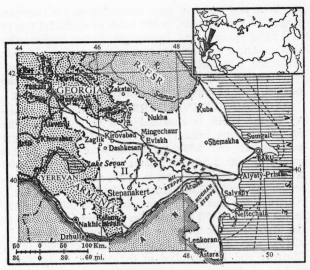

Azerbaijan SSR
(I–Nakhichevan ASSR; II–Nagorno-Karabakh Autonomous Oblast)

Kirovabad (116,000). The average density of pop. is 111 per sq. mi.

Nature and Climate. High mountain chains of the Caucasus cut across the N.E. and the S.W. part of A, leaving the Kura plain at the center, the Lenkoran plain in the S.E. and the Apsheron Peninsula in the E. The Kura plain has a hot, dry temperate climate with an average temperature in Jan. of 34°F and in July 80°F, and an average yearly rainfall of 8–12 in. The subtropical Lenkoran plain has an annual precipitation of 40–68 in. Mountain areas are much colder, the degree depending on elevation. The Kura, most important river, and its tributaries are used for irrigation (a necessity in the Kura plain) and as a source of hydroelectric power. A is rich in oil, natural gas, minerals, and salt. The sea provides a variety of fish.

National Economy. Oil and oil products, natural gas, and cotton are A's main items. Iron ore and aluminum are also extracted; tea, tobacco, fruit, wine, and caviar are produced. Industry and mining account for 90 per cent of A production.

Oil is drilled in the Apsheron Peninsula and around Siyar, Neftechala, and Ali-Bayramli. Offshore oil accounts for 30 per cent of production. Medicated oil is extracted in Naftalan. Since the end of World War II, the oil production of Baku has remained constant at about 16 mill. tons per year (as against 24 mill. on the eve of the war). Most of the oil is processed in Baku refineries; some oil, however, goes to Batumi (on the Black Sea in Georgia) by pipeline.

Heavy industry includes machine building, chemical works, and construction; light industry includes textiles, canneries, tobacco, dairy products and wines.

Half of A's land is arable, and is divided equally between pasturage and cultivation; 60 per cent of the arable land is irrigated. The main crops are cotton, tobacco, wheat, fruit, nuts, and wine grapes. There are abundant cattle, goats, and sheep.

History. The first state-unit on the territory of A was Mana (first millennium B.C.). From the 7th to the 2nd century B.C., A was part of either Persia or Media. In the 4th century B.C., the Caucasian state of Albania was formed on A territory. Feudal life came to A in the 3rd and 4th centuries A.D., together with the new Persian domination. In the 7th century, A was conquered by the Arabs and, after initial resistance, Islam became the official religion. Local states, created in the middle of the 9th century, after the Khalife of Bagdad had been weakened, succumbed to a Turkish invasion in the 11th century. In the 13th century, A was in turn conquered by the Mongols, but at the beginning of the 15th century was again associated with Persia.

Between 1723 and 1735 Russia temporarily occupied E. A and only a century later (1813, 1823) was able to take the territory now known as Azerbaijan SSR away from Persia. During the second half of the 19th century, A went through the early phases of a modern economy. A land reform was instituted in 1870 and at the turn of the century Baku was a large industrial center producing over half of the world's oil (its share is now much smaller).

During the 1905 revolution a Soviet of Workers' Deputies was created in Baku and among the prominent Bolsheviks active there in the years following were: A. Dzhaparidze, S. Ordzhonikidze, S. Shaumyan, J. Stalin, the Yenukidze brothers, and K. Voroshilov.

The Bolsheviks took over in Baku a week after the October revolution (Nov. 13, 1917), but soon thereafter A became part of the anti-Bolshevik Transcausian Federation which broke up in May 1918. Independent for a short time, A was then occupied by Turkish troops in the summer and by British troops at the end of the year. After the British withdrawal a communist coup ended A's independence and a Soviet Republic was organized by Kirov, Ordzhonikidze, and Shaumyan and served as a base for Soviet Russia to recover all of Transcaucasia. In 1922, A was included in the Soviet Transcaucasian Federation. Forced collectivization led in 1930–31 to peasant uprisings which were suppressed by the Red Army. On Dec. 5, 1936, A became a union republic. The great purge of 1936–37 decimated the ranks of A officials, intellectuals, and educators. Thousands (including the head of state, Dr. Sultan Medzhit Efendiev, and the premiers, Dadash Buniyatzade and Gusein Rakhmanov) were shot, imprisoned or deported. Nationalist elements, whether Communist or not, were eradicated; A history was rewritten and distorted; tsarist R. colonial conquest of the area was presented as a progressive event favored by the Azeris themselves.

Culture. Ancient A literature is part of the common literary heritage of the Turkic people. Many works are written in Arabic and Persian. The epic, *Kitabi Dede-Korkud* (10th century) was written in Turkic; 12-th century poetry in Persian. Nizami (author of *Hamsa*, 12th century), Nesimi (14th to 15th century), Fizuli (16th century), Vidali and Vagif (18th century) are considered part of the Azeri literary heritage, but they may just as well be included with Turkish or Persian literature depending on the language used. After the annexation of A by Russia, the pioneers of modern A literature were A. Bakhikhan,

Mirza-Shafi-Vazikh and Mirza-Fatali Akhundov. Akhundov's writing influenced Melikov-Zordabi, Vezirov, Mamedkulidze, Akhverdov, and other writers at the turn of the century. During the Soviet period poets Hussein Djavit and Ahmed Djevat, novelist Sultan Medjit Ganizade, and others were liquidated in 1936–37. Among those remaining, one can mention the playwright D. Dzhabarly, the poet S. Vurgun, and the novelist M. S. Ordubardy. The A alphabet, like other Turkic alphabets of the USSR, was replaced first by a Latin one (in the mid-1920's) and then ten years later by a Cyrillic alphabet.

The history of A art is closely associated with that of N. Iran. Stone carving, mosaics, metal ornamentation, ceramics, rug weaving, all date from the Middle Ages. Miniature and decorative art prevailed as the style in painting. The oldest architectural monuments are caves and tombs. Some old forts date from the 6th and 7th centuries. Architecture flourished in the 11th to the 13th century, and numerous fortresses, mosques, mausoleums, and palaces still remain from that time.

A music is characterized by a complicated system of seven tones and half tones, a highly developed melodic structure, and a unique rhythm. Solo voice prevails in popular singing. The first A opera by U. Gadzhibekov was performed in 1908. A has an Opera theater, a Symphonic Orchestra, a Musical Comedy, and seven drama theaters. The first A films were made in the 1920's. A has several institutions of higher learning. The Ac. of S. of A was founded in 1945.   M. R.

AZGÚR, Zair Isáakovich (1908–), sculptor. A native of Byelorussia, he trained at the Academy of Fine Arts and Kiev Art Institute. His work consists mainly of portraits of public figures and historical personalities. His sculptures of several prominent R. scientists are displayed at the Moscow University campus.

AZHÁYEV, Vasily Nikolayevich (1915–), novelist. His first book was published in 1937. Graduated from the Institute of Literature of the Union of Soviet Writers. His popular novel *Far From Moscow* (1948) was awarded the Stalin prize (1949).

AZÓV, CAMPAIGNS OF (1695–1696), by Peter I, during the struggle of Russia with Turkey for an outlet to the Sea of Azov and the Black Sea. During the second campaign Azov was taken (July 18, 1696). This was the first important R. victory carried out by united forces of army and fleet.

AZÓV, city in Rostov Oblast, RSFSR, a port on Sea of Azov; pop. 37,400 (1956). Important fisheries, shipyards, agricultural machinery plant. A is one of the oldest cities of the Black Sea, founded on the site of the ancient Tanais.

AZÓV, SEA OF (Latin *Palus Maeotis*), in the S. of USSR, connected to the Black Sea by the Kerch Strait; area about 14,700 sq. mi.; depth up to 50 ft.; the Don, Kuban, Mius, Kalmius rivers flow into it. The coastal area freezes in winter for 2 to 3 months. Important ports are Rostov-on-Don, Zhdanov (Mariupol), Taganrog, Kerch; extensive fisheries and shipping (grain and ore). Sivash Sea is its W. branch.

B

BABAYÉVSKY, Semyón Petróvich (1909–), novelist. Best known for the collection of stories *Tales of the Kuban* (1940), *The Cavalier of the Gold Star* (1947), and *Light over the Land* (1949). Stalin prizes (1949, 1950, 1951).

BÁBEL, Isáak Emmanuílovich (1894–1941), story writer, born in a Jewish family in Odessa. B started to write for the journal *Letopis* (Annals) in 1915, published by Maxim Gorky. He joined the revolutionary movement at an early age. During the civil war, already a member of the CP, he served in the First Cavalry Army as a party worker. His impressions and observations of that period are reflected in a cycle of stories under the title *Cavalry Army*, also known in its English translation as *Red Cavalry*. These stories were published over a period of eight years from 1924 to 1932. B portrayed the civil war with realism and cruel objectivity.

B is also known for his autobiographical stories: *The Story of My Pigeon-house and Odessa Stories*. During the later 1920's B became a dramatist and motion picture scenario writer. His best-known plays are *The Sunset* (1928); *Benya Krik* (1926), the story of a Jewish gangster in Odessa whose exploits terrorize the police; and a scenario for the film *Chinese Windmill* (1929). Some critics are of the opinion that a later play, *Maria,* written by B in 1934–35 and banned from the Soviet stage as alien to Soviet art, actually was his outstanding dramatic work.

In the 1930's B was appointed to supervise collectivization in S. USSR, but became disgusted with the widespread use of violence and was removed from his post after being accused of "rotten liberalism." He left for France but soon returned to the USSR. His experience with collectivization provided material for a novel, *The White Jar*. While the manuscript of the novel has been completed, only brief excerpts have been published to date. According to Ilya Ehrenburg, in 1939 B was arrested and perished in a Soviet concentration camp. Following Stalin's death, B was posthumously rehabilitated and his works, which were banned in 1939, are now being re-edited and re-published.

BABÚKHIN, Aleksándr Ivánovich (1835–1891), histologist and physiologist. Graduate (1859), professor (1865), Moscow University. Discovered the origins of electrical organs in fish (1869) and proved that nerves transmit stimuli in both directions. B's research greatly contributed to the development of the physiology of the nervomuscular system. Inventor of the "Babukhin microscope stand."

BÁBUSHKIN (f. Losino-Ostrovskaya), city in Moscow Oblast, RSFSR, 7 mi. from Moscow; pop. 112,000 (1959). Electro-mechanical plant, knitting mill.

BÁBUSHKIN, Iván Vasílyevich (1873–1906), prominent Bolshevik, Lenin's disciple. He was arrested many times, exiled, and imprisoned. He was a participant in the 1905 revolution; and in 1906 he was shot during the punitive expedition of Gen. Meller-Zakomelsky.

BAER, Karl Maksímovich (1792–1876), naturalist. Fellow, St. Petersburg Ac. of Sc. (1830). Graduate, Dorpat University (1814); professor, Königsberg University (1817–34); Medical and Surgical Ac. in St. Petersburg (1841–52). A pioneer in the study of embryonic development of animals, he repudiated Darwin's theory of evolution, particularly in reference to natural selection. Founder of embryology in Russia. Cofounder of the Geographical Society.

BAGRAMYÁN, Iván Khristofórovich (1897–), marshal of the USSR, born into a worker's family in Armenia. During World War I he volunteered for the R. army and fought for the Bolsheviks in the civil war. He graduated from the Frunze Military Academy in the late 1920's and from the Voroshilov General Staff Academy in 1938. He held several command posts during World War II; was named commander of the Baltic military district at the end of hostilities; and from 1946 to 1948 took part in the suppression of resistance movements in the Baltic republics. Since 1952, he has been a candidate member of the Central Committee of the CPSU; a member of the central committee, Latvian CP, 1954–55; was given the rank of marshal of the Soviet Union in 1955; and appointed deputy minister of defense and director of the Voroshilov Military Academy in 1956.

BAGRATIÓN, Pyotr Ivánovich (1765–1812), prominent army leader, hero of several wars including those against Napoleon. He was victor at Eylau (Prussia) in 1807; killed in the battle of Borodino in 1812.

BAGRÍTSKY (Dzyúbin), **Eduárd Geórgievich** (1895–1934), poet. Born into a poor Jewish family in Odessa, he participated in the civil war. Although his early works were influenced by the symbolist movement in the beginning of the century, the heroes of his later poems are generally strong-willed and hard-working individuals of the revolutionary period. Among the dominant themes are the pathos of the revolution and of the civil war and the idea of the emancipation of mankind. Occasionally B idealizes the image of the wanderer, of extreme individualism and the freedom from all ties, coloring this anarchist striving in romantic hues. In his best poems B's language conforms to the traditions of folk poetry and is both simple and harmonious. His most important work is the poem *The Elegy on Opanas* (1926), which depicts the civil war in the Ukraine. His poem *Death of a Pioneer Girl* is dedicated to youth. B also translated from English poetry, including Burns and Scott.

BAKÁL, city in Chelyabinsk Oblast, RSFSR, pop. 25,400 (1959). Has one of the best iron-ore deposits in the world, mechanized mining. Ore-concentration plant.

BAKÁYEV, Iván Petróvich (1887–1936), Bolshevik. Joined the revolutionary movement in 1905 and the Bolshevik party in 1906. Spent six years in prison. During the October revolution, was secretary of the Petrograd Soviet of the Workers' and Peasants' Deputies: political commissar on several fronts during the civil war. In 1919–20, was chairman of the Cheka, first in Petrograd, then in S.E. Russia. In the twenties, B became a member of the Zinoviev-Kamenev opposition. In 1936, B was tried at the first show trial and, with Zinoviev, Kamenev and others, was sentenced to death.

BAKHCHISARÁY, city in S. Crimea; pop. 9,900 (1956). Former residence of Crimean Khans; palace of 16th century preserved.

BAKHCHISARÁY, TREATY OF, 1681, a 20-year armistice between Russia, Turkey, and Crimea concluding the wars of the 1670's. It established the Russian-Turkish border along the Dnieper, and a neutral zone between the Bug and Dnieper rivers. The towns of Kiev, Tripolye, Vasilkov, and Stayki became part of Russia, as well as the E. Ukraine.

BAKHMÉTEFF, Borís Aleksándrovich (1880–1951), engineer and diplomat. Born in Tiflis, he became a hydraulic engineer, professor of hydraulics at the Polytechnic Institute, St. Petersburg, 1908–1917. During World War I B was active in the War Industries Committees. After the revolution of February 1917 B was assistant minister of trade and commerce; in May 1917 appointed ambassador to the United States, a position which he retained until 1922. From 1931 B was professor of civil engineering at Columbia University and chairman of the board of the Lion Match Company.

BAKHMÚT: see ARTYOMOVSK.

BAKHÚRIN, Iván Mikháylovich (1880–1940), geophysicist and mine surveyor. Corresponding member, Ac. of S., USSR (1939). Graduate (1909), professor, St. Petersburg Mining Institute. Developed a method of determining the size and depth of magnetic deposits according to magnetic prospecting data. Founder and director, Central Scientific Research Bureau of Mine Surveying. Author of *A Course of Magnetic Prospecting* (1933), *Shifting of Rock under the Effects of Mining* (1946).

BAKSÁN RIVER, in the Caucasus, right tributary of the Malka (Terek basin); length 105 mi.; not navigable; hydroelectric power station.

BAKST, Leoníd Samóylovich (1868–1924), painter and decorator, associated with Diaghilev, Benois and others in the *Mir Iskusstva* group, sharing their debt to the French impressionists. He is best known as a decorator. During the first decade of the century, he designed settings for the St. Petersburg Imperial Theater productions of *Le Coeur de la Marquise, Hyppolitus,* and *Œdipus.* He gained international renown when Diaghilev took R. ballet and opera to Paris in 1909.

BAKÚ, capital of Azerbaijan SSR, the chief oil center of USSR, and a port on Caspian Sea; pop. 971,000 (1959). Oil-drilling equipment, machine-tool, chemical, and food ind. Is the seat of Azerbaijan Ac. of S., has numerous schools of higher education and a university. Russian since 1806.

BAKÚNIN, Mikhaíl Aleksándrovich (1814–1876), radical philosopher and writer, and anarchist revolutionary. He led a very adventurous life. Born at Torzhok (Tver province) into a wealthy noble family, he was educated in Russia and Italy and became a guard officer. He resigned in protest against tsarism (1834) and

after studying German philosophy and making radical friends in Moscow in the 1830's, went to W. Europe in 1840, where he developed his anarchistic theories of revolutionary violence and "pan-destruction," and became friendly with Marx, Proudhon and the German revolutionary Weitling. For his defiance of the R. government's summons to return home, his estates were confiscated. B practiced what he preached. Dreaming to unite all the Slavs in one republic, he participated in insurrections in Prague (1848), and Dresden (1849). Caught by the Saxon reaction, he was condemned to death, imprisoned, and handed over to the Austrian government, which again condemned him to death, imprisoned him, and extradited him to the R. government. After six years of imprisonment in Peter and Paul and Schlüsselburg fortresses, during which time he lost his teeth and much of his health, B was exiled to Siberia (1857), from which he made an astonishing escape to Japan and America, reaching Europe by 1861. In prison he wrote his "Confession"—an extraordinary document where he tried to justify his revolutionary activities. Plunging again into revolutionary politics, B tried to help the Polish uprising (1863), to stir R. exiles to extremism, and to foment disturbances in Italy (1864–68). Moving to Switzerland (1868), B made himself "dictator" of a minuscule but ambitious revolutionary "Alliance of Socialist Democracy" and joined the First International, in which he carried on a vehement factional struggle with Marx until the latter secured B's expulsion in 1872 at the cost of fatally weakening the organization. His chief principles were anarchism, collectivism, and atheism. He advocated violent revolution and rejected political action and a "socialist state." In the 1870's B was largely concerned with promoting anarchism among the watchmakers of the Swiss Jura, and the R. students at Zurich, and took part in revolts in Lyons (1871) and Bologna (1874). B died in Berne but his name and legend arouse passion to this day. Bakuninism struck roots in Spain, Italy, and Russia. B wrote many books and pamphlets including *God and the State; Marxism, Freedom and the State; The Social Revolution.* (*See also* ANARCHISTS.)
BIBLIOGRAPHY: E. H. Carr, *Michael Bakunin,* New York, 1937.

BALAKHNÁ, city in Gorky Oblast, RSFSR, port on the Volga; pop. 30,500 (1956). Paper mill, cardboard factory, tannery, peat-fed power station; technical schools.

BALÁKIREV, Miliy Alekséyevich (1837–1910), composer, pianist, and conductor. Born in Nizhny-Novgorod, B first won prominence as a pianist. In 1855, he met Glinka who exercised a great influence on him. Shortly afterwards, B became leader of the group of composers known as "The Mighty Five" (the other members were Borodin, Cui, Musorgsky, and Rimsky-Korsakov). He was also associated with the eminent music critic Stasov. A founder of the Free School of Music, St. Petersburg, B did much to assist young composers. In 1869 he became director of the Imperial Chapel Choir and five years later conductor of the Russian Music Society. He retired from these activities in 1874 to devote himself exclusively to creative work.

In his compositions, B gave prominence to folk themes, and published transcripts of R. folk songs. An oriental influence is evident in his piano fantasy *Islamey* and the tone poem *Tamara* (after Lermontov). Other compositions include the overture *In Bohemia* (1867) and *Chopiniane* (1910). B wrote incidental music for Shakespeare's *King Lear* (1859–61), and numerous romances. His work, though sometimes criticized as uneven, is characterized by a passionate lyricism.

BALAKLÁVA, town in S. Crimea, on the Black Sea, 10 mi. from Sevastopol; pop. 7,100 (1956). Fisheries, limestone, mining, vineyards; ruins of 14th-century Genoese fortress.

BALANCHÍNE, George (Balanchivadze) (1904–), choreographer, born in St. Petersburg. He graduated from the Petrograd ballet academy in 1922, and produced his first avant-garde work in 1923 independently of the State Theatre. He left Russia with a group of dancers in 1924 and joined the Diaghilev company where he remained from 1925 to 1929. Later staged for Ballet Russe de Monte Carlo (1932 and 1941), Les Ballets (1933). Came to the United States to participate in the founding of the School of American Ballet (1934) and to organize the American Ballet and Ballet Caravan, Ballet Society and subsequently the New York City Ballet which grew out of these companies. Currently (1960) he is art director and chief choreographer of the New York City Ballet. Among his major works are *Apollo* (Stravinsky, 1928), *The Prodigal Son* (Prokofyev, 1929), *Serenade* (Tchaikovsky, 1935), *Concerto Barocco* (Bach, 1941), *Ballet Imperial* (Tchaikovsky, 1941), *Danses Concertantes* (Stravinsky, 1944), *Symphony in C* (Bizet, 1947), *Four Temperaments* (Hindemith, 1946), *Symphonie Concertantes* (Mozart, 1948), *Orpheus* (Stravinsky, 1948), *Bourrée Fantasque* (Chabrier, 1949), *Firebird* (Stravinsky, 1950), *The Nutcracker* (Tchaikovsky, 1954), *Gounod's Symphony* (1957), *Agon* (Stravinsky, 1957), *Figure in the Carpet* (Handel, 1960).

BALÁNDIN, Alekséy Aleksándrovich (1898–), chemist. Fellow, Ac. of S., USSR (1946). Graduated from Moscow University (1923) and became professor (1934). Chief of laboratory at the Institue of Organic Chemistry (1935). Advanced the theory on structural and energetic correlation between molecules and solid catalysts, applicable to catalytic hydrogenation and dehydrogenation. Author of *Catalytic Dehydrogenation of Hydrocarbons and Its Application for Synthesis of Rubber from Gas* (1942); *The Theory of Organic Catalysis* (1947); *Theory of Selective Catalysis* (1956); *Kinetics of Dehydrogenation of Alcohols* (1957). Received the D. Mendeleyev prize from the Ac. of S. (1936), S. V. Lebedev prize (1945), and Stalin prize (1946).

BALASHÍKHA, city in Moscow Oblast, 10 mi. east of Moscow; pop. 58,000 (1959). Textile ind.; laboratory for fur-animal breeding; children's sanatorium.

BALASHÓV, city in Saratov Oblast, RSFSR, on Khoper River; pop. 64,000 (1959). R.R. station; machine building, food processing.

BALÉY, city in Chita Oblast, RSFSR; pop. 29,200 (1956); gold-mining center.

BALKHÁN RANGES, Large and Small, mountains in W. Turkmen SSR; elevations: Large B, 6,166 ft., Small B, 2,624 ft.

BALKHÁSH, city in Karaganda Oblast, Kazakh SSR, on N. shore of Lake Balkhash; pop. 53,000 (1959). One of the biggest copper-smelting plants; metallurgical mining school.

BALKHÁSH, lake in S.E. of Kazakh SSR, with elevation of 1,115 ft.; area about 7,300 sq. mi.; depth 85 ft. It has fresh water in W. part, salt water in the E.; is covered with ice for 120–140 days. Ili, Karatal, Aksu, Lepsa, and Ayaguz rivers empty into it. Navigable; fisheries (carp, perch). Copper center Kounrad near its N. shore.

BALLET. Russia had an imperial school of ballet from 1738. Empress Anna had engaged the Frenchman Jean Baptiste Landet in 1734 to teach manners and dancing to the cadets of the Military School for Nobles. So successful was M. Landet that four years later he was ordered to organize a separate ballet school —for dancers.

Empress Elizabeth and after her Catherine the Great and Paul I continued to take a lively interest in ballet. As a boy Paul took ballet lessons from Franz van Hilverding, who was ballet master in St. Petersburg in the 1750's and '60s. Paul later danced in ballets in the Court Theater. In 1786 Charles Le Picq came to St. Petersburg from France as first dancer, and ten years later became chief ballet master.

Along with the ballet's growth as a spectacle for the capital's high society, it was also developing in the house theaters of the wealthy landowners and serf-owners on their estates and in city mansions. The beginning of these theaters dates back to the middle of the 18th century. They were very popular and multiplied so rapidly that toward the end of the century there were thousands of them in the country and twenty or more in Moscow alone. The dancers were selected among the serfs and were trained by teachers and ballet masters usually imported by the landowners from abroad. Toward the middle of the 19th century, house theaters began to decline in number. The imperial theaters bought most of the outstanding dancers from their owners and freed them from serfdom.

Russian B was guided in its development by foreign ballet masters until the end of the 19th century. Among these were such great masters as Charles Louis Didelot, Jules Perrot, Arthur Saint-Léon, and Marius Petipa. Of these, Petipa stayed longer in Russia than any other ballet master, and contributed more than anyone else to the greatness of R. B. He arrived in St. Petersburg as a dancer in 1847, at the time when the Romantic period was nearing its end in W. Europe, when ballet was beginning to lose favor, and when the center of interest in ballet was shifting to Russia. In 1862, with the production of his monumental *The Daughter of Pharaoh*, Petipa became ballet-master-in-chief of the St. Petersburg Imperial Theater, a position he held until 1903. His achievements were prodigious and ballet owes a debt to him which is often acknowledged by the revivals of his ballets the world over. Among his great original ballets were *Don Quixote, La Bayadère, Talisman, The Sleeping Beauty, Raymonda, The Seasons, Swan Lake* (Acts 1 and 3; Acts 2 and 4 were staged by Lev Ivanov). His restaging of ballets of other choreographers included *Giselle, Le Corsaire, Coppélia, Les Sylphides, The Humpbacked Horse,* and others.

It was under Petipa's regime that Lev Ivanov, the first Russian ballet master of the 19th century, came into his own and choreographed, among other works, *The Nutcracker,* which, with the above-mentioned Petipa ballets, is still performed in almost every European country, as well as in the United States and in several Latin American countries. It was also during this period that R. ballerinas began to gain prominence, replacing the Italian, French, and German ballerinas who had held sway in R. B for nearly a century. Among the great R. ballerinas of the period were Olga Preobrazhenska, Mathilda Kshessinska, Vera Trefilova, Lyubov Yegorova, Anna Pavlova, Tamara Karsavina.

During the first decade of the 20th century, the Russification of the R. B was complete; coincidentally, ballet reached its zenith in Russia. But the ballet was a grand and elegant spectacle, a magnificent entertainment, and little more. It had to wait until nearly the end of the decade to become an art form. The transformation came with the organization of the "Ballet Russe" by Serge Diaghilev, the impresario of genius, who knew how to surround himself with the exquisite talents of his generation.

The first performance of the Diaghilev ballet took place May 18, 1909 at the Théâtre du Châtelet in Paris. The company included Anna Pavlova, Tamara Karsavina, Bronislava Nijinska, Michel Fokine, Adolph Bolm, Vaslav Nijinsky, Mikhail Mordkin, and Laurent Novikov, in addition to a *corps de ballet* assembled from the St. Petersburg Mariinsky and Moscow Bolshoy theaters. The repertoire consisted of *Les Sylphides* (Chopin), *Cleopatra* (Arensky and others), *Le Pavillon d'Armide* (Tcherepnine), *Prince Igor* (Borodin), all staged by Michel Fokine, the young choreographer who was creating a revolution in ballet. The painters who designed the scenery and costumes were Alexandre Benois and Léon Bakst. The Diaghilev Ballet was a revelation to Paris, as it would have been to St. Petersburg.

Season followed season in W. Europe, new and exciting productions followed one another, and everything that was talented in Europe—in music and painting—flocked to work with or at least be near to the Diaghilev company. The collaboration of choreographers like Michel Fokine and later Bronislava Nijinska, Leonide Massine, and George Balanchine, composers like Nicholas Tcherepnine and later Igor Stravinsky, Claude Debussy, Francis Poulenc, Georges Auric, and Erik Satie, painters like Benois and Bakst and later Picasso, Matisse, Dérain, Marie Laurencin, Michael Larionov, and Nathalie Goncharova, and the dancers mentioned above and those who followed them—this collabora-

tion, uninhibited by official rules and opinions, could not help but produce the most talented and most exciting works of art.

The Diaghilev ballet never returned to Russia after 1911. With the exception of two visits to the United States and one to South America the company continued to dance in Europe until the death of Serge Diaghilev in 1929. The Diaghilev company left an artistic heritage which is still feeding ballet companies in Europe and the United States, and former members of the Diaghilev company are still contributing their talents and skills to ballet companies the world over. At least three of the choreographers who staged their ballets for the Diaghilev company—George Balanchine, Leonide Massine, and Bronislava Nijinska—continue to be in the forefront of choreographers in the United States and Europe.

The ballet in the USSR is a direct continuation of the 19th-century classic ballet, given form by Jules Perrot, Arthur Saint-Léon, Marius Petipa, and Lev Ivanov. Although Michel Fokine, the reformer of contemporary ballet, began his career as choreographer in Russia, he achieved his greatness outside Russia, mainly in the Diaghilev company, and the imprint he left on ballet in Russia was very modest. The only Fokine ballet being performed in the Soviet Union is *Les Sylphides,* known there under its original title *Chopiniana.* The modernization of ballet, as we understand the term, has never touched Soviet Russia.

The Soviet revivals of classic ballets seen in the United States or in W. Europe, such as *Swan Lake* and *Giselle,* are well produced and excellently danced. Their style of dancing is much more influenced by the loose Moscow style of prerevolutionary Russia rather than the restrained and elegant St. Petersburg style. Most new ballets, as well as most of the revivals, are full-evening productions, the plots very elaborate and related in great detail, with a number of subplots and many quasi-folk dance elements, which in their total amount to a superabundance that to the Western eye appears as a superfluity.

Until the early '30s, all new Soviet ballets were of a propaganda nature. The subject matter and the message were there, but ballet art was lacking. It became clear that in spite of excellent dancing, in spite of music by the outstanding Soviet composers, in spite of fine décor, the Soviet ballet was not progressing.

In 1934 the Leningrad Kirov Theater (formerly, the Mariinsky) took the first step toward a new direction in ballet. It produced *The Fountain of Bakhchisaray,* based on a poem by Alexander Pushkin, with choreography by Rostislav Zakharov to music by Boris Asafiev. This may be considered the first new nonpolitical ballet produced in the Soviet Union. Although several ballets on contemporary and propaganda themes have been staged in the USSR since then, the main tendency of the Soviet ballet is classic and traditional, more traditional than anywhere else. Significant in the new repertoire, in addition to *The Fountain of Bakhchisaray,* are Sergey Prokofiev's three ballets, *Cinderella, Romeo and Juliet,* and *Stone Flower,* and Reinhold Glière's *The Bronze Horseman.*

The Soviet ballet, as the imperial ballet before it, is rich in dancers. Galina Ulanova, the prima ballerina of the Soviet Union, is a great dancer by any standard. Maya Plissetskaya, Raisa Struchkova, Marina Kondratieva, and Nina Timofeyeva are ballerinas of a high caliber. Among the men Nikolay Fadeyechev, Yury Zhdanov, Georgy Farmanyants, Boris Khokhlov, Aleksandr Lapauri, and Vladimir Vasilyev are in the front rank.

BIBLIOGRAPHY: Alexandre Benois, *Reminiscences of the Russian Ballet*, London, 1941; S. L. Grigoriev, *The Diaghilev Ballet, 1909–1929*, London, 1953; Tamara Karsavina, *Theatre Street*, New York, Revised edition, 1950; Mathilde Kschessinska, *Dancing in Petersburg*, Garden City, N.Y., 1960; Prince Peter Lieven, The *Birth of Ballet-Russe*, Boston, 1936.   A. C.

BALMASHÉV, Stepán Valeriánovich (1882–1902), student-revolutionary who, on April 2, 1902, killed the minister of interior Sipyagin. On May 3, he was hanged in Schlüsselburg Fortress.

BÁLMONT, Konstantín Dmítrievich (1867–1943), one of the first and most popular symbolist poets of his time. He studied history, philosophy, and philology at the University of Moscow and mastered European and Oriental languages. His translations of foreign poets into Russian (W. Whitman, E. Poe, Calderon) are numerous. His poetry, rich in sound, is superficial and shallow. Heavy sensuality and the theatrical pose like that of the High Priest of Beauty give his poems the flavor of banality. His collections of verses are: *Under Northern Skies* (1894), *Buildings of Fire* (1900), *Let Us Be as the Sun* (1903). B greeted the revolution of 1905 and joined the Social Democratic party. Forced to leave Russia, he traveled extensively in distant exotic lands, and wrote about Mexico, South Africa, and the Pacific Islands—a genre relatively rare in R. literature. He returned to Russia and left it again after the Bolshevik Revolution. He died in France poor and forgotten.

BALTIC SEA, arm of Atlantic Ocean, indenting N. Europe. Area 153,250 sq. mi. (incl. gulfs of Bothnia, Finland, and Riga); shallow water (1,500 ft. maximum); freezes partly in winter; fisheries (herring, salmon, and others). Ports in the USSR: Leningrad, Riga, Tallin, Liepaja, Klaipeda, Kaliningrad.

BALTÍYSKY: see PALDISKI.

BALTRUSHÁITIS, Jurgis (Yúri Kazímirovich) (1873–1945), a symbolist poet of Lithuanian origin. He studied mathematics at the University of Moscow. With S. Polyakov, he founded the publishing house Scorpion. His books reflected his favorite theme of the loneliness of man, isolated in the universe. He also translated works of Ibsen, Hauptmann, and D'Annunzio.

BANKING AND CREDIT. In prerevolutionary Russia the first banks were established by the government in 1754—one for the landed nobility and one for commerce. In 1860 the government established a central bank, and a few years later, in 1864, the first private joint-stock bank was founded. In the course of the next fifty years 47 commercial banks with 743 branches were established, as well as a state-owned savings bank, cooperative banks, and mutual credit societies. A considerable share of the banks' resources consisted of foreign capital (42% stock of leading commercial banks).

In 1917 the banks were nationalized and plans were made to utilize the banking system to control the activities of the still numerous privately owned enterprises. This was postponed, however, by the subsequent unanticipated decision to nationalize all enterprises without delay, as well as by the runaway inflation of the period of the civil war. During the recovery period, after 1921, when the nationalized enterprises were generally operated on a commercial basis, both the newly organized State Bank and the new regional and functional banks operated essentially along traditional commercial lines. A radical change in this regard, however, occurred following the adoption of the first Five Year Plan as a result of the banking and credit reforms of 1930–32.

The functions of the reorganized banking system included not only the holding of the savings of individuals and the making of loans, but the redistribution to enterprises and other organizations of funds originating in the state budget (the major source of capital) and the controlling of all financial transactions among individual units to ensure that expenditures would be made only for purposes that conform to the carrying out of the yearly plans. This control function, which is a basic element in the Soviet method of planning and which corresponds to the principle of "economic calculation" for enterprises and other organizations (*khozraschot*), was assigned to the State Bank (*Gosbank*). Until the reform of 1959 the distribution of funds for investment to individual branches of the economy was carried out by the Industrial Bank (*Prombank*), the Agricultural Bank (*Selkhozbank*), the Trade Bank (*Torgbank*) (discontinued in 1956), and the Municipal Bank (*Tsekombank*). The Bank for Foreign Trade (*Vneshtorgbank*) has provided credits in the sphere of foreign trade and together with the State Bank has performed foreign exchange operations.

The activity of the State Bank as a financial transfer agent has been the most important one from the point of view of individual enterprises, since all payments have been effectuated through that bank's bookkeepers upon receipt of the proper (nontransferable) paper instruments. Within the State Bank's own structure, mutual clearing bureaus have been established in key areas. The use of currency in the Soviet economy has thus been confined to the payment of wages, including the monetary receipts of collective farmers, and to the subsequent use of these wages by the population for the purchasing of consumers' goods and services.

In addition the State Bank has been the basic source of short-term credit for all enterprises and other organizations. It has also acted as the government's fiscal agent, receiving all taxes and other payments to the state; issued money and withdrawn it from circulation; kept supplies of precious metals and of foreign currencies owned by the government; and handled settlements with foreigners through its accounts with correspondent banks abroad.

The loans granted by the State Bank have usually been for specific purposes and for fixed periods; they have been returnable, and they have carried interest charge. They have been granted within the limits established by the enterprises' credit plan, except in cases of emergency or other unanticipated situations. Enterprises that have failed to fulfill their obligations to the State Bank have had sanctions applied to them, such as the denial of further credit and the sale of commodities offered as securities.

The total volume of credit issued by the State Bank has been limited by a Credit Plan approved quarterly by the Council of Ministers. The reserves upon which the Bank has drawn in issuing credit have included, aside from its original charter capital, accumulated reserves from profits and other special funds, including funds from the state budget; the funds deposited in the Bank by the enterprises and other organizations that are required to have accounts in it; and also money printed by the Bank. The Bank's freedom to print money has been checked, however, by the government's Cash Plan, which is worked out in concordance with the Credit Plan. The State Bank, accordingly, has been incapable of independently causing inflation by issuing an excess of currency or credit.

In Jan. 1959 the funds lent out by the State Bank amounted to 320 bill. rubles—a sevenfold increase since 1952. Of this sum 41 per cent was lent to manufacturing enterprises (16.8 per cent of the producers' goods sector), 1.2 per cent to transport and communications, 9.7 per cent to financing of agriculture and procurement activities, 38.7 per cent to the distributive trades, and 6.5 per cent to supply and marketing organizations.

The four major long-term investment banks were essentially concerned with providing funds for capital construction to different economic organizations, mostly in the form of nonreturnable grants. Most of these funds were allocated to the banks by the government from its budget. The additional resources of the investment banks included the obligatory amortization allowances accumulated by economic organizations; funds from the profit tax; and the capital funds of collective farms. The investment banks exercised strict control over the execution, progress, quality, and financial discipline of construction projects. This control was usually far more detailed than that exercised by the State Bank over recipients of short-term loans.

The Industrial Bank has made grants to industrial, transport, communications, and road-building organizations. It has also made long-term credits available to local and provincial industrial enterprises to help them organize or expand the output of consumers' goods, food manufactures, construction materials, and fuel.

The Municipal Bank provided credits and nonreturnable grants to local municipal governments for housing, public utilities, and related construction. It also granted long-term credits to demobilized soldiers, war invalids, families of dead soldiers, and needy families of persons serving in the armed forces. It worked in cooperation with a system of local municipal banks.

The Trade Bank provided funds for capital investment to domestic and foreign trade enterprises, organizations of the Ministry of Procurement, and cooperatives. Cooperatives were required to repay credits from this bank, but government organizations received nonreturnable grants, as in other areas of the economy.

The Agricultural Bank provided long-term credits to collective farms for construction, repair of buildings, purchase of equipment or cattle, irrigation works, and so forth, as well as some short-term loans of less than a year's duration for similar purposes. It also made some long-term loans to individual members of collective farms and to other individual borrowers, particularly invalids of the last war and families of soldiers. Government agricultural organizations, such as state farms, were also financed by this bank.

These investment banks generally financed only construction projects that had been specifically authorized by the government, and usually, too, only those for which complete cost estimates had been prepared. Financing has been provided only within the limits of the estimated costs for different types of work. The banks may refuse to provide funds in cases when costs exceeded estimates, or in cases when they observe a wasteful utilization of the funds and resources made available for construction. They generally follow closely the progress of each construction project, analyze the balance and other accounting records of each, and inform responsible organs of economic control when they find abnormalities. To facilitate control over the cost and progress of construction work, such activity has usually been carried on, not by the enterprises that eventually operate the new plants, mines, or other productive facilities being built, but by separate construction organizations that perform their function on a contractual basis. When enterprises do carry on their own construction activity, all funds available for construction are kept in separate accounts.

In 1955, 71.3 per cent of the total capital investment was provided by the Industrial Bank, 16.8 per cent by the Agricultural Bank, 9.5 per cent by the Municipal Bank, and 2.4 per cent by the Trade Bank.

Individuals are encouraged by the Soviet government to save money for future needs. There exists a wide network of Savings Banks for this purpose (62,800 offices as of Jan. 1, 1960) and 3 per cent interest is paid on the savings deposits of individuals. Because the great majority of such deposits are very small, however, this represents an insignificant source of income for most depositors. In 1960 there were 50 mill. depositors with total deposits of 100.5 bill. rubles. This represented a twelvefold increase since 1941 that was particularly pronounced in rural localities (21 per cent of total deposits in early 1959, as opposed to 13.4 per cent in 1952). The average deposit was 2,005 rubles.

In April 1959, the banking system was reorganized so as to conform more closely to the earlier regrouping of enterprises into regional economic councils (*sovnarkhozy*). The Agricultural Bank and the Municipal Bank were dissolved and their investment functions were transferred partly to the Industrial Bank, renamed the Construction Bank (*Stroybank*), and partly to the State Bank.

BIBLIOGRAPHY: PREREVOLUTIONARY PERIOD: P. I. Lyashchenko, *History of the National Economy of Russia*, N.Y., 1949; J. Mavor, *An Economic History of Russia*, N.Y., 1914. SOVIET PERIOD: M. I. Bogolepov, *The Soviet Financial System*, L., 1945; A. Z. Arnold, *Banks, Credit, and Money in Soviet Russia*, N.Y., 1937; R. W. Davies, *The Development of the Soviet Budgetary System*, Cambridge, England, 1958. P. I. M.

BAPTISTS, religious sect which originated in 17th century in England as a branch of Anabaptism. B appeared in Russia in the 1870's. There is a Baptist Union in the USSR.

BAR ASSOCIATIONS are attorneys' associations which both regulate the profession and organize legal aid to clients. Tsarist BA, having survived the Feb. 1917 revolution and the period of the Provisional Government, were abolished in Nov. 1917 by the Soviet regime which attempted unsuccessfully to dispense with the services of professional attorneys. From 1918 to 1932 varying restrictions were imposed on the professional freedom of attorneys and their rights to receive private fees. Between 1932 and 1939 there evolved the present system of attorneys' BA (*kollegii advokatov*). But no general professional legal association exists for all jurists: scholars and teachers, judges, prosecutors, investigators, notaries, legal experts of security and other state agencies, all of whom play a part in formulating, developing, and applying Soviet law under the direction of the CPSU.

One BA may be formed in each oblast, republic without provincial subdivisions, or major city. BA, supposedly "self-governing" voluntary "public" (non-state) organizations, are actually under the administrative control of the republic ministries of justice and the political surveillance of the CPSU. They organize legal aid to individuals and organizations. They maintain legal standards and discipline through their regulation of the admittance, expulsion, penalizing, and further training of their members, the attorneys. Each BA establishes legal aid offices with the permission of its republic minister of justice. In the legal aid offices, attorneys meet their clients, give them legal aid and advice, arrange to represent them in civil cases or to defend them in criminal trials.

Attorneys receive fixed fees; e.g., 10 rubles for simple oral advice, 75 rubles for drafting petitions such as divorce petitions, up to 500 rubles or sometimes more as set by the BA for defending in the most complex criminal cases. Clients pay the fees to the legal aid offices which transfer them to their respective BA, where 25–30% of the fees are deducted for operating expenses, vacations, social security funds, and free legal aid, after which the remaining 70–75% are returned to the attorneys who earned them.

Some attorneys, especially experts in civil law (q.v.), are loaned out on contract as counsels to state and cooperative enterprises. (*See also* ARBITRATION, THE COURT SYSTEM, CRIMINAL LAW, LEGAL TRAINING, SOVIET LAW.)   P. H. J.

BARÁBA STEPPE, forested steppe on Ob-Irtysh divide, Novosibirsk Oblast, RSFSR; area about 45,000 sq. mi. Severe continental climate. Lakes and marshes. A major region of dairy and grain farming; large areas of virgin lands under cultivation.

BARÁBINSK, city in Novosibirsk Oblast, RSFSR; pop. 37,000 (1957). Railway-car repair shops, building materials, food processing.

BARÁNOV, Aleksándr Andréyevich (1746–1819), R. trader, founder and governor of R. possessions in N. America (Alaska).

BARÁNOVICHI, city in Brest Oblast, Byelorussian SSR; pop. 58,000 (1959). Food, metalworking, clothing, shoe ind.; pedag. inst.; large R.R. junction.

BARÁNSKY, Nikoláy Nikoláyevich (1881–), geographer and cartographer. Corresponding member, Ac. of S., USSR (1939). Professor of Moscow University (1929). Published economic-geographical works on the Soviet Union and other countries. Stalin prize (1952).

BARATÝNSKY (Boratýnsky), **Yevgény Abrámovich** (1800–1844), outstanding poet of the Pushkin group, author of brilliant poetry: *Two Fates, Truth, Waterfall,* poems *Eda* (1826), *Festivals* (1826), *Ball* (1828), and others. After the defeat of the Decembrist movement he became philosophically contemplative and his poetry was influenced by pessimistic feelings of solitude and doom (*Goethe's Death, The Last Death, Useless Days,* and others). He is at his best as an elegist.

BARCLÁY DE TÓLLY, Mikhaíl Bogdánovich (1761–1818), army leader, field-marshal. During the war of 1812 against Napoleon, he commanded the first R. Army and, being minister of war, was actually commander in chief of R. armies until the nomination of M. I. Kutuzov. After the latter's death (1813), he was reinstated as commander-in-chief and invaded France in 1815.

BÁRDIN, Iván Pávlovich (1883–1960), leading Soviet metallurgist and administrator. Fellow (1932), vice president (1942), Ac. of S., USSR. Hero of Socialist Labor (1945). Deputy to the Supreme Soviet (1937, 1946, 1950, 1954). Graduated from Kiev Polytechnic Institute (1910). Worked in a steel plant at Gary, Indiana, USA (1910–11); returned to Russia (1911). After the 1917 revolution he occupied a number of executive positions in the steel industry. Supervised the building of Kuznetsk Metallurgical Combine (1929). Director, Central Scientific Research Institute of Ferrous Metallurgy (1944). Head of the Ac. of S. mobilization project for the E. part of the USSR (1941–45). Supervised postwar reconstruction of metallurgical plants (1946). Chairman, Soviet Committee for the International Geophysical Year (1955). Research concerned the modernization of the steel industry. Stalin prizes (1942, 1948) and Lenin award (1958).

BARENTS SEA, arm of Arctic Ocean, between N. Europe and the islands of Spitzbergen, Franz Josef Land and Novaya Zemlya; area 542,300 sq. mi.; up to 1,300 ft. deep; its S.W. part (Kola Peninsula) does not freeze. Has considerable fisheries (cod, herring, haddock). Main port is Murmansk.

BARGUZÍN RANGE, mountain range along N.E. shore of Lake Baykal; elevation 9,315 ft.

BARGUZÍN RIVER, in Buryat ASSR, flows into Lake Baykal. Length 248 mi.; landing at Mogayto.

BARNAÚL, city in Altay Kray, RSFSR, port on the Ob River; pop. 305,000 (1959). One of the most important industrial and grain-growing centers of Siberia. Machine works, ship repairs, sawmills, textiles, leather factories, food processing.

BÁRSHCHINA. The cultivation of the estates of the nobility was carried on under the system of either *barshchina* or *obrok* (q.v.). Under the B system only a portion of the land of an estate, and usually the smaller portion, was divided into allotments and farmed by the peasants on their own account, while the bulk of the land was managed directly by the owner and was cultivated by labor of the same peasants. Under the B system the peasant paid no monetary tribute to the landlord but discharged his obligations toward him by working on his fields and by rendering other services, whereas the landlord paid the poll tax (q.v.). The prevailing system was to work three days a week for the lord and three days on the peasant's own allotment.

After the emancipation of 1861 this system survived in a modified form. Arrangements were made under which peasants paid for the right to farm a portion of the neighboring estate by cultivating for the benefit of the owner another portion with their own horses and implements. Some estates were farmed on a cropsharing basis, the landowner providing the land and the peasant the labor.

BÁRSOVA (Vladimirova), **Valéria Vladímirovna** (1892–), opera singer (lyric coloratura soprano), People's Artist of USSR. Her main roles: Antonida, Ludmila (*Ivan Susanin* and *Ruslan and Ludmila*, by Glinka), Rosina (*The Barber of Seville*). Member of the CPSU since 1940. Stalin prize (1941).

BARSUKÍ, Large and Small, two sand deserts in Kazakh SSR, north of Aral Sea. Large B is about 125 mi. long; Small B, 60 mi.

BASHKÍR ASSR, part of RSFSR; area 55,400 sq. mi.; pop. 3,342,000 (1959): Bashkirs, Tatars, Russians. Cities: Ufa (capital), Beloretsk, Ishimbay, Oktyabrsky, Sterlitamak, Chernikovsk, Baymak, Belebey, Birsk, Blagoveshchensk, Davlekanovo, Kumer Tau. It has forests and steppes with black soil, and a continental climate. Principal rivers are the Belaya and Ufa. Minerals: oil, coal, peat, iron, copper, gold, zinc, bauxite, salt, sulfur. Because of its very rich oil fields, it is called the "Second Baku"; besides the oil ind., it has metallurgical and machine-building plants. Its agr. area is 7,500,000 hectares, with crops of wheat, rye, oats, buckwheat, hemp, flax. Several schools of higher education, research institutes, theaters, philharmonic orchestra; considerable development of Bashkir national art and literature. Est. 1919.

BASKUNCHÁK, a salt lake in Astrakhan Oblast, RSFSR; area 40 sq. mi.

BATÁLOV, Nikoláy Petróvich (1899–1937), actor. Made his first stage appearance at the Moscow Art Theater in 1916; was at the same time (1916–24) an actor of the 2nd Studio of the MKhAT (Moscow Academic Art Theater). His stage successes include the roles of Figaro in Beaumarchais' *Le Mariage de Figaro,* Vaska Okorok and sailor Rubtsov in Ivanov's *Armored Train 14–69* and *Blocade,* Lopakhin in Chekhov's *The Cherry Orchard,* and others. Vivid temperament, genuine humor, and sincerity distinguished the acting and creativeness of B. In 1923 B began to appear in moving pictures and starred in *Aelita, The Mother, A Start in Life, Three Comrades,* and others.

BATALPASHÍNSK: *see* CHERKESSK.

BATÁYSK, city in Rostov Oblast, RSFSR, 6 mi. south of Rostov-on-Don; pop. 52,000 (1959). Large R.R. junction.

BATÚ KHAN (died 1255), grandson of Genghis Khan, Mongolian Khan whose invasion marks the beginning of the Tatar domination of Russia. In 1236 B conquered Russia and in 1241 advanced into Poland, Hungary, and the Balkans but unexpectedly reversed his course, returned to S. Russia and established a Mongol state, the Golden Horde, on the lower Volga. Its capital was Sarai.

BATÚMI, capital of Adzhar ASSR, important port on Black Sea; pop. 82,000 (1959). Connected by pipeline with Baku, it is an important oil-refining and shipping center. Humid, subtropical climate. Citrus fruit, tea. World-renowned botanical garden of subtropical flora, pedag. inst., Scientific Research Institute of Adzharia, museums. Is an ancient city; was under Turkish domination in the 18th and 19th centuries; became Russian in 1878.

BÁTYUSHKOV, Konstantín Nikoláyevich (1787–1855), poet, author of patriotic poetry (*To Dáshkov, Prisoner*). Member if the literary circle "Arzamas." His subjects were pagan joys of the earth, love, and friendship. He developed a literary language near to conversational (*Essays in Poetry and Prose,* 1817). As officer participated in the war against Napoleon. In 1821 he became insane.

BÁUMAN, Nikoláy Ernéstovich (1873–1905), revolutionary, prominent Bolshevik, organizer of the paper *Iskra* (The Spark), staunch supporter of Lenin. Was arrested many times and exiled. Killed in Moscow by a political antagonist in 1905. His funeral was transformed into a huge political demonstration.

BAYDÁR GATE, mountain pass across main range of Crimean mountains, connecting Sevastopol and Yalta.

BAYDARÁTA BAY, in S. part of Kara Sea; length 110 mi.; Kara River flows into it.

BAYKÁL, largest fresh-water lake in Eurasia. Altitude 1,486 ft., area 12,160 sq. mi., world's deepest lake (5,700 ft.), has more than 300 tributaries; its only outflow is the Angara River. Freezes in January, opens up in May; navigable. Rich fauna; fisheries (seals); used for floating timber; hydroelectric power station built at Irkutsk. Ports: Baykal, Listvyanka, Turka, Ust-Barguzin, Nizhne-Angarsk.

BAYKÁL RANGE, along N.W. shore of Lake Baykal, with elevations over 8,200 ft.

BAYKÓV, Aleksándr Aleksándrovich (1870–1946), physical metallurgist. Fellow, Ac. of S., USSR (1932). Professor, St. Petersburg Polytechnic Institute (1903). Research concerned the theory of metallurgical processes, physics, corrosion, refractories, ferrous and cuprous sulfide binary alloys and pyritic smelting. Proved the existence of austenite by hydrogen chloride etching of iron at high temperatures. Stalin prize (1943).

BAYMÁK, town in Bashkir ASSR; 75 mi. S.W. of Magnitogorsk; pop. 13,500 (1956); nonferrous metallurgy.

BAYRÁM-ALÍ, city in Mary Oblast, Turkmen SSR; pop. 20,300 (1956). Cotton processing, butter, rugs; sanatoriums (kidney ailments).

BAZHÁN, Mikóla (Nikoláy) **Platónovich** (1904–), Ukrainian poet, born in Kamenets-Podolsk, son of a military topographer. B attended the gymnasium in Uman. His first book of poetry, *The 17th Patrol*, appeared in 1927. Other known works of B are: *The Carved Shadow* on Ukraine's past; *A Trilogy of Passions; Mickiewicz in Odessa* (1957). He was elected to the presidium of the Ukrainian Writers' Union and awarded the order of Lenin in 1934 and joined the Communist party in 1940. From 1943 to 1949, B was vice-chairman of the Ukrainian Council of People's Commissars, and he has served as a deputy to the USSR Supreme Soviet three times. B has translated into Ukrainian the works of many authors, including Pushkin, Mayakovsky, N. Tikhonov, Rustaveli, Tsereteli, and Heine. Stalin prize (1946).

BAZHÉNOV, Vasíly Ivánovich (1737–1799), architect and teacher. Born to a family of a deacon, he went to school in Moscow; in 1755 transferred to St. Petersburg Academy of Fine Arts. In 1760 B received a stipend for studying abroad and went to France and Italy. Received academic rank at the Academy of Fine Arts of Bologna and that of Florence. In 1765 returned to Russia, was conferred the rank of academician, but not allowed to teach in the Academy. Author of many projects that were carried out by other architects. The most important is the project of the Kremlin Place (1773) that would have encompassed the entire Kremlin hill in one architectural complex. The project did not materialize. Author of important treatise *A Brief Discourse on the Kremlin Architecture* and report on reorganization of the Academy of Fine Arts. Laid foundation for classical tradition in R. architecture, which paved the way for the golden age of St. Petersburg architecture.

BÉDNY, Demyán (Pridvórov, Yefím Alekséyevich) (1883–1945), writer and propagandist. Born in Kherson,  he started writing in 1900. His first poetry showed extreme right political views. He soon veered to the left, however, becoming a Bolshevik as early as 1912, and a regular contributor to the newspaper *Pravda*. From the time of the Bolshevik Revolution in 1917 until the early 1930's, he wrote propaganda-type poetry. He enjoyed the personal support of both Lenin and Stalin, and in 1923 was awarded the order of the Red Banner. His poem *Climb Off the Stove,* however, and the dramatic poem *Heroes of Antiquity* (1933–34), written as a libretto for a comic opera, signaled his downfall. The latter play is a satire on ancient R. heroes, at a time when the princes and tsars were again treated with respect. During the war B received Stalin's pardon and returned to *Pravda.*

BÉGICHEV ISLAND, in S. part of the Laptev Sea; length 40 mi., width 35 mi.; hunting.

BEGOVÁT, city in Tashkent Oblast, Uzbek SSR, port on Syr Darya; pop. 30,600 (1956). Important industrial center; metallurgical plant, Farkhad hydroelectric power station, cement, bricks, concrete.

BÉILIS (BEYLIS), Mendel, defendant in the sensational "ritual murder" trial held in Kiev in 1913 at the instigation of the R. government, with the support of anti-Semitic organizations. B, a Jew and superintendent of a brick kiln, was accused of having killed the boy Andrey Yushchinsky in order to use his blood in Passover rituals. He was acquitted by the jury. After the trial B went to Palestine and eight years later to New York City where he led a retired life, first, as owner of a printing shop, and, later, as an insurance agent. He died in Saratoga Springs in 1934.

BÉKHTEREV, Vladímir Mikháylovich (1857–1927), neuropathologist, psychiatrist, psychologist, and physiol-ogist. Graduate, Medical and Surgical Academy (1878); professor of psychiatry and neuropathology, Kazan University (1885), Military Ac. of Medicine (1894), and the Medical Institute for Women (1897). Founder and director, Institute of Psychoneurology (1908), Institute for the Study of the Brain and Nervous Activity (1918), the Kazan Society of Neuropathologists and Psychiatrists. Research concerned the structure of the higher nervous system, the effects of the cerebral cortex on the functions of different organs, the origins of emotion. Suggested the treatment of alcoholism by hypnosis; described and diagnosed a number of nervous diseases. Promulgated reflexology aiming to replace psychology as a discipline. In his quest for an "objective psychology," he affirmed the inaccessibility of the psyche to knowledge, and stressed "associated reflexes" responsible for human behavior. Author of more than 500 papers including *The Transmitting Path of the Spinal Cord and the Cerebrum* (2nd ed., 1896–98); *Basic Theories on the Functions of the Brain* (1903); *A Guide to an Objective Study of the Human Personality* (4th ed., 1928); *Selected Works* (1954).

BÉLAYA RIVER, (1) in Bashkir ASSR, left tributary of the Kama; length 880 mi.; navigable from Sterlitamak. **(2)** in Buryat ASSR and Irkutsk Oblast, RSFSR, left tributary of the Angara; length 186 mi. **(3)** in Krasnodar Kray, RSFSR, left tributary of the Kuban; length 142 mi.

BÉLAYA TSÉRKOV, city in Kiev Oblast, Ukrainian SSR; pop. 71,000 (1959). Tractor-repair plant, furniture, flour mills, butter, meat and poultry combine, shoe factory; agricultural and pedag. inst. Dates back to 14th century.

BÉLGOROD-DNESTRÓVSKY (f. Akkerman, Rum. *Cetatea Alba*), city in Moldavian SSR, 12 mi. from Black Sea; pop. 21,600 (1956). Fisheries, flour mills, butter, wine; pedag. inst., technical schools. Founded as *Tyras* in 7th century B.C. by Greeks.

BÉLGOROD OBLAST, RSFSR, situated in the S. part of the central Russian heights; area 10,460 sq. mi.; pop. 1,227,000 (1959). Principal cities: Belgorod (adm. center), Stary Oskol, Valuyki. Rivers: N. Donets, Oskol, Vorskla, Tikhaya Sosna. Moderately continental climate, black soil. Minerals: iron ore (Kursk Magnetic Anomaly). Agr.: wheat, rye, sugar beets, sunflower crops. Ind.: chalk and iron-ore mining, flour mills, construction materials, sugar.

BELÍNSKY, Vissarión Grigóryevich (1811–1848), radical philosopher, critic, and journalist. Son of a poor and vicious army surgeon, B had great difficulty securing an education, but was finally able to study philology at the University of Moscow (from 1829). Introduced to German philosophy and radical protest, B  was expelled (1832) for writing a play against serfdom. Henceforth he supported himself by tutoring, translation, and editorial work, but lived for his writing and for discussions with his distinguished circle of friends, which included Botkin, Goncharov, Dostoyevsky, Bakunin, Herzen, Nekrasov, Kavelin, and Turgenev. B's intellectual pilgrimage was long and interesting. A radical by overpowering sentiment, his readings of Fichte, Schelling, and especially Hegel persuaded him to give intellectual assent to the regime of Nicholas I (mid-1830's). Moving to St. Petersburg in 1839, he found release from this dilemma first in a left Hegelian position, and then (from 1842) in French socialism, just at the time he was becoming well known for his writings in the liberal journal *Otechestvennya Zapiski* (Notes of the Fatherland). His most influential writings were his essay on the Battle of Borodino (1839), his analysis of Pushkin (1844), his extravagant praise of Dostoyevsky's *Poor Folk* (1846), and his blast at Gogol's moralistic writings (1847). B's heavy emphasis on the social purpose of literature, as well as his own diffuse style, has had immense influence on R. literary criticism to this day. Since much of B's literary criticism was thinly concealed political criticism, he had increasing difficulties with the censors. His health drove him to the S. of Russia (1845) and to a German spa (1847), but he returned to Russia to die (1848) apparently just in time to avoid arrest during the police terror of that year. B was the first major R. radical of the 19th century to come not from the nobility but from a lower social stratum. He was the first of a long line of radical journalists who spoke for much of the intelligentsia. Through his many friends, the journal *Sovremennik* (The Contemporary) which he helped to reorganize (1846), and his writings, B influenced three generations of R. radicals.

BIBLIOGRAPHY: T. G. Masaryk, *The Spirit of Russia*, Vol. I, rev. ed., London, 1955; E. Lampert, *Studies in Rebellion*, New York, 1957; Herbert E. Bowman, *Vissarion Belinsky*, Cambridge, 1954.

BELLINGSHÁUSEN, Faddéy Faddéyevich (1778–1852), famous navigator, R. admiral, head of around-the-world expedition to Antarctica in 1819–21. In Jan. 1820 he discovered Antarctica and many islands in polar and tropical zones; he also made important oceanological explorations.

BELOBORÓDOV, Aleksándr Geórgievich (1891–?), revolutionary. Joined the Bolshevik party in 1908. In 1918 was elected a member of the Central Committee. As chairman of the Ural Soviet, B organized the assassination of the tsar and his family in Yekaterinburg. In 1919 was deputy chief of the political department of the Red Army. In 1923 was appointed people's commissar of internal affairs. As a member of the Trotskyite opposition, was arrested and shot in the late 1930's.

BELOKÚRIKHA, balneological resort in Altay Kray, RSFSR, 45 mi. from Biysk; warm radioactive alkaline springs; treatment of joint, artery, gynecological diseases.

BELOMÓRSK, town in Karelian ASSR, White Sea port, end point of White Sea–Baltic Canal; pop. 11,800 (1956). Fishing industry, sawmills.

BELOPÓLSKY, Aristarkh Apollónovich (1854–1934), astronomer and astrophysicist. Fellow, Ac. of S. (1903). Graduated from Moscow University (1877). Director (1917–19), Pulkovo Observatory, which he joined in 1891. Extensive research on the orbit of Jupiter, spectrums of stars and comets. Author of numerous papers on the rotation of the sun. Awards of the Paris Ac. of S. (1908, 1918).

BELORÉTSK, city in Bashkir ASSR; pop. 59,000 (1959). One of the oldest metallurgical centers of S. Urals in the Komarovo-Zigazinsky iron-ore area. Wire and cable plant. Founded 1762.

BELOTSÁRSK: *see* KYZYL.

BELOÚSOV, Vladímir Vladímirovich (1907–), geologist. Corresponding member, Ac. of S., USSR (1953). Head of the Laboratory of Theoretical Tectonics (1943); professor of Moscow University (1953). B suggested methods of investigating the history of oscillations of the crust of the earth which greatly contributed to the study of the geological development of the Russian Plateau. Advanced a radiomigrational geotectonic theory (1951) to the effect that the evolution of the earth is based upon differentiation processes which affect its substance. Author of *Principles of Geotectonics* (1954).

BELÓV, Nikoláy Vasílyevich (1891–), crystallographer. Fellow, Ac. of S., USSR (1953). Graduated from Leningrad Polytechnic Institute (1921). Joined the Institute of Crystallography (1938). Professor, Gorky (1946) and Moscow universities (1953). Vice president, International Society of Crystallography (1957). Work concerns geometrical crystallography, X-ray diffraction analyses, practical application of the Fedorov groups of symmetry. Co-founder of the crystallochemical museum in Moscow and Leningrad. Author of over 160 publications including *The Structure of Ionic Crystals and Metallic Phases* (1947), *Crystalline Structure of Turmalin* (1949), *Progress of Structural Mineralogy* (1950). Stalin Prize (1952).

BELOVÉZHA PÚSHCHA (the Bialowieza Forest), a national reserve and sanctuary of zúbry (R. bison) and other rare animals and plants. It is situated in W. Byelorussian SSR in the Brest and Grodno oblasts. Area, 184,000 acres.

BELÓVO, city in Kemerovo Oblast, RSFSR; pop. 66,800 (1956), 107,000 (1959). Major industrial center of Kuzbas, with zinc and coal ind. R.R. workshops.

BÉLOYE ÓZERO: *see* WHITE LAKE.

BELOZÉRSK, town in Vologda Oblast, RSFSR, landing on canal connecting Beloye Ozero (White Lake) to the Volga-Baltic water system; pop. 10,300 (1956). Fish cannery. Ancient R. town.

BÉLTSY, city in Moldavian SSR, on Reut River (tributary of Dniester); pop. 67,000 (1959). R.R. station; distilleries, beet-sugar, food-processing factories.

BELÚKHA, highest peak (14,780 ft.) of Altay mountains in the Katun Range; covered with glaciers.

BÉLY, Andréy (Borís Nikoláyevich Bugáyev), (1880–1934), leading symbolist poet, writer, and literary critic. He studied philosophy and mathematics at the University of Moscow. Like Blok he hailed the revolution of 1917 and identified it with Christ in the poem *Christ Is Risen* (1918). He soon rejected Bolshevism and emigrated in 1921. He returned in 1923 and died in the Soviet Union in 1934.

The "symphonic" poetry of B never became popular, and his linguistic experiments and mannerisms make his prose very difficult for translation. He often treats the world in a fantastic manner. Chaos always prevails, and only a symbol, created by art, could bridge the gap between the man's soul and the world. B's first novel, *The Silver Dove*, was published in 1910. Its theme is typical of this period; an unsatisfied poet joins the sect of peasants, called the White Doves, and returns, frustrated, to his former life. Another novel, *St. Petersburg* (1913), shows the influence of Gogol and Dostoyevsky. The most interesting work of B is *Kotik Letayev*. The gradual organization of the experience of a child and the change of language are mastered with great skill. Other works by B are: *The Crime of Nikolay Letayev* (1921), *Memoirs of a Crank* (1923), *Moscow* (1926), and *Masks* (1930–32). In this period the extravagant polyphonic experimentations of B were still tolerated. The four volumes of his memoirs *Recollections of Alexander Blok* (1922), *On the Border of Two Centuries* (1929), *The Beginning of a Century* (1932), and *Between Two Revolutions* (1933)—are a valuable record of the history of symbolism.

BÉLY, island in Kara Sea, in Tyumen Oblast, RSFSR; area 735 sq. mi.

BELYÁNKIN, Dmítry Stepánovich (1876–1953), geologist. Fellow, Ac. of S., USSR (1943). Graduate, Yuryev (Dorpat) University (1901); joined St. Petersburg (Leningrad) Polytechnic Institute (1903), professor (1920–35). Affiliated with the Petrographic and Geological Institute (1930). Member of the editorial staff of *Bolshaya Sovetskaya Entsiklopedia* (Large Soviet Encyclopedia). Research concerned the geology and petrography of the Urals, the Caucasus, and the N. part of the European USSR. Studied rock-forming minerals, i.e. feldspar, mica, minerals of clay, and rare minerals; also investigated refractories, ceramics, abrasives, glass. One volume of his *Selected Works* was published in 1956.

BELYÁYEV, Mitrófan Petróvich (1836–1903), a rich industrialist who devoted himself to promoting R. music. He established a music publishing house in Leipzig, organized concerts of symphonic and chamber music in St. Petersburg. Composers gathered at his house ("The Belyayev Circle"), among them Rimsky-Korsakov. In 1898 B was elected chairman of the St. Petersburg Society of Chamber Music.

BELYÁYEV, Nikoláy Ilyích (1903–), party and government official, born in Bashkiria, a CP member since 1921. He finished at the Moscow Agricultural Institute in 1925 and held party posts in W. Siberia, at Novosibirsk; in 1943 he was named chairman of the Altay Kray Executive Committee and then first secretary of the Altay Kray Party Central Committee; was elected a member of the Central Committee, CPSU, in 1952, at the 19th Party Congress. He was deputy to the USSR and the RSFSR Supreme Soviets; vice-chairman of the RSFSR Bureau of the Central Committee, 1956–57. He was elected a member of the Presidium of the Central Committee in 1957 but was relieved of these duties in May 1960. He was also first secretary of the Kazakhstan CP Central Committee from Dec. 1957 to Jan. 1960. He was criticized for failures in agricultural policies and demoted to first secretary of the Stavropol Kray Committee, but held this post only until June 1960.

BENDÉRY (Rum. *Tighina*), city in Moldavian SSR; pop. 45,000 (1957). Canned food, clothing, and shoe factories; many gardens and vineyards in suburbs; ruins of ancient 14th-century fortress.

BENKENDÓRF, Aleksándr Khristofórovich (1783–1844), general, one of the most reactionary of statesmen, head of the police during the reign of Nicholas I. He participated in the investigation of the Decembrists; from 1826 was chief of the Corps of Gendarmes and of the Third Department (political police).

BENOIS, Aleksándr Nikoláyevich (1870–1960), painter, writer, and art critic. Son of the architect, Nikolay Benois, he studied law at the University of St. Petersburg and attended art classes at the Academy of Art. His first water colors were exhibited in 1896. From 1896 till 1899, B studied art in Paris. Upon his return to Russia, he took an active part in the *Mir Iskusstva* movement and was one of the editors of the art magazine published under the same title. From 1901 till 1903 he was the editor of the magazine *Art Treasures of Russia*. His water colors show his deep love for France of the 17th and 18th centuries. B created stage designs for the operas and ballets: *Boris Godunov, Pavillon d'Armide, Götterdämmerung,* and others. His illustrations of Pushkin's works (*Bronze Horseman, Pique Dame*) reflect his appreciation of the austere beauty of St. Petersburg. In 1915, B was head of the art department of the Moscow Art Theater. His books *School of Russian Painting* and *History of Paintings of All Times and Nations* were published in Russia before the revolution. From 1926 B lived in France, where he continued to work as a stage designer and painter of water colors. His memoirs were published by the Chekhov Publishing House in New York.

BERDÍCHEV, city in Zhitomir Oblast, Ukrainian SSR; pop. 66,000 (1939), 53,000 (1959). Machineworks, food, beet sugar, shoe, leather ind.; R.R. junction. Pedag. inst.

BERDSK, city in Novosibirsk Oblast, RSFSR, on the Ob River; pop. 26,600 (1956). Flour mills; sanatoriums, rest homes.

BERDYÁNSK (f. Osipénko), seaport town in Zaporozhye Oblast, Ukrainian SSR, a resort on the N. shore of Sea of Azov; pop. 58,700 (1956). Ind.: machine mfg., food processing; large salt lagoons in vicinity.

BERDYÁYEV, Nikoláy Aleksándrovich (1874–1948), philosophical Marxist and religious thinker. Born in Kiev and well educated, B was one of many young Russians who in the 1890's were attracted to Marxism by its social protest and program. Trained in critical phi-

losophy, he could not accept Marxist materialism or ethics, and consequently made a very interesting attempt to combine Marxist socialism with neo-Kantian ethics and metaphysics. As this proved unsatisfactory to him, he abandoned his critical position, moving in the 1900's toward his own kind of nonconformist Orthodox Christianity. Having been exiled (1899) to the N. of Russia for criticizing the church's subservience to the regime, he continued his protests which kept him in difficulties that culminated in his trial (1914) for attacks on the Holy Synod. Although after the Revolution B became a professor of philosophy at the University of Moscow, he was twice jailed by the Bolsheviks and expelled from Russia in 1922 for criticizing Marxism and the regime. In 1924 he established himself at Clamart near Paris, where he presided over his own religious academy, and wrote the books of religious speculation that have given him a considerable vogue among enthusiasts for the revival of religion, existentialism, and Dostoyevsky's ideas. Although B is now best known for his later efforts, his significance lies more in the dissidence and ethical protests of his R. period. His principal works include: *The Beginning and the End,* London, 1952; *The Divine and the Human,* London, 1949; *Dostoyevsky: An Interpretation,* New York, 1934; *Dream and Reality,* London, 1950; *Freedom and the Spirit,* London, 1935; *The Meaning of the Creative Art,* New York, 1954; *The Meaning of History,* London, 1936; *The Origin of Russian Communism,* Ann Arbor, 1960; *The Realm of Spirit and the Realm of Caesar,* New York, 1952; *The Russian Revolution,* London, 1931; *Slavery and Freedom,* New York, 1944.

BIBLIOGRAPHY: O. F. Clarke, *Introduction to Berdyayev,* London, 1950; D. A. Lowrie, *Rebellious Prophet;* a life of Nikolay Berdyayev, New York, 1960; M. A. Vallon, *An Apostle of Freedom:* life and teachings of Nikolay Berdyayev, New York, 1960.

BEREZINÁ RIVER, in Byelorussian SSR, right tributary of Dnieper, length 365 mi.; navigable for 300 mi. In November 1812 last remnants of Napoleon's army were destroyed here.

BEREZNIKÍ, city in Perm Oblast, RSFSR, landing on Kama River; pop. 106,000 (1959). Is important center of chemical ind. (fertilizers); has vast reserves of common and potassium salts.

BERÉZOVO, town in Khanty-Mansi National Okrug, RSFSR; pop. 12,900 (1959). Landing on N. Sosva River; fisheries, trapping, lumbering; experimental station for arctic agriculture. In 1728 Prince Menshikov was exiled to B.

BERG, Áksel Ivánovich (1893–), radio engineer. Fellow, Ac. of S., USSR (1946). Submarine navigator, and navy commander (1914–22). Graduated simultaneously from Military Naval Academy and Naval Engineering School (1925), Leningrad. Teaches at military naval schools in Leningrad and the Institute of Electrical Engineering. Chairman of the All-Union Scientific Council of Radiophysics and Radio Engineering.

BERG, Lev Semyónovich (1876–1950), geographer, biologist, president of the Geographical Society of the Soviet Union (1940). Was the author of many important works on ichthyology, geography, history, geographical discoveries, and climatology. Stalin prize (1951).

BÉRGELSON, David (1884–1952), Yiddish novelist and short-story writer. An impresisonist, he gained recognition with his novelettes *Arum Vokzal* (Around the Railway Station, 1909) and *Noch Alemen* (All Is Ended, 1913). After the Soviet revolution, he joined the Bolsheviks and published a number of novels and short stories in the "proletarian" manner. B was arrested during the "purge" of Jewish intellectuals in 1948 and was executed in Aug. 1952.

BERGHÓLTS, Ólga Fyódorovna (1910–), poet, born in St. Petersburg. Graduated from the philological faculty of Leningrad University, 1930. Her first book was published in 1934. Her husband, the poet Boris Kornilov, was arrested in 1937, and subsequently died in a concentration camp. She is the author of lyrics, narrative poems, children's books, short stories, and songs: *Poems; February Diary; Leningrad Poem* (1934); *Leningrad Notebook* (1942); *Leningrad; In Memory of the Defenders;* a play, *They Lived in Leningrad* (1944); *Your Path* (1945); *Poems* (1946); *Selected Works* (1948); a play, *On Our Earth* (1947); *On Stalingrad Soil* (1952). During the "thaw" she published for the first time a number of poems written in the late 1930's which hint at how she was forced to "repudiate" her husband: "and the soul will writhe with fear and anguish." Poems written after Stalin's death frequently dealt with loneliness of women in a Soviet village, left desolate of men by the war; or the return of concentration camp prisoners, arrested unjustly in the 1930's: "Few of them returned—seventeen years—always seventeen years!"

BÉRIA, Lavrénty Pávlovich (1899–1953), leading Bolshevik and head of the security police, son of a Georgian peasant. In 1915 he entered a technical school in Baku and graduated in 1919. Joined the Bolshevik party in 1917. In 1921 B started service in the security police, and soon became head of the Georgian and later Transcaucasian OGPU. In 1931 he was a rising member of the party hierarchy as first secretary of the Transcaucasian party committee, and in 1934 was elected member of the Central Committee of the CP of the USSR. In 1935 B published a book on the history of the Bolsheviks in Transcaucasia.

In 1938 he was transferred to Moscow and appointed deputy chief of the NKVD, under Yezhov. After Yezhov's ouster in Dec. 1938, B was appointed chief of the NKVD. His task was to eliminate the now admitted "excesses" of the *yezhovshchina,* and to restore "normalcy" in the work of the police. He carried out a thorough purge of the police personnel which was made the scapegoat for the "excesses" and improved the qualifications of the newly trained personnel. Yet terrorism, forced labor, and other aspects of the NKVD's activities continued on a vast, though reduced, scale. In 1939 B was made candidate member, and in 1946 full member of the ruling Politburo, the first security police chief to reach this position. In 1941 he was appointed deputy chairman of the Sovnarkom and member of the State Defense Committee; in 1945 he was elevated to the military rank of marshal. He abandoned the posts of minister of the MVD and MGB, but retained supreme responsibility for the two police agencies. Because of security aspects of atomic research, B was put in charge of this sensitive work.

In the unsettled situation following Stalin's death Beria's power apparently became a menace to Stalin's successors. B was accused of having been a British agent since 1919, of plotting to seize power, of subverting farm collectivization, and sponsoring nationalist feeling among Soviet minorities. He was allegedly tried in Dec. of 1953, sentenced to death, and executed together with six aides; but, according to some information, he had been shot and killed in the spring of 1953 at a stormy session of the Politburo.

BERING SEA, between Siberia, Alaska, Aleutian and Commander Islands; area 884,700 sq. mi., depth about 15,650 ft. Considerable fisheries (salmon, herring, cod); mammals: whale, seal, walrus. Northern Seaway passes through it.

BERING STRAIT, between N.E. Asia and N. America; width 52 mi., depth 130–160 ft. Two Diomedes Islands are in center of it; between them runs the boundary line between USSR and U.S.

BERLIN CONGRESS (1878) of European States. The conditions of the San Stephano Treaty signed after the Russo-Turkish War (1877–78) were reconsidered and revised by the Berlin Treaty of 1878. The Berlin Treaty confirmed the independence of Serbia, Montenegro, and Rumania; and ratified the occupation of Bosnia and Herzegovina by Austro-Hungary.

BERNSHTÉYN, Sergéy Natánovich (1880–), mathematician. Fellow, Ac. of S., USSR (1929). Graduate of  Paris (1902) and Goettingen universities. Professor of Kharkov University (1920). Co-founder of Ukrainian Scientific Research Institute of Mathematical Sciences (1928). Professor of Leningrad Polytechnic Institute and Leningrad University (1934–41). Honorary member, Moscow Mathematical Society (1942); honorary degrees from the universities of Algiers (1944) and Paris (1945). Extensive research on the theories of differential equations, approximations of functions by polynominals, and the theory of probabilities applicable to physics and statistics. Author of *The Theory of Probabilities* (4th ed., 1946); *On the Sums of Dependent Variables with Near Zero Correlation.* Stalin prize (1942).

BERSÉNEV (Pavlishchev), **Iván Nikoláyevich** (1889–1951), actor and producer, People's Artist, USSR. He began his acting career in Kiev (1907), joined the company of the Moscow Art Theater (1911) and in 1924 was appointed art director of the 2nd MKhAT (Moscow Academic Art Theater). In 1938 B became art director and leading actor of the Lenin Komsomol Theater where he produced Gergey's and Litovsky's *My Son* (1939) and *A Fellow from Our Town* (1944), Simonov's *Let It Be So* (1944), Korneychuk's *Battle-Front* (1942), and Ibsen's *A Doll's House.* B played Protasov

in L. Tolstoy's *The Living Corpse,* and Cyrano de Bergerac in Rostand's play.

BESKIDS, Western and Eastern, range of Carpathian Mountains along the frontier line of Poland, Czechoslovakia and USSR, elevation about 5,650 ft.

BESTÚZHEV, Aleksándr Aleksándrovich, pen name  Marlinsky (1797–1837), writer, Decembrist, cavalry officer. Together with K. F. Ryleyev, he published the almanac *Polyarnaya Zvezda* (The Polar Star). Was exiled to the Caucasus where he was killed in the war against mountain tribes. His Caucasian novels and military stories (*Ammalat-Bek,* 1832, *Mulla-Nur,* 1835–36, and others) contain many colorful ethnographic details.

BESTÚZHEV, Nikoláy Aleksándrovich (1791–1855), writer and scientist, naval officer. One of the publishers of *Polyarnaya Zvezda* (The Polar Star), Decembrist. He was condemned to forced labor for life, his sentence later commuted to 20 years.

BESTÚZHEV-RYÚMIN, Count Alekséy Petróvich (1693–1766), statesman and diplomat. He began his service under Peter I; was chancellor from 1744; adversary of Prussia and supporter of the alliance with England and Austria. Was exiled during the Seven Years' War, but rehabilitated by Catherine II.

BESTÚZHEV-RYÚMIN, Konstantín Nikoláyevich (1829–1897), historian. A graduate of Moscow University, he was for seventeen years prof. of history at the University of St. Petersburg. He opposed historical determinism, suggesting that history could be explained only in terms of a variety of interrelated factors. In 1868 he published his monograph on the R. chronicles before the 14th century. His history of Russia to the 16th century (1872, 1875) paid particular attention to cultural developments.

BESTÚZHEV-RYÚMIN, Mikhaíl Pávlovich (1803–1826), leader of the Southern Society of Decembrists, a convinced republican. Executed July 13, 1826.

BETÉKHTIN, Anatóly Geórgievich (1897–), geologist and mineralogist. Fellow, Ac. of S., USSR (1953). Graduated from Leningrad Mining Institute (1924), where he remained as professor. Since 1956 affiliated with the Institute of Geology of Ore Deposits, Petrography, Mineralogy, and Geochemistry. Author of about 200 books on the theory of ore formation and mineralography. Received the Stalin prize (1947) for his *Industrial Manganese Ores of the USSR* and the Lenin prize (1958) for *Main Problems in the Study of Magmatic Ore Deposits.*

BET-PAK-DALÁ, (R. *Severnaya Golodnaya Step*— Northern Hunger Steppe), in central part of Kazakh SSR, area about 28,500 sq. mi. Its development started during Soviet rule, it now has karakul-raising state farms, an experimental cattle-breeding station, beginnings of agriculture.

BETSKÓY, Iván Ivánovich (1704–1795), educator. Son of a nobleman, he traveled widely, was an admirer of Locke and Rousseau, and became education minister in 1764. He sought to regenerate society by giving children of the nobility a well-rounded education away from the crude atmosphere of their homes. This and other similar experiments were not always successful, but they were important because they pioneered in emphasizing equality of education for girls and boys, the necessity for individualized instruction, and the universal value of a liberal education.

BEZBORÓDKO, Aleksándr Andréyevich (1747–1799), statesman and diplomat. He participated in the conclusion of international pacts of Russia in the last quarter of the 18th century. Became chancellor in 1797.

BÉZHETSK, city in Kalinin Oblast, RSFSR; pop. 24,700 (1956). Agricultural implements, equipment for peat exploitation, distilleries; agricultural technical school. Dates from 12th century.

BÉZHITSA, formerly town in Bryansk Oblast, RSFSR; in 1956 merged with Bryansk (q.v.).

BEZYMÉNSKY, Aleksándr Ilyích (1898–), poet, born in Zhitomir. In his own words, "First a party member—then a poet." He was one of the founders of the "October" group and active collaborator on the journal *Na Postu* (On Assignment). At one time he was a follower of Trotsky, but changed his political allegiance in time to avoid persecution by writing a series of poems known as "stones that were hurled at Trotskyism." His best-known poems are *Komsomolia* (1924), dealing with communist youth of which B was a keen observer; *Feliks* (1927), about Dzerzhinsky and the early "Chekists"; *Tragic Night,* and *Night of the Chief of the Political Department* (1934). B is the author of a satirical poem *The Shot,* written as a play for Meyerhold's theater in the late 1920's. After World War II B published *Notebook from the Front.*

BÍBIKOV, Aleksándr Ilyích (1729–1774), general. He participated in the Seven Years' War (1756–63); in 1773–74, he was commander of the troops sent for the suppression of Ye. Pugachov's mutiny.

BILÍBIN, Iván Yákovlevich (1876–1942), painter, graphic artist, and stage designer. Studied in Munich and St. Petersburg (under Repin). Contributed to the magazine *Mir Iskusstva* (World of Art). In his conventionally stylized illustrations of R. folk tales he continued the tradition of Polenov (illustrations of Pushkin's folk tales and epic poems). B developed a style of his own, two-dimensional and ornate, greatly influenced by R. folk art and by old R. miniatures.

BIOCHEMISTRY: see BIOLOGICAL SCIENCES.

BIOLOGICAL SCIENCES. The end of the 17th century and the early 18th century mark a rapid development of experimental biology, particularly after the foundation of the Ac. of S. (1724). Initial information on the fauna and flora of the Arctic Seas and the Ural Mountains was obtained by members of the Kamchatka expedition (1725–43) as well as in the course of subsequent explorations. M. V. Lomonosov advanced his law on the development of nature (1750). In 1767, K. F. Wolf renounced the theory of preformation and hypothesized the theory of evolution. Experimental data refuting the self-generation of microorganisms were published (M. Terekhovsky, 1775) and the study of hybridization and selectivity was carried on (A. T. Bolotov, 1778). K. M. Baer was the forerunner of modern embryology (1828–37).

During the second half of the 19th century biological science benefited by the theories of I. M. Sechenov and I. P. Pavlov (*see* PHYSIOLOGY). In the 1860's A. O. Kovalevsky and I. I. Mechnikov expanded the principles of evolutionary embryology; K. A. Timiryazev studied natural selection, the nature of heredity, and Michurin's theories of hybridization in the 1880's. Mechnikov postulated the theory of phagocytosis and D. I. Ivanovsky (1892) the existence of filtrating viruses. Complex problems of the physiology of the nervous system and psychology were studied and a bold attempt made at establishing physiological bases for psychic processes which, in turn, led to an objective investigation of higher nervous activity (I. M. Sechenov, 1863). S. P. Botkin's physiological trends in clinical medicine were adopted and developed by I. P. Pavlov.

After the revolution biological sciences have for a number of years been under strict ideological party control (*see* I. V. MICHURIN, T. D. LYSENKO, GENETICS). In recent years restrictions have been eased and followers of classic genetics are no longer subjected to reprisals. Biological research has developed in the following major directions:

BIOCHEMISTRY. Biochemical research is conducted by means of tracer techniques, chromatographic adsorption analysis and other modern methods. It has become a leading branch of the biological sciences and is closely linked with different fields of biology and medicine. The versatile study of proteins and their effects is conducted by V. A. Engelhardt, M. N. Lyubimov, and A. N. Belozersky who have found that the structure of nuclear substance in all modern organisms is related. Nitrogen metabolism in plants and animals was investigated by D. N. Pryanishnikov, V. S. Gulevich, and A. Ye. Braunshteyn. Research concerned the biochemistry of respiration and fermentation of the correlation between these processes, the theory of plant respiration, photosynthesis, and so forth. A. V. Palladin and G. Ye. Vladimirov obtained interesting results on the biochemistry of the brain and nervous excitation. A. I. Oparin suggested a theory on the origin of plant life based on biochemical research. A. N. Bakh contributed greatly to the development of a new branch of biochemistry, i.e. industrial biochemistry which deals with such matters as storing conditions for sugar beets, the drying of grain, technological process in the baking, wine, tea and tobacco industries, and the production of organic acids from tobacco leaves and cotton.

Research is conducted at the Ukrainian Biochemical Institute (1925); the Institute of Biochemistry, Ac. of S., USSR (1935); the Institute of Biological and Medical Chemistry, Academy of Medical Science USSR (1945); the Laboratory of Physiological Chemistry (1943), in addition to various universities and research laboratories.

BIOPHYSICS. On the basis of the ionic theory of excitation of living tissues the adaptation process of vision was formulated. Problems of eye sensitivity to various spectral rays in the presence of external stimuli are studied in S. V. Kravkov's laboratory. Physiological acoustics (S. N. Rzhevkin), optics (N. T. Fedorov, N. D. Nurnberg), effects of ultrashort electro-magnetic waves on organisms (S. Ya. Turlygin), the nature of biological phenomena and electrical properties of tissues (D. N. Nasonov), and the action of ionizing radiation on the organism (M. N. Meysel, Ye. Ya. Grayevsky, A. M. Kuzin), are major fields of study. New physical methods of biological investigation and X-ray examinations of molecular substances are arousing wide interest. Most research is carried out at the Institute of Biological Physics, Ac. of S., USSR, the Academy of Medical Science, and at universities and scientific institutes.

BOTANICS. The classic series on *The Flora of the USSR* is being published since 1934; so far 24 volumes have appeared. Extensive research on cultural plants is conducted at the All-Union Institute of Plants (formerly under N. I. Vavilov who also organized a great many expeditions throughout the USSR, Asia, Africa, and Latin America). Vavilov suggested a new theory of the origin of plant life. Industrial crops including new varieties of rubber (*koksagyz, tau-sagyz*), gutta-percha and tanning trees, medical plants, useful weeds, and so forth were discovered. A theory of acclimatization advanced by I. V. Michurin proved of particular importance in introducing plants to arctic and mountainous regions. Morphology, anatomy, cytology, and embryology of plant life are being extensively investigated (B. N. Kozo-Polyansky, K. I. Meyer, N. P. Krenko,

V. G. Aleksandrov). A variety of geobotanic maps is available. Particular attention has been given to plant physiology for the purpose of improving agricultural crops (K. A. Timiryazev, D. I. Ivanovsky, D. N. Pryanishnikov, V. I. Palladin). Large-scale irrigation projects also required special plant studies. The effects of environment on plant development were investigated (V. I. Razumov, T. D. Lysenko). Research is primarily carried out at various institutes of the Ac. of S., USSR, universities, the K. A. Timiryazev Academy in Moscow, and in agricultural laboratories and institutes.

MICROBIOLOGY. The general development of technological processes in different branches of industry, the intensification of agriculture and the struggle with infectious diseases enhanced the research in all the subdivisions of microbiology: general, geological, technical, agricultural, medical and veterinary, and also virology. Geomicrobiology originated with the study of microbes as geological factors. V. L. Omelyansky's theory on microbiological methane formation led to the development of research of petroleum microbiology (V. S. Butkevich, L. D. Shturm, and S. I. Kuznetsov). A series of studies was dedicated to the role of microorganisms in the chemical changes of sulfur, iron, and calcium salts, to the morphological changes in the process of ontogenesis of Nitrobacter *Bacillus megatherium*, *Granulobacter pectinovorum*, and others (B. L. Isachenko, L. I. Rubenchik, A. A. Bachinskaya, N. A. Krasilnikov, V. I. Kudryavtsev, A. A. Imshenetsky).

Studies of cytology of microorganisms have shown that bacteria have no separate nucleus and that chromatin is diffusely distributed within the cell (A. A. Imshenetsky). Research was done on the problem of gigantic forms of bacteria; of physiology and biochemistry of microbes in connection with their environment, including creation, under the influence of X-rays, of mutations of yeasts sharply different from the original culture (G. A. Nadson, 1926). Work on comparative morphology of microorganisms and their ecology made it possible to form a system of actinomyces and microbacteria (N. A. Krasilnikov), yeasts (V. I. Kudryavtsev), and others. S. P. Kostychev studied the chemistry of alcohol fermentation and found that acetaldehyde is an intermediate product of fermentation. V. V Pervozvansky discovered that the oxidation of carbohydrates was promoted by *Bact. pseudomonas*. Research is continued on the role of bacteria of sulfur, iron and hydrogen. The biological fixation of nitrogen is a most important study in general and soil microbiology (V. L. Omelyansky, M. V. Fedorov, and others). The development of industry stimulated the study of technical microbiological production of lactic acid, acetone, and vinegar. The improvement of technology and work on the physiology of yeasts brought about the rational production of liquor, beer, wine, yeast, and bread. Research in soil microbiology explored the role of microorganisms in the metabolism of substances in the soil and methods of direction of microbiological processes for the increase of the fertility of the soil.

In medical microbiology and epidemiology special attention was given to the ecology and spreading of disease-causing organisms, and to the prevention and treatment of infectious diseases. Vaccines against Siberian ulcer, plague, tularemia, brucellosis, and others were introduced. Fundamental research in medical microbiology was done by L. A. Tarasevich, D. K. Zabolotny, and N. F. Gamaleya.

The main institutions in USSR for the study of microbiology are: The Institute of Microbiology of the Academy of Sciences, the Institute of Microbiology and Epidemiology of the Acad. of Medic. Sciences, the Institute of Agricultural Microbiology.

SOIL SCIENCE. The physical chemistry of soils has been studied by K. K. Gedroyts whose theories on the absorbability of soil had a decisive influence on practical aspects of pedology (I. N. Antipov-Kratayev, A. N. Sokolovsky). Methods to combat erosion and drought are based on chemistry, mineralogy, and hydrology of soils (Ya. V. Peyve, B. B. Polynov, N. I. Gorbunov, G. N. Vysotsky). Great progress was made in the field of soil fertility, improvement, and reclamation (D. N. Pryanishnikov). A series of soil maps was compiled under L. I. Prasolov and work continues in that direction. Research is conducted at the Institute of Pedology, Ac. of S., USSR, and in a number of universities and agricultural institutes.

ZOOLOGY. The study of Soviet fauna, especially in remote and coastal regions, is conducted by the Institute of Zoology, Ac. of S., USSR and Ukrainian SSR, the Leningrad Museum of Zoology, the Moscow Research Institute of Helminthology, and others. The Biological Research Centers in Sevastopol (Black Sea) and in Murmansk (Barents Sea) are engaged in the study of sea fauna. A wealth of material was compiled by Ye. N. Pavlovsky and K. I. Skryabin who studied taxonomy, geographical distribution, ecological conditions, and biological cycles of parasites. Health campaigns were launched and many diseases reduced to a minimum (filariasis, malaria, and others).

Important contributions to science were made by expeditions to the Barents and Kara seas on the schooner *Persy* (1923–41), expeditions initiated by the Arctic Institute and K. M. Deryugin (1925–32), the Institute of Oceanography (1949–55), and the Ac. of S. (1955). The results of these expeditions made it possible to describe numerous species, genera, families, and larger groups of animals, establish new charts of the life in vertical zones and characterize the ultra-abyssal fauna of the ocean. The study of ichthyology in fresh and salt

waters contributed to the development of the Soviet fish industry. Interesting zoogeographical and paleofaunistic generalizations resulted from the study of Caucasian and Uralian subterranean fauna. The introduction of Far Eastern bees in the European part of the USSR was a valuable aid to apiculture. *The Fauna of the USSR*, a series which started in 1935, and *The Key to the Fauna of the USSR*, another series launched in 1927, are major publications of the Institute of Zoology.

BIOPHYSICS: *see* BIOLOGICAL SCIENCES.

BÍRMAN, Serafíma Gérmanovna (1890–), actress, producer for the Lenin Komsomol Moscow Theater, People's Artist, USSR. B has appeared on the stage since 1911. Among her best roles are: Vassa Zheleznova in Gorky's play of the same name and Major Grech in Simonov's *Let It Be So*. In moving pictures she played the part of Staritskaya in *Ivan Grozny*.

BIROBIDZHÁN: *see* JEWISH AUTONOMOUS OBLAST, JEWS.

BIROBIDZHÁN, city, adm. center of Jewish Autonomous Oblast, on Bira R., part of Khabarovsk Kray, RSFSR; pop. 41,000 (1959). Lumber mill, furniture, plywood, meat combine, clothing, mining; railroad technical school. Founded 1928.

BÍRON (Bühren), **Ernst Johann** (1690–1772), favorite of Empress Anna Ivanovna and *de facto* ruler of Russia although his only official position was that of chamberlain. In 1730 B was made Count of the Holy Roman Empire, in 1737 Duke of Courland. His rule from 1730 to 1740 was called *Bironovshchina;* it is associated with a clique of German adventurers who exploited the state resources. B was made regent upon the death of Empress Anna but this lasted only 22 days. He was deposed by his arch enemies Ostermann and Münnich with the help of the guards. B was exiled to Pelym in Siberia in Nov. 1740, but was amnestied, returned to St. Petersburg under Peter III, and in 1763 was restored by Catherine II to the throne of Courland. He abdicated in 1769.

BIRTH RATE: *see* MEDICAL SYSTEM, POPULATION.

BÍYA RIVER, within Altay mountain range, forming together with Katun the Ob River; flows from Lake Teletskoye. Length 188 mi.; navigable for 140 mi.

BIYSK, city in Altay Kray, RSFSR, landing on Biya River; pop. 145,000 (1959). Machine building, meat, sugar, distilleries, tobacco, leather, woodworking. Founded 1709.

BLACK HUNDREDS, a reactionary and anti-Semitic organization which was founded in the revolution of 1905. Its chief aim was to fight the revolutionaries and the Jews. The BH were particularly active in the years of Stolypin's premiership, 1906–1911.

"BLACK REPARTITION" (*Chorny Peredel*), the anti-terrorist wing of the populist *Zemlya i Volya* (Land and Liberty) organized after the Voronezh congress, in June 1879, by G. Plekhanov, P. Akselrod, V. Zasulich and other future Marxists. In the first issue of the underground paper published under this name Plekhanov argued that "history has taught us" that political *coups d'état* have "nowhere and at no time" been able to secure economic and political freedom for the people. Only an economic revolution on the land, with its repartition among the peasants, will inevitably bring with it the overturning of all other social relations. To preach general, political aims to the people, which they could not understand, would only have the effect of turning them against all revolutionary activities. *Chorny Peredel* ceased publication with its 4th issue, in Sept. 1881. By that date the founders of the movement had all emigrated and had become converted to the doctrines of Marx and Engels.   V. Su.

BLACK SEA (R. *Chornoye More*, ancient *Pontus* or *Pontus Euxinus*), sea between Europe and Asia; area 159,000 sq. mi.; mean depth 4,166 ft., greatest 7,363 ft. (in S.); connected with Aegean Sea through the Bosporus, Sea of Marmara, and Dardanelles, and with the Sea of Azov; receives many rivers including the Danube, Dniester, Bug, Dnieper, Kuban (in Europe), Kizil Irmak (in Asia). Salt content is 16.5 to 18.5 per cent, increasing with depth and reaching 25 per cent at 300 ft. Hydrogen sulfide at greater depth prevents marine life. There are several small islands in the shallow N.W. part. There are storms and fogs in the fall and winter. Fish are not very abundant. Is important means of transportation for the USSR and for other countries along its coast. Major Soviet ports: Odessa, Sevastopol, Novorossiysk, Tuapse, Poti, Batumi.

BLACK SOILS: *see* CHORNYE ZEMLI.

BLAGODÁT, mountain in the Urals, Sverdlovsk Oblast, RSFSR, elevation 1,246 ft.; rich iron-ore deposits.

BLAGONRÁVOV, Anatóly Arkádyevich (1894–), expert in mechanics, ballistics, and armament. Lieutenant general of artillery. Fellow, Ac. of S., USSR (1943). Graduated from Military Technical Academy (1929) and became professor (1938). President of the Academy of Artillery, USSR (1946–50). Deputy, Supreme Soviet, RSFSR (1947). Director, Institute of Machine Science, (1953). Head of Soviet delegation at the Conference on Rockets and Satellites of the International Geophysical Year (1957). Author of publications on mechanics and armament. Awarded the Stalin prize (1941) for *Principles in Design of Automatic Weapons*. Holder of three Lenin orders and other decorations.

BLAGOVÉSHCHENSK, city, adm. center of Amur Oblast, RSFSR; pop. 95,000 (1959). R.R. station; landing on Amur. Shipbuilding, ship repairs, match factory, food processing.

BLAGOVÉSHCHENSK, town in Bashkir ASSR, port on Belaya River; pop. 12,200 (1956). Machine-building and metalworking plants.

"BLAT": *see* INDUSTRIAL MANAGEMENT AND ORGANIZATION.

BLOK, Aleksándr Aleksándrovich (1880–1921), symbolist poet. His parents were divorced, and the tragic figure of his father is portrayed in the poem "Retaliation" which Blok never completed. He studied philology and graduated from the University of St. Petersburg in 1906. In 1903 he married Lyubov Dmitrievna Mendeleyeva, daughter of the famous scientist. His first collection of poems, *Verses about the Beautiful Lady*, was published in 1903. His adoration of the Divine Wisdom and the medieval worship of the feminine hypostasis of that wisdom, which he bestowed upon his

wife, were soon dispelled. The romanticism of B turned into despair when it met the reality of human suffering in the big city. The lyrical dramas (*The Puppet Show, The Unknown Woman,* and others) and poems (*Snow Mask*) show the collapse of B's mystical symbolism in this period following the Revolution of 1905.

His poems are very musical, sounding like nostalgic gypsy songs in his early period. He introduced new rhythms and contributed to a variety of R. poetical forms. Another cycle of poems which sprang from his deep love of Russia, *The Field of Kulikovo* (1908), depicts the victory of the Russians over the Tatars in 1380. B's undoubted masterpiece is his poem on the October revolution—*The Twelve* (1918). It is full of images of the doomed old order. The twelve Red Guardsmen march along shooting, headed by Christ crowned with white roses—the image into which B cast all his poetical vision of Russia purified through suffering. The poem *The Scythians* (1918)—an outcry charged with gloomy prophecies—was the last of the poet's achievements.

B greeted the revolution of 1917 with joy and hope, which soon waned, leaving him silent and melancholy. He almost ceased to write, and died three years later in 1921. Because B accepted the revolution, the Soviet critics accepted him. However, he remained alien to the Bolsheviks with his culture, mysticism, and tragic forebodings. Similar to the R. poet Vladimir Mayakovsky, B had his own conception of the revolution, whose outcome and reality distressed him.

BLOODY SUNDAY, the name given to the massacre of workers in St. Petersburg which took place on Sunday, Jan. 9, 1905. A wave of strikes in St. Petersburg had in part been directed by the Assembly of R. Workingmen, a group sponsored and financed by the police, and headed by a priest, Father G. Gapon, who apparently was both a police agent and an idealist for the workers' cause. Gapon, having informed the authorities, arranged a march of workers from their various quarters toward the Winter Palace, to present to the tsar respectfully worded petitions listing economic and political grievances and wishes, the most radical of which was a request for a constituent assembly, included over Gapon's protest. The groups of marchers, carrying icons and portraits of the tsar, bore the peaceful aspect of religious processions. Nicholas II was not in St. Petersburg. The authorities became alarmed. The Grand Prince Vladimir (an uncle of the tsar), in charge of the security forces, apparently hoped, through a display of force, to nip a revolution in the bud. He ordered his troops to halt the marchers and, when this proved difficult, to fire into the crowds. The snow ran red with blood. The government later admitted 130 dead and several hundred wounded; although other estimates usually placed the deaths at 500–600 with several thousand wounded. Gapon fled abroad and denounced the tsar as a hangman. The BS had a major part in stirring up the Revolution of 1905, of which it was the first violent episode.

BLUCHER, Vasíly Konstantínovich (1889–1938), marshal of the Soviet Union, born into a peasant's family. Joined the revolutionary movement in 1910; was arrested for leading a strike. In 1914 was mobilized and became a noncommissioned officer. Joined the Bolshevik party in 1916. In the civil war, fought against General Dutov, Admiral Kolchak, and General Wrangel. In 1921–22, was commander-in-chief of the Far East Republic, and in 1924–27 the main military adviser to the Chinese revolutionary government in Canton, known under the name of Gen. Galin. In 1936 B was commander of the Special Far East Army and in the same year was promoted to marshal. Together with Tukhachevsky, Yakir, Uborevich, Eideman and others, B was arrested and disappeared. Posthumously rehabilitated in 1956.

BOBORÝKIN, Pyótr Dmítrievich (1836–1921), novelist. In 1863–65 edited the magazine *Biblioteka dlya chtenia* (Reading Library) and contributed to the liberal magazine *Vestnik Yevropy* (European Messenger). Wrote many novels: *Evening Sacrifice* (1868), *Shady Dealers* (1872–73), *Chinatown* (1882), *Vasily Terkin* (1892), *The Mountain Pass* (1894), and *He Grew Wiser* (1890). Most of his works describe the life of the R. middle class. Is credited with coining the term "intelligentsia" which became current in the sixties.

BOBROV, town in Voronezh Oblast, RSFSR; pop. 6,800 (1956). Food industry, brick factory.

BOBRÚYSK, city in Mogilev Oblast, Byelorussian SSR, landing on the Berezina River; pop. 97,000 (1959). Sawmills, wood-working, machine-building, food and clothing ind. Dates back to 16th century.

BÓCHVAR, Andréy Anatólyevich (1902–), physical metallurgist. Fellow, Ac. of S. (1946). Hero of Socialist Labor. Graduate, School of Technology in Moscow (1923); professor, Institute of Nonferrous Metals and Gold (1934). Introduced an industrial method of casting complex components with crystallization under pressure proving porosity in aluminum alloys. His theory of casting properties of alloys led to the discovery of new alloys. Author of *Principles of Heat Treatment of Alloys* (1940), *Physical Metallurgy* (1956). Stalin prize (1941).

BODÁYBO, town in Irkutsk Oblast, RSFSR, landing on Vitim River; pop. 14,600 (1959). Center of Lena gold mining area. Scene of Lena Goldfields Massacre 1912 (q.v.).

BOGDÁNOV (Malinovsky), **Aleksándr Aleksándrovich** (1873–1928), philosopher, economist, and revolutionary. His *Short Course* (1896) and two-volume *Course* (1910) were standard works on Marxist economics. In Feb. 1904 he joined Lenin and became a leader of the Bolsheviks. In 1905–06 he published *Empiriomonism* which showed the influence of Mach and Avenarius and was criticized by Plekhanov and, later, Lenin. B opposed Bolshevik participation in the Duma elections of 1907. He broke away from Lenin in 1909 when, together with A. Lunacharsky and Maxim Gorky, he organized a party school at Capri (Italy) and edited

Vpered (Forward). The latter became the organ of the *otzovists* (*see* OPPOSITION), opposing Leninist views and tactics. In 1913 B published the first volume of *Tectology* or "universal organizational science" (final edition, 1922). A certified physician, he served as a military surgeon during World War I. Though outside the Bolshevik party, he exercised some influence after 1917 as a theorist of the literary group "Proletkult." From 1923 he devoted his time to the problem of blood transfusion, died following an experiment on himself.

BOGDÁNOV (Olénich), **Borís Ósipovich** (1884–1956), Social Democrat and trade-union leader. During World War I was secretary of the labor section of the Central War Industries Committee. Was arrested on the eve of the February revolution. One of the founders and leaders of the Petrograd Soviet of the Workers' Deputies. A right-wing Menshevik, B was arrested after the October revolution and for many years was confined in concentration camps.

BOGDÁNOV-BELSKY, Nikoláy Petróvich (1868–1945), genre painter, adhered to the R. realistic school of painting. Peasant children were his favored subject. Illustrated Aleksey Tolstoy's *Peter I*; designed stage settings for the operas *Boris Godunov* and *Ruslan and Ludmila*. Lived abroad for some time. Perished during the siege of Leningrad in World War II.

BOGOLÉPOV, Mikhaíl Ivánovich (1879–1945), economist, corresponding member, Ac. of S., USSR (1939), specialist in financial questions. Published about 200 scientific works. Most important are: *State Debt* (1910); *War, Finances and National Economy* (1914); *Soviet Financial System* (1945).

BOGOLYÚBOV, Nikoláy Nikoláyevich (1909–), mathematician. Fellow, Ac. of S., USSR (1953). Professor at Kiev and Moscow universities (1936–50). Extensive research in calculus of variations and approximation methods of mathematical analysis. Advanced the theory of invariant measure in dynamic systems. Developed a sequential microscopic theory of superfluidity and superconductivity. Author of *Statistical Methods in Mathematical Physics* (1945) and *Problems of Dynamic Theory in Static Physics* (1946) for which he was awarded the Stalin prize (1947); *New Methods in Calculus of Variations* (1932); *Asymptotic Methods in the Theory of Nonlinear Oscillations* (1955); *New Methods in the Theory of Superconductivity* (1957); *Introduction to the Theory of Quantum Fields* (1957). Lenin prize (1958).

BOGOMÓLETS, Aleksándr Aleksándrovich (1881–1946), pathophysiologist. Fellow (1929), president (1930–46), Ac. of S., Ukrainian SSR; vice president, Ac. of S., USSR, (1944); fellow, Ac. of S., Byelorussian SSR (1939), Ac. of Med. S., USSR (1944); honorary member, Ac. of S., Georgian SSR (1944). Honored Scientist, RSFSR (1935); Hero of Socialist Labor (1944). Graduate, Novorossiysk University in Odessa (1906); professor, Saratov University (1911–15), Moscow University (1925–31). Director, Institute of Hematology and Blood Transfusion,

Institute of Experimental Biology and Pathology, Institute of Clinical Physiology (the last two are named after B) (1926–46). Research concerned physiology, endocrinology, vegetative neural system, diathesis. Advanced the theory on the decisive influence of reactivity of the human body on the origin of disease. Studied the functions of connective tissues and their part in combating disease. Developed "AtsS," a antireticular-cytotoxic serum widely used during World War II. Author of *Manual of Pathological Physiology* (3 vols., 1935–37), *Extending Longevity* (1938); *Selected Works* (1956).

BOGORÓDITSK, town in Tula Oblast, RSFSR; pop. 21,750 (1957); coal-mining center; zoo-veterinary technical school.

BOGORÓDSK, city in Gorky Oblast, RSFSR; pop. 27,500 (1958). Ancient center of leather ind.

BOGORÓDSK: *see* NOGINSK.

BOGORÓDSKY, Fyódor Semyónovich (1895–1959), painter. Corresponding member, Ac. of Fine Arts, USSR (1947), professor (1938). Best known are his paintings: *Sailors in Ambush* (1927), *Little Brother* (1932). Stalin prize (1946).

BOGOSLÓVSK: *see* KARPINSK.

BOGOSSKY RANGE, N. slope of Greater Caucasus in Dagestan ASSR, elevation exceeds 13,000 ft., covered with large glaciers.

BOGUCHÁRSKY (Yákovlev), **Vasíly Yákovlevich** (1861–1915), liberal politician and historian of the populist movement in Russia. In the 1890's a legal Marxist, he later was a member of the Union of Liberation.

BOKHARA: *see* BUKHARA.

BOKSITOGÓRSK, town in Leningrad Oblast, RSFSR; pop. 19,200 (1956). Bauxite mining, alumina plant; founded 1935.

BÓKY, Borís Ivánovich (1873–1927), mining engineer. Graduate (1895), professor (1908), St. Petersburg Mining Institute. Member, Scientific Technical Council, Main Mining Administration, RSFSR (1921). Research concerned mining ventilation, safety engineering, and analytical methods of mine design.

BOLOGÓYE, city in Kalinin Oblast, RSFSR; pop. 26,500 (1958). Important R.R. junction, half-way between Moscow and Leningrad. Sawmill, brick and tile factories, tie impregnating, meat production.

BOLÓTNIKOV, Iván Isáyevich (died in 1608), leader of the peasant revolt of 1606–07. He was supported for a time by members of the service class (Istoma Pashkov and P. P. Lyapunov), who deserted him later and went over to tsar V. Shuysky. B was captured at Tula after bitter fighting, was exiled to Kargopol and there blinded and drowned.

BÓLOTOV, Andréy Timoféyevich (1738–1833), scientist, writer and a founder of Russian agronomic science. A self-taught student of philosophy, history and natural science, B experimented with methods of improving agricultural practice. His book *The Separation of Fields* (1771) suggested methods of crop rotation. B is also known as a pioneer of hybridization and selectivity, inventor of agricultural machinery and the discoverer of dichogamy. Author of the memoirs *The Life and Adventures of Andrey Bolotov as Written by Him-*

self for his Descendants (1816) which gave a vivid picture of Russian life and society of that period.

BOLSHEVIK: *see* COMMUNIST.

BOLSHEZEMÉLSKAYA TÚNDRA, in N.E. European part of USSR, part of the Nenets National Okrug of Archangel Oblast and Komi ASSR. Extends from Pechora River to the Urals, area 38,600 sq. mi. Reindeer breeding; rich coal deposits in Vorkuta area.

BOLSHÓY FERGANSKY KANÁL, (Great Fergana Canal), important irrigation canal. Goes through Uzbek SSR, Kirghiz SSR, and Tadzhik SSR; length 204 mi., depth 13 ft., feeds from Naryn River, irrigates S. part of Fergana Valley. Improved irrigation of 500,000 hectares of cultivated land. Built 1939.

BONCH-BRUYÉVICH, Vladímir Dimítrievich (1873–1955), Old Bolshevik. Joined the revolutionary movement in the 1880's. From 1896 to 1905, he lived abroad where he was associated with Lenin, specializing in the publication of Bolshevik literature. He contributed to *Iskra* and later to *Pravda*. After the October revolution, became secretary of the Council of People's Commissars. In later years, he was the director of the Museum of History of Religion and Atheism.

BOOK PUBLISHING. The publication, printing, and selling of books, pamphlets, and periodicals in the USSR are state monopolies; therefore they are operated by government agencies. Over-all supervision of these activities is now vested in the Main Administration for Literary Affairs and Publishing at the Council of Ministers of the USSR. There are over 200 publishers in the USSR, many of them specializing in various fields of literature, for instance, *Gospolitizdat* for political literature; the Publishing House of the Academy of Sciences of the USSR, which in 1957 published 524 titles of books and 67 magazines; the Publishing House for Foreign Literature, which publishes translations of both scientific books and belles-lettres. Some ministries, especially the Ministry of Culture, labor unions, and other permitted organizations have their own publishing houses.

The amount of printed material in the USSR increases every year. In 1950 the total of published books and pamphlets amounted to 43,600 titles with 820,-529,000 copies, and in 1959 to 69,100 titles and 1,169,-000,000 copies. Books were printed in 89 languages of Soviet nationalities, and 46 foreign languages. Much of this literature is published in compliance with decisions of the planning agencies and not with the readers' demands: according to Soviet statistics, the large book trading organization *Glavknigotorg* alone had to destroy 100 mill. rubles worth of books and pamphlets in 1956, and almost twice as much in 1957. The average circulation of single books amounted (in thousands) to:

	1950	1956
Political, social, economic literature	29.5	28.4
Science and mathematics	30.5	32.8
Agriculture	9.0	7.5
Contemporary Soviet belles-lettres	31.6	41.9
Pre-Soviet belles-lettres	60.0	78.6
Translations of foreign literature	48.7	91.9

This official table shows a striking increase in the publication of belles-lettres, especially of prerevolutionary and foreign literature, obviously reflecting a great demand for it. In 1956 works of pre-Soviet classics were published in 61 mill. copies, some of them in excellent editions. During 1956 and 9 months of 1957, almost 35 mill. copies of translations of French books were published, mainly by Victor Hugo, Alexandre Dumas, Emile Zola, Anatole France, with Alexandre Dumas far in front. The total number of translations published during that period reached 132.2 mill. copies. The extraordinary demand for these books reflects the readers' attempt to escape from the monotony of Soviet literature and their interest in western writers.

Though freedom of the press is guaranteed by the Soviet Constitution, no publication can appear without approval by a censor. The Main Administration for Literary Affairs and Publishing (*Glavlit*), established at the People's Commissariat for Education by a decree of June 6, 1922, was to carry out "preliminary examination of all works to be published"; the law prescribed that one of the two deputy chiefs of *Glavlit* should be a representative of the security police. A law of 1931 redefining the duties of *Glavlit* stated that the agency had been established "for the carrying out of all kinds of political, ideological, military and economic control of printed matter." On the basis of this law, secret lists of items (*perechen*) which censors were to prevent from appearing were issued and were frequently revised. Among economic items listed were data on crop yields, unless published by *Pravda*, export losses, foreign loans; among political items were data on crime, security police activities, attacks on Soviet officials, election disorders, epidemics. A law of 1932 stated that printing establishments of any kind "may be opened only by government agencies, cooperatives and public organizations," the latter, of course, approved by the government.

To make censorship more strict, it is carried out in two stages: pre-publication censorship guarantees that no undesirable book is published, and post-publication censorship sees to it that the book is published in the approved form and with the censor's corrections. In recent years, a few religious books, among them the Orthodox Bible, but mostly calendars, probably less than ten titles a year, have been permitted for publication by church organizations, while numerous antireligious books and pamphlets are published for mass circulation. Exempt from normal censorship are publications of the central and local party committees.

Supreme ideological supervision of book publishing and censorship are the responsibility of the Literature Sector of the Propaganda and Agitation Department of the Party Central Committee. Each local committee has a corresponding department. The duty of the censors is not confined to suppression of anti-Soviet views; the censors have to guarantee that all published works are in accord with the currently prevailing party trends in a given area.

BIBLIOGRAPHY: A. Inkeles, *Public Opinion in Soviet Russia*, Cambridge, 1950; B. Gorokhoff, *Publishing in the USSR*, Bloomington, 1959; M. Fainsod, "Censorship in the USSR," in *Problems of Communism*, 1956, No. 2. S. W.

BOR, city in Gorky Oblast, RSFSR, on left bank of Volga, opposite the city of Gorky; pop. 36,400 (1956). Glass, silicates, woodworking, felt ind.

BORATÝNSKY: *see* BARATYNSKY.

BORÉTSKY, a boyar family, posádniks (administrators) of Novgorod in 15th century: Isaak B., his widow Márfa Posádnitsa, and their sons, Dmítry and Fyódor were at the head of riots, the aim of which was to gain the independence of Novgorod from Moscow.

BORÍS GODUNÓV: *see* GODUNOV.

BORISLÁV, city in Lvov Oblast, Ukrainian SSR; pop. 32,200 (1957). Industrial and oil center of W. Ukraine; mfg. of oil industry equipment. Seat of Carpathian Geological Research Institute.

BORISOGLÉBSK, city in Voronezh Oblast, RSFSR; pop. 54,000 (1959). Car-repairing plant, meat cannery, flour mills; technical schools. Founded in the middle of 17th century.

BORÍSOV, city in Minsk Oblast, Byelorussian SSR, landing on Berezina River; pop. 59,000 (1959). Sawmills, plywood, furniture, matches, glass, food ind.; pedag. inst. Dates back to 12th century.

BORISYÁK, Alekséy Alekséyevich (1872–1944), geologist and paleontologist. Fellow, Ac. of S., USSR (1929). Graduate (1896) and professor (1911–30) of the Mining Institute in St. Petersburg. As the director of the Institute of Paleontology (1930–44) B organized many major expeditions. He advanced the theory of geosynclines as a key toward the understanding of the tectonic structure of the earth crust and the stages of its development. Stalin prize (1943).

BORODÍN, Aleksándr Porfíryevich (1833–1887), composer and scientist. Born in St. Petersburg, B received a good education including training in the flute and piano. He first specialized in science, majoring in chemistry at the St. Petersburg Medical Academy and becoming professor of chemistry there in 1862. Subsequently B established himself as an important scientist with 40 studies on various aspects of chemistry. A meeting with Balakirev in 1862 led to the revival of his interest in music and he became a member of the group of composers known as the "The Five" (the other members were Musorgsky, Cui, Rimsky-Korsakov, and Balakirev). B's first symphony came in 1867. His second symphony in B minor is particularly well known as is his opera *Prince Igor* which was left unfinished but was completed posthumously by Rimsky-Korsakov and Glazunov. B also wrote two quartets and numerous romances. His work is characterized by a feeling for rhythm, vigor, lyricism. The influence of oriental music is often evident. While B's output was relatively small, his place as a master of 19-th century R. music remains unchallenged.

BORODÍN (Grúsenberg), **Mikhaíl Markovich** (1884–1953), Comintern agent. Born in Vitebsk, spent his youth in Latvia. Here he joined the Jewish Bund but in 1903 transferred his allegiance to the Bolsheviks. After being arrested during the revolution of 1905, he emigrated to the United States where he continued his studies at Valparaiso University. He then taught at the Progressive Preparatory School in Chicago and was active in American socialism. In July 1918, B returned to Russia and quickly became a prominent Bolshevik diplomat. After expulsion from Great Britain, he turned to Asian affairs and became Comintern advisor to the Kuomintang. Chiang Kai-shek's anti-Soviet stand ended this activity and he returned to Russia where he held minor posts until his death in 1953.

BORODINÓ, famous battle during the Franco-Russian War (1812). Both sides suffered great losses. The battle is considered by some historians as the turning point of the war.

BOROTBÍSTY, a Ukrainian party, formed in May 1918 by former Left Socialist Revolutionaries (q.v.). B applied for membership in the Comintern, and upon refusal were suppressed in 1920. Many former B (among them Lyubchenko, Grinko and Shumsky) joined the CP and subsequently played an important role in the Soviet Ukraine. However, most of them were purged in the 1930's.

BOROVICHÍ, city in Novgorod Oblast, RSFSR; pop. 48,000 (1958). Refractories, paper, woodworking, knitting, leather goods; coal mining.

BOROVIKÓVSKY, Vladímir Lukích (1757–1825), one of the first Russian portraitists. Taught by his father, he first worked at religious subjects. When he moved to St. Petersburg from his native Mirgorod, he began painting sentimental portraits, chiefly of women. They had an elegiac and dreamlike quality, for the sitters were usually represented in unrealistic parks. His famous portrait of Catherine II (1795, Russian Museum) shows her in a simple dress in a garden. He became an academician in 1795.

BOROVÓYE, resort in Kokchetav Oblast, Kazakh SSR, in Kokchetav mountains, covered with pine woods; pop. 5,200. Kumyss (mares' milk), climatic station for tuberculosis; salt and mud lakes.

BÓROVSK, city in Perm Oblast, RSFSR, landing on Kama River; pop. 37,000 (1957). Large pulp-paper plant; prefabricated houses; wharf.

BORSHCHÓVOCHNY RANGE, in Chita Oblast, RSFSR; highest point is Sokhondo Peak, 8,140 ft.; zinc, lead, tin, silver, gold.

BORTNYÁNSKY, Dmítry Stepánovich (1751–1825), composer, born in Ukraine. Director of the St. Petersburg court choir. Author of the operas *The Falcon* (1786), *The Son Rival* (1787). He composed religious choir music, piano sonatas, and chamber music. His mass and other church music were popular.

BORZHÓMI, town, spa and climatic station in Georgian SSR at an altitude of 2,624 ft. on Kura River; pop. 15,600 (1956). Carbonated springs, beneficial for intestinal and liver diseases.

BOTANICS: *see* BIOLOGICAL SCIENCES.

BÓTKIN, Sergéy Petróvich (1832–1889), physician. Graduate, Moscow University (1855) and the Medical

and Surgical Ac. in St. Petersburg (1860) of which he became professor (1861). In the early part of his life B was close to the circle of A. I. Herzen and V. G. Belinsky. Participated in the Crimean War under N. I. Pirogov. Founder of the first R. clinical experimental laboratory (1860–61) where he studied the physiological and pharmacological effects of drugs and which was to become the Institute of Experimental Medicine. Introduced the first free medical consultation service (1861) and hospital (1880) in Russia. As personal physician of Alexander II, B took charge of the health conditions of the army during the Russo-Turkish War (1877–78), inspected hospitals, and so forth. Founded the Institute of Sanitation, Institute for Sanitation Training. Chairman of the Commission for the Improvement of Sanitary Conditions and the Reduction of Mortality in Russia (1886). B considered medicine a related branch of natural sciences and gave rise to a new direction referred to by I. P. Pavlov as "nervism." Investigated circulatory and cardiac disorders, typhoid fever. Diagnosed "Botkin's disease."

BÓTKIN, Vasíly Petróvich (1812–1869), literary critic and publicist. Contributed to the leading magazines of the time, *Otechestvennya Zapiski* (Notes of the Fatherland) and *Sovremennik* (Contemporary). Traveled in Europe and described his impressions in *Letters from Spain* (1847); was also known as a music critic and translator. B was one of the rare writers who, at that time, advocated "art for art's sake."

BOTVÍNNIK, Mikhaíl Moiséyevich (1911–), chess player. Grand Master of Chess; world champion from 1948 to 1957 and from 1958. Member of the CPSU since 1940. B is an engineer by profession.

BOYARS' DUMA. A council, presided over by the prince, formed in ancient times by those boyars who occupied the highest state positions. It apparently had no formal constitution and no definite membership, but it included the most influential members of the boyar class. Since the prince had to consult the Duma as a matter of practical necessity, its powers were broad and ill-defined. As a result of the imposition of the obligation of state service on estate owners by the Muscovite autocracy in the 16th century, the boyars' economic independence waned and their freedom to refuse to serve the ruler came to an end. With this loss of independence went a loss of influence. Under Ivan III and Vasily III the BD suffered an eclipse in that its ability to express opinions adverse to those of the rulers was curtailed sharply. The creation of the *zemsky sobor* as another consultative body by Ivan IV further undermined the BD. It remained an ineffectual body appointed by the tsar, giving advice when consulted and performing administrative tasks when permitted, but ceased to function at the end of the 17th century without being formally abolished.

BOYCOTTERS: *see* OPPOSITION.

BRATSK, city in Irkutsk Oblast, RSFSR, landing on Angara River; pop. 51,000 (1959). Gigantic power station; woodworking, concrete. Fortress founded in 1631,

BRÉDY, settlement in Chelyabinsk Oblast, RSFSR; pop. 13,000 (1956); coal mining and production of building materials.

BRENNA, Vincenzo (1745–1820), Italian architect and *plafond* painter of the transitional period from baroque to classicism. Worked in Russia; one of the builders of Engineers' Castle; built a palace in Pavlovsk.

BRÉSHKO–BRESHKÓVSKAYA, Catherine (Yekaterína Konstantínovna) (1844–1934), a well-known or-ganizer and leader of the Populist movement and Socialist Revolutionary party who supported the methods of terror against tsarism. B-B was arrested several times (in 1874, 1907, 1910, 1914) but never ceased to be active in the revolutionary struggle. In the factional differences in the Socialist Revolutionary party she sided with the moderate wing. After the Bolshevik seizure of power she fought against the Bolsheviks. Later B-B went into exile where she continued to be active politically in anti-Soviet organizations and campaigns. B-B was nicknamed the "granny" of the Russian revolution.

BREST (f. Brest-Litovsk), city in Byelorussian SSR, port on right side of W. Bug River; pop. 73,000 (1959). Clothing, footwear, food processing; pedag. inst., railroad technical school. Known since 1017. 1918 peace treaty with Germany.

BREST-LITÓVSK: *see* BREST.

BREST-LITÓVSK TREATY, peace treaty signed on March 3, 1918 between Soviet Russia and the Central Powers (Germany, Austria-Hungary, Bulgaria, and Turkey). One of the first acts of the new Bolshevik government, which had come to power promising "bread, land and peace," was to open negotiations for the cessation of hostilities with Germany (Nov. 20, 1917). The Allies, who were informed and invited, refused to participate and protested against any separate peace talks. On Nov. 22, 1917, a temporary agreement for the cessation of hostilities was concluded and, on Dec. 2, an armistice (which was later extended) was signed for ten days to permit negotiations for a peace treaty. The peace conference began on Dec. 22, 1917, in Brest-Litovsk with the German delegation headed by von Kühlmann and Russia represented by Ioffe and Kamenev (later, Trotsky) as well as by a worker, a sailor, a soldier, and a peasant. Austria-Hungary, Turkey, and Bulgaria were also represented. The Bolsheviks were demanding a "peace without annexations and indemnities." However, their position was weak and was further complicated by sharp differences of opinion within the Soviet government. While Lenin was for accepting the harsh German terms in order to consolidate the victory of the revolution, Trotsky advocated a policy of "no war, no peace," meaning the cessation of hostilities without the signing of a peace treaty. On Feb. 10, 1918, Trotsky interrupted the peace talks and on Feb. 18 the German offensive began. The rout of the R. troops and the danger to the R. capital resulted in a victory of Lenin's policy: The Germans were informed that Russia was ready to sign a dictated peace.

BREST-LITOVSK PEACE TREATY

Russia lost 1,300,000 sq. miles of territory
with a population of 62 mill.

The main provisions of the treaty were the following: Russia had to give up her Polish, Baltic and part of her White Russian provinces, as well as the districts of Kars, Batum, and Ardagan (to Turkey). The independence of the Ukraine (occupied by Germany) and Finland was recognized. There were provisions dealing with demobilization, disarmament and trade. A supplementary treaty stipulated that Russia had to pay 300,000,000 gold rubles as compensation for the losses suffered by Germans. The treaty was set aside by article 15 of the armistice of Nov. 11, 1918, concluded between the Allies and Germany, and was formally abrogated by Article 116 of the Treaty of Versailles. The Soviet government annulled it on November 13, 1918.

BIBLIOGRAPHY: J. W. Wheeler-Bennett, *The Forgotten Peace: Brest-Litovsk, March 1918,* London, 1938.

BREST OBLAST, in Byelorussian SSR; area 12,585 sq. mi.; pop. 1,205,000 (1959). Cities: Brest (adm. center), Kobrin, Pruzhany, Kossovo, Bereza, Vysokoye, Pinsk, Baranovichi. Is a plain irrigated by the W. Bug; climate mildly continental; podzol soil, mixed forests of birch, fir, pine, oak. Agr.: rye, barley, oats, buckwheat, wheat, potatoes, flax, hemp. Ind.: food, dairy, peat. Has a national park and animal reservation, Belovezha Pushcha. Est. 1939.

BRÉZHNEV, Leoníd Ilyích (1906–), chairman of the Presidium of the USSR Supreme Soviet, born in Dne-

prodzerzhinsk, a CP member since 1931. He graduated from Dneprodzerzhinsk Metallurgical Institute in 1935. During World War II he was active in party work in Ukraine; in 1946 he was elected first secretary of the Zaporozhye Oblast Party Committee and in 1947 first secretary of the Dnepropetrovsk Oblast Party Committee; in 1950 he was named first secretary of the Moldavian CP Central Committee; and at the 19th Party Congress, 1952, he was elected a member of Central Committee, CPSU. In 1954 he was elected secretary of the Central Committee of the Kazakhstan CP, and in 1956 was made secretary of the Central Committee, CPSU. He was named candidate member of the Central Committee Presidium in Feb. 1956 and full member in June 1957, but was relieved of these duties in May 1960 to replace Voroshilov as USSR's President.

BRÍTSKE, Érgard Víktorovich (1877–1953), chemist and metallurgist. Fellow, Ac. of S., USSR (1932) and member of the executive board (1939). Graduated from Riga Polytechnic Institute (1903); professor of the institute (1910) and the Institute of National Economy (1919). Cofounder and director of the Institute of Applied Mineralogy and Institute of Fertilizers. Member of the All-Union Academy of Agricultural Sciences (1934). Research on the processing of metallurgical raw materials and minerals. Lenin and Stalin prizes.

BRÓDSKY, Aleksándr Ilyích (1895–), physical chemist. Corresponding member, Ac. of S., USSR (1943); fellow, Ac. of S., Ukrainian SSR (1939). Graduated from Moscow University. Director, Institute of Physical Chemistry (1938). Introduced the study of chemical reactions by isotopes. Author of textbook *Physical Chemistry* (2 vols., 6th ed., 1948). Stalin prize (1946).

BRÓDSKY, Isáak Izráilevich (1883–1939), painter, pupil of Repin. Rector of the Academy of Fine Arts in Leningrad. Specialized in group and individual portraits. His best-known Soviet period paintings are *Lenin at the Putilov Factory* as well as various portraits of Lenin, Stalin, Voroshilov (Tretyakov Gallery, Lenin Museum, Red Army Museum in Moscow; Russian Museum in Leningrad and others).

BRONSHTÉYN, Davíd Iónovich (1924–), Grand Master of chess (1948). Contended for world championship (1951) against M. M. Botvinnik but game ended in a draw.

BRUK, Isáak Semyónovich (1902–), electrical engineer. Corresponding member, Ac. of S., USSR (1939). Graduated from Moscow School of Technology (1925); joined Institute of Power Engineering (1935). Director, Laboratory of Computers and Computing Systems (1956). Designed first Soviet computer for integration of ordinary differential equations (1936) and M-1, M-2, and M-3 digital computers (1950–55). Since 1948 engaged in research on high-speed electronic computers.

BRÚNI, Fyódor Antónovich (1799–1875), son of a court painter, an artist in the classical tradition. In 1818, B was sent abroad. He copied Raphael's frescoes in Rome, and painted his own compositions of which *Death of Camilla, Bacchante with Amor,* and *The*

Agony in the Garden were famous in his day. In 1836, he returned to St. Petersburg and together with Bryullov took part in the decoration of the St. Isaac Cathedral. From 1849 to 1864, he was curator of the Hermitage.

BRUSÍLOV, Alekséy Alekséyevich (1853–1926), general, who distinguished himself as a cavalry officer in the Russo-Turkish war. By 1914, he was commander of the Eighth Army in the Galician offensive against the Austrians. As commander of R. armies in the S., he led the great offensive that began in April 1916. He was appointed supreme commander May 22, 1917, but was replaced July 18. However, he remained in service under the Bolsheviks, commanding the Polish campaign of 1920 and the forces in S. Russia in 1921. He was named inspector of cavalry in 1924.

BRÚSNEV, Mikhaíl Ivánovich (1864–1937), organizer of one of the first Marxist groups in St. Petersburg (1881) and of the first May Day celebration (1891). In 1892, his group was arrested and sent into exile in E. Siberia. Upon his return, he retired from active participation in revolutionary work.

BRUYÉVICH, Nikoláy Grigóryevich (1896–), machine engineer. Lieutenant general of the Engineering Corps. Fellow, Ac. of S., USSR (1942). Graduate of Moscow University (1923) and Moscow Institute of Aviation (1930). Teaches at N. Ye. Zhukovsky Military Air Academy and the Institute of Machine Sciences. Developed methods for the analysis of two- and three-dimensional mechanisms (1930), and a precision theory for mechanisms to determine the rational design and production of machines and precision instruments. Head of air force research during World War II. Author of *Kinetostatics of Three-Dimensional Mechanisms* (1937); *Precision Mechanisms* (1946); *Computers* (1954).

BRYANSK, city in RSFSR; port on Desna River; pop. 207,000 (1959). Important industrial center; machine construction, road-building machinery, sawmills, automobile-repair plants; forestry institute, technical schools. Known since 12th century. In 1956 the city of Bezhitsa was merged with Bryansk.

BRYANSK OBLAST in W. RSFSR, irrigated by the Desna; area 17,300 sq. mi.; pop. 1,550,000 (1959). Cities: Bryansk (adm. center), Klintsy, Novozybkov. Is a rolling agricultural and forest region with podzol soil. Agr.: rye, wheat, buckwheat, hemp, flax, sugar beets. Ind.: machine building, locomotives, road-building machinery, glass, cement, textile and shoe manufacturing; phosphorites, peat, white clay. Several schools of higher education.

BRYULLÓV, Karl Pávlovich (1799–1852), painter. Born in St. Petersburg, died in Italy. From 1809 to  1821, he studied in the Academy of Fine Arts in St. Petersburg; from 1823 to 1834, worked in Italy; was professor in the Academy of Fine Arts in St. Petersburg from 1836; in 1849 went back to Italy. His paintings *Italian Noon* and *Virsavia* already distinguished themselves by their sincerity and richness of color. B's better-known painting is *The Last Day of Pompeii* (1830–33). His unfinished historical canvas, *The Siege of Pskov* (1839–43), as well as his other paintings are in the Tretyakov Gallery in Moscow.

BRYÚSOV, Valéry Yákovlevich (1873–1924), one of the leading symbolist poets. He studied history and philology at the University of Moscow. His lyrics were published in the first volume of the almanac *Russian Symbolists* in 1894. The collections of verses, *Urbi et Orbi* and *Stephanos*, followed in 1903 and 1905. B's great erudition is blended with strong but cold eroticism. As a founder of a review, *Vesy* (Scales) (1904–09), B became the leader of the Moscow symbolists. His novels, *The Fire Angel* (1907), a story of witchcraft in the time of Luther, and *The Republic of the Southern Cross*, are as coldly erotic and ornate as his poetry. After the October revolution, B joined the Bolsheviks and taught the art of poetry to young Soviet poets. His work was not liked by Communists, but he was tolerated as a scholar of considerable merit, as a translator, and as editor of the collected works by Pushkin.

BUBNÓV, Andréy Sergéyevich (1883–1940), a leading Bolshevik, born in Ivanovo. B joined the revolutionary movement in 1900 and became an ardent supporter of Lenin. Arrested several times. He collaborated in *Pravda* and was a member of the Central Committee before the revolution. In 1917 B helped to organize the Revolutionary Military Committee responsible for the October uprising. A member of the first Politburo, he was active in the civil war and participated in the suppression of the Kronstadt revolt of 1921. B was a historian of the Bolshevik party and an editor of *The History of the Civil War in the USSR*. Before his arrest and disappearance during the purges of the 1930's he was people's commissar of education. B was posthumously rehabilitated after the 20th Party Congress

BÚBNOV, Iván Grigóryevich (1872–1919), naval engineer. Graduate, School of Naval Engineering (1891) and Naval Academy (1896); professor, St. Petersburg Polytechnic Institute (1909), Naval Academy (1910). Designer of the first submarine (1902). B's theories on the structural mechanics of submarines became the basis for shipbuilding in Russia.

BUCHAREST, TREATY OF: (1) 1812 between Russia and Turkey which concluded the war of 1806–12. By it Serbia was granted autonomy and Russia obtained Bessarabia and areas in Transcaucasia. **(2)** 1913, which concluded the Second Balkan war. Under it Southern Dobrudja passed from Bulgaria to Rumania and Macedonia was divided between Serbia and Greece.

BUDGET. Nearly half of the national income in the USSR passes through the central B each year, which is prepared by the Ministry of Finance and includes the separate budgets of the member republics and of the provincial, city, and rural government units.

Expenditures. The government's ownership of all industrial enterprises and its direct involvement in the planned development of the economy as well as in the provision of social and cultural services have made the over-all scope of budgetary expenditures in the USSR considerably wider than it is in such countries as the United Kingdom or the United States. The state B is the major source of funds for new capital investment. The national system of socialized medicine is financed entirely through the B. In so far as tuition fees, ticket sales, and the like are insufficient to meet the costs of such social institutions as schools, universities, theaters, museums, newspapers, and book publishing houses, their operations, too, are financed through budgetary grants.

Of 744.8 bill. rubles to be spent at all levels of government in 1960, 34 per cent were directed to the financing of economic development; 33 per cent to financing social and cultural services; 13 per cent to military procurement (exclusive of capital investment in military industries); and 1.5 per cent to meeting the costs of public administration.

The appropriations for the national economy cover a large share of the cost of new investments in productive facilities in the economy (plants, railroads, machinery), and of additions to working capital. Newly established enterprises receive funds from the state to meet the costs of their initial stock of capital equipment; existing plants may receive additional funds when they expand their activities; enterprises that operate at a deficit may receive budgetary grants to make up their losses.

The appropriations for socio-cultural measures include separate appropriations for education (102 bill. rubles in 1960), health (47.5 bill.), and social security and insurance (97.9 bill.). Expenditures on education include not only those for schools of all types, but also the cost of political propaganda, of military academies. scientific research institutes, museums, expositions, all newspaper and book publishing, theaters, and orchestras. The health appropriation includes expenditures not only for medical personnel and hospitals, but also for the maintenance of some kindergartens and children's homes. Social security expenditures are primarily those made to persons invalided during the war and to their families. Social insurance expenditures, on the other hand, provide for persons unable to work because of illness or accident, for funeral expenses, for pensions to permanently incapacitated or retired elderly workers, and for the maintenance of sanatoria, rest homes, and parks.

As in the case of industrial enterprises, the activities of the organizations financed by the socio-cultural appropriations of the B are coordinated with the relevant major obectives of the national plan. The institutions —hospitals, schools, rest homes, and so on—submit to administering authorities estimates of their financial requirements that are calculated on the basis of standardized norms for personnel and for material resources for each type of activity. The administering authorities, in turn, make such changes as they deem desirable in the light of major national objectives before allocating the necessary funds.

The expenditures of the union republics. The distribution of expenditures among the different levels of government is established by the Constitution of the USSR and reflects the different functions that are assigned to them. The All-Union B provides for the financing of military expenditures, some socio-cultural services, and the investment requirements of those enterprises and economic organizations that are subordinated to the All-Union Council of Ministers. The union republics' budgets finance the investment of those enterprises and economic organizations that are subordinated to them (e.g., the regional Economic Councils), as well as social and cultural measures. The share of the republics' budgets in the over-all B of the Soviet Union has been growing steadily since 1950, especially in connection with the decentralization of economic activity. In 1960 it was approximately 50 per cent. Although the union republics' governments may increase or reduce their budgets without consulting the All-Union government, this freedom is limited by the power of the Supreme Soviet to determine which sources of revenue will be assigned to the republics.

BUDGETARY EXPENDITURES IN THE USSR
Combined Expenditures of the All-Union, Union Republics' and Local Governments

Year	Economy	Socio-Cultural	Administr.	Military	Misc.	Total (bill. r.)
	%	%	%	%	%	
1940	33	24	4	33	6	174.3
1950	38	28	3	20	11	413.2
1956	44	29	2	17	8	563.5
1958	45	33	2	15	5	642.3
1960(pl.)	34	33	1.5	13	18.5	744.8

Revenue. The major part of the budgetary revenue has been derived from levies on the operations of enterprises. In 1960 the tax on the turnover of enterprises was scheduled to provide 41 per cent of the planned revenue for that year, and deductions from the profits of enterprises, 20 per cent. In addition, 2.8 per cent was scheduled to come from taxes on the incomes of collective farms and cooperatives, and 7.4 per cent from taxes on personal income.

The tax on the turnover of enterprises is essentially a tax on sales, even though it is collected from the enterprises themselves, rather than from the purchasers of their products. It has been imposed at varying but usually heavy rates upon all significant articles of consumption, and, particularly in earlier years, upon the products of heavy industry as well. It may be imposed as a percentage of the price at retail, as a percentage of the wholesale price, as a specific sum per unit of commodity, or on some other base. Rates of taxation on the same good may vary in cities and in rural areas, as well as in different regions. They are changed from time to time by the Ministry of Finance.

The deductions from the profits of enterprises, whose role as a source of revenue has been increasing in recent years, also vary considerably from industry to industry and from year to year. In levying this tax the needs of each industry for reinvestment are taken into consideration by the government, and a relatively larger share of their profits is usually left to enterprises that are expected to develop rapidly.

The tax on incomes has been levied on persons employed by the state (including both workers and executives); at a higher rate, on persons employed by industrial cooperatives; and at a still higher rate on individual artisans as well as on members of the profes-

sions who receive incomes other than their official salaries. It has also been levied on the personal income of members of collective farms. For each of these groups the rate of taxation has been progressive. A program for the gradual abolishing of taxes on income by 1965 was initiated in 1960.

The minor sources of revenue include local taxes on buildings (both dwellings and plants) and on non-agricultural land as well as customs duties. Since 1938 the payments made by enterprises to social insurance funds have been included in budgetary revenues. Money deposited in savings banks is also counted as state revenue.

Although the sale of government bonds came to an end in 1958, when the repayment of the existing debt was also postponed for twenty years, their sale to banks and other institutions as well as to individuals had provided an appreciable additional source of revenue until that time.

The revenues of union republics. Unlike the assignment of types of expenditures, which is established by the Constitution, the assignment of specific sources of revenue to different levels of government falls within the competence of the Supreme Soviet, and may accordingly be revised through legislation initiated by the Ministry of Finance. In 1960 existing legislation assigned the following sources of revenue to the All-Union government: (a) the turnover tax on all enterprises and other economic organizations, except for a share assigned in advance to the governments of union republics; (b) deductions from the profits of those state enterprises and other economic organizations that are subordinated to the All-Union Council of Ministers; (c) a share (determined by the All-Union Council of Ministers) of the deductions from the profits of enterprises and other economic organizations that are subordinated to the regional Economic Councils; (d) 50 per cent of the tax on incomes; (e) customs duties and other revenue specified by legislation. The sources of revenue assigned to the union republics' governments included: (a) deductions from the profits and other receipts of enterprises and other economic organizations under the republics' jurisdiction, except for the share assigned to the all-Union B; (b) income from lumbering enterprises, and taxes on the incomes of collective farms and co-operative enterprises; (c) taxes on agriculture; (d) 50 per cent of taxes on income; (e) revenues from customs duties, local taxes, and other revenues laid down by legislation; (f) allotments from the turnover tax collected by the All-Union government as fixed annually by the Law on the State Budget.

BUDGETARY REVENUE IN THE USSR
Combined Revenue of the All-Union, Union Republics', and Local Governments

Year	Tax on turnover	Deductions from profits	Tax on personal incomes	Misc.	Loans	Total
	%	%	%	%	%	(bill. r.)
1940	59	12	5	18	6	180.2
1950	56	10	9	18	7	422.8
1956	44	18	9	21	8	585.9
1958	45	20	8	25	2	672.3
1960(pl.)	41	26	7	26	0	772.1

(*See also* CREDIT AND BANKING)

BIBLIOGRAPHY: R. W. Davies, *The Development of the Soviet Budgetary System*, London and New York, 1958; F. D. Holzman, *Soviet Taxation*, Cambridge, 1955.   P. I. M.

BUDYÓNNY, Semyón Mikháylovich (1883–), Bolshevik hero of the civil war, marshal of the Soviet Union; born in Rostov Province, son of a poor peasant. He began military service in 1903 in the Far East; participated in the February revolution; and became a CP member in 1919. He formed a cavalry detachment in Feb. 1918 to fight Whites in the N. Caucasus and by March 1919 he commanded a cavalry division. He played an important role in defeating Denikin and Wrangel. He also participated in the Polish campaign in 1920, and from 1919 to 1924 he commanded the First Cavalry Army. In May 1921 he was named a member of the Revolutionary War Soviet and in 1922 deputy commander of the forces of the N. Caucasus military district. From 1924 to 1937 he was inspector of cavalry of the Soviet Army; in 1932 he finished at the Frunze Military Academy; in 1937 was named commander of forces of the Moscow military district; and in 1940 was first vice-chairman of the People's Commissariat of Defense. At the beginning of World War II he commanded the S.W. front, but was soon replaced. Since 1937 he has been a deputy to the USSR Supreme Soviet. He is also a member of the Presidium of the USSR Supreme Soviet and at the 19th and 20th Party Congresses, he was elected candidate member of the Central Committee.

BUG (Southern), river in S.W. Ukrainian SSR, flows into Black Sea; length 532 mi.; navigable up to Voznesensk.

BUG (Western), river along the USSR-Polish border and right tributary of Vistula in Poland; length 478 mi.; navigable 190 mi.; connected by a canal with the Dnieper.

BUGULMÁ, city in Tatar ASSR; pop. 25,000 (1939), 61,000 (1959). Egg, meat, flour and grain production; poultry farms; new oil region.

BUGURUSLÁN, city in Orenburg Oblast, RSFSR; pop. 39,600 (1957). Important center of oil production. Pedag. inst.

BUILDING MATERIALS INDUSTRY. This industry produces bricks, cement, structural components, pipes, and related items. In 1960, 45.5 mill. tons of cement, 34 bill. bricks, and 147 mill. sq. m. of window glass were produced (in the United States in 1958, 54.8 mill. tons of cement and 6.5 bill. bricks; in the United Kingdom, 11.9 mill. tons of cement and 6.4 bill. bricks).

During the prewar Five Year Plans (1928–40) existing facilities were modernized and expanded and new large plants were constructed. Of the cement produced in 1940, 20 per cent came from plants in the Urals, Siberia, Central Asia, and Kazakhstan.

As a result of further improvements and new construction after the war the amount of cement produced in 1950 was 1.8 times greater than in 1940; of window glass 1.9 times; of bricks 1.3 times; of slate 1.3 times; and of cement pipes 2.8 times. A more intensive program of modernization was carried out during the Fifth Five Year Plan (1950–55), in which the use of assembly-line methods and the production of new types of blocks and of prefabricated structures was emphasized. This resulted in a further doubling of output.

The Seven Year Plan (1959–65) calls for increasing the production of cement to 75–81 mill. tons; of precast reinforced concrete parts to 42–45 mill. cu. m.; of slate to 6 bill. standard pieces; of soft roofing to 1.3 bill. sq. m.; and of window glass to 220 mill. sq. m.

PRODUCTION OF BUILDING MATERIALS IN THE USSR

Year	Cement (mill. tons)	Concrete parts (mill. cu. m.)	Bricks (bill. units)	Slate (mill. units)	Soft roofing (mill. sq.m.)	Window glass (mill. sq.m.)
1913	1.8	—	3.4	30.4	8.8	23.7
1928	1.9	—	2.8	—	19.2	34.2
1932	3.5	—	4.9	59.0	66.0	29.5
1937	5.5	—	8.7	142.1	161.4	79.3
1940	5.7	—	7.5	173.3	127.1	44.7
1945	1.8	—	2.0	—	—	—
1950	10.2	1.3	10.2	222.5	285.5	76.9
1955	22.5	5.3	20.8	472.1	503.7	99.8
1958	33.3	18.9	28.3	662.5	647.5	132.9
1959	38.8	25.8	32.0	—	—	—
1960	45.5	32	34.0			147
1965 (pl.)	75–81	42–45	—	6 bill.	1.3 bill.	220

P. I. M.

BUKHARÁ (BOKHÁRA), city in Uzbek SSR, in the Zeravshan valley; pop. 69,000 (1959). Processing of karakul furs, silk, cotton; light industry, handicrafts: silk knitting, gold embroidering, copper embossing, famous rugs. Pedag. inst., agr. technical school. One of the oldest cities in Central Asia and a center of Islamic culture. It was the capital of the emirate of B, which comprised parts of Uzbekistan, Tadzhikistan and Turkmenistan. Accepted R. suzerainty in 1868. Has wonderful architectural monuments.

BUKHARÁ OBLAST in Uzbek SSR; area 45,350 sq. mi.; pop. 585,000 (1959). Cities: Bukhara (adm. center), Kagan, Gizhduvan. Is a plain situated around lower course of the Zeravshan River and adjoining the Kyzylkum desert; has arid continental climate; gray earth, meadows, and salt plains; fields need irrigation. Its minerals are salt, sulfates, asbestos; agr.: cotton, silk, animal breeding (karakul lambs), vineyards; ind.: metalworking, silk spinning, cotton. Pedag. inst. Est. 1938.

BUKHÁRIN, Nikoláy Ivánovich (1887–1938), Bolshevik leader, economist, and theorist, born in Moscow in a schoolteacher's family. He studied economics in Moscow University but did not graduate. In 1906, he joined the Bolshevik party and for five years worked as propagandist and organizer, being arrested several times.

In 1911, B went to Germany and later to Austria. In the fall of 1912, he joined Lenin in Cracow and was invited by him to collaborate on *Pravda*. In Vienna B studied at the university, wrote polemical articles, worked on his *Political Economy of the Leisure Class,* and assisted Stalin in preparing his study on the national question. After the outbreak of World War I, B was arrested as a "Russian spy" but was soon released and expelled to Switzerland. In 1915, provided with a false passport, B went to Sweden but was there arrested as an undesirable revolutionary and expelled to Norway. In 1916, he went illegally to Denmark and from there to New York, where he edited a R. paper *Novy Mir* (New World) along the lines of Lenin's policy.

After the February revolution in 1917, B returned to Russia via Japan, and was one of the Bolshevik leaders in Moscow. In Dec. 1917, he became editor of *Pravda* but resigned during the Brest-Litovsk treaty negotiations and became one of the leaders of the "left-wing Communists" who opposed the treaty. After the *Putsch* of the left-wing Socialist Revolutionaries in July 1918, B resumed the editorship of *Pravda* and retained this post until 1929. In 1920, he wrote (in collaboration with Preobrazhensky) his most popular work, the *ABC of Communism,* which was followed, in 1921, by the *Theory of Historical Materialism.* After the establishment of the Communist International, in 1919, B became one of its leaders and, in 1926, replaced Zinoviev as the chairman of its executive committee. At that time, B was one of Stalin's principal collaborators in his struggle against Trotsky, Zinoviev, and Kamenev, and editor of the *Large Soviet Encyclopedia* where in a 13-page biography he was described as one of the leading participants of the October revolution, an outstanding theorist of communism, economist, and sociologist. Two years later, B (together with Rykov and Tomsky) was proclaimed a leader of the "rightist deviation" (*see* OPPOSITION, PURGES) in the party and a "falsifier of Marxism," and was removed from all his posts. After the 17th Party Congress, in Feb. 1934, he became editor of the official organ of the Soviet government, *Izvestia,* but in March 1937 was accused of being a "Trotskyite" and expelled from the party. In March 1938, at the last public trial of the great purges (*see* SHOW TRIALS), B, together with 20 other prominent old Bolsheviks, was tried, found guilty of high treason, condemned to death and executed.

BIBLIOGRAPHY: Sidney Heitman, *An Annotated Bibliography of N. I. Bukharin's Published Works,* Fort Collins, 1958; L. Schapiro, *The Communist Party of the Soviet Union,* New York, 1960.

BUKHTARMÁ RIVER, in Kazakh SSR, right tributary of the Irtysh, length about 250 mi.; used for log floating.

BUKOVÍNA, a historical territory. The northern part is now the Chernovtsy Oblast, Ukrainian SSR, formerly a part of Rumania; area 2,316 sq. mi.; pop. over 500,000. Occupied by Ukrainian SSR in 1940. The southern part is a province in N. Rumania; area about 1,500 sq. mi.; pop. 338,895 (1943). B belonged to Kievan Russia (10th–13th centuries), Hungary and Poland (14th–16th centuries), Turkey (16th–18th centuries), Austria-Hungary (1775–1918), Rumania (1920–40). Population is largely Ukrainian. B is an agricultural country (grain crops, potatoes, flax and hemp); also has manganese mining.

BULÁVIN, Kondráty Afanásyevich (c. 1660–1708), Don Cossack, leader of a peasant uprising which began in 1707 in the Don region but spread to the Volga and Azov area. It was ruthlessly suppressed and B shot himself when surrounded by government troops.

BULGÁKOV, Mikhaíl Afanásyevich (1891–1940), novelist and playwright. He graduated from the medical faculty of the University of Kiev in 1916, but forsook a medical career for that of a writer. His first comedies were staged in 1919, but his first real success came with two satirical stories, *Deviltry* (1923) and *The Fatal Eggs* (1924). These stamped B as one of the sharpest

and boldest postrevolutionary satirists. He wrote two comedies, *Zoyka's Apartment* (1920) and *The Crimson Island* (1927). The first is a penetrating satire on contemporary Soviet Union, while the second presents, in very unusual form, a satire on the story of the February and October revolutions. B's most successful novel, *White Guards,* was published in 1925. It is a masterful and objective portrayal of the doom of the White (anti-Bolshevik) movement during the civil war, and was reworked by the author as a play under the title *Days of the Turbins.* The play was staged by the Moscow Art Theater.

BULGÁKOV, Sergéy Nikoláyevich (1871–1944), religious philosopher, born in Livny, province of Orel, in the family of a priest. In his youth B was a legal Marxist. He studied law and political economy and taught at the universities of Kiev and Moscow. In 1901 B became a defender of Orthodoxy. In 1905, he founded with N. Berdyayev the journal *Novy Put* (New Path), and later, the journal *Voprosy Zhizni* (Problems of Life). In 1918 B was ordained a priest, and in 1922 exiled by the Soviet government. He lived in Prague and later in Paris where he taught gomatic theology at the Russian Orthodox Theological Institute. His principal publications are (in Russian): *From Marxism to Idealism* (1904), *Two Cities* (1911), *The Light That Never Wanes* (1927); *The Tragedy of Philosophy* (1927, in German), and *The Philosophy of Language* (1953, in French).

BULGÁNIN, Nikoláy Aleksándrovich (1895–), Soviet leader, son of an office worker, born and educated in Nizhny-Novgorod (now Gorky). He joined the party in 1917 and during the civil war worked in the Cheka (1918–22, in Nizhny-Novgorod, Moscow, and Turkestan), later in the Supreme Council of National Economy (1922–27). In 1927–31, B was  manager of the Moscow electric plant; in 1931–37, chairman of the Moscow City Soviet; in 1937–38, chairman of the Council of People's Commissars of the RSFSR; in 1938–41, chairman of the board of the USSR State Bank and deputy chairman of the USSR Council of People's Commissars. During the war, he was promoted to the rank of general and was a member of the military councils on several fronts, then member of the State Defense Committee and, from 1944, deputy people's commissar for defense. In July 1944, B was sent as a representative to the Soviet-sponsored Lublin Committee of National Liberation in Poland. He was decorated with several orders and medals, and in 1947 was made a marshal.

B has been a member of the party's Central Committee since 1934, and a member of Politburo since 1948. After the war, B was deputy chairman of the Council of Ministers (1947–55), and simultaneously defense minister (1947–49, and again 1953–55). After Stalin's death, B was at first a secondary figure in the new collective leadership, but after Malenkov's downfall in Feb. 1955, he became chairman of the Council of Ministers and for some years was, in the USSR, second only to Khrushchev, with whom he traveled widely. From the middle of 1957 this close cooperation with Khrushchev ended, but B kept his post for one more year. Dismissed in March 1958, he was named chairman of the board of the State Bank but soon was sent to a secondary post of chairman of a provincial council of national economy in Stavropol. At the December Plenum of the Central Committee in 1958, B was officially included in the membership of the "anti-party group." In 1960 he resigned from his post in Stavropol and was allowed to retire as a pensioner in Moscow.

BULGÁRIN, Faddéy Venedíktovich (1789–1859), editor of the reactionary paper *The Northern Bee*. He attempted a polemic with Pushkin who ridiculed him. His novel *Iván Výzhigin* (1829) and others are superficial and mediocre.

BUNAKÓV, I. (Ilyá Isidórovich Fondamínsky) (1879–1942), member of the Socialist Revolutionary party and publicist. Participated in the revolutionary movements of 1905 and 1917. After the October revolution, he lived in Paris where he became one of the editors of the journals *Sovremennye Zapiski* (Contemporary Notes) and *Novy Grad* (New City). Was killed by the Germans during World War II. Before his death, B was converted to Greek (Russian) Orthodoxy.

BUND, a Jewish labor and socialist party in Russia, Poland, and Lithuania, founded illegally in Vilna in 1897. Its founders and leaders were A. Kremer, I. Aizenstadt, and V. Kossovsky. The program drafted by the B asked for the abolition of all discrimination against Jews, the transformation of the multi-national Russian empire into a federation of autonomous nationalities, and national-cultural autonomy for the Jews. In 1903–05, under the impact of the anti-Jewish pogroms (Kishinev, Gomel, and others) the B was active in organizing self-defense groups. In 1903 the B participated in the 2nd Congress of the Russian Social Democratic party, which split into Bolsheviks and Mensheviks. The B left the congress when its request to recognize the B as the sole representative of the Jewish working masses was rejected. Having reentered the Social Democratic party in 1906–07, it was, in later years, under the ideological and political influence of Menshevism. Under the leadership of Mark Liber, R. Abramovich, and V. Medem, the B, with a membership of 30,000, played an important role in the revolutions of 1905 and 1917. In April 1920, at its twelfth conference, the B split. The majority, which adopted a communist program, recommended its members to join the CP. The leaders of the majority, R. Weinstein, E. Frumkin and others, were later liquidated in the Yezhov purges. The minority, under Abramovich, founded a social-democratic B which, however, soon ended its existence owing to the Bolshevik terror. The B became active once again in independent Poland between the two world wars. Its leaders, Henryk Erlich and Wiktor Alter, were shot by the Soviet police when they fled to Russia in 1939 from Hitler-occupied Poland. G. A.

BÚNGE, Nikoláy Khristiánovich (1823–1895). Economist and statesman. He was prof. of economics at Kiev University, 1850–80, and helped with the financing of the emancipation of the serfs. As an economist, he criticized Marx and opposed excessive state intervention. He became minister of finance in 1881 and president of the committee of ministers in 1886. Relatively liberal in outlook, he paved the way for monetary reform, promoted labor legislation, opposed the land tenure laws of 1893–94, and favored some reduction in protective tariffs.

BÚNIN, Iván Alekséyevich (1870–1953), poet, novelist, and short-story writer. His first published works (1887) were poems, of which a collection, *Fallen Leaves*, appeared in 1901. They describe in idealized terms and in accordance with the principles of "art for art's sake" the beauties of nature and the quiet peacefulness of life on the rapidly vanishing country estates of the landed gentry. At the same time they express a mood of sadness for that which is fading away. B's first short stories, which were concerned with the everyday life of hard-pressed but socially insignificant individuals, were published in the early 1890's. Subsequently B associated for a time with a circle of progressive writers centering on M. Gorky, and with the editors of *Znanye*.

The poems of his second period abound in biblical themes. Its prose works, on the other hand, reflect an attitude toward the peasantry that emerged only after the revolution of 1905, when B abandoned his earlier beliefs concerning the possibility of harmonizing the interests of the peasants with those of the landed gentry. His novel, *The Village* (1910–11), which describes the plight of the peasants, is one of thorough gloom unrelieved by any trace of hope concerning the future. A similar mood permeates his other works concerning village life, such as the short stories *Dry Valley* (Sukhodol), *A Nocturnal Conversation*, and *Everyday Things*. While B's masterful use of the written word earned him the praise of critics, it was also suggested at the time that the many merits of his style did not compensate sufficiently for a distinctly prejudiced outlook on what was then regarded as Russia's basic social problem.

An earlier tendency on the part of B's realism to pass into naturalism manifested itself clearly during World War I when he wrote the stories *Brothers* and *The Gentleman from San Francisco* (1915). The latter, which acquired considerable popularity and was considered a masterpiece, contains a convincing, yet clearly formal treatment of the inner emptiness and insignificance of the life of rich persons who "decide upon the destinies of the world while smoking a cigar." Both works reflect strongly, as well, a mood of pessimism and of mystical resignation.

B's attitude toward the Bolshevik Revolution was highly negative from the first. In 1918 he wrote articles for the press of the White army that called for the defeat of communism. After his emigration to France, he continued to write articles and literary works that reflected an irreconcilable hatred for the new regime in Russia. Although B's works of the period of his emigration suffer even more than his earlier ones from a hopeless pessimism, they too possess great literary mer-

its. This is particularly true of the stories *Mitya's Love,
The Case of Cornet Yelagin,* and *Sunstroke.* Other significant works of B are: *Life of Arsenyev* (1927), a
semi-autobiographical novel (*The Well of Days* in English translation), and his *Reminiscences* (*Memoirs and
Portraits* in English) about R. writers, including Gorky,
Chekhov, and others.

　B's works include a masterful translation into Russian
of Longfellow's *The Song of Hiawatha,* as well as of
Byron's *Cain, Manfred,* and *Heaven and Earth.* In 1933,
B was the first R. writer to receive the Nobel Prize
for literature.　　　　　　　　　　　　　　　　C. P. K.

　BURÉYA RANGE, in Khabarovsk Kray, RSFSR;
highest peak 7,150 ft.

　BURÉYA RIVER, in Khabarovsk Kray and Amur
Oblast, RSFSR, a left tributary of the Amur; length
445 mi.; navigable; irrigates in its lower course a
fertile valley.

　BÚRTSEV, Vladímir Lvóvich (1862–1942), historian
of the revolutionary movement. In his youth was a
populist and was arrested. Later became known when
he exposed the *agents provocateurs* in the revolutionary
underground, among them Ye. Azef, the chief of the
terrorist organization of the Socialist Revolutionary
party. From 1900 to 1904 and from 1908 to 1912 B
edited *Byloye* (The Past), a journal devoted to the history of the R. revolutionary movement. In his later
years he evolved to the right. In 1917 B accused Lenin
and other Bolsheviks of being agents of Germany. After
the October revolution, B worked with the White armies. Died in Paris.

　BURYÁT ASSR (f. Buryat-Mongolian ASSR), part
of RSFSR; situated between Lake Baykal and Yablonovy
Ridge, it borders on Mongolian People's Republic. Area
135,600 sq. mi.; pop. 673,000 (1959), 30 per cent urban
(Buryats, Russians, Evenki). Cities: Ulan-Ude (capital),
Babushkin, Kyakhta, Zakamensk. Rivers: Selenga, Barguzin, Upper Angara and Vitim. Mountainous country,
with 70 per cent of its area covered by forests; continental climate. Minerals: lignite, graphite, shales, iron
ore, tungsten, molybdenum, gold, tin, mercury. Huge
hydroelectric reserves. Agr. is mainly animal breeding,
fur farming, sugar beets. Considerable ind.: locomotive
building, boat repairs, sugar refining, textiles, rare metals, coal mines. Several schools of higher education,
museums, theaters. Area annexed by R. in the 17th
century. Est. 1923, renamed in 1958.

　BUS TRANSPORTATION. Apart from urban transportation, where buses and trolley-buses play a large
and impressive role, intercity BT in the USSR is just
beginning to show rapid growth. Regular scheduled
routes now exist between Moscow and Leningrad, between Moscow and the Crimea via Kharkov, and
among many provincial centers. Intercity bus lines
grew from 1,942 in 1950 to 6,115 in 1959, with an
overall length of 83,000 mi. (1950), 384,000 mi.
(1959); the amount of passengers grew from 51.9 mill.
(1950) to 574.2 mill. (1959).

　BÚTLEROV, Aleksándr Mikháylovich (1828–1886),
chemist. Fellow, St. Petersburg Ac. of S. (1874). Graduate (1849), professor (1857), Kazan University. Head,
Dept. of Organic Chemistry, St. Petersburg Univer-

sity (1869–86). Carried out extensive
research in theoretical and experimental
chemistry. Discovered formaldehyde
polymer. Advanced the theory of the
structure of organic compounds which
is the base of modern organic chemistry. Also made a name for himself in
the field of apiculture. D. I. Mendeleyev referred to B as "one of the
most outstanding Russian scientists." Author of a *Complete Study of Organic Chemistry* (1866; translated into
German, 1867), *Fundamentals of Chemistry* (1886),
Bees, Their Life and Principles of Efficient Apiculture
(1871; 10th ed., 1905), *How to Keep Bees* (1885; 12th
ed., 1929).

　BUTURLÍN, Count Aleksándr Borísovich (1694–
1767), general, field marshal. Began his career under
Peter I but rose to power under the reign of Elizabeth
Petrovna. In 1760–61 he was commander in chief of
Russian Army in the war with Prussia (Seven Years'
War).

　BUYÁLSKY, Ilyá Vasílyevich (1789–1866), surgeon.
Graduate (1814), professor (1821–44), Medical and
Surgical Academy in St. Petersburg. Pioneer in the application of anesthesia; introduced new surgical techniques. His charts *Anatomical and Surgical Tables Explaining the Ligation of the Large Arteries* (1828) and
Anatomical and Surgical Tables of the Excision of Urinary Calculi and Lithotomy (1852) were translated
into many languages. Founder of "sculptural" and "ice"
anatomy, i.e. the application of cold in the treatment
of anatomic material.

　BUYNÁKSK (f. Temir-Khan-Shura), city in Dagestan ASSR; pop. 29,600 (1956). Important canning ind.;
technical schools.

　BUZULÚK, city in Orenburg Oblast, RSFSR; pop.
55,000 (1959). Has machine-building, distillery, flour
mills, sewing and knitting ind.; technical schools.
Founded 1736.

　BYELORUSSIAN SOVIET SOCIALIST REPUBLIC was officially established Jan. 1, 1919. Located in
the W. section of the European part of the USSR, it
borders on Poland and is divided into 6 oblasts (Brest,
Gomel, Grodno, Minsk, Mogilev, Vitebsk). Capital—
Minsk. Area, 80,100 sq. mi.

　The population of B is 8,055,000 (1959 census).
Of this total, Byelorussians account for 80 per cent
(6,440,000); Russians, 9.1 per cent (729,000); Poles,
6.7 per cent (539,000); Ukrainians, 1.9 per cent
(150,000); Jews, 1.9 per cent (150,000) and others,
0.4 per cent (32,000). Before
the war Jews constituted 8.2 per
cent of the pop. (1933 census)
but were annihilated during the
German occupation. The average pop. density is 100 per sq.
mi. The central area is the most
densely populated, Polesye the
most sparsely. The populations

of important cities are: Minsk, 509,000; Gomel, 168,-
000; Vitebsk, 148,000; Mogilev, 121,000; Bobruysk,
97,000; Brest, 73,000; Grodno, 72,000.

Nature and Climate. B is a plain with numerous lakes, swamps, and marshes. The B ridge, a low hill country lying roughly between Vilna (Vilnius) and Smolensk, is divided into several uplands. The highest point (1,168 ft. above sea level) is located in the Minsk heights. The S. section of B is a low, flat marshland—Polesye. The climate is temperate (average temperature in Jan. is 23°F; in July, 66.5°F.) and quite humid (average yearly precipitation 22 to 26 in.). The vegetative period lasts from 175 (N.E.) to 205 (S.W.) days. Turf-podsolic soil forms 60 per cent of the land, marshes, 25 per cent. Forests cover 30 per cent of the territory.

National Economy. B has an important timber and chemical industry; also machine building, metalworking, power, and food. B has important peat reserves (close to 5 bill tons). and among minerals, dolomites and dolomitized limestones, quartz gravel, chalk, refractory clay, some rock and potassium salt, phosphorite, and marl. There are also modest amounts of oil and coal. Machine building and metalworking account for one fourth of the total industrial output and are concentrated on the production of tractors, trucks, machine tools, and agricultural machinery. B also produces radios, televisions, watches, sewing machines; peat extracting, road building and meliorative equipment; bearings, bicycles, motorcycles, moving cranes, and metalcutting instruments. During the postwar period a shipbuilding and ship-repair industry developed in river harbors.

The most important agricultural products are potatoes and flax. Animal husbandry concentrates on hog and beef farming. One-third of the land is arable.

B has 67.6 mi. of R.R. per 1,000 sq. mi.; 2,175 mi. of navigable rivers and only 8,400 mi. of highways.

History. The first E. Slavic tribes appeared in B probably in the 7th century and by the 9th century had settled over the area, pushing the Lithuanians toward the Baltic Sea. From the 9th to the 11th century, when local principalities were loosely connected parts of the old Kievan state, the first cities were built and river trade and crafts developed. During the invasion of Kievan Russia by the Mongols (13th to 14th century), B was peacefully absorbed by Lithuania and Byelorussian became the official language of the B-Lithuanian state. When the Grand Duchy of Lithuania was united with Poland in the 16th century, B lost its relative importance in the new union and Polish replaced B as the official language of the area. The strengthening of serfdom and the concentration of B land in the hands of the Polish-Lithuanian nobility took place in the 15th and 16th centuries. However, R. serfs escaping from the Muscovite state still found more freedom in B than in their own country. Polish efforts to force

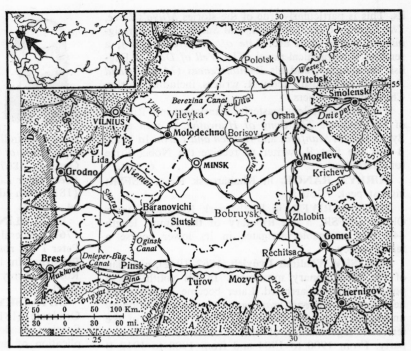

Byelorussian SSR

Catholicism on the Greek Orthodox B pop. awakened national consciousness and hastened the formation of the B nationality. During the 17th century, the condition of B serfs grew worse and several peasant revolts, aggravated by the religious issue, took place. As a result of three consecutive partitions of Poland, B became part of the R. Empire by the end of the 18th century.

The 19th century saw the development of cities, industry, trade, and agriculture. Nevertheless, dissatisfaction continued among the serfs, especially toward the middle of the century. The Polish insurrection of 1830–31 found no support among B peasants, but the 1863 revolt was echoed in B by an uprising led by K. Kalinowski. The 80's and 90's were years of strong economic development; timber, tobacco, vodka, and the match industry prospered and R.R. construction increased. At the beginning of the 20th century there were several factories with over 1,000 workers each, but independent craftsmen still predominated in industry. By 1913 the number of industrial workers reached 40,000 and the volume of industrial production doubled as compared to 1903. In agriculture, 38.5 per cent of the tillable land was in the hands of big landowners and only 23.8 per cent was owned by poor and average peasants, with 62 per cent of the peasant families owning one or no horse.

In 1915 part of B was occupied by the German army. The B Rada, which was established after the February revolution of 1917, was overthrown by a Bolshevik Military Revolutionary Committee. A few weeks later the Germans, according to the Brest-Litovsk Treaty, occupied B and established a "Rada" of their own. After the disintegration of the German armies, the Soviets took over again and proclaimed the establishment of the BSSR. During 1919 a federation was contemplated of the B and the Lithuanian Soviet republics, but in April 1919 the Polish advance put an end to the Soviet regime in Lithuania. The Poles also occupied a large part of B, including Minsk. During the Polish retreat B fell again into Soviet hands, but the Polish-Soviet armistice of 1920 and the Riga treaty of 1921 gave the W. part of B to Poland. The Soviet policy in B was relatively liberal in the 1920's. Purges of the intelligentsia began in 1930 and developed into a general purge in 1936–38, during which all actual and potential opposition to Stalin's dictatorship was liquidated. In 1939, according to the Molotov-Ribbentrop agreement defining the partition of Poland, the Soviets received W. Byelorussia. Between 1941 and 1944 B was under Nazi occupation. After its liberation the Curzon Line became the frontier between B and Poland.

Culture. The beginnings of B written language can be traced to the 13th-15th centuries, but B literature appeared only in the 16th century with Ivan Melesko and with the first translation of the Holy Scriptures into B by G. Skorina. The famous Simeon from Polotsk came from B to Moscow in the 17th century. In the 19th, B literature is represented by V. Dunin-Martsinkevich and F. Bogushevich, and later by Maksim Bogdanovich and the writers of the "Our Sky" circle. The best-known modern B writers were Yakub Kolas and Yanka Kupala.

For centuries B has been known for its crafts: wood carving, ceramics, embroidery, and painting of icons. Earliest architectural monuments date from the 11th century (St. Sophia Cathedral in Polotsk), many others date from the 12th. B songs are humorous and lyrical. National instruments are cymbals, the pipe and the violin. Professional music began only in the 20th century. The B State Theater in Minsk was established in 1933, the State Philharmonic Orchestra in 1937, the Conservatoire in 1932. The B theatre originated at rural country fairs. By the end of the 18th century there were a few theaters with serfs as artists and in the 19th century amateur theaters appeared. The first professional theater was established by V. Dunin-Martsinkevich in 1905. Theaters are now found in all the oblast centers, and also in Mozyr, Baranovichi, and Bobruysk. The first moving picture studio was opened in Minsk in 1939, although several B films were produced in Leningrad between 1925 and 1939. The Academy of Sciences of the BSSR was established in 1929.

M. R.

C

CADETS, Corps of, a military school in St. Petersburg designed to prepare children of commissioned officers for military careers or for admittance to higher military schools. Founded in 1732, it was abolished in 1918.

CALENDAR. Until Feb. 14, 1918, Russia adhered to the Julian, or Old Style, calendar, although other European countries, including Poland, had long since adopted the Gregorian, or New Style, calendar introduced by Pope Gregory XIII in 1582. The Julian itself superseded the old Muscovite calendar in 1699. It was ten days behind the Gregorian during the 17th century, eleven days during the 18th, and twelve days during the 19th; and by March 1, 1900, the difference had increased to thirteen. Thus the Soviet decree (Jan. 26, 1918), adopting the Gregorian calendar, fixed Feb. 1, 1918, Old Style, as Feb. 14; and the anniversary of the Revolution (Oct. 25, O.S.) now became Nov. 7, though that event continued to be known as the "October Revolution."

CAMEL BREEDING. Many two-humped camels are bred, in Kazakhstan, Turkmenia, and Kirgizia. Besides being used in transport and in field work, they provide valuable wool, meat, and milk. Prior to World War I, Russia accounted for 32% of the world's total number of camels. Between 1913 and 1928 herds rose from 1.6 to 1.8 mill. Forcible collectivization during the early 1930's was accompanied by mass destruction of camels, the number of which declined to 277,000 by 1935, a major blow to the nomadic population which largely depended on camels for a living. No more recent statistics are available.

CANALS. Russia caught the canal fever from W. Europe in the 18th and 19th centuries. As the elevations within the Eur. part of the USSR are rather low, the sources of rivers flowing in opposite directions are in many instances very close to each other. Several C were built to connect the headwaters of rivers in central European Russia, especially the Mariinsky system joining the Volga via several connections to the Neva. This tradition continued under Stalin who built the notorious White Sea–Baltic Canal in the 1930's, and the Moscow Canal connecting Moscow with the Upper Volga, and also completed the Volga-Don Canal, west of Stalingrad, in 1952. Moscow is called a "port on five seas." At present an extensive system of canals connects the rivers draining into the Arctic Ocean and into the Baltic, Black and Caspian seas. The Dnieper basin is connected with the rivers belonging to the Baltic basin. Of greatest importance is the Dnieper-Bug Canal joining the Dnieper and the Vistula. The Volga-Don Canal is very important for navigation. Nevertheless, freight traffic on Soviet internal waterways increased only threefold from 1913 to 1958, while rail traffic grew seventeenfold. At present, the ancient network of irrigation C in Soviet Central Asia is being reconstituted at certain points, and there is talk of a C to draw the headwaters of the Pechora (in the N. European Russia) south into the Kama, so as to bring additional water via the Volga to check the falling level of the Caspian Sea.

CANNING INDUSTRY. The canning industry in the USSR is regarded as a branch of the food industry. It produced 4,800 mill. (standard) cans in 1960.

Canned foods were first produced in the 1860's. Several canning factories were established in Simferopol (Crimea) in 1877. By 1913 the annual rate was 95.1 mill. cans, of which 71% contained meat products.

During the 1930's nearly all existing plants were re-equipped and several hundred new plants were established in all parts of the country. By 1940 the canning of food had increased tenfold by comparison with 1913, while the canning of fruits and vegetables increased 28 times. For the first time dairy products were canned. The types of foods canned in large quantities included fruit juices, vegetables and fruits, condensed milk, cream, and cocoa and tea as well as meat and fish products.

The very considerable effects of wartime destruction were overcome by 1950. The construction of 200 additional plants is contemplated during the period 1959–1965.

FOODS CANNED IN THE USSR
(mill. of standard cans)

Year	Cans
1913	95
1928	125
1940	1113
1945	558
1956	3602
1958	4100
1959	4322
1960	4800

CAPITAL. Moscow became the "capital" of Russia following the decline of Kiev in the 12th century and of the Mongol power, centered at Sarai, in the late 14th and 15th. It remained the seat of the government until Peter the Great moved the capital to St. Petersburg in 1712. This new capital city, situated on the Gulf of Finland, was for Peter the symbol of a new western-oriented Russia as opposed to the Asiatic backwardness he associated with Moscow. In 1914, the name St. Petersburg was Russified to Petrograd. On March 12, 1918, for reasons of military security, the Soviets retransferred the government to Moscow which later was formally named C of the USSR. In Nov. 1941, the German advance forced the evacuation of government departments to Kuybyshev on the Volga, though Stalin remained in the Kremlin. This emergency arrangement ended late in 1942.

CAPITAL PUNISHMENT: *see* CRIMINAL LAW.

CAPITATION TAX: *see* POLL TAX.

CARDÍS, PEACE OF, concluded at Valiesar 1658, confirmed in Cardis 1661, to put an end to the Russo-Swedish War of 1656. The simultaneous involvement in war with Poland for the possession of the Ukraine and White Russia compelled Russia to accept unfavorable conditions resulting in a return of all her acquisitions in Livonia to Sweden.

CASPIAN SEA (ancient *Caspium Mare* or *Hyrcanum Mare*), salt lake between Europe and Asia, largest inland body of water in the world; borders on RSFSR, Azerbaijan, Kazakhstan and Iran. Area 152,000 sq. mi.; about 92 ft. below sea level; greatest depth is in the S. (3,200 ft.); N. is shallow (max. 33 ft.) with a great number of islands. Large amounts of hydrogen sulfide inhibit life at 1,300 ft. depth. Salt content varies betw.

0.3 per cent (N.) and 14 per cent (S.E.). Fed by Volga, Ural, Kura, Terek, Kuma, and other rivers. Has no outlet; loses more by evaporation than it receives from the streams. Major gulfs are Kara-Bogaz-Gol and Krasnovodsk Gulf. Is important in Soviet economy because of fishing ind. (sturgeon, beluga, pike, perch, and other fish); as a source of oil and a convenient waterway. Major ports: Astrakhan, Baku, Makhachkala, Krasnovodsk, and Pehlevi (in Iran). In recent years the water level has receded (by 8 ft. from 1929 to 1956) complicating water transportation and fishing. A special plan is being developed to control the sea level. In the Middle Ages the CS was important as a part of the Mongol-Baltic trade route.

CATHERINE I (Yekaterína Alekséyevna) (1684–1727), empress of Russia (1725–27), second wife of Peter I. During her reign the Supreme Privy Council was established in 1726. She was a commoner of Lithuanian origin.

CATHERINE II, THE GREAT (Yekaterína Alekséyevna) (1729–1796), empress from 1762. Born Princess of Anhalt-Zerbst, C married Peter (later Tsar Peter III), son of Tsarevna Anne and Charles Frederick, Duke of Holstein, in 1745; seventeen years later, with the help of the guards regiment, she mounted the throne. Imbued with the ideas of the enlightenment, C instituted many reforms. A degree of decentralization was introduced in local government (1775), and the police system was reformed (1782). She revised the administrative framework of Russia's division into provinces and laid down the principle of unitary ministerial power by abolishing several administrative "colleges" and by concentrating executive authority in the hands of the procurator-general of the Senate. The constitutional position of the nobility and the urban population was revised in 1785; the former was organized into legally constituted corporations at the apex of the social hierarchy, while the foundations were laid for the creation of a guild system and municipal self-government. But C's liberal  views were out of harmony with Russian life, and her social reforms were not consummated by any improvement in the position of the peasantry. The Legislative Commission of 1767–74, for which C wrote a well-known *Instruction* (*Nakaz*), accomplished nothing; the institution of serfdom was strengthened, C herself contributing to the increase in the number of serfs by lavish distributions to her favorites of land formerly populated by state peasants (q.v.). Widespread popular discontent culminated in the peasant war of 1773 led by Yemelyan Pugachov.

In foreign policy C added substantially to the national territory at the expense of Turkey and Poland. The treaty of Kuchuk-Kainarzh, which ended the 1768–74 war with Turkey, gave Russia the southern steppe (to the Bug River) and many other gains; the rivalries of the following decade confirmed Russian possession of the Crimea, as well as Taman and Kuban, after the second Russo-Turkish war (1787–91), and recognized the Dniester River as the Russo-Turkish frontier. New cities sprang up in S. Russia and there was a massive movement of settlers to the newly acquired provinces. C was active in Polish affairs: she was instrumental in the three partitions of Poland (1773, 1793, 1795), which finally extinguished Poland leaving Russia holding Lithuania and Kurland.

C has a great reputation for brilliance, partly owing to the zeal with which she cultivated leaders of European thought (Voltaire, Diderot, Grimm, D'Alembert), and her voluminous correspondence with numerous key personalities. C made favoritism a quasi-official institution: she had ten official favorites in her 34 years' reign, all treated munificently. Three of them—Orlov, Potemkin, Zubov—had a major influence in domestic and foreign affairs.

Not only was serfdom legally and institutionally consolidated under C, but her many grandiose political projects—conquest of India, expulsion of the Turks from Europe—never approached realization. Her reign, marked by the wholesale adoption by the gentry of French language and theories, helped widen the gulf between the upper class and the bulk of the people. Though C never entirely abandoned her "republican" outlook, her horror at both the American and the French revolutions brought about a reaction against the somewhat rhetorical liberalism of the first half of her reign. Her ruthless persecution of A. Radishchev (q.v.) and N. Novikov (q.v.) gives the measure of her devotion to the cause of the enlightenment. C was the author of memoirs, comedies, comic operas, and fairy tales.

CATTLE BREEDING. The January count of cattle was, in mill.:

	1916*	1928	1934	1941	1946	1953	1960
Cattle	58.4	60.1	33.5	54.5	47.6	56.6	74.2
(incl. cows)	28.8	29.3	19.0	27.8	22.9	24.3	33.9

* Present boundaries.

The damages of collectivization (when the number of cows declined by 45% between 1928 and 1935 as the result of mass slaughter) were not repaired until 1957. Despite continuous efforts to expand state- and collective-owned herds, in 1959 only 9.8% of all cows were owned by state farms, 34.6% by collective farms, while 55.6% were privately owned (38.2% by collective farmers on their household plots, and 17.4% by workers and employees). Nevertheless, collective farms accounted for as much as 62% of milk marketings, state farms for 22%, and individuals for only 16%.

A drive to considerably expand cattle herds was launched by Premier Khrushchev in 1957, in connection with his announced policy to overtake the United States in per capita production of meat and dairy products. It is doubtful, however, whether the fodder base will expand at the required rate. The United States had 67.4 mill. head (or by 15% more than the Russians) in 1916, and 96.9 mill. (or by 37% more) in 1959.

Gross output of milk and milk products, in mill. tons, was officially reported as follows:

1913*	1928	1940	1959
29.4	31.0	33.6	61.7

(U.S. 1958 output of cow milk: 56.8 mill. tons).

* Present boundaries.

Annual milk yield per cow was reported as 1,017 kg. in 1940, 1,016 in 1954, and 2,004 in 1959 (collective farms only). The sensational rise in milk output and yields during the late 1950's may, however, possibly be due in part to changes in statistical coverage.

CAUCASIAN MINERAL RESORTS (R. *Kavkazskie mineralnye vody*), a group of health resorts comprising Kislovodsk, Yessentuki, Pyatigorsk, Zheleznovodsk, on N. slopes of the Caucasus Mountains; famous for sanatoria, convalescent homes, clinics, and hospitals.

CAUCASUS (CAUCASIA), mountain system between Europe and Asia, extending 745 mi. from Black Sea S.E. to Caspian Sea. The main range, the Greater Caucasus divides the area into Ciscaucasia (N. Caucasus), and Transcaucasia (Zakavkazye). Majestic scenery of wild grandeur with snow-capped peaks Elbrus (18,476 ft.), Shkhara (17,059 ft.) and Kazbek (16,554 ft.). Mamison, Daryal passes. Rivers: Kura, Sulak, Terek, Kuma (Caspian Sea); Rioni, Inguri, Kodori, Bzyb (Black Sea); Kuban (Sea of Azov). Climate: continental in Ciscaucasia, changing at altitudes, subtropical in Transcaucasia, arid in E. Forested mt. slopes, alpine meadows. Subtropical flora, steppes in Transcaucasian valleys. Rich mineral resources include oil, manganese, nonferrous metals, coal, etc. Foothills and lowlands are densely populated by a mottled mosaic of nationalities and tribes of a complex ethnical structure due to centuries of invasions and migrations. Numerous resorts along the Black Sea coast. Ciscaucasia and N. mt. range belong to the RSFSR; Transcaucasia is divided into the Azerbaijan, Georgian and Armenian SSR's. Caucasus was known to the ancient Greeks: here Prometheus was chained, Jason sought Golden Fleece. It was the area of obstinate resistance by the Moslem population to R. colonization (Shamyl wars).

CENSORSHIP: *see* BOOK PUBLISHING, PRESS.

THE CENTRAL COMMITTEE of the Communist party, elected by the Party Congress, is in theory the executive arm of the party instructed by the party rules to direct the whole work of the party between intervals of the Party Congress. Under Lenin the CC was an important decision-making body which it ceased to be under Stalin who sharply increased its membership, purged and coopted members at will and who in later years failed to schedule meetings regularly. The real power was concentrated in the Secretariat (q.v.) and Presidium (q.v.) of the CC. Under Khrushchev the CC has regained some prestige but in the main has remained a ratifying body for important party policies which are promulgated in its name. At the end of 1960 the CC was composed of 133 full and 122 alternate members; its meetings are held at least once every six months as stipulated by the party rules.

MEMBERS OF THE CENTRAL COMMITTEE (as of May 1, 1961): Pavel N. Alferov, Andrey A. Andreyev, Averky B. Aristov, Nikolay E. Avkhimovich, Nikolay K. Baybakov, Nikolay I. Belyayev, Ivan A. Benediktov, Boris P. Beshchev, Nikolay I. Bobrovnikov, Ivan P. Boytsov, Dmitry D. Brezhnev, Leonid I. Brezhnev, Nikolay A. Bulganin, Vasily Ye. Chernyshev, Abdurakhman D. Daniyalov, Pyotr V. Dementyev, Georgy A. Denisov, Boris I. Deryugin, Pavel I. Doronin, Nikolay P. Dudorov, Givi D. Dzhavakhishvili, Yekaterina A. Furtseva, Bobodzhan G. Gafurov, Anton I. Gayevoy, Fyodor S. Goryachev, Ivan T. Grishin, Viktor V. Grishin, Andrey A. Gromyko, Semyon D. Ignatyev, Nikolay F. Ignatov, Nikolay G. Ignatov, Ivan G. Kabanov, Ivan G. Käbin, Nikifor T. Kalchenko, Janis E. Kalnberzins, Ivan V. Kapitonov, Mikhail V. Khrunichev, Nikita S. Khrushchev, Aleksey I. Khvorostukhin, Aleksey I. Kirichenko, Andrey P. Kirilenko, Nikolay V. Kisilev, Vasily K. Klimenko, Boris N. Kobelev, Yevgeny P. Kolushchinsky, Ivan S. Konev, Aleksandr E. Korneychuk, Demyan S. Korotchenko, Aleksey N. Kosygin, Maria D. Kovrigina, Frol R. Kozlov, Vladimir Kucherenko, Dinmukhamed A. Kunayev, Otto V. Kuusinen, Vasily V. Kuznetsov, Nikolay V. Laptev, Ivan S. Latunov, Ivan K. Lebedev, Leonid I. Lubennikov, Rodion Ya. Malinovsky, Ivan T. Marchenko, Vasily S. Markov, Vladimir V. Matskevich, Kirill T. Mazurov, Nikolay A. Mikhaylov, Anastas I. Mikoyan, Mark B. Mitin, Kirill S. Moskalenko, Vasily A. Moskvin, Nuritdin A. Mukhitdinov, Zinnyat I. Muratov, Imam D. Mustafayev, Vasily P. Mzhavanadze, Yadgar S. Nasriddinova, Nikolay N. Organov, Nikolay S. Patolichev, Nikolay M. Pegov, Mikhail G. Pervukhin, Konstantin D. Petukhov, Nikolay V. Podgorny, Dmitry S. Polyansky, Panteleymon K. Ponomarenko, Boris N. Ponomarev, Pyotr N. Pospelov, Vasily A. Prokofev, Aleksandr M. Puzanov, Konstantin G. Pysin, Sadykh G. Ragimov, Iskhak R. Razzakov, Aleksey M. Rumyantsev, Maksim Z. Saburov, Zinovy T. Serdyuk, Ivan A. Serov, Aleksandr N. Shelepin, Aleksey M. Shkolnikov, Terenty F. Shtykov, Nikolay M. Shvernik, Antanas J. Snieckus, Vasily D. Sokolovsky, Mikhail M. Stakhursky, Aleksey I. Struyev, Mikhail A. Suslov, Viktor M. Suslov, Sergey M. Tikhomirov, Fyodor E. Titov, Vitaly N. Titov, Suren A. Tovmasyan, Dmitry F. Ustinov, Boris L. Vannikov, Aleksandr M. Vasilevsky, Aleksandr P. Volkov, Gennady I. Voronov, Kliment E. Voroshilov, Ivan E. Yakovlev, Mikhail A. Yasnov, Leonid N. Yefremov, Mikhail T. Yefremov, Georgy V. Yenyutin, Pavel F. Yudin, Aleksandr N. Zademidko, Ivan K. Zhegalin, Arseny G. Zverev.

CHAADÁYEV, Pyótr Yákovlevich (ca. 1794–1856), officer in the guards, philosopher, and essayist. In his youth, he was close to the Decembrists and a friend of Pushkin. In the 1820's he came under the influence of the Catholic Church. In 1936, CH published in the *Teleskop* (The Telescope) the "Philosophical Letter" which was ruthlessly critical of R. history and questioned the very right of the R. people to a future. The letter was a bitter attack on serfdom and the government retaliated by having CH declared insane. Nadezhdin, the editor of *Teleskop,* was exiled and the journal was suppressed. In a later work, *Apology of a Madman,* CH modified his thesis and suggested that Russia, having emerged late on the scene of history, would not commit the errors of W. Europe. CH had turned mystic. He lived quietly in Moscow where, in spite of his official disgrace, he was popular in aristocratic circles.

CHALIAPIN: *see* SHALYAPIN.

CHANÝ LAKE, in Baraba Steppe (W. Siberian lowland); area 825 sq. mi.; 33 ft. deep.

CHAPÁYEV, Vasíly Ivánovich (1887–1919), civil  war commander. At the head of a Bolshevik division, he fought the Czechoslovak Legion and the Kolchak forces. Was killed in action. In the early 1920's, a book was published on CH, written by his political commissar, the writer, D. Furmanov. The famous motion picture *Chapayev* produced in 1934 by the brothers Vasilyev, is based on Furmanov's novel.

CHAPÁYEVSK (f. Ivashchenkovo, later Trotsk), in Kuybyshev Oblast, RSFSR; pop. 83,000 (1959). Agr. center and mfg. town; chemicals, explosives, clothing, food processing.

CHAPLÝGIN, Sergéy Alekséyevich (1869–1942), mechanical engineer, physicist, and mathematician. Fellow, Ac. of S., USSR (1929). Hero of  Socialist Labor (1941). Graduate of Moscow University (1890). Professor of mechanical engineering, Moscow Women's College (1901), and of applied mathematics, Moscow School of Technology (1903). CH's theories were greatly influenced by N. Ye. Zhukovsky with whom he founded the Central Insitute of Aerohydrodynamics (1918). CH's early research concerned hydromechanics, particularly the motion of solids in fluid; also studied gas dynamics. His work was instrumental in the development of high-speed aviation which required the study of the forces acting upon the aircraft at subsonic speeds. The Chaplygin-Zhukovsky postulate on the impact of flow upon a streamlined body is widely applied in aerodynamics. His *Collected Works* in 4 volumes were published in 1948.

CHAPÝGIN, Alekséy Pávlovich (1870–1937), writer. Born into a family of Old-Believers in the Olonets region. He was a shepherd and house painter. He began to publish in 1903, but he first attracted attention with the novel *The Snow-Covered Retreat* (1913), a poetic description of peasant life in the north. Much of his writing is colored by his upbringing as an Old-Believer. Such are *Olonets Notes,* only excerpts of which have been published, and the autobiographical novels *My Life* (1929), *Along Trails and Roads* (1933), and the unfinished *A Fragment of the Same Mirror* (1933–35). CH is also known for historical novels, *Razin Stepan* (1926–27) and the unfinished *Roving People* (1935). CH wrote scenarios for two films: *Mountains of Gold* (1931) and *Stepan Razin* (1939).

CHARDZHÓU (f. Chardzhuy), city, adm. center of Chardzhou Oblast; pop. 66,000 (1959). Important railriver transfer point at the intersection of the Amu Darya and Transcaspian R.R.; has cotton-ginning and silk mills, knitting factories, food-processing plants, repair shops for agr. machinery and excavators.

CHARDZHÓU OBLAST, Turkmen SSR, on the left bank of the middle course of Amu Darya; area 36,100 sq. mi.; pop. 320,000 (1959): Russians, Turkmen, Uzbeks. Cities: Chardzhou, Kerki. Part of it is the Kara Kum desert, with outspurs of the Gissar mountain ridge cutting into the territory in the extreme S.E. Continental, dry climate. Cotton, wheat, and melons are grown in the irrigated river valley; sericulture and rearing of karakul sheep are other important features of the rural economy. Potash, common salt, sulfur, copper, and coal are mined. Principal ind. are cotton- and silk-processing. Construction has begun on the Kara Kum Canal, which will open a new era for agriculture. Est. 1938.

CHARÚSHIN, Yevgény Ivánovich (1901–), painter and author. First became known as illustrator of children's books including works of Gorky and Marshak. An able painter of animals he did decorative painting based on R. fairy tales. He has written numerous books for the young, among them *Seven Tales* (1930) and *Nikita and His Friends* (1938).

CHAYKÓVSKY, Nikoláy Vasílyevich (1850–1925), populist leader. As a student at St. Petersburg CH organized "the Chaykovsky Circle" which played an important role in the populist movement. CH left the "Circle" when it changed from peaceful propaganda to violent methods. In 1875 he led an agricultural socialist settlement in Kansas which lasted only two years. Later CH settled in London, where he again became active in the revolutionary movement. He collected funds for it and published a nonparty revolutionary newspaper for distribution in Russia. Meanwhile he abandoned his earlier anarchistic views and joined the Russian Socialist Revolutionary party. After 1907 CH returned to Russia and dedicated his energies to the cooperative movement. Following the October revolution CH fought against the Bolsheviks and became the head of the provisional government at Archangel. After its collapse CH in 1920 offered his services to General Denikin. He died in Paris.

CHAYKOVSKY, Peter Ilyich: *see* TCHAIKOVSKY.

CHEBOKSÁRY, city, adm. center of Chuvash ASSR; pop. more than tripled, from 31,000 (1939) to 104,000 (1959). River port on the Volga; center of local ind.; important producer of electrical equipment, lumber, leather and textile fabrics, flour, alcohol, and processed foods. Has a number of higher technical schools.

CHEBOTARYÓV, Nikoláy Grigóryevich (1894–1947), mathematician. Corresponding member, Ac. of S., USSR (1929). Honored Scientist, RSFSR (1943). Graduate of Kiev University (1916); professor, Kazan University (1928). Did research on modern algebra; solved Frobenius problem and generalized Dirichlet theorem on integer numbers in arithmetic progression (1924). Stalin prize (1948).

CHEBYSHÓV, Pafnúty Lvóvich (1821–1894), mathematician and mechanical engineer. Fellow, St. Petersburg Ac. of S. (1859), member of many  foreign Ac. of S., including the Royal Society of London. Graduate of Moscow University (1841); professor, St. Petersburg University (1850). CH's original methods contributed to the development of mathematics, mechanics, and related sciences in Russia. Author of papers on the theory of probability and mechanisms, the number theory, mathematical analyses; specialized in the theory of hinged mechanisms. Medals awarded by the Ac. of S., USSR, for outstanding achievements in mathematics and mechanics are named after CH. Founder of the St. Petersburg School of Mathematics.

CHECHÉN-INGÚSH ASSR, on the N. slope of central Greater Caucasus, RSFSR; area 7,450 sq. mi.; pop. 710,000 (1959). Capital: Grozny. In 1922 the area, inhabited by the Moslem Chechens, formerly part of the Dagestan ASSR, later incorporated in Ordzhonikidze Kray, was organized into an autonomous oblast. Two years later the Ingush people, belonging to the same ethnic group, were given similar autonomy. The two regions were integrated in 1934, and the territory raised to the status of republic in 1936. During World War II both nationalities were accused of treasonable collaboration with the Germans and deported from their homeland, and the region was reorganized as Grozny Oblast. After Stalin's death the Chechen-Ingush ASSR was restored.

CHEKA: *see* SECURITY POLICE.

CHEKHOV PUBLISHING HOUSE: *see* RUSSIAN STUDIES.

CHÉKHOV, Antón Pávlovich (1860–1904), dramatist and short-story writer, was born and brought up in

 Taganrog on the Sea of Azov, where his father, a former serf, owned a grocery store. In 1876 the family moved to Moscow, Anton CH remaining in Taganrog for two more years in order to complete his studies at a secondary school. In 1879, he came to Moscow and in 1844 graduated from the Moscow University school of medicine. To support himself and the family CH turned to journalism and contributed humorous stories to Moscow popular magazines and, later, to the more influential and better paying St. Petersburg journals under the pseudonym "Antosha Chekhonte," and others. These stories were exuberantly gay, mischievous, but still somewhat crude (*Night Before the Trial, Romance with the Double-Bass, Daughter of Albion*). Meanwhile CH was becoming more exacting and truer to life in the early stories *Horsey Name, He Forgot, Surgery,* and *Death of a Government Clerk;* several tales about children revealed both a delicate sense of humor and a rare gift for characterization—*The Cook's Wedding* and *Children.* CH's talent achieved early maturity and originality in the amusing, but deeply moving *The Beggar, The Chorus Girl,* and *Vanka,* while in *Sergeant Prishibeyev, The Witch, A Nightmare, In Court,* and *Woe,* there are depths of tragicomedy and effective social satire.

CH's popularity grew rapidly; in 1886 he was invited to contribute to *Novoye Vremya* (New Times), an influential conservative newspaper, and became a friend of its editor, A. Suvorin. The novelette *The Steppe* (1888) enhanced CH's reputation. It is the story of a boy journeying by wagon across the steppes of S. Russia to a town where he is to go to school. His trivial adventures, the characterization of the drivers and of various people met on the journey, changes of weather, and the variety of "moods" of the steppe are fused—nature, animals, and men—into a harmonious and poetic whole. In 1888 CH was awarded the Pushkin prize by the Ac. of S.

CH began to practice medicine in 1884, mostly in the rural areas of the Moscow province. Gradually his literary work became more professional, but also sadder and more melancholy in tone, reflecting the poverty and ignorance of the peasantry and the drabness, callousness, and pettiness of much of R. life. The novelettes *Dreary Story* (1889), *The Duel,* and *Ward No. 6* (1891) are masterpieces of conciseness and vividness of portrayal, but sad and almost hopeless in their outlook.

In 1890 CH undertook a difficult and, at times, dangerous journey across Siberia to the island of Sakhalin. His object was to study prison conditions of the island. The result was a book on medical ethnography, *The Island of Sakhalin.* He returned to Russia by sea, via Japan, Singapore, Ceylon, and Odessa.

By that time CH's talent had received full recognition and he was admired by the older writers, including Korolenko and Tolstoy. After 1892 a measure of optimism is noticeable in his stories together with an element of protest against Russia's political order. It is observable in *An Anonymous Story*, in the pathetic *Rothschild Fiddle*, in *Teacher of Literature*, even in the bleak and harrowing *The Peasants* (1897) which with its harsh realism provoked keen polemics; the liberal and satirical note is struck in the admirable portrayal of a petty local tyrant in *The Man in a Case*. In 1897 CH broke with Suvorin and his conservative paper over the Dreyfus affair. In the same year he became ill with tuberculosis and for the next seven years lived for the most part in the Crimea or French health resorts. In 1901 he married Olga Knipper of the Moscow Art Theater. He died in 1904. The stories of CH's last six or seven years reached a high level of perfection. A note of poetic symbolism and hope is discernible in *Doctor's Visit, On Love, The Darling*, and even in the tragic and overpowering *In the Ravine*. The sad and tender tale *The Bishop* (1902) may be considered as the writer's symbolic swan song.

CH's dramatic work falls in two periods, before and after 1896. During the first period he wrote amusing and successful short plays: *The Bear, The Proposal, The Swan Song,* and the drama *Ivanov.* They were written in the traditional realistic manner of the R. 19th-century drama. By mid-1890's CH became dissatisfied with the routine of the R. stage, with its costume plays, ranting melodramas and "cape and sword" plays. The elements of allusiveness, mood of inner, invisible drama, which he had used with such success in his stories seemed to call for a similar experiment in the theater. The result was the now famous plays (1896–1904) *The Seagull, Uncle Vanya, The Three Sisters,* and *The Cherry Orchard.* After the initial failure of *The Seagull* in St. Petersburg, the play was produced by the young Moscow Art Theater and, brilliantly interpreted, was the theatrical event of 1898. His other plays were equally successful. Both the R. and the W. theaters were to be deeply affected by his art.

CH's letters were published several years after his death; their verve, gayety, and the shrewdness of his judgments of books, plays, and people assure him of an honorable place among the letter-writers of the 19th century.

BIBLIOGRAPHY: W. H. Bruford, *Chekhov and His Russia*, London, 1947; David Magarshack, *Chekhov, A Life*, London, 1952.

I. L. T.

CHÉKHOV, Mikhaíl Aleksándrovich (1891–1955), actor, nephew of Anton Chekhov. Upon completing his studies at the school of dramatics of the A. S. Suvorin Theater in St. Petersburg, he joined the company there but in 1912 transferred to the Moscow Art Theater. He was particularly successful in his work at Studio One of that theater which in 1924 became, under his leadership, the Second Moscow Art Theater. A high-strung individual, a convinced anthroposophist and an opponent of Bolshevik materialism, CH sought to counter the analytical method of Stanislavsky and its principle of "affective memory" by his own synthetic method of acting in which intuition, imagination, fantasy, and inspiration interact powerfully. An actor on the stage, according to CH, is a dual personality, one of which is the performer while the other is the spectator; one "I" performs while the other "I" observes. Of his many memorable portrayals (Khlestakov, Eric XIV, King Lear), the

best was his Hamlet. Growing conflicts with the Soviet leadership forced CH in the mid-1920's to go abroad, where he acted brilliantly in German at the Max Reinhardt Theater, toured Paris, Latvia, and the United States, and appeared in motion pictures. Toward the end of his life he was a director and dramatic coach in studios in California. He has left an interesting autobiography, *An Actor's Technique*.

CHELKÁR-TENGÍZ LAKE, in central Kazakh SSR; area 714 sq. mi.; salty, drying up, desert area to S.

CHELYÁBINSK, city, adm. center of Chelyabinsk Oblast, RSFSR, on Miass River and Trans-Siberian R.R.; pop. 689,000 (1959). Fast-growing ind. community, with many important plants including a giant tractor, metallurgical, ferroalloy, zinc and chemical works, aircraft factory, cement mills; hydroelectric station. Has a number of higher educational and cultural institutions.

CHELYÁBINSK OBLAST, W. Siberia, RSFSR; area 33,930 sq. mi.; pop. 2,982,000 (1959). Main cities: Chelyabinsk (adm. center), Magnitogorsk, Zlatoust. A highly ind. region of major importance, on E. slopes of Middle and S. Urals; its E. sector occupies part of W. Siberian lowlands; drained by upper Ural, Miass, Uy, and others. Precipitation dwindles sharply eastward. Ample deposits of peat and lignite in the forested zone provide the fuel base for high-grade ferrous and nonferrous metallurgy, machine-building and mining ind., drawing on vast mineral resources, including iron and titanium ores, ferroalloys (tungsten, manganese, nickel, chrome), bauxite, copper-zinc, building materials (dolomite, limestone, magnesite, refractory clays). Among the outstanding ind. plants are the Magnitogorsk Metallurgical Combine, tractor and metallurgical works at Chelyabinsk, automobile factory at Miass. The agr. area was drastically reduced when a large sector of fertile black-earth steppes in the E. was incorporated in the newly formed Kurgan Oblast. Wheat and sunflowers are the chief crops of the remaining agr. zone. Truck and dairy farming are important in urban areas. Est. 1934.

CHEMICAL INDUSTRY. The products of this industry include basic chemicals (sulfuric acid, nitric acid, chlorine, soda ash), agricultural fertilizers and insecticides, synthetic rubber and rubber products (*see* RUBBER INDUSTRY), plastics, artificial fibers, photographic materials, aniline dyes, paints, varnishes, and pharmaceutical and medical preparations.

During the period that preceded World War I, plants producing heavy chemicals (acids, alkali, salts) were few, small in size, and unsuited for large-scale production. By 1921, most of them had been destroyed in the civil war or were worn out, and only in 1927 was the 1913 level of production reattained. Already in the early 1920's, however, far-reaching plans were prepared for the further development of this industry and a number of scientific institutes were established for the carrying out of the fundamental research in applied chemistry (e.g., the Karpov Institute of Physics and Chemistry, and the Institute of Applied Chemistry).

Official data indicate that there was a tenfold increase in the output of the CI between 1930 and 1940. This was made possible by the discovery of large deposits of basic chemical raw materials, the construction of many new plants employing modern equipment, the importation of foreign equipment, and the technical assistance of American, German, and other foreign technicians. By 1935 the new branches of chemical production that did not exist in 1913 included synthetic ammonia and related chemicals (e.g., nitrates and nitric acid); coke by-products; synthetic resins; rayon; potassium salts; phosphate fertilizers from apatite; methanol; butanol; acetone; synthetic rubber; and many pharmaceutical products.

During this period chemical plants were built in many parts of the USSR, frequently near sources of raw materials. Production of ammonium sulfate, benzol, toluol, and other coke by-products were integrated with the metallurgical coke industry at various iron and steel plants. Synthetic rubber plants using the Lebedev process were located in potato growing areas (e.g., at Yaroslavl, Voronezh, Yefremov in Tula Oblast, and Kazan), since the basic alcohol employed is made from potatoes. Among the major fertilizer plants built in the 1930's were the superphosphate plants at Voskresensk in Moscow Oblast, at Konstantinovka in the Donbas, and in Leningrad (the Neva Chemical Combine); the Solikamsk Potassium Works in the Urals; and the nitrogenous fertilizer plants producing ammonium sulfate in the major iron and steel centers. The plastics industry was concentrated near Moscow, Leningrad, Vladimir, and Kalinin, while pharmaceutical production centered largely in Moscow, Leningrad, Kharkov, Kiev, Baku, and Chimkent in Kazakhstan.

Although many chemical plants were destroyed or seriously damaged during World War II, others were successfully evacuated to eastern areas. Within the remaining plants the output of such products as ammonia and nitric acid grew rapidly and exceeded the 1940 levels of production, while the output of fertilizers, for example, was sharply reduced. Because the output of pharmaceutical products during this period was insufficient to meet wartime requirements, large quantities were imported from the United States, Great Britain, and Canada under Lend-Lease and the Mutual Aid Program.

The further development of the CI continued to proceed rapidly during the postwar period, as the government sought to keep abreast of modern technological developments and to attain a maximum degree of self-sufficiency in this field. According to official data the output of the CI increased fivefold during the period 1940–58. Among the newly created branches of the CI were those producing sulfa drugs, antibiotics, and radioactive isotopes. In recent years, particular emphasis has been placed on increasing the production of fertilizers and of artificial fibers.

The objectives of the Seven Year Plan (1959–65) provide for a further tripling of the general volume of output of the CI as a whole, and for the completion of 140 large chemical enterprises and the modernization of 130 others. It is expected that the production of synthetic fibers will be 12 or 13 times greater by the end of this period, while that of plastics and of synthetic resins will increase seven times and that of mineral fertilizers—three times.

PRODUCTION OF THE CHEMICAL INDUSTRY

Year	Sulfuric Acid (th. of tons)	Fertilizers (th. of tons)	Artif. Fibers (th. of tons)	Tires (th.)	Rubber Footwear (mill. of pairs)
1913	145	89.0	–	–	38.9
1928	211	135.4	.2	85	36.3
1932	552	920.8	2.8	553	64.7
1937	1,369	3,240.0	8.6	2,698	84.6
1940	1,587	3,237.7	11.1	3,007	69.7
1945	–	1,121.2	–	–	–
1950	2,125	5,497.1	24.2	7,401	110.8
1955	3,799	9,669.2	110.5	10,190	134.6
1958	4,804	12,419.5	166.6	14,395	158.7
1959	5,100	13,900.0	179.0	15,500	–
1960	5,400	13,800.0	211.0	17,200	

P. I. M.

CHEMISTRY. After the first systematic work by M. V. Lomonosov and some of his contemporaries around the middle of the 18th century, the study of C progressed gradually in Russia for the next 100 years. In the second half of the 19th century there appeared a group of chemists who made contributions of great significance. The periodic system proposed by D. I. Mendeleyev in 1869 was spectacularly confirmed within less than a decade. Gallium, scandium, and germanium, three elements whose existence and properties had been predicted on the basis of the periodic system were discovered and their properties were found to be identical with those predicted. The structural theory of organic compounds, introduced by A. M. Butlerov in 1861, included concepts which proved to be fundamental in the development of organic C: tautomerism and the influence of structure on reactivity. Butlerov was also first to study the polymerization of olefins. His school trained such eminent chemists as A. M. Zaytsev, S. N. Reformatsky, and Ye. Ye. Wagner. These and others developed the reduction of metal oxides with aluminum, the oxidation of olefins with weak solutions of potassium permanganate, the peroxide theory of slow oxidation, and the concept of ion hydration. In 1891, V. A. Kistyakovsky determined the differences in the heats of formation of isomeric organic molecules. In 1910, S. V. Lebedev obtained a rubberlike material on polymerization of butadiene.

After the revolution, under the guidance of prominent chemists, some new research institutes were founded. There are a number of Institutes of the Ac. of S.: those of general and inorganic C, physical C, organic C, high-molecular-weight compounds, geochemistry, analytical C, and silicate C. Chemical research is also carried out by many institutions of higher learning and by the D. I. Mendeleyev All-Union Chemical Society. There are also institutes connected with various industries, devoted to the study of more specific fields.

In the field of **physical chemistry** thorough studies of the structure of matter, the nature of chemical bonding, and the mechanisms of the basic chemical processes were carried out. Various spectroscopic, electrical, and magnetic methods furnished detailed information about dissociation energies, interatomic distances, and vibrational frequencies.

The photolysis of vaporized salts was discovered. The new optical method of measuring reactions in gas layers absorbed on surfaces of solids found wide application. V. N. Kondratyev studied the behavior of free radicals and reaction intermediates in the gas phase. In the 1920's and 1930's the study of kinetics was applied primarily to gas-phase chain reactions. The modern theory of chain reactions developed by N. N. Semyonov (co-recipient of the 1956 Nobel prize) and his co-workers on radicals represents an important stage in this work. Later work correlated the structure of free radicals with their reactivity. Many industrial processes involve formation and reactions of free radicals: synthesis of ammonia, catalytic oxidation of carbon monoxide and sulfur dioxide, hydrogenation of ethylene, chlorination, and polymerization.

One of the important points in the study of catalysis was the development of the multiple theory (A. A. Balandin, 1929). This theory takes into account not only the various thermodynamic parameters, but also the relation between the spatial distribution of atoms and bonds of the reacting molecule and the geometric parameters of the crystal lattice of the catalyst, which form the active centers. L. V. Pisarzhevsky demonstrated the importance of the electronic configurations of the solid catalysts. The development of new catalytic methods proved to be of great importance to industry (synthetic rubber, fuel, and others).

In thermochemistry, the equation of A. F. Kapustinsky pertaining to the lattice energy of ionic crystals proved to be of great importance: if the composition and the ionic radii of the compound are known, the heat of formation of the crystal from individual ions can be calculated directly.

The C of solutions was studied intensively by many investigators. Studies of ion solvation resolved some existing contradictions between the chemical and the physical treatment of the theory of solutions. Experimental work showed that electrolytic conductance of many solutions is not always determined by the dielectric characteristics of the components, but rather by the formation and the decomposition of complexes.

The development of colloid C has been of great importance to the leather-tanning, textile, and food industries. The lyophobic colloidal systems were studied by A. V. Dumansky and N. P. Peskov, the founders of the Russian school of colloidal C.

Adsorption phenomena were investigated primarily because of their numerous industrial applications.

General and Inorganic Chemistry. The work of N. S. Kurnakov, dealing with the graphic representation of phase composition, influenced greatly the subsequent development of inorganic C. It has found application in the C of metallic alloys, aqueous salt solutions, fused salts, silicates, as well as in analytical and organic C. The main center of physico-chemical analysis is the Institute of General and Inorganic Chemistry of the Ac. of S. of the USSR.

In the C of complexes, the work of L. A. Chugayev extended the concepts of the Werner theory, especially in regard to the complexes of the platinum metals,

cobalt and nickel (the Chugayev rule of the stability of five- and six-membered rings). B. V. Nekrasov studied the molecular rearrangements of complexes; I. A. Kazarnovsky, that of hydrides and peroxides. Widely studied were: the C of hydration and hardening of concrete; various properties of glass, by A. A. Lebedev and others; theoretical foundations of a number of metallurgical processes, especially the affinity of metals for oxygen, sulfur, selenium, hydrogen, and halogens, as well as the reduction of oxides, sulfides, and phosphates. In recent years a number of new methods were introduced in analytical C, such as polarography, spectrometry, electroanalysis, potentiometry, luminescence and X-ray spectroscopy, as well as isotope dilution. Organic reagents are being used more and more extensively. One of the important problems of analytical C is the study of the less common elements, including the rare earths. Increased demand for nuclear fuels requires methods for the purification of thorium and uranium. Germanium of high purity, used for the production of semiconductors, can now be prepared. The problem of preparing ultra-pure silicon has recently been solved.

Organic Chemistry was developed along the guide lines laid out by the early investigators in that field. A great deal of work was devoted to the study of isomerization, tautomerism, formation of free radicals, polymerization, and decomposition of organic compounds. The extensive study of organic C gave rise to new industries: dyes, petrochemicals, coke, synthetic rubber, plastics, synthetic and artificial fibers, synthetic fuels, cellulose, and photographic materials. Organic chemists realized the syntheses of many important organic compounds: vitamins, hormones, and others. Catalysis, high-pressure techniques, and other physical methods of investigation find wide application in modern organic C. The most important contribution to the C of hydrocarbons was made by A. Ye. Favorsky and his school. N. A. Domnin studied the possibility of the existence of compounds containing triple bonds in five-membered carbocyclic rings. The study of organic compounds containing metals and nonmetals, such as P, S, Si, developed into an important branch of organic C. The C of phosphorus-containing organic compounds was studied by A. Ye. Arbuzov and B. A. Arbuzov as well as their students. New methods were developed for the preparation of high-molecular-weight organosilicon compounds, resins, lacs, liquids with high thermal stability and with desirable dielectric properties. New methods of synthesis utilizing organolithium compounds were developed by K. A. Kocheshkov and others. A. N. Nesmeyanov and others made important contributions to the C of organometallic substances. Compounds of tin, lead, thallium, antimony, bismuth, magnesium, zinc, cadmium, aluminum, and arsenic have been prepared. A general method of preparation of organomercury compounds was developed. An important contribution was made by I. N. Knunyants to the C of fluorine-containing organic substances. A great deal of work was devoted to the development of the C of heterocyclic compounds; the amination and hydroxylation of pyridine (A. Ye. Chichibabin and co-workers). The C of pyrimidine and inidazole derivatives as well as of other biologically important compounds has been studied; also the structure and properties of alkaloids. Systems of classification of alkaloids based on the carbon-nitrogen skeleton were proposed by A. P. Orekhov. Recently high-molecular-weight substances—rubber, proteins, cellulose, and synthetic polymers—acquired great importance. Ion-exchange resins and various films find progressively greater application.

V. S.

CHEREMISS: *see* MARI.

CHEREMKHÓVO, city in Irkutsk Oblast, E. Siberia, RSFSR; pop. 56,000 (1939), 123,000 (1959); rail town on the Trans-Siberian line; center of the coal mining district N. of Irkutsk.

CHERENKÓV, Pável Alekséyevich (1904–), physicist. Graduated from Voronezh University (1928). Associated with the Institute of Physics, Ac. of S., USSR (since 1930). Discoverer of the "Cherenkov-Vavilov effect" (1934). Based on "Cherenkov radiation" various devices for measuring the velocity of charged particles have been developed; known as "Cherenkov counters," they have been decisive in the discovery of antiprotons (1955). For the discovery and explanation of the "Cherenkov effect" he was awarded in cooperation with I. Ye. Tamm and I. M. Frank the Stalin prize (1946) and Nobel prize (1958).

CHERÉPOVETS, city in Vologda Oblast, RSFSR; pop. nearly tripled, from 32,000 (1939) to 92,000 (1959). Major R.R. station and inland port on recently completed Rybinsk reservoir, at the estuary of Sheksna River; fast-growing steel center, with shipyards, railway repair and servicing shops, and a number of light industry and food-processing plants. Horse and hog breeding.

CHERKÁSOV, Nikoláy Konstantínovich (1903–), one of the best known movie actors of the older generation. People's Artist USSR (1947). Graduated from the Leningrad Institute of Scenic Arts (1926) and has been in the movies ever since. His main roles: Professor Polezhayev in *Baltic Deputy* (1937), tsarevich Alexis in *Peter I* (1937–39). His title roles in *Alexander Nevsky* (1938), *Ivan the Terrible* (1945), *Don Quixote* (1956) brought him fame. Stalin prizes (1941, 1946, 1950, twice 1951).

CHERKÁSSY, city, adm. center of Cherkassy Oblast, Ukrainian SSR; pop. 83,000 (1959). River harbor on the Dnieper and R.R. station; the site of various ind., including machine-building, sugar-refining, and tobacco-processing plants, sawmills, clothing and leather factories, cannery, brewery. Pedag. inst. and several schools for specialized technical training.

CHERKÁSSY OBLAST, Ukrainian SSR; area 7,950 sq. mi.; pop. 1,504,000 (1959). Principal cities: Cherkassy (adm. center), Uman, Smela, Shpola. The W. sector lies on the Dnieper upland, merging into lowlands in the E. Mineral building materials and lignite deposits are located in the broad-leaved forest belt (mainly oak and witch-elm groves). Wheat farming and sugar-beet cultivation predominate, based on fertile black earth and gray podsolized soils and moderate continental climate; rearing of dairy and meat livestock.

Metal- and woodworking, light mfg., sugar, tobacco and food-processing ind. Navigation on the Dnieper. Est. 1954.

CHERKÉSSK (f. Batalpashinsk), city, adm. center of Karachai-Cherkess Autonomous Oblast, Stavropol Kray, RSFSR; pop. 41,000 (1959). R.R. town on the Kuban River. Chemical, clothing, furniture, and footwear factories; building-materials and food-processing plants.

CHERNÍGOV, city, adm. center of Chernigov Oblast, Ukrainian SSR; pop. 89,000 (1959). Rail junction and harbor on right bank of the Desna; light mfg. (clothing and leather goods, wool processing, furniture factories), metalworking and chemical plants. Pedag. inst. and several schools for specialized technical training. Dates from early 10th century. The Spassky Sobor (Byzantine cathedral, built 1024), was destroyed in World War II.

CHERNÍGOV OBLAST, Ukrainian SSR; area 12,160 sq. mi.; pop. 1,553,000 (1959). Principal cities: Chernigov (adm. center), Nezhin, Priluki, Bakhmach. Its slightly elevated level plains are watered by the Desna, bounded by the Dnieper on W. The N. zone is occupied by mixed deciduous and coniferous forests growing on turf podsols; black earth and gray podsolized soils predominate in the S. Mineral deposits include peat, marl, clays, phosphorites. Of the basic crops, rye, buckwheat, and oats are emphasized in the N.; potatoes in central section; sugar beets, tobacco, and mint farther S. Extensive dairy and meat livestock raising. Heavy ind. (road-construction machinery, tractor parts, fire-fighting equipment) are centered in larger towns, light mfg. based on local produce. Est. 1932.

CHERNÍGOVSKY, Vladímir Nikoláyevich (1907–), physiologist. Fellow, Ac. of S., USSR (1960); fellow (1950) and vice president (1953–57), Ac. of Medical S. Graduate of Perm University (1930). Senior scientist (1937–41) and professor (1944), Division of General Physiology, All-Union Institute of Experimental Medicine, Leningrad. Director, Institute of Physiology, Ac. of S. (1953). Research concerns the mechanism of introceptive reflexes and the functional correlation between the cerebral cortex and internal organs. Identified new reflexes and characterized the introceptive analyzer. Author of *The Afferent System of the Internal Organs* (1943); *Problems of Neural Regulation of the Hematic System*, in collaboration with A. Ya. Yaroshevsky (1953). I. P. Pavlov award of the Ac. of S. (1943).

CHERNOGÓRSK, city in Khakass Autonomous Oblast, Krasnoyarsk Kray, E. Siberia, RSFSR; pop. rose from 11,000 (1939) to 51,000 (1959). Center of the Minusinsk coal-mining district.

CHERNÓV, Dmítry Konstantínovich (1839–1921), metallurgist. Graduate, Institute of Applied Technology in St. Petersburg (1858); professor, St. Petersburg Artillery Academy (1889–1917). Discovered critical temperatures for steel (1866), laying the foundation of physical metallurgy in Russia. Advanced theories on crystallization of steel ingots (1878), heat treatment, cold plastic deformation (1884), oxidation. Member of numerous societies including the American Institute of Mining Engineers and the Royal Society of

Arts; honorary vice president of the British Iron and Steel Institute.

CHERNÓV, Víktor Mikháylovich (1873–1952), radical thinker and leader of the Socialist Revolutionary party. Son of a rural school teacher in Tambov, CH was expelled from the University of Moscow after a student strike (1894) and became a professional revolutionary. A friend and disciple of N. K. Mikhaylovsky, CH organized revolutionary groups among the peasants of Tambov, and in European exile. The relative freedom obtained after Oct. 1905 permitted CH and other neo-populists to hold a full-scale organizational Congress of the Socialist Revolutionary party at Imatra in Finland (Dec. 1905–1906) at which CH wrote the party platform calling for a two-stage revolution (democratic and then socialist) and for the "socialization of land" (abolition of property in land, freedom for peasants to enjoy all crops grown with their own hands, democratic village communes), which proved popular among the R. peasants. As a leading Socialist Revolutionary, CH was ambivalent toward his party's terrorists until the exposure of the double-spy Azef (1908), but bitterly opposed Prime Minister Stolypin's "capitalist" agrarian program (q.v.) (1906–14). Exiled in W. Europe during World War I, CH in Aug. 1914 developed a "third force" program, according to which European socialists should defend their countries, but seize power (first in Russia) and end the "imperialist" war. Returning to Russia after the Feb. Revolution, CH presided weakly over the fast-growing but deeply divided Socialist Revolutionary party. He was minister of agriculture in the Provisional Governments of Lvov and Kerensky (May 5–Sept. 1, 1917) but was unable to secure enactment of the socialization of land. CH could not prevent the Bolshevik seizure of power or the ensuing split-off of the Left Socialist Revolutionaries from his party, but his Right Socialist Revolutionaries won a plurality of seats in the Constituent Assembly (q.v.), which elected CH chairman during its one-day meeting (Jan. 5, 1918). During the Civil War, CH was associated with the Socialist Revolutionary government at Samara, was arrested and released by Adm. Kolchak's forces, fled Russia and thereafter lived in exile in Central and W. Europe, and finally in New York. (*See also* SOCIALIST REVOLUTIONARIES)

BIBLIOGRAPHY: V. M. Chernov, *The Great Russian Revolution,* New Haven, 1936; O. Radkey, *The Agrarian Foes of Bolshevism,* New York, 1958.

CHERNÓVTSY (Rum. *Cernauti*), city, adm. center of Chernovtsy Oblast, Ukrainian SSR; pop. 145,000 (1959). R.R. junction and river port on upper Prut. Metallurgical, chemical, and textile plants, food processing; has a university and various institutions of higher academic and specialized training.

CHERNÓVTSY OBLAST, Ukrainian SSR; area 3,100 sq. mi.; pop. 776,000 (1959). Principal cities: Chernovtsy (adm. center), Storozhinets, Khotin, Novoselitsa. Formerly a province of Bukovina in N. Rumania, extending along upper Prut and Dniester rivers. Predominantly an open hilly terrain bordered by the outcroppings of Carpathian Mountains in the S.W.; the beech forests of the mountainous country growing on turf podsols and brown soils merge with the wooded steppe and podsolized black earth of the E. section. Sheep raising and lumbering are the principal occupations in the mountains; basic grains, potatoes, and sugar beets are grown extensively in the S., orchards and vineyards predominate along the Dniester valley. Recently developed heavy ind. plants (machine, motor and rolling stock repair shops) are centered in urban areas, as well as light mfg. and processing establishments based on local produce. Est. 1940.

CHERNOZEM: *see* SOILS.

CHERNYAKHÓVSKY, Iván Danílovich (1906–1945), Red Army general, twice awarded the title of Hero of the Soviet Union. Member of the CP from 1928. During World War II, he was commander of an infantry division, later of a tank corps. In 1944 put in command of all troops operating on the third Byelorussian front. Voronezh, Kiev, Kursk, Minsk, Vilnius, Kaunas and other key cities taken by the Germans were recaptured by Soviet troops under his command. Died in Feb. 1945, from wounds sustained during a close combat, in E. Prussia.

CHERNYÁYEV, Ilyá Ilyich (1893–), chemist. Fellow, Ac. of S., USSR (1943). Graduate (1915) and professor (1932), Leningrad University and the Moscow Petroleum Institute (1935–41). Since 1918 associated with the Institute for the Study of Platinum; director, Institute of General and Inorganic Chemistry (1941). Research concerns complex compounds and refining of platinum metals. Stalin prizes (1946, 1952).

CHERNYSHÉVSKY, Nikoláy Gavrílovich (1828–1889), radical journalist, philosopher, and literary critic. Born in Saratov, the son of a poor priest, CH experienced the difficulties of those in old Russia who rose from low status through education. First trained for the priesthood, his linguistic talents enabled him to go

to the University of St. Petersburg, where he became a radical. Briefly a teacher in Saratov, CH returned to St. Petersburg and joined the staff of the noted journal *Sovremennik* (The Contemporary) (1854). Through its pages he broadcast his philosophical and social views, which were influenced by Hegel, Feuerbach, Bentham, James Mill, and the French socialists. He preached a thoroughgoing materialism and, independently of Marx, combined it in some ways with Hegelian dialectics. Although he believed in a deterministic universe, he urged "egoism," by which he meant a kind of utilitarian self-development involving radical activity. As a literary critic, CH emphasized R. works, opposed both romanticism and art-for-art's-sake, and favored novels and poetry with a socially critical purpose. Though his writings passed the censors, his denunciations were so sweeping in manner and content that his critics seized on Turgenev's word "nihilism" (q.v.) to describe CH's position. In 1862 CH was arrested and imprisoned for two years in the Fortress of Peter and Paul. There he wrote the popular didactic novel, *What is to be Done?*, in which "positive" heroes and heroines discuss and exemplify his views of the rational and socialist life. In 1864 he was sentenced to fourteen years in the mines of Siberia, and lived in exile there. CH's productive life was over; only in 1883 was he allowed to return to Astrakhan, and in 1889 to his native Saratov, to die. Lenin learned from and admired CH above all other non-Marxist R. radicals, and sometimes attributed to CH his own conversion to materialism, the dialectics, and socialism, and his views on literature. Therefore CH has had a great vogue in Communist Russia.

BIBLIOGRAPHY: N. G. Chernyshevsky, *What is to be Done?*, 4th ed., New York, 1909; T. G. Masaryk, *The Spirit of Russia*, London and New York, 1955.

CHERNYSHÓV, Aleksándr Alekséyevich (1882–1940), electrical engineer. Fellow, Ac. of S., USSR (1932). Graduate of St. Petersburg Folytechnic Institute (1907) where he remained until the end of his life. Was also associated with the Petrograd Institute of Physics and Technology, the Institute of Power Engineering, and the Committee of Automation and Telemechanics. Research concerned high-voltage techniques and radio engineering, methods of obtaining high power outputs with a high-voltage maximum of one million volts by means of cascade connections, ranges of radio-telephone transmission, television, electrification of railroads. Lenin prize (1930).

CHERNYSHÓV, Feodósy Nikoláyevich (1856–1914), geologist and paleontologist. Fellow, Ac. of S. Graduated from St. Petersburg Mining Inst. (1880). Director of the Geological Museum of the Ac. of S. (1900). His field surveys led to the study of the stratigraphy of paleozoic deposits in the Urals. Directed the initial mapping of the Donbas area (1892), and compiled geological maps of the S. Urals and the Timan. Honorary member of Russian and foreign learned societies.

CHERVONETS: *see* MONETARY SYSTEM.

CHIATÚRA, city in Georgian SSR; pop. 19,200 (1956). Rail town in Transcaucasia, on the Kvirila River, N. of Kutaisi; one of the world's richest manganese-mining centers.

CHICHÉRIN, Borís Nikoláyevich (1828–1904), historian, political philosopher. Professor of legal history, University of Moscow, until 1868, when differences with the university administration caused him to resign. He served as mayor of Moscow, 1881–1883, losing that position at the emperor's behest after calling on local governments to unite in promoting a better Russia. Considered a precursor of the Kadet party which was formed the year after his death. In such books as *Essays in the History of Russian Law* (1858) and *Property and the State* (1882–83) he showed the influence of Hegel and Savigny, treating the state as the supreme expression of community life and the national spirit. Thus, for him, the central factor in the history of Russia was the development of Moscow as the core of a burgeoning national state.

CHICHÉRIN, Geórgy Vasílyevich (1872–1936), Soviet diplomat. Born into the aristocracy, he joined the

foreign service after graduation from the University of St. Petersburg. Became a Social Democrat (1905). Left Russia in 1907, and later settled in England, where after 1914, he participated in anti-war activities. He was imprisoned by the British after the Bolshevik Revolution and expelled from England, Jan. 1918. Returning to Russia, he succeeded Trotsky as commissar for foreign affairs in March 1918. He advocated closer relations with Germany; was chief Soviet delegate to the Genoa conference of 1922; and signed the treaty of Rapallo with Germany in April of that year. Improved relations with Near East countries, particularly Turkey, became another object of his policy. He remained head of the foreign ministry until 1930, when he was succeeded by Litvinov.

CHICHIBÁBIN, Alekséy Yevgényevich (1871–1945), chemist. Member, Ac. of S., USSR (1928). Left the USSR (1930) and died abroad. Research concerned organic chemistry; developed the "Chichibabin pyridine synthesis" and the "Chichibabin reaction" (1914). Made valuable contributions to the development of the chemical and pharmaceutical industry in Russia. Lenin prize (1926). Author of *Fundamentals of Organic Chemistry*, two vols. (6th ed., 1954–58).

CHIGIRÍN CONSPIRACY, (1877), an attempt, led by a group of populists, to organize a peasant uprising against the large estate-owners in the Ukraine. Pretending to be acting as fully authorized "tsar's envoys," the populist leaders Yakov Stefanovich and Lev Deutch succeeded in recruiting a "Secret Militia" numbering a few hundred peasants, in the Chigirin county of the Kiev province. The attempt was promptly crushed by the government.

CHIGÓRIN, Mikhaíl Ivánovich (1850–1908), outstanding chess player, one of the founders of the R. school of chess. Winner of numerous international tournaments, including New York (1889), Budapest (1896), Vienna (1903), All-Russian tournaments in 1878 and 1893. C had decisive influence on the development of chess-playing in Russia.

CHILD CARE AND EDUCATION. The youngest children are taken care of in the babies' homes (*domá rebyonka*) which take babies and children up to the age of 3. By a decree of the Presidium of the Supreme Soviet of the USSR dated July 8, 1944, these homes accept also the children of unmarried mothers.

The children's homes (*detskie domá*) take care of orphaned children aged from 3 to 14. They are of four different types: preschool, school, mixed, and special. Unusually gifted children are permitted to remain in these homes until they complete their secondary education. All children's homes are run by the government. They have taken the place of the children's shelters (*detskie priyuty*) of prerevolutionary Russia, some of which were run by the government and others by religious, charitable, and other institutions.

Creches and day nurseries (*detskie yasli*) are attached to factories, collective farms, and so forth, and take care of children of working mothers, aged from 3 to 6 years. Their personnel includes a doctor and a nurse. Normally, the child is kept in them during the mother's working shift, but some nurseries are open 24 hours a day.

Kindergartens (*detskie sady*) educate children aged between 3 and 7 years. (*See also* EDUCATION)

CHIMKÉNT, city, adm. center of S. Kazakhstan Oblast; pop. 153,000 (1959). Important rail, ind. and trading center of a cotton- and fruit-growing area; its ind. include nonferrous metallurgy (smelting of lead ores mined in Karatau), a pharmaceutical plant, cotton gins, and fruit canneries. Building Materials Technological Institute.

CHIRCHÍK, city in Tashkent Oblast, Uzbek SSR; pop. more than quadrupled, from 15,000 (1939) to 65,000 (1959). Recently developed, fast-growing ind. community, on the Chirchik River, right tributary of the Syr Darya; major center of electro-chemical industry; important producer of nitrogen fertilizer, chemical machinery and equipment. Hydroelectric station.

CHÍRIKOV, Yevgény Nikoláyevich (1864–1936), novelist. In his early works, he described the life of the intelligentsia—*The Invalids, The Foreigners*. A follower of M. Gorky, at first sympathized with the Marxi.t viewpoint but by 1905 he changed his mind. After the revolution, he emigrated and wrote books critical of the Soviet regime.

CHÍRIN, Prokópy (died in 1621 or 1623), icon painter. His *Ivan Voin* (Ivan the Warrior) is at the Russian Museum in Leningrad; and *Nikita Muchenik* (Nikita the Martyr) at the Tretyakov Gallery, Moscow.

CHÍSTOPOL, city in Tatar SSR; pop. 51,000 (1959). On the left bank of Kama River; drydocks, watch factory, woodworking, clothing, leather and knitted goods.

CHISTYAKOV, Pável Petróvich (1832–1919), painter. Taught painting and drawing at the Academy of Fine Arts in St. Petersburg. Among his pupils were Repin, Surikov, Vasnetsov, and Serov. His better-known pictures are *A Rome Beggar, Boyarin,* and *Sophie*.

CHISTYAKÓVO, city in Stalino Oblast, Ukrainian SSR; pop. 49,000 (1939), 92,000 (1959). Railway junction; major mining center in the Donets coal basin.

CHITÁ, city, adm. center of Chita Oblast, RSFSR; pop. 172,000 (1959). Major rail and ind. hub; locomotive and rolling-stock repair shops, meat-packing, sawmills, sheepskin and leather factories. Medical school, pedag. inst., and various schools for specialized technical training. Founded 1653.

CHITÁ OBLAST, E. Siberia, RSFSR; area 166,560 sq. mi.; pop. 1,036,000 (1959). Principal cities: Chita (adm. center), Petrovsk-Zabaykalsky, Nerchinsk, Sretensk. Includes the Aga (Aginsky) Buryat National Okrug; borders on Mongolia and China in the S.; walled off by Yablonovy range on N. Predominantly a high plateau crossed by several mountain ridges (highest peak, 8,000 ft.) alternating with broad valleys; drained by the Amur with its headstreams Shilka and Argun, and by the Olekma and Vitim of the Lena basin; very cold, dry climate, the amount of precipitation declining sharply eastward. The larger portion of the region is covered by dense pine forests, merging into the wooded

steppe in the S. The vast and varied mineral resources of the oblast, primarily lead-zinc, include also coal, iron, gold, molybdenum, tungsten, and tin. Agriculture is limited to the river valleys and the steppe belt along the S. border, with most of the acreage under hardy grains, flax, and hay, but dairy farming is very important. Timbering and hunting are also essential occupations. Recent industrial development has followed the location of the chief mineral deposits. Est. 1937.

CHIZHÉVSKY, Nikoláy Prokópyevich (1873–1952), metallurgist and chemist. Fellow, Ac. of S., USSR (1939). Graduate of St. Petersburg University (1899), Mining Academy of Leoben (1902), and Kiev Polytechnic Institute (1904. Professor, Tomsk Institute of Technology (1910–23), Moscow Mining Academy and Moscow Steel Institute (1923). Joined the Institute of Mineral Fuels (1935). Investigated the effects of nitrogen, carbon, manganese, and silicon on the mechanical properties of iron and steel; suggested boronization of steel; advanced principles of metallography of nitrided steel, vacuum treatment of steel, a theory of coke oven design, and new methods of coal coking. Stalin prize (1943).

CHÍZHIKOV, Davíd Mikháylovich (1895–), metallurgist. Corresponding member, Ac. of S., USSR (1939). Graduate, Moscow Mining Academy (1924); professor, Moscow Institute of Nonferrous Metals and Gold (1933–41). Chief engineer for the design and building of the Konstantinovka Zinc Plant, Donbas (1928–30). Cofounder and director, Scientific Research Institute of Nonferrous Metallurgy (1930). Research concerns the theory and technology of nonferrous and rare metal production, chlorination of polymetallic and tin ores, and electrolysis of sulfide materials. Author of *Metallurgy of Nonferrous Heavy Metals* (1948), *Metallurgy of Zinc* (1938), *Metallurgy of Lead* (1944). Stalin prizes (1942, 1950); Order of Red Banner of Labor.

CHKÁLOV: *see* ORENBURG.

CHKÁLOV, Valéry Pávlovich (1904–1938), outstanding flier, hero of the Soviet Union, deputy to the Supreme Soviet. In 1936 he made a 56-hour nonstop 5,800-mile flight, Moscow–Franz Josef Land–Cape Chelyuskin–Petropavlovsk-Kamchatsky–Udd Island (renamed Chkalov Island). In 1937, together with pilots G. F. Baydukov and A. V. Belyakov, he made the first nonstop flight Moscow-USA over the N. Pole. He was killed Dec. 15, 1938, while testing a new type of plane.

CHKHEÍDZE, Nikoláy Semyónovich (1864–1926), Menshevik leader in Georgia and Russia. Deputy to the third and fourth Dumas where he led the Menshevik faction. After the February revolution in 1917 he was the first chairman of the Petrograd Soviet. In 1918 he went to Georgia where he was elected chairman of the Constituent Assembly. In 1921, after the conquest of Georgia by the Bolsheviks, he emigrated. Committed suicide in 1926.

CHKHENKÉLI, Akáky Ivánovich (1874–1959), Georgian Menshevik leader. Deputy to the fourth Duma. From 1918 to 1921 was minister of foreign affairs in independent Georgia. After 1921 was active among Georgian *émigrés* in Paris.

CHÓRNY, Sásha (Aleksandr Mikhaylovich Glückberg) (1880–1933), humorist and satirical poet. His poems are parodies of the symbolist poets. Left the Soviet Union in 1920. In his later years he wrote satirical anti-communist poetry and verses for children.

"CHORNY PEREDEL": *see* "BLACK REPARTITION."

CHÓRNYE ZÉMLI, (Black Soils), semi-barren area, W. of Volga, S.W. Caspian lowland; 4 mill. hectares, fit only for winter pasturing.

CHRISTIANIZATION OF RUSSIA. Christianity began to filter through to E. Slavs as far back as the 5th or 6th century. By the 9th century the Christian faith was practiced on a limited scale in Russia. A century later (in 988–989) the R. people were Christianized by order of Prince Vladimir, son of Svyatoslav (Vladimir the Saint). The acceptance of Christianity by the old pagan Russia was a gradual process. The conversion met with some resistance and occasional open rebellion. On the other hand, it brought Russia closer to the family of more civilized nations, through contact with Byzantine culture.

CHU RIVER flows from Tien Shan Mountains, Kirghiz SSR, via Kazakhstan into Saumal-Kul Lake. Not navigable; 640 mi. long. Irrigation and climate cause summer drying.

CHUBÁR, Vlas Yákovlevich (1891–1941), Bolshevik leader in the Ukraine. Born of a poor peasant family, he joined the Bolshevik movement in 1907. He first became prominent after the Bolshevik Revolution as commissar of artillery. Subsequently he filled important posts in the Ukraine and RSFSR, becoming a candidate member of the Politburo and a member of the Communist party Central Committee in the late 1920's. CH appears to have led a movement against Stalin within the Central Committee and this probably explains his disappearance in 1938. He was posthumously rehabilitated after the 20th Party Congress in 1956.

CHUDAKÓV, Yevgény Alekséyevich (1890–1953), automobile and mechanical engineer. Fellow (1939), vice president (1939–42), and member of the executive board (1942–53), Ac. of S., USSR. Graduate (1916) and professor (1926), Moscow School of Technology. Founder of the Scientific Laboratory of Automation (1918), the Scientific Institute of Automation (1921), and the Institute of Mechanical Engineering (1938), Ac. of S. Research concerned the design of the automobile and its traction qualities, problems related to mechanical engineering, strength, friction and wear. In 1949, joined the editorial board of *Bolshaya Sovetskaya Entsiklopedia* (Large Soviet Encyclopedia). Author of *The Theory of Automobile Design* (1935; 2nd ed., 1950); *Atlas of Designs of Soviet Automobiles* (5 vols., in cooperation with Ya. E. Malakhovsky 1948–54). Stalin prizes (1943, 1951).

CHUDSKÓYE LAKE (PEIPUS LAKE), divides Estonian SSR and W. Pskov Oblast, RSFSR; extends N. to S. for 90 mi.; area 1,390 sq. mi. (including Lake Pskov). Consists of two basins connected by a strait: in the N. called Lake Peipus and the S. extension Lake Pskov. The strait is known as Teploye Ozero. The lake receives over 50 streams and rivers; its outlet is the Narova River which flows into the Gulf of Finland.

The lake has several islands; has an abundance of fish; is navigable. Scene of a battle in 1242 when Alexander Nevsky defeated Teutonic knights; center of heavy fighting during World War II.

CHUFÁROV, Grigóry Ivánovich (1900–), physical chemist. Corresponding member, Ac. of S., USSR (1953). Graduated from the Urals Polytechnic Institute (1928). Director, Chemical Institute of the Ural Branch, Ac. of S. (1939–46); Dean of Ural University (1946–56). Since 1956 has been working at Ural Branch, Ac. of S., on physical and chemical problems of metallurgical and related processes, including the mechanism and kinetics of the dissociation and reduction of metal oxides.

CHUGÁYEV, Lev Aleksándrovich (1873–1922), chemist. Graduated from Moscow University (1895). Professor in Moscow and St. Petersburg. Founder and director (1918) of the Institute for the Study of Platinum and Other Precious Metals. CH's research concerned biochemistry, bacteriology, and organic chemistry of terpenes and camphor. Made valuable contributions to the chemistry of complex compounds.

CHÚKCHI (R. *Chukotsky*) **NATIONAL OKRUG,** part of Magadan Oblast, Soviet Far East, RSFSR; area 284,750 sq. mi.; pop 47,000 (1959), predominantly Chukchi, Eveny, and Yakuts. Principal settlements: Anadyr (adm. center), Ugolny, Providenie, Chukotskaya Kultbaza. Formerly incorporated in Khabarovsk Kray, it occupies the N.E. tip of the Asiatic continent, washed by the E. Siberian and Chukchi (Chukot) seas, and is separated from Alaska by the Bering Strait. The territory comprises the Chukchi Peninsula and adjacent region in the Anadyr River basin, mountainous country crossed by the Kolyma range extending parallel to the coastline. Severe climate, with short, cool summers, limits the major occupations to reindeer breeding, hunting valuable fur-bearing animals, and fishing. Coal for local needs is mined near Anadyr and Ugolny, and there are lead-zinc deposits on the N. coast. Commercial seal and walrus hunting. Est. 1930.

CHUKCHÍ PENINSULA, N.E. extremity of Asia, culminating in Dezhnev Cape. Juts into Chukchi Sea which extends W. to Wrangel Island and is linked to Bering Gulf. Area 224,000 sq. mi. Tundra; much wild life and seal and walrus.

CHUKHÁNOV, Zinóvy Fyódorovich (1912–), expert in the field of heat power engineering, power chemistry, and gasification. Corresponding member, Ac. of S., USSR (1939). Graduate of Moscow Institute of Chemical Technology (1932). Associated with the All-Union Institute of Heat Power Engineering (1931–34), State Institute of Nitrogen (1932–37), and the Institute of Power Engineering (1938). Research on the theory and development of new methods of fuel combustion, gasification of solid fuels, heat exchange, and diffusion.

CHUKÓTKA: *see* CHUKCHI.

CHUKÓTSKY: *see* CHUKCHI.

CHUKÓVSKY, Kornéy Ivánovich (1882–), literary critic and writer for children. He contributed to the journals *Russkaya Mysl* (Russian Thought), *Rech* (Speech), *Vesy* (Scales). In *Faces and Masks* (1914) he gave impressionistic portraits of literary figures. He also translated from Walt Whitman and Oscar Wilde. His witty verses for children are still popular.

CHULKÓV, Mikhaíl Dmítrievich (ca. 1743–1792), writer and journalist who assembled R. folk songs and fairy tales published in two collections: *The Scoffer* (1766–68) and *Collection of Various Songs* (1770–74). His best-known original work is, perhaps, the satirical novel *The Fair Cook* (1770). In 1771–78 he published a seven-volume treatise *Historical Description of the Commerce of Russia.*

CHULÝM RIVER: (1) Flows through Krasnoyarsk Kray and Tomsk Oblast. Right tributary of Ob; length 1,154 mi.; timber floating. **(2)** In Novosibirsk Oblast, flows into Lake Chany; length 140 mi.

CHURCH: *see* ORTHODOX CHURCH.

CHUSOVÁYA RIVER, left tributary of the Kama River, originates in the Ural Mountains. Length 456 mi., of which 250 mi. are navigable; used for floating timber.

CHUSOVÓY, city in Perm Oblast, RSFSR; pop. 60,000 (1959). Railway junction, on the Chusovaya River; major metallurgical center in the Middle Urals.

CHUVÁSH ASSR, middle Volga region, RSFSR; area 7,065 sq. mi.; pop. 1,098,000 (1959). Cities: Cheboksary (capital), Alatyr, Kanash, Mariinsky Posad, Shumerlya, Yadrin. In the 15th and 16th centuries it was part of the Kazan Khanate. Under the Soviets, it was organized as an autonomous oblast in 1920, raised to the status of republic five years later. The Chuvash natives, an ethnic strain affected by Bulgarians and Tatars, constitute about 80 per cent of the population. The region extends along the right bank of the Volga, through forest and wooded steppe zones. Fertile black-earth and podsolized soils support extensive farming, featuring rye, oats, and, more recently, potatoes, fodder, and technical crops such as hemp, flax, and tobacco. Lumbering and allied ind. and cattle and hog raising for the dairy and meat market are of vital importance. Phosphorite, oil shale, and peat deposits provide the basis for other essential ind. Heavy mfg. and processing plants are centered in Alatyr, Shumerlya, and other larger cities. Peasant handicrafts are source of substantian auxiliary income. Est. 1925.

CHUYKÓV, Semyón Afanásyevich (1902–), painter. His early work displayed modernist leanings (*Evening in the Mountains,* 1927). Official praise came only when, after moving to Kirgizia (1932), he began painting historical subjects (*Kirghiz Rebellion of 1916*). Thereafter a realist, he produced patriotic pictures during World War II (*For the Motherland*) and, later, portrayals of Kirghiz scenes.

CHUYKÓV, Vasíly Ivánovich (1900–), marshal of the Soviet Union. He volunteered for the Red Army in  1918. He graduated from the Frunze Military Academy in the mid-1920's, and later from the eastern faculty of that institution. He was Soviet military adviser to Chiang Kai-shek from 1926 to 1937. During World War II he commanded important army units; in 1949 he became commander in chief of Soviet military forces in Germany and

in 1950 was made a full general. He was appointed commander of the Kiev military district in 1953 and marshal of the Soviet Union in 1955. CH was elected deputy to the USSR Supreme Soviet, member of the central committee of the Ukrainian CP in 1955, and candidate member of the Central Committee of the CPSU in 1952 and 1956.

CINEMA: *see* MOVING PICTURES.

CIRCASSIANS: *see* KARACHAI-CHERKESS A.O.

CITIZENSHIP was legally or *de facto* unequal up to 1936 for capitalists, those living on unearned incomes, monks and priests, former members of the tsarist police and royal family, and some of the old intelligentsia (*lishentsy*). Their rights to education, food rations, and housing were curtailed and they were disenfranchised. Peasants received less representation in the soviets than did urban voters, and the deported peasants who had resisted collectivization lost civil rights for several years.

Until 1938, foreigners (if workers, peasants not hiring others for labor, political refugees) could vote and gain office in elections, and could acquire Soviet C through local soviets with a minimum of "annoying formalities." Laws of Soviet C were tightened and emptied of class provisions in Stalin's later years. Under the law of Aug. 19, 1938, still in effect, foreigners lost the rights to vote and to be elected to office. Simplified acquisition of Soviet C by workers and peasants was discontinued. Up to 1938, persons living in the USSR without proof of foreign citizenship became automatically citizens of the USSR, but under present rules they are considered stateless. Marriage to foreigners was forbidden from Feb. 15, 1947 to April 26, 1954.

Today, Soviet citizens are those who (1) were subjects of the Russian Empire up to Nov. 7, 1917 and did not lose Soviet C subsequently; (2) acquired C legally in the past. *Emigrés* were deprived of Soviet C but it was restored to those who returned voluntarily to the USSR during and after World War II. Soviet C is granted by the Presidiums of the USSR and republic supreme soviets. It may be lost through court sentence or special individual edicts of the Presidium of the USSR Supreme Soviet.

CIVIL AVIATION appeared in the USSR during the middle 1920's as an adjunct to the defense forces. It was greatly stimulated by the Second World War and is rapidly becoming an important factor in long-distance passenger transportation. In 1958, this traffic was recorded as some 3.29 bill. passenger-miles; by 1960 it had reached about 7 bill. The Soviet government plans to make air travel the dominant means of domestic long-distance travel. Until recently a two-engine aircraft similar to the Convair 440 was the mainstay of Aeroflot operations. The two-engine jet TU-104 was put into service in 1956; in 1958 a four-engine TU-110 appeared, along with the AN-10 (Ukraina) and IL-18 (Moskva), both four-engine turboprop aircraft. The TU-114 (Rossiya) four-engine turboprop of 1959 can carry 120 passengers, de luxe, or 220 passengers, tourist-class, nonstop between Moscow and New York. The USSR is gradually extending Aeroflot routes to foreign capitals and permitting reciprocal

SOVIET CIVIL AIRLINES

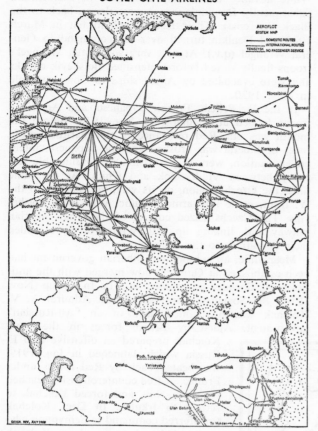

flights by foreign airlines to Moscow, though at present no foreign airlines are permitted to cross the whole Soviet territory.

CIVIL LAW regulates primarily property relations, while criminal law (q.v.), the other major branch of Soviet law (q.v.), is concerned with the prevention and punishment of crime. Subjects of CL may be either legally competent people, or legally competent organizations ("juridical persons"). CL is divided into a general part and a particular part. The general part of any of the republic CL codes outlines who may enter into CL relations and how they may do so, which goods, services, inheritances, inventions, and so forth, may be objects of the relations, and what the time limitations are on suits. The particular part of the codes covers the subdivisions: (1) property (q.v.)—the rights and duties and nature of state, collective farm-cooperative and personal property; (2) liability law (q.v.), including contracts and torts; (3) inheritance (q.v.); (4) authorship and invention (q.v.). Labor, collective farm, land, and family law (q.v.) are treated as branches of law separate from CL, but cases under all these branches of law are heard under similar rules of civil procedure.

Soviet CL contains recognizable provisions from Russian tsarist and Western European law, and also provisions characteristic of the special social and economic policies of the present regime. CL was eclipsed during the repressive, confiscatory period of war communism (q.v.), 1918–1921. It was first codified for the RSFSR in 1922. The RSFSR and other republic codes have been much amended and supplemented by central and local laws and directives. During the NEP period, CL contained provisions for regulating private, capitalist enterprise in small-scale manufacturing and in trade. When Stalin had pushed through the collectivization of the peasantry and the expropriation of remaining capitalists (1928–1936), some sections of the codes fell into disuse. Such radical changes in CL testify that Soviet property rights are not held to be sacred and eternal, but, rather, to be justified in terms of their current social functions. CL has become more stable, nevertheless, and the court judges and attorneys more competent to apply it properly. It promotes the efficiency of a growingly complex system, not only by enforcing social and economic policies of the CPSU, but also by enabling citizens to seek remedies for many damages, thus increasing the security of property and thereby raising incentives to work so as to accumulate that property.   P. H. J.

CIVIL WAR. Alienated by the Bolshevik seizure of power and, particularly, by the harsh policies of the new Soviet government, many dissident elements in Russia joined forces and challenged the authority of the new regime. Supported to some extent by the Allies, these opposition groups fought against the Bolsheviks on numerous fronts.

The CW began in the S. with the Don Cossack revolt of Dec. 1917 and the formation of a volunteer army under Gen. Kaledin and Gen. Kornilov. General Denikin took command after Kaledin's suicide (Feb. 1918) and Kornilov's death in battle (April 1918). With Cossack support, Denikin cleared the Bolsheviks out of the Don and N. Caucasus regions during the summer of 1918.

Meantime a Red Army was in process of formation. Trotsky became Soviet commissar of war in March 1918 and, under his leadership, a highly organized effective fighting force based on conscription was sent into action. Trotsky remained the directing genius of the Soviet war effort, with M. V. Frunze, A. I. Yegorov, K. Ye. Voroshilov, M. N. Tukhachevsky, I. P. Uborevich, V. K. Blücher, G. D. Gay, G. I. Kotovsky, V. K. Putna, S. K. Timoshenko, V. I. Chapayev, I. E. Yakir, F. Raskolnikov, S. Budyonny, V. Stalin, and former tsarist officers S. S. Kamenev, and B. M. Shaposhnikov, directing individual operations.

After the peace treaty between the newly independent Ukraine and Germany (Feb. 1918), control of this territory changed hands nine times in 23 months. The Ukraine was occupied successively by the Bolsheviks in Feb. 1918; the Germans, who in March set up Hetman Skoropadsky as puppet ruler; the Ukrainian Socialists who under Petlyura overthrew Skoropadsky in Nov.; the Bolsheviks in Feb. 1919; Denikin in the fall of 1919; the Bolsheviks again in Dec. 1919; the Poles in May 1920; and finally the Bolsheviks in Dec. 1920.

In the Baltic region, the Germans continued to predominate even after the Nov. 1918 armistice. However, a White army under General Yudenich was repulsed in its attempt to seize Petrograd by a force under Trotsky (Oct. 1919). In 1920, the Soviet government recognized the independence of Estonia, Latvia, Lithuania, and Finland.

Attempting to reopen the E. front and to protect their supplies, Allied troops landed in Murmansk and Archangel in the summer of 1918. Unable to agree among themselves on the extent of their intervention, their activities were scattered and disorganized. There was some fighting between the Allies and the Bolsheviks during the spring of 1919. But the W. troops were withdrawn in the autumn, the Bolsheviks recapturing the two N. ports, Sept.–Oct. 1919.

In the S., efforts by the Bolsheviks in Jan. 1919 to reconquer Armenia, Georgia, and Azerbaijan (which had declared their independence, Apr.–May 1918) were defeated by the White army under Denikin. Both Britain and France had troops in this area, Britain in Batum and Baku, and France in Odessa. The French troops, however, were of little value, as their will to fight was sapped by Bolshevik propaganda. From the British, Denikin received supplies and, thus bolstered, began his 1919 offensive north in the direction of Moscow. His path was barred by the Bolshevik garrison at Tsaritsyn (now Stalingrad) which, under the command of Stalin, Voroshilov, and Budyonny, delayed the

White advance and fatally exhausted its momentum. Subsequently Denikin's troops were driven back to the Black Sea coast. Their last stronghold fell in March 1920 and Denikin turned over his command to General Wrangel (q.v.). At first very successful, Wrangel's troops finally wilted before intensified Bolshevik attacks and were evacuated by Allied ships to Constantinople in Nov. 1920.

In the E., British, French, Japanese, and American troops landed at Vladivostok, Aug. 1918. Before the month was out, Red resistance in the maritime provinces of Siberia was crushed and the Japanese, intent on annexation, were in possession of considerable territory between Vladivostok and Chita. At the same time, the Czech Legion, on its way, via Siberia, to the W. front, came into armed conflict with local Bolsheviks. The Czechs seized control of the Trans-Siberian railway and, linking up with White forces, extended their operations to the Volga area.

Meanwhile, an autonomous Siberian government had been established at Omsk. It now merged with the anti-Bolshevik Socialist government at Ufa. In a coup (Nov. 1918), the Socialists were ousted and Admiral A. V. Kolchak was proclaimed head of an "All-Russian" government. Aided by British forces in the area, Kolchak prepared an offensive into E. Russia which, launched in Jan. 1919, was beaten back by Red forces under Frunze. A Red counteroffensive reached Omsk in Nov. and forced Kolchak to retreat to Irkutsk. In Dec., Kolchak transferred command to Semyonov who was routed a short time later. Kolchak himself was captured and executed by the Bolsheviks, Feb. 1920.

The White disaster brought withdrawal of all Allied forces from Siberia, with the exception of the Japanese who remained until Oct. 1922. The French and British withdrew from the Ukraine and the Caucasus in the spring of 1919. With the Allied evacuation of the N. front later in 1919, foreign intervention in the CW came to an end. By 1920 the Bolsheviks were everywhere victorious. Their superior numbers, unified and skillful command, and control of the railways were of immense advantage, while the feebleness of the Allied intervention added still further to the plight of the White forces already plagued by lack of cohesion.

Map of the Russian Civil War (1918-1920)

BIBLIOGRAPHY: John Bunyan, ed., *Intervention, Civil War and Communism in Russia; April-December 1918 Documents and Materials*, Baltimore, 1936; W. H. Chamberlin, *The Russian Revolution, 1917–1921*, Vol. II, New York, 1952; Anton Denikin, *The White Army*, London, 1930; George F. Kennan, *Soviet American Relations, 1917–1920*, Princeton, Vol. I, *Russia Leaves the War* (1956), and Vol. II, *The Decision to Intervene* (1958); Elena Varneck and H. H. Fischer, eds., *The Testimony of Kolchak and Other Siberian Materials*, Stanford, 1935.

M. S.

CLASSES, SOCIAL: *see* SOCIAL STRATIFICATION.

CLASSICISM: *see* LITERATURE, PAINTING, ARCHITECTURE.

CLASS STRUGGLE: *see* MARXISM-LENINISM.

CLIMATE. A diversity in climatic conditions of the USSR is explained by the vastness of its territory stretching from the frozen Arctic Ocean in the N. to the subtropical zone in the S., and by the complicated and diverse relief characteristics. All the basic C types of the earth are found within the USSR, except the climates of tropical forests and of savanna. All the C varieties in the USSR are characterized by a marked difference between the cold and the warm seasons. However, the degree of contrast between winter and summer, the duration of these seasons, and their nature are different in various regions. Everywhere, except the Taymyr Peninsula and the Arctic islands, the maximum summer temperature may attain $+86°$ F and higher. In the winter, the freezing temperatures of $—20°$ F and lower are possible everywhere except the Black Sea coast in the Crimea and the Caucasus.

The C of **the European part of the USSR** is greatly influenced by the Atlantic Ocean. Although situated several hundreds of miles west of the USSR, the Atlantic succeeds in sending air masses which cause an increase in temperature in winter and cool weather in summer. The degree of continentality of C, which is characterized by the range between summer and winter averages of temperatures, rapidly grows in the eastward direction. This difference in Minsk equals $43°$ F, in Moscow $52°$ F, and in Sverdlovsk $59°$ F. The amount of annual precipitation varies between 8 and 28 in., the maximum coming in summer, mainly in July, the minimum in spring. In the N. the snow cover starts in Oct., and in the southernmost areas in late Dec. The snow cover disappears in March-May. The most important agricultural areas, on the average, are free from snow late in March or early in April. The average maximum snow cover varies from 4–8 in. in the S. Ukraine and the N. Caucasus to 24–32 in. in the N.E. (the Komi ASSR). The duration of the snow cover increases from 40–60 days in the S. to 220 days and more in the extreme N.E. Common features of the C of the European part of the USSR are: snow cover in winter with freezing temperatures of $—5°$ F and lower; more cloudiness in winter than in summer; more precipitation in summer than in winter. In summer the precipitation, largely of Atlantic origin, decreases from W. toward the S.E., i.e. in the direction of the arid steppes of the Volga-Ural watershed. In places evaporation exceeds precipitation; there the areas are subjected to periodic droughts.

In **W. Siberia** the continentality becomes more accentuated, as the influence of the Atlantic is reduced. The difference between summer and winter averages changes from $59°$ F in the W. to $72°$ F in the E. The daily changes of temperature are very great. The annual precipitation, which is largely brought from the Atlantic, varies from 16–20 in. in the middle reaches of the Ob and the Yenisey rivers down to 8–12 in. in the extreme S. and N.W. of W. Siberia. There is more precipitation in summer than in winter. In the N. the snow cover sets in Sept., and in the S. in Nov. It thaws in April and May; in the extreme N. the snow cover disappears in early June. The average maximum snow cover in the low reaches of the Ob and the Yenisey rivers attains 32–36 in.; only in the extreme S. does it decrease to 12–16 in. The duration of the snow cover varies from 140 to 260 days and more. The extreme S of W. Siberia lies in the dry zone. The humidity grows northwards and is excessive in the middle reaches of the Ob and the Yenisey rivers.

E. Siberia is the region experiencing about the same, rather slight, influence from both the Atlantic and the Pacific oceans. It has the maximum difference between the summer and the winter averages of temperatures, and the coldest winter, as compared with other areas of the USSR. The amount of annual precipitation lies within the range 4–16 in. The continentality of C is sharply manifested: in Yakutia the difference between the averages of the warmest and the coldest months reaches $108°–117°$ F, mainly owing to the very severe winter. The lowest temperature in the whole world ($—93.6°$ F) was registered at the Verkhoyansk-Oymyakon cold pole. The maximum quantity of precipitation falls in July-August. The snow cover sets late in Sept. and in Oct. The snow thawing continues from late April to early June. The average maximum snow cover on most of the territory is 16–24 in., decreasing to 8–12 in. in the area of the cold pole and to 4 in. in the southernmost areas of E. Siberia. The duration of snow cover varies from 140 days in the S. to 260 days and more in the N. Although the whole region lies within the zone of sufficient humidity, droughts are observed in some years in S. areas.

The **Far East** presents a strip of 300–600 mi. wide, stretching along the Pacific coast. This region has the monsoon C. In winter the wind blows steadily from the N. along the coast. Surface winds blow predominantly from the continent (up to 80–90 per cent of all the winds). Hence, the moderating influence of the Pacific is so small that in Vladivostok, lying at the same altitude as Sochi, winter is colder than in Moscow. In summer the cyclones move along the coast; surface winds prevail from the S. and S.E. Only a relatively narrow coastal region is influenced by the maritime air with respect to temperatures. The precipitation is brought from the Pacific. Summer is rainy and humid. The annual precipitation varies from 4–8 in. on the Chukchi Peninsula to 28–40 in. on the S.W. Kamchatka and in the Maritime Kray where the amount of precipitation in Aug. and Sept. is 10–11 times more than in Jan. and Feb. The snow cover sets on Chukchi Peninsula late in Sept., in the Maritime Kray early in Nov. The snow begins to thaw in May and disappears on Kamchatka and the Chukchi Peninsula in June. The maximum depth of snow cover is 32–40 in. on Sakhalin and exceeds 48 in. on the S.E. coast of Kamchatka. However, the depth of snow rapidly decreases toward the continent and the S. coastal areas. In the Maritime Kray the snow cover does not exceed 8–16 in., and on the coast of the Okhotsk Sea, 16–20 In. The duration of snow cover varies from 100

CLIMATIC REGIONS OF THE USSR

Arctic regions	
Next coldest	
Hottest	
Dryest	
Sufficient precipitation	

1. Arctic climate: long, severe winters, short cool summers. 2. Long winters, warmer summers. 3. Cold winters, warm summers with sufficient precipitation. 4. Dry winters, damp summers. 5. Raw stormy winters, rainy summers. 6. The steppe region: cold winters, long hot dry summers. 7. Semidesert. 8. Subtropical regions, mild winters, hot summers with abundant rainfall. 9. The "cotton belt," hot, dry, irrigated. 10. Mountain climate.

days in the Vladivostok area to 220–260 days on the Chukchi Peninsula.

Kazakhstan and Central Asia are considerably isolated from the ocean influence. Because of extremely hot summers, the range between summer and winter averages of temperatures is large. There is very little precipitation. The annual amount does not exceed 4–8 in. in most of the territory, and there are localities with less than 4 in. Only in the mountains is the annual amount higher, attaining 28–32 in. in places lying at altitudes exceeding 6,500 ft. The annual course of precipitation is very peculiar: the maximum falls in spring; but in summer there is practically none on the plains, where there is only a slight probability of cloudy sky. Under the influence of heavy insulation all the moisture accumulated in winter and spring rapidly evaporates and all the sun's energy is used for the heating of soil and air. The highest average monthly temperature in the USSR is in Termez (88.5° F in July). Thus there is extreme aridity in summer: in deserts the amount of sun heat obtained during the year is 8 to 10 times more than is necessary for the evaporation of the annual precipitation. Therefore irrigation must be used for agriculture. There is practically no snow cover in the Kara-Kum and Kyzyl-Kum deserts: its maximum depth is less than 4 in.; its duration does not exceed 20 days. Beginning with the latitudes of the Aral Sea, the duration and the depth of the snow cover grow rapidly toward the N., attaining in N. Kazakhstan 160 days and 8–16 in., respectively.

Transcaucasia and the S. coast of Crimea have subtropic C. This is due to the high mountain barriers which prevent the access of cold air from the N., as well as to proximity to the sea and to low altitudes. Summer heat is moderated by the influence of the sea. The range between summer and winter temperature averages is smaller than in the European part of the

USSR. In Sevastopol it equals 70.4° F, in Batumi 85° F, and in Baku 85.4° F. W. Georgia and the Lenkoran area at the Caspian coast are the most humid regions in the USSR, with the warmest winter. In W. Transcaucasia the annual precipitation exceeds 80 in., the largest amount in the USSR being recorded on the mountain slopes there— some 160 in. In E. Transcaucasia the amount is much lower (some 16 in.), while on the S. coast of Crimea it is within the range of 12–24 in., attaining 40 in. in the mountains. The average temperature of the coldest month is close to 32° F, and in places is higher. Sometimes, under the influence of foehns, the temperature in winter rises to 68° F. There is seldom any snowfall and the snow cover usually lies for only several days.

The Arctic. Particular features of the Arctic C are determined by the following factors: (1) no sun heat comes during the polar night, therefore the winter negative radiation balance has a considerable magnitude; (2) large masses of floating ice are typical for summer. Average monthly temperatures of air above the seas of the Arctic Ocean diminish in the W. to E. direction. The average temperature of the coldest month is in the range of 17.6° to 15.8° F at the coast of the Barents Sea, and —13° F to —22° F at the Chukchi Sea. Respective summer averages are 50° F to 59° F, and 35.6° F to 37.4° F. In the center of the Arctic, temperatures of the coldest month are lower than —22° F to —31° F; of the warmest month, close to 32° F. Although winter temperatures are lower in E. Siberia, winter is more uncomfortable in the Arctic, because of the strong winds. The annual precipitation is not high and is mostly within the range of 2.8 to 6 in. There are many days with precipitation, and fog is common, particularly in summers.

BIBLIOGRAPHY: Lev S. Berg, *Natural Regions of the USSR*, John A. Morrison and C. C. Nikiforoff, Eds. New York, 1950.

L. D.

CLODT (CLODT VON JURGENSBURG), Baron Peter Karlovich (1805–1867), sculptor of classical style; prof. of the Academy of Fine Arts. His best works: bronze horse tamers on the Anichkov bridge (1833–50) and the I. A. Krylov Monument in the Summer Garden, both in Leningrad.

COAL. Soviet sources claim that the USSR has the world's largest coal reserves, deposits of economic importance being found in almost all areas. In 1927 the C reserves were calculated for the entire USSR. According to international regulations, these calculations took into account all the C reserves believed, on the basis of geological considerations, to lie down to 1,800 m. below the surface. Thus the total reserves of C to this depth are estimated by Soviet authorities to be 8,669 bill. tons—believed to be about 57 per cent of the world's C reserves—while the measured and indicated reserves total 155 bill. tons. Some 90 per cent of the reserves are found in the E. regions of the USSR, where C basins and deposits, owing to geological conditions, have seams of large thicknesses lying close to the surface, thus favoring open-pit mining in many cases.

In European part of the USSR, the Donets basin, with its coal-bearing strata of Carboniferous age, is of the greatest economic importance, as it contains most of the reserves of the Ukraine and all those of N. Caucasus. All the basic categories of C are encountered there, including coking C and anthracite. In the European N., in the Pechora basin of Lower Permian age, lie rich deposits, which include, among other categories, also coking C. The Carboniferous sedimentary strata which compose the Moscow basin abound in lignite. Numerous Tertiary lignite deposits are found in the Ukraine, W. from the Dnieper River, and on the W. slope of the Urals, and C deposits of Carboniferous age in the Urals, in the Kizel, Yegorshino, and other districts. The principal C deposits in the Caucasus are in Tkvarcheli and Tkibuli. Among numerous and rich deposits of Kazakhstan, the Karaganda coal basin is of greatest importance; it contains also coking C. The Kushmurun and other deposits of the Ubagan basin in the Kustanay Oblast of Kazakhstan supply C for Ural industry. Many deposits of C and lignite of Jurassic age are found in Central Asia. The principal C base in Siberia is the Kuznetsk basin which contains Carboniferous, Permian, and Jurassic high-grade C of various categories, including coking C, its measured reserves being 22 per cent of the total Soviet reserves. Also of great importance is the vast Tungus C-bearing area in the basin of the Angara, and the Middle and Lower Tunguska rivers; as well as the rich deposits of the Irkutsk (Cheremkhovo) basin, suitable for metallurgy, gasification, and the extraction of liquid fuels. Vast reserves of lignite are concentrated in the Lena basin. Numerous C deposits are found in Transbaykalia, for example, Bukachacha, Gusinoye Ozero, and Kharanora. The Far East, Sakhalin, and Kamchatka also abound in coal deposits, the most important of which are: the reserves along the Bureya River, making up the so-called Bureya basin; the Kivda-Raychikhinsk; the Suchan; and the Sakhalin.   L. D.

COAL MINING. Coal mining provided 56% of the total energy resources in the Soviet economy in 1959. Of 506 mill. tons mined in that year 365 mill. tons were bituminous coal (including 79 mill. tons of anthracite) and 141 mill. tons were lignite (compared with 388 mill. tons of bituminous coal in the United States and 209 mill. tons in the United Kingdom). The principal deposits are those of the Donets basin (36% of total production in 1958); of the Kuznetsk basin (15%); the Ural deposits (12%); the Moscow deposits (9%); and the deposits of E. Siberia (7%). Among the less important deposits are those of Karaganda (5%); of the Far E. provinces (4%); and of the Pechora basin (3%). Despite more than a sevenfold increase in production since 1913, the share of the Donbas in the national coal output has declined from 87% in 1913 to 36.5% in 1959, because of the shift to the east. The rapid growth of coal production (a more than tenfold in-

crease during the planning period 1928–58) has been achieved through an extensive mechanization of individual processes and an emphasis on open-pit mining (20% in 1959) as well as through the exploitation of new deposits.

COAL OUTPUT IN USSR
(thous. tons)

	1913	1940	1956	1959
TOTAL	29,117	165,923	429,174	506,557
including:				
Donets Basin	25,288	94,319	154,120	185,060
Kuznetsk Basin	774	22,487	66,154	79,857
Ural	1,217	11,956	52,305	61,886
E. Siberia	847	9,229	28,915	36,543
Moscow Basin	300	10,093	42,198	47,076

P. I. M.

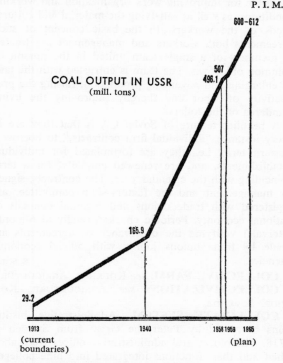

COAL OUTPUT IN USSR
(mill. tons)

600–612

507
496.1

165.9

29.2

1913 (current boundaries)   1940   1958 1959 1965 (plan)

COEXISTENCE POLICY: *see* FOREIGN POLICY.
COLD WAR: *see* FOREIGN POLICY.
COLLECTIVE AGREEMENTS. During the first decade of the postrevolutionary era Soviet CA bore a certain external resemblance to those of W. Europe. The Soviet Labor Code promulgated in 1922 defines the collective agreement as a contract stipulating terms of employment and working conditions for industrial establishments, economic enterprises and institutions, singly or in a group. In time CA lost their original significance with respect to all matters directly regulated by law, or by administrative rulings based thereon. They had become mere paper records which reiterated the content of the existing labor laws but made no provisions for any possible improvements. Thus CA in the Soviet Union had very early been divorced from the pioneering function they performed in the West, where they often anticipated progressive labor legislation. In the matter of wages, however, which could not be fully regulated by law, the collective agreement retained for a long time the nature of an authentic labor contract between two independent parties. In the early thirties wage administration was placed under exclusive juris-

diction of central economic agencies, which rendered the collective agreement meaningless (*see* TRADE UNIONS). During 1933–35 CA had gradually disappeared from practice and were not revived until 1947, when they became associated with different objectives.

In its present form the collective contract, in Soviet practice, is an agreement between factory management and trade-union committee stipulating commitments by both parties, including the entire working force and salaried personnel of the establishment, to fulfill and over-fulfill the planned production schedule. By the terms of agreement the management is also made responsible for improving work organization and working conditions, as well as satisfying the material and cultural needs of the workers. In the basic concept of such agreements both workers and management are treated as members of a single team united in the pursuit of common objectives. The team is entrusted with the task of enlarging and advancing production, raising the productivity of labor and thereby improving the living standards of the toilers.

A peculiar feature of Soviet CA is that they are in every instance "individual firm contracts," to borrow a western term, i.e., they are formulated for individual establishments, and are renewed annually, for a term coinciding with the calendar year. The contracts, signed by management and the factory-shop committee, are registered with trade unions and regional councils of national economy. Periodic checks (usually at 6-month intervals) verifying the observance of agreements are made by trade unions jointly with official economic agencies.   S. SCH.

COLLECTIVE FARM: *see* KOLKHOZ, AGRICULTURE.

COLLECTIVIZATION: *see* AGRICULTURE, KOLKHOZ, SOVKHOZ.

COLLEGIATE SYSTEM. Administrative institutions borrowed by Peter the Great from Sweden in 1718. The old central administrative offices were abolished and their functions integrated into nine colleges, each operating under the direction of a collegiate board. The system did not function well and was abolished by Alexander I in 1802.

COMBINE: *see* INDUSTRIAL MANAGEMENT AND ORGANIZATION.

COMECON: *see* COUNCIL FOR ECONOMIC MUTUAL ASSISTANCE.

COMINFORM. The Cominform (Communist Information Bureau, Informbureau) was set up at a meeting in Poland, Sept. 22–27, 1947, attended by representatives of the CPs of the Soviet Union, Bulgaria, Czechoslovakia, Hungary, Poland, Rumania, Yugoslavia, France and Italy. Belgrade was chosen as its headquarters. "The task of the Information Bureau will be to organize interchange of experience among the Parties, and if need be to coordinate their activities on the basis of mutual agreement." It had no statutes, and did not claim to be a single international party, as the Comintern had. Its establishment reflected the new "hard" line that was then shaping Soviet foreign policy, with the final breakdown of attempts at postwar cooperation among the Allies, and the realization in Moscow that independent action by the governments in its E. European sphere of influence might embarrass its own policy or take forms of which it disapproved. The conference decided, "in view of the negative effect caused by the absence of contacts among the Parties represented . . . to set up an Information Bureau." Czechoslovakia and Poland had had to be dissuaded from attending the conference from which the Marshall Plan emerged (the Soviet Union had decided not to attend, fearing an opening for the United States in E. Europe), and Bulgaria and Yugoslavia had considered the possibility of federation, which might well have extended to neighboring countries and led to a Balkan Federation excluding and relatively independent of the USSR.

The two main reports at the conference were given by A. A. Zhdanov and Gomulka; from these, and the resolutions based on them, CPs could deduce their policy. In the six E. European countries their first task was to consolidate their leadership; this meant the elimination of independent socialist and peasant parties (in Czechoslovakia the policy was crowned by the Communist coup of Feb. 1948). The French and Italian parties had to regain their leading positions in the labor movement; they were severely criticized for having let slip the opportunity to seize power offered by their strong position after the war. The French and Italian delegates admitted their errors, and on their return home concentrated on the organization of industrial strikes and propaganda against United States action in Europe. The resolutions elaborated the theme of "two world camps," and asserted that as the United States had begun to organize the capitalist world for its aggressive plans, the socialist states had to defend themselves and defeat the aggressor.

At a meeting in Jan. 1948 in Yugoslavia the Bureau appointed the Soviet journalist-philosopher P. F. Yudin as editor of the paper, *For a Lasting Peace, For a People's Democracy*, first issued in Nov. 1947.

The only memorable event in the Cominform's brief and inglorious career was the expulsion of the Yugoslav CP. This was announced in a communiqué dated June 28, 1948. The resolution, passed in the absence of the Yugoslavs who refused to attend the meeting of the Bureau, accused them of deviations from Marxism-Leninism, of unfriendliness toward the USSR, and of incorrect policies at home. The policy of the Yugoslav leaders, described as disgraceful, bureaucratic, and terrorist, "threatened the very existence of the CP of Yugoslavia." The basis of their mistakes was the dominance won by "nationalist elements" who thought they could "curry favor with the imperialist states." The members of the Yugoslav party were summoned to replace them by new "internationalist" leaders. It was stated that the Bureau's headquarters had been transferred to Bucharest.

It is clear from the Yugoslav statement of June 29, 1948 which rejected all the charges, and from the preceding correspondence between Moscow and Belgrade which was published shortly afterwards, that the dispute went back to 1945, and arose from Yugoslav resistance to Soviet efforts to assert comprehensive control over Yugoslav policies; resistance was regarded as "anti-Soviet."

Immediately, in the communist press throughout the world, an intense campaign was mounted against Yugoslavia, in which its leaders were vilified and the population called on to revolt against them; economic pressure was also applied by the USSR and its European allies, counteracted to some extent by economic aid from the W. powers. The unscrupulous violence of the campaign led to a number of resignations from CPs outside the Soviet bloc.

The repercussions of the dispute were severe. Moscow was bent on eliminating those leaders in the E. European CPs suspected of sympathy with Tito's stand for independence. Subservience to Moscow, described as "proletarian internationalism," became the touchstone of orthodoxy. This eventually led to a series of demotions, arrests, and trials in which a number of prominent Communists disappeared. Some, like Rajk in Hungary, Kostov in Bulgaria, Xoxe in Albania, and Slansky and thirteen others in Czechoslovakia, were executed; others, like Gomulka in Poland, were disgraced and imprisoned. Bierut, leading the attack on Gomulka, accused him of failing to understand the implications of the polarization of world forces. "Now, more than ever, the attitude towards the USSR becomes the touchstone of loyalty to the cause of socialism."

The Bureau met again in Hungary in Nov. 1949 and passed a resolution on "The CP of Yugoslavia in the Power of Assassins and Spies" which stated that "the Tito fascist nationalist clique have become agents of international imperialist reaction" and "spies in the service of the imperialists." The dispute continued unabated until the death of Stalin in March 1953 made it possible for the new Soviet leaders to discard a policy which had failed. Reconciliation was demonstrated by Khrushchev's visit to Belgrade in 1955. The Bureau does not appear to have met after 1949 except to dissolve itself. Mikoyan announced its dissolution on April 17, 1956. In an interview given shortly afterwards, Togliatti said the decision had been taken during the CPSU congress in Feb. and then ratified by the central committees of the parties concerned; the Cominform had not been an entirely satisfactory body, its biggest mistake was to expel Yugoslavia; contacts between CPs would be maintained by ad hoc conferences and bilateral meetings. The dissolution was clearly designed as a moral indemnity paid to Tito, and as a gesture which would be appreciated by the neutralist countries whose good will the USSR was out to win. (*See also* COMINTERN, CPSU)

BIBLIOGRAPHY: Royal Institute of International Affairs, *The Soviet-Yugoslav Dispute*, London, 1948; Denis Healey, ed., *The Curtain Falls*, London, 1951; E. Halperin, *The Triumphant Heretic*, London, 1958; *Meeting of the Information Bureau of Communist Parties*, Published by the Journal *For a Lasting Peace, For a People's Democracy*, 1950.
                                                              J. D.

COMINTERN: *see* COMMUNIST INTERNATIONAL.

COMMANDER (*Komandórskie*) **ISLANDS,** a group of islands S. of Kamchatka Peninsula in S.W. Bering Sea, part of Kamchatka Oblast; area 713 sq. mi.; chief islands Bering (on which the explorer Vitus Bering died in 1741) and Medny, several small islands (Topor-

kov and others); pop. Russians, Eskimos. Hilly tundra; maritime climate with cool summers and temperate winters. Hunting ground for blue fox, fur seal, sea beavers; fur tanning, fishing. Named after Bering as he held the rank of a commander.

COMMITTEE FOR THE SALVATION OF THE COUNTRY AND THE REVOLUTION, organized in late Oct. 1917 by the municipal administration of Petrograd under the leadership of Abram R. Gots. It was composed of representatives of the municipal council, of the Soviets of Workers', Soldiers', and Peasants' Deputies, and of all the socialist groups opposing Bolshevik rule. In an appeal to the people the committee urged them not to comply with the orders of the Bolsheviks and to support the overthrown Provisional Government; an unsuccessful uprising of the cadets in the military schools was organized. Committee broke up in November of the same year.

COMMUNE: *see* PEASANTS, POPULISM, AGRICULTURE.

COMMUNIST, THE, a publication. *See* KOMMUNIST.

COMMUNIST ACADEMY. On June 25, 1918, the Soviets established an Academy of Social Science to study and teach the social and related sciences in line with scientific socialism and communism. The name was changed to Communist Academy in 1923. The Academy was directed to defend Marxism-Leninism, advocate dialectical materialism in the social and natural sciences, and obliterate the last vestiges of "idealism," all under the supervision of the party's Central Committee. Soon problems connected with the five year plans became the Academy's main concern. It set up several institutes, among which the Agrarian, established in 1933 to study collective farm reconstruction, was particularly important. In 1935, the Communist Academy was dissolved and its institutes transferred to the Academy of Sciences.

COMMUNIST INFORMATION BUREAU: *see* COMINFORM.

COMMUNIST INTERNATIONAL. The Communist International (Comintern, CI) was founded in March 1919, 16 months after the Bolsheviks seized power in Russia. Lenin had contemplated the step from the outbreak of war in 1914, when the Second (Socialist) International virtually broke down into its constituent parties, each supporting its government. The idea was embodied in his "April (1917) theses" (q.v.), the first document he produced in Russia after his return from exile in Switzerland. The Bolsheviks believed that the proletariat, particularly in Europe, were in a revolutionary mood and were being held back from direct action only by the timidity and cowardice of their leaders who were preparing to cooperate with the capitalists to restore the old order. If the industrial workers could be rescued from the influence of these leaders (described as social-patriots, social-chauvinists, traitors, and capitalist lackeys) and given conscious revolutionary leadership, they would move forward to the conquest of political power. The Bolsheviks also believed that the young Soviet state could not survive unless successful revolutions elsewhere brought them aid. On both counts, therefore, world revolution was their goal.

The appeal, "to convene the first congress of a new revolutionary International," signed on behalf of the Bolsheviks by Lenin and Trotsky, was published Jan. 24, 1919. Conditions in Europe were extremely disturbed, and only five delegates specifically sent for this purpose reached Moscow. The others were Russians or foreigners present in Russia. The congress met March 2–6, 1919, with 35 voting delegates representing 19 organizations, and 19 nonvoting participants. The German delegate Eberlein had been instructed by the recently formed German CP (KPD) to oppose the formation of a new International as premature, and to suggest the drafting of a provisional platform to be used to ascertain the strength of like-minded forces in other countries, but he was persuaded to abstain from voting when on March 4 the resolution to constitute the meeting the first congress of the Third (Communist) International was carried. It adopted a platform aimed at the destruction of the bourgeois capitalist order by "methods of mass action leading logically to direct clashes with the bourgeois state machine in open struggle," and a resolution condemning the re-formed Socialist International as "a yellow strike-breaking International which is and will remain nothing but a tool of the bourgeoisie"; it issued an appeal to the workers of all countries to act against foreign intervention in Russia and to agitate for the recognition of the Soviet government, and a manifesto which, surveying the origins and consequences of the war, linked the struggle in Europe with the aspirations of nationalist movements elsewhere. "Colonial slaves of Asia and Africa! The hour of proletarian dictatorship in Europe will also be the hour of your own liberation." Zinoviev was elected president of the Comintern. In Oct. 1919 it began to issue its own periodical, *The Communist International,* in a number of languages. CPs were established in a number of countries, some from already existing organizations and groups (as in England), others by a breakaway from the main Socialist party (as in France).

The second congress (July 19–Aug. 7, 1920) was attended by 217 delegates from 41 countries. (The figures should not be taken too seriously; many so-called CPs then existed only on paper, or were small ill-organized groups.) It agreed on conditions of admission to the CI (known as the "21 points") and adopted statutes making the CI a highly centralized body; it was to be "a single communist party of the entire world" with national sections whose aim was "to fight by all available means, including armed struggle, for the overthrow of the international bourgeoisie and the creation of an international Soviet republic" as the only way "to liberate mankind from the horrors of capitalism. . . . In its ranks the white, the yellow, and the black-skinned peoples—the working people of the entire world—are fraternally united." The statutes also envisaged the formation of a revolutionary trade-union International (Profintern, RILU) (q.v.), set up the same year. Comintern trade-union policy, always ambiguous and at times contradictory, led to many difficulties, the chief dispute being whether Communists should work in "reformist" trade unions and try to capture them, or break away and start separate unions. The colonial theses

drafted by Lenin laid the foundation for communist strategy in colonial and dependent countries. Between congresses authority was vested in an Executive Committee (ECCI) composed of representatives of the sections; it had a large permanent staff in which Russians, Germans, and Hungarians predominated. After a number of reorganizations the work of the ECCI was arranged by regional secretariats controlled by a presidium, which was in fact if not in theory controlled by the Russian CP.

By the time the third congress met a number of events had shown that the period of acute postwar disturbance and sporadic uprisings was over. In Russia herself the government had retreated into the moderate New Economic Policy after the Kronstadt uprising (q.v.); in Germany the failure of the attempted insurrection in March 1921 had dashed revolutionary hopes. The congress (June 22–July 12, 1921), attended by 509 delegates from 48 countries, had to reshape CI policy. If the leadership of the workers could not be captured for immediate revolutionary purposes, Communists had to adapt themselves to the new conditions. Lenin used a military analogy: the CI must turn from tactics of assault to tactics of siege, and the CPs had to work to win leading positions in socialist parties and trade unions and wean the workers from their "democratic illusions." These infiltration tactics were embodied in the theses on the united front adopted at the end of 1921 and endorsed by the fourth congress a year later. At this congress (Nov. 5–Dec. 5, 1922) there were 408 delegates from 58 countries. In 1924, when the fifth congress met (June 17–July 8; 510 delegates from 49 countries) the debates were dominated by the quarrels which arose after the abortive attempt at insurrection in Germany in Oct. 1923, and by the disputes in the Russian CP, following Lenin's death, which were then coming into the open. Their repercussions involved the fall of Trotsky, the dismissal of Zinoviev from the post of Comintern president (the post itself was abolished) in 1926, and sweeping changes in the leadership of a number of CPs. "Trotskyism" (q.v.) became the chief heresy. United front tactics, exemplified in the alliance with the Kuomintang in China and the Anglo-Soviet trade-union committee, both of which ended in failure, held the field until 1928, when the sixth congress ratified the "class against class" tactics adopted earlier in the year by the ninth plenary session of the ECCI. At this congress (July 17–Sept. 1; 532 delegates from 57 countries), the CI adopted its program, drafted by Bukharin. On the grounds that labor and socialist parties were no longer representative of the working class, but "the left wing of the bourgeoisie," while the rank and file were moving to the left in a situation that was growing steadily more revolutionary, the CI adopted a position of outright and unconcealed hostility to all such parties and decided to run Communist against labor candidates in elections, and so forth. Again, the change in the Comintern line paralleled a similar change inside the USSR, where NEP gave way to forced industrialization and collectivization, leading to the disappearance of the small farmer, trader, and citizen, "the liquidation of the kulaks as a class," and elimination of Bukharin and others who opposed these measures. The new policy created great uneasiness in some parties (e.g., the French and British) and had disastrous results in Germany where, in the attempt to destroy their socialist rivals and to weaken the "bourgeois-democratic" Weimar Republic, the KPD played straight into the hands of Hitler. Even in 1932, less than a year before the Nazis came to power, the ECCI and the KPD were declaring their "chief fire" had to be directed against the Socialist party, which was a greater danger to the workers than the Nazis. After Hitler's triumph, and with the realization of the threat he represented to the USSR, a gradual reorientation of policy introduced "popular front" tactics, first adopted in France in 1934 and later extended to the entire International at its seventh and final congress in 1935. Popular front tactics envisaged cooperation with all anti-fascist groups and organizations and had considerable success in a number of countries, particularly in France and Spain. In a local variant, these tactics were adopted in China as representing national opposition to Japanese aggression. It was a counterpart to the change in Soviet foreign policy represented by the entry of the USSR into the League of Nations, by its pacts of mutual assistance with France and Czechoslovakia, and by the reestablishment of diplomatic relations with Kuomintang China.

On the outbreak of war in 1939 the CPs were in a more than usually equivocal position. This was the war against fascism which was the logical goal of their popular front policy, but since the USSR had entered into friendly agreements with Hitler a mere week before war broke out, the CPs had to swing into line, withdraw their original statements in support of the war, and condemn it as "imperialist" (the dilemma of the Polish party would have been even more acute but its leaders, in exile in the Soviet Union, had been "liquidated" in 1938), although few Communists went so far as to repeat Stalin's assertion that the W. allies were responsible for the war, or Molotov's remark that fascism was a matter of taste.

With the German attack on Russia the CPs recovered from their disarray and again swung into line. The war was now a just war against fascism and in defense of democracy, the working class, and civilization. This too had its embarrassing features. In India, for example, the CP, in contrast to the national independence movement, came out in support of the imperialist British government, Russia's ally, which it had from the beginning proclaimed the arch enemy.

On May 22, 1943 it was suddenly announced in Moscow that the Comintern had been dissolved. The statement said the ECCI Presidium had met on May 15 and, because of the increasing complexity of the situation, which put insuperable obstacles in the way of directing work from an international center, the CI form of organization had "become a drag on the further strengthening of the national working class parties." The step was primarily a gesture of conciliation toward Moscow's allies (recently shaken by the Soviet rupture of relations with the Polish government-in-exile in London); Stalin commented that it was designed to "expose the calumny of the adversaries of communism" who asserted that CPs "act not in the interests of their people but on orders from outside" and the Nazi lie that Moscow intended to interfere in other countries. Formal dissolution followed on June 10, after agreement had been received from 31 sections and objections from none. (*See also* COMINFORM, CPSU)

BIBLIOGRAPHY: F. Borkenau, *The Communist International*, London, 1938; E. H. Carr, *A History of Soviet Russia*, New York, Vol. 3, 1953, Vol. 4, 1954; J. Degras, ed., *The Communist International 1919–43: Documents*, London and New York, Vol. 1, 1956, Vol. 2, 1960; H. Seton-Watson, *Pattern of Communist Revolution*, London, 1953; R. H. S. Crossman, ed., *The God That Failed*, London, 1950.

J. D.

COMMUNIST PARTY OF THE SOVIET UNION (CPSU).

The origins of the Communist Party of the Soviet Union can be traced to the development of industry and the simultaneous decline of populism as a political movement toward the end of the 19th century. Two factors characterized the revolutionary movement before 1917. First, because of constant harassment by the tsarist police, political activity, for most of the period, had to be conducted illegally. This led to a dichotomy. Leaders of Marxist groups faced arrest and imprisonment and upon release or escape were forced to direct revolutionary activity from abroad. Second, the Social-Democratic Party, once established, split irrevocably into two major factions. Despite repeated attempts at reconciliation, the division, caused primarily by personality and sectarian differences on strategy and tactics, remained permanent.

Prerevolutionary Period. Russian Marxism as a political movement developed in the last two decades of the 19th century. A disillusioned populist, G. V. Plekhanov, together with P. B. Akselrod, V. Zasulich, and L. Deutsch, Russian revolutionaries in exile, formed the first Russian Marxist group, "The Emancipation of Labor," in Geneva in 1883. Its primary aim was to form a Social-Democratic Party in Russia and to focus attention not on the peasants, as the Populists had, but on the proletariat as the instrument of revolution.

In Russia growing workers' discontent, manifested in a wave of strikes, caused the organization of workers' groups in various cities and sections of the empire. A Polish Socialist Party was formed in 1888. In St. Petersburg, capitalizing on workers' unrest, Lenin and Martov founded the "Union of Struggle for the Emancipation of the Working Class" in 1895, because of which Lenin was arrested and exiled to Siberia. Jewish Social Democrats in W. and S.W. Russia organized the "Bund" in 1897. An attempt to consolidate these and other groups in one party was made in 1898 when the 1st Congress of the Russian Social-Democratic Labor Party (RSDLP) was held in Minsk. The meeting of nine delegates, who were soon to be arrested, was far from representative and the Congress exercised little practical influence.

In 1900, Lenin finished his penal exile and went abroad to play a prominent role in the Marxist movement, unyielding, despite continuous opposition, in his determination to lead the party along his chosen revolutionary path. On Lenin's initiative a newspaper, *Iskra* (The Spark) was founded with Lenin, Martov, Potresov (the three representing the younger Marxists), Plekhanov (the most influential R. Marxist), Zasulich, and Akselrod members of the editorial board. Despite quarrels among the editors they were united in opposing the "Economists," R. Marxists whose organ *Rabocheye Delo* (Workers' Task) was accused by *Iskra* of emphasizing the realization of immediate economic gains for workers, and minimizing the political struggle.

During this period Lenin developed the principles on party organization which were to have a profound influence in determining the nature of the party. In *What Is to Be Done?*, published in March 1902, Lenin stressed the necessity, if the revolution were to succeed, for organizing a small, centrally controlled, and disciplined party of professional revolutionaries to lead the workers' movement.

The 2nd Congress of the RSDLP, held in Brussels and London, July-August 1903, may be considered the constituent congress of the party. It also gave birth to the Bolshevik and Menshevik factions which irrevocably split the party despite repeated attempts at reconciliation through the years. The Congress was not called until the *Iskra*-ites were certain of a safe majority to carry through their program. At the Congress, however, a split developed within the *Iskra* group when Lenin and Martov disagreed on the nature of the party membership. Lenin advocated that membership should be restricted to a small number of dedicated revolutionaries, while Martov desired a broad party open to all who accepted the party program and who were willing to obey the central leadership. Lenin's proposal was defeated 28–23. Martov, however, soon lost his majority, which had depended upon five Bundist and two Economist delegates, when they walked out of the meeting in protest over action taken by the Congress. The Bundists walked out because the Congress rejected the Bund's claim to autonomy. The Economists left the Congress because Congress decided that the *Iskra* group was to be the sole representative of the party abroad.

By the accident of their departure Lenin received a working majority which he exploited in order to elect himself and his supporters to the central party organs: the editorial board of *Iskra* with only Plekhanov (who supported Lenin at the Congress), Lenin, and Martov as editors; a Central Committee to function in Russia which was entirely composed of Bolsheviks; and a Party Council of five members (two from *Iskra,* two from the Central Committee, and one elected by the Congress) to settle any disputes which might arise. It was this victory which gave Lenin's supporters the name Bolsheviks (majority) while his opponents were called Mensheviks (minority). The appellations remained even when the Mensheviks were in the majority at future party meetings.

Lenin's success was of short duration. Plekhanov, desirous of healing the breach with Martov, acceded to the latter's demand that the original six-member editorial board of *Iskra* be reinstated. Lenin, in protest, resigned and *Iskra* became a Menshevik organ in Nov. 1903. Lenin was further isolated. He lost support in the Central Committee—his request to call a new Party Congress (an attempt to regain control over all party organs) was refused by that committee.

Rallying the remnants of his support, Lenin formed the Bureau of the Committees of the Party Majority to rival the Central Committee, and by the end of 1904 published a new paper, *Vpered* (Forward), with the help of A. A. Bogdanov. Lenin finally succeeded in calling a 3rd Party Congress (London, April–May 1905) which, however, the Mensheviks boycotted by holding their own meeting in Geneva at the same time.

The revolution of 1905 drew the Bolsheviks and Mensheviks closer together. Joint committees were formed in many R. cities as thousands of new members flocked to the party, unconcerned with past differences. Despite the fact that most of the party leaders returned to Russia, the RSDLP in the main could only encourage but not lead the workers' movement. It was, however, active in organizing and participating in Soviets of Workers' Deputies which sprang up in various parts of the country. The most striking party figure during the revolution was L. D. Trotsky (he was aligned with neither faction) who at the age of twenty-six became chairman of the St. Petersburg Soviet and the party's most eloquent speaker. The revolution came to an end when a Bolshevik-inspired uprising failed in Moscow in Dec. 1905.

The 4th or "Unity" Party Congress which was held in Stockholm (April 1906) met in a spirit of optimism. The party had greatly increased its membership and some 36,000 workers took part in electing 111 voting delegates of which 62 were Mensheviks and 49 were Bolsheviks. The Mensheviks dominated the Congress, elected a Central Committee composed of seven Mensheviks and three Bolsheviks, and determined the program and resolutions which were passed. Although the Congress adopted the Leninist concept of a disciplined, centralized party organization, Lenin was unsuccessful in determining the rest of the program. An important organizational development was the admission of the Bund and the Polish and Latvian Social Democratic parties, giving them the balance of voting power at future congresses.

The unity achieved at the 4th Congress was precarious. The Bolsheviks never ceased in their aggressive opposition, for almost immediately Lenin made plans to call for a new congress. A secret Bolshevik Center was formed to direct activity, a Bolshevik paper maintained, and efforts to capture local committees from Menshevik control continued.

In numbers of delegates, the Bolsheviks had a slight advantage over the Mensheviks when the 5th Congress assembled in London (May 1907). The Bolsheviks, however, were not able to establish a dependable majority because the decisive votes rested with the Bund and the Polish and Latvian Social Democrats. Nevertheless Lenin succeeded in having the Congress condemn the Menshevik policy of cooperating with the Kadets in the Duma and in defeating the Akselrod proposal that the RSDLP should be transformed into a mass labor party. The Bolsheviks themselves suffered defeat when their policy of expropriation (armed robbery as a source of party income) was decisively censured. Despite the disapproval, raids of expropriation were not immediately abandoned by the Bolsheviks and were to cause Lenin further embarrassment during the next few years.

From 1907 on the party went into years of decline as the tsarist regime increased its repressive measures. The Social Democratic members of the 2nd Duma were arrested and imprisoned, and the legal party newspapers were shut down. Arrests decimated party ranks and police spies infiltrated those cells which remained. Party membership dropped precipitously from an estimated high of 100,000 to less than 10,000.

In addition to the renewed tsarist repression both factions were rent by internal dissension. The Menshevik ranks were split into several groups, the largest number distributed between those who advocated the abandoning of illegal activity to work openly for a mass party (called Liquidators by Lenin) and those who stressed the necessity of continuing illegal organization. Lenin found his leadership of the Bolshevik faction challenged by the Boycotters, the *Otzovists* (Recallers), and the Ultimatists (all three of whom to different degrees opposed the participation of the Social Democrats in the Duma) and by those who spawned the philosophical heresies of God-Constructing and Empiriocriticism which were alien to Lenin's interpretation of Marx. Lenin was successful in having these groups denounced at a Bolshevik conference in June 1909 and their leaders expelled. The dissidents formed a new group, the *Vpered*-ist Bolsheviks and had the distinction of organizing the first party school in Capri in 1909, a feat which Lenin was not able to duplicate until 1911 when he conducted a party school at Longjumeau, a suburb of Paris.

Lenin was less successful in overcoming the opposition of the Conciliators, certain Bolsheviks who desired a united party and peace with all factions. At a plenary meeting of the party's Central Committee in Paris, Jan. 1910, Lenin found himself in the minority of the party and of the Bolshevik faction. The conference voted to unite and to cooperate on leading party committees in and outside of Russia and to publish a single party paper, *Sotsial Demokrat,* dissolving the separate factional organs.

The attempt at unity failed as new exacerbations, stemming from past differences, soon developed. Mensheviks, distrustful of Bolshevik motives, refused to cooperate with them inside Russia. Lenin on his part denied Martov, an editor of *Sotsial Demokrat,* (and leader of the majority of the last party conference), the right to publish signed articles in what was supposed to be the paper of a united party. Martov retaliated and widened the split by publicly accusing Lenin of complicity in Bolshevik raids of expropriation.

Lenin spent most of 1911 plotting for a final break with all those who opposed his policies. To this end Lenin, without authorization, called an All-Russian Party Conference which met in Prague in Jan. 1912. The hand-picked "Rump Parliament" which assembled was composed of only fourteen voting delegates, constituted itself as a party conference, passed a number of resolutions, and elected an all-Bolshevik Central Committee to replace the multi-factional one elected at the 5th Party Congress. It included Lenin, Zinoviev,

Ordzhonikidze, Spandaryan, and Malinovsky (who turned out to be a police agent). Stalin, who did not attend the conference, was soon thereafter co-opted to the Central Committee by Lenin. The Prague Conference marked the decisive rupture between the Menshevik and Bolshevik factions. Various attempts to restore unity failed including the endeavor to place the dispute before a Congress of the Second International for arbitration. The Congress, which was scheduled to convene in August 1914, never met because war intervened.

With the advent of war the tsarist government increased its repressive measures which made agitational and underground activity difficult. The Social Democratic organs, the Bolshevik *Pravda* (Truth) and the Menshevik *Luch* (Ray), which had been published legally since 1912 were closed. The Bolshevik Duma deputies (both Bolshevik and Menshevik representatives had voted against the regime's war budget) were arrested at the end of 1914. Although Lenin maintained contact with the Bolshevik organizations in Russia through the Russian Bureau of the Central Committee, consisting of Shlyapnikov and Molotov, their activity was limited.

Seizure of Power. Lenin-Trotsky Period. The Bolsheviks played no significant role in fomenting the February revolution of 1917. Yet within eight months they succeeded in seizing power. Before Lenin's return to Russia, the Bolsheviks, led by Kamenev and Stalin, both back from exile since March, urged a conciliatory policy regarding the Provisional Government, to which Lenin was vigorously opposed. Upon his arrival in Russia, April 3 (16 N. S.) 1917, which was made possible by the German General Staff which provided Lenin with a sealed train to go from Switzerland through Germany, Lenin called for "All Power to the Soviets" which in effect was a demand for immediate socialist revolution. Lenin's program at first met strong opposition within his own party. Kamenev and others believed that Russia had just entered the bourgeois phase and was not ready for socialist revolution. Before long, however, Lenin won over the Bolsheviks, and at the All-Russian Party Conference, which met April 25 to 30 (May 7 to 12 N. S.), with 151 delegates representing over 70,000 party members, his policy to press for revolution was adopted.

The chances for immediate success were remote. Despite registering gains in party membership among workers the Bolsheviks were still a minority in the Petrograd Soviet. Consequently Lenin urged caution and restrained the overzealous in his ranks, calling off a Bolshevik demonstration planned for June 9 (22 N. S.) when so ordered by the 1st All-Russian Congress of Soviets. Lenin was apprehensive of uniting the Soviet and the Provisional Government against his party by striking prematurely.

Exactly this, however, came to pass during the July riots, July 3–4 (16–17 N. S.). Unruly and armed crowds of workers and soldiers demonstrated against the Provisional Government, calling on the Soviets to seize power. The Provisional Government, which had the support of the majority of the Petrograd Soviet, took forceful action against the Bolsheviks, accusing them of attempting to stage a *coup d'état* and charging Lenin and others with being German agents. Lenin and Zinoviev were forced to flee to escape arrest, but other prominent Bolsheviks, including Trotsky (who had recently joined their party), Kamenev, and Lunacharsky, were imprisoned.

With Bolshevik fortunes at low ebb the 6th Party Congress met *sub rosa* in Petrograd on July 26 (Aug. 8 N. S.). In the absence of many party leaders Stalin and Bukharin were the major figures. Necessarily the policy of "All Power to the Soviets" was abandoned but the party's commitment to insurrection decisively reaffirmed.

Within a month the tide had turned in the Bolsheviks' favor. The Kornilov mutiny helped further to discredit the inept Provisional Government of Kerensky. In Sept. and Oct. the Bolsheviks, for the first time, gained a majority for their resolutions in the Petrograd and Moscow Soviets, as well as in other cities.

In Sept. Lenin (from his Finnish retreat) pressed for an immediate seizure of power by the Bolsheviks, but he was unable to convince the Central Committee until Oct. 10 (23 N. S.) when by a vote of 10–2 it approved the resolution to support immediate insurrection. Kamenev and Zinoviev who voted against the resolution continued their opposition at an enlarged meeting of the Central Committee on Oct. 16 (29 N. S.) after which Kamenev resigned from the body. On Oct. 18 (31 N. S.), to the exasperation of Lenin, Kamenev committed a breach of party discipline by publishing in M. Gorky's *Novaya Zhizn* (New Life) a statement declaring that Zinoviev and he were opposed to an armed uprising. Lenin, angry at the revelation, asked that both be expelled from the party. On Oct. 20 (Nov. 2, N. S.), at a meeting of the Central Committee which Lenin did not attend, Zinoviev and Kamenev were severely censured but not expelled. Since both refrained from any further public declaration they regained favor and Kamenev was taken back into the Central Committee on Oct. 24 (Nov. 6 N. S.), the day before the insurrection.

With Lenin still in hiding Trotsky played the leading role in seizing power. On Oct. 20 (Nov. 2 N. S.) a Military Revolutionary Committee (wholly Bolshevik controlled) of the Petrograd Soviet was organized with Trotsky as chairman. It controlled the Red Guard and other revolutionary detachments. Oct. 25 (Nov. 7 N. S.) was decided upon as the day for insurrection, to coincide with the meeting of the 2nd All-Russian Congress of Soviets. On that day a detachment under the command of the Military Revolutionary Committee seized the Winter Palace and other public buildings, overthrowing the Provisional Government. The Bolsheviks, riding the wave of chaos of revolution, were in power.

Once in control the Bolsheviks were faced with the alternative of governing by minority rule or of sharing power with the two major Socialist parties. Refusal to share power with the Socialist Revolutionaries and the Mensheviks made the prospects for civil war, the suppression of opposition, and the use of terror almost inevitable. Coalition government on the other hand represented a threat to Bolshevik supremacy. In the Central Committee the majority, led by Lenin and Trotsky, favored single party dictatorship, permitting the inclusion of other parties only if Bolshevik hegemony were to be maintained. The majority view was adopted despite the opposition of Zinoviev, Kamenev, and others which led to their resignation from the Central Committee on Nov. 4 (17) for a brief period.

The party leadership was more seriously split on whether to accept the harsh peace terms offered by the Central Powers at Brest Litovsk. Only after a long debate was Lenin's policy, to accept the peace terms in order to preserve Bolshevik rule, adopted at a Central Committee meeting of Feb. 23–24. In March 1918 the hastily summoned 7th Party Congress (only 34 delegates representing 270,000 party members attended) voted to ratify the peace treaty, despite the bitter opposition of N. I. Bukharin and the Left Communists. The Congress also voted to change the party's name to the All-Russian Communist (Bolshevik) Party.

The period of War Communism (1917–21) severely tested the party's ability to survive. The defeat of the White forces, interventionist armies of the Allied Powers, anti-Bolshevik nationalist movements, and a Polish invasion became the paramount consideration. A rapidly deteriorating military and economic situation also forced the party leaders to discard many utopian aspects of Marxian theory. The policy of workers' control of industry (factories run by committees of workers) proved disastrous, and there developed appreciation for the complexity of industrial management and respect for technical skills. The need for incentives to raise labor productivity was recognized, as the attempted transformation from capitalism to socialism created far more serious problems than were anticipated. Within the party, opposition groups formed which were critical of party policies and of the increasing tendency toward centralization which they regarded as a threat to party democracy.

The 8th Party Congress (March 1919) convened immediately after the founding Congress of the 3rd International. It approved important organizational changes. The *Politburo* was reconstituted (it had existed briefly at the time of the seizure of power) to decide all urgent policy matters. An *Orgburo* (Organizational Bureau) was created to make decisions regarding organizational matters which were to be carried out by the *Secretariat*. All three bodies were in theory responsible to the Central Committee which consisted of 19 full members at the time. A new party program was adopted which has not yet been replaced (Summer 1961), although a new program has been promised since 1939. The Congress defeated the proposal of the Military Opposition, a group which opposed the employment of former tsarist officers and the formation of a standing army. The 8th Party Congress also authorized the first large-scale purge to cleanse the party of opportunists who had joined in the wake of the Bolsheviks' triumph and this resulted in the expulsion of approximately half of the 250,000 party members.

The drop in party membership was temporary. New recruits were needed as the tempo of the civil war increased. Party membership reached 612,000 (all party figures of the early period are only an approximation) by the time the 9th Party Congress met in March and April of 1920. At the Congress the role of trade unions was discussed but not resolved. Trade-union supporters objected to Lenin's proposal of introducing one-man management in industry and also viewed with disfavor Trotsky's notion of forming labor armies—but both proposals were adopted by the Congress. Here also the Democratic Centralists emerged as an opposition group calling for more intra-party democracy. The Congress appointed a Secretariat which included: N. N. Krestinsky, Ye. A. Preobrazhensky, and L. P. Serebryakov.

The 10th Party Congress (March 1921) was a turning point in party history. The Congress met amid serious economic crisis, political insurrection, and factional dissension within the party. The civil war had ended, leaving Russia economically exhausted. The radical economic measures of the War Communism period—an attempt to establish communism in one thrust—had failed. Lenin, faced with a bankrupt economy, with production at a near standstill, with a recalcitrant peasantry refusing to deliver grain to the cities, proposed the New Economic Policy (NEP) which was adopted by the Congress. NEP represented a retreat, permitting a return to limited private enterprise and abolishing compulsory grain deliveries hated by the peasants.

The Kronstadt rebellion which took place at the time of the Congress and severely shook the party was symptomatic of widespread dissatisfaction with party policies. The rebellious sailors formed a Provisional Revolutionary Committee (it lasted 15 days) which demanded basic rights that had been denied: free and secret elections to the Soviets; freedom of speech, press, and assembly; the liberation of political prisoners; and the abolition of special privileges for the CP. The mutiny was ruthlessly suppressed by the Bolsheviks and branded counterrevolutionary.

After Kronstadt (the most serious internal threat since the revolution) Lenin was in no mood to countenance factional disputes, chiefly regarding the role of trade unions which had divided the party for some time. At the Congress the *Workers' Opposition* proposed that all matters concerning industry be decided by trade unions. Trotsky countered by advocating that trade unions be incorporated by the state. Finally, Lenin's intermediate program permitting some trade-union autonomy while retaining economic responsibility for the party was overwhelmingly adopted.

The most significant result of the 10th Party Congress was that two resolutions were passed: the first condemning the Workers' Opposition; the second "On Party Unity" ordering all factions to disband at the threat of expulsion. The latter was to have far-reaching consequences. It gave complete sanction to the party leader(s) who controlled the party machinery and denied the opposition the right to organize.

The Congress also replaced the Secretariat with Molotov, Yaroslavsky, and Mikhaylov—the first two, as it happened, staunch supporters of Stalin. A Central Control Commission was also established with the alleged purpose of checking party functionaries. This was later, under Stalin, transformed into an agency which enforced party discipline.

Stalin Period. The next years were marked by Lenin's illness and death and Stalin's rise to power. The 11th Party Congress (March 1922) was the last that Lenin attended. Soon thereafter he suffered the first of three strokes (the last of which in March 1923 effectively terminated his political career) and he died in January 1924. Lenin did not choose a successor although he did, in Dec. 1922, dictate a "Testament" in which he analyzed the merits and weaknesses of the leading Bolshevik candidates. In a Postscript to the Testament Lenin was severely critical of Stalin and advised his removal as General Secretary of the party—a position to which Stalin had been appointed in April 1922. Lenin openly broke with Stalin by letter over the latter's treatment of the Georgian Communists in March 1923, but soon thereafter he suffered his third stroke. This break between Stalin and Lenin was not made public nor was Lenin's Testament used by Trotsky at the time to discredit Stalin. The Testament was read to party leaders in May 1924 but was not published in the Soviet Union until 1956. Thus spared by secrecy, Stalin used every opportunity to don Lenin's cloak and pose as his faithful disciple.

Stalin's triumph represented the victory of the *apparatchiki* (men of the apparatus) over the more colorful party intellectuals who had spent the years before the revolution in *émigré* disputation abroad. Stalin was the only Bolshevik leader to be a member of the three most important party bodies: the Politburo, the Orgburo, and the Secretariat. As General Secretary he was able to place his followers strategically throughout the apparatus including the Central Committee and the Central Control Commission (the latter body sat jointly with the Central Committee after the 12th Party Congress and both were enlarged periodically and packed with Stalin's functionaries), giving him a decisive advantage in controlling the party organization even before Lenin's death.

The fact that Stalin did not yet control the Politburo, and the prestige of Trotsky, who as a revolutionary leader ranked second only to Lenin, caused Stalin to form an alliance with Zinoviev and Kamenev against Trotsky—although he shrewdly stayed in the background during the early part of the controversy which ensued. When Trotsky was successfully removed as commissar of war in Jan. 1925 Stalin turned on his associates and formed a new alliance with the Right-wing members of the Politburo until Trotsky, Zinoviev, and Kamenev were expelled from the party in the fall and winter of 1927. The new Politburo which was elected by the 15th Party Congress (Dec. 1927), consisting of Stalin, Voroshilov, Kalinin, Kuybyshev, Molotov, Rudzutak, Bukharin, Rykov, and Tomsky, gave Stalin a safe majority which he now used to defeat the Right. By the time of the 16th Party Congress (June–July 1930) Bukharin, Tomsky, and Rykov had lost their positions of power and Stalin was in undisputed control of the party.

Ideological factors also entered into the struggle for succession. Stalin's doctrine of "Socialism in One Country" (q.v.), first announced at the end of 1924, clashed with Trotsky's thesis of "Permanent Revolution." In addition Stalin provoked the enmity of the Right by the adoption of his program of rapid industrialization and collectivization in 1928–29 (Bukharin and others believed that the continuance of NEP with a lenient policy as regards the peasantry was essential for the future of socialism in Russia). This program ushered in an era of the five year plans and launched Russia on a new economic and social revolution.

During the 1920's party membership increased significantly, though not consistently. A decline was registered in the early twenties from 730,000 members and candidates in March 1921 to 472,000 by Jan. 1924. Immediately after Lenin's death the trend was reversed. The party embarked on a recruitment drive which saw the membership climb to 1,078,185 by Jan. 1926. The period of the five year plans caused a further rapid expansion of membership which reached a total of 1,674,910 by Jan. 1930 and slightly over 3,500,000 in 1933.

Under Stalin the party became even more sharply centralized and bureaucratized. The General Secretary tightly controlled the party apparatus through a nexus of party secretaries located at various levels of party administration throughout the country. The party ceased being an organ which formulated policies; it was responsible only for their execution. The Party Congress, once a deliberative body, met with decreasing frequency—the 15th Congress in 1927, the 16th Congress in 1930, the 17th Congress in 1934, the 18th Congress in 1939, the 19th Congress in 1952—and was used primarily as a forum to extol the dictator and to propagandize his directives.

The ruthlessness which had become manifest in the application of Stalin's economic program was in the 1930's turned against the party itself in a series of brutal purges, the severest of which was the period of the Great Purge (1936–38), touched off by the assassination in Dec. 1934 of S. M. Kirov, Politburo member and Secretary of the Leningrad party organization. Stalin used the assassination as an excuse to eliminate all real and imagined centers of opposition. The years of stark terror which followed saw a decimation of party ranks and a ravaging of all strata of Soviet society. No group remained untouched; thousands were executed and hundreds of thousands imprisoned, including the most prominent Bolsheviks.

The 18th Congress, a cowed and servile body, meeting in the aftermath of the purges (March 1939) elected a Politburo consisting of Stalin and those of his lieutenants who had weathered the purges: Molotov, Kaganovich, Voroshilov, Mikoyan, Andreyev, Zhdanov, and Khrushchev, with Beria and Shvernik as alternate members. G. V. Malenkov, who at this time was already a member of the Secretariat, became an alternate in 1941 and a full member of the Politburo in 1946.

With the outbreak of the war Stalin fused the party and governmental machinery by creating a State Committee of Defense (June 30, 1941) which lasted for the duration of the war, consisting of himself, Molotov, Malenkov, Beria, and Voroshilov. Mikoyan, Voznesensky, Kaganovich, and Bulganin were later co-opted to it. This war cabinet exercised absolute power and authority over the party and the government to direct the war effort.

Stalin, although unchallengeable, nevertheless used the effective practice of encouraging rivalries among his subordinates, realizing that a divided group presented a minimum threat to himself. Thus he was probably well aware of and encouraged the conflict that arose between Malenkov and Zhdanov in the 1940's. Upon Zhdanov's return to Moscow in 1945, after having spent most of the war in Leningrad where he was Party Secretary, his increasing influence temporarily dislodged Malenkov and his protégés from favor. Following Zhdanov's sudden death in Aug. 1948 Malenkov regained his lost prestige and presumably was instrumental in having Zhdanov's closest associates ruthlessly purged in what has come to be known as the Leningrad case.

Stalin's rule remained uncontested until his death. The enormous powers concentrated in his hands diminished the importance of the higher party organs. No new party congress was called until October 1952 and full Politburo as well as Central Committee meetings ceased to be held on a regular basis.

Party membership, which had declined to 1,920,000 members and candidates in 1938 rose rapidly after the 18th Party Congress, reaching 3,876,885 by Feb. 1941. With the advent of war, conditions for admitting members were relaxed to facilitate mass recruitment. Over two million joined in 1942 alone. By Jan. 1945 party membership totaled 5,760,000. After the war the party continued to expand, but at a slower pace, to 6,300,000 by Sept. 1947 and 6,882,145 by Oct. 1952. Admission was again carefully regulated, and an attempt was made to weed out unsuitable war recruits.

The 19th Party Congress met in Oct. 1952. It was the last under Stalin's dominance. At the Congress the Politburo and the Orgburo were abolished and replaced by an enlarged Presidium of twenty-five full members and eleven alternates. Evidence coming to light since Stalin's death strengthens the speculation that Stalin, with the possible aid of Malenkov, was preparing to purge most of the Politburo members appointed during the 1930's. Increasing the size of the former Politburo with new appointees may have been the first step. The Central Committee was also enlarged to 236 members and candidates, almost twice the size of the Central Committee elected in 1939. The name of the party was changed to the Communist Party of the Soviet Union, casting off the historic name "Bolshevik."

Three months after the Congress met the doctors' plot was announced. Nine leading doctors were accused of murdering Zhdanov and plotting to eliminate leading military figures. In addition to the anti-Semitic character of these allegations—six out of the nine doctors were Jews—admitted to be a fabrication in April 1953 after Stalin's death, the "conspiracy" had the familiar earmarks of a purge which, according to

Khrushchev in 1956, had as its intended victims Molotov, Mikoyan, and Voroshilov. Other evidence indicates that Beria also was scheduled for elimination when Stalin died on March 5, 1953.

Post-Stalin Period. With Stalin's death a new struggle for succession ensued. Judging by the nature of the party and government reorganization which was announced on March 7, 1953, Malenkov appeared to be Stalin's heir. He headed the list of the party Presidium now reduced to ten members (Malenkov, Beria, Molotov, Voroshilov, Khrushchev, Bulganin, Kaganovich, Mikoyan, Pervukhin, and Saburov), retained his position in the Secretariat, and was named chairman of the Council of Ministers, thus combining the most important party and government positions. However, Malenkov's early advantage was to be temporary. On March 14, the Central Committee granted his "request" to be released from the party Secretariat. It is not known whether Malenkov was forced out of the Secretariat or whether he was given an alternative and chose the government position because he thought it had become more important. In any case Malenkov's subsequent downfall dates from this period. Control progressively slipped from his hands. In Feb. 1955 he "resigned" as chairman of the Council of Ministers, though still retaining his seat in the party Presidium.

The first victim actually to fall in the power struggle was L. P. Beria. On July 10, 1953 Beria's arrest was made public—in December, his execution. Among the charges leveled against him was the fantastic allegation that he had been a British agent since 1919. The removal of Beria undoubtedly signified that because of his control of the security apparatus he was a threat to the supremacy of the party apparatus and had to be eliminated.

Following the pattern of Stalin's rise to power, Khrushchev, leading member of the Secretariat after Malenkov's resignation from that body and named First Secretary in Sept. 1953, was able within four years to eliminate all opposition from the Presidium. Through Khrushchev's adroit handling of the party apparatus, he controlled important appointments, packed the Central Committee, and progressively restored party supremacy over the government bureaucracy which under Stalin had to some extent been diminished. Party Congresses and meetings of the Central Committee were again held on a regular basis. Not the least of Khrushchev's success was due to his capacity for developing new programs and to a certain measure of political daring. His most daring undertaking, which almost defeated him, was the vigorous de-Stalinization campaign.

The downgrading of Stalin which had begun slowly after Stalin's death reached its zenith in Feb. 1956 when Khrushchev in a secret address to the 20th Party Congress (which became rapidly known in and outside of Russia) accused Stalin of fostering a "cult of personality," charging him with brutal and arbitrary acts of terror and persecution of party members, extensively documenting his accusations with facts and figures. Khrushchev's speech was not, however, a wholesale castigation of Stalin's rule. He neither vindicated Trot-

sky or the Right Opposition of Bukharin, nor criticized Stalin for his ruthless implementation of the policies of forced collectivization and rapid industrialization.

Khrushchev's denunciation of Stalin was an attempt to disassociate himself and the party from past acts of terror and irrationality by laying the blame on the dictator rather than on the system which had been created by Lenin. Although the revelation of the speech may have aided Khrushchev in his power struggle against his opponents, Molotov, Malenkov, and Kaganovich, by indirectly implicating them as Stalin's accessories, the speech had far greater impact on the Soviet bloc and on foreign Communists than he anticipated. It was no coincidence that the Polish riots and the Hungarian revolution which challenged Soviet control in Eastern Europe broke out in 1956. (Unrest in this area was also stimulated by Khrushchev's policy of reconciliation with Yugoslavia and his statement made at the 20th Party Congress that there were various roads to socialism.)

Khrushchev significantly extended his influence over the party apparatus at the 20th Party Congress. Although still uncertain of commanding a majority in the Presidium, Khrushchev as a result of decisions reached by the Congress was able to place his supporters in important posts by supersedure (approximately 30 per cent of the full members and 60 per cent of the candidates elected by the Central Committee in 1952 were replaced) and by enlarging the existing party bodies. Four candidate members were added to the Presidium, the Secretariat was increased to eight, and the Central Committee was enlarged to 133 full and 122 alternate members.

Another indication of Khrushchev's growing influence was the establishment, by the Congress, of the Bureau of RSFSR Affairs to which Khrushchev was elected chairman. The Bureau, attached to the Central Committee, was placed in charge of party work in the largest and most important republic of the USSR.

The First Secretary's control of the apparatus served him well when in June 1957 he was opposed by a majority of the Presidium which was critical of his foreign and domestic policies. The immediate issue of controversy was Khrushchev's program calling for a drastic reorganization of the economy. Outvoted and faced with removal as First Secretary, Khrushchev with the help of Marshal Zhukov (who was appointed alternate member in Feb. 1956) was able to call a special session of the Central Committee upon which he could count for support.

On June 29, after seven days of deliberation, the Central Committee issued a resolution condemning the opposition of the Anti-Party Group of Molotov, Malenkov, Kaganovich, and Shepilov, and expelling them from the Presidium and Central Committee. Saburov and Pervukhin (who probably voted against Khrushchev) were also demoted, the former was dropped from the Presidium, the latter reduced to alternate status. Khrushchev was now master of the Presidium which was enlarged to fifteen full members. Only five of the eleven, apart from Khrushchev who had been elected by the 20th Party Congress (Mikoyan, Suslov, Kirichenko, Bul-

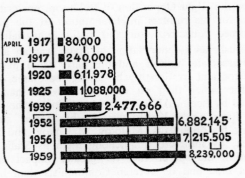

Numerical growth of the CPSU

ganin, and Voroshilov), survived the change. Five alternate members—Brezhnev, Shvernik, Zhukov, Mme Furtseva and Kozlov—were rewarded by being elevated to full membership, as were Aristov, Belyayev, Kuusinen, and Ignatov, who were promoted either from the Secretariat or from the Central Committee.

In Nov. 1957 Marshal Zhukov, who had supported Khrushchev against his opponents, was unceremoniously ousted from the Presidium. His place was taken by Mukhitdinov in Dec. 1957. At that time Mukhitdinov, Kirichenko, and Ignatov were also added to the Secretariat giving that body a majority of ten of the fifteen-member Presidium.

The altering of the Presidium, in addition to being a personal triumph for Khrushchev, was a conclusive victory for the representatives of the party apparatus over the government bureaucracy. On the Presidium formed in the aftermath of Stalin's death Khrushchev (after Malenkov's resignation from the Secretariat) had been the sole representative of the central party apparatus. By the end of 1957 the tables were turned, the *apparatchiki* again clearly predominated.

Khrushchev further consolidated his powers when in March 1958 he became chairman of the Council of Ministers. By the time the 21st Extraordinary Party Congress met in Jan.-Feb. 1959, Khrushchev had eliminated every serious opponent—Bulganin, also linked with the Anti-Party Group, had been expelled from the Presidium in Sept. 1958.

The Congress was expressly convened to publicize and to approve the Seven Year Plan (1959–1965). Khrushchev, delivering the major address, declared that with the Seven Year Plan the USSR, having entered the stage of constructing communism, would within decades be transformed into the world's foremost industrial power giving the Soviet people a high standard of living. Party membership increased steadily, and by the 21st Party Congress it totaled 8,239,131 as compared to 7,215,505 at the 20th Party Congress.

Following the 21st Party Congress further changes in the top party bodies were recorded, the most significant of which were announced on May 5 and July 17, 1960. Kirichenko and Belyayev were removed from the Presidium and replaced by Kosygin, Podgorny, and Polyansky—all three of whom had been alternate members. Voroshilov retired, leaving Khrushchev and Mikoyan the sole surviving members of the Presidium which had been formed in March 1953. The Secretariat

was reduced to five members, consisting of Khrushchev, Suslov, Kuusinen, Mukhitdinov, and Kozlov.

Although several differing explanations have been offered for the most recent changes, some preliminary conclusions may be drawn. Khrushchev apparently has increased his personal power at the expense of his colleagues. The Secretariat no longer holds a majority of seats in the Presidium, thus giving Khrushchev singular control over the four most important bodies in the USSR: the party Presidium, the Secretariat, the party Bureau for RSFSR Affairs, and the Council of Ministers. He alone is member of all four. All other important leaders are limited to holding simultaneously either two party positions, or one party position and one government position. (*See* OPPOSITION, PURGES, HISTORY OF USSR, MARXISM-LENINISM, MARXISM RUSSIAN, MENSHEVISM, TROTSKYISM)

BIBLIOGRAPHY: Leonard Schapiro, *The Communist Party of the Soviet Union*, New York, 1960; John S. Reshetar, Jr., *A Concise History of the Communist Party*, New York, 1960; Merle Fainsod, *How Russia Is Ruled*, Cambridge, 1953. H. W. M.

COMPUTERS: *see* AUTOMATION, MATHEMATICS.

COMÚCH, a committee organized in Samara on June 6, 1918, by Socialist Revolutionaries, former members of the Constituent Assembly, dispersed shortly after the seizure of power by the Bolsheviks. Two days later, after Samara fell to the Czechoslovakian Corps, C proclaimed itself the legitimate government of the region. Within the next two months C gained control of large territories along the Volga and in the Urals, setting up local agencies of rural and municipal administration. On Sept. 23, a rival organization, the Directorate, was established in Ufa City. C was reorganized as the Congress of Members of the Constituent Assembly. Two months later, on Dec. 3, it was disbanded by commander in chief of White army forces in Siberia, Admiral Kolchak.

CONCENTRATION CAMPS. Origin. Soviet concentration camps were at first established primarily for anti-Soviet elements. After the revolt in Penza in Aug. 1918, Lenin ordered suspects put in camps, though there was no legal basis for this measure. But a decree of May 17, 1919 ordered that "in all provincial capitals . . . camps are to be organized for at least 300 persons each," and on Sept. 5, 1919 it was decreed that the Cheka (q.v.) was to be vested with the unlimited power to confine persons to camps because "it is necessary to safeguard the Soviet Republic from class enemies by isolating them in concentration camps." The Cheka, accordingly, organized camps for members of anti-Soviet political parties, landlords and capitalists, hostages, and other political groups. On Oct. 16, 1924 a Corrective Labor Code of the RSFSR was published which contained detailed regulations for the administration of camps, in which both political offenders and common criminals were to be confined.

Thus concentration camps became an essential element of the Soviet penal system, based on the communist legal doctrine according to which crime is a product of social antagonisms, and since no such antagonisms existed in the "classless" Soviet society, crime would rapidly disappear in the USSR; its remnants would be eradicated in places of confinement by education and "socially useful labor," that is, work in state enterprises. In reality, criminal activities throughout the 1920's showed a strong upward trend, and the camp population increased steadily. A vast system of forced labor came into being.

Forced labor. The system expanded greatly during the early 1930's, the initial period of industrialization, farm collectivization, and militarization. Rapid industrialization required raw materials, rich deposits of which were available in the northern regions of European Russia and Siberia. It also needed highways, railways, and canals. On the other hand, farm collectivization yielded great numbers of forced laborers, since well-to-do peasant families were subject to deportation; according to official data, there were 5,889,000 such families in 1928; a few years later there were none. Mounting terrorism, the Great Purge, and delinquency further swelled the camp population. Sentences to forced labor, according to Soviet data, increased from 21 per cent of all sentences in 1927 to 58 per cent in 1958. On the island of Solovki, where formerly a centuries-old monastery and in the 1920's one of the most important camps were situated, the number of prisoners rose from about 4,000 in 1923 to 7,000 in 1925, 20,000 in 1927, and 100,000 in 1930. Statistics on crime and prisoners have always been con-

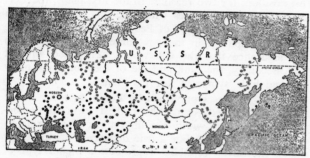

Soviet slave-labor camps (based on data gathered by the American Federation of Labor)

sidered a state secret in the USSR. According to best estimates, based on the testimony of numerous released inmates, especially foreigners repatriated after World War II, the number of camp laborers amounted to 12 to 15 million men and women.

Among the most important projects operated by forced labor were: the Vorkuta coal mines; Kolyma, one of the largest gold-producing areas of the world; the Belomor Canal between the White Sea and the Baltic, on which 300,000 persons worked; the Moscow-Volga Canal, 80 miles long; the building of Magnitogorsk, a new center of the iron and steel industry. The projects, all operated by the NKVD, were directed by many arrested engineers, economists, and so forth.

Working, living, and food conditions in the camps were appalling. Prisoners were housed in filthy, vermin-infested barracks which gave little protection against the rigors of the northern climate. Practically unlimited working hours, utterly inadequate food rationed according to the work norm fulfilled by each prisoner, primitive medical care, and harsh treatment,

including shooting, beating and solitary confinement, turned the helpless prisoners into emaciated human beings almost incapable of doing any work. New mass arrests replenished the ranks of prisoners that were steadily reduced by the appalling mortality rate. These conditions, aggravated by the lack of legal protection for prisoners, constitute a main difference between forced labor, as practiced in Soviet camps, and the obligation to work which obtains in prisons in the West.

During World War II the camp population decreased, but in the late 1940's a new expansion set in. Large numbers of "disloyal" persons, suspects, Ukrainian and other minority nationalists, priests, returned war prisoners, *Ostarbeiter* (q.v.), and others swelled the camp population. However, political prisoners were now separated from common criminals and placed in "special regime" camps. It was realized that the low productivity of enforced labor and the high incidence of sickness and death constituted a waste of manpower incompatible with the ambitious plans of postwar rehabilitation and industrialization, especially since manpower had been reduced by war losses. Beginning in 1948 more humane methods were introduced in the camps.

Post-Stalin period. The trend was strengthened after Stalin's death. Also, information on Soviet forced labor, which had leaked out and become the subject of careful studies by, among others, the United Nations and the American Federation of Labor, had been damaging to Soviet prestige. Under the amnesties of 1953 and 1955 large numbers of prisoners were released. Reduced terrorism further diminished the number of convicts. Stalin's death and Beria's execution inspired hope in the convicts and created confusion among the security police; this led to riots in several large camps. Such riots were reliably reported to have occurred in May 1953 at camp Norilsk, where 1,500 of the 2,500 rioters were killed or wounded; in Karaganda in 1953 and 1954; in Kolyma (150,000 inmates) in May 1954, when 200 convicts were killed and 180 wounded; and in several other camps. These events resulted in further easing the regime in the camps.

Since then significant reforms have been enacted. An unknown but considerable number of prisoners were set free or permitted to live outside the camps; many camps were disbanded; housing, food, and sanitary conditions improved; working hours were reduced and the treatment of prisoners became less brutal. But the system of concentration camps, now designated "colonies," with their compulsory labor, persists. The Foundations of Criminal Law, published on Dec. 25, 1958, provides for two places of confinement, prisons and "corrective labor colonies," with prisons as the more rigorous place of punishment. As regards political prisoners, it has recently been reported that special camps have been organized for them in the far north, where prisoners are cut off from any contact with the outside world. (*See also* SECURITY POLICE)

BIBLIOGRAPHY: D. Dallin and B. Nicolaevsky, *Forced Labor in Soviet Russia*, New Haven, 1947; Paul Barton, *L'Institution Concentrationnaire*, Paris, 1959; Unto Parvilahti, *Beria's Gardens*, New York, 1960; J. Scholmer, *Vorkuta*, London, 1954; A. Weissberg, *The Accused*, New York, 1951.   S. W.

CONCILIATORS: *see* OPPOSITION.

CONSTANTINOPLE, TREATY OF, concluded between Russia and Turkey in 1879 to regulate financial, commercial, and other conditions left undetermined by the Treaty of Berlin in 1878. It established the compensation to Russia and the indemnity for losses incurred by R. subjects and business in Turkey.

CONSTITUENT ASSEMBLY, THE. The idea of calling a CA which would establish in Russia a form of government based on self-rule of the people dates back to the 19th century, as a concept developed in Russian revolutionary circles. Nevertheless, the demand for immediate convocation of a CA was actually incorporated in programs adopted by revolutionary parties or middle-of-the road liberals (Constitutional Democrats, and others) only in the 1905 revolution and, especially, in the February revolution in 1917. The Bolsheviks, who engineered the dispersal of the CA after the very first session, began as its most ardent supporters. It was the Bolsheviks who from Lenin's arrival in Petrograd in April 1917 accused the Provisional Government of deliberate procrastination in promulgating the Election Law, charging the "capitalist ministers" with sabotaging the convocation of the CA.

For the first time in its history a country involved in a world war, handicapped by the paucity of passable roads, lacking experience and the necessary technical means, 60 per cent of its people practically illiterate, found itself facing the task of holding national elections on the basis of universal, direct, equal, and secret suffrage. Such conditions created incredible complications in the matter of preparations for the elections. Everyone kept a wary eye on the preliminaries to make sure that all the safeguards of proper electoral proceedings would be duly complied with.

Elections to the CA, scheduled originally by the Provisional Government for Sept. 17, were postponed by agreement with the Soviet of Workers', Soldiers' and Peasants' Deputies following the Bolshevik demonstrations in June and July. The date of Election Day was fixed for the 12th and the 26th of Nov. (O.S.).

In the elections based on proportional representation, one deputy was elected for about 219,000 inhabitants on the home front and 100,000 men in active service. (The Navy, and some sparsely populated outlying regions, elected their representatives by straight majority vote.)

The elections, held as scheduled, despite the October coup carried out by the Bolsheviks a few weeks earlier, brought the following returns:

Of the 36,265,560 voters who went to the polls in 54 electoral districts, 20,900,000, or 58 per cent, voted for the Socialist Revolutionaries (16,500,000 votes cast for the Russian Socialist Revolutionary party and the balance polled by the Socialist Revolutionaries of other nationalities—Ukrainian, Moslem, and so on). The Mensheviks received 668,064 votes; the People's Socialists, 507,000; the Unity (Plekhanov's) group, 25,000; leaders of the cooperative movement, 51,000; Ukrainian Socialists, 507,000; German Socialists, 44,000; and Finnish Socialists, 14,000; 1,800,000 Socialist votes in all. The Bolsheviks captured 9,023,963 votes; the Kadets (Constitutional Democrats), 1,856,639, although

this total can be raised to 4,000,000, by expanding it to include the votes polled by the "League of Landowners and Landholders," the old believers, the national minority groups—Jews, Moslems, Bashkirs, Latvians, Poles, Cossacks, Byelorussians—and a list of miscellaneous groups and organizations.

The total of 703 deputies elected to the CA included 380 Socialist Revolutionaries and 38 Left Socialist Revolutionaries, 168 Bolsheviks, 18 Mensheviks, 77 representatives of the national minority groups, and 17 Kadets, and 4 Popular Socialists. Thus, 75 per cent of the voters cast their ballots against the Bolsheviks. Yet, in Lenin's words, "The proletariat had inflicted a crushing defeat upon the bourgeoisie." "The city," wrote Lenin, "is never the equal of the countryside. The city inevitably *leads the village*. The village inevitably *follows the city*." Now the majority of the proletariat had, according to Lenin, voted for the Bolsheviks, including nearly half of the armed forces, the proletariat of both capitals, and men in active service quartered near the center. In other words, the pro-Bolshevik vote was cast at a decisive moment in the strategic areas; hence, they must be acknowledged as the victors.

When the outcome of the elections had been ascertained, Lenin felt that the CA should not be summoned at any time. He was, however, compelled to abandon his position, for two reasons. In the first place, the Left Socialist Revolutionaries whom he had invited to join the *Sovnarkom* (Council of People's Commissars) made their participation in the government contingent upon his assurance that the CA would be opened without fail. Secondly, the rank and file of the Bolshevik party showed little sympathy for his plans.

In the 19 theses published by Lenin on Dec. 29 the CA is acknowledged as "the highest form of democracy"—but only "within the limitations of an ordinary bourgeois republic." For a true democrat, on the other hand, the Soviet republic "represents a higher type of democratic institution, which alone can ensure a less painful transition to socialism."

The first and only session of the CA was held on Jan. 5 and 6, 1918 and lasted 17 hours in all. At that time the Tauride Palace where the session took place became an armed camp crowded by soldiers and sailors brandishing their rifles, pistols, and hand grenades. The Bolsheviks, backed by the Left faction of the Socialist Revolutionaries, served an ultimatum upon the CA, demanding a wholesale approval of their proposals. After this request had been turned down, the sailors were given orders to break up the meeting. This was followed by an "official" dissolution decree published on the same day.

Time and again, during the remaining years of his life, Lenin came back to the matter of the CA and its liquidation. To justify the dispersal, Lenin pointed out that the lists of nominees, compiled before the October uprising, represented a "relationship of political forces which no longer existed." The Bolsheviks, however, made no attempt at any time to elect a new CA with full powers, on the same basis and with the same electoral guarantees as those secured for the elections to the All-Russian CA.

It is characteristic of the political climate prevalent in that era that the liquidation of the CA was hailed enthusiastically also by the Right-wing leaders of society. Admiral Kolchak, one of the heads of the White movement, felt that "if nothing else, the Bolsheviks must be credited with breaking up the Constituent Assembly." "It was a ghastly night—a night that had spelled out Russia's destiny for many years to come," wrote V. M. Chernov, Chairman of the CA as he recalled the time of its dissolution. "Today I see ever more clearly that this dreadful night had decided the destinies not of Russia alone but of Europe and of the entire world as well."

BIBLIOGRAPHY: O. H. Radkey, *The Election to the Russian Constituent Assembly of 1917*, Cambridge, 1950; Mark Vishniak, *The All-Russian Constituent Assembly*, Paris, 1932.   M. V.

CONSTITUENT REPUBLICS: *see* ADMINISTRATIVE AND TERRITORIAL DIVISIONS.

CONSTITUTIONAL DEMOCRATIC PARTY, also called the Party of People's Freedom (Kadet Party), was founded under the leadership of Paul Milyukov in Oct. 1905—as a result of the fusion of the Union of Liberation and the Zemstvo Militants.

At their first two congresses (Oct. 1905 and Jan. 1906) the Kadets adopted a platform calling for a variety of moderate reforms. The party advocated, among other things, a constitutional monarchy along English lines, a program of land redistribution with compensation for the dispossessed landowners and the eight-hour working day. For a time, when not completely curbed by government restrictions, the Kadets were a rallying point for the forces of R. liberalism. Strong support came from the professional and business classes as well as from the progressive gentry. Party membership in these years had reached a peak of 70,000.

Among the party's leaders, in addition to Milyukov himself, were: V. A. Maklakov, I. V. Gessen, S. A. Muromtsev, Prince P. D. Dolgorukov, Prince Ye. N. Trubetskoy, P. Struve, V. Nabokov, F. Rodichev, M. Vinaver, N. V. Nekrasov, A. I. Shingaryev and F. D. Kokoshkin.

The Kadets displayed great vigor in the election campaign for the first Duma early in 1906. With their slogan "Political Freedom and Social Justice," they won 179 seats or 37.4 per cent of the House, sufficient to dominate the legislature. Indicative of their triumph was Muromtsev's election as speaker. But within months the Duma was dissolved. About 120 Kadet deputies joined in the Vyborg Appeal calling on the people not to pay taxes and to refuse to obey the conscription law until the rights of the Duma had been restored. The signatories were tried and received light sentences which, however, involved disfranchisement and made them ineligible for elective office (Dec. 1906).

Thus disorganized, the party found itself confronted with elections for a new Duma, Jan.-Feb. 1907. The Kadets fought the election in the face of much official harassment and considerable hostility among groups to their left. As a result, the party's strength in the second Duma fell to 98 out of a total of 478 seats. Hoping to avoid a second sudden dissolution, the Kadets mollified their criticism of government policies.

This tactic was to no avail, however, as Stolypin dissolved the new assembly before the year's end.

The electoral law of June 1907 helped reduce Kadet representation in the third Duma (Nov. 1907-June 1912) to 53. In the fourth Duma (1912–1917), the Kadets numbered 58 and participated with the Octobrists and other Right-wing groups in the Progressive Bloc. This coalition of moderate opposition elements, formed in Aug. 1915, was loud in its criticism of the government's handling of the war situation. The Bloc declared that victory could be achieved only through the establishment of a new ministry more representative of the broad mass of the people. In addition it advocated a variety of reform measures designed to win the loyalty and wholehearted participation of all citizens in the struggle against the Central Powers. As the military situation grew worse, parliamentary criticism was intensified, and, in Nov. 1916, Milyukov and Maklakov delivered speeches in the Duma of unprecedented vehemence.

During the war the Kadets had played a prominent role in the Industrial War Committee.

After the revolution of February 1917, the Kadets were one of the most conservative groups in R. politics. Milyukov at first strove to save the monarchy, but finally agreed to the establishment of a republic. His party constituted a majority in the first Provisional cabinet formed under Prince Lvov on March 2. Among the Kadets participating were Milyukov who, long an expert in international affairs, became foreign minister, and N. V. Nekrasov, minister of transport. But Milyukov's refusal to alter the nation's war aims or its agreements with the Allies led to his resignation, May 2. In the coalition ministry organized May 5, Nekrasov and several other Kadets were among the nine non-socialists participating. Kadet influence was on the wane, however, and in the last Provisional cabinet under Kerensky (Sept. 25) the party controlled only two portfolios. In the election to the Constituent Assembly the Kadets got nearly 2,000,000 votes and 17 deputies.

With the Bolshevik Revolution, the significance of the party as an active political force was almost at an end. Nevertheless Kadets participated in some of the White political committees and, after the civil war, Kadet groups continued to function in exile. In 1921 the unity of the movement was shattered as two distinct groups emerged. One, led by Milyukov, was centered in Paris and called itself the "Democratic Group of the Party of People's Freedom." Its official organ was the paper *Poslednie Novosti* (Latest News). The other section was established in Berlin under the leadership of I. V. Gessen. Its views were disseminated through the journal *Rul* (Rudder).   C. J. F.

CONSTITUTIONS. In contrast to the Western democratic tradition, C in the Soviet system do not serve as limitations upon the exercise of governmental power. The Soviet C provides an air of legitimacy to the system, and is in part a means by which the regime caters to the democratic aspirations of the population. While the Soviet constitutional system is democratic in form, it is limited by totalitarian controls which assure that effective power never passes out of the hands of the leaders of the Communist party.

Throughout the 19th cent., the efforts of the R. liberals were directed towards the establishment of a constitutional monarchy. Formal success did not come, however, until 1905 and the October manifesto, which —together with the Fundamental Laws of 1906—can be considered the first and only constitutional document of the R. Empire.

1918 Constitution. After the Bolshevik revolution of Nov. 1917 and the dispersal of the Constituent Assembly in Jan. 1918, the Bolsheviks sought to embody their assumption of power in constitutional form. The Constitution of the Russian Soviet Federated Socialist Republic (RSFSR) was approved on July 10, 1918 by the fifth All-Russian Congress of Soviets. The new governmental structure, which had already come into existence more or less spontaneously, was a highly centralized and discriminatory system with the party in actual control. According to the C, the workers, and their representatives in the soviets at each level, became the repository of all authority. Freedom of speech, of press, of assembly, and of association were restricted to the working class. Church and state were separated. National minorities were to form autonomous units and were to enter the RSFSR on a federal basis. Universal military service was established, but non-working-class elements were exempt because of their anti-regime attitude. The duty to work was proclaimed: "He who does not work shall not eat."

The All-Russian Congress of Soviets became the highest body. It was to be weighted in favor of the workers as against the peasantry; it was composed of representatives of the urban soviets on the basis of one deputy for every 25,000 *voters* and representatives of provincial congresses of soviets on the basis of one deputy for every 125,000 *inhabitants*. Between sessions of the All-Russian Congress, supreme power was vested in a Central Executive Committee of not more than 200 members elected by the Congress. The Central Executive Committee was to appoint a Council of People's Commissars to direct the executive branch of the government. The C also provided for a hierarchical system of local soviets and congresses of soviets. The highest bodies determined their own authority, with the local organs subject to the control of the superior bodies. No reference was made in the C to the real source of authority, the party.

Federal Constitution. With the establishment of the USSR in 1922, a new constitutional structure became necessary. The C of the USSR was ratified by the second All-Union Congress of Soviets on Jan. 31, 1924, and came to be known as the "federal constitution." Part II of the C contained the treaty of unification by which the separate republics agreed to unite, and in which was set forth the new governmental structure. The federal government was given authority in questions of war and peace, foreign relations and foreign trade, fiscal policy, armed forces, and other matters. In addition, it was given wide powers of planning for and control over the national economy. There was no bill of rights; each republic was left to develop its own

electoral law; no changes were made in the pre-unification civil, criminal, family, land and labor codes of the republics, nor were the codes of criminal and civil procedure changed. The authority of the constituent republics was limited to such powers as were not given to the federal government, which were very few.

The Congress of Soviets remained the supreme authority, and the Central Executive Committee was made bicameral to reflect the federative character of the C: a Council of Union to be selected on the basis of population, and a Council of Nationalities made up of five delegates from each constituent republic and autonomous republic and one delegate from each autonomous *oblast*. The forms of national autonomy, while circumscribed within narrow bounds, were preserved to placate national feeling and to encourage support from the national minorities in Central Asia and the Far East.

The C also set up three categories of commissariats under the Council of People's Commissars: all-union, union-republic, and republic. A Supreme Court and a procurator, both subordinate to the Central Executive Committee, were also created. As was the case in 1918, the 1924 C made no reference to the Communist party.

Stalin Constitution. The next major constitutional development was the adoption of the "Stalin Constitution" in 1936, at a time when the USSR was seeking support from the Western democracies against the growth of fascism. Stalin evidently felt that more support could be engendered for alliances with the USSR if the Soviet system appeared more democratic. Also, the new C was in part a reflection of the new conditions in the USSR after the introduction of the Five Year plans, accelerated industrialization, and collectivization of agriculture. This new C, which was adopted on Dec. 5, 1936 by the Extraordinary Eighth All-Union Congress of Soviets, is still in force.

The political structure outlined in the C is so heavily centralized that it almost completely negates the federal pattern on which the government is formally constructed. The Congress of Soviets and the Central Executive Committee are eliminated, the highest body being the directly elected bicameral Supreme Soviet. Executive and administrative authority remained in the Council of People's Commissars (after 1946, Council of Ministers), to be appointed by the Supreme Soviet, and the three types of commissariats (ministries) were retained. The C also describes the governmental structure of the constituent republics and the local organs of state authority.

Chapter X is a statement of the fundamental rights and duties of citizens; these rights, however, are not, as in the United States, in the form of limitations on the power of the government, but rather are in the form of guarantees, the fulfillment of which is dependent upon the good faith of the government. The rights of free speech, free press, and free assembly are qualified by the statement that they must be exercised "in conformity with the interests of the working class, and in order to strengthen the socialist system," and it is the Communist party which decides what is in the interest of the working class. Other provisions of Chapter X define the duties of Soviet citizens: to abide by the C, to observe the laws, to maintain labor discipline, to safeguard and fortify public socialist property, and to defend the country. These duties have been given substance through specific legislative enactments.

Other chapters are concerned with the electoral system and the procedures for amending the C. In the 1936 C, the role of the party is acknowledged for the first time. It is described as "the leading core of all organizations . . . , both public and state."

Since 1936 the Soviet C has been amended many times. Most of the amendments are of minor significance, such as the admission of new constituent republics or the rearrangements of commissariats or ministries. A major change took place, however, in Feb. 1944 when the constituent republics were given "the right to enter direct relations with foreign states and to conclude agreements and exchange representatives with them," and the right to have their own military forces. These amendments were made during the negotiations for the creation of the United Nations, and seem to have been a maneuver to gain the admittance of all of the then sixteen constituent republics into the United Nations. Although the Ukrainian SSR and the Byelorussian SSR have been admitted to the United Nations, these amendments have never been given any substance. (*See also* SOVIETS, ELECTORAL SYSTEM, CENTRAL GOVERNMENT, REVOLUTION OF 1905)

BIBLIOGRAPHY: Merle Fainsod, *How Russia Is Ruled*, Cambridge, 1953; John N. Hazard, *The Soviet System of Government*, Chicago, 1960.
P. H. J.

CONSUMPTION. Increases in C in the Soviet economy have been relatively modest since the revolution. The prerevolutionary level of C was probably not achieved again until the late twenties following recovery from the war and postwar dislocations. Collectivization of agriculture and drought brought about a serious deteriorization of C levels during the First Five Year Plan. Consumers' goods production improved somewhat in the course of the Second Five Year Plan at the end of which C apparently reached its prewar peak though it was still below the 1928 level. Defense expenditures cut into C beginning in 1938 and, following the German attack in 1941, C levels fell to new lows. Since World War II, there seems to have been a steady improvement in C levels with perhaps an average annual increase of 5% currently being achieved.

It is a basic law of Soviet economic development that the expansion of consumers' goods production (Group B industries) must proceed at a slower pace than the increase in heavy industry (Group A industries). Briefly after the death of Stalin some Soviet economists suggested that the output of both consumers' and producers' goods might expand at similar rates, but they were soon silenced with the fall of Premier Malenkov.

Before World War II there was chronic falling short of the targets of both the agricultural and consumers' goods industries generally. After World War II the consumers' goods sector, while still falling short of their targets more frequently than the producers' goods branches, have been showing an improved performance. Even

agriculture, the basis of much of Soviet C, has made considerable progress since the introduction of greater incentives for collective farmers although the agricultural targets for the current Seven Year Plan seem likely not to be reached.

The Russians have generally relied on freedom of choice to distribute most goods and services to consumers. Formal rationing has been resorted to only during the exceptional years of the first half of the thirties and during and after World War II until 1948. No attempt is made by the planners to follow consumers' sovereignty, however, in determining either the total amount of C or the structure of consumers' goods produced. As is the case with most countries, hard liquor is highly taxed to discourage its consumption.

Most consumers' goods are distributed to urban inhabitants through the government system of state and cooperative trade, selling consumers' goods at centrally fixed prices. About 10 per cent of all food, however, is still purchased on the collective farm markets. The individual collective farmers are able to grow considerable food on their own plots of land, a portion of which is sold on the collective farm market, the remainder being consumed by the farmers in kind. Collective farmers also receive part of their earnings on the collective farm in the form of produce.

In comparison with most industrialized economies, the Soviet C levels seem low, although they are probably higher than levels throughout most of the Soviet bloc, with the exception of Czechoslovakia.

Comparisons of Soviet levels of living with those in the West, particularly in the United States, are extremely difficult to make. A larger share of the average R. budget is spent on food and clothing and a smaller share goes for housing, health services, education, and transportation.

There seems to be a higher proportion of cereals in the R. diet in comparison with the West and a lower share of proteins. Recently, however, there has been a tendency for grain C to fall off and there have been some significant improvements in the per capita C of milk, butter, and meat.

Clothing, especially woolen, is very expensive, and it accounts for a large share of budgetary expenditures.

Rent is relatively inexpensive, accounting for about 5 per cent of the average family income. But the housing space obtained for this nominal rent has until recently been—and often still is—extremely cramped. Public transportation is comparatively well developed and inexpensive, while private ownership of automobiles is exceptional.

Medical and dental services are provided freely by the state, although drugs must be purchased by outpatients. In general the quantity and distribution of medical services are more impressive than their quality.

Education is also free and stipends are given to most students who are accepted by higher institutions of learning.

In all respects but housing, urban levels of C are higher than they are in rural areas. There may have been some narrowing of the gap between urban and rural levels of living since 1953. Because of this gap, the mere fact that Soviet industrialization has meant the transfer of large numbers of rural inhabitants to the cities has meant some improvement in over-all levels of living.

Marketing of consumers' goods in the USSR displays all of the characteristics of seller's markets generally. The quality of consumers' goods is low by western standards and the range of choice is very limited. Advertising is largely restricted to informative notices. Installment credit can be used for only a limited number of expensive consumers' goods and repayment must be made within six months. Despite severe penalties, speculation in scarce commodities is quite common.

BIBLIOGRAPHY: Colin D. and Rosemary G. Campbell, "Soviet Price Reductions for Consumer Goods, 1948–54," *American Economic Review*, September, 1955; Janet Chapman, "Real Wages in the Soviet Union, 1928–52," *Review of Economics and Statistics*, May, 1954; Norman Kaplan and Eleanor Wainstein, "A Comparison of Soviet and American Retail Prices in 1950," *Journal of Politic Economy*, December 1956; Alec Nove, "Toward a 'Communist Welfare State'?" *Problems of Communism*, January-February 1960; Lynn Turgeon, "Levels of Living, Wages and Prices in the Soviet and United States Economies," in: *Comparison of the United States and Soviet Economies*, Part I, Washington, 1959.   L. Tu.

CONTRACTS: *see* LIABILITY LAW.

COOPERATIVES. The extension of market relationships and the growth of small-scale enterprise that followed the liberation of the serfs in 1861 resulted in a gradual and at first uneven establishment of credit, consumers', and agricultural cooperatives. This development, which embraced the towns and cities as well as the rural areas, became pronounced, however, only after the turn of the century. The credit cooperatives sought to provide financial resources for small-scale ventures not served by the large banks. The consumers' cooperatives, which, by contrast, represented a defense against the rapid extension of market relationships, generally sought to by-pass private merchants by establishing direct channels to the sources of supply and bargaining with them from a position of relative strength. Agricultural cooperatives established jointly-owned facilities for the processing and storing of marketable agricultural products (e.g., flour), as well as joint organizations for their marketing. All three differed from the less numerous and less stable producers' artels that developed in fields that did not require large investments (e.g., the making of furniture, shoes, and wearing apparel, wrought iron goods, silver products, handicrafts, and dairy products), and that were essentially associations of manual workers for the joint fulfillment of contractual commitments.

The formation of cooperatives was encouraged by individual members of the landed gentry, by intellectuals, and by the land councils (*zemstvos*), as well as by the government. In 1895 the government permitted credit cooperatives to borrow from the State Bank. Shortly afterwards (1904), this privilege was extended to all types of cooperatives, while in 1910 the cooperatives were also permitted to draw on the considerable financial resources of the government-operated network of savings banks. At the same time (1904), the zemstvos were permitted to issue charters to new cooperatives on their own responsibility and with a minimum of formalities. In 1898 the centralized purchasing of products by the consumers' cooperatives was made possible by the establishment of the Central Union of Consumers' Cooperatives (*Tsentrosoyúz*). It is only after these measures were taken that a rapid development of the cooperative movement took place. In 1901 there were still only 837 credit cooperatives, 600 consumers' cooperatives, and 137 agricultural cooperatives. In contrast, by 1915 there were 14,000 credit cooperatives, 11,000 consumers' cooperatives, and 5,000 agricultural cooperatives, as well as slightly more than 100 producers' artels.

Early Soviet Policy toward the Cooperatives. Although the central cooperative bank (the Moscow People's Cooperative Bank, established 1912), like all other banks, was nationalized by the Soviet government shortly after it came to power, the activities of the cooperatives themselves were not discouraged. As private trade declined, the channels provided by the consumers' cooperatives for the distribution of goods were regarded by Lenin as a provisional alternative to the all-embracing system of "social accounting," centering on the banks, that he envisioned. Accordingly, during the short period that preceded the civil war the property of cooperatives was generally protected from confiscation.

During the civil war the consumers' cooperatives, and later the agricultural and the producers' cooperatives, too, were subordinated directly to the Food Commissariat, which also assumed responsibility for the financing of their activities, while the membership of the consumers' cooperatives was extended to include the entire population. The original policy toward cooperatives was resumed after 1924, however. At that time, even though they were declared to belong to the socialist sector of the economy, membership in the cooperatives once again became voluntary and responsibility for financing their activities was returned to the cooperatives themselves. Two cooperative banks (*Vsekobank* and *Ukrainbank*) were established. In 1929 there were 10,000 credit cooperatives in existence, embracing 9.5 mill. members; 28,000 consumers' cooperatives, with 28.8 mill. members; and 13,000 producers' cooperatives, with approximately 1 mill. members.

The Functions of the Cooperatives under the Five Year Plans. The subsequent position of cooperative organizations within the general framework of the Soviet economy was largely determined by the decision of the government to extend the principle of cooperation beyond the sphere of trade and of small-scale manufacturing to all of agricultural production as well. The replacement of individual peasant holdings by collective farms employing the equipment of Machine Tractor Stations was viewed in part as a method for changing the traditionally hostile attitude of peasants to socialism. The immediate stimulus to the establishment of collective farms, however, came from the insufficiency of exchange-motivated food deliveries to the cities at a time when a decision had been adopted to proceed rapidly with the country's planned industrialization.

The establishment of collective farms naturally led to the dissolution of agricultural cooperatives of the earlier type. It also led, however, to the dissolution of the credit cooperatives, since all financing in the field of agriculture was now assumed by the government banks (the newly created Agricultural Bank and the State Bank). At the same time it influenced considerably the activities of the consumers' cooperatives and of *Tsentrosoyúz,* their central union, whose selling activities were restricted to rural areas following the abandonment of rationing in 1935.

The close association of the consumers' cooperatives with the collective farms has provided them with a function that has steadily increased their importance. In 1958 there were 18,800 consumers' cooperatives operating 291,000 stores that served 37.4 mill. members. The value of the goods that they distributed amounted to 30 per cent of the value of all goods sold at retail in the USSR. According to official estimates the number of cooperative stores should increase by 62,000 in 1965, and the volume of their trade by 65–70 per cent. Among the new functions assumed by consumers' cooperatives in recent years there is the operation of local bakeries as well as of restaurants and the selling on distant markets of surplus goods produced by individual farmers on their own plots.

Producers' cooperatives, on the other hand, which continue to exist in such fields as the production of clothing, knitted goods, shoes, and handicrafts, have declined in importance since 1956. At that time they operated 54,700 workshops and other enterprises in which 1.8 mill. members were employed. The subsequent transfer (in 1956) of the larger workshops to the sphere of state-owned industry and of their trading enterprises to the consumers' cooperatives or to state trading organizations has reduced their membership by 600,000 persons. (*See also* DOMESTIC TRADE, KOLKHOZ, AGRICULTURE)

BIBLIOGRAPHY: M. Dobb, *Soviet Economic Development Since 1917,* London, 1948.   P. I. M.

COPECK: *see* KOPECK, MONETARY SYSTEM.

COPYRIGHT: *see* AUTHORSHIP AND INVENTION.

CORRESPONDENCE SCHOOLS AND CLASSES are intended to offer education to working men and women. There exists a network of correspondence schools on the secondary and university levels, in addition to the correspondence courses offered by many universities, *technikums,* pedagogical institutes, schools. The external student can obtain, through correspondence schools and classes, degrees that are fully equivalent to degrees obtained through ordinary study at educational institutions. In 1957–58 school year there were 401,000 students in secondary, and 779,300 in university correspondence schools. There are 24 correspondence colleges, and 430 correspondence departments. The All-Union Correspondence Polytechnical Institute is the largest and has an enrollment of 32,000 students in 62 fields. In 1957, 1,350 engineers graduated from the institute.

COSSACKS. The name—*Kazaki* in Russian—was applied to populations of the R. Empire which were granted certain privileges in return for military service. The C were originally frontiersmen and their name is probably derived from a Turkic word meaning "Adventurer."

The C originated in the frontier areas between the Slavs and the Turkic peoples. The first C were refugees who fled the oppressive policies of Muscovy, Lithuania and Poland. By the 16th century they established themselves on the shores of the Dnieper and Don in free military communities organized on democratic lines, with elected officers (*atamans, sotniks, esauls*). They invaded the neighboring states of Poland, Crimea, and Muscovy, and were occasionally employed by them as frontier guards. Zaporozhian C formed in 16th-17th centuries strong military organizations and under the atamans Nalevayko, Sahaydachny, Doroshenko, Gonta, etc. took part in many rebellions. Their original independence was at first restricted and then vanished in the 17th century when the Cossack state established by Bohdan Khmelnitsky, after a rising against Poland, united with Muscovy. From then on, the C formed part of the R. Empire and new Cossack communities were set up on Russia's European and Asian frontiers, and played an important role in conquering Tatar territories and Siberia for Russia (Yermak Timofeyevich).

The C took part in peasant risings of the 17th and 18th centuries (Bolotnikov's, Razin's, Bulavin's, Pugachov's) but the remnants of their political autonomy gradually disappeared and they were incorporated in the army, and often used to suppress revolutionary movements. In the 19th century there were 11 communities of C (*voysko*)—the Don, Kuban, Terek, Astrakhan, Ural, Orenburg, Siberian, Semirechensk, Amur, Ussuri, and Zabaykalye—of which the Don C were the largest. They occupied an area of 230,000 sq. mi. with a pop. of 8 mill. of which 3 mill. were C.

The primary unit of C organization was the village (*stanitsa*) which held land in common, but the statute of 1869 provided officers and officials in C areas with individual land allotments, while maintaining the communal regime for the rank and file. The village assembly consisted of all householders in the smaller villages and of elected representatives in the larger ones. Military service of 20 years beginning at the age of 18 was compulsory for C. The non-Cossack population (*inogorodnie*) of the areas resented the C's privileged position. There were also tensions between officers and the rank and file.

The Soviet government leveled the C communities with the rest of the pop. by the decree of June 12, 1918. C fought on both sides in the civil war and 30,000 of them emigrated with the defeated White army. A modified form of C organization was restored under Soviet rule in 1936, but without political autonomy, or privilege. C lands were subject to forced collectivization. C units fought prominently in World War II, some of them on the side of the Germans. Among prominent C in modern times are the writer M. Sholokhov and the politician G. M. Malenkov.

BIBLIOGRAPHY: W. P. Cresson, *The Cossacks,* New York, 1919.

COTTON CROPS. Cotton is the major textile fiber and an important oil-bearing crop in the USSR. Output of unginned C rose, in mill. tons, from .74 in 1913, to .82 in 1928, 2.24 in 1940, and 4.68 in 1959. Yields were considerably improved: from 1.08 tons per hectare in 1913 to double that figure, 2.17, in 1959, by far the best such performance of any major Soviet crop. Large-scale investment in irrigation works and abundant use of fertilizers were two major sources of progress.

While C is traditionally grown on irrigated lands in Central Asia (which accounts for almost 90% of all Soviet production), persistent efforts were made from the 1930's on to grow C on unirrigated lands. These plantings made up over one-fourth of all area sown to C as late as 1950 but the method was highly inefficient and was completely abandoned by 1953.

Another important and more successful innovation was the introduction of long-staple Egyptian C, which was previously not grown in Russia. Production of C in the USSR runs at present at about 60% of the U.S. level; and productivity lags still far behind: in seed cotton it took, in 1958, 428 man-hours to produce one ton on Soviet collective farms as against 188 in the United States.

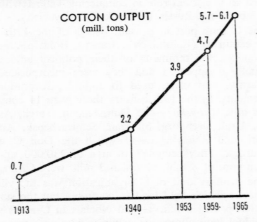

COTTON OUTPUT
(mill. tons)

0.7   2.2   3.9   4.7   5.7 – 6.1
1913   1940   1953   1959· 1965

COUNCIL FOR ECONOMIC MUTUAL ASSISTANCE (CEMA) (*Soviet Ekonomicheskoy Vzaimopomoshchi,* SEV)—the Soviet bloc's international economic organization for cooperation in planning and trade; sometimes referred to as "Comecon."

CEMA is an intergovernmental organization of European communist states. Its foundation was announced from Moscow, Jan. 25, 1949; a formal charter was not adopted until Dec. 14, 1959. The member governments are: USSR, Bulgaria, Czechoslovakia, Hungary, Poland, Rumania (founding members), Albania (joined Feb. 1949), and E. Germany (joined 1950). Asian communist governments have been represented at C meetings by observers since 1956, but membership is formally restricted to European states. C is nominally open to European countries outside the Soviet orbit. However, the sole applicant, Yugoslavia, was rejected.

The organization's present importance and activity are of relatively recent development. Its role during the first five years of its existence appears to have been extremely limited. Although C was publicized in 1949 as an eastern version of the Marshall Plan, and seen by critics as a Soviet device for dictating an economic "master plan" for E. Europe, it apparently performed neither function (except, possibly, in armaments production). National planning in the member states continued to be individual and even autarchic, with much duplication of effort. Mutual trade and dependence did

increase, but this was due partly to the simultaneous western embargo on strategic goods shipments to communist countries. The available information on members' trade during 1949–53 suggests less multilateral consultation than purely bilateral negotiations, with perhaps some one-sided "coordination" to the advantage of the USSR.

Until 1956, C's organizational structure consisted of only three units: (1) the Session of the Council, attended by representatives of all member countries, and constituting the highest organ of C, (2) the Conference of Representatives, to consult between sessions, and (3) a permanent Secretariat, located in Moscow. Council Sessions rotate among the members' capitals and the 1959 charter now requires two meetings a year. During C's first five years, however, there were only three plenary sessions: two in 1949, one in 1950, and none 1951–53.

Activity resumed with two sessions in 1954, annual meetings in 1955–57, and two a year since, as well as with substantial additions to C's organizational structure in the form of a series of permanent commissions, each with its own secretariat, to deal with specific branches of economic activity. The known commissions, and the locations of their headquarters are: Agriculture (Sofia), Electric Power (Moscow), Coal (Warsaw), Machinery (Prague), Petroleum and Gas (Bucharest), Ferrous Metals (Moscow), Nonferrous Metals (Budapest), Chemicals (East Berlin), Foreign Trade (Moscow), Transportation (Warsaw), Construction (East Berlin), Food and Consumers' Goods (Prague), General Economic Questions (Moscow). Of these, the first nine were established by decision of the seventh plenary Council Session in May 1956 and the last four by the ninth and tenth sessions in 1958. An atomic energy commission was formed in mid-1960.

C's revival after Stalin's death coincided with a change in E. European economic policies toward patterns of development more suitable to individual national resources, and C has been working since 1954 toward some of the purposes originally claimed for it: facilitating exchanges of technical information and standardization of products, fostering national specialization according to cost advantages, reducing uneconomical duplications of effort. Initially, discussions centered on the problems created by the strenuous policies of Stalin's era, which had produced critical shortages of industrial raw materials in E. Europe, as well as deteriorating standards of living. The area of consideration has since broadened to the general coordination of the long-term plans of the member countries, with a view to achieving a more efficient international division of labor.

Progress in implementing this aim has, as of 1960, been only moderate. C members have concluded some agreements to specialize in specific areas of production, including an important agreement on types of machinery, but none has given up any significant branch of output. Similarly, there are several joint investment projects in operation, of which the most spectacular is an international oil pipeline from the USSR to Poland, East Germany, Hungary, and Czechoslovakia, but broad investment plan coordination is reportedly still under discussion.

Full plan coordination and the close economic integration it would bring are handicapped by the lack of any objective criteria for comparing costs among countries. The controlled prices used in the centrally planned communist economies do not necessarily reflect real values, and their exchange rates do not express relative purchasing power. For this reason, despite the economic and ideological drawbacks, C members have for years conducted their mutual trade through rigid bilateral agreements negotiated with reference to prices in the markets of the noncommunist world. Although a uniform price system would enable both more flexible, multilateral trade and rational decisions as to which country could best produce a given product, the problem is technically complex and deeply involved with established tenets of Soviet Marxist theory. Both coordinated investment planning and a system for general multilateral clearing of foreign trade accounts continue under discussion.

The USSR clearly remains the dominant member of C. The superiority of Soviet economic and military resources logically conditions the meaning of the charter clauses providing "respect for equal rights, national interest, and mutual advantage" and stating that Council decisions depend for their implementation on the consent of the member government. Since Stalin's death, however, and especially since the 1956 revolts in E. Europe, Soviet economic policy toward the smaller C members has become somewhat more equitable. The advantages which the planned division of labor will bring to the individual members nonetheless depend on the degree to which superior Soviet bargaining power is exercised, though more rational coordination under C should advance their efficiency and productivity, as well as that of the area as a whole.

E. M.

COUNCIL OF LABOR AND DEFENSE. A coordinating body formed in April 1920 for defense and economic activities. It was made a permanent commission of the Council of People's Commissars in Dec. 1920 during the eighth congress of Soviets. It continued to serve as the operative body controlling the Soviet economy until it was abolished in Nov. 1937, when its work was shifted to the newly created Economic Council, also a permanent commission of the Council of People's Commissars.

COUNCIL OF MINISTERS: *see* GOVERNMENT CENTRAL.

COUNCIL OF NATIONALITIES: *see* SOVIETS.

COUNCIL OF PEOPLE'S COMMISSARS: *see* GOVERNMENT CENTRAL.

COUNCIL OF THE UNION: *see* SOVIETS.

COURLAND (or Kúrland), Duchy of, founded in the 16th century on the territory of the present Latvian SSR, a hereditary vassal of Poland. It passed to Russia as a result of the Third Partition of Poland in 1795.

(THE) COURT SYSTEM comprises general courts, military tribunals, and arbitration (q.v.), plus any special or quasi-courts which may be added. The Soviet regime in 1917 scrapped the tsarist CS which the Pro-

visional Government (q.v.) had merely reformed. During the terror and counterterror of the Civil War period, 1918–20, the stopgap CS of general courts, revolutionary tribunals, and *Cheka* (q.v.) units dispensed summary and arbitrary justice. The outline of the present general courts emerged in the 1920's with increasing centralization under Stalin when the old native Moslem courts in the Caucasus and Central Asia were abolished (about 1930), transport courts reintroduced (1934), and special boards of the security police were organized (1934) to send Stalin's purge victims to exile, prison, or death. Purge procedures of the police and general courts, which, as Khrushchev confirmed in 1956, included false charges, confession under torture, punishment without trial, contrasted strangely with the attempts to systematize and stabilize the administration of justice. Purges of judges continued to debase their originally low competence. In 1941 only 23.5% of judges in intermediate courts had higher legal training and 23.5% had no legal training, although about 90% were party members.

Post-Stalin reforms include the devolution in 1956–57 of some operative controls on the CS to the Union republics and to the courts themselves. All the republic CS and the USSR Supreme Court conform to the 1958 Fundamental Principles of the CS of the USSR and republics. Republics are in the prolonged process of passing their own laws on their CS and of revising their codes of civil and criminal procedure, laws which will deviate only in small detail from one republic to another.

People's courts hear the bulk of general court cases. In the larger republics having oblasts, krays, autonomous republics, and large cities, one court in each of these areas acts as an intermediate court, hearing the final stage of divorce, and some other civil, more serious criminal cases. There is a one-step appeal of decisions, from people's courts to intermediate courts and no further, or in smaller republics straight to the supreme courts, and from decisions of the intermediate courts to the republic supreme courts and no further. Republic supreme courts act mostly as courts of appeal and review. The USSR Supreme Court hears no appeals except from military tribunals to its military collegium. It hears cases probably even more rarely than do the republic supreme courts. But it does consider protests on decisions of the lower courts by the USSR Procurator-General or by its own president, only, however, when decisions of the lower courts contravene USSR laws or hurt the interests of another republic.

Although a suspect is not to be arrested without an order signed by a prosecutor or court, he can be held incommunicado during the "preliminary investigation" which precedes the trial and gathers most of the evidence for it. The investigation is conducted by investigators under the control of the procurator, or, for political and possibly other crimes, by agents of the central government's Committee of State Security (KGB), the security police arm since 1954. The accused has right to defense counsel only when the investigation—which under Soviet procedure seems more decisive than the court trial itself—is over, and the accused is presented with the record (counsel is permitted earlier for minors or the incapable). The investigation is vital because judges depend heavily on it during the trial. Even this limited right of counsel since the 1958 reforms is an improvement over the previous procedure when the accused had right of counsel only in court. The defense counsel, who may be an attorney, a relative, or a representative of a trade union or other public organization if the accused wishes, is supposed to put up a stiff defense of his client, but he is hampered by widespread misunderstanding of the role of a defense counsel. For example, in spite of strong advocacy by Soviet jurists, presumption of innocence was not explicitly written into the new 1958 Fundamental Principles of criminal procedure, although it was implicit in the rule that burden of proof of guilt lies with the prosecutor. Moreover, counsel must not put the interests of his client ahead of the search for the "truth" of the exact degree of guilt, or ahead of the interests of Soviet society. He is not to "whitewash" his client. Current practice, at least away from the distant provinces, is for counsel to fight hard to have exonerated a client he believes to be innocent, or, if he believes the client committed the act in question, to obtain for him the lightest possible sentence. Trials are public, except when state secrets are involved, or where the court rules otherwise. Since political crimes, as also sex crimes, are tried usually *in camera*, we do not know but can only suspect that defense tends to be less vigorous in political trials. It used to be virtually nonexistent. Civil procedure differs from the above criminal procedure.

Both criminal and noncriminal cases are heard in first instance by a judge and by two nonprofessional people's assessors who have equal rights with the judge during hearings and in reaching decisions but who usually leave active conduct of the trial to the judge. Appeals and protests are heard by three judges. Judges are proclaimed independent and subordinated "only to law." Their independence is in doubt, at least relative to their non-Communist continental European counterparts, because they are accountable to the Communist party, procurators, and higher court officials who may check on their work and reopen cases nominally already closed, where decisions have already gone into effect. One would have more faith in the independence of judges if the strictly centralized USSR procuracy under the Procurator-General did not combine the job of checking on the legality of court decisions with prosecution of criminal cases and representing the interests of the state in civil cases. Judges serve five-year terms after elections, which means really selection by the judicial and party machines. The impression is that CS procedures are fairest in civil cases, which are now 80% of all cases, less just in ordinary criminal cases, least just in political cases.

Justice became more uniform after the abolition of the special security police boards (1953) and the reduction of police power, the elimination of the special transport courts (1957), and the ending of summary special procedures in political trials for "terrorism" (1956). Exceptions to uniformity remain, however. Civilians are tried for espionage in military tribunals. Military tribunals hear all cases under martial law, and try civilians under certain other conditions. Attempts are being made to supplement the regular system of police and courts with various forms of public participation in maintaining law and order. Anti-parasite laws passed during 1957–58 in most of the border republics provide that loafers, vagrants, and other undesirable persons may be sentenced by open, majority vote of meetings of majorities of local residents, subsequently approved by the local soviets, to from 2 to 5 years' exile from their place of residence accompanied by compulsory labor at place of exile. Opposed by many Soviet jurists, these laws might possibly lapse into disuse in the next few years. A once-praised anti-parasite law project for the RSFSR was quashed without ever being adopted. "People's detachments" of civilian volunteers were formed in 1959 alongside the smaller existing "Brigades to Help the Militia," the job of these not always too scrupulous *druzhiniki* being to apprehend disorderly or criminal elements. Under the new system of "guardianship," non-hardened criminals may be put not in confinement but on probation in the care of the state and public organizations at their places of work, where they are to be reformed into honest workers. "Comradely courts" existed apart from the regular court system in the 1930's and were revived in 1957. Organized in factories, villages, farms, and dwelling places, they apply moral force of the "collective" and minor material sanctions in handling misdemeanors and disputes. (*See also* BAR ASSOCIATIONS, CIVIL LAW, CRIMINAL LAW, SOVIET LAW.)

BIBLIOGRAPHY: Harold J. Berman, *Justice in Russia,* Cambridge, 1950; John N. Hazard, *Settling Disputes in Soviet Society,* New York, 1960; Boris A. Konstantinovsky, *Soviet Law in Action: The Recollected Cases of a Soviet Lawyer,* Cambridge, 1953; Herbert McClosky and John E. Turner, *The Soviet Dictatorship,* New York, 1960.
P.H.J.

CP: *see* COMMUNIST PARTY OF THE SOVIET UNION.

CPSU: *see* COMMUNIST PARTY OF THE SOVIET UNION.

CREDIT: *see* BANKING AND CREDIT.

CRIMEAN KHANATE, kingdom on the Crimean peninsula. It was annexed by the Tatars in the 13th century, a vassal of Turkey in late 15th century, and passed to Russia in 1783.

CRIMEAN MOUNTAINS, a range along S.E. coast of Crimea Peninsula; highest peaks in the S. ridge, Roman-Kosh (5,067 ft.) and Chatyr-Dag (5,000 ft.). Formation processes caused earthquake in 1927. Forested gentle slopes in N. with steep slopes in S.; orchards, vineyards, tobacco fields in valleys; subtropical resort area along the Black Sea coast.

CRIMEAN OBLAST, Ukrainian SSR; area, 9,880 sq. mi.; pop. 1,202,000 (1959). Occupies the Crimean Peninsula; borders on Kherson Oblast in the N.; on the Black Sea, bounded by the Sea of Azov in the N.E. and Kerch Strait in the E. Cities: Simferopol (adm. center), Sevastopol, Kerch, Yevpatoria, Feodosia, Yalta, Alupka, Alushta, Balaklava, Bakhchisaray, and numerous other resorts. Its steppe is drained by streams, including the Salgir River; Crimean Mountains are along the S. coast.

Mild climate becoming subtropical in S. Sheep raising in mountains, fruit orchards along S. coast; fisheries; wheat, corn, sunflowers, tobacco, vineyards (in steppe); heavy metallurgy (Kerch), food processing, tourism. Est. 1945.

CRIMINAL LAW defines crimes and prescribes punishments. Its official purpose is to protect the Soviet state and social system, citizens, and the socialist legal order. Protection of the state was the main task of CL during the real emergency of 1918–20, and the Stalin-created emergency following the assassination of Kirov in 1934, from which year date many of the oppressive CL measures annulled under post-Stalin reforms. CL was the first branch of Soviet law to be systematically recodified since the 1920's. The 1958 legislation yielded new Fundamental Principles—of the court system, of CL, of criminal court procedure—which the republics then applied in greater detail to the redrafting of their codes of CL and criminal procedure. The USSR has reserved the right to legislate exclusively on military law and tribunals, and on the definition and punishment of state crimes, as defined in a new 1958 law which will be part of the republic codes.

Criminal codes contain a general part, which includes, for example, definitions of crime, and such rules as: intention is more serious than negligence; insanity or derangement at the time of the crime exempts from punishment, as does necessary self-defense or extreme need of other action in order to prevent a crime. Sentences are more severe for crimes against minors, the old, and the helpless, lowered for pregnant women and in cases of extreme provocation or dire need, and so on. Sentences range from public censure to death. Maximum confinement was lowered in 1958 from 25 to 15 years, but this was countered by stricter policies on release before completion of sentence. Capital punishment was abolished briefly Jan.–May 1920 and May 1947 to Jan. 1950, when it was reinstated for serious political crimes; in April 1954 it was applied also to intentional murder under aggravated circumstances, with much more severe sentencing than before 1917, or 1947 when 10 years was the top sentence. Pregnant women and minors under 18 are exempted. "Aggravated circumstances" has been broadly interpreted to apply to unpremeditated intentional homicide without rape or cruelty.

The special part of CL defines crimes against the state in a manner more precise than before 1958, prescribing penalties up to 15 years or death, plus confiscation of property, for treason, espionage, and terrorism (murder or attempt on life of official as an official). Treason includes flight abroad and refusal to return to the USSR. Anti-racial agitation, serious smuggling, and propaganda for war are classified as less serious crimes against the state. Of these crimes only banditry and refusal to be mobilized in wartime may be capital offenses. In May 1961 the death penalty was broadened to include cases of large-scale embezzlement of Socialist property, and severe punishments were imposed for reporting fraudulent statistical data of production plan fulfillment.

CL reflects the regime's concern for the vast sector of socialist (state and public) property (q.v.). Theft, destruction, or misuse of socialist property is more severely punished than are crimes against personal property in spite of the post-Stalin removal of criminal penalties for several managerial lapses and for sale of surplus equipment to another enterprise. Productive property is the key to power and a potential disruptor of the economy. Moreover, private enterprise is condemned in ideology. Actions which may not be considered crimes in non-communist CL, such as buying goods with the intention of reselling at a profit (called "speculation"), trading in land, or certain failures of economic administrators to fulfill economic tasks—e.g., the "localism" of not making promised deliveries outside of one's own economic region—are subject to criminal penalties. Until 1955 the courts were restricted to high sentences of 5 to 25 years for theft of socialist property (in 1932 the penalty was death, a much-abused measure originally intended against "kulaks"). Since 1955 there has been prescribed for petty theft a maximum penalty of three months' confinement or six months to a year of "corrective labor" (up to 25% cut in pay at place of work without confinement)—a frequent type of punishment for lesser crimes—and, since 1957, lower penalties are specified for petty speculation. Social controls were liberalized by the abolition of penalties for abortion (1955) if performed in medical centers, but tightened in 1956 by an edict ordering Gypsies to end their nomadic ways and take steady jobs, on pain of up to five years' exile with compulsory labor.

Punishment without legal crime was common in Stalinist and pre-Stalinist CL. Relatives of servicemen who escaped abroad were held collectively responsible from 1934 until recently—even relatives who did not know of the flight were exiled to distant parts of Siberia for five years. Special boards of the secret police from 1934 to 1953 were authorized to exile people deemed "socially dangerous." Under the general principle of analogy, a suspect could be punished for an act nowhere specified as a crime by the application of sections of the criminal code describing acts which resembled the act of the suspect. The CL reforms of 1958 ended analogy. Now, in theory, punishment may be meted out only for crimes directly specified by law. (*See also* SOVIET LAW, BAR ASSOCIATIONS, THE COURT SYSTEM)

BIBLIOGRAPHY: Harold J. Berman, *Justice in Russia*, Cambridge, 1950; V. I. Lenin, *et al.*, *Soviet Legal Philosophy*, Hugh W. Babb, trans., Cambridge, 1951; *Fundamentals of Soviet Criminal Legislation, the Judicial System and Criminal Court Procedure*, Moscow, 1960.
                                                              P. H. J.

CRYSTALLOGRAPHY: see PHYSICS.

CUI, César Antónovich (1835–1918), Russian composer and musical critic of French origin. A graduate of the Academy of Military Engineering, he pursued his musical studies at home. Became professor of fortifications and retired with the rank of a major-general; taught engineering to members of the imperial family. Under the influence of Balakirev whom C met in 1857, he became an advocate of R. national music and composed the operas *The Prisoner of the Caucasus* (first performed in 1859), *Feast During the Plague*, and

Captain's Daughter, which, however, did not enjoy the success of his romances. His compositions for orchestra include *Marche Solenelle, Tarantella, Petite Suite;* he also wrote numerous pieces for the piano. As a musical critic C contributed to the success of Balakirev, Musorgsky, Borodin, and Rimsky-Korsakov.

CULTURAL EXCHANGE. Almost immediately after the death of Joseph Stalin in March 1953, his successors proclaimed that they favored the "free development of contacts" between the Soviet Union and all other countries. Partly in response to the Soviet "cultural offensive" the term "cultural diplomacy" came into increasing use in the West to describe exchanges of persons, particularly those of scientific eminence, and of cultural materials, conducted with political objectives or at least with an awareness of their possible political consequences.

In terms of human and financial resources involved, the effort with which we are here concerned represents a new dimension of the Kremlin's diplomacy and propaganda. In its ultimate purposes, however, it is squarely in the revolutionary Lenin tradition which Khrushchev sought to revive after his discrediting of Stalinism in 1956. It also bears many marks of the heritage of Stalin, who himself, especially before the great purges of 1936–38, was an energetic practitioner of cultural diplomacy.

Many of Stalin's actions reflected his belief that the display of Soviet achievements to foreign visitors in the USSR, or to all who were interested abroad, was of great political significance. He often interrupted his busy schedule to play host to delegations of labor leaders, artistic and literary figures, and other foreign notables. Not infrequently he took the trouble to receive individually such personages as H. G. Wells, George Bernard Shaw, Emil Ludwig, Lion Feuchtwanger, and many others. In a statement to the 14th Congress of the Russian Communist Party in 1925 Stalin revealed a basic motive for this policy. He told the Congress that visits of groups from India, Egypt, and China, as well as of delegations of workers from the W., constituted "the best, most forceful and active propaganda for the Soviet system against the capitalist system." In a somewhat similar vein, Khrushchev, during his visit to the United States in Sept. 1959, professed a desire for "the broadest possible cultural and scientific exchange" between Russia and America, and linked such exchange to peaceful competition between rival social systems.

In 1925, VOKS, the All-Union Society for Cultural Relations with Foreign Countries, was established. In Feb. 1958, VOKS dissolved itself and was replaced by the Union of Soviet Societies for Friendship and Cultural Relations with Foreign Countries. Although Soviet sources stated that the methods employed by VOKS had become outmoded, there appears to be no essential difference between its activities and those of its successor organization which, like VOKS, is officially described as a "voluntary, public organization" and is carefully distinguished in Soviet terminology from such state agencies as the Ministry of Foreign Affairs or the State Committee for Cultural Relations with Foreign Countries, established in 1957. Like VOKS, the Union of Friendship Societies operates mainly on a nominally nongovernmental level. It invites artistic, literary, and, sometimes, scientific delegations to visit the USSR and arranges for formal meetings between such groups and Soviet colleagues. It also is active in the dissemination of Soviet publications to foreign scholars and intellectuals.

The State Committee for Cultural Relations with Foreign Countries, to the chairmanship of which Georgy A. Zhukov, former *Pravda* foreign editor, was appointed upon its establishment, played a major role in Khrushchev's expansion of cultural diplomacy. The State Committee has negotiated a number of cultural agreements and treaties with foreign countries, including the United Kingdom (1959), the German Federal Republic, India, France, the United Arab Republic, and Afghanistan. Of particular interest to Americans is the United States-Soviet Agreement on Educational, Scientific and Cultural Exchanges, signed in Jan. 1958, and extended for two years in Dec. 1959. In addition to negotiating over-all agreements, the State Committee takes a hand in negotiation of important individual cultural exchanges, working often with other Soviet agencies, such as the Ministry of Culture.

Another organization which plays an important part in the Soviet system of guided culture contact is Intourist, the official tourist agency. Founded in 1928 as one of several Soviet-style "joint stock" companies, and still so organized, Intourist had, as of 1957, some five thousand employees, according to an article in the Soviet English language magazine for Americans, *USSR.* Its staff has probably grown considerably since then, if one can assume some proportionality between its size and the swelling dimensions of tourist travel to the USSR. In the case of the United States, for example, about 2,500 tourists visited the Soviet Union in 1956, while estimates for 1960 were in the neighborhood of 25,000. With its network of hotels and restaurants and its staffs of interpreters, chauffeurs, and so forth, Intourist has shepherded and guided, served, helped, and sometimes obstructed thousands of foreign tourists, teachers, students, businessmen, and others who have over the years come to the "land of socialism" to observe, to marvel, or to compare impressions based on printed sources with whatever aspects of Soviet reality they were able to see and appraise for themselves. Most foreign visitors to Russia, with the exception of such categories as diplomats and journalists on long-term assignments, must use the facilities of Intourist by virtue of its monopoly control over indispensable services. With the recovery of the Soviet economy from the effects of World War II and the partial reopening of the USSR to foreign contact that followed Stalin's death, the services of Intourist were expanded and improved. However, it is fair to say that the Soviet system of official tourism of which Intourist is a part still serves to render travel in Russia highly restricted by free world standards. The consequences of this situation, in terms of concealing aspects of Soviet life which the Kremlin does not wish to disclose, are of course significant if, as is usually the case, foreign visitors do not have a working knowledge of the Russian language.

The main professed purpose of Soviet cultural exchange policy has always been the "struggle for peace." For example, Nikolay Mikhaylov, Soviet minister of culture, wrote in *Pravda* for April 2, 1956, that "the development of cultural relations between the Soviet Union and Great Britain will undoubtedly contribute to the noble aims, common to both peoples, of consolidating peace." It is significant also that the post-Stalin cultural campaign was launched in June 1953, at the Budapest meeting of the major international communist-front organization, the World Peace Council, which has continued to coordinate its activities with those of the Soviet cultural apparatus. This aspect of Soviet cultural diplomacy appears to be intended to strengthen the desired image of the USSR and the Soviet bloc in general as champions of peace, while at the same time casting the United States in the role of chief warmonger. Furtherance of Soviet disarmament policy and hindrance of American defense efforts are corollary themes of much of the Soviet propaganda disseminated in connection with major Communist cultural exchange projects, such as the mammoth Moscow Festival of Youth and Students (1957) and the next in this series, held in Vienna in 1959.

Because it is the chief rival of the USSR in the world-wide propaganda and power struggle, the United States is also a major target of Soviet cultural diplomacy. While W. Europe has consistently held first priority in the Soviet program, at least in terms of numbers and quality of the Soviet personnel involved, some of the Soviet Union's most elaborate and costly projects, such as the Soviet Exhibition of Science, Technology and Culture, displayed in the New York City Coliseum for six weeks in 1959, were designed to impress Americans. Later, however, this Exhibition was displayed in Mexico and then in Cuba. Besides peace, the Soviet Exhibition stressed such propaganda themes as full employment, free education and medical care and other social services, Soviet scientific progress, and, perhaps most conspicuously of all, the abundance of Soviet machinery.

In contrast, the American National Exposition, held in July, Aug., and early Sept. 1959 in the Moscow Sokolniki Park, placed its main emphasis on the glittering gadgetry of American consumer goods and on the easy availability to the average American of a wide range of services, comforts, and luxuries. There is no doubt that the more than one million Americans who saw the Soviet Exhibition and the more than two and one-half million Soviet visitors to its American counterpart had many valuable opportunities to increase their knowledge and deepen their understanding of one another's social and political system, culture, and way of life.

Many other developments of a kind inconceivable in the late Stalin era came about in Soviet-American cultural relations following the signature of the Jan. 1958 Agreement. It should not be forgotten, however, that even the relative freedom of contact of recent years has not permitted the degree of informality and spontaneity

which characterized personal and professional relations between citizens of the two countries in the 1920's and early 1930's. Perhaps the most interesting and potentially useful of the exchanges that followed the 1958 Agreement was a modest, and thus far slowly growing, exchange of graduate students between American and Soviet universities. Further expansion and improvement of this type of exchange, which involved numerous difficulties for both sides in view of great differences of institutional, cultural, and ideological backgrounds, might do more than almost any other kind of communication to facilitate, if not agreement, at least mutual comprehension and respect.

In addition, there were Soviet-American exchanges in almost every conceivable field in the post-Stalin years, especially after conclusion of the official Agreement in 1958, but also before this, as in the important case of the first exchange of agricultural delegations in 1955, which brought to the United States the astute Vladimir Matskevich, later to become minister of agriculture. Many leading Soviet and American artists and art groups performed successfully in one another's countries. However, incompatibilities between American "show business" and the Soviet cultural bureaucracy shaped the somewhat constricted pattern of these exchanges.

Although Moscow has devoted less of its cultural resources to the underdeveloped countries than to W. Europe and the United States, it is perhaps in the less industrialized lands that Soviet cultural diplomacy has the greatest potential for future influence. Africa and Latin America have not been neglected by the Kremlin cultural strategists. Beginning in 1955 the Soviet authorities undertook a revival of Oriental studies which led to development of a substantial, growing program of teaching and research on the history, languages and literatures, and the economic and political conditions of the peoples of the non-industrialized countries. At both the 20th Congress of the CPSU in 1956 and the Extraordinary 21st Congress in 1959 such toprank-ing party Presidium members as, respectively, Anastas Mikoyan and Mikhail Suslov demanded that Soviet scholars produce works which would be useful in carrying the Soviet message to these areas.

The visit by Nikita S. Khrushchev and Nikolay Bulganin to India, Burma, and Afghanistan in 1955 and Khrushchev's visit in 1959 to Indonesia and other S.E. Asian countries, again including India and Afghanistan, lent impetus to Soviet efforts at cultural penetration in these and neighboring countries. Mikoyan's visits and speech-making in Mexico and Cuba in 1959 reminded North Americans that the Soviet Union did not intend to refrain from persuasion and subversion in the W. hemisphere. A significant move, which may for some time be difficult to evaluate, was taken in 1960 when Khrushchev announced in Indonesia that the Soviet government had decided to open, in Moscow, a special Peoples' Friendship University (q.v.), primarily for students from Asia, Africa, and Latin America. According to *Sovetskaya Kultura* (Soviet Culture), the newspaper of the Ministry of Culture, for Feb. 25, 1960, the new university was to be under the joint sponsorship of the "Soviet Committee for Solidarity of the Countries of Asia and Africa," the already-mentioned Union of Friendship Societies, and the All-Union Council of Trade Unions. (*See also* TRAVELING AND TOURISM)

BIBLIOGRAPHY: Frederick C. Barghoorn, *Soviet Cultural Diplomacy*, Princeton, 1960; Frederick C. Barghoorn, with the assistance of Paul W. Friedrich, "Cultural Relations and Soviet Foreign Policy," *World Politics*, Vol. VIII, No. 3 (April 1956); Walter Z. Laqueur, ed., "Cultural Exchanges," *Soviet Survey*, No. 31, Jan.–March 1960; Ruth Emily McMurry and Muna Lee, *The Cultural Approach*, Chapel Hill, 1947; Louis Nemzer, "The Soviet Friendship Societies," *Public Opinion Quarterly*, Vol. XIII (Summer 1949).   F. C. B.

CUMÁNS (Pólovtsy), nomads of Turkic origin. They founded the nomadic state of Desht-i-Kipchak (middle of the 11th to early 13th century) in the steppes along the Black Sea; they repeatedly attacked R. principalities and often interfered in the feuds of R. princes. C were conquered by Tatars in the 13th century and joined the Golden Horde.

CURRENCY: *see* MONETARY SYSTEM.

CURZON LINE. Named for the then British Foreign Secretary, it was first proposed as the frontier between Russia and Poland in 1920 as part of an attempt by the Allies to end hostilities between the two countries. The line ran from Grodno through Bialystok south to Brest-Litovsk, from there along the Bug River to a point near Sokoly and south past Przemysl to the Carpathians. At the time both Soviets and Poles rejected the proposed border and, in the Treaty of Riga, determined on a line well to the E. But in 1944 at Teheran, the Big Three recognized the CL as the new frontier between Poland and the Soviet Union, though with minor rectifications. Poland was compensated for her substantial territorial loss by the extension of her W. border to include Silesia and a portion of East Prussia.

CYBERNETICS: *see* MATHEMATICS.

CYRIL and METHODIUS (Kiríll and Mefódy), two brothers from Thessalonica in Macedonia, Christian missionaries in Moravia in the 9th century. They are credited with the invention of the Slavonic alphabet to which they adapted the Greek speedwriting of their time "kirillitsa," the Cyrillic alphabet. Cyril (Constantin before he took monastic vows, 827–869) preached Christianity to the Khazars, and with Methodius (885) created a Slavonic literary language which was used by a considerable number of western and eastern Slavic tribes. In 1708 Peter I simplified and changed the Slavonic alphabet into the so-called "civilian alphabet"

used at present with small changes. The Slavonic alphabet and language are still used by the Orthodox Church. (*See* ALPHABET).

CZARTORYSKI, Prince Adam Jerzy (1770–1861), scion of an aristocratic Polish family, patriot and statesman. Educated in Edinburgh, he fought for his country during the war of the second partition following which his estates were confiscated by Russia and he was sent as a hostage to St. Petersburg. C, however, gained the confidence and friendship of young Alexander, the future emperor of Russia, and after his ascension was appointed R. minister of foreign affairs. For a number of years he was Emperor Alexander I's trusted adviser. The champion of the restoration of a united autonomous Poland (in 1772 boundaries) under the scepter of the R. tsars, C distrusted and opposed Napoleon's policy and devised a comprehensive plan for an Anglo-Russian league and a new order in Europe. In 1806 C resigned as minister of foreign affairs. At the Congress of Vienna, as a member of Alexander I's entourage, C favored the creation of an autonomous constitutional kingdom of Poland under the Russian Crown. Contrary to expectations, he was not appointed viceroy of the new kingdom. C had an active part in the Polish insurrection of 1830–31 and was for a short time the head of the provisional (later national) Polish government. Following the defeat of the Poles by the Russians, C was sentenced to death but fled to Paris where his residence, Hotel Lambert, became a political center of Polish *émigrés*.

CZECHOSLOVAK LEGION. Formed in 1914, the Legion consisted of Czech and Slovak prisoners-of-war and deserters from the Austro-Hungarian army anxious to fight against the Central Powers for their country's independence. Soon it numbered upwards of 40,000 men. After the Russian Revolution, the Legion determined to continue fighting the Germans on the W. front, a destination it hoped to reach via Vladivostok. The Soviets granted it permission to leave in March 1918, but a clash between the Legion and local Bolsheviks at Chelyabinsk, Siberia, in May brought a government order that the former be disarmed and detained. Further clashes followed. By mid-1918, the Czechs controlled all the principal cities along the Trans-Siberian Railway from the Urals to the Pacific. They were regarded as the mainstay of the anti-Bolshevik forces, but they grew progressively more passive as Allied intervention languished, and they finally withdrew from Russia in 1919.

D

DAGESTÁN ASSR, part of RSFSR, situated between the Caucasus Mountains and the Caspian Sea. Area 19,415 sq. mi.; pop. 1,063,000 (1959), consisting of 30 nationalities belonging to 5 main groups: Avars, Dargins, Lezgins, Kumyks, Laks. Cities: Makhachkala (adm. center), Derbent, Buynaksk, Khasavyurt, Kaspiysk, Izberbash. On the slopes of the mountains are

forests and semidesert plains; climate is moderately warm and dry. Minerals are oil, coal, siderites, natural gas; has considerable oil and chemical ind.; agr.: wheat, corn, barley, vegetables, cotton, vineyards; fishing, hunting. Several schools of higher learning, pedag. inst., museums, branch of Ac. of S. USSR; considerable development of national art and literature. Est. 1921.

DAGŒ: *see* KHIUMA.

DAIRY FARMING: *see* CATTLE BREEDING.

DAL (Dahl), Vladímir Ivánovich (1801–1872), writer,  ethnographer, and linguist. Honorary member of the St. Petersburg Ac. of S. (1863). He is the author of the monumental *Comprehensive Dictionary of Living Great-Russian Language* (4 vols., 1863–66) which it took him 53 years to compile; collected in *Proverbs of Russian Folk* (1862) about 30,000 proverbs; published also songs, novels, and essays.

DAN (Gurvich), Fyodor Ilyich (1871–1947), Menshevik leader. Joined the social-democratic movement in 1894; was active in the St. Petersburg "Union of Struggle for the Liberation of the Working Class" (q.v.). In 1902 became a contributor of *Iskra* (q.v.). Repeatedly arrested and exiled. After 1906, was a permanent member of the Menshevik Central Committee. In World War I was mobilized as a physician. After the February revolution, D was one of the influential leaders in the Executive Committee of the Soviets. Was arrested by the Bolsheviks in 1921. In 1922 D emigrated abroad where he became an editor of the *Sotsialistichesky Vestnik* (Socialist Courier), first in Berlin, then in Paris; and the Menshevik representative to the Second International. In 1940, he settled in New York where he died. D is the author of *The Origin of Bolshevism* (New York, 1946).

DÁNIELSON, Nikoláy Frántsevich (1844–1918), publicist who signed his writings "Nikolay-on." An ideologist of the liberal populist movement in the 1860's and the 1890's, he translated into Russian the first volume of Marx's *Capital.* He considered the doctrine of Marx inapplicable in Russia, an opinion for which he was severely criticized by Lenin.

DANILÉVSKY, Grigóry Petróvich (1829–1890), author of many historical novels and stories: *Miróvich* (1879), *Moscow Burned* (1886), *The Black Year* (1888–89), and others describing Pugachov's mutiny, Napoleon's invasion, and so forth.

DANILÉVSKY, Nikoláy Yákovlevich (1828–1885), prominent publicist, an advocate of naturalist philosophy. In his youth an enthusiastic member of Petrashevsky's circle (q.v.), D later became an eloquent exponent of R. nationalism. His principal work, *Russia and Europe,* advanced the theory of unique and distinctive patterns of national culture, with special reference to Slavic cultural heritage as inherently incompatible with the European tradition. In *Darwinism,* published shortly before his death, D's non-receptive attitude toward contemporary western thought was demonstrated even more clearly in the valiant, if unsuccessful, attempt to refute Darwin's theory of evolution.

DANUBE (R. *Dunáy*), river in Europe, second in size after the Volga; length, 1,770 mi.; navigable. Rises in Germany, flows through Austria, Czechoslovakia, Hungary, Yugoslavia, Rumania, Bulgaria, USSR. Port in USSR: Izmail.

DARGHINS: *see* POPULATION.

DARGOMÝZHSKY, Aleksándr Sergéyevich (1813–1869), composer and pianist. Son of a government offi-

 cial, he studied violin and piano at home, entered the civil service (1831), and did not become seriously interested in music until he met Glinka (1834) after which he devoted himself entirely to music. His only theoretical training was derived from copying Glinka's notebooks containing exercises in harmony. D's compositions include the operas *Esmeralda* (1847) and *The Mermaid,* produced in 1856 with considerable success in St. Petersburg and which has remained his best-known work; *The Stone Guest,* posthumosuly completed (1872) by his colleagues; orchestral music; 90 pieces for voice and piano; and 15 vocal duets.

DARVÁZA RANGE, in Tadzhik SSR, length about 115 mi.; highest peak 19,950 ft.; covered with perennial snow and glaciers; pastures.

DARYÁL (R. *Daryálskoye Ushchélye*), gorge in Caucasus, E. of Mt. Kazbek, formed by Terek River; depth about 5,900 ft. Crossed by Georgian Military Road. Famed for wild grandeur and immortalized by Lermontov.

DÁSHKOVA, Princess Yekaterína Románovna (1743–1810). From 1783 to 1796 she was director of the Petersburg Academy of Sciences and president of the newly founded R. Academy for the Development of the Russian Language. She was instrumental in the palace coup in 1762 which brought to power Catherine II.

DASHNAKTSUTYÚN, Armenian nationalist party propagating agrarian-socialist ideas, similar to those advocated by the Socialist Revolutionaries (q.v.). The party was organized in Turkish Armenia in the 1890's. Its activity was tolerated by the tsarist government until the party began to enlist R. Armenians with the aim of creating an independent state of Great Armenia. The R. government incited the Transcaucasian Moslems (Tatars) to violence against the Armenians; the latter retaliated and bloody riots resulted. In 1917 the Dashnaks supported the Provisional Government and opposed Bolshevik rule. The D was banned after the Soviets took over. The leaders of D were: Kh. Mikaelyan, S. Zavaryan, R. Zoryan, Kh. Malumyan, and others.

DÁUGAVA: *see* DVINA, WESTERN.

DÁUGAVPILS (f. Dvinsk, Ger. *Dünaburg*), city in Latvian SSR, on Daugava (W. Dvina); pop. 52,000 (1939), 65,000 (1959). R.R. junction; locomotive and car-repair shops. Founded in 13th century.

DAVIDÉNKOV, Nikoláy Nikoláyevich (1879–), mechanical engineer. Fellow, Ac. of S., Ukrainian SSR (1939). Graduate, Institute of Railroad Engineering in St. Petersburg (1902); professor, Leningrad Polytechnic Institute; head, Department for the Study of Mechanical Properties of Metals, Institute of Physics and Technology (1925). Research concerns the behavior of metals under high-velocity impacts, cold brittleness, plastic deformation, theory of strength with three dimensional state of stress, residual stress, metal fatigue. Stalin prize (1943). Author of *Fatigue of Metals* (1949).

DÁVYDOV, Denis Vasilyevich (1784–1839), hero of the war of 1812, poet, and military writer. He organized partisan units to fight the French during the invasion. He was the author of *Essay on the Theory of Partisan Action* and several collections of patriotic verse: *The Hussar Feast, Contemporary Songs,* and others.

DAVÝDOV, Vladímir Nikolávevich (Gorélov, Iván Nikoláyevich), (1849–1925), actor. Made his debut in the provinces to become a leading actor at Aleksandrinsky Theater in St. Petersburg (1880). His acting, in the tradition of R. realism, showed psychological insight and he was widely acclaimed for his brilliant characterizations. D took the leading parts in plays by Griboyedov, Gogol, and others. Author of the memoirs *Tale of the Past,* published posthumously in 1931.

DEATH RATE: *see* MEDICAL SYSTEM, POPULATION.

DEATH TAX: *see* INHERITANCE.

DEBÁLTSEVO, city in Stalino Oblast, Ukrainian SSR; pop. 32,500 (1956). Important R.R. center in Donets coal basin; machine building and mining.

DEBÓRIN (Ioffe), **Abrám Moiséyevich** (1881–), Soviet philosopher and historian. Joined the Bolsheviks in 1903; later became a Menshevik; from 1928, again a Bolshevik. In the 1920's, D was the editor of the magazine *Pod Znamenem Marksizma* (Under the Banner of Marxism) and secretary of the historical section of the Ac. of S. In 1931, D was criticized for his "idealism" and faded into relative obscurity.

DECEMBRISTS. The Decembrist insurrection took place on Dec. 14 (Dec. 26, N.S.) 1825. It was organized mainly by members of the R. upper classes affiliated with the secret societies that had sprung up in Russia after the Napoleonic War of 1812–15. The desire for change was stimulated by economic stagnation, high taxation, and the realization of the need for thoroughgoing reform. Some of the more socially-minded representatives of the upper classes were deeply disappointed in the reactionary policies pursued by Alexander I during the latter part of his reign, by the military settlements of Arakcheyev, and by the tsar's cooperation with Metternich. Most of the Decembrists had been educated on the ideas of the French and German philosophers, which had penetrated Russia in many ways. The French Revolution (1789) had had a considerable impact on educated Russians. Many sons of the privileged classes had gone to W. European universities and had brought home new ideas about political order and social organization. Army officers abroad during the war and during the subsequent occupation of France had had an opportunity to see the changing social patterns of the West. Moreover, an important role in the intellectual formation of the R. opposition was played by the new R. literature, which was full of moral and social protest against R. backwardness. Among the writers were Nikolay Novikov, Aleksandr Radishchev, the poets Pushkin and Griboyedov, and many others.

While at the beginning of the 19th century Free Masonry in Russia was weak and carefully avoided engaging in political activity, some of the D were affiliated with Masonic groups, and the secret political societies were undoubtedly influenced by the Masonic movement. The first secret society, the Union of Salvation, was founded in St. Petersburg in 1816. Its

membership included Prince Sergey Trubetskoy, Matvey and Sergey Muravyov-Apostol, Aleksandr and Mikhail Muravyov, and Pavel Pestel. This group led later to the creation of the Union of the Public Good (1818), which was subsequently dissolved (1821) and re-established under the name of the Northern Society (1822). The leading members of the Northern Society included Nikita Muravyov, Prince Sergey Trubetskoy, Prince Yevgeny Obolensky, Nikolay Turgenev, and the poet Kondraty Ryleyev. Another secret group, the so-called Southern Society, was founded in Tulchin, Ukraine, in 1821 by Pestel, who was stationed with his regiment in the south of Russia. A third group, the Society of the United Slavs, founded in 1823 by Pyotr Borisov, and aiming at the creation of a federation of Slavic peoples, merged with the Southern Society in 1825. While both the Northern and Southern societies aimed at the abolition of the autocracy and the liquidation of serfdom, there were profound differences between the two groups. Notwithstanding some internal dissension, the Northern Society was on the whole more conservative in its social program and tended toward a constitutional monarchy. The uncompleted constitutional project prepared for the Society by Nikita Muravyov, while guaranteeing the equality of all citizens before the law, imposed property qualifications on the right to vote and the right to seek elective office. It postulated the emancipation of the serfs and small land apportionments, but at the same time emphasized the rights and interests of the landed classes. On the other hand, the "Russian Truth," a constitutional project of the Southern Society, drawn up by Pestel, was much more radical in both its social demands and the contemplated political set-up. Pestel, a pupil of the French Jacobins, contemplated the establishment of a rigidly centralized democratic republic with a dictatorial provisional government taking charge during the period of transition. The project proclaimed also the necessity of emancipating the serfs and appropriations of land sufficient to support the liberated peasants. Significantly, this comprehensive project foresaw the annexation of many neighboring territories, including Moldavia, additional lands of Caucasia, and areas inhabited by Mongols and Kirghiz. Pestel also demanded a total assimilation of all these different peoples into one R. nation, and did not recognize the right of secession. There were two exceptions to this far-reaching program of expansion and Russification: one was Poland, where it was contemplated to establish an independent state provided that it would be patterned on the system prevailing in Russia; the other was the Jews, who, Pestel believed, had to be treated in an especially strong fashion because of their resistance to assimilation. Expulsion of the Jews from Russia, however, appeared to him more desirable, and he envisaged the establishment of a Jewish state in Asia Minor.

There were a number of moves toward reaching understanding between and coordination of practical plans of the Northern and Southern societies, but substantial differences regarding the character and role of the provisional government, the land program, and so on remained.

The date of the insurrection was not determined

in advance. The sudden death of the childless Alexander I (Nov. 19, 1825), the unwillingness of his brother Constantine to take the throne, and the confusion over the succession forced the hand of the secret societies. The leaders of the Northern Society fixed the date for the insurrection as Dec. 14, 1825, the date on which the oath of loyalty to the new emperor, Nicholas I, was to be taken. The organizers of the insurrection hoped that the soldiers would refuse to take the oath to Nicholas and that in the ensuing chaos it would be possible to force a call for a constituent assembly and the establishment of a provisional government. In fact, only some 3,000 soldiers and sailors followed the rebellious officers, refused to take the oath, and revolted. The rebellious regiments proceeded to the Senate Square in St. Petersburg and stood there, without effective leadership and unprepared for action. The Governor General of St. Petersburg, Nikolay Miloradovich, who tried to negotiate with the rebels, fell victim to a bullet fired by one of the officers, Pyotr Kakhovsky. Meanwhile, even earlier, the tsar had accepted the oath of the Council of State and the Senate, and substantial army forces loyal to him were brought to the Senate Square, where they surrounded the rebels. After some artillery fire the hesitating soldiers surrendered and the insurrection of St. Petersburg was over.

The St. Petersburg insurrection was followed, on Dec. 29, 1825, by the rebellion of the Chernigov regiment, which offered little resistance and was liquidated by government troops on Jan. 3, 1826 near the village of Kovalevka, in Ukraine.

Repression was immediate and far-reaching. Speransky, the erstwhile liberal, was one of the members of the trial tribunal. Altogether 579 individuals involved in the D uprising were investigated; 79 per cent of them were army personnel. One hundred twenty-one D were brought to trial. Five—Pestel, Muravyov-Apostol, Bestuzhev-Ryumin, Kakhovsky, and Ryleyev—were hanged; thirty-one went into penal servitude, and the rest were deported to Siberia. Many of the rebellious soldiers were forced to run the gauntlet. The entire Chernigov regiment was sent to Caucasia, where there was a local war in progress.

Thus ended the first organized rebellion against the tsar in modern times. While it was easily crushed and shattered, it nevertheless marked the beginning of the modern R. revolutionary tradition. The ideas of the D were taken over and influenced the ideological development of generations of the R. intelligentsia in the 19th century and beyond.   L. SH.

BIBLIOGRAPHY: A. G. Mazour, *The First Russian Revolution, 1825*, Berkeley, 1937.

DEGÁYEV, Sergéy Petróvich (1854–1908), a member of the terrorist "People's Will" and a police agent. In 1881 he participated in an attempt on the life of the tsar. After his arrest, he became an *agent provocateur*. When his double role became known, the revolutionaries forced D to assassinate the police chief Sudeykin.

DEGTYARYÓV, Vasíly Alekséyevich (1879–1949), major general. Expert in the design of artillery arms. Doctor of technical sciences. Of humble origin, he rose from the ranks and worked at various ammunition factories from the age of ten. After the 1917 revolution he designed machine guns and automatic weapons used for Soviet rearmament. Deputy to the Supreme Soviet, USSR (1937, 1946). Hero of Socialist Labor (1940). Chief of the Office of Armament Design. Stalin prizes (1941, 1942, 1944, 1946).

DEKHTERYÓV, Borís Aleksándrovich (1908–), illustrator and graphic artist. His reputation stems mainly from his illustrations for books by N. A. Ostrovsky and F. Gladkov and editions of the R. classics; also known for his stage settings. He has taught graphic arts at the State Art Institute since 1948. Stalin prize.

DÉLVIG, Baron Antón Antónovich (1798–1831), poet, and friend of Pushkin, his classmate at the *lycée* of Tsarskoye Selo. Descendant of an old German family, D was a leading member of Pushkin's "Pleiade" (circle), and the chief organizer of its literary activities. D wrote a few poems in the classical manner and songs on popular themes. In 1830 he began publishing the *Literaturnaya Gazeta* (Literary Gazette) but was prevented from continuing by censorship.

DEMÍDOV FAMILY. The founder of the family was Nikita Demidovich Antufyev (Demidov, since 1702) (1656–1725), a Tula blacksmith who received land grants from Peter I on which he established iron works. In the 18th century the Demidovs controlled a vast empire comprising 55 enterprises, of which 40 were in the Urals; they produced over 40 per cent of the total output of R. cast iron in the 18th century, and about 25 per cent in the early 19th century. The family was raised to nobility in 1726 and the title of Prince San Donato was purchased in Italy by Anatoly Nikolayevich Demidov (1812–70) who was married to Matilde, daughter of Jerome Bonaparte and a niece of Napoleon I. The title was officially recognized in 1872. The Demidovs played an important part as patrons of arts and sciences.

DEMOCRATIC CENTRALISM is advanced as the guiding principle of the organizational structure of the CP and is defined in the party rules as follows: (a) the election of all leading party bodies, from the lowest to the highest; (b) periodic reports of the party bodies to their party organizations; (c) strict party discipline and subordination of the minority to the majority; (d) the absolutely binding character of the decision of higher bodies upon lower bodies. In practice intra-party democracy does not exist. The party leaders are promoted by designation from above rather than by elections from below. Discussion and criticism are encouraged only within carefully defined limits. Substantive party policies and decisions may not be criticized or rejected. No mechanism exists through which the rank-and-file party members may voice their opposition to party policy and suggest alternatives, nor may they form factions to oppose of the leadership.   H. W. M.

DEMOCRATIC CONFERENCE, a consultative body convoked in Petrograd on Sept. 27, 1917. The failure of the Moscow State Conference and the following Kornilov "mutiny" (q.v.) caused the resignation from the Provisional Government of the ministers representing the liberal groups. At the same time the moderate Left had lost its majority in the Petrograd, Moscow, and some other Soviets. In this situation a new consultative conference was called, from which all the propertied elements were excluded, the largest representation being accorded to the Soviets, to municipal and zemstvo assemblies, to cooperatives and trade unions. Of the 1,775 delegates some 10 per cent were Bolsheviks. After four days of discussion, on Oct. 2 the main political question of the day came up before the DC: whether a new government should be based on a coalition of the socialist and nonsocialist elements. On the vote, 766 delegates were for a coalition, 688 against, with 38 abstaining. However, an amendment excluding the Kadets (members of the Constitutional Democratic party) from the coalition won a majority: 595 against 493, with 72 abstaining. Since the Kadets constituted the sole nonsocialist party of any size or significance, the formula "coalition without Kadets" was meaningless; and when it was put to a vote, it was defeated by 813 to 183, with 80 abstaining. The DC had thus proved unable to solve the crisis. Before dispersing, the DC appointed from its members a body of about 350 delegates to form the Council of the Republic or Pre-Parliament which was to represent the nation until the convocation of the Constituent Assembly.　　v. su.

DEMOCRATIC REFORM PARTY, a moderately liberal grouping that separated itself from the Constitutional Democratic party shortly after its formation (in 1905). Unlike the Constitutional Democratic party it supported the bicameral parliamentary system, opposed the extension of the right to vote to women, and manifested an ambivalent attitude with regard to the granting of autonomy to Poland. It existed for only a short time. Its leaders included several personalities highly respected in academic circles, such as Prof. M. M. Kovalevsky, K. K. Arsenyev, M. M. Stasyulevich.

DÉMUT-MALINÓVSKY, Vasíly Ivánovich (1779–1846), sculptor, partisan of R. classicism of the early 19th century. Graduated from the Academy of Fine Arts in 1800. In 1803 was sent to Italy. On his return he worked on sculptural decoration of buildings designed by the best architects of the period, such as Zakharov, Voronichin, Stasov and Rossi. His best works executed in monumental classical style are: sculptural decoration of the Military Headquarters (1828–29), executed in collaboration with Pimenov, statue of St. Andrew in the Kazan Cathedral, 44 bas-reliefs in Mikhailovsky Castle (1823–25), sculptural decorations of the Aleksandrinsky Theater (1831–32), the Senate and the Synode, all in St. Petersburg.

DENÍKIN, Antón Ivánovich (1872–1947), Lt. General, one of the organizers of the White (anti-Bolshevik) Army during the civil war of 1918–1920. From peasant stock, mother Polish. After the February revolution of 1917, he was appointed chief of staff; later, commander in chief for the S. and S.W. fronts. Arrested in 1917 as an active supporter of the unsuccessful uprising led by Gen. Kornilov, D escaped to the Don region where, together with Kornilov and Alekseyev, he began to organize the White army. Serving as Gen. Kornilov's aide during the first anti-Soviet campaign, in 1918, D took over the command after Kornilov had been killed in action. The White army, led by D, including the Kuban and Don Cossack troops headed by Generals Shkuro and Krasnov, occupied N. Caucasus and started to advance toward Moscow, in the direction of Voronezh and Orel. In the summer of 1919 the White army took Kharkov, Kiev, Voronezh, and, for a brief time, captured Orel, but was routed by the Bolsheviks, in Oct. 1919, and retreated to the S. of Russia. In March 1920, the remainder of D's troops were brought over to Crimea and placed under the command of Gen. Wrangel. D spent the remaining years of his life in France, where he published a *History of the Civil Strife in Russia.* in 5 volumes.

DERYÁGIN, Borís Vladímirovich (1902–), physicist. Corresponding member, Ac. of S., USSR (1946). Graduated from Moscow University (1922). Head of the Laboratory of Surface-Active Forces, Institute of Physical Chemistry. Proposed the theories of coagulation of dispersed systems in electrolytes (1935–41), of external friction of solid bodies (1934), and of electrical adhesion. Author of *New Ideas in the Field of Aerosol Studies* (1949), *The Nature of Friction* (1952).

DERYÚGIN, Konstantín Mikháylovich (1878–1938), zoologist. Graduate (1905), professor (1910–38), St. Petersburg (Leningrad) University. Founder of research centers on the White Sea and the Pacific Ocean. Discovered underwater currents in Bay of Finland and established nomenclature of zones. Author of the series *Investigations of the Seas of the USSR*, 25 volumes; *Fauna and Flora of the Kola Peninsula.*

DERZHÁVIN, Gavríla Románovich (1743–1816), greatest poet of the 18th century, the direct predecessor  of A. S. Pushkin. In solemn odes in honor of Catherine II (*Felitsa*, 1783, and others) D sharply criticized court life. He lampooned unjust bureaucrats, parasitic aristocracy (*The Courtier*, 1776, *To the Potentates and Judges*, 1780). In his patriotic odes commemorating victories of R. armies, he created grandiose portraits of R. army leaders. His poetry is characterized by a remarkable though uneven mastery of language. His best works are: *The Death of Prince Meshchérsky*, 1779–83, and *The Waterfall*, 1791–94.

DESNÁ RIVER, in Smolensk and Bryansk oblasts, RSFSR; Chernigov and Kiev oblasts, Ukrainian SSR, left tributary of Dnieper; length 700 mi.; navigable to Novgorod-Seversky. Cities on it: Bryansk, Chernigov.

DÉTSKOYE SELÓ: *see* PUSHKIN.

DEUTSCH, Lev Grigóryevich (1855–1943), revolutionary. In 1876 joined the populists in Kiev; was arrested but soon escaped. In 1877 participated in the Chigirin conspiracy (q.v.). Together with Plekhanov and Akselrod, D was a founder of the populist Black Repartition (q.v.) and later of the first R. Marxist group abroad, known as Liberation of Labor (q.v.). Arrested in Germany in 1884, D was handed over to the R.

government which condemned him to 16 years of hard labor. In 1903, D became a Menshevik. In 1906 was again arrested after having participated in the 1905 revolution. Lived in W. Europe and the U.S. where he edited the Socialist paper *Novy Mir* (New World). Took a patriotic stand in World War I. In 1917 joined the Plekhanov group "Yedinstvo" (q.v.). D is the author of memoirs, *Sixteen Years in Siberia*.

DEYNÉKA, Aleksándr Aleksándrovich (1899–), painter and sculptor. After study in Kharkov and Moscow, he painted industrial and sports scenes (*Soccer*, 1924) and also took sports as the main subject of his sculptures. He painted the mural for the Soviet pavilion at the Paris World's Exhibition (1937) and did much decorative work for Moscow subway stations. Paintings since the war include *Opening of the Kolkhoz Power Plant* (1956).

DIALECTICAL MATERIALISM. The philosophic underpinnings of Marxism-Leninism (q.v.), hence the philosophic doctrine of Soviet and world communism. Marx and Engels broke away from Hegelian philosophy, which to them was *the* philosophy, with the determination to fulfill philosophy by transcending it through political action. Their doctrine thus contains a positivistic, pragmatist, and antiphilosophic strain, while simultaneously trying to integrate philosophy into social science. Their followers nonetheless abstracted from their writings a more or less systematic philosophic doctrine which after many decades of controversy involving all of its elements took on its present shape as the philosophic dogma of communism.

DM purports to be the most abstract set of statements that can be made about reality. Its scope is universal in that there is no realm of inquiry to which it is not applicable. At the same time it transcends science by dealing with those laws which apply to reality as a whole and to all fields in common.

DM contains a theory of knowledge, in which consciousness is defined as the reflection of objective reality. By implication, therefore, and indeed quite explicitly, it is realistic, asserting that the world and its various phenomena exist objectively, independently of our senses. This objective reality can be known completely by man. DM goes on to describe reality as consisting of, or being reducible to, matter. Matter, in turn, is eternal and has no creator. One of its most important attributes is motion, which also has no cause; it is automotion, an inherent quality of all matter. There is no prime mover of the universe. The material universe, moreover, is one of infinite complexity, in which all phenomena are related to each other in multiple fashion. One might describe DM as an ontology of complex relationship. It is also an ontology of process or change. The so-called laws of dialectics may in fact be called a morphology of change and interrelationship. In final analysis, all change is explained by the dynamic attribute of all matter, which is related to the contradictory nature of all phenomena—the fact that all phenomena contain within themselves opposite forces (thesis and antithesis), resulting in a new and higher stage of development (synthesis). This dynamic

nature of all matter makes DM suspicious of formal (Aristotelian) logic, which is usually condemned as excessively static.

Echoing Marx's endeavor to fulfill and transcend philosophy by political action, DM postulates the unity of theory and practice, in which philosophy acquires political significance while political action becomes part of philosophic method. In line with this, it affirms the partisan nature of all philosophic inquiry, and indeed of all scientific research as well, insisting that the search for knowledge will bear fruits only as long as it is conducted in full sympathy with the struggle of the proletariat and its vanguard, the Communist party. As a consequence, findings and hypotheses in natural or social science are acceptable to communist scholars only if they do not conflict with the dogmas of DM. DM proclaims its chief antagonist in philosophy to be idealism, which connotes a variety of errors: the belief in the primacy of spirit over matter; the belief in a creator or any other higher being; any doubts about the objective reality of the universe or about man's ability to gain absolute knowledge; and any tendencies toward a dualistic separation between subject and object, mind and matter, or fact and value. Another enemy is vulgar materialism which substitutes simple mechanistic models for the subtle and elusive relationships of dialectics.

Certain branches of philosophy, as defined by Western philosophers, are not included in DM, but in historical materialism, which is the philosophy of man and society, and includes ethics as well as aesthetics. (*See also* PHILOSOPHY)

BIBLIOGRAPHY: Gustav A. Wetter, *Dialectical Materialism*, New York, 1958; J. M. Sommerville, *Soviet Philosophy*, New York, 1946.
A. G. M.

DIÁGHILEV, Serge (1872–1929), great Russian impresario and patron of the arts, who organized the seasons of R. ballet in W. Europe beginning 1909 in Paris. Among his collaborators were the composers Nicholas Tcherepnine, Igor Stravinsky; the painters Alexandre Benois, Leon Bakst; choreographers Michel Fokine, Leonide Massine, Bronislava Nijinska, George Balanchine; dancers Anna Pavlova, Tamara Karsavina, Felia Doubrovska, Alexandra Danilova, V. Nijinsky,

 Adolph Bolm, Mikhail Mordkin, Laurent Novikov. In its twenty-one years of existence, the D Ballets Russes produced nearly all of the major works of Michel Fokine, among them *Le Pavillon d'Armide* (Tcherepnine), *Les Sylphides* (Chopin), *Prince Igor* (Borodin), *Cleopatra* (Arensky and others), *Scheherazade* (Rimsky-Korsakov), *Carnaval* (Schumann), *Firebird* and *Petrouchka* (both Stravinsky), *Le Spectre de la Rose* (von Weber), *Daphnis and Chloe* (Ravel); and the early works of Massine, Nijinska and Balanchine, and the only ballets of Nijinsky; *L'Après-midi d'un Faune* and *Jeux* (both Debussy) and *Sacre du Printemps* (Stravinsky). In its later years the D company veered toward W. European art rather than R., and the R. composers were replaced by Ravel, Poulenc, Auric, and Satie; and the painters by Picasso,

Matisse, Derain, and Marie Laurencin. The chief attributes of D were his impeccable taste and his ability to recognize genius and surround himself with the most talented people in the various arts which contributed to the emergence of a new art form—ballet—which became a synthesis of the contributing elements.

BIBLIOGRAPHY: S. L. Grigoriev, *The Diaghilev Ballet*, Baltimore, 1960.

DÍBICH, Iván Ivánovich (1785–1831), field marshal in wars with Napoleonic France and in Russo-Turkish war (1829). In 1831 during the Polish insurrection he was appointed commander-in-chief of the R. expeditionary force.

DICTATORSHIP OF THE PROLETARIAT: *see* MARXISM-LENINISM, CPSU.

DIKÚSHIN, Vladímir Ivánovich (1902–), mechanical engineer. Fellow, Ac. of S., USSR (1953). Graduate, School of Technology in Moscow (1928); joined the Experimental Research Institute of Metalcutting Machine Tools (1932). Supervised design of unit machine tools and of the first Soviet automated plant. Stalin prizes (1941, 1951); Order of Lenin and of the Red Banner of Labor.

DÍKY, Alekséy Denísovich (1889–1955), actor and producer. People's Artist, USSR. Began his career at the Moscow Art Theater (1910). In 1913 D joined the MKhAT (Moscow Academic Art Theater); in 1922 he became producer. Among his productions are: Fayko's *The Man with the Briefcase* and Vishnevsky's *The First Cavalry Army*. In 1943 he played at Vakhtangov's Theater the role of Ivan Gorlov in Korneychuk's *The Battle Front* and others. In 1919 D began to appear in the movies, where he created the part of M. N. Kutuzov in the film of that name; P. S. Nakhimov in *Admiral Nakhimov*; and Stalin in *The Third Blow*.

DIMÍTRY IVÁNOVICH DONSKÓY (1350–1389), —from 1359 Prince of Moscow and from 1363 Prince

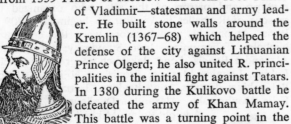

of Vladimir—statesman and army leader. He built stone walls around the Kremlin (1367–68) which helped the defense of the city against Lithuanian Prince Olgerd; he also united R. principalities in the initial fight against Tatars. In 1380 during the Kulikovo battle he defeated the army of Khan Mamay. This battle was a turning point in the relations between the Russians and the Tatars.

DIMÍTRY SHEMYÁKA (1420–1453), Prince of Galich, cunning and treacherous grandson of Dimítry Donskoy. He blinded Vasily II Temny when fighting for the control of Moscow. Became Grand Duke of Moscow in 1446 but had to escape as he failed to gain the support of the Moscow population. Died in Novgorod.

DIMÍTRY, TSARÉVICH (1582–1591), son of Ivan IV, died in Uglich. According to the official version his death was due to accident, but according to another version he was assassinated by hirelings of Boris Godunov. Impostors who assumed the name of Tsarevich Dimitry played an important part in the events of the Time of Troubles (q.v.).

DÍNNIK, Aleksándr Nikoláyevich (1876–1950), mechanical engineer. Fellow, Ac. of S., Ukrainian SSR,

(1929), and Ac. of S., USSR (1946). Honored Scientist and Technologist, Ukrainian SSR (1943). Professor, Mining and Metallurgical Institute, Dnepropetrovsk (1911–41), Kiev University (1944). Research on theory of elasticity and its application.

DISABILITY INSURANCE: *see* SOCIAL INSURANCE.

DISCRIMINATION: *see* NATIONALITIES, JEWS.

DIVORCE: *see* FAMILY LAW.

DMÍTRIEV, Iván Ivánovich (1760–1837), poet-sentimentalist, author of court and monarchistic odes and solemn messages, also proverbs and fables, humoristic satires about contemporary morals, lyrical poetry, and imitations of folk songs. He withdrew from literature in 1803.

DNEPRODZERZHÍNSK (f. Kamenskoye), city in Dnepropetrovsk Oblast, Ukrainian SSR, landing on the Dnieper; pop. 194,000 (1959). Ind.: large metallurgical, machine-building, chemical plants. Metallurgical institute.

DNEPROGÉS, the V. I. Lenin Dnieper hydroelectric power station in Zaporozhye, Ukrainian SSR, was built in 1932; destroyed during World War II, rebuilt and enlarged after the war, it supplies power to numerous heavy industry plants in the vicinity. The power of the station is 663,000 kw.

DNEPROPETRÓVSK (f. Yekaterinoslav), city, adm. center of Dnepropetrovsk Oblast, Ukrainian SSR; pop. 660,000 (1959). Port on the Dnieper; one of the most important centers of metallurgical industry. Numerous colleges, including university. Founded 1783.

DNEPROPETRÓVSK OBLAST, in Ukrainian SSR along the middle course of the Dnieper; area 12,350 sq. mi.; pop. 2,705,000 (1959). Cities: Dnepropetrovsk (adm. center), Dneprodzerzhinsk, Krivoy Rog, Nikopol, Pavlograd, Marganets, Novo-Moskovsk, Pyatikhatki, Sinelnikovo. Is a plain with black earth and moderate continental climate; iron, manganese; wheat, barley, corn, cattle raising; major heavy-industry and ferrous-metallurgy center; mining, mining equipment, railroad rolling stock, coke products. Numerous schools of higher education. Est. 1932.

DNIÉPER (ancient *Borýsthenes*), river, starts in Valday highland, Smolensk Oblast, RSFSR, crosses Byelorussia and Ukraine, flows into Black Sea; length 1,420 mi.; navigable from Dorogobuzh. Third largest river in Europe (after the Volga and the Danube). Main tributaries: (left) Sozh, Desna, Sula, Psyol, Vorskla; (right) Berezina, Pripyat, Ingulets. Main cities on its course: Smolensk, Orsha, Mogilev, Kiev, Dneprodzerzhinsk, Dnepropetrovsk, Zaporozhye, Kherson. Is historically of great economic importance, forming part of the route between the Baltic and Black seas. Lenin Hydroelectric Power Plant near Zaporozhye built in 1932; floating of timber, shipping of grain.

DNIEPER-BUG CANAL, in Byelorussian SSR; connects river Mukhavets, right tributary of W. Bug, of the Vistula basin, with Pina, left tributary of the Pripyat of the Dnieper basin; length 58 mi.

DNIEPER-BUG ESTUARY, bay in Black Sea, mouth of Dnieper and S. Bug rivers, in Nikolayev and Kherson oblasts, Ukrainian SSR; large fisheries.

DNIESTER, (ancient *Tyras*), river in Ukrainian SSR and Moldavian SSR. Rises in Carpathian Mountains, flows into Black Sea; length 875 mi.; partly navigable. Tributaries: Stry, Bystritsa, Zbruch, Seret.

DOBROLYÚBOV, Nikoláy Aleksándrovich (1836–1861), literary critic and spokesman for the radical in-

telligentsia. Born in Nizhny-Novgorod (now Gorky), D was the son of a priest and studied, first, in a theological seminary and, later, history and philosophy at the University of St. Petersburg. He was influenced by the philosophy of Feuerbach and by the writings of V. G. Belinsky. In 1856 he met Chernyshevsky who became his teacher and friend. In 1857, at the completion of his studies, D became a contributor to *Sovremennik* (Contemporary), then its chief critic and, consequently, co-editor with Nekrasov and Chernyshevsky. He believed in the necessity of reforms to improve the lot of the people. The real significance of literature, according to D, was to educate and to teach. He did not believe in "art for art's sake" but wanted art to be effective in order to convey its message. His major literary essays dealt with the work of Turgenev, Ostrovsky, and Goncharov. He also wrote on political and educational topics and edited a satirical magazine. D is considered one of the forerunners of populism. His writings had a tremendous influence on generations of R. progressive intelligentsia.

DOBUZHÍNSKY, Mstislav Valeryánovich (1875–1957), painter, stage designer, etcher, illustrator. Chairman of *Mir Iskusstva* (q.v.). A native of St. Petersburg, D, fascinated with the splendor and squalor of the R. metropolis, was illustrator of Dostoyevsky's *White Nights*. Designed stage settings for Serge Diaghilev's *Ballet Russe*. After the revolution he settled in Paris and New York and worked primarily for the theater as a stage designer, including the Metropolitan Opera House in New York.

THE DOCTORS' PLOT. In Jan. 1953 it was announced that nine distinguished doctors of the USSR, of whom at least six were Jewish, had confessed to the murder of A. A. Zhdanov and to having plotted the elimination of high army officers with the intention of weakening the country's defense. It was alleged that some of the doctors were agents of the American intelligence service and had established contact through the American Joint Distribution Committee, a Jewish charity organization. Shortly after Stalin's death, in April 1953, it was officially conceded that the charges had been falsified and that the confessions had been obtained through torture.

DOKTORÁNT, previously a candidate for the degree of Doctor of Sciences (in humanities or natural sciences) who was studying in a *doktorantura* of a higher school. The title *doktorant* and the *doktoranturas* have been abolished. The degree of Doctor of Sciences (*Doktor nauk*) continues to be awarded to persons usually more mature than United States recipients of doctoral degrees.

DOKUCHÁYEV, Vasíly Vasílyevich (1846–1903), naturalist. Graduate; St. Petersburg University (1872).

Member, St. Petersburg Mineralogical Society. Research concerned the black-soil areas in Russia. Compiled a soil map of the European part of Russia (1876–77), the Caucasus, and the northern hemisphere (1900). Founder of the Permanent Commission for the Study of Soil in Russia (1888). Sent specimens of R. soil to the world fairs in Paris (1889) and Chicago (1893) showing the development of soil science in Russia. D's findings proved of great value in the study of agronomical sciences, physical geography, geobotanics. Author of *The Black Soil in Russia* (1883) and numerous other publications on the subject. The Soil Institute of the Ac. of S. has been named after D as well as an award for the most outstanding work in the field (1946).

DOLGÁNO-NÉNETS NATIONAL OKRUG: *see* TAYMYR N.O.

DOLGORÚKY, Prince Vasíly Lukích (1670–1739), diplomat under Peter I. Was Ambassador to Denmark (1707–20), minister in Paris (1720–22); also a member of the Supreme Privy Council and in favor of "Conditions" presented to Empress Anna Ivanovna limiting the power of the monarch in favor of the nobility. Was later executed.

DOLGORÚKY, Prince Vasíly Vladímirovich (1667–1746), general, field marshal. One of closest collaborators of Peter I, he suppressed the mutiny of Bulavin (1707–08). During the reign of Elizabeth Petrovna, he was president of the War College (Ministry).

DOLGÚSHIN, Aleksándr Vasílyevich (1848–1885), revolutionary populist, organizer of propaganda and of a secret printing plant. In 1874, he was condemned to forced labor; in 1884, he was transferred to the Schlüsselburg Fortress where he died. He wrote *Buried Alive*.

DÓLINSK (prior to 1946, Otiay), town in Sakhalin Oblast, RSFSR; pop. 16,200 (1957). Pulp and paper plants and sawmills. Experimental forestry station.

DOLMATÓVSKY, Yevgény Arónovich (1915–), poet. His first volume of poetry, *Lyrics*, was published in 1934. Then followed *The Day* (1935) and *Far-Eastern Poetry* (1939). D became one of the most popular Soviet poets during and after the war. He is the author of many well-known songs, e.g. *The Beloved City* (Lyubímy Górod). Stalin prize (1950).

DOMESTIC TRADE. Trade is an integral part of the centrally planned Soviet economy. With the increasing choice of consumer goods it has assumed the task of controlling production quality and transmitting consumer preferences to planners in addition to distribution. Goods are traded for monetary prices fixed by law; thus, prices often do not reflect availability or desirability. The bulk of producer goods is not traded but directly allocated to manufacturing units; only few enter trade channels.

The present complex trading organization has developed from earlier experimentations and subsequent adjustments. The period of War Communism (1917–20) failed to build communism through expropriations, prohibition or private trade, compulsory cooperatives, and so forth, but disrupted production and trade. The NEP period (1920–28) started with a temporary revival of private trade; but after 1924 a gradual socialization developed by expanding trading consumer cooperatives and "syndicates" (wholesale trading organizations of state-owned industries), by direct delivery contracts between industries and cooperatives, and by discrimination against private trade through exorbitant prices and taxation.

The present period of socialized trade began with the prohibition of private trade enterprises (1930); since then trade has been carried on in three forms: (1) *state trade,* the most significant and, according to communist doctrine, the "highest" form (at present it caters mainly to the urban population); (2) *cooperative trade,* also a socialized form, since 1936 confined to rural areas, except for a brief period after World War II; (3) *unorganized trade,* conducted by farmers who freely sell their surplus after making deliveries to the state. Prices of farmers' markets are set by supply and demand.

TABLE 1
RELATIVE IMPORTANCE OF THE THREE BRANCHES
OF TRADE
(percentage of total turnover)

Years	1932	1940	1956	1958
State trade	30.9	60.7	67.4	62.5
Cooperatives	53.4	23.0	28.4	29.1
Farmers	15.7	14.3	7.2	8.4

Volume and Character of Soviet Trade. Chronic underproduction of consumer goods to foster rapid industrial growth resulted in scarcity and poor quality of consumer goods and marketing services and facilities (see tables 3 and 4); a high turnover tax is used as a demand-regulating device leading to high retail prices as compared with wages. Trade in food items predominates (see table 5). In 1959, the USSR maintained 519,300 retail outlets with 844,000 employees and an annual turnover of 745.2 bill. rubles (see table 2). Heavy emphasis was placed on retail trade specialization and low distribution cost (see table 6).

Socialized trade on all levels is conducted in accordance with a central plan that fixes its physical and monetary volume. Planning work begins with estimates of trade enterprises revised and coordinated in a broader plan by the planning organs of local soviets, by *sovnarkhozy* (regional economic councils), and finally reach the republic gosplans (planning committees of the Council of Ministers). The All-Union Gosplan coordinates republican plans upon approval by the USSR Council of Ministers and the Presidium of the CPSU. On this level only basic trade targets are fixed (total retail turnover, intra-republican distribution quotas, and so on). Such data are submitted to the republican gosplans which break them into component elements; these are forwarded to agencies on lower levels for further elaboration. Planned figures are used on various levels to draw up "delivery contracts" between producers and/or distributors. Theoretically, everything is planned; in fact, many decisions remain with subordinate agencies, the degree of freedom depending upon their importance. A detailed and tight credit and monetary control of plan fulfillment is additionally provided through the local branches of the State Bank.

Trade operations are the responsibility of the trade ministries of the union republics which act through commercial departments of the various territorial soviets. Before 1953, trade was directed by departments

(chief administrations, *Glavki*) of numerous USSR ministries; thereafter, most of this work was taken over by the Trade Ministry of the USSR; since its dissolution (1958) its functions are performed by the *Glavki* of the trade ministries of the republics. *Glavki* are usually commodity-specialized (*Glav-textil-torg* and so on); others are recipient-oriented (*Glav-kurortotorg* —recreation resort supplies). A *Glav-ORS* coordinates all labor supply departments (ORS) of the various ministries. Some ministries retain their own specialized retail organizations.

The State Trading System. Since 1958 wholesale operations of the state trading system are conducted by the following networks of usually specialized warehouses and depots (*bazy*): (a) The bulk of consumer goods (67.3% in 1959) is distributed by the *Glav-torgy,* departments of the trade ministries of the republics and a network of their branches (*kontory* and *bazy*). (b) Similar departments (*Glav-snab-sbyty*) of the republic gosplans and their bases (*prom-bazy*) distribute traded products of the heavy industries. (c) A chief administration (*soyuz-glav-torg*) of the USSR Gosplan directs a network of intra-republic distribution bases. (d) Goods of local significance are sold either directly to retail organizations by the sales departments of various industrial agencies, or through departments (*glav-sbyty*) of the *Sovnarkhozy* (regional economic councils).

The retail network consists basically of organizations and enterprises controlled by the trade ministries and *Sovnarkhozy,* other ministries, and worker supply departments (ORS).

Similar retail stores in an area are organized in local *torgy.* The country's 1156 local *torgy* are supervised by the local soviets; the district *torgy* by *sovnarkhozy,* and so on. *Torgy* are governmental agencies with departments for planning, purchasing, financing. Similarly, the 130,900 restaurants, cafés, and other public eating places, are organized in 296 *Tresty* (1959). Retail enterprises consist of stalls, stores, restaurants, and so forth; specialized outlets account for 45% of retail turnover. Most units are poorly equipped except a few in big cities including the 300 department stores (*univer-mag*) with about 20,000 employees (the "model *univer-mag* GUM" in Moscow, with 4,000 employees in 130 departments, services over 150,000 customers daily). In periods of rationing (1930–35 and 1941–47) special "commercial stores" freely sold scarce commodities at very high prices.

The ORS network, which took 28% of total state trade in 1956, developed from the closed labor cooperatives (SRK), dissolved in 1932. In order to secure more consumer goods for their workers, ministries and local industrial organizations set up restaurants and shops; there were 2,061 ORS in the USSR (1959), as compared with 7,700 in 1945. With more consumer goods available their significance is declining. In the specialized trading network of the ministries, the drugstores, operated by the Ministries of Health and the bookstores under the Ministries of Culture are important.

The Cooperative Trading System. After nationalization of urban cooperative shops (1935), the cooperative trade, which is centrally planned at various administrative levels, mainly services rural areas. The 37 mill. members of 21,000 consumer cooperative societies legally own the system (1958). It operated 290,000 retail outlets; 11,000 were located in cities; 33,500 were restaurants, canteens, cafés, and so on. In recent years its significance has been increasing: it distributes certain producer goods to the farmers (construction materials, trucks, and so forth), and sells farm surplus on a commission basis (1954). Some cooperatives produce goods, mainly for their own trade.

The basic unit is the village cooperative, *selpo*, its members comprising almost all adults of a community. A *selpo* usually has 1,000 to 2,000 members. Theoretically, they freely elect their officers and the delegates to the district associations (*ray-soyuzy*), which, in turn, send elected delegates to the *oblast-soyuzy, kray-soyuzy* and the republican associations. The All-Union *Tsentrosoyuz* in Moscow resembles a union-trade ministry in regard to functions and organizational structure. The *selpo* usually purchases from district warehouses (*ray-bazy*) operated by *ray-soyuzy,* which sign delivery contracts with the state wholesale organizations and collective farms; large *selpo* may also sign such contracts. In few instances the superseding *oblast-soyuzy* or *kray-soyuzy* maintain intra-district wholesale bases (260, in 1959); generally they perform only supervisory and administrative functions. The retail outlet of a *selpo* is one (or more) village store (*sel-mag*), restaurant, or the like, operated by hired personnel; usually a *sel-mag* is poorly equipped and is seldom specialized. District department stores (*ray-magy*) are operated by the *ray-soyuzy.*

The Unorganized (Kolkhoz) Trade. Farmers and collective farms, after meeting their obligations to government procurement agencies, may sell their surplus to consumers. Until 1953 no middlemen were permitted; thereafter, cooperatives were directed to sell farm surplus on a commission basis using their marketing facilities (collect, transport). There were over 8,600 farmers' markets (1956) in urban areas, supervised by local soviets. Only a few are well organized (the farm market in Kiev rents 1,200 stalls, mainly to farmers). Of this trade 60% consists of vegetables, 34% of animal products. The *kolkhoz* trade is of great importance: it provided 17.4% (1958) of the urban food supply and is a major source of the farmers' monetary income (29.2% of total sales volume in 1957). Prices are free and vary considerably depending largely upon supply and prices in the socialized markets.

TABLE 2
TOTAL RETAIL TURNOVER IN BILLION* RUBLES
(prices are not adjusted)

Years	1940	1950	1951	1952	1954	1956	1958	1959
Socialized	175.1	359.6	379.8	393.6	481.9	547.2	677.2	745.2
Farmers	25.1	49.2	50.8	53.7	49.0	42.5	38.3	

* A billion = a thousand million.

TABLE 3
GROWTH OF PHYSICAL TRADE TURNOVER
(percentage of 1940)

1940	1950	1952	1958
100	110	139	274

TABLE 4
GROWTH OF TRADING NETWORK (Retail)

Year	1940	1958
Number of retail outlets (in 1,000)	407.2	529.3
Percentage	100	127

TABLE 5
ROLE OF FOOD ITEMS
(percentage of total value of retail turnover)

1940	1950	1958
63.1	58.4	54.6

TABLE 6
DISTRIBUTION COST
(percentage of total value of retail turnover)

1940	1950	1957
10.9	9.21	7.61

(*See also* COOPERATIVES, PRICES)

BIBLIOGRAPHY: Gregory Grossman, ed., *Value and Plan: Economic Calculation and Organization in Eastern Europe,* Berkeley, 1960; Marshal I. Goldman, "Marketing: A Lesson for Marx," *Harvard Business Review,* Jan. 1960; Marshal I. Goldman, "Retailing in the Soviet Union," *Journal of Marketing,* April 1960; Michael Kaser, "Changes in Planning Methods During the Preparation of the Soviet Seven-Year Plan," *Soviet Studies,* April 1959; Robert W. Campbell, *Soviet Economic Power: Organization, Growth and Challenge,* Cambridge, 1960.
          G. D.

DON RIVER (anc. *Tánais*), rises in Moscow Oblast, RSFSR, flows into Sea of Azov; length 1,224 mi. Tributaries: (right) Sosna, Donets Seversky; (left) Voronezh, Bityug, Khoper, Medveditsa, Sal, Manych. Considerable fisheries. Navigable for 840 mi.; used for shipping coal and grain. Navigation improved because of Volga–Don Canal.

DONBÁS, Donets coal basin, in the Ukrainian SSR and partly in RSFSR (Rostov Oblast). Area over 23,000 sq. mi.; geological coal reserves estimated at 260 bill. ton (1957). Is one of most important mining and metallurgical areas of USSR, with machine building, ferrous and nonferrous metallurgy, coke-chemical ind., large power stations. Main cities: Stalino, Lugansk, Gorlovka, Makeyevka, Zhdanov, Kramatorsk. (*See also*: STALINO, LUGANSK, ROSTOV OBLASTS.)

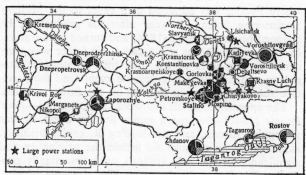

Industrial centers of the Donets Basin and Dnieper Region

DONÉTS, ancient R. town (11th-13th centuries), near Kharkov. Mentioned in 1185 in "Tale of the Host of Igor," is a center of archaeological excavations.

DONÉTS BASIN: *see* DONBAS.

DONÉTS SÉVERSKY (Northern Donets River), in E. Ukrainian SSR and S.W. RSFSR, right tributary of the Don; length 630 mi.; navigable. Supplies water to Donbas (q.v.).

DORODNÍTSYN, Anatóly Alekséyevich (1910–), geophysicist and mathematician. Fellow, Ac. of S.,

USSR (1953). Graduate of Grozny Petroleum Institute (1931); professor, Institute of Physics and Technology (1947); director, Computing Center, Ac. of S. (1955). Research on aerodynamics and applied mathematics. Contributed to the development of the design of sweepback airplane wings and delta wings. Author of *Boundary Layer of Compressible Gas* (1942); *Effect of the Earth Crust Relief on Air Currents* (1950); *Asymptomatic Distribution Laws for Certain Types of Differential Equations of Second Order* (1952). Stalin prizes (1946, 1947, 1951).

DÓRPAT: *see* TARTU.

DOSAÁF USSR, abbreviation for *Vsesoyúznoye Dobrovólnoye Obshchestvo Sodéystvia Armii, Aviátsii i Flótu* (All-Union Voluntary Society for Cooperation with the Army, Air Force, and Navy)—paramilitary civilian defense agency founded 1951. United three independent agencies (DOSARM, DOSAV, DOSFLOT). Participation, particularly by Komsomol members, prepares for service in Soviet armed forces. Activities include shooting practice, air raid drills, parachute and glider training, first aid, long marches, and political instruction stressing the need for military preparedness.

DOSTOYÉVSKY, Fyódor Mikháylovich (1821–1881), novelist, political and religious thinker. Appropriately, the future author of the *Poor People* was born in the Moscow Hospital for the poor where his father was the head physician. The family was of modest clergy origin. The father was a stern disciplinarian, suspicious, stingy,  and an alcoholic. Nevertheless, the children (four boys and four girls) were given a good education. The father's alcoholism apparently told on his children: two of D's brothers were alcoholics; he himself was sickly, highly nervous, and subject to epileptic fits. In 1837, the two older boys, Michael and Fyodor, were sent to St. Petersburg where Fyodor was admitted as a cadet to the Military Engineering School. A year after his graduation, he resigned his commission (1844) and turned to literature. In 1839, when D was still a cadet, his father was murdered by the serfs of his own little estate—for despotism and cruelty. The gruesome event (and the parricide theme) left a deep imprint on the future novelist.

The appearance of his first work, a short novel—*Poor People* (1846)—became a major literary event. It was a popular success, and the leading R. critic, Belinsky, explained in an enthusiastic article the originality and significance of the new author's work, practically predicting D's future development. The elements of pity, human suffering, and deep understanding of the contradictions of the human soul are all present in D's first literary effort. The story: a timid and elderly little government clerk, Makar Devushkin, is trying to help a remote relative, a young penniless girl exposed to the pitfalls and heartless exploitation of the big city. He falls in love with her, but, in the end, the girl is compelled to marry a rich brute who can "provide" for her. There is more than an echo of Gogol's masterpiece—*The Cloak*—in *Poor People*, but it is deeper in social perspectives and more complex in psychology.

It is somewhat gauche and overwritten, but there are scenes of "tears of things" worthy of the later D (the scene with the torn-off button). D woke up famous and almost affluent. For the next two or three years, he rushed off with a number of long and short stories, but most of them were hasty, forced, and, hence, more imitative and less convincing than *Poor People*. *The Double* evokes, in a pedestrian fashion, Gogol's *The Nose*; *The Landlady* is a clumsy imitation of Gogol's sinister *The Terrible Vengeance*. Readers and critics voiced their disappointment. Hypersensitive, suspicious, and once more harassed by debts (always over-generous, a careless spender, and an incipient gambler, he was for the rest of his life to suffer from poverty, frequently abject and humiliating), D felt keenly the reversal of fortune. But the real catastrophe was yet to come.

D, a liberal with vague socialist overtones, joined a group of young intellectuals (the Petrashevsky Circle) who were discussing Russia's evils of the time—serfdom, censorship, and autocracy with its corrupt officialdom. Few of them went beyond asking for peaceful reforms, though some had revolutionary leanings. In 1849, Nicholas I, frightened by the revolutions of 1848 in Europe, ordered the imprisonment and trial by courtmartial of the Petrashevsky group. Twenty men, including D, were sentenced to death. On a cold December day the prisoners were brought to the Semyonovsky Square in St. Petersburg, where the death verdict was read to them, the firing squad called out–when an imperial ukase "granting them their lives" was read. D was sentenced to four years at hard labor in a Siberian penitentiary with subsequent service as a private in a Siberian regiment. There followed four years of inferno in "the house of the dead" in Omsk, with five more years of "purgatory" as a private soldier. Prison conditions wrecked D's health; epileptic fits became more frequent and harrowing. The inner transformation was much deeper. In prison he discovered *man, God* and *the Russian people*. Man proved to be more complicated, contradictory and, in his polarity, more extreme for good and for evil—not at all the placid and reasonable creature imagined by the rationalistic and materialistic radicals of the time. Man is a tragic being. He needs God and without God he is a beast or on the way to become one. D was deeply impressed by the religious feeling and humility of the Russian people. He fell in love with Christ and the "God-fearing" Russian people. He was now a liberal Christian and nationalist.

In 1859 D was amnestied by the new tsar, Alexander II. Now married, he returned to the capital. In 1860, together with his brother Mikhail, he established in St. Petersburg a magazine, *Vremya* (The Time), a literary and financial success. He resumed his creative activity in 1859–61 with two long tales *A Friend of the Family* and *Uncle's Dream*—and a rather pale novel, *The Insulted and Injured*. These had a friendly, but moderate reception from both critics and readers. They represented a transition from his earlier Gogolesque and satirical manner of the forties to the later "deeper" D. With the *House of the Dead* (1861–62) there began the series of masterpieces: *Notes from Underground, The*

Gambler, Crime and Punishment, The Idiot, The Possessed, Brothers Karamazov, and the much weaker *Raw Youth. The House of the Dead* was immediately acclaimed as the greatest book ever written about men in captivity and servitude. The scenes and portraits of prison life and prisoners equal in vividness and penetration the army scenes of Tolstoy's *War and Peace.* Both Turgenev and Tolstoy admired the book for its craftsmanship and the depth of its humaneness. The next short novel (or tale), *Notes from Underground,* is crucial for the further development of D: it opens the series of "disturbed" people struggling with problems of human destiny and torn with inner conflicts. The unheroic hero is an average man (. . . "I am an unpleasant person"), petty, but frustrated and embittered by his own insignificance, by the pettiness and emptiness of our modern life. Hence, he is infuriated by the radicals and their optimistic, rationalistic promises of mechanized "progress" and a "crystal palace" on earth. He rebels against the "multiplication table." Man is an irrational, tragic being: Perhaps he is just as fond of his sufferings as of his well-being. In this moving, eloquent book D challenged the whole philosophy of materialistic radicalism and socialism of his time. He turned more and more from his former liberalism to a fusion of ardent nationalism and religious ("orthodox") mysticism. The trend was probably accelerated by a series of personal disasters; the closing by the government (through a misunderstanding) of the brothers' magazine (1863), the death of Mikhail, financial ruin and crushing debts, the death of his wife (1864), illness and disastrous gambling.

Crime and Punishment is perhaps D's most famous novel. If we are all potential criminals, how does a good man become a criminal? Raskolnikov, a brilliant and terribly poor student, in his intellectual pride considers himself a superman before Nietzsche (humanity is divided into a majority—the herd who must obey the law —and a small chosen minority of superior men—"the extraordinary, special men," the Keplers, Napoleons, Mahomets who are above or beyond the law, who must break the old law in order to realize their new discoveries and visions). In order to test himself, Raskolnikov must kill the old woman, a usurer. The fierce struggle between his conscience and the idea-obsession is depicted in its "dialectics" (ebb and flow) with a hypnotizing power. After the crime, Raskolnikov feels himself isolated, excommunicated from the rest of humanity, and realizes the sterility of his "superman" doctrine. His encounters with those who represent the Christian (the "Russian") ideal of humility and submission to the law of God (the poor sinners, the drunkard Marmeladov and his daughter, the saintly prostitute, Sonya) do not convert him, but disturb him. In the end, he confesses and expiates his crime in a Siberian penitentiary. An Italian critic called D the Russian Dante and the novel a portrayal of the *Inferno* which every man carries within himself.

The next three great novels only further accentuated D's mature and disturbing genius. *The Possessed* (1871) is his most controversial novel since it satirized the Russian revolutionary movement of the time. The radicals were perhaps right in calling it a caricature, but D was more concerned with the future than with his time, with his startling prophecy that a successful revolution in Russia will bring about not freedom, but "total" tyranny (Shigalev's paper). The two protagonists—young Verkhovensky, the cynical nihilist, and the demoniac, but "empty," Stavrogin—are unforgettable.

In *The Idiot* (1868), a moving, but uneven novel (with touches of melodrama), Myshkin, the representative of the "Russian idea" with his universal pity, humility, and Christian mysticism is opposed as it were to the Raskolnikovs corrupted by the "western idea" with its intellectual pride, and godless materialism. The novel is further marred by the writer's growing nationalistic pride and religious intolerance (toward the Catholics, and "an atheist cannot be a Russian"). The two principal characters of the novel—the earthy, primitive Rogozhin with his animalistic passions and the pure, almost angelic Myshkin—effectively represent the polarity of man.

The vast *Brothers Karamazov* (1879–80) is D's swan song and a summing up of his lifelong literary experience and intellectual pilgrimage. Written in the comparative comfort of his last few years, it is free from the hastiness and unevenness of *The Gambler, The Idiot,* and the decidedly weak *Raw Youth.* The provincial town, the Karamazov family (the dissolute and sly father, his sons—three legitimate and one illegitimate), with their friends, enemies and acquaintances, are a vision of D's "disturbed" Russia of the 1870's, atheistic and religious; Slavophile-patriotic and cosmopolitan-radical. The theme of parricide dominates the novel. Of his sons, Ivan is a further extension of Raskolnikov, is also tormented by his intellectual pride, by his rejection of God and of God's world; Mitya, with his carnal passions and hatred for his father-rival, is a more spiritualized Rogozhin with touches of old Marmeladov; Alyosha is a more realistic and healthier Myshkin; Smerdyakov (the illegitimate) is the Russian Caliban, the vulgarization of the "western" revolt and radicalism idea. The two ideals, the Madonna ideal and that of Sodom and Gomorrah (materialistic welfare and moral dissolution), are in violent conflict. Among the several famous monologues and dialogues in *Brothers Karamazov,* the "Legend of the Grand Inquisitor" alone, with its strange depths, has created a little literature of its own. The father is killed, Mitya is suspected and sentenced to a long term in the penitentiary, but the actual murderer is Smerdyakov.

In 1866, D married Anna Smitkina, his stenographer. The marriage brought happiness and affection to both of them. His second wife had all the qualities of orderliness, attention to money matters and careful management—so lacking in the novelist himself. To escape the pressure of his debts the newlywed couple went abroad where they stayed until their return in 1871. Debts were gradually paid off, and, in the last seven or eight years of his life, D knew both domestic happiness and a measure of comfort. His health, however, was deteriorating, and a few months after his famous speech on Pushkin (Moscow, June 1880) he died, Feb. 1881.

After his return to Russia and until his death D

was publishing a one-man magazine *Dnevnik Pisatelya* (A Writer's Diary). His numerous articles there on a variety of current subjects—literary, political, and social—are of great interest as they elucidate his views and teachings of his last phase. Among his shorter works the best-known are: *The Eternal Husband, Bobok, The Peasant Marey, Heavenly Christmas Tree*, and *A Gentle Spirit.*

His fame and influence, first in Russia and, from the beginning of this century, in the western world, have been ever increasing and make him one of the world's greatest novelists and dynamic thinkers.

BIBLIOGRAPHY: Avrahm Yarmolinsky, *Dostoyevsky: His Life and Art*, New York, 1957.   I. L. T.

DOTSÉNT, an academic title derived from the German *Privatdozent*, granted to persons teaching at universities and institutes. It ranks above *assistént* (assistant) and *prepodavátel* (instructor) but below "professor."

DOVZHÉNKO, Aleksándr Petróvich (1894–1956), film director. People's Artist of RSFSR (1950). He was a teacher and a painter before he started his movie career in 1926 in Odessa. His *Arsenal* (1929) and *Earth* (1930) brought him fame but also official criticism. His other best known pictures are *Shchors* (1939), *Michurin* (1949), and *Poem of the Sea* (completed in 1958). Stalin prizes (1941, 1949).

DRAGOMÁNOV (Drohomanov), **Mikhaíl Petróvich** (1841–1895), Ukrainian historian and publicist. Leader of the "Federalists," a moderate Ukrainian group which advocated national and cultural autonomy, he was dismissed from Kiev University, where he taught history, because of his nationalistic leanings. From 1870 to 1889 lived abroad, mostly in Switzerland and Bulgaria. Edited the Ukrainian collection *Hromada*. D was the author of several books on Ukrainian etnography. Jointly with the historian V. B. Antonovich, D published a two-volume *Songs of the Ukrainian People.*

DRAGOMÍROV, Mikhaíl Ivánovich (1830–1905), general and military writer; author of numerous works on tactics, education and training of troops.

DRESS: *see* NATIONAL DRESS.

DROGÓBYCH, city in Lvov Oblast, Ukrainian SSR; pop. 42,000 (1959). Center of oil industry; oil refineries, chemical ind., metalworking, woodworking, meat processing.

DROGOBYCH OBLAST, Ukrainian SSR, abolished May 1959, incorporated into Lvov Oblast.

DROHOMANOV: *see* DRAGOMANOV.

DRÓZHZHIN, Spiridón Dmítrievich (1848–1930), poet, born of peasant stock. Lived most of his life in his native village where he died. His first verse appeared in print in 1873. His poetry, which was greatly influenced by folklore and the work of Nekrasov (q.v.), describes the bleak life of the peasants. It contains many descriptions of the R. countryside—*In a Peasant Cottage* (1882), *Autumn Holiday* (1886), *Give Me Wings* (1905). After 1917 D extolled changes in village life—*Centuries of Wicked Slavery Are Past* (1918). In 1938 a Drozhzhin Museum was opened in the Soviet Union.

DRUZHÍNA, military forces attached to the prince and participating in the wars and in the administration of the principality, as well as in the personal household of a prince. They were: senior *druzhína*—boyars and prince's men, and junior *druzhína—grid, ótroki* (youth)—who were military servants of the prince.

DUAL POWER, split of the state authority and sovereignty between the Provisional Government and the Soviets during the first period of the Russian Revolution in 1917. On March 12, 1917, two institutions were established in Petrograd simultaneously but independently one of the other: the provisional committee of the Duma (q.v.) and the Soviet of the Workers' and Soldiers' Deputies. Neither wanted to take into its hands the state power. The majority of the Duma and of its committee were for reform, not for the revolution. The majority of the Soviet at that time adhered to the idea that the Soviet should not take power itself but should give "conditional" support to the government for which the middle-class parties should have political responsibility. After some days of hesitation a Provisional Government was established which promised to be guided in its activity by some specified principles. Although the Executive Committee of the Soviet, in a declaration published on March 16, 1917, stated that, "in the measure in which the government . . . will act in the direction of realizing these obligations and of decisive struggle with the old power, the democracy must support it," two days earlier it has published the so-called "Order Number One" which, in fact, ruined the discipline in the army. Several similar acts of authority on the part of the Soviets created the situation of DP, that is, the authority of the Provisional Government was limited and "conditioned" by the support given (or refused) by the Soviets.   V. Su.

DUBÍNIN, Mikhaíl Mikháylovich (1901–), physical chemist. Fellow, Ac. of S., USSR (1943). Graduate of Moscow Polytechnic School (1921); professor, Military Academy of Chemical Defense (1933). Secretary of the Department of Chemical Sciences, Ac. of S. (1957). Research on the absorption of gas and methods for separating vapor mixtures, also in the field of chemical defense. Author of *Physicochemical Principles of Sorption Techniques* (1935); *Physicochemical Principles of Gas Defense* (1939); *Sorption and Structure of Activated Carbons* (1947, 1949, 1950). Stalin prizes (1942, 1950).

DUDÍNKA, city in Taymyr National Okrug of Krasnoyarsk Kray, RSFSR; pop. 20,000 (1958). Landing on the lower course of Yenisey River.

DUDÍNTSEV, Vladímir Dmítrievich (1918–), novelist, born in Kupyansk. Graduated from the Moscow Institute of Law. During World War II he was an infantry officer and was seriously wounded in 1941 near Leningrad. From 1942 to 1945 he was defense counsel with a military tribunal in Siberia. His first publication appeared in 1938. From 1946 to 1951 D was a staff contributor to *Komsomolskaya Pravda* in which his articles and short stories appeared. His other publications include: a collection of short stories (1952); *Not By Bread Alone* (1957); *A New Year's Tale* (1960). *Not By Bread Alone* enjoyed great success in the USSR and was translated into many languages. It was interpreted as a penetrating criticism of the Soviet system. The CP organized thoughout the USSR a series of conferences to censure D's novel. Khrushchev condemned it.

DUKHOBORS ("spirit fighters"), religious sect of nonconformist peasants founded in 18th century, now called Christians of the Universal Brotherhood. Their teaching is based on absolute equality of men and they oppose all authority if it comes in conflict with their conscience. For their resistance to military conscription they endured persecution and banishments in Russia. In late 1890s with the help of Leo Tolstoy and the Quakers most of them emigrated to Canada. Trouble with the school authorities led to "nudist demonstrations" and part of them recently returned to USSR. Their leader is Peter Verigin.

DUKHÓNIN, Nikoláy Nikoláyevich (1876–1917), general. One of the youngest generals in the Imperial Army, he was commander in chief of all R. forces at the time of the Bolshevik Revolution. After abetting the escape south of a number of imprisoned generals, he refused to obey a Bolshevik order to begin truce negotiations with the Germans and was shot (Nov. 1917) by the mutineering soldiers.

DUMA: *see* STATE DUMA.

DUMÁNSKY, Antón Vladímirovich (1880–), chemist, one of the originators of colloidal chemistry in Russia. Fellow, Ac. of S., Ukrainian SSR (1945). Graduated from Kiev Polytechnic Institute (1903) where he remained until 1913. Founder (1913) and head of the Laboratory of Colloidal Chemistry in Voronezh which developed into the All-Union Scientific Research Institute of Colloidal Chemistry. Director, Institute of General and Inorganic Chemistry, Ac. of S., Ukrainian SSR (1946). Applied physical methods of investigation to colloidal chemistry and suggested application of powerful centrifuge for size determination of colloidal particles. His research greatly contributed to agronomy, sugar production, the study of fermentation processes. Founder and editor (1935) of *Kolloidny Zhurnal* (The Colloidal Journal).

DUENABURG: *see* DAUGAVPILS.

DUNAYÉVSKY, Isáak Ósipovich (1900–1955), composer of popular songs. Studied piano and violin with Joseph Achron at the Kharkov Conservatoire. Graduated in 1919 and went to Leningrad, devoting himself to popular music which made him famous. At one time he experimented with jazz. D wrote scores for films, the first Soviet composer to enter this field. His better-known compositions are *The Knives* (1928), *The Golden Valley* (1937), *Road to Happiness* (1941), *The Circus* and *Volga* (the two latter brought him the Stalin prize, 1941); and the films *The Good Fellows* and *Captain Grant's Children*. D's song *For the Fatherland* enjoys great popularity.

DUNGAN: *see* POPULATION.

DURABLE CONSUMERS' GOODS PRODUCTION. The durable consumers' goods produced in the USSR in 1960 included 4.2 mill. radios, 1.7 mill. television sets, and 26 mill. watches and clocks, as well as 529,000 refrigerators and 953,000 washing machines. (In 1959 the United States produced 15.9 mill. radios and 5.9 mill. television sets; the United Kingdom 1.8 mill. radios and 2.8 mill. television sets.)

Until 1953 the development of industries producing non-vital consumers' goods was accorded a low priority in the national investment programs. In addition the practice of assigning the production of durable consumers' goods to plants primarily concerned with making industrial and military equipment tended to reduce the actual level of their output still further. In 1937 13,000 motorcycles, 541,000 bicycles, and 510,000 sewing machines were produced.

The subsequent conversion of industrial plants to the production of military equipment resulted in an appreciable decline in this level of output even before 1941. After the completion of the postwar reconstruction program, however, output rose to 143,000 motorcycles, 1.9 mill. bicycles, and 993,000 sewing machines by 1953. During this period, too, the mass production of vacuum cleaners, television sets, and washing machines was started.

A substantial increase in the production of all major types of durable consumers' goods occurred after the adoption of the Fifth Five Year Plan (1953–58). The production of radios, television sets, cameras, and watches approximately tripled during this period, to the levels indicated above, while the production of vacuum machines, and refrigerators increased even more rapidly.

The objectives of the Seven Year Plan (1959–65) provide for a further increase of 84% in the production of radios, phonographs, and television sets; 317% of refrigerators; and 365% of washing machines.

PRODUCTION OF DURABLE CONSUMERS' GOODS
(thousands)

Year	Motorcycles and motor scooters	Bicycles & motor bicycles	Sewing machines	Watches	Cameras
1913	.1	4.9	271.8	—	—
1928	—	10.8	285.6	—	—
1932	.1	125.6	318.8	65	29.6
1937	13.1	540.7	510.1	533	353.2
1940	6.8	255.0	175.2	816	355.2
1950	123.1	649.3	501.7	2,150	260.3
1955	244.5	2,883.8	1,610.9	8,731	1,022.5
1958	400.1	3,651.0	2,685.8	15,215	1,472.3
1959	500	3,300.0	2,900.0	26,200	1,600.0
1960			3,100.0	26,000	
1965 (pl.)		4,200.0			

Year	Radios	Television	Vacuum cleaners	Refrigerators	Washing machines	Electric irons
1940	160.5	.3		3.5	—	420.0
1950	1,072.4	11.9	6.1	1.2	.3	507.7
1955	3,549.4	494.7	130.9	151.4	87.0	5,290.5
1958	3,801.2	979.3	245.3	359.6	538.3	2,130.4
1959	4 mill.	1.3 mill.		426.0	724.0	
1960	4.2 mill.	1.7 mill.		529.0	953.0	
1965 (pl.)				1,500.0	2,500.0	

P. I. M.

DÚTOV, Aleksándr Ilyích (1864–1921), White commander. In 1917, a colonel, he was ataman of the Ural Cossacks. He opposed the Bolshevik Revolution and undertook to organize all Cossack elements in the service of Admiral Kolchak; but his force was defeated by the Reds and he and his adherents were compelled to flee into Chinese Turkestan (1920), where he was killed by discontented members of his own entourage.

DVINÁ BAY (R. *Dvínskaya Guba*), in S.E. part of White Sea (Beloye More), 80 mi. wide. Northern Dvina River flows into it; fishing.

DVINÁ, NORTHERN (R. *Sévernaya Dviná*), river in Archangel Oblast, RSFSR, formed by confluence of the Sukhona and Yug; length about 453 mi. Tributaries: (right) Pinega; (left) Vaga. Navigable; used for floating timber. Ports: Kotlas, Archangel.

DVINÁ, WESTERN (R. *Západnaya Dviná,* Lett. *Dáugava, Ger. Düna*), river. Rises in Pskov Oblast, RSFSR, flows through Byelorussia and Latvia into Gulf of Riga; length 633 mi. Tributaries: (right) Drissa; (left) Mezha, Kasplya, Ulla, Disna. Ports: Vitebsk, Daugavpils, Riga.

DVINSK: *see* DAUGAVPILS.

DYÁKONOV, Pyotr Ivánovich (1855–1908), surgeon. Graduate, Medical and Surgical Academy in St. Petersburg (1879); professor, Moscow University (1893). Research concerned with oncology, antisepsis, asepsis, and hernia operations. Organized Russian and International Congresses of Surgeons. Edited *Letopisi Khirurgicheskogo Obshchestva v Moskve* (The Annals of the Surgical Society in Moscow) and, with N. V. Sklifosovsky, the journal *Khirurgicheskie Letopisi* (Annals of Surgery) (1891–95) and *Khirurgia* (Surgery) (1897).

DYÁTKOVO, town in Bryansk Oblast, RSFSR; pop. 18,000 (1957). Ind.: crystal glass, prefabricated houses.

DYBÉNKO, Pável Yefímovich (1889–1938), Soviet leader. Joined the party in 1912 and being a sailor in the tsarist navy, organized sailors of the Baltic Fleet on the eve of the Bolshevik revolution. He was appointed people's commissar of the navy. Active in the Ukraine during the civil war, he narrowly escaped execution by the Germans. During the 1920's he was prominent in the training of artillerymen. He wrote several books on the revolutionary movement in the tsarist navy. His career was cut short by the purge of the Red Army in 1937. After Stalin's death D was rehabilitated.

DYULTYDÁG, mountain range and peak in Caucasus, in Samur River basin, elevation 13,548 ft.; covered with perennial snow.

DYUSHAMBÉ: *see* STALINABAD.

DZAUDZHIKÁU: *see* ORDZHONIKIDZE.

DZERZHÍNSK (f. Shcherbinovka), city in Stalino Oblast, Ukrainian SSR; pop. 103,000 (1939), 164,000 (1959). Center of coal-mining industry; coke, chemical and ceramic plants.

DZERZHÍNSKY, Feliks Edmundovich (1877–1926), Soviet leader of Polish origin, born in Vilna province of a gentry family. In 1895, as a student of high school in Vilna, D joined the social democratic movement and was active in Kovno (1897) and in Warsaw (1899) where he reorganized the social democratic organization  and inaugurated the SDKPiL (Social Democracy of Kingdom of Poland and Lithuania). Arrested several times, he escaped abroad in June 1902. Being a partisan of one united all-Russian party, D took part in the R. Social Democratic party's congress in Stockholm (April 1906), and was elected to its Central Committee. From Aug. 1906, he was active in St. Petersburg as well as in Warsaw but, in 1908, was arrested and imprisoned in Warsaw; while in detention he wrote his *Prisoner's Diary.* Banished to Siberia, he soon escaped abroad. In Sept. 1912, again arrested in Warsaw, D was imprisoned until the February revolution in 1917. Elected to the Bolshevik Central Committee in Aug. 1917, D took an active part in the preparation of the October revolution. On Dec. 20, 1917, he was nominated by Lenin as the head of the Extraordinary Commission for Fighting the Counterrevolution (Cheka, in 1922 renamed OGPU), the post he held until his death. In the summer of 1920, he combined this post with that of people's commissar for the interior and, from April 1921, with the post of people's commissar of transport in which capacity he reorganized and improved the Soviet railway system. From Feb. 1924, D became also chairman of the Supreme Council of National Economy and was largely responsible for the development of Soviet heavy industry. Simultaneously he was chairman of the commission for liquidating the *bezprizornye* (homeless children). In the internal party fights D generally supported Stalin although he had some sympathy with the rightist opposition of Bukharin. He died of a heart attack during the 14th Party Congress in July 1926.

DZERZHÍNSKY, Iván Ivánovich (1909–), composer. In 1930, entered the Leningrad Conservatoire. Among his early works were a piano concerto and the *Spring Suite* for piano. His importance in developing Soviet program music lies chiefly in his operas: *Quiet Flows the Don* (1935) and *Soil Upturned* (1937), both based on novels by M. Sholokhov, and *Far from Moscow* (1954).

DZHAMBÚL DZHABÁYEV (1846–1945), Kazakh poet. Came from a poor nomad family. His prerevolutionary writing reflected the thoughts and hopes of the Kazakhs and their hardships. He wrote lyrical and satirical songs on everyday themes, epic poems and tales—*Bay Kadyrbay's Dog, Black Decree, Song of an Angry Heart* and others. After the revolution, D wrote patriotic poetry and eulogies of the Bolshevik leaders.

DZHAMBÚL (f. Aulie-Ata), city, adm. center of Dzhambul Oblast in S. Kazakhstan; pop. 97,900 (1957). Fertilizers, distilleries, sugar, leather, meat ind. Known in 7th century as Taraz or Talas, ancient architectural monuments.

DZHAMBÚL OBLAST in Kazakh SSR; area 56,050 sq. mi.; pop. 562,000 (1959). Adm. center, Dzhambul. Its S. part is on the slopes of Kirghiz Alatau; its N. is the Muyunkum desert. Rivers: Chu, Talass, Ass are not navigable, but used for irrigation; has arid continental climate. Its minerals are phosphorites, salt, marble, coal. Agr. (irrigated): wheat, tobacco, kendyr, kenaf, sugar beets, orchards and vineyards; animal raising. Ind.: mining, superphosphate, sugar. Est. 1939.

DZHIMARÁY-KHÓKH, (or Gimaray-Khokh), peak in Caucasus, Georgian SSR, 15,672 ft.

DZHUGDZHÚR RANGE, mountains in Khabarovsk Kray, RSFSR; highest elevation 6,560 ft.

DZUNGÁRIAN ALATÁU (SEMIRECHENSKY ALATAU), mountain system in S.E. part of Kazakh SSR, between the Ili River and Lake Alakol; length about 250 mi.; elevations reach 14,750 ft.

DZUNGÁRIAN GATES, mountain pass on the border of the USSR and China, between Dzungarian Alatau and Barlyk mountain ranges.

E

EAST EUROPEAN PLAIN (Russian Plain), a land mass from the Vistula River to the Urals and from the North Arctic Ocean to the Black Sea and Sea of Azov.

EAST KAZAKHSTAN OBLAST in Kazakh SSR; area 37,550 sq. mi.; pop. 735,000 (1959). Cities: Ust-Kamenogorsk (adm. center), Leninogorsk, Zyryanovsk, Zaysan. Situated in S.W. Altay in the basin of upper Irtysh, it has sharply continental climate; black-earth soil in the N., alpine pastures on mountain slopes, a desert-like depression in the S. Field crops are wheat, rye, oats, partly irrigated; minerals: copper, zinc, tin, lead, coal, silver, gold; ind.: important nonferrous metallurgy, power stations, mining. Est. 1932.

EAST SIBERIAN SEA, part of the Arctic Ocean between the shores of Siberia, New Siberian and Wrangel islands; area 337,750 sq. mi.; depth in southern part about 100 ft.; hazardous for navigation; considerable fisheries, walruses, seals. Kolyma and Indigirka rivers empty into it.

ECCI: *see* COMMUNIST INTERNATIONAL.

ECONOMIC DEVELOPMENT, PREREVOLUTIONARY. Ancient times. According to tradition, the beginnings of the R. state go back to the middle of the 9th century. The territory of Kievan Russia, as that state was known from the 9th to the middle of the 12th century, was relatively small and comprised an area in E. Europe controlled by several cities of which the more important were Kiev, on the Dnieper River, and Novgorod on the Volkhov. Little is known about Russia's economic conditions during the earlier centuries of her history. It is believed that the population consisted chiefly of freemen who engaged in agriculture, hunting, and fishing. There were also slaves drawn from among the conquered tribes but this group was presumably economically unimportant. The opinion has been advanced by both prerevolutionary R. historians and by the Soviet historians of the 1930's–1950's that Kievan Russia achieved high levels of cultural and economic development and had a sizable body of skilled artisans. Such statements are speculations based on linguistic and archeological data and inspire little confidence. Whatever elements of culture and skill existed in Russia during these early centuries were derived from foreign sources—Byzantine and Scandinavian.

Of great importance, both politically and economically, was Russia's foreign trade which was carried along the two principal water routes linking the Baltic littoral with the Black Sea and Byzantium, on the one hand, and with the Arabic East, on the other. This trade to which Russia contributed slaves as well as the products of the forest—furs, honey, wax, amber—came to a standstill with the appearance of the Cumans in the Black Sea steppes (middle of the 11th century). However, Novgorod, an outpost of the Hanseatic League, retained its position as a leading trading center until its absorption by Muscovy in the latter part of the 15th century.

Of lasting significance was the evolution of land tenure. It is believed that private ownership in land existed at the dawn of Russia's history and that during the earlier stage land was cultivated by farmer-owners. From the 11th century on, however, there came into being large estates owned by members of the princely dynasties, the upper classes (boyars), and the church. The source of landownership was at first occupation and, later, inheritance, purchase, and princely grants. Large estates were originally farmed by free tenant farmers who soon found themselves in a position of increasing dependence on their landowners. This change of status may be traced to two main causes: the growing indebtedness of the tenants to their lords and the restrictive legislation of the state which was vitally interested in preventing evasion of taxes and army draft. It is from these two roots that gradually evolved the institution of serfdom.

Middle of the 12th to the End of the 17th Century. Inter-princely feuds and the pressure of the Cumans, and later of the Tatars from the S., brought about the decline and fall of Kiev and the shift of the center of political authority to the N.W., first to the principality of Rostov-Suzdal-Vladimir (second half of the 12th century), and then to Moscow (latter part of the 15th century). During the Rostov-Suzdal-Vladimir period economic conditions were not vastly different from those of the Kievan era, except for the drastic contraction of foreign trade. The Mongol occupation of Russia, which lasted from the middle of the 13th to the end of the 15th century, retarded her economic progress; the subjugated people had to pay heavy tributes to the conqueror and to serve in his armed forces, but otherwise the Tatars did not interfere directly with the working of the political and economic institutions of their vassals. On the other hand, the unification of the formerly autonomous R. principalities under Moscow and the emergence of a highly centralized bureaucratic state had far-reaching effects upon social and economic conditions.

The 14th to the 17th centuries witnessed a great expansion of the R. territory when vast areas in the W., S., and E. were brought under the scepter of the tsars. In the 16th century the Russians began the conquest of Siberia which three centuries later led them to annex the shores of the Pacific. Territorial aggrandizement generally means war; Muscovy was indeed engaged in intermittent warfare with the German Knights and Poland-Lithuania in the W., with the Tatars and later the Turks in the S., and with the native tribes in the E. Wars are costly and require armed forces which in Muscovy were financed by a system of land grants. Gradually all the members of the upper land-owning class (the nobility or *dvoryanstvo*) became subject to the obligation of army service, their landed estates which were held in service tenure being known as *pomestye*. The right of the peasant tenants to relinquish tenancy and move elsewhere was at first curtailed and by the end of the 16th century disappeared altogether without being formally abolished. The peasants became attached to the land which they farmed. They fell broadly into two main groups: state peasants who settled on state land and serfs who lived on the estates of the nobility. Unlike the state peasants, the serfs were in personal bondage to their master and could be sold, or otherwise disposed of, without the land. In this respect their status was similar to that of slaves but, unlike the latter, they paid taxes, were drafted into the armed forces, and performed other obligations toward the state. The law contained practically no provisions regulating the relationship between the serfs and their lord. The above legal situation came about piecemeal in the 16th and early 17th century and was confirmed by the Code of 1649.

Although in the 16th and 17th centuries Russia was a predominantly agricultural country and progress of urban life was exceedingly slow, there was much internal commerce as well as beginnings of industrial development. Under the provisions of the Code of 1649, domestic trade was the exclusive prerogative of the burghers (who paid a special tax) but in actual practice this rule was frequently infringed. In 1553 Richard Chancellor, an adventurous Englishman, landed inadvertently on the shore of the White Sea and made his way to Moscow—an accident that led to the founding by London merchants of the Muscovy Company upon which Ivan IV conferred valuable privileges. The trade link with England proved lasting and until the latter part of the 19th century that country remained Russia's principal trading partner. Industry made little progress. The Muscovite rulers of the 15th century and their successors resumed the practice that possibly existed in Kievan Russia of importing foreign craftsmen, especially architects and masons. A small colony of expatriates skilled in arts and crafts existed in Moscow as early as the 16th century. In 1632 the Dutch merchant, Andrew Vinius, established armament works in Tula, perhaps Russia's first large-scale enterprise. The bulk of industrial production, covering a wide range of articles—woodwork (spoons, bowls, plows, harrows), weaving and spinning, felt boots, sheepskin coats, metalware (axes, knives)—was carried on by artisans by the methods of domestic (cottage) industry.

On the eve of the accession of Peter I, Russia was a medieval country with a primitive backward economy.

18th to Middle of 19th Century. The pace of Russia's territorial expansion was accelerated in the 18th and in the first half of the 19th century when the empire (a title claimed by the R. government since 1721) established itself on the shores of the Baltic and the Black seas and acquired large sections of Poland as well as Finland and vast areas in the E. The reign of Peter I (first quarter of the 18th century) is traditionally regarded as a major turning point in R. political and economic history. However, the changes in Rus-

sia's international position and political institutions were much greater than those in the structure of her economy. Both were primarily due to the exigencies of the protracted Russo-Swedish war (1700–1721) and to Peter's predilection for European methods and policies. The basic social and economic institutions inherited from the 17th century—predominance of the nobility and its total dominion over the servile population living on its estates—were retained, except that the nobility was relieved of the obligation of compulsory service (1762). The poll tax which was imposed in 1723 became the earmark of servile status even though it survived the emancipation of the serfs and was not repealed until the 1880's. The secularization of ecclesiastical estates in 1764 finally deprived the Church of its vast landholdings which since the beginning of the 18th century had actually been administered by lay agencies.

The modernization of the army, the creation of a navy, and the drastic remodeling of the dress and social habits of the upper classes which lay behind the Petrine reforms brought forth a new demand which imports and the existing industries could not meet. The exigencies of the economic situation were reinforced by the prescripts of the mercantilist doctrine which had gained acceptance in Muscovy in the 17th century. State intervention, which took the form of bounties, subsidies, exemption from taxation and government service, high tariff protection, and occasionally the monopolistic control of the market, resulted in the establishment of large industrial enterprises engaged in the manufacture of armaments and military and naval stores, as well as of brocades, silks, woolens, hosiery, and other consumers' goods. Although these enterprises employed hundreds and even thousands of workers, production was carried on by the methods of cottage industry, that is, in the workers' own cottages. The entrepreneurs were chiefly merchants, with a sprinkling of the nobility. It is a much disputed issue whether the capital invested came from the owners or was provided by the state treasury, but the latter theory is more plausible. The great difficulties in securing industrial labor were only partly resolved by the creation of *possessionary* serfs who were permanently attached to industrial enterprises. Most of the labor force in industry during the entire period under review in this section consisted of the state peasants and serfs paying their masters an annual tribute (*obrok*) and permitted to seek outside employment; that is, industry was predominantly manned not by the serfs of the entrepreneur but by hired workers. By the end of Peter I's reign the number of large industrial enterprises was perhaps 200; many of them, however, were forced to close their doors during the subsequent decades. Production of pig iron which was concentrated in the Ural region rose from 15,000 poods in 1700 to 1,000,000 poods (19,000 tons) in 1725, exceeding for a while by a narrow margin that of England. Among the more progressive industries of the late 18th and early 19th century were cotton textiles and sugar. Although no precise figures on the size of the labor force in industry are available, it is believed that at the beginning of the

19th century it was about 200,000; in 1860 it rose to 800,000, or slightly more than 1 per cent of the total population. Approximately two-thirds of this number were hired workers.

Other noteworthy developments were the decline of Archangel, on the White Sea, as Russia's chief port and the shift of foreign trade to the ports of the Baltic and Black seas; the relatively slow growth of foreign trade which represented from 3 to 4 per cent of world trade both at the beginning and in the middle of the 19th century; and the introduction in 1768 of paper currency which almost immediately became depreciated and was not stabilized until the end of the 19th century.

To sum up: There was little economic progress during the century and a half preceding the reforms of Alexander II. It is believed that in the middle of the 19th century Russia passed through an acute economic crisis which made the emancipation of the serfs practically a necessity, but this theory is not universally accepted.

Imperial Russia's Modern Age, 1860–1914. The emancipation of the serfs in 1861, for all its inequities and imperfections, was a decisive turning point in R. history without which the economic progress of the subsequent decades could not have taken place. The Stolypin land reform of 1906–1911 was another major step toward the removal of the legal and economic disabilities of the peasantry. The other so-called great reforms of Alexander II served similar objectives, i.e., the modernization of Russia's social and economic structure. Nevertheless the anticipated change was often slow in coming; in farming, for instance, it remained for decades a promise rather than an actual gain. The yield of crops per acre showed little improvement and was considerably lower than in the W. European countries. But there was a great and potentially important reduction in the landholding of the nobility which by 1911 contracted to about half of its 1860 area.

Industry fared better than agriculture, especially after 1890. Industrial employment grew steadily and in 1913 reached some 3 mill. which however was still but 2 per cent of the total population. The value of industrial production rose from 1,500 mill. rubles in 1890 to 5,700 mill. in 1913. The largest gains were made by the cotton, coal, iron and steel industries. Beginning in the 1890's rapid expansion took place in the development of the Donets basin, a region in the S. of European Russia rich in coal and iron ore. There was a great deal of concentration of production: in 1914 about 56 per cent of the workers engaged in manufacturing industries were employed in enterprises with 500 or more workers. Industrial growth was fostered by a comprehensive program of railroad building, by the powerful flow of foreign capital, and by an aggressive protectionism which reached exorbitant heights by the end of the 19th and early 20th century.

The financial situation improved vastly. The state budget was unified (1862) and made available to the public (1866). A comprehensive system of private banks was created, none of which existed before 1860. In 1897 Russia, the last major European country to link its currency to gold, introduced the gold standard which was maintained, although not without difficulties, until 1914. There was, however, a dark side to this heartening picture of economic advancement. On the eve of World War I nearly four-fifths of the state revenue was still derived from indirect taxation and more than one-fourth was supplied by the state monopoly of spirits. While the average annual value of foreign trade (exports and imports) rose from 432 mill. rubles in 1861–1865 to 2,780 mill. rubles in 1911–1913, the excess of exports over imports which was essential to the working of the gold standard (because of the smallness of the other credit items in Russia's balance of payments) was achieved by forcing the export of grain irrespective of the level of prices and conditions of supply, even in years of poor harvest and actual famine. Figures of national income are not available, but there is no question that the standard of living of the peasants, workers, and the vast majority of Russians in every walk of life was substantially below that of their opposite numbers in W. Europe.

War and Revolution. Russia's backwardness notwithstanding, her economy reacted to the impact of war in a manner similar to that of the more advanced countries. Loss of foreign markets, enemy occupation of the industrial W. provinces, mobilization of millions of men, breakdown of the transport system, huge war expenditures—these and other factors inherent in wartime conditions had their inevitable consequences: imbalance of international accounts, suspension of the gold standard, inflation, decline in productivity, shortage of supplies especially in the larger cities, rising prices, and general impoverishment. It was symbolic that the uprising of the Petrograd populace which led to the revolution of Feb.-March 1917 originated in queues of disgruntled householders waiting in front of foodshops. The revolutionary upheaval accelerated the process of economic disintegration and introduced powerful new disruptive elements: seizure of large landed estates, occupation of the factories by the workers, and the general feeling of insecurity which dealt the final blow to the tottering economy of imperial and bourgeois Russia. The economic structure which the Bolsheviks wrested from their predecessors had reached a state of advanced disintegration even though it contained the elements of industrial organization and technical skill and know-how that provided the indispensable base for the huge program of economic development upon which the Soviet government was soon to embark.

BIBLIOGRAPHY: M. T. Florinsky, *Russia: A History and an Interpretation*, 2 vols, New York, 1953; V. O. Klyuchevsky, *A History of Russia*, 5 vols, New York, 1911–31; P. T. Lyashchenko, *History of the National Economy of Russia to the 1917 Revolution*, New York, 1949; M. S. Miller, *The Economic Development of Russia, 1905–14*, London, 1926.   M. T. F.

ECONOMIC DEVELOPMENT, SOVIET. The history of the Soviet economy since 1917 may be divided into six periods, each characterized by distinctive features. The periods are: (1) War Communism, which lasted until early 1921; (2) the New Economic Policy, or NEP, 1921 to about 1927–28; (3) Five Year Plans before World War II, from 1928 to early 1941;

(4) World War II, from the Nazi invasion of June 1941 to mid-1945; (5) the recovery after World War II and then expansion under Stalinist rule, from mid-1945 to Stalin's death in early 1953; and 6) the economic expansion, from Stalin's death to the present (late 1960). We shall examine each of these.

War Communism. The infant Soviet regime was struggling for its existence against the armed forces of its domestic enemies (supporters of the deposed tsar, minority nationalists in the Ukraine and elsewhere, and others) as well as against foreign military forces. In addition, during this period the Bolsheviks were trying to impose some of the more radical tenets of Marxism interpreted in a naive manner. It was a time of chaos and hardship. Military setbacks as well as a growing inflation disrupted normal economic relationships. Industrial production fell off rapidly as factories were cut off from normal sources of raw materials and as urban workers fled the cities in large numbers to escape the hunger which ruled in large communities. Such industrial production facilities as remained were concentrated on producing supplies for the Red Army. Food was often seized from the peasants by armed force assisted by groups of poor peasants. Industry, banks, public utilities, land, and other natural resources were nationalized.

NEP. Inauguration of the NEP was made possible by Red Army's military victories over the Soviet regime's enemies, but it was also forced by the threat of catastrophic consequences if War Communism were continued. Peasant resentment at the regime's exactions was expressed by armed resistance and by a sharp diminution of normal agricultural production caused by absence of normal incentives to produce. The Kronstadt rebellion in early 1921 showed that disaffection had spread to the armed forces.

Essentially, the Soviet government during the NEP period followed a twofold policy. On the one hand it sought to harness the forces of private enterprise and of individual incentive to spur economic recovery. Private trade and private industry were once again permitted; the policy of confiscating peasant output was abandoned and replaced by a policy that sought to provide production incentives by requiring peasants to surrender only a portion of their produce to the state while permitting them to sell the rest on a free market. On the other hand the Soviet government kept control over the "commanding heights" of the economy, mainly large-scale industry, the banking system, foreign trade, and the like. This was a period in which the Soviet Union had a "mixed economy" and in which both private businessmen and government action combined swiftly to heal the wounds of the preceding period so that by 1927 or so production was back to levels of before World War I. During this period, too, inflation —which had reached enormous proportions—was ended by institution of a new dual monetary system, including the *chervontsy* (backed in part by gold and foreign currency) and a new ruble currency.

Five Year Plans, 1928–40. From 1928 to 1940, the Soviet Union operated under the first three Five Year Plans. It was a tempestuous, stormy period of great changes in all areas of economic life. In industry a massive program of capital investment— particularly into heavy industry—swiftly sent production of metals, fuels, machinery, chemicals and the like soaring. Millions of people were transplanted from farms to factories and mines as the country strove feverishly to build the economic strength for anticipated war. The capital for this great transformation of the Soviet economy and society had to be squeezed out of the people by forcing them to submit to sharply lower living standards. In the cities this was done by imposing a strict rationing system and sharply reducing the purchasing power of the ruble. In the countryside, the need to extort capital from the peasantry led Stalin to destroy the system of 25,000,000 or so peasant farms which had existed in the mid-1920's and institute collectivization instead. In the early 1930's government forces and peasants waged a bitter battle, and both force and economic pressure were used to dragoon the peasants into the collective farms. The economic significance of the state victory here—a victory achieved at great cost because the peasants destroyed much of their livestock and other capital—was that it permitted the government to requisition annually large parts of the peasant output at a small fraction of its real value, the profit subsequently arising from this expropriation providing much of the capital for industrialization.

World War II. In the four years that followed Hitler's invasion of Russia, the country suffered tremendous human and material losses. Much of the richest agricultural and industrial area of the country—in the regions west of the Leningrad-Moscow-Stalingrad line —was bitterly fought over and badly damaged. Part of the machinery in the occupied regions was saved by being moved eastward before the German invader, but even so production fell precipitously. The country survived economically because of two reasons: (1) all energies were focused upon production for the front and the population accepted a very rigid rationing system and accompanying catastrophically low standard of living, and (2) the aid provided by the Soviet Union's allies —principally from United States Lend-Lease—in the way of key types of machinery, essential medicines, meat and other high protein, high fat foodstuffs, and other commodities in dangerously short supply. Compensating somewhat for the great losses in the occupied western regions and the terrible deprivation of the Soviet population, was the progress made during this period in building up industry and agriculture in the areas east of the Volga, to the Urals and beyond.

Postwar Recovery, 1945–53. Draconian methods were applied by Stalin in the years immediately after World War II to rebuild the shattered Soviet economy despite the enormous human and material losses of the struggle. Within the country the population was kept at work under what amounted to military discipline, the basic workweek was set at 48 hours, and internal capital accumulation was pursued intensively by permitting only relatively slow improvement of the standard of living. Wartime inflation and the gains of profiteers were both liquidated by the drastic currency reform of Dec. 1947 whose key component

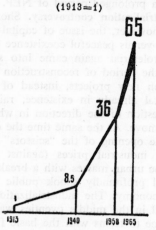

GROSS INDUSTRIAL OUTPUT
(1913=1)

65

36

8.5

1

1913   1940   1958 1965

was the wiping out of much of the purchasing power of the currency in circulation. First priority was put on rebuilding factories and other production facilities which had been destroyed and damaged, with new investment being pushed particularly intensively into scientific research and construction of facilities designed to wipe out the West's lead in military technology. The burden fell particularly heavily upon farmers who had to deliver most of their produce for payment whose purchasing power was negligible, while the goods farmers bought showed the inflationary influence of World War II upon Soviet prices. From outside the Soviet Union, Stalin seized capital—machinery, livestock, raw materials, and so forth—in the areas occupied by the Soviet Army from East Germany to Manchuria and North Korea, the total capital thus acquired amounting to billions of dollars in original value. The result of this economic policy was a steady and rapid rise in industrial production to the point where it was well above prewar levels by the time Stalin died. But after an initial rise agricultural production remained stagnant for years as farmers lacked production incentives and as the farm labor force consisted mainly of women, old men, and children, having lost vigorous male workers to death during World War II or to the better paying urban factories. Though improved substantially over the worst of the 1941–45 period, Soviet living standards at Stalin's death, particularly in the area of housing, were extremely poor.

Post-Stalin Period. In the last period, 1953–60, rapid growth continued, though at a lower rate than in Stalin's era, in Soviet industrial output, but much more attention was paid to agriculture, housing, and output of consumer goods. The tensions generated under Stalin were vividly shown in the rapidity with which his immediate successor, Premier Malenkov, espoused a line-giving. Though Malenkov was defeated by Khrushchev on this issue and forced to resign as premier in early 1955, the latter hastened in turn not long afterward to identify himself with consumer aspirations, at least publicly, though without cutting back on intensive heavy industrial development. Many steps were taken to rationalize and normalize Soviet economic life in this period. Workers' hours were reduced to 41 or 42 hours a week by late

1960, minimum wages and lowest pension levels were raised substantially, and workers were given the right to change jobs without employer permission. In agriculture substantial success in raising output was achieved by a variety of measures: capital investments in farming were increased, trained workers and technicians were sent to the farms, peasant production incentives were increased by raising prices paid for farm produce and by greatly simplifying the formerly complex farm price structure. The institutional setting of Soviet agriculture was sharply altered by amalgamating collective farms into very large units (a move begun in 1950 but pushed intensively after Stalin's death), by abolishing the machine tractor stations and selling their equipment to collective farms, and by converting the poorest collective farms into state farms. In addition the pattern of Soviet agricultural activity was sharply altered by such moves as the opening of the "virgin lands" for extensive grain culture in W. Siberia and Kazakhstan, and by the enormous expansion of corn plantings to augment the supply of livestock feedstuffs. In all fields the post-Stalin era saw intensive efforts made to study foreign, especially American, experience and practice in production and to borrow and adapt for Soviet use ideas, methods, and machines which had proved themselves abroad. Important gains in both Soviet economic power and in the Soviet standard of living were made during 1953–60—despite the forced abandonment of the Sixth Five Year Plan in 1957, after less than two years of its scheduled five-year term—but in both areas the Soviet Union still remained far behind the United States.

The cyclical variation of Soviet production of some key commodities over the different periods discussed above is shown below:

Commodity	1913	1921	1928	1940	1945	1953	1959
Electricity*	2.0	.5	5.0	48.3	43.3	134.3	264.0
Steel**	4.2	.2	4.3	18.3	12.3	38.1	59.9
Oil**	9.2	3.8	11.6	31.1	19.4	52.8	129.5
Shoes***	60.0	N.a.	58.0	211.0	63.1	238.1	389.0
TV Sets****	0	0	0	.3	0	84.1	1,278.0

* Billion kw-hr. ** Million metric tons. *** Million pairs.
**** Thousand units, N.a.—Not available.

BIBLIOGRAPHY: Harry Schwartz, *Russia's Soviet Economy*, N.Y., 1958; Harry Schwartz, *The Soviet Seven Year Plan*, London, 1960; Donald R. Hodgman, *Soviet Industrial Production 1928–1951*, Cambridge, 1954; Gregory Grossman, ed., *Value and Plan*, Berkeley, 1960.
H. S.

ECONOMIC THEORY. The history of economic thought in Soviet Russia is largely the story of a perpetual struggle to remold and vindicate the Marxist inheritance in the face of historical changes which constantly threatened to impair, if not to destroy, its practical relevance. Political victory over capitalism deprived the Marxian theories of their old functions of exposure and indictment, while the economic tasks of reconstruction confronted them with new demands for positive guidance which—in their original state, at least—they were quite unable to meet. Initially, therefore, the economist, torn between the call to preach what was no longer necessary and the need to teach what was not yet possible, lost his claim to a separate identity, and abdicated his functions to the politician and ideologist on the one hand and the engineer and statistician on the other.

Lenin's contribution. Only Lenin was able to keep in touch with both sides and to bring a measure of coherence to their disjointed efforts. His adaptation of Marxism and Hobson's theory of imperialism provided the original justification for the overthrow of capitalism in backward Russia, where the Marxian preconditions for revolution were further from being met than anywhere in the West. At the same time his clear-cut conception of "socialism" as a transitional order between capitalism and "communism," and of "state capitalism" as a first step toward it, furnished the concrete precepts of action for the crucial period between the seizure of power and his death in 1924. From his basic diagnosis of Russian backwardness and isolation he derived the three fundamental prescriptions which have pervaded all subsequent Soviet thinking and, even when honored in the breach, are always firmly associated with his name: the need for peace and a permanent alliance between proletariat and peasantry (*smychka*); the need to use Soviet power to continue and intensify the process of capital accumulation which capitalism had initiated; and the need for material incentives, cost control, and all the paraphernalia of capitalist accounting as a spur to socialist production. None of these principles can be described as purely *economic* insights, but Lenin was too concerned with the unity of theory and practice to abandon himself to any one discipline of the social sciences. His contribution lay rather in the fact that he was able to distill these principles from a historical situation of bewildering complexity which would have paralyzed many a deeper and more specialized mind, and that he knew exactly at what moment any of them needed to be given precedence or had to be sacrificed to the others temporarily.

When the dust of civil war had settled and wider prospects opened up, Lenin let himself be guided by his vision of nation-wide long-term planning for capital accumulation. His definition of communism as "Soviet power *plus* electrification" inspired the famous GOELRO plan, the first coherent set of economic projects to cover a whole country, and a period as long as 15 years. The same vision, taken up and developed by Trotsky, called into life the State Planning Commission (Gosplan) which survived all subsequent changes of economic policy and is as powerful as ever today. When it became clear after the Kronstadt rising that the wartime system of grain procurement (by confiscation from the peasants) could not be retained without immediate danger to the regime, Lenin did not hesitate to sound the retreat from the principle of rigid state control for maximum capital investment. The inauguration of the New Economic Policy (NEP) in 1921 marked the return to the first of his prescriptions, the need to keep the peace between peasantry and proletariat, and the readmittance of the free market where state control had signally failed in this task. In the years that followed it was again a contribution from Lenin, his special theory of the mixed economy (renouncing the frontal assault on capitalism in favor of a policy of promoting in each economic sector the *workable* social order judged to be the most "advanced" by Marxist standards), which eventually succeeded in doing ade-

quate justice to the real situation and reconciling the orthodox to a prolonged period of NEP.

The industrialization controversy. Shortly after Lenin's death, however, the issue of capital accumulation for socialism versus peaceful coexistence between peasantry and proletariat again came into sharper relief. The end of the period of reconstruction and the need to embark on new projects, instead of merely reactivating capital already in existence, raised with full force the question of the direction in which the economy was to move. At the same time the ominous crisis caused by the opening of the "scissors" between agricultural and industrial prices (against the peasants) threatened the urban masses with a breakdown in food supplies, and profoundly shook public confidence in the mixed economy. The industrialization controversy which ensued in the middle twenties was the first attempt to come to terms with the basic facts of life in a country dominated by subsistence farming and rural overpopulation which neither Marx nor Lenin had adequately taken into account. The Right-wing faction, headed by Bukharin, argued for a policy of fostering peasant prosperity until such time as the annual food surplus had reached sufficient levels to sustain a voluntary shift of resources into industry. This was strenuously opposed by the Left wing, inspired by Preobrazhensky, Smilga, and Pyatakov, who took their stand on the need for industry to embark immediately on its "primitive accumulation" of capital through the deliberate exploitation of peasant agriculture, much as a metropolitan country was alleged to exploit its colonies, or an emergent social order in the Marxian scheme of things was said to draw its initial fund of strength by parasitic action on the predecessor which it was about to supplant. The intellectual weapons of the chief contestants were historical analogy and dialectic materialism rather than the analytic tools of the professional economist, but the controversy found its reflection on a more technical level inside the State Planning Commission and other bodies where the economic and planning implications of alternative policies occupied the forefront of attention.

The planning controversy. The older school of economists, led by such impressive figures as Kondratyev, Groman, and Bazarov, advocated—and practiced—what came to be known as "geneticist" planning. Essentially, they took their starting point from a forecast of the harvest (as the least controllable variable in the economy) with the consequent surpluses available for urban consumption, and built around these estimates a balanced system of performance indicators (output, employment, investment, and so forth) for the guidance of the urban and the rural economy alike. The indicators were presented as feasible ideals to be aimed at rather than as binding targets, and their mutual consistency was tested by means of structural "coefficients" derived from the experience of normally functioning unplanned economies, including that of prerevolutionary Russia. The opposing "teleological" school, in which Strumilin was steadily gaining in prominence, rejected such procedures as a retreat from the "conscious choices" made possible by socialism toward voluntary submission to the "elemental forces" at work in lower-type economies, and advocated a method of planning which was to take its starting point from the final aims, rather than the initial possibilities, that characterized the period to be covered. It was the planners' task to single out the "leading links" in the economy whose development was desired by the party on political or social grounds, and to draw up the concrete investment projects to serve them. From these were derived the targets for output or other performance which the rest of the economy would have to meet to support the postulated investment program. Over-all consistency was tested by a system of supply-and-requirements "balances" drawn up separately for each key commodity or commodity-group with the aid of technological input norms. If the original program turned out to be unrealizable with existing resources, this was remedied by further shifts from consumption to investment, a tightening of input norms or, as a last resort, a lowering of the initial targets; but at each stage of the adjustment process the "leading links" were assured of absolute priority.

As the twenties wore on, the annual economic plans or "Control Figures" (which were issued from 1925–26 onward) became more and more oriented toward the "teleological" school, and by the end of the decade the advocates of "geneticism" had completely lost out or disappeared in political purges.

The Stalin period. Meanwhile the party leadership had veered abruptly to the left, and the country was radically transformed by the forced collectivization drive of 1929–32. Henceforth the food surplus exacted from the peasants passed under the political control of the government, the risks of the harvest devolved entirely on the rural population, and the terms of trade between country and town could be dictated at will without endangering the supply situation, present or future. Accordingly, the crucial questions concerning the pace of industrialization, the rate of investment and consumption, and so forth, ceased to be debated in *economic* terms (i.e., as choices between competing ends, given scarce means), and largely assumed the character of *technological* or *military* problems in which the ends were preconceived and unassailable, and only the means to their fulfillment remained open to choice. Stalin's famous speech to business executives in 1931 delimited the area in which economic thinking was henceforth to move. It was to concern itself with organizational problems of labor recruitment, the allocation of managerial responsibilities, incentive schemes for labor and management, cost accounting, and the nature of statistical returns—all geared to the maximization of industrial output and capital accumulation. For the next two decades economic journals, textbooks, and learned debates, in so far as they departed from descriptive or technical studies of particular regions or industries, were almost exclusively devoted to problems of this sort. There were some outstanding exceptions in the field of social accounting (*tableaux économiques*), investment choice, and Marxian growth models, associated with the names of Strumilin, Tsagolov, Notkin, Turetsky, and others, but the

traditional concerns of economic theory, such as general resource allocation, price formation, or financial policy, had become the preserve of specialized organs of state which wielded their weapons with an eye to administrative or planning efficiency and ease of "fulfillment" control rather than purely economic criteria. It seems probable that the unprecedented upsurge in industrial output and productivity was due to the coercive austerity measures of a determined political dictatorship and owed little, if anything, to the basic teaching or current advice of professional economists, whether Marxist or otherwise.

This is not to say, however, that the regime's attitudes and policies were not constantly being rationalized in the language of Marxian economics. Thus, the long-delayed recognition that administrative decision-taking should not infringe the basic dictates of economic consistency received its official imprimatur in the form of a pronouncement by Stalin that the "Law of Value" continued to be operative under socialism (*Economic Problems of Socialism in the USSR,* 1952). Similarly, the long-established policy of giving absolute priority to the growth of instrumental branches of production (Marx's "Department I"), and within that to the branches supplying other instrumental branches, was often justified by invoking an obscure tract by Lenin (*Concerning the so-called Question of Markets,* 1893) in which this was asserted to be the *sine qua non* of all industrial growth. A number of later attempts to give a rigorous proof, particularly with the aid of simple models of the accelerator type (e.g., Strumilin in 1954), yielded barely convincing results, but the proposition assumed such importance as an article of faith that it was eventually incorporated as an integral part in the "Law of Planned Proportional Development of the National Economy." The standard textbook in political economy which, though published after Stalin's death (1955–57), most clearly bears the imprint of his personality and sanction describes the socialist system as an ideal order obedient to a number of such laws (including the Basic Economic Law of Socialism). These appear to be hardly more than reformulations of the Marxian vision of the communist society, specially adapted to a demonstration that Soviet policies, past and present, were moving in the right direction, and could not in the nature of things do otherwise.

The post-Stalin period. After Stalin's death the forces of change were able to assert themselves, and with them the awareness that the constant draining of resources into industry had begun to be self-defeating and needed to be tempered by some compensation to the *drained* sectors of the economy, notably agriculture, whose surplus manpower (especially at higher levels of skill) and "exploitability" were gradually approaching exhaustion. The resulting policy changes under Khrushchev opened the way for a somewhat timid, but unmistakable, comeback of economic thinking in the proper sense of the word. Once it was recognized that labor had acquired a scarcity value, and that only a judicious choice of capital investment (possibly *outside* industry) would enable it to be more efficiently deployed, the traditional need for criteria of optimality and the balancing of economic advantage against economic cost could not but reassert itself. Economists are therefore again suffered, and even encouraged to cast about for some way of meeting this need.

As a consequence the arguments on the operation of the "Law of Value" moved from the sphere of shadowboxing into that of practical price policy. The longstanding dissatisfaction with the Soviet system of industrial prices (*ex tax*), based—in intention at least—on the full cost principle (average unit cost *plus* a percentage markup on *total cost*), was at least given fully articulate form in connection with Strumilin's advocacy of a return to the true labor values of Marx (average unit cost *plus* a percentage markup on *wage cost*). This created, or brought into the open, two kinds of analytic preoccupation which have since pervaded Soviet economic literature: the search for the nature and preconditions of consistent labor-cost accounting on a national scale, and the probe into the fitness of such accounting for the rational allocation of resources at the present stage of Soviet development. The first line of thought stimulated interest in general macro-economics, national income categories, and input-output analysis, thus sanctioning the open or implied use of matrix algebra in economic argument. The second, and much more iconoclastic, line raised the problem of how the claims on scarce factors *other than labor* could be taken into account without obvious affront to the Marxian orthodoxy. The Soviet debates on differential rent and notional interest rates are of somewhat longer standing, but the postwar contributions of Novozhilov, Lurye, and Strumilin and, more recently, of Khachaturov, Malyshev, and others brought a new approach, at once pragmatic and analytic, with the Marxian profession of faith scaled down to a passing obeisance. Economists now seem to be aware that their theoretical findings are treated with increasing seriousness by politicians and operational planners. All of them are in search of meaningful criteria of effectiveness for alternative capital projects, locational patterns in agriculture, timetables for the retirement of equipment, automation, and so forth. The recent changes in the structure of managerial incentives (now largely geared to cost reduction rather than output volume) also bear the clear imprint of the new climate in economic thought.

Meanwhile the mathematical school, associated chiefly with the name of L. Kantorovich, has staged a comeback from the limbo in which the Marxian economists had kept it for so long. The elements of linear programing and computer techniques form increasingly frequent subjects of expository articles in learned journals, and much attention is paid to Western (chiefly American) progress in these fields. The very fact that Professor Leontief's input-output analysis is claimed as an originally Soviet contribution, and that the inception of linear programing is traced back to the early work of Kantorovich rather than to the well-known American pioneers, demonstrates the Soviets' increasing respect for and, possibly, practical dependence on these methods. While serious objection is still being taken to the marginalist views which are implicit in the linear programing approach, especially as expounded by Kan-

torovich, this no longer seems to require a public recantation, or even abandonment, of the methods criticized.

While it could hardly be claimed that Soviet economic thought has so far contributed anything of outstanding value to economic analysis as we know it in the West, there is little doubt that it is beginning to have a greater and more respected place in practical affairs.

BIBLIOGRAPHY: A. Erlich, *The Soviet Industrialization Debate, 1924–1928*, Cambridge, 1960; O. Lange, "Marxian Economics in the Soviet Union," *American Economic Review*, March 1945; A. Zauberman, "Economic Thought in the Soviet Union" in *The Review of Economic Studies*, 1949–50, pp. 1, 102, 189; S. G. Strumilin, "The Time Factor in Capital Investment," translated in *International Economic Papers*, issue No. 1, and discussed in *Soviet Studies*, Vol. I, No. 2, p. 119; A. Nove, *Communist Economy Strategy: Soviet Growth and Capabilities*, The National Planning Association, Washington, 1959.
F. S.

"ECONOMISM": *see* MARXISM RUSSIAN, CPSU.

EDUCATION. Kievan and Muscovite Russia. The beginnings of public education in R. date from the period immediately following the adoption of Christianity. The chronicle of Nestor mentions the foundation of schools for some 300 children in Kiev (988) and Novgorod (1028). The most important educational agencies in both Kiev and Muscovite R. were religious institutions, church and monastery schools, and, as in contemporary medieval Europe, education was largely confined to the clergy.

The first moves towards broader popular education were also religious in impulse. During the 16th and 17th centuries, the Orthodox Church in the Ukraine and Byelorussia had to contend with the rivalry of the Catholic Church. The Orthodox religious fraternities (*bratstva*) founded schools as a defensive measure. The first school was opened at Lvov in 1586 and the first institution of higher learning was created in 1631 when the Kiev school was reorganized as the Kievan-Mogilian Academy. Secondary schools followed, with the creation of the colleges (*kollegia*) of Kharkov and Chernigov. The influence of these institutions spread well beyond the Ukraine and far into Muscovy, especially after Kiev became part of R. by the treaty of Andrusovo (1667).

In Muscovy, the church and monastery schools taught reading, writing and arithmetic in addition to religious subjects. The language of instruction was Church Slavonic, the counterpart in the Russian Orthodox Church to Latin in the West. In 1686, the Slav-Greco-Latin Academy was opened in Moscow to provide better education for clergy. It offered some secular subjects in addition to religious instruction and the three languages. Secular education was also provided by private tutors (*mastera gramoty*) employed by families, especially in the cities.

The 18th Century. Education was given new impetus by the reforms of Peter the Great, as the government began to supplement the efforts of the Church. A modernized Russian alphabet replaced Church Slavonic, and the government opened public schools to train the educated men it needed in all its services. The School of Mathematics and Navigation was founded in Moscow in 1699 and was soon followed by schools of Engineering, Artillery and Surgery. In addition, a Foreign Language Academy provided instruction in the rudiments of western learning. The government also opened Theological Seminaries in a number of towns to educate a clergy more amenable to the Tsar's reforms, and the seminaries served as secondary schools as well. The Naval Academy of the new capital, St. Petersburg, was created in 1715. The whole structure was crowned by the Academy of Sciences founded there in 1725, already after Peter's death, with a university and a secondary school attached to it. Education for the sons of the nobility was provided through the Corps of Pages, Cadets and Midshipmen.

Moscow University was founded in 1755, due to the efforts of the scientist M. V. Lomonosov for whom it is now named. Secondary boarding schools (*internaty*) were opened in a number of towns. Two of them, the Smolny in Moscow and the Yekaterininsky in St. Petersburg, were for women, the first of their kind in Russia. They were created in 1764 by Catherine the Great who had the philosopher Diderot among her educational advisers. Catherine's initial enthusiasm for education was considerably dampened by Russian peasant risings and the French Revolution. She came to feel that "the mob (*chern'*) must not be given education because when they know as much as you and I they will no longer obey us as they do now." Her School Act of 1786 nonetheless established two types of national schools, with five- and two-year courses, respectively. By the beginning of the 19th century, there were 315 of these schools with 19,915 pupils, including 1,787 girls. There were also vocational schools, including the Mining Inst. founded in 1774, and missionary schools (for non-Russians converted to Orthodoxy). Foreign tutors, who were predominantly French, provided an additional source of education.

The 19th Century. The School Act of 1804, under Alexander I, responded to a demand for reforms, put forward by men such as N. I. Novikov, who founded the first newspaper for children. The Act established 4 levels of schools:

1. Parish Schools (1 year)
2. County Schools (2 years)
3. Secondary Schools (*gimnazia*) (4 years)
4. Universities (4 years)

The new system was strong at the top—new universities were opened at Kazan and Kharkov (1804)—but weak at the bottom, since it was all but impossible to give a child even the rudiments of education in a single year. In 1811, the secondary school curriculum was extended to 7 years. The need for teachers was met by the Pedagogical Institute in St. Petersburg, which was raised to university rank in 1819. Elementary education, starved of government funds, was supplemented by the "Bible Societies."

The tendency towards a dual system of education, one for the rich and another for the poor, became accentuated under Nicholas I, who succeeded his brother Alexander in 1825. Nicholas' Minister of Education, Uvarov, fostered classical education for the upper classes, tightened school discipline, and summarized his reactionary policies with the formula "autocracy, orthodoxy and nationality." Under the latter, the school system was given the task of Russifying the non-Russian peoples of the Empire. Vocational education was strengthened, and the St. Petersburg Technological Inst. was founded in 1828. The growth of the school system under Nicholas I is shown in Table 1.

TABLE 1
NUMBER OF SCHOOLS

	1830	1840	1850
Parish Schools	718	983	1106
County Schools	416	439	439
Secondary Schools	62	73	76
Universities	6	6	6

The government's critics, such as Herzen, Belinsky, Chernyshevsky, Dobrolyubov and Pisarev, strongly opposed Uvarov's system and developed very different educational theories, as did the famous educator Pirogov and the novelist Count L. N. Tolstoy. Their efforts bore fruit in the first half of the reign of Alexander II (1855–81).

The universities were reformed under a law of 1863, and a new one was created at Odessa, while a Polytechnic Institute was established in Riga. In 1864, two acts were passed to improve elementary and secondary education. With the exception of the church schools, all the elementary schools were brought under the supervision of the Ministry of Education, and three types of secondary schools (*gimnazia*) were created:

1. Classical, with Greek and Latin.
2. Classical, with Latin only.
3. Modern (*realnaya*).

Education for women was now made available in addition to the institutions reserved to the daughters of the nobility, with secondary schools offering three- and six-year courses. Adult education was given attention for the first time, and 200 evening and Sunday schools were opened.

These changes were, however, undermined in the last years of Alexander II and under Alexander III (1881–94), when the Ministry of Education was in the hands of Count D. A. Tolstoy. In 1871, a decree made the modern *gimnazia* revert to classical curricula. A series of administrative measures excluded thousands of students from the universities for political reasons. Secondary education became more expensive, and access to it was restricted for children of non-noble origin, with quotas established for Jewish pupils. In 1894, 56.7% of the children in secondary schools were of noble birth. In 1872, modern schools of a vocational rather than a general type were set up in addition to town schools. Both were designed for non-noble children and did not provide access to the universities. An unforeseen result of these measures was that many children were sent abroad for their education, especially to foreign universities and technical schools. Thousands of young Russians left to study in Western Europe and returned with ideas of which their government disapproved.

Elementary schools were placed under the control of the nobility by a law of 1874, which made the local marshal of the nobility the ex-officio chairman of the school board in his district. The number of parish schools was increased and by 1905 they constituted 46.5% of the elementary schools.

These trends were somewhat mitigated by the schools established by the provincial councils (*zemstvos*). Over the decade 1864–74, the *zemstvos* opened some 10,000 elementary schools on modern pedagogical lines, in addition to teachers' seminaries. The vocational schools underwent reform in 1887–89, and commercial schools also began to make progress in the 1890's. Both were encouraged by increasing industrialization. Education for national minorities, however, became once again a means for their Russification. The school system evolved as of 1895 is shown in Table 2.

TABLE 2

Type of School	No. of Schools	Number of Students
Universities	9	13,976
Gimnazia and		
Pro-Gimnazia*	225	64,711
Modern Schools	107	26,002
Women's Gimnazia	325	68,029
Elementary Schools	29,241	1,937,076
(Not including		
parish schools)		

*The *pro-gimnazia* were similar to the *gimnazia*, but on a lower level.

The Last Years of Tsarism. According to the 1897 census, the percentage of literate population throughout the Russian Empire was 21.1. But literacy was very unevenly distributed; the rate was 33.7% among men and only 11.7% among women, with far higher rates in the cities and in European Russia than in the countryside and in the Asian parts of the Empire. Literacy rates were as low as 1.6% among the Uzbeks, 0.7% among the Turkmenians and Yakuts, and 0.6% among the Kirghiz.

In the last years of Tsarism, considerable efforts were made to spread education to the people who had not hitherto benefited from it. From 1895 to 1904, the number of technical schools rose from 51 to 93, vocational schools from 91 to 237, and commercial schools from 6 to 139. Libraries and evening classes were organized in both towns and villages by the government, the *zemstvos*, private organizations and individual citizens, participating in a general effort to bridge the gap between Russia and the West. The past emphasis on classicism was largely abandoned in 1902 and a law providing for compulsory school attendance was enacted in 1908.

By 1915, there were about 122,000 schools with 8,122,000 pupils. The number of children in elementary schools of all kinds was estimated at 7,260,000. Secondary schools had 764,600 pupils, and professional and technical schools had 93,200 on the elementary level and 35,000 on the secondary level. Higher educational institutions numbered 39, including 10 universities, and had 62,225 students. The 19 technical institutes had 22,379 students, and 9 agricultural institutes had about 6,000.

Although the progress shown by these figures had been considerable, the achievement was still inadequate. Schools were still not available to everybody, and 57.1% of the students in the universities were drawn from the upper and middle classes.

The Early Revolutionary Years. The communists were fully conscious of the importance of education. The program adopted by the Eighth Party Congress in 1919 called for "the transformation of the school system from a weapon of bourgeois class rule into a weapon for the complete abolition of the division of society into classes, into a weapon of the communist rebirth of society." The party program went on to define the principles governing the new, communist "unified labor school" (*Yedinaya Trudovaya Shkola*): instruction in native languages, co-education, separation of school and church, and an indissoluble linking of education with economic life through technical education.

The communists set out to remodel the R. school system in line with Lenin's definition of the functions of Soviet education: "To give to youth the fundamentals of knowledge and the capacity to form communist opinions for themselves; to make them educated people." (*Works*, 4th Ed., Vol. 31, pp. 270). Among the urgent tasks, Lenin emphasized the need to spread education among the workers and peasants, to raise the educational level of backward nationalities and to introduce general compulsory school attendance, first at the primary and then at the secondary level. The entire school system was to be re-modelled along communist lines. In practice, Lenin defined communist education as comprising "basic scientific knowledge of both nature and society, the world outlook of scientific materialism, communist morality, physical exercise for good health, close links between study and productive labor." Of all the branches of the system, the elementary schools seemed to Lenin the most important as molders of communist men and women.

Although the country was in chaos from civil war and foreign intervention, the Soviet government rapidly set about giving its school system a legal foundation. Education was assigned to People's Commissar A. V. Lunacharsky, with a Special Commission. A decree "On the Separation of Church and State and Church and School" was published on February 5, 1918. A further decree of the Council of People's Commissars, published June 5, 1918, put all types of schools, including pre-schools and adult institutions, under the People's Commissariat of Education. Thus full state control over all schools was established in law and put into practice as soon as the communists obtained full control of the country.

In October 1918, the Unified Labor School was established by statute as the only type of institution for the RSFSR at the elementary and secondary school levels. Its curriculum had two stages, first a five-year stage for children from 8 to 13, and then a four-year stage for children from 13 to 17. The universities and other institutions of higher learning were also brought under the control of the government and the party.

One of the first major educational efforts was the campaign against illiteracy. Lenin took a prominent role in the First Congress on Adult Education held in May, 1919, and a decree of the Council of People's Commissars of December 26, 1919 made it compulsory for all illiterates between the ages of 8 and 50 to learn to read and write. The effects of this decree were delayed, for circumstances did not allow its serious implementation until the late 1920's. It is estimated, however, that some 50 million adults learned to read and write between 1920 and 1940.

In reality, conditions were chaotic in the first few years after the revolution. The school system suffered the great loss, by death or emigration, of thousands of teachers and professors, including some scientists of first rank. Others stayed on, while new teaching cadres grew up to supplement them. The general relaxation of discipline affected the schools, as did the competing educational theories. The confused conditions of the early 1920's are well described in Nikolay Ognyov's novel *Kostya Ryabtsev.* It was during this period that A. S. Makarenko developed and applied his pioneering methods to educate the *bezprizorny,* the homeless children roaming the countryside and living by their wits.

Moreover, although education was universal in theory, there was considerable discrimination in practice. Children from the former ruling classes, who were not of worker or peasant origin, or whose parents were not party members, were excluded from some schools, and especially from universities. Some parents even resorted to forging false personal documents to ensure their children's education. It was not until December 1935 that a decree abolished the ban on admitting young people of "undesirable social origin" to the universities. Meanwhile, there was pressure to train "new cadres of Red specialists," which intensified with the beginning of the five-year plans in 1928. In the rush, quality of training, traditional methods, discipline, and basic theory were neglected in favor of quantity, progressive methods, practical work training and political zeal.

One further innovation made during the revolutionary period, and maintained to the present day, was the thoroughly political orientation of all the schools. Marxist dialectics, communist party history, and other political subjects are taught as part of the regular curriculum at all levels. The goal of the Soviet school system became, and remains, the development of communists.

The Intermediate Years. After 1928, rapid industrialization made it necessary to extend education to the entire population, with special emphasis on technical training. An expanded school program was inaugurated with a party central committee decree of July 25, 1930 "On Universal Compulsory Elementary Education." In 1934, the Central Committee and the Council of People's Commissars passed a further decree "On the Structure of the Elementary and Secondary School in the USSR," which provided the basis for making the seven-year school the general rule in Soviet education. The 18th Congress of the CPSU in 1939 resolved to establish the seven-year schools in all villages and secondary schools in all towns and cities. The implementation of this decision was hampered by the war and the German occupation, but even during the war, special schools for workers in factories, mines, and railroads were opened in 1943, and special schools for peasant children in 1944. It has been estimated that by 1956–57 some 50 million people were attending Soviet educational institutions of all types.

With universal compulsory education, there came a general tightening of school discipline. The teacher's authority was increased. Curricula were made uniform.

As the thirties and forties progressed, some of the traditional patriotic and national R. values were reincorporated in teaching. The libertarian innovations of the revolution were abandoned and the new privileged classes began to make their position felt in the schools as in other aspects of Soviet life.

The first change in this direction came from a party central committee decree of September 5, 1931, which pointed out "certain serious defects" in Soviet schools and introduced uniform curricula. Strict rules for examinations were established by a further decree of August 25, 1932, and general school discipline was greatly tightened by a decree of May 16, 1934.

Education ceased to be free for everyone at all levels when, on October 2, 1940, the Council of People's Commissars introduced tuition fees for the last three years of secondary schooling and for all higher education. Some exemptions were later granted, to students at military and art schools, but for the majority tuition was required until the fees were abolished by a law of June 10, 1956.

An effort was also made to abolish co-educational schooling at the secondary level. The decree of July 16, 1943, calling for separation of schools according to sex, was never, however, fully implemented.

In effect, the changes of the 1930's established the basic structure of the Soviet school system which was to endure without major modification until 1956. Its general outline and quantitative growth are shown in Table 3.

TABLE 3

NUMBER OF STUDENTS
(thousands)

Type of Institution	1914–15	1945–46	1956–57	1958–59	1959–60
General schools (elementary, seven-year, eight-year, secondary)	9,656	26,808	30,127	31,483	33,351
Vocational and factory schools	106	945	1,365	904	991
Specialized secondary schools	54	1,008	2,021	1,876	1,907
Higher educational institutions (including correspondence and evening courses)	127	730	2,001	2,179	2,260
TOTAL	9,943	29,491	35,505	36,442	38,509

The general schools established, with non-specialized curricula, were of three types. There were four-year primary schools for children aged 7–11, seven-year schools for children 7–14 (recently expanded into eight-year schools), and secondary schools (the equivalent of the old *gimnazia*) providing a ten-year course for children 7–17.

The vocational, factory, and specialized schools formed a system parallel to the general schools and provided specialized courses at the elementary and secondary levels. There are also trade schools, railroad schools, factory apprenticeship and collective farm schools with one or two-year courses at the elementary level. It is estimated that between 1940 and 1956 these schools supplied over eight million skilled workers. The intermediate specialized schools, or *technikums,* at the secondary level combine general education with vocational training.

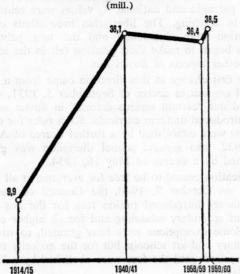

NUMBER OF STUDENTS
(mill.)

38,1   36,4   38,5

9,9

1914/15   1940/41   1958/59 1959/60

Soviet higher educational institutions are also divided into two types: universities, and technical or professional institutes. The institutes concentrate on advanced specialized courses, offering four to six years of training for engineers, agricultural experts, doctors, and such. The universities, whose number has risen since 1917 from 14 to 40, are concerned more broadly with study and research in the sciences and humanities. Originally, there were also special "workers' faculties" (*rabfaki*), established in line with the Communist Party Program of 1919 which called for "opening the university lecture halls to all who want to learn." These were, however, incorporated into the general school system in the early 1940's and since then, efforts have been made to give workers access to the universities through evening and correspondence courses, and by providing scholarships for poor students.

Training for teachers is provided by specialized teachers' colleges, of which there were 222 in 1956 with some 700,000 students. In addition, many university graduates go to teaching posts.

Finally, in addition to the regular schools, there are the kindergartens and preschools. Their increase in numbers and attendance is shown in Table 4.

TABLE 4

Year	Preschools	Children	Teachers
1914	275	7,000	—
1927	2,155	107,525	6,132
1955	31,596	1,730,941	143,834

Recent Changes. Since 1956, the school system described above has been undergoing change, with a series of government measures intended to adapt it to new conditions. For example, while the quantitative achievements of the system have been impressive, some doubts have been raised on whether the quality of the various types of training is uniformly high. There has also been criticism to the effect that the Soviet school system has tended to re-establish educational privileges for the children of the new upper class.

An important factor in the background of the current

reforms is the virtual abolition of illiteracy, (shown in Table 5). The data of the 1959 census show literacy rates on a par with those of Western Europe and the United States.

TABLE 5

PERCENTAGE OF LITERATE PERSONS IN
URBAN AREAS

(AGE GROUP: 9–49)

Year	Men	Women	Both sexes
1897	65.5	43.1	55.6
1926	88.0	73.9	80.9
1939	97.6	91.0	94.2
1959	99.5	98.1	98.7

PERCENTAGE OF LITERATE PERSONS IN
RURAL AREAS

(AGE GROUP: 9–49)

1897	34.3	9.6	21.7
1926	67.3	35.4	50.6
1939	93.7	79.2	86.3
1959	99.1	97.5	98.2

PERCENTAGE OF LITERATE PERSONS IN
TOTAL POPULATION

(AGE GROUP: 9–49)

1897	39.1	13.7	26.3
1926	71.5	42.7	56.6
1939	95.1	83.4	89.1
1959	99.3	97.8	98.5

At the other end of the educational scale, enrollment at the secondary and university levels appears to be comparatively low. The number of students in Soviet universities and institutes, measured per thousand of population, has doubled between 1939 and 1959, from 5.2 to 10.5. The USSR also graduated 94,000 engineers in 1958, compared to 35,000 in the United States. Yet, according to the Report of the National Education Fund to the U.S. Congress on April 14, 1960, higher education is provided to only 7% of the secondary school graduates in the Soviet Union, in contrast to 15% in the United States. Similarly, 60 out of every 100 Americans receive secondary schooling, while the figure for the Soviet Union is 30. The elementary, secondary, and higher schools together taught 46,102,-000 young people during 1958–59 in the United States, and only 36,442,000 in the Soviet Union, which has much the larger population (209 million, compared to 180 in the U.S.). The United States has 2,000 universities, colleges and advanced institutes with over three million students, whereas the Soviet Union has 40 universities and 726 technical and specialized institutes with slightly over two million students.

Some of the recent changes in the school system have been designed to improve educational standards, and others affect the social role of the schools. An early innovation, in 1956, was the establishment of boarding schools, for boys and girls separately. In the first year of their enrollment, 1956–57, the boarding schools (*shkoly internaty*) had 56,000 pupils, and it has been proposed that they should eventually become the most common type of secondary school. The abolition of tuition fees, as noted above, also came in 1956.

Reforms have been made, beginning in 1956 and continuing in 1960, in the *aspirantura* system of graduate and research work in the universities and institutes. The system had proved too lenient in evaluating students' work and awarding degrees, and there had been abuses in admitting unqualified students with influential parents. In 1956, the *aspirantura* was restricted to students with at least two years of experience in their field of specialization and proven research ability. Publication of a major portion of the aspirant's dissertation was made the criterion for awarding the degree of Candidate of Sciences. In 1960, the standards for defending both candidate and doctoral dissertations were stiffened. The Higher Attestation Commission of the USSR Ministry of Higher and Specialized Secondary Education was also given the power to revoke the degrees of persons whose later work proved unworthy.

As the reforms have progressed, purely pedagogical and technical problems have become entangled with economic considerations and with renewed attempts by the party to reduce class stratification in education. Two major social problems were discerned. First, the officials and the intelligentsia held a low opinion of manual labor as a career for their children, and parents resorted to personal influence or even bribery to secure a child's entrance into an advanced school or university, thence to white-collar employment. Secondly, relatively few young people from workers' or peasants' families went on to higher education after secondary school. In a speech to the 13th Congress of the Communist Youth Organization in 1958, Khrushchev denounced the "shameful situation" in which education was easily available to the children of party members and others in favored positions, while most of the children of workers, peasants, and subordinate employees were compelled to go to work after finishing secondary school. Khrushchev declared that this contradicts "the democratic principles of socialism." Less explicitly stated, there was also the need to adapt the school system to growing requirements for highly skilled labor.

After Khrushchev's speech, the pace of reform increased. In December 1958, a law was passed "For Strengthening the Ties of the Schools with Life and Further Developing the System of Public Education in the USSR." This law, followed by related measures, set forth the following outline of reform:

1) Admission to higher schools is to be determined by merit, and the trade unions and the communist youth organizations are to participate in the selection. Priority in fields other than the arts and natural sciences is to be given to candidates who have had two years of practical working experience, and especially to those sent for advanced training by their place of employment.

2) Advanced technical schools are to be organized in connection with factories, so that young people may acquire higher education while at work.

3) Both higher and intermediate agricultural schools are to be moved from urban locations to rural areas. Admission to them is to be limited to students who actually intend to work in agriculture.

4) Practical, on-the-job instruction is to be increased in the regular higher schools, and evening and correspondence courses on both the secondary and advanced levels are to be greatly expanded. The latter increase was begun immediately, so that in the school year 1959–60, 1,115,000 undergraduates out of a total of 2,260,000 studied in evening and correspondence courses while holding regular jobs.

5) The seven- and ten-year school courses are to be increased by one year so that the regular curriculum can be combined with practical work training in shops, factories, at experiment stations and on collective and state farms. Thus the basic, compulsory school unit will be an eight-year school, for ages 7–15. The secondary schools are to work in close connection with economic organizations, acting as "feeders." Graduation certificates will include a clause on labor skills.

It is too soon to judge the results of these reforms. Many are still in the early stages of implementation. The shift to eight- and eleven-year schools, for example, is expected to take from five to seven years to complete. It should be noted that the combination of general education with factory or farm work is not without precedent in the Soviet Union, and a similar requirement was made of the schools for a while under the Labor Reserves Law of October 2, 1940.

The Soviet education system in general has recently attracted considerable interest in countries outside the Soviet orbit. Western political, military and pedagogical experts have visited the Soviet Union and studied its schools with a view to assessing their share in the USSR's technological achievements and to estimate their merits and demerits. These observers have called particular attention to the emphasis on scientific and technical subjects in Soviet curricula. The interest is not, however, entirely unilateral. Soviet educational experts have made reciprocal visits to study western schools and reported valuable exchanges of experience.

BIBLIOGRAPHY: Michael T. Florinsky, *Russia: A History and an Interpretation*, New York, 1953; George S. Counts, *The Challenge of Soviet Education*, New York, 1957; George C. Kline, ed., *Soviet Education*, New York, 1957; Alexander G. Korol, *Soviet Education for Science and Technology*, New York, 1957; George Z. F. Bereday and Jaan Pennar, ed., *The Politics of Soviet Education*, New York, 1960.
G. DEN.

EHRENBÚRG, Ilyá Grigóryevich (1891–), writer, critic, poet, and translator. Studied in the first Moscow gymnasium. He left Russia for France in 1908, following his arrest for participation in a revolutionary organization. Was war correspondent for the newspaper *Utro Rossii* (Russia's Dawn), 1914–17, on the western  front and in Europe. Before and during the October revolution E was an anti-Bolshevik, but from 1923 on he became the European correspondent of *Izvestia*. Following several visits to Russia, he returned and remained there permanently. E served as war correspondent for *Izvestia* in the Spanish civil war, 1936–37. During World War II, he wrote numerous patriotic articles calling upon the Soviet soldiers to "kill the German." He was a member of the Jewish anti-fascist committee in World War II, but resigned shortly before its members were arrested and liquidated. After the death of Stalin, E favored moderately liberal reforms. He was a frequent visitor to European countries and America. Many thousands of his articles have been published in various collections: *Time as a Visa* (1931), *England* (1932), *My Paris* (1933), *War* (1942–44).

E's principal creative works, however, are his numerous novels: *The Love of Jeanne Ney* (1924), *In the Open Alley* (1927), *The D.E. Trust*, and *Ruination of Europe* (1923); *The Extraordinary Adventures of Julio Jurenito* (1921–22), a sharp and witty criticism of communist ideology; *The Life and Death of Nicholas Kurbov* (1923), a psychological novel of the era of war communism; *Without Drawing a Breath* (1934–35), dealing with discontent among the Soviet youth. This theme is again the subject of his novel *The Thaw* (1954–56). E is also the author of *The Second Day* (1933), *The Fall of Paris* (1941–42), *The Storm* (1947), and *The Ninth Breaker* (1951–55). His poems include *A Prayer for Russia* (1918) and *In the Hour of Death* (1919). He translated from French the poetry of François Villon and the prose of André Malraux. As a critic, E is best known for his *And Yet She Rotates* (1922), *On the Labor of a Writer* (1953), *Rereading Chekhov, Lessons of Stendhal*, and *Recollections of Tolstoy*. E is a member of the Supreme Soviet and a recipient of many awards. He is also member of the Presidium of World Peace Council.   v. z.

ÉIDEMAN, Róbert Petróvich (1895–1937), general, joined the Bolsheviks in 1917. Party worker in Siberia where he commanded the Bolshevik troops during the civil war. In 1924, E was appointed commander of the Red Army in Siberia and, in March 1925, head of the Frunze Military Academy. He was the editor-in-chief of the Soviet *Military Encyclopedia*. In June 1937, E was executed for alleged participation in the Tukhachevsky affair. He was exonerated after Stalin's death.

EIKHE, Róbert Índrikovich (1890–1940), Communist leader, born in Latvia of a poor peasant family. As a youth, he participated in the revolution of 1905–07. Subsequently, became a Bolshevik leader in Latvia. In 1918, during the Bolshevik regime in Latvia, E was people's commissar of supplies. Afterwards, he went to Russia where he became a member of the Central Committee of the CPSU. In 1940 he was shot, having been suspected by Stalin of opposition activities. At the 20th Party Congress of Feb. 1956, Khrushchev disclosed in his secret speech that the case against E was fabricated.

EISENSTEIN, Sergey Mikhaylovich (1898–1948), motion picture producer. Professor, All-Union State Institute of Motion Picture Art (1937); director of the First Workers' Theater in Moscow (1921–24). Associated with motion pictures since 1924. Among his best-known productions are *The Strike* (1925) and *The Battleship Potemkin* (1925), a picture on the mutiny in 1905 which has brought E international recognition. E studied the techniques of motion picture production in the United States (1929–31) where he worked on the unfinished picture *Long Live Mexico*. His motion picture *Bezhin Lug*, banned because of "formalistic errors," was followed by the successful production of

the monumental pictures *Aleksandr Nevsky* (1941) and *Ivan the Terrible* (part I, 1945; part II, released in 1958). Introduced such advanced techniques as montage, color pictures, stereoscopy. Stalin prizes (1941, 1946); Order of Lenin.

EKIBASTÚZ, city in Pavlodar Oblast, Kazakh SSR; fast-growing mining town, center of a new rich coal basin.

ELBRÚS, highest peak in Caucasus, in Georgian SSR; 18,476 ft.; glaciers.

ELECTORAL SYSTEM. Elected representative assemblies were introduced in Russia for the first time in 1906 after the revolutionary activities of the preceding year. Previous to this time the limited rights of the electorate were restricted to the selection of local officials, with negligible powers, and to the indirect selection of the rudimentary bodies of local government, the zemstvos and the municipal councils. These elections were conducted on the basis of a narrow franchise, with the mass of the population having a limited voice and being highly underrepresented.

The ES which was created for the elections to the State Duma in 1906 was regulated so as to favor those elements which supported the tsarist regime. While the suffrage was wide, the elections were not universal; the minimum age was 25, and women, soldiers, sailors, students, and certain other categories were not enfranchised. Voters in a district did not vote as a whole, but were divided into five classes (*curiae*) of voters with the large landowning class holding the preponderance of power. The members of the State Duma were indirectly elected through electoral assemblies, which were themselves partially subject to indirect election. Since the government bureaucracy had a leading role in the electoral process, it could, and did, influence the elections by administrative action. Perhaps the most significant control exercised by the regime was the administrative and police interference with the campaigning for the candidates when nominated.

When the Bolsheviks took power in 1917 they thus inherited a tradition and technique of general elections

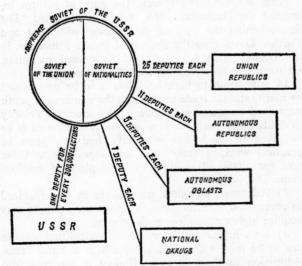

Elections to the Supreme Soviet of the the USSR

which presumed discrimination in voting privileges and manipulation of voting procedure by administrative action. The only exception to this had been the elections in the fall of 1917 to the Constituent Assembly (q.v.), the first and only relatively free expression of choice by the R. people. Until 1936, all popular elections in the USSR were for local state bodies only, each constituent republic having its own electoral laws. The higher state bodies were elected by the lower bodies. There was great discrimination in the suffrage, as those classes or groups which were assumed to be against the regime were disenfranchised. All persons, including noncitizens, of the working class 18 years of age or over could vote and be elected unless deprived of electoral rights by law; but those who hired labor for the purpose of making a profit, those who lived on income not derived from their own labor, and those who were engaged in trade had no electoral rights. There were also many specific exclusions (e.g., certain former government officials under the old regime, particularly the police, and all religious personnel). In practice it was found necessary to make many exceptions to these provisions for exclusion.

Under the USSR constitution of 1936, the franchise became universal and all state bodies which were designed to represent the people were subject to direct election. For the first time the electoral rights of Soviet citizens were defined in the union constitution. Since 1936, elections to the various soviets have been secret, with printed ballots being used and privacy for marking the ballot provided. These forms of democratic procedure are offset, however, by controls which prevent the election to state bodies of anyone who might be unwilling to accept the guidance of the Communist party.

The most important of these controls is the provision in the constitution which establishes the Communist party as the sole political party. There is no free selection of candidates within the one-party system, and there are no primaries in the USSR. While the nominating procedure provided by law appears to make possible the naming of more than one candidate for each position, all the organizations which may propose candidates are in fact under the control of the party. Factions and groups which might be in opposition to the policies laid down by the party elite, and which might like to nominate their own candidates, are not tolerated (they are explicitly prohibited within the party).

Voting procedures also offer a means of controlling the electoral process. Only one name appears on the ballot for each place. The voter has the option of depositing the ballot unmarked in the receptacle, crossing out the name inscribed, or writing in another name. Since folding the ballot unmarked in plain view of the poll watcher has been encouraged, the use of the curtained booths to mark the ballot in privacy becomes in effect a sign of disloyalty to the regime.

The Soviet leaders make full use of the electoral process for several reasons: elections are an essential element in a modern democratic system, and have to be made a part of the Soviet system in order to complete the democratic forms in which it is cloaked; elections create in the population an illusion of participation in public affairs; and elections serve as a form of national mobilization, for they provide a demonstration, to both the outside world and the Soviet people, which purports to show that the regime has the solid support of the people. (*See also* CONSTITUTIONS, SOVIETS, STATE DUMA, ZEMSTVO.)

BIBLIOGRAPHY: George Barr Carson, Jr., *Electoral Practices in the USSR*, New York and London, 1956; John N. Hazard, *The Soviet System of Government*, Chicago, 1960. R. C.

ELECTRIC POWER STATIONS. In 1960, 292 bill. kw-hr of electric power were produced, of which about one-fifth came from hydroelectric stations (in 1959, the United States produced 795 bill. kw-hr, one-fifth of which came from hydroelectric stations; the United Kingdom 121 bill. kw-hr, of which 3 per cent came from hydroelectric stations).

A plan to expand the production of electricity rapidly was adopted by the government in 1921 immediately after the civil war. The direct purpose of this initial program, which provided for the construction in various regions of the USSR of 30 large thermal and hydroelectric stations with an aggregate capacity of 1.7 bill. kw. in the course of ten to fifteen years, was to lay the basis for a subsequent program of general industrializa-

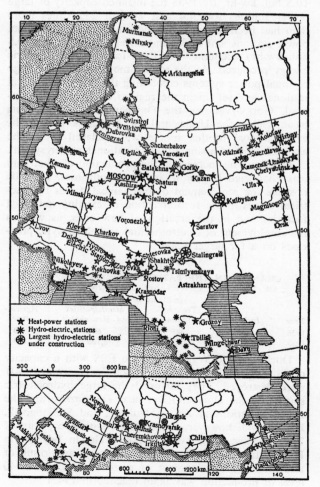

Electrification of the USSR

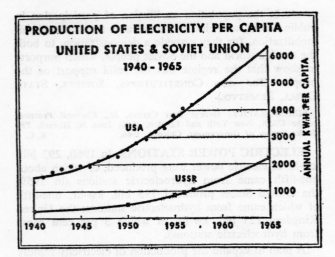

PRODUCTION OF ELECTRICITY PER CAPITA
UNITED STATES & SOVIET UNION
1940 - 1965

tion (GOELRO—State Commission for the Electrification.

The implementation of this program was carried out more rapidly than had been expected. By 1931 the installed capacity of the large regional stations reached 2.1 mill. kw. (it had been .2 mill kw. in 1913), and the production of electric power reached an annual rate of 10.5 bill. kw-hr. By 1935 the installed capacity of large power stations was 4.4 mill kw., or 2½ times more than had been initially planned, and the large regional power stations and major industrial power plants (19.5 bill. kw-hr) accounted for three-fourths of all electric energy produced. At the same time a number of large regional power systems combining the power of several stations were set up in the regions of Moscow, Leningrad, Gorky-Ivanovo, the Dnieper basin, the Donets basin, Baku, the Urals, and the Kuznetsk basin. The eventual goal in this sphere was declared to be the establishment of a single unified national power system.

The resulting increase in the production of electricity was channeled largely to industrial purposes. It made possible the replacement of mechanical drives by electrical drives in the reconstruction of existing industrial facilities and in the creation of new ones, as well as the employment of electrothermal and electrolytic processes on a far larger scale.

TABLE I
CHANGES IN THE PATTERNS OF CONSUMPTION OF ELECTRIC POWER BEFORE WORLD WAR II
(mill. kw-hr)

Year	Industry	Transportation	Municipalities and Households	Agriculture
1926	2,430	90	660	30
1935	17,970	570	3,766	190

During World War II 60 large EPS with a capacity of 58 mill. kw. (44 per cent of total capacity in 1940) were destroyed. They included the large hydroelectric station on the Dnieper River near Zaporozhye and the regional stations at Zuyev, Dubrov, and Stalinogorsk. In 1942–44, however, new stations with a capacity of 3.4 mill. kw. were built in the Urals, in Siberia, in Kazakhstan, and in Central Asia. Largely as a result of this intensive development of eastern areas, the 1940 level of production was again reached in 1945.

An emphasis on the development of electric power in eastern areas continued during the post-war years, when the rate of increase in the production of electricity became particularly rapid. This is indicated, for example, by the fact that already by 1951 areas east of the Volga valley produced nearly as much electricity as was produced in the entire country in 1940.

By 1953 both the installed capacity of the EPS of the country as a whole and the output of electricity had tripled by comparison with 1945. It is this that made possible the general postwar upsurge in Soviet industry, especially in the production of nuclear weapons, aluminum, and magnesium. During this period the development of electricity production was marked in part by a tendency toward the building of larger stations (e.g., thermal stations of 600,000 kw. and a hydroelectric station of 2.1 mill. kw. at Kuybyshev). At the same time the earlier trend toward the development of larger unified power systems continued to progress. In addition, a policy directed at encouraging the utilization of local fuels in thermal stations was implemented. In 1955, only 9% of the electric power produced in thermal stations derived from fuels imported from other regions.

In 1955 the value of electric power production and of transmission equipment represented 14% of the value of all industrial equipment, while the cost of operations of EPS represented 6% of expenditures on all industrial production. By far the largest share (67%) of the 160 bill. kw-hr of electric power produced in that year was again directed to industrial uses.

TABLE II
CONSUMPTION OF ELECTRIC POWER BY INDIVIDUAL SECTORS OF THE ECONOMY IN THE POSTWAR PERIOD
(bill. kw-hr)

Year	Total Electricity Produced	Consumption in Industry	Consumption in Transp.	Other Sections
1940	48.3	32.1	1.6	8.6
1950	91.2	60.6	2.6	16.5
1955	170.2	113.3	5.4	30.3

TABLE III
ELECTRIC POWER CAPACITY OF INDUSTRIAL ENTERPRISES IN THE USSR
(mill. kw.)

Year	Capacity of Machine-driving Motors mech.	elect.	total	Capacity of electrical equip.	Elect. capacity serving ind. processes
1928	1.0	2.0	3.0	.02	2.0
1932	1.2	4.3	5.5	.2	4.5
1937	2.1	10.2	12.3	1.4	11.6
1940	2.7	14.2	16.9	2.0	16.2
1950	4.1	26.4	30.5	5.2	31.6
1955	5.7	46.3	52.0	9.2	55.5

The extent to which this led to the further electrification of industrial processes is indicated by the changes, in the various industries, in the coefficient of electrification of power processes.

TABLE IV
COEFFICIENT OF ELECTRIFICATION OF POWER IN INDIVIDUAL INDUSTRIES (%)

Year	all ind.	fer. met.	nonfer. met.	chem.	mach. build.	paper & wood-work	lt. ind. text.	food
1928	64.9	51.3	79.3	73.4	85.3	55.2	62.4	24.7
1932	78.0	62.7	94.1	90.3	90.5	74.2	78.2	42.6
1937	82.8	73.8	91.4	83.1	91.6	84.5	82.5	56.7
1940	83.8	75.1	92.1	91.8	87.4	85.1	62.5
1950	86.7	81.6	96.6	95.3	96.3	86.3	91.7	68.8
1955	89.0	83.4	96.2	97.6	98.1	93.6	96.0	78.8

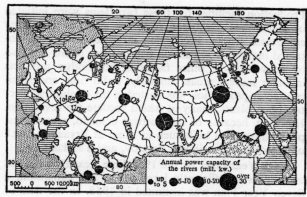

USSR hydro resources

Hydroelectric power. Official estimates place the potential hydroelectric power capacity (of 1,477 rivers) of the USSR at 340 mill. kw., and the corresponding potential for the production of hydroelectricity at 3,400 bill. kw-hr. In spite of a pronounced emphasis on the development of hydroelectric power stations, however, by far the largest share of electric power production until the present time (86% in 1955) has come from thermal stations.

Among the large hydroelectric stations constructed during the prewar period are the very large station on the Dnieper near Zaporozhye, with a capacity of 500,000 kw. before World War II; the stations at Volkhov and on the Svir River near Leningrad; at Shcherbakov and at Uglich, on the Volga; at Chirchik and on the Chu River in Central Asia; and on the Tuloma, Niva, and Suna rivers in Karelia and the Kola Peninsula. Altogether 32 regional hydroelectric stations were built during the First and Second Five Year Plans.

Between 1946 and 1950, 47 more large hydroelectric stations with a capacity of 2.3 mill. kw. were constructed. By 1955 the total number of regional hydro-

electric stations reached 84 and their aggregate capacity 5.3 mill. kw. Among the largest are the stations at Kuybyshev and at Stalingrad on the Volga, each with a planned annual production of 10 bill. kw-hr.

A 5,000 kw. atomic power plant of an experimental character began to produce electricity for industrial and agricultural needs in 1954 and it has been announced that similar plants with a capacity of 50,000 and 100,000 kw. are being projected.

The objectives of the Seven Year Plan (1959–65) provide for increasing the installed capacity of both thermal and hydroelectric stations by 58–60 mill. kw. (to 113–115 mill. kw.) and the production of electric power by 257–287 bill. kw-hr annually (to 500–520 bill. kw-hr). Although it is expected that the large hydroelectric stations at Bratsk, Stalingrad, Kremenchug, Votkinsk, and Bukhtarma will be completed during this period, most of this increase is to come from the construction of new thermal stations.

TABLE V

PRODUCTION OF ELECTRIC POWER IN THE USSR

Year	Installed cap. (thous. kw.)	Elect. power (mill. kw-hr)	Installed capacity	Hydroelect. power prod
1913	1,141	2,039	16	35
1921	1,228	520	18	10
1929	2,296	6,224	126	462
1931	3,972	10,686	130	592
1932	4,677	13,540	504	812
1937	8,235	36,173	1,044	4,184
1940	11,193	48,309	1,587	5,113
1945	11,124	43,257	1,252	4,841
1950	19,614	91,226	3,218	12,691
1955	37,246	170,225	5,996	23,165
1958	53,367	235,350	10,856	46,487
1959	——	265,112	——	
1960		292,000		
1965 (pl.)				
113–115 mill. kw.		500–520 bill. kw-hr.		P. I. M.

ELECTRICAL ENGINEERING: *see* TECHNICAL SCIENCES.

ELECTRICAL MACHINERY INDUSTRY. The main products of this branch of heavy industry are thermal and hydraulic generators, various types of electric motors, and electric locomotives. They also include, however, such durable consumers' goods as washing machines, electric fans, vacuum cleaners, and phonographs. In 1960 generators with an aggregate capacity of 7.9 mill. kw. and 435 electric locomotives were produced.

The production of electrical equipment was initiated in the 19th century in plants that were affiliated with W. European and especially with German firms. The plants in existence in 1913 included the Siemens-Schuckert, Elektrik, Elektroapparat, and Svetlana plants in St. Petersburg (Leningrad), the Dynamo plant in Moscow, and the Kharkov Electromechanical Works in Kharkov. Their output was limited, and it met only a small fraction of current requirements. In particular such items as large generators, transformers, and electrical measuring instruments were imported from other countries.

The production of large generators and electric motors as well as of electric locomotives was first undertaken during the prewar Five Year Plans. At that time existing plants were reconstructed and expanded and their output became specialized. The newly con-

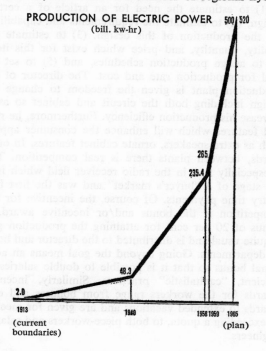

PRODUCTION OF ELECTRIC POWER (bill. kw-hr)

500 | 520
265
235.4
48.3
2.0

1913 (current boundaries)
1940
1958 1959 1965 (plan)

structed plants included the Moscow Electric Motor Plant, the Yaroslavl Electrical Equipment Plant, the Kharkov Turbo-Generator Plant, and the Ural Electrical Instruments Plant in Sverdlovsk.

The further development of this industry was particularly rapid during the years that followed World War II. According to official data the annual rate of output of electrical equipment was eight times higher in 1955 than it had been in 1940, and included a variety of new products. A measure of the technological improvements that were made during this period is provided by the production, in recent years, of a hydrogen-cooled turbogenerator with a capacity of 150,000 kw. (by the Elektrosila plant at Leningrad); of hydraulic turbines for the station at Kuybyshev with a capacity of 105,000 kw.; of hydrogen-cooled automatic transformers, designed for the long-distance transmission of power between Kuybyshev and Moscow, with a capacity of 75,000 kw.; and of an electric locomotive with a power of 4,300 kw.

The objectives of the Seven Year Plan provide for increasing the production of thermal and hydraulic generators to an annual rate of 17.5–18.4 mill. kw. It has been estimated that a yearly addition of this size to installed generator capacity would make possible a yearly increase of 80–100 bill. kw-hr in the amount of electricity produced.

PRODUCTION OF ELECTRIC GENERATORS, ELECTRIC MOTORS, AND ELECTRIC LOCOMOTIVES IN THE USSR

Year	Generators (mill. kw.)	Large electric motors (over 100 kw.) (mill. kw.)	Small electric motors (mill. kw.)	Electric locomotives
1913	—	—	—	—
1928	.08	.06	.2	—
1932	10.9	.3	1.4	3
1937	.6	.6	1.2	32
1940	.5	.5	1.3	9
1950	.9	2.5	4.2	102
1955	4.5	2.2	6.6	191
1956	5.2	2.5	7.3	216
1958	5.2	3.3	10.4	344
1959	6.5	181,000 units	2.5 mill. units	435
1960	7.9	—	—	396
1965 (pl.)	17.5–18.4	—	—	—

P. I. M.

ELECTRONICS. Activity and production in electronics have existed since before the revolution. In fact, in 1895 Aleksandr S. Popov, who was working as an instructor for the tsarist admiralty, experimented in wireless telegraphy. Thus he was active in the field concurrently with Marconi and others, and successfully received wireless messages transmitted from one ship to another over a distance of 700 meters in 1897. In 1945, there was formed the Popov Society (correctly known as The All-Union Scientific-Technical Society of Radio Engineering and Electrical Communication). It has about 15,000 members with a membership fee of 12 rubles per year.

However, broadcast transmission and reception were quite inactive during the twenties and production of receiving sets did not start until 1931. The value of broadcasting as a means of mass communication over the vast extent of the Soviet Union was readily realized and production increased tremendously after World War II as shown in Figure 1. This also shows the rapid increase in television production in the past ten years.

Production facilities for these two items were initiated in established electrical factories such as telephone equipment plants. Production increases have been obtained mainly by expansion within these plants but also by conversion of other factories from other products in other market areas. Similarly, radio tube and semiconductor production was started in the established electric lamp plants, many of which predate the revolution. However, because of the postwar demand, several new plants have been built such as those at Fryazino, north of Moscow, Novosibirsk, Saratov, and Tashkent.

Seven Year Plan. As the 1955 Five Year Plan did not encompass a sufficiently large production expansion, a Seven Year Plan was instituted in 1958. In the field of electronics, this plan required a production increase of 400–500 per cent by 1965 except in the field of radio receivers, which was planned at only 110 per cent. The reason for this was that the market was approaching saturation (6 to 25 persons per receiver versus the ratio of 1.8 in the United States) and required the institution of time payments to revitalize this market.

Production and Planning. Production design and planning are under the control of the State Committee for Radio-Electronics which is part of the Ministry of Communications. Its two main functions are engineering and economic planning. Under the former, they assume the responsibility for the detailed design, e.g., for a radio receiver, they develop the circuit, the schematic and even the cabinet, and specify the complete bill of materials. As economic planners, they decide the production quantity and cost for each plant under their jurisdiction, taking into account the labor supply, production equipment, and so on.

Ideally, this State Committee functions as the coordinating liaison between the research institutes of the Ac. of S. and of the ministries concerned with this field, and the production plants. Actually, its function is (1) to estimate the need for an article of a certain design, (2) to estimate the requirements and capabilities for the production of this design, (3) to estimate the quality, quantity, and price which exist for this item, (4) to assign production schedules, and (5) to set the goal for production rate and cost. The director of the production plant is given the freedom to change the design including both the circuit and cabinet so as to increase his production efficiency. Furthermore, he may add features which will enhance the consumer appeal, such as extra speakers, ornate cabinet features. In other words, between plants there is real competition. This is especially true in the radio receiver field which is in the stage of a "buyer's market" and was the first field to try time payments. Of course, the incentive for this competition is the bonus and/or incentive award. A bonus of 20 per cent for attaining the production goal is quite usual and is distributed to the director and heads of departments. Going beyond the goal means an additional bonus so that it is possible to double salaries by efficient, "capitalistic" practices. Similarly, incentive awards for the workers range from bonuses and cash awards to extended vacations and are given for meeting or exceeding a quota, to both piece-workers and salaried engineers.

Design and Engineering. In the following discussion of the assemblies, devices, and components, it must be remembered that the economy of the Soviet Union is a "seller's market" and that this dictates the advances that are required to satisfy the consumer and is one of the causes of the considerable time delay between development and production.

Radio Receivers. Receiving sets are produced as portable, table, and console models with a limited production of large console combination receivers. In general, the engineer specifies overcapacity of components with emphasis on inspection of all connections. As set failure and repair are chargeable to the factory of origin, the engineer must assure reliability. This is attained mainly by "brute-force" techniques (e.g., higher power resistors) rather than by refining the components themselves. One reason for this reliability need is the scarcity of technicians competent to make repairs in the field. For the same reason printed circuit boards, on which it is very difficult to make repairs, were considered by the design engineer, but were not used in production until this last year. In general, the sensitivity, stability, and quality of the receivers are very good but they are complicated by usually including not only AM and FM but also all-wave for foreign reception. They are of the W. Europe design and appearance. It should be mentioned that there is some export of both Russian and Chinese receivers to S. and S.E. Asia.

Television Receivers. Television broadcasting uses 625 lines with a 50-cycle vertical scan and a bandwidth of 6.5 mc between picture and audio signals. Broadcasting is further complicated by the immense distances between population centers, lack of broadband communication facilities and the multiplicity of languages and cultures within the Soviet Union. Transmittal of a program from point of origin to the various transmitters is mostly by microwave linkage even within a city. Television receiver production is predominantly of the 17-inch (43 cm.) tube but some 21-inch (53 cm.), 90° deflection sets are being produced. These sets all have 12 channels although the maximum number of channels for any city was two in 1958. Design emphasizes redundancy as an approach to reliability as with radio receivers, e.g., use of resistors of twice the wattage required. Also the factory of origin is responsible for repair or malfunction.

Receiving Tubes. While western tubes and type numbers have been duplicated and produced, the Russians have evolved their own type numbering system using a numerical, alphabetical sequence similar to that used in this country, as shown in Table I.

Without our competitive engineering, and with the advantage of state control, their total number of receiving tube types was about 260 in 1958 in comparison with our 1,500 types. Most of our innovations, both in materials and design, are found in their types, e.g., multielement tubes. It may be mentioned that the E. German production uses western designs and type numbers although the Russian types are made throughout the Union and even in the Chinese People's Republic. In quality of design and materials the Soviet and western tubes are quite comparable, even including the con-

TABLE I
RUSSIAN NUMBERING SYSTEM
RECEIVING TUBES

1. First Numerical Portion
    Heater voltage in volts
2. Second Alphabetical Portion

Diodes	D or Ts
Duodiodes	Kh
Triodes single	S
Triodes twin	N
Triodes with diodes	G
Tetrodes	E
Pentodes	P, K or Zh
Pentodes with diodes	B
Pentodes with triodes	F
Pentagrid converters	A
Pentagrid with triode	I

3. Third Numerical Portion
    A series number for the type.
4. Fourth Alphabetical Portion

Glass tubes, subminiature	A or B
Glass tubes, miniature	P
Glass tubes, other	S
Glass tubes, lock-in	L
Glass tubes, disc seal	D
Glass tubes, acorn	Zh
Metal tubes	M
Ceramic tubes	K

struction and workmanship. The latter comparison is valid despite the lack of advanced equipment and jigging. It is believed that the techniques and refinements for reliability have not been advanced appreciably. Total production of tubes is estimated at about 100 million per year, of which about 20 million are metal tubes and perhaps 10 million are subminiature tubes.

Semiconductors. The development and production of diodes and transistors have advanced slowly as the art has progressed. The annual production rate is estimated at about 30 million. The evolution of design started quite independently of practices in this country but of late the design is similar to ours. The designs include high-power and high-voltage diodes and high-power and high-frequency transistors (e.g. f_{max} of 500 mc/s). However, there appears to be a considerable delay between development and volume production. All the advanced techniques are in use but not all the refinements have been worked out or applied. For this reason, production has a wider scatter of characteristic values. While Russian transistorized radios were exhibited at the Coliseum in New York City in July 1959, none were available for consumer use. Similarly, the Russians have developed transistorized telephone switchboards and computers but have no production of these items.

Other Devices and Components. Cathode ray tubes, compatible with western types for both television and oscilloscope use, have been designed and produced. Because of the large demand for 17″ television tubes, round metal cone tubes are in production because (1) there is a producing facility in operation and (2) the metal cone can be reused more easily than a glass one. Dual gun oscilloscope tubes as well as triple gun color tubes are in development and some of the former are in production. Vidicons and iconoscopes are produced for television broadcast and closed-circuit plant control and also for research in undersea and space applications. Power and microwave devices are in small-scale or even custom production as befits their small demand. Generally they are similar to western designs but are not

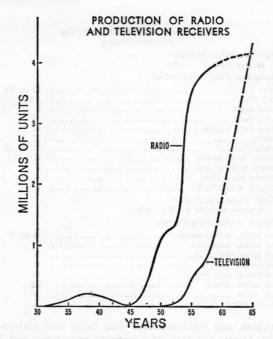

PRODUCTION OF RADIO AND TELEVISION RECEIVERS

MILLIONS OF UNITS

RADIO

TELEVISION

YEARS

very advanced. Other devices cover the range of modern needs and are in small-scale production. Photographers use a high-voltage gaseous flash tube rather than the metal-oxygen single flash bulbs. Resistors have been standardized in the wire and deposited-carbon types. Capacitors are available with paper, electrolytic, plastic-film, ceramic, and oil dielectrics. The shortage of tantalum ore precludes the production of "tantalytic" capacitors.

Design Data. Because of state control and design of assemblies, product data sheets are not issued by the producing factories. Instead the state issues a handbook listing characteristics of devices and components together with dissertations on their functioning. Also the magazines have tables and articles on "new products." However, the system design engineer is severely limited by this lack of data, at least by our standards. While some maximum and minimum values are shown, in many cases the publication of only typical values limits him further. Where reliable systems are required (e.g., for computers), considerable testing of the devices and components is necessary and must lead to duplication of effort.

BIBLIOGRAPHY: Norman M. Kaplan and R. H. Moorsteen, *Indexes of Soviet Industrial Output*, The RAND Corporation, 1960 (processed); *Handbook on Vacuum-Tube and Semi-conductor Devices*, State Publishing House for Communications and Radio, Moscow, 1957 (re-published, processed, U.S. Joint Publication Research Service, Washington, D.C., 1958); P. E. Green, Jr. and D. B. Sinclair, *Trip Report*, 1958 (processed). C. P. M.

ELEKTROSTÁL, city in Moscow Oblast, RSFSR; pop. 43,000 (1939), 97,000 (1959). Major producer of high-grade steel.

ELISTA, (f. Stepnoy), city, capital of Kalmyk ASSR, RSFSR; pop. 23,000 (1959). Trading center of important cattle- and sheep-raising area, with processing ind. based on local produce.

ELIZABETH (Yelizavéta Petróvna), (1709–1761), Empress of Russia (1741–61). E was the daughter of Peter the Great and Catherine I. She gained the throne by a *coup d'état* effected by the nobles and officers opposed to the German influence which had dominated the court during the reign of Anna Ivanovna and her successor, Ivan VI. E never married but had many lovers, including a long liaison with Alexis Razumovsky, an illiterate but handsome Cossack lad whom she made a count and a field marshal. E was politically keen, but dissolute and lax, and her reign left no imprint on the structure of the government or social conditions. It saw the development of learning and science, with the foundation of the first Russian university at Moscow and the Academy of Fine Arts at St. Petersburg. Foreign policy, under the guidance of Alexis Bestuzhev-Ryumin, was based on alliance with Austria and England, with a view to R. expansion at the expense of Sweden, Poland, and Turkey. War against Sweden (1741–73) resulted in territorial gains in Finland. Participation in the Seven Years' War (1756–63) brought temporary R. occupation of Berlin, but came to an abrupt end because of E's death and her succession by an admirer of Prussia, Peter III.

EMANCIPATION OF THE SERFS. The Crimean War (1853–55) revealed the backwardness of the R. economy and military technology and the ineptness of the Russian Army. The oppressed opposition, which was immobilized under Nicholas I, became stronger again and demanded reforms. The peasants, who had believed a false rumor that voluntary enlistment in the army would lead to emancipation, continued mass uprisings when their hopes were shattered by punitive military expeditions.

The accession of Alexander II was received with great hopes by all believers in reforms. His conservative views were not generally known and he was regarded as a reformer and the champion of E. This was not true, for in reality the young emperor was compelled by circumstances to believe that only E from above could prevent a peasant revolution from below.

While Alexander II decided for E in principle, he continued to regard the landed noblemen as the mainstay of the throne and endeavored to persuade the aristocracy to give its consent to E and share the credit for it. This explains why five years passed between the young emperor's manifesto of March 19, 1856, which contained the first indication of coming reforms, and the proclamation of the end of serfdom on Feb. 19, 1861. The conservative serf-owners, although recognizing the necessity for E, deliberately postponed the day of reforms.

The Manifesto of March 19, 1856 vaguely hinted a program of internal reforms. The noblemen reacted to it with alarm or inertia. To this the government responded at the end of 1856 by appointing a secret committee composed mainly of large landowners opposed to E. The committee after long considerations stated that serfdom was an evil but it should be abolished gradually and with the greatest caution. On Aug. 18, 1857 the committee officially reported that E should proceed in three stages. The second stage alone—a period of transition—should be not less than ten years. Fortunately in the meantime Alexander had read some of the circulated manuscripts (e.g., by Yury Samarin) urging speedy E and pressure was put on him by the partisans of E (e.g., Grand Duke Constantine whom the tsar appointed on Aug. 18, 1857 as chairman of the committee) to favor a more urgent reform. A petition by the landowners of the Lithuanian provinces presented the tsar with an opportunity for hastening matters. In an imperial rescript he approved the initiative and demanded establishment of provincial committees of noblemen to elaborate within six months detailed proposals for "the betterment of the conditions of the serfs." This rescript, and a similar one to the Governor-General of St. Petersburg, were published in the press on Dec. 17, 1857. For the first time the government had announced publicly its intentions to proceed with E and thus the stage was set for E. In the next four months committees were established in every province. Although the committees had approximately 1,400 members, less than one-tenth participated actively in their work. They reflected the opposition of the noblemen to E and endeavored to secure for themselves the best possible terms. For two years a great variety of recommendations (because of diverse economic conditions in various parts of Russia) was presented to the central committee (the former secret committee, renamed on Jan. 8, 1858). Two editorial commissions were established on Feb. 17, 1858 to draft the E statutes. Some of their members (e.g., Prince F. I. Paskevich, Count P. A. Shuvalov) were opponents of E, but the appointed chairman, General J. I. Rostovtsev, among others, believed in the need for E. However, Rostovtsev died in Feb. 1860 and his successor, Count V. N. Panin, was a known opponent of E. General Rostovtsev, among others, is credited with making the original draft of the statutes more favorable to the peasants than the recommendations by the provincial committees. This draft was revised three times in favor of the landowners: first, by the editorial commissions under the pressure of the provincial committees; later by the central committee; and then by the State Council.

The statutes were solemnly proclaimed on Feb. 19, 1861 in an insincere manifesto written by Metropolitan Philaret, a well-known enemy of E. The statutes consisted of twenty-two enactments published in a volume of 360 pages. They contained numerous inconsistencies and in general gave no adequate solution to the enormous difficulties created by the bewildering complexity of the reform. To some degree that was corrected, however, by many amendments in later years.

E was to proceed gradually in three stages. During the first stage the 22.4 mill. serfs were to receive their personal liberty, e.g., were free to marry, engage in trades, buy and sell property. For two years—through a protracted and complicated process—inventories were prepared specifying the area of land for each peasant and the annual payments and services due from him. The second stage was to begin on Feb. 19, 1863. During it the peasants were temporarily obligated to the noblemen and were to continue the annual payments and services determined by the inventories. The final stage was to follow with redemption payments for land allotted to the peasants. No time limit was established

for the period of temporary obligations and the statutes did not provide a revision of the inventories till 1881. By 1880, however, settlements had been made on 85 per cent of the allotments. By the law of Dec. 28, 1881 the redemption of the remaining allotments was made compulsory beginning in 1883. The government advanced to the landowners approximately three-fourths of the total indemnification while the peasants provided the balance and often additional payments. The peasants were to repay the government by annual instalments. Because the allotments were overvalued and burdened by heavy interests, the peasants usually could not keep up their obligations, which caused repeated reassessment of the accumulated redemption debts. Finally on Nov. 3, 1905, forced by the revolution, all redemption payments were canceled.

The allotments were considerably smaller than the peasant holdings before E. The peasants were unable to utilize their full labor power on their own land nor consequently to secure their livelihood from the income of it. That compelled them to seek employment either with the large landowners or in the urban industries. The inevitable result was a dissatisfied peasantry.

The statutes of Feb. 19, 1861 retained the village commune. All peasants were compelled to belong to it. They could not absent themselves from the village without a passport. The village commune was jointly responsible for taxes and other obligations of its members. The village elders wielded wide disciplinary powers over peasants. The influence of the village commune was stifling and did not allow a sound development of peasant farming.

E was a great and important reform which, together with other reforms that followed, was intended to modernize Russia. But for all their importance the great reforms were only halfhearted concessions to avoid a peasant revolution. E failed to solve the peasant problems. The peasants remained a class separate from the other classes. Socially they were at the bottom of the society. They remained subject to corporal punishment. They were taxed by the government per capita, not according to their income. Usually half of the arable land of an estate, and all the non-arable land, remained in the hands of the noblemen. In addition, the landlords received the more fertile land, and the peasants had to pay for their land more than its market price. As a result the peasants were unable to solve the problem of their livelihood and remained impoverished. Above all, the peasant bitterness continued. Only a few months after the E, troops had been needed to suppress 337 uprisings. There were innumerable insubordinations caused by the refusal of the peasants to accept the "inventories." The disturbances were quelled by executions, floggings and deportations to Siberia. The dissatisfied peasantry was a strong factor in all consecutive revolutionary developments in Russia. (*See also* AGRICULTURE, BARSHCHINA, OBROK, PEASANTS)

BIBLIOGRAPHY: Michael T. Florinsky, *Russia: A History and an Interpretation*, Vol. II, New York, 1953; Geroid T. Robinson, *Rural Russia Under the Old Regime*, New York, 1932.

K. R. P.

ÉMBA RIVER, Kazakh SSR, flows from W. Mugodzhar mts., S.W. via Aktyubinsk and Guryev oblasts, ending in a delta on Caspian Sea; 384 mi. long; rich oil region.

EMIGRÉS: *see* RUSSIANS ABROAD.

ENCYCLOPEDIA. The European success of Diderot's *Encyclopedia* gave rise in R. to the compilation of dictionaries on different subjects. Leading articles from the work of Diderot were translated into R. and published. In 1730, V. N. Tatishchev completed a *Lexicon of Russian Historical, Geographical, Political and Civil Matters;* F. Polunin in cooperation with the historian G. F. Miller published a *Geographical Lexicon of the Russian State* (1773). In 1803–06, the Ac. of S. charged N. M. Yanovsky with the compilation of the *New Dictionary of Words,* a voluminous E of foreign words in R. usage. In the years 1823–25, S. A. Selivanovsky published his *Encyclopedia,* the first comprehensive dictionary in Russia. However, since its author sympathized with the Decembrists and many of its distinguished contributors belonged to the movement (W. K. Kuchelbeker and others), the series was suppressed by the government.

The *Encyclopedic Dictionary* by A. A. Plyvshar was completed in 1835–41. V. N. Maykov and later M. V. Petrashevsky edited the *Pocket Dictionary of Foreign Words* in 1845–46. A *Reference Dictionary for All Branches of Knowledge,* the work of F. G. Toll, was distinguished by democratic tendencies (1863–66). Only six volumes of A. A. Krayevsky's *Encyclopedic Dictionary* appeared between 1861 and 1863. The first complete E, *Russian Encyclopedic Dictionary,* by I. N. Berezin, carried articles by the eminent scientists of the time (1873–79). This publication was followed by 82 volumes of the *Encyclopedic Dictionary* by Brockhaus and Efron (1890–1907) which counted outstanding scholars among its contributors. The E written on a high level enjoyed great success; however its second edition (1911–16) remained incomplete. Another widely used series was the *Great Encyclopedia* by S. N. Yuzhakov (1902–09) and the *Encyclopedic Dictionary* (1892–1910), by the brothers Granat. In 1910, a new edition appeared under the name *Encyclopedic Dictionary Granat, 7th ed.*; it is styled after the *Encyclopedia Britannica* and contains detailed articles and vast bibliographies.

The widely used *Large Soviet Encyclopedia* (*Bolshaya Sovetskaya Entsiklopedia*) first appeared in 1926 (N. Bukharin, editor); its 66 volumes including one devoted entirely to the USSR were completed in the 1940's. A second edition in 50 volumes with supplements came out in the 1950's (B. A. Vvedensky, editor). The concise *Encyclopedic Dictionary* in three volumes was published by the same editor (1953–55). The equally popular *Small Soviet Encyclopedia* (*Malaya Sovetskaya Entsiklopedia*) has come out in three editions, the first (10 volumes) in 1928–31, the second (11 volumes) in 1933–47, and the last (10 volumes) in 1957–60. Furthermore, a great many specialized encyclopedias are available, such as *Technical Encyclopedia, Agricultural Encyclopedia, Large Medical Encyclopedia, Dictionary of Physics.*　　　　T. D.

ENGELHÁRDT, Vladímir Aleksándrovich (1894–), biochemist. Fellow, Ac. of S. (1953) and Academy of Medical Sciences, USSR (1944). Graduate (1919) and professor (1936), Moscow University. Since 1933 associated with various institutes of the Ac. of S. Secretary of the Department of Biological Sciences, Ac. of S. (1955). Research concerns the transformation of organic phosphorous compounds in the process of cell metabolism and the biochemistry of vitamins. Substantiated the physiological aspects of the interaction between respiration and fermentation. Member of Soviet and foreign learned societies. Editor-in-chief (1944) of the publication *Biokhimia* (Biochemistry). Stalin prize (1943).

ÉNGELS (f. Pokrovsk), city in Saratov Obl., RSFSR; pop. 69,000 (1939), 90,000 (1959). Rail town and river port on the left bank of the Volga; railway cars, Diesel engines, textiles.

ENGINEERING: *see* TECHNICAL SCIENCES.

ENTENTE, THE. Involving Russia, Britain and France, the E came into existence gradually after the Franco-Russian Dual Alliance of 1894. The British emerged from their isolation in 1904 to conclude an "understanding" with France on problems which had divided the two countries for many years. With French encouragement, Russia (defeated by Japan and anxious for new allies) and Britain (alarmed by the growing strength of Germany) signed a "convention" in 1907 settling their differences, chiefly with regard to Persia. But this series of agreements did not become a formal military alliance until Sept. 5, 1914, when the three powers vowed not to make a separate peace and to refrain from offering peace terms without prior agreement.

ERDMAN, Nikoláy Robértovich (1902–), playwright and satirist, author of satirical verse and short stories. His comedy *The Mandate* (1925) was very successful, as were his other plays; his epigrams on Soviet leaders, including Stalin, were widely circulated. In 1937 E was arrested. After his release in 1954 he contributed a short story to *Ogonek.*

ERENBURG: *see* EHRENBURG.

ÉRISMAN, Fyódor Fyódorovich (1842–1915), hygienist. Born in Switzerland, studied ophthalmology in Zürich, Würzburg and Prague. Moved to Russia (1869) but returned to Germany to study hygiene (1872–77). Professor, Moscow University (1882–96). He introduced hygiene as a popular science in Russia. Research concerned sanitary conditions in slum areas and factories, and problems of canalization and irrigation in Moscow. Founder of the first Laboratory of Sanitation in Russia (1891) which was to become the F. F. Erisman Institute of Hygiene.

ERIVÁN: *see* YEREVAN.

ÉRTEL, Aleksándr Ivánovich (1855–1908), populist author. His novel *The Gardenins, Their Retainers, Their Adherents, and Their Foes* (1889) gives a broad description of peasantry, middle class, and gentry. Leo Tolstov praised E's language for its force and beauty.

ESENIN: *see* YESENIN.

ESPIONAGE: *see* INTELLIGENCE.

ESTONIAN SOVIET SOCIALIST REPUBLIC (ESTONIA) is in the western part of the European USSR and borders on RSFSR and Lake Peipus in the E., Latvia in the S., the Baltic Sea in the W., and the Gulf of Finland in the N. Area, 17,400 sq. mi. (after the cession of Pechory (Petseri) area to the RSFSR in 1945), includes the islands of Saarema (Oesel) and Hiiuma (Dagö). Capital: Tallin (Tallinn, Reval, or Revel). Lowlands occupy the major part of E, while the hills spread in the south and in the east. The climate is moderately continental.

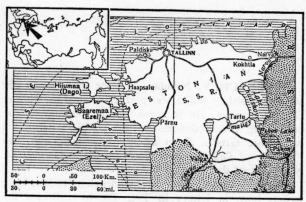

Estonian SSR

Population according to the 1959 census is 1,197,000 as against 1,126,000 in 1934. The national composition (1934 figures in parentheses) is as follows: Estonians 873,000 or 72.9% (88.25); Russians 260,000 or 21.7% (8.5%); Finns 17,000 or 1.4%; Ukrainians 16,000 or 1.3%; Byelorussians 11,000 or 0.9%; Jews 5,000 or 0.5%; others 15,000 or 1.3% (2.1%); Germans, 1.2% in 1934, left E in 1940. Main cities: Tallin (280,000), Tartu (74,000). Before World War II the population was four-fifths Lutheran and one-fifth Greek-Orthodox.

National Economy. The mainstay of E agriculture is dairy farming. Fishing, poultry and hog raising are next in importance. Textiles, shipping, paper-milling, and metalworking dominate in industry. Oil shale deposits found betwen Lake Peipus and the Gulf of Finland and hydroelectric stations along the Narva River constitute the fuel basis of E economy.

History. Early E tribes failed to create their own state units and were conquered by Danes (north) and Germans (south) in the first quarter of the 13th century. In 1346 Denmark sold her part of E to the German Livonian Knights. During the Livonian wars (1558–83), Polish and R. troops invaded E, but Sweden managed to keep her hold over E until the beginning of the 18th century. In 1710, R. armies of Peter the Great took Tallin and in 1721, by the Nystad treaty, Sweden ceded E to Russia. Throughout the Swedish and R. rule, German barons continued to keep a dominant position in the country and rule over their E serfs. The abolition of serfdom took place in 1817, but without land redistribution. From 1881 to 1905 a policy of Russification was followed by tsarist authorities.

During and after the February and October revolutions of 1917, the German nobility was inclined to unite with Prussia, while nationalist Estonians under the leadership of K. Päts and J. Poska leaned toward independence. Russia ceded E to Germany at Brest-Litovsk, but the collapse of the latter brought about the independence of E with Päts as prime minister. On Dec. 31, 1919 the independence of E was acknowledged by R. The long-overdue land reform distributed more than half of the arable land to farmers, cutting thus the economic power of the landowning classes.

A communist putsch led by J. Anvelt, on Dec. 1, 1924 was easily crushed. In 1934, in line with similar events in many other countries of east-central Europe (including Lithuania and Latvia), a "strong hand" regime replaced the original Scandinavian-style democracy. A partial democratization of the regime took place in 1937. The fate of E was decided by the Soviet-Nazi agreement of Aug. 1939. In September she was forced to accept Soviet bases and on July 16–17, 1940 Soviet troops ended her independence. Shortly thereafter E was incorporated into the USSR. During the 1941–44 German occupation thousands of Estonians perished at the hands of the Nazis; tens of thousands of others were deported to Siberia and N. Kazakhstan by the Soviets in 1940 and 1944–49. At least 60,000 E refugees remained in W. Europe after World War II. The annexation of E has not been recognized by the U.S.

Culture. The E language belongs to the West-Finnish group of the Finno-Ugrian family. The first book in the E language was printed at Lübeck (Germany) in 1553. The University of Tartu (Dorpat or Yuryev) was founded by the Swedes in 1632. Among early writers are the religious author H. Stahl and the educator B. Forselini (17th century). Secular literature appeared with Hans Käsu (end of 17th, beginning of 18th century). In the 19th century F. R. Kreutwald collected the E national epic poem *Kalevipoeg*, E. Ahrens reformed E orthography and Prof. Fählmann introduced the teaching of the E language at Tartu University. In the 19th century prominent are: the publicist J. Jannsen and his daughter, L. Koidula, and C. Jakobson, the editor of the E newspaper *Sakala*. Among modern E writers A. Jakobson, M. Under, A. Gailit, E. Vilde, A. Tammsaare, should be mentioned.   M. R.

EUPATORIA: *see* YEVPATORIA.

EVÉNKI NATIONAL OKRUG, part of Krasnoyarsk Kray, E. Siberia, RSFSR; area 287,500 sq. mi.; pop. 10,000 (1959), predominantly Evenki (Mongol tribe of the Tungus family). Principal settlements: Tura (adm. center), Noginsk, Baykit, Vanavara. The region, lying on the mid-Siberian plateau, in the tayga and forested tundra belts, is drained by the Nizhnyaya Tunguska and Podkamennaya Tunguska, of the Yenisey basin. Reindeer raising, fishing, and fur trapping are the basic occupations. Timbering is important, and truck farming is being developed for local markets. Coal and graphite are mined in the Noginsk area. Est. 1930.

EXCHANGE RATE: *see* FOREIGN TRADE AND AID.

F

FADEYECHEV, Nikolay, premier danseur of the Moscow Bolshoy Ballet and partner of prima ballerina Galina Ulanova. He is considered to be one of the oustanding classic dancers in the USSR. Among his ballets are *Giselle, Swan Lake, Chopiniana,* and *The Fountain of Bakhchisaray.* He is noted for his elegant, lyric style of dancing.

FADÉYEV, Aleksándr Aleksándrovich (1901–1956), writer, born in Kimry in Tver Province. Joined the CP in 1918. At the 18th and 19th party congresses was elected a member of the Central Committee. Was a deputy to the Supreme Soviet and a propagandist of the Communist-sponsored World Peace Council. F participated in the civil war against Kolchak. In 1923 he published his first novel *Overflow* and the story *Against the Current.* In 1927 his popular novel *The Rout* appeared. In these works as well as in the unfinished novel *The Last from the Udege* (1926–36 and 1941), F depicts the civil war and the Red partisan movement. During World War II he wrote the well-known *Young Guard* in which he portrayed the underground work of young Communists against the Nazis (Stalin prize, 1946). Under the pressure of the party, he was compelled to "correct" this novel several times. F was one of the leaders of the Soviet Writers' Union. Very close to the Communist rulers, he rarely defended his numerous colleagues who perished during the purges. F committed suicide in Peredelkino, residence of many writers, in 1956.

FAMILY ALLOWANCES. Financial help to large families was first introduced in 1936. Financial assistance was rendered only from the seventh child on and amounted to 2,000 rubles a year payable up to the fifth birthday. In 1944 more generous payments were introduced, but were cut in half by a decree in 1947, which is still in force. According to these rates a mother receives at the birth of her third child a premium of 200 rubles, at the birth of the fourth child a premium of 650 rubles and a monthly allowance of 40 rubles up to the fifth birthday of the child. These rates increase up to the birth of the tenth child when a mother may receive a premium of 2,500 rubles and a monthly allowance of 150 rubles.

FAMILY LAW is a separate branch of Soviet law (q.v.) regulating marriage and divorce, the rights and duties of parents and children, adoption, and guardianship. The Soviet regime annulled tsarist FL in Dec. 1917, as one of its first major social reforms. It aimed to combat "reactionary" influences over the family and children by breaking the legal religious controls, and loosening family ties. FL reforms were hailed by Bolsheviks who scorned the "bourgeois" family, or shared Mme. Kollontay's (q.v.) belief that the family was superfluous and would wither away under socialism. By late 1917, registration of births, marriages, and deaths was transferred from religious to state authorities, women gained legal equality with men, divorces were removed from religious courts and greatly simplified, and illegitimate children no longer suffered legal discrimination. Following further liberalizations in 1926, unregistered marriages—steady cohabitation—were equated by law with registered marriages, establishing full rights to alimony, inheritance (q.v.), and share of communal property upon separation. Divorces could be had by registration of one party, or by the simple fact of separation. Stalin's regime began a reversion to conservative FL in 1936 because it felt that juvenile delinquency was caused by loose and broken family ties. Moderate divorce fees and stricter alimony were introduced. Abortions were banned, but allowed again in 1955.

Present law on marriage and divorce dates back to 1944 when legal bonds of the family were radically tightened after war had aggravated problems of delinquency. Divorce is more difficult and costly than before, with three main stages: (a) publication (fee 400 rubles) after wait of several months from petition; (b) conciliation hearing in people's court; (c) hearing and decision in higher court (fee 500–2000 rubles if granted, which usually happens). Alimony is paid for a year after divorce to disabled husband or wife. Parent left with custody of children receive support payments from former spouse. There is no claim for paternity of illegitimate children, whose unwed mothers may accept a small state allowance or lodge their offspring free in state homes. Spouses may no longer inherit, claim alimony or a share of communal property on the basis of cohabitation alone; their marriage must be registered in order to have legal force. Many people have urged that the impending Fundamental Principles of FL simplify divorce and liberalize present rules on illegitimate children who cannot now take their fathers' names, even when the fathers acknowledge them. At present, family ties are backed also by official praise of the family, approval of romantic love, and firm material foundations based upon rules of responsibility for dependent children or parents, community property, inheritance, paid maternity leaves. (*See also* CIVIL LAW, AUTHORSHIP AND INVENTION, THE COURT SYSTEM) P. H. J.

FAR EAST. The Soviet Far East stretches along the entire Pacific coastline of the USSR and comprises the Maritime and Khabarovsk krays, and the Amur, Magadan, Kamchatka and Sakhalin oblasts. Its area is 1,250,000 sq. mi.; population (1959) 4,400,000: Russians, Ukrainians, remnants of the indigenous Evenki (Tungus) and other East Asiatic tribes (3% of the population). The area was gradually colonized by Russia from 1649. It has been a place of banishment and concentration camps. In the Soviet period the population more than doubled but the area is still very thinly populated: while it occupies one-seventh of the territory of the **USSR,** its population equals only 2% of the Soviet population. The large pre-war Japanese, Chinese and Korean population was driven out after 1945. The main natural resources consist of forests (valuable trees and fur-bearing animals: squirrel, sable, fox, ermine, polar fox), waters (abounding in fish and sea animals), hydroenergy of the swift mountain rivers, and rich mineral deposits: coal and lignite, oil, iron ore, gold, rare and nonferrous metals. The climate is severe and cold. The land is exposed to cold currents and winds, hampering agriculture. Fifty per cent of the population live in the cities and are employed in the ever-growing industry.

FAVÓRSKY, Vladímir Andréyevich (1886–), artist and critic. After study in Moscow and Munich, he produced both sculptures (*Chess,* 1910) and paintings (*Self-Portrait*). He gained considerable prominence after 1920 as artist and critic, but fell into disfavor during the 1930's for his alleged "formalism." His later work includes subway decorations in Moscow, book illustrations, stage settings. Has done wood cuts of Dostoyevsky, Lermontov, Kutuzov and illustrations for Russian classics.

FEBRUARY REVOLUTION—events culminating in the collapse of the tsarist regime in Feb. and early March 1917. Poverty and the injustices of tsarism had induced the desire for revolutionary changes in most social groups in the R. Empire. The military disasters of World War I and the widespread opinion that these were due to the incompetence, corruption, and perhaps treason of the imperial circle led even the bureaucratic and military pillars of the regime to think of replacing Nicholas II in order to save the war effort and the monarchy.

All seemed surprisingly quiet, both at the front and at home, at the beginning of 1917. The Fourth Duma (q.v.), conservative at its election in 1912 but now articulately restive in its concern about the mismanagement of the war, was in session from Feb. 14. On Feb. 22 Nicholas II left Petrograd for army headquarters at Mogilev. On Feb. 23 food riots of undetermined origin broke out in Petrograd. Very possibly a rude baker, by slamming the door of his empty shop in the faces of workers' wives who had waited on line for hours, touched off the R. Revolution. The riots spread throughout the workers' quarters and into the center of the city. Barricades went up. On Feb. 24–25 the police and troops seemed to be containing if not putting down the riots, but on Feb. 26 violence increased and some of the troops of the Petrograd garrison (no longer the pride of the R. army, but poorly trained reserves and ill-disciplined elements) defected to the rioters. Alarmed, the government prorogued the Duma, but on Feb. 27, the Duma decided to elect a Provisional Committee of its moderate, liberal, and radical leaders, which met in the Tauride Palace. That afternoon, in another wing of the Palace, revolutionaries and strikers organized, in the tradition of the revolution of 1905, the Petrograd Soviet (Council) of Workers' Deputies. The Menshevik N. S. Chkheidze was president and the Socialist Revolutionary A. Kerensky was one of the vice-presidents. Meanwhile (Feb. 27) the bulk of the Petrograd garrison went over to the insurgents' side. At the cost of about 1,500 lives, the capital was secured for the revolution.

On Feb. 28 the Soviet grew rapidly, especially by addition of soldiers from the garrison (chiefly peasants in origin, a link between the FR and the countryside). Its agents, by evening, had arrested most of the tsar's ministers and high bureaucrats, and interned them in the now overcrowded Tauride Palace. In view of these events, the president of the Duma, the conservative M. V. Rodzyanko, begged the tsar (by telegram) to grant representative government and abdicate. That night Nicholas entrained for Petrograd, but striking railway workers allowed his train to proceed no further than Pskov, a strong indication of the breakdown of authority. On March 1 Rodzyanko tried vainly to persuade the railway workers to let him go to the tsar. Meanwhile at Pskov Nicholas was urged by the Grand Duke Nicholas, Chief of Staff M. V. Alekseyev, and others to abdicate to save the monarchy.

March 2 proved to be the climax of the FR. The Petrograd Soviet (now of Workers' and Soldiers' Deputies) had grown to an unwieldy body of 1,300 delegates with immense but undefined authority. Its Executive Committee was negotiating with the Provisional Committee of the Duma for the establishment of a new government. This resulted in the promulgation of the Provisional Government (q.v.), for which the Soviet leaders, on socialist principle, declined to take any large degree of responsibility, because it was a largely bourgeois government. Prince G. Ye. Lvov, the liberal leader of the zemstvos, became prime minister; A. I. Guchkov, leader of the (moderate) Octobrist party, minister of war and navy; P. Milyukov, leader of the (liberal) Kadet party, foreign minister; M. I. Tereshchenko—finance; Chkheidze was minister of labor, but resigned that afternoon at the insistence of the Soviet. A. F. Kerensky, by now the oratorical hero of the FR, persuaded the Soviet to approve his participation as minister of justice. The Soviet concluded its day's work by reaffirming the aloofness of socialists from any bourgeois government (thereby confirming the "dual power" which so weakened both Provisional Government and Soviet), and by issuing its Army Order No. 1, which called for the establishment of soviets in army units to control the actions of officers in the interests of the R (a procedure that greatly hastened the disintegration of the army). Meanwhile, on March 2 (March 15 N.S.) in Pskov the tsar abdicated in favor of his son Alexis, and drew up documents to that effect. That evening Guchkov and V. V. Shulgin, a strongly nationalist conservative, were allowed by the railway workers to reach Pskov on a mission from the Provisional Government. They supported the tsar in his change of mind to abdicate in favor of his brother, the Grand Duke Michael. Nicholas abdicated without displaying undue emotion, and slept soundly that night in the train that carried him to Tsarskoye Selo.

Guchkov and Shulgin returned to Petrograd with the news and documents on the morning of March 3. The Provisional Government consulted Michael, who demanded personal protection if he were to accept the throne. Since protection could not be guaranteed, Michael declined. Thus the thousand-year-old R. monarchy ended, to the consternation of conservatives, and even of the moderates and some liberals in the Provisional Government, but to the great joy of most of the people. The Provisional Government, with the support of the Soviet, issued its program on March 6: civil liberties and full democracy, the convocation of a Constituent Assembly, but also the continuation of the war to victory (which boded ill for the future). The FR was successful, and Russia became, on paper, the freest country on earth. The astonishing ease with which a not very violent revolt in Petrograd alone brought down the tsarist regime suggests that by Feb. 1917 the regime had virtually lost its once formidable power.

BIBLIOGRAPHY: W. H. Chamberlin, *The Russian Revolution, 1917–1923*, Vol. I, New York and London, 1952; V. M. Chernov, *The Great Russian Revolution*, New Haven, 1936; L. Trotsky, *History of the Russian Revolution*, Vol. I, Ann Arbor, 1957.   F. B. R.

FÉDCHENKO GLACIER, in Pamir, Tadzhik SSR, one of the world's largest; 44 mi. long, 9 mi. wide. Discovered by A. P. Fedchenko in 1878.

FÉDIN, Konstantín Aleksándrovich (1892–), Soviet author. Graduated from a commercial trade school and from 1911 to 1914 attended courses at the Moscow Commercial Institute. His first journalistic efforts dating from 1913 were interrupted by his internment in Germany throughout World War I. He returned to Russia  in 1918 and worked as a journalist for various Red army papers. He tried at first to avoid involvement in politics but was profoundly disturbed by the apparent triumph of the forces of destruction after the revolution. This anxiety is clearly felt in the collection of short stories, *Voidness* (1923), and in the novel *Cities and Years* (1924). The latter work portrays the doubts and difficulties of R. intellectuals who were reluctant to accept the realities of life under communism. F was severely criticized but returned to the theme of the position of the intellectuals in postrevolutionary Russia; however, his novel *Brothers* (1928), dealt with a submissive intellectual who had no strength left to fight against the coming vulgarization and eventual doom of R. culture. In 1923–28 F wrote the short novels *Morning at Vyazhnoye, Peasants,* and *Transvaal* which depicted the coming struggle between the farmers and the party. He was again the target of Soviet critics who accused him of idealizing the "kulak" whom the government was bent on exterminating.

From the 1930's on F appears to have become reconciled to the inevitability of the new order. Some literary critics view his later writings as indicative of a compromise by which, willingly or unwillingly, F sacrificed his integrity on the altar of party politics. His earlier literary efforts during this period were undistinguished. His novel *The Rape of Europe* (1932–35), was an attempt to contrast the decadent West with the progressive land of the Soviets. The results were ideologically unconvincing and literarily weak. F's recent writings, which are his best, won him a place among the outstanding authors on the contemporary Soviet scene. His novels *First Joys* (1945–46), *An Unusual Summer* (1947–48), and *The Campfire* are the work of a master. (Only a few chapters of *The Campfire* have been published to date.) The three novels give evidence of the new F who, having conquered his detestation of the Soviet order, has adopted the safest road of peaceful compromise with communism. F's acceptance of the Soviet way of life has fully restored his position in Soviet political and literary circles as evidenced by the fact that he is now the head of the Writers' Union, and member of the Ac. of S.

FEDOR (Fyódor Ivánovich) (1557–1598), tsar, son of Ivan IV. Ascended the throne after the death of his brother Ivan (1584). Because of ill health and incapacity, F did not govern Russia which was actually ruled by his brother-in-law, Boris Godunov. Foreign policy was reasonably successful with Russia regaining the southern shores of the Gulf of Finland and concluding the allegedly "eternal" peace with Sweden (1595). A major factor in domestic policy was the establishment of patriarchate (1589). Tsar F died childless and was the last descendant of Ryurik to occupy the R. throne.

FÉDOROV, Sergéy Petróvich (1869–1936), surgeon. Graduated, Moscow University (1891); professor of surgery, Military Medical Academy in Leningrad (1903). Research concerned surgery of urinary and biliary tracts, and treatment of tumors. He was a pioneer in introducing aseptic methods of surgery, cystoscopy, and ureteral catheterization, thus laying the foundation of urology in Russia, and in resorting to blood transfusion.

FÉDOROV, Yevgény Konstantínovich (1910–), geophysicist. Fellow, Ac. of S., USSR (1960). Hero of the Soviet Union (1938). Graduated from Leningrad University (1932). Worked as magnetologist at the polar stations of Franz Josef Land (1934–35) and as geophysicist and astronomer at the first Soviet drifting station "North Pole" (1937–48). Associated with the Geophysical Institute, (1947–55) and director of the Institute of Applied Geophysics (1955). Research concerns magnetology, metereology and practical astronomy. Author of "Metereological Instruments and Observations," *Trudy dreyfuyushchey stantsii "Severny Polyus"* (Research of the Drifting Station "North Pole") Vol. 2, 1941–45; "The Effect of Atomic Explosions on Metereological Processes," *Atomnaya energia* (Atomic Energy, No. 5, 1956.

FÉDOROV, Yevgráf Stepánovich (1853–1919), crystallographer, mineralogist, and geologist. Fellow, Ac. of S. (1919). Graduate, Military School of Engineering (1872); professor, Moscow Agricultural Institute (1895–1905); first director of the Mining Institute in St. Petersburg (1905). Investigated the geology of the N. Urals (1885–90); research concerned the symmetry and structure of crystals. Author of about 500 papers on crystallography, geometry, petrography, mineralogy and geology, including the *Symmetry of Regular Systems of Figures* (1890) in which F describes three-dimensional groups of figures known as "Fedorov groups." An award of the Ac. of S. for the most outstanding work on crystallography has been named after F (1944).

FEDÓTOV, Geórgy Petróvich (1886–1951), writer and philosopher, born in Saratov. In 1905 he joined the Social Democratic party; was arrested and exiled. After the October revolution, he became a religious socialist. In 1925, F left Russia, contributed to *émigré* publications, and was professor at the Institute of Orthodox Theology in Paris. In 1940 F came to tne U.S. and was professor at the St. Vladimir Seminary in New York (1943); associated with Yale University (1941–43). He is author of *The Russian Church Since the Revolution* (1928), *The Russian Religious Mind* (1946), *A Treasury of Russian Spirituality* (1948).

FEDÓTOVA, Glikéria Nikoláyevna (1846–1925), actress, People's Artist, USSR, and a leading member of the company of the Moscow Maly Theater which she joined in 1862. She was greatly admired as Lady Macbeth; Cleopatra, in *Antony and Cleopatra;* Beatrice, in *Much Ado About Nothing*; and Elizabeth in Schiller's *Mary Stuart*. In 1905 F withdrew from the stage because of illness.

FÉFER, Itsik (Isaac) (1900–1952), Yiddish poet. A Bolshevik, he fought in the civil war of 1917–20. He held important offices in the government, but was arrested during the "purge" of Jewish writers in 1948 and was executed in Aug. 1952.

FELDSHER: *see* MEDICAL SYSTEM.

FEMALE LABOR. Contemporary Soviet Union is a country in which female labor outside the domestic household has become uniquely prevalent, more so than in any other country in the world. This is the result of 40 years of deliberate policy, but it is also a product of objective factors: the low general level of earnings, which do not assure a family's support if only the head of the family works for pay, and the unfavorable balance between the number of men and women, which became especially acute during World War II and in the postwar years.

For twenty years, the Soviet government pursued a policy of increasing the attraction of women to paid work for humanitarian and social reasons, in an endeavor to raise women's social position and secure their independence. With the inception of policies of vigorous industrialization in 1929, there was a rapid reduction of the available labor reserves, and extensive measures to draw women into paid work came to be—and are to this day—dictated by primarily economic motives, motives of labor market policy to secure the necessary working force for the national economy.

As early as World War I, women comprised almost 25% of the total number of factory workers. By 1929 the percentage employed in industry had risen to 28, in 1940 to 41, and in 1945 to 51, so that women accounted for a majority of the factory proletariat. After the war, this percentage began to fall. It reached 45 in 1950 and has held that level since. At the same time, there was an enormous influx of women into other branches of employment which was substantially more intensive than the flow of women into industry. Specifically, the percentage of women employed was:

	1929	1940	1945	1958
Construction	7	23	32	30
Transportation	9	21	40	27
Communications	28	48	70	63
Trade and Public Dining	19	44	69	67
Health and Medicine	65	76	85	85
Education	54	58	73	63
Government Administration	19	35	59	52

And women's share in the total number of workers and employees rose from 27% in 1929, to 38% in 1940, and 55% in 1945, then declined to 45% in 1954, held that level for three years, and rose again to 46% in 1957 and 47% in 1958. The total number of female workers and employees rose to 25.6 mill. in 1958 and they were distributed among the various branches of employment as follows:

PERCENTAGES OF TOTAL NUMBER OF FEMALE
WORKERS AND EMPLOYEES

Industry	40	Education	10
Agriculture	8	Health and Medicine	14
Transportation and		Government Administration	3
Communications	8	Other Branches	6
Trade and Public Dining	11		

The low figure for women working in agriculture shown in the above table by no means indicates that their participation in agriculture is insignificant. The vast majority of the agricultural working force (the collective farmers) are not included in the count of workers and employees and are not covered by the table. In agriculture too, especially during the war and in the postwar years, the role of women was quite considerably larger than in industry.

Another noteworthy feature of the development of female labor in the Soviet Union during the past 20 years is the advancement of women into types of work and positions to which until recently very few women had been attracted. It is no longer unusual to find female workers in the metallurgical, metalworking, machine building, mining, and construction industries, holding jobs which were considered traditionally men's work a quarter of a century ago. Many women occupy executive positions in industry and construction and there are even more in educational and health institutions where female labor had an established position earlier. Thus in industry, according to 1957 data, 13,100 women held positions as directors of enterprises, chief engineers, other chief specialists, or as their deputies. These were predominantly in branches of industry with a high percentage of female labor, and they comprised 10% of the group of employees at this level in industry as a whole. Among shop superintendents and their assistants, women accounted for 14%; of heads of departments and factory management offices and their assistants, 26%; of engineers, 38%; technicians, 59%; foremen, 21%; chief and senior accountants, 44%.

The extensive influx of women into paid employment has been accompanied by legislation protecting the interests of the working woman. In principle, women must receive pay equal to a man's; in practice, the average earnings for women in the overwhelming majority of enterprises and institutions are significantly lower than the average male earnings as a result of preferential hiring of men for the better paid jobs. Also there is frequently purely verbal observance of the group of directives on not allowing women to do exceptionally hard work, on maximum norms for loads and weights to be moved, on special adaptations to facilitate women's working, for example, as tractor drivers or chauffeurs, and so forth. Until 1940, there was a formal prohibition against employing women at underground work, but it was widely violated. In 1940, it was fully revoked and female labor underground became very widespread during the war years, especially in the coal industry. After the war, the use of women workers underground declined sharply, but the general prohibition has not been reestablished so far and has merely been mentioned, with reservations, in the projects for new legislation.

In contrast, there is reality as well as great practical meaning in the special regulations protecting pregnant women and nursing mothers and generally in the regulations protecting motherhood. Women workers and employees have leave from work for 8 weeks before and 8 weeks after giving birth and receive allowances of social insurance in amounts of $2/3$ or more of their full pay, depending on the length of time they have worked and of their membership in the trade union (the majority get full pay). In addition, there is a lump-sum grant when the mother plans to give up work to care for her child. These rules are firmly in force and play an important role in the lives of women workers and employees. Legislation also stipulates a series of other rules (not always observed) on guaranteeing pregnant and nursing mothers against dismissal, on lightening their work, and so forth.

Women's participation in paid employment is facilitated by the availability of child-care institutions, such as creches and kindergartens. These have been greatly expanded, but they are still far from covering the actual need. Thus, according to data for 1959, by an optimistic count, 4 mill. children were attending creches and kindergartens and about 3 mill., mostly in rural areas, were in seasonal creches and playgrounds, whereas the total number of children of preschool age (up to 6, inclusively) is above 31 mill. Women's participation in paid work ought also to be facilitated by the development of consumer services, such as public eating places, laundries, and repair shops, but the achievements in this field are modest and, to be precise, lag far behind the level of development of child-care institutions. The still acute inconvenience of material existence requires that women workers and employees do much supplementary work at home. As the chairman of the All-Union Central Council of Trade Unions, V. V. Grishin, observed on May 6, 1960 in the USSR Supreme Soviet, "the woman worker who has children spends, on the average, up to 4 hours on housework on workdays, and even more on her days off."

BIBLIOGRAPHY: Solomon M. Schwarz, *Labor in the Soviet Union*, New York, 1952. S. SCH.

FEODÓSIA, city in the Crimea; pop. 50,100 (1959). Ancient Greek colony founded on the S.E. shore of the Black Sea in the 6th century B.C.; thriving Genoese trading town during the Middle Ages (*Kaffa*); seized by the Turks in 1475; ceded to Russia in 1774. Is an important grain-shipping and fishing port; a center of tobacco and fruit-growing district, with flour mills, tobacco factories, wineries and food-processing ind. (including caviar-packing plants); a noted seaside and health resort.

FERGANÁ (f. Novy Margelan, later Skobelev), city, adm. center of Fergana Oblast, Uzbek SSR; pop. 80,000 (1959). Has large power and hydrolysis plants, cotton and silk mills, meat-packing and canning ind., cottonseed oil presses; important deposits of ferganite (a uranium mineral) are worked near the city.

FERGANÁ OBLAST, Uzbek SSR; area 4,600 sq. mi.; pop. 1,135,000 (1959). Principal cities: Fergana (adm. center), Margelan, Kokand, Kuvasay. Climate is characterized by hot, dry summers and mild winters. Extensive sericulture and cotton cultivation on well-irrigated gray soils; vineyards and orchards in the S.; cattle and fat-tail sheep are raised in the desert area near the Syr Darya. Large ind., recently developed, are based on local reserves of oil (near Chimion, with an oil-cracking plant at Kuvasay), sulfur and ozocerite (at Shor-Su), phosphates (Kokand); metallurgical and chemical plants, cotton and silk mills, food-processing plants centered in the larger cities. The Bolshoy Fergana Canal, built in 1939, has transformed the oblast into an important agr. region. Est. 1938.

FERGANÁ RANGE, portion of Tien Shan Range between Kara Darya and Naryn rivers. Altitude 15,000–16,500 ft.; length 235 mi.

FERGANÁ VALLEY, area W. of Tien Shan Mountains, mostly in Uzbek SSR. Many rivers and warm climate ensure fertile soil (cotton, grapes, and fruit are grown). Minerals include oil, coal, and rare metals; one of the major cotton-growing areas in the USSR.

FÉRSMAN, Aleksándr Yevgényevich (1883–1945), noted mineralogist and geochemist. Fellow, Ac. of S. (1919). Graduate of Moscow University (1909); studied in Paris and Heidelberg. Explored mineral deposits on the Kola Peninsula, in Fergana, Kara-Kum, Transbaykalia, and the Urals as well as in Scandinavia, Italy, Germany, Belgium, and Switzerland. Founder (with V. I. Vernadsky) of geochemistry in Russia. Suggested aerial photography for the study of natural resources. Author of *Pegmatites* (1931); *Geochemistry*, 4 vols. (1933–39); and the series *Mineralogy as a Hobby* and *Geochemistry as a Hobby* (1950). Lenin and Stalin prizes (1942); W. H. Wollaston Award of the Royal Geographic Society (1943).

FERTILIZERS. The use of commercial F was greatly expanded since collectivization of agriculture. Output (in thousand tons) rose from 89 in 1913, when main reliance was on imports and application of manure, to 135 in 1928, 3,238 in 1940, and 12,900 in 1959 (of which less than 20% was exported). Production of nitrogen and potassium F lags considerably behind that of phosphates. The expansion of commercial F was partly offset by the diminished amount of manure because of large-scale losses of livestock following collectivization.

Commercial F are allocated almost exclusively to high priority technical crops, such as cotton, sugar beet, and fiber crops. These preferential policies contribute indirectly to low grain and potato yields, especially in areas where the decline in the availability of manure was most pronounced. The use of peat for bedding is encouraged to supplement mineral F. Crop rotation serves similar purposes.

FESÉNKOV, Vasíly Grigóryevich (1889–), astrophysicist. Fellow, Ac. of S., USSR (1935), Ac. of S., Kazakh SSR (1946). Graduate, Kharkov University (1911). Pioneer in the field of photometric study of zodiacal light and originator of the dynamic theory of this phenomenon. Developed a criterion of the tidal stability of celestial bodies which explains characteristics of the structure of the solar system and the formation of galactic objects. Suggested hypothesis of star formation from gas-dust nebulae. Member, International Astronomical Union.

FET (Shénshin), **Afanásy Afanásyevich** (1820–1892), a leading poet of the 19th century. He studied at the University of Moscow and began to publish his poems in 1840. Two other volumes of verse appeared in 1850 and 1856. As he was a Parnassian poet of conservative political views, he was severely criticized and silenced by the left-wing critics of the sixties. His next volumes of poetry, *Evening of Lights,* did not appear until 1883. Fet had a platonic conception of unified reality, and identified his self with nature. His dreamy poetry was close to the symbolists.

FIBER CROPS. The main fiber crops in the USSR are cotton (q.v.), flax, and hemp fiber. In addition, some kenaph (about 90,000 acres) is grown mainly in Uzbekistan and about 8,000 acres are planted to jute.

Gross output of flax fiber, a traditional R. peasant crop, amounted, in thousand tons, to: 401 in 1913 (within present Soviet boundaries), 324 in 1928, 349 in 1940, 386 in 1959. Reliable information on gross output of hemp fiber is not available but marketings, which presumably reflected the trend in gross output, amounted to 66,000 tons in 1958 as against 95,000 in 1928.

Fiber flax is grown chiefly in central and N. Russia and in Byelorussia. The expansion in its production did not materialize in the desired proportions despite the great emphasis put upon it under Five Year Plans, preferential allocation of fertilizers, some mechanization of flax processing, and relatively profitable delivery terms. The highly labor-intensive crop did not fare well under the collective farm system and, although area planted rose by some 30% between 1913 and 1959, yields declined by one-fourth.

Hemp is grown chiefly in S. and central Russia. The area planted to it declined by about one-third since 1928.

FÍGNER, Véra Nikoláyevna (1852–1942), populist revolutionary. Studied medicine in Zurich, Switzerland (1872–77). She became a member of the Executive

Committee of "the People's Will" in 1879. She was condemned to death in 1884, but her sentence was commuted to penal servitude for life and she was incarcerated in the Schlüsselburg Fortress for 20 years. She was then a political exile for the decade 1906–15. After the Revolution she wrote her valuable memoirs, *Records of a Life's Work. Collected Works* in 7 vols. (1932).

FILARÉT, Patriarch (Fyódor Nikítich Románov, c. 1560–1633), father of Michael, first tsar of the Romanov dynasty. During Michael's reign F was made Patriarch and Great Lord Sovereign and was the actual power behind the throne.

FILÁTOV, Nil Fyódorovich (1847–1902), pediatrician. Graduate (1869), professor (1891–1902), Moscow University. Associated with the Pediatric Hospital in Moscow (1875–81) which has been named after him. A pioneer of pediatrics in Russia, F studied contagious diseases and their prevention by vaccination, diagnosed *rubeola scarlatinosa,* known as "Filatov Disease," and nervous afflictions in children. Founder and president of the Society of Pediatricians (1892–1902).

FILÁTOV, Vladímir Petróvich (1875–1956), ophthalmologist. Fellow, Ac. of S., USSR (1944); Ac. of Medical S. Graduate, Moscow University (1897); professor, Medical Institute in Odessa (1911). Director, V. P. Filatov Institute of Ophthalmology (1936). Developed a method of keratotomy (1924) and designed special instruments for that operation; suggested skin grafting methods. Author of *Tissue Therapy (Treatment by Means of Biogenic Stimuli)* (1945); *My Path in Science* (1955). Stalin prize (1941); Hero of Socialist Labor (1950); I. I. Mechnikov gold medal (1951).

FILÓNOV, Pável Nikoláyevich (1883–1941), painter, an outstanding modernist in R. postrevolutionary painting. From 1929 to 1935 he was a professor at the Leningrad Academy of Fine Arts. In 1935 as a result of attacks on modernism F was forced to resign. He died in 1941, during the blockade of Leningrad. In *Revolutionary Formula* and *Formula of the Leningrad Proletariat,* and also in his hitherto suppressed works, which were reproduced for the first time in the March 28, 1960 issue of *Life,* New York, F portrays postrevolutionary Russia as a land of apocalyptic visions, as a nightmare become reality, as a country in the grip of a destructive demon. Apart from private collections (the largest being in the possession of the painter's sister) F's pictures are to be found mainly in the Tretyakov Gallery in Moscow and the Russian Museum in Leningrad. Since 1935, however, they are not on public exhibit.

FINLAND, GULF OF, arm of Baltic Sea, extending from W. to E. for nearly 260 mi.; greatest width 75 mi.; S. of Finland and N. of Estonian SSR; at E. end narrows to Kronstadt Bay. Numerous small islands along N. shore. Freezes during 4 to 5 months. Receives many rivers (Neva, Narva, Luga, and others); consequently, the salt content is very low. Chief islands: Hogland, Lavansaari, and Kotlin (Kronstadt). Chief cities (in USSR): Leningrad, Tallin, Vyborg, Narva.

FISHERIES: *see* PISCICULTURE.

FLÉROV, Geórgy Nikoláyevich (1913–), physicist. Corresponding member, Ac. of S., USSR (1953). Graduate, Leningrad Industrial Institute (1938); associated with various institutes of the Ac. of S. Research concerns nuclear physics and cosmic rays. Proved the discharge of secondary neutrons during fission (1940) and discovered (jointly with K. A. Petrzhak) the spontaneous fission of heavy nuclei. Stalin prize (1946).

FLOR, Solomón Mikháylovich (1908–), Soviet chess player of Czech origin. Became Soviet citizen in 1942; Grand Master of chess. Tournament with M. M. Botvinnik ended 6 : 6 (1933). Shared first and second place with M. M. Botvinnik at International Chess Tournament in Moscow (1935).

FLORICULTURE was developed mainly in the relatively few areas where climate favored industrial flower-growing in the open air, such as Crimea, Caucasus, and Central Asia. Specialized enterprises maintain nurseries and hothouses in a number of cities such as Sochi and Batum where subtropical plants, palms, and bulb plants are grown on a large scale. Scattered efforts are made by state and collective farms as well as by pharmaceutical and soap enterprises which grow flowers for their own use. Associations of flower growers organize periodical flower shows, while educational and research work in F is done mainly in botanical gardens and research institutes.

FLÓRIN, Víktor Anatólyevich (1899–), power engineer. Corresponding member, Ac. of S., USSR (1953). Graduate, Petrograd Institute of Railway Engineering (1922); professor, Leningrad Polytechnic Institute (1943). Joined the All-Union Research Institute of Power Engineering (1942–48), Institute of Mechanics (1950). Developed design methods of constant and variable rigidity plates placed on linearly deformable foundation; suggested the theory of compacting water-saturated grounds, filtration in a medium of variable density, compressibility of water, stability of foundations.

FODDER CROPS. Despite considerable expansion of sown grass and silage crops during the last two or three decades, natural hay and pastures still account for 70% of all hay supply and 90% of green forage. The area under various FC, in mill. hectares, is shown below:

	1928	1940	1958
Grain crops: barley, oats and corn	28.9	35.1	32.6
Root crops and fodder melon crops	.3	1.0	1.4
Silage crops	—	.8	8.1
Sown grass (hay and green)	3.6	16.3	37.0
Natural hay	51.1	59.2	54.9

The area under rotation hay rose more than tenfold between 1928 and 1958, a deliberate policy motivated by shortages of natural hay and by the allegedly beneficial effects of rotation grass on soil fertility, especially in areas with little rainfall. The main emphasis in this policy was on perennial grasses, the area under which was increased from 2.5 mill. hectares in 1928, to 12.1 mill. in 1940 and 14.3 mill. in 1958. This process was accompanied by a decline in rotation hay yields which were (in tons per hectare) 2.9 in 1928, 1.9 in 1935, and presumably not appreciably higher at present. At the same time, emphasis on rotation hay led to neglect of natural hay, much of which is being wasted owing often to considerable delays in haying and to the low priority accorded natural meadows in work schedules of collective farms and MTSs. Yields of natural hay which had been low to start with declined from 1.3 tons per hectare in 1928 to 1.0 ton in 1932 and are estimated at some .8 ton in 1959.

Total FC production in collective farms was estimated, in mill. tons fodder conversion units, at 62.8 in 1940 and 107.3 in 1956, a highly inadequate base for the planned drastic expansion of livestock herds. As the main remedy to this situation, silage crops, especially corn, have been stressed in recent years. Corn silage stocks rose from almost none in 1950 to 52 mill. tons in 1957 and 114.0 mill. in 1959. Unsuitable climatic conditions and low yields of corn in most of the Soviet territory make the ultimate success of the current campaign questionable.

FÓFANOV, Konstantín Mikháylovich (1862–1911), lyric poet who wrote about nature, human emotions, and feelings in a manner unrelated to reality. Some of his poetry was put to music in songs which are still popular.

FOK, Vladímir Aleksándrovich (1898–), physicist. Fellow, Ac. of S., USSR (1939). Graduate (1922) and professor (1932), Petrograd University.  Associated with the Institute of Optics (1919–23, 1928–41), Leningrad Institute of Physics and Technology (1924–36), Institute of Physics, Ac. of S. (1934–41, 1944–53), Institute of Physical Problems (since 1954). Extensive research on quantum mechanics and electrodynamics, light diffraction, propagation of radio waves, the theory of relativity, mathematics, and mathematical physics. He is mentioned in the well-known relativistic scalar equation of Klein-Fok. Author of *The Theory of Space, Time, and Gravitation* (1955); *Research on the Quantum (Field) Theory* (1957). Lenin prize (1960).

FÓKINE, Michel Mikháylovich (1880–1942), the father of modern ballet, who began his career in the Mariinsky Theater as dancer and later became a teacher and choreographer. Among his ballets were *Acis and Galatea, Le Pavillon d'Armide, Chopiniana* (later called *Les Sylphides*), *Egyptian Nights* (later called *Cleopatra*), *Carnaval*, and others. His choreographic talent came to fruition in the Diaghilev company for which he restaged the above-mentioned works and also *Scheherazade, Prince Igor, The Firebird, Petrouchka, Le Spectre de la Rose, Daphnis and Chloe.* After  leaving Diaghilev he staged among other ballets, *Don Juan, Le Coq d'Or,* and *Paganini.* F saw the necessity of freeing the ballet from the arbitrary academic limitations which hampered its development. He coordinated the choreography of his ballets with the music to which they were planned and the period and locale in which they were laid. While the classical tradition was apparent in everything he created, he knew how to separate the true tradition from the barnacles of pseudo-tradition. The influence of F on ballet was tremendous, not only because he was a great reformer, but also because he was a choreographer of genius, active to the very last weeks of his life, brilliant in most of his creations. Ballets like *Les Sylphides, Firebird, Le Spectre de la Rose, Scheherazade* survive to this day.

FONDAMÍNSKY: *see* Bunakov.

FONVÍZIN, Denís Ivánovich (1745–1792), outstanding playwright of the 18th century. His comedy *The Minor*, first staged in 1783 and pub-lished the following year, is a classic. It portrays an ignorant teen-age lout whose adoring but bullying and brutish mother has her own ideas of what is good for her son's education. The boy's name—Mitrofan, or its diminutive, Mitrofanushka—has become in Russia the synonym of a dolt, an ignorant fool. F's second play, *The Brigadier*, written in the 1760's and first published in 1786, is a satire on the then current fascination in Russia with everything French, especially by those who knew no French and understood little about France.

FOOD AND DRINK. In medieval Russia most food was farinaceous. To this day many different types of pancakes (*bliny, oladii, blinchiki*, and others) are popular. French cuisine introduced to Russia in the 18th century has remained for the upper classes and gourmets; boeuf Stroganoff, for instance, was prepared by a French chef in Paris for Count Stroganoff who took the recipe to Russia.

Much of the food consumed by the rural and provincial population consists of salted and pickled vegetables, mushrooms, berries; garlic, onions, and saffron are used as spices. Cabbage is the ingredient of many dishes, including *golubtsy* (stuffed cabbage rolls). Soups are eaten regularly and some are known abroad, i.e. *borshch* (made of beets, cabbage, meat, vegetables), *shchi* (the classic soup of the army), and *rassolnik* (made of pickled cucumbers). Cooked buckwheat, millet, and barley as well as dark bread are the daily food of the Russian population much like the potato in W. Europe. Sunflower oil and sour cream are used in preference to butter. In the 16th century only cabbage-filled *kulebyaki* (pies) were known but over the centuries many other varieties have been added (meat, fish, carrot, mushroom, rice, chicken, and other fillings); patties with different fillings are called *pirozhki*. *Kotletki* is the R. counterpart of the United States hamburger. Fish is abundant and ranges from high-cost sturgeon to herring; pickled herring, as well as, economic circumstances allowing, caviar, is a popular companion of vodka. There is a great variety of regional dishes; among the best-known are Siberian *pelmeni* (meat dumplings) which are prepared to last throughout the winter and stored in the snow; Caucasian *shashlyk*, pieces of mutton roasted on a spit; Ukrainian *galushki*,

and their northern cousin *vareniki*, curd or fruit dumplings. It should be pointed out that "Russian dressing" is unknown in Russia and is in no way associated with the Russian cuisine.

Coffee is considered an outlandish drink and tea is generally preferred; it is usually taken in glasses with a silver or metal holder. *Kvas* is a summer drink made by pouring water on rye or barley and letting it ferment. In addition to common vodka (ethyl alcohol and water) there is *ryabinovka* (ashberry brandy), *zubrovka* (vodka with herbs) and many other kinds. *Nalivka* is a fragrant cherry liqueur. Soda, mineral, and fruit water also enjoy considerable popularity. Wines, cognac, and champagne are made in the Caucasus and the Crimea.

The Russian Easter feast merits special mention. Originally, the Easter midnight meal terminated a seven-week period of fasting. In accordance with the economic conditions and social standing of a family the Easter table traditionally abounds in food, including such old-time favorites as ham, Easter lambs, sucklingpigs, multicolored eggs, *zakuski* (hors d'œuvres), different varieties of smoked, jellied, and pickled fish, *kulichi* (Easter cakes), and *paskha*, a delicious concoction of cottage cheese, butter, cream, sugar, and eggs. Vodka, wines, and liqueurs are, of course, the traditional drinks.   T. D.

FORCED LABOR: *see* Concentration Camps.

FOREIGN AID: *see* Foreign Trade and Aid.

FOREIGN EXCHANGE RATE: *see* Monetary System, Traveling and Tourism, Foreign Trade and Aid.

FOREIGN POLICY SINCE 1945. The end of World War II found the Soviet Union, for all the destruction it had suffered, as the only major military power on the Eurasian continent, and second on the world stage only to the United States. Despite the recent alliance, Stalin continued to see relations with the noncommunist world as dominated by inevitable antagonism.

Immediate Postwar Policy. The *immediate postwar policy* of the Soviet Union strove to use its ready military strength both for extracting the maximum amount of "war booty" and reparations from the occupied territories, and for extending its permanent control by means of Communist governments. Meanwhile Soviet diplomacy and Communist propaganda aimed to prevent any concerted Western resistance to those moves. In *Eastern Europe,* by the end of the war, dictatorial Communist governments were in power in Yugoslavia, Poland, Rumania, and Bulgaria. A Soviet promise to "broaden" the last two with representatives of democratic parties, given in Dec. 1945 at the Moscow meeting of the Council of Foreign Ministers, was never carried out.

In Hungary and Czechoslovakia, the Soviets were at first content with coalition governments in which the Communists controlled the police, the army, and the propaganda machine. But when the Hungarian Communists gained only 17 per cent of the vote in Nov. 1945, the Soviet authorities joined almost at once with the police in "purging" government and majority par-

172

ties from independent leaders, and finally in arresting or deporting the opponents of sole Communist control. Only in Czechoslovakia, where the Communists emerged as the strongest party from elections held in spring 1946, did a true multiparty system last several years; elsewhere in E. Europe, all independent democratic leaders who had not escaped abroad were under arrest by the summer of 1947. In zonally divided *Austria*, the elections of Nov. 1945 showed the Communists as an insignificant minority, and led to a clearly noncommunist government. Immediately afterwards, the policy of enforcing Sovietization of their own zones was adopted by the Russians in both *Germany* and *Korea*.

More tentative were Soviet attempts at postwar expansion in the *Mediterranean and Middle East*. The Soviets asked for a trusteeship over the former Italian colony of Tripolitania. They urged that the Montreux convention on the Turkish straits should be revised to put them under the sole control of the Black Sea powers, to be enforced by a Soviet base in the Dardanelles. Soviet wartime occupation of parts of N. Iran was prolonged beyond the agreed data, and used to proclaim and protect a pro-Soviet "autonomous government" of Persian Azerbaijan in Dec. 1945. Soviet armies in *Manchuria* also stayed beyond the agreed time and tended to favor the Chinese Communists; but here, the Soviets officially recognized only Chiang Kai-shek's government, from which they were seeking to obtain a permanent share in the control of those Manchurian industries they had not dismantled as war booty.

From the spring of 1946, however, awareness that this all-round expansion was causing growing opposition of the United States led the Soviet government gradually to drop some of their claims and to open a propaganda campaign against the alleged Anglo-American striving for "world domination." In March the Soviets announced their readiness to leave Iran. Early in April, they agreed to leave Manchuria and were actually out by May 23. In June-July, they dropped their claim to Tripolitania and offered a compromise on Trieste which fell short of the Yugoslav demands. Their attitude on the *Axis Peace Treaties* changed from obstructive refusal to hard bargaining, by which they obtained Western recognition of the Communist Bulgarian government as well as some Italian reparations. On February 10, 1947 peace treaties were signed in Paris with Italy, Rumania, Hungary, Bulgaria and Finland.

Conflict with the West: Europe. Yet during the same period, there began the internal discussions between Soviet and Balkan Communist leaders which later led to the founding of the "Communist Information Bureau" (Cominform). The strain caused by Soviet and Soviet-bloc pressures on Greece and Turkey led to the proclamation of the "Truman doctrine" of support for both by the President of the United States on March 12, 1947. Also since the spring of 1946, Soviet comments on the *Chinese* civil war changed from earlier approval of General Marshall's mission of mediation to denunciation of it and to demands for the withdrawal of the United States marines from China.

The situation in *Germany* led to inevitable conflict, because of the crucial importance of Ruhr for W. European recovery. As late as March 1946, the Soviets and the West had agreed to a low limit for the level of German industry which would leave much of the remaining capacity to be dismantled for reparations, but as the Soviets broke the agreement which excluded reparations from current production, deliveries of reparations to the Soviet Union from the United States zone were stopped on May 3. By July, Molotov began to combine insistence on Russia's demand for $10 bill. worth of German reparations with pressure for four-power control of the Ruhr, and with a bid for German support on the issue of political unity. Before the year was out, the Western powers created the Anglo-American Bizone, and the U.S. secretary of state made his counterbid for German support in Stuttgart in September. The first full-scale discussion of a German settlement by the Council of Foreign Ministers—in Moscow, March-April 1947—failed to make progress on the restoration of German unity. The United States offer to aid a joint European recovery program, which developed into the *Marshall Plan,* was the direct outcome of this failure; and the Soviet government's decision to refuse cooperation in this effort (announced by Molotov at the Paris preliminary conference on July 2, 1947) proved a turning point in Soviet foreign policy. The *Cominform,* founded in Sept. 1947 as an association of ruling E. European CP's with the French and Italian Communists under Soviet leadership, started from the fact of the existence of "two camps" in world affairs, and designated as its principal task the foiling of the Marshall Plan by every means. The Greek Communist guerrillas proclaimed in December a counter-government in the mountains. Within the bloc, Stalin had forced the Czechoslovak government to reverse its initial willingness to join the Marshall Plan, the breach thus opened in the Czech government coalition ending in the imposition of full Communist control by the *Prague coup* of Feb. 1948.

But the fate of the Marshall Plan depended on *Germany,* and here the Soviets had to act directly. They appointed a German Economic Commission for their own zone and eliminated the last independent party leaders there, and at the London meeting of the Council of Foreign Ministers in Dec. 1947 charged the Western powers with planning to "split Germany." After Secretary of State Marshall adjourned the Council, the Soviets withdrew from the Allied Control Council (March 20, 1948) and began to interfere with allied military traffic to Berlin. Following the publication of the London recommendations and the introduction of the Western Deutsche Mark in June, the Soviets first tried to make the E. German currency compulsory for the whole of Berlin; and when the Deutsche Mark was nevertheless introduced into the western sectors of the four-power city, the Soviets declared that the Western powers had forfeited their rights there by "breaking the Potsdam agreement," and began the *Berlin Blockade* on June 24, 1948.

In subsequent negotiations with the Western ambassadors in Moscow, Stalin and Molotov insisted on terms which would have made the position of the West in Berlin untenable. But when the West preferred to defy the blockade by the airlift, the Soviets were not prepared to stop it by force at the risk of war, and when it was kept going successfully through the winter, they accepted defeat. It was agreed in New York in April 1949 that the blockade and the allied countermeasures should stop simultaneously on May 12 and that a conference of foreign ministers should meet afterwards. When it convened in Paris on May 23, the W. German constitution had already been promulgated. The chief aim now pursued by Vyshinsky (who had taken over as Soviet foreign foreign minister from Molotov in March) was to subject the new state to a restored allied four-power control and to prepare an early peace treaty which was to lead to a withdrawal of all occupation forces within a year. For, in the meantime, the North Atlantic Treaty Organization had been formed and Stalin was now more concerned to deprive it of its German glacis than to fight the Marshall Plan. The conference merely achieved a modus vivendi between the powers now occupying the separated eastern and western parts of Germany.

Meanwhile Stalin had taken action to crush the germ of a rival center for Communist E. Europe. Early in 1948 he had forced the Yugoslav and Bulgarian leaders to disavow plans for a federation of all the "People's Democracies." Feeling that the root of the trouble was the independence and unity of the *Yugoslav* party leadership, he then pressed for an immediate Yugoslav-Bulgarian federation. When the Yugoslav leaders stalled, the CPSU circulated a general indictment of the CP of Yugoslavia among all Cominform parties. The Yugoslav CP was expelled from the Cominform on June 28—a few days after its representatives had still taken part in a Warsaw conference of Soviet-bloc governments. The failure of this expulsion to shake the Tito regime led during 1948–49 to a breach of diplomatic and economic relations with Yugoslavia by the entire bloc, and to the winding up of the insurrection by the Greek CP before the end of the year. The Soviet postwar offensive in Europe was at an end.

Conflict with the West: Asia. In *Asia*, however, it was only beginning. At first the Communists in Vietnam and Indonesia had been advised by Moscow to aim at a national emancipation by agreement with France and Holland rather than by violent struggle. But by the end of 1947 the Cominform effort at weakening the "imperialist camp" coincided with the power vacuum created by the British withdrawal from India and with the growing successes achieved by the Chinese Communists in their civil war. Though Soviet diplomacy continued to recognize the Kuomintang government, Soviet representatives at Asian Communist conferences began to endorse, from early 1948, the "Chinese model" for the conquest of power. Within the next two years, Communist guerrilla warfare, directed not only against the retreating "imperialists" but also against the new governments of the "national bourgeoisie," started in Burma, Malaya, S. India, and S. Korea, and revived in the Philippines, in addition to an abortive coup in Indonesia and to Cominform pressure for similar action in Japan. But in contrast to

Vietnam, none of these movements scored major successes.

In *China* the Soviets seem to have advised against an all-out offensive as late as July 1948. Only in the beginning of 1949, when the Communists were about to take Peking, did the Soviet press begin to give them full support, and only in May was the Soviet ambassador to Chiang "recalled for consultation." By then the Chinese Communists had announced their intention to side with Russia in any future war. When on Oct. 1 Mao Tse-tung proclaimed his "Chinese People's Government" as the only legal government of China, the Soviets accorded recognition on the following day. In December a Chinese delegation headed by Mao arrived in Moscow; after two months of negotiation it returned with a treaty of friendship, alliance, and mutual assistance, modeled on Russia's 1945 treaty with Chiang. The new treaty included a clause about mutual consultation on major foreign policy questions affecting both countries. Under another agreement, the Soviets promised to renounce their rights in Port Arthur and over the Manchurian railway not later than the end of 1952, while under a third they pledged substantial economic aid.

The first test of the new alliance came in *Korea*. There, opposite regimes had developed in North and South ever since the attempt to unify the country under a four-power trusteeship had broken down in the spring of 1946. After a second attempt at unification failed in Aug. 1947, the Soviets refused to admit UN supervision over separate zonal elections and proposed the early withdrawal of all foreign troops. In May 1948 they announced their decision to withdraw unilaterally, and in September recognized a new Northern government as representative of the whole of Korea; the last Soviet troops left by the end of the year, and in March 1949 an agreement on economic and cultural cooperation with N. Korea was signed in Moscow.

After the American withdrawal from the South had also been completed by mid-1949, Northern-directed guerrilla activity soon started in the South. On June 7, 1950, the N. Korean "United Patriotic Front" issued an appeal calling for nation-wide elections in August; when this was ignored by the South, the North issued on June 19 a demand for an immediate merger of N. Korea and S. Korea. Six days later N. Korean forces attacked across the 38th parallel. The attack was carried out with the help of Soviet military equipment and backed by Soviet propaganda and diplomacy. The first decisions by the UN Security Council, condemning the aggression and recommending assistance to S. Korea, were taken in the absence of the Soviets, who were boycotting the Council on account of China; the Soviets then claimed that the decisions were "illegal" and constitued intervention in a "civil war." While the Northern offensive was successful, the Soviets rejected all proposals for negotiations unless Communist China was first admitted to the Security Council; when the counterattacking UN forces under United States command crossed the 38th parallel in October, the Soviets left it to the Chinese to stop them. From Nov. 1950 to Jan. 1951, while the Chinese "volunteers" were advancing, the Soviets backed Peking's refusal of any cease-fire without simultaneous agreement on the withdrawal of "all foreign troops" from Korea and Formosa, and the exclusive recognition of the Peking regime. Only after the second Chinese offensive, launched in April, had failed to yield decisive results, did the Soviets propose that the military commands should start cease-fire talks without political conditions. This led to the Panmunjon meetings beginning in July 1951.

The war had thus failed to change Korea's frontiers. It had established Communist China as a major military power. It also led to the decision of the United States to go ahead with the *Japanese* peace treaty. The Soviets, unable to influence the occupation regime in Japan, had urged since mid-1947 that this treaty should be worked out speedily by the Council of Foreign Ministers and not by the Far Eastern Commission. They had even tried to enlist Chiang's support by proposing a Council meeting on his territory in Jan. 1948. Since the formation of NATO, they were increasingly concerned with the danger of a United States-Japanese alliance. The Soviet-Chinese alliance of 1950 proclaimed an early peace treaty between Japan and all the victors as one of its objectives. But when the United States circulated its outline proposals for a peace with Japan, the Soviets replied, in November, objecting to the provisions that left for future decision the sovereignty over Formosa and the Pescadores, and over S. Sakhalin and the Kuriles; and they demanded clauses to ensure the disarmament of Japan, the end of the occupation, and a ban on her joining any alliance directed against any of the signatories. In July 1951, after further exchanges, the Soviets found themselves confronted with an invitation to sign the final Anglo-American draft at San Francisco in September. They decided to attend in order to submit their counterproposals for the record, but not to sign the treaty. A year later, a Soviet-Chinese agreement restored to China control of the Manchurian railways, but extended the use of Port Arthur as a joint base of the Communist powers.

In *Europe*, the Soviets tried to consolidate their own sphere. In Jan. 1949, the Council for Mutual Economic Aid was created to coordinate the economic policies of the satellites. In September, the campaign of the "World Peace Movement" for a five-power peace pact and a ban of nuclear weapons was launched just after the first successful atomic explosions in Russia. In October 1949, the German Soviet zone was proclaimed as the "German Democratic Republic."

Anti-NATO Policies. Yet the effect of the Korean war, and of E. German threats that *Germany* might become "another Korea," was to put the rearmament of W. Germany within NATO on the agenda of Western policy. From the fall of 1950, Stalin's European policy strove vainly to reverse this trend and to stop the growth of a ring of NATO bases around Soviet E. Europe. In the spring of 1951, deputy foreign ministers of the four occupying powers met in Paris to prepare another meeting of the Council of Foreign Ministers, but failed to agree on its agenda. In the autumn, following the Western foreign ministers' decision to negotiate with the German Federal Republic the res-

toration of its sovereignty and its integration in a European Defense Community, a Soviet-backed E. German note offered to discuss unification by all-German elections, but a W. German proposal to have these elections supervised by the UN was rejected. Finally, Stalin proposed on March 10, 1952 that a peace treaty should give an all-German government a limited national army but bind it to neutrality. The offer, which did not specify how the all-German government was to be formed, failed to prevent the signature of the Bonn and Paris treaties in May.

Relaxation of Tension and the New Offensive. After *Stalin's death* in March 1953, his heirs embarked on a seemingly more conciliatory policy—reduction of military pressure and the creation of more tolerable conditions in E. Europe. This "relaxation of tension" was attributable in part to a thermonuclear explosion in Russia later that year which freed the Soviets from the fear of a deliberate attack by the West. The Chinese premier Chou En-lai, after a visit to Moscow, modified the Chinese stand on the exchange of prisoners in *Korea,* and an armistice was agreed in July. Following some major Communist successes in *Vietnam,* the Western powers met in 1954 at Geneva with both R. and Chinese Communist delegates and negotiated an armistice which, while ending French rule throughout Indochina, gave to the Communists N. Vietnam, leaving S. Vietnam under an anti-Communist government and Laos and Cambodia under neutral governments. A Korean peace treaty, however, proved impossible, while the terms agreed on for the future of Vietnam and Laos have never been carried out.

In Europe, the relaxation of military pressure culminated in 1955 in the signing of the *Austrian* peace treaty, guaranteeing the neutrality of the country and ending the Soviet occupation; in the evacuation of the Soviet base of Porkkala in *Finland;* and in the Geneva conference of the United States, Soviet, British, and French heads of government. This *first summit conference,* while achieving no concrete agreement, established an understanding of the existence of a "balance of terror." From that time onward, the Soviet contribution to the UN debates on *disarmament* became more concrete.

Also in 1955, Soviet support for the *Afro-Asian* conference at Bandung, the travels of the Soviet leaders to India and other uncommitted countries, and the granting of substantial *development credits* to neutrals showed a novel approach designed to prevent the newly formed SEATO alliance from creating a NATO-like ring around the Communist powers in Asia. At the *20th Congress of the CPSU* in Feb. 1956, the Soviets declared that world war was no longer inevitable, while the new importance of the uncommitted Asian nations was acknowledged in the slogan of a "zone of peace" that was to comprise them as well as the "Socialist camp."

The congress also proclaimed the concept of the Soviet bloc itself as a "socialist world system," founded on a partnership of equals. In fact, the forms of Soviet control had been modified in *Eastern Europe* since Stalin's death. The "new course" had begun with economic concessions to the peoples of E. Germany and Hungary, and a slowing down of forced industrialization and collectivization continued for some years throughout the region. The "mixed companies" were wound up; Soviet control of the satellite administrations and economies was reduced; police terror was relaxed, and some of the surviving victims of Stalin's purges rehabilitated. With this went a normalization of Soviet-Yugoslav relations which culminated in Tito's triumphant tour of the Soviet Union in 1956. The aim of these reforms was not, however, to abandon Soviet control of the area, but to consolidate it on a more rational basis. The Council for Economic Mutual Assistance began serious work on a bloc-wide division of labor. The *Warsaw Pact,* setting up a joint military command under a Soviet marshal, was signed in May 1955.

The inclusion of E. Germany in this policy of consolidation proved an obstacle to the parallel efforts to prevent W. German rearmament within NATO. Soviet proposals for *Germany* at the Berlin four-power conference of 1954 asked that an all-German government with peace-signing powers should be formed *before* all-German elections, which the Soviets knew to be unacceptable to the West. The real Soviet objective then was a "European security pact" which would have barred the "two German states" from joining any military alliance. Only after the agreements for W. German entry into NATO had been signed in Oct. 1954 did the Soviets offer to "reexamine" the Eden plan for free all-German elections under international supervision; the Soviets insisted that German unity could only come about by a *rapprochement* between the "two German states." On this basis, no progress on Germany proved possible at Geneva. In Sept. 1955, the Soviets established diplomatic relations with the Federal Republic, but concluded a formal treaty with the E. German state and made it a full member of the Warsaw Pact.

Soviet cooperation with Communist *China* was put on a more equal basis by revision of the alliance treaty, negotiated in Oct. 1954. The Soviets agreed to withdraw from Port Arthur and to resell their share in the mixed companies, and the alliance ceased to be directed primarily against Japan. Despite the beginning of Japanese rearmament, Soviet negotiations with *Japan* led in fact to the resumption of diplomatic relations in 1956, and to Japan's entry into the UN with Soviet consent. In *South Asia,* the coexistence policy succeeded in keeping most of the new nations out of SEATO. In the *Middle East,* Soviet diplomacy had shown a noncommittal sympathy for Arab nationalism. Early hopes for a pro-Soviet orientation of Israel had been disappointed in 1948–49, leading to a wave of "anti-Zionist" trials throughout the Soviet bloc. The Baghdad Pact of 1954, linking Iraq with Turkey and Britain, became the starting point for a more definite Soviet attempt to support the Egyptian nationalist regime. The 1955 arms deal with Nasser, by encouraging him to nationalize the Suez Canal, became the prelude to the *Suez crisis* of the following year. The Soviets backed Egypt diplomatically both before and after the Anglo-French-Israeli attack.

The Hungarian Uprising and After. Those events coincided with the "October crisis" of 1956 in *Eastern Europe,* where the new Soviet policy had combined with Khrushchev's attack on the Stalin myth to produce a dramatic loss of Soviet authority. In *Poland,* an inner-party upheaval restored Gomulka to the leadership; the Soviet leaders reluctantly accepted his claim for increased autonomy in domestic affairs in return for assurances that he would preserve the party dictatorship and continue unconditional support for Soviet foreign policy. In *Hungary,* where the Stalinists had retained control of the party in the face of rising criticism, a popular revolution backed by most of the armed forces swept them away and forced Imre Nagy to proclaim a democratic multiparty regime and military neutrality. The Soviet government, after announcing on Oct. 30 its readiness to negotiate a withdrawal of its troops from any country that asked for it, moved in on Nov. 4 to crush the revolution with armed force.

During the following year, the Soviets succeeded in restoring disciplined unity in the bloc. They were greatly helped by the Chinese Communist leaders, who joined with them in a declaration of common principles for maintaining unity in the "Socialist camp with the Soviet Union at the head," which was adopted by twelve ruling CP's at the *Moscow conference* of Nov. 1957. One price they had to pay was a renewed conflict with Tito's Yugoslavia. When in the following spring the Yugoslavs adopted a new party program justifying their "nonaligned" position, fraternal relations were definitely broken; but there were no serious repercussions. The E. European "reorganization crisis" thus ended at the same time as the post-Stalin succession struggles inside Russia reached their conclusion with the achievement of undisputed one-man rule by Khrushchev; and this was also the moment when the success of the first Sputniks greatly increased the self-confidence of the Soviet Union. Now the Soviets could afford to use the threat of force far more boldly to exploit or even produce crisis situations in parts of the globe which up to then had been "safe" spheres of Western influence. Yet they still wished to limit the risks and retained a defensive interest in ending the political vulnerability of their own E. European sphere by getting it recognized. This delicate balance of risks and opportunities came to be reflected diplomatically in the alternation of bids for new summit negotiations with the creation of crises and with threats of rocket intervention, and ideologically in the alternation of emphasis on "peaceful coexistence" with that on the prospects of revolutionary advance.

Thus Russia stopped cooperation in the UN *disarmament* subcommittee in July 1957 and after her Sputnik successes walked out of the committee. But during the following months she sought to prevent the introduction of nuclear arms into Germany by endorsing the Polish *"Rapacki Plan"* for keeping them out of a Central European zone including Poland and Czechoslovakia as well as the two German states. From 1958, the Soviets sought to prevent the establishment of American medium-range missile bases in Europe by threatening notes to the countries concerned. But they also took the initiative in suspending *nuclear tests* in March of that year, and later agreed both to technical talks on test control and to a moratorium during political negotiations on a permanent ban. They repeatedly announced substantial reductions in their conventional forces, and submitted to the 1959 UN Assembly a plan for "general and complete disarmament," but they again walked out of the committee dealing with it in June 1960, on the eve of the submission of the counterproposals of the West for which they had asked. The test-ban negotiations, however, were kept in being all the time.

In the *Middle East,* the Soviets used the coup of 1957 in Syria which preceded that country's union with Egypt to accuse *Turkey* of plans for military intervention. But when after the *Iraqi* revolution of 1958 United States and British forces landed in Lebanon and Jordan respectively, the Soviets did not commit themselves to aid the new Iraqi regime but called for a special summit meeting and only drew back when Western recognition of the regime showed that the danger was past.

In the *Far East,* a Chinese Communist bombardment of *Quemoy and Matsu* was launched with R. diplomatic support within a few weeks of Khrushchev's 1958 visit to Peking. But when Chiang's forces resisted with modern United States weapons, the attack petered out. When in 1959 the chronic trouble between the *Laos* government and the still "unintegrated" Communist guerrillas there flared up in armed clashes, the Soviets backed their partisans only by diplomatic notes. A year later, however, when a "neutralist" group had first formed a government after a military coup, and had then been ousted by an anti-Communist counter-coup and linked up with the Communists, the Soviets decided to treat the joint Communist and neutralist units as the "legitimate government" and to supply them with arms and ammunition.

In Europe, Khrushchev launched, in Nov. 1958, demands for a withdrawal of Western garrisons from W. *Berlin,* for its neutralization as a "free city," and for the conclusion of peace treaties with the "two German states," threatening to annul the rights of the West in Berlin by concluding his own treaty with E. Germany if no agreement was reached within six months. But he extended the time limit when a conference of foreign ministers met in Geneva in spring 1959; and he dropped it altogether, after he had been invited to the United States by President Eisenhower and been promised a *summit meeting* in the spring of 1960. When, despite the "coexistence atmosphere" created by this American visit, the summit conference seemed unlikely to grant his demands, Khrushchev called it off at the last moment on the ground of the President's refusal to apologize for the *U2 flights* over Soviet territory; yet he still attempted no unilateral change in Berlin but announced his intention to reach a settlement with Eisenhower's successor. During the same period, Soviet development aid and political intervention extended to Africa and Latin America. Having long given the *Al-*

gerian nationalist rebels purely propagandist support, the Soviets in the fall of 1959, during the period of summit preparations, welcomed President de Gaulle's offer of self-determination following a cease-fire; but during the 1960 session of the UN Assembly Khrushchev took up *de facto* relations with the Algerian "Provisional Government" and began to speak of its "just war." In black Africa, where the Soviets gained an early foothold in Guinea, they exploited the *Congo* crisis by charging in July 1960 that Belgian intervention there was part of a general "Western plot" to restore colonial rule throughout the continent. Their own insistence on giving direct support to one Congolese faction led first to conflicts with the UN machinery there and then to expulsion of the Soviet mission by another faction; the Soviets reacted with an attack, conducted by Khrushchev in person, on the secretary general of the UN as a "servant of colonialism" and with proposals for replacing him by a tripartite secretariat acting under the unanimity rule, which they did not, however, press to a vote. Altogether, the Soviets used the *1960 UN session* more to try to rally the ex-colonial nations for a joint struggle against Western "colonialism" than to submit any proposals for negotiation with the West.

The *Cuban* revolution of 1959 had been supported by the Communists only in its final phase; but as Castro became involved in economic and political conflict with the United States, the Soviets supported him by economic agreements, by mutual high-level visits, and by generally proclaiming Cuba as the model for anti-United States "national revolutions" throughout Latin America. In July 1960 Khrushchev even threatened rocket retaliation against any United States attack on Cuba, but by the turn of 1960–61 Castro was apparently advised by the Soviets not to rely on those "symbolic" threats.

The inherent difficulty of maintaining the right balance between the exploitation of revolutionary chances and the diplomatic limitation of risks was aggravated for the Soviets by the growing opposition of their *Chinese* allies to the latter. Chinese anxiety about the dangers of a Soviet-American understanding and Chinese discontent with the extent of Soviet economic and military aid had been noted since 1958; they led to Chinese criticism of "illusions about United States imperialism" after Khrushchev's 1959 visit to the United States. Yet Khrushchev maintained his attitude throughout the winter of 1959–60, and used a new journey in *neutral Asia* in Feb. 1960 to assure his hosts not only of his backing in their conflicts with Western or Western-allied countries (as with Indonesia against Holland and Afghanistan against Pakistan), but also of his neutrality in India's and Indonesia's disputes with China. Chinese pressure then took the more serious form of accusing the Soviets before the world communist movement of an "opportunist" tendency to sacrifice revolutionary struggles to their desire for peace with the "imperialists" and their excessive fear of nuclear war. Though rebutting the attack with countercharges of "dogmatism" and "sectarianism," the Soviets now found themselves forced to compete with the Chinese for authority over revolutionary movements in critical areas. The militancy of Soviet foreign policy in the second half of 1960 was probably influenced by that situation; it certainly contributed to the relative Soviet victory embodied in the new *Moscow declaration* adopted by 81 Communist parties in Dec. 1960.

But while that declaration endorses the Soviet formulations on peaceful coexistence, the possibility of eliminating world war, the primacy of the peace campaign, and the seriousness of the effort for disarmament, it also establishes the obligation for all Communist states to give support to revolutionary movements and "just wars of liberation" everywhere. Moreover, while the Soviet Communists are recognized as the "vanguard" of the world movement, they have not recovered their former monopoly of ideological authority. The 1957 formula of the Soviets' role "at the head of the Socialist camp" has been dropped at their own request, and there is growing emphasis on the need to preserve unity between the two great Communist powers despite inevitable differences of opinion. The Chinese impact on the delicate balance of Soviet foreign policy is thus unlikely to disappear.

BIBLIOGRAPHY: Hugh Seton-Watson, *The East European Revolution*, London, 1952; Boris Meissner, *Russland, die Westmaechte und Deutschland*, Hamburg 1953; Hamilton Fish Armstrong, *Tito and Goliath*, New York, 1951; Max Beloff, *Soviet Policy in the Far East 1944–51*, London, 1959; David J. Dallin, *Soviet Foreign Policy After Stalin*, Philadelphia, 1961.   R. L.

FOREIGN TRADE AND AID. Foreign trade probably represents no more than 3% of total Soviet gross national product. Although relatively insignificant in terms of over-all Soviet economic activity, foreign trade has been increasing in importance since World War II. The USSR has found foreign trade to be a useful instrument for consolidating its control in Communist countries and for strengthening its influence in non-Communist nations. Moreover, since Stalin's death in 1953, the Soviet leadership has shown increasing appreciation of the economic advantages to be derived from international specialization and trade, particularly in areas where Soviet political power is dominant.

Commercial Organization. Like most other economic activities in the Soviet Union, foreign trade is closely planned and controlled by the government. A government monopoly of foreign trade was instituted in 1918 and has been in effect ever since. The monopoly is vested in the Ministry of Foreign Trade in Moscow which maintains a specialized commercial apparatus at home as well as a far-flung network of trade missions and commercial agencies abroad. The commercial apparatus in the Soviet Union is made up of state-trading corporations (*vsesoyuznye obyedinenia*). In 1959, the Ministry had 27 such corporations, each of which is authorized by special charter to operate in one clearly defined sector of the commercial field. Most of the state-trading corporations are engaged in the purchase and sale of specific groups of commodities.

In its operations abroad the Ministry of Foreign Trade is represented by one of three types of commercial agencies. In countries where the scale of trade is substantial, the Soviet government maintains an officially accredited trade delegation, forming part of the Soviet Embassy. Its three chief officials have diplomatic status. The delegation represents the export and import corporations, acts as their agents, makes market surveys for them, and negotiates contracts with buyers and sellers for commodities offered or required by export-import organizations. In areas of lesser commercial importance, Soviet foreign trade operations are often handled by a trade agency or by a member of the regular diplomatic mission acting as commercial counselor or attaché.

A third form of commercial representation has evolved in the United States which began trading with the USSR long before the Soviet government had been accorded official recognition. In 1924 representatives of the Soviet government were permitted to organize a company known as the Amtorg Trading Corporation to handle Soviet commercial transactions in the United States. While the company was formed under the laws of the state of New York, all its stock is owned by the Bank for Foreign Trade in Moscow. The company performs the same functions as trade delegations in other countries but does not enjoy their official or diplomatic status.

All financial transactions with foreign countries pass through the State Bank. It has correspondent banks all over the world which credit and debit its account as transactions take place. When necessary to balance accounts it can transfer convertible foreign exchange, gold or other precious metals from one country to another. The State Bank is in a position to check into and control the activities of the Ministry of Foreign Trade and its subordinate agencies.

Tariffs. The Soviet government maintains a system of tariffs on most imports and some exports. Soviet tariffs, however, while generally high, serve no real protective function as do tariffs in a free-enterprise society. The Soviet monopoly of foreign trade is a much more effective barrier against imports which might compete with domestic industry. Soviet tariffs have real significance only for the limited amount of goods brought into the Soviet Union through nongovernmental channels, for example, parcel post, goods brought in in the luggage of visitors, goods imported by the diplomatic missions, and the like.

Foreign Exchange Rate. Since the late 1920's the export and import of the ruble have been prohibited. Actual payments and receipts between the USSR and other countries have been made in foreign currencies or gold. As far as commercial transactions are concerned, the Soviet exchange rate has been little more than an accounting device for converting foreign currency prices of Soviet exports and imports into rubles. As far as noncommercial transactions are concerned, such as those involving tourists or diplomatic missions in the USSR, the exchange rate set by the Soviet government does have some limited significance. The more rubles foreign visitors or residents in the USSR obtain per unit of foreign currency, the better off they are. In general, the rate of exchange set by the Soviet government has overvalued the ruble in terms of foreign currency.

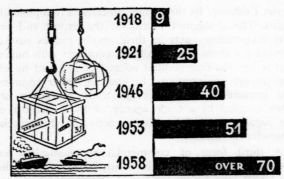

Number of Foreign Countries Trading with USSR

Despite the largely fictitious character of the ruble exchange rate, the Soviet government has seen fit, from time to time, to make exchange rate adjustments. In 1950, for example, the ruble was revalued upward by 32.5%. The gold content was defined as 0.222168 grams, which implies a ruble-dollar ratio of four to one. In April 1957 the rate for tourists and diplomatic missions in Moscow was raised from four to ten rubles per dollar but the official rate, used to convert commercial transactions into rubles, remained four to one. As of Jan. 1, 1961, the gold content of the ruble was redefined as .987412 grams and the exchange rate between the ruble and dollar set at 90 kopecks per dollar or $1.11 per ruble. In addition, effective Jan. 1, 1961 all prices, wages and other money incomes, taxes, savings deposits, government bonds, and assets and liabilities of Soviet enterprises were reduced to one tenth of their former level. The only external effect of the 1961 changes was a slight increase in the expense to foreigners of traveling and residing in the USSR. Internally, however, they may have had the effect of reducing fictitious losses of export organizations and fictitious profits of import organizations stemming from the former grossly overvalued ruble exchange rate. At the former exchange rate and internal price level, Soviet export organizations fell short, by a wide margin, of covering the domestic ruble cost of their deliveries abroad with foreign exchange earnings. Import organizations, on the other hand, chalked up handsome ruble profits.

Bilateral Trading Arrangements. Before World War II Soviet foreign trade was generally conducted on a multilateral basis. In the postwar period, however, bilateralism has become a hallmark of Soviet commercial policy. In 1959 the USSR had bilateral trading arrangements with most bloc countries and with 38 free world countries.

Bilateral trade agreements concluded with the USSR usually specify an equal value of trade for both countries at a given level. The agreements often contain quotas, expressed in value or quantity terms, for individual commodity exports and imports. Such quotas are target figures and are not legally binding. The trade agreements are usually accompanied by payments agreements which specify the financial arrangements under which trade is to be conducted. The payments agreements typically provide for the establishment of clearing accounts in the appropriate financial institutions of the trading partners. As trade between two countries will never balance precisely at all times, there is usually provision for swing credits, which allow for a certain percentage of trade imbalance without an interest charge. Should the trade imbalance exceed the limit set, the creditor country may request payment of the excess in gold or convertible currency.

Bilateral trading arrangements tend to increase the dependence of the USSR's trading partner on Soviet sources of supply. Since, under such arrangements, trade must be generally balanced in both directions, a country wishing to expand its exports to the USSR must increase its imports from the USSR, often diverting them from other sources of supply. Similarly, under such arrangements, a country may be compelled to import higher priced or poorer quality Soviet products in order to maintain or increase its exports to the USSR.

Soviet Gold Policy. Soviet gold reserves have been variously estimated at from $3 to $8 bill. Annual production has been put at $250 to $850 mill. Whatever the actual figures for Soviet gold production and reserves may be, there is no question but that they are very substantial.

The USSR uses gold to meet planned deficits in its balance of payments, to make purchases abroad to correct maladjustments in the plan, to make payments under bilateral clearing agreements, to extend credits to friendly nations, and the like. Annual sales of gold by the USSR, mainly through the Swiss and London markets, are shown for the period 1953 to 1958 in the following table:

TABLE I.
(in millions)

Year	Ounces	Dollars
1953	4.3	150
1955	2.0	70
1956	4.3	151
1957	7.5	263
1958	6.0	210

SOURCES: International Monetary Fund, *International Financial News*, March 29, 1957; *The New York Times*, March 11, 1959.

Pricing in Soviet Foreign Trade. The USSR appears to enjoy a price advantage in its trade with some bloc countries. Statistical data contained in the 1958 and 1959 supplements to the Soviet foreign trade journal *Vneshnyaya Torgovlya* (Foreign Trade), for example, suggest that prices of the bulk of Soviet exports to bloc countries in E. Europe are above world market levels while prices of the bulk of Soviet imports from these countries are below world market levels.

The USSR generally trades with free world countries at the prices prevailing on world markets. There have been a number of highly publicized exceptions, however. In 1958, for example, the USSR sold substantial quantities of aluminum and tin in free world countries at prices below those prevailing in world markets. It has sold petroleum to free world countries at prices above, equal to, or at a discount from those quoted on world markets.

Council for Economic Mutual Assistance. An organization known as the Council for Economic Mutual Assistance (q.v.), consisting of the USSR and its European satellites, was formed in 1949 on Soviet initiative. Representatives of Asian-bloc countries frequently take part in the meetings of the Council or its subordinate agencies in the capacity of observers. The purpose of the Council was officially stated to be "the exchange of experience in the economic field, the rendering of technical assistance to each other and the rendering of mutual economic assistance with respect to raw materials, foodstuffs, machinery, equipment, etc." Over recent years the Council has been charged with the task of coordinating the long-term economic plans of member countries. Countries having a cost advantage in certain lines of production are urged to specialize in these lines, exporting their surplus output to meet the requirements of other Council members.

LEVEL, COMMODITY COMPOSITION, AND GEOGRAPHIC DISTRIBUTION OF SOVIET FOREIGN TRADE

Interwar Period. In the 20-year period 1919–38 Soviet foreign trade failed to regain the level of tsarist Russia in 1913 (Table II). Annual exports averaged $274 mill. and annual imports averaged $279 mill. during this period. Foreign trade of the USSR averaged less than 1.5% of world trade from 1921 through 1938.

TABLE II.
SOVIET FOREIGN TRADE DURING THE INTERWAR PERIOD
(millions of dollars)

Year	Exports	Imports	Total Trade Turnover
1913	773	722	1,495
1924	171	131	302
1925	309	428	737
1928	412	490	902
1929	474	454	928
1930	536	546	1,082
1931	418	572	990
1932	299	361	660
1933	318	223	541
1934	362	198	560
1935	322	209	531
1936	270	268	538
1937	326	253	579
1938	255	272	527

The following ruble-dollar ratios were used to compute the dollar values given above: 1913 — 1.94 rubles to the dollar; 1924 — 1.99 rubles to the dollar; 1925–32 — 1.94 rubles to the dollar; 1933 — 1.57 rubles to the dollar; 1934 — 1.16 rubles to the dollar; 1935 — 1.15 rubles to the dollar; 1936 — 5.03 rubles to the dollar; 1937–38 — 5.30 rubles to the dollar.

SOURCE: Tsentralnoye Statisticheskoye Upravlenie pri Sovete Ministrov SSSR, *Narodnoye Khozyaystvo SSSR v 1958 godu*, Gosstatizdat, Moscow, 1959, p. 798.

Industrial products accounted for about 60% of the reduced volume of the USSR's exports in the interwar period. The most important increase occurred in exports of petroleum and petroleum products which made up 15% of the value of total exports and averaged four times the pre-1914 quantity of petroleum exports. Although in small quantities, the USSR began to export coal, which had been mainly an import in the pre-1914 period. Exports of grain during the interwar period were far below pre-1914 levels and accounted for less than 15% of Soviet exports.

The relative importance of machinery, iron and steel products, and nonferrous metals in Soviet imports rose, reflecting the launching of the USSR's forced-draft industrialization in the early 1930's. The USSR's imports of cotton dropped sharply in the 1930's, reflecting the successful expansion of cotton cultivation in Soviet Central Asia.

The regional distribution of Soviet foreign trade in 1931 and 1937 is shown in the following table:

TABLE III.
REGIONAL PATTERN OF SOVIET FOREIGN TRADE

Region	Exports 1931 (% of total)	Exports 1937 (% of total)	Imports 1931 (% of total)	Imports 1937 (% of total)
Central Europe	16.9	7.9	42.1	17.1
Western Europe	47.6	58.6	11.4	31.7
Northern Europe	3.6	3.6	4.0	1.8
Balkan Countries	1.4	0.8	0.1	0.4
Near East, Middle East, and Far East	16.7	15.7	12.7	15.5
American Continent and British Dominions	3.1	8.0	22.0	25.9
Baltic Countries	6.0	2.5	4.5	2.1
Japan	2.4	0.7	1.2	4.0
All Others	2.2	2.1	2.0	1.5
Total	100.0	100.0	100.0	100.0

Based on data in Gerschenkron, *Economic Relations with the USSR*, 1945, p. 33.

Soviet Foreign Trade during World War II. World War II resulted in a striking transformation of the Soviet foreign trade pattern. A summary view of this change is given by the data below:

TABLE IV.

Year	Exports	Imports
	(millions of dollars)*	
1938	255	272
1940	266	274
1942	94	528
1943	94	1,623
1945	270	2,794

* A ruble-dollar ratio of 5.3 to 1 was used to convert ruble values to dollar values.

SOURCES: Voznesensky, *The Economy of the USSR during World War II* (in Russian), p. 73; Tsentralnoye Statisticheskoye Upravlenie pri Sovete Ministrov SSSR, *Narodnoye Khozyaystvo SSSR v 1958 godu*, Gosstatizdat, Moscow, 1959, p. 798.

The sharp increase in the USSR's import surplus reflected the impact of World War II. To meet the urgent Soviet requirement for immediate outside aid, the American Lend-Lease and the British and Canadian Mutual Aid programs were set up, under which the USSR received tremendous amounts of commodities of all kinds at no current cost. Almost $13 bill. worth of goods were received by the USSR from the three major Western allies during World War II, of which about $11.2 bill. worth came from the United States.

TABLE V.
SOVIET FOREIGN TRADE AND WORLD TRADE, 1947–59
(billions of dollars)

Year	World Trade Exports	World Trade Imports	Soviet Foreign Trade Exports	Soviet Foreign Trade Imports
1947	47.4	47.4	0.4	0.5
1948	52.9	58.5	0.9	0.8
1949	60.7	62.0	1.0	0.9
1950	61.7	64.8	1.1	1.0
1951	82.3	87.6	2.0	1.5
1952	80.4	86.7	2.6	2.6
1953	82.2	83.9	2.9	2.9
1954	85.7	87.8	3.1	3.2
1955	93.8	97.6	3.5	3.1
1956	103.8	107.9	3.6	3.6
1957	105.4	110.0	4.4	3.7
1958	104.4	108.9	4.3	4.4
1959*	114.4	119.2	5.4	5.1

* Preliminary.

SOURCES: *Foreign Commerce Weekly*, Vol. 62, No. 15, October 12, 1959, p. 3; *World Trade Information Service*, Part 3, No. 60–8; *New York Times*, June 18, 1960.

Soviet Foreign Trade after World War II. In 1946 and 1947 Soviet foreign trade dropped sharply from its abnormally high wartime levels. In 1947 the USSR's foreign trade amounted to about $.9 bill. and accounted for about 1% of world trade (Table V). After 1947, however, Soviet foreign trade rose steadily, amounting to $10.5 bill. in 1959 or more than 4% of the world total.

Soviet Trade with Bloc Countries. A large portion of the increase in the USSR's foreign trade has been with other countries in the Soviet bloc (Table VI). Be-

TABLE VI.
SOVIET FOREIGN TRADE WITH BLOC AND FREE WORLD COUNTRIES 1952–59
(millions of dollars)

YEAR	TOTAL SOVIET FOREIGN TRADE	SOVIET FOREIGN TRADE WITH BLOC COUNTRIES		SOVIET FOREIGN TRADE WITH FREE WORLD COUNTRIES	
		Value	Percent	Value	Percent
1952	5,200	4,160	80	1,040	20
1953	5,750	4,750	83	1,000	17
1954	6,250	4,875	78	1,375	20
1955	6,300	4,900	78	1,400	22
1956	7,225	5,300	74	1,875	26
1957	8,320	6,000	70	2,320	30
1958	8,650	6,375	74	2,275	26
1959*	10,500	7,800	74	2,700	26

* Preliminary.

SOURCE: *Foreign Commerce Weekly*, Vol. 62, No. 15, October 12, 1959, p. 22; *New York Times, March 10, 1960*.

fore World War II these countries accounted for only 12% of Soviet foreign trade. By 1949, however, about two-thirds of Soviet foreign trade was with bloc countries. The share of the bloc in the USSR's foreign trade reached a peak of 83% in 1953, declining thereafter, despite rises in trade volume, to about 74% in 1959. Communist China and East Germany are the USSR's principal trading partners within the bloc. They are followed by Czechoslovakia, Poland, and Rumania in order of importance (Table VII).

TABLE VII.
GEOGRAPHIC PATTERN OF SOVIET TRADE WITH BLOC COUNTRIES 1955–1958

	EXPORTS		IMPORTS	
	1955	1958	1955	1958
Country	% of total	% of total	% of total	% of total
Albania	0.6	1.4	0.2	0.4
Bulgaria	4.0	6.5	5.1	6.4
Czechoslovakia	13.0	14.6	15.6	15.6
East Germany	17.6	26.0	20.8	25.8
Hungary	4.3	6.5	6.1	5.1
Poland	15.7	12.2	11.9	8.6
Rumania	10.2	8.1	9.3	7.3
Europ. Bloc Total	65.4	75.3	69.0	69.2
Communist China	27.8	20.3	27.1	27.3
Mongolia	4.5	2.0	2.2	1.5
North Korea	1.9	1.9	1.8	1.5
North Vietnam	insig.	0.3	insig.	0.3
Asian Bloc Total	34.2	24.5	31.1	30.6
GRAND TOTAL	100.00	100.00	100.00	100.00

SOURCES: Ministerstvo Vneshney Torgovli SSSR, Planovo-Ekonomicheskoye Upravlenie, *Vneshnyaya Torgovlya SSSR za 1956*, Vneshtorgizdat, Moscow, 1958; *Vneshnyaya Torgovlya SSSR za 1958*; Vneshtorgizdat, Moscow, 1959.

Machinery and equipment have played an important role in Soviet exports to bloc countries, accounting for about 20% of the total in 1958. Communist China is a major importer of Soviet machinery and equipment, absorbing more than 50% of Soviet shipments

of these products to bloc countries in 1958. Other important Soviet exports to bloc countries include iron ore, manganese, chrome, cement, petroleum products, coke, fertilizers, timber, woodpulp, newsprint, cotton, ferrous and nonferrous metals, grain, seeds, sugar, meat, butter, and fish products.

Machinery and equipment also figure prominently in Soviet imports from bloc countries. In 1958 East Germany alone supplied the USSR with machinery and equipment valued at $450 mill. In addition to machinery and equipment, the USSR imports substantial quantities of nonferrous metals from bloc countries. Communist China, the most important bloc supplier of nonferrous metals, furnishes tin, tungsten, bismuth, molybdenum, cobalt, mercury, and antimony. Other important Soviet imports from bloc countries include potash, coal, wool, jute, silk, hides, leather, cork, meat, fruit, sugar, oils, and vegetables.

Soviet Trade with Free World Countries since World War II. As Soviet political relations with the West worsened after World War II, the USSR's trade with free world countries fell off, reaching a low of $.6 bill. in 1950. The imposition of controls on exports of products considered to be of strategic value to the USSR by the United States and its allies in W. Europe and countermeasures of a similar character taken by the USSR gave impetus to the decline. Since 1950, however, there has been a fairly steady rise in Soviet trade with free world countries as a whole (Table VI), reflecting some easing of political tensions and the USSR's efforts to increase its influence in the less-developed countries outside the Soviet orbit through increased trade and programs of economic and military assistance. Soviet trade with the United States, however, has remained at very low levels since 1948 (Tables VIII and XI).

TABLE VIII.
U.S. TRADE WITH THE USSR, 1935–40 (AVERAGE), 1947–59
(millions of dollars)

Year	Exports	Imports
1935–40	57.9	24.2
1947	149.1	77.1
1948	27.9	86.8
1949	6.6	39.1
1950	0.8	38.3
1951	0.06	27.4
1952	0.02	16.8
1953	0.02	10.8
1954	0.2	11.8
1955	0.3	16.9
1956	3.8	24.6
1957	4.5	16.8
1958	3.4	17.3
1959	7.4	28.3

SOURCES: *Statistical Abstract of the United States*, p. 928 and data from the Department of Commerce.

The bulk of Soviet trade outside the bloc is concentrated in W. Europe. Despite substantial increases in Soviet trade with W. Europe in recent years, however, the share of this area in Soviet trade with non-bloc countries has declined (Table IX). While in 1953, for example, 89% of Soviet non-bloc exports went to W. Europe, in 1956 this percentage stood at 82, and in 1958 at 78. The share of W. Europe in Soviet non-bloc imports also tended to decline during this period.

TABLE IX.
GEOGRAPHIC PATTERN OF SOVIET TRADE WITH FREE
WORLD COUNTRIES, 1955, 1958

Region	1955 % of total	1958 % of total
	EXPORTS	
Europe, excluding Bloc	83.1	78.2
Near East & Africa	5.9	9.8
Far East	1.7	7.8
Oceania	0.3	0.2
Western Hemisphere	9.0	4.0
Total	100.0	100.0
	IMPORTS	
Europe, excluding Bloc	69.9	64.0
Near East & Africa	12.6	14.9
Far East	3.8	13.8
Oceania	1.1	0.2
Western Hemisphere	12.6	7.1
Total	100.0	100.0

* Preliminary.

Based on East-West trade tabulations prepared in the International Analysis Division, Bureau of Foreign Commerce, Department of Commerce.

The decline in the importance of W. Europe in the non-bloc trade of the USSR was accompanied by a rise in the importance of the less-developed countries of the free world. Over the period 1954 to 1958 the value of Soviet trade with these countries rose nearly 150% as shown in the following table:

TABLE X.

	1954	1955	1956	1957	1958
	(in thousands of dollars)				
Soviet exports to less-developed countries	71,775	94,236	123,843	175,833	183,678
Soviet imports from less-developed countries	131,148	166,700	146,050	286,848	315,058

Based on East-West trade tabulations prepared in the International Economic Analysis Division, Bureau of Foreign Commerce, Department of Commerce.

The shift in the geographic pattern of Soviet trade with free world countries from 1954 to 1958 is discernible in data on the composition of Soviet imports from these countries. While the value of Soviet imports of machinery and transport equipment from free world countries in 1957 and 1958 was substantially the same as in 1954 an 1955, the share of these products in Soviet imports from free world countries declined from 27% to 15%. This change is in line with the reduced importance of W. Europe—an important supplier of machinery and equipment to the USSR —in Soviet imports. On the other hand, there was a sharp rise in Soviet imports from free world sources of fruit and vegetables, tea and coffee, hides and skins, cereals, rubber and cotton over this period. This change reflects the increased importance of the less-developed countries in Soviet imports.

Soviet imports of copper from free world sources of supply rose from $6.4 mill. in 1954 to $53.2 mill, in 1958. This sharp rise is attributable to relaxation of W. controls on the export of copper to the USSR during this period.

There have been marked shifts in the composition of Soviet exports to free world countries over recent years. The most conspicuous change has been a steep rise in Soviet shipments of petroleum to the world market. Deliveries of petroleum rose from $56 mill. in 1954 to $208 mill. in 1958, making petroleum the leading Soviet export to non-bloc countries.

The Soviet Union has also stepped up its exports of lumber products, shipments rising from $74 mill. in 1954 to $139 mill. in 1958. In 1958 lumber was the USSR's second most important export to free world countries, accounting for about 13% of the total.

Grain, which was a major export of tsarist Russia and a leading Soviet export throughout much of the interwar period, ranked third in importance in 1958. The value of grain exports to non-bloc countries rose from $50 mill. in 1955 to $110 mill. in 1957 but declined in 1958 to $87 mill.

Bloc Aid to Underdeveloped Countries. From 1954 through April 15, 1960, Soviet-bloc countries concluded agreements with 21 of the less-developed nations outside the Soviet orbit providing for the extension of $3.8 bill. in intermediate and long-term credits and grants for goods and services to be supplied from the bloc. Of the total about $800 mill. consists of credits for the purchase of Soviet-bloc arms extended to Egypt, Syria, Iraq, Yemen, Indonesia, Afghanistan, and Guinea. The remaining $3.0 bill. is for economic purposes. Communist China is the only bloc country providing grants of any magnitude. Recipients of Communist Chinese grants, totaling about $190 mill., include Cambodia, Ceylon, Nepal, and Egypt.

The USSR is providing about $2.9 bill. or 76% of the total bloc assistance; the European satellites about $700 mill. or 19% of the total; and Communist China nearly $200 mill. or 5% of the total. The USSR has concentrated its activities on a relatively small number of major deals involving $100 mill. or more with Afghanistan, Argentina, Cuba, Indonesia, India, Yugoslavia, Egypt, and Syria.

The drawings under these credits and grants are generally spread over several years. Drawings on as-

TABLE XI.

U.S.-USSR TRADE, 1946-1960
(Thousands of U.S. Dollars)

	Exports of U.S. to USSR	% of Total U.S. Exports	Imports of U.S. from USSR	% of Total U.S. Imports	Turnover (Exports & Imports)	% of Total U.S. Turnover	% of Total USSR Turnover
1946	358,539[1]	3.7	100,548	2.0	459,087	3.1	30.1
1947	149,092	1.0	77,104	1.3	226,196	1.1	15.2
1948	28,003	0.2	86,840	1.2	114,843	0.6	4.6
1949	6,646	0.1	39,200	0.6	45,846	0.2	1.6
1950	752	[2]	38,300	0.4	39,052	0.2	1.2
1951	55	[2]	27,456	0.3	27.511	0.1	0.6
1952	20	[2]	16,818	0.2	16,838	0.1	0.3
1953	19	[2]	10,791	0.1	10,810	[2]	0.2
1954	216	[2]	11,929	0.1	12,145	[2]	0.2
1955	252	[2]	17,139	0.2	17,391	0.1	0.3
1956	3,819	[2]	24,468	0.2	28,287	0.1	0.4
1957	11,491	[2]	16,772	0.1	28,263	0.1	0.3
1958	19,495	[2]	17,504	0.1	36,999	0.1	0.4
1959	7,398	[2]	28,317	0.2	35,715	0.1	0.3
1960	39,192	0.2	22,635	0.2	61,827	0.2	[3]

[1] Includes $152,124,403 Lend Lease Shipments. [2] Negligible. [3] Not available.

SOURCE: Foreign Commerce and Navigation of the United States, 1946. U.S. Department of Commerce; Value Series, 1947-1960 Free World Exports and Imports, International Economic Analysis Division, Bureau of Foreign Commerce, U.S. Department of Commerce; Narodnoye Khozyaystvo SSSR v 1958 godu, Moscow, 1959, Vneshnyaya Torgovlya SSSR 1959.

sistance of a military character generally proceed at a more rapid pace than drawings on assistance of an economic character.

The interest charges on Soviet and other bloc credits are low, typically 2% to 2.5%. Many of the major Soviet credit agreements provide for future negotiations to establish lists, prices, and quantities of goods to be delivered in repayment. In its more recent credit accords the USSR has agreed to defer repayments until completion of its own deliveries of equipment and services.

In conjunction with their aid programs the USSR and other bloc countries extend technical assistance to less-developed countries of the free world. Bloc specialists and technicians are sent to the less-developed countries to assist in constructing capital projects and to train local personnel in their operation. Students and technicians from the less-developed countries also go to the bloc countries for study and training in connection with these projects.

Virtually all bloc technical assistance is extended on a bilateral basis. The USSR does, however, provide a token amount of assistance through the UN.

Soviet Aid to Bloc Countries. The Soviet Union took its first steps in the field of economic assistance in its relations with other bloc countries. In his report to the 20th Party Congress in Feb. 1956 Khrushchev stated that the USSR had granted a total of 21 bill. rubles in long-term economic credits to the "people's democracies." At the official rate of exchange this amounts to a sum of $5,250 mill. Published records of credits through Feb. 1956 show a total of only $1,772 mill. The discrepancy may be due in part to the inclusion in Khrushchev's total of the satellite debts to the USSR incurred by the liquidation of some of the "joint companies" in late 1954. China alone would account for $1.4 bill. of these and Hungary for $700 mill.

On the whole, it seems reasonable to conclude that Soviet credits to bloc countries did not exceed $2 bill. through early 1956. This is, of course, a gross figure which does not take account of the very considerable Soviet benefits extracted from the bloc countries in such forms as war booty, reparations payments, profits of "joint companies," and Soviet-dictated prices in commercial trade or the repayment of credits.

Following the political upheavals in E. Europe in 1956, the USSR sharply expanded its economic assistance to the satellite countries. In 1956 and 1957 a series of new credit agreements was concluded with these countries and in a number of cases outstanding debts were cancelled. During the seventeen months following the 20th Party Congress, the USSR extended $1,542 mill. in new credits to members of the bloc. (*See also* MONETARY SYSTEM, COUNCIL FOR ECONOMIC MUTUAL ASSISTANCE)

BIBLIOGRAPHY: Harry Schwartz, *Russia's Soviet Economy,* New York, 1954; Joseph S. Berliner, *Soviet Economic Aid,* New York, 1958; U.S. Bureau of Foreign Commerce, *The USSR—Summary of Basic Economic Information,* Washington, 1959 (mimeographed); Ernest Rubin, "USSR Trade over Past Half Century Reflects Changing Economy," *Foreign Commerce Weekly,* Vol. 62, No. 15 (October, 1959), p. 3, p. 22.   R. C. H.

FORESTS: *see* PLANT LIFE.

FORMALISTS, a group of writers and linguists which considered the form as the most important essential in literary work. They united in *Opoyaz* (The Society for the Study of Poetic Language) and published the *Periodical on the Theory of Poetic Language* (1916–17) and *Poetica* (1919). They rejected poetry as thinking in images; tried to divorce literary work from the person of its author, and proclaimed the thesis of art as the method of presenting the literary material. Representatives of formalism are: V. Shklovsky, B. Eichenbaum, Roman Jacobson, Yu. Tynyanov, and others.

After 1927 most of the F were under pressure of the Marxist critics. They tried to create a new formalist-socialist method of writing, bringing literature closer to life. New groups of writers were formed—"Serapion Brothers" and "Lef"—but they were defeated by socialist realism. Everything in art and literature that is different from socialist realism is today called "formalism" by the Soviet critics.

FORSH, Ólga Dmítrievna (1875–), novelist, born in the Caucasus. Her father was the military governor of Central Dagestan. Graduated from an institute for daughters of the nobility, she later studied in two art schools. Her first works were about R. rural life (1908–09): *Pioneers, After the Firebird, Panfamil the Bear.* After visiting Paris and Munich F was attracted by occultism and wrote *Children of the Earth* (1920). Her other and more important works are *Clad in Stone* (1908–09), *The Burning Workshop* (1927), *The Raven* (1934), *The Jacobin Leaven* (1934), *The Squiress of Kazan* (1935), *The Pernicious Book* (1939); scenarios, *Pugachov* (1937) and *The Mikhaylov Castle* (1946); and *The Firstlings of Liberty* (1953), a novel about the Decembrists. F has received several Soviet awards, including the order of Lenin. As the oldest Soviet female author, she opened the Second Congress of the Soviet writers in 1954.

FORTUNÁTOV, Filípp Fyódorovich (1848–1914), philologist, authority on linguistics and comparative grammar of Indo-European languages. Author of books on Slavic and Baltic phonetics, including *Comparative Linguistics* (1897), *Comparative Phonetics of Indo-European Languages* (1901).

FOUNDRY: *see* METALLURGY.

FRANCO-RUSSIAN ALLIANCE, 1894. Germany's refusal to renew the Russian-German "reinsurance treaty" of 1887 and her improved relations with Britain after 1890 led the R. government to seal recent Franco-Russian cooperation with a formal agreement. On Aug. 27, 1891, Russia and France agreed to attempt an understanding on measures to be taken in the event of a threat to the peace. A supplementary military agreement was initialed Aug. 17, 1892, providing for mutual action against Germany if France were attacked by Germany or by Italy with German support, or if Russia were attacked by Germany or by Austria with German support. Mobilization by the Triple Alliance meant mobilization by France and Russia. Coordination between the two general staffs was provided for, and neither party was to sign a separate peace. The agreement would end only on termination of the Triple Alliance. It was ratified by Russia Dec. 27, 1893 and remained secret until 1918.

FRANK, Ilyá Mikháylovich (1908–), physicist. Corresponding member, Ac. of S., USSR (1946). Graduate (1930) and professor (1944), of Moscow University. Associated with the Institute of Physics, Ac. of S. (1934). Research concerns neutrons. Jointly with I. Ye. Tamm developed the theory of the Cherenkov-Vavilov effect. Stalin (1946) and Nobel (1958) prizes.

FRANK, Simon Ludvigovich (1877–1950), philosopher. Was born in Moscow and studied sociology and philosophy at Moscow, Berlin, and Heidelberg universities. He taught at the University of Saratov and then of Moscow. In 1922 he was exiled by the Soviet government. After living in Germany and in France he settled in London. F's principal works are (in Russian) *The Object and Its Cognition* (1915, also in French), *The Human Soul* (1917), *The Methodology of the Social Sciences* (1922), *The Spiritual Foundations of Society* (1930), *On the Inconceivable* (1939), *Light in the Darkness* (1939) and *God with Us* (1946).

FRANKÓ, Iván Yákovlevich (1856–1916), Ukrainian writer and poet. Was born in W. Ukraine under  Austrian domination. His best known stories and novels are: *Borislav* (1877), *Boa Constrictor* (1878), *Laughing Borislav* (1882); poems, *Quarry* (1878), *The Death of Cain* (1889), *Moses* (1905). His collections of verses enjoyed a tremendous success. He also wrote plays (*Stolen Happiness*) and made translations. In 1910 he published an *Essay on the History of Ukrainian-Russian Literature,* and in 1913, *Ukrainian Folk Songs, a Study.* Published journals *Hromadsky Druh* (The Society's Friend), *Dzvin* (The Bell), *Zhitie i Slovo* (Life and Word). The prevailing motif of his writings was national and social liberation of the Ukrainian people. In 1939 the Lvov University was named after him, as well as the Ukrainian Drama Theater in Kiev.

FREEMASONRY. Freemasonry was introduced in Russia in the 1730's. The order, composed chiefly of members of the gentry and the intelligentsia, gained momentum in the latter half of the 18th century as Masonic lodges were formed in St. Petersburg, Moscow, Riga, and other cities attracting prominent persons to its ranks. Empress Catherine, who at one time had favored the order, in 1794 fearing the spread of revolutionary ideas from France withdrew her protection and most of the lodges ceased holding meetings. Tsar Paul, who succeeded Catherine, continued the interdict against Masons as did Alexander I for a brief period. In 1803 Alexander I permitted the order to meet again. The brief renaissance of F which ensued saw the development of two Grand Lodges: Astrea and the Provincial Lodge. The order also attracted a number of officers who were to form the leading core of the Decembrist uprising in 1825. In Aug. 1822 Alexander I, persuaded by one Senator Kushelev, a former Grand Master, of the dangers of F, ordered all Masonic lodges closed. The attempt to revive the order after the revolution of 1905 met with little success.

FRÉNKEL, Yákov Ilyich (1894–1952), physicist. Corresponding member, Ac. of S., USSR (1929). Graduate, Petrograd University (1916); professor, Institute of Physical Technology, Leningrad Polytechnic Institute (1921–52). Developed quantum theory of electron movement in metals, theory of ferromagnetism, light absorption by dielectrics. Author of *Kinetic Theory of Fluids* (1945).

FROST, Andréy Vladímirovich (1906–1952), physical chemist. Professor, Moscow University (1942). Research on the thermodynamics and kinetics of thermal and catalytic conversion of hydrocarbons and other organic compounds; the development of statistical methods for the calculation of various parameters in thermodynamics; and the theory of petroleum origin, chemistry of petroleum refining processes, chemistry of phosphorus and its compounds.

FRÚMKIN, Aleksándr Naúmovich (1895–), physical chemist and electrochemist. Fellow, Ac. of S., USSR (1932). Educated abroad; returned to Russia and graduated from Odessa University (1915). Professor, Institute of Popular Education, Odessa (1920–22); associated with the Karpov Institute of Physical Chemistry, Moscow (1922–46). Lectured on colloidal chemistry at the University of Wisconsin (1928–29). Director, Institute of Physical Chemistry and Institute of Colloidal Chemistry, Ac. of S. (1939–49). Research on surface phenomena, electrocapillary phenomena, diffusion processes, flotation, heterogeneous catalysis, and colloidal chemistry. F's ideas and theories have found application in Soviet electrochemistry. Author of *Achievements in Chemistry* (1949); *Adsorption Phenomena and Electrochemical Kinetics* (1955). Lenin prize (1931) and Stalin prize (1941).

FRÚNZE, city, capital of Kirghiz SSR. Formerly Pishpek, a R. fortress, it is the birthplace of M. Frunze, Bolshevik leader in the civil war, for whom it was renamed. Pop. 220,000 (1959). Lies in the center of the Chu River valley in the N. foothills of Kirghiz Range. It is a fast growing industrial and cultural community, on the Lugovoy-Rybachye branch of the great Turkestan-Siberian R.R., with a number of higher educational institutions; site of the Kirghiz Division of the Ac. of S., USSR. Its ind. include agr. mach., Diesel engines, textiles, leather goods, canneries, food- and tobacco-processing plants.

FRÚNZE, Mikhaíl Vasílyevich (1885–1925), Soviet military leader, born in Kirghizia in a family of R.  settlers. F studied in St. Petersburg Institute of Technology and, in 1904, joined the Bolshevik party. In 1905 he took part in the 3rd Party Congress in London. Arrested in 1907, F was sentenced to 8 years at hard labor and in 1915 was banished to Siberia. During the 1917 revolution, he was politically active first in Byelorussia (Minsk) and then in the Moscow region. During the civil war, in 1918, he took part in the suppression of the Yaroslavl rebellion; in 1919–20, he commanded the Red forces in Turkestan against Kolchak, and, in 1920, defeated Wrangel in the Crimea. In Dec. 1921, F headed a Soviet military mission to Turkey, and later was sent to the Ukraine to fight the Makhno peasant rebellion. In 1921, at the 10th Party Congress F was elected a member of the Central Committee, and, in 1924, at the 13th Party Congress, a deputy member of the Politburo. Shortly afterwards, in 1925, he replaced Trotsky as the head of the Soviet military forces. In Oct. 1925, F was called by Stalin to Moscow and ordered to undergo a surgical operation, during which he died. The circumstances of his death had inspired Boris Pilnyak to write a short story *The Death of the Komandarm* (*The Story of the Unextinguished Moon*). F's works on military topics were published in 3 volumes in Russian in the 1920's.

FUNDAMENTAL LAWS OF 1906. A codification of the principal laws bearing on the constitutional structure of the Empire. It was issued in April 1906 shortly before the opening of the First Duma. Unlike other statutes, the FL could be amended only on the initiative of the Crown. This provision was unnecessary since the tsar had an absolute veto over all legislation, but it prevented the State Duma from taking legal steps for the revision of the constitutional arrangements. Under Article 87, the tsar was empowered to promulgate emergency decrees while the State Duma was in recess, subject to subsequent ratification by that body. This method was used frequently to impose the will of the government on the State Duma. Certain functions, such as the conduct of foreign affairs, were reserved to the Crown under the FL.

FUR ANIMAL BREEDING was initiated under the First Five Year Plan. By 1932, 20 large state farms were organized, specializing in FAB. Their number rose to 45 by the late 1950's. The largest farms keep up to 20,000 caged animals. Silver-black fox, blue fox, sable, martin, and beaver are the most widely bred animals. Platinum fox and mink, snow-white mink, and other rare fur varieties were obtained by selective breeding. Efforts were made to standardize the quality of furs and to meet other export requirements since most of the output of FAB farms is exported. The USSR occupies the first place in Europe as regards the number of caged fur animals.

FÚRMANOV, Dmítry Andréyevich (1891–1926), Soviet writer who first achieved notoriety as a journalist.  In 1914 he joined the army as a volunteer and wrote several "Sketches from the Front" which, in 1916, were published in the leading Russian daily *Russkoye Slovo*. He joined the CP in 1918 and served as a political commissar attached to the guerrilla forces of Chapayev. His novel *Chapayev*, written in 1923, is largely a description of this experience. His other stories and novels are *Red Sortie* (1922), *Riot* (1923–25), and the unfinished novel *Writers*.

FÚRTSEVA, Yekaterína Alekséyevna (1910–), member of the Presidium of the CPSU and state official, born in a worker's family in Kalinin Oblast. Studied at the Leningrad Higher Academy of Civil Aviation (1935), the Moscow Institute of Chemical Technology (1942) and took a correspondence course at a higher party school of the Central Committee of the CPSU (1948). F was active in the Komsomol (Young Communist League) and has been a member of the CPSU since 1930. In 1942–50, F was secretary of the Frunze district committee of the CP in Moscow; in 1950, second secretary of the Moscow city committee of the CPSU, and in 1954–57, first secretary. At the 20th Party Congress (1956) F was elected member of the Central Committee of the CPSU; in Feb. 1956, candidate member of the Presidium and secretary of the Central Committee and of the Moscow city committee of the CPSU. In June 1957 she became a member of the Presidium of the Central Committee of the CPSU. In May 1960 F was appointed minister of culture of the USSR and relieved as secretary of the party's Central Committee. F is also a deputy to the Supreme Soviet of the USSR and of the Supreme Soviet of the RSFSR. She seems to be in great favor with Khrushchev whom she accompanied to Peking in 1954. She was the first woman to appear on the reviewing stand with members of the Presidium at the May Day Parade 1955.

FUTURISTS. Adherents to a formalistic movement in art and literature that also developed in France, Italy, and England shortly before World War I. The F sought to create a "dynamic" "art of the future," original to an extent never yet seen. This striving was frequently associated with a cult of technology, machines, and large industrial cities, as well as with a defense of the ugly and the hideous. At the same time it entailed an unreserved negation of the artistic heritage, culture, and morality of the past. They rejected the view that a logical meaning must attach to words, and that sentences must conform to rules of syntax.

The principal associations of futurist poets in prerevolutionary Russia were "Gilea," a group of cubofuturists that included D. D. Burlyuk, V. V. Khlebnikov, V. V. Kamensky, A. E. Kruchonykh, and B. Lifshits; and "The Centrifuge," which was headed by P. Bobrov. Mayakovsky was closely associated for a time with a group of cubofuturists, while B. L. Pasternak and N. N. Aseyev were briefly associated with "The Centrifuge." Several collections of poems, as well as of statements of principle, were published by the cubofuturists. They include *A Slap on the Face of Public Taste, Rider of Judges, The Dead Moon, The Word as It Is,* and *The Roaring Parnassus.*

Unlike many of the W. European F, the representatives of R. futurism did not develop a pronounced cult of technology. Some of them displayed, instead, a preference for primitivism, for early Russian Orthodox culture, and for the ideal of an elemental, natural life (Khlebnikov).

Although the majority of the F had been indifferent to political problems before the October revolution, their struggle for radicalism in art subsequently led some of them to ascribe to themselves a status of revolutionaries in a social sense as well. A futurist newspaper, *The Art of the Commune*, was published between 1918 and 1919. In the 1920's, remaining futurist influences centered on the journal *Lef* (Left Front).

C. P. K.

G

GABRICHÉVSKY, Geórgy Norbértovich (1860–1907), physician. Graduate of Moscow University (1886); studied under I. I. Mechnikov, Robert Koch, E. Roux, and Paul Ehrlich (1889–91). One of the founders of microbiology in Russia. Founded a bacteriological laboratory which was to develop into the G. N. Gabrichevsky Institute of Bacteriology in Moscow. Research concerned epidemic diseases; discovered *Streptococcus scarlatinae* as the cause of scarlet fever and introduced a preventive vaccine; established the transmission of malaria by mosquitoes and introduced anti-diphtheria serum in Russia with N. F. Filatov.

GAGÁRIN, Yúry Alekséyevich (born March 9, 1934). Major Gagarin became the first man to circle  the world in an earth satellite on April 12, 1961 aboard a rocket, the Vostok. Up to the time of his flight he was an unknown Soviet Air Force officer. According to R. sources, he was born on a collective farm near Smolensk, the son of a carpenter. He began his education there in 1941, but his schooling was interrupted by World War II. Later he attended a vocational school to become a qualified molder and foundry man. Simultaneously, he attended evening school for Communist youth. Still later he enrolled at a technical school at Saratov on the Volga, and in 1955 he was graduated with honors. At that time he joined the Saratov Aeroclub for flying lessons. Next he went to a Soviet Air Force school at Orenburg in the Urals. There he met Valentina, a young medical student whom he later married and who bore him two daughters, Galya and Yelena. He became an airman in 1957, again with honors, and presumably entered training as an astronaut within a year or two after that. He joined the Komsomol in 1959 and the CPSU in June 1960. According to the official report submitted to the International Aeronautical Federation, Major Gagarin started at the cosmodrome at Baykonur, in W. Siberia and landed near the village of Smelovka, Saratov Oblast, 400 mi. southeast of Moscow. Duration of flight, 108 minutes; maximum altitude, 203 mi. The rocket had 6 engines with a total boost of 20,000,000 HP.

GAGAUZ: *see* MOLDAVIAN SSR.

GÁGRA (f. Gagry), town in Abkhaz ASSR, Black Sea resort in Caucasus, 37 mi. S. of Sochi; pop. 16,000 (1957). Warm, pleasant climate, subtropical vegetation.

GALAKTIÓNOV, Stepán Filíppovich (1779–1854), painter, graphic artist and lithographer. His best-known works are prints of St. Petersburg and its environs, mostly made from his own drawings (*The New Cascade in Peterhof, The Italian Fountain*, and others). He devoted much time to book illustration.

GALYÓRKIN, Borís Grigóryevich (1871–1945), engineer. Fellow, Ac. of S., USSR (1935). Honored Scientist, RSFSR (1934). Graduate, St. Petersburg Institute of Technology (1899); head, Department of Structural Mechanics, Leningrad Polytechnic Institute. Research concerned problems of structural mechanics, theory of elasticity and of shells (1942). Developed method of approximate solution of boundary value problems (1915). Stalin prize (1942).

GAMALÉYA, Nikoláy Fyódorovich (1859–1949), microbiologist. Fellow, Ac. of S., USSR (1940), Ac. of  Medical Sciences (1945). Honored scientist, RSFSR (1934). Graduate, Novorossiysk University in Odessa (1880) and the Military Medical Academy in St. Petersburg (1883); professor, Moscow Medical Institute (1938–49). With I. I. Mechnikov, G investigated the bacteriology of tuberculosis and anthrax. Studied under L. Pasteur in Paris (1886). Founded (with I. I. Mechnikov) the first R. bacteriological laboratory in Odessa (1886); the Bacteriological and Physiological Institute (1899). Combated plague (1901–02) and cholera in Transcaucasia, St. Petersburg, and Odessa. Research concerned rabies, inflammatory and epidemic diseases. The Institute of Microbiology, Ac. of Med. S., has been named after G.

GAMÁRNIK, Yan Borísovich (1894–1937), prominent Bolshevik military leader. He began his revolutionary activities by organizing student circles in Kiev in 1914. Two years later he became a Bolshevik, carrying out party assignments in Kiev. A commander in the civil war, G later rose to become head of the political administration of the Red Army. From 1927 to 1934 he was a member of the Central Committee. In May 1937, he committed suicide, supposedly to avoid arrest and trial for treason. He was posthumously rehabilitated after the 20th Party Congress in 1956.

GÁMBURTSEV, Grigóry Aleksándrovich (1903–1955), geophysicist. Fellow, Ac. of S., USSR (1953). Graduate of Moscow University (1926). Director, Geophysical Institute (1948). Research in geophysics of the earth crust, gravimetry, and seismography. Developed a theory of and designs for seismographs; investigated methods of predicting earthquakes.

GANDZHÁ: *see* KIROVABAD.

GAPÓN, Geórgy Appollónovich (1870–1906), priest, social worker, police informer. After ordination, he went to St. Petersburg to work among the poor. His purpose seemed to be the neutralization of revolutionary influences among the workers through organizing loyal working men into patriotic fraternities; hence his establishment of the Assembly of Russian Workingmen (1904) and his alliance with Zubatov and the secret police after 1902. On Jan. 9, 1905 ("Bloody Sunday"), he led the mass demonstration of workers to petition the tsar at the Winter Palace, the bloody dispersal of which helped bring revolution. He now became vehement in his denunciation of the tsar, the administration, and the army; consequently he was unfrocked and left Russia. While abroad he joined the Socialist Revolutionaries. Returning to St. Petersburg later in 1905, he re-established his former connection with the police. He was hanged by order of the Socialist Revolutionary central committee in March 1906. The assassination was organized by P. Rutenberg. (*See also* BLOODY SUNDAY, REVOLUTION OF 1905.)

GÁRIN (Mikhaylóvsky), **Nikol** **Geórgievich** (1852–1906), a writer known mostly for his autobiographical novels, *Tyoma's Childhood, Schoolboys, University Students,* and *Engineers* written over the period from 1892 to 1908. They give a portrayal of education in Russia of his days. Also compiled a collection of Korean tales.

GARMENT INDUSTRY is classified as a branch of light industry. In 1960, 111 mill. pieces of knitted outerwar, and 471 mill. pieces of knitted underwear were produced.

During the prerevolutionary period, garments were made largely on a handicraft basis, while factory production was concentrated mainly around Moscow and St. Petersburg (Leningrad). In 1921 there were 279 nationalized enterprises in which 40,000 workers were employed.

During the prewar Five Year Plans (1928–40) rapid progress in the volume and variety of machinery available made possible the modernization and expansion of existing enterprises and the construction of new ones. Of the new plants 40 per cent were located in the republics of Central Asia and of the Caucasus.

Approximately one-third of the productive capacity of the GI was destroyed during World War II, including large plants in Kiev, Kharkov, Stalino, Vitebsk, Gomel, and Mogilev. In the postwar period its further development resulted largely from the modernization of the larger plants and the construction of additional facilities in eastern regions. According to official data there were 450 large plants in 1955, employing 260,000 workers, as well as smaller enterprises under local jurisdiction and producers' cooperatives employing 240,000 additional workers. The value of the output of the larger plants in that year was 30 bill. rubles. The number of overcoats produced was 2.6 times larger than in 1940; of suits 2 times; and of dresses 1.1 times. As a result of technological innovations 20 per cent of the machines employed were special-purpose machines (compared to 12 per cent in 1950), and the number of conveyor belt installations was 3 times higher than in 1946.

Important factors in the postwar development of the GI have been the existence of specialized curricula in technical schools; the establishment, in 1947, of the All-Union Scientific Research Institute of the Garment Industry; and the establishment of Houses of Modeling in Moscow, Leningrad, Kiev, Tashkent, Minsk, Tbilisi, Novosibirsk, Lvov, and Riga.

The Seven Year Plan (1958–65) calls for the production of 1,250 mill. pairs of hosiery, 160 mill. pieces of knitted outwear, and 780 mill. pieces of knitted underwear in 1965. P. I. M.

GÁRSHIN, Vsévolod Mikháylovich (1855–1888), popular writer belonging to the landed gentry. His short stories, *Four Days* (1877), *The Coward* (1879), and *Reminiscences of Private Ivanov* (1883) express his feelings against the war. *The Red Flower* (1883) is a symbolic expression of the fight against injustice and evil. His best works are motivated by the idea of the fight for the liberation of personality, but they are morbid and full of pessimistic notes. He committed suicide by throwing himself down a stair well in a fit of insane melancholia.

GÁTCHINA, city in Leningrad Oblast, 27 mi. from Leningrad, RSFSR; pop. 33,300 (1956). Former summer residence of the tsars. Sights: palace, built in 1766–81 by A. Rinaldi; remarkable collection of furniture, china, bronzes, paintings, and sculpture; picturesque parks with pavilions. Palace was damaged during World War II, is now a museum.

GÁUYA, (f. Aa), river in Latvian SSR, flows into Gulf of Riga; length about 235 mi.

GDANSK BAY, in S. part of Baltic Sea in USSR and Poland. The Vistula flows into it. Ports: Gdansk, Gdynia (Poland), Baltiysk (USSR).

GE, Nikoláy Nikoláyevich (1831–1894), a religious and historical painter, illustrator of works by Leo Tolstoy, whose thinking influenced his art. While in Florence G painted *The Last Supper* for which the Academy awarded him the title of professor. Later he turned to historical subjects and painted *Peter I and Tsarevich Alexis, Catherine at the Tomb of Elizabeth,* and *Pushkin in the Village of Mikhaylovskoye,* also portraits of Herzen, Nekrasov, Tolstoy.

GEGECHKÓRY, Yevgény Petróvich (1879–1954), of Georgian peasant origin, graduated as a lawyer. G was a member of the third State Duma, belonging to the Menshevik faction of the Social Democratic party. In 1917 he was a member of the Presidium of the All-Russian Soviet of Workers', Peasants', and Soldiers' Deputies. After the October revolution, G returned to Georgia and became minister of foreign affairs; later he was president of the Transcaucasian government. G emigrated in 1921, after Georgia was taken over by the Soviets, and was a member of the Georgian government-in-exile.

GELENDZHÍK, town in Krasnodar Kray, RSFSR, resort on Black Sea, 27 mi. from Novorossiysk; pop. 12,800 (1956). Mud baths.

GÉLFAND, Izraíl Moiséyevich (1913–), mathematician. Corresponding member, Ac. of S., USSR (1953). Specialized in functional analysis; developed theory of integration of functions the values of which are elements of any linear normalized spaces (1935) and theory of normalized rings used by mathematicians in various fields of mathematics (1940). Research in quantum mechanics led to valuable results in regard to Lie groups. Stalin prize (1951).

GÉLFOND, Aleksándr Ósipovich (1906–), mathematician. Corresponding member, Ac. of S., USSR (1939). Professor, Moscow University (1931). Research concerns the theory of numbers and of a complex variable. Developed methods of investigation of transcendental numbers, logarithms, and algebraic numbers. Established relationship between analysis and arithmetic. Author of *Calculation of Finite Variables* (1952).

GENETICS, the scientific study of heredity and variation, has undergone its chief development in the 20th century. The chief impetus was given by the discovery by Gregor Mendel (1822–1884), an Augustinian monk in Brünn (now in Czechoslovakia), of the first general laws of heredity. Although published in 1866, Mendel's chief work lay unappreciated until the principles were rediscovered by biologists in Germany, Austria, and Holland in 1900. Then his theory that heredity is transmitted by discrete living particles, now known as genes, underwent a rapid development, largely in W. Europe and America. By 1915 proof had been obtained, chiefly through the work of T. H. Morgan, E. B. Wilson, and their school at Columbia University, that the chromosomes of the cell nucleus consist of thousands of these elements, each with its own location in a linear order which can be specified in a map. This provides the physical mechanism of Mendelian heredity.

In Russia, a strong school of G began to develop at the time of the First World War; and in the period 1920–1939 the USSR rapidly became a leading center of research in both theoretical G and its applications to agriculture, chiefly plant breeding. The Institute of Applied Botany in Leningrad, reconstituted in 1920 by Lenin and directed by Nikolay Ivanovich Vavilov (1887–1943), a leading geneticist and authority on the origin of cultivated plants, became, together with the Lenin All-Union Academy of Agricultural Sciences, also directed by Vavilov, the center of the most extensive research in seed selection and plant breeding in the world. It quickly developed a network of experimental and testing stations spread over the USSR and manned by some 20,000 scientific and technical workers. The guiding principles were those of Mendelian heredity expanded and applied by R. geneticists.

From these institutes came, in 1926, the first experimental proof, by Karpechenko, of the origin of a new species, Raphanobrassica, from a cross of radish (Raphanus) by cabbage (Brassica). By a process of chromosome doubling (allopolyploidy) it transmitted the chromosomes and contained genes of both parent species, fertile in matings within the new species but separated from each parent by sterility. Filipchenko had initiated the genetical analysis of race differences in plants and Chetverikov the analysis of concealed genetic variability in natural populations of insects which in the hands of Dubinin, Dobzhansky, Timofeyev-Ressovsky and others led to the development of a new branch of G (population G) which has come to constitute the most fruitful experimental approach to the study of evolution. Koltsov, Navashin, and other cytologists became leading figures in the interpretation of the physical basis of heredity in the chromosomes, while Serebrovsky and Dubinin supplied both ideas and experimental results which contributed to the modern interpretation of the finer structure of the genetic material. Rapaport at Moscow first demonstrated the production by specific chemicals of characters imitating the effects of mutant genes, now known as chemical phenocopies. Schmalhausen, primarily an embryologist, had developed his theory of stabilizing selection which provided new insights into the manner which natural selection acts upon the genetic variability in populations of animals and plants.

All in all, the work initiated by Soviet geneticists played an important part, during the 20's and 30's, in the development of modern G, integrated closely with the research proceeding apace in W. Europe, America, and Japan.

Then in the mid-30's there arose a new school descended, not from the foundations laid by Mendel and expanded greatly by his successors, but rather from the ideas and methods of I. V. Michurin (1855–1935), a R. horticulturist and practical plant breeder who had played a leading role in the introduction and adaptation for R. conditions of crop plants and fruit trees. The leader of what came to be called "Michurinist biology" was the agronomist Trofim Denisovich Lysenko who in 1935, together with the philosopher Prezent, published a book On the Laws of Phasic Development of Plants. In this and in a spate of publications by Lysenko and his followers which preceded and followed it were set forth the evidence and principles of the "New Biology" which were destined to supplant the principles of G in giving direction and guidance to Soviet biologists. These were summarized in Lysenko's book Heredity and Its Variability which appeared in R. in 1943 and in English translation in 1946. The work of this school was painstakingly and objectively examined and reported for English readers by two English plant breeders, Hudson and Richens, in 1946. This excellent review should be consulted for a full account, together with the accounts by Huxley (1949) and the translations of some original documents in Zirkle (1949) and the articles by Dobzhansky (1947 and 1951).

Although it is not possible to summarize briefly the voluminous statements of the Michurinist position, in which philosophical, political, and scientific arguments are mingled, it is at least clear that it represented a revolt from and a rejection of the principles of modern G and a return to views about heredity which had been current in the 19th century. Chief of these was that heredity was malleable, subject to influences from the environment which were assimilated by organisms in their development, and then transmitted to their descendants. This view, for which the catch phrase is "inheritance of acquired characters," had been repeatedly subjected to experimental tests, none of which had provided evidence of its validity, nor was cogent new evidence for it obtained by the Michurinists. On the other hand, conclusive disproof of it would require proof of a universal negative not attainable by experimental methods. It had been abandoned because unnecessary, the origin of changes in heredity having been shown to be due to random changes (mutations) in the heredity elements, genes and chromosomes. These, according to the evidence of G, can be caused to change by environmental agencies, but the changes produced bear no constant or adaptive relations to the agencies that call them forth, X-rays, heat, chemicals, and other physical forces, all producing similar changes, which become, or fail to become, part of the hereditary patrimony of the species as natural selection or other evolutionary forces may determine.

The Michurinists correctly saw that the inheritance of acquired characters and inheritance by genes were mutually incompatible. They chose to reject the genic alternative and in 1936 and 1939 challenged the "Mendelian-Morganist" geneticists in public debate. It is significant that, to the description of their opponents, the Michurinists usually added the accusative terms "bourgeois idealists," thus indicating the political and philosophical tendencies of their arguments. Both sides spoke their minds in these debates, and active research and publications of both schools continued until the war intensified what was called the "crisis in biology."

The climax and resolution were reached in the great and final debate of July 31–Aug. 7, 1948, before the plenary sessions of the Lenin Academy. By this time Lysenko had replaced Vavilov as director of the Academy and of the Institute of Genetics, and Vavilov had died in exile in 1943 in the Soviet Arctic. The chief scientific and administrative posts in the biological institutions were held by Michurinists and these constituted the great majority of the 56 persons who spoke. Only a half-dozen spoke in favor of G, some of these only after the violence of the denunciation forced them to their feet. At the end of the debate Lysenko announced that the Central Committee of the Communist Party had examined his report and approved it as the line of the party before the debate began. All except two who had defended G thereupon recanted their errors and submitted to the line. The few geneticists still remaining in positions of authority were removed from them, the rubric "genetics" disappeared from the publications of the USSR Ac. of S., and the victory of Michurinist biology was declared to be complete.

Although 1948 apparently marked the end of G in the USSR, there have been some indications of revival since the death of Stalin. Reviews of the progress of G in other countries appeared in *Botanichesky Zhurnal* in 1957, although these were followed later by the dismissal of the editorial board. "Genetics" has been retained in the titles of certain Institutes of the USSR Ac. of S. although its content appears to have been altered to conform to the official Michurinist line. At the tenth International Congress of Genetics held in Montreal in 1958, the dozen delegates from the USSR were all Michurinists, as judged by the contents of the papers which they presented, although papers by others, who did not attend, had been submitted. Articles again appear in *Doklady Akademii Nauk* under the heading "Genetics" and some of these are by geneticists who were discredited after the 1948 decisions of the Central Committee CPSU. But as of mid-1960 it is fair to say that the scientists of the USSR have not resumed their position of the 1930's as major contributors to G which has moved ahead rapidly in non-Communist countries.

BIBLIOGRAPHY: Th. Dobzhansky, *Russian Genetics: Symposium on Soviet Science*, Washington, D. C., 1951; P. S. Hudson and R. H. Richens, *The New Genetics in the Soviet Union*, Cambridge, 1946; J. S. Huxley, *Heredity East and West*, New York, 1949; Conway Zirkle, *Death of a Science in Russia*, Philadelphia, 1949; S. S. Chetverikov, "On Certain Aspects of the Evolutionary Process from the Standpoint of Modern Genetics," Translation with note by I. M. Lerner, *Proceedings of the American Philosophical Society*, Vol. 105, April 1961; David Joravsky, "Soviet Marxism and Biology before Lysenko," *Journal of the History of Ideas*, Vol. 20, January 1959.
L. C. D.

GENÍCHESK, town in Kherson Oblast, Ukrainian SSR, landing, Sea of Azov; pop. 14,300 (1956). Fish cannery, foundry, brick and textile plants.

GEOCHEMISTRY: *see* GEOLOGICAL SCIENCES.

GEODESY. In 1919, the Higher Geodesic Administration was founded and eventually reorganized into the Main Administration of Geodesy and Cartography (GUGK). The Central Scientific Research Institute of Geodesy and Aerial Mapping and Cartography (TsNIIGAK) in Moscow is the leading scientific geodesic institution in the USSR. Upon the initiative of F. N. Krasovsky the state triangulation network was established. A. A. Mikhyalov, M. S. Molodensky developed geodesic gravimetry.

GEOGRAPHIC ZONES. Broad natural belts of latitude differing one from another, each possessing its own more or less uniform climate, soil, and vegetation, gradually change on plains and medium plateaus. In mountain regions the natural zones usually have a vertical distribution. The following geographic zones are distinguished from N. to S.: arctic tundra, shrub tundra, wooded tundra, forests, forest steppe, steppe, semideserts of temperate zone, deserts of temperate zone, and subtropics. The wooded tundra, forest steppe, and the semideserts belong to the transitional zones, the others to the principal zones.

The Arctic Tundra is found on most of the large islands of the Arctic Ocean (Franz Josef Land, Severnaya Zemlya, and others) and on the N. of the Taymyr Peninsula, where the climate is severe. The mean temperature of the warmest month is close to 32°F (35°, 37°), and the average annual precipitation 8–10 in. Perennial permafrost covers the area. Vegetation in general is extremely scant: there are large expanses of spotty tundra; trees and shrubs are absent, with only small shrub willow in places. Mosses and lichens predominate, but there are some flowering plants. The soil horizon is thin, and the polygonal ground is widely distributed. Birds are abundant. Of the mammals, white bears are typical, also Arctic foxes, lemmings, and in places reindeer.

The Typical or Shrub Tundra lies mostly along the shores of the Arctic Ocean, reaches the Pacific Ocean, and occurs on some S. islands of the Arctic Ocean (Kolguyev, Vaygach, Bely, and others). The climate is somewhat warmer than that in the Arctic tundra; the mean temperature of the warmest month ranges from 40°F to 50°F, and even reaches 53.5°F. The average annual precipitation fluctuates from 16 in. in the European part to 8–10 in. in Eastern Siberia and 12–20 in. in the Far East. The permafrost is almost continuous, and bogs are numerous. Trees are very seldom found in the river valleys. The lichen-moss societies predominate, as well as shrubs (dwarf arctic birches and willows) and bog plants. In the central and S. areas the vegetation is partly continuous, partly interrupted by clayey patches. There occur gley soils, in the N.—latent gley soils. Characteristic are the Arctic fox, two types of lemmings, reindeer, wolf, and varying hare, as well as numerous migratory waterfowl, the willow and tundra ptarmigan, and the snowy owl. In

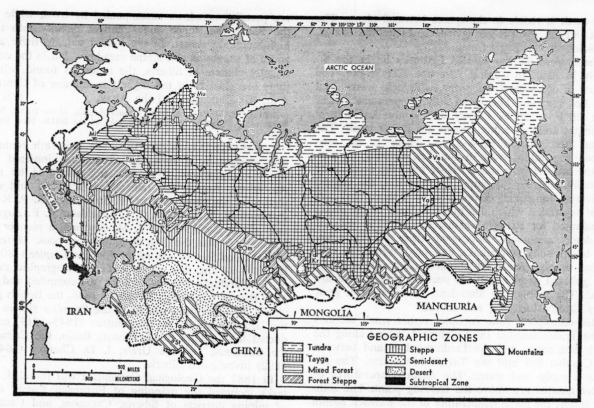

both the shrub and wooded tundras there are very many blood-sucking insects: mosquitoes and gadflies.

THE WOODED TUNDRA has a somewhat higher range of mean temperature of the warmest month (from 50°F to 57°F). Snowfall and freezing temperatures may come in this zone in any month. The average annual precipitation is 8–12 in., and the permafrost is almost continuous. The vegetation is characterized by a combination of tundra and forest and by the presence of particularly thin forests. The tundra-podzol and peat-bog soils predominate. Tundra animals are most numerous, but there are also forest animals, such as the elk, bear, glutton, squirrel, and others.

The Forest Zone occupies about one-half of the total area of the USSR. The climate is temperate. While the winter is severe and relatively long, the summer is warm, the mean summer temperature reaching 68°F. Permafrost is widespread in eastern areas. Annual precipitation is 20–24 in. in W. areas, around 8 in. in Central Siberia, and 20–36 in. in the Far East. The tayga or coniferous forests are most extensive. There occur also spruce, larch, fir, Siberian stone pine, and common pine. Deciduous species are of secondary importance. In the mixed forests the so-called "broad-leaved" species appear together with the conifers. In European Russia, oak, linden, maple, hornbeam, and ash predominate in forests; in the Far East, Mongolian oak, maple, and Manchurian ash are common. The podzol and bog soils are found in the tayga; the gray forest soils predominate in areas of mixed and broad-leaved forests. There is a great diversity of fauna. The squirrel, varying hare, fox, and ermine are common in the tayga, the elk, marten, and bear less com-

mon. In the mixed forests there are elk and the roe deer; in the broad-leaved forests, bear, fox, lynx, wolf, badger, ermine, and squirrel. The tiger and the panther are found in the Far East.

THE FOREST STEPPE is a zone of transition from the forest in the N. to the steppe in the S. In the typical forest steppe landscape, large masses of forest alternate with vast sections of steppe, or there are coppices scattered in patches over a background of steppe. The climate is temperate, but the summer is hot, with the average July temperature ranging from 68°F to 71.5°F. There are 14–22 in. of annual precipitation. The gray forest soils and chernozems are predominant.

The Steppe Zone is distinguished by a dry continental climate. The mean temperature for July ranges from 70°F to 73.5°F. The annual precipiation is 18 in. in the N. and 10 in. in the S. Droughts are common in the S.E. areas. The herbaceous vegetation predominates, with forests found only in the river valleys and in ravines. The chernozems and chestnut soils predominate, but there occur also the solonets soils. Small mammals are typical in the steppe, such as marmot, hamster, social meadow mouse, jerboa, and others. This zone and the forest steppe provide the best natural conditions for plant breeding.

THE SEMIDESERT ZONE constitutes the transition from the steppe to the desert. The climate is continental and dry. The winter is cold; the summer long and hot, with the average July temperature reaching 80°F. The annual precipitation is 8–12 in. and is exceeded by evaporation. The vegetation includes steppe (feather-grass) and desert (polyn, saltbush) forms; annuals ("ephemerals") are very prominent. In the semidesert bare earth is visible in the spaces between plants. The plant and soil cover is variegated, light chestnut, brown, and solonets soils being found.

The Deserts of the Middle Latitudes lie in the S., chiefly in Asia: in Central Asia and Kazakhstan. The climate is continental, very dry, with cold winter and very hot summer. The mean July temperature ranges from 80°F to 90°F. Clayey and sandy deserts predominate; areas of stony deserts are rather small. The annual precipitation is 4–8 in. There is no continuous vegetation cover in summer, autumn, or winter; the area of bare soil is larger than the area under vegetation. During the spring rainy season, the ground is covered, sometimes completely, by a short-lived carpet of vegetation which dies quickly. Many of the plants are adapted for struggle against dryness. The soils of the desert are poorly developed; there are serozems, gray-brown soils, solonchaks, and sandy soils. The desert has unique fauna. Of animals, saiga antelope, jerboa, goitered gazelle, and the peculiar barkhan cat are found. The reptiles are abundant, among them a great many lizards, tortoises, and snakes.

The subtropical zone occupies rather small sections of the Transcaucasus: the Colchian Lowland along the Black Sea coast, and the Lenkoran Lowland between the Caspian Sea and the Talysh Mountains. The climate is moist and warm. The mean temperatures of winter months are above the freezing point. The summer is hot: the mean temperature of the warmest month is 73°–75°F. There is much precipitation, more than 40 in. annually—in some places as much as 100 in. Plant life is unusually luxuriant; broad-leaved forests have an admixture of evergreen plants, and a profusion of vines and ferns. Brown forest soils predominate, but there also occur red soils on the foothills. Of animals, wild boars, porcupines, and panthers should be mentioned. Along the S. coast of the Crimea and the W. coast of the Caucasus, there are sections of subtropics which lie on the N. outskirts of the region with Mediterranean climate. The summer is dry and hot, the winter rainy. Small areas of dry subtropics are located in Central Asia.

Vertical zones are found in mountainous regions, such as the Caucasus, the Pamir Mountains, the Tien Shan, the Altay, and others. These zones differ one from other in their climate, soils, vegetation, and fauna. The lower zone usually is a continuation of the zone adjoining the foothills of a corresponding mountain system, e.g., the steppe zone on the N. slope of the Caucasus Range, the desert zone on the Tien Shan, the forest zone on the Sikhote-Alin, and so on. On these mountains the vertical distribution of zones approximates in altitude that of more northerly latitudes. Thus, in the central section of the N. slope of the Caucasus Range, the steppe zone gives place in a higher altitude to the forest steppe, and this in turn to the forests. Or, as in the Tien Shan, the desert zone changes into the semidesert, and still higher the semidesert into the steppe. However, the order of zones differs in these ranges, because of local climatic conditions. For example, owing to low precipitation, the forests are absent in many sections of the Tien Shan, but there

are peculiar meadows accompanied by trees, while in the Pamir the steppe zone changes directly into the high-mountain desert. In the humid climate there are zones of subalpine and alpine meadows; but in the continental climate of Siberia, the tundra is found, while there are glaciers in the highest mountains of Central Asia, the Caucasus and the Altay.   L. D.

BIBLIOGRAPHY: L. S. Berg, *Natural Regions of the USSR*, New York, 1950; Theodore Shabad, *Geography of the USSR*, New York, 1951.

GEOLOGICAL SCIENCES. The late 18th century was marked by a series of expeditions initiated by M. V. Lomonosov (1711–65) and sponsored by the Ac. of Sc. Among the outstanding travelers and explorers of the time were M. F. Soymonov, S. P. Krasheninnikov, P. S. Pallas, I. I. Lepekhin, V. F. Zuyev, and others. Academician V. M. Severgin, a pioneer of Russian G, was the first to publish a book *Mineralogical Land Description of the Russian Empire* (1809). In 1789–94 the first geologic and petrographic map of the Nerchinsk Mining District was compiled and in 1829 that of the Donets Ridge. In 1846, the British geologist R. Murchison described the Permian system in the Urals. Prof. A. A. Inostrantsev (1843–1919) conducted field studies in the Donets Basin, the Crimea, the Caucasus, and the Urals; I. D. Chersky (1845–1892) investigated Siberia.

In 1882 the Geological Committee was founded; its tasks included the mapping of European Russia and of mining districts of Siberia, Caucasus, and Central Asia. Such eminent geologists of the late 19th and early 20th century as A. P. Karpinsky, F. N. Chernyshev, N. I. Andrusov, V. A. Obruchev, and L. I. Lutugin participated in the work of the Geological Committee. Schools of G at Moscow and Kazan universities were established toward the end of the 19th century.

In the 1890's, the Geological Committee headed by L. I. Lutugin (1864–1915) initiated a geological survey of the Donets Basin. Important geological investigations were conducted along the Trans-Siberian R. R. and in the gold-bearing areas of Siberia. V. A. Obruchev who participated in these projects is the author of numerous papers on tectonics and ore deposits in Asia, permafrost and glacial deposits. The oil fields of Caucasus were surveyed by N. I. Andrusov (1861–1924) and I. M. Gubkin (1871–1939). The Geological Committee was also engaged in the publication of papers on regional G and paleontology. A. P. Karpinsky (1846–1936) was one of the most prominent theoreticians and the author of numerous books on tectonics, stratigraphy, paleontology, petrography, and mineral resources. These achievements inspired a statement made by Academician F. N. Chernyshev at the 7th International Geologic Congress in St. Petersburg: "At this congress Russian geological investigations have proved to be equal to West European and American geological studies which begun much earlier. We may assume that Russia will become a source of information for the solution of numerous problems of modern geology."

Soviet industrialization with its requirements of tremendous amounts of coal, petroleum, and metals called for a rapid development of geological investigations.

Geological institutions were reorganized. In 1930, the Geological Committee was transformed into the Chief Administration of Geology and Prospecting, to become in 1946, the All-Union Ministry of Geology and Mineral Resources. The Ac. of S. gradually expanded its geological research and now includes numerous research institutions engaged in the geological investigations (Geological Institute, Institute for the Study of Geology of Ore Deposits, Petrography, Mineralogy, and Geochemistry, Petroleum Institute, and others). Geological investigations are also carried out by institutes of Ac. of Sciences of national Soviet republics, by research institutes attached to ministries, by universities and branches of the Ac. of S.

In 1957 some 98% of the territory of the USSR was covered by the geological surveys. Hundreds of deep core holes were drilled to yield data on a variety of major geological problems. More than a hundred core holes reached the Precambrian basement of the East European Platform. Geological maps of the USSR at the scales 1:5,000,000 and 1:2,500,000 were published. A new tectonic map of the USSR was compiled in 1956. Soviet geologists have published a number of theoretical studies, generalizing the accumulated new data.

Modern methods have been introduced in all fields of geology. Pore-pollen analysis, micropaleontological investigations and the radiocarbon method have been widely applied to stratigraphy whose achievements are summarized in *Stratigraphic Dictionary of the USSR*, 1956. Detailed geological studies of mountainous regions contributed to the development of tectonics. New theories of orogenesis were advanced (M. Tetyayev, V. A. Obruchev, M. A. Usov, and V. A. Belousov). Modern ideas in the field of tectonics are summarized in Belousov's *Fundamental Problems of Tectonics* (1954).

MINERALOGY. The development of mineralogy was closely associated with the development of mining in Russia. The Urals was the cradle of Russian mineralogy. M. V. Lomonosov who studied mineralogy in Freiberg, Saxony, was a pioneer in this field; he organized the mineralogical collection of the Ac. of S. and planned the mineralogical studies throughout all the territory of the Russian Empire. In 1773 the School of Mining (later the Institute of Mining) was founded in St. Petersburg. Simultaneously the All-Russian Mineralogical Society was organized.

In the 19th century, the mineralogical studies in Russia were concentrated around these two institutions. The most prominent mineralogists were S. S. Kutorga, N. I. Koksharov, P. V. Yeremeyev, A. P. Karpinsky, A. A. Inostrantsev, and F. Yu. Levinson-Lessing. Ye. S. Fedorov (1853–1919) introduced new methods of microscopic mineralogical studies.

Mineralogical investigations in the USSR have been devoted to many practical and theoretical problems such as genetic mineralogy (V. I. Vernadsky, A. Ye. Fersman, N. M. Fedorovsky, and others), the study of mineral associations and processes of mineral formation: pegmatites (A. Ye. Fersman), the weathered crust (I. I. Ginzburg), mineralogy of clays (P. A. Zemyatchensky), mineralogy of sedimentary rocks (N. M. Strakhov and Ye. K. Lazarenko), colloidal mineralogy (F. V. Chukhrov). Modern instrumental methods of investigations were used. Many important publications appeared, as *Minerals of the USSR*, 2 volumes, 1940; *Minerals of Khibiny and Lovozero Tundras*. 1937; *Mineralogy of the Urals*, 1941, and others.

GEOCHEMISTRY V. I. Vernadsky (1863–1945), professor of mineralogy at the University of Moscow, was the first to formulate early in the 20th century the scope and the tasks of modern geochemistry. He developed ideas of genetic mineralogy and advanced concepts of a leading role of radioactive disintegration in energetic processes transforming the earth.

The geochemical studies in the USSR have been closely associated with the work in the field of economic geology. Many theoretical problems were developed, such as the theory of migration of chemical elements under various conditions of the earth's crust, the study of individual agents influencing migration of elements (A. Ye. Fersman, D. S. Korzhinsky, N. V. Belov, A. F. Kapustinsky, V. V. Shcherbina). Geochemical peculiarities of certain natural processes were studied, such as the formation of pegmatites (A. Ye. Fersman), hydrothermal (A. N. Zavaritsky, S. S. Smirnov, A. G. Betekhtin) and hypergenic (B. B. Polynov, S. S. Smirnov, I. I. Ginzburg) processes. Biogeochemistry developed into an independent science (V. I. Vernadsky, Ya. V. Samoylov, A. P. Vinogradov). Geochemical methods (metallometry, hydro- and biogeochemical methods) of search for mineral reserves were developed and have been widely applied. Many important publications appeared such as, V. I. Vernadsky, *Essays on Geochemistry (Selected Works*, Vol. I, 1954); A. Ye. Fersman, *Geochemistry*, 4 volumes, 1933–39; A. P. Vinogradov, *Geochemistry of Rare and Disseminated Elements in Soils*, 1950; A. A. Saukov, *Geochemistry*, 2nd. ed., 1951; V. V. Shcherbina, *Geochemistry*, 1939.

PETROGRAPHY. In the field of petrography, of great importance are regional-petrographic studies of vast areas in Asia. Detailed works were carried out on the Kola Peninsula, the Ukrainian Crystalline Shield, the Urals, and the Caucasus. Volcanic phenomena were studied on Kamchatka, the Kuril Islands, and in Transcarpathia. Many theoretical problems related to magmatism, petrotectonics, metamorphism, and others were elaborated.

Demands of oil, coal, and chemical industries facilitated the studies of sedimentary rocks. Physical properties of oil-reservoir rocks have been widely studied. Yu. A. Zhemchuzhnikov contributed to the development of coal petrography and elaborated the method of facies cyclic analysis. Modern instrumental methods have been applied to the study of clay minerals. Many theoretical problems were studied related to the conditions of sediments accumulation and contributing to a better understanding of geologic history (A. D. Arkhangelsky, N. M. Strakhov, L. V. Pustovalov, N. S. Shtatsky, and M. S. Shvetsov).

PALEONTOLOGY. Voluminous material has been accumulated in the field of paleontology. Paleozoological investigations covered all the groups of fossils, being concentrated on morphological and taxonomic studies, as well as on the clarifying of stratigraphic significance of certain organisms. New fields of research were developed. A. V. Martynov was a pioneer in paleoentomological studies. Of many expeditions, that to the Mongolian People's Republic (1946–49, I. A. Yefremov) is of special importance: valuable material on Mesozoic reptiles and tertiary mammals were collected, significant for the further development of the evolutionary theory. The most important paleobotanical works were conducted by A. N. Krishtofovich who, on the basis of his studies of the Mesozoic and Tertiary floras of the USSR, advanced hypotheses on the history of the Palearctic flora, and by M. D. Zalessky who studied Paleozoic floras, especially in the Donets Basin. Numerous laboratories engaged in micropaleotological investigations and pore pollen analysis meet demands of petroleum geology and contribute data for the elaboration of the problems of stratigraphy. Beginning with the mid-thirties, *Paleontology of the USSR* has been published, planned as a series of monographs describing all fossil animals and plants found in the USSR.

GEOPHYSICS. Several research institutions (the most important belong to the system of the Ac. of S. of the USSR) are engaged in geophysical investigations which comprise both the basic research and the elaboration of problems having a practical importance. Important achievements were made in the study of the earth's interior where modern theories related to the physics of solid body were applied. The influence of the radioactive heating on the thermal history of the earth has been studied (Ye. A. Lyubimova). An expanding network of seismic stations contributed to the development of seismology. Principles of nuclear physics have been applied to the investigation of composition of rocks penetrated by drilling holes. Geophysical surveying has been widely applied using gravimetric, magnetometric, seismic, electric, and electronic methods. Soviet scientists took an active part in the International Geophysical Year, 1957–58.

ECONOMIC GEOLOGY has been the field of rapid progress. Theoretical investigations related to the ore formation were conducted and new regularities in the ore occurrence established. They facilitated a discovery of many new deposits of metals: platinum, tin, copper, lead, zinc, iron, manganese, and others; the largest in the world deposit of potassium salts was discovered in Solikamsk (Urals region), apatite-nepheline rocks were discovered on the Kola Peninsula; diamonds were found in Yakutia in 1954. The regularities in the coal formation and in the distribution of coal basins were studied. It was established that the reserves of the Donets Basin stretch far beyond the area with the outcrops of coal seams. The Pechora, Kuznetsk, and Karaganda coal basins were explored in detail. New coal reserves were discovered in the Tunguska Basin, on the Taymyr Peninsula, in Yakutia and in Khabarovsk Kray. New oil fields were discovered and put in operation as a result of systematic geological and geophysical explorations and prospecting; the most important oil fields are located within the Volga-Ural oil region.

Many research institutions have been engaged in hydrogeological investigations, hydrogeological surveying and observation of ground water regime in many areas. New artesian basins were discovered in several semi-arid areas of the USSR. A theory of hydrogeological zonality was advanced by F. P. Savarensky.

The construction program carried out in the USSR during the last few decades has stimulated development of engineering geology and soil mechanics. Voluminous field studies were conducted, theoretical investigations carried out in laboratories, and observational data on formerly constructed structures have been collected and evaluated.

The science of frozen deposits (geocryology) came into being in connection with the necessity of building large industrial structures on frozen soils. The investigations of frozen soils have been concentrated in the Permafrost Institute of the Ac. of S. of the USSR. M. I. Sumgin and N. A. Tsytovich are pioneers in this field.

BIBLIOGRAPHY: D. V. Nalivkin, *The Geology of the U.S.S.R.* A short outline. Translation from Russian. New York, 1960; N. S. Shatzki and A. A. Bogdanoff, "Explanatory Notes on the Tectonic Map of the USSR and Adjoining Countries," *International Geology Review*, Vol. 1, No. 1, 1959, Washington.   N. E.; L. D.

GEOLOGICAL STRUCTURE. There is great diversity of geologic conditions in the USSR—diversity of constituent rock formations, of their distribution and structural arrangements, and of the mineral deposits which they contain. Geological history witnessed a transformation of ancient geosynclinal regions into platforms, whose areas increased, gradually forming a huge massif which occupies now the greatest part of the USSR. Every important rock system is represented. Geologically the USSR may be divided into six large regions, differing from one another in their structure and geological history: the E. European and Siberian platforms, the Ural-Altay, Maritime-Chukchi, Alpine, and the Pacific Coast. Two of these regions—the E. European and Siberian platforms—have Precambrian folded basements built of the older sedimentary rocks which had been metamorphosed partly into gneisses and schists, and pierced by many intrusions, mostly of granites—these processes ending in Precambrian times. The folded basements are overlain by sedimentary almost horizontal strata of the Paleozoic, Mesozoic, and Cenozoic eras; in places these strata are slightly dislocated. Two other regions have folded basements of younger age: the Ural-Altay resting upon the Paleozoic foundation, and the Mesozoic basement underlying the Maritime-Chukchi region which includes N.E. Siberia, E. Transbaykalia, the Maritime Kray, and low reaches of the Amur River. These four regions cover the greatest part of the area of the USSR. From the S. they are ringed by the zone of Alpine folding, in which are the Carpathians, the Crimea, the Caucasus, Kopet Dagh, and the Pamir. From the E., the platform region of N.E. Asia borders on the zone of the most recent folding of the Pacific coast, to which the Koryak Range, Kamchatka, Sakhalin, and the Kuril Islands belong. Prevailing opinion among geologists now is that these two zones of recent folding present "live" geosynclinal regions. All the strata within these zones, including the Upper Tertiary rocks, are folded; the contemporary tectonic activity is shown in the form of intensive recent vertical movements, volcanism and earthquakes.

The E. European platform occupies a large part of European Russia. The surface of its folded basement is uneven. Occasionally the ancient rock formations are exposed, forming the Baltic and the Ukrainian crystalline shields. There are the Voronezh, Byelorussian, Volga-Ural, and Timan uplifts where crystalline rocks lie close to the surface and in places form outcrops. Of numerous depressions (synclises) in the basement of the platform, the Moscow and the Caspian synclises are the largest. The immense *Moscow Basin* contains mainly Paleozoic rocks with some Mesozoic deposits, the thickness of these sedimentary rocks being 1–2 mi. But the depth of the Caspian synclise is 3.7–6 mi. There are also the Polish-Lithuanian, Dnieper-Donets, Black Sea, and Pechora synclises. Many depressions have slopes complicated by terraces and ridges. The ridges of the Volga-Ural area are associated with the oil and gas fields. Salt domes occur in the central parts of the Dnieper-Donets and Caspian synclises. In the latter they are associated with the *Ural-Emba oil fields*. The E. European platform is separated from the folded structures of the Urals by a deep trough filled with Carboniferous and Permian rocks. The latter are associated with deposits of potassium salts (Solikamsk), oil (Ishimbayevo), and coal (Vorkuta). A similar trough was discovered by the borings in the Astrakhan area. *The Donets Basin* (q.v.) forms a continuation of this trough which penetrates into the E. European platform, and is built of Carboniferous coal-bearing rocks and Permian rocks which are salt-bearing in places.

The Siberian platform covers the greatest part of E. Siberia. The surface of the folded basement forms uplifts and depressions. The Baykal-Aldan shield occupies the Baykal area, W. Transbaykalia, and the Aldan plateau. On the W. edge of the platform, the folded basement outcrops in the crests of large uplifts striking N. across the Yenisey River. The Anabar uplift lies in the N. The Tunguska synclise is the largest depression and is filled with Cambrian, Ordovician, and Silurian marine deposits, in the N.—with Devonian and Low Carboniferous marine sediments, as well as with coal-bearing deposits of the Tunguska series (Carboniferous and Trias). The Angara-Lena depression is filled with Cambrian sediments, including deposits of rock salt, and with Ordovician and Silurian deposits. The Khatanga depression rings the platform in the N. and is filled with Paleozoic and Mesozoic sediments, where salt domes occur.

The Ural-Altay region lies between the E. European and Siberian platforms and encloses the Urals, Central and E. Kazakhstan, Tien Shan, Altay, the Salair Ridge, the Kuznetsk Basin, the Kuznetsk Alatau Mountains, the S.W. slope of the E. and W. Sayan Mountains, the Minusinsk depression, Tuva, and the Taymyr Peninsula. The folded basement of this region is built of the Precambrian and Paleozoic metamorphized sedimentary rocks, as well as of effusives and magmatic intrusions. The rocks form complicated folded structures—anticlinal uplifts and synclinal depressions with different orientations; e.g., in the Urals they are oriented meridionally, but in Tien Shan stretch mostly in the latitudinal and N.W. direction. All the folded structures were formed in the Paleozoic era. Some of them belong to the older Caledonian folded formations, such as the Sayans, the Kuznetsk Alatau, and the E. part of Tuva; the others belong to the younger Hercynian folded formations, such as the

Urals, Kazakhstan, Tien Shan, Taymyr. The Urals are an example of one of the largest linear folded systems with a consistent strike of its principal structural elements. The anticlinorium Ural-Tau built of schists stretches most of the length of the Urals. In the Urals, iron ore is abundant; there are also extensive copper deposits with combinations of zinc, lead, silver, and gold; and platinum and gold are found in placers. The Altay Mountains, which are rich in polymetallic ores, have a folded basement lying at a considerable depth within the depressions. The Minusinsk depression is filled with slightly dislocated Devonian and Carboniferous rocks, as well as Permian rocks with which several coal deposits are associated. The coal-bearing Jurassic sediments occur widely in the Chulym-Yenisey depression. Two large depressions—the Naryn and Fergana—lie between the ranges of Tien Shan and the Alau mountain systems. The brown coal deposits of the Jurassic age and the Upper Tertiary oil fields occur within the Fergana depression. The Karaganda coal basin is located in a synclinorium within the E. Kazakhstan folded system. The depression of the *Kuznetsk Basin* (q.v.) is filled with the thick accumulation of continental Carboniferous and Permian coal-bearing sediments, as well as with Triassic, Jurassic, and Cretaceous rocks.

The Maritime-Chukchi region lies to the E. from the Siberian platform. Its basement is built of Mesozoic folded structures. The Okhotsk Sea divides it into two parts: the Verkhoyansk-Chukchi, which occupies almost all the N.E. corner of Asia; and the Amur-Maritime, which includes E. Transbaykalia, low reaches of the Amur, and the Maritime Kray. The Verkhoyansk-Chukchi part is complex in structure, containing a number of ancient inner blocks surrounded by systems of large folded zones, The largest block is the Kolyma massif in the extreme W. A huge folded arch stretches from the Chukchi Peninsula to the W., along the coast of the E. Siberian Sea, then turns to the S. and S.E., and approaches the Okhotsk Sea. It consists of several mountain chains, including the Polousny and Chersky Ranges. Numerous anticlinal structures stretch parallel to the arch, having cores of Paleozoic rocks and, in places, of Precambrian schists. Their flanks, and areas between anticlinaria, are built of Triassic, Jurassic, and here and there Low Cretaceous rocks. These rocks also fill the deep depressions. The Amur-Maritime part is divided into two sections. One—the East Transbaykalian—rings the Siberian platform at the S.E. and has the N.E. orientation. The second, the maritime section, stretches from the low reaches of the Amur River through the Sikhote-Alin Range to the coasts of the Japanese Sea. These two sections are separated by the Bureya massif built of folded Precambrian and Paleozoic rocks covered by Cretaceous and Tertiary continental deposits. The Bureya coal-bearing basin lies at the N.E. edge of the massif. In E. Transbaykalia, Jurassic marine and continental sediments, together with Paleozoic and Precambrian rocks, form complicated folded structures with granite intrusions. Tin and polymetallic deposits of Transbaykalia are associated with these intrusions. In the maritime section

there occur numerous folded structures, of which the largest are: the anticlinal uplifts of Sikhote-Alin, Ussuriysk, Maritime, and the Komsomolsk area. Mostly Permian and Carboniferous rocks outcrop in their cores, although Precambrian rocks are present in places. The separating synclinal structures are filled with Triassic, Jurassic, and Low Cretaceous deposits which are coal-bearing in places. Low Tertiary brown coal deposits are found in some depressions.

The Alpine region. A part of the N. edge of the Alpine geosynclinal region stretches from the Carpathians in the W. to the Pamir in the E. A system of large troughs or depressions is found in this region adjoining the chain of the anticlinal uplifts lying along the N. edge and including the E. Carpathians, the mountainous Crimea, the Main Caucasus Range, the Great Balkhan and Kuvadag ranges (E. of the Caspian Sea), the Turkmen-Khorasan Mountains, Kopet Dagh and N. Pamir. A system of marginal troughs separated by gentle transverse uplands lies in the N. between the anticlinal uplifts and the platforms. In the S. the uplifts border on two large and deep troughs filled by the Black Sea and the S. part of the Caspian Sea. The continuation of the Black Sea depression is found in the trough occupied by the Rion Lowland; the S. Caspian depression continues as the Kura-Araks Lowland. Southwards there lies the Little Caucasus which belongs to the inner zone of the Alpine geosynclinal region, just as the S. and Central Pamir. The Great Caucasus is the largest of the anticlinal uplifts. Its core consists of Precambrian and Paleozoic rocks; its limbs built of Jurassic, Cretaceous, and Tertiary rocks; its E. and W. ends submerged. The oil fields of the Apsheron Peninsula are associated with the E. region of submergence. N. of the Caucasus lie two narrow marginal troughs separated by the Stavropol Plateau. The Grozny and Kuban oil fields are associated with these troughs. The Crimean anticlinorium is built by Jurassic, Cretaceous, and Low Tertiary rocks, its S. flank subsided under the sea level. The Precambrian or Paleozoic schists outcrop in the E. Carpathians. Their E. limbs consist of a Flysch formation of Cretaceous and Paleocene, associated with the Boryslav oil fields. On the E., the Carpathian uplift borders on the narrow foreland trough filled with the Upper Tertiary formations bearing deposits of gases and potash (Dashava). E. of the Caspian Sea is situated the uplift of the Great Balkhan whose W. part lies under sea level. The Kopet Dagh forms the N. margin of the complicated system of the Turkmen-Khorasan Mountains in Iran. The N. Pamir is a very complicated system built mostly of Paleozoic rocks. To the S. there lies the synclinal structure of the Central Pamir built of folded Mesozoic sediments. Still further S. the second large uplift of the S. Pamir is located, built of the schists and other Precambrian and Paleozoic rocks. An immense Tadzhik depression, filled with the Mesozoic and Tertiary sediments, stretches between the Pamir and the Tien Shan. The Alpine region is evidently in the final stage of the geosynclinal development, as this region is considerably uplifted and ringed by marginal troughs which always appear in the final stage of the existence of geosynclines.

The Pacific Coast. The extreme E. part of the USSR contains the most recent geosynclinal formations associated with Cenozoic folding of the Pacific belt. Just as in the Alpine region, here are found several large anticlinal uplifts and depressions. Two parallel uplifts lie in Kamchatka: the Central and the E. anticlinoria separated by the syncline. The extinct volcanoes are associated with the Central uplift and the active ones with the E. uplift. The anticlinoria are continued in the N. in the folded structures of the Koryak Range, and in the S. in the Kuril Islands Ridge. The latter presents an uplift consisting of two crests separated by an elongated depression. These crests evidently are contemporaneous geoanticlines: the cones of acting volcanoes tower on the W. crest above sea level forming the chain of islands, whereas mostly submarine volcanoes are found on the E. crest. These uplifts are adjoined by depressions in the sea bottom which present deep synclinal troughs. Sakhalin contains two large anticlinoria separated by an intermediate synclinorium built of the Cretaceous and Tertiary sediments including the coal-bearing formations. Contrary to the Alpine region, the Pacific Coast region is now in an early stage of the geosynclinal development.

BIBLIOGRAPHY: D. V. Nalivkin, *The Geology of the U.S.S.R. A short outline.* Translation from Russian. New York, 1960; N. S. Shatzki and A. A. Bogdanoff, "Explanatory Notes on the Tectonic Map of the USSR and Adjoining Countries," *International Geology Review*, Vol. 1, No. 1, 1959, Washington.   L. D.

GEOPHYSICS: *see* GEOLOGICAL SCIENCES.

GEORGIAN MILITARY ROAD through Caucasus mountains (Krestovy pass, 7,830 ft.) from Ordzhonikidze to Tbilisi; length 128 mi. Bus communication; excellent vistas; tourism.

GEORGIAN SOVIET SOCIALIST REPUBLIC (GEORGIA, R. *Grúzia*, Georgian *Sakártvelo*, ancient *Ibéria*), is located in the central western part of Transcaucasia and borders on Turkey and the Armenian SSR in the S., Azerbaijan SSR in the E., and the N. Caucasian areas of the RSFSR in the N. It includes

the Abkhaz and the Adzhar Autonomous SSR's and the South-Ossetian Autonomous Oblast. Area, 26,900 sq. mi. Capital, Tbilisi (Tiflis) (695,000); other cities, Kutaisi (128,000), Sukhumi (64,000), Batumi (82,000), Chiatura (19,200).

Population of G is 4,044,000 (1959); out of this total, 2,558,000 (63.3%) are Georgians, 443,000 Armenians (11%), 141,000 Ossetians (3.5%), 71,000 Abkhazians (1.8%). Russians constitute 10.8% (438,000); they were only 4.9% in 1917, and 8.7% in 1939. Among other groups are: Azeri Turks, 157,000 (3.9%); Greeks, 73,000 (1.8%); Ukrainians, 52,000 (1.3%); Jews, 52,000 (1.3%); Kurds, 16,000 (0.4%); misc., 43,000 (0.9%). Density of population is 150 per sq. mi.

Nature and Climate. G is bounded by the chains of the Greater Caucasus in the N., by the Lesser Caucasus in the S., and by the Black Sea in the W. The littoral and the Rion plains are warm and humid and enjoy a subtropical climate, with over 80 inches of yearly rainfall, and an average temperature of 42.8° F in Jan., 73.4° in July. The E. part has a continental climate —20°F in Feb., 75° in July—and is considerably drier, with about 20 inches of yearly precipitation.

National Economy. G is almost the only region of the USSR where subtropical crops like tea and citrus can grow (on the littoral). It also produces tobacco, almonds, wine, silk, non-citrus fruits as well as corn and sugar beets. There is sheep and goat farming in mountain pastures.

The Chiatura manganese mines are second in the world. Hydroelectric stations, coal mines, and oil refineries (processing mostly Baku oil) provide a sound energetic base for the G economy. Metallurgy, machine building (including a truck factory), and the building-material industry are of recent origin but growing rapidly.

History. The first G state emerged in the 4th century B.C. after the destruction of the Persian empire by Alexander the Great. In the 1st century B.C. Roman "friendship" was imposed upon G. Christianity was introduced in the 4th century A.D. and since the 5th century the G church has been independent from Byzantium. Beginning with the 6th century G was involved in the Persian-Byzantine struggle and was independent for short periods only. As a result of Arab invasion an emirate was established in Tiflis in the 7th century. The local Bagrat dynasty grew in power, however, and during the 11th century managed to restore the unity of the country. The first invasion by Seljuk Turks put an end to G independence. The crusades forced the Turks to turn their attention elsewhere and David II, The Restorer, liberated Tiflis in 1122 and extended the borders of G. A century later (1220) Genghiz-Khan's hordes appeared at G borders and in 1236 the Mongols conquered the country. In the first part of the 14th century G freed herself again, but in 1386 Timur, master of Central Asia, entered Tiflis and plundered the country. After another attempt at unity and independence (beginning of 15th century), G was divided into several principalities; these managed to survive throughout the 16th and 17th centuries because of Turkish-Persian rivalries. After 1639 Kartlia and Kakhetia remained under Persian protectorate while the rest of G had to accept Turkish domination. In 1772 Russians appeared at G borders, by which time the kings of Kakhetia had managed to unify Kakhetia and Kartlia. In 1783 Irakli II of Kakhetia, for the price of a military alliance, recognized R. suzerainty. A Persian invasion (1795) left Tiflis in ruins, but at Irakli's death in 1801 both Kartlia and Kakhetia were incorporated into the Russian Empire. During the next three-quarters of a century Russia took away one by one and annexed all G lands under Turkish control: Imeretia (1810), Guria (1830), Mingrelia (1857), Svanetia (1864), Abkhazia (1867), and Samtshke (1878).

By the end of the 19th century nationalist movements developed in G headed by Ilia Chavchavadze and George Tsereteli. In 1893 a social-democratic group was organized by Noah Zhordania and Karlo Chkheidze under the name of "Mesame-Dasi." In 1898 V. Ketskhoveli, A. Tsulukidze, I. V. Dzhugashvili (Stalin), and their friends formed the extremist wing of the movement.

The February revolution of 1917 and the collapse of R. armies resulted in the formation of the Transcaucasian Federation (Georgia, Armenia, and Azerbaijan) headed by Akaky Chkhenkeli, who signed a separate peace treaty with Germany. After the German defeat of 1918, the Federation broke down. The Menshevik Zhordania formed the new G government which gained allied and Soviet recognition in 1920. In Feb. 1921 G faced both Turkish and Soviet intervention. Soviet troops entered Tiflis, and a Soviet-Turkish treaty was signed in March 1921, establishing the present borders between the two countries. A G Revkom (Revolutionary Committee) was established with P. Makharadze as chairman. The real ruler of the country was, however, Sergo Ordzhonikidze, political commissar of the 11th red army. On his and Joseph Stalin's initiative (Stalin was then People's Commissar for Nationalities in Moscow), Makharadze, Mdivani, and their friends were ousted as too nationalistically-minded. The Transcaucasian Socialist Federated Soviet Republic was formed in Dec. 1922 and immediately joined the USSR. The 1924 anti-Soviet rising led by K. Cholokashvili was put down by the Red Army. During the purges of 1930 and those that followed, many prominent Soviet G leaders were liquidated, including M. Orachelashvili, A. Yenukidze, B. Mdivani, and S. Eliava.

In 1952 K. Charkviany, secretary of the central committee of the Georgian CP and several other high officials were purged for nationalist deviation. After Stalin's death, Beria carried out two more purges in G. The "thaw" of 1956 was reflected in G by political demonstrations in the streets of Tbilisi.

Culture. The oldest literary monument of the area —the Amirami epic—dates back to the second millennium B.C. The first written inscriptions (5th century A.D.) were in Aramean script. The old G script was in use between the 5th century and the 11th century, when religious literature flourished. The new script came into existence in the middle of the 11th century with the development of secular literature. The most important G epic—*The Knight in the Tiger Skin*—was written in the 12th century by Shota Rustaveli. Best known writers of the 17th and 18th centuries are S. Orbeliani and D. Guramishvili; of the 19th century, N. Baratashvili, A. Chavchavadze, and G. Orbeliani. I. Chavchavadze and A. Tsereteli wrote at the turn of the century. At the beginning of the 20th century both symbolist (T. Tabidze) and proletarian literature (I. Evdoshvili) developed. Among writers of the Soviet period one can mention L. Kiacheli, N. Lordkipanidze, G. Tabidze, N. Nadiradze, S. Chikovani, G. Leonidze, A. Mirtskhulava. Greatest modern G poets Paolo Yashvili and Titian Tabidze perished during the purges of 1937–38.

G. decorative art dates back to the second and the first millennia B.C. and consists of gold, silver, and bronze ornaments. Small sculpture and ceramics came next, followed by stone sculpture; stone carvings and

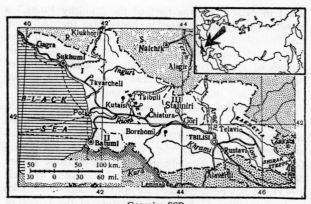

Georgian SSR
(I—Abkhaz ASSR; II—Adzhar ASSR; III—S. Ossetian Aut. Obl.)

miniatures in the middle ages. (The most famous G miniaturist was Tevdore in the 11th century.) Metal stamping flourished in the 11th to the 13th centuries. Since the 19th century, R. influence has been predominant. In architecture, some old ruins date back to the first millennium B.C. During the 4th and 5th centuries A.D. a number of stone churches were built (such as Bolni and Sion basilicas); sculpture flourished in the 7th century in the center dome-shaped temples (Dzhvari, Vana). During the 9th and 10th centuries cross dome-shaped temples were built, such as the Sveti-Tskhoveli Cathedral in Mtskhet and the Alaverdi Cathedral in Kakhetia. The structures erected in the 12th and 13th centuries were poorer. During the 16th to the 18th centuries several forts (Anamuri and others), bridges, and other secular structures were built, with brick replacing stone as building material. Starting with the 19th century, the R. influence has dominated the architecture.

G music is generally polyphonic. Church music began in the 4th century, church singing in the 9th. Between the 9th century and the 17th century little progress was made, but the 18th century brought a revival of old G music. Professional music was introduced in the 19th century and the Tiflis Opera opened in 1851. Among well-known contemporary G composers are Kiladze, Mshvelidze, and Taktakishvili. Folk dances are widespread in G.   M. R.

GERÁSIMOV, Aleksándr Mikháylovich (1881–), painter, studied under Konstantin Korovin. G's early work included portraits (*V. A. Gilyarosky,* 1912) and landscapes (*Winter Troyka,* 1914). After the revolution he turned to political subjects, particularly the glorification of Stalin: *Stalin and Gorky, V. I. Lenin on the Tribune,* portraits of Molotov, Nehru. A member of the Communist party since 1950, has been twice elected deputy to the Supreme Soviet. In 1952 he was elected chairman of the Union of Soviet Artists. For many years G was Stalin's "court painter"; he was criticized after the 20th Party Congress for having advanced the "cult of personality."

GERÁSIMOV, Mikhaíl Prokófyevich (1889–1939), poet and prose writer. An old Bolshevik, he had lived in exile in Europe for many years. Appointed to an executive position in the CP (1918); resigned (1921) in disagreement with its policies. Arrested in 1938, G perished in prison. G was part of the "Smithy Poets," a Moscow group of proletarian poets who seceded from the *Proletkult* (1920). He extolled the October revolution in ecstatic hymns and resorted to certain cosmic images of symbolism to celebrate the achievements of industrialization. His collected poems *Black Froth* (1921–22) are marked by disillusion.

GERÁSIMOV, Sergéy Vasílyevich (1885–), painter. After studying under Korovin and others, he painted chiefly still life and portraits. Later he dealt with peasant themes (*Village Soviet*, 1925) and the revolution (*October*, 1932). Despite this and the patriotic nature of his work during World War II (*A Partisan's Mother*, 1943), he has been rebuked for impressionist tendencies by Soviet critics. G has been secretary of the Union of Soviet Artists since 1957.

GÉRMAN, Aleksándr Petróvich (1874–1953), mining engineer. Fellow, Ac. of S., USSR (1939). Graduate of St. Petersburg University (1897) and Mining Institute (1903); professor, St. Petersburg Mining Institute (1907). Developed theoretical principles of mining mechanics.

GÉRMAN, Yúry Pávlovich (1910–), novelist and story writer. Author of *Our Friends* (1936). The novel *A Lieutenant Colonel of the Medical Corps*, published in instalments in *Zvezda* (1949), has never been completed.

GERMAN OCCUPATION OF THE SOVIET UNION, 1941–1944. The German occupation of Soviet territory, beginning on June 22, 1941, rapidly covered Byelorussia, Lithuania, Latvia, Estonia, much of the Ukraine, and the W parts of the RSFSR. After the standstill and Soviet counterthrust during the following winter, German occupation reached its maximum expanse in the summer of 1942, when it extended to the Crimea, N. Caucasus, and the area between the Don and the Volga. Thereafter the Germans were increasingly on the defensive, until by late summer of 1944 Soviet territory had been substantially cleared of foreign troops.

Most of the occupied Soviet soil remained under German military rule in the form of "rear areas" of the army groups stationed at the front to the E. Farther away from the front lines, civilian rule prevailed. The three Baltic states and Byelorussia constituted General Commissariats which jointly formed the Reich Commissariat Ostland, headed by Heinrich Lohse. That part of the Ukraine which was turned over to corresponding civil government, under Erich Koch, constituted the Reich Commissariat Ukraine. Neither reached the full scope envisaged in Berlin; and the additional Reich Commissariats, intended for Muscovy and the Caucasus, were never brought into being. A confusing multiplicity of German civil, military, police, and economic agencies with overlapping and ill-defined functions operated at cross-purposes throughout the occupied lands. Their clashes reflected not only conflicts of personalities and power elites but also differing conceptions of the occupation itself.

Hitler expected Russia to be defeated by a *Blitz* campaign that made no allowance for failure or delay. The war was not expected to require the use of or the appeal to Soviet citizens. No political warfare was contemplated. So far as the Nazi leadership was concerned, the aim of the "Eastern campaign" was not merely the elimination of Russia as a power and as the seat of victorious Bolshevism, but also the extension of effective and permanent control over the Soviet Union and its economic and manpower resources. Nazi racist policies and German colonial aspirations led to the assignment to the Slavs, and especially Russians, of the ultimate status of inferiors—*Untermenschen*, as Nazi propaganda called them. Educational, cultural, and medical opportunities were to be substantially denied them; politically and socially they were to be atomized; while the E. territories (as the USSR was referred to in Nazi parlance) were to become the settling ground for many millions of Germans and other Nordic peoples.

In practice, these schemes had scant opportunity for realization. Yet even short of this, the initial attitude of the occupation authorities was predominantly one of colonial hostility and derogation. The so-called Commissar Decree, the indiscriminate liquidation of suspects by German security units, the subsequent wholesale extermination of the Jewish population and other "undesirables," public hangings of would-be Bolsheviks and saboteurs, the cruelties that accompanied antipartisan warfare, and the draft of millions of Soviet citizens for forced labor in Germany (as *Ostarbeiter*) —all these contributed to an atmosphere of terror and despair in wide areas of German-held territory. Such a mood, coupled with wide-spread shortages and occasional famine in the cities, would have made it impossible for the Germans to win the wholehearted support of a sizable part of the population. Initially, no such effort was made.

The occupation was marked by bitter disputes which, behind the scene, revealed considerable diversities of outlook and attitude from top to bottom of the German political and military machine. Adolf Hitler, Martin Bormann, and Erich Koch were among those who propounded the extreme anti-Russian position, "against the Kremlin and against the people." The Foreign Office and the military command included, along with fanatics, a number of advocates of a more moderate and "practical" course which would use Russians not only as helpers but as allies against Stalin. As the war dragged on and German setbacks multiplied, the sincere advocates of such a German-Russian entente were joined by an increasing number of officials who favored appeasing the population on occupied soil, so as to use it for anti-Soviet propaganda and arm it to fight on the German side—solely for the sake of winning the war and without political commitments for the future. In the final stages of the war, Heinrich Himmler sided with the advocates of tactical concessions to the point of permitting political warfare by the Vlasov movement (q.v.). In practice, the policy of conciliation and blandishments was too transparently insincere and belated, and was contradicted by too many contrary experiences, to have a significant impact on military events or popular attitudes in the occupied USSR.

A second major conflict among German policy makers concerned the nationality question. Alfred Rosenberg,

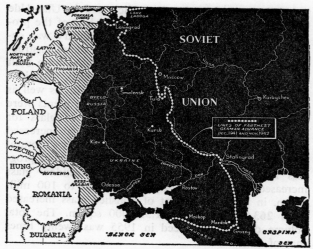

Area left of dotted line shows German occupied territory

as Reich Minister for the Occupied Eastern Territories (a position which concealed the fact that he in fact wielded little influence), was a major advocate of German leadership over the non-Russian peoples of the USSR. He strove for a sharp differentiation in policy between these peoples—notably, Ukrainians, but also Byelorussians, Caucasian and Turkic nationalities—whom he would have sustained in a state of dependency on the Reich, and the Great Russians, whom he was prepared to write off in impotent isolation. This selective policy found little application, but it reflected a dominant trend in German thinking. It was lost in the struggle between the colonialist fanatics and the moderates who claimed that "it takes a Russian to beat a Russian."

The remaining population was not a fair cross section of Soviet society. Many males were under arms; officials, many intellectuals, some skilled and unskilled labor, and others left wherever time and opportunity for evacuation existed before the Germans arrived. In the countryside, "stragglers" roamed in considerable numbers. In 1941, those who had remained at their places had often been prepared to be shown a desirable alternative to Soviet rule. That chance Nazi Germany missed completely. By the following winter, the fluidity of popular attitudes had begun to yield to an irreversible hardening.

The available evidence shows no substantial variation in loyalty among the residents of Slavic areas of the USSR. In the non-Slavic areas and those more recently annexed (1939–40), centrifugal elements were apparently more virulent, ubiquitous, and outspoken. Given their ideological preoccupations with national and racial categories, the Germans showed themselves first unwilling and later unable to capitalize on real social, economic, and political grievances and fissures in Soviet society. The sole exception was agriculture. Here the reform decreed on Feb. 15, 1942 transformed the collectives into communes and, at least on paper, foresaw a reorganization into cooperatives. Another decree on June 3, 1943 sanctioned private land ownership. Both measures were halfhearted compromises, as Nazi ideology frowned on Russians or Ukrainians as

landowners and since the increasing severity of food shortages in Nazi Europe compelled forcible requisitions, which were easier to exact from collective rather than individual farms.

Yet, even in economic terms the occupation was a dismal failure, netting little for the use of German civilians and military. It was manifestly a military failure. It wrought untold devastation and claimed millions of lives in vain. It was a political failure as well. Having failed to capitalize on the severe crisis of confidence that Soviet society experienced during the initial months of the campaign, German policy and behavior thereafter helped forge a new bond between Soviet leaders and citizens. (*See also* WORLD WAR II, PARTISAN MOVEMENT, VLASOV MOVEMENT)

BIBLIOGRAPHY: Alexander Dallin, *German Rule in Russia, 1941–1945*, New York, 1957; Gerald Reitlinger, *The House Built on Sand*, New York, 1960; John A. Armstrong, *Ukrainian Nationalism, 1939–1945*, New York, 1955.   A. D.

GERSEVÁNOV, Mikhaíl Nikoláyevich (1830–1907), civil engineer. Graduated from the Main School of Engineering in St. Petersburg (1851). Cofounder and vice president of the Russian Technical Society (1885–92). Research concerned hydraulics and hydrotechnical structures.

GERSHENZÓN, Mikhaíl Ósipovich (1869–1925), critic, literary historian, and editor. Graduated from the history and philology faculty of Moscow University. After the revolution, he lectured in the Literary Art Institute in Moscow and was chairman of the department of literature of the Academy of Arts and Sciences. His works as a literary critic include: *Griboyedov's Moscow* (1910), *The Wisdom of Pushkin* (1919), and *The Dreams and Thoughts of Turgenev* (1919). His publication *Source Material on the History of Russian Literature* is a major contribution to the history of R. letters. G also wrote numerous articles and letters bearing on the philosophy of religion.

GERSHGÓRIN, Semyón Arónovich (1901–1933), mathematician. Professor, Leningrad Polytechnic Institute. Research concerned numerical and mechanical integration of partial differential equations. Designed model for approximate integration of Laplace equation.

GERSHÚNI, Grigóry Aleksándrovich (1870–1908), revolutionary, founder of the "Workers' Party for the Political Liberation of Russia." Later organizer and leader of the first terrorist group of Socialist Revolutionaries which was responsible for numerous acts of violence directed against men in high office in the tsarist regime. Arrested in 1903, G was sentenced to death, but the sentence was commuted to penal servitude for life. Transferred from the Schlüsselburg fortress to Akatuy, he escaped and died abroad, in 1908.

GÍLELS, Emíl Grigórievich (1916–), pianist. People's Artist of the USSR (1954). Member of the CPSU since 1942. Graduated from Odessa conservatoire (1935). Winner of the All-Union Contest of Performing Artists (1933) and of the International Contest of Pianists in Vienna (1936, second prize). G has been teaching at Moscow conservatoire since 1936, became professor in 1954. Stalin prize laureate (1943). Is widely known through his concert appearances in the United States, Mexico, and Europe.

GILYAKS: *see* NIVKHI.

GIMARÁY-KHÓKH: *see* DZHIMARAY-KHOKH.

GIMNAZIA: *see* EDUCATION.

GIPPIUS: *see* HIPPIUS.

GISSÁR RANGE, in Central Asia, Tadzhik SSR and Uzbek SSR; elevation above 18,000 ft.; numerous glaciers.

GLACIERS. Alpine glaciers occupy some 5,400–6,200 sq. mi. of the USSR. The main regions of glaciation are in the mountains of Central Asia, the Caucasus, the Altay, and E. Siberia; but small G also occur in the Sayan Mountains, in the Urals, and on Kamchatka Peninsula. The most intensive glaciation is found in Central Asia: the Fedchenko Glacier in the Pamir is the longest in the USSR (44.2 mi. long); the Yuzhny Inylchek in the Tien Shan Mountains, the next largest (some 37 mi. long). Second in importance is the Caucasus, the chief region of G being in the central Caucasus between the Elbrus and Kazbek summits. Ice sheets covering about 21,000 sq. mi. are found on the islands in the Arctic region of the USSR.

GLADKÓV, Fyódor Vasílyevich (1883–1958), a Soviet writer of peasant origin, born in Saratov Oblast. He started career as a teacher and journalist. He joined the CP in 1920 and achieved considerable notoriety at home and abroad with his first novel *Cement,* written in 1924–25. It is the story of the rehabilitation of a  cement factory, wrecked during the civil war. Critics in W. Europe hailed Gladkov in those days as the Emile Zola of the Russian Revolution. The popularity of the novel in the Soviet Union was due primarily to the sincere and frank portrayal of human types, and the minimizing of the prevalent "slogan-type" language in Soviet literature. To the western world it was the first insight into the economic ruin and the start of reconstruction in postrevolutionary Russia. The same sincere treatment of many painful problems in the daily life of Soviet people is seen in G's other literary works such as the novel *The Drunken Sun* (1927) and the critical study *By Blood from the Heart* (1928), concerned with the lack of sincerity in postrevolutionary literature. G's lengthy novel *Energy* (1930–36), designed as a continuation of *Cement,* is a story of the construction of the Dneprostroy.

GLASS-MAKING INDUSTRY. According to official data 147 mill. sq. m. of window glass were produced in 1960. The first glass-making factory in Russia was established in 1635. In 1880 there were 207 glass-making enterprises of the craft type in which 15,000 workers were employed. By 1913 the number of workers increased more than fourfold (to 62,000), although the number of plants increased only slightly (to 259), During the prewar Five Year Plans (1928–40) the production of glass increased threefold, to 3 mill. tons annually, and the importation of glass ceased. Existing facilities were modernized and large mechanized plants were constructed in Konstantinovka, Gusev (Vladimir Oblast), Gomel, Gorky, Chagoda (Ladoga region), Kherson, Kamyshin, and Ordzhonikidze, as well as in

Ashkhabad (Turkmenian Republic) and in Ulan-Ude (Buryat Autonomous Republic). About half of the productive capacity of the glass-making industry was destroyed during World War II. Following the reconstruction of destroyed plants, additional facilities were built at Anzhero-Sudzhensk (Kemerovo Oblast), Skopinsk (Ryazan Oblast), Magnitogorsk, and Kutaisi, as well as in other cities, while some of the existing plants were considerably expanded. The production of glass for automobiles and for optical instruments increased rapidly during this period, and production for structural purposes was begun. Partly as a result of further progress in mechanization, the output of window glass increased from 77 mill. sq. m. in 1950 to 100 mill. sq. m. in 1955, while that of polished glass increased from 263,000 sq. m. to 1,520,000 sq. m. The total volume of glass produced in 1955 was twenty times that of 1913.

The Seven Year Plan (1959–65) calls for a further increase in the annual output of window glass to 220 mill. sq. m.

PRODUCTION OF WINDOW GLASS
IN THE USSR
(mill. sq. m.)

1913	23.7
1928	34.2
1932	29.5
1937	79.3
1940	44.7
1950	76.9
1955	99.8
1958	133.1
1959	139.8
1960	147.0
1965 (pl.)	220.0

P. I. M.

GLAVLIT: *see* PUBLISHING.

GLÁZOV, town in Udmurt ASSR; pop. 16,000 (1939), 59,000 (1960). Large mechanical plant, distilleries, furniture. Pedag. inst.

GLAZUNÓV, Aleksándr Aleksándrovich (1891–), electrical engineer. Honored Scientist and Technologist, RSFSR (1942). Graduate (1917), professor (1920), Moscow School of Technology. Participated in preparing the "State Plan for the Electrification of the Republic" (GOELRO) and in the design of large power systems and electric power plants. Author of *Operation and Calculation of Lines and Cables* (1956). Stalin prize (1943).

GLAZUNÓV, Aleksándr Konstantínovich (1865–1936), composer and conductor, born in St. Petersburg  in the family of a book publisher. Studied piano since childhood. Graduated from St. Petersburg conservatoire where he studied under Rimsky-Korsakov. At the age of 16 G wrote a symphony which was successfully performed under the baton of Balakirev. G often sought the advice of Tchaikovsky, Balakirev, Borodin, and Rimsky-Korsakov. In 1890 he became professor of instrumentation at the St. Petersburg conservatoire and served as its director from 1902 to 1912. His main compositions include 8 symphonies (of which the 2nd written in 1886 is the best known), symphonic poems (*Stenka Razin, The*

Kremlin), 3 string quartets, ballet suites, cantatas, and orchestrations of popular themes. Collaborated with Rimsky-Korsakov on the final version of *Prince Igor*. He personally conducted his compositions abroad. Was awarded honorary degrees by Cambridge and Oxford Universities in 1907. From 1928 he lived in France.

GLIERE, Reinhold Moritsevich (1875–1956), composer, conductor, and teacher. Studied violin and composition at Moscow conservatoire, graduated with honors (gold medal) in 1900. Taught music (S. Prokofiev was a pupil); professor of the Kiev conservatoire (1913–20) and of the Moscow conservatoire (1920–41). In 1920–33 G conducted many of his own compositions. Wrote numerous operas and ballets. Is best known for his romances; wrote incidental music for plays and motion pictures. Three Glinka prizes, 3 Stalin prizes.

GLÍNKA, Konstantín Dmítrievich (1867–1927), mineralogist and soil scientist. Fellow, Ac. of S., USSR (1927). Graduate of St. Petersburg University (1889); dean of the Leningrad Agr. Inst. and first director of the Soil Science Inst., Ac. of S. (1922–27). Organizer and participant of major geographical and soil study expeditions to Siberia and Central Asia which led to the initial mapping of soil zones in the Asian part of the USSR. G. made a major contribution to paleogeography by introducing "paleosoil science."

GLÍNKA, Mikhaíl Ivánovich (1804–1857), composer, pioneer of R. "national" music. Son of a landowner of Smolensk Province, the music of which was to influence his later compositions. A good education in St. Petersburg was followed by musical studies in Italy and Berlin. G returned to Russia in 1834 where he  made the acquaintance of young composers, the music critic Stasov, the poet Pushkin, and the painter Bryullov. His first success was the patriotic opera *Ivan Susanin* produced in 1836 under the title *Life for the Tsar*. The work marked the beginning of the "national" movement in R. music. Less successful was his second opera, *Ruslan and Ludmila*, based on Pushkin's fairy tale, which followed six years later. R. folk themes dominate G's one symphony (in B minor) and *Kamarinskaya*. A visit to Spain (1844–46) resulted in the *Overture Espagnole* and *Summer Nights in Madrid*, orchestral works making much use of Spanish folk music. G also wrote romances based on the poetry of Pushkin and others, as well as piano and instrumental pieces. He was a well-known teacher and for a time served as imperial chapel-master and conductor of the St. Petersburg opera. He died suddenly in Berlin while engaged on a study of church music.

GLUSHKO, Valentín Petróvich (1908–), heat power engineer. Fellow, Ac. of S., USSR, (1958). Research in the field of liquid fuels for jet engines since 1930. In 1930–32 designed liquid-fuel jet engines which work on liquid oxygen, nitric acid, and other liquids.

GOD-CONSTRUCTING: *see* OPPOSITION.

GODUNÓV, Borís Fyódorovich (1551–1605), tsar of Russia 1598–1605. G belonged to the lesser nobility and combined great ability with shrewd political sense.

He became a favorite of Ivan IV (the Terrible) and the actual ruler during the reign of Ivan's feeble-minded son Fedor (1584–98). Under G's regency, wars with the Crimean Tatars (1591), Sweden (1595), and Poland were successful, and some of Ivan IV's more disastrous enterprises were liquidated. Also, Russia's first patriarch, Job, was established at Moscow in 1589. Little, however, was done to alleviate the peasant problem. G was nonetheless popular as regent because of his public largesse and promises of a better future. In 1598, when Fedor's death ended the established dynasty, G was elected tsar by the *zemsky sobor* (q.v.). His power was soon undermined by the plots and intrigues of the boyar opposition. His reign was characterized by deportations, spying, and confiscations of property. It also marked the solidification of serfdom in Russia, by the 1601 limitation on the peasant's right to move from one estate to another. The famine of 1601–03 added to acute rural unrest and the growing opposition to G's rule. A new candidate for the throne appeared, claiming to be Ivan's youngest son, Dimitry (who had died as a child in 1591 under circumstances which warranted the suspicion that G had murdered him). G's death ushered in the era of anarchy in Russia known as "The Time of Troubles." G's career is the subject of a play by Pushkin and an opera by Musorgsky based on the play.

BIBLIOGRAPHY: S. Graham, *Boris Godunov*, New Haven, 1933.

GOELRO: *see* ELECTRIC POWER STATIONS, POWER ENGINEERING.

GÓGOL, Nikoláy Vasílyevich (1809–1852), one of the greatest Russian writers and dramatists, was born on March 19, 1809 in Sorochintsy, Poltava Province, son of a Ukrainian landowner and author of Ukrainian plays. From 1821 to 1828 Gogol studied at the Nezhin *lycée*. Upon graduation he went to St. Petersburg  dreaming of a career "in the service of humanity." His first published work, a romantic poem, *Hanz Kuechelgarten*, met with no success. He went abroad; on his return he tried unsuccessfully to get on the stage in St. Petersburg, but became a history teacher at the Girls' school instead. The first volume of his Ukrainian tales *Evenings on a Farm Near Dikanka* was published in 1831 and made him famous overnight. His interests were now divided between history and literature. In 1834–35 he was a prof. of world history at the University of St. Petersburg. In 1835 four volumes of his works appeared: *Mirgorod* (including *Taras Bulba*), a continuation of *Evenings*, *Arabesques*, containing scholarly articles in addition to the St. Petersburg novelettes. He then began to work on his best comedy *The Inspector General* and on a large-scale novel which he called "a poem," *Dead Souls*.

Dissatisfied with the reaction to *The Inspector General* and with its production, Gogol left Russia in 1836 for Rome, which was to become his second home. When the first volume of *Dead Souls* appeared in 1842, it was acclaimed in Russia. Work on the second volume proceeded slowly. In 1846 Gogol sent to Russia the manuscript of his new book *Selected Passages from a Correspondence with Friends*, which contained his moral, social, and political views. As they were in sharp conflict with those of the R. intelligentsia of the time, they caused great indignation. Some critics and biographers even today consider this book an expression of Gogol's spiritual crisis, or even of his "religious mania" and the end of his literary career. The consistency in Gogol's spiritual and moral make-up went unnoticed at the time. The aesthetic essays in the book attracted no attention. Disheartened by this reception of his work, Gogol went to the Holy Land (1848), then returned to Russia. He lived an intense religious life and tried to complete *Dead Souls*. Deeply depressed by the death of a friend, in Feb. 1852 he burned the second volume of *Dead Souls* together with some papers intended for burning. He explained it as the influence of an "evil spirit" upon him. It was the beginning of his grave illness which together with excessive fasting, led to his death on Feb. 21, 1852 at the age of less than 43.

Data of his life are of little help toward understanding this controversial writer whose effect upon the development of R. letters is unique. Misunderstood and misinterpreted by his contemporaries and by posterity, in spite of his fame, Gogol was considered for a long time to be the founder of R. realism and was imitated as such. However, neither Gogol's unique creative gift nor his language, which he forged out of very diverse elements into a perfect musical unity, could ever be duplicated. Gogol's ideology, which was markedly out of tune with that of his time, was more understood by the R. religious thinkers of the 20th century. It is clear now that realistic, satiric, and humoristic elements in Gogol's work have been grossly overstressed. All the new evidence suggests that ultimate understanding of Gogol can be gained only through careful study of his spiritual life, the religious drama of his life. His extraordinary insight into the depths of human nature, the highly symbolic texture of his work, his spiritual searchings, and his completely original vision of the world as expressed in his unique language—all these made him a forerunner of the modernist trends in R. letters.

BIBLIOGRAPHY: Janko Lavrin, *N. V. Gogol*, London, 1951; David Magarshack, *Gogol*, New York, 1957.   Z. Yu.

GOKCHÁ: *see* SEVAN LAKE.

GOLD POLICY: *see* FOREIGN TRADE AND AID, MONETARY SYSTEM.

GOLD STANDARD: *see* MONETARY SYSTEM.

GOLDEN HORDE (R. *Zolotáya Ordá*, Mong. *Ulus Dzhuchi*), Mongolian state established in the conquered lands of E. Europe during the first half of the 13th century. The actual founder was Batu, the son of Dzhuchi. The GH encompassed S. Russian steppes around the Black Sea, the agricultural districts of Volga-Bulgaria, Crimea, Caucasus, and N. Khorezm. The capital of the GH initially was Saray-Batu (near Astrakhan), but Uzbek-Khan (1312–42) transferred it to Saray-Berke (near Stalingrad). The rise of Moscow principality stimulated the fight of Russians for liberation from the Tatar yoke. The Kulikovo battle, on Sept. 8,

1380, under Dimitry Donskoy, dealt a severe blow to the GH, and interior feudal strifes further hastened its decay. The khanates of Crimea, Siberia, and Nogay seceded from the GH, and in the middle of the 16th century, Ivan IV conquered the remainder of it (the khanate of Kazan in 1552 and the khanate of Astrakhan in 1556) which was incorporated into the R. state.

GOLDEN HORN BAY (R. *Zolotóy Rog*), harbor of Vladivostok; length 3.7 mi.; width 0.5 mi.

GÓLDENWEISER, Aleksándr Borísovich (1875–1946), composer and pianist, pupil of Alexander Zilotti. Noted teacher; director of the Moscow Conservatoire, 1939–42; teacher of D. Kabalevsky. Author of numerous compositions, which show the influence of Taneyev, Arensky, and Ippolitov-Ivanov. People's Artist of the USSR. Wrote operas and symphonies.

GOLDI: *see* NANAI.

GÓLIKOV, Filíp Ivánovich (1900–), general. Member of the CP since 1918. In 1933 G graduated from the Frunze Military Academy. In 1940–41, he was deputy chief of staff; in 1943–50, deputy people's commissar of defense. Since 1958, chief of the Political Administration of the Red Army.

GÓLIKOV, Iván Ivánovich (1735–1801), merchant and "amateur" historian. He was an ardent Westerner and admirer of Peter the Great. Between 1788 and 1797 he published 30 volumes of source materials connected with Peter's reign.

GOLÍTSYN, Prince Dmítry Mikháylovich (1665–1737), conservative statesman, adversary of radical reforms of Peter I. He was governor of Kiev (1707–18), president of Kamer-College (Finance Ministry), and member of the Supreme Privy Council (1726–30). For his attempt to limit the powers of Anna Ivanovna he was sent to Schlüsselburg fortress and died there.

GOLÍTSYN, Prince Mikhaíl Mikháylovich (1675–1730), talented strategist, field marshal during the reign of Peter I. He took part in many battles with Sweden (Narva, Poltava, Noteburg, Vyborg, and other places). He was also president of the War College (Ministry), senator, and member of the Supreme Privy Council.

GOLÍTSYN, Prince Vasíly Vasílyevich (1643–1714), foreign secretary while Sofia Alekseyevna was regent during the childhood of Peter I and his brother Ivan. He was supreme commander of the R. Army in the Crimean campaigns of 1687 and 1689, but was exiled after the overthrow of Sofia.

GOLÓDNAYA STEP (Hunger Steppe): **(1)** Severnaya (N.) GS or Bet-Pak-Dala—desert in central part of Kazakh SSR. **(2)** Yuzhnaya (S.) GS—plain in S.E. part of Kyzylkum in Kazakh SSR. Area about 3,850 sq. mi. Largest part of steppe is irrigated by Kirov Canal; cotton-growing area.

GOLOVÁNOV, Nikoláy Semyónovich (1891–1953), conductor, People's Artist of USSR, four time Laureate of Stalin prize. After 1948 G was conductor of the Bolshoy Theater. Author of two operas and symphonic music.

GOLOVÍN, Aleksándr Yákovlevich (1863–1930), landscape and portrait painter, stage designer. G adhered to the impressionist movement of the early 20th century. Designed theatrical settings for several productions (*Don Juan, Marriage of Figaro,* plays of Ibsen, and others). Painted landscapes and portraits, mostly water colors and tempera.

GOLOVÍN, Fyódor Alekséyevich (1650–1706), statesman, diplomat, general, admiral. In 1689 he signed the Nerchinsk Treaty with China; was second ambassador of the "Great Mission" of Peter I (1697–98). He helped to create the R. navy and to shape R. foreign policy.

GOLÓVKIN, Gavriíl Ivánovich (1660–1734), statesman and diplomat, collaborator of Peter I; first Russian Chancellor (appointed in 1709).

GOLOVNÍN, Vasíly Mikháylovich (1776–1831), outstanding navigator and vice admiral who made two round-the-world voyages. He was captured by the Japanese (1811–13) while surveying the Kuril Islands and described his stay in Japan and travels.

GOLÚZIN, Gennády Mikháylovich (1906–1952), mathematician. Professor, Leningrad University (1938). Research on the theory of analytical functions and single-valued functions of a complex variable. Determined final form of the "theorem of rotation." Stalin prize (1948).

GÓMEL, city, adm. center of Gomel Oblast, Byelorussian SSR, landing on Sozh River; pop. 168,000 (1959). Ind: machine building, machines for peat extraction, matches, woodworking, clothing, footwear. Pedag. inst. and numerous technical schools. Dates back to 12th century.

GÓMEL OBLAST in S.E. Byelorussian SSR; area 15,500 sq. mi.; pop. 1,357,000 (1959). Cities: Gomel (adm. center), Rechitsa, Dobrush, Zhlobin, Rogachev, Vetka. Is a plain irrigated by the Dnieper and its tributary, the Sozh; has mildly continental climate; podzol soils, alluvial near rivers. Agr.: rye, oats, buckwheat, wheat, potatoes, flax, hemp, makhorka; ind.: peat, agr. machinery, glass, condensed milk. Est. 1938.

GONCHARÓV, Iván Aleksándrovich (1812–1891), novelist, born in Simbirsk. Of his three novels—*A Common Story* (1847), *Oblomov* (1859), and *The Precipice* (1869)—*Oblomov* has become a classic. An expansion of a previously published fragment, *Oblomov's Dream* (1849), it tells the story of an intelligent and liberal landowner  whose inability to overcome his inborn laziness destroys a love affair and causes him to withdraw from the world and die in an atmosphere of apathy and sloth. The impression of inertia is predominant; it actually takes the hero some seventy pages to get out of bed. In contrast to the laziness of Oblomov are the energy and industry of his friend Shtolts, who was probably intended by the author to serve as a model. The novel met with great success. The critic Dobrolyubov invented a term which has become proverbial—*oblomovshchina* or "oblomovism." It has come to signify the inability of R. intellectuals to take action.

BIBLIOGRAPHY: Janko Lavrin, *Goncharov*, New Haven, 1954.

GONCHARÓVA, Natália Sergéyevna (1883–), painter. Studied in the Moscow School of Painting, Sculpture and Architecture; adhered to several schools of painting in the early 20th century; followed the path of generalization and fragmentation of color and form (impressionism, cubism) and later turned to neoimpressionism proceeding from the technique of icon painting. Since 1915 G has been working in Paris devoting her time to easel painting and stage designing.

GORBÁTOV, Borís Leóntyevich (1908–1954), novelist, poet, and journalist, born in the Donbas. In 1926 he moved to Moscow where he worked as secretary for the All-Union Association of Proletarian Writers, and wrote verses for Moscow newspapers and magazines. He later returned to the Donbas to write his first book, *Cell,* about Donbas young communists. *Cell* was a success, ran to ten editions and was translated into German. As a *Pravda* correspondent, he traveled through the USSR, visiting factories, and lived in the Urals. He wrote essays for *Pravda* and published books, including *Masters* and *The Comintern.* G's book *My Generation* appeared in 1934. He spent a year flying in the Arctic, which produced *The Ordinary Arctic.*

G was a war correspondent during World War II and wrote *Stories of the Soldiers' Spirit, Letters to a Comrade,* and the volume, *The Unsubdued,* which was issued in over one million copies and has been translated into 23 languages. It won a Stalin prize (1943–44), one of nine government awards G received.

GORCHAKÓV, Prince Aleksándr Mikháylovich (1798–1883), statesman. Member of a distinguished family, he joined the foreign office in 1821 and served in R. embassies throughout Europe. He conducted the preliminary peace negotiations at Vienna, 1854–55; was appointed foreign minister April 1856 and chancellor 1867. His aim was to restore Russia's position in the face of the setbacks suffered in the Crimean war and the peace that followed. The result was closer relations with Prussia, a policy confirmed by Bismarck's acquiescence in the crushing of the Polish rebellion of 1863. At the Congress of Berlin (1878) he claimed Germany had failed to support Russia; thus he agitated for abandonment of the German alliance. He retired from active participation in affairs, 1882. His unrivaled command of diplomatic French and long period in office were primarily responsible for his becoming a leading figure in European diplomacy.

GORCHAKÓV, Nikolay Mikháylovich (1898–), Soviet producer; joined the company of the Moscow Art Theater in 1924, and was later made Honored Art Worker of the RSFSR. G participated in producing the plays: *The Earth* by N. Ye. Virta, *Navy Officer* by A. A. Kron, and others. He is the author of the book *K. S. Stanislavsky's Lessons in Production* (1950), for which he obtained the Stalin prize (1951).

GORDÓN, Patrick (1635–1699), army leader, R. general, emigrant from Scotland. Served the Swedish, Polish, and, from 1661, the R. crown; he also participated in Crimean and Azov campaigns. He enjoyed the friendship of Peter I.

GOREMÝKIN, Iván Lógginovich (1839–1917), statesman. Born into the minor gentry, G became a lawyer and entered government service. He was appointed assistant minister of justice (1891), minister of the interior and, upon convocation of the first Duma in

1906, prime minister. But the Duma refused to co-operate with G's government and he was forced to resign. He again served as a premier, 1914–16, by now an aged incarnation of "reaction" indifferent to mounting criticism. Milyukov's (q.v.) violent attack upon him and the empress in the Duma resulted in his dismissal.

GÓREV, Aleksándr Aleksándrovich (1884–1953), electrical engineer. Graduate (1907), professor (1919), St. Petersburg Polytechnic Institute. Participated in preparing the "State Plan for the Electrification of the Republic" (GOELRO). Member, State Planning Commission. Consultant of state electric power institutions. Specialized in electric power transmission, design of powerful pulse generators, lightning protection. Author of *Transition Process of a Synchronous Device*. Stalin prize for the design of high-power equipment for high-voltage installations (1948).

GÓRI, ancient town in Georgian SSR on Kura River; pop. 33,100 (1956). Ind.: cotton, canned food, sawmills. Birthplace of I. V. Stalin; his house is now a museum.

GÓRKY, Maksím (Peshkóv, Alekséy Maksímovich, 1868–1936), short-story writer, novelist, playwright, born in Nizhny Novgorod (now Gorky). Lost parents as a young child, was raised by grandparents. Left home at the age of twelve and wandered, mostly on foot, over Russia for more than a decade, often as a vagabond, working on various odd jobs, also in a bakery as a servant, a scullery boy, ship loader, an icon seller, office clerk. G had no formal education.

During his wanderings he published his first short story, *Makar Chudra* (1892). In 1895 Vladimir Korolenko discovered G and helped him to publish the story *Chelkash* which made G famous overnight. Other short stories followed in which G depicted in a romanticized way the life of the poor, downtrodden and homeless. After 1898 G abandoned the romantic style for realism. Several novels followed: *Foma Gordeyev* (1899), *A Confession* (1908), and *The Mother* (1906). He founded the publishing house *Znanie* (Knowledge) which published the works of some of Russia's greatest contemporary authors—Kuprin, Andreyev, and Bunin. G wrote several plays, including the famous *Lower Depths* (1902), where life of vagabonds at a night refuge for the homeless was realistically depicted. G's autobiographical trilogy—*Childhood, In the World*, and *My Universities*—is considered one of his best literary creations. During the two closing decades of his life G wrote several novels and plays. The best-known were: *The Artamonovs' Business, The Town Okurov, The Life of Matvey Kozhemyakin*, the dramas *Yegor Bulychov, Dostigayev*. G's longest novel is an unfinished four-volume family chronicle *The Life of Klim Samgin* (1927–36). Of great literary value is his book of reminiscences about Tolstoy, Chekhov, Andreyev, and Blok.

G took an active part in politics both as a writer (his *Song of the Stormy Petrel* was popular during the revolution of 1905), as well as a member of the Russian Social Democratic party. He helped Lenin to provide financial means for the Bolshevik faction of the party.

G was arrested in 1905, but soon released because of world-wide protests. He left Russia and, after touring Europe and the United States, settled in Capri, Italy. As a result of his trip to the United States he published a series of stories about New York, *The City of the Yellow Devil* (1906), which is still being used by Khrushchev and other Soviet leaders as a source of anti-American propaganda. G returned to Russia in 1917. At the beginning he was critical of the Bolsheviks. During the years of revolution and civil war G saved many writers, artists, journalists, and other intellectuals from starvation. He left Russia in 1921 for Germany and Italy, but returned in 1928 and 1936. After 1928, G publicly supported Stalin's policies, including forced collectivization. G died while under medical treatment "murdered by the Trotsky-Bukharin gang," according to the official Stalin version. During the twenties, G was proclaimed by Soviet literary authorities as the father of so-called socialist realism and of proletarian literature.

BIBLIOGRAPHY: Alexander Kaun, *Maxim Gorky and His Russia*, New York, 1931.
E. N.

GÓRKY (f. Nizhny Nóvgorod), city, adm. center of Gorky Oblast, RSFSR; pop. 644,000 (1939), 942,000 (1959). Important port on the Volga. Major industrial center: automobiles, shipbuilding, Diesel engines, rolling stock, machine tools, radio sets, woodworking. Nizhny Novgorod was founded in 1221, and the old citadel (kremlin) is preserved; in 1611, during the "Time of Troubles" K. Minin and D. Pozharsky formed a people's army in the city. Site of famous fairs. Is the birthplace of M. Gorky, and was renamed after him in 1932. Is a picturesque city with many old monuments. Has numerous colleges (one university), theaters, museums, including the Gorky Museum.

GÓRKY OBLAST in Central European RSFSR; area 28,950 sq. mi.; pop. 3,590,000 (1959): Russians, Tatars, Mordvinians, Chuvash, Mari, and others. Cities: Gorky (adm. center), Dzerzhinsk, Balakhna, Bogorodsk, Pavlovo, Vyksa, Arzamas, Bor, Kulebaki. Navigation on the Volga, Oka, Vetluga, Sura; landings at Gorky, Lyskovo, Vasilsursk, Pavlovo. Rolling country with mixed forests and podzol soil; moderately continental climate. Agr.: wheat, flax, hemp, potatoes, cattle breeding. Ind.: largest automobile plant in the USSR, machine tools, chemical, paper, woodworking, Gorky hydroelectric station on Volga. Numerous schools of higher education, museums, theaters. Est. 1936.

GORLÓVKA, city in Stalino Oblast, Ukrainian SSR; pop. 181,000 (1939), 293,000 (1959). As a center of Donbas coal region, its ind. are equipment for coal mining, machine-building, chemical plants. Mining institute.

GÓRNAYA SHÓRIYA, mining area in S. Kemerovo Oblast, RSFSR; iron-ore base for Kuznetsk metallurgical combine (Stalinsk). Iron ores, gold mines, coal, lumber (Tashtagol, Telbes, Temir-Tau).

GÓRNO-ALTÁY AUTONOMOUS OBLAST, in the S.E. Altay Kray, RSFSR; borders Mongolian People's Republic and China. Area 35,750 sq. mi.; pop. 157,000 (1959): Russians, Oyrots, Temut, Kumand. Adm. center: Gorno-Altaysk; main river Katun. Covered with forests, alpine meadows; continental climate; fertile valleys with black earth and podzol soils; about 2 per cent arable land. Mainly animal farming: horse- and cattle-breeding; many deposits of nonferrous metals and lignite. Pedag. inst. Est. 1922.

GÓRNO-ALTÁYSK (f. Oyrot-Tura, and before that Ulala), city in Gorno-Altay Autonomous Oblast, RSFSR; pop. 27,000 (1959). Ind.: butter- and cheese-making, brick and lime plants. Pedag. inst., school for veterinarians, medical and trade schools.

GÓRNO-BADAKHSHÁN AUTONOMOUS OB-LAST, part of Tadzhik SSR bordering China; area 24,-600 sq. mi.; pop. 73,000 (1959): Kirghiz, Russians. Adm. center Khorog. Highly mountainous country in Pamir, with the highest peaks of the USSR: Lenin and Stalin peaks. E. part has continental climate; western, milder. Minerals are salt, iron ore, gold; mining, home ind. (carpets, metalworking, shoes); agr.: vegetables and wheat. Is the seat of Pamir Biological Station and Pamir Botanical Garden. Est. 1925.

GORODÉTS, city in Gorky Oblast, RSFSR, landing on the Volga; pop. 26,400 (1956). Shipbuilding and ship-repair ind.; site of the Gorky hydroelectric station. Founded 1183; Aleksandr Nevsky died here in 1263.

GORODÉTSKY, Sergéy Mitrofánovich (1884–), poet. Brought out the collections *Vital Sap* (1907) and *Wild Freedom* (1908) which are interesting for their arrangement of R. folklore themes. He was, with Gumil-yov, one of the early acmeists. After the revolution he turned to writing political poetry, but had little success.

GOROZHÁNKIN, Iván Nikoláyevich (1848–1904), botanist. Graduate (1871), professor (1881), Moscow University. Research concerned the morphology of green algae and gymnospermas. Forerunner of the comparative morphological approach to botany in Russia.

GORYÁCHKIN, Vasíly Prokhórovich (1868–1935), agricultural engineer. Honorary member, Ac. of S., USSR (1932). Honored Scientist and Technologist, RSFSR (1935). Graduate, Moscow University (1890) and the School of Technology (1894). Director, Institute of Agricultural Mechanics (1929). Initiated organization of Moscow Institute of Mechanization and Electrification of Agriculture. Founder of a new branch of science—agricultural mechanics.

GOSIZDAT: *see* PUBLISHING.

GOSPLAN: *see* PLANNING.

GOTS, Abrám Rafaílovich (1882–1937), (younger brother of Mikhail G), leading Socialist Revolutionary. G was born in Moscow in a wealthy Jewish family, was a member of the terrorist organization and of the Central Committee of the Socialist Revolutionary party. In 1907 he was condemned to eight years of hard labor. In 1917 he returned from Siberia and was active in the Executive Committee of the Petrograd Soviet; later he tried to organize the resistance to the Bolsheviks. In 1920 he was condemned to death with eleven other members of the Socialist Revolutionary party, but his sentence was commuted to five years' imprisonment. Released in 1927, he worked in various Soviet economic planning agencies. In 1936 he was rearrested and according to reliable information was executed in 1937.

GOTS, Mikhaíl Rafaílovich (1866–1906), one of the founders of the Socialist Revolutionary party and member of its Central Committee. Born in Moscow in a wealthy Jewish family, G participated in the revolutionary movement from his student days. Arrested in 1886, he was deported in 1888 to E. Siberia for eight years. There he took part in an armed rising in 1889, was severely wounded and condemned to hard labor. He was released in 1895 and emigrated in 1900. In exile, G dedicated himself to the work of the Socialist Revolutionary party. The money he received from his relatives and friends financed the activities of the party; his house in Geneva became its headquarters and G its central figure. He published, together with N. S. Rusanov and I. A. Rubanovich *Vestnik Russkoy Revolyutsii* (Messenger of the Russian Revolution) and wrote many articles and essays.

GOUL (GUL), Román Borísovich (1896–), writer. Participated in the civil war and subsequently described his recollections in *The Ice Campaign*. Left Russia in 1919, lived in Germany and France; settled in the United States (1950). Author of *A Scythian in Europe,* a biography of M. A. Bakunin (1931); *The Red Horse* (1952), an autobiographical novel; and *Azef,* translated into English, French, German and other languages. One of the editors of the R. quarterly *Novy Zhurnal* (New Review) in New York.

GOVERNMENT. The conduct of the economy as one firm has demanded high managerial skill and reliable discipline. The conspiratorial party of the revolution has been converted to mobilize the former and enforce the latter. The soviets of workers' deputies, picked up as a device of revolutionary tactics, have provided a form for part of the chain of management and endowed it with the prestige of legend and a useful public relations machinery. Organization and administrative areas have been in perpetual flux to accommodate changing needs and notions, from which only the areas based on recognized linguistic "nationalities" have—with exceptions, mainly during Hitler's war—been largely exempt. All enterprises, organizations, and units of habitation are within the state-firm, though differing in their "subordination" (*podchinenie*)—the link of the chain to which they are attached.

The soviets, though not they alone, symbolize mass participation in, and support for, G, convey information to higher authority—sometimes circumventing the officials—and help mobilize popular effort; their individual members are encouraged to hear, and as far as possible redress, grievances. These purposes have made them large (over 800 for Moscow city soviet), and detailed management of production and local services has had to be left to smaller bodies selected from among their membership (sometimes, irregularly from outside it) by form of election. To these bodies the administrative staff is ascribed.

In soviets of *oblast* (or *kray*) level and below, this inner body is styled executive committee (*ispolkom*). Moscow city executive committee, as elected in 1959, has a chairman, two first vice-chairmen, four vice-chairmen, and a secretary, all supervising groups of departments, six of the 31 department heads, of whom one—the chairman of the city's planning commission—also supervises other departments, the first and second secretaries of the Communist party for the city and nine other members. The nine members having supervision of groups of departments apparently form a further inner body, the presidium of the executive committee. This seems usual in at least all the larger units.

In any unit having the title of republic the popularly elected body is styled Supreme Soviet and the inner body presidium. The Union presidium is the titular head of state and formally enacts certain measures decided elsewhere, which powers are in practice exercised by its chairman or chairman and secretary. In subordinate republics the presidium possibly also exercises general supervision over administration. A more effective management board is the Council of Ministers, also formally elected by the Supreme Soviet (casual changes being made by the presidium), though not exclusively from among its members. Apart from chairman, first vice-chairmen, and vice-chairmen—who at times have formed an inner body (bureau or presidium)—most members formerly headed ministries controlling enterprises in the several industries. Since mid-1957, ministries represented have been reduced to 15 in all in a membership of 67 (as against 52 out of 65 in 1956, much as under Stalin) and replaced by chairmen of specialized development committees and heads of divisions of Gosplan and others personally invested with the title of minister. The councils also contain, at Union level, the chairmen of the union republic councils of ministers and, at union republic level, many or all chairmen of the councils of national economy.

A Union Council of Ministers decree of May 22, 1957 gave chairmen and department heads of the newly formed councils of national economy the powers of Union ministers (without, apparently, actual membership at Union level) and department heads. They are ministers with some difference. Instead of running a whole industry throughout the country (sometimes from Union level through another ministry at republican level) a council runs all economic life for a limited area—apart from agriculture and perhaps a quarter of other economic activity continuing under central agencies or entrusted to local soviet executive committees of various degrees. Formerly the minister, as a specialist, often went deeply into technical details; now allegedly his successor cannot.

A council of national economy itself closely ressembles in apparent composition and function the "collegium" of department heads and others with whose advice, though not necessarily consent, any minister is supposed to work. Attached to it, much as to the ministries, is an auxiliary "technical-economic council" of several hundred practical and academic experts, managers, and workers of approved inventive and other attainments. It usually works in specialized sections.

In the RSFSR the council areas are those of the 49 *oblasts* less two—merged for that purpose with another—the 6 *kray* areas, the 14 autonomous republics and the city of Moscow. In the Ukraine the *oblasts* are

grouped into 14, and in Kazakhstan into 9 such areas; other union republics have (July 1960) only one council each.

Their introduction, while connected with Khrushchev's contest with his rivals, responded to concern at the length, slackness, and mutual exclusiveness of the ministry chains of command; working to correct these they incur accusations of "localism." Difficulties also arise in dealing with the republican Gosplan—previously overshadowed by the federal body—now developed as coordinator of councils of national economy and, in effect, ministry of everything in general.

Soviet administrative theory prescribes "dual subordination" for executive units—outward through representative bodies to the public and upward toward higher authority of their own kind or branch. The latter line has persistently proved the stronger. Certain branches, particularly internal affairs (police, civil registration, internal passports, and so on) have always acted in substantial independence of the executive committees to which they are attached. Though these have latterly been allowed greatly increased powers over this branch it seems unlikely that all such privilege is ended. Apart from such agencies, the structure is elaborated in a great variety of committees—some attached to, though not represented in, councils of ministers, some emanating from supreme soviets, from soviet executive committees, ministries, academies of sciences, trade unions, and so on—all about the state's business.

For general coordination—the most intractable problem—there are many inspecting networks, including the Commission of Soviet Control (having ministerial rank), certain agencies of the Ministry of Finance, the State Bank, the *arbitrazh* (industrial courts) and the procurators (public prosecutors, guardians of recognized legal rights, and general management inspectors with a shifting and disputed competence, responsible only at Union level). There is also the police and security machinery, offering a temptingly easy way round obstructions to the realization of the desirable.

Councils of ministers, ministries, councils of national economy, and soviet executive committees compensate for the legislative inactivity of supreme soviets and soviets. Their legislation consists of specific assignment of tasks, often to a named person and with date prescribed for performance, rather than delimitation of powers. It is supplemented by the soviet form of contract, which defines, instead of creating, obligations and can be amended by the *arbitrazh* for not defining correctly.

The principal network of general management, the *corps d'élite* of the whole administration, is the professional staff, or "apparatus" of the party. Of the party membership of some 8¼ millions (1959) the full-time paid professionals, an élite primarily of educational attainments, are perhaps one in thirty. Holders of almost all leading posts elsewhere in the administration and the economy are party members, and the most successful have commonly held a post, at least for a time, in the apparatus. Holders of high and scarce professional qualifications seem able to achieve eminence without such service or, as with some leading natural scientists, without accepting the burdens of membership at all.

The party's territorial organization corresponds to that of the state administration from *rayon* or city upward, though autonomous republics are called *oblasts* for party purposes, and the RSFSR, unlike other union republics, lacks the acknowledgment implied by a titular party of its own. The party committee (*raykom* in the *rayon*, *obkom* in the *oblast*, and so on) or central committee (in Union or union republic) has an inner body of seven or more called the bureau (or, for the Union and the Ukrainian union republic, the presidium) consisting of several secretaries, the chairman of the soviet executive committee (in republics the chairmen of the council of ministers and of the supreme soviet presidium), and others. The party's first secretary takes precedence over all other officials in his area, including the chairman of the executive committee, even in formal state business.

Apart from formal supervision by party officials, the party maximizes its influence by requiring members in any organization to operate in concerted groups and under discipline.

The party staff at *rayon* level seems now commonly to be divided into two departments—one for propaganda and agitation, the other for organization and instruction. In the latter the head is assisted by officials called instructors who are in fact general inspectors, each responsible for the work of a representative selection of the enterprises and institutions in the area. At higher levels the staff is organized in specialized departments for the several industries and activities. At Union level most are duplicated, with one for the RSFSR, under a special bureau of the central committee, and one for all the other union republics.

The party has its own supervision and rechecking networks and, in effect, its system of party courts. Its educational system, closely related in standards to that of the state, trains all leading soviet and journalistic, as well as party, staffs.

Committees and central committees seem rather briefing sessions—and usually also organs of general publicity—than deliberative bodies. Most speakers at recent plenary sessions of the central committee at Union level of which proceedings have been published (i.e., since Dec. 1958) have been not members of that body but specially introduced experts on the subjects under discussion. The conferences (congresses at the level of the CPSU and the 14 parties of union republics) which nominally elect the committees are similar in role. Khrushchev may have mobilized the central committee against its presidium, but it would hardly be possible to mobilize a congress against the central committee, and such maneuvers locally are unthinkable.

As local soviets by local party officers, so the central government is supervised by the central committee apparatus. The presidium of the central committee, or the narrower group of the secretariat within it—in any case the First Secretary's entourage—rather than any presidium of the council of ministers, is the true inner cabinet. The First Secretary, Nikita Khrushchev, announced in March 1958 his assumption of the chairmanship of the Council of Ministers also, but the latter office adds little to the power of the former, and at times has been entrusted to a relatively minor figure. In strong hands, however, it could conceivably be a rival force.

For propaganda the party is peculiarly responsible—it trains, appoints, and controls all newspaper editors, has a monopoly of education in the social sciences, and defines the faith. In other fields some other agency always shares responsibility, though the party alone is responsible for everything. Chief among the areas in which it acknowledges its concern as predominant is cadres work—all appointments, whether within its own ranks or in state agencies, trade unions, collective farms, or wherever projects which authority holds important may be furthered or impeded, whether the posts are nominally filled by election or not. Each bureau has a list of posts within its gift subject to approval by higher authority, but as in other fields this does not limit its responsibility for shortcomings.

The party staff is strictly charged to activate but not to duplicate or override soviet or other administrative agencies, to persuade, not to dictate. Yet it is by material results, the party proclaims, that it judges its agents. Inevitably, they often dictate. Whether other motives may have counseled reorganization of industrial management in 1957, the expression of satisfaction by *oblast* party secretaries seemed unmistakably genuine; whereas previously, they said, their power to direct had been limited by orders declared by ministries in Moscow, they would now be free to settle matters with organs under their own control. They would acquire influence where they already had responsibility.

BIBLIOGRAPHY: Merle Fainsod, *How Russia is Ruled*, Cambridge, 1953; John N. Hazard, *The Soviet System of Government*, Chicago, 1957; Herbert McClosky and John E. Turner, *The Soviet Dictatorship*, New York, 1960; Derek J. R. Scott, *Russian Political Institutions*, New York, 1958; Julian Towster, *Political Power in the USSR*, New York, 1948.   D. J. R. S.

GOVERNMENT, CENTRAL. The political history of Russia, from the establishment of the absolute monarchy in the 16th cent. until the present time, has been one of strong central government, with no real popular representation and very limited traditions of local autonomy. The powers of the Crown were limited for the first time, formally by the constitutional developments of 1905, but in fact the Crown continued to wield absolute power right up to its overthrow in March 1917. The governmental system created by the Bolsheviks follows the prerevolutionary tradition of a strong CG and an extensive bureaucracy.

The machinery of the CG in the 16th and 17th centuries was cumbersome and unmanageable. Supreme legislative, executive, and judicial authority became concentrated in the person of the tsar, with the boyars' duma and the *zemsky sobor* serving periodically as consultative bodies. The central administration was composed of a large number of haphazardly established government departments (*prikazy*) with overlapping duties and jurisdictions. In the early years of the reign of Peter the Great, the administrative and financial ap-

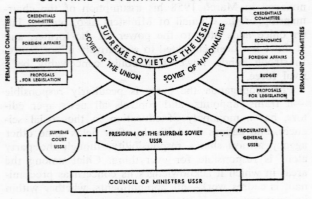

CENTRAL GOVERNMENT OF THE USSR

paratus was decentralized in an attempt to improve its efficiency. The result, however, was even greater chaos. With the creation of St. Petersburg as the new capital in 1712, the institutions of CG were reinforced and the central administration reformed on the model of the Swedish system of administrative colleges; nine colleges were established in Dec. 1717 (foreign affairs, state revenue, justice, state control, army, admiralty, commerce, extractive industry and manufactures, and state expenditures). These new central departments exercised their respective powers over the entire territory of Russia, while the former *prikazy* were often organized so as to fulfill all government functions within a given area. Each college was governed, in theory, by a board headed by a president, with decisions to be by a majority vote. In 1721 the colleges were made subordinate to the Senate, which had been created by Peter in 1711 to serve as an executive body in his absence. The Senate was in theory the chief administrative organ under the tsar. Its powers fluctuated over the years, especially after the creation of the procurator-general in 1722. The procurator-general at that time was the chief of the Senate chancery and represented the Crown at meetings of the Senate.

Continuous efforts were made over the years by the autocracy to reorganize the machinery of the CG in order to improve its efficiency. It was towards this end that Catherine the Great decentralized the administration through the local government reforms of 1775. By these reforms, the institutions of the CG lost many of their former functions. The position of the Senate as the chief administrative organ became weakened, and that of the procurator-general strengthened. Towards the end of the reign of Catherine, the procurator-general became an independent organ of state administration and no longer functioned as an officer of the Senate. He was in effect a combined minister of finance, justice, and the interior, and for all practical purposes the Crown's prime minister. In later years the procurator-general ceased to play an important role, his sole function being that of minister of justice. Catherine also introduced the Imperial Council, which acted as the chief advisory body to the monarch and consisted of the higher officers of State. By the end of Catherine's reign, the three principal agencies of the CG under

the Crown were the Imperial Council, the Senate and the procurator-general.

Under Alexander I, the Imperial Council was abolished and replaced by a "permanent council" of twelve elder statesmen. In addition, in 1802 the administrative colleges were abolished, a committee of ministers established, and the executive functions divided among eight ministries (war, navy, foreign affairs, justice, interior, finance, commerce, education). These ministries were reorganized, in 1810–11: the number of ministries was increased, personal responsibility was imposed upon the ministers, and the functions of each ministry carefully delimited. Also in 1810, a State Council was created to draft legislative bills and to advise the monarch. Throughout the 19th cent. and up to the revolution of 1905, the most important organs of the CG remained the State Council, the Senate, and the committee of ministers, all of which were instruments of the Crown. The administrative apparatus remained notoriously inefficient.

As a result of the revolutionary activities of 1905, the first representative assembly, the State Duma (q.v.), was introduced. While this body reflected to some degree public opinion, at least until 1907 and the Third Duma, it had very limited legislative powers. The executive functions remained in the hands of ministers appointed by and responsible only to the tsar. Although a council of ministers, with but little collective character, was also established in 1905 to perform the functions of the earlier committee of ministers, the tsar continued to deal with the ministers individually, thus hampering efforts at administrative unification.

With the revolution of March 1917, the liberal elements took control of the CG apparatus and the Provisional Government became the supreme organ of state authority. In fact, however, the Provisional Government shared power with the Petrograd Soviet from March until the Bolshevik revolution in November.

The second All-Russian Congress of Soviets, held immediately after the Bolshevik seizure of power and acting as the chief legislative authority, created the Council of People's Commissars (*sovnarkom*) as the new chief executive agency. The portfolios of the former Council of Ministers of the Provisional Government were divided among its members. Under the constitution adopted after the formation of the USSR in 1924, each union-republic had its own *sovnarkom*. Three types of commissariats (as the old ministries were renamed) were set up: all-union, which existed only at the USSR level and dealt with matters of concern to the USSR as a whole (e.g., foreign affairs, military and naval affairs, foreign trade, and posts and telegraph); union-republic, which existed in the governments of both the USSR and the union-republics, with the general supervisory functions found in the former and the execution of policy the responsibility of the latter; and republic, found only in the governments of the republics to deal with activities which could be left to the local level (e.g., justice, education, health and welfare).

In 1946 the Council of People's Commissars was renamed the Council of Ministers and the commissariats

THE SOVIET GOVERNMENT
(as of July 1, 1961)

COUNCIL OF MINISTERS: *Chairman*, Nikita S. Khrushchev; *First Deputy Chairmen*, Aleksey N. Kosygin, Anastas I. Mikoyan; *Deputy Chairmen*, Nikolay G. Ignatov, Vladimir N. Novikov, Dmitry F. Ustinov, Aleksandr F. Zasyadko.

MINISTRIES: Transport Construction: Yevgeny F. Kozhevnikov; Merchant Marine: Viktor G. Bakayev; Electric Power Station Construction: I. T. Novikov; Foreign Trade: Nikolay S. Patolichev; Railroad Communications: Boris P. Beshchev; Minister without portfolio: Ivan G. Kabanov; Foreign Affairs: Andrey A. Gromyko; Defense: Rodion Ya. Malinovsky; Finance: Vasily F. Garbuzov; Postal Services and Telecommunications: Nikolay D. Psurtsev; Geology and Mineral Resource Conservation: Pyotr Ya. Antropov; Health: Sergey V. Kurashov; Agriculture: Mikhail A. Olshansky; Higher Education: Vyacheslav P. Yelyutin; Culture: Yekaterina A. Furtseva.

DEPARTMENTS AT MINISTERIAL LEVEL: *Chairman:*
State Committee for Aviation Technology — Pyotr V. Dementyev
State Committee for Automation and Machine Building — Anatoly I. Kostousov
State Scientific and Economic Council — Aleksandr F. Zasyadko
State Committee for Foreign Economic Relations — Semyon A. Skachkov
State Committee for Questions of Labor and Wages — Aleksandr P. Volkov

State Committee for Defense Technology — Leonid V. Smirnov
State Committee for Radio and Electronics — Valery D. Kalmykov
State Committee for Shipbuilding — Boris Ye. Butoma
State Committee for Chemistry — Viktor S. Fedorov
Board of State Bank — A. K. Korovushkin
State Committee for Cultural Ties with Foreign Countries — Georgy A. Zhukov
State Committee for Sound and Television Broadcasting — S. Kaftanov
State Committee for the Use of Atomic Energy — V. S. Yemelyanov
State Committee for Coordination of Scientific Research Work — Konstantin N. Rudnev
State Control Commission — Georgy V. Yenyutin
Committee for State Security — Aleksandr N. Shelepin
State Committee for Building Affairs — Ivan A. Grishmanov
State Committee for State Purchases — Nikolay G. Ignatov
State Committee for Vocational and Technical Training — Gendrikh I. Zelenko
State Planning Commission (Gosplan) — Vladimir N. Novikov
Head of the Central Statistical Administration — Vladimir N. Starovsky

reverted to the designation of ministry. This system has continued, with frequent modifications, up to the present time. Previous to 1957, the Council of Ministers of the USSR was composed of the heads of the important all-union and union-republic ministries. In 1957 it was reorganized to include, in addition to the USSR ministers whose number was initially reduced, the chairmen of the Council of Ministers of each union-republic and the chairmen of a number of important state committees (e.g., Gosplan). At the head of each ministry is the minister and a number of deputy ministers. A small collegium composed of high officials of the ministry advises the minister, but can interfere with the minister's power of decision only by means of appeal to the Council of Ministers. The number and functions of the commissariats and ministries have been continually changing. Since 1957, the number of ministries is smaller than before the reorganization of that year, since economic activities are primarily under the control and supervision of regional economic councils (*sovnarkhozy*).

While the Supreme Soviet is the formal legislative body, the Presidium of the USSR Council of Ministers exercises supreme policy-making authority and coordinating responsibility. The exercise of governmental authority by the Council of Ministers is qualified, however, by the fact that the ultimate power of decision resides in the top party organs. Since most of the top leaders in the state apparatus, including the Council of Ministers, are members of the higher party organs, conflicts of policy always remain within the party and presumably take the form of differences between the representatives of the party bureaucracy and those of the state bureaucracy. As in prerevolutionary Russia, the USSR today is plagued by the conflicting needs of centralized control and efficient administration.

R. C.

GOVERNMENT, LOCAL. Local administration in the 17th cent. was carried on by appointed military governors (*voyevoda*), who were the chief representatives of the Crown in the cities and rural areas and for all practical purposes the masters of the territory under their jurisdiction. Their powers were as broad as they were ill-defined. Such institutions of local self-government as existed at this time functioned side by side with the *voyevoda* and under his close control and supervision. The duties of local self-government became those of providing the central authorities with officials for the collection of taxes.

In 1707 Peter the Great divided Russia into provinces (*gubernia*) under appointed governors. Although created for the purpose of bringing army units in close relation to the groups of taxpayers who provided for their maintenance, the new provinces also furnished the territorial framework for the organization of all governmental activities and lasted until the Bolshevik revolution. Later in Peter's reign the provinces were further divided into counties (*provintsia*), which were each divided into several districts (*uyezd*). The county became the basic unit of local administration, and was headed by a *voyevoda*. The administration of the cities was made subject to the close supervision of that of the county, and the latter to the provincial governor.

During most of the 18th cent., the administrative practice in the 17th century was carried out within the framework of the territorial-administrative structure of LG introduced by Peter. Under the pressure of the nobility for a greater voice in the conduct of local affairs, Catherine the Great increased considerably the number of provinces. Local administration was to be conducted on the principles of decentralization, separation of functions within the organs of LG, the filling of administrative and judicial offices partly by appointment and partly by election, and the granting of predominance in local affairs to the nobility, merchants, and free peasants (Law of 1775). These LG reforms of Catherine proved a failure. Election of local officials was abolished by Paul in 1800 but restored by Alexander in 1801; nevertheless by the mid-19th cent. local administration in Russia was in the hands of notoriously corrupt petty bureaucrats appointed by the central government.

Catherine also began the vigorous enforcement of the principle of administrative unification and "Russification" which was to continue until the revolutions of 1917. National autonomy was sharply curtailed, with the various national areas being absorbed administratively into the R. Empire. The case of Finland was the only major exception to this practice in later years. During the reign of Nicholas I, local institutions dealing with local economic problems (provincial road commissions, committees on provisioning, and committees on local dues and charges) came into being. These bodies played a subordinate role, but are often regarded as the precursors of the local self-government act of 1864.

The emancipation statutes of Feb. 1861 retained the village commune as the basic unit of peasant organization, and created a new administrative-territorial division, the township or rural district (*volost*). The *volost* was composed of one or more village communes and dealt exclusively with the affairs of the peasantry. Both the village commune and the *volost* enjoyed in theory some degree of self-government. The actual administration of peasant affairs was carried on by the village and *volost* elders, who were subordinated to appointed administrative and police officials vested with comprehensive disciplinary powers. The reform of the system of LG established by Catherine followed from the emancipation statutes. A statute of 1864 created a system of zemstvos which were the institution of LG until the Bolshevik revolution in 1917. The autonomy of the zemstvos was continually restricted, and these bodies were increasingly subjected to central government interference. After Nov. 1917, the soviets exercised the functions of LG. As the Bolshevik regime consolidated its power, the local soviets came to be instruments by which the masses were mobilized to carry out the policies decided upon by the leaders of the Communist party. (*See also* ZEMSTVO, SOVIETS, MUNICIPAL GOVERNMENT.)

BIBLIOGRAPHY: Michael T. Florinsky, *Russia: A History and an Interpretation*, New York, 1953.

GOVERNMENT, MUNICIPAL. The urban settlements of Russia before Peter the Great were backward and very poor. In 1720 an organ of the central government was set up to oversee municipal affairs. This body enacted a charter of municipal institutions in 1724, organizing the urban population on a corporate basis and dividing it into three "guilds": (1) the wealthy merchants and other prosperous elements, (2) the small merchants, traders, and artisans, (3) the balance of the population. A municipal council was elected by the first two guilds, but its members came only from the first. The main function of the municipal council was to collect taxes, but its activities extended to police, judicial, and other administrative matters. By 1727, these rudimentary institutions of municipal government had been integrated into the bureaucratic structure of local administration.

In 1785, Catherine the Great endeavored to rebuild the moribund municipal government structure by issuing a Charter of the Cities. The urban population was divided into six groups: (1) property owners, (2) mer-

chants, (3) artisans, (4) nonresidents and foreign merchants, (5) "distinguished citizens," a category which included bankers, former officials, intellectuals, and other leading personages, and (6) unskilled workers and small traders. All groups participated in the election of a municipal council. The city was to be run by an executive board of six members, one from each group, chosen by the municipal council. The police powers remained in the hands of an official appointed by the Crown. These institutions exercised no real influence, the business of the city government continuing to be conducted by appointed officials according to a system which had no basis in law.

A bill on the reorganization of the municipalities to replace the charter of 1785 was promulgated in June 1870. Provision was made for a municipal council, and an executive board and mayor elected by the council. The electorate was divided according to tax assessment, with the large taxpayers being represented far out of proportion to their numbers. The functions and powers of the municipal institutions were restricted primarily to local economic and social needs. There was no executive power, only a limited right of taxation, and considerable control by officials of the Crown. The municipal government act of June 1892 further restricted the franchise and tightened bureaucratic controls. Despite their limitations, the new municipalities succeeded in carrying through many progressive measures designed to alleviate the economic and social problems of the time, especially in the fields of education and public health. During the short reign of the Provisional Government, the composition of the municipal councils became completely revolutionary through the forced resignation of the former members. Under the Bolsheviks, the city, town, and village Soviets became the institutions of municipal government. (*See also* SOVIETS.)

BIBLIOGRAPHY: Michael T. Florinsky, *Russia: A History and an Interpretation*, New York, 1953.

GOVERNOR: *see* GOVERNMENT LOCAL.

GOVERNOR-GENERAL: *see* GOVERNMENT LOCAL.

GÓVOROV, Leoníd Aleksándrovich (1897–1955), Soviet military leader, marshal of the Soviet Union. Born in a peasant family in the Kirov Oblast, he fought in the civil war and joined the Red Army in 1919. He took part in the Soviet-Finnish War of 1939–40 and became a member of the CPSU in 1942. During World War II he was, first, in charge of the army at the western front and, later, commanded the army defending Leningrad. In 1944, he was made marshal of the Soviet Union.

GPU: *see* SECURITY POLICE.

GRABÁR, Igor Emmanuilovich (1871–1960), art historian, architect, and painter of impressionistic landscapes (*Blue February*, 1904; *Snow in March*, 1904; *Birches*, 1939). A pupil of Repin, he joined the group *Mir Iskusstva* (World of Art) (q.v.). In 1909–16 he wrote and edited the first comprehensive *History of Russian Art*, still a classic, of which five volumes have appeared. G was curator of the Tretyakov Gallery from 1913 to 1925, head of the Department of Protection of Historical Monuments, and from 1944 to his death, director of the Institute of Fine Arts of the Ac. of S. As a leading Soviet artist G painted many iconographic portraits of Lenin and other Soviet figures. He also wrote several art monographs (*Andrey Rublyov,* 1925; *Ilya Repin,* 1937).

GRADÓVSKY, Aleksándr Dmítrievich (1841–1889), prof. of public law, University of St. Petersburg, and contributor to the periodical *Golos* (Voice). He believed in the rule of law and the preservation of individual liberties, while reserving a positive function for the state.

GRÁFTIO, Génrikh Ósipovich (1869–1949), power engineer, a pioneer of Soviet hydrotechnical power construction. Fellow, Ac. of S., USSR (1932). Graduate, Novorossiysk University in Odessa (1892), St. Petersburg Institute of Railway Engineering (1896). Professor, Leningrad Institute of Electrical Engineering (1921). Designed and built railways and streetcar lines (1900–17); planned electrification of railways and hydroelectric power plants. During World War II participated in the building of power plants in the E. part of the USSR.

GRAIN CROPS accounted for 64.0% of the total area sown in 1958, a decline from 88.5% in 1913 and 81.6% in 1928. The main GC cultivated in the USSR are: wheat (53% of the area planted to GC in 1958), rye (14%), oats (12%), barley and corn, (7% each). Gross output of GC amounted, in mill. tons, to 86.0 in 1913 (within present Soviet boundaries), 73.3 in 1928, 95.5 in 1940, 47.3 in 1945, and 124.8 in 1959.

Grain products are a basic component of the Russian diet; grain is also an important feed and industrial raw material. It was tsarist Russia's main export, accounting for 45% of the value of all agricultural

BARN HARVEST OF GRAIN CROPS
(bill. poods; 1 pood = 36.11 lbs.)

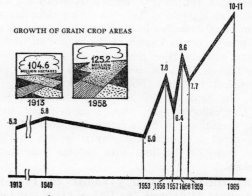

GROWTH OF GRAIN CROP AREAS

exports over the period 1911–15. Exports of grain were also used to finance purchases of machinery in the early 1930's. Raising and controlling the marketed share of the output of GC were therefore a central issue in Soviet economic policy. The marketed share declined at first from 26% of gross output in 1914 to only 11% in 1928, as the result of fragmentation of holdings and growth of subsistence farming. Collectivization raised it to 39% by 1937 and 41% in 1939. With the exception of negligible amounts traded in *kolkhoz* markets, the state has a monopoly over marketings of grain.

Collectivization was less successful in raising the

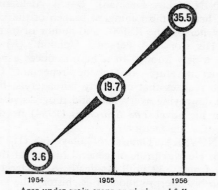

Area under grain crops on virgin and fallow lands (mill. ha.)

output of GC which, until Stalin's death, increased but little (73.6 mill. tons over the 1928–32 average, against 80.9 mill. over the 1949–53 average). Yields improved insignificantly (from 334 to 343 lb. per acre over the same period). A considerable increase in the output of GC was achieved since 1954, primarily owing to the putting under cultivation of the so-called virgin lands—mainly steppe land situated in Kazakhstan, W. Siberia, and adjacent areas. Some 81.5 mill. acres (or 31% of the total area under GC in 1953) were ploughed between 1954 and 1958, most of it being allocated to GC, especially wheat. Most of the new lands were organized as state farms, raising the latter's share in total marketings of grain from 10% in 1953 to 36% in 1958. The impressive expansion of GC into the virgin lands has been the main source of increased grain output in recent years (113.1 mill. tons annual average over the 1954–58 period). The long-run success of this program will depend on the effects of wind erosion, droughts, and possible decline in soil fertility —phenomena characteristic for the areas in question.

Collectivization changed the methods of grain production by substituting, on a large scale, machinery for horses in field work. As for 1958, 98% of spring ploughing and 97% of sowing were done by tractor and 92% of harvesting was done with the use of combines. Nevertheless the overall efficiency of Soviet grain farming and especially labor productivity are low. According to Khrushchev, it took, in 1958, 73 man-hours of labor for each ton produced in *kolkhozy*, against 18 on state farms, and 10 on an average farm in the United States.

L. S.

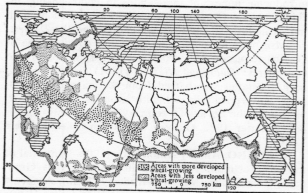

Areas under wheat

GRÁNIN, (alias German), **Daniíl Aleksándrovich**, (1919–), head of the Leningrad branch of the Union of Soviet Writers of the RSFSR and author of many short stories. His story "A Personal Opinion" (*Novy Mir*, 1956) is widely known. In it he introduces a new type into Soviet literature—that of the "repentant" Communist, who realizes that old party bureaucrats, like himself, are destroying every new and progressive development. In his novel *The Searchers* (1954) he describes the life of a big factory.

GRANÓVSKY, **Timoféy Nikoláyevich** (1813–1855), historian. He was prof. of general history at the U. of Moscow from 1839 until his death. A moderate "westerner" in his interpretation of R. history, he combined an awareness of organic development, derived from Hegel and Savigny, with a liberal-humanist orientation inspired by Guizot and Thierry.

GRÁVE, **Dmítry Aleksándrovich** (1863–1939), mathematician. Fellow, Ac. of S., Ukrainian SSR (1919); honorary member, Ac. of S., USSR (1929). Graduate, St. Petersburg University. Founder of the first R. algebraic school of thought (Kiev) which had a major influence on the development of Soviet algebra. Simplified the theory of Galois. After the 1917 revolution, his research concerned primarily applied mathematics and mechanics.

GREBENSHCHIKÓV, **Ilyá Vasílyevich** (1887–1953), chemist. Fellow (1953) and member of the executive board (1947), Ac. of S., USSR. Graduate of St. Petersburg University (1910); professor of physics, chemistry, and the theory of electrochemistry, St. Petersburg Institute of Electrical Engineering (1922–32). Cofounder of the State Institute of Physical Optics in Leningrad; founder and director of the Chemical Laboratory of Silicates (1933) which was to become the Chemical Institute of Silicates (1948). G's research concerned the effects of ultrahigh pressures on crystallization temperatures of organic compounds and binary eutectic system, and the use of transparent plastics in the optical field. Author of *The Chemical Stability of Glass* (1931); *The Physical Chemistry of Ternary Systems* (1949). Stalin prizes (1941, 1942).

GRECHANÍNOV, **Aleksándr Tikhónovich** (1864–1956), composer, pupil of Arensky and Rimsky-Korsakov. His "Lullaby" sold millions of copies. G wrote 355 songs and romances on texts by Pushkin, Lermontov, Baudelaire, and others. He composed several masses introducing important innovations in choir singing, including *Missa Oecumenica* which can be used by both the Orthodox and the Catholic church and the *Demestvennaya* mass for piano and voice. His *Credo* is one of G's masterpieces. He wrote also five symphonies and two operas: *Dobrynya Nikitich* (1901) and *Sister Beatrice;* the latter was barred from the stage by the imperial government on religious grounds and was forbidden by the Soviets as contrary to their antireligious policy. After 1922 G lived abroad and died in New York.

GRÉCHKO, **Andréy Antónovich** (1903–), marshal of the Soviet Union. Participant in the civil war. Graduated from Frunze Military Academy (1936), Academy of the General Staff (1941). During World War II was division, corps, and army commander. In 1953 was named chief commander of Soviet troops in Germany, and in Nov. 1957, first deputy minister of defense and commander in chief of land forces. In 1960 became commander in chief of the unified armed forces of the Warsaw Treaty Powers. Deputy to the Supreme Soviet, Hero of the Soviet Union.

GREEK ORTHODOXY: *see* ORTHODOX CHURCH.

GRÉKOV, **Borís Dmítrievich** (1882–1953), historian. Author of monographs on the development of feudal relationships in Russia. Member of the Ac. of S. (1935) and recipient of three Stalin awards. G was a professor of history at Moscow University.

GRÉKOV, **Mitrofán Borísovich** (1882–1934), battlefield painter. Graduated from the Academy of Fine Arts in St. Petersburg in 1911. Fought in the First Cavalry Army in the civil war. Made a series of pictures of the cavalry men (*Machine-Gun Cart, Trumpet-Players, Battle at Tsaritsyn,* in Tretyakov Gallery, Museum of the Red Army, and others).

GRIBOYÉDOV, **Aleksándr Sergéyevich** (1795–1829), leading playwright of the early 19th century. Son of  an officer, he studied science and law at the University of Moscow, then served in the army during the Napoleonic Invasion of 1812. After the war he entered the civil service in the ministry of foreign affairs; in 1818 he was sent to Persia as secretary to the Russian mission; in 1826 he was arrested on the charge of association with the Decembrists but was released and returned to his diplomatic post. He negotiated the peace treaty of 1828 that ended the Russo-Persian war, and was appointed minister to Persia. He perished when attacked by the mob in the Russian legation in Teheran during riots. He wrote a number of comedies in prose and in verse and a few lyric poems, but is known as the author of one great Russian comedy *Woe from Wit* or *The Mischief of Being Clever,* 1822–24, comprising an extensive gallery of satirical portraits (Eng. translation by B. Pares, 1925). Its hero, Chatsky, is the prototype of the so-called superfluous man, who criticizes social and political conditions in his country but does nothing to bring about a change. The play is written in rhymed verse; many of the lines have become proverbial expressions.

GRIGORÓVICH, **Dmítry Vasílyevich** (1822–1899), prose writer. His novels *The Village* (1846) and *Anton Goremýka* (1847) depict sympathetically the hard peasant life; *Country Roads* (1852) and *Settlers* (1855–56) are rich in ethnographical material.

GRIGÓRYEV, **Apollón Aleksándrovich** (1822–1864), critic and poet, born of a middle-class family. He studied at the University of Moscow, became editor of the journal *The Muscovite* in 1850, and later joined the staff of *Time* under the editorship of Dostoyevsky with whom he became close friends. As a critic, G rejected the literary views of Belinsky and believed that art has its own laws. His beliefs in everything distinctly R. made him close to the Slavophiles. His Bohemian poetry is now forgotten, except his *Two Guitars* which became a song.

GRIN, Aleksándr (Aleksándr Stepánovich Grinévsky) (1880–1932), author of fantastic novels. Was a Socialist Revolutionary and suffered persecution both before and after the revolution. G's works may be divided into two groups. The first includes the novels *The Adventures of Ginch* (1914), *The Rat-Catcher* (1925), and *An Autobiographical Tale* (1929–31), the final chapters of which have never been published. In these works the action takes place in Russia. In the novels, stories, and tales of the second group, the action moves to an imaginary land. G's work was influenced by Edgar Allen Poe and Herman Melville.

GRÍNBERG, Aleksándr Abrámovich (1898–), chemist. Corresponding member, Ac. of S., USSR (1943). Graduate, Leningrad University (1924); professor, Lensovet Institute of Technology in Leningrad (1936). Research concerns acid basicity and oxidation and use of tagged atoms in complex compounds, their equilibrium in aqueous solutions. Author of *Introduction of Complex Compounds into Chemistry,* two vols. (1951). Stalin prize (1946).

GRÓDNO, city, adm. center of Grodno Oblast, Byelorussian SSR, landing on Neman River; pop. 49,000 (1939), 72,000 (1959). Ind.: metal, woodworking, tobacco, leather, shoes, textiles. Ped. inst. Founded at the end of 11th century.

GRÓDNO OBLAST, in W. Byelorussian SSR; area 9,650 sq. mi.; pop. 1,077,000 (1960). Cities: Grodno (adm. center), Lida, Volkovysk. Is a rolling plain in the basin of Neman which is used for timber floating; has mild climate, podzol and meadow soil. Agr.: rye, oats, buckwheat, wheat, flax, hemp. Ind.: textiles, rubber, shoes, lumber, food processing. Pedag. and agr. inst. Est. 1944, absorbed part of Molodechno Oblast 1960.

GRÓMOV, Valerián Innokéntyevich (1896–), geologist. Research concerns the application of paleontological methods for the stratigraphy of Quaternary deposits. Formulated the chronology of the basic stages in the making of prepatrimonial society and suggested the most ancient forms of the patrimonial system. Author of *Paleontological and Archeological Substantiation of the Stratigraphy of Continental Deposits During the Quaternary Period of the Territory of the USSR* (1948). Stalin prize (1948).

GROMÝKO, Andréy Andréyevich (1909–), Soviet diplomat. Graduate of the Minsk Agricultural Institute and the Moscow Institute of Economics; candidate of economics, and senior scientific associate of the Institute of Economics, Ac. of S. Member of the CP since 1931. G began his diplomatic career in 1939 as head of the American Department of People's Commissariat for Foreign Affairs; in 1939–43, counselor of the Soviet Embassy in the USA. In 1943–46 G was ambassador to the United States, and simultaneously ambassador to Cuba. G participated in the Teheran, Yalta, and Berlin conferences, was a member of the Soviet delegation to the San Francisco conference; headed the Soviet delegation to

Dumbarton Oaks and took part in the foreign ministers' conferences. In 1946–48 G was the permanent Soviet representative to the Security Council; in 1946–49, deputy minister of foreign affairs, in 1952–53, ambassador to Great Britain, in 1953–57, first deputy minister of foreign affairs; and in 1957 was appointed minister of foreign affairs. G is a deputy to the Supreme Soviet of the USSR.

GROSSGÉYM, Aleksándr Alfónsovich (1888–1948), botanist. Fellow, Ac. of S., USSR (1946), Azerbaijan SSR (1945). Graduate, Moscow University (1912); professor, Baku (1929) and Leningrad universities (1947–48). Research concerned classification and distribution of plants in the Caucasus. Author of *The Flora of the Caucasus* (1934), *Plant Resources of the Caucasus* (1946). Stalin prize (1948); V. L. Komarov prize (1946).

GRÓSSMAN, Leoníd Petróvich (1888–), novelist, poet, and scholar. Of his many works, the most interesting are those written during the NEP period: *Method and Style,* a collection; *Studies on Pushkin; Three Contemporaries; Tyutchev, Dostoyevsky; Appolon Grigoryev; The Poetics of Dostoyevsky*; and others. From the 1930's on, G wrote mostly biographies of R. writers, including Leskov (1945) and Pushkin (1958). As a novelist, G brought out *The Confessions of a Jew* (1924) and two historical novels about the time of Pushkin and Dostoyevsky. G's poetry shows the influence of Kuzmin and Voloshin.

GRÓSSMAN, Vasíly Semyónovich (1905–), novelist and playwright. Graduated in physics and mathematics from Moscow University. His first novel, *Glückauf,* written in the early 1930's, deals with the life of Donets basin miners. His second, *Stepan Kolchugin* (1937–40), presents a rather distorted picture of prerevolutionary Russia and of the revolutionary movement. In 1946 he completed the play *If We Were to Believe the Pythagorians,* which, however, was banned as being "ideologically unacceptable." In 1949–52 G worked on the first chapters of the novel *For a Just Cause.* However, these chapters got G into trouble with the literary critics of Stalin's era. He was accused of dwelling excessively on the hardships and privations of the people. In 1960 G completed his new novel *Life and Destiny.*

GRÓZNY, city, capital of Chechen-Ingush ASSR, RSFSR, on Sunzha River; pop. 172,000 (1939), 240,000 (1959). Major oil center, second only to Baku, connected by pipelines with Makhachkala on the Caspian Sea and with Tuapse and Rostov-on-Don. Founded as a frontier fortress in 1818.

GRUM-GRZHIMÁYLO, Grigóry Yefímovich (1860–1936), explorer. Graduated from St. Petersburg University (1884). Studied the Pamirs and the Tien Shan Mountain range (1884–87); led major expedition of the Russian Geographical Society to Central Asia (1889-90). Discoverer of the Turfan depression; collector of valuable botanical and zoological material. N. M. Przhevalsky award of the Russian Geographical Society (1891), P. A.

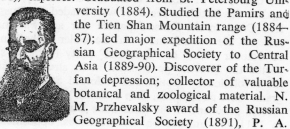

Chikhachev prize of the Paris Academy (1893). Author of numerous publications on the geography, history, botany, zoology and ethnography of Central Asia.

GUARDS, term used in olden times for the personal guard of the monarch or army commander, later for the more privileged troops. The oldest R. Guard regiments, the Preobrazhensky and Semyonovsky, were founded by Peter I at the end of the 17th century. The title of "guards" was reintroduced in Russia during World War II and was awarded to several divisions which had distinguished themselves in the defense of Moscow.

GUBÁKHA, city in Perm Oblast, RSFSR, center of coal mining in the Kizel coal basin; pop. 65,000 (1958). Coke-chemical plant.

GUBERNIA: *see* GOVERNMENT LOCAL, ADMINISTRATIVE AND TERRITORIAL DIVISIONS.

GÚBKIN, Iván Mikháylovich (1871–1939), geologist and statesman. Father of S. I. Gubkin. Fellow, Ac. of  S. (1929). Graduate, St. Petersburg Mining Institute (1910). After the 1917 revolution returned to Russia from the USA. Professor (1920), principal (1922–1930), Moscow Mining Academy. Initiated organization of Moscow Petroleum Institute (1930) and State Petroleum Research Institute (1924) which was reorganized into Institute of Mineral Fuels, Ac. of S. (1934). Founder of Soviet petroleum geology. Deputy, Supreme Soviet USSR (1937). Vice president, Ac. of S. (1936), and president, Azerbaijan Branch, Ac. of S. (1937). Head of the Soviet delegation to the 16th session of the International Geological Congress in Washington and president of the 17th session of this Congress in Moscow (1937). In his classic work *Science of Petroleum* (1932) G summarized the results of his studies on the origin of petroleum and conditions of petroleum deposits formation.

GÚBKIN, Sergéy Ivánovich (1898–1955), physical metallurgist. Fellow, Ac. of S., Byelorussian SSR (1947). Graduate, Mining Ac. in Moscow (1928); professor, Moscow Institute of Nonferrous Metals and Gold (1932); Director, Institute of Physical Technology (1948); affiliated with the Institute of Metallurgy, Ac. of S. (1944–53). Research concerned the theory of plastic deformation; plastic working; theory of metal flow; principles of forging, stamping, extrusion, and drawing. Author of *Plastic Deformation of Magnetic Alloys* (1955), *Photoplasticity* (1957).

GUCHKÓV, Aleksándr Ivánovich (1862–1936), political leader, born into a family of wealthy Moscow merchants. After studying philosophy and history at the University of Moscow G traveled extensively, fought against the British in the Boer war, headed the Russian Red Cross in the Russo-Japanese war and was made prisoner. He was a founder and the leader of the "Union of October 17th," or "Octobrist" party (q.v.). G supported the imperial government in its struggle against the revolutionary groups and endorsed Stolypin's program, "first pacification, then reforms." In 1910 G was elected president of the third State Duma but resigned in 1911. G's attitude on defense issues, opposition to

Rasputin and criticism of court circles antagonized the emperor. During World War I he headed the Red Cross and later was president of the Central War Industries Committee. A severe critic of the imperial regime, G went to Pskov in March 1917 to secure the abdication of Emperor Nicholas II; he was the first minister of war and navy in the Provisional Government but was forced to resign in May 1917. He left Russia soon after the Bolshevik Revolution and lived in Paris where he was active in anti-Soviet movements.

GUDTSÓV, Nikoláy Timoféyevich (1885–1957), physical metallurgist. Fellow, Ac. of S., USSR (1939). Honored Scientist, RSFSR. Graduate, St. Petersburg Polytechnic Institute (1911); professor, Leningrad Polytechnic Institute (1930), Moscow Steel Institute (1943). Affiliated with the Leningrad Institute of Metals (1928–39), Institute of Metallurgy, Ac. of S. (1939). Research concerned the application of alloy steel in the automobile industry, crystallization phenomena, X-ray examinations. Stalin prize (1943).

GUIDED MISSILES: *see* ROCKETRY.

GUMILYÓV, Nikoláy Stepánovich (1886–1921), one of the founders of the acmeist movement (q.v.) in R. poetry and one of the leaders of R. modernism. He traveled widely and repeatedly in W. Europe and in Africa, and studied in Paris at the Sorbonne. He was executed in 1921 for supposed participation in a conspiracy against the Soviet government—the Tagantsev Affair.

After publishing a series of theoretical articles under the title "Letters Concerning Russian Poetry" in the journal *Apollon*, G organized, in 1911, The Poets' Workshop, which united an important group of writers who were repelled, as he was, by extreme symbolism. In 1913 he published a manifesto concerning the principles of acmeism.

G's poems are permeated with color, exotic imagery, and musical effects, and are tinged with romanticism. His published collections include: *The Path of the Conquistador* (1905); *Romantic Flowers* (1908); *Pearls* (1910); *A Foreign Sky* (1912); *Quiver* (1916); *Gondola*, a drama in verse (1916); *To a Deep-Blue Star* (published posthumously); *The Camp Fire* (1918); the African poem *Mic* (1918); the collection of Chinese poems *The Porcelain Pavilion* (1918); *The Tent* (1921); *The Pillar of Fire* (1921). G's work also include a Russian translation of *Hilgamet* (a Babylonian epic) and of Coleridge's *Rime of the Ancient Mariner*.

GUMILYÓVSKY, Lev Ivánovich (1890–), novelist and journalist. Before the revolution wrote stories and essays in a liberal vein. After the revolution, following Artsybashev's footsteps, he gained prominence by treating a subject matter rare in Soviet literature: sex. His novels *Dogs' Alley* (1925–26) and *Playing at Love* (1927–28) caused quite a stir. G also became known for his adventure novels *The White Soils* (1928) and *The Land of Hyperborea* (1929). Later worked on the popularization of scientific discoveries. In 1958 he published, in the magazine *Voprosy literatury* (Problems of Literature), his *Writer's Journal*, which indicts the lack of sincerity in Soviet literature.

GURÉVICH, Mikhaíl Iósifovich (1892–), aeronautical engineer. For two years studied at Department of Physics and Mathematics, Kharkov Univeristy. During 1917 revolution he emigrated to France but returned to Kharkov in 1921. Graduate of Kharkov Institute of Technology (1925). For several years was designing various types of gliders. Since 1929 has been associated with the aircraft industry. In cooperation with A. I. Mikoyan designed the MIG-1 and other MIG-type aircraft. At present is engaged in improving rocket fighters. Stalin prizes (1941, 1947, 1948, 1949).

GURILYÓV, Aleksándr Lvóvich (1803–1858), composer, son of the composer L. S. Gurilyov, of peasant origin. Wrote popular and folk songs, and music for piano.

GÚRKO, Iósif Vladímirovich (1828–1901), general, field marshal. He became famous in the battles of Tyrnov, Shipka, and Gorny Dubnyak during the wars of 1877–78 with Turkey. While Governor General of Poland, he carried out a policy of Russification and suppressed revolutionary movements.

GÚRYEV, city, adm. center of Guryev Oblast, Kazakh SSR at the mouth of Ural River; pop. 41,000 (1939), 78,000 (1959). Center of oil industry; fisheries. Terminus of pipeline to Orsk. Founded in 17th century.

GÚRYEV OBLAST in W. Kazakh SSR around lower course of the Ural River and at the Caspian shore; navigation on the Caspian Sea and the Ural; area 107,540 sq. mi.; pop. 288,000 (1959): Kazakhs, Russians, and Tatars. Cities: Guryev (adm. center) and Fort Shevchenko. Semidesert lowlands; minerals are oil, coal, potassium salts, iron, copper, manganese, borates; when irrigated, wheat and rice are grown; animal breeding, karakul lambs; oil-refining, borates, fish-canning ind.; pedag. and med. institutes. Est. 1938.

GÚRYEVSK, city in Kemerovo Oblast, RSFSR; pop. 30,600 (1956); metallurgical and cement plants.

GURZÚF, sea resort in the Crimea, Ukrainian SSR, 10 mi. N.E. from Yalta; pop. 4,800 (1956).

GÚSEV, Vladímir Nikoláyevich (1904–1956), electrochemical engineer. Graduated from Leningrad Polytechnic Institute (1930). Worked at "Bolshevik" plant (1930–36), Scientific Research Institute (1936–56). Research concerned electrical methods of metal machining widely used in the USSR. Author of *Mechanical Anodic Treatment of Metals* (1952). Stalin prizes (1942, 1948, 1949).

GUS-KHRUSTALNY, city in Vladimir Oblast, RSFSR; pop. 53,000 (1959). Ancient center of glass ind. and crystal works.

GVÓZDEV, Alekséy Alekséyevich (1897–), construction engineer. Fellow, Ac. of Construction and Architecture, USSR (1956). Graduate (1922), professor (1933), Moscow Institute of Railway Engineering; instructor, Moscow Military Engineering Ac. (1932–41), Moscow Institute of Civil Engineering (1942). Supervised research on prefabricated reinforced-concrete structures. Stalin prize (1951).

GVOZDYÓV, Kuzmá Antónovich (1883–), a Menshevik leader. In tsarist Russia he was repeatedly arrested and exiled for revolutionary activity. During World War I G headed a labor group in the Central War Industries Committee. After the February Revolution became one of the leaders of the Executive Committee of the Petrograd Soviet. In 1917 he was appointed minister of labor in the Provisional Government. He opposed Bolshevik rule but, later, withdrew from active political life and held minor posts in the Soviet economic apparatus.

GYDÁ GULF, in Kara Sea, deep inside Gyda Peninsula.

GYDÁ PENINSULA, in N. Siberia, between Ob Bay and Yenisey Gulf; tundra and forests; reindeer breeding, hunting, fishing.

GYDÁN: *see* KOLYMA RANGE.

H

HANIECKI (Fürstenberg), **Yákov Stanislávovich** (1879–1937), Polish socialist and Bolshevik. A founding member of the Polish Social Democratic party (SDKPiL), he spent many years in Switzerland and Germany participating in several socialist congresses including Zimmerwald where he supported Lenin. Wrote under the pseudonyms "Kuba," "Henryk." During World War I, he appears to have been involved in some dubious negotiations with the Germans. H joined the Bolsheviks in 1917. In the 30's he held numerous diplomatic posts negotiating treaties with Finland, Latvia, and Poland. From 1935 he was director of the Museum of the Revolution.

HAYDAMÁKI: (1) Cossack and peasant troops in Ukraine in the 18th century acting against Poland, who reached their highest development in 1768 under the leadership of Zheleznyák and Gónta; **(2)** in 1918–19 troops of Ukrainian Rada of Hetman Skoropadsky.

HEALTH INSURANCE: *see* SOCIAL INSURANCE.
HERMITAGE: *see* MUSEUMS.
HÉRZEN (Gértsen), Aleksándr Ivánovich (1812–1870), radical journalist, philosopher, and literary critic—in the opinion of many, the greatest and noblest of the R. radicals. Born in Moscow, the illegitimate son of a wealthy noble, H suffered an uncertain and troubled childhood, but he read widely, found a lifelong friend in N. P. Ogarev, and secured a sci-entific education at the University of Moscow. An admirer of the Decembrists (q.v.), H was arrested for his part in a radical discussion group, and was exiled (1834) to Vyatka. During military service, he eloped romantically with a cousin (1838), and returned to live chiefly in St. Petersburg and Moscow. His father's death (1846) left him a fortune of half a

million rubles, with which he escaped from Russia (Jan. 1847) to spend the rest of his life in exile in W. Europe. He greeted the revolutions of 1848 with enthusiasm; their failure, conjoined with his wife's unfaithfulness, plunged him into a depression. From these events came *From the Other Shore* (1850), a denunciation of reactionary *and* revolutionary violence in "bourgeois" Europe, and his lengthy *Memoirs* (1855–56) of his childhood, marriage, and wanderings. H settled in London (1852) where he was joined by his friend Ogarev and moved in a distinguished circle of Englishmen, R. and European exiles, notably Mazzini. There, chiefly at his own expense, he published a review, *Polyarnaya Zvezda* (The Polar Star) (1855–62), and the celebrated fortnightly journal, *Kolokol* (The Bell, 1857–67), which he and Ogarev wrote largely themselves. During its first five years, *Kolokol* was the most influential journal in R. history. Most of its copies, which never exceeded 3,000 an issue, were smuggled into Russia and were read by everyone of importance, including Alexander II. H had contacts high in the government who sent him information that made *Kolokol* the only public source of news about the progress of bills for the emancipation of the serfs and other reforms which were being drafted in secret by government committees. H's ringing editorials in favor of reform attracted wide support, as did his denunciations of the inadequacy of emancipation when it came ("The people need *land and freedom!*"). But he favored the Polish insurrection of 1863 (q.v.), and thereby killed most of *Kolokol's* influence and circulation (which fell to 500). A move to Geneva (1865) failed to revive it. H came to feel increasingly out of touch with the younger and more extreme R. radicals, and died in Paris (1870).

H's intellectual pilgrimage was long and complicated. Influenced when young by such diverse thinkers as Feuerbach and Swedenborg, he passed, after 1848, through a period of Byronic pessimism. In his maturity (from 1852) he asserted now materialism and now the independence of the human spirit, ending life as a "skeptical Christian." His emphases on the diversity of the universe and the pricelessness of man's freedom and development are not reducible to any set doctrine. His social and political views can be called both "liberal" and "socialist." He was most important as a critic, castigating both the R. regime and "bourgeois" Europe, but after the failures of 1848, most of the time he opposed revolutionary action and violence, especially in Russia. In some ways a R. messianist, H defended Russia against European contempt, dwelt on the R. village commune as a collective institution morally superior to "bourgeois" Europe, and suggested that Russia might well skip capitalism and move directly to socialism, a guide for Europe to follow. But he feared that technology in an unfree Russia would produce a doubly dangerous "Genghis Khan with telegraphs."

BIBLIOGRAPHY: A. Herzen, *From the Other Shore and Memoirs* (*My Past and Thoughts*); T. G. Massaryk, *The Spirit of Russia*, London and New York, 1955; E. Lampert, *Studies in Rebellion*, London and New York, 1957.

HÉSSEN, Iósif Vladímirovich (1866–1943), one of the leaders of the Constitutional Democratic party. Editor of the daily *Rech* (Speech), 1905–18. After the October revolution, H emigrated to Berlin where he edited the daily *Rul* (Rudder) and the *Archives of Russian Revolution* (22 volumes).

HETMAN: (1) In the 16th century, the elected commander of Zaporozhye Cossack army; in the 17th-18th centuries, ruler of the Ukraine, East of the Dnieper. This office was abolished by Catherine II. (2) In the Polish-Lithuanian state of the 16th-18th centuries, supreme commander of all armed forces. (3) Title assumed by Skoropadsky in 1918.

HIIUMAA: *see* KHIUMA.

HÍPPIUS (or GIPPIUS), Zinaída Nikoláyevna (1867–1945), symbolist poet and writer. Married D. S. Merezhkovsky in 1890; was a member of The Religious and Philosophical Society. A beautiful *femme fatale*, she presided over a literary salon in St. Petersburg which became a meeting place for the younger symbolists. Emigrated in 1919 and lived in Paris. She was much preoccupied with her own morbid and many-sided personality, and struck a pose of Satanism. Her political verses are sardonic, while her lyrics reflect her sad and sensual, feminine nature. Under the pseudonym of Anton Krayny, H wrote critical essays and left reminiscences of her literary friends published in the volume *Living Faces* (1925).

HISTORY, PREREVOLUTIONARY. Russian history was quite recently regarded as beginning in the 9th century A.D. with the appearance of the state and nation called *Rus*. Now, historians are returning to the views of the 18th century, according to which the times of the Scythians, Sarmatians, Goths, Huns, and Khazars, known from Herodotus and other ancient authors, are as much part of R. history as the epoch of Kiev and Moscow. In the recent literature, there is a growing view that the ethnographic material of European Russia was the unchanging basis of all the states formed there from the 7th century B.C. into the Christian era. From time immemorial, a complex of geopolitical factors has been operative in the region of the future European Russia, and its effect continues to the present day. All the states which have arisen in that area have been distinguished by several common characteristics: vast territory, centralization of power, weak popular social and political activity, and variegated national composition. The stimulus as well as the economic basis for their formation was the collection of tribute. The secret of the huge size of these ancient states lay in the ease of imposing tribute on the inhabitants of the R. plain, who lived thinly scattered and isolated from each other. From the beginnings of history, the people were situated in unfavorable conditions for contending with an organized power.

Even four thousand years ago, agriculture existed in the south of present-day Russia. In Herodotus' time, wheat, barley, oats, and hemp were planted and such a quantity of grain was produced that it was exported over the sea to Greece. Domestic animals were also raised. The people wove coarse cloth and engaged extensively in hunting and fishing. Side by side with this, there was also a nomadic, semi-productive, semi-brigand form of existence. But all the traces of higher culture discovered by archaeologists or witnessed by ancient writers were products of foreign influences—often Iranian, but predominantly Hellenic. From the 7th century B.C. up to the Christian era, Greek city-colonies began to arise on the northern shores of the Black Sea. Their trade ties with the Scythians brought gold and silver vases, goblets, precious diadems, bracelets, and necklaces of the wonderful workmanship of Greek master craftsmen into the barbarians' tents. The Greek language, customs, and even religion spread. Whole tribes living near the cities became Hellenized. The Scythians, however, were too numerous for the Black Sea cities to civilize them rapidly. In the course of time, they fell victim to the onslaughts of the wild nomadic elements and the Hellenized population along the Black Sea shores perished with them, or reverted to barbarity.

The Kievan State (9th–13th Centuries). The thousand years between the epoch of the ancient colonies on the north shore of the Black Sea and the arrival of a new cultural influence from Byzantium are the darkest period in the history of that region. Only scraps of written information have been preserved, and while archaeology has shed some light on the economy, culture, and ethnography of future Russia during this time, its political history remains almost unknown. As of the 8th–9th centuries, what became R. territory was divided in two major parts, under the Varangians in the north and the Khazars in the south. Then toward the end of the 9th century, these merged into the single Kievan state under the rule of the Varangian dynasty. The founder of the dynasty was Ryurik (862–879), of whom no records but chronicle legends have survived. In contrast, the next three princes, Oleg (879–913), Igor (913–946), and Svyatoslav (946–971), are to some extent documented both in the R. chronicles, in Scandanavian and Byzantine sources, and in the treaties they concluded with the Byzantine Empire.

Under the early princes the Kievan state, like its predecessors, was a conglomeration of tribes and peoples, in various stages of development. Presently, however, the influence of the state began to be felt. A class of administrators, soldiers, and merchants emerged from the tight clan-tribal groupings and formed state leadership. It was to these groups, primarily, that the term *Rus* applied. Their government was concerned not simply with exacting tribute, but also with administration, organization, and defense. Thus under Prince Vladimir (980–1015), a line of fortified outposts was built to fend off the attacks of the nomads of the steppes.

The struggle against the nomads began under Vladimir's father Svyatoslav, who was killed by the Patzinacs (Pechenegs), and continued for almost 300 years. After the Patzinacs, the even more rapacious Cumans (Polovtsy) cut Russia off from the Black Sea, seized the steppes, and systematically ravaged the southern parts of the state. These wars gave birth to a consciousness of the unity of the land, which was reflected in the chronicles and contemporary poetry.

A hardly less vital factor for unification and centralization was the acceptance of Christianity. Religion in the Kievan state originally consisted of animistic beliefs.

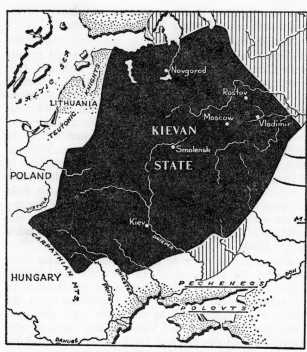

Kievan State at Its Height in 1054

According to tradition, Prince Vladimir, dissatisfied with heathenism, sought another religion. His choice fell on Greek Orthodoxy. For the barbarians of the east, Byzantium provided a center of attraction such as Rome exercised in the west. Vladimir's grandmother, Princess Olga, had visited Constantinople in 957 and accepted the Orthodox faith. Thus the new religion was known in Rus well before Vladimir's time. What evidently appealed to him was the role of the emperor as the head of the church, which he himself intended to play in Rus. He treated Christianization as a state measure and imposed it by force, including punitive expeditions.

The introduction of Christianity nonetheless marks the beginning of education and culture. Orthodoxy brought to Russia the arts of stone architecture and iconography. Wooden architecture had existed in Russia from ancient times and the first Orthodox churches, such as the large cathedral of St. Sophia in Novgorod, were built of wood. For stone churches Greek craftsmen were initially used. The Russians apparently mastered early the new techniques. According to some accounts, the R. master Peter in 1119 built the Yuryev Monastery's cathedral, the finest building in Novgorod after St. Sophia. The names of other early allegedly R. builders have been preserved. By the end of the 11th century, the Russians appear to have had their own architects, and in the 12th century the elements of a specifically R. style became discernible. Iconography took root rapidly and the Russians made noteworthy achievements in this field. The Byzantine system of church jurisprudence familiarized the Russians with western legal notions and promoted the codification of local customary law. The earliest version of *Russkaya*

Pravda (Russian Truth), appeared presumably in the early 11th century under Yaroslav the Wise.

With these benefits, Orthodoxy brought to Russia the historical misfortune of a thousand years of enmity with Catholic Europe. As early as the 12th and 13th centuries the antagonism between the churches became so bitter that the Catholic world sent crusades against eastern Europe, first the Swedes and then the Teutonic knights. With the passing of centuries, animosity between the churches reached a stage when it may be regarded as one of the major causes of Russia's alienation from western civilization. It is believed that in Kievan times, R. ties with Europe were still strong. According to some reports there were dynastic links between the R. princes and the ruling houses of Europe. There was considerable commerce with Europe, and colonies of foreign merchants existed in Kiev and other larger cities.

Kievan power came to an end with the Tatar invasion, but the disintegration of the state had actually begun earlier. It was partly due to the proliferation of the ruling family. While the family remained small, the power was concentrated, as under the early princes—Oleg, Igor, Svyatoslav, and Vladimir. But Yaroslav, who ruled with full power from 1017 to 1054, divided his realm among his sons. Thereafter divisions grew, each prince regarding his domain as the exclusive property of his family. The authority of the Kievan prince declined progressively, until Prince Andrey Bogolyubsky in 1169 subjected Kiev to a devastating raid which dealt a final blow to its traditional political supremacy. Andrey intended the city of Vladimir-on-Klyazma to be the new capital, but this city was not destined to restore the unity of "the Ryurik empire." The process of political disintegration continued in the 13th and 14th centuries.

The Tatar Invasion. The Tatar invasion in 1237–42 was the greatest catastrophe in R. history. It brought unprecedented extermination of population, with half killed or led into captivity and the rest forced to flee into the forests and marshes. Populous Kiev had not more than 200 households after the massacre. The chronicle recounts the burning of churches filled with icons, books, and valuables brought there for safekeeping. Almost all the fruits of three hundred years were destroyed, for only Novgorod and its northern provinces were spared. Initially, there was some hope that the Tatars would depart after they finished plundering, as their predecessors had. But at the end of the campaign, Khan Batu established the capital of the new state of the Golden Horde on the Volga. He required the surviving R. princes to take an oath of allegiance to the Mongol power, and imposed on Russia heavy taxes, which were to bleed the nation white for more than two centuries. The most frightful aspect of the Tatars' rule, however, was not exactions nor the inroads of the khan's officials, but the periodic mass slaughters. Seizing some pretext, or intervening in a dispute between princes, the Tatars would conduct punitive expeditions into Russia which depopulated entire regions. They were, however, solely concerned with maintaining their own power and did not destroy the traditional R.

order, her laws, customs, morals, or religion. The Orthodox Church and clergy were taken under the khan's protection. It is arguable that the common view that there was considerable Mongol influence on the life and character of the R. people is greatly exaggerated. The Tatar regime, moreover, was not truly Mongolian. The majority of the Mongols returned to the region beyond Lake Baykal immediately after the campaign, leaving only a handful of leaders and a few soldiers, members of the imperial household. Their army and administration were composed almost entirely of Cumans, the Russians' old enemies, who were predatory nomads like the Mongols themselves. The language, writing, and general culture of the Golden Horde soon became "Cumanized." Thus Russian-Tatar relations were actually a continuation of the tragedy of the Kievan era. Only the roles were reversed, and, whereas Russia held sway over the steppes in the 11th and 12th centuries, the steppes now ruled over urban and agricultural Russia.

The Lithuanian-Russian State (1248–1569). An important consequence of the Tatar occupation was that Russia became divided into two parts, northeastern and southwestern. The Tatar avalanche had swept across Russia, into Poland, Hungary, Romania, Bulgaria, and eastern parts of Germany and Austria. Batu, however, withdrew from the western countries, so that only Russia remained in the hands of the conquerors. There the full force of Tatar oppression and exploitation concentrated in the northeastern regions, while the lands across the Dnieper felt it in lesser degree. For some unexplained reason, the Tatars were significantly weaker in the areas now known as the Ukraine and Byelorussia, allowing the local princes and populations to free themselves more easily from the tribute payments and other burdens. Tatar raids were less frequent in this region. These conditions favored effective resistance, but they also meant that the southwestern areas broke off from the other R. lands. The outstanding example was Galicia which succeeded in freeing itself from the Tatars in 1336–49, a century after the invasion, but at the price of being annexed by Poland. The other R. regions beyond the Dnieper which wished to escape Tatar captivity without losing their faith and nationality, as Galicia had, gradually came to be controlled by the Lithuanian princes who headed a new state, the Grand Duchy of Lithuania. This state was characterized from the very beginning by national dualism, resulting from the Lithuanian and the R. strains in its population. Its capital was first Novgorodok and later Vilna. Originally a rather small territory under the rule of Prince Mindowh (1248–63), Lithuania grew rapidly until, under Gedimin (1316–41) and his son Olgerd (1341–77), it became a large and powerful state. Lithuanian expansion was due to the absorption of R. lands, and R. ethnic elements became predominant in the population of Lithuania. Russian was the state and court language and R. cultural influence was strong. Many Lithuanian princes were converted to Orthodoxy and married into R. princely families. Following the absorption by Lithuania of the lands of Polotsk and Kiev, the Lithuanian-Russian state continued to expand on the left bank of the Dnieper and acquired the Chernigov region during Olgerd's reign. Under Prince Vitovt (1392–1430), the Lithuanian boundaries extended from the Baltic Sea to the Black Sea and, with the annexation of the Smolensk principality, came close to the territory of Moscow. Lithuania's borders in the 15th century were along the Ugra River, next to Moscow's possessions, and its political influence extended to Tver and Ryazan. At one point, it appeared as if Moscow, too, would be absorbed and that Russia would be reunited under the Lithuanian crown. After Vitovt's death, however, the power of Lithuania declined. In 1569, by the Act of Lublin, Lithuania was incorporated into the kingdom of Poland. From that date to the middle of the 17th century, the southwestern R. lands were separated from the R. northeast. Until the 14th century, there were few religious, cultural, or language differences between the two. But after the southwest was incorporated into Lithuania-Poland, its language showed marked Polish influence and this territory became known as Little Russia or Ukraine.

The Moscow State. Eastern Russia remained under the "Tatar yoke" until the end of the 15th century. Its liberation came with the rise of Moscow. Moscow's existence was recorded as early as 1147, but until the very end of the 14th century it was a small town of no consequence. Historians have offered many reasons for its rise to success, but no single explanation fully accounts for it. It is possible only to outline accidental circumstances which played a part in Moscow's good fortune. First and foremost, there was the energy of the two Danilovich brothers, Princes Yury and Ivan (Kalita). They won the long-standing dispute for the title of grand duke, a dignity which made its possessor first among R. princes and gave him the right to collect the Tatar tribute. It was secured by using bribery in the Golden Horde, by denunciations, intrigues, and a bloody struggle with the princes of Tver which lasted a quarter of a century, from 1304 to 1328.

Another important occurrence which gave the obscure town prominence was the move of the metropolitan's see to Moscow. The original residence of the head of the R. Church had been Kiev, but in 1300 Metropolitan Maxim had moved north to Vladimir and his successor Peter shifted his residence to Moscow.

A further cause of Moscow's success was the policy toward the Tatars established by the founder of the Moscow dynasty, Prince Alexander Nevsky. He deprecated a provocative attitude toward the Tatars and chose instead a policy of loyalty and service, and this policy was continued by his grandsons and great-grandsons. A. N. Nasonov in *The Mongols and Russia* (1940) advocates the revision of the theory advanced by Karamzin (q.v.) and Kostomarov (q.v.) that the advent of the Moscow state and the power of its tsars grew out of the policies of the Golden Horde, as though a continuation of it. According to this theory, the Tatars facilitated the unification of Russia and the rise of Moscow. Close investigation, however, suggests that Tatar policy had for its object to prevent the formation of a unified R. state. The historical achievement of Muscovy and its leaders is the creation of a strong

state despite Mongol opposition. The methods used to bring about unification were the same as elsewhere in Europe and Asia: conquest, purchase, advantageous marriages, inheritance, and acceptance of the fealty of small princes and landed boyars as vassals.

At the time of Dmitry Donskoy's reign (1359–89), Moscow had not yet succeeded in uniting even half of northeastern Russia within its borders, but it stood out as the political leader of Russia. Prince Dmitry refused to pay the Tatar tribute and this brought Khan Mamay down upon Muscovy with a huge army in 1380. R. forces met him on the upper reaches of the Don River and there was a great battle at Kulikovo field in which the Tatars were defeated. The effects of this victory were inconclusive. It is true that Khan Tokhtamysh reimposed tribute two years later, but from that time on, the tribute became uncertain and irregular. The Tatars began to fear Moscow and under Dmitry's grandson, Prince Vasily II, many of them transferred to the service of Moscow, heralding the internal disintegration of the Golden Horde. By the time of Ivan III (1462–1505), the Tatars' power had become largely nominal and interfered little with the grand duke's undertakings.

The final demise of Tatar power in 1480 hastened Moscow's expansion. More lands were added during the last three decades of the 15th century than during the preceding 200 years. The Tver and Ryazan principalities came over to Moscow without military struggle, and Novgorod, although it gave some opposition, was subjugated without great difficulty between 1471 and 1478. "Great Lord Novgorod" and its satellites Pskov and Vyatka were governed ostensibly by *veche*, a medieval republican institution, though in actuality they were *boyar* oligarchies. The conquest of these lands thus meant the elimination in Muscovy of a form of government at variance with absolutism.

Ivan III was then ruler of one of the territorially largest states in Europe. There was an appropriate transformation in the appearance of his capital. Churches and palaces were erected and the Kremlin was rebuilt on a far more ambitious scale than before. Ivan's work of reconstruction was continued under his son, Vasily III, who like his father imported architects from Italy.

There were other changes. Ivan III married Sophia Paleologue, a Byzantine princess, and in 1493 he assumed the title "Sovereign of all Russia."

Further territorial acquisitions during the 16th century were not large. Kazan and Astrakhan were conquered (1552–56). The main development of Russia in the 16th century was not in external growth but in internal consolidation. The upper class, though greatly weakened as a social class in the process of territorial unification, did not abandon their political ambitions. Assembled at the court of the grand duke as servitors, they nonetheless longed for a part in government that would limit the grand ducal powers. Ivan III's successors struggled determinedly with this social group. Sharp clashes with the aristocracy began under his son, Vasily III (1505–33), but the real onslaught against the boyars was conducted by his grandson, Ivan IV, called the Terrible (1533–84). In 1564 Ivan IV created the *oprichnina*, a military-administrative apparatus with which he physically exterminated the aristocracy and simultaneously confiscated their land holdings. Over six or seven years he made fearful inroads into the ranks of the boyars, and distributed their estates, as small holdings to his obscure servitors.

At the same time measures were taken to increase the prestige of the crown. The grand duke officially assumed the title of tsar, which was conferred upon Ivan at a magnificent coronation ceremony held in 1547. The genealogy of the house of Ryurik was revised, in a curious attempt to establish his descent from Byzantine and Roman emperors, specifically from Augustus. The divine character of their rule was attributed to the tsar's as well.

The primitive material and cultural basis of the state, however, contrasted sharply with these pretensions. Neither its trade nor its crafts could compare to Europe in development, let alone its art and learning. Moscow's court could not equal the Viennese in brilliance, or even the courts of German electors and Italian dukes. Ivan the Terrible was aware of these limitations and sought to improve economic conditions. He was interested in trade with Europe and attracting skilled artisans. Moscow, however, was cut off from Europe by a circle of hostile countries and lacked access to the sea. The Black Sea had been a Turkish lake since the

middle of the 15th century and Sweden and Livonia prevented Russia from reaching the Baltic. In 1553 an English captain, Chancellor, opened a route to Moscow through the Barents and White seas and inaugurated Russia's trade and diplomatic ties with England. The northern route, however, was inconvenient, and in 1558 Tsar Ivan began the Livonian war to win a port on the Baltic. He gained the Baltic shore fairly rapidly, but could not hold it.

The Livonian war aroused concern in Europe. An anti-Russian coalition was formed and agitation by Poland, Livonia, and the Vatican conjured up the specter of a R. menace to the world. England and Holland, however, continued to trade with Russia, supplying everything from weapons to engravings, musical instruments, exotic plants, and rare animals. Toward the end of the 16th century and increasingly in the 17th, foreigners, including many military specialists, physicians and jewelers, as well as merchants, settled in Moscow. The R. government favored contacts with Europe primarily because they catered to military and state requirements. The privileges granted to foreigners, however, were deemed detrimental to R. commerce and brought complaints from the R. merchants.

Pressing military needs explain in part the sweeping changes which brought the peasantry into the state of serfdom. In the west, serfdom had grown out of slavery and conquest, in the course of the development of the feudal system. In Russia, however, contrary to the official Marxist view, feudalism did not exist and serfdom was created by a series of government measures. In principle, bondage in service applied to the landowners as well as the peasantry. Both were obligated to serve the state in their assigned roles, the landowner by fighting and the peasant by providing for him, so that the government could count on ready military forces without expense to the treasury. With the passage of time, of course, the landowners came to treat the peasants as their personal bondsmen, but legally they were themselves considered "serfs" obligated to serve the state, until the second half of the 18th century. The process of restricting the peasants' freedom was begun at the end of the 15th century and was completed by the end of the 16th.

The enslavement of the peasantry, economic dislocations from the violent disturbances wrought by Ivan the Terrible's *oprichnina,* by the Crimean Khan, Devlet Girey's terrible raids in 1571, by the Livonian war, and the extinction in 1598 of the old dynasty descended from Ryurik—all combined to create an unprecedented crisis and brought the so-called "Time of Troubles" which threatened the very existence of the Moscow state. Utter chaos ruled in the country and on the throne from 1605 to 1613. There were peasant uprisings, civil war, multiple rulers creating a vacuum of authority, invasions by Poles, Swedes, and Cossacks, resulting in seemingly hopeless confusion. Finally, once the Poles were driven out and Michael Romanov was elected tsar in 1613, it became possible to restore a measure of normalcy.

The history of the 17th century did not differ radically from that of the preceding years except in the growth of the size of the R. state. As early as 1582, the first R. conquistador, Yermak, had presented Ivan IV with a Siberian kingdom in the basin of the Irtysh and the Ob. From then on enterprising merchants, Cossacks, and settlers streamed eastward, sometimes on their own initiative and sometimes with government support, adding one area after another to Moscow's territory. The tsar's soldiers followed, building towns and forts in the lands seized, and behind the soldiers a few peasant colonizers came to settle and establish agriculture in Siberia. In this fashion, the Russians reached the Bering and Okhotsk seas as early as 1676. To the government and the society of the time, however, these lands appeared less important than the increase in western territory which occurred in the middle of the century, that is, the addition of the Ukraine, which was formally sanctioned by the Pereyaslavl Rada in 1654.

The Russian Empire. The larger Moscow's territory grew, the more obvious its internal weaknesses became. The major problem was the absence of a rational state administrative and military structure, and the inevitable remedy was to adopt European methods. The virtues of European culture had been recognized in the 16th and 17th centuries, but the real change in Russia's attitude did not come until the reign of Peter the Great (1682–1725). Prior to Peter, elements of technique and arts had been borrowed from Europe, but everything that might shake the Russian Church's outlook had been avoided. Peter undertook to adopt European enlightenment in all its aspects, from the secularization of science and philosophy to worldly manners and dress. He was the first R. tsar to go abroad, departing in 1697 to travel "incognito" for a year and a half in Germany, Holland, England, and Austria, and he returned convinced of the necessity for rapid Europeanization.

The reforms Peter introduced over a period of 26 years were, however, conducted not according to any plan so much as according to exigency, determined largely by the course of the Great Northern War (1700–21). In the twenty years of this difficult struggle, Sweden was defeated on land and sea and ousted from possession of the Baltic littoral. Russia gained the whole shore from Riga to Vyborg. As a symbol of the new European era for Russia, St. Petersburg was founded on the banks of the Gulf of Finland in 1703 and the capital of the state was moved there. The progress and incidents of the war so affected the order and character of Peter's reforms that some historians prefer to regard them as primarily military reforms, arguing that the creation of a regular army and navy gave rise to all the other economic, social, and cultural changes. Be that as it may, Peter's measures, although introduced in no particular order, present cumulatively a pattern of radical transformation. Under Peter, improved organs of government were created, including the Senate (1711), the administrative colleges which resembled the later ministries (1718), and the procurator-general's office which carried out the tsar's will in the Senate (1722). Radical changes were made in the church's administration. The church had previously been dependent on the government to a considerable degree, but in 1721 Peter deprived it of the last vestige of independence by abol-

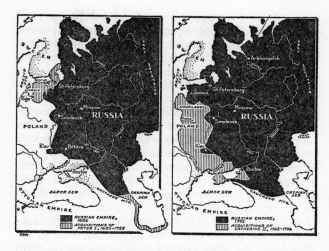

ishing the patriarchate and instituting a Synod directly subordinate to himself through the chief procurator. Provincial administration was reformed with the creation of the provinces (*gubernia*) in 1708, and their modification along Swedish lines in 1718. Peter also admired W. European forms for city governments, which inspired the institution of the chief magistracy in 1720. This series of state reforms was crowned by Peter's assuming the title of Emperor in 1721.

These major reforms were accompanied by many decrees affecting other areas of R. life. A new calendar system was introduced as of Jan. 1700 and Arabic numerals replaced letter indications of numbers. In 1714 compulsory schooling was decreed for the children of nobility and the naval academy was founded. In 1718 an engineering school was started and in 1724 a decree was issued to establish the Academy of Sciences. Book publishing grew to an unprecedented extent, young people were sent abroad to study, a wave of foreign specialists poured into Russia, and the very texture of urban life began to change.

A revolution of sorts was definitely achieved, but the results of Peter's effort to acclimatize Russia all at once to the civilization Europe had built cumulatively over the centuries were necessarily superficial. After his death, Europeanization was nearly undone by the opponents of his work, but Russia nonetheless continued to make progress, albeit with interruptions, in the directions set by Peter's reforms. Enlightenment continued to penetrate further into R. life and not only Europe's techniques but its literature and philosophy found converts in higher social groups.

Europe's teaching on state and political systems found such fervent adepts in Russia that only five years after Peter's death there was an attempt to limit the supreme power. In 1730, people who had until recently regarded the tsar's power as divine endeavored to have the Empress Anne sign a set of "conditions" which would have deprived her of important royal prerogatives. The attempt failed, but the fact that it was made was symptomatic of the penetration of European political ideas into Russia.

Wartime conditions aggravated the severity with which Peter introduced his reforms and the nation and the aristocracy both suffered. The main burden, however, fell on the peasant serfs. Peter turned the rural administrative and police powers over to the landowners, making them the representatives of the state on their own lands. In practice this meant that slavery was introduced in the countryside. Under the weak empresses who ruled throughout the 18th century, the landowners also succeeded in using guard regiments composed of people from their own "estate" to effect palace revolutions and exert a decisive influence on politics, the court and the crown. They enforced Peter's measure twice over where the dependence of the peasantry was concerned and used all possible means to increase their own prerogatives. Eventually, they obtained the abolition of their state service obligations in the manifesto on the liberty of the nobility (1762) and the "Charter of the Nobility" (1785). On the whole, the 18th century was the golden age of the R. nobility, but, on the other hand, no other century experienced such a great peasant uprising and slaughter of landowners as occurred in 1773–75 under the leadership of Yemelyan Pugachov.

Domestic antagonisms notwithstanding, the 18th century was one of the more brilliant periods in Russia's foreign affairs. Under Empresses Elizabeth (1742–60) and Catherine II (1762–96) successful wars were fought and crushing defeats were inflicted by Saltykov, Rumyantsev, and Suvorov. The northern shore of the Black Sea was conquered, the Crimea was subdued in 1783, and five years later Ochakov fortress fell, ending the era of Turkish hegemony in southern Russia. The legacy, however, was the Balkan wars which continued through most of the 19th century, and a struggle to subdue the Caucasus (although Georgia, was incorporated in Russia in 1801) which lasted from the reign of Catherine II into the 1860's. Between 1772 and 1795 the three partitions of Poland added substantially to R. territory. The R. eastward movement reached Alaska and America in the 18th century and in 1798 the "Russian-American Company" was granted monopoly rights by Emperor Paul I to trade in and develop the lands on the American continent. In 1805 Fort Novo-Arkhangelsk was built in Alaska and in 1812 Fort Ross was established in California. All these possessions were later ceded to the United States (Fort Ross in 1840 and Alaska in 1867).

The Russian Empire, however, in contrast to the Moscow state, did not have its own clear foreign policy doctrines. While the wars with the Turks conformed to real national interests and made historical sense (despite the fact that they also redounded greatly to the benefit of Austria), Russia's entire policy in the west was dependent on and determined by the interplay of European politics. This applies to Russia's participation in the Seven Years' War (1757–61) and the Polish partitions. From the end of the 18th century to the middle of the 19th, R. policies in Europe had no positive aims and were governed by the abstract idea of suppressing revolutions. In 1799 Emperor Paul I (1796–1801) sent Suvorov's army to fight the French Directory and his son Alexander I (1801–25) was drawn into the wars against Napoleon for no particular purpose, by similarly abstract motives. Among all of Alexander's

conflicts, only the war of 1812 was Russia's war rather than purely the tsar's. From Ryurik to Nicholas II, 99 per cent of the R. people remained outside of politics and few could have understood why Alexander I concluded an alliance with Austria and Prussia and fought the French at Austerlitz and Prussian Eylau. But when Napoleon intruded into the depths of Russia, the whole nation rose to the danger. As soon as the enemy was driven out and R. soldiers moved on to Paris, Alexander's policy again lost its national character and became legitimist. When the Holy Alliance was formed, the R. emperor was the sole participant who fully accepted its principles of "legitimacy." Alexander's successor and brother, Nicholas (1825–55), was enthusiastic in suppressing revolts for other monarchs who could not cope with them—Mekhmet-Ali's revolt in 1833, the Krakow uprising in 1846, and the Hungarian revolt in 1849. This activity brought great harm to Russia and her reputation.

It was nevertheless under Alexander I and Nicholas I that an active revolutionary movement began in Russia herself. The movement displayed Jacobin tendencies from the very beginning, with proposals for the overthrow of the monarch and even the physical extermination of the ruling family. Two armed uprisings were staged in Dec. 1825, one in St. Peteresburg on the 14th and the other on the 28th in the Vasilkov region in the S.; hence the movement's participants were called Decembrists. Neither the common people nor the soldiers commanded by the revolt's leaders understood the reasons for it, for the Decembrist movement was, in part, an offshoot of W. European ideology, applied to R. conditions. The same was true of the Herzen-Ogarev group active in the 1830's and of Petrashevsky's circle (1848–49). They were enamored of European utopian socialism and dreamed of reforming Russia according to the prescriptions of Saint-Simon and Fourier.

Nicholas I, having been greeted by a guard's revolt on the day of his succession to the throne, hunted sedition for the next 30 years of his reign. Militarist and police methods of government reached their apogee, and since Nicholas regarded European revolutionary ideas as a product of education, he thought it necessary to put restrictions on the schools and universities. Many new schools and higher institutions were opened during his reign, especially in technical fields, but teaching was severely hampered by police supervision. Science and art labored under similar difficulties and literature suffered greatly from censorship.

There was virtually no educated civil service in Russia and people of the caliber of Speransky (Alexander I's adviser and minister) were the exception in Russia. Speransky's contribution in the first decade of Alexander's reign lay less in his project for government reforms than in his work in current administrative affairs. The effect of Nicholas' regime on the government and the army was catastrophic. When his injudicious policies precipitated the Crimean War (1854–56), the army proved backward compared to the English and French armies in technical equipment and even in military skill. There were no trained, capable generals and Rus-

sia's defeat revealed the bankruptcy of Nicholas' policies. His regime perished with its creator who, according to some accounts, committed suicide.

The Reforms. Reforms were made mandatory by the Crimean military catastrophe, which was caused by Russia's cultural backwardness and the ineptness of the government. The first reactions to the defeats came from leading groups in the form of handwritten pamphlets. Even before the war ended, Pogodin's *Political Letters* and Valuyev's *A Russian's Thoughts* appeared, criticizing the old order and calling for change. The new emperor, Alexander II (1855–81), recognized the need for reform and alluded to it in the manifesto on the conclusion of the peace.

The central reform was the abolition of serfdom. This institution had been blatantly unjust since the liberation of the nobility from their former obligations to the state in 1762 and 1785, which had turned serfdom into a class system of domination of the peasantry by the landowners. The more enlightened members of the nobility had long since advocated its abolition, and even the government had mentioned the possibility and made a few timid steps in that direction, such as the law on free farmers in 1803, and the secret commissions' work under Nicholas I. No decision, however, had been taken affecting the basic system. Nicholas I's attitude was that "Serfdom is an evil, but I regard changing it as an even greater one." There were many reasons for hesitation, but the major one was fear that the nobility would be ruined and the crown's chief support thus destroyed. After the Crimean War the impossibility of further delay was admitted and the peasants were freed in 1861.

Following the abolition of serfdom, there was the zemstvo reform, which created organs of local self-government, as well as judicial reforms which logically arose from it (1864). A new university statute was devised in 1863, the municipal government reform came in 1870, and, finally, the military reform in 1874. Some of these, such as the military and judicial reforms, were aptly worked out on the basis of W. European experience and learning. The university statute, which freed higher education from bureaucratic supervision, was equally enlightened. However, the peasant and zemstvo reforms were so framed as to offend the peas-

antry and betrayed their expectations. There were over a thousand peasant disturbances in the two years following the reform. The landowner's personal power over the peasant was also preserved to a significant degree. The inadequacy of the measures to liberate the peasants and allot them land produced a state of constant underlying tension which broke out at every revolutionary crisis.

To complete its failures, the government eventually became mistrustful of its own reforms and moved to liquidate some of them. This affected the judicial, zemstvo, and even the military reforms, not to mention censorship and the university statute. The reaction first set in under Alexander II, but it became even more severe during the reign of his son, Alexander III (1881–94). To some degree, it was provoked by the conduct of the revolutionary intelligentsia, who managed to utilize the zemstvo, courts, and universities for their own ends and threatened to turn them into organs of opposition to the autocrat. The radical intelligentsia formed in the 1860's took no part in implementing the reforms and pursued the goal of reconstructing Russia in line with their socialist ideals, for which they proclaimed the autocracy's downfall as the first prerequisite. Terroristic acts were begun against prominent officials and the tsar himself. The revolutionaries counted on the assassination of Alexander II to produce a shock which would lead to a revolution. Nothing, however, came of their schemes. When, after several abortive attempts, Alexander II was assassinated on March 1, 1881 (O.S.), the people failed to rise.

Alexander III's punitive policies and the generally reactionary character of his regime were explained as self-defense from red terror. Under the new tsar, the chief procurator of the Synod, Pobedonostsev (q.v.), became extraordinarily influential. He was convinced that popular education, technical progress, and social evolution were dangerous and labored to protect Russia from them. Pobedonostsev forced teaching into the mold of obscurantism, suppressed manifestations of free thought, created an intellectually gray epoch, and termed it all "prolonging Russia's youth."

An industrial revolution was nevertheless achieved in Russia during the reign of Alexander III. The machinery industry began to expand rapidly and commerce and banking acquired significance in the economy. The financial reform carried out by ministers Vyshnegradsky and Witte aided capitalist growth considerably and made the ruble a stable foreign exchange currency. S. Yu. Witte was not only a competent financier, but also a talented director for the whole economy. His name is connected with the building of the Trans-Siberian Railway which was the greatest railroad of its day. He also influenced foreign policy and it was due considerably to him that the reign of Alexander III passed without a war, unless the completion of the conquests of Khiva and Turkestan begun under Alexander II are counted.

The bulk of the growth of R. territory during the 19th century was in Asia. In 1850 Captain Nevelsky raised the empire's flag at the mouth of the Amur River, and in 1860 the Ussuri region and the northern half of Sakhalin were acquired under the Peking treaty. Southern Sakhalin was subsequently acquired from Japan in exchange for the Kuril Islands. Acquisitions in Europe consisted of the annexation of Finland (1809), Bessarabia (1812), and the Kingdom of Poland in 1815. Finland was given autonomy from the start and a basic constitution was devised for her. Poland was granted a constitution, but it was revoked after the Polish uprising of 1830–31.

Although the majority of Russia's possessions lay in Asia, her fate was nonetheless decided in Europe. Under Alexander III, a deterioration of relations with Germany pressed Russia into an alliance with France (1891–93) which formed the political bond that drew Russia into the Entente and hence into the war in 1914.

The tragedy of World War I, which ended in the destruction of the Russian Empire and dynasty, fell in the reign of Nicholas II (1894–1917). Although the manufacturing industry was expanding rapidly, its development was still inadequate and the sparse distribution of population, combined with scarce means of communication, made Russia little more mobile than in Muscovite or Kievan times.

Nicholas II, however, proved an incompetent ruler. With no experience in government, he displayed an ability for surrounding himself with nonentities, to whose influence he easily succumbed. A group of irresponsible advisers, headed by Bezobrazov, Abaza, and Admiral Alekseyev, managed to involve the emperor in the foolish adventure in the Far East which resulted in the war with Japan in 1904.

In this totally useless war, Russia suffered a defeat which had tragic consequences. It strengthened the revolutionary movement. The radical intelligentsia, which had been driven underground, renewed the struggle against tsarism with even greater fanaticism and bitterness. Having failed to rouse a revolution by populist (q.v.) terror and propaganda among the peasantry, they turned to Marxism and the Social Democrats, and some of the Socialist Revolutionaries sought to organize a workers' movement in the towns. Their success, however, was again slight; for, while the propagandists sometimes were able to draw workers out on political strikes, their activity did not find a broad response among the proletariat. An official of the security police, Zubatov, realized that workers' organizations of the European type would be the least dangerous to the autocracy and could be a means for deterring a revolution. Through his agents, notably the priest G. Gapon, he made some progress, especially in St. Petersburg and Moscow. Zubatov's ideas, however, received no support from above while the movement organized by Gapon ended in a bloody massacre on Jan. 9, 1905 (O.S.) when workers carrying icons and portraits of the tsar marched to the Winter Palace and were met with rifle volleys. The country was swept with demonstrations against the senseless slaughter of Jan. 9th. Strikes broke out and grew gradually into a general strike. Disturbances flared in the Black Sea fleet and an armed uprising in Moscow broke out in December. Unrest in the cities was accompanied by agrarian disorder as peasants burned manor houses and seized large estates.

RUSSIAN EASTWARD EXPANSION, 1801-1914

The government succeeded in averting a revolution with great difficulty, not a little assisted by the Peace of Portsmouth signed with Japan on Aug. 23, 1905 (O.S.), which had been concluded through the good offices of President Theodore Roosevelt. Peace freed the government's hands. The army, returned from Manchuria, was used to put down disturbances, which brought the turning point in the struggle against the revolution. Another important factor was a government manifesto published on Oct. 17, 1905 (O.S.), promising that civil liberties would be granted and that a representative legislative assembly would be called promptly.

The Constitutional Monarchy. The disturbances had no sooner ceased than work was begun to assemble the State Duma which was to bring an era of R. parliamentarianism. An electoral law was promulgated on Dec. 11, 1905 (O.S.) and the Duma opened on April 27, 1906 (O.S.). Most of the socialists greeted both the government's earlier manifesto and the Duma with extreme hostility and urged the people to boycott it. Extreme right-wing groups, represented by the organization "United Nobility," behaved with equal hostility toward the Duma. Moderate and liberal groups, however, such as the Constitutional Democratic party (Kadets), the October 17th Union, and the St. Petersburg Society of Industrialists and Manufacturers, welcomed it and counted on it to fulfill their hopes for reform. These also comprised a majority in the first Duma, with the Kadets alone winning 170–180 seats out of 524. The first Duma, however, lasted less than two and a half months and was then dissolved by a decree of July 9, 1906 (O.S.).

The October manifesto had allotted the Duma a modest role. It had no power of control over the executive and was not even allowed to pass on some parts of the budget. In addition, a State Council was put above it to function as an upper house, without whose sanction no Duma legislation could come into force. Finally, the emperor retained the right of veto.

In view of the fact that the Duma's powers were so limited, some members of the government, as well as the left-wing groups, did not consider the Duma a parliament and similarly did not refer to the system established by the October manifesto as "constitutional." However, historians nowadays, including Americans, perceive in it the rudiments of constitutionalism, including, above all, recognition of the principle of popular representation for discussing government policies. No law could be promulgated without the consent of the Duma, and by this alone the emperor restricted his power and ceased to be an unlimited monarch. The Duma also had many other channels for influencing the government policy. In addition, the Duma period was marked by an unprecedented expansion of civil liberties. One of the leaders of the Kadet party and a historian of the Duma, V. A. Maklakov, acknowledged thirty years later that wise use of the legal opportunities offered by the Duma could have brought social and political progress, that "Liberal reform in Russia had become possible without revolution." However, the revolutionary atmosphere of 1905 had made even the moderate groups more radical and the Duma consequently did not keep within the bounds prescribed by the October manifesto. After the first Duma was dissolved, a second Duma was convoked on Feb. 20, 1907 (O.S.) and this time there was a majority of left-wing elements —the Labor Group, the Socialist Revolutionaries, and the Social Democrats. They turned the Duma into an anti-government propaganda forum and the Social Democratic faction was even charged with sedition. On June 3, 1907 (O.S.) this Duma, too, was dissolved and the electoral law was then strenuously revised to enable the government to influence the elections. The third Duma was consequently thoroughly conservative and lasted from the end of 1907 until 1912. It was called Stolypin's Duma after P. A. Stolypin (q.v.) who was prime minister from 1906 to 1911. His government combined severe measures against revolutionary tendencies with agrarian reforms designed to remove the cause of the peasants' discontent, which was their land poverty. The essence of his reform amounted to abolishing the communal system of land holding, and it offered hope of solving the agrarian problem. Stolypin, however, was assassinated in 1911 by a terrorist (who was simultaneously an agent of the security police). Three years later Russia entered World War I.

Russia in World War I. The assassination of the heir to the Austrian throne at Sarajevo on June 28, 1914 changed the fate of the world. Russia was one of the first countries to be affected by the Austrian-Serbian conflict. Her intercession for Serbia led to Germany's declaring war on Russia on Aug. 1. Austria followed on Aug. 6, and on Oct. 29 and 30, without any declaration of war, the Turkish navy bombarded the R. Black Sea ports of Odessa, Sevastopol, Feodosia, and Novorossiysk. None of the powers that entered the war was properly prepared for it, least of all Russia. Bad generals, shortage of officers, backward military doctrines and lack of war plan—such were the main defects of the R. war machine. But the weakness of the military industries and the railroad network proved especially lethal. All these combined caused a debacle. Within two or three months of the start of military action, there were shortages of shells and cartridges, and then of rifles. At the end of August, the annihilation of General Samsonov's army of a hundred thousand in E. Prussia made an especially depressing impression throughout the country. The effect of this

catastrophe was not effaced by the R. soldiers' brief success in occupying Galicia, all the less so since they did not succeed in holding it and were driven out by General Mackensen's counteroffensive in May 1915 along the front from the Vistula to the Rumanian border. The Russian Army fell rapidly into an exposed position and was forced to make a general retreat, surrendering large areas to the enemy. The withdrawal of this huge army had an extremely discouraging effect on both the people and the leaders. At a cabinet session in July 1915, War Minister Polivanov declared, "The fatherland is endangered." The recognition of the danger and the sense of outraged patriotism brought inquiry as to who was responsible for the failures and, with growing frequency, the autocracy was charged with inability to conduct the war. This idea became a subject of discussion in Duma circles. At the start of the war, all the Duma factions, right down to the Labor group whose leader was Kerensky, consumed with patriotic sentiments, had avowed their loyalty as subjects to the tsar. Now, after the failures at the front, the old tensions revived. Public leaders wished to participate in the conduct of the war and they demanded the creation of war industries committees which would work along with government departments to provide the army with arms and supplies. Other organizations with analogous purposes arose, including the Union of Zemstvos and the Union of Towns. These soon became refuges for elements opposed to the autocracy. They were all closely connected with the leaders in the Duma and the Duma consequently became the spokesman for an enfranchised public opinion and began to be contrasted to the government as an organ which had the confidence of the country.

The Duma's prestige was enhanced by Nicholas II's decision in Sept. 1915 to take personal command of the army. It was believed that his departure for the front would mean a transfer of power to the anonymous government headed by Empress Alexandra Fyodorovna. The tsarina had always been unpopular and, once the war started, her German origin gave grounds for unwarranted talk of her being a traitor. The most unfortunate circumstance for her and the tsar was their intimacy with Rasputin (q.v.). When he began interfering in government affairs, nominating and removing ministers, not only the general public but even official circles became aroused. Behind Rasputin there was a clique of unscrupulous favor-seekers. By joining the army, the tsar left Russia at the mercy of this band.

Nicholas' departure touched off anti-dynastic agitation. V. A. Maklakov's newspaper articles compared him to a mad chauffeur "driving both himself and us to destruction." Even Brusilov's offensive in the summer of 1916 did not relieve the tension, though it was the sole significant R. success of the war. General Brusilov's forces on the southwestern front broke through the line in May and advanced on a wide front. Around half a million Austrians were taken prisoner and over a million and a half were killed or wounded, but the results attained were not decisive and the R. offensive soon came to a halt.

In Nov. 1916, the Kadet leader P. N. Milyukov (q.v.)

made a speech in the Duma in which he mentioned the name of the empress in connection with treason. Although suppressed by censorship, this speech was given wide circulation. Then on Dec. 7, 1916 (O.S.) there was an even greater sensation over the murder of Rasputin, in which a grand duke and a Duma member participated. This was the harbinger of a court revolution, which began to be considered in earnest both in higher society and in the army. Conspiracies began to form which included Duma deputies, army and naval officers, large industrialists, and grand dukes. The aim of the plotters was not to abolish the monarchy but to remove the incompetent tsar, put the heir on the throne and establish a regency.

On Feb. 24, 1917 (O.S.) crowds formed in the streets of Petrograd protesting food shortages and demanding bread. The disturbance grew the next day and the day after. The red flag appeared, and on Feb. 27 (O.S.) the soldiers of the Petrograd garrison began to go over to the side of the insurgents. By the 28th the capital was in the grip of revolutionary fever, and while the tsar was on his way from general headquarters to Petrograd, events reached such a pass that there was no longer any question of keeping him in power. On March 2 (O.S.), in Pskov, he signed his abdication and a Provisional Government was formed in Petrograd. Thus the fateful moves were accomplished in the capital alone. At the military front and in the provinces the news met no opposition.

The Provisional Government. The State Duma remained active, but it could not head the new order, so a provisional committee was chosen from its membership and, in turn, appointed the Provisional Government. It was composed of leaders of the liberal opposition. The left-wing elements were represented by A. F. Kerensky who became minister of justice. Prince G. Ye. Lvov was the prime minister, P. N. Milyukov became minister of foreign affairs and A. I. Guchkov of war. In a declaration drafted jointly with the Soviet, the Provisional Government proclaimed freedom of speech, press, association, assembly; the right to strike; abolition of all class, religious, or nationality discrimination; prompt preparations for a Constituent Assembly elected by universal, equal, direct, and secret ballot; and elections of local government organs on the same basis.

The masses, however, dreamed less of freedom of speech and assembly than of peace. On April 18 (O.S.), Milyukov had informed the allies of the "nation-wide effort to bring the world war to a decisive victory and of the Provisional Government's intention to observe the obligations undertaken with regard to our allies." The publication of this note brought street demonstrations of protest. The result was the removal of Milyukov and Guchkov from the government.

The tragedy of the new order was that power was divided. While the Provisional Government was being formed at the Taurida Palace, the Soviet of Workers' and Soldiers' Deputies was meeting in the same building. Although created "spontaneously," the Soviet regarded itself as an authoritative assembly and exerted constant pressure on the Provisional Government, acting as a second decisive organ of power. On March 2 (O.S.) it

published Order No. 1 which played a vital role in the disintegration of the army. In fact, it abolished the authority of the officers and substituted for it that of the soldiers' committees. The Soviet acquired its own armed force: the Petrograd garrison undertook to obey no orders from any other authority. In exchange, the Soviet guaranteed that the units of the garrison would not be sent to the front.

At first, the Bolsheviks commanded little support. Their influence was insignificant in the Soviet which was dominated by the Mensheviks and the Socialist Revolutionaries. Only Lenin's arrival on April 3 (O.S.) made the Bolsheviks into a powerful political force. Lenin formulated the party program in his April Theses (q.v.). His slogans demanding immediate peace and the distribution of land were particularly successful and had a magical effect upon the soldiers. The Bolsheviks were accused of having conducted propaganda to break up the army because they received funds from the Germans. An investigation was begun, but it was interrupted by the October revolution. Recently the question was raised anew by the availability of the German archives, which fell into English hands during World War II and proved to contain documents supporting the contention that the Bolsheviks were subsidized by Germany.

In their effort to overthrow the Provisional Government, the Bolsheviks in July organized street demonstrations which ended in their rout. Lenin went into hiding in Finland while Trotsky and other leaders were arrested. In the Soviet, the Mensheviks and Socialist Revolutionaries ruled as before, wary of danger from the "right," fearing the revival of the monarchy or "bourgeois-landowner reaction." They did not, however, anticipate the destruction of democracy from the left.

At the end of August, an episode occurred which struck panic in the socialist camp and precipitated it into an alliance with the Bolsheviks. It was caused by the catastrophic conditions at the front and in the rear. After the fall of the monarchy, the war had not gone better, as expected, but worse, and the R. armies were in retreat. The offensive launched in June was a failure. The soldiers did not wish to fight, deserted, fraternized with the enemy, and refused to obey their officers. Anarchy was mounting throughout the country, and the Provisional Government was paralyzed. A State Conference (q.v.) was summoned to Moscow in August to discuss the situation but it produced no results. In these circumstances, the commander in chief, General Kornilov (q.v.), decided to move some troops from the front to the capital with a view to creating a strong government (see KORNILOV "MUTINY"). There followed an extraordinary misunderstanding between Kornilov and Kerensky with the result that Kornilov was removed from his command (Aug. 27 O.S.) by Kerensky's order, which he defied, denouncing the Provisional Government as a tool of the Bolsheviks and the German General Staff. He was accused of mutiny and arrested.

These events produced a sharp change in the political climate of Petrograd. Kornilov was arrested on Sept. 1 (O.S.) and on the 4th Trotsky was released from jail and became the head of the Petrograd Soviet. The

Bolsheviks began to take over important positions in the capital and at the front. Trotsky subsequently said that, having decided to overthrow the government, the Bolsheviks "openly, before the eyes of the public and its government, prepared the armed force for that revolution." World history, in his words, has not seen another uprising "publicly set in advance for a designated date and accomplished on the day indicated, with victory."

Indeed, the government did nothing to prevent the impending explosion. The Military-Revolutionary Committee and the Petrograd Soviet, where the Bolsheviks had a majority, had become the centers of the conspiracy. The leaders of the uprising waited only for the opening of the second All-Russian Congress of Soviets in order to get its sanction for their seizure of power, and meanwhile made the technical preparations for the revolution. Commissars from the Military-Revolutionary Committee were sent to the units of the Petrograd garrison and the soldiers were directed to obey no one else's orders. Thus military power in the capital was actually transferred to the Bolsheviks by Oct. 22 (O.S.). On the evening of Oct. 24, a cruiser of the Baltic fleet whose crew supported the Bolsheviks entered the Neva and the sailors occupied the bridges commanding the Winter Palace where the government was in session. Kerensky, finding himself in a hopeless position, contrived to leave Petrograd on the morning of Oct. 25 (O.S.) in a United States Embassy car, flying the American flag, to obtain reinforcements at the front. Meanwhile, in the evening, the second congress of Soviets opened at Smolny and gave the Bolsheviks a majority of 40 votes. The Mensheviks, Socialist Revolutionaries, and other socialist representatives withdrew. The Bolsheviks, left the masters of the session, obtained all the resolutions they needed and simultaneously started action in the streets. At two in the morning the Winter Palace was taken by Bolshevik forces and the Provisional Government was arrested. A new era of R. history was begun.

BIBLIOGRAPHY: G. Vernadsky, *Ancient Russia*, New Haven, 1943; G. Vernadsky, *Kievan Russia*, New Haven, 1948; M. T. Florinsky, *Russia: A History and an Interpretation*, New York, 1953; M. T. Florinsky, *The End of the Russian Empire*, New York, 1931; V. O. Klyuchevsky, *A History of Russia*, 5 vols., New York, 1960.
N. I. Ou.

HISTORY, SOVIET.

I. The Consolidation of Bolshevik Rule.

FIRST STEPS (Nov. 1917—March 1918). Bolsheviks and their Left Socialist Revolutionary allies gained complete control of the 2nd All-Russian Congress of Soviets of Workers' and Soldiers' Deputies meeting in Petrograd on the afternoon of Nov. 7 (Oct. 25, O.S.), 1917. The minority opposition of Mensheviks and Right Socialist Revolutionaries withdrew in protest against the "October Revolution," that is, the violent overthrow of the Provisional Government, then nearing its climax in the same city. Lenin appeared before the Congress on Nov. 8, the day of victory in Petrograd, proposing decrees on peace and land which were enthusiastically confirmed. The Decree on Peace appealed for immediate peace without annexations or indemnities and repudiated secret diplomacy. The Decree on Land nationalized natural resources and land, much of which was

to be turned over to the peasants for cultivation without hired labor. An All-Bolshevik government, the Council of People's Commissars, was approved, including Lenin as chairman, Trotsky as commissar of foreign affairs, and Stalin as commissar of nationalities. Left Socialist Revolutionaries numbered a third of the less powerful Central Executive Committee, and entered the Council of People's Commissars in coalition with the Bolsheviks in December. The Bolshevik regime gained political control over the R. heartland by the end of 1917, although faced with German advances in the west, separatism in the borderlands, and a wide spectrum of political opposition. Resistance in Moscow ended after a week of bloody fighting. Kerensky fled abroad after the failure of his attempt at a military counterblow. Most opposition newspapers were suppressed (Nov. 9); the Kadet party outlawed (Dec. 11); the tsarist Senate abolished (Dec. 7) and a month later also the *zemstvos* (q.v.). The old court system was dismantled and the *Cheka* was organized under Feliks Dzerzhinsky. The long-awaited Constituent Assembly might have survived, and the Provisional Government along with it, had the Provisional Government convoked it months earlier. In the elections of Nov. 25, 1917, the Bolsheviks gained majorities in and near most major cities, but the Socialist Revolutionaries received by far the largest over-all vote and a majority of the seats, so that when the Constituent Assembly met on Jan. 18, 1918, it refused to adopt Bolshevik measures and was dissolved the next day, when Chernov, Tsereteli, Chkheidze, Dan, and other anti-Bolshevik leaders were unable to evoke massive counterforce in its defense. The first RSFSR constitution was passed by the Congress of Soviets (July 10, 1918), performing the task many had hoped would be completed by the Constituent Assembly.

Sweeping changes in family law and legal separation of the church from the state and the school from the church struck at church power. In a tightening of economic controls, a Supreme Economic Council was organized (Dec. 14, 1917) and the banks nationalized soon after. Members of the formerly privileged classes who did not join the large emigration faced prosecution, political repression, and legal discrimination.

WAR COMMUNISM (1918–21). Soviet Russia remained in the World War against the Central Powers after the October revolution. But after an armistice (Dec. 15, 1917) and protracted negotiations at Brest-Litovsk, and renewed German advances, Lenin's view prevailed that the demoralized Russian Army could neither fight a "revolutionary war" nor continue as an ally of the West. The harsh peace of Brest-Litovsk (Mar. 3, 1918) between Russia and the Central Powers stirred Allied enmity, prompted a Socialist Revolutionary rising in Yaroslavl, made enemies of the Left Socialist Revolutionaries, who withdrew from the government and carried out assassinations. One victim was the German ambassador, von Mirbach (July 6). Lenin was wounded by Dora Kaplan, a Socialist Revolutionary, on the same day that others killed Uritsky, chief of the Petrograd Cheka (Aug. 30). The Bolsheviks proclaimed the "Red Terror."

After Brest-Litovsk came three years of War Communism marked by stringent economic measures; the growth of a powerful, conscripted, disciplined Red Army under War Commissar Trotsky; and by civil war, which began with the campaigns of the White Russian Volunteer Army and the Don Cossacks in S. Russia at the end of 1917. Britain, France, the United States, and other allies began to intervene against the Bolsheviks in March 1918, landing supplies, military advisers to the Whites, and troops at Murmansk, Archangel, and Vladivostok. They acted on mixed motives which included a desire to restore the eastern front and to prevent allied war stores and Caucasian oil from falling into German hands, and a growing dislike of Bolshevism. After the armistice of Nov. 11, 1918 Allied intervention continued, but the troops began to withdraw in the spring of 1919.

An important addition was made to the anti-Bolshevik forces when the stranded Czech legion, on its way to embark at Vladivostok for the western front, refused Trotsky's order to disarm after growing misunderstandings (May 25, 1918), and seized part of the Trans-Siberian R.R. in W. Siberia. As Czechs marched on Yekaterinburg (Sverdlovsk), local Bolsheviks murdered the tsar and his family in the cellar of the house in Yekaterinburg where they were imprisoned (July 16).

Threats from four directions were repulsed by the Bolsheviks in 1919. Fighting with short, interior supply lines and the unifying political direction of the Communist party against a disunited, far-flung foe, they were assured of victory by early the following year. Admiral Kolchak and his Czech allies moved west from Siberia, but were stopped and turned back in May. General Miller, operating from his base at Archangel was unable to establish contact with him. Denikin and his Volunteer Amy drove north from the Crimea as far as Orel on the road to Moscow (Oct.), while Yudenich, advancing southeast from Estonia, was repulsed in the suburbs of Petrograd. The defeated former "Supreme Ruler" Kolchak was executed by the Red regime at Irkutsk (Feb. 1920). East of Irkutsk the Bolsheviks created a buffer Far Eastern Republic (Apr.). When the Japanese had evacuated Vladivostok (Oct. 1922), the Far Eastern Republic was absorbed into the RSFSR (Nov.).

Poland launched a war against Russia on April 20, 1920, soon after the Bolshevik victory in the Civil War. Invading Polish forces took Kiev (May 6) which was soon recaptured in a strong Red counteroffensive. Tukhachevsky (q.v.) advanced to the gates of Warsaw, spurred on by Lenin, Zinoviev, and Kamenev, who believed mistakenly that the Polish masses would rise in support of the Red Army. His defeat at the gates of Warsaw ended for the time being Bolshevik hopes of establishing a communist regime in Poland, from which communism was to have spread to Germany. The peace of Riga with Poland (Mar. 18, 1921) freed Red troops to deal with Denikin's successor, Wrangel. Overwhelmed by superior numbers, Wrangel evacuated 150,000 soldiers and civilians (Nov. 1920).

Some former R. borderlands emerged independent in the aftermath of the civil war. Poland, Finland, Lat-

via, Lithuania, and Estonia became free states. Parts of W. Ukraine and Byelorussia went to Poland. Bessarabia reverted to Rumania. Most of this land, excluding W. Poland and the larger part of Finland, was later regained (1939–45). The rich Ukraine had been savagely contested. Its capital, Kiev, had ten successive regimes in just over three years: a moderate Ukrainian nationalist Rada government (3 times); the reactionary German puppet, Hetman Skoropadsky; Denikin and the White Russians; the Poles; and the Bolsheviks, who came to stay the fourth time, proclaiming a Ukrainian Soviet Republic (1921).

Soviet reconquest of the Caucasus was facilitated by a *rapprochement* with Kemalist Turkey (1920–21), a historic reversal of centuries of Russo-Turkish discord. Azerbaijan, Georgia, and Armenia lost their independence by April 1921. They were reorganized as the Transcaucasian Soviet Socialist Republic (Dec. 13, 1922), which was united with the Ukrainian, Byelorussian, and Russian Federated SSR's into the newly formed Union of Soviet Socialist Republics (Dec. 30, 1922), whose constitution was approved by the 2nd USSR Congress of Soviets (Jan. 13, 1924). Control in the central Asian part of the former Russian empire was gained by 1926.

Civil war and allied blockade intensified the economic crisis which had been precipitated by World War I. Life was made even more difficult by the extreme Bolshevik economic measures, including nationalization of industry. Forced requisitions of grain provoked peasant risings, notably in Tambov. Popular unrest culminated in the uprising of the sailors in the fortress of Kronstadt near Petrograd which the Bolsheviks bloodily suppressed (March 7–18, 1921).

II. The New Economic Policy (1921–28).

LENIN'S LAST YEARS (1921–24). Faced with popular unrest, economic ruin, and the Kronstadt uprising, Lenin proposed to the 10th Party Congress then meeting initial measures of the economic retreat which became the New Economic Policy (NEP). There were two major compromises involved in NEP. One was with the peasantry. Grain requisitions were abolished and replaced with a proportional tax in kind which left peasants a surplus to trade in the open market. Limited hiring of labor and leasing of land were permitted by the NEP land decree of 1922. Agricultural recovery was marred by the famine of 1921–22, when Herbert Hoover organized famine relief.

The second major NEP compromise was with the principles of socialism. Private entrepreneurs ("Nepmen") were allowed to own small industrial enterprises and to conduct most retail trade. The state retained the "commanding heights": major factories, transport, communications, banking, and the monopoly of foreign trade.

Meanwhile the dictatorship of the Communist party was completed with the final elimination of openly organized political opposition.

The problem of dictatorship *within* the Communist party remained. Lenin pushed through the 10th Congress a resolution, aimed at the "workers' opposition" faction, which forbade separately organized ideological groupings in the party. (*See* OPPOSITION, COMMUNIST PARTY.) Factional strife continued, however, becoming a struggle for power after Lenin had been incapacitated by strokes which he suffered in May and Dec. 1922. He died after a fourth stroke, Jan. 21, 1924. After elaborate ceremonies, in which Stalin was careful to play the leading part, Lenin's embalmed remains were placed in the newly-built mausoleum on Red Square. Petrograd was renamed Leningrad.

STALIN BECOMES DICTATOR. A triumvirate of Zinoviev, Kamenev, and Stalin assumed leadership in 1923. Zinoviev, head of the Comintern and chief of the Petrograd party organization, and Kamenev, head of the Moscow party organization, underestimated the threat to their own position presented by Stalin and the power he had gained as secretary general. The triumvirate, which Stalin used against Trotsky, broke up in 1925 when Stalin allied himself with the "right" group of Bukharin, Tomsky, and Rykov, who advocated economic gradualism and material incentives for the peasantry. Zinoviev and Kamenev joined Trotsky. Their "left opposition" favored rapid industrialization at the expense of a collectivized peasantry. Trotsky opposed also his theory of "permanent revolution" to Stalin's major theoretical postulation, "socialism in one country," in which Stalin declared (late 1924) that socialism could and must be built in the USSR alone without the aid of communist revolutions in other countries. Trotsky was removed from the post of commissar for war (1925). In the rout of the "left opposition," he was also removed from the Politburo (1926) and the Central Committee (1927). After leading a street demonstration (Nov. 7, 1927), he was expelled from the party and then exiled to Alma-Ata. Ultimately deported (Jan. 1929) he took final refuge in Mexico, where he was murdered (Aug. 20, 1940).

Having used the "right" to defeat the "left," Stalin now appropriated much of the "left's" economic program, defeated the "right," and brought NEP to an end with the inauguration of the First Five Year Plan.

III. Soviet Foreign Policy, 1920–32.

Communism has infused Soviet diplomacy with a dynamism, universalist appeal, and a sense of alienation from the noncommunist state system. Simultaneously, Soviet communism acted through its own channels, such as the Communist (Third) International (q.v.) which became an arm of Soviet foreign policy.

Faced with the failure of communist uprisings in Germany and E. Europe before and during the early NEP period, and the impossibility of communizing Poland or the Baltic states, the Soviet leaders turned to diplomatic means of strengthening Russia's position against Britain and France. On the one hand, they looked east. A congress of peoples of the east in Baku under Zinoviev's leadership led picturesquely nowhere (Sept. 1920). But treaties with Afghanistan and Iran followed (Feb. 1921), and a treaty of friendship with Kemalist Turkey (Mar. 16, 1921). Control of Outer Mongolia passed from the Chinese to the USSR (1921). Diplomatic relations were established with Japan in 1925, when Japan agreed to evacuate N. Sakhalin but to retain an oil concession there. A tiny communist

party appeared in China. Stalin supported a policy of communist cooperation with the Chinese national revolutionary Sun Yat-Sen and his Kuomintang party. Sun and competing governments in Peking and Manchuria were all impressed by Soviet denunciation of tsarist "unequal" treaties with China. Soviet envoy, Ioffe, met Sun Yat-Sen for cordial talks (Jan. 1923). His successor, Karakhan, concluded agreements with Peking and Manchuria's warlord, Chang So-lin (1924), whereby the USSR and China shared operative controls of the Chinese Eastern R.R., formerly under tsarist domination. Many Chinese came to study in the USSR, including the young Chiang Kai-shek, who returned to head the new Whampoa Academy of the Kuomintang. A Soviet military mission headed by Blücher aided Chiang. The Comintern agent Borodin arrived with money, specialists, and military experts to help Sun's movement. Thus, communism and Chinese revolutionary nationalism entered a temporary partnership.

Soviet diplomacy, conducted until 1930 under the aristocratic Foreign Commissar Georgy Chicherin, yielded its first relatively long-lasting agreement in the treaty with Estonia, followed by similar treaties which recognized the independence of Lithuania, Latvia, and Finland (1920). During Soviet participation in the unsuccessful Genoa economic conference (April-May 1922), Chicherin and Germany's foreign minister, Walter Rathenau, surprised all with the Soviet-German Treaty of Rapallo (Apr. 16). Both sides renounced war claims and close political and economic ties were initiated. Apart from the Rapallo Treaty, secret agreements between the Reichswehr and the Red Army provided for the training of German pilots and tank crews on Soviet soil in circumvention of the military restrictions imposed on Germany by the Versailles Treaty. Good diplomatic relations with the Weimar Republic did not prevent attempts of the Soviet-dominated Comintern to undermine it. Diplomatic relations were established with Britain, Italy, and France (1924). Soviet espionage, propaganda, and subversive activities in the West and in Asia engendered discord and tension which reached a climax in 1927. British police raided Arcos, the Soviet trade mission (May 21). Britain and Canada broke off relations. Soviet ambassador to Poland, P. Voykov, was shot in Warsaw by a R. *émigré* (June 7). Trouble came also in the east. Chiang Kai-shek, Sun Yat-Sen's successor as Kuomintang leader, turned on the communists, purging them (April). Chinese police raided the Soviet embassy in Peking (May) and other Soviet missions. A bloody communist rising in Canton failed (Dec.). Soviet troops had to be used in 1929 to rescue arrested Soviet officials of the Chinese Eastern R.R. and to restore Russia's share in its operation under the 1924 agreement. Japan's seizure of Manchuria and creation there of the puppet regime of Manchukuo (March 9, 1932) caused Russia and China to patch up their quarrels with a nonaggression pact (June 29, 1932). Russia eventually sold the R.R. to Japan in a conciliatory move (March 1935).

Litvinov took charge of Soviet diplomacy in 1929 and became foreign commissar in 1930. He sought security in the west as a bolster against Japan's threat in the east. Nonaggression pacts were concluded in 1932 with Finland, Poland, Latvia, Estonia, and France.

IV. Stalin's Prewar Rule and the Five Year Plans (1928–41).

FIRST FIVE YEAR PLAN (1928–32). NEP ended in 1928, by which year the economy was restored approximately to its prewar level. Stalin was in control of the party apparatus, the army, and the formidable OGPU (security police, q.v.). He was in a position to end the concessions and compromises of NEP by launching a "revolution from above," a mighty and costly effort at rapid industrialization beginning with the First Five Year Plan (Oct. 1, 1928–Dec. 31, 1932). Survivals of private enterprise were rapidly eliminated. The "right opposition" in the party was routed. This led to the complete subordination of the trade unions to be an obedient arm of the state whose main task was to secure increased production. Heavy industry was to be given clear priority over the consumer goods industry. The Five Year Plan called for 20 per cent collectivization of the peasantry. But in 1929, Stalin rejected conciliation of the peasants with consumer goods in favor of coercion and full collectivization. During the nightmarish winter of 1929–30, urban communists, army and OGPU troops poured into the countryside to bring the peasants in line. By 1932 collectivization was 60 per cent complete, and by 1936 over 90 per cent complete. Some peasants worked on state farms, but the majority on collective farms (*kolkhozy*) which received mechanical services and much of their political controls through Machine Tractor Stations (MTS). Members of *kolkhozy* gave up all large farm utensils, retained household garden plots and some livestock in quantities depending on the region. Basic work was to be in the communal sector. Peasants were paid from farm profits left after expenses and compulsory deliveries to the state. Millions died in the collectivizations, deportations, and resulting famine of 1932–33. Desperate peasants destroyed about half of all livestock and much other agricultural inventory. For this cost, the regime was able to finance heavy industrialization with the food it could now extract from the peasants at low prices and sell to the urban consumers.

With the Five Year Plan came rationing, tighter discipline, the elimination of all cultural freedom, the expansion of state domination in economic and social life, and the consolidation of Stalin's autocracy. Dictatorship of the party had been transformed into the total dictatorship of one man.

At the end of NEP, there began a series of show trials. Forerunners of more lethal purge trials of the late 1930's, they were aimed at scapegoats, primarily among noncommunist and foreign technicians: Donbas engineers at Shakhty (1928), "Industrial party" (1930), Mensheviks, including Groman and Sukhanov (1931), Metro-Vickers engineers (1933).

Conservatism of method if not of goal began to appear. In 1931 Stalin stopped the persecution of "bourgeois" specialists. All talent was needed. He condemned also "petty-bourgeois leveling" of wages, approving highly stratified rewards. Traditional examinations, teaching methods, and discipline were restored in schools (1931–32).

THE SECOND AND THIRD FIVE YEAR PLANS (1933–41). The country seemed to be approaching a breathing spell during the Second Five Year Plan (1933–36). Industrial production rose rapidly and living standards modestly, although life was still harder for most people than it had been during NEP. The party declared that "socialism" had been built in the USSR by 1936. Under "socialism" large wage differentials continued. To spur output, workers were paid widely by the piece, not by the hour. Stakhanovism—bonuses and medals for outstanding workers whose records were then used to raise everybody's norms—became another form of incentive (1935). Labor discipline was greatly tightened before the war (1938–40). A new, "Stalin" constitution of the USSR outlined the new order (Dec. 5, 1936). The constitution mentioned the leading role of Communist party members in all organizations; that is, in effect, a totalitarian political system. The bicameral USSR Supreme Soviet was set up to replace the old, unwieldy Congress of Soviets as the top representative and legislative organ, the "highest organ of state power." Previously existing class restrictions and weighting of voting against the peasantry were eliminated, and secret, direct suffrage replaced open, indirect suffrage. Improved suffrage was meaningless in the controlled elections to the controlled Supreme Soviet. There is an impressive bill of rights in the constitution. But it does not permit political opposition, and it did not prevent the purges.

The purges of 1935–39 were set off by the assassination of Sergey Kirov, Leningrad party boss (Dec. 1, 1934). It was used by Stalin as a pretext for what Khrushchev called (1956) "mass repressions and brutal violations of socialist legality." Terror reached a peak in 1936–38, the so-called *Yezhovshchina*, named after police chief Yezhov. The world's main attention focused on five major public trials, mostly of "old Bolsheviks," —including Bukharin, Zinoviev, and Kamenev—and top army commanders, Tukhachevsky and Yegorov. The procurator general, Andrey Vyshinsky, used fabricated evidence and presumably forced confessions of treason, espionage, terrorism, "Trotskyite" conspiracy, and other "counterrevolutionary" crimes. Most victims, who numbered in the millions, received sentences of death or, more frequently, exile to forced labor camps, not at public trials but at secret hearings of NKVD special boards. Purges hit high and low, among party and state officials, the police itself, including its chiefs Yagoda and Yezhov, military officers, intellectuals, foreign Communists including most of the Polish, Hungarian, and German Communist parties, and ordinary citizens. Great talent was lost, and the army weakened. But posts were opened up for a new breed of tough, efficient young *apparatchiki*, including Khrushchev, who stood by Stalin. As war approached some prisoners such as General Rokossovsky were released as indispensable.

Heavy industry in the period 1929–40 grew out of all proportion as compared with light consumer industry, or with agriculture where production actually declined.

Yearly output of steel increased from 4.3 mill. to 18.3 mill. tons, of coal from 35.5 mill. to 165.9 mill. tons, of machine tools from 2,000 to 58,400, while the rates of production of means of production in total output increased from 39.5 per cent to 61.2 per cent.

The great economic changes under Stalin were accompanied by the destruction of the relative cultural freedom of NEP, and by rigid imposition through total controls of methods of "socialist realism" and "partyness," while art of the national minorities had to be "national in form but socialist in content." The internationalism of early Bolshevism acquired increasingly nationalist overtones, traceable from Stalin's doctrine of "socialism in one country" (1924, q.v.) to the condemnation of Pokrovsky's Marxist school of history and the glorification of the R. historical tradition beginning in the middle 1930's.

V. Foreign Policy, 1933–41.

Hitler's advance to power in 1933, repression of the German Communist party, and hostility to the USSR caused the Kremlin to reverse its pro-German policy. The establishment of closer ties with the West included a long delayed recognition of the Soviet government by the United States (Nov. 17, 1933). Mutual aid pacts were concluded with France (May 2, 1935) and with Czechoslovakia (May 16), to which the USSR promised aid in case of an attack, but only if France also intervened. It entered the League of Nations which it had once condemned (Sept. 18, 1934). "Popular Front" tactics of collaboration with Socialists were tried by French Communists (Feb.-July) in response to the changing diplomatic situation, with such success that the 7th (last) Comintern Congress officially abandoned militant hostility to the noncommunist left and ordered communist parties to ally themselves with anti-fascist groups (1935).

"Collective security" suffered setbacks in the face of increasing German, Italian, and Japanese aggression and the "appeasement" policies of England and France, whose nonintervention in the Spanish Civil War (Mar. 1936–Mar. 1939) left the field free to the USSR. It helped and infiltrated the losing Republican side against Franco's Nationalists who received German and Italian support. When the West agreed at Munich, in talks with Hitler to which the USSR was not invited, that Czechoslovakian Sudetenland should go to Germany (Sept. 1938), the USSR found itself isolated once again. After the fall of Czechoslovakia (March 1939), Molotov replaced Litvinov as commissar of foreign affairs. The USSR conducted unsuccessful talks with Britain and France on common measures for defense while its representatives were negotiating secretly with the Nazis. Resumption of a pro-German policy was signaled by the signing of the Nazi-Soviet nonaggression pact (Aug. 23, 1939). Hitler was now free to attack Poland (Sept. 1). Britain and France lived up to their obligations to Poland and declared war on Germany (Sept. 3). Russia and Germany partitioned Poland, which Soviet troops entered Sept. 17, occupying Poland up to the Bug River. After the startlingly rapid fall of France (June 1940), the USSR annexed Latvia, Lithuania, and Estonia as union republics, and took Bessarabia and N. Bukovina

from Rumania (July). Soviet western borders now resembled those of the Russian empire, excluding Finland. When the USSR attacked Finland to enforce territorial demands, stubborn Finnish resistance pointed up the weakness of the Red Army, but numbers prevailed in the short Soviet-Finnish war (Nov. 30, 1939–Mar. 12, 1940). Finland had to yield Karelia, land near Leningrad up to and including Vyborg, and sites for bases. Russia was expelled from the League of Nations (Dec. 14, 1939).

The Japanese invasion of China (July 1937) prompted a Sino-Soviet pact (Aug. 29, 1937) after which the USSR began to supply arms and advisers to Chiang Kai-shek. Tension grew with Japan. There were border incidents, along the Manchurian and Outer Mongolian borders (1937–39). But war did not suit either side. A Soviet-Japanese nonaggression pact (April 13, 1941) lasted four years until broken by the USSR.

Although Russia lived up faithfully to all the vital trade agreements with Germany, Hitler began formulating plans of attack on Russia in 1940, which gathered momentum after Molotov, who succeeded Litvinov as foreign minister in 1939, and the German foreign minister, Ribbentrop, failed to agree over future divisions of spheres of influence (Nov. 1940). Stalin became premier in May 1941, replacing Molotov. Ignoring British warnings, he seemed taken by surprise when "Operation Barbarossa," the German invasion of Russia, began June 22, 1941, a year to the day after the Franco-German armistice.

VI. The "Great Fatherland War," 1941–45.

Germany, Italy, Rumania, and Slovakia declared war on Russia on the day of invasion. Finland (June 25) and Hungary (June 27) followed. As Nazi panzer divisions launched an offensive swiftly and confidently into the Soviet Union, Churchill promptly promised aid, and the United States offered lend-lease supplies. Soviet war leadership was concentrated in the State Committee of Defense with the Politburo members Stalin, Molotov, Malenkov, Beria, and Voroshilov. Stalin delivered on July 3 a nationalistic speech which justified the Nazi-Soviet pact as having given 18 months' breathing space and called for a "scorched earth" policy.

The Germans advanced in three prongs aimed at Leningrad, Moscow, and Kiev. Kiev fell (Sept. 19), Kharkov (Oct. 24), and Crimea including Sevastopol after a heroic siege resistance (Nov. 15, 1941–July 2, 1942). The Soviet government left Moscow for Kuybyshev, Stalin remaining in the panicky capital. Millions of Soviet troops deserted or were captured. But Hitler missed his main goals: Moscow and a quick victory. Moscow repelled the attack (Nov.-Dec.). Leningrad withstood a long siege in which 600,000 are said to have died of starvation. There were massive casualties among the Germans in the exceptionally severe winter, recalling the winter of 1812 which ravaged Napoleon's army. (*See* WORLD WAR II, GERMAN OCCUPATION.)

Some of the people, especially in the Ukraine, welcomed the Germans, but were soon disillusioned. The most striking instance of disaffection was General Vlasov's movement (q.v.). Stalin stirred the people to resistance by emphasizing German atrocities and by appealing to their patriotism rather than to communist fanaticism. Memories of Russia's heroes were evoked. The regime rewarded army officers with new orders and medals, mass promotions, the creation of guards and Cossack regiments, the re-introduction of epaulettes, and the demotion of political commissars to the rank of deputy commanders for political affairs. There was a reconciliation with the church (q.v.), and the Comintern was dissolved (1943).

Early in the war the regime deported the Volga Germans. It moved later similarly to obliterate the Crimean Tatars, Kalmyks, Chechen-Ingush, Karachais, and Balkars. In his secret speech, 1956, Khrushchev condemned, and blamed Stalin for, the "mass deportations . . . of whole nations, together with all Communists and Komsomol members without exception," did not mention the Volga Germans or the Crimean Tatars, but added that the Ukrainians "avoided meeting this fate only because there were too many of them." Partial rehabilitation of the deported nationalities began in 1956.

Stalin frequently reproached the West for delaying the opening of a "second front." But he had no cause to complain about the material aid shipped at considerable risk to Archangel, Murmansk, Vladivostok, and through Persia. The United States sent to Russia 16½ mill. tons of vitally needed war matériel and food under lend-lease, valued at $11 bill., of which 15 mill. tons arrived safely. Struggling to overcome a loss of more than half their prewar industrial production, the Soviets moved thousands of plants to safety in Siberia.

German forces in 1942 thrust toward Caucasian oil, but failed to capture Baku or Grozny because Hitler diverted troops from this goal in his determination to take Stalingrad. The battle of Stalingrad (Sept. 15, 1942–Feb. 2, 1943) ended in total defeat of the Germans and the capture of their commander, Marshal von Paulus, with shattered remnants of his troops.

VICTORY AND ITS PROBLEMS, 1943–45. Well coordinated offensives carried Soviet armies across the prewar borders of the USSR in 1944 and into its E. European neighbors. The Polish-born General Rokossovsky halted his army on the Vistula in Warsaw's Praga suburb. As a result the noncommunist Home Army under the Polish resistance leader Bor-Komorowski, which had risen in Warsaw expecting Soviet liberation and which had held out for nine weeks, was destroyed by the Germans who razed Warsaw (Oct. 5) in retaliation against the rising. Rumania was forced out of the war (Aug. 24), then Bulgaria (Aug. 26), and Finland (Sept. 19). Soviet forces helped to liberate Belgrade (Oct. 20), and entered Budapest (Feb. 13, 1945). American and Soviet forces met on the Elbe (April 25, 1945), after an American decision to hold back and allow the Soviets to take Berlin (April 20–May 3). As a result of a similar American decision, the Soviets, not the closer Americans, entered Prague (May 8). Meanwhile Hitler committed suicide, and at midnight, May 8, the war in Europe ended.

Stalin's first wartime diplomatic concern was to make agreements and pacts on mutual aid with the allies.

But post-war problems loomed already in 1943. The USSR broke with the Polish government-in-exile, London (April), over the latter's demand for investigation of the 1940 Katyn massacre of 15,000 Polish war prisoners, for which it is now widely believed that the USSR was responsible. The meeting of Roosevelt, Churchill, and Stalin at Teheran, Persia (Nov. 28–Dec. 1, 1943), was the first of several momentous summit meetings, at each of which Stalin scored notable successes. Stalin at Teheran vetoed Churchill's plan for a Balkan "second front"; obtained agreement on a landing in France; agreed to declare war on Japan, but only after Germany's defeat. Soviet diplomats participated in planning for the United Nations Organization (Dumbarton Oaks, Oct. 1944, and San Francisco, April-June 1945).

The Yalta (or Crimean) conference (Feb. 7–12, 1945) left Stalin well satisfied. The Byelorussian and Ukrainian republics were to be admitted to the UN. France would have a German occupation zone, but carved out of the western zones. It was agreed that representatives of the London Polish government-in-exile would be included in Poland's Soviet-sponsored Lublin regime, and that there should be free elections (provisions which did not prevent the communization of Poland). The Curzon line was to be Poland's eastern boundary but her western frontier remained undefined. The Yalta "Declaration of Liberated Europe," expressing the belief that problems of the liberated and former Axis satellite countries should be solved "by democratic means," turned out to be meaningless for E. Europe, which was Stalinized within three years after the end of the war. A secret Far E. agreement provided for Russia's eventual declaration of war on Japan; the USSR was to annex the Kurile Islands and S. Sakhalin, to control Port Arthur and Dairen, and to share in the management of the Manchurian R.R.

When Truman, Churchill, and Stalin met at the Potsdam conference (July 17–Aug. 2), hopes for Soviet-Western cooperation had begun to fade because of Soviet policy in E. Europe. Neither Attlee and Bevin, who replaced Churchill and Eden during the conference, nor President Truman and Secretary of State Byrnes had been at Teheran or Yalta, which added to their difficulties.

Among the Potsdam agreements was the proviso that Germany, although divided into four zones of occupation, be administered as one unit. In fact, Germany soon emerged split between East and West. The three western zones united into the Federal German Republic and the Soviet zone became the German Democratic Republic (1949). Reparations were agreed on in principle, but East and West disagreed on amounts and sources, and the West began pumping wealth into the W. German economy while the USSR was still draining the economy of E. Germany (German Democratic Republic). Germany was to be denazified, demilitarized, and democratized. Denazification was clumsy and incomplete, demilitarization a brief interlude before partial rearmament, and democratization carried out only in W. Germany. Soviet-supported Polish occupation of former E. German lands up to the Oder and Neisse

TERRITORIAL GAINS OF THE USSR, 1939—45

Territory	Date	Area (sq. mi.)	Population (est. 1939)
IN EUROPE:			
W. Ukraine and W. Byelorussia (from Poland)	Sept. 28, 1939	65,000	10,800,000
Karelia and Petsamo-Pechenga (from Finland)	March 12, 1940	17,600	450,000
Bessarabia and N. Bukovina (from Rumania)	June 28, 1940	19,450	3,700,000
Lithuania (including Vilnius and Klaipeda)	Aug. 3, 1940	25,175	3,000,000
Latvia	Aug. 5, 1940	25,400	1,950,000
Estonia	Aug. 6, 1940	18,350	1,122,000
Sub-Carpathian Ruthenia (from Czechoslovakia) ...	June 20, 1945	4,875	731,000
East Prussia (N. part) (from Germany)	Aug. 2, 1945	4,250	1,187,000
TOTAL EUROPE		180,100	22,940,000
IN ASIA:			
Tannu Tuva People's Republic	Oct. 11, 1944	65,800	120,000
S. Sakhalin (Karafuto)	Feb. 11, 1945	13,950	400,000
Kurile Islands (from Japan)	Sept. 2, 1945	6,000	17,500
TOTAL ASIA		85,750	537,500
GRAND TOTAL		265,850	23,477,500

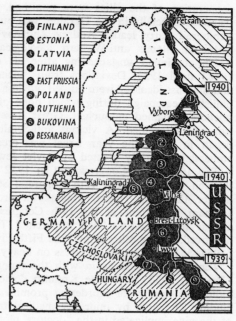

rivers and expulsion of millions of Germans presented the West with a *fait accompli* at Potsdam. The West refused to recognize permanent Polish possession, and agreed only to temporary Polish administration of these lands. Poland claims these territories as her own, which are in effect compensation for Soviet annexation of her former E. provinces, and which remain potentially serious sources of discord. By one ill-fated Potsdam decision, a jointly occupied but segmented Berlin was almost isolated in E. Germany, with only restricted and vulnerable access from the West. (Communist pressure continued in 1960–61 for the end of western occupation in W. Berlin and its conversion into a "free city.") By the Potsdam agreement, a council of foreign ministers of the USSR, the United States, Britain, France, and Nationalist China was to meet periodically to discuss inter-allied problems and draft peace settlements. Its meetings ended often in East-West stalemate. The council worked out treaties of peace with Hungary, Rumania, Bulgaria, Italy, and Finland (signed Feb. 10, 1947). An Austrian peace treaty was signed finally in 1955. No peace treaty had been signed with Germany by 1961.

After a gruelling campaign in the Pacific against Japan, the United States dropped a devastating atomic bomb on Hiroshima (Aug. 6, 1945). The USSR declared war on Japan (Aug. 8). Another atomic bomb was dropped, on Nagasaki (Aug. 9). Japan soon capitulated, signing the surrender agreement on the battleship *Missouri* (Sept. 2). Soviet forces swiftly occupied Manchuria. They saw to it that Chinese Communists rather than Chinese Nationalists received surrendered Japanese weapons. The Soviets dismantled valuable factories and shipped them back to the USSR. Korea was partitioned at the 38th parallel between a N. Korean communist regime and a S. Korean government sponsored by the West.

VII. Reconstruction and Reaction, 1945–53.

War damage and German occupation caused serious setbacks in Soviet economic development. About 25 million people died and births were perhaps 15 million below normal, which meant an approximate total loss in population of 40 million because of the war. But the defeat of Germany and Japan and the weakening of Britain and France, together with Soviet military successes, increased military strength, and sizable annexations (not only those of 1939–40 but also part of E. Prussia including Königsberg [Kaliningrad], the Kurile Islands and S. Sakhalin), meant that Soviet Russia's power in the world had grown enormously. There was a Soviet satellite empire in E. Europe. Later, communism was to make large gains in the Far East. (*See* FOREIGN POLICY SINCE 1945.)

Stalin promised little of the better life and relaxation so eagerly awaited by his war-weary people when he addressed them in an election speech (Feb. 9, 1946), one of the first signs of the "cold war," pointing out that the danger of war will continue as long as capitalism exists. He set high 15-year goals for heavy industry which were indeed more than reached. The Fourth Five Year Plan of reconstruction (1946–50) brought industrial production above prewar levels. Rationing was ended in Dec. 1947 and a currency reform wiped out cash savings, especially of peasants who had not banked profits from open-market sales of food during the war. Collective farms were amalgamated to increase administrative efficiency and political control. But agriculture continued to suffer from overcentralization, underinvestment and lack of material incentives. (*See* AGRICULTURE.)

A major attack was launched by the government, during and after the close of the war, on actual, potential, or imagined disloyalty. Returning soldiers were reindoctrinated and DP's repatriated by force with the cooperation of the allies were punished. Partisan resistance, especially in the Ukraine, was put down. The Leningrad party leader Andrey Zhdanov initiated in 1946 an intense anti-Western ideological campaign, which continued unslackening after his death (Aug. 1948) until 1953. Deviations from "socialist realism" and Stalinist ideology were hunted out in a chauvinistic, philistine campaign during which none of the arts or sciences remained untouched. Great Russian nationalism was intensified. A vicious anti-Semitic campaign began in 1948, the year Israel was created and its ambassador warmly greeted by Soviet Jews.

The 19th Party Congress met in 1952 (Oct. 5–15), thirteen years after the 18th Congress; Stalin did not deliver the main report. Malenkov's prominent role as main rapporteur at the 19th Congress made him appear to be Stalin's "heir apparent." The Congress approved, among other things, the Fifth Five Year Plan (1951–55) with continued stress on heavy industry.

Tension increased again with the report in *Pravda* (Jan. 13, 1953) that nine Kremlin doctors had been indicted allegedly for murdering prominent leaders including Zhdanov, by improper medical treatment. Six of the nine implicated in the "doctors' plot" were Jews, and there were charges of "cosmopolitanism and Zionism." Jews were not the only intended victims. Beria's MVD was blamed for carelessness. Perhaps Beria was to be purged by his rivals. Khrushchev implied in 1956 that Stalin was planning a general purge of his principal lieutenants.

But purges were stopped short by the momentous news of Stalin's death (March 5, 1953).

VIII. "The Thaw" and the Rise of Khrushchev.

So great was the shock of Stalin's death that his top lieutenants warned the people against "panic and disorder." They promptly concentrated controls back in their hands by reducing the size of the Presidium and Secretariat to the dimensions of before the 19th Congress. Voroshilov was named chairman of the USSR Supreme Soviet's Presidium (or "president" of the USSR, a ceremonial post held by Kalinin, 1938–46, Shvernik, 1946–53, Voroshilov, 1953–60, Brezhnev, 1960–). Ministries were amalgamated. "Collective leadership" was proclaimed. But Malenkov was clearly on top. He was both premier (chairman of the USSR Council of Ministers) and senior secretary in the Secretariat, as well as member of the party Presidium. Next came Beria, head of the security police. The third member of the leading triumvirate was Molotov, one of the surviving "old Bolsheviks." Kaganovich, Mikoyan, Voroshilov, Suslov, Khrushchev, Bulganin, Saburov, and Pervukhin completed the membership of the party Presidium. Malenkov soon yielded to Khrushchev his place in the Secretariat (March 14). The Stalin cult faded in a matter of weeks, most leaders probably relieved to be rid of Stalin and anxious to disassociate themselves from his rule. Worship centered ever more exclusively in Lenin. The "doctors' plot" was exposed as a hoax by Beria's MVD (April), while Beria posed as the champion of legality in the reforms of Soviet law which were gaining momentum. Beria was the only top leader to be physically purged. His arrest (late June)

was justified on charges that he had been an agent of British intelligence and had tried to seize power through the MVD. When his execution with his associates was reported (Dec.), he was not widely mourned. In the next two years, many top police and party protegés of Beria were demoted, some of them liquidated. Meanwhile unrest stirred in the Soviet empire with strikes in Czechoslovakia (early June), the rising in E. Berlin (June 17) which spread in E. Germany and could be suppressed only with the aid of Soviet troops, and the strikes among the forced laborers of Vorkuta.

Malenkov's "new course" offered economic concessions in the form of increased stress on consumer goods, for whose greatly expanded production, said Malenkov (Aug. 8), heavy industry now presented an adequate base. Malenkov proclaimed for the peasantry lower taxes and reduced quotas as well as higher prices for some compulsory deliveries. Foreign policy was more conciliatory and military budgets lower. But the explosion of a Soviet H-bomb (1953) marked increasing military power. Terror abated, while, as part of the downgrading of the security police, notorious special boards of the MVD were abolished by secret decree (Sept. 1953). The "thaw," or general relaxation, affected art in 1953–54, when voices were raised among writers and artists criticizing the dull, stereotyped Soviet works, asking for more creative freedom, and even questioning party controls over art.

While battling Malenkov's threat to the priority of heavy industry, Khrushchev acted in the field of agriculture. He disclosed frankly what most Russians knew, that farming was in a lamentable state. There was less livestock than there had been before the revolution (Sept. 1953). He launched the bold move to conquer the "virgin lands," causing hundreds of thousands of youth and experts to be sent to pioneer in W. Siberia and Kazakhstan. His name became associated with corn, which he persistently stressed as good livestock feed. As first secretary since Sept. 1953, he was able to advance his own supporters within the party. By 1955 he was strong enough to force Malenkov to resign as premier (Feb. 8). Bulganin succeeded him.

The 20th Congress (1956) brought to a climax de-Stalinization and planned for economic, administrative, and social reforms. The Sixth Five Year Plan (1956–60) was approved. Khrushchev, who played the leading role at the Congress, declared obsolete the thesis of the inevitability of wars while imperialism existed, and declared that communist revolutions could win sometimes by peaceful parliamentary means. Advance notice was given of impending increase in lower pensions and wages, shortening of the work day, and elimination of the tuition fees for secondary school and higher schools imposed in 1940 (1956). Decentralization and increase of competence of the republics were called for. Most important, in a secret speech to the Congress, Khrushchev denounced the "cult of Stalin's personality" in by far the strongest terms used up to and since then, illustrating Stalin's incompetence, paranoiac suspicion, and purge brutality. In 1956, a year of unrest, Poland gained more national freedom under Gomulka and a Hungarian revolution was suppressed by Soviet troops

(Oct.-Nov.). Artistic ferment was again apparent. The party criticized Dudintsev's controversial novel, *Not by Bread Alone,* limiting it to a small edition, while banning altogether the publication of Boris Pasternak's *Doctor Zhivago,* which appeared only abroad. Open condemnations of *Doctor Zhivago* did not appear until Oct. 1958, after Pasternak had been awarded the Nobel Prize which the party then compelled him to refuse. Unrest took political forms at home too. Soviet students evidenced disquiet over Hungary. Demonstrations in Tbilisi, Georgia, on the anniversary of Stalin's death were broken up with loss of life. In December, Khrushchev's rivals challenged his power. Khrushchev was able to launch in 1957 over their opposition a major economic reorganization which abolished most economic ministries, transferring their enterprises to new regional economic councils. The reform not only aimed at increased efficiency, but also gave to Khrushchev's supporters, the regional and republic party secretaries, greater control over industry at the expense of the former ministers from whom Khrushchev's rivals seemed to derive support. Rebounding from defeat in the Presidium to victory in the Central Committee (June 1957), Khrushchev obtained the expulsion from the Presidium of the "anti-party group of Malenkov, Molotov, and Kaganovich, and Shepilov who joined them." Defense Minister Marshal Zhukov was rewarded for his support with promotion to full membership in the Presidium, but was soon expelled and denounced (Oct.). That summer, Moscow was gay with the huge International Youth Festival, which provided many Soviet young people with their first uncensored contact with foreign cultures and ideas.

Khrushchev took over the position of chairman of the USSR Council of Ministers (premier) from Bulganin, Malenkov's successor (March 1958), who suffered successive demotions, confessed membership in the "anti-party group" and eventually retired. Khrushchev was indisputably leader of the USSR as head of the party and the government.

Agricultural reforms of 1958 included abolition of the MTS's and sale of their machinery to the collective farms. Modest legal reforms and sweeping educational reforms were confirmed (Dec.).

The 21st Party Congress (Jan.-Feb. 1959) approved an ambitious Seven Year Plan to replace the Sixth Five Year Plan. It charted accelerated housing construction, industrial automation, continuing priority for heavy industry, and a 40 per cent rise in living standards. Khrushchev proclaimed a period of "full-fledged building of communism," predicted that by 1970 the USSR would surpass the United States as the world's leading industrial power, and asserted that "capitalist encirclement" was over because of the strength and size of the system of "socialist" states. He asserted, however, that the state must remain, even under future communism, not "withering away," as long as there was danger of attack by "imperialists." The Congress endorsed the transfer of some state functions to (nominally) non-state organs; e.g., the "people's police" and "comradely courts." It envisaged the eventual "merging of collective farm-cooperative and public (state) forms

of property"—a hint that collective farms would be transformed into state farms.

In the optimistic year, 1959, the USSR sent up three moon rockets; Moscow was host to an American exhibition and New York to a Soviet exhibit; and expectations of understanding rose to a peak in Russia during the visit to the United States of Nikita Khrushchev —the first R. ruler to come to America. The projected return visit of President Eisenhower to the USSR in 1960 did not take place. United States-Soviet relations deteriorated rapidly. An American U-2 jet reconnaissance aircraft crashed or was downed on May Day, 1960, over Sverdlovsk in the heart of Russia. The Paris summit conference collapsed (May 16-17). A spy-scare campaign for vigilance preceded and accompanied the trial and sentencing of the U-2 pilot, Francis Gary Powers. When Khrushchev visited New York in September, one year after his first trip to America, in order to attend the 15th session of the UN General Assembly, there was no sign of deviation from the renewed hard line in Soviet foreign policy.

During the Soviet period, Russia advanced from fifth to second rank among nations in terms of gross industrial production. Modernization still contrasted sharply in 1960 with prerevolutionary vestiges, especially in the countryside where just over half the population still lived. The post-Stalin regime, in which Khrushchev consolidated his leadership (1955–58), has repudiated the purge terror and adulation associated with "the cult of Stalin's personality." People live in less fear of arbitrary arrest and greater comfort than they did under Stalin. But there has been no repudiation of centralized planning and its enforcement of the primacy of heavy industry over the production of consumer goods, of industrial over agricultural investments, and of collectivized over private farming. Lines of political control branch out from the leadership of the Communist party through the party apparatus to the core of party members in the state bureaucracy and non-state organizations in an attempt to harness all phases of Soviet life to the goals which the party sets. The Soviet regime led by Khrushchev has made the USSR an increasingly formidable political competitor on a world scale. It has introduced, within the limits of party control, some of the administrative flexibility and personal security which seem to be needed for rapid growth in advanced stages of industrialization, while conducting a determined diplomatic, economic, and psychological offensive in underdeveloped and "uncommitted" nations.

BIBLIOGRAPHY: Max Beloff, *The Foreign Policy of Soviet Russia, 1921–41,* 2 vols., New York and London, 1947 and 1949; Merle Fainsod, *How Russia Is Ruled,* Cambridge, 1953; Louis Fischer, *The Soviets in World Affairs,* 2 vols., Princeton, 1951; James Meisel and Edward Kozera (eds.), *Materials for the Study of the Soviet System,* Ann Arbor, 1953; Frederick Schuman, *Russia since 1917,* New York, 1957; Donald W. Treadgold, *Twentieth Century Russia,* Chicago, 1959; George F. Kennan, *Russia and the West under Lenin and Stalin,* New York, 1961.   P. H. J.

HÓFSTEIN, David (1889–), Yiddish poet. Wrote poetry in Yiddish, Hebrew, Russian, and Ukrainian. In 1919 H came in conflict with the Bolshevik authorities in Moscow, fled to Berlin, then went to Palestine. As his family was left behind in Soviet Russia, he came back and made his peace with the Soviets. He was arrested during the purge of Jewish writers in 1948; became insane in a Soviet prison. His collections of poems are: *Bei Vegn* (By the Roads), *I Believe,* collected works, and others.

HOG BREEDING. The January count of hogs was, in mill.: 23.0 in 1916 (within present Soviet boundaries), 27.7 in 1928, 27.5 in 1941, 53.3 in 1960. Gross output of pork (carcass weight) was reported to be, in mill. tons, 1.8 in 1913, 1.4 in 1928, 1.7 in 1940, 3.6 in 1959. In 1959, 21.4% of all hogs were owned by state farms, 47.5% by collective farms, the remainder belonging to collective farmers and employees. Twelve breeds are raised, regional specialization being promoted. The number of pedigreed animals rose from 5.8 mill. in 1939 to 11.9 mill. in 1955. Average carcass weight rose from 118 lb. in 1928 to 137.7 lb. in 1956.

HORSE BREEDING was well developed in tsarist Russia. Well-known breeds, such as the Orlov trotter, were created. Selective breeding was carried on mainly on large estates and suffered a severe setback during the period of War Communism, when most breeding animals were destroyed. According to January counts, there were 38.2 mill. horses in 1916 (within present Soviet boundaries), 36.1 mill. in 1928. Their number was more than halved during the early collectivization years. Recovery was slower than in the case of other livestock since, given the goal of mechanization and the grain shortage, no serious effort was made to encourage HB. There were 21.0 mill. horses in 1941, and only 10.7 mill. in 1946 as the result of war losses. The herds numbered 11.5 mill. in 1959 and had been continuously declining since 1954, partly as the concomitant of a progressing mechanization of field work. The decline of Soviet HB since 1928 has been a logical and partly anticipated result of collectivization. The losses of draft power and manure which were associated with it have, however, to be borne in mind as a partial offset to the Soviet policies of promoting mechanization and the use of artificial fertilizers.

HORTICULTURE CROPS. Frost hazard and moisture shortage make most of the Soviet territory ill-suited for HC. Major producers are Ukraine (42.3% of its area under HC), Moldavia, Georgia, and Central Asian Republics. Horticulture picked up impetus after the abolition of serfdom, with the general intensification of R. agriculture. The first fruit-tree nurseries, of which about 5,000 exist now, were then set up, mainly on large estates. The area under fruit and berry crops rose (in thousand acres) from 1,600 in 1913, to 2,580 in 1928, 3,780 in 1938, and 7,400 in 1958. According to the 1959 census, 32% of that area belonged to collective farms, 10% to state farms, 44% to collective farmers' household plots. Seed fruit varieties accounted for 54% of all trees, stone fruit for 40%. Soviet researchers emphasized breeding frost-resistant strains, pushing HC to the N., but neglected pruning and training practices.

Fruit is relatively short in Russia. The annual crop amounted to 2.2 mill. tons over the 1925–28 period, resulting in per capita consumption of some 22 pounds.

The 1958 crop was about 20 pounds per capita, as against some 150 pounds in the United States.

HOSPITALS: *see* MEDICAL SYSTEM.

HOTELS: *see* TRAVELING AND TOURISM.

HOUSING REGULATIONS contained in Soviet civil law (q.v.) govern the renting and ownership of living space. Uniform in important details for all Union republics, tight HR are necessary because housing has been so short in the USSR that it has been discussed in terms of square meters, not rooms; living space, not apartments. Although there is a "sanitary norm" of 9 sq. m. (96.8 sq. ft.) per person, the national average is closer to 5 sq. m. (54 sq. ft.). Changing HR have reflected Soviet experiments with various ways of maintaining and distributing existing housing. After the Oct. Revolution, housing of the rich was requisitioned and masses of workers were moved in. Larger town houses were confiscated in 1918. Rent-free occupancy was tried in 1921, and subsequently the most common form of administration was through building cooperatives and renting cooperatives. The government dissolved renting cooperatives and all but a few building cooperatives in 1937. Housing is administered now either through local soviets or through the factories and other state or public organizations which maintain living quarters for their employees. Seekers of either form of rental housing wait their turn for permission from the soviets, factories, etc. When they have permission, they may sign their leases with the building superintendent. Rents are low, at most 1.32 rubles per sq. m.(=10.76 sq. ft.). Rental for a given living space depends on its size, on the amount of the tenant's salary, and on whether a tenant is entitled to a reduction as a serviceman, invalid, hardship case, or because his housing is dark, in a basement, lacking in utilities or plumbing. There are extra payments for central heating, utilities and other special comforts. But total payments are usually less than 5% of a family's budget, even for the rarer separate apartments which are reserved for privileged intellectuals, managers, officers, officials, artists, and exceptional workers. People's courts play a vital role in settling housing disputes. Renewal of leases is assured and evictions impossible, save for nonpayment of rent, destructiveness, unbearable annoyance to other tenants in the same apartment, or illegal occupancy. But if occupancy of a tenant in factory housing was made legally conditional on his working in that factory, he must move if he gives up his job or is dismissed, unless through no fault of his own he lost his job by layoff, illness, or at convenience of the plant. In this case, eviction proceedings must be taken to a people's court, and the evicted tenant must be given equivalent housing elsewhere, as must all occupants evicted through no fault of their own (because of demolition, major renovations, or commandeering of the building for other uses). Absent tenants retain housing rights for six months. But they may be away as long as necessary without losing their living space when they leave for medical treatment, for compulsory military service, or on work assignments abroad and in hardship posts such as the Arctic. Subletting is allowed, and in practice vacationers at holiday resorts or urban boarders pay up to 300–400 rubles a month for a room, or far above the regular rental fee. Housing construction has greatly increased recently under an ambitious long-term program. It will be years, however, before most families have their own apartments, without four persons to a room. When the shortage eases, so may the government controls on migration to big cities. (*See* PASSPORTS.)

Houses may be owned as personal property, acquired by inheritance, as a gift, by purchase from state organizations with a minimum of 20% down payment, or by construction with bank loans up to 50%, or sometimes 70%, of building costs. Private houses must not be built with more than five rooms, and on plots of (state) land larger than 300–600 sq. m. (3,200–6,500 sq. ft.) in cities or 700–1,200 sq. m. (7,500–13,000 sq. ft.) in the country. To prevent speculation, a family is forbidden to own more than one house, except through inheritance. Nor may it sell its house until it has held it for three years. A peasant's house in a collective farm is the joint property of the collective farm household. (*See also* PROPERTY, INHERITANCE, THE COURT SYSTEM, URBAN HOUSING) P. H. J.

HRUSHÉVSKY, Mikhaíl Sergéyevich (1866–1934), Ukrainian historian and political leader. His advocacy of Ukrainian nationalism forced him to leave the University of Kiev and settle in Austria (1894). There he taught and worked on his ten-volume *History of the Ukraine* (1903–36). He became chairman of the Ukrainian National Council (Rada) in March 1917, emigrated in 1918, and returned in 1924 to Kiev where he worked in the Ac. of S., Ukrainian SSR.

HUNGER STEPPE: *see* GOLODNAYA STEP.

HUNTING AND TRAPPING. All hunting terrains have been nationalized. Most of them are utilized by state and collective farms specializing in HT; some are open to individuals. Professional and amateur hunters and trappers number about 2 mill. While indiscriminate deforestation had an adverse effect on numbers of game in some areas, a wide variety of game still exists, including about 100 animals and 200 birds. Ever since the 15th century, but especially since the conquest of Siberia, HT provided Russia with her traditional export article, furs. In the 1930's, Russia accounted for 90% of the world's trade in squirrel furs, 95% in sable, 68% in ermine. According to official statistics, output amounts to over 150 mill. furs a year, making Russia the world's largest producer. All output is delivered to the state. Squirrel accounts for 22%, fox for 12%, of all deliveries.

HYDROELECTRIC POWER: *see* ELECTRIC POWER STATIONS, TECHNICAL SCIENCES.

HYDROENGINEERING: *see* TECHNICAL SCIENCES.

I

ICON PAINTING, a form of easel painting for worship purposes, which was extensively used in Russia, Georgia, and S. Slavic countries, where independent schools were formed. R. icons are notable for loveliness of colors and harmonious composition. In the 11th-12th centuries an outstanding icon painter was Olimpey. In the 12th-13th centuries icon painting centered in the cities of Novgorod, Vladimir, Pskov, and Yaroslavl. In the late part of the 14th century precedence goes to Moscow. The end of the 14th and beginning of the 15th centuries saw several outstanding icon painters: Theophanus Grek, Prokhor of Gorodets, Daniil Chorny, and Andrey Rublyov. In the late 15th century and early 16th century, the leading icon painter was Dionisyus. The 16th century was the period of the Stroganov school distinguished by calligraphic accuracy and meticulous refinement of draftsmanship. In the 17th century there were signs of three-dimensional treatment of form and perspective. In the 18th century icon painting degenerated to the level of a handicraft and was practiced predominantly in the regions of Mstera, Kholuy, and Palekh. (*See also* PAINTING)

IGÁRKA, city in Krasnoyarsk Kray, RSFSR, port on the Yenisey River; pop. 15,200 (1956). Center of timber ind. and floating. Sawmills, fisheries.

IGNÁTOV, Nikoláy Grigóryevich (1901–), party and government official; born in Don Province; a CP member since 1924. He served from 1917 to 1921 as volunteer in the Red Army. Until 1932 he worked in agencies of Cheka and OGPU; was party official in Leningrad until 1937, then went to Kuybyshev, becoming first secretary of Kuybyshev Oblast party committee; in 1940 he was appointed secretary of the Orel Oblast party committee; in 1949, secretary of the Krasnodar Kray party committee. He became a member and secretary of the Central Committee, CPSU, in 1952, and candidate member of the Presidium. In 1953 he was first secretary of the Leningrad City party committee; in 1954, first secretary of the Voronezh Oblast party committee, in 1955, first secretary of the Gorky Oblast party committee; in 1956 was approved as a member of the Central Committee's Bureau for the RSFSR. In July 1957, he was elected a member of the Presidium of Central Committee, but in May 1960 he was relieved of his duties as secretary of the Central Committee and appointed Vice-Chairman of the USSR Council of Ministers.

IGNÁTYEV, Count Nikoláy Pávlovich (1832–1908), diplomat, and statesman. Was Ambassador to Turkey, and from 1881 minister of internal affairs. He actively promoted the reactionary policies of Alexander III.

IGNÁTYEV, Semyón Denísovich, party and government official. A CP member since 1926, he has held party posts in Buryat Mongolia, Bashkiria, Uzbekistan, and Byelorussia. From 1951 to April 1953 he was USSR minister of state security. He was elected a member of the Central Committee in 1952 and of the Presidium at the Central Committee plenum following the 19th Congress. He was shifted on March 6, 1953, to Central Committee secretary, but was dismissed from this post and from the ministry of state security in April 1953, for "political blindness" in the notorious doctors' plot. Early in 1954 he was again made first secretary of the Bashkir ASSR party committee and was elected a member of the Central Committee at the 20th Congress. In June 1957, he was appointed first secretary of the Tatar ASSR party committee.

ÍGOR, prince of Kiev, according to chronicles, son of Ryurik. He waged war twice against Byzantium (941–944) and concluded a treaty with the Greeks (944); subjugated the tribes of Ulichí, Drevlyáne, and Pechenégi to the power of Kiev-Russia. He was killed by Drevlyáne in 945.

ÍGOR, Tale of the Host of (*Slóvo o Polkú Igoreve*), an outstanding work of old R. literature and a unique monument of the spoken R. language of the 13th century. Most probably it was written by one of the warriors who took part in the campaign of Prince Igor Svyatoslavovich of Novgorod Seversky against the Cumans (Polovtsy) in 1185. The only 16th-century copy of the manuscript was discovered in 1795 in the library of Count Musin-Pushkin. A faulty translation into modern R. was made, as well as a copy. The original was destroyed in the Moscow fire of 1812. The Igor tale provided the subject matter of Borodin's opera *Prince Igor*. Modern R. paraphrases of the Igor tale have been made by the poets Zhukovsky and Maykov. There is much controversy as to many obscure passages of the tale but its authenticity appears established.

IGÚMNOV, Konstantín Nikoláyevich (1873–1948), pianist and teacher, People's Artist of USSR, laureate of Stalin prize, professor of the Moscow conservatoire.

IKRÁMOV, Akmal (1898–1938), Uzbek CP leader. One of the defendants in the trial of the "Bloc of Rights and Trotskyites" of the March 1938 purges, he was accused of engaging in espionage and wanting to restore capitalism, was convicted and executed. Other defendants in the trial included Bukharin, Rykov, Yagoda.

ILF (Fáynzilberg), **Ilyá Arnóldovich** (1897–1937), writer whose humorous stories and satires were widely published. In these he collaborated with Ye. P. Petrov, their articles appearing under various pseudonyms as The Cool Philosopher, Tolstoyevsky, and others. Many of these stories and his newspaper commentaries were reproduced in collections entitled *Indifference* (1933), *How Robinson Was Created* (1933), *and Tonya* (1937). Both authors acquired considerable popularity at home and abroad, following the publication of their two satirical novels *Twelve Chairs* (1928) and *The Golden Calf* (1932), and the travel essays *One-Story America* 1936).

ILÍ RIVER, in Central Asia, begins in China, flows through Kazakh SSR into Balkhash; length about 870 mi.; navigable in its middle course.

ILÍM RIVER, in Irkutsk Oblast, RSFSR, right tributary of the Angara River; length about 372 mi.

ILLEGITIMACY: *see* FAMILY LAW.

ILLITERACY: *see* EDUCATION.

ÍLMEN, shallow lake in Novgorod Oblast, RSFSR, with an area of 235 to 810 sq. mi., depending on water levels. Receives Pola, Msta, Lovat, and other rivers; the Volkhov River flows out of it. Is navigable; has considerable fisheries.

ÍLMEN MOUNTAINS, E. spurs of S. Ural mountains, with an elevation of about 2,460 ft.; has deposits of many rare and valuable minerals.

ILYÍCH, town in South Kazakhstan Oblast; pop. 19,100 (1956); cotton growing and processing.

ILYÚSHIN, Alekséy Antónovich (1911–), physicist. Corresponding member, Ac. of S., USSR (1943). Graduate (1934), professor (1938), Moscow University. Director, Institute of Mechanics, Ac. of S. (1953). Research concerns the theories of elasticity and plasticity including elastic-plastic flow and its stability for metals (1936–38); minor elastic-plastic deformations (1942–48); stability of plates and shells beyond the limit of elasticity (1948); modeling for processes of plastic working of metals (1951–52). Stalin prize (1948).

ILYÚSHIN, Sergéy Vladímirovich (1894–), aeronautical engineer. General, Engineering Technical Corps. 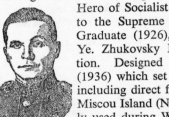 Hero of Socialist Labor (1941). Deputy to the Supreme Soviet, USSR (1937). Graduate (1926), professor (1948), N. Ye. Zhukovsky Military Ac. of Aviation. Designed twin-engine bomber (1936) which set several world records, including direct flights from Moscow to Miscou Island (N.B.) and was extensively used during World War II; armored fighter IL-2 (1939); four-engine passenger airplane IL-12 (1946), IL-14 (1954) and four-engine 75 passenger turboprop IL-18 (1957). Seven Stalin prizes.

IMAGINISTS, adherents of a formalistic movement in poetry that originated in England shortly before World War I. In R. poetry imaginism developed in the early 1920's as an open imitation of the W. European initiative. The first imaginist manifesto was published in Feb. 1919 . The leading I included V. Shershenevich, N. Klyuyev, A. Mariengof, and V. Kusikov. Collections of imaginist poems were published, such as *The Tempest's Cavalry* (1920) and *Pedlars of Happiness*. The early works of S. Yesenin reflect the influences of imaginism. As in the other formalist movements in poetry (acmeism, futurism, dadaism), imaginism is characterized above all by an emphasis on the expressiveness of individual elements in a poem—in this case images—at the expense of its over-all content. Closely associated with this is a disregard for the requirements of logical consistency, as well as an indifference for the social and political issues of the times. The I defended individualism to the point of anarchism, and idealized the vanishing past. One of the central themes of their poetry is the daily life of the traditional peasantry. They tended to describe it in a stylized manner, with the aid of unexpected comparisons, and also of an affected vulgarity. The poet Mayakovsky described the I as "poets playing at being peasants." I faded away by 1924.   C. P. K.

ÍMANDRA, lake in Murmansk Oblast, RSFSR; area about 350 sq. mi. Niva River flows out from it. Abounds in fish.

ÍNBER, Véra Mikháylovna (1890–), poet, born in Odessa. She began to write verse as a child. Her first collection, *Sad Wine*, was published in Russian in Paris in 1912. *Bitter Delight* and *Fragile Words* were published later in Russia and *Goal and Way* appeared in 1923. During the war, she lived through three years of the siege of Leningrad. She joined the Communist party in 1942. Under the siege, she wrote the poem *The Pulkovo Meridian* and published her diary *Nearly Three Years*. Stalin prize (1946).

INDIGÍRKA RIVER, in N.E. Yakut ASSR; length about 1,100 mi.; is navigable from the mouth of Moma River.

INDUSTRIAL MANAGEMENT AND ORGANIZATION. At the apex of the Soviet industrial pyramid is the Council of Ministers of the USSR, the highest executive body of the Soviet government. The central ministerial council supervises the over-all work of Soviet industry, issues necessary orders, and approves the long-term, annual, and quarterly economic plans directing the operations of industry during each time period. The Council's membership includes the chairmen of the ministerial councils of the 15 Union Republics, representatives of the central planning agency (Gosplan), and representatives of a number of committees or ministries charged with the over-all supervision of key sectors of industry (defense production, electric power, and chemical) or with specific matters affecting industry as a whole (like automation and coordination of wage policy). Other important subgroups with representation on the Council include the Central Statistical Administration, the Committee for State Security, and the Committee for Building Affairs. The central ministerial council, in practice, is subordinate to the Presidium of the Central Committee of the Communist Party. The Presidium makes the basic decisions that are executed by the central ministerial council.

The republic ministerial councils are charged directly (or indirectly) with the supervision of the more than 100 regional economic councils (*sovnarkhozy*) located throughout the country. Each republic has at least one regional economic council; the Russian Federation has about 70. (In republics with more than one regional economic council there may be an intermediate administrative link between the republic ministerial council and the several regional economic councils known as the republic economic council.) The regional economic councils are charged with the detailed everyday operation and supervision of most Soviet industrial enterprises.

The regional economic council is an innovation in the Soviet industrial hierarchy dating from 1957. Prior to that year, the everyday operation of industry was entrusted to a large number of industrial branch ministries, each of which was represented in the central ministerial council. (In 1957 there were 36 such ministries.)

A complex of political and economic factors appears

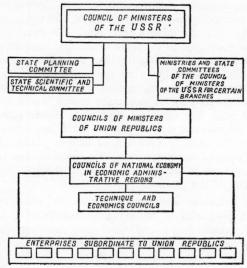

Structure of Industry Management

to have influenced the decision to abolish most of the industrial branch ministries and to replace them with regional economic councils. One factor cited frequently in Soviet sources was the difficulty inherent in administering a rapidly expanding and increasingly complex industrial organization from a single center—Moscow. Another factor cited for the decision involved the tendencies of the former branch ministries toward self-sufficiency and empire-building, which had adverse effects on the location of industry and inter-enterprise relationships.

As things have turned out, the new regional economic councils have shown similar tendencies and the central government has had to take vigorous measures to counteract them. Such tendencies appear to be accentuated in the USSR because of the great pressure and strain under which the economy operates. Economic officials simply do not trust the planning system to provide them with the supplies they need in the right quantity and quality at the right time. They prefer to develop their own sources of supply. Tendencies toward self-sufficiency and empire-building may be reinforced under the new system by considerations of regional and ethnic loyalties.

The ultimate unit in the Soviet industrial structure is the enterprise. The basic chain of command is from the director, to the shop chiefs, to the foremen, to the brigade leaders. The director has a number of functional departments—for planning, finance, payroll, personnel, technical control, supply and sales—and a number of assistants of whom the most important is the chief engineer. Enterprises in a given area producing one or a group of related products are often integrated into what is known as a combine or trust.

The enterprise director and his assistants have two main tasks. The first is the preparation of the so-called technical-industrial-financial plan for the enterprise (*tekhpromfinplan*). This plan covers matters such as the following in great detail: estimated number of workers to be employed; estimated payroll; production-cost plan; estimated requirements for fuel, electric power, raw materials, semifinished products, and equipment; distribution of the plant's products; introduction of new processes; details of plant expansion; cooperation with other enterprises; and the like. The plan also covers the financial results to be sought by the management during the long-term, annual, quarterly, or monthly period covered by the particular technical-industrial-financial plan. The plan is submitted to higher authority for amendment and approval. Once approved, it becomes the concrete program of action, guiding the management of the enterprise. The second main task of management is the fulfillment and, if possible, overfulfillment of the plan.

Most industrial enterprises operate in accordance with the principles of economic accountability (*khozraschot*), which means essentially that each enterprise is considered as an independent quasi-corporation endowed with certain resources. Relationships between enterprises are commercial relationships, that is, they are sales or purchases for money at prices set by higher authorities.

The Soviet government has used bonuses extensively as a managerial incentive. Bonuses received by some managers have reportedly been double their base pay. Prior to 1960 managerial bonuses were awarded primarily for plan fulfillment or overfulfillment. This arrangement tended to stimulate increases in production with little regard to cost. In Jan. 1960 a new arrangement was introduced in a large number of industries under which the size of bonuses depends, to a significant extent, on success in cutting costs. As prices are fixed by higher authority, this, in effect, means that managerial bonuses are now more closely dependent upon enterprise profits than in the past. The new arrangement should increase the efficiency of industry generally and encourage the adoption of innovations. The old arrangement tended to discourage innovations because their adoption, which is painstaking and time-consuming, interferes with the fulfillment of production plans.

In theory, the enterprise director has complete charge of all activities and personnel under him. In fact, however, there is a great deal of extraneous interference in enterprise affairs. The activities of enterprise officials are subject to the immediate and intimate supervision of the regional economic councils. This supervision is perhaps greater and more detailed than that which the more remote ministries could exercise. The Ministry of Finance, through the State Bank, also constantly checks the financial aspects of industrial operation and thereby the actual conduct of enterprises. (Soviet sources refer to this as "control by the ruble.") In 1959 party control commissions were set up in industrial and commercial enterprises to check into and control fulfillment of production, cost-reduction, and other plans. The trade unions, the Committee for State Control, the Committee for State Security, and the Central Statistical Administration also exercise important control functions. Newspapers frequently carry articles pointing up shortcomings in the work of enterprise

and other economic officials based on information gathered by their correspondents in the field. Those criticized are expected to defend themselves, or, if the charges are true, to acknowledge their errors and indicate how they propose to correct them.

Although the scope for independent decision-making by the manager is severely circumscribed, his job is by no means easy or routine. Higher authorities are prone to set production and other targets at very high if not impossible levels, given the availability of materials, labor, and capital. The manager must exercise great ingenuity, often including the resort to quasi-legal or illegal methods, in order to keep the targets within reach and to meet or appear to meet them.

Among the time-tested techniques he employs is the deliberate concealment of plant capacity in order to assure that plan targets are attainable. Often by slightly altering the product mix, the plant manager can appear to have met his production target, although, in fact, he has not. In certain types of production, for example, such as metals, the production target is expressed in terms of tons; in such cases the manager can order his shop to curtail the production of lightweight products (special and quality metals) and to throw more men and materials into production of heavier products. In some cases he can borrow from the future by reporting that his production was higher in the immediately preceding period than it actually was and attempt to make up the shortfall in the next period. In order to meet production plans, he can also cut corners in terms of quality: fewer stitches in the garment, fewer screws in the piece, more impurities in the metal, and the like.

On the supply side, he often increases the labor available by ordering overtime work in violation of existing regulations. He often hoards labor, working capital, and fixed capital. The low interest charge on working capital and the complete absence of an interest charge on fixed capital encourage such hoarding.

An effective technique used by managers to assure their supply of materials involves the employment of special supply expediters called *tolkachi* or "pushers." The table of organization does not provide for this occupation, yet the need is so great that enterprises manage in one way or another to employ these people. The chief job of the expediter is to assure that his enterprise gets the materials it needs when it needs them. He spends much of his time on the road visiting his enterprise's suppliers, handing out gifts here and there to assure that his orders are expeditiously handled, and picking up supplies of one kind or another that his enterprise may be able to use or trade for other goods. Much of this activity is associated with the black market, that is, obtaining materials for which no allocation order has been issued.

The generic term for influence in the USSR is "blat." Blat can be acquired in innumerable ways, including bribery, special favors, friendship, family ties, and the like. It represents an invaluable, intangible asset for any enterprise.

Given the various forms of supervision and control

in the economy, it may be asked how Soviet managers get away with practices such as those outlined above. They do not, of course, always get away with them. However, there appears to be a high degree of solidarity and interdependence among bureaucratic officials at the lower levels of the industrial hierarchy. The career of the chief party official in the enterprise, for example, depends in part upon the success or apparent success with which the enterprise meets its plan targets. He is therefore not inclined to report misdemeanors of the enterprise director if the latter is successfully meeting production and other plans. Similarly, officials in the regional economic council may be reluctant to dismiss a manager who employs quasilegal or illegal methods if he is meeting plan targets. A more law-abiding enterprise director might not be able to meet the targets, which would reflect adversely on the work of the economic council.

Many of the imperfections in the Soviet industrial machine outlined above stem from the fact that the economy is operating under full steam. They are reminiscent, to some extent, of shortcomings which developed in the United States economy during World War II.

BIBLIOGRAPHY: Harry Schwartz, *Russia's Soviet Economy*, New York, 1954; Joseph F. Berliner, "Managerial Incentives and Decision-making: A Comparison of the United States and the Soviet Union," *Comparisons of the United States and Soviet Economies: Papers Submitted by Panelists Appearing Before the Sub-Committee on Economic Statistics*, Joint Economic Committee, Congress of the United States, Washington, 1959. R. C. H.

INDUSTRIAL PARTY, allegedly a group of the intelligentsia who had been bribed by France to wreck the First Five Year Plan and restore capitalism in Russia. Numerous technical specialists, notably Prof. Leonid Ramzin and P. I. Palchinsky, were tried and convicted on this count in 1930. The death sentence was commuted to 10-year imprisonment. The trial and condemnation of the IP were used as a pretext for eliminating Rykov and other members of the Bolshevik "Right" from the Soviet government. Many others who had opposed the pace of the Five Year Plan's industrialization program were accused of belonging to the IP and punished accordingly.

INDUSTRIALIZATION: *see* ECONOMIC DEVELOPMENT, INDUSTRY, AGRICULTURE.

INDUSTRY has been the dynamic heart of Soviet economic development over the past four decades. Its remarkable expansion had a sound foundation in its prerevolutionary progress.

Prerevolutionary Period. The latter part of the 19th and the beginning of the present century saw the emergence of a vigorous and—at least in part—up-to-date R. industrial body. Its core was formed by two regions, grown around the old and the new capitals, and supplemented by a third, the Ukrainian, famous for the marriage of the Krivoy Rog iron and the Donets coal. The Moscow and St. Petersburg regions alone were responsible for about half the national industrial output. The former specialized primarily in textiles, while the latter was the nursery of R. engineering, but in output value it was outstripped by the well-developed Polish region which was soon to be lost when Poland regained her

independence. Fertile agricultural lands formed the basis of the food industries in the S.W. Fuel, metal, and other mineral wealth were the basis of the four remaining regions, the Ukrainian, the Urals metallurgical center still in infancy, the oil region of Baku (Azerbaijan), and the small peripheral Trans-Caucasian manganese and hard-coal basin.

RUSSIAN INDUSTRIAL OUTPUT 1896, BY REGIONS

Moscow	Petersburg	Polish	S. Russian Ukrainian	Urals	Baku	South-western	Trans-caucasian
(mill. rubles)							
755	317	336	246	85	82	135	—

Almost three-fifths of factory employment was concentrated in only 8 of the 63 provinces (*gubernia*) of European Russia. With a relatively small fuel consumption the country had a coal deficit and, being still, in the 1890's, responsible for half the world's output, Russia had a sizable export of oil. In spite of her natural wealth she was importing considerable quantities of both pig iron and steel. R. I enjoyed strong support from the state's financial and tariff policies. It had intimate international links: about a third of all joint-stock capital was foreign held. Foreign investment was particularly heavy in mining, engineering and chemicals, where its share amounted to about nine-tenths, two-fifths and a half, respectively.

The cataclysms of World War I, defeat and enemy occupation of large territories, of revolution and civil war, produced a fast spiral of industrial decline. After the Bolshevik revolution—partly under the pressure of chaotic conditions and partly because of an ideological nostalgia—the economic model degenerated into that of War Communism (1918–21). A decree of Nov. 1917 established in I a mixed regime of management shared by owners and workers. Under War Communism successive partial measures of expropriation culminated in wholesale nationalization of industrial enterprises (June 1918). The state—ill-equipped as it was for the purpose—took over the control and direct running of industries, with a virtual exclusion of market for their products. By 1920 industrial output reached an all-time low: it dropped to less than a fifth of the prerevolutionary peak level; production of pig iron amounted to 3 per cent of that of 1913.

The New Economic Policy (NEP) was embarked upon in 1921 to stop the disintegration of economic life. It left with the state the control of the bulk of I as one of the "commanding heights" of the economy but private enterprise was permitted to operate, though primarily on the small-scale periphery of I. Links with international capital were resumed: certain "concessions" were granted to foreign entrepreneurs (their assets represented about 1 per cent of total capital of Soviet I). More autonomy was granted to the state-owned enterprises and their "trusts." Cost calculation—*khozraschot*—was made compulsory for them. Market relations were restored. Within a few years considerable progress was made, especially in textiles and other light industries; broadly speaking, by 1928 the 1913 structure of I was restored, prewar levels of over-all output having been regained somewhat earlier. As rehabilitation proceeded, the "public hand" strengthened its hold over I. Toward the end of the twenties a policy of discrimination reduced the share of private enterprise to almost nil; it fell from 22–25 per cent in the first years of NEP (4–5 per cent in large-scale industry) to about 5 per cent in 1928; within the two following years it dropped to a mere fraction of 1 per cent of output. Before the decade came to its end the NEP interlude was closed: the plan era was inaugurated when the First Five Year Plan (1928–32) was embarked upon.

Five Year Plans. Gradually the broad lines of the economic grand strategy of the new era crystallized. Throughout the era the whole emphasis has been laid on a fast industrialization inspired partly by the vision of economic advancement and partly by the goal of a profound transformation of the society—of strengthening its proletarian core. These objectives have been reflected in a drastic increase in the ratio of savings to national income and a policy of massive and highly centralized capital formation. In this way the channeling of the bulk of investment toward I has been secured. Over the three decades between the start of the plan phase and the late fifties, I shared by as much as 70 per cent in the state's "productive" investment and by two-fifths in the total investment (gross fixed, 1928–58). Between the outbreak of World War I and the late fifties the share of I in the nation's stock of fixed capital increased fourfold. Between the end of the reconstruction period (1928) and the end of the fifties fixed industrial capital increased 33-fold, and by 1960 it accounted for 45 per cent of all fixed man-made productive capital of the country (nearly a half if construction is included).

Furthermore, massive investments have been used to impart to I a specific direction of growth. This corresponds to the precept that, in order to preserve a balanced growth, output of producer goods must outpace that of consumer goods; and also to the partly overlapping rule that heavy industries, i.e., those providing energy, metals, building materials, and chemicals, and the metal-working I, should outpace light industries. (About 88 per cent of all industrial gross

fixed investment was directed to heavy I during 1928–1958.) At times the assumption of such strategy has been an increasingly closed economy. However, until well on in the thirties Soviet I had still to rely on substantial supplies of foreign equipment with the accompanying advanced technologies and technical services (paid for with exports of food, raw materials, and gold). The latecomer's advantage—access to accumulated technological wealth of industrial nations, the opportunity to by-pass the costly road from the researcher's laboratory to technical solution—has been indeed one of the most powerful elements in Soviet industrial development. For a time also the finance of industrial growth was supplemented, if modestly, by commercial foreign credits—the great depression which sharpened the competition for Soviet outlets helped to obtain them (on the other hand W. capital proved unwilling to avail itself of the opportunities of long-term investments under the system of concessions, still offered by the Soviet government at the beginning of the thirties). Toward the end of the interwar period the USSR was nearest to economic insulation: the share of net imports in the total supply of machinery fell to a fraction of 1 per cent (from 44 per cent and 30 per cent in 1913 and 1927–28, respectively).

Viewed in greater detail the policy of preferential support of producer-good branches has called for pushing ahead with particular vigor in selected "leading links" of I. Iron and steel has been looked upon as the principal growth industry. It has been feeding the engineering branches considered as the apex of industrial structure, with special accent on its machine tool sector: the machine tool branch was created virtually anew in the thirties. Metals and metal-processing between them have been absorbing up to one-third of all investment in heavy I. Compared with the proportion at the outbreak of World War I the share of metal-working in industrial manpower was doubled by the end of the fifties, while that of light and food industries was halved (in 1913, 14 per cent and 52 per cent; in 1958, 31 per cent and 25 per cent, respectively). Engineering has been expected to expand even faster than the supporting ferrous and nonferrous metallurgy. Energy supplies—part of the price of industrial growth—have had to be developed as yet another "leading link" at a correspondingly fast pace. The goal of increasing efficiency in fuel economy has been pursued by a rapid expansion of electric—thermal and hydro—capacities.

Stress on Heavy Industry. In the strategy of subordinating all other sectors of the economy to the dominating aim of industrial growth, the countryside has had the assigned role of the supplier of manpower, and—at a price as depressed as possible—of food to the industrial "crews." In this sense it has had to finance industrial growth: at the beginning of the plan era agriculture was restructured and policies were given a slant to

INDUSTRIAL PRODUCTION: Tsarist Russia, Soviet Union, and United States 1870—1955

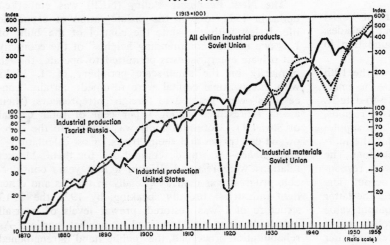

accord with these objectives. Such policies enabled the rapidly growing I to tap an ample pool of labor. Industrial manpower was trebled between the start of the plan era and the outbreak of World War II and almost doubled in the following two decades (labor employed directly in production amounted to 3.8, 11.0, and 21.0 mill. in 1928, 1940, and 1960, respectively; construction excluded).

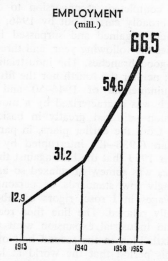

EMPLOYMENT
(mill.)

66.5

54.6

31.2

12.9

1913   1940   1958 1965

In such an economic environment, at least until the latter part of the 1950's, capital was only parsimoniously substituted for human hands (but over a long period skills were also a bottleneck factor). Capital-intensity of industrial processes has been promoted only where imperative as a means of imparting to I a required tempo of technological progress. At least until the last war a far greater part of the increase in industrial output was obtained through the growing number of workers than through the increased average worker's production. But as more energy was provided and more modern mechanisms installed per man, and skills of the new recruits to I improved, output per man tended also to rise faster.

Generally, owing to the pattern of prime-factor endowment, Soviet I has been aiming at a maximum performance from its stock of fixed capital—per unit of space, or unit of equipment: typical is the attention paid to, and the world records achieved in, output of pig iron and steel as related to the capacities of furnaces. On the other hand manual labor has been relied upon in auxiliary operations such as maintenance, intra-plant transport, and handling of materials to a degree far higher than in most industrialized countries.

This is but one of the factors which have tended to swell the manpower of an average Soviet enterprise. By the mid-fifties manufacturing enterprises with over 10,000 workers each formed 14 per cent of the total, and those with over 3,000, 37 per cent (as against a sixth in the USA). A highly specialized basic industrial unit has been the aim; at the same time, however, large firms have tended to combine as many stages of fabrication as possible, including a ramified auxiliary production as often as not rather remotely connected with the main line of the enterprise (such

attitudes have stemmed partly from the managers' desire to insure themselves against the unreliability of supplies).

The policy of fast capital accumulation, the bias against the consumer-good producing branches, the acute housing shortage in the swelling industrial centers (owing to concentrating the bulk of construction in productive assets rather than homes)—all these tended over a long period to depress industrial real wages. To offset the impact on productivity, intensive incentives combined with emulation were built into the system of remuneration. These were supplemented by measures of hard labor discipline. A Draconian legislation—consistent with the political climate of the period—was enforced at the threshold of the forties. The clouds gathering on the international horizon were invoked as a justification of this policy.

The influence of military considerations on industrial policies has been potent and manifold throughout the Soviet era. It is hardly measurable in precise terms: military production may be estimated to have accounted for two-fifths of Soviet metal-working in 1939, and for about a half in the year the USSR became formally a belligerent; little can be said about its share in subsequent periods. More generally, it may be safely presumed that military considerations have worked in two partly opposite directions: military requirements have competed with other uses of resources, but at the same time they have spurred scientific research and technological advancement in, and preferential allocation to, the leading "growth branches" of I.

Eastward Shifts. Considerations of military strategy have also been one of the several (sometimes conflicting) elements in the Soviet industrial locational policy. Other determining factors have been the geographical distribution of undeveloped natural wealth, the desire to link up sources of supply with consuming areas, the tendency to relieve the overburdened transport system without freezing too much capital in its expansion, the availability of labor, and so on. The general aim has been to reduce cost of production and transportation; however, in some cases this objective has been more or less deliberately sacrificed to achieve others. The interwar period saw a rise in the industrial weight of the E. regions. The most significant feat from this angle was the creation of the second metallurgical "base"—the development and integration of the Magnitogorsk ore-mining and the Kuznetsk coal basin (Kuzbas). However, at the end of the interwar era about four-fifths of Soviet industrial production was still coming from the areas West of the Urals. At the same time the profile of the old industrial regions underwent a marked change: in particular, while the traditional industries of the Moscow area suffered a decline, the region acquired a sizable metallurgical industry. The size and output range of engineering in the Leningrad area was vastly enlarged. The first metallurgical "base" grew sufficiently to feed its own expanding metal-working as well as to supply other regions.

After the abandonment of the semicommercial model under the NEP, the organizational framework of I was reshaped, largely by trial and error. The "functional" principle originally adopted gave place to what was termed "territorial productive" subordination; during the thirties a rigid command system was built up in I which survived with little change until the middle of the fifties. Decision-making in matters of both current operation and investment outlay was tightly centralized on vertical lines, converging in all-Union branch ministries. Prices lost most of their relevance as a guide in choice-making: planning and control of I relied primarily on physical-term computations and directives. Planning prices were conventionalized; inter-industrial prices were divorced from them; they ceased to reflect comparative costs and indicate opportunities. Industrial managers, otherwise severely restrained in their freedom of maneuver, were encouraged to aim at maximum output and over-fulfillment of plans with little consideration for cost. Success was primarily measured by quantitative performance, giving management a vested interest in inflating gross-output values. This is but one of various elements which favored quantity at the expense of quality. It may be fairly believed that the very nature of the economic mechanism created a serious dilemma of quality versus quantity.

In spite of such deficiencies the framework "institutionalized" industrial growth. New industrial centers were created. Production expanded and its range was widened. Progress was interrupted by the German invasion.

There is little doubt that, after the initial chaos and in spite of blunders of policy, Soviet I well withstood the historical test of the Second World War. A feat of decisive importance was the mass transfer of productive capacities: by mid-1942, 1,360 industrial plants were evacuated from the areas threatened by the enemy. This migration was to have a lasting effect in so far as it accentuated the locational drive eastward. By the end of the war industrial output of the E. regions was nearly twice that of 1941. Industrial capacities which were newly commissioned in E. areas corresponded to about one-tenth of the prewar national total: they included coal mines and steel-making furnaces with an annual output of 30 and 2½ mill. tons, respectively. The single-mindedness of the war exertions strengthened the concentration of industrial effort on the key branches and efficiency in some of them improved (thus between 1940 and 1943 the cost of manufacturing a cannon shell was cut by two-thirds). An important factor in wartime industrial expansion was the enormous, never repaid, United States Lend-Lease aid ($11 bill.) and British Mutual Aid. Not only did they secure war matériel and consumer goods for troops and civilian population, but they provided also a substantial quantity of industrial and other productive equipment and reopened the contact with W. technological know-how which tended to dry up in the years of the growing autarchy.

Postwar Period. By the same token the postwar inclusion of a substantial part of industrialized central Europe into the USSR's sphere of political and economic control was a contributing factor to the future industrial development of the country. Of im-

mediate help for the swift rehabilitation and reconversion of Soviet I was a wide flow of equipment secured from the new orbit of influence under the heading of war reparations, or obtained otherwise on exceptionally favorable terms. Formally the rehabilitation was embarked upon when the Fourth Five Year Plan (1946–50) was put into operation. By the end of the 1940's the task of restoring the prewar industrial capacities was broadly completed: reconversion to civilian production was broadly carried out by 1946; prewar output levels were regained and surpassed in producer-good industries the following year, and three years later in consumer-good branches. The industrialization drive was resumed; neither the fourth nor the fifth plans covering the quinquennia of 1946–50 and 1951–55—most of which was characterized by a mounting international tension—differed greatly in basic tendencies and features from the earlier plans, in particular from the third plan (1938–42) interrupted by the war. It was only after 1953 that the bias against the consumer-good branches was somewhat relaxed so as to improve the distressingly low standards of personal consumption. Real wages in I rose; rigors of labor discipline were gradually relaxed. The line thus readjusted was continued and industrial expansion went on unabated under the Sixth Plan in the second half of the 1950's. It was in this period that the world at large became growingly aware of the USSR's advancement to the rank of one of the leading industrial powers of the world. It was also around the mid-fifties that the Soviet leadership became alive to the fact that certain structural forms of their economy had become anachronistic. Moreover, certain major readjustments in the strategy of industrialization became imperative. It was presumably with these considerations in mind that the implementation of the Sixth Five Year Plan was stopped in mid-course in 1957—a move with no precedent in peacetime (though previous plans had been subjected to major—politically or economically motivated—revisions; this was the case in particular with the First Plan). When the rethinking matured—under the Seventh Plan (1959–65)—a new phase was opened. (Its seven years are considered as the start of a longer period—of 15 to 20 years—devoted to what is termed the establishment of the material and technical basis of a communist society; a master-plan with this horizon is under elaboration. Only a few tentative industrial targets for the early 1970's have been revealed.)

At that stage the Soviet Union could look back to three decades of spectacular industrial performance. However, although not affected by major setbacks, cyclical or otherwise (except for that caused by a world war), the rhythm of industrial growth was neither unique in the industrial history of the world nor smooth, as it is sometimes claimed to be. In fact, a certain deceleration is borne out by the official index series; but toward the end of the fifties the pulse of I settled down at a level still high by standards of industrial nations.

AVERAGE YEARLY RATES OF INDUSTRIAL GROWTH
(official indices — % per annum)

1928–29	1930–40	1941–45	1947–58	1952–58	1959	1960
21.0	16.5	−1.7	15.4	11.4	11	10

GROWTH OF SOVIET INDUSTRY

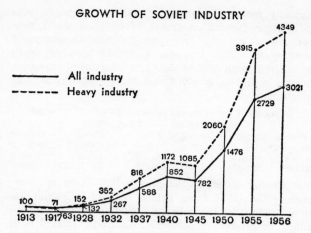

The tempo of growth reflected in this table corresponds to the official Soviet claim that between 1913 and 1960 industrial production increased 41 times within the present boundaries of the USSR (44 times within the pre-1939 territory, and 36 times when comparison is made with the old Russian Empire).

GROWTH OF INDUSTRIAL GROSS OUTPUT
(OFFICIAL CLAIM)

a) 1913 (Pre-1939 territory) = 100

1917	1921	1928	1932	1937	1940	1946	1950	1955	1959 over	1960 over	1965 (plan) over
71	31	132	267	588	852	652	1476	2729	40	44	77

b) GROWTH OVER PLAN PERIODS

1932 (1928 = 100)	1937 (1932 = 100)	1950 (1945 = 100)	1955 (1950 = 100)	1965 (1958 = 100)
202	220	189	185	180 (7 years)

There is, however, a common consensus of opinion among independent students that the Soviet official index series is affected by an inherent very strong upward bias (because it reflects gross rather than net output, and does not allow for a varying degree of duplication, one industry's outputs appearing again as inputs of another; and because it is based on distorted prices). When trying to deflate the index W. experts arrived at differing results, ranging from about a 5½ to a 12 times increase (within present boundaries) for the period bracketed by the start of the plan era and the mid-fifties, as against a 21 times increase officially claimed. A middle-of-the-road school of thought of W. experts would accept a third of this figure to be nearest to the (inevitably relative) truth. Accordingly a realistic estimate would presumably accept that productivity of Soviet manpower rose roughly 2½ times over the same period as against the official claim that it increased more than 8 times (12 times by 1960, on per man-year basis).

It is fair to say that some contributors to the most recent Soviet literature on the subject are more ready to admit that the industry's progress would be somewhat reduced when measured by the value-added rather than gross-output on Soviet definition. (The distinguished Academician, S. Strumilin, suggests in 1959 that net industrial production increased only 14.7 times between 1928 and 1956, the concept however, being defined in a specific way.)

These calculations are obviously relevant for locat-

ing the USSR in the world's map of industrial powers. Soviet sources claim that in 1959 the USSR's industrial output equaled about ⅗ of the USA. (Productivity of Soviet industrial labor equalling 40–50 per cent of that of the USA.) This has been found an exaggeration by all independent inquiries: according to various methods applied they have arrived at proportions varying from ¼ to ⅖ of the USA level.

To portray the economic progress more adequately such calculations must be supplemented by data on the industry's technological level. No doubt it rose enormously during the past few decades. A more than forty fold increase in the industrial consumption of electric power during the three decades that followed the start of the plan era (3.3 and 154.2 bill. kilowatt-hours in 1928 and 1958, respectively) is a telling indicator. Mechanization of industrial processes made very substantial progress especially in metal-working whose stock of equipment was greatly increased (by the end of the fifties half of it was less than 10 years old).

METAL-WORKING EQUIPMENT — STOCK

	1908	1940	1955	1958
		(thousand units)		
Metal-working machine tools	75	710	1699	1915
Forging and pressing machines	18	119	345	394

But there are areas of technological backwardness: they are partly due to deliberate neglect of some industrial branches, partly also to deliberate disregard over long periods of wear and tear and obsolescence.

Decentralization Reforms. One of the signal features of the new phase of industrial development is the organizational remodelling. Its beginnings go back to the mid-fifties. It culminated in the 1957 reforms which carried out a substantial decentralization in the running of I. The institutional frame was rebuilt: only a few all-Union industrial ministries survived. Most of the administration of I was entrusted to more than a hundred newly created regional authorities (sovnarkhozy). At the same time guarantees were built into the system to secure the effectiveness of central planning and control, although central plans are less detailed than hitherto. Moreover, direct allocation of specifically listed key commodities is reserved for central agencies. This system of checks is strengthened by measures of strict centralized financial control. At the lowest, the enterprise echelon of the I, more operational elbowroom is provided for the plant manager. The devolution of managerial decision-making, under the strongly centralized and still comprehensive planning, implied some shift in the tools of command from direct physical-term fiats to more indirect guidance by means of centrally shaped prices. However, a reform aiming at a rational intra-industrial price system came up against serious obstacles, doctrinal as well as technical. No less serious impediments were encountered in attempts to graft on to the rather crude planning techniques in I, modern mathematical methods for checking the consistency of the plan and choosing the most efficient program among feasible alternatives.

The Seven Year Plan and Future Targets. The new organizational model has been construed by its architects with an eye to the locational aspirations of the

Seven Year Plan. The plan envisages a forceful intensification of the territorial spread, the eastward shift of I. The E. regions are to receive about two-fifths of the planned all-national addition to manpower and of investment. Their share in the all-national industrial output is expected to rise during the plan period from about a quarter to about a third.

EASTERN REGIONS — SHARE IN INDUSTRIAL GROSS
OUTPUT AND MANPOWER
(% of national total)

	1930	1940	1955	1958	1965
Gross output	9	15	27	26	33
Industrial (productive) manpower	11	20	30	29	

The leading objectives are: the building of the third ferrous metallurgical "base" (Taishet, Karaganda); the expansion of nonferrous metallurgy combined with exploitation of deposits in Kazakhstan, Central Asia, the Urals, and Transbaykalia, the stepping-up of Siberian power generation, relying to a considerable extent on open-cast coal mining (the formation of integrated power grids is envisaged for Central Siberia as well as for European Russia), the expansion of Central Asian chemical industry. Both the chemical industry and the fuel economy are to benefit from natural gas conveyed by a new pipe network from the North Urals and Uzbekistan to industrial centers of the Urals.

SHARE OF EASTERN REGIONS IN OUTPUT OF CERTAIN
BASIC MATERIALS
1965 targets

Coal	Steel	Copper refined	Aluminum	Electric power	Cement	Timber (sawn)
			% of national total			
50	48	88	71	46	42	52

A far-reaching shift away from coal toward petroleum and natural gas is indeed one of the signal features of the plan: between them they are expected to meet by the mid-sixties nearly half of the consumption needs (20 per cent and 28 per cent in 1951 and 1958, respectively).

Substantial reshaping of industrial input and output patterns is a general tendency of the plan which aims at increasing gross production by four-fifths (8.6 per cent per annum). True, engineering remains the pinnacle of the industrial structure and its output is to be doubled (yet the USSR may be expected to remain a net importer of engineering products; in particular it will remain dependent for heavy imports of equipment on the Central European industrially developed countries of its orbit). Targets for steel, crude and finished, have been set accordingly: if the upper limit of the goal is attained, Soviet consumption of crude steel will reach nearly 400 kilograms per capita (it should be noted, however, that in relation to value Soviet engineering production appears to be rather exceptionally steel-absorbing). While these elements preserve a traditionalist look for the plan, the production pattern will be almost revolutionized by the shift from coal to oil and gas, already mentioned, and the exceptional emphasis on the creation of a modern chemical industry—especially that of petrochemicals—the lag in which has increasingly handicapped Soviet economy. Half the capital allotted to chemicals is to be earmarked for plants expected to provide a wide flow of techno-

logically more advantageous modern man-made substitutes for "natural" materials—for metals, wood, rubber, fibers. For the first time the hitherto axiomatic primacy of metals in Soviet industrial structure is to be shared with chemicals, now the most dynamic branch of I. This is well illustrated by the direction of investment.

DIRECTION OF INDUSTRIAL INVESTMENT, 1959–1965
A: bill. rubles; B: 1952–58 = 100

	Ferrous metallurgy	Chemicals	Oil and gas	Coal	Power generation	Machine industry
A.	100	100–105	170–173	73– 78	125–129	118
B.	245	502–528	235–240	122–127	166–172	180

Yet another aspect of the plan is the accent on overcoming the USSR's lag behind leading industrial nations in the mechanization, automation, and electrification of productive processes; electronic control is to be applied on a wide scale; in engineering 400,000 machine tools are to be modernized and 1,300 automated production lines installed. This tendency is partly connected with the tightness in the supply of industrial labor, which is real and growing even if only in a relative sense, in a country where almost half the nation's labor resources are tied up in food production at very low levels of productivity. Roughly three-quarters of the scheduled increase of industrial output is expected to be obtained from gains in productivity (though the rate of increase in per-man output—5½ to 6 per cent per annum—is scheduled to be slower than the claimed average for the fifties).

The changes in I's profile, its geographic spread, its technological transformation, its difficulties in securing adequate labor supply, all combine to entail a greater expenditure of capital as related to output than has hitherto been the case (indeed, these phenomena are to some extent causally interconnected; e.g., it is the newly opened-up regions which suffer from the greatest labor deficit and require generous labor-saving investment). It has been estimated that over a third (37 per cent) more capital will be required relatively to add one ruble's worth of industrial output under the Seven Year Plan that it was in the previous corresponding period (computed as the rise in investment related to growth of output).

The relatively growing cost of progress may prove of signal impact on economic—and indeed perhaps also on political—developments, in what, in many respects, appears to be a new phase of industrial revolution. However, in the view of highly authoritative Western students of the subject—as summarized recently by Prof. Simon Kuznets—Soviet economic growth must be considered capable of being sustained for some indefinite period: (See also ECONOMIC DEVELOPMENT, INDUSTRIAL MANAGEMENT AND ORGANIZATION, INVESTMENT, PLANNING, STATISTICS, ECONOMIC THEORY)

BIBLIOGRAPHY: A. Bergson, ed., Soviet Economic Growth, New York, 1953; Economic Commission for Europe, Economic Survey of Europe for successive years from 1948 to 1960; M. T. Florinsky, Towards an Understanding of the USSR, New York, 1951; P. I. Lyashchenko, History of the National Economy of Russia to the 1917 Revolution, translated by L. M. Herman, New York, 1949; Harry Schwartz, Russia's Soviet Economy, New York and London, 1954.
A. Z.

INFANT MORTALITY: see MEDICAL SYSTEM.

INFLATION: see MONETARY SYSTEM.

INGÁL, Vladímir Iósifovich (1901–), sculptor. After training at the Academy of Fine Arts, Leningrad, he collaborated with V. Ya. Bogolyubov in a number of monuments (*Rimsky-Korsakov*, Leningrad, 1948; *Lenin*, Riga, 1950; and others). His own work is chiefly monumental. Notable is his memorial to Stalin in Leningrad.

INGÓDA RIVER, in Transbaykalia; forms, together with Onon River, the Shilka River which is a part of the Amur; length 377 mi.

INGULÉTS RIVER, in Ukrainian SSR, right tributary of Dnieper; length 340 km.; navigable for 67 mi. Town on it is Krivoy Rog.

INGUSH: *see* POPULATION.

INHERITANCE of personal property (q.v.), regulated by civil law (q.v.) is almost unrestricted and untaxed. It was condemned by Marx, Engels, and early Soviet theorists but never disappeared entirely in Soviet Russia. Tsarist I laws applied until their annulment in 1918. The amount and the circle of legal heirs of I were restricted, but liberalization began in the mid-1920's. By 1936 the new constitution declared I of personal property to be the right of all Soviet citizens. Soon I was officially praised because, it was said, "socialist" I could not mean the perpetuation of a class of capitalist exploiters, since private capital had been nationalized, and citizens could inherit only personal property. I was credited with strengthening family ties, and with increasing work incentives because people knew that the fruits of their toil could be passed on after their death to their near and dear survivors.

Under the final liberalizations of 1945, the death tax takes the form of a mildly progressive notary registration fee which increases from small fixed sums on modest estates to a maximum of 10% of any estates worth more than 10,000 rubles. Exemptions from tax cover government bonds, insurance policies, savings accounts, incomes from copyrights, which may amount together to sizable fortunes.

"I by law" covers estates or portions of estates not mentioned in a valid will. Heirs of unwilled property fall into three priorities of relationships to the deceased: the spouse, legitimate children, disabled parents or dependent household member; able-bodied parents; finally, brothers and sisters.

"I by will" covers the estate mentioned in a valid will (where the author was of sound mind, not under coercion or defrauded, and the will was notarized). An estate may now be willed to anyone, provided that minor children and dependents receive the shares to which they are entitled under "I by law." Savings bank accounts are exempted, and may be left to any beneficiary simply by signing a form at the bank.

Joint property of peasant collective farm households is subject to a special system of I dating back to tsarist customary law. When a member of a peasant household dies, his share of the joint property cannot be willed, but passes automatically to the surviving members. Ordinary laws of I apply only to personal property. But when the last member of a peasant household dies, the household property—building, furnishings, livestock, small tools, plants—is then treated as personal property and passes on through "I by will"

or "I by law." (*See also*: SOVIET LAW, AUTHORSHIP AND INVENTION)   P. H. J.

INOSTRÁNTSEV, Aleksándr Aleksándrovich (1843–1919), geologist. Corresponding member of the St. Petersburg Ac. of S. (1901). Graduate (1867) and professor (1873) of St. Petersburg University. A pioneer in the field of microscopic rock examination. Author of a detailed study of the dwelling place of the primitive man on the shore of Lake Ladoga (1882). Conducted geological field studies in the Donets Basin, the Crimea the Caucasus and the Urals.

INOZÉMTSEV, Fyódor Ivánovich (1802–1869), physician. Graduate, Kharkov University (1828); professor, Moscow University (1846–69). Rejected R. Virchow's "cellular pathology" and emphasized the participation of the nervous system in cellular and tissue metabolism. Introduced *Guttae Inozemtsev* for the treatment of cholera.

INSTITUTE OF MARXISM-LENINISM of the Central Committee of the CPSU, main party institute for research and publication of the works of Marx, Engels, Lenin, and Stalin. The Institute of K. Marx and F. Engels, founded in 1920, and the Lenin Institute, founded in 1924, were merged in 1931 and formed the Institute of Marx-Engels-Lenin (later, Marx-Engels-Lenin-Stalin) in Moscow. Its present name was adopted in 1956. The main tasks of the I are: to collect and safeguard documents about and works of the Communist leaders; to carry out research and publish biographies of the leaders and their collaborators. The I also encourages the collection and publication of documents on the history of the CPSU, the First International and the Paris Commune. Collected works of Marx and Engels (28 volumes) as well as selections of their work have been published. The collected works of V. I. Lenin have appeared in four editions. The publication of a multi-volume collection of the works of Stalin was announced. Volume I appeared in 1946 and was followed by others through volume XIII, in 1955. None have been published since.

INTELLIGENCE. Soviet intelligence activities and military espionage started in the early 1920's. While Soviet espionage, like that of any other nation, aims at obtaining foreign military secrets, their efforts have a dual purpose: gathering secret political, industrial, and scientific information, and also countering anti-Soviet trends abroad, winning agents and sympathizers, promoting local Communist parties, and undermining existing regimes. The foremost task of these activities is to serve Soviet foreign political objectives. Until World War II, the main targets of these efforts were European powers, especially France and Germany, and sometimes small neighboring nations, such as Iran, Turkey or Poland, that at one time or another became important to Soviet political strategy. Since the early war years, the main target has been the USA.

The main agency responsible for I and espionage is the Foreign Administration of the Security Police. An important role in espionage is played by the Intelligence Administration of the Army General Staff, known by its Russian abbreviation GRU (*Glavnoye Razvedyvatelnoye Upravlenie*). This work is considered so important that its supreme direction and evaluation are vested in a special Central Information Department at the Presidium of the Central Committee of the Communist party.

Two important traits are peculiar to Soviet I: its unparalleled size, and the unique opportunities it derives from the cooperation of local Communist parties. Extensive I and espionage work is usually carried out by a few specially designated prominent party leaders who also help in enlisting native agents and establishing hide-outs and "contact points"; local Communists are used for infiltration into government offices, industrial enterprises, educational institutions, and so forth. Some of them work, not for money, but out of devotion to the USSR, as was the case of the repented American spy Elizabeth Bentley or the French Communist leader Jacques Duclos who admitted in 1954 that he had obtained highly secret records of the French National Defense Committee. The Canadian Royal Commission on Espionage disclosed that a Miss Willsher, a Communist employed in the office of the British High Commissioner, supplied, through her party chiefs, information on the correspondence between the Canadian Ambassador to Moscow and the Prime Minister; she pleaded guilty. Another Canadian Communist, Fred Rose, member of Parliament, reported on secret sessions of Parliament; after serving his sentence, he went to Poland. Many cases of this kind have been exposed and tried in all western nations.

For purposes of I and espionage Moscow has organized a far-flung network, operating in the underground under trained agents and well equipped to meet the requirements of conspiratorial work. A special laboratory at the Committee of State Security in Moscow is engaged in manufacturing false foreign passports, visas and documents. Agents are supplied with modern devices, such as tiny but powerful cameras, two-way radios, and noiseless guns. A U.S. State Department report, released in June 1960, stated that in recent years "some 360 individuals in eleven different countries of the free world have been convicted of espionage for the Soviet Union." The testimony of defendants at these trials, information received by western counterintelligence, and carefully sifted reports of Soviet agents who defected to the West and of some former Communist leaders have revealed many aspects of the Soviet espionage system.

The basic method of Soviet I is strict centralization of a large number of small groups working in the same place, but unaware of one another. Therefore, if one group is broken up, the others remain intact. The groups are headed by "residents," appointed and supervised by Moscow. "Residents" are kept under constant and minute control: the recruitment of a new agent, the establishment of a new hide-out, even trivial assignments require explicit approval from Moscow. This strict centralization causes resentment among the "residents" and frustrates their initiative.

Diplomatic, UN and consular services are amply used for purposes of Soviet I. Military, naval, and air attachés are often agents of the GRU, while the Security Police has its own representatives attached to the Embassies under the guise of secretaries, clerks or chauffeurs. Thus, the defecting Security Police representative in Australia, Vladimir Petrov, was "third secretary" of the Embassy, and his wife, Evdokia, a captain in the Security Police, held the rank of Embassy "accountant." These representatives use the diplomatic pouch, have their own codes for communication with their superiors in Moscow, and are not subordinated to the ambassador. One of their tasks is to enlist, through "go-betweens," the collaboration of useful nationals. Thus, among the agents of Major Rogov of the Soviet Embassy in Canada were officials of the National Research Council, a professor of mathematics specializing in artillery, new weapons, and explosives, and an engineer employed by the Ammunition Production Branch. In July 1960, Pyotr Y. Yezhov, "third secretary" of the Soviet Embassy in Washington, was expelled from the USA for having engaged a photographer to take pictures of United States Navy installations and other strategic target areas, but the photographer was an FBI agent who denounced the major. Yezhov was the twelfth Soviet diplomat expelled from this country since 1950 for espionage. The FBI reported in 1960 that dozens of aerial photographs of major United States cities and vital areas had been gathered by Soviet agents; in secret meetings during 1958 in a darkened parking lot in Scarsdale, N.Y., aerial maps of New York City and Chicago were turned over to Soviet employees of the UN, and attempts were made to obtain aerial pictures of Portland, Seattle, San Diego, and San Francisco. Soviet diplomats are assisted in work by satellite Embassies.

In other Soviet agencies in the West, such as foreign outlets of the Ministry of Foreign Trade or offices for cultural exchanges, one or more officials are usually entrusted with work of which even their colleagues are not aware. An outstanding example was the wartime Soviet Purchasing Commission in Washington which handled Lend-Lease orders in the USA and had access to the largest American industrial enterprises; some of its high officials were actually MVD representatives, as was disclosed by a member of the Commission, Victor Kravchenko.

After World War II a new major task arose for Soviet I in the field of nuclear research, which had been started in the USSR before the war. But the USSR lagged far behind Britain and the USA. An extensive spying operation was launched. Some outstanding German physicists were kidnapped and made to work in the USSR. The German-born and British-naturalized atomic physicist, Klaus Fuchs, who worked on secret nuclear projects in Los Alamos, Birmingham, and Glasgow, testified, after his arrest, that he had established contact, through British Communists, with Soviet military attaché Kremer, and in 1944, after his arrival in the USA, with Anatoly Yakovlev, a Soviet "viceconsul," in charge of atomic espionage in the USA. Vasily Zubilin of the Soviet Embassy in Washington, with several Soviet and American assistants, conducted effective I activities at the Radiation Laboratory at Berkeley, California. A number of such rings in the USA,

Britain, and Canada were broken up. The top-secret information thus obtained enabled the brilliant team of Soviet physicists to achieve results which otherwise would have been impossible in so short a time.

The Soviet I system is by far the largest in the world. However successful some of its operations, many ended in failure or defections. In the words of a defecting Soviet I agent, "the weak point of Soviet intelligence is the low level of intelligence and insufficient ability of its personnel"; some of its chiefs, however, have shown remarkable skill and intelligence. Another weakness is the inability of the Moscow central agency, because of Communist prejudices and misunderstanding of western ways and psychology, correctly to evaluate information obtained. (*See also* SECURITY POLICE)

BIBLIOGRAPHY: D. Dallin, *Soviet Espionage*, New York, 1955; W. Chambers, *Witness*, New York, 1952; E. Bentley, *Out of Bondage*, New York, 1951; V. and E. Petrov, *The Empire of Fear*, New York, 1956; I. Gouzenko, *The Iron Curtain*, New York, 1948; *Report of the Royal Commission on Espionage*, Sydney, 1956, and Ottawa, 1946.
S. W.

INTELLIGENTSIA, which has been defined as "the part of a nation that aspires to independent thinking" (*Concise Oxford Dictionary*), originated in Russia in the middle of the 19th century. It is probably correct to say that while the Russian I, which drew its following from every social group, had no coordinated economic and political program the vast majority of its members held liberal or radical views and participated in the opposition to the imperial government and in the revolutionary movement. (*See also* PHILOSOPHY, POPULISM, RUSSIAN MARXISM, NIHILISM, RAZNO-CHINTSY)

BIBLIOGRAPHY: Richard Pipes, ed., *The Russian Intelligentsia*, New York, 1960.

INTERNATIONAL LAW has been accepted by the USSR as treaties and customs by which fully sovereign states agree voluntarily to bind themselves. Soviet leaders at first rejected IL as serving the ends of colonialism and exploitation. "Unequal" tsarist treaties and the tsarist debts were repudiated, foreign economic interests in the Russian republic confiscated, and institutions of IL and diplomacy viewed with contempt by the first foreign commissar, Trotsky. He, Lenin, and other Bolsheviks hopefully awaited the world revolution which would sweep away all bourgeois states and their IL. The counter-trend of activities of Russia as an active subject of IL came first with the much-opposed signing of the Treaty of Brest-Litovsk with the Central Powers, March 3, 1918, which was annulled by the armistice of Nov. 11, 1918. The first more permanent agreement was the Peace Treaty with Estonia of Feb. 2, 1920, which was later violated. Failure of the Polish campaign, 1920–21, and of attempts at communist revolution elsewhere forced the USSR in its own interest to undertake a growing variety of international obligations, to seek diplomatic recognition, and eventually to alter its theory of IL whereby Soviet jurists, not ceasing to point out the alleged "class nature" of IL, conceded that, used selectively, it can benefit the USSR, in the period of its "peaceful competitive coexistence" with "capitalist imperialist" states. The USSR recognizes traditional institutions of IL such as territorial sovereignty, freedom of the seas, diplomatic customs and immunity, laws of war, neutrality, principles of international organization. It subscribed to the postwar Geneva convention on war prisoners, and has its own theory of "just" and "unjust" wars to which its diplomatic adversaries are not willing to subscribe. "Just wars" are wars of national liberation, revolutionary wars, all wars which further the cause of communism.

In its search for "collective security" against fascism, the USSR made many treaties of nonaggression and mutual aid, and in 1934 entered the League of Nations which the first congress of the Communist International in 1919 had labeled "the holy alliance of the bourgeoisie for the suppression of the proletarian revolution." As a founding member of the UN in June 1945, the USSR ignored its own IL doctrine of equality of states by negotiating for a veto for the five permanent members of the Security Council, but not for the nonpermanent members. It participates in the work of some UN agencies such as UNESCO, and in the UN's International Law Commission and International Court of Justice, on which the Soviet judge has been, successively, Sergey B. Krylov, Sergey A. Golunski, Fyodor I. Kozhevnikov, Vladimir M. Koretsky, all distinguished jurists. The USSR is a party to many international agreements of an administrative-economic nature, e.g., Universal Postal Union, also increasingly to treaties involving Soviet economic aid.

Soviet jurists claim a "new, socialist IL" is growing out of the relations among the members of the Soviet bloc. The USSR, anxious to maintain the appearance of legitimacy in its relations with its satellites, has masked unequal relations with legal frills and with praise of the "cooperation and mutual aid" between itself and the people's democracies.

Union republics, still in Soviet theory sovereign units, received in 1944 the right to conduct diplomatic relations and to have their own armed forces. On this basis, Ukraine and Byelorussia became separate members of the UN, and the Ukraine signed the all-Communist convention on Danubian navigation, Aug. 18, 1948.

Space IL is of growing importance in an age of orbital and cosmic flight. The Soviet aviation code of 1935 claimed Soviet sovereignty of the air space over territory of the USSR. No objections of violation of IL were raised to flights of United States satellites over the USSR, including the cloud-photographing Tiros, in spite of the furor over the U-2 reconnaissance airplane. Future objections are possible. It remains to be seen whether outer space can be internationalized as were the seas.

Private IL, which involves relations among persons and organizations in different states, has a key problem of "conflict of laws," that is, of deciding in a given case which laws of which country are to apply. The USSR recognizes marriages of foreigners as long as they conform to the rules of the countries where they were performed. Foreign law is valid within the USSR only where such law does not conflict with Soviet law, and with the interests of the Soviet state, which, of course, coincide. Its courts have rejected numerous claims of foreign authors for royalties on their works reprinted or translated in the USSR. Disputes between the corporations of the government's foreign trade monopoly and foreign states or concerns are heard as a rule under voluntary arbitration (q.v.) by the Foreign Trade Arbitration Commission, Moscow, on the basis of Soviet law (q.v.). (*See also* AUTHORSHIP AND INVENTION)

BIBLIOGRAPHY: John N. Hazard, *Law and Social Change in the USSR*, Toronto, 1953; Alvin Z. Rubinstein, *The Foreign Policy of the Soviet Union*, New York, 1960; Rudolf Schlesinger, *Soviet Legal Philosophy*, London, 1951.   P. H. J.

INTERNATIONAL ORGANIZATION. Soviet attitudes toward international organization developed under the influence of the customary blend of ideological dogmatism and pragmatic flexibility. During the first years of Soviet power, doctrinal precepts and political expediency seemed to coincide. Orthodox Marxism-Leninism pointed to the incompatibility of a revolutionary socialist regime with the established society of capitalist states. For a while, world revolution looked like the only salvation for the embattled Russian Commune, and the revolutionary overthrow of the existing governments in the W. appeared more relevant than relations with these governments or with the League of Nations, seen as the tool of France and Britain, Soviet Russia's main antagonists. "The so-called League of Nations is nothing but an insurance policy in which the victors mutually guarantee each other their prey," said Lenin in 1920.

The end of the civil war and foreign interventions made the new regime face a more or less protracted period of internal reconstruction in the absence of a European or world revolution. With the New Economic Policy (NEP) went the admission that some forms of "coexistence," albeit temporary, with capitalist powers were both possible and necessary. This laid the foundation for a policy of seeking *de jure* recognition and trade treaties with capitalist states. There was at first no similar change, however, in the attitude toward IO. The League was still considered a potential enemy, and attempts were continued to combine efforts with Germany, the other "outcast" of the Versailles system. The Rapallo Treaty with Germany (1922), suddenly announced in the midst of the Genoa Economic Conference, was a symbol of this policy.

League of Nations. New trends appeared when the Locarno Treaties (1925) and Germany's entry into the League (1926) threatened to completely isolate Soviet Russia. This prompted limited Soviet participation in the activities of the League, primarily in the economic field and that of disarmament (the International Economic Conference and the Preparatory Commission for the Disarmament Conference). In 1928 Soviet Russia endorsed the Briand-Kellogg Pact, and in 1929 she signed with Poland, Estonia, Rumania, and Latvia the Moscow Protocol on its immediate implementation. The trend became increasingly pronounced as the process of rapid industrialization and forcible collectivization of agriculture went into full gear. To shield the experiment, Russia needed peace at any price. In 1931 Stalin emphatically pointed out to Soviet industrial managers gathered for their first conference that Russia was fifty or a hundred years behind the advanced countries. Backwardness meant defeat, he said, and, with surprising precision, he even set the time limit for catching up industrially with the advanced countries—not more than ten years—if Russia was not to be beaten again in a new war. Russia's participation in the activities of the League, including the Disarmament Conferences of 1932 and 1933, remained limited and admittedly based on considerations of expediency. Hostility to the League abated only when the realization was brought home that Nazism in Germany (as well as Japanese militarism) represented that very threat of war which the Soviets wanted to avoid. As long as the rulers of the Soviet Union viewed Germany as a breach in the Versailles system—a hostile combination from which only they feared warlike action—the main danger was seen not in the revanchism of the Nazi movement but in the pro-Western liberal forces in Germany. As soon, however, as it appeared that Hitler represented something else, namely, the immediate menace of a new war, most likely against the Soviet Union, an entirely new period of Soviet diplomacy was initiated. The old tactics of the German Communist party and of the Comintern were set aside while the Soviets began to court non-fascist bourgeois states of yesterday's Entente, seeking means of avoiding war or, should that objective be defeated, of avoiding isolation in a war. USSR joined the League of Nations on Sept. 18, 1934. Foreign commissar Litvinov stepped to the front in Geneva to become the champion of collective security and of the principle of indivisibility of peace. With the usual singleness of purpose, an attempt was also made to create popular support for the diplomatic alliance forged by Litvinov. The Comintern once more became a factor of some importance in a new and rather unusual role of protagonist of national unity against fascism.

The desire to build up an anti-Nazi coalition was the main, if not the only, concern of the Soviets. Functional cooperation and the League's economic and social activities scarcely interested them. "Decisions regarding traffic, assistance to refugees, establishment of an international system of signaling at grade crossings" were scorned by Litvinov in Sept. 1938: "What have all the questions, important as they are in themselves, in common with the maintenance of peace, with the main object for which the League was set up?" The Soviets were after an ironclad coalition which, in their thinking, presented a good chance of intimidating Hitler and thus averting the danger of war he represented. When developments in world politics made such an outcome unlikely and a war appeared inevitable, the very essence of Soviet policy changed. To the fore came the technique which Robert Strausz-Hupé and Stefan T. Possony once termed "chestnut strategy" and which, according to their picturesque definition, consists "in stacking the cards in such a manner that the kibitzer wins the game," and should the kibitzer be compelled to participate in the game, entering it "at the last possible moment when the others have already lost their pants and when he still has a big heap of chips." The Rapallo coup of the twenties was repeated on a world-shaking scale, in the form of the Nazi-Soviet pact of Aug. 1939. The brief episode of Soviet participation in the League was ended, and, after the attack on Finland, the finishing touch was added when, on Dec. 14, 1939, the Soviet Union was expelled from the League of Nations.

United Nations. The wartime alliance of the Soviet Union, Britain and the United States once again gave rise to plans for Soviet participation in an international organization to be formed after the Second World War. The policy of the Soviets in this respect was founded on the interaction of two conflicting premises: their obvious desire to achieve a postwar projection of the wartime coalition; and wariness caused by doctrinal preconceptions and the humiliating experience with the League of Nations. Out of this arose a conception of the United Nations Organization which Soviet representatives maintained throughout all the preliminary consultations and negotiations and which, to a very considerable extent, affected the actual make-up of the new world organization formed in Dumbarton Oaks and San Francisco. From the Soviet point of view, the world organization was to be primarily a security organization. International cooperation in the economic and social fields was to be separated from the security tasks of the envisaged organization. (At a later stage, the objections against the plan of one comprehensive organization were withdrawn.) The world security organization was not to go beyond the point within which its legal constitution would correspond to the actual power structure of international society. The new system had to remain within the limitations set by conflicting national interests of the powers: "Such organizations materially facilitate relations between states . . . they do not put an end to the contradictions which exist in the capitalist world" (from a Soviet textbook on international law). Consequently, the principle of sovereignty was to remain the basic premise of international relations, and Soviet Russia opposed any atempt to limit national sovereignty aiming at endowing international institutions with authority and influence over and above that of the members composing them. The greatest precautions were taken by the Soviet representatives during these negotiations against the possibility that the Soviet Union might be bound in the new organization by a majority vote. Hence, the insistence on the veto or, in the official definition which the Soviets clearly prefer, the unanimity rule of the permanent members of the Security Council. The Security Council was to be the political organ of the Great Powers for the settlement, by mutual consent, of international disputes and for the adjustment of the interests of the powers themselves. This idea was impressed upon the earlier drafts and remained basically intact even after the metamorphoses suffered by the original idea of a Great-Power nucleus on different stages of development after the Moscow Declaration

of Oct. 30, 1943. The Dumbarton Oaks draft, the Yalta voting formula, and the final provisions of the San Francisco Charter did not do away with the basic idea that the major powers were to maintain in peace the controlling power they had in war. The Yalta formula, with its refinements which Harry Hopkins obtained from Stalin in dramatic direct conversations, only endeavored to reconcile the position of the Great Powers with the susceptibilities of the smaller ones. Created as a projection of the wartime coalition, with strong overtones of Concert of Powers philosophy in its structural pattern, the Organization reflected, immediately and sharply, the postwar end of the "concert" between the leading powers. Signs of future difficulties could have been discerned even before the Organization was founded. The Soviets clearly had misgivings about the unprecedented commitments UN participation involved for them in conditions of an assured numerical preponderance of non-Communist members. The three votes the Soviet Union obtained (Soviet Union, Byelorussia, Ukraine), after the rejection of their demand for separate representation for all sixteen constituent Republics, did not dispel these misgivings. Nor did the much more effective right of veto. At one point during the San Francisco Conference, a deadlock ensued; and the Charter was ultimately signed, as John Foster Dulles relates, only when the United States made it clear that, unless the Soviets agreed to the proposed draft, the conference would vote its text, leaving the Russians to withdraw if they wished. Despite these dubious beginnings, the opening of the first General Assembly in Jan. 1946 was reasonably harmonious. The atmosphere deteriorated decisively after Mr. Gromyko's famous walk-out during the discussion of the Iranian complaint in the Security Council in the spring of 1947. Having been forced to withdraw from Iran under the impact of a hostile majority in the UN, the Soviets thereafter began to exercise their veto right freely to the purpose of thwarting the wishes of the majority of the Security Council and preventing the Council from taking action. The first such veto was cast in the Syria-Lebanon case and has since been used on a wide range of subjects including a series of vetoes cast to turn down new members.

Consolidation of Two Hostile Blocks. The "Thaw." The following decade, the period of consolidation of two hostile blocs, was one of virtual paralysis for the UN. During this period, both the United States and the Soviet Union increased their activity outside the UN. In March 1947 the Truman Doctrine was announced, and in July the Marshall Plan was inaugurated. The Soviets, on their part, concentrated on the complete separation of their E. European allies from the non-Communist world. In Sept. 1947 the Cominform was constituted. Tension increased from year to year, and with the withdrawal of the Soviet delegation from the Security Council over Chinese representation in Jan. 1950, the Soviets reverted to the tactics employed in the earlier League of Nations, namely, abstention from the activities of what they began to consider a hostile organization. Indeed, the war in Korea brought about unprecedentedly forceful UN action in a new capacity: minus the Soviet Union, the UN proved fairly effective as an instrument of rallying anti-Communist forces. In Aug. 1950, the Soviet representative returned and successfully stalled further Security Council action, but was unable to stop the military action initiated in Korea and continued under the aegis of the General Assembly. There ensued an era of the veto, of vituperative speeches, and of ineffectual wranglings. As Anthony Eden said (in 1953), many began "to regard the UN as a simple instrument in the cold war." This trend was interrupted by the post-Stalin "thaw" which became especially pronounced in 1955 and culminated in the Geneva Summit Conference. During this period, after the cessation of hostilities in Korea, the Soviet Union began to step up its participation in UN activities. For the first time it accepted participation in the work of the UN Technical Assistance Program; joined the UNESCO (April 21, 1955); and in May 1955, after almost seven years of stalemate, talks on disarmament and controls were resumed. The new tentative trends seemed in danger under the impact of the events in Hungary in 1956, the failure of the London disarmament subcommittee in 1957, the Berlin crisis in 1958. However, in these and later controversies, including the Congo crisis, Soviet tactics in the UN veered away from earlier walk-outs. Communist representatives mercilessly attack the Secretary General, use filibuster tactics and seek to introduce the veto into the structure of the UN Secretariat. They nevertheless remain and attempt to bring UN weight to bear in favor of the Soviet stand on respective issues (for instance, Suez, disarmament or colonial issues).

The new composition of the organization, with the considerably increased number of Asian and African states and neutralist influences, makes such uses practicable. Some observers see in it a transformation of the original Soviets' concept of the UN. Instead of a security organization, they are said to view it as a "forum for a Soviet effort to mobilize opinion against Britain and America" (Alexander Dallin quoting Adlai Stevenson). Be this as it may, the IO is now part and parcel of universal diplomacy to such an extent that, whatever the uses the Soviet bloc may ascribe to it from time to time, it has become impossible to view the UN as expendable like the League of Nations. The Soviet Union, perhaps reluctantly and without theoretical substantiation, seems to have factually joined a single international system. This does not, by any means, involve acceptance by the Soviet Union of limitations of sovereignty or compulsory international jurisdiction. The Soviets still maintain that the "prospects of the International Court of Justice contributing to the peaceful regulations of international relations are extremely meager" (S. B. Krylov, one-time Soviet member of the International Court in the Hague). Nor does it signify doctrinal conclusions portending the propagation of "one world" concepts. To the contrary, faced with implications of the fact of the existence, recognized also by Soviet theorists, of universally binding norms of international law, the Soviets endeavor to establish a

dividing line between the universal system of states and that in process of formation in the Communist orbit. The principle of "proletarian internationalism" is brought out as the distinctive feature of the latter, in contrast to the former. But, while concepts of struggle, albeit nonmilitary, between the two worlds are still propagated, Soviet diplomacy increasingly makes appeal to the binding norms of the UN system and often seeks refuge behind them.

As an ancillary development in the same process, there is a noticeable increase in Soviet participation in the functional and technical aspects of UN activity. After years of negative attitude to these organizations, the Soviet Union joined the International Labour Organisation in 1954, UNESCO in 1955, and resumed in 1956 membership in the World Health Organization (from which it withdrew in Feb. 1949). It has increased collaboration on technical problems (maintained to an extent even during the years of the "cold war" in the UN); joined the Technical Assistance Program; and become increasingly active in the Economic and Social Council endeavors, especially in the Economic Commission for Europe, where it is said at present to have the initiative. The Soviet Union is also one of the leading powers in the Agency for the Peaceful Uses of Atomic Energy in Vienna. It has remained hostile, however, toward the International Monetary Fund and the International Bank for Reconstruction and Development. (*See also* HISTORY, FOREIGN POLICY SINCE 1945, COMINTERN, COMINFORM, WORLD WAR II)

BIBLIOGRAPHY: *The Year Book of World Affairs, 1954,* London Institute of World Affairs; Alexander Dallin, *The Soviet View of the United Nations,* Cambridge, Mass., 1959; G. M. Mason, "Toward Indivisible International Law? The Evolution of Soviet Doctrine," *Social Research,* Spring 1956.

INTERVENTION: *see* CIVIL WAR, HISTORY.

INTOURIST: *see* TRAVELING AND TOURISM, CULTURAL EXCHANGE.

INVENTIONS: *see* AUTHORSHIP AND INVENTION.

INVESTMENT. The over-all rate of investment is a political decision in the USSR made in the top echelons of the party and government. Since 1928, when the USSR embarked on a program of forced-draft industrialization, a very high rate of gross I has been maintained, as shown in the following table. (Comparable data for the United States are presented below.)

GROSS INVESTMENT AS A PERCENT OF
GROSS NATIONAL PRODUCT

	1928	1937	1940	1944	1948	1950	1955
USSR	23.2	22.9	16.6	13.5	25.6	23.3	26.9
U.S.	18.9	16.6	18.4	6.4	18.9	20.0	18.7

Source: *Soviet Economic Growth: A Comparison with the United States,* Washington, 1957.

The rate of net I (gross I minus capital consumption) has also been very high in the USSR (exceeding the corresponding rate in the USA), in part because of the Soviet policy, pursued until very recently, of employing capital equipment until it was physically unusable (in other words, ignoring obsolescence). Under conditions of extreme capital scarcity, such as existed in the USSR in the 1930's, this policy was, perhaps, justifiable. As the supply of capital has increased, relative to labor and other factors of production, however, the policy of disregarding obsolescence has become less and less tenable. In response to changes in factor supply, the Soviet government has been adopting a more resolute policy of scrapping obsolete equipment, which will, among other things, tend to lower the rate of net I.

Like the over-all rate of I, the allocation of I to different sectors and branches of the economy, and often to specific projects within a sector or branch, is a political decision in the USSR. As the Soviet leadership has been concerned primarily with building up the country's political-military might and economic power, it has concentrated I in industry, the heavy engineering branches in particular. Over the period 1928–58, about two-fifths of total Soviet I went into industry (q.v.), other sectors such as agriculture, transport, housing, and services being relatively neglected. Of total I in industry, the heavy industrial branches, such as machine-building, metallurgy, fuel and power, accounted for 88 per cent over the same period.

While decisions about *what* will be produced are essentially political and highly centralized decisions in the USSR, decisions about *how* and where things will be produced are essentially economic decisions, which may or may not be made in a centralized fashion. Decisions of this latter type involve a wide range of practical problems. Should, for example, a given electric power requirement be met by constructing a hydroelectric plant, which requires much capital, or several thermal power plants which require less capital but have higher operating costs? Would it be more economical, in terms of total resources, to locate a steel mill in Karaganda or Magnitogorsk? Should a given railroad gradient be made less steep, which would require more capital, or more steep, which would require less capital but entail higher operating expenses?

To solve such problems Soviet engineers and design-makers employ a "pay-off" period calculation, similar to that used in the United States and other W. countries. The Soviet "pay-off" period formula takes various forms, one of the most common of which is shown below. (This particular version of the formula is generally used when there are only two variants of a given project to be compared and when the time pattern of the I outlays required by the two variants is identical.)

$$\frac{I_2 - I_1}{E_1 - E_2} < T$$

where I_2 and E_2 are the capital and average annual operating costs of the more capital-intensive variant and I_1 and E_1 are the capital and average annual operating costs of the less capital-intensive variant. T is the maximum acceptable "pay-off" period for the branch of industry in question.

If the "pay-off" period of the more capital-intensive variant, calculated according to the above formula, is shorter than the maximum acceptable period which has been set for the branch of industry in question, the more capital-intensive variant is selected. If the "pay-off" period of the more capital-intensive variant is longer than the maximum acceptable period for the branch, the less capital-intensive variant is chosen.

Soviet sources are not very explicit about the criteria used to establish maximum acceptable "pay-off" periods for different industrial branches. They are probably set, for the most part, quite arbitrarily. In general, the maximum acceptable "pay-off periods" are longer in the heavy than in the consumer branches of industry, reflecting, in part, the government's more generous allocations of capital to the former. There are indications that the periods have been set longer in certain key branches of industry with the express purpose of encouraging technological advances in these branches.

When more than two variants of a given project are being compared, the above formula is recast into the following mathematically equivalent but less cumbersome form:

$$\frac{I}{T} \text{ plus } E = \text{minimum}$$

The variant having the lowest capital and operating costs, calculated by the above formula, is selected.

In order to take into account differences in the time pattern of capital outlays and in operating costs of project variants the formula is sometimes used in the following form:

$$\frac{I}{(1+p)^t} + \frac{E}{(1+p)^t} = \text{minimum}$$

where p is the reciprocal of the maximum acceptable "pay-off" period (called the coefficient of effectiveness) and t refers to the years in which capital outlays and operating costs are incurred.

The Soviet "pay-off" period formula is more sophisticated than its western counterpart, in that it calls for the inclusion of depreciation charges in the calculation of operating costs. The results obtained with the formula, however, are often suspect, as Soviet economists themselves readily admit, because of the arbitrary character of Soviet prices, which must, of course, be used in the formula.

The "pay-off" period formula, which involves an implicit interest charge, has had a long and stormy history in the Soviet Union. It was first employed, more or less surreptitiously, by Soviet engineers and design-makers in the 1930's when the use of explicit interest charges, for choosing among project variants, came under heavy fire from theoretical Soviet economists. The latter, in fact, argued that capital costs should be disregarded entirely when choosing among project variants. In effect, they recommended that project variants be chosen according to the following formula:

$$E = \text{minimum}$$

where E represents annual operating costs.

It is perhaps no coincidence that tendencies toward "gigantomania," that is, preference for large-scale project variants, were most marked in the USSR in the 1930's when the influence of these theoreticians was strongest.

The "pay-off" period formula has only recently achieved some official recognition in the USSR. In 1956 the State Committee for Technology advocated the use of the formula in making certain types of I decisions. In 1958 the formula's legitimacy was reinforced by a recommendation of the Ac. of S. of the USSR that it be used, along with other criteria, for choice among project variants.

It should be emphasized, however, that while an implicit interest charge is generally employed in selecting project variants, the Soviet banking system allocates fixed capital to enterprises free of such a charge.

There is, therefore, little monetary incentive for Soviet management to economize in the use of fixed capital. Moreover, the absence of an interest charge contributes to the distortion of Soviet prices, which, in turn, compounds the difficulties of I choice.

BIBLIOGRAPHY: Norman Kaplan, "Capital Formation and Allocation," ed. by A. Bergson, *Soviet Economic Growth,* White Plains, N. Y., 1953; Gregory Grossman, "Scarce Capital and Soviet Doctrine," *Quarterly Journal of Economics,* August 1953.　　R. C. H.

INYLCHÉK, Northern and Southern, glaciers in Central Tien Shan, N.E. Kirghiz SSR; length of N. about 21 mi., S. about 37 mi.

IOFÁN, Borís Mikháylovich (1891–), architect. Graduated from the Higher Institute of Fine Arts in Rome (1916). He was the architect of the Soviet pavillions at the world fairs in Paris (1937) and New York (1939).

IÓFFE, Abrám Fyódorovich (1880–1960), physicist. Fellow, Ac. of S., USSR (1920); honorary member of the American Academy of Arts and Sciences, Boston; corresponding member of Goettingen and Berlin Ac. of S. Honorary doctor of California, Bucharest, Paris, and other universities. Graduate of St. Petersburg Institute of Technology (1902) and Munich University (1905). Worked for W. K. Roentgen (1902–6). Professor, St. Petersburg Polytechnic Institute (1913), and director, Institute of Physics and Technology (1918–51). Research on quantum theory of light, mechanical properties of crystals, and electric properties of semiconductors. Stalin prize (1942), two Lenin orders, and other decorations.

IÓFFE, Ádolf Abrámovich (1883–1927), leading organizer of the Bolshevik Revolution and diplomat. Born of a wealthy family, I became a member of the Menshevik party in 1903. In 1908, he joined Trotsky in Vienna and a few years later helped to organize the "August Bloc." In 1912, I went to Odessa and was immediately imprisoned. Together with Trotsky, he joined the Bolsheviks in Aug. 1917. After the revolution, I initiated peace negotiations with Germany at Brest-Litovsk and became ambassador to Germany in 1918. He also carried out diplomatic assignments in Geneva (1922) and in China (1923). During the intra-party struggle, I strongly supported Trotsky. In 1927, when Trotsky appeared to have lost, I, long under psychiatric treatment, committed suicide.

IPPOLÍTOV-IVÁNOV, Mikhaíl Mikháylovich (1859–1935), composer and conductor, People's Artist of USSR. His style is in the tradition of R. classical music. Author of the operas *Ruth* (1887), *Asya* (1900); completed Musorgsky's opera *The Marriage* by finishing the 2nd, 3rd and 4th acts. Composer of *Treason, Caucasian Sketches, The Voroshilov March.* Was director of the Moscow conservatoire. I continued the traditions of Tchaikovsky and was considered a master of orchestration.

IRBÍS-TÚ, peak in Altay Mountains, covered with glacier of same name; elevation about 13,120 ft.

IRBÍT, city in Sverdlovsk Oblast, RSFSR; pop. 42,-100 (1957). Motorcycle, technical glass and ceramic plants.

IRGÍZ BOLSHÓY, river in Saratov and Kuybyshev oblasts, RSFSR, left tributary of the Volga; length 371 mi.; navigable.

IRGÍZ RIVER, in Kazakh SSR; length about 350 mi.; flows into Chelkar-Tengiz Lake.

IRKÚTSK, city, oblast adm. center, RSFSR, on Angara River; pop. 250,000 (1939), 365,000 (1959). Important economical and cultural center of E. Siberia. Ind.: heavy machine-building, auto repairs, electrotechnical and machine-tooling plants, mica, woodworking, food, processing, light industry such as furs and skins. Has numerous colleges, including one university, and is the seat of the E. Siberian Branch of the Ac. of S. Founded in 1652; important trade point and administrative center. Starting with 18th century it became a place of political exile.

IRKÚTSK OBLAST in E. Siberia near Lake Baykal, RSFSR; comprises Ust-Orda Buryat National Okrug. Area 296,400 sq. mi.; pop. 1,976,000 (1959), consisting of Russians, Buryats, Yakuts, Tofas, Evenki. Cities: Irkutsk (adm. center), Cheremkhovo, Tulun, Tayshet, Zima, Bodaybo, Usolye Sibirskoye. Rivers: Angara, Nizhnyaya Tunguska, Lena, Vitim, with navigable waterways of 2,000 mi. Has a continental climate and is mostly covered with forests (pine, cedar, larch). Mineral wealth: coal, gold, iron, mica, salt. Agr.: rye, wheat, oats, cattle breeding; fisheries, fur-bearing animals. Ind.: mining, hydroelectric power stations, woodworking, machine-building, lumber, food, clothing. University, schools of higher education, E. Siberian Branch of the Ac. of S., USSR, scientific research institutes, theaters. In tsarist times used as area of political exile. Est. 1937.

IRON ORE: *see* METALS, IRON AND STEEL INDUSTRY.

IRON AND STEEL INDUSTRY. The amount of pig iron produced in 1960 was 46.8 mill. metric tons, and of steel 65.3 mill. tons (as compared with 84.7 mill. tons of steel produced in 1959 in the United States, 20.5 mill. tons in the United Kingdom, and 25.8 mill. tons in W. Germany).

The principal centers of ferrous metallurgy are located in the Ukraine (Donbas), in the Urals (Magnitogorsk), and in Siberia (Kuznetsk basin). Smaller production facilities exist in the Far E. Provinces, in Uzbekistan, in Kazakhstan, and in Georgia. The establishment of an additional large center in Siberia has been projected for the period 1958–1972.

The smelting of iron in factories was first undertaken in the 17th century. It developed rapidly in the 18th century as a result of the reforms of Peter the Great and of the large requirements for metal of the newly established national army and fleet. In the 1730's Russia became the world's leading producer of pig iron, and throughout the 18th century she continued to export a large share of her domestic production to the countries of W. Europe, especially England. The principal center of production at that time was in the Urals. A century later (1885), as a result of the rapid development of production in W. European countries which was made possible by radical technological advances, the share of Russia in the world's production of pig iron declined

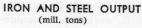

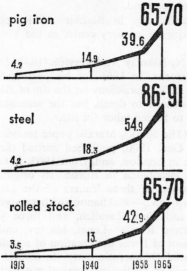

IRON AND STEEL OUTPUT
(mill. tons)

to less than 3 per cent, while one-third of domestic needs were met by imports.

Subsequently the construction of railroads led to the opening of a new center of production in the S. based on the iron-ore deposits at Krivoy Rog and equipped with relatively advanced technology. This was followed, once again, by a rapid growth in the production of metal, 2.3 mill. tons of steel being produced in 1900, and 4.2 mill. tons in 1913.

Following the nationalization of the iron and steel industry in 1917, production declined drastically at first, particularly during the years of the civil war. It regained the 1913 level, however, by 1929.

In view of the strategic position of ferrous metallurgy both in the construction of modern machines and in the production of military equipment, the highest priority was accorded to its further development in the 1930's. As a result more than 80 per cent of the 18.3 mill. tons of steel produced in 1940 came from plants entirely reconstructed or else built only since the industry had been nationalized. An emphasis on the introduction of modern equipment was reflected in the increasing size of the blast furnaces and open-hearth furnaces as well as in their productivity. In contrast to 1900, when 200 small blast furnaces were in operation, producing 2.9 mill. tons of pig iron, there were only 92 blast furnaces in operation in 1940 producing 14.9 mill. tons of pig iron. As the average productivity of blast furnaces increased fivefold during the period 1928–40, efforts were also made to introduce such improvements as the automatic controlling of all stages of iron and steel production; the use of modern methods of rolling, including the continuous strip mill technique; and the increasing of the share of scrap iron and steel in the industry's raw materials.

In addition, strong emphasis was placed on the construction of new centers of production in the E. regions of the country. Among the largest steel plants built in the 1930's there were those at Magnitogorsk and at Novotagilskoye in the Urals; at Kuznetsk, in Siberia; and

at Komsomolsk, in the Far East. Of particular significance was the close association of the productive facilities of the Urals, which had large deposits of iron ore, with those of the Kuznetsk basin, which had an abundance of coal but lacked iron ore.

During the Second World War 62 blast furnaces and 213 open-hearth furnaces were destroyed in the areas occupied by the Germans. In the E. regions, however, 13 blast furnaces capable of producing 2.3 mill. tons of steel and 28 rolling mills with an annual capacity of 17 mill. tons of finished steel began operations in 1942 and 1944. The productive capacity in the E. regions increased by 60% during the period 1941–45. This played a decisive role in altering the traditional locational pattern of the industry. In spite of this new construction, however, the production of steel in 1945 had fallen 66% compared with 1940.

Between 1945 and 1955 the destroyed facilities in the S. were rebuilt and the production of the E. centers was expanded still further. In 1950 the 1940 level of steel production was exceeded by nearly 50%. In 1955 the production of steel had increased by another 66%. A considerable share of this increment stemmed from the further introduction of such improvements as the use of automatic controls in furnaces and rolling mills, the use of pure oxygen in smelting, and the employment of (lower grade) ores from sources closer to production. At the same time there was considerable improvement in the quality and variety of the special-purpose steels that were produced. Although a still more pronounced shift of production to E. regions occurred once again during this period, the industry as a whole continued to be concentrated in a relatively few areas.

The objectives of the Seven Year Plan (1959–65) provide for the production of 65–70 mill. tons of pig iron in 1965, and 89–91 mill. tons of steel. In addition they provide for the creation of new large metallurgical facilities in Siberia, as well as for an increased emphasis on the production of special-purpose steels (heat-resistant, rust-resistant, precision, electrotechnical, bimetallic sheets, cold-rolled sheets). (*See also* ECONOMIC DEVELOPMENT, INDUSTRY, METALS, METALLURGY.)

PRODUCTION OF IRON AND STEEL IN THE USSR
(mill. metric tons)

	Pig Iron	Steel	
1900	2.6	2.3	
1913	4.2	4.2	
1929	4.0	4.9	
1940	14.9	18.3	
1945	8.8	12.2	
1955	33.3	45.2	
1959	43.0	59.9	
1960	46.8	65.3	
1965 (pl.)	65–70	86–91	P. I. M.

IRRIGATION. One of the crucial disadvantages of the climatic conditions in the USSR is the lack of adequate rainfall over large areas of the country; hence, the importance of I. In the prerevolutionary period larger I works were completed principally in the Central Asiatic cotton-producing regions. In 1917 the irrigated area in the R. empire amounted to 10.08 mill. acres. In the first decade of the Soviet power I works were rather neglected and by 1929 land under I increased by only 963,700 acres as compared to 1917. With the collectivization of agriculture and the availability of man power in the countryside I works on a larger scale were done in the Uzbek, Tadzhik, Turkmen and Kirghiz Republics, in the S. part of Kazakhstan and in Azerbaijan. Consequently, the area under I increased from 11.04 mill. acres in 1929 to 13.88 mill. in 1937, 15.19 mill. in 1940, and in 1957 to about 27 mill. acres, of which 17.3 were irrigated by underflowing.

The table below presents the geographic distribution of irrigated land in the USSR in 1957:

	Thous. of hectares	Thous. of acres
USSR, total	11,080	27,378
of which		
RSFSR	1,481	3,660
Ukrainian SSR	223	551
Uzbek SSR	2,887	7,134
Kazakh SSR	2,055	5,078
Georgian SSR	319	788
Azerbaijan SSR	1,580	3,904
Moldavian SSR	30	74
Kirgiz SSR	1,146	2,832
Tadzhik SSR	425	1,050
Armenian SSR	213	526
Turkmen SSR	721	1,781

Cotton is the main crop produced on irrigated land. In 1940, 74 per cent of the total area sown under cotton was irrigated; but in 1953 and in the following years 100 per cent was irrigated.   A. K.

IRTÝSH RIVER, left tributary of the Ob, rises in China, flows in Kazakh SSR, Omsk and Tyumen oblasts, RSFSR; length, 2,745 mi.; navigable; has fisheries. Chief tributaries: (left) Ishim, Tobol, Vagay, Konda; (right) Om, Tara, Demyanka. Towns on its banks: Ust-Kamenogorsk, Semipalatinsk, Pavlodar, Omsk, Tobolsk. Ust-Kamenogorsk and Bukhtarma electric power plants.

ISAKÓVSKY, Mikháil Vasílyevich (1900–), poet, born in Smolensk Oblast into a poor peasant family.

 He became a CP member in 1928. His first book of verse, *Wire in the Straw*, came in 1927, and was followed by *The Province, Masters of the Land, Selected Poems, Poems and Songs,* and *Song of the Motherland.* I's verses are almost entirely in the folk song manner and usually on rural themes. Many became widely known abroad, as well as in the USSR; e.g., *Katyusha, And Who Knows Him, Departure,* and *The Border Guard Leaves the Service.* He received Stalin prizes in 1943 and 1949 and was awarded the Orders of Lenin and of the Red Banner of Labor. He has been a deputy to the RSFSR Supreme Soviet since 1947.

ISÉT RIVER, in Sverdlovsk and Tyumen oblasts, RSFSR, left tributary of the Tobol; length 301 mi.; navigable in its lower course.

ISHLÍNSKY, Aleksándr Yúlyevich (1913–), mechanical engineer. Fellow, Ac. of S., Ukrainian SSR (1960). Professor, Moscow University (1945). Director, Mathematical Institute, Ukrainian Ac. of S., and professor, Kiev University (1948–55). Research on automation and guidance. Advanced theories on interspace gyroscopes, elasticity and plasticity, vibration, and general mechanics.

ISHÍM, city in Tyumen Oblast, RSFSR; pop. 43,100 (1956). Has R.R. workshops, machine-building, sewing-knitting and food ind.

ISHIMBÁY, city in Bashkir ASSR; pop. 44,400 (1956). Major oil-industry center in the Volga-Ural oil region.

ISHÚTIN, Nikoláy Andréyevich (1840–1879), populist and terrorist. In 1866 for his participation in the attempt of D. V. Karakózov on the life of Alexander II, he was sentenced to death, but the sentence later was commuted to forced labor for life.

ÍSKRA (The Spark), Marxist paper founded by Lenin and, after Dec. 1900, published abroad (first in Germany, then in London, and, from 1903, in Geneva) for clandestine circulation in Russia. Its original editorial board consisted of three leaders of the Liberation of Labor group (q.v.)—Plekhanov (with two votes), P. B. Akselrod, and Vera Zasulich, and three young new emigrants from Russia—Lenin, Martov, and Potresov. The main aim of I was the creation of a well-organized Russian Social Democratic party. In several articles its editors (Lenin in particular) worked out both the main ideas of a political program and the general principles of the organization of the party. In fact, *Iskra* became not only the ideological but also the organizational center of the new party, through its network of agents working underground in Russia. The "Iskrites" were in the majority among the delegates to the 2nd Party Congress (convoked in July-August 1903 in Brussels and then transferred to London), and *Iskra* became the main official organ of the party. However, a split occurred at the congress between Lenin ("Bolshevik") and Martov ("Menshevik") over the problem of the composition of I's editorial board. On Lenin's proposal, the majority of votes were for the reduction of the board to three persons—Plekhanov, Lenin, and Martov. Martov had refused cooperation and, from Aug. till Nov. 1903, I was edited by Plekhanov and Lenin. Then Plekhanov suggested the cooptation of all the original editors but Lenin did not agree and withdrew. The 52nd issue of I, dated Nov. 7, 1903, was edited by Plekhanov alone, and the following sixty numbers (until Oct. 1905) by all the original editors, except Lenin.
V. Su.

ISSÝK-KÚL, lake in Tien Shan mountains, in Kirghiz SSR. Elevation 5,278 ft.; area 2,400 sq. mi.; navigable; does not freeze. Abounds in fish.

ITELMEN: *see* POPULATION.

IVÁN I KALITÁ (Iván Danílovich), (died 1340), Grand Duke of Moscow (1325). Endeavored to unite R. principalities around and under Moscow. In 1327, he defeated the principality of Tver with the help of the Tatars and subsequently became Grand Duke of Vladimir and Moscow. Ivan's policy was one of caution in regard to the Golden Horde, trying to use the khans for his own purposes. Ivan enlarged his domain by subduing other R. principalities and by purchases of land. During his rule, Moscow became the residence of the Metropolitan of the Russian Orthodox Church.

IVÁN II, Ivánovich (1326–1359), Grand Duke of Moscow (1353–59), son of Ivan I and father of Dimitry

Donskoy. Ivan's brief reign was filled with internal strife and international disturbances which endangered the still precarious unity of Muscovy.

IVAN III, Vasílyevich (1440–1505), Grand Duke of Moscow and all Russia. He united the principalities surrounding Moscow into a single R. state; freed Russia from the Mongol-Tatar yoke (1480); fought successfully against Livonia, Poland, and Lithuania; and enhanced the political prestige of Russia. He also published the first code of law.

IVÁN IV THE TERRIBLE (Iván Vasílyevich) (1530–1584), tsar, son of Vasily III and Helen Glinsky. Ivan, the first R. ruler to assume officially the title of "Tsar" (1547), had the longest reign in R. history. He is known primarily for cruelty, debauchery, and piety; he also had an unusual memory and considerable literary gifts. Next to Catherine the Great he was perhaps the most articulate of R. sovereigns.

He was responsible for a number of basic reforms of R. institutions, notably the legal reform embodied in the Code of 1550, and the reform of local administration of 1555. He also instituted the so-called *oprichnina*, which has been defined as an all-powerful security police. It was under his direct control; it shattered the political influence of the landed aristocracy, replacing it with men, generally parvenus, selected by Ivan. The headquarters of the *oprichnina*, and thus the capital of the country, was a sort of fortified monastery near Moscow; he ran it like a monastic order, where he and his favorites divided their time between lengthy church services and extravagant orgies punctuated by visits to the torture chambers. Ivan was successful in the struggle against the Tatars: he annexed Kazan in 1552 and Astrakhan in 1556, thus acquiring almost the entire Volga region. In the west, however, he was checkmated in his effort to secure a vantage point on the Baltic Sea, the "window" on Europe, as Peter the Great was to call it. The inconclusive Livonian war (1558–83) involved Ivan in war with Poland (1562) and Sweden (1567). Though an English explorer, Richard Chancellor, had discovered a northern sea passage to Russia via the White Sea, thus establishing trade relations with England, the Baltic Sea was a more rapid channel for the engineers, doctors, and artisans whom Ivan was anxious to get from Europe. In 1581–83 he annexed W. Siberia, launching Russia on her long march eastward. Another potentially far-reaching reform of Ivan's was the convocation in 1566 of the *zemsky sobor* (q.v.) an embryonic representative institution, which he needed as a link to the populace, to "authorize" his wars and to assess financial and other burdens.

The number of Ivan's wives is estimated variously at between five and seven; his mistresses have never been counted. His first wife, Anastasia, the only woman he is supposed to have had any affection for, was poisoned, according to him, by enemies of his, as were two of her successors; two others were forced into nunneries, while another was drowned on his orders. In 1581, in a fit of anger, Ivan murdered his son and heir Tsarevich Ivan, and on his death bed he took monastic vows as was customary at the time.

BIBLIOGRAPHY: H. von Eckhardt, *Ivan the Terrible*, New York, 1949; S. Graham, *Ivan the Terrible*, New Haven, 1933.

IVÁN V, Alekséyevich (1666–1696), son of Tsar Alekséy Mikháylovich from his first wife (Miloslávskaya). He reigned conjointly with his brother Peter I from 1682. The regent was their sister Princess Sofia; she was deposed in 1689.

IVÁN VI, Antónovich (1740–1764), nominally emperor from 1740 to 1741. He was the son of Anna Leopoldovna (niece of Empress Anna Ivanovna) and Duke Anton of Brunswick. In 1741 he was deposed by the guards and imprisoned in Schlüsselburg Fortress; later he was stabbed to death by his wardens during an attempt by officer Mirovich to liberate him.

IVÁNOV, Aleksándr Andréyevich (1806–1858), a religious painter deeply preoccupied with spiritual values; the first R. artist to treat them in western terms. Educated at the Imperial Academy of Fine Arts from the age of eleven, he spent six years in Rome studying medieval, Renaissance and romantic religious painting. In 1836 he began his famous *Appearance of Messiah to the People*. Completed thirty years later, this huge canvas was intended to surpass in spirituality all previous religious paintings. Generally it is regarded as a noble failure, but I's preliminary sketches (some 275) even today seem modern and have strongly influenced subsequent R. painters.

IVÁNOV, Geórgy Vladímirovich (1894–1958), poet. A follower of Gumilyov, he became a leading acmeist. His first book of poems appeared in 1912. Emigrated after the revolution. In 1937 published a volume *Sailing off to Tsitera*, which contained poems written between 1916 and 1936. His collections *Heather* (1923), *Gardens* (1924), and *Portrait without Resemblance* (1950) showed I to be one of the best R. poets of the past few decades. He also wrote a story entitled *Disintegration of the Atom*, a book of memoirs and brilliant critical essays on Gumilyov and Yesenin. Died in Paris.

IVANÓV, Konstantín Konstantínovich (1907–), conductor. People's Artist of the USSR (1958). Graduated from Moscow conservatoire (1937). From 1941 to 1946, was conductor of the Great Symphony Orchestra of the All-Union Radio Network; in 1946, chief conductor of the State Symphony of the USSR. Received the Stalin prize (1949). Performed in the United States (1959).

IVANÓV, Víktor Semyónovich (1909–), poster artist. After gaining prominence in the 1930's, he produced numerous patriotic posters during World War II (*Our Flag—Flag of Victory*, and others). Since 1945, he has dealt mainly with the theme of "Peace." Many of his estimated 200 posters are reproduced in *The Soviet Political Poster* (1952).

IVÁNOV, Vsévolod Vyacheslávovich (1895–), a postrevolutionary writer. His varied experience as a sailor, actor, juggler in a traveling circus, and typesetter is reflected in his writings. In the 1920's he joined the literary society, Serapion Brothers. As a writer, he attained prominence with his stories *The Partisan* (1921),

Colored Winds (1922), *Blue Sands,* and *Armored Train 14–69* (1922). The last-named story was later dramatized under the title *Vision.* In these stories, the author makes a distinction between the popular Russian-type revolutionary upheaval and communism, and expresses the thought that Bolshevism succeeded in harnessing the upheaval and identifying itself with it, but still remained essentially inimical to it. He wrote a novel *End of Zheleznaya* (1925–26) and a volume of short stories *Mystery of Mysteries* (1927). His principal plays, written in the 1930's, were *The Compromise of Naib Khan, Twelve Young Lads from a Snuffbox,* and *The Pigeons See the Departing Cruisers.* In 1934–35, I wrote an autobiographical novel *The Adventures of a Fakir,* based on his early experience in the circus. His wartime novels were *My Fatherland* (1941), *On the Field of Borodino* (1943), and *Uncle Kostya.* In 1947 he published interesting memoirs *Meeting with Gorky.*

IVANÓV, Vyacheslác Ivánovich (1866–1949), symbolist poet. He studied classics and ancient history at the universities of Moscow and Berlin. After his first volume of poems, *Pilot Stars* (1903), he was proclaimed the leading symbolist poet. In his lodgings, surnamed "The Tower," the St. Petersburg symbolists met to read and discuss poetry. As an acknowledged arbiter of his craft, Ivanov discovered new talents, and was the first to recognize Anna Akhmatova. In 1924, he left the Soviet Union and lived in Italy, where he taught classical subjects at several universities. He died in Italy in 1949. He published the following volumes of poems: *Eros* (1907), *Cor Ardens* (1911), *Tender Mystery* (1912), *Childhood* (1918), *Winter Sonnets* (1920). I's poetry suffered from excessive erudition and labored literary form. The goal of art for him was the creation of religious myths. He also wrote prose and carried on an interesting correspondence with the literary historian Gershenzon.

IVÁNOV-RAZÚMNIK (Razúmnik Vasílyevich Iván-ov), (1878–1946), writer and literary critic of the populist trend. I-R became known before the revolution as the author of a *History of Russian Social Thought* and of a *History of the Russian Intelligentsia,* and also as a frequent contributor to populist and Socialist Revolutionary publications. He headed the *Scythians,* a group of writers and intellectuals who believed in the peculiar destiny of Russia as a Eurasian nation. After the revolution I-R became close to the Left Socialist Revolutionaries. In the twenties and early thirties he worked on monographs on M. Ye. Saltykov-Shchedrin and A. A. Blok. He was frequently arrested by the Soviet police as an "ideologist of populism." In 1941 he was arrested by the Germans in Pushkin and deported to a concentration camp in Prussia. Released in 1943, he wrote a book about his experiences in the various Communist prisons and places of exile. This book was published in Russian, in New York (1953).

IVÁNOVO (f. Ivanovo-Voznesensk), city, adm. center of Ivanovo Oblast, RSFSR; pop. 335,000 (1959). Is an old and important center of the textile ind. which dates back to the beginning of the 18th century, called the "Soviet Manchester"; also manufactures peat-processing machinery. It has a large power plant; and numerous colleges and scientific research establishments. Was an active center of revolutionary movement in tsarist era.

IVÁNOVO OBLAST in Central European RSFSR between the Klyazma and the Volga; area 9,260 sq. mi.; pop. 1,322,000 (1959). Cities: Ivanovo (adm. center), Kineshma, Shuya, Vichuga, Furmanov, Rodniki. Is a plain with mildly continental climate, and podzol soil on which are grown rye, wheat, oats, flax, and potatoes; one of the most important textile centers in the USSR, cotton mills, textile machinery, peat processing, power plants. Has numerous schools of higher education. Est. 1929.

IVÁNOVO-VOZNESÉNSK: *see* IVANOVO.

IVANÓVSKY, Dmítry Iósifovich (1864–1920), botanist and microbiologist. Graduate (1888), professor (1895), St. Petersburg University; professor, Warsaw University (1903). Research concerned diseases of tobacco plants. Experimentally established the existence of the pathogenic agent of tobacco mosaic (1892). Pioneer in the study of viruses in Russia.

IVASHCHÉNKOVO: *see* CHAPAYEVSK.

ÍVDEL, town in Sverdlovsk Oblast, RSFSR; pop. 12,100 (1956). Forestry and mining.

ÍYA RIVER, in Irkutsk Oblast, RSFSR, left tributary of the Oka; length 363 mi. Its main tributaries are the Kirey, Ikey, and Ilir.

IZBERBÁSH, town in Dagestan ASSR; founded in 1932 in connection with the discovery and production of oil.

ÍZHEVSK, capital of Udmurt ASSR; pop. 176,000 (1939), 285,000 (1959). One of the oldest centers (1759) of the metallurgical industry in the Urals; also mfg. of motorcycles, machine-building, steel mills and arms mfg.; sawmills, wood-chemical, food-processing ind.

ÍZHMA RIVER, in Komi ASSR, left tributary of the Pechora; length 317 mi.; navigable from Ust-Ukhta.

IZMAÍL, city in Odessa Oblast, Ukrainian SSR, port of Kilia arm of the Danube; pop. 43,000 (1956). Ship-repair plant, food processing. It was a former Turkish fortress which was taken by the R. army in 1790.

IZVÉSTIA (News), official organ of the Supreme Soviet and leading government newspaper in USSR. A daily of about four pages published in Moscow, it had a 1960 circulation of 2,300,000. The second most influential newspaper in USSR, but not in any sense *Pravda*'s equal in this respect. First published in 1917 in Petrograd as *News of Petrograd Soviet of Workers' Deputies,* it was published under varying titles in Petrograd and Moscow in the early days. Before World War II its circulation was second only to *Pravda* but the postwar rise of *Pravda* and *Komsomolskaya Pravda* dropped it to third place. Under the editorship of Alexey Adzhubey, Khrushchev's son-in-law, *Izvestia* has been enlivened with the use of more pictures, feature stories, cartoons, big headlines, and similar devices found in the western press. Still, because of its official nature, *Izvestia* must publish the full text of laws, announcements, government decisions, and speeches by Soviet figures. Since March 1960 *Izvestia* has been publishing a weekly supplement *Nedelya* (Week).

IZVÓLSKY, Aleksándr Petróvich (1865–1919), diplomat and statesman. Graduate of the Alexander Lycée; entered diplomatic service holding junior appointments at Bucharest, Washington, and the Vatican; subsequently minister plenipotentiary at Belgrade, Munich, Tokyo, and Copenhagen; appointed minister of foreign affairs in May 1906. He favored a pro-Japanese and pro-English orientation of R. foreign policy, with which he had some success. His Balkan policy failed, perhaps because of his principal opponent, the Austrian states-man Aehrenthal. In the celebrated interview at Buchlau (Sept. 15–16, 1908) Izvolsky recognized Austria's right to annex Bosnia-Herzegovina, expecting in return the opening of the Dardanelles to Russia. But he was taken by surprise in October when Austria annexed the two provinces, whereupon, despite Serb protests and R. agitation, he was compelled by the pressure of London to advise the Serbs to accept the annexation. In Sept. 1910 he was dismissed as minister of foreign affairs and was appointed ambassador to Paris. In 1914 he played a role that led many to charge him with responsibility for the war. He retired as ambassador in June 1917.

J

JASIENSKI, Bruno: *see* YASENSKY.

JÁSSY, TREATY OF, signed on Jan. 9, 1792, ending the second Russo-Turkish War of 1787–92, during the reign of Catherine the Great. A new boundary along the Dniester River was established and the annexation of the Crimea to Russia confirmed.

JÉLGAVA: *see* YELGAVA.

JEWISH AUTONOMOUS OBLAST (BIROBI-DZHAN), in Khabarovsk Kray, RSFSR; situated on the Amur and its tributaries, the Bira and Bidzhan; area 13,900 sq. mi.; pop. 163,000 (1959), consisting of Jews and Russians. Cities: Birobidzhan (adm. center) and Obluchye. Has iron, gold, granite, lignite, marble deposits; its ind. are mining, metalworking, building materials, clothing, footwear, lumber; its main agr. crops, wheat, oats, soybeans, potatoes. Est. 1934.

JEWS. Political and Economic Conditions Under the Tsars. From the beginning the attitude of the rulers of Muscovy toward the very few Jews who lived or visited their realm was a mixture of contempt, fear, and aversion. Thus Empress Elizabeth barred Jewish traders from her dominion as carriers of spiritual pollution, even though R. merchants had pleaded the usefulness of the Jews as promoters of trade. It was Catherine the Great who, by instituting in 1791 the "Pale of Settlement," a limited southern and western portion of the empire beyond which Jews were not permitted to live, initiated the process of restrictive legislation which, carried on by successive tsars, grew into an elaborate strait jacket, constricting and repressing the Jews until the downfall of tsardom. It was the desire of all the rulers of Russia to convert the Jews from their religion to Christianity and from the "parasitic" occupation of commerce to "useful" toil. This endeavor pursued fitfully and with clumsy ruthlessness bore no fruit; and the recalcitrant people was kept in appropriate subjection.

The reign of Alexander I was marked by a mixture of meager benevolence and oppression, that of Nicholas I by inept brutality. He ordered that Jewish youth be conscripted into the army at the age of 12 for a period of 25 years during which they should be encouraged by peaceful persuasion and the rod to abandon the faith of their fathers. The liberal dispensation of Alexander II, admitting the Jews to the institutions of higher learning and benefiting the Jewish upper classes, was succeeded by the severity of Alexander III whose intolerance was inflamed by the procurator of the Holy Synod, Pobedonostsev. The reign of Alexander III was inaugurated by violent outbursts (pogroms) of bands which, incited and guided by agents of the government, threw themselves upon Jewish communities looting, beating, and raping. In the scheme of the authorities the pogroms were designed to serve as a safe outlet for the explosive discontent of the lower orders; and this motive was later joined by the purpose of intimidating the Jews whose youth had shown a growing tendency to enlist in revolutionary movements. In 1903 a pogrom in the city of Kishinev claiming 40 lives spread waves of horror in the western world which had not yet grown inured by the mass exterminations of succeeding decades. The summer and autumn of 1905 saw another wave of large-scale violence sweeping over the Jewish communities. The restrictive legislation imposed upon the Jews may be divided into the following rough categories: laws restricting the residence of the great majority of Jews to the Pale of Settlement; laws excluding Jews from holding most public offices; laws requiring Jews to serve in the army for longer terms and under more rigorous conditions than other subjects of the tsar; laws, feebly enforced and largely ineffective, designed to further the Russification of the Jews by prohibiting or rendering difficult the observance of their faith and the fostering of their cultural tradition; quotas restricting the number of Jewish students in secondary and higher schools. Although 400,000 Jews served in the tsarist army during World War I, tsardom crowned the last years of its existence by banishing whole communities from the western war zone on the ground that they were engaging in espionage on behalf of Germany. The Provisional Government, installed after the revolution of 1917, abolished all the disabilities of the Jews by a decree promulgated with deliberate symbolism on the first day of the Jewish holiday of Passover, March 11, 1917.

The constricting legislation bred a depressing scene of economic misery in the Pale of Settlement. Commerce and inn-keeping had been the traditional occupations of the Jews of Russia. The law of May 1882, barring the Jews from the villages where they had hitherto served as the suppliers of peasants, drove thousands into the overcrowded towns where they eked out a precarious existence bordering on starvation. The most eloquent description of conditions in the Pale is provided by the fact that 30 per cent of all Jews were sustained by philanthropic relief; 54 per cent fell into the vague category of traders, middlemen, and persons of undefined occupation; 18.4 per cent were artisans. According to the census of 1897, 5,215,800 Jews lived within the confines of the Russian Empire.

The R. intellectual community, comparatively free from anti-Semitism, admitted Jews into its ranks as equals. R. liberals and radicals alike were committed to the abolition of the inferior status to which the Jews were condemned by the autocracy.

Culture. Until the middle of the 19th century religious orthodoxy commanded the unquestioning obedience of the Orthodox Jews, isolating them culturally and spiritually from the surrounding Gentile world. The Hassidic movement which arose in the 18th century as a reaction against the excessive intellectualism of orthodoxy to dignify the emotional communion and ecstatic abandon of the untutored as acceptable ways of worshiping God never transgressed the sacred bounds of Orthodox Law. It was the Haskalah (enlightenment), preaching the radical purging of the Judaic legacy of all those elements which stood in the way of the integration of Jews in R. society, that presented a serious challenge to tradition. From now onward, orthodoxy was to recede, giving way to the deepening inroad of secularism. The disappointment of the hopes in Russification caused by the pogroms of 1881 drove many of the adherents of the Haskalah to embrace Zionism which grew rapidly to become the largest Jewish political movement in Russia (300,000 members in 1917). It stimulated the rebirth of the Hebrew language as a spoken tongue and the creation of a secular Hebrew literature. Alongside Zionism several other political movements emerged, imparting to the R. Jewish scene a diverse political hue. In the northwestern regions, in the midst of the largest concentration of Jewish proletarians, there arose the "General Jewish Workers' Bund of Russia and Poland" (founded 1897). Raising the banners of Marxism, it worked for the realization of a socialist commonwealth in which the Jews, living in harmony with all other nations, would enjoy "national cultural autonomy" of a secular character and with Yiddish as their national language. Opposing nationalism, the Bund waged an ideological war against Zionism. Three lesser socialist parties, small in numbers but distinguished by scintillating intellectual leadership, competed for recognition: the Jewish Socialist Labor party (SERP); the Zionist Socialist Labor party (SS), and the Poale Zion. The first worked for the establishment of a self-governing Jewish assembly (Seym) as a necessary prelude to the concentration of the Jews on an autonomous territory; the second affirmed the immediate need for Jewish statehood on a territory other than Palestine; and the third sought to jusitfy a "proletarian Zionism" from orthodox Marxist premises. All socialist parties favored the use and the fostering of Yiddish—the language of the masses whom they re-

vered. In this respect they were close to the Yiddishist movement which had proclaimed Yiddish as the national language of the Jews, defending it against the Hebraists who abused it as an ugly and ignominious tongue unworthy of a proud people—the mark of exile and degradation. This love for Yiddish begot a rich and remarkable Yiddish literature. Among the numerous Yiddish writers three distinguished themselves by considerable literary talent and moral influence: Mendele Mokher Sforim (S. J. Abramovitz), 1837–1917; Sholom Aleichem (S. Rabinowitz), 1850–1916; I. L. Peretz, 1851–1915.

A small but growing number of Jews who had adopted Russian as their intellectual medium made noticeable contributions to R. literature, art, and jurisprudence; and some achieved prominence in the liberal and socialist movements: M. Vinaver in the Constitutional Democratic party; M. and A. Gots and G. Gershuni in the Socialist Revolutionary movement; L. B. Akselrod, L. Martov, and M. Liber in Menshevism; L. Trotsky, Ya. Sverdlov, L. Kamenev, and G. Zinoviev in Bolshevism.

Social and Economic Conditions in Soviet Russia. Although Bolshevik ideology had found few adherents in the Jewish community, the ordeal of the civil war drove the Jews to seek the protection of the Red Army against the fury of the anti-Bolshevik soldiery which, having inscribed anti-Semitism on its banners, massacred and pillaged the Jewish communities in their path. In the Ukraine almost 100,000 noncombatant Jews perished at the hands of the forces of Denikin and of the Ukrainian nationalistic chieftain, Petlyura, leaving 300,000 children orphaned and homeless.

The economic dispensation of communism spelled ruin for the overwhelming majority of Jews. The abolition of commerce plunged hundreds and thousands of shopkeepers and traders into unemployment and misery. Many sought to turn to the soil; but at first the scarcity of land and of implements and the resistance of the local peasantry set severe limits to this endeavor. In 1924 the Soviet government set up organizations to direct and guide the settlement of the Jews on the land; and assisted by the Agro-Joint, a branch of the American Joint Distribution Committee, 100,000 Jews were wedded to agriculture in the Ukraine and in the Crimea. The need for a large expanse of land upon which to settle large numbers of destitute Jews combined with the desire to impress Jewish opinion abroad induced the Soviet government to proclaim in 1928 its intention of creating a Jewish "Republic" in the Far Eastern region of Birobidzhan; and in 1934 that area was invested with the promising title "Jewish Autonomous Region" (Oblast). But the official enthusiasm attending the proclamation of this project failed to stir the Jewish masses who viewed with cold skepticism the remote region with its inhospitable clime which, moreover, unlike Palestine, was for them a historical void. Only a small number responded to the call and today of the 165,000 inhabitants of Birobidzhan probably no more than 30,000 are Jews. Although lacking a predominant Jewish character the region has incongruously retained its official "Jewish" name.

But agrarianization provided only a partial remedy. It was not until the advent of large-scale industrialization under the Five Year Plans that a solution was found for the chronic unemployment afflicting the Jewish community. A large number of Jews streamed into the expanding industrial economy; and by 1939, 70 per cent of all gainfully employed Jews were engaged as wage-earners or salary-earners. The socioeconomic structure of R. Jewry had undergone a radical transformation.

Cultural Life. The standards of Soviet policy toward national minorities, though at first uniformly applied to all groups, dealt a particularly heavy blow to the integrity and viability of Jewish culture. By attacking the religious and Hebraic tradition Bolshevism struck at the lifeblood of Jewish culture. A fierce antireligious campaign destroyed thousands of religious schools, exiled or imprisoned numerous rabbis, and made the observance of religion, though not formally proscribed, the object of official derision and obloquy. Zionism was outlawed and denounced as a nationalistic movement serving British imperialism, and the teaching and fostering of the Hebrew language, intimately linked to Zionism, was proscribed. It must be emphasized that this assault on the traditional modes of expressing Jewish identity sprang not from anti-Semitism but from the general precepts governing Bolshevik conduct. In their stead the regime encouraged the cultivation of the Yiddish language which was raised to the status of a national language of the Jews. A growing network of Yiddish schools was erected comprising at its high-water mark, in 1930, 100,000 Jewish students. Three daily Yiddish newspapers were published, a Yiddish theater was subsidized, and Yiddish literature and linguistics were encouraged and introduced as academic subjects in universities. A large and prolific Yiddish literary community supported by the government, while laboring under the constricting demands of the official literary canons, created some works of enduring value which have become part of the world-wide Jewish literary heritage (P. Markish, D. Hofstein, L. Kvitko, I. Fefer, I. Kharik, D. Bergelson, M. Erik, and others). This cultural endeavor, Yiddish in form but predominantly Bolshevik in spirit, failed to command the affection or even the sustained interest of the nationally-minded or religious Jews who tended to regard its official promoters as traducers of the authentic tradition. The destruction of the institutions which had served to perpetuate Jewish culture set in motion a process of cultural dissolution hastened by the growing concentration of Jews in large cities where the powerful hold which the tradition ethos had exercised in the smaller, closely knit communities was greatly weakened. Russification and intermarriage were rampant. In 1897, 97 per cent of the Jews in Russia declared Yiddish as their mother tongue, in 1926, 72.6 per cent, and in 1959, 20.8 per cent. But the consciousness of identity remained alive even in those Jews who had embraced Russification, fed by the events of the war and by the disabilities and the terror which enveloped the Jews during the last years of Stalin's rule.

Jewish religious life survives in a vestigial form. No more than several scores of synagogues served by a diminishing number of aging rabbis are to be found within the confines of the Soviet Union in which, according to the census of 1959, 2,250,000 Jews live. A small theological school for the training of rabbis was recently established.

World War II. The Nazi design of extermination of European Jewry embraced the Jews in the territories of the Soviet Union conquered by the German Army. Some had fled with the retreating Soviet Army, but the majority remained in their homes to perish at the hands of special execution squads after a short confinement in ghettoes and concentration camps. It has been estimated that of the 3,000,000 Jews living within the Soviet boundaries of 1939, 1,000,000 were exterminated.

Behind the Soviet lines anti-Semitism reared its head nourished by the fearful suffering of the war; and the Soviet government, eager to secure the allegiance of the populace, chose not to combat it. This consideration also prompted it to cast a veil of silence over the singularity of the tragedy of the Jews under Nazi rule. The identity of the Jewish victims was obscured by referring to them by the general term "Soviet citizens"; and their mass graves were left unmarked and unhonored.

Anti-Semitism. Bolshevik ideology denounced anti-Semitism as incompatible with the socialist tenet of the brotherhood of all nations and as a tool serving the *bourgeosie* to divert the proletariat from its real enemies. During the civil war and the 1920's anti-Semitism was suppressed as an enemy of the Soviet cause. But from the early 1930's onward the dictates of expediency overrode adherence to the principle of enmity to anti-Semitism. The Soviet government, anxious to placate anti-Semitic sentiments, began to restrict the number of Jews in certain branches of the bureaucracy and in the universities. This policy of exclusion grew in 1948 into one of cultural obliteration. In that year Stalin, suspecting that Soviet Jews had now transferred their allegiance to the newly created state of Israel, of whose creation the Soviet Union had approved, resolved upon the extirpation of the residual cultural substance of the Jewish community. The Jewish anti-Fascist Committee created during the war was dissolved, the Yiddish theater was abolished, the publication of Yiddish books was suspended, and hundreds of Yiddish writers were imprisoned and the more prominent ones executed after a secret trial in Aug. 1952. All this took place to the accompaniment of a scarcely veiled campaign of distrust and calumny of the Jews; culminating in Jan. 1953 in the Doctors' Plot in which nine doctors, six of whom were Jews, were accused of having conspired at the behest of Western Powers and Jewish agencies to poison leading Soviet personalities. The death of Stalin put an end to the terror. Stalin's heirs, while repudiating the repressive measures of the past, including the Doctors' Plot, seem, however, to have retained Stalin's view of the Jews as inherent security risks. Continuing to pursue the objective of assimilating the Jews, they have refused to restore Jewish cultural institutions and to lift the ban on Yiddish literary activity. Only two volumes destined for foreign consumption have been published.

The treatment of the Jewish community by the Soviet government is conspicuously different from that accorded to other national minorities. Singled out for restrictions, smarting from the memories of the terror of Stalin's last years, exposed to the suspicion and ill-will of the Soviet leaders, the Jews, Russified and Yiddish-speaking alike, are keenly aware of their separate identity. The policy of enforced assimilation, far from achieving its aim, tends to strengthen Jewish consciousness. But apart from a handful of synagogues, any organized form of expression of that consciousness is proscribed. Such is the unique position of the Jews in the rich mosaic of Soviet national minorities.

BIBLIOGRAPHY: S. Dubnov, *A History of the Jews in Russia and Poland*, New York, 1916; Solomon Schwartz, *The Jews in the Soviet Union*, Syracuse, 1951; Editors of The New Leader, "Jews in the Soviet Union," *The New Leader*, Sept. 14, 1959; H. Levy, *Jews and the National Question*, New York, 1958.   E. G.

JUDAIZERS (*zhidóvstvuyushchie*), religious sect at the end of the 15th century in Novgorod. They were against church landed property, its hierarchy and monks. The J movement was suppressed at the beginning of the 16th century.

JOHVI: *see* YYKHVI.

JULY DAYS, 1917. The Provisional Government was unable to satisfy the demands of the peasants, soldiers, workers, and national minorities. In mid-July there came a crisis, the "bourgeois" ministers resigned, the crisis remained unsolved for several days. On July 1 delegates of several regiments in Petrograd demanded that the Bolshevik party lead an armed demonstration against the Provisional Government. At first the Bolsheviks considered the attempt premature and apparently hesitated to lead it, but as the demonstration progressed the Bolshevik Central Committee reversed its stand. On July 17 columns of soldiers, sailors and workers marched under the slogan "All Power to the Soviets." In various places government troops clashed with the demonstrators, and about 400 people were killed or wounded. The Mensheviks and the Socialist Revolutionaries urged the demonstrators to disperse, and the movement petered out. On July 18 the charge was officially made that Lenin and the demonstrators were guided by the German General Staff. "Neutral" regiments came out in support of the Provisional Government, while pro-Bolshevik soldiers shifted to "neutrality"; government troops occupied strategic points in Petrograd, raided Bolshevik organizations and arrested some of their leaders. Lenin fled to Finland. The Bolsheviks suffered a setback and their influence temporarily declined.   K. R. P.

K

KABALÉVSKY, Dmítry Borísovich (1904–), composer, born in St. Petersburg, graduated from Moscow conservatoire in composition (1929) but continued piano studies. Has been teaching at Moscow conservatoire since 1932. His first compositions were written in 1922. A prolific composer, K has produced piano concertos, quartets, ballet suites, sonatas, symphonies, romances, violin concertos, and scores for plays and motion pictures. Composed over 70 operas (*In the Fire; The Tarasov Family*, after a novel by Gorbatov; *The Invincible*). K's music is marked by melodic lilt, dynamic rhythm, and rich orchestration. Stalin prizes (1946, 1949, 1951).

KABARDÍNIAN-BALKÁRIAN ASSR, in the central part of the N. slopes of Caucasus Mts., part of RSFSR; area 4,825 sq. mi.; pop. 420,000 (1959): Kabardinians, Balkars, Russians, Ukrainians. Cities: Nalchik (capital), Prokhladny and others. Rivers: Terek, Malka, Baksan. Its mountains include some of the highest peaks of the Caucasus: Dykh Tau (17,050 ft.), Shkhara Tau (17,059 ft.), and Koshtan Tau (16,070 ft.). Agr.: cattle raising, horses, corn, millet, vegetables, vine. Has forests; tourism; resorts and mineral sources; a hydroelectric station on the Baksan River. Grozny-Almavir R.R., with branch to Nalchik. The total length of highways is over 1,000 mi.

KABLUKÓV, Iván Alekséyevich (1857–1942), physical chemist. Fellow, Ac. of S., USSR (1932). Professor, Moscow University (1903). Greatly contributed to the development of physical chemistry in the USSR.

KACHÁLOV (Shverubovich), **Vasíly Ivánovich** (1875–1948), noted actor; son of a priest, born in Vilna.

Studied law in St. Petersburg. In 1896 he became a member of the Society of Literature and Art in St. Petersburg, and in 1900 joined the company of the Moscow Art Theater, where he remained for the rest of his life. K's art is notable for its psychological depth and finesse of performance. He gave memorable characterizations of Tuzenbakh and Trofimov in Chekhov's *The Three Sisters* and *The Cherry Orchard*, Protasov in Gorky's *The Children of the Sun*, and in the parts of Julius Caesar and Hamlet in Shakespeare's plays, and Ivan Karamazov in the stage version of Dostoyevsky's novel.

KACHENÓVSKY, Mikhaíl Trofímovich (1775–1842), Russian historian and critic. He was editor of the periodical *Vestnik Yevropy* (The Messenger of Europe) and professor at Moscow University. A classicist in literature, he opposed romanticism. In history he was a pragmatist who doubted the veracity of the medieval chronicles.

KADETS: *see* CONSTITUTIONAL DEMOCRATIC PARTY.

KÁDIEVKA, city in Lugansk Oblast, Ukrainian SSR; pop. 180,000 (1959). Large ind. center of Donbas, with metalworks, beneficiation plants, coke and chemical factories.

KAFÁN, city in Armenian SSR; pop. 19,100 (1959). Has extensive mining and beneficiation of copper-zinc ores, Zangezur deposits; R.R. station.

KÁGAN, Veniamín Fyódorovich (1869–1953), mathematician. Honored Scientist, RSFSR (1929). Graduated, Kiev University (1892); professor, Moscow University (1923). Founder of Soviet school of tensor analysis in differential geometry. Author of *Principles of the Theory of Surfaces in Tensor Representation* (1947–48). Stalin prize (1943).

KAGANÓVICH, Lázar Moiséyevich (1893–), party and government official, born in Kiev Province of Jewish parents. In 1911, he joined the Kiev organization of the Bolshevik party; was an active participant in the Bolshevik revolution; and rose rapidly in party and government organizations. He was elected candidate  member of the Central Committee in 1923; a full member in 1924. From 1925 to 1928 he was first secretary of the Central Committee of the Ukrainian CP; in 1930 he became a member of the Politburo; 1930–35 was first secretary of the Moscow party committee. At the 17th CP Congress, 1934, he was elected chairman of the Party Control Commission which was responsible for carrying out the great purges which followed. By the end of the 1930's he had power not only in the party but also in the government, having control of transportation, heavy industry, oil and fuel industries, and was known as a strong organizer, planner, and "trouble shooter" in these fields. He played an important role in defense in World War II. As a member of the State Defense Committee in 1947, he was sent to the Ukraine to strengthen party cadres. In the post-Stalin reorganization, 1953, he was named first deputy chairman of the USSR Council of Ministers, and member of the Central Committee Presidium. His influence began to decline with Malenkov's loss of power and he was demoted from policy-making to administration. From May 1955 to June 1956 he was head of the State Labor and Wages Committee; in Sept. 1956 he became minister of the building materials industry. In June 1957 he was expelled from membership in the Presidium and Central Committee of the party for belonging to the "anti-party" group of Molotov, Malenkov, and Shepilov and was released from all government posts. Together with Molotov, he was considered a die-hard "Stalinist."

KAKHÓVKA, city in Kherson Oblast, Ukrainian SSR, on Dnieper River; pop. 19,200 (1956). Has R.R. station and hydroelectric power plant.

KAKHÓVSKY, Pyótr Grigóryevich (1797–1826), Decembrist of republican trend. He actively participated  in preparing the insurrection of Dec. 14, 1825, was an advocate of resolute actions such as seizing the Winter Palace and arresting the tsar's family, and mortally wounded General-Governor Miloradovich during the insurrection on the Senate Square. He was sentenced to death and hanged July 13, 1826.

KALÉDIN, Alekséy Maksímovich (1861–1918), tsarist general. A Cossack by origin, he took command of a cavalry division in Galicia shortly after 1914. In 1916 he led the 8th Army offensive at Lutsk. However, he soon found himself in disagreement with the policy of the Provisional Government and resigned in May 1917.

Returning to his native Don, and elected ataman of the Don-Cossack troops, he headed the anti-Bolshevik campaign, seized Rostov-on-Don but realizing his failure shot himself (Feb. 1918).

KALATÁ: *see* KIROVGRAD.

KALÍNIN (prior to 1931 Tver), city, adm. center of Kalinin Oblast, RSFSR, on left bank of the Volga at the confluence with the Tvertsa; pop. 261,000 (1959). R.R. station. Extensive ind.: railway-car building, textiles, leather goods, machine mfg., artificial fiber. There was mention of the city in the early 12th century. It was the capital of Tver principality for two centuries and was annexed by Moscow in 1485.

KALÍNIN, Mikhaíl Ivánovich (1875–1946), Bolshevik party and state leader, born in Tver Province in a  peasant family. From 1893, he worked in St. Petersburg at the Putilov factory. He joined the revolutionary movement in 1898. One of the first adherents of Lenin in Russia, K was repeatedly arrested. In 1912, he was elected candidate member of the Central Committee of the Bolshevik party. He was an organizer and active participant of the October revolution, and in March 1919, after the death of Ya. M. Sverdlov, he was appointed chairman of the All Russian Executive Committee of the Soviets, a post which corresponded to that of the head of state. In 1919, K was also elected a member of the Central Committee and, from 1926, a member of its Politburo. From 1938 to 1946, K was chairman of the Supreme Soviet of the USSR. A figure popular with party members, he was one of the rare old Bolsheviks who was not involved in opposition strife in the 1920's and 1930's, although he was said to be sympathetic with the rightist opposition of N. Bukharin and A. Rykov.

KALÍNIN OBLAST, RSFSR, N.W. of Moscow, on both banks of the upper Volga River; area 32,000 sq. mi.; pop. 1,802,000 (1959): Russians and Karelians. Cities: Kalinin (adm. center), Vyshny Volochek, Kimry, Rzhev, Torzhok, Ostashkov, Bezhetsk. Lowland, crossed by the Valday upland; mixed forests; temperate continental climate, podsol soils. Mineral resources: peat, lignite, building materials. Many lakes (the largest is Seliger Lake), pastures, forests; drained by the upper Volga and its tributaries. Specialized agr.: flax, potato growing, animal husbandry. Ind.: machinery, lumbering, textiles, leather goods, distilleries, flax processing (large combine at Rzhev). Crossed by a canal system connecting the Baltic Sea with the Volga. Est. 1935.

KALININGRÁD (f. Königsberg), city, adm. center of Kaliningrad Oblast, RSFSR, on Pregola River, a port on the Baltic Sea; pop. 204,000 (1959). Ind.: shipyards, railway-car and machine mfg., paper mills, food processing, textiles, chemicals, ironware, tobacco, brewery, distillery, cement. Was assigned to the USSR by the Potsdam Conference in 1945. Founded 1255; member of Hanseatic League 1365; birthplace of the philosopher Immanuel Kant.

KALININGRÁD OBLAST, RSFSR, S.E. coast of the Baltic Sea; area 5,828 sq. mi.; pop. 610,000 (1959). Cities: Kaliningrad (adm. center), Sovetsk, Chernyakhovsk. Pronounced glacial formations, numerous lakes known as the Masurian Lakes. Drained by the Neman, Pregola and other rivers. Maritime to temperate continental climate; heavy forested podsol soils. Mineral resources include peat, building materials, amber. Highly developed ind.: machine building, lumbering, food processing. Major agr.: dairy cattle, hog breeding, grain, fodder and vegetable crops, horticulture. Dense network of R.R.; highways, maritime and river transportation. Est. 1946, formerly part of E. Prussia, Germany.

KALÍNNIKOV, Vasíly Sergéyevich (1866–1901), composer. In 1892 graduated from the music school of the Moscow Philharmonic Society. The product of his early years was a symphonic poem, *The Nymphs* (1889). After graduation he composed *The Cedar and the Palm*, the overture *Tsar Boris*, and a prelude *In the Year 1812*; also *John of Damascus*, a cantata, and many romances. He became ill with tuberculosis and died in Yalta.

KÁLISH (Polish *Kalisz*), **TREATY OF**, concluded between Russia and Prussia in a coalition against Napoleon on Feb. 28, 1813 as a consequence of the French defeat in Russia and liberation movement in Prussia. It stipulates the restoration of Prussia within the 1806 boundaries, the independence of German states, and the commitment not to conclude separate peace with Napoleon.

KALMYK ASSR (KALMYKIA), RSFSR; area 29,-400 sq. mi.; pop. 183,000 (1959): Kalmyks, Russians. Capital: Elista. Has continental climate with hot summers and cool winters. Agr.: millet, wheat, corn; animal husbandry. Ind.: processing agr. products, construction material, light ind. In 1935, Kalmyk Autonomous Oblast was transformed into Kalmyk ASSR as part of RSFSR. In 1943 the Republic was liquidated, in 1957 restored as Kalmyk Autonomous Oblast, and in 1958 again transformed into Kalmyk ASSR.

KÁLNBERZINSH, Jánis Eduárdovich (1893–), party and government official, born near Riga. A CP member since April 1917, he took active part in the establishment of the Latvian Soviet Republic, 1919; then served as volunteer in the Red Army. After the civil war he studied in the Communist University in Moscow; then returned to Latvia as a party worker, leading the revolutionary underground work of Riga Communists. He was arrested and imprisoned in Riga (1939). After the occupation of Latvia by Soviet troops in 1940, he was released and elected first secretary of the Central Committee of the Latvian CP. During World War II he was one of the organizers of a Latvian Infantry Division. He was elected a member of the Central Committee, CPSU, at the 19th and 20th Congresses and in June 1957 was chosen candidate member of the Presidium. In Nov. 1959 he was relieved of his duties as first secretary of the Latvian CP Central Committee and in May 1960 was appointed deputy chairman of the Presidium of the Supreme Soviet of the USSR.

KALÚGA, city, adm. center of Kaluga Oblast, RSFSR, on left bank of the Oka; pop. 133,000 (1959). R.R. station. Ind.: R.R. equipment, machine mfg., match and furniture factory, pianos and accordions, sawmills. Dates back to 1389; was included in Moscow principality in 1518.

KALÚGA OBLAST, RSFSR, in Ugra-Oka river basin, between the Smolensk-Moscow upland (N.) and Central Russian upland (S.); area 11,500 sq. mi.; pop. 936,000 (1959). Cities: Kaluga (adm. center), Lyudinovo, Kirov, Borovsk, Kondrovo. Has hilly surface; pine, oak, birch, and aspen cover 20 per cent of its area. Mineral resources: lignite, peat, quartz. Agr.: basic crops, coarse grain, potatoes, hemp; dairy farming and cattle raising. Ind.: machine building, glass, leather, food processing, woodworking, papermill. Est. 1944.

KALYÁYEV, Iván Platónovich (1877–1905), member of the Socialist-Revolutionary terrorist group. He participated in the assassination of V. K. Plehve, minister of internal affairs, in 1904, and assassinated the general-governor of Moscow, Grand Duke Sergey, by throwing a bomb in 1905. He was executed in Schlüsselburg May 1905.

KÁMA RIVER, largest tributary of the Volga, about 1,260 mi. long; rises in N. border of Udmurt ASSR, flows N. in Kirov Oblast, in Perm Oblast, along W. slope of Middle Urals and in Tatar and Bashkir ASSRs to the Volga. Navigable; important part of Soviet transportation system and major source of water supply to regional chemical combines. Hydroelectric resources are considerable with Kama Hydroelectric Power Plant (near Perm), Votkinsk Hydroelectric Power Plant, and a plant in the Lower Kama region. Medium-size and small power plants are under construction along its tributaries, the Belaya, Vyatka, Chusovaya, Vishera.

KAMCHADALS: *see* ITELMEN.

KAMCHÁTKA: (1) Peninsula in N.E. Asia, 750 mi. long, extending S. between Sea of Okhotsk and Bering Sea to Cape Lopatka. Area, about 135,000 sq. mi.; drained by Kamchatka, Vacha, Bolshaya. Its mountain system, the Kamchatka Mountains, consists of two main ranges: the E. Range with about 100 volcanoes, 22 of them active (Klyuchevskaya, 15,900 ft., highest in Siberia), and the Central Range (R. *Sredinny Khrebet*) extending along the peninsula. Abounds in hot mineral sources; the only area in the Soviet Union where geysers occur. Mineral resources include sulfur, peat, coal. Cold humid climate. S. I. Krasheninnikov who lived in K from 1737 to 1741 greatly contributed to the study of its nature and population. **(2)** River of the peninsula, 478 mi. long; rises in Central Range, flows into the Pacific Ocean. Rapid current and an abundance of hot springs. **(3)** Bay, part of Pacific Ocean, at E. shore of peninsula, greatest depth 650 ft.

KAMCHÁTKA OBLAST, RSFSR, includes Koryak National Okrug, occupies the Kamchatka Peninsula, Commander Islands and several small islands; bounded by the Bering Sea (N.W.), Pacific Ocean (S.E.), and the Sea of Okhotsk (W.). Area 179,500 sq. mi.; pop. 220,000 (1959): Russians, Koryaks, Evenki, Aleuts. Adm. center Petropavlovsk-Kamchatsky, which was founded in 1740 by V. Bering. Est. 1932.

KÁMEN-ON-THE-OB (R. *Kamen-na-Obi*), city in Altay Kray, S.W. of Novosibirsk, RSFSR; pop. 24,400 (1959). Port on Ob River; food processing.

KÁMENETS-PODÓLSKY, city in Khmelnitsky Oblast, Ukrainian SSR, on Smotrich River, left tributary of the Dniester; pop. 33,300 (1956). R.R. station; agr. center. Ind.: food processing, lumbering, construction materials, tool mfg. Dates back to 12th century.

KÁMENETS-PODÓLSKY OBLAST: *see* KHMEL-NITSKY OBLAST.

KÁMENEV (Rosenfeld), **Lev Borísovich** (1883–1936), outstanding Bolshevik leader, born in Moscow of a middle-class family. Joined the Social Democrats in 1901 and became a Bolshevik. Arrested several times, K emigrated in 1908, together with G. Ye. Zinoviev, became a close associate of Lenin. Lenin sent him to  St. Petersburg to take over the editorship of *Pravda* and to assume the leadership of the Bolshevik members of the Duma. Early in World War I, K was directed by Lenin to organize a defeatist declaration by the Bolshevik deputies in the Duma. However, he was arrested on Nov. 4, 1914 and, together with all the Bolshevik deputies, sentenced to banishment for life to Siberia. After the February revolution, K returned to Petrograd and in company with Stalin led the Bolshevik party until Lenin's return from abroad. Being opposed to Lenin's policy of seizing power and advocating instead the establishment of a coalition government of all the socialist parties, K resigned from the Central Committee. However, after the October revolution, he returned and became first chairman of the Central Executive Committee of the Soviets.

K was also chairman of the Moscow Soviet (1919–26) and deputy chairman of the central Soviet government. From 1919 to Dec. 1925 he was a full member of the Politburo and from the latter date to Oct. 1926 a deputy member. During Lenin's illness and after his death, K, with Zinoviev and Stalin, formed a triumvirate to lead the party and state. In Nov. 1924, K and Zinoviev were attacked by Trotsky for their anti-Leninist and "defeatist" stand in 1917. After Trotsky's defeat, K was himself deprived of party and governmental power. He joined Trotsky and Zinoviev in the "new" anti-Stalin opposition. In 1926–27, he was Soviet ambassador to Italy. He was twice expelled from the party (1927 and 1932), but each time was readmitted upon recantation of his "heretical" views. After the assassination of S. Kirov (q.v.), K was sentenced in 1935 to five years' imprisonment for "moral complicity" in the murder. In 1936 he was re-arraigned at the first show trial of the period of purges, was condemned to death and executed. (*See also* OPPOSITION, PURGES, SHOW TRIALS, COMMUNIST PARTY OF THE SOVIET UNION)

KÁMENEV, Sergéy Sergéyevich (1881–1936), former tsarist colonel. He was one of the first who joined the Bolsheviks and became a commander of the Red Army during the civil war. From 1919 to 1924, he was commander in chief of the armed forces of the RSFSR; in 1925, chief inspector of the Red Army; and from 1927, deputy people's commissar of military and naval affairs.

KÁMENSK-SHÁKHTINSKY, city in Rostov Oblast, RSFSR, in Donets Basin; a port on the N. Donets River; pop. 58,000 (1959). R.R. station. Ind.: coal mining, agr. machine mfg., construction materials.

KÁMENSK-URÁLSKY, city in Sverdlovsk Oblast, RSFSR; pop. 51,000 (1939), 141,000 (1959). R.R. junction (Sinarskaya). Ind.: aluminum, pipe, metalworking, electrical plants. Founded at the end of 17th century.

KÁMENSKOYE: *see* DNEPRODZERZHINSK.

KAMÓ (Semyón Arshakovich Ter-Petrosyán) (1882–1922), a daring Communist "expropriator." Was in the revolutionary movement from 1897 and a Bolshevik from 1903. Repeatedly arrested and escaped. Was active in transporting weapons and in organizing escapes of Bolsheviks from prisons. In 1907, organized (under Stalin's supervision) robberies of banks in Tiflis and Kutais. In 1907 was arrested while transporting explosives and weapons in Berlin. In order not to be surrendered to the R. government, K simulated insanity for four years. In 1912 K was again arrested while attempting to rob a tax office. Was sentenced to death four times. After the October revolution K worked with the Cheka (*see* SECURITY POLICE) and in the Red Army. In 1922 he perished in an automobile accident.

KAMÝSHIN, city in Stalingrad Oblast, RSFSR, port on Volga River; R.R. station; pop. 55,000 (1959). Ind.: glassmaking, canning, meat processing, clothing. Major river-railroad reloading point (grain, salt, oil). Known since the 17th century.

KANDALÁKSHA, city in Murmansk Oblast, RSFSR; port on the White Sea; R.R. station; pop. 32,800 (1956). Extensive fishing. Ind.: aluminum, lumbering, fish canning, hydroelectric stations.

KANDIDAT NAUK, a graduate student who, after achieving the rank of *aspirant* (q.v.), has passed examinations and publicly defended a thesis.

KANDINSKY, Vasíly Vasílyevich (1866–1944), painter, a pioneer of abstract art. Studied law and economics at Moscow University. At the age of 30 he decided to devote himself to art and study painting under Franz von Stuck at the Academy of Munich. Founded a school of painting and a group known as "The Phalanx" (1902). After extensive travels (1904–08) K came to realize the significance of tone and form exclusive of subject matter in painting. His first nonobjective canvases created a sensation at the Sonderbund Exhibition (1912). Member of the "Blue Rider" group which included Klee, Marc, Macke, and others. Upon his return to Russia (1914) he was appointed professor at Moscow University and Academy. K continued his experiments in color organization and the relating of color and form to space in Germany (1921). Was professor at the Weimar Bauhaus and, with Klee, Jawlensky, and Feininger, member of the "Blue Four" group. Author of *The Art of Spiritual Harmony* (1912), *Point, Line and Plane* (1921). Flayed as "decadent" painter by the Nazis (1933), K moved to France where he spent the remainder of his life. Represented in the leading galleries of Europe and the United States.

KANSK, city in Krasnoyarsk Kray, RSFSR, on tributary of the Yenisey and on the Trans-Siberian R.R.; pop. 74,000 (1959). Near lignite and iron deposits. Ind.: cotton ginning, metalworking, sawmills. Founded 1640.

KANTEMIR, Prince Antiókh Dmítrievich (1708–1744), writer and philosopher, born in Constantinople. He contributed to the development of R. literary language and poetry. He wrote a philosophical treatise *Letters on the Nature of Man* (1742) and several fables. His main literary work consisted of nine satires in which he was a protagonist of education and public enlightenment. They were first published in 1762, eighteen years after the author's death.

KANTONISTS, sons of soldiers destined for military service from their birth. Peter I founded in 1721 schools for the education and military training of youths of this group. In 1798 these schools were renamed War Orphan Institutions and in 1805 their pupils received the name of K. Later the K were included in the so-called "military colonies," in which all boys from 7 to 18 were classified as K. In 1836 a few selected K were placed in schools for noncommissioned officers. Most of the K became soldiers at the age of 20. In the middle of the 19th century there were about 378,000 K. The K were abolished in 1856.

KANTORÓVICH, Leoníd Vitályevich (1912–), mathematician, specializing in techniques applicable to economic problems; corresponding member, Ac. of S., USSR (1958). K is a Soviet pioneer of linear programing, a mathematical technique for solving complex problems in economic analysis and planning. In 1939, K formulated the basic ideas of linear programing in a pamphlet on *Mathematical Methods for the Organization of Planning and Production*, but little attention was paid to his work. Linear programing was meanwhile independently rediscovered in the United States and developed into wide use, in conjunction with input-output analysis, with many potential applications for Soviet economic planning. Official Soviet interest in it, however, is still limited, and K's methods have not yet found acceptance with the State Planning Commission. K himself has recently been criticized by several Soviet economists for "slipping into the path of error" in his recent book, *The Economic Calculation of the Optimum Utilization of Resources* (1959) which provides a systematic exposition of general principles of rational resource allocation. Stalin prize (1949).

KAPELYÚSHNIKOV, Matvéy Alkunovich (1886–1959), petroleum engineer. Corresponding member, Ac. of S., USSR (1939). Honored Scientist and Technologist, RSFSR (1947). Graduated from Tomsk Institute of Technology; with Research Institute at Baku (1914–37). Suggested turbine well drilling (1922). Designed and built first Soviet cracking plant (1924–31). Clarified conditions of petroleum migration and formation of deposits.

KÁPITSA, Pyotr Leonídovich (1894–), physicist. Fellow, Ac. of S., USSR (1939), British Royal Society (1929). Honorary member, British Institute of Metals (1943); Franklin Institute, USA (1944); Danish and Irish Ac. of S. (1946); worked with A. F. Ioffe until 1921. Left USSR (1921) and worked at Cambridge University with E. Rutherford (1921–30); was assistant director, Cavendish Magnetic Research Laboratory (1924); director, Cambridge University laboratory (1930–34). Returned to USSR (1934) and was not

permitted to leave again. Director, Institute of Physical Problems, Ac. of S., USSR (1935–46 and since 1955). His initial research dealt with electron inertia and properties of radioactive emission. Designed equipment for powerful magnetic fields and observed splitting of spectral lines in magnetic fields of 320,000 gauss; discovered linear increase of metal resistivity as a function of magnetic field, and studied magnetostriction of diamagnetic bodies in these fields. Invented equipment (turbodetander) for temperatures near absolute zero to be used for the production of large quantities of liquid helium and oxygen. Developed hydrodynamic theory of bearing lubrication. After the invention of the atomic bomb K joined the Commission for the Study of Cosmic Radiation. In 1955 he suggested the hypothesis of spherical lightning. Supervises laboratories and experimental projects for development of atomic and hydrogen bombs and military use of cosmic ray energy. Author of *Turbodetander for Obtaining Low Temperatures and Its Application for Air Liquefaction* (1939); *Heat Transfer and Superfluidity of Helium II* (1941). Stalin prizes (1941, 1943).

KAPUSTÍNSKY, Anatóly Fyódorovich (1906–), chemist. Corresponding member, Ac. of S., USSR (1939). Graduate, Moscow University (1929); professor, Gorky University (1934–37), the Moscow Steel Institute (1937–41), Kazan University (1941–43), Institute of Chemical Technology in Moscow (1943). Associated with the Institute of Applied Mineralogy (1929–41), the Institute of General and Inorganic Chemistry, Ac. of S. (1941). Research concerns physical chemistry of metallurgical reactions, thermodynamics of chemical reactions, chemical technology, the history of R. chemistry. Member of the editorial board of *Bolshaya Sovetskaya Entsiklopedia* (The Large Soviet Encyclopedia) (1948).

KARABÁKH MOUNTAIN AREA: *see* NAGORNO-KARABAKH AUTONOMOUS OBLAST.

KARABÁSH, city in Chelyabinsk Oblast, RSFSR; pop. 25,400 (1959). R.R. station; copper mining and smelting.

KARÁ-BOGÁZ-GOL, large gulf, an inlet of E. Caspian Sea, on coast of Turkmen SSR, almost entirely enclosed on W. by a narrow strip of sand; area 7,000 sq. mi. Salt content over 30 per cent. Rich source of sulfates, sodium and magnesium chlorides, and bromium.

KARACHAI-CHERKESS AUTONOMOUS OBLAST, part of Stavropol Kray, RSFSR; on N. slope of Caucasus Mountains, bounded on S. by Georgia; area 5,500 sq. mi.; pop. 277,000 (1959): Karachai, Circassians (Cherkess), Russians. Center: Cherkessk. Mountainous, with lowlands in N.; fertile soils, temperate humid climate. Drained by the upper Kuban River and its right tributaries Maly and Bolshoy Zelenchuk. Min.: coal, copper, lead-zinc ores, barite. Agr.: wheat, rye, corn, horticulture, dairying, sheep raising. Ind.: food processing, coal mining, ore beneficiation. Est. 1922. In 1944 Karachai Autonomous Oblast was abolished but restored in 1957 combined with Circassian (Cherkess) National Okrug.

KARAGANDÁ, city, adm. center of Karaganda Oblast, Kazakh SSR; pop. 397,000 (1959). Third-largest Soviet coal-mining center, it supplies coal to S. Urals and other areas. Ind.: steel milling, mining-equipment mfg., concrete, brick plants. Has school of mining, and medical institute.

KARAGANDÁ OBLAST, Kazakh SSR, occupies most of the Kazakh desert and part of the Turan lowland; area 155,300 sq. mi.; pop. 1,022,000 (1959). Cities: Karaganda (adm. center), Dzhezkazgan, Kounrad, Temir-Tau, Balkash. Dry steppes and semidesert; is watered by the Nura and Sary-Su rivers. The Karaganda coal basin is third largest in the USSR; other minerals are copper, iron ore, manganese, molybdenum, corundum, lead, zinc. Ind.: ferrous metallurgy, machine building, structural material. Agr.: millet, wheat; sheep, camel, and cattle breeding. The Trans-Kazakhstan R.R. passes through Akmolinsk-Karaganda-Balkash with a branch to Baykonur. Est. 1932.

KARA GATES (R. *Kárskie Voróta*), strait between Novaya Zemlya and Vaygach Islands, connects Barents Sea with Kara Sea; width 30 mi.; frozen most of the year.

KARAGÍN ISLAND, W. Bering Sea, off E. coast of N. Kamchatka Peninsula; area 770 sq. mi. Tundra flora; reindeer breeding, fishing, hunting of fur-bearing animals.

KÁRA-KALPÁK ASSR (KARA-KALPAKIA), part of Uzbek SSR, S.E. of Aral Sea and N. of the Khiva oasis along the right bank of the Amu Darya and in the delta; area 60,500 sq. mi.; pop. 510,000 (1959): Kara-Kalpaks, Uzbeks, Kazakhs. Cities: Nukus (adm. center), Turtkul, Khodzheyli, Chimbay, Takhia-Tash. Much of it is desert (S.W. part of the Kyzyl Kum) with fertile regions along the river; dry continental climate. Agr.: cotton, rice, alfalfa in artificially irrigated areas; Kara-Kalpak sheep are bred in desert pastures; fishing in Aral Sea and the Amu Darya delta. Ind.: cotton ginning, alfalfa processing, canning. In the 16th century the Kara-Kalpaks were vassals of the khanate of Bukhara; until the middle of the 18th century they lived in the Syr Darya valley which was overrun by Dzhungars in 1723. Became Russian as part of Turkestan in 1867. Est. 1932.

KARAKHÁN, Lev Mikháylovich (1889–1937), Soviet diplomat, born in Kutais province. Joined the revolutionary movement in 1904. After the February revolution, was a member of the Presidium of the Petrograd Executive Committee of the Soviet of Workers' Deputies. In 1918, participated in the peace negotiations at Brest-Litovsk; in 1923, appointed ambassador to China. From 1917 to 1920, a member of the Central Committee. In 1937, accused of opposition activities and executed.

KARÁ-KIRGHÍZ: *see* KIRGHIZ.

KARAKLÍS: *see* KIROVAKAN.

KARAKÓL: *see* PRZHEVALSK.

KARAKÓZOV, Dmítry Vladímirovich (1840–1866), member of the Ishutin terrorist group. He made an abortive attempt at Alexander II in April 1866, for which he was tried and executed.

KARA-KÚL, lake on Pamir plateau, N.E. Gorno-Badakhshan Autonomous Oblast, E. Tadzhik SSR; area 140 sq. mi.; altitude 12,840 ft.

KÁRA-KUM: (1) Literally the "Black Desert," a desert area about 120,000 sq. mi., S. of Aral Sea, W. of the Amu Darya, including most of Turkmen SSR; drained only in S.E. by the Murgab and Tedzhen with large oases along these rivers. Pop. Turkmen. Rich source of sulfur; some oil. Cattle breeding (sheep, camels). **(2)** Aral K, sandy desert in Kazakh SSR, N.E. of Aral Sea, about 15,000 sq. mi. **(3)** Canal 60 mi. long; main irrigation system in S. Uzbek and Turkmen SSR's. Begins at the Amu Darya running W. to the Murgab and Tedzhen oases; designed to irrigate the S.E. part of the desert. Extension to Ashkhabad is planned.

KARAMZÍN, Nikoláy Mikháylovich (1766–1820), Russian historian and novelist born in the village of Mikhaylovka in the Orenburg province. After some studies in Moscow, K traveled in Europe in 1789, visiting Germany, France, Switzerland, and England. On his return, he published his *Letters of a Russian Traveller*, which were afterwards published  separately in six volumes (1797–1801). It was also in the *Moscow Journal* that K first published his prose stories, including *Poor Lisa*, Russia's first sentimental novel. In 1798 K published *The Pantheon,* a collection of translations of classics of world literature; and in 1802 he founded the monthly *Vestnik Yevropy* (The Messenger of Europe). From 1819 to 1826 K worked on his *History of the Russian State.* The *History* was left unfinished, and stops with the accession of Michael Romanov in 1613. It has been the subject of many criticisms—including some sarcastic ones by Pushkin—but it remains a landmark in R. history and literature. K's researches were pioneering. His sympathies were patriotic and monarchist, his style romantic and influenced by French writers.

KÁRA SEA, between the islands of Novaya Zemlya and Vaygach Island; greatest depth 2,000 ft.; area 340,000 sq. mi.; sharp changes in weather and heavy fogs. Main port: Dikson.

KÁRA-TAU: (1) mountain ranges in S. Kazakh SSR: N.W. spur of Tien Shan Mountains; highest peak, Mynzhilgi, 7,150 ft.; major deposits of phosphorites and nonferrous ores. Name derived from the Kazakh "kara" (black), and "tau" (mountain). **(2)** Mountain ridge on Mangyshlak Peninsula, Guryev Oblast, Kazakh SSR; highest peak, Besshoki, 1820 ft.; argillaceous slates, limestone, and sandrock.

KARAVÁYEVA, Ánna Aleksándrovna (1893–), lecturer and author, born in Perm, daughter of a minor government official. During the civil war she lectured to the Red Army and taught in Siberia. There she published her first story, *Under the Sparks,* and later *The Wing, Guest,* and *Red Color,* among others. In 1922 she joined the Communist party. K's story *Golden Beak,* about Altay workers in the 18th century, appeared in 1923, her novels *Lumber Mill* in 1928 and *Lena from* *the Cranes' Grove* in 1938. She also wrote a trilogy entitled *Native Land*. Stalin prize (1951).

KÁRSKIE VORÓTA: see KARA GATES.

KARDÓVSKY, Dmítry Nikoláyevich (1886–1943), painter, studied at St. Petersburg Academy of Fine Arts where he was Repin's pupil, and later in Munich. Specialized in book illustration (illustrated the works of Chekhov, Griboyedov, L. M. Leonov, and Aleksey Tolstoy). K produced numerous paintings, water colors, drawings, representing the era of Peter I, and that of Pushkin.

KARÉLIAN ASSR (KARELIA), in the N.W. part of the RSFSR; area 66,540 sq. mi.; pop. 649,000 (1959): Karelians, Finns, Russians. Cities: Petrozavodsk (capital), Sortavala, Belomorsk, Segezha, Kondopoga, Kem. Bounded on the N. by Murmansk Oblast, on the E. by the White Sea and the Archangel Oblast, on the S. by Vologda and Leningrad oblasts, and on the W. by Finland. It has low hills, numerous lakes, marshes and streams; abundant forests, cold climate, poor soil; hunting and fishing; hydroelectric stations on Kem and Suna rivers; rich fauna (wolf, brown bear, reindeer, fox). The Kirov R.R. and the White Sea-Baltic Canal run through its territory. Agr.: dairy and meat farming. Ind.: sawmills, pulp and paper, timber, furniture, prefabricated houses. Annexed by Moscow in 1478; in 17th century ruled by Sweden. The foundation of St. Petersburg was an important factor in the economic development of Karelia. Est. 1923.

KARÉYEV, Nikoláy Ivánovich (1850–1931). Russian historian. Studied at Moscow University. In 1879 K published *The Peasants and the Peasant Question in the French Revolution,* a pioneering study which revealed the distinctions between poor and well-to-do peasants, and attacked the thesis of Tocqueville that the prerevolutionary peasants were relatively well-to-do. In *The Chief Questions of the Philosophy of History* (1883–90) and *Essay on the History of the Reformation in Poland* (1886), his views were less radical. K was a prominent liberal and leader of the Constitutional Democrats. Under the Soviet regime, he returned to the study of the French Revolution. He became member of the Acad. of Sc. in 1929.

KARGÍN, Valentín Alekséyevich (1907–), chemist. Fellow, Ac. of S., USSR (1953). Graduate of Moscow University (1930). Associated with the L. Ya. Karpov Institute of Physics and Technology. Research on colloidal chemistry and high-molecular compounds; properties and composition of aluminum silicate compounds; thermodynamic, mechanical properties and viscosity of polymers. His findings are widely applied in synthetic fiber and rubber production. Three Stalin prizes and other decorations.

KARNAÚKHOV, Mikhaíl Mikháylovich (1892–1955), metallurgist. Fellow, Ac. of S., USSR (1953). Graduate of St. Petersburg Polytechnic Institute (1914); professor, Leningrad Polytechnic Institute (1927). Chief of the laboratory at the Institute of Metallurgy (1953). Research on physicochemical principles of steel smelting, particularly acid open-hearth furnace processes. Author of *Metallurgy of Steel.* Stalin prize (1943).

KARPÍNSK, (f. Bogoslovsk), city in Sverdlovsk Oblast, RSFSR, center of Bogoslovsk coal basin; pop. 48,300 (1958). Has R.R. station; extensive coal mining, machine mfg. plant; school of mining.

KARPÍNSKY, Aleksándr Petróvich (1846–1936), geologist. Fellow (1896) and first president-elect (1917),  Ac. of S. Graduate (1866) and professor (1877), Institute of Mines in St. Petersburg. Director, Geological Committee (1885–1903). Permanent representative at all international geological congresses. President, Mineralogical Society (1899–1936). Versatile research included paleontology, paleogeography, tectonics, mineral deposits, and petrography. Compiled geological maps of the Urals and the European part of Russia. Suggested the theory of the structure of the Russian Plateau which was to become a classic for the investigation of pleateaus, in general. Exerted considerable influence on the development of W. European geology. K's studies of paleobotanics (at the age of 60) led to invaluable discoveries in that field. Many geographical areas and research institutes bear his name, including a town in Sverdlovsk Oblast, a volcano in the Kuril Islands, a mountain in the N. Urals, the Geological Museum in Leningrad, and so forth.

KARPÓVICH, Mikhaíl Mikháylovich (1888–1959), historian. Born in Tiflis, studied at the Sorbonne, Paris, graduated from Moscow University. In May 1917 K came to the United States as a secretary of the R. embassy. From 1927 he was lecturer and, later, professor of R. history at Harvard University. Author of *Imperial Russia 1801–1917* (1932). K was editor of the Russian language *Novy Zhurnal* (New Review), New York. He played an important part in the promotion of Slavic, especially Russian, studies in the United States.

KARPÓVICH, Pyotr Vladímirovich (1875–1917), Socialist Revolutionary terrorist. K was expelled from the University of Moscow for participating in revolutionary student movements and went to study abroad. In Feb. 1901, soon after his return to Russia, K assassinated the minister of education, N. P. Bogolepov. He was sentenced to 20 years at hard labor, but in 1907 fled abroad and joined the Terrorist Organization of the Socialist Revolutionaries.

KARSÁVINA, Tamara (1885–), great ballerina of the Imperial Mariinsky Theater of St. Petersburg. She joined the Diaghilev (q.v.) Ballet from its inception, dancing the principal roles in most ballets, among them *Les Sylphides, Carnaval, Petrouchka, Giselle, Le Spectre de la Rose, Firebird, Daphnis and Chloe, Le Tricorne.* She has been living in London since 1917 and is the author of *Theatre Street,* an autobiography (1930).

KARSHÍ, city in Surkhan-Darya Oblast, Uzbek SSR, in Karshi oasis, drained by Kashkadarya River; pop. 30,000 (1959). R.R. station. Extensive agr., wheat, cotton, sericulture, orchards, and vineyards; ind.: cotton ginning, food processing. Residence of Tamerlane.

KARTASHÓV, Antón Vladímirovich (1875–1960), professor of church history and one of the founders of the Religious-Philosophical Society. K was a member of the Constitutional Democratic party. In 1917 he headed the department of Church Affairs in the Provisional Government. In 1919 he emigrated to France where he played a leading role in the training of young Russians for the priesthood. Author of a history of the R. church.

KASHÍRA, city in Moscow Oblast, RSFSR, on Oka River; pop. 22,200 (1956). R.R. station; ind.: plywood, railway servicing, boat mfg., macaroni plant; the Kashira Thermal Power Plant is one of the oldest in the USSR. Founded in 14th century.

KASHKÁ-DARYÁ OBLAST, Uzbek SSR, abolished Jan. 1960, incorporated into Surkhan-Darya Oblast.

KASSÍL, Lev Abrámovich (1905–), writer. His well-known book *Conduit* (1930), dealing with school life prior to the revolution, appeared in the magazine *Pioneer*; whereupon K joined its editorial board and began to write for children. His success as a journalist was due to his satirical sketches, which were bright, sharp, and apt. Many terms and phrases which he coined became part of everyday language in the Soviet Union. His publications include the book *Shvambrania* (1931), a sports novel *Goalkeeper for the Republic* (1937), *Cheremysh, the Hero's Brother* (1938), *Mayakovsky Himself* (1940), *My Dear Boys* (1944), and short stories, *The Street of the Younger Son* (1949, Stalin prize 1951), *Early Rising* (1953), and *A Grandson's Business* (1958). K's writings are romantic, heroic and humorous.

KASTÁLSKY, Aleksándr Dmítrievich (1856–1926), composer, choral conductor, and musicologist. A pupil of Tchaikovsky, Taneyev, and Hubert at the Moscow conservatoire (1875–82). In 1911 made an extended European tour and visited Warsaw, Vienna, Dresden, Florence, Rome, and other places. K taught conducting at the Moscow Philharmonic Institute (1912–22) and in 1923 was appointed professor of choral singing at the Moscow conservatoire. His compositions include: opera *Klara Milich* (after Turgenev) in 1916, *Requiem* (1916), *Rustic Symphony* (1925), *Stenka Razin* (1918)

KATÁYEV, Valentín Petróvich (1897–), novelist. Son of a high-school teacher in Odessa, his early poetry was published in local papers. Served in the artillery during World War I, and from 1918 to 1920 in the Red Army. In 1925 he wrote the novel *The Father* which deals with one of the tragic problems engendered by the revolution—the increasing conflict between sons and fathers. His next novels, *Embezzlers* (1926) and *Squaring the Circle* (1928), are light, witty, and amusing comedies, in which K kindheartedly depicts Russia and her people during the period of the NEP.

In 1932 he published the novel *Time Forward,* one of the few literary works in which the beginnings of industrialization are treated artistically and objectively. In 1936 K published a romantic and lyrical story, *The Lonely White Sail,* followed in 1937 by *I Am the Son of the Working People.* His wartime novels *Son of the Regiment* (1945, Stalin prize, 1946) and *For the Power of the Soviets* show him as a sincere and objective writer. His more popular plays are: *The Road of Flowers* (1934), *The Family House* (1944), *Day of*

Rest (later 1940's), and *The Electrical Machine* (1943).

KATKÓV, Mikhaíl Nikifórovich (1818–1887), journalist. After five years as professor of philosophy, Moscow University, he became editor of the paper *Moskovskia Vedomosti* (Moscow News) (1851). From 1856 to 1887 he published the magazine *Russky Vestnik* (Russian Courier), but returned to the *News* in 1863 to remain with it until his death. He came to exercise an influence in government circles unmatched by any other journalist of his time. Though a disciple of Belinsky in his youth, K became a reactionary and a nationalist in response to the rise of nihilism after 1861 and the Polish insurrection of 1863. Alexander II was greatly impressed by K's views.

KATTÁ-KURGÁN, city in Samarkand Oblast, Uzbek SSR; pop. 30,100 (1956). R.R. station. Extensive agr. center on Zeravshan River, with cotton growing, orchards, vineyards, wheat crops. Ind.: cotton ginning, oil extraction, engine-repair factory. Tremendous reservoir for irrigation of Samarkand and Bukhara oblasts.

KATÚN RIVER, in Altay Kray, RSFSR; source in Katun Range, Gorno-Altay Autonomous Oblast, flows N., joins the Biya to form the Ob. About 400 mi. long. Tributaries: Argut, Chuya, Syema. Gold, asbestos, copper, silver, and lead deposits in valley.

KÁTYN: *see* HISTORY.

KÁUFMAN, Konstantín Petróvich (1818–1882), general prominent in the conquest of Middle Asia. K began his military career in the Caucasus in the 1840's; from 1867 he was commander of the army of the military district of Turkestan. In 1868, he occupied Samarkand; in 1873, he conducted the campaign against the Khanate of Khiva; in 1875–76, he brought about the annexation of the Khanate of Kokand by Russia and was appointed governor-general of Turkestan.

KÁUNAS (f. Kovno), city in Lithuanian SSR, on the Neman River; pop 152,000 (1939), 214,000 (1959). Important R.R. junction. Ind.: metalworks, lumbering, paper mills, food processing, breweries, also has hydroelectric power plant. Founded in 11th century, it was the capital of Lithuania between the two World Wars; is seat of national university.

KAVÉLIN, Konstantín Dmítrievich (1818–1885), historian and political philosopher. He taught legal history at the University of Moscow and elsewhere from 1857 to his death. He considered the rise of Moscow historically inevitable. In his view the central R. state was not a result of popular initiative, but rather was imposed from above on the inert peasant mass; therefore he advocated a strong monarchy in his own time.

KAVÉRIN (Zilber), **Veniamín Aleksándrovich** (1902–), writer. Studied Oriental languages. Graduated from Petrograd University. Attempted to combine the modern approach with fantasy reminiscent of Hoffmann and Gogol, in the story *The Eleventh Axiom.* In 1927–28 K worked on the novel *The Unknown Artist,* in which he combined "psychological realism" with grotesque imagery traceable to Gogol. The book was a protest against the slavish subservience of art to communist ideology. In his further works—*The Ruffian, or Evenings on Vasily Island* (1928) and *The Fulfillment of Desires* (English translation—*The Larger View*)

(1935–36)—K marries "critical realism" with the style of a detective story. In his later works K returned to romantic subjects—*Two Captains* (1940–45, Stalin prize, 1946), and *Open Book* (1952–54).

KAVKÁZSKIE MINERÁLNYE VÓDY: *see* CAUCASIAN MINERAL RESORTS.

KAZAKH SOVIET SOCIALIST REPUBLIC (KAZAKHSTAN), the second largest republic of the USSR (1,062,500 sq. mi.), occupies the N. part of Soviet Central Asia and borders on China in the E., Siberia in the N., European Russia and the Caspian Sea in the W.,

and on the Turkmen, Uzbek, and Kirghiz SSR's on the S. It is divided into 1 kray (Virgin Lands Kray, R. *Tselínny Kray,* including Kokchetav, Kustanay, North Kazakhstan, Pavlodar oblasts, and the territory of former Akmolinsk Oblast under its jurisdiction); and Aktyubinsk, Alma-Ata, Dzhambul, East Kazakhstan, Guryev, Karaganda, Kzyl-Orda, Semipalatinsk, South Kazakhstan, and West Kazakhstan oblasts. Capital, Alma-Ata (456,000); other large cities are Karaganda (397,000), Semipalatinsk (156,000), Chimkent (153,000), Petropavlovsk (131,000).

Population (1959) is 9,310,000 (density 8.8 per sq. mi.); this includes 4,014,000 Russians (43.1%), 2,755,-000 Kazakhs (29.6%), 762,000 Ukrainians (8.2%), 192,000 Tatars (2.1%), 137,000 Uzbeks (1.5%), 108,-000 Byelorussians (1.2%), 74,000 Koreans (0.8%),

60,000 Uygurs (0.6%), 53,000 Poles (0.6%), 10,000 Dungans (0.1%), and 1,145,000 unaccounted for (12.2%). Since even such small native groups as the Dungans were counted, almost all the unaccounted people should be considered non-natives. The largest group among them is probably the Germans deported during World War II from the then liquidated Volga German Republic. Chechen, Lithuanian, Latvian, Estonian, and other deportees cover the rest of the "unaccounted" persons. In all about two-thirds of the K population is non-native and Kazakhstan should now be regarded as a basically R. area. Not only did Kazakhs become a minority group in their "own" republic, but between 1926 and 1939 their number decreased by about one million. Resistance to forced collectivization, disappearance of the old nomad Kazakh way of life, and increasing immigration of outside elements (deportees, industrial workers, technicians, "virgin land" pioneers) are the main causes for such a drastic shift in the national structure of K.

Nature and Climate. K is a large lowland, bordered by mountain chains in the S.E. and by the Caspian Sea in the W. The Caspian depression and the Turan lowland occupy the S.W. part of K; the central K upland, the central and the E. parts. In the N., along the Ishim and Irtysh rivers, the Siberian-type black-soil steppes begin; in the N.W. are located the Mugodzhary mountains which connect with the S. Urals. Various types of desert (sand, clay, salt, and stone) and "hungry" (dry) steppes occupy most of the territory, while the arable lands are confined to the extreme N. and N.E. ("virgin

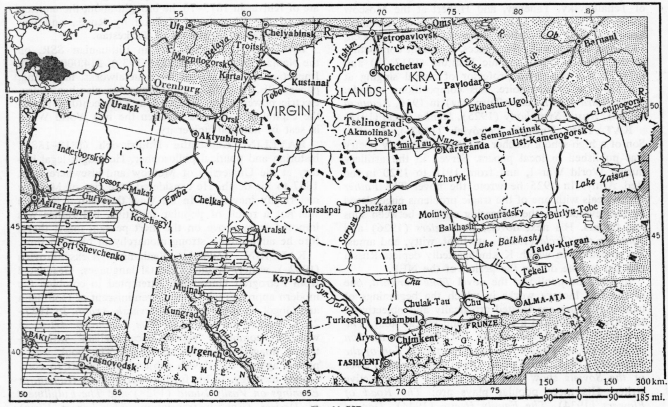

Kazakh SSR

lands") and to the S.E. (irrigated areas, along the Syr Darya, Arys, Talas, Chu, Ili, and Kara-Tal rivers). Most of the rivers belong to several inland basins: the Ural and Emba flow into the Caspian Sea; the Syr Darya into the Aral Sea (the fourth largest inland lake in the world, 25,475 sq. mi.), bordering on both K and Uzbekistan; Ili into Lake Balkhash; the Talas and the Chu flow into the desert, and only the Irtysh and its tributaries flow north through W. Siberia to the Kara Sea and the Arctic Ocean. The climate everywhere is very dry. The average Jan. temperature is below freezing; the average in July is 82° F in the S., 68° F in the N. The rainfall decreases from north to south leaving the greater part of K without sufficient precipitation.

National Economy. The main branches of industry are: ferrous and nonferrous metallurgy, coal mining, and oil, metalworking, chemical, light, and food industries. The agricultural emphasis is on grain (in the N. and N.E.) and cattle breeding (in the center, S., and S.W.). The irrigated land in the S. produces cotton and sugar beets. K produces more than three-fourths of all the lead extracted in the USSR, two-fifths of all the zinc and copper. Gold, silver, molybdenum, and other rare metals are also found. The nonferrous metallurgy is concentrated in the East Karaganda, South K, and Alma-Ata oblasts; the ferrous metal industry in Karaganda, Pavlodar, and Kustanay oblasts. K has large iron ore reserves. Coal is extracted in the Karaganda and Ekibastuz basins, oil in Guryev and Aktyubinsk oblasts. It is also very rich in phosphorite deposits. The arable lands increased several-fold since 1913. Recently, Soviet efforts have been concentrating on developing the "virgin lands" of northern K. Hundreds of thousands of young settlers were induced to migrate to that area from European Russia. Cattle breeding is of great importance, but it has still failed to recover from the heavy losses suffered during the forced collectivization when over 85 per cent of the cattle perished. (For history and culture, *see* TURKESTAN.)   M. R.

KAZALÍNSK, town in Kzyl-Orda Oblast, Kazakh SSR, on Syr Darya River; pop. 7,800 (1957); agr. center (rice, wheat), fish-canning, brick factories.

KAZÁN, capital of Tatar ASSR, on the left bank of the Volga; pop. 647,000 (1959). Ind. and cultural center, with chemicals, pelting, felt boots, leather, textiles, soap, food processing, machine mfg. ind.; a university, and a branch of the Ac. of S., USSR. Founded in 13th century, it was the capital of the Kazan Khanate in the 15th century; has numerous historical monuments. Lenin and the outstanding mathematician Lobachevsky studied at the University of K.

KAZÁN, KHANATE OF. Founded about 1438 after the disintegration of the Golden Horde. Its independent existence lasted little over a century, until its conquest and incorporation in Russia by Ivan IV in 1552.

KAZÁNSKY, Borís Aleksándrovich (1891–), organic chemist. Fellow, Ac. of S., USSR (1946). Graduate (1918), professor (1935), Moscow University. Founder and director, Laboratory of Catalytic Synthesis, Institute of Organic Chemistry (1936); director, Institute of Catalytic Synthesis (1954). Research concerns catalytic conversion of hydrocarbons; suggested conversion of five-membered hydrocarbons into structure of paraffin hydrocarbons; and aromatization reactions with various catalysts. Stalin prize (1949).

KAZARNÓVSKY, Isáak Abrámovich (1890–), chemist. Corresponding member, Ac. of S., USSR (1939). Graduate of Zurich University, Switzerland (1914). Associated with the Karpov Institute of Physical Chemistry, Moscow (1922). Research on formation and structure of chlorides and metal oxides. Discovered several higher oxides and explained their structure. Developed an industrial method for the regeneration of air. Stalin prize (1941).

KAZBÉK, peak in central Caucasus Mts., Georgian SSR, (16,554 ft.). An extinct volcano with a double-summit cone, steep slopes, towering above the Daryal Gorge; has eight glaciers; first climbed 1868; subject of many legends.

KÁZIN, Vasíly Vasílyevich (1898–), poet. Has been publishing since 1914. After the revolution he joined the *Kuznitsa* (Smithy) group. In 1922 K brought out a collection entitled *Workers' May* which was hailed by Soviet critics as "the most poetic page in proletarian literature." Nevertheless, for the poem *The Fox-Fur Coat and Love* (1925–26) and the collection *Confessions* (1928), the official critics branded K "decadent" and "renegade." Since the death of Stalin, some of his poems have appeared in Soviet magazines but they are rather weak and colorless.

KEBIN, Iván (Johannes) Gustavovich (1905–), Estonian communist, born into a farm family. He moved to St. Petersburg in 1910; studied in the Leningrad Soviet Party School in 1925–26; graduated from the Moscow Institute of Red Professors in 1938; held several posts in the propaganda apparatus; in 1941 became deputy chief of the propaganda department, central committee, Estonian CP. Since 1948 he has been secretary of the central committee of the Estonian CP; since 1950, first secretary. He was elected to the Central Committee, CPSU in 1952 and 1956; elected a member of the Presidium, CPSU, in 1956. He is also deputy of the USSR Supreme Soviet.

KÉLDYSH, Mstislav Vsevolodovich (1911–), mathematician and mechanical engineer. Fellow, Ac. of S.,  USSR (1946). Professor, Moscow University and Moscow School of Technology. Director, Department of Applied Mathematics, Mathematical Institute Ac. of S. (1960). Research on vibration, aerodynamics, wave propagation. Author of *Vibrations of Wings with Inclined Supports in the Air Current* (1938); *On the Representation of Functions of a Complex Variable by Series of Polynominals in a Closed Domain* (1945); *Shimmy of the Front Wheel of the Tricycle Landing Gear* (1945). Stalin prizes (1942, 1946). In May 1961 K was elected President, Ac. of S.

KÉLLER, Borís Aleksándrovich (1874–1945), botanist and ecologist. Fellow, Ac. of S., USSR (1931). Honored Scientist, RSFSR (1929) and Turkmen SSR

(1944). Graduate, Kazan University (1902); professor, Voronezh Agricultural Institute and University (1913). Director, Botanical Gardens (1937–45); Turkmen branch of the Ac. of S. (1941–45). Research concerned new techniques for the study of the interaction between plant and its environment. Introduced the geographical concept "semidesert" and classified the flora of the steppe and semidesert. Author of *The Study of the Evolution of Plant Life* (1948).

KEM, city in Karelian ASSR, in delta region of the Kem River; pop. 16,000 (1956); a port; also has a R.R. station, and extensive lumbering. Site of Uspensky Cathedral (1714).

KÉMEROVO (f. Shcheglovsk), city, adm. center of Kemerovo Oblast, RSFSR; pop. 133,000 (1939), 278,-000 (1959). On Tom River in Kuznetsk Basin; R.R. station connected to Trans-Siberian RR. Has extensive mining, coke-chemical ind., coal, machine mfg.; power plant; school of mining.

KÉMEROVO OBLAST, RSFSR; area 36,860 sq. mi.; pop. 2,788,000 (1959): Russians, Shors. In S.E. of West Siberia, between the Salair Ridge and Kuznetsk Ala-Tau; crossed by Trans-Siberian R.R. Cities: Kemerovo (adm. center), Stalinsk, Prokopyevsk, Leninsk-Kuznetsky, Anzhero-Sudzhensk, Belovo, Guryevsk, Salair. Has hilly steppes and heavy forests, continental climate, and is watered by the Tom and Kiya rivers. Is a highly developed industrial area, with coal production in Kuzbas (Kuznetsk Basin, the second largest coal basin in the USSR); also iron ore, zinc, gold, dolomite, chemicals, ferrous and nonferrous metallurgy, machine building. Agr.: dairy farming, grain crops, cattle raising; lumbering, fur trapping. Est. 1943.

KERCH, city in E. Crimea, Ukrainian SSR, pop. 104,500 (1939), 99,000 (1959). Active seaport on Kerch Strait, also a R.R. terminus, has large iron-ore deposits; its ind. includes extensive mining, machine mfg., tobacco plants, canning, metalworks, shipyards, construction materials, fishing (herring). One of the oldest S. cities, it was founded by the Milesians 600 B.C. as Greek colony Panticapaeum, part of the Kingdom of Bosporus. It was conquered by Pontus, held by Huns, Khazars, and others; from the 14th to 15th centuries it was held by Genoese as a trading port, eventually seized by Turks; conquered by Russia in 1774. Extensive archaeological excavations in vicinity; metallurgical school.

KERCH PENINSULA, extending E. of the Crimea, Ukrainian SSR; area about 1,160 sq. mi. Hilly, variegated clays, limestone; salt lakes and mud springs; rich iron deposits, natural gas fields.

KERCH STRAIT (ancient *Bosporus Cimmerius*), lies between the Kerch Peninsula in the W. and the Taman Peninsula in the E.; connects the Black Sea with the Sea of Azov.

KÉRENSKY, Aleksándr Fyódorovich (1881–), lawyer, member of the State Duma, and president of the Provisional Government. Born in Simbirsk, K studied in Tashkent and upon graduation from the University of St. Petersburg in 1904 became a lawyer. He joined the Socialist Revolutionary party, probably in 1905,

and later attracted attention as a public speaker and defense counsel in political cases. In 1912 he was elected to the fourth State Duma as a representative of the Labor Group (q.v.). During the revolution of February-March 1917 K became deputy chairman of the Petrograd Soviet and minister of justice in the Provisional Government. In June 1917 he was made president of the Provisional Government and simultaneously held the portfolios of war and navy. In Sept. 1917, following the Kornilov affair (q.v.), K became commander in chief. On Oct. 25, 1917 (O.S.), when the Bolsheviks overthrew the Provisional Government, K escaped from Petrograd in an unsuccessful attempt to organize resistance to the Soviets. Soon thereafter he went abroad, where he carried on anti-Soviet activities.

K published in English *Prelude to Bolshevism* (1919), *Allied Policy Towards Russia* (1920), *The Catastrophe* (1927), and *The Crucifixion of Liberty* (1934); his reminiscences of 1917 have appeared in German (1928) and in French. He published in Russian *The Kornilov Affair* (1918) and a collection of essays *From Afar* (1922). K was the editor of the newspaper *Golos Rossii* (Voice of Russia, Berlin) and of the journals *Dni* (Days, Berlin and Paris) and *Novaya Rossiya* (New Russia, Paris). Shortly before World War II K came to the United States where he contributed to Russian-language publications and was active, especially since 1945, in organizing Russian *émigrés*, both old and new. In the late 1950's K directed at Stanford University a research project bearing on the history of the Russian Revolution. Three volumes of documents dealing with the Provisional Government were reported ready for publication at the end of 1960.

KÉRES, Pavel (Paul) **Petróvich** (1916–), chess player, Grand Master of chess since 1940; champion of the USSR (1947, 1950, 1951).

KÉRZHENTSEV (Lébedev), **Platón Mikháylovich** (1881–1940), historian and politician, member of CP from 1904, and Soviet diplomatic representative in Sweden (1921–23) and Italy (1925–26). In the thirties he occupied a prominent post in the Soviet radio and the government commission for the fine arts. He wrote the *Irish Struggle for Independence* and *History of the Paris Commune of 1871.*

KET RIVER, in Tomsk Oblast, RSFSR; rises N. of Krasnoyarsk, flows W. into Ob River at Kolpachevo, 505 mi. long; navigable.

KGB: *see* SECURITY POLICE.

KHABÁROVSK, city in Khabarovsk Kray, Soviet Far E., RSFSR; pop. 207,000 (1939), 323,000 (1959). Major river-rail transfer point on the Trans-Siberian line, at the confluence of the Amur and the Ussuri. In the past an agr. and fur-trading town, it is now the center of many essential ind., including machinery and shipbuilding, oil refining, woodworking, food processing, and light goods.

KHABÁROVSK KRAY, Far E., RSFSR; area 318,-500 sq. mi.; pop. 1,143,000 (1959). It includes the Jewish Autonomous Oblast. Cities: Khabarovsk (adm.

center), Komsomolsk-on-Amur, Sovetskaya Gavan, Birobidzhan, Nikolayevsk. It is washed by the Sea of Japan and the Okhotsk Sea. It is largely a heavily forested mountainous country crossed by the Sikhote-Alin, Dzhugdzhur, and other mountain ranges extending parallel to the seacoast. Main rivers: Amur, Bira, Bidzhan, Amgun, Ussuri, Bureya. A distinct monsoon climate, with some local variations. An economic region of major importance, it ranks first in seal hunting and reindeer breeding, second as fish and fur producer, and third in gold mining. New, extensively mechanized ind. have been developed, including oil refining, metalworking, machine-making, shipbuilding, timbering, food processing, and light mfg. Recent advances in agr. techniques mark increased acreage under grains and fodder crops, rapid growth of truck farming and cattle breeding for milk and meat. Next to the Trans-Siberian R.R. crossing the kray, river and sea transport is of vital importance for the regional economy, as well as air routes linking the remote sections with the center. Est. 1938.

KHACHATURYÁN, Aram Ilyich (1903–), composer, born in Tbilisi. In 1921 entered the Gnesin Musical School Moscow. Studied cello and composition. Graduated from Moscow conservatoire (1934). His trio and piano *Toccata* followed by the *Danse Suite* brought him recognition in 1932. Completed his First Symphony in 1934. K's piano concerto composed in 1937 abounds in Armenian folklore themes. The violin concerto written for David Oistrakh (q.v.) is internationally known. The ballet *Spartacus* was completed in 1953. K's music is marked by a richness of tonal shades and original rhythms. He also composed romances, a concerto for cello, and scores for moving pictures. Stalin prizes (1941, 1943, 1946, 1950), Lenin prize (1959).

KHAKÁSS AUTONOMOUS OBLAST, E. Siberia, RSFSR; area 23,700 sq. mi.; pop. 414,000 (1959): Russians and Khakass. Cities: Abakan (adm. center), Chernogorsk. Occupies the S.W. sector of Krasnoyarsk Kray, extending along the left bank of the Yenisey upon the wooded slopes of Kuznetsk Ala-Tau and the Sayans, in the W. portion of the Minusinsk depression. The region is rich in mineral resources, including the Minusinsk coal basin, iron, barite, and gold placers. Timber and the lumbering ind. based on coniferous mountain forests are the main occupations of the Khakass natives, as well as livestock breeding for hides, wool, and meat. Recently developed irrigation farming emphasizes basic grains and fodder crops. Navigation is maintained on the Yenisey and its tributary, the Abakan River. Est. 1930.

KHALTÚRIN, Stepán Nikoláyevich (1856–1882), revolutionary. He organized the Workers' Union of North Russia in 1878; later he joined a populist group engaged in terrorist activity. In 1880 he attempted to kill Alexander II by trying to blow up the Winter Palace (residence of the tsar). In 1882 he was executed for participating in the assassination of Strelnikov, Military Procurator of Odessa.

KHÁMAR-DÁBAN RANGE, S. of Lake Baykal, Buryat ASSR; greatest altitude 9,050 ft.; iron, gold, mica among deposits.

KHÁNKA, lake along Soviet-Chinese border in Maritime Kray; area 1,700 sq. mi.; much fish.

KHANKENDY: *see* STEPANAKERT.

KHAN-TÉNGRI MOUNTAIN, highest in Tien Shan range on the Soviet-Chinese border; height 22,950 ft.

KHANTÝ-MANSÍ NATIONAL OKRUG, in Tyumen Oblast, W. Siberia, RSFSR; area 227,000 sq. mi.; pop. 124,000 (1959): Khanty (Ostyaks), Mansi (Voguls), Russians, and others. Principal cities and settlements: Khanty Mansiysk (adm. center), Kondinskoye, Berezovo, Samarovo, Laryak. Formerly the Ostyak-Vogul National Okrug, it is a vast marshland region in the tayga belt of the W. Siberian lowlands, part of the lower Ob and Irtysh river basin. Timbering (largely mechanized in recent years), fur trapping, and fishing (motorized fleets) are the major occupations. Reindeer, meat and dairy cattle are raised extensively. Potato farming and truck gardening are important, with increased acreage under grain cultures. Rock crystal, platinum, and Iceland spar are mined on the N. slopes of the Urals. Fish canneries, sawmills are centered in Khanty-Mansiysk. Est. 1930.

KHANTÝ-MANSÍYSK (f. Ostyako-Vogulsk), city, adm. center of Khanty-Mansi National Okrug, W. Siberia, RSFSR; pop. 22,000 (1959). A recently developed town, at the junction of the Ob and Irtysh rivers, it is the focal point of all regional air routes.

KHARITÓN, Yúly Borísovich (1904–), physicist and physical chemist. Fellow, Ac. of S., USSR (1953). Deputy to the Supreme Soviet, USSR (1954, 1958). Graduate of Leningrad Polytechnic Institute (1925). Worked under E. Rutherford in England (1927–28). Associated with the Institute of Physical Chemistry, Ac. of S., since 1931. Research on the condensation of molecular beams of metallic vapors under vacuum on cooled surfaces and development of the theory of condensation. Discoverer of the phenomena of lower limit of ignition of phosphorus vapors which served as a basis for further investigations of chain reactions in splitting uranium. Determined relation between explosive capacity of substances and speed of chemical reaction.

KHÁRKOV (Ukr. *Kharkiv*), city, adm. center, Kharkov Oblast, Ukrainian SSR; pop. 934,000 (1959). Sixth largest city of the USSR, it is a major ind., distributing, and cultural center, with vital rail connections. Has a large number of higher educational institutions including a noted university founded in 1805. Besides light mfg. and food processing, the city's great ind. plants turn out turbine generators and tractors, Diesel engines, coal-mining and oil-drilling equipment, locomotives, harvester combines, ball bearings and machine tools. The principal air routes connect it with Moscow, Kiev, Odessa, and Baku. Founded in 1654, was capital of Ukrainian SSR 1921–34.

KHÁRKOV OBLAST, Ukrainian SSR, N.E. sector; area 12,160 sq. mi.; pop. 2,517,000 (1959). Cities: Kharkov (adm. center), Kupyansk, Izyum. It is a highly industrialized region occupying the N. outspurs of the Donets ridge and the S.W. outliers of the Central R.

plateau, largely in the black-earth belt, and is drained by the N. Donets with its left tributary, the Oskol, and by the Orel and Samara rivers, of the Dnieper basin. Has moderate continental climate; mixed broad-leaved and pine forests in the N.W. section. Technical crops (sugar beets in the N., sunflowers in the S.) and basic grains are cultivated extensively in the steppes of the S. sector; peat, phosphorites, building materials are mined. Light mfg. and heavy ind. are concentrated in Kharkov and other regional centers. Est. 1932.

KHÁTANGA RIVER, in Krasnoyarsk Kray, formed through the merger of Kotuy and Kheta rivers. Empties into the Khatanga Gulf of the Laptev Sea. Length 715 mi.; navigable.

KHAZÁRS, an ancient people, composed of many different tribes but, predominantly, of Turkic origin. The K formed a large, independent state in the seventh century which extended from the lower Volga to the Caucasus and the Crimea (cities, Belendzher, Itil, Sari-cel). The K state developed trade between the Far East and Arabia and the Slavic countries. The dynasty and ruling class of the K embraced Judaism (746). The K state fell in the second half of the 10th century after Svyatoslav, duke of Kiev, defeated Itil (969). Some R. Jews are supposedly descendants of K.

BIBLIOGRAPHY: Douglas M. Dunlop, *The History of the Jew-ish Khazars,* Princeton, 1954.

KHEM-BELDYR: *see* KYZYL.

KHEMNÍTSER, Iván Ivánovich (1745–1784), writer of fables. Most of them depict such common human failings as pride, cupidity, arrogance, and selfishness.

KHERÁSKOV, Mikhaíl Matvéyevich (1733–1807), writer of the pseudo-classical school and a versatile author. He wrote comedies, dramas, novels, odes, poem *Rossiáda* (1779) which depicts the conquest of Kazan by the Tsar Ivan the Terrible. The theme of another poem, *Vladimir Reborn* (1785), is the introduction of Christianity into Russia.

KHERSÓN, city, adm. center of Kherson Oblast; pop. 158,000 (1959). Situated on the right bank of the Dnieper near its mouth in the Black Sea, it is an important river port and terminal of the new R.R. connecting the region with the Crimea. Manufactures agr. machinery and road-construction equipment, building materials, glassware; has extensive shipyards and R.R. repair shops, flour mills, canneries, and food-processing plants.

KHERSÓN OBLAST, Ukrainian SSR, S. sector; area 10,460 sq. mi.; pop. 824,000 (1959). Cities: Kherson (adm. center), Genichesk, Kakhovka. Dry flatlands in lower Dnieper region bordering on Black Sea and Sea of Azov, with fertile black earth and chestnut soils supporting extensive cultivation of grains and technical crops (wheat and sunflowers predominating). Orchards and vineyards, livestock breeding, and poultry farming are an important sector of the rural economy. Mineral resources include building materials (limestone, sand-stone, refractory clays), sodium, and magnesium salts; fishing industries, river and seacoast shipping are essential; heavy machine-building plants are centered in Kherson city. Est. 1944.

KHIBINOGÓRSK: *see* KIROVSK.

KHÍNCHIN, Aleksándr Yákovlevich (1894–1959), mathematician. Fellow, Ac. of Pedagogical Sciences (1944). Professor, Moscow University (1922). Research on the application of the theory of probability to statistical physics, mechanics, technology. Author of 151 publications on the theory of probability, number theory, theory of functions of a real variable, mathematics and methods of teaching it, quantum statistics. Stalin prize (1941).

KHINCHÚK, Lev Mikháylovich (1868–?), Soviet diplomat. In the revolutionary movement from 1889. In 1903 he was a Menshevik. In 1905 K was one of the organizers of the St. Petersburg Soviet. After the February revolution, was chairman of the Moscow Soviet. In 1920 K joined the Bolsheviks. He held important positions in the economic apparatus, and was made ambassador to England in 1926, and ambassador to Germany in 1930.

KHÍUMA (Hiiumaa, Dagö), Estonian island in Moonzund Archipelago, Baltic Sea; area 370 sq. mi.; fishing, farming, livestock.

KHIVÁ, city in Khorezm Oblast, Uzbek SSR; pop. 16,700. Ancient oasis town in the lower Amu Darya region, known before the 7th century. Former capital of the Khorezm exclave, and of the Khiva khanate. Is noted for the excellence of local handicrafts (rug making, wood carving). Cotton-ginning plants and creameries principal ind. Historical monuments.

KHIVÁ KHANATE, a feudal kingdom in central Asia formed in the 16th century along the lower reaches of the Amu Darya. It was populated by Uzbeks, Turkmen, Karakalpaks, and others. In 1873 it was incorporated into the R. Empire.

KHLÉBNIKOV, Víktor (Velémir) Vladímirovich (1885–1922), writer. Founder of Russian futurism. He changed his first name to the old Slavonic surname *Velemir.* Prior to World War I, K created nonobjective poetic vocabulary in an attempt at freeing words from their meanings. His first "etymological" poem (1910) concerned newly invented variations of the word "laughter" (*smekh*). After World War I, he renounced abstract images and wrote pacific antimilitaristic poems ("War in a Mouse Trap," "Night in a Trench"). K exerted a strong influence on R. prerevolutionary literature.

KHLÓPIN, Vitály Grigóryevich (1890–1950), chemist. Fellow, Ac. of S., USSR (1939). Honored Scientist and Technologist, RSFSR (1940). Graduate of Goettingen University (1911) and St. Petersburg University (1912). Associated with the Radiological Laboratory (1915–21) and the Radium Institute (1922), Ac. of S., of which he became director (1939). Directed the establishment of the first Soviet radium plant (1918–21); determined the law governing the distribution of microcomponents at the solid-liquid interface which bears his name. Research in chemistry and geochemistry of radioactive elements. Developed several methods of gas, volumetric, gravimetric, and calorimetric analyses. Studied conditions of migration of radioactive elements in the crust of the earth and applied the results to determine the earth's age. Founder of the school of Soviet radiochemists. Stalin prizes.

KHLYSTÝ (flagellants), religious sect dating back to the 17th century. "Khlystovshchina" (distorted "Khristovshchina," the True Faith of Christ) was based on the belief in perpetual rebirth and reincarnation of Christ. The sect as a distinct religious group ceased to exist in the 1860's.

KHMELKÓ, Mikhaíl Ivánovich (1919–), painter, known mainly for his patriotic pictures: *For the Great Russian People*, 1947; *Triumph of the Victorious Motherland*, 1949; *N. S. Khrushchev and N. F. Vatutin at the Approaches to Kiev*. Two Stalin prizes.

KHMELNÍTSKY, Bogdán Mikháylovich (1595–1657), hetman of the Ukraine, Ukrainian leader, sol-  dier, and patriot. In 1648–54 he led a successful war against Poland. Under K's command the insurgents defeated the Poles at Korsun, Pilyavtsy, Zborov, and Batog. The war was over, but the concessions won by the Zborov (1649) and Belaya Tserkov (1651) agreements did not satisfy the Ukrainian leaders striving for complete political and religious freedom. K, however, realized that a fully autonomous Ukraine, exposed to Turkish aggression in the S. and threatened by the Poles in the W., could not long maintain its independence. He favored a union with Russia, which was achieved at the Pereyaslav Rada, in Jan. 1654, but led eventually to the destruction of Ukrainian autonomy by the R. state.

BIBLIOGRAPHY: G. Vernadsky, *Bogdan, Hetman of Ukraine*, New Haven, 1940.

KHMELNÍTSKY (f. Proskurov), city, adm. center of Khmelnitsky Oblast; pop. 62,000 (1959). Busy river port and rail center on upper S. Bug. The city's ind. include machine-tool building, sugar refineries, breweries, clothing, footwear and furniture mfg., food-processing plants.

KHMELNÍTSKY OBLAST, (f. Kamenets-Podolsky Oblast), Ukrainian SSR, S.W. sector; area 8,050 sq. mi.; pop. 1,609,000 (1959). Cities: Khmelnitsky (adm. center), Kamenets-Podolsky, Slavuta, Shepetovka. It occupies part of the Volyn-Podolian plateau, and is predominantly a wooded steppe in the black-earth belt, drained by the Dniester and S. Bug. Moderate continental climate and fertile soils favor extensive farming, with wheat, rye, corn, sugar beets, and tobacco the principal crops. Lumber and paper are milled; peat and phosphorite deposits are mined in the forested N. zone; light mfg. and some heavy ind. are centered in the larger cities. Est. 1937.

KHODASÉVICH, Vladisláv Felitsyánovich (1886–1939), poet, became known as a symbolist (1908) but changed his style after the revolution. Emigrated to France and wrote witty satires in verse.

KHODÝNKA DISASTER. Occurred on May 18, 1896, when enormous festive crowds gathered on Khodynskoye pole (field) in Moscow to celebrate the coronation of Nicholas II. Because the necessary precautionary measures had not been taken by the city and police administration, the throngs surging into the field were finally stampeded. Over two thousand persons were killed, and many more seriously injured in the ensuing panic.

KHODZHÁYEV, Fayzúla Abayduláyevich (1896–1938), a Bolshevik leader in Turkestan; a member of the Central Committee from 1917. Chairman of the Young Bukhara Group which joined the CP in 1920. From 1922 to 1924 was chairman of the Soviet government in Bukhara. Led the struggle against the Basmach movement. From 1925 was chairman of the Soviet government in Uzbekistan. In March 1938, K was suspected of opposition to Stalin and was executed.

KHODZHÉNT: *see* LENINABAD.

KHOLMOGÓRY, port about 50 mi. S.E. of Archangel, on N. Dvina River. Dates back to 14th century. Fishing and dairy farming are among its industries. The writer and scientist M. V. Lomonosov was born here in 1711.

KHOLOP (slave): *see* PEASANTS.

KHOMYAKÓV, Alekséy Stepánovich (1804–1860), landowner and army officer, social and political writer, poet and philosopher, founder of the Slavophile doctrine. Assuming that historical processes are governed by religion, K theoretically advocated "universal Christianity," i.e. the union of all the Christian churches, but this actually meant to him the supremacy of the Greek (Russian) Orthodoxy over Catholicism and the reformed churches. Inexorably opposed to western ideology and ways of life which he called "dying" or "rotten Occident," he preached the political supremacy of R. autocracy among Slavic states, considering this a special mission of "Holy Russia," and praising her military victories over her neighbors. His philosophical position may be characterized as mystical idealism, which led him to exaggerate the significance of Russia's national culture and her role in human history.

KHOPÉR RIVER, flows from S. of Penza to become left tributary of the Don in Stalingrad Oblast; 630 mi. long.

KHORÉZM OBLAST, Uzbek SSR; area 1,740 sq. mi.; pop. 380,000 (1949). Cities: Urgench (adm. center). Khiva. It extends along the left bank of the lower Amu Darya in the Khiva (Khorezm) oasis. Cotton, rice, lucerne, fruit, melons, and truck produce are grown on irrigated farmlands in the valley; karakul sheep, camels, cattle are bred for meat, wool, and hides; sericulture is an essential occupation. Ind. include cotton ginning and silk processing. The navigable Amu Darya, the Chardzhou-Kungrad R.R. crossing the region, and motor highways are the main arteries of transportation. Est. 1938.

KHORÓG, town, adm. center of Gorno-Badakhshan Autonomous Oblast, Tadzhik SSR; pop. 8,000 (1959). Is the terminal point of important highways to Stalinabad and Osh.

KHOVÁNSKY, Prince Iván Andréyevich (died 1682). He participated in many campaigns against Poland and Turkey. Head of the Streltsy (sharpshooters). After the uprising which put Tsarevna Sofia Alekseyevna in power, he plotted against her and was executed.

KHOZRASCHOT: *see* BANKING AND CREDIT, INDUSTRY, INDUSTRIAL MANAGEMENT AND ORGANIZATION.

KHRÉNNIKOV, Tíkhon Nikoláyevich (1913–), composer. Graduated in composition from Moscow conservatoire (1936). Deputy to the Supreme Soviet RSFSR (1941–56); secretary general of the Union of Soviet Composers (1948); People's artist, RSFSR (1954); member of the CPSU since 1947. K traveled widely abroad. His compositions include operas, two symphonies, concertos for piano, romances, and scores for plays (*Much Ado About Nothing*) and motion pictures.

KHRÉNOV, Konstantín Konstantínovich (1894–), welding engineer. Corresponding member, Ac. of S., USSR (1953). Fellow (1945) and member of the executive board (1953), Ac. of S., Ukrainian SSR. Honored Scientist and Technologist. Graduate of St. Petersburg Institute of Electrical Engineering (1918); professor, Moscow Institute of Electro-Mechanics (1933–47) and Kiev University (1947). Research on the development of methods for electric welding of metals under water. Author of numerous publications on related subjects. Stalin prize (1946).

KHRISTIANÓVICH, Sergéy Alekséyevich (1908–), mechanical engineer and mathematician. Fellow (1943) and member of the executive board (1946–56), Ac. of S., USSR. Graduate of Leningrad University (1930). Associated with the Central Institute of Aerodynamics and Hydrodynamics (1937–53) and the Institute of Physical Chemistry (1956). Research on hydrodynamics, aerodynamics, and aviation technology. Stalin prizes (1942, 1946, 1952).

KHRUSHCHÉV, Nikíta Sergéyevich (1894–), chairman of the Council of Ministers of the USSR, member of the Presidium and first secretary of the Central Committee of the CPSU. K was born in the village of Kalinovka in Kursk *gubernia* (province). His father was a miner and K as a small boy worked as a shepherd. In  1911, he went to work as a locksmith and mechanic in Kharkov and elsewhere in the Donets basin. K participated in the revolution in 1917 and in December of that year was elected to the Lugansk city soviet. He joined the CP in 1918 and fought in the civil war. He then studied under the workers' faculty of Kharkov University and went on to party propaganda work in the Ukraine, where his abilities attracted the attention of L. Kaganovich, who was then highly influential. In 1929, K was sent for further study at the Moscow Industrial Academy. In 1931, he was elected secretary of the Bauman party district in Moscow and then rose consecutively to second and first secretary of the Moscow city party committee, and, in 1935, to first secretary of the Moscow *obkom* (oblast committee). He had been made a member of the CPSU Central Committee in 1934, and became a candidate member of the Politburo in 1938 and a full member in 1939. In 1938, K was sent to the Ukraine as first secretary of the Ukrainian CP, which was considered unreliable and which he ruthlessly purged. During the war, he was a member of the war councils on various fronts and took part in organizing the defense of Stalingrad. In 1947–49, he was in the Ukraine again, first as chairman of the Council of

Ministers, then once more as first secretary of the Ukrainian party. He returned to Moscow in 1949 as a secretary of the Central Committee of the CPSU and also resumed the post of first secretary of the Moscow oblast committee. After Stalin's death in March 1953, K dropped the Moscow oblast committee post "to concentrate on the work of the secretariat of the Central Committee," and in Sept. 1953, he became first secretary of the Central Committee of the CPSU. In Feb. 1956, was appointed chairman of the special bureau of the Central Committee for the RSFSR. In 1958, he became the chairman of the Council of Ministers of the USSR, and was indisputably the most powerful member of the party's "collective leadership."

More than "the first among equals," K has been victorious over his rivals and opponents. It should, however, be stressed that he fought not only for personal power, but for his political line, the "de-Stalinization" or "liberalization" expressed in his striking "secret speech" to the 20th Party Congress in 1956, which has not been published in the Soviet Union. Unlike Stalin, who rarely traveled abroad, K has visited many countries, including India, Yugoslavia, England and has visited the United States twice. His main political slogans which he widely publicized were "coexistence" of the two systems (Capitalism and Socialism) and "peace." However, he was instrumental in wrecking the Summit Conference in Paris in 1960.

From his youth, K has displayed unusual energy and efficiency in all his undertakings, subordinate, however, to Stalin's will until the latter's death. Since then, K has struggled successfully for the power to enable him to carry out his own ideas for changes, innovation, and reconstruction. Under his direction, there has been one reform after another, especially in agriculture. K is undoubtedly of great, though purely pragmatic, intelligence. He is not burdened by theoretical considerations and scruples, and although he is a Communist believer and certainly quite sincerely considers himself a consistent Marxist-Leninist, he appears to have reduced the ideology to a few rather primitive propositions. A certain primitiveness and even straightforward crudity have often been expressed in his speech and action.

BIBLIOGRAPHY: Myron Rush, *The Rise of Khrushchev*, Washington, 1958; L. Pistrak, *The Grand Tactician*, New York, 1961; K. Kellen, *Khrushchev, a Political Portrait*, New York, 1961.

G. P. D.

KHRUSTALÉV-NOSÁR, Geórgy Stepánovich (1879–1918), a lawyer. K-N was elected chairman of the St. Petersburg Soviet of Workers' Deputies in 1905. In 1906, he was exiled to Siberia. In 1907 he emigrated abroad where he was active among the Mensheviks. In 1914, he returned to Russia and was again arrested. During the civil war K-N opposed the Bolsheviks in the Ukraine and collaborated with Petlyura. He was shot by the Bolsheviks.

KHUTOR: *see* AGRARIAN REFORMS, PEASANTS.

KHVÓLSON, Orest Danilovich (1852–1934), physicist. Honorary member, Ac. of S., USSR (1920). Hero of Socialist Labor (1926). Graduate (1873) and professor (1891), St. Petersburg University. K was an outstanding lecturer and pedagogue. Research on light diffusion (1886–89) and solar energy (1892–96). Inventor of the actinometer which was widely used at R. meteorological stations. His philosophic views, considered as idealistic, were flayed by Lenin. Author of *A Course of Physics* (4 vols., 1892–1915), translated into German, French, and Spanish.

KHVOROSTÍNIN (Starkóvsky) **Prince Iván Andréyevich** (died in 1625), prominent in the political and military history of the early 17th century; author of the *Chronicle of Moscow Tsars and Church Dignitaries* covering the period beginning with Boris Godunov and up to 1612.

KIBÁLCHICH, Nikoláy Ivánovich (1854–1881), revolutionary and inventor. Member of the revolutionary party "People's Will." He was imprisoned in 1881, and executed for participation in the assassination of Alexander II. While in prison, he originated the idea of an aircraft based on the principle of jet-propelled movement.

KÍBEL, Ilyá Afanásyevich (1904–), mathematician and hydromechanical engineer. Corresponding member, Ac. of S., USSR (1943). Graduate, Saratov University (1925); associated with the Main Geophysical Observatory (1925–43); professor (1949). Central Institute of Weather Forecasts. Research on weather forecasts and theory of climates. Author of *Introduction of an Expedient Weather Forecast into Hydrodynamic Methods* (1957). Stalin prize (1941).

KÍBRIK, Yevgény Ádolfovich (1906–), illustrator and draftsman. Gained recognition in the 1930's for his book illustrations of Romain Rolland, Gogol, and others. During World War II K specialized in pencil drawings (*Stalingrad,* 1943, and others). More drawings followed after the war (*Lenin in Razliv,* Stalin prize, 1948), as well as graphic compositions, e.g., *Architects of Communism* (1952).

KÍEV, capital of Ukrainian SSR, adm. center of Kiev Oblast; pop. 1,104,000 (1959); third largest city in USSR; junction of several R.R.s and of an extensive highway network; mechanized river port, airport. Scenically located on the Dnieper, it is one of the loveliest Soviet cities, abounding in gardens and parks; has many old buildings, including the Cathedral of St. Sophia (about 1037), the church of St. Andrew, built by V. V. Rastrelli and I. F. Michurin, 1744–67, the Pechersky Monastery (about 11th century), a sacred place of pilgrimage. It was heavily damaged during World War II but was rebuilt and expanded. Is the seat of the Ukrainian Ac. of S.; has numerous schools of higher learning, including a university, research institutes, museums, theaters. Ind.: machine mfg. for chemical, sugar refining and tanning plants, smelting works, tobacco factories, flour mills, refineries, distilleries, printing; extensive light ind. such as footwear and knitwear. A fuel gaspipe Dashava-Kiev was built in 1948. The oldest of large R. cities, it is known as "The Mother of Cities"; mention of a town on the Dnieper called "Metropolis" is found in Ptolomeus (2nd century A.D.). Was at the height of its prosperity and cultural and political significance as the capital of the Varangian principality (9th century). A trading center down the Dnieper to Black Sea, on route from Scandinavia and Constantinople, it was the object of rivalry among princes; was ruined by

Tatar invasion 1240; annexed by Lithuania in the 14th century; transferred to Poland in 1569; seized by Bogdan Khmelnitsky, incorporated by Russia in 1654 and formally annexed in 1686.

KÍEV OBLAST, Ukrainian SSR; area 11,200 sq. mi.; pop. 2,821,000 (1959): Ukrainians, Russians. Located along the banks of the Dnieper and the Desna lowland; watered by the Dnieper and its affluents. Cities: Kiev (adm. center), Cherkassy, Uman, Belaya Tserkov, Fastov. Wooded steppe area in N., hilly plains in S.; has moderate climate, podsolic and black soils. Agr.: flax, wheat, corn, potatoes, buckwheat, sugar beets; orchards; dairy-cattle raising. Ind.: lignite, peat, distilleries, flour mills, sugar refineries, construction materials, light ind. Est. 1932.

KIKÓIN, Isáak Konstantínovich (1908–), physicist. Fellow, Ac. of S., USSR (1953). Graduate of Leningrad Polytechnic Institute (1931); professor, Moscow Institute of Physical Engineering (1944). Research on electrical and magnetic properties of metals and semiconductors, galvanomagnetic phenomena in and electrical resistance of liquid metals, gyromagnetic coefficients for superconductors. Author of *Physics of Metals.* Stalin prize (1942).

KÍMRY, city in Kalinin Oblast, RSFSR, on the Volga; pop. 39,900 (1956). R.R. station. An old tanning center in the 17th century, it now leads in shoe and leather production; also metalworks, knitwear mfg.

KÍNESHMA, city in Ivanovo Oblast, RSFSR, on right bank of the Volga; pop. 85,000 (1959). R.R. station. Is an old textile center, cotton and flax factories, paper making machinery, lumbering, food processing. Scenically located on steep right bank of the river, surrounded by forests.

KIPPER, Aksel Yanovich (1907–), astrophysicist. Fellow, Ac. of S., Estonian SSR (1946). Graduate (1930), professor (1946), Tartu University; at Tartu Astronomical Observatory (1930–44). Vice president (1946–50), director (1950), Institute of Physics and Astronomy, Ac. of S., Estonian SSR. Research concerns astrophysics and quantum mechanics. Author of *Nonstationary Stars* (1955).

KIPRÉNSKY, Orést Adámovich (1782–1836), gifted romantic portrait painter. He was a serf and the illegitimate son of a nobleman. Given freedom from serfdom he went to the Academy of Fine Arts in 1788, where he studied with Levitsky (q.v.). K's best-known work is a portrait of Pushkin dramatically draped in Scotch tartan, now in the Tretyakov Gallery. Also noted are the painting *Dmitry Donskoy,* the portrait of the poet and partisan Davydov and a self-portrait.

KIREYÉVSKY, Iván Vasílyevich (1806–1856), Slavophile writer. Influenced by the German idealistic philosophy, K was, in his youth, a westerner. In 1832, after a short stay abroad, he founded the review *Yevropeyets* (European) which was suppressed after the second issue. Soon thereafter K's ideas changed radically. He became a follower of the R. church and one of the first exponents of the philosophy of Slavophilism (*see* PHILOSOPHY).

KIRGHIZ RANGE (f. Aleksandr Range), extreme N. range of the Tien Shan Mountains, N. Kirghiz SSR;

extends W. from Issyk-Kul; its highest peak at E. end, Mt. Semenov (15,990 ft.).

KIRGHIZ SOVIET SOCIALIST REPUBLIC (KIRGIZIA) is located in Soviet Central Asia (formerly known as Turkestan, the land of the Turks). It borders on China in the E., Kazakh SSR in the N., Tadzhik SSR in the S., and Uzbek SSR in the W. It contains  2 oblasts: Osh and Tyan-Shan. Area, 76,500 sq. mi.; capital, Frunze (220,000).

Population of K is 2,066,000 (1959) including 837,000 Kirghiz (until 1925 called Kara-Kirghiz) or 40.5%, 219,000 Uzbeks (10.6%), 56,000 Tatars (2.7%), 20,000 Kazakhs (1.0%), 15,000 Tadzhiks (0.7%), 14,000 Uygurs (0.7%), as well as 624,-000 Russians (30.2%), 137,000 Ukrainians (6.6%), and 144,000 others (7%). Since all the "others" belong to various non-native groups transplanted from the European part of the USSR, the "European" pop. of K is now over 45% of the total, as compared with 18.8% in 1926, and therefore K cannot any longer be considered an Asian area from the point of view of national development. The Slavic pop., in addition to being the majority in the main urban centers, is also engaged in agriculture in N. K where the climatic conditions are more favorable for colonization.

Nature and Climate. The territory of K is covered by mountain ranges between 13,000 ft. and 15,750 ft. in elevation. Most of the valleys lie at 6,500 ft. to 10,000 ft. and only the Chu and the Talas valleys (1,300 ft. to 1,575 ft.) and the basin of Lake Issyk-Kul have the relatively warm climate and sufficient rainfall necessary for agriculture.

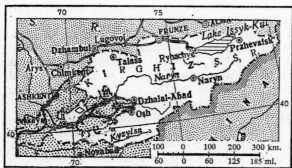

Kirghiz SSR

National Economy. The main branches of K economy are mining (coal, oil, lead), nonferrous metallurgy (mercury [first place in the USSR], antimony), dairy farming, cotton, tobacco, grain and sugar production, and sheep breeding. Over 60 per cent of industry is con-

centrated in and around the capital city of Frunze, the remainder (especially coal and oil) in Osh Oblast. K is the main coal supplier for all the other Soviet republics of Central Asia (except for Kazakhstan). Among the other industries are machine building and repair (agricultural machinery), textiles (cotton and silk), leather, clothing, food (meat and dairy), canneries. Almost three-fourths of the animal stock perished during the forced collectivization, and the 1929 level of cattle breeding was to be reestablished only in 1960. (For history and culture, *see* TURKESTAN)   M. R.

KIRICHÉNKO, Alekséy Illariónovich (1908–), party and government official, born in Kherson Province. CP member since 1930. In 1936 he graduated from the Azov-Black Sea Institute for mechanized agriculture, in 1938 was assigned to party work in the Ukraine, and during World War II did political work in the army with the rank of major general. In 1944 he returned to the Ukraine and rose through the party organization, holding posts of first secretary of Odessa Oblast CP Committee and Odessa City party committee; elected second secretary of Ukraine CP Central Committee in 1949 and first secretary June 1953, replacing Melnikov. K's support was a factor in the rise of Khrushchev. He was elected a member of Central Committee at the 19th Congress, 1952; was named candidate member of the Presidium 1953 and full member July 1955; and Central Committee secretary Dec. 1957. He declined in power May 1960 when he was removed from the Central Committee Secretariat and Presidium. Until his decline he was considered a trusted aide of Khrushchev.

KIRILÉNKO, Andréy Pávlovich (1906–), party official. He held several party posts during his early career; was elected and reelected a member of the central committee, Ukrainian CP, in 1949, 1952, and 1954; was first secretary of the Dnepropetrovsk Oblast party committee, 1950–55; since Dec. 1955, he has been first secretary, Sverdlovsk Oblast party committee. Several times he was elected deputy to the USSR Supreme Soviet; was appointed a member of the Central Committee, CPSU, in 1956, and candidate member of the CPSU Presidium in June 1957.

KIRÍLLOV, Vladímir Timoféyevich (1889–1939), poet. An old Bolshevik, after the revolution he became one of the leaders of the *Kuznitsa* (Smithy) group. He hailed the revolution in rather old-fashioned, rapturous verse. There is an overtone of disillusionment in his later poems. Arrested by the security police in 1937, he was never heard of again.

KÍROV (f. Vyatka), city, adm. center of Kirov Oblast, RSFSR, on the Vyatka River; pop. 252,000 (1959). Important R.R. junction. Ind.: transport equipment, tanning, footwear mfg., lumbering, match factory, food processing; also has extensive dairy farming. Founded about 1174 as Khlynov, renamed Vyatka 1780, Kirov, 1934; it was plundered twice by Tatars (14th and 15th centuries). Agric. and pedag. inst.

KÍROV OBLAST, RSFSR; area 46,650 sq. mi.; pop. 1,919,000 (1959), mainly Russians, also Mari, Tatars, Udmurt, Komi. Located in Vyatka River basin, is lowland, bordered on the N. by the N. Urals and crossed N.-S. by Vyatka Uval. Cities: Kirov (adm. center),

Kotelnich, Urzhum, Slobodskoy, and others. It has podsolic and argillaceous soils; forests and peat marshes; a continental climate; iron ore, phosphorite. Agr.: dairy farming, flax, rye, oats. Ind.: metallurgy, machine mfg., fur processing, tanning, shoe and match factories, chemicals, toys.

KÍROV (Kostrikov), **Sergéy Mirónovich** (1886–1934), Bolshevik leader, born in Urzhum (Vyatka, now Kirov Oblast). He graduated from a two-year technical school in Kazan in 1904 and went to work in Tomsk in Siberia where he joined the Bolshevik party. In 1910, K migrated to the Caucasuus, still carrying on his political activities for which he was several times arrested by the police.

After the October revolution in 1917, K was active in establishing Soviet power in the Caucasus. In 1919, he organized the Red troops in Astrakhan and in 1921 was a member of the Soviet delegation for the peace negotiations with Poland in Riga. In March 1921, K was elected a deputy member of the party's Central Committee, and a year later promoted to full membership. From 1921 till 1925, he was Communist boss in the Azerbaijan and one of the leaders of the Trancaucasian Federation. After the stormy 14th Party Congress of 1925, K, together with Molotov, Voroshilov and Kalinin, was sent by Stalin to Leningrad which was then a stronghold of the anti-Stalin opposition. After 1926, K replaced Zinoviev as the head of the Leningrad party organization. In 1926, he became a deputy member, and in 1930 a full member, of the Politburo. Officially a close collaborator of Stalin in his fight against all opposition factions; in fact K allegedly became Stalin's rival, especially after the 17th Party Congress had elected him as one of the secretaries of the Central Committee in Feb. 1934. He was preparing to move from Leningrad to Moscow, when, on Dec. 1, 1934, he was assassinated in his office in Leningrad by a certain Nikolayev, a party member and presumably an instrument of the security police. K's assassination was the signal for the wave of terror that culminated in the great purges during which, according to Khrushchev's "secret" speech at the 20th Party Congress in Feb. 1956, 1,108 (out of 1,966) delegates to the 17th Congress were arrested, and 70 per cent of the members of the Central Committee elected at it were executed.

KIROVABÁD (f. Gandzha, Yelisavetpol), city in Azerbaijan SSR, second largest after Baku; on Gandzha-Chay River, at foothill of Shakh Dag ridge; pop. 116,000 (1959). Has extensive cotton milling, dairy production, cloth factory; orchards and vineyards, sericulture; rug weaving. S.W. of the city are iron-ore (Dashkesan) and alunite (Zaglik) deposits. Is an old Armenian town, birhtplace of the Persian poet Nizami (1141); annexed by Russia 1813.

KIROVAKÁN (f. Karaklis), city in Armenian SSR; pop. 50,000 (1959). Center of chemical, textile and food-processing ind.

KIROVGRÁD (f. Kalata), city in Sverdlovsk Oblast, RSFSR; pop. 21,500 (1956). Major center of nonferrous metallurgy, copper-smelting and beneficiation plant.

KIROVOGRÁD, (f. Zinovievsk, Yelizavetgrad), city, adm. center of Kirovograd Oblast, Ukrainian SSR, on Ingul River; pop. 127,000 (1959). Ind.: machine building, metal working, food processing, flour milling, knitwear. Founded as a fortress 1754; renamed after 1917 Revolution for G. Ye. Zinoviev who was born there; again renamed in 1935 after Sergey Kirov.

KIROVOGRÁD OBLAST, Ukrainian SSR; area 9,300 sq. mi.; pop. 1,218,000 (1959): Ukrainians, some Russians and Moldavians. On the right bank of the Dnieper; bounded by the Volyn-Podolian upland in the W.; watered by the Dnieper, Ingul, and Ingulets rivers. Cities: Kirovograd (adm. center), Aleksandria, Znamenka, and others. A hilly lowland with black soil, it has a moderately continental climate. Agr.: wheat, sugar beets, sunflowers, potatoes, flax, poultry and dairy farming. Ind.: agr. machinery, food processing, chemicals, sugar refining, flour milling; lignite mining.

KÍROVSK (f. Khibinogorsk), town in Murmansk Oblast, RSFSR, on Kola Peninsula, beyond the Arctic Circle; pop. 22,100 (1956). R.R. station. "Apatite" combine, beneficiation plant; Kola branch of the Ac. of S.; school of mining and chemistry.

KIRPICHÓV, Mikhaíl Víktorovich (1879–1955), heat power engineer. Fellow, Ac. of S., USSR (1939). Graduate of St. Petersburg Institute of Technology (1907); professor, Leningrad Polytechnic Institute (1919–34) and Moscow Institute of Power Engineering (1937–49). Research and development of the theory of simulation.

KIRSÁNOV, Semyón Isaákovich (1906–), poet, born in Odessa in a Jewish family. His first works appeared in the early 1920's. He was close to Mayakovsky and a member of the Left Front in Literature—a futurist movement. His major works are: *Comrade Marx* (1933), *A Poem about Labor* (1934), *Cinderella* (1935), *Your Poem* (1936), *The Precepts of Foma Smyslov, a Russian Veteran* (1943), *Aleksandr Matrosov* (1946), *Makar Mazay* (1950, Stalin prize, 1951). He has translated the poetry of the Chilean poet, Pablo Neruda, and of Louis Aragon, Eluard, Broniewski, and Bertolt Brecht. During the "thaw," he published the poem *Seven Days of the Week* (1956), which was sharply critical of the bureaucratic attitudes, callousness, and inhumanity bequeathed by the Stalin era.

Created is the light, the land—
The only thing that lacks is man!

For this poem K was attacked by party leadership and the official critics. He was accused of revisionism, compelled to "repent," and to state publicly that his poem was a "mistake."

KIRSÁNOV, town in Tambov Oblast, RSFSR; pop. 15,400 (1956). R.R. station. In an iron-mining area, it has a foundry, smelting works; also food-processing ind.

KIRSHÓN, Vladímir Mikháylovich (1902–1938), dramatist and critic. Became a party member in 1920, was a friend of Yagoda (q.v.), and that led to his arrest at the time of Yagoda's fall. K died in a cell of the NKVD in 1938, but after the death of Stalin he was posthumously rehabilitated.

K was a leading member of RAPP (Russian Association of Proletarian Writers). His best-known play *Bread*, written in 1930, deals with the extermination of the kulaks, who resisted the policy of collectivization. He was co-author of the play *Konstantín Teryókhin* (1925–26), written in collaboration with Uspénsky. K's lesser works are *The Rails Are Humming* (1927), *The Windy City* (1929), and *The Miracle Alloy* (1934).

KIRZHÁCH, town in Vladimir Oblast, RSFSR; pop. 17,600 (1956). Has cotton and silk ind.

KISELÉV, Count Pável Dmítrievich (1788–1872), statesman. Advocated moderate reforms. Author of the "organic statute" (constitution) of Moldavia and Wallachia under the Treaty of Adrianople (1829). Member of the secret committees on the abolition of serfdom (1835). As head of the Ministry of State Domains (1837), K introduced the "Reform on the Administration of State Peasants" which somewhat benefited the peasantry (1838–40). Ambassador to France (1856–62).

KISELÉVSK, city in Kemerovo Oblast, RSFSR; pop. 44,000 (1939), 130,000 (1959). R.R. station. Major center of the Kuznetsk Basin coal ind. with coal-machinery plants; school of mining.

KISHINÉV (Rum. *Chisinau*), capital of Moldavian SSR; pop. 112,000 (1939), 216,000 (1959). A commercial city on the Yassy-Odessa R.R., has extensive food-processing ind., winemaking, tobacco, canning, flour milling, tanning, lumbering; metalworking and machine-tool plants; orchards and vineyards. Founded 1436; it was acquired in 1812 by Russia. Known for pogrom in 1903. Seat of the Moldavian branch of Ac. of S., USSR.

KISLOVÓDSK, city in Stavropol Kray, RSFSR; pop. 79,000 (1959). A health spa in N. Caucasus, famous for its mineral springs, primarily for coronary ailments; has lovely mild climate with year-round season.

KISTYAKÓVSKY, Vladímir Aleksándrovich (1865–1952), chemist. Fellow, Ac. of S., USSR and Ukrainian SSR (1929). Graduate of St. Petersburg University (1889); professor, St. Petersburg Polytechnic Institute (1903–34). Director, Laboratory of Colloidal Electrochemistry, reorganized into the Institute of Colloidal Electrochemistry (1934–39). Extensive research on thermodynamics of fluids. Numerous discoveries in electrochemistry, colloidal and physical chemistry, metal corrosion.

KITAYGORODSKY, Isáak Ilyích (1888–), physical chemist. Graduate, Kiev Polytechnic Institute (1910); professor, Moscow Institute of Chemical Technology (1933). Research concerns method of glass production, glass composition, ceramic metal-cutting tools. Author of *Glass and Glassmaking* (2nd ed., 1957). Stalin prizes (1941, 1950).

KIVÁCH, waterfall on Suna River, Karelian ASSR. The water falls 36 ft.; the energy is partly used for the Kondopoga Hydroelectric Plant.

KIZÉL, city in Perm Oblast, RSFSR; pop. 60,000 (1959). R.R. station. Center of the Kizel coal basin; mining ind.; beneficiation plant; a school of mining. Large electric power plant supplies Kizel and Berezniki ind. centers.

KIZEVETTER, Aleksándr Aleksándrovich (1866–1933), historian and publicist. Taught history at Moscow University. In 1905, became an editor of the review *Russkaya Mysl* (Russian Thought) and a member of the Union of Liberation (q.v.). In 1906, K was elected to the Central Committee of the Constitutional Democratic party (q.v.) and to the second Duma. After the October revolution, K was deported from Soviet Russia and lived in Prague where he was professor of history at Prague University.

KIZLYÁR, city in Dagestan ASSR, on Terek River, with R.R. connecting Caucasus with the Volga region; pop. 24,800 (1956). Surrounded by gardens and vineyards, it is famous for wines.

KLAIPEDA (f. Memel), city in Lithuanian SSR, an ice-free port on the Baltic Sea at the mouth of the Neman River; pop. 47,189 (1938), 89,000 (1959). A major commercial and mfg. city, with fishing, lumbering, chemicals, soap, wood pulp, textile, agr. products ind.

KLASSÓN, Róbert Eduárdovich (1868–1926), electrical engineer. Graduated from St. Petersburg Institute of Technology (1891). Research in transmitting electric power by means of three-phase alternate current. Supervised the building of electric power plants at Moscow and St. Petersburg and of the first peat-fed power plant at Noginsk.

KLIN, city in Moscow Oblast, RSFSR, on Moscow-Leningrad R.R.; pop. 28,000 (1939), 53,000 (1959). Ind.: glassmaking, metalworking, textiles. Has the Tchaikovsky Museum, the composer's home 1892–93.

KLINTSÝ, city in Bryansk Oblast, RSFSR; pop. 33,400 (1956). R.R. station; textiles, footwear, metalworking; peat cutting near the town.

KLUKHÓR PASS, leads through the Caucasus Mountains, connects the upstream areas of the Teberda and Kodori rivers, runs W. of Mt. Elbrus to Sukhumi; height, 9,250 ft.

KLYCHKÓV (Leshenkov), **Sergéy Antónovich** (1889–1942), novelist, poet, translator, critic; of peasant stock. The best of his collected poems are *Songs of Home* (1923) and *Guest of the Storks* (1930). Between 1925 and 1931, he produced four novels in which realism and the fantastic are interwoven in a fanciful and original way. Gorky called K the Soviet "successor of Gogol and Leskov." As a translator K introduced the poetry of the Voguls and the Chuvash to R. readers. In 1937, K was arrested and, according to some witnesses, perished in a forced-labor camp.

KLYUCHÉVSKAYA SÓPKA, highest active volcano on Kamchatka Peninsula, 15,580 ft.; covered by permanent snow and ice.

KLYUCHÉVSKY, Vasíly Ósipovich (1841–1911), historian. Son of a village priest, K entered the University of Moscow in 1861, where his teachers included S. Solovyov and B. Chicherin. In early studies of church-state relations and of the Boyar Duma, he emphasized social and economic factors, an approach maintained  in his later writings on serfdom and early representative assemblies. In 1879 K succeeded Solovyov as professor of history at the University of Moscow. His lectures, published as *A Course in Russian History* (1904–21), end with the reign of Nicholas I.

A pioneer of the sociological approach in R. history, K stressed the role of the peasantry and the gentry in the development of society. He interpreted the country's history from the "Great Russian" point of view and saw Russia's steady territorial expansion as a key factor in the rise of a strong central state. Attempting a synthesis of Slavophile and western opinion, he criticized Slavophile "myths" but also expressed opposition to excessive western tendencies in national life after Peter the Great. As a scholar K was noted for the scrupulous care of his research. His literary style won him wide acclaim and a place among R. historians comparable to that of Michelet in France. A brilliant lecturer, he attracted large and enthusiastic audiences at the University of Moscow.

KLYUYEV, Nikoláy Alekséyevich (1887–1937), poet of the peasant, reared among the Old-Believers in the Onega region, northeast of St. Petersburg. At one time member of the sect of flagellants (*khlystý*), but broke with them after becoming interested in the theories of the Socialist Revolutionaries. K could not agree with the policies of collectivization of the peasants in the 1930's, and offered a desperately unyielding opposition to these policies. He was arrested for "idealizing" the kulaks as a class, and interned in a concentration camp. He died of typhus in 1937, in the train that was returning him home after serving out his sentence. K was a master at portraying the R. folklore and the tragic fate of Russia's post-revolutionary peasantry. His early poems have been published in a two-volume edition entitled *The Songwriter* (1919). His major poems of later years are *Lament over Yesenin, The Village,* and *The Burnt Out Remains.*

KNÍPPER-CHÉKHOVA, Ólga Leonárdovna (1868–1959), actress. People's Artist of the USSR, wife of A. P. Chekhov. Graduated from the School of Music and Drama, the Moscow Philharmonic Society, and had a part in organizing the Moscow Art Theater. Her success dates from her roles in Chekhov's plays: Arkadina, in *The Sea Gull;* Yelena Andreyevna, in *Uncle Vanya*; Masha, in *The Three Sisters*; Madame Ranevsky, in *The Cherry Orchard*; and in plays by Gorky: Yelena, in *The Smug Citizen*; and Nastya, in *The Lower Depths*. Stalin prize (1943).

KNUNYÁNTS, Iván Ludvigovich (1906–), organic chemist. Fellow, Ac. of S., USSR (1953). Graduate of Moscow School of Technology (1928). Since 1931 associated with the Institute of Organic Chemistry. Research and development of methods for the introduction of fluorine into organic compounds, methods for obtaining antimalaria cultures, antibiotics, vitamins. Inventor of photosensitizers, caprone, and atebrin which are widely used in Soviet industry. Author of over 130 publications. Three Stalin prizes (1943, 1948, 1950) and other decorations.

KOCHESHKÓV, Ksenofónt Aleksándrovich (1894–), chemist. Corresponding member, Ac. of S., USSR (1946). Graduate (1922) and professor (1935), Moscow University. Research on the chemistry of organometallic compounds. Developed methods for the synthesis of or-

ganic compounds of lead, tin, silicon, zinc, thallium, antimony, and bismuth, and for the use of organometallic catalysts. Co-author of *Synthetic Methods in the Field of Organometallic Compounds.* Stalin prize (1948).

KÓCHIN, Nikoláy Yevgráfovich (1901–1944), mechanical engineer and mathematician. Fellow, Ac. of S., USSR (1939). Graduate of Petrograd University (1923). Director, Institute of Theoretical Meteorology (1933–34), head of the chair of mechanics at the Institute of Mechanical Engineering, Ac. of S. (1939–44). Research on gas, hydrodynamics and areodynamics, mathematics, and theoretical mechanics.

KÓCHINA, Pelagéya Yákovlevna, (Polubarinova-Kochina), (1899–), hydrodynamic engineer. Fellow, Ac. of S., USSR (1958). Graduate (1921), professor (1934), Petrograd (Leningrad) University. Associated with the Institute of Mathematics and Mechanics, Ac. of S. Research concerns the theory of filtration, the movement of ground waters and petroleum in porous environment, dynamic meteorology. Author of *Life and Work of S. V. Kovalevskaya* (1950). Stalin prize (1945).

KOCHUBÉY, Vasíly Leóntyevich (1640–1708), eminent member of the Ukrainian Cossack Elders. He informed Peter I of a plan harbored by Hetman Mazepa to detach E. Ukraine from Russia; was executed by order of Mazepa.

KÓGAN, Leoníd Borísovich (1924–), violinist. People's Artist, RSFSR. Graduated from Moscow conservatoire (1948). Awarded first prize at the Queen Elizabeth International Contest of Violinists in Brussels (1951). Has been teaching at the Tchaikovsky Conservatoire in Moscow since 1952. Toured the United States and W. European countries.

KOKÁND, city in Fergana Oblast, Uzbek SSR; pop. 105,000 (1959). R.R. junction. Ind.: chemical, cotton ginning, linseed-oil production, footwear mfg., metalworking, meat canning, superphosphate plant. One of the most ancient Uzbek towns, from the end of the 18th century to 1876 it was the capital of Kokand khanate.

KOKÁND, KHANATE OF. At the height of its power in the 18th century and about 1760 it recognized Chinese sovereignty. It was the last Central Asian khanate to be conquered by Russia (1873–76); was made a province of Turkistan under the ancient name of Fergana; is now a part of the Uzbek SSR.

KOKCHETÁV, city, adm. center of Kokchetav Oblast, Kazakh SSR; pop. 17,000 (1939), 40,000 (1959). R.R. station; food-processing ind.; and metalworking plants.

KOKCHETÁV OBLAST, in N. part of Kazakh SSR; area 30,500 sq. mi.; pop. 491,000 (1959): Russians, Ukrainians, Kazakh. Cities: Kokchetav (adm. center), Shchuchinsk, Stepnyak. A wooded steppe, hilly lake region, it is watered by the Ishim River and lakes Teke, Selety-Tengyz; has a continental climate. Agr.: wheat, oats, millet, sunflowers; cattle and sheep raising; gold mining. The Trans-Kazakhstan R.R. crosses it N.–S.

KÓKHMA, town in Ivanovo Oblast, RSFSR; pop. 18,600 (1956). R.R. station; one of the oldest centers of the textile ind.; cotton, flax.

KÓKHTLA-YÁRVE, city in Estonian SSR; pop. 28,600 (1958). R.R. station. Is a center of oil slate production, and a starting point for gaslines to Leningrad and Tallin.

KOKÓSHKIN, Fyódor Fyódorovich (1871–1918), a liberal democrat, prof. of constitutional law at Moscow University. K joined the Union of Liberation and was very active in zemstvo organizations. In 1905 he was one of the founders of the Constitutional Democratic party. In 1917 he was appointed state controller by the Provisional Government. Imprisoned by the Bolsheviks, he was assassinated by drunken sailors while in a prison hospital.

KOKÓVTSOV, Count Vladímir Nikoláyevich (1853–1942), statesman. As a young lawyer K entered government service, becoming state secretary (1902) and finance minister (1906). In the latter capacity, K found himself torn between the demands of the Duma and those of the reactionary elements at Court. He became premier (Sept. 1911) after the assassination of A. P. Stolypin, but he was unable to assert his control over the Court circles and was dismissed in Jan. 1914. Author of interesting memoirs which are available in an English translation.

KOKSHÁAL-TAU, range of the Tien Shan Mountains; extends S.W. from the Tengri Khan Mountains to the Altay Range along the border of the Kirghiz SSR and China. Pobeda Peak is highest (24,400 ft.); covered by glaciers.

KOK-YANGÁK, town in Dzhalal-Abad Oblast, Kirghiz SSR; pop. 16,500 (1956). R.R. station; coal mining.

KOLA BAY, inlet of Barents Sea, about 37 mi. long; fed by Kola, Tuloma and other rivers. Murmansk is at its head. Does not freeze.

KÓLA PENINSULA, projecting E. on N.W. coast of RSFSR, between the White Sea and the Barents Sea; about 39,000 sq. mi.; drained by turbulent rivers with numerous rapids (Tuloma, Kola, Niva). The N. shore has a milder climate than the center of the peninsula and does not freeze because of a N. Atlantic current. Forested tayga in the S., tundra in the N.; minerals, apatites, iron ore, nickel.

KOLCHÁK, Aleksándr Vasílyevich (1873–1920), Admiral and anti-Soviet leader. He served in the Russo-Japanese war; later he commanded torpedo forces in the Baltic Sea (1914) and, as a rear admiral, took command of the Black Sea fleet in 1916. After the October Revolution, he established an anti-Bolshevik government at Omsk, Siberia, assuming absolute control as "Supreme Ruler of All Russia" in Nov. 1918. His troops launched a major offensive into E. Russia in 1919 but were forced to retreat by Red counterattacks. After the fall of Omsk (Nov. 1919), he fled to Irkutsk where he resigned his office (Jan. 4, 1920). He was captured by the Bolsheviks and shot, Feb. 7, 1920.

KOLCHÚGINO, city in Vladimir Oblast, RSFSR; pop. 36,200 (1958). R.R. station. Nonferrous metal plants, cable mfg., breweries.

KOLCHÚGINO: *see* LENINSK-KUZNETSKY.

KOLGÚYEV, island in Barents Sea, N.E. of Kanin Peninsula, Archangel Oblast; about 1,450 sq. mi. Chiefly tundra with hills in the N.; many lakes, streams, and marshes. Inhabitants are Nenets and Russians; reindeer breeding, hunting, fishing.

KOLKHOZ—the abbreviated form of *kollektivnoye khozyaystvo* (collective farm)—is in theory an agricultural producers' cooperative jointly operated by its membership. Each member of the K shares in its output in proportion to the quantity and quality of labor days (*trudodni*) worked. Some part of the annual output of the K is sold or delivered to the state procurement organizations. Additional allotments are made for capital and reserve stocks as well as for special funds, seeds, fodder, insurance, and so on. The remainder is distributed among the K members, partly in money payments and partly in kind.

Beginning with the industrialization drive in 1929, the Soviet authorities exerted a strong administrative pressure in order to induce the independent Soviet peasants to join the K. In less than two years the resistance of the peasantry, which was extremely strong in the Ukraine and N. Caucasus, was broken by drastic and brutal police measures, and by 1931 the overwhelming majority of Soviet peasants were absorbed by the K system.

As a partial concession to the farmers the authorities allowed the K members to exercise direct control over private household plots (*priusadebnoye khozyaystvo*) as a rule not exceeding more than one-third of a hectare. In the thirties, these plots were—and to a lesser extent are even now—an important source of subsistence for the majority of *kolkhozniki* in the collective farms of the prevalent *artel* type.

The forced method of collectivization brought an acute shortage of capital in the countryside. This scarcity coupled with the lack of material incentives on the part of the collective farmers contributed largely to the more than twenty-year period of stagnation of Soviet agricultural output. The decline was most extreme in animal husbandry. In the formative stage of the K system the horse and cattle population diminished considerably. Furthermore, the state industry was still unable to provide tractors and combines in the greater amounts needed. This resulted in the man-made famine of 1932–33 and in an acute shortage of dairy and meat products in the succeeding years.

Until after World War II the K were small in size, comprising not more than one village with a working membership not exceeding 70–80 persons. In 1937 the number of collective farms amounted to 243,500 with an average number of 76 households and 591 hectares of arable land per K. In 1949 the Soviet authorities started a drive for amalgamation of K, bringing under one management several of the previously independently operated collective farms. At the end of 1959 the number of K was reduced to 54,800 (including fishermen's cooperatives), the average number of households belonging to the K increased to 342 while the average size of collective farm land increased to 5,500 hectares (= 13,590 acres).

In the post-Stalin period, a number of far-reaching

reforms were initiated which drastically changed the management and operation of the collective farm system. These reforms, closely connected with other reforms of Khrushchev, can be briefly characterized as follows:

The management of the K obtained a larger degree of freedom in planning their own output. State obligatory deliveries which in the past deprived the K of a considerable part of their produce were abrogated. The Ministry of Agriculture prescribes each year the quotas of specific commodities which the K are obliged to sell to the state procurement organizations. Instead of a multiple system of agricultural prices, a uniform price was introduced for all state purchases, a price which takes into account the working cost of the product.

Prior to 1958 the proper operation of the K system suffered from a peculiar dualism. On one hand, the labor force engaged in the K was under the management of the K administration; on the other hand, the machinery actually used in the work of the K was under the management of the machine tractor stations (MTS) administration (q.v.). This led to frictions, misuses, and waste. In 1958 the machine tractor stations were abolished and their stock sold to the K. In this way, the burden of investment in agricultural machinery which previously fell on the state-operated and state-sustained MTS is now the responsibility of the K.

The abolition of the MTS brought into the membership of the collective farms over 3 mill. skilled workers (engineers, tractor drivers, and others) and this *inter alia* led to considerable changes in the remuneration obtained by members of the K. As a cumulative effect of the reforms mentioned above the money income of the K greatly increased, from 34.2 bill. rubles in 1950 to 131.8 bill. in 1958. Some of the K started to pay their members fixed money wages which as a rule are not higher than the wages of workers employed in the state-operated farms (*sovkhozy*, q.v.).

	1928	1932	1940	1950	1953	1958	1959
Total number of K (incl. fishing and handicraft) (thous.)	33.3	211.7	243.5	123.7	93.3	69.1	54.8
of which Agricultural artels	33.3	210.6	235.5	121.4	91.2	67.7	53.7
K households (mill.)	0.4	14.7	18.7	20.5	19.7	18.8	18.6
Total sown area (mill. hectares	1.4	91.5	117.7	121.0	132.0	131.4	130.3
Collectivized livestock (mill. head)							
Cattle	0.4	8.8	20.1	28.1	27.8	32.1	36.9
Hogs	0.1	3.1	8.2	12.3	13.6	23.1	26.8

It is too early to evaluate the long-run effect of the new administrative set-up of the K system. It is obvious that these reforms contributed to an increase in agricultural output. But at the same time the reforms led to a rapid differentiation of the K. In 1959, 22 per cent of the total number of K had a money income of 20 to 120 rubles per acre of agricultural land, while 19.8 per cent of collective farms had an income of 400 to more than 800 rubles per acre. In order to diminish differences between rich and poor K propositions recently have been made to create territorial associations of collective farms. As of today the K are under the jurisdiction of the central ministry and are not subjected to the controls of the regional economic councils. (*See also* AGRICULTURE, MTS)

A. K.

KOLLONTÁY, Aleksándra Mikháylovna (1872–1952), Bolshevik and Soviet diplomat. Daughter of a tsarist general, K rejected her privileged status and became an active propagandist among working women. At first a Bolshevik, she broke with Lenin and became a Menshevik. Eventually she was reconciled with Lenin and rejoined the Bolshevik party in 1915. Wrote to Lenin constantly from the United States where she carried on pacifist agitation in 1916. Participated in international socialist congresses. Member of the Central Committee of the Bolshevik party, K was in the early 20's a leading figure in the Workers' Opposition. (*See* OPPOSITION.) From 1923 she was assigned to diplomatic posts in Norway, Mexico, and Sweden. K was also the author of several novels in which she was an advocate of free love.

KOLMOGÓROV, Andréy Nikoláyevich (1903–), mathematician. Fellow, Ac. of S., USSR (1939). Graduate (1925), professor (1931), Moscow University. Research concerns the theory of probability, application of the theory of functions of a real variable, functional analysis, statistical theory of turbulence, statistical methods of mass production control, automation. Author of *Limit Distributions of Sums of Independent Random Values* (1949). Stalin prize (1941).

KOLÓMNA, city in Moscow Oblast, a river port on R.R. near confluence of the Moskva and Oka; pop. 100,000 (1959). Ind.: locomotive and machine-mfg. plants, R.R. workshops, engine-repair factory, hardware, lumbering. Founded in 12th century, it was destroyed by Tatar invasions.

KÓLPINO, city in Leningrad Oblast, RSFSR, suburb of Leningrad; pop. 28,700 (1956). Metal working and machine mfg.; Izhora plant produces equipment for heavy ind.

KOLTSÓV, Alekséy Vasílyevich (1809–1842), lyric poet, whose basic themes were nature, peasant life, and  the countryside. Much of his poetry has been set to music. He was born in Voronezh in the family of a modest cattle trader. His verse breathes of the nostalgic dreams, hopes, and simple creed of the R. peasant. It includes such short poems as *The Murmur of the Rye Fields, Song of the Plowman,* and *Man with the Scythe.*

KOLTSÓV, Mikhaíl Yefímovich (1898–1942), writer and journalist, born in Kiev, son of a craftsman. He attended a secondary school in Belostok and entered Petrograd University in 1915. K participated in the October revolution, working on Lenin's staff at Smolny. From 1922 on, *Pravda* frequently carried his pieces: satirical sketches, essays, letters, articles, reviews. His style was light and incisive. In 1936, K went to Spain where he fought in the civil war against General Franco. After returning to Russia, he was deputy to the RSFSR Supreme Soviet, member of *Pravda*'s editorial board, member of the governing board and chairman of the foreign commission of the Union of Soviet Writers, editor of *Ogonyok* and of *Krokodil,* and corresponding member of Ac. of S., USSR.

His major works include *The First Circle: Studies of the Revolution* (1922), *Ideas and Shots* (1924), *Startling Encounters* (1931), *I Want to Fly* (1931), *The Soul is Sick* (1932), *Spanish Spring* (1933), *Spanish Diary* (1938). His collected works were published in six volumes in 1933–36 and in three volumes in 1957. In 1938 K was arrested and he either died or was shot in a concentration camp. After Stalin's death, he was rehabilitated and a book *Soviet Writers* published in 1959 states that K "perished by the foul hand of the concealed enemies of the people."

KOLYMÁ RANGE (f. Gydan), in N.E. Siberia, Magadan Oblast, in the upstream area of Omolon River; highest peak 6,435 ft.

KOLYMÁ RIVER, N.E. Yakut ASSR and Magadan Oblast; rises S. of Chersky range and on E. slopes of Verkhoyansk range, flows into E. Siberian Sea; about 1,600 mi. long. Navigable to Verkhnekolymsk; gold diggings worked along its course; chief tributaries Omolon and Anyui. Discovered by Cossacks ca. 1640.

KOMARÓV, Vladímir Leóntyevich (1869–1945), botanist, geographer, and explorer. Fellow (1920), vice president (1930–36), president (1936–45), Ac. of S., USSR. Hero of Socialist Labor (1944). Deputy to the Supreme Soviet (1937). Graduate (1894), professor (1918), St. Petersburg University. Studied the flora of Central Asia (1892–93), Manchuria (1896), and North Korea (1897). Initiated the publication of the 24-volume encyclopedia *Flora of the USSR.* Gold medal of the Russian Geographical Society. Stalin prizes (1941, 1943). The Botanical Institute of the Ac. of S. was named after K (1940).

KÓMI ASSR, in N.E. European part of RSFSR; area 162,100 sq. mi.; pop. 804,000 (1959): Komi (formerly Zyryans) and Russians. Cities: Syktyvkar (capital), Vorkuta, Ukhta, Pechora. Heavily forested lowlands (over 70 per cent), tundra in N., Ural mountain slopes in E.; its rivers are the Pechora and Vychegda; has a continental climate. Minerals: coal, oil, natural gas, iron ore, salt. Agr.: cattle, deer breeding in N.; lumbering ind. It has the Pechora R.R. and Kotlas-Salekhard air transportation. Est. 1936.

KÓMI-PERMYAK NATIONAL OKRUG, part of Perm Oblast, RSFSR, W. of Ural Mountains; area 12,650 sq. mi.; pop. 220,000 (1959): Komi, Permyaks, and Russians. Adm. center: Kudymkar, in basin of Kama River. Forests cover 80 per cent of the territory. Chief occupations are lumbering, fishing, hunting; some agr. including grain crops, flax, dairying.

KOMISSARZHÉVSKAYA, Véra Fyódorovna (1864–1910), actress and producer, daughter of the singer F. P. Komissarzhevsky. K began her career in 1894, appearing in Novocherkassk, Vilna, and Aleksandrinsky Theater in St. Petersburg (1896–1902). Among her parts: Rosi, in Sudermann's *The Battle of the Butterflies;* Nina Zarechnaya, in Chekhov's *The Sea Gull;* Larisa, in Ostrovsky's *The Dowryless.* In 1904 K organized the Theater of Drama (St.

Petersburg) and played Varvara Mikhaylovna and Liza in Gorky's *The Summer Residents* and *The Children of the Sun,* and Nora in Ibsen's *A Doll's House.* Her acting was notable for sincerity, psychological depth, and lyricism. K made extensive tours of Russia and foreign countries.

KOMMUNIST (The Communist), theoretical and political journal of the Central Committee of CPSU. Published bi-monthly in Moscow, with a circulation of over 500,000, and an average issue of 125 pages. Editor-in-chief is F. V. Konstantinov. Published from 1924 to Oct. 1952 as *Bolshevik.* It deals chiefly with problems of Marxism-Leninism, party affairs, foreign relations, particularly those of satellite countries.

KOMSOMOL. The Komsomol (The Young Communist League) is an important satellite organization of the CP which is organized for the purpose of realizing party objectives among Soviet youth. Although specific party goals for the youth have changed from era to era under Soviet rule, five basic objectives have remained permanent features of the communist youth organization: controlling Soviet youth, indoctrinating them in the ideals and ideology of communism, channeling their energy to attain party goals, preventing the formation of competing and dissident youth groups, and recruiting the most active K members into party ranks.

The present age group for the K is between fourteen and twenty-seven. Members exceeding the age limit may remain within the organization with a consultative vote if they are elected to leading organs (at the 13th congress in 1958, 52 per cent of the delegates were older than twenty-six, the age limit at that time). Admission to the K is effected at the general membership meeting of the local organization after the candidate has received the recommendations of two members and the approval of a city or rayon K committee. Organizationally, the K is modeled after the party, with primary organizations (of which there were 384,000 in 1958) in schools, factories, collective and state farms, and military units. K units on all administrative levels (cities, rayon, oblast, kray, republic) hold conferences and congresses each of which is guided by its respective committees, bureaus, and secretaries.

At the top of the pyramid is the All-Union Congress of the Komsomol which is to meet every four years. The congress "elects" a central committee of 103 full and 47 candidate members. The committee in turn "elects" a bureau of 13 full and two candidate members to direct the work between sessions. The central committee also establishes a secretariat to conduct the day-to-day affairs of the organization. This secretariat, which is really the core of the organizational structure, and through which control is effected, is currently composed of a first secretary and six additional secretaries.

The K had its antecedents in the Socialist League of Working Youth, founded in 1917 (to combat a rival youth organization, Work and Light). In the fall of 1918 the constituent congress of the K met in Moscow, representing 22,100 members. The first congress was Bolshevik-inspired and controlled but did contain some nonparty youth delegates as well as representatives from left-wing groups. The bond between the party and K was tightened by the time of the second congress (1919), representing 96,000 members. The K professed complete adherence to the program of the Russian CP and declared its own central committee subordinate to the party's Central Committee.

The K's major effort during the civil war period was concentrated on mobilizing its members for front duty where thousands served as agitators, commissars, and shock troops. In the later stages of the civil war, with Bolshevik victory in sight, membership increased significantly, exceeding 400,000 by the time of the third congress in Oct. 1920.

At this time the K, like the party, was not yet as tightly controlled as was later to be the case. Opposition groups developed within the movement, including one led by V. Dunayevsky who advocated special youth sections in the trade unions; another was the so-called "Ukrainian Opposition" which principally opposed the increasing central controls imposed by the K hierarchy. These opposition groups were sharply denounced by the third congress.

The highlight of the third congress was Lenin's address. With the end of the civil war in sight, Lenin called on the youthful generation to seek proficiency in the more prosaic tasks of study and work to help build a communist society, an appeal which met with unenthusiastic response by the membership, still afire from the heroic days of the civil war. Disillusionment with party policy deepened with the announcement of the New Economic Policy in March 1921. Substituting a mixed economy for War Communism was considered by many young people to be a serious retreat from the principles of socialism for which the K had fought. Spirit further declined as many K members failed to gain employment after hostilities had ceased.

By the time of the fifth congress (Oct. 1922) K membership had dropped precipitously to 247,000. Strenuous efforts were now made to recapture the loyalty and affection of Soviet youth. The congress provided for the organization of Pioneers (q.v.), a party-inspired organization to attract youngsters of pre-Komsomol age and to prepare them for K membership.

As a result of these and other efforts K membership was again reversed as numbers mounted to 400,000 by Jan. 1924, one million by 1925, and two million by 1927. During this period the intra-party struggle, particularly Trotsky's appeal for world revolution, did not leave the K unaffected. The purge of the Left Opposition, which also saw the rise of A. Kosarev to prominence as a K leader (he became secretary general of the K in 1929 replacing N. Chaplin who had served in that capacity since 1924), left some wounds which were quickly healed by the advent of the Five Year Plans in 1928 which evoked tremendous zeal and fervor among the youth. The K members were invested with important tasks as thousands were mobilized to build industrial units in the Ukraine, the Urals, and Siberia; to liquidate the kulaks and to initiate collectivization. K members were also at the forefront of party-sponsored drives to eliminate illiteracy and to spread antireligious propaganda.

This period, however, also proved disillusioning to some in the K as their initial expenditure of energy and enthusiasm was dissipated and alienated by continued hardships in working and living conditions, by the brutality of enforced collectivization, and by a series of purges whose tentacles reached from the party down into the K. Membership which had topped the 5 million mark in the early thirties was reduced to 4½ million by Oct. 1933. Kirov's assassination in 1934 further accelerated the rate of expulsion as membership dipped to 3,623,000 by Jan. 1936.

The ninth Komsomol congress meeting in April 1936 called for fundamental policy changes. A new membership policy was adopted which was to transform the K from an elite, which had limited membership to children of workers and poor peasants, into a mass organization with admission no longer dependent upon social origin. Further, a new program was adopted which called for an intensified campaign of political indoctrination of youths (this had been neglected during the Five Year Plan period with its emphasis on economic construction) and for an extension of the K's cultural and recreational activities. The new admission policy, despite the great purge, bore fruit as K membership reached five million by 1938 and jumped to eleven million by 1941.

The great purge of 1936–38 laid a heavy hand on the K as thousands of K leaders, including A. Kosarev, were purged, accused of fantastic crimes. (N. Mikhaylov, who unlike Kosarev had had no direct experience as a rank-and-file K member, was selected by Stalin as Kosarev's replacement.) Although the purge left a legacy of bitterness among many of the youth, it did provide an opportunity for surviving activists to fill important positions left vacant in the party and K hierarchy.

With the advent of war the K was enlisted to serve in various capacities, from participation in guerrilla warfare to mobilization of youth on the home front in support of war production. During this period admission policy was relaxed to permit millions of servicemen as well as civilians to join the K and the membership rolls reached fifteen million by Oct. 1945.

After the war the failure of many former servicemen to register with their local organization and infraction of rules by others resulted in a sharp drop in membership. By the time of the eleventh congress meeting in 1949 (the first since 1936), membership had declined to 9,283,289. After the congress an intensive recruitment campaign to implement the renewed party policy of mass membership for extensive political indoctrination of youth yielded positive results. By the time of the twelfth congress which met in 1954, membership had doubled, reaching 18,825,327. This figure remained fairly constant for the rest of the decade. The K, however, is still subject to a high turnover rate. Although ten million joined between 1954 and 1958, the total membership has not exceeded nineteen million. In addition, despite continuous membership drives, K members are heavily concentrated in urban centers; in 1956 only three million lived in rural areas.

The post-Stalin years have not altered the essential nature of the communist youth organization. The K is still called upon to realize specific party tasks, to form shock brigades, and to stimulate socialist production. In the virgin lands campaign of 1954–55, over 350,000 K members participated.

K direction and leadership are still subjected to direct party control. K secretaries of cities, rayon, and higher administrative levels are required by K statutes to be party members. Further, local K organizations continue to be guided by corresponding party groups on their respective levels. Party functionaries continue to lead the K and are generally appointed, rather than elected, in violation of the K rules. (In 1952 A. Shelepin replaced N. Mikhaylov as K leader. He was succeeded for a short while by Ye. Semichastny in 1958, who in turn was followed by S. Pavlov in 1959, the current first secretary.)

The necessity of maintaining tight controls over the K has exacted from the party a heavy toll. It has substantially reduced the enthusiasm and zeal of many members and accounts for a high turnover in membership. Although the party in recent years has attempted to infuse a new spirit into the youth movement it has been singularly unsuccessful in solving the problem of how to exercise despotic control without stifling initiative.

BIBLIOGRAPHY: Merle S. Fainsod, *How Russia Is Ruled*, Cambridge, 1953; Ralph T. Fisher, Jr., *Pattern for Soviet Youth: A Study of the Congresses of the Komsomol, 1919–1954*, New York, 1959.   H. W. M.

KOMSOMÓLSK-ON-AMÚR, city in Khabarovsk Kray, RSFSR, on left bank of Amur; on branch of the Trans-Siberian R.R.; pop. 71,000 (1939), 177,000 (1959). Modern city, founded 1932 by the Young Communist League (Komsomol); a major ind. center in the Far East, with steelworks, large shipyard, oil refinery, power plants, R.R. workshops, lumbering, building materials.

KONCHALÓVSKY, Pyotr Petróvich (1876–1956), painter. Studied in Paris, Rome and St. Petersburg. He soon drifted away from official academism and in 1910 was among the founders of the *Bubnovy Valet* (Jack of Diamonds). He was still chairman of that group when it was dissolved in 1926. K's best-known prerevolutionary pictures were: *Oranges* (1908), *Woman in White* (1909), *Fruit, Billiard Balls* (1915)—all formalistic, vigorous, and bold paintings. By the late twenties, his style and subject matter began changing, and he started painting nostalgic scenes of old Russian fairs (*Fair*, 1927) and Caucasian landscapes (*Kazbek*, 1928; *Mtsyri*, 1928). His much praised *Red Cavalry* (end of 1927) was an almost perfect example of socialist realism. In 1942 he received the Stalin prize.

KONDRÁTENKO, Román Isídorovich (1857–1904), lieutenant general. Hero of the defense of Port Arthur during Russian-Japanese War (1904). He was commander of the fortress.

KONDRÁTYEV, Víktor Nikoláyevich (1902–), physical chemist. Fellow, Ac. of S., USSR (1953). Graduate, Leningrad Polytechnic Institute (1924); associated with the Institute of Chemical Physics, Ac. of S. (1913); professor, Institute of Physical Engineering in Moscow. Research concerns chemical kinetics, structure of substances, molecular spectrosopy, and photochemistry.

Proved experimentally the chain reaction theory, determined the geometrical structure of various molecules, developed an optical method for the study of the unstable state of molecules, and demonstrated the photochemical dissociation of molecules. Stalin prize (1944).

KONÉNKOV, Sergéy Timoféyevich (1874–), sculptor. After study in Russia and abroad, he first molded peasant figures and portraits (*Chekhov*, 1908) and then turned to subjects from Slavic and Greek mythology. In 1924, K settled in the United States, where he executed numerous portraits (*Mayakovsky*, 1927; *Gorky*, 1928; *Dostoyevsky*, 1933). Returning to Russia in 1945, K produced portrait studies and busts (*Chaliapin*, 1952; *Musorgsky*, 1953; *Socrates*, 1955).

KÓNEV, Iván Stepánovich (1897–), marshal of the Soviet Union, born in Kirov Oblast in a peasant family.  He has been in the Soviet Army since Aug. 1918, and a CP member since 1918. He was also an active participant in the civil war. In 1926 he graduated from the Frunze Military Academy and in 1934 from a special faculty of this academy. During World War II he commanded forces of the W., Kalinin, and the first and second Ukrainian fronts, and they were victorious in battles in Ukraine, Poland, Germany, Czechoslovakia. After the war he commanded Soviet occupation forces in Austria and Hungary. In 1946 he became commander of land forces and deputy minister of war; in 1950, chief inspector of the Soviet Army; in May 1955, commander of the Warsaw Pact forces; and in March 1956 first deputy minister of defense. He was elected candidate member of the Central Committee, CPSU, in 1939, and a full member in 1952. He was twice named Hero of the Soviet Union. In July 1960 he was replaced as military commander of the Warsaw Pact forces by Marshal Andrey Grechko.

KÓNI, Anatóly Fyódorovich (1844–1927), outstanding lawyer and writer, honorary member of the Ac. of S. (1900). Presided over the Court of St. Petersburg that acquitted Vera Zasulich (in 1878), which evoked the indignation of the government and reactionary circles. He is the author of memoirs *On the Road to Life* (5 volumes, 1912–29) which contain interesting information on outstanding public figures and writers. After the October Revolution of 1917 he became professor at Leningrad University.

KŒNIGSBERG: *see* KALININGRAD.

KONOTÓP, city in Sumy Oblast, Ukrainian SSR; pop. 53,000 (1959). As a R.R. junction in a rich farming area, on the Kiev-Moscow line, it exports much grain. Ind.: locomotive repair works, food processing.

KONOVÁLOV, Aleksándr Ivánovich (1875–1948), industrialist and public figure, member of the Progressive Bloc of the fourth State Duma. During World War I, he was vice president of the Central War Industries Committee. In March 1917, he was appointed minister of trade and industry in the Provisional Government. He was deputy chairman of Kerensky's last cabinet. After the October revolution, he emigrated and died in New York.

KONSTANTÍNOV, Borís Pávlovich (1910–), physicist. Fellow, Ac. of S., USSR (1960). Graduate and professor (1947), Leningrad Polytechnic Institute. Associated with the Leningrad Institute of Electrophysics (1939), the Institute of Physical Technology, Ac. of S. (1940). Research concerns theoretical and applied acoustics and physical chemistry; including self-induced vibrations and sound formation processes in musical instruments and signaling devices (1935–43); effects of sorption of sound in organic media. Suggested quantitative theory of propeller sound (1934).

KONSTANTÍNOVKA, city in Stalino Oblast, Ukrainian SSR, in the Dnieper bend; pop. 89,000 (1959). R.R. junction. Large ind. center in the Donbas, metallurgical, chemical, glassmaking, and ceramic plants.

KÓONEN, Alísa Geórgievna (1889–), actress, People's Artist, RSFSR (1935). In 1905–13 K appeared at Moscow Art Theater. Played the parts of Mitil, in Maeterlinck's *The Blue Bird*; Verochka, in Turgenev's *A Month in the Country*; and Masha, in L. Tolstoy's *The Living Corpse*. From 1914 to 1949 K was the leading actress of the Moscow Chamber Theater.

KOPECK: *see* MONETARY SYSTEM.

KOPET DAGH, mountain range extending N.W. to S.E. along border between N.E. Iran and Turkmen SSR, E. of S. end of Caspian Sea. In the Turkmen SSR at the foothills, oases are crossed by R.R. Sheep breeding in mountains; horticulture and vineyards in valleys. Highest point 10,223 ft. (in Iran).

KOPÉYSK, city in Chelyabinsk Oblast, RSFSR; pop. 60,000 (1939), 161,000 (1959). R.R. station (Sergo-Ufaleyskaya). Coal-mining center of Chelyabinsk coal basin. Machine mfg. includes mining and R.R. equipment, farming machinery; ore beneficiating.

KÓRKINO, city in Chelyabinsk Oblast, RSFSR; pop. 12,000 (1939), 85,000 (1959). R.R. station. Main coal-mining center of Chelyabinsk coal basin; has school of mining.

KORNEYCHÚK, Aleksándr Yevdokímovich (1905–), Ukrainian playwright and politician. Member of the Central Committee of the Ukrainian CP. Ukrainian minister of foreign affairs at the end of World War II. K gained fame as a lauder of the Bolshevik party; at the same time, he has always pointed out the disastrous consequences of social revolutions and turmoils. His boldest play, *Platon Krechet*, concerns the conflict between party and intelligentsia. Five Stalin prizes.

KORNILOV "MUTINY" (August 1917). In the quest for a strong and more stable regime, the name of General Lavr Georgievich Kornilov (1870–1918) was often mentioned as a possible alternative to Alexander Kerensky as head of the Provisional Government. Kornilov, regarded by many as a hero, was made supreme military commander on July 18. He was determined to check the disintegration of the army and in this had the support of Kerensky. But the strength of Kornilov's determination was sufficient to alarm the prime minister and those who feared the possibility of counterrevolution and army dictatorship. Kornilov despised the Soviets, wishing particularly to curb the army committees for which they were responsible. Many of his fellow-officers professed an aversion for Kerensky

personally. Thus a rift developed between the government, which enjoyed a measure of support on the Left, and the officer corps, which was favored on the Right. Military events brought the impending crisis to a head. After Aug. 18, the German drive on Petrograd seemed ever more threatening. Yet the government continued to resist Kornilov's demands for corrective measures, fearing protests by the Soviets. Kornilov therefore despatched a cavalry corps to Petrograd as a first step in the establishment of a new and "stronger" regime. Kerensky, sensing a Kornilov coup, dismissed the supreme commander from office on Aug. 26.

Meantime the cavalry corps advancing on Petrograd was slowed and scattered by the obstruction of railway workers. The soldiers themselves soon became mutinous and, after the suicide of their commander, General Krymov, formally defected to the government, Aug. 31. With Kerensky now commander in chief as well as prime minister, Kornilov surrendered peacefully (Sept. 1) and was jailed together with a number of other officer-conspirators. The attempted "counterrevolution," probably impossible from the start, was over. Subsequently Kornilov escaped and, after the Bolshevik revolution, took command of the White army in S. Russia. He was killed while leading the White attack on Yekaterinodar, April 1918.

KORNÍLOV, Vladímir Alekséyevich (1806–1854), vice-admiral, organized the defense of Sevastopol in 1854. He was fatally wounded during one of the first bombardments.

KOROLÉNKO, Vladímir Galaktiónovich (1853–1921), novelist, journalist and editor. K was born in  the town of Zhitomir in the family of a civil servant. He studied at the University of St. Petersburg and later at the Agricultural Academy in Moscow; following his participation in a "populist" student movement he was expelled from the Academy and exiled (1879). In exile he began to write short stories. In 1884 he was permitted to return to European Russia, and settled in Nizhny Novgorod (now Gorky). In the late 1890's K became literary editor of the review *Russkoye Bogatstvo* (Russian Wealth). K's better-known works include the short story *Makar's Dream* (1885), the novel *The Blind Musician* (1886), and the autobiographical novel *The Story of a Contemporary* (1906–22).

KORÓSTEN, city in Zhitomir Oblast, Ukrainian SSR; pop. 34,000 (1956). Key R.R. junction on the Leningrad-Odessa and Kiev-Warsaw lines. Ind.: peat cutting and transportation equipment, porcelain, sewing-machine factory, food processing, metalworking.

KORÓVIN, Konstantín Alekséyevich (1861–1939), painter and stage designer. Studied in Moscow; adhered to the realistic school of painting; painted genre pictures and landscapes (*Bridge Near the Terrace*, 1886; *In Winter*, 1894, at the Tretyakov Gallery). Created a new type of stage settings: a colorful pageant closely related to musical themes (*Konyok Gorbunok* 1901, *Life for the Tsar* 1904, *Khovanshchina* 1912, *Coq d'Or* 1909, at the Moscow Bolshoy Theater). In the late 19th century

K turned to impressionism. In 1917 he settled in Paris and lived there until his death.

KORÓVIN, Sergéy Alekséyevich (1858–1908), painter of realistic trend. Studied in Moscow (1876–86); pupil of Perov. Continued traditional R. realistic style of genre painting (*Before Punishment*, 1884, in Museum of the Revolution, Moscow; *In the World*, 1893, Tretyakov Gallery). His favorite themes are army life and pilgrims on their way to holy places.

KORSÁKOV (f. Otomari), city in Sakhalin Oblast, RSFSR, port at Aniwa Bay; pop. 35,900 (1957). R.R. station; fishing center.

KÓRSAKOV, Sergéy Sergéyevich (1854–1900), psychiatrist. Graduate, (1875), Moscow University, and professor (1890) of its Psychiatric Clinic which was named after him. K is one of the founders of psychiatry in Russia. At the International Congress of Psychiatrists in Moscow (1897), polyneurotic psychosis which K diagnosed was called "Korsakov Disease." K opposed restraint of mental patients and campaigned against prejudice in connection with mental illnesses.

KORSÚN, BATTLE OF, May 16, 1648, in which Cossack Hetman Bogdan Khmelnitsky defeated the Polish Army imprisoning Polish Hetman Potocki. After a decisive victory at the Zholtye Vody and Korsun the war expanded throughout the W. Ukraine and Byelorussia.

KORYÁK NATIONAL OKRUG, RSFSR, N.W. third of the Kamchatka Peninsula; area 116,400 sq. mi.; pop. 28,000 (1959): Koryaks, Chukchi, Evenki, and Russians. Comprises mountainous area on the coast of the Bering Sea, including Karagin Island; is watered by the Penzhina River; is tundra, forested tundra, and tayga; has Arctic climate. It is the center of air communication routes of E. Siberia. Vegetables and potatoes; coal and peat; reindeer breeding, hunting, fishing. Adm. center: Palana Village. Est. 1930.

KORYÁK RANGE, extends S.W. to N.E. for over 500 mi. along the shores of the Bering Sea, from Kamchatka to Cape Navarin; highest point 8,200 ft.

KORYÁK SOPKA, volcano, 11,336 ft., at S. end of eastern range, Kamchatka Peninsula, N. of Petropavlovsk.

KÓSAREV, Aleksándr Vasílyevich (1903–1937), leader of the Komsomol. Became a Bolshevik in 1919 and joined a group of young volunteers to fight Yudenich. Later he became active in the Komsomol movement, becoming general secretary of the Leningrad Komsomol in 1929. At the 16th Congress of the CPSU he was made a candidate member of the Central Committee. Then he became secretary of the Komsomol. In 1937, at the peak of his career, he disappeared in the purges.

KOSHELYÓV, Aleksándr Ivánovich (1806–1883), publicist and Slavophile. K played a leading role in the liberal opposition and participated in the framing of many reforms including the emancipation of the serfs in 1861. In accordance with the Slavophile doctrine, K advocated the convocation of a representative consultative assembly. His book *Zapiski* (Notes) was published in 1884.

KOSIÓR, Stanisláv Vikéntyevich (1889–1939), Bolshevik leader in Ukraine. As a factory worker, K joined the Bolsheviks in 1907. He carried out revolutionary agitation throughout Ukraine, being intermittently jailed until 1917. In 1918 he joined the left communists in opposition to the Treaty of Brest-Litovsk. Restored to favor, he held miscellaneous party offices culminating with his appointment as secretary of the Central Committee in 1925. He was a member of the Central Committee and the Politburo in the thirties. In 1937 he was purged. In 1956, K's execution became the focal point of Khrushchev's attack on Stalin. After the 20th Congress of the CPSU, K was posthumously rehabilitated.

KOSMODEMYÁNSKAYA, Zóya Anatólyevna ("Tanya"), (1923–1941), member of the Young Communist League and student of a Moscow high school. She volunteered for service in the Soviet Army during World War II, and while on partisan duty behind the enemy lines was taken prisoner by the Germans in Petrishchevo, a village of Moscow Oblast, Nov. 1941; then tortured and hanged. The title of the Hero of the Soviet Union was conferred on her posthumously.

KOSTÉNKO, Mikhaíl Polievktovich (1889–), electrical engineer. Fellow, Ac. of S., USSR (1953). Honored Scientist and Technologist, Uzbek SSR. Deputy to the Supreme Soviet (1958). Graduate (1918), professor (1930), Petrograd (Leningrad) Polytechnic Institute; professor, Tashkent Industrial Institute (1942–44). Research concerns the theory and design of electrical machinery. Generalized the theory of transformers, developed design methods of long-distance electric power transmissions. Numerous inventions in electrical machinery. Stalin prizes (1949, 1951); Lenin prize (1958).

KOSTOMÁROV, Nikoláy Ivánovich (1817–1885), historian. In 1846 he began to teach at the University of Kiev. Arrested in 1847 for agitation on behalf of the emancipation of serfs and Ukrainian autonomy, K was exiled to Saratov. Returning in 1857, he lectured in history at the University of St. Petersburg, but was forced to resign his university position in 1862. Thereafter he published studies on the Ukrainian struggle against Poland and Russia, democratic tendencies among the early Slavs and Stenka Razin. He interpreted the history of the early state from the Ukrainian point of view and opposed Russo-Ukrainian union.

KOSTROMÁ, city, adm. center of Kostroma Oblast, RSFSR, on the left bank of the Volga at the mouth of Kostroma River; pop. 172,000 (1959). R.R. station. Old center of textile ind., it is noted for fine linen since the 16th century. Ind.: extensive lumbering, mfg. of woodenware, machinery, cotton goods, footwear, metalworking. Founded in 1152, it is one of the oldest cities of Russia; its cathedral, built in 1239, is a fine example of early R. architecture. In the 13th century it was in the Rostov-Suzdal principality; in the 15th century it was annexed by Moscow; was frequently invaded by Tatars. Has research institutes and a museum.

KOSTROMÁ OBLAST, RSFSR; area 23,350 sq. mi.; pop. 919,000 (1959). Located on the upper Volga and in the basins of its affluents, the Kostroma, Unzha and Vetluga, it is bordered on the N. by the N. Uvals. Cities: Kostroma (adm. center), Buy, Nerekhta, Sharya, Galich. A forested lowland, watered by numerous rivers and lakes, it has a continental climate; peat and phosphorite deposits. Ind.: lumbering, sawmilling, veneering.

Agr.: flax predominant, potatoes, dairy farming, wheat. Est. 1944.

KÓSTYCHEV, Pável Andréyevich (1845–1895), soil scientist. Born in the family of a serf in Moscow, K became one of the founders of modern soil science. Graduate (1869) and professor of the St. Petersburg Agr. Inst. and University. His research dealt with the biological principles of soil formation, geobotanics and fertility. Author of the first Russian textbook on *Soil Science*, 3 vol. (1887).

KOSTYLYÓV, Valentín Ivánovich (1884–1950), author. His first works appeared in 1903. He achieved recognition after the revolution. His main work consists of patriotic historical novels among which are *Pitirím, Kozma Minin,* and *A Fortunate Encounter,* written, respectively, in 1936, 1939, and 1947. The last-named is a novel based on the October revolution and the civil war. K's most important work is a trilogy *Ivan the Terrible* (1943–46) for which he was awarded the Stalin prize (1948).

KOSÝGIN, Alekséy Nikoláyevich (1904–), party and government official, born in St. Petersburg in a worker's family. In 1919, K joined the Red Army as a volunteer. After the civil war, he studied cooperatives in Siberia, finally joining the CPSU in 1927. In 1936 he became director of the October Textile Factory in Leningrad. In 1939 he was promoted to people's commissar of textile industries. During World War II he served as deputy chairman of the Council of People's Commissars, continuing in the post until the death of Stalin. He also held concurrent party posts, being a member of both the Politburo and the Central Committee. He did, however, suffer a political setback in 1952, when he was not appointed to the newly organized Presidium of the Central Committee. After Stalin's death, K regained his prominence and in 1957 he finally did become a member of the Presidium. He was also reappointed deputy chairman of the USSR Council of Ministers. Since 1957 he has been particularly prominent, speaking on economic matters with an authority second only to Khrushchev and Mikoyan. He has also been considered by observers as a possible successor to Khrushchev.

KOTÉLNICH, city in Kirov Oblast, RSFSR; pop. 27,000 (1956); port on Vyatka River, also major junction. Ind.: metalworking, sawmills, textile, food processing, weaving, knitwear, repair shop.

KOTÉLNIKOV, Vladímir Aleksándrovich (1908–), radio and electronic engineer. Fellow, Ac. of S., USSR (1953). Graduate (1931), professor (1947), Moscow Institute of Power Engineering. Director, Institute of Radio Engineering and Electronics, Ac. of S. (1954). Research concerns suppression of interferences and design of radio communication equipment. Supervised the design of a multichannel telephone-telegraph line working on one sideband. Currently used in the USSR on a large scale. Author of *The Theory of Potential Interference Resistance* (1956). Stalin prizes (1943, 1946).

KOTÉLNY, island, 4,750 sq. mi.; largest of New Siberian Islands, in W. part of the group, Yakut ASSR. Arctic climate; tundra vegetation; blue fox, reindeer,

many bird species in the summer; bones of prehistoric animals found in the soil. Discovered by I. Lyakhov, a Yakutsk merchant, in 1773.

KOTLÁS, city in Archangel Oblast, RSFSR; pop. 37,000 (1956). At the confluence of the Vychegda and N. Dvina rivers. Is a port on N. Dvina; a key R.R. junction; important river-rail lumber-reloading point. Grain-shipping center, with lumbering, shipyard, ship-repair shops, chemical ind., and paper mills.

KÓTLIN, island in Kronstadt Bay, E. end of the Gulf of Finland, 15 mi. from Leningrad; area 6 sq. mi.

KOTLYARÉVSKY, Iván Petróvich (1769–1838), Ukrainian writer and a founder of the literary Ukrainian language, born in Poltava. His satirical poem, *Aeneid* (1798), depicted life and social conditions in the Ukraine at the close of the 18th century. His famous play *Natalie from Poltava,* first acted in 1819 and published in 1838, is still produced in the Soviet Union.

KÓTOV, Aleksándr Aleksándrovich (1913–), chess player. Grand Master since 1939. Winner of international tournaments (1950, 1952). K is by profession a mechanical engineer.

KOTÓVSKY, Grigóry Ivánovich (1881–1925), prominent partisan leader and hero of the civil war (1918–21). He was organizer of the Moldavian SSR, and an early participant of the revolutionary movement. He joined the CP in 1920. Was assassinated near Odessa in 1925.

KOTSYUBÍNSKY, Mikhaíl Mikháylovich (1864–1913), leading Ukrainian writer, born in Vinnitsa. His novel *Fata Morgana,* published in two parts in 1904 and 1910, is concerned with revolutionary propaganda among the peasantry in 1905–06. Some of his short novels, also based largely on the revolutionary events of the early 1900's, are *Laughter, He Is Coming* (1906), and *On the Road* (1907).

KOTZEBUE, Otto von (1788–1846), scientist and navigator. In the course of three sea voyages around the world, he discovered nearly 400 islands in the Pacific Ocean and the Kotzebue Sound on the Alaskan coast.

KOVALÉVSKAYA, Sófia Vasílyevna (1850–1891), mathematician and writer. First female professor in  the world. Corresponding member, St. Petersburg Ac. of S. (1889). Born in the family of Lt. Gen. V. V. Korvin-Krukovsky, K showed an extraordinary ability in mathematics at an early age. Took up the study of mathematics in St. Petersburg (1866), but being a woman was barred from entering the university. Studied at the universities of Heidelberg (1869), Berlin (1870) and Göttingen (1874). Unable to find work in her field K embarked upon a literary career. Accepted position as professor of mathematics at Stockholm University (1883–91). Member of the editorial board of the journal *Acta Mathematica.*

KOVALÉVSKY, Aleksándr Onúfrievich (1840–1901), biologist. Fellow, Ac. of S. (1890). Graduate (1865), professor (1891–94), St. Petersburg University. Studied invertebrates in the Adriatic (1867), Mediterranean (1864–95), the Caspian (1869) and Red (1870) seas,

La Manche (1892), and described many new species. Discovered phagocytic organs in invertebrates (1893).

KOVALÉVSKY, Maksím Maksímovich (1851–1916), sociologist, lawyer and historian, professor of state and constitutional law at Moscow and St. Petersburg, and, after his dismissal by the government, lecturer at foreign universities (Stockholm, Oxford, and Paris). After his return to Russia in 1905 he resumed teaching in R. universities and served as a member of the legislative assemblies (1906–16). A convinced Westerner, he rejected Marxism and favored the introduction of a truly democratic constitutional regime. His views were strongly criticized by Lenin. From 1909 on, K was editor of *Vestnik Yevropy* (European Messenger).

KOVALÉVSKY, Vladímir Onúfrievich (1842–1883), paleontologist. Translator of books on Darwinism into Russian. Graduated from the University of Jena (1872) and St. Petersburg (1875). K's monographs on the paleontology of ungulates formed the basis of a new science known as "evolutionary paleontology." His geological studies deal with geological synchronization and zoo-geography; mapped out paleographic zones of the Upper Jura and Lower Cretaceous. Established the "Kovalevsky Law" which governs the historical development of animal life.

KÓVEL, city in Volyn Oblast, Ukrainian SSR; pop. 27,000 (1957). R.R. junction; railway-repair works, garment, butter, peat.

KÓVNO: *see* KAUNAS.

KOVPÁK, Sídor Artémyevich (1887–), partisan leader and Soviet official. K has been a member of the CPSU since 1919. During the civil war, he organized a unit which fought against the Whites in the Ukraine. In 1941–45, he was one of the organizers and head of the partisan movement in the Ukraine causing great losses to the Germans. K became deputy chairman of the Presidium of the Supreme Soviet of the Ukrainian SSR in 1947, and is a deputy to the Supreme Soviet USSR.

KOVRÓV, city on Klyazma River, Vladimir Oblast, RSFSR; pop. 100,000 (1959). R.R. junction. Ind.: clothing, textiles, food processing, machine mfg.

KÓVTYUKH, Yepifán Ióvich (1890–1943), veteran of the civil war. K joined the CP in 1918. He fought with the Red Army in the civil war, and led the evacuation of army units and civilians from the encircled Taman Peninsula (described by A. Serafimovich in *Zhelezny potok* [The Iron Torrent]). In 1936, K was appointed inspector of the White Russian military district. In 1937 he was arrested on charges of treason and participation in the alleged Tukhachevsky conspiracy. Apparently he was rehabilitated after Stalin's death.

KOZLÓV: *see* MICHURINSK.

KOZLÓV, Frol Románovich (1908–), member of the party Presidium and since May 1960 a secretary of the Central Committee of the CPSU. K was born in a village in Ryazan province, the son of a poor peasant. He started working in a textile factory at 15. Within a year, in 1924, he joined the Komsomol (Communist Youth League), and in 1926 he became a member of the CP. Like many an

able young man with good party standing, he was sent to study in Leningrad, in the workers' faculty of the Mining Institute, and at the Polytechnical Institute. In 1936, he began working as an engineer at a metallurgical plant in Izhevsk (Ural) where he gradually shifted to full-time party work and became secretary of the Izhevsk Gorkom (party city committee) in 1940. After 1944, his party career included three years in Moscow in the apparatus of the Central Committee, about two years in the party secretariat of Kuybyshev Oblast and then, starting in 1949, various positions in Leningrad, culminating with the post of second secretary in the Leningrad Oblast and election to the CPSU Central Committee in 1952. After Stalin's death K lost his Leningrad post temporarily, but was soon reinstated as first secretary of the same oblast committee. There he proved a staunch Khrushchev supporter and laid the foundations for his subsequent rise in the party and government. In Feb. 1956, he became a member of the Central Committee Bureau for the RSFSR, newly formed under Khrushchev's chairmanship, and a candidate member of the party Presidium. In June 1957, after Khrushchev's victory over the "anti-party" group, he was made a full Presidium member. K became chairman of the RSFSR Council of Ministers in Dec. 1957, and first vice-chairman of the USSR Council of Ministers in March 1958. In May 1960 he left the government for a position as secretary of the party Central Committee. Khrushchev has reportedly mentioned K privately as his successor. Like many of his generation of Communists, K shows little originality or imagination, and is more a political businessman, inclined to practicality and calculation, although he can undoubtedly be tough and ruthless as well. K visited the United States in 1959.

KOZLÓV, Pyotr Kuzmich (1863–1935), explorer. Fellow, Ac. of S., Ukrainian SSR (1928). Joined Przhevalsky's expeditions (1883–85 and 1888–90) in the course of which he compiled rich orographic, geological, and botanical material. Acquired world fame as the head of an expedition to Mongolia and Tibet (1899–1901) described in his book *Mongolia and Kam* (1905–06). During an expedition to the Gobi desert, he discovered the 13th-century city Khara-Khoto; excavations produced over 2,000 ancient manuscripts in addition to valuable material on the culture of the peoples of Asia. Other major discoveries include the burial mounts of eastern Huns and the ancient Chinese city Shun-uy-Khoto, both made during his last expedition to Mongolia and Tibet (1923–26). Received the highest award of the Russian Geographical Society (1902), the medal of the British Geographical Society (1911), and the P. A. Chikhachev Prize of the Paris Ac. of S. (1913). Honorary Member of the Dutch (1896), Russian (1910), and Hungarian (1911) Geographical Societies.

KOZLÓVSKY, Mikháil Ivánovich (1753–1802), sculptor. Studied at St. Petersburg Academy of Fine Arts (1764–73); worked in Italy and France (1774–90). His style, classic in form, combines the emotional elements with the idyllic, heroism with lyrics. Subjects are taken from mythology, history and literature (low reliefs in the Marble Palace, 1787; *Night Watch of Alexander the Great; The Hymen,* 1796; *Amour,* 1797, all marble;

terra-cotta sketches on subjects from *The Iliad,* 1790; equestrian figure of Yakov Dolgoruky, 1797). Best-known are K's monumental statues of *Suvorov* (in Leningrad) and *Samson* (in Petrodvorets).

KOZMÁ PRUTKÓV, a collective pseudonym created in the 60's of the 19th century by A. K. Tolstoy and his cousins, the brothers A. M. and V. M. Zhemchuzhnikov, for their jointly written satirical aphorisms, epigrams, poems, and proverbs. Most of these are nonsense poetry, but many are cleverly designed to ridicule the mores and customs of the time. Many of these witticisms have entered into Russian usage as proverbs.

KRAMATÓRSK, city in N. Stalino Oblast, Ukrainian SSR, in central Donbas; pop. 115,000 (1959). Ind. city of recent development; a center of ferrous metallurgy and heavy machinery mfg.

KRAMSKÓY, Iván Nikoláyevich (1837–1887), painter. Born in Strogozhsk, province of Voronezh, worked as retoucher and photographer. In 1857 enrolled in the Academy of Fine Arts. Leader of a movement towards realism among young painters, who refused in 1863 to participate in the graduation contest on the prescribed subject and withdrew from the Academy. K considered art as a means of serving the people; stressed the social factor and the realization of national character in works of art. His earlier works shown at the newly-founded Society of Circulating Exhibitions (*Peredvizhniki*) were *Mermaid* and *Christ in the Desert* (1872). K painted numerous portraits: Tolstoy (1873), Antokolsky (1876), Nekrasov (1878), Saltykov-Shchedrin (1879); also genre pictures: *Inspection of an Old House* (1873), *Moonlit Night* (1880), *Inconsolable Grief* (1884), *Nekrasov in the Period of His Last Songs* (1877), *Unknown Woman* (1883).

KRÁSIN, Leoníd Borísovich (1870–1926), engineer and Soviet diplomat. A specialist in the construction of electric plants, he worked for four years in Baku, being at the same time involved in revolutionary activities, especially in the running of the clandestine printing office which reprinted *Iskra* (q.v.). In 1904, K moved to Moscow and became a close friend of the millionaire, Savva Morozov, who showed great generosity to revolutionaries. In April 1905, K took part in the party congress in London as a deputy chairman and was elected to the Central Committee. At that time K was one of Lenin's closest assistants in the leadership of the Bolsheviks. In particular, he was responsible for the provision of funds through Morozov and other wealthy Russians, and through the organization of the "expropriations" (armed robberies) in the Caucasus. In 1907 K moved to St. Petersburg where he was arrested. In 1908 he went to Berlin and continued his engineering studies. Employed as a highly paid specialist by the firm of Siemens and Schuckert, K renounced revolutionary activities and was sent back to Russia as managing director of the St. Petersburg branch. After the October revolution, K returned to political activity. He took part in the Brest-Litovsk peace negotiations and then became chairman of a Special Commission for Army Supply, people's commissar for industry and trade and, in 1919, also people's commissar for transportation. In Dec. 1919, K signed the peace treaty with Estonia. In 1920,

he was head of the Soviet mission to London and, in March 1921, signed the first Anglo-Soviet agreement. In 1922, K took part in the Genoa and The Hague international conferences. He was nominated people's commissar for foreign trade which he organized as a strict state monopoly. In May 1924, K was elected by the 13th Party Congress as a member of the Central Committee and at the end of 1924 nominated as Soviet envoy to Paris. In 1925, he became Soviet ambassador in London where he died.

KRASNODÁR (f. Yekaterinodar), city, center of Krasnodar Kray, RSFSR; pop. 193,000 (1939), 313,000 (1959). Port on the Kuban River, on the Rostov-Novorossiysk R.R. Is a major cultural and industrial center, with extensive food processing, oil refinery, machine mfg., light ind., coal mining, fishing, textiles, tobacco ind.; institutions of higher learning, scientific institutes, theaters.

KRASNODÁR KRAY, RSFSR; includes Adygey Autonomous Oblast; area 32,300 sq. mi.; pop. 3,766,000 (1959). On the N.W. Caucasus, it borders on the Black Sea and Sea of Azov, and is watered by the Kuban River. Cities: Krasnodar (adm. center), Armavir, Novorossiysk, Tuapse, Yeysk, Kropotkin, Maykop, Sochi. Fertile black soil; in the S. the mountains and foothills of the Caucasus; moderate climate, mild along the shores of the Black Sea and the Sea of Azov; oil and gas deposits; also mineral resources. Ind.: oil, metalworking, machinery, concrete, food processing, tobacco, flour milling, textile, timber. Agr.: wheat, rye, corn, rice, sunflowers, tobacco, sugar beets, vegetables, fruit, wine, citrus fruit, tea, dairy farming, cattle raising, fishing. Has famous resorts, vast network of highways, maritime transport; is crossed by several R.R. lines. In the Middle Ages it was under Tatar khanates. Est. 1937.

KRASNODÓN (f. Sorokino), city in Lugansk Oblast, Ukrainian SSR; pop. 35,200 (1956). Coal mines.

KRASNOKÁMSK, city in Perm Oblast, RSFSR; pop. 54,000 (1959). Port on the Kama River. R.R. station. It has paper and cellulose mills, oil refineries. Founded 1930.

KRASNOKOKSHÁYSK: *see* YOSHKAR-OLA.

KRASNOTURYÍNSK (f. Turyinskie Rudniki), city in Sverdlovsk Oblast, RSFSR, on Turya River; pop. 62,000 (1959). R.R. station. Aluminum plant operating on the basis of the bauxite deposits "Krasnaya Shapochka"; coal mining. Memorial museum of A. S. Popov who was born here.

KRASNOURÁLSK, city in Sverdlovsk Oblast, RSFSR; pop. 45,000 (1959). Founded 1925 as a result of development of copper mining.

KRASNÓV, Pyotr Nikoláyevich (1869–1947), tsarist general, leader of the anti-Soviet Cossacks during the civil war. In Oct. 1917 K was appointed by Kerensky as commander of a Cossack force to fight the Bolshevik Red Guards. In May 1918, he was elected Ataman of the Don Cossacks and participated in the war against the Bolsheviks. K tried to take Tsaritsyn (now Stalingrad) in Oct. 1918. After the civil war, he emigrated to Germany where he was active among right-wing *émigrés*. During World War II K fought on the side of the Germans against the Bolsheviks, was captured by the Soviet army after the war, and was executed in 1947. K is the author of several novels on the civil war.

KRASNOVÍSHERSK, town in Perm Oblast, RSFSR, on Vishera River (left tributary of the Kama); pop. 15,000 (1956). Founded 1930 with the construction of a large cellulose and paper plant; also lumbering ind.

KRASNOVÓDSK, city, port on Krasnovodsk Gulf of Caspian Sea, Turkmen SSR; pop. 38,000 (1956). Is a transshipment point, as Ashkhabad R.R. terminus (grain, lumber). Exports oil, cotton, fruit; also has extensive fishing.

KRASNOYÁRSK, city, adm. center of Krasnoyarsk Kray, RSFSR, on left bank of the upper Yenisey River and on the Trans-Siberian R.R., E. of Novosibirsk; pop. 190,000 (1939), 412,000 (1959). A major industrial and cultural center, with scientific and research institutes, it is also a center of a gold-mining district. Its ind. include mining equipment, farm machinery plants, large paper mill, footwear and pencil mfg., food processing. A large hydroelectric power plant is under construction S of Krasnoyarsk. It has developed rapidly since the construction of the Trans-Siberian R.R. Founded in 1628.

KRASNOYÁRSK KRAY, RSFSR; area 927,000 sq. mi.; pop. 2,614,000 (1959): Russians, Evenki, Khakass, Nenets, Dolgans. Lies in Asia, in W. Central Siberia, and includes Khakass Autonomous Oblast, Taymyr and Evenki National Okrugs. Bounded on the N. by the Arctic Ocean, on the E. by Irkutsk Oblast and Yakut ASSR, on the S. by Tuva Autonomous Oblast, on the W. by Kemerovo and Tomsk oblasts. Cities: Krasnoyarsk (center), Achinsk, Igarka, Norilsk, Minusinsk, Kansk, Yeniseysk. Watered by the Yenisey River, it is tundra, hilly in central part, mountainous in S. Minerals: coal, iron, gold, manganese, graphite, nonferrous metals, slate. Ind.: heavy machinery, building materials, timber, flour milling, fish canning. Agr.: rye, wheat, oats; dairy farming, animal husbandry, reindeer breeding; hunting and fishing. Crossed by the Trans-Siberian R.R.

KRÁSNOYE SELÓ, town in Leningrad Oblast, RSFSR, suburb of Leningrad; pop. 14,100 (1956). R.R. station; paper factory.

KRÁSNY LUCH, (f. Krindachevka), city in Lugansk Oblast, Ukrainian SSR; pop. 59,000 (1939), 94,000 (1959). Is a major coal mining center in Donbas (primarily anthracite); has large power plant, metalworks, lumbering ind., machine mfg.

KRÁSNY SULÍN, (f. Sulin), city in Rostov Oblast, RSFSR; pop. 36,200 (1956). R.R. station. One of the oldest metallurgical centers in Donbas, it has coal-mining, food-processing, power plant.

KRAVCHÍNSKY, Sergéy Mikháylovich (pen name, Stepnyak), (1851–1895), participant of the populist movement of the 1870's, journalist, writer. He joined the Chaykovsky Group 1872; propagated revolutionary ideas among peasants; was arrested, fled abroad 1873; then participated in the rebellion of Serbs against Turks in Bosnia and Herzegovina, 1875. He became editor of the journal *Land and Freedom* upon his return to St. Petersburg. After assassinating Mezentsov, Chief of Police, he fled abroad. He is the author of the novels

Andrey Kozhukhov (written 1889, pub. in Russia 1893) and *Underground Russia* in which he idealized terrorist heroes.

KRAY, administrative-territorial unit. There are seven krays: Altay, Khabarovsk, Krasnodar, Krasnoyarsk, Maritime, Stavropol, all of them forming a part of RSFSR, and the recently established Virgin Lands Kray, part of Kazakh SSR. The largest is Krasnoyarsk Kray (area 927,000 sq. mi.); the smallest, Stavropol Kray (31,000 sq. mi.).

KREMENCHÚG, city in Poltava Oblast, Ukrainian SSR; pop. 90,000 (1939), 86,000 (1959). Port on the Dnieper and R.R. junction; ind. city in black-soil region, it has extensive trade in grain, lumber, tobacco; mfg. of transportation machinery, cloth factories; granite works in vicinity. Founded 1571.

KREMLIN, The (Russian "citadel"). The oldest and most imposing structure in Moscow consisting of a large triangular fortress on the Moskva River, with Red Square to the W., it was the residence of the ruling family from the early 14th century until 1712. At present, it serves as the meeting place of administrative councils and houses government offices. The first wooden walls were erected in 1156; in 1367 the fortress was surrounded by stone walls and towers; and in 1485–95 brick structures were added. The K harbors fine examples of 15th to 17th century R. architecture such as the Cathedral of the Assumption (1475–79), the bell tower known as "Ivan the Great" (1505–08), the Hall of Facets (1487–91), the Chambers (1635–36), and the

The Moscow Kremlin

Armory added in the early 18th century. The Senate building completed by 1788 houses the government of the USSR. The Great Kremlin Palace was built in the 19th century. Among the many towers of the K the best-known are Spasskaya, Nikolskaya, Troitskaya, Borovitskaya (all of them with gates), and Vodovzvodnaya which were adorned with five-pointed ruby stars in 1937.

BIBLIOGRAPHY: D. D. Duncan, *The Kremlin*, Greenwich, 1960; Arthur Voyce, *The Moscow Kremlin*, Berkeley, 1954.

KRESTÍNSKY, Nikoláy Nikoláyevich (1883–1938), joined the revolutionary movement in 1901 and the Social Democrats in 1903; from 1907 was a Bolshevik. Repeatedly arrested. After the October revolution, was people's commissar of finance, and from 1919 to 1921, one of the secretaries of the Central Committee of the CP. In Oct. 1921, was appointed Soviet ambassador to Germany. In March 1938, K was tried, together with Bukharin and Rykov, and as a right-wing oppositionist was sentenced to death and executed.

KRESTÓVY PASS, leads through Caucasus Mountains to Georgian Military Road; altitude 7,832 ft.

KRINDACHEVKA: *see* KRASNY LUCH.

KRISHTOFOVICH, Afrikan Nikoláyevich (1885–1953), paleobotanist. Corresponding member of the Ac. of S., USSR (1953), and fellow of the Ac. of S., Ukrainian SSR (1945). Graduated from Novorossiysk University in Odessa (1908). Associated with the Main Botanical Garden in Leningrad (1924) which has become the Inst. of Botanics. Conducted paleobotanical investigations in USSR, China, Korea and Japan. Disproved the theory of the uniformity of climate on earth during the Carboniferous period. Author of *Paleobotanics* (3rd edit. 1945) which earned him the Stalin prize (1946).

KRIVÍTSKY, Walter (Samuel Ginsburg) (1889–1941), chief of the Soviet Military Intelligence in W. Europe. In 1937, while in Paris, he defected and revealed numerous secrets of Soviet intelligence. Scheduled to appear before a U.S. Congressional Committee, K committed suicide. Author of *In Stalin's Secret Service* (1939).

KRIVÓY ROG, city in Dnepropetrovsk Oblast, Ukrainian SSR, on Ingulets River (right tributary of the Dnieper); pop. 189,000 (1939), 388,000 (1959). R.R. and ind. center in the midst of rich iron mines and on E. edge of the Donets Basin; has metallurgical plants, foundries, chemical works.

KRONSTÁDT or **KRONSHTADT,** city in Leningrad Oblast, RSFSR (subordinated to Leningrad Municipal Council); pop. 43,400 (1956). Founded by Peter I in 1703 as a fortress. Has a fine harbor but is blocked by ice five months of the year; is also an important naval base. Scene of mutinies in 1825, 1882, 1905, 1921. During World War II was a bulwark in the defense of Leningrad.

THE KRONSTADT UPRISING occurred March 7–18, 1921, in the major naval base and fortress of Kronstadt in the Gulf of Finland within sight of Petrograd (Leningrad). Its garrison hailed and supported the October Revolution. But strikes and demonstrations of Petrograd workers in 1921 against labor regimentation and food shortages found ready response among the Kronstadt sailors. Under the slogan, "Soviets without Bolsheviks!," they demanded greater economic and political freedom for workers and peasants. After attempts at pacification had failed, Trotsky and Tukhachevsky led a military attack across the ice. The uprising was suppressed and the survivors of the garrison of 14,000 shot or imprisoned. Lenin interpreted the uprising as a warning of the need for concessions. He proposed to the 10th Party Congress then meeting the economic retreat which was later called the New Economic Policy.

KROPÓTKIN, city in Krasnodar Kray, RSFSR, pop. 54,000 (1959). On Kuban River; a R.R. junction; center of food-processing ind., also has grain trade, flour mills, canneries.

KROPÓTKIN, Prince Peter Alekséyevich (1842–1921), theorist of anarchism, geographer, and traveler.  Graduate of the Corps of Pages in St. Petersburg, he served as officer in Siberia, where he took part in two geographical expeditions. In 1867 he became attached to the Russian Geographical Society and published important papers about his discoveries. In 1872 he joined the Bakunist movement, was arrested and imprisoned. He escaped in 1876 and went to W. Europe. He was active in Switzerland, France and in 1886 settled in London where he devoted himself to the development of his doctrines of Communist anarchism. Being opposed to the Darwinian notion of struggle for existence and to the tsarist regime, he developed a theory of mutual aid and a vision of a society based on a voluntary organization of producers' associations. He opposed Marxism, the Socialist state, and the dictatorship of the proletariat. K enjoyed a considerable personal respect and popularity. In June 1917 he returned to Russia where he died in 1921. His works include: *Paroles d'un révolté* (1884); *La conquête du pain* (1888); *L'anarchie: sa philosophie, son idéal* (1896); *The State, Its Part in History* (1898); *Fields, Factories, and Workshops* (1899, 1919); *Mutual Aid, a Factor of Evolution* (1902); *Memoirs of a Revolutionist* (1900), and others. A mountain range in S. Patom plateau, a city in Krasnodar Kray, a settlement in Irkutsk Oblast, a street and square in Moscow are named after him.

KRUCHÓNYKH, Alekséy Yeliséyevich (1886–), poet and member of the Cubo-Futurist group. With Khlebnikov (q.v.) developed a so-called "trans-sense language" (*zaumny yazyk*) in which new and original words were invented or derived from known words.

KRUG, Karl Adólfovich (1873–1952), electrical engineer. Corresponding member, Ac. of S., USSR (1933). Honored Scientist and Technologist (1937). Graduate, Moscow School of Technology (1898) and Moscow University (1903).

KRÚPSKAYA, Nadézhda Konstantínovna (1869–1939), wife of V. I. Lenin, revolutionary and leader in  education after 1917; born in St. Petersburg to an officer's family. She joined the first Marxist circle there in 1891 and met Lenin in 1893 or 1894. She was arrested 1896 and sentenced to three years' exile in Ufa Province in N. Russia. She was permitted to join Lenin in Siberia where they were married in July 1898. She was secretary of *Iskra* (q.v.). In 1905–07 K and Lenin lived in Finland, while K frequently visited St. Petersburg to carry on organizational work. In 1907 they went abroad but returned to Russia in April 1917. After the advent of the Bolsheviks to power K was made a member of collegium of People's Commissariat of Education and in 1929 assistant vice commissar of education. She was one of the organizers of the Pioneer movement; a member of the Central

Control Commission of the CP, 1924, and a member of the Central Committee, 1927. Author of a book of reminiscences of Lenin and of several books on education.

KRUZENSHTÉRN, Iván Fyódorovich (1770–1846), admiral and explorer. Honorary member, St. Petersburg Ac. of S. (1806). Headed the first Russian sea voyage around the world (1803–06) in the course of which numerous islands were discovered and valuable information gathered on the geography and ethnography of Pacific islands. Author of *Voyage Around the World in 1803, 1804, 1805 and 1806 on Board the Nadezhda and Neva* with maps (1809–12). Cofounder and member of the Russian Geographical Society, member of the Royal London Society.

KRYLÉNKO, Nikoláy Vasílyevich (1885–1938?), leading Communist. Graduated from the juridical and historico-philological faculties of St. Petersburg University. During the 1905 revolution, K was one of the popular student leaders and was several times arrested. Formally a Bolshevik, in 1909 he published a book *In Search of Orthodoxy* which betrayed syndicalist deviations. During World War I, K was conscripted into the army. After the February revolution, he organized the Bolshevik propaganda in the army and was arrested by Kerensky's government. After the October revolution, Lenin included K in his government (as a member of the War Commissariat), and on Nov. 25, 1917 appointed him commander-in-chief of all armed forces, replacing Gen. Dukhonin. In 1918, K organized the revolutionary tribunals, and from 1922 was deputy commissar (from 1931, commissar) of justice of the RSFSR and chief public prosecutor of the supreme court in which capacity he took part in the earlier political trials (*Shakhty, Prompartia,* and so forth). K was author of several books on Soviet criminal law and the organization of courts. In 1933 he received the orders of Lenin and the Red Banner. In 1936, he was appointed commissar of justice of the USSR, but disappeared without trial during the great purges in 1937.

KRYLÓV, Alekséy Nikoláyevich (1863–1945), mathematician, mechanical and aeronautical engineer. Fellow, Ac. of S. (1916). Hero of Socialist Labor (1943). Graduate (1890), professor (1892–1940), St. Petersburg Naval Academy. Research concerned the theory of aeronautical design, mathematics, mechanics, artillery, ballistics, and the theory of gyroscope. Designed and built the first R. device for integrating differential equations as well as numerous other devices and instruments. Author of *Vibration of Ships* (1908). Stalin prize (1941).

KRYLÓV, Iván Andréyevich (1769–1844), noted Russian fabulist. His fables, which have been translated  into many languages, are widely known in Russia. They are written in the colloquial language of the common people and moralize the practical consequences of such petty failings as laziness, vanity, and hypocrisy. Born in the family of a poor army officer, K spent his early childhood in the houses of wealthy benefactors. Upon arriving in St. Peters-

burg in 1792 he began to write satirical poems, comedies, and comic operas dealing with the corruption, stupidity, and lawlessness of the gentry. He also founded and edited satirical reviews. His sharp wit had made him many enemies and he was soon forced to leave the capital. K worked in the provinces for many years as tutor and secretary. He returned to the literary scene in 1805 by translating into Russian some of the fables of La Fontaine. Subsequently, 9 volumes of his own fables were published (1809–41) and received immediate recognition. In 1812 K became librarian in the Public Library of St. Petersburg.

KRYLÓV, Nikoláy Mitrofánovich (1879–1955), mathematician. Fellow, Ac. of S., USSR (1929). Honored Scientist, Ukrainian SSR (1939). Graduate, (1904), professor (1912), St. Petersburg Mining Institute. Head, Department of Mathematical Physics, Ac. of S. (1922). Research concerned the theory of interpolation, approximated integration of differential equations, equations of mathematical physics and nonlinear mechanics. Collaborated with N. N. Bogolyubov from 1932.

KRÝMOV, Aleksándr Mikháylovich (1871–1917), tsarist general. Participated in a conspiracy against the tsar on the eve of the February revolution. Under the Provisional Government he commanded the Third Cavalry Corps and was ready to support Kornilov's rebellion by direct military action. When his troops refused to obey and A. F. Kerensky censured him for mutinous action, K committed suicide.

KRZHIZHANÓVSKY, Gleb Maksimiliánovich (1872–1959), revolutionary, specialist in energetics.  Born in Samara; he graduated from the St. Petersburg Institute of Technology in 1894. While still a student, he organized, with Lenin, the Union of Struggle for the Liberation of the Working Class in 1893. Joined the Social Democratic party; was elected to the Central Committee at the 2nd Party Congress. He took active part in the revolution of 1905–07. After the October revolution, he was head of the State Power Commission (GOELRO) (1920). From 1921 to 1930, he directed the work of the Gosplan (State Planning Commission); later, he was head of the Central Power Administration. From 1930, he was director of the Institute of Energetics. From 1929 he was a member of the Ac. of S., USSR, and vice president from 1929 to 1939.

KSHESSINSKA, Mathilda (Princess Krassinska-Romanovska) (1872–), ballerina of the Imperial Mariinsky Theater of St. Petersburg. She was a great dancer, who could have held sway over the Mariinsky on her talent alone, but used her court connections to exercise additional authority. She was the first of the R. ballerinas to begin the gradual replacement of foreign ballerinas in the Imperial Theater. She married Grand Duke Andrey Vladimirovich in 1921 in Cannes, France, having borne him a son, Vladimir, in 1902, in Strelna, near St. Petersburg. Since 1920 she has been living in Paris where she still teaches in her ballet school (1960). Author of interesting memoirs published in 1961.

KUBÁ, town, N.E. Azerbaijan SSR, on E. slopes of

Caucasus Mountains; pop. 15,600 (1957). Center of large vine- and orchard-growing area; food-processing ind., rug weaving.

KUBÁN RIVER (ancient *Hypanis*), 563 mi. long, navigable for over 180 mi. Rises in the Caucasus Mountains, S.W. of the Elbrus Mountain; flows through Stavropol and Krasnodar krays into a wide marshy delta with three mouths—two on the Sea of Azov and one on the Black Sea. Major left tributaries include Teberda, Bolshoy and Maly Zelenchuk, Laba, Urup, Belaya rivers. Abounds in fish; part of its water is used for irrigation.

KÚBENA LAKE, Vologda Oblast, 143 sq. mi., outlet of the Sukhona River, a tributary of the N. Dvina. Connected by N. Dvina Canal with the Sheksna River, thus joining the N. Dvina and the Leningrad-Volga (Mariinsk Canal) systems.

KUCHELBEKER, Wilhelm Karlovich (1797–1846), romantic poet. An ardent R. patriot in spite of his German origin, K was a classmate of Pushkin at the *lycée* of Tsarskoye Selo and became his close friend. Because he took part in the unsuccessful Decembrist uprising, he was arrested and sentenced first to prison and then to exile in Siberia. His first poems, which reflect the influence of the classical poets Derzhavin and Zhukovsky, were published in the almanac *Mnemozina* (1824–25). They express a love of liberty and a pantheistic view of the universe. K also wrote an autobiography and literary essays.

KUDÝMKAR, city, adm. and cultural center of Komi-Permyak National Okrug, Perm Oblast, RSFSR; pop. 20,000 (1956). At the confluence of the Inva and Kuva rivers (Kama River basin). Ind.: flax and food processing, lumbering, metalworking.

KÚINDZHI, Arkhíp Ivánovich (1842–1910), landscape painter noted for his experimentation with light effects. His decorative theatrical landscapes formed a transition from the naturalism of the Society of Circulating Exhibitions (*Peredvizhniki*) school to the lyrical, intimate landscapes which were popular at the turn of the century. His paintings are in the Tretyakov Gallery, Moscow, and the Russian Museum, Leningrad.

KUKÁRKIN, Borís Vasílyevich (1909–), astronomer. Professor, Moscow University (1951). Director, State Astronomical Institute (1952–56); vice president, International Astronomical Society (1955). Editor of the publication *Peremennye Zvezdy* (Variable Stars) (1928).

KÚKOLNIK, Néstor Vasílyevich (1809–1868), playwright, author of ultra-patriotic historical plays; among them are *Prince Mikhail Vasilyevich Skopin-Shuysky* and *The Hand of the Almighty Protects the Fatherland.*

KUKRYNÍKSY, pen name used jointly by three Soviet caricaturists: Kupriánov, Mikhail Vasilyevich (1903–), Krylóv, Porfiry Nikitich (1902–), and Sokolov, Nikolay Aleksandrovich (1903–). They have worked together since 1926 as caricaturists, illustrators, and poster artists. They painted satirical portraits of writers and artists, derided survivals of the past in *The Old Moscow* and exposed fake "shock" workers and ineffectual and corrupt bureaucrats in *Pravda.* Were illustrators of Gorky's *Klim Samgin* and Ilf's and Petrov's *12 Chairs.*

KULAK: *see* AGRICULTURE, NEP.

KULEBÁKI, city in Gorky Oblast, RSFSR; pop. 40,000 (1956). Ferrous metallurgy.

KULEBÁKIN, Víktor Sergéyevich (1891–), electrical engineer. Fellow, Ac. of S., USSR (1939). Graduate, Moscow School of Technology (1914); professor, Military Academy of Airforce Engineering (1923). Cofounder of the Moscow Institute of Power Engineering, the All-Union Institute of Electrical Engineering, and the Institute of Automation and Telemechanics, Ac. of S., with which he has been associated since 1939. Research concerns theory and design of electric machinery, theory of automatic control, and electrical equipment for aircraft. Stalin prize (1950).

KULIKÓVO, BATTLE OF, Sept. 8, 1380, between hordes of Mongolian Tatars under Khan Mamay and Russians led by Dimitry Ivanovich, Grand Duke of Moscow, surnamed Donskoy. The battle was waged on Kulikovo plain near the source of the Nepryadva River (tributary of the Don) and was a major victory over Tatars.

KULYÁB, city in Tadzhik SSR; pop. 39,600 (1959). Ind. include cotton ginning, butter plant, machine repair shops, building materials.

KUMÁ RIVER, 366 mi. long; rises on the slope of the Caucasian Mountains, at an altitude of over 6,500 ft., flows E. to Caspian Sea through Stavropol Kray, borders downstream on Kalmyk ASSR and Dagestan ASSR; reaches the sea only during flood season. Used for irrigation of rice, vegetable fields, vineyards, orchards. The completion of the Terek-Kuma Canal will make possible the cultivation of large areas of fertile soil in the Kuma valley.

KURGAN: *see* ARCHAEOLOGY.

KUNGÉY ALA-TAU, mountain range in Tien Shan, Kirghiz SSR, rises in the form of an immense wall almost without foothills along the N. shore of Issyk-Kul Lake, extending for 180 mi. The highest peak, Choktal Mountain, (15,650 ft.) has 10 glaciers.

KUNGRÁD, settlement in Kara-Kalpak ASSR, in the delta of Amu Darya; pop. 9,600 (1956). Terminus on Chardzhou-Kungrad R.R. Cotton ginning, fishing.

KUNGÚR, city in Perm Oblast, RSFSR, at the confluence of the Iren and Sylva (left tributary of the Chusovaya); pop. 36,000 (1939), 65,000 (1959). R.R. station. Center of agr. district, it is rich in gypsum and kaolin, also famous for leather goods. Kungur ice cave on the bank of the Sylva River is tourist attraction. Founded 1648.

KÚNTSEVO, city in Moscow Oblast, RSFSR; pop. 61,000 (1939), 128,000 (1959). R.R. station. Center of wool and metalworking ind.

KUPÁLA, Yánka (Lutsévich, Iván Dominíkovich) (1882–1942), a popular poet of Byelorussia, member  of the Ac. of S. of the Byelorussian SSR and Ukrainian SSR. His works were first published in 1905. His later writings, issued in 1908, 1910, and 1913, depicted life of peasants in his native Byelorussia. K's best prerevolutionary poems are *Dream on a Burial Mound* (1912), *A Lion's Grave,* and *The Ravaged Nest* (1913). In 1914 K became editor of the Byelorussian daily *Nasha niva* (Our fields). Following the revolution, K continued to write poetry dealing with life in Byelorussia: *The Son Came for a Visit* (1935), *On the Oressa River* (1933), and others. At the outbreak of World War II K wrote the patriotic poems *To the Byelorussian Partisans* and *The People Rise* (1941).

KUPRÍN, Aleksándr Ivánovich (1870–1938), novelist. He studied in military school in Moscow, and served as an officer in the army. He emigrated after the revolution and returned to the Soviet Union shortly before his death. Of his numerous writings, the best-known are *Moloch* and *The Duel* (1905–6). His novel *The Pit* (1909–15) deals with the life of prostitutes, and his story *Gambrinus* (1907) with anti-Semitism.

KURÁ RIVER, (ancient *Cyrus*, Turkish *Kora*), 940 mi. long, the largest in Transcaucasia; rises in N.E. Turkey at an altitude of over 8,850 ft., flows N. into Georgian SSR and then E.S.E. into Azerbaijan SSR to the Caspian Sea S. of Baku. Tributaries: (left) Aragvi, Alazan with Iori; (right) Khrami, Shamkhor, Araks. Navigable; used for irrigation and log floating; supplies hydroelectric power; fed by many mountain streams, it has rapid current in upper course. A large hydroelectric station has been built at Mingechaur, a network of irrigation canals under construction will increase the cotton-growing area.

KÚRBAS, Lev Stepánovich (1887–?), leading Ukrainian actor, born in Galicia. He was educated in Europe and made his debut in Kiev in 1915 in the nationalethnic Ukrainian theater of M. Sadowsky. Working with a young Ukrainian troupe, he became from 1916 on one of the greatest innovators and reformers of the Ukrainian theater, bringing to it a repertory of W. European classics and new plays. After the 1917 revolution, K organized the Berezil Theater and a number of affiliated studies, where productions were staged in expressionist and constructionist styles and new theatrical cadres received solid training. Toward the end of the 1920's, conflicts arose between the freedom-loving K and the party, culminating in 1933 with the shutting down of Berezil as a "bourgeois nationalist" organization. K was suppressed and died in a concentration camp. His significance in the Ukrainian theater is comparable to that of Meyerhold in the Russian theater.

KÚRBSKY, Prince Andréy Mikháylovich (1528–1583), prominent boyar. While commander in Livonia he abandoned his army and joined Lithuanian forces. He is the author of a controversial correspondence with Ivan IV in defense of the nobility and of a book *History of the Grand Duke of Moscow*.

KURCHÁTOV, Ígor Vasílyevich (1902–1960), nuclear physicist. Fellow, Ac. of S., USSR (1943). Graduate, Crimean University in Simferopol (1923); professor, Leningrad University (1925–60); director, Institute of Atomic Energy. Deputy to the Supreme Soviet (1950, 1958). Early research concerns electric properties of Rochelle salt; K became a leading nuclear physicist in 1933. Observed nuclear chain reactions under neutron bombardment (1934); investigated artificially-induced radioactivity of several elements. In the study of neutron capture by boron atoms, K discovered nuclear iso-

merism phenomena in artificial radioactive isotopes; suggested the theory of nuclear isomerism and clarified processes which occur in atomic nuclei. Split heavy nuclei and discovered the spontaneous fall-out of uranium. Organized research for a wider scientific and technical application of nuclear power in the USSR. Participated in the first Soviet atomic bomb project as a member of A. S. Alikhanov's team. Member of the Soviet delegation to the International Conference on the Peaceful Use of Atomic Energy in Geneva (1955) and in England (1956). Author of *Splitting the Atom* (1935); *Problems of the Development of Nuclear Power Engineering in the USSR* (1956); *The Possibility of Inducing Thermonuclear Reactions in Gas Discharge* (1956). Stalin prize.

KURGÁN, city, adm. center of Kurgan Oblast, RSFSR, on Tobol River and Trans-Siberian R.R.; pop. 53,000 (1939), 145,000 (1959). As it is in rich agr. plain E. of the Urals, it is a trade center for dairy products, including butter, cattle and grain; also has agr. machinery, chemical machinery, bus mfg., food processing plants. Russ. "kurgan" means "tumulus," a name derived from numerous ancient burial mounds in the vicinity. Founded in 17th century.

KURGÁN OBLAST, RSFSR; area 27,050 sq. mi.; pop. 1,002,000 (1959). Borders on Sverdlovsk (N.) and Chelyabinsk (W.) oblasts and on Kazakh SSR (S.), part of West Siberian plain. Cities: Kurgan (adm. center), Shadrinsk, Dalmatovo, Kataysk, Petukhovo, Shumikha, Shchuchye. Its lowland is watered by the Tobol, Iset, and Miass; has numerous fresh- and mineral-water lakes; dry continental climate with occasional drought. Rich black-soil agr.: wheat, dairy farming, horse breeding, apiculture; food-processing ind. Is crossed by the Trans-Siberian RR., and has direct air connection to Moscow. Est. 1943.

KURGÁN-TYUBÉ, town in Tadzhik SSR, on Vakhsh River; pop. 22,000 (1958). R.R. station. New irrigation system made the town into a highly productive area (cotton, rice, alfalfa, vineyards, horticulture).

KURÍL or KURILE ISLANDS, group of about 32 islands extending from Cape Lopatka (S. end of Kamchatka Peninsula) to Hokkaido (Japan), 800 mi., separate the Sea of Okhotsk from the Pacific Ocean. Area about 6,000 sq. mi. All islands are of volcanic origin, some still having active volcanoes. Severe climate, frequent storms and fogs, cold winters. N. islands mostly tundra; S. have forests. Fur-bearing animals, fish, fur seal.

KURNAKÓV, Nikoláy Semyónovich (1860–1941), chemist. Fellow, Ac. of S. (1913); Honored Scientist, RSFSR (1940). Graduate (1882), professor (1893), St. Petersburg Mining Institute; chairman, Chemical Association, Ac. of S. (1930–34). Research concerned metal alloys, viscosity of binary systems and thermal analysis. Invented self-recording pyrometer (1903). A pioneer in physicochemical analysis, K greatly contributed to the development of platinum refining, aluminum and magnesium production, the use of mineral fertilizers and domestic minerals. Lenin prize (1928); Stalin prize (1941).

KUROSH, Aleksándr Gennádievich (1908–), mathematician. Graduate, Smolensk University (1928); professor, Moscow University (1937). Research concerns group theory, and the theory of rings and structures. Author of an extensive monograph translated into many languages, *The Theory of Groups* (2nd ed., 1953); and of *A Course of Higher Algebra* (5th ed., 1956).

KURSK, city, adm. center of Kursk Oblast, RSFSR, on the N. bank of Seym River; pop. 120,000 (1939), 205,000 (1959). Is a R.R. junction, and a major ind. city with mfg. of machinery, chemicals, food processing, sewing machines, footwear, building materials; pedag. and medical inst. Founded in 11th century. Scene of major battle in World War II.

KURSK OBLAST, RSFSR, in central R. plateau; area 11,500 sq. mi.; pop. 1,481,000 (1959): Russians and Ukrainians. Cities: Kursk (center), Lgov, Dmitryev-Lgovsky, Fatezh, Rylsk. Crossed by Seym River and is source of Donets and tributaries of the Donets and Dnieper. In N. part of black-earth (chernozem) belt; temperate continental climate. Mineral resources include iron ore deposits (Kursk Magnetic Anomaly), phosphorite, structural materials. Developed agr. (wheat, rye, oats, sugar beets, millet, potatoes, flax, sunflowers, hemp), horticulture. Ind.: food processing (flour mills, canning), machinery.

KÚRSKY, Dmítry Ivánovich (1874–1932), Communist lawyer. In the revolutionary movement from the 1890's. In 1904 he joined the Bolsheviks and in 1905 participated in the uprising in Moscow. Was people's commissar of justice of the RSFSR from 1918 to 1928; Soviet ambassador to Italy, 1928–32.

KÚSHVA, city in Sverdlovsk Oblast, RSFSR, on Kushva River (right tributary of the Tura), near Blagodat Mt.; pop. 40,000 (1957). Has R.R. station. Iron-ore mining and ferrous metallurgy plant. Founded 1735.

K U S K Ó V A (Esipova), Yekaterína Dmítrievna (1869–1958), journalist. In the 1890's K became a leader of the "Legal" (moderate) Marxists and joined the Social Democratic movement. In 1899 she published a declaration known as the "Credo" expressing the view of the "Economists" that the Social Democrats should fight mainly for the economic betterment of the working class and not exclusively for the overthrow of the autocracy. The "Credo" was sharply attacked by such orthodox Marxists as Plekhanov, Lenin, Akselrod and others. In 1902–03, K was one of the founders of the Union of Liberation (q.v.). In the revolutions of 1905 and 1917, she was a leading spokesman for the liberal intelligentsia. During the famine of 1921, she tried, together with her husband S. N. Prokopovich and N. M. Kishkin, to organize help for the starving population, but was arrested and later exiled by the Soviet government. A controversial figure in the emigration, K believed in the evolution and gradual democratization of the Soviet regime.

KUSTANÁY, city, adm. center of Kustanay Oblast, Kazakh SSR, on Tobol River (left tributary of the Irtysh); pop. 34,000 (1939), 83,000 (1959). Has extensive agr. in fertile black-soil area; and rapidly developing ind., such as an electric plant, flour mills, footwear factories. Est. 1880.

KUSTANÁY OBLAST, Kazakh SSR; area 76,000 sq. mi.; pop. 703,000 (1959): Kazakh, Russians, Ukrainians. Borders in the W. on the foothills of the S. Urals and on following oblasts: Kurgan and Chelyabinsk (N.), Karaganda (S.), Akmolinsk and Kokchetav (E.). Cities: Kustanay (adm. center), Dzhetygara, Rudny. Black soil area in the N. with dry steppe changing into semidesert in the S., it is drained by the Tobol River and its affluents and by Turgay and Ulkayak; in the center is the Turgay Valley; has continental climate. Rich agr.: dairy and poultry farming, sunflowers, hemp, wheat and other grain crops, vegetables, sheep, goat and hog raising, horse breeding. Minerals are iron ore, titanium, bauxite, lead, asbestos, lignite. Ind.: food processing; gold mining at Dzhetygara; ore beneficiation combine under construction at Rudny on the Tobol River. Crossed by the Trans-Siberian R.R. Est. 1936.

KUSTÓDIEV, Borís Mikháylovich (1878–1927), painter, graphic artist, and stage designer. Contributed to the magazine *Mir Iskusstva* (World of Art). Began as a romantic painter idealizing the life of the provincial merchant class; designed colorful stage settings. After the October revolution K painted chiefly heroic revolutionaries. His best-known postrevolution picture is *Bolshevik*, Russian Museum in Leningrad. K illustrated the works of Pushkin, Nekrasov, and others.

KUTAÍSI, city in Georgian SSR, on both banks of the Rioni River; pop. 78,000 (1939), 128,000 (1959). On a branch of the Tbilisi-Poti R.R. Important trading center, with versatile ind. including automobile plant, textiles (silk, cloth), winemaking, tobacco factories; orchards; a large hydroelectric power plant in the vicinity (Rionges); coal and barite mining (Tkibuli). A very ancient city, it was the capital of Abkhazia in 792; annexed by Russia in 1810.

KUTÚZOV (Goleníshchev-Kutúzov), Prince Mikhaíl Illariónovich (1745–1813), field marshal and one of the  founders of R. military science. He participated in the Russo-Turkish Wars of the 18th century under the command of P. A. Rumyantsev and A. V. Suvorov and gained fame by the seizure of Izmail (1790). He was commander of the R. Army in Austria in the war of the Third Coalition (Russia, Austria, England) against Napoleon; defeated the Turkish Army 1811–12 which resulted in a favorable peace treaty at Bucharest. As commander in chief of the R. Army in the Napoleonic war of 1812, he practiced cautious strategy and, after the battle of Borodino, retreated behind Moscow. Until his death (in April 1813) he led the R. Army in the liberation of European countries from the rule of Napoleon. In 1942–43 the Order of Kutuzov was established in his honor.

KÚUSINEN, Otto Vilgelmovich (1881–), leader of the CP in Finland and the CPSU. Graduate of the faculty of philosophy and history, Helsinki University (1905). K began his political career in 1905 when he headed the left wing of the Finnish Social Democratic party. He took part in the revolution of 1905–06 and led the Social Democratic party which he represented

in the Finnish Diet. In 1918 K was member of the revolutionary government and became the founder and chairman of the CP of Finland. In 1921–39 K was secretary of the executive committee of the Comintern. After the banning of the CP in Finland (1930) he lived in Moscow. In 1939 he became the head of the new, Soviet-supported Karelo-Finnish government; in July 1940, chairman of the Presidium of the Supreme Soviet of Karelo-Finnish Socialist Soviet Republic. After 1952 member of the Presidium. In 1953 K left the Presidium of the Central Committee of CPSU, but at the 1957 Plenum of the Central Committee he was appointed secretary and Presidium member of the Central Committee of the CPSU. K has been deputy to the Supreme Soviet of the USSR since 1940; he has published several books; and was awarded the order of Lenin three times. Fellow, Ac. of S., USSR (1958).

KÚYBYSHEV (f. Samara), city, adm. center of Kuybyshev Oblast, RSFSR, an important port on the left bank of the Volga and on main R.R. to the Urals, Siberia, and Central Asia; pop. 390,000 (1939), 806,000 (1959). A major industrial center: transportation machinery, tool construction, oil industry and power-plant equipment, light and food ind.; Kuybyshev Hydroelectric Power plant has a capacity of over 2 mill. kw. Scenically located on the steep bank of the Volga, surrounded by forests, parks, gardens; has schools of higher learning, scientific institutes, theaters, museum. Est. 1596, it was the scene of Pugachov's rebellion against Catherine II in 1774; since the 18th century, it has been a trading center with Kirghiz Steppe region and cities of Turkestan. During World War II it became the temporary capital of the USSR when Moscow was threatened by the German advance. In 1935 it was renamed in honor of the Bolshevik leader V. V. Kuybyshev.

KÚYBYSHEV OBLAST, RSFSR; area 20,700 sq. mi.; pop. 2,257,000 (1959): Russians and Tatars. In the middle Volga valley, at the Samara bend in the W. (Zhiguli Mts.), it is bounded in the E. by the foothills of the S. Urals; and is drained by the Samara, Sok, Greater Kinel, and Greater Irgiz rivers. Cities: Kuybyshev (adm. center), Syzran, Stavropol, Chapayevsk, Kinel, Mukhanovo. Its forested elevated plain is known as the Volga Upland on the right bank of the Volga with humid climate; its lowland with dry climate and steppe vegetation is on the left bank; has black soil. Mineral resources: petroleum, oil shale, phosphorite, sulfur, cement rock, limestone. Rich agr.: wheat, hemp, sunflowers, corn, potatoes, barley, sugar beets, orchards; cattle and hog raising. Ind.: oil and food processing, tanning, flour and sugar milling, machine mfg., building materials, chemical, lumber sawing. Has a well-developed rail and road network; commercial traffic on the Volga facilitates export. Kuybyshev Power Plant is near Zhigulyovsk on the Volga. Est. 1935.

KÚYBYSHEV, Valerián Vladímirovich (1888–1935), a prominent Bolshevik. He was born into an officer's

family in Omsk and spent most of his youth in Siberia. Here he joined the Bolshevik party in 1904. His revolutionary agitation led to his expulsion from the Military-Medical Academy in St. Petersburg, and to many arrests. Thereafter he devoted himself entirely to party affairs. During the period of revolution and civil war, K was the organizer of the armed revolt in Samara (now Kuybyshev) and served as commissar on several military fronts. In 1922 he entered the Central Committee and supported Stalin in the latter's struggle with Trotsky. K was rewarded with a promotion to the Politburo and leadership of Gosplan. His sudden death in 1935 occurred under suspicious circumstances.

KUZBÁS: *see* KUZNETSK BASIN.

KUZMÍN, Iósif Iósifovich (1910–), party and government official. He was born in Astrakhan and joined the CPSU in 1930 as a machinist in a Leningrad factory. The party sent him to the Budyonny Electrical Engineering Academy. In 1940 he became deputy chairman of the party control commission. In 1956 he achieved some prominence by accompanying Khrushchev and Bulganin to England. In 1957 he was named chairman of the State Planning Committee (*Gosplan*) and Deputy Premier. Ambassador to Switzerland (1959).

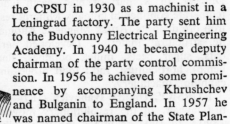

KUZMÍN, Mikhaíl Alekséyevich (1875–1936), poet whose work reflects his interest in the sect of Old-Believers. Much of it is in the form of poetic songs of love with overtones of homosexuality. Sexual perversion is also the subject of some of his short novels, including the erotic novel *Wings* (1907) and the novel *Travelers by Land and Sea* (1915).

KUZNÉTSK, city in E. Penza Oblast, RSFSR, near source of Sura River, on Tula-Kuybyshev R.R.; pop. 38,000 (1939), 57,000 (1959). Has extensive trade in leather goods; wool; textile-machinery mfg.

KUZNÉTSK: *see* STALINSK.

KUZNÉTSK BASIN (KUZBAS), Kemerovo Oblast, in the basin of the Upper Tom River, betwen Salair ridge and Kuznetsk Ala-Tau. Second-largest Soviet coal deposits; has been converted into great independent industrial area; rich iron-ore deposits at Tamir-Tau, S. of Stalinsk. Rapid development of nonferrous metallurgy and machine manufacturing. Ind. centers: Stalinsk, Kemerovo, Prokopyevsk, Leninsk-Kuznetsky, Anzhero-Sudzhensk.

KUZNETSÓV, Nikoláy Gerasímovich (1902–), Soviet admiral. Graduate of the Naval Training School in Leningrad (1926) and the Voroshilov Naval Academy (1932). K has been a member of the CPSU since 1925. In 1937, he was appointed commander of the Pacific fleet; 1939–45, was people's commissar of the navy and commander in chief of USSR naval forces; 1946, first deputy minister of war and commander in chief of USSR Navy. In 1948 he was demoted and appointed deputy commander in chief. In 1953, K was first deputy minister of defense. Since 1957, he has been serving in the central apparatus of the Ministry of Defense. K was elected member of the Central Committee of the CPSU in 1939 and 1952; is deputy to the Supreme Soviet USSR, Hero of the Soviet Union. He has four Lenin orders and many other medals. K is credited with the development of a powerful submarine fleet.

KUZNETSÓV, Vasíly Vasílyevich (1901–), party and government official. Born in Gorky Oblast, studied at Leningrad Polytechnical Institute, 1921–26. He held several metallurgical engineering positions until, in 1940, he was appointed deputy chairman of the USSR State Planning Commission (Gosplan). During World War II he was also a member of the State Defense Committee on metallurgical matters; held several trade-union posts during the war and was appointed a member of the general council of the executive committee and vice chairman of the World Federation of Trade Unions. He also headed the Soviet trade-union delegations at international congresses. He was elected deputy to the Council of Nationalities, USSR Supreme Soviet in 1950 and 1954; has been member of the Central Committee, CPSU, since 1952; was named second deputy minister of foreign affairs and ambassador to Communist China. In 1953 he became deputy minister of foreign affairs. In this capacity he represented the USSR at international conferences and in the UN.

KUZNETSÓV, Vladímir Dmítrievich (1887–), physicist. Fellow, Ac. of S., USSR (1958). Honored Scientist, RSFSR (1934). Hero of Socialist Labor (1957). Graduate, St. Petersburg University (1910); professor, Tomsk University (1920). Founder and director, Siberian Institute of Physical Engineering (1929). Research on physics of solids, surface energy, properties of crystals, internal and external friction, tool wear, strength and plasticity of single and polycrystals, metal machining, plastic working of metals. A pioneer in substantiating the possibility of high-speed metal machining theoretically and experimentally. Author of *Physics of Solids* (5 vols., 1937–49); *Surface Energy of Solids* (1954). Stalin prize (1942).

KVIRILY: *see* ZESTAFONI.

KVITKÓ, Leib Moiséyevich (1895–1952), Yiddish poet. His first book *Trit* (Steps) was published in 1919. Its folkish romanticism reflected the pathos of revolutionary strivings. An important part of his writing was his poems for children. These were translated into many languages of the peoples of Soviet Russia. K was arrested in 1948 during the purge of the Yiddish writers and executed in Aug. 1952.

KYÁKHTA (f. Troitskosavsk), city in S. Buryat ASSR, at the Mongolian border E. of the Selenga River; pop. 11,000 (1956). Connected with Ulan-Ude by a branch of the Trans-Siberian R.R. Leather and weaving factories. Until the middle of the 19th century it was the leading trade center between Russia and China.

KYSHTÝM, city in Chelyabinsk Oblast. RSFSR; pop. 32,300 (1958). R.R. station. Is an important center of nonferrous metallurgy; mechanical, refractory, copper smelting, kaolin, graphite plants.

KYZÝL (f. Belotsarsk, then Khem-Beldyr), city, adm. center of Tuva Autonomous Oblast, RSFSR, on Yenisey River; pop. 10,000 (1939), 34,000 (1959). Leather factory, timber, and furniture plant.

KYZYL-KÚM, desert (mostly sand), S.E. of Aral Sea, in Uzbek and Kazakh SSR's; area 116,000 sq. mi.; covers a large area between Amu Darya and Syr Darya. Very dry continental climate. In river valleys, along artificial canal systems in oases, cotton, rice and wheat growing; orchards; in semi-desert, sheep (karakul), camel, horse and cattle breeding. Mineral resources: coal, polymetallic ores, asbestos, graphite. Traversed by caravan routes. Name derived from the Turkic "kyzyl" (red) and "kum" (sand).

KZÝL-ORDÁ (f. Ak-Mechet, Perovsk), city, adm. center of Kzyl-Orda Oblast, Kazakh SSR, on N. bank of Syr Darya, with branch to Orenburg-Tashkent R.R.; pop. 47,000 (1939), 66,000 (1959). Ind.: rice processing, machine mfg., meat canning; has pedag. inst., agricultural and technical schools, is seat of the Kazakh Ac. of S. Name is derived from the Kazakh "kzyl" meaning red and "orda," settlement; annexed by Russia 1853.

KZYL-ORDÁ OBLAST, Kazakh SSR, on Aral Sea, in the Syr Darya basin; area 89,500 sq. mi.; pop. 329,000 (1959): Kazakhs, some Russians, Ukrainians, Koreans. Cities: Kzyl-Orda (adm. center), Aralsk, Kazalinsk. Sandy deserts, Aral Kara-Kum and Kzyl-Kum; continental climate. Irrigated agr.: rice, cotton; sheep and camel raising. Has fisheries along Aral Sea coast; salt, saltpeter deposits. Is crossed by Trans-Caspian R.R. Est. 1938.

L

LABIAU: *see* POLESSK.

LABOR GROUP (Trudoviki) in the State Duma, predominantly representatives of the peasantry associated ideologically with the populist movement. At the time of the February revolution the LG allied itself and partly fused with the Popular Socialists. In the first Duma the group had 107 deputies whose leaders included A. F. Aladin, I. V. Zhilkin, and L. M. Bramson; in the second Duma,104; in the third and fourth Dumas the number declined sharply (to 14 and 9, respectively) as a result of a change of the electoral law. The leader of the LG in the fourth Duma was A. F. Kerensky. The LG was consistently democratic in its political program; in agrarian matters it was close to the Socialist Revolutionary party. (*See also* SOCIALIST REVOLUTIONARIES)

LÁCHA, lake, area about 130 sq. mi., source of the Onega River, Archangel Oblast; has abundance of fish.

LÁDOGA, (R. *Ladozhskoye Ozero*, ancient *Nevo*), lake, largest in Europe, formerly divided between USSR and Finland, in Karelian ASSR and Leningrad Oblast;

area 7,100 sq. mi.; depth in N. 770 ft., shallow in S. Fed by about 70 streams mostly in Finland, in the S. by the Volkhov and Syas, on the E. by the Svir, an outlet of Lake Onega; its outlet is the Neva, from the S.W. corner through Leningrad to the Gulf of Finland. Frozen from October to April. Has about 500 islands. Abundance of fish. Chief towns on its shores are Petro-krepost (f. Shlüsselburg), Novaya Ladoga, Sortavala, Priozersk (Keksgolm). Played important role in Russian history, being on the route from the Baltic to the Black Sea. During World War II a R.R. built across the ice of the lake supplied besieged Leningrad.

LÁDOGA CANAL, follows the S. and S.E. shores of Lake Ladoga from the source of the Neva River to the mouth of the Svir River in Leningrad Oblast.

LAKES. There are more than 250 thousand lakes in the USSR. The largest of them are:

	Area in sq. mi.	Greatest depth in ft.
Caspian Sea	152,000	3,200
Aral Sea	25,475	225
Baykal	12,160	5,700
Balkhash	7,300	85
Ladoga	7,100	770

The fresh-water lakes in the N. are formed by the abundant precipitation, cool temperatures, and the presence of depressions in the relief. Numerous lakes in the arid Aralo-Caspian landlocked basin, in W. Siberia, and in Kazakhstan are located in shallow depressions filled with water during the melting of the snow in spring. In the N.W. of the European part of the USSR lies the so-called "lake plain" with thousands of long, shallow, winding lakes often connected by rivers; of these Onega, Ladoga, Imandra, Ilmen, and Umbozero are the largest and deepest. Lakes are also abundant in the tundra zone. The largest above the arctic circle is Lake Taymyr in Siberia. There are some lakes in the Polesye and the Meshchera Lowlands in the valleys and flood plains of large rivers. On the shores of the Black Sea, the Sea of Azov, and the Caspian Sea, so-called limans are found which were formed as a result of flooding of the low reaches of the rivers which later became completely separated from the sea by spits. The most important lakes of this type are Khadzhibey, Kuyalnik, Molochne, Eya. Large lakes in the Caspian Lowland (Baskunchak, Inder, and others) are rich in different salts. Of the many lakes in the lowlands of W. Siberia and in the steppe and semideserts of N. Kazakhstan, some are fresh; others, farther S., have brackish water, and still others are salty. In the deserts of Central Asia are found the largest inland salty lakes in the world: in the W., the Caspian and the Aral Seas; in the E., smaller lakes, such as Balkhash, Issyk-Kul, Sasykkol, and Alakol. There are groups of small lakes in the Central Yakutian Lowland, in the low reaches of the Yenisey River, in Transbaykalia, on the Kamchatka Peninsula, and in other regions. Large lakes are encountered in some mountainous regions of the USSR. Lake Sevan is in the Caucasus; Teletskoye Lake in the Altay Mountains; Lake Issyk-Kul in Central Asia; Baykal Lake, in E. Siberia.

LAKS: *see* POPULATION.

LANCERET, Yevgény Yevgényevich (1875–1946), painter and illustrator. Member of *Mir Iskusstva* (World of Art) group. After 1917 lived in Georgia. In his paintings he developed oriental themes. Is well known for his murals in Kazan railway terminal in Moscow.

LAND TENURE: *see* AGRICULTURE, PEASANTS.

LANDÁU, Lev Davídovich (1908–), physicist. Fellow, Ac. of S., USSR (1946). Graduated from Leningrad University (1927); affiliated with the Institute of Physical Problems, Ac. of S. (1937). Research concerns the theory of solids, low temperature physics, superconductivity, thermo-dynamic theory of phase transformations in solids, nuclear physics and cosmic rays. Developed macroscopic theory of superfluidity of liquid helium at temperatures close to absolute zero (1940–41). Stalin prize (1946).

LÁNDSBERG, Grigóry Samuilovich (1890–1957), physicist. Fellow, Ac. of S., USSR (1946). Graduate, Moscow University (1913); professor, Moscow Physicotechnic Institute (1951); affiliated with the Institute of Physics, Ac. of S. (1934–57). Research concerned molecular dispersion of light and spectral analysis, spectral analysis of metals and design of instruments for this purpose. Developed method of spectral analysis of organic compounds including engine fuels. Author of *Optics* (4th ed., 1957). Stalin prize (1941).

LANGUAGES. More than 120 separate and distinct L and numerous dialects are spoken by peoples inhabiting the territory of the USSR. Some of these languages, like Russian, Ukrainian, and Byelorussian, for example, are used by native populations numbering many millions of people. Others, like the Ginukh, Karagassian (Tofalar), and Vodian tongues, are spoken by only a few hundred persons. Some L have been spoken and written since ancient times and are highly developed from a literary standpoint, while others are still in the formative stages of development and have no written form. In some instances the process of combining several separate tribal tongues of a single nationality group into one language used by all tribes of the nationality is still continuing. It is impossible, therefore, to determine the precise number of different L that do in fact exist in the USSR at the present time.

By far the most prevalent and highly developed language in the USSR is Russian. This is the mother tongue of 114,000,000 native Russians, and is the official "inter-nation" language of the nationalities that form the Soviet state. It has its origins in the language used by groups of nomadic tribes that roamed much of the territory of present-day European USSR during the pre-Christian and early Christian eras, and were known collectively as Slavs. Originally, the language of the Slavs must have consisted of a series of dialects, each of which developed under the influence of L spoken by the ethnic groups that lived in close geographic proximity to the various Slavic tribes. Thus, in the N. there was close contact with the Baltic and Germanic peoples. In the S., the vast expanse of the open steppe facilitated periodic invasions of the lands of the S. Slavs by the Mongolian hordes of E. and Central Asia. In addition, the Greeks established a number of trading posts and colonies along the N. shores of the Black Sea and in the Crimean peninsula. As the many Slavic dialects gradually became unified into a single language, its basic Indo-European lexical stock became enriched with the addition of Germanic, Greek, and Mongolian terms. This process continued after Russia's emergence in history, as a result of the introduction of Christianity into Russia from Byzantium in the 10th century and the Tatar yoke of the 13th and 14th centuries. Until the close of the 17th century virtually all literature in the R. language was in the Old Slavonic Church script, and the spoken language was not very different from the Slavonic used in the religious ceremonies in the Orthodox Church, where it has been preserved to this day.

At the start of the 18th century, following the "westernization" of Russia under Peter the Great, increased contacts between Russians and the nations of W. Europe resulted in the entry into R. language of many terms of W. European L (French and English, especially), and the gradual development of the R. language, as distinct from the old Slavonic. Mikhail Lomonosov, a writer, scientist, and statesman of the early 18th century, did much to develop the R. language. Through his many works on grammar and his scientific writings, Lomonosov was the first to lay down a definite distinction between R. and Slavonic. Such writers of the golden era of R. literature as Karamzin, Pushkin, Turgenev, Lermontov, and many others during the late 18th and 19th centuries helped establish the modern R. language.

The process of additions to the lexical stock of the R. language has continued in recent years. Under the Soviets there has been a tendency for the coining of new words from a number of abbreviations (such as "Gosizdat," from Gosudarstvennoye Izdatelstvo—State Publishing House). Since World War II with the rapid advance in science and technology, many foreign (mostly American) words and expressions have been Russianized and included in the R. language.

Russian, both literary and spoken, is a rich and flexible L. Although there are 33 letters in the R. alphabet, this does not make it a more difficult language than others with fewer letters, since its 33 letters represent all the sounds that in other languages must be formed by a combination of two or more letters. The many guttural sounds in R.—to a large extent a legacy from the Tatars—present some difficulty to the student of R. On the other hand, R. words contain no letters that are not pronounced (similar to the combination "gh" in the English language, for example), with the result that a student of R. who first learns to recognize and pronounce each letter of the R. alphabet, could read R. fluently even before fully understanding the text. Nouns in R. have three genders and are not preceded by an article, which fact adds to the expressiveness of the language. Nouns also have declensions with different endings for cases. Adjectives too have three genders and endings corresponding to the genders and cases of the nouns. Verbs have three tenses, but can be made to express fine shades of meaning by the use of the perfect and imperfect moods (for example: "gulyát"

—to walk; "pogulyát"—to take a walk). A peculiarity of the R. language is the large variety and frequent use of diminutives and augmentatives that add extraordinarily to its expressiveness. The R. language is heavily accented, which fact lends it a certain cadence that makes it especially adaptable to the poetic form. Rhyming R. is helped also by considerable similarity between the endings of nouns and adjectives for the same genders and declension cases. One of its difficulties is the absence of fixed rules for accenting of syllables. On the other hand, this very fact allows considerable freedom for the poetic form.

Two of the other leading L in the USSR are Ukrainian and Byelorussian. Both belong to the same E. Slavic group of L as R., and until recent years were regarded as little more than separate dialects of R. Both L have undergone especial development under the Soviets. They are characterized by a relatively greater admixture of Polish and Germanic terms than R. Ukrainian (from the R. "u kraya"—at the border) is the language of Ukrainians, who inhabit the S. and S.W. regions of European USSR, where for several centuries they lived "on the borders" of Poland and other W. Slavic lands. Ukrainian is spoken by more than 35,000,000 citizens of the Soviet state, and possesses a large and well-developed literature of its own. Byelorussian is the language of Byelorussians (White Russians), inhabiting the W. region of European USSR. The sources of the Byelorussian language are the dialects of the ancient Slavic tribes that roamed the region of the W. Dvina and the upper Dnieper rivers. Much of this territory, during the period of the Tatar yoke, was annexed for some time by the ancient kingdom of Lithuania; hence the relatively greater influence of Polish and Lithuanian on the Byelorussian language as compared to R.

Most of the other languages now spoken in the USSR were developed extensively under the Soviets. The exceptions in this respect are Armenian and Georgian —two of the world's most ancient tongues. Both Armenian and Georgian have preserved their own writing, while others, with the active encouragement of the Soviet government, have adopted the Latin or R. (cyrillic) alphabets. This has been the case particularly with a number of the L of the Turkic group that only recently employed Arabic characters. In addition, many L, that until a few years ago had no written form, are now being developed to the point where many national groups speaking these L have their own schools, theaters, and printed matter in their own native tongue. (*See also* NATIONALITIES, POPULATION)   A. B. T.

LA PÉROUSE STRAIT, also **SOYA STRAIT,** channel about 27 mi. wide between N.W. Hokkaido Island, Japan, and S. tip of Sakhalin Island. Named after French navigator who discovered the strait in 1787.

LÁPPO-DANILÉVSKY, Aleksándr Sergéyevich (1863–1919), historian. Professor of history at the University of St. Petersburg, he was much influenced by Klyuchevsky. He devoted numerous monographs to the socio-economic history of the 17th and 18th centuries, including works on the Muscovite tax system (1890) and the status of the serfs (1901).

LÁPPO-DANILÉVSKY, Iván Aleksándrovich (1895–1931), mathematician. Corresponding member, Ac. of S., USSR (1931). Graduated from Leningrad University (1925). Suggested theory of functions from matrices applicable for the solution of differential equations. Author of *Theory of Functions from Matrices and Systems of Linear Differential Equations* (3 vols., 1936).

LAPPS: *see* Sami.

LÁPTEV, Dmítry Yákovlevich (date of birth and death are unknown), Arctic explorer. As a navy lieutenant, commanded a detachment in the Great Northern Expedition of 1736 in the course of which the maritime coast of the Lena River and other rivers in that area was initially mapped. L retired from the navy with the rank of vice admiral (1762). Numerous geographical areas were named after him.

LÁPTEV SEA, part of Arctic Ocean along the coast of Asia, between Taymyr Peninsula, Severnaya Zemlya on W. and New Siberian Islands. Covered by ice almost throughout the entire year; area 250,000 sq. mi.; shallow waters in the S., reaching 9,800 ft. depth in the N. Ports: Tiksi in the mouth of the Lena River and Nordvik in Khatanga Bay. Named after the participants of the Great Arctic expedition (1733–1743), lieutenants Khariton and Dmitry Laptev who explored the sea coast.

LÁPTEV STRAIT (R. *Lapteva Dmitria proliv*), passage about 30 mi. wide, between mainland of N. Yakut ASSR and Bolshoy Lyakhov Island; connects E. Siberian Sea and Laptev Sea.

LÁRIN, Yu. (Lúrye, Mikhaíl Aleksándrovich) (1882–1932), Communist economist. Joined the Social Democrats in the Crimea in 1902. Arrested and condemned to eight years of exile in Siberia. In 1904, escaped and joined the Mensheviks. L became a member of the Bolshevik party in 1917. After the October revolution, he held high positions in the economic apparatus and was the author of the program of nationalization of industry and the monopoly of foreign trade.

LATVIAN SOVIET SOCIALIST REPUBLIC (LATVIA). Located in the W. part of European USSR, L borders on Estonia in the N., the RSFSR in the E., Lithuania and Byelorussia in the S., and the Baltic Sea in the W. Area, 24,600 sq. mi. Capital: Riga.

Population is 2,093,000 (1959 census). Out of this total (1935 figures given in parentheses), Latvians are 1,298,000 or 62% (1,473,000 or 75.5%); Russians 536,000 or 26.6% (206,000 or 10.6%); Byelorussians 61,000 or 2.9%; Poles 60,000 or 2.9% (49,000 or 2.5%); Jews 37,000 or 1.7% (93,000 or 4.8%); others 81,000 or 3.9%. Sixty two thousand Germans left L in 1940 and again in 1944; most of the Jews were exterminated by the Nazis; over one hundred thousand Latvians were deported to Kazakhstan and elsewhere, and another hundred thousand left the country following the German retreat in 1944. Cities: Riga, capital (605,000), Liepa-

ja (71,000), Daugavpils (65,000), Jelgava (31,700), Ventspils (26,200).

Nature and Climate. Most of L is a fertile lowland country, with morainic hills covering parts of Kurland and Livonia ("Livonian Switzerland"). The coast line is covered by sandy beaches and dunes. Over one-third of the territory is covered by forests. The climate is between maritime and continental: average Jan. temperature from 28.4° F to 21.2° F; July, from 60° F to 65° F. Rainfall, 28 to 32 in.

National Economy. Peat and hydroenergy form the main fuel base for L. Principal industries: machine building and metalworking, timber, light industry, food, dairy, and hog industries. Riga harbor is open 10–11 months a year, Liepaja and Ventspils the year round. The Dvina River is navigable throughout the entire territory of L.

History. Early Baltic tribes (Latgals, Zemgals, and Kurs) were known in the area as early as the 9th century. During the 10th-12th centuries the first towns appeared in L and during the 12th century the first principalities. A Latvian state could not develop, however, since the Germans (Order of Livonian Knights) founded Riga in 1201 and soon extended their domination to all of L. The reformation took place in L in the 1520's and today only the Latgals (about 20% of the population) remain Catholic. In 1561 the German Order of Livonian Knights disintegrated and L became the object of struggle between Poland, Sweden, and Russia. Latgale fell into Polish hands; Riga (after Polish occupation from 1581 to 1621) and northern L (Vidzeme) into Swedish hands (1621 and 1629). In the middle of the 17th century new wars began for L. In 1721, according to the Nystad treaty, northern L fell into R. hands. In 1722, as a result of the first partition of Poland, Russia received Latgale and in 1795 (third partition) Kurland. Thus all of L became part of the R. Empire. Serfdom was abolished in L in 1817 and 1819, but all the land remained in the hands of German landlords. L peasants were first given the right to settle in towns and only in 1861 did they have the right to buy land for themselves. Riga soon became an important harbor for R. products and the L economy developed.

After World War I L became independent and a peace treaty was signed with the RSFSR on Aug. 11,

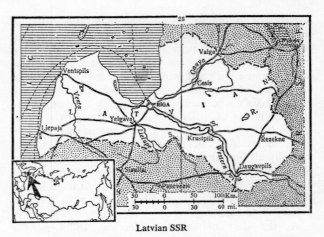

Latvian SSR

1920. On Feb. 16, 1922 the Latvian Republic was officially proclaimed with a Scandinavian-style democratic regime. L pursued a policy of friendship with her Baltic neighbors as well as with Poland, also signing a non-aggression treaty with Russia in 1932. In 1934 Ulmanis took full power into his own hands and ruled L until World War II. In Oct. 1939, following the Molotov-Ribbentrop agreement, L was forced to accept Soviet army, air, and naval bases under the Soviet-imposed treaty of mutual assistance. On June 20, 1940, L's government was overthrown by Soviet troops moving from their bases in L and A. Vyshinsky arrived in Riga to carry on the sovietization of the country. A Soviet regime was officially established on July 21 and L was incorporated into the USSR on Aug. 5, 1940. The annexation of L has not been recognized by the U.S.

Culture. L script was introduced in the 16th-17th centuries by the German clergy. The 17th-century writers were: poet Cr. Fuereccus, writer G. Mancelius, and translators of religious writings E. Gluck and J. Reiters. Secular literature began in the 18th century with G. F. Stender. In the second part of the 19th century a "young L literary movement" awakened an interest in L language and folklore, bringing it closer to modern literary currents. Among the most active writers of this group are the poets J. Alunans and A. Pumpurs, and the publisher of L folklore, Kr. Barons. The first L novel describing the life of L peasants was written by the brothers R. and M. Kaudzites, and the L realist school was represented by R. Blauman and Poruks. The best-known L writer was the poet-playwright J. Rainis (1865–1929). His wife Aspazia (pseud.) was also a talented writer. Among modern authors are: poets K. Skalbe and E. Virza; novelists J. Jausundrabins, A. Upit, and V. Lacis; playwright M. Ziverts.

Decorative art is centered in wood carving, metal and ornamentation, embroidery, and ceramics. Among the 19th-century artists are painters J. Feddlers, K. Gun, J. Rosental, V. Purvit, and A. Baumanis, and sculptors G. Shilter and T. Zalkaln, while among the modern painters we find O. Skulme, E. Kalnyn, and sculptor A. Briedis.   M. R.

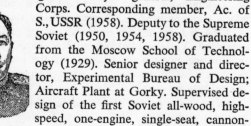

LÁVOCHKIN, Semyón Alekséyevich (1900–1960), aeronautical engineer. Major general, Engineering Corps. Corresponding member, Ac. of S., USSR (1958). Deputy to the Supreme Soviet (1950, 1954, 1958). Graduated from the Moscow School of Technology (1929). Senior designer and director, Experimental Bureau of Design; Aircraft Plant at Gorky. Supervised design of the first Soviet all-wood, high-speed, one-engine, single-seat, cannon-equipped fighter LaGG-1, and fighters VK-105R, LaGG-3, La-5, La-7, La-9 (1938–45). These fighters were mass produced and widely used in World War II. Worked on experimental design of jet and rocket fighters (1946). Supervised design of the lightest Soviet all-metal jet fighter La-15 (1947). Stalin prizes (1941, 1943, 1946, 1948).

LAVRENYÓV, Borís Andréyevich (1891–1959), writer, futurist poet. His stories about the civil war in

Russia (*The Wind*, 1924; *The Forty-First*, 1926; *The Seventh Satellite*, 1927) are romantic and idealize heroism and noble feeling; later stories are fantastic. Best known for a short-story *The Wood-Engraving* (1928) and a play *The Voice of America* (1949) in which he attacks American radio propaganda. Stalin prizes (1946, 1950).

LAVRÉNTYEV, Mikhaíl Alekséyevich (1900–), mathematician. Fellow (1939), vice-president (1945–48), Ukr. Ac. of S. Fellow, Ac. of S., USSR (1946). Deputy to the Supreme Soviet. Director, Inst. of Mathematics and Mechanics (1939–48); Inst. of Precision Mechanics and Computing Techniques (1950–53). Academy secretary, Division of Physical and Mathematical Sciences, Ac. of S. (1951–53 and 1955–57). Research concerns the theory of functions of a complex variable, mechanics of continuous media, hydromechanics. Stalin prizes (1946, 1949).

LAVRÓV, Pyotr Lávrovich (1823–1900), philosopher, ideologist of populism. He understood progress as the uninterrupted rise of the critical consciousness of individuals accompanied by the growing solidarity of society. A society is well balanced if the interests of the majority may be identified with the ideals of the most conscious and progressive minority. The "critically-minded individuals," i.e. the intellectuals, owe, according to L, a moral debt to the toiling peasantry. Such views were considered by the tsarist regime as revolutionary, and L, without ever being tried, was deported to the E. provinces, but escaped and went to France. There he developed the ideology of peasant movements and became one of the founders and editors of the clandestine quarterly *Vpered* (Forward), which was distributed to revolutionary populist groups in Russia. His principal work, the *Historical Letters*, was published under the pseudonym of P. L. Mirtov.

LAVRÓVSKY, Leoníd Mikháylovich (1905–), principal choreographer of the Moscow Bolshoy Ballet since 1944. Educated at the St. Petersburg Imperial School of Ballet and Leningrad Music School, he was the artistic director of the Leningrad Kirov (formerly Mariinsky) Ballet from 1938 to 1944. Among his ballets are *Fadette* (1934), *Katerina* (1935), *Prisoner of the Caucasus* (1938), *Romeo and Juliet* (1940, 1946), *The Stone Flower* (1954). He holds the chair of choreography at the Moscow Institute of Theatrical Art. Stalin prizes (1946, 1947, 1950).

LAW, PREREVOLUTIONARY. The earliest known R. law collection, compiled by churchmen for ecclesiastical courts, took the Byzantine manuals for its model and constituted a precedent when, centuries later, custom gave way to written law and state legislation. A legislative collection *Russkaya Pravda* (*Russian Truth*) dates from as early as the 13th century. Not until 1497 was a first attempt at codification made in Russia, though this contained merely the scantiest provisions for a more equitable administration of justice. A new code followed in 1550 aimed primarily at improvements in judicial procedure and the replacement of immemorial customs by written law.

Much more comprehensive was the code (*Ulozhenie*) of 1649. This was a summation of the laws of the previous hundred years, with special emphasis on consolidation of those laws and decrees enacted since the establishment of the Romanov dynasty. Implied in its provisions was the complete subordination of the individual to the state. Its attempted definition of the law on serfs reflected this general orientation, guaranteeing the landlord the labor of his peasants while making him responsible for the collection of peasant taxes. Thus hereditary serfdom received formal recognition. In this and other respects, the Code of 1649 remained the framework of the R. legal system until 1833.

It was by no means, however, an ideal arrangement. Peter the Great expressed his dissatisfaction and proposed a revision of the Code in 1700 and 1718. His attempts were in vain, as were those of the Empress Elizabeth. Catherine II decided that mere revision was not enough. She envisioned an entirely new code incorporating the most advanced legal theories the age had to offer. For this purpose she summoned a legislative commission Dec. 14, 1766 and, though knowing little of R. law herself, published an *Instruction* for their benefit, a restatement of the ideas of such western thinkers as Montesquieu and Beccaria. Catherine urged modest improvement in the legal and economic status of the peasantry, but there were to be no changes in the position of the nobility.

Bearing such regal generalities in mind, the commission assembled July 30, 1767. It continued in existence until 1774, but with no results. Not for half a century was the cause of recodification revived. Then, in 1826, Nicholas I appointed Count Mikhail Speransky to lead Section II of His Majesty's Own Chancery charged with the task of compiling a new code. In 1833, Speransky's group published: (1) a complete collection of the laws of the R. Empire, from those in the Code of 1649 to those issued prior to Jan. 1, 1830; and (2) a code of laws of the R. Empire covering all the laws in effect. The latter was modeled on Justinian's *Corpus Juris,* but was marred by inconsistencies and lack of integration.

Speransky was also responsible for a new criminal code (1845) and several collections in such specialized areas as army and navy regulations and taxation laws. The Code of 1833 was extended to the W. and S.W. provinces of the Empire in 1840, another stage in the process of unification and Russification characteristic of this period. But while steps were taken to mitigate the harshness of the penal system, the judiciary, reform of which Speransky strongly advocated, remained untouched for many years. The R. judiciary, inequitable and corrupt, complex and cumbersome in its operation, arbitrary and secretive, with personnel of low moral and educational standards, finally came under official scrutiny in 1850 when a committee was appointed to draft reform legislation. It was led first by Count D. N. Bludov and, after 1861, by S. I. Zarudny and D. N. Zamyatin.

The requisite law finally materialized Nov. 20, 1864. It provided for equality of all before the law; the right to be heard by impartial tribunals; implementation of the principle, *nullum crimen, nulla poena sine lege;* a uniform and simplified judicial procedure; separation of the judicial from the legislative and executive arms of government; irremovability of all judges except those found guilty of misconduct; open proceedings; trial by jury; representation by qualified members of the bar; election of lower court judges; and exclusion of police from preliminary investigations, which were now to be carried out by magistrates. Justices of the peace were to be elected by the zemstvos in country districts, and by the city councils in Moscow and St. Petersburg. As a further step toward ensuring justice where previously the landowner had supreme sway as local magistrate, the decisions of justices of the peace could now be appealed to county sessions. More important cases went to district courts and appeals to local higher courts. Both latter sets of judges were to be appointed by the Crown from candidates nominated by the judiciary.

A law of April 1863 abolished capital punishment in its worst forms, revised the penal system but allowed flogging to continue under certain circumstances. The main reform went into effect in Moscow and St. Petersburg in 1865 and soon thereafter in other areas. Independence of the courts now was an accepted principle and there arose in Russia a progressive and well-educated legal profession that was to play a uniquely significant role in the life of the country.

Soon, however, inroads were being made on the achievements of the reformers. Military, ecclesiastical, and township courts dealing with petty cases involving peasants were retained. Government officials accused of offenses committed in line of duty were tried under special rules. The bureaucracy continued to take arbitrary action against "undesirables" while retaining control over certain members of the judiciary. Unqualified men were often appointed to the bench and trial by jury dropped in "crimes against the state." In 1881, the jurisdiction of military tribunals and the extrajudicial powers of administrative officials were extended. The minister of justice received additional disciplinary powers over judges and other law officers. The office of justice of the peace was abolished in 1889 and Jews excluded from the judiciary except under special permission from the government. Wide use of the powers of appointment, transfer, reward, and advancement which were granted the justice minister under the law of 1864 led to further undermining of judicial independence. Yet the work of Bludov, Zarudny, and Zamyatin was not wholly vitiated and the judicial system remained much superior to what it had been before the reform act was passed.   C. J. F.

Soviet Law is called by Soviet theorists "a new, higher type of law." It is not only, they say, the totality of rules of behavior backed by the coercive force of the Soviet state; it has its origins in the will of the working class and of all the Soviet people. Its function, they assert, was never exploitatory. In the first years of the regime it was mainly repressive as long as hostile classes opposed the government. Now its main functions are: (1) to educate Soviet citizens to be patriotic, disciplined in their work and devoted to their system; (2) to transform society, at the present stage from a socialist into a communist society; e.g., by regulating the future transition of collective farms into state farms; (3) to guard the Soviet state and social system; (4) to protect the property and personal rights of citizens. Their definition needs to be tested against Soviet reality.

SL originates not in the will of the Soviet people, who have no practical means of controlling legislation, but rather in the will of the CPSU, which claims to express the will of the people and which proclaims openly its control over making and executing SL. SL educates as does the law in many lands. In the USSR, however, jurists and agitators are enlisted for lectures on law to the masses. From its first days the Soviet regime used law as a protective, politicized, flexible means of repression of enemies and of social transformation. It abolished in 1917 the tsarist legal institutions which its predecessor, the Provisional Government (q.v.), had merely reformed. Laws of the Russian Imperial and Provisional governments were to be applied only where not otherwise annulled. Citation of these laws was forbidden in 1918, and, for the next few years, poorly qualified judges applied as best they could sketchy government decrees and the first labor and family codes, filling the lacunae with the dictates of their "revolutionary conception of justice." The repressive and confiscatory content of SL during war communism (q.v.) faded during the NEP period of limited concessions to capitalism for the sake of restoring a strife-shattered economy whose ruin had been hastened by Bolshevik extremes. Codification of criminal, civil, and other SL was rushed to completion.

The rights of citizens under law have been more emphasized since Stalin. These rights, however, have never been treated by Soviet theorists as sacred immutable categories. Early Soviet theorists such as P. I. Stuchka and N. V. Krylenko inherited from Marx the view that all law is "class law," preserving certain social relationships; e.g., capitalistic private ownership of the means of production, in the interests of the ruling class, and therefore not a permanent set of moral, divine, or logical truths. Marx and Engels had conceded some primary action of law and will back on the basic, causative economic relations in society, but were basically economic determinists. Lenin, himself a trained lawyer, implicitly rejected Marxist determinism in the context of Russian backwardness, and stressed the necessary creative and transforming as well as repressive functions of state and law. The eminent E. B. Pashukanis deviated from Lenin with the embarrassing and politically inconvenient theory that *all* law, even SL, is bourgeois law because it grew out of and reflects the commodity exchange of the market place. There can be no socialist law, he believed. Law will "wither away" under socialism, together with the state and its coercive power, to be replaced by administrative rules. This theory was interestingly paralleled by contemporary theories of the withering away of the family, the school, and so forth. Stalin, believing it impossible soon to dispense with coercion and the courts, countered theories of the imminent "withering away" of state and

law. They would grow stronger before they withered (1930). His later (1939) indefinite postponement of the withering away of the state even under communism is still in force, buttressed by the concept that state and law will exist as long as there remains any danger of attack from a capitalist country. Pashukanis was purged in 1937, long after his partial recantation, following an attack on him by P. Yudin. Andrey Vyshinsky became spokesman for the official view that Soviet socialist law was "a new, higher type of law," unlike bourgeois law.

As the procurator general he denied the necessity of establishing by the court the objective truth in each case and admitted the possibility of conviction of the defendant solely on the basis of the probability of the facts submitted to the court's appraisal or just on the basis of the defendant's personal confession (often extorted by tortures, false promises of mercy, spurious appeals to "confess" for the sake of the party).

After Stalin's death in 1953, the relaxation of terror and shift of emphasis from physical to administrative-economic coercion resulted in significant, although not necessarily irreversible, legal reforms. Police chief Beria and his supporters were arrested and mostly shot in summary secret proceedings reminiscent of the Stalin era. But for the ordinary citizen SL became less harsh, and more uniform and predictable. Special boards of the security police, Stalin's chief purge instruments, which conducted secret trials before three secret police officials were abolished (Sept. 1953), and security police functions shifted to a Committee of State Security under the central government. More uniformity of justice within the regular courts was secured by ending special closed court proceedings without appeal in trials of "terrorism" (1956) and abolition of special railroad and water transport courts (1957). Special judicial commissions were set up to rehabilitate purge victims, often posthumously. The procuracy, supposedly guardian of legality, was given fortified powers of surveillance over places of detention and the security police (1955–56). Vyshinsky's theories of proof were repudiated. The so-called principle of analogy under which a person could be tried and convicted for some act not specifically prohibited by the law just on the ground that the act was analogous to some specifically prohibited behavior, has also been eliminated (1958).

Western specialists generally believe that in spite of the reforms of 1953–58, Soviet legal practice still assures defendants appreciably less protection than they would receive under Western law. They note that in Soviet law there is no writ of *habeas corpus*. They question that judges can be "independent" of political controls when they are subjected to tight party discipline and administrative supervision, especially in political trials, which are usually closed to the public, except when there is a propaganda point to be made, as in the trial of Francis Powers, the American U-2 pilot (Aug. 1960). In criminal cases, normal adult defendants still may not have defense counsel until after the first major stage, the investigation, and before the second major stage, the trial. Soviet authorities rejected suggestions to include specific mention of presumption of innocence in the codes of criminal procedure. Western specialists are concerned also about dubious innovations in the form of "public participation" in law enforcement through such non-state agencies which bypass the courts as the "public meetings." Under "anti-parasite" laws passed in many border republics (not the RSFSR), these party-controlled local gatherings may sentence idlers, suspected speculators, etc. to up to five years' exile, subject to approval of the local soviets.

Government and legislation in the USSR are federally decentralized in form, but politically unified in fact in all important principles. Uniformity of lawmaking and law enforcement is assured by the centralized controls of the CPSU and the USSR procuracy, by administrative controls (q.v.), and by the constitutional authority for All-Union legislation of basic principles of criminal law (q.v.), civil law (q.v.), family law (q.v.), labor law (q.v.), the court system (q.v.), land, collective farm, labor social security and educational law. The central organs pass the national plan and budget, rules on USSR citizenship (q.v.) and the rights of aliens and laws on state crimes.

The branch of SL called civil law is not to be confused with the general descriptive term, civil law, which refers to "civil-law" countries, which, like the USSR, France, and other continental countries, rely on codified law in contrast to the "common-law" countries such as Great Britain and the United States (except Louisiana) which rely heavily on the common law built out of precedents of judicial decisions, though some law is codified. Codes, laws, and other acts of SL have to be interpreted by the courts to fit concrete cases. But the experience of application of SL by the courts is not binding on the courts, except in the cases where the government and the supreme courts issue directives. In the directives certain specific cases are summarized as examples of how to or how not to judge. When, then, an attorney prepares a case for his client —and some cases can be quite complex—he researches among the statutes, codes, and directives on court practice. He has no voluminous court reports to comb as do lawyers in common-law countries.

Recent legal reforms have brought guarantees in the Soviet legal system closer to those guarantees in other civil-law countries. But certain procedural guarantees are still lacking, and SL continues to bear the stamp of Communist party inspired goal-directedness.
(See also ARBITRATION, AUTHORSHIP AND INVENTION, BAR ASSOCIATIONS, HOUSING REGULATIONS, INHERITANCE, INTERNATIONAL LAW, LEGAL TRAINING, LIABILITY LAW, PASSPORTS, PROPERTY, ADMINISTRATIVE LAW)

BIBLIOGRAPHY: Hugh W. Babb and John N. Hazard, Soviet Legal Philosophy, Cambridge, 1951; Harold J. Berman, Justice in Russia, Cambridge, 1950; Vladimir Gsovski, Soviet Civil Law, 2 vols., Ann Arbor, 1948–49; V. Gsovski and K. Grzybowski, eds., Government, Law and Courts in the Soviet Union and Eastern Europe, New York, 1959; J. N. Hazard, Law and Social Change in the USSR, London, 1953; Hans Kelsen, The Communist Theory of Law, New York, 1955.
P. H. J.

LAW SCHOOLS: see LEGAL TRAINING.
LAZARÉNKO, Borís Románovich (1910–), inventor. Graduated from Moscow University (1936). Associated with the All-Union Institute of Electrical Engineering

(1935–42), Research Institute of the Ministry of Electrical Industry (1942–48); director, Central Research Laboratory of Electric Methods of Metal Machining (1948). Suggested a new method of metal coating (1943). Collaborated with N. I. Lazarenko in the discovery of electrospark metal machining and a method of production of current conducting powder (1943). Stalin prize (1946).

LAZARÉNKO, Natália Ioasafovna (1911–), inventor. Graduated from Moscow University (1936). Associated with the Central Elemental Laboratory (1936–42). Since 1942 collaborates with B. R. Lazarenko with whom she has invented a method of electrospark metal machining and production of current conducting powder (1943). Stalin prize (1946).

LÁZAREV, Mikhaíl Petróvich (1788–1851), famous naval commander, admiral, scientist, Arctic explorer. Between 1813 and 1835 he made three trips around the world including an Antarctic expedition on the sailing boat *Mirny* (1819–21) as a member of the first R. Antarctic explorer team under F. F. Bellingshausen.

LAZHÉCHNIKOV, Iván Ivánovich (1792–1869), writer of historical R. novels. He is best known for *The House of Ice* (1835) which deals with the era of Biron. L also wrote novels on Peter I and Ivan III and a volume on V. Belinsky.

LAZÓ, Sergéy Geórgievich (1894–1920), partisan leader in the civil war (1918–20), commander of the Transbaykalian front, 1918. He joined the CP in 1918; was leader of partisan groups in the Far East and chairman of the Revolutionary War Council of the Maritime (Primorsky) Kray. He was caught by the Japanese in April 1920 and burned alive in the firebox of a locomotive at the Muravyovo–Amurskaya R.R. station (renamed Lazo station) in May 1920.

LEATHER AND SHOES INDUSTRY. The leather products industry includes such items as belts, leather coats and jackets, handbags, and saddles, as well as shoes and boots. In 1960, 418 mill. pairs of footwear were produced (compared to 582 mill. pairs in the United States in 1958, and 138 mill. pairs in the United Kingdom).

The first large leather factories were constructed in the towns of Ostrakhov (Kalinin Oblast) in 1739, and in St. Petersburg in 1847; the first shoe factory was established in St. Petersburg in 1896. Of 60 mill. pairs of shoes and boots produced in 1916 only 20% were made in factories. Their quality, however, as well as the quality of the other hand-made leather products, was generally high.

During the 1930's existing leather and shoe factories were reconstructed and reequipped, and many new ones were established. The production of tanning agents on an industrial basis was initiated, and new types of leathers (chrome leathers) as well as high-quality leather substitutes were produced for a time. The establishment of a native shoe machinery industry subsequently made possible a continuous growth in the level of mechanization of existing plants. In 1958, according to official data, 60% of all operations in shoe factories were performed by machines, while 85% of all transfers were effected by conveyor belts. The objectives of the Seven Year Plan (1959–65) provide for the production of 515 mill. pairs of footwear in 1965.

PRODUCTION OF LEATHER AND OF SHOES IN THE USSR

Year	Rough leather (thous. tons)	Shoes and boots (mill. pairs)
1913	—	60
1928	—	58
1940	70.3	211
1955	84.8	225
1958	113.9	356
1959	—	389
1960	—	418
1965 (pl.)	—	515

P. I. M.

LEAGUE OF NATIONS: *see* INTERNATIONAL ORGANIZATION.

LÉBEDEV, Aleksándr Alekséyevich (1893–), physicist. Fellow, Ac. of S., USSR (1943). Hero of Socialist Labor (1957). Deputy to the Supreme Soviet, USSR (1950, 1954). Graduate and professor (1916), St. Petersburg (Leningrad) University. Developed a method of determining annealing rates for optical glasses. A leading Soviet expert in electronic optics. Designer of an electronic microscope (1947) and an electric camera (1949). Author of *Polarization Interferometer and Its Application* (1931), *Structural Transformations in Glass* (1953). Stalin prizes (1947, 1949).

LÉBEDEV, Sergéy Alekséyevich (1902–), electrical engineer. Fellow, Ac. of S., Ukrainian SSR (1945) and USSR (1953). Hero of Socialist Labor (1956). Graduate, Moscow School of Technology (1928); professor, Moscow Institute of Physical Technology (1952). Director, Institute of Electrical Engineering, Ac. of S., Ukrainian SSR (1946–51); Institute of Precision Mechanics and Computation Technology, Ac. of S., USSR (1953). Proposed a theory of artificial stability of synchronous machinery. Research concerns automation of power systems and computers; designer of a high-speed computer. Stalin prize (1950).

LÉBEDEV, Sergéy Vasílyevich (1874–1934), chemist. Fellow, Ac. of S., USSR (1932). Graduate (1900), professor (1902), St. Petersburg (Leningrad) University where he founded the Laboratory for Petroleum Refining (1925); professor, Military Medical Academy (1916), Director, Laboratory of Syntehtic Rubber (1928–30). Research concerned polymerization of unsaturated compounds. Developed production method for synthetic rubber (1928–31) which has become the base of the Soviet rubber industry.

LEFÓRT, Francis (1656–1699), Swiss, friend of Peter I. He headed the delegation abroad in 1697–98, of which Peter was a member.

LEFT COMMUNISM: *see* OPPOSITION.

LEGAL MARXISM: *see* MARXISM RUSSIAN.

LEGAL TRAINING is supervised according to party and government directives by the USSR Ministry of Higher and Specialized Secondary Education, through its Chief Administration for Universities, Economic and Law Higher Schools and its Higher Attestation Commission, the latter concerned particularly with final approval of higher degrees and academic promotions. LT is also under party surveillance through the party and *Komsomol* (q.v.) bureaus in each law department. It is offered mainly at the undergraduate level, with over 36,000 students at about 23 of the 40 universities, the 3 law institutes which offer more practical training for those with experience in law and administration, and the All-Union Juridical Correspondence Institute. Only about one-third of the students study by day, the rest in evening and correspondence courses of lower quality than in the day courses. There are about 250 graduate students in three-year courses; their candidate's degree is helpful if not essential for a successful career in teaching and research in the schools, the Institute of Law of the Ac. of S. or other research institutes. School reforms beginning in 1958 have barred day studies to almost all applicants without work experience of two years. They have caused practical work to increase a total of eight months, with five months of this in the fifth (i.e. last) year, working preferably at their future specialty in the court system (q.v.), procuracy and investigations office, militia, Committee of State Security, bar associations (q.v.), notary offices, ministries, local soviets. Only the brightest graduates with a minimum of two years of law work will then be admitted to graduate school. Students have the typically heavy Soviet schedule of at least 30 class hours a week. In their lectures, seminars, yearly written work, and diploma theses based on their practice, they do not follow the "case method" typical of American law schools although individual cases are cited to illustrate theoretical points. They study the branches of law and their subdivisions from texts which outline the theory of civil, criminal, land, collective farm, international, administrative, state law, and so on, from the viewpoint of Marxism-Leninism which permeates LT; technical and theoretical problems; sources such as codes and statutes; and the problems of interpretation and proper application of the codes as exemplified in court practice. They study also criminology, logic, Latin, Roman law, comparative state law, political theory, foreign languages, and the ideological courses of the history of the CPSU, dialectical materialism, and political economy required for all Soviet students. Their studies are not mentally exacting; they develop technical competence, but permit no questioning of the basic party line as embodied in legal provisions. When the CPSU wishes reforms of Soviet law (q.v.), the leading scholars and legal officials can influence the content of new codes, as they did for criminal law (q.v.) in 1958.

P. H. J.

LEKAR: *see* MEDICINE.

LEMBERG: *see* LVOV.

LÉMESHEV, Sergéy Yákovlevich (1902–), lyric tenor, People's Artist of USSR. Graduated from the Moscow conservatoire, began his career in the provinces. From 1931 was soloist of Bolshoy Theater in Moscow. Known for his interpretation of the roles of Lensky (*Eugene Onegin*), Levko (*May Night*), the Duke (*Rigoletto*), Alfred (*Traviata*). Gave concerts and played in the motion picture *The Musical Story*. Stalin prize (1941).

LÉNA GOLDFIELDS MASSACRE of workers by tsarist troops occurred on April 4, 1912 on the Lena goldfields in Siberia. In March 1912 a strike was organized by the mineworkers in the Lena goldfields to obtain better working conditions. On April 4, to protest the arrest of their leaders and to present their demands, 2,000 workers marched toward the administration buildings. The demonstrators were met by fire and hundreds of participants were killed or wounded.

LÉNA RIVER, one of the longest rivers of the USSR; length 2,650 mi.; has its source near Lake Baykal; flows through Irkutsk Oblast, Yakut ASSR, and empties into the Laptev Sea. It has many tributaries, the largest being Kuta, Vilyuy, Kirenga, Olekma, Aldan, and Vitim. It is frozen seven or eight months of the year. There is gold as well as other minerals in its basin. Landings: Bulun, Zhigansk, Yakutsk, Olekminsk, Kirensk, Ust-Kut.

LEND-LEASE. Act of March 11, 1941 (H.R. 1776) gave the president power to make available war supplies to nations whose defense was vital to the United States. By the end of the war the USSR received from the United States over $11 bill. worth of supplies. After the war the recipients were expected to settle their obligations under L-L on terms satisfactory to the president of the United States. In spite of prolonged negotiations no arrangement was reached with the Soviet Union. The United States reduced eventually its claim to $800 million while the USSR offered $300 million.

LÉNIN (Ulyánov), **Vladímir Ilyich** (1870–1924), founder and leader of the CP and the Communist International, first head of the Soviet government. Born in Simbirsk (now Ulyanovsk) on the middle Volga, son of a schoolmaster, married to the daughter of a physician by the name of Blank. His older brother, Aleksandr, 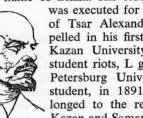 was executed for an attempt on the life of Tsar Alexander III, in 1887. Expelled in his first year of study at the Kazan University for participation in student riots, L graduated in law at St. Petersburg University as an external student, in 1891. In 1887–93, L belonged to the revolutionary circles in Kazan and Samara, moved to St. Petersburg in 1893, and there joined a Marxist circle. In 1894 he met there his future wife, Nadezhda Krupskaya, and wrote his first mimeographed pamphlet against the populists (q.v.). In 1895, L went abroad and, in Switzerland, came in touch with Plekhanov and his "Group for the Liberation of Labor." On his return to St. Petersburg, L, jointly with Martov organized "The Union of Struggle for the Liberation of the Working Class," which was soon discovered by the police who arrested its leaders. After 14 months in prison, L was banished for three years to Siberia, in 1897. In 1898, Krupskaya joined him and they were married. In Siberia, L wrote *The Tasks of Russian Social Democrats,* published in 1898, and *The Development of Capitalism in Russia,* published in 1899 in St. Petersburg under the name of "Ilyin." Later he used the pen name "Nikolay Lenin." In 1900, L went abroad where, together with Martov and Potresov, and with the

aid of Plekhanov's group, he published a paper *Iskra* (Spark); its slogan was "From Spark to Conflagration." In 1902, L wrote *What Is To Be Done?* in which he postulated the formation of a strictly centralized organization of professional revolutionaries, with the aid of which he promised to turn Russia "upside down." In 1903, *Iskra* organized a congress of the R. Social Democrats in Brussels, which later moved to London. The 40-odd delegates, after several weeks of discussions, mostly on organizational matters, split up into a majority group (Bolsheviks) with L and Plekhanov, and a minority group (Mensheviks) with Martov and Trotsky. After the congress both sides published pamphlets vilifying the other. Soon, however, Plekhanov changed sides, and L found himself in a minority. In spite of this, he held on firmly to his "majority" title and "rights" and, as *Iskra* became Menshevik, in Jan. 1905 started publishing a new paper *Vpered* (Forward) in Geneva.

During the 1905 revolution, L returned to Russia and bitterly fought the Mensheviks as well as the then newly established *Soviets,* sponsored by Mensheviks as "organs of workers' self-government." L was against the election to the first Duma (q.v.). In the fall of 1906, L moved to Finland and, in Dec. 1907, to Switzerland. In 1908–12, L seconded by Kamenev and Zinoviev, attacked the "revisionist" tendencies and "idealistic" deviations (so-called *Bogostroitelstvo*—"the building of God,") which became popular among some of the Bolsheviks. He started to study philosophy and, in 1909, published *Materialism and Empiriocriticism.* In 1908–10, L edited his own paper *The Proletarian,* and later collaborated with the Mensheviks on *Sotsial-Democrat.* When the quarrels of the factions within the party had practically paralyzed all the activities of its central organs, L made a spectacular *coup d'état.* In Jan. 1912, he called, in Prague, a conference of 15 of his adherents who "expelled" from the party all other groups, "elected" a new, purely Bolshevik Central Committee, and set up a special bureau to work in Russia, where a generous gift of Tikhomirov, the heir of a Volga millionaire, made it possible to start publishing a daily paper *Pravda,* after May 1912. In order to be nearer Russia, L moved to Cracow in July 1912, spending the summers in the little mountain village of Poronin, near Zakopane. There the conferences of his adherents in Russia were held in 1912–13.

With the outbreak of World War I, L was arrested by the Austrians and, after a fortnight's detention, was exiled to Switzerland. There, on Sept. 6, 1914, L published a resolution condemning the attitude of socialists in the belligerent countries and appealing to the workers "to transform the imperialist war into a civil war." At the international conferences of the left-wing socialists in Zimmerwald (Sept. 1915) and in Kienthal (April 1916) L proposed the creation of a Third International, but remained in a minority. In 1916, L wrote *Imperialism, the Highest Stage of Capitalism* and started to work on *The State and Revolution.* In April 1917, L came, with the help of the German military authorities, through Germany and Sweden, to Petrograd, where he radically changed the politics of the Bolsheviks and proclaimed the struggle against the Provisional Government (q.v.) for the establishment of the Soviet government. Following the unsuccessful uprising, in July 1917, L went into hiding and moved to Finland. There he completed *The State and Revolution* and wrote a pamphlet to prove the possibility of the Bolsheviks taking power and keeping the state power in Russia.

On Oct. 20, 1917, L illegally returned to Petrograd and, against the opposition of Kamenev and Zinoviev, but with the full support of Trotsky and Stalin, forced through a resolution for the immediate seizure of power. On Nov. 7, L issued a proclamation announcing the fall of the Provisional Government. On Nov. 9, L formed the first Soviet government and became its chairman, a position which he held until his death. When, in Feb. 1918, the Germans resumed their offensive in Russia, the Soviet government moved to Moscow, and L took up residence in the Kremlin. Overcoming the opposition of Trotsky, Bukharin and others, L concluded a formal peace treaty with the Germans, on March 3, 1918 (*see* BREST-LITOVSK PEACE TREATY).

In Aug. 1918, L was seriously wounded by the Socialist Revolutionary terrorist, Dora (Fanny) Kaplan, but quickly resumed political activities. On March 6, 1919, he opened the 1st congress of the Communist International in Moscow. After the Kronstadt uprising (q.v.), L changed his policy and, in March 1921, at the 10th Party Congress, proclaimed the New Economic Policy (NEP, q.v.). In May 1922, L had a stroke but returned to work in Oct. On Nov. 20, 1922, he delivered his last public speech. On Dec. 16, 1922, he had a second stroke which paralyzed his right side. On Dec. 22, 1922, L dictated his political "Testament" giving the characterization of the main party leaders. On Jan. 4, 1923, he added a postscript recommending Stalin's removal from the office of secretary general of the party. During Jan. and Feb. 1923, L dictated articles in which he was desperately seeking for a remedy against the "cancer of bureaucratism." On March 4, 1923, L's last article "Better Less But Better" was published in *Pravda*. In March also, L dictated a letter to Stalin threatening to break off all personal relations with him. On March 9, 1923, L had a third stroke and lost the power of speech. In the middle of May 1923, he was taken to Gorky, 20 miles from Moscow. By Oct. he could walk but could not speak, and on Jan. 21, 1924, he had a fatal stroke. His embalmed body was placed in a specially built mausoleum in the Red Square in Moscow, where, in March 1953, Stalin's body was also placed.

The literature about L is vast, written both by supporters and by adversaries, the former becoming the more and more hagiographic with the years. The 5th edition of L's *Works* is being prepared in Moscow in 50 volumes. In English the most complete *Selected Works* in 12 volumes was published in New York in 1943.

BIBLIOGRAPHY: N. K. Krupskaya, *Memories of Lenin*, 2 vols., New York, 1930; L. Trotsky, *Lenin*, New York, 1925; David Shub, *Lenin*, New York, 1948; Bertram D. Wolf, *Three Who Made a Revolution*, Boston, 1955.

V. SU.

LENINABÁD (f. Khodzhent), city, adm. center of Leninabad Oblast, Tadzhik SSR, on Syr Darya River; pop. 46,000 (1939), 77,000 (1959). R.R. station. Ind.: food processing, cotton ginning, fruit canning, sericulture. It is the oldest town in Central Asia, on an ancient caravan route from China to W. Asia.

LENINABÁD OBLAST, in N. Tadzhik SSR; area,

10,075 sq. mi.; pop. 666,000: Tadzhiks, Uzbeks, Kirghiz and Russians. Bounded on the N. by Uzbek SSR, on the E. by Kirghiz SSR, and on the S. by Gissar range; it projects N.E. across the Turkestan range; is drained by the Syr Darya and Zeravshan rivers. Cities: Leninabad (adm. center), Kanibadam, Sovetabad, Ura-Tyube, Isfara. It has a dry continental climate in the valleys; steppe, desert vegetation is predominant. Agr.: cotton, wheat, grapes (mostly in Fergana Valley), sericulture, cattle, sheep and angora goat raising (in mountains). Minerals: coal (Shurab), oil (Kim, Nefteabad), nonferrous ores (Kansay, Kara-Mazar), vanadium, bismuth, arsenic, tungsten. Ind.: mining on the S. slope of the Kurama range, fruit canning and drying, mfg. of building materials. Est. 1939.

LENINAKÁN (f. Aleksandropol), city in Armenian SSR; pop. 68,000 (1939), 108,000 (1959). An ind. center and R.R. junction, mfg. carpets, textiles, and machinery, and has meat-canning and bicycle factories. There are rich pumice and tuff deposits in the vicinity.

LENINGRÁD (f. St. Petersburg, 1914–24 Petrograd), second largest city after Moscow, adm. center of Leningrad Oblast, RSFSR; pop. 3,321,000 (1959). A seaport on the Gulf of Finland, and a key R.R. junction. A spacious city of classical beauty planned by French and Italian architects, it became a cultural, scientific and industrial center. It has highly developed ind. with emphasis on metalworking, electro-technical, chemical, lumbering, light, and food ind. Is a leading cultural center, with universities, institutes, outstanding theaters, museums (including the Hermitage), and the M. Ye. Saltykov-Shchedrin Library which is one of the largest public libraries in the world; has fine 18th-century architecture, such as the Winter Palace and Smolny Monastery by Rastrelli, the Academy of Fine Arts by de la Motte, Kazan Cathedral, Peter and Paul Fortress; also has beautiful suburban areas with palaces and parks—Petrodvorets, Gatchina. Founded 1703 by Peter the Great as a "window on Europe," it was made the capital of Russia in 1713. It was the scene of the Decembrist revolt in 1825 and of the 1905 revolution, and the original center of the October revolution of 1917. The capital was moved to Moscow in March, 1918. It was renamed Petrograd in 1914, and Leningrad in 1924 after Lenin's death. It suffered heavily in World War II.

THE LENINGRAD CASE. Following the death (to all appearances by natural causes) of A. A. Zhdanov, Politburo member and leader of the Leningrad party organization, in Aug. 1948, his closest associates including N. A. Voznesensky, member of the Politburo, A. A. Kuznetsov, a secretary of the Central Committee, M. I. Rodionov, chairman of the RSFSR Council of Ministers, P. S. Popkov, secretary of the Leningrad party organization, and others were ousted from their positions on various charges and, as later revealed by Khrushchev, in his secret address to the 20th Party Congress in 1956, were executed. Khrushchev blamed L. P. Beria and his associate, V. S. Abakumov, for fabricating this so-called "Leningrad Case," for which Abakumov was executed in 1954. G. M. Malenkov's complicity in this affair, although he was never openly accused, is suspect since he stood to gain most by the death of Zhdanov and the elimination of his closest supporters; moreover, V. M. Andrianov, who carried out the purge of the Leningrad party organization and who succeeded Popkov as first secretary in Leningrad, was closely associated with Malenkov throughout his career.

LENINGRAD OBLAST, RSFSR; area 33,300 sq. mi.; pop. 4,561,000 (1959): Russians, Finns, Estonians, Karelians. Bounded on the W. by the Estonian SSR, on the E. by the Vologda Oblast, on the S. by Pskov and Novgorod oblasts, on the N.W. by Finland. Cities: Leningrad (adm. center), Volkhov, Vyborg, Tikhvin, Gatchina, Pushkin. It is watered by the Neva, Luga, Vuoksa, Volkhov, Svir and other rivers; borders on the Gulf of Finland; has a series of canals partly built in the 18th and 19th centuries (the Mariinsky, Tikhvin and Vyshnevolotsk water system), and a dense rail network and extensive waterways connecting with the Volga and the White Sea. Heavily forested (pine, spruce) lowland, with the N. part of the Valday upland in the E., it has numerous lakes (Onega, Ladoga); humid continental climate; podsolic soil and marshes. Mineral resources: peat, oil shale, dolomite, bauxite, marble. Ind.: peat-fed power plants, lumbering, paper milling (Antropshino, Krasnoye Selo), aluminum plant (Volkhov), metalworking (Vyborg), mfg. of building material. Agr.: potatoes, vegetables, flax, fodder crops, cattle raising. Est. 1927.

LENIN HILLS (prior to 1935, Vorobyov Hills), elevation on the right bank of Moskva River in the S.W. section of Moscow, with a net of deep ravines. 100–160 ft. above river level. Site of Moscow University.

LENINISM: *see* MARXISM-LENINISM.

LENINOGÓRSK (f. Ridder), city in E. Kazakhstan Oblast, Kazakh SSR, on Ulba River (right tributary of the Irtysh R.); pop 67,000 (1959); on a branch of the Turkmen-Siberian R.R. Is a center of Altay ore deposits, including lead, zinc, silver, copper, gold; has a school of mining.

LENINOGÓRSK (f. Novaya Pismyanka), city in Tatar ASSR; pop. 41,200 (1958). A modern oil-production center.

LENIN PEAK, 24,400 ft., highest in Trans-Alay range, between Kirghiz SSR and Gorno-Badakhshan Oblast, N.E. Tadzhik SSR, second-highest peak in the USSR (highest, Stalin Peak). Discovered by the famous traveler and explorer of Central Asia, A. P. Fedchenko in 1869.

LENIN PRIZES for outstanding works in the fields of science, engineering, letters, and arts were established by the Soviet government on June 23, 1925. From 1935 to 1956 the Lenin prizes were superseded by Stalin prizes. In Sept. 1956 the Lenin prizes were restored and every year on Lenin's birthday 50 prizes of 75,000 rubles each are awarded. Special international honorary awards for outstanding achievements in the struggle for peace, *Lenin's International Awards "For Strengthening Peace Among Nations,"* are being distributed each year. The award consists of 100,000 rubles, a diploma, and a gold medal engraved with Lenin's bust. There are about ten recipients annually. Until 1956 this award, too, bore Stalin's name; the designation was changed by a decree of the Presidium of the Supreme Soviet USSR.

LÉNINSK-KUZNÉTSKY (f. Kolchugino), city in W. Kemerovo Oblast, RSFSR, on Tom River; pop. 83,000 (1939), 132,000 (1959). A mining town in the center of the Kuznetsk Basin; R.R. station.

LENKORÁN, seaport city in S.E. Azerbaijan SSR, on S.W. shore of the Caspian Sea near the Iranian border; pop. 30,000 (1958). Exports citrus fruit and tea. Ind.: lumbering, fishing, canning. There is a sulfur-spring resort in the vicinity.

LÉNSKY (Vervitsiotti), **Aleksándr Pávlovich** (1847–1908), actor, producer, and teacher. His stage activity began in 1865. In 1876 L joined the Moscow Maly Theater. He appeared as Chatsky and later Famusov in Griboyedov's *Woe from Wit,* Glumov and Paratov in Ostrovsky's *Even a Wise Man Stumbles,* Hamlet and Benedict in Shakespeare's *Hamlet* and *Much Ado About Nothing,* Nicholas in Ibsen's *The Pretenders.*

LEONÍDOV (Volfenzon), **Leoníd Mirónovich** (1873–1941), actor, People's Artist, USSR. L is said to have been one of the greatest tragedians of the first half of the 20th century. Before the revolution he played the parts of Cassius in Shakespeare's *Julius Caesar,* Lopakhin and Soleny in Chekhov's *The Cherry Orchard* and *The Three Sisters,* Dimitry Karamazov in the dramatization of Dostoyevsky's novel. Under the Soviets L created the part of Pugachov in Trenev's *Pugachovshchina,* and that of Plyushkin in Gogol's *Dead Souls.* In 1918 L began to appear in films and played Ivan the Terrible in *The Wings of the Bondman,* and other leading roles. L was professor and art director of the Lunacharsky Institute of Theatrical Art in Moscow.

LEÓNOV, Leoníd Maksímovich (1899–), leading Soviet writer and dramatist, born into a peasant family. Several of his works reflect the influence of Dostoyevsky. During a visit to the United States in 1960, L admitted to being influenced by Theodore Dreiser.

L was a graduate of the gymnasium and studied at Moscow University. After the revolution, he served for three years in the Red Army. He began writing poetry in 1922, but is best known for his novels.

L's early writings are influenced by romanticism and R. folklore. The fairy tale influence is evident in such stories as *Tuatamur, The Wooden Queen, The Jack of Diamonds, Valya's Doll,* and *The Death of Yegorushka.* Then follow *The Breakthrough at Petushinino* and the novel *The Badgers,* in which romantic tendencies give way to psychological realism. *The Badgers,* written in 1924, depicts the class struggle among the peasantry during the civil war. *The Thief* (1927) is L's most notable work. It is the story of a man who becomes disillusioned with the revolution and its mass killings for which he cannot find justification. He ends by doubting the revolution itself, becomes an outcast and a gangster.

From the early 1930's on, L's writings show evidences of his growing allegiance to the regime. A novel, known in English as *Soviet River* (1930), describes the impact of the new technical civilization on ignorant and backward Russia. It was followed by *Skutarévsky* (1932), in which the compromise between R. intellectuals and communism is portrayed. The lengthy and complicated novel *Road to the Ocean* (1936), attempts a picture of the life of the future as visualized by the communist leaders. Its publication resulted in much adverse criticism in the Soviet press. In his latest novel, *Russian Forest* (1953), L has succeeded in camouflaging sharp criticism of the communist tendency to ravage the rich natural resources of the country in order to impose the new technical civilization. L's apparent "rehabilitation" is exemplified by the fact that he was three times chosen a deputy to the Supreme Soviet of the USSR and was awarded the order of Lenin.

L wrote several plays of which the better known was *Invasion* (1942, Stalin prize, 1943). This play and *Lyonushka* (1943) picture the psychological change wrought in the national consciousness of the Russians by the war. Other plays are *Untílovsk* (1928), *The Orchards of Polovchansk* and *The Golden Carriage* (both 1953).

LEONTÓVICH, Mikhaíl Aleksándrovich (1903–), physicist. Fellow, Ac. of S., USSR (1946). Graduate (1923), professor (1934–45 and since 1955), Moscow University. Worked with the Commission for the Investigation of Kursk Magnetic Anomaly; associated with the Institute of Physics (1934–41 and 1946–52); Institute of Atomic Energy, Ac. of S. (1951–). Research concerns electrodynamics, optics, statistical physics, radiophysics, ultrasonics, powerful impulse discharges for the production of high-temperature plasma (1958). Awarded A. S. Popov gold medal (1952); Lenin prize (1958).

LEÓNTYEV, Konstantín Nikoláyevich (1831–1891), writer, critic, and philosopher. Son of a landowner, L first practiced medicine, then served as consul in Greece (1863–73). From 1880 to 1887 L was censor in Moscow. In 1887 he retired to the Optina Monastery and, shortly before his death, became a monk. L was an individualistic, original thinker who rejected the ideals of European industrialization and bourgeois democracy. He looked to aesthetic values and to Christian faith for the salvation of mankind. L believed in the special destiny of Russia, and in that respect shared the views of the Slavophiles. However, he took his inspiration from the Byzantine rather than from the Slavic past. He advocated unlimited autocracy and militant Greek Orthodoxy. A collection of his essays *The East, Russia and Slavdom* was published in 1885–86. L also wrote novels and literary criticisms.

LEPÉKHIN, Iván Ivánovich (1740–1802), explorer and naturalist. Fellow, St. Petersburg Ac. of S. (1771). First permanent secretary of the All-Russian Academy (1783). Headed an expedition to the Volga area, the Urals, and the N. of the European part of Russia (1768–72). Research concerned the changes in the surface of the earth, cave formation, effects of environment on plant and animal life.

LEPESHÍNSKAYA, Olga Vasílyevna (1916–), dancer, one of the principal ballerinas of the Moscow Bolshoy Ballet, which she joined in 1933. Her repertoire includes *Swan Lake, Sleeping Beauty, La Fille Mal Gardée, La Bayadère, Don Quixote, Mistress into Maid*, and others. Is a People's Artist (1937), and recipient of four Stalin prizes.

LEPESHÍNSKY, Panteleymón Nikoláyevich (1868–1944), member of the "Old Bolshevik Guard." Active since his student years in the "People's Will" movement. Expelled from St. Petersburg University and banished from the capital, he returned in 1894 to resume revolutionary work as a Social Democrat and Marxist. Three years later, he was exiled to Siberia, where he became a close associate and follower of Lenin. Deported to Siberia for the second time, he escaped to Switzerland. After the October revolution worked on school reform in the commissariat of Public Education. One of the organizers of "Istpart"—Commission for the Study of the History of the Communist Party. Author of historic memoirs.

LÉRMONTOV, Mikhaíl Yúryevich (1814–1841), great R. poet, second only to Pushkin as a lyricist. After studying at the University of Moscow and a military school in St. Petersburg, L became a commissioned officer in the Hussars of the Guards. The publication of his poem *The Death of a Poet* in 1837, which was evoked  by Pushkin's death in a duel and presented an indictment of the court circles, led to his arrest and his exile to the Caucasus, where he participated in military operations against the mountain tribes. He was permitted to return to the capital in 1838, but following a duel with the son of the French ambassador he was exiled to the Caucasus a second time in 1840. He returned to St. Petersburg again for three months in 1841, but was sent to the Caucasus for a third time, where he was killed in a duel with a fellow officer, N. Martynov.

The great poetic talents of L were recognized during his lifetime. The R. critic, V. G. Belinsky, ranked him with Pushkin and Gogol, and this appraisal has not been altered to this day. L's early death did not permit his genius to reach the full scope of its potentialities. Nevertheless he succeeded in creating an impressive literary heritage that included lyrical and other poems, dramas, and a novel. While L was one of the leading representatives of the romantic and specifically of the Byronic movement in Russia, his works also contain a strong emphasis on realism. His lyrical poetry expresses a passionate protest against injustice, the emptiness of life of the upper class, as well as a deep concern with the fate of his own generation whose inactivity and "indifference to good and evil" he condemned. To the decadence of the upper class he opposed the moral health of simple and honest people, and this led him to idealize primitive life (e.g., in the poem *Mtsyri*). The leading theme in his works is the conflict between ideals and reality, the rejection of reality in the name of ideals, proud solitude in a world that one scorns, and thirst for action.

L's romantic perception of reality was combined with a broad reliance on realistic elements characterized by historical accuracy and faithfulness to national culture, both in the past (*Boyarin Orsha*, 1835, and *A Song about Tsar Ivan Vasilievich*, 1838) and in the present (in his Caucasian works). L has produced such outstanding examples of R. lyric poetry as *The Sail, The Cliff, The Debate, The Prophet, The Poet,* and *Clouds in the Sky*. The realistic element appears most successfully in the poems *Native Land* and *Borodino*. L's long poem *The Demon* (1839) expresses L's rebellious strivings. In it an enormous inner strength is combined with tragic impotence, a striving to overcome loneliness and unite with the good, and the inability to achieve this. In L's plays, the author's attention centers not on the unfolding of the plot, but on the monologues. His *Masquerade Ball* (1835–36), in spite of its somewhat melodramatic character, is one of the best works of R. drama. In *A Song about Tsar Ivan Vasilyevich*, which derives from the wellsprings of traditional folklore, the theme of man's struggle for his rights, independence, and dignity is strongly expressed. The psychological novel *A Hero of Our Times* (1840) has played an important role in the development of R. prose. Its hero, Pechorin, whose name has since become a byword, belongs to the type of "superfluous men." In this novel L revealed himself as a master of psychological realism.

The influence of L on R. literature has by no means come to an end. He was "rediscovered" toward the end of the 19th century by the symbolist poets and he continues to remain one of the R. classics both in poetry and in prose. His works have been translated into many languages. C. P. K.

LÉSGAFT, Pyotr Frántsevich (1837–1909), educator, anatomist, and physician. Graduated from the Medical and Surgical Academy in St. Petersburg (1861). Founder of a biological laboratory (1893) which was to become the P. F. Lesgaft Research Institute (1918). Research concerned functional anatomy or, as he termed it, "directed exercise" and its effects on physical education and moral and intellectual development; the education of preschool children. The Institute of Physical Culture in Leningrad bears his name.

LESKÓV, Nikoláy Semyónovich (1831–1895), writer. After graduating from secondary school L joined the civil service for a short time. Subsequently, he traveled widely through Russia as the business agent for an English relative, and then became a journalist before finally turning to literature.

His first novels, *No Way Out* (1864), *The Ones Passed By* (1865), *The Islanders* (1866), and *At Daggers Drawn* (1870), centered on critical representations of nihilist intellectuals and served to illustrate his convictions that a genuinely moral person could find, in an urban setting, no task to which he could fully devote himself. Following the condemnation of these writings by the radical critics, L turned to portrayals of traditional characters from provincial life (priests, peasants, merchants, craftsmen). His treatment of the central figures in *The Cathedral*

Folk (1872), *The Sealed Angel* (1873), and *The Enchanted Wanderer* (1873) emphasized the depth and social significance of their concern with morality as well as the close association of traditional forms of social morality with the national element in R. culture. It is above all the descriptive aspects of these works, however, in which the life, speech, and attitudes of the traditional classes were vividly portrayed, that brought L wide recognition.

L turned next to short works concerned with "virtuous men" (*pravedniki*) from among the lower classes, whose humble and unnoticed deeds explained, in his view, the positive course of R. history (the short stories *One Track Mind*, 1879; *The Immortal Golovan*, 1880; *The Left-Handed Smith*, 1881; and *The Sentry*, 1887). There followed religious tales based on folklore and the tradition of the Church. L is regarded as one of the leading stylists in R. fiction. His style has influenced the writings of authors in the early 20th century, including Gorky, Remizov, Zamyatin, Leonov, and Zoshchenko. I. M.

LEVITÁN, Isáak Ilyich (1861–1900), landscape painter, born in Lithuania. Studied in the School of Painting, Sculpture and Architecture, Moscow; pupil of Savrasov and Polenov. His landscapes, conveying a feeling of lyrical melancholy, depict mainly the Central Russia and Volga regions. The better known of these pictures—*Quiet Haven, Evening, At the Pool, Dusk, March, Vladimir Highway, Quiet Forever,* and *The Golden Autumn*—are in the Tretyakov Gallery, Moscow, and the Russian Museum, Leningrad. L is regarded as a forerunner of R. impressionists.

LEVÍTOV, Aleksándr Ivánovich (1835–1877), writer of populist tendencies. He depicted the tragic lot of peasants and the sordid life of the poor and destitute in the cities. His principal novels are *The Reckoning* (1862), *Village Pictures* (1870), and *Moscow Burrows and Slums* (1866). L took an active part in the student revolutionary movement.

LEVÍTSKY, Dmítry Grigóryevich (1735–1822), portrait painter, born in Ukraine, son of a priest. He studied art with Antropov and Valeriani. Became a member of the Academy of Fine Arts in 1770. L left an impressive gallery of portraits among which *Architect Kokorinov, Nikita Demidov,* and *Madame Lvov* are the best.

LEYBENZÓN, Leoníd Samuílovich (1879–1951), mechanical and petroleum engineer, geophysicist. Fellow, Ac. of S., USSR (1943). Graduate, Moscow University (1901), School of Technology (1906); professor, Tbilisi (1919), Baku (1921) Polytechnic Institute, Moscow University (1922–51). Research on hydraulics, aerodynamics, petroleum extraction and refining, and geophysics. Author of *Variational Methods in Solving Problems of the Theory of Elasticity* (1943). Stalin prize (1943).

LÉYKIN, Nikoláy Aleksándrovich (1841–1906), humorist whose prolific writings had an important influence on his famous contemporary Chekhov. Most of his writings make fun of the merchant class. His best-known work is *Our People Abroad* (1890).

LEZGHINS: *see* POPULATION, AZERBAIJAN SSR.

LIABILITY LAW is the part of Civil Law (q.v.) covering contracts, torts (injury to persons and property), and some other obligations involving property. It differs from non-communist LL in the restrictions which it places on contracts and on remedies for torts. These restrictions stem largely from Soviet socialization of means of production and the nature of economic controls through a central inclusive national plan.

Contracts between private traders and manufacturers ended almost completely when private capital was expropriated during the First Five Year Plan (1928–32); but contracts continued between state and other organizations. Contracts are praised for combining the principle of planning with that of economic accountability and for facilitating control over plan fulfillment. When one enterprise does not fulfill a contract to deliver goods or to perform services, it may be taken by the other party to arbitration (q.v.) if it does not volunteer proper compensation. Officials involved may also be liable to criminal penalties in case of "localism," that is, failure to fulfill planned deliveries outside one's own economic region. Freedom of contract is limited by the dictates of the economic plan, fixed prices, compulsory model contracts, lack of choice between suppliers and compulsory arbitration of precontractual disputes. Contracts may be made between individuals, as when one buys in the collective farm market, or rents a room from the occupant of an apartment or *dacha* (summer home), or buys a private house; or they may be between individuals and organizations, as in the purchase of a 50-kopeck subway ticket or goods in a state store. Apart from conventional restrictions on fraudulent and coerced contracts, there is a ban on contracts involving private hire of labor for profit, or private purchase of goods for resale at a profit.

Soviet tort law recognizes no liability to a person who has been insulted, caused mental anguish, libeled or slandered. Such actions are punished as crimes, and fines involved go to the state. Courts do not award huge compensations for injuries, but only sums or goods necessary to cover material losses. Until the early 1930's it was easier than at present to receive such full compensation, since there was liability without cause. An employer had to pay enough to his employees who were injured on the job to make up the difference between their social security (q.v.) payments and their regular wages, even if he was not negligent. Now he pays such supplements only if he is criminally negligent, in which case he may be sued by the insurance organization for its payments to the injured. The law provides exceptions to this which cover especially dangerous operations and their operators: railroads, tramways, factories, dealers in inflammable material, keepers of wild animals, building and construction projects, and, by later rulings, civil aviation, cars, ships, motor boats, and so on. Persons injured by es-

pecially dangerous operations must be paid the supplements necessary to make up their full regular wages, even if no negligence is involved, unless it can be shown that injury was due to *force majeure,* or to willful or gross negligence of the injured persons. Injured employees of organizations conducting extra-hazardous operations do not come under these special provisions for liability without cause. Even if injured on the job, they receive only social security payments, unless the employer was criminally negligent. (*See also* ARBITRATION, COURT SYSTEM, PROPERTY, SOVIET LAW)

P. H. J.

LIBÁVA: *see* LIEPAJA.

LIBEDÍNSKY, Yúry Nikoláyevich (1898–1959), writer. A member of the CP (1920), L portrayed party leaders. Author of *The Week* (1922), a novel on the crushing of a White revolt; *The Birth of a Hero* (1930); *The Guards* (1942). One of the leaders of the Russian Association of Proletarian Writers, he was expelled from the Union of Soviet Writers in 1936 and reinstated in 1958.

LÍBER (Goldman), **Mikhaíl Isáakovich** (1880–1937), leader of the Bund and the Mensheviks. Joined the revolutionary movement at the age of 16. Participated in the 2nd Congress of the Russian Social Democratic party in 1903. Was repeatedly arrested. In 1912 was, together with Trotsky, one of the organizers of the August Bloc (q.v.). After the February revolution, L was, with F. Dan and I. Tsereteli, one of the most influential leaders of the Executive Committee of the Soviets. Belonged to the right wing of the Mensheviks and Bund. After the October revolution L was arrested and then liberated and assigned to a minor post in the economic apparatus. In 1937, during the great purges, L was, together with the Socialist Revolutionary leader Abram Gots, arrested and executed.

LIBERATION OF LABOR, the first R. Marxist organization formed in Switzerland, in 1883, by former members of the populist "Black Repartition" (q.v.). Its leaders were G. Plekhanov, P. Akselrod, L. Deutsch, and V. Zasulich. The members of the LL translated several works of Marx and Engels into Russian and organized their distribution in Russia. In their own writings (especially in two drafts of the political program —first in 1884, and second in 1888) Plekhanov and his associates went over to the Marxist viewpoint in their interpretation of R. developments and expressed a number of ideas which subsequently figured in the ideology of the Russian Social Democratic movement. Among these ideas were the leadership of the working class in the struggle against tsarism and the seizure of state power by the working class as the goal of the revolutionary movement. In 1888, the LL initiated a Russian Social Democratic Union abroad which, in 1894, was reorganized into a Union of Russian Social Democrats. In 1900, the LL seceded from the Union, the majority of the latter being on the side of "economists" (*see* MARXISM, RUSSIAN). Shortly afterwards the LL, together with the new, young emigrants from Russia— Lenin, Martov, and Potresov—started to publish *Iskra* (q.v.) which prepared and organized a congress of the

Russian Social Democratic Workers' party in Brussels and London, in 1903. After this congress all the members of the LL joined the Russian Social Democratic Workers' party, and the LL was officially dissolved.

V. Su.

LÍDIN (Gomberg), **Vladímir Germánovich** (1894–), writer. Studied eastern languages in Moscow. Author of many short stories about Soviet life, including the novel *The Renegade* (1928), *Great or Pacific?* (1932) dealing with the Far East and the development of socialism. Criticized in recent years because of individualistic tendencies.

LÍEPAJA (f. Libava), seaport city in Latvian SSR, on Baltic Sea; pop. 53,000 (1939), 71,000 (1959). Is a R.R. junction; a major ind. center, with heavy machinery, food processing, linoleum, wood and metal products, mining equipment. Founded by the Teutonic Knights 1263, it came under Lithuanian rule in 1418, and under Prussian rule in 1560; was captured by Charles XII of Sweden in 1701 and in 1795 by the Russians.

LIFÁR, Serge (1905–), dancer, choreographer, and author, born in Kiev. He joined the Diaghilev Ballet in 1923 and became premier danseur in 1925. After Diaghilev's death L joined the Paris Opéra as premier danseur and maître de ballet, and later became professor. He staged more than thirty-five ballets for the Opéra (among them, *Icare, David Triomphant, Le Roi Nu, Alexandre le Grand, Suite en Blanc*; and *Chota Rustavelli* and others for Nouveau Ballet de Monte Carlo). His books include *La Danse* (1937), *Diaghilev* (1939), *L'Histoire du Ballet Russe* (1945), *Le Livre de la Danse* (1954), *Au Service de la Danse* (1958), and others. Currently (1960) he is free-lancing as choreographer and instructor in Paris.

LIFE EXPECTANCY: *see* MEDICAL SYSTEM.

LÍLINA, Mária Petróvna (1866–1943), actress. People's Artist, RSFSR; wife and associate of K. S. Stanislavsky. Played in the Moscow Art Theater since 1898. The versatility of L's talent allowed her to appear in both lyric and dramatic roles. Among her best impersonations were the Snow Maiden, in Ostrovsky's play of that name; Sonya, in Chekhov's *Uncle Vanya*; Liza, in Griboyedov's *Woe From Wit;* and Korobochka, in Gogol's *Dead Souls*.

LÍNNIK, Vladímir Pávlovich (1889–), physicist. Fellow, Ac. of S., USSR (1939). Graduate, Kiev University (1914); associated with the State Institute of Optics (1926); professor, Leningrad University (1926–41). Research concerns optics, optical instruments, X-ray examination of crystals. Inventor of the double microscope (1929), microinterferometer and microprofilometer (1933) and others. Stalin prizes (1946, 1950); two Lenin orders.

LÍPETSK, city, adm. center of Lipetsk Oblast, RSFSR, at the confluence of the Lipovka and Voronezh rivers; pop. 67,000 (1939), 157,000 (1959). Has a R.R. station, metallurgical plants (at Lipetsk iron-ore deposits), also tractor, radiator, and silicate plants. It is noted since the 18th century for chalybeate mineral springs and mud baths.

LÍPETSK OBLAST, RSFSR; area 9,650 sq. mi.; pop. 1,144,000 (1959). Is on the Central Russian and Oka-Don upland, in the N. part of the black-soil region. Cities: Lipetsk (adm. center), Yelets, Gryazi. It is watered by the affluents of the Don; has temperate continental climate; iron-ore deposits. Agr.: potatoes, wheat, sugar beets, dairy farming, cattle and hog raising. Ind.: metallurgical plants, machine building, food processing. Est. 1954.

LIQUIDATORS: *see* CPSU.

LISHENTSY: *see* CITIZENSHIP.

LÍSHEV, Vsévolod Vsévolodovich (1877–), sculptor. After training at St. Petersburg Academy of Fine Arts, he produced monuments (*Peter the Great*, 1914) and busts (*Marx*). In later years he continued in the same realist vein with group studies (*Stalin and Voroshilov*, 1933) and monuments (*Chernyshevsky*, 1942) as well as works inspired by the war (*In the Streets of Leningrad*, 1942–43).

LISICHÁNSK, city in Lugansk Oblast, Ukrainian SSR, on N. Donets River; pop. 35,000 (1956); R.R. station. It is a major center of the Donbas coal and chemical ind. and has a large N. Donets power plant.

LISYÁNSKY, Yúry Fyódorovich (1773–1837), explorer. Participated in the first Russian sea voyage around the world (under I. F. Kruzenshtern) and collected valuable material on oceanography and ethnography. Discoverer of Lisyansky islet. A peninsula at the N. coast of the Sea of Okhotsk and a mountain on Sakhalin Island were named after L.

LITERATURE, PREREVOLUTIONARY. Kievan Period—the Middle Ages (11th–15th centuries). Although Russian L did not enter the European scene till the middle of the 19th century it has had a long if not unbroken tradition dating back to the 11th century.

Along with Christianity (988) the E. Slavs received from Byzantium the gift of letters. At first Slavic (mostly Bulgarian) translations of the ecclesiastic books were used in Kiev, then spiritual and secular L as well was translated anew in the reign of Yaroslav the Wise (1019–54).

More original works than writers are known to us from this period. One of the few is a monk by the name of Nestor, allegedly author of the earliest Lives of the Russian Saints. He has also been credited with the Primary Chronicle (up to 1118), the final editing of which was probably done by Sylvester of Vydubitsky Monastery. Much interesting material—tales, sermons, instructions, letters—had been incorporated into the Chronicle along with the historical entries. It also affords us a glimpse into the earliest Slavic epic of pre-Christian times, partially preserved in the N. Great-Russian poetry, so-called *byliny* or *stariny*. Other authors of the period are Ilarion, metropolitan of Kiev (11th century) and Daniel the Abbot, who left us the first description of a pilgrimage to the Holy Land. Prince Vladimir Monomakh (1113–1125) wrote an *Instruction to His Children* and an autobiography. A compilation of 1076 (*Izbornik*) is important because of its partly original contents, especially rhymed aphoristic expressions.

The Primary Chronicle, written in a simple, unadorned style, has been copied in regional collections and continued in the Kievan Chronicle until the year 1200, and further in the Galician-Volynian Chronicle, renowned for its secular biographies of the local princes and its richly ornamented style, characteristic of the period. Other literary monuments of interest are the Kievan Paterikon (a spirited and at times dramatic exchange of letters between two ascetics) and *Supplication of Daniel the Prisoner,* with many interesting proverbs, but the most important monument of this period is the epic, *The Tale of the Host of Igor,* describing the disastrous expedition of Prince Igor Svyatoslavich against Polovtsy in 1185. The exquisite beauty of the tale does not lie in its contents. Its fine poetic and symbolic style skillfully blends Christian and pagan elements.

The Kievan advancement of letters and culture was not duplicated in the new literary centers such as Suzdal, Tver, Ryazan, Pskov or Novgorod or, finally, Moscow—which replaced it after the fall of Kiev in the second half of the 12th century. Then came the Tatar domination which lasted for over 200 years.

Literary activity continued in the N. of the E. Slavic territory, though only slowly and mostly through hagiographic works. Outstanding lives of saints were written in the 14th century by Epiphany the Wisest, the decorative style reminiscent of late medieval tradition. Though severed from Byzantium and Europe, Russia did not lose her connection with the Balkan Slavs and, in the 14th century, she experienced the so-called "second S. Slavic influence" (the first being the borrowing of the ecclesiastic literature from Serbians and Bulgarians at the beginning of the Kievan period).

Muscovite Isolationism (16th–17th centuries). The rise of Moscow as a political power marks the emergence of a new period in L, which one is tempted to call the period of Muscovite isolationism because of its severance of all cultural ties with the rest of the world. Periods of political consolidation are rarely blessed with a literary flowering as well. Moscow, which after the fall of Constantinople in 1453 had begun to look upon itself as the "Third Rome," was preoccupied with the development of such L as would be appropriate to its political ideology and the union it had achieved between church and state. The characteristic (and most vital) L of the time is that inspired by two controversies, the first theological, between Nil Sorsky (1443–1508), a proponent of the ascetic movement, and Iosif Volotsky (1439–1515) who with the support of the church defended Muscovite autocracy, and the victory of whose party was to have far-reaching consequences on the future of R. intellectual history. The other controversy took the form of an exchange of angry letters between Ivan the Terrible (1530–84), who was not only the newly created tsar, but an effective writer as well, and Prince Andrey Mikhaylovich Kurbsky (ca. 1528–83), who had fled to Lithuania.

Cycles of historical songs have come down to us from this time, celebrating the military victories of Ivan the Terrible. From this time also dates the compilation, by Makary, metropolitan of Moscow and author of the *Stepennaya Knüga,* a genealogy, of the lives of the Saints (including many old theological writings), which served as the official calendar of the Russian Church until the time of Peter the Great. The writing and rewriting of the chronicles continued with the addition of some folklore motifs (as in the Nikonovskaya Letopis), attesting a revival of the epos. A nonliterary work of this time is the *Domostroy,* an extensive manual on proper conduct, which still makes interesting reading today for the picture it gives of the manners and morals of the Muscovite family of the day.

In belles-lettres, the 16th and 17th centuries were not very productive. There were some translations, and the two genres of miracle plays and school plays made their appearance, largely as a result of renewed contacts with the west through Poles, Byelorussians, and Ukrainians, dating from the Polish invasion of Moscow in 1612 and later.

The greatest manifestation of the Muscovite style and spirit is found in the writings of Priest Avvakum (1621–82), the spiritual leader of the Old-Believers after the great schism during the reign of Tsar Alexis, especially in his autobiography, vividly and expressively written in colloquial Russian of the time interspersed with Old Church Slavonic quotations.

Baroque and Classicism. Toward the middle of the 17th century, a new literary style, to which an ever-increasing number of scholars are giving the name of baroque, was introduced to Moscow by graduates of the Kievan Theological Academy: the Byelorussian Simeon of Polotsk (1629–80), preacher, scholar, poet, and the initiator of syllabic versification in Moscow; the Ukrainian St. Dimitry of Rostov (1651–1709), writer of sermons, poet, dramatist; Stefan Yavorsky (1655–1722), a master of the sermon; Feofan Prokopovich (1681–1736), outstanding teacher, writer of spiritual dramas and of syllabic poetry, and eloquent defender of the reforms of Peter the Great.

The reform of R. verse is the work of two outstanding scholars and writers, the scientist and first academician M. V. Lomonosov (1711–65), and V. K. Trediakovsky (1703–69), secretary to the Russian Academy, who rejected the syllabic verse in use in Russia at the time, introducing instead accentual versification (similar to English). Trediakovsky translated Fénelon's *Aventures de Télémaque* into rather ponderous hexameters and inaugurated a productive tradition of the so-called tonico-syllabic versification. Neither of them can be considered a real poet, but Lomonosov's odes still preserve a certain grandeur.

Another poet, Prince Antiokh Kantemir (1709–44), R. ambassador to London and Paris, is spoken of as the "first deliberate and artistically conscious realist in Russian literature" (D. Mirsky); however, his satires (written in syllabic meter) were not published until long after his death and so had no part in shaping the L of his day. Lomonosov and Trediakovsky still inclined toward the baroque, but classicistic principles already characterized the dramatic, poetic, and critical writings of A. P. Sumarokov (1718–77). M. M. Kheraskov (1733–1807) wrote fables and songs, and the epics *Rossiada* and *Vladimir.* The first author of stature to write satirical comedies of manners was D. I. Fonvizin (1744–92) with his *Brigadir* and *Nedorosl* (The Minor). The better-known poet of the 18th century was G. R. Derzhavin (1743–1816). In his odes full of rich effects of sound and color, he combined classical and baroque elements; then, having by irony and parody successfully undermined the dignity of the classical style, he switched to pre-romanticism.

In the late 60's and early 70's there appeared satirical journals modeled on the English *Tatler* and *Spectator*. For a time these enjoyed the protection of Catherine II, but their radical and oppositional tendencies became more pronounced and they were finally suppressed. *A Journey from St. Petersburg to Moscow* (1790) was also suppressed by the Empress because it contained severe criticism of R. serfdom, and its author, A. N. Radishchev (1749–1802), was imprisoned and committed suicide afterwards.

A development of importance was the linguistic reform largely brought about by N. M. Karamzin (1760–1826), the champion of the new movement known as sensibility, and his followers, though the way for it was to some extent paved by the editor of one of the satirical journals under Catherine II, N. Novikov. Karamzin's modernization of the R. language consisted chiefly from numerous adoptions of foreign expressions, chiefly from French and German, and some new modes of expression appearing in his *Letters of a Russian Traveler* (influenced by Sterne) and in the story *Poor Liza.* His most ambitious work was a *History of Russia* in 12 volumes.

Karamzin's school included the gifted I. I. Dmitriev (1760–1837), writer of lyrical verse of quality, witty fables, epistles, epigrams; the Ukrainian V. Kapnist (1757-1823), author of the rhymed satirical comedy *Yabeda* (chicane) as well as idyllic and erotic poetry; V. L. Pushkin (1767–1830) (uncle of A. S. Pushkin), popular because of his polemical letters, fables, and epigrams defending the innovations of Karamzin; V. Ozerov (1770–1816), the author of psychologically effective tragedies written in verse (*Fingal, Dmitry Donskoy,* both 1807), and, departing from the classicist tradition in violating the unities of place and action, introducing local color, choruses, and even ballet. A somewhat later follower of Karamzin was V. T. Narezhny (1780–1825), with his picaresque novels, which incidentally anticipate some of the plots used later on by N. Gogol (e.g. *The Bursar, Russian Gil Blas*).

The influence of Karamzin and his school can be discerned in the work of I. A. Krylov (1768–1843), who wrote comedies and satirical prose as well as the fables that made him famous. These grew up out of the rich folk tradition, and often became proverbs. Only a few are original in content, but Krylov's place in R. letters rests on his masterful handling of the living colloquial language and on the lexical and phraseological riches he has handed down.

The Romanticists. A score or so of Karamzin's followers, including Zhukovsky, Batyushkov, Prince Vyazemsky, Uvarov, and the young Pushkin, banded together to form *Arzamas,* a literary society dedicated to propagating and defending the innovations of Karamzin against the conservative classicists, led by Admiral A. Shishkov (1753–1841). Of these, the pre-romantic K.

Batyushkov (1787–1855) was notable chiefly for his attempt to give to his poetry the melodiousness of Italian verse; while V. Zhukovsky (1783–1852) soon began to incorporate romantic themes and motifs into his work. His greatest contribution was as a translator, and it was through his superb translations that whole generations of Russians absorbed the English and German poetry of the age.

However, the first to excite real interest in romanticism was Russia's greatest poet, A. S. Pushkin (1799–1837), with his Byronic poems *The Caucasian Captive, The Gypsies, Poltava.* Pushkin was deeply imbued with the spirit of the classicist tradition, but he was too great a genius to be swallowed up in any one literary movement. His literary work was eminently successful, bringing about what many R. writers and poets before him had striven for: the fusion of the living and the literary languages, not an imitation of the mannerisms of folksy speech, but the preservation of the true spirit of the living, spoken language.

Pushkin is the author of the first R. national drama, *Boris Godunov,* in which, under the influence of Shakespeare, he abandoned the three unities (of time, place, and action) prescribed by the classicists; of the first R. social novel of everyday life, and of a great novel in verse, *Eugene Onegin.*

A hundred and twenty-five years after his death his lyrics are still inimitable, in their unity of content and form.

Pushkin stands out above a cluster of contemporary poets, of whom he especially admired three, Ye. Baratynsky (1800–44), a philosophical poet of a bent very different from his own; N. Yazykov (1803–46), and Baron A. Delvig (1793–1831). Other contemporaries, all to a greater or lesser extent affected by romanticism, were Denis Davydov (1794–1836), bard of war and love; F. Glinka (1786–1880); D. Venevitinov (1805–27), of exceptional intellectual and poetic promise; Prince P. A. Vyazemsky (1792–1878), noteworthy as a critic. There was also a circle of "Lovers of Wisdom" centered in Prince V. Odoyevsky (1803–69) and devoted to the study of German philosophy, especially Schelling, and the philosophy of romanticism. Romanticism did not necessarily go with modernism; perhaps the finest exponent of the romantic world view and the first fully romantic poet in Russia (as well as a talented philosophical poet) was F. I. Tyutchev (1803–73), whose poetry, however, is archaic in form and saturated with idioms of Church Slavonic. A similar archaism pervades the sparkling classical comedy of Moscow society, *Gore ot uma* (Woe from Wit, known also as *The Mischief of Being Clever*) by A. S. Griboyedov (1795–1829), which nevertheless uses the resources of archaic language to achieve faultless intonation, delightful diction, and flawless and expressive rhyme.

A gifted romantic poet of the younger generation was M. Yu. Lermontov (1814–41), (allegedly descendant of a Scotch bard) who wrote beautiful lyrics. He derived his romantic inspiration from the Caucasus, and described himself as Byron with a Russian soul; like a true (Russian) Byron, he rebelled against society, God, and the universe. His heroes delight in tempting fate (for instance in the dramatic poems *Demon* and *Mtsyri* [The Novice]). In addition to a large body of lyric poetry, Lermontov has left some historical poems that preserve the genuine flavor of the folk epic, and the first R. psychological novel, *The Hero of Our Time*, written in a terse, concise prose style that has served as a model to many a R. writer of a later generation, Chekhov among others.

The wild romantic scenery of the Caucasus was the inspiration for the novels and tales of the Decembrist A. Bestuzhev-Marlinsky (1797–1837), technically modeled on contemporary western romantic writing. The romantic influence is also traceable in the work of the talented novelist, playwright, and lyric poet, Count K. Tolstoy (1817–75), and in the poetry of Karolina Pavlova (1807–93).

Although N. V. Gogol (1809–52), a writer of great distinction, does not fit into the romantic mold, his first (unsuccessful) poem *Hans Kuechelgarten*, and for that matter his whole outlook on life, was definitely in that tradition, as can be seen in his Ukrainian tales and is explicitly stated in some of his essays and in letters to friends. Attracted to the imaginary and fantastic, and longing for unexpressed beauty, he found the reality about him banal and base and mean, and used his gift of suggestion to distort it, hoping to awaken in his readers his own longing for a purer and better world.

Natural School and Realism. Gogol became the founder (around 1840) of a new school in Russian L often called the "Natural School" (not to be confused with naturalism). Representatives of the Natural School (Vladimir Dahl, 1801–72, Ya. Butkov, Count Vladimir Sollogub and others) borrowed from Gogol his artistic methods but not his (primarily romantic) ideology. They excluded the sphere of supernatural and the more refined aspects of life, concentrating on a grotesque portrayal of the lower strata of human society and human experience. They delighted in exaggerated, almost physiological descriptions of the everyday activities of their heroes. The school included fledgling efforts of Dostoyevsky and Turgenev, who however soon outgrew this stage and passed on to realism, the movement that was destined to rule over Russian L for many decades to come and earn it world-wide fame.

With V. G. Belinsky (1811–48), literary criticism began to play an important role in the development of L and in particular of the Natural School and the realist movement.

Belinsky was a Westerner and opposed the Slavophiles who believed in Russia's peculiar destiny. The lead of Belinsky was followed by Chernyshevsky, Pisemsky, Dobrolyubov, and others. They tended to regard L as merely a mirror of life and a vehicle for the ethical and political controversy that censorship otherwise suppressed. This was the intellectual climate in which realism came to the fore.

There were two Russian writers of the 19th century who kept alive the traditional R. faith in a higher sphere of reality to which one might aspire, in visions, and in dreams. These two were Gogol and Dostoyevsky. In his early work Dostoyevsky was preoccupied with stylistic effects, in his later work, "with the drama of ideas."

His early work is directly dependent on Gogol: his Petersburg resembles closely one aspect of Gogol's Petersburg, as portrayed in his *Petersburg Tales*—a city-phantom, wrapped in fog and darkness, breeding strange creatures who live in a complete isolation, in a world of strange and terrible, sometimes mad, dreams. The names of Dostoyevsky's novels read like a catalogue of the great books of human history: *Notes from the Underground, Crime and Punishment, The Idiot, The Possessed, A Raw Youth,* and *The Brothers Karamazov.* They represent stages in the development of the psychological and the philosophical novel. Dostoyevsky's style of psychological writing, the type of insights into the hidden nature of man, was influential in that exploring of the "underworld" of the subconscious which still constitutes the main bulk of the novel-writing since Dostoyevsky. Although his tradition is followed rather by French writers (Mauriac, Bernanos) than by Russians, he nevertheless remains one of the most popular writers with the young Russians of today. For political reasons his work has not been published for a long time in the Soviet Union, except recently in abridged form and without *The Possessed.*

While Dostoyevsky's prose—especially in his early period—is studded with the stylistic devices of the Natural School and even of the sentimentalists, the style of his contemporaries A. I. Goncharov (1812–91) and A. F. Pisemsky (1820–81) is realistic in the full sense of the word. Goncharov especially re-created life in all its breadth and complexity, with each minute detail (as he had learned from Gogol) appearing before the reader with astonishing vividness. As one symbolist critic put it, he did not *describe* Oblomov, he *found* him stretched on his sofa and wrapped in his Oriental dressing-gown.

Oblomov became a symbol of the indolent and weak, though generous and kind R. intellectual, utterly ineffectual and incapable, and unwilling to lead an active, practical life; Oblomovism became the name for a state of mind. Goncharov wrote other books, *An Ordinary Story, The Precipice,* a lengthy novel, and a travel-book *The Frigate Pallada,* but only *Oblomov* became a classic. Pisemsky, a severe but unjust critic of Pushkin, himself left a few novels and a drama, *The Hard Lot,* which was popular in his time. In the same realistic vein—describing reality in every smallest detail but without the brilliancy of the great masters of R. prose—there were a score of "lesser lights," as N. G. Pomyalovsky, F. M. Reshetnikov, V. A. Sleptsov, N. Uspensky, A. I. Levitov. Much more original and talented were M. I. Saltykov-Shchedrin (1826–89) and G. I. Uspensky (1840–1902) both of whom combined social and "civic" motives with genuine humor to create a powerful satire of the pre-reform Russia. Saltykov's social novel *The Golovlyov Family* must be considered his greatest achievement. P. I. Melnikov-Pechersky (1819–83) created a very vivid, semi-ethnographic description of the life of the Old-Believers.

N. S. Leskov (1831–95) stands apart because of his striking use of the R. language, whose spirit he understood more fully than did others, and whose possibilities he knew how to exploit to the best advantage.

Leskov was a good story-teller and his tales make interesting and enjoyable reading. He was not very popular during his lifetime since he did not share the radical views generally accepted by the R. intelligentsia of his time, but he has been rediscovered several times since then.

I. S. Turgenev (1813–83) came to the fore during the "age of the R. novel" (that is, from the 1840's to the 1880's). Like Dostoyevsky, he owes much to Gogol and the Natural School, but his style is different, even and flowing in movement, on the whole easy to read and also easy to translate. He devoted much attention to the R. landscape and the R. peasant and fought for the abolition of serfdom (his *Sketches of a Huntsman* played a role similar to that of *Uncle Tom's Cabin*). Later his ambition was to describe the R. social and political scene and the changes he saw in R. society. He described a score or so of "superfluous men" of various types and from various walks of life, beginning with Rudin (in the novel of the same name) and ending with *Fathers and Sons*, and picturing the "nihilism" that was beginning to spread among the R. intelligentsia. One of his best novels is *A Nest of Gentlefolk*. Turgenev was the first R. writer to become known in the West and the first to have personal contacts with western literary figures such as Henry James.

Another Westerner in both life and literature was A. I. Herzen (1812–70), writer of realistic short novels and of highly significant memoirs (*The Past and Thoughts*), containing many acute characterizations of his contemporaries and their activities. He was an accomplished essayist and political writer, as is evidenced in a series of pamphlets "From the Other Shore," his letters and his articles in the paper *Kolokol* (The Bell) which he founded and published in England.

The period of the rise of realistic prose was a period of definite decline in poetry. A notable poet of the period was N. A. Nekrasov (1821–77) who introduced into R. poetry new motifs (mostly social), new rhythms (primarily dactylic), and even journalistic jargon. According to his own appraisal, his "civic" activities were in conflict with his poetic output, and his poems interfered with his status as a progressive fighter for human rights and dignity. He advocated the preeminence of the first over the second. "You do not have to be a poet, but you are obliged to be a citizen." This was the attitude of many of his contemporaries. Only a few poets, especially A. N. Maykov (1821–97) and L. A. Mey (1822–62), managed to stay away from the "political evil" of the day.

Count L. N. Tolstoy (1828–1910) had embodied this prevalence of the moral pathos over everything else especially in his later period, when he wrote primarily philosophical and religious work. However, his early work shows a preoccupation with moral issues as well. R. realistic writing reached its height in his autobiographical *Childhood, Boyhood, Youth* and especially in the prose epic of the Napoleonic wars, *War and Peace,* and in *Anna Karenina.* Tolstoy's endless quest for freedom, for truth, for simplicity found a most adequate expression in his writings, which are accessible to the most sophisticated and to the uneducated masses.

Tolstoy had achieved complete command over words and was able to re-create most convincingly not only "reality" and the world of the historical past, but the hidden motives of the human heart as well, anticipating the psychological insights of European novelists (even of Freud) of a later epoch. The language of Tolstoy's novels and tales is remarkable; he reproduced the speech of the society to which he belonged with an unerring feeling for the right word and the right place for that word. Tolstoy is rightly regarded as one of the greatest novelists of the last century. His moral and religious teachings in a highly artistic form have endeared him to millions all over the world, and his works have been widely translated into numerous languages, including the most exotic ones.

In the 80's, just after Tolstoy's conversion and Dostoyevsky's death, the progress of Russian L was temporarily interrupted. Turgenev died in 1883, Nekrasov in 1877, Pisemsky in 1881, A. N. Ostrovsky, the leading realist dramatist, in 1886. Goncharov did not produce anything. The political atmosphere was not favorable to literary thought.

Chekhov, Bunin, Gorky. New writers who appeared at the time on the literary scene were A. P. Chekhov (1860–1904), V. G. Korolenko (1853–1921), and V. M. Garshin (1855–88). However, Chekhov at the beginning of his literary activity wrote mostly humorous stories in a light vein which appeared in second-rate periodicals. Korolenko continued the line of Turgenev with his delicate and poetic depictions of Siberian landscape (*Makar's Dream*) and spent much time working as a publicist. Garshin committed suicide after having written a volume of emotionally saturated impressionistic prose, which was highly praised by contemporary critics and readers alike. At the end of the 80's Chekhov created a new type of impressionistic short story, in which he substituted a general mood for definitely formulated thoughts and judgments and masterfully exposed "the lack of correspondence between external causes and inner experiences, and between experiences and the decisions which follow them." Chekhov's non-humorous longish short stories, such as "My Life," "Three Years," "Steppe," "The Duel," reveal him as a great artist with universal appeal. His plays, *The Seagull, Three Sisters, Uncle Vanya, The Cherry Orchard,* are written in the same intentionally casual, impressionistic style, which was preparing the dissolution of realism. It manifested itself earlier in the works of L. Tolstoy, and especially in the poetry of A. A. Fet-Shenshin (1820–92) who was appealing more to the recollective power of the reader than to his perception with moody, mosaic-like depictions of nature.

In spite of these impressionistic tendencies, R. realism died hard. There was I. A. Bunin (1870–1953) who wrote lucid and lyrical prose in the great R. tradition, a superb stylist and a most discriminating artist with an unerring feeling for *le mot juste.* His handling of peasant themes in *Sukhodol* (Dry Valley) and in *The Village* is remarkable for economy of means and the power of observation and evocation. (Bunin, who became an *émigré*, was awarded the Nobel Prize in literature in 1933.) There was Maksim Gorky (pen name of Aleksey Maksimovich Peshkov, 1868–1936) who had a fabulous career in Russian letters by introducing a parade of romantic rebels and philosophizing vagabonds as opposed to the "smug citizens" (*meshchane*) found in all social strata and in all walks of life. He wrote about crude harsh realities, poverty, sickness and death, and other "indelicate" subjects. His early stories, published in two volumes in 1898, were an immediate success. Though Gorky started as an impressionist and sympathized with symbolism, he later developed such a realistic love of detail as shown in his portrayal of characters, that he was finally hailed as the greatest master and even father of socialist realism. His first novel *Foma Gordeyev* (1899), depicting the decay of the merchant class, is considered also his most successful one. *Mother* (1907), a proletarian novel, is one of his weakest. Gorky is at his best in his autobiographical writings such as *Childhood* (1913), *In the World* (1916) and others. Gorky's publishing enterprise *Znanie* (Knowledge) attracted a score of lesser talents like Ye. M. Chirikov, V. Veresayev (V. V. Smidovich), I. Shmelyov, Skitalets (S. G. Petrov), A. Serafimovich (A. S. Popov), in addition to Bunin, A. I. Kuprin (1870–1938), a talented portrayer of army life and a master of the plot of intrigue, and Leonid Andreyev (1871–1919), who enjoyed immense popularity with his pessimistic and sensational writings on death and sex. Next to Andreyev stands Artsybashev, author of a "bestseller" of the time, *Sanin*.

Symbolism, Acmeism, Futurism. The success of Andreyev and Artsybashev in prose, of Nadson and Apukhtin in poetry, shows a marked decline in Russia's taste, owing largely to political causes, and an infatuation with positivism and materialism. However, when the "enlightened ideas" of the 60's were found to be an illusion, new foundations were eagerly sought for politics and aesthetics. "Modernism," "decadentism," "symbolism," or "neoromanticism" in Russia started—partly under western (French and German) influence—with a pamphlet of D. S. Merezhkovsky (1867–1941), "On the causes of the decline of contemporary Russian literature" (1893). Merezhkovsky, a very perceptive critic, was backed by his wife, the poetess Zinaida Gippius (1869–1945). A very important predecessor of symbolism was the prominent philosopher and poet Vladimir Solovyov (1854–1901). He was one of the first to "recognize symbolical worth, and prize it highest" (Carlyle). Symbolists were looking for new metaphysical and aesthetic values; they strove toward new ways of expression, as opposed to realistic artistic methods; they valued the word primarily as a symbol of other realities, and saw in everything external only a reflection of other spheres of being. Goethe's "All that is passing is but a symbol" well suited their taste. Subsequently the symbolists reevaluated the R. literary heritage in the light of their new aesthetics, and rediscovered such poets as Tyutchev, Baratynsky, Fet, and even Pushkin. They had a new interest in philosophy—Nietzsche, Schopenhauer, Kant—and in the poetic achievements of the western symbolists and Parnassians. Their art was esoteric, highly subjective and egocentric. The first volumes of new poetry called *Russian Symbolists* and edited by

Valery Bryusov appeared in 1894 and 1895. V. Ya. Bryusov (1873–1924) and K. D. Balmont (1867–1943) are considered the most important of the older generation of the symbolists. To the enrichment of R. poetic technique they contributed new rhythms, unusual rhymes, and a new musical quality. The younger generation of the symbolists, A. A. Blok (1880–1921), possessing an exceptional lyrical gift, and Andrey Bely (nom de plume of Boris Nikolayevich Bugayev, 1880–1934), an ingenious experimenter with the R. language and a brilliant theoretician of poetry, raised symbolism to new heights. Both had profound mystical experiences which they expressed in a highly refined and original form. Bely created a new form of musical prose which he called "symphony," and to which he did not hesitate to apply the rules of counterpoint. His highly modern and difficult style, which has been compared to that of James Joyce and Pablo Picasso, did not create a school in Russia, but had a profound influence on several R. writers, among them A. M. Remizov (1876–1959), a highly talented prose writer and stylist. Blok is considered one of the greatest R. poets of any school. Besides poetry he wrote also "lyrical dramas" (*The Puppet Show, The Stranger*). Another leading symbolist lyricist and philosopher was Vyacheslav Ivánov (1866–1950), a classical scholar, who attempted to bring into R. poetry the splendor of Byzantium and often achieved it in his exquisite verse saturated with philosophical and metaphysical implications. More loosely associated with symbolists was another classical scholar and poet, I. F. Annensky (1856–1909), author of dramas on classical subjects and excellent renderings of Euripides. F. K. Sologub (Teternikov, 1863–1927) like Bryusov was a master of classical form but with a predilection for unusual subjects. His rejection of the vulgar world around us in favor of one created by his poetic fantasy found highly artistic expression in both his poetry and his prose. He said: "I take a piece of life coarse and grey and create a legend out of it." Sologub showed himself a master in the satiric depiction of the petty life of a provincial town by means of symbols; Peredonov, the hero of one of his novels, *Melky Bes* (The Minor Demon), acquires universal dimensions as a symbol of everything mean, base, and trite.

Close to the symbolists was another prose writer, V. V. Rozanov (1856–1919), who developed an original, intimate style (he said: "I do not write, I speak aloud. . . .") in which he wrote his autobiographical revelations. Rozanov is known also for his acute critical essays (on Gogol, Dostoyevsky, and others).

The philosophical quest or "metaphysical thirst" of the symbolists often led them toward religious problems. Thus besides an aesthetic revolt they brought about a religious revival among the intelligentsia. In St. Petersburg D. S. Merezhkovsky founded the Religious-Philosophical Society, which was intended as a forum and a meeting place for R. intellectuals and members of the R. clergy, who had long been estranged.

The achievements of the R. symbolists could be summed up as an aesthetic revival in L and thought which led toward perfection of poetic technique and discoveries in the realm of poetic theory, rejuvenation of R. prose and prosody, and the emergence of a new criticism, not obscured by political and sociological considerations. The symbolist movement is often called the Russian Renaissance and the Silver Age of R. poetry as contrasted with the Golden Age of Pushkin. The reverberations of symbolists' discoveries and innovations in L and criticism have been felt through all succeeding generations, even though they have often been subject to severe criticism. The main objection has usually been the obscurity of their metaphors and diction and the vagueness of their symbols. The first to bring this criticism openly were the members of the movement itself, N. S. Gumilyov (1886–1921) and Sergey M. Gorodetsky (1884–), who founded a new school of poetry, called Acmeism or Adamism, protesting against metaphorization and symbolization, and advocating a concretization of the word and liberation of the concrete world of things from its mystic captivity. The acmeists formed the Guild of Poets in St. Petersburg and advocated as their main objectives perfection of form and thorough craftsmanship in poetry. In this they were continuing the symbolists' work without their metaphysical aspirations and implications. After Gumilyov, Anna Akhmatova (1888–) and Osip Mandelshtam (1892–1945) were the most prominent exponents of the acmeism. Anna Akhmatova, who regarded Annensky as her teacher, has remained true to the legacy of symbolism and acmeism, polishing her feminine, emotional, and dramatic verse to a delicate and highly enjoyable perfection. Osip Mandelshtam (also a prose writer and essayist) was a poet with a diction all his own, who often succeeded in making R. verse sound like Latin. He knew how to make it sing and sparkle with vivid color and how to enliven it with original images.

Another new school which revolted against symbolism was that of futurism. The name was borrowed from the Italian (Marinetti). The founder of this new movement was Viktor-Velemir Khlebnikov (1885–1922), who has been more highly valued by the linguists than by critics for his daring inventiveness in R. wordformation and syntax and by other poets for his inventive imagination and complete freshness of vision. Another strikingly original futurist poet was V. V. Mayakovsky (1894–1930), who rebelled with all the power and passion he could muster against any and every literary tradition and convention, revamping the R. language and R. prosody to suit his whim, enriching it with new types of rhyme, prosaisms and neologisms, uncommon metaphors and hyperboles. In one of the futurist associations, called the "Centrifuge," there appeared in 1913 the first book of verse by Boris Pasternak. However, Pasternak soon outgrew all schools because of his unique freshness, depth, originality, and musicality.

No matter how much all these new groupings might seem to be in opposition to symbolism, they could not have existed without its innovating tendencies which once and for all revolutionized taste and sensitivity and set high standards for literary achievement for many a decade to come.

The development of Russian L was forcibly disrupted by the October revolution of 1917. The Russian Renaissance of the 20th century still awaits its final appraisal.

BIBLIOGRAPHY: D. S. Mirsky, *A History of Russian Literature*, New York, 1949; Marc L. Slonim, *The Epic of Russian Literature, from Its Origins through Tolstoy*, New York, 1950. Z. Yu.

LITERATURE, SOVIET. The term Soviet literature is used to refer to imaginative literature produced in the Soviet Union from 1917 to the present and its use implies a break at that point in the continuing traditions of R. literature. Although the break was far from complete it is generally regarded as sound to make a division at this date. The Bolshevik Revolution and the transformation of R. society which followed it created radically new conditions for the writing of literature. While these changes did not occur immediately, it soon became clear that R. literature, the creation of an independent intelligentsia, was giving way to a new product, collective in its outlook and aimed at the widest possible mass appeal. On the other hand, the break at 1917 is an artificial one as far as the development of literary styles and genres is concerned: the literary schools which occupied the center of the stage in the early Soviet period merely continued prerevolutionary movements in poetry and prose, often in proletarian or communist habiliments.

The history of Soviet literature may conveniently be treated under three chronological divisions: (1) the period of relative liberalism, 1917 to 1932; (3) the period of "socialist realism," 1932 to 1953; and (3) from the death of Stalin to the present.

(1) **From 1917 to 1932.** During the earliest period, especially after the liberalization signalized by NEP in 1921, an effort was made in the literary milieu to maintain the literary profession as a free activity independent of government control. Both the Proletkult, which proposed the forced creation of a proletarian class literature, and the futurists, who sought a complete break with the art of the past in all its forms, were shorn of authority by the government itself, and as the country recovered from war and revolution a degree of private enterprise was readmitted in the literary field as well as in other areas of Soviet life. A policy of relatively liberal forbearance, effected in practice since 1921, was solemnly confirmed after an intra-party debate, by the Resolution on Belles-Lettres promulgated in 1925. However, under the pressures generated by the First Five Year Plan which began in 1928, the liberal policy was gradually eroded, until, in 1932, all independence of centralized party control disappeared.

The years from 1921 to 1932 were the richest of the Soviet period in the quality and variety of the literary product. Soviet literature had during those years many points of contact with the West, and shared with western writers an experimental approach to the medium of literature. The new state was revolutionary, and innovation was the order of the day: symbolists, futurists, imagists, constructivists, and other radical groups flourished and for a time dominated Soviet literature. Aleksandr Blok, Andrey Bely, and Valery Bryusov, each of whom was identified with the prerevolutionary symbolist movement, continued to write, and the influence of their stylistic experimentation was felt even by proletarian poets. The futurist poet Vladimir Mayakovsky was a supporter of the Bolsheviks and an ardent literary propagandist of the new regime. Prominent in those years were the Bolshevik party-poet Demyan Bedny, the very talented lyrical peasant poets S. A. Yesenin and N. A. Klyuyev, as well as E. G. Bagritsky and the younger "proletarian" poets A. I. Bezymensky, A. A. Zharov, Mikhail Golodny, M. A. Svetlov and Iosif Utkin. A number of young writers, most of whom later gained fame, formed a group known as the Serapion Brothers, whose chief tenet was that literature should be free of ideological supervision. The group included many of the most important Soviet novelists: Konstantin Fedin, Boris Pilnyak, Venyamin Kaverin, Vsevolod Ivanov, and Mikhail Slonimsky, as well as an eminent Soviet poet, Nikolay Tikhonov. One of their guides and teachers was Yevgeny Zamyatin, author of the futuristic novel *We* (1924). To this group, and to other writers who, though sympathetic to the revolution, were neither proletarian nor Communist, the term "fellow-traveler" (*poputchik*) was customarily applied. The latter included men of greatly varying political and aesthetic creeds, who produced during the twenties a number of important and original works. Pilnyak's *Naked Year* (1922) presents vivid scenes from the civil war period; Fedin's *Cities and Years* (1924) deals with the problems of an intellectual at odds with his time; Olesha's *Envy* (1927) presents in expressionistic style the conflict between a poet and a Babbitt of the new order; Kaverin's *Artist Unknown* (1931) develops the theme of the artist's need for freedom; Babel's *Red Cavalry* (1926) describes in ornamental prose the bloody violence of the revolution; a typical representative of the fellow travelers was L. M. Leonov, author of *The Badgers* (1925) and *The Thief* (1927).

The fellow-travelers in literature of the twenties tended to be "modern" and to favor experimentation; the proletarians, on the other hand, tended to be conservative and to favor traditional realism. Yury Libedinsky's *The Week* (1922) describes an anti-communist peasant uprising from the viewpoint of the Communist leaders themselves; Aleksandr Fadeyev's *The Rout* (1927), written under the influence of Tolstoy, deals with the struggle and ultimate defeat of a small band of red partisans; Fyodor Gladkov's *Cement* (1925), a mixture of romanticism and traditional realism, had as its main theme the revival of industry under proletarian auspices; and Mikhail Sholokhov's *The Quiet Don* (1928–40), probably the most famous of Soviet novels, presents, again after the manner of Tolstoy, a panoramic picture of war and revolution in the Don Cossack country.

Worth mentioning are also the following works belonging to this period: D. A. Furmanov's *Chapayev* (1923) and *Revolt* (1925); A. S. Serafimovich's *The Iron Torrent* (1924); K. A. Trenyov's *Lyubov Yarovaya;* Vsevold Ivanov's, *Armored Train No. 14–19;* B. Lavrenyov's, *The Forty First,* (1924); and the stories of the widely read Soviet satirists M. A. Zoshchenko, and Ilf and Petrov.

(2) **From 1932 to 1953.** Beginning in the late twenties during the First Five Year Plan the Communist party exercised increasing hegemony in all cultural fields with the conscious aim of using art and literature as its own instruments of education and propaganda. Under Stalin's inspiration a style known as "socialist realism" was cultivated in all the arts. For literature the term signified socialism in content and realism in form. In practice what was called for was the production of works which would inculcate certain approved viewpoints in a mass audience. The works characteristic of the period are not only tendentious, but simple, direct, and traditional in language and literary form, their overriding purpose being to make the socialist message intelligible to the broad masses. During this period a number of new writers emerged who had been formed in the Soviet schools and whose work conformed closely to the requirements of the day. Among these might be mentioned Konstantin Simonov, Margarita Aliger, Yury Krymov, Nikolay Virta, V. P. Katayev, M. S. Shaginyan, F. I. Panfyorov, A. T. Tvardovsky. Writers of an older generation were obliged to conform to the demands of the party and to produce useful educational works on various topical themes.

Two works especially popular with the young Soviet reader during the thirties were N. A. Ostrovsky's *How Steel Was Tempered* (1935) and A. Makarenko's *Pedagogical Poem* (1934). The following should also be mentioned: A. Novikov-Priboy, O. D. Forsh, A. P. Chapygin, Yu. N. Tynyanov, V. Ya. Shishkov, S. N. Sergeyev-Tsensky and Aleksey N. Tolstoy, author of *Peter The First.*

As a result of the demands made officially on literary men the literary product of those years, even when technically competent, lacked individuality and creativity. The deterioration increased sharply after 1946, when Andrey Zhdanov, a political leader close to Stalin, became the party spokesman in literature. The demand for tendentious works was expressed by him and by his lieutenants in crude, direct terms, and the abuse of deviant writers reached new extremes of harshness.

(3) **From 1953 to the Present.** Since the death of Stalin there have been important changes in the official policy for literature. While the direction of movement has been toward more liberal policies, there has not been a consistent, steady development, but rather a pattern of vacillation: liberalization has been followed by reaction and reassertion of party control, to be followed again by relaxation, and a repetition of the cycle. There have been two high points of literary freedom. After the death of Stalin there was an almost immediate movement among literary men to escape from the burden of party tutelage and this movement rose to a climax during the early months of 1954. A number of authors attempted to discard the established patterns of "socialist realism" and to move in new directions. This tendency was best expressed by a young critic named Pomerantsev, who in an article entitled "On Sincerity in Literature" wrote: "What's needed is a statement of what the author really feels instead of this constant preachment and propaganda. Men are bored by lessons and arguments." Works typical of the new liberalism were Vera Panova's *The Four Seasons* (1954), whose theme is the career of a Communist leader corrupted by power; Leonid Zorin's play *The Guests*

(1954), an ironical portrait of a Soviet official and his family; and Ilya Ehrenburg's *The Thaw* (1954) which honestly faced the task of transmuting into words and literary images the experience of individual human beings in the USSR. Indeed one of the main themes of this new literature was the rediscovery of the individual human being with his unique and particular feelings and thoughts.

Such works were, in part, a reflection of the liberalization of Soviet life introduced by the successors of Stalin, but a number of writers seem to have gone beyond the bounds of what was considered permissible. There was severe criticism of both Vera Panova and Ilya Ehrenburg. Zorin's play *The Guests* was banned after a single performance. The name of the critic Pomerantsev soon disappeared from the pages of Soviet magazines. At the 2nd Congress of Soviet Writers in Dec. 1954, the party representatives once more asserted the doctrine of "socialist realism."

A new surge of unconventional writing followed the 20th Congress of the Communist Party in Feb. 1956, where Khrushchev exposed the criminal deeds of the Soviet government under Stalin. The effect of these exposures was shattering to many writers and led to renewed efforts on their part to free themselves from the ideological guidance of the party. A number of articles, stories, and novels which appeared in late 1956 and 1957 are typical of this stage in the post-Stalin developments. Daniel Granin's *Personal Opinion* (1956) and Dudintsev's *Not by Bread Alone* (1957), both expose the dangers of blindly conforming to approved patterns of thought. In the collection *Literary Moscow* (1956) a number of stories presented unsavory aspects of Soviet life. It was in the summer of 1956 that Boris Pasternak presented his novel *Doctor Zhivago* to the editors of *New World*, a literary magazine, in the hope that they would consider publishing it. That act was probably the highest point of optimism to be reached since Stalin's death. The letter of rejection to Pasternak from the editors of *New World*, while stern and serious, was politely worded: it was only after the novel became a weapon in the international political struggle that violent personal attacks on Pasternak were made. His novel is unquestionably one of the finest products of the Soviet period. Written over a period of about twenty years, it is a sensitive artistic judgment on the experiences of those years. It is the judgment of a poet whose aim it has been to preserve the purity and originality of his own idiom in a world of cant and jargon.

After the brief upsurge of 1956 and early 1957 there was again a period of repression initiated by Khrushchev himself who, in a series of speeches to writers' groups during 1957, attacked by name some of the writers responsible for the collection *Literary Moscow*, and other intellectuals identified with the mild rebellion of 1956. In 1958 there appeared a novel by Vsevolod Kochetov, editor of the *Literary Gazette, The Brothers Yershov*. This work was a primitive and savage attack on liberal intellectuals, both in the Soviet Union and outside of it, and to some it seemed to represent the thinking of the party hierarchy regarding recent events in Soviet literature. For the second time since 1953 the cycle—liberalization, reaction, repression—had been completed.

But during the year 1959 there was again an "easing of tension" in the Soviet literary world, and the conditions under which writers worked improved noticeably. For example, Dudintsev, the author of *Not by Bread Alone*, was mentioned favorably by Khrushchev in a speech delivered at the 3rd Congress of Writers in 1959. Khrushchev in that speech announced a new era of forgiveness and reconciliation and he rehabilitated a number of writers whose reputations had been damaged during the previous year.

BIBLIOGRAPHY: Mark L. Slonim, *Modern Russian Literature*, New York, 1953; Gleb Struve, *Soviet Russian Literature*, Norman, 1951; E. J. Brown, *The Proletarian Episode in Russian Literature, 1928–1932*, New York, 1953; V. Zavalishin, *Early Soviet Writers*, New York, 1958. E. J. B.

LITHUANIAN SOVIET SOCIALIST REPUBLIC (LITHUANIA, Lith. *Lietuva*, Russ. *Litvá*) was annexed by the USSR in June 1940 and made a Soviet Republic one month later. It is located at the USSR's W. borders and has common frontiers with Latvia in the N., Byelorussia in the E. and S.E., Poland  in the S.W., former German East Prussia (now Kaliningrad Oblast of the RSFSR) and the Baltic Sea on the W. Area, 25,140 sq. mi. Capital Vilnius (Wilno or Vilna); other cities, Kaunas (Kovno), Klaipeda, Šiauliai, Panevezys.

Population of L is 2,711,000 (1959); in 1939 it was 3,132,000 within the present-day borders. The national composition is as follows (1939 figures in parentheses): Lithuanians 2,151,000 or 79.3% (2,193,000 or 71%), Poles 230,000 or 8.5% (447,000 or 14%), Jews 25,000 or 0.9% (278,000 or 9%), Russians 231,000 or 8.5% (76,000 or 2.4%), Byelorussians 30,000 or 1.1%, Ukrainians 18,000 or 0.7%, unspecified 26,000 or 1% (32,000 or 1% plus 106,000 Germans or 3.4%). These figures include Klaipeda, German from 1939 to 1944 (1938 pop. 154,000, including 86,000 Lithuanians, 59,000 Germans, 9,000 Jews), and the Vilnius (Wilno) area (1939 pop. 549,000, including 369,000 Poles, 84,000 Jews, 61,000 Lithuanians, 17,000 Russians, 15,000 Byelorussians and 3,000 others). Changes in the national composition of L are due to the following causes: (1) deportation of numerous politically unreliable or socially "undesirable" Lithuanians, Poles, and Jews by Soviet authorities; (2) extermination of about 98% of L Jews by the Nazis in 1941–44; (3) repatriation of former Polish citizens of Polish and Jewish descent to Poland (since 1945); (4) arrival of a large number of Russians from the RSFSR starting with 1944.

Nature and Climate. L is a lowland, with morainic hills in its western (Zhmud) and eastern sections. Numerous lakes are found in the E. Forests occupy over 22 per cent of the land. Turf-podsolic and swamp-podsolic soils predominate. The climate is moderately continental: 23° F in Jan., 67° F in July; yearly rainfall from 22 to 34 in.

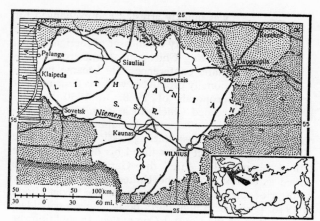

Lithuanian SSR

National Economy. The main crops are rye, oats, and potatoes. Dairy farming serves as the basis of the food industry; sugar mills use local sugar beets. Hog raising and poultry raising are extensive; fisheries exist around the harbor of Klaipeda. Industry consists of tanneries, lumber and paper mills, glass, cement, brick and furniture factories, peat power plants. L also produces machine tools, bicycles, electrical machinery, and various specialized tools.

History. Lithuanian, Latvian, and Prussian ancient Baltic tribes were already heard of in the first centuries A.D. In the 9th century, L began to organize into state-units. In the 13th century the Germanic Order of Teutonic Knights exterminated the Prussians, brought the Latvians into submission and constantly clashed with L principalities. To face the German threat, Lithuanians united under Mindaugas (Mindove, Mendog). At the same time Tatars invaded Kievan Russia and the Grand Dukes of L started to annex R. lands. The process of absorption was a peaceful one, L rule being preferable to Tataro-Mongol domination. Gediminas (Gedymin), 1316–39, Algirdas (Olgerd), 1345–77, and Keitutas (Kiejstut) built the L empire. Between the 13th and the middle of the 15th century, the entire territory of today's Byelorussia, the bulk of today's Ukraine up to the Black Sea, and the W. part of Great Russia proper fell into L hands. This included such important R. principalities as Polotsk, Smolensk, Chernigov, Kiev, Volynia. R. (Byelorussian) cultural influence was strong in L and pagan Lithuanians showed remarkable political skill and religious tolerance. L expansion eastward was arrested by the growth of the Moscovite state. In the W., Teutonic Knights by 1378 had conquered the entire Zhmud (Zemaitija or Samogitya) area, the cradle of the L people; at the same time they menaced Poland. Because of the common danger, Poland and L united in 1385 (Union of Krewo). Jagela (Jagiello), Grand Duke of L, married Jadwiga (Hedwig), Queen of Poland (1387), and accepted Catholicism for the entire L nation. On July 15, 1410 the Teutonic Knights were defeated at Grünewald near Tannenberg by the combined Polish-Lithuanian army. In 1569 the personal union between Poland and L was transformed into a complete one (Union of Lublin). Common religious ties between Byelorussia and Mos-

cow came into conflict with Polish-Lithuanian Catholicism. Starting with the 17th century, L began to lose some of her E. land to growing Moscow. During the first partition of Poland (1772) L lost all of her Byelorussian lands to Russia. During the third partition (1795) L proper was annexed. In 1805 R. tsars took the title of Grand Duke of L. A Russian governor-general was appointed to reside in Vilna. Unsuccessful Polish uprisings in 1830–31 and 1863 spread to L. In 1840 a R. code replaced the old L code and from 1864 to 1905 a policy of Russification was enforced. L nationalist renaissance, apart from Polish movements, began in the 1880's with the publication of the first L newspaper *Ausra* (*Dawn*) by Jonas Basanavicius. In the 1890's social-democratic circles formed in Vilna. In 1897 the Jewish social-democratic movement *Bund* was organized there. During the 1905 revolution all social-democratic groups (Bolsheviks, Mensheviks, *Bund*) as well as Polish and L nationalists showed a great deal of activity. The latter pressed for national autonomy for L. During World War I, L was occupied by the Germans who supported the L nationalist movements. In Sept. 1917 a L congress gathered in Vilna under the leadership of Antanas Smetona, S. Kairys, and J. Savlys, electing a national council (*Taryba*). The idea of federation with Poland was rejected and L independence was proclaimed. On Feb. 7, 1918 a L government was formed with Prof. Augustinas Voldemaras as premier. In Jan. 1919 Soviet troops entered L and installed their own government (Premier Mickevicius-Kapsukas). The nationalist government fled but in April 1919 Polish troops chased the Soviets from Vilna, thus enabling L nationalists to re-enter Kaunas (Kovno). During the Soviet-Polish war of 1920, Vilna fell again into Soviet hands. In August retreating Soviet troops ceded Vilna to L nationalists. In October, on Pilsudski's orders, Polish troops under Gen. L. Zeligowski entered Vilna and, backed by the Polish majority in the city, set up a pro-Polish government of Central Lithuania. The latter united with Poland in 1923. The main part of L, with Kaunas (Kovno) as capital, remained independent until June 1940, with A. Smetona in power during most of those years. In foreign affairs, the young L state pursued a policy of alliance with the other Baltic states (Latvia and Estonia), but Polish-Lithuanian relations remained at the lowest point. In 1938 L was forced to acknowledge the loss of Vilna and in 1939 to cede Klaipeda (Memel) to Germany. A treaty of non-aggression with the USSR was signed in 1926. According to the Soviet-Nazi agreement of Aug. 1939, however, L was to be included within the German sphere of influence. A month later she was traded by the Soviets in exchange for the Lublin district of Poland, originally assigned to the USSR. Following the new arrangement, L was forced to sign a treaty of mutual assistance with the USSR and to accept Soviet land and air bases on her soil (Oct. 10, 1939). After a brief period of limited occupation, L independence was ended by Soviet troops on June 15, 1940. President Smetona fled; other high officials (Premier A. Merkys, Stulginskis, and many others) as well as over 30,000 Lithuanians were deported to Siberia. In July, L was officially incorporated into the USSR. (G. Britain and the U.S. refused to recognize the annexation of Lithuania.) From 1941 to 1944 L was in German hands. Made part of the Ostland province, L lost about 700,000 citizens during the occupation. Soviet troops under Gen. I. D. Chernyakhovsky reconquered all of L between Aug. 1944 and Jan. 1945. Deportations of "unreliable elements" began almost immediately. Forced collectivization of agriculture was completed in 1949.

Culture. The first written documents in L were chronicles written in Byelorussian in the 14th to 16th centuries. The first book in the L language is the Catechism of M. Mažvydas, printed in Königsberg in 1547. The University of Vilna was founded in 1579. The first dictionary of the L language was written by K. Sirvydas (1629). While most of the works published in the 17th century were of a religious nature, secular books began to appear in larger numbers in the 18th century (among them *The Four Seasons* by K. Donelaitis, printed in 1818). S. Stanevicius, D. Poska, S. Valyunas, and A. Strazdas are among the L writers of the 19th century who were active in creating a L literary language. The prohibition of printing L books or of using the Latin script (1864–1905) shifted L publishing activity to East Prussia. Among the writers of that time are Bishop A. Baranauskas, J. Mačiulis-Maironis, V. Kudirka (author of the L national anthem), J. Zemaite, and Basanavicius. Among 20th-century writers are J. Grusas, A. Vienuolis, J. Savickis, P. Cvirka, V. Krevé-Mickevičius, I. Seinius, A. Vaiciulaitis; among poets, V. Putinas-Mykolaitis, S. Neris, B. Brazdzionis, A. Miskinis, J. Aistis, and others. O. V. Milosz-Milasius, L by origin, is well known in modern French literature. Jurgis Baltrušaitis (1873–1944) became famous both as L and R. lyric poet.

Ceramics, metal and wood carving, embroidery, and religious sculpture are popular in L. Among 20th-century painters are M. Ciurlionis, P. Kalpokas, A. Galdikas, and A. Zmuidzinavicius; among sculptors, P. Rimsa, J. Mikenas, V. Kasuba, and P. Aleksandrovicius are best known. L music is lyrical, with some epic songs. Until the middle of the 18th century solo singing was predominant. Folk dancing is rich and varied. The traditional material of L architecture was wood. Stone buildings began in the 13th–14th centuries (Vilna and other castles) but some 18th-century wooden churches still exist. Several gothic monuments are preserved from the 16th century. Few are in the Renaissance style. In the 16th to 18th centuries the baroque style predominated. There are numerous 19th- and 20th-century buildings but their style is rather modern and without originality.   M. R.

LITTLE RUSSIA: *see* UKRAINIAN SSR.

LITVÍNOV (Wallach), **Maksím Maksímovich** (1876–1951), soviet diplomat, born in Belostok. Joined the Social-Democratic party, 1898. From 1903 a Bolshevik. As a young revolutionary, L traveled throughout Europe in the Bolshevik cause. As a result of these activities, he was successively expelled from France and Great Britain. In the Bolshevik underground L was known as "Papasha" and "Feliks." After the Bolshevik Revolution, L was sent to England where he

was quickly arrested and exchanged for Bruce Lockhart. During the 1920's he was deputy commissar of foreign affairs, assisting Chicherin at numerous diplomatic conferences. He became internationally prominent with his disarmament proposals of 1928. In 1930 he succeeded Chicherin as commissar of foreign affairs. He became an advocate of collective security against Nazi aggression. However, the 1939 Nazi-Soviet pact necessitated his dismissal and he retired temporarily. After the German invasion he served as ambassador to the United States, and deputy minister of foreign affairs, returning to the Soviet Union in 1946. L also held high party posts, being a candidate and member of the Central Committee. In addition, he served as deputy to the Supreme Soviet.

"LIVING CHURCH": *see* ORTHODOX CHURCH.

LIVING SPACE: *see* URBAN HOUSING, HOUSING REGULATIONS.

LIVÓNIAN WAR (1558–1583), abortive attempts made by Russia at winning an outlet to the Baltic Sea which caused Ivan IV to open hostilities against the Livonian Order, Poland, Sweden, and Denmark. As a result, the R. fortresses at Narva and Yuryev (Dorpat, Tartu) were regained; the rest of Livonia was divided among Poland, Denmark, and Sweden. The position of Russia was greatly impaired by the peace treaty between Sweden and Denmark (1563–70), the unification of Lithuania and Poland in 1569 (the Lublin Union), and the election of Stefan Batory to the throne of the Polish-Lithuanian state. Batory seized several R. frontier towns and Polotsk in 1579, but his advance was arrested at Pskov. Sweden occupied Narva and Karelia in 1581. Ivan IV was compelled to conclude a peace treaty for 10 years with Poland in 1582. Russia regained frontier towns, but lost Livonia. By a three-year truce concluded with Sweden in 1583, Russia lost Koporye, Yam, and Ivangorod.

LIZOGÚB, Dmítry Andréyevich (1850–1879), populist who helped organize and contributed substantial sums of money to the revolutionary party "Land and Freedom." He was arrested in Odessa and hanged.

LOBACHÉVSKY, Nikoláy Ivánovich (1792–1856), noted mathematician, born in Nizhny Novgorod (Gorky). Graduate (1811), professor (1822),  dean of the Department of Physics and Mathematics (1820–21, 1823–25), and rector (1827–46), Kazan University which he made into a leading educational institution. Acquired world-wide fame by creating non-Euclidean geometry which is known as "Lobachevsky's geometry" in Russia. His first textbook was subjected to severe criticism and barred from publication (1823). *Exposition succincte des principes de la géometrie avec une demonstration rigoureuse du théorème des parallèles*, submitted to the Department of Physics and Mathematics, was his initial contribution to the theory of non-Euclidean geometry. Author of *Principles of Geometry* (1829–30); *Imaginary Geometry* (1835); *Application of Imaginary Geometry to*

Some Integrals (1836); *Geometrische Untersuchungen zur Theorie der Parallellinien* (1835–38), translated into English under the title *Geometrical Investigations on the Theory of Parallels* (1891; 2nd ed., 1914); *Algebra or Calculation of Finite Series* (1834); *Convergence of Infinite Series* (1841); *Pangeometry* (1855) which summarizes the results of his lifelong studies of geometry. Founder of the publication *Uchonye Zapiski Kazanskogo Universiteta* (Learned Papers of Kazan University).

LOBÁNOV, Pável Pávlovich (1902–), Soviet official. Graduate of Agricultural Timiryazev Academy. Member of the CPSU since 1927. In 1938, L became people's commissar of agriculture, RSFSR; in 1946, first deputy minister of agriculture, USSR; 1953, first deputy chairman of Council of Ministers, RSFSR; 1955, first deputy chairman of Council of Ministers, USSR; since 1956, president of the All-Union Lenin Academy of Agriculture. L was elected deputy to the Supreme Soviet USSR and chairman of Council of the Union in 1954. Since 1956, he has been a candidate member to the Central Committee of the CPSU.

LOCAL GOVERNMENT: *see* GOVERNMENT LOCAL.

LOCOMOTIVE AND RAILWAY CAR INDUSTRY. Production in 1959 was: 1,000 diesel locomotives, 435 electric locomotives, 38,600 freight cars, and 1,800 passenger cars (U.S. production in 1954: 1,000 diesel locomotives, 1,100 electric locomotives, 38,300 freight cars, and 585 passenger cars; United Kingdom: 583 steam locomotives, 687 diesel locomotives, 62,000 freight cars, and 2,400 passenger cars).

The production of locomotives was initiated in 1846 in St. Petersburg. By 1880, after several more plants had been established in that city, approximately 2,000 locomotives of various types had been produced. Following the construction of additional plants in other parts of the country the annual production of locomotives reached 1,200 in 1906, but began to decline after that year. During the entire period from 1846 to 1917, 21,000 locomotives of all types were manufactured.

The losses in productive capacity sustained by the industry during the years of the First World War and of the civil war were overcome only toward the end of the 1920's. During the 1930's existing facilities were modernized and new facilities were constructed, e.g., at Lugansk (Voroshilovgrad), and the production of new models, including some electric and diesel locomotives, was initiated. Steam locomotives of the types FD 1–5–1 and IS 1–4–2 were made on a serial basis. Altogether 12,000 locomotives were produced from 1929 to 1940, of which a considerable number were freight locomotives of the types FD and SO. During the same period 516,000 freight cars and 11,000 passenger cars were manufactured.

Among the facilities destroyed during the Second World War were the locomotive works at Bryansk, Voroshilovgrad, and Kharkov, and the railway car plants at Kryukov, Dneprodzerzhinsk, and Kaluga.

During the postwar period the reconstruction of destroyed facilities was accompanied by the introduction of new models of steam locomotives (e.g., the freight models L 1–5–0 and L 1–5–1 and the passenger model P–36:242). After 1950, however, when the prewar annual level of production was reached once again, the production of steam locomotives began to decline, and in 1956 it ended altogether. During the same period the production of electric locomotives and also of diesel locomotives (e.g., models TE–1, TE–2, and TE–3), which until then had been limited, increased rapidly. In terms of horsepower, although not of numbers, the output of long-distance electric locomotives and the output of long-distance diesel locomotives were equal in 1958 (1.4 mill. horsepower).

THE PRODUCTION OF LOCOMOTIVES AND OF RAILWAY CARS IN THE USSR

	Steam locom. (units)	Electr. locom. (units)	Diesel locom. (units)	Freight cars (thous.)	Pass. cars (thous.)
1913	477	—	—	9.7	1.0
1928	479	—	—	7.9	.4
1932	827	3	1	15.2	1.1
1937	1,172	32	4	29.8	.9
1940	914	9	5	30.9	1.1
1950	985	102	125	50.8	.9
1955	654	194	134	34.4	1.8
1959	none	435	1,002	38.6	1.8
1960	none	396	1,303	—	—

P. I. M.

LOKHVÍTSKAYA, Mírra Aleksándrovna (married name: Zhiber) (1869–1905), poetess. First collection of poems appeared in 1888. Her musical love poems are steeped in emotion and full of brilliant metaphors. Her first two volumes of verse reflect her joy of living, but in the third notes of pessimism creep in, and the fourth and fifth turn to mysticism. The latter volumes contain medieval dramas as well as lyric poetry.

LOMONÓSOV (f. Oranienbaum), city in Leningrad Oblast, RSFSR, harbor on the Gulf of Finland (opposite Kronstadt); pop. 24,000 (1958). R.R. station. It is a popular summer resort which developed from a small village where Menshikov, aide of Peter I, built a suburban mansion with fountains and a park in 1714. It was renamed in 1948 after M. V. Lomonosov.

LOMONÓSOV, Mikhaíl Vasílyevich (1711–1765), outstanding scientist and man of letters. Born near Kholmogory (Archangel) of peasant parentage, he learned to read at an early age and devoured all books available in and around his village. Prompted by the desire to continue his education, L went to Moscow on foot  (1730) where he studied classic languages, particularly Latin. A brilliant student, he was given the opportunity to enter the Institute of the St. Petersburg Ac. of S. (1736). Studied humanities at Marburg University (1736–39), and chemistry, mining, and metallurgy at Freiburg. Returned to Russia (1741) and became professor of chemistry at the university attached to the Ac. of S. and member, St. Petersburg Ac. of S. His scientific work was many-sided, including natural sciences, mining, metallurgy, physics, chemistry, optics, astronomy, geography, philology, history, and poetry. He is credited with the initial discovery of the "law of conservation of matter" during chemical reactions (1752) and Lavoisier with its rediscovery (1770). Famous for his achievements in science, particularly in the field of chemistry and physics, his influence was even greater upon Russian letters. He reformed R. literary language, adopting the syllabo-tonic versification system. As a poet, he was a leading representative of R. classicism. He revived the art of mosaics and played an important role in the development of R. historiography. His works were published by the Imperial Ac. of S. (1892–1902). Moscow University (Moscow State University), founded in 1755, bears his name. Elected member, Swedish Ac. of S. (1760), honorary member, Bologna Academy (1764). Author of *Comments on the Origin of Light Representing a New Theory of Color* (1756); *Comments on the Origin of Metals from Earthquakes* (1757); *Russian Grammar* (1757); *Brief Russian Chronicle* (1759); *Fundamentals of Metallurgy or Mining* (1763); *Ancient Russian History up to the Year 1054* (1766); *Complete Works* in 10 volumes (1950–57).

BIBLIOGRAPHY: B. N. Menshutkin, *Russia's Lomonosov*, Princeton, 1952.

LOPÁTIN, Gérman Aleksándrovich (1845–1918), revolutionary, involved in the Karakozov case. He organized the escape of P. L. Lavrov in 1870; then fled to France. He was a friend of Karl Marx; was elected to the General Council of the First International; and translated Volume I of *Das Kapital* into R. In 1872, he arrived clandestinely in Siberia in an attempt to arrange the escape of I. G. Chernyshevsky. He became a member of the revolutionary party, "People's Will," in 1884; was arrested and tried. The original death sentence was eventually changed to life imprisonment in 1887, and he served his time in solitary confinement at Schlüsselburg. He was liberated by the 1905–07 revolution.

LOPÁTINO: *see* VOLZHSK.

LORÍS-MÉLIKOV, Count Mikhaíl Tariélovich (1825–1888), statesman. In 1880, L-M was appointed minister of interior. As the chief advisor of the tsar, he made an attempt at a liberalization of the regime. L-M submitted a project of constitutional changes which gave the institutions of local government a part in discussing legislation. The project was in principle favored by Alexander II and was to be examined by the Council of Ministers on March 4, 1881. The assassination of the tsar which took place three days earlier killed the project. The new tsar, Aleksander III, inspired by Pobedonostsev, rejected it. In May 1881, L-M was dismissed.

LOSÉNKO, Antón Pávlovich (1737–1773), painter. Studied with I. P. Argunov in St. Petersburg, also in Paris and Rome. A member and professor in the Academy of Fine Arts in St. Petersburg. His paintings, *Vladimir and Rogneda* and *Hector and Andromache,* had an important influence on the development of early R. art.

LOSINO-OSTRÓVSKAYA: *see* BABUSHKIN.

LÓSSKY, Nikoláy Onúfrievich (1870–), philosopher. L was born in the province of Vitebsk, and studied at the University of St. Petersburg, where he subsequently taught philosophy. After being exiled by the Soviet government he lived in Prague until 1942, and then in Bratislava, in Slovakia. In 1946 he came to the United States. His principal publications are *The Intuitive Basis of Knowledge* (1906, in Russian, German, and English), *The World as an Organic Whole* (1918, in Russian and

English), *Freedom of Will* (1927, in Russian and English), *Value and Existence* (1931, in Russian and English), *Intuition* (1938 in Russian, German, and English), *The Conditions of Absolute Morality* (1949, in Russian), *Dostoyevsky's Christian Philosophy* (1953, in Russian), and *A History of Russian Philosophy from Its Origins to 1950* (1954, in Russian, French, and English).

LOWER TUNGÚSKA RIVER (R. *Nizhnyaya Tunguska*), about 1,640 mi. long, rises in N. central Irkutsk Oblast and flows N., crossing into Evenki National Okrug through Irkutsk Oblast and Krasnoyarsk Kray; flows W. into the Yenisey River at Turukhansk. Tura, capital of Evenki National Okrug is on it.

LOZÓVSKY (Dridzo), **Solomón Abrámovich** (1878–1949?), Bolshevik trade-union leader. L joined the Social Democratic party in 1901 and participated in revolutionary work in Kazan. Police persecution forced him to emigrate in 1909 and he did not return until 1917. Was active in trade-union work in France. After the Bolshevik Revolution, L became secretary of the textile unions and one of the most prominent trade-union leaders. He was secretary-general of the *Profintern* (international of the communist trade unions). He was also active in Comintern and diplomatic work, heading several delegations and becoming vice commissar of foreign affairs. After the German invasion of 1944, L became assistant director of the Soviet Information Bureau. He was purged in 1949 by Stalin during his anti-Semitic drive. His rehabilitation was announced in 1956.

LUCHÍTSKY, Vladímir Ivánovich (1877–1949), geologist and petrographer. Fellow, Ac. of S., Ukrainian SSR (1945). Graduate (1899) and professor (1913–22, 1945–49) of Kiev University and Moscow Mining Academy (1923); director of the Inst. of Geological Sciences, Ac. of S., Ukrainian SSR (1947–49). Pioneer in the field of Ukrainian and Crimean hydrogeology and first one to map out geological and hydrogeological regions. Author of the textbook *Petrography*, 2 vols. (6th edition, 1949).

LUGÁNSK, (Voroshilovgrad 1935–1958), city, adm. center of Lugansk Oblast, Ukrainian SSR, on Lugan River (right tributary of the N. Donets); pop. 275,000 (1959). It is the oldest center of the Donbas coal-mining region; founded in 1796 as a settlement around the first Ukrainian foundry. It is one of the leading ind. centers in USSR: engineering plants, mfg. of mining equipment, tool, machinery, and food-processing factories; has colleges, libraries, theaters.

LUGÁNSK OBLAST (f. Voroshilovgrad Oblast), Ukrainian SSR; area 10,300 sq. mi.; pop. 2,457,000 (1959): Ukrainians, Russians. Is in the N.E. part of the Donets basin, along the left banks of the N. Donets and the S. slopes of the Central Russian upland. Cities: Lugansk (adm. center), Kadievka, Krasny Luch, Krasnodon, Rovenki. It is drained by the N. Donets and its affluents; is a hilly lowland with Donets Ridge in the S.; with fertile black soil; continental climate. Its rich mineral deposits include coal, limestone, quartz sands, refractory clays. Agr.: wheat, rye, corn, millet, sunflowers, sugar beets. One of the major industrial areas of the USSR, its ind. include coal mining (Bokovo-

Antratsit, Kadievka, Krasnodon), steel (Lugansk), chemicals, machine building, glass, cement, food processing. Est. 1938.

LUKÍRSKY, Pyotr Ivánovich (1894–1954), physicist. Fellow, Ac. of S., USSR (1946). Associated with the Roentgenological and Radiological Institute (1918); Radium Institute (1943); professor, Leningrad Polytechnic Institute (1945). Research concerns electrical conductivity of crystals, X-rays, electronics, nuclear physics.

LUNACHÁRSKY, Anatóly Vasílyevich (1875–1933), leading Bolshevik, literary critic, born in Poltava. L  was active in the revolutionary movement as early as 1892 and joined the Russian Social Democrats in 1897. Although he sided with Lenin in the party split of 1903, the two men later quarrelled over religion and Marxist ideology. L participated in the *Vpered* group. During World War I he became reconciled with Lenin and returned to Petrograd in 1917 a convinced Bolshevik. After the Bolshevik Revolution, he became commissar of education. Together with Gorky, he tried to convince Lenin to preserve the art and architecture of the tsarist regime. In 1929 L was relieved of his post. His death (1933) came just after he was named ambassador to Spain. L was also a dramatist and literary critic, writing fourteen plays mainly on historical themes.

LUNIK: *see* SPACE SCIENCE, ROCKETRY.

LUNTS, Lev Natánovich (1901–1924), writer and critic. Member of the literary circle The Serapion Brothers. He wrote one of the best characterizations of that group in 1922. A budding reformer, he criticized R. literature for its isolation from the west.

LUTSK (Pol. *Łuck*), city, adm. center of Volyn Oblast, Ukrainian SSR, on Styr River; pop. 49,000 (1959). R.R. station. It has food-processing and light ind. Founded 1085, it is one of the oldest towns in Volynia, and was especially wealthy in the 15th century. It declined in the wars between Russia and Poland 1557–82; was taken by Russia 1791 and was part of Poland after World War I; was seized by the USSR in 1939.

LÚZHSKY, Vasíly Vasílyevich (1869–1931), actor and producer. Joined the Moscow Art Theater in 1898. Among his best roles are Ivan Shuysky, in A. K. Tolstoy's *Tsar Fyodor Ioannovich*, and Bubnov, in Gorky's *The Lower Depths*. L was the co-producer with K. S. Stanislavsky and V. I. Nemirovich-Danchenko of numerous plays, among them Ibsen's *An Enemy of the People*, Gorky's *The Smug Citizen*, and Trenev's *Pugachovshchina*.

LÚZIN, Nikoláy Nikoláyevich (1883–1950), mathematician. Fellow, Ac. of S., USSR (1929). Professor, Moscow University (1917). Research concerned the theory of functions of a real variable, differential equations, differential geometry, mathematical analysis. Introduced a descriptive theory of functions. Many outstanding Soviet mathematicians are his followers and former students.

LVOV, (Ukr. *Lviv*, Pol. *Lwów*, Ger. *Lemberg*), city, adm. center of Lvov Oblast, Ukrainian SSR; pop.

340,000 (1939), 411,000 (1959). A major R.R. junction. It has a university, polytechnic institute, colleges, museums, libraries, picture galleries, theaters. Ind.: agr. machinery, automobile and bus factory, food processing, sugar refinery, breweries, distilleries. It was founded in 1241 by a Galician prince, Daniil Romanovich; captured by Poles in 1340 and became a trading center of medieval Europe. It passed to Austria in 1772 and was renamed Lemberg. After World War I it was taken by Poland; retaken by the Russians in 1939. Is the seat of a branch of the Ukrainian Ac. of S., has many historical monuments.

LVOV OBLAST, Ukrainian SSR; area 8,375 sq. mi.; pop. 2,108,000 (1959). It occupies the W. of the Volyn-Podolian upland, borders W. and N.W. on the Polish People's Republic. Cities: Lvov (adm. center), Zolochev, Brody, Rava-Russkaya, Vinniki, Borislav. It is drained by the upper Bug, Styr, and the affluents of the Dniester and San; has podsolic and black soil, and continental climate. Mineral resources: lignite, peat, limestone, refractory clay, gypsum, quartz sands. Extensive agr.: wheat, rye, potatoes, sugar beets, flax, hemp, dairy farming. Ind.: coal mining, machine mfg., building materials, chemicals, food processing, light ind., brewing, distilling, flour milling. Dense rail and highway network. Est. 1939. In 1959 absorbed Drogobych Oblast.

LVOV, Prince Geórgy Yevgényevich (1861–1925), head of the first Provisional Government and zemstvo leader. In 1905 joined the Constitutional Democratic (Kadet) party and was elected deputy to the first Duma. In World War I, L was president of the All-Russian Union of the Zemstvos and a leader of Zemgor (Union of Zemstvos and Towns). He took an active part in the Organization of the Relief of Sick and Wounded Soldiers. After the February revolution he was president of the Provisional Government (March–July 1917). After the Bolshevik revolution, L was arrested. He managed to escape, and for a while was active in the organization of the White armies. He finally settled in Paris where he died.

LYÁDOV, Anatóly Konstantínovich (1855–1914), composer. Admitted to the St. Petersburg conservatoire at an early age, he was a pupil of Johansen and Rimsky-Korsakov. In 1894 he became conductor of the Russian Musical Society and made an extensive study of folk songs for the Russian Geographical Society. His pieces for orchestra *Bába-Yagá, The Fairy Lake, Kikímora*, are based on folk songs and are noted for their instrumentation.

LYAPUNÓV, Aleksándr Mikháylovich (1857–1918), noted mathematician and mechanical engineer. Fellow,  Ac. of S. (1901). Graduate, St. Petersburg University (1880) where he studied under P. L. Chebyshov; professor, Kharkov University (1892). Developed a general method of solving stability problems of nonlinear and time-dependent dynamical systems. Carried out extensive research on figures of the equilibrium of uniformly rotating fluids, the particles of which are attracted according to the theory of gravitation; studied mathematical physics, the theory of probability, and mathematical analysis. His *Collected Works* in two volumes were published in 1956.

LYAPUNÓV, Prokópy Petróvich (died 1611), popular leader during the "Time of Troubles." He eventually joined the peasant movement under Bolotnikov but defected and participated in the suppression of the revolt in July 1611. He was killed by Zarutsky's Cossacks.

LYÁSHCHENKO, Pyotr Ivánovich (1876–1955), economist, scholar, and teacher, specializing in agrarian subjects and economic history. L was born in Saratov and studied at the University of St. Petersburg. He was professor of political economy and statistics at the University of Tomsk, 1913–17.

L was a "legal Marxist" of established academic position before the revolution, and never became a Communist party member. After the revolution, he was a professor at the Don University, and simultaneously Rector of the Economics Institute in Rostov-on-Don and a senior fellow of the Economics Institute of the USSR Ac. of S. From 1943, he was a corresponding member of the Ac. of S., USSR and from 1945 a member of the Ukrainian Ac. of S.

L published some 120 scholarly works on various subjects. These included *Essays on the Agrarian Evolution of Russia* (1908), *Grain Trade in the Internal Markets of European Russia* (1912), *History of the Russian National Economy* (1927, 2nd. ed. 1930) and *History of the National Economy of the USSR* (1939, 2nd ed. in two vols. 1947–48, 3rd ed. 1952). The last, while it inevitably makes obeisance to Stalinist dogma, remains one of the most informative works on the subject and was issued in English by the American Council of Learned Societies in 1949. The second edition was awarded a Stalin prize in 1949.

LYSÉNKO, Trofim Denisovich (1898–), biologist and agriculturist. Fellow, Ac. of S., Ukrainian SSR (1934), All-Union Ac. of Agricultural S. (1935); fellow and member of the executive board, Ac. of S., USSR (1939). Hero of Socialist Labor (1945). Since 1937, member of the Supreme Soviet and vice chairman of the Council  of the Union. Graduate of the Poltava School of Horticulture (1917) and the Institute of Agriculture (1925) in Kiev. Associated with the Kirovabad Experimental Selective Center (1925–29); head of the All-Union Institute of Genetics in Novorossiysk and of the Institute of Genetics, Ac. of S. (1940), President of the All-Union Academy of Agricultural Sciences (1938). A disciple of V. I. Michurin, L became known for his vernalization process of seeds of spring wheat which, he claimed, endowed it with characteristics of winter wheat. L's doctrine that characteristics acquired through environmental influences are inherited has become a highly controversial subject. He opposed and rejected the theories of heredity accepted by most geneticists ("Weismanism-Mendelism-Morganism"). Being in line with the Marxian ideology, he won the support of the party. The teaching of biology in the USSR was adjusted to L's theories. The peak of L's power was reached in 1948, when a great conclave was summoned at the Lenin Academy of Agricultural Sciences on July 31 to "consider the situation in the biological sciences." Stalin gave his personal support to L and, at the time, any scientist who was opposed to L's doctrine became subject to reprisals. His most renowned opponent, Nikolay I. Vavilov, the leading geneticist in the Soviet Union, died in a Siberian concentration camp during World War II. Presently, L has moved to the background and other theories are officially accepted. Author of *Heredity and Its Variability* (1943; English, 1946); *The Science of Biology Today* (English, 1949); *Problems of Genetics, Selection, and Seed Processing* (6th ed., 1952); *Stage Development of Plants* (1952). Stalin prizes (1941, 1943, 1949), six Orders of Lenin, Order of the Red Banner of Labor, and others. (*See also* GENETICS.)

LÝSVA, town in Perm Oblast, RSFSR; pop. 73,000 (1959). R.R. station. Metallurgical plant, est. 1784, enamel and zinc-ware mfg.

LYÚBECH CONFERENCE (1097), convened as a result of feuds among R. princes. At it the hereditary rights of each prince to succeed his father in ruling were consolidated.

LYÚBERTSY, city in Moscow Oblast, RSFSR; pop. 46,000 (1939), 93,000 (1959). Major center of agr. machinery ind.

LYUBLINÓ, city in Moscow Oblast, RSFSR; pop. 86,000 (1959). R.R. station. Mechanical and foundry works, woodworking plants.

LYÚLKA, Arkhíp Mikháylovich (1908–), aeronautical engineer. Graduate, Kiev Polytechnic Institute (1931); worked at Kharkov Turbogenerator Plant (1931–33); professor, Kharkov Institute of Aviation (1933–39). Research concerns the application of gas turbines for aircraft; the theory, design, and characteristics of high-altitude, high-speed turbojet engines; substantiated the expedience of using such engines for jet aircraft. Designer of the first experimental Soviet turbojet engine (1937–39). Supervised the design of the powerful turbojet engines AL-3 and AL-5 in the postwar years.

M

MACHAJSKI, Waclaw: *see* MAKHAYSKY.

MACHINE MAKING INDUSTRIES. Under the system of classification employed in the USSR this term refers to all industries producing industrial equipment, machines, and mechanisms. It includes enterprises producing locomotives, ships, aircraft, armaments, automobiles, and durable consumers' goods as well as machine tools, lathes, presses, and electric turbines. In over-all volume the output of these industries in 1960 exceeded that of the United Kingdom or Germany, although not of the United States. The principal centers of production are in the regions of Moscow and Leningrad, in the Ukraine, along the Volga, in the Urals, and in W. Siberia.

Enterprises making machines were first established in the 18th century. In 1861 there were approximately 100 such factories and there were 1,400 at the turn of the century. In 1913 their products included internal combustion engines, steam turbines, simple metal-cutting lathes, locomotives, railway cars, and agricultural equipment. Most of the country's industrial equipment, however, and especially the equipment needed for heavy industry, continued to be imported from the countries of W. Europe.

Following the adoption of a policy directed toward making the industrialization of the USSR independent of vital imports, a rapid growth in the production of machines first began to take place in the period that immediately preceded the First Five Year Plan. According to official data the output of machinery increased 3.6 times from 1925 to 1929. It was at this time that the production of tractors was initiated. In the course of the First Five Year Plan (1928–32) the rate of growth of the machine-producing industries was particularly pronounced, and a number of important types of machines were produced for the first time. Among the major new facilities established during this period were large tractor plants at Stalingrad and at Kharkov, and automobile and machine-tool plants at Gorky and in Moscow. The new industries established included those producing aircraft, metallurgical and mining equipment, electric turbines and generators, and equipment for the production of chemicals. The pace at which the production of machine tools increased was especially rapid, while subsequently emphasis was also placed on their diversification. About 200 types and sizes of machine tools were produced during the Second Five Year Plan (1933–37), and about 500 in 1940.

Following the reconstruction of plants destroyed during the Second World War, strong emphasis was placed on the technological modernization of the machine-making industries, as well as on the further diversification of their output. In 1958, according to official data, the over-all volume of production of machines was 240 times larger than in 1913, (that of all industrial production was 36 times larger). During the period 1940–57 the number of metal-cutting lathes produced increased 2.6 times, and of forge presses 3.2 times. From 1950 to 1955 an average of 1,000 types of machines and other industrial equipment was produced each year. Within the machine-making industries themselves considerable progress had been achieved in introducing assembly-line methods of production, and the full automation of individual processes had also begun.

The objectives of the Seven Year Plan (1959–65), which rest in part on the reequipment and further technological modernization of existing industries, provide for a doubling in the production of machines. Emphasis is to be placed on the production of heavy machinery, precision instruments, and electric and electronic equipment.

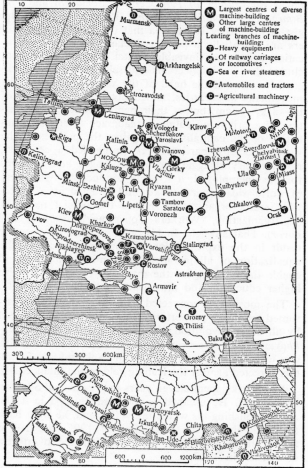

Machine-making industries

PRODUCTION OF METAL-CUTTING LATHES IN THE USSR

(thousands of units)

1913	1.8
1929	4.3
1932	19.7
1937	48.5
1940	58.4
1945	38.4
1950	70.6
1958	138.6
1959	145.9
1960	154.0

P. I. M.

MACHINE TRACTOR STATIONS: *see* MTS, AGRICULTURE.

MAGADÁN, new port (founded in 1933) on N. shore of the Sea of Okhotsk, adm. center of Magadan Oblast, RSFSR; pop. 27,000 (1939), 62,000 (1959). Center of a large gold-mining area, also has automobile-repair and other plants.

MAGADÁN OBLAST, RSFSR, includes the Chukchi National Okrug; area 463,200 sq. mi.; pop. 236,000 (1959). In the extreme N.E. of the USSR, it borders on the Yakut ASSR on the N., on the lower Amur Oblast on the W., and on the Koryak National Okrug in the S.E.; and is bounded by the Chukchi Sea (on the N.) and the Sea of Okhotsk (on the E.). Adm. center: Magadan. Has pine-covered mountain ranges (Kolyma, Chukchi); is drained by the Kolyma and Anadyr rivers; has tundra and tayga vegetation, severe nordic climate. Lumbering, fishing, gold mining, fur pelleting, reindeer breeding. Has highway to Yakut ASSR.

MAGNITOGÓRSK, city in Chelyabinsk Oblast, RSFSR, on the left bank of the Ural River and the E. slopes of the S. Urals, at the foothill of Magnitnaya Mt.; pop. 146,000 (1939), 311,000 (1959). R.R. junction. Is a leading iron and steel producing city, developed in connection with the building of the Magnitogorsk Metallurgical Combine (1932); has numerous plants. The electric R.R. Magnitogorsk–Sterlitamak–Abdulino is under construction linking the Kuznetsk Basin directly with the S. Urals and the Volga. For centuries it was a village inhabited by Bashkirs and Kirghiz engaged in cattle raising.

MAIL: *see* POST AND MAIL.

MAKÁRENKO, Antón Semyónovich (1888–1939), Soviet pedagogue and writer. Best-known for his edu-cational experiment in the 1920's when he organized the social redemption of the *bezprizorny*, homeless children who roamed the countryside in gangs, committed crimes and were generally considered intractable. M's successful treatment of them is described in his *Pedagogical Poem* (1933–35, English translation called *The Road to Life*), which was made into a movie by Nikolay Ekk. In the Soviet Union, the present tendency is rather to stress his pedagogical theories which emphasize the collective nature of the educational process that trains the child to be, first and foremost, a member of his community.

MAKÁROV, Stepán Ósipovich (1848–1904), outstanding naval commander, vice admiral, scientist, Paci-fic and Arctic explorer. He sailed twice around the earth and made important scientific discoveries. He wrote numerous scientific works on navigation, shipbuilding, hydrography, geography, and similar subjects. He was commander of the cruiser *Constantin* in the Russo-Turkish War (1877–78) and used torpedo boats to attack Turkish ironclad men-of-war. He was the founder of the R. torpedo boat fleet; he designed the first powerful ice-breaker *Yermak*, which was built under his supervision; and he invented the armor-piercing point for projectiles. He was commander of Russian Pacific Fleet in the Russo-Japanese war (1904–05) and perished on his flagship *Petropavlovsk* which was torpedoed in April 1904.

MAKÉYEVKA, city in Stalino Oblast, Ukrainian SSR; pop. 242,000 (1939), 358,000 (1959). Is a great ind. center in the Donbas, with extensive steel production (Kirov Metallurgical Plant), coal mining, large machine-mfg. plants; metallurgical and technical schools.

MAKHACHKALÁ (f. Petrovsk-Port), capital of Dagestan ASSR; pop. 119,000 (1959). Port on the Caspian Sea; a key R.R. junction, and terminus of the R.R. running N.W. of Rostov. As it is linked to Grozny by pipelines, it has extensive oil and oil-products exports. Has fishing, cotton, fish-canning ind.; sulfur springs in the vicinity; colleges, research institutes, and the Dagestan branch of the Ac. of S., USSR. Est. 1844 as a fortress; was renamed in 1921 after Makhach, a Dagestani national hero.

MAKHÁYSKY, Vátslav Konstantínovich (1866–1926), Polish-Russian revolutionist and social theorist, was the originator of a theory and a movement which in Russia has been referred to as *Makhayevshchina* (Makhayevism). His works, written between 1898 and 1905, include *The Intellectual Worker,* published under the pen name of A. Volsky, and the anonymous pamphlets *Bankruptcy of 19th Century Socialism* and *The Bourgeois Revolution and the Workers' Cause.* The gist of his theory is the idea that the intellectual workers are essentially a privileged class, their higher education being their invisible capital. From this he concluded that the intellectuals and self-educated ex-workers who were at the head of the various anti-capitalist movements and parties, aimed not at the abolition of the class system, but at their own elevation to a position of a privileged ruling bureaucracy after the elimination of the capitalists. As against the policies of the various socialist parties he recommended a ceaseless, revolutionary struggle for higher wages and for jobs for the unemployed; a struggle conducted in the form of world-wide general strikes and directed by a world-wide secret organization. Hence the official name of his organization, "Workers' Conspiracy" (*Rabochy Zagovor*). That struggle, in his opinion, would eventually result in the expropriation of the capitalists and the equalization of all incomes. Economic equality would enable the offspring of the manual workers to acquire higher education and thus usher in a claseless society.

The movement connected with M's name never assumed any large proportions. It was bitterly denounced by all other revolutionary schools, and the name *Makhayevshchina* has been generally applied even to this day to all those manifestations of rank-and-file discontent directed against the leading role of the intellectuals.

Makhaysky spent eleven years in prisons and Siberian banishment. He escaped to Western Europe in 1903. After publishing his works in Switzerland, he went back to Russia during the Revolution of 1905, but had to flee again in 1907. He returned after the overthrow of tsarism in 1917.

BIBLIOGRAPHY: Max Nomad, *Rebels and Renegades*, New York, 1932; Max Nomad, *Aspects of Revolt*, New York, 1961.

MAKHNÓ, Néstor Ivánovich (1889–1934), partisan leader in the Ukraine during the civil war. Of peasant origin, M joined the anarchists in 1905. In 1908 he was arrested and condemned to hard labor. After the February revolution, M was elected chairman of the local Soviet in Gulyay Pole (Ukraine). In 1918 he formed a guerrilla group and fought the Germans, Petlyura, the Whites and, later, the Reds. His main associates were the anarchists Volin and Arshinov. Personally opposed to anti-Semitism, he was unable to prevent anti-Jewish excesses perpetrated by his troops. In the spring of 1919, when Denikin started his offensive, M joined forces with the Bolsheviks and called the peasants and workers to establish "Free Soviets." In 1920 the Red Army once again concluded an agreement with M against the White forces of Wrangel. However, after the defeat of the latter, the Reds liquidated the M guerrillas. M himself escaped to Rumania, was tried and acquitted in Poland, and afterwards settled in Paris where he died of tuberculosis. (*See also* ANARCHISM, CIVIL WAR, HISTORY OF THE USSR)

BIBLIOGRAPHY: P. Arshinoff, *Histoire du Mouvement Makhnoviste*, Paris, 1924; Max Nomad, *Apostles of Revolution*, Boston, 1939.

MAKLAKÓV, Vasíly Alekséyevich (1870–1959), statesman and lawyer. Son of a professor, he studied the natural sciences, history, philology, and law at Moscow University. In 1895 he took up the practice of law, and became well known in 1905–07 as a defense lawyer in political trials. From 1906 on M was a member of the Central Committee of the Constitutional Democratic party (q.v.). He was Moscow deputy to the second, third, and fourth Dumas. As a prominent liberal of moderate views, M was a partisan of collaboration with the tsarist regime. In a speech in the fourth Duma in 1912, he coined a phrase that evoked the enthusiasm of the conservative newspaper *Novoye Vremya*: "Let Russia not be divided into two camps—the country and the government." After the February revolution of 1917, M was made ambassador to France, where he remained after the Bolsheviks took over. Hs was active in Paris in relief work among the *émigrés*. M published in Russia his memoirs and a book on Leo Tolstoy.

MAKÓVSKY, Konstantín Yegórovich (1839–1915), painter, brother of Vladimir Ye. Makovsky. He began to study art at the age of twelve and received the gold medal award in 1862 for the painting *Agents of False Dimitry Kill the Son of Boris Godunov*. His large and colorful paintings depicting the life of boyars and the common people in old Russia, weddings, feasts and scenes from R. fairy tales were very popular.

MAKÓVSKY, Vladímir Matvéyevich (1870–1941), heat power engineer. Graduated from Kharkov Institute of Technology (1894). Founder of the chair of turbine construction at Kharkov Institute of Mechanical Engineering (1930) and of the first Soviet gas-turbine laboratory (1933). Designer of a 1,000 hp gas turbine built at the Kharkov turbogenerator plant. His research greatly contributed to the development of gas turbines.

MAKÓVSKY, Vladímir Yegórovich (1846–1920), an active member of the Society of Circulating Exhibitions (*Peredvizhniki*) and a genre painter. He studied art at the Moscow School of Painting and received the gold medal award for the picture *Peasant Boys Guarding Horses*. Another picture *Lovers of Nightingales*, now at the Tretyakov Gallery, made him a member of the Academy of Fine Arts. Was appointed prof. of genre painting at the Academy in 1894. His pictures deal with the life of the common people of his day.

MÁLAYA VÍSHERA, city in Novgorod Oblast, RSFSR, on the Moscow-Leningrad R.R.; pop. 14,100 (1956). Extensive glass ind.

MÁLENKOV, Geórgy Maksimiliánovich (1902–), Soviet leader of Cossack origin, born in Orenburg, son of a government official. During the civil war, M joined the Red Army and, as a party member (from 1920), became a political commissar. In 1921, he was demobilized and for four years studied in the Moscow  high technical school. He was the secretary of the school's party cell and bitterly fought all anti-Stalin oppositionists. Stalin became interested in the efficient young man and, in 1925, took him into the party's Central Committee apparatus. In 1934–39, M was head of the department dealing with senior party personnel and, in this capacity, was one of the chief perpetrators of the great purges. In 1939, he became a member and a secretary of the party's Central Committee and the head of its administration of cadres; in 1941, a deputy member of the Politburo, and in 1946, a full member. During World War II, M was a member of the State Defense Committee responsible for the technical equipment of the army and air force, and high-ranking political commissar on various fronts. In 1943, he was appointed chairman of the committee for rehabilitation in former German-occupied territories. In Nov. 1945, M was decorated with the order of Lenin, and appointed a secretary of the party's Central Committee and deputy chairman of the Council of Ministers. In 1952, he received the second order of Lenin and, at the 19th Party Congress, presented the party's Central Committee report, which was normally done by Stalin. After Stalin's death, in March 1953, M became chairman of the Council of Ministers and formally the most prominent member of the "collective leadership," but he was forced to cede his post as secretary of the party's Central Committee to Khrushchev. In July 1953, M formally took the lead in denouncing Beria, but, in Feb. 1955, he himself was compelled to resign under the most unpleasant circumstances, having confessed his ignorance of and disregard for Lenin's teaching on the priority of heavy industry. For some time M was minister of electric power plants but, in July 1957, together with Molotov and Kaganovich, was expelled from the Central Committee as a member of "anti-party group." Nominated director of an obscure electric power plant in the Urals, M disappeared from the public scene.

BIBLIOGRAPHY: Martin Ebon, *Malenkov: Stalin's Successor*, New York, 1953.

MALGOBÉK, town, center of a newly developed oilfield area, North Ossetian ASSR; pop. 12,800 (1958).

MÁLIK, Yákov Aleksándrovich (1906–), diplomat. Graduate of the Kharkov Institute of Economics (1930) and of the Institute for Diplomatic and Consular Officials (1937). M served in the Press Department of the People's Commissariat for Foreign Affairs in 1937–39; 1939–42 he was counselor to the Soviet embassy in Japan. In 1942 he was appointed ambassador to Japan. After the rupture of diplomatic relations with Japan M served in the Ministry of Foreign Affairs; 1946, political adviser to Allied Council for Japan. In Aug. 1946, deputy minister for foreign affairs; 1948, representative of the USSR in the Security Council; 1953, appointed ambassador to Great Britain. Was twice awarded the order of Lenin. M joined the Communist party in 1938. Since 1956 candidate member of the Central Committee of the CPSU.

MALINÓVSKY, Rodíon Yákovlevich (1898–), marshal of the Soviet Union, minister of defense, born near  Odessa as son of a Ukrainian laborer. At 15 he ran away to join the tsarist army, was wounded and upon recovery was sent to France with R. troops to fight on the western front. In 1919 he was shipped to Vladivostok where he joined the Red forces as a machine-gun instructor, and took part in the civil war. He joined the CP in 1926; graduated from the Frunze Military Academy in 1930. In World War II he led the southern part of the Stalingrad encirclement. From Feb. 1943, he commanded the southern and then the third Ukrainian fronts, recaptured the Donets Basin and fought in the W. Ukraine. In 1944 he was appointed marshal, and captured Budapest and Vienna. From 1945 to 1956 was commander in chief of the Far E. military district and representative of the Soviet General Staff with Red Chinese military leaders. Has been a member of the Supreme Soviet since 1946, and of the Central Committee since 1954. In 1956 he was appointed commander in chief of the Soviet land forces, replacing Konev who was transferred to the Warsaw Pact Organization. In Oct. 1957, on the demotion of Zhukov, he was appointed minister of defense.

MALINÓVSKY, Róman Vikéntyevich (1878–1918), tsarist police agent and Bolshevik spokesman in the Duma. Born in the Plock region (Poland) of a working-class family. In his youth M committed some criminal offenses and was arrested. Released, he moved to St. Petersburg where, during the 1905 revolution, he took part in the organization of the trade unions and became popular among workers. In 1909, M was arrested and at that time was recruited by the police. In 1912, he participated in the Bolshevik Prague Conference and was elected to the new Central Committee. He was the main organizer of *Pravda* and became the leader of the six-man Bolshevik faction in the fourth Duma. Lenin vigorously defended M in spite of the widespread rumors about his double role, especially after M suddenly resigned from his post in the Duma, in May 1914, and left for Germany. In Nov. 1918, M appeared in Moscow, but was arrested, tried in camera, sentenced to death and executed.

MALOYAROSLÁVETS, town in Kaluga Oblast, on Kiev-Moscow R.R.; pop. 15,900 (1956). Orchards.

Scene of an important battle in 1812. In World War II, an outer defense of Moscow, occupied by Germans in 1941, retaken in 1942. Founded late in the 14th century.

MÁLTSEV, Anatóly Ivánovich (1909–), mathematician. Fellow, Ac. of S., USSR (1958). Honored scientist RSFSR (1956). Member of the Supreme Soviet RSFSR (1951) and USSR (1954–58). Graduate of Moscow University (1931). Since 1932 has been associated with the Ivanovo Pedagogical Institute; professor (1943) at the Institute of Mathematics, Ac. of S. M is a leading authority on algebra, mathematical logic, and theory of continuous groups and rings. Author of numerous publications including *Fundamentals of Linear Algebra* (2nd edition, 1956). Stalin prize (1946).

MALYÁVIN, Filíp Andréyevich (1869–1940), painter, pupil of Repin, after the revolution he lived abroad. M painted in broad strokes forming colorful decorative patterns of dynamic quality (*Peasant Women*). Most of his pictures are rather large (*Whirlwind*, in Tretyakov Gallery, Moscow).

MÁLYSHEV, VyacheslÁv Aleksándrovich (1902–1957), leading planner and engineer, high party official. M was a member of the CP from 1926. During 1939–52, he held the following positions: people's commissar for the tank industry, minister of transportation machinery and heavy machinery, chairman of the state commission of the Council of Ministers for the introduction of new technology, and minister of shipbuilding industry. After the reorganization following the removal of Beria in 1953, M was appointed minister of medium machine building industry of the USSR (presumably in charge of Soviet nuclear weapons development), and, simultaneously, deputy chairman of the Council of Ministers of the USSR. In 1956, he was promoted to first deputy chairman of the State Economic Commission.

MALÝSHKIN, Aleksándr Geórgievich (1890–1938), Soviet writer, whose novels deal almost exclusively with the civil war, and postrevolutionary reconstruction. The better-known are *Fall of the Dair* (1922), *Sevastopol* (1929–30), and *People of the Provinces* (1937–38).

MALYÚTA SKURÁTOV (Grigóry Lukyánovich Bélsky), leader of the oprichnina movement and influential figure under Ivan IV. He was executed in 1572.

MAMÁY, Khan of the Golden Horde. He was defeated by Russians under Prince Dmitry Donskoy at the battle of Kulikovo, Sept. 8, 1380; he then fled to the Crimea and was assassinated in Kaffa (Feodosia).

MÁMIN-SIBIRYÁK, Dimítry Narkísovich (1852–1912), writer, known for his stories portraying life in  the Ural Mountains and Siberia. Born in a priest's family, he graduated from the Perm theological seminary (1872). In 1877–91 he lived in Yekaterinburg (now Sverdlovsk). His best-known novels are: *The Privalov Millions* (1883), *The Mountain Nest* (1884), *Gold* (1892), *Bread* (1895), and *Tales of the Urals* (1888–89). In these novels he portrays the stormy economic development of the Urals at the end of the 19th century.

MAMISÓN PASS, mountain pass over central Caucasus on boundary between South and North Ossetia; altitude 9,280 ft. Crossed by Ossetian Military Road.

MANGANESE PRODUCTION. Manganese is used primarily in metallurgy, but also in the chemical and the pharmaceutical industries, in the production of dry cells, of ceramics, and of glass. In 1958, 2.4 mill. tons of M were produced in the USSR (world production in 1958, 4.9 mill. tons; India, 545,000 tons; Union of South Africa, 302,000 tons).

The M reserves of the USSR have been estimated at 786 mill. tons (1938), including 230 mill. tons of measured reserves, and are the largest in the world.

M was first produced in Russia in the 18th century, in the Urals (Bogoslovsk region). Production increased considerably in the second half of the 19th century, when open-hearth furnaces and the Bessemer process began to be employed in the making of steel. Production at the large deposits at Chiatura (Georgia) was started in 1879 and was channeled primarily into export. In 1886 production was also begun at Nikopol (Ukraine), largely in connection with the development of the iron and steel industry of the Donets basin. Partly because of the relatively low grade of ores, the output of M in the Urals region and in Siberia was inadequate in 1913, even for meeting the requirements of local iron and steel production. By far the largest share of the total output of M ore in 1913 was exported (1,195,000 tons of a total of 1,245,000 tons).

The production capacity of the M mines was increased during the 1920's through the technological modernization of ore removal and transportation, and through the centralization of ore-enriching facilities. In 1930 in the two main centers 1,581,000 tons of enriched M ore were produced (27 per cent more than in 1913). A further and much larger increase in production occurred in the same two centers during the 1930's, once again in connection with the rapid growth of the steel industry. In 1940, 3,377,000 tons of M ore were produced.

The loss of the mines at Nikopol to the Germans during World War II and the transportation difficulties associated with supplying the eastern metallurgical facilities with ore from the mines at Chiatura accelerated considerably the implementation of an earlier government decision (taken in 1939) to develop additional manganese-producing facilities in the eastern regions. Among the eastern mines whose production developed rapidly during this period were new mines in the N. Urals, in Central Kazakhstan, and in W. Siberia.

Following the reconstruction and modernization of the mines at Nikopol and the further modernization of the mines at Chiatura, the pre-war level of production of M was exceeded by over 1 mill. tons at the end of the Fourth Five Year Plan (1950). Since that time, partly in connection with the introduction of new methods of ore enrichment, the annual rate has nearly doubled. In recent years, research concerning new improvements has centered on the finding of new uses for M (for example as fertilizers), and on the finding of more effective methods for the refining of low-grade ores. (*See also* METALS.)

PRODUCTION OF MANGANESE ORE AND OF MANGANESE IN THE USSR

Year	M ore (mill. tons)	M (mill. tons)
1913	1.2	—
1928	.7	—
1940	2.5	—
1948	—	1.0
1950	3.4	1.5
1955	4.7	2.1
1956	4.9	2.2
1957	5.1	2.3
1958	5.4	2.4

P. I. M.

MANDELSHTÁM, Leoníd Isáakovich (1889–1944), physicist. Fellow, Ac. of S., USSR (1929). Graduate of Strasbourg University; professor of Odessa Polytechnic Institute (1918) and Moscow University (1925). Research concerned optics, the theories of vibration and probability, radiophysics, statistical and quantum mechanics. Proved the fallibility of the molecular theory of light dispersion and suggested the nonlinear theory of vibration dealing with the problems of self-induced vibrations which has found application in radio engineering and automation. In 1945, the Ac. of S. established two prizes bearing his name for outstanding works in radio and physics.

MANDELSHTÁM, Ósip Emílyevich (1892–1940?), poet of the early decades of the 20th century who belonged to the acmeists (q.v.). He became widely known, however, only after 1922, following the publication of a collection of poems entitled *The Stone*. In the 1930's M was arrested and sent to a concentration camp, where it is thought that he died shortly after the beginning of World War II. His works include poems that were published in the journal *Apollon* (1911); two collections of poems, *The Stone* and *Tristia* (1922); several volumes of articles and essays; an autobiographical novel, *The Egyptian Stamp* (1928); and several translations. M's poetry is concerned with themes from fantasy or from past history. It is colored by pessimism, as well as by aloofness from the life that he describes. His neoclassical treatment of themes from antiquity (*Troy, The Odyssey*) met with objections on the part of some critics concerning his use of a "latinized Russian." In spite of the presence in it of archaic elements, however, a conspicuous feature of M's poetry is its simultaneous modernism, which reflects the influences of dadaism and of cubo-futurism, as well as of acmeism.

MÁNIZER, Matvéy Génrikhovich (1891–), sculptor. Graduated (in mathematics) from the University of St. Petersburg in 1914 and from the Academy of Fine Arts in 1916. Among his works, mostly in bronze, are the monuments to V. Volodarsky (Leningrad, 1925); the victims of Jan. 9, 1905 (Obukhovo, 1931); Chapayev (Kuybyshev, 1932); V. I. Lenin (Petrozavodsk, 1933); the statue of Lenin at the World's Fair in Brussels in 1958, and others. M has been vice president of the Russian Academy of Fine Arts since 1947. Stalin prizes (1941, 1950, 1953).

MANUÍLSKY, Dmítry Zakhárovich (1883–1959), leading communist. M joined the Bolsheviks in 1903. For participation in the Kronstadt uprising in 1906, he was exiled to Siberia. From 1907 he was abroad where he collaborated with Trotsky. Published pamphlets and articles under the pseudonym Bezrabotny. After the

Revolution M was a secretary of the Ukrainian Communist party. Member of the Central Committee of the CPSU in 1922; he was also active in the Comintern and supported Stalin against Trotsky. After the disgrace of Bukharin in 1928, M succeeded to the leadership of the Comintern, becoming Stalin's official spokesman there. After the Comintern was dissolved in 1943, M was given various diplomatic posts. From 1944 to 1952 M was foreign minister of the Ukrainian SSR. In this capacity he represented the Ukrainian SSR in the UN.

MÁNSELKYA, wide forested watershed along the Soviet-Finnish boundary, separates the basin of the White Sea from the basin of the Gulf of Bothnia; highest point 2,440 ft.; tundra in N. part.

MANSI: *see* KHANTY-MANSI.

MARGELÁN, city in Fergana Oblast, Uzbek SSR; pop. 46,000 (1939), 68,000 (1959). Is an ancient city, with many old monuments. Largest silk industry center in USSR; homespun Uzbek folk fabrics.

MARI ASSR, part of RSFSR; lies on the left bank of the Volga; area 8,950 sq. mi.; pop. 648,000 (1959): Mari (Cheremiss), Russians, Tatars, Chuvash. It borders on the Chuvash ASSR, Tatar ASSR, Gorky and Kirov oblasts. Cities: Yoshkar-Ola (capital), Volzhsk, Kozmodemyansk. Is heavily forested; its agr. includes wheat, rye, corn, potatoes, dairy farming; has timber, cotton-ginning, paper. Est. 1936.

MARITIME (PRIMÓRSKY) **KRAY,** Soviet Far E., RSFSR; area 64,000 sq. mi.; pop. 1,381,000 (1959). Cities: Vladivostok (adm. center), Ussuriysk (f. Voroshilov), Artyom, Nakhodka, Suchan. The region forms a wedge between Manchuria and the Sea of Japan, N. of Korea. Dense tayga forests, predominantly of the broad-leaved type, are supported by podsol, gray and brown soils. East of the Sikhote-Alin range hugging the rocky seaboard strip lie fertile lowlands watered by the Ussuri River and Lake Khanka, where rice, soybeans, the Chinese varieties of millet, sugar beets, watermelons, and squash are grown on irrigated farm fields. Milk and dairy cattle are raised, and commercial apiculture is emphasized in the Ussuri valley. Timbering, fur trapping, and fishing are likewise essential. There is an important coal-mining ind., with major centers at Artyom and Suchan. Iron, lead, zinc, gold, silver, and tin are mined in the mountains, and iodine processed on the sea littoral. Shipbuilding, heavy mfg. and food-processing ind. are centered at Vladivostok, Russia's most important all-year seaport on the Pacific, the terminal point of the Trans-Siberian R.R. and the Northern Sea Route. The region has a number of higher educational institutions and specialized technical schools. Est. 1938.

MARIÚPOL: *see* ZHDANOV.

MÁRKISH, Pérets Davídovich (1895–1952), Yiddish poet. The first collection of his verse *Shveln* (Thresholds) was published in 1919. He immediately became popular and several volumes of his poems followed. In 1926 he joined the CP and was one of the most prolific Yiddish poets in the Soviet Union until he was liqui-

dated during the purge of Jewish writers. He was arrested in 1948 and executed in Aug. 1952.

MÁRKOV, Andréy Andréyevich, Jr. (1903–), mathematician. Corresponding member, Ac. of S., USSR (1953). Professor, Leningrad University (1935). Research concerns topology, topological algebra, theory of dynamic systems. By methods of mathematical logic M proved the impossibility of solving some problems of the associative system theory and problems of integral matrices.

MARR, Nikoláy Yákovlevich (1864–1934), Orientalist, linguist, and archeologist. Fellow, Ac. of S., USSR. Initiated the archeological excavation of Ani, ancient capital of Armenia. Suggested a "Japhetic theory" which approaches Marxism closely. His basic doctrine concerns the interrelationship of languages and the connection between the development of languages and thought as they, in turn, are affected by the evolution of material culture and economy. M was posthumously flayed in a *Pravda* article of June 1950 that "exposed the non-Marxist essence of Marr's doctrine." However, in *Marxism and Problems of Linguistics* Stalin stated (1952): ". . . N. Ya. Marr has, indeed, tried to be a Marxist. He was merely a simplifier and vulgarizer of Marxism. . . . " M published numerous papers on Armenian and Georgian philology and linguistics. Order of Lenin.

MARRIAGE: *see* FAMILY LAW.

MÁRTENS, Fyódor Fyódorovich (1845-1909), jurist, authority on international law, prof. at St. Petersburg University. In 1884, he was president of the European Institute of International Law, a participant of the International Peace Conferences at The Hague, in 1899 and 1907; and a permanent member of the International Court of Arbitration. His principal works are: *Russia and England in Middle Asia* and *International Law Among the Civilized Nations of Our Time.* He was also editor of the widely used collection of international treaties (15 vols.).

MÁRTOS, Iván Petróvich (1752–1835), sculptor, born in a Cossack family in the Ukraine. Studied at the Academy of Fine Arts in St. Petersburg 1764–73, and in Rome in 1774–79. Is the outstanding sculptor of the classical school. In 1804, M began to work on the monument to Minin and Pozharsky which is in the Red Square in Moscow (in bronze, unveiled in 1818).

MÁRTOV, L. (Yúly Ósipovich Tséderbaum) (1873–1923), Menshevik leader, born in Constantinople into a Russian-Jewish family. Joined the revolutionary movement in 1891. In 1893–95 as an exile in Vilna, M participated in the Bund (q.v.). Later, along with Lenin, M was one of the organizers of the "Union of Struggle for the Liberation of the Working Class." In 1896, M was arrested and exiled to Siberia. After three years of exile, he went abroad where he edited, jointly with Lenin, Potresov, Plekhanov and others, the *Iskra.* At the 2nd Congress of the Social Democratic party (1903), M opposed Lenin's attempt to transform the party into a rigidly centralized organization, favoring a democratic party of the western model. From 1905 to 1907 he led the Menshevik faction in Russia and in the emigration. Opposed the tendency among the Mensheviks who wished to liquidate the underground socialist organization. During the war, M took part in the Zimmerwald and Kienthal conferences. Unlike Lenin's extreme position of favoring defeat of Russia in the war, M advocated peace without victory. After the February revolution, M was in opposition to his own party's policies on the most important issues. Being against a coalition government with the moderate parties, M and his group (The Internationalists) asked for immediate peace and for a coalition government of all socialist parties, including the Bolsheviks. After the October revolution, M was hostile to Lenin's dictatorship, protested against the red terror and capital punishment. On the other hand, he also opposed the Whites and the foreign intervention, fearing that this would bring about a counterrevolutionary regime. In 1920, he left Russia and founded *Sotsialistichesky Vestnik* (Socialist Courier) in Berlin.

M is the author of several books, including an autobiography, *The Annals of a Social Democrat*.

MARTÝNOV (Picker), **Aleksándr Samóylovich** (1865–1935), revolutionary. M began his revolutionary activities in the ranks of People's Will (1884); later he joined the Social Democrats, and became one of the leaders of the "economists" (*see* MARXISM). He was repeatedly arrested and exiled. After the 2nd Party Congress (1903), M joined the Mensheviks and contributed to the *Iskra*. In 1923, M joined the CP and became a member of the editorial board of the journal *Communist International*.

MARTÝNOV, Leoníd Nikoláyevich (1905–), poet, born in Omsk. His first works were published in 1921. Writes historical narrative poems and lyrics. After Stalin's death M published a number of poems that became popular in the USSR. In one of them, *Results of the Day* (1956), he compares life around him to darkness of night before dawn, when "rubbish and litter" are carted away to the "back yard," that is, "erroneous conceptions and piles of pseudo-axioms."

MARXISM-LENINISM is the official ideology of the CP and the Soviet government, which claim to be following the ideas of Marx and Engels and their adaptation to changed conditions by Lenin. Marxism is one of the several schools of socialism, all of which arose in response to the social dislocation and misery that accompanied the development of modern industrialism in W. Europe. The central idea of both Marxism and Leninism is the notion of the inevitability of socialism. It is based on the following considerations:

(1) The nature of capitalism. Marx defined capitalism as that type of market economy in which human labor power itself had become a marketable commodity. He saw a number of trends in capitalism which inevitably would cause it to collapse: an incessant urge to accumulate more and more capital; an increasing concentration of the means of production in the hands of fewer and fewer monopolists, accompanied by the ruination of the majority of businessmen; a steady fall in the rate of profit in relation to capital investment; and an increase in the misery of the working class. On the basis of these trends, he developed a theory of the business cycle in which each depression would be more

disastrous than the last, until finally the last crisis would bring about the collapse of capitalism.

(2) Marxism holds that the purposeful activity of production is the most human of all pursuits and that social institutions can be understood only as part of society's ever improving production machinery. Progress has not been smooth, however, because the human relationships corresponding to any given state of development in the "forces of production" have a tendency to outlive their functionality. These human relations are not only the class structure, but also the legal, political, and cultural institutions, traditions, and beliefs which develop as a "superstructure" out of the class structure. The superstructure always corresponds to and reinforces the prevailing "relations of production," and it has to be destroyed before mankind can move on to any higher mode of production. Progress can be achieved only by revolutions.

(3) Man's economic progress, by creating relationships of domination and exploitation, has been accompanied by the increasing dehumanization of the individual. History has stifled, repressed, and distorted everything human, including man's power to reason and know. In turn, socialism will be a society without domination, repression, exploitation, or alienation. Marx and Engels believed that such a society could be created at once. The industrial base created by capitalism could provide abundance as soon as private property in the means of production was abolished. The proletariat was fit, they thought, to exercise rational management. The alienation to which capitalism had subjected the workers was compelling them to gain rational understanding of the mainsprings of the entire society.

(4) While this social and political doctrine represents the essential core of Marxism, a number of ideas on a great variety of topics are usually considered part of it, especially dialectical materialism (q.v.). Orthodox Marxism sees in dialectical materialism a philosophic doctrine valid for all fields of inquiry, including natural science. In actual fact, dialectical materialism should be described as a sociological variation of Hegel's philosophy of history, applying therefore only to social phenomena.

Leninism is the Bolshevik method of applying Marxist doctrine to 20th-century R. conditions. It might be summarized as follows:

(1) As against populism (q.v.), Lenin asserts that Marxist doctrine fully applies to Russia, even though the overwhelming predominance of the peasantry, the weakness of capitalism, and autocratic tsarism called for modifications in social-democratic strategy. Among these modifications, the following are the most important: (a) In Russia the bourgeois revolution would have to be first on the agenda of the movement. In it, however, the proletariat, not the *bourgeoisie*, would have to exercise hegemony, because in Russia only the proletariat was genuinely interested in attaining the liberal program. (b) While the *bourgeoisie* was regarded as a class that would betray its own values, the peasantry was regarded as a valuable ally in the bourgeois revo-

lution; and so were the dissatisfied national minorities of the R. empire. The party's slogans were adjusted so as to attract them. (c) While Leninism distinguishes between the bourgeois and the proletarian revolutions, it also seeks to shorten and weaken as much as possible the expected bourgeois phase through which Russia would have to go; ideally the bourgeois and proletarian revolutions should merge into one. (d) Against those Marxists who asserted that the proletarian revolution must be the product of mature and well-developed capitalism, Leninism maintains that backward countries such as R., where capitalism is still weak, might be the first to fall into the hands of the proletariat; such an event would set off a world-wide chain reaction of proletarian revolutions.

(2) While Mensheviks and W. European Marxists tended to lay great stress on the idea that revolutionary activity makes sense only when conditions are mature, Leninism revives Marxist ideas of consciousness as the driving force of history. In contrast to Marx, however, it asserts that the proletariat, by itself, is unable to attain consciousness; this quality is possessed, instead, by small numbers of bourgeois intellectuals, who will become professional revolutionaries, and constitute the party, functioning as the general staff of the revolution. To be successful, however, the party needs a mass following of proletarians, and it seeks to acquire this by two methods. The first is persuasion, both through simple slogans and battle cries (agitation) and through a thorough educational process (propaganda) which aims to raise the workers to full consciousness. The second is organization. Used skillfully, organization becomes a system of transmission belts by which the will of the leaders is imparted to the masses.

(3) M-L seeks to combine the traditions of party democracy with the bureaucratic command structure of a military unit in a synthesis called "democratic centralism." It was to ensure full democratic rights to all party members in the discussion of issues while giving the party leadership the assurance that obedience and discipline would prevail once a decision had been taken. In practice, the centralist tendencies have won over the democratic ones. In the realm of tactics too, M-L tries to steer between two heresies (deviations). One of these would be premature action, taken before conditions are favorable or the masses are ready to follow, which therefore will end in defeat and disaster. The other is that of insufficient resoluteness: either opportunism, which is excessive responsiveness to given conditions or to the spontaneous mood of the masses; or reformism, which is an excessive reliance on gradual improvements in the conditions of the working class. The most serious deviation, however, is a breach of party discipline.

(4) In the theory of imperialism, M-L seeks to explain why some of the predictions made by Marx and Engels did not come true, but at the same time tries to reaffirm the inevitability of socialism. The theory asserts that in the 20th century capitalism has spread all over the globe, thus prolonging its existence but also transferring its structural defects onto a global lev-

el. This has transmuted them, the most important new feature being the sharp antagonism between the industrial world of the W. and the underdeveloped nations. M-L through this theory links the plight of the industrial workers to that of colonial natives, provides a challenging theory of backwardness, and becomes an important ideological element in the revolution of our time.

(5) While Lenin was preoccupied with the conditions and actions leading to the seizure of power by the CP, M-L as developed since 1917 also generalized about the organization and function of the Soviet government. This theory of state is summarized as follows: The revolution establishes the dictatorship of the proletariat which socializes the means of production and destroys all classes and individuals opposed to its rule. When the old order is destroyed and economic planning begins, society will enter socialism, an era in which it will devote all its efforts to building the country's industrial base (Stalin's "law of industrialization"). In such a society class differences would persist, but class conflict will have disappeared. Workers, peasants, and intelligentsia will collaborate freely to the utmost of their ability. Yet, in order to provide incentives for this, differences of reward and status have to be stressed.

Though socialism has been reached, the state will not wither away. Instead, institutions of domination and repression have to be strengthened. The state will plan and manage the economy, educate the population, guard against outside enemies (capitalist encirclement), and intensify the domestic class struggle against remnants of the old order and foreign agents. Socialism, when confined to one country, thus will diverge from the Marxian image; nor will its attainments be secure until a major part of the globe has been added to the socialist camp; and yet it would be heresy to deny that socialism can be built in an isolated backward country like Russia.

N. S. Khrushchev has meanwhile stated that capitalist encirclement is a feature of the past. With this, Stalin's main justification for totalitarian government has disappeared. Since, moreover, Soviet society has succeeded in building a strong industrial base, the CP now holds that the transition from socialism to communism has begun and, with it, the gradual withering-away of inequality and government. The CP, however, is expected to persist even in the communist era.

(6) M-L elevates the dialectical materialism of Marx and Engels to a dogma and has, furthermore, shown great reluctance to abandon the terminology of Marx and Engels in other areas. The boldness of some of its changes is therefore concealed by orthodox Marxist terminology, which makes the language of M-L cumbersome and handicaps scientists and philosophers who are compelled to use it. (*See also* MARXISM RUSSIAN, DIALECTICAL MATERIALISM, CPSU)

BIBLIOGRAPHY: Alfred G. Meyer, *Marxism: The Unity of Theory and Practice*, Cambridge, Mass., 1953; Alfred G. Meyer, *Leninism*, Cambridge, Mass., 1957; Edmund Wilson, *To the Finland Station*, Garden City, 1947; John Plamenatz, *German Marxism and Russian Communism*, New York, 1954; Herbert A. Marcuse, *Soviet Marxism: A Critical Analysis*, New York, 1957.　　　　A. G. M.

MARXISM, RUSSIAN. The radical R. intelligentsia studied the writings of Marx and Engels with the same eagerness with which they had studied their liberal and socialist precursors, and R. was the first foreign language into which *Das Kapital* was translated. The influence of this doctrine went far beyond the circle of orthodox Marxists; many populists and left-of-center liberals freely acknowledged their debt to Marx and Engels.

Orthodox M in Russia was born in 1883, when Georgy V. Plekhanov, Vera Zasulich, Pavel B. Akselrod (q.v.), A. N. Potresov (q.v.), and others abandoned the populist belief that the peasantry, inspired by the intelligentsia, would lead Russia into socialism. Their group, the "Liberation of Labor" (q.v.), sought to combat populist ideas by preaching that salvation for Russia lay in following the footsteps of the W. by developing capitalism and a revolutionary proletariat, and that such a development was inevitable in any event. Their propaganda work bore fruit only a decade later. In the years between the great famine of 1891 and the accession of Nicholas II in 1894, a whole generation of young intellectuals, including such men as Lenin, Martov, Struve, and Tugan-Baranovski, were converted to M and formed discussion and agitation circles throughout the R. empire. At the same time the working class in Russia and her Caucasian, Polish, and Baltic provinces began to organize spontaneously. Strike waves began to shake R. industry. In time, the workers' organizations and the intellectual circles merged, though not without friction, to form the R. Marxist movement. A Russian Social-Democratic Workers party (R.S.-D.R.P.) was formally created at the Minsk congress of 1898, which was attended only by second-rank leaders, the more important figures being in exile in Siberia or W. Europe.

M having originated in the industrial nations of the W., its application to R. conditions created problems, disputes, and rival political schools. Under the influence of Eduard Bernstein's revisionism, "Legal Marxists" such as P. B. Struve and S. N. Bulgakov renounced revolutionary activity, holding that socialism could and would be reached by gradual reforms obtained within the framework of liberal constitutional government. "Legal Marxism" freely re-interpreted most of the basic ideas of Marx and Engels, did not attract substantial numbers of intellectuals, and lived only very briefly in the late 1890's. Its spokesmen were quickly absorbed in the liberal and conservative movements. Another school, the "Economists," were more influential, dominating for a while the Union of Social Democrats Abroad. Their views, expressed most clearly in the "Credo" published by Ye. D. Kuskova in 1899, were that in Russia, where capitalism was as yet in its infancy, political activity by the working class was senseless, and that the proletariat should concentrate all its efforts on the more immediate and practical struggle for improvements in its economic conditions, while joining hands with the liberals in political activity. While the policies they proposed were not radically different from accepted Marxist practices, Economism was sharply attacked as a heresy by orthodox Marxists, who insisted that in the fight for democratic freedoms the R. proletariat should assume a leading role. Two or three years after these views were expressed, a wave of political unrest gripped R. students and workers and led to the emergence of the working class as a political force. This more than the arguments of the orthodox Marxists led to the decline of "Economism."

In 1900, two young orthodox Marxists, Yu. O. Martov and V. I. Lenin, who were released from exile in Siberia, joined the group around Plekhanov in W. Europe, and helped it rout the Economists. The foundation of the newspaper *Iskra* (q.v.) and the drafting and discussion of a party platform were among the major achievements. The creation and activities of *Iskra*'s editorial board constituted, in effect, the emergence of the R.S.-D.R.P. as a serious political party.

The party congress of 1903, held in Brussels and London, might be said to have been the victory congress of orthodox M. But orthodoxy emerged from the congress in the form of two factions which were destined to become irreconcilable and to find themselves on opposite sides of the barricades—the Mensheviks led by Martov, Dan, Akselrod, and others, and Lenin's faction, the Bolsheviks.

The differences between Bolshevism and Menshevism may be summarized as follows: The Mensheviks desired a party of comparatively loose structure and thoroughly democratic procedure, in which policies would be formulated in close response to the wishes of the working-class membership. They argued that a social-democratic party could operate only on the basis of freely given consent of the workers; and that any revolutionary activity undertaken without such consent would be premature and end in disaster. They had confidence in the working class, believing that the conditions of capitalism would make them fully class-conscious sooner or later. Bolshevik party organization, in contrast, was based on the axiom that the proletariat, by itself, would never attain class consciousness; that therefore a small, tightly organized elite of professional revolutionaries composed of truly conscious intellectuals was required to educate the workers and to function as the general staff of the revolutionary movement. Any concessions made to grass-roots opinions would threaten to lead the party into a betrayal of its revolutionary goals.

Both Bolshevism and Menshevism distinguished between maximal and minimal goals of the movement, the former denoting the proletarian revolution, and the latter the overthrow of tsarism and the establishment of "bourgeois democracy." But the Mensheviks tended to stick more closely to the timetable of revolutions established by Marx and Engels and to the W. European model of development; this led them to postpone all thought of the proletarian revolution into the distant future. Bolsheviks in contrast was the more impatient school, which sought to make use of particular R. conditions and political constellations for the purpose of skipping or shortening the capitalist phase and making the proletarian and bourgeois revolutions merge with each other. The Mensheviks in this took their cue from the Economists, while Bolsheviks showed certain affinities with populist ideas. Again, both factions agreed that the small R. proletariat needed allies in the bourgeois revolution, i.e., in the fight for political freedom. But while the Mensheviks tended to look to the liberals as their natural allies, the Bolsheviks came to rely on the support of the peasantry, in which they saw greater revolutionary potential; in addition, they laid far greater stress on the idea that even in the bourgeois revolution the proletariat should maintain hegemony.

Similarly, the Mensheviks insisted that R. revolutionary developments would have to be coordinated with, and follow in the footsteps of, the proletarian revolution in W. Europe, while the Bolsheviks came to believe, in time, that the revolution in Russia might serve as a spark which might kindle a proletarian revolution in the W. Both factions claimed to be the orthodox interpreters of Marx and Engels. But the Mensheviks stressed the morphology of development outlined in Marxist writings and clung to the founders' methods and policies. Bolsheviks laid greater stress on the goals to be reached and the peculiar obstacles to be overcome. Menshevism was more optimistic, humanitarian, and soft; Bolshevism was secretly pessimistic, impatient, and hard.

On many questions, differences of opinion within the R.S.-D.R.P. overlapped the factional alignment. One instance was the troubling problem of how the Georgian, Jewish, Polish, and other national Marxist organizations were to fit in with the all-R. party, and what the nationality platform in the party's program should be. Moreover, there were party leaders such as Trotsky who refused to be identified with either of the two factions.

During the revolution of 1905 factional differences were blurred, not only because the actual struggle tended to draw all Marxists close together, but also because most of the intellectual leaders did not manage to reach the scene. Actual leadership often was in the hands of local organizers who had little interest in the factional conflict. But the differences were emphasized at the Stockholm party congress of 1906, which analyzed the causes of the failure of the revolution and sought to define strategies and tactics for the future. Moreover, in the course of the next six years, the gulf between Bolsheviks and Mensheviks grew steadily wider.

The bitterness with which some of the party leaders conducted their disputes was not only based on ideological considerations, but was sharpened by the misery and pettiness of émigré life and by the wave of disappointment following the revolution. Like other R. revolutionary movements, M was at a low ebb. Many of its veterans turned their backs on politics altogether. Police infiltration into the highest revolutionary circles was extremely disruptive.

The years of reaction gave rise to several new factions. On the left wing of the party there were those who refused to participate in the newly created State Duma. They argued in favor of boycotting the elections (Boycottists) or of recalling the social-democratic deputies (Otzovists) from an institution which they considered a mockery of constitutional democracy. On the right wing of the Mensheviks, a sizable number of leaders, taking up arguments previously advanced by the Economists, wished to concentrate their efforts henceforth in legally permitted work primarily with labor unions, and so to build up a strong working-class movement from the grass roots. Because some of them favored the liquidation of the party's underground machine, which they considered to be either ineffectual or harmful, the Bolsheviks called them Liquidators. Finally, philosophic revisionism acquired new adherents who wished to reconcile Marxist ideas with prevailing Kantian, pragmatic, or even religious thought.

Until 1912, Bolsheviks and Mensheviks continued as factions of the same party, even though the Bolsheviks sought to maintain their own organization and caucus for at least six years before that. The formal break between the two factions was made in 1912, when at the Prague congress the Bolsheviks formally established their organization as a separate party.

RM was further split by the problem of what attitude to take toward the war of 1914. A minority including Plekhanov came out in support of the R. war effort. Lenin and some of his Bolshevik colleagues developed the theory of revolutionary defeatism (*porazhenchestvo*), according to which every class-conscious proletarian must work for the defeat of his own bourgeois state with the aim of transforming the war into a proletarian revolution. Most other R. Menshevik leaders occupied positions in between the two extremes. The bitterness of feeling over this issue on the part of Lenin and other Bolshevik leaders made the break between the two factions irremediable and transferred it onto an international plane. The dispute over the attitude toward war and peace was therefore a direct cause of the establishment, after the war, of the Third International and the rivalry between socialism and communism.

After the beginning of the revolution of 1917, one more major issue was added to the controversy between Bolshevism and Menshevism: the attitude to be taken toward the Provisional Government. While the Mensheviks and other moderate socialists were prepared to support and join it, as long as they could wield influence over it, the Bolsheviks were determined to destroy it and replace it by a Soviet government. Even though, after the Kornilov "mutiny" (q.v.), most Mensheviks collaborated with the Bolsheviks for the purpose of defending the revolution, the October revolution placed power exclusively into the hands of the Bolsheviks. They thus turned into a government party, while the Mensheviks became an opposition which was quickly driven underground and soon eliminated from Russia altogether. R. Marxism entered into the postrevolutionary phase. (*See also* CPSU, HISTORY, MARXISM-LENINISM, MENSHEVISM, TROTSKYISM)

BIBLIOGRAPHY: Leopold H. Haimson, *The Russian Marxists and the Origins of Bolshevism*, Cambridge, Mass., 1955; Donald W. Treadgold, *Lenin and His Rivals*, New York, 1955; Bertram D. Wolfe, *Three Who Made a Revolution*, New York, 1948; Nicholas Berdyayev, *The Origins of Russian Communism*, London, 1948; Leonard Schapiro, *The Communist Party of the Soviet Union*, New York, 1960.

A. G. M.

MARÝ (f. Merv), city, adm. center of Mary Oblast, Turkmen SSR, in an oasis on the Murgab River; pop. 48,000 (1959). Is a R.R. junction; a center of a rich cotton-producing area; has orchards. Cotton and wool processing. Ancient town, it is believed to be the Paradise in Hindu, Parsi, and Arab tradition. Was the center of a province of ancient kingdoms; under the Arabs (646–847); invaded by the Turks in 1040; seized by Mongols in 1221; conquered by Russians in 1883.

MARÝ OBLAST, Turkmen SSR, the southernmost oblast of the USSR, in the Murgab River basin, bordering on Afghanistan (S.); area 45,800 sq. mi.; pop. 417,-000 (1959): Turkmens, Russians, Uzbeks, Kazakhs. Cities: Mary (adm. center), Bayram-Ali, Iolotan. Dry continental climate, desert vegetation, pistachio groves along Afghanistan border; intensive cotton growing in irrigated fertile Murgab R. valley; karakul-sheep, camel and goat raising in the desert. Ind.: cotton ginning, cottonseed-oil extraction, silk production, food processing, rug weaving. Has highway network; and the Trans-Caspian R.R. crosses Murgab oasis. Est. 1939.

MÁSLOV, Pyótr Pávlovich (1867–1946), Marxist economist. Joined the revolutionary movement in the 1890's. In 1905, M was the author of the Social Democratic program of "municipalization" of the land. He was one of the editors of the 5-volume Menshevik collective work on the social movement in Russia. After the Bolshevik Revolution, M worked as an economist and teacher under the Soviets. In 1929, he was elected a member of the Ac. of S. of the USSR. M is the author of several books including: *The Agrarian Problem in Russia; The Foundations of the Cooperative Movement.*

MASSINE, Leonide (1896–), choreographer and dancer, born in Moscow. Graduated from the Moscow Imperial School of Ballet (1912) and joined the Diaghilev (q.v.) Ballet, eventually to replace Vaslav Nijinsky (q.v.) as dancer and choreographer. A very limited list of the ballets which he staged would include *La Boutique Fantasque* (1919), *The Three-Cornered Hat* (1919), *Les Présages, Choreartium, Le Beau Danube* (all in 1933), *Symphonie Fantastique* (1936), *Beethoven's Seventh Symphony, Saint Francis, Gaité Parisienne* (all in 1938). He also staged ballets in musical comedies. Currently (1960) he does staging for various European ballet companies.

MATERIAL BALANCES: *see* PLANNING.

MATERNITY BENEFITS: *see* SOCIAL INSURANCE.

MATHEMATICS. The founding of the Academy of Sciences (1724) brought the Swiss mathematician Daniel Bernoulli to St. Petersburg, followed (1727) by his friend Leonhard Euler (1707–83), who spent the rest of his life at the Academy except from 1741 to 1766. Euler created formal algorithmic solutions and methods in number theory, mathematical physics and mathematical analysis, as well as other fields, publishing many papers in the first R. scientific journal (1725), *Commentarii Academiae Scientiarum Imperialis Petropolitanae.* Euler left no serious students, and the 19th century dawned with no firmly established R. mathematical traditions. In 1829, in Kazan, N. I. Lobachevsky (1792–1856) constructed the first non-Euclidean ge-

ometry, one of the principal sources of the rigorous abstract mathematics of the late 19th and 20th centuries, but had no immediate impact on R. or world mathematical thought. At this time, the return from Paris of the probabilist V. Ya. Bunyakovsky (1804–89) and the mathematical physicist and analyst M. V. Ostrogradsky (1801–61) set the stage for the creation of the St. Petersburg Mathematical School.

In 1874, P. L. Chebyshov (1821–94) arrived in St. Petersburg, having written his master's dissertation on probability in Moscow. Chebyshov, obtaining beautiful results and suggesting many problems to his students, created the St. Petersburg Mathematical School. While editing Euler's number-theoretical papers in 1849, Chebyshov became interested in prime number theory, and obtained the best results on prime number distribution since Euclid, proving Bertrand's Postulate and obtaining sharp estimates indicating the validity of the Prime Number Theorem (proved in 1896). In probability theory, Chebyshov conjectured two basic theorems, proving the Law of Large Numbers and creating the method of moments in an attempt at proving the Central Limit Theorem. Chebyshov also created the first problem of *best* approximation of functions by polynomials and solved it. Sofia V. Kovalevskaya (1850–91), who studied and worked outside Russia because women could not attend R. universities, produced profound results on partial differential equations and the motion of a rigid body about a fixed point. Chebyshov could not open the doors of a R. university to her, but finally obtained for her a corresponding-membership in the Academy. A. A. Markov (1856–1922), a Chebyshov student, developed Chebyshov's method of moments (using it to prove the Central Limit Theorem), introduced Markov chains into probability theory, and did significant work in number theory. A. M. Lyapunov (1857–1918), another brilliant Chebyshov student, generalized Chebyshov's Central Limit Theorem and contributed basic results on equilibrium figures of homogeneous rotating fluids, but his greatest contribution was the creation of a general theory of stability of dynamical systems, which, with the work of the great French mathematician Henri Poincaré, forms the basis of the theory of general dynamical systems and the qualitative theory of differential equations. S. N. Bernshteyn (1880–), another important Chebyshov student, solved Hilbert's 19th problem (of the 23 most difficult and important problems of the 20th century proposed by the great German mathematician David Hilbert in 1900) on the analyticity of solutions of partial differential equations of elliptic type in 1903, and in 1908 solved Hilbert's 20th problem on a generalization of Dirichlet's problem. Bernshteyn then turned Chebyshov's theorem on the best approximation of continuous functions into a whole theory of the approximation of functions of a real variable, which is now called "the constructive theory of functions."

Moscow was mathematically quiet until 1864, when the Moscow Mathematical Society was formed, which then founded the first mathematical journal, *Matematichesky Sbornik* (Mathematical Papers), in 1865. Moscow became a center for mechanics as a result of the work of N. Ye. Zhukovsky (1847–1921) and his student S. A. Chaplygin (1869–1942). In 1911, D. F. Yegorov (1869–1930) and his student N. N. Luzin (1883–1950), impressed by the importance of Henri Lebesgue's new theory of measure and integration, initiated the Moscow School of Function Theory. Luzin made basic contributions to the metric theory of functions (measure-theoretic properties of sets and functions), the theory of trigonometric series, and the descriptive theory of functions (non-measure-theoretic properties of sets and functions). Yegorov's seminar of 1914 produced Luzin's first group of students: P. S. Aleksandrov (1896–) and M. Ya. Suslin (1894–1919) in the descriptive theory of functions; D. Ye. Menshov (1892–) and A. Ya. Khinchin (1894–) in the metric theory of functions. In 1916, P. S. Uryson (1848–1924) joined them. After the revolution, the doors of Soviet universities opened wide, and the conditions of the Kovalevskaya tragedy vanished. The second generation of Luzin's students included A. N. Kolmogorov (1903—), M. A. Lavrentyev (1900–), L. A. Lyusternik (1899–), and Nina K. Bari (1901–) in the metric theory of functions; P. S. Novikov (1901–) and Lyudmila V. Keldysh (1904–) in the descriptive theory of functions. V. V. Golubev (1884–1954), another of Yegorov's students, initiated, in his study published in 1916, the application of the metric theory of functions of a real variable to analytic functions of a complex variable. In 1917, Luzin and another of Yegorov's students, I. I. Privalov (1891–1941), began publishing work on the boundary values of analytic functions using the new methods and ideas. They were followed by Menshov, Lavrentyev, and A. O. Gelfond (1906–).

In 1921, Uryson initiated the study of set-theoretic topology in the Soviet Union, and was joined in the following year by P. S. Aleksandrov. Uryson contributed basic ideas and results to dimension theory and the theory of topological spaces. In 1925, P. S. Aleksandrov formed the topology seminar among whose participants were his students A. N. Tikhonov (1906–), V. V. Nemytsky, and L. S. Pontryagin (1908–), as well as Lyusternik, Kolmogorov and L. G. Shnirelman (1905–38). Problems arising in the study of the dimension theory of metric spaces could not be solved by set-theoretic methods, and hence P. S. Aleksandrov initiated the modern investigation of combinatorial topology, and applied it to dimension theory. Pontryagin proved his famous Duality Theorem, Kolmogorov obtained important results in cohomology theory, and P. S. Aleksandrov then obtained a general duality theory of homology. Pontryagin made substantial contributions to the theory of topological and Lie groups. Recently, basic work of M. M. Postnikov in homotopy theory has excited great interest.

In 1919, the mathematical physicist V. A. Steklov (1863–1926), Lyapunov's only student, became vice president of the Academy of Sciences and organized its Physico-Mathematical Institute. In 1934, when the Academy moved from Leningrad to Moscow, the Physico-Mathematical Institute was divided into three parts, one becoming the Steklov Mathematical Institute.

The move carried several academicians with it, breaking up the traditions of the St. Petersburg Mathematical School.

Many classical problems have been attacked and solved by new methods since the revolution. In 1928, Lyusternik and Shnirelman applied homology theory to the calculus of variations, proving, in particular, that any closed convex surface has at least three closed geodesics on it. In the 1930's, another Yegorov student, V. V. Stepanov (1889–1950), and Nemytsky applied topological methods to the study of the qualitative theory of differential equations, while N. M. Krylov (1879–1955) and his student N. N. Bogolyubov (1909–) applied measure theory to the study of nonlinear dynamical systems. In the 1940's, A. D. Aleksandrov (1912–) (rector, Leningrad) created a beautiful modern theory of convex surfaces. In the 1950's, S. N. Mergelyan (1928–) completely solved the problem of characterizing functions in the complex plane which can be approximated arbitrarily closely by uniformly convergent sequences of polynomials.

In a more classical vein, in the early 1930's, I. A. Lappo-Danilevsky (1895–1931) created the theory of analytic functions of matrices for application to the study of systems of ordinary differential equations, and I. G. Petrovsky (1901–) (rector, Moscow) introduced a fruitful classification of systems of partial differential equations. In a less classical vein, in the 1930's, S. L. Sobolev (1908–) developed a theory of generalized solutions of partial differential equations, and Lavrentyev introduced a theory of quasi-conformal mappings (a generalization of conformal mappings) which is a useful tool in the study of the properties of solutions of partial differential equations. For more than thirty years, a school of mathematicians in Tbilisi, dedicated to solving the differential and integral equations of mathematical physics (elasticity, in particular), has been growing around N. I. Muskhelishvili (1891–). One of its brightest stars, I. N. Vekua (1907–) (rector, Novosibirsk), obtained many new results in a theory of generalized analytic functions closely related to the work of Sobolev and Lavrentyev.

Even number theory was affected by the Moscow Function Theory School, when Khinchin began to work, in 1922, on diophantine aproximation, i.e. the approximation of real numbers by rationals, continued fractions, and so on, using the ideas of the metric theory of functions, thereby creating the metric theory of diophantine approximation. Academician Christian Goldbach, writing to Euler in 1742, conjectured that every integer greater than three is the sum of at most three primes. Shnirelman attacked this untouched problem in 1930, proving every integer is the sum of at most a certain number of primes, by a powerful new method based on the concept of the density of a sequence of positive integers. In 1934, Gelfond created a powerful method which solved Hilbert's 7th problem (a generalization of an unproved conjecture of Euler) concerning a class of transcendental numbers. In 1937, I. M. Vinogradov (1891–), a St. Petersburg number theorist who had moved to Moscow with the Academy in 1934, had developed his fifteen-year-old trigonometric sum method to the point where he could attack Goldbach's problem, proving that every sufficiently large odd integer is the sum of three odd primes. Vinogradov's student N. G. Chudakov (1905–) and Yu. V. Linnik (1915–) have done further extensive work in number theory using various methods, and Linnik has applied the trigonometric sum method to probability problems. In 1960, Linnik solved the 1923 Hardy-Littlewood Problem, proving every sufficiently large integer is the sum of a prime and two squares, by a modification of the basic idea of the trigonometric sum method.

Although O. Yu. Shmidt (1891–1956) had worked on group theory in Moscow since 1912, modern algebraic theories had a weak position in Soviet mathematics until the visit of the important German woman algebraist Emmy Noether in 1929. In 1930 Shmidt organized the Moscow Algebraic Seminar, the basis of the Moscow Algebraic School, which produced the group theorist A. G. Kurosh (1908–) and A. I. Maltsev (1909–) in the 1930's and I. R. Shafarevich (1923–) in the 1940's.

The Soviet School of Functional Analysis, starting in the 1930's, has several branches, centering in Sobolev, Lyusternik, Kolmogorov, Kolmogorov's brilliant student, I. M. Gelfand (1913–) in Moscow, L. V. Kantorovich (1912–) in Leningrad, and M. G. Kreyn (1907–) in Odessa. Kreyn's co-workers and students operate in many fields. Kantorovich's group works on the application of functional analysis to approximation methods and the theory of partially ordered spaces. The group around Sobolev works on new formulations and solutions of mathematical physics problems. Lyusternik's group is concerned with problems of nonlinear analysis, and variational problems in particular. Gelfand operates a seminar which deals with almost all parts of functional analysis and its applications, and this seminar has created and developed new directions in functional analysis: normed rings, infinite dimensional representations of classical groups, spectral theory of differential operators, generalized functions, and so on. Gelfand's principal co-workers are G. E. Shilov and M. A. Naymark.

The St. Petersburg tradition in probability was continued by Bernshteyn, in 1917–27, who created the first systematically developed axiomatization of probability theory, proved the central limit theorem for independent random variables in such generality that the conditions turned out to be essentially sufficient, proved the applicability of the Central Limit Theorem to dependent random variables under very general conditions, and gave the first rigorous proof of a multidimensional limit theorem. The Moscow School of Probability was initiated in 1924 by Khinchin and Kolmogorov, who applied the methods of metric function theory to probability, proving Khinchin's Law of the Iterated Logarithm, formulating necessary and sufficient conditions for the applicability of the Law of Large Numbers to sums of independent random variables, finding very general conditions for the applicability of the Strong Law of Large Numbers, and proving necessary and sufficient conditions for the convergence of a series of independent random variables. In 1934, Kolmogorov introduced the simplest known axiomatization of probability theory, one intimately associated with measure and metric function theory. Kolmogorov initiated the study of Markov processes (a generalization of Markov chains) that led to stochastic differential equations, which were intensively studied by Bernshteyn, Khinchin, and Petrovsky. In the 1930's, Khinchin began the study of the spectral and ergodic theory of general stationary processes. In the 1940's and 1950's, Khinchin gave beautiful rigorous treatments of statistical mechanics, information theory, and queuing theory.

Mathematical statistics had been relatively undeveloped in the Soviet Union until the early 1930's, when the influence of the probabilists was felt. In 1933, Kolmogorov found an exact asymptotic characterization of the maximum deviation of the nth empirical distribution function from the continuous distribution function of a random variable, which is used as a criterion verifying correctness of the distribution function. Then N. Y. Smirnov carried out a series of investigations in similar directions, leading to many results including the Cramer-Mises-Smirnov criterion for correctness of the distribution function and a criterion for two different empirical distribution functions to correspond to the same distribution function. In recent years, Kolmogorov has developed a general viewpoint on the role of unbiased estimates of unknown parameters and their connection with sufficient statistics, while E. B. Dynkin, in his investigations of sufficient statistics, has introduced the notion of necessary statistics.

Serious Soviet interest in **mathematical logic** dates from the mid-1940's although of the four leading mathematicians in this field, Kolmogorov, Novikov, A. A. Markov (1903–) and N. A. Shanin, the first three showed an interest, in the 1930's, in *intuitionistic* logic, called *constructive* logic in the Soviet Union. In 1955, Novikov proved the algorithmic unsolvability of the general word problem in groups. Novikov is interested in foundations of mathematics and constructive mathematical logic; Markov in foundations of mathematical logic, the theory of algorithms, and constructive mathematical logic; Shanin in constructive mathematical logic and constructive mathematical analysis.

Systematic scientific work in **mathematical cybernetics,** the science of control and communication, came to the Soviet Union in 1950. At the newly formed Institute for Precision Mechanics and Computer Technology (IPMCT) of the Ac. of S., work by mathematicians on programing problems was started under Lyusternik, on the initiative of Lavrentyev (director of IPMCT, 1950–53; now vice president of the Ac. of S.), with no digital computing machines available. The BESM I computer was completed at IPMCT in 1953, and a transistorized copy BESM II will probably be in serial production in 1961. The STRELA computer was completed at IPMCT in 1953, a number of copies were then produced, and an advanced transistorial model is expected very soon. A new miniature vacuum tube computer KIEV was recently completed at the Computing Center of the Ukrainian Ac. of S. and a new ferrite core miniaturized computer SETUN is expected momentarily at Moscow University. Large Soviet universities now have four areas of mathematics specialization: pure mathematics, mechanics, astronomy, and *computer mathematics (including mathematical logic)*. Sobolev is head of the computer mathematics group at the new Siberian Academy of Sciences Center in Novosibirsk. Theoretical investigations into programing center on Kantorovich, M. R. Shura-Bura, and A. A. Lyapunov. Since 1955 extensive theoretical and empirical investigations into machine translations to and from various languages have been carried out at IMPCT and at the Steklov Mathematical Institute (around Lyapunov). In 1939, Kantorovich had introduced the method of steepest descent to create optimal economic plans, and a group concerned with linear programing now centers on him. Because computer mathematics is part of the formal structure of the mathematical life of the Soviet Union, Soviet mathematicians are more interested in computers; and, hence, more and better mathematicians are connected with computers in the Soviet Union's computing centers than anywhere else in the world.

S. K.

MATSÉSTA, resort near Sochi, on Black Sea, Krasnodar Kray, RSFSR, with highly concentrated hydrogen sulfide springs.

MATÚLIS, Yuozas Yuozasovich (1899–), chemist. Fellow (1941) and President (1946), Ac. of S., Lithuanian SSR. Honored scientist, Lithuanian SSR (1945). Member of the Supreme Soviet USSR (1950, 1958). M's research concerns photochemistry, electrochemistry, and kinetics of reactions in solutions.

MATVÉYEV, Andréy Matvéyevich (1701–1739), painter. In 1716 M was sent by Tsar Peter I to study art in Holland. He returned to Russia in 1727 and was commissioned to decorate the Cathedral of Peter and Paul in St. Petersburg. His *Self Portrait with Wife* (1729, Russian Museum, Leningrad) is an outstanding example of 18th-century art.

MAUSOLEUM OF V. I. LENIN AND I. V. STALIN, monumental structure in the Red Square in Moscow near the Kremlin Wall in which are placed the coffins containing the embalmed bodies of V. I. Lenin and I. V. Stalin. A temporary wooden mausoleum was erected for Lenin's funeral on Jan. 27, 1924 according to plans by the member of the Academy, A. V. Shchusev. In 1930 the permanent M, a replica of the temporary one, was built in granite, marble, labrador, and porphyry. By virtue of a decree of March 7, 1953, the remains of Stalin were placed next to those of Lenin.

The Lenin-Stalin Mausoleum

On national holidays Soviet troops and civilians parade in the Red Square in front of the M.

MAXIM THE GREEK (Mikhail Trivolis) (ca. 1480–1556), a learned Greek divine who was invited by Vasily III of Moscow to translate religious books for the Russian Orthodox Church. He left several treatises in Russian in which he criticized the administration of the R. church. In 1525 a council of R. bishops condemned him to exile at the Volokolamsk Monastery. His sermons and writings were published in 1859–61.

MAYAKÓVSKY, Vladímir Vladímirovich (1893–1930), leading Soviet poet; born in Georgia. His first poems appeared in 1912, in collections published by the futurists whose most vociferous leader he was for a time. Although his poems of this period reflect formalistic tendencies of an experimental character, they also  show concern with social justice. M already sought to create a "poetry of the streets and public squares," directed at the masses of the people. To this period belong: autobiographical tragedy *Vladimir Mayakovsky* (1914); *The Cloud in Trousers* (1915); *War and Peace* (1916); *The Man* (1917). After 1917 M devoted himself to the revolutionary cause and to the popularization of its ideals. In the play *Mystery Bouffe* (1918) he sought to convey the sense of the historical significance of the revolution. *Ode to the Revolution* (1918) and *The Left March* (1919) are an enthusiastic welcome to the new era. His striving to reach the widest possible audience was assisted by his use of satirical genre that he developed while working on posters for the Russian Telegraphic Agency (ROSTA), as well as by use of a variety of stylistic elements from traditional folklore. The most striking qualities of his writings are his unusual drumlike rhythms, powerful metaphors, rhythmical irregularity of stresses, and typographical breakdown of lines. His long poem *150 million* in which Ivan opposes Woodrow Wilson was criticized by Lenin while his satire on red tape and bureaucracy *Lost in Conference* (1922) met with the latter's high praise. In 1923 he was one of the founders of LEF ("Left Front"), a futurist literary group. He dealt with such eternal themes as love, death, and nature from the standpoint of a new approach to life which is associated with socialism (e.g. in the poems *I Love* and *Concerning That*). His work of this period includes the long poem *Lenin* (1924), the satirical plays *The Bedbug* (1928) and *The Bathhouse* (1929), and the group of poems entitled *My Discovery of America*. The last, which followed a visit to the United States, reflects, as does the long poem *Khorosho* (1927), admiration for his native land. Tragic love and increasing disillusion brought him to suicide (1930). His works have been published in 40 million copies and translated into 57 USSR languages and 38 foreign languages.

MAYKÓP, city, adm. center of Adygey Autonomous Oblast, Krasnodar Kray, RSFSR; pop. 56,000 (1939), 82,000 (1959). Lies in the foothills of the W. spurs of Greater Caucasus on the shore of Belaya River; on R.R. between Armavir and Tuapse. Has tanning-extracts, food-processing, furniture, tobacco, canning ind.; mineral springs; and is the center of oil fields.

MÁYKOV, Apollón Nikoláyevich (1821–1897), poet influenced by Greek and Roman mythology. His best poetry, however, is devoted to the portrayal of R. scenery. His better-known poems are *Summer Rain* and *It's Spring!*

MÁYKOV, Valerián Nikoláyevich (1823–1847), literary critic and publicist, brother of the poet. He defended the views that literature should be above the social and political struggles of the day. He was close to the Petrashévsky circle (q.v.); also prominent as the literary editor of *Otechestvennya Zapiski* (Notes of the Fatherland).

MÁYSKY (Lyakhovétsky), **Iván Mikháylovich** (1884–), Soviet diplomat. Graduate of the faculty of economics of the University of Munich. Before the revolution M was a Menshevik; he was frequently arrested and twice exiled to Siberia for his revolutionary activity; he spent nine years in England, Germany, and Switzerland. From 1925 to 1932, M served in the foreign service. From 1932 to 1943 M was ambassador to Great Britain; 1943–46, he was deputy minister for foreign affairs and in 1946 was elected member of the Ac. of S. M represented the USSR in many international negotiations. He took part in the Yalta and Potsdam conferences; he signed agreements on the establishment of diplomatic relations with Canada, the Netherlands, and other countries. M published many books including: *Contemporary Mongolia* (1921), *Contemporary Germany* (1924), *Foreign Policy of the RSFSR 1917–22* (1923), and *Spain 1808–1917* (1957).

MAZÉPA, Iván Stepánovich (1644–1709), hetman of the Ukraine (1687–1709). He betrayed Peter I to the Swedes (1708) by joining the forces of Charles XII in order to separate the Ukraine from Russia. After the battle of Poltava (1709), he fled with Charles XII to Bendery and Turkey.

MECHANICS: *see* TECHNICAL SCIENCES.

MÉCHNIKOV, Ilyá Ilyích (1845–1916), prominent zoologist, biologist, bacteriologist. Honorary member,  St. Petersburg Ac. of S. and of most Ac. of S. in the world. Graduated from Kharkov University and continued studies in Germany (1867) and Italy (1868). Professor of zoology and comparative anatomy, Odessa University (1870). Resigned with the purpose of devoting himself entirely to research (1882). Worked with L. Pasteur in Paris whom he succeeded as director of the Pasteur Institute (1895). Research concerned intercellular digestion, phagocytosis, and blood diseases. Author of numerous publications including *The Comparative Pathology of Inflammation* (translated into French in 1892 and into English in 1893); *Immunity of Infectious Diseases* (French 1901, English 1905); *The Nature of Man* (French 1903, English 1904). Shared with Paul Ehrlich the Nobel prize for physiology and medicine (1908).

MEDICAL SYSTEM. The medical system of a society has three basic mandates: the search for medical knowledge, its application, and its transmission to new generations of medical personnel. In the Soviet Union these tasks are regarded essentially as functions of the state, administered by the government through specially designated organs, performed by salaried state employees, financed from the central and local budgets, and carried out within the general framework of the plans, programs, and priorities of the CPSU.

Basic Principles of Soviet Health Protection. The official cornerstone of the Soviet MS is that of *prophylaxis* through the protection of health and the prevention of illness and injury. The bulk of medical activities, however, is still directed to clinical rather than preventive services, and is based on the following principles:

1) The protection of health, like any other activity, must be *planned*.

2) There must be *unidirectionality* in the protection of health.

3) Health protection is a *free* social service financed by the state.

4) *The health of the people is a responsibility of the people* and the widest popular participation should be encouraged.

5) There must be *unity of theory and practice*.

6) The principle of *priority treatment for certain groups of the population* means that medical efforts must be directed first toward the treatment of those whose functions are most critical to the state and party.

Administration. The over-all administrative responsibility for the operation of the Soviet MS rests with the Ministry of Health for the USSR, and its subordinate republican health ministries, regional, provincial, district, and city health departments. At each administrative-territorial level, the health authorities are responsible both to the corresponding executive organs of the government (and of course the party) and to their immediately superior health authority.

There are, in addition to the Health Ministry's facilities, some *closed* medical administrations that do not fall directly under the supervision of the Ministry and provide for the medical services of the personnel of such organizations as the armed forces, railroad transportation, internal affairs, and others. These facilities are said to be governed by the same principles as those of the Health Ministry.

Functions of the Medical System.

A. MEDICAL SERVICES.

(1) In urban communities the following types of services are generally available: (a) out-patient care, in a variety of general and specialized out-patient clinics and dispensaries; (b) home care, given by the physicians of the medical institutions of the town; (c) emergency care in case of accident or sudden illness, given either by physicians of emergency stations, or by medical duty officers where such stations do not exist; (d) hospital care, in either general or specialized hospitals. Access to medical care is through either the *residential* or the *occupational* principle. Individuals are assigned, on the basis of residence, to a medical district (*rayon*) which is further subdivided into medical sectors (*uchastok*) of about 4,000 inhabitants each. Tables of organization provide the following number of medical positions and hospital beds per sector:

STRUCTURE OF THE SOVIET URBAN MEDICAL SECTOR (*UCHASTOK*) FOR 4,000 PERSONS

Specialty	Number of Medical Positions by Specialty	Approximate number of Hospital beds by Specialty
Internal medicine	2.00	10.0
Pediatrics	1.25	5.4
Surgery	0.90	7.6
Obstetrics and gynecology	1.00	7.2
Ophthalmology	0.25	1.0
Otolaryngology	0.20	0.6
Neurology	0.25	0.8
Phthisiology	0.6	4.2
Dermatovenerology	0.4	1.6
TOTAL	6.85	38.4

In factories and industrial plants with a large number of workers and employees, medical care is available to them on an *occupational* basis from a network of medical institutions existing within the plant.

(2) In rural communities: the same principles that apply to urban medical care apply to the rural population but are adapted and modified to the special circumstances of the countryside (great distances, low population density, and so on). The health authorities appear to experience difficulties in staffing the countryside with physicians, and a substantial amount of rural medical work is performed by junior personnel, particularly *feldshers* (see below). A system of air ambulances sometimes permits the flying either of patients to medical facilities or of medical personnel to patients.

(3) Public health, anti-epidemiological and sanitary services: preventive services are part of the network of medical facilities. Locally the direction of preventive work rests with the Sanitary Epidemiological Station and its staff of public health physicians, epidemiologists, assistants, and inspectors. The typical SES has its own laboratories.

(4) Other services: the Health Ministry also has general supervision over the following services: (a) sanatoria, rest cures, houses of rest, resorts, and organizations of rest; (b) physical culture and medical control over sports; (c) health education of the population; (d) the production and distribution of pharmaceuticals and instruments.

Medical Facilities. The growth of medical facilities in total number of beds and beds per constant units of the population shows sizable progress since 1913:

NUMBER OF HOSPITAL BEDS (EXCLUSIVE OF THE MILITARY) 1913–1959, USSR

(in thousands)

	1913	1940	1956	1958	1959
Number of beds	207.6	791	1,361	1,533	1,620
Number of beds per 10,000 of population	13	40	68	73	76

Soviet health authorities consider the present number of beds as still inadequate and aim at about 110 beds per 10,000 of population by 1965.

B. MEDICAL RESEARCH.

The over-all direction of medical research belongs to the Academy of Medical Sciences founded in 1944. The Academy is the research arm of the Ministry and receives its general directives and support from it. In addition the following organizations may have their own research institutes: (1) The Health Ministry of the USSR; (2) the health ministries of the constituent republics; (3) the departments of health of regions or provinces, cities, and districts.

A recent report of the World Health Organization points out that, while medical research is widespread and covers every conceivable field, it does appear that this network is centralized in its planning and choice of research projects, and that it is somewhat rigid functionally.

C. EDUCATION AND TRAINING OF PERSONNEL.

(1) Medical personnel: education of senior medical personnel is the responsibility of the Health Ministry. The future Soviet physician begins his medical training at the age of 18 after having completed ten years of elementary and secondary schooling or its equivalent. In 1956 there were 77 medical institutes (68 in medicine, 2 in dentistry, and 7 in pharmacology). A medical institute may have one or more *faculties* giving instruction, from the beginning, in five basic undergraduate medical fields: (a) general medicine (66 faculties); (b) pediatrics (25 faculties); (c) public health (22 faculties); (d) dentistry (12 faculties); (e) pharmacology (16 faculties).

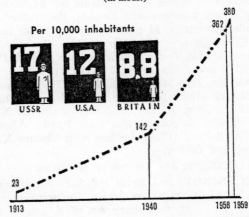

NUMBER OF PHYSICIANS
(in thous.)

Per 10,000 inhabitants

17 USSR   12 U.S.A.   8.8 BRITAIN

23 — 1913   142 — 1940   362 / 380 — 1958 1959

Medical education lasts six years except in dentistry and pharmacology where it is shorter. At the age of 23 or 24 the young Soviet medical student becomes a *vrach* or physician. The term "doctor" is formally reserved for those professionals who acquire an advanced academic degree, first as a candidate of medical sciences and then a doctor of medical sciences. Possession of such a degree enables the physician to pursue an academic career in teaching and research. Others may go to an institute to acquire a specialty. Those who remain in general practice may, at regular intervals, be sent to refresher courses to become acquainted with the latest techniques and to improve their qualifications. Clinical positions are available to physicians at outpatient clinics, hospitals, or both. Private practice still exists on a small scale.

The growth of the medical contingent since the revolution is truly one of the most impressive achievements of the Soviet regime:

NUMBER OF PHYSICIANS (EXCLUSIVE OF THE MILITARY)
1913–1959, USSR
(in thousands)

	1913	1940	1956	1958	1959
Number of physicians	23	142	329	362	381
Number of physicians per 10,000 of population	1	7	16	17	18

This increase was made possible by the widespread training of women physicians. Before the revolution, only 10 per cent of doctors were women, in 1940 60 per cent of all physicians were women, and in 1958, 75 per cent.

(2) Junior personnel: there are eight types of junior medical personnel presently trained in the Soviet Union. Access to training is generally after seven years of primary and secondary schooling. Training usually lasts two or three years. The following table lists the categories of such personnel and the increases since 1940:

NUMBER OF JUNIOR MEDICAL PERSONNEL (EXCLUSIVE
OF THE MILITARY)) 1940–1958, USSR
(in thousands)

	1940	1950	1955	1958
Feldshers-midwives	82.2	160.2	183.2	267.4
Midwives	12.8	42.1	66.5	75.9
Assistants to public health physicians and epidemiologists	68.1	66.6	83.6	117.5
Nurses	9.7	18.5	20.5	27.3
Laboratory technicians	227.7	325.4	462.5	568.5
X-Ray technicians	11.7	25.3	38.3	47.9
Dental technicians	3.6	7.5	12.2	17.0
Disinfectors	4.9	6.8	10.2	12.0
Feldshers (physicians' assistants)	15.9	27.0	36.6	46.3
Total	472.0	720.3	955.9	1,233.5

A *feldsher* is the civilian equivalent of the army non-commissioned medic. When a physician is not available, the *feldsher* performs most medical functions except major elective surgical procedures. He is expected, of course, to refer cases beyond his competence to the proper medical facilities and personnel.

(3) Other health personnel: it can be estimated that there are, in addition to the categories of medical personnel listed above, an additional 1.5 mill. individuals engaged in the different aspects of the medical system. Altogether in 1959, 3,256,000 persons were employed by the Soviet MS, or slightly over 5 per cent of all salaried employees in the USSR (exclusive of collective farmers).

Vital Statistics are a fairly good index of medical and public health progress, and the following figures on birth and death rates indicate the magnitude of Soviet accomplishments since 1913:

CRUDE BIRTH AND DEATH RATE, NATURAL INCREASE
OF THE POPULATION, AND INFANT MORTALITY,
1913–1958, USSR

	1913	1940	1950	1955	1958
Births per 1,000 of population	47.0	31.3	26.7	25.7	25.3
Deaths per 1,000 of population	30.2	18.1	9.7	8.2	7.2
Natural increase per 1,000 of population	16.8	13.2	17.0	17.5	18.1
Infant mortality per 1,000 births, under one year of age	273	184	81	60	40.6

Life expectancy has more than doubled since the end of the 19th century as the following figures indicate:

AVERAGE LIFE EXPECTANCY AT BIRTH OF POPULATION,
BY SEX, PREREVOLUTIONARY RUSSIA AND USSR (1896–1958)

	1896–1897 (50 provinces of European Russia)	1926–1927 (European part of USSR)	1957–1958 (All of USSR)
Average life expectancy of males	31	42	64
Average life expectancy of females	33	47	71
Average life expectancy, total population	32	44	68

Summary and Conclusions. The Soviet regime has established, over the last four decades, a system of medical care and preventive medicine dispensed as a public service the scope of which goes beyond anything ever attempted in this field on a national scale. This system has both the advantage and the drawbacks of being centrally planned, controlled, and administered, and its growth is in theory geared to the general development of the society. It is financed by the state and does not depend for its sustenance on fees for services or voluntary and charitable contributions. This undoubtedly permits long-range programing and some flexibility in the sense that human and material resources can be mobilized and shifted to meet medical problems as they arise. The emphasis in the medical system has been primarily a quantitative one, but there is little doubt that the quality of services, research, and education will improve in the future as the industrialization drive levels off and more resources can be devoted to this area. At the same time, the bureaucratic and centralized nature of the medical system has the general problems of such structures: red tape, inertia, some loss of individual motivation and initiative, depersonalization of services, the avoidance of personal responsibility, heavy administrative overheads, and the "formal" fulfillment of orders and directives. Yet the total balance is undoubtedly a positive one and represents one of the most impressive achievements of the regime and the health authorities. The Soviet MS provides a realistic and workable solution to the provision of medical services to the Soviet population.

BIBLIOGRAPHY: Henry E. Sigerist, *Medicine and Health in the Soviet Union*, New York, 1947; Mark G. Field, *Doctor and Patient in Soviet Russia*, Cambridge, 1957; *Health Service in the USSR*, World Service Organization, Geneva, 1960. M. G. F.

MEDICINE AND MEDICAL SCIENCE. Before the Revolution. For centuries, Russian medicine was primitive and folk medicine, an amalgam of empirical knowledge, magic rituals and religious beliefs. Historically the origins of M in Russia can be traced as far back as the 11th and 12th centuries when physicians first made their appearance in Kievan Russia. They came mostly from the east (Byzantium, Syria, Armenia). At that time the care and support of the sick and the destitute were mostly the responsibility of the churches, which sometimes maintained asylums or hostels for them. The 13th and 14th centuries were the years of the Mongol domination over Russia, and no significant medical developments took place.

With the rise of Moscovy in the 15th century and the transfer of the center of government to Moscow, physicians began arriving from the west in Russia. Indeed, until the middle of the 18th century, the practice of M as well as medical research remained mostly in the hands of foreigners. As contacts between Russia and the West increased in the 16th and 17th centuries, more W. European physicians (mostly from England, Holland, Germany, and France) came to Moscow to serve the court and the tsar. They were well paid and if they did not dabble in politics could expect to return home wealthy men. The demand for physicians, and particularly surgeons, increased during the 17th century because of the growth of the army and the background of warfare in the south and in the drive toward the Baltic Sea. Many of the foreign regiments that served in Russia would not fight without surgeons. These surgeons were not, any more, the personal servants of the tsar or the court, but servants of the state hired to provide medical and surgical services to a designated group of individuals. The pattern of the employment of physicians as civil servants became established as a result of the growing needs of the state, and particularly the armed forces, and has remained the predominant pattern to this day.

In 1581 a private pharmacy to serve the needs of the Kremlin was established by an English apothecary, James Frencham. Another pharmacy was later built in town to serve the population (1672). Since drugs can, and often do, contain poison, a formal office was established in 1620 to control the work of the Kremlin pharmacy and particularly the importation of pharmaceuticals from abroad. This office, which was first known as the *Aptekarsky Prikaz* (Apothecary Board), soon outgrew its original mandate and became the central medical authority in Russia, thereby establishing another important pattern in Russian M: state direction, financing, administration, and centralization of medical services. The Board appointed physicians and surgeons to the army and outfitted field pharmacies. Foreign physicians presented their credentials to it, and later were examined by it. In 1654 the Board established a school to train *lekars* (a *lekar* or "treater" was the equivalent to the barber-surgeon in the west who treated patients but knew very little M; a doctor, by contrast, knew M but did not usually treat patients). These *lekars* trained from 4 to 6 years and then served in the army. This school, however, existed only for a short period of time. Military hospitals began functioning in 1656 in Smolensk and in 1678 in Moscow. The Apothecary Board became the Apothecary Chancellery in 1707, was moved to St. Petersburg in 1712, renamed the *Medical* Chancellery in 1725 and the Medical Collegium in 1763.

Peter the Great's efforts to modernize and westernize Russia also bore fruit in the development of science in general and medical science in particular. For example, in the military (1716) and naval (1720) rules, and in the regulations of 1721–22 there are many references to the need to maintain and strengthen the health of the men and the necessity to provide medical personnel for this purpose. In 1692 Peter sent a young Russian named Posnikov to Padua and another one, Volkov, in 1698. They were the first Russians to go abroad to study M.

In 1707 a military general hospital, patterned after the Greenwich Hospital in England, was opened in Moscow. The term "general" meant that a medical school was attached to the hospital. Dr. N. Bidloo directed the training of students in medicine and surgery. Similar hospitals (with medical schools) began operating in St. Petersburg (1719) and Kronstadt (1720) for the navy, and in 1733 for the army (also in St. Petersburg). The schools were called at first "hospital schools" and later "medico-surgical schools."

In 1721 a licensing system began in Russia; the state reserved to itself the right to determine who had the competence to practice M; in addition, since in most cases the state paid the physician, it wanted to know what the physicians did.

Peter the Great laid the foundation for scientific work by importing scientists, books, collections from Europe including many relating to M, and by suggesting the foundation of an Academy of Sciences. The Academy, which began its work shortly after Peter's death, had a physician, Lorenz Blumentroost, as its first president and in the years that followed, many distinguished medical men were among its members: Duvernoi, Gmelin, Weibrecht, Schreiber, Amman, Kaau-Boerhaave, Hebenstreit, Gorter, Pallas, and others. The mass importation of scientists of all types placed Russia in the 18th century on an equal footing with the rest of Europe in scientific achievements: the history of Russian M then became part of the history of European M.

Another important milestone was the founding of Moscow University in 1755 and of a medical faculty at the university in 1764. The first *academic* medical degree was granted in 1794 to F. I. Barsuk-Moiseyev. Prior to that time, the right to bestow such a degree in M was reserved to the Medical Chancellery or Collegium. M. V. Lomonosov, on whose initiative the university had been founded, took great interest in the medical situation in Russia, in increasing the number of medical students, and in measures that would foster the health of the population. He greatly influenced S. G. Zybelin (1735–1802) who taught therapeutics, pediatrics, and hygiene; N. M. Ambodik-Maksimovich (1744–1812) who taught obstetrics; the epidemiologist D. S. Samoilovich (1745–1805); the surgeons K. I. Shchepin and A. M. Skumliansky who in 1788 wrote a thesis on the structure of the kidneys. In 1798 a Medical-Surgical Academy was founded in St. Petersburg with a branch in Moscow. New universities and medical schools (faculties) were founded in Yuryev (Dorpat, now Tartu) in 1802, in Kazan (1804), Kharkov (1805), and Kiev (1834). In 1775 as part of measures introduced to strengthen local governments, boards of social assistance were established; their jurisdiction embraced all charitable and medical institutions. The position of *uyezdny* (district) physician was also instituted, and in 1797 there were medical departments in all provincial towns and district medical administrations to provide some modicum of medical assistance to the needy population.

At the beginning of the 19th century, there were 1,519 physicians instead of 150 a century before. In 1803 the Medical Collegium was replaced by the Medical Department of the Ministry of Internal Affairs and remained in charge of medical matters until tsarism fell. At the same time, some ministries and administrations had their medical institutions catering to the medical needs of their own personnel. As such Russia did not have a central planning and coordinating medical system for the nation.

Russian M came of age in the 19th century, as the result of the general flowering of cultural and scientific life that followed the Napoleonic war and increased contact with the West. Medical students and physicians who wanted to complete special studies, postgraduate work, or do research often went abroad, particularly to Germany, Austria, and to a lesser degree France. Physiology attracted many R. students, the better known being I. M. Sechenov (1829–1905) who is usually credited with having started the R. physiological school. Sechenov studied under von Helmholtz, Müller, Du Bois-Reymond, and Ludwig in Germany, and Claude Bernard in France and was thus influenced both by the mechanistic, materialistic approach of the so-called German school and by the deterministic outlook of the French school. His work on the central nervous system has become classic, and laid the foundation for further work by A. Danilevsky (1838–1923), N. Ye. Vvedensky (1852–1922), A. Ukhtomsky (1875–1942), and I. P. Pavlov (1849–1936).

Sechenov's work on central neural inhibition contributed to the development of the Pavlovian concepts of the conditioned reflex and of higher nervous activity in the behavior of the whole organism. Pavlov's work had actually begun with Botkin's concept of "nervism" which stressed the management of all processes of the body by the central nervous system and the means whereby the animal and man adapt effectively to their environment. The first half of Pavlov's career was devoted to work on the digestive glands, for which he received the Nobel Prize in medicine in 1904. An extension of his work by a study of psychic secretion led to the development of objective conditioned reflex methods for the study of the activities of the cerebral hemispheres, for which he is best known. In Pavlov's ultimate formulation, the unconditioned reflex served the organism's adaptation to its environment in phylogeny, whereas the conditioned reflex played this role in ontogenetic development.

Another important figure in M of the 19th century was N. I. Pirogov (1810–81), the first great Russian physician and military surgeon. He pioneered the use of anesthesia on a large scale on the battlefield, the use of plaster of Paris for the fixation of fractures, and measures against wound infection. He founded the first anatomical institute at the St. Petersburg Military Medical Academy and it is largely due to his efforts that the Academy became the best medical school in Russia.

In clinical M, the outstanding person was S. P. Botkin (1832–89) who in contrast to the anatomical orientation of his day laid the foundation for an experimental, physiological orientation in clinical practice. At the basis of an understanding of the concept of disease he placed not only morphological changes but also and primarily functional changes with particular attention to disturbances of nervous activity.

Botkin had many students and influenced the course of clinical M in Russia. Other outstanding representatives of clinical M were G. A. Zakharin (1829–97), and A. A. Ostroumov (1844–1908) who was particularly interested in the importance of the milieu in the etiology of illness and its treatment and who, just like Botkin, tried to bring the university clinic closer to the ordinary hospital and the hospital closer to the outpatient clinic.

In psychiatry, S. S. Korsakov (1853–1900) investigated the mental symptoms of alcoholic polyneuritis and described the symptom now known as Korsakov's psychosis. He is considered a pioneer in organic psychiatry and contributed greatly to the treatment of the mentally ill by introducing a system of nonrestraint in 1881. Another important figure in psychiatry was V. M. Bekhterev (1857-1927) who did voluminous research in such fields as neuroanatomy, reflexology, and psychiatry.

In microbiology and immunology, the work of I. I. Mechnikov (1845–1916) is world renowned. In 1888 he had to leave Russia because of political pressures and it was at the Pasteur Institute that he made his great contributions for which he also received a Nobel Prize in medicine. Other important figures in microbiology and immunology were L. S. Tsenkovsky (1822–77), N. F. Gamaleya (1859–1949), G. N. Gabrichevsky (1860–1907), and D. K. Zabolotny (1866–1929). D. I. Ivanovsky (1864–1920) and Gamaleya are credited with the discovery of viruses.

Some of the most significant developments in Russian M and medical organization in the 19th century were the medical functions assumed by the zemstvos (q.v.) introduced in 1864. The zemstvo system inherited the medical institutions of the boards of assistance, a small and inadequate network of hospitals and asylums, the majority of which were in a dilapidated state. The zemstvo medical system grew unevenly since there was no over-all, nation-wide coordinated program applicable to the whole of Russia. Furthermore there were zemstvo assemblies in only 54 of the 89 provinces that made the Russian Empire. And yet zemstvo M made a very important contribution to social M. It was *public medicine* financed from tax contributions and with the physician cast in the role of a public salaried servant. At the same time, zemstvo M was a part of the populist movement of the 19th century and the zemstvo physician the prototype of the devoted and humanitarian professional intellectual who sacrificed personal comfort and financial gain to render service to the people. This conception of medical services removed, officially at least, the stigma of charity from medical care giving everyone a claim to medical attention as a service society "owes" the individual. The principle of "public practice" was therefore favorably regarded by physicians as part of a cultural tradition upheld by the most respected members of the prerevolutionary medical profession. By contrast, private M was often looked upon as a commercial practice unworthy of the high calling of physician.

Another aspect in the development of M and the medical profession in the 19th century was the formation of medical societies and the publication of medical journals. The Medico-Physical Society was formed in 1808 and had its journal. The Society of Russian Physicians in Moscow was founded in 1861 by F. I. Inozemtsev and published the *Moscow Medical Gazette*. The most important medical journal *Vrach* (Physician), founded by V. A. Manassein in 1880 (after 1902 *Russky Vrach* [Russian Physician]), was published until 1918. By far the most influential national medical association was the Society of Russian Physicians in memory of N. I. Pirogov, which in 1886 succeeded the Moscow-St. Petersburg Medical Society, founded in 1883. This society played a vigorous role in welding together the medical profession, in calling attention to the deplorable health situation of the population, particularly in the countryside, and in demanding reforms. These calls for change often went beyond the strictly medical framework and spilled over into the political arena.

By the end of 1913, there were about 24,000 physicians in the Russian Empire.

The Soviet Period. Intensive reorganization and expansion of the Soviet medical system took place after the assumption of power by the Bolsheviks (*see* MEDICAL SYSTEM). The first efforts of Soviet M were directed against the epidemics that were raging then in Russia, particularly typhus and influenza. In 1918 the first Soviet medical research institute was established by N. A. Semashko, the People's Commissar of Health (The State Research Institute of People's Health Protection). It was followed by institutes of tuberculosis, nutrition, biochemistry and others. In 1923 an Institute of Social Hygiene, of the Protection of Mother and Childhood, and of Professional Diseases (*Obukh Institute*) was founded. In 1926 the Institute of Blood Transfusion was formed. An important step in medical research was the formation in 1932, on the initiative of Maxim Gorky, of the All-Union Institute of Experimental Medicine based on the former Institute of Experimental Medicine in St. Petersburg. This institute served as the core of the future Academy of Medical Sciences that was founded in 1944. An important reason behind the formation of the Academy was the recognition, born of the experiences of the first three years of the war, that Soviet M suffered from deficiencies in medical technology, surgical instruments, and drugs. These deficiencies stemmed in large part from the isolation from the West and from ideological factors that affected M after the revolution. It was felt that a central institution directing, supervising, coordinating, and controlling the work of leading medical scientists and of medical research institutes would be the answer to these deficiencies. The Academy is a highly centralized medical research organization, in effect the research arm of the Health Ministry to which it is subordinate and from which it draws its administrative and financial support.

While the war opened up channels of communications between Soviet scientists and their colleagues, these channels were soon closed after the war and remained generally so until after Stalin's death. From 1955 there has been increased activity in exchanges of personnel and visits to and from the Soviet Union. Impressive Soviet achievements have also been re-corded in the translation and dissemination of western medical research materials.

Present Soviet medical and research efforts are directed at the elimination of infectious diseases (particularly influenza which leads in the incidence of illness), tuberculosis (which is still an important health problem), and the cardio-vascular diseases and cancer (whose importance increases as the proportion of older members in the population increases). Pavlov's work has been continued by his students, and generally serves as the theoretical base of Soviet medical research and practice.

Since Pavlov and Mechnikov received the Nobel Prize in medicine, no such prizes have been awarded to R. medical scientists to date.

BIBLIOGRAPHY: Fielding H. Garrison, "Russian Medicine under the Old Regime," *Bulletin of the New York Academy of Medicine*, 1931, vol. VII; W. Horsley Gantt, *History of Russian Medicine*, New York, 1937; Henry E. Sigerist, *Medicine and Public Health in the Soviet Union*, New York, 1947. M. G. F.

MEDNOGÓRSK, city in Orenburg Oblast, RSFSR; pop. 39,000 (1957). R.R. station; founded 1939 in connection with the development of copper smelting.

MEDVÉDEV, Sergéy (1885–?), joined the social-democratic movement in 1901. From 1903 a Bolshevik. Repeatedly arrested. In 1920 was elected chairman of the Metal Workers Trade Union. In the early 1920's M was one of the leaders of the Workers' Opposition (*see* OPPOSITION). In the 1930's M was arrested and disappeared.

MEDVÉDITSA RIVER, 430 mi. long, left tributary of the Don River, rises in Saratov Oblast, flows S.S.W. to the Don in Stalingrad Oblast; not navigable.

MEDVEZHYEGÓRSK, town in Karelian ASSR; pop. 13,300 (1956). R.R. station and harbor on N. shore of Lake Onega; has R.R. servicing-equipment plants, lumbering ind.

MÉKHLIS, Lev Zakhárovich (1889–1953), leading Bolshevik, colonel general; born in Odessa. He had been  a member of the Communist party since 1918; brigade and division commissar during the civil war of 1918–20. After 1921, he worked in the Workers' and Peasants' Inspection; later, in the administration of the Central Committee. After graduation from the Institute of Red Professors in 1930, he was a member of the editorial board of *Pravda*. In 1937, he became head of PURKKA (Political Administration of the Workers' and Peasants' Red Army); later (1940), head of the State Control, USSR. From 1938 to 1952, he was a member of the organizational bureau, Central Committee, CPSU. He also was an active organizer during World War II.

MELEKÉSS, city in Ulyanovsk Oblast, RSFSR; pop. 51,000 (1959). R.R. station; flour milling, flax and grain processing, foundry. Pedag. inst.

MELGUNÓV, Sergéy Petróvich (1879–1956), historian and journalist; born in Moscow. M graduated from the historical-philological faculty, Moscow University, 1904, and subsequently joined the university staff. His books include *Church and State in Russia* (1905–07) and *On the History of Religious Movements* *in Russia, 17th to 19th Centuries* (1919–22). From 1914 to 1922 he contributed to several collective works: *The Great Reforms, The Patriotic War of 1812, Serfdom* and *Masonry, Past and Present.* He also edited the historical review *Golos Proshlago* (Voice of the Past). During the civil war, M was arrested by the Bolsheviks. An exile after 1922, he wrote many books on the history of the revolution, including: *The Red Terror in Russia* (1926); *The Way Towards a Palace Revolution* (1931); *The Tragedy of Admiral Kolchak* (1930–31); and *How the Bolsheviks Seized Power* (1953). He was a leader of the moderate People's Socialist party. After World War II, he attempted to unite old and new members of the R. emigration.

MELITÓPOL, city in Zaporozhye Oblast, Ukrainian SSR, on Molochnaya River, on the main R.R. from Kharkov to Sevastopol; pop. 95,000 (1959). Ind.: metalworking, food processing, clothing, footwear, fishing.

MÉLNIKOV, Nikoláy Vasílyevich (1909–), mining engineer. Corresponding member, Ac. of S., USSR (1953). Graduate of Sverdlovsk Mining Institute (1933); professor, Academy of Coal Industry (1950–56); assistant director, Mining Institute, Ac. of S., USSR (1953). Developed new methods of mining technology, particularly open-pit mining. Stalin prize (1946).

MÉLNIKOV, Pável Ivánovich (pen name Andréy Pechérsky, 1818–1883), novelist who wrote about the Old-Believers and their settlements in the Volga region. His better-known novels are *In the Woods* (1868–74) and *On the Mountains* (1875–78). M published documents on the Schism (1860–63).

MÉMEL: *see* KLAIPEDA.

MENDELÉYEV, Dmítry Ivánovich (1834–1907), distinguished chemist; born in Tobolsk, Siberia. Well known for his periodic system on the basis of which he was able to predict the properties of then unknown elements. Corresponding member, Ac. of S. (1876) and honorary member of numerous Russian and foreign  scientific societies. Graduated in physics and mathematics, Main Pedagogical Institute in St. Petersburg. At Heidelberg (1859), he studied physical chemistry and discovered the existence of critical temperature points. Professor, St. Petersburg Institute of Applied Technology (1864). In compiling his periodic system of chemical elements M corrected the atomic weight of nine elements including beryllium, indium, uranium, thorium and cerium. In 1869, predicted the existence of four new elements and established their atomic weight. Research concerned viscosity, thermal expansion and capillarity of fluids, metrology, meteorology and air transportation; designed a differential barometer, initiated the development of agricultural chemistry, developed methods for the manufacture of smokeless gunpowder and other industrial processes. Author of numerous publications, including *The Principles of Chemistry* (1868–70), translated into English (1905). Soviet scientific societies, chemical schools, chemical congresses, and awards of the Ac. of S. bear his name.

BIBLIOGRAPHY: Daniel Q. Posin, *Mendeleyev: The Story of a Great Scientist,* New York, 1948.

MENGLÍ-GIRÉY, khan of Crimea from 1468 to 1514 (intermittently). He allied himself with Ivan III, Grand Duke of Moscow, against the Golden Horde and Lithuania.

MENSHEVIK TRIAL. Following a succession of trials for industrial sabotage, the MT took place in March 1931. A group of Mensheviks were accused of organizing a conspiracy to restore capitalism in the Soviet Union. Most of the accused (Sukhanov, Groman, Sher, Ikov, Rubin, Ginzburg) were economists, some of whom held high posts in Gosplan. The accused confessed to conspiring with Menshevik *émigrés* abroad, but there was no doubt in the western world that the "confessions" were extorted by the security police. The accused were sentenced to long prison terms. They may well have been executed, however, for none have ever been seen since.

MENSHEVISM. Democratic faction of Marxist socialism in Russia. Initiated as the result of a split at the Second Congress of the Russian Social Democratic Labor party, which opened in Brussels and was concluded in London (1903). At this Congress the followers of V. I. Lenin received a majority of the votes for the directing organs of the party, and hence were called Bolsheviks (from the Russian meaning "majority"). The opposing group, which was in the minority, came to be known as the Mensheviks ("minority").

Both the Mensheviks and Bolsheviks fought against the fundamental populist belief in an original R. socialism based on the peasant community. In accordance with prevailing Marxist doctrine, both emphasized the existence of objective social and economic conditions leading to the development in Russia of an industrial-capitalist economy. There were, however, deep-seated differences between them in their concepts of the role of the workers' party and their views of the structure of the party organization. The Mensheviks strongly opposed the Bolshevik emphasis on the predominant role to be played in the party by "professional revolutionaries" and the "active conscious minority," which, according to the Bolsheviks, must lead the proletarian masses to victory. Anticipating the development in Russia of an open democratic mass labor movement, the Mensheviks were opposed also to Lenin's concept of "organizational centralism." In their view, "organizational centralism," coupled with the necessity of working under conspiratorial conditions, presented the risk of placing direction of the party in the hands of a small disciplined group of power-hungry individuals and possibly divorcing the party from the wishes and needs of the working masses. This ideological split in the Russian Social Democratic Labor party became apparent during the discussion of Paragraph 1 of the party regulations, dealing with rules governing party membership; Lenin's followers wanted membership to be limited to individuals actively participating in party underground work.

The Mensheviks, headed by P. Akselrod, A. Potresov, V. Zasulich, L. Martov, and, later, G. Plekhanov, defended a broader concept of a proletarian socialist party, based on participation of all who shared the party's political ideas and cooperated in its activities.

The real impact and implications of these differences were not fully understood until later, but as time went on it became apparent that Menshevism was ideologically akin to the W. European social-democratic movement. While up to 1912 the Mensheviks continued to belong to the Russian Social Democratic Labor party (along with the Bolsheviks), already during the Russo-Japanese War (1904), and in the course of 1905, their political policy and strategy had all the characteristics of a distinct and separate political formation. The Mensheviks were opposed to the Bolshevik idea of a centrally directed preparation of the workers for an armed rebellion. While they, too, foresaw the possibility of a rebellious movement, their activities were essentially focused on the development, through organization and propaganda, of wider democratic structures both in the labor camp and outside it. They saw in the coming revolution a necessary phase of the historical development that would bring to political power the maturing R. capitalism. They believed that this period should be used for the education and organization of the workers to prepare them for the future fight for a socialist revolution under the freer conditions of a bourgeois-democratic regime.

In 1905 the St. Petersburg Soviet of Workers' Deputies was headed by Mensheviks. In the extensive debate concerning the projected Duma (Parliament), the Mensheviks defended participation in this limited representative body as an important step in the fight for democratization of the regime and as a forum for the expression of political opinions by broader strata of R. society. Among the leaders of social-democratic groups in the various Dumas were the Georgian Mensheviks I. Tsereteli, A. Japaridze, K. Chkheidze, and A. Chkhenkeli. Using opportunities created by the revolution, the Mensheviks initiated the establishment of a network of trade unions, cooperatives, cultural and publishing organizations, and so forth, without neglecting the illegal fight against tsarism.

The differences of view on the character of the war of 1914 and its consequences occasioned a split among the Mensheviks. One group, the *Oborontsy*, under Potresov, shared the patriotic "my country first" attitude of the majority of the various European socialist parties on both sides of the conflict. The second group, among whom were P. Akselrod and L. Martov abroad, and T. Dan and I. Tsereteli in Russia, represented the Menshevik internationalists who saw in the war the beginning of the coming socialist revolution. It participated in the Zimmerwald-Kienthal congresses and demanded an immediate ending of the war and the conclusion of peace "without annexations and indemnities." During the February 1917 revolution the Mensheviks played a leading role in both the coalition government and in the Soviet of Workers' and Soldiers' Deputies (I. Tsereteli, K. Chkheidze, M. Liber, T. Dan). With respect to the war, the Mensheviks demanded that pressure for peace be exerted by all democratic forces in all the belligerent countries and by concerted international action. They insisted, however, on respect for treaties and were faithful to Russia's allies.

After the October 1917 revolution and the begin-

ning of the Bolshevik terror, the Menshevik organization was persecuted, and Menshevik leaders were arrested. As, under these circumstances, the organization could not continue its publishing activities in Russia, in 1921 *Sotsialistichesky Vestnik* (Socialist Courier) began to appear in Berlin under the direction of L. Martov and R. Abramovich. It was later transferred to Paris and is now issued in New York.

BIBLIOGRAPHY: Donald W. Treadgold, *Lenin and His Rivals: The Struggle for Russia's Future, 1898–1906*, New York, 1955; Leopold H. Haimson, *The Russian Marxists and the Origin of Bolshevism*, Cambridge, Mass., 1955; Leonard Schapiro, *The Origin of the Communist Autocracy: Political Opposition in the Soviet State, First Phase 1917–1922*, Cambridge, Mass., 1955; Leonard Schapiro, *The Communist Party of the Soviet Union*, New York, 1959; John S. Reshetar, Jr., *A Concise History of the Communist Party of the Soviet Union*, New York, 1960.
L. SH.

MÉNSHIKOV, Prince Aleksándr Danílovich (1673–1729), closest associate of Peter I, general and statesman, commander in chief of the R. Army. He was the first governor of St. Petersburg (1703) and supervised the building of St. Petersburg and Kronstadt Fortress. Peter's factotum and an unscrupulous businessman; he fell into disgrace under Peter II and was exiled to Berezov (W. Siberia) in 1727.

MENZHÍNSKY, Vyacheslác Rudólfovich (1874–1934), head of the security police. Of Polish origin, M  was born in St. Petersburg. Well educated, M graduated in law at St. Petersburg University, and was well known in literary ("decadent") and revolutionary circles. He joined the social democrats in 1902, and was active during the 1905 revolution. The years 1907 to 1917 M spent in W. Europe. Belonged to the "Vpered" group. After the October revolution, M first was appointed people's commissar of finance, then sent as Soviet consul general to Berlin (1918). From 1919, M was head of the special department in the Soviet Intelligence Service and a member of the collegium of the Cheka, and later Dzerzhinsky's deputy. He succeeded the latter on his death in 1926 as chief of the OGPU, a post which he held until his own death, allegedly engineered by his deputy and successor, Yagoda.

MERETSKÓV, Kiríll Afanásyevich (1897–), marshal of the Soviet Union, born in a peasant family, Moscow Oblast. In 1918 he volunteered for the  Red Army; in 1921 graduated from the Red Army Military Academy, later from the Frunze Military Academy; has held several command and staff positions. He led troops in the Finnish invasion. Organized the breakthrough of the Mannerheim Line and was made Chief of Staff in 1941; later was replaced by Zhukov. In World War II he took active part in the defense of Leningrad; in 1945 M commanded the troops against Japan. He was named commander of the Moscow military district, 1946, and of the Northern military district in 1947. Several times he was deputy, USSR Supreme Soviet; until 1954 a member of the Central Committee, Karelo-Finnish CP; elected candidate member, Central Committee, CPSU, 1952; since

1955 deputy Defense Minister for higher military education. Member, Central Auditing Commission, CPSU. Chairman, Soviet Committee of War Veterans.

MEREZHKÓVSKY, Dmítry Sergéyevich (1865–1941), writer and critic. Together with his wife, the poetess Zinaida Hippius (q.v.), he became a member of The Religious and Philosophical Society in 1903. After his violent attack on the tsarist system during the revolution of 1905, M was forced to leave Russia and live in France, where he stayed until 1912. He returned to Russia and emigrated again after the Bolshevik Revolution. The rest of his life was spent in France.

M's historical views were expounded in his trilogy *Christ and Antichrist*: *Julian the Apostate* (or *The Death of the Gods*) (1896); *Leonardo da Vinci* (or *The Gods Reborn*) (1901); and *Peter and Alexis* (1905). M saw the goal of history in the synthesis of the Hellenic principle of the purity of the flesh and the Judeo-Christian principle of the purity of the spirit. Among his novels *Leonardo da Vinci*, with its ornate setting, enjoyed a measure of popularity. *Peter and Alexis*, however, is better written, although its theme strays from the basic idea of the trilogy. M also wrote a historical novel *Alexander I* and critical essays on Lermontov, Gogol, and Tyutchev. In an interesting essay *Tolstoy and Dostoyevsky* (1901–02), M characterized the former as "the great seer of the flesh" and the latter as "the great seer of the spirit." M's poetry is almost entirely forgotten, but his historical novels have been translated into foreign languages, and are still read.

MERKÚROV, Sergéy Dmítryevich (1881–1952), sculptor. Studied in the Polytechnical Institute in Kiev, at the University in Zurich, and at the Academy of Arts in Munich. His works: statues of Leo Tolstoy (1911–13), K. A. Timiryazev (1922–23), and V. I. Lenin (1939). Member of the Academy of Fine Arts (1947).

MERTSÁLOV, Nikoláy Ivánovich (1866–1948), mechanical engineer. Honored Scientist and Technologist, RSFSR (1944). Graduate of Moscow University (1888) and Moscow School of Technology (1894). Professor of engineering (1920) at the K. A. Timiryazev Agricultural Academy which became the Institute of Mechanization and Electrification of Agriculture (1930). Extensive research on thermodynamics, gyroscopes, and development of hydrodynamic theories of lubrication. One of the originators of theory of three-dimensional hinged mechanisms.

MERV: *see* MARY.

MESHCHÉRSKY, Iván Vsevolodovich (1859–1935), mechanical engineer. Graduate of St. Petersburg University (1882); professor, St. Petersburg Polytechnic Institute (1902). Research on mechanics of bodies with the variable mass as a scientific basis for the solution of problems of jet aircraft, celestial mechanics. Author of *Collection of Problems on Theoretical Mechanics* (1st ed., 1911; 24th ed., 1958).

METALLURGY. Metallurgical research is carried out by the following organizations: the Institute of Metallurgy of the Ac. of S., USSR; Institute of Ferrous Metallurgy, Ac. of S., Ukrainian SSR; Institute of Metals and Mining, Ac. of S., Georgian SSR; Institute of Metallurgy and Beneficiation, Ac. of S., Kazakh SSR; State Institute of Rare Metals; State Institute of Non-ferrous Metals; Institute of Metallurgy and Institute of Physics of Metals, Ural Branch of the Ac. of S., USSR; Ukrainian Institute of Metals (Kharkov); and others; as well as by various universities. Scientific investigations are devoted to the search for new production methods, treatment of metals and alloys, improvement of currently used technology and determination of laws governing the metallurgical processes.

In 1937, A. P. Afanasyev and L. Ya. Gabrielyan suggested the use of wet blast to increase the productivity of blast furnaces. B. I. Kitayev studied heat exchange processes in blast furnaces, I. P. Bardin, L. M. Tsylev and A. N. Rudneva slag formation, and I. P. Bardin, A. N. Ramm and M. A. Shapovalov coke combustion and oxygen-enrichment of the blast. The Leningrad Polytechnic Institute and Institute of Metallurgy of the Ac. of S., USSR, developed the essential principles of blast furnace melting under pressure originally suggested by P. M. Yesmansky in 1915. In 1957 over 50 blast furnaces producing about 70 per cent of Soviet cast iron were working at increased gas pressure. In 1932 I. V. Raspopov and others launched fluxed sinter production. By 1957, 70 mill. tons of sinter including 36 mill. tons of fluxed sinter were produced. At the suggestion of P. I. Kanavets in 1955 institutes of the Ac. of S., USSR, developed a method of strengthening iron ore concentrate pellets without calcination.

The First Five Year Plan marks the launching of experimental studies in the field of production of high-quality steels and ferroalloys as well as the use of large capacity open-hearth furnaces. In the 1930's the thorough study of physicochemical principles of steel smelting process was further amplified and was elaborated after World War II. The introduction of modern laboratory equipment resulted in the increased accuracy of industrial and laboratory analyses. By means of radioactive isotopes used in postwar years data were obtained showing the mechanism of melting of the charge and alloying elements and characterizing the hydrodynamics of the steel bath. The study of the basic reaction of the steel smelting process revealed that the concentration of oxygen in metal during the boil period is limited only by the carbon content. Modern methods of high-speed steel smelting with the introduction of gaseous oxygen are based on that study. The effect of nitrogen and hydrogen on the processes of steel smelting was investigated. These experiments and the data showing the effect of temperature and slag composition on the distribution of gases between slag and metal phases played an important part in improving steel quality in the USSR.

The publications of A. D. Kramarov, A. N. Morozov, A. I. Stroganov and others contain the theoretical and practical results of investigations of steel deoxidation processes.

In 1940, A. M. Samarin and L. M. Novikov developed a method of degassing molten steel by means of vacuum treatment either in the ladle before pouring or

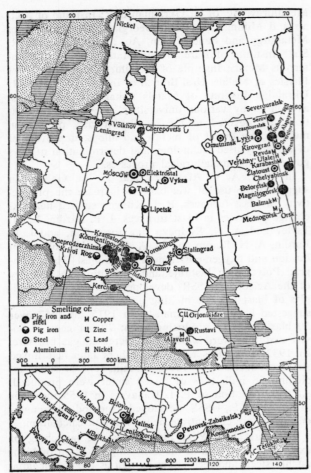

Main centers of ferrous and nonferrous metallurgy

Smelting of:
⦿ Pig iron and steel   M Copper
● Pig iron   Ц Zinc
◉ Steel   C Lead
A Aluminium   H Nickel

tion of alumina from bauxites and nephelines, and electrolysis of alumina in molten carnallite, have been developed. Conversion of carnallite into metal and chlorine is based on the investigation of magnesium production.

Soviet physical metallurgy dates back to the work of P. P. Anosov and D. K. Chernov. Toward the end of the 19th and in the beginning of the 20th century the work of N. S. Kurnakov and his numerous students and associates played an important role in the study of equilibrium diagrams. S. S. Shteynberg assumed a leading part in the study of phase transformations during heat treatment of steel, and of the mechanism and kinetics of these transformations. His followers studied the transformation in alloys during heating and cooling as well as temper brittleness. Many new heat treatment methods have been developed, including isothermal annealing, interrupted and isothermal quenching, continuous annealing, quenching resulting in minimal deformation, thermomagnetic treatment.

N. T. Gudtsov, N. A. Minkevich and others originated a theory of metal alloying. Systematic study of complex systems by A. A. Bochvar and associates made it possible to create several valuable light alloys. There were important achievements in creating alloys with special physical properties (magnetic, electric, thermal) as well as high-strength steels and cast irons, light alloys, stainless steels and alloys, heat and oxidation resistant alloys.

Soviet accomplishments in the field of metallurgy are epitomized in I. P. Bardin's *Metallurgy of the USSR 1917–1957* (1958); as well as in the periodical publications: *Mining Journal; Steel; Nonferrous Metals; Plant Laboratory; Coke and Chemistry; Physical Metallurgy and Heat Treatment of Metals; Physics and Physical Metallurgy; News of the Ac. of S. USSR*, Series of Technical Sciences (most of them available in English translations).   s. s.

FOUNDRY PRODUCTION. Russian foundry tradition is illustrated by such examples as "The King of the Cannons" (1586), and "The King of the Bells" (1735). Works of 19th and 20th century scientists (A. S. Lavrov, P. P. Anosov, D. K. Chernov, V. Ye. Grum-Grzhimaylo) laid the cornerstone of this tradition. By 1914 the total output of R. foundries was about 550,000 ton per year as against 12 mill. ton in 1957. In 1926 plans were made for an extensive development of foundry production. Old plants were modernized and new foundries built. At present, Soviet foundry production occupies a leading place in Europe. Such modern methods as chill mold, pressure-die, continuous, centrifugal shell mold, and investment casting are widely practiced.

MINING. Research in the field of mining is carried out at the mining institutes of the various branches of the Ac. of S. and at research institutes and mining colleges. The prevention of mine destruction under the action of rock pressure occupies an important place in this research.

The improvement of ore and coal mining productivity required the determination of qualitative and quantitative relationships between the main geological, technical and economical factors that affect mining methods. A theoretical substantiation of mine design led to the determination of rational parameters by means of mathematical analysis of functional relationships between technical and economical mining parameters.

Much attention is devoted to the decrease or elimination of underground labor and to open-pit mining (N. G. Dombrovsky and B. I. Satovsky). Investigations based on mechanization, automation and remote control of underground mining machinery are carried out by the following institutions: Donets Research Institute, State Experimental Institute of Design and Construction for the Coal-Machinery Industry and Kuznetsk Research Coal Institute.

Mechanized mining transport is the subject of special study.

Mining sanitation and safety engineering (A. A. Skochinsky) are a major field of study including ventilation (V. N. Voronin, V. B.

in the mold during pouring. At the same time, they proposed a method of steel pouring in a protective atmosphere (argon). Investigations of melting titanium ores were initiated in the 1930's. Various methods of titanium production were developed by G. G. Urazov, K. Kh. Tagirov, B. A. Borok.

Owing to the construction of numerous nonferrous metallurgical plants, extensive scientific research has been conducted in various fields of nonferrous metallurgy. Preliminary beneficiation of complex ores to obtain separate concentrates required prolonged studies in the field of flotation (V. Ya. Mostovich, S. M. Yasyukevich, I. N. Plaksin). Investigations of slags and matte determined the optimal conditions of pyrometallurgical conversion of copper and copper-nickel ores (V. Ya. Mostovich, N. P. Diev). Investigations of the deoxidation of metal oxides by carbon contributed to the technology of lead production as well as to the electrothermal method of lead, zinc, and tin smelting from ore concentrates (D. M. Chizhikov, G. I. Chufarov). Rationalization of calcination of sulfide concentrates in a fluidized bed called for a study of mechanism and kinetics of oxidation of sulfide minerals (D. M. Chizhikov, G. S. Frents, G. Ya. Leyzerovich). Nickel, cobalt and copper were produced from complex ores and electrolytically refined. Original technology of produc-

Komarov), air conditioning (A. F. Voropayev), and estimation of gas saturation in coal deposits (G. D. Lidin, I. M. Pechuk).

WELDING. A large-scale industrial application of welding dates back to the 1920's (V. P. Vologdin). The theory, technology and design of welding equipment are investigated at the Institute of Electric Welding, Ac. of S., Ukrainian SSR, the Central Research Institute of Technology and Machinery, the Bauman School of Technology in Moscow, the All-Union Research Institute of Welding Equipment and at various colleges and industrial plants. Properties of welding arcs, electric contacts and welding torches are subjects of investigation (K. K. Khrenov, V. P. Nikitin, A. A. Alekseyev, N. N. Klebanov). The laws governing heating and cooling processes during welding (N. N. Rykalin) and calculation methods for the selection of welding rates were established. Due to the work of the Institute of Electric Welding and its founder Ye. O. Paton, the Soviet Union has occupied a leading position in the field of submerged automatic arc welding techniques and electroslag welding.

METALS. Metals are classified in four groups: ferrous (*chornye*—"black"), nonferrous (*tsvetnye*—"colored"), precious, and rare and radioactive. Within each group they are arranged in alphabetical order.

FERROUS METALS

Chromite. The USSR has large deposits of high-grade C ores, reserves being estimated to be 25 to 30 mill. tons. The C deposits, concentrated in the southernmost section of the Urals and in W. Kazakhstan, are the most important; the Kempyrsay deposits in W. Kazakhstan are also of great significance. The Sarany group of deposits in the Urals has been known for a long time; while the Khalilovo, S. Akkarga and Verblyuzhya Gora deposits were discovered later. Several large deposits of high-grade C ore were put in operation in Aktyubinsk Oblast just before World War II. Many small deposits are found in the Urals and in Transcaucasia.

Iron Ore. The Soviet Union claims to have enormous IO resources, allegedly the largest in the world, 40 per cent of the world reserves. Although the USSR has but limited quantities of top-grade ore, its resources are abundant, provided reasonable attention is given to ore-dressing technology. More than 50 per cent of the All-Union measured IO reserves lie in the Ukraine and Central Russia: the Krivoy Rog basin, the Kerch deposit, the Kursk magnetic anomaly, and the Belgorod iron-bearing area. About 16 per cent of the IO reserves are in the Urals and 18 per cent in Kazakhstan; around 10 per cent in Siberia and the Far East: in Krasnoyarsk Kray (the Low-Angara deposit and IO in Khakassia), the Angara-Ilim group, deposits in the S. part of the Yakut ASSR and Transbaykalia, the Khingan area. There are also deposits in N.W. Russia (the Kola Peninsula and the Karelian ASSR). Up to the present time the IO has come principally from the Urals and the Ukraine.

The IO is characterized by a diversity in quality and in properties for its industrial use. High-quality ores with metal content exceeding 46 per cent and requiring no dressing total more than 12 per cent of the measured reserves in the USSR. The largest part of the reserves (some 57 per cent) consist of rather easily dressed ores, including magnetites, with iron content exceeding 25–30 per cent, magnetite quartzites (25–33 per cent of iron), and titano-magnetites (16–30 per cent of iron). About 30 per cent of reserves consist of ores requiring the use of complicated methods of dressing.

The enormous reserves of IO in Krivoy Rog in the Ukraine come in the form of hematite and ferruginous quartzites, estimated at 51.3 bill. tons, constituting the basis for the development of Ukrainian metallurgy. IO deposits of the Kursk magnetic anomaly are in the form of magnetite and ferruginous quartzites. Reserves were estimated at about 200 bill. tons; but in 1957, as a result of exploration, there was a significant increase in measured reserves of the Belgorod iron-bearing area lying S. from the Kursk magnetic anomaly. This is believed to be one of the world's largest deposits of high-grade IO. Ores of sedimentary origin are found in the vicinity of Tula, Lipetsk, in the basin of the Khoper River, and in the Omutninsk rayon of Kirov Oblast. The Kerch Peninsula in the Crimea abounds in limonite of marine origin, the ore reserves being estimated at over 2.7 bill. tons. The Urals constitute an exceptionally rich depository of various IO. In the mountains Magnitnaya (485 mill. tons), Vysokaya, and Blagodat are found important deposits of magnetite; at Bakal, siderite IO (over 176 mill. tons); and in the Komarovo-Zigazinsky group of deposits ore in the form of limonite (over 100 mill. tons). In the areas of Alapayevsk and Kamensk IO deposits are associated with the Jurassic and Cretaceous sedimentary rocks where the ore is in the form of limonites and siderites. In the S. Urals the IO in places contains chromium and nickel (Khalilovo). In Transcaucasia, the Dashkesan magnetite deposit is located in the Kirovabad area. In Kazakhstan, in addition to the Kustanay Oblast, there are several important deposits of magnetite which have served as the basis for the development of metallurgy in the Karaganda area. S. of the Kuznetsk basin in the region of Gornaya Shoriya (in the Altay) and in the Khakassia lie several deposits of magnetite used by the Kuznetsk steel works. Considerable reserves of magnetite ores, partly borax-bearing, were discovered and explored in S. Yakutia, a location close to coking coal of the Aldan Basin which favors the development of metallurgy in this area. High-grade magnetite ores are found within the E. Siberian platform in the basin of the Ilim River (an Angara tributary) and in other areas. The Angara-Ilim group contains more than 400 mill. tons of IO. Magnetite ores, partly borax-bearing, as well as deposits of siderite and limonite, were discovered in Transbaykalia; in the Far East, ferruginous quartzites have been found in the region of the Little Khingan Mountains. Recently a new large deposit of magnetite ores was explored (Garinsky deposit). (*See also* IRON AND STEEL INDUSTRY, METALLURGY, MINING.)

Manganese. The USSR claims to be the world's largest producer of M and to have the largest reserves, totaling in 1938 786 mill. metric tons, including 230 mill. metric tons of measured reserves. About 93 per cent of the total reserves are ascribed to two deposit groups: Nikopol in the Ukraine and Chiatura in Georgia, both containing high-grade ores. M-ore deposits occur also in the Urals, W. Siberia, and Kazakhstan. (*See* MANGANESE PRODUCTION.)

NONFERROUS METALS

Aluminum. Bauxite is the most important raw material for the production of A. The first deposit of bauxites was discovered in the USSR in 1917: the Tikhvin, which became a basis for the development of the A industry. Then bauxite deposits were discovered and explored in many areas, including the Urals, Kazakhstan, the Ukraine, E. and W. Siberia. Soviet sources claim that the USSR has the world's largest measured bauxite deposits. W. specialists estimate that in 1942 these reserves totaled 41.4 mill. metric tons, containing 10.0–10.7 mill. metric tons of A. All the Soviet bauxite deposits are associated with sedimentary rocks of different age, the largest being vast beds of marine origin, such as the Petropavlovsk belt of deposits in the N. Urals.

In addition to bauxites, nepheline ores are important for the A industry. These ores are found in the complex apatite-nepheline rocks of the Kola Peninsula; nepheline syenites, in Krasnoyarsk Kray and in Armenia. Alunites occur in Azerbaijan and Kazakhstan. (*See also* ALUMINUM INDUSTRY)

Antimony. The USSR has considerable reserves of A, exceeding 400,000 metric tons, according to data of 1953. The largest deposit is Kadamzhay in the Kirghiz SSR. Important deposits are also in the Tadzhik SSR, Krasnoyarsk Kray, the Kazakh SSR, and Transcaucasia.

Copper. The Soviet Union claims to have the world's largest measured reserves of C—probably totaling 18 to 20 mill. metric tons as of Jan. 1, 1948. A large part of these reserves consists, however, of very low-grade and refractory ores, as well as the C content of zinc ores, and the C output cannot meet the needs of the economy. Kazakhstan, the Urals, Central Asia, and the Caucasus are the principal C-bearing regions. The largest deposit, Dzhezkazgan in Kazakhstan, is a group of massive pyritic replacement bodies in Carboniferous sandstones. The Kounrad deposit in Central Kazakhstan is a source of raw material for the Balkhash C refinery; several other significant deposits are found in Kazakhstan. The oldest region of C production, the Urals, is still very important. These deposits are almost all associated with volcanic deposits of Silurian and Devonian age, chalcopyrite being the most common ore. Deposits stretch in two strips along the E. slope of the Urals. Polymetallic deposits of Rudny Altay also contain considerable amounts of C. The Almalyk group of deposits in Uzbekistan is of importance; the Transcaucasian deposits have been known for a long time. A considerable amount of C is found at the Norilsk copper-nickel-platinum deposit (N. of Krasnoyarsk Kray) and a large deposit of C-bearing sandstones was recently discovered at Chita, in E. Siberia.

Lead and Zinc. Soviet sources claim that the USSR has the world's largest L reserves; but the estimates by W. specialists are much more moderate. The reserves of 1947 were estimated at 3.5 mill. metric tons of content. The principal L-bearing areas are in Kazakhstan and Central Asiatic republics. L comes in the form of complex ores containing zinc, copper, gold, silver, and some rare elements, Ridder in Altay and Sadon in N. Caucasus being well-known deposits of complex ores. Soviet Z resources, which are largely concentrated in the Kazakh SSR, the Urals, and W. Siberia, are small.

Most Z deposits are associated with L, some with copper.

Mercury. The USSR has considerable reserves of M which are well in excess of 20,000 metric tons. Nikitovka in the Ukraine has been mined since 1878. After the Revolution, the Khaydarkan deposit in the Kirghiz SSR was discovered and explored; other deposits were discovered in the W. Ukraine, the Caucasus, Central Asia, the Altay, and Kamchatka.

Molybdenum. Although Soviet sources claim large reserves of M, the USSR has imported considerable amounts of this metal. The principal M-bearing areas are Transcaucasia, the N. Caucasus, Central Kazakhstan, Krasnoyarsk Kray, and Transbaykalia. In 1940, 90 per cent of measured and 70 per cent of the total M reserves were ascribed to Tyrny-Auz in the N. Caucasus. In many deposits, for example, at Kounrad (Kazakhstan), M is contained in copper ores.

Nickel and Cobalt. Soviet sources claim that the USSR is among the countries having the largest reserves of N and C. As of 1948, Soviet N reserves totaled about 1,300,000 metric tons of content, 25–30 per cent being ascribed to the Petsamo and Monchegorsk deposits on the Kola Peninsula and in N. Russia. The Norilsk deposit in Krasnoyarsk Kray is the largest in the USSR; the ore contains also copper, cobalt, and platinum. There are N reserves also in the S. Urals and in N.E. Kazakhstan. C production has been a postwar phenomenon linked to the rise of the N industry, the Soviets having based their output on by-products from N deposits. The reserves of C are estimated (1953) at some 25,000 metric tons of content. The largest sources of C appear to be the nickel-silicate deposits of N.W. Kazakhstan and of the S. Urals. There are also several deposits of proper C ores, of which the Khovu-Aksinsk in the Tuva Autonomous Oblast and Elizavetinskoye in the Urals are of the greatest importance.

Titanium. Soviet sources claimed in 1939 that the T reserves were at least 10.2 mill. metric tons. Deposits of T ores of different genesis are found in several regions. The economically most important titano-magnetite ores are associated with gabbro-intrusions in the Urals and in the Karelian ASSR. Recently T-bearing minerals, rutile and ilmenite, were discovered in placers in the Ukraine, W. Kazakhstan, and other areas.

Tin. There was no production of T in the USSR before 1926; then deposits of T ores were discovered and explored. These deposits may be divided into pegmatic, hydrothermal, and placer types. In 1953, T reserves were estimated to be over 100,000 metric tons of metal content. Principal deposits are found in E. Siberia and the Far East: in the Yakut ASSR, Magadan and Chita oblasts, in Maritime and Khabarovsk krays. Since the major deposits are located in remote areas, operating conditions are difficult.

Tungsten (Wolfram). Soviet sources claim that the USSR has the world's largest measured deposits of T, but many data indicate that it has been a heavy importer of T. In 1940, reserves were estimated to equal 40,000 metric tons. The principal T-bearing areas are: Central Kazakhstan, the N. Caucasus, Central Asia, the Buryat ASSR, and others. The T ores come mostly in quartz-wolframite veins, as in deposits of Transbaykalia, Kolyma, and Kazakhstan, or in sheelite ores in skarns, as in the Tyrny-Auz deposit in the N. Caucasus, in deposits of Central Asia and Siberia.

PRECIOUS METALS

Gold. Official statistics on the production of G have long been withheld, but it is clear that Soviet reserves are large. G deposits of economic importance are in E. areas of the USSR: the Urals, Kazakhstan, E. Siberia, and the Far East; while the most important G fields lie in the Upper Lena and Kolyma regions. G comes in lodes and placers and is also produced from polymetallic deposits, especially in Kazakhstan.

Silver. No data are available on Soviet S reserves which are rather extensive. S is produced mostly from polymetallic ores (zinc, tin, and silver) and from chalcopyrite. The main regions of S-bearing ores are Altay, the Urals, Central Asia, the Caucasus, and Siberia.

Platinum Metals. The USSR is among the world's largest producers of P and platinoids (Osmium, Iridium, Palladium) which have been continuously exported. For a long time the only area of P production was the Urals, where it is derived from ultrabasic and basic rocks and placers. Since the 1930's it has also come from Norilsk (Krasnoyarsk Kray) where it is associated with nickel deposits. Some P has been recovered as a by-product of gold-mining operations in E. Siberia.

RARE AND RADIOACTIVE METALS

Beryllium. B deposits are associated with granitic pegmatites. The most important is in the Urals, at the great emerald mines in *Izumrudnye Kopi;* another significant deposit is in the Transbaykal region, and some are in E. Siberia, the Altay, and the Pamirs.

Niobium (Columbium) and Tantalum. The production of these metals began only within the past two decades, and there are no statistics on Soviet reserves. The most important deposit is Lovozero on the Kola Peninsula; another is in the Urals.

Radioactive Minerals: Uranium and Radium. Authentic data on Soviet U output and reserves are lacking. There are low-grade but possibly extensive uranium-vanadium deposits in the Fergana Valley in Central Asia, and very small but good betafite deposits in the area of Lake Baykal and in other regions N.E. to the Aldan shield. In addition to extraction from U ores, radioactive waters at Ukhta in N. Russia provide a source of R.

Vanadium. At least until 1944–45 the USSR depended overwhelmingly upon imports and stockpiles for ferrovanadium, essential for manufacturing high-speed tool steels. At home, the V concentrate was produced from the Kerch iron ore and from the Ural titano-magnetites. In recent years Soviet V supplies have increased because of the discovery of a vanadium-mica deposit in Kazakhstan.

Zirconium. Not until 1946 were deposits of Z mentioned. It is produced in the Mariupol area in the Ukraine, in the Urals, and in the Far East.

BIBLIOGRAPHY: Demitri B. Shimkin, *Minerals, a Key to Soviet Power,* Cambridge, 1953.

L. D.

MEY, Lev Aleksándrovich (1822–1862), poet and dramatist known for his two historical poems *The Tsar's Bride* (1849) and *The Maiden from Pskov* (1860). Both were used as libretti for the operas of Rimsky-Korsakov. Many of M's lyrics were put to music by Tchaikovsky, Musorgsky, and Borodin. He is also known for his translations of Anacreon, Byron, and other authors.

MEYERHÓLD, Vsévolod Emílyevich (1874–1942), highly influential avant-garde director. In 1896 he transferred from the university to the Moscow Philharmonic Dramatic School, and two years later his teacher, Vladimir I. Nemirovich-Danchenko, invited him to join the newly organized group of MKhT (Moscow Art Thea-ter). During the years 1906 and 1907 he worked in the St. Petersburg theater of the noted actress V. F. Kommissarzhevskaya, producing symbolist plays and attempting to bring to fruition his concept of "conditional" theater. Astounding the public with the extravagance of his productions, M at the same time deprived actors of their independence, turning them into marionettes to be manipulated by the director. After his break with Kommissarzhevskaya, M became director of the St. Petersburg imperial theaters of drama and opera, staging highly stylized productions (e.g., Molière's *Don Juan* and Lermontov's *Masquerade*). After the October revolution, M joined the Communist party and stood at the vanguard of the "theatrical October." Daringly experimental and possessing remarkable inventiveness with scenic forms, M was fascinated first by constructivism and then by "biomechanics," a system of special physical training for actors; he injected into the dramatic theater elements of revue, circus, and cinema as well as unusual interpretations of plays by the classical writers in which he made his own additions and changes in the scripts. M is particularly noted for the strongly satirical tone of his productions (e.g., in the plays of Mayakovsky), the ruthlessness of his grotesques and the hyperbole of his mask images. M's productions frequently gave rise to arguments and scandals. By the mid-1930's he began to be accused of formalism; conflict increased between him and the Soviet leadership, culminating in the destruction of his theater and his own arrest in 1939. He died in a concentration camp. The influence of M—a paradoxical personality, but indisputably a director of the highest gifts—is felt beyond the borders of the USSR.

P. E. YE.

MEZÉN RIVER, in Komi ASSR, about 565 mi. long; rises in the S.W. slopes of Timan ridge, flows through central Archangel Oblast into Gulf of Mezen, an arm of the White Sea; navigable in its lower course.

MEZHDURÉCHENSK, city in Kemerovo Oblast, RSFSR; pop. 55,000 (1959). R.R. station; center of major Tom-Usa coal deposits. Founded 1955.

MEZHRAYÓNTSY, a group of Russian Social Democrats, who tried to unite the different factions into one party. Their leaders were L. Trotsky, D. Ryazanov, A. Lunacharsky, and S. Uritsky. First organized in 1913, they succeeded in building up a strong organization which was influential with the workers of St. Petersburg and Moscow. The M carried propaganda in the armed forces and fought against the War Industries Committee. In 1917 they gradually established closer relations with the Bolsheviks and in August of the same year joined the CP.

MGB: *see* SECURITY POLICE.

MIÁSS, city in Chelyabinsk Oblast, RSFSR, on Miass River; pop. 38,000 (1939), 99,000 (1959). Has an automobile plant (built 1944), tool mfg., rich mineral and gold deposits in the vicinity.

MICHAEL (Mikhaíl Fyódorovich (1596–1645), first tsar of the Romanov dynasty, son of the Patriarch Filaret. Was elected tsar by a *zemsky sobor* (q.v.) in Feb. 1613 at the end of the "Time of Troubles." M was a man of limited ability, who was guided by his father. Under his rule, order was gradually restored. At the same time, serfdom was strengthened. At the beginning of the reign the *zemsky sobor* met frequently; however, it did not develop beyond the status of a consultative assembly.

MICHÚRIN, Iván Vladímirovich (1855–1935), biologist and horticulturist. Honorary member, Ac. of S.,

USSR (1935); member, Ac. of Agricultural S. and Forestry (1935). Honored Scientist and Technologist, RSFSR (1934). Started horticultural experiments while working as an office clerk at Kozlov (1872) (renamed Michurinsk in 1932). Founder (1875) and director (1918) of a nursery which was expanded to include a horticultural experimental institute, a research laboratory, and other scientific institutions (1928). M made a name for himself by experimental grafting which resulted in the production of superior fruit trees. He produced over 300 new types of fruit trees and berries in support of his theory that hereditary changes can be artificially induced and subsequently inherited. The theory was elaborated by T. D. Lysenko. The Soviet government outlawed the teachings of Mendel (1948), replacing it by what was termed "Michurin Science" (*Michurinism*) and lending it an official status. All agricultural and genetic research was subjugated to M's ideas. However, his research and results, summed up in his *Selected Works* (4 vols., 1948), have been questioned by western scholars.

MICHÚRINSK (f. Kozlov), city in Tambov Oblast, RSFSR, on the Voronezh River; pop. 80,000 (1959). R.R. junction point. It has a large horticultural station and the Michurin Research Institute; locomotive mfg., metalworking, automobile-repair, and textile plants; experimental distillery. Founded 1636 as a frontier fort against the Crimean Tatars, it was renamed in 1932 after I. V. Michurin, who lived there.

MICROBIOLOGY: *see* BIOLOGICAL SCIENCES.

MIKHÁYLOV, Aleksándr Aleksándrovich (1888–), astronomer. Corresponding member, Ac. of S., USSR (1943). Graduate (1911), professor (1918–50), Moscow University. Chairman, Astronomical Council (1918–50), Moscow University. Chairman, Astronomical Council (1939), and director, Pulkovo Astronomical Observatory (1947). Vice president, International Astronomical Council (1946–48). Advanced a theory of solar and lunar eclipses and compiled calculation charts; developed a method of determining the shape of the earth. Led five expeditions for the observation of total solar eclipses. Initiated a general gravimetrical survey of the USSR (1932). On the editorial board of *Bolshaya Sovetskaya Entsiklopedia* (Large Soviet Encyclopedia) and the *Journal of Astronomy*.

MIKHÁYLOV, Aleksándr Dmítrievich (1855–1884), Russian revolutionary, one of the founders of the party "Land and Freedom." Eventually he joined the party "People's Will" and participated in terrorist acts. He was sentenced to death in 1882, but the sentence was commuted to life imprisonment and he died in the Peter and Paul Fortress.

MIKHÁYLOV, Nikoláy Aleksándrovich (1906–), communist leader. Member of the CPSU (1930) and Secretary of the Central Committee (1952). Deputy to the Supreme Soviet (1950). First Secretary of the Komsomol (1938–52). On the editorial board of *Pravda* and *Komsomolskaya Pravda*. Ambassador to Poland (1954). Minister of Culture (1955). Order of Lenin (1956). Order of the Great War for the Defense of the Fatherland.

MIKHÁYLOV, Timoféy Mikháylovich (1859–1881), revolutionary, member of the party "Land and Freedom." He was executed in April 1881 together with Zhelyabov, Perovskaya, Kibalchich and Rysakov for participation in the assassination of Alexander II.

MIKHAYLÓVSKY, Nikoláy Konstantínovich (1842–1904), radical journalist, philosopher, sociologist, and literary critic. Born near Kaluga into a family of lesser gentry, M received the education of a mining engineer, but chose to devote his life to writing for radical journals especially *Otechestvennya Zapiski* (Notes of the Fatherland) (1868–84) and *Rus-*

skoye Bogatstvo (Russian Wealth) (from 1892). Political moderation and luck enabled him, alone among the important radicals who rose in the 1860's, to live and publish legally in European Russia through the end of the century, which added greatly to his influence. As a critic, M was important in introducing many European writers and thinkers to the R. public, notably Darwin and Marx. As a thinker, M was influenced by Belinsky, Proudhon, and Comte, and by his friends N. D. Nozhin and G. Z. Yeliseyev, but when he wrote his first and most important book, *What is Progress?* (1869–70), he had already formulated the chief elements of the doctrine he later called "critical populism." He believed neither in a god nor in atomic materialism, and opposed all deterministic philosophies. He insisted that the center of all philosophical, historical, and political concern should be the human individual, whose growth should be fostered until he becomes an "integral personality," a super-Michaelangelo who fulfills all the potentialities of life. M divided history into three stages in which technology became more complex while human beings, fragmented by increasing division of labor, became more oppressed by giant systems such as Christianity, the tsarist state, and European capitalism. Only the R. peasant, he asserted, retained in many ways the older, more well-rounded way of life, and only the R. village commune might serve as a model for the future, small-scale, democratic, socialist communities after the passing of tsarism and capitalism. Although a radical, M usually opposed terrorist activity to overthrow the regime. In his last decade, he spent much time controverting R. Marxists. His influence survived chiefly among the Socialist Revolutionaries, especially V. M. Chernov.

BIBLIOGRAPHY: J. H. Billington, *Mikhaylovsky and Russian Populism*, Oxford, 1958; T. G. Massaryk, *The Spirit of Russia*, London and New York, 1955.

MIKHÉYEV, Mikhaíl Aleksándrovich (1902–), heat power engineer. Fellow, Ac. of S., USSR (1953). Graduate, Leningrad Polytechnic Institute (1927). Associated with the Institute of Physics and Technology and the Steam Turbine Institute (1925–34), the Moscow Institute of Power Engineering (1936), and the Institute of Power Engineering, Ac. of S. (1953). Research concerns problems of heat transfer and thermal simulation. Author of *The Simulation of Heat Power Equipment* (1936) and of a textbook *Principles of Heat Transfer* (2nd ed., 1949). Stalin prizes (1951, 1951).

MIKHÓELS (Vovsi), **Solomón Mikháylovich** (1890–1948), gifted actor-director of the Jewish State Theater of the USSR (GOSET). Upon completion of his university education in 1919, M entered the Jewish Theatrical Studio of St. Petersburg which, merging with the Moscow Jewish Studio, soon grew into the model theater known as GOSET. A series of remarkable and original portrayals in the plays of Gutskov, Sholem Asch, Goldfaden, Sholom Aleichem, Peretz and other Jewish writers advanced M to the front ranks. After passing through several interesting expressionist and formalist phases which were condemned by party critics, M scaled the heights in his portrayal of the king in Shakespeare's *King Lear* in 1935. Stalin prize (1946).

As chairman of the Jewish Anti-Fascist Committee, M in 1942 participated in an appeal to the Jews of the world to aid the Red Army with financial contributions, medical and scientific aid. In May 1943, he led a delegation which visited the Jewish communities of England and America appealing for more assistance to the Red Army. The committee was dissolved in 1948. In January of that year, M was killed under mysterious circumstances. By mid-1949, the Moscow Jewish State Theater, the last remaining Yiddish theater in the Soviet Union, was closed.

MIKOYÁN, Anastás Ivánovich (1895–), member of the Presidium of the CPSU and first vice-chairman of the Council of Ministers of the USSR.  M was born near Tbilisi in a middle-class Armenian family. He studied at a theological seminary and joined the liberal Constitutional Democratic party while a student, then switched to the Bolsheviks in 1915. M was first politically active in Baku and Tbilisi, then moved on after 1920 to Nizhny-Nov-

gorod (now Gorky) and Moscow. He was elected to the party Central Committee in 1923 and became a candidate member of the Politburo in 1935. In 1926, he was made commissar for foreign and domestic trade and he has been actively associated with these fields almost constantly since then, directing the various trade commissariats or ministries, or supervising them as vice-chairman of the Council of Ministers without portfolio. M has acted as a sort of commercial foreign minister, representing the USSR in major foreign trade negotiations. Foreign negotiators have been impressed by his bargaining skill, his exact knowledge of detail, and his capacity to combine formal propriety with stubborn insistence on Soviet demands. The "stone-hard" communists, on the other hand, have sometimes suspected him of being too liberal and, by his own account, his career and even his life have been in jeopardy on occasion. He told the American writer, Louis Fischer, that he had come close to suicide during the 1930's and that his life was in danger in the last months before Stalin's death. M's speech to the 20th Party Congress was the sharpest and most passionate in denouncing the consequences of the so-called "personality cult" of Stalin. M has been a staunch follower of Khrushchev's political line and is known to have been one of the three Presidium members (with Suslov and Kirichenko) who supported Khrushchev against the majority in the "anti-party group" crisis of June 1957. M travels widely abroad; he visited the United States in 1959.

MIKOYÁN, Artém Ivánovich (1905–), aircraft designer. Major general. Corresponding member, Ac. of S.,  USSR (1953). Deputy to the Supreme Soviet, USSR (1950, 1954, 1958). Director and chief designer of the Experimental Design Bureau, Ministry of Aircraft Industry. Graduate of Zhukovsky Military Aircraft Academy (1936). In 1939–40 he designed (in cooperation with M. I. Gurevich) the single-seat high-altitude fighter MIG-1, which was modified and as a MIG-3 used extensively during World War II. In 1945, head of a team of Soviet engineers who studied wartime German jet aircraft designs in East Germany. Subsequently, studied jet technology in England and obtained blueprints of Rolls-Royce jet engines. A pioneer of jet aviation in USSR, M designed the first Soviet turbojet fighter MIG-9, as well as MIG-5, MIG-9A, MIG-11, MIG-15, MIG-17 and MIG-19 (with M. I. Gurevich). Has been working on supersonic jet fighters since 1954. Three Stalin prizes and other decorations.

MIKÚLIN, Aleksándr Aleksándrovich (1895–), aeronautical engineer. Fellow, Ac. of S., USSR (1943). Major General, Engineering and Technical Service. Hero of Socialist Labor (1940). Associated with the Scientific Institute of Automotive Engines (1932). Designed the 750 HP aircraft engine AM-34 used by the Soviet pilots Chkalov and Gromov for non-stop flights USSR-USA via the North Pole (1937), and another 1,200 HP engine for high-speed MIG-1 fighters. During World War II, M was in charge of designing AM-38 aircraft engines for IL-2 fighters. He developed the first Soviet turbocompressor and variable-pitch screw propeller. Since 1946 M directs the design of jet engines.

MILITARY OPPOSITION: *see* OPPOSITION.

MILLER, Gerard Friedrich (1705–1783), Russian historian of German extraction, was the originator of scientific historic research in R. primary sources. M was sent by the Ac. of S. to Siberia where he collected historical documents. He did not create an original historical school, but he has contributed to the advancement of R. historiography.

MILORÁDOVICH, Mikhaíl Andréyevich (1771–1825), general who fought in the war against Napoleon under Suvorov and Kutuzov. In the Borodino battle, M was in command of an army corps; during the R. counteroffensive in 1812, he was in charge of the avantguard of the main army. In 1818, he was appointed governor-general of St. Petersburg. He was fatally wounded by the insurgents during the Decembrist revolt.

MILYUKÓV, Paul Nikoláyevich (1859–1943), historian and leader of the Constitutional Democratic (Kadet) party. M studied history and the humanities at Moscow University. His dissertation for a higher degree, perhaps his most important book, was later published as *Financial Administration of Russia in the First Quarter of the 18th Century and the Reform of Peter the Great.* A lecturer at the Moscow University, he was dismissed in 1895 on political grounds. His *Studies in the History of Russian Culture* and *Chief Trends in Russian Historical Thought* appeared in the same year.

M spent the years 1902–04 in W. Europe and the United States, where he lectured on R. history. He was active in the Union of Liberation and on the review *Osvobozhdenye* (Liberation) edited by Pyotr Struve, and was a founder of the Constitutional Democratic party in 1905. His failure to satisfy the residence requirements of the electoral law prevented his seeking election to the first and second Dumas. He was not therefore among the signatories of the Vyborg appeal (1906) which led to the trial and disfranchisement of the other leaders of the Constitutional Democratic party. M was the principal Kadet spokesman in the third and fourth Dumas (1907–17), and an expert on foreign affairs.

With the outbreak of World War I, M advocated close cooperation with the Allies and war to a victorious end. He was a severe critic of the inefficiency of the imperial government in conducting the war. In Aug.-Sept. 1915 the Kadets joined a coalition of political parties known as the Progressive Bloc (q.v.) which called for the creation of a ministry enjoying public confidence. M nevertheless supported the institution of the monarchy and urged Grand Duke Michael to accept the crown after the abdication of Nicholas II (March 1917). M was minister of foreign affairs in the first Provisional Government under Prince Lvov.

M interpreted the February revolution as a protest against the tsarist regime's conduct of the war. He favored a continuation of the struggle against the Central Powers in order to achieve Russian annexation of Constantinople and the Straits, liberation of the Slavs under Hapsburg domination, and the absorption by Russia of the Ukrainian provinces of Austria-Hungary. This position brought him into conflict with the executive committee of the Soviet of Workers' Deputies and forced his resignation from the cabinet early in May 1917. Following the Bolshevik Revolution, M fled first to German-occupied Kiev and then to W. Europe. After a period in London, he settled in Paris, where he edited the daily *Poslednie Novosti* (Latest News) which became a forum for democratic anti-Bolshevik elements.

In exile, M published numerous works on history. Among them were: *A History of the Second Russian Revolution* (1921–23); *Russia's Catastrophe* (1927); and a revision of his earlier study on Russian culture (1930–37). During World War II M advocated support for the Soviet Union against Germany.

MILYÚTIN, Count Dmítry Aleksándrovich (1816–1912), field marshal and statesman. As minister of war (1861–81), he was responsible for the progressive shortening of the term of service in the armed forces and the introduction of the universal compulsory military service which was enacted in 1874. An ardent admirer of Suvorov and Kutuzov, M published numerous works on R. military history.

MILYÚTIN, Nikoláy Aleksándrovich (1818–1872), high official, statesman, assistant minister of the interior, 1859–61. A man of moderately liberal views, M was responsible for the reform of municipal government enacted in the 1840's, and took a prominent part in framing the emancipation acts of Feb. 19, 1861, which terminated serfdom. An ardent Russian nationalist, M was chairman of the Russian commission entrusted with the liquidation of the Polish uprising of 1863 and author of the statute of Feb. 19, 1864, which reorganized rural Poland and favored the Ukrainian peasants at the expense of the Polish landowners.

MILYÚTIN, Vladímir Pávlovich (1884–?), member of the Bolshevik party from 1910 and member of its Central Committee from 1917. After the February revolution, was elected member of the executive committee of the Soviet of Workers' and Soldiers' Deputies, and deputy chairman of the Petrograd Duma. He was people's commissar of agriculture in the first Soviet government. Subsequently, he held high positions in the economic apparatus and was elected deputy chairman of the Communist Academy. In 1928, he was appointed director of the Central Statistical office. Author of several works on economic problems, including *The New Period in World Economy, The Agrarian Policy of the USSR* and *The History of Economic Development of the USSR*. During the purges in the 1930's, M was arrested and disappeared.

MINERALOGY: *see* GEOLOGICAL SCIENCES.

MINERALS. Soviet resources of nonmetallic minerals are generally large, especially in andalusite, asbestos, bromine, fire clays, fluorspar, graphite, gypsum, kaolin, the micas, magnesite and dolomite, magnesium salts, phosphate rock, potassium and sodium salts. They are weak in borax, corundum, probably strontium, and high-grade talc. The Ukraine, the Urals, Central Asia, and E. Siberia have large and varied resources of non-metallic minerals. Many regions have not as yet been properly investigated.

Potassium. Soviet sources claim that the USSR has the world's largest measured reserves of P salts. The Solikamsk deposit discovered in 1925 is one of the world's largest accumulations of P salts, holding an estimated 18.5 bill. metric tons of K_2O content. Considerable reserves of P salts are found in the W. Ukraine on the N.E. slope of the Carpathians (the Kalush-Volynian and Stebnik deposits), totaling approximately 50 mill. metric tons of K_2O content. Large deposits of P salts were discovered in Byelorussia and near Aktyubinsk (Kazakhstan). There are also deposits in Central Asia, in Orenburg and Saratov oblasts, and in the Bashkir ASSR.

Salt (Sodium Chloride). The S reserves of the USSR aggregate many bill. of tons and may be considered inexhaustible. Deposits are found in many areas, with measured reserves totaling 37 bill. tons, and may be grouped into the following categories: rock salt, salt lakes, salt springs, brine wells, and salt basins associated with marine inlets. Large deposits have been known in the Ukraine for a long time. The Artemovsk rock-salt deposit and salt springs at Slavyansk, in the Donets basin, are associated with the Lower Permian S-bearing sediments. These deposits are a basis for the development of the soda industry. Another center of S production in the Ukraine is in the Transcarpathian Oblast. There are large reserves in Byelorussia; an important Verkhnekamsky deposit of rock S in Molotov Oblast; an important S dome at Iletsk in the Urals; and the Yar-Bishkadar and other deposits in the Bashkir ASSR. The vast Lena-Angara S basin containing large deposits of rock S and brines is located within Irkutsk Oblast; the Dus-Dag deposit is in the Tuva Autonomous Oblast. Considerable deposits of rock S are found in the Yakut ASSR. A S dome was discovered at Nordvik in the polar region of Siberia. A significant Nakhichevan rock-salt deposit is in Transcaucasia; other large deposits are also known in the Tadzhik, Uzbek, and Turkmen SSR. The most significant S lake is Lake Baskunchak in Astrakhan Oblast.

Gypsum and Anhydrite. Soviet reserves of these minerals are very large. There are some 300 deposits with measured reserves which, according to Soviet sources, in 1936 totaled 1.25 bill. metric tons. Numerous deposits are in the N. part of European Russia, in the Tadzhik SSR and in Krasnodar Kray, with many of economic importance in the Donets basin.

Glauber Salt. The largest deposit of natural sodium sulfate in the world is the Gulf of Kara-Bogaz-Gol at the E. coast of the Caspian Sea. This inlet acts as a natural evaporating basin drawing off the water of the Caspian Sea and depositing salt along its shores. In addition to sodium sulfate, the brines of Kara-Bogaz-Gol contain magnesium and bromine salts, as well as sodium chloride. Because of the GS deposits, a large chemical plant was constructed. Considerable reserves of sodium sulfate, magnesium salt, and sodium chloride are found also in salt lakes in the Aral Sea area.

Borax. The Inder group of deposits of B in Kazakhstan is the most important in the USSR. Its discovery in 1934 ended importation of B. Another deposit of importance is Klyuchevsko-Dmitrievskoye in the Transbaykal region of E. Siberia. Boron is also associated with oil fields.

Phosphate Rock and Apatite. The USSR has large reserves of these minerals, but their distribution is very irregular. P resources total at least 9 bill. metric tons, the measured reserves of 1957 being equal to 1.5 bill. tons. The Khibiny deposit of apatite-nepheline ores on the Kola Peninsula is the largest in the world, being associated with an intrusive massif of alkali rocks. The Khibiny mines supply ore to numerous factories producing superphosphates. In addition to A, the ore contains nepheline suitable for aluminum production, and also vanadium. Deposits of high-grade phosphates are concentrated in the Kazakh SSR comprising 54 per cent of Soviet reserves. In 1933–36, the largest P deposit in the world was discovered in the Kara-Tau Range in S. Kazakhstan. Other large reserves were discovered in the central areas of the USSR, the most important being the Vyatka-Kama deposit in Kirov Oblast and the Kingisep deposit in Leningrad Oblast. There are also deposits in the Ukraine, the Volga region, and in Bryansk, Orel, and Kursk oblasts.

Barite and Witherite. The principal deposits of B and W are in W. Siberia, Transcaucasia, and the Urals. In W. Siberia, Salair near the Kuznetsk basin and Zmeinogorsk in Altay Kray are the most important. In Transcaucasia, some areas of the Georgian and the Azerbaijan SSR have possibilities for further development of B production, as has also the Dzhalair deposit in Karaganda Oblast (Kazakh SSR). There are some 50 B—W deposits in Turkmen SSR.

Magnesite. Soviet reserves of M are among the largest in the world, totaling 630 mill. tons, according to a Soviet source in 1946. Principal deposits are found in the Urals, in Siberia, and in the Far East. The Satka group of deposits in Chelyabinsk Oblast is one of the largest in the USSR and is noted for the high quality of crystalline M. The smaller Khalilovo deposit in Orenburg Oblast contains amorphous M.

Graphite. The USSR has extensive G reserves, although many deposits lie in remote regions of Siberia and the Far East. The most important producers of G have been several deposits in the Ukraine. Deposits of Chelyabinsk Oblast are also of importance, as is Tashkazgan deposit which was recently discovered in the Uzbek SSR.

Diamonds. Until recent times, the USSR's very inadequate output of industrial D was secured from the Urals, with consumption dependent upon imports. Recently, however, large deposits were discovered in the Yakut ASSR, associated with basic igneous rocks and presented by placers. Now Soviet sources claim that the USSR is a leading country in D reserves.

Native Sulfur. The principal deposits of NS are in the Volga region, in Central Asia, and in the Carpathians. Of greatest economic importance are the Vodinsk and Alekseyevskoye deposits in Kuybyshev Oblast.

Large deposits were recently discovered in the Carpathians (W. Ukraine), while smaller deposits are in the Crimea, Dagestan, Kazakhstan, and Khabarovsk Kray. Deposits of sulfur of volcanic origin are known on the Kuril Islands.

Fluorspar. Soviet F ore reserves, averaging about 50 per cent F content, totaled 13.6 mill. metric tons as of Jan. 1, 1937. The largest F deposits are found in the Far East, E. Transbaykalia, and Central Asia; smaller deposits in the Tuva Autonomous Oblast, E. Siberia, Kazakhstan, and Kirgizia.

Piezooptical Materials. Here belong P quartz crystals, icelandic spar, and optical fluorite, which are used for electronic and optical purposes. Deposits of P quartz are found in the Pamirs, E. Siberia, Kazakhstan, the Urals, and the Ukraine; deposits of icelandic spar in Siberia and the Tuva Autonomous Oblast; optic fluorite primarily in Kazakhstan and the Tadzhik SSR.

Mica. Soviet sources claim that the USSR has the world's largest M reserves. The principal varieties of economic importance are muscovite and phlogopite. The largest M deposits are found in E. Siberia, where they are associated with Precambrian schists. The group of deposits at the Mama River in Irkutsk Oblast is of first importance, producing high-grade muscovite for the electrical industry. The Slyudyanka deposit of phlogopite which lies at the S. tip of Lake Baykal has been known since the late 18th century, while the vast Aldan phlogopite-bearing area was discovered only during the Soviet regime. Some M deposits are also found in the Urals, the Karelian ASSR, and the Ukraine.

Asbestos. The high-grade Soviet reserves of this mineral are believed to be the greatest in the world, the principal deposits being found in the Urals, in the territory of Sverdlovsk Oblast. The Bazhenov open-pit mine is overwhelmingly the most important, having produced 95 per cent of all Soviet A in 1939. There are smaller deposits in Sverdlovsk, Chelyabinsk, and Orenburg oblasts, as well as in the Bashkir ASSR. Economically important deposits are also the Ak-Dourak (Aktovrak) in the Tuva Autonomous Oblast and the Dzhetygara in Kazakhstan; several still smaller ones are found in Siberia, Central Asia, and the N. Caucasus.

Abrasives. Natural corundum, emery, and garnet are principal abrasive raw materials. Soviet sources claim that total reserves at the end of World War II aggregated a few thousand tons of corundum and about 100,000 metric tons of emery. Semiz-Bugu in Kazakhstan has been the primary source of corundum, but now it is considerably depleted. Corundum and cyanite from deposits of the Yakut ASSR are of high quality. The largest emery deposits are found in the Urals; garnet in the N. of European Russia.

Fire Clays and Refractory Materials. Reserves of FC in the USSR are large: 482 mill. metric tons measured and 1,041 mill. metric tons total, as of 1939. The principal deposits are associated with sediments of lakes and swamps and are often found in places of coal deposits. FC occur widely in the Moscow coal basin, in the Donets and Kuznetsk basins, and in the Kazakh SSR. The largest deposits are in Novgorod Oblast, with

important deposits also in Tula Oblast (Suvorov group of deposits), in Voronezh Oblast, in the Urals, and in the Ukraine (Chasov Yar).

Raw materials for the production of refractories are abundant in the USSR. Quartzites used for the production of dinas bricks occur in many localities. Economically the most important are in the Urals, the Ukraine, and W. Siberia. There are also numerous deposits of andalusite and related aluminum silicates used in high-temperature industrial processes. The most important are: the Aktash diaspore deposit in S. Kazakhstan, and the cyanite deposits in Murmansk Oblast and the Karelian ASSR.

Kaolin. According to Soviet sources, measured reserves of K were over 176 mill. metric tons in 1939; total reserves 535 mill. metric tons. K production is centered in the Ukraine, where it occurs in numerous economically important deposits. The Prosyanaya deposit is the largest in the USSR; there are also significant deposits in the Urals; and smaller deposits in Siberia and in Kazakhstan.

Building Materials. Various carbonate rocks (limestones, chalk, and marls) and clayey deposits (clays and shales) are used as raw materials for the manufacturing of cement, varieties of marls with mixtures of clay materials and lime being of greatest value. Measured reserves of raw materials used for cement production are recorded in 400 deposits located mostly in European Russia. Extensive marl deposits in the W. of the N. Caucasus supply raw materials for the Novorossiysk group of cement plants. Limestones are found almost everywhere in the USSR. Numerous deposits of chalk occur in many areas, 175 having been explored in detail, mostly in European Russia. Chalk is used as a high-grade raw material for the Volsk group of cement plants and plants in Stalingrad, Bryansk, Belgorod, and other oblasts.

Natural BM are abundant. They embrace various intrusive, sedimentary, and metamorphic rocks which may be used for construction purposes. Of importance are rocks used for decoration, such as granites, syenites, gabbro, marbles, dolomites, and quartzites. Rich deposits of decorative and BM are found in the Ukraine, the Urals, and the Karelian ASSR; beautiful colored marbles in the Caucasus and Central Asia.

BIBLIOGRAPHY: Demitry B. Shimkin: *Minerals, A Key to Soviet Power*, Cambridge, 1953. L. D.

MINGECHAÚR, town in Azerbaijan SSR; pop. 24,500 (1956). Has a large modern power plant on the Kura River which supplies power to ind. areas (Baku and Kirovabad); water reservoir is used for irrigation of the dry Kura valley. There have been numerous archaeological discoveries in the vicinity dating from the Bronze Age to the Middle Ages, such as ruins of settlements, graves, money, treasures. Archaeological excavation since 1946.

MÍNIKH (Munnich), **Burkhard Christopher** (1683–1767), R. field marshal of German origin. He commanded the Russian Army in the Russo-Turkish war (1735–39), and was an active member of the ruling circle in 18th-century Russia after the death of Peter I.

MÍNIN (Sukhoruk), **Kozmá,** merchant, zemsky elder of Nizhny Novgorod. He was the organizer of the People's Army 1611–12, and with Prince Pozharsky freed Moscow from Polish rule. He was given a seat in the boyar duma (council) and awarded a nobility title in 1613. He died in 1616. The monument to Minin and Pozharsky on Red Square in Moscow was erected in 1818.

MINING: *see* METALLURGY.

MINISTRIES: *see* GOVERNMENT CENTRAL.

MINKÉVICH, Nikoláy Anatólyevich (1883–1942), metallurgist. Honored Scientist and Technologist, RSFSR (1934). Graduate, St. Petersburg Polytechnic Institute (1907); professor, Moscow Mining Academy (at which he founded the chair of metallurgy) and Moscow Steel Institute (1930). M's research on thermal and thermochemical treatment of steel contributed to the modernization of technological processes in the building of machinery and equipment. Author of *Heat Treatment of Steel and Cast Iron* (1935), *New Low-Alloy High-Speed Steels* (1940). Stalin prize (1941).

MINSK, capital of Byelorussian SSR, adm. center of Minsk Oblast, on both banks of the Svisloch River; pop. 237,000 (1939), 509,000 (1959). It is the largest city on Warsaw-Moscow R.R., and an important commercial and ind. center, producing machinery, lumber, clothing, automobiles, tractors, bicycles, watches, radios, instruments. Seat of Byelorussian Ac. of S., university, colleges, research institutes. It was known in the 11th century; was occupied by Lithuanians, Russians, Poles, Swedes; invaded by Tatars in 1505; and partially destroyed by Napoleon in 1812.

MINSK OBLAST, Byelorussian SSR, area 15,826 sq. mi.; pop. 2,037,000 (1959): Byelorussians, Russians, Ukrainians, Jews, Poles. Cities: Minsk (adm. center), Borisov (a port), Slutsk, Nesvizh, Cherven, Dzerzhinsk. In the basin of the Berezina and its left affluents, the Pripyat and upper Neman. A forested upland; has podsolic and argillaceous soils; temperate continental climate. Agr.: potatoes, grain crops, hog and sheep raising, cattle breeding, apiculture, poultry and dairy farming. Ind.: machine mfg., lumbering, peat cutting, food processing, glassmaking, leather tanning, match production (Borisov). Crossed by three R.R. lines, the Moscow-Minsk highway; has waterways. Est. 1938, expanded 1954, now includes parts of Baranovichi and Bobruysk oblasts; in 1960 absorbed part of Molodechno Oblast.

MÍNSKY (Vilenkin), **Nikoláy Maksímovich** (1855–1937), poet, essayist, playwright, and translator. Took a law degree at St. Petersburg University. Three collections of essays: *In the Light of Conscience* (1890), *Religion of the Future* (1905), and *Essays on Public Subjects* (1909). In 1905 M worked on the editorial board of the Bolshevik newspaper *Novaya zhizn* (New Life). Soon, however, a rift developed between him and his Bolshevik colleagues. This was to some extent reflected in his three plays, *The Iron Ghost* (1909), *Minor Temptation* (1910), and *Chaos* (1912). After 1917, emigrated and died in Paris.

MINTS, Aleksándr Lvóvich (1894–), radio engineer.

Fellow, Ac. of S., USSR (1958). Graduated from the Don University (1918). Professor, Leningrad Institute of Communications (1930–38). Director, Laboratory of Radio Engineering, Ac. of S. (1946). Associated with radio engineering and scientific institutions of the Soviet Army (1920–28) and industry, and worked on the planning of high-power radio stations (1928–43). Research concerns the theory and calculation of modulation systems, high power in broadcasting stations, systems of antennas for long- and short-wave stations, application of radio engineering and electronics to the acceleration of elementary particles, design and building of radio stations. A. S. Popov Gold Medal, Ac. of S. (1950), Stalin prizes (1946, 1951), Lenin prize (1959).

MINUSÍNSK, city in Krasnoyarsk Kray RSFSR, near Abakan R.R. station, a river port on right bank of the Yenisey; pop. 34,000 (1956). It is the center of a rich agr. area; has coal mining; flour mills, sawmills, sugar factory, distillery, breweries. Archaeological excavations indicate its origin in prehistoric times.

MIR: *see* PEASANTS, POPULISM.

MÍRGOROD, town in Poltava Oblast, Ukrainian SSR, on Khorol River; pop. 23,600 (1957). R.R. station; center of oil and gas ind., also food processing; is a resort with mineral springs.

MIR ISKÚSSTVA (The World of Art), an art movement, organized in the 1890's by a group of St. Petersburg painters who opposed the democratic and naturalistic art of the Society of Circulating Exhibitions and the theories of Chernyshevsky, who emphasized the social function of art. "Art for art's sake" was the slogan of the new movement. Admiration for old France and old Russia inspired the graceful stylized paintings and drawings by the members of the group, which was founded by S. P. Diaghilev and A. N. Benois and comprised Somov, Bakst, Lanceret, Dobuzhinsky, Serov, Roerich, Korovin, and others. Too aloof and romantic to create great historical art, *Mir Iskusstva* contributed to the advancement of the graphic arts, book illustration, and stage designing. The revival of interest in icon painting and in the work of the R. masters of the 18th century was also due to this movement. It published the art magazine *Mir Iskusstva*, 1899–1904. The writings of Bryusov, Bely, Rozanov, Filosofov, and others appeared in its columns as did the reproductions of the work of its members.

MÍRNY, Panás (Rudchénko, Afanásy Yákovlevich) (1849–1920), a leading Ukrainian writer of leftist tendencies. Was under the influence of Shevchenko. His novel entitled *Do the Oxen Howl When the Manger Is Full?* (1880) was translated into Russian. M is also the author of *Lost Strength* and other stories about Ukrainian peasantry.

MISSILES: *see* ROCKETRY.

MITÁVA: *see* YELGAVA.

MÍTIN, Mark Borísovich (1901–), Soviet philosopher. M joined the CPSU in 1919. In the 1930's he became a writer, justifying Stalin's policies in the light of Marxist theory and exalting Stalin as a theoretician. He later specialized in history and was one of the early editors of the postwar journal *Voprosy Istorii* (Problems of History). He is chairman of the All-Union Society for the Dissemination of Political and Scientific Knowledge and a member of the Central Committee of the CPSU. Fellow, Ac. of S., USSR. Stalin prize (1943).

MITKÉVICH, Vladímir Fyódorovich (1872–1951), electrical engineer. Fellow, Ac. of S., USSR (1929). Honored Scientist and Technologist, RSFSR (1938). Graduate, St. Petersburg University (1895); lecturer, St. Petersburg (Leningrad) Polytechnic Institute (1902–38). Associated with the Institute of Power Engineering; the Department of Communications, Ac. of S. (1938). Participated in the organization of electrical engineering plants and patented several inventions in wire and wireless communications. Author of *Magnetic Flux and Its Transformations* (1946); his *Selective Works* were published in 1956. Lenin prize (1928) and Stalin prize (1943).

MIXED COMPANIES: *see* FOREIGN POLICY.

MIXED ECONOMY: *see* ECONOMIC DEVELOPMENT.

MLODZEYÉVSKY, Boleslav Kornelievich (1858–1923), mathematician. Graduate (1880), professor (1892), Moscow University. President, Moscow Mathematical Society (1921). Research concerned differential and algebraic geometry, mathematical analysis, mechanics, astronomy. Suggested the theory of differential invariants of diversities. Author of *Bending of Peterson Surfaces* (1904).

MNÍSZEK, Marína (1588–1614), daughter of Jerzy Mniszek, a Polish magnate, and wife of Pseudo-Dmitry I. After his murder, she recognized Pseudo-Dmitry II as her husband. She was captured by the Muscovites and died in prison.

MOCHÁLOV, Pável Stepánovich (1800–1848), actor-tragedian and representative of romanticism in the R. theater. Son of an actor, M began to appear on the Moscow stage in 1817. He played the parts of Hamlet, Othello, and King Lear in Shakespeare's tragedies; Ferdinand and Karl Moore in Schiller's *Cabal and Love*; Chatsky in Griboyedov's *Woe from Wit*. His acting, in the grand manner, exerted great influence upon the development of R. dramatic art.

MOGILÉV, city, adm. center of Mogilev Oblast, Byelorussian SSR; pop. 121,000 (1959). A port on right bank of the Dnieper, and a R.R. junction; has metalworking, machine building, chemical, leather, silk, furniture, food-processing plants, flour mills. Pedag. inst. Probably founded in the early 13th century, it has several old churches and a tower built by the Tatars.

MOGILÉV OBLAST, Byelorussian SSR, in Dnieper lowland; area 11,080 sq. mi.; pop. 1,132,000 (1959), mostly Byelorussians. Cities: Mogilev (adm. center), Bobruysk, Osipovichi, Krichev, Shklov, Bykhov. Drained by the Dnieper and its affluents, the Sozh, Berezina, Drut; it has podsolic soils, temperate continental climate; forests occupy 26 per cent of its area. Mineral resources: limestone, dolomite, phosphorite, peat. Agr.: flax, grain crops, potatoes, hog and cattle raising, dairy farming. Ind.: peat cutting, chemicals, machine mfg., building materials, lumbering, food processing, flour milling. Has R.R. and highway network, waterways. Est. 1938.

MOGILÉV-PODÓLSKY, city in Vinnitsa Oblast, Ukrainian SSR, on the Dniester; pop. 19,000 (1956). Has R.R. station, agr. trade, flour mill, sugar refinery, food-processing plants, limestone quarries. Founded at end of the 16th century, it was the scene of heavy fighting between Cossacks, Poles, Turks.

MOISÉYENKO (Moiseyenok), **Pyótr Anísimovich** (1852–1923), revolutionary, weaver, member of the Northern Union of Russian Factory Workers, and one of the organizers of the strike at the Morozov textile factory in Orekhovo-Zuyevo. He joined the Russian Social Democratic Workers' party in 1905 and was an active participant in the 1905–07 revolution. He also served during the civil war of 1918–20. He is the author of *Memoirs, 1873–1923*, published in 1924. (*See also* MOROZOV STRIKE)

MÓKSHA RIVER, right tributary of Oka; originates in the Volga uplands; length 435 mi. Its largest tributary is the Tsna River.

MOLDAVIAN SOVIET SOCIALIST REPUBLIC (MOLDAVIA) occupies the major part of Bessarabia (area between the Prut and Dniester rivers). It borders on the Ukrainian SSR and Rumania. Area, 13,100 sq. mi. Capital, Kishinev (pop. 216,000); other cities, Beltsy, Tiraspol, Bendery.

Population of M is 2,885,000 (1959). Out of the total, Moldavians or Moldavian Rumanians constitute 65.4% (1,887,000); Ukrainians, 14.6% (421,000); Russians, 10.2% (293,000); Gagauz, 3.3% (96,000); Jews, 3.3% (95,000); Bulgars, 2.1% (62,000). Before World War II Russians accounted for about 7%, Ukrainians 10%, Jews 10%. The large majority of Jews were exterminated during the Nazi occupation; a number of Russians and Ukrainians settled in the area after the war.

Nature and Climate. The territory is a hilly plain, broken by river valleys and ravines. It is one of the warmest regions of the European USSR: the average July temperature is 67° F in the N., 73° F in the S.; in January 22° F and 26.6° F respectively.

National Economy. The main activity is agriculture (corn and other grains, fruit, grapes, vegetables, tobacco) and cattle breeding (dairy cattle and hogs in the north, sheep and goats in the south). Food-processing plants, wine distilleries, and tobacco factories predominate in industry.

History. The early and medieval history of today's M SSR is closely connected with that of Rumanian M. Under Turkish domination from the 16th to the end of the 18th century, Eastern M (or Bessarabia) was annexed by R. in 1812. Western M, independent since 1829, united with Wallachia in 1859. Both principalities severed remaining nominal ties with Turkey and in 1866 took the name of Rumania. In 1856, as a result of the Crimean war, R. lost S. Bessarabia to M (Rumania), but recovered it at the Congress of Berlin (1878). In Feb. 1918 Bessarabia passed into Rumanian hands; the USSR refused to recognize it and in 1924 the Soviets formed a M Republic of their own—the Moldavian ASSR on the Ukrainian side of the river Dniester in an area populated mostly by Ukrainians

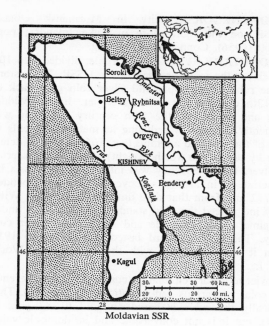

Moldavian SSR

(48.5%), but also containing Moldavian Rumanians (30%) and Jews (12%). In June 1940, after prior agreement with Germany, a Soviet ultimatum forced Rumania to cede Bessarabia (and N. Bukovina) to the USSR. S. Bessarabia, the Kotovsk-Balta area of the former Moldavian ASSR and N. Bukovina were given to Ukraine. The bulk of Bessarabia and the remaining part of the former Moldavian ASSR were united and made a Union Republic (Moldavian SSR). During World War II Rumanian troops occupied M from June 1941 to Aug. 1944.

The Culture of M is closely related to both Rumania and the Ukraine. The M language (a dialect of Rumanian) belongs to the eastern group of Romance languages, but is now written in Cyrillic script.   M. R.

MOLODÉCHNO, city in Byelorussian SSR; pop. 7,000 (1939), 26,000 (1959). Food, lumbering, footwear, meat-canning plants, foundry.

MOLODÉCHNO OBLAST, Byelorussian SSR, abolished Jan. 1960, territory divided among Minsk, Vitebsk, and Grodno oblasts.

MOLÓGA RIVER, about 280 mi. long, in Kalinin and Vologda oblasts, formerly a left tributary of the Volga, flowing now into the Rybinsk Reservoir; navigable.

MOLOKÁNS, members of a religious sect which sprang up in Russia in the late 18th century. They advocate moral self-improvement and reject all church rites. The name derives from *molokó* (milk) which they drink during fasts.

MÓLOTOV (Skryábin), **Vyacheslávĭ Mikháylovich** (1890–), Soviet government official. Former chairman of the Council of Ministers, foreign minister, and representative to the International Atomic Energy Agency in Vienna, as of Sept. 1960. M was born in a small town in Vyatka Province, now Kirov Oblast, son of a storekeeper, related to the composer A. N. Skryabin. He was sent to Kazan to be educated at the gymnasium. M participated in the revolution of 1905, at the age of 15, and in 1906 he joined the Social Democratic party, which in Kazan was entirely Bolshevik, and took the party name Molotov (Hammerman). In 1909, when M was about to graduate from the gymnasium, he was arrested and exiled to Vologda Province for two years. On his return, he studied briefly at the faculty of economics of the St. Petersburg Polytechnical Institute. In 1912, the Bolsheviks in St. Petersburg founded the daily newspaper *Pravda,* financed by Victor Tikhomirov who was a former schoolmate and close friend of M's. M became the secretary and acting editor of *Pravda,* which was supervised by Stalin as the representative of the party's Central Committee.

After the revolution, M carried out several responsible missions in various parts of Russia and in March 1921 he became a candidate member of the party Politburo and one of three secretaries of the Central Committee, a post he retained when Stalin became Secretary General the following year. Lenin characterized him as "the best file clerk in Russia." M was made a full Politburo member in 1926 and was first secretary of the Moscow Party Committee during 1928–30, when he played a leading role in the purge of the Moscow party organization. In Dec. 1930, M became chairman of the Council of People's Commissars and in May 1939 he also took over the portfolio of commissar for foreign affairs, replacing Litvinov. A few months later, he signed the agreement with Hitler's Germany which became known as the Molotov-Ribbentrop Pact. Stalin himself took over the chairmanship of the Council of People's Commissars in May 1941, but M continued in charge of foreign affairs through the war and until March 1949. He visited England and the United States during the war, participated in Teheran (1943), Yalta (1945), and Potsdam (1945) conferences, and represented the USSR at the 1945 San Francisco conference which founded the UN.

From 1949 to Stalin's death in 1953, M was first vice chairman of the Council of ministers, and after Stalin's death he again became minister of foreign affairs. His replacement three years later by Shepilov marked the beginning of his political decline. In June 1957, he was expelled from the Central Committee as a member of the "anti-party group," actually an anti-Khrushchev group, which had threatened to control the Presidium. M was probably the only member of the group whose opposition was exclusively based on principle. He could hardly be characterized as a pure "Stalinist," but, for him, Khrushchev's "de-Stalinization" had gone too far, his domestic policies were too "liberal," his economic reforms were too unorthodox, and, last but not least, Khrushchev's foreign policy was not sufficiently uncompromising, and therefore dangerous. On his expulsion from the Central Committee, M was "exiled" to Outer Mongolia as ambassador. In Sept. 1960, he was transferred to Vienna to represent the USSR in the International Atomic Energy Agency.

BIBLIOGRAPHY: Bernard Bromage, *Molotov: The Story of an Era,* London, 1956.   G. P. D.

MÓLOTOV: *see* PERM.

MOLOTOV-RIBBENTROP PACT: *see* HISTORY.

MONARCHY, ABSOLUTE AND CONSTITUTIONAL. The autocratic R. monarchy developed its absolute political power on the foundations laid by Vasily II in the mid-15th century. Vasily concentrated in his hands, and in those of his descendants, the political power formerly scattered among the numerous Russian principalities. While local independence had not yet been completely overcome by these centralizing efforts, the trend had begun. Ivan III and Vasily III, son and grandson of Vasily II, completed the work of creating the absolute state, expanding considerably the area under the control of the Muscovite dynasty.

In 1547, Ivan IV became the first ruler of Russia to be crowned tsar, openly espousing for the first time the doctrine of absolutism. The absolute character of the Crown survived the "Time of Troubles" (q.v.) at the turn of the 17th century, and when Michael, the first Romanov, accepted the Crown in 1613 he assumed all the unlimited powers built up by the monarchy in the previous century and a half. During the reigns of Catherine I and Peter II (1725–1730), the absolutism of the monarchy was in eclipse, with actual power being exercised by the Supreme Privy Council. In 1730 the autocracy was restored to preeminence and Anne became the custodian of the traditional Muscovite absolutism.

Catherine the Great attempted to liberalize the concept of the absolute monarchy in the latter part of the 18th century; she believed that absolute monarchy was the only form of government suited to Russia, but that it must be based on strict observance of the law, of which the Crown was the sole source. This concept of "legal paternalism" was continued by Paul. Alexander I, however, brought a vacillating liberalism to the throne in 1801. The early years of his reign were marked by liberal experiments and plans for constitutional reform. These projects came to naught as Alexander grew more conservative after 1812.

Russian absolutism reached its fullest development in the period 1825–1855 under Nicholas I, who added an emphasis on dynasticism and religion to the idea that the monarch was, "by the Grace of God," the source of all law and the actual head of the administration. This concept was upheld by his successors. While Alexander II introduced many reforms, he would not agree to any curtailment of the powers of the Russian Crown. The brief reign of Alexander III (1881–94) brought a conservative reaction to the reforms of his predecessor.

When Nicholas II was forced to grant constitutional concessions in 1905, Russia formally became a limited constitutional monarchy. The tsar however granted concessions resentfully and with the feeling of betraying his "sacred trust." He was never reconciled to the status of a constitutional monarch. The inability of the R. monarchy to compromise with the developing liberal, constitutional spirit in Russia eventually led to its downfall in 1917.

BIBLIOGRAPHY: Michael T. Florinsky, *Russia: A History and an Interpretation*, New York, 1953.

MONCHEGÓRSK, city in Murmansk Oblast, RSFSR, on the right shore of Lake Imandra; pop. 28,500 (1956). Copper-nickel mining.

MONETARY SYSTEM. The ruble, divided into 100 kopecks, is the monetary unit of the USSR. The history of the ruble as a copper and silver coin goes back to the 13th century and perhaps earlier. In the Middle Ages and as late as the 18th century the ruble was frequently debased by reducing its metallic contents in spite of the repeated attempts (e.g. 1667, 1689) to determine by statute the worth (weight) of the ruble in terms of silver. Paper currency was introduced in Russia by Catherine II, in 1768. Its convertibility was suspended in 1777 and from that date until 1897, when S. Witte (q.v.) introduced the gold standard, Russia lived under a regime of inconvertible and depreciated paper currency. The gold standard lasted from 1897 to 1914 when it was suspended with the outbreak of World War I.

Soviet monetary circulation comprises paper currency and coins of various denominations (see table 1). Theoretically the ruble is based on gold (0.987 gm., in 1961), but it is not convertible and its domestic value is determined by government fiat, while prices are fixed by administrative agencies. Trade in gold and foreign exchange transactions are government monopolies. The export and import of rubles are prohibited except for very small quantities.

TABLE 1

DENOMINATION OF MONETARY TOKENS

Bank notes	10	25	50	100
Treasury notes	1	3	5	
Coins	1 ruble; 1, 2, 3, 5, 10, 15, 20, and 50 kopecks.			

Development of the Soviet Monetary System. The early attempts of the Soviet government to build a moneyless economy (1917–20) failed; the extensive use of forced labor paid in kind, requisitions, and the uncontrolled issue of paper money (*sovznaki*) led to galloping inflation (see table 2) and widespread barter.

TABLE 2

STATE BUDGET AND CURRENCY ISSUES (1917–21)
(in billion rubles)*

Years	1917	1918	1919	1920	1921
Budget deficit	22.6	31.1	166.4	1,055.6	21,936.9
Issue of paper currency	16.4	33.6	164.2	943.6	16,375.3

* Billion–a thousand millions.

However it soon became clear to the Soviet government that money was necessary and that it could be made into a tool of planning and control during the period of transition to a communist society.

Under the New Economic Policy (1921–28) the Soviet State Bank (*Gosbank*) was organized (1921) and the *monetary reform* (1922–24) laid down the basis of the present monetary system. The State Bank issued a new currency unit, *chervonets*, equal to 10 prerevolutionary gold rubles; it was backed by precious metal (25 per cent) and by easily marketable commodities or short-term industrial loans (75 per cent). However, the government continued to print *sovznaki* rubles to meet budgetary needs; it was not until 1924 that the *sovznaki* were replaced by treasury notes, by law accepted for gold payments. The 1923 rubles were convertible into the new rubles at the rate of 50,000:1

and the 1922 rubles at the rate of 50 bill. :1. Notes in denominations of 1, 3, and 5 rubles were issued. Eventually, the 10, 15, 20, and 50 kopeck silver coins were replaced by nickel coins (1927) and the copper coins (1, 2, 3, and 5 kopecks) by bronze coins (1929). During this period treasury bills had no gold backing, their issue depending exclusively on budgetary needs. However, soon after the reform the state budget was balanced and the State Bank was directed to issue treasury bills and maintain a fixed ratio between the volume issued and the banknotes in circulation (1925) (see table 3).

TABLE 3
CURRENCY CIRCULATION (1924–37)
(in billion rubles)

Years	Total rubles (average) annual	Banknotes as of January	Treasury notes & coins as of January
1924	0.3		
1925	0.7	0.4	0.3
1926	1.3	0.7	0.5
1927	1.4	0.8	0.6
1928	1.8	1.0	0.7
1929	2.4	1.1	0.9
1930	3.6	1.9	1.3
1931	4.8	2.1	2.2
1932	6.6	2.8	2.9
1933	7.2	3.4 (July)	3.5 (July)
1934	7.3	3.4	3.4
1935	8.6	3.8	3.9
1936	10.2	5.9	3.9
1937	11.3	8.0	3.2

No figures are available after 1937.

The increasing rate of gold production and grain exports raised gold reserves, stabilizing temporarily the foreign exchange value of the ruble. However, the following period of forced industrialization, financed through credit and currency expansion, caused rapid depreciation, a growing imbalance of international payments, and the ruble export (1926) and import (1928) embargo. The 1936 devaluation linked the ruble to the United States dollar ($1:5.3 rubles) and set its gold content at 0.168 gm.

After 1928, the centrally planned Soviet economy was widely operated through the medium of money which had become a vital factor of economic planning, direction, and control. Consequently, money per se was not intended to exert an independent influence on economic processes. The volume of output and investment and the level of prices and wages were determined by the central economic plan. As a result, money, credit, and fiscal policies had become the integral part of an overall financial plan and could no longer be considered as independent factors. Other functions performed by the Soviet money are similar to those found in market economies; thus, the ruble is a *means of payment* and a *legal tender*; it also serves as a *standard of value* and a *unit of account* for cost and price calculations, including those of non-traded investment goods. In fact, only a highly developed monetary cost accounting system enables the Soviet planners to control performance, productivity, profitability, and so forth by way of comparison between planned and actual cost.

Soviet money is a *circulation medium* inasmuch as it directs the movement of goods along the channels predetermined by the plan, even when goods are shifted from one state enterprise to another without changing ownership. Owing to its deferring effect on consumer purchases, the function of money as a *means of saving* is important; private savings cannot be used to acquire means of production; money is saved through bank savings accounts (with payments of 2 per cent interest for call-deposits) and—up to 1959—through usually compulsory purchase of government bonds; after the 1947 conversion which cancelled about ⅔ of the state loan, interest on loans was reduced to 2–3 per cent; bonds were issued for a period of 20 years. Subscriptions were solicited "collectively," i.e. by withholding a part of wage earnings. In 1957 the Soviet government declared that the cost of redeeming earlier loans and raising new state loans had reached a point where it absorbed about 35 per cent of the total amount collected and would continuously increase. In order to stop this vicious circle, the Soviet government declared a moratorium on all state loans outstanding (approximately 260 billion rubles) and on all interest thereon for a period of 20–25 years. At the same time the government promised not to solicit new loans after 1958. Assets of the State Savings Bank (see table 4) as well as funds "mobilized" through "mass subscriptions" (see table 5) are considered to be current budgetary revenues which give planners control over large amounts of "temporary free" purchasing power. In fact, the number and volume of state bonds were determined by the balance of monetary revenue and expenditure of the population.

TABLE 4
BANK SAVINGS ACCOUNTS IN SELECTED YEARS
(in billion rubles)

1933	1938	1941	1951	1955	1957	1959
1.0	4.5	7.3	18.5	48.0	63.0	105.0

TABLE 5
GOVERNMENT LOANS DURING THE FIVE YEAR PLANS AND WORLD WAR II
(in billion rubles)

First 1929–32	Second 1933–37	Third 1938–40	World War II	Fourth 1946–51	Fifth 1951–55
9.5	24.3	27.4	125.4	132.9	173.1

After the credit reform of 1930–31 the State Bank became the issue, credit, accounting, and cash center of the USSR; it directs and closely controls two forms of "monetary resources," i.e. the currency and the deposit (banking) money. Currency is primarily confined to consumer income and spending; deposit money is circulated in the socialized sector of the economy inasmuch as transactions among enterprises and organizations must be negotiated through the State Bank. For this purpose the State Bank holds deposits of all Soviet enterprises and organizations, receives their cash remittances daily, and is the only authorized source of short-term credit. Thus, most transactions among enterprises are settled by book entries while the instruments used include bank-approved orders-to-pay and letters of credit. Thus, most transactions among enterprises are settled by book entries while the instruments used include bank-approved orders-to-pay and letters of credit. For small, local transactions (not over 1,000 rubles) checks are acceptable. Most accounts are settled by nation-wide clearing operations of the State Bank, which almost completely eliminates cash transactions from the socialized sector (see tables 6 and 7).

TABLE 6
CIRCULATION OF CURRENCY AND DEPOSIT MONEY IN SELECTED YEARS
(in billion rubles)

Years	1950	1956	1958
Currency turnover as indicated by consumer spendings	408.8	589.7	715.5
Deposit money turnover—as indicated by the payments of enterprises for goods and services through the *Gosbank*	1,537.7	2,368.6	2,834.7

TABLE 7
STRUCTURE OF THE DEPOSIT MONEY CIRCULATION IN SELECTED YEARS
(in billion rubles)

Years	1940	1950	1956	1958
Total Turnover	555.6	1,537.7	2,368.6	2,834.7
1. Accepted orders-to-pay	432.7	905.1	1,185.8	1,429.5
2. Settlement by clearing	59.8	483.9	1,111.3	1,339.4
3. Check operations	21.3	61.8	42.2	30.1
4. Letters of credit and special accounts	41.8	86.9	29.3	35.6

The State Bank is in charge of the execution of the financial plan (the monetary counterpart of the national production plan), the outlining of the credit plan which determines its credit operation, and responsible for the currency volume, circulation, emission or withdrawal (see table 8).

TABLE 8
STRUCTURE OF THE BANK CASH PLAN

INCOME	EXPENDITURES
Receipts from	*Payments* (outgo) *for*
Trade enterprises, etc.	Wage funds and related payments
Transportation	Agriculture procurement offices
Tax payment and collections	Subsidies to the post office
Rents and other communal receipts	Subsidies to savings banks
Local transport	Pensions and insurance claims
Collective farms	Individual home constructions and household goods loans
Government bonds and lotteries	Cash reserves of enterprises
Post office	Other payments in cash
Savings banks assets	
Entertainment enterprises	(income exceeding expenditures= withdrawal of currency)
Cultural services	
Others	

(expenditures exceeding income= currency emission)

Despite strict monetary control during World War II and large payments made by the population (a total of 270 billion rubles), currency expanded four times and the rate of spending increased considerably resulting in a 12 to 13 times increase of the prices obtained by the farmers on the free market. This inflation which occurred in the postwar reconstruction period was checked by the monetary reform of Dec. 1947 which redeemed the old rubles at the ratio of 1:10, with preference for small savings (1:1 up to a maximum of 3,000 rubles), kolkhoz accounts (1:5), and government bonds (1:4 and 1:5).

TABLE 9
VOLUME OF NOTES IN CIRCULATION, 1938–1948
(Estimated by the Bank of International Settlements)
(in billion rubles)

1938	40	:	1944	260
1939	65	:	1945	340
1940	85	:	1946	385
1941	100	:	1947	420
1942	115	:	1948	42 new rubles
1943	175	:		

TABLE 10
CHANGES IN MONETARY SUPPLY AS A RESULT OF THE 1947 REFORM
(Estimated by the Bank of International Settlements)
(in billion rubles)

	Old rubles	Cancelled by reform	New rubles
Notes in circulation	420	378	42
State obligations	150	100	50
Savings accounts	10	2	8
	580	480	100

After the reform the "control over the ruble" was tightened along with the developing trend toward decentralization. The State Bank, operating 170 regional and 4,690 district offices (as of 1958), gained a close control over the use of cash funds of enterprises such as wage funds which account for 80 per cent of the total cash outlay of the State Bank and constitute the main source of the monetary income of the population. In order to have a tighter control of the circulating currency the union republics and other territorial governments had to submit to the Council of Ministers of the USSR an annual plan outlining the monetary income and expenditures of their population (1959). Similar centralized approval is required for the quarterly cash plans of the State Bank before they are forwarded to the territorial governments. To stimulate efficiency and plan fulfillment the State Bank was permitted to differentiate terms of short-time credits (1959).

The postwar split of the world market through the creation and economic integration of a Soviet bloc made the ruble the basic intra-bloc monetary unit; in 1950 the U. S. dollar basis of the ruble was renounced and the official gold content raised to 0.222 gm. corresponding to U. S. $.25. However, since the domestic purchasing value was much lower, a special "tourist ruble" was available at the exchange rate of 1 ruble for U. S. $.10 for all noncommercial transactions (1957). As of Jan. 1961 a new ruble with a 10 times higher nominal value was introduced, exchangeable for old rubles at a rate of 1:10 for a three-month transit period. Simultaneously, all prices were cut to 1/10 of their prereform level. As against the tenfold domestic value increase, the gold content increase was only fourfold (0.987 gm.) resulting in a new U.S. dollar exchange rate of $1.00 to 0.9 rubles. Thus, the long-time discrepancy between the foreign rate (which was grossly overvalued) and the domestic purchasing value of the ruble has been almost eliminated by this devaluation and the official new ruble course has come close to the former "tourist ruble" exchange rate; this eliminated the necessity of maintaining a special ruble rate.

BIBLIOGRAPHY: Mikhail V. Condoide, *The Soviet Financial System*, Columbus, 1951; Donald R. Hodgeman, "Soviet Monetary Controls Through the Banking System," in Gregory Grossman, ed., *Value and Plan*, Berkeley, 1960; Franklyn D. Holzman, *Soviet Taxation: The Fiscal and Monetary Problems of a Planned Economy*, Cambridge, 1955; Alexander Baykov, *The Development of the Soviet Economic System*, New York, 1947; Harry Schwartz, *Russia's Soviet Economy*, New York, 1960.   G. D.

MONTFERRAND, August Augustovich (1786–1858), architect of the classical school. A native of France, M came to Russia in 1816 and from that date resided in St. Petersburg. His best-known work is the Alexander Column (1830–34) erected to commemorate the victory over Napoleon in 1812. It forms the center of the Palace Square in Leningrad. M designed the Isaac Cathedral, which, however, was built later.

MORDVINIAN ASSR (MORDOVIA), part of RSFSR; area 10,100 sq. mi.; pop. 999,000 (1959): Mordvinians, Russians, Tatars. Cities: Saransk (capital), Temnikov, Ardatov. Rivers: Moksha, Sura, Alatyr. Has forests (15 per cent of total area) growing on black soil; climate is humid and continental. Mineral resources:

oil shale, phosphorite. Agr.: wheat, hemp, potatoes, rye, oats, sunflowers, dairy farming, apiculture. Ind.: food processing, flour milling, distilling, timber, electr. equipment, agr. machinery, metalworking. Has good R.R. and highways; several schools of higher education and research institutes. Est. 1934.

MORÓZOV, Nikoláy Aleksándrovich (1854–1946), revolutionary, scientist, poet. He participated in the organization "Land and Freedom" and in the executive committee of "People's Will." He went abroad to establish contacts with the leaders of the First International, returned to Russia illegally, was arrested, and sentenced in 1882. He served 21 years in the Schlüsselburg Fortress and was liberated by the 1905–07 revolution. While imprisoned he continued his scientific activities in the fields of chemistry, physics, astronomy, and mathematics. He is the author of the autobiographical *Stories from My Life* (latest revised edition was published in 1947) and a book of poetry.

MORÓZOV STRIKE, Jan. 7–17, 1885, large-scale strike of textile workers at the Morozov factory in Orekhovo-Zuyevo. It was the turning point in the history of the revolutionary movement in Russia. From 1882 to 1884 workers' wages were decreased five times and fines constituted 25 per cent of their wages. The strike was staged by 8,000 workers under the leadership of Pyotr Moiséyenko, but was suppressed by the armed forces. However, the government was forced to issue a law on fines in 1886.

MORSHÁNSK, city in Tambov Oblast, RSFSR, on Tsna River; pop. 40,600 (1956). Is an ind. town on the main R.R. line from Tula to Penza and Kuybyshev, with large cloth factory, glass, tobacco, brick, and butter plants, sawmills, food processing.

MORTALITY RATE: *see* MEDICAL SYSTEM, POPULATION.

MOSCOW, (R. *Moskvá*), capital of the USSR and RSFSR, adm. center of Moscow Oblast; pop. 4,183,000 (1939), 5,046,000 (1959). Situated on Moskva River, it is the largest city in the Soviet Union and its political, economic, scientific, and cultural center. It is a key R.R. point, an international and domestic airport (Vnukovo); after the opening of the Moscow-Volga Canal (1937) it became a port for five seas and is serviced by three river ports. Has heavy ind., giant machine mfg. plants, Likhachev Automobile Plant, "Ordzhonikidze," "Krasny proletary," "Kalibr," "Frezer," plants mfg. ball bearings, machine tools; "Serp i Molot" metalworks, "Dinamo" electrotechnical plant, chemical, pharmaceutical, aniline dyes, rubber, perfumery, cosmetic, textile, shoe factories; production of silk, wool, cotton, jersey; A. I. Mikoyan Meat Canning Combine, and many others. Although it has a powerful electric station, since 1956 power has also been supplied by the Kuybyshev Hydroelectric Plant; gaslines extend to Saratov, Dashava, Kiev, Stavropol. The city has bus, trolley bus, street car, and subway service; most suburban trains are electric. There are also passenger boats on the Moskva River.

History. First mentioned in chronicles 1147, but archaeological data indicate earlier settlement (9th–10th centuries). In the 13th century it was the capital of the feudal principality of Muscovy, was destroyed by Tatars in 1237, and restored toward the end of the 13th century. It was the largest trade and cultural center in the 16th century; the cradle of R. printing, and the political center of Russia from the 15th century to 1713, when Peter I transferred the capital to St. Petersburg. It was occupied by Napoleon in 1812, but his retreat from it was a turning point in the history of the Franco-Russian War. Became capital again in 1918. It has fine examples of old R. architecture. The most imposing is the Kremlin (built from the 14th to the 17th century), a large triangular fortress on the Moskva with the Red Square to the W.; for centuries the residence of R. rulers (to 1712), it is now the headquarters of the Communist Party's Central Committee, the meeting place of Congresses of the CPSU, of sessions of the Supreme Soviet of the USSR, and so forth; and the headquarters of the Soviet government. The city has the All-Union V. I. Lenin Public Library, as well as other libraries, numerous colleges, research institutes, cathedrals, palaces, 49 museums (Tretyakov Gallery), 26 theaters (Moscow Art Theater and the Bolshoy), the M. V. Lomonosov State University (largest and oldest in Russia) which was founded 1755. It is also the seat of the Ac. of S. of the USSR.

MOSCOW CANAL (R. *Kanal imeni Moskvy*, until 1947 Moscow-Volga Canal) connects the Volga and Moskva rivers; 80 mi. long. Built from 1932 to 1937, as part of an over-all plan to rebuild Moscow, making it into a port for five seas. Begins at the right bank of the Volga, near Ivankovo; has 9 sluices and 5 pumpworks; several hydroelectric plants were built. The Moscow-Leningrad waterway has been shortened by 700 mi. Main ports: Khimki, Dmitrov, Ivankovo. Reliable water supply to Moscow. Renamed on the occasion of the 800th anniversary of the city of Moscow.

THE MOSCOW LOMONOSOV STATE UNIVERSITY, generally referred to in the Soviet Union by its R. initials MGU, oldest R. university. It was founded in 1755 by Count I. I. Shuvalov with the aid of the scientist M. V. Lomonosov, who helped to work out its curriculum. Some of the greatest R. scientists taught at Moscow University, and its graduates include names distinguished in R. literature: Griboyedov, Lermontov, Belinsky, Herzen, Turgenev, and Chekhov. In 1940 it was named after M. V. Lomonosov and granted the order of Lenin. Its original building was burned down

The Moscow University

in the fire of Moscow in 1812. It was soon rebuilt and at present occupies a number of sites, the most important being a complex of buildings on the Lenin Hills on the outskirts of Moscow. There are 27 main and 30 subsidiary buildings with 168 auditoriums, 1,700 laboratories, and living quarters for 184 professors and 5,755 students. The chief building, a skyscraper, is a well-known Moscow landmark. The present enrollment is 22,000 undergraduates, including 6,000 students of extension courses, with a faculty staff of over 2,000. The university is divided into 12 faculties: mechanico-mathematical; physical; chemical; biological and soil; geographical; geological; historical; philosophical; philological; economical; juridical; and journalism. Associated with it are many institutes, libraries, museums, observatories, laboratories.

MOSCOW OBLAST, RSFSR; area 18,100 sq. mi.; pop. 10,949,000 (1959). Central European USSR, occupies E. part of the Central Russian upland, in the Oka-Volga watershed. Cities: Moscow (capital), Podolsk, Serpukhov, Klin, Orekhovo-Zuyevo, Kolomna, Mozhaysk, Kashira, Noginsk, Stalinogorsk. Drained by the Klyazma, Moskva (and its affluents), Oka and other rivers, it also has lakes. Hilly plain with Klin-Dmitrov Ridge (stretching from W. to E.) cut by the Moscow Canal; has mixed forest vegetation (pine, spruce, oak, maple). Climate varies: severe (N.), mild (S.), maritime (W.), continental (E.). Mineral resources: peat (E. of Moscow), phosphorite (Voskresensk), brick clays, lignite (Moscow basin). Largest ind. center (20 per cent of total Soviet ind.): machine mfg., chemicals, light and food ind., lignite and peat-fed power plants, steel, textile, clothing and knitting mills, handicraft works (toys, haberdashery, weaving), structural materials. Agr.: dairy farming, milk center, hog raising, vegetables, berries, corn crops. Has a dense rail and highway network. Est. 1929.

MOSCOW UNIVERSITY: *see* MOSCOW LOMONOSOV STATE UNIVERSITY.

MOSKVÁ RIVER, in Moscow Oblast, over 310 mi. long; flows E. through Moscow to join the Oka River just below Kolomna. Navigable from Moscow; has several sluices. Chief tributaries: Ruza, Istra, Yauza (left); Pakhra, Koloch (right). After the opening of the Moscow Canal, has acquired primary importance.

MOSLEMS: *see* NATIONALITIES.

MOSKVÍN, Iván Mikháylovich (1874–1946), actor, People's Artist, USSR. Graduated from the School of  Music and Drama, Moscow Philharmonic Society; later he joined the Korsh Theater in Moscow; and in 1898, the Moscow Art Theater. M was an exceptionally talented and versatile actor. Before the revolution he gave revealing impersonations of Tsar Fyodor, in A. K. Tolstoy's *Tsar Fyodor Ioannovich;* Protasov, in L. Tolstoy's *The Living Corpse;* Snegirev, in Dostoyevsky's *The Brothers Karamazov;* and Luka, in Gorky's *The Lower Depths.* Under the Soviets M created the parts of Pugachov, in Trenev's *Pugachovshchina;* Nozdrev, in Gogol's *Dead*

Souls; Khlynov, in Ostrovsky's *The Warm Hearth.* From 1919 he appeared in a number of films.

MOSTÓVICH, Vladímir Yákovlevich (1880–1935), metallurgist. Honored Scientist and Technologist, RSFSR (1934). Graduate, Riga Polytechnic Institute (1903); professor, Tomsk Institute of Technology (1912) and Institute of Mining and Metallurgy, in Ordzhonikidze (1931). Research on problems of nonferrous metallurgy, particularly those involved in investigations of gold ores; studied the theory of copper and lead smelting and selective flotation of cuprous pyrites.

MOVING PICTURES. The cinema film is a binding element in the structure of the Soviet Union. Lenin called it "for us the first of the arts" and fully appreciated its importance as a medium of information and persuasion. For him and his successors entertainment was strictly secondary, a useful jam to coat the pill. Regular MP shows are given in remote farms, fishing settlements, educational centers, and engineering projects, when the story film is only intermittently the climax of the program. Political, technical, scientific, and artistic achievements are habitually recorded on a scale far more lavish than commerce would justify. The image aroused by the efforts of Soviet MP is of a group of nations vastly interested in their own endeavors and devoted to reaching the goal of international communism.

Before the 1917 Revolution the influence of MP was slight in the tsarist Russian empire. More than 70 per cent of the population was both poverty-stricken and illiterate and thus unable to read the captions on silent films. After the French invention of screen projection, two French cameramen-projectionists brought their apparatus to St. Petersburg in 1896. The first film studio was opened in Moscow in 1908. By 1917 there were seven studios, twenty-four production concerns (among them Ermoliev, Khanzhonkov, Neptune, and Russ), and some seventy distribution firms and 1,045 MP theaters, situated in the larger towns, with an average seating capacity of 350. Entertainment provided by local production was largely escapist, sentimental, romantic, scarcely adult. The better subjects were adaptations of R. classics. Among names which have deserved to survive are those of Ladislas Starevich, the earliest master of puppet films, Meyerhold who at times combined film with his stage productions and introduced MP to Eisenstein, the directors Bukhovetsky, Granovsky, Turzhansky, Volkov, Protazanov, and Ivan Mozhukhin, who was also a famous actor. Other outstanding players were Kolin, Rimsky, and the actresses Kovanko, Lissenko, and Desny, all of whom had fled the country by the end of 1919, and only Protazanov returned.

On Aug. 27, 1919, the Soviet Government nationalized the film industry and trade and began to bend it into a rigid implement of Communist propaganda. The process took ten years to become effective and during that time enthusiasm for the revolution and shortage of trained personnel and of technical equipment fired and fused a revolution in techniques and story method. A training school was founded; new masters of MP—S. M. Eisenstein, V. I. Pudovkin, A. P.

Dovzhenko, and others—emerged and successfully experimented with the flexibility of the medium. Their work created widespread interest and sympathy abroad. Lenin rejected escapism and encouraged the factual film, but the demand for fiction persisted and a new realism emerged, triggered by lack of negative stock which led to the invention of the compilation film, old negatives reassembled in new ways. Influenced by D. W. Griffith's American film, *Intolerance,* Eisenstein's genius discovered the dramatic shock inherent in the clash of contrasting images, and this discovery provoked him to visualize, not merely a particular story as Pudovkin achieved in *Mother* and *The End of St. Petersburg,* but political theories—in fact to generalize. Out of his films, *Potemkin, October, The General Line,* grew the documentary film movement which has spread across the world to mankind's lasting benefit. This ten-year period of trial and experiment came to a sudden end with the inception of the first of the Five Year Plans in 1928 and the innovation of the sound film. The experimental work in silent films was denounced as formalism.

The planners took too active an interest in the film industry by imposing an ever-narrowing political censorship, with the result that it took forty years, from 1917 to the late 1950's, to restore the quantity of feature film production to the tsarist level of more than 100 feature films a year. The situation in the last years of Stalin was so acute that in 1952 only five fiction films were released out of the hundreds planned. The emergence of occasional masterpieces like Donskoy's film for children, *The Childhood of Maxim Gorky,* or Eisenstein's historical pageant, *Alexander Nevsky,* in 1938 only served to throw the surrounding situation into deeper gloom. Contemporary subjects on Soviet themes were almost impossible to achieve. All artistic expression was confined in the cold grasp of socialist realism, the same restraint which has forced Soviet painting and sculpture back into the styles of the pre-photographic age. For war subjects and those which exalt the native at the expense of the foreign, this restraint was less apparent; and, since all nations voluntarily accept disciplines during times of emergency, the quality of Soviet MP seemed to improve during the Second World War. But for works capable of more imaginative treatment and of adult and subtle approach, this firm control acted as a choke.

Meanwhile, the simple factual film for general information contrived to flourish. Popular science, current events, children's entertainment, cartoon, and educational subjects were filmed in abundance.

The planners developed the physique of the industry and, when much of their work, located in the war zone, was overrun and destroyed by enemy action, they rebuilt and then continued to expand. They constructed studios in all constituent republics, designed and built equipment for production and laboratory work, increased cinema installations to nearly 40,000 in MP theaters and public halls, introduced improvements in sound and color photography, created the only three-dimensional film which can be viewed by the naked eye, adequately copied the wide and giant and triple-screen systems of the W. world. By 1950, the industry was using more than half a billion feet of positive film per year, a popular production needing as many as 2,000 prints and 20 language versions to meet the demand.

Payment of personnel is threefold: by basic half-pay all the year round, by full pay during production, and by premium for commercially successful results. For example, creative workers—writers, directors and composers—share some 2½ per cent of the gross receipts of their work. For one musical, the receipts approached 5,000 per cent of the film's cost and the director became a ruble millionaire.

No one is admitted to the technical and creative departments of the industry without five years of training, during which period a stipend is paid. For over forty years the All-Union State Institute of Cinematography has taken students from high schools and after military service and continued their general education as well as grounding them in the special techniques of writing, directing, acting, camerawork, art direction, and film history and appreciation. Applicants are rigorously examined by panels of experts and some 120 are accepted every year, 600 being the current total at the Institute. The leaders of the profession take turns teaching courses in the intervals between their own productions. Student directors and actors largely share the same courses; consequently leading actors give the fruits of their experience to budding actors and directors alike, as also do established directors. Apparatus is professional, and innumerable short films are made of which only the very cream are preserved.

The influence of Eisenstein and his contemporaries of the early experimental days has created the tradition that the creative work of film editing is the concern of the director. The manual work is done by artisans who never become film editors. Indeed, there is no separate category of film editor in the Soviet Union. Scarcely ever has a film director completed more than one film in a year, since he is also involved in the script-writing and the general preparation of design, casting, and the planning of shooting which is often elaborate. Subjects are graded, not by their commercial possibilities, but by their ideological importance. Films glorifying Communist achievements, particularly in the Second World War, have been staged with scenes as elaborate as those of the most massive historical spectacles of Italy and the U. S., but at far inferior cost, since there is no commercial competition and virtually only one employer.

After the removal of the bans imposed during Stalin's lifetime, it took some years for the film industry to flex its muscles and regain the use of its limbs and brains. One stimulus was the encouraging reaction abroad to S. I. Yutkevich's noble *Othello,* played by S. F. Bondarchuk who was later to begin directing, and G. M. Kozintsev's *Don Quixote,* played by N. K. Cherkasov, the greatest living Soviet film actor. G. N. Chukhray's war film, *The Forty-First,* came closer to the human interpretation of contemporary life, and the new approach was established by *The Cranes Are Flying,* directed by M. K. Kalatozov, which won international approval for its revelation of character and its faint regard for propaganda.

A nation's MP are as good a long-distance reflection of that nation's condition as any other. By these standards, conditions are better in the Soviet Union of 1961 than they have been since 1917. On the other hand, there is less freedom for self-expression of the individual talent than in the old days.

ANNUAL MOVIE ATTENDANCE

FILM PROJECTING INSTALLATIONS
(in thousands, as of Jan. 1)

	1914*	1941	1960
TOTAL	1.5	28.0	90.9
Stationary	1.5	15.5	59.0
Mobile	—	12.5	31.9
RURAL	0.14	19.5	73.6
Stationary	0.14	8.0	43.8
Mobile	—	11.5	29.8
Attendance (mill.)	106	883	3,522

* Present day boundaries.

Film-projecting Installations (thous.)

As of Jan. 1, 1960 there were 35 studios in the USSR, including the Mosfilm and Gorky studios (Moscow), Lenfilm (Leningrad), the Dovzhenko Studio (Kiev), Gruzia-Film (Tbilisi), Armen-Film (Yerevan), the Tashkent, Riga and other studios. Production rose from 54 features in 1940 to 145 in 1959, and from 198 short subjects to 750, respectively.

BIBLIOGRAPHY: Thorold Dickinson and Catherine de la Roche, *Soviet Cinema,* London, 1948; Jay Leyda, *Kino,* a history of the Russian and Soviet film, New York, 1960; John Rimberg, *The Soviet Film Industry,* New York, 1956; Marie Seton, *Sergey M. Eisenstein,* London, 1952.   TH. D.

MOZDÓK, town in N. Ossetian SSR, on the Terek River; pop. 24,500 (1959); has a R.R. station, vineyards, orchards, horticulture, furniture and brick factories, food processing.

MOZHÁYSK, town in Moscow Oblast, RSFSR, on Moskva River; pop. 12,600 (1956). R.R. station; brick and clothing factory. In 1812 the battle of Borodino between Napoleon and the R. Army was waged there.

MÓZYR, city in Gomel Oblast, Byelorussian SSR, harbor on the right bank of the Pripyat River; pop. 30,000 (1959). R.R. station; ind.: lumbering, food processing, furniture factory. Founded in 12th century.

MRAVÍNSKY, Yevgény Aleksándrovich (1903–), conductor; People's Artist of the USSR (1954). Graduated from Leningrad conservatoire (1931). Served as conductor of Kirov Opera and Ballet Theaters (1932–38). Became chief conductor of Leningrad Philharmonic Orchestra in 1938. M has conducted most of the first performances of Shostakovich's symphonies. Awarded Stalin prize in 1946.

MSTÁ RIVER, about 275 mi. long, central Novgorod Oblast; rises in Kalinin Oblast, flowing N.W. and W. into N. end of Lake Ilmen; navigable.

MSTÉRA, town on Klyazma River in Vladimir Oblast, RSFSR. A major center of popular art; once famous for icon painting, now miniature paintings, artistic embroidery.

MTS—abbreviated form of *Mashinno-Traktornye Stantsii,* machine-tractor stations—state enterprises which for a fixed fee paid in kind carried out for the kolkhozes specific agricultural operations (such as ploughing and harvesting), requiring the use of tractors, combines, and other agricultural machinery.

In 1932–58 the overwhelming part of the stock of agricultural machinery was concentrated in the MTS. In 1957 out of 1,635,000 tractors in agriculture (in terms of 15 HP), 1,044,000, or 64 per cent, belonged to the MTS.

The fee drawn by the MTS was determined as a fixed amount of centners of grain per hectare of cultivated land according to the service rendered. Payments in kind to the MTS were transferred to the state procurement organizations. In 1937, a year of a record harvest, out of 32 mill. tons of grain collected by government agencies about 9 mill. tons were derived from work done by the MTS.

The organization of the MTS as separate from the productive units of the kolkhozes may, on one hand, be explained by the prevailing conditions in the initial period of the kolkhoz system (small size of the kolkhoz, lack of skilled labor as tractor drivers, etc.), and on the other, by the desire of Soviet authorities to keep a stricter control, through the MTS, over the nearly quarter of a million collective farms.

It is worth noting that throughout the total period of their existence the MTS were never operated under conditions of economic accounting (*khozraschot*), being directly supported by means drawn from the state budget; hence, very few incentives, if any, existed for a rational utilization of the machine stock by the management of the MTS. Furthermore, the duality of control by the management of the MTS over machinery and equipment and by the kolkhoz management over the labor force led to frictions, malpractice, and waste.

On March 31, 1958 the Supreme Soviet of the USSR promulgated a law which prescribes the liquidation of the MTS and the sale of their machine stock to the collective farms. Some of the MTS will continue to operate as repair shops and trade centers for gasoline and spare parts—RTS—*Remontno-Tekhnicheskie Stantsii* (3,500 as of Jan. 1, 1960).

By the end of 1959 the bulk of tractors and combines belonging previously to the MTS became the property of the kolkhozes. The burden of investment in new machinery and equipment was put henceforth on the collective farms and this brought an accelerated differentiation between the more successful, rich and the poor, backward collective farms. In 1958–59 the collective farms purchased agricultural machinery and implements for 32 bill. rubles. (*See also* AGRICULTURE, KOLKHOZ)

A. K.

MTSKHÉTA, town in Georgian SSR, at the confluence of the Aragva and Kura rivers, on the Transcaucasian R.R. and the Georgian Military Road; pop. 5,100 (1956). Match, ceramic, brick factories, sawmills. It was the ancient capital of Georgia (Iberia) before the 6th century B.C.; excavations revealed ruins of a palace and tombs of Iberian kings, and there are outstanding examples of Georgian architecture (Sveti-Tskhoveli).

MUDRÓV, Matvéy Nikoláyevich (1776–1831), physician. Graduate (1800), professor (1809), Moscow University. Introduced the system of recording case histories of patients, emphasized the diagnosis of the causes of disease. A pioneer of military hygiene and disease-prevention in the army. Participated actively in anti-cholera campaigns in Saratov and St. Petersburg. Died of cholera.

MUKDÉN, BATTLE OF, 1905, the last major land battle (Feb. 6 to Feb. 25, 1905) in the Russo-Japanese War. The Russian Army in Manchuria which was threatened by encirclement was forced to retreat and took up positions at Telin (Sypingay positions). The defeat of the Russian Army at Mukden and the annihilation of the Russian Fleet in Tsushima Strait greatly discredited the R. government and culminated in the revolution of 1905.

MÚKHINA (Zamkova), **Véra Ignátyevna** (1889–1953), sculptress. Studied in Moscow (1909–11) and Paris (1912–14). In 1918–20, worked on the projects of the so-called "monumental propaganda." In 1937 M finished the group (in stainless steel), *The Worker and the Kolkhoz Girl*, which was shown in the Soviet Pavilion at the World Exhibition in Paris in 1937. Received the Stalin prize in 1941. M sculpted portraits and designed monuments (Gorky, Tchaikovsky) as well as stage settings.

MUKHITDÍNOV, Nuritdin Akramovich (1917–), Soviet official. Member of the CPSU since 1942. In 1949, member of the central committee of the CP of Uzbekistan; 1950, first secretary of the Tashkent Oblast committee of CP; 1951–55, chairman of Council of Ministers of Uzbek SSR; 1955, first secretary of the central committee of the Uzbek SSR. At the 19th and 20th Congresses of the CPSU, M was elected member of the Central Committee of the CPSU; 1957, member of the Presidium of the Central Committee of the CPSU. He is a deputy to the Supreme Soviet USSR and Supreme Soviet of Uzbek SSR. In 1956–58, chairman of the Commission for Foreign Affairs of the Council of Nationalities.

MUNICIPAL GOVERNMENT: *see* GOVERNMENT MUNICIPAL.

MUNKÚ-SARDÝK, highest peak (11,450 ft.) in the Sayan Mountains, on boundary between Buryat ASSR and the Mongolian People's Republic. Has minor glaciers.

MUNNICH: *see* MINIKH.

MURADÉLI, Vano Ilyich (1908–), composer, graduated from Tbilisi and Moscow conservatoires. Author of the opera *The Great Friendship* (produced in 1947), two symphonies, and many popular songs: *The Hymn of the International Students' Union, Song of Fighters for Peace, Moscow-Peking*. Stalin prizes (1946, 1951).

MURÁLOV, Nikoláy Ivánovich (1877–1937), born in Taganrog of a peasant family. In 1903, joined the Bolshevik party. After the February revolution, was very active in the Moscow Soviet; was one of the chief organizers of the Bolshevik uprising in Moscow in 1917. In the civil war M commanded Bolshevik detachments. In 1921, was commander of the Red Army in the Moscow district; in 1924, commander of the Red Army in the North Caucasian military district. In 1937, as an oppositionist to Stalin, M was condemned to death and executed.

MURAVYÓV-AMÚRSKY, Count Nikoláy Nikoláyevich (1809–1881), governor general of E. Siberia (1847–1861). He concluded the Aygun Treaty with China (1858) which established the Russian-Chinese border along the Amur River.

MURAVYÓV-APÓSTOL, Sergéy Ivánovich (1796–1826), outstanding Decembrist, colonel of the Chernigov Regiment. Graduated from the St. Petersburg Institute of Communications. Took part in Napoleonian campaign. In 1816 he was cofounder of the "Union of Salvation" and leader of the Decembrist organization in S. Russia. A republican, he led the revolt of the Chernigov Regiment; was hanged in July 13, 1826, in St. Petersburg.

MURAVYÓV, Mikhaíl Artémyevich (1880–1918), lieutenant colonel in the Imperial Army, joined the Socialist Revolutionary party. In Oct. 1917 he led the Bolshevik troops against General Krasnov and then fought the Whites in Ukraine and on the Don. However, he later supported the uprising of the left-wing Socialist Revolutionaries against the Bolsheviks in Moscow in July 1918. Surrounded by troops faithful to the Bolsheviks, M allegedly committed suicide.

MURAVYÓV, Count Mikhaíl Nikoláyevich (1796–1866), statesman, defender of serfdom. He suppressed the revolt in Poland in 1863; was nicknamed "Muravyov-the-Hanger."

MURAVYÓV, Nikíta Mikháylovich (1796–1843), prominent member and ideologist of the Decembrist movement, one of the leaders of the Northern Society, and author of a draft constitution of the R. state. He was condemned to death, but his sentence was commuted to 20 years of hard labor in the Nerchinsk mines. Died in Irkutsk Province.

MURGÁB RIVER, in N.W. Afghanistan and S.E. Turkmen SSR; 530 mi. long. Rises in W. slopes of the Hindu Kush and flows W. and N.W. until lost in the sands of the Kara-Kum Desert. Used for artificial irrigation in the S. part of the Turkmen SSR.

MÚRMANSK, city, adm. center of Murmansk Oblast, RSFSR, in the N.W. part of Kola Bay (Barents Sea); pop. 119,000 (1939), 222,000 (1959). A large ice-free port all year round, and terminus of the R.R. to Leningrad; extensive fishing; fish-canning combine, refrigeration plant, shipyard; and the Arctic Institute of Pisciculture and Oceanography. Its name was derived from the Lapp words "mur," sea, and "ma," land.

MÚRMANSK OBLAST, RSFSR; area 56,000 sq. mi.; pop. 567,000 (1959): Russians, Lapps, Nenets, Komi. Borders on Norway and Finland in the W., Karelian ASSR in the S.; bounded by Barents Sea in the N., including the Kola Peninsula. Cities: Murmansk (adm. center and port), Monchegorsk, Kandalaksha, Polyarny, Kirovsk. Drained by dense network of rivers, such as Niva, Tuloma, Ponoy; has numerous lakes (Imandra, Umbozero, Lovozero); podsolic soils; tundra vegetation, with birch, spruce, and pine forests. Its humid climate is influenced by the Gulf Stream which passes the ice-free Barents Sea. Mineral resources: apatite, nephelite, nickel ores (Pechenga), granite, basalt, peat. Ind.: non-ferrous metallurgy, lumbering, fish canning, shipbuilding, mfg. of structural materials. Agr.: dairy farming, grain crops, potatoes, vegetables, reindeer and cattle raising, apiculture, breeding of fur-bearing animals. Has extensive rail and waterway network. Est. 1938.

MÚROM, city in Vladimir Oblast, RSFSR, on Oka River; pop. 40,000 (1939), 73,000 (1959). Is a key R.R. junction and a river port; an ind. center with large factories, including textile, machine mfg., linen, cotton goods, woodworking. First mentioned in the 9th century.

MÚROMTSEV, Sergéy Andréyevich (1850–1910), professor of law at the University of Moscow, one of the founders of the Constitutional Democratic party, and president of the first State Duma. After the dissolution of the Duma, M signed the Vyborg appeal, was tried and served a prison sentence.

MUSEUMS. In medieval Russia valuables and art objects were collected in monasteries and churches (Monastery of the Caves in Kiev, Cathedral of St. Sophie in Novgorod). In the 16th century the Kremlin armory was used for storage of weapons, silverware, and armors. The palaces of St. Petersburg and of its environment—Tsarskoye Selo (now Pushkin), Peterhof (now Petrodvorets), Oranienbaum, and Pavlovsk—house important art collections. The first scientific museum in Russia, *Kunstkamera*, was founded by Peter the Great in 1714; Peter was primarily interested in curios, but he also acquired works of art. The first important collection of paintings was purchased by Catherine II in 1764, the official date of the founding of the Hermitage Museum in the present Leningrad. It consists today of several buildings, the oldest being the Winter Palace. In 1768, a small mansion designed by Vallin de la Motte and called "The Hermitage" was built next to the Winter Palace to house art collections. In 1852, it was opened to the public. After the October revolution The Hermitage was greatly enriched by the incorporation of private collections which had been nationalized. The State Hermitage Museum houses a large collection of paintings by Rembrandt, El Greco, Van Dyke, Rubens, Watteau, and many others; prints, drawings, antiquities, precious stones, and coins.

Next to the Hermitage is the Russian Museum (1895) located in the former Mikhaylov Palace and containing over 226,000 specimens of R. art.

There are many other M in Leningrad: the Peter the Great Museum of Anthropology and Ethnography (1878), the Museum of Ethnography of the Peoples of the USSR, the Darwin and Zoological Museum (affiliated with the Ac. of S., USSR), the Theatrical Museum, the All-Union A. S. Pushkin Museum, the Central Museum of Communications, and the Museum of R.R. Transportation.

Moscow comes second: the Tretyakov State Gallery, founded by R. M. Tretyakov, who donated his vast collection of 18th- and 19th-century R. painters to the city of Moscow in 1892. The Gallery has also an important collection of icons. The A. S. Pushkin Museum of Fine Arts (1912) owns about 600,000 items and specializes in restoration work. The Museum of the Revolution was inaugurated in 1924. The Museum of Eastern Cultures (1918) has a fine collection of applied and decorative art. Furthermore, Moscow has numerous specialized museums, such as the Industrial and Polytechnic Museum, the Museum of Earth Studies, the K. A. Timiryazev Biological Museum (both affiliated with Moscow State University), the State Museum of Literature, the M. I. Glinka Central Museum of Musical Culture, the A. N. Skryabin Museum, the L. N. Tolstoy Museum, and the A. A. Bakhrushin Theatrical Museum.

The Museum of Ukrainian Art (1899) in Kiev owns some 9,000 specimens of Ukrainian national decorative and applied art. The establishment of the Museum of Western and Eastern Art in Kiev (1919) was followed by the inauguration of the Museum of Russian Art (1922) which has some 6,000 specimens of the pre-revolutionary and postrevolutionary periods. The residences of outstanding writers and musicians have been converted into national shrines: the Pushkin House, a museum of literature in Leningrad; the house of L. N. Tolstoy in Yasnaya Polyana; the residences of A. P. Chekhov in Moscow and Yalta; the M. Yu. Lermontov House in Pyatigorsk and his country residence in Lermontovo, Penza Oblast; the P. I. Tchaikovsky Museum in Klin, near Moscow; the T. G. Shevchenko Museum in Kiev; the Gorky Museum in Gorky; the Pushkin Memorial Park in Pskov Oblast, and many others.

There was a total of 907 M (1960) in the Soviet Union (213 in 1913), including about 122 art M, with an attendance of 43 mill. visitors (1959).   T. D.

MUSHKÉTOV, Iván Vasílyevich (1850–1902), geologist and geographer. Graduate (1872) and professor

(1896), St. Petersburg Mining Institute. On numerous exploratory trips M discovered a number of mineral deposits in N. Tien Shan and the Kuldzha region. Research concerned the geological structure of Central Asia, the glaciers of the Caucasus, the coal and manganese deposits in the Rioni River basin and the Upper Don. Studied the causes and consequences of the 1887 earthquake and based his research projects on tectonic and seismographic processes. The Nan Shan ridge, the volcanic foundation of the Vitim River, glaciers of the Tien Shan and the Kara Tau ridges bear his name.

MUSIC. Russian musical art was introduced to the western world in the first decade of this century. In 1907 Serge Diaghilev brought to Paris the composers Rimsky-Korsakov and Glazunov, the singers Chaliapin, Smirnov, and Feliya Litvin, and the orchestra of Mariinsky opera house, with Nickisch, Blumenfeld, and Rachmaninoff as conductors. With these distinguished artists concerts and recitals were given at which were performed compositions by Glinka, Musorgsky, Borodin, Tchaikovsky, Rimsky-Korsakov, Glazunov, Taneyev, Lyadov, Balakirev, Cui, and others. In 1908 and 1909 Diaghilev organized in Paris R. opera seasons. The entire company of the St. Petersburg Mariinsky opera house was brought to the French capital. R. operas, virtually unknown in the West, were presented to Paris audiences for the first time, in the stage settings by distinguished artists. Diaghilev's "Russian seasons" were a great success and continued until 1913.

The recognition of R. musical art came rather late; it had been delayed by several decades—in the case of Glinka, for example, by nearly three-quarters of a century. His *Ivan Susanin* was written in 1836 and produced at the imperial opera house in the same year. Glinka's second opera, *Ruslan and Lyudmila*, was composed and staged in 1842. The history of R. music, however, does not begin with Glinka, whose work is still little known in the West.

Russian love of music is reflected in the folk songs. The influence of the Tatars, Khazars, Mongols and other nomads inhabiting medieval Russia injected oriental color into the melodic structure of the R. folk song and intercourse with Russia's near-eastern neighbors left its imprint. These alien elements were assimilated by the R. folk song, in creating a distinctive style of its own. Its rhythmic structure allows occasional 5/4 and 7/4 deviations from the conventional 3/4 or 4/4 time, and its melodic line is based primarily on the pure pentatonic scale.

Musical instruments had been in general use since the earliest time of R. history. *Gudok,* a bow instrument, is mentioned in R. annals dating back to the 11th century. *Gusli* (psaltery) was a pizzicato instrument. There were small horns, pipes, the clay ocarina, *zhaleyka* (a reed instrument resembling the clarinet), *surna,* a kind of oboe. The more commonly used percussion instruments included the drums, kettledrums, and tambourines. The *domra* (a kind of mandolin) did not come into existence before the 16th century. The 12th century marks the appearance of professional entertainers (*skomorokhi*) performing simultaneously as minstrel singers, acrobats, and clowns. There were a

few foreign musicians in the service of the R. princes. Some were engaged to play on festive occasions, when war victories were celebrated, or in the homes of the wealthy. The troops had their brass bands, which blared forth "military" music.

During the reign of Ivan III (1462–1505), a court choir was formed in which church deacons appeared as the principal singers. In the 18th century a permanent Court Capella was founded and in 1721, at the time of Peter the Great, the Moscow Synodal Choir.

With the annexation of Byelorussia and the Ukraine in the 17th century, polyphonic singing in the manner of western chorals was brought to Russia. Concertos with many vocal and solo parts were composed; canticles and psalms were sung. Religious plays based on Biblical subjects were performed in the German settlement, a Moscow suburb. During the time of Peter the Great counterpoint singing, military bands, and dance orchestras were common. A few foreign musicians visited Russia. In 1730 operas by Sarti, Galuppi, and Cimarose were produced in Russia by Italian opera companies. Some Italian composers spent a few years in Russia, where they conducted performances, or furnished the music for stage shows. In the last third of the 18th century several composers rose to local prominence. M. Berezovsky (1745–77) wrote operas in the Italian style. D. Bortnyansky (1752–1825), a competent musician, exerted an influence upon the development of church music. His works are still sung at the divine service in R. churches. Ivan Khandoshkin (1740–1804), a former serf and self-taught musician, was a gifted composer. A good violinist, Khandoshkin was the author of original compositions based on R. folk tunes and written in the grand virtuoso style. M. Matinsky (1750–1820) was the author of numerous operas. The work of Daniil Kashin (1769–1841), who studied with Sarti, enjoyed considerable popularity. E. Fomin (1761–1800), a pupil of Padre Martini, had a part in the development of R. operatic music. I. Kozlovsky (1757–1831), a versatile musician and craftsman, had mastered the European techniques of composition. A. Zhilin (1760–1848), a blind musician, was the author of many lyric songs of merit. Fyodor Dubyansky (1760–96), wrote romantic songs in the popular vein. Vasily Pashkevich (1742–1800) was a conductor and composer. S. Degtyarev (1766–1813) composed Russia's earliest oratorios and cantatas. S. Davydov (1777–1825), pupil of Sarti, wrote operas, ballet, and orchestral pieces.

K. Cavos (1776–1840) was an Italian conductor and composer who had come to Russia in 1797 and lived there for 40 years, working as teacher, composer, and conductor in charge of operatic performances. His better-known work is the opera *Ivan Susanin,* built around the same theme as Glinka's opera of that name. A. Alyabev (1787–1851), author of many operas, incidental music for Shakespeare's *Tempest,* symphonic overtures, wrote also 150 romances. His *Nightingale* is sung outside Russia. A. Varlamov (1801–48) is credited with having written about 150 romances which were widely popular in his time. A. Gurilev (1802–56) composed numerous piano pieces as well as romantic and popular songs, in a manner anticipating that of Tchaikovsky. Among the better-known composers preceding Glinka was A. Verstovsky (1799–1862), author of the opera *Tomb of Askold,* which was revised by Jacommo Rossini.

M. I. Glinka (1804–57) was at first a wealthy amateur amusing himself with occasional fiddling or piano playing, composer of quadrilles and fantasies on Italian folk melodies, who had produced little beyond musical trifles. At the age of thirty-four he wrote an opera *Life for the Tsar* (renamed *Ivan Susanin* after the Soviet revolution), which showed imagination and originality and met the technical standards of western operatic art. His other opera was *Ruslan and Lyudmila.* His compositions included church and chamber music and many romances. A. Dargomyzhsky (1813–69) was nine years younger than Glinka. His operas, *The Mermaid* (*Rusalka*) and *The Stone Guest,* especially the former, were and still are popular in Russia. While continuing Glinka's tradition, Dargomyzhsky introduced novel elements into R. music. A. Serov (1820–71), composer and music critic, was the author of numerous operas, including *Judith, Rogneda, The Mighty Foe.* Anton Rubinstein (1829–94), a celebrated pianist, left more than 200 compositions, of which the 4th piano concerto and the *Songs of Persia* are still played today. Of his operas, the most successful was *The Demon.* Nicholas Rubinstein (1835–81) was a pianist of no lesser distinction than his brother Anton. He was a composer of promise but wrote little.

M. Balakirev (1836–1910) founded a group known as "The Five," which included Musorgsky, Rimsky-Korsakov, Borodin, and Cui. His symphonic poems *Tamara, Rus* and *Islamey* are important musical works. Caesar Cui (1835–1918) wrote the operas *Ratcliff, The Caucasian Prisoner, The Mandarin's Son,* as well as a number of compositions for voice and piano.

M. Musorgsky (1839–81) is one of Russia's most important composers. His operas *Boris Godunov, Khovanshchina, The Fair of Sorochinsk,* his orchestral work *Night on Bald Mountain,* and the piano composition *Pictures at an Exhibition* have become the standard part of the operatic and concert repertory in every country. The influence of Musorgsky's musical language is felt in the creative work of western composers. A. Borodin (1833–87), a professor of chemistry, called himself a "Sunday composer," since he seldom had an opportunity to write music. His opera *Prince Igor,* both his symphonies, the symphonic poem *In the Steppes of Middle Asia,* and his quartets are well known. N. Rimsky-Korsakov (1844–1908) is the author of 15 operas, the symphonic poems *Scheherazade* and *Antar, Cappriccio Espagnol,* and other important works. Musorgsky's *Boris Godunov* was revised and orchestrated by Rimsky-Korsakov, and in this version has won world recognition. Together with Glazunov, he completed Borodin's opera *Prince Igor.* The work of Rimsky-Korsakov, who taught two generations of R. composers, influenced the musical art of W. Europe. P. I. Tchaikovsky (1840–93), perhaps the best known of all R. composers, wrote 8 operas, 6 symphonies, 3 ballets, and a great many other works. A.

Arensky (1861–1906), a pupil of Rimsky-Korsakov, left the opera *Nil and Damayanti* and a number of chamber works. The compositions of A. Lyadov (1855–1914), author of symphonic poems *Baba Yaga* (The Witch), *Kikimora* (The Incubus), show strong poetic imagination, good taste, and true craftsmanship. A. Glazunov (1865–1936), who wrote his first symphony at the age of 16, left eight symphonies, ballet music, symphonic poems, and a highly popular violin concerto. A. Grechaninov (1864–1956) produced an opera *Dobrynya Nikitich,* a large body of church music, four symphonies, a few quartets, and numerous romances. V. Kalinnikov (1866–1901) wrote two symphonies. Nikolay Cherepnin (1873–1939), composer and conductor, is the author of ballet music and other works. S. Taneyev (1856–1915), a master of counterpoint, wrote four symphonies, quartets, and the opera *Oresteya.* A. Skryabin and S. Rachmaninoff were pupils of Taneyev. Aleksandr Skryabin (1872–1915), the most popular composer in Russia during the last fifteen years of his life, is less appreciated in the West. I. Stravinsky (1882–), a noted composer, despite his advanced age continues to surprise the world with his novel musical ideas. S. Rachmaninoff (1873–1943), a distinguished pianist, was also a prolific composer whose piano concertos have won a permanent place in the repertory.

Sergey Prokofyev (1891–1953), a pupil of Rimsky-Korsakov, Lyadov, and Cherepnin, left over 140 compositions. Next to Stravinsky's, his work must be considered the most important manifestation in the R. musical art of our time. R. Glière (1875–1957), distinguished teacher and prolific composer, was a master of orchestration. N. Myaskovsky (1881–1947), the author of more than 25 symphonies, taught several generations of Soviet composers. Glière, Myaskovsky, and Prokofyev belong to both the pre-Soviet and Soviet periods. All of them by 1917 had been fully developed as composers. Unlike Rachmaninoff, Glazunov, Cherepnin, or Grechaninov, they remained in Russia, where they continued their creative work and their artistic activities to the last. Prokofyev lived abroad for nearly a decade, but in the thirties returned to Russia where during the remaining 25 years of his life he produced a number of important musical works.

On the initiative of Anton Rubinstein the Russian Music Society (*Russkoye Muzykalnoye Obshchestvo*) was established in 1859 "to advance music culture and education . . . and to encourage local talents." The Society organized symphonic concerts and in 1862 founded the St. Petersburg Conservatoire, with Anton Rubinstein as its director. Among the early graduates of the Conservatoire was Tchaikovsky (1865). The Conservatoire had a distinguished faculty and has trained many outstanding musicians. In 1866 Nikolay Rubinstein, Anton's brother, founded the Moscow Conservatoire. These two great music schools powerfully contributed to the advancement of music not only in Russia but throughout the world.

Chamber music was popular in Russia from the end of the eighteenth century. Early in the nineteenth chamber music recitals and symphonic concerts were fairly common in the larger cities and were sponsored by well-to-do music lovers. With the organization of the Russian Music Society concerts given by symphony orchestras became a regular feature of the music life of St. Petersburg, Moscow, Kiev, Odessa, and Kharkov. Today both Moscow and Leningrad have several excellent orchestras and there are several hundred more in the various cities of the Soviet Union. Russian conductors—E. F. Napravnik, V. I. Safonov, Aleksandr Ziloti, Glazunov, Rachmaninoff (to mention only a few) —have won the acclaims of the world.

Among composers of the Soviet period, first mention should be made of D. Shostakovich (1906–), whose ability was recognized by Glazunov in the early years of the revolution. Aram Khachaturyan, Dmitry Kabalevsky, Ivan Dzerzhinsky, Yury Shaporin, Vissarion Shebalin and Tikhon Khrennikov are perhaps the best known among Soviet composers. Next to Shostakovich, Aram Khachaturyan (1904–) is the most colorful and original. He is a Russian Armenian, and the oriental blood flowing in his veins makes itself felt in his music —whether a violin or piano concerto, or a symphonic work. D. Kabalevsky (1904–), a pupil of Myaskovsky, author of several operas, piano compositions, ballet music, is known in the West mainly because of his piano sonatas, frequently performed at recitals. Few Europeans are acquainted with the work of Dzerzhinsky (1909–), Shaporin (1889–), Khrennikov (1913–), and the list is far from complete. Only musicologists who follow Soviet literature know the names of Mariana Koval (1907–), A. Davidenko (1899–1934), Aleksey Zhivotov (1904–), Irakly Muradeli, the Georgian composer (1908–), Dmitry Zhelobinsky (1913–), Samuil Feinberg (1890–), L. Knipper (1898–), pianist and teacher, author of 7 or 8 symphonies, B. Lyatoshinsky (1893–), pupil of Glière, an excellent orchestrator, author of several operas, Boris Shekhter (1900–), specializing in the music of the Soviet Far East.

In the past 40 years hundreds of operas, thousands of orchestral works, and many thousands of folk songs and romances have been published in Soviet Russia —some of these by such composers as Isaak Dunayevsky or the Pokrass brothers. A good deal of music is written by the "regional" composers, natives of Georgia, Armenia, Azerbaijan, and other regions. In the early period the music of the national minorities had been elaborated by such veteran Soviet composers as Glière, Kreyn, Shekhter, and others, but recent years mark the emergence of distinct native talent. No really great composers have come to the fore in the W. of Russia, nor in the Soviet E., but the work carried on in this field merits attention. Of the Jewish composers who had created the neo-Jewish school of musical art in St. Petersburg shortly before World War I, Milner, Achron, Saminsky, Gnesin, Engel, and Kreyn died. Aleksandr Veprik and Grigory Kreyn are still living and continue to write music, but very few people in Russia, for the past 30–35 years, have been aware of their work.

The R. composers living abroad continue to work actively at their calling. Stravinsky took up residence in California. Aleksandr Cherepnin is a professor teaching in Chicago; his symphonies, ballets, and operas are produced, or performed, both in the United States and in Europe. Igor Markevich lives in Paris, where he conducts and writes music, between concert tours abroad. Nikolay Nabokov lives in America, but has another permanent residence in Paris; his opera *Rasputin* has been favorably received in Europe. Vladimir Dukelsky (Vernon Duke) is a resident of California, as is Mikhail Levin, who writes background music for motion pictures, under the name of Michel Michle. Dmitry Temkin, a graduate of the St. Petersburg Conservatoire, is a highly successful composer of film music. Vladimir Fogel, who settled down in Switzerland, writes music, frequently performed in Europe. Nikolay Lopatnikov holds a professorship in Pittsburgh; his compositions enjoy a measure of popularity in the United States.

Mischa Elman, Jascha Heifetz, Nathan Milstein, and Stern, the celebrated Russian-born virtuosi, have gone on frequent tours in the United States and abroad. Vladimir Horowitz continues making recordings. Grigory Pyatigorsky is still heard in an occasional appearance before the public. Alexander Schneider has participated in every international music festival directed by Pablo Casals. Efrem Zimbalist holds a professorship in Philadelphia, as does Lea Luboschitz.

Of singular importance were the activities of Sergey Koussevitzky (1874–1951), the former virtuoso double-bass player who became an internationally renowned conductor. He established in 1910 in Moscow his own admirable symphony orchestra which toured frequently other Russian cities. Koussevitzky also headed a publishing house which published the scores of the leading Russian composers. In 1920 he left Russia and lived in Western Europe and in the United States. He was for twenty-five years the conductor of the Boston Symphony Orchestra and frequently led orchestras in Europe and Latin America. He was the founder of the Berkshire Music Center in Tanglewood.

In the meantime a whole galaxy of brilliant instrumentalists has advanced into the limelight in Soviet Russia: pianists (Richter, Gilels, Oborin); violinists (David Oistrach and his son Igor, Leonid Kogan, Busya Goldstein, Liza Gilels); cellists (Rostropovich, Shafran); conductors (Kondrashin, Rakhlin, Samosud, Ivanov), as well as others. Musicology has reached a high level of development in the Soviet Union, and while the general approach is seldom free from the inevitable tendentiousness, much of the published material is on a high level of scholarship.

A few words should be said concerning the Soviet choirs. Before the revolution a number of high-caliber choral groups had existed in Russia, such as the Court Capella, Moscow Synodal Choir, the choir of St. Sophie Cathedral in Kiev, Metropolitan Choir; the choruses of Mariinsky and Bolshoy opera houses, and others. In the Soviet era these choirs had ben variously reorganized, functioning under such names as "State Academic Capellas" and the like. Among the newly formed choral groups there is the remarkable "Red Banner Ensemble of Song and Dance," organized by the late A. Aleksandrov, now led by his son, as well as the Pyatnitsky Choir or "State Russian Folk Choir," Voronezhsky, and Uralsky choirs. The "Red Banner" ensemble is known in the West through recordings.

In the past four decades there have been some changes in the policy of the Soviet government with respect to music. Shostakovich's opera *Lady Macbeth of Mtsensk* brought the official wrath upon the composer, who was reinstated in grace only when the late writer Aleksey Tolstoy interceded in his behalf before Stalin. The party has frequently given unsolicited and ill-considered counsel to the composers, who could scarcely ignore such "suggestions." The future historians of musical art in Russia will record that in many instances a completed composition was rewritten at the bidding of a party official.

BIBLIOGRAPHY: M. D. Calvocoressi, *Survey of Russian Music*, New York, 1944; R. A. Leonard, *History of Russian Music*, New York, 1956; M. D. Calvocoressi, *Masters of Russian Music*, New York, 1936; V. I. Seroff, *The Mighty Five*, New York, 1948; A. Olkhovsky, *Music Under the Soviets: the Agony of an Art*, New York, 1955.   G. Sw.

MUSKHELISHVÍLI, Nikoláy Ivánovich (1891–), mechanical engineer and mathematician. Fellow (1939) and member of the Executive Board (1957), Ac. of S., USSR. President, Georgian Ac. of S. (1941). Hero of Socialist Labor (1945). Member of the Supreme Soviet USSR (1937–58), and of its delegation to the United Kingdom (1956); head of the Soviet delegation to the Ninth International Congress of Applied Mechanics, Brussels (1956). Graduated from St. Petersburg University (1914). Professor, Tbilisi State University and Polytechnic Institute (1922). Founder of the Institute of Mathematics (1935) at Tbilisi. Research concerns the theory of elasticity, integral equations, boundary value problems of the theory of functions, the application of the theory of functions of a complex variable to elasticity theory problems, etc. Author of *Singular Integral Equations* (1946); *Course of Analytical Geometry* (1947); *Fundamental Problems of the Mathematical Theory of Elasticity* (1949). Stalin prizes (1941, 1947) and other awards.

MÚSORGSKY, Modést Petróvich (1839–1881), great R. composer, born in Karevo, Pskov Province, son of a landowner. M studied music, especially piano, as a child. He attended a military school and upon graduation served in the army until 1858. Friendship with Balakirev, Vladimir Stasov, and others led him to become a professional composer. However the impoverishment of his family prevented him from obtaining proper musical training, and he never acquired full command of the technique of his craft. Nevertheless M was recognized as the greatest of the group of composers known as "The Five" (the other members were Balakirev, Borodin, Cui, and Rimsky-Korsakov). After early experiments in dramatic music, with *King Oedipus* (1858), he composed

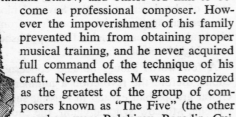

Boris Godunov (1868–69), perhaps the greatest R. opera. In 1872 came his second major work, the opera *Khovanshchina*. Later M composed the comic opera *Fair at Sorochinsk*. This score, like his other compositions, remained unfinished. The orchestration of M's operas was largely done by Rimsky-Korsakov. M wrote many piano pieces, including the very popular *Pictures at an Exhibition*. Acclaimed as Russia's greatest "national" composer, M nevertheless exercised great influence abroad.

BIBLIOGRAPHY: Oskar von Riesemann, *Musorgsky*, English translation, New York, 1935; M. D. Calvocoressi, *Musorgsky: His Life and Works*, New York, 1951, London, 1956.

MVD: *see* SECURITY POLICE.

MYAKÓTIN, Venedikt Aleksándrovich (1867–), historian and one of the leaders of the People's Socialist party (q.v.). From 1893, a writer in the populist review *Russkoye Bogatstvo* (Russian Wealth). After the October revolution, he emigrated. He is the author of *The Peasant Problem During the Partitions of Poland*, and other monographs.

MYASKÓVSKY, Nikoláy Yákovlevich (1881–1950), composer, People's Artist of USSR (1946); graduated from the St. Petersburg conservatoire where he studied under Lyadov. Professor of the Moscow conservatoire, M wrote 27 symphonies, a concerto for violin, string quartets, and sonatas. Best known for his 5th symphony (1918) which deals with folk life; the 6th symphony (1923) on the October revolution; the 12th symphony on kolkhoz themes; and the cantata, *Kreml at Night* (1947). Several Stalin prizes.

MYASOYÉDOV, Grigóry Grigóryevich (1835–1911), painter. Studied in the Academy of Fine Arts in St. Petersburg (1859–62), became member of the Academy in 1893. Active in the Society of Circulating Exhibitions (*Peredvizhniki*). Among his pictures are *The Flight of Grigory Otrepyev* (1862), *The Zemstvo at Dinner* (1872), *The Reading of the Manifesto* (1873). M is represented at the Tretyakov Gallery, Moscow, and the Russian Museum, Leningrad.

MÝSHKIN, Ippolít Nikítich (1848–1885), revolutionary, organizer of a clandestine printing shop in Moscow. He attempted to free Chernyshevsky in 1875, but was arrested and sentenced to 10 years of forced labor. He was executed for protesting against the brutal treatment of prisoners at the Schlüsselburg Fortress.

MYTÍSHCHI, city in Moscow Oblast, RSFSR; pop. 60,000 (1939), 99,000 (1959). A large machine-mfg. center, brick plant.

MZHAVANÁDZE, Vasíly Pávlovich (1902–), party and state official, member of the CP since 1927. M worked as a political commissar during the war with Finland and World War II. From 1953, first secretary of the Central Committee of the Georgian CP; since 1956, member of the Central Committee of the CPSU and, since 1957, candidate member of its Presidium.

N

NABÓKOV, Vladímir Dmítryevich (1869–1922), leader of the Constitutional Democratic party (Kadets) and chairman of its Central Committee. In 1905, N. was elected to the first State Duma. After the dissolution of the Duma, N, who signed the Vyborg appeal, was imprisoned for three months. He was one of the editors of the newspaper *Rech* and contributed to other party publications. In 1917 he became the executive secretary of the Provisional Government. After the October revolution, N left for S. Russia where he acted as General Wrangel's minister of justice, until he had to flee with the remnants of the White army. In exile he was one of the editors of the paper *Rul* in Berlin. He was killed by a White Russian, who was aiming at P. N. Milyukov.

NABÓKOV, Vladímir Vladímirovich (pen-name Vladimir Sírin) (1899–), writer. Graduate of Cambridge University, lived in Berlin and Paris. Settled in the United States (1940) and stopped writing in Russian. Associated with Cornell University. Wrote poetry in his youth. His writings include the novel *The Luzhin Defense* (1930); the macabre *Invitation to a Beheading* (1938), *The Real Life of Sebastian Knight* (1941), *Conclusive Evidence, Pnin,* the controversial *Lolita,* first published in France and then in the United States, an essay on Gogol (1944); he translated into English the epic *The Tale of the Host of Igor* from old Slavonic.

NADÉZHDIN, Nikoláy Ivánovich (1804–1856), critic, journalist, and ethnographer, best known as the editor of *Teleskóp* (The Telescope) from 1831 to 1836, when that journal was closed and N was arrested and exiled to Ust-Sysolsk for publishing Chaadayev's (q.v.) *Philosophical Letter.* Upon his return from exile N pursued historical, ethnographical, and geographical studies.

NADÉZHDINSK: *see* SEROV.

NÁDSON, Semyón Yákovlevich (1862–1887), lyrical poet. His poetry is largely the nostalgic lament of a young artistic soul tormented by the harsh realities of everyday life, and by the seemingly inexorable tragic fate of those who struggle for beauty in a humdrum existence. Among his best lyrics are *No, Muse, Do Not Call Me* and *Painters Liked to Portray Her.*

NAGÍBIN, Yúry Márkovich (1920–), fiction writer, born in Moscow. Graduated from All-Union Institute of the Cinema. His first publications appeared in 1942. During World War II N was war correspondent for the newspaper *Trud.* He is the author of short stories; among them are *Khazar Ornament* and *Light in the Window* (1956). In these stories N criticizes the inhumanity of the party leaders and their aloofness from the people. He introduced a new character into Soviet literature—the "repentant" Communist.

NAGÓRNO-KARABÁKH AUTONOMOUS OBLAST (Karabakh Mountain Area), part of Azerbaijan SSR; area 1,700 sq. mi.; pop. 131,000 (1959): Armenians, Azerbaijanis. Cities: Stepanakert (adm. center), Shusha. Is a heavily forested mountainous area, watered by tributaries of the Kura, with climate moderate at the foothills and cold at altitudes; has alpine and subalpine pastures. Ind.: silk, distilleries, carpet weaving, food, timber. Agr.: wheat, rye, tobacco, fruit; animal husbandry, horses, apiculture. Est. 1923.

NAKHICHEVÁN, city, adm. center of Nakhichevan ASSR, on the Araks River, part of Azerbaijan SSR; pop. 25,000 (1959). Has a R.R. station; food processing, winemaking, leather factory, cotton-ginning ind., with salt extraction in the vicinity. One of the oldest cities of Transcaucasia, often invaded by Persians, Mongols, Armenians, it was occupied by Russia in 1828.

NAKHICHEVÁN ASSR, part of Azerbaijan SSR, Transcaucasia, in S.W. mountainous part in bend of Araks River; area 2,100 sq. mi.; pop. 142,000 (1959), predominantly Azerbaijani (84.5%), Armenians (10.8%). Cities: Nakhichevan (adm. center), Dzhulfa, Ordubad. Rivers: Araks, Nakhichevanchay, Arpa. Dry climate. Mineral resources: salt, zinc, lead, molybdenum, building materials, sulfur. Agr.: cotton, tobacco, vineyards, orchards, silkworm breeding, cattle raising. Ind.: cotton ginning, canning, winemaking. One of the most ancient areas in the USSR. In the 8th century B.C., part of the Kingdom of Media, later conquered by Alexander of Macedon; in the 1st century B.C. overrun by Romans; in the early 3rd century A.D. taken by Persians, in the 7th century A.D. by Arabs; suffered from Tatar invasion in the 13th century. The period between the 13th and 16th century marked by unrelenting struggle against Mongolian, Turkish, and Persian invaders. Nakhichevan destroyed upon an order of Persian Shah Abbas in 1747. Under Persian rule until 1828 when it was taken over by Russia. Est. 1924.

NAKHÍMOV, Pável Stepánovich (1802–1855), outstanding naval commander, admiral, pupil of Admiral  Lazarev. He circumnavigated the globe on the frigate *Cruiser,* 1822–24; participated in the sea battle of Navarino in 1827; was commander of frigate *Pallada,* 1832–33; served in the Black Sea Fleet in 1834. In the Crimean War (1853–56) he destroyed a Turkish squadron and captured its commander at the sea battle of Sinop, Nov. 18, 1853. From Oct. 3, 1854, after Admiral Kornilov's death, he led the defense of Sevastopol. He was mortally wounded at Malakhov redoubt June 28, 1855. The Nakhimov Order and Medal was established March 3, 1944.

NAKHÓDKA, seaport city, in Maritime Kray, RSFSR, on Sea of Japan; pop. 63,000 (1959). R.R. terminus; has marine servicing shops, fishing, food processing.

NALBANDYÁN, Dmítry Arkádyevich (1906–), painter. Early work in films and as cartoonist was followed by paintings of Stalin and other political leaders. During World War II, he painted battle scenes (*Stalingrad,*

1944) and landscapes (*Winter in Yerevan*, 1943) as well as more paintings of Stalin. His most ambitious work is the monumental picture *Power to the Soviets —Peace to the World* (1950).

NÁLCHIK, capital of Kabardinian-Balkarian ASSR, on the Nalchik River; pop. 48,000 (1939), 87,000 (1959). R.R. terminus, and a scenic health resort in a mountain valley. It has a machine-mfg. factory, sawmill, food-processing ind., flour mill.

NALÍVKIN, Dmítry Vasílyevich (1889–), geologist and paleontologist. Fellow, Ac. of S., USSR (1946); Presidium chairman of the Executive Board (1946–51) and Honorary member, Ac. of S., Turkmen SSR (1951). Graduate (1915) and professor (1920) of Petrograd Mining Institute. Associated with the Geological Committee renamed the All-Union Scientific Research Institute (1917–49). Director, Laboratory of Limnology, Ac. of S. (1946–53). N participated in expeditions to Central Asia, the Urals (1921), and the Pamirs (1927–32) and in the mapping of geological regions (1937). His research on poleography and stratigraphy contributed to the discovery of Ural bauxites and petroleum deposits. N's studies of facies enhanced the rapid development and practical application of this branch of science. Author of *The Study of Facies. Geographical Conditions of the Formation of Precipitations*, two volumes (1955–56); *Brief Synopsis on the Geology of the USSR* (1957). A. P. Karpinsky Gold Medal, Ac. of S., USSR (1949). Stalin (1946) and Lenin (1957) prizes, other decorations.

NAMANGÁN, city in Andizhan Oblast, Uzbek SSR, in the Fergana Valley; pop. 80,000 (1939), 122,000 (1959). Ind.: cotton gins, production of silk and cotton goods, weaving factory, winemaking.

NAMANGÁN OBLAST, Uzbek SSR, abolished Jan. 1960, territory divided between Andizhan and Fergana oblasts.

NAMÉTKIN, Sergéy Semyónovich (1876–1950), organic chemist. Fellow, Ac. of S., USSR (1939). Honored scientist and technologist, RSFSR (1947). Associated with the State Petroleum Research Institute (1926–34) and Institute of Mineral Fuels, Ac. of S. (1934–48), director of the Petroleum Institute (1948). Research concerned the chemistry of hydrocarbons. Studied the compositions of various deposits in the USSR, developed methods of petroleum synthesis and various additions to engine fuels and lubricants. Author of the monograph *The Chemistry of Petroleum* (1932–35). Stalin prizes (1943, 1949).

NANAI: *see* POPULATION.

NANI: *see* OROCHI.

NARÓDNAYA, highest peak in the Urals (6,212 ft.), in N. Ural extending N.E. along the boundary between Komi ASSR and Tyumen Oblast.

"NARODNAYA VOLYA" (People's Will): *see* POPULISM.

NÁRVA, city in Estonian SSR, on Narova River; pop. 27,000 (1958); R.R. station. Is a major center of the textile ind., with cotton, jute, woolen, flax mills. Founded 1256, it was captured by the Swedes in the 16th century; recaptured by Russia in 1704.

NARYÁN-MAR, city, adm. center of Nenets National Okrug, Archangel Oblast, RSFSR; pop. 11,400 (1958). Has sawmill, fisheries, food processing; reindeer breeding. Airport, seaport, landing on Pechora River.

NARÝN, city, adm. center of Tyan-Shan Oblast, Kirghiz SSR, on the Naryn R. (upper tributary of the Syr Darya); pop. 5,000 (1939), 15,000 (1959). Is the center of sheep breeding and irrigated crop grains; has lumber mill, brick factory.

NATANSÓN, Mark Andréyevich (pseudonym: Bobrov), (1850–1919), revolutionary. Was one of the founders of the populist organization Land and Freedom and of the People's Right party. N was repeatedly arrested, exiled, and imprisoned in the Peter and Paul Fortress. In 1902, N was instrumental in founding the Socialist Revolutionary party, and from the beginning was a member of its Central Committee. During World War I, he was an internationalist and participated in the Zimmerwald conference. After the revolution, he sided with the left wing Socialist Revolutionary party and cooperated with the Bolsheviks. He died in Switzerland.

NATIONAL ANTHEM. After the Bolshevik Revolution, the "International" replaced the traditional "God save the Tsar" ("*Bózhe, tsaryá khraní,*" words by V. Zhukovsky, music by A. F. Lvov) as Russia's national anthem. With words by Eugène Pottier (1871) and music by Adolphe Degeyter (1888), the "International," (Russian words by A. Ya. Kots, 1902) remained the country's anthem until 1944. The dissolution of the Comintern and the increasingly "patriotic" orientation of the regime led to the replacement of the "International" in that year by a new "Hymn of the Soviet Union." This anthem was the work of Sergey V. Mikhalkov and El-Registan, music by A. V. Aleksandrov. Its central theme was the grandeur of the R. homeland as transformed by Lenin and Stalin. The "International" is now retained as an official party song.

NATIONAL DRESS. The dress common in 11th- and 12th-century Russia was influenced by Byzantine fashions and included loose silver- and gold-embroidered garments and leather boots. Women wore tunics.

In Siberia two types of fur garments are used: one-piece overalls (Eskimos, Nenets, Chukchi) and fur coats cut open in front (Evenki, Yakuts, Buryats).

The ND in N. and S. Russia is similar to that worn by other Slavic peoples; for women in S. Russia it consists of a richly embroidered long chemise and panel skirt open on the sides (*paneva*). In the Ukraine girls adorn themselves with flower wreaths, beads, and multicolored ribbons. In N. and central Russia a sleeveless dress (*sarafan*) is worn over a blouse. Originally, boyar women wore costly *sarafans*, embroidered with precious stones and trimmed with sable, mink, or ermine. In winter a fur-lined velvet jacket (*dushegreyka*) was worn over it. Headdresses (*kokoshnik*) were also set with precious stones and richly embroidered with silk, silver-thread, and pearls. Peter the Great introduced western fashions, and eventually simplified versions of the *sarafan* remained the traditional dress of only peasant women. Presently, *sarafans* are still popular in Archangel, Vologda, Kursk and other areas. On holidays, women wear *sarafans* with multicolored beads, gay kerchiefs. Men wear full trousers tucked into leather boots, and shirts with side-fastening; the stand-up collar, bottom and sleeves are often embroidered in cross-stitches. A sheepskin coat gathered in folds around the waist is used in winter.

Bast shoes (*lapti*) and strips of cloth wrapped around the feet (*onuchi*) are worn in the Baltic states, the Volga, Kama and other eastern and western areas. Felt boots (*válenki*) are worn in the villages in winter time.

The peoples of the Caucasus (Georgians, Circassians, Ossets and others) wear quilted jackets (*beshmet*) with high collars under collarless long-waisted outer garments (*cherkeska*). Length, color, and ornaments vary in every area. A sheepskin hat (*papakha*) completes the costume. The traditional dress of women is a long dress, taken in at the waist, which has a wide skirt embroidered in silver-thread, wool, silk. Silver jewelry is artistically made in the Caucasus and enjoys great popularity.

Clothes worn by the population of central Asia have the following basic style: tunic-like shirts, wide trousers, oriental robes, embroidered skull caps, turbans or fur hats. Women wear wide dresses with a tight-fitting top. Color, ornaments, the type of kerchiefs, and the design of the fabric vary according to the region.

The rural and provincial population has adapted the ND to present-day living and economic conditions, climate and occupation.   T. D.

NATIONAL INCOME AND PRODUCT. Rate of Growth.

Official Soviet statistics put the USSR's national income in 1959 at more than 24 times the level of 1913, implying an average annual increase of 7 per cent. Since 1928, when the USSR embarked on a program of rapid industrialization, the official index of NI has risen at a much higher average annual rate (except in war years)—16 per cent in the period 1928–37 and 10 per cent in the period 1950–59. Taken at face value, these rates are very impressive, but several factors should be kept in mind when considering them.

In the first place, the Soviet concept of NI differs from the concept generally accepted in western countries by excluding income generated in most service industries. The inclusion of income stemming from the service industries, in accordance with western practice, would tend to depress the rate of growth of the official index, because of the lag in the development of these

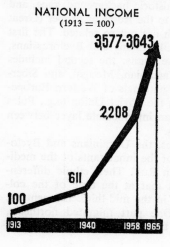

NATIONAL INCOME
(1913 = 100)

3,577-3,643

2,208

611

100

1913   1940   1958 1965

industries compared with that of other sectors of the Soviet economy. Secondly, the Soviet index until 1950 was weighted (although, as noted below, not consistently) by prices of 1926–27 vintage. (Since 1950, prices of 1951 have been used as weights.) An index weighted by prices of an earlier year is likely to show a higher rate of increase during a period of industrial-

ization than an index weighted by prices of a later year. As output of new products increases, their prices fall relative to those of other products, the new output of which is increasing more slowly. Thus an index weighted by prices of an earlier year gives more emphasis to rapid increases in output of new products and less emphasis to slower increases in output of other products. Thirdly, although the prices used as weights until 1950 are supposed to be of 1926–27 vintage, they are, in fact, by no means entirely of these years. New products have often been included at their current prices, rather than at their estimated 1926–27 prices. Since the Soviet economy has, at times, been characterized by severe inflation, this practice has given an upward bias to the index of NI. Moreover, the prices of new products added to the index have often been those of the initial stages of production, reflecting the higher costs of that period; this has also tended to inflate the index. Other factors known to impart an upward bias to the official index of NI include inadequate measurement of small, private production in the 1920's and earlier, inadequate adjustment for changes in territorial boundaries, and changes in the methods employed to measure crop output.

Non-Soviet scholars have made independent estimates of the growth of Soviet NI which point to an average annual rate of increase of 6 or 7 per cent in both the 1928–37 and 1950–59 periods. Although the western estimates point to lower rates of growth of Soviet NI than the official Soviet index, these rates are still impressive. (The long-term rate of growth of U.S. national income since 1929 has been 3 or 4 per cent per annum.)

Structure of Soviet Product. The relatively rapid rate of growth of Soviet NI stems in part from the large share of investment in gross NP. (NI differs from gross NP in that the former excludes, while the latter includes, an allowance for depreciation of capital assets.) As shown in the table below, the proportion of Soviet gross NP devoted to investment in 1955 substantially exceeded the corresponding figure for the United States. (Moreover, because of the relatively lower age of much of its capital stock and other factors, the USSR did not devote as large a share of gross investment to replacement.) Of at least equal importance is the fact that a much larger proportion of investment in the USSR went into the growth-inducing producers' goods industries than in the United States.

GROSS NATIONAL PRODUCT BY END USE
IN THE USSR AND THE U.S., 1955

End Use	Per Cent of Total*	
	USSR**	U.S.
Consumption	58,9	66.3
Investment	25.2	20.3
Defense	13.0	10.2
Government Administration	2.9	3.2
Gross National Product	100.0	100.0

* The value figures used in these calculations were adjusted to approximate factor costs by deducting indirect taxes and adding subsidies.

** The figures for the USSR are for gross domestic product, exclusive of the net effect of transactions with foreign countries.

Relationship of Soviet to U.S. Gross National Product. According to authoritative western estimates, Soviet gross NP rose from a little less than half of U.S. gross NP in 1950 to about two-thirds in 1958 if both Soviet

Where does the ruble go?   Where does the dollar go?

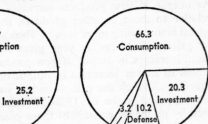

and U.S. gross national products are valued at U.S. prices. If both are valued at Soviet prices, Soviet gross NP increased from one-fifth of U.S. gross NP in 1950 to about one-third in 1958. In terms of the geometric average of the two types of comparison, Soviet gross NP grew from about one-third of the U.S. level in 1950 to a little less than half in 1958. In 1959 Soviet gross NP was about one-half of U.S. gross NP (in terms of the geometric average comparison).

The higher relationship of Soviet to U.S. gross NP found when both products are valued at U.S. prices and the lower relationship of Soviet to U.S. gross NP found when both products are valued at Soviet prices reflect the generally negative correlation of relative prices and quantities in the two countries. Goods and services with lower relative prices in the United States (than in the USSR) are generally produced in larger

GROSS NATIONAL PRODUCT

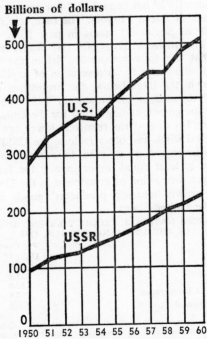

relative quantities in the United States (than in the USSR) and goods and services with lower relative prices in the USSR (than in the United States) are generally produced in larger relative quantities in the USSR (than in the United States). Hence, if the two national products are valued at U.S. prices a greater relative

price weight is given to goods and services which are more heavily produced in the USSR than if Soviet prices are used. Similarly, if two products are valued at Soviet prices a greater relative price weight is given to products which are more heavily produced in the United States than if U.S. prices are used.

Prospects for Future Soviet Growth. It is problematic whether Soviet NI and NP will continue to grow at the relatively high rates of the past. Impediments to future growth include growing limitations on the supply of labor and natural resources, the increasing need to replace worn-out and obsolete machinery, and diminishing opportunites for borrowing technology as the USSR approaches western technological levels. On the other hand, there is still much room for improvements in Soviet planning and administration. Such improvements, if realized, could at least partially offset factors tending to depress the future rate of growth. A reduction in the Soviet defense effort, which would release additional resources for growth-inducing investment, would have a similar effect, but such a reduction does not appear imminent.

BIBLIOGRAPHY: Morris Bornstein, *A Comparison of Soviet and United States National Product,* Papers Submitted by Panelists Appearing before the Subcommittee on Economic Statistics of the Joint Economict Committee, 86th Congress, 1st session, Washington, 1959; Gregory Grossman, "National Income," in Abram Bergson, ed., *Soviet Economic Growth,* Evanston, 1953.   R. C. H.

NATIONALISTS. A group of deputies of moderate right-wing orientation in the third and fourth State Dumas. There were 26 N in the third Duma and 88 in the fourth. Toward the end of the existence of the fourth Duma, however, and especially during the period when the Progressive Bloc (q.v.) was being formed, a number of "left-wing" or "independent" members under the leadership of V. V. Shulgin withdrew from the nationalist faction. Other prominent leaders among the N were Count V. A. Bobrinsky, Bishop Evlogy, P. N. Krupensky, and V. N. Lvov (subsequently chief procurator of the Holy Synod). The evolution of the N toward an agreement with liberal elements took place under the influence of military defeats at the front and of a sharp conflict between the State Duma on the one hand, and the government and the court, on the other.

NATIONALITIES. The national minorities of the Soviet Union can be divided into two principal groups: those which by virtue of historic background, race, and culture are closely related to the Russians proper (Great Russians), and those which are not so related. The first category consists of the Ukrainians and Byelorussians, and to some extent of the Finns; the second includes Turkic, Iranian, Baltic, Caucasian, Mongol, and Siberian groups. The Jews and nationals of Western European ethnic groups living in the Soviet Union (e.g., Poles and Germans) constitute an intermediate layer between these two main categories.

Like the Great Russians, the Ukrainians and Byelorussians are descendants of the inhabitants of the medieval Russian state, Kievan Rus'. Their ethnic differentiation is due to the fact that at the time of the collapse of the Kievan state in the mid-thirteenth century, its population divided. One part migrated northeast, into the forest zone of the mid-Volga and mid-Oka, where it fused with the local Finnic population, and eventually established a powerful new state centered on Moscow. This in time became the Great Russian nationality. Another part—that which today constitutes the Ukrainian and Byelorussian nationality–came under Lithuanian and Polish rule for some five hundred years, in the course of which it was exposed to Catholic culture and became accustomed to political and civil rights unknown to the Great Russians. As a consequence, by the time the Russian Empire acquired these areas in the partitions of Poland (second half of the eighteenth century) their inhabitants had developed their own ethos that precluded a simple fusion with their Great Russian neighbors.

The Finnic population of the Soviet Union (5.6 million in 1959) consists largely of the descendants of the original inhabitants of the forest zone of Russia. While not directly related to the Russians, they have close affinities with them because of identity of religion, and because during and after the mass-migrations into their regions which attended the collapse of Kiev they freely intermarried with Russians. They are divided into a number of ethnic sub-groups (Mordva, Cheremis, Karelians, Votyaks, etc.), and inhabit the areas to the north and east of the center of Russia.

The other national minorities consist of groups which differ radically from the Russians in respect of origin, race, and culture. They constitute a dependent colonial population which in most cases has been conquered and is today retained by force.

The most numerous group in this category consists of Muslims. Soviet Muslims are concentrated in three principal areas which are separated from one another either by natural frontiers or by Russian settlements. The first of these areas to have come under Russian rule is the Volga-Ural region, inhabited by the descendants of the original Turco-Mongol conquerors of Kiev. They are known today as the Volga Tatars and Bashkirs (5 million and 1 million respectively in 1959) and were subjugated by Russia in the mid-sixteenth century. Next, in the first half of the nineteenth century, the Russians acquired partly from Persia, partly from the Ottoman Empire, and partly by conquest of independent peoples, the Muslims inhabiting Transcaucasia (the Azeri Turks, numbering 3 million in 1959) and the mountains of the Caucasus (nearly 2 million). Finally, in a series of conquests that began in the eighteenth century and ended in 1882, the Russians seized the vast areas of Central Asia, inhabited almost entirely by Muslims of Turkic or Persian stock (Uzbeks, Kazakhs, Kirghiz, Turcomans, Tadzhiks) (13 million in 1959). The bulk of the Soviet Muslims consists of Sunni Turks, but there is one major Iranian group the Tadzhiks (1.4 million), while the Azeri Turks are Shiite. Until the twentieth century these Muslims were not differentiated into precisely defined nationalities, but since then, partly from contact with the West, and partly under Soviet pressure, they have become administratively separated into a number of distinct national groups. Their total number in the Soviet Union in 1959 was around 25 million.

The Georgians (2.7 million) and Armenians (2.8 million) are Christian inhabitants of Transcaucasia who came under Russian rule at the beginning of the nineteenth century. Racially and linguistically they are not related either to the Russians or any other major ethnic group in the Soviet Union.

The Lithuanians (2.3 million) and Latvians (1.4 million) also are not directly related to any major nationality in the USSR. Located on the shores of the Baltic, they had been acquired by Russia in the eighteenth century, and lost in 1918 when they gained independence. In the course of World War II, the Soviet Union occupied and then annexed them.

Among the other groups one may mention the Mongols (Buryats, Kalmyks), Koreans, and Chinese, as well as a number of smaller nationalities (e.g. Yakuts) inhabiting the vast territories of Siberia.

The Jews, most of whom Russia acquired from Poland at the end of the eighteenth century, constitute a special ethnic category. Racially and religiously distinct from the remainder of Soviet population, they nevertheless do not constitute a national group in the sense in which the others do, because they lack a clearly defined territory of their own. Moreover, the Jewish intelligentsia tends to assimilate and to adopt Russian culture as its own. The same rule applies to other Western European groups, such as the Poles (1.4 mil-

THE ETHNIC STRUCTURE OF THE SOVIET UNION, 1926–1959

ETHNIC GROUP OR NATIONALITY	1926		1959	
	in millions	% of total population	in millions	% of total population
I. EASTERN SLAVS	113.8	77.3	159.4	76.2
1. Great Russians	77.8	52.9	114.6	54.8
2. Ukrainians[1]	31.2	21.2	37.0	17.7
3. Byelorussians[2]	4.7	3.2	7.8	3.7
II. OTHER EUROPEANS	5.6	3.8	12.1	5.8
1. Jews[3]	2.7	1.8	2.3	1.1
2. Lithuanians and Latvians[4]	0.2	0.1	3.7	1.8
3. Others[5]	2.7	1.8	6.1	2.9
III. FINNS AND CHUVASH	4.3	2.8	5.6	2.6
IV. MUSLIMS	18.5	12.6	24.7	11.8
1. Turkic peoples	15.9	10.8	21.0	10.0
2. Iranian peoples	1.4	1.0	1.9	0.9
3. N. Caucasians	1.2	0.8	1.8	0.9
V. TRANSCAUCASIAN GROUPS	3.4	2.3	5.5	2.6
1. Georgians	1.8	1.2	2.7	1.3
2. Armenians	1.6	1.1	2.8	1.3
VI. MONGOLS AND OTHER ORIENTAL PEOPLES	0.5	0.3	0.8	0.4
VII. OTHERS	1.0	0.7	1.0	0.5
TOTAL	147.0	100.0	209.0	100.0

[1] [2] During World War II the Soviet Ukrainian and Byelorussian population increased by an estimated 4–6 million and 3–4 million respectively as a result of the annexation of eastern Poland. This must be taken into account in comparing the 1926 and 1939 census percentages.

[3] The Jewish population of the USSR first increased with the annexation of eastern Poland, and then decreased from German massacres.

[4] The annexation of Lithuania and Latvia brought the USSR 5 million inhabitants, that of Estonia 1 million.

[5] Includes 2.2 million Moldavians acquired during World War II.

FIVE LARGEST NATIONALITIES OF THE USSR
(1959 census, in thous.)

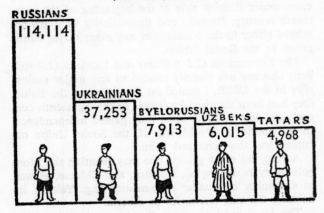

RUSSIANS
114,114

UKRAINIANS
37,253

BYELORUSSIANS
7,913

UZBEKS
6,015

TATARS
4,968

lion), and somewhat less to the Germans (1.6 million).

The demographic relationship between the Great Russians and the national minorities fluctuates, depending on the movement of frontiers and the varying rate of growth of the various ethnic groups. In 1897 the nationalities constituted 55 per cent of the country's total population; in 1926 this figure stood at 47 per cent, in 1940 at 49 per cent, and in 1959 45 per cent. The Great Russians thus are historically more dynamic than the minority population.

The peculiar nature of what in the Soviet Union is known as the "national problem" derives from the fact that the relationship between the Russians and their subject peoples does not involve all the elements customary in such a relationship elsewhere. There is no color line or racial prejudice, neither of which is much known in Russia. Nor is there a clear line dividing the metropolis from the colony. Both these features are lacking because the colonial dependencies of Russia are contiguous to the mother country with the result that the conquering and conquered nation have always lived in close proximity, and that the process of building and administrating the imperial domain cannot be clearly distinguished from that of building and administering the metropolis. As a result, neither the Russian government nor the Russian intelligentsia has ever developed a conscious attitude, let alone policy, toward its subject peoples. Another peculiarity of the Russian treatment of the minorities is that insofar as they inhabit a state that was and continues to be extraordinarily centralized, the minorities have been on the whole denied territoral and national self-rule.

The tsarist state, although officially called an "Empire," did not constitutionally acknowledge its multinational structure, and never evolved a consistent policy towards its minorities. Except for occasional periods of religious or national intolerance, it tended to leave them to their own devices, content to maintain peace and order, and to derive from them and their territories the maximum of strategic and economic advantage. As a result, in the century preceding the revolution, the minorities (except for the Jews) were free to engage in the same cultural, social and political activities as the Great Russians. On the eve of the revolution nearly all the major political groups had their own political parties.

In the course of the revolution, many of the national minorities, largely in an effort to escape Communism and the civil war, formed autonomous and in some instances even independent governments. But except for those which were strongly supported by the West (the Baltic states, Poland, Finland), they were not able to withstand the pressures of the new Soviet state, and were one by one occupied and incorporated into it.

Of all the parties operating in prerevolutionary Russia, save for those of the extreme right, the Bolsheviks had had the most centralist program and were least inclined to make concessions to minority nationalism. Their platform did contain a clause conceding all nationalities the "right of national self-determination"; but they interpreted it in a manner which gave the minorities no choice between full separation (which none save the Poles and inhabitants of Finland demanded), and complete integration. In particular, the Bolsheviks opposed federalism and cultural autonomy. But in view of the unexpected disintegration of the Russian Empire which attended their seizure of power, the Bolsheviks were compelled radically to alter their program. First of all they made a formal concession to federalism by constructing in Russia a pseudo-federal structure in which the state (but not the Communist Party, the ruling institution) was divided into constituent republics. Secondly, they granted the minorities considerable cultural autonomy which, at its height in the 1920's, led to a rapid growth of national consciousness in areas where it had been weak or lacking altogether.

After his rise to a position of unchallenged power, Stalin introduced certain changes in this policy. He left the pseudo-federal structure devised by Lenin intact (though he tightened it considerably); but he abolished, for all practical purposes, the extensive cultural autonomy which the minorities had enjoyed in the 1920's, leaving them in the end with little more than the right to use their language (but not necessarily their alphabet) and to enjoy folk art. Stalin based himself to a large extent on Russian national sentiment and for that reason felt impelled to discriminate against the minorities not only in the matter of state and party appointments, but also in cultural affairs. This discrimination was particularly intense in the last decade of Stalin's life, and found its most appalling expression in the deportation in 1944 of several national groups to Central Asia and Siberia. After Stalin's death, his successors softened somewhat this policy, but they did not alter it in any of its essentials.

Soviet nationality policy may be characterized as a temporary device meant to allow the regime to keep the national minorities under control at home, and at the same time to exploit national discontent abroad until such time when the expected world-wide triumph of Communism will eliminate nationalism as a factor in politics. The nature of the problem facing the Soviet rulers suggests that they cannot solve it by any simple formula. Repression at home has adverse reactions abroad, especially in Asia. The replacement of political self-rule with cultural autonomy, howsoever limited, tends to stimulate national consciousness. The encouragement of education in the borderland areas, vitally necessary for the further growth of the Soviet economy, produces a native intelligentsia which tends to identify itself with its own nationality, and thus indirectly stimulates nationalism as well. The same applies to the settlement of nomadic populations and the official sponsorship of local nationalism as a counterweight to various Pan-Islamic or Pan-Iranian movements. The dilemmas of Soviet nationality policy are most clearly manifested in the treatment of the Jewish population. The official policy of identifying Jews as a national minority (every Jew being identified as such in the passport all Soviet citizens are required to carry) is accompanied by a refusal to grant them cultural autonomy and a steady pressure to assimilate.

The reaction of the nationalities to these policies is subject to differing interpretations. Some scholars believe that the Communist regime is gradually succeeding in absorbing the nationalities, and dissolving various local nationalisms in an all-embracing "Soviet" nationalism. Others (to whom belongs the author of this essay) argue, on the contrary, that Soviet policies have resulted in the intensification of national self-consciousness and the emergence of a number of modern nationalities. Evidence presently available does not permit a solution of this question. Ethnographic and linguistic data provided by the 1959 census do, however, reveal some very significant trends. They suggest that the major ethnic groups tend to become linguistically more cohesive, while the smaller ones either dissolve or else assimilate with that minority group which is closest to them racially and culturally. Thus, the number of nationalities seems to be steadily decreasing but the major, dynamic nationalities (such as the Georgians in the Caucasus, and Uzbeks in Central Asia) consolidate and assume leadership in their respective regions. The status of the Ukrainians and Byelorussians seems particularly uncertain. Time alone will tell whether they will succeed in maintaining their identity, or merge with the Great Russians. Census data indicate a considerable gain of the Great Russian nationality at the expense of the Ukrainian. The future of the Jews, on the other hand, seems predetermined by the discrimination to which they are constantly subjected, and which precludes their assimilation.

On the whole, the Communists cannot be said to have "solved" the nationality question in any sense. All that can be said is that thanks to their uniquely centralized political system and a political philosophy which imposes no constraints on the methods employed, they have succeeded better than the other imperial powers in neutralizing the nationalism of their subject peoples.

BIBLIOGRAPHY: M. Hrushevsky, *History of the Ukraine*, New Haven, 1941; N. P. Vakar, *Belorussia; the making of a nation*, Cambridge, 1956; S. Zenkovsky, *Pan-Turkism and Islam in Russia*, Cambridge, 1960; W. E. D. Allen, *The History of the Georgian People*, London, 1933; S. Dubnow, *A History of the Jews in Russia and Poland*, 3 vols., New York, 1916; R. Pipes, *The Formation of the Soviet Union*, Cambridge, 1954. R. P.

NATURAL GAS. In 1940, the measured reserves of NG were stated to be 54 bill. cubic m., with total reserves of 985 bill. cubic m. The most important are found in the N. Caucasus (Stavropol and Krasnodar krays), at Dashava in the W. Ukraine, and at Saratov on the Volga River. Other important NG deposits are in Shebelinka near Kharkov, Berezovskoye in W. Siberia, and reserves of the Azerbaijan and the Turkmen SSR. In 1957 new deposits were discovered in Irkutsk Oblast, the Yakut ASSR, and the Uzbek SSR.

NATURAL GAS PRODUCTION. In 1958, 28.1 bill. cubic meters of natural gas were produced, as well as 1.8 bill. cubic meters of coal gas; and in 1960, 47 bill. cubic meters of gas of both types (U.S. in 1959: 341 bill. cub. m.; Canada: 12.1 bill. cub. m.) Among the advantages of natural gas over other sources of heat are its low cost of production (8½% of that of coal) and its low labor requirements (5% of that of coal).

The production of natural gas in the USSR first developed in the 1930's as a by-product of the rapid growth of petroleum production. At that time a number of cities located near centers of oil, including Baku, Grozny, Ufa, Kazan, and Krasnodar, began to be supplied with natural gas, and the production of synthetic derivatives from natural gas was also initiated. The natural gas industry was developed on a large scale only during the postwar period, however, following the discovery of very large deposits in a number of regions and the construction of long-distance pipelines. By 1950 more than 170 major deposits had been found, with reserves of more than 1,000 bill. cubic meters. Among the regions that are particularly well endowed in this respect are parts of W. as well as of E. Ukraine (24% of total reserves in 1958), of the N. Caucasus (44%), of the Volga region—in the Saratov, Kuybyshev, and Stalingrad oblasts — (16%), of Uzbekistan, Turkmenia, and Azerbaijan (4%), of the Komi Autonomous Republic (4%), and of W. Siberia (2%). In 1958 the total length of long-distance pipelines carrying natural gas was 7,450 mi. The diameter of some of the pipelines was 2.7 ft. while for some of the newest ones it was 3.35 ft.

The first pipeline, that between Buguruslan and Kuybyshev (100 mi.), was constructed in 1943, and the first long-distance pipeline, that between Saratov and Moscow (497 mi.), was completed in 1946. In 1948 the line Dashava-Kiev (310 mi.) was constructed and in 1949 it was extended to Moscow (new length: 826 mi.). In 1956 the first pipeline between Stavropol and Moscow (807 mi.) was also completed. As a result the production of natural gas increased from 3.2 bill. cubic meters in 1940 to 28.1 bill. cubic meters in 1958. At that time over 150 towns and cities as well as 300 small settlements were supplied with natural gas, including Moscow, Leningrad, Kiev, Kuybyshev, Stalingrad, Ufa, Kazan, and Gorky. In Moscow 500,-000 apartments were supplied with gas for cooking purposes, and by 1960, 70% of all heat was also scheduled to come from that source.

The objectives of the Seven Year Plan (1959–65) provide for increasing the production of natural gas to 150 bill. cubic meters and for increasing its share in

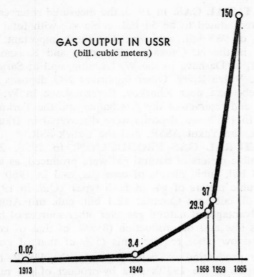

GAS OUTPUT IN USSR
(bill. cubic meters)

PRODUCTION OF NATURAL GAS IN THE USSR
(bill. of cubic meters)

	Natural gas	Coal gas	Total
1940	3.2	.2	3.4
1945	3.3	.1	3.4
1950	5.8	.4	6.2
1956	12.1	1.6	13.6
1958	28.1	1.8	29.9
1959	—	—	37.2
1960	—	—	47.0
1965 (pl.)	—	—	150.0

P. I. M.

the total consumption of energy from 4% to 21% in the USSR as a whole, and to a still larger proportion in the case of individual regions: from 37% to 61% in the Caucasus; from 7% to 27% in the Moscow region; from .8% to 28% in the Urals; from 0 to 25% in the N.W. regions; and from 0 to 18% in the W. regions. Official estimates indicate that 6.5 mill. apartments will be supplied with gas in 1965, as opposed to 1.7 mill. in 1957. At the same time a considerable increase has been scheduled in the utilization of natural gas as a raw material for the making of such synthetic products as nitrates and artificial rubber.

NATURAL RESOURCES of the USSR are very abundant and diversified. Due to intensive and planned prospecting many new deposits—some of primary importance—have been discovered in the last four decades. USSR is rich in basic mineral resources necessary for the development of national economy: oil, coal, ferrous and nonferrous metals, as well as potassium and phosphate fertilizers. Its self-sufficiency would be complete but for the deficit in copper and tin. (*See:* COAL, OIL, METALS, MINERALS).

BIBLIOGRAPHY: Demitri B. Shimkin, *Minerals, a Key to Soviet Power*, Cambridge, 1953; Heinrich Hassman, *Oil in the Soviet Union*, Princeton, 1953; S. S. Balzak, V. F. Vasyutin, and Ya. G. Feigin, *Economic Geography of the USSR*, New York, 1949.

NATURALIZATION: *see* CITIZENSHIP.

NAVÁSHIN, Sergéy Gavrílovich (1857–1930), biologist. Fellow, Ac. of S., Ukrainian SSR (1924). Graduate, Moscow University (1881); professor, Kiev (1894–1915) and Tbilisi (1918–23) universities. Cofounder (1923) and director of the K. A. Timiryazev Institute of Biology in Moscow. Research concerned plant cytology and embryology. Discoverer of the dual fertilization in angiospermous plants (1898).

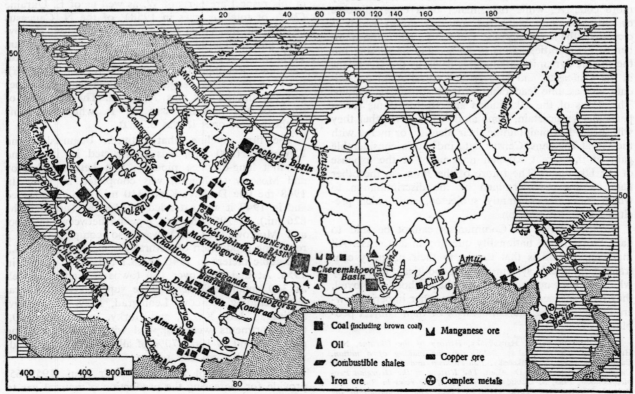

Main Mineral Resources of the USSR

NAVY: *see* Armed Forces.

NAZI-SOVIET PACT: *see* History.

NEBÍT-DÁG (Neftedag), city in Ashkhabad Oblast, Turkmen SSR, at the foothill of Bolshoy Balkhan ridge; pop. 30,400 (1956). Oil industry center.

NECHÁYEV, Sergéy Gennádievich (1847–1882), revolutionary. As a part-time student of St. Petersburg University, N was one of the leaders of students' disturbances in 1868–69 and then fled abroad. In Switzerland, jointly with Bakunin (q.v.), N published *The Revolutionary's Catechism* proclaiming the principle that all means are justified in furthering the cause of revolution. In the fall of 1869, N returned to Russia, and, pretending to be a leader of a powerful revolutionary organization, started to organize the students of the agricultural academy in Moscow into clandestine five-man rings, known as People's Avenge. When the strict discipline he imposed met some opposition, N falsely accused the main oppositionist, a student, Ivanov, of being a police spy, and ordered the other members of the ring to kill him. After the murder on Nov. 21, 1869, N left Moscow and went to St. Petersburg to continue his activities. When Moscow police discovered the murderers, N fled abroad. In Aug. 1872, he was arrested by Swiss police and extradited to Russia as a common murderer. In 1873, N was tried in Russia for Ivanov's murder, and condemned to 20 years at hard labor. He was imprisoned until his death in the Peter and Paul Fortress in St. Petersburg. N's case inspired Dostoyevsky to write the novel *The Possessed.*

NEDÉLIN, Mitrofán Ivánovich (1902–1960), marshal of artillery. N joined the Red Army after the civil war and became an artillery specialist at the Dzerzhinsky Artillery Academy, Moscow. A member of the Communist party since 1922, he was a candidate and member of the Central Committee after 1952. In 1936 he was sent to Spain as adviser to the Loyalists. Upon his return, he was charged with the supervision of the Moscow area artillery. During the war, his artillery played a prominent role in the battle of Moscow and later on the western front. He enjoyed rapid promotion, becoming a marshal in 1953. Since then he served as deputy to the Supreme Soviet and was extensively decorated and repeatedly commended for his wartime efforts. In 1955 he became deputy minister of defense of the USSR. N was the Soviet missile chief. He was killed in an airplane accident in October 1960.

NEFTEDAG: *see* Nebit-Dag.

NEFTEGÓRSK, town in Krasnodar Kray, near Maykop, RSFSR; pop. 9,600 (1959). A rapidly developing center of oil ind.

NEKRÁSOV, Aleksándr Ivánovich (1883–1957), mechanical engineer. Fellow, Ac. of S., USSR (1946). Honored Scientist and Technologist, RSFSR (1947). Graduate (1906) and professor (1937) of Moscow University. Assistant Director, Central Institute of Aerodynamics (1930–38) and director, Division of Aerohydromechanics, Institute of Mechanical Engineering, Ac. of S. (1945). Research concerned settled waves of finite amplitude on the surface of incompressible fluid, problems of airfoils with various profiles in a stream of compressible and incompressible fluid, diffusion of

vortex in viscous fluid, wing flutter, etc. Author of the monograph *Precise Theory of Settled-Type Waves on the Surface of Heavy Fluid* (1951). Stalin prize (1952).

NEKRÁSOV, Borís Vladímirovich (1899–), chemist. Corresponding member, Ac. of S., USSR (1946). Graduated from the Plekhanov Institute of National Economy (1924). Associated with the Moscow School of Technology, Military Academy of Chemistry, and Moscow Textile Institute. Dean of the chair of Nonferrous Metals and Gold at the Kalinin Institute in Moscow. Research concerns the structure and properties of chemical compounds. Investigated the transeffects in complex compounds (1935). Proposed a theory on the structure of borons (1940), equations for the polarity of bonds and atomic charges in certain molecules.

NEKRÁSOV, Nikoláy Alekséyevich (1821–1878), poet, journalist, and editor. N began his literary career as a hack writer. He suffered three years of starvation in St. Petersburg before his talents were noticed. He then (1848) became the editor and the publisher of the most important literary journals of his day: *Sovremen-*  *nik* (The Contemporary), founded by Pushkin, and later (1868) *Otechest-vennye Zapiski* (Notes of the Fatherland). N's journals represented the extreme in liberalism and he was constantly harassed by the government. An attempt to appease the authorities by publicly praising the reactionary minister Muravyov cost him the friendship and respect of many of the radicals and liberals. He continued to publish their works, and, had he never written an original word himself, he nevertheless would have a secure place in the history of R. literature, as the leading writers of his time—to mention only a few, Turgenev, Dostoyevsky, and Tolstoy—contributed to his journals.

N's poetry is concerned mainly with the sufferings of the peasants. It includes both the traditional forms, such as satire, elegy, lyric poetry, love poems, as well as the folk song. Among his best narrative poems of peasant life are: *Vlas* (1854), *Frost the Red-Nosed* (1863), *Russian Women* (1871–72). His most famous work in the folk style, *Who Is Happy in Russia?*, describes the wanderings of seven peasants. Their encounters with various characters give a vigorous, humorous, and satirical picture of peasant life in the R. countryside of the 19th century.

NEKRÁSOV, Nikoláy Visarionovich (1879–), leader of the Constitutional Democratic party. Mayor of Tomsk and professor of the Tomsk Technological Institute, N was a member of the third and fourth Dumas. In the Provisional Government N served as minister of communications (March-June 1917), minister without portfolio (July), and minister of finance (from July 24th). N was one of the closest collaborators of Kerensky. After the October revolution, N remained in Russia and worked in the Soviet economic apparatus.

NEKRÁSOV, Víktor Platónovich (1911–), novelist. Graduated from the School of Architecture, University of Kiev; later studied dramatics. Spent most of World War II at the front as an officer in the engineers. His first novel, *In the Trenches of Stalingrad*, is one of the better Soviet war novels. After Stalin's death N's novel, *Native Town* (1954) appeared and voiced the disillusionment among former servicemen who had had hopes that democracy would be introduced in the USSR after the war.

NÉMAN RIVER, (Ger. *Memel*, Pol. *Niemen*, Lith. *Nemunas*), about 580 mi. long, navigable for most of its length; rises in Byelorussian SSR, S. of Minsk, in Minsk Oblast, flows N. into Grodno Oblast, and Lithuanian SSR and W. between Lithuanian SSR and Kaliningrad Oblast, into the Baltic Sea. Tributaries: Vilia (right), Shchara, Svisloch (left). Connected by Oginsky Canal with Pripyat. Hydroelectric power plant near Kaunas (Kovno).

NEMIRÓVICH-DÁNCHENKO, Vasíly Ivánovich (1848–1936), a prolific writer of popular travel sketches and novels. He was the brother of Vladimir Ivanovich N-D, the founder of the Moscow Art Theater. His writings total more than one hundred volumes.

NEMIRÓVICH-DÁNCHENKO, Vladímir Ivánovich (1858–1943), prominent playwright, director, producer, People's Artist of the USSR. After leaving the university in 1879, he devoted himself to literature and the theater. From 1891 to 1898 he headed the drama classes of the Moscow Philharmonic Society. As a dramatist, N-D  was disturbed by what he considered the stagnating routinism of the metropolitan and provincial theaters; he dreamed of creating a model progressive theater. Having taken notice of the work of the young actor and avant-garde director, K. S. Stanislavsky, N-D offered him the opportunity to organize jointly a young group unspoiled by routine. In 1898 the MKhT (Moscow Art Theater, later Moscow Art Academy Theater, or MKhAT) was opened by them under a strict regime in which only first-class works were admitted into the repertory and the role of director was placed on a very high plane. It was N-D who discovered the dramatic genius of Anton Chekhov; it was he also who extended a helping hand to the young Maksim Gorky and who always made room for young actors. The possessor of rare administrative tact, N-D supported the MKhT during periods of crisis and temporary internal dissension. After 1917, N-D was honored several times by the Soviet government. With the support of Stanislavsky, he steadfastly held to the basic style of MKhT—psychological realism. His productions of the classics (Pushkin, Gogol, Turgenev, Leo Tolstoy, Dostoyevsky in dramatized form, Ostrovsky, Gorky, Chekhov, and others) were especially original and outstanding as was his direction of several Soviet plays. In 1919 he became interested in the creation of a musical theater (named after him in 1926), for the training of "singing actors," seeking to do away with "operatic clichés of acting" prevalent in operetta and chamber opera. In the 1930's he worked for a short while in Hollywood. A considerable number of faithful followers have assured the permanence of his creative legacy in MKhT. P. E. YE.

NENÉTS NATIONAL OKRUG, part of Archangel Oblast, RSFSR; area 68,200 sq. mi.; pop. 45,000(1959): Nenets (Samoyeds), Russians, Komi. Along the shores of the Arctic Ocean, tundra coast N. of Komi ASSR. Cities: Naryan-Mar (center), Amderma. It is a lowland, watered by the Pechora River, with arctic climate, numerous rivers and minor lakes; fishing and hunting; reindeer farming; fur-bearing animals. Transportation is by river, reindeer and air. Est. 1929.

NEP. Abbreviation for "New Economic Policy" proclaimed by Lenin in March 1921, in the wake of the Kronstadt revolt and the spreading peasant uprisings. Lenin recognized that, in a fundamentally peasant society, the Communist Revolution would not survive without the *smychka*, union of the urban proletariat and the peasantry, which had been jeopardized under War Communism by forcible grain requisitions and other policies. The NEP's two major goals accordingly were: (1) to safeguard the *smychka* by granting the peasant a relatively free use of land and of its produce, (2) "to increase at all cost the quantity of output" (Lenin) so as ultimately to expand large-scale industry and thus provide an economic basis for "the dictatorship of the proletariat." Economic recovery was to be achieved by authorizing, within limits, private enterprise in agriculture, trade, and small-scale industry while keeping the "commanding heights" of the economy (large-scale industry, banking, foreign trade) in the hands of the state. The mixed economy thus brought into existence was characterized by Lenin as "state capitalism," private enterprise being severely restrained by the political and economic power of the state.

Rapid recovery of private enterprise within these limits was followed by its gradual suppression and liquidation. By 1930, with collectivization of peasant farming, the period of coexistence of private and socialized enterprise was terminated. Private trade revived fast and, in 1922–23 accounted for 75.2% of all retail sales. Preferential government policies favoring cooperative and state trade organizations, and then ruthless suppression, brought its share down to 22.4% in 1927–28, and 5.6% in 1930. In 1931, private trade was declared an "economic crime." Private industry and handicraft accounted at first for one-fourth of gross industrial output and produced most consumer goods. As state-owned large factories were gradually restored, its share fell to 20% in 1925–26, and 13% in 1927–28. By 1930, discriminatory taxation and confiscations drove it virtually out of existence.

The major issue of the NEP period was the size of and control over agricultural marketings, especially grain. Prior to the revolution, landed estates and well-to-do peasants (the kulaks) accounted, respectively, for 12% and 38% of grain production but for as much as 21.6% and 50% of grain marketings. Other peasants, while producing one-half of grain output, supplied only 28.4% of the marketed share. The landed estates were partitioned among peasants (only 6–7% of their area was preserved as state or collective farms). In turn, the kulaks lost much of their land to the village poor (the *bednyak*) and divided much of the remaining land among relatives so as to escape persecution under War Communism. The number of farmsteads rose from 18 mill. in 1916 to 25.6 mill. in 1928. Changes in land tenure thus favored a shift from production for the market to subsistence farming. An aggravating factor was the so-called "scissors crisis": the relationship between prices received and paid by farmers, which in 1922 was at about the 1913 level, shifted then increasingly against the farmers, owing primarily to the high cost of state-produced manufactures. Unfavorable terms of trade reinforced the tendency on the part of the peasants to consume their produce rather than market it. The 1926–27 output of grain fell short by only 5% of the prewar level but marketings amounted then to only 48.5% of the prewar figure and grain exports to about 5%.

Meanwhile, in 1925, the party committed itself to a rapid industrialization program. In an economy where 76% of the population depended for its living on the agricultural sector, the ambitious investment program had to be financed mainly by the latter. An expanding industrial labor force had to be fed, and agricultural raw materials were needed for industry, also for exports to pay for imports of machinery. After the "leftist" and "rightist" solutions to this problem were rejected (see AGRICULTURE), and after the grain shortage became more acute in the late 1920's, Stalin adopted the policy of an all-out collectivization of peasant farming, thus giving the government control over the agricultural marketings. This was the last step on the road from the NEP to the period of forced industrialization that followed.

BIBLIOGRAPHY: A. Baykov, *The Development of the Soviet Economic System*, New York, 1947; M. Dobb, *Soviet Economic Development since 1917*, New York, 1948; S. N. Prokopovicz, *Histoire Economique de l'URSS*, Paris, 1952; A. Erlich, *The Soviet Industrialization Debate, 1924–1928*, Cambridge, Mass., 1960.   L. S.

NÉRCHINSK, town in Chita Oblast, RSFSR; pop. 11,600 (1956). R.R. station; market for furs, tea, cattle; has gold mining, iron-ore deposits. Founded as a fort 1653, for two centuries it was one of Russia's outposts in the Far East; formerly used for exile of political prisoners.

NÉRCHINSK HARD LABOR CAMP, founded in the 18th century in Transbaykalia. The Decembrists were the first political prisoners. Later, the participants in the Polish uprising of 1863 and members of the revolutionary movement of 1905 were detained there. The regime at N was noted for its cruelty.

NÉRCHINSK, TREATY OF, 1689, the first treaty between any European power and China. It checked the R. advance in the Amur River valley and served as a basis for relations with China until 1858 (modified 1727 and 1768).

NESMEYÁNOV, Aleksándr Nikoláyevich (1899–), organic chemist. President of the Ac. of S., USSR (1951–61). Member of the Supreme Soviet USSR (1950, 1954, 1958). Graduate (1922) and professor (1935) of Moscow University. Co-founder and director of the Laboratory of Organic Chemistry at the Institute of Fertilizers, Insecticides, and Fungicides (1934) and of the Laboratory of Organometallic Compounds at Moscow University; associated with the Institute of Organic Chemistry, Ac. of S. Director, Institute of Organometallic Compounds (1939). Chairman, Stalin Prize Award Committee for Science and Inventions of the Council of Ministers USSR (19497), member of World Peace Council and the Soviet Committee for the Defense of Peace. Director, Institute of Scientific Information, Ac. of S. (1953). Research concerns organometallic and organo-elemental compounds. Developed the "Nesmeyanov diazo-method" for the mercury synthesis of organometallic thallium, tin, lead, germanium, antimony, arsenic and bismuth compounds. Founder of the school of Soviet metal-organic chemists. Author of *New Method of Synthesis of Aromatic Mercury* (1934); *Organo-Elemental Compounds and Periodic System of Elements* (1945); *Coupling of Simple Bonds* (1950); *Dual Reactive Ability and Tautomerism* (1955) and others. Stalin prize (1943) and other awards.

NESSELRÓDE, Count Karl Vasílyevich (1780–1862), minister of foreign affairs 1816–56 (served in R. embassies from 1801). He became a member of the State Council in 1821, and State Councillor in 1845. He was a conservative and a champion of the Holy Alliance.

NÉSTEROV, Mikhaíl Vasílyevich (1862–1942), painter. Member of the Academy of Fine Arts from 1898. Member and exponent of the Society of Circulating Exhibitions (*Peredvizhniki*). His genre pictures, *The Expert, The Hermit*, and others are in the Tretyakov Gallery in Moscow.

NÉSTOR, THE CHRONICLER, ecclesiastical author of the second half of the 11th century and monk in the Monastery of the Caves, Kiev. He was long regarded as the compiler of the chronicle containing the account of the founding of the R. state. Later studies, however, do not support this hypothesis.

NEUHAUS, Génrikh Gústavovich (1888–), pianist and teacher. Studied with his father G. V. Neuhaus. In 1914 N graduated from the Vienna Master-School of piano. In 1922 became professor at the Moscow Conservatoire. Among his pupils are E. Gilels, Ya. I. Zak, and S. Richter.

NEVÁ, BATTLE OF, July 15, 1240, between Swedes and Novgorodian forces led by Prince Alexander Yaroslavich, at the confluence of the Neva and Izhora rivers. The Swedes were defeated and Prince Alexander was given the surname "Nevsky."

NEVÁ RIVER, about 46 mi. long, navigable, N.W. Leningrad Oblast, flowing from S.W. corner of Lake Ladoga into the Gulf of Finland through several mouths. Chief tributaries: Tosna, Izhora (left), Okhta (right). The delta is divided into Bolshaya Neva, Bolshaya Nevka, and Malaya Nevka. Occasional floods due to low banks. Connected by canals and other waterways with the White Sea in the N. and the Volga and Caspian Sea in the S.E. Usually frozen Nov. to April. Leningrad is in its delta.

NEVÉROV (Skobelev), Aleksándr Sergéyevich (1886–1923), writer of peasant origin. His tales are marked by the 19th-century populist trend and deal with the oppression of the peasant class. After the revolution he depicted the struggle between the poor and the rich peasants (*kulaks*). Best known for his story *Tashkent, the City of Bread* (1923).

NÉVSKY (Krivobókov), **Vladímir Ivánovich** (1876–1937), Bolshevik historian and a participant in the October revolution. In 1897 he organized in Rostov-on-Don a Social Democratic group. In 1903, joined the Bolsheviks. Repeatedly arrested. After the February revolution, N created, together with N. Podvoysky, the military organization of the Bolsheviks. In the October days, was a member of the Military Revolutionary Committee. After the October revolution, was people's commissar of communications and the rector of the Sverdlov University. N was editor of the review *Krasnaya Letopis* (Red Annals) and the author of several books. As chairman of the Society of the Old Bolsheviks N protested against the executions of Zinoviev, Kamenev and other aides of Lenin. Soon afterwards, he was arrested and disappeared.

NEW ECONOMIC POLICY: *see* NEP.

NEW OPPOSITION: *see* OPPOSITION.

NEW SIBERIAN ISLANDS, group in Arctic Ocean between Laptev Sea and E. Siberian Sea, a part of Yakut ASSR. Chief island groups: Lyakhov Islands, New Siberian or Anzhu Islands (Kotelny, Belkovsky, Zemlya Bunge, Faddeyevsky, and Novaya Sibir Island), De Long Islands (Bennett, Henrietta, and Zhokova). Total area about 15,300 sq. mi.; largest island is Kotelny. Climate very severe; winter lasts from August to June. First visited in 1773.

NEW STYLE (N.S.): *see* CALENDAR.

NEWSPRINT: *see* PAPER AND NEWSPRINT INDUSTRY.

NEZAMÉTNY: *see* ALDAN.

NEZHDÁNOVA, Antonína Vasílyevna (1873–1950), lyric soprano, People's Artist of USSR. Graduated from the Moscow conservatoire in 1902. For 30 years on the stage of Bolshoy Theater, N combined vocal mastery with convincing acting. After 1943 taught at Moscow conservatoire. Stalin prize (1943).

NÉZHIN, city in Chernigov Oblast, Ukrainian SSR; pop. 44,900 (1959). R.R. junction on the Kiev-Moscow line; as the center of a vegetable-growing area, it has a food ind. Founded in 12th century.

NGANASANS: *see* POPULATION.

NICHOLAS I (Nikoláy Pávlovich (1796–1855), Emperor of Russia (1825–55), third son of Paul I and Maria Fyodorovna, formerly Princess of Württemberg. His reign started with the Decembrist conspiracy which he crushed, and he became the "gendarme" of Europe. He suppressed the Polish uprising of 1830–31 with an iron hand and used R. troops to quell the Hungarian revolution of 1848. In domestic affairs, his attitude was summed up by his minister of education, Uvarov, in a famous formula: "Orthodoxy, autocracy, and nationality." He ruled the country through the "Third Section" of his personal chancellery and persecuted every trace of progressive thought. Pushkin, Lermontov, Shevchenko, Belinsky, Herzen were persecuted by him. Against the background of the disaffection then sweeping Europe, his conservatism, fear of the masses, and determination to shield the landed nobility turned the paternalism he professed into a stifling police tyranny. N's reign did not produce a single substantial reform.

He was acute enough to perceive the need for change, especially with respect to serfdom, but he could find no way out. Russia's defeat in the Crimean war proved the rottenness and weakness of his regime.

BIBLIOGRAPHY: C. de Grunwald, *Nicholas I*, New York, 1954.

NICHOLAS II (Nikoláy Aleksándrovich) (1868–1918), the last emperor of Russia (1894–1917). He was the eldest son of Alexander III and Maria Fyodorovna, a princess of Denmark. Before he mounted the throne his participation in state affairs was limited to perfunctory attendance of official meetings; his father considered his judgment immature. This opinion is fortified by the diary assiduously kept by N throughout his life; the diary displays a triviality of mind that contrasts ironically with the turbulent events N was fated to live through.

Notable points in R. foreign policy during N's reign were the reinforcement of the Franco-Russian alliance, initiated by Alexander III; the construction of the Trans-Siberian R.R., and the military penetration in the Far East, one of the causes of the rupture that led to the disastrous Russo-Japanese war of 1904; estrangement from Germany; rapprochement with England; and finally World War I.

Despite N's ultraconservatism, the defeat of Russia in the Japanese war and the pressure of the liberal and the revolutionary movement which led to the revolution of 1905 forced the tsar to grant a limited parliamentary regime the cornerstone of which was the new Russian parliament, the State Duma (1905).

His marriage to Alexandra Fyodorovna (q.v.), a German princess and a granddaughter of Queen Victoria, was ideally happy, though marred by her ill health and the hemophilia of their son and heir, Alexis, which gave Rasputin, an illiterate peasant and debauchee, a great ascendancy over the Imperial family. N assumed command of the army in 1915, but he remained an essentially passive figure, while in his absence from the capital the empress wielded her sinister authority more and more extravagantly.

After the February revolution of 1917 N was forced to abdicate. He was imprisoned first at Tsarskoye Selo palace, then at Tobolsk. On July 16, 1918 N, together with his whole family, was shot in a cellar at Yekaterinburg (now Sverdlovsk) by order of local Soviet authorities.

J. C.

NICHOLAS, Nikoláyevich (1856–1929), grand duke, grandson of Emperor Nicholas I. In 1914 he was commander of the Imperial Guards; appointed commander in chief of the army after the outbreak of World War I; in Aug. 1915 transferred to the Caucasus as viceroy and commander of the Caucasian front. After the February revolution of 1917, he escaped abroad and died in exile.

NIHILISM, a philosophical movement among R. intellectuals that centered on the negation of traditional values, moral principles and cultural heritage. The term "nihilist" was first used by Nadezhdin in the 1830's in connection with Pushkin's poetry. It was revived and made popular by Turgenev in his novel *Fathers and Sons* (1862), the hero of which, Bazarov, is a typical *raznochinets*, or intellectual of non-noble origin. During the few years that followed, nihilist characters presented in either a negative or a positive light, were depicted by a number of authors. They include Pomyalovsky's Chervanin (in *Molotov*), Chernyshevsky's Lopukhov, Kirsanov and Rakhmetov, Sleptsov's Ryazanov (*Difficult Times*), and the heroes of Pisemsky's *Turbulent Sea*, of Leskov's *Nowhere to Go*, and of Klushnikov's *Marevo*. The closest study of the psychology of N is in Dostoyevsky's description of Raskolnikov in *Crime and Punishment*. Turgenev's initial representation of the R. nihilist as a person having no positive values served to strengthen the position of conservative circles in their condemnation of the scientifically-minded revolutionaries. This led to strong attacks on Turgenev on the part of radical critics as well as to an attempt by Chernyshevsky to present a positive interpretation of the nihilistic tendencies among the revolutionaries. In *What Is to Be Done?* (1863), Chernyshevsky ascribed their excesses to the lack of opportunity, under conditions then existing, to devote one's life fully to the cause of social reform. I. M.

NIJINSKY, Vaslav (1890–1950), ballet dancer. Graduated from the St. Petersburg school of ballet and joined the St. Petersburg Imperial Ballet company; partner of famous ballerinas, among them Pavlova and Karsavina. A dancer of prodigious technique and great style, N created a sensation when he first  appeared with the Diaghilev (q.v.) ballet in Paris in 1909. His greatest successes were scored in *Le Pavillon d'Armide, Les Sylphides, Scheherazade, Le Spectre de la Rose, Carnaval*, and *Petrouchka* (all by Fokine, q.v.), and *Giselle*, and *L'Après-midi d'un Faune*, one of the three ballets which he choreographed. While the Diaghilev company was appearing in S. America in 1913 but in Diaghilev's absence, N married Romola de Pulszky, a dancer in the corps de ballet. Diaghilev immediately dismissed N and his wife. N's marriage virtually terminated his career as a dancer. On his return to Europe N lived in Switzerland and soon began to display symptoms of a mental ailment from which he never recovered. He died in London in 1950.

BIBLIOGRAPHY: F. Reiss, *Nijinsky, A Biography*, New York and London, 1961.

NIKÍTIN, Iván Sávvich (1824–1861), poet-realist  whose principal theme was the hopeless lot of the peasant and people of the lower middle class. Son of a small trader, N was one of Russia's most popular lyricists. Among his notable lyrics and poems are *Kulak*, the story of a poor peasant driven by misery to exploiting other peasants, *Hopeless Lot, The Village Pauper*, and *Burlak*.

NIKÍTIN, Nikoláy Nikoláyevich (1895–), writer, member of the Serapion Brothers group. His early novel *Kirik Rudenko's Crime* (1926) treats sexual freedom and other ethical problems faced by Communist youth of the 1920's. *The Lost Rembrandt* deals with organ-

ized suppression of creative freedom. Later writings including *Aurora Borealis* (1950) are strongly marked by a reversion to socialist realism.

NIKÍTIN, Vasíly Petróvich (1893–1956), electromechanical and welding engineer. Fellow (1939) and member of the executive board (1939–42, 1947–53), Ac. of S., USSR. Honorary member (1951), Ac. of S., Turkmenian SSR. Honorary Scientist and Technologist, RSFSR (1949). Graduate of St. Petersburg Polytechnic Institute (1914). Professor, Dnepropetrovsk Mining Institute (1925–29), Moscow Mining Academy (1929–32), Moscow Steel Institute (1930), and Moscow School of Technology (1933). Research on physical processes in an electric arc and the development of equipment for electric arc welding. Author of *Electric Machines and Transformers for Electric Arc Welding* (1937); *Electric Arc Welding, a Russian Invention* (1952).

NIKOLÁYEV, city, adm. center of Nikolayev Oblast, Ukrainian SSR, on Black Sea estuary, at the confluence of the Bug and Ingul rivers; pop. 169,000 (1939), 226,000 (1959). Is a modern port; R.R. junction; and a major ind. center: agric. machinery, ship repairs, food processing.

NIKOLÁYEV OBLAST, Ukrainian SSR, in Black Sea lowland, bounded S. by Black Sea; area 9,600 sq. mi.; pop. 1,015,000 (1959). Cities: Nikolayev (adm. center), Voznesensk, Ochakov, Pervomaysk. It is drained by the lower S. Bug, Ingul and Ingulets rivers; has fertile black soil; temperate continental climate (dry summers). Agr.: wheat, corn, rye, sunflowers, orchards, vineyards, livestock, fishing (Black Sea inlets). Ind.: shipyards, machine mfg., fish canning, food processing, sugar refining; mining of granite. Has extensive R.R. network. Est. 1937.

NIKOLÁYEVSK-ON-AMUR, seaport city in E. Khabarovsk Kray, RSFSR, near Amur River delta. Pop. 35,600 (1958). Steamer lines to Komsomolsk, Blagoveshchensk, Khabarovsk, Vladivostok; harbor closed by ice for six months of the year. Regional center for salmon fishing and canning; shipbuilding and repair.

NIKOLÁYEVSKY, Borís Ivánovich (1887–), Menshevik, historian, and journalist. In Russia, N worked in historical archives and on the editorial board of several Menshevik newspapers, including *Luch* (Ray) (1912–14). In 1922, he was exiled. As an *émigré*, N was a member of the editorial board of the Menshevik review *Sotsialistichesky Vestnik* (Socialist Courier) and contributed to scholarly publications. Author of *History of a Traitor* (*Azef*) (1932) and *A. N. Potresov* (1937), a biography. N edited the letters of P. B. Akselrod, G. V. Plekhanov, and Yu. O. Martov and is a co-author, with David Dallin, of *Forced Labor in Soviet Russia* (1947).

NÍKON, Moscow Patriarch (Nikita Minov), (1605–1681). His church reforms affected the rites of public worship and brought about a schism in the Russian church; he also attempted to subordinate secular power to the church. He was deposed by Tsar Alexis and died in exile. The reforms of N resulted in secession from the church of the Old-Believers, who were condemned by the church as schismatics.

NÍKOPOL, city in Dnepropetrovsk Oblast, Ukrainian SSR, on right bank of the Dnieper; pop. 81,000 (1959). R.R. station. Center of Nikopol manganese region; has machine mfg. and metalworking ind., large pipe-rolling plant. Founded 1781; a strategic crossing point of the Dnieper.

NIL SÓRSKY (1433–1508), born in a peasant family and known under the name of Maykov. Prior to entering the Kirillo-Belozero monastery he copied books. He protested against ownership of land by monasteries as contradictory to Christian ideals. He was the author of a statute for monasteries in 12 volumes. He founded the monastic movement of the so-called "Volga Hermits" (*zavolzhskiye startsy*) which comprised monks from the Belozero and Vologda monasteries who shared his predilection for the hermiatge type of monasticism.

NIVKHI: *see* POPULATION.

NIZHNEÚDINSK, city in Irkutsk Oblast, RSFSR, on the upper Uda River; pop. 44,000 (1959). Is a rapidly developing ind. city on the Trans-Siberian R.R., with slate-processing plant and chemical ind. Founded 1648.

NÍZHNY NÓVGOROD: *see* GORKY.

NÍZHNY TAGÍL, city in Sverdlovsk Oblast, RSFSR, on Tagil River, at the foothill of Vysokaya Mt.; pop. 160,000 (1939), 339,000 (1959). Major center of heavy ind. in the Urals since 1725; giant metallurgical and railway-car mfg. plants; rich iron, copper, gold and platinum deposits in vicinity.

NKGB: *see* SECURITY POLICE.

NKVD: *see* SECURITY POLICE.

NOBILITY: *see* ECONOMIC DEVELOPMENT, HISTORY, EMANCIPATION OF THE SERFS.

NOGAIS: *see* POPULATION.

NOGÁYSK ORDA (Horde), a feudal state founded in late 14th century by Nogay, grandson of Genghiz Khan, following the disintegration of the Golden Horde. It occupied a vast territory extending between the Volga and Irtysh rivers and from the Aral and Caspian seas to Kazan and Tyumen regions, with an administrative center at Saraychik, on lower Yaik River, in the Urals. Was populated largely by nomad cattle-breeders, of a Turkic-Tatar ethnic strain. In the late 16th century, it broke up into the Great Orda (N. of the Caucasus), Lesser Orda (E. of the Volga), and Altyulskaya Orda. In the 18th century the Nogays were driven out of most of their territories by Cossack settlers.

NOGÍN, Víktor Pávlovich (1878–1924), Bolshevik, joined the revolutionary movement in the 1890's and the Bolshevik faction in 1903. Contributed to *Iskra*. From 1907 to 1917 was a member of the Central Committee. After the October revolution N was a partisan of a Soviet government which would have included the Mensheviks and other Socialist parties. Subsequently he was people's commissar of trade and industry, and later of labor. In 1920 N was a member of the Soviet delegation to Great Britain.

NOGÍNSK, (f. Bogorodsk), city in Moscow Oblast, RSFSR, on Klyazma River; pop. 93,000 (1959). Old textile industry center; cotton ginning.

NÓLDE, Baron Borís Emmanuílovich (1876–1948), international lawyer, historian. Graduated from the St. Petersburg University; professor at St. Petersburg Poly-

technic Institute, 1903; chief legal adviser, Ministry of Foreign Affairs, 1914. Drafted, with V. Nabokov, the text of the abdication of Emperor Nicholas II, March 1917. Undersecretary of state for foreign affairs and professor at the Petrograd University, 1917. Emigrated in 1919 and lived in France. Professor at the Academy of International Law, The Hague; president of the Institute of International Law. Author of numerous books and articles on legal and historical subjects. Principal publications: in Russian, *Permanently Neutral States* (1905), *Russian Constitutional Law* (1911); in French, *L'ancien régime et la révolution russe* (1929), *L'Alliance Franco-Russe* (1936); in English, *Russia in the Economic War* (1928).

NORDVIK, bay, a large inlet of Laptev Sea just E. of the mouth of Khatanga River, N.W. Yakut ASSR; bounds on Nordvik Peninsula in E. Ice-free in July for 8 to 10 weeks. On its N.W. shore is the port Nordvik.

NORÍLSK, city in Krasnoyarsk Kray, RSFSR; pop. 108,000 (1959). One of the northernmost cities in the world. Founded in 1935 as center of a rich nonferrous metals region (nickel, copper, cobalt).

NORTHEAST PASSAGE, connecting Atlantic and Pacific along N. shores. First navigation by Nordenskjöld 1878–79. Regular shipping route for Siberian ports.

NORTH-KAZAKHSTÁN OBLAST, Kazakh SSR; area 15,860 sq. mi.; pop. 457,000 (1959): Russians, Kazakhs, Ukrainians. Petropavlovsk, adm. center. Is an unbroken level plain watered by the Ishim River, with black-earth soils and steppe vegetation. Wheat, millet and sunflower emphasized in planting of grains and technical crops; virgin and fallow land is being broken for cultivation. Cattle breeding for milk and meat. Its main ind. are limited to processing of agr. produce. Est. 1936.

NORTH OSSETIAN ASSR, S. European RSFSR; area 3,880 sq. mi.; pop. 451,000 (1959): Ossetians, Russians, Armenians, Ukrainians, Georgians and related Caucasian ethnic groups. Cities: Ordzhonikidze (capital), Malgobek, Alagir, Beslan, Mozdok. The major portion of N. Ossetia lies on the slopes and foothills of the Great Caucasus range, with lowlands in the N. drained by the navigable Terek River. It has a continental climate, with distinct altitude zones. The low steppes, with black-earth soils, largely under cultivation, are succeeded, at the next level, by the forest belt, where dense broad-leaved and coniferous woods growing on brown soils alternate with alpine and sub-alpine meadow lands. The region abounds in useful minerals such as oil, iron, copper, nonferrous metals, and building materials. Major ind. include the lead-zinc mines of Sadon, the ore concentrating plant at Mizur, the new smelting works of Ordzhonikidze, the petroleum center at Malgobek, the metalworking plants of Mozdok and Alagir, and the giant processing kombinat of Beslan, where starches, molasses, cattle feed, and glucose are produced from corn, the chief agr. crop of the region. Wheat and corn are grown largely in the N. plains. Truck farmnig and the rearing of livestock are likewise essential. The largest population group, the Ossetians, are of the Indo-Iranian strain, and have inhabited the region since the 5th century B.C. The republic is crossed by the Georgian Military Road and the Ossetian Military Road. Est. as autonomous oblast in 1924, raised to the status of republic in 1936.

NORTHERN UNION OF RUSSIAN WORKERS, founded in 1878 in St. Petersburg by S. N. Khalturin, cabinet maker, and V. P. Obnorsky, mechanic. Only men actually engaged in manual labor were admitted to the Union. While the ultimate goal of its founders was the overthrow of the existing political order, their immediate objective was fighting for better economic conditions and basic civil rights (freedom of the press, freedom of assembly, and so forth). During the few years of its existence the Union gained a membership of 200, organized an underground printing shop, put out one issue of *Rabochaya Zarya* (The Worker's Dawn), fomented a wave of unrest and strikes (1878–79), issuing leaflets and proclamations addressed to the working class. The organization was suppressed by the government in 1880–81.

NORTHERN WAR (1700–1721), between Russia and Sweden. In Nov. 1700, the Swedes defeated the R. troops under Narva, but R. victory followed in 1701 by the capture of the Noteburg Fortress, renamed Schlüsselburg (now Petrokrepost). In 1703, the town of St. Petersburg was founded at the delta of the Neva River as a R. stronghold on the Baltic Sea. Other R. victories followed, including the occupation of Derpt, Narva, and Ivangorod. After the defeat in 1708 of Augustus II of Saxony and Poland, who was an ally of Russia, Charles XII of Sweden invaded R. territory in an attempt to reach Moscow through Smolensk. Under the impact of the Russian army under Peter the Great, the Swedes turned south toward the Ukraine where they had a secret ally, the Ukrainian Hetman Mazepa. On June 27, 1709, the Russian army scored a decisive victory at Poltava. Charles XII fled to Turkey. In 1710, the Russians occupied Riga, Revel, Vyborg, and Keksholm and in 1713 Abo. In 1714, the Russian navy defeated the Swedish navy. Under the threat of a R. advance toward Stockholm in 1720, the Swedish government was compelled to sign the Treaty of Nystad, Aug. 30, 1721, by which Russia restored Finland, and Sweden ceded certain regions to Russia. The Northern War marked the decline of Sweden and the beginning of R. influence in the Baltic Sea.

NÓVAYA LÝALYA, town in Sverdlovsk Oblast, RSFSR; pop. 17,700 (1956). R.R. station; center of pulp ind.

NÓVAYA PISMYÁNKA: *see* LENINOGORSK.

NÓVAYA ZEMLÝA, a group of islands between the Barents and Kara seas in the Arctic Ocean; area 31,900 sq. mi. Tundra in the S. and ice covered in the N. Animals: reindeer, white bear, fox, walrus, seal. Population (Nenets) is engaged in fishing and hunting.

NÓVGOROD, city, adm. center of Novgorod Oblast, RSFSR, on both sides of the Volkhov River, N. of Lake Ilmen; pop. 61,000 (1959). Harbor, key R.R. junction. Ind.: woodware, boat-repair, match, porcelain and food-processing factories. One of the oldest Russian cities, it is mentioned in the 9th-century chronicles. It originated as a military and trading town, then was con-

quered by Ryurik and became the capital of the principality Great Novgorod in the 12th–15th centuries. With a highly developed trade with the Orient, Constantinople, and Hansa towns, it controlled many dependent lands in N. Russia. It was seized by Ivan III in 1478, and declined rapidly. Has 11th-century Kremlin, St. Sofia Cathedral, and other outstanding examples of early R. architecture. It suffered severely during World War II, but restoration work and archaeological excavations are now under way.

NÓVGOROD OBLAST, in N.W. European RSFSR; area 21,350 sq. mi.; pop. 736,000 (1959). Cities: Novgorod (center), Borovichi, Staraya Russa, Valday, Chudovo. It is drained by numerous rivers including the Volkhov, Msta, Lovat. Heavily forested (50 per cent of total area, with spruce, oak, birch), it also has lowlands with N. Valday Hills in the E.; over 1,000 lakes of which Ilmen, Valday, Uzhinskoye are the largest; marshes; clayey and sandy soils; temperate humid climate. Mineral resources: lignite (Komarovo, Zarubino), mineral sources (Staraya Russa), peat, refractory clays. Agr.: flax, dairy farming, rye, potatoes, wheat, livestock, orchards. Ind.: lumbering, saw and paper milling, veneering, glassworking, peat cutting, ceramics, textiles, food processing, porcelain mfg. (Krasnofarforny). It is on the Leningrad-Moscow R.R., and has a highway network. Est. 1944.

NÓVGOROD-SÉVERSKY, town in Chernigov Oblast, Ukrainian SSR, on right bank of the Desna River; pop. 11,000 (1959). Has hemp, butter, weaving, limestone factories. One of the oldest Russian towns, it was founded in the early 11th century; early in the 13th century it became part of the Bryansk principality and in 14th century of the Grand Duchy of Lithuania.

NÓVGOROD THE GREAT, medieval principality, 11th–13th centuries, covering the extensive region of all N. Russia from Lake Peipus and Lithuania to the Urals. Its capital, Novgorod, escaped the Mongol invasion of 1237–40. It was ruled by Prince Alexander Nevsky from 1238 to 1263; it developed economically from its favorable location by trade with the Orient and Constantinople and with the Hanseatic towns; it became the rival of Moscow, with many dependent towns in N. Russia; its population was estimated in the 14th century at 400,000. It was not subject to Tatars and fought successful wars with the Germans and Swedes, but was overpowered by Ivan III (1471–78) and laid waste by Ivan IV (1570). It declined on the rise of St. Petersburg. It has a Kremlin of the 11th century and several churches, cathedrals, and monasteries dating from the period of its supremacy.

NÓVIKOV, Iván Ivánovich (1916–), physicist. Corresponding member, Ac. of S., USSR (1958). Graduate, Moscow University (1939); professor (1950), director (1956), Moscow Institute of Physical Engineering. Associated with naval research institutes (1940–48). Acting learned secretary of the executive board, Ac. of S., USSR (1954–57); director, Institute of Thermal Physics, Siberian Branch, Ac. of S (1957). Research concerns thermodynamics of gas, heat transfer, gas dynamics, application of the theory of similarity to the study of thermophysical properties of substances, and problems of atomic power engineering. Editor-in-chief of the periodical *Atomnaya Energia* (Atomic Energy) (1956). Co-author of *Equations of the State of Real Gases* (1948); *Liquid-Metal Heat-Transfer Carriers* (1958). Stalin prize (1951).

NÓVIKOV, Nikoláy Ivánovich (1744–1818), writer, journalist, publisher, and social worker. An enthusiastic believer in the enlightenment, N dedicated himself and his fortune to the advancement of elementary education. His publishing houses which operated first in St. Petersburg and then in Moscow issued numerous books, including textbooks, as well as several journals, and were eminently successful. N was a pillar of the Friendly Learned Society which raised funds for educational purposes. His activities and success annoyed Empress Catherine II who regarded education as her special preserve. In 1791 N's publishing business was closed by the authorities; he was arrested but never tried and was sentenced by imperial decree to detention in the fortress of Schlüsselburg for 15 years. He was released on the accession of Emperor Paul, in 1796, but came out of prison a broken man.

NÓVIKOV, Pyotr Sergéyevich (1901–), mathematician. Fellow, Ac. of S., USSR (1960). Graduated from Moscow University (1927). Since 1934, N has been associated with the Mathematical Institute, Ac. of S. His research concerns the theory of sets and mathematical logic; expounded in his paper *The Consistency of Certain Theses in the Descriptive Theory of Sets*. Lenin prize (1957).

NÓVIKOV-PRIBÓY, Alekséy Sílych (1877–1944), Soviet writer about the sea. Served in the navy during the Russo-Japanese war. Author of *Stories of the Sea* (1917); *The Sea Calls* (1919); *The Submariners* (1923) and others. His better known novel is *Tsushima*, a fictional account of Russia's naval disaster in 1905 (Stalin prize, 1941).

NOVOCHERKÁSSK, city in Rostov Oblast, RSFSR, on a delta arm of the Don; on Rostov–Voronezh R.R.; pop. 94,000 (1959). Ind.: R.R. machinery, tool mfg., mining and building equipment, food processing. A cultural center, it has colleges and research institutes. Founded 1805 by Don Cossacks.

NOVOKÚYBYSHEVSK, city in Kuybyshev Oblast, RSFSR; pop. 63,000 (1959). Founded in 1952 in connection with development of oil industry; petroleum processing, synthetic alcohol, building materials.

NOVO-KUZNÉTSK: *see* STALINSK.

NOVONIKOLÁYEVSK: *see* NOVOSIBIRSK.

NOVOROSSÍYSK, seaport city in W. Krasnodar Kray, RSFSR, on Black Sea; pop. 95,000 (1939), 93,000 (1959). Terminus of branch R.R. from Krasno-dar. Largest center of Soviet cement ind.; R.R. car and boat repairs, food processing; resorts in vicinity.

NOVOSHÁKHTINSK, city in Rostov Oblast, RSFSR; pop. 104,000 (1959). Coal mining, coke-chemical, clothing, food ind., building materials.

NOVOSIBÍRSK (f. Novonikoláyevsk), city, adm. center of Novosibirsk Oblast, RSFSR, on navigable Ob River; pop. 404,000 (1939), 886,000 (1959). Is a large R.R. junction; terminus on Trans-Siberian R.R. and an airport. Largest Siberian ind. center, with agr. machinery, metallurgy, food and light ind., lumbering, textile mfg.; Novosibirsk Hydroelectric Plant. Has colleges, research institutes; the Siberian division of the Ac. of S. of the USSR. Founded 1893.

NOVOSIBÍRSK OBLAST, in W. Siberia, RSFSR; area 68,800 sq. mi.; pop. 2,299,000 (1959): Russians, Ukrainians. Bounded on the S. by the Kazakh SSR, on the S.E. by the Altay Kray. Cities: Novosibirsk (adm. center), Kuybyshev, Tatarsk, Berdsk, Iskitim, Cherepanovo, and others. Drained by the Ob, Om, Tara, it is a lowland W. of the Ob; Baraba Steppe in the S., with black soil, hilly forest steppe and tayga, Salair Ridge E. of the Ob. Has continental climate, with long severe winters, hot summers, and drought. Mineral resources: coal, clays, sands, powdered quartz, peat, salt. Agr.: dairy farming, wheat, flax, sunflowers, potatoes, vegetables. Ind.: machine mfg., metal working, cement, food processing. There is a large power plant under construction on the Ob. Transportation is by Trans-Siberian R.R. (E. to W.) and waterways. Est. 1937.

NOVO SIBIRSKIE OSTROVA: *see* NEW SIBERIAN ISLANDS.

NOVOTRÓITSK, city in Orenburg Oblast, RSFSR, on Ural River; pop. 57,000 (1959). R.R. station. Major center of S. Urals ferrous metallurgy, between the Khalilovo iron and nickel mines and the city of Orsk. A new city founded during World War II.

NÓVY MARGELÁN: *see* FERGANA.

"NO WAR, NO PEACE": *see* BREST-LITOVSK TREATY.

N.S. (NEW STYLE): *see* CALENDAR.

NUKÚS, capital of Kara-Kalpak ASSR (part of Uzbek SSR); on right bank of the Amu Darya River at head of delta; pop. 10,000 (1939), 38,000 (1959). Major ind. and cultural center; largest Soviet alfalfa-processing plant, auto repairing, brick, timber, food processing, printing; fishing.

NYSTÁD, TREATY OF, Aug. 30, 1721, between Russia and Sweden ending the Northern War (q.v.) by the victory of Peter I. Russia obtained Livonia, Estonia, Ingermanland, part of Karelia, Vyborg, the islands of Œsel and Dagö and secured a firm position on the Baltic Sea. Both parties committed themselves to restore freedom of trade.

O

OB, river in Asia, about 2,700 mi. long (with the Irtysh 3,450 mi. long), flowing N.W. and N. through Novosibirsk and Tomsk oblasts and Khanty-Mansi and Yamal-Nenets National okrugs into the Gulf of Ob. Formed by junction of Biya and Katun rivers. Main tributaries: Irtysh, Tom, Chulym, Ket, Vakh. Navigable; has an abundance of fish. Chief towns on its banks: Novosibirsk, Barnaul, Salekhard, Khanty-Mansiysk. Large hydroelectric power plant just above Novosibirsk.

OBDÓRSK: *see* SALEKHARD.

ÓBLAST, administrative-territorial unit, usually formed on the principle of economic integration. The O areas and borders change frequently following economic development. As of Jan. 1, 1961, there were forty-nine oblasts in RSFSR, twenty-five in the Ukrainian SSR, six in the Byelorussian SSR, eight in the Uzbek SSR, fourteen in the Kazakh SSR, one in Tadzhik SSR, three in Turkmen SSR. The largest is Tyumen Oblast of RSFSR (544,000 sq. mi.), i.e. the combined size of California, Arizona and Texas), the smallest is Khorezm Oblast in Uzbek SSR (1,740 sq. mi., i.e. less than the area of Delaware).

OBNÓRSKY, Víktor Pávlovich (1852–1920), factory worker, revolutionary. He was active in the "Land and Freedom" movement, in St. Petersburg. In 1878 he founded the Northern Union of Russian Workers, together with S. N. Khalturin. He was arrested in 1879 and sentenced to 10 years of forced labor.

OBOLÉNSKY, Prince Yevgény Petróvich (1796–1865), Decembrist, lieutenant in the Finland Regiment of the Body Guard. He was a leader of the Northern Society, together with Ryleyev and Nikita Muravyov. He participated actively in the uprising of December 14, 1825, for which he was condemned to death, but his sentence was changed to exile in Siberia.

OBÓRIN, Lev Nikoláyevich (1907–), pianist and teacher. People's Artist of the RSFSR. Graduated from Gnessin's School of Music (1921) and the Moscow Conservatoire (1926); studied piano with Igumnov. O toured Russia and abroad. An accomplished piano player, his repertory comprises nearly every type of composition. In 1927 O was awarded the first prize at the International Chopin Contest in Warsaw.

"OBORONTSY": *see* MENSHEVISM, SOCIAL REVOLUTIONARIES.

OBRAZTSÓV, Vasíly Parmyónovich (1851–1920), therapeutist. Graduate, Medical and Surgical Academy in St. Petersburg (1875); professor, Kiev University (1893). Introduced palpation techniques in Russia and auscultation directly by ear without a stethoscope. In 1910 with N. D. Strazhesko, O described the obstruction of coronary arteries.

OBRÉIMOV, Iván Vasílyevich (1894–), physicist. Fellow, Ac. of S., USSR (1958). Graduated from Petrograd University (1915). Associated with the Leningrad Institute of Physics and Technology (1924) and director of its Ukrainian Branch (1929). Research concerns the physics of crystals, molecular spectroscopy, plastic deformation and optical properties of single crystals, crystal spectroscopy at subzero temperature, etc. Developed the "Obreimov method" for the estimation of dispersion. Stalin prize (1946); M. V. Lomonosov Gold Medal (1960).

OBRÓK, an ancient term, means two different things: (a) consolidated tax payment; and (b) annual payment by serfs to their masters, or by state peasants (q.v.) to the government, for the use of their land allotments. (a) It was an ancient and common practice traceable to the 14th century to consolidate all taxes into one payment. This privilege was usually granted in letters patent issued by the prince to the owner of an estate who was empowered to collect the taxes and to deliver them to the appropriate authority, thus relieving the tenants of the estate of the duty to deal directly with the tax officials. (b) Under the O systems of estate management most of the land of the estate was farmed by the peasants on their own account; they paid the owner an annual sum known as O. It was customary to supplement monetary payments by deliveries in kind or occasional services. As a rule, peasants under O enjoyed greater freedom than those under the *barshchina* system (q.v.). It is estimated that in the 18th century about 44 per cent of the peasants lived under the O system. (*See also* PEASANTS, STATE PEASANTS)

ÓBRUCHEV, Vladímir Afanásyevich (1863–1956), geologist, geographer, and explorer. Fellow, Ac. of S., USSR (1929). Hero of Socialist Labor (1945). Honored scientist RSFSR (1927). Honorary president of the Geographical Society of the USSR (1947). Graduated from St. Petersburg Mining Institute (1886). Professor, Tomsk Institute of Technology (1901–12), Simferopol University (1919–21), Moscow Mining Academy (1921–29). He explored Central Asia, Siberia, and other regions of the USSR. Participated in numerous expeditions to Mongolia and Northern China; made geographical and geological discoveries. Author of publications and papers on geology, geography, travel, neo- and geotectonics as well as fiction including *Over the Hills and Steppes of Central Asia* (1948). Numerous awards including gold medals of the Geographical Society and the Ac. of S., USSR, the French Ac. of S., and Lenin and Stalin prizes.

OBÚKHOV, Aleksándr Mikháylovich (1918–), geophysicist. Corresponding member, Ac. of S., USSR (1953). Graduate, Moscow University (1940); joined the Geophysical Institute. Director, Institute of Physics of Atmosphere (1956). Research concerns the application of the statistical theory of turbulence to meteorology, atmospheric turbulence, certain problems of dynamic meteorology, and the theory of probability. With A. N. Kolmogorov, O advanced a theory of the local structure of turbulence.

OCHÁKOV, seaport town in Nikolayev Oblast, S. Ukraine, on the Black Sea between Odessa and Kherson; pop. 7,700 (1958). Has extensive fishing, fish-canning ind. It was the site of the ancient Greek town Alektor in 7th-6th centuries B.C.; became Tatar fort Kara-Kermen 1492, seized by Turks; the scene of many battles between R. and Turkish fleets; it was finally conquered by Russia 1791.

OCTOBER REVOLUTION—the name given by the Bolsheviks to their seizure of power on Oct. 25 (Nov. 7 N. S.) 1917, which has passed into common usage. By Oct. the Provisional Government (q.v.) headed by A. Kerensky had lost most of its authority, and many elements and institutions of R. society were rapidly disintegrating. In these circumstances the Bolsheviks, a relatively small but determined and well-organized group strategically concentrated in Petrograd and Moscow, were able to seize military control of the two cities, with little resistance from the rest of the country.

The Provisional Government, which had been inaugurated with such high hopes in March, failed to solve the four most pressing problems: 1. The traditional chains of authority emanating from the tsar had been snapped in Feb. No Provisional Government could inspire the same automatic obedience, and through Oct. none had seen fit to summon the promised Constituent Assembly (q.v.), representative of all the peoples of Russia, which might have commanded such respect. 2. The Provisional Government had no military strength to drive the German army from Russia and had neither the will nor the political strength to end the war on German terms. Consequently the war continued month after month, a major disintegrating factor on the R. scene. 3. The Provisional Government had no agrarian policy that would allow the peasants to take over the land of the gentry, state, and church. While the Government was preparing constitutional and orderly agrarian reforms, the peasants became impatient and they began increasingly to seize these lands illegally and violently, in disregard of the orders of the Provisional Government. 4. The war and the disorders in the countryside interfered with the supply of food to the cities. The Provisional Government failed to maintain the urban food supply and to control inflation, corruption, black markets, and profiteers, all of which contributed to its downfall.

Since May, the strong man in successive provisional governments was A. F. Kerensky. On June 1 the third congress of the Socialist Revolutionary party (q.v.) failed to elect him to the party's Central Committee by two votes. This confirmed the breach between Kerensky and the party's organization headed by V. M. Chernov, the minister of agriculture. The position of Kerensky was greatly weakened in late June and early July when the offensive on the Galician front collapsed dismally, revealing the warlike intentions of the Provisional Government to the unwilling soldiers, and the hopeless condition of the R. army to the world. The "mutiny" (late Aug.) of the Command. in Chief Gen. L. G. Kornilov accompanied by the resignation of most of Kerensky's important colleagues from the Provisional Government, marked the falling away of much of the prime minister's remaining support. Meanwhile, the chaos resulting from mass desertions

from the army, agrarian disorders, urban economic crises, and administrative breakdown was increased by separatist movements among national minorities on all fringes of the former R. Empire, notably in Finland, the Baltic provinces, the Ukraine, and Transcaucasia, which were largely independent of the Provisional Government by Oct.

Amid this social disintegration, Lenin and the Bolsheviks saw their chance to seize power. Lenin believed that World War I was to lead to the breakdown of world capitalism, that the Feb. revolution was the first step on the way to a socialist Russia, that the strikes and naval mutinies in Germany signified the imminence of the world revolution, and that a workers' victory in Russia would touch off the final battle for socialism all over Europe. He further believed that only his Bolshevik party had the true Marxist ideology and effective combat organization to guide the R. workers to victory. The questions for Lenin, then, were when and how the Bolsheviks might best seize power. By Oct. he thought the time had come. The Bolshevik party had grown from about 14,000 before Feb. to over 200,000 by Oct. (chiefly intelligentsia, workers in the two capital cities, and soldiers of the Petrograd garrison and on nearby fronts). Unlike the Socialist Revolutionaries, the Bolshevik organization had not been disrupted by growth. The Kornilov "mutiny" had led many waverers to support the Bolsheviks, who used the crisis to gain control of the "Red Guard" which was mobilized by the Petrograd Soviet to protect the city from Kornilov. Economic difficulties and reaction to the mutiny secured majorities for the Bolsheviks in the Petrograd Soviet (Aug. 31) and the Moscow Soviet (Sept. 6). The appearance of these majorities determined Lenin on the seizure of power "for the Soviets" while Bolsheviks controlled them, and before the Bolshevik stronghold of Petrograd fell to the threatening Germans. The second All-Russian Congress of Soviets was scheduled for Oct. 25. Lenin decided to seize power before that date; hence the actual date of the rising: the night of Oct. 24–25. Lenin insisted that the seizure of power must come about through armed insurrection. Other methods, he believed, would be too slow, would fail to overcome the resistance of the Provisional Government, and would not permit a thorough crushing of the opposition. Lenin had great difficulty, through Sept. and early Oct., in persuading his Bolshevik colleagues to accept these views. He had been hiding in Finland since the unsuccessful Bolshevik rising in July, but on Oct. 20 he slipped into Petrograd in disguise to attend a meeting of the Bolshevik Central Committee. Twelve out of twenty-one members were present. Some protested that the proposed uprising would fail, but Lenin held that the peasant soldiers of Petrograd were for the insurrection and would make it succeed. After a stormy discussion that lasted for ten hours, Lenin's resolution for an armed insurrection was approved by a 10–2 vote—Zinoviev and Kamenev dissenting.

The actual seizure of power proved surprisingly easy, for the Provisional Government was far weaker than anyone thought, and the other revolutionary parties, the Socialist Revolutionary and the Menshevik (q.v.), were too split internally, intent on the forthcoming elections to the Constituent Assembly, and contemptuous of the Bolsheviks to counter the threat. Trotsky, in jail since the July rising, had been released (Sept. 4) and had been made president of the Bolshevik-dominated Petrograd Soviet (Sept. 23). On Oct. 9 the Bolsheviks seized on a Menshevik proposal and formed a Military Revolutionary Committee of the Soviet, which under the lead of Trotsky and Sverdlov became the group that prepared and carried through the Bolshevik insurrection. Meanwhile Zinoviev and Kamenev continued their opposition to the rising so vocally that most details of the plan became widely known, and were even published in the press. Yet Kerensky no longer had the police power to arrest the plotters. The Military Revolutionary Committee began to operate on Oct. 20, with the organization of garrison troops to act as insurrectionary units. Bolshevik commissars were appointed to displace the commander of the garrison (Oct. 21). The Provisional Government at last decided to bring in loyal troops to suppress the Bolsheviks (Oct. 23), but could only persuade some military cadets to occupy a few key points and shut down two Bolshevik presses for a few hours (Oct. 24) before a successful counter-attack by Bolshevik troops. Lenin returned to Petrograd, and the insurrection moved into the open on the evening of Oct. 24. Units of armed Bolsheviks (Trotsky estimated that not more than 30,000 participated in the seizure of power) occupied public buildings and communications centers, including the crucially important telephone exchange, meeting little resistance. The next morning (Oct. 25) Kerensky left Petrograd, in a last attempt to secure loyal troops. Petrograd was now in Bolshevik hands save for the Winter Palace, where the remaining members of the Provisional Government were blockaded. A surrender ultimatum (6.30 p.m.) was ignored. Clumsy bombardment of the Winter Palace from the cruiser *Aurora* and from the Fortress of Peter and Paul failed to inflict damage. A troop of Bolsheviks led by V. A. Antonov-Ovseyenko finally infiltrated the building and arrested the ministers of the Provisional Government at 2.10 a.m., Oct. 26.

The new Bolshevik government was announced at the Petrograd Soviet and proclaimed at the All-Russian Congress of Soviets (Oct. 25). At the latter meeting Mensheviks, rightwing Socialist Revolutionaries, and others denounced the Bolshevik uprising and withdrew, leaving the Bolsheviks and the left-wing Socialist Revolutionaries (who were soon to split openly with their own party and form a short-lived coalition with the Bolsheviks) in control. At Lenin's instance, the rump congress passed resolutions favoring peace without annexations and taking over the land for the benefit of the peasants (appropriating temporarily the Socialist Revolutionaries' land program). It also confirmed an all-Bolshevik government of People's Commissars headed by Lenin. Meanwhile Kerensky succeeded in securing the support of the Cossack Gen. P. N. Krasnov whose troops moved to Gatchina, 10 miles from Petrograd. Trotsky mobilized the workers and Krasnov was defeated. Kerensky fled abroad. After sharp fighting, Moscow was captured by Bolsheviks by Nov. 2. Army headquarters at Mogilev were taken on Nov. 19. Most other cities and towns, save in areas of minorities, submitted by the end of the year. Lenin's "October Revolution" had gained power for the Bolsheviks in most of Russia, but it did not touch off a world revolution. With limited resources, Lenin and the Bolsheviks had to face the Germans at the front and to deal with a restive and still disintegrating society throughout all Russia.

BIBLIOGRAPHY: E. H. Carr, *The Bolshevik Revolution, 1917–23*, New York, 1951; W. H. Chamberlin, *The Russian Revolution*; D. Shub, *Lenin*, New York, 1948; N. N. Sukhanov, *The Russian Revolution, 1917: A Personal Record*, London and New York, 1955; L. Trotsky, *The History of the Russian Revolution*, Vol. III.

F. B. R.

OCTOBRISTS. Founded in November 1905 as the "Union of October 17," the Octobrist Party (*Oktyabristy*) demanded nothing more than the fulfillment of the promises made in the imperial manifesto from which it took its name. Alexander Guchkov, who became leader of the new party, had strongly opposed the Kadet program regarding land redistribution. Thus the Octobrists adopted a moderate conservative position to the right of the Kadets. While they favored the idea of a constitutional monarchy with a Duma enjoying full legislative powers, they rejected the English concept of an executive responsible to the legislature. The Octobrists wanted instead a strong executive responsible to the monarch himself.

The group drew most of its support from the "enlightened" country gentry and leading members of the bureaucracy. For a time, however, it was not a party in the strict sense of the word. Discipline was at a minimum, members enjoying greater latitude than did their counterparts among the Kadets. Only under the leadership of Guchkov in the Third Duma (1907–12) did the Octobrists begin to take on the conventional features of a parliamentary party.

They controlled only 12 seats in the First Duma (1906) but increased their strength to 32 in the Second (1907). From the beginning they supported the Stolypin government. This probably explains their resounding success under the terms of the new electoral law of June 1907 (so detrimental to the Kadets) in the elections for the Third Duma. The Octobrists won 150 seats or roughly one-third of the total membership and were now the largest single group in the house. Three Octobrists were to serve as speakers during the lifetime of the Third Duma: N. A. Khomyakov (1907–10); Guchkov (March 1910–March 1911); and M. V. Rodzyanko (1911–12). Rodzyanko was also speaker for the duration of the Fourth Duma.

As the Third Duma convened, Guchkov reaffirmed the party's support for Stolypin as a means of preventing the Premier's becoming a captive of the "reactionaries." However, the alliance soon deteriorated. The Octobrist leader did not hesitate to criticize government policies, notably in matters of military organization and education. The reactionaries were thus able to increase their pressure on Stolypin for an end to his collaboration with the Octobrists. The final break came in the spring of 1910. Thereafter the government swung to the right, while the Octobrists tended leftwards ever closer to the Kadets.

This tendency continued in the Fourth Duma where Octobrist strength fell to 97 seats. Finally the military setbacks of 1915 and the government's indifference to criticism led the Octobrists to join with the Kadets and other groups in the "Progressive Bloc" (August 1915) (q.v.). The Bloc insisted that the war effort could be saved only through the formation of a more representative government and a program of reforms designed to win the loyalty of all the people. The government rejected these suggestions and opposition criticism mounted still further. Guchkov, chairman of the War Industries Committee and prominent in Red Cross activities, had first-hand knowledge of the military situation. Thus he bitterly attacked the policies of the war minister, General Sukhomlinov, forcing the latter's resignation (June 1916).

Despite his pro-monarchist sympathies, Guchkov himself became war minister in the first Provisional Government (March 1917). He was one of the two Octobrists in Prince Lvov's first cabinet. However his violent disagreements with the Soviets regarding army organization forced his resignation at the end of April. The role of the Octobrists as a significant force in Russia was thus terminated.   C. J. F.

ODÉSSA, city, adm. center of Odessa Oblast, Ukrainian SSR; pop. 667,000 (1959). Large port on Black Sea, N.E. of the Dniester delta on Odessa Bay, the town is built on terraced hills and noted for its beauty; is a cultural and ind. center, with a university, conservatoire, Research Institute for Ophthalmology, colleges, public library, theaters, museums; a resort area. Ind.: machine mfg., metalworking, sugar refineries, tobacco, leather and chemical plants; grain elevators; exports grain, lumber, coal, wool, sugar, cattle; imports oil and oil products (from the Caucasus), coal (Donbas), concrete (Novorossiysk) for transportation to Ukraine, Byelorussia, and further N. Airport. Region early colonized by Greeks; the present town was founded 1794; name is derived from ancient Greek colony Odessos which was in vicinity. Scene of the revolution of 1905.

ODÉSSA OBLAST, Ukrainian SSR; area 12,800 sq. mi.; pop. 2,028,000 (1959): Ukrainians, Russians, Moldavians. In S.W. European USSR, a Black Sea lowland rising (N.) to the Volyn-Podolian upland; bounded on the S. by the Black Sea, on the W. by the Moldavian SSR. Cities: Odessa (adm. center), Balta, Pervomaysk, Kotovsk, Ananyev, Izmail. Drained by the S. Bug, Dniester, Danube, and numerous streams; has steppe, hills in the S.; fertile black soil; mild climate. Extensive agr.: wheat, rye, corn, millet, sunflowers, orchards; livestock (cattle, sheep, horses). Ind.: machine mfg., chemicals, textiles, food processing, flour milling, distilling, sugar refining, fish canning, tanning. Est. 1932.

ODÓYEVSKY, Aleksándr Ivánovich (1802–1839), poet and Decembrist, born in St. Petersburg in an aristocratic family. Much of his poetry is patriotic. Arrested and condemned to 8 years at hard labor in Siberia after the uprising of Dec. 1825. When freed, he served as a private in the army in the Caucasus and died of fever.

ODÓYEVSKY, Vladímir Fyódorovich (1804–1869), writer and musical critic, and founder of the circle of "Lyubomúdry," a group favoring philosophic idealism, which was dissolved after the Decembrist uprising in 1825. Author of philosophical fantasies *Russian Nights* (1844), novels, and noted articles on the composer Glinka (q.v.).

ŒSEL: *see* SAREMA ISLAND.

OGARYÓV, Nikoláy Platónovich (1813–1877), revolutionary publicist and poet, son of a wealthy landowner.

O joined the revolutionary movement in his student days and was very closely associated with Herzen. Was expelled from the Moscow University, arrested, and exiled to the estate of his father. In 1856, O left Russia and lived the rest of his life abroad, mostly in London. He was co-editor with Herzen of *Kolokol* (The Bell) and one of the organizers of the populist group *Zemlya i Volya* (Land and Freedom) in the 1860's. O was a partisan of farreaching reforms but was hostile to a bloody revolution. O wrote also lyrical poetry which expressed melancholy and disenchantment.

OGNYÓV, Nikoláy (Mikhail Grigorievich Rozanov) (1888–1938), novelist, journalist, and educator. His works were first published before the revolution. Came to prominence with his two novels written during the NEP period, *The Diary of Kostya Ryabtsev* (translated into English under the title *The Diary of a Communist Schoolboy*) and *Iskhod Nikpetozh* (translated as *The Diary of a Communist Undergraduate*), a sincere description of Soviet education during that period. In the early 1930's, O incurred official disapproval for his novel *The Three Dimensions*.

OGPU: *see* SECURITY POLICE.

OIL. The USSR is one of the world's most important O countries. Estimates of Soviet reserves by Western specialists vary between 14 and 20 bill. tons; estimates by Gubkin, the well-known R. petroleum scientist, in 1938 were 8.64 bill. tons, or some 65 bill. barrels.

The most important deposits lie W. of the Ural Mountains. The O area of Baku lies on the Apsheron Peninsula in the Azerbaijan SSR and is the oldest in the Soviet Union, the output dating from 1869. In 1901 it supplied half the world's output. O is associated with Pliocene sands. Several important O deposits were recently opened in coastal waters of the Caspian Sea off Baku. After the Revolution of 1917 new fields were discovered and put in operation as a result of systematic geological and geophysical explorations and prospecting. The most important fields are located within the Volga-Ural O region, and Soviet sources claim that this is one of the world's richest O reservoirs ("*Second Baku*"). It lies in a quadrangle formed by the cities of Kirov and Perm in the N., and Saratov and Orenburg in the S. Adjacent to it on the N. is the Ukhta-Pechora O region, and on the S., the Emba. The Ural Mountains form the E. borders and the Volga River forms the W. border. O fields are found in the Tatar, the Bashkir and the Udmurt autonomous repub-

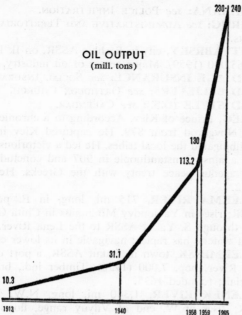

OIL OUTPUT
(mill. tons)

230-| 240

130

113.2

31.1

10.3

1913 1940 1958 1959 1965

lics and in Kirov, Penza, Perm, Orenburg, Ulyanovsk, Saratov, Stalingrad, and Kuybyshev oblasts. Beginning in 1944 large deposits were almost simultaneously discovered in the Devonian rocks of W. Bashkiria and at the Volga around Kuybyshev, the richest being the deposits of Devonian age, followed by the Carboniferous and finally by the low-Permian deposits. O and natural gas occur at depths from 590–820 ft. up to 4,900–5,600 ft. The world's oldest O fields are in W. Ukraine, lying on the E. slope of the Carpathians roughly in the triangle formed by Przemysl, Lvov, and Chernovtsy. The city of Boryslav is the commercial O center. O is associated with the Lower Tertiary rocks. Vast deposits are found in areas along the N. slope of the Great Caucasus where almost all Tertiary sediments are O-bearing. The principal O fields are in Krasnodar Kray (Maykop area), around Grozny, in the N. Ossetian ASSR, and in the Dagestan ASSR. The Emba O-bearing area lies mainly in W. Kazakhstan. O is found in Permo-Triassic, Jurassic, and Cretaceous rocks, being associated with salt domes. The most important O deposits are Kulsara, Koschagyl, and Karaton. The industrial O regions of Central Asia are concentrated principally in the Fergana Valley (Andizhan, Palvantash, Izbaskent, and others), where they are associated with the Lower Tertiary sediments. Small O deposits are found in the S. Tadzhik depression. In the Turkmen SSR O is found in the Middle and Upper Pliocene sediments (Cheleken, Nebit-Dag, and Kum-Dag). The fields of Sakhalin Island are of special importance as they supply O to the army in the Far East, to industry there, and to navigation in the Pacific. O is associated here with the Miocene sediments.

In September 1960 Soviet sources indicated that new oilfields were found in Central Asia and Kazakhstan comparable with the oilfields of the Near and Middle East. (*See also* NATURAL GAS, OIL SHALES, PETROLEUM INDUSTRY, PIPELINES.)

BIBLIOGRAPHY: Heinrich Hassmann, *Oil in the Soviet Union*, Princeton, 1953.   L. D.

OIL-BEARING CROPS. Fourteen OC are cultivated in the USSR, the main of which are sunflower (70% of the area planted), flax (9%), soybean (7.9%), mustard (5.4%), rape (4.6%). Prior to World War II, OC were mainly cultivated in the S. Ukraine, N. Caucasus, and central chernozem region, but the area of cultivation is being constantly expanded, especially into Kazakhstan and W. Siberia. Gross output of oilseed was (in mill. tons) 1.0 in 1913, 3.22 in 1940, 3.34 in 1959; that of the sunflower seed, the most important OC, was .75 in 1913, 2.2 in 1928, 2.6 in 1940, and 2.9 in 1959. Inter-regional specialization in varieties of sunflowers most suited for a given area is promoted, i.e. by the All-Union Research Institute for OC in Krasnodar. Thirty-five varieties of sunflowers are bred, with emphasis on insect- and disease-resistant varieties and on high oil contents. While sunflower oil is destined mainly for human consumption, other OC are used by industry. Among these, castor beans are undergoing a large-scale expansion. In 1957, the USSR produced, in thousands of tons, 989 of sunflower oil, 343 of cottonseed oil, 80 of soybean oil, 30 of linseed oil.

OIL SHALES. The total OS reserves are estimated at about 55 bill. tons. Deposits are widely distributed over the territory of the USSR and are associated with

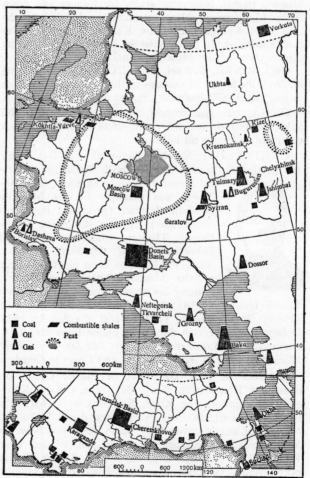

Fuel Resources of the USSR

rocks of different age. The largest reserves are Kokhtla-Yarve in the Estonian SSR; Gdov in Leningrad Oblast; Kashpir and Undor shales, and Obshchy Syrt in the Volga region. The Kendyrlik deposit of OS is in Kazakhstan; OS also occur in Siberia, in the S. part of the Timan ridge, along the W. slope of the Urals, in the Carpathians, the Caucasus, and Central Asia. Output in 1959 was 13.7 mill. tons.

ÓISTRAKH, Davíd Fyódorovich (1908–), violinist, born in Odessa. Graduated from the Odessa conservatoire (1926). Played Glazunov's concerto under the baton of the composer. Has been living in Moscow since 1928. Won first prize at the All-Union Contest for Young Performing Artists. Became professor at Moscow Conservatoire in 1934. In 1937, awarded first prize at the Ysaye International Contest of Violinists in Brussels. Frequently tours Europe, the United States, and S. America. Taught many young violinists including his son Igor and V. Pikayzen.

OKÁ RIVER, 912 mi. long, European USSR, right tributary of the Volga. Rises in N. part of Kursk Oblast, in central Russian upland, flows N. and N.E. with several bends through Orel, Kaluga, Tula, Moscow, Ryazan, Vladimir, and Gorky oblasts; received by the Volga at Gorky; navigable for most of its length. Main tributaries: Klyazma, Ugra, Zhizdra, Moskva (left), Upa, Moksha (right). Important artery for lumber and grain trade. Many ancient Russian cities are located on the Oka (Orel, Kaluga, Serpukhov, Kashira, Kolomna, Ryazan, Kasimov). It has gained in importance since the construction of the Moscow Canal.

OKÁ RIVER, 610 mi. long, Irkutsk Oblast, flowing N. from the Sayan Mountains to the Angara River; rises in Buryat, ASSR; has many rapids and is navigable.

OKHÁ, city and seaport on the N.E. coast of N. Sakhalin Island, RSFSR; pop, 26,000 (1956). Major center of Sakhalin oil industry.

OKHLÓPKOV, Nikoláy Pávlovich (1900–), actor and producer. People's Artist, USSR. Began his theatrical career in 1918 as an actor. In 1930–36 O was manager of the Moscow  Realistic Theater (produced Pogodin's *Aristocrats*); in 1938–43 of the Vakhtangov Theater, where he produced Solovyov's *Field Marshal Kutuzov.* Since 1943 O has been chief producer of the Moscow Theater of Drama. Among his productions were Fadeyev's *Young Guard* (1948); Shteyn's *The Law of Honor* (1948); *Hotel Astoria* (1956); and *Hamlet.* In 1924 O began to appear in films. His major films are *Alexander Nevsky, Summer in October, The Story of a Real Man, A Long Way from Moscow,* and *Lenin in October.*

OKHÓTSK, SEA OF, inlet of Pacific Ocean on coasts of Khabarovsk Kray, Magadan Oblast, Kamchatka Peninsula, the Kuril, Sakhalin, and Hokkaido islands. Area 615,000 sq. mi.; greatest depth 11,200 ft. N. part of sea is covered by heavy ice from Nov. to May. Abundance of rare species of fish; whales; near Kamchatka Peninsula large-scale crab fishing. Soviet ports: Ayan, Okhotsk, Magadan. Main traffic outlets: Tatar Strait, Soya Strait, and Kuril Strait.

OKHRANA: *see* POLICE INFILTRATION.

OKRUG: *see* ADMINISTRATIVE AND TERRITORIAL DIVISIONS.

OKTYÁBRSKY, city in Bashkir ASSR, on Ik River; pop. 65,000 (1959). Major center of oil industry.

OLD AGE INSURANCE: *see* SOCIAL INSURANCE.

OLD BELIEVERS: *see* ORTHODOX CHURCH.

OLD STYLE (O.S.): *see* CALENDAR.

OLÉG, Prince of Kiev. According to a chronicle, he ruled Novgorod from 879. He captured Kiev in 882 and subjugated the local tribes. He led a victorious campaign against Constantinople in 907 and concluded an advantageous peace treaty with the Greeks. He died in 912.

OLÉKMA RIVER, 715 mi. long, in E. part of RSFSR; rises in Yablonovy Mountains in Chita Oblast; flows through S. Yakut ASSR to the Lena River. Turbulent waters, has rapids; navigable in its lower course.

OLÉKMINSK, town in Yakut ASSR, a port on the Lena River, pop. 7,000 (1956). Timber ind., building materials; founded 1635.

OLENÉK RIVER, 1,340 mi. long, N.W. Yakut ASSR; rises at W. end of Vilyuy range, flows N.E. into Laptev Sea W. of the Lena River. Has an abundance of fish. Discovered by Russian Cossacks in 1637. Town of Olenek on it, trading in furs.

OLÉSHA, Yúry Kárlovich (1899–1960), journalist and playwright. Attended school in Odessa and there wrote his first poetry. Moved to Moscow in 1922, where, in collaboration with Ilf and Petrov, edited the newspaper *Gudok* (The Whistle) and translations of captions for silent foreign films, especially American films, with Charlie Chaplin, Buster Keaton, and Harold Lloyd. In 1927, his remarkable and controversial novel *Envy* appeared, followed in 1928 by a romantic fairy tale *The Three Fat Men.* Severely criticized, he "confessed his errors." His plays include *A List of Blessings* (1931) and *The Black Man* (1931–34). More recently O wrote short stories (1944–45), sketches in *Literaturnaya Moskva* (Literary Moscow), and film scenarios for such classics as Dostoyevsky's *The Idiot.*

ÓLGA (Yeléna), Russian princess, wife of Igor, prince of Kiev. She was baptized in the Greek Orthodox faith and visited Constantinople in 957. She died in 969.

OLKHÓN ISLAND, in Lake Baykal, 280 sq. mi., extends for 45 mi. at a width of 6 to 9 mi.; mountain ridge; part of Irkutsk Oblast. Pine forests in the center of the island; stony, sandy soil along coast; fur-bearing animals, fish.

OLMÍNSKY (Aleksándrov), Mikhaíl Stepánovich (1863–1933), revolutionary, Bolshevik historian. In his youth, he was a participant in the "People's Will" movement. In 1898 exiled to the Yakut region in Siberia, where he joined a Social Democrat group. In 1904, while living abroad, he became a follower and close associate of Lenin. In the interim between the two revolutions (1905–1917), wrote for and edited a number of important revolutionary publications. Took active part in the October revolution. From 1920, he was chairman of *Istpart* (Commission for the Study of the History of the Communist Party).

OLÓNETS, town in S. Karelian ASSR, near the E. shore of Lake Ladoga, on the Olonka River; pop. 5,000 (1958). An old town, mentioned in the 12th century; in 1649 a fortress was built as defense against the Swedes. Peter I established ironworks.

OM RIVER, 475 mi. long, W. Siberia; rises in Novosibirsk Oblast, flowing through Omsk Oblast to join Irtysh at Omsk; navigable in its lower course.

OMOLÓN RIVER, 715 mi. long, in Yakut ASSR, right tributary of Kolyma River, rises on N.W. slopes of Gydan range, flowing through Magadan Oblast. Steep banks, forested valleys; has an abundance of fish.

OMSK, city, adm. center of Omsk Oblast, RSFSR, at the confluence of the Irtysh and Om rivers, on the Trans-Siberian R.R.; pop. 289,000 (1939), 581,000 (1959). Major cultural center with colleges, research institutes, public library, museums, theaters. Ind.: chemical, food processing, light ind., timber; extensive machine mfg., including electrical and agr. machinery, precision instruments. Oil for its large oil refinery is supplied by pipeline from Tuymazy, Bashkir ASSR. Founded 1716 as a fort.

OMSK OBLAST, RSFSR; area 54,000 sq. mi.; pop. 1,646,000 (1959): Russians, Ukrainians, Kazakhs, Tatars. In Asiatic USSR, on W. Siberian Plain, it occupies the Irtysh River basin, and is drained by the Irtysh, Ishim, Om. Cities: Omsk (adm. center), Tara, Isil-Kul, Tyukalinsk, Kalachinsk. It has lowland sloping toward the S.; forested Baraba Steppe (E.) and Ishim Steppe (W.), tayga; black-soil zone in the S., mixed forest in the N.; continental climate (cold winters). Mineral resources: clays, peat, sands, lignite. Extensive agr.: grain crops, dairy farming, sunflowers, flax (Tara), livestock. Ind.: lumbering (N.), machine mfg., chemicals, light ind., food processing, oil refining, flour milling. On the Trans-Siberian R.R., it also has waterways. Est. 1934.

OMÚTNINSK, town in Kirov Oblast, RSFSR; pop. 23,000 (1959). Has a metallurgical plant, lumbering.

ONÉGA BAY, at S.W. end of the White Sea, 124 mi. long. Has numerous granite islands; in the northern part of the gulf are the Solovetsky Islands. The White Sea-Baltic Canal system begins in Onega Bay at Belomorsk.

ONÉGA CANAL, along S. shore of Lake Onega, in Vologda and Leningrad oblasts, connects the Vytegra and the Svir rivers; is part of the Volga-Baltic Sea waterway system.

ONÉGA, city and port in Archangel Oblast, on right bank of Onega River at its mouth; pop. 18,000 (1958); R.R. station; extensive lumber ind. Founded in 15th century.

ONÉGA, lake, second largest in Europe, in N.W. part of the USSR; area 3,800 sq. mi.; greatest depth 360 ft. N. shores are rocky, have numerous islands, arms and inlets; frozen over six months of the year. Connected with Lake Ladoga by the Svir River, with the Volga River by the Volga-Baltic Sea waterway, and with the White Sea by the White Sea-Baltic Canal system. Fed by Vytegra, Vodla, and Suna rivers. Has valuable fisheries; much timber is cut near its shores.

ONÉGA RIVER, about 260 mi. long; in W. part of Archangel Oblast. Rises in Lake Lacha, flowing N. to Onega Bay. Rapids prevent navigation along its entire length.

ONÓN RIVER, 570 mi. long, in Chita Oblast and N.E. Mongolian People's Republic; flowing N.E. to unite with Ingoda River and form the Shilka (left tributary of the Amur). Rare species of fish and crawfish; lead deposits along its banks.

OPRÍCHNINA, an administrative and economic policy (introduced in 1565) involving a vast redistribution of landholding. It was directed against the landed nobility and aimed at strengthening the powers of the Crown. (*See also* IVAN IV, HISTORY)

OPPOSITION. Opposition is an all-inclusive term used here to describe those groups within the Bolshevik faction, later the Communist party, which unsuccessfully opposed the leadership of Lenin, Stalin, and Khrushchev. Only the more important groups which challenged the leaders are mentioned.

The Boycotters. This was an ultra Left-wing group among the Bolshevik faction, led by A. A. Bogdanov which opposed Lenin in 1907. They were against participation in the third Duma.

Otzovists (Recallers) and **Ultimatists.** In 1908, displeased with the conduct of the Social Democratic group in the third Duma, many of the former Boycotters split into *Otzovists* and *Ultimatists.* The Otzovists demanded the immediate recall of the Duma delegates. Somewhat less extreme, the Ultimatists, led by A. A. Bogdanov, G. A. Aleksinsky, and A. V. Lunacharsky, urged the serving of an ultimatum on the Duma group calling upon them to obey *unconditionally* instructions from the Central Committee or resign. Lenin opposed both groups.

Empiriocriticism and **God-Constructing.** These were philosophical heresies of A. A. Bogdanov, A. V. Lunacharsky, M. Gorky, V. Bazarov and others. Empiriocriticism, principally propounded by Bogdanov, was an attempt to modernize Marx by injecting new thoughts into his theories. Influenced by the philosophical writings of E. Mach and F. Avenarius, Bogdanov expounded views on the nature of sense perception which Lenin criticized as contradicting historical materialism. God-Constructing, advocated principally by Lunacharsky and Gorky, was a romanticized notion that if socialism were to have mass appeal it would have to have the attributes of a religion, while at the same time denying the existence of God. In June 1909 at an enlarged editorial conference of *Proletary,* the Bolshevik paper, Lenin had the necessary votes to denounce Boycottism, Otzovism, Ultimatism, and the philosophical heresies, and formally expelled Bogdanov and Lunacharsky. The expelled members, calling themselves the true Bolsheviks, formed an O group, established a newspaper, *Vpered* (Forward), and were known as *Vperedist Bolsheviks* through the following years.

Conciliators. Those Bolsheviks, notably I. F. Dubrovinsky, V. P. Nogin, A. I. Rykov, who at a plenum of the Central Committee of the party, held in Paris Jan. 1910, called for unity with the Mensheviks and reconciliation with the expelled faction over the opposition of Lenin, who was in the minority, were called

Conciliators. The unity achieved was of short duration.

The Waverers. Ten days after the seizure of power, G. Ye. Zinoviev, L. B. Kamenev A. I. Rykov, V. P. Nogin, and V. P. Milyutin, fearing that the Bolsheviks could not maintain themselves without forming a coalition government with the Mensheviks and Socialist Revolutionaries, resigned from the Central Committee on Nov. 4 (17), 1917 and made public the reason for their opposition. The opposition was short-lived. Party censure, in terms of a Central Committee ultimatum to submit to party discipline, had the desired effect. Zinoviev and the others relented and were re-admitted to the Central Committee.

Brest-Litovsk and Left Communism. The party leadership was seriously divided as to whether the harsh peace terms dictated by the Germans at Brest-Litovsk should be accepted. At one point the Central Committee was divided into three factions. Lenin advocated the acceptance of the German terms in order to preserve the Bolshevik regime; Trotsky advocated a "no war, no peace" solution; while N. I. Bukharin and his group of Left Communists—which included G. I. Lomov, A. S. Bubnov, M. S. Uritsky, A. M. Kollontay, S. V. Kossior, V. V. Kuybyshev, E. A. Preobrazhensky, and others—called for a revolutionary war, terming the proposed peace a betrayal of internationalism. The issue, debated at the Central Committee meeting (Feb. 23–24, 1918) and won by Lenin, was carried to the rank and file where the Left Communists at first received some support. They published an O paper, *Kommunist* and captured control of the Moscow party organization. At the hastily summoned 7th Party Congress (March 1918) the Brest-Litovsk peace was debated and the Left Communists were outvoted.

Military Opposition. Led by former Left Communists, this group strongly opposed the employment of former tsarist officers as military specialists in the Red Army, the forming of a standing army (they were for a people's militia), and the introduction of professional military discipline. The Military Opposition was defeated at the 8th Party Congress, held in March 1919, although its members were able to muster 95 votes (against 174 for the majority) for their resolution.

Democratic Centralists. Opposing Lenin on the nature of the party organization and led by T. V. Sapronov and V. V. Osinsky (Obolensky), the Democratic Centralists were for the most part former Left Communists. At the 9th Party Congress (March 1920) they charged that the party was run by a bureaucratic clique; that party elections were not democratically conducted; and that party members who disagreed with the Central Committee were arbitrarily reassigned from Moscow.

Workers' Opposition. In the summer and fall of 1920 growing workers' discontent crystallized in the form of the Workers' Opposition. Its leading spokesmen, Aleksandra Kollontay, A. G. Shlyapnikov, and S. P. Medvedev, called for trade-union control of industry (which would have severely restricted party dictatorship) and for greater party democracy. At the 10th Party Congress (March 1921) the role of the trade unions was debated. Lenin, whose program was adopted by an overwhelming majority, advocated some trade-union autonomy while retaining economic responsibility for the party. The Congress, which met during the Kronstadt crisis, condemned the Workers' Opposition, but despite the threat of expulsion, this O continued to agitate for its program and submitted an appeal to the Executive Committee of the Comintern, "The Declaration of the Twenty-Two" (Feb. 1922), which was rejected. The 11th Party Congress (March 1922), despite a special commission recommending expulsion, only administered a stern warning to Kollontay, Shlyapnikov, and Medvedev, although lesser members of the O were expelled.

Trotsky Opposes the Triumvirate of Stalin, Zinoviev, and Kamenev. In the fall and winter of 1923, Trotsky publicly criticized the triumvirate of Stalin (who was General Secretary and controlled the party apparatus), Zinoviev (leader of the Leningrad party organization), and Kamenev (head of the Moscow party organization), attacking their economic policy and their bureaucratic control of the party machine. At the 13th Party Conference (Jan. 1924), which Trotsky did not attend because of illness, Stalin accused Trotsky of placing himself above the party and the Central Committee. The conference condemned Trotskyism (q.v.) as a petty bourgeois deviation. Subsequently many important supporters of Trotsky were removed from strategic party and government positions. At the 13th Party Congress (May 1924) Zinoviev demanded that Trotsky recant his errors. Trotsky in a conciliatory speech declared that the party was always right, yet refused to admit that his criticism had been mistaken. In the fall of 1924 Trotsky published *Lessons of October* which was particularly critical of Zinoviev and Kamenev. The acrimonious debate which ensued was damaging for all principals concerned (except for Stalin, who was not directly involved), and led to Trotsky's dismissal as commissar of war in Jan. 1925.

Zinoviev and Kamenev Oppose Stalin. With Trotsky disarmed Stalin moved against Zinoviev and Kamenev, and aligned himself with the Right wing of the Politburo, N. I. Bukharin, M. Tomsky, and A. I. Rykov. At the 14th Party Congress (Dec. 1925) Stalin, in full control of the party apparatus, except for the Leningrad organization (which was purged of Zinoviev supporters following the Congress), was able to smash the O forces of Kamenev and Zinoviev.

The New Opposition Against Stalin and the Right. Defeated and stripped of their power base Zinoviev and Kamenev in 1926 joined forces with Trotsky and supported his economic program of rapid industrialization. Stalin, determined to eliminate the O, had Zinoviev expelled from the Politburo in July 1926. In Oct. the O leaders sued for peace, declaring their readiness to submit to party discipline. Stalin responded by ousting Trotsky and Kamenev from the Politburo. In 1927, Trotsky, Zinoviev, and their supporters published the "Platform of the Eighty-Three," which criticized Stalin for recent domestic and foreign policy failures. Severely censured at the plenum of the Central Committee (summer 1927) the O again promised to submit to party discipline and thus escaped expulsion from the Central

Committee. The truce was short-lived. In a last desperate effort the O leaders held secret meetings, established an underground press, and held public demonstrations to discredit Stalin and his supporters. On Oct. 23, 1927 Trotsky and Zinoviev were removed from the Central Committee and on Nov. 14, 1927 they were expelled from the party. The 15th Party Congress (Dec. 1927) marked the end of the Trotskyist Opposition. Seventy-five followers of Trotsky including Kamenev, Lashevich, Pyatakov, Radek, Rakovsky, and Smilga were expelled from the party.

Stalin and the Right Opposition. Stalin now turned on the so-called Right Opposition of Bukharin, Rykov, and Tomsky who were critical of Stalin's policy switch to rapid industrialization and forced collectivization. The Right Opposition, outnumbered in the Politburo and in the Central Committee, had some support in the Moscow party organization headed by N. A. Uglanov, in the trade unions and in the government bureaucracy. In Sept. 1928 Bukharin published *Notes of an Economist* in which he documented the benefits realized as a result of the New Economic Policy, advocating its continuance. It was a veiled criticism of the new Stalinist policy. Stalin moved against the O by removing Uglanov from his post in Nov. 1928. In April 1929 at a plenum of the Central Committee the Right Opposition was condemned for factionalism and threatened with expulsion. After Stalin's program was adopted at the 16th Party Congress (April 1929) he publicly accused the Right of collaborating with capitalist elements and of attempting to form a bloc with former Trotskyites—both serious offenses. In June Tomsky was removed as head of the trade unions and in July Bukharin lost the chairmanship of the Comintern. In Nov. 1929 Bukharin was expelled from the Politburo, as were Tomsky and Rykov despite their public recantation.

Minor Opposition Groups. Syrtsov and Lominadze, supporters of Stalin for many years, were accused of forming Right-wing factional groups within the party and were expelled from the Central Committee in Dec. 1930. In 1932 two groups headed by Ryutin and Eismont were known to have been very critical of Stalin's policy of forced collectivization and rapid industrialization, circulating manifestos to that effect. Ryutin, Eismont, and their supporters were sent into penal exile in 1933.

The Anti-Party Group. The opposition against Khrushchev came to a head in June 1957. The immediate issue was Khrushchev's proposal for reorganizing the economy. Outvoted in the Presidium and threatened with removal from the Secretariat, Khrushchev was able to call a special session of the Central Committee, on which he could count for support. On June 29, 1957, Georgy M. Malenkov, Vyacheslav N. Molotov, Lazar M. Kaganovich, and Dymitry T. Shepilov were accused by a Central Committee resolution of having formed an anti-party group with the intention of changing the membership of the top party organs and of opposing Khrushchev's domestic and foreign policy (particularly the reorganization of the economy, the agricultural program, and reconciliation with Yugosla-

via) and were expelled from the Presidium and from the Central Committee. (*See also* PURGES, SHOW TRIALS, COMMUNIST PARTY OF THE SOVIET UNION, HISTORY OF THE USSR, TROTSKYISM.)

BIBLIOGRAPHY: R. V. Daniels, *The Conscience of the Revolution* (Communist Opposition in Soviet Russia), New York, 1960.

H. W. M.

OPTICS: *see* PHYSICS.

ORÁNIENBAUM: *see* LOMONOSOV.

ORBÉLI, Leon Abgarovich (1882–1958), noted physiologist. Fellow (1935) and vice president (1942–46), Ac. of S., USSR; fellow, Ac. of S., Armenian SSR (1943), and Ac. of Medical S., USSR (1944). Colonel general, Army Medical Corps. Disciple of I. P. Pavlov. Graduate of the Military Academy (1904); professor, Leningrad Medical Institute (1920–31) and Military Medical Academy (1925–50). Director, Institute of Physiology, Institute of Physiology and Pathology of Higher Nervous Activity (1936–50), and Institute of Evolutionary Physiology (1956). O's research concerned the physiology of nervous systems, i.e. the effects of the sympathetic nervous system on skeletal muscles, cerebrospinal coordination, the cerebrum, kidneys, and digestion; he also investigated problems of applied physiology, particularly under conditions of high-altitude flights and great water depths. Flayed for his reconciliatory attitude toward W. European and American theories and deviations from the teachings of Marx and Engels (1950), O was rehabilitated in 1955. Author of *Problems of Higher Nervous Activity* (1945). Stalin prize (1941); I. I. Mechnikov Gold Medal (1946); Order of Lenin (1957).

ORDERS OF MERIT (decorations). Under the Soviet Constitution (article 49) OM are awarded by the Presidium of the Supreme Soviet, USSR, for outstanding achievements in socialist labor and the building of socialism; for raising industrial productivity; for distinguished service in defending the Soviet fatherland, as well as for achievements contributing to the good of the country. The highest award is the Order of Lenin (given together with the title Hero of the Soviet Union or Hero of Socialist Labor). Other orders are the Red Banner, the Red Banner of Labor, the Red Star, the Badge of Honor. The armed services rewards are the order of the Patriotic War; of Suvorov; of Kutuzov; of Alexander Nevsky; of Bogdan Khmelnitsky; of Victory; and of Glory. The order of Ushakov and that of Nakhimov are reserved for the Navy. There is also the order of Mother Heroine, of Glory of Motherhood, as well as various other medals. Most of the orders are subdivided into two or three classes.

ORDÝN-NASHCHÓKIN, Afanásy Lavréntyevich (1605–1681), Tsar Alexis' adviser on foreign affairs, advocated closer contacts with W. countries.

ORDZHONIKÍDZE, Grigóry Konstantínovich (1886–1937), leading Bolshevik, born in Kutaisi Oblast. O became a Bolshevik in 1903 and was active in the Georgian revolutionary movement. In the underground he was known as "Sergo" and was arrested and jailed several times. In 1912, after the Prague Conference, he became a member of the party Central Committee.

O took an active part in the Bolshevik Revolution and the civil war. In cooperation with Stalin he forced the incorporation of Georgia into the Soviet Union (1922). Throughout the intraparty struggle of the 1920's he sided with Stalin against Trotsky, but was never fully committed to Stalin's support. O was one of the organizers of Soviet industry during the first two five year plans. In 1930 he entered the Politburo. He sought to limit the scope of the purges, and his sudden death may well be attributable to his attempts to save some of the victims.

ORDZHONIKÍDZE (f. Vladikavkaz, Dzaudzhikau 1944–54), city, adm. center of N. Ossetian ASSR, on Terek R.; starting point of Georgian Military Road leading to Tbilisi; pop. 164,000 (1959). Ind.: nonferrous metallurgy, metal working, food, knitwear. Has colleges, theaters, philharmonic orchestra; founded 1784.

ORÉKHOVO-ZÚYEVO, city in Moscow Oblast, RSFSR, on the Klyazma River and on the Moscow-Gorky R.R.; pop. 108,000 (1959). One of the oldest and largest cotton-ginning centers in the USSR.

ORÉL, city, adm. center of Orel Oblast, RSFSR; on the left bank of the Oka River and the R.R. line to Moscow; pop. 150,000 (1959). Has colleges, public library, theaters. Ind.: agr. and textile machinery, leather, weaving factories. Founded as a fort against the Crimean Tatars in 1566, on Orlik River; after a fire in 1673 it was rebuilt on the present site.

ORÉL OBLAST, RSFSR, in Central Russian upland, including the Upper Oka River basin; area 9,500 sq. mi.; pop. 929,000 (1959). Cities: Orel (adm. center), Bolkhov, Dmitrovsk-Orlovsky, Livny. Drained by the Oka and Sosna and their affluents, it is hilly steppe with fertile black soil (E.), forested steppe with podsolic soil crossed by deep elongated ravines (W.); humid continental climate. Mineral resources: limestone, dolomite, clays, sands, phosphorite, peat, iron ore. Agr.: buckwheat, wheat, rye, millet, potatoes, hemp, sugar beets, orchards, extensive hog and cattle raising, horse breeding, dairy farming. Ind.: metalworking, food and hemp processing, milling, distilling. Has a R.R. and highway network, major R.R. junction at Orel. Est. 1937.

ORENBÚRG, city, adm. center of Orenburg Oblast, RSFSR, on the Ural River and the Kuybyshev–Tashkent R.R.; pop. 172,000 (1939), 267,000 (1959). Ind.: machine mfg., silk weaving, meat combine, tanning plant. Colleges, scientific institutes, theaters. Founded as a fort in 1735.

ORENBÚRG OBLAST (f. Chkalov Oblast), in S. Urals, RSFSR; area 47,800 sq. mi.; pop. 1,831,000 (1959): mainly Russians, also Ukrainians, Mordvinians, Tatars, Kazakhs. Cities: Orenburg (adm. center), Orsk, Novotroitsk, Sol-Iletsk, Buguruslan. Drained by the Ural, Sakmara, Samara, Greater Kinel, Ilek rivers; a lowland with Obshchy Syrt hills (W.) and foothills of S. Urals (E.); has predominantly black soil, steppe vegetation; dry climate (severe winters, hot summers). Its rich mineral deposits (highly developed ind. around Orsk-Khalilovo), include coal, limonite, hematite, nickel, cobalt, chromite, lignite, jasper, limestone, salt, oil (Buguruslan),

asphalt, gold, oil shale, phosphorite, gypsum, copper, sulfur (Mednogorsk), refractory clays. Extensive agr.: wheat, rye, millet, sunflowers, livestock, dairy farming. Ind.: mining, ferrous and nonferrous metallurgy, machine mfg., oil refining, saltworks, food processing, flour milling, meat canning, textiles, wool weaving (famed wool kerchiefs). It has R.R. and highway networks, also waterways. Est. 1934.

ORÉSHNIKOV, Víktor Mikháylovich (1904–), painter. He first achieved prominence after World War II with works on the revolution (*Petrograd Defense Headquarters, November 1917,* 1949) and portraits (*V. V. Lishev, Sculptor,* 1952). Director of the Institute of Painting, Sculpture and Architecture, Leningrad (1953). Stalin prizes (1948, 1950).

ORGBURO, the Organizational Bureau of the Central Committee of the Communist party, was organized on instructions of the 8th Party Congress in March 1919 and was authorized to direct all organizational work of the party. It was soon superseded in importance by the Secretariat, a body which although theoretically under the jurisdiction of the O shortly took over its functions. The O was abolished by the 19th Party Congress, 1952.

ORLÓV, Count Alekséy Grigóryevich (1737–1807), officer in the guards and brother of Grigory, who was a favorite of Catherine II. Rose to prominence through the palace revolution in 1762, which brought Catherine II to the throne.

ORLÓV, Count Grigóry Grigóryevich (1734–1783), officer in the guards and favorite of Catherine II, and chief organizer of the palace revolution of 1762.

ORLÓV, Sergéy Mikháylovich (1911–), sculptor. His earlier works, chiefly in porcelain, were based on popular mythology and historical epics (*The Hunchback Pony,* 1945; *Alexander Nevsky,* 1943). In recent years he has specialized in monuments; for instance *Yury Dolgorukov,* Moscow, 1954. Stalin prize (1946).

ORLÓV, Yúry Aleksándrovich (1893–), paleontologist and histologist. Fellow, Ac. of S., USSR (1960). Honored Scientist, RSFSR (1946). Graduate of Petrograd University (1917); professor, Leningrad University (1933–41) and Moscow University (1943). Joined the Institute of Paleontology (1929), of which he became director (1945). Research concerns the nervous system of invertebrates.

OROCHI: *see* POPULATION.

ÓRSHA, city in Vitebsk Oblast, N.E. Byelorussian SSR, on Dnieper River and on Minsk–Moscow R.R. line with junctions to four other lines; pop. 64,000 (1959). Center of agr. region; its ind.: food processing, flour mills, flax weaving, meat factories, metalworking; large peat-fed power plant in vicinity. Mentioned as "Rsha" in 1067.

ORSK, city in Orenburg Oblast, RSFSR, at the mouth of the Ora (left tribuatry of the Ural River); pop. 65,800 (1939), 176,000 (1959). Key R.R. junction point. Center of Orsk-Khalilovo ind. area with rich iron-ore, copper, nickel, and coal deposits; machine mfg., ferrous and nonferrous metallurgy, large meat combine. As it is the terminus of oil pipelines from Guryev and other oil ports at the N. of Caspian Sea, it has oil refineries. Founded 1735 by famous cartographer I. K. Kirillov.

ORTHODOX CHURCH. In 987, by order of Vladimir, Grand Duke of Kiev, the Greek Orthodox religion became the official R. faith. As Russia looked to the Greeks for religious inspiration and regarded the Catholics of Central Europe as schismatics, Russia thus was outside the stream of W. civilization.

At first Greek clergy dominated the Russian church and educated the people, but by the 15th cent. the church became independent of the Greeks. The temporary Greek acceptance of papal authority in 1439, which the Russians furiously rejected, and the subsequent fall of Constantinople to the Turks, convinced the Russians that Moscow was the "Third Rome," the holy city that had replaced Rome and Constantinople as the City of God. In the late 16th cent. the Metropolitan of Moscow received the rank of Patriarch, which further raised R. self-esteem.

In the early 16th cent. there was a bitter struggle between Nil Sorsky, a monk who wanted the R. church to be poor and independent of the state, and Joseph of Volokolamsk, a monastic defender of church landholding, who relied strongly on the ruler for suppression of heresy. Joseph's victory tied the church more closely to the civil power. For a period in the 17th cent. weak rulers permitted churchmen to dominate, but two acts of Patriarch Nikon led to an increase of the government's power over the church. First Nikon provoked a deep schism among the believers, thereby weakening the church and forcing it to seek state support. Later, Nikon quarreled with tsar Alexis and arrogantly claimed supremacy, which led to the deposition of the prelate in 1667. Both developments enhanced the power of the government.

The schism (*raskól*) was caused by Nikon's correction of R. ritual practices, using Greek service books as models. Many believers regarded this as the work of Antichrist and faced death rather than accept such minor changes as using three fingers instead of two when making the sign of the cross. Nikon's tactlessness aroused stubborn resistance by the Old Believers —a denomination that still exists.

Peter I further subordinated the church. When Patriarch Adrian died in 1700, Peter kept that office vacant and then, largely because of clerical opposition to his reforms, in 1721 he created the Holy Synod (q.v.) to take the place of a patriarch. The tsar picked the Synod's members and named a lay Over Procurator to supervise their actions. He also issued detailed Regulations for the church which practically deprived it of independence. Catherine II continued this tendency by taking the lands of the church in 1763 and by giving state salaries to bishops, which made them even more dependent upon the crown.

From 1825 to 1855 the church felt the powerful hand of Nicholas I. This devout and active supporter of Orthodoxy ruled the church through the Over Procurator and made it a branch of the state administration, whose duty was to preach complete submission to the tsar, "the Anointed of God," and to condemn his foes. After Nicholas, the rule of the monarch bore less heavily upon the church, but in 1881 it came under Konstantin Petrovich Pobedonostsev, Over Procurator. For 25 years this powerful man guided the tsars along the path of reaction and combatted liberalism. Under him the church strongly upheld the autocracy and disciplined liberal-minded clergy. Pobedonostsev also worked to repress Old Believers, sectarians, and Jews.

The official church had weaknesses. Intellectuals regarded it as a foe to progress, and many of the factory workers were hostile. Although the peasants were devout, often their religion was a matter of form, with little spiritual content. The Orthodox church did little effective teaching or preaching. One of its gravest weaknesses was the attitude of the parish clergy, who, being married, could never become bishops and who resented episcopal haughtiness. Many of the seminary students were cynical and rebellious, as they had taken pastoral training because no other road was open. Such seminarians made lackluster priests.

The church had noble men, with fine minds, chiefly in the theological academies. Most of them, however, devoted themselves to religious mysticism and rejected rationalism, so that they had little influence in the affairs of the church.

During the Revolution of 1905 the hierarchy strongly supported the tsar and condemned the "Liberation Movement," while some of the leading prelates joined the *Union of the R. People* (q.v.), which sponsored violence against liberals and organized brutal anti-Jewish pogroms. Many parish priests also supported the government by word and deed. Some of the clergy supported the revolution, but the church dealt sternly with them. In the first two Dumas a handful of priests took the side of the people, but were severely disciplined by the Synod. In the conservative later Dumas larger groups of priests, and two bishops, ardently backed the government against the liberals.

In the years before 1914 the weaknesses of the church remained. Efforts to call a reforming church council failed. Hostility persisted between priests and bishops, and there was a growing shortage of pastors. In addition, the debauched Grigory Yefimovich Rasputin (q.v.), having gained influence over the neurotic Empress, was able to exert his power over the Synod. When the war came in 1914, the church preached patriotism and vigorous support for the war; but as the R. losses mounted the attitude of the church lost popularity. Furthermore, the obvious power that Rasputin had over the Synod in 1915 and 1916 was a scandal which boded no good for the church.

When the Imperial government fell in March 1917, there was little change in the church. The new Over Procurator promptly ousted the discredited members of the Synod and replaced them with more respected clerics. For a short time the parish priests in a number of dioceses took hostile measures against their bishops, but the clergy quickly became more conservative and closed their ranks. As before, the church ardently supported the war and warned against radical agitators.

In Aug. 1917, a church council (*Sobór*) met in Moscow. It was very conservative, as it contained large numbers of bishops, and laymen from the upper strata of society. It immediately condemned the growing popular radicalism and gave warm support to the vain attempt of Gen. Lavr Georgievich Kornilov to set up a military dictatorship. Finally, after bitter opposition from the liberal members, the Sobor decided to elect a patriarch to lead the people and to serve as a rallying-point against the radical movements. On Nov. 18, 1917, Metropolitan Tikhon of Moscow (Vasily Ivanovich Bellavin) was chosen and on Nov. 29 he was enthroned in the Kremlin cathedral. The Soviet authorities did not interfere.

The Patriarch and other clergy at once tried to arouse the people against the Soviet regime, by messages, proclamations, and condemnations of its leaders, as well as by public processions and demonstrations. The masses, however, did not respond, and the Soviet leaders avoided clashes with the churchmen. Instead, the new government sought to weaken the church by taking its lands, halting state subsidies, and nationalizing its schools, including theological seminaries. On Feb. 5, 1918, the government published a decree of separation of church and state, which nationalized all church buildings and their contents, although groups of parishioners were permitted to use them for divine worship. Thus religious services were maintained. The authorities also closed monasteries and convents and made use of the buildings. Some violence was done to churchmen in the first months, mostly by mobs or irresponsible persons; the Soviet government executed only those few clerics who were actively against it.

By the end of 1918 the churchmen, seeing that they could not destroy the Soviet regime, were hoping that the rising anti-Soviet or White armies would do so. A number of bishops and priests in areas held by the Whites energetically aided the anti-Soviet forces, by calling on the people to enlist, by serving as chaplains with the White armies, and by condemning the Soviet regime and all its works. Several groups of churchmen appealed to ecclesiastics in other countries to back the anti-Soviet efforts. By 1920, however, the White armies had collapsed, and the Soviet regime was in control. For a time there was a truce between the government and the hostile Orthodox clergy.

In 1921 a great famine swept Russia. Both government and church appealed at home and abroad for aid to the millions of sufferers, but mutual suspicion prevented cooperation, especially as a gathering of emigré churchmen in Yugoslavia had urged that no aid be given to R. By early 1922 the Soviet press was demanding that gold and silver articles of the church be used for famine relief. The Patriarch, who was unwilling, finally sent a secret message to the parish clergy telling them to oppose the seizure of such articles, on the grounds that the government would misuse them. In a number of places violence broke out when officials sought to collect the treasure, and some rioters were killed by troops. The government arrested and tried a number of clerics on grounds of counterrevolutionary incitement and executed some, including the Metropolitan of Petrograd. Patriarch Tikhon was arrested in May 1922, on similar charges.

At this point some liberal priests, among them Dean Alexander Ivanovich Vvedensky, persuaded the Patriarch to resign and let them manage current church affairs until his replacement, Metropolitan Agafangel, could take over. The latter, however, was arrested and could not come. These priests thereupon formed the Temporary Higher Church Administration and under the name of the Living Church ran Orthodox affairs and cooperated with the government. They deposed hostile bishops and consecrated new ones, and for a time they held full sway, because of the arrest of many of their opponents. The Living Church proclaimed the deposition of Patriarch Tikhon, who remained under arrest, with his trial set for April 1923. Suddenly, however, in June 1923 he was released, after having signed a statement admitting his guilt and repenting of his actions. He at once resumed control of the R. church, warmly welcomed by the believers, whom he advised to be loyal to the Soviet government. The Living Church under Vvedensky still existed, but it was much weakened by defections to Tikhon. Upon his death in April 1925 Tikhon left a Testament urging his followers to support the Soviet government and to cease all hostility to it.

After Tikhon, however, anti-Soviet feeling rose among the believers. Efforts to install a locum tenens failed, as the government arrested all the candidates for hostility. Finally, after much negotiation, in 1927 Metropolitan Sergii (Ivan Nikolayevich Stragorodsky) obtained permission to set up a church administration upon his promise to be loyal to the government. The church then entered a more peaceful period.

During the 1920's an active anti-religious campaign had developed. At first crude and inept, under the League of Militant Godless, it grew in size and effectiveness, reaching 5 million members in 1932. In the 1930's numerous churches closed and Orthodoxy lost many followers. Religion did not die out, however, as the Godless had hoped, and, indeed, in 1935 the status of the clergy improved, although anti-religious propaganda continued.

When Germany attacked in 1941 the R. church urged its followers to fight the invaders. In 1942 Metropolitan Sergii hailed Stalin as the nation's "divinely anointed leader." In return, in Sept. 1943 Stalin met with Sergii and gave permission for his election as Patriarch. Later the Orthodox church rebuilt damaged churches with government aid and opened theological seminaries and began publication of a periodical.

After Sergii's death in 1944, a Sobor met in 1945 to elect Metropolitan Alexy of Leningrad as Patriarch, amid official expressions of good will. Two E. Patriarchs and representatives of other Orthodox churches were present. Nevertheless, in 1944 anti-religious propaganda revived, declaring that religion is unscientific and outmoded. Strong efforts were made to win the children to atheism. In spite of this, however, relations between church and state have remained good. R. clergy have been able to travel abroad and to receive foreign churchmen in the USSR. More churches and theological schools have opened and there has been a substantial religious revival. The government has supported the efforts of the church to extend its influence. In turn, the church has furthered Soviet foreign policy, especially in the great peace campaigns. It has also condemned "American imperialism and aggression" in Korea and Lebanon and denounced NATO and American bases surrounding the USSR. Thus the strange compromise begun by Metropolitan Sergii in 1927 is still in effect. (*See also* HISTORY, RUSSIANS ABROAD)

BIBLIOGRAPHY: Paul B. Anderson, *People, Church, and State in Modern Russia*, New York, 1944; John Shelton Curtiss, *Church and State in Russia*, New York, 1940; G. P. Fedotov, *The Russian Church since the Revolution*, London, New York, 1928; Matthew Spinka, *The Church in Soviet Russia*, New York, 1956; N. S. Timasheff, *Religion in Soviet Russia, 1917–1942*, New York, 1942.   J. S. C.

O.S. (OLD STYLE): *see* CALENDAR.

OSH, city, adm. center of Osh Oblast, Kirghiz SSR, on Akbur River; pop. 33,000 (1939), 65,000 (1959). Ind.: silk, cotton ginning, foundry, food processing.

OSH OBLAST, Kirghiz SSR; area, 28,525 sq. mi.; pop. 871,000 (1959): Kirghiz, also Uzbeks, Tadzhiks, Russians. Borders S.E. on China, including the S. fringe of Fergana Valley and mountain range S. of it. Cities: Osh (adm. center), Dzhalal-Abad, Uzgen, Kyzyl-Kia, Sulyukta. Drained by the Kara-Darya R. and its affluents; has rich mineral deposits of coal, oil, antimony, mercury, nonferrous metals; dry climate (hot summers, mild winters); semidesert vegetation. Agr.: cotton growing (Fergana Valley), vineyards, sericulture, orchards, tobacco, wheat, rice, corn, livestock. Ind.: extensive mining, cotton ginning, silk processing, food canning, oil. It is on a R.R. and the Osh–Khorog highway. Est. 1939, in 1959 incorporated Dzhalal-Abad Oblast.

OSÍNNIKI, city in Kemerovo Oblast, RSFSR, in Kuzbas, on Kondoma River; pop. 68,000 (1959). Coal mining.

OSÍNSKY (Obolénsky), **Valeryán Valeryánovich** (1887–?), revolutionary. Joined the Bolsheviks in 1907. Arrested and exiled several times. After the October revolution, he was chairman of the Committee of National Economy and commissar of agriculture. In 1918, O denounced the Treaty of Brest-Litovsk. In 1919, he joined the opposition group of democratic centralism which fought for intra-party democracy. After completing several diplomatic assignments, such as the World Economic Conference in 1927, he disappeared during the purges of the 1930's.

OSIPÉNKO: *see* BERDYANSK.

ÓSIPOV, Víktor Petróvich (1871–1947), psychiatrist. Corresponding member, Ac. of S., USSR (1939); fellow, Ac. of Medical S. (1944). Lt. General, Medical Corps. Honored Scientist, RSFSR (1933). Professor, Kazan University (1906); director, V. M. Bekhterev Brain Institute (1929). A disciple of V. M. Bekhterev, O was an advocate of pathological trends in psychiatry. Research concerned somatic and endocrine disturbances in depressive psychosis and war psychiatry. Author of *Guide to Psychiatry* (1931).

OSKÓL RIVER, 287 mi. long, left tributary of N. Donets, rises near Tim in Kursk Oblast, RSFSR, flowing S.; not navigable.

OSOAVIAKHIM: *see* RED ARMY.

OSORGÍN, Mikhaíl (Mikhaíl Andréyevich Ilyin) (1878–1942), author, journalist, and critic. Before the revolution contributed to *Russkie Vedomosti* (Russian News) for many years. Expelled from Russia in 1922. His most important works, written in the 1920's and 1930's, are *Sivtsev vrazhek* (translated into English as *Quiet Street*) (1928) and *An Eye-Witness to History* (1932). In his collection of short stories, *Miracle on the Lake* (1931), and in the volume, *Events in the Green World*, O showed his subtle understanding of nature.

OSSETIA: *see* NORTH OSSETIAN ASSR and SOUTH OSSETIAN AUTONOMOUS OBLAST.

OSSETIAN MILITARY ROAD, through Caucasus mountain range (Mamison pass), from Darg-Kokh station in N. Ossetia to Kutaisi in Georgia; very picturesque; length 170 mi.; altitude 9,280 ft. Built 1889.

OSTARBEITER, "Eastern workers," Soviet citizens, sent for forced labor in Germany during World War II from German-occupied territories of the USSR. Because of acute manpower shortage the German government on Dec. 19, 1941 ordered that "all residents of occupied Eastern territories are subject to obligatory labor." In charge of the O's was the Gestapo which allocated them to industrial and agricultural enterprises. Considered as racially inferior, they were actually turned into slaves. Their food, housing, sanitary and labor conditions were appalling, and the rate of mortality and sickness very high. Failure to comply with mobilization orders was punished by whipping or burning down of their homes. Escapees were sentenced to death or concentration camps. In 1944, when German defeat became probable, the treatment of O's became more humane. Altogether about 2.8 million men and women were made O's. When they were liberated by the western armies, many thousands of O's refused to return to the USSR and became displaced persons.   s. w.

OSTÁSHKOV, town in W. Kalinin Oblast, RSFSR, a tourist resort on S. shore of Lake Seliger, at the source of the Volga; pop. 18,400 (1956). R.R. station; leather factory and a fishing ind.

ÓSTERMAN, Andréy Ivánovich (Heinrich Johann) (1686–1747), statesman. He arrived in Russia from Westphalia in 1704; participated in the Aland (1718–19) and Nystad (1721) congresses; was a member of the Supreme Council (1726–30); and helped Anna Ivanovna to ascend the throne. After the accession of Elizabeth, in 1741, he was arrested and exiled to Beryozov.

OSTROÚKHOV, Ilyá Semyónovich (1858–1929), landscape painter, member of the Society of Circulating Exhibitions (*Peredvizhniki*). Painted realistic, emotionally saturated dynamic landscapes (*Siverko*, 1890, in Tretyakov Gallery). Owner of a rich collection of R. art, which passed in 1918 to the Tretyakov Gallery.

OSTROÚMOV, Alekséy Aleksándrovich (1844–1908), therapeutist. Graduate (1871), professor (1879–1903), Moscow University. Research concerned disturbances of the nervous system and their effect on morphology. Introduced extensive therapy, physiotherapy and treatment in resorts and under favorable climatic conditions. A Moscow hospital was named after O.

OSTROÚMOVA-LÉBEDEVA, Anna Petróvna (1871–1955), engraver and painter. Studied in the Academy of Fine Arts (1892–1900); was a pupil of Repin. Member of the *Mir Iskusstva* (q.v.) group. Revived interest in original R. engravings (also in colors) on wood; painted water colors and made lithographs. Basic work: poetical landscapes mostly of St. Petersburg and environs (color engravings, *Column of the Stock Exchange Building and the Fortress*, 1908; *Summer Park in Hoar-Frost*, 1929; water color, *Champs de Mars*, 1922).

ÓSTROV, town in Pskov Oblast, N.W. RSFSR, on the Velikaya River; pop. 13,600 (1958). R.R. station; food- and hemp-processing ind., building materials.

OSTRÓVSKY, Aleksándr Nikoláyevich (1823–1886), playwright, son of a government clerk, born and brought up in the merchant section of Moscow. Studied law in Moscow University, but did not take a degree; entered the civil service as a clerk in the Moscow commercial court. His first play, *The Bankrupt* (1847), was pro-hibited by censorship. O was forced to resign and was kept under police surveillance. He was the founder of the society for the protection of the rights of playwrights. Shortly before his death, O was appointed director of the Moscow Theatrical School. Author of some forty plays in prose and eight in blank verse, he was Russia's most prolific dramatist. In his plays he presented a telling and unflattering picture of the R. middle class. The use of colloquial R. practically precludes the translation of O's plays into foreign languages. *The Bankrupt* was first performed in 1850, and was followed by *Poverty Is No Crime* (1854), *The Ward* (1859), and *The Thunderstorm* (1859) which was praised by the radical critic Dobrolyubov in a noted article entitled "A Sun Ray in the Kingdom of Darkness." O's solitary fairy tale, *The Snow Maiden* (1873) was used as the libretto of an opera by Rimsky-Korsakov.

OSTRÓVSKY, Nikoláy Alekséyevich (1904–1936), writer connected with the Bolshevik underground during  the civil war, born in Volyn in a worker's family. In 1919 O joined the Red Army as a volunteer and became a party member in 1924. His active life ended when he became blind and almost completely paralyzed. Author of two popular novels, *How Steel Was Tempered* (Eng. translation, *The Making of a Hero*, 1932–34) and *Born in the Storm* (1934–36). His books were translated into many languages and dramatized for the theater and screen.

OSTYAKS: *see* KHANTY.

OTOMARI: *see* KORSAKOV.

OTRÉPYEV, Grigóry (Pseudo-Dimitry), allegedly a monk of Chudov Monastery who during the Time of Troubles assumed the name of Dimitry, son of Ivan IV, and for a short time ascended the Moscow throne. He was killed during a Moscow uprising in 1606.

OTRUB: *see* AGRARIAN REFORM, PEASANTS.

OTZOVISTS: *see* OPPOSITION.

OVER-PROCURATOR: *see* ORTHODOX CHURCH.

OVSYÁNIKO-KULIKÓVSKY, Dmítry Nikoláyevich (1853–1920), literary critic, professor of R. literature in the universities of Kazan, Kharkov, and St. Petersburg. He was editor of the *History of Russian Literature in the Nineteenth Century* (5 vols., 1908–11), and author of *History of the Russian Intelligentsia* (2 vols., 1906–07) and monographs on R. classics.

OYROT-TURA: *see* GORNO-ALTAYSK.

ÓZEROV, Vladisláv Aleksándrovich (1769–1816), dramatist, and author of plays in the form of classical tragedies, *Œdipus in Athens* (1804), *Fingal* (1805), *Polixenes* (1809). His play *Dmitry Donskoy* (1807) is a patriotic tale based on the life of the R. hero of the period of the Tatar invasion.

P

PÁHLEN, Count Pyótr Alekséyevich (1745–1826), military governor of St. Petersburg, one of the organizers of the plot to assassinate Emperor Paul I.

PAINTING. Russia's historical development gave her P a specific character and a unique place among European creative arts. Both medieval and modern Russia had to absorb quickly foreign art disciplines. Each time native traditions were uprooted and thrown upon a new and foreign course, first under St. Vladimir and then under Peter the Great. Long before Kievan Russia imported and developed the Byzantine tradition, the vast plains of E. Europe had seen the influence of Greek art, of Cymerian, Scythian, Sarmatian and Avar civilizations. The Ante and the Nordsmen also left many traces. Thus when Russia stepped into history, she already had a rich heritage. With her conversion to Christianity in 988, religious P was brought to Russia and was, until the end of the 16th century, almost the only P Russia knew. It manifested itself in four forms: mosaics, frescoes, icons, and illuminated manuscripts. Though essentially Byzantine in iconography and treatment, this art soon developed many local stylistic traits and gave birth to several regional schools.

Before Peter the Great. KIEVAN RUSSIA (988–1160). *Mosaics* art was short-lived in Kiev. The better known mosaic was the huge *Orans Virgin* (11th century) of Byzantine tradition in the St. Sophia Cathedral in Kiev. Religious art quickly turned to frescoes, many of which can still be seen in St. Sophia. They depict, in an illusionistic style, scenes of the life of Prince

Yaroslav, builder of the cathedral. Frescoes at Kiev's Dime Church were reminiscent of Hellenistic portraits, while those of St. Mikhail of Golden Domes (1108) and of the Monastery of the Caves followed the Byzantine pictorial-illusionistic style.

St. Vladimir, who converted Russia to Christianity, brought many icons to Kiev. The famous icon of *Our Lady of Vladimir* (11th century) survived and became not only the source of inspiration for future generations of painters but also one of the most venerated holy images of Orthodox Russia. The *Ustiuzh Annunciation* icon (12th century), which was illusionistically painted, also survived. Both are now at the Moscow Tretyakov Gallery.

VLADIMIR SUZDALIAN RUSSIA (1156–1240). In Vladimir, the frescoes of St. Demetrius Cathedral (1194–97) were in a Byzantine illusionistic style, tempered by almost impressionistic effects of heavy, shadowed eyes and melting contours. The French art historian, Louis Reau, thought that they were "superior to those of Cappadoce."

NOVGOROD RUSSIA (13th–15th centuries). Mural P developed in Novgorod. As early as the 11th century, the St. Sophia Cathedral of Novgorod was painted in Byzantine style by order of the Kievan bishopric. The most remarkable series of frescoes of that period was that of the Spas Nereditsa Church (1199), the walls of which were covered with monumental frescoes. They escaped many subsequent "restorations" and thus provided art historians with one of the best examples of the formative style of medieval Russia. Spas Nereditsa, unfortunately, was destroyed during World War II.

Of the very great number and variety of frescoes in Novgorod the outstanding were those in the Dormition Church of Volotovo (1363), which were painted in a pictorial style with such realistic touches that the Soviet critic, Lazarev, characterized them as "very Russian." They showed much violent emotion, complicated composition, powerful lines and clear forms. Colors were brilliant: yellow, purple, turquoise, light green. This church also suffered a great deal during the last war. Another outstanding monument was the Church of Fedor Stratilat (c. 1370), where many a saint looked like a Novgorod citizen. The figures, full of movement, were dressed in light vestments. The composition frequently was asymmetrical. Nereditsa and Stratilat frescoes are often ascribed to the talented painter Theophanes the Greek who was then working in Novgorod. But latest Soviet studies seem to prove the contrary. It is certain, however, that Theophanes painted some sections of Novgorod's Church of Transfiguration on Ilyin Street (1378), with dynamic and well modeled figures.

Novgorod is internationally known for its icons. Their bright color schemes, their spirituality with emphasis on eyes—as receptacles of mind—their peculiarly elongated figures, and their wonderful inner rhythm contributed to make them outstanding works of art. Best examples are: *The Prophet Ilya* of the 14th century, now in the Tretyakov Gallery but formerly of the I. S. Ostroukhov collection. *Life of Fedor Stratilat* (end of the 15th century) with its great spirituality and perfect coloring; *The Descent from the Cross* and *Entombment* (Ostroukhov collection, Tretyakov Gallery), end of 15th century, both of which are most fortunately composed and balanced. Theophanes also painted many icons. The best known were executed in Moscow, in 1405, for the *Deësis* of the Annunciation Cathedral, where his pupil and disciple, Andrey Rublyov worked with him. Rublyov's *Old Testament Trinity* (now in the Tretyakov Gallery) used to be the most venerated R. icon after *The Virgin of Vladimir*. Its unusual circular rhythm, its pastel coloring, its blending of Byzantine traditions with mysticism make it a truly outstanding work. With the ascendancy of Moscow, Novgorod P deteriorated, but was kept alive for a while by a rich Novgorod merchant family of Stroganov who made icons en masse.

MOSCOW RUSSIA (14th–17th centuries). To the great icon painters who started first in Novgorod and then worked in Moscow, the name of Dyonisius should be added. He and his sons painted the *Therapont Monastery* near Novgorod (1470), with wonderful elongated figures, impressionistic in treatment. In 1482 Dyonisius painted the superb *Deësis* in the Kremlin's Dormition Cathedral.

The Stroganov School painters also worked in Moscow in the 16th and 17th centuries. They were liked for their ornate, detailed, minute effeminate style and the abundant use of gold. Simon Ushakov, Prokopy Chirin, and Nikifor Savin were the best representatives of that school.

In the beginning of the 16th century outside influences slowly began to make their way into Muscovy. The icon became an easel painting, and the miniatures, which were used to illustrate church books and biographies, became extremely popular. From Byelorussia and the Ukraine, Moscow acquired the art of engraving. When the *Stoglav* Church Council met in 1551 it put out a series of rules which forbade any changes in the iconography of religious paintings, prescribed exactly how to paint and even how to care for the icons. Thus died the free art of the icon. In its stead, portrait P began to come to the fore, especially under Tsar Alexis (1645–76), though often portraits looked like icons.

The Baroque. In love with everything foreign, Peter I brought to Russia many W. European portrait painters and architects. But he was chiefly interested in architecture and built St. Petersburg and many palaces in a baroque style somehow reminiscent of Moscow's Naryshkin baroque, which he knew and loved in his childhood. Empress Elizabeth also continued to rely on foreign artists, chiefly Italians. During her reign, the Academy of Fine Arts was created and modern painters made their appearance. Ivan Firsov painted the first genre painting *In an Art Studio* (mid 18th century); Anton Losenko (1737–73) painted the first picture with a national and historical subject, *Vladimir before Rogneda*, while Aleksey Antropov and Ivan Argunov concentrated on portraiture.

Russian Classicism (1762–1825). Under the enlightened classicism of Catherine II (1762–96) many painters came to the fore. Fyodor Rokotov (1740–1810) painted Catherine II; elegant Vladimir Borovikovsky concentrated on women's portraits; Dmitry Levitsky (1735–1822), a portraitist of European stature, painted Diderot (1773). Landscape P also made its appearance with Simon Shchedrin (1745–1804).

Romantic Painting flourished in Russia chiefly during the reign of Tsar Nicholas I. Felice Bruni (1800–75) painted *Brass Snake,* a huge tasteless picture, and the frescoes of St. Isaac Cathedral in St. Petersburg. *The Last Days of Pompeii* by Karl Bryullov (1799–1859), an outsized canvas which today looks very theatrical and artificial, was eulogized by Walter Scott and inspired Bulwer-Lytton's famous novel. Although Romanticism brought back religious P, forgotten since the reign of Peter the Great, Aleksandr Ivanov was the only outstanding religious painter of the first half of the 19th century.

With Aleksey Venetsianov (1780–1847) realistic genre P was born in Russia and the peasant was introduced into art. In 1849 Pavel Fedotov (1815–1853) painted *Newly Decorated Knight,* which was the first canvas banned by the government. Fedotov's satirical art was well in advance of his time—he wanted to expose as well as paint.

Ideological Realism and the "Peredvizhniki." On May 10, 1865 N. G. Chernyshevsky's university thesis, *The Esthetic Relation between Art and Reality,* was published and immediately became the center of violent controversy. "Because of conflicting claims of naturalism and idealism," said G. H. Hamilton, an American art critic, "R. art was faced with a dilemma: which to choose?" N. A. Nekrasov coined a phrase: "You need not be a poet, but you must be a citizen" (one hundred years later Bolshevik Russia came back to this formula). Belinsky and Pisarev joined in, and under these influences the subject matter became all important in P. It was the idea that counted, not technique or artistic truth. The father of such purposeful realism of genre P was Vasily Perov, disciple of Fedotov, who created a long series of didactic canvases. He was backed, as were many others afterwards, by the gifted art critic Vladimir Stasov.

In 1863, a trivial event occurred at the Academy of Fine Arts, but it changed the course of R. art. Following the literary lead and V. G. Perov's paintings, thirteen academy students headed by Ivan Kramskoy refused to paint the required final examination subject, *The Banquet of Gods at Valhalla,* and demanded that they be allowed to paint any subject they wanted. When they were refused, they resigned. The breach with official academicism was complete. But in its place the Kramskoy group put so much "literariness" and "purpose" that their canvases soon became cluttered and untidy. Yet, they were very successful and formed the Society of Circulating Exhibitions (*Peredvizhniki*). Under Kramskoy, Vasily V. Vereshchagin, Grigory V. Myasoyedov, and others, the Society dominated R. representative art for thirty years. In that they were helped by collector Pavel V. Tretyakov.

Although not all R. painters were members of the *Peredvizhniki* group, many were affected by its ideas one way or another, and often exhibited at its shows. Among these were the landscape painters Isaac Levitan,

Arkhip Kuinzhi, A. K. Savrasov, *The Rooks have Come,* and the seascape painter Ivan Ayvazovsky, as well as the religious and Slavophile painters V. M. Vasnetsov and Mikhail Nesterov and finally the historical painters Vasily Surikov and A. P. Ryabushkin. But the hollowness of literary realism and the mediocrity bred by the notion of civic expression in art slowly gave way to what became known as artistic realism. Painters began to pay more attention to drawing and color. Though the development of Russian landscape brought this forth with painter V. Polenov, Ilya Repin was the dominant member of the movement.

R. Impressionism, which followed, lasted until the 1920's. But though it was represented by such gifted painters as M. V. Vrubel, Konstantin Korovin, A. Golovin (1863–1930), a talented painter for the theater, Valentin Serov, and Nicholas Roerich, it never met with general acceptance. When the *Peredvizhniki* collapsed as an ideological movement, and the impressionists were feeling their way in Moscow, a new group was formed in St. Petersburg (1898) around Serge Diaghilev, Alexander Benois, and Leonid Bakst under the name of *Mir Iskusstva* (q.v.) or World of Art. Fighting for "art for art's sake," they established a link between R. art and the W. They created theatrical scenery, book illustrations, graphic arts, and they revived interest in Russia's past, especially through the study of icons and old portraits. In 1910, both the impressionists and the World of Art were overshadowed by the development in Moscow of R. futurism led by the "Russian Cézanne," P. P. Konchalovsky, and the "Russian Gauguin" Pavel Kuznetsov. They formed various competing groups: The Jack of Diamonds, the Blue Rose, the Donkey Tail, and so on. The years before the Revolution of 1917 were alive with new movements—the Imaginists, Rayonists (M. Larionov and N. Goncharova), Suprematists (Kazimir Malevich), and the Constructivists (V. A. Tatlin, A. Pevzner and Gabo).

Soviet Art (1918). Thus, because P was vigorous at the time of the Bolshevik revolution, it was quickly brought into the service of the new regime. "Art belongs to the people," said Lenin. "It must be understood and liked by them." Though many painters had left Russia, the young futurists took up the challenge. A. V. Lunacharsky, a people's commissar, headed the arts. A "Collegium" tried to keep together "the Right" and "the Left," and Vasily Kandinsky directed the Department of Fine Arts set up in 1922. With Malevich and Gabo, Kandinsky fought the "non-objectivist painters" Tatlin and Rodchenko, while he wanted a more speculative art. But the leftists (LEF) were sneered at by the masses. With Lenin's New Economic Policy realism began creeping back. The newly formed AKhRR (Association of Artists of Revolutionary Russia) proclaimed the birth of socialist realism by declaring: "We reflect daily life—of the Red army, of the workers, of the heroes of labor . . . content will form its own style." In 1930 the government declared that all groups should get rid of bourgeois elements and, in 1932, a decree reorganized all existing literary and artistic groups, put an end to free creation, and firmly established "the art of social command." The artist became a state functionary. By that time many "futurists" had already emigrated (Gabo, Pevzner, Marc Chagall, V. Kandinsky). Those who remained and compromised (V. A. Tatlin, K. Malevich, A. Filonov, D. Lissitsky) lived in abject poverty or sank into obscurity.

Socialist Realism. "The creation of the image of a positive hero," said the socialist realists, "is the principle of Soviet Art." Chernyshevsky's ideas and the *Peredvizhniki* were referred to constantly. Thus the circle was completed, the only difference being that in the 19th century the painters chose what they wanted, while in the 20th century they were told what to choose. Portrait P became paramount. Izrail Brodsky, Igor E. Grabar and Aleksandr M. Gerasimov painted many portraits of Lenin, Stalin and Voroshilov. One of the most famous works of Gerasimov was a huge canvas *Stalin and Voroshilov in the Kremlin* (1947); V. Yefanov specialized in group portraits of party leaders (*Stalin, Molotov and Voroshilov at Gorky's Bed*). D. Nalbandian, N. Zhukov, I. Pavlov and P. Vasilyev created many Stalin portraits which, according to critic Zamochkin, "rendered the soul's magnitude and heart's simplicity of the leader, dear to millions of people." There were exhibits in Moscow in which half of the paintings represented Stalin. Boris V. Ioganson (*At a Ural Factory*) was the painter of the proletariat. Sergey Malyutin, G. Ryazhsky, G. Vereysky, D. Shmarinov, A. Pakhomov and N. Zhukov painted the new Soviet man showing determination to form the new socialist society. The landscape P of A. Plastov, T. Gaponenko and others showed the changing village and the new *kolkhozes*.

Two forms of artistic expression play an extremely important part in the new Soviet society, because of their great visual appeal and propaganda value—the poster (P. Apsita, D. Moor, A. Radakov, Vladimir Mayakovsky and his *ROST window* propaganda agency, M. Cheremnykh and others) and the political cartoon (B. Yefimov, Kukryniksy, Yu. Ganf, A. Deineka, A. Kokorekin and others). World War II gave birth to many battle painters, the best of whom were P. Sokolov-Skalya, A. Avilov, F. Bogorodsky, A. Deineka and K. Finogenov. During the first thirty years of Soviet art, historical P played an important role with I. Brodsky (*The Second Congress of the Comintern*), M. Grekov (*Comrades Stalin and Voroshilov near Tsaritsyn*), G. Savitsky (*First Days of October*), and V. Serov (*Lenin Proclaims the Soviets;* 1947). Despite all the conformism, "the dust of formalism" clung to some painters, and, in 1948, party theoretician A. Zhdanov called all arts to order.

After Stalin's death in 1953, a "thaw" was proclaimed. The magnificent collections of western paintings of Shchukin and Mamontov, which had been relegated for decades to various storerooms, were brought out and shown to the public. Exhibits of Western 20th century painters also were organized in Moscow. K. Malevich and N. Roerich were shown. The result was that again the young painters of Moscow began using various advanced techniques. For the past several years these painters have produced a whole crop of "closet" paintings which are all abstract and non objective. They have not yet been shown in public. But some of these works by Ergoshina, Dmitry Krasnopevtsev, Yury Vasilyev and Zverev have been reproduced in the Western world. They show amazing freedom of expression, though the examples they follow are some fifty years old. Also at the Spring Exhibition of Moscow Painters of 1960, although there was a greater variety of techniques, the titles and subject matter were the same as before—*The Cow-Milking Girls* by G. Korolev, *My Country* by N. Sapozhnikova.

Said Sergey Gerasimov—Secretary of the Union of Painters—just after the 21st Party Congress: "Inspired by the Congress, the artists are aware that the chief subjects of the representative arts should be the Soviet people's builder, the people's hero, who brings forth new ways to mankind."

BIBLIOGRAPHY: C. G. E. Bunt, *Russian Art from Scyths to Soviets,* New York, 1956; G. K. Lukomsky, *History of Modern Russian Painting,* London, 1945; Juri Jelagin, *Taming of the Arts,* New York, 1951. V. K.

PAKHÓMOV, Alekséy Fyódorovich (1900–), graphic artist. Portrayals of children's activities and illustrations for books by Turgenev, Mayakovsky and others. Lithographs of Leningrad under blockade (1941–44) were followed by studies of the city in process of reconstruction. Stalin prize (1946).

PÁLDISKI (f. Baltiysky), seaport in N.W. Estonian SSR, at S. entrance to Gulf of Finland; pop. 10,100 (1956). Ice-free except for very severe winters.

PALE OF SETTLEMENT: *see* JEWS.

PALECKIS, Justas Ignovich (1899–), Lithuanian CP official. He studied at Kaunas University. From 1915 to 1940 he was worker, clerk, teacher, translator, journalist, writer; was arrested in 1939 by the Lithuanian goverment for communist activities. In 1940, after the Soviet troops entered Lithuania, was appointed prime minister. He became chairman of the Lithuanian Supreme Soviet; and candidate member, Central Committee, CPSU, in 1952 and 1956.

PÁLEKH MINIATURES, a form of Russian folk art—or miniature painting—chiefly on lacquered surfaces, such as boxes, trays, and so forth, usually made of papier-mache. Palekh is a small village in Ivanovo Oblast, which became known in the 16th century as an icon painting center. Its style was akin to that of the Stroganov school. In the 17th century Palekh peasants began applying their folk technique to secular objects. After the revolution Palekh turned to contemporary subjects, fairy tales, peasant lore, while maintaining the traditional elaborate and decorative style.

PALEONTOLOGY: *see* GEOLOGICAL SCIENCES.

PALLÁDIN, Aleksándr Vladímirovich (1885–), biochemist. Fellow, Ac. of S. (1942) and Ac. of Medical S., USSR (1944). Honorary member, Ac. of S., Byelorussian SSR (1950). President, Ac. of S., Ukrainian SSR (1946). Hero of Socialist Labor (1925). Member, Supreme Soviet (1946–58). Graduate of St. Petersburg University (1908). Professor, Kharkov Institute of Agriculture and Forestry (1916) and Kiev University (since 1934). Founder and director of the Ukrainian Biochemical Institute (1925). Research and development of problems of intermediate chemical transformations in the metabolic process including the biochemistry of muscular and nervous systems. Established the importance of creatine and its formation. Developed a vitamin preparation known as "Viscasol." Author of *A Study of the Biochemistry of Muscles and Nervous System Under Various States* (1946); *Metabolism in the Brain Under Various Functional States* (1952).

PAMIR (the Pamirs), called by natives Bam-i-Dunya (Roof of the World), a high-altitude region of Central Asia, mostly in Tadzhik SSR, borders with Sinkiang, Kashmir, and Afghanistan. Highest peaks: Kongur (25,320 ft.), Stalin Peak (24,584 ft.); many glaciers. The climate is dry and severe. Roads lead to Fergana Valley and Stalinabad. Agr.: rye, oats, wheat, cattle breeding in the state of development. Prospecting.

PANFYÓROV, Fyódor Ivánovich (1896–1960), Soviet writer and dramatist of peasant origin. He began writing in 1920; joined the CP in 1926. His early works are *From the Farm Fields* (1926) and *The Early Predawn* (1927). P is one of the best portrayers of farm peasant life in postrevolutionary Russia, especially in the lengthy novel *Chunks of Wood*, written over a period of 9 years, from 1928 to 1937. He also wrote two novels, *Great Artistry* (1949–54) and *Mother Volga* (1953), and the play *When We Are Handsome* (1952). Stalin prizes (1948, 1949).

PÁNIN, Count Nikíta Ivánovich (1718–1783), prominent Russian diplomat and statesman; ambassador to Denmark (1747), Sweden (1748–60); Catherine II's chief diplomatic adviser (1763–80). P favored close cooperation with England, Prussia, Sweden and Denmark. He also advocated the appointment of a permanent "Imperial Council" that would advise the Crown.

PANJ RIVER: *see* PYANDZH RIVER.

PANKRÁTOVA, Ánna Mikháylovna (1897–1957), historian. She graduated from the Novorossiysk University in 1917 and from the Institute of Red Professors in 1925. Author of almost 200 monographs, mostly on the history of the R. labor movement and *History of Diplomacy*. From the late 1930's, she was considered an official historian. Stalin prize (1946).

PANÓVA, Véra Fyódorovna (1905–), novelist, playwright, and journalist. Her novels *Traveling Companions* (1946), *Kruzhilikha* (1947), and *Seasons of the Year* (1953), the last flayed for its lack of "party spirit," are widely read in the Soviet Union. Stalin prizes (1947, 1950).

PAN-SLAVISM is a movement to unite all the people speaking Slavic languages for common political, economic, and cultural purposes. This movement gained strength in 19th-century Russia among nationalist R. intellectuals who saw in P a means for enhancing Russia's great power position in Europe. For a brief time, especially in the war against Turkey in 1877, P was also officially used to supply a moral justification to R. war efforts.

P was, however, not of R. origin. Before and at the beginning of the 19th century the Russians paid little attention to the W. Slavs. The religious element in R. thought was then stronger than an emphasis on linguistic or racial ties. Little was known about the W.

Slavs with the exception of the Poles, and the fact that the W. Slavs were Roman Catholic did not make them more interesting to the Greek Orthodox Russians. At that time Russia, in her drive against the Ottoman Empire, tried to enlist the sympathy of the Christian subjects of the Sultan by emphasizing the religious, not the linguistic, ties.

P developed among the W. and S. Slavs at the time of their national awakening at the beginning of the 19th century. These small Slav peoples sought strength in Slav solidarity. The first modern Pan-Slav writers arose among the Czechs and Slovaks, and Prague became the first center of P, where in 1848 the first Pan-Slavic congress met. This congress was held under the leadership of the Czech historian František Palacký, not to proclaim any tie with Russia, but to strengthen Austria as a bulwark against German and R. expansion and to strengthen, through their close cooperation, the position of the Slav peoples in Austria.

Russian P gained in importance only in the 1860's. Among the reasons which contributed to its rise were the Crimean War (q.v.) in which Russia believed herself facing a Europe united against her, the German unification in the second half of the 1860's, and the disillusionment of the Austrian Slavs in their ability to determine Austria's future. One of the earliest R. Pan-Slavists was Mikhail Petrovich Pogodin (1800–75) who was professor of history at the Moscow U. and visited the W. Slav nations six times. He regarded the unification of the Slavs under R. leadership as a condition not only for Russia's ranking great-power position but also the fulfillment of Russia's historical mission.

He shared the conviction of the Slavophiles that the time of the European nations was past and that their strength was running out, whereas the future belonged to the Slavs (whom he, like most R. Pan-Slavists, identified with the Russians) who would serve and guide mankind. In 1854 Pogodin exhorted Russia to liberate all Slav peoples and to create a Slavic union which would act as a buffer between Russia and Europe. This union was to include not only the Slavs but other central E. and S.E. peoples like the Magyars, the Rumanians, and the Greeks.

The leading R. Pan-Slav writer, a more systematic thinker than Pogodin, was Nikolay Yakovlevich Danilevsky (1822–85). His *Russia and Europe: A View of the Cultural and Political Relations of the Slavic with the Germano-Roman World* appeared first in a periodical in 1869 and in book form in 1871. It was enthusiastically hailed as the bible of R. Pan-Slavists and fervently supported by Dostoyevsky who in his novels and in his journalistic writings was one of the most extremist supporters of Slavophilism and P.

Danilevsky and the other R. Pan-Slavists, among whom the great poet Fyodor Ivanovich Tyutchev (1803–75) and the influential journalist Mikhail Nikiforovich Katkov (1818–87) should be mentioned, started from the supposition that a deep-rooted antagonism existed between Russia and Europe, which sooner or later inevitably would lead to a decisive struggle. Out of this, Russia, with which the salvation of mankind rested, would emerge victorious and then establish a lasting reign of peace and social justice. To this end Russia needed the support of the Slav peoples who were living under non-R. domination and who served Russia's enemies against their will. The Pan-Slavic union could establish the only firm foundation on which an original Slav civilization could grow. Through the liberation of the kindred Slavs from the German, Austrian, Hungarian, and Turkish yokes, Russia would fulfill her political and spiritual destiny. "In this divine and perhaps unique coincidence of moral motives and obligations with political advantage and necessity, we must see a guarantee for the fulfillment of Russia's great task. Otherwise our world would be only a miserable chain of accidents and not the reflection of supreme reason, right and goodness."

The jarring note in R. 19th-century P was sounded by the two Slav peoples who found themselves under Great Russian domination, the Poles and Ukrainians. The Ukrainians were generally disregarded by the R. Pan-Slavists and their existence as a nationality was denied. The Poles were considered "traitors" to the Slav cause and agents of European and Catholic imperialism. The absence of the Poles from the Pan-Slavic congress held in Moscow in 1867 showed up the weakness of the Pan-Slavic movement. R. insistence on undisputed leadership among the Slavs, on the R. language, and on the Orthodox faith as a cementing link did not help to strengthen Russia's appeal among the W. Slavs. The Pan-Slavic congress in Moscow ended without a follow-up.

The R. government gave little official encouragement to P except in the 1870's, when Count Nicholas Pavlovich Ignatyev (1832–1908) was Russia's envoy in Turkey and used P for the support of Russia's attempt to control the Balkans with the help of the Slavic peoples, the Bulgars and Serbs. He wished to solve the "eastern question" by establishing R. control over Constantinople and the Straits and organizing all Slav peoples in the Austrian and Turkish empires in autonomous states bound to Russia by indissoluble bonds.

After the Congress of Berlin (1878) P ceased again to form an important element in official R. policy. With the advance of R. liberalism and constitutionalism at the beginning of the 20th century, P de-emphasized its link with Slavophilism. A movement called Neo-Slavism stressed R. domination less than the voluntary cooperation of the various Slav peoples who were to be regarded as equals. In W. Europe the suspicion that P was a tool of R. policy continued, however. World War I, in which Russia fought Austria, Hungary, and Turkey, rekindled the embers of P in R. writings. Among the Austrian Slavs, many Czechs looked hopefully to Russia to help establish Czech independence from Austria.

P in Russia seemed definitely ended when the Bolsheviks seized power and rejected officially the nationalist, Orthodox, and tsarist heritage of R. history. For twenty years the Soviet government showed neither friendship nor any special interest in the W. Slavs.

This attitude changed only in the late 1930's when, under the influence of the rise of national socialism to power in Germany, the national roots and purposes of the R. Revolution were discovered. From 1936 on, Stalin appealed simultaneously to the class consciousness of socialism and the traditional emotionalism of nationalism.

In spite of the fact that the Soviet government had done everything possible to maintain good relations with Germany and had condoned Hitler's aggression against Slav peoples, it appealed to P after the German attack on the Soviet Union in June 1941. Two months later a Pan-Slav committee was formed in Moscow under the chairmanship of the Soviet General Aleksandr Semyonovich Gundorov. At the second meeting of this committee in Moscow in April 1942 the R. composer Shostakovich declared: "I am proud to be a Russian, I boast of being a Slav. . . . May all the spiritual forces, all the intellectuals of the glorious family of the Slavonic nations fearlessly fulfill the great mission entrusted to them by history!" For the first time P was extended not only to the Slav peoples living in their homelands but also to the descendants of Slav peoples who were citizens of non-Slavic countries, including the United States. An American Slav Congress was established, which was listed in 1948 as a subversive agency by the Attorney General of the United States.

The end of World War II did not immediately put an end to the new P. In 1945 R. Communist influence became predominant in all countries inhabited by Slav peoples, and the political goals set by Pogodin and Danilevsky seemed achieved, though under the guise of a different Moscow-centered ideology. A Pan-Slavic congress met in Belgrade in Dec. 1946 and marked the triumphant affirmation of Moscow's hold over the Slavic world. But the resolutions unanimously adopted by the Belgrade congress came to naught as had those of the previous Pan-Slavic congresses. In 1948 the Yugoslav Communists defected from the Communist Slav "family of nations." Yugoslavia became now, what Poland had been in the 19th century, a "traitor" to the Slav cause and a "tool" of "western scheming" against Moscow. P receded quickly again into the lumber box of history as it had in 1918.

BIBLIOGRAPHY: Hans Kohn, *Pan-Slavism: Its History and Ideology*, New Edition, New York, 1960; Michael Boro Petrovich, *The Emergence of Russian Panslavism, 1856–1870*, New York, 1956; B. H. Sumner, *Russia and the Balkans, 1870–1880*, Oxford, 1937; Waclaw Lednicki, "Panslavism," *European Ideologies*, ed. by Feliks Gross, New York, 1948.

H. K.

PAPER AND NEWSPRINT PRODUCTION. In 1958, 1.8 mill. tons of paper and 389,000 tons of newsprint were produced, and 2.3 mill. tons of paper of both types in 1959. (In 1958 the United States produced 11.9 mill. tons of paper and 1.6 mill. tons of newsprint; and the United Kingdom 1.8 mill. tons of paper and 624,000 tons of newsprint.)

The paper industry began to develop rapidly during the second half of the 19th century, after the process for making paper from wood had been discovered. Over 170 paper-producing enterprises had been established by 1900, and by 1913 this number reached 212, employing 41,000 workers. About half of the 197,000 tons of paper, 20,000 tons of cardboard, and 41,000 tons of cellulose made that year were produced in the N.W. regions of the country. Domestic production was insufficient to meet all needs, however, and considerable amounts of paper as well as paper-making equipment and auxiliary raw materials were imported.

Following the reconstruction, during the 1920's, of the productive facilities destroyed in the course of the First World War and of the civil war, existing plants were expanded and modernized, a number of large new plants were constructed (e.g., at Balakhna, Kamsk, and Solikamsk), and the making of new grades of paper was initiated. In 1940, 812,000 tons of paper were produced, of which 55% was newsprint and writing paper. The by-products of the paper industry included alcohol, tanning agents, and turpentine.

After the reconstruction of facilities destroyed during the Second World War the production of paper continued to expand rapidly during the 1950's, partly because of the continuous modernization of technological processes. Annual production reached 2 mill. tons in 1956. The new plants established during this period include those at Kamenogorsk (Leningrad Oblast), Sverdlovsk (Vologda Oblast), and Neman (Kaliningrad Oblast), and the cardboard-producing plants at Zhidachov (Drogobych Oblast), Rakhov (Transcarpathian Oblast), Lvov, and Klaipeda. Among the new paper-producing regions of the postwar period are those of S. Sakhalin. In recent years the production of fine grades of paper and of paper for packing purposes has been emphasized.

The objectives of the Seven Year Plan (1959–65) provide for the production of 3.5 mill. tons of paper and of 2.8 mill. tons of cardboard in 1965.

PRODUCTION OF PAPER AND OF CARDBOARD
IN THE USSR
(thousands of tons)

Year	Paper	Cardboard
1913	197	20
1928	285	47
1932	471	73
1937	832	144
1940	812	151
1945	321	56
1950	1,193	292
1955	1,863	545
1958	2,238	720
1959	2,300	—
1965 (pl.)	3,500	2,800	P. I. M.

PAPKÓVICH, Pyótr Fyódorovich (1887–1946), shipbuilding engineer. Professor, Leningrad Shipbuilding Institute and Military Naval Academy (1934–40). Research on structural mechanics of ships. Development and improvement of methods for the calculation of modern ship construction with dynamic and static loads. Study of general theorems of stability of elastic systems. Author of *Structural Mechanics of a Ship* (2 vols., 1945–47). Stalin prize (1946).

PARENÁGO, Pável Petróvich (1906–), astronomer. Corresponding member, Ac. of S., USSR (1953). Graduate (1929), professor (1938), Moscow University. Since 1922, P has been investigating variable stars; suggested the theory of light absorption in interstellar space, laws governing various characteristics of stars; studied the dynamics of stellar systems. Author of *The Structure of the Galaxy*, for which he was awarded the F. A. Bredikhin prize by the Ac. of S., USSR (1950).

PARIS, TREATY OF, signed on March 30, 1856 at the Congress of Paris by the representatives of France, Austria, England, Prussia, Sardinia, and Turkey with Russia; it marked the termination of the Crimean War (1853–56). Russia and Turkey exchanged mutually occupied territories, and the Black Sea was declared neutral territory. Under the stipulation of the Treaty no R. or Turkish warships were to sail on the Black Sea and no fortifications were to be built on its shores. A separate convention closed the Dardanelles and the Bosporus to warships of all foreign nations. Russia lost the Danube delta and part of S. Bessarabia and her protectorate over Danubian principalities was replaced by a joint guarantee of the signatory powers.

PARKHÓMENKO, Aleksándr Yákovlevich (1885–1921), old Bolshevik, veteran of the civil war of 1918–20. The son of a poor peasant, P, as a youth of 16, found employment at the locomotive works in Lugansk, where he soon became active in underground organizations. In 1904 he joined the Bolsheviks and participated in the revolutionary events of 1905–07. After the October revolution in 1917, P fought against the Whites and the German occupation troops in Ukraine.

PARTISAN MOVEMENT IN WORLD WAR II. The partisan movement was a skillfully organized and centrally directed arm in the Soviet struggle against the Germans. It was neither an underground movement nor a spontaneous mass rising. While Soviet military doctrine as well as earlier experience (e.g., the R. and Chinese civil wars) had prepared for guerrilla warfare behind enemy lines, the Soviet forces in June 1941 were caught unprepared for its large-scale employment. During the initial weeks of the campaign, Moscow improvised the formation of NKVD-run "destruction battalions" and ordered a selected number of CP stalwarts to stay behind in the areas being surrendered to the Germans. On the whole, the small bands and teams which operated in the German rear in 1941 were ineffectual; many melted away within weeks. They were generally untrained, their efforts uncoordinated, initially lacking popular support, and deprived of supplies, reinforcements, and instructions from the Soviet side. They were of no military value to the Red Army.

The Soviet partisans began to become an effective force in early 1942, thanks to the coincidence of several developments: the change in popular attitudes toward the Germans, owing to both their terror and their failure to win a rapid victory; the large number of "stragglers" from the Red Army who, cut off from their units in the giant encirclement battles, roamed the forests fearing to surrender to the Germans and provided the nuclei of partisan units with professional cadres; the tightening of Soviet controls and establishment of radio and later air communications with a few partisan units, as well as their reinforcement with men and matériel from the Soviet side; the deteriorating fortunes of the Germans, which not only reduced popular willingness to side with them but also forced them to denude their security troops in the "rear areas."

Propitious terrain was essential for the growth of the PM. The wooded and swamp areas of Byelorussia, the W. RSFSR, and the N. Ukraine provided good cover and concealment. Open stretches, such as the S. steppe, did not permit partisan units to survive. By the same token, the locale of partisan units was no index to pro-Soviet sentiment among the population.

Another prerequisite to success was systematic Soviet direction. The units which proved ultimately successful began essentially as nonspontaneous nuclei supported from the outside. From the spring of 1942 on, the Central Staff for Partisan Warfare was attached to the Soviet High Command, and corresponding staffs existed at the level of each Soviet army group in liaison with partisan units in the sector across the front lines. As time went on, many of the key leaders and much of the decisive equipment were brought in from the Soviet side. Modern technology—radio and aviation—were preconditions for partisan effectiveness.

The expanding partisan units gradually absorbed other autonomous bands and "sovietized" them; they attracted the support of theretofore neutral civilians and of defectors from collaborator units. By 1943–44 the guerrillas were a substantial force which the Soviet command chose to use for military and political purposes. The major military assignment was to harass the German rear areas and especially communications. The "battle of the rails," which commanded highest priority, diverted some German forces, caused moderate casualties, delayed and destroyed some supplies, and made German troops and command nervous. At times, partisan operations were closely coordinated with military action at the front. Yet in the total picture the impact of the partisans on the course of the war was marginal; economic sabotage was slight and largely at the expense of the local residents; and the value of intelligence gathered by the partisans was uncertain.

On the political side, the partisans came to represent and reassert Soviet authority and administration in wide areas behind the lines. Here they operated as the eyes and ears of Moscow, and as the "long arm" of Soviet justice. In addition to their own territory—such as the Bryansk forests and large parts of Byelorussia—they played a decisive role in the "twilight areas," where neither they nor the Germans were strong enough to hold constant sway; here raids and retributions by both would alternate.

Finally, by 1943–44 some units were strong enough to stage ambitious demonstrative raids across otherwise partisan-free territory (such as Kovpak's raid across the Ukraine to the Carpathians). A primary function of all these endeavors was to engender a sense of omnipresent Soviet power and a reminder of imminent Communist return, and to neutralize non-Communist partisans (such as Ukrainian nationalists). They importantly contributed to the polarization of attitudes and loyalties, making "neutralism" on occupied soil virtually impossible.

German anti-partisan warfare was singularly unsuccessful, both politically and militarily. The partisans' ground was apparently undercut politically in those areas where a more tolerant regime emerged. In Ru-

manian-held Odessa, where a more permissive course avoided the extremes of Nazi abuse, and in the N. Caucasus, where German policy allowed local authorities greater independence, no partisan units managed to gain ground.

The spread of a guerrilla movement on a mass scale involved encouraging "spontaneity" in a fashion which ran counter to long-range Soviet concepts of control. The gamble was made less risky by strict adherence to the commissar system for all partisan units as well as a re-emerging network of CP organizations and discipline; by prompt screening of returnees to the Soviet side; and by limiting the size of any one partisan unit. On the whole, the flexible propaganda line of the war years, which played down Communist orthodoxy and hegemony, was even exceeded in the PM, where talk of drastic postwar changes was apparently sanctioned from above (including in at least some instances, the prospect of ending one-man dictatorship and dissolving collective farms). Such concessions from weakness were eliminated as, by 1944, controls and victories made the PM a powerful fighting arm of the Soviet armed forces. Its development—and its greater political, rather than military, impact—could not have been foreseen by either the Soviet or the German command.

BIBLIOGRAPHY: N. Galai, "The Partisan Forces," in B. H. Liddell-Hart, ed., *The Red Army*, New York, 1956; Edgar Howell, *The Soviet Partisan Movement, 1941–1944*, Washington, D.C., 1956; Aubrey Dixon and Otto Heilbrum, *Communist Guerilla Warfare*, New York, 1954.

A. D.

PARTÍYNAYA ZHIZN (Party Life)—semimonthly journal of the Central Committee of CPSU devoted to propagandistic and organizing work of CP members, founded 1919. Published under present title since Nov. 1946, when it superseded the journal *Partiynoye Stroitelstvo* (Party Construction). In 1960 it had a circulation of about 400,000; has about 80 pages per issue.

PARTY CONTROL COMMITTEE OF THE CENTRAL COMMITTEE, CPSU which in 1934 succeeded the Central Control Commission, and since 1952 is appointed by the Central Committee, supervises discipline of party members, and takes action against Communists who violate party ethics.

PARTY OF PEOPLE'S FREEDOM: *see* CONSTITUTIONAL DEMOCRATIC PARTY.

PÁRVUS (A. L. Gelfand) (1869–1924), Russian and German Marxist theorist. Joined the R. Social Democrats in the 1890's; soon emigrated to Germany where he became one of the leaders of the left-wing Social Democrats. In 1902 contributed to *Iskra* (q.v.). After the split of the R. Social Democrats in 1903, P backed the Mensheviks. In 1905, was one of the leaders of the St. Petersburg Soviet of Workers' Deputies. Author, jointly with Trotsky, of the theory of "permanent revolution." After his arrest and release, P returned to Germany where he amassed considerable wealth in stock speculation. He identified himself with the right-wing of the German Social Democratic party and supported the Imperial German Government in World War I. P was instrumental in persuading the German government to allow Lenin to pass through Germany in the "sealed train" in 1917. After World War I, P became economic adviser to Frederick Ebert, the Socialist president of the German Republic.

PASHUKÁNIS, Yevgény Bronislávovich (1891–1938?), Soviet lawyer of Lithuanian peasant origin. Studying law at St. Petersburg University P joined the Bolshevik party. After the October revolution in 1917, P worked in the People's Commissariat of Justice under Stuchka. Upon the death of Stuchka, P became the most prominent Marxist theorist of law, director of the Moscow Law Institute, vice-chairman of the Communist Academy and deputy people's commissar of justice of the RSFSR. His main work, *The General Theory of Law: A Critical Test of Basic Juridical Notions*, had several R. editions and was translated into foreign languages. P disappeared during the purges in 1938.

PASKÉVICH, Iván Fyódorovich (1782–1856), general, field marshal. He participated in the war against France, 1812; was commander of R. troops in the war against Persia, 1826–28; and suppressed the Polish uprising 1830–31. He also was viceroy in Poland from 1832 until his death.

PASSPORTS are a means of personal identification obligatory for Soviet citizens aged 16 and over if they live in urban areas; all of Latvia, Lithuania, Estonia, and Moscow Oblast; 10 districts in Leningrad Oblast; and restricted border zones. Rural inhabitants outside these areas do not have P unless they leave their own districts for more than 30 days, except on business or to convalesce or rest. In the latter case they do not need P but must have travel documents from their local soviet. A P shows its bearer's name: date and place of birth; nationality, that is, ethnic origin—Jewish, Russian, Uzbek, and so on; social status—worker, peasant or employee; military status; and name of the police official who issued it. Marriages, births, children, and changes of employment must be registered in the P. P help the government and the police to follow and control the movements of the population. Before a citizen leaves on a journey of more than one and a half months (unless for his summer home or vacation and convalescence or temporary job assignment), moves to another residence in the same locality, enters military service, or leaves for exile or a term of prison, he must be signed out by his house management and, through the house management, by the local police. The police indicates its permission of the moves or departures in both the P and the house registry.

When a traveler arrives at a destination where he intends to stay more than three days, he is supposed to sign in with the police within three days in cities and border areas, within seven days in the country, or, if staying in a village no more than 30 days, with the village soviet.

Police permission for permanent residence, the precious *propiska* in one's passport, will be very hard to obtain in large cities such as Moscow as long as the housing shortage there continues. It seems that thousands risk fines of 100 rubles or up to two years in prison by living in such cities without *propiski*, even without passports.

When a citizen wishes to travel abroad, he should exchange his internal P for a traveling P with proper visa, making the exchange in the reverse order when he returns to the USSR.   P. H. J.

PASTERNÁK, Borís Leonídovich (1890–1960), poet and novelist, born in Moscow, the eldest of four children of the painter, Leonid Osipovich P. He grew up in an art-saturated atmosphere, graduated from a Moscow gymnasium, and studied philosophy in Moscow and Marburg. His early collections of poems—*A Twin in the Clouds* (1914), *Over the Barriers* (1917), and *My Sister My Life* (1922), of which the last was particularly popular—reflected the influence of the symbolist movement. Subsequently, after writing another collection of lyrical poems *Themes and Variations* (1923), and an autobiographical long poem, *Spektorsky* (1926), P turned briefly, in the long poems *Lieutenant Schmidt* (1926) and *The Year 1905* (1927), to the contemporary revolutionary themes and to the concept of selfless service to the revolution's ideals. In 1932 he published a new collection of lyrical poems, *The Second Birth*. Still other collections, *On Early Trains* (1943) and *The Terrestrial Expanse* (1945) published during World War II, are concerned with patriotic themes.

His poems reveal P as a profound individualist, whose favorite themes are a philosophical perception of the world, the lyricism of love, and images of nature. His cosmic representations of nature are similar in some respects to those of Tyutchev. They are frequently animistic, and represent attempts to reenact, as it were, the miracle of the first day of creation. Partly because his poetry is so personal, however, it is often difficult to identify clearly the meaning of the images and associations that P employs. Their subtlety and refinement, as well as the refinement of his language, have led many persons to regard P as an unsurpassed master of his craft. They have also led others, however, and particularly critics representing the official Soviet position, to accuse P of formalism and egocentrism as well as of aloofness from reality. It is this official condemnation of P's own poetry, presumably, that led him to turn increasingly in his last period, to the making of translations of such works as Goethe's *Faust*, Shakespeare's tragedies (*Hamlet, Othello, Macbeth, Antony and Cleopatra, Henry IV, King Lear*), the works of the Hungarian poet S. Petöfi, and also of Georgian poets (the collection *Georgian Poets*, 1946).

Until the publication abroad of *Dr. Zhivago* (1957), P's prose works had been of secondary significance. His only collection of short stories, which included *The Childhood of Luvers* and *Air Ways*, was published in 1925. Also, *Safe Conduct*, an autobiographical account of the poet's youth, was published in 1931. *Dr. Zhivago* brought world fame to P as well as the Nobel Prize for literature in 1958, but the harsh reaction of the Soviet government and of the Soviet critics to his presentation of the negative aspects of the early postrevolutionary years caused P to decline the Nobel Prize. In the view of many critics the world over, the artistic as well as the moral, religious, and philosophical merits of *Dr. Zhivago* have made it one of the important works of modern times.   C. P. K.

PASTERNÁK, Leoníd Ósipovich (1862–1945),

painter. Born in Odessa, died in London. Artist of the realistic school. Painted in oil and water colors. Was also an illustrator of L. Tolstoy's books. Member of the Academy of Fine Arts in St. Petersburg from 1905. His paintings of the 1880's and 1890's, i.e. *Meditations, A Letter from Home, By a Jug of Beer*, and others, are in the art galleries of Moscow and Leningrad. P sometimes used Jewish subjects in his pictures (*The Musicians, Etude*); he also painted portraits (Leo Tolstoy, Klyuchevsky, Chaliapin, Rachmaninov, Einstein). After 1921, P lived in Germany and England. His son is the poet, Boris Pasternak.

PATENT: *see* AUTHORSHIP AND INVENTION.

PATÓLICHEV, Nikoláy Semyónovich (1908–), minister of foreign trade, party official, born in Zolino, Vladimir Oblast in a peasant family. He studied at the Moscow Technological Institute, 1931–37; also at a military academy. He has been a party organizer since 1938; in 1939 he became first secretary of Yaroslavl Oblast party committee, then in Chelyabinsk; in 1946 he was named secretary of the Central Committee, CPSU; from 1947, secretary of the central committee, Ukrainian CP; 1950–56 he was first secretary of the central committee, Byelorussian CP; elected in 1954 to the Foreign Affairs Commission, Council of the Union, USSR Supreme Soviet; in 1956 was named deputy minister of foreign affairs, and in 1958, minister of foreign trade.

PATÓN, Yevgény Oskarovich (1870–1953), welding and bridge-construction engineer. Fellow, Ukrainian Ac. of S. (1929). Honored Scientist, Ukrainian SSR (1943). Hero of Socialist Labor (1943). Deputy to the Supreme Soviet, USSR (1950–53). Graduate of St. Petersburg Institute of Railway Engineering (1896). Founded the Scientific Research Institute of Electric Welding (1930) which was named after him (1945). Research on automation of welding processes, submerged arc welding techniques, and problems of strength of welded joints. During World War II investigated methods of welding special types of steel for the defense industry. Participated in designing the first Soviet production lines for the welding industry including electro-slag welding, pipelines, and reservoirs; supervised the construction of the all-welded bridge over the Dnieper River which bears his name. Author of *Bare Submerged-Arc Welding* (1940). Stalin prize (1941).

PATRIARCHATE, Russian, the see of the patriarch, where the supreme authority of the Orthodox Church was located; founded 1589 and abolished by Peter I in 1721 who entrusted church administration to the Synod; reinstated by the Church Assembly in 1918; Patriarch Sergey was elected 1943 and followed by Metropolitan Aleksey, 1945; there are also Georgian, Serbian, Rumanian and Bulgarian P.

PATRONYMIC, a customary form of address in Russia formed by adding the suffix, in most cases "ovich" (males) or "ovna" (females), to the father's first name. In combination with the first name of a person it has been known in 12th-century Russia and is part of the full legal name. According to Soviet law any birth register includes the P. In the birth certificate of a child born out of wedlock the mother is free to indicate a P of her choice.

PAUL I (Pável Petróvich) (1754–1801), tsar, son of Catherine II and Peter III. Paul was brought up by Empress Elizabeth and distrusted his mother who tried to keep him away from the affairs of state. After the death of his first wife, a marriage with a German princess was arranged for him. On his visit to Germany P was very impressed with the Prussian army and his favorite occupation became that of drilling soldiers (he was famous for having sent entire regiments into exile for mistakes in drilling). In 1796, P ascended the throne. The chief concern of the monarch was to consolidate his rule which, he felt, was threatened by popular unrest, scheming nobles, and the influence of the French Revolution. P introduced a law to regulate the order of succession (1797), made the censorship more rigorous, and interrupted cultural exchanges with the West (prohibiting the import of books, and so on). P issued an order limiting serf labor for the landowner to three days a week and, simultaneously, abolished some of the privileges granted by Catherine II to the nobility. In his foreign policy, P opposed the French revolutionary forces. He sent an army, under General Suvorov, and a naval expedition, under Admiral Ushakov, to assist Austria against France. Later, he reversed R. foreign policy in breaking relations with England. A conspiracy was organized, led by Count V. Pahlen, and on March 11, 1801 P was strangled in his bedroom (with the knowledge of his son Alexander I).

PAUSTÓVSKY, Konstantín Geórgyevich (1892–), postrevolutionary writer. He studied in the Moscow and Kiev universities; worked as a laborer, street car conductor, sailor, and reporter. Although his works have been published since 1911, he became a professional writer only after 1926–27. In his writings, romanticism is closely associated with a realistic portrayal of R. life, especially evident in his early collections, *Minetoza* (1927), *Naval Sketches* (1927–28), *Ships that Were Met* (1928), and *The Romanticists* (1929–30). His later writings tend to be more realistic; among them are: *Notes of Vasily Sedykh* (1930), *Valuable Cargo* (1931), and the novels *Karabugaz* (1932), *Kolkhida* (1934), and *The Black Sea* (1936). P is an outstanding stylist and master of lyrical portrayal of nature. In 1948 he published a novel *Overcoming Time* that depicts the struggle of machinery versus nature. He is now working on an autobiographical trilogy *The Story of a Life*. He is the author of historical novels; the best known among them is *The Fate of Charles Lonseville* (1933). P is also a critic and a biographer. His biographies include those of the artists Isaac Levitan and Orest Kiprensky and the poet Taras Shevchenko. P is the authors of plays on Lermontov and Pushkin.

PAVLÉNKO, Pyotr Andréyevich (1899–1951), writer. He wrote books on Soviet Turkmenistan, *The Desert* and *Travels in Turkmenistan*, both published in 1932; the novels *In the East* (1936) and *Happiness* (1947); as well as scripts for the films, *Alexander Nevsky* (1938), *The Oath* (1946), and *The Fall of Berlin* (1948). P was a member of the Supreme Soviet of the USSR. Stalin prizes (1941, 1947, 1948, 1950).

PAVLODÁR, city, adm. center of Pavlodar Oblast, N.E. Kazakh SSR, on right bank of Irtysh River; pop. 29,000 (1939), 90,000 (1959). In rich agr. area, about halfway on Akmolinsk–Barnaul R.R., has flour mills, wool factories, tanning and food processing ind. Construction of aluminum, ferrosilicon, and combine plants is under way, making it into a leading ind. center of Kazakhstan.

PAVLODÁR OBLAST, Kazakh SSR, occupies Irtysh River valley; area 49,300 sq. mi.; pop. 455,000 (1959): Kazakhs, Ukrainians, Russians. N. part of oblast belongs to S.E. of W. Siberian plain, Kazakh Hills (S.W.). Cities: Pavlodar (adm. center), Ekibastuz. Drained by Irtysh River, has salt lakes, continental climate (hot dry summers, cold winters); steppe with forested black-soil area predominant. Cultivation of virgin soil program made oblast into leading Soviet wheat producer; also millet, rye, barley, sunflowers, orchards, dairy farming. Ind.: flour milling, tanning, coal, gold, copper mining (Maykain), chemicals, food processing, machine mfg., salt extraction.

PÁVLOV, Iván Petróvich (1849–1936), famous physiologist. Born in the family of a priest, P had been preparing for a clerical career but became interested in natural sciences. Graduate, St. Petersburg University (1875) and Ac. of Medicine (1879) where he was awarded a gold medal for outstanding experiments. Pro-

fessor, St. Petersburg Academy of Medicine (1890–1925); head of the Department of Physiology at the Institute of Experimental Medicine (1891) which he helped organize and where he spent 45 years of his life. Fellow, Ac. of S. (1907), P advanced the theory of conditioned and unconditioned reflexes which he observed in his famous experiments with dogs. P found that a conditioned reflex could be established by applying sound stimuli to an animal before the intake of food over a period of time and that a flow of saliva would be evoked by a reapplication of such stimuli even after food was no longer given. His contribution to physiology is invaluable; he developed methods of treating animals, established the existence of enzymes of ferment in the gastric juices and made revolutionary discoveries in regard to the higher nervous system. Author of a series on the physiology of digestion which appeared in *Les Archives des Sciences Biologiques* (1892–97); a monograph in German, *Die Arbeit der Verdauungsdrüsen* (translated into English, French and other languages) (1902); *Conditioned Reflexes* (1926); *Complete Works* in six volumes (1951–52). Nobel Prize in physiology and medicine (1904); Copley Medal (1915). Member of R. and foreign learned societies, including the British Royal Society (1907), the Royal College of Physicians in London (1928). Received honorary degrees from numerous universities.

BIBLIOGRAPHY: Boris P. Babkin, *Pavlov: A Biography*, Chicago, 1960.

PÁVLOV, Mikhaíl Aleksándrovich (1863–1958), metallurgist. Fellow, Ac. of S., USSR (1932). Hero of Socialist Labor (1945). Graduate, St. Petersburg Mining Institute (1885); professor, St. Petersburg (Lenin-

grad) Polytechnic Institute (1904–41), Moscow Mining Academy (1921–30), and Moscow Steel Institute (1930–41). Research concerned puddling furnaces, gas generators, and the use of hot blast in steel melting. Introduced anthracite-fired furnaces, a method for the calculation of furnace dimensions, and modernized blast furnaces. Author of *The Metallurgy of Cast Iron* (1948), *Calculations of Furnace Charges* (6th ed., 1951). Stalin prizes (1943, 1947).

PÁVLOV-SILVÁNSKY, Nikoláy Pávlovich (1869–1908), historian. His books *Feudalism in Medieval Russia* (1907) and *Feudalism in Appanage Russia* (1910), undermined the myth of the "uniqueness" of early R. society. They substituted a schematic account which endeavored to show the close resemblance between R. feudalism and its W. European counterpart. Other works of his include monographs on Peter I, Radishchev, and the Decembrists.

PÁVLOVA, Ánna Pávlovna (1881–1931), the greatest R. dancer of the first quarter of the 20th century, was

a graduate of the St. Petersburg Imperial Ballet School and a ballerina of the Mariinsky Theater. She danced on the Mariinsky stage from 1899 to 1913, then resigned and left Russia never to return. She was the first ballerina of the Diaghilev (q.v.) Ballet in 1909 in Paris, and in 1910 danced in New York and in London with Mikhail Mordkin as her partner. After her resignation she settled in London and in 1914 formed her own company. She spent the war years traveling in N. and S. America and returned to Europe in 1920. The next eleven years she danced in every European country except Russia, as well as in America, Asia, Africa, Australia, and New Zealand. She died at The Hague, The Netherlands, on Jan. 23, 1931 of double pneumonia. Her body was taken to England and cremated. She was married (1914) to Victor Dandré, a wealthy R. landowner and balletomane, who organized and managed her tours. P was a great artist who was able to elevate to a high artistic level even some of the trite choreographic pieces which often formed part of her repertoire. The repertoire of P included *Chopiniana, Dying Swan, Les Preludes* (all by Fokine, q.v.), *Giselle, Swan Lake,* as well as variations and *pas de deux* from the old classic ballets. P was a phenomenon and her success was due to her genius, which was a purely personal one, unique, inalienable, inimitable: the sum total of a divine gift, an active mind, a perfect body, and superb craftsmanship.   A. C.

PÁVLOVO, city in Gorky Oblast, RSFSR, on Oka River; pop. 46,500 (1959). R.R. station. Old center of iron and steel handicraft; automobile, metalworking and food ind.

PAVLÓVSKY, Nikoláy Nikoláyevich (1884–1937), hydraulic engineer. Fellow, Ac. of S., USSR (1932). Graduate (1912), professor (1919), St. Petersburg Institute of Railroad Engineering, the Institute of Forestry, and Petrograd Polytechnic Institute (1921). Research concerned hydraulic engineering projects at various research institutes; new principles of designing hydrotechnical structures; a theory of pressure and pressure-less motion of ground water and a method of electro-hydrodynamic analogies (for seepage calculation). Participated in the design and building of several large power plants and the Moscow subway.

PAVLÓVSKY, Yevgény Nikanórovich (1884–), zoologist. Fellow, Ac. of S. (1939); Ac. of Medical S., USSR (1944); honorary member, Ac. of S., Tadzhik SSR (1951). Lt. General, Medical Corps. Honored Scientist, RSFSR (1935) and Tadzhik SSR (1943). President, Soviet Geographical Society (1952). Graduate (1908), professor (1921–), Military Medical Academy; director, Zoological Institute (1942); Department of Parasitology and Medical Zoology at the Institute of Epidemiology and Microbiology (1946).

PÁVLOVSKY-POSÁD, city in Moscow Oblast, RSFSR, on the Klyazma River; pop. 55,000 (1959). R.R. station; old center of textile ind. (cotton, silk, wool); known in 18th century.

"PEACEFUL COEXISTENCE": *see* Foreign Policy.

PEASANT BANK. The chief agency for the sale of land to the peasants, the State Peasant Bank, was founded in 1882. It financed purchases of land by peasants, granting loans on part of the cost. In 1895 the bank was permitted to purchase land on its own account. By laws of Nov. 3, 1905 and Nov. 15, 1906, loans to the full amount of the land bought were granted and the rate, including amortization over a period of fifty-five years, was reduced to 4.5 percent, which was below that charged by other credit institutions. The aggregate acreage sold to the peasants through the bank increased from 2.4 mill. desiatines in 1883–1895 to 5.3 mill. in 1896–1905 and to 8.5 mill. in 1906–13. Between 1905 and the end of 1914 the area of peasant holdings in forty-seven provinces increased by 9.6 mill. desiatines.

The lending policies of the PB reflected the changing attitude of the government toward communal tenure. From 1883 to 1894, 98.7 per cent of the loans went to village communes and peasant associations, whereas in 1912, 82.9 per cent went to individual owners, the ratio of individual borrowers gradually increasing from 1906.

The expansion of peasant acreage through land purchases was one way to deal with the problem of the shortage of land.

The PB was abolished after the advent of the Soviets.

PEASANTS. It is believed that in the R. principalities of the 11th and 12th centuries the free P comprised a majority of the population. They enjoyed self-administration, elected their elders, divided their taxes and services. Their chief pursuits were hunting, beekeeping, and agriculture in which they engaged either on the land they owned or as tenant farmers, on the estates of the princes and other large owners.

At the bottom of the social pyramid of that time were the slaves or *kholopy*. This unhappy status was the normal fate of prisoners of war, but it could also be acquired by birth, bankruptcy, or agreement. The *Russian Truth*, the only R. legal code of the 11th and 12th centuries, shows particular interest in that class, suggesting that it was numerous.

In the 13th to 15th centuries four causes slowly developed leading toward a gradual enslavement of the free peasantry: the growth of the landholding by the princes, the church, and the boyars; taxation privileges conferred on large estate owners; restrictions limiting the tenant's right to relinquish his tenancy; and indebtedness of the P.

In the 12th to 15th centuries when the acquisition of estates progressed, the majority of the free farming population was already working on land owned by the princes, the church, or other large landowners. The spreading of the estate system tended to reduce the number of small farmers. Moreover, many small holders were seeking the protection of landowners, partly because of taxation privileges conferred upon large estates by the princes, and partly because of the feeling of insecurity generated by Mongol rule. Tenancy had its disadvantages since the tenant, besides his obligation to pay taxes, had to give part of his produce to his lord. But as a free man, he enjoyed the unrestricted right to give up his tenancy.

P living on land owned by princes enjoyed greater freedom in self-administration than those living on privately owned estates. Other P lived on the land owned by the state. They were known as state P.

The object of the first legal restrictions in the landlord-tenant relationship was to limit the opportunity of the free tenant to exercise his right to leave. The codes of 1497 and 1550 forbade tenants to relinquish their tenancy except during the two weeks preceding and following St. George's Day (Nov. 26) and subject to the fulfillment of certain conditions.

One of the powerful causes working against the development of a free peasantry was the burden of indebtedness. The tenant, who paid taxes as well as rent to his landlord for use of land and farm buildings, often obtained subsidies from the latter at a high rate of interest. As a free man the tenant could leave, provided he had repaid his entire debt. As this was usually impossible, the right to relinquish tenancy gradually became inoperative.

Cadastral surveys carried out in the 16th century registered tenants as residing on estates and militated against their freedom of movement. This and the reshuffling of landlords on a gigantic scale by Ivan the Terrible, as well as the conversion of large tracts of newly acquired land into *pomestie*, i.e. estates held in service tenure, contributed to the acceleration of the enslavement process. The burdens of the peasantry increased and forced many of them to flee beyond Russia's eastern and southern borders.

To safeguard the landlords against the flight of their tenants it became customary in the 17th century to exact from the tenants a written undertaking—*krestyanskaya krepost*—stating that they would continue to live on the allotments assigned to them until their death. The extreme mobility of the farming population led to a series of measures enacted in the 16th and the early 17th century which provided for the forcible return of tenants who had left their tenancy "unlawfully."

By the middle of the 17th century the once free tenant-farmers were attached to their land allotments as well as to the person of their lord. The once clear line between the P and the *kholopy* (slaves) tended to disappear until the decree of Peter the Great of Jan. 19, 1723 finally wiped it out by making the entire peasant population subject to the poll, or capitation, tax.

In the 18th century there were four groups of P: serfs or P in possession of the nobility; state P; P living on land owned by the Crown; and "possessionary" P. There were some basic differences in the legal status of these groups.

The serfs or P in possession of the nobility could be sold with the land or apart from it. The noble landowner paid their poll tax and provided them with land allotments for which they performed services under either the *barshchina* (q.v.) or the *obrok* (q.v.) system. In the 18th century, according to reliable estimates, in Great Russia 44 per cent of the serfs lived under the *obrok* system and 56 per cent under the *barshchina* system. Serfdom was a hereditary status. It could be terminated by emancipation voluntarily granted by the owners or by deportation to Siberia for criminal offenses under the terms of a decree of 1760. A decree of 1737 provided that the serfs could not acquire land or business enterprises except in the name of their lord. In spite of these restrictions some P owned estates and industrial enterprises, which, however, were registered in the names of their masters.

State P as well as P settled on the estates of the Crown paid taxes through their village administration. They could not be separated from the land and enjoyed certain rights of self-government. Their obligations consisted of the poll tax and the *obrok*.

"Possessionary" P were permanently attached to industrial enterprises. Their conditions of employment were regulated by the state and they could not be sold separately from the enterprise.

No significant change in the position of the peasantry occurred in the first half of the 19th century. Not all the landed proprietors, however, were blind to the realities of the peasant situation and the dangers it presented. In 1833 the breaking up of peasant families through sales, and sales of serfs without land at public auctions were prohibited. A law of April 2, 1842, on the "obligated" P permitted the noble landowners to enter with their serfs into voluntary agreements transferring to the serfs' use land allotments in return for suitable compensation. By 1855 the number of serfs emancipated under this law was merely 24,000.

The rural population (both sexes), which is roughly identical with the peasant population, increased from 12.7 mill. or 97.7 per cent of the total population in 1722, to 54.7 mill. or 96.4 per cent in 1796; to 69.8 mill. or 94.3 per cent, in 1859; and to 112.7 mill. or 87.4 per cent, in 1897. In 1859, on the eve of the emancipation, the number of serfs and of state P (males only) was, respectively, 10.7 mill. and 12.8 mill.

Stagnation in agriculture, impoverishment of the landed nobility, peasant uprisings, and Russia's defeat in the Crimean War paved the way for the emancipation of 1861. Beginning in 1856 various committees were engaged in making plans for the abolition of serfdom. The emancipation statutes were proclaimed on Feb. 19, 1861. The emancipation was to be put into

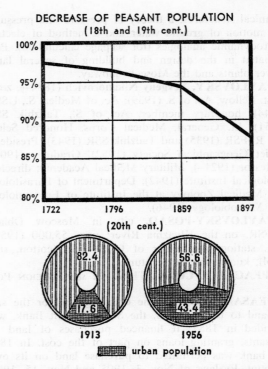

DECREASE OF PEASANT POPULATION
(18th and 19th cent.)

(20th cent.)

1913   1956

▓ urban population

effect gradually in three stages. During the first stage the serfs received their personal liberty, and "inventories" —documents stating the rights and obligations of the liberated bondsmen—were prepared. The second stage was to begin on Feb. 19, 1863. During this stage the P were "temporarily obligated" to the noblemen and were to continue the annual payments and the performance of services determined by the inventories. The final stage followed with redemption payments for the land allotted to the P. The legislation of 1861 retained the village commune as the basic unit of peasant organization. It was jointly responsible, as before, for taxes and other obligations of its members.

In the post-emancipation period outbursts of agrarian unrest were due to a variety of causes: smallness of the allotments and the growth of the peasant population, arrears on account of tax and redemption payments which were excessively high, impoverishment of the landed nobility, recurrent failures of crops, and the low yield of land. An early measure to remedy this situation was the repeal of the poll tax as of Jan. 1, 1887. To compensate the treasury for the loss of revenue the excise on spirits was raised and redemption payments were extended to the former state P. But by a manifesto of Nov. 3, 1905, all redemption payments were canceled.

The land reform initiated by P. A. Stolypin was inaugurated on Nov. 9, 1906. It was a complex piece of legislation with different rules for the village communes holding land in repartitional tenure and in hereditary household tenure. Every householder in the commune with repartitional tenure (about three-quarters of the total number) was entitled to claim his share of arable land as his individual property, a claim the commune was bound to grant. The communes with hereditary household tenure were declared to have passed to the regime of individual ownership without even the formality of consulting the wishes of their members. A law of 1911 permitted the partition among the householders of pastures and grazing land which, by earlier legislation, were left under communal control. Another major aspect of the reform was the abolition of the ancient institution of joint family ownership. The household elder was recognized as the sole owner of the allotment land of the household. Thus the P became the owners of the land on which they had worked for generations.

Abolition of communal tenure was accompanied by enclosures, that is, the consolidation of scattered strips of land into compact holdings. Between 1907 and 1913 almost 5 million P applied for consolidation of their holdings, but by the end of 1915, when the work of the land organization slowed down because of the war, only 2.4 million projects were completed. The two types of farms favored by the government were the *khutor* and the *otrub*. The *khutor* was the farm with the farmhouse adjoining the fields; the *otrub*, a system where the farmhouse remained in the village, the cultivable land being consolidated into one or two plots of arable land and pastures.

Russian agrarian policy after 1906 comprised also measures for internal colonization and increase of the area of peasant landholdings. The chief agency for the sale of land to the P was the State Peasant Bank (q.v.) founded in 1882.

During World War I the economic position of the peasantry rapidly deteriorated. The P also bore the main burden of the huge war losses. Their long-suppressed desire to divide among themselves the estates of the large owners, skillfully exploited by Lenin, was a major factor in the triumph of the Bolshevik Revolution. (*See also* AGRARIAN REFORMS, AGRICULTURE, EMANCIPATION OF THE SERFS.)

BIBLIOGRAPHY: M. T. Florinsky, *Russia: A History and an Interpretation,* 2 vols., New York, 1953; P. L. Lyashchenko, *History of the National Economy of Russia to the 1917 Revolution,* New York, 1949; G. T. Robinson, *Rural Russia Under the Old Regime,* New York, 1932; A. N. Antsiferov, *et al., Russian Agriculture During the War,* New Haven, 1930.   H. P.

PECHENEGS: *see* HISTORY.

PECHÓRA RIVER, originates in the W. slopes of the N. Urals and empties in the Barents Sea; length 1,120 mi. Tributaries: Usa, Izhma. Coal deposits in its basin around Vorkuta and oil in the Ukhta coal basin.

PEDAGOGICAL INSTITUTE: *see* TEACHERS' TRAINING.

PÉGOV, Nikoláy Mikháylovich (1905–), party and government official. He was factory worker in Moscow, studied at the Molotov Industrial Academy, and became director of various plants in Gorky, Moscow, and Uzbekistan; in 1938 he was active as a party official in the Far E. provinces. He was elected to the Central Committee, CPSU in 1939, 1952, and 1956; since 1947 he has held several important positions in the central party apparatus; appointed secretary of the Central Committee, CPSU, in 1952; was elected to the Presidium, USSR Supreme Soviet in 1953; elected a member of the Council of the Union, USSR Supreme Soviet, in 1954, but was relieved of that post in 1956 and appointed ambassador to Iran.

PEIPUS LAKE: *see* CHUDSKOYE LAKE.

PÉNZA, city, adm. center of Penza Oblast, RSFSR, on left bank of the navigable Sura River; on Tula–Kuybyshev R.R..; pop. 160,000 (1939), 255,000 (1959). Has many schools and ind. plants; bicycle, watch, and other factories, light ind., lumbering, food and paper plants. Founded 1666.

PÉNZA OBLAST, RSFSR; situated W. of Volga Hills; area 16,675 sq. mi.; pop. 1,510,000 (1959): Russians, Mordvinians, Tatars. Cities: Penza (adm. center), Kamenka, Kuznetsk, Sursk, Nikolsk. Drained by Sura and Moksha rivers and their affluents; the left-bank section of the Sura has treeless black soils, right bank is heavily forested (oak, linden, maple), with podsolic soil; temperate continental climate. Mineral resources: peat, clays, gravel, phosphorites. Extensive agr.: rye, wheat, oats, corn, potatoes, hemp, sunflowers, sugar beets, hog raising, horse breeding; flour milling, distilling, food processing, tanning, sawmilling, glassworking, machine mfg. Has well-developed R.R. and highway network. Est. 1939.

PEOPLES' FRIENDSHIP UNIVERSITY, established in Moscow solely for students from underdeveloped countries. In 1960, the first year of its existence, there was an enrollment of 500 students. Soviet authorities forecast an eventual student body of three to four thousand.

PEOPLE'S SOCIALIST PARTY, founded 1906. Its leaders included N. F. Annensky, V. A. Myakotin, and A. V. Peshekhonov, grouped around the populist review *Russkoye Bogatstvo* (Russian Wealth). At first they formed part of the Socialist Revolutionary party. But their opposition to terrorism prompted a break after the first Socialist Revolutionary congress in 1906. The party's program called for general democratic reforms, regional autonomy, separation of church and state, an eight-hour working day and the nationalization of land. While the party did not enjoy wide popular influence, it attracted membership from the intelligentsia active in the zemstvos and the radical press. Sixteen People's Socialists sat in the second Duma, forming part of the Labor (*Trudoviki*) group. After the February revolution (1917), several members of the PS participated in the Provisional Government, including Peshekhonov who served as minister of supply.

"PEREDVIZHNIKI": *see* PAINTING.

PEREKÓP ISTHMUS (5 to 14 mi. wide, 18 mi. long) connecting the Crimea with the Russian mainland. Numerous salt lakes (Perekop Lakes). Scene of fighting during the civil war (1920) and World War II.

PERESLAVL LAKE: *see* PLESHCHEYEVO.

PERESLÁVL-ZALÉSSKY, town in Yaroslavl Oblast, RSFSR, on Pleshcheyevo Lake; pop. 22,200 (1956). Textile, food, and other ind. Fine examples of 12th-14th century architecture. Founded 1152 by Yury Dolgoruky.

PERESVÉTOV, Iván Semyónovich, 16th-century essayist and writer. He is the author of two petitions addressed to Ivan IV and of political pamphlets, such as *Story of the Turkish Tsar Mahmet, Story of the Polotsk Voyvod Pyotr.* He criticized the arbitrary rule

of the boyars and was a partisan of a centralized absolute monarchist power supported by the gentry.

PEREYÁSLAV-KHMELNÍTSKY (f. Pereyaslav),
town in Kiev Oblast, N. Ukrainian SSR, on Trubezh
River (left tributary of the Dnieper); pop. 9,000 (1956).
Founded 922 by Prince Vladimir, it was an important
strategic point during Cossack Wars 1648–1712, headquarters of Bogdan Khmelnitsky; here the Pereyaslav
Rada decided to unite Ukraine with Russia.

PEREYÁSLAV RADA (1654), national council of
the Ukrainian people, summoned at Pereyaslav on Jan.
8, 1654, to decide upon the union with Russia. The
delegates representing the Cossacks, townsmen, and
other groups of the population heard a plea by Hetman
Bogdan Khmelnitsky, who described the perilous situation of the country, exposed to aggression by its powerful neighbors—Turkey and the Crimean Khanate in the
S., Poland in the W.—and asked for union with Muscovy. The Russian envoy, V. V. Buturlin, then read a
message of consent from Tsar Alexis. The Ukraine was
incorporated in the Muscovite state, but retained her
autonomous institutions. They were later destroyed by
the Russians.

PERM (f. Molotov), city, adm. center of Perm Oblast, RSFSR, on left bank of Kama River; pop. 306,000
(1939), 629,000 (1959). One of the leading ind. centers
of the Urals and the USSR. Ind.: machine building
(engines, boats, mining and transportation equipment),
chemical, timber sawing, leather, matches. Hydroelectric power plant on Kama River contributed to rapid
ind. development. University, colleges, libraries, museums, theaters. Founded 1568; copper-smelting plant
established in early 18th century; named Perm in 1781.

PERM OBLAST (f. Molotov Oblast), RSFSR, in N.
foothills of the Urals and in Kama River basin; includes
Komi-Permyak National Okrug; area 62,750 sq. mi.;
pop. 2,993,000 (1959): Russians, Tatars, Komi-Perm-
yaks. Cities: Perm (adm. center), Krasnokamsk, Kizel,
Verkhne-Chusovskiye Gorodki, Berezniki, Solikamsk,
Chusovoy, and others. Drained by the Kama and its
affluents; has heavily forested (pine) lowland with hills
toward the E.; podsolic soils; cool humid climate. Rich
mineral resources: salt, potash (leading in USSR),
chromites, lignite, bituminous coal, oil, gold, iron, gypsum, limestone, peat; unexploited hematite, magnetite,
titanium, vanadium deposits (N. Urals). A major mining region, includes the Solikamsk potash district, the
Kizel coal basin; its ind. are: Krasnokamsk oil cracking,
steel, pig-iron production, lumbering, chemicals (potash-
phosphorous fertilizers, aniline dyes), pulp mfg. (Krasnokamsk, Krasnovishersk), machine mfg., food processing.
Large thermal power plants; the Kama Hydroelectric
Plant (N. of Perm) supplies Perm and Sverdlovsk oblasts with electricity. Agr. largely based on lumbering,
dairy farming (S.), flax, orchards, rye, oats, wheat, clover (Kungur), livestock; hunting in tayga (N.). Has
R.R.s and waterways. Est. 1938.

PERMANENT REVOLUTION: *see* CPSU, TROT-
SKYISM.

PERNÓV: *see* PYARNU.

PERÓV, Vasíly Grigóryevich (1833–1882), painter
of the naturalistic school. Studied at the School of

Painting, Sculpture, and Architecture,
Moscow. His most popular works are
satirical genre paintings which provide
a revealing comment on the various
classes of contemporary Russia. His
best and most characteristic work was
done in the late 1860's, after his return
from abroad (*Supper in a Convent,
Troyka, Arrival of a Governess in a
Merchant House, Scene at the Railroad, Tavern at the
Tollgate*). In the 1870's P painted chiefly non-contro-
versial (*Bird-Catcher, Fisherman, Resting Hunter*) and
historical subjects. His portraits (Dostoyevsky, Anton
and Nicholas Rubinstein) are noted for likeness and
restrained manner of painting.

PERÓVO, city in Moscow Oblast, RSFSR; pop.
63,000 (1939), 143,000 (1959). R.R. station in suburban
Moscow; machine-mfg. ind.

PEROVSK: *see* KZYL-ORDA.

PERÓVSKAYA, Sófia Lvóvna (1853–1881), R. revolutionary, leader of the organization
"People's Will." She participated in
plotting the assassination of Alexander
II on March 1, 1881 and was executed
in April of that year.

PERVOMÁYSKY, Leoníd (Gurévich, Ilyá Shlyómovich) (1908–),
Ukrainian poet and dramatist, born in
Krasnodar, Kharkov Oblast, son of a
bookbinder. P joined the Komsomol in 1924. His first
small book of poems appeared in 1925. In 1929 he published a volume of poems, *Sour Apples,* and a play
Young Communist. Collections of his verses issued
before the war include *Salute to the Mountain,* about
travels in Pamir (1932), *New Lyrics,* and others. Since
the war he wrote a novel in verse, *Brother's Youth*
(1947), the poems *On Steep Banks* and *My Father,*
and a book of verse, *Happiness for All.* Stalin prize
(1946).

PERVOURÁLSK, city in Sverdlovsk Oblast, RSFSR,
on Chusovaya River; pop. 44,000 (1939), 90,000 (1959).
R.R. station; major pipe-rolling ind.

PERVÚKHIN, Mikhaíl Geórgievich (1904–), party
and government official, ambassador to East Germany;

born in Chelyabinsk Oblast. He joined
Komsomol and the CP in 1919; studied
at the Moscow Institute of National
Economy, graduated from its faculty
of electrical industry in 1929; during
the 1930's he was engineer and administrator at various power plants; in
1938 he was named deputy, later first
deputy commissar of heavy industry;
in 1939 he was appointed people's commissar of electric
power plants and electrical industry; in 1946 named
minister of chemical industry; in 1950 became deputy
chairman, USSR Council of Ministers; Presidium member of the Central Committee after the 19th and 20th
Party Congresses. In 1955 he was appointed first deputy
chairman, USSR Council of Ministers; in 1956 named
chairman, USSR State Economic Commission; for participation in the "anti-party" group he was demoted in

1957 to minister of medium machine construction; appointed ambassador to E. Germany in 1958.

PESHKÓV, Alekséy Maksímovich: *see* GORKY, M.

PÉSTEL, Pável Ivánovich (1793–1826), a leader of the Decembrists. In 1811 graduated from an aristocratic  school, the "Corps of Pages." Participated in the Franco-Russian war of 1812. One of the founders of the secret Southern Society, and author of the *Russian Truth*, the revolutionary program of the Southern Society. P was a fervent partisan of the overthrow of the autocracy, liquidation of serfdom, and the establishment of a republic. Worked out a plan wherein the land was to be confiscated from the nobility and turned over to the peasants. P was arrested on the eve of the Decembrist uprising and was hanged, on July 13, 1826.

PETER I THE GREAT (Pyotr Alekséyevich) (1672–1725), tsar, fourteenth child of Tsar Alexis and first-born of his father's second wife, Nathalie Naryshkin. Known as the Tsar-Reformer, P was largely a self-made man. Because of the tangled dynastic situation at his father's death, when P was three, he received scarcely 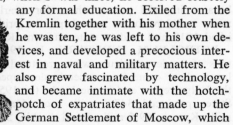 any formal education. Exiled from the Kremlin together with his mother when he was ten, he was left to his own devices, and developed a precocious interest in naval and military matters. He also grew fascinated by technology, and became intimate with the hotch-potch of expatriates that made up the German Settlement of Moscow, which for P was a model of W. Europe. Throughout his life, indeed, P copied the look and manner of the Dutch seaman he first met there. Boundlessly energetic, P wrote and rewrote in his own hand nearly all legislative acts, which rapidly increased in number, as well as most of the diplomatic communications signed by his ministers. He became tsar in 1682 jointly with his half-brother Ivan V, with his half-sister Sophie as regent, but in 1689 seized the throne for himself.

After a successful impromptu campaign in Turkey, P decided in 1697 to see W. Europe for himself, ostensibly in order to launch a Christian alliance against Turkey and the Khan of Crimea. Though this aim was never achieved, P's obsession with western technology was confirmed, and many hundreds of technicians were imported into Russia. P's first trip to W. Europe, on which his great physical bulk, bizarre appearance, repellent untidiness, and barbaric coarseness left a strange impression everywhere, was interrupted in 1698 by a revolt of the *streltsy*, a semimilitary formation of 17th-century Moscow that lived in special settlements and plied various trades. Though the revolt did not amount to much, the frightful vengeance taken by P was directed at the significance of the *streltsy* as a symbol of the Old Russia he was determined to transform. P's variegated reforms began with a campaign against the way Russians looked and dressed: in April 1698 he clipped the beards and moustaches of court notables; beards were then allowed, but taxed, by a ukase of Sept. 1698. Ancient Muscovite costume was also forcibly replaced by foreign models.

From 1700 on P was preoccupied by his war against Sweden, which lasted 21 years; after varying fortunes P won the pick of the Baltic Provinces, which enabled him to build St. Petersburg and a navy. In 1721 he assumed the title of emperor. War took up all but the last year of P's 35-year reign; there were only 13 months of peace during the remainder. It was war, in fact, that was directly responsible for P's multiplicity of reforms, which were aimed primarily at building up an efficient armed force. But the absence of any central idea, the empirical, *ad hoc* genesis of most of these reforms, in the sphere of administration, the promotion of industry and education, and social development, very largely canceled themselves out. Perhaps his most lasting reforms were the institution of the "Table of Ranks," which, by bureaucratizing the source of *anoblissement*, shackled the aristocracy to the service of the state, and lasted until the revolution of 1917; and also the police regime that has never vanished from Russia since.

P's pleasures, taken in a motley company, revolved around hard drinking mingled with debauchery. P contributed an elaborate and imaginative ritual, with a zeal quite unlike his capriciousness in other matters. When about 28 he instituted the "Most Drunken Assembly of Fools and Jesters," an obscene travesty of the Roman Catholic and Greek Orthodox Churches, which P kept up with unflagging concentration all his life, accompanied by enforced public participation. P's family life was highly informal. After an abortive early marriage and countless liaisons, he formed an attachment to an illiterate Lithuanian peasant girl, who eventually became Tsarina Catherine I. In 1718 he carried out the execution of Tsarevich Alexis, P's son by his first wife whom the tsar did not like and whom he suspected of opposing the reforms.

Though P's "superhuman" role is generally assented to by historians, as well as by R. patriotic sentiment, the verdict of the masses who bore the extravagant sacrifices of his various enterprises was different. It may be said that P helped promote the process, begun long before him, of assimilating European technique, and did it with unprecedented ferocity though without corresponding effectiveness.

BIBLIOGRAPHY: H. Schuyler, *Peter the Great*, New York, 1884; C. de Grunwald, *Peter the Great*, London, 1956; Ian Grey, *Peter the Great*, Philadelphia, 1960.

PETER I BAY, inlet of the Sea of Japan at S. end of Maritime Kray. Its two arms in the N. are Amur Bay and Ussuri Bay flanking Muravyov-Amursky Peninsula on which Vladivostok is situated.

PETER I ISLAND, off Antarctica in Bellingshausen Sea N.E. of Thurston Peninsula; area 100 sq. mi., elevation 4,000 ft. Always covered by ice and snow. Discovered in 1821 by a Russian team under Faddey F. Bellingshausen.

PETER I RIDGE, one of the highest in the Pamirs, extending for 125 mi. along the left bank of the Surkhab River. Height increases in eastward direction reaching 22,250 ft. (Moscow Peak). The Stalin Peak (24,584 ft.) lies between Peter I Ridge and Academy of Sciences Ridge. Has many large glaciers.

PETER II (Pyotr Alekséyevich) (1715–1730), Russian Emperor, 1727–30; grandson of Peter I. In reality, the Secret Supreme Council ruled for him.

PETER III (Pyotr Fyódorovich) (1728–1762), Russian Emperor, 1761–62, son of the Duke of Holstein-Gottorp and Anna, daughter of Peter I. His neglect of R. affairs, his boundless admiration for Prussia and his hostile atttitude toward the Russian Guard led to the *coup d'état* of 1762 and the accession of his wife Catherine II to the throne. He was assassinated with Catherine's consent.

PETIPÁ, Marius (1822–1910), French-born dancer and choreographer who came to the St. Petersburg Imperial Mariinsky Theater as premier danseur in 1847, was appointed choreographer-in-chief in 1862 and remained active until 1903. During his half-century at the Mariinsky he produced more than fifty ballets, establishing the style, form, and structure of what is called classic ballet. In all his work he always considered that choreography proper took precedence over all other artistic expressions, such as music, libretto, and decor which, with choreography, are part of the art of ballet. He elevated to new prominence the ballerina, who became the focal point of the whole ballet. Under his artistic direction the R. ballet produced its greatest dancers, among them Kshessinska, Preobrazhenska, Pavlova, Gerdt, Legat, Fokine, and many others. Considered one of the greatest choreographers of all time, P added to his choreographic talent exhaustive research and detailed preparations for every ballet he staged. Among his greatest ballets are *The Sleeping Beauty, Raymonda, Giselle, Coppelia, Le Corsaire, La Sylphide, Swan Lake* (Acts 1 and 3), *La Bayadère, The Humpbacked Horse.* The great R. choreographers of our time, Fokine, Massine, Balanchine, Lavrovsky, were brought up on P's choreography.   A. C.

PETLYÚRA, Símon Vasílyevich (1877–1926), Ukrainian nationalist leader. Formerly a socialist, P became the secretary of war, and finally, the chief of the Ukrainian Central Rada in 1917–18. Defeated by the Bolsheviks, he concluded an agreement with Poland's Marshal Pilsudski and took part in the Polish-Soviet war of 1920. After the Polish-Russian Treaty of Riga, by which the Ukraine was left under the domination of the Soviets, he emigrated to France. In 1926 he was fatally shot in Paris by Shalom Schwarzbard, who acted in retaliation for the pogroms against the Jews perpetrated by P's army.

PETRASHÉVSKY CIRCLE, the name given to a group of (mostly young) radical writers and thinkers who met, from 1845 to 1848, to discuss philosophical and political issues in the home of the nobleman M. Butashevich-Petrashevsky in St. Petersburg. Petrashevsky, a publicist and convinced disciple of Fourier and Saint-Simon, tended to center discussions of his own favorite ideas and projects. But the members of his circle, which included Belinsky until his death, Dostoyevsky, the later Slavophile Danilevsky, the poet A. Maykov and his brother the critic V. Maykov, and many others, were able to cover all the pressing topics of the day. When the European revolutions of 1848 frightened Nicholas I into launching a campaign of police terror against "subversive elements," most of the PC were arrested and tried. Some, notably Dostoyevsky, were condemned to death and made to prepare for execution before being reprieved and sent for years of penal servitude in Siberia. The innocence of the group, the harshness of the treatment meted to the arrested men, and the accounts thereof by Dostoyevsky have made the PC a symbol of liberal aspiration brutally crushed by police tyranny.

PETRODVORÉTS (f. Petergof or Peterhof), town on S. shore of Kronstadt Bay, N.W. Leningrad Oblast, RSFSR; subordinated to the Leningrad Municipal Council; pop. 40,000 (1958). Developed around palace built by Peter I in 1711 and rebuilt 1746 (by Rastrelli), has other palaces, gardens, fountains. Was partly destroyed during World War II but has been restored.

PETROGRÁD: *see* LENINGRAD.

PETROKRÉPOST (f. Shlüsselburg), town in Leningrad Oblast, RSFSR, on exit of Neva River at S.W. corner of Lake Ladoga; pop. 6,400 (1956). A Novgorodian fortress founded 1323 under the name ot Oreshek, was renamed Schlüsselburg in 1702. It later became imperial prison where for nearly 200 years many noted prisoners were kept; the prison was abolished 1917 and made a state museum. Renamed 1944.

PETROLEUM INDUSTRY. In 1960, 148 mill. tons of crude petroleum were produced, of which the larger share came from recently developed deposits in the Volga region and in the Urals. (In 1959 the United States produced 347.9 mill. tons; Venezuela, 147.9 mill.; Kuwait, 69.5 mill.; Saudi Arabia, 54.2 mill.; Iran 45.0 mill.)

In the prerevolutionary period the production of petroleum centered in the Baku area and in the region near Grozny, and was developed largely by W. European enterprise. It was also carried on, on a small scale, in the Kuban, Taman, Fergana, and Emba regions. For a short time (in 1901) the annual rate of production of petroleum in Russia exceeded that of any other country (11.6 mill. tons).

Following partial destruction during the civil war, there was some modernization of existing production facilities in the late 1920's. As a result of new construction and of further modernization during the 1930's the 1913 rate of petroleum production was exceeded threefold in 1940. During this period existing refineries at Baku and at Grozny were considerably expanded, and new ones were established on the Black Sea shore of the Caucasus, in the Ukraine, in Moscow, in Saratov, in Bashkiria, and in the Far East.

Subsequently, in accordance with a decision adopted by the government in 1939 to create a new center of petroleum production in the region between the Volga and the Urals, additional facilities were established in the Bashkir Autonomous Republic and in the Kuybyshev, Orenburg, and Perm oblasts. New and very considerable deposits in this general area were found in 1943–48, and it is predominantly there that the postwar development of the petroleum industry has occurred (*Second Baku*).

The major technological innovations of the postwar period have included the extensive use of turbodrills in drilling operations, and the production of petroleum under pressure. The new refineries include those in Bashkiria, in the Kuybyshev, Irkutsk, Omsk, Gorky, Stalingrad, and Perm oblasts, and in Uzbekistan. In the early 1960's additional refining facilities were being established in the Moscow and Krasnoyarsk regions, and in Kazakhstan and Byelorussia. The transportation of petroleum through pipelines has been developed to a considerable extent. In 1957, the annual rate of petroleum production of 98.3 mill. tons represented 11.2% of the world's petroleum production.

The objectives of the Seven Year Plan (1959–65) provide for a doubling of the petroleum output by 1965 (to 230–240 mill. tons). As a result it is expected that the share of petroleum and natural gas in the total consumption of energy will increase from 31% in 1959 to 51%, while that of coal will be reduced from 60% to 43%. A further doubling of petroleum production is envisaged for the period 1965–72. (*See also* OIL)

OIL OUTPUT IN THE USSR
(mill. tons)

Year	Volga Region and Urals	Total
1913	—	9.2
1922	—	4.7
1927	—	10.3
1932	.01	21.4
1937	1.0	28.5
1940	1.8	31.1
1946	3.9	21.7
1950	11.0	37.9
1955	41.2	70.8
1956	52.6	83.8
1957	64.8	98.3
1958	76.6	113.2
1959	—	129.5
1960	—	148.0
1965 (pl.)	—	230–240

P. I. M.

PETROPÁVLOVSK, city, adm. center of North-Kazakhstan Oblast, Kazakh SSR, on Ishim River and Trans-Siberian R.R.; pop. 131,000 (1959). Agr. center; has flour mills, food-processing ind.; trades in corn, cattle and cattle products, wool, cotton, furs, tea. Founded 1752.

PETROPÁVLOVSK: *see* SEVEROURALSK.

PETROPÁVLOVSK-KAMCHÁTSKY, city, adm. center of Kamchatka Oblast, RSFSR, on Avacha Gulf of the Pacific Ocean, has a fine wind-sheltered harbor (icebound 3 months); pop. 35,000 (1939), 86,000 (1959). Shipyard, fishing ind., sawmills, fish- and crab-canning plants. Founded 1740; there was an abortive attempt of Anglo-French troops at seizing it 1854; monuments to V. Bering, J. F. Laperouse and to the 1854 defense of the town.

PETRÓV, Borís Nikoláyevich (1913–), electrical engineer. Fellow, Ac. of S., USSR 1960). Graduated from the Moscow Institute of Power Engineering. Associated with the Institute of Automation and Telemechanics (1939). Lecturer (1944) and professor (1948), Moscow Institute of Aviation. His research concerns primarily problems of automatic control, and the approximate integration of differential equations.

PETRÓV, Geórgy Ivánovich (1912–), mechanical engineer and physicist. Fellow, Ac. of S., USSR (1958).

A graduate of Moscow University (1945), he has been associated with various scientific research institutes. P's research on hydro-aeromechanics and gas dynamics concerns the stability of vortical layers, propagation of vibrations in viscous fluid, and disintegration of laminar flow. He proved the convergence of the Galyorkin method with a wide variety of equations, particularly those of vibrations in viscous fluid.

PETRÓV, Geórgy Nikoláyeivch (1899–), electrical engineer. Honored Scientist and Technologist, RSFSR (1942). Graduate, Moscow School of Technology (1924); professor, Moscow Institute of Power Engineering (1933). Research concerns the design and building of electrical equipment; participated in the development of powerful rectifying transformers and transformers with a new current balancing system. Stalin prizes (1942, 1952).

PETRÓV, Ósip Afanásyevich (1806–1878), eminent basso and founder of the Russian vocal school. The range and volume of his voice brought him fame and recognition. He knew Glinka, who greatly influenced the development of his talent. P was one of the first to interpret the leading basso parts in the operas of Glinka, Dargomyzhsky, and Musorgsky.

PETRÓV (Katáyev), **Yevgény Petróvich** (1903–1942), writer, younger brother of Valentin Katayev. He began as a writer in the provinces, then moved to Moscow and became literary editor of the daily *Gudok*. There he met Ilya Ilf and became his lifelong collaborator. Together P and Ilf wrote two popular satirical novels, *Twelve Chairs* (1928) and *The Golden Calf* (1930–31). The hero of both novels, the adventurer Ostap Bender, typifies the unscrupulous profiteer who has adapted himself to the realities of Soviet life. Following a visit to the United States, the two authors wrote *One-Story America* (1936). After the death of Ilf, P continued to write essays. He was killed in the Crimea during the siege of Sevastopol.

PETRÓV-VÓDKIN, Kuzmá Sergéyevich (1878–1939), painter. Studied in Moscow. For many years his work was greatly influenced by impressionism. Wrote several autobiographical books.

PETRÓVSK-PORT: *see* MAKHACHKALA.

PETRÓVSK-ZABAYKÁLSKY (f. Petróvsky Zavód), city in Chita Oblast, RSFSR, on trans-Siberian R.R.; pop. 27,600 (1956). Founded 1789 around a small foundry, it is an ind. center of ferrous metallurgy.

PETRÓVSKY, Grigóry Ivánovich (1878–1958), old Bolshevik; born in Kharkov in a poor artisan family. In 1897, P joined the revolutionary movement and became a Bolshevik. In 1912, he was elected as Yekaterinoslav workers' deputy to the Duma. In this capacity he took part in several conferences with Lenin and in Nov. 1914 was arrested and banished to Siberia. After the October revolution in 1917, P was people's commissar for internal affairs, 1918–19, and later for twenty years the nominal head of the Soviet Ukrainian Republic. He was a member of the party Central Committee, 1921–39, and a deputy member of the Politburo, 1926–39. In 1939, P disappeared from the political scene and became a deputy director of the Museum of Revolution in Moscow. He was rehabilitated after the 20th Party Congress.

PETRÓVSKY, Iván Geórgievich (1901–), mathematician. Fellow, Ac. of S., USSR (1946). Graduate (1927), professor (1933), and rector (1951), Moscow University. Research on differential equations with partial derivatives, algebraic geometry, qualitative theory of differential equations, theory of probability, and other fields. Author of *Ordinary Differential Equations* (1939); *Lectures on the Theory of Integral Equations* (1948); *Lectures on Partial Differential Equations* (1950). Several of his books and papers were translated; e.g. "On the Topology of Real Plane Algebraic Curves," *Annals of Mathematics* (Princeton, 1938). Stalin prizes (1946, 1952).

PETRÓVSKY-ZAVÓD: *see* PETROVSK - ZABAYKAL-SKY.

PETROZAVÓDSK, capital of Karelian ASSR, on N.W. shore of Lake Onega; pop. 70,000 (1939), 135,-000 (1959). Ind. city on Leningrad–Murmansk R.R.; has a university, colleges, scientific institutes, and the Karelian branch of the Ac. of S., USSR. Ind.: machine mfg., sawmills. The settlement developed around foundry and ammunition plant established by Peter I in 1703; became town 1777.

PETRUNKÉVICH, Iván Ilyích (1844–1928), one of the founders of the Union of Liberation and of the Constitutional Democratic party. P, a descendant of landowning nobility, devoted much of his time to work in the zemstvo organizations. In 1905 P was a member of a delegation of zemstvo leaders to the tsar which asked for reforms. A year later he was elected deputy to the first Duma. Because he signed the Vyborg appeal, which urged the people not to pay taxes and to refuse obedience to the government, he was imprisoned. After 1907 P published the periodicals *Rech* (The Speech) and *Sovremenny Mir* (Contemporary Word). He emigrated in 1920.

PHARMACEUTICAL INDUSTRY. The PI, which is a major branch of the chemical industry, produces synthetic medical preparations, antibiotics, and medical preparations from herbs. Only a few pharmaceutical plants were in existence in 1913. In 1920 the All-Union Chemical-Pharmaceutical Scientific Research Institute was established, and subsequently a program directed at the rapid development of the PI was started. A substantial rate of output for most of the basic medical products, however, was attained only in 1940, following the expansion and modernization of existing plants and the construction of important new facilities during the prewar Five Year Plans (1928–40). During World War II the PI production changed considerably in response to the new character of the needs, and additional plants were built in the E. regions (in Novosibirsk, Kemerovo, Anzhero-Sudzhensk, Tyumen, Tomsk, Irbit and elsewhere). The aggregate level of production, however, was insufficient to meet the wartime requirements, and large amounts of pharmaceutical products were imported from the United States, the United Kingdom, and Canada under Lend-Lease and the Mutual Aid Program. After the war the reconstruction and modernization of destroyed facilities were followed by a rapid expansion both in the volume and in the assortment of production. According to official data the increase in the annual output of the PI was approximately tenfold during the period 1940–60, and over 115 new products were introduced between 1946 and 1955, including antibiotics, new types of remedies for heart conditions, and preparations from hormones.   P. I. M.

PHILOSOPHY. Russian philosophy as an intellectual discipline arose in the late 18th century. Its focus was upon questions of ethics, social and political philosophy, and philosophy of history, rather than logic, theory of knowledge, and metaphysics. R. philosophers have been concerned with good and evil in individual and social life, the "meaning of history," the relation of national to universal culture rather than the nature of being and knowledge, or the presuppositions of science. And they have tended to regard theoretical knowledge as, ideally, part and function of the total life-activity of integral human beings. This emphasis upon man in his wholeness was shared by widely varied thinkers—"Slavophiles" and "Westerners," mystics and atheists, Populists and Marxists.

The first R. philosopher was Gregory Skovorodá (1722–94), a Ukrainian by birth, who has been called "the Russian Socrates." A poet and theologian, Skovoroda traveled widely and was at home in many languages. In a series of brilliant "Platonic" dialogues he developed both a critique of pure empiricism and a dualistic metaphysics with a pantheistic coloring. Skovoroda's theory of man, while broadly Christian, anticipated in some respects later psychological and philosophic theories of the unconscious. His writings are shot through with moving poetry and striking philosophic insights, but he was not a systematic philosopher. Skovoroda's resemblance to his lonely contemporary, William Blake, is more than superficial.

The R. secular intelligentsia, during the late 18th century, was much influenced by French rationalism, skepticism, and deism—especially through the works of Voltaire—and by Freemasonry (q.v.), chiefly from German sources. These W. influences followed in the wake of Peter the Great's forced "Europeanization" of R. life and thought. Diderot's visit to the court of Catherine II in 1773–74 offers a concrete symbol of the penetration into Russia of the ideas and attitudes of the French Enlightenment. Many 18th century R. followers of the *philosophes* defended the theory of "natural law" and "natural rights"; however, after 1789 such doctrines became officially suspect as "alien and subversive," and certain university professors were dismissed for defending them. R. theorists of natural law include the learned historian Vasily N. Tatishchev (1686–1750), the first Russian to sketch a utilitarian ethical theory; the anticlerical Prince M. M. Shcherbatov (1733–90, who defended "natural religion"; and the many-sided humanist Aleksandr N. Radishchev (1749–1802), whose *Journey from Petersburg to Moscow* (1790) was to become a model of social criticism for later R. radicals. Its publication—within a year of the outbreak of revolution in France—brought its author a death sentence, later commuted to ten years' exile. In this respect, too, Radishchev set the pattern for subsequent oppositionist thinkers, most of whom spent a portion of their adult lives in St. Petersburg prison cells or in Siberian exile.

The early 19th century was marked by a shift from French to German influence. After an initial enthusiasm for Schelling's aesthetics and nature-philosophy, many R. intellectuals turned to Kant and Fichte. Kant's *Critiques* were forbidden by the censorship as subversive of religion and morals, but they circulated widely in manuscript translations among university and even divinity-school students. Hegel was the dominant influence; his chief impact upon R. thought dates from the late 1830's, but his philosophic presence continued to dominate the Russian intellectual—not merely academic —scene for many years.

The chief R. Schellingians were D. M. Vellansky (1774–1847); D. V. Venevitinov (1805–27), a gifted poet and philosopher who died very young and left few writings; and Prince V. F. Odoyevsky (1804–69). Odoyevsky, who later turned from Schelling's nature-philosophy to the working out of a philosophy of man and history, was one of the first R. thinkers to formulate the idea, and ideal, of "organic wholeness" which was to be a central tenet of the Slavophiles. He was the first Russian to offer a systematic critique of W. culture. The W., he insisted, cannot achieve a full or harmonious development until it finds its own Peter the Great who will open a window upon Russia and infuse Europe with the "fresh and powerful saps of the Slavic East."

The "Slavophiles," who emerged during the 1840's as a dominant force in R. intellectual life, are often represented as politically conservative and religiously Orthodox, and contrasted in these respects with the anticlerical and politically radical (or, at the least, liberal) "Westerners." Such generalizations are undercut by the obvious counterexamples of (1) P. Ya. Chaadayev (ca. 1794–1856), who was—in his early works at any rate—an outspoken critic of Russia and warm admirer of the W., yet a deeply religious and political-conservative thinker, and (2) Mikhail Bakunin (1814–76), an enthusiastic pan-Slavist, who ended as an anarchist, atheist, and revolutionary nihilist.

Chaadayev, who was influenced by Schelling (they met in Germany in 1825) as well as by Kant and Hegel, developed a philosophy of history reminiscent in many respects of St. Augustine's, and a doctrine of man which repudiated "fragmented individualism," asserting the "collective nature of human consciousness." A. S. Khomyakov (1804–60) is best known for his doctrine of *sobornost* ("conciliarity" or "organic togetherness") and his emphasis on the integral individual. He was sharply critical of philosophic rationalism (especially Hegelianism) and he identified it, rather confusingly, with the alleged "cultural rationalism" of Roman Catholicism. Khomyakov's emphasis on "total reason" and the communal nature of the act of knowing was echoed by the other Slavophiles, especially I. V. Kireyevsky (1806–56).

The "Westerners" or "Westernizers" (*zapadniki*) exhibit a passion for Hegelian philosophy, usually following upon a brief infatuation with Schelling and Fichte, and giving way in turn to a more stable union with Feuerbach and the Hegelian Left.

V. G. Belinsky (1811–48), a brilliant and influential literary critic and essayist, reacted strongly (in the early 1840's) against the impersonalism of Hegel's philosophy of history, repudiating the Hegelian doctrine that the individual is only a partial manifestation, a means or instrument for the self-realization of Absolute Spirit. "The fate of the individual person," he wrote, "is more important than the fate of the whole world . . . including Hegel's *Allgemeinheit*." Like A. I. Herzen (1812–70), Belinsky turned toward Utopian socialism as a defense of the individual person. Herzen himself later moved from his early political radicalism toward a moderate reformism. In philosophy of history, he repudiated his early Hegelian rationalism and determinism, stressing the "whirlwind of chances" and the "tousled improvisation" of history. In his later years, disillusioned by W. political developments after 1848, Herzen placed his hope for the future in the R. peasant and village commune. In this, he anticipated a central doctrine of the later "Populists."

M. A. Bakunin, after a brief flirtation with Fichte, became a convinced and dogmatic Hegelian; he was the first to exploit the Hegelian dialectic in a systematic way (in his essay *Reaction in Germany*, 1842) as a theoretical justification of violent revolution. But Bakunin soon repudiated Hegel, turning from theoretical philosophy to political activity, and (in middle life) embracing atheism, materialism, and anarchist socialism. He is associated, along with S. G. Nechayev (1847–82), with the first detailed formulation (in 1869) of "revolutionary Machiavellianism": the doctrine that the "good" end of revolution justifies—even "sanctifies" —any means which may be necessary to its realization.

N. G. Chernyshevsky (1828–89) and N. A. Dobrolyubov (1836–61), both philosophic materialists and atheists, were leaders of the radical Nihilists (q.v.) of the 1860's. (Both, incidentally, were sons of R. Orthodox priests.) Under the influence of Feuerbach, Comte, Fourier, and Mill, Chernyshevsky developed a utilitarian doctrine of "rational egoism" as the foundation of morality. However, he combined it with a "revolutionary Machiavellianism" which, though it would have been distasteful to Mill, was in fact at least as consistent with the "greatest happiness" principle as Mill's own moderate liberalism. Chernyshevsky also made influential contributions to esthetics and literary criticism. Dobrolyubov was a talented literary critic, but not a major theorist. Chernyshevsky's social and political views, especially his emphasis on the R. village commune as a seedbed of socialism, and his doctrine that Russia could avoid the evils of industrial capitalism by moving directly from primitive to advanced socialism, were taken over by the Populists during the 1870's and 1880's.

Certain of Chernyshevsky's views were further developed by Dmitry I. Pisarev (1840–68), who left substantial works in literary criticism and social philosophy at his untimely death (at twenty-eight). However, Pisarev modified Chernyshevsky's utilitarianism by introducing the principle of "economy of intellectual energies." In Russia, he held, where "intellectual capital" was scarce, energy could not be spared for idle luxuries—"art for art's sake," "speculative philosophy," "abstruse science." Indeed, Pisarev anticipated Tolstoy's moralistic-utilitarian critique of art and science: both should be related directly to the "living needs" of men. Poets, he declared, must become "Titans, shaking the mountains of age-old evil"; otherwise they remain mere "insects, burrowing in flower-dust." In his early works, Pisarev laid central stress on the emancipation of the individual from the restraints of mob opinion, superstition, ignorance, and even moral norms and ideals. Along with Lavrov, he gave currency to the expression, "critically-thinking individual."

The Populists, especially P. L. Lavrov (1823–1900) and N. K. Mikhaylovsky (1842–1904), developed further the social and historical views of Belinsky, Herzen and Chernyshevsky—stressing the uniqueness of the village commune, Russia's "special path" to socialism, the debt (and even guilt) of the intellectuals vis-a-vis the common people. Both were critical of the philosophic foundations and historical doctrines of Marxism, as these were being defended during the 1890's by G. V. Plekhanov (1856–1918) and V. I. Lenin (1870–1924). In opposition to the Marxists' "objective method" of studying history and society, they developed a "subjective method." "Observation of social phenomena," Mikhaylovsky held, "neccesarily involves moral evaluation." The Populists stressed the role of individual volition and subjective goals in social development. They insisted on measuring historical progress by ethical criteria, and defended "freedom" and "individuality" as absolute ethical values. But at the same time they accepted sociological relativism, emulated the methods of the natural sciences, and endorsed Comte's positivistic critique of speculative philosophy. Their "semi-positivism" is an inconsistent combination of philosophic positivism and a very unpositivistic ethical idealism. Lavrov regarded the theoretical problem of free will as insoluble, but he insisted that man's "sense of freedom" is real and causally efficacious; man does—and should—set goals for himself "as though" he were free.

Mikhaylovsky criticized specialization and division of labor as destructive of the wholeness of the individual person. He viewed history as moving from an "objectively anthropocentric" stage to an "exocentric" stage (marked by specialization, alienation, and exploitation), and toward a "subjectively anthropocentric" stage, in which human needs, ideals and aspirations will be given a central place.

Among the outstanding religiously-oriented thinkers of the late 19th century we note K. N. Leontyev (1831–91)—often called the "Russian Nietzsche" because of his esthetic "amoralism" and biting critique of egalitarianism and "shopkeeper morality"—and V. V. Rozanov (1856–1919), famed for his theological heresies and his "metaphysics of sex." Both men were brilliant stylists and both strongly influenced Nikolay Berdyayev (1874–1948), the best-known of contemporary R. religious philosophers.

Vladimir S. Solovyov (1853–1900), the most influential of 19th century R. religious philosophers, turned—under the influence of Spinoza, his "first philosophic love"—from an early positivism and atheism toward a metaphysics of "positive total-unity." His system has been described as "the most full-sounding chord in the history of philosophy," and it is indeed a grandiose, if not always successful, attempt at what he called an "organic synthesis of religion, philosophy and science in the interests of the integral life." Solovyov wrote penetrating critiques of positivism, Hegelianism, and Tolstoyianism (i.e., the doctrine of nonresistance to evil).

Almost all of the major R. religious thinkers of the 20th century were directly influenced by Solovyov: among others, D. S. Merezhkovsky (1865–1941), Berdyayev, S. L. Frank (1877–1950), and S. N. Bulgakov (1871–1944). Most of these men, together with N. O. Lossky (1870–), who elaborated Solovyov's doctrine of "intellectual intuition" into an intuitivistic theory of knowledge, spent their later years in exile in W. Europe and America. Of these, the most significant philosophically is probably S. L. Frank.

Marxism became an intellectual influence in Russia in the early 1890's, and Marxists split almost immediately into three separate and opposed philosophic groupings. The most productive of these "deviations," philosophically speaking, was the "Nietzschean" Marxism represented by A. A. Bogdanov (1873–1928), A. V. Lunacharsky (1875–1933), V. A. Bazarov (1874–1936?), and S. A. Volsky (1880–1936?). These thinkers—and Maxim Gorky was associated with them for a time—felt that Marxism as a theory of history and society was essentially sound, but lacked an adequate ethical theory and had no real theory of knowledge. In effect, they repeated the earlier reaction of Belinsky and Herzen against the "impersonalism" of Hegel's philosophy of history, turning to Nietzsche for a morality which rejected duty and obligation and stressed individual freedom, spontaneous impulse, the "artistic" shaping of values and ideals. However, they were not a monolithic group: they ranged from the extreme individualism of Volsky to the "collectivism" of Bazarov. For a theory of knowledge to supplement Marxism, the "Nietzschean" Marxists turned to Mach and Avenarius, but here they were less original and interesting than in their development of a Nietzschean ethics.

The second group, "Kantian" Marxists, saw similar deficiencies in Marxism, but turned to Kant for both a theory of knowledge and an ethical theory. The members of this group were Berdyayev, Bulgakov, and P. B. Struve (1870–1944); all of them later abandoned Marxism for an idealistic and religiously-oriented philosophy sympathetic to R. Orthodoxy. (Bulgakov became a priest in 1918 and subsequently devoted himself to theological writing.)

The "orthodox" Marxist position was defended by Plekhanov, L. I. Akselrod (Orthodox) (1868–1946) and A. M. Kollontay (1872–1952)—the last two being women philosophers—and, of course, by Lenin. But "deviations" became apparent even within this group: Plekhanov developed a theory of "hieroglyphs," which Lenin criticized as a concession to Kantianism in theory of knowledge. And Lenin himself defended a very un-Marxian doctrine of "absolute and objective truth." He also "deviated" in his philosophy of history from Marxian determinism toward an acceptance of human freedom and volition as factors shaping historical events. Lenin followed Bakunin in his violent anticlericalism, and his assertion of atheism as the "religion of the proletariat." Like Bakunin, he held that the disjunction "idealism or materialism" is both exclusive and exhaustive. It was the attempt of the R. "Machians" (Bogdanov, *et al.*) to assert a third (positivist) position, neither idealism nor materialism, which evoked the impatient hammer blows of Lenin's *Materialism and Empiriocriticism* (1909).

In the early Soviet period tension between the two heterogeneous components of Marxism-Leninism—classical materialism and the Hegelian dialectic—issued in a lively dispute between the "Mechanists," headed by L. I. Akselrod, who emphasized the materialism, and the "Menshevizing Idealists," headed by A. M. Deborin (1881–), who stressed the dialectic. This long struggle culminated in 1930 in the official repudiation of "Mechanism," followed a year later by the official repudiation of "Deborinism." The new "orthodox" position established in 1931 was an attempt to balance the two elements. It also marked the effective termination of relatively free philosophic discussion in the Soviet Union; all subsequent philosophic disputes have been settled "from above," e.g., by Zhdanov in 1947, and Stalin in 1950. The "politicalization" of Soviet philosophy may be traced in detail through ethical theory, logic, esthetics, theory of knowledge, and even philosophy of history.

In the post-Stalin period there have been very few concessions to intellectual freedom: one of these is an increased hospitality to the ideas of non-Marxist-Leninist thinkers. Thus, Soviet philosophy journals have recently published discussions—critical, to be sure—of the thought of Solovyov, Kant, and Whitehead. Detailed treatment of such thinkers—however critical—was unheard of between 1931 and the mid-1950's. Unfortunately, there has been no sign of any genuine loosening of the doctrinal strait jacket of Marxism-Leninism as a philosophy in the Soviet Union. (*See also* POPULISM, MARXISM RUSSIAN, MARXISM-LENINISM, DIALECTICAL MATERIALISM)

BIBLIOGRAPHY: T. G. Masaryk, *The Spirit of Russia* (tr. by E. & C. Paul), two vols., London and New York, 1919; N. O. Lossky, *History of Russian Philosophy*, New York, 1951; V. V. Zenkovsky, *A History of Russian Philosophy* (tr. by G. L. Kline), two vols., New York, 1953; G. A. Wetter, *Dialectical Materialism: A Historical and Systematic Survey of Philosophy in the Soviet Union* (tr. by P. Heath), New York, 1958.
G. L. K.

PHYSICS. Soviet physics has been the most outstanding of all the branches of Soviet science. It has a notable tradition going back to the days of Peter the Great. The intellectual giant of 18th-century Russia, Mikhail Lomonosov (1711–65), had very advanced ideas for his time on the conservation of matter, kinetic theory of gases, and other physical phenomena. Leonard Euler (1707–83), the great mathematician, spent twenty-seven years of his life at St. Petersburg and developed there not only various branches of mathematics but also the dynamics of motion of rigid bodies.

The famous Swiss mathematicians and physicists John Bernoulli (1667–1748) and Daniel Bernoulli (1700–82) also worked in St. Petersburg and developed the basic theory of hydrodynamics. In the 19th century the outstanding physicists were E. K. Lenz (1804–65) known for his discovery of heat generated by an electric current and his law of electromagnetic induction, B. S. Jacobi (1801–74) for his development of galvanoplastics, G. I. Wild (1833–1902) for his meteorological investigations, and B. B. Golitsyn (1862–1916) for his work in seismology. P. N. Lebedev (1866–1912) received world recognition for his measurement of the pressure of light. The revolution of 1917 found P well taught in all the universities of Imperial Russia with such outstanding teachers as O. D. Khvolson (1852–1934) and Ya. I. Frenkel (1894–1952). The leaders of P in the early years of the Soviet regime were D. S. Rozhdestvensky (1876–1940) who studied the anomalous dispersion of light, P. P. Lazarev (1878–1942) who studied the action of light on dyes, and A. F. Ioffe (1880–1960) who was the leader in the field of solid state P. The great accomplishments during the last forty years of Soviet P were the work in quantum mechanics of V. A. Fok (1898–), the solid state theory of I. Ye. Tamm (1895–), and the theoretical P work of L. D. Landau (1908–). Outstanding was also the experimental work of P. L. Kapitsa (1894–), who on his return from England in 1935 studied low temperature phenomena, liquefaction of gases, and inexpensive production of oxygen. The solid state field was distinguished by the work of Ioffe, of B. M. Vul (1903–) on the dielectric material barium titanate, and by studies of photoelectric surfaces. In 1924 G. S. Landsberg (1890–) and L. I. Mandelshtam (1879–1944) discovered the scattering of light in crystals which had been found somewhat earlier in liquids by the Indian scientist Raman and for which the latter received a Nobel Prize. In this period there was extensive work in luminescence led by S. I. Vavilov (1891–1951). P. A. Cherenkov, his student, discovered a very important phenomenon of luminescence of liquids under the action of high energy radiation known throughout the world as the Cherenkov effect. This notable discovery was explained theoretically by I. Ye. Tamm and I. M. Frank (1908–); and in 1958 Cherenkov, Tamm, and Frank received the first Nobel Prize to be given Russians in the field of P. In 1940 G. N. Flerov (1913–) and K. A. Petrzhak proved experimentally that the uranium nucleus undergoes spontaneous fission. In the field of accelerators V. I. Veksler (1907–) showed how to construct an accelerator that would take care of the variation of the mass of the particle with velocity. This principle was discovered at about the same time in the United States by E. MacMillan. From 1945 to 1951 the president of the Ac. of S. of the USSR was the physicist S. I. Vavilov.

Research in P is carried out in the institutes of the USSR Academy, in the P departments of the most important universities, in the institutes of the State Committee of the Council of Ministers for Utilization of Atomic Energy, and in some of the laboratories of the various ministries. The mathematical-physics section of the Ac. of S. USSR is responsible for the P institutes of the Academy: in Moscow, the Lebedev Physical Institute, the Vavilov Institute of Physical Problems, the Institute of Semiconductors, the Institute of Theoretical and Experimental Physics, the Electrophysical Laboratory, the Acoustical Institute, the Institute of Crystallography, Institute of Precision Mechanics and Computor Engineering, the Computing Center, Institute of Physics of High Pressure; in Leningrad, the Physico-Technical Institute; in Kharkov, the Ukrainian Physico-Technical Institute; in Tomsk, Siberia, the Siberian Physico-Technical Institute; in Sverdlovsk, the Institute of the Physics of Metals; in Novosibirsk, Siberian sections of the Academy with Institutes of Physics, Institute of Heat Physics, Institute of Radiophysics and Electronics. An important research institute is the combined Institute of Nuclear Research at Dubna near Moscow where the communist bloc nations carry out research in nuclear P. The P faculties (departments) of the Universities of Moscow, Leningrad, Kiev, Kharkov, and other cities are centers not only of instruction but also of research. The following is a characterization of the most important institutes.

Fizichesky Institut Imeni P. N. Lebedeva (Lebedev Physical Institute) in Moscow was organized in 1932 by the Soviet physicist S. I. Vavilov on the basis of the Physical Cabinet of the Academy and its various successors in Leningrad. It was moved to Moscow in 1934. It has been concerned with a wide range of investigations. Particle accelerators are designed for attaining high energy to produce various nuclear transformations. Cosmic rays are studied to elucidate their primary nature and to understand the phenomenon of shower formation which they cause. These studies are supplemented with theoretical work on the nature of nuclear forces. Yearly expeditions are sent to the Pamir Mountains to study cosmic rays. An investigation of electrical discharges in gases is coupled with work on the controlled thermonuclear reaction. Radio wave propagation along the earth's surface is examined and applied to the determination of distances. There is a section of radio astronomy which studies the radio waves received from space and which has a radiotelescope in Crimea. The institute workers have discovered unusual propagation of sound in oceans. In the field of solid state, work is carried out on semiconductors and dielectrics. The phenomenon of luminescence of solids has been of great scientific interest to the Physical Institute. This was the field of interest of the founder S. I. Vavilov and various aspects of the phenomenon (preparation of luminescent materials, the laws of excitation and those of decay of light) were pursued for several decades. Spectroscopic investigations, both in the optical and in the radio frequency range, were also extensively examined. The Physical Institute was used as the basis for a number of institutes. The Seismological Institute was formed by separation of some of the scientists from the Physical Institute in 1928 and this in turn was incorporated into the Geophysical Institute. In 1953 the acoustical laboratory was reorganized into the Acoustical Institute, while in 1937 the laboratory of surface phenomena, the laboratory of surface layers, and the laboratory of disperse systems were transformed into the Colloidal Electrochemical Institute which in 1945 became the Institute of Physical Chemistry. The director of the Lebedev Physical Institute is the Academician D. V. Skobeltsyn.

Institut Fizicheskikh Problem Imeni S. I. Vavilova (Vavilov Institute of Physical Problems) was founded in Moscow in 1951. Its basic interests are the production of low temperature, liquefaction of gases, and the study of the behavior of substances at low temperatures. Studies are also carried out on the P of polymeric materials. It is equipped with many machines for the liquefaction of air, hydrogen, and helium. The new phenomena that were studied at the Institute of Physical Problems were the superfluidity of helium II, second sound in helium II, phase transformations in helium II, superconductivity of pure metals and alloys, development of turbine method of liquefying gases. The director of the institute is Peter L. Kapitsa.

Fiziko-Tekhnichesky Institut (Physico-Technical Institute) in Leningrad was founded in 1919 as an institute of the Commissariat of Higher Education by A. F. Ioffe and was transferred to the Academy in 1939. Its director and guiding spirit until 1951 was A. F. Ioffe. Scientific research was conducted in a number of fields of P. In the field of nuclear research, investigations were made on the spontaneous fission of uranium, isomerism in nuclei, electron and positron pair formation from gamma rays, and observations of cosmic rays in the Wilson cloud chamber. An important field of interest of

the Institute is that of solid state. Work is carried out on the preparation and properties of semi-conductors and dielectrics; electrical breakthrough of crystals, exciton spectra and rectification at the boundaries of two semi-conductors have been extensively studied. X-rays are used to study the deformation of crystals. Rupture of solids is carried out at low temperatures and at very rapid deformation velocities. The technical aspects of the work of the institute are the production of small-scale models of power installations, the development of methods of measuring stress and residual strain in metallic samples, the development of thermoelements, rectifiers and phototubes, improvement of properties of synthetic rubber, and application of gaseous dielectrics in electrical equipment. The institute has been a great training institution for Soviet physicists and physico-chemists. The following prominent Soviet scientists worked there at one time or other: A. P. Aleksandrov, A. I. Alikhanov, A. I. Alikhanyan, L. A. Artsimovich, I. K. Kikoin, P. P. Kobeko, V. N. Kondratyev, G. V. Kordyumov, I. V. Kurchatov, P. I. Lukirsky, N. N. Semyonov, D. V. Skobeltsyn, Ya. I. Frenkel, Yu. B. Khariton, A. A. Chernyshev, A. I. Shalnikov. The following institutes were organized by former associates of the Physico-Technical Institute: the physico-technical institute of Kharkov (1928–30), Tomsk (1928), Sverdlovsk (1932–36), Dnepropetrovsk (1933), and also the physico-agronomical institute of Leningrad (1932). The director of the Physico-Technical Institute in Leningrad is Academician B. P. Konstantinov.

Fiziki-Tekhnichesky Institut Akademii Nauk Ukr. SSR (Ukrainian Physico-Technical Institute) at Kharkov was organized in 1928 by workers from the Leningrad Physico-Technical Institute and members of the P faculty of the University of Kharkov. The main areas of research are the P of the atomic nucleus, P and engineering of accelerating charged particles, P of low temperatures and of solids, radiophysics and theoretical P. The first electrostatic accelerators in the Soviet Union and the first low temperature laboratory were built at the Ukrainian Physico-Technical Institute. The institute constructed powerful vacuum pumps so necessary for the operation of particle accelerators. In the field of radiophysics investigations led to the construction of a variety of magnetrons and other generators of electromagnetic radiation. In the field of low temperature and solid state, investigations are being carried out on optical, mechanical, thermal electrical, magnetic and galvanomagnetic phenomena, on superconductivity and on the properties of liquid helium. Theoretical studies are made on the theory of phase transitions, theory of superconductivity, theory of the solid state, theory of elementary processes and theoretical electronics.

Sibirsky Fiziko-Tekhnichesky Institut (Siberian Physico-Technical Institute) at Tomsk, Siberia, was founded in 1928 on the basis of the P faculty of the Tomsk State University. The institute is devoted to the study of solids: theory of mechanical properties, theory of structure of crystals and experimental investigation of the hardness, surface energy, plasticity, and strength of metals, the P of cutting metals, polishing and friction. In the defect laboratory, apparatus is constructed for finding defects and flaws in railroad rails. There is a spectroscopic laboratory where studies are carried out on the luminescence of phosphors. Dielectric behavior of solids including electrical breakthrough is investigated. Work is carried out on the theory of propagation of radiowaves in the ionosphere, on the theory of vibrations, and on the electrodynamics of radiating systems.

Fiziki Metallov Institut (Institute of the Physics of Metals) of the Ural Branch of the USSR Ac. of S. in Sverdlovsk was organized in Jan. 1932 by scientists of the Leningrad Physico-Technical Institute and since 1939 has been under the administrative control of the Ural branch of the USSR Ac. of S. It has a section of theoretical P and laboratories: diffusion, physical metallurgy, mechanical properties, magnetic materials, electrical phenomena, technical electromagnetism, magnetic structural analysis, high pressures, optics of metals, and spectral analysis, low temperatures. The following areas have been stressed in recent years: quantum theory of the solid state with consideration of interaction of electrons, theoretical and experimental study of ferromagnetism, diffusion in solids, theoretical and experimental study of the optical, mechanical, and electrical properties of polycrystalline solids, phase transformations, theory of thermal treatment of metals, magnetic and gamma ray methods for determining defects in solids. Apparatus was designed, constructed, and placed in production for carrying magnetic measurements and for the determination of structural faults by magnetic and gamma ray examination.

The important **theoretical physicists** of the Soviet Union are the following: V. A. Fok in 1930 developed an important approximate solution to the many particle problems in quantum mechanics now widely known as the Hartree-Fok Method. He also worked on the propagation of electric waves around the earth. L. D. Landau worked in many branches of theoretical P and is the author of many treatises. His main contributions are in the fields of quantum theory of solids, nuclear forces, superfluidity second sound and superconductivity. N. N. Bogolyubov (1907–), a student of the famous R. mathematical physicist N. M. Krylov (1879–1955), has made significant contributions to the theory of non-linear mechanics, statistical mechanics, superconductivity and nuclear forces. I. Ye. Tamm was awarded the Nobel Prize in P for his theory of the Cherenkov effect and is widely recognized as an outstanding theoretical physicist. In the thirties he predicted the existence of the "Tamm surface states" in solids. In 1950 together with A. D. Sakharov he proposed a scheme for containing with a magnetic field a plasma for carrying out a thermonuclear reaction. Tamm has also worked in the field of nuclear forces. M. A. Leontovich (1903–) has worked in statistical mechanics and in the theory of antenna.

One of the great accomplishments of Soviet theoretical P is the theory of **non-linear vibrations.** Initiated by the work of L. I. Mandelshtam and N. D. Papaleksi, the new discipline was developed by A. A. Andronov, A. A. Vitt, G. S. Gorelik, S. M. Rytov, S. P. Strelkov, S. E. Khaykin. The work was started at the Physical Institute of the Ac. of S. and Gorky University. The result was the study of non-linear vibrations of great significance to radiation P. A. A. Andronov related the problem of non-linear vibrations to the qualitative theory of differential equations. N. M. Krylov and N. N. Bogolyubov also developed mathematical methods for the theory of non-linear vibrations.

Cosmic rays are extensively investigated in the Soviet Union. In 1929 D. V. Skobeltsyn showed that cosmic rays can be detected in a Wilson cloud chamber and the nature of the particles further determined by the action of a magnetic field. In 1936–38 S. N. Vernov (1910–) used balloons for registering cosmic ray intensity at an altitude of 25 kilometers and used a radio transmitter on the balloon to obtain information during the flight. He established the latitude effect of cosmic rays in the stratosphere and showed that the main component of the primary particles in the cosmic rays are protons. He is now actively engaged in using Soviet satellites for the study of cosmic rays. In 1944–45 the physicists A. I. Alikhanov and A. I. Alikhanyan (1908–) studied cosmic rays on the Mountain Aragats in Armenia and claimed to have found a large number of elementary particles. At the same time another group of Soviet physicists under the direction of D. V. Skobeltsyn, namely V. I. Veksler, N. A. Dobrotin, G. T. Zatsepin, studied cosmic rays in the Pamir Mountains and showed that the cosmic ray showers are due to the action of neutrons and protons on the nuclei of the atmosphere. The Soviet physicist A. P. Zhdanov in 1935 used photographic emulsions for the study of cosmic rays.

In the field of **particle accelerators**, the first cyclotron on the continent was built before World War II at the Radium Institute in Leningrad. At that time Leningrad was the center of nuclear research led by I. V. Kurchatov (1903–60). At the Physico-Technical Institute, Kurchatov discovered in 1935 the isomerism of nuclei. After World War II M. G. Meshcheryakov (1910–) constructed a 680 MEV accelerator at Dubna near Mos-

cow and this accelerator was used to study elementary particle interactions. In April 1957 a 10 BEV accelerator was put into operation at Dubna but to date it had not produced any particularly important results. Recently the CENR (Central European Nuclear Research) group at Geneva has been operating an accelerator at 25 BEV and the United States Atomic National Laboratory at Brookhaven has one also operating at the same energy.

The leader of the Soviet atomic effort I. V. Kurchatov, together with A. I. Alikhanov (1904–), A. P. Aleksandrov (1903–), D. I. Blokhintsev (1908–), and N. A. Dollezhal, constructed many experimental nuclear reactors for research purposes and for production of both weapons and power. Considerable effort is being devoted by Soviet P to attain control of the thermonuclear reaction. The directors of this research are L. A. Artsimovich (1909–) and M. A. Leontovich (1903–).

There has been a long tradition of research in the **solid state** associated with the school of A. F. Ioffe. In recent years it has produced a highly effective thermoelectric device that has received wide publicity. But Soviet solid state P did not produce the very important breakthrough in this area of science—the discovery and development of the transistor. The fame for this work rests with the American physicists. However, during the period of World War II and after, the accomplishments of Soviet solid state work were theoretical papers on almost every aspect of solid state theory, the discovery in 1944 of the unusual dielectric properties of barium titanate by B. M. Vul, the work on photosurfaces made of cesium oxygen and cesium antimony by P. V. Timofeyev (1902–), P. I. Lukirsky (1894–1954), N. D. Morgulis, and work on exciton spectra by Ye. F. Gross (1897–).

In the field of **magnetism** Ye. K. Zavoysky in 1944 made the important discovery of the electron spin resonance. This effect has been exploited in physical and chemical research far more extensively in the United States and England than in the Soviet Union. Considerable theoretical work has been carried out on ferromagnetism by Ya. I. Frenkel in 1928, L. D. Landau in 1930, and S. V. Vonsovsky (1910–).

The leader of the Soviet school of **acoustics** is N. N. Andreyev (1880–). Soviet experts in this field work on the problems of propagation of sound in heterogeneous and layer media, of the refraction and focusing of acoustical waves, and of filling open spaces with sound. The director of the Institute of Acoustics is L. M. Brekhovskikh (1917–).

The strong tradition in **crystallography** in the Soviet Union stems from the work of the great crystallographer Ye. S. Fyodorov (1853–1919) who developed the mathematical theory of crystal lattice symmetry. His work has been continued by A. V. Shubnikov (1887–), N. V. Belov (1891–), and the mathematician B. N. Delone (1890–). X-ray structure examination of crystals so widely developed in England and the United States has been limited in the Soviet Union to a small group consisting of N. V. Belov, G. S. Zhdanov, G. B. Boky (1909–), and A. I. Kitaygorodsky (1914–). The work of Z. G. Pinsker on electron diffraction by crystals has been outstanding. Production of synthetic crystals so important in various branches of P has been organized by A. V. Shubnikov.

Research on **low temperature and the liquefaction of gases** has been carried out in many countries since World War I. The two important centers in the Soviet Union are the Institute of Physical Problems in Moscow under the direction of P. L. Kapitsa and the cryogenic laboratory of the Ukrainian Physico-Technical Institute in Kharkov. Kapitsa's investigations dealt with the construction of a highly efficient gas liquifier. This laboratory model was developed into an industrial machine for cheap production of oxygen. Kapitsa and his collaborators studied the remarkable properties of helium II. V. P. Peshkov verified experimentally the theoretical predictions of L. D. Landau on the existence of second sound in helium II and A. I. Schalnikov (1905–) in an excellent experiment confirmed the existence of superconducting layers in solids near the superconducting temperature that Landau also predicted. In 1957 N. N. Bogolyubov published a theory of superconductivity which is a very good variant of a theory presented previously by J. Bardeen of the United States.

The accomplishments of Soviet P in **spectroscopy** are based on the development during the Soviet regime of the optical glass industry and instrument making, and also on the theoretical foundations laid by D. S. Rozhdestvensky, S. I. Vavilov, L. I. Mandelshtam, and G. S. Landsberg. Recent important work is that of A. N. Terenin (1896–) on spectroscopy of absorbed molecules, the work of V. L. Levshin (1896–), P. P. Feofilov, and V. V. Antonov-Romanovski on luminescence, the work of A. S. Davydov on the theory of spectra of organic crystals, and the discovery of exciton spectra in the cuprous oxide of Ye. F. Gross.   J. T.

PHYSIOLOGY. Soviet physiology has a far-reaching heritage. I. M. Sechenov contributed to R. physiology original and fruitful ideas which led to the creation of two schools of thought: one of I. P. Pavlov and the other of N. Ye. Vvedensky. At the beginning of the Soviet era Vvedensky fully developed his theories about the rhythmical character of the activity of tissues and organs and about the genetic connection between stimulation and inhibition. At the same time, Pavlov completed his work on digestion and blood circulation and started his research on higher nervous activity. I. F. Tsion, I. R. Tarkhanov, N. A. Mislavsky, V. Ya. Danilevsky, V. M. Bekhterev, B. F. Verigo, and others contributed valuable facts to physiological research. Soviet papers on physiology are characterized by the trend of investigating physiological phenomena in the light of developments and conditioning of changing environment. This synthetic method is based on Pavlov's investigations of conditioned reflexes which led to the theory of higher nervous activity. In the first place, Pavlov established a system in cortical processes which reflects the synthetic activity of the cerebral cortex. The study of regularity in the formation of complexes of nervous processes led Pavlov to the theory of the dynamic stereotype. The cortical activity was conceived as a system of stimulation and inhibition processes. Pavlov attached

major importance to the investigation of inhibition as a means of prevention of excessive exploitation of the nervous apparatus (protective inhibition).

Another major discovery made by Pavlov was the principle of nervous activity applicable only to human beings and concerning the perception of reality by speech or writing which he called the "second signal system of reality." While the speech function provides a link with the environment, it also causes a detachment from reality, i.e., the ability to generalize and conceive abstract ideas. Furthermore, Pavlov studied the evolution of higher nervous activity. He found several types of nervous systems characterized by strength, balance and mobility, and had to solve the problem of their genesis. He also searched for an explanation of neuroses.

Pavlov suggested the conception of analyzers which interact in the cerebral cortex. His pupil, K. M. Bykov, and his assistants proved the regulating influence of the cortex on the activity of all internal organs and even on such processes as the chemistry of the liver and tissue oxidation. Furthermore, they discovered special receptors in all internal organs, in blood vessels and lymphatic vessels and in all body tissues, and suggested the regulation of cell metabolism by impulses which stimulate the activity of a nerve cell as a result of a reflex reaction.

L. A. Orbeli and his assistants have determined the stimulating effects of the sympathetic nervous system on the activity of muscles, receptors, the functional condition of the central nervous system, and the cerebellum as an autonomic center.

I. P. Razenkov, Yu. V. Folbort, and others continued Pavlov's research on the physiology and pathology of digestion. N. I. Krasnogorsky studied the gradual development of the cortex in infants. According to A. D. Speransky, the trophic effect of the central nervous system enhances the resistance of the organism to factors that cause pathological processes. Many other scientists are Pavlov's followers, including P. K. Anokhin, Ye. A. Asratyan, D. A. Biryukov, A. G. Ivanov-Smolensky, P. S. Kupalov, M. K. Petrov, N. A. Rozhansky, V. V. Savich, and Yu. P. Frolov.

The work of Vvedensky has been continued since the revolution. He made a major contribution to the study of inhibition by his theory of parabiosis. He established an interrelation between stimulation and inhibition and formulated a law of regularity of their reciprocal transition. His follower, A. A. Ukhtomsky, suggested the theory of a dominant which he believed to be the formation of a group of nerve centers on a certain level of stationary stimulation. Ukhtomsky interpreted Vvedensky's problem of instability as an "appropriation of rhythm" and a basic factor in the regulation of physiological activity. A. F. Samoilov and his assistants studied electrophysiology. V. Yu. Chagovets, P. P. Lazarev, and others worked on the ionic theory of stimulation.

In the Soviet era emphasis has been placed on two new physiological branches, i.e. the physiology of sport and of work. In sport, much attention is given to the formation of motion habits, muscle strength and stamina; in work, studies concern the organization of work under conditions of mass production, rationalization of work and recreation, and vocational training (K. Kh. Kekcheyev, M. I. Vinogradov, M. V. Leynik).

L. M.

PILNYÁK (Vógau), **Borís Andréyevich** (1894–1942?), revolutionary writer and journalist. Graduated in 1920  from the Moscow Institute of Commerce. His first collection of stories, *The Past,* was published in 1919. He wrote numerous stories of the civil war and the era of militant communism; the better-known are: *The Naked Year* (1920), *Machines and Wolves* (1923–24), *Time Wasted* and *The Snowstorm.* His writings draw a clear distinction between the popular upheaval that knows no bounds and the carefully organized terror machine of the Communists. From an aesthetic standpoint, P is an outstanding example of postrevolutionary R. ornamentalism. His writings give evidence of considerable political courage, especially true of the novel *Story of the Unextinguished Moon* (1926), which is based on a version of the death of the army commander Frunze, allegedly poisoned on the orders of Stalin; and of the novel *Red Wood,* published in Berlin in 1929. The latter publication caused P to be removed from his post of chairman of the All-Russian Union of Writers. His novel, *The Volga Flows into the Caspian Sea* (1930), deals with the Five Year Plan. P traveled extensively in Europe, and visited Japan and America, describing his experiences in *The Roots of Japan's Sun* and *Okay.* According to reports, he was arrested in 1938 and died in a concentration camp in 1942.

PÍMENOV, Yúry Ivánovich (1903–), painter and engraver, was awarded the Stalin prize twice (1947, 1950) for paintings on the subject of Soviet life and Moscow during World War II. Also known as a designer of stage settings.

PÍNEGA RIVER, in Archangel Oblast, right tributary of the N. Dvina; 400 mi. long; navigable.

PINSK, city in Brest Oblast, Byelorussian SSR, on left bank of Pina River, connected with the Neman R. by waterway; in the center of Pinsk Marshes; pop. 41,000 (1958). Ind.: furniture, match, food factories. Ancient town, in 11th century was part of Kiev principality.

PIONEER ISLAND, belongs to the group of islands known as Severnaya Zemlya; area 580 sq. mi.

PIONEERS, mass organization of children, age nine to fifteen, designed to inculcate the political and social ideas of the CP. Closely linked with the Young Communist League (Komsomol) whose members are aged fifteen to twenty-seven, the P were founded in 1922 by a resolution of the second All-Russian Conference of the Komsomol. Today there are 19,000,000 P and a unit is at almost every school and children's institution. Pioneer membership is practically universal, unlike the Komsomol, which is more selective. The basic unit of five to ten members is called a *zveno* (link); several links make up an *otryad* (detachment) with about thirty to forty members; all the detachments in the school or institution make up the *druzhina* (brigade). There are Pioneer organizations paralleling the administrative divisions of the government. On the central level, *Pionerskaya Pravda* (Pioneers' Truth) and other children's newspapers and magazines are published. The symbol of membership is a three-cornered red tie signifying the three generations of Soviet citizens—Pioneer, Komsomol, Communist party.

Pioneer activities vary according to the age and special interest of the group. Under the supervision of adult workers (usually Komsomol members), children receive political instruction, stressing patriotism and the identification of the interests of party and state with society. The importance of socially useful labor is emphasized through work projects in the classroom, gardens, community, and special summer camps. In addition, P participate in athletics, nature study, dramatics, music, crafts, and so forth. Special houses of P are set aside as centers for activities. At the age of fifteen, a Pioneer can, upon fulfilling the membership requirements, join the Komsomol, which has more intensive and rigorous activities, but the same goals.

C. L.

PIPELINES. Transportation of petroleum and natural gas by underground P has begun to assume importance in the USSR after over fifty years of neglect. A 548-mi., 8-inch diameter line between Baku and Batumi was the only P from 1906 to 1928; by 1940 some 2,550 mi. were handling 2.36 bill. ton-mi. of petroleum (about 6% of all domestic petroleum traffic). With the economy shifting from coal to oil, and with supplies of both coal and natural gas rapidly increasing, P construction has spurted in the last decade. In 1959, about 10,370 mi. of pipeline carried 25.9 bill. ton-mi. of crude oil, petroleum products, and natural gas (about one-seventh of total domestic petroleum traffic). As part of a developing oil-export program, a large crude-oil line joining the Middle Volga fields with E. Europe is to be completed by 1963.

PIROGÓV, Nikoláy Ivánovich (1810–1881), physician, military surgeon, and educator. Corresponding member, St. Petersburg Ac. of S. (1847). Graduate, Moscow University (1828); studied in Germany (1833–35); professor, Derpt (Tartu) University (1836) and St. Petersburg Medical and Surgical Academy (1841). Founder of the first Institute of Anatomy (1846). Participated in the Caucasian and Crimean campaigns and used ether anesthesia under field conditons for the first time in Russia (1847); introduced first aid and corps of women nurses (1854), plaster casts, specially designed surgical instruments for the army; suggested different methods of ether administration and was a pioneer in osteoplastic operations. Originated the practice of anatomical examination by dissection and the study of medicine by applied anatomy. P was profoundly interested in educational problems and founded the first Sunday school in Russia (1859); he campaigned for active methods of study including literary clubs, discussions, lectures.

PÍSAREV, Dmítry Ivánovich (1840–1868), literary critic. In contrast to the social reformers of the first half of that decade, P was concerned with the individual-ethical aspects of socio-economic reforms, with family problems, and with the difficult position of women in society. He developed a theory of reasonable egoism.

 P's parents were members of the land-owning nobility. After studying history and philology first at Moscow University and then in St. Petersburg, P became an ideological leader of the literary political journal, *Russky Mir* (The Russian World) (1862–66). His articles on Plato and Metternich, and especially the article "Scholasticism of the XIX century" (1861) caused him to be regarded as an outstanding literary critic. In 1862 he was arrested for writing an article critical of the government. It was while in solitary confinement in the Petropavlovsk Fortress during the next four and a half years that he wrote his important works. This included the long article "Realists" (1864), "Notes on the History of Labor" (1863), "The Historical Ideas of Auguste Comte" (1865), and "Pushkin and Belinsky" (1865). Upon regaining his freedom P contributed articles to the journals *Delo* (The Task), and *Otechestvennya Zapiski* (Notes of the Fatherland), which was edited at that time by Nekrasov. P drowned in the Gulf of Riga in 1868.

PISARZHÉVSKY, Lev Vladímirovich (1874–1938), chemist. Fellow, Ac. of S., USSR (1930) and Ukrainian SSR (1925). One of the founders of electronic chemistry in Russia. Organizer of the first plant for the extraction of iodine from algae (1915–17); founder of the University (1918) and the Institute of Chemistry and Technology (1930) in Dnepropetrovsk. Lenin prize (1930).

PISCICULTURE (FISHERIES). The first fish ponds were created as early as the 13th century, mainly in cloisters. Expensive fish such as sterlet, bream, pike, and carp were produced. Since the middle of the 19th century river and lake fisheries have been in operation. They put at present, each year, over 6 billion young fish into rivers and lakes, mainly salmon and sturgeon. Special efforts are made to introduce some varieties of fish in areas in which they did not live before. Thus, for example, the black mullet was re-settled from the Black Sea into the Caspian Sea; and Far E. breeds were brought from the Amur into rivers of European Russia. The development of Soviet P is being increasingly hampered by the lack of adequate conservation laws and by damages owing to the prevailing practice of dumping industrial refuse into rivers and lakes. As industrialization progresses, losses on that count are reported to be increasingly heavy.

Soviet fisheries appear to be the world's third largest (after the U.S. and China). Fish ponds occupied an area of some 123,500 acres in 1937 and have probably expanded since then. Inland fishing is mainly carried on by collective farms, about 1,800 of which specialized in fishing in 1955. The catch of sturgeon alone amounted to 2 mill. tons, or about 95% of the world's total.

Total fish haul in the USSR (including whales) was: 10.2 mill. tons in 1913; 14 mill. tons in 1940; 17.5 mill. tons in 1950; and 29 mill. tons in 1958.

PÍSEMSKY, Alekséy Feofilaktovich (1820–1881), novelist and playwright. Born in the family of an impoverished nobleman, P studied mathematics at Moscow University and graduated in 1844. He became a member, in that year, of the staff of the conservative journal *Moskvich* (The Muscovite). P's major works include the short stories, *Sketches of Peasant Life* (1852–55), the novels *Boyarshchina* (1858) and *A Thousand Souls* (1858), and the play *A Bitter Lot* (1859). From 1857 to 1862 P was editor of the journal *Biblioteka Dlya Chtenia* (Library for Reading). In 1863 his novel, *Troubled Sea*, was strongly condemned by leading radical critics, and this led him to move from St. Petersburg to Moscow. P's style is characterized by a conservative's pessimism and a realism that is close to naturalism. His characters are powerfully drawn and there is more manly vigor in his narrative art than in that of most of his contemporaries.

PISHPÉK: *see* Frunze.

PLÁKSIN, Igor Nikoláyevich (1900–), hydrometallurgist. Corresponding member, Ac. of S., USSR (1946). Graduate, Far-East Univeristy (1926); professor, Institute of Nonferrous Metals and Gold in Moscow (1930). Joined the Institue of Mining (1944). Research concerns the theory and technology of hydrometallurgy, particularly the modernization of beneficiation processes, application of microantoradiography, radiometry. Author of *Flotation Beneficiation of Pyrite-Arsenate Ore* (with G. A. Myasnikova and A. M. Okolovich, 1955). Stalin prizes (1951, 1952).

PLANNING. National Economic Plans. Since the late 1920's detailed centralized P has been the chief coordinating mechanism in the Soviet economy. The national economic plan outlines the tasks to be accomplished during the period it is in effect and directs the allocation of all resources toward the achievement of the goals which have been set. It prescribes the total national income objective and the physical volume of production for all major commodities. The plan determines the division of the national income between investment and consumption and the relative share in consumption to be enjoyed by each significant group of the population. The volume and composition of both domestic and foreign trade are governed by the plan as are the prices of most of the commodities bought and sold. All money in circulation is taken into account in the plan, which estimates how much of the population's income will go for purchases of consumer goods, for bank savings, for taxes, and the like. The annual government budget is an important component of the financial portions of the plan. In short, the Soviet economic plan is a gigantic, comprehensive blueprint that attempts to regulate the economic activities and interrelations of all persons and institutions in the USSR as well as the economic relations between the USSR and other countries.

The Planning Mechanism. At the top of the P hierarchy is the State Planning Committee, which is subordinate to the Council of Ministers of the USSR (*see*

INDUSTRY). This committee is broken down into two
types of departments: branch departments (*otraslevye
otdely*), which plan the development of individual
branches and sectors of the economy, and summary
departments (*svodnye otdely*), which deal with more
general problems affecting the economy as a whole,
such as wage, price, and cost determination. Attached
to the State Planning Committee are the main administrations for inter-republic deliveries. (These are the
former main administrations for sales which were under
the ministries before the latter were abolished in 1957.
They have been consolidated and reduced in number.)

At the next lower step in the P hierarchy are the
republic state planning committees, which are smaller
duplicates of the central planning committee. The chain
of command then passes to the regional economic
councils which have P departments and ultimately to
individual enterprises which also have such departments. (In republics where there are republic economic
councils the latter also may have some P and coordinating functions.)

In preparing economic plans, particularly the shorter-
term operational ones, the Soviet government seeks to
combine centralized direction with local initiative. Enterprises reportedly now initiate their plans, submitting
them to the regional economic council for amendment
and coordination with those of other enterprises in the
same region. (Prior to 1958 the central authorities gave
enterprises detailed guidelines for the preparation of
their initial plans.) The regional economic councils pass
the amended and coordinated plans on to the republic
P authorities for further amendment and coordination.
(In republics with republic economic councils the latter
may perform some of this work.) As the plans move
up through the hierarchy their production, investment,
and other targets are expressed in increasingly generalized and aggregate terms. Once the plans have been
amended, coordinated, and integrated by the central
planning committee, the resulting comprehensive document is submitted to the Council of Ministers of the
USSR for endorsement. The plan must also, of course,
have the endorsement of the top party leadership. The
latter occasionally makes very substantial and far-
reaching alterations in the plan submitted by the central
planning committee. Once the plan has been approved
by the Council of Ministers and top party leadership it
is disseminated downward through the hierarchy with
an increasing amount of disaggregation and detail. It
then has the force of law and must be met, or, if possible, exceeded.

Planning Techniques. In free enterprise-type economies decentralized production units are charged with
responsibility for achieving rough balance between the
future demand for an individual product and the future
supply of an individual product, utilizing indicators
provided by the market mechanism. In the USSR such
balance is brought about, or is supposed to be brought
about, by the P apparatus with little or no assistance
from the market mechanism. The balance between projected demand and supply must be a realistic one if
serious bottlenecks in key branches and sectors of the
economy are to be avoided. The task is a formidable

one for any bureaucracy and the Soviet P apparatus
has not always accomplished it successfully. The most
conspicuous failure occurred in connection with Sixth
Five Year Plan, which was discarded in 1957, primarily
because it overcommitted available resources.

The task of achieving consistency between the projected demand for and the projected supply of individual products is made a little more manageable by dividing products into a number of categories and assigning
responsibilities for P the supply and distribution of each
category to a different level of the P hierarchy. The
central planning committee has responsibility for achieving balance between projected demand for and supply
of those products which are considered of most importance for the economy as a whole, those which are
seriously deficit, and those which are used in several
republics. The republic P authorities have responsibility
for planning the supply and distribution of the commodities of lesser importance and those which are produced either wholly or largely within one republic.
The regional economic councils plan the supply and
distribution of those commodities considered of least
importance and those which are produced wholly or
largely within a single economic-administrative region.

Method of Material Balances. To reconcile the projected demand for and the projected supply of individual products the method of "material balances" is used.
A material balance is essentially a balance sheet showing the projected supply of and demand for a given
product. At the central planning committee a separate
balance is made out for each of the centrally allocated
products. (The ensuing discussion relates to procedures
followed by the central planning committee only. Procedures at lower levels of the P hierarchy are thought
to be analogous, however.) On the left side (see table
below) are listed the sources of the product and on the
right side, the uses of the product. On the sources side
the most important category is "production." It often
accounts for as much as 95 per cent of the total supply
of a product. The "imports" category is usually insignificant. The "other sources" category is of varying importance. "Stocks" include only those at suppliers.
Stocks at users, if they are above normal levels, are
taken into account by subtracting them from enterprise
requirements (*zayavki*) when the latter are made up.

The important categories on the distribution side
are "production-operation needs" (which include maintenance requirements) and "construction." The "market
fund" category refers to that part of the output of the
product which is distributed more or less without further processing to satisfy the consumption needs of the
population. The two "reserves" have different functions. The "State Reserve" is a permanent one, built up
as a protection against national disaster. The "Reserve
of the Council of Ministers" is an operational reserve
to be utilized over time by enterprises which are going
above their output targets and are in need of additional
input materials and by enterprises which did not get
supplies which had been allotted to them because of
supply failures. The "production" categories on the
sources side, and on the distribution side before the
reorganization of industry in 1957 were broken down

by producing and consuming ministries; they are now broken down by republics.

MATERIAL BALANCE
PRODUCT X

Sources	*Distribution*
1. Production	1. Production-operation needs
(a) by major producing ministries (now republics)	(a) by major consuming ministries (now by republics)
2. Imports	2. Construction
3. Other sources	(a) by major consumers
4. Stocks at suppliers (beginning of period)	3. Market fund
(a) by major supplier ministries (now by republic)	4. Exports
	5. Increase of State Reserves
	6. Increase of Reserves of Council of Ministers
	7. Stocks at suppliers at end of period
	(a) by major supplier ministries (now by republics)

The crucial problem is how to bring sources and distribution into balance when at first there is an imbalance. Usually an imbalance stems from an excess of demand over the supply of a product.

According to Soviet sources, the "easy" way out of such an imbalance—a lowering of the output target of a given branch because of a shortage in the supply to it of a deficit commodity—is generally not adopted. Instead, efforts are made to increase the supply of or to reduce the demand for the deficit commodity. On the supply side, there are several alternatives. The possibility of cutting stocks at suppliers may be investigated. The planned level of imports may be raised. Most importantly, the projected level of production of the deficit commodity may be increased. To the extent possible, an effort is made to increase production within the framework of existing capacity without ordering additional supplies, that is, through greater efficiency. This method is preferred in part because an expansion in capacity or the ordering of additional supplies upsets other material balances. If, for example, additional supplies are ordered, this may require additional output of the supplies (if they cannot be drawn from stocks), which, in turn, may require additional production of the inputs required by the additional supplies, and so on down the line.

On the demand side, efforts may be directed toward economizing in the use of the deficit product or substituting for it non-deficit products. Throughout the balancing process, the priority principle is applied. Whenever possible it is the sectors of secondary importance (the consumer sectors) which have their allocations cut or are called upon to use substitutes.

The adjustments made to remove an imbalance in projected demand and supply, it will be observed, are generally such as to increase the over-all tautness of the plan. This is a principal cause of the frequent supply failures in the Soviet economy.

Over recent years Soviet economists and mathematicians have been investigating the possibility of using input-output techniques to achieve balance in their plans. It is possible that these techniques will eventually be adopted, at least as a supplement to the method of material balances.

Pay-off Period Calculation. As indicated in the section on investment, Soviet economic authorities often employ a "pay-off" period calculation to determine what productive facilities should be constructed and where they should be constructed in order to meet a future output requirement. The results of this type of calculation are presumably secured prior to preparing the final material balances of an economic plan and are utilized in working up these balances.

The main difficulty associated with the application of the "pay-off" period calculation stems from the arbitrary character of many Soviet prices. As there are no genuine markets for most producers' goods (they are simply allocated to users by the P apparatus), the prices attached to these products often bear a very tenuous relation to demand and supply conditions. They do not adequately reflect opportunity costs. To be sure, the central P authorities occasionally adjust the prices of very deficit products upward to encourage economy at lower levels of the industrial and P hierarchy but such adjustments are generally crude and do not alter the general picture.

Need for Market Research Techniques in Consumer Sector. Up to this point it has been tacitly assumed that the P authorities could predict future demand. The discussion has been in terms of achieving consistency between projected demand and supply and how best to meet projected demand and supply requirements. Until very recently Soviet P authorities had little difficulty in predicting demand. The requirements of the state were and still are determined by the top party leadership. On the other hand, because of their relatively low standard of living, consumers were prepared to purchase almost anything turned out by the productive machine at almost any price. Over recent years, however, particularly since Stalin's death in 1953, the standard of living has risen steadily, albeit modestly, and consumers have become increasingly selective in their purchases. Stocks of unwanted and overpriced products have tended to rise and the government has had to resort to the extension of consumer credit, price reductions, increased advertising, and the like to clear consumer markets. The P authorities will apparently have to follow developments in consumer demand much more closely in the future than in the past if substantial wastes are to be avoided. They may well resort to market research techniques similar to those used extensively in western countries.

Broad Regional Concepts in Planning. In the late 1930's the USSR was divided into 13 so-called "basic" (*osnovny*) or large (*krupny*) economic regions, which were to be utilized in P new investment and the like. Despite numerous suggestions for change, this network of "basic" economic regions is in effect today. The regions are: the Center, the North West, the North, the West, the South, the Northern Caucasus, the Volga area, the Urals, the Trans-Caucasus, Kazakhstan and Central Asia, Western Siberia, Eastern Siberia, and the Far East. At least in theory, each region is characterized by specialization in one or more branches of industry or agriculture considered of national importance. Enterprises in these branches or sectors form a nucleus about which a closely integrated economic complex is supposed to develop.

It is not known to what extent these concepts have

been operationally significant for Soviet P. Sporadic criticism in the press of the P agencies for disregarding or underestimating the importance of these broad regional concepts suggests they have not been very significant from an operational standpoint. However this may be, the broad regional concepts appear to have been designed in part to avoid duplication of effort and other wastes associated with the autonomous tendencies of Soviet economic and administrative units. During the period, for example, when Soviet industry was run on the branch principle by a large number of more or less self-contained ministries, it was quite possible for one ministry to propose the construction of productive facilities in a given area where, in fact, its needs could be met by a nearby plant belonging to a different ministry. The P authorities, employing the concept of highly integrated "basic" economic regions, could forestall this and similar types of costly errors. Under the new system of industrial organization, inaugurated in 1957, the P authorities can use the broad regional concept to avoid similar mistakes by the 100-odd regional economic councils. (There are a number of regional economic councils in each of the "basic" economic regions.) The broad regional concept may also, of course, be of some military or strategic significance. (*See also* ECONOMIC DEVELOPMENT, INDUSTRY, INDUSTRIAL MANAGEMENT AND ORGANIZATION, INVESTMENT)

BIBLIOGRAPHY: Harry Schwartz, *Russia's Soviet Economy*, New York, 1954; Herbert S. Levine, "The Centralized Planning of Supply in Soviet Industry," *Comparisons of the United States and Soviet Economies*, Joint Economic Committee, Congress of the United States, Washington, 1959.
R. C. H.

PLANT LIFE. About 17,000 kinds of seed-bearing plants and ferns grow in the Soviet Union. Most of them belong to the following families: Compositae, Leguminosae, Gramineae, Mustard, Parsley, Sedge, Rose, and Crowfoot.

The territory of the USSR may be divided into several vegetation zones: arctic deserts, tundra, forests, steppes, and deserts.

The Arctic Deserts Zone occupies the bare land of the N. islands, the areas which are free of ice, on Franz Josef Land, the N. island of Novaya Zemlya, Severnaya Zemlya, New Siberian Island, Wrangel Island, and the very N. of the Taymyr Peninsula.

The tundra soil which is dissected into polygons by the shrinking action of the ground frost is only partly carpeted with sea weeds, lichens, and liverworts. The flowering plants, the leafy moss, and bushy lichens are restricted to cracks or depressions, where the snow accumulates.

The Tundra Zone occupies the N. edge of European Russia, the N. part of Asia and the islands of the Arctic Ocean. Most of this area is covered by moss and lichens, the commonest of which are: among the mosses —Aulacomnium, Dicranum, Drepanocladus, Hylocomium, Pleurozium, Polytrichum, Rhacomitrium; and among the lichens—Cetraria, Cladonia, Alectoria, and others.

The vegetation changes from the N. to the S., forming several subzones. On the shores of the Arctic Ocean, from Ukotsk Shar to Chukchi Peninsula, lies a zone transitory between the arctic zone and the moss-lichen

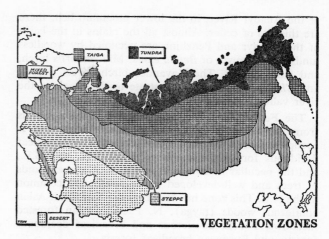

VEGETATION ZONES

tundra. Here the large patches of vegetation are stretched among the stone-strewn and the barren soil. The moss prevails: *Tomenthypnum nitens (Camptothecium trichoides), Dicranum elongatum, Hylocomium alascanum, Oncophorus Wahlenbergii, Polytrichum alpestre, Ptilidium ciliare*. The moss is partly mixed with the lichens. Among the grass, the plants of the sedge family are the commonest: the common sedge (*Carex stans*), and the cotton grass (*Eriophorum angustifolium*). Farther to the S. lies the zone of the moss-lichen tundra, which extends from the Kola Peninsula to the Kolyma River. The vegetation cover is continuous. The moss is abundant, preponderantly *Aulacomnium turgidum, Tomenthypnum nitens, Dicranum elongatum, Hylocomium alascanum, Polytrichum strictum, Ptilidium ciliare*, and others. The grass-bush range is represented by the sedge, arctic poa, often together with the creeping bushes of *Dryas octopetala* and *D. punctata*, arctic willows, Labrador tea (*Ledum decumbens*), Alpean bearberries (*Arctous alpina*), dwarf birches (*Betula nana*), and to the E. from the Yenisey River, *Betula exilis*, cranberries, and crowberries. The lichen tundra occupies the sandy plains where either Cladonia lichens (*Cladonia mitis, C. rangiferina, C. alpestris*) or Alectorian lichens (*Alectoria ochroleuca, A. nigricans, Bryopogon divergens, Cetraria nivalis*) are present. The depressions are occupied by grass-hypno, lichen-spagnous hummocks, and flat hummock marshes.

To the S. lies the forest tundra with well-developed bushes, usually dwarf birch, and to the E. of the Yenisey, *Betula exilis*, swamp Labrador tea, willows (*Salix pulchra, S. arbuscula, S. glauca*). To the E. of the Ural Mountains the tundra is covered by thickets of dwarf willows and alder bushes (*Alnus fruticosa*) with marshes in the depressions. The cotton grass and the sedge (*Carex lugens*) prevail to the E. of the Lena River.

On the S., in the river valleys and on the S. slopes, is the subzone of sparsely forested and wooded tundra, but here and there the woods give way to swamps. Birches, larch trees, and cedars are common in the woods.

The Kuzmichev's birch predominates on the Kola Peninsula; the Siberian larch tree is mostly found between the Ural and the Pyasina River, the Dahurian larch prevails from the Pyasina to Anadyr; and to the S.

of the Anadyr River, in the lower mountain belt, there are thickets of cedar. Almost all the plains in the basin of the Anadyr and Penzhina are occupied by woodless tundra with growth of *Betula exilis*, Middendorf's birch, and alder bushes. The Kayander birch, sweet poplar, and *Chosenia macrolepis* penetrate to the N. along the river valleys.

The Forest Zone, the largest in the USSR, extends from the W. boundaries to the Pacific coast and is occupied mostly by coniferous forests. The broadleaf deciduous forests predominate in the S.W. and S.E., and the peculiar narrow leaf woods, with sparse stands of trees and well-developed undergrowth, are common in the N.E. This zone has four regions: European-Asian coniferous woods (tayga), N. Pacific Ocean forested meadows, Far E. coniferous and broadleaf deciduous forests, and European broadleaf forests.

The European-Asian region extends from the N.W. boundaries of the USSR to the Okhotsk Sea. It may be divided into three subzones: northern, central, and southern tayga. Sparse stands of trees with rich underbrush are typical of the northern tayga. The woods are denser and the underbrush absent in the central tayga; the undergrowth consists of blueberries, cranberries, northern linnaea, wood sorrel, pyrola, and others. The moss cover is well developed, with bright green moss (*Hylocomium splendens, Eutodon Schreberi, Ptilium crista-castrensis*). The lichens are less abundant and grow mostly on sandy soil and pebbles. The woods are more or less dense and the grassy undergrowth is thick in the southern tayga, but the moss-lichen cover is poorer. The southern or continental tayga lies to the E. of the Ural Mountains and middle Amur. The characteristic flora consists of coniferous forests of pine trees, or of deciduous forests with undergrowth of meadow-forest plants.

From W. to E. the tayga is divided into three groups: European-Siberian with dark coniferous forests; E. Siberian with light coniferous forests; and Far E. (S. Okhotsk) again with dark coniferous forests.

The European-Siberian part of the tayga extends from the W. boundaries of the USSR to the E. of the Yenisey River, including the Yenisey mountain range and the W. Sayans. *Picea exelsa* predominates in the W. half of the European region, *P. obovata* in the E. half of Siberia. Deciduous forests with Siberian larch trees and Siberian Sukachev's elms are widely spread, especially in the mountains. The birch woods extend from the southern limits of the tayga to the W. Siberian forested steppes, and occupy a wide stretch in the W. Siberian and partly in the central Siberian plains. The mixed forests with firs, pines, oaks, lindens, and maples are widely spread in the S.W. of European Russia. The E. Siberian part of the tayga includes the most continental Siberian regions, and extends from the Yenisey to the Okhotsk Sea. The S.W. territory of this area is almost entirely occupied by Siberian and Dahurian larch trees. The pine trees are to be found along the middle part of the Lena River on sandy soil. The Siberian cedars and the silver firs are limited to the mountains of E. Sayan, the Baykal regions, and S.E. parts of the tayga. The vegetation of the steppes penetrates far to

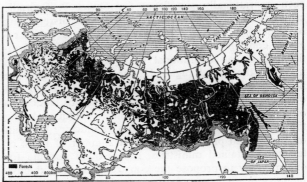

Forested areas of the USSR

the N. along the valleys of the Lena, Yana, and Indigirka. The Far E. or S. Pacific tayga occupies a smaller territory in the regions bordering the Amur River on the N., some areas of the Sikhote-Alin, central and S. parts of Sakhalin Island, and the Kuril Islands. The Ayan firs mixed with the white bark silver firs are common on the mainland, and the Sakhalin silver firs on Sakhalin Island. Through man's activities the flora of the tayga is being changed, with meadows, which are used as pastures, replacing woods, and fields of corn and cereals replacing the forests of Europe and the S. Asian tayga.

The N. Pacific forested meadow area includes Kamchatka, the Commander Islands, the N. and central Kuril Islands. This is the region of sparse birch woods with rich grass in the meadows. The stone birch predominates on the Kamchatka Peninsula, at the altitude of 1,800–2,000 ft. The woods become sparser at 650 ft., and the undergrowth here is formed, not by gramineous plants, but mostly by the plants of the parsley family. The woods of Ayan firs, often mixed with Okhotsk larch trees, grow in the valley of the Kamchatka River. The meadows prevail on the Commander Islands and cedars on the N. and central Kuril Islands. Sparse birch woods, Kurilean bamboo, and thickets of Maksimovich's alders and grass meadows are found on Uruppu, Shimushiro, and Ketoy islands of the Kuril archipelago.

The Far E. coniferous-broadleaf deciduous area includes the regions of the S. Amur and the sea coast. Here the plains and lower mountain belt are occupied by oak forests, mostly by Mongolian oaks mixed with birches, and in the undergrowth with hazel nuts and lespedeza. Elms, Manchurian ash trees, and nut trees predominate in the valleys. Mixed woods of cedars and broadleaf trees occupy the central and part of the lower belts of the mountains and mixed woods of silver firs and broadleaf trees are at the sea coast. The most common coniferous trees growing in the mountains are Korean cedar and silver fir; the most abundant deciduous trees, linden, yellow birch, elm, Manchurian ash tree, Manchurian hazel nut, and, in the S., maple and hornbeam. The well-developed undergrowth consists of *Philadelphus tenuifolius*, hazel nuts, wild pepper, and other plants. Ayan firs and silver firs occupy the upper limit of the mixed forests, and stone birches are still higher, at the edge of the mountainous woods. Because of man's activities the original woods give way to birch and oak groves, and in the river valleys to meadows.

The European broadleaf wood region covers the S.W. of European Russia, the Carpathian Mountains, the Volyn-Podolian heights, most of Polesye and the regions further to the E., up to the Volga River. The oaks and beech woods prevail in the lowlands, yet vast areas formerly covered by woods are now cleared for fields and meadows. Common pine trees and oaks are spread on the plains of Polesye; uniform pine forests grow only on poor, sandy soil. The forests of the R. plains consist of oaks, ash trees, lindens, maples, elms, and common hornbeams. Hazel nuts, prickwood, and rock cherries are common in the undergrowth. The areas which are cleared of woods are being used for the cultivation of wheat, sugar beets, sunflowers, and other plants.

The Steppe Zone extends from the lower Danube to the Altay and Saur and penetrates from Mongolia to Transbaykalia. There are also two isolated areas in Siberia—Minusinsk and Tuva. This zone has three distinct subzones: forested or meadow steppe, typical steppe, and semidesert.

The subzone of forested steppe lies to the N. of the steppe zone, bounding the forest zone. It is usually spotted with large forested areas. There are two kinds of steppes in this area: the mixed herbaceous and the meadow. Mesophyte grass is characteristic of the mixed herbaceous steppe. The narrow leaf poa, beech grass, bent grass, *Festuca sulcata*, the tough feather grass, and also pulsatilla herb, multi-flower buttercup, six-leaf meadowsweet, mountain clover, and cheese rennet are very common. The plants of the meadow steppe are moderate xerophyte, usually sod-forming Gramineae, such as the tough feather grass (John's, narrowleaf, and hairy), *Festuca sulcata*, koeleria, *Helictotrichon desertorum*, and also some species with underground stems. Thickets of bushes are also common; usually they include steppe cherries, low almonds, *Spiraea crenata*, *S. hypericifolia*, and on the S. of the forested steppe the false acacia. The steppe black thorn and the Russian cytisus grow only in European Russia. Large groves of oak woods are common on the elevations.

The typical steppe and the semidesert zones are woodless, except for the ravines and valleys.

The typical steppes of the Black Sea and Kazakhstan regions are carpeted with sod-forming Gramineae, such as the tough feather grass (Ukrainian, red one, Lessing's, hairy, and others), *Festuca sulcata*, Becker's fescue grass, *Helictotrichon desertorum*, koeleria, snake root, and others. Xerophyte brushwood and also sod-forming Gramineae are characteristic of the semidesert. The tough feather grass (Lessing's and especially Sarepta), *Festuca sulcata*, the wormwood (Tauride, white, and Lercheana), milfoiled pyrethrum, and shrubs are very abundant. The saltwort (black, saline anabasis) and the wormwoods usually grow on the saline spots of the soil. Some perennial ephemeral plants, such as bulbous root poa, tulips, hyacinths, star of Bethlehem, and also a few annual ephemeral plants, such as the darnel, borage, fluellin, are rather common. The Dahurian Mongolian steppes, extending along the Selenga, Onon, and Argun rivers, penetrate north, up to Ulan-

Ude and Nerchinsk. Here the tough feather grass and the ephemeral plants are replaced by *Stipa decipiens*, *Aneurolepidium pseudoagropyrum*, and snake roots, which are typical of the Dahurian Mongolian steppes. These steppes and the steppes of Khakass, Minusinsk, Tuva, and Barguzin have a very similar vegetation.

The flora of the steppes is constantly being changed. In the European part the original flora remains only in the reservations, in the barren steppes of the Caspian Sea, and in Yergeni. Legumes, cereals (mostly wheat), root crops, and melons have replaced the original plants.

The Desert Zone occupies a vast area in Asia: E. Transcaucasia, the plains of the W. and N. Caspian regions, the Turanian lowlands, and the S. part of the volcanic hills in Kazakhstan. There are two types of vegetation—desert brushwood and desert shrubs. The plants of the Compositae family, such as wormwood, goosefoot, *Eurotia*, *Nanophyton erinaceum*, and *Halocnemum strobilaceum*, are characteristic of the desert brushwood. The desert shrubs grow in dry river beds with underground water. The dendroid goosefoot, *haloxylon*, *Salsola Richteri*, *Calligonum*, *Ammodendron*, and ephedra are very common. The ephemeral plant communities are typical of the desert. Occasionally tulips, gagea, ferula, numerous species of darnels and borage are seen, and toward the S., ragweeds, poa bulbosa var. vivipara, and sedges are found.

The desert zone may be divided into three subzones: northern desert, typical desert, and southern desert. The northern subzone lies in the N. of the desert zone, at the limits of the steppes. It is the wormwood steppe desert with *Artemisia Lercheana*, *A. gracilescens*, *A. sublessingiana*, and also sod-forming grass, such as *Festuca sulcata*, the desert tough feather grass of Sarepta, and others. The typical desert subzone occupies the central part of the desert zone and extends from the N. regions of the Caspian Sea to Dzungarian Ala-Tau and to the border of China. The wormwoods and saltworts (larch-tree-leaved kali, saline echinochloa, leafless echinochloa) are common plants of this subzone. The southern desert subzone lies in the S. part of Central Asia and also in E. Transcaucasia. The sandy deserts of Kara Kum and Kyzyl Kum occupy most of the territory. Numerous ephemeral plants, especially bulbous poa and sedges, are typical of the brushwood and shrub desert. Different wormwoods such as *Artemisia herba alba* prefer gravelly soil. *Artemisia Meyeriana* and *A. fragrans* are limited to Transcaucasia; *Salsola gemmascens* grows on the saline soil of Central Asia and *Salsola dendroides*, *S. nodulosa*, *S. ericoides* in Transcaucasia. *Haloxylon persicum*, together with sedges and, in the depressions, *Haloxylon aphyllum*, predominates on the sands of Kara Kum and Kyzyl Kum. Richter's saltwort is also abundant on the sand. As a result of the destruction of Haloxylon for firewood and also because of overgrazing, large areas are almost bare. The sparse bushes which still remain are mostly Calligonum, ephedra, sand acacia, and Eremosparton flaccidum. Saltwort (sarsazan), Halocnemum, the Caspian potash plant, and *Halostachys caspica* occupy the bottoms of the saline basins and the shores of the salt lakes. Reeds and

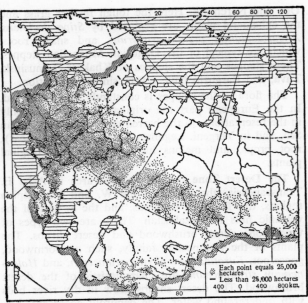

Areas under cultivation

the peculiar inundated forests (tugay) of different poplar trees, Babylonian narrow-leaf willows, tamarisks, and *Halimodendron halodendron* are common in the meadows of the Syr Darya and Amu Darya rivers. Grass communities of subtropical Gramineae prevail in the S. of Central Asia. Cotton and rice fields, orchards, and vineyards are replacing the wild plants in the irrigated areas.

The Vegetation of the Mountains is different from that of the plains. The Carpathians belong to the European broadleaf zone. The lower and central belts are occupied by European beech tree woods, which also grow on the heights of Volyn-Podolia. The coniferous forests with silver and common firs and some broadleaf trees are in the higher region, above the beech tree woods. Sparse fir woods with cedars and Polish silver firs occupy the upper limit of the forests; above them are carpets of sphagnous moss, juniper berries, subalpine *Pinus mughus*, and, on the steep slopes, thickets of alder trees. The rhododendron bushes are almost on the top of the mountains, and the meadows with matgrass, fescue grass, and sedges are still higher.

The S. slopes of the Crimean Mountains and the shores of the Black Sea, between Anapa and Tuapse, belong to the Mediterranean forest zone. Sparse woods of Mediterranean junipers and pubescent oaks occupy the lower mountain belt. The Crimean fir tree woods mixed with groves of cliff oaks are in the central belt of the Crimean Mountains, and pine trees with Crimean beech trees in the higher regions. Vineyards, orchards, and parks are in the lower mountain belt.

The N.W. Caucasus belongs to the Mediterranean zone, while the main mountain range of the Caucasus, Transcaucasia, with neighboring forested mountains of the Minor Caucasus, are in the European broadleaf zone. The forested steppes cover the lower mountains of the N. Caucasus; cliff oaks, beech trees, and pine trees predominate on the N. slopes of the Great Caucasus, while silver and common firs grow in the basin of

Kuban. Woods of Georgian oaks, and Caucasian hornbeams, with undergrowth of azalea, are mostly found in the lower and central belts of Transcaucasia. Woods of Gartviss' and Imeretian oaks, with vines and lianas on the outskirts, are found in the hilly regions of Transcaucasia, and Colchis, while chestnuts, eastern beech trees, Caucasian hornbeams, alder trees, and some of the oaks occupy the lowlands. The undergrowth of this forest usually consists of evergreen bushes, such as Buxus colchica, ponteus rhododendron, laurel cherries, and Colchis ash trees. Dark coniferous forests with Caucasian silver firs, eastern firs mixed with broadleaf trees, occur in the W. part of the Great Caucasus and on the edge of the Minor Caucasus. The growth of *Rhododendron caucasicum* and, in the dryer regions, *Juniperus depressa* belong to the subalpine zone, as do the meadows. The wormwood and saltwort deserts are to be found in E. and S. Transcaucasia, in the Kura-Araks lowland, and in the valley of the Araks. East Indies bluestem covers the hilly regions; the sod-forming Gramineae and the xerophytes, such as astragals or the brushwood of the Labiatae family, are to be found in the central and in part of the lower mountain belts.

A sharp difference in the vegetation of each mountain belt is characteristic of the S.E. Kazakhstan and Central Asian mountains. The grassy steppes cover the central belt of Dzungarian Ala Tau and N. Tien Shan. Coniferous forests, mostly Tien Shan firs, are found in the upper part of this belt. The subalpine and alpine meadows, with large communities of Cobresia, lie in the higher mountain belt; the junipers, mostly *Juniperus turkestanica*, replace Cobresia in the lower part. Peculiar ephemeral plants, usually the bulbous poa and sedges, prevail in the hilly regions of the W. Tien Shan, Pamir, Altay, and Kopet Dagh. Sod-forming Gramineae with pubescent couch grass, bulbous barley, and other ephemeral plants cover the lower region of the central mountain belt. The mountainous meadows, the steppes of half-savannas are found in the central mountain belt. There are brushwood thickets of eglantine, hawthorn, junipers, and communities of prickled Compositae, such as astragals, sainfoin, Acanthaceae, thyme, and other plants. The woods of apples, maples, and hazel nuts are now rare, and the pistachio woods, formerly widely distributed, are almost annihilated. High mountainous deserts occupy almost the whole Pamir region, in which Skornyakov's wormwood and the common tansy are abundant. The interference of man has greatly reduced the number of forests in Central Asia.

The mountains of S. Siberia include the coniferous forests of the Altay and the woodless S.E. areas of the Altay, which are transitory to the mountainous steppes of Mongolia. Dark coniferous forests, mostly Siberian firs, grow in the central mountain belt of the W. and N.W. areas. Deciduous or mixed woods with Siberian larch trees and Siberian cedars are in the inner and N. parts. The steppes usually occupy the river valleys; the mountainous tundra, with thickets of dwarf birches, lies in the high mountain belt. The woods of cedar and silver fir cover the lower part of the Sayan Mountains.

The Water Vegetation consists of angio-spermae plants, ferns, mosses, weeds, and a few species of mushrooms. The geographical distribution of the fresh-water weeds has not yet been well studied. Usually the aquatic territory of the USSR is divided into three regions: the N. where the Desmodus weeds predominate; the lakes of the central plains with numerous blue-green algae and diatoms; and the S.E. region where the blue-green and green weeds, the diatoms, and peridials form large communities. The duckweed is cosmopolitan.

The flora of the White and Barents seas is the same as in the Atlantic Ocean. The littoral flora consists mostly of fucus; the sublittoral of laminaria, alaria, and, deeper in the water, of desmateria and numerous red weeds. The flora of the Baltic Sea is limited in species. Numerous weeds grow on the underwater ice of the arctic seas. Diatoms predominate in the phytoplankton. Sea weeds grow everywhere along the coast, but the richest vegetation is in the W. part of the ocean. Diatoms and blue-green weeds predominate in the Far E. seas. Sargassum is found in the Sea of Japan and nowhere else. The bottom weeds are more abundant in the cooler part of the Pacific Ocean. The flora of the Black and Azov seas is the same as in the Mediterranean, but is much poorer in the Caspian and Aral seas. Diatoms, especially *Rhizosolenia calcar-avis* and the blue-green algae, are numerous in the Caspian Sea, and among the peridial sporophores, *Exuviella cordata* is the best known. The blue-green algae prevail in the brackish water of the N. part of the Caspian Sea, and blue-green weeds are common on the bottom.

Uses of the Plants. The forests are important in construction work and are also used as firewood. The lumber of firs, pines, and larches is considered the best for the construction industry. The pulp of firs and some grasses of Kazakhstan and Central Asia are used in the cellulose industry. The bark of oaks, firs, larches, and numerous willows contains tannic acid, which is also found in the bushes of myrtle leaf sumach, the roots of saxifrage, Central Asian buckwheat, and other plants. Ropes, mats, and brushes are often made from wild sugar cane, chia, barbateg grass, and other species. The rosin and gum of some astragals from S. Transcaucasia and Kopet Dagh and of pine trees, silver firs, and larch trees are used in the textile industry. Some plants, as dandelion *kok-sagyz*, the viper grass *tau-sagyz*, and a few evonymus, contain India rubber; many, as silver firs, yield invaluable oils. Sages, mints, cat mints, snake roots, and S. Siberian Corulia geoides are used in the perfume industry. Many plants are toxic and are applied as insecticides, the most common of which are anabasis and pyrethrum. Vitamins are prepared from the acerose leaves of some coniferous trees, some eglantines, and the berries of black currant. The best-known medicinal plants are lily of the valley, foxglove, valerian, *Atropa belladonna*, and *Ephedra distachya*. There are 224 kinds of wild fruit-bearing trees and bushes which are used in the food industry, as well as some bulbous herbs, sea weeds, and mushrooms. Timothy grass, fox tail, poa, fescue grass, couch grass, barley and, from the legume family, clover, alfalfa, sainfoin, astragal and blue vetch are common in natural pastures.   T. D. G.

PLATÓNOV, Sergéy Fyódorovich (1860–1933), historian. Graduated from the historical-philological faculty of the St. Petersburg University. P was well known as a historian, and many of his books are translated into foreign languages. Of great value is his study on *The Times of Troubles in the Moscow State* (1899). P was a disciple of V. O. Klyuchevsky and considered that economic factors greatly influenced social and political history. In 1917, he became chairman of the Historical-Archeological Commission which published much valuable source materials on R. history. In 1920, P participated as an expert at the negotiations of the Riga Peace Treaty between Poland and Soviet Russia. In 1930, together with a group of historians, P was arrested. After a year in prison, he was exiled to Samara (now Kuybyshev) where he died.

PLÉHVE, Vyacheslável Konstantínovich (1846–1904), statesman, one of the most reactionary figures of the autocratic regime of Tsar Nicholas II. Chief of the security police (gendarmerie), director of police department, governor general of Finland and, finally, the most feared and hated minister of the interior. Notorious as ruthless "Russificator" of national minorities and a stern enemy of the revolutionary movement. Is said to be an instigator of the Russo-Japanese War of 1904. Murdered by the Socialist Revolutionary Yegor Sozonov.

PLEKHÁNOV, Geórgy Valentínovich (1856–1918), Marxist theoretician, one of the founders of the R. Social Democratic party. P was born in Tambov Province of a gentry family. Joined the populist movement as a student of the Mining Institute of the St. Petersburg University in 1875; he soon became one of the chief  populist writers and organizers. P was co-author of the program of Land and Freedom (*see* POPULISM). In 1876 he led the student and workers' demonstration in the Kazan Square in the capital. In 1879 when a majority of the populist leaders decided to adopt terrorist methods in the struggle against autocracy, P seceded and with a small group of populists (P. Akselrod, L. Deutsch, V. Zasulich) formed a new populist group, Black Repartition (q.v.). In 1883, as an *émigré*, in Switzerland, P renounced populism, and became a Marxist. He founded the first R. Marxist group, Liberation of Labor (q.v.).

During the forty years which P spent in exile, he wrote many books and pamphlets and became the intellectual leader of the R. social-democratic movement. Most of his books, written in the 1880's and 1890's, were directed against the populists: *Socialism and Political Action* (1883), *Our Differences* (1884), *Anarchism and Socialism* (1895). However, he also published studies on the history of materialism which were highly praised in the Marxist circles outside Russia.

In 1900, P jointly with a group of younger R. Marxists (V. Lenin, L. Martov, and A. Potresov) started the publication of *Iskra* (q.v.). In 1903 he prepared, jointly with Lenin, the program which was adopted at the 2nd Congress of the Social Democratic party. At the congress itself, P supported Lenin; however, he soon broke with the Bolsheviks and joined the Mensheviks. P was a defeatist during the Russo-Japanese War. After the revolution of 1905, he was close to the Bolsheviks on many issues, particularly on the question of participation in the Duma and that of illegal activities of the Social Democratic party. However, with the outbreak of World War I, P pleaded for support of the Allies and the defense of Russia. In 1917, after the February revolution, P returned to Russia where he was warmly greeted by the Petrograd Soviet of Workers' Deputies. Outside of both Marxist factions, he became the leader of a group *Yedinstvo* (q.v.) which had little influence on the course of the revolution. Actively supporting the Provisional Government against the Bolsheviks, P remained an irreconcilable opponent of the Bolsheviks until his death in Finland.

P's contributions to Marxist theory, philosophy, and esthetics are numerous. Besides a variety of books on Marxism, P published monographs on V. Belinsky and N. Chernyshevsky and an unfinished social history of Russia.

PLESHCHÉYEV, Alekséy Nikoláyevich (1825–1893), poet, born in Kostroma in a family of landed gentry. He was sentenced to hard labor in 1849 for participation in the Petrashevsky circle. His poetry reflects love of freedom and his *Forward! Without Doubts or Fears* (1846) became a revolutionary song. He also wrote poetry for children and translated Heine and others.

PLESHCHÉYEVO or PERESLAVL, lake in S. Yaroslavl Oblast, RSFSR. Pereslavl-Zalessky is on E. shore. Area 20 sq. mi.; its water is transparent; has sandy and hard bottom. Receives Trubezh River, an outlet for the Veksa. The first vessels of the Russian navy were built on the lake by Peter the Great (1691).

PLETNYÓV, Pyotr Aleksándrovich (1792–1865), poet and critic. Prof. of R. literature and later rector of the University of St. Petersburg. From 1838 to 1846, he was editor of the *Sovremennik* (Contemporary), a leading literary journal. P was a friend of Pushkin.

PLEVE: *see* PLEHVE.

PLISÉTSKAYA, Máya Mikháylovna (1925–), dancer, daughter of a dramatic dancer and niece of Asaf Messerer, teacher and choreographer of the Moscow Bolshoy Ballet. Graduated from the Moscow State School of Ballet in 1943, she is now one of the principal ballerinas of the Bolshoy. She has a highly developed lyric and dramatic style, is the possessor of a beautiful line, an excellent technique, and a very high elevation and good ballon. Her roles include the leading parts in *Swan Lake, The Nutcracker, The Fountain of Bakhchisaray, The Stone Flower, Walpurgis Night,* and others. She is a People's Artist of the USSR.

POBÉDA PEAK, Kokshal-Tau range in the Tien Shan mountain system, on Soviet-Chinese border; 24,400 ft.

POBEDONÓSTSEV, Konstantín Petróvich (1827–1907), jurist and statesman. Was professor of civil law at the University of Moscow (1859). He moved to St. Petersburg in 1865 on being summoned to teach law to the older sons of Alexander II. In 1872 he was appointed member of the State Council. Procurator of the Holy Synod from April 1880 to October 1905, he became, under Alexander III and at the beginning of Nicholas II's reign, one of the most important reaction-

ary advisers to the tsar on internal policy. Imbued with the panslav spirit, P created an imaginary ideal of the R. people and the old R. culture. Something of a mystic (he translated Thomas à Kempis' *Imitation of Christ* into Russian), taking his inspiration from the R. form of Christianity, the Orthodox Church, and absolutist government, P was fanatically behind the unity of the church and the power of the tsar.

An enemy of western liberal rationalism, while scrupulous in his choice of means and disinterested personally, he was a consistent ultra conservative; he fought tenaciously against a constitution, trial by jury, freedom of the press. His chief argument in favor of autocracy was the historical fact of its existence.

PODGÓRNY, Nikoláy Víktorovich (1903–), Soviet state and party official. Presidium member of the Central Committee of the CPSU and chairman of the Council of Ministers of the Ukrainian SSR. Accompanied N. S. Khrushchev to the General Assembly Session of the UN in New York in Sept.-Oct. 1960. Has been a member of the CPSU since 1930. In 1939, was deputy people's commissar for the food industry in the Ukraine; 1950, elected first secretary of the Kharkov Oblast committee of the CP of the Ukraine; 1953, second secretary of the CP of the Ukraine; 1957, first secretary of the CP of the Ukraine. At the 20th Congress of the CPSU (1956) P was elected candidate member of Central Committee of the CPSU; in 1958 candidate member of the Presidium of the Central Committee of the CPSU. P is a deputy to the Supreme Soviet USSR and member of the Presidium of the Supreme Soviet.

PODÓLSK, city in Moscow Oblast, RSFSR, on Pakhra River; pop 72,000 (1939), 124,000 (1959). A major ind. center; machine mfg., cement and lime factories, R.R. repair shops.

PODVÓYSKY, Nikoláy Ilyích (1880–1948), revolutionary. From 1901, a member of the party; in 1905, P participated in organizing strikes in Ivanovo-Voznesensk and in Yaroslavl. After emigrating in 1906, he soon returned to Russia and worked underground in St. Petersburg. Following the February revolution in 1917, P became a leader of the military organization of the Bolshevik party, and one of the organizers of the Red Guard. As a secretary of the military revolutionary committee of the Petrograd Soviet, P took a prominent part in the preparation of the October revolution. Later he worked in the People's Commissariat for Army and Navy and took part in the organization of the Red Army. In 1919, P was people's commissar for army and navy in the Soviet Ukraine. Since the early 1930's, P has not been heard of, but he was rehabilitated after the 20th Party Congress. His reminiscences of the events of 1917 were published in Moscow in 1958.

PODZOL: *see* SOILS.

POGÓDIN, Mikhaíl Petróvich (1800–1875), historian and journalist. The son of a serf, P taught at the University of Moscow and, as journalist, became prominent because of his extreme nationalism. His *Early History of Russia* (1871) was a rather formless compendium of facts. A panslavist, he often suggested the hand of God at work in R. history preparing the nation for a great mission of peace and order.

POGÓDIN (Stukálov), **Nikoláy Fyódorovich** (1900–), dramatist, born on the Don. P began by writing poetry and at the age of 20 became a correspondent for *Pravda*. His first play, *Tempo* (1929), dealt with the construction of a Stalingrad tractor factory. His second play, *Impertinence*, was accepted by the Moscow Art Theater as part of its permanent repertory. Many more followed, including *Song of the Axe* (1930), *My Friend* (1932), *Aristocrats* (1934) which was very successful, and a trilogy of plays about Lenin: *Man with a Gun* (1937), *Kremlin Chimes* (1940, reworked in 1955), and *The Third is Pathetic* (1958). The trilogy won a Lenin prize. In addition to some 30 plays, P has written film scenarios, including *Conclusion, Kuban Cossacks*, and the film version of *Man with a Gun*. Two of his more recent works, *We Three Went to the Virgin Lands* (1955) and *Petrarch's Sonnet* (1956), were attacked by party critics for their candor and "revisionist spirit." Stalin prize (1941).

POKRÓVSK: *see* ENGELS.

POKRÓVSKY, Mikhaíl Nikoláyevich (1868–1932), Communist historian. Graduated from Moscow University in 1891. Was a pupil of V. O. Klyuchevsky and P. Vinogradoff. In 1903–04, participated in the zemstvo liberal movement but in 1905 joined the Bolshevik party. From 1908 was abroad and returned to Russia in Aug. 1917. After the October revolution he was chairman of the Moscow Soviet; in May 1918, was appointed deputy people's commissar of education. P was also the chairman of the Central Archives, of the Marxist Historians' Society, director of the Institute of Red Professors, and editor of many historical reviews.

P was instrumental in lowering the standard of teaching of R. history. From 1929 to 1935, he actually abolished the teaching of history in the Soviet high schools and universities. P's attitude toward history, which, according to him, had to serve the goals of the Communist party, was very utilitarian. His best-known books, which were textbooks in R. schools in the 1920's, were *Concise Russian History, Russian History from Ancient Times* (4 volumes), and *Outline of the History of Russian Culture*. In the 1920's and early 1930's, P was the official Soviet historian. However, in 1936, his historical "conception" was proclaimed "anti-Marxist" and "anti-Leninist."

POLÉNOV, Vasíly Dmítrievich (1844–1927), painter. Son of an archaeologist, P received an excellent education in Russia and in Paris. Member of the Society of Circulating Exhibitions (*Peredvizhniki*) from 1878. P painted historical subjects (*The Right of the Master*, 1874) as well as genre pictures (*The Sick Woman*), landscapes, and portraits. His pictures are in the Tretyakov Gallery in Moscow.

POLÉSSK (f. Labiau), town in Kaliningrad Oblast, RSFSR; pop. 6,600 (1956). Fish and food ind., breweries.

POLEVÓY (Kampov), **Borís Nikoláyevich** (1908–), novelist and journalist. War correspondent for *Pravda* (1941–45). His best-known novel, *The Tale of a Real Man* (1946) concerning the war exploits of a Soviet pilot, received wide acclaim in the Soviet press. Author of short stories, including *We—The Soviet People*; and

novel, *Gold* (1949–50). A propagandist for the communist cause during his visits to the United States (1958, 1959, and 1960). Stalin prize (1949).

POLEZHÁYEV, Aleksándr Ivánovich (1805–1838), poet and revolutionary. His poems were inspired by the Decembrist movement and bore titles such as *Song of the Doomed Swimmer* and *The Prisoner*. In 1826, P wrote the satirical poem *Sáshka* which brought upon him the punishment of a term of service as private in the army. He died of tuberculosis in the Caucasus.

POLICE INFILTRATION. The placing of secret agents by organs of the political police (*Okhrana*) for the "internal illumination" of the activities of revolutionary organizations was already practiced in Russia in the 1880's. At that time the leaders of the Okhrana, P. Rachkovsky, Sudeykin, Ratayev, and others, attached great importance to information attained from secret agents working within "The People's Will." These included Sergey Degayev (1854–1908), a prominent member of this organization, who was recruited into the Okhrana by Sudeykin and who participated in one of the attempts on the life of Alexander II. Subsequently, Degayev sought to atone for his guilt by killing Sudeykin. He then fled the country and lived in the United States under an assumed name as a professor of mathematics. Another secret agent of the political police who became prominent during this period was Arkady Harting (also known as Hekkelman and as Landensen) who provided information on the activities of the populist leader Lavrov, among others. He had become an agent of Rachkovsky in 1884. Later he was head of the foreign agents of the R. police. Wide renown was also acquired by Zubatov who was at first a revolutionary and then became an agent of the Okhrana. Zubatov lent his name (*Zubatovschina*) to an organized attempt on the part of the police to provide the labor movement with leaders who would be loyal to the government. With the help of some participants in socialist groups that he was able to bring to his side in 1900–03 Zubatov succeeded in creating a legal "Independent Labor Party." It is the ideas of Zubatov that led the priest Gapon (who turned out to have been an agent of the Okhrana) to organize a march of factory workers bearing a petition to the tsar on Jan. 9, 1905. This action was transformed, by the course of events, into the beginning of the first Russian Revolution (*see* BLOODY SUNDAY). Zubatov committed suicide in 1917.

Of the police infiltrators who were active in the 20th century, the greatest fame attaches to Yevno Azef, who was a member of the Central Committee of the Socialist Revolutionary party and chief of its terrorist group, and who personally directed several acts of terrorism. Azef enjoyed the full confidence of both his colleagues in the party and of the Police Department. It is curious that after the publication of the Manifesto of Oct. 17, 1905, he recommended to the Central Committee of the Socialist Revolutionary party that the Okhrana building be blown up so that "no evidence would remain." The unmasking of Azef was carried out by V. L. Burtsev with the aid of two former members of the Okhrana —Bakay and Menshchikov. Their information was confirmed by a former director of the Police Department, A. A. Lopukhin (who on Jan. 19, 1909 was sentenced to 5 years of hard labor, subsequently commuted to exile, for this indiscretion). In 1908 Azef was tried in Paris by a court that consisted of old participants in the revolutionary movement: V. N. Figner, P. A. Kropotkin, and Herman Lopatin.

The police infiltrators who provided information concerning the activities of the social democrats included M. I. Gurovich, the editor of one of the first Marxist journals *Nachalo* (The Beginning) (1899); Dobroskok ("Nikolay—Golden Glasses") who was active during the years 1902–05; I. M. Kaplinsky (Langsam), who worked in the Bund and who was exposed in Feb. 1909; Miron Chernomazov, editor of the Bolshevik *Pravda* in 1912–13 (committed suicide by taking poison after his arrest in April 1917); Dr. Zhitomirsky, M. Brandinsky, and A. Romanov, who were prominent among the Bolsheviks; and V. M. Abrosimov, a worker and a Menshevik, who was exposed in 1917. The greatest renown was obtained by R. V. Malinovsky (1878–1918), a worker who became a member of the Okhrana in 1910 and a member of the fourth State Duma representing Moscow. Malinovsky was a Bolshevik leader, a member of the Russian Bureau of the Bolshevik Central Committee, and a person who enjoyed the confidence both of Lenin and of Beletsky of the Police Department.

After the coming to power of the Bolsheviks the use of police infiltrators became a widely used method for combating anti-Soviet movements both within Russia and among *émigré* circles abroad. Special organizations were established by the foreign department of the security police in the 1930's (e.g., the "Trust") in order to entice opponents into Russia (e.g. in the case of B. Savinkov in 1924) and in some instances to carry out the kidnapping of individual influential leaders (e.g. Gen. Kutepov and Gen. Miller). The best-known police infiltrators carrying out this type of assignment included Yakushev, Operput, Gen. Skoblin, the singer Plevitskaya, and S. Tretyakov.   G. A.

BIBLIOGRAPHY: A. T. Vasilyev, *The Okhrana*, Philadelphia, 1930.

POLISH UPRISINGS, 1768, 1794, 1830–1831, 1863, were directed against the pressure brought to bear upon Poland by her neighbors, but especially against Russia. Their object was to throw off the foreign yoke. Strong anti-Russian feeling in Poland was in evidence early in the 18th century. The first real uprising occurred during the reign of Empress Catherine II of Russia and is known as the Bar Confederation (1768–72). It led to war with Russia and was largely provoked by the brutal policies of the R. ambassador to Warsaw, Prince Nicholas Repnin, and his interference with the internal affairs of Poland. The uprising was defeated and brought about the first partition of Poland in 1772. Next, the proclamation on May 3, 1791 of the new Polish constitution, which was reasonably democratic and aimed at overcoming Poland's internal disorders, was again opposed by Russia and led to the Kosciuszko uprising in 1794. The Poles were defeated by the overwhelming R. forces and Poland lost her independence (1795). Napoleon's plans for E. Europe included the creation of the Polish Duchy of Warsaw (1807); this arrangement

was superseded, under the provisions of the treaty of Vienna (1815), by the establishment of the Kingdom of Poland under the suzerainty of the R. tsars. The constitution granted to Russian Poland by Emperor Alexander I was liberal according to the standards of the time but it was never properly applied. Tension increased with the accession of Emperor Nicholas I (1825) and in Nov. 1830 a Polish uprising broke out which extended to the Lithuanian provinces and lasted nearly a year. The Poles, in spite of their gallant resistance, were defeated. The constitution of 1815 was abrogated and the R. government retaliated with great ruthlessness. The last uprising against imperial Russia occurred in 1863. The memories of the Crimean war being still alive, the insurgents found much encouragement in England and France but no effective action was taken on their behalf. The uprising was again defeated. Poland lost the last remnants of her autonomy and there were mass trials followed by heavy prison sentences and massive deportations to Siberia.   J. W.

POLITBURÓ (the Political Bureau of the Central Committee of the Communist Party) was organized on Oct. 23, 1917 as a small standing committee capable of prompt decision. Its members were Lenin, Zinoviev, Kamenev, Trotsky, Stalin, Sokolnikov, and Bubnov. It was dissolved after the seizure of power by the Bolsheviks but revived in March 1919 when the 8th Party Congress made it a permanent organ; its members were then Lenin, Trotsky, Stalin, Kamenev, and Krestinsky. Soon the P became the central policy-making body and in part supplanted the Central Committee. In 1926, after the 14th Party Congress, Trotsky, Kamenev, and Zinoviev were expelled and replaced either by Stalin's supporters or by followers of the Bukharin-Rykov-Tomsky group. In 1929–30 the leaders of the Right opposition were also expelled, and the P fell entirely under Stalin's control. It was rarely convened in the later period of Stalin's rule. At the 19th Party Congress in October 1952, the P was reorganized as the Presidium of the Central Committee of the CPSU.

POLITBURO MEMBERS 1919–1952

Lenin, Vladimir I.	1919—1924	Died 1924
Stalin, Joseph V.	1919—1952	Died 1953
Sverdlov, Yakov M.	1919—1919	Died 1919
Trotsky, Lev D.	1919—1926	Murdered 1940
Bukharin, Nikolay I.	1919—1929	Executed 1938
Kamenev, Lev B.	1919—1926	Executed 1936
Krestinsky, Nikolay N.	1919—1921	Executed 1938
Rykov, Aleksey I.	1919—1929	Executed 1938
Tomsky, Mikhail P.	1919—1929	Suicide 1936
Zinoviev, Grigory Ye.	1923—1926	Executed 1936
Molotov, Vyacheslav M.	1925—1952	
Voroshilov, Kliment Ye.	1925—1952	
Kalinin, Mikhail I.	1926—1946	Died 1946
Kuybyshev, Valerian V.	1927—1935	Died 1935
Rudzutak, Yan E.	1927—1931	Disappeared 1938
Kaganovich, Lazar M.	1930—1952	
Kirov, Sergey M.	1930—1934	Murdered 1934
Kosior, Stanislav V.	1930—1938	Disappeared 1938
Ordzhonikidze, Grigory K.	1930—1937	Died 1937
Andreyev, Andrey A.	1932—1952	
Chubar, Vlas Ya.	1935—1938	Disappeared 1938
Mikoyan, Anastas I.	1935—1952	
Khrushchev, Nikita S.	1939—1952	
Zhdanov, Andrey A.	1939—1948	Died 1948
Beria, Lavrenty P.	1946—1952	Executed 1953
Malenkov, Georgy M.	1946—1952	
Voznesensky, Nikolay A.	1947—1949	Executed 1951

BIBLIOGRAPHY: George K. Schueller, *The Politburo*, Stanford, 1951.

POLITICAL COMMISSARS: *see* ARMED FORCES.

POLL TAX was a capitation tax paid by every male peasant and by the lower strata of the urban population —artisans and burghers (*meshchane*). It was introduced by the decree of Jan. 19, 1723. Throughout the 18th and most of the 19th century liability to the PT was, in the case of the rural inhabitants, the earmark of servile status, even though the tax survived the abolition of serfdom in 1861. The original annual rate of the tax was 74 kopecks for each male serf (the serfs lived on privately owned estates and had to pay in addition to the tax a tribute to their master) and 1.20 rubles per state peasant (q.v.). The accumulation of arrears on account of the tax forced the government to lower the rate in 1725, in 1742, and again in 1750–58. The rate of the tax for each serf was increased to 70 kopecks in 1760 and to one ruble in 1794. The PT was the principal single source of state revenue. Its yield was 5.7 mill. rubles in 1763; 24.7 mill. in 1796; 38 mill. in 1869; and 52 mill. in 1879. In the second half of the 18th century the PT provided about one-third of the total state revenue, and in the 1860's to the 1880's it accounted for about 45 per cent of the aggregate revenue from direct taxation. The PT was partly removed in 1883 and 1884 and was repealed as of Jan. 1, 1887. It was an apportioned tax; it was assessed on each community on the basis of the assumed number of taxpayers who were jointly responsible for the payment of the tax. This arrangement, which also applied to redemption payments (q.v.) was one reason for the fostering of the village commune by the government and for the retention of this form of landholding after the emancipation of 1861.

POLÓNSKY, Yákov Petróvich (1819–1898), poet. Some of his verses were put to music by Tchaikovsky, Taneyev, and Rubinstein. P's most successful work was the allegorical poem *The Cricket-Musician* (1859).

PÓLOTSK, city in Vitebsk Oblast, Byelorussian SSR, on right bank of the W. Dvina River; pop. 38,100 (1956). Key R.R. junction; oil refining, flax-weaving, timber ind. One of the oldest cities in Russia, it is mentioned in Scandinavian sagas and in Nestor's chronicle 862. Capital of Polotsk principality from the 11th to early 14th century when it was incorporated in Lithuania. Occupied by R. 1563–79, then under Polish rule until annexed by R. in 1772; partly destroyed by Napoleon 1812. Has many architectural monuments.

PÓLOTSK, PRINCIPALITY OF, occupied area along the W. Dvina and Polot rivers. Its decline was marked by the breakup into several principalities in the 12th century. It was incorporated into the Grand Principality of Lithuania in the 14th century.

PÓLOTSKY, Simeón (Samuíl Yemelyánovich Petróvsky-Sitnianóvich) (1629–1680), learned monk and writer; native of Byelorussia. He advocated secular education and planned to organize a Slavic-Greek-Latin Academy. He wrote sermons, poetry, a play, *The Fable of the Prodigal Son*, in syllabic verse which gives a vivid picture of life in 17th-century Russia.

PÓLOVTSY: *see* CUMANS.

POLTÁVA, BATTLE OF, June 27, 1709, which ended in R. victory under Peter I over the Swedish Army of Charles XII. Heavy casualties were suffered by the Swedes (9,000 men), their entire artillery being wiped out, and 2,500 men being taken prisoner. The remnants of the defeated Swedish army (16,000) surrendered on June 30 to General Menshikov at Perevolochnaya on the Dnieper. Charles XII was wounded and fled to Turkey in the company of Hetman Mazepa. The battle was decisive for the outcome of the Northern War (1700–21) and marks the beginning of R. influence in Europe.

POLTÁVA, city, adm. center of Poltava Oblast, Ukrainian SSR, on right bank of Vorskla River; pop. 141,000 (1959). Key R.R. junction; has colleges, scientific institutes, historical museum, V. G. Korolenko museum (domicile of writer 1903–21). A center of rich agr. region, is a grain-collection point; raises grain, sugar beets, tobacco, fruit; has extensive leather mfg. Origin dates back to 12th century; annexed by Lithuania in 14th century; under Khmelnitsky a Cossack stronghold; scene of victory of Peter I over Charles XII of Sweden 1709.

POLTÁVA OBLAST, in Dnieper lowland, Ukrainian SSR; area 11,200 sq. mi.; pop. 1,632,000 (1959). Cities: Poltava (adm. center), Kremenchug, Mirgorod, Piryatin. Drained by the Dnieper and its affluents, the Sula, Psel, Vorskla; has black soils (70 per cent), some podsolic soils; mild continental climate. Extensive agr.: wheat, corn, rye, barley, sugar beets, potatoes, sunflowers, livestock, dairy farming, orchards, flowers, apiculture and sericulture, horse breeding (Piryatin). Ind.: machine mfg. (Kremenchug, Poltava), food processing (sugar refining), light ind., distilling, meat packing, flour milling (Mirgorod), cigarets. R.R. and highway network. Est. 1937.

POLYÁNSKY, Dmítry Stepánovich (1917–), party and state official, born in the Donbas of a peasant family. In 1939 he graduated from the Kharkov Agricultural School. In the same year, he became a member of the CP. He worked as a party secretary in the provinces and in the 1940's was given a position in the Central Committee of the CP. In 1949, he was appointed second secretary and in 1953 first secretary of the Crimean Oblast. In 1956, he was elected to the Central Committee. In March 1958, P was appointed chairman of the Council of Ministers of the RSFSR. In this capacity, he accompanied Khrushchev to the United Nations session in New York in 1960. Since May 1960 member of the Presidium.

POMYALÓVSKY, Nikoláy Gerásimovich (1835–1863), promising writer, whose career was ended at an early age by death due to alcoholism. Once a student in a theological seminary, he related his experience in *Seminary Sketches* (1862–63). His two novels *Bourgeois Happiness* and *Molotov*, both published in 1861, described conditions among low-born intellectuals.

PONIATÓWSKI, Stanislaw August (1732–1798), favorite of Catherine II with whose help he was elected King of Poland (1764–95). Under his reign Polish prestige deteriorated steadily, resulting in the partition of Poland.

PONOMARÉNKO, Panteleymón Kondrátyevich (1902–), party and government official, born in Kuban.

He served in the Red Army, 1919; worked as mechanic in the oil industry and on railroads; graduated from the Moscow Institute of Transport Engineers in 1932. In 1938 he became first secretary of the central committee, Byelorussian CP. During the war he was active in the partisan movement. In 1944 he became chairman of the Byelorussian SSR Council of Ministers; from 1948 to 1952 he was secretary of the Central Committee, CPSU; in 1952 Presidium member, Central Committee, CPSU; was appointed minister of supplies in 1950; minister of culture, 1953–54; elected first secretary of the central committee, Kazakh CP, in 1954; named ambassador to Poland in 1955; ambassador to India in 1956; concurrently envoy to Nepal, 1957. Several times he was deputy to the USSR Supreme Soviet; and a member of the USSR Supreme Soviet Presidium, 1954.

PONÓY RIVER, largest on Kola Peninsula, 255 mi. long; rises in marshland, flows in deep valley forming many rapids, empties into the White Sea; timber floating.

PONTRYÁGIN, Lev Semyónovich (1908–), mathematician. Fellow, Ac. of S., USSR (1958). Lost his eyesight at the age of 14. Graduate (1929) and professor (1935), Moscow University. Research on topology and continuous groups. In 1932, made an important contribution to modern topology by discovering the general law of duality. Originator of theories on reflections, dimensionality, and related subjects. The results of his work are adduced in his monograph *Continuous Groups* (1938). Author of works on algebra, the theory of Lie groups, and differential geometry. Stalin prize (1941) and other decorations.

POPÓV, Aleksándr Stepánovich (1859–1905), mathematician and physicist. Claimed by the Russians to be  the inventor of radio communication (1895) before G. Marconi had patented his invention. Graduate, St. Petersburg University (1882); head, Department of Physics (1901), and director (1905), St. Petersburg Institute of Electrical Engineering. Early research concerned problems of physics and electrical engineering. Realizing the importance of wireless communications, P devoted himself entirely to research in that field (1893). Correlating the results achieved by the physicists E. Branly and O. Lodge, P built an experimental device and established wireless ship-to-shore communication over a distance of 750 ft. (1896), 1,950 ft. (1897), and 3 mi. Suggested radiotelegraph communication between Russia and Bulgaria (1903). Honorary member of engineering societies; honorary degree and Gold Medal awarded at the Fourth World Congress of Electrical Engineering (1900).

POPULAR FRONT: *see* COMMUNIST INTERNATIONAL.

POPULATION. The population of USSR is, according to the January 15, 1959 census, 208,826,650. This makes USSR the third-largest (after China and India) state on earth as regards population. This population is distributed among the constituent republics as follows:

TABLE 1
POPULATION OF THE USSR
(Current boundaries. In thousands)

Republic	Jan. 17, 1939	Jan. 15, 1959
USSR	190,678	208,827
RSFSR	108,379	117,534
Ukrainian SSR	40,469	41,869
Byelorussian SSR	8,910	8,055
Uzbek SSR	6,336	8,106
Kazakh SSR	6,094	9,310
Georgian SSR	3,540	4,044
Azerbaijan SSR	3,205	3,698
Lithuanian SSR	2,880	2,711
Moldavian SSR	2,452	2,885
Latvian SSR	1,885	2,093
Kirghiz SSR	1,458	2,066
Tadzhik SSR	1,484	1,980
Armenian SSR	1,282	1,763
Turkmen SSR	1,252	1,516
Estonian SSR	1,052	1,197

The analysis of the above figures tells the drama of the tremendous industrial and cultural effort of the USSR, the human cost of the gigantic experiment and the tragic war losses. The distribution of population has been affected by recent population shifts, e.g., the wartime transfers of population eastward due to the relocation of many industrial enterprises, and also to the postwar cultivation of virgin and idle lands in these regions. While the population of the USSR as a whole increased 9.5% in the period from 1939 to 1959, the population of the Urals increased 32%, of W. Siberia 24%, of E. Siberia 34%, of the Far East 70%, Central Asia and Kazakhstan 38%. Due to this inner migration the percentage of Kazakhs in their republic decreased from 38 in 1939 to 30 in 1959, and the percentage of Russians and Ukrainians grew in Kazakhstan from 33 to 51, and in Kirgizia from 12 to 30.

The figures in Table 1 reflect, on the other hand, the enormous war losses of the USSR. Its population now exceeds that of U.S. by only 18%, whereas before the war the margin was 46% which corresponds to a

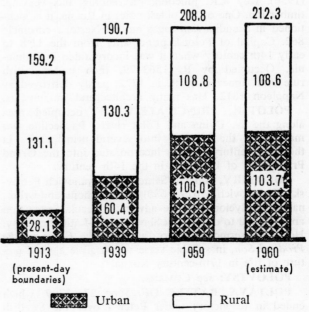

POPULATION OF THE USSR
(in mill.)

Urban   Rural

deficit of at least 40 million persons. The human costs of World War I, the Revolution and the famine in the civil war years are evaluated at 12 million excess civilian deaths, 2 million refugees, and a birth deficit of nearly 10 million. To these should be added the direct military losses of some 2 million during World War I. The years between the first and second national censuses in 1926 and 1939 encompass the collectivization of the agriculture and the human costs of this period are evaluated at as high as 20 million.

The World War II losses resulted also in a striking disparity between the sexes. The 1959 census shows 94,050,000 or 45% men, and 114,776,000 or 55% women. In 1950 this shortage amounted to 23.5 million males, and in 1959 this deficit has declined to 20.7 million.

TABLE 2

MALES PER 100 FEMALES IN USSR

	(All ages)	(Ages 15–59)	In USA (All ages)
1926	93	90	103.1
1940	92	91	110.8
1950	77	68	
1959	82	77	98.0

In order to replace the deficient male labor to the growing industry the Soviet Government was forced to resort to an extraordinarily high employment of women. In 1957 women composed 53% of Soviet labor force. A second source of manpower was the draining of the schools by the recent educational reforms. The next source was the continuing migration of the rural population to the cities, as shown in Table 3.

TABLE 3

POPULATION OF THE USSR, BY URBAN-RURAL RESIDENCE, SELECTED YEARS, 1913–59
(In millions)

Year	Total	Urban	Rural	Percent urban
1913				
Current boundaries	159.2	28.1	131.1	18
Boundaries prior to Sept. 17, 1939	139.3	24.7	114.6	18
1926				
Population census of Dec. 17, 1926 (boundaries prior to Sept. 17, 1939)	147.0	26.3	120.7	18
1939				
Population census of Jan. 17, 1939 (boundaries prior to Sept. 17, 1939)	170.6	56.1	114.5	33
Estimate, including western oblasts of the Ukraine and Byelorussia, plus Moldavia, Lithuania, Latvia, and Estonia	190.7	60.4	130.3	32
1959				
Population Census of Jan. 15, 1959	208.8	99.8	109.0	48

This shift of population from the countryside to the cities, due primarily to industrialization, resulted also in the tremendous growth of cities.

It is to be noted that the number of cities with a population of over 500,000 rose from 3 in 1926 to 11 in 1939 to 25 in 1959; cities from 100–500 thousand rose from 31 in 1926 to 78 in 1939 to 123 in 1959, and 50–100 thousand from 60 to 94 and then to 151 (see Table 4, p. 445).

The revolution has also produced very considerable changes in the occupational structure of the population. The substance of these changes is given in percentage form in Table 5.

TABLE 5

OCCUPATIONAL STRUCTURE OF THE POPULATION

	1913	1928	1937	1958
Industry and Construction	9.0	8.0	24.0	31.0
Agriculture	75.0	80.0	56.0	42.0
Education and Health	1.0	2.0	5.0	10.0
Public Administration and Cooperatives	4.0	5.0	6.0	5.0
Trade and Services	9.0	3.0	4.0	5.0
Transport and Communications .	2.0	2.0	5.0	7.0
TOTAL	100.0	100.0	100.0	100.0

Another important change occurred in the rates of birth, death and population increase (Table 6).

TABLE 6

POPULATION INCREASE

	1913	1940	1950	1958
Birth rate per 1,000 of population	47.0	31.7	26.5	25.3
Death rate per 1,000 of population	30.2	18.3	9.6	7.2
Natural increase per 1,000 of population	16.8	13.4	16.9	18.1

The death rate, according to the census of 1959, sunk to 7.2 per 1000 in 1958. This is claimed to be the lowest mortality rate in the world.

TABLE 7

POPULATION OF THE USSR BY AGE

	No. of persons (thousands) 1939	1959	% of total pop. 1939	1959	1959 in % of 1939
Total population including:	190,678	208,827	100.0	100.0	109.5
0– 9 years	43,476	46,363	22.8	22.2	107
10–15 years	28,365	17,133	14.9	8.2	60
16–19 years	13,030	14,675	6.8	7.0	113
20–24 years	15,786	20,343	8.3	9.7	129
25–29 years	18,520	18,190	9.7	8.7	98
30–34 years	15,598	18,999	8.2	9.1	122
35–39 years	12,958	11,590	6.8	5.6	89
40–44 years	9,603	10,408	5.0	5.0	108
45–49 years	7,776	12,264	4.1	5.9	158
50–59 years	12,533	19,146	6.6	9.2	153
60–69 years	8,535	11,736	4.5	5.6	137
70 years and over	4,462	7,972	2.3	3.8	179

The overwhelming majority of the population of the USSR — 151,000,000 persons, or almost ¾ of the total — consists of people born after the October revolution.

Illiteracy has been practically eradicated, as shown in Table 8. It still shows almost 2 million people in the 9–49 age group who are illiterate.

TABLE 8

GROWTH OF LITERACY IN AGE GROUP 9–49
(In % to population)

1897*	26.3	1939*	89.1
1926*	56.6	1959	98.5

* 1939 boundaries.

The density of the population varies considerably. It is highest in the industrialized regions of European Russia and the Ukraine and is very low in the desolate arctic wastelands.

Finally, the population of the USSR is distributed, ethnically, among over 100 nationalities, large and small. They range from the Russians, who form the majority of the Union's population, to peoples like the Tofalar, who number 600, according to the census of 1959. The distribution of the nationalities over the different parts of the USSR has changed considerably of late. Some of the population shifts were voluntary, due to such causes as movement from the countryside to the cities. But there have also been considerable compulsory population shifts on an ethnical basis. Thus, the Volga Germans were moved to an unknown destination as a war-time preventive measure; several peoples, e.g., the Crimean Tatars, Chechens, Ingush, Balkars, were similarly removed after the war as punishment for alleged collaboration with the Nazis. The classifications of the Soviet census have been subject to some criticism. Thus, the figure given for the Jews (2,268,000) is said to be too small because it does not include all persons of Jewish ethnic origin. It is estimated that only a small minority of the Jews lives in the "Jewish Autonomous Oblast" in Birobidzhan (from 20,000 to 30,000).

A considerable majority of the population of the USSR belongs to the Slavs. The Russians alone number 114,114,000 and are to be found throughout the USSR, while practically all the other peoples are more or less geographically confined to one or two constituent republics. It is to be noted that 10,200,000 persons of non-Russian origin gave Russian as their native language, according to the 1959 census.

The Ukrainians number 37,253,000 of whom 31,-852,000 live in the Ukrainian SSR where they form 76.1% of the population. Ukrainians are also second only to the Russians in their Union-wide dsitribution.

The Byelorussians, 7,913,000, are to be found mostly within the confines of the Byelorussian SRR. (*See also* NATIONALITIES, LANGUAGES.)

TABLE 9

ETHNIC COMPOSITION OF THE POPULATION

	No. of persons of given nationality	% who consider language of given nationality their native language
TOTAL USSR POPULATION	208,827,000	94.3
Russians	114,114,000	99.8
Ukrainians	37,253,000	87.7
Byelorussians	7,913,000	84.2
Uzbeks	6,015,000	98.4
Tatars	4,968,000	92.1
Kazakhs	3,622,000	98.4
Azerbaijanians	2,940,000	97.6
Armenians	2,787,000	89.9
Georgians	2,692,000	98.6
Lithuanians	2,326,000	97.8
Jews	2,268,000	20.8
Moldavians	2,214,000	95.2
Germans	1,620,000	75.0
Chuvash	1,470,000	90.8
Latvians	1,400,000	95.1
Tadzhiks	1,397,000	98.1
Poles	1,380,000	45.5
Mordvinians	1,285,000	78.1
Turkmenians	1,002,000	98.9
Bashkirs	989,000	61.9
Estonians	989,000	95.2
Kirghiz	969,000	98.7
Peoples of Dagestan incl.:	947,000	95.9
Avars	270,000	97.2
Lezghians	223,000	92.7
Darghin	158,000	98.6
Kumyks	135,000	98.0
Laks	64,000	95.8
Nogais	41,000	84.3
Tabasarans	35,000	99.2
Aguls	7,000	99.4
Rutuls	7,000	99.9
Tsakhurs	7,000	99.0

	No. of persons of given nationality	% who consider language of given nationality their native language
Udmurts	625,000	89.1
Mari	504,000	95.1
Komi and Komi-Permyaks	431,000	88.7
Chechen	419,000	98.8
Ossetians	410,000	89.7
Bulgarians	324,000	79.4
Koreans	314,000	79.3
Greeks	309,000	41.5
Buryats	253,000	94.9
Yakuts	237,000	97.5
Kabardians	204,000	97.9
Kara-Kalpaks	173,000	95.0
Karelians	167,000	71.3
Hungarians	155,000	97.2
Gypsies	132,000	59.3
Peoples of the North incl.:	127,000	75.2
Evenki	24,500	55.5
Nenets	23,000	84.7
Khanty (Ostyaks)	19,400	77.0
Chukchi	11,700	93.9
Eveny	9,400	81.8
Nanai (Goldi)	8,000	86.3
Mansi	6,400	59.2
Koryaks	6,300	90.5
Selkup	3,800	50.6
Nivkhi (Gilyaks)	3,700	76.3
Ulchi	2,100	84.9
Saam (Laps)	1,800	69.9
Udege	1,400	73.7
Eskimos	1,100	84.0
Itelmen (Kamchadals)	1,100	36.0
Ket	1,000	77.1
Orochi (Neni)	800	68.4
Nganasans (Tawgi)	700	93.4
Yukagirs	400	52.5
Aleuts	400	22.3
Gagauz	124,000	94.0
Rumanians	106,000	83.3
Kalmyks	106,000	91.0
Ingush	106,000	97.9
Tuvinians	100,000	99.1
Uygurs	95,000	85.0
Finns	93,000	59.5
Karachai	81,000	73.9
Adighe	80,000	96.7
Abkhaz (Abkhazians)	65,000	95.0
Kurds	59,000	89.9
Khakass	57,000	86.0
Altayans	45,000	88.5
Balkars	42,000	97.0
Turks	35,000	82.2
Cherkess (Circassians)	30,000	86.6
Chinese	26,000	69.3
Czechs	25,000	49.0
Aissors	22,000	64.3
Dungan	22,000	95.1
Iranians	21,000	44.7
Abaza	20,000	94.8
Veps	16,000	46.1
Shors	15,000	83.7
Slovaks	15,000	61.2
Tates	11,000	70.8
Arabs	8,000	34.1
Beluchi	7,800	94.9
Karaites	5,700	13.8
Yugoslavs	5,000	66.6
Albanians	4,800	78.1
Udins	3,700	92.6
Spaniards	2,400	67.8
Afghans	1,900	71.8
Mongols	1,800	86.6
Italians	1,200	32.6
Izhora	1,100	34.7
Frenchmen	1,100	56.4
Japanese	1,000	69.5
Vietnamese	800	99.3
Tofalar (Karagas)	600	89.1
Other nationalities	17,000	60.3

During the 1959 census a total of 124,100,000 persons indicated Russian as their native language, including 113,900,000 Russians and 10,200,000 persons of other nationalities.

TABLE 4

MAJOR CITIES IN THE USSR BY THE CENSUSES OF 1939 AND 1959

City	Population (thous.) Jan. 17, 1939	Jan. 15, 1959	% of 1959 to 1939	City	Jan. 17, 1939	Jan. 15, 1959	% of 1959 to 1939
Moscow	4,183	5,046	121	Lugansk (Voroshilovgrad)	215	275	128
Leningrad (Petrograd, St. Petersburg)	3,385	3,321	98	Orenburg (Chkalov)	172	267	156
Kiev	847	1,104	130	Kalinin (Tver)	216	261	121
Baku	775	971	125	Archangel	251	256	102
Gorky (Nizhny Novgorod)	644	942	146	Penza	160	255	160
Kharkov	833	934	112	Kirov (Vyatka)	145	249	172
Tashkent	550	912	166	Tomsk	144	252	176
Novosibisrk (Novonikolayevsk)	404	886	219	Grozny	172	242	140
Kuybyshev (Samara)	390	806	206	Vilnius (Vilno)	215	236	110
Sverdlovsk (Yekaterinburg)	423	779	184	Nikolayev	169	226	134
Stalino (Yuzovka)	466	700	150	Stalinabad (Dyushambe)	83	224	271
Tbilisi (Tiflis)	519	695	134	Murmansk	119	222	186
Chelyabinsk	273	689	252	Frunze (Pishpek)	93	220	237
Odessa	602	667	111	Kishinev	112	216	193
Dnepropetrovsk (Yekaterinoslav)	527	660	125	Kaunas (Kovno)	152	214	141
Kazan	398	647	163	Ryazan	95	214	225
Perm (Molotov)	306	629	206	Bryansk	174	207	119
Riga	385	605	170	Ulyanovsk (Simbirsk)	98	206	210
Rostov-on-Don	510	600	118	Kursk	120	205	171
Stalingrad (Tsaritsyn)	445	592	133	Kaliningrad (Königsberg)	—	204	—
Omsk	289	581	201	Taganrog	189	202	107
Saratov	372	581	156	Samarkand	136	196	144
Ufa	258	547	212	Shakhty (Aleksandrovsk-Grushevsky)	135	196	146
Minsk	237	509	215	Dneprodzerzhinsk (Kamenskoye)	148	194	131
Yerevan (Erivan)	204	509	250	Simferopol	143	186	131
Alma-Ata (Verny)	222	456	206	Rybinsk (Shcherbakov)	144	182	126
Voronezh	344	448	130	Kadievka (Sergo)	135	180	134
Zaporozhye (Aleksandrovsk)	282	435	154	Komsomolsk-on-Amur (Permskoye)	71	177	250
Krasnoyarsk	190	412	217	Orsk	66	176	266
Lvov	340	411	121	Ulan-Ude (Verkhneudinsk)	126	175	139
Yaroslavl	309	407	132	Tambov	106	172	162
Karaganda	156	397	254	Chita	121	172	142
Krivoy Rog	189	388	205	Kostroma	121	172	142
Stalinsk (Novo-Kuznetsk)	166	377	227	Ashkhabad (Poltoratsk)	127	170	134
Irkutsk	250	366	146	Gomel	139	168	121
Makeyevka	242	358	148	Ordzhonikidze	131	164	126
Nizhny Tagil	160	339	212	Dzerzhinsk (Rastyapino)	103	164	159
Ivanovo (Ivanovo-Voznesensk)	285	335	118	Zlatoust	99	161	162
Khabarovsk	207	323	156	Kopeysk (Kopi)	60	161	267
Tula	272	316	116	Kherson	97	158	163
Krasnodar (Yekaterinodar)	193	313	162	Lipetsk	67	157	235
Magnitogorsk	146	311	213	Semipalatinsk	110	156	142
Barnaul	148	305	206	Vladimir	67	154	230
Astrakhan	254	296	117	Chimkent	74	153	206
Gorlovka	181	293	161	Ust-Kamenogorsk	20	150	747
Vladivostok	206	291	141	Tyumen	79	150	190
Izhevsk	176	285	162	Orel	111	150	136
Zhdanov (Mariupol)	222	284	128	Syzran	83	149	179
Prokopyevsk	107	282	263	Vitebsk	167	148	89
Tallin (Revel)	160	282	176	Sevastopol	114	148	130
Kemerovo (Shcheglovsk)	133	278	209	Smolensk	157	147	94

Source: *Narodnoye Khozyaystvo SSSR, 1959.*

POPULISM (Naródnichestvo), a social movement that agitated Russia from about 1860 to 1895. Populist theories were based on the conviction that it was possible for Russia to bypass capitalist development by utilizing the peasant commune, which was regarded as the embryo of socialism. P was a variety of utopian socialism adapted to the conditions of a predominantly agricultural country, a complex of variegated phenomena comprising different tendencies and nuances. Beginning as a form of revolutionary democracy, it eventually took both a terroristic and a liberal turn. The sources of P go back to the end of the 1840's. Among its founders were Herzen (q.v.) and Chernyshevsky (q.v.). Herzen saw socialism in the emancipation of the peasant who should receive land allotments, in the communal form of land tenure, and in the peasant concept of a "right to land." After the abolition of serfdom the "conscience-stricken" noblemen who had been the leaders of the liberal and radical opposition were followed by a motley group of plebeians (*raznochintsy*), and P became the dominant ideology of the discontented elements. Herzen's ideas were developed by Chernyshevsky, who was far more consistent and aggressive.

During the 1860's and 1870's P was encouraged by the embitterment of the peasantry disappointed by one peasant reform of 1861. The idea of a peasant *revolution* was merged with the current theories of utopian socialism; it entailed the abolition of the autocracy, the introduction of agrarian reforms, and the establishment of a socialist society based on the peasant commune. The earlier populists considered the peasantry and the revolutionary intelligentsia the chief force in the transformation of society. The populists of the 1870's carried on the tradition of the revolutionaries of the 1860's (Chernyshevsky, Dobrolyubov, and others), which was developed into a campaign of incitement of the peasantry. On the philosophical side, however, there was a substantial difference.

Chernyshevsky, Herzen, and their most consistent followers were, philosophically, materialists: they accepted a materialist theory of knowledge, acknowledged the existence of objective social laws and believed in the active role of the masses in history. They thought a revolution could be accomplished only by the positive will of the people.

From the end of the 1860's, however, it was the idealistic theories of M. A. Bakunin, P. L. Lavrov, and P. N. Tkachov that exercised the major influence. In particular, the question of the historical role of the masses came to be assessed differently. Lavrov advanced the theory that certain "critically thinking individuals" were the movers of history; N. K. Mikhaylovsky had a theory of "heroes" and "crowds"; Tkachov propounded the theory of the seizure of power through a conspiracy of the revolutionary intelligentsia without the participation of the masses of the people. Bakunin, with his anarchistic theories, considered the immediate organization of a "peasant uprising" possible. On a number of philosophical questions some populists went over to the positions held by positivism and neo-Kantianism; they did not believe that social life was governed by objective laws, and in sociology adopted a subjective method.

The populists expressed their views in a number of illegal periodicals published abroad: Lavrov's *Vpered* (Forward) (1873–77); Bakunin's *Rabotnik* (The Worker) (1875–76) and *Obshchina* (The Land Commune) (1878–79); the Tkachovist *Nabat* (The Tocsin) (1875–81).

Though the populists of the 1870's considered capitalism in Russia a regression, for the first time they confronted public opinion with the question of capitalist development, and in comparison with the 1860's broadened the circle of participation in the revolutionary movement by involving in it the representatives of the progressive intelligentsia and the more aware workers. A number of populists of the 1860's actively took part in the First International, the Paris Commune, and other events in the international revolutionary movement. In 1870 some populists, followers of Chernyshevsky (N. I. Utin, A. D. Trusov, V. I. Barteneva, *et al.*) founded in Geneva the Russian section of the First International. Populists were familiar with the works of Marx and Engels, and translated *Das Kapital* into Russian, though they considered Marxism a "western" doctrine inapplicable to Russia.

By the 1860's revolutionary circles and organizations had begun springing up. The P. G. Zaichnevsky and P. E. Argiropulo circle was active in 1861–62, disseminating revolutionary propaganda among the people. In 1861–64 a secret society, *Zemlya i Volya* ("Land and Freedom"), started its revolutionary work: Chernyshevsky was its inspirer. The organizers of this society were A. I. Herzen, N. P. Ogaryov, the brothers N. A. and A. A. Serno-Solovyevich, A. A. Sleptsov, N. N. Obruchov, V. S. Kurochkin, and others. *Land and Freedom* aimed at a peasant uprising. The Ishutin circle (1863–66), in addition to its plans for assassinating the tsar, made an attempt to organize producing

associations, and to scatter revolutionaries among the people to study their life and to carry on revolutionary propaganda.

In 1869 S. G. Nechayev founded a secret conspirational student organization (*Narodnaya Rasprava*) which was destroyed by the police in December of the same year. Nechayev's tactics were regarded as adventurist by many populists, including the Russian section of the First International, and were also combated by Marx and Engels. The Chaykovsky circle was a large populist organization (1869–74) in St. Petersburg, with sections in Moscow, Odessa, Kiev, and other cities. Its active members were M. A. Natanson, S. M. Kravchinsky, N. A. Charushin, P. A. Kropotkin, and Sophie Perovskaya. Beginning with self-education and revolutionary propaganda among students, the Chaykovsky circle proceeded to revolutionary activities among factory workers, designed to prepare them for propaganda work among peasants. In the 1870's, especially the spring and summer of 1874, the campaign of "going to the people" was intensified: a view was current that the Volga, Don, Dnieper, and Ural regions had a strong revolutionary tradition that could be of use. But despite its extraordinary enthusiasm, the movement in fact proved a fiasco. By the end of 1874 more than 1,000 of those "going to the people" were arrested, and tried in the "Trial of the 193" (1877–78). The failure of this movement caused the populists to change their tactics, and to found a secret centralized organ.

In 1875 the "All-Russian Socialist-Revolutionary Organization" sprang up in Moscow, and spread revolutionary propaganda among the workers of Moscow, Ivanovo-Voznesensk, Tula, and some other cities. It was discovered the same year; its members were tried in the "Trial of the 50" (February-March 1877).

In 1876 a new populist organization was founded in St. Petersburg, and in 1878 it was given the old name of *Zemlya i Volya* (Land and Freedom). G. V. Plekhanov, the future Marxist leader, was one of its members, as well as A. D. Mikhaylov, O. V. Aptekman, D. A. Lizogub, and A. F. Mikhaylov. *Land and Freedom* published an illegal review in St. Petersburg (1878–79). It dropped the tactic of despatching roving propagandists among the people, and instead concentrated on the establishment of settlements of revolutionaries in the hope of inciting the peasants to revolt. Links were forged with factory workers, who were expected to play an auxiliary role in the forthcoming peasant revolution. Despite the self-sacrificing zeal of the *Land and Freedom* its methods failed, and a new tactic—individual terror—was decided. By 1878 significant numbers of populists had embraced this new policy.

Land and Freedom split on this question into two organizations (1879): the supporters of the former *Land and Freedom* platform (Plekhanov, V. I. Zasulich, and L. G. Deutsch) formed a new group called *Chorny Peredel* (i.e., "The Total Reapportionment of Land"); in 1883 these three broke finally with the populists and founded in Geneva the first Russian Marxist organization, the "Liberation of Labor" group. The new tendency (A. I. Zhelyabov, A. D. Mikhaylov, V. N. Figner, M. A. Frolenko, and others) founded a new party, *Narodnaya Volya* (People's Will), which published an illegal periodical of the same name from 1879 and 1885; it set as its goal the overthrow of autocracy and the establishment of a democratic republic based on "people's will." This party was the first to raise the question of the necessity of a political struggle (demand for a constitution, freedom of speech, press, and so on), which they linked to the tactic of individual terror. *People's Will* aroused great enthusiasm in revolutionary circles in Russia and abroad through its selfless heroism, but in the end it proved to be futile.

On March 1, 1881 (O.S.) *People's Will* assassinated Alexander II, but the act led to nothing. The perpetrators—A. I. Zhelyabov, Sophie Perovskaya, N. I. Kibalchich, T. M. Mikhaylov, and N. I. Rysakov—were arrested and executed. The party asked Alexander III for an amnesty and some liberties in return for a promise of legal behavior, but the arrests and emigration that followed the assassination bled *People's Will* white. During the 1880's, to be sure, further acts of terrorism took place, such as the attempt to murder Alexander III made by a group headed by A. Ulyanov (brother of Lenin). There were again mass trials, but the active elements of P were soon absorbed by the Socialist Revolutionary party (q.v.), which became the chief antagonist on the left of the Marxist movement that began developing toward the end of the 19th century. Alongside of the terrorist activities of the populists, there was also the so-called "liberal populism" whose chief representatives were N. K. Mikhaylovsky and V. P. Vorontsov.

In the 1860's–1880's P exercised a great influence on literature, the plastic arts, and music, and had a following among the intellectual leaders of Russia's national minorities.

BIBLIOGRAPHY: Michael T. Florinsky, *Russia: A History and an Interpretation*, New York, 1953; Franco Venturi, *The Roots of Revolution*, New York, 1960.   J. C.

PORÁY-KÓSHITS, Aleksándr Yevgényevich (1887–1949), chemist. Fellow, Ac. of S., USSR (1935). Honored Scientist and Technologist, RSFSR (1947). Graduate (1903) and professor (1918), St. Petersburg University. Head of the chair of organic dyes, Kazan University (1941–44), and Laboratory of Intermediate Products and Dyes, Institute of Organic Chemistry, Ac. of S. Research on organic chemistry, particularly chemistry and technology of dyes. Established a chemical interaction between dyes and proteinaceous fibers. Suggested a method for the production of furfural; developed a single-phase method for azo-dyes and vat dyes.

PORTSMOUTH, TREATY OF, concluded between Russia and Japan, Sept. 5, 1905 in Portsmouth, New Hampshire, USA. It ended the war of 1904–05 in which Russia suffered severe defeat and lost Port Arthur and S. Sakhalin to Japan. The R. delegation was headed by Serge Witte, who was rewarded with the title of count.

POSKRÉBYSHEV, Aleksándr Nikoláyevich (1891–?), Communist, was close to Stalin. In 1931 he assumed command of Stalin's personal secretariat and appears to have retained close contact with the security police over the years. From 1928 P was chief of the "Special Section" of the party secretariat. In this capacity he played

a major role in the purges of the 1930's. Deliberately inconspicuous, he held great power as the liaison man with Stalin. In 1939 P was elected a member of the Central Committee. On the day of Stalin's death, P disappeared and has not been seen since.

POSOSHKÓV, Iván Tíkhonovich (1652–1726), peasant-author and amateur economist; great admirer of Peter I and believer in mercantilism. His remarkable book *On Poverty and Riches,* written about 1725, was not published until many years later. P advocated the establishment of guilds and strict regulation of the relationship between masters and serfs.

POSPÉLOV, Pyótr Nikoláyevich (1898–), Communist theorist, secretary of the Central Committee of the CPSU, member of the Ac. of S. (1953). Graduate of the Moscow Academy of Agriculture, the Communist Academy and the Institute of Red Professors. P, who was born in Tver, has been a member of the Communist party since 1916. In the 1930's, he was a member of the Central Control Commission of the CPSU, and worked as a propagandist and editor. From 1940 to 1949, he was editor of *Pravda* and, in 1949–52, director of the Marx-Engels-Lenin Institute. At the 19th and 20th Party Congresses, P was elected member of the Central Committee of the CPSU and, in 1953, one of its secretaries. Since 1957 P has been candidate member of the Presidium of the Central Committee of the CPSU. P has been a deputy to the Supreme Soviet of the USSR. He has published several books on party history and has served on the editorial board of the *Bolshaya Sovetskaya Entsiklopedia* (Large Soviet Encyclopedia). P received the Stalin prize for his contribution to the *History of the Civil War*.

"POSSESSIONARY" PEASANTS. The nobility and —since 1721—merchants, who owned industrial enterprises, had the right of purchasing peasants for employment in those enterprises on two conditions: that the servile population and the enterprise were to be considered as an entity; and that they were not to be disposed of separately. The peasants were thus attached to the industrial establishment in which they were to work and were known as "possessionary" peasants. But the rights of the owners were also subject to important limitations: "possessionary" enterprises were under the supervision of the government which regulated production, the conditions of employment, and the remuneration of labor. The number of PP remained small. According to the census of 1762–66 they represented about 0.7 per cent of the peasant population. Possessionary enterprises created a new and harsh form of serfdom, which survived until the emancipation of 1861.

POST AND MAIL. Prerevolutionary post and mail services carried a relatively light volume of material by Western standards, reflecting Russia's long distances and low level of general literacy. Especially in the countryside, communications were slow, but there has been substantial improvement over the last forty years. Soviet data record an especially marked rise in the number of newspapers and journals handled by the postal system; from 358 mill. in 1913, to 6.7 bill. in 1940 and 13.1 bill. in 1959. The number of letters sent per year rose from 615 mill. to 4,103 mill. between 1913 and 1959. Postal connections with rural areas have improved markedly in recent years, both because the network of post offices has grown, and because collective farms have been merged. Soviet post offices, totaling 61,000 in 1959 (8,000 in 1913)—48,000 of them rural—also handle packages and money orders, though another organization deals with savings accounts. In 1956, there were 211,200 mail carriers.

PÓSTYSHEV, Pável Petróvich (1888–1940), old Bolshevik; born in Ivanovo-Voznesensk of a worker's family. Joined the Bolshevik party in 1904; arrested in 1908 and sentenced to four years at hard labor. An active participant in the October revolution and in the civil war, P was made a member of the Politburo in 1926 and the secretary of the CP in the Ukraine. In 1931, he became a secretary and a member of the Orgburo of the Central Committee. In 1938 P was replaced in this office by Khrushchev and in the same year was arrested and later executed. At the 20th Party Congress, Khrushchev disclosed that P was condemned on false evidence.

POTATO CULTIVATION. Large-scale cultivation started in Russia about 1840 as the government compelled the peasants to plant P despite their violent resistance. The crop then became highly popular and is a far more important component of R. than of Western diet: consumption per capita amounted to 286 lb. in 1928 (312 in villages) and rose under the early Five Year Plans, following shortages of more nutritive foods. Gross output of P was, in mill. tons, 31.9 in 1913 (within present Soviet boundaries), 46.4 in 1928, 75.9 in 1940, 86.4 in 1959. The 1958 marketings amounted to 13.7 mill. tons. P are cultivated all over the country, the main areas being Central Russia which accounts for about one-third of total output, Ukraine, one-fourth, and Byelorussia, one-tenth. Besides the food and feed uses, P are also a major industrial raw material: 2.3 mill. tons were processed into alcohol in 1957, and smaller amounts were used in the making of starch, and other products.

Mechanization of PC progresses, the number of tractor-drawn potato planters having risen from 18,000 to 66,000 between 1940 and 1957. Nevertheless, a considerable portion of the crop continues to be grown by highly primitive, labor-intensive methods on collective farmers' tiny household plots and in "victory gardens" allotted to urban dwellers. These two categories of producers accounted for over 45% of the total area under potatoes and vegetables in 1958.

POTEBNYÁ, Aleksándr Afanásyevich (1835–1891), Russian and Ukrainian philologist. Professor at Kharkov University. P introduced a new method of teaching grammar and linguistics. His papers on the historical grammar of the R. and other Slavic languages are particularly valuable. Author of *Notes on the Russian Grammar* (1874–1941, 4 parts), *Thought and Language* (1862), and other books.

PÓTI, seaport city in Georgian SSR, on Black Sea at mouth of Rioni River; pop. 48,000 (1959). R.R. con-

nection to Tbilisi. Has food, machine mfg. ind.; export trade in lumber, Chiatura manganese, grain; mild and humid climate; on drained land in the vicinity, eucalyptus and citrus growing. Site of ancient Greek colony Phasis; annexed by Russia 1829.

PÓTRESOV, Aleksándr Nikoláyevich (1869–1934), Social Democrat, born into a family of gentry. His father was a high official in the judiciary in Kharkov. One of the founders of the St. Petersburg Union of Struggle for the Liberation of the Working Class, P was a Russian delegate to the International Socialist Congress in London in 1896. Thereafter P was arrested and exiled. In 1903, he was jointly with Lenin and Martov and Plekhanov, a founder of *Iskra*. After the revolution of 1905, he became the leader of the right-wing Mensheviks. During World War I, took a patriotic stand. After the October revolution P broke with the Menshevik party and edited a journal *Annals of the Social Democrats* in Paris. He often used the pen name "Starover."

POTYÓMKIN, Grigóry Aleksándrovich (1739–1791), Prince of Tavrida, statesman and diplomat, general field marshal (1784), favorite of Empress Catherine II. He participated in the Russo-Turkish War of 1768–74 and commanded the Russian army in that of 1787–91. His influence with the empress, especially in international affairs, was great.

BIBLIOGRAPHY: G. Soloveytchik, *Potemkin*, New York, 1947.

POTYÓMKIN, Vladímir Petróvich (1878–1946), Soviet historian, diplomat. Joined the CP in 1919; member of the Central Committee from 1939. Participated in the civil war of 1918–20. For over two decades P held important diplomatic posts; was ambassador to Greece (1929–32), Italy (1932–34), France (1934–37). In 1937–40, was first deputy minister of foreign affairs; people's commissar of public education, 1940–46. Fellow, Ac. of S., USSR. Co-author and editor of the *History of Diplomatic Relations* (3 vols., 1941–45) for which he was twice awarded the Stalin prize.

"POTYÓMKIN," battleship of the Black Sea Navy. Its crew took up arms in mutiny June 14–24, 1905, shot the most-hated officers, hoisted a red flag, and sailed into Odessa harbor. Not being supported by the crews of other ships, they were compelled to seek asylum in Rumania (Port of Constanza) on June 25, 1905. Eventually some sailors returned to Russia. They were tried and sentenced to death or penal servitude.

POTSDAM (BERLIN) CONFERENCE, (July 17–Aug. 2, 1945) was held by Stalin, Truman, and Churchill (later Attlee). The conference saw further deterioration in Allied unity. Charges of Soviet misconduct in E. Europe were denied by Stalin and the conference reaffirmed the necessity for democratic government in all liberated countries. Germany was to remain under a single Allied Control Council; but with four-zone occupation, the country was in effect divided for an unspecified time. Each power could collect reparations in its own zone, with Russia permitted additional industrial plant from other zones. Poland was to "administer" former German territory E. of the Oder-Neisse line and all Germans in the area were to be expelled.

Russia received, in addition to Ruthenia, the E. part of East Prussia, including Königsberg.

BIBL.: Herbert Feis, *Between War and Peace* (The Potsdam Conference), Princeton, 1960.

POULTRY FARMING. Total holdings of P were (in mill.) 210 in 1913, 215 in 1928, declined to 110 by 1932 following collectivization but were reestablished at 216 by 1938. Chickens accounted for some 92% of all P in 1928 but a shift toward geese and ducks took place in later years. Turkey farming has been unimportant. Gross output of eggs (in billions) was 11.9 in 1913 (present territory), 10.8 in 1928, 4.4 in 1932, 12.2 in 1940, 24.8 in 1959. Output of poultry meat amounted to 290,000 tons in 1928; statistics for later years were not published.

As of 1953, there were in operation 90,000 collective poultry farms owning 83.2 mill. poultry, 2,500 incubator stations with a capacity of some 200 mill. eggs, 143 specialized state farms keeping 2.3 mill. poultry, and 9 so-called "poultry factories," the largest of which kept 141,000 birds. Despite preference for large-scale production methods, state farms and "poultry factories" progressed little after 1930–31 when they were first organized. Most poultry continues to be privately owned and consists mainly of chickens kept on collective farmers' household plots, which accounted for 87% of the output of eggs in 1956.

POWER ENGINEERING: *see* TECHNICAL SCIENCES.

POZHÁRSKY, Prince Dmítry Mikháylovich (1578–1641), leader of the struggle against the Polish-Swedish intervention in Russia. He defeated  Polish-Lithuanian forces at the village of Vysokoye (near Kolomna) in 1608, and retrieved Zaraysk from the Cossacks of the second pretender Dimitry in 1609. He was elected *voivoda* (commander) of the People's Volunteer Army of Nizhny Novgorod in 1612; and, together with Minin, freed Moscow in Oct. 1612. He also participated in the Russo-Polish wars of 1617–18 and 1632–34.

PRÁVDA (Truth), official organ of the Central Committee of CPSU and leading newspaper in the USSR, with 1960 circulation of 6,300,000. Published daily in Moscow; Pavel A. Satyukov, editor-in-chief. The anniversary of its founding, May 5, 1912, is celebrated throughout the country as Press Day. First published in St. Petersburg as the organ of Bolsheviks. Its early history was marked by repeated closings by tsarist police and courts; at times it was published as an illegal underground newspaper. Molotov was editorial secretary; Stalin was associated with the paper from earliest days. The paper was primarily a forum for political arguments, debates over revolutionary tactics, Marxist doctrine. The publication was suppressed July 1914, resumed March 1917 under the Provisional Government, suspended again in July. Its preeminence came in the 1930's with Stalin's consolidation of party power as he established the policy of choosing *Pravda's* editors. Today *Pravda* keynotes major changes in policy, initiates campaigns, sets the tone and approach for other newspapers. Content of its six to eight pages reflects current concerns of CPSU, both domestic and foreign. Material

from *Pravda* is distributed throughout the country by Tass news service and is reprinted, often verbatim, by provincial newspapers.

PRECISION INSTRUMENTS INDUSTRY. This branch of the precision machinery industry produces a wide variety of instruments for the measuring and control of technological and other processes (instruments for the measuring of time, weight, heat, electricity; meteorological and navigation equipment; telescopes; electronic computing machines).

The first large enterprises producing measuring instruments were established in the 1920's. They included the plants: "Aviapribor" (1923) which made clocks and subsequently instruments for the aircraft industry; "Termoelektropribor" (1925) which made pyrometers and other instruments for measuring high temperatures; "Metron" (1925) which made testing instruments and precision scales; "Lamo," which made precisions instruments for medical purposes; and the First and Second Watch Plants in Moscow. Additional plants for optical, mechanical, navigational, and electronic instruments were constructed during the prewar Five Year Plans (1928–40).

After World War II, following the modernization of existing enterprises and the construction of additional facilities a variety of new types of precision instruments began to be produced. This included manometers for the measuring of very high pressures; electronic potentiometers; optico-acoustical and magnetic gas analyzers; electronic computing machines; and new types of optical instruments. Important factors in their development have been the scientific research institutes such as the State Optical Scientific Research Institute; the All-Union Scientific Research Institute in Experimental Electrotechnology; the Dzerzhinsky All-Union Thermoelectric Institute; the Central Boiler and Turbine Institute; the Institute for the Construction of Laboratory Equipment; the All-Union Institute of Meteorology; and the Institute of Automation and Telemechanics of the USSR Academy of Sciences.   P. I. M.

PREDVODÍTELEV, Aleksándr Savvich (1891–), physicist. Corresponding member, Ac. of S., USSR (1939). Graduate (1915), professor (1930), Moscow University. Head of laboratory, Institute of Power Engineering, Ac. of S. (1938). Research concerns molecular physics, hydrodynamics, and thermal physics, including combustion processes, wave propagation in fluid and gas media, problems of gas dynamics of reacting media, physical properties of fluids. His theory of heterogeneous combustion which establishes the relationship between chemical and physical processes is widely used in technology. Author of *The Combustion of Carbon* (1949). Stalin prize (1950).

PREOBRAZHENSKA, Olga (1871–), R. ballerina (1898–1917) of the St. Petersburg Mariinsky Theater, who left Russia in 1921 and established a ballet school in Paris where she is still teaching (1960). She is considered one of the greatest teachers of ballet and her school is a mecca for dancers and students from Europe and America.

PREOBRAZHÉNSKY, Yevgény Alekséyevich (1886–?), revolutionary and economist. Became a Bolshevik in 1903, but for many years gravitated toward Trotsky rather than Lenin. P fought in the civil war and in 1920 was named a secretary of the party. One of the leading Bolshevik economists, he was demoted in the late 1920's because of his opposition to NEP. During the intra-party struggle, P strongly supported Trotsky and called for massive development of heavy industry. In 1927 he was expelled from the party but, after recantation, was readmitted in 1929. He disappeared during the purges of the 1930's and was presumably liquidated. P wrote many books and pamphlets. Best known are: *Paper Money During the Era of the Proletarian Revolution*; *From NEP to Socialism*; and, in collaboration with Bukharin, *The ABC of Communism*.

PRE-PARLIAMENT or Provisional Council of the Republic, an ingeniously constructed deliberative and consultative body which, on the eve of the October revolution, was to represent the nation until the convocation of the Constituent Assembly. Most of the P—350 delegates—were appointed from the members of the Democratic Conference (q.v.). The additional 200 delegates were the representatives of nonsocialist parties and groups which had been excluded from the Democratic Conference. The 53 Bolsheviks, at the first session of the P, Oct. 20, 1917, walked out after having read a strongly worded declaration. During its fortnight existence, the P mostly debated on the questions of war and peace. The various parties having sent their best representatives of the P, its debates were on a high academic level but without any relation to R. reality. On Nov. 5, 1917 (N.S.), the President of the Council of Ministers A. F. Kerensky suddenly took the rostrum and, after describing the Bolshevik preparation for seizing state power, declared that the government intended to put down the uprising with stern measures. When he concluded with the demand that "the Provisional Government should on this very day receive a reply from you at to whether it can fulfill its duty with confidence in your support," the answer of the majority of the P was no. By a vote of 113 to 102, with 26 abstentions, the P adopted a resolution, offered by L. Martov (q.v.), which censured the impending armed outbreak and tried to prevent it by politico-ideological measures: immediate transfer of the land to the public administration and decisive moves to begin peace negotiations. On the next day, in the early afternoon of Nov. 6, the assembly room of the P was surrounded by Bolshevik troops and its members ordered to leave the building. Though they registered a formal protest against being ordered out, they were never to meet again.   V. Su.

PRESIDIUM OF THE CENTRAL COMMITTEE (formerly the Politburo) of the Communist party was so named by the 19th Party Congress in October 1952 and at the end of 1960 consisted of 14 full members. After Stalin's death (March 1953) the Presidium was reduced to 10 members and 4 candidates. In the reduced Presidium only the closest lieutenants of Stalin remained: Malenkov, Beria, Molotov, Voroshilov, Khrushchev, Bulganin, Kaganovich, Mikoyan, Saburov, Pervukhin. However, very soon most of the them were purged. Beria was expelled in July 1953, Malenkov, Kaganovich, Molotov, Saburov and Pervukhin in 1957

and Bulganin in 1958. In 1960 only two members—Khrushchev and Mikoyan—remained from the Presidium nominated after Stalin's death. The purged were replaced by supporters of Khrushchev. The Presidium is theoretically the chief policy-making body of the party since, according to the party rules it directs the work of the Central Committee when that body is not meeting. In practice, however, the first secretary, Khrushchev, since June 1957 has to all appearances dominated the policy-making functions of the Presidium.

MEMBERS OF THE PRESIDIUM (as of May 1, 1961): Averky B. Aristov, Leonid I. Brezhnev, Yekaterina A. Furtseva, Nikolay G. Ignatov, Nikita S. Khrushchev, Aleksey N. Kosygin, Frol R. Kozlov, Otto V. Kuusinen, Anastas I. Mikoyan, Nuritdin A. Mukhitdinov, Nikolay V. Podgorny, Dmitry S. Polyansky, Nikolay M. Shvernik, Mikhail A. Suslov.

PRESNYAKÓV, Aleksándr Yevgényevich (1870–1929), historian. P taught at the University of St. Petersburg. His *Formation of the Great Russian State* (1918) is a masterly study of the rise of Moscow. His writings dealt chiefly with ancient and medieval R. history, but he is also known for studies of the Decembrists (1926) and of the 19th century.

PRESS. *Kuranty* (The Chimes), the earliest periodical in Russia, dates back to 1621. It was carefully handwritten to be read by the tsar and his courtiers. In 1702, Peter I founded *Vedomosti Moskovskogo Gosudarstva* (Gazette of the Muscovite State); he perused the Dutch press, marked items for translation, and read the proofs personally. The publication with a circulation of about 1,000 copies carried two to seven pages in Slavonic. Taken over by the Ac. of S. in 1728, it was issued four times a week under the title *Sankt Peterburgskie Vedomosti* (St. Petersburg Gazette) and made into a daily in 1815.

Moskovskie Vedomosti (Moscow Gazette), an organ of the gentry, was founded by the writer M. M. Kheraskov of Moscow University (1756) and appeared regularly until 1917.

In the late 18th century specialized weekly reviews and literary, artistic and satirical publications had become quite popular.

A major influence on the development of journalism and the shaping of public opinion was exercised by A. N. Radishchev, whose views were reflected in I. A. Krylov's *Pochta Dukhov* (The Courier of the Spirits) (1782) and *Zritel* (The Spectator) (1792). At the same time, N. M. Karamzin, the outstanding literary figure at the turn of the century, edited and published *Moskovsky Zhurnal* (Moscow Journal) (1791) and *Vestnik Yevropy* (European Messenger) (1820).

The order on the closing of private printing establishments issued by Paul I in 1796 drastically decreased the number of periodicals. However, at the beginning of the 19th century, journalism was anew on the road toward recovery with 70 publications issued regularly, including *Moskovsky Merkury* (The Moscow Mercury) (1802), *Severny Vestnik* (The Northern Messenger) (1804), *Zhurnal Rossiyskoy Slovestnosti* (Journal of Russian Literature) (1805), *Otechestvennye Zapiski* (Notes of the Fatherland) (1818).

The military events of 1812–15 revived the circulation of both the *Sankt Peterburgskie Vedomosti* and

Moskovskie Vedomosti; the daily *Russky Invalid* (The Russian Veteran) (1813), which at its inception published only military communiqués, became the official press organ of the Ministry of War (1847). *Severnaya Pchela* (The Northern Bee) (1825), the first privately published literary and political review, approached the standards of modern journalism and favorably competed with the bureaucratic style of the above-mentioned three publications. On the other hand, the widely read journal *Dukh Zhurnalov* (Review of Reviews) was suspended (1821) after printing articles on the constitution of the United States of America and on representative government. *Polyarnaya Zvezda* (The Northern Star) (1823) openly sympathized with the Decembrist movement and, later, with A. I. Herzen. The rigid censorship law of 1826 was amended in 1828. However, censorship restrictions began to pile up anew after the French Revolution (1830). The progressive *Teleskop* (Telescope) (1831–36) had to close after the publication of a sensational article by P. Ya. Chaadayev ("A Philosophical Letter"). The foundation of *Sovremennik* (The Contemporary) (1836) by A. S. Pushkin, who was succeeded by N. A. Nekrasov (1847), was a major event in the history of journalism.

The Crimean War imparted new vigor to the P. In the period 1845–54 six newspapers and nineteen reviews were granted publication licenses; from 1855 to 1864 the number of the former increased to 66 and of the latter to 156. *Otechestvennye Zapiski* had become an influential publication of populist trend which was to mark journalism until the late 1890's. It was taken over by N. G. Chernyshevsky and N. A. Dobrolyubov, the editors of *Sovremennik*, and, after the suspension of the latter, by N. A. Nekrasov (1868).

Slavophile ideas frowned upon by the government were the vogue and found expression in *Moskovsky Sbornik* (Moscow Articles) (1852), which was suspended after the second issue, and I. S. Aksakov's *Den* (The Day) (1861–65); it was not until 1880–87 that Aksakov was permitted to publish his Slavophile daily *Rus* (Russia). In the period from 1861 to 1896 a galaxy of outstanding literary figures contributed to the P— V. G. Belinsky, N. G. Chernyshevsky, N. A. Dobrolyubov, D. N. Pisarev, and M. Ye. Saltykov-Shchedrin, who represented the progressive elements in journalism. *Russkie Vedomosti* (Russian Gazette) rose to the ranks of a leading periodical under the able management of a team of Moscow University professors assisted by N. M. Mikhaylovsky, V. G. Korolenko, D. N. Mamin-Sibiryak, and K. S. Barantsevich.

The abolition of preliminary censorship for city publications (1865) and such novel features as paid advertisements and retail sales at newsstands and in railroad stations promoted the circulation of periodicals in the 1860's. By 1868, the liberal *Novoye Vremya* (The New Times) had two daily editions and a circulation of about 60,000 copies. Tabloids also enjoyed vast popularity; news highlights, scandals, and even camouflaged criticism of the government enhanced their sales. *Vestnik Yevropy* had developed into a leading press organ of liberalism. Edited by N. K. Mikhaylovsky and V. G. Korolenko, *Russkoye Bogatstvo* (Russian Wealth)

(1897), followed populist lines. On the eve of World War I the following publications were widely read: *Novoye Vremya* (1868–1917), taken over by A. S. Suvorin (1876) and made into a publication of the gentry; *Rech* (The Speech) (1908–18), the mouthpiece of the Constitutional Democratic party, edited by I. V. Hessen and P. N. Milyukov; *Utro Rossii* (The Morning of Russia) (1908–18), a financial newspaper; *Russkie Vedomosti* (1863–1918), the voice of the liberal intelligentsia; *Golos Moskvy* (The Voice of Moscow), of moderately liberal trends; and *Russkoye Slovo* (The Russian Word) (1904–18) which catered to the lower middle class.

Although the preliminary censorship of periodicals was abolished (1905–06), issues of journals containing matters allegedly in contravention of the law could be subjected to reviewing by the courts and severe penalties inflicted for such ill-defined offenses as "the spreading of false information concerning state agencies and officials," "favorable comments on criminal acts." Nevertheless, publishers, editors, and authors were willing to take the risk. In fact, from 1906 to 1914 the status of the P was the nearest approximation to one of freedom Russia had ever experienced.

By 1912, 2,167 periodicals in 33 languages were published in 246 cities reflecting almost every shade of political thought. *Niva* (The Cornfield) was a popular illustrated weekly with a circulation of 200,000 copies.

Revolutionary Press prior to 1917. In 1857, A. I. Herzen began the publication of the monthly and in 1858 the bimonthly journal *Kolokol* (The Bell) in London (later in Geneva). *Kolokol* was to exercise exceptional influence on R. thought over a number of years. The publication advocated the emancipation of serfs, freedom of the press, and the abolition of corporal punishment. *Narodnoye Delo* (The People's Cause) (1868), also published in Geneva, became the organ of the R. section of the First International. In *Narodnaya Rasprava* (The People's Wrath), of which only two issues had appeared, S. G. Nechayev propagated a popular revolution of the peasants. The legal journal *Vpered* (Forward) (1873–77), edited by a group of Kievan social democrats under P. L. Lavrov, defended populist views and advocated the theoretical propagation of socialist ideas. *Nabat* (The Tocsin) founded by P. N. Tkachov (1875–81) in Geneva called for a radical revolution. The R. anarchist group in Geneva printed fifteen issues of the periodical *Rabotnik* (The Worker) followed by the social revolutionary organ *Obshchina* (The Commune) which survived only nine issues. The four issues of the revolutionary journal *Nachalo* (The Beginning), also published in Geneva, were widely distributed in Russia. Other underground publications were *Zemlya i Volya* (Land and Freedom) (1876), edited by G. V. Plekhanov, and *Listok Zemli i Voli* (News of Land and Freedom) (1879). An abortive attempt was made at printing the labor publications *Rabochaya Zarya* (The Worker's Dawn) and *Rabochy* (The Worker) in Russia (1885).

The semi-Marxist publication *Zhizn* (Life) was initially published in Russia (1897) and transferred abroad (1901) by V. A. Posse and V. Bonch-Bruyevich; *Iskra* (The Spark) and *Zarya* (The Dawn) to which Lenin contributed have disseminated Marxist ideas. Socialist ideas were reflected in the clandestinely distributed newspaper *Revolyutsionnaya Rossiya* (Revolutionary Russia) (1901), the central organ of the Social Revolutionary party. P. B. Struve published *Osvobozhdenie* (Liberation) (1902), the review of R. liberals abroad. After the 1905 revolution *Nachalo* (The Beginning) and *Nevskaya Gazeta* (Neva Gazette) were circulated in St. Petersburg, Moscow, and other industrial cities by Mensheviks. Other publications were *Syn Otechestva* (Son of the Fatherland) (1904–05), the Bolshevik weekly *Zvezda* (The Star) (1910), *Pravda* (1912–14), *Mysl* (The Thought), *Prosveshchenie* (Enlightenment) (1911–14), and others.

During World War I the following publications appeared abroad: *Prizyv* (The Call), a Socialist Revolutionary newspaper; the Menshevik and semi-internationalist *Golos* (The Voice); *Nash Golos* (Our Voice); *Nashe Slovo* (Our Word). These were strongly opposed by the Bolshevik publications *Sotsial Demokrat* (The Social Democrat) and *Kommunist* (The Communist). Despite censorship restrictions *Nasha Gazeta* (Our Gazette), a Bolshevik periodical, was published in Saratov (1915).

T. D.

Soviet Press. The Soviet press is a powerful political weapon designed to mold public opinion and to implement the decisions of the Communist party and Soviet government. A major editorial in *Pravda* and a notice on a wall newspaper are similar in that they both fulfill the concept of the P's role in Soviet society as, in Lenin's words, "a collective propagandist, collective agitator, and collective organizer." Because this purpose is vital to the continuance of the Soviet regime, the P has grown rapidly in size and scope since the Revolution. At the beginning of 1960, there were 10,603 newspapers published in the USSR, with a combined circulation of 62,300,000, while in 1913 there were only 1,055 newspapers with a circulation of 3,300,000; and this growth has been accompanied by a strict party control of the P at all levels.

The administrative and party hierarchy characteristic of Soviet society is mirrored in the P. The party is the publisher or co-publisher of the majority of newspapers, the leading paper being *Pravda* (Truth), the official organ of the CP Central Committee. The government hierarchy of newspapers is headed by *Izvestia* (News), with a circulation of 2,300,000 per issue, considerably less than *Pravda*'s 6,300,000. Among the other central, Moscow-published newspapers, *Komsomolskaya Pravda* (Young Communist League Truth), the organ of the Komsomol, is popular and influential, and has a circulation of 3,400,000. It is brighter in tone and livelier than the typical Soviet newspaper.

Under the central papers are the regional papers, broken down into republic, provincial, territory, district, and city newspapers. As these newspapers decrease in importance and area covered, they tend more and more to concentrate on purely local issues, leaving the national problems to *Pravda* and *Izvestia*. The number of papers published in non-Russian languages has increased, but Russian is still the dominant language in the P. Over 2,500 newspapers appear in 81 languages, including 20 languages of non-Russian peoples who had no written language before 1917.

Not to be overlooked are newspapers published at enterprises, construction projects, and collective farms. On the most basic level, wall newspapers are a widely used and effective propaganda measure.

In addition to this breakdown of newspapers by administrative district, there are also many specialized presses which print central and local newspapers for particular interests and vocations. For example, there is a large trade-union press, headed by *Trud* (Labor), a military press, led by *Krasnaya Zvezda* (Red Star), literary and cultural papers, papers dealing with pedagogy, agriculture, transport, technology, railroads, sports, youth interests, and so on.

Periodical literature is also broad in scope and circulation. In 1960 there were 908 different journals with a total circulation of 515,000,000. These cover a wide range of interests, with titles such as *Radio* and *Nauka i Religia* (Science and Religion), a new monthly atheistic publication. The format of the journals also is diversified. Those directly related to the propagandizing and organizing work of the CP are serious in content, as are the scientific and technical journals. At the other end of the spectrum are magazines such as the popular weekly *Ogonyok* (Little Flame), with its illustrations and feature articles, the humorous *Krokodil,* and the children's *Murzilka* (The Little Rascal). The most widely distributed magazine in the country is *Rabotnitsa* (Woman Worker) which has a circulation of 2,400,000 per issue.

Party control of the P is absolute. Despite the fact that not all papers are published by party groups, the party, through the local executive committee, must approve the selection of the editor of a newspaper. This decision must be then approved by the next higher executive body. For the higher level of newspaper, the Central Committee must approve the editor. Though the staff may include non-party men, it is chosen not only on the basis of journalistic ability, but also on political reliability. In addition, the party issues general and detailed directives to editors, telling them what types of material they are supposed to publish and in what forms. Their fulfillment of these directives is regularly checked by the press section of the party group, which checks the publications to see that nothing has been published which does not meet their approval. They can demand explanations from the editor if all is not to their satisfaction. The P itself is always on the lookout for slips by its colleagues. A common practice is for a newspaper to publish a criticism of another paper, always, of course, one of lesser importance. Only *Pravda* is exempt from these "Reviews of the Press."

All these checks and controls are necessary to maintain the peculiarly Soviet function of the P. The fact that the party plays such an important part in every aspect of the P is an indication of the power it can wield on the Soviet citizen.

Because of this control and this purpose, the Soviet

P is quite unlike its western counterpart. A typical Soviet newspaper would seem to an American, first of all, quite small, because of the lack of advertising. Next, it would appear dull in make-up, because there are not as many feature pictures or big headlines. The typical front page may present only one or two pictures, probably of a group of Soviet leaders or outstanding workers, and then solid blocks of type devoted to the latest speech of a Soviet leader or a new party proposal. Because the criterion for inclusion is its importance to the party, an article need not be interesting, newsworthy, or objective—and it need not be written to sell newspapers. A recent trend in Soviet newspapers has been to enliven the pages with sprightlier treatment of articles, more cartoons, pictures, and so forth, particularly notable in the change in *Izvestia*. However, so much material must be included that does not fit these treatments that a drastic revision of style is unlikely.

Soviet newspapers give the impression of uniformity because so much of the material is distributed by Tass, the only news service. *Pravda*'s editorials and main articles are reprinted in full throughout the country. The main differences are to be found in the space devoted to purely local topics.

Feuilleton are short, often sarcastic articles exposing some type of anti-social activity. Those dealing with foreign affairs are particularly biting in tone. The "Letters to the Editor" section is a forum where a Soviet citizen may complain about injustices or incompetence in many fields. The limits of criticism are strictly proscribed and complaints deal only with the execution of policy and never with the policy itself. In the heat of a nation-wide campaign on a certain subject, such as farm policy, hooliganism, all papers devote a great deal of space to the topic, usually following *Pravda*'s lead.

Thus, the Soviet citizen is exposed to the party line through all of these devices and through a complex network of press organs. C. L.

PRIAMÚRYE: *see* AMUR REGION.

PRICES. Most commodities and services are officially priced in the Soviet Union. Once a price has been decreed by the price-fixing authorities, it ordinarily remains unchanged for a number of years. Price decrees are legal documents and violators are subject to sanctions. The auditing of accounts by the State Bank is the chief control on the observance of price controls.

The P of commodities sold on the collective farm markets represent the principal exception to the above general policy of fixed official P. In these markets for agricultural produce the forces of supply and demand establish ever fluctuating P at a level above the controlled P for the same item sold through the state and cooperative trading network. Collective farm market P differ from one locality to the next or even from one day to the next in the same market. In the winter time or in a wartime situation these P considerably exceed the official fixed P for the same commodity.

Fixed P of most producers' goods in the long run seem to be based on cost of production as defined by Soviet accounting practices. The principal components of production cost are: direct and indirect labor, including wages, salaries, and social security payments; auxiliary and basic materials, including fuel and power; and amortization. Although some rent and short-term interest payments for working capital may also be included in the cost of production, in comparison with western cost accounts, rent and interest are largely omitted from Soviet cost calculations.

The fixed P of most producers' goods are initially set to include a relatively small profit margin of from 3 to 5 per cent, as well as some marketing expenditures by the sales agency (*sbyt*). In a growing number of cases, P of producers' goods have been established on a f.o.b. station of consignee basis. In such instances the P include the average transportation costs involved in delivering the product to final users.

Since the fixed P of producers' goods have been revised very infrequently, two possible situations have arisen. During the early thirties, production costs rose primarily because money wages were allowed to rise at a faster rate than the increase in labor productivity. Rather than change the official P to reflect the new higher costs of production, the government chose to allocate substantial direct subsidies from the government budget to enable most industries to meet their obligations. Following the 1936 wholesale price reform, the practice of subsidizing became less widespread in the late thirties only to be reinstituted during the war and immediate postwar years.

Since 1949 the reverse development has generally taken place throughout Soviet industry. Production costs have generally fallen, owing to the fact that money wage increases have ordinarily been smaller than the increases in labor productivity. As a consequence, there has been a progressive tendency for profits to increase beyond the small margin planned when the official P were initially decreed. The profit margin is again substantially reduced whenever there is a major revision of P. The last major revision of producers' goods P was made on July 1, 1955, but a major revision is scheduled for 1961.

Until 1949 nominal turnover taxes were included in the P of most producers' goods primarily as a control device. At present substantial turnover taxes are included only in the official P for refined petroleum products and electric power.

The fixed P of most consumers' goods sold in the state and cooperative trading network also include substantial turnover taxes, as well as retail distribution costs. In exceptional cases, however, the P of certain consumers' goods may be set near or below cost of production to stimulate consumption.

The P of producers' goods seldom ration the supply. As a result, the central planners allocate directly the supplies of "deficit" items in critically short supply. In rare cases the P of some producers' goods (tin or lead) may be established at levels considerably above production costs to encourage economies in the use of these goods as well as the substitution of other materials. On the other hand, artificially low P may be established on new types of machinery or materials to stimulate their adoption.

The official P of consumers' goods are set with the objective of rationing the purchase of them. To the extent that food P are set too low, the supplies of the state stores are quickly exhausted and the remainder of consumer demand must be satisfied on the collective farm market at considerably higher P. The P of some non-foods (automobiles) have been set far too low to ration supply effectively, with the result that waiting lists are kept and an informal rationing takes place.

Such P as are set on the factors of production are also centrally established. Various types of labor are paid according to centrally determined rate structures, although there is some variation in the wage and salary payments whenever individual workers exceed their norms or managers pay varying amounts of premiums for output above the targets.

Capital has in most instances been distributed without cost to users, although amortization is charged on capital equipment as it is used in the productive process. Regarding the recent disbanding of the machine tractor stations, however, the collective farms have been required to purchase their agricultural machinery from the state at officially decreed P.

Interest charges are only nominal and are confined largely to borrowing of working capital by the enterprises. Some interest is also paid on savings accounts held by individual citizens. Low interest charges have also been made in connection with the recent introduction of installment buying, as well as with the international lending activities of the Soviet Union.

Rent is charged in the extraction of peat, while stumpage fees are levied and included in the cost of timber. These latter charges are greatest in areas where forests are easily accessible or where they have been depleted, and smallest in remote timber-producing areas.

Transportation charges are designed to effect a more rational utilization of the carriers, and do not bear much relation to costs.

For both producers' and consumers' goods, price zones are used in the transfer and sale of some items. Among producers' goods, the largest number of zones is found in connection with timber sales where there are twelve zones. Cement and oil P are divided into five zones each, while there are three price zones for engineering steel. For consumers' goods, the highest price zones for items not sold at all-Union P are found in Siberia and remote areas generally.

The charges for electric power vary from network to network, reflecting variations in production costs in the different regions. Certain users such as aluminum or chemical plants receive special low "privileged" rates. Hydroelectric power is generally much cheaper than thermal power. Users of electric power for consumption purposes pay a much higher uniform all-Union rate, while the highest charges of all are reserved for religious institutions.

The P for products of extractive industries such as iron ore, nonferrous metal ores, and coal vary from region to region, reflecting both differential production costs and the richness of the deposits. Most finished products, whether they be producers' or consumers' goods, are sold at all-Union P.

P for the same product also vary in accordance with quality. Most products are classified into three grades with price discounts for commodities considered to be lower than first quality.

Although it was planned to lower P generally in a secular fashion as early as 1926, in actual practice there was considerable over-all price and cost inflation in most commodities between 1930 and 1949. Since that time the P of most producers' goods with the exception of timber have fallen. Production costs of coal have been rising recently and it is probable that coal P will have to be increased in 1961. Consumers' goods P fell in a series of annual price reductions between 1948 and 1954, but since that time price stability has been the rule for consumers' goods. During this period of over-all price stability, there have been occasional price cuts for selected items, as well as price increases in the case of automobiles and vodka.

Publication of cost-of-living indexes is limited to the years before 1930 and after 1940. According to these official claims, consumers' goods P in 1960 were about 40 per cent above the prewar level in the state and cooperative stores and at about the same level on the collective farm markets as they were at the end of 1940. Official indexes of the P of producers' goods are withheld from publication. However, western studies of Soviet price movements have brought out the uneven nature of the relative price changes.

The price increases for consumers' goods have been considerably in excess of those for most producers' goods with perhaps an average over-all increase of between 13 and 16 times from 1928 to 1960. Variation in the over-all price increase is associated with different weighting systems, the greatest gains resulting from early year weights. Producers' goods P on the average have risen approximately fivefold, while wages have increased about 13-fold.

These variations in the relative price movements undoubtedly reflect Soviet modification of the so-called law of value. According to this "law," commodities tend to exchange in proportion to their labor content. In the Soviet Union at the present time the P of consumers' goods considerably exceed their average labor costs, while producers' goods are priced close to their average labor costs, including both live and "stored-up" labor.

The P of agricultural products sold directly by the collective farms to the state are also determined centrally. Until 1953, the P of these compulsory deliveries of agricultural products were virtually unchanged from their earlier levels. Since the retail P of agricultural products rose sharply during the planning period, the turnover tax rates were very high. According to one study, the average rate of turnover tax as a percentage of consumers' goods P amounted to roughly 60 per cent in the latter half of the thirties. Substantial increases in procurement P have taken place since 1953 and some efforts are also being made for the first time to calculate various agricultural production costs.

Some decentralization of price determination occurred after the creation of the regional economic councils (sovnarkhozy) in 1957. Decentralized price-fixing seems to apply primarily to consumers' goods produced exclusively in particular localities.

In weighting the index of gross industrial production, a set of "constant" 1926–27 ruble P was used to value the products of Soviet industry until after 1950. In many cases, particularly in the fast-growing machine-building branch, these unchanging P were set at the time the commodity was first produced and reflected a relatively much higher level of production costs. Since these new products were also the ones with the most rapid rate of growth, these "constant" P imparted an upward bias to the Soviet claims of industrial growth.

In their international trade agreements both within and outside the Soviet bloc, commodities exchanged are believed to be valued at world market P rather than at P prevailing internally in the Soviet economy. (*See also* CONSUMPTION, DOMESTIC TRADE, AGRICULTURE, IN-DUSTRY)

BIBLIOGRAPHY: Abram Bergson, et al., "Prices of Basic Industrial Products in the USSR, 1928–50," *The Journal of Political Economy*, August 1956; Robert W. Campbell, "Accounting for Cost Control in the Soviet Economy," *Review of Economics and Statistics*, February 1958; Gregory Grossman, "Industrial Prices in the USSR," *The American Economic Review*, May 1959; M. C. Kaser, "Soviet Planning and the Price Mechanism," *The Economic Journal*, March 1950; Lynn Turgeon, "Cost-Price Relationships in Basic Industries During the Soviet Planning Era," *Soviet Studies*, October 1957.
L. Tu.

PRIESTLESS (*Bezpopóvtsy*), one of the chief sects of the Old Believers of the Russian Orthodox Church, who did not recognize the clergy and the church hierarchy.

PRIMÓRSKY KRAY: *see* MARITIME KRAY.

PRINTING AND PUBLISHING INDUSTRY. According to official data 64,000 book titles (1.1 bill. copies), 3,800 periodicals (637 mill. copies), and 10,400 newspapers (13 bill. copies) were published in 1958. The United States figures for 1958 are: 13,400 book titles (888 mill. copies), 8,400 periodicals, and 11,300 newspapers (20 bill. copies).

The output of the printing and publishing industry had already become very substantial in Russia before the revolution: 30,000 books (99 mill. copies), 1,400 periodicals, and 1,100 newspapers were published in 1913. The majority of the 2,654 printing establishments in existence at that time, however, were small in size. Their concentration as well as the specialization of individual enterprises in particular types of production was one of the first measures carried out by the Soviet government.

Existing facilities were modernized and a number of large new printing plants were constructed under the prewar Five Year Plans. In Moscow the new plants included the facilities of the newspapers *Pravda, Red Star,* and *Moscow Pravda,* as well as those of the publishing house *Molodaya Gvardia.* Large printing establishments were also constructed in Leningrad (for the newspaper *Leningradskaya Pravda*), Tbilisi, Kiev, Kharkov, Baku, and in other cities. After the war similar plants were built in Yaroslav, Saratov, Minsk, and Kalinin. Altogether by 1957 there were 6,230 printing establishments in the USSR in which the type-setting process had become largely mechanized.

The Seven Year Plan calls for the construction of additional facilities in Chekhov (Moscow Oblast), Kalinin, Novosibirsk, Kaluga, and Kryukov (Moscow Oblast), and for further modernization. It is expected that by 1965 the number of books published each year will increase to 1.6 bill. units, that there will be twice as many periodicals and 1½ times as many newspapers. (*See also* BOOK PUBLISHING, PRESS) P. I. M.

PRÍPYAT (PRIPET) **RIVER,** in the Ukraine and Byelorussia, right tributary of Dnieper; 500 mi. long. Main tributaries: Stokhod, Styr, Horyn, Uzh (right), Yaselda, Sluch (left). Landings: Pinsk, Mozyr.

PRÍSHVIN, Mikhaíl Mikháylovich (1873–1954), an agronomist by education. He combined knowledge of natural sciences with considerable talents as a writer and student of the R. language and folklore. His writings range from the autobiographical novel *The Chain of Kashchey* (1923–36), to the highly specialized and sci-entifically prized paper *Potato Cultivation on Field and Truck Farms.* He made a reputation as an ethnographer and a naturalist. P's scientific publications include *Among Friendly Birds* (1905), *Tyan-Shan* (1932), and *The Forest* (1940–43).

PRIVÁLOV, Iván Ivánovich (1891–1941), mathematician. Corresponding member, Ac. of S., USSR (1939). Graduate, Moscow University (1913); professor, Saratov (1918) and Moscow (1922) universities. Expert in the theory of functions of a complex variable. In his monograph *Cauchy Integral* (1918) P advanced theorems on boundary properties of a function reflecting domains with a rectifiable property boundary, and discusses boundary properties of Cauchy integrals. In his investigations P used methods of metrical theory of functions of a real variable. Author of *Subharmonic Functions* (1937).

PROFESSIONAL EDUCATION is given in the Soviet Union on three levels:

(1) lower, in factory and collective farm schools, railroad training institutions, vocational schools;

(2) intermediate, in *technikums* (vocational schools on the secondary level), music and art schools, pedagogical schools, training establishments for nurses, midwives and pharmacists, courses for instructors in physical culture, and so on;

(3) higher, in universities and institutes.

PE had made some progress in prerevolutionary Russia, especially since the turn of the last century. It was very much extended in the Soviet period, in connection with the growing industrialization of the country. (*See also* EDUCATION)

PROFINTERN: *see* RED INTERNATIONAL OF LABOR UNIONS.

PROGIMNAZIA: *see* EDUCATION.

PROGRESSISTS, a group of moderate liberal deputies in the State Duma, first organized in 1908. It consisted of 28 deputies in the third Duma, and 48 in the fourth, some of which had come from the Octobrist (q.v.) faction. Several prominent political figures, including I. N. Yefremov, A. I. Konovalov, and I. P. Ryabushinsky, initially came from this group. In the last two Dumas the P entered into a coalition with the Constitutional Democrats, and in the fourth Duma they participated in the creation of the Progressive Bloc (1915) (q.v.). At the beginning of the February revolution Yefremov was appointed state controller in the Provisional Government while Konovalov (who subsequently joined the Constitutional Democrats) was appointed minister of trade and industry.

PROGRESSIVE BLOC. The military setbacks of 1915 and the growing discontent of the leaders of the Duma with the government's conduct of the war led to the formation (August 1915) of a coalition of opposition groups designed to give unified expression to the demands for change. This "Progressive Bloc" included moderate deputies from three parties, notably the Kadets, the Octobrists, and the Progressive Nationalists, constituting three-quarters of the membership of the Fourth Duma. Also represented were three of the less reactionary groups in the State Council.

In its appeal to the tsar and his advisers, the PB insisted on the formation of a new government more representative of the public at large. Only in this way, it declared, could the active cooperation of all citizens be enlisted in the nation's war effort. While the PB, solicitous of the feelings of its more conservative members, did not demand a ministry responsible to the Duma, it did call for elimination of "the distrust of public initiative." This was to be achieved by enforcement of the rule of law, less military interference with the conduct of civilian affairs, staff changes in local administrative bodies, and repeal of the worst of those measures inspired by racial, religious, or class discrimination.

Some of the ministers in Goremykin's government sympathized with these proposals, but Goremykin himself denounced them as "unconstitutional" by reason of the restrictions they placed on the powers of the monarch. He advised Nicholas II to this effect and the tsar prorogued the Duma, Sept. 2, 1915. Thus was ended all possibility of a Russian *union sacrée* and a peaceful solution to the country's internal problems. The PB joined in the increasingly bitter criticism of the government as 1916 brought further evidence of colossal mismanagement at the top. In November 1916 the Kadet leader Paul Milyukov, speaking for the entire PB, delivered a stinging attack in the Duma. It was disclosed later that some leaders of the PB had taken part in abortive attempts of a palace revolution.

C. J. F.

PROHIBITION: see ALCOHOLISM.

PROKÓFIEV, Sergéy Sergéyevich (1891–1953), composer and conductor. P's musical training began at the age of five when he took piano lessons from his mother. He entered St. Petersburg conservatoire in 1904 and graduated in composition, which he studied under Lyadov, in 1909; and as pianist and conductor, in

1914. His first piano recital was given in 1911. From 1918 to 1932 P lived abroad and toured the United States, Japan, and Europe. He became a People's Artist of the RSFSR (1947), member of the St. Cecilia Academy in Rome, and the Swedish Royal Academy of Music (1947). He was decorated with the Order of the Red Banner (1943), two Soviet medals, six Stalin prizes, and a gold medal

of the London Philharmonic Society (1944). A prolific composer, P's best-known works include the operas *The Love of Three Oranges* (1919) and *War and Peace*, the ballets *Romeo and Juliet* and *The Stone Flower*, the oratorio *Alexander Nevsky*, the symphonic tale *Peter and the Wolf*, scores for motion pictures (*Lieutenant Kizhe Suite, Ivan the Terrible*) and plays (*Boris Godunov, Hamlet*), ballet suites (*The Scythian Suite*), 5 piano, 2 violin, and 2 cello concertos and numerous other pieces for flute, oboe, cello. Although P has never been officially disgraced, he was repeatedly reprimanded for "formalism" and some of his compositions were suppressed in the Soviet Union.

BIBLIOGRAPHY: Israel V. Nestyev, *Prokofiev*, New York, 1960.

PROKÓFYEV, Aleksándr Andréyevich (1900–), poet, born in a fishing village on Lake Ladoga, near Leningrad. His first verse, *Songs of Ladoga*, was published in 1927. During the early 1930's, he brought out a number of collections of poems, including *Noon, Street of the Red Dawns*, and *The Temporary*. P was in Leningrad in 1943–44, during the siege, and wrote the lyric poem *Russia* which won a Stalin prize (1946). P has made extensive translations of Ukrainian and Byelorussian poets.

PROKÓPOVICH, Sergéy Nikoláyevich (1871–1955), economist, minister of the Provisional Government in 1917. P received his university education in Germany, Switzerland, and Belgium. In the 1890's he joined the Social Democrats. Together with his wife Ye. D. Kuskova (q.v.), P was one of the ideologues of the "economists." One of the leaders of the Union of Liberation, he was also an outstanding figure in the R. cooperative movement. In the Provisional Government, P was minister of trade and industry and later of supply. Arrested by the Bolsheviks, he later went into exile. P was a pioneer in the study of R. national income. He wrote many books and pamphlets on economic and social problems. Best known among them are: *To the Critique of Marx* (1901); *The Economic Conditions of Soviet Russia* (1924); and *The National Economy of the USSR* (2 vols., 1952).

PROKOPÓVICH, Theophan (1681–1736), outstanding theologian, essayist, and public leader. At one time, he was head of the Kiev-Mogilyansk Academy; later, the Bishop of Pskov, vice president of the Holy Synod, and Archbishop of Novgorod. He was an advocate of autocracy and absolute state, and an active supporter of the radical reforms instituted by Peter the Great. His best-known literary works are *A Discourse on the Power and Glory of the Tsars* and the tragicomedy *Vladimir*.

PROKÓPYEVSK, city in Kemerovo Oblast, W. Siberia, RSFSR; pop. 107,000 (1939) 282,000 (1959). Major mining center of high quality coking coal in Kuznetsk coal basin, with important rail connections; has large shops for repair of mining equipment.

PROLETKULT: see LITERATURE.

PROPAGANDA has normally been one of the most important activities of all communist parties. Lenin, in *What is to be Done?*, first published in 1902, and still regarded as one of the most important "classics of Marxism-Leninism," emphasized the crucial significance of P. Lenin urged his followers to go "among all classes of the population," as "theoreticians, propagandists, agitators and organizers." Despite the many changes and developments which have occurred in the 60-odd years since Lenin laid down the basic principles of Bolshevism, his successors in the leadership of Soviet and international communism continue to regard P as of central significance for the success of their self-imposed mission of world revolution.

The highest executive body of the CPSU, its Central Committee, has always had a section for P and agitation. This section, often referred to as "agitprop," determines policy and issues directives for all phases of domestic and foreign P, agitation and cultural activity carried on by party, state, and public organizations in or under the control of the Soviet Union. Major CP newspapers such as *Pravda* and magazines such as *Kommunist* (formerly *Bolshevik*) take their "line" from agitprop. Operating through the Ministry of Culture of the USSR, agitprop also controls the Soviet theater, cinema, and other cultural media. Such Soviet leaders as Mikhail Suslov or the late Andrey Zhdanov made their careers primarily as propagandists. The importance of P is spelled out in the statutes of the CPSU, which require members to engage in P efforts inside the party and among the nonparty "masses" to facilitate achievement of party objectives.

The term "agitprop" reflects the distinction drawn by Lenin between P and agitation. In the Soviet view, P consists in the dissemination, to relatively small audiences, of ideas and theories requiring detailed explanation. Agitation, in contrast, is defined as political activity intended to influence the "consciousness and mood" of "broad masses" of people by disseminating ideas and slogans. Both P and agitation are viewed by Soviet leaders as instruments of class struggle. Following Lenin in *What is to be Done?*, contemporary Soviet writers depict the "working classes" of so-called capitalist countries as victims of bourgeois propaganda disseminated by governments, churches, educational institutions, and other agencies of communication. It is the duty of the international communist movement to "liberate" the peoples of the world from bourgeois ideological domination. This task is said to have already been accomplished in the countries of the "socialist commonwealth."

However, the leaders of the Soviet and other communist parties which have achieved state power believe that the inculcation of "socialist consciousness" in the populations they control still remains an unfinished task of tremendous proportions. In broadest terms, one might describe the ultimate mission of domestic P activity in communist-ruled countries as the transformation of "capitalist man" into "socialist man." For many years the Soviet regime has conducted a struggle to inculcate into the minds of Soviet school children and youths the precepts of "communist morality," which prescribe such traits as "socialist patriotism," "proletarian internationalism," and a "collectivist" attitude toward labor. The major agency of this struggle is the Soviet school system but many other party and state instrumentalities, including the Young Communist League (Komsomol), the Young Pioneers, children's theaters, and so forth are involved.

Not all propaganda for the home front in communist-controlled countries is concerned with the inculcation of communist ideals, political loyalty, and other primarily political goals. Almost from the inception of the Soviet state, Lenin and his colleagues stressed the importance of various "practical" day-to-day missions for P and agitation. Khrushchev, in the section of his report to the 20th Party Congress in 1956 entitled "Problems of Ideological Work," emphasized that P must be "practical" and must not confine itself to "studying and lecturing on the principles of communism." Throughout the history of the USSR one of the most important "practical" tasks of P has been that of mobilizing the Soviet labor force for the rapid fulfillment of the production quotas set by the Kremlin. From time to time the party high command has assigned to the vast coordinated communications mechanism at its disposal other tasks such as the popularization of science and technology, the struggle against "religious prejudices," and, with varying degrees of emphasis depending upon the domestic and the international situation, the inculcation of patriotism and of hatred for whatever "capitalist" or "imperialist" government or group of governments was regarded at the time by the party leadership as the chief threat to Soviet security or the main obstacle to the further extension of communist power in the world.

Turning to Soviet "foreign" P, perhaps the first point to be stressed is that domestic P and foreign P are, in Soviet practice, inextricably interconnected. The content, planning, and strategy of both domestic and foreign P change in unison on the command of the top party leadership. However, Soviet foreign P exhibits the same continuity of purpose as does Soviet domestic P. The ultimate objective, for Lenin, for Stalin, and for Khrushchev has been world revolution. This is not, however, the sole objective of Soviet foreign policy and P. The survival of the Soviet regime, and in particular of its leadership, has always been the most immediate concern of all Soviet political activity, and therefore a determining influence on P. Between this first priority and the distant dream of world communism lie many intermediate objectives. They may, perhaps, be broken down into two main categories. Soviet P seeks, on the governmental level, to facilitate the foreign policy purposes of the Soviet leadership operating as a state in a world of nation-states. Even in pursuit of its most "normal" nation-state interests, however, the Soviet Union employs unconventional methods, such as appealing to the citizenry of "capitalist" states over the heads of their governments.

Normally, the top leadership both of the Soviet government and of the CPSU has been, if not always formally, at least for practical purposes, in the hands of one man. Stalin, although he did not until 1941 assume formal leadership of the Soviet state, dealt with foreign statesmen as, in fact, the supreme political dictator that he was. One consequence of this interlocking leadership at the pinnacle of state and party power is that the supreme leader, whether Lenin, Stalin, or

Khrushchev, has been not only the major P policy maker of the Soviet Union but also the living symbol of both state and party P "lines." Khrushchev, in particular, has engaged in a peculiarly active form of personalized face-to-face P and agitation. Much of Khrushchev's activity during his sojourns in foreign countries, particularly at the 1960 United Nations General Assembly Session, could more aptly be described as agitation than as P. Partly because of a very different personality, but perhaps more because of the relative weakness and enforced defensive position of the Soviet Union during most of his political lifetime, Stalin employed a P style which differed from Khrushchev's flamboyantly agitational one. However, Stalin also made very effective use of personal P on both state and party levels. He was able, apparently at will, to capture world press headlines whenever he deigned to grant one of his relatively rare interviews to a representative of the "capitalist" press.

In addition to the dimension of personal P just described, the Soviet government operates abroad through a wide range of mass media, such as foreign radio broadcasting, the export of newspapers, magazines and books, and so on. It has, in fact, devoted greater effort and resources to such activities than has any other government in history. In addition, the Soviet state has made very effective use of exchanges of persons and other aspects of "cultural diplomacy." It has for many years operated the world's largest national tourist monopoly and has set up many other agencies for the conduct of politically significant international exchanges.

Important as the above-mentioned "conventional" P activities are, they are probably subordinate in the Soviet scheme of things to P designed to build foreign communist parties, to exercise Moscow leadership over these parties, and to help foreign communist parties ultimately to gain control of the societies in which they operate. Moscow's "state" and "party" P activities are two sides of the same coin. Direct P from Moscow and display of Soviet achievements at international trade fairs, for example, strengthen the morale of foreign Communists and assist them in their recruitment activities. Such activities as Khrushchev's trips to India or Indonesia are doubtless calculated, in part, to weaken resistance to the eventual accession of communist parties of those countries to state power.

However, for purposes of analysis it is useful to distinguish between the direct P activities of the Soviet state and the P which Moscow indirectly conducts or inspires as the leading party of a network of communist parties throughout the world. The Soviet CP assists and guides other communist parties by personal contacts of top party leaders, by joint participation in international communist conferences, such as the major conferences held in Moscow in 1957 and 1960, and in many other ways, including a preponderant role in laying down the "general line" for international communism and the preparation of authoritative works on communist party history, on the fundamentals of political economy and on the basic tenets of Marxist-Leninist philosophy. It would be a mistake to assume that this process, especially since the death of Stalin, has always been one of dictation from Moscow. On the contrary, and particularly in recent years, consultation and discussion have played important roles in the process of interaction at the top levels of international communism.

Also, communication of the "party line" does not take place exclusively, or perhaps not even mainly, through secret directives dispatched by couriers from Moscow or via Soviet diplomatic channels. Although much, of course, is obscure in the whole area of interparty communications, there is considerable evidence to indicate that Moscow normally exercises leadership over foreign communist parties and other communist countries and thus determines their propaganda output, mainly by virtue of its prestige and through such media as short wave radio broadcasts or by articles in authoritative journals of international communism such as *World Marxist Review,* published in Prague (in Russian, *Problemy Mira i Sotsializm*), which since 1958 has been a substitute for the former Cominform journal *For a Lasting Peace, For a People's Democracy!*

For the coordination of international communist P the Soviet Communists have created centralized organizations such as the Comintern (Communist International) which functioned from 1919 until May 1943, and the Cominform which functioned from 1947 until April 1956. In addition, there always have been and are today many communist "fronts" which to a greater or lesser extent disguise the Soviet control of communist-inspired organizations and attempt to adapt the activities and P of these organizations to national, cultural, occupational, and other characteristics of various target groups. Among the most important international communist "fronts" since the end of World War II, the World Peace Council (WPC) and the World Federation of Trade Unions (WFTU) should be mentioned. Also important are the World Federation of Democratic Youth (WFDY), the International Union of Students (IUS), and the Soviet-controlled international network of "friendship societies."

Into this vast communications network, only the barest outlines of which are sketched here, Moscow feeds an endless series of messages, adapted to the ever-changing world political situation. Perhaps the most important single theme of the P disseminated directly by the Soviet state, and indirectly through communist parties and communist fronts, has been Soviet "peace" P. The Soviet leaders have vigorously and at times almost hysterically sought to convince the world that mankind can free itself from the scourge of war only by accepting Soviet leadership and ultimately by replacing the "capitalist" with the "socialist" political and social system. Soviet P agencies have also exploited international rivalries and ethnic, cultural, racial, and religious divisions within nations. They have proclaimed that the only final cure for these "contradictions of capitalism" is Soviet-style—and no other style—"socialism."

In the presentation of these themes Soviet propagandists have displayed energy and skill. They have been adept in combing the "capitalist" press for statements which, quoted out of context, would tend to confirm Soviet P assertions. They have utilized the testimony of noncommunist foreign visitors to Russia and of Soviet "eyewitness" reporters sent on missions to foreign lands to lend credibility to the Soviet P line. Perhaps most striking of all has been their success in exploiting the "bourgeois" press to draw attention to and as far as possible to confirm Soviet claims.

BIBLIOGRAPHY: Alex Inkeles, *Public Opinion in Soviet Russia*, Cambridge, 1951; Evron Kirkpatrick, ed., *Year of Crisis*, N.Y., 1957; V. I. Lenin, *What is to be Done?*, available in English editions.

F. C. B.

PROPERTY ownership in the USSR involves the Roman law rights of possession, use, and disposal, as regulated by the national economic plan, administrative and civil law (q.v.). It is classified by the Constitution (q.v.) and the laws as "socialist" P and "personal" P. "Socialist" P, in turn, may be either state P or the P of non-state organizations such as the CPSU, trade unions, and cooperatives. In spite of the recent increase in cooperative property by the transfer of farm machinery in 1958 from the abolished Machine Tractor Stations to the collective farms, the Soviet regime has not abandoned its ultimate aim of transforming collective farms into state farms. State P, the preponderant form of P, is described in the Constitution as: land, subsoil, water and forests, factories, plants, mines, railroads, water and air transport, banks, post and telegraph, public broadcasting facilities, telephones, state farms, public utilities, and most urban housing. Soviet P relations are noteworthy for wide state ownership, socialization of most means of production, centralized planned controls over the use of "socialist" P, and the restrictions on the acquisition and disposal of "personal" P. Private P in the means of production, which communist ideology associates with exploitation of one class by another and which in practical terms meant a challenge to total Soviet power, all but disappeared during the expropriations of the remaining capitalists and collectivization of the peasants in the late 1920's and early 1930's. Means of production remaining in private possession are considered part of "personal" P and consist of individual craftsmen's small tools; the subsidiary economies of collective farm households connected with the use of a garden plot, i.e., small tools, some livestock and poultry and the produce of the plot; and similar economies of nonfarm families centering on their kitchen gardens. Most legal "personal" P is nonproductive; i.e., earned income and savings, personal effects, private houses, home furnishings and utensils, and private cars. "Personal" P is permitted as a material spur to the all-important greater labor and productivity. Further P incentives take the form of liberal inheritance (q.v.), generous rights of authorship and invention (q.v.), and the current abolition of income taxes. The regime denies that inequality of "personal" P ownership is unsocialistic, rejects equalitarian "leveling" (although extreme differences in pensions and wages have been recently reduced), and insists that under socialism people must still be paid according to their work.

"Personal" P may not be used in connection with private hiring of labor for profit. There are limits on the size, acquisition, and sale of private houses (see HOUSING REGULATIONS). Usury and gaining of profit from the use of private cars are forbidden. Goods must not be bought privately for resale at a profit, on pain of prosecution for "speculation," the only legal private sales for profit being by vendors in "bazaars" and collective farm markets. Black markets will continue, however, as long as there are shortages and price controls. (*See also* SOVIET LAW)

P. H. J.

PROSKÚROV: *see* KHMELNITSKY.

PROSTITUTION was legalized in tsarist Russia; police and medical regulation began in 1843. Prostitutes were supposed to carry "yellow tickets" of registration in place of passports, and to work in registered "public houses." Under tsarist divorce law, the mere presence of one's wife in a "public house" was not grounds for divorce. Specific acts of adultery had to be proved in the regular manner. P, now defined in the USSR as "the sale of one's body, chiefly by women, as a means of livelihood," is not directly penalized by law, perhaps in line with the communist view that prostitutes are the exploited victims of pre-Soviet social-economic systems. But compelling a woman to prostitute herself, running a house of P, and procuring or recruiting women for the purpose of P are punishable by up to five years' confinement and confiscation of all or part of the property of the convicted. P is officially eliminated in the USSR. It is still in evidence, however.

PROTODYÁKONOV, Mikhaíl Mikháylovich (1874–1930), mining engineer. Graduated St. Petersburg Mining Institute (1899). Supervised lead mine (1900). Teacher (1904), professor (1908), Dnepropetrovsk Mining Institute. Founder of Turkestan University (1918). Professor, Moscow University (1925). Works concern rock pressure, mine supports, ventilation, norming in mining industry.

PROTOPÓPOV, Aleksándr Dimítryevich (1866–1918), last minister of the interior under Nicholas II, an appointee of Empress Alexandra and Rasputin. Member of the Octobrist party in the third and fourth Dumas. During World War I he was suspected of favoring a separate peace with Germany. Arrested after the revolution and executed by the Bolsheviks in 1918.

PROVINTSIA: *see* LOCAL GOVERNMENT, ADMINISTRATIVE AND TERRITORIAL DIVISIONS.

PROVISIONAL COMMITTEE OF THE DUMA was elected by the Duma's Council of Elders after receiving the tsar's decree dissolving the Duma on March 12, 1917 (N.S.). It included the representatives of all parties in the Duma, except the extreme Right and Bolsheviks whose deputies were in Siberian banishment. Its chairman, the president of the Duma, Rodzyanko, and the majority of its members desired to see the monarchy in Russia reformed, but not abolished by the revolution. Thus the original functions of the committee were defined as the restoration of order in the capital and the establishment of relations with public organizations and institutions. When, however, on one side, the tsar and his government were not inclined to make any reasonable concessions, and, on the other, the capital passed completely into the hands of the revolutionaries and the Soviet of Workers' and Soldiers' Deputies was organized, the committee extended the scope of its authority.

It took "into its hands the restoration of state and public order and the creation of a government corresponding to the desires of the population and capable of enjoying its confidence." After having reached, on March 15, 1917 (N.S.), a tentative agreement with the representatives of the Soviet as to the conditions on which the Soviet would support the Provisional Government created by the provisional committee, such government was established and formally assumed office on March 16. After that the committee passed into oblivion.

V. Su.

PROVISIONAL GOVERNMENT. On March 2, 1917, after much negotiation with the Petrograd Soviet, the provisional committee of the Duma announced formation of a Provisional Government under the leadership of Prince George Lvov. Lvov, a wealthy landowner, zemstvo leader, social reformer, and Slavophile, also served as minister of the interior. Chief among his colleagues were P. N. Milyukov, historian and leader of the Kadets, minister of foreign affairs; A. I. Guchkov, founder and leader of the Octobrist party, minister of war and navy; M. T. Tereshchenko, one of Russia's richest men, minister of finance; N. V. Nekrasov, an obscure Kadet, minister of transport; and Alexander Kerensky, leader of the non-Marxist Labor group in the fourth Duma, minister of justice. The new cabinet's main domestic task was the convocation of a constituent assembly, while it also announced its intention to remove restrictions on civil liberties, democratize local government, and institute a broad political amnesty.

The Petrograd Soviet associated itself with this statement of policy. But in reality its attitude toward the Provisional Government was ambiguous. It merely promised to support the government in so far as Lvov's policies corresponded to the interests of the proletariat and the broad democratic masses of the people. A contact committee was formed between the two bodies, but conflicts were quick to develop. Disagreement arose first over the question of army organization. Guchkov did not conceal his detestation of the new system of army committees and other such revolutionary changes in military organization that followed the decree of Order No. 1 by the army section of the Soviet on March 2.

Further friction ensued when Milyukov, in his note of April 18 to the Allies, denied any intention of making a separate peace and reiterated Russia's faithfulness to her war agreements in the fight against the Central Powers. The Soviet, on the other hand, demanded changes in the war agreements and the publication of those that were secret. There were further demands for peace without annexations or indemnities, an end to the war, and Milyukov's resignation. Inability to cope with factory seizures and the explosive agrarian revolution, labor unrest, general economic dislocation, collapse of the army, and disintegration of the Empire undermined the government.

The end of the first PG came after Guchkov resigned April 30 and Milyukov on May 2. The cabinet, branded as "capitalist" and "imperialist" by Lenin in his *April Theses,* was replaced by a coalition government, May 5.

More to the left in orientation than its predecessor, the new ministry consisted of ten non-socialists, three Socialist Revolutionaries and two Mensheviks. Prince Lvov remained as premier and minister of the interior; Tereshchenko became minister of foreign affairs; Kerensky took over the war and navy portfolio; and the most radical member of the cabinet, Victor Chernov, was minister of agriculture. The government promised peace without annexations or indemnities and preliminary steps to revise Russia's war-aim agreements with the Allies. But this was not enough to assuage the Petrograd Soviet or to diminish the hostility of the Bolsheviks, while the government's difficulties were compounded by internal dissensions.

Though making a brave show of force in dealing with the July Uprising, Lvov resigned because of his opposition to what he considered the excessive radicalism of his colleagues; and on July 24 Kerensky formed a second coalition government. The new premier continued as war minister, Tereshchenko as foreign minister, Chernov in agriculture, with Nekrasov vice-premier and minister of finance, and the Menshevik I. G. Tsereteli minister of the interior. In all, the non-socialists were a minority. Kerensky himself was the dominant figure, making eloquent appeals for iron rule, unity, and enthusiasm. But he was unable to rely on a representative popular assembly and suffered further setbacks with the continued deterioration of the war effort and the collapse of central authority. The Kornilov "counter-revolution" of Aug., which ended with Kerensky's assumption of the office of commander in chief, further hastened the end of the government.

A third coalition government, headed by Kerensky, was formed Sept. 25. There were ten socialist and six non-socialist ministers, and policies were enacted which were designed to placate Kerensky's Left-wing supporters. But on Oct. 24 came the uprisinng led by Lenin and Trotsky. The next day Kerensky left Petrograd. On the 26th all ministers, with the exception of Kerensky and S. N. Prokopovich, were arrested. The PG was no more. (*See also* DUAL POWER, JULY DAYS, FEBRUARY REVOLUTION, KORNILOV "MUTINY")

C. J. F.

PRUT RIVER, flows along Moldavian SSR-Rumanian border, emptying into Danube; 370 mi. long, of which 120 mi. are navigable. Landings: Kolomiya, Chernovtsy.

PRYÁNISHNIKOV, Dmítry Nikoláyevich (1865–1948), agrochemist and plant physiologist. Fellow, Ac. of S., USSR (1929). Hero of Socialist Labor (1945). A student of K. A. Timiryazev. Graduate, Moscow University (1887) and the Moscow Agricultural Academy (1889) where he was a professor (1895–1948). Research concerned plant nutrition and the use of chemical fertilizers in agriculture. Developed and clarified the role of nitrogenous metabolism in plant and animal life which had great significance for the study of evolution of living organisms. Initiated the large scale introduction of mineral fertilizers in the USSR. Honorary member of foreign academies and learned societies. Several experimental stations and the Agricultural Institute in

Perm are named after P. Lenin prize (1926); Stalin prize (1941); K. A. Timiryazev award (1945).

PRZHEVÁLSK (f. Karakol), city, adm. center of Issyk-Kul Oblast, Kirghiz SSR; pop. 35,000 (1959). Its ind. include flour mills, sunflower-oil presses, brewery, bread factory, footwear, woodworking; has several higher technical schools. Renamed in commemoration of the famous explorer, Nikolay Przhevalsky, who died in the city in 1888.

PRZHEVÁLSKY, Nikoláy Mikháylovich (1839–1888), explorer and geographer. Honorary Fellow, Ac. of S. (1878), Russian Geographical Society (1864), and other Russian and foreign learned societies. Graduated from the St. Petersburg Academy of the General Staff (1880). Major general. As a result of five major expeditions to Central Asia (1867–88) he described climatic conditions, waterways, and the fauna and flora of Mongolia, N. China, the Gobi desert, and the Tien Shan Mountains. He was the first to climb the Kunlun Shan Mountain range; discovered that the Nan Shan Mountains were part of a chain. Left a remarkable collection of plants, fish, and stuffed animals. A Russian Geographic Society award and a gold medal of the Soviet Geographic Society were named after P (in 1880 and 1946, respectively). The town where he died is known as Przhevalsk (formerly Karakol). Furthermore, a mountain range, a glacier, a bay, as well as many animals and plants discovered by him bear his name. His books written with considerable literary talent have been translated into many languages.

PSEL (PSYOL) RIVER, flows S. from Belgorod region mostly through the Ukraine; left tributary of Dnieper; 450 mi. long.

PSEUDO-DIMITRY: *see* OTREPYEV.

PSKOV, city, adm. center of Pskov Oblast, on Velikaya River near its estuary in Lake Peipus; pop. 81,000 (1959). Once a "free city," of ancient fame dating back to 903. Ind.: agr. and textile machinery; linen and rope mills. Important R.R. junction. Famous for its architectural monuments, museums, churches.

PSKOV LAKE, in Pskov Oblast, connected with Gulf of Finland by Narva River and Lake Chudskoye; area 275 sq. mi.

PSKOV OBLAST, RSFSR, N.W. sector; borders on Estonian and Latvian SSR's; area 21,300 sq. mi.; pop. 952,000 (1959). Cities: Pskov (adm. center), Gdov, Dno, Velikie Luki. Wooded lowland on Lake Peipus drained by Velikaya River; has mixed and pine forests growing on clayey glacial soils; humid climate. Important flax-growing region; grains, fodder crops (rye, oats), potatoes extensively cultivated; has dairy farming, lumbering, peat works, quartz and dolomite quarries. Ind. plants around Pskov city. Est. 1944.

PSYCHIATRY. Psychiatry in the Soviet Union is a branch of medicine, having historical antecedents that are W. European as well as Russian, but exhibiting special features that reflect the vicissitudes of development within the Soviet context. The efforts in the decade or so after the revolution to construct a "materialist psychiatry," based on dialectical materialism, led to aborted attempts at the amalgamation of Freudianism and Marxism, on the one extreme, and, on the other, to formulations in accord with the reflexological principles of V. M. Bekhterev who, in a recent review of 40 years of Soviet P, was declared the actual "founder of Soviet psychotherapy." By the early thirties, however, psychoanalytically influenced publications had ceased, although individual interest in psychoanalysis was still manifest, and reflexological principles were replaced by principles developed by I. P. Pavlov who for a number of years had been conducting research on psychiatric problems and who had continued to do so until his death in 1936.

Pavlov viewed mental disturbances as primarily disruptions in the normal interrelationships between the excitatory and inhibitory processes and had developed therapeutic methods such as sleep and hypnotherapy, the former reflecting in particular his theory of "protective inhibition." However, Pavlov's influence on P was in actual fact limited, and allegiance to his principles and theories was more declarative than active, that is, until 1949 when signs began multiplying that Pavlov was due for official canonization. As a matter of fact, Pavlovian theory encountered considerable apathy and even resistance among Soviet psychiatrists, among whom there were those who saw in it only a "verbal husk" and a "huge mechanistic peril." In actual practice P during this period, with the exceptions noted above, pursued a conservative course, with psychotherapy, as such, reduced in the main to encouraging, common-sense talk.

A cross section of psychiatric practice in 1949, on the eve of the Pavlovian reform, shows that at the time at least four basic therapies were explicitly recognized: work therapy, physiotherapy, psychotherapy, and "active therapy," the last including therapies based on chemical, electrical, and surgical methods. Among these, active therapy predominated by far. Physiotherapy, while appreciated, was slighted owing to insufficiency of equipment and lack of trained personnel. Work therapy, when practiced, was frequently assigned a secondary role. Inadequate space allotment, overcrowding, lack of raw materials, limited trained personnel, as well as an "overenthusiasm for active therapy"—all contributed to the neglect of work therapy in spite of theoretical stress on its psychotherapeutic role. The least developed of the therapies was psychotherapy. Its "application in both hospitals and dispensaries bore a fortuitous character" and "was frequently carried out on a low level."

Active therapy carried the major therapeutic burden. This form of therapy included, in the main, insulin shock therapy, electro- and pharmaco-convulsive therapy, sulphotherapy, and sleep therapy. However, in spite of steady improvements in both personnel and matériel (many hospitals were, for example, without X-ray apparatus and sufficient supplies of insulin), in any given hospital the number of patients undergoing active therapy during 1949 still varied by as much as 3 per cent to 50 per cent among the over 100 hospitals designated as equipped to undertake such therapy in the Soviet Union. By 1949 insulin shock therapy had come to be preferred to electroconvulsive therapy, while sleep therapy ran a poor third to both of them. Surgical therapy in the form of leucotomy, introduced into general practice in 1947, was in 1949 undergoing gradual abandonment in anticipation of the official ban, decreed in 1950.

Such was the general picture of P on the eve of the Pavlovian reform, foreshadowed by the "Jubilee Scientific Session, Dedicated to the 100th Birthday of Academician I. P. Pavlov." On Sept. 27, 1949 the participants of this celebration directed a message to Stalin, declaring that "thanks to [his] personal concern and instructions the triumph was guaranteed of the materialist theory of I. P. Pavlov on higher nervous activity as the only scientific and progressive direction in natural science for the study of psychic phenomena" and that they would "apply every effort to connect even more deeply and more directly Soviet physiology with the real needs of [Soviet] medicine." In Dec. 1949 S. I. Vavilov wrote of Stalin's great interest in the development of Pavlovian theory "as part of the very foundations of a materialist theory of nature," and in March 1950 A. D. Speransky, summarizing the widely held discussions aimed at showing "Pavlovism" to be the "only right direction," wrote that Pavlovianism "not only can, but ought to be the basis of development for Soviet medical science"—an admonition amplified in May 1950 by O. Ostry who flatly declared that the "time had come for the full victory of the Pavlovian direction in Soviet medicine." When the "Pavlovian Sessions" took place one month later, the "triumph of Pavlovism" was a foregone conclusion. Soviet P, which, according to V. A. Gilyarovsky's confession at these sessions, was not Pavlovian, was now to become Pavlovian.

As a result, the language of P became Pavlovian, its major research programs took on a physiological orientation, sleep therapy became more widespread, and psychotherapy was assigned a larger role. Pavlov's theory of the "second signal system," which Pavlov actually did not get around to developing to any extent, became the theoretical basis of psychotherapy because, in contradistinction to the "first signal system" whose activators are physical stimuli, the activating stimuli of the "second signal system" are words—and words *are* used in psychotherapy.

By 1957 the Pavlovianization of P by fiat had led to some recognized "dogmatic vulgarization of Pavlovian theory" whereby "everything is explained with the help of general formulas from Pavlov's theory on higher nervous activity." Among a number of Soviet psychiatrists there even appeared public dissatisfaction with the "preconceived confirmation of Pavlovian propositions on the character of changes in higher nervous activity in all kinds of pathological states and psychic illness." This dissatisfaction, along with the influence of foreign psychiatric literature, apparently introduced among those psychiatrists who had "related themselves skeptically to the importance of I. P. Pavlov's theory for psychiatry" a number of "revisionist tendencies," seen as manifested in an "eclectic union of Pavlovian

theory with Freudism and various psychomorphological conceptions."

Sub rosa "revisionism" in P had evidently become widespread enough to constitute a problem. In Oct. 1958, accordingly, a conference on the "ideological struggle with contemporary Freudism" was held, one of whose aims was to "overcome the remnants of Freudism, existing in our midst." This was accomplished by taking over many of the major conceptions of Freud and programing them for development in Pavlovian terms. Thus, "the consequences of affective conflict," "the role of unconscious factors in behavior," "the functional tension of unconscious effects," and "the pathogenic role of motivational conflicts" are explicitly recognized. F. V. Bassin, who was assigned an important role in this conference, stated that, because of the great cumulation of clinical and experimental evidence, one simply had to admit the reality of unconscious urges and motives, their conflict, and influence on behavior, but that the "psychological problem of the unconscious" had to date been given a "distorted, idealist, and pseudoscientific treatment" on the basis of a "monopolizing" Freudism. In other words, it was time to seize the problem from those under the influence of the latter and, not denying its reality, to give it the proper treatment which Freudism cannot provide.

The problems, explored by Freud, are now seen as real, but their solution is still being sought within the frame of Pavlovian conceptions in spite of the many complications which recent findings on subcortical functioning have brought. Soviet P, which has in fact functioned conservatively over the years in a highly organized network of specialized hospitals and dispensaries (inpatient and/or outpatient clinics), appears ready to move in new directions, however reluctant officially its disengagement from and disenchantment with the widespread "Pavlovian scholasticism which freezes Pavlovian theory at the point where it was when Pavlov died" and which "dictates to the clinicians what they ought to see and do." (*See also* MEDICINE, PHYSIOLOGY, PSYCHOLOGY.)

BIBLIOGRAPHY: F. V. Bassin, "Freudism in the Light of Contemporary Scientific Discussions," *Soviet Survey*, 1929, No. 27; Mark G. Field, "Approaches to Mental Illness in Soviet Society: Some Comparisons and Conjectures," *Social Problems*, 1960, No. 7; I. D. London, "Therapy in Soviet Psychiatric Hospitals," *American Psychologist*, 1953, No. 8; J. Wortis, *Soviet Psychiatry*, Baltimore, 1950; *Scientific Session on the Physiological Teachings of Academician I. P. Pavlov*, Moscow, 1951.   I. D. L.

PSYCHOANALYSIS: *see* PSYCHIATRY.

PSYCHOLOGY in the Soviet Union is an area of research, theorization, and application shared by several disciplines, only one of which is recognized as P proper. This results in a P which from W. habit and point of view is narrowly conceived and considerably restricted, because of preemption of much of its traditional themes and problems by disciplines ancillary to it and to deliberate neglect of still others through hostile attitudes and outright proscription. Congruency of Western P with a Soviet counterpart is, accordingly, incomplete and must be sought in a truncated psychology supplemented by those relevant areas of Soviet biophysics, physiology, medicine, pedagogy, and so forth, as are seen by Westerners as within P. It is best to view P in the Soviet Union in precisely this way, especially in view of the long-time stepchild status of Soviet P and its dependent and deferential relationship to physiology and pedagogy in particular that have obtained at intervals over so much of the Soviet period.

P in the Soviet Union has had a hectic and spotty development. By 1923 traditional Russian P had disappeared from the scene under the combined attack of a hostile Marxism, which sought to cleanse P of idealism, and a militant reflexology, which aimed to replace P *in toto* as a discipline. The latter was promulgated by V. M. Bekhterev as a separate discipline and actually did succeed in displacing P in many institutions. Bekhterev, in his quest for an "objective psychology," affirmed the inaccessibility of the psyche to knowledge and stressed in its stead "external behavior" which, when viewed as "associated reflexes" in proper combinations, could, according to him, account for all properties and special characteristics of human behavior, including the social. Rival to Bekhterev's reflexology and destined to provide in the fifties the major basis for Soviet P was the Pavlovian school. Although I. P. Pavlov and his disciples conducted their research on the conditioned reflex and related conceptions strictly within the framework of physiology, the influence of their work was projected into P by the followers of Soviet behaviorism and others who saw in it great possibilities for P, conceived as the science of behavior, as opposed to an inadmissible P, conceived as a science of the psyche. Concurrently, there developed a strong contender for attention in the guise of reactology, proposed by K. N. Kornilov as a Marxist version of P and seen essentially as a synthesis of behaviorism and introspectionism. However, party-inspired attacks, culminating in 1931, forced reflexology, behaviorism, and reactology from the psychological scene as crudely mechanistic theories, unwilling to recognize or unable to cope with the leading role of consciousness in man's behavior. At the same time foreign P was anathematized—Gestaltism, American behaviorism, and psychoanalysis in particular.

The scope of Soviet P underwent thereupon considerable constriction with only psychotechnique and pedology flourishing—the former a form of vocational and industrial P, the latter a form of P concentrating on the all-round genetic development of the child. Both made considerable use of psychological measurement and testing and were banned in 1936 for presuming the fatalistic dependence of the individual's destiny on biological and social factors, that is to say, on the influence of a blind heredity and some sort of "irrevocable environment"—all of which was seen as in "howling contradiction to Marxism and to the whole practice of socialist construction, successfully transforming people in the spirit of socialism." This ban on pedology in 1936 initiated the still continuing large-scale hostility to "testology" as a reactionary American importation and the long neglect of statistical procedures in general which is only now being studiously overcome in Soviet P. With these developments Soviet P was almost reduced to the position of mere handmaiden

to pedagogy and increasingly took on a functionalistic cast. But its work was, as always, supplemented elsewhere. Thus, conditioned-reflex experimentation continued and research in the psychophysiological aspects of man took place under biophysical and physiological auspices as well as elsewhere.

The period which followed produced no major developments in Soviet P prior to 1950 except for the call in 1947 to reaffirm ideological trueness and partisanship in psychological theory. This call, along with the triumph of Lysenko in genetics and the wide celebration in 1949 of the 100th anniversary of Pavlov's birth, set the stage for the Draconian introduction a year later of a doctrinaire version of Pavlovian theory as its necessary basis and guide. Accordingly, Soviet P, which before either ignored Pavlovian theory or paid, at the most, lip service to it, now operates within a Pavlovian framework, however traditional and even old-fashioned some of its psychological categories continue to be. While a major portion of Soviet P continues to be pedagogically oriented—a situation which has become sharply accentuated since the Khrushchevian school reforms—the last decade has seen a considerable expansion of research beyond previous narrow confines, many of its new problems being suggested by Pavlovian theory. Thus, much work is now being done on verbal conditioning because of the emphasis given to Pavlov's conception of the "second signal system" where verbal stimuli substitute for physical stimuli in the classical conditioning paradigm and serve thereby to elicit calculated responses. This Pavlovian conception has also served to restore psychotherapy to good repute because by its very nature psychotherapy must operate through the medium of words, that is, verbal stimuli or cues. However, the reintroduction of psychotherapy has not been into Soviet P proper, but into medicine, one of whose subdivisions is psychiatry. Along with the Pavlovian impetus to explore new problems have also come many domestic and foreign-inspired new interests: personality theory, engineering P, information theory, and so forth—all heretofore very weakly represented in contemporary Soviet P, if at all. While the conscious continues, as before, to play a dominant role in Soviet P, recent developments have brought a publicized recognition of the role of the unconscious in behavior (at least to the extent of calling it the automatic regulatory aspect of consciousness) and a call to rescue the problems of unconscious motivation, conflict, and so forth from the "reactionary Freudians" who have been "monopolizing" these conceptions.

Since Soviet P is required to have a philosophically sound base in dialectical materialism, considerable effort continues to be devoted to finding acceptable formulations. The most recently acclaimed formulation is that of S. L. Rubinshteyn, who makes traditional use of Lenin's theory of reflection. In Lenin's theory the brain is viewed as a "reflecting organ, reflecting an objectively existent external reality," and the psyche, resident in the brain, is viewed as presenting an *ideal* copy of a reflected *material* world. Rubinshteyn, however, introduces into the reflective process *refraction* within the individual, by which is meant that, through inter-action within the "inner conditions" of an individual, "outer causation," working on him, results in a medi-ated and individualized reflection of objective reality, rather than one in simple correspondence with the ma-terial world. In other words, reflection is *intra*person-ally refracted and, accordingly, must always be tested and corrected in conscious action.

BIBLIOGRAPHY: I. D. London, Instrumentation in Soviet psycho-logical research, *Journal of Social Psychology*, 1960; N. O'Connor, (Ed.) *Recent Soviet Psychology*, New York, 1961; I. P. Pavlov, *Ex-perimental Psychology and Other Essays*, New York, 1957; B. Si-mon, (Ed.) *Psychology in the Soviet Union*, Stanford, 1957; R. Winn, (Ed.) *Soviet Psychology*, New York, 1961. I. D. L.

PUBLIC HEALTH: *see* MEDICAL SYSTEM.

PUBLIC LIBRARIES. A network of state public libraries has been established in the cities of the Soviet Union, headed by the Lenin Library in Moscow and the Saltykov-Shchedrin Library in Leningrad. They often include special children's rooms, reading rooms, and lecture halls.

GROWTH OF LIBRARIES
IN THE USSR

Year	Number (thous.)	Volumes (mill.)
1913	13.9	9.4
1922	16.6	46.3
1940	95.4	184.8
1945	47.4	109.1
1950	123.1	244.2
1959	134.6	800.0

The Lenin Library has 19 mill. books and periodi-cals; Library of the Ac. of S., 12 mill. books and pe-riodicals; Saltykov-Shchedrin Library, 12 mill.

PUBLISHING INDUSTRY: *see* PRINTING AND PUB-LISHING INDUSTRY, BOOK PUBLISHING.

PUDÓVKIN, Vsevolod Illarionovich (1893–1953), motion picture producer. Associated with motion pic-tures since 1920, first as an actor then as a producer. Directed the documentary *Mechanics of the Brain* (1926) and the pictures, *Mother* after the book by Maxim Gorky (1926), *Storm Over Asia* (1927), *Minin and Pozharsky* (1939), *Suvorov* (1940), *In the Name of the Homeland* (1943), *Admiral Nakhimov* (1946), *Zhukovsky* (1950), *The Return of Vasily Bortnikov* (1953). Stalin prizes (1941, 1947, 1951); two Orders of Lenin.

PUGACHÓV, Yemelyán Ivánovich (1742–1775), Don Cossack, veteran of three wars (the Seven Years'  War against Prussia, the Polish cam-paign of 1764, and the Russo-Turkish War in 1768–74), and leader of the important peasant uprising against serf-dom in 1773–75. Starting in the Urals, the rebellion rapidly spread over a vast territory. Pugachov's troops succeeded in capturing Kazan, Penza, Saratov, and other major cities, but the insurrection finally collapsed. Pugachov was delivered to the authori-ties by Cossack elders and executed in Moscow on Jan. 10, 1775.

PÚLKOVO, town 10 mi. S. of Leningrad, seat of the famous Pulkovo Astronomical Observatory; founded 1839.

PURGES. The device of the purge has been a meth-od of continuous party purification. It has taken vari-ous forms, from reassignment and expulsion to ex-treme terror resulting in torture, imprisonment, and liquidation of party members. The nature, scope, and severity of each purge have differed from period to period.

Soon after the seizure of power, in March 1919, the 8th Party Congress ordered the re-registration of the entire party membership to weed out the unworthy—careerists and class enemies—who had joined the party in the flush of a victorious revolution. Consequently 100,000 members were expelled. In Aug. 1921 a new purge was ordered. Attempting to reinforce the prole-tarian element in the party the purge was primarily directed against former members of other political par-ties and party bureaucrats. Approximately 170,000 were expelled. During the 1920's supporters of Trot-sky, of the New Opposition, and of the Right Opposi-tion suffered reassignments and expulsions as Stalin successively eliminated his opponents.

The decade of the 1930's was marked by a series of severe P which culminated in the terror of the Great Purge 1936–38. In 1933 the Central Committee of the CPSU ordered a verification and purge of the party membership. A Central Purge Commission with local affiliates was set up as the entire party member-ship was subjected to a public purging process. With-in months 800,000 were expelled, and an additional 340,000 in 1934. Recent party recruits (primarily among collective farm workers and new industrial workers of peasant origin as well as a number of na-tionality groups) were particularly hard hit.

The assassination of S. M. Kirov, Politburo mem-ber and head of the Leningrad party organization, in Dec. 1934 prepared the way for the Great Purge of 1936–38. The *Yezhovshchina* as it was also called (after N. I. Yezhov, People's Commissar of Internal Affairs) differed from preceding P not only in the severity of the terror which ravaged all areas of So-viet life but in that it was initiated by Stalin against the party and the Central Committee, and caused a radical transformation. Of 139 members elected to the Central Committee by the 17th Party Congress (1934) 98 were shot; of 1,966 delegates attending the Congress 1,108 were subsequently charged with committing anti-revolutionary crimes and were arrested. Approximate-ly 36% of the members, 850,000, were removed from the party roster.

A dramatic feature of the Great Purge was the show trials of former Bolshevik leaders. Fifty-four were tried in three public trials: 16 (including Zinoviev, Kame-nev, and Smirnov) in Aug. 1936, 17 (including Radek, and Pyatakov) in Jan. 1937, and 21 (including Buk-harin, Rykov, Krestinsky, and Yagoda) in March 1938. The accused confessed to most of the crimes charged; the charges became more serious with each trial, and embraced conspiracy with Trotsky to overthrow the regime, acts of sabotage, and espionage activity on be-half of Germany and Japan. In June 1937 the mili-tary command was purged. Marshal Tukhachevsky,

Chief of Staff, and seven prominent generals were tried *in camera* and executed.

In the years following the war no general purge was ordered (mass P were abolished by an amendment of the Communist party charter in 1939), although there were wholesale dismissals and transfers of lower party functionaries. The top party leadership remained relatively stable with one notable exception. Upon A. A. Zhdanov's death in 1948 (he was an important party leader and headed the Leningrad party organization) his closest supporters, including A. A. Kuznetsov, N. A. Voznesensky, P. S. Popov, and M. I. Rodionov, were liquidated, presumably by the orders of Malenkov. This has been called the Leningrad Case (q.v.).

A few months before Stalin's death the uncovering of the so-called doctors' plot (q.v.) (later revealed to have been a fabrication) indicated that a new wave of terror was threatened, with Molotov, Mikoyan, Voroshilov, and Beria singled out as its first victims. With the dictator's death (March 1953) the intended purge was halted.

In Dec. 1953 the liquidation of Beria was accompanied by a purge of his supporters from key positions in the party and in the Security Police hierarchy. Characteristic of the postwar period, this did not lead to a violent mass purge but affected only those party officials who were Beria appointees. (*See also* OPPOSITION, SHOW TRIALS, HISTORY OF THE USSR, CPSU, SECURITY POLICE, TROTSKYISM)

BIBLIOGRAPHY: Z. K. Brzezinski, *The Permanent Purge*, Cambridge, 1956; N. Leites and E. Bernaut, *Ritual of Liquidation*, Glencoe, Ill., 1954.
H. W. M.

PURISHKÉVICH, Vladímir Mitrofánovich (1870–1920), monarchist leader, influential in the extreme right wing of the second, third and fourth Dumas. Earlier, P was special aide to the minister of internal affairs, V. K. Plehve. Founder of the Union of the Russian People, later head of the Union of Michael the Archangel, both notoriously anti-Semitic organizations. Together with Grand Duke Dimitry Pavlovich and Prince Yusupov, P participated in the assassination of Rasputin in Dec. 1916. After the February revolution P fought for the restoration of the monarchy. Later fled to the Caucasian region; died in Novorossiysk.

"PUSHERS": *see* INDUSTRIAL MANAGEMENT AND ORGANIZATION.

PÚSHKIN, Aleksándr Sergéyevich (1799–1837), Russia's foremost poet, dramatist, and master of prose fiction. The Pushkins were an old though somewhat impoverished family of Russian gentry. The father (Sergey) and a more talented uncle (Vasily) were minor poets with the then usual French training of the 18th  century: P knew both French and Italian languages from childhood. The house attracted the literary notables of the time, including I. I. Dmitriev (poet), N. M. Karamzin (writer and future historian), and V. A. Zhukovsky, romantic poet and older contemporary of P. P had apparently some African blood: his mother, née Hannibal, was the granddaughter of Abram Hannibal, an Abyssinian page and, later, an engineer officer in the army of Peter the Great.

In 1811 P entered the recently founded *lycée* at Tsarskoye Selo (an aristocratic school), graduated in 1817. Precocious, his lyrics, witty, mischievous, bold or melancholy, began attracting attention of readers and poets alike, while he was still at school. The resounding success of his first important work—*Ruslan and Lyudmila* (1817–20), a long narrative poem with a folk fairy tale background, in the light and graceful vein of Ariosto and Voltaire—confirmed the young poet's fame.

Officially, P was a junior clerk at the Foreign Affairs department in St. Petersburg. Young, healthy, passionate, he plunged into the pleasures (and dissipations) of the capital's gilded youth. There was a serious side: his devotion to literature, his eager study of contemporary romantic poets, French, German and, later, English. Also, P formed friendships with a number of liberal and radical officers of regiments recently returned from campaigns against Napoleon (1812–15). These, dissatisfied with the reactionary policies of the government, began forming secret revolutionary societies. The young poet became their voice: in his poems and epigrams he attacked serfdom (*The Village*), autocracy (*Ode on Liberty*), censorship—satirizing the highest dignitaries and the tsar, Alexander I, himself. Surreptitiously, these poems were spread and avidly read. In 1820 P was arrested and banished to South Russia (Kishinev, later to Odessa). He was now the Russian Byron: a romantic poet, a rebel, an exile. The Byronic influence was strengthened by P's study of English. Byron's influence is obvious in P's narrative poems of 1820–24 (*The Prisoner of the Caucasus, The Fountain of Bakhchisaray, The Gypsies*) as well as in his lyrics. The poet's talent gained in maturity and psychological depth. After *The Gypsies*, P turned to Shakespeare and away from Byronic romanticism to an ever increasing realism. He began his novel in verse *Eugene Onegin* (1823–30) and wrote the historical drama *Boris Godunov* (1824), both to become national models of the realistic novel and historical drama.

In 1824 P was removed from the civil service and banished again, this time from the south to his father's estate in the province of Novgorod: the charge was atheism. Here, under the close supervision of the local police, he languished till 1826, but wrote some of his best-known works. Banishment probably saved his life. In Dec. 1825, his political and personal friends, the Decembrists, staged the first revolutionary armed rebellion in modern R. history. The rebellion was crushed, its leaders were hanged or sent to Siberian prisons or banished.

P expected further persecution. Instead, in 1826, the new tsar, Nicholas I, summoned the poet to Moscow, pardoned his past "offenses" and promised to be his personal censor. P thus returned to civilization and apparent freedom. It is possible that the tsar was quite sincere in expecting the poet to support the government in exchange for imperial kindness. But the stern and exacting autocrat and the freedom-loving and independent poet were too incompatible in temperament for the imperial idyll to last long. P was subjected to petty annoyances, censorship was irritating—P's letters were opened by the authorities—and the poet was driven once more into opposition. Several of his writings of that period came to be known, in part or in full, only years after his death (*Message to the Decembrists, The Monument,* the 10th canto of *Eugene Onegin*). From a literary viewpoint the last ten years of P's life represent the highest development of his genius. He turned increasingly to prose fiction and to deeper psychological realism. In 1831 he wrote the five *Belkin Stories*, simple, lucid tales of ordinary people, of which the moving *The Stationmaster* is considered as the beginning of realism in R. literature. The psychological *Queen of Spades* (1834) foreshadows Dostoyevsky's *Crime and Punishment*.

P's love for and keen sense of history, Russian and European, came to the fore in the period 1826-37. The powerful narrative poem *The Bronze Horseman* (1833) raised the problem of the individual crushed by the all-powerful state established by Peter the Great. No less important is P's last prose novel *The Captain's Daughter* (1836), for this dealt with a dangerous historical subject, the Pugachov Cossack and peasant rebellion during the reign of Catherine II. The picture of R. provincial life of the 1770's, the landlords, peasants, Cossacks, army officers and soldiers, and the Cossack leader Pugachov, are drawn with precision, vividness and humor, at times grim, especially in the scenes of civil war with cruelty on both sides. Behind P's deliberate objectivity, there is an implied lesson in this small novel: the enserfed peasants had their grievances and, unless given freedom, another *jacquerie* was possible.

In the 1830's P turned to the psychological and, again, to the historical drama. The short plays in blank verse, *The Avaricious Knight, Mozart and Salieri, Don Juan,* are gems of psychological dynamism, dramatic verve, and compactness. No less remarkable are the unfinished historical dramas: *The Mermaid* and *Scenes from Knighthood Times*. P's charming folk tales in verse, *Tsar Saltan, The Golden Cockrel* and others, belong to this period.

P was mortally wounded in a duel with a French officer in the R. service, George Heckeren d'Anthès who, by his attentions to the poet's wife, had aroused P's jealousy.

P's letters to friends, fellow-writers, and acquaintances are a treasure of wit, observation and literary criticism and make him a master of the epistolary art.

BIBLIOGRAPHY: Janko Lavrin, *Pushkin and Russian Literature,* London, 1947. I. L. T.

PÚSHKIN, (f. Tsarskoye Selo, then Detskoye Selo), city in Leningrad Oblast, RSFSR; subordinated to the Leningrad Municipal Council; pop. 38,200 (1956). As Tsarskoye Selo (Tsar's Village), for two centuries is was the summer residence of the tsars; world renowned for the sumptuousness and beauty of the imperial palaces and parks, including the Yekaterininsky palace built by Rastrelli.

PUZÁNOV, Aleksándr Mikháylovich (1906–), party and government official, born in Ivanovo Oblast. He became chairman of the village soviet at the age of 18; studied at the Agricultural Technicum, 1926–1930. From 1940 to 1944 he was deputy commissar of state control; 1946–1952, first secretary of the Kuybyshev Oblast party committee; in 1952 named chairman of the RSFSR Council of Ministers; ambassador to the Korean People's Democratic Republic since 1957.

PUZDYUNIN, Valentín Lvóvich (1883–1948), mechanical engineer and expert in ship building. Fellow, Ac. of S., USSR (1939). Graduated from St. Petersburg Polytechnic Institute (1908) and the Naval Engineering School at Kronstadt. Professor (1920) at the Leningrad Ship Building Institute (1930). Director of the Department of Hydraulics at the Institute of Mechanics (1941).

PYANDZH (PANJ) RIVER, flows from E. Hindukush Mountains, Afghanistan, to become left tributary of the Amu Darya; 500 mi. long.

PYÁRNU (f. Pernov), city in Estonian SSR; pop. 38,000 (1959). Ice-free seaport and mud resort near the mouth of the Pyarnu River in Pyarnu Bay (inlet of the Gulf of Riga). Dates back to early 13th century. Is an important shipping point for local products (lumber, wood pulp, flax) and center of fishing ind.; has machine bldg. plants, match and furniture factories, paper mills, flax processing.

PYATAKÓV, Grigóry (Yury) Leonídovich (1890–1937), leading Bolshevik. As a youth, P favored anarchism but in 1910 became a Bolshevik. Was twice sentenced to prison and Siberian exile. He often disagreed with Lenin but was reconciled with him in 1917. Active in the revolution of 1917, he later took part in the civil war in the Ukraine. Subsequently P was one of the leaders of Soviet industry and in 1927 an ambassador to France. He sided with Trotsky in 1927 and was expelled from the party. In 1928 he recanted, returning to his post as director of the Gosbank (State Bank). In 1937 he became a leading defendant in the trial of the so-called "Trotskyite Center" and was sentenced to death. In his "Testament" Lenin praised P as a man of remarkable will and ability.

PYATIGÓRSK, city in Stavropol Kray, RSFSR; pop. 69,000 (1959). Mountain resort on N. slopes of the Caucasus range, long famous for its warm sulfur springs and mud baths. Principal ind. include creameries, distilleries, milk plants, clothing and footwear factories, mfg. and repair shops for agr. implements and machinery. Has several specialized colleges and technical schools. In 1841 the poet M. Lermontov was killed near P.

PÝATNITSKY CHOIR, the State Russian People's Pyatnitsky Choir was founded by Mitrofan Yefimovich Pyatnitsky (1864–1927). A good singer and an imaginative interpreter, he gave recitals of folk songs which were highly successful. He then organized a choir in which prominent folk-song artists took part and which he conducted. The PC made its debut in 1911 and won immediate acclaim; its performances included folk dancing as well as singing.

PYPIN, Aleksándr Nikoláyevich (1833–1904), literary critic and historian. Contributor to the review *Sovremennik* (The Contemporary) and *Vestnik Yevropy* (European Messenger). P is the author of monographs on R. folklore, a biography of V. Belinsky, a 4-volume *History of Russian Literature*, books on the history of literature of other Slavic peoples, and a 4-volume *History of Russian Ethnography*.

R

RABINÓVICH, Isáak Moiséyevich (1894–), painter and stage designer. Since 1911 has worked chiefly for the theater. He designed the productions of Aristophanes' *Lysistrata* (1923), Pushkin's *Eugene Onegin* (1933), and Gutzkov's *Uriel Acosta* (1940). Since 1955, R has been chief stage designer of the Vakhtangov Theater in Moscow, where he staged Dostoyevsky's *The Idiot* and Shakespeare's *Hamlet*, both in 1958.

RABFAKI are educational institutions attached to factories and colleges and offering day or evening classes to working men and women to prepare them for universities and other institutions of higher education. They were established in 1919. In the 1930's, they were gradually absorbed in the general educational system.

RABÓTNOV, Yúry Nikoláyevich (1914–), mechanical engineer. Fellow, Ac. of S., USSR (1958). Graduate of Moscow University (1935). Lecturer at the Moscow Institute of Power Engineering (1935–46). Professor of Moscow University (1947). R's research is devoted to the theory of shells, creep, and plasticity. Author of the textbook *Strength of Materials* (1950).

RACHMÁNINOFF, Sergéy Vasílyevich (1873–1943), pianist, composer, and conductor, son of a captain of 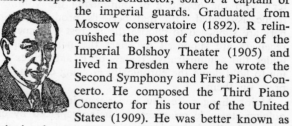 the imperial guards. Graduated from Moscow conservatoire (1892). R relinquished the post of conductor of the Imperial Bolshoy Theater (1905) and lived in Dresden where he wrote the Second Symphony and First Piano Concerto. He composed the Third Piano Concerto for his tour of the United States (1909). He was better known as a pianist than as a composer. R returned to Russia in 1910 and left again in 1917, never to return. He toured the United States each season, but lived in Switzerland and Paris. He wrote two symphonies, four piano concertos, préludes, études, romances, and cantatas. His music is marked by romantic pathos, dynamic strength, and lyrical moods. R died in California.

BIBLIOGRAPHY: S. Bertensson and J. Leyda: *Rachmaninoff*, New York, 1956; V. I. Seroff: *Rachmaninov*, New York, 1950.

RÁDEK (Sobelsohn), **Karl Bernhardovich** (1885–1947), Communist, born in Lvov province under Austrian rule, in a middle-class family. Prior to World War I, R was active in the Polish and German Social Democratic parties. A brilliant political writer renowned for his wit. Lenin, who knew R in 1915, publicly dis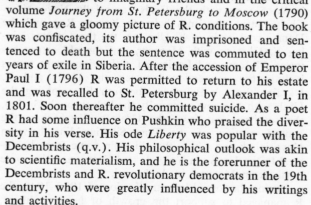agreed with him on the questions of nationalities and of the self-determination of dependent nations. After the February revolution, R came with Lenin to Russia through Germany in the "sealed train." He joined the Bolshevik party and was sent to Sweden in 1917, and to Germany in 1918, where he was arrested for revolutionary activities. After 1921, R settled in Moscow and became secretary of the Communist International. In 1925, he was rector of the Sun Yat-sen Communist University for Chinese and other Oriental students in Moscow. An outstanding member of the Trotskyite opposition, R was known as the author of many political anecdotes. In Dec. 1927, at the 15th Party Congress, R was expelled from the party and banished to the Urals. However, he was soon reinstated, after writing a panegyric about Stalin (*The Architect of Socialist Society*). In the 1930's R was the chief foreign affairs commentator in the leading Soviet papers. In 1937, during the purges, R was tried in the second of the big show trials and sentenced to 10 years' imprisonment. During the war, in 1941, there were rumors (unconfirmed) about his release and employment in anti-German propaganda. He probably died in a prison or in a concentration camp in the 1940's. R is the author of many books, including *The German Revolution* (3 vols.), *Five Years of the Comintern* (2 vols.), R's chief publication in English is *Portraits and Pamphlets* (London, 1935).

RADIO RECEIVERS: see ELECTRONICS.

RADÍSHCHEV, Aleksándr Nikoláyevich (1749–1802), philosopher and poet; born in Moscow. Student  in Germany at the University of Leipzig. R was greatly influenced by the peasant uprising of 1773–75 and the ideas of the Encyclopedists. He was one of the first to advocate the revolutionary transformation of R. society, aimed at the abolition of serfdom and autocracy. He presented his views in "letters" to imaginary friends and in the critical volume *Journey from St. Petersburg to Moscow* (1790) which gave a gloomy picture of R. conditions. The book was confiscated, its author was imprisoned and sentenced to death but the sentence was commuted to ten years of exile in Siberia. After the accession of Emperor Paul I (1796) R was permitted to return to his estate and was recalled to St. Petersburg by Alexander I, in 1801. Soon thereafter he committed suicide. As a poet R had some influence on Pushkin who praised the diversity in his verse. His ode *Liberty* was popular with the Decembrists (q.v.). His philosophical outlook was akin to scientific materialism, and he is the forerunner of the Decembrists and R. revolutionary democrats in the 19th century, who were greatly influenced by his writings and activities.

RAGÓZIN, Vyacheslác Vasílyevich (1908–), chess player. Grand master of chess since 1946; civil engineer by profession.

RAILROADS. Over the last century, R have come to dominate R. and Soviet transportation. Construction of R lines since 1838 has served the needs of national defense, heavy industry, and agriculture. Especially during the late 19th century, railroad building led the rapid movement toward industrialization, while under the Soviet regime R have been made to support industrial growth without sharing its primacy.

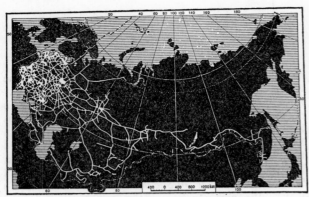

Density of railway network in the USSR

Early rail lines connected Russia's major cities, reached out to the national frontier at various points, and extended into new agricultural hinterlands. Coal and iron ore in the E. Ukraine were joined to initiate a domestic industrial base. Similar lines were laid in the Ural region. Grain-collecting lines were extended first from Baltic Sea ports southeastward into European Russia, and later from Black Sea ports north and east into fertile wheat-growing regions. By the end of 1913, a network totaling 71,475 km. (44,400 mi.) of first main track had been built in the Russian Empire. Two-thirds of the railways were state-owned. All but 3,700 km. (2,300 mi.) had a 5-foot gauge, 3½ inches wider than W. European standard gauge.

Under Soviet auspices, the R system grew from a total of 73,987 km. (45,946 mi.) (for first main track at the end of 1924), to 106,102 km. (65,890 mi.) at the end of 1940 (including the line taken over along the W. frontier), and to 124,400 km. (77,252 mi.) at the end of 1959. The heaviest freight traffic densities are now found on the lines connecting the Kuznetsk basin in W. Siberia with the Urals (especially Novosibirsk-Chelyabinsk), the lines between Krivoy Rog and the Donets coal basin in E. Ukraine, the three routes joining E. Ukraine with Moscow, and the old artery between Moscow and Leningrad. Other important routes include the connection between the Urals and E. Ukraine through Balashov, the four lines joining the Urals with Moscow (especially the link through Gorky), the southern exit from the Urals to Kuybyshev, the central portion of the Trans-Siberian line between Novosibirsk and Chita, the old main route from Leningrad to the Urals via Vologda and Kirov, and the route north from Moscow to Archangel.

During the forced industrialization of 1928–1940, the R managed to support the growth of heavy industry, though large backlogs of unshipped freight hampered growth between 1931 and 1934. Rail freight ton-mi. rose from 58 bill. in 1928 to 260 bill. in 1940. The R were expected to be a weak spot in Soviet defenses during World War II, but they proved capable of handling wartime traffic, and backing up the Soviet drive to Berlin. After the initial retreats of 1941–42, a hastily built rail line, west of the Volga from near Kazan southward over 600 mi. to the Stalingrad region, was instrumental in bringing matériel for the great battle that turned the tide of the war. Since the war,

freight traffic has continued its steady expansion, rising from 196 bill. ton-mi. in 1945 to 814 bill. in 1958.

Soviet R handle 93 per cent of all intercity passenger traffic. The service is offered in "hard" and "soft" classes, at speeds up to 50 mi. per hour (on the Moscow-Leningrad run), with an over-all average in 1958 of 27.3 mi. per hour, excluding stops, and 24.22 mi. per hour including them. Compartments with berths, and dining cars, are available on the principal express trains, though it is the general practice to obtain food at local stops en route. Departures from train schedules are recorded, and apparently lateness is not a serious problem. In addition to the 1958 total of 251 mill. long-distance passengers, carried an average distance of 300.5 mi., the R also carried 1583 mill. suburban passengers, on trips averaging 14.3 mi.

Since 1917 all main-line R have been nationalized under the Ministry (formerly People's Commissariat) of Means of Communication. Other carriers are administered by other Ministries, making this one in fact the Ministry of Railways. Operating responsibilities are delegated to territorial administrations (35 of them in 1960), each supervising all the track in its territory. Motive power and rolling stock are separately assigned to each R administration, though national needs will determine their place of use, and the evidence suggests that the resulting degree of friction is not serious. Shipment plans are drawn up annually (revised each quarter), with the objective of minimizing the volume of traffic associated with that period's production. Shippers are supposed to choose the nearest customer, and receivers are supposed to select the nearest supplier, under the administrative review of R authorities seeking to hold down the chronically growing demands that press on them.

Major changes are now under way in Soviet R technology: steam locomotives are being replaced by electric and diesel-electric motive power, and related changes in line facilities are being put through. In 1958 some 11,000 steam locomotives, 1,000 electric locomotives, and 900 diesel-electric locomotives were in road freight service; by 1965 the intention is to reduce the steam number to around 3,300 while raising the others to 3,100 and 3,500 units. Soviet freight cars have at long last been fully equipped with automatic couplings

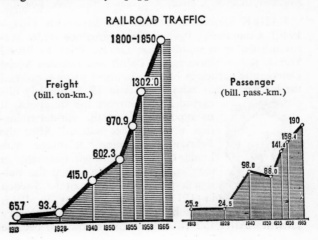

RAILROAD TRAFFIC

and automatic air brakes; some three-quarters of them are now of the large 4-axle variety. In 1955 their capacity was divided by type as follows: 36.1 per cent gondolas, 32.1 per cent boxcars, 17.8 per cent flatcars, 11.3 per cent tank cars, and 2.7 per cent refrigerated cars. At the end of 1958, first main track administered by the Ministry of Railroads totaled 122,800 km. (76,260 mi.); second tracks came to about 32,000 km. (19,872 mi.) and yard tracks to about 57,000 km. (35,400 mi.).

The freight traffic carried by Soviet R reflects the economy's emphasis on heavy industry; consumer goods and highly fabricated products play a very small role, there being in particular a very small volume of less-than-carload-lot shipments. In 1958, coal and coke accounted for 26.8 per cent of total freight ton-mi.; timber, 13.7 per cent; oil and oil products, 11.8 per cent; mineral building materials, 8.8 per cent; iron and steel, 7.0 per cent; grain and flour, 6.2 per cent; ores 4.6 per cent; and a variegated "all others" category, the remaining 21.1 per cent. The average length of haul for total freight traffic was 815 km. (506 mi.).

Soviet R in recent years have been highly profitable, achieving reduced unit costs with increased traffic densities, and accumulating substantial net income in spite of lowered freight tariffs. Both the freight and passenger services cover all operating costs, including an inadequate depreciation charge. Most of the profits are siphoned off into the general state budget for investment wherever the regime sees fit. The R thus generate the income to finance their own expansion, and the expansion of other carriers too, if added transportation capacity is needed, but under present policy this sector of the economy seems to be a net provider of funds to the state.

BIBLIOGRAPHY: Holland Hunter, *Soviet Transportation Policy*, Cambridge, 1957; Ernest W. Williams, Jr., *Freight Transportation in the Soviet Union*, New York, 1959; U.S. Congress, Joint Economic Committee, *Comparisons of the United States and Soviet Economies*, Washington, 1959, Part I, pp. 177–99; James H. Blackman, *Transport Development and Locomotive Technology in the Soviet Union*, Columbia, South Carolina, 1957; George Kish, *Economic Atlas of the Soviet Union*, Ann Arbor, 1960.   H. H.

RAILWAY CAR INDUSTRY: see LOCOMOTIVE AND RAILWAY CAR INDUSTRY.

RAKHMATÚLIN, Khalil Akhmedovich (1909–), mechanical engineer. Fellow, Ac. of S., Uzbek SSR (1947). Graduate (1934) and professor (1944), Moscow University. Associated with the Institute of Mechanical Engineering (1943). Research on gas dynamics, the aerodynamics of a permeable body, and elastic-plastic waves. Modernized precision instruments and machines. Stalin prize (1949).

RAKÓVSKY, Christián Geórgievich (1873–19??), revolutionary and political leader. Of Bulgarian origin, he became a Rumanian citizen after the second Balkan war (1913). Educated in W. Europe, taking a French medical degree, he joined the socialist movement and, under the name of "Insarov," collaborated in Lenin's *Iskra* and, later, Trotsky's *Pravda* in Vienna. Returning to Rumania, R organized and led the Rumanian socialist party. He was arrested in 1916 and because of Rumania's defeat was taken to Russia where he was imprisoned in Bessarabia. Liberated after the February revolution, R joined the Bolshevik party and became a prominent Bolshevik leader. Premier of the Soviet Ukraine during the civil war, R was also active in military operations against Denikin and in the Ukrainian Cheka. In 1919 he became a member of the All-Russian Party's Central Committee and in 1923–24 negotiated with the British Labor government for *de jure* recognition of the Soviet government. He conducted similar negotiations with France and, after French recognition was announced, R was named Soviet ambassador to Paris (1925–27).

In Dec. 1927, the 15th Party Congress expelled R from the party as a Trotskyite. He was banished first to Astrakhan and in 1929 to Barnaul in Kazakhstan. Unlike other Trotskyites, R held firmly to his anti-Stalinist position and wrote several papers to the party authorities explaining his point of view. R retracted only in 1934, upon Hitler's rise to power in Germany, and was readmitted to the party. However, he was arrested during the great purge, arraigned at the third trial (March 1938), found guilty of high treason, and sentenced to 20 years' hard labor.

RAMZÍN, Leoníd Konstantínovich (1887–1948), heat power engineer. Graduate (1914), professor (1920), Moscow School of Technology, and Institute of Power Engineering (1944). Founder and director, All-Union Institute of Heat Power Engineering (1921–30). Simultaneously worked at the Bureau for the Design of Uniflow Boilers. In 1930, R was convicted in the case of the Industrial party (q.v.) but restored in his rights "for research work essential to the national economy." His research concerned boiler modernization; thermal, aerodynamic, and hydrodynamic calculations of boiler installations; the theory of radiation in furnaces; and the study of characteristics and properties of fuel. Stalin prize (1943).

RAPALLO TREATY (April 16, 1922), signed by RSFSR and Germany in Rapallo, Italy, during the Genoa Conference. (Agreement signed in Berlin on Nov. 5, 1922 extended this treaty to the other Soviet republics.) This treaty established friendly diplomatic and economic relations between the two countries. The RT, negotiated secretly during the Genoa Conference by W. Rathenau and G. Chicherin, produced a great surprise among the Western Powers. Articles 1 and 2 of the RT stipulated that both Russia and Germany renounced their claims for compensation of war losses and costs; that Germany renounced any claim for restitution for enterprises nationalized by the Soviet Union, provided similar claims of other states were not satisfied. Articles 3 and 4 dealt with the renewal of diplomatic and consular relations and economic cooperation. The RT was considered a diplomatic success for Russia and led to a close cooperation with the Weimar Republic.

RAPP (Russian Association of Proletarian Writers): *see* LITERATURE.

RASHÍDOV, Sharaf Rashidovich (1917–), party and government official. Born in Uzbekistan, he graduated from a pedagogical technicum in 1936; attended the philological faculty, Uzbek State University, 1937–41; was wounded while in the army in World War II. He was one of the secretaries of the Samarkand Oblast party committee, 1944–47; was elected Presidium chairman, Uzbek Supreme Soviet, and deputy chairman, USSR Supreme Soviet in 1950; became bureau member of the central committee, Uzbek CP in 1951; elected as candidate member of the Central Committee, CPSU in 1956.

RASKÓLNIKOV, Fyódor Fyódorovich (1892–1939). Joined the Bolshevik party in St. Petersburg in 1910. Contributed to *Pravda* and other Bolshevik newspapers. In 1917, was a leader of the Kronstadt Soviet. After the October revolution, R commanded Red troops and in 1918 was appointed deputy people's commissar of the navy. In 1921–22 was envoy to Afghanistan and from 1936 was envoy to Estonia, Denmark, and Bulgaria. In April 1938, R was recalled to Moscow. Aware of the purges taking place, R refused to return and instead fled to Belgium. In July 1939, he wrote an open letter to Stalin in which he accused him of tyranny, disregarding the Soviet Constitution, and degrading socialism. In September of the same year, R died under very suspicious circumstances in Southern France.

RASPUTIN, Grigóry Yefímovich (1872–1916), born in Tobolsk, a Siberian peasant who acquired great political influence from 1905 to 1916. R was a *starets*, that is, an unordained religious teacher, roving from  place to place and living by his wits. R's somewhat inchoate doctrine revolved around the need to sin in order to achieve humility and hence eternal salvation. Sin was primarily a synonym for sexual license, and R's powerful physique, forceful character, and oracular speech gained him a following among neurotic St. Petersburg society women in quest of excitement. He was also sponsored by a number of highly placed churchmen.

R gained access to the imperial family in 1905 because of the tsarina's distress over the hemophilia of Alexis, the infant heir apparent. In addition to having allegedly been trained by a professional medium, R seems to have had healing powers; credible witnesses agree that he stopped Alexis' bleeding several times. His mysterious success seemed miraculous to the tsarina. Moreover, R was the living embodiment of the tsarina's conception of the mystic union of the Crown and the People.

R acquired immense power over the tsarina, the tsar, and the government, especially after the tsar's departure for army headquarters in 1915. He used his influence on behalf of venal ecclesiastics, bureaucrats, financiers, and adventurers. The situation grew more and more scandalous until R was assassinated, in Dec. 1916, by V. M. Purishkevich, an ultraconservative Duma deputy, Grand Duke Dmitry Pavlovich, a nephew of the tsar, and Prince Felix Yusupov, a relative by marriage of the imperial family.

RASTRÉLLI, Bartolomeo (1700–1771), famous Italian architect who worked in Russia. R was an exponent of the baroque style. His most important works are the palaces of Peterhof (now Petrodvorets) and Tsarskoye Selo 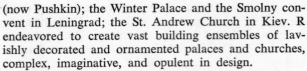 (now Pushkin); the Winter Palace and the Smolny convent in Leningrad; the St. Andrew Church in Kiev. R endeavored to create vast building ensembles of lavishly decorated and ornamented palaces and churches, complex, imaginative, and opulent in design.

RAYÉVSKY, Nikoláy Nikoláyevich (1771–1829), general. Served with distinction in military campaigns against Turkey, Poland, Persia, France (1805–07) and Sweden (1808–09). During Napoleon's invasion of Russia in 1812 R won fame as the defender of Smolensk against superior enemy forces. He distinguished himself in the battle of Borodino and in the European campaigns of 1813 and 1814.

RAYON: *see* ADMINISTRATIVE AND TERRITORIAL DIVISIONS.

RAZDÁN (ZANGA) RIVER, flows through Armenian SSR, left tributary of Araks; 90 mi. long. Many power stations (Kanaker, Sevan, Gyumush, Yerevan). Armenian capital Yerevan is on it.

RÁZIN, Stepán Timoféyevich (died in 1671), Cossack, native of the Don region, leader of a major  peasant rebellion against serfdom and oppression (1667–71). The insurgents, joined by runaway serfs and recalcitrant tribesmen along the Volga, captured Tsaritsyn, Astrakhan, and Saratov, and were approaching Simbirsk, but were finally routed by the government troops. Razin was executed in Moscow on June 6, 1671.

RAZNOCHINTSY. A term used to refer to intellectuals of lower- and middle-class origin in the middle and second half of the 19th century. The word literally means "persons of various classes." Their appearance may be attributed to the establishment of universities open to all classes in Russia, and to the subsequent influence of western and especially of German philosophy. Already by 1840 the intellectuals in Russia had formed themselves into two camps: the Slavophiles, on the one hand, who opposed the abandonment of certain fundamental national and religious traditions, and the Westerners, who were influenced above all by their faith in rational progress along European lines. The most prominent R were Westerners who were revolutionary rather than gradualist in their basic disposition, and who were passionately concerned with the task of bringing about the liberation of the serfs and with the establishment of a democratic political order. Although their early leaders, the literary critics V. Belinsky, (1811–48), N. Chernyshevsky (1828–89), N. Dobrolyubov (1836–61), and D. Pisarev (1840–68), adhered to the principles of social utilitarianism, a greater emphasis on nonfunctional aspects of social ethics came to prevail during the 1870's in connection with the emergence of populism. The writers of *raznochintsy* origin include N. Pomyalovski, I. Nikitin, N. Uspensky, and F. Reshetnikov. The R played an important role in the development of Russian culture in the 19th century.

RAZUMÓVSKY, Alekséy Grigórievich (1709–1771), favorite of Empress Elizabeth Petrovna. He was an active participant in the palace revolution which put her on the throne in 1741. The son of a Ukrainian Cossack, he supported the restoration of hetmanship, and later succeeded in getting his brother, Kirill Grigorievich, appointed hetman (the last) of the Ukraine.

REBINDER, Pyótr Aleksándrovich (1898–), physical chemist. Fellow, Ac. of S., USSR (1946). Graduate of Moscow University (1924); professor, Liebknecht Pedagogical Institute (1929) and Moscow University (1942). Head of the Section of Dispersed Systems, Institute of Physical Chemistry, (1934). Extensive research in physical and colloidal chemistry, and molecular physics including the study of surface adsorption layers at the solid-liquid interface and their effect on dispersed and colloidal systems. R contributed to the development of the theory of mineral flotation and such industrial processes as well-drilling, metal machining, plastic metalworking. Stalin prize (1942).

RED CROSS, mass public organization affiliated since 1934 with the International League of Red Cross Societies. Aids sick and wounded in time of war and disaster and performs other social services. Soviet organizations were united in 1925 in the "Union of Societies of Red Cross and Red Crescent." Chairman of the Executive Committee is professor G. A. Miterev who is at the same time vice-president of the International League of Red Cross Societies. As of Jan. 1, 1960 the Soviet Red Cross had 359,000 locals with over 32,000,000 members.

THE RED INTERNATIONAL OF LABOR UNIONS (RILU), also known as the *Profintern,* was formed in Moscow in July 1921, primarily to implement point 10 of a 21-point program adopted by the 2nd Congress of the Comintern in 1920. Point 10 called upon all parties of the Comintern to carry on a stubborn struggle against the International Federation of Trade Unions (IFTU), formed in 1919, which had a membership of 23 mill. organized workers in 22 countries and was the successor to the pre-war international trade-union organization with headquarters in Amsterdam.

The principal tactic pursued by the RILU between 1921 and 1928 was a "United Front" policy which called for Communists not to break up existing trade unions but to bore from within, capture the trade-union leadership and then affiliate with the RILU. In 1928 the "United Front" policy was dropped by the Comintern and its subsidiary the RILU. Communists were now urged to form competing unions under their own leadership. The Communist tactic of attacking the IFTU and of attempting to break up existing trade unions was not successful. When the Comintern announced a "Popular Front" policy at its 7th Congress in Aug. 1935 urging united action with socialist and liberal parties and non-Communist labor unions against the menace of Fascism the RILU, which had greatly exacerbated international labor relations, was allowed to lapse, which it did in late 1937 and early 1938.

During its tenure the RILU received its financial support from the Soviet Union with its headquarters in Moscow, and a Russian Communist, Arnold Lozovsky, was the general secretary. The bulk of the RILU membership came from the Soviet Union. In 1929 out of a total membership claim of 17 mill. over 10 mill. were

Soviet members. China listed over 2 mill., France over 500,000, Czechoslovakia 200,000, and Norway, Finland and other countries somewhat lesser numbers. By 1935 the international membership shrank to a mere ½ mill.; the remainder (19½ mill.) were Soviet trade unionists.   H. W. M.

RED TERROR: *see* HISTORY, SECURITY POLICE.

REDEMPTION PAYMENTS are payments through which the former serfs eventually were to become owners of their allotment in accordance with the emancipation statutes of Feb. 19, 1861. According to this legislation the government advanced to the landowners interest-bearing securities to the amount of 75 to 80 per cent of the total indemnification to which they were entitled. Governmental advances to the landowners were to be repaid by the peasants in annual installments extending over 49 years and equal in amount to the share of the advance assessed on each allotment, plus interest.

The charges were far too high and the redemption operation proved impracticable. Because of the impoverishment of the peasantry and revolutionary disturbances the government abandoned this scheme and by a manifesto of Nov. 3, 1905 all redemption payments were cancelled.

REFORMÁTSKY, Sergéy Nikoláyevich (1860–1934), chemist. Corresponding member, Ac. of S., USSR (1928). Graduate of Kazan University (1882); professor, Kiev University (1891). Research on organometallic synthesis. Development of a synthesis method for beta oxyacids known as the "Reformatsky reaction."

REGIONAL ECONOMIC COUNCIL: *see* INDUSTRIAL MANAGEMENT AND ORGANIZATION.

REICHSTADT AGREEMENT, secret agreement between Russia and Austria-Hungary, concluded on June 26 (July 8 N.S.), 1876, in Reichstadt (Bohemia), where emperors Franz Josef and Alexander II, accompanied by their ministers of foreign affairs Andrassy and A. M. Gorchakov, met in an attempt to reach a compromise in the conflicting interests of the two Powers in the Balkans. While Russia guaranteed noninterference in the Serbian-Turkish war, which had started a few weeks earlier, consented to the annexation by Austria-Hungary of Bosnia and (according to Andrassy) Herzegovina, and gave assurances that no move would be made toward the creation of a strong Slav state in the Balkans, Austria-Hungary agreed to return the S.W. part of Bessarabia, lost by Russia under the Treaty of Paris of 1856, and consented to the annexation of Batum to Russia.

REINDEER BREEDING. Spread over an area of some 3.9 mill. sq. mi., RB represents the main branch of agriculture in the Far North, where 1.8 mill. reindeer were bred in 1938; it is also important in the Altay, Sayan, and Far E. regions. R are bred for meat, fur, and milk and serve as a means of transport in the tayga. Thirty state farms specializing in RB were in operation in 1952 and accounted for 20% of all animals; collective farms accounted for 64%. A typical herd numbered 1,200 to 1,500 head in the tundra regions, and some 250 to 600 head in the tayga.

RELIEF. The surface of the USSR is characterized by a great variety of land forms. Vast plains and lowlands occupy the W. part of the country; uplands and plateaus predominate in the S.E. The belt of high mountain ranges stretches almost continuously along the S. and E. boundaries of the country. The highest point in the USSR, Stalin Peak (24,584 ft.), lies in the Pamir; the lowest, on the Mangyshlak Peninsula, is 433 ft. below sea level.

EUROPEAN USSR AND THE CAUCASUS

European Russia occupies the E. half of Europe including several groups of islands in the Arctic. Franz Josef Land, an archipelago of some 800 islands, has elevations up to 2,400 ft. The R of Kolguyev and Vaygach islands is generally level, up to 545 ft. in elevation.

The Kola-Karelian region occupies the extreme N.W. part of European Russia. The highest elevations are found in the central sections of the Kola Peninsula, where the plateau-like Khibin massifs and the Lovozero tundra rise to 3,300–4,000 ft. The massifs are often divided by deep depressions which are covered with large lakes, such as Imandra, Umbozero, and others. The R of the Karelian ASSR shows predominantly a hilly lowland with elevations generally lower than 650 ft., but elevations of some 2,000 ft. are found in the W. and N.W. parts (the Manselkya ridge).

The E. European plain occupies the largest part of the E. European territory. In the S., it is bordered by the Carpathians, the Crimean mountains, the Caucasus, and the Black and Caspian seas; to the E. are the Ural River and the Urals; and in the N. the plain is washed by the Barents and White seas. The average elevation of the plain is around 560 ft.; but some highlands rise to 1,300 ft. and more. The N.W. part of the plain is characterized by land forms of glacial accumulation. There are several long and relatively narrow ridges presenting terminal or recessional moraines, with elevations sometimes exceeding 1,000 ft. Swampy depressions and lakes occur in areas between hills. The N.E. part of the plain is also covered by moraine deposits, but the R is much smoother, flat plains prevailing in the N. coastal areas. The Timan ridge (highest point, 1,520 ft.) dominates above the plain which rises somewhat toward the S. and is limited by the belt of Severnye Uvaly up to 964 ft. in elevation. In the S., the Dnieper upland occupies the watershed between the Dnieper and the Southern Bug, the elevation being from 400 to 1,060 ft. The Volynian-Podolian upland lies on the watershed between the Dniester and the Dnieper. It has features of a plateau rising to the W. (maximum elevation of 1,550 ft. is in the Lvov area) and gradually sinks to the E. The surface is extensively dissected by deeply incised valleys and ravines. Toward the E. this upland passes into the Azov upland (1,050 ft.) lying at the left bank of the Dnieper River, to the N. from the Sea of Azov. The wide Dnieper lowland (165–425 ft.) separates the Volynian-Podolian upland from the Central R. upland which stretches in an almost meridional direction between the Dnieper and the Don. It is characterized by an erosive R with numerous young, intensively increasing gulleys. Its average elevation is 750–820 ft.—the highest points (within the Tula Oblast) reaching 950 ft. Further S. lies the Donets ridge

presenting a slightly undulating upland with gentle slopes and young valleys. Although its average elevation is 800–1,000 ft., the highest point is 1,200 ft. The wide Oka-Don lowland (525–600 ft.) lies between the E. slopes of the Central R. upland in the W. and the Volga upland (1,050–1,150 ft.) in the E. The latter stretches almost meridionally along the right bank of the Volga from Gorky to Stalingrad. At the point where the Volga turns sharply to the S.E., the Volga upland merges into the Yergeni heights (500–650 ft.). A meridional lowland, called the Low Trans-Volga, borders the Volga upland in the E. In the S.E. part of the E. European plain, beyond the Volga, three flat uplands are found: the Upper-Kama, Bugulma-Belebey, and Obshchy Syrt, with elevations from 800 to 1,000 ft. The Black Sea lowland as a rather narrow strip stretches along the N. coast of the Black Sea and the Sea of Azov, including also the flat part of the Crimea. The elevations seldom exceed 300 ft. The Caspian lowland occupies the extreme S.E. of the E. European plain along the N. and partially W. coast, of the Caspian Sea. Its surface is flat, with elevations not exceeding 150 ft., and a considerable part of it lying below sea level.

The Urals are an old range stretching in a general meridional direction from the Arctic Ocean to the Kazakh steppes, along the E. edge of the E. European plain, and form the natural frontier between Europe and Asia. The length of the Urals exceeds 1,250 mi., the width is 35 to 95 mi. The system is formed of a number of parallel ranges, massifs, and ridges. The highest point is Narodnaya Mountain (6,212 ft.).

Southern mountain systems. S. of the E. European plain lie folded mountains—the E. Carpathians, the Crimean mountains, and the Caucasus. The section of the Carpathians lying within the USSR territory is called the Ukrainian Carpathians. They are some 150 mi. long and 60–75 mi. wide, forming several rather low parallel ridges which stretch from S.E. to N.W. The elevations of individual massifs are between 1,640 and 6,500 ft., while the highest Hoverla Mountain rises to 6,760 ft. The Crimean mountains occupy a rather narrow strip in the S. of the Crimean peninsula. They are about 100 mi. long, 25–30 mi. wide, and consist of three parallel ranges. The southern or coastal range is the highest, with elevations reaching 4,000–5,000 ft.; the other two are considerably lower (2,000–2,600 ft.). The Caucasus is a vast mountain country occupying a con-

USSR HIGHEST AND LOWEST POINTS

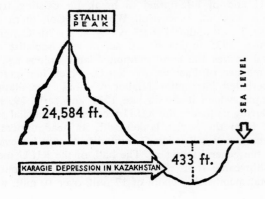

siderable part of the area between the Black and Caspian seas. In the central part of the plains forming the N. Caucasus foreland the Stavropol plateau rises (average elevations 1,200–2,000 ft., the highest point 2,730 ft.) which separates the Kuban-Azov lowland in the W. and the Terek-Kuma lowland in the E. The latter's section adjacent to the Caspian Sea is below ocean level. The Great Caucasus is a complicated system of folded chains stretching from N.N.W. to S.S.E. from Anapa on the Black Sea to the Caspian Sea coasts. Its length is 950 mi., the maximum width in the region of Mount Elbrus is 110 mi. The highest elevations occur between the extinct volcanoes Elbrus (18,476 ft.) and Kazbek (16,554 ft.), where the crest of the Water Divide Range rises to 11,500–13,000 ft. The Transcaucasus plains are separated by a rather low Suram range and form the Colchian or Rioni lowland and the Kura-Araks lowland. Ranges of the Little Caucasus rise in the S. above these lowlands and have elevations exceeding 8,200 ft., the highest point being 12,200 ft. These ranges form the external N. zone of the Transcaucasus mountain country whose central part lies at elevations of 5,000 to 6,500 ft. The Aragats Mountain (13,430 ft.) is the highest peak in the Transcaucasus.

ASIATIC USSR

Central Asia occupies the S.W. corner of the territory of Asiatic Russia. In the W. its border runs along the Ural River and the E. coast of the Caspian Sea; in the N., along the N. foothills of the Turgay tableland and of the Central Kazakhstan low hills region; in the S. and E., along the boundary between the USSR and Iran, Afghanistan, and the Chinese People's Republic.

THE TURANIAN LOWLAND stretches from the Caspian depression in the W. to piedmont plains in the S. and E., being almost entirely in the desert and semidesert zones. Barchans, ridged sands, *takyrs* (flat clayey spaces), and solonchaks are common. Elevations do not exceed 650 ft.; only the altitudes of some marginal sections and separate monadnocks attain 1,000 ft. In the N. there prevail slightly dissected high plateaus: (1) the Turgay tableland (1,000–1,300 ft.); (2) the Ust-Urt plateau lying between the Caspian and Aral seas and reaching an elevation of 1,214 ft.; (3) Trans-Unguz Kara-Kums (325–725 ft.) which are separated from the Ust-Urt by the Sarykamysh basin and the dry channel of the Uzboy River, with the major part of the surface occupied by sand massifs; (4) the W. part of the Bet-Pak-Dala plateau (Golodnaya steppe) built of tertiary clays and sandstones, with an average elevation of 1,000–1,200 ft. A considerable part of the Turanian lowland is covered with vast sandy deserts of which the Kara-Kum and Kyzyl-Kum are the largest.

THE UPLAND OF CENTRAL KAZAKHSTAN occupies the vast territory extending from the W. Siberian lowland to Lake Balkhash in the S., and from the Turgay tableland in the W. approximately to the Turksib railroad in the E. The average altitude is 1,000–2,000 ft. Characteristic of this region are scattered rocky hills and ridges, whose relative heights mostly do not exceed 160–200 ft. Numerous isolated massifs are also found with elevations up to 4,250 ft.

MOUNTAINS OF CENTRAL ASIA are a part of the vast mountain belt of Asia. Several mountain systems may be distinguished. The Caspian system includes the relatively low desert Mangyshlak Mountains (the highest point 1,820 ft.), the Krasnovodsk plateau, and the isolated Great Balkhan massif (6,166 ft). The Kopet Dagh and Pamir mountains constitute a complicated system of young folded uplands, the W. link of which, the Kopet Dagh, is built of parallel ranges with flat summits. The highest peak within the boundaries of the USSR is the Reza Mountain (9,650 ft.). The Pamir, the highest upland in the USSR, lies in the extreme S.E. of Central Asia. It is divided into a W. part which constitutes a strongly dissected mountain country, and an E. part in which high plains predominate. Elevations of all the ranges of W. Pamir exceed 16,500–20,000 ft. Stalin Peak, the highest point in the USSR, 24,584 ft., is in the Academy of Sciences Range, whose elevations almost everywhere exceed 20,000 ft. While the absolute elevations of the massifs in the E. Pamir reach 18,000–20,000 ft. in places, the elevations above depressions separating these massifs usually do not exceed 3,300–5,000 ft. The Alay mountain system includes ranges lying between the Pamir in the S. and the Fergana lowland in the N. In the E. there lies the high Alay range (elevations up to 19,500 ft.), whose branches in the W. are the Turkestan, Zeravshan, and Hissar ranges. The Tien Shan occupies a considerable part of the mountainous belt of Central Asia and constitutes a complicated system of high ranges which diverge westward from a comparatively narrow section in the E. The highest peaks are concentrated in the E. of the Soviet Tien Shan (Pobeda Peak, 24,400 ft.; Khan-Tengri Peak, 22,950 ft.). From here, the highest ranges of the region diverge to the W. and S.W., with elevations of ridges exceeding 13,000–16,000 ft. N. from the intermontane valley of the Ili River, there lie mountains of the Dzungarian Alatau and the Tarbagatay which are divided by the intermontane Balkhash-Alakol depression (1,100–1,650 ft.). Two main ranges of the Dzungarian Alatau stretch in an almost latitudinal direction. In the E. the ridges lie at elevations of 11,500–15,000 ft.; to the W. the ranges become lower.

Siberia occupies the greatest part of N. Asia between the Urals in the W. and the E. mountain ranges which form the divide between the basins draining into the Arctic Ocean and into the Pacific. In the N. its shores are washed by the Arctic Ocean and in the S. it borders on the dry steppe of Kazakhstan and on the frontiers of the Mongolian People's Republic.

WESTERN SIBERIAN LOWLAND occupies the area from the shores of the Arctic Ocean to the Kazakhstan steppe and Altay, and from the Urals to the Yenisey. Its meridional length is almost 1,550 mi.; its width between 600 mi. in the N. and 1,250 mi. in the S. All of this area presents an extremely level plain with very small differences in elevation. The lowest altitudes of 300–450 ft. lie in the N. and in the central part of the lowland. Flat and very wide watersheds predominate over other land forms of the W. Siberian lowland. Swamps are usual on their surface. Morainal hills occur in the N.

CENTRAL SIBERIA is a vast area bounded by the valley of the Yenisey River in the W., by the E. Sayan, Baykal, and N. Trans-Baykal mountains in the S., and by the foothills of the Verkhoyansk range in the E. It includes the archipelago Severnaya Zemlya (N. Land) which consists of four rather large islands. The N. part of the Taymyr Peninsula is occupied by the Byrranga Mountains (the highest elevation some 3,600 ft.) which are built of 2–3 parallel ranges with flat summits. Between the Byrranga Mountains and the Central Siberian plateau lies the N. Siberian lowland whose surface presents a rolling plain with a rather dissected relief. The Central Siberian plateau occupies the greater portion of Central Siberia and is bounded by the Yenisey and the Lena rivers, the N. Siberian lowland, and the foothills of the S. mountains of Siberia. Different resistance of rocks to weathering results in terraces on the slopes and in rapids in the river valleys. The average elevation of the plateau is 1,650–2,300 ft. The highest elevations (5,000–5,600 ft.) are found in the Putorana Mountains lying in the N.W. section. While summits of the Yenisey ridge, located in the S.W., have average elevations of 2,600–2,950 ft., the highest point is 3,620 ft. A considerable part of the territory of the Central Siberian plateau lying within the basins of the Low Tunguska, the Angara, and the upper reaches of the Vilyuy River is characterized by a more smooth and gentle relief. The Central Yakutian (Lena-Vilyuy) lowland (250–650 ft.) occupies a tectonic depression in the valley of the middle Lena River and in the lower reaches of its two affluents, the Vilyuy and the Aldan. Within this lowland, the flat watersheds alternate with river valleys which have widths of 12–18 mi. The Aldan plateau lies in the S.E. section of Central Siberia. In the N. gentle flat-topped plateaus prevail with average elevations of 1,600–2,600 ft.; to the S. the elevations gradually increase and attain 5,000–6,500 ft.

Mountains of Southern Siberia form a high barrier separating plains and plateaus of Siberia from plateaus of Central Asia. The Altay, which forms the westernmost link of these mountains, is composed of several ranges, the highest of which have elevations of 11,500–13,000 ft.; the highest peak, Belukha, rising to 14,780 ft. The Salair-Kuznetsk mountainous region adjoins the Altay in the N. and N.E. and is constituted by the Salair range which is rather low and not well defined and by the Kuznetsk Alatau which is rather a group of mountains. The average elevation of the Salair is 1,300–1,650 ft. The Kuznetsk Alatau is much higher; some peaks in its S. portion rise to 5,250–6,500 ft., the highest point being 7,144 ft. Between the Salair range and the Kuznetsk Alatau there lies the Kuznetsk basin (q.v.). E. of the Altay and the Kuznetsk Alatau, along the S. edge of Siberia, stretch the Sayan and the Tuva mountains. The rocky summits of the main range in the W. part of the Sayans reach more than 8,200–9,500 ft. The E. Sayan system begins on the left bank of the Yenisey above Krasnoyarsk and extends S.E. from there almost to the Baykal; its highest peaks have elevations of 9,585 ft. and 11,450 ft. In the N.E. of the Tuva Autonomous Oblast there lies at the elevation of 2,800–6,500 ft. the intermontane Todzha depression; to the S. is the E.-Tuva upland, the central section of which is occupied by the Academician Obruchev range.

The vast intermontane Tuva depression (2,000–3,000 ft.) lies in the central and W. sections of Tuva. The mountains of the S. Tuva form a huge arc, with the middle part convex to the N., and consist of the W. and E. Tannu-Ola ranges, some peaks of which reach 10,000 ft. The Sangilen plateau is the southernmost portion of the mountains of the S. Tuva and has elevations up to 10,750 ft. In the area of Lake Baykal the mountainous belt of S. Siberia becomes much wider; the mountain ranges of the Baykal region and of Transbaykalia extend over all the area of S.E. Siberia between the Lena River in the N. and the boundary with the Mongolian People's Republic in the S. Predominant are the mountains of middle elevations (5,000–6,500 ft.), in no place reaching the snow line. There are also extensive areas of high plateaus (the Vitim plateau and others) and of intermontane depressions; the latter present slightly dissected plains of steppe or swamp character. The ranges of Transbaykalia mostly lie parallel to each other and have a generally E.N.E.-W.S.W. orientation; they are separated by tectonic depressions having the same orientation. One of them, Lake Baykal, is the deepest lake in the world, its greatest depth 5,700 ft.

Mountains of N.E. Siberia lie between the Lena River in the W. and the Kolyma range in the E. The Verkhoyansk range (elevations 8,200–9,200 ft.) in the W. and S. and the Kolyma or Gydan range in the E. form a huge arc embracing mountain chains and high plateaus. The Chersky range, lying parallel to the Verkhoyansk range, is the highest in N.E. Siberia. Here lies the Pobeda Mountain (10,322 ft.), the highest peak of the region. A large part of the area of N.E. Siberia is occupied by plateaus, with rolling plains with individual dome-shaped peaks. The mountainous country borders on the coastal area of the Arctic Ocean. Between the Buorkhaya Bay and the mouth of the Kolyma River this coastal area and the neighboring Novosibirsk Islands present vast lowlands built of soft deposits often with layers and lenses of ice.

The Far East (within the USSR) occupies the E. part of the N. Asia from the coast of the Chukchi sea in the N. to the southernmost maritime region and faces the seas of the Pacific Ocean—the Bering, the Okhotsk, and the Sea of Japan. The Far East embraces also the Commander Islands, the Shantar Islands, the Kuril Islands, and the island of Sakhalin. It is predominantly mountainous, with rather small areas occupied by plains. The easternmost sections, the Kamchatka Peninsula and the Kuril Islands, are still subjected to orogenic processes manifested by volcanis eruptions and earthquakes.

The N. (Chukchi-Okhotsk) region is mountainous with ranges having different orientations. The Chukchi (Anadyr) range is located on the watershed divide between the rivers flowing into the Arctic and the Anadyr basin. In its center the range reaches elevations of some 5,900 ft., but in the marginal massifs the altitudes of the crest do not exceed 3,300–4,000 ft. In the S.W. the S. slope of the Anadyr range borders on the Anadyr plateau (2,300–3,000 ft.) which gradually drops eastward to the vast Anadyr lowland whose elevations do not exceed 650 ft. In the S.W. this lowland merges with the smaller Penzhina lowland. Above the Anadyr-

Penzhina depression there rises in the S. a complicated system of the Koryak range, whose elevations are 5,000 to 6,500 ft. The mountains of the N. coast of the Okhotsk Sea drop steeply to the sea, the average elevation being 1,600–5,000 ft., but the highest reaching 9,200 ft.

In the AMUR AND MARITIME REGIONS the ranges of different orientation (from meridional to latitudinal) interchange with areas of high plains and with vast lowlands. In the N.E. section of the maritime region there stretch in an almost latitudinal direction the S. chain of the Stanovoy range (up to 7,900 ft.) and the system of the Yankan-Tukuringra-Dzhagdy ranges (elevations 5,000–5,300 to 6,040 ft.). S. of these mountains lies the vast Zeya-Bureya lowland adjoining the Amur River. Above the E. margin of this lowland rises the Khingan-Bureya mountain system. The Bureya range begins near the Amur River valley as a system of low heights (650–1,650 ft.), then rises in a N.N.E. direction with elevations over 6,500 ft. in its N. part. Still higher altitudes (8,640 ft.) are found on the Badzhal range which is the spur of the Bureya range. To the N., the latter merges into the meridional massifs of high ranges, the Dusse-Alin and the Yam-Alin (5,250–6,550 ft.; the highest point the Gorod Makit Mountain, 7,530 ft.). A great tectonic depression occupies the vast area of the maritime region. It is bordered by the E. spurs of the Bureya range and the W. slopes of the Sikhote-Alin mountain system. The Khanka and the Lower Amur lowlands lie within this depression and are drained by the Amur River and by its right tributary, the Ussuri. These lowlands are very flat, their surface altitudes being mostly lower than 325 ft. There are many swampy areas. The Sikhote-Alin is an intensively dissected mountainous country whose slopes drop steeply to the E., toward the Sea of Japan and the Tatar Sound. The average elevation is some 2,600–3,300 ft.; the highest peaks are the Tardoki-Yani Mountain (6,815 ft.) and a nameless massif in the upper reaches of the Bikin River (6,573 ft.).

KAMCHATKA is the largest peninsula in the Far East, the R mostly mountainous. It consists essentially of two parallel ranges, with the central Kamchatka intermontane depression between, having a width up to 37 mi., and elevations generally not exceeding 650 ft.. The W. or inner range extends throughout the entire length of Kamchatka. The average elevations of the ridge are 3,300 to 5,250 ft.; but the highest point of the range, the extinct volcano, Ichinskaya Sopka, reaches 11,875 ft. The parallel E. range has average elevations 5,000–6,500 ft. Between the E. range and the Bering Sea, on a hilly plain (2,300–4,300 ft.) there is located the most spectacular volcanic region of Kamchatka. Numerous cones of extinct and active volcanoes rise above the plain. At present some 180 volcanoes are known in Kamchatka, 23 of them active, one of which Klyuchevskaya Sopka (15,580 ft.), is the highest point on the peninsula.

THE KURIL ISLANDS form a chain of more than thirty islands between the S. tip of Kamchatka and the islands of Japan. The R is almost always of mountainous character, while the average elevation of the islands forming the Large Kuril Ridge is 1,650–3,300 ft., the highest point, the Alaid Volcano on the Atlasov (Alaid) Island, reaches 7,672 ft. More than 100 volcanoes are known on the Kuril Islands, 38 of them active.

THE ISLAND OF SAKHALIN is over 560 mi. long, with an average width of some 60 mi. Mountain ranges lie along each coast. The average elevations of the W. Sakhalin mountains are 1,300–3,600 ft., although the highest peak, the Zhuravlyov Mountain, is 4,342 ft. high. The E. Sakhalin mountians are higher, the Lopatin Mountain (5,275 ft.) being the highest point. The swampy Tym-Poronay lowland lies between the E. and W. Sakhalin mountains. The N. tip of Sakhalin, which is called Schmidt Peninsula, is formed by small mountain massifs of which the Vtoroy Brat Mountain is 1,975 ft. high.   L. D.

RÉMIZOV, Alekséy Mikháylovich (1877–1958), novelist and essayist. Took a degree in natural science at Moscow University. Traveled widely in Russia, visiting monasteries and observing the way of life of Old-Believers. Emigrated after the revolution. Died in France. Revolution and religion are the central themes of R's work. The dying-out of religious principles and the unleashing of animal instincts in the people alarmed him. For R the Russian revolution was a savage debauch, the work of a satanic, evil force. He developed these ideas both in his novels and in articles. They are to be found in his early novel, *The Pond* (1905–06), in the pamphlet *Of Man, Stars and Swine* (1919) and in *The Lay on the Destruction of the Russian Land* (1918), as well as in *Russia Afire* (1921) and *Whirlwind Over Russia* (1926–27). In the last period of his life, R worked on autobiographical novels. R. influenced the Soviet authors Yevgeny Zamyatin, Boris Pilnyak, Artyom Vesyoly, and Vsevolod Ivanov.

REMOTE CONTROL: *see* AUTOMATION.

RÉNNENKAMPF, Pável Kárlovich (1854–1918), tsarist general. He played an important part in crushing the popular uprising of 1905–07. It is generally conceded that he was largely responsible for the defeat of the R. troops in E. Prussia during the early stage of World War I.

RÉPIN, Ilyá Yefímovich (1844–1930), noted painter of the naturalistic school. Born in Chuguyevo, province of Kharkov. Studied at the Bunakov art school. Moved to St. Petersburg and enrolled at the Academy of Fine Arts, 1863. Became close friend of Kramskoy and Stasov, under whose influence he adopted the ideas  and technique of the school of ideological naturalism. In 1872 he wrote in a letter: "Now the peasant is judge—and we must comply with his interests." The better-known work of this period is *The Volga Burlaki*. Lived abroad on a stipend 1873–76. Upon his return painted portraits of peasants. Joined the Society of Circulating Exhibitions (*Peredvizhniki*). Works of this period are: *At the District Center, On the Way Home, Hero of the Last War, Seeing Off Recruits, Religious Procession in Kursk Province* (1877–83), all at the Tretyakov Gallery. Advocated political tendencies in art, 1880 (*Under Escort*, 1876, *Arrest of a Revolutionary*, 1870–92; *Confes-*

sion Refused, 1879–85, at the Tretyakov Gallery). The best work of this period is *Unexpected* (1884, Tretyakov Gallery). Also painted portraits of the outstanding men of his time, and historical pictures: *Ivan the Terrible Kills His Son Ivan* (1885); *Zaporozhye Cossacks* (1890–91). In the 1890's he was attracted for a time to the *Mir Iskusstva* (World of Art) group. Between 1890 and 1900 painted portraits as well as the large canvas *Session of the State Council* (1901, Russian Museum). Paid tribute to impressionism in his pictures *Dumb Joseph* (1903, Russian Museum); and *Self-Immolation of Gogol* (1909, Tretyakov Gallery). From 1909 until his death R lived in Kuokkala, a Finnish resort near the Russian border.

REPUBLICS, AUTONOMOUS: *see* Administrative and Territorial Divisions.

REPUBLICS, CONSTITUENT: *see* Administrative and Territorial Divisions.

REPUBLICS, UNION: *see* Administrative and Territorial Divisions.

RESHÉTNIKOV, Fyódor Mikháylovich (1841–1871), novelist of populist leanings who presented an unadorned picture of the life of workers and peasants. His novel *Under the Linden Trees* (1864) deals with peasants of the Perm region and the barge haulers along the Kama River. R's other novels *Miners* (1866) and *The Glumovs,* portray the life of workers in the mines of the Urals, while the novels *Where Is It Better* (1867), and *His Own Bread* (1870) describe the lot of urban workers.

RÉVDA, city in Sverdlovsk Oblast, RSFSR, in the middle Urals; pop 55,000 (1959). Rail center, and the site of the noted Sredneuralsk copper smelting plant.

RÉVEL: *see* Tallin.

REVOLUTION OF 1905. The name given to the cycle of disturbances in cities and countryside, and to the consequent concessions by the regime, during 1905 and early 1906. Poverty and the injustices of the tsarist regime induced the desire for revolutionary changes in many social groups throughout the R. Empire. The withdrawal of much of the army from European Russia to the Far East to fight the Japanese (from Jan. 1904) made successful risings temporarily possible. The regime's loss of prestige from the military disasters in Manchuria, combined with the weak direction of the police after revolutionary terrorists killed Minister of the Interior Plehve (Aug. 1904), precipitated the crisis.

Diverse groups, from the zemstvos to the terrorists, organized and agitated with increasing boldness throughout the latter half of 1904. A widespread strike in St. Petersburg culminated on Jan. 9, 1905, when crowds of petition-bearing workers, led by G. Gapon, a priest and police agent, were fired on by the military near the Winter Palace, which resulted in the death of about 200 persons. Revulsion against this "Bloody Sunday" (q.v.) increased all agitation for reform. The regime responded, as it was to do for most of the year, with concessions too small to satisfy the revolutionaries, but large enough to give the appearance of weakness and thereby encourage further agitation. On Feb. 18 the government promised to receive petitions of grievances (which led to disturbances in the countryside) and to summon elected representatives of the people to aid in the discussion of legislative bills (which encouraged strikes and agitation by liberal and radical groups). A decree of April 17 ended the worst persecution of dissenting Christian sects. Another wave of strikes, further terrorist bombings, and the mutiny of the sailors on the battleship *Potemkin* in the harbor of Odessa (June 14) increased unrest, while the sinking of the R. fleet in the Straits of Tsushima (May) led to the humiliating Peace of Portsmouth with Japan (Aug.) and increased the exasperation of the public.

On Aug. 6 the government announced the procedures for election to the promised consultative body, to be known as the State Duma (q.v.). Liberals and radicals demanded "universal, direct, equal, secret suffrage" but the government proposed a complicated indirect suffrage weighted in favor of the gentry and the supposedly loyal peasantry, and against the urban workers and middle classes. A further concession (Aug. 27) granted autonomy to the universities, which, under the circumstances, merely freed more student shock troops for the revolution. In protest against the government's election plans, strikes and agitaiton increased during Sept., supported by majorities of all social groups throughout the empire save the gentry and the bureaucrats, who were split. A railroad strike on Oct. 7 expanded rapidly into an astonishingly effective general strike in most large cities accompanied in many cases by lockouts on the part of factory owners and by barricades in the workers' quarters. The police, surprised, were unable to deal with the strike, and even the government's communications were partly shut down. At first the strikers in St. Petersburg demanded a genuine constituent assembly, the repeal of many police powers, civil liberties, and the eight-hour day. As professional revolutionaries took over the strike, demands went further: a democratic republic, amnesties, and the surrender of police and military arms to workers. The first workers' soviet (council) to guide the strike was formed in Ivanovo-Voznesensk, but most important was the St. Petersburg Soviet, formed on Oct. 13, which grew to 562 members, and was led by a Menshevik, G. S. Khrustalev-Nosar, and then by a more radical revolutionary, Trotsky. The general strike proved to be the climax of the R of 1905.

When the general strike began, Nicholas II, isolated in his Baltic palace at Peterhof, called on S. Witte who had gained new respect and a title by negotiating the end of the Japanese war (q.v.). Witte, in the strike, reached Nicholas with difficulty by sea, and advised him to choose between a military dictatorship and a real constitution. Nicholas preferred the former, but could not find a dictator to act in his place, so he reluctantly entrusted Witte with a mandate to grant a constitution in order to suppress the revolution. Witte wrote and Nicholas signed the October manifesto (Oct. 17) (q.v.) which proclaimed civil liberties, broadened the franchise for elections to the Duma, and announced that no law would be valid without the consent of the Duma. These moves effectively divided the opposition. Moderate liberals, especially industrialists (the core of the future Octobrist party), were satisfied, reopened their factories, and rallied behind Witte. Liberal professional people (the core of the future Kadet party) and the entire revolutionary intelligentsia remained intransigent, but were unable to topple the monarchy, or to prevent the striking workers (many of whom believed themselves triumphant, and all of whom were running out of funds) from returning to work during the next few weeks. Witte bided his time and arrested the leaders of the soviets five to six weeks later. He also negotiated a loan from France, which strengthened the government's hand in the months to come.

The crest of the R had broken, but disturbances continued. The October manifesto seemed to paralyze the police, but the confusion was a short-lived one; with the tsar's blessing the reactionary *Union of the Russian People* was formed, and a wave of pro-tsarist demonstrations and anti-Jewish pogroms organized by the police followed.

A brief Bolshevik-supported rising flared in Moscow (Dec.). Peasants burned manors, killed landlords, and seized lands until June 1906, especially in the Volga, Central, and Baltic provinces. Mutinies in the army in the Far East prevented the transfer of troops to European Russia till the end of Jan. With the return of the army in Feb. the government recovered much of its armed force and its nerve, and was prepared to encroach upon the liberties wrested from it the previous autumn. Save for rural disorder and some scattered strikes, the Revolution of 1905 was over. But the Kadet party under P. Milyukov, the Socialist Revolutionary party under V. M. Chernov, and the two factions of the Social Democratic party firmly organized in the months of freedom after the October manifesto, and the institution of the Duma itself, remained to trouble the regime.

BIBLIOGRAPHY: M. T. Florinsky, *Russia, A History and an Interpretation*, New York, 1953; Ch. 39; H. Seton-Watson, *The Decline of Imperial Russia, 1855–1914*, Part II, London and New York, 1952; G. T. Robinson, *Rural Russia under the Old Regime*, New York, 1932; S. Witte, *Memoirs*, Berlin, 1922–23; L. Trotsky, *1905*, Moscow, 1922.
F. B. R.

RÉYZEN, Mark Ósipovich (1895–), singer, basso, People's Artist of USSR. In 1925 he was soloist of the Leningrad Opera House; from 1930 to 1954 on the stage of Bolshoy Theater in Moscow. Teaches at the Musical Pedagogical Institute. Several Stalin prizes.

RÍCHTER, Svyatosláv Teofílovich (1914–), pianist. People's Artist of the RSFSR (1955). Graduated from Moscow conservatoire (1947). Stalin prize (1950); was awarded first prize at the Third International Contest of Performing Artists (1945). Toured the United States for the first time in 1960.

RÍDDER: *see* LENINOGORSK.

RÍGA, capital of Latvian SSR; pop. 385,000 (1939), 605,000 (1959). Is a major Baltic port and R.R. terminal on the W. Dvina, about 10 miles above its mouth in the Gulf of Riga. An ancient town founded in the late 12th century at the crossing of important sea and land trade routes, it was later a member of the Hanseatic League. Successively under Polish, then Swedish domination, it finally fell under Russia's Peter the Great.

Today it is a center of many important ind., including shipyards and heavy machine-building plants (machine tools, railway, subway and trolley cars, electrical motors and machinery, radio and telephone equipment), superphosphate and paper mills, chemical plants, bicycle factories; glassware and rubber goods, paints and cement, clothing and footwear are manufactured also on a large scale. It is the site of Latvian branch of the Ac. of S. USSR, and has a number of higher educational institutions, including a university; also is famous for its seaside resorts.

RIGA, GULF OF, in N.E. Baltic Sea; area 7,350 sq. mi. Major ports are Riga and Pyarnu. There are also a number of resorts, as Kemeri, Maiori, Bulduri.

RIGA, SOVIET-POLISH TREATY OF (1921). By Sept. 1920, the Soviets had given up hope of establishing communism in Poland and were anxious to concentrate on defeating the last White forces under General Wrangel. They thus offered the Poles concessions and succeeded in negotiating a peace treaty, the final version of which was signed by A. Ioffe for the Soviet Union and Dombski for Poland, on March 18, 1921. The treaty extended Poland's frontiers east of the projected Curzon Line, giving her an additional 51,762 sq. mi. (including much of the Ukraine and Byelorussia) containing 3,600,000 people. Both signees foreswore aggression and intervention and guaranteed the religious and cultural rights of national minorities. Russia was to return Polish treasures taken after 1772.

RIGHT OPPOSITION: *see* OPPOSITION.

RILU: *see* RED INTERNATIONAL OF LABOR UNIONS.

RÍMSKY-KÓRSAKOV, Nikoláy Andréyevich (1844–1908), composer and conductor, born in Tikhvin, near Novgorod. Graduated from the St. Petersburg Naval Academy in 1862. His first symphony (1865) was written during a cruise. Like R-K's *Fantasia on Serbian Themes*, the first symphony made use of folk themes  in which the composer was much interested as evidenced by the publication of two volumes of R. folk songs which he collected. Among his orchestral works *Capriccio Espagnole* and *Scheherazade* (both 1887), the latter on the subject from *Thousand and One Nights*, are particularly popular. R-K wrote 15 operas which were influenced by Glinka and employed R. idioms and oriental melodies. Favorites of the Russian operatic stage are his *Sadko* (1895); *The Tsar's Bride* (1898); *The Tale of Tsar Saltan* (1900) built around a poem by Pushkin; and *Le Coq d'or* (1907), a satire on autocracy. R-K also wrote cantatas, choral pieces, romances, and chamber music. He was a member of a group of composers known as "The Five" (its other members were Borodin, Balakirev, Cui, and Musorgsky) and orchestrated Musorgsky's operas and Borodin's *Prince Igor*. R-K was a prominent conductor and professor at the St. Petersburg conservatoire where he taught Glazunov and Stravinsky. The influence of his work, particularly of his instrumentation and program music, was great both in Russia and abroad.

BIBLIOGRAPHY: G. E. H. Abraham, *Rimsky-Korsakoff*, London, 1954; N. A. Rimsky-Korsakov, *My Musical Life*, New York, 1942.

RINALDI, Antonio (1710–1794), architect. Of Italian origin, R settled in Russia (1752). Designed palaces and parks including the Chinese Palace in Oranienbaum (1762–68), the Palace in Gatchina (1766–81), the Orlov Gates (1773–76), and the Marble Palace in St. Petersburg (1768–83).

RIÓNI (RION) RIVER, flows from Greater Caucasus through Transcaucasia into Black Sea near Poti, 185 mi. long; provides electric power.

RÍTSA LAKE, in Abkhaz ASSR, at an altitude of 3,100 ft.; small but deep; a tourist center.

RIVERS. The USSR has some 150,000 R longer than 6 mi., with a total length of 1,860,000 mi., and the portions suitable for navigation and floatage exceeding 300,000 mi. Soviet sources claim that the USSR has the world's largest reserves of water power and estimate that the potential power only of large rivers equals 300 mill. kilowatts, of which some 85% are located in Siberia and the Far East. The R of the USSR belong to the basins of the Arctic, the Pacific, and the Atlantic oceans. In addition, there is the vast Aralo-Caspian region which is a landlocked basin. The R differ greatly in length, basin area and volume of water. The Ob (2,700 mi.), Amur (2,700 mi.), Lena (2,650 mi.), and Yenisey (2,565 mi.) are the longest in the USSR; the Volga is the greatest in Europe, as to length (2,290 mi.), basin area, and volume. Then follow: Syr Darya (1,775 mi.), Kolyma (1,600 mi.), Ural (1,572 mi.), Dnieper (1,419 mi.), Don (1,224 mi.).

The drainage basin of the Arctic Ocean has the greatest area, occupying more than one half of the territory of the USSR. Twelve important R enter seas of the Arctic Ocean. Their lengths and the areas of their basins increase in the W. to E. direction, approximately to the Baykal meridian. The R of the Kola Peninsula and the Karelian ASSR, flowing to the White and the Barents seas, are short (only 125–200 mi.) and swift, with many rapids. In spite of their small drainage areas (up to ten thousand sq. mi.), these rivers have large volumes, and because of steep gradients and lakes along their courses, they also have powerful water resources. N. of the E. European plain, the Pechora and the N. Dvina are quiet and slow. The R of Siberia, of which the Ob, the Yenisey, and the Lena are the most important, are distinguished by their great length and volume. The steep gradients and large volumes of the chief Siberian R make them important sources of hydroelectric power measured in tens of mill. kilowatts.

The basin of the Pacific Ocean includes R of N.E. Siberia, the Far East, the Kamchatka Peninsula, and Sakhalin Island. The R empty into the Sea of Japan, the Okhotsk and Bering seas. The Amur River basin occupies 58% of the area under consideration. The Amur and its tributaries, the Shilka, the Argun, and the Zeya, have steep gradients and thus have much hydroelectric power. The Anadyr is the next in importance.

In the **basin of the Atlantic Ocean** there is a great diversity of the numerous river systems. They comprise the R of the N.W. having lakes along their courses, the slow R of the middle and S. parts of the E. European plain, the mountainous rivers of the Carpathians, the Caucasus and the Crimean mountains. The streams flow W. and N. to the Baltic Sea and S. and W. to the Black Sea and the Sea of Azov. Of those emptying into the Baltic Sea, the Neva, the Narva, the W. Dvina, and the Neman are the most important. In their basins there are many lakes, of which the largest are Ladoga, Onega, and Ilmen. The Danube, the Dniester, the Dnieper, the Rion, and others flow to the Black Sea; the Don and the Kuban to the Sea of Azov. While only the low reaches of the Danube, the largest R emptying into the Black Sea, are within the boundaries of the USSR, its large tributaries, the Tisa, the Prut, and the Seret, rise in the Carpathians, within the Soviet territory. The Dniester's sources are on the E. slopes of the Carpathians. The high reaches of all the R flowing from the Carpathians are mountainous. The chief R of the Black Sea-Azov basin, the Dnieper and the Don, rise on the uplands of the W. and central portions of the E. European plain, the Dnieper flowing across the vast Polesye and Dnieper lowlands. To the Black Sea-Azov basin also belong numerous R of the N. and W. portions of the Caucasus. These are mostly short (up to 20 mi.), rapid, and rich in hydroelectric power. The Rion and the Ingur are the largest. There are very few rivers in the steppe portion of the Crimea; the water network is developed somewhat better in the Crimean mountains, but the R are characterized by sharp fluctuations in volume.

The landlocked Aralo-Caspian basin includes regions with very diverse natural conditions: a part of the E. European plain, mountains of the Caucasus, Tien

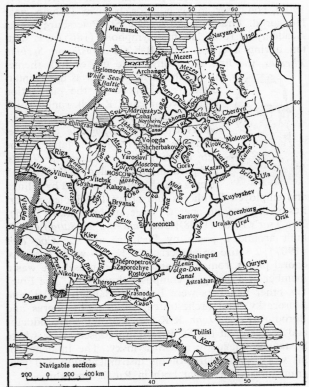

Inner waterways of European USSR

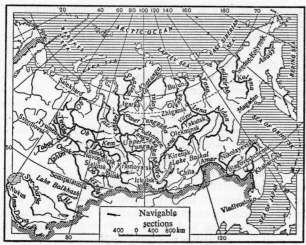

Inner waterways of Asiatic USSR

Shan, and Pamir, deserts of Kazakhstan and Central Asia. There is a flow on only approximately half of the Aralo-Caspian basin, no surface streams being found within the other half. Some R carry transit waters from other areas. About 10% of the whole volume of flow in the territory of the USSR is locked in the Aralo-Caspian basin. The Caspian Sea has the largest drainage area; of this 70% is the Volga basin which—except for the high reaches of tributaries of the Kama River, where the elevations attain 3,300 ft.— lies in the plain, with elevations not exceeding 650–1,000 ft. Gradients are gentle and the R are slow, except for the Ural tributaries which are like mountain R. A branching R network comprising the Oka and Kama systems is found in the upper part of the Volga basin which is covered with forests. After the Volga receives the Kama, it flows across the forest-steppe and steppe zones and has only small and shallow tributaries, with none below Stalingrad. The Volga and its tributaries are of great economic importance. The total length of navigatory network in the basin is 11,000 mi. The Kura River is the most important of numerous Caucasian R entering the Caspian Sea from the W. The basin of two more landlocked water bodies—the Aral Sea and the Lake Balkhash—lies to the E. from the Caspian Sea. The R rise in mountainous regions, but in their low reaches they flow through deserts and lose their water. The Syr Darya and the Amu Darya are the largest R of the region.   L. D.

RIVER TRANSPORTATION. Until the last decades, rivers maintained their traditional importance in Russia. Although even in S. Russia they froze for at least three months every year, rivers provided cheap means of freight movement, typically using serf-power and towropes along the broad slow streams. Traffic on the Volga is still heavy, involving southbound movement of timber and other commodities, together with northbound movement of grain. Petroleum traffic was mainly northbound from Baku, until the appearance in recent years of an even larger southbound movement from the new fields east of the middle Volga. The Ob, Yenisey, and Lena rivers of Siberia have helped in the opening up of the Soviet N.E., though the an-

nual volume of traffic has remained very small. Multi-purpose dam projects are increasing the usefulness of many Soviet rivers by increasing their depth and controlling their flow, but long freezing periods remain a hindrance to their use. The combined length of exploited waterways is 85,000 miles.

Freight volume			Passenger transportation
bill. ton-km.	mill. ton		(mill.)
		Year	
28.9	35.1	1913*	11.5
15.9	18.3	1928	17.8
35.9	72.9	1940	73.0
45.9	91.5	1950	53.6
70.2	146.8	1956	81.7

* Present-day boundaries.

FREIGHT TRAFFIC ON SOVIET RIVERS
(bill. ton-km.)

ROADS. Soviet records show a 1913 estimate of some 900,000 miles of R available in all of Russia, of which 15,000 mi. were paved. Since then, though the total has grown little, if at all, paved R increased to 146,500 mi. in 1959, of which 41,360 mi. had an asphalt or concrete surface. (There are more than 2,400,000 miles of paved roads in the U.S.). Spring and fall rains still cause grave difficulties on most Russian R. Low priority has been given to improvement of the road system, since heavy industrial growth does not depend on it, but gradual modernization of R is in prospect. Freight transportation by truck has been confined to short trips within metropolitan areas or between collective farms and R.R. stations; the average haul for such shipments has risen from 6 to 8 mi. in the last thirty years.

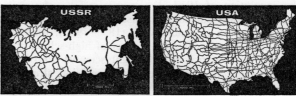

Comparative density of road network

ROCKETRY. The first mention of war rockets in R. literature dates back to 1607 when Onisim Mikhaylov, a master of gunnery, wrote about "cannonballs that run and fly." The news of such marvels might have reached Muscovy from China, the land of the earliest use of rockets. In the late 17th century R. tsars ordered the making of rockets for fireworks, also for signaling in combat. *Raketnoye Zavedenie,* or Rocket Works, was established in Moscow in 1680. Tsar Peter I moved it to St. Petersburg in the early 1700's, expanding this enterprise considerably. In 1733, Empress Anna decreed a festival for which 2,000 of her Rocket Works artisans toiled for 10 weeks to shoot fiery castles and fountains into the St. Petersburg sky. From 1742 to 1762, Major General Abram Hannibal (Alexander Pushkin's ancestor) was in charge of creating pyrotechnic rockets for Empress Elizabeth.

As warhead rockets made their first important mark in the Napoleonic Wars. Alexander I appreciated the role of these weapons in the battle of Leipzig in 1813, rewarding their improver, Britain's William Congreve, with the R. Order of St. Anne. The British had discovered rockets as arms in India, and in 1815, the Russian artillery officer Alexander Zasiadko based his blueprint of "a fighting rocket" on the British adaptation of India's heaven-blazing weapon (most likely brought to India from China). In 1826, at Zasiadko's suggestion, Nicholas I ordered the formation of Russia's first rocket company of soldiers. The unit was attached to the St. Petersburg Rocket Works. Under General Zasiadko's guidance, warhead rockets were used with occasional success in the Russo-Turkish War of 1828–29. Later they were employed by Russian armies also in the Crimean War of 1853–56, and to some extent in the conquest of the Caucasus through the middle of the 19th century.

Zasiadko was followed by Konstantin Konstantinov, likewise an artillerist and mathematician. But the sizable experimental data collected by both Zasiadko and Konstantinov did not lead to any logical or complete theory of rocket flight. "This is a science yet to be created," General Konstantinov admitted in the 1860's.

Use of rockets as propulsion engines for human flight was first proposed in Russia in 1849 by I. I. Tretesky, a captain of engineering troops in the Caucasus. A similar suggestion came from Admiral Nikolay Sokovnin in 1866. The modern idea of jet planes, carrying pilots and passengers, and rising into the air vertically with the aid of rocket thrust, was diagrammed in his prison cell in 1881 by a revolutionary plotter, Nikolay Kibalchich, as he awaited hanging for his part in the assassination of Alexander II. Kibalchich was executed in April 1881, and his project came to light only after the revolution of 1917.

But the most outstanding Russian pioneer in rocketry was Konstantin E. Tsiolkovsky (1857–1935), for many years an obscure provincial teacher of high-school physics and mathematics, a self-taught scientist who began to speculate and write on rocket propulsion already in the 1880's–90's. The literary output of his long and busy life was enormous, but of uneven quality. His first important paper on rockets was published in 1903; his second, in 1911. His Soviet biographers insist that Tsiolkovsky was among the very first to discuss the multi-stage rocket principle, to propose the use of solar energy in the earth's artificial satellites of the future, and to draw diagrams of such a satellite as well as a space platform. On the other hand, Western experts point out that America's Professor Robert H. Goddard anticipated Tsiolkovsky in the multi-stage principle by some 15 years. Still, it is recognized in the West that in suggesting liquid propellants (although not in actual use of them in rockets) Tsiolkovsky did antedate the Germans—particularly Dr. Hermann Oberth—by 20 years, and was ahead of Goddard by some 14 years. Tsiol-

kovsky's priority is also generally conceded in the efforts to control the direction of a rocket's motion.

But Tsiolkovsky's work was in theorizing and diagramming far more than in practical experimenting. The reason was simply the extreme poverty of so many of his creative years. He lacked money for materials and equipment; for long decades he failed to gain from his fellow Russians any financial aid. And so, in the actual building of liquid-fuel rockets Goddard was first, beginning his work in 1920; the Germans came next in 1930; while the Russians managed to fire their very first liquid-fuel rocket as late as 1933.

Despite the recent Soviet claim that immediately after the revolution of 1917 Tsiolkovsky and other R. scientists received from the government all the help they needed, in reality assistance to pure research in Soviet Russia had a slow start. The initial Communist interest in rocketry in the early 1920's was not for the purposes of higher science, but in the very utilitarian direction of war weapons. The old combat-rockets of Zasiadko and Konstantinov were re-examined, and gradually, as the result of much experimentation, the first multiple rocket-launcher was designed for Soviet planes and field artillery. Its ground-use version was called Katyusha. Ready for mass production just before Hitler's invasion of the Soviet Union, the new Russian rocket gun made its first appearance against the advancing Nazi armies in July 1941. The Katyusha gun, however, played a psychological role rather than any decisive military part in Hitler's eventual defeat.

The collapse of Nazi Germany gave Russia the shambles of Peenemünde, Hitler's chief rocket site (occupied by Soviet troops on May 5, 1945). From these and other ruins, Stalin's marshals and secret police officers salvaged important specimens of the Nazi V-2 rocket, also some German blueprints and models of further war-rocket improvements. Although the Soviets captured or otherwise engaged a lesser number of German rocket specialists than such experts were at the time found on the American side, the Russian high command used its German contingent of rocket men far more intensively and secretively than such employment distinguished the United States rocketry of the immediate postwar period.

Russia's skilled use of German blueprints and captive engineers, but above all the Russians' own early interest and knowledge in the realm of rockets, resulted in the sensational Soviet break-through in the great new field in 1957.

Warning signals about the imminent Red conquest of outer space had been issued by Moscow to the largely unheeding world for nearly four years. On November 27, 1953, Professor Aleksandr N. Nesmeyanov, president of the Soviet Academy of Sciences, declared to the World Peace Council gathered in Vienna: "Science has reached a point where it is realistic for us to speak of sending a stratoplane to the Moon and of creating an artificial satellite for the Earth." In 1954, in Moscow, the Interdepartmental Commission on Interplanetary Communications was established, and this proved to be the first co-ordinating agency for all Soviet space research and production. In 1955, President Dwight D.

Eisenhower announced that the United States would launch an earth satellite during the International Geophysical Year of 1957–58. It was generally, in most countries, expected that an American satellite would indeed be the first to circle this globe.

Yet it was the Soviets who first placed their satellite into its orbit. Russia anticipated the United States by several months, achieving at that a stronger rocket thrust, which resulted in a heavier rocket payload than Americans could accomplish. On October 4, 1957, Moscow's rocket men astonished mankind by their successful launching of Sputnik I. This weighed 184 pounds, and reached a maximum height of 560 miles. Its carrier-rocket lasted 60 days, and Sputnik I itself orbited for 94 days. On November 3, 1957, Sputnik II was launched, with a live passenger inside—a female dog named Layka. This satellite's weight was 1,120½ pounds; its maximum altitude, 1,037 miles; and it whirled around the Earth for 163 days, completing 2,370 orbits, a total of 62,500,000 miles. The dog lived only a week.

Americans finally joined the celestial race by launching Explorer I on January 31, 1958, and Vanguard I on March 17 of the same year. The Soviets followed their successes with Sputnik III on May 15, 1958. This weighed 2,925½ pounds, reached its maximum height of 1,168½ miles, and lasted in its orbit 691 days. But Vanguard I's maximum altitude, 2,453 miles, remained higher, and its life expectancy much longer. Presently, from both countries, came rocket shots aimed at the Moon, some of them going wide of that body, in the direction of the Sun. Russia's Lunik I, its payload weighing 796½ pounds, was successfully launched on January 2, 1959, but the American Pioneer IV made its journey only two months later, with a mere 13.4 pounds of payload. However, American scientists with their better radio communications traced their Pioneer IV for a distance of 407,000 miles, or some 32,000 miles beyond the Russian loss of contact with Lunik I. Lunik II was fired in the Soviet Union on September 12, 1959. It hit the Moon on September 13, at 2 minutes and 24 seconds past midnight Moscow time. For political reasons this triumph of the Soviets was timed to coincide with Premier Khrushchev's arrival in the United States on his first trip to this country. On October 4, 1959, to mark the second anniversary of Sputnik I, the Soviets launched Lunik III. This satellite orbited both the Earth and the Moon and, on October 7, accomplished an unprecedented feat: it photographed and televised back to Earth the far side of the Moon. On May 15, 1960, to celebrate the second anniversary of Sputnik III and to impress the abortive Summit Conference then gathering in Paris, the Soviets launched "a spaceship-satellite," also known as Sputnik IV. Its so-called "cabin" contained "a weight equal to that ot a human being" as a prelude to the first Soviet man-into-space experiments. The latter were further advanced on August 20, 1960, when Sputnik V or "second spaceship" was decelerated after 17 globe-circlings totaling 435,000 miles. This brought back to earth the satellite's capsule with its two dog passengers Belka and Strelka, also its assorted rats, mice, flies, land and water plants, fungi and seeds, all safe and sound, all to be examined by Russian scientists for the effects of outer space on this live matter.

The Soviet superiority in rocket thrust and in the weight of the rockets continued to excite mankind's awe. Already Sputnik III weighed 100 times more than any of the four United States satellites launched up to late July 1958. In the outer-space events of 1959 the final stage of Lunik I, minus fuel, was 3,245.2 pounds, and its total launching weight may have been about 250 tons. The last stage of Lunik II was 3,342 pounds minus fuel. In Lunik III the final stage weighed 3,423 pounds without fuel. Already for Lunik I, Dr. Wernher von Braun estimated a propulsion system of some 750,000 pounds of thrust, or twice the most powerful rocket boosters then available in America. In 1959–60 the United States placed more satellites into orbit than the Soviets had achieved by then, yet, in early October 1959, a Washington source calculated that the aggregate payloads of Russia's first three Sputniks and first two Luniks were some five times heavier than the combined weight of instruments taken aloft by America's 12 satellites and three space probes.

In military rocketry, the American Polaris, a 1,500-mile solid-fuel missile that can be fired from a submerged submarine, was thought to have been superior to anything the Soviets might have developed by late 1960. Yet, in 1958–60, the Soviet Union was generally recognized to be ahead of the United States in the quantity (although not necessarily in quality) of ICBMs, or intercontinental ballistic missiles, and IRBMs, or intermediate ballistic missiles. In January and July 1960 the Soviets advertised their ICBM capacity by shooting such missiles for more than 7,600 miles, all the way from their Central Asian or Siberian launching sites to targets in the middle of the Pacific Ocean.

In either late 1959 or early 1960 (a more precise time is not ascertainable), Russia's military rocketry was elevated into a separate service of the Soviet armed forces. On May 6, 1960, Marshal Andrey A. Grechko in a speech to the Supreme Soviet in Moscow praised the new command as "actually the main branch of our Armed Force." Two days before, on May 4, it was revealed that Marshal Mitrofan I. Nedelin was chief of all the Soviet rocket units. But in late October 1960 he was killed in an airplane accident, and his post as supreme comander of rocket arms was given to Marshal Kirill S. Moskalenko.

The top civilian agency co-ordinating all of the USSR's outer-space research and production is the Interdepartmental Commission on Interplanetary Communications, established in 1954, and officially responsible to the Presidium of the Soviet Academy of Sciences.

The Commission is headed by Professor Leonid I. Sedov, a noted astrophysicist. Typical of other Soviet scientists prominent in this field are Professors Georgy I. Pokrovsky and Anatoly A. Blagonravov. Both combine their academic standing with military posts: the former as a major general of the engineering-technical armed service, the latter a lieutenant general of artillery.

We may assume that a higher Soviet central office rules both the military rocket service commanded by Marshal Moskalenko and the civilian agency led by Professor Sedov. Such an overall office probably has total powers covering the entire work of Russia's astrophysicists and rocket and missile specialists, but the identity of such a top agency and its personnel is apparently kept secret.

That some of the foremost Soviet rocket experts are completely unknown to the general public at home and abroad was hinted by Nikita S. Khrushchev in his speech at the Electrochemical Kombinat (factory) at Bitterfield, East Germany, on July 9, 1958. On that occasion he said that in due time his government would indeed honor "the scientists-engineers working in the field of the atomic and rocket technology," but, for reasons of security, their names and photographs could not be published—"for the surrounding world they are, for the time being, anonymous." Russia's rocket bases must remain equally secret, the Soviet government declares—and for the same reason of ensuring safety from prying foreign eyes. In November 1960 Marshal Andrey I. Yeremenko, a deputy defense minister, asserted that the Soviet superiority in rockets was partly due to the better secrecy with which the USSR blanketed its space-age installations, and that, conversely, the American vulnerability to rocket attack was in part the result of the greater publicity given to their missile bases by Americans themselves.

However, Western intelligence sources, trying to pinpoint the hidden Soviet rocket establishments, insist that the largest of such bases are Tyuratam in Central Asia, near the Aral Sea; also at Krasny Yar and Kapustin Yar near Stalingrad and the Caspian Sea. (*See also* SPACE SCIENCE.)

BIBLIOGRAPHY: A. Kosmodemyansky, *Konstantin Tsiolkovsky, His Life and Work*, (English), Moscow, 1956; F. J. Krieger, *Behind the Sputniks, A Survey of Soviet Space Science*, Washington, D.C., 1958; Albert Parry, *Russia's Rockets and Missiles*, New York, 1960; *USSR Missiles, Rockets and Space Effort, 1956–60*, Washington, D.C., 1960; Alfred A. Zaehringer, *Soviet Space Technology*, New York, 1961. A. P.

RÓDICHEV, Fyódor Izmáylovich (1856–1933), born in a wealthy family of landed gentry, was active in zemstvo organizations. He was a member of the Union of Liberation and one of the founders of the Constitutional Democrattic party, a member of its central committee and one of its best speakers. He was a deputy to all four State Dumas. Under the Provisional Government, R was commissar on Finnish affairs. He emigrated after the October revolution.

RODZYÁNKO, Michael (Mikhaíl Vladímirovich) (1859–1924), statesman. R was a leader of the Union of October 17 or Octobrist party (q.v.), a wealthy landowner, and president of the third and fourth Dumas, 1911–17. A man of limited intellectual gifts and conservative disposition, R in World War I supported the territorial ambitions of the imperial government. When the February revolution of 1917 broke out, R by virtue of his office headed the provisional committee of the Duma, which approved the Provisional Government in which, however, he had no part. After the October

revolution R fled south, joined the Volunteer Army, and made an attempt to unify all anti-Bolshevik forces under the leadership of a "National Council" which was to comprise the members of the four Dumas. Following the defeat of the anti-Soviet armies in 1919–20, R emigrated and died in Yugoslavia. His memoirs, which are not notable for accuracy, were published in English in 1927 under the title *The Reign of Rasputin*: *An Empire's Collapse*.

ROERICH, Nikoláy Konstantínovich (1874–1947), painter, stage designer, and archaeologist. His early works are poetical in character (*Messenger*, 1897, in the Tretyakov Gallery). Later R was attracted by decorative stylization and symbolism (*The Heavenly Battle*, 1909, in the Russian Museum). From 1920 R lived in the USA and India; participated in archaeological expeditions to the Orient. His pictures have emotional quality and striking color effects (*Remember*, 1945). Designed the stage settings for *Prince Igor* (1909), and many other productions.

ROKOSSÓVSKY, Konstantín Konstantínovich (1896–), marshal of the Soviet Union. Born in Warsaw,  R became a Bolshevik in 1919. He fought in the civil war and rose rapidly through the ranks of the Red Army. His career nearly ended during the purge of the Red Army in 1937 but he was subsequently released. In World War II, R led a Soviet army through Poland where his Polish origin was widely exploited—despite his failure or unwillingness to take Warsaw during the Home Army's uprising (1944). In 1949 he became minister of defense in the Polish Communist regime. In 1956 he was the chief target of Polish communists, supporters of Wl. Gomulka, who forced his recall to the USSR. Back in Moscow, R became deputy minister of defense.

RÓKOTOV, Fyódor Stepánovich (1732–1808), portrait painter who shared with Levitsky and Borovikovsky the distinction of painting contemporary Russians with ease and charm. His portraits of women, *Countess Branicki, Countess Orlov* and others, are especially attractive. R was a pupil of Le Lorrain and Count Rotari and became a member of the Academy of Fine Arts in 1760.

ROMÁNOV, Grand Duke Konstantin Konstantinovich (1858–1915), poet who published his works under the pen name "K. R." Wrote romantic and lyrical poems. Was translator of English and German poetry, notably of Shakespeare's *Hamlet*.

ROMÁNOV DYNASTY, tsars and emperors, rulers of Russia for three centuries (1613–1917). Genealogically, the Romanov lineage is traced back to boyar Roman, in the service of Vasily III of Moscow (16th century). On Feb. 21, 1613, following a period of internal strife and foreign intervention, the *zemski sobor* (q.v.) elected Michael Romanov, the 16-year-old son of Fyodor Romanov (later Patriarch Filaret), as tsar of Russia. Michael Fyodorovich (1613–1645) was succeeded by Alexis Mikhaylovich (1645–1676); Fedor Alekseyevich (1676–1682); Ivan Alekseyevich (Ivan V, 1682–1696); Peter Alekseyevich (Peter I or Peter the

Great, 1682–1725; assumed the title of emperor in 1721; in 1682–1696 Ivan and Peter were co-rulers); Catherine I, wife of Peter I (1725–1727); Peter II, grandson of Peter I (1727–1730); Anna Ivanovna, daughter of Ivan V (1730–1740); Ivan Antonovich (Ivan VI, great-grandson of Ivan V, 1740–1741); Elizabeth, daughter of Peter I (1741–1761); Peter III, grandson of Peter I (1761–1762); Catherine II (Catherine the Great, wife of Peter III, 1762–1796); Paul I, son of Peter III and Catherine II (1796–1801); Alexander I, son of Paul I (1801–1825); Nicholas I, son of Paul I (1825–1855); Alexander II, son of Nicholas I (1855–1881); Alexander III, son of Alexander II (1881–1894); Nicholas II, son of Alexander III (1894–1917). After the February revolution, on March 2 (15 N.S.), 1917, Nicholas II abdicated. On July 17, 1918, the former tsar and his family were executed in Yekaterinburg (now Sverdlovsk), by order of the regional Ural Soviet.

ROMÁNOV, Panteleymón Sergéyevich (1884–1938), postrevolutionary writer of aristocratic origins. He first attracted attention by the novels *Without Cherry Blossoms* and *Three Pairs of Silk Stockings*, written in 1926 and 1930, which dealt with the sexual problems of young people who regarded love purely as a biological necessity. His best literary efforts are the essay "The Right to Life, or the Problem of No Party Allegiance" and the novels *New Decalogue* and *Property*. The former is a defense of the spiritual values of R. and world culture against the onslaught of the party line that seeks to replace spiritual values in literature with ideological communist dogma. The *New Decalogue* sets up age-old human reactions to political party doctrines. R is the author of a lengthy novel *Russia*, in 5 parts, written over a period of 10 years, from 1926 to 1936.

ROMANÓVSKY, Vsevolod Ivanovich (1879–1954), mathematician. Fellow, Ac. of S., Uzbek SSR (1943). Graduate, St. Petersburg University (1906); professor, Warsaw (1911–15), Rostov (1915–18), and Tashkent (1918) universities. Research concerned mathematical statistics, the theory of probability (arrived at important results on Markov chains), and the integration of partial differential equations.

ROMANTICISM: *see* LITERATURE, PAINTING.

ROSSOLÍMO, Grigóry Ivánovich (1860–1928), neuropathologist. Graduate (1884), professor (1917), Moscow University. Research concerned neuropathology, psychiatry, the application of surgical methods in the treatment of nervous diseases and child psychology. Cofounder of the Society of Neuropathologists and Psychiatrists.

ROSTOPCHÍN, Count Fyódor Vasílyevich (1763–1826), military governor of Moscow at the time of Napoleon's invasion of Russia.

ROSTÓV, city in Yaroslavl Oblast, Central RSFSR; pop. 29,200 (1956). An ancient city on Lake Nero mentioned in the 9th century. For four centuries it was the center of the Rostov-Suzdal principality and came under Moscow rule in 1474. Among its many prominent monuments of early architecture is the famed Uspensky Cathedral. Metal foundries, flax and food-processing ind.

ROSTÓV OBLAST, RSFSR, S.E. sector; area 39,000 sq. mi.; pop. 3,312,000 (1959). Cities: Rostov-on-Don (adm. center), Taganrog, Novocherkassk, Shakhty. Rivers: Don, and its left tributaries, Sal and Manych. Predominantly level plains in the fertile black-earth belt; somewhat arid in the E. (chestnut soils), is cattle and sheep country, with rich alluvial pastures; wheat and corn farming; sunflower, tobacco, mustard plant cultures; large orchards and vineyards in the S.; commercial fishing in the Don delta and Sea of Azov; coal mines (Shakhty, Novoshakhtinsk); metallurgical and pipe-rolling mills, boiler works (Taganrog). Heavy concentration of ind. at Rostov; footwear, furniture, canning, food-processing plants distributed through the region. Est. 1937.

ROSTÓV-ON-DON, city, adm. center of Rostov Oblast; pop. 600,000 (1959). Is a major ind. city, R.R. center, and port on lower Don, near its mouth at the Sea of Azov; harbors the giant Rostselmash agr. machine works, shipyards; has aircraft, automobile-assembly, machine-tool plants. Founded 1761.

ROSTÓV-SÚZDAL, GRAND DUCHY OF, medieval principality extending between the Volga and Oka rivers, with the center at Rostov. Formed by secession from Kievan Russia in the 11th century, it grew in power and attempted to reduce the Great Novgorod and Kiev to a state of political dependence. In the late 12th century Vladimir became the capital of the Duchy.

RSFSR: *see* RUSSIAN SOVIET FEDERATED SOCIALIST REPUBLIC.

RÓVNO, city, adm. center of Rovno Oblast; pop. 57,000 (1959). Important R.R. junction; ind.: lumber, chemicals, agr. machinery, clothing, breweries, confectionery mfg., foundry.

RÓVNO OBLAST, Ukrainian SSR, W. sector; area 7,850 sq. mi.; pop. 927,000 (1959). Cities: Rovno (adm. center), Dubno, Sarny, Ostrog, Zdolbunov. The N. section lies in Polesye, the region of mixed deciduous-coniferous forests and Pripet marshes; it is drained by the Goryn, Sluch, and Stry of the Dnieper basin; has moderate continental climate. Flax, rye, potatoes are grown on the turf-podsol soils; lumbering, raising of meat and dairy cattle important; granite, cement rock, and slate quarries. In the S. section, on the Volyn-Podolian upland (the Rovno plateau), fertile black-earth and gray podsolized soils support grain and garden crops, hops, tobacco and sugar-beet cultures. Large ind. concentrated in Rovno city. Est. 1939.

ROSTÓVTSEV, Mikhaíl Ivánovich (1870–1952), historian and archaeologist, professor at St. Petersburg University (1901–18). After the October revolution he went to England and then to the United States. Professor at Yale University, U.S.A., after 1925. Principal publications: *Ancient Decorative Painting in Southern Russia* (1913–14); *The Social and Economic History of the Hellenistic World* (3 vols., 1941); *A History of the Ancient World* (2 vols., 1945); and many others, translated into various languages.

ROZHDÉSTVENSKY, Robért Ivánovich (1932–), poet, born in Kosishat, in the Altay. His first verses were published in 1949. In 1956 R graduated from the Gorky Literary Institute in Moscow. He published three volumes of poetry: *Spring Flags* (1955), *Temptation* (1956), and *My Love* (1956). His work tends to be lyrical, but with a noticeable social-conscious note. During the "thaw" he published the poem *Morning* (1956). It presented the Stalin era as a dark night, which "nevertheless cannot drown out the dawn"—"morning" will soon come.

ROZHKÓV, Nikoláy Aleksándrovich (1867–1927), historian. At the University of Moscow, he was a student of Vasily Klyuchevsky; hence, perhaps, the nature of his early studies, such as *The Origin of Absolutism in Russia* (1906). In 1919, he commenced publication of his 12-volume survey of R. history. Here he attempted a Marxist interpretation. Other works include: *Agriculture in Muscovite Russia in the 16th Century* (1899), *Town and Village in Russian History* (1902).

RUBBER INDUSTRY. The products of the RI, which is regarded as a branch of the chemical industry, include tires, conveyor belts, insulating materials, rubber consumer goods, and medical items. It has been estimated that 350,000 tons of synthetic rubber were produced in 1955 (in 1959 the United States produced 1,401,000 tons of synthetic rubber; Canada 102,000 tons; the United Kingdom 58,000 tons).

The first rubber plant in Russia was built in St. Petersburg in the 1830's and produced primarily rubber footwear. In 1860 a second and larger rubber factory was erected in that city; subsequently additional rubber plants were constructed in Moscow ("Bogatyr" 1887), Riga ("Provodnik" 1889 and "Russia" 1896), and elsewhere. In 1913 the RI in Russia employed 15,000 workers.

The rapid development of the RI during the Soviet period began in the late 1920's in connection with the production of automobiles. According to official data four times as many rubber goods were produced in 1932 as in 1913, and 10 times as many in 1940 when 3 mill. automobile tires and 70 mill. pairs of rubber footwear were produced. At that time tires represented 45% of all rubber goods produced; footwear, 17%, and products for industrial uses, 38%.

The first large synthetic rubber plant, based on the divinyl (Lebedev) process, began operations in 1932, and by 1937, 70% rubber produced was synthetic rubber.

The RI continued to develop during World War II, particularly in the eastern regions. Its further development became especially rapid, however, after the completion of a program of expansion and intensive technological modernization during the Fourth Five Year Plan (1946–50). It has been estimated that approximately 200,000 tons of synthetic rubber were produced in 1950, when, according to official data, 7.4 mill. automobile tires and 111 mill. pairs of rubber footwear were made. By 1958 the number of automobile tires produced reached 14.4 mill., and of rubber footwear, 159 mill. pairs.

PRODUCTION OF RUBBER GOODS
IN THE USSR

Year	Automobile tires	Rubber footwear
1913	—	38.9 mill. pairs
1928	.085 mill.	—
1940	3.0	69.7
1950	7.4	110.8
1958	14.4	158.7
1959	15.4	—
1960	17.2	—

P. I. M.

RUBINSTEIN, Antón Grigóryevich (1829–1894), composer and pianist, pioneer of musical education in Russia. Unlike "The Five," R adhered to classical western musical forms, and is considered the head of the "western" school, which included his pupils Tchaikovsky, Arensky, Rachmaninoff and others. R was a prolific  composer in the manner of Mendelssohn and Schumann. His most important compositions are the operas *The Demon* (1875), *The Children of the Steppes, Maccabees,* and *Nero.* He wrote five concertos for piano, six symphonies and symphonic poems, quartets, trios, a multitude of piano pieces, 165 songs for voice and piano. At the age of ten R gave piano concerts in Europe and America. His "Historical Concerts" in St. Petersburg, Moscow, and in W. Europe comprised compositions ranging from Bach to Liszt. R had little regard for contemporary composers and denied their merits. He founded the Imperial Musical Society (1859), and the first conservatoire in St. Petersburg (1862) which had a distinguished body of teachers. R was its director and professor of piano and composition for many years.

RUBINSTEIN, Nikoláy Grigóryevich (1835–1881), brother of Anton R., pianist, composer, conductor, and teacher. Better known as a pianist and teacher than as a composer; he wrote but a few short pieces for piano which were soon forgotten. In 1860 R founded the Moscow branch of the Russian Musical Society and in 1866 established the Moscow Conservatoire of which he was the director until his death. Dissipation undermined R's health and led to an untimely death.

RUBLE: *see* MONETARY SYSTEM.

RUBLYÓV, Andrey (ca. 1360–1430), outstanding icon painter, noted for idealism, purity of line, compositional eurythmy and freshness of color. He was first mentioned in 1405 when, together with Theophanus the Greek, he executed the frescoes in Moscow's Assumption Cathedral. In 1408, with Daniil Chorny, he painted the murals of the Dormition Cathedral in Vladimir, notably the very large representation of the Last Judgment. R's outstanding work is the icon of the *Trinity* (1408?) in which R. romanticism is blended with Byzantine severity. Its three Angels representing the Three Persons and combining triangular forms into the unity of a circle, are painted with wonderful light blues and lilac shades and sum up R's consummate mastery and feeling.

RUBTSÓVSK, city in Altay Kray, W. Siberia, RSFSR; pop. 38,000 (1939), 111,000 (1959). A recently developed ind. town, on Aley River and Turkestan-Siberian R.R.; it is a large-scale producer of tractors, agr. machinery, and electrical equipment; also flour mills, dairies and meat-packing plants.

RUD, Gerasím Yákovlevich (1907–), Moldavian party and government official. He spent his early years as a farm laborer; attended the Rybnitsa Horticultural and Viticultural Technicum, 1924–28, and the Moscow Academy of Agriculture, 1928–31. From 1939 to 1944 he held increasingly important Moldavian SSR government posts; was commissar of foreign affairs, Moldavian SSR, 1944–46; became chairman of the Moldavian SSR Council of Ministers, 1946. In 1952 he was appointed a member of the Central Auditing Commission, CPSU; deputy of the USSR Supreme Soviet; in 1956 was elected candidate member of the Central Committee, CPSU; in 1958 was released as bureau member of the central committee, Moldavian CP, and as chairman of the Moldavian SSR Council of Ministers.

RÚDNEV, Lev Vladímirovich (1885–), architect. Designed the Frunze Military Academy in Moscow, and the government building in Baku. R was director and chief architect of the project for the construction of the Moscow State University and the Warsaw Palace of Culture.

RÚDNEV, Vadím Vasílyevich (1874–1940), Socialist Revolutionary. As a student, took part in the armed revolt in Moscow in 1905; thereafter was active in the Socialist Revolutionary party. In 1917, after the February revolution, R became mayor of Moscow. In this office he attempted to resist the victorious Bolsheviks. After the October revolution, he left Russia and confined himself to literary and editorial work. For many years R had been an editor of the R. journal *Sovremennya Zapiski* (Contemporary Notes) in Paris.

RUDZUTÁK, Yan Ernestovich (1887–1938), born in Latvia to a poor peasant family. He joined the revolutionary movement in 1905. Arrested and sentenced to fifteen years at hard labor. Was active in the October revolution. From 1920, was a member of the Central Committee and from 1923 a secretary of the Central Committee of the CP. Was one of the party's specialists on the trade-union movement. Later he held high positions in the economic apparatus. From 1924 to 1930 R was people's commissar for communications. In 1938, R was arrested and disappeared. In 1956, he was rehabilitated by Khrushchev in his "secret speech" at the 20th Party Congress.

RUMYÁNTSEV (Rumyantsev-Zadunaysky), **Pyótr Aleksándrovich** (1725–1796), field marshal, general, distinguished statesman and military leader, one of the founders of the R. school of military art. Under his leadership the R. armies won a number of brilliant victories in the Seven Years' War against Prussia (1756–63) as well as in the Russo-Turkish Wars of 1768–74 and 1787–91. Author of the *Articles of Military Service*, he did a great deal toward better organization and greater fighting capacity of Russia's armed forces.

RUSÁNOV, Nikoláy Sergéyevich (1859–?). A populist and member of the Executive Committee of the "People's Will," R was one of the organizers of the Socialist Revolutionary party. He emigrated the first time in 1882; returned to Russia in 1905; fled again in 1908; and returned in 1917. In Russia and abroad R contributed to Socialist Revolutionary and populist publications, *Vestnik Narodnoy Voli* (Messenger of People's Will), *Russkoye Bogatstvo* (Russian Wealth) and others. R wrote under the pseudonyms of K. Tarasov and N. Kudrin.

RUSSIAN-AMERICAN COMPANY: *see* HISTORY.

RUSSIAN MUSIC SOCIETY: *see* MUSIC.

RUSSIAN MUSEUM: *see* MUSEUMS.

RUSSIAN SOCIAL-DEMOCRATIC LABOR PARTY: *see* CPSU, MENSHEVISM.

RUSSIAN SOVIET FEDERATED SOCIALIST REPUBLIC (RSFSR) is the largest of the 15 union republics of the USSR. It was formed on Oct. 25 (Nov. 7 N.S.), 1917. It is situated in E. Europe and N. Asia.

It has frontiers in the N.W. with Norway and Finland, in the W. with Poland and with the Estonian, Latvian, Lithuanian, and Byelorussian SSRs, on the S. with China, Outer Mongolia and with the Kazakh, Azerbaijan, Georgian, and Ukrainian SSRs. It occupies a territory of 6,591,000 sq. mi. that constitutes over three-fourths of the entire territory of the USSR. It is surrounded on the N.W., N., and E. by the waters of the Atlantic, Arctic, and Pacific oceans.

In 1960 the RSFSR included 15 autonomous soviet

EUROPEAN RSFSR: ADMINISTRATIVE-TERRITORIAL MAP

OBLASTS: 1. Archangel 2. Astrakhan 3. Belgorod 4. Bryansk 5. Gorky 6. Ivanovo 7. Kalinin 8. Kaliningrad 9. Kaluga 10. Kirov 11. Kostroma 12. Kursk 13. Kuybyshev 14. Leningrad 15. Lipetsk 16. Moscow 17. Murmansk 18. Novgorod 19. Orel 20. Orenburg 21. Penza 22. Perm 23. Pskov 24. Rostov 25. Ryazan 26. Saratov 27. Smolensk 28. Stalingrad 29. Tambov 30. Tula 31. Ulyanovsk 32. Vladimir 33. Vologda 34. Voronezh 35. Yaroslavl.
AUTONOMOUS OBLASTS: [1] Adygey [2] Karachai-Cherkess. NATIONAL OKRUGS: 1A. Nenets 22A. Komi-Permyak. KRAYS: 1K. Krasnodar 2K. Stavropol. ASSRs: I. Bashkir II. Chechen-Ingush III. Chuvash IV. Dagestan V. Kabardinian-Balkarian VI. Kalmyk VII. Karelian VIII. Komi IX. Mari X. Mordvinian XI. North Ossetian XII. Tatar XIII. Udmurt.

ASIATIC RSFSR: ADMINISTRATIVE-TERRITORIAL MAP

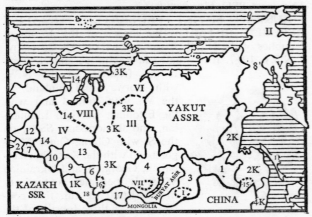

OBLASTS: 1. Amur 2. Chelyabinsk 3. Chita 4. Irkutsk 5. Kamchatka
6. Kemerovo 7. Kurgan 8. Magadan 9. Novosibirsk 10. Omsk 11. Sakhalin 12. Sverdlovsk 13. Tomsk 14. Tyumen. AUTONOMOUS OBLASTS:
15. Jewish 16. Khakass 17. Tuva 18. Gorno-Altay. NATIONAL OKRUGS:
I. Aga Buryat II. Chukchi III. Evenki IV. Khanty-Mansi V. Koryak
VI. Taymyr VII. Ust-Orda Buryat VIII. Yamal-Nenets. KRAYS: 1K. Altay 2K. Khabarovsk 3K. Krasnoyarsk 4K. Maritime.

socialist republics (ASSR): Bashkir, Buryat, Chechen-Ingush, Chuvash, Dagestan, Kabardinian-Balkarian, Kalmyk, Karelian, Komi, Mari, Mordvinian, North Ossetian, Tatar, Udmurt, and Yakut; 6 territories (kray): Altay, Khabarovsk, Krasnodar, Krasnoyarsk, Maritime (Primorsky), and Stavropol; 49 oblasts: Amur, Archangel, Astrakhan, Belgorod, Bryansk, Chelyabinsk, Chita, Gorky, Ivanovo, Irkutsk, Kalinin, Kaliningrad, Kaluga, Kamchatka, Kemerovo, Kirov, Kostroma, Kurgan, Kursk, Kuybyshev, Leningrad, Lipetsk, Magadan, Moscow, Murmansk, Novgorod, Novosibirsk, Omsk, Orel, Orenburg, Penza, Perm, Pskov, Rostov, Ryazan, Sakhalin, Saratov, Smolensk, Stalingrad, Sverdlovsk, Tambov, Tomsk, Tula, Tyumen, Ulyanovsk, Vladimir, Vologda, Voronezh, and Yaroslavl; 6 autonomous oblasts: Adygey, Gorno-Altay, Jewish, Karachai-Cherkess, Khakass, and Tuva; 10 national regions (okrugs): Aga (Aginsky) Buryat, Chukchi, Evenki, Khanty-Mansi, Komi-Permyak, Koryak, Nenets, Taymyr, Ust-Orda Buryat, and Yamal-Nenets.

Moscow, the capital of the USSR, is also the capital of the RSFSR. There are 876 cities in the RSFSR and 1,557 urban-type settlements.

The population of the RFSFR numbers 117.5 millions (1959), consisting of many nationalities, among which the Russians predominate. Population density averages 18.2 per sq. mi. The most densely populated areas are the central, followed by the W. and S. areas of European USSR. In the Asiatic portion of the Republic, the most densely populated areas are in the S. Some of the largest cities of the Republic (and their population according to the census of 1959) are: Moscow (5,046,000), Leningrad (3,321,000), Gorky (942,-000), Novosibirsk (886,000), Kuybyshev (806,000), Sverdlovsk (779,000), Chelyabinsk (689,000), Kazan (647,000), Perm (629,000), Rostov-on-Don (600,000), Stalingrad (592,000), Omsk (581,000), Saratov (581,-000), Ufa (547,000), Voronezh (448,000), Yaroslavl (407,000), Irkutsk (366,000), Tula (316,000). During the succession of five year plans, many new large cities

came into being, among them: Magnitogorsk (311,000), Komsomolsk-on-Amur (177,000), Dzerzhinsk (164,000), Norilsk (108,000), Stalinogorsk (107,000), Magadan (62,000), and others. (See also ECONOMY, INDUSTRY, AGRICULTURE, TRANSPORTATION, HISTORY, LITERATURE, SCIENCE, EDUCATION)   A. B. T.

RUSSIAN STUDIES OUTSIDE THE USSR. The mysteries of Russia have been the subject of fascinated observation and explanation by western travelers and writers for over five centuries, dating back at least to such early first-hand accounts as those of the German diplomat von Herberstein and the English adventurer Chancellor in the 16th century and extending to the spate of contemporary books and press reports by recent western visitors to the Soviet Union. Systematic, scholarly study of Russia, however, began in the West only during the last sixty or eighty years and, on an intensified basis, only since World War II. In Asia, R. studies are a relatively new field of inquiry developing in Japan, India, and Turkey primarily in the past decade.

Before World War I academic study of Russia in W. Europe and the United States was pursued only sporadically, and was focused chiefly in the traditional fields of language and literature, philosophy, and history. The R. revolutions of 1917, the Allied and American intervention in Russia, and the bold challenge to the West of the Soviet system greatly stimulated popular and, to some extent, scholarly interest in Russia. These events also brought to W. Europe and the United States a number of R. scholars. The latter, together with a small group of western scholars, contributed to the slow but steady development of R. studies outside the USSR during the 1920's and 1930's. Several scholarly journals were established, and important monographs were published. In the United States, a Committee on Slavic Studies was appointed in 1938. In England, the School of Slavonic and East European Studies was founded at the University of London by the late Sir Bernard Pares in the 1920's.

World War II provided a powerful impetus to the development of R. studies in W. Europe and especially in the United States. The need for accurate information concerning Russia's performance and intentions, the shortage of well-trained specialists on Russia, and the low level of public understanding of the Soviet system made clear the urgency of extending and improving the West's knowledge of Russia, particularly in the light of the Soviet Union's growing power and emerging influence in world affairs. During the war a significant number of English and American diplomatic and military officials received intensive training in the R. language under government auspices, and in the United States the first R. "area studies" program—an effort to examine together R. history, institutions, culture, and thought-patterns and to view the society as a whole—was established at Cornell University. The handful of specialists on Russia developed before the war did yeoman service staffing the various language and area training programs subsequently supported by the government, as well as fulfilling research, intelligence, and diplomatic functions for various government agencies.

Buttressed by this wartime experience and ever more convinced of the need to expand our knowledge of Russia, a group of American scholars, university administrators, and foundation officials cooperated at the close of the war in the establishment of major university area programs for graduate study of Russia. Staffed by the scholars developed before and during the war, and benefiting from enlightened leadership and an influx of students, area programs undertook the urgent tasks in research and training necessary to provide knowledge about the Soviet Union and to prepare American specialists on Russia. Despite severe handicaps resulting from the virtual closing of the Soviet Union to outsiders between 1947 and 1954 and from the general paucity of data and materials available on the Soviet Union, the area programs provided a solid foundation for a rapid growth of R. studies in the United States in the postwar years.

Between 1946 and 1960 over 600 Americans received one- or two-year training to the master's level in R. studies, including at least a reading command of the R. language. Approximately 100 students obtained doctoral degrees in various disciplines with specialization on Russia. In addition, the area programs educated a considerable number of government officials and foreign students and scholars. Over 75 per cent of the students majored in history, political science, and language and literature, although the overwhelming majority also studied two to five other disciplines as applied to the Soviet Union. Very few students were prepared in such disciplines as geography, sociology, education, philosophy, fine arts, and the history of science, and little training was provided on the non-Russian peoples and cultures of the Soviet Union.

In research, the field of R. studies made substantial strides during the postwar years, both in the United States and W. Europe. At least 150 monographic studies relating to Russia and the Soviet Union were published, a great many more scholarly articles were written, and upwards of a dozen collective works were issued. Important in this effort in the United States were several group or cooperative research projects which drew strength from the interaction of various disciplinary approaches to a given problem, notably the Harvard Refugee Interview Project, the study of Russia in Asia at the University of Washington, and the Research Program on the History of the Communist Party of the Soviet Union. In addition, the contributions of refugee scholars from the Soviet Union were made available through the Research Program on the USSR and the Chekhov Publishing House, and through the American-supported Institute for the Study of the USSR in Munich. Further light on the Soviet Union was shed in unclassified and published research undertaken under contract with the United States government, especially in studies sponsored by the Rand Corporation, in the work and publications of the Human Relations Area Files on the Soviet area, and in research at the Center for International Studies of the Massachusetts Institute of Technology. A comprehensive translation program of Soviet scientific and technical literature is being carried out under the auspices of the National Science Foundation and Office of Technical Information, Department of Commerce.

R. studies in the United States have been greatly assisted by the support of the Carnegie Corporation, the Ford Foundation, and the Rockefeller Foundation, as well as by the major contributions of the universities themselves. In addition, guidance and planning have been provided by the Joint Committee on Slavic Studies, a body of scholars appointed by the American Council of Learned Societies and the Social Science Research Council, whose chairman in 1961 was Professor Abram Bergson of the Department of Economics at Harvard University. This committee, among other things, initiated a program for the reprinting and translating of R. books, has published since 1949 the weekly *Current Digest of the Soviet Press*, and supervised, in 1957–58, an over-all appraisal of the present condition and future direction of R. studies in the United States. One of the important results of this appraisal was the establishment in 1960 of a national professional organization for those engaged in the study of Russia and E. Europe. This body, the American Association for the Advancement of Slavic Studies, Inc. (AAASS), had by the end of 1960 almost 700 members from a variety of academic disciplines. Supported by university contributions and membership dues, the AAASS, whose secretary in 1961 was Professor Ralph Fisher of the Department of History at Illinois University, publishes an expanded quarterly, the *Slavic Review*, formerly the *American Slavic and East European Review*, and a periodic newsletter, and sponsors an annual bibliography of American publications in Slavic studies. It complements such older organizations as the American Association for Teachers of Slavic and East European Languages (AATSEEL) and the subgroups on Russia of the American professional associations in economics, history, literature, and political science.

Between 1955 and 1960 R. studies in the United States received a new impetus, stemming largely from three factors. Beginning in 1954 the Soviet government permitted brief visits to the Soviet Union by Westerners, and four years later the Soviet Union and the United States signed a cultural exchange agreement. As a result, approximately 300 American scholars specializing on Russia visited the Soviet Union for periods of up to ninety days between 1955 and 1960. In addition, in 1958–60 sixty-six American graduate students studied at Moscow and Leningrad universities, and sixty-five Soviet students studied at sixteen American universities. Countries in W. Europe also carried out exchanges and visits with the Soviet Union in this period. These developments greatly stimulated and broadened western training and research respecting Russia. Second, the National Defense Education Act, passed by the United States Congress in 1958, has provided assistance to training and research on Russia. Through 1960, approximately 225 fellowships for study of the R. language and area were awarded under the Act, and 11 Soviet and E. European languages and area centers were established. Finally, between 1955 and 1960 American public concern to know more about Russia grew enormously. In 1960 more than 600 colleges and 500 high schools taught the R. language, a manifold increase since 1955. Many colleges introduced or planned to start courses dealing with various aspects of Soviet history and society. In 1958 4,055 students were studying the Russian language in American public schools while a year later the figure had almost doubled, reaching 7,513 (excluding the schools of Texas). Between 1958 and 1959 the number of college students studying the Russian language jumped from 16,214 to 25,459, an increase of over 50% in one year.

In 1961 R. studies in the United States are a vital, vigorous, and rapidly expanding field. Larger area programs at the universities of California (Berkeley), Columbia, Harvard, Indiana, and Washington are supplemented by new or developing programs at such universities as California (Los Angeles), Chicago, Colorado, Fordham, Illinois, Michigan, Michigan State, Princeton, Stanford, Syracuse, Texas, Wayne, Wisconsin, and Yale. In Canada graduate study of Russia is carried on at the universities of British Columbia, McGill, and Toronto. Major library collections on Russia exist in the United States at the Library of Congress, Columbia, Harvard, the New York Public Library, California, and the Hoover Institution at Stanford. In addition to fellowship programs administered under the National Defense Education Act by the United States Office of Education, financial assistance for students of Russia is available through the national Woodrow Wilson Fellowships and the Foreign Area Training Fellowships of the Ford Foundation, as well as through many of the universities having area programs. Support for post-doctoral visits to Russia or for graduate study there is administered through the Inter-University Committee on Travel Grants, located in 1961 at Indiana University. Grants-in-aid to post-doctoral scholars for research, publications, and conferences are sponsored by the American Council of Learned Societies. Among the major scholarly journals are the recently expanded *Slavic Review*, the *Russian Review*, the *Slavic and East European Journal*, and the more topical *Problems of Communism*.

In W. Europe and Asia, R. studies have not grown as rapidly as in the United States during the postwar years. In England, where the concept of the area program has not been adopted, a major center for research and instruction is the School of Slavonic and East European Studies at the University of London. The study of Russia is also vigorously pursued at the universities of Oxford, Cambridge, Birmingham and, more recently, Glasgow. The British Museum remains one of the greatest R. library collections in the world, and British scholars have contributed some of the most significant and challenging books on Russia published in the postwar period. A team of specialists is grouped around the publication *Soviet Survey*.

On the continent, W. Germany has taken the lead in research and instruction concerning Russia, with important centers of activity in Berlin, Hamburg, Kiel, Mainz, Marburg, Munich, and Stuttgart.

In France, the destruction of several important library collections during the war delayed the revival of R. studies. The main center now is in the Sorbonne, where the area approach has been adopted and where a new generation of young scholars is being created. The old emphasis upon literature is being gradually reduced, and at the same time a new interest in 20th-century and contemporary problems is emerging. Italy, Switzerland, Belgium, Holland, Denmark, and Norway all have a number of important but isolated scholars studying Russia. The Slavic Institute at Uppsala in Sweden has one of the most significant R. programs on the continent, outside of W. Germany.

In Asia, only Japan developed a marked interest in R. studies before World War II. Japan now has approximately fifty scholars interested in Russia, mostly in literature and political science, and often left-wing in political attitude.

Among the leading periodicals published in Canada and W. Europe are the *Canadian Slavonic Papers, Soviet Survey, Est et Ouest, Soviet Affairs, Europe de l'Est et Union Soviétique, Revue des Etudes Slaves, Osteuropa, Jahrbücher für Geschichte Osteuropas, Die Slavische Rundschau, Die Welt der Slaven, Slavonic and European Review*, and *Soviet Studies*.

BIBLIOGRAPHY: Harold H. Fisher, ed., *American Research on Russia*, Bloomington, Ind., 1959; Cyril E. Black and John M. Thompson, eds., *American Teaching About Russia*, Bloomington, Ind., 1959; "An Appraisal of Russian Studies in the United States," *American Slavic and East European Review*, October, 1959; Henry L. Roberts, "Exchanging Scholars with the Soviet Union," Columbia University *Forum*, Spring, 1958. J. M. T.

RUSSIANS ABROAD. While R. expatriate groups existed long before the First World War both in Europe and in the United States, the social identity of the immigrants changed drastically since 1918. Before the revolution of 1917 Paris, London, and Geneva were the principal centers where the old-time revolutionaries struggling against the tsarist regime found a haven. The *émigrés* who had made their home in Europe left Russia for purely political reasons. The emigration toward America, since the early 19th century, was prompted rather by personal, human, economic, and social factors. A great many emigrants were poor peasants from the outlying regions of W. Russia who had looked to the New World in quest of a better life. Along with them came hundreds of thousands of R. and Polish Jews fleeing from the pogroms of 1903–1905.

The exodus from Russia, halted by the outbreak of war in 1914, resumed with renewed vigor immediately after the October revolution. The flight from communism, civil strife, and starvation took on mass proportions as White army troops were routed on the battle fronts of the civil war. The last step following the crushing defeat of the White army was the evacuation of the Crimea in 1920. On Nov. 19, 1920, 126 R. ships, of the navy and merchant marine fleet, carrying General Wrangel's troops and civilian refugees from Southern Russia, 150,000 persons all told, arrived in Istanbul. Another refugee wave followed the retreating troops of Admiral Kolchak, settling down in Shanghai, Kharbin, and Tientsin. Some of these refugees later on made their way to the United States, where they took up residence on the W. coast, largely in San Francisco. To this mass of voluntary escapees should be added the native R. population of Poland, Latvia, Estonia, and Lithuania.

The Istanbul Stage. Istanbul was the first stage of the R. refugee peregrination. Close to 60,000 officers and men of General Wrangel's army were shipped to military camps in Gallipoli and on the island of Lemnos. Thirty R. ships carrying refugees were dispatched to Bizerte by the Allied Command.

The White Army Command at that time was convinced that the downfall of the Bolshevik rule was imminent and that the army must be kept in battle trim for the sake of future Russia. It soon became evident, however, that R. military forces could not indefinitely remain on foreign territory. Thus began an organized migration to the Balkan States. Young refugees eager to complete their education went on to Czechoslovakia. The last of the R. refugees remaining in Istanbul started on their way, individually and in groups, hoping to reach Paris or Berlin. Several thousand Russians looking for work came to the United States in 1923.

In Yugoslavia the Russians found a sponsor in the person of King Alexander. The government of Czechoslovakia, at the suggestion of President Masaryk, instituted the so-called "Russian action" designed to provide higher education to 3,000 students, the State Treasury footing the bill. Prof. P. I. Novgorodtsev founded a Russian Law School in Prague. In the same city were established the Russian Historic Archives, a unique collection of documents, *émigré* periodicals, and so forth.

The actual number of refugees was never accurately estimated, but there is little doubt that during the 1920–1930 decade the population of "Refugee Russia" numbered several hundred thousand men, including the holders of Nansen's passports and the "stateless" Russians. The American writer W. Chapin-Huntington, in his book *Russia out of Russia,* speaks of a million men as a probable figure. The refugee ranks were continually swelled through the influx of escapees who had managed to cross the Soviet border illegally. During the period of the New Economic Policy many Russians were given an opportunity to leave the country legitimately—among these, the natives of Poland and the Baltic States. In 1922 a group of leading intellectuals was exiled from Russia by the Soviet government, including such prominent men as S. N. Prokopovich, Ye. D. Kuskova, N. A. Berdyayev, Rev. Sergy Bulgakov, G. P. Vysheslavtsev, I. A. Ilyin, N. O. Lossky, F. A. Stepun, S. L. Frank, A. A. Kizevetter, M. A. Osorgin, and others.

Between 1920 and 1930 Berlin was a major R. refugee center, where close to 50 R. publishing houses were active, and two large dailies were issued regularly, *Rul* (*The Rudder*) under the editorship of I. V. Hessen and V. D. Nabokov, and *Dni* (*Our Days*), a Socialist Revolutionary paper edited by A. F. Kerensky.

Paris. Beginning with the mid-twenties and up to World War II Paris had been the undisputed center of "Russia outside Russia." As early as 1921 a National Congress was held in Paris which brought together the moderate and the rightist R. political groups; subsequently a National Committee was founded, pre-

sided over by A. V. Kartashev. The liberals and the Constitutional Democrats (Kadets) were represented by Paul N. Milyukov's United Democratic Republicans. Equally active were the monarchists, following the line adopted by the Grand Duke Kirill Vladimirovich who had proclaimed himself "custodian" of the R. throne. The Supreme Monarchist Council was headed by Markov II and P. Skarzhinsky. Among the prominent Socialist Revolutionaries residing in Paris were A. F. Kerensky, N. D. Avksentyev, O. S. Minor, V. Chernov, M. V. Vishniak, V. M. Zenzinov; the Paris colony included also a Menshevik group led by F. I. Dan, R. A. Abramovich, and B. I. Nikolayevsky; and the People's Socialist group was represented by S. P. Melgunov, V. Myakotin, and M. A. Aldanov.

The largest military organization was the Russian Servicemen Union (*Obshchevoinsky Soyuz*) formed by ex-soldiers of the White armies. Close to forty military associations had been founded, in which officers who had served in the same regiment, or graduates of the same military schools, were united. It can hardly be doubted that the existence of this "extraterritorial" army was a matter of grave concern to the Soviet government, which planted its own undercover men in these organizations and kept them under close surveillance. As a result of the work of the double spies, General Kutepov, head of the Russian Servicemen Union, was kidnapped in broad daylight from a Paris street, in Jan. 1930. Seven years later, on Sept. 22, 1937, his successor, General E. K. Miller, became the victim of a similar Soviet plot. He was lured into a trap by his closest associate, General Skoblin, who turned out to be an agent of the Soviets. Skoblin disappeared, but his wife, the popular singer Nadezhda Plevitskaya, was brought to trial and sentenced. Another victim of Communist duplicity was the former Socialist Revolutionary Boris Savinkov. Duped by the provocateurs, he went to Moscow, where he was promptly incarcerated, and allegedly "committed suicide" shortly thereafter. V. V. Shulgin, the noted monarchist, made a "secret" trip to the USSR, and came back safe and sound. It was disclosed at a later date that the entire journey had been prearranged by the GPU (Soviet security police).

In 1923 the first congress of Russian monarchist youth abroad was held in Munich. The result was the emergence of a Young-Russian Youth movement (*Mladorosy*) led by A. L. Kazem Bek, whose catchwords were both "The Tsar" and "The Soviets." In Sept. 1939, the Russian Youth League, infiltrated by Soviet agents, was disbanded by order of the French Home Office. Kazem Bek departed for the United States. In 1957 the former "leader" of the young R. patriots left the country secretly to go back to the Soviet Union.

In addition to political groupings, there were numerous public and purely professional organizations existing in Paris and in other large *émigré* centers. Among these may be mentioned the Association of the Zemstvo and Municipal Workers, Russian Red Cross, associations of Russian writers and journalists; physicians', engineers', and lawyers' societies; students' leagues, and so on. Legal defense of refugees' rights was taken up by the Ambassadors' Council headed by V. N. Kokovtsov. After his death the legal work was carried on by the Refugee Committee and its head, V. A. Maklakov. The Committee actually performed consular functions inasmuch as it issued the necessary documents, and the like.

In France certain occupations became specifically associated with the Russians. At one time there were 3,000 Russian taxi drivers, mostly ex-army officers, registered in Paris. Thousands of Russians worked at the Renault automobile plant in the suburbs of Paris. The women found work in the fashion trades. An inner drive toward the land led to gradual resettlement of the Russians in the country, especially in the farming districts near Nice and Toulouse.

Russian Refugees and DP's in World War II. During the Second World War some of the *émigrés,* primarily the extreme Right-wingers, stayed where they were and during the occupation made an attempt to collaborate with the Germans. From the ranks of such "collaborationists" Hitler's Military Administration recruited interpreters for the occupied zones, informers for the Gestapo, and staff writers for the Nazi newspapers published in Russian—*Parizhsky Vestnik* (*The Paris Herald*) and *Novoye Slovo* (*The New World*) published in Berlin.

Other *émigrés* took the patriotic defensist stand, being convinced that at a time when Russia is attacked by the enemy, all forces must unite for the defense of the mother country. Such was the position shared not only by liberals of the type of P. N. Milyukov or V. A. Maklakov but by the former head of the White armies General Denikin as well. A number of R. *émigrés* took an active part in the Resistance movement against the Germans.

During the first few months of "Blitzkrieg" on the E. front ca. two million Soviet soldiers—officers and privates—had been taken prisoner by the Germans. Beginning with 1942 the German Headquarters used these men in forming a "Russian Army of Liberation" under the command of General Vlasov. Toward the end of the war there were over a million Soviet citizens scattered through Europe, including General Vlasov's men, and the *Ostarbeiter* deported by the Germans from Russia for compulsory labor. According to the Yalta Agreement, the former Soviet citizens were to be repatriated following termination of the war; as a result of this agreement, many thousands of "recent" refugees were forcibly handed over to the Soviet Repatriation Commission by the Allies.

The Second World War marks the emergence of new political groups, such as the "Solidarists," with a center at Munich, where *Grani* (*The Ultimate Boundaries*), *Posev* (*The Planting of the Seed*), *Mosty* (*The Bridging Over*), and other periodicals are published. The city harbors a Russian Scientific Institute and Radio Liberty —a broadcasting station sponsored by the American Committee of Liberation. General Vlasov's followers formed a "League for the Liberation of the Peoples of Russia" (SBONR).

After the Second World War the center of Russian *émigrés*' activities was transferred from Paris to New York, where a number of political and other organizations have been in existence. Most prominent among these are the Writers' Fund (*Literaturny Fond*) dating from 1920, the ROOV (Mutual Aid Fraternity) with a membership of over 3,000 Russian-Americans, and others. On the political scene, the refugee activities have been on the wane in the postwar period, though an attempt to integrate the Right-wing circles was made in 1959 by Prince S. S. Beloselsky, the author of a project envisioning the creation of a central agency representing the R. refugees in the U.S.

By 1960 the overwhelming majority of "recent," i.e. postwar, expatriates residing in W. Europe or in the United States have gained a measure of financial security. Those who could not find work in their special fields learned new trades. Fifteen years after the end of the war the handful of Russians still remaining in the refugee camps of Europe (Germany and Austria) are for the most part the aged, the invalids, and the chronically ill.

The Russian Press Abroad. The most influential and widely read daily newspaper published abroad was *Poslednie Novosti* (*The Latest News*), in Paris of which Prof. P. N. Milyukov had been editor-in-chief since 1921. The publication had ceased to exist two days before Paris was occupied by the Germans, in June 1940. Despite the fact that the general tenor of the paper leaned farther to the left than the political sentiments of the majority of its readers, *Poslednie Novosti* continued to grow both in influence and in circulation. In 1925 a rival R. daily *Vozrozhdenie* (*The Renaissance*) was started in Paris. Financial difficulties were responsible for the demise of such publications as *Obshcheye Delo* (*Our Common Cause*) of V. L. Burtsev, the Socialist Revolutionary organ *Dni* (*Our Days*), *Rossiya i Slavyanstvo* (*Russia and Slavdom*) founded by P. B. Struve.

Beginning with 1920 and up to the time of German occupation several quarterly and monthly publications appeared regularly in Paris; foremost among them was the journal *Sovremennye Zapiski* (*Contemporary Notes*) edited by M. V. Vishniak, A. I. Gukovsky, V. V. Rudnev, N. D. Avksentyev, and I. I. Fondaminsky. While members of the editorial board were Socialist Revolutionaries to a man, the publication became the rallying point for writers and publicists of every political creed and had played an essential part in the cultural life of the refugees. After the war, when the political center of the *émigrés* was shifted to the United States, another publication, *Novy Zhurnal* (*The New Review*), under the editorship of Prof. M. M. Karpovich, was started in New York. Among the monthly publications the best known and oldest is *Sotsialistichesky Vestnik* (*Socialist Courier*) founded in 1920 in Berlin by the Menshevik leader Yu. O. Martov, presently edited by R. A. Abramovich.

Other journals published abroad during the period between the two wars should be mentioned: *Russkaya Mysl* (*Russian Thought*) edited by P. B. Struve; the Socialist Revolutionary organ *Volya Rossii* (*Russia's Will*); M. P. Mironov's *Illustrirovannaya Rossia* (*Russia Illustrated*), and so forth. Of the larger dailies, *Se-*

vodnya (*Today*) appeared in Riga; *Za Svobodu* (*For Freedom*), in Warsaw. In Belgrade the monarchist paper *Novoye Vremya* (*The New Time*) was published under the editorship of M. A. Suvorin. There were several R. dailies published in Kharbin and Shanghai.

The oldest R. daily abroad, *Novoye Russkoye Slovo* (*The New Russian Word*), published in New York by M. Ye. Weinbaum and V. I. Shimkin, celebrated its fiftieth anniversary in April 1960. In the same year there were two more R. dailies published in New York, the monarchist publication *Rossiya* (*Russia*) and the pro-Soviet *Russky Golos* (*The Russian Voice*). San Francisco has two daily newspapers, *Novaya Zarya* (*The New Dawn*) and *Russkaya Zhizn* (*Russian Life*). In postwar Paris two R. publications came into existence: *Russkaya Mysl* (*Russian Thought*) edited by S. Vodov; and the pro-Soviet weekly paper *Russkie Novosti* (*Russian News*). In Germany a Soviet publication *Za Vozvrashchenie na Rodinu* (*Back to Motherland*) was started by General Mikhaylov, Chairman of the Committee for Repatriation, and as a result of this propaganda a number of refugees went back to the USSR.

Educational and Cultural Activities. Russian universities, institutes, and elementary, secondary, and technical schools have been organized in Paris. Back in 1920 a Russian High School was founded which is still in existence; a year later the People's University was established, and in 1925, the School of Business Administration. The following year marks the opening of the Russian Technical Institute; and the Russian Theological Seminary dates from 1924. In the field of musical education, there is the Rachmaninoff Conservatoire. During the first decade in exile over 7,000 young refugees in various countries were awarded university diplomas. Worthy of mention are the numerous primary and parish schools where children are taught the R. language and history, and receive religious instruction. Summer camps for youngsters have been built by the Boy Scouts, the Russian Christian Movement, the St. Vladimir Youth, and similar organizations. According to a report by the Russian Scientific Institute in Belgrade, there were, in 1930, 472 scientists, 140 university professors, and 327 research men working abroad, who had published a total of 7,088 studies in their respective fields.

In France S. N. Vinogradsky, D. P. Ryabushinsky, and K. N. Davydov were elected to the Academy of Sciences; B. Unbegaun became a member of Brussels and German Academies; in Rome the Academy of Sciences elected B. Shmurlo. B. Yu. Pregel was President of New York Academy of Sciences in 1958. Among the prominent persons working abroad the following must be mentioned: in the field of theology, S. N. Bulgakov, A. V. Kartashev, Metropolitan Antoniy, N. S. Arsenyev, Rev. A. Shmeman, G. P. Fedotov; in philosophy, N. A. Berdyayev, Lev Shestov, N. O. Lossky, B. P. Vysheslavtsev, S. L. Frank, L. P. Karsavin; historians, Sir Paul Vinogradoff, B. Shmurlo, P. N. Milyukov, M. I. Rostovtsev, G. F. Vernadsky, M. T. Florinsky, M. M. Karpovich, P. B. Struve, B. E. Nolde, S. P. Melgunov, D. Dallin; in the history of

art, academician N. P. Kondakov, G. Lukomsky, A. N. Benois, P. Muratov; philologists and literary critics, G. Losinsky, M. Hoffman, B. Schlezer, V. Khodasevich, G. Adamovich, R. O. Yacobson, Mark Slonim, Gleb Struve; in sociology and economics, P. Vinogradov, M. V. Bernadsky, N. S. Timashev, Pitirim Sorokin.

In other fields the following should be mentioned: D. P. Ryabushinsky, an authority on aerodynamics; V. A. Bakhmetev, the hydraulics expert; the chemists V. N. Ipatyev and A. E. Chichibabin; Prof. V. Zvorykin, the father of television; the airplane designers Sikorsky and Seversky; and V. N. Yurkevich, designer of ships. Research work in the Mechnikov tradition was carried on at the Pasteur Institute in Paris by S. I. Metalnikov, S. N. Vinogradsky, and L. Kepinov. Among the other notables who are members of the Ac. of S. are K. N. Davydov, the zoologist; Prof. M. M. Novikov, former President of Moscow University; Andrusov and Agafonov, zoologists. In the United States Prof. Kistyakovsky has served President Eisenhower as special adviser on scientific matters.

Among the expatriates were many outstanding writers of the older generation: I. A. Bunin, academician, recipient of the Nobel prize in literature; D. S. Merezhkovsky, Z. Hippius, F. A. Stepun, M. A. Osorgin, B. K. Zaytsev, I. S. Shmelev, A. I. Kuprin, Count A. N. Tolstoy, A. I. Remizov, A. B. Amfiteatrov, M. A. Aldanov, Leonid Andreyev, Semyon Yushkevich, R. B. Goul, N. A. Teffi, Arkady Averchenko, and Don Aminado. Two of these writers, Tolstoy and Kuprin, went back to Russia. Among the noted poets were K. D. Balmont, Marina Tsvetayeva, and V. F. Khodasevich.

The Creative Arts. The political influence of R. *émigrés* upon the world had been rather limited, whereas in the fields of science, literature, and art, in particular, the penetration into foreign environment proved quite extensive. The writings of R. authors have been translated into many languages. Some of the younger *émigré* writers are now celebrated literary masters of France—among these are the recipients of the *Prix Goncourt*, Joseph Kessel, R. Gary, and Henri Troyat (Tarasov). Another *émigré* author, Sirin, has written a number of novels in English, using his real name Vladimir Nabokov, which brought him wide renown both in the United States and in Europe.

The ballet shows produced by S. P. Diaghilev, an expatriate since 1918, created a revolution in choreography, bringing world fame to such artists as Anna Pavlova, Nijinsky, Karsavina, Fokine, and Sergey Lifar. Diaghilev's influence was felt not only in ballet interpretations but also in designing theatrical scenery and stage settings. His collaborators in this field were such noted masters as A. N. Benois, Dobuzhinsky, Sudeykin, Bilibin, and Korovin. *The Bat*, a theater of miniature skits created by N. F. Balieff, brought to the W. world the vivid colors and earthy humor of R. folk art, in a series of strikingly original stage productions.

F. I. Chaliapin, an expatriate since 1921, worked and died abroad. Of the composers, Prokofiev alone went back to the Soviet Union. Stravinsky has become an American citizen; S. V. Rachmaninoff, A. K. Glazunov, and A. T. Grechaninoff died abroad. A few artists—Bilibin, Shukhayev, the noted sculptor Konenkov—may be named among the "returnees," but Marc Chagal, Chaim Soutine, A. Yakovlev, Sudeykin, Naum Aronson, and many others remained in their adopted countries.

In the world of music Vladimir Horowitz, the pianist, Nathan Milstein, the violinist, Gregor Piatigorsky, the cellist, have won universal acclaim; S. A. Koussevitzky had been the conductor of the Boston Symphony Orchestra for two decades. The roster of Russian-born artists could be considerably expanded, except that some of them—for instance, Jascha Heifetz or Mischa Elman—can scarcely be expected to identify themselves with the expatriate group.

Less satisfactory was the situation in the realm of dramatic art. Only the so-called Prague group, which had split off from the Moscow Art Theatre during one of its trips abroad, remained in existence for several years. In this group were V. I. Kachalov, who later returned to the USSR, M. N. Hermanova, M. Chekhov, Gr. Chmara, and Akim Tamirov. A permanent theater existed in Riga (Russian Dramatic Theater). A few R. performers such as the film actor Ivan Mozzhukhin, the popular singer Alexander Vertinsky (later returned to the Soviet Union), and others rose to considerable prominence in their particular fields.

The Church. From the first days in exile the majority of R. refugees rallied around the Church as their spiritual center. In the 20's the head of West-European Eparchy was Metropolitan Yevlogiy. With his blessing parishes were organized, and houses of worship erected. The Russian Orthodox Church abroad is divided into three spheres of ecclesiastic jurisdiction. The so-called "patriarchal" Church, both in Europe and in the United States, is distinct from the others, being under the canonic authority of the Patriarch in Moscow. The West-European Eparchy, headed until 1959 by Metropolitan Vladimir, is under the canonic jurisdiction of the Patriarch in Istanbul. In a number of countries the Russian Church came under the influence of the "Orthodox Synod Abroad" established at Sermski Karlovtsy in Yugoslavia by Metropolitan Antoniy, in 1920.

In 1924 the Fourth All-American Church Council in Detroit declared the "autonomy" of the Russian Orthodox Church in America, conferring upon Archbishop Platon the title of "Metropolitan for All Americas and Canada." Some of the parishes came under the canonic authority of the Orthodox Synod Abroad founded by Metropolitan Antoniy. In 1935 the new "Metropolitan for All Americas" Feofil went to Yugoslavia, where a reconciliation with the Orthodox Synod Abroad was effected. Archbishop Vitaliy, representing the Synod, came to the United States to carry on his missionary work. The reconciliation proved a short-lived one. The Seventh Ecclesiastic Council convening at Cleveland in 1946 resolved that all relations with the Orthodox Synod Abroad must be broken off, and that the Moscow Patriarch Aleksiy must be recognized as the spiritual head of the Orthodox Church in America, with a stipulation that the American Church will remain independent in administrative matters.

The resolution adopted by the Cleveland Council has never materialized, nor were the ties with the Patriarch in Moscow ever restored. In 1960 four major spheres of ecclesiastic jurisdiction were in existence: The West-European Eparchy (under the authority of the Patriarch in Istanbul); the North-American Metropoly administered by Metropolitan Leontiy, comprising 350 parishes; the church domain under the jurisdiction of the Orthodox Synod Abroad (renamed "The Orthodox Church Abroad"), with 300 parishes; and a relatively small number of parishes under the jurisdiction of the Patriarch in Moscow.   A. S.

"RÚSSKAYA PRÁVDA" ("Russian Truth"), laws of Kievan Russia codified in the 11th and 12th centuries. Based on common law, court practice, and legislative acts promulgated by the rulers of various principalities, this ancient code (the "short," "expanded," and "abridged" versions) provided the basis of later legislation of medieval Russia.

RUSSO-JAPANESE WAR, 1904–5. Japanese expansionism and Russo-Japanese rivalry in Manchuria and Korea helped to bring war between the two countries. The war began with the surprise Japanese attack on R. ships at Port Arthur and Chemulpo, Feb. 8, 1904. The Russians at first underrated their opponents, and the strength of their war effort suffered accordingly. Port Arthur fell to the Japanese after a 148-day siege, Dec. 19, 1904. The main Manchurian campaign, involving great numbers of troops, culminated in the staggering defeat of the Russians under General A. N. Kuropatkin at Mukden, late in Feb. 1905. Almost 90,000 Russians were lost, although the army as a whole survived.

At sea, a R. fleet attempting to break out of Port Arthur was obliterated by the Japanese, Aug. 10, 1904. A similar fate awaited the R. Baltic fleet when, after its departure in Oct. 1904 en route to Vladivostok, it reached the Straits of Tsushima (May 27, 1905). The Japanese sank sixteen of Admiral Z. P. Rozhestvensky's ships, captured five others, and allowed only three to reach Vladivostok. The defeat inclined Russia to make peace. In the Treaty of Portsmouth, New Hampshire, Sept. 5, 1905, Russia acknowledged Japan's primacy in Korea, while ceding to Japan S. Sakhalin together with the lease of the Liaotung Peninsula (including Port Arthur and Talienwan), the Kurile Islands and a portion of the S. Manchuria Railway. Both powers promised to evacuate Manchuria and restore China's exclusive administration there.

RUSTÁVI, city in Georgian SSR; pop. 62,000 (1959). A recently developed, rapidly growing mfg. town of major importance, lying astride the Kura River; the center of the steel ind. in Transcaucasia.

RUTULS: *see* POPULATION.

RÚZSKY, Nikoláy Vladímirovich (1854–1918), tsarist general. During World War I, he was commander of the third army in the battle of Galicia; directed the critically important Lodz operation on the northwestern front. In March 1917 at his headquarters in Pskov Nicholas II signed his abdication. In Oct. 1918 R was shot by the Bolsheviks, together with other generals and high officials.

RYÁBUSHKIN, Andréy Petróvich (1861–1904), historical genre painter. Painted pictures of R. daily life of the past with striking colors and keen sense of composition. His best works are:*They Are Coming, Moscow Women and Girls of the 17th Century at Church, Tea Drinking, The Village.* K is regarded as an outstanding representative of R. realism.

RYAZÁN, city, adm. center of Ryazan Oblast, on the right bank of the Oka; pop. 214,000 (1959). Manufactures farm implements and machinery; lighting fixtures; footwear and clothing; textile and leather goods; wooden products. Founded 1094.

RYAZÁN, GRAND DUCHY OF, principality situated along the middle Oka and upper Don, with a capital at the old town of Ryazan, later at Pereyaslavl-Ryazansky (now Ryazan city). It dates from the early 12th century; was devastated by the Mongol-Tatar hordes invading Russia in 1237; came under Moscow domination in the 15th century; and annexed to Great Russia in 1520.

RYAZÁN OBLAST, Central RSFSR; area 15,300 sq. mi.; pop. 1,445,000 (1959). Cities: Ryazan (adm. center), Ryazhsk, Kasimov, Sasovo. The mixed forests, lakes, and swamps of Meshchera depression, N. of Oka River, are replaced by fertile Oka–Don plain and wooded steppe upon E. outliers of the Central R. plateau farther S. Dairy and poultry farming are essential; breeding of livestock is based on fodder crops of Oka flood plain; hog-raising in the N. is supported by potato-growing on poor podsols; wheat, rye, millet are cultivated on gray and black-earth soils in the S.; large acreage sown with flax, hemp, tobacco. There are peat, lignite and iron deposits. Ind.: machine building, metal and wood working, leather, textiles. Est. 1937.

RYAZÁNOV (Goldendakh), **Davíd Borísovich** (1870–1938), Marxist theorist and founder of the Marx-Engels Institute. Born in Odessa where he joined the revolutionary movement in 1890. One of the organizers of the R. trade unions in 1906–07, R formed a close friendship with Trotsky in 1908 and joined the Bolsheviks in July 1917. His opposition to the NEP cost R his trade-union post. His undisguised contempt for Stalin brought accusations of Menshevik sympathies and expulsion from the party. He disappeared from public life, dying in exile. R was considered the foremost Russian and international expert on Marxism. As such he edited the journal *Annals of Marxism* and wrote a number of books.

RYBÁCHY PENINSULA, N.W. extremity of USSR in Barents Sea N. of Murmansk. Industries include herring fishery and cod-liver oil.

RYBÁLKO, Pável Semyónovich (1894–1948), marshal of the Tank Corps. He joined the CP in 1919 and during World War II held high military positions. He is credited with the liberation of Prague.

RÝBINSK (f. Shcherbakov), city in Yaroslavl Oblast, RSFSR; pop. 182,000 (1959). It is an important rail town and inland port at the junction of Volga and a recently completed reservoir; a center of lumbering, shipbuilding and machinery (printing, road-building), match mfg. First mentioned 1137.

RÝBINSK RESERVOIR, in N. central RSFSR, mostly in Yaroslavl Oblast between Mologa and Sheksna rivers; formed from dam on upper Volga; 1,750 sq. mi.

RYKÁLIN, Nikoláy Nikoláyevich (1903–), welding engineer. Corresponding member, Ac. of S., USSR (1953). Gradute of the Far-Eastern University in Vladivostok (1929). Associated with the Far-Eastern Polytechnic Institute (1930–36), Moscow School of Technology (1937–53), Institute of Mechanical Engineering and Department of Electric Welding and Electrothermal Technology (1939–53), and Metallurgical Institute (since 1953). Research on methods of calculating thermal processes during welding.

RÝKOV, Alekséy Ivánovich (1881–1938), prominent Bolshevik party and state leader. Born in Saratov into a peasant family, R became a member of the first Bolshevik Central Committee. Was arrested several times and left Russia in 1910. Returning in 1914, he was again arrested but escaped. One of the leaders of the  Bolsheviks in Moscow, R was known as a moderate in 1917, advocating a coalition government of Bolsheviks, Mensheviks, and other socialist parties. After the revolution, R became commissar of the interior, one of the most powerful positions in the government. Subsequently he headed the Supreme Council of the National Economy, playing a major role in the implementation of NEP. Concurrently he held high posts in the Central Committee and the Politburo.

In 1924, R, by then a prominent contender for power, assumed Lenin's post as chairman of the Council of People's Commissars. Lacking Lenin's prestige and influence, he became a secondary figure in the intra-party struggle. As one of the leaders of the "rightist" group, he allied with Stalin against Trotsky. After the latter's defeat, R and his colleague Bukharin were attacked by Stalin as "rightist deviators" and removed from their high posts. In 1931, R recanted his opposition to Stalin and was restored to favor, but only after public humiliation at the 17th Party Congress. Nevertheless, the congress made him a candidate member of the Central Committee. In 1938, together with Bukharin, he was tried and executed on the charge of treason.

RYLÉYEV, Kondráty Fyódorovich (1795–1826), poet and a leader of the Decemberist movement. Born in the family of an army officer, R, too, became an officer and served in units stationed in W. Europe after the defeat of Napoleon's armies. Upon returning to St. Petersburg he became active in a variety of social and political circles, and in 1823 joined the secret Northern Society, whose objective was to bring an end to the traditional form of the monarchy through revolutionary means. He played a leading role in organizing the mutiny of the military units in St. Petersburg that occurred on Dec. 14, 1825 (O.S.). Following his arrest he was tried and executed. With the exception of his earliest works R's poems are romantic in style. Their themes reflect his patriotic sentiments and his concern with the course of R. history.

RÝNDIN, Vadím Fyódorovich (1902–), stage designer. Originally a "constructivist," he first worked with the Bolshoy and Moscow Kamerny theaters (1919–34). Thereafter he designed stage settings for several theaters, including the Moscow Art Theater. Among his productions are *Much Ado About Nothing* (1936) and Gorky's *Dostigayev* (1938). In 1953 R became chief stage designer for the Academic Bolshoy Theater, Moscow.

RYÚRIK—according to legend—a Varangian (Scandinavian) prince who came to Great Novgorod in 862 with his brothers Truvor and Sineus, at the head of a small army of Norsemen, and settled in the country. The subsequent rulers of Kievan Russia are traditionally referred to by historians as "Ryurikovichi" (the Descendants of Ryurik).

RZHEV, city in Kalinin Oblast, Central RSFSR; pop. 46,600 (1959). R.R. junction, on both banks of the Volga; has flax retting and linen-processing mills, foundries, brickyards, prefabricated houses, and other ind. Dates from the 11th century.

S

SAAREMAA: *see* SAREMA ISLAND.

SABSÁY, Pinkhos Vladímirovich (1893–), sculptor, member, Ac. of Fine Arts (1947). A realist, he has specialized in portraits and monuments. He first achieved prominence with his sculpture of the Baku commissars (1928). Notable are his monument of S. M. Kirov and, since World War II, statues and busts of Lenin. Stalin prize (1942).

SABÚROV, Maksím Zakhárovich (1900–), Soviet engineer and planner, party and state official, graduate  of Moscow Bauman Machine-building Institute and the Communist University. S was born in a worker's family in Donbas and joined the CPSU in 1920. In the thirties, he held executive positions in Soviet industrial management. In 1938, he was deputy chairman of the State Planning Commission and, in 1941–44, deputy chairman of the Council of People's Commissars; in 1947, deputy chairman of the Council of Ministers of the USSR; and in 1949, upon Voznesensky's removal, chairman of the State Planning Commission. In 1952, S was elected member of the Presidium of the Central Committee of the CPSU and in 1955, first deputy chairman of the Council of Ministers and head of the State Economic Commission. In 1957, S was implicated in the "anti-party" activity of the Molotov-Kaganovich-Malenkov group and was dropped from the Presidium and removed as first deputy chairman of the Council of Ministers. In 1957 he was appointed deputy chairman of the State Committee for Foreign Relations.

SADÓVSKY, Mikhaíl Próvych (1847–1910), actor, son of P. M. Sadovsky whose traditions he continued. Among his famous parts were: Shchastlivtsev and Karandyshev in Ostrovsky's *The Forest* and *The Dowerless*; and Khlestakov in Gogol's *The Inspector-General*.

SADÓVSKY, Ólga Ósipovna (1850–1919), actress. Wife of M. P. Sadovsky, she joined the company of the Maly Theater in 1881. A master of elocution and a favorite of Ostrovsky, S gave memorable interpretations in *The Forest, Guilty though Guiltless,* and in L. Tolstoy's *The Power of Darkness*, where she played the part of Matrena.

SADÓVSKY, Prov Mikháylovich (1818–1872), actor. Gained recognition as interpreter of A. N. Ostrovsky's plays at the Moscow Maly Theater. His greatest successes were scored in *It's a Family Affair, The Storm,* and *A Profitable Place.*

SADÓVSKY, Prov Mikháylovich (1874–1934), actor and producer, son of M. P. and O. O. Sadovsky, People's Artist, USSR. Began his career with the Maly Theater in 1895. Appeared in plays by Schiller, Shakespeare, Griboyedov, Ostrovsky, and others. Among his productions were: Ostrovsky's *The Snow Maiden* and *The Busy Place* and Griboyedov's *The Misfortune of Being Wise.*

SADÓVSKY, Yelizavéta Mikháylovna (1870–1934), daughter of M. P. and O. O. Sadovsky. Joined the Maly Theater in 1894.

SAFÓNOV, Vasíly Ilyích (1852–1918), pianist, conductor, and teacher. In 1880 S made his debut with the Imperial Russian Music Society in St. Petersburg. From 1889 to 1905 he was director of the Moscow Conservatoire. S was the first R. conductor to dispense with the baton. He appeared as guest conductor with the leading orchestras in Europe and in the United States, where he won acclaim. On his return to Russia he was appointed conductor at the Imperial Russian Music Society in St. Petersburg.

SAKHALÍN ISLAND, in W. Sea of Okhotsk between USSR and Japan; area 29,500 sq. mi.; pop. 420,000: Russians, Evenki. Mountainous and lacking good harbors, but wealthy in fish, oil, coal, and forest. Annexed in 1875; southern portion ceded to Japan 1905; reannexed by R. 1945.

SAKHALÍN OBLAST, Far E., RSFSR; area 33,650 sq. mi.; pop. 649,000 (1959). Cities: Yuzhno-Sakhalinsk (adm. center), Aleksandrovsk, Okha. Separated from Soviet mainland by Tatar Strait, Sakhalin is washed by Sea of Japan and Sea of Okhotsk. Inclement climate and rugged terrain restrict the scope of agriculture, but dairy farming, sugar beets, leguminous and fodder crops are important. Main ind.: coal, petroleum, lumber; extensive commercial fishing; shipbuilding, pulp and paper milling centered in the S. Est. 1932.

SAKI, Crimean resort town; pop. 16,100 (1956). Salt lake, mud baths.

SAKMÁRA RIVER, flows from Ural Mountains S. and W. through Bashkir ASSR to form branch of Ural River; 435 mi. long.

SAL RIVER, flows through Rostov steppe into Don River; 500 mi. long.

SALAÍR RIDGE, a mountain range N. of Altay; altitude up to 2,000 ft.; rich in gold and other mineral resources.

SALAVÁT, city in Bashkir ASSR, on Belaya River; pop. 61,000 (1959). A new city, founded in 1949 as a petroleum-industry center; machine building, auto-repair shops.

SALEKHÁRD, (f. Obdórsk), city, adm. center of Yamal-Nenets National Okrug, W. Siberia, RSFSR; pop. 22,000 (1959). It is a river port at the confluence of the Poluy and Ob; has large fish-canning, boat-building and repair ind.; several higher technical institutes.

SALSK, city in Rostov Oblast, RSFSR; pop. 35,700 (1959). R.R. center and food products.

SALTYKÓV, Fyódor Stepánovich (died in 1715), aide of Peter the Great, and Russia's naval envoy in London. At one time, he was head of the nascent ship-building industry; advocate of enlightenment; and author of numerous projects aimed at the development of industry and trade.

SALTYKÓV, Mikhaíl Yevgráfovich (1826–1889), novelist, pen-name Shchedrin, best known for satirical sketches of the life of the upper classes in provincial Russia. Born in a family of the gentry, S attended an aristocratic school at Tsarskoye Selo and in 1844 entered the civil service. Close association with members  of the Petrashevsky group (q.v.) led him to acquire an interest in French socialist doctrines. Following the appearance of his novels *Contradictions* (1847) and *A Complicated Matter* (1848), in which he had presented the established social order in a highly critical light, S was transferred, as a civil servant, from St. Petersburg to Vyatka. It was there that he acquired much of the first-hand knowledge of life in the provinces that was reflected in his subsequent writings. His *Provincial Sketches* (1856–57), in particular, met immediately with a wide success and caused S to be regarded as one of the leaders of radical social thought. After retiring from the civil service in 1862, S devoted himself to the editing of progressive literary journals—first of *Sovremennik* (The Contemporary) (1863–64) and then, with the poet Nekrasov, of *Otechestvennya Zapiski* (Notes of the Fatherland) (1868–84). Most of his best-known works were written during this period. They include *The History of a City* (1869–70), *The Gentlemen of Tashkent* (1869–72), *Well Intentioned Speeches* (1872–76), and *The Golovlyov Family* (1875–80). The names of many of their leading characters have since come into general use in conversation and writing. The later writers influenced by the work of S include Chekhov, Gorky, and the poet Mayakovsky.

SALTYKÓV, Count Pyótr Semyónovich (1698–1772), field marshal. For a brief time R. commander in chief during the Seven Years' War, he defeated the Prussians at Kunersdorf in 1759.

SAMÁRA: *see* Kuybyshev.

SAMÁRA RIVER, flows from Stalino Oblast through Kharkov Oblast, entering Dnieper near Dnepropetrovsk; 190 mi. long.

SAMÁRA RIVER, flows from Orenburg Oblast to become tributary of Volga near Kuybyshev; about 360 mi. long.

SAMÁRIN, Aleksándr Mikháylovich (1902–), metallurgist. Corresponding member, Ac. of S., USSR (1946). Graduate (1930), professor (1938), Moscow Steel Institute. Deputy director, Institute of Metallurgy, Ac. of S. (1955). Research concerns electrometallurgy of steel and ferro-alloys. Author of *Deslagging in Melting of Multi-Carbon Ferrochromium* (1935).

SAMÁRIN, Yúry Fyódorovich (1819–1876), writer and leading Slavophile, born into a family of landed nobility. He graduated from the University of Moscow in 1844. In 1840 he had met Khomyakov (q.v.), who strongly influenced his views. From 1844 to 1852 S was in government service. After 1852 he devoted himself entirely to writing and work in connection with emancipation of the serfs. S was a member of the agency which drafted the emancipation statutes and in which he defended the more liberal point of view. S was a theorist of Slavophilism. He extolled the peasant commune in which he saw both economic and moral virtues and he upheld R. nationalistic policies in the borderlands.

SAMARKÁND, city, adm. center of Samarkand Oblast; pop. 196,000 (1959). Dates from the 4th century, b.c.; laid waste by Alexander the Great 329 b.c. and by Ghengis Khan in 1220; later it was the capital of Tamerlane's empire. The palace and tomb of Tamerlane are among the many monuments of ancient and medieval architecture for which the city is famous. At present, it is one of the major cultural and economic centers of Central Asia. Next to the old city there is a new city with a university and several research institutes, machine building, cotton ginning, silk weaving, food-processing ind.

SAMARKÁND OBLAST, Uzbek SSR; area 14,500 sq. mi.; pop. 1,151,000 (1959). Cities: Samarkand (adm. center), Dzhizak, Katta-Kurgan. The region, drained by the Zeravshan River, includes the Turkestan mountain ridge, the W. slopes and spurs of the Zeravshan ridge, the Nura-Tau and Ak-Tau mountains. Has hot, dry summers; semidesert and steppe vegetation (above 2,500–3,000 ft.), almond groves and leafy forests in high altitudes; soils predominantly gray in low country, brown or chestnut in the mountains. Irrigation farming is essential. Cotton growing, sericulture emphasized in river valleys; orchards and vineyards, upon foothills. Wheat and barley crops are produced by dry farming; cattle, karakul, and fat-tail sheep are reared extensively. Ind.: cotton ginning and silk milling; sugar refineries; canning and meat-packing plants; clothing and footwear mfg.; tractor, auto accessories. Gigantic water reservoir built in Katta-Kurgan. Est. 1938.

SAMARKÁNDSKY: *see* Temir-Tau.

SAMI: *see* Population.

SAMOYEDS: *see* NENETS.

SAN STEFANO, TREATY OF, ending the Russo-Turkish War of 1877–78, signed at the village of San Stefano near Istanbul, on March 3, 1878. By it, Ardahan, Kars, Batum, Bayazet (Turkish Armenia) and part of Bessarabia were ceded to Russia; Serbia, Rumania and Montenegro were recognized by Turkey as fully independent states; and Bulgaria was granted what amounted in effect to an independent status. Soon thereafter, under pressure from the Western powers, particularly Britain and Austria-Hungary, the San Stefano T was set aside and replaced by the Treaty of Berlin (1878).

SAPÓZHNIKOV, Leoníd Mikháylovich (1906–), fuel engineer. Corresponding member, Ac. of S., USSR (1946). Graduate of Dnepropetrovsk Mining Institute (1930); professor, Dnepropetrovsk Coal-Chemical Institute and Dnepropetrovsk Institute of Technology (1935); chief, Laboratory of Mineral Fuels, Ac. of S. (1937). Research on the process of coal coking. Author of several publications on coal processing and of *New Techniques of Coking and Concentration of Coal* written together with A. Z. Yurovsky (1956).

SAPRÓNOV, Timoféy Vladímirovich (1887–?), a member of the Bolshevik party from 1912. Worked as party organizer and propagandist in Moscow, St. Petersburg, Saratov, Nizhny-Novgorod, and Tula. In October 1917 he was one of the leaders of the Bolshevik uprising. After the Bolshevik revolution, he occupied important party and governmental positions and was a leader of the group of "Democratic Centralism" which fought against violating intra-party democracy. In the 1930's, S was arrested and vanished without trace.

SARÁNSK, city, adm. center of Mordvinian ASSR; pop. 41,000 (1939), 90,000 (1959). Modern ind. plants built after World War II include metalworking and machine building (electrical equipment), canned milk and meat-packing, pharmaceuticals, starch factory, hemp and jute mills. Has several higher technical colleges and schools. Founded 1641.

SARÁPUL, city in the Udmurt ASSR, an old city on the Kama River; pop. 42,000 (1939), 68,000 (1959). The center of an agr. area in the middle Urals; also has ind.: machine-building and metalworking plants, footwear and leather goods factories, rope mills. Has several higher technical colleges and schools.

SARÁTOV, city, adm. center of Saratov Oblast; pop. 581,000 (1959). After World War II, it became a major ind. and cultural center; has oil refineries, iron foundries, ball-bearings, harvester combine, precision instrument plants. Important river port on Volga waterway and a transfer point for Baku oil; has a university, medical and agr. institutes, and museums. Founded 1590.

SARÁTOV OBLAST, RSFSR; area 38,500 sq. mi.; pop. 2,163,000 (1959). Cities: Saratov (adm. center), Engels, Balashov, Kamyshin, Volsk. Northernmost of lower Volga regions, in E. part of Central R. plateau, its N. tip wedges into the zone of broad-leaved forests. Volga uplands forming the elevated right bank slope down to low, treeless steppe E. of the river. Black-earth soils predominate in the W.; chestnut, with occasional salt marshes, in the E. Prominent farming area, despite dry climate, with spring wheat the main crop, also raises sunflowers, sugar beets, bean and mustard plants, tobacco cultures. Cattle are raised in the Volga flood valley; sheep and hog raising is widespread; also has extensive cement milling, oil-shale mining, phosphorites extraction, based on rich local deposits. Pipeline completed in 1947 supplies natural gas to Moscow ind. A large number of metallurgical, chemical, and textile plants have been built since 1920. Est. 1934.

SÁREMA ISLAND (Est. *Saaremaa*, Ger. *Oesel*), in E. Baltic off W. coast of Estonian SSR, near mouth of Riga Gulf; area 1,050 sq. mi.; fishing and farming. Mudbath resort named Kingissep.

SARMATIANS: *see* HISTORY.

SARYKÓL RANGE, along border of Tadzhik SSR and China; highest peak 20,500 ft.

SATPÁYEV, Kanysh Imantayevich (1899–), geologist and expert on ore deposits. Fellow, Ac. of S., USSR and president of the Ac. of S., Kazakh SSR (1946–52 and since 1955), honorary member, Ac. of S., Tadzhik SSR (1951). Graduated from the Tomsk Institute of Technology (1926). Participated in expeditions (1926–41). S's research concerns the exploration of Central Kazakhstan and the utilization of minerals in national economy and proved of major importance in the discovery of vast copper ore and other mineral deposits in the Ulutau–Dzhezkazgan region. S was also instrumental in mapping mineral deposit areas. Stalin prize (1942).

SÁVIN, Gúry Nikoláyevich (1907–), engineer. Fellow (1948) and vice president (1952–57), Ac. of S., Ukrainian SSR. Graduate of Dnepropetrovsk University (1932); professor, Dnepropetrovsk Institute of Civil Engineering (1941) and Kiev University (1951); rector, Lvov University (1948–51). Research on and development of the theory of elasticity, concentration of stresses near apertures in machine parts, and effects of corner fillets on stress concentration. Investigation of contact strength and dynamics of mine hoisting cables. Stalin prize (1952).

SÁVINA, Maria Gavrílovna (1854–1915), prominent actress. After 1874, the leading actress of the Aleksandrinsky Theater in St. Petersburg. Her art was much admired. S gave memorable performances of the parts of Maria Antonovna in Gogol's *The Inspector-General*, Verochka and Natalia Petrovna in Turgenev's *A Month in the Country*, and Akulina in Tolstoy's *The Power of Darkness*.

SAVINGS BANKS: *see* BANKING AND CREDIT.

SÁVINKOV, Borís Víktorovich (1879–1925), revolutionary and author. He joined the Socialist Revolutionary party in exile and became a leading member of its terroristic organization. He was responsible for the planning of daring feats of terrorism carried out by the organization: the assassination of V. Plehve (1904), the assassination of Grand Duke Sergius Aleksandrovich (1905), and others. During World War I S was an ardent supporter of the Russian war effort and under Kerensky's Provisional Government, he was appointed assistant minister of war. However, he participated in the abortive "mutiny" of General Kornilov and was dismissed by Kerensky. S opposed Bolshevik rule and joined the counter-revolutionary armies. He was the organizer of the Yaroslavl revolt in July 1918. In 1924, he was arrested in Soviet Russia where he had gone secretly. He was sentenced to death but his sentence was commuted to ten years of hard labor. His death, a year later, was attributed by the Soviets to suicide. S wrote several novels under the pseudonym V. Ropshin dealing with his experiences as a terrorist. His better-known books are *Pale Horse* (1909) and *What Never Happened* (1913). S also wrote poetry.

SAVRÁSOV, Alekséy Kondrátyevich (1830–1897), landscape painter. Studied at the school of Painting and Plastic Art in Moscow. Was made a member of the Academy of Fine Arts in 1854 in recognition of his picture *Landscape Near Oranienbaum*. His *The Rooks Are Back* and other works are in the Tretyakov Gallery in Moscow.

SAYÁN MOUNTAINS, between Angara and Upper Yenisey rivers, S.E. Siberia; altitudes range from 8,000 to 11,450 ft. Minerals include asbestos, graphite, mica, and gold.

SAYÁNOV, Vissarión Mikháylovich (1903–1959), poet and prose writer. His first book of poems, *The Years at the Front*, appeared in 1926; in the 1930's he published two two-volume novels, *Lena* and *Sky and Earth*. Starting in 1929, S worked for a number of magazines, and was editor of *The Poet's Library*. He joined the army during the Finnish war in 1939 and served until 1945 while writing poems, sketches, verses, plays, dialogues, and letters, some of which were published in the collection *Soldiers' Conversations* and later in the book *Leningrad Diary*. Stalin prize (1949).

SAZÓNOV, Sergey Dmitrievich (1861–1927), diplomat and statesman, born into a family of landed nobility, studied at the Alexander Lycée. He entered the diplomatic service in 1883, was attached to the London embassy in 1904–6, and from 1906 to 1909 was minister resident at the Vatican. In 1909 S was recalled to St. Petersburg and succeeded Izvolsky (q.v.) as minister of foreign affairs in Oct. 1910. He was a brother-in-law of Stolypin which may account for his rapid advancement. S has among western historians the reputation of a warmonger, which is unwarranted. Nor does S deserve the reproach, which is often made, that by insisting on the mobilization of the Russian Army in July 1914 he made the war inevitable. S was faithful to the cause of the Allies, opposed a separate peace; he was dismissed from office in July 1916. He was appointed ambassador to London but was prevented from taking his post by the revolution. Eventually he made his way to Paris where he was active among the *émigré* anti-Soviet groups. A man of personal charm and a good conversationalist, S left a volume of colorless memoirs *Fateful Years, 1909–1916*, which is available in English.

SCHISM (Raskol): *see* ORTHODOX CHURCH.

SCHLUSSELBURG: *see* PETROKREPOST.

SCHMIDT, Ótto Yúlyevich (1891–1956), mathematician, astronomer, geophysicist, and explorer. Fellow (1935) and vice president (1939–42), Ac. of S., USSR; fellow, Ac. of S., Ukrainian SSR (1934). Hero of the Soviet Union (1937). Member of the Supreme Soviet (1937). Graduate of Kiev University (1913); professor, Institute of Forestry Engineering (1920–23) and Moscow University (1926). Chairman of the Lenin Prize Award Commission (1926–33). Head of the State Publishing House (1921–24). Founder (1938) and director (1938–49) of the Geophyiscal Institute. S's research concerned mathematics in general and the theory of groups, in particular. He advanced the isomorphic theorem of the direct expansion of infinite operational groups with a finite principal series (1928). Moreover, S, a pioneer in the exploration of the Arctic region, is the discoverer of Schmidt Island. He headed several Arctic expeditions: Icebreaker *Sedov* (1929), *Sibiryakov* (1932), *Chelyuskin* (1933–4). In his late years, he advanced a novel hypothesis on the origin of the earth. Author of *The Abstract Theory of Groups* (1914; 2nd ed., 1933); *The Origin of the Planets and of Their Satellites* (1950). Chief editor of several scientific publications including *Bolshaya Sovetskaya Entsiklopediya* (The Great Soviet Encyclopedia) (1924–41) and the journal *Priroda* (Nature).

SCHMIDT, Pyótr Petróvich (1867–1906), lieutenant, in the Russian Imperial Navy. One of the leaders of the sailors' mutiny on the cruiser *Ochakov* of the Black Sea fleet, in Oct.-Nov. 1905, he was court-martialed and executed on Berezan Island, March 6, 1906.

SCHOLARSHIPS (*stipendii*) are granted by the government to pupils and students of secondary and vocational schools, universities, and institutes as well as to graduate students. Nearly 80% of all students have scholarship aid which may be considerable, particularly in the cases of specially gifted youths. The scholarship system has been a major factor in extending education to the less favored classes. However, it has not been free of abuses. Favoritism often prevails in the apportioning of scholarships and the general level of the aid—as opposed to special cases— barely covers living expenses.

SCHOOL AGE in the Soviet Union is from 7 to 17 years. It is divided into three periods: younger, from 7 to 12 years; intermediate, from 12 to 14 years; older, from 14 to 17 years. Since the reforms of 1958, secondary schooling has been undergoing reorganization into an eight-year school, ages 7–15 (intended to be compulsory), and three senior years, ages 15–18.

SCHOOLS FOR ILLITERATES AND SEMI-LITERATES. Schools for illiterates, offering a six-months' course, were established by the decree on the liquidation of illiteracy passed by the Council of People's Commissars of the RSFSR on Dec. 26, 1919. They were stopped in the 1930's, when their objective was allegedly attained.

Schools for semi-literates were schools that offered a general education to adults who could read and write but lacked knowledge of subjects taught at elementary schools. They were established in the 1930's and were gradually abandoned with the spread of elementary schools.

SCIENCE. Science during the last three decades has become an important activity of the Soviet state. The development of atomic weapons and intercontinental missiles is the most spectacular result of the work of Soviet scientists and technologists. This has given the Soviet government a position of a first class military nation and brought Soviet science world-wide recognition. In a less spectacular way Soviet scientists are developing various other aspects of sciences and technology to bolster and develop the economy of the Soviet state.

Soviet science has its roots in two and a half centuries of Russian history. Peter the Great (1672–1725) was impressed by Western science during his visits to England, France and Holland. Using the scientific apparatus that he brought back with him from his travels, he established the first scientific museum in St. Petersburg. Emulating the example of the Western rulers he founded the St. Petersburg Academy of Sciences (1724). He and his successor, Catherine I (1727) staffed it with prominent Western scholars such as Leonard Euler (1707–83) who spent twenty-seven years in St. Petersburg, John Bernoulli (1667–1748) and Daniel Bernoulli (1700–82). These men and others of lesser prominence gave the Academy prestige in Western Europe and trained native Russian followers. The most prominent Russian scientist of the eighteenth century was Mikhail Lomonosov (1711–65) whose many sided genius contributed significant discoveries in chemistry, metallurgy, physics, astronomy, literature and grammar and has subsequently served as the idol of Soviet science. The nineteenth century saw a gradual development both in the extent and depth. The establishment of universities in the various parts of the Russian Empire, the rise in the cultural level of the landowners, merchants and the professional classes, the formation of the class of intelligentsia—all fostered the development of both science and scientists. At the beginning of the twentieth century Imperial Russia had a corps of scholars that were not only effective teachers in almost every branch of science but also competent researchers whose contributions to their specialties were appreciated and valued by the West. At least three such Russian scientists: Lobachevsky, Mendeleyev and Pavlov won world-wide recognition. The concepts that they introduced became part of the cultural heritage of the world. During this period there was a ready interchange between the Russian scientists and those of the West. Young Russian scholars studied in Western European universities, scientists of established reputation presented their achievements at international meetings and published their investigations in European journals. The Baltic provinces, which later became Latvia and Estonia, furnished many Russian university professors and these in turn became the connecting link between East and West. The World War I, the Revolution of 1917 and the Civil War that followed raised havoc with science in the newly establisihed Soviet state. The general breakdown of the economic life of the country, the mass emigration of the upper middle class, the loss of many prominent scientists to the West brought scientific work in Communist Russia to a very low level. With the betterment of economic conditions

and with the recognition by the Communist Party of the importance of science and technology for building up the Communist state, the old Imperial Academy of St. Petersburg was reorganized in 1925 into the Academy of Sciences of the USSR and established legally as the highest scholarly institution in the Soviet Union. It reported directly to the Council of People's Commissars (subsequently the Council of Ministers) and coordinated its activities with the activities of the Gosplan. In 1929 it was expanded to include a new membership of engineers and in 1934 it was transferred from Leningrad to Moscow.

During the period 1924–35 science expanded. The academy carried out important government assignments such as the investigation of the iron-ore deposits in the Kursk region and the phosphate deposits in the Kola peninsula. New institutes were established. Individual Soviet scientists studied, visited and lectured in Western Europe and America. A number of European and American scientists worked in Soviet laboratories. Several scientific journals were published in English and German to make the results of Soviet scholars available to scientists who could not read Russian. In 1935 difficulties of communication between Soviet science and that of the West began. The retention in the Soviet Union of Peter L. Kapitsa who though a Soviet citizen had been for many years a professor at Cambridge University, the disappearance of prominent pro-Western Soviet scholars from the Soviet scientific scene, the return to Europe of western scholars who had worked in the Soviet Union all presaged the future isolation of Soviet science from the West. World War II took a heavy toll from the Soviet science. Its normal academic activity was converted to war work, and many of its laboratories were destroyed by invading armies, scientific equipment and museum contents were sent to Germany as war booty. The Soviet government transferred the academy from Moscow to Kuybyshev on the Volga and its institutes to Kazan, Sverdlovsk, Frunze, Tashkent, Alma Ata. The Ukrainian Academy of Sciences was moved to Ufa. The ten year period after the end of World War II was characterized by reconstruction of the destroyed scientific establishments, work on the atom bomb and on missiles, and isolation from the West. The laboratories and educational institutions were rebuilt all over the Soviet Union. A massive set of buildings was erected on a hill outside of Moscow for the science faculties of the Moscow university. These were outfitted with the best scientific equipment that the state could obtain. Dominating the Soviet skyline, the university of Moscow impresses everyone in the city with the importance that the Soviet government assigns to scientific training and serves as a show place to all foreign visitors. Soviet work on atomic weapons was started immediately after the fall of Berlin and was carried out under the direct supervision of L. Beria. Its rapid rate of progress was disclosed in the first Soviet atom bomb explosion in September 1949. Since that time Soviet progress in the field of atomic weapons was punctuated with periodic bomb tests and culminated in the development of a hydrogen bomb in August 1953. This work was paralleled with research and development of intercontinental missiles. The magnitude and the success of this program was not appreciated by the West until the first sputnik was launched dramatically in October 1957. The post war decade was also marked by a great ideological struggle in Soviet science. Though it was concentrated in science of genetics, its repercussions were felt in many fields. It first flared up just before World War II in a struggle between N. I. Vavilov, the champion of Western point of view, and T. Lysenko representing the Marxist "science." Vavilov was arrested and disappeared just before the war broke out. During the war the controversy was dormant, but in 1948 it broke out violently at the meeting of the Lenin All-Union Academy of Agricultural Sciences in July 1948. An ex cathedra decision of the Central Committee of the Communist Party established Lysenko's Marxist genetics as the "true science" and proscribed the adherents of the genetics universally adhered to in the West. This policy decision affected other branches of science in the Soviet Union and they underwent thorough search for any evidence of idealism, non-appreciation of Soviet achievements, and pro-Westernism. During the Stalin period many prominent scientists were arrested and Soviet science lost its prestige in the West. Communication between Soviet science and the rest of the World was for all practical purposes nonexistent.

The death of Stalin and the subsequent thaw in the political climate of the Soviet Union had its repercussions in Soviet science. Some of the Soviet scientists came out of exile, more and more from the Communist countries came to Western Europe to attend scientific conferences. The first major conclave between atomic scientists of the West and those of the East was at the Geneva Conference of the United Nations on the Peaceful Uses of Atomic Energy in September 1955. At this conference scientists showed the world that identical scientific resultts can be obtained on either side of the Iron Curtain and that scientists could discuss them without getting involved in ideological or political disputes. A second conference on the same subject was held successfully in Geneva in the Fall of 1958. In the meantime in February of 1958 an agreement was signed between the United States and the Soviet Union on a program of cultural exchanges and this resulted in visits of scientists and students of both countries to the other country.

Scientific investigations are carried out in the Soviet Union under the direction of the USSR Academy of Sciences, the academies of sciences of the constituent republics, educational institutions, special committees of the council of ministers and the various ministries.

The USSR Academy of Sciences is by law the highest scientific organization in the Soviet Union. The ruling body of the Academy is the General Assembly of the academicians. A scholar is elected to the rank of academician by the following procedure. He is first nominated by either a scientific organization or by a group of scientists and the list of such nominations is published in the daily press. There are two stages of election. The nomination must win a two thirds majority of all academicians of the section present in the Soviet Union and then it must receive a majority vote of all academicians. The status of an academician

carries not only great prestige in the Soviet Union but also a 5000 rubles per month salary for life, good living quarters in an academy apartment house, a country home in an academy settlement, a car with a chauffeur. As of Jan. 1, 1960 there were 158 active members (fellows).

Corresponding members of the academy are elected in a similar way, do not enjoy quite as high a prestige and receive a stipend of 3000 rubles per month for life. They have no voting rights in the academy. There are 344 corresponding members, 55 foreign members.

The membership of the academy is divided into nine sections: physics and mathematics; chemistry; biology; geology and geography; technical sciences; historical studies; economics, philosophy and legal studies; literature and linguistics; and also a Siberian section of the academy which unites the academicians and corresponding members carrying out work in the scientific establishments of Siberia and the Far East. Each of the sections has a secretary academician and a committee of academicians and corresponding members. In recent years the individual sections have been given more administrative independence.

The executive authority of the academy is vested in the Presidium which consists of the President of the Academy, the Vice-Presidents, the Academician-secretary, the secretaries of the individual sections and a number of academicians elected by the General Assembly. The Presidium, assisted by its staff, carries out the decisions of the General Assembly and administers science in the Soviet Union. The President of the Academy is a man of great importance in the Soviet Union and is elected for five years. Since the reorganization of the academy this post has been held by the botanist V. L. Komarow (1896–1945) from 1936 to 1945; the physicist S. I. Vavilov (1881–1951) from 1945 to 1951; the chemist A. N. Nesmeyanov (1899–) from 1951 to 1961; and by the mathematician M. V. Keldysh (1911–). The vicepresident is often the mouthpiece of the academy and at present such role is played by A. V. Topchiev (1907–), an organic chemist. The secretary academician is Ye. K. Fedorov (1910–), a geophysicist who has been the chairman of the Soviet delegation to the Geneva Conference on Detection of Atomic Explosions. This position was occupied for a long time (1949–58) by A. V. Topchiev.

In 1959 the academy had 136 institutes, and 25 independent laboratories, sections and scientific councils. In addition it has a number of scientific research stations, botanical gardens, museums, expeditions, bases and libraries. In 1958 the staff of the academy consisted of 1466 scholars with a doctor's degree and 6788 with that of a candidate. In the spring of 1957 the Council of ministers announced the creation of a Siberian section of the academy with headquarters in a new "science city" on the river Ob near Novosibirsk. It will occupy the area of four and a half square miles. Thirteen academicians and twenty-eight corresponding members have volunteered to be the nucleus of the scientific corps of this ambitious method to spur rapid development of science in a new region. The mathematical physicist M. A. Lavrentyev is the secretary academician of this new section of the academy.

The academy has a number of filials (branches) throughout the Soviet Union: the Bashkir Filial in Ufa, the Dagestan Filial in Makhachkala, the Karelia Filial in Kivorsk, the Komi Filial at Syktyvkar, the Moldavian Filial in Kishenev. The filials have sixty-four research institutes.

The various constituent republics also have their own academies of sciences in which local scientists and scholars work on problems peculiar to their region of the country. The names of the various academies with the place of their headquarters and the date of establishment of the academy are as follows: Armenian in Yerevan (1943), Azerbaijanian in Baku (1945), Byelorussian in Minsk (1929), Estonian in Tallin (1946), Georgian in Tbilisi (1941), Kazakh in Alma Ata (1946), Kirghiz in Frunze (1954), Latvian in Riga (1946), Lithuanian in Vilnius (1941), Tadzhik in Stalinabad (1951), Turkmenian in Ashkhabad (1951), Ukrainian in Kiev (1919), Uzbek in Tashkent (1943). The most important of these academies is that of the Ukrainian republic. It has five sections, 40 institutes, 90 academicians and 113 corresponding members.

A recent development in the organizational structure of science is the creation of a series of State committees at the Council of Ministers for important branches of science. There are for examples, the State Committee of the Council of Ministers for Science and Technology, one for Chemistry, another for the Utilization of Atomic Energy. These committees are not only involved in the policy formulation but also coordinate the application of the scientific results for the needs of the Soviet state. Some of them, as the Atomic Energy Committee, have their own institutes.

Various ministries also carry out scientific and development work and have their own institutes such as the Karpov Institute of Chemistry in Moscow of the Ministry of Chemical Industry. The Ministry of Medium Machine Construction is engaged in the production of atomic weapons and has its own laboratories.

There are forty universities in the Soviet Union (1961) and all of them to some degree or other carry out scientific and scholarly work. The larger universities, those of Moscow, Leningrad and Kiev, are very well equipped with scientific laboratories and a number of world-famous scientists serve on their faculties and carry out research in conjunction with graduate work called in the Soviet Union "aspirantura." It should be pointed out that the Academy of Sciences has the right to grant advanced degrees and graduate work is carried out in its institutes.

In April 1961 a new super-agency, the State Committee for Coordination of Scientific Research Work, was created. Headed by Konstantin Nikolayevich Rudnev (1911–), former chairman of the State Committee of the Council of Ministers for Defense Technology, the new agency is in control of all scientific research and international scientific contacts. It appears to curtail the power of the Ac. of S. and to reduce the scope of its activities. A number of research institutes have been shifted to other agencies. The main function of the Committee is to improve coordination of research, avoid duplication, narrow the gap between research and production, and enhance the utilization of science

for military purpose. (*See also* ACADEMY OF SCIENCES, BIOLOGICAL SCIENCES, CHEMISTRY, GEOLOGICAL SCIENCES, PHYSICS, PHYSIOLOGY, TECHNICAL SCIENCES, TECHNOLOGY)

BIBLIOGRAPHY: Ruth C. Christman, Ed., *Soviet Science*, arranged by Conway Zirkle and Howard A. Meyerhoff, Washington, 1952; Alexander Vucinich, *The Soviet Academy of Sciences*, Stanford, 1956; John Turkevich, "The Progress of Soviet Science," *Foreign Affairs*, April, 1954; John Turkevich, "The Scientist in the USSR," *Atlantic Monthly*, January, 1958.   J. T.

SCULPTURE. Prior to the 18th century, the art of S was virtually nonexistent in Russia as a result of the traditional iconoclasm of the Orthodox Church. It was only during the reign of Peter the Great that S first became an accepted art form. Peter was determined to people the newly constructed parks and gardens of his capital city with statuary in the western style. For this purpose he engaged the service of the Venetian-born Count Carlo Rastrelli (1716). Father of the celebrated architect, "Rastrelli the Elder" did his best work in Russia. His portrait busts render considerable psychological insight with studied exactitude. A bronze bust of Peter (1724) in the Winter Palace and an equestrian statue of the tsar at Leningrad are perhaps his best-known works.

Only in the reign of Catherine II did native R sculptors begin to appear in any number. The first to gain prominence was Fyodor Shubin (1740–1805), a former fisherman from the White Sea region. Shubin studied under Nicholas Gillet at the Academy of Fine Arts and traveled widely in Europe. With this background, he was able to temper a vigorous realism with a classicism appropriate to the century. The height of his achievement is to be found in portrait busts, such as those of Paul I and Potemkin.

Another outstanding student of Gillet was Mikhail Kozlovsky (1753–1802) who was also much influenced by the visiting French sculptor Falconnet. Kozlovsky ultimately adopted a classical heroic style best exemplified by his statue of Samson and the Lion (1800) in the Grand Cascade, Peterhof. Fyodor Shchedrin (1751–1825), who cultivated a particular admiration for the style of the Greeks, was the third native Russian to achieve prominence in this early period. He did much decorative work for such buildings as the Admiralty in St. Petersburg (1806–11) and is also remembered for his statue of Marsyas now in the Academy of Fine Arts, Leningrad.

The later years of the 19th century saw an attempt at conveying the national spirit by the romanticist, Count Theodore Tolstoy (1783–1873). Working in a naturalist vein were the sculptors Mark Antokolsky (1843–1902) and Kamensky. But, on the whole, this was a period of relative decline broken only toward the end of the century when some degree of revival became discernible in portraiture and ornamentation. In this connection the name of the painter-sculptor Mikhail Vrubel (1856–1910) is noteworthy. Vrubel's sculptural works were few and limited in their range, but are reminiscent of Rodin.

Since the Revolution, grandiosity and realism have emerged as the two most common characteristics of Russian S. Sergey Merkurov's statue of Stalin and A. T. Matveyev's figure of Karl Marx (1918) in Leningrad are examples of this, although Matveyev is also known for smaller works of considerable lightness and delicacy. I. D. Shadr's *1905,* reputedly one of the greatest works of Soviet S, is marked by undiluted realism. In the same realistic vein, portrait heads of revolutionary personalities abound. V. I. Ingal and I. M. Chaykov have been prominent in this genre while N. A. Andreyev is particularly well known for his statues of Lenin (*Bust of Lenin Writing,* and others).

A. Archipenko has produced work reflecting the influence of cubism, but more significant in the development of modern Russian S has been that offshoot of futurism, "constructivism." With its use of paper, glass, steel, and concrete to convey the feeling of a great revolutionary industrial effort, constructivism was really a combination of painting and S. Examples are to be found in N. A. Altman's *Russia* and V. A. Tatlin's monument to the Third International. The influence of this movement can also be discerned in the work of the sculptor Chaykov. Meanwhile, working in a different tradition, I. G. Frikh-Khar has drawn on the subject matter of Central Asia to provide some of the most interesting works of contemporary Soviet S. Among the other known sculptors are two women: V. I. Mukhina and S. D. Lebedeva, and Z. I. Azgur, E. V. Vuchetich and Ya. I. Nikoladze.   C. J. F.

SEA-BORNE TRANSPORTATION. Maritime carriers have long been used in Russia and the USSR for both freight and passenger transportation, though recently they have accounted for less than a tenth of all transportation activity. At least half the total sea-borne freight traffic has been carried on the Caspian Sea, where there has been a heavy movement of petroleum from Baku northward for over half a century. Coastwise traffic on the Black and Azov seas is substantial, and some appears also along the Soviet Baltic coast. Soviet sea-borne foreign trade originates or terminates primarily at Black and Baltic seaports, together with relatively minor flows to and from Murmansk, an all-year outlet near Norway, and Vladivostok, across from Japan. During most of the last twenty-five years, annual convoys, both eastbound and westbound, have sought to use the "Great Northern Sea Route," between the Barents Sea, above European Russia, and the Soviet Pacific coast below the Bering Strait. The volume of traffic carried, however, has been small. Similarly, small amounts move between the Black Sea and the Pacific coast, via the Suez Canal and the Indian Ocean.

SEA-BORNE TRAFFIC

Passengers (in mill.)	Year	Freight (in bill. ton-miles)
3.7	1913*	12.6
1.5	1929	6.5
3.1	1940	14.8
3.2	1950	24.7
8.2	1956	51.2

* Present-day boundaries.

SEAS of the USSR belong to the basins of the Arctic, the Pacific, and the Atlantic oceans.

The S on the Arctic Ocean are the Barents, the White, the Kara, the Laptev, the East-Siberian, and Chukchi, which are located within the continental shelf and are shallow, with a depth seldom exceeding 650 ft. Almost all these S are ice-covered, not only in winter, but nearly all year, making navigation difficult. Almost all are rich in fish, especially the Barents Sea; and the White and the Kara seas are rich in valuable marine animals. Archangel, Murmansk, Dikson, and Tiksi are the largest seaports.

On the Pacific coast are the Bering and the Okhotsk seas, and the Sea of Japan, which extend from the Arctic Circle up to 35° N. The influence of the Asiatic continent and a relatively free access to the Pacific Ocean condition the climatic and hydrologic peculiarities of the Far East seas. They are of oceanic type and are very deep, with a maximum depth of 15,525 ft. in the Bering Sea. In winter the ice cover is found on the Bering and the Okhotsk, and partly on the Sea of Japan; in summer they are free from ice. Prolonged fogs are characteristic of the Sea of Japan in summer and autumn. These S are very rich in valuable marine animals and in fish. Vladivostok, Magadan, and Petropavlovsk-Kamchatsky are the principal seaports.

Of primary importance are the S of the Atlantic Ocean which extend deep into the land. Within the territory of the USSR lies the E. part of the Baltic Sea which serves as the shortest route to the Atlantic Ocean and the overseas countries. This is a shallow sea, with prevailing depths of 200–500 ft., the greatest being 1,475 ft. The largest Soviet ports of the Baltic Sea are Leningrad, Riga, Tallin, and Kaliningrad. The Black Sea in the S. of European Russia is an inland sea. The greater part is deep, the maximum depth being 7,350 ft. One peculiar aspect of the Black Sea is that its deep waters are almost devoid of living organisms because of the presence of hydrogene sulfide. The Sea of Azov which is connected with the Black Sea by the Kerch Strait is a shallow body of slightly saline water with maximum depths up to 42 ft. Odessa, Novorossiysk, and Zhdanov are the principal ports of these two S. seas.

SCYTHIANS: *see* HISTORY.

SECH: *see* ZAPOROZHYE SECH.

SÉCHENOV, Iván Mikháylovich (1829–1905), physiologist. Honorary member, Ac. of S. (1904). Graduate,  St. Petersburg School of Engineering (1848) and the Medical Faculty of Moscow University (1856); professor, Novorossiysk University in Odessa (1870–76), St. Petersburg University (1876), and Moscow University (1891–1901). Resigned from the last to "open the path for new forces." Carried out research under H. L. F. Helmholtz, E. DuBois Reymond, and K. F. W. Ludwig in Germany. Founder of the R. physiological school of thought and pioneer in the preparation of materialistic ideas in science. I. P. Pavlov referred to him as the "Father of Russian Physiology" and was greatly influenced by his book *The Reflexes of the Brain* (1863). His collected works (1956) include two volumes, *Physiology and Psychology* and *The Physiology of the Nervous System.* The First Institute of Medicine in Moscow was named after S.

SECRET POLICE: *see* SECURITY POLICE.

**SECRETARIAT OF THE CENTRAL COMMIT-
TEE** of the Communist party, USSR, was formed by
the Central Committee on instruction of the 8th Party
Congress in 1919 to execute administrative decisions of
the Orgburo. Under Stalin, appointed general secretary
in April 1922, the S was transformed from an administrative organ into one of party guidance which in the
course of the 1920's supplanted the Politburo as the
locus of party power. By virtue of his position as
general secretary, Stalin was able to establish his dictatorship over the party. Under his leadership the S
became the nerve center of the party controlling appointments and dominating the apparatus through a
network of party secretaries. In the post-Stalin era the
S has retained its primacy in party affairs and Khrushchev's rise to power can be traced to his appointment
as first secretary of the CPSU in Sept. 1953. From
this position Khrushchev was able to place his supporters strategically within the party apparatus and
succeeded in defeating the serious oppositon of the
so-called "anti-party group" in June 1957.

MEMBERS OF THE SECRETARIAT: *First Secretary*, Nikita S.
Khrushchev; *Secretaries*, Frol R. Kozlov, Otto V. Kuusinen, Nuritdin A. Mukhitdinov, Mikhail A. Suslov (May, 1961).

SECURITY POLICE. Origin and functions. The
Soviet SP was established on Dec. 20 (7), 1917, six
weeks after the advent of the Soviet regime, under
the name All-Russian Extraordinary Commission for
Combatting Counterrevolution, Speculation and Delinquency in Office (known by the R. abbreviation
Cheka). Its first head was Felix Dzerzhinsky. The
functions of the Cheka were defined as follows: "To
hunt out and liquidate all counterrevolutionary [and]
sabotage attempts and actions . . . to carry out preliminary investigation only." In reality, the Cheka,
from the start, was neither an "extraordinary" nor a
merely investigative agency; it arrogated to itself the
right to carry out arrests, imprisonment and executions.
On Feb. 23 (10), 1918 the Cheka ordered the shooting
of "enemy agents, counterrevolutionary agitators, speculators, organizers of uprisings," and other opponents
of the regime.

Terrorism on a large scale began after the Yaroslavl
uprising (q.v.) in July 1918 and an attempt on Lenin's
life on Aug. 30, 1918. A proclamation of Sept. 3
introduced "mass terror" and the taking of hostages,
and a decree of Sept. 5 established concentration camps
for "enemies of the people." The weekly bulletin of
the Cheka, published toward the end of 1918, approved
the application of torture for the extortion of information and confessions. The Cheka soon extended its
control to all spheres of Soviet life: administration,
economy, transportation, armed forces, and so forth,
and became the main agency for espionage.

After the introduction of the New Economic Policy
in 1921 the sinister record of the Cheka became incompatible with the stabilizing elements of the NEP.
A decree of Feb. 1922 abolished the Cheka, but established in its place a State Political Administration
(GPU) in the Commissariat of Internal Affairs
(NKVD). The decree provided that the GPU was

either to free arrested persons within two months or
obtain special permission to continue the detention;
the latter of course presented no difficulty.

With the formation of the USSR in 1923, the GPU
was taken out of the NKVD and transformed into
a Unified State Political Administration (OGPU) attached to the *Sovnarkom* (Council of People's Commissars) of the USSR, in which its chairman had a
deliberative vote. By now the SP was officially recognized as a permanent and important element of
the Soviet system, rooted in the constitution. Art. 61
of the constitution of 1924 vested the OGPU with
the duty to conduct "the struggle with political and
economic counterrevolution, espionage and banditry."

Throughout its existence, the SP, under its changing
names and despite its tremendous powers, was a faithful
instrument of the collective or individual dictator, never
deviating from the prescribed party line. In 1934, after
the 17th Party Congress, a special section was formed
in the Secretariat of the Party Central Committee for
liaison with the SP.

Consolidation. The OGPU period of the SP, when
it was consolidated, coincided with the consolidation
of the totalitarian elements of the Soviet state. Its
personnel occupied a privileged position and enjoyed
the highest standard of living. It built up its own
army, estimated at 700–800 thousand carefully selected
men highly trained to carry out raids, street fighting,
and so forth, including aviation and tank units. In the
early 1930's it was a powerful instrument in enforcing
farm collectivization. It also played a prominent role
in staging "show trials" (q.v.) and suppressing the
intraparty opposition to Stalin. Then and later, the
basic operational principle of the SP was to repress
not only actual offenders, but also potential opponents
of the Soviet regime. In order to reach these opponents
the SP established a vast network of spies and informers who infiltrated each factory, village, government office, army unit, and dwelling house.

The NKVD and the Great Purge. Dzerzhinsky died
in 1926 and was replaced by Vyacheslav Menzhinsky
(q.v.), who headed the OGPU until his death in 1934.
He was succeeded by Genrikh G. Yagoda, during
whose tenure a new reorganization of the SP took place.
By a decree of July 10, 1934, the OGPU was abolished
and its functions were transferred to the NKVD,
within which a Main Administration of State Security
(GUGB) was formed. The judicial "collegium" of the
OGPU was replaced by a Special Board in the NKVD
which had the right to pass administrative sentences
of up to five years in exile or "corrective labor camps."
Defendants had no right to counsel, and sentences were
passed *in absentia*. In reality, the Special Board, particularly during the great purge of 1936–38, sentenced
a great number of persons to terms of up to 25 years.
Among the main divisions of the GUGB were: the
Secret-Operational Administration, which carried out
raids, arrests, and so forth; the Economic Administration; the Military Administration, which supervised the
Special Sections in the armed forces; the Division for
the Protection of Leaders; and the Foreign Administration, in charge of espionage and subversion abroad.

In Sept. 1936 Yagoda was removed from the NKVD and was replaced by Nikolay I. Yezhov, a high official of the central party apparatus. Yezhov's task was to carry out Stalin's great purge, during which terror, executions, and the power of the SP reached unprecedented heights. After two years of the purge it became obvious that terror had not only crushed the last vestige of overt opposition, but had also begun to wreak havoc with the morale of government officials and army officers. The NKVD was accused of "excesses" perpetrated by wreckers and saboteurs who had allegedly infiltrated its ranks. A bloody purge of the NKVD followed, and in Dec. 1938 Yezhov was replaced by Lavrenty Beria.

World War II. Under Beria the NKVD curbed the "excesses" and reverted to its "normal" activities. With the outbreak of World War II, new tasks fell to the NKVD. On Sept. 17, 1939 the Red Army marched into Poland. Mass deportations of Poles to Siberia and a stubborn fight with resistance forces were carried on by the NKVD. In the following years, similar deportations on a large scale and with great brutality were conducted by the NKVD against actual and potential opponents in Latvia, Estonia and Lithuania after their annexation by the USSR.

In Feb. 1941 the GUGB was transformed into a separate People's Commissariat of State Security (NKGB), with V. N. Merkulov as its chief; Beria remained head of the NKVD. After the German invasion of the USSR the two commissariats were reunited under Beria, but in April 1943 they were again divided into NKGB and NKVD.

In wartime the SP reinforced espionage activities abroad, controlled Soviet partisans behind the German lines, took charge of prisoners of war camps, and greatly strengthened its efforts in the armed forces. Its Special Sections in all army units were transformed into an organization called SMERSH ("Death to Spies"), whose official functions, expressed in its name, were only a minor part of its duties. Its main efforts consisted in political supervision of the army through a vast network of informers and the elimination of opposition in Soviet-occupied territories. At home the NKGB somewhat relaxed its normal activities in view of the great upsurge of patriotic feelings, but it hit hard wherever it suspected opposition to the regime. Thus, the Volga German Autonomous Republic, inhabited by 600,000 descendants of German immigrants, was abolished and its population was deported to Siberia; in 1943–45 the NKGB carried out wholesale deportations of several small Soviet nationalities— Chechens, Ingushi, Balkars, Karachi, Kalmyks and Crimean Tatars. The gradual liberation of Soviet territories from German occupation was followed by mass punishment of real and alleged collaborators.

Postwar activities. The postwar period, until Stalin's death, was marked by mounting terrorism, reminiscent of the years immediately preceding the great purge. The NKGB was put in charge of screening demobilized army personnel, repatriated POW's and *Ostarbeiter* (q.v.). The contacts which these three groups had had with Westerners made them suspect, and many of them were sentenced by the special board to long terms in forced labor camps. The *kolkhoz* regime, somewhat relaxed during the war, was tightened. To increase even more the remarkable success of postwar reconstruction, numerous engineers and managers were rounded up by the SP as saboteurs or foreign spies. A purge of intellectuals accused of deviation from the party line extended to all fields of intellectual activities. An important task of the NKGB (designated MGB in 1946, when People's Commissariats became Ministries) was suppression of nationalist trends which had developed in wartime among some Soviet national minorities. Though there is no reliable information that any serious anti-Soviet activities were carried on at that time, suspects were subjected to harsh sentences, and the camp population, according to released inmates, greatly increased. On Jan. 13, 1953 it was announced that the MGB had discovered a plot of several doctors, most of them Jews, to assassinate some high party and army leaders at the bidding of "Jewish nationalism" and "American imperialism." In the newly formed satellite nations the foreign division of the MGB was the main instrument for suppression of all forms of opposition and for keeping in power the small minorities of native Communists. MGB "advisers" directed the activities of the satellite SP, especially in Poland, East Germany, and China, and trained native police cadres working on the MGB pattern. The MGB, highly organized and well fitted for keeping state secrets, was also put in charge of massive atomic research; for this purpose it built special laboratories in which outstanding physicists were put to work, some of them as forced laborers.

The post-Stalin period. The period of mounting terrorism ended with Stalin's death. Members of the new, still unstable, government were anxious to clear themselves of responsibility for Stalin's domestic policy. Curtailment of the MGB was an obvious step in this direction. The MGB was first merged with the MVD, but a year later, in March 1954, it was transformed into a new agency, the Committee of State Security (KGB), which was subordinated directly, as was earlier the OGPU, to the Council of Ministers. The chief of the KGB was General Ivan A. Serov, a veteran official of the SP, who had been responsible for some of its most brutal operations. In 1956 Serov was promoted to membership in the party Central Committee. On Dec. 25, 1958 he was replaced by Aleksandr N. Shelepin, formerly leader of the Komsomol and a high official of the central party apparatus, thus personifying the continuing dependence of the SP on the party Presidium rather than on the Council of Ministers.

A month after Stalin's death, on April 4, 1953, it was announced that the "doctors' plot" had been a "frame-up" staged by wreckers among MGB officials. The doctors were rehabilitated, and in press comment it was admitted that in other cases, too, frame-ups and torture had been resorted to by the MGB. Beria and a number of high-ranking police officials both in Moscow and in the union republics were executed. This was a hard blow to the MGB, whose powers were reduced. Fear among the population subsided and a period of "political thaw" followed. On April 1, 1953 the Special Board of the MVD was abolished.

Though the activities of the SP have been considerably restricted, it remains an important element of the Soviet regime. In Feb. 1956 Khrushchev stressed the need "to strengthen the organs of State Security." The reduced personnel of the agency consists of a highly trained and reliable staff which is kept in constant readiness. This was attested to during the celebrations of the 40th anniversary of the Cheka, in Dec. 1957, when the SP received high official praise as the "sword of the revolution," ever vigilant since 1917. A resolution adopted by a conference of high KGB officials in May 1959 declared: "We, Soviet Chekists, fully realize that the restriction of [our] punitive functions within the country does not mean that we have less work and that the activities of our enemies have weakened." (*See also* CONCENTRATION CAMPS, PURGES, SHOW TRIALS, INTELLIGENCE.)

BIBLIOGRAPHY: Merle Fainsod, *How Russia Is Ruled*, New York, 1953; F. Beck and W. Godin, *Russian Purge and the Extraction of Confession*, New York, 1951; S. Wolin and R. Slusser, *The Soviet Secret Police*, New York, 1957; A. Orlov, *The Secret History of Stalin's Crimes*, New York, 1953; P. Deriabin and F. Gibney, *The Secret World*, New York, 1959. S. W.

SÉDOV, Leoníd Ivánovich (1907–), mechanical engineer. Fellow, Ac. of S., USSR (1953). Graduate (1931) and professor (1937) of Moscow University. Associated with the Central Aerodynamics Institute (1931) and Central Institute of Aircraft Engine Construction (1947). President of the International Astronautical Federation and head of the Interdepartmental Commission for Organization and Control of Theoretical Scientific Research on Interplanetary Communication. Research on plane hydromechanics of incompressible fluid;  d e r i v e d formulas for aerodynamic forces during unsettled wing motion. Generalized N. Ye. Zhukovsky's theorem for random motions of the wing and elaborated new mathematical methods for the solution of problems of an airfoil in the air gas flow, and of percussions of bodies against water, ricoshetting, and other problems of hydrodynamics of heavy fluid. Investigated several problems of astrophysics. Author of *Plane Problems of Hydrodynamics and Aerodynamics* (1950); *Methods of Analogy and Dimensionality in Mechanics* (2nd edition, 1951). Stalin prize (1952).

SÉGOZERO, lake in Karelian ASSR; area 300 sq. mi.; Segezha River links it with Lake Vygozero from which the Vyg River takes its waters to White Sea.

SELKUPS: *see* POPULATION.

SELVÍNSKY, Ilyá Lvóvich (1899–), poet. Served in the Red Army from 1918 to 1920. In 1923 graduated from the Moscow University Law School. Was one of the founders of the *Constructivist* group. He gained prominence with the poem *The Ulyalayev Story* (1927), in which he shows the spontaneously anarchistic element that was inherent in the Russian revolution as it had been in the Pugachov and Razin uprisings. In *The Fur Trade* (1928) and *The Second Army Commander*, S continued to develop his epic style. In the latter the poet touches upon the collapse of revolutionary idealism. In the former he expressed his fears that the end of NEP (q.v.) would hamper all private initiative. S wrote the poem *Chelyuskiniana* (1937–38), followed by two historical tragedies, *Knight John* (1927–39) and *The Livonian War* (1944), and the philosophical drama *Reading Faust* (1952).

SEMÁSHKO, Nikoláy Aleksándrovich (1874–1949), old Bolshevik, physician, member of Academy of Medical Science, USSR, an authority on problems of social hygiene. Active in the revolutionary movement from his student years. Joined the CP in 1893. Took part in the revolution of 1905. After the October revolution played an important part in the organization of public health agencies of the Soviet Union. In 1918–30, was the first people's commissar of public health of RSFSR. After 1921, was prof. of social hygiene at Moscow University.

SEMENOV–TYAN SHANSKY (until 1906 Semé-nov), Pyotr Petróvich (1827–1914), geographer, statistician, botanist and ethnologist. Honorary member, St. Petersburg Ac. of S. (1873), and Academy of Fine Arts (1874). President (1860–73) and vice president (1873–1914), Russian Geographic Society; president, Russian Ethnological Society (1889); director, Central Committee of Statistics (1864–75); president, Statistical Council (1875–97); member, State Council (1897). Graduated from St. Petersburg University (1848) and studied in Berlin, Switzerland, and Italy. Explored the Tien Shan Mountains (1856) and refuted A. von Humboldt's theory on their volcanic origin. Discovered vast glaciers at the source of the Sary Dzhaza River. Left a valuable collection of minerals, plants, insects, and ethnographic material. Determined the law governing the vertical distribution of vegetation in the Tien Shan Mountains. He made important contributions to the development of statistical sciences in Russia. Organized the first Russian Statistical Congress (1870) and supervised the first Russian census of the population (1897). Donated a fine collection of Flemish and Dutch paintings (700 paintings and 3,500 prints) to the Hermitage Museum. Author of *Geographic and Statistical Dictionary of the Russian Empire*, five volumes (1863–85); *Russia: A Complete Geographical Description of our Country*, 19 volumes (1899–1914); *Studies on the History of Dutch Painting* (1885–90).

SEMÉVSKY, Vasíly Ivánovich (1848–1916), historian. A member of the faculty of the University of St. Petersburg, he was barred from teaching as a result of his populist opinions (1884). However, he continued his studies of the peasant question as it developed during the century prior to emancipation.

SEMIPALÁTINSK, city, adm. center of Semipalatinsk Oblast, Kazakh SSR; pop. 156,000 (1959). Located on the right bank of the Irtysh River. Light industry and fruit-processing center, meat cannery. Founded 1718.

SEMIPALÁTINSK OBLAST, in Kazakh SSR situated on both banks of the Irtysh River and in the valley between lakes Zaysan and Alakol. Area 68,500 sq. mi.; pop. 520,000 (1959). Agr.: dairy cattle, sheep, grain culture; melons and grapes in the S. Food processing and light industry in Semipalatinsk.

SEMIRÉCHENSKY ALATÁU: *see* DZUNGARIAN ALATAU.

SEMYÓNOV, Grigóry Mikháylovich (1890–), White commander. A Cossack officer, he took over, after the Bolshevik Revolution, the leadership of the East Siberian Cossacks (March 1918) and placed them in the service of Admiral Kolchak's White regime. His forces, with Japanese aid, gained control of the region east of Lake Baykal, but in Nov. 1920, they were driven into China by Bolshevik troops.

SEMYÓNOV, Nikoláy Nikoláyevich (1896–), physicist and physical chemist. Fellow, Ac. of S., USSR (1932). A graduate of Petrograd University (1917), he was associated with the Leningrad Institute of Physics and Technology. Professor, Leningrad Polytechnic Institute (1928) and Moscow University (1944). Scientific  manager (1931) and director of the Institute of Physical Chemistry, Ac. of S. and academical secretary of its Division of Chemical Sciences (1957). Research concerned molecular physics and electronic phenomena pertaining to electric disruption of dielectrics. S applied his theory of dielectric disruption to the theory of thermal explosion of gas mixtures. His work on chain reactions in the course of which he discovered a new type of chemical process known as "branching chain reactions" is a major contribution to science. As a result a comprehensive theory of both branching and non-branching chain reactions was suggested. Author of *Chain Reactions* (1934); *Thermal Theory of Combustion and Explosion* (1940); *Problems of Chemical Kinetics and Reaction Capacity* (1954). Stalin (1941) and Nobel prizes (1956).

SEMYONOVA, Yekaterína Semyónovna (1786–1849), actress. Distinguished herself in the tragedies of Racine and Voltaire; was highly praised by Pushkin.

SENATE. Originally created in 1711 by Peter the Great to serve as an executive body in his absence, it became a permanent body and the chief administrative organ and highest judicial authority under the tsar. In 1802 it was given the right to issue decrees, subject to veto by the tsar, and to criticize imperial decrees. It exercised supervision over the administrative machinery through the procurator-general. Its power fluctuated over the years, and it was finally abolished in Nov. 1917.

SERAFIMÓVICH (Popov), **Aleksándr Serafímovich** (1863–1949), novelist. Of Don Cossack origin, S attended the physical-mathematical faculty of St. Petersburg University in 1883, and joined a revolutionary group. He was arrested and banished to the northern regions of the country and began his literary career in exile. His first novel, *City in the Steppe,* was written over a period of three years (1907–10) and published

in 1912. Some of his early writings were issued by Maksim Gorky's publishing house *Znanie.* His best-known novel *The Iron Stream* (1924) glorifies the Red Army commander Kovtyukh in the person of the novel's hero Kozhukh. During the 1930's S worked on a large novel *The Struggle.* It has remained unfinished and only excerpts have been published. Stalin prize (1943).

SERAPION BROTHERS: *see* LITERATURE.

SERDOBÓL: *see* SORTVALA.

SEREBRYAKÓV, Leoníd Petróvich (1890–1937), leading Communist, born in Samara (now Kuybyshev) on the Volga, son of a metalworker. In 1905 he joined the Bolshevik party, was subsequently arrested several times and was banished for two years to the Vologda region. In 1910–11, S made a tour of the R. underground organizations preparing (in company with Ordzhonikidze) for the Bolshevik conference in Prague, and took part in this conference. After returning to Russia, he was arrested and sentenced to three years' banishment in Narym, E. Siberia. S was one of the Bolshevik leaders who prepared the October revolution. In 1919–20, he was a secretary of the party Central Committee and the secretary of the Central Executive Committee of the Soviets. In 1921–22 he served as deputy commissar of transportation. A leading member of the Trotskyite group, 1921–27, he was expelled from the party in Oct. 1927. He retracted in June 1929, was readmitted in 1930 and given work in the Commissariat of Transportation. Arrested during the great purge, S was arraigned at the second show trial, condemned to death and executed.

SERGÉYEV-TSÉNSKY, Sergéy Nikoláyevich (1875–1959), R. writer. In 1901 he published a volume of poetry *Thoughts and Dreams* followed by the popular novels *Forest Swamps* (1905), *Babayev* (1905), *The Mourning Fields* (1909), *The Corner* (1905), and *Diphtheria* (1904); and a psychological novel *Valya* (1914). Following the revolution, he wrote some politically unpopular stories, *Brilliant Life* and *How to Hide from Life.* Between 1928 and 1935, he wrote a series of fragments of a single panorama, entitled *Transfiguration of Russia,* as separate novels: *Condemned to Destruction, The Cannon Are Heard, The Regiment at the Ready* and *Fierce Winter.* His best-known recent works are: *To Search, Always to Search; The Trials of Sevastopol;* and *The Brusilov Breakthrough.*

SERGÉYEVICH, Vasíly Ivánovich (1835–1911), legal historian. S was a prof. of the St. Petersburg and Moscow universities and a member of the State Council. His most important work is a collection entitled *Antiquities of Russian Law,* published in 1890–1903.

SÉRGIEV: *see* ZAGORSK.

SÉRGY RADONÉZHSKY (ca. 1319–1392), prominent leader in the early history of the Russian church, founder of the Troitsk-Sergiev monastery at Zagorsk.

He was an active supporter of Prince Dmitry Donskoy in his struggle against Tatar oppression and was canonized by the Russian Church.

SÉRNO-SOLOVYÉVICH, Nikoláy Aleksándrovich (1834–1866), revolutionary active in the populist movement, born in St. Petersburg, son of a government official. In 1860, influenced by Chernyshevsky, Dobrolyubov, and Herzen he resigned, went abroad, and became a contributor to *Sovremennik* (The Contemporary). Back in Russia, S-S joined the revolutionary organization "Land and Freedom." He was arrested in June 1862, together with Chernyshevsky, and incarcerated in the Peter and Paul Fortress. In 1865, he was exiled to Siberia, where he died.

SERÓV, Aleksándr Nikoláyevich (1820–1871), composer and critic. Initially a music critic, S became a leading figure in R. journalism. On one of his visits abroad he met Wagner whose ardent admirer he became and whose ideas he advocated in R. publications. Composer of the operas *Judith* and *Rogneda.*

SERÓV, Iván Aleksándrovich (1905–), general and security police chief. Born of a peasant family in Sokol, Vologda Province, S at the age of 18 became leader of a village soviet. He then served in the Red Army, joined the CP in 1926, and started a rapid career in the security police. During the Soviet occupation of the Baltic states in 1940, S, with extraordinary brutality, planned mass deportation of natives suspected of anti-Soviet sentiment. From 1939 to 1941 he worked in the Ukraine under Khrushchev, and became chief of the Ukrainian security police. In 1940 he was elected member of the Ukrainian party central committee. From 1941 he served under Beria, and in 1944 planned and executed wholesale deportations of several small nationalities, suspected of disloyalty to the Soviet government, from the Caucasus and Crimea to Siberia. In 1945 S was made general of security troops, and in 1945–47 was Soviet deputy commander in Germany. After Beria's arrest in 1953, S was appointed deputy minister of the Ministry of Interior, and in 1954 chairman of the Committee of State Security. In 1952 S was elected candidate member, and in 1956 full member of the party Central Committee of the USSR; in 1955 he became general of the Army. During the suppression of the Hungarian uprising in 1956, S was reported to have been present in Budapest. In 1955–57 S accompanied Khrushchev in his trips to India, London, and Finland. On Dec. 9, 1958, S was relieved of his post as chairman of the Committee of State Security, and probably appointed chief of intelligence of the General Staff.

SERÓV, Valentín Aleksándrovich (1865–1911), outstanding artist, master of portrait painting. Born in St. Petersburg in a family of musicians. Studied at the Academy of Fine Arts, 1880–85. While still in his early twenties S created pictures which made his reputation: *Girl with Peaches* (1887), *Girl in Sunlight* (1888), *Pond Overgrown, in Domotkanovo* (1888). Affiliated with the *Mir Iskusstva* (World of Art) group. S painted the portraits of  the members of the family of Alexander III and, later, those of prominent personalities—Gorky, Yermolova, Fedotov, Shalyapin and others. Still later he became interested in modern art and in antiquity and produced historical paintings and drawings (*Peter I* and *Elizabeth*) as well as illustrations for the fables of Krylov. Most of S's work is at the Tretyakov Gallery, Moscow, and the Russian Museum at Leningrad.

SERÓV, Vladímir Aleksándrovich (1910–), painter. An accomplished craftsman, he first won recognition with paintings of scenes from the revolution (*Lenin's Arrival in Petrograd, 1917*, 1937). During World War II, he produced posters and historical pictures such as *The Winter Palace Is Taken.* His other works include portraits of Soviet leaders and illustrations for editions of Tolstoy, Gorky, Nekrasov. Stalin prizes (1948, 1951).

SERÓV (f. Nadezhdinsk), city in Sverdlovsk Oblast, in Urals. RSFSR; pop. 98,000 (1959). A fast growing ind. community in recently developed steel-milling district.

SEROZEM: *see* Soils.

SÉRPUKHOV, city in Moscow Oblast, RSFSR; pop. 105,000 (1959). R.R. town, on the Oka River; major producer of cotton goods, woolens, and linen fabrics, metalworking.

SESTRORÉTSK, city in Leningrad Oblast; RSFSR; pop. 24,600 (1956). R.R. town and seaside resort on the Gulf of Finland. Metalworking is chief ind.

SEVÁN (GOKCHA) LAKE, Armenian SSR, largest in Caucasus; area 540 sq. mi.; altitude 6,275 ft. Source of hydroelectric power.

SEVASTÓPOL, city in Crimean Oblast, Ukrainian SSR; pop. 148,000 (1959). A major naval base and port on the Black Sea (Sevastopol Bay), in the S.W. part of the Crimean Peninsula, has one of the best natural harbors in Europe; rail terminal; center of electrotechnical ind. developed in the past decade. Its history goes back to antiquity; it was settled by Greek traders in the 5th century B.C. Site of the famous siege in Crimean War (1854–56).

SÉVERNAYA DVINÁ: *see* Dvina, Northern.

SÉVERNAYA ZEMLYÁ (North Land), archipelago in Arctic Ocean, off the Asian mainland at Taymyr Peninsula; polar regions; area 14,000 sq. mi. Islands include October Revolution, Pioneer, and Bolshevik.

SEVERODVÍNSK (f. Molotovsk), city in Archangel Oblast on Dvina Bay, White Sea; pop. 79,000 (1959). Industries include shipbuilding.

SEVEROURÁLSK (f. Petropavlovsk), town in Sverdlovsk Oblast, RSFSR; pop 24,300 (1959). Important center of bauxite mining in the newly developed ind. region of the middle Urals.

SÉVERSKY DONÉTS: *see* Donets, Seversky.

SÉVERTSOV, Alekséy Nikoláyevich (1866–1936), biologist. Fellow, Ac. of S., Ukrainian SSR (1925). Graduate (1890), professor (1911–30), Moscow University. Research concerned the study of the relationship between the autogenesis and the phylogenesis. Developed a theory of the biological and the morphophysiological progress. Founder of the Laboratory of Evolutionary Morphology (1930) which has become the A. N. Severtsov Institute of Animal Morphology. His numerous publications deal with the problems of evolutionary morphology and the laws of the evolutionary process. *Collected Works* in five volumes published in 1950.

SEVERYÁNIN, Igor (Igor Vasilyevich Lotarev), (1887–1942), poet and founder of the so-called "Ego-Futurism." Combined the opulent style of symbolism with a brilliant command of rhythm and with subjects and new words taken from the world of technology. Author of *The Thunder-Seething Cup* (1913), *Pineapples in Champagne* (1915), *Victoria Regia* (1915). After the revolution, S emigrated to and died in Estonia during the German occupation. He wrote anti-fascist poetry, including a fine poem dedicated to the violinist Sara Rashina, who was killed in a German prison.

SEYFÚLLINA, Lídia Nikoláyevna (1889–1954), postrevolutionary writer of Tatar origin. She was a teacher, 1906–09, and an actress on the provincial stage, 1909–14. First achieved recognition as writer following publication in the journal *Sibirskie Ogni* (The Lights of Siberia) of her story *Transgressors of the Law* (1922), an objective portrayal of homeless children. This was followed by two novels *The Compost* (1922) and *Virineya* (1925). Her longest novel *Cain's Tavern* (late 1920's), depicts the peasant uprising in Siberia during the civil war. S wrote plays including *The Black Cliff* (1931) and *Traveling Companions* (1933), and a postwar novel *On Native Soil* (1946).

SHADR (Ivanov), **Iván Dmítrievich** (1887–1941), sculptor and portrait painter, son of a carpenter. Studied art at Yekaterinburg and St. Petersburg, and later (1911–12) in Paris and Rome. In 1922 S made the dies —*The Sowers, The Red Army Man, The Peasant*, and *The Worker*—which were used on Soviet coins. He made busts and statues of Lenin, prepared sketches of monuments to Gorky and Pushkin (1938 and 1940), and painted numerous portraits.

SHÁDRINSK, city in Kurgan Oblast, W. Siberia, RSFSR; pop. 52,000 (1959). R.R. town, on Iset River, tributary of the Tobol. Has machine-building plant, leather factories, hemp and flax processing mills.

SHAFÍROV, Baron Pyótr Pávlovich (1669–1739), of Jewish-German extraction, vice cancellor and senator under Peter I; later tried and exiled but was pardoned by Empress Anne and reappointed to the Senate.

SHAFRÁN, Daniíl Borísovich (1923–), cellist, laureate of Stalin prize. First prizes at the All-Union Competition of Pianists, Violinists and Cellists (1937); Competition of the International Festival of Democratic Youth and Students in Budapest (1949), O. Vigan International Competition of Cellists in Prague (1950).

SHAGINYÁN, Mariétta Sergéyevna (1888–), poet and novelist. She gave up poetry after the revolution. Author of the mystery stories *Laurie Lane* (1925), *Mess Mend or the Yankees in Petrograd* (1926), the latter published under the pen name "Jim Dollar," supposedly an American worker in Russia; *The Hydroelectric Plant* (1931), describing the building of a power plant in Armenia; *The Ulyanov Family* (1938), concerning Lenin's family. Stalin prize for *A Voyage through*

Soviet Armenia (1950). S also wrote short stories about life in England and Czechoslovakia; and biographies, including *Taras Shevchenko* (1946), *Goethe* (1950), *Recollections of Rachmaninoff* (1957). Two Orders of the Red Banner.

SHÁKHMATOV, Alekséy Aleksándrovich (1864–1920), historian and philologist. He utilized the historical method of textual criticism to determine the original version of the Nestor Chronicle. By similar techniques, he cast new light on the sources of these materials. His main works include: *Studies in Ancient Russian Chronicles* (1908), *Outline of the History of the Ancient Period of the Russian Language* (1915).

SHÁKHTY (f. Aleksandrovsk-Grushevsky), city in Rostov Oblast, RSFSR; pop. 196,000 (1959). It is one of the principal coal-mining centers in the Donets Basin; thermal power plant; important producer of leather, textiles, and processed foods.

SHAKHTY TRIAL. In May 1928, a group of non-communist specialists employed in the industrial center of Shakhty (in Donbas) were accused of sabotaging production. French, Polish, and German capitalists were supposed to have ordered this sabotage. Eleven of the accused were sentenced to death; others were sentenced to prison terms and four were acquitted. The death sentence of six of the accused was later commuted to ten years in prison. The ST, coming immediately after the introduction of the Five Year Plans, became the focal point of a purge of non-communist technicians throughout the USSR and signified the end of the privileges they had enjoyed under the NEP.

SHAKLOVÍTY, Fyódor Leóntyevich (died in 1689), head of the *streltsy* (q.v.) and leader of the abortive conspiracy against Peter I aimed at putting the tsar's sister Sofia on the throne. He was executed in 1689.

SHALYÁPIN, Fyódor Ivánovich (1873–1938), noted bass singer, born in Kazan to a poor family. Was by  turns porter, shoemaker, and street sweeper. Studied under Usatov in Tiflis, where he made his first appearance in *Life for the Tsar.* He then sang at the Mariinsky Theater in St. Petersburg (1894), Mamontov's private opera company in Moscow (1896), Bolshoy Moscow Theater (1899), and from 1901, in Milan, Paris, London. He visited the United States in 1908 and 1922–23. His powerful voice and superb dramatic genius brought him world fame. Among his best-known parts are: Susanin in Glinka's *Life for the Tsar*, the Miller in Dargomyzhsky's *Mermaid*, Ivan the Terrible in Rimsky-Korsakov's *Maid of Pskov*, Mephisto in *Mefistofele*. Was friendly with Gorky, who had great influence on his artistic development. In 1921 emigrated from Russia, died in Paris. Author, *Pages from My Life,* New York, 1927.

SHAMÍL (1789–1871), of legendary fame, Third Imam (religious and secular head) of Dagestan, organizer of a strong nationalist movement among the Moslem mountaineers of N. Caucasus. For a quarter of a century Russia's drive toward the conquest of the rich Caucasian region and ultimate subjugation ("pacification") of its warlike people was all but frustrated by S, who under the slogan of *ghazawatt* (holy war upon infidels) rallied his followers for a determined armed resistance to Russian penetration. In 1834 S founded an independent state (imamate) which he ruled with ruthless efficiency. In 1859 the imamate was overrun and devastated by the Russians. S was captured and deported to Kaluga. A decade later he was permitted to leave for a pilgrimage to Mecca, where he died the following year (1871).

SHAPÓRIN, Yúry Aleksándrovich (1887–), composer, born in the Ukraine. Began piano lessons at the age of six, composing at ten. Graduated from St. Petersburg conservatoire (1918). S wrote the opera *The Decembrists*, a symphony *The Kulikovo Field*, sonatas, romances, scores for plays and motion pictures. His music is characterized by lyricism, harmony, and polyphonic richness. The performance of his *Ten Days That Shook the World* requires a symphonic orchestra of 120, a piano, a brass band, and a chorus of 50. This composition was performed in London, Boston, and elsewhere. Three Stalin prizes.

SHÁPOSHNIKOV, Borís Mikháylovich (1882–1945), Soviet marshal and military theorist. Graduate of the  Academy of the General Staff (1910); head of the Frunze Military Academy and the Voroshilov Military Academy. S, born in Zlatoust, was originally a tsarist officer who defected to the Bolshevik side during the civil war. He held high positions in the Soviet Army and became a member of the CPSU in 1930. In the 1930's he was chief of the General Staff and deputy people's commissar for defense. In 1939 he became a candidate member of the Central Committee of the CPSU. In 1941–42, S was again Chief of Staff and in 1943 was appointed head of the Voroshilov Military Academy. He published many books on military theory and was awarded three Lenin orders and many other decorations.

SHATELEN, Mikhaíl Andréyevich (1866–1957), electrical engineer and educator. Corresponding member, Ac. of S., USSR (1931). Hero of Socialist Labor (1956). Honored Scientist and Technologist, RSFSR (1934) and Uzbek SSR (1943). Graduate (1888), lecturer (1891), St. Petersburg University and St. Petersburg Mining Institute; professor, St. Petersburg Institute of Electrical Engineering (1893–1901). Founder and professor, St. Petersburg (Leningrad) Polytechnic Institute (1901–57). President, Main Bureau of Weights and Measures (1929); member (1929–49) and honorary member of the International Bureau of Weights and Measures (1948), the French and British Societies of Electrical Engineers; honorary secretary, American Institute of Electrical Engineers. S's research concerned general problems of electrical engineering, lighting technology, metrology, and the history of technology. Stalin prize (1949).

SHÁTSKY, Nikoláy Sergéyevich (1895–1960), geologist. Fellow, Ac. of S., USSR (1953). Grad. Moscow Mining Academy (1929). Professor, Moscow Institute of Geological Prospecting (1932); associated with the Institute of Geological Sciences (1934–55). Research on problems of stratigraphy, regional and general tectonics, and general geology. Established basic features of tectonics of the Siberian platform, W. Siberian lowland, and Central Kazakhstan. Compiled the first general tectonic map of the USSR (1952) and studied geology and tectonics of the R. platform. Author of *Outline of Tectonics of the Volga-Ural Oil-Bearing Area and the Adjacent Part of the Western Slope of Southern Urals* (1945); *Comparative Tectonics of Ancient Platforms* (1947–48). Stalin (1946), Lenin (1958) prizes.

SHATÚRA, city in Moscow Oblast, RSFSR; pop. 20,000 (1956). Site of the noted thermal power plant supplying power to the Moscow ind. district.

SHAUMYÁN, Stepán Geórgievich (1878–1918), Communist leader, pupil and close associate of Lenin.  Born in Tiflis, where he graduated from secondary school, S developed an early interest in Marxism, was active in the local workers' movement from 1898. Expelled from Riga Polytechnicum in 1900, S was deported to his native Caucasus, where he continued revolutionary work, joining the Social Democratic party a year later. In 1905–07 S together with Stalin guided the revolutionary uprising in Transcaucasia. At the 6th Party Congress (1917), S was elected to membership in the Central Committee of the party; made chairman of the Council of People's Commissars in Baku, April 1918. Executed by the British with a group of 25 leading Bolsheviks (the so-called Baku Commissars) in Sept. 1918.

SHÁVLI: *see* ŠIAULIAI.

SHAYN, Grigóry Abrámovich (1892–1956), astronomer. Fellow, Ac. of S., USSR (1939). Graduate of Perm University (1919). Associated with Pulkovo Observatory (1922–25) and its Simeiz branch (1925–45); director of the Crimean Astrophysical Observatory (1952). Research concerned astral spectroscopy and physics of gas nebulae; investigated changes in the spectra of variable stars and the content of carbon isotopes in the atmospheres of cold stars. Discoverer of a new comet, about 150 new gas nebulae and interstellar magnetic fields. He studied double stars, small planets, meteor showers, solar corona. Author of *Atlas of Diffuse Gas Nebulae* (1952). Honorary member of various foreign scientific institutes.

SHCHÁPOV, Afanásy Prokófyevich (1830–1876), historian, born in Siberia, the son of a priest. His thesis for Kazan University dealt with the church schism of the 17th century which he interpreted as a popular protest against state policies in some ways connected with contemporary peasant disturbances. A "federalist" in his interpretation of R. history generally, he opposed state absolutism in his own time and expressed populist views. This brought his dismissal from the faculty of Kazan University (1861) and banishment to his native Irkutsk. There he did work on Siberian history and, altering his former position, came to attribute Russia's development to western influences first introduced under Peter the Great.

SHCHEDRÍN, Silvéster Fyódorovich (1791–1830), landscape painter. S went to Italy in 1818 and never returned. His Italian landscapes are well painted and pleasing, and the works of "Signor Silvestro" were highly valued by his contemporaries. He died of consumption and was buried at Sorrento.

SHCHEGLOVÍTOV, Iván Grigóryevich (1861–1918), jurist and statesman. Appointed minister of justice in the Goremykin government (1906), he held that post for nine years. He became increasingly reactionary, abetting the anti-Semitic excesses of the years after 1906. He was the instigator of the prosecution of Beylis (q.v.) on the charge of ritual murder. His mounting unpopularity finally forced his removal (summer 1915). Made president of the Council of State (Jan. 1917) he was swept from influence by the February revolution and executed by the Bolsheviks the following year.

SHCHEGLÓVSK: *see* KEMEROVO.

SHCHÉLKIN, Kiríll Ivánovich (1911–), physicist. Corresponding member, Ac. of S., USSR (1953). Graduated from Simferopol Pedagogical Institute (1932) and joined the Institute of Physical Chemistry, Ac. of S. Research concerns physics of combustion and explosion. S adduced experimental proof of the influence of the turbulent flow of a starting combustible mixture on the acceleration of combustion and subsequently suggested the transition of slow combustion to detonation.

SHCHÉPKIN, Mikhaíl Semyónovich (1788–1863), prominent actor. A serf until 1821, S began his theatrical career in 1805. In 1822 made his debut on the Moscow stage. S was the founder of the realistic school in R. acting, and was a friend of Herzen, Gogol, Belinsky, and Shevchenko. S was noted for his interpretation of the leading parts in the plays of Griboyedov and Gogol.

SHCHERBAKÓV, Aleksándr Sergéyevich (1901–1945), government and CP official, born near Moscow in a worker's family. Joined the CP in 1918. Active in Komsomol in Turkestan, 1918–22. In 1921–24 studied at CP university in Sverdlov, and in 1930–32 at party historical institute; secretary of Union of Soviet Writers, 1934; first secretary of Moscow city and oblast party committees, 1938–45; made a member of the party Central Committee at 18th Party Congress 1939, and secretary of the Central Committee 1941; candidate member of the Politburo, 1941. Held important posts during World War II, achieving the rank of Colonel General, 1943; head of Main Political Administration of the Red Army and Deputy-Commissar of Defense, 1942. His death in 1945 was later ascribed to the "doctors' plot."

SHCHERBAKÓV, Dmítry Ivánovich (1893–), geologist and geochemist. Fellow, Ac. of S., USSR (1953). Graduate of Simferopol University (1922); worked at the Institute of Geology (1939–54). Simultaneously lectured at Leningrad University and Polytechnic Institute. Academy Secretary, Division of Geology and Geography, Ac. of S. (1953). Participated in expeditions to Transbaykalia, Kazakhstan, the Crimea, the Kola Peninsula, and the Central Urals. Studied mineral deposits in Central Europe and Sicily (1927).

SHCHERBAKÓV: *see* RYBINSK.

SHCHÉRBAN, Aleksándr Nazárovich (1906–), mining engineer. Fellow (1957), academic secretary of the executive board (1953–57), and vice president (1957), Ac. of S., Ukrainian SSR. Graduate of Dnepropetrovsk Mining Institute (1933). Assistant director of the Mining Institute (1946–53). His research on heat transfer problems in mines served as a basis for the development of mining thermodynamics, a new branch of science. Inventor of a device for the automatic determination of methane in the mine atmosphere.

SHCHERBÁTOV, Prince Mikhaíl Mikháylovich (1733–1790), historian and essayist, and wealthy landowner of wide cosmopolitan culture. His *Russian History from Earliest Times* (1770–91) in 7 volumes stressed the role of the nobility and was the first to utilize archive materials as well as the chronicle.

SHCHERBÍNOVKA: *see* DZERZHINSK.

SHCHIPACHÓV, Stepán Petróvich (1899–), poet, born in the Ural area, of a poor peasant family. He was drafted into the army in 1917, served with the White forces in 1918, then deserted to the Red Army's Chapayev Division. He became a Communist party member in 1919 and served in the Red Army as a political officer until 1931, when he entered the Institute for Red Professors in Moscow. S began writing poetry in 1915. His themes were the war, rural life, wounded soldiers, and, in 1917, "the bloodsucking tsar" and "bourgeois vampires." His first book of poetry, *On the Graves of the Ages*, was published in the Crimea in 1923. Later published collections were *One Sixth* (1931) and *Disregarding Pages* (1932). His long poem *Frontliners* also appeared in 1932. During World War II, S was a war correspondent and published a book of poems from the front in 1941, the poem *The Cottage in Shushensky* about Lenin (1944), and the long poem *Pavlik Morozov* (1950). S visited the United States as a member of the delegation of Soviet journalists. Stalin prizes (1949, 1951).

SHCHÓRS, Nikoláy Aleksándrovich (1895–1919), commander of the Red Army during the civil war in the Ukraine. One of the organizers of partisan detachments against the Germans. Was killed in action.

SHCHÚKIN, Aleksándr Nikoláyevich (1900–), radio engineer. Fellow, Ac. of S., USSR (1953). Major general, engineering and technical corps. Graduate (1927) and professor (1939), Leningrad Institute of Electrical Engineering. Simultaneously lectured at the Leningrad Naval Academy (1933–45) and in other scientific institutes. Research concerns the propagation of short waves; advanced a theory and calculation methods for long-distance short-wave communication and developed a new system of radio-telegraph transmission including methods of interference control. Author of *Propagation of Radio Waves* (1940).

SHCHÚKIN, Borís Vasílyevich (1894–1939), actor. People's Artist of the USSR. Made his debut in 1920 in a studio directed by Vakhtangov and remained with the Vakhtangov Theater until his death. S appeared on the Soviet screen and played the leading parts in *The Aviators* and in *The Generation of Victors*. Particularly notable were his interpretations of the part of

Lenin in the films *Lenin in October* (1937) and *Lenin in 1918* (1939).

SHEEP BREEDING. The January count of S. was, in mill., 89.7 in 1916 (within present Soviet boundaries) and rose to 104.2 by 1928. The herds then declined almost two-thirds by 1934, as the result of collectivization losses, and were partly restored, to 79.9 mill., by 1941. The 1960 count was 136.0 mill., of which about 57% were owned by collective farms, 21% by state farms, the remainder being privately owned.

Wool output amounted, in thousand tons, to 192 in 1913, 182 in 1928, 161 in 1940, and 322 in 1959. The average quality of wool improved considerably over time, the number of fine-fleeced S having increased 4.7 times between 1940 and 1958. The annual wool clip per sheep was 2.7 kg. in 1958.

An effort was made to expand selective breeding in some 70 state farms where pedigreed S are bred. Artificial insemination was promoted and about 13.4 mill. S were so treated in 1940. Since 1951, the government introduced regional specialization: the most suitable variety of S was selected for each region, in which its breeding is supposed to be promoted in preference to other varieties. About 40 breeds are being raised.

SHÉIN, Mikhaíl Borísovich (died in 1634), army commander whose troops defended Smolensk for 20 months against Poland and Lithuania (1609–11). During the unsuccessful retaliation war against Poland in 1634, he was accused of treason and executed.

SHELÉPIN, Aleksándr Nikoláyevich (1918–), Komsomol leader and security police chief. Graduated from the Moscow Institute of History, Philosophy and Literature. During the Soviet-Finnish war, 1939–40, Shelepin was at the front, in 1940 joined the CP, and became a Komsomol official. During 1940–43 S rose from instructor to head of section and to secretary of the Moscow committee of the Komsomol. In 1943 he was transferred to the Central Committee of the Komsomol as one of its secretaries, and in 1952 became its first secretary. At the 19th and 20th Party Congresses he was elected member of the Central Committee of the CP, and in 1954 member of the Supreme Soviet of the USSR and member of the Foreign Affairs Committee of the Soviet of Nationalities. In 1957 he became vice president, executive committee, World Federation of Democratic Youth. In 1958 Shelepin was appointed chairman of the Committee of State Security.

SHELGUNÓV, Nikoláy Vasílyevich (1824–1891), a frequent contributor to the outstanding publications of his time—*Sovremennik* (The Contemporary), *Russkaya Mysl* (Russian Thought), later *Russkoye Slovo* (The Russian Word). An eloquent advocate of general education and enlightenment, emancipation of women, and western culture, he became a close friend and follower of Herzen in the 1850's, during his stay abroad. Together with L. M. Mikhaylov, he published a "Proclamation" addressed to the younger generation, which led to his arrest. Best known of his writings are *Sketches of Russian Life*.

SHÉLIKHOV GULF, extreme N. of Okhotsk Sea; area 108,000 sq. mi.; Penzhina and Gizhiga rivers empty into it.

SHÉLLER-MIKHÁYLOV, Aleksándr Konstantínovich (1838–1900), novelist, son of an Estonian musician. In 1864 his novel *Rotting Swamp* appeared in the magazine *Sovremennik* (The Contemporary). This was followed by many other books— *Shypov's Life, They Cut Wood and the Chips Fly* (1877) and others. He expressed the views of those in the 1860's and the 1870's who advocated active participation in practical and cultural affairs and believed in training the young as engineers and technicians. Was opposed to serfdom.

SHEMYÁKIN, Mikhaíl Mikháylovich (1908–), organic chemist. Fellow, Ac. of S., USSR (1958). Graduate of Moscow University (1930). Associated with the Scientific Research Institute of Organic Intermediate Products and Dyes (1930–35) and the All-Union Institute of Experimental Medicine (1935–45). Professor, Moscow Textile Institute (1942). Joined the Institute of Biological and Medical Chemistry (1945), and has been associated with the Institute of Organic Chemistry since 1958. Research concerns the chemistry of antibiotics, vitamins, and other natural and biologically active substances. Developed methods of the synthesis of several organic compounds, including chloromycetine, vitamin K_3, and others.

SHÉNFER, Klávdy Ippolítovich (1885–1946), electrical engineer. Fellow, Ac. of S., USSR (1932). Graduate (1910) and professor (1917), Moscow School of Technology. Professor, Institute of Power Engineering (1930) where he founded and headed the electromechanical laboratory. Research on new designs for electrical equipment, and electromagnetic processes. Designed a new type of induction motor. Stalin prize (1943).

SHEPÍLOV, Dimítry Trofímovich (1905–), Soviet journalist and diplomat, born in Ashkhabad. Corresponding member, USSR Ac. of S., Department of Economics, Philosophy and Law (1953). During World War II S was political commissar of the Ukrainian front working under Khrushchev. In 1948, director of propaganda and agitation department of the Central Committee of CPSU; 1950, deputy to Supreme Soviet; 1952–56, editor of *Pravda;* 1952, member of the Central Committee of CPSU, and 1954, secretary; 1954, chairman of Council of Nationalities and of Foreign Affairs Commission of the Supreme Soviet USSR; 1955–56, member of Soviet delegations to England, Germany, Yugoslavia, Egypt; 1956–57, minister of foreign affairs. In 1957 was dismissed as minister of foreign affairs because of "anti-party" activity; the Central Committee Plenum in June 1957 removed S from the positions of secretary and member of the Central Committee of CPSU. Since then has been head of a Scientific Institute in Kirghiz Republic. S is the author of a textbook on political economy.

SHEREMÉTEV, Borís Petróvich (1652–1719), field marshal, general, and outstanding diplomat, participant in the N. war against Sweden.

SHESTOV (Schwartzman), **Lev Isákovich** (1866–1938), religious philosopher, existentialist. S was born in Kiev and studied law in Moscow. After the revolution he settled in Paris. His principal works include: *Dostoyevsky and Nietzsche* (1903), *The Idea of the Good* *in Tolstoy and Nietzsche* (1907), *The Power of the Keys* (1923), *The Night of Gethsemane* (1925), and *Athens and Jerusalem* (1938 in German).

SHEVCHÉNKO, Tarás Grigóryevich (1814–1861), Ukrainian poet and playwright, of peasant origin and a serf whose liberty was "purchased" in 1838. He was an ardent Ukrainian patriot and leader of those who opposed Russia's rule over his native land. His early poetry, published under the title of *Kobzár* in 1840,  described the sufferings of the Ukrainian peasantry and the tragedy of Ukrainian womanhood denied even the few civic rights available to peasants under serfdom. His poetry and virtually all of his literary work are marked with a hatred of the Moscovites and a yearning for a free and independent Ukraine. His poem *Gaydamáki* (1841) portrays the peasant uprisings of 1768, when the peasants and Cossacks of W. Ukraine rose against the overlordship of the Poles. S's satirical poem *The Dream* (1844) is an attack on autocracy. In 1847 S was arrested as a member of a secret revolutionary society and sent to serve as an army private at Orenburg, in the Ural region. In 1850 he was exiled to Novopetróvsk (now Fort Shevchenko) where he remained until 1857. He wrote poems while in exile, in the Ukrainian language, and novels in Russian. Returning to St. Petersburg in 1858, he collaborated with Chernyshevsky and Dobrolyubov and wrote poems which, together with his other writings, form the basis of the literary Ukrainian language. S was also a painter, known for his portraits and landscapes. A large number of his works are preserved in the museum bearing his name in Moscow. Among other known works of S are the play *Nazar Stodolya*, the poem *The Caucasus*, the novels *The Musician* and *The Princess*. Of high interest is his diary.

SHEVYAKÓV, Lev Dmítryevich (1899–), mining engineer. Fellow, Ac. of S., USSR (1939). Graduate (1912) and professor (1920), Yekaterinoslav (Dnepropetrovsk) Mining Institute. He was associated with the Siberian Institute of Technology (1929), Sverdlovsk Mining Institute (1932), Moscow Mining Institute (1944–52), and Mining Institute, Ac. of S. (since 1952). Member of the State Planning Commission and chairman of its technical council. Basic line of scientific activity and research concerns the application of analytical methods to problems of mining as summarized in his *Principles of the Theory of Coal Mine Planning* (1950), translated into Hungarian and Chinese. Author of *Draining Mines* (4th ed., 1954). Stalin prize (1942).

SHEVYRYÓV, Stepán Petróvich (1806–1864), literary historian, critic, poet, prof. of Russian literature at Moscow University. His early enthusiasm for the romanticist notions of contemporary German philosophers, particularly Schelling and Schlegel, gave way to extreme nationalism in his mature years. Out of his unwavering faith in the church, the tsars, and the people of Russia grew a vision of Russia's supreme destiny in the family of European nations.

SHIDLOVSKY COMMISSION, appointed by the government on Jan. 29, 1905 (O.S.), with Senator V. N. Shidlovsky at its head, for the purpose of "investigating the causes of discontent among the workers in the St. Petersburg area." The move came as a result of the wave of strikes and revolutionary unrest which followed the shooting down of workers during a peaceful demonstration led by Father Gapon three weeks earlier on Jan. 9 (O.S.). The efforts of the commission found some support among the more moderate leftist groups, but were bitterly denounced by the Bolsheviks as "an attempt to deceive the workers, by diverting their attention from the revolutionary class struggle." The commission, whose activities lasted less than a month, was dissolved in Feb. 1905.

SHIFRÍN, Nísson Abrámovich (1892–), stage designer. Began his professional career in Kiev in 1919; stage manager of the Moscow Central Theater of the Red Army since 1934. His best productions are *The Taming of the Shrew*, A. P. Stein's *The Admiral's Flag*, and *The Stalingraders* by V. P. Chepurin.

SHILKA RIVER, in Chita Oblast, RSFSR; left tributary of Amur River; length 340 mi.

SHIMÁNSKY, Yulián Aleksándrovich (1883–), shipbuilding engineer. Fellow, Ac. of S., USSR (1953). Graduate of Naval Engineering School (1905) and Military Naval Academy (1910); professor, Scientific Research Institute of the Shipbuilding Industry (1938). Research on various problems of structural mechanics, the theory of ships, and general problems of shipbuilding. Other studies concern the history of mechanics, theory of magnetic and pyroscopic compasses, artillery, mathematical physics, and ballistics. Developed norms of permissible stresses for strength calculations of ship construction. Author of *Dynamic Calculation of Ship Constructions* (1948); *Design of Intermittent Connections of Ship Hulls* (1948); *Collection of Articles on Shipbuilding* (1954). Stalin prize (1941).

SHINGARÉV, Andréy Ivánovich (1860–1918), leader of the Constitutional Democratic (Kadet) party. S, a physician, was an active worker in the zemstvo organizations and member of the second, third, and fourth State Duma. Under the Provisional Government he was minister of finance (March-May 1917) and minister of agriculture (May-July 1917). After the October revolution, S was arrested by the Bolsheviks and, while under arrest, assassinated by soldiers together with another Kadet leader, Kokoshkin.

SHIPBUILDING INDUSTRY. According to unofficial estimates the Soviet Navy included, in 1959, 25 cruisers, 125 destroyers, and 420 submarines, while the merchant fleet apparently consisted of about 1,190 ships of 3,486,000 gross tons. Of the latter some 430,000 tons (282 ships) were fishing and whaling craft, and 157,000 tons (166 ships) were auxiliaries such as tugs and ice-breakers. 844 of the merchant ships (2,231,000 tons) were built between 1945 and 1959, leaving 346 (1,255,000 tons) of wartime and prewar construction. The greater share of the merchant ships, however, was built in foreign shipyards. Of the 2,175,000 tons of new tonnage acquired in 1951–59 only a third was produced in the Soviet Union; another third was produced in Poland, Hungary, and East Germany, and 13% was produced in Finland.

The SI was first developed in Russia in the early 18th century under Peter the Great. It remained weak up to the period of World War I, and most of the R. ships in use at that time were imported from countries of W. Europe.

In 1921, a program was initiated that aimed at the reconstruction and further development of both the military and the merchant fleets. It was only in 1929, however, that the SI again attained its 1913 level.

During the first two Five Year Plans (1928–37) the production of ships was four times larger, according to official data, than it had been in years 1904 to 1913. The larger ships built during this period included six freight and passenger ships of the "Smolny" type, a number of lumber-carrying ships, several types of freighters and tankers designed for use in the Caspian Sea, several diesel-powered ships for use in the Black Sea, and several ocean-going tankers. At the same time existing production facilities were modernized, and new facilities created. This made possible a very considerable increase in production during the three years that preceded World War II. According to official data five times more shipping was produced in 1938 than in any earlier year, and more in 1939 than in the entire period 1903 to 1913.

Another large-scale program of modernization and further expansion was adopted after the termination of World War II. It emphasized the building of more modern types of ships, the standardization of models, and such improvements in the techniques of production as the automatic gas cutting and cold shaping of metal parts, the replacing of riveting by welding, the construction of hulls from large pre-equipped sections through assembly line methods, the simultaneous working on the hull, on details and the installation of equipment, and the specialization of individual plants and shops in the making of individual models and parts. According to official data these measures resulted in a doubling of the productivity of labor by 1955 (by comparison with 1940), while the annual rate of production of sea-going freighters and tankers rose nearly 300 per cent during the period 1951–55; of ships for the fishing fleet, 250 per cent; and of river-going steamships, 87 per cent.

Particular emphasis has been placed in recent years on the construction of submarines, rather than of large surface ships; on the construction of large numbers of fishing and whaling ships; and on increasing the size and power of the larger freighters and tankers. The First Seven Year Plan (1959–65) provides for a doubling of the total tonnage of the merchant fleet, with a slightly greater emphasis on dry cargo ships (2.2 times) than on tankers (1.8 times). These tonnage increases, together with the statement that the average size of the ships will increase by 20%, indicate that there should be 1,070 dry cargo ships (4,540,000 tons) and 160 tankers (1,010,000 tons) in 1965. The net increase in tonnage over the seven years will then be approximately 3 mill. tons.

The first nuclear ship, the ice-breaker *Lenin*, was launched in 1959.   P. I. M.

SHÍPOV, Dimítry Nikoláyevich (1851–1920), leader in the zemstvo movement, moderate liberal. A wealthy landowner, graduated from the University of St. Petersburg, he was active in public affairs from 1877. From 1893 to 1904 he was chairman of the executive board of the Moscow provincial zemstvo and was a leader in the movement for constitutional reform. In June 1905 S was invited by the tsar to form a liberal cabinet which did not materialize because of the opposition of the Constitutional Democratic party. In Nov. 1905 S founded, together with A. I. Guchkov and others, the "Union of October 17," which, however, he left in 1906. In 1906 he was elected member of the State Council where he represented the Moscow zemstvo. S retired from public life in 1911. In 1918 he published a volume of reminiscences.

SHIRSHÓV, Pyótr Petróvich (1905–1953), oceanographer, hydrobiologist, and arctic explorer. Fellow, Ac. of S., USSR (1939). Hero of the Soviet Union (1938). People's commissar and minister of the navy, USSR (1942–48). Joined the first Soviet drifting station "North Pole-1" as a hydrobiologist and participated in expeditions on the SS's *Sibiryakov* (1932) and *Chelyuskin* (1933–34). Research concerned the plankton of arctic seas; established laws which govern the propagation of warm waters from the Arctic Ocean to the polar basin.

SHÍSHKIN, Iván Ivánovich (1832–1898), landscape painter, designer, and engraver. Member of the Society of Circulating Exhibitions (*Peredvizhniki*). He painted *Noon Near Moscow, Rye, Forest Distances, Morning in a Pine Forest, Rain in an Oak Forest, Naval Grove.*

SHISHKÓV, Aleksándr Semyónovich (1754–1841), vice-admiral of the fleet and minister of education from 1824 to 1828, an amateur philologist and would-be reformer of the R. language. In *Talks Among Friends of the Russian Language* and *Discussion on the Old and the New in the Russian Language* (1803), he opposed the linguistic innovations introduced by Karamzin, and argued that new words should be evolved from R. roots rather than adapted from foreign languages.

SHISHKÓV, Vyacheslív Yákovlevich (1873–1945), novelist. Graduated from a technical college in Vyshny Volochok. Was a land-surveyor and hydrologist. Traveled much and knew Siberia especially well. His story *Tayga* is one of his best prerevolutionary works. During the first years of NEP, he published *The Band* (1924), *Lake Peipus* (1925), and the cycle *Playful Stories* (1922–27). Between 1918 and 1932 he wrote the novel *Sullen River*. During the last years of his life S worked on a panoramic historical work, *Yemelyan Pugachov* (1938–45). Stalin prize (1946).

SHKIRYÁTOV, Matvéy Fyódorovich (1883–1954), leading Communist. S became a Bolshevik in 1906 and was active in Moscow politics in 1917. In 1922 he was appointed to the party Control Commission and soon became prominent in that position as a favorite of Stalin. In 1939 S was elected to the Central Committee of the CPSU where he became the representative of the Control Commission in 1952.

SHKLÓVSKY, Iósif Samuílovich (1916–), astrophysicist. A graduate of Moscow University (1938), he has been associated with P. K. Shternberg State Institute of

Astronomy since 1944. S developed the theory of ionization of the solar corona and classified the radiation of galactics quantitatively into thermal and non-thermal types; he studied the origin of cosmic rays in the shells of new stars, and the infrared radiation of night sky and the aurora australis and borealis. Author of *The Solar Corona* (1951); *Cosmic Radiation* (1956).

SHKLÓVSKY, Víktor Borísovich (1893–), critic, writer, and a literary theorist. A leading formalist, he was one of the founders of *Opoyaz* (Society for the Study of Poetic Language). His theory of the distortion of reality by literary devices influenced the R. writers of the twenties—Zamyatin, Olesha, and Kaverin. His autobiography, *A Sentimental Journey*, was published in 1923.

SHLYÁPNIKOV, Aleksándr Gavrílovich (1883–193?), Bolshevik, leader of the "Workers' Opposition." Joined the revolutionary movement in the 1890's. After several arrests, he emigrated in 1908 and spent most of the next decade on assignments abroad for the Bolsheviks. After 1915 he was a member of the Bolshevik Central Committee and was active in the Soviets and during the October revolution. Chairman of the Metal Workers' Union, S became the first commissar for labor after the October revolution. However his leadership of the "Workers' Opposition" cost him this post and he was expelled from the Bolshevik party. Condemned as a "syndicalist," he was presumably liquidated in the purges of the 1930's.

SHMAKÓV, Pável Vasílyevich (1885–), radio and television engineer. Honored Scientist and Technologist, RSFSR (1948). Graduate of Moscow University (1913); professor, Leningrad Electrotechnical Institute of Communications (1937). First one to establish radio communication between a moving train and a car in the Soviet Union (1924). Introduced long-distance phototelegraph communication between Moscow and Berlin (1927). Developed low-definition television (1931) and a system of prospecting oil wells by means of TV. Research on color and three-dimensional television. Several inventions and patents.

SHMÁLHAUZEN, Iván Ivánovich (1884–), zoologist. Fellow, Ac. of S., USSR (1935) and Ukrainian SSR (1922). Graduate, Kiev University (1907); professor, Moscow University (1938–48). Director, Institute of Zoology and Biology, Ac. of S., Ukrainian SSR (1930–41); A. N. Severtsov Institute of Animal Morphology (1938–48); presently associated with the Zoological Institute, Ac. of S. Research concerns evolutionary morphology, comparative anatomy and the origin of vertebrates. Author of *Problems of Darwinism* (1946).

SHMELYÓV, Iván Sergéyevich (1875–1950), author. Became known with his story *The Man from the Restaurant* (1911). A profound knowledge of the life of the people and a rich and brilliant style marked S prerevolutionary writing. After the revolution he emigrated. The most important of his books are *A Love Story* (1929), *Summer of the Lord* (1933), *The Pilgrimage* (1935), and *Heavenly Paths* (1937–38). In addition, S wrote a novel called *The Soldiers* of which only fragments were published, and many articles and stories. During the revolution and the civil war, S was drawn to people who searched for a mercy to counteract anger and violence. The Russian Orthodox Church, particularly its ritual, formed a basic theme of his work.

SHMIDT, Vasíly Vladímirovich (1886–?,) Bolshevik party member from 1905. Secretary of the Petrograd Party Committee and the Petrograd Council of Trade Unions. Active participant in the October revolution. After October, was secretary of the Central Committee of the All-Russian Trade Unions, then people's commissar of labor. In the thirties, S was arrested and disappeared.

SHNÍRELMAN, Lev Genrikhovich (1905–1938), mathematician. Corresponding member, Ac. of S., USSR (1933). Graduate, Moscow University (1925); professor, Don Polytechnic Institute, Novocherkassk (1929); joined the Mathematical Institute, Ac. of S. (1934). Developed qualitative methods of variation calculus and solved (with L. A. Lyusternik) the Poincaré problem; suggested general metric methods in the number theory.

SHOES INDUSTRY: *see* LEATHER AND SHOES INDUSTRY.

SHOLEM ALEICHEM (Solomon Rabinovich) (1859–1916), Yiddish humorist (known in America as  "The Jewish Mark Twain"). Born in Pereyaslav, a small town in the Ukraine, died in New York. The so-called *World of Sholem Aleichem* includes many hundreds of distinct types—and characters —some of whom have become proverbial, such as Menachem Mendel. Many of his works were translated into English: *The Old Country, Tevye and His Daughters, Wandering Stars, Motel, the Son of Peise the Cantor,* and others. His "monologues," "Tales of Jewish Children," as well as his numerous other short stories are brilliant and his humor mixes with the tragic which often reminds one of Cervantes, Molière, and Gogol. He also wrote novels and plays.

SHÓLOKHOV, Mikhaíl Aleksándrovich (1905–), outstanding novelist, born and brought up among the Cossacks of the Don. He attended the parish and the high school in his native "stanitsa" (large Cossack village), and participated in the civil war on the side of the Reds. He joined the CP in the early 1920's and  began writing in 1922. In his very first literary efforts, many of them unpublished, S plunged into the description of the civil strife in the Don region, picturing it as part of the tragedy of Cossack life, the fratricidal struggle within the Cossack community. This tragedy is the theme of his two early collections published under the titles *Tales of the Don* (1925) and *The Azure Steppe* (1926). These books, together with other early works, both published and unpublished, must be viewed as sketches of his masterpiece *Quiet Don* (1926–40). *Quiet Don* (also known in the English translations as *Quiet Flows the Don* and *The Silent Don*) is an epic of the civil war. In its descriptive portions as well as in its treatment of the action, *Quiet Don* is reminiscent of Tolstoy's *War and Peace*. The masterful portrayal of the love story of Grigory and Aksinya, a love that triumphs over all social tragedies and catastrophes unleashed by the revolution, is one of the best in R. literature. This, together with the poetic description of the scenery of the Don country and the vivid battle scenes, is what makes *Quiet Don* the outstanding novel it is.

Book One of his second novel, *The Virgin Soil Upturned* was published in 1932 and was followed by Book Two, published complete in 1959–60. This is a novel about the collectivization. S's third and unfinished novel, *They Fought for Their Country* of which only a few excerpts have been published to date, is a story of World War II. Among his recent writings is the tale *Man's Destiny*. S is the recipient of many awards, member of the Ac. of S., and deputy to the Supreme Soviet. In 1960 he accompanied Khrushchev to the United States.

SHORS: *see* POPULATION.

SHOSTAKÓVICH, Dmítry Dmítryevich (1906–), composer, born in St. Petersburg, in the family of a chemical engineer. At the age of 11 S wrote his first composition. Started piano lessons at the age of 9; studied piano and composition at the St. Petersburg conservatoire and graduated in 1925. His first symphony  composed at the age of 19 won him international acclaim; it was performed in 1926 in Leningrad and, eventually, conducted by Toscanini, Stokowski, and Bruno Walter. S, a very prolific composer, by 1958 had completed eleven symphonies, two piano concertos, six string quartets, a concerto for violin and orchestra, piano music, compositions for motion pictures, songs, music for plays, oratorios, cantatas, orchestral suites. His opera *Lady Macbeth from Mtsensk* was flayed in a *Pravda* editorial (1936) entitled "Confusion Instead of Music" and, as a consequence, the composer fell into disgrace. His ballet suite *Limpid Stream* was suppressed by the Soviet government as deviating from traditional R. music and being too sensational. During World War II S was rehabilitated but banned again in postwar years. His final rehabilitation came in 1956.

S is a master of polyphony following in the wake of J. S. Bach and the R. polyphonists Taneyev and Glazunov. It was said of S that "his orchestra pulsates like a live body." His musical roots originate with Bach, Beethoven, Glinka, Tchaikovsky, Musorgsky, Mahler, and Prokofiev. His music has influenced many modern composers including the young generation of musicians in the Soviet Union.

BIBLIOGRAPHY: V. I. Seroff, *Shostakovich*, New York, 1943.

SHOW TRIALS. The first public trials of "treasonous" elements initiated by the Soviet government took place in 1928–29. They were part of Stalin's plan to supplant the old technical elite with fresh, more trustworthy personnel. Thus, 47 engineers from the Donets Basin were tried and convicted (May 18–July 5, 1928) on charges of "sabotaging" the national industrial effort. Five were executed, while six others received commutations of their death sentences (*see* SHAKHTY

TRIAL). In May 1929 similar charges were brought against another group of technicians, all of whom went to their deaths. The following year further contingents of experts were arraigned for alleged "wrecking" and counterrevolutionary activities. One such group was the "Industrial Party" (q.v.). In this case the accused confessed and recanted with grotesque enthusiasm. They were duly liquidated. Supposed "saboteurs" from the staff of the Gosplan met the same fate. In 1931, a "Menshevik spy ring" (q.v.) was allegedly exposed and annihilated.

With the inauguration, in the mid-1930's, of the great Stalinist purge, the ST assumed the central place in the ritual of condemnation and death. The ST of 1935–38 were preceded (Dec. 28–29, 1934) by the trial, *in camera* at the Military Collegium, of Nikolayev and others allegedly involved in the assassination of S. Kirov. Nikolayev, Kotolynov, Rumyantsev, Mandelstam, and Levin were all found guilty of Kirov's murder and were executed.

The initial show trial took place before the Military Collegium at Leningrad, Jan. 15–16, 1935. Involved were members of the "Moscow Center," notably G. Ye. Zinoviev and L. B. Kamenev, accused of "moral" responsibility for Kirov's death. Others accused were G. E. Yevdokimov and I. P. Bakayev. All were found guilty. Zinoviev received ten years of imprisonment and Kamenev five years, while Yevdokimov and Bakayev were each sentenced to eight years.

In the trial of the "Trotskyite-Zinovievite Terrorist Center" (Aug. 19–24, 1936), A. Ya. Vyshinsky acted as state prosecutor and the Moscow court was under the presidency of V. V. Ulrich. Sixteen defendants were accused of plotting to assassinate party and government leaders. The defendants were Zinoviev, Kamenev, Yevdokimov, I. N. Smirnov, I. P. Bakayev, V. V. Ter-Vaganyan, S. V. Mrachkovsky, E. A. Dreitser, E. S. Holtsman, I. I. Reingold, R. V. Pickel, V. P. Olberg, K. B. Berman-Yurin, Fritz David, M. Lurye, and N. Lurye. The first seven were found guilty of Kirov's assassination, the other nine of membership in the "Trotskyite-Zinovievist Center." All confessed and were shot.

The next trial, that of the "Anti-Soviet Trotskyite Center," took place before the same court in Moscow, Jan. 25–30, 1937. Vyshinsky conducted the prosecution of seventeen defendants charged with attempting to overthrow the Soviet government by way of a secret organization in the capital established on orders from Trotsky. The accused were Y. L. Pyatakov, K. B. Radek, G. Y. Sokolnikov, L. P. Serebryakov, N. I. Muralov, Y. A. Livshitz, Y. N. Drobnis, M. S. Boguslavsky, I. A. Knyazev, S. A. Rataychak, B. A. Norkin, A. A. Shestov, M. S. Stroilov, Y. D. Turok, I. Y. Hrashche, G. E. Pushin, and V. V. Arnold. Thirteen were shot. Of the four who escaped death, Sokolnikov and Radek were found guilty of "criminal activities" but not of the actual organization and execution of the crimes themselves. Thus their punishment was limited to ten years' imprisonment. Arnold too received ten years, since he had only "attempted" terrorist acts. Stroilov was found to have carried out "certain commissions," but nothing more. Consequently his sentence was imprisonment for eight years.

Twenty-one members of the "Anti-Soviet Bloc of Rightists and Trotskyites" went on trial in Moscow, March 2–13, 1938, with the same officials as before presiding. Arraigned on the now-familiar charges were N. I. Bukharin, A. I. Rykov, G. G. Yagoda, N. N. Krestinsky, Ch. G. Rakovsky, A. P. Rosengolts, V. I. Ivanov, M. A. Chernov, G. F. Grinko, I. A. Zelensky, S. A. Bessonov, I. Ikramov, F. Khodzhayev, V. F. Sharangovich, P. T. Zubarev, P. P. Bulanov, L. G. Levin, D. D. Pletnev, I. N. Kozakov, V. A. Maksimov-Dikovsky, and P. P. Kryuchkov. Eighteen of these were sentenced to death. Pletnev was given 25 years' imprisonment, Rakovsky 20 and Bessonov 15.

Between June 1937 and March 1938, the trials of numerous Red Army officers took place. The first and most significant of these was held *in camera* before a special session of the USSR Supreme Court, June 11, 1937. The accused were Marshal Tukhachevsky and Generals Yakir, Kork, Uborevich, Eideman, Feldman, and Primakov, together with Major Putna. All were given the death penalty for alleged spy work on behalf of "hostile foreign powers" (particularly Nazi Germany) and a variety of supposed conspiracies against the leaders and workers of the Soviet Union. Yan Gamarnik, chief of the political department of the Army, committed suicide. (*See also* PURGES, OPPOSITION, CPSU)

BIBLIOGRAPHY: Zbigniew K. Brezinski, *The Permanent Purge: Politics in Soviet Totalitarianism*, Cambridge, 1956.

C. J. F.

SHTERN, Lína Solomónovna (1878–), physiologist. Fellow, Ac. of S., USSR (1939), and Ac. of Medical S., USSR (1944). Honored Scientist, RSFSR (1934). Born in Libava (Latvia). Graduate (1903) and professor (1917–25), Geneva University. In 1925, S came to the USSR and became professor of the Second Medical Institute and director of the Institute of Physiology (1925–49). Since 1954, has been associated with the Institute of Biological Physics, Ac. of S. Her research concerns the chemical bases of the physiological processes in the organism, primarily in the central neural system. After a close study of the hematoencephalic barrier controlling the formation and composition of cerebrospinal fluid, S developed a method for the treatment of neural diseases with antibiotics administered into the cerebrospinal channel. In 1953, her name was linked with the "exposure" of an alleged conspiracy by a number of Jewish physicians ("the doctors' plot") to poison Soviet leaders. Stalin prize (1943).

SHTÉRNBERG, Pável Kárlovich (1865–1920), astronomer. Graduate (1887) and professor (1916–17) of Moscow University. Carried out scientific work at the observatory of Moscow University and lectured on astronomy and geodesy. Throughout his life S was engaged in political work and active in government service. Renown for his research on gravimetry and photo-astrometry. Led an expedition to observe total solar eclipse (1914). The State Institute of Astronomy at Moscow University is named after him.

SHTÉYNBERG, Lev Petróvich (1870–1945), conductor and composer. People's Artist of the USSR (1937). Since 1892 S appeared as opera conductor in St. Petersburg as well as in provincial cities. Made a guest appearance in London (1914), where he conducted (for the first time in Europe) Borodin's *Prince Igor,* with F. I. Chaliapin in the cast. After the revolution S organized symphony orchestras and operatic companies in the Ukraine. In 1928 S became conductor at the Bolshoy Theater in Moscow and in 1941, professor at the Moscow Conservatoire. He wrote several symphonies.

SHTÉYNBERG, Maksimilián Oséyevich (1883–1946), composer and teacher. Studied with Glazunov and Rimsky-Korsakov at the St. Petersburg Conservatoire. In 1934 S was appointed director of the Leningrad Conservatoire. Among his pupils were Shostakovich and Shaporin. He wrote *Metamorphoses*; a ballet *La Princesse Maleine,* after Maeterlinck; *Heaven and Earth,* after Byron; *Turksib,* on the occasion of the inauguration of the Turkestan-Siberian Railway. S edited Rimsky-Korsakov's *Foundation of Orchestration.*

SHTÉYNBERG, Sergéy Samóylovich (1872–1940), metallurgist. Corresponding member, Ac. of S., USSR (1939). Professor, Ural Polytechnic Institute (1925). Joined the Ural Branch, Ac. of S. (1932); director, Ural Institute of Metallurgy and Physics of Metals (1939). S's research on heat treatment and alloying, kinetics and structural mechanism of phase transformations in heating and cooling of steel greatly contributed to the development of Soviet metallurgy. Author of *Heat Treatment of Steel, Selected Articles* (1950).

SHÚBNIKOV, Alekséy Vasílyevich (1887–), crystallographer. Fellow, Ac. of S., USSR (1953). Graduate of Moscow University (1912); porfessor, Ural Mining Institute in Sverdlovsk (1920–25) and Moscow University (1953). Chief of the Crystallographic Laboratory (1937) and director of the Institute of Crystallography (1944), Ac. of S., which was founded on his initiative. Research concerns processes of crystal growth (electrical and optical properties of crystals), symmetry, applied crystallography (piezoelectrical properties, methods of cleaving, cutting, and polishing). Member of the All-Union Mineralogical Society (1919); honorary member of the British (1945) and French (1947) Mineralogical societies. Author of *A Study of Piezoelectric Textures* (1955); *Crystals in Science and Technology* (1956). Stalin prizes (1946, 1950).

SHULÉYKIN, Vasíly Vladímirovich (1895–), geophysicist. Fellow, Ac. of S., USSR (1946). Cofounder of the marine department, Moscow Hydrometeorological Institute (1930), the chair of oceanographic physics, Moscow University (1945), and of other hydrophysical centers and laboratories. He advanced theories of the thermal balance of the sea, the thermal interaction between the ocean, the atmosphere, and the continent, and a theory of sea waves; and invented instruments for oceanographic investigation. Author of *The Theory of Sea Waves* (1952), *Oceanographic Physics* (1953). Stalin prize (1942) and other awards.

SHULGIN, Vasíly Vitályevich (1871–), political leader. Graduate of the law faculty of Kiev University; editor of the daily *Kievlyanin;* member of the second, third and fourth State Dumas; right-wing nationalist.

During World War I S was the leader of the progressive (independent) nationalists in the fourth Duma. He joined the Progressive Bloc and played an important role therein. After the revolution of 1917, S was a member of the provisional committee of the State Duma and together with A. I. Guchkov went to Pskov to secure Nicholas II's abdication. During the civil war, S was active in the white armies. S left Russia and lived in the Balkans, in France and also Yugoslavia, where he was caught, at the end of World War II, by the Soviet Army; brought back to the USSR he spent almost ten years in concentration camps. According to some reports, S now lives, at liberty, in Russia. While abroad, S published several books on the revolution of 1917 and on the White armies: *Days, The Year 1920*. In 1926, he went, illegally, to Soviet Russia. Later it was alleged that this trip was pre-arranged by the Soviet security police. As a result of this trip, he wrote the book *Three Capitals* (1927).

SHUMÍLOV, Pyotr Pávlovich (1901–1942), inventor. Studied problems of hydraulics, heat transfer, and drilling at the State Petroleum Institute. Designed multistage turbodrill. Was killed during the testing of a new-type nuclear weapon of his own design. Stalin prize (1942 and twice posthumously in 1947).

SHUVÁLOV, Pyótr Ivánovich (1710–1762), head of state administration during the reign of Empress Elizabeth, daughter of Peter the Great. He organized Russia's army and military defenses at the time of the Seven Years' War, and introduced major improvements into artillery warfare, including a perfected type of Howitzer gun.

SHÚYA, city in Ivanovo Oblast, RSFSR; pop. 64,000 (1959). R.R. town and port on the navigable Teza River, in the Moscow textile district.

SHÚYSKY, an old R. boyar family. Played important political roles during the reigns of Ivan IV, Boris Godunov and The Time of Troubles. From 1606 to 1610, Vasily Shuysky was the tsar of Muscovy.

SHVÉRNIK, Nikoláy Mikháylovich (1888–), leading communist. S became a Bolshevik during the revolution  of 1905 and subsequently was arrested several times. After the Bolshevik Revolution, S was head of the Samara city soviet and participated in the civil war. In 1925 he was promoted to the Central Committee of the CPSU and in 1930 to the Orgburo. In 1929 became president of the Metallurgical Workers' Union, and in 1930, secretary of Trade Union Federation. In 1939 he became member of the Politburo, and 1946–53 was president of the Presidium of Supreme Soviet. Apparently he lost much of his influence after the death of Stalin in 1953. Yet he had retained some of his power and since 1957 has been a member of the Central Committee and of the Presidium of the CPSU.

SIAULIAI (f. Shávli), city in Lithuanian SSR; pop. 31,000 (1939), 60,000 (1959). R.R. junction; mfg. and trading center of a lumbering and flax-growing district; light ind., food production.

SICH: *see* ZAPOROZHYE SECH.

SIMBÍRSK: *see* ULYANOVSK.

SIMEON GORDY (died 1353), Grand Duke of Muscovy (1340–1353), son of Ivan Kalita. He was the successful defender of the young R. state against Lithuania.

SIMFERÓPOL, city, adm. center of Crimean Oblast, Ukrainian SSR; pop. 186,000 (1959). A major junction on Kharkov–Sevastopol R.R.; center of truck-farming and fruit-growing area. Its chief ind. are vegetable, fruit and fish canneries, tobacco and wheat processing plants; also canning equipment. Its history dates back to the first century B.C.; originally a small Scythian settlement; came permanently under R. domination in 1784.

SÍMONOV, Konstantin (Kiril) **Mikháylovich** (1915–), poet and writer. His first works appeared in 1934. The long poem, *Pavel Chorny*, was concerned with the building of the White Sea–Baltic Canal. The long poems, *Battle on the Ice* and *Suvorov*, which dealt with historical themes, were concerned with the love of the R.  people for their land and their fortitude under trying conditions. In 1940 S wrote the play *An Ordinary Story* (later renamed *A Story of Love*). Another long poem, *Far Away in the East*, and the play *A Young Man from Our Town* both dealt with the military operations against the Japanese in Mongolia.

During World War II, as a correspondent for the army newspaper *Red Star*, S wrote the narrative essays and short stories subsequently published under the title *From the Black Sea to the Barents Sea*, in which he described the life of front-line soldiers. His novel *Days and Nights* describes the siege of Stalingrad. His later novel, *Comrades in Arms* (1952), describes the war against Japan in Mongolia in 1939. Some of his wartime lyrical-philosophical poems acquired a very great popularity. S's plays *Russians, The Russian Problem*, and *Under Prague's Chestnut Trees* are concerned with postwar political themes. Stalin prizes (1943, 1947, 1950).

SÍMONOV, Nikoláy Konstantínovich (1901–), actor. People's Artist of the USSR. In 1924 S became a member of the company at the Leningrad Theater of Drama. Among his best roles are Protasov in Tolstoy's *The Living Corpse* and Muravyov in Chirsky's *The Victors*. S has appeared in moving pictures since 1924. He won acclaim in the title part in *Peter I*.

SÍMONOV, Rúben Nikoláyevich (1899–), actor and producer. People's Artist of the USSR. Became production manager of the Vakhtangov Theater in 1939. He gave memorable interpretations of Benedick in Shakespeare's *Much Ado About Nothing*, and of the title role in Rostand's *Cyrano de Bergerac*. S appeared on the screen and produced Korneychuk's *The Battle Front*.

SINÉLNIKOV, Nikoláy Nikoláyevich (1855–1939), producer. People's Artist of RSFSR. Began his theatrical career in 1873. The years of 1899–1909 S spent at the Korsh Theater, Moscow. The last years of his life he played in Kharkov. S contributed greatly to the development of R. provincial theater.

SINÓP, THE BATTLE OF (Nov. 1853), a naval encounter in which a R. fleet under Admiral Nakhimov defeated a Turkish squadron in the Bay of Sinop, on the Anatolian coast of the Black Sea. The battle was an element in the outbreak of the Crimean War.

SÍRIN: *see* NABOKOV, V. V.

SIROTÍNSKY, Leoníd Ivánovich (1879–), electrical engineer. Honored Scientist and Technologist, RSFSR (1942). Graduate, Institute of Electrical Engineering at Liège, Belgium (1930), professor, Moscow School of Technology (1917) and Institute of Electrical Engineering (1930). Cofounder of the All-Union Institute of Electrical Engineering and consultant to its High-Voltage Department. An authority on problems of lightning-arresting safety devices for electrical installations. Participated in the development of rectifier-type dischargers (1950). Author of textbook *High-Voltage Technology* (3 vols., 1939–45). Stalin prize (1950).

SISAKYÁN, Norayr Martirosovich (1907–), biochemist. Fellow, Ac. of S., USSR (1960). Graduate of the K. A. Timiryazev Agricultural Academy in Moscow (1932); associated with the Institute of Biochemistry, Ac. of S. (1939). Research concerns the laws governing the action of ferments in the process of metabolism, biochemical properties of protoplasms, the chemical nature and biochemical functions of plastids, biochemistry of viniculture, and the biochemical nature of plant sensitivity to drought. Author of *The Biochemistry of Metabolism* (1954). A. N. Bakh (1949) and A. I. Mechnikov (1950) awards; Stalin prize (1952).

SIVÁSH (PUTRID) SEA, salt lagoons and marshes in N.E. Crimea; separated from Sea of Azov by Arabat land tongue, from Black Sea by Perekop Isthmus; area about 1,000 sq. mi.

SKITÁLETS (Petróv), **Stepán Gavrílovich** (1868–1941), writer of realistic tales, *Court Martial* (1905) and *The Forest Burned* (1906), dealing with the peasantry in the revolutionary years of 1905–7. S also was a minor poet and wrote autobiographical novels, the lengthy novel *The House of the Chernovs* (1935), and reminiscences of L. Tolstoy and A. Chekhov.

SKLIFOSÓVSKY, Nikoláy Vasílyevich (1836–1904), surgeon. Graduate, Moscow University (1859); professor, Kiev University (1870); Medical and Surgical Academy (1871); dean, Medical Faculty at Moscow University (1880–93). A follower of N. I. Pirogov, S studied related problems and introduced new surgical techniques as well as antiseptic and aseptic methods during numerous military campaigns in which he participated (1866, 1870–71, 1877–78). The Institute of First Aid in Moscow was named after him.

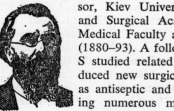

SKÓBELEV: *see* FERGANA.

SKÓBELEV, Matvéy Ivánovich (1885–?), revolutionary, born of a wealthy family. S joined the Social Democrats in 1903 and worked as a propagandist and organizer for the party in Baku. In 1912 he was elected deputy to the fourth State Duma as representative of the Menshevik faction. After the February revolution, he was chairman of the Petrograd Soviet, and later minister of labor in the Provisional Government. After the October revolution he withdrew from political life and emigrated in 1920. However, in 1921–23, he was instrumental in re-establishing trade relations between the Soviet Union and France. In 1922, he was accepted into the CPSU. In 1924 he became a member of the Soviet Trade Delegation to London, and in 1926–30 he worked in the Soviet economic apparatus. He was later demoted and disappeared in the 1930 purges.

SKÓBELEV, Mikhaíl Dmítrievich (1843–1882), general. He distinguished himself during the Khiva campaign (1873) and in the battle ol Plevna (Russo-Turkish War of 1877–78).

SKOBELTSÝN, Dmítry Vladímirovich (1892–), physicist. Fellow, Ac. of S., USSR (1946). Deputy to the Supreme Soviet USSR (1954, 1958).  Member of the Foreign Affairs Committee. Graduate of Petrograd University (1915). Director of the Institute of Physics, Ac. of S. (1951). Chairman of the Lenin Prize Award Committee (1950). Headed the Soviet delegation at the International Conference on the Peaceful Use of Atomic Energy in Geneva (1955). First Soviet scientist to study beta and gamma-rays by means of a Wilson cloud chamber. His research on cosmic ray showers led to the assumption that the ionization of the earth atmosphere is caused by cosmic rays. S's investigations have exerted a decisive influence on the study of cosmic rays in the USSR. Recipient of Vavilov Gold Medal. Stalin prize (1951).

SKOCHÍNSKY, Aleksándr Aleksándrovich (1874–1960), mining engineer. Fellow, Ac. of S., USSR (1935). Hero of Socialist Labor (1954). Honored scientist and technologist RSFSR (1934). Graduate (1900) and professor (1906–30) Leningrad and Moscow Mining Institutes. Founder and director of the Mining Institute, Ac. of S. (1938–60) and of its West-Siberian Branch. Member of the Stalin Prize Award Committee. Participated in the planning of the industrial development of Donbas (1921–22), and its rehabilitation after World War II. Research concerned mine ventilation, thermodynamics, safety engineering, hygiene, mechanization and automation of mining operations and aerodynamic resistance in several types of mining. Two Stalin and five Lenin prizes, and other awards.

SKOPÍN-SHÚYSKY, Prince Mikhaíl Vasílyevich (1587–1610), R. military leader during the "Time of Troubles."

SKOPTSÝ, religious sect preaching renunciation of wordly pleasures. Members of this sect, which came into existence in late 18th century, had to subject themselves to voluntary castration.

SKOROPÁDSKY, Pável Petróvich (1873–1945), general in the Russian imperial army, born in Ukraine, into a wealthy family of landed gentry. For a brief period (April 29 through Dec. 14, 1918), Hetman of Ukraine, head of a puppet government set up by the Germans in an attempt to win over the strongly nationalist elements among the Ukrainian people. S's regime fell after the defeat of the Central Powers. S escaped to Germany.

SKRYÁBIN, Aleksándr Nikoláyevich (1871–1915), composer. Studied composition under Taneyev and

piano under Safonov. His musical life is divided into three distinct creative periods. His early music is reminiscent of Chopin and strives to achieve structural perfection (Etudes, Op. 8 and Prélude, Op. 9). Then S turned to symphonic composition. His First Symphony was written in the process of transition from the first to the second phase and reveals a new conception of harmony (*The Tragic Poem, The Satanic Poem* for piano, sonatas No. 4 and No. 5, *The Poem of Ecstasy* for orchestra belong to the second period). During his third period S conceived the end of the world in terms of musical mystery (*Prometheus,* a symphonic poem for piano and orchestra, sonatas No. 9 and No. 10, *Vers la Flamme, Flammes Sombres*). He died at the height of his career and is considered a forerunner of modern music.

SKRÝPNIK, Nikoláy Alekséyevich (1872–1933), Bolshevik leader in Ukraine, born in Donbas. S was an active Bolshevik for many years, spending much of the time prior to the Bolshevik Revolution in Siberia. In 1918–20 S was instrumental in establishing a Soviet regime in the Ukraine. As a leader of the Ukrainian Communist party and of the Ukrainian government, S promoted a peculiar combination of nationalism and communism. He encouraged derussification and nationalism and appears to have sought real sovereignty for a Soviet Ukraine. In 1933, faced with an impending purge of Ukrainian communists, S committed suicide.

SKVORTSÓV-STEPÁNOV, Iván Ivánovich (1870–1928), Bolshevik publicist, historian, and economist. S, son of a petty official, graduated from Moscow University in 1890 and joined the populist movement. He was arrested and exiled several times. In 1905, he joined the Bolshevik party. S was very active in the preparation of the October revolution. In 1917–18, he was editor of *Izvestia;* in 1924, assistant editor of *Pravda;* and in 1926, director of the Lenin Institute. S translated Marx and wrote on political and economic topics.

SLÁVGOROD, city in Altay Kray, W. Siberia, RSFSR; pop. 36,100 (1959). Agr. town in the Kulunda steppe; processing and distributing center for the local farm produce.

SLAVOPHILES: *see* PHILOSOPHY.

SLAVYÁNSK, city in Stalino Oblast, Ukrainian SSR; pop. 83,000 (1959). Salt mining town, on Torets River, tributary of the Donets, in Donbas ind. region; other ind. include soda works and limestone quarries; porcelain, glass and graphite mfg. plants. Long known as a health resort, with mineral waters and mud baths.

SLONÍMSKY, Mikhaíl Leonídovich (1897–), writer. Member of the Serapion Brothers group (1920). Initially author of grotesque stories but gradually embraced psychological realism. Best known are his stories *Emery's Machine* (1923), *The Lavrovs* (1926), *Foma Kleshnyov* (1931), and *First Years* (1949), a revision of *The Lavrovs* and an attempt to correct his "ideological errors" by emphasizing the importance of the October revolution. Also: *Engineers* (1950), *Friends* (1954).

SLUCH RIVER, in Byelorussian SSR, flowing S. to become left tributary of Pripyat River; 140 mi. long.

SLUCH RIVER, in Ukrainian SSR, flowing N. from Volyn-Podolian upland to become right branch of Goryn River; 305 mi. long.

SLUTSK, city in Minsk Oblast, Byelorussian SSR; pop. 21,000 (1956). R.R. station, on Sluch River; has foundries, electrical motor repair shops; sawmill, creameries and cheese dairies, flour mills and meat packing plant.

SLYUDYÁNKA, city in Irkutsk Oblast on Lake Baykal; pop. 20,000 (1959). Mica production.

SMERSH: *see* SECURITY POLICE.

SMÍLGA, Iván Ténisovich (1892–?), revolutionary, born in Latvia. S became a Bolshevik in 1907 and was arrested several times. In April 1917, elected to the party Central Committee. S took an active part in the bolshevization of Finland and was prominent in the civil war. During the 1920's he held various posts in the Soviet economy. S supported Trotsky in the intra-party struggle and consequently was expelled from the party in 1927. He was readmitted in 1929, but disappeared a few years later. Author of a book on the civil war.

SMIRNÓV, Iván Nikítich (1881–1936), member of the Social Democratic Labor party from 1899 and of the Bolshevik party from 1903; worked as party organizer and propagandist in many cities. One of the organizers of the Moscow uprising in 1905. Repeatedly arrested. After the February revolution, was a member of the Executive Committee of the Soviet of Workers' and Soldiers' Deputies in Tomsk. In October 1917 he was in Moscow. Then, a member of the revolutionary military Soviet of the eastern front, chairman of the Siberian revolutionary committee; in 1920, member of the Central Committee and secretary of the Petrograd committee and the northwestern bureau of the Central Committee of the party. S was involved in opposition activities and was shot in August 1936.

SMIRNÓV, Nikoláy Vasílyevich (1900–), mathematician. Corresponding member, Ac. of S., USSR (1959). Graduate, Moscow University (1926); professor, Lenin Pedagogical Institute (1937), Pedagogical City Institute in Moscow (1943). Joined the Mathematical Institute, Ac. of S. (1938). Research concerns the theory of probability and mathematical statistics. Cofounder of the theory of non-parametrical methods in mathematical statistics. Author of *The Theory of Probabilities and Mathematical Statistics in Technology* (with Dunin-Barkovsky, 1955). Stalin prize (1951).

SMIRNÓV, Sergéy Sergéyevich (1895–1947), geologist and mineralogist. Fellow, Ac. of S., USSR (1943). Graduate (1919), and professor (1930) of the Leningrad Mining Institute. Associated with the Geological Committee which was to become the All-Union Scientific Research Institute of Geology. Director of the Ore Department at the Institute of Geological Sciences (1945). S studied ore deposits in the Southern parts of Baykal and Transbaykal regions. His investigations of the processes of mineral formation in the oxidation zone are of major importance. Founder of the school of Soviet geologists and mining experts. Member (1924) and chairman (1925) of the All-Union Mineralogical Society. Stalin prize (1946).

SMIRNÓV, Vladímir Ivánovich (1887–), mathematician. Fellow, Ac. of S., USSR (1943). Graduate (1910) and professor (1926), St. Petersburg University; professor, St. Petersburg (Leningrad) Institute of Railway Engineering (1912–30). At the Institute of Mathematics and Seismology (1929–35). Research on functions of a complex variable and differential equations. In collaboration with L. S. Sobolev, S developed new methods for the solution of various problems of wave propagation in elastic media with plane boundaries, and investigated the vibration of elastic ring and sphere induced by external excitation. Author of *A Course of Higher Mathematics* (5 vols., 1924–47). Stalin prize (1948).

SMOLÉNSK, city, adm. center of Smolensk Oblast; pop. 147,000 (1959). R.R. junction, an important distribution center for lumber, flax and grain, at the head of Dnieper waterway; manufactures machinery and has smelting furnaces, and a large textile ind. Has a number of higher educational institutions. Founded in the 9th century.

SMOLÉNSK OBLAST, RSFSR; area 19,250 sq. mi.; pop. 1,143,000 (1959). Cities: Smolensk (adm. center), Vyazma, Roslavl. The Smolensk–Moscow upland extending through the E. section forms a watershed between the W. Dvina, Volga, and Dnieper rivers: lowlands are in the W. Has podsol clayey soils, mixed forests; humid climate; a highly developed flax economy. Potato and dairy farming, grains, and fodder crops are essential; peat, lignite, building materials. Est. 1937.

SMYCHKA: *see* AGRICULTURE, NEP.

SMYSLÓV, Vasíly Vasílyevich (1921–), chess player. Grand Master of chess since 1941; second in the world championship tournament of 1948. In a match with M. M. Botvinnik for world championship (1954) the game ended in a draw 12 : 12.

SNEČKUS, Antanas Juozovich (1903–), Lithuanian party and government official. He went to school in Vilna and Voronezh, then returned to Lithuania after World War I. He worked as a telegraph engineer but was arrested for communist activity. He was appointed secretary of the central committee in 1936; arrested in 1939; released the following year by Soviet occupation forces; was named head of state security in Lithuania in 1940; was appointed secretary of the central committee of the Lithuanian CP in 1940. He was deputy, USSR Supreme Soviet, and member, Foreign Affairs Commission.

SNEGIRYÓV, Vladímir Fyódorovich (1847–1917), gynecologist. Graduate (1870), professor (1875) Moscow University. Initiated the study of gynecology as an independent discipline. Founder of the first gynecological clinic in Russia (1889) and the Gynecological Institute (1896).

SÓBOLEV, Sergéy Lvóvich (1908–), mathematician. Fellow, Ac. of S., USSR (1939). Graduate, Leningrad University (1929); joined the Institute of Seismology and the Institute of Mathematics, Ac. of S. (1932); professor, Moscow University (1935). Research concerns dynamics of elastic bodies; advanced a theory of plane waves in elastic half-space with a stress-free

boundary and determined the general concept of surface waves. With V. I. Smirnov, S developed a method for the integration of linear and nonlinear equations with partial hyperbolic-type derivatives with predetermined initial conditions. Author of *Applications of Functional Analysis in Mathematical Physics* (1950), *Equations of Mathematical Physics* (1954). Stalin prize (1941).

SÓBOLEV, Vladímir Stepánovich (1908–), petrographer and mineralogist. Fellow, Ac. of S., USSR (1958). Graduate (1930) and professor (1939) of the Leningrad Mining Institute, Irkutsk (1941–45), and Lvov Universities (1945). Associated with the All-Union Scientific Research Institute of Geology (1930–41) and Geological Institute of Minerals, Ukrainian SSR. S's research concerns rock-forming minerals and the laws governing the crystallization of trappean magma. He discovered rare minerals, explored ore deposits at the Siberian platform, studied foreign diamond deposits, and suggested the occurrence of diamond deposits in the North Siberian platform. Stalin prize (1950).

SÓCHI, port town and prominent health resort on the Black Sea, Krasnodar Kray, RSFSR; pop. 95,000 (1959). Famous also for Matsesta sulfur springs in the vicinity of the city.

SOCIAL INSURANCE. The beginnings of SI in Russia go back to 1903 when disability insurance against work-accidents was first introduced. A broader health and accident insurance policy, obligatory for mechanized enterprises with more than 20 workers, was enacted in 1912. It was financed by employers and payroll deductions. Special boards were organized to deal with all problems of the insured worker's health and compensation.

In accordance with communist slogans, efforts were made to broaden the democratic organization of SI in 1917–18. But these efforts clashed with the dictatorial system of the communist government. In 1918 self-governing insurance agencies were closed. The Soviet government took over SI, financing it from the national budget. All different forms of SI were united into one system.

As this organization proved to be unsuccessful the Soviet government authorized the already Communist-controlled trade unions to build up a new insurance system in 1922. At that time *health* and *maternity* insurances were given preference to *unemployment, disability or invalidity* insurances, *workmen's compensation, old age,* and *survivors* insurances.

With the start of the Five Year Plans in 1928 the basic principles of SI were revised. Every field of life and labor was now geared to increase economic production. In Nov. 1930 the 7th All Union Conference of Labor Agencies accepted a resolution stating that "the task of social insurance lies in the many-sided, unremitting daily struggle for increasing the productivity of labor."

Since 1933 the All Union Central Trade Union Council is the central body of SI and draws up the annual insurance budget which is approved by the Council of People's Commissars. The unions are insurance carriers for their respective industries. Shop committees and insurance councils serve as agents.

In Jan. 1931 the All-Union Central Trade Union Council, following government policies, started to apply SI as a means of increasing production. Benefits were now to be determined by the length of employment, union membership, and quality and quantity of work. On Dec. 28, 1938 these same ideas were incorporated in strict regulations to combat labor turnover and enforce labor discipline. Insurance benefits of 100 per cent were now to be paid only after 6 years of continuous work at one place of employment. The amount of payments rapidly decreased with shorter employment periods. Workers were also deprived of their insurance benefits for violation of work discipline and nonunion members received only 50 to 25 per cent of the benefit they would be eligible for if they had been union members.

On Aug. 9, 1948 another act was passed introducing even more rigid limitations along the same lines and requiring a worker to be employed at least 8 years at one place of work before he is eligible to receive 100 per cent of SI benefits.

On July 14, 1956 some reforms were introduced into the Soviet SI. A new scale of benefit payments was put into effect. This brought a reduction of higher pensions and some improvement of benefit payments for the lower groups of wage- and salary-earners as well as those suffering permanent disability of varying degrees, but the eligibility requirements were raised considerably. All these regulations enacted during the last three decades either by the Soviet government or by the All-Union Central Trade Union Council prove that, although SI is supposedly extended to all working people, it is being used by the government to draw very definite lines between workers especially useful to the regime and those of minor economic or political interest to the government.

One of the essential features of Soviet SI is that no payments are deducted from payrolls. Under a rigidly controlled Soviet "socialized" wage system this practically amounts to dividing wages into two parts: one paid to the wage- and salary-earners directly and the other to SI agencies. SI contributions are graded according to "hazards and dangers of work." The scale of SI contribution varied at different times. In the 1920's it amounted to some 16 to 20 per cent of the payroll and was then constantly reduced until it reached about 6.9 per cent of the aggregate payroll in 1940 just before World War II. In the postwar years attempts were made to increase the amount of SI contributions. In the early 1950's it averaged 9 to 10 per cent of the payroll. In 1958 it averaged from 4.4 per cent to 9.0 per cent of the payroll. Excess of expenditures were always covered by the government.

Compared with the standard of living, benefits of the different insurance plans are low. It is these benefit rates and the severe eligibility requirements which reduce the practical significance of Soviet SI.

SI policies in the Soviet Union, where the government is the sole employer as well as insurance agent, can hardly be identified with those in a democratic country.

Workmen's Compensation. Disability insurance covering individuals incapacitated by work accidents was first introduced in Russia on June 2, 1903. Financed by the employer, it made the latter responsible for accidents that occurred at work.

In 1912 a new insurance plan was enacted and made compulsory for all mechanized enterprises with 20 or more workers. Its budget came from employers and payroll deductions. Special boards had to deal with all problems of the insured worker's compensation.

The Soviet Labor Code of 1922 neglected workmen's compensation considerably. After 1931 the payments of workers' benefits were made conditional upon the length of time worked at one enterprise, as well as union membership. Since 1938 only workers employed six years and over at one enterprise are eligible for 100 per cent benefit. Benefits of those employed less were greatly reduced. Violation of work discipline automatically deprived a worker of his benefits, and nonunion members received only 50 per cent or even 25 per cent, of the benefit they would have been eligible for as union members. In 1948 more rigid rules were enacted in the same direction.

The social insurance reform of July 14, 1956 introduced a new scale of payments. A worker receives for temporary disability 100 per cent of his wages—a minimum of 300 rubles in towns and 270 rubles in rural areas; for partial disability, 65 per cent of 400 rubles plus 10 per cent of higher earnings; for permanent disability, either 90 per cent of 450 rubles plus 10 per cent of higher earnings or, if constant attendance is required, 500 rubles plus 10 per cent of higher earnings. In all instance persons working underground or performing unhealthy work receive higher rates. Qualifying conditions for 100 per cent benefit are 12 years employment at one place of work—or the benefit might be reduced up to 50 per cent if the worker was employed three years or less—and union membership is essential. Survivors depending on the earnings of a worker deceased because of work injuries may, depending on their age and the eligibility of the deceased, receive from 260 rubles to 1,200 rubles.

Old Age Insurance was first introduced in the Soviet Union in 1928, but did not cover all categories of workers. Payments of benefits were made conditional upon an employment record of 25 years for men and 20 years for women. The worker was not supposed to be employed at the time of application and had to prove continuous employment for at least one year preceding the date of retirement.

Old age pension regulations of Feb. 29, 1932 provided, until 1956, the basis of premium calculations. The workers were divided into four categories receiving from 60 to 50 per cent of the last income; these included one category—later abolished—which did not have any right to benefits. Only in 1937 were all workers and employees covered by old age insurance.

At the present time old age premiums are regulated by the 1956 reform. This provides for a minimum of 300 rubles a month and a maximum of 1,200 rubles. The amount is calculated by the average earnings of the last twelve months or the best five years in the last ten years. Qualifying conditions are for men 60 years and 25 years of employment and for women 55 years and 20 years of employment. If those conditions are not met the pension may be decreased even to 25 per cent. For difficult and underground work there are special regulations with lower age requirements, as well as for women with more than five children. There is an increment of 10 per cent for continuous employment of 35 years for men and 30 years for women. But if pensioners continue to work their pensions are reduced to approximately 150 rubles a month.

Health Insurance. Health insurance was established in Russia in 1912 and made obligatory for all mechanized enterprises over 20 employees. It was financed by both employers and payroll deductions. Special boards were organized to deal with all problems of the insured worker's health.

Under the Labor Code of 1922 all workers and employees were entitled to HI benefits. The upper limit was fixed in 1927 at 120 to 180 rubles a month and was increased to 150 to 180 rubles in 1929. But these sick benefits could be reduced by reclassifying the worker as temporarily incapacitated or, in case of insufficient social insurance funds, payments could be discontinued.

In 1931, with labor productivity as the chief consideration in deciding on the eligibility for sick benefits, new rules were gradually laid down requiring union membership and at least six years of continuous employment at one place of work to qualify for 100 per cent benefit. Nonunion workers received 50 to 25 per cent of their wages. In 1938 violation of work discipline and voluntary quitting of employment deprived a worker of sick benefits for at least the first six months at the new place of work. In 1948 the number of years required for a 100 per cent benefit was raised to eight.

The present sick benefit rates are regulated by a law of July 14, 1956. The insured worker now receives, only after twelve years of continuous employment at one place of work, 90 per cent of his wage and this decreases gradually to 50 per cent if employed three years or less. For care in rest homes and sanatoria preference is given, as before, to union and party members as well as special categories of workers.

Hospitalization, operations, treatments in hospitals and out-patient departments as well as most medicines are free. There are almost no private physicians.

Disability Insurance. This is an insurance covering general disability or invalidity caused by illness or accidents not connected with the occupation of the insured. A system of DI was set up in the course of the 1920's. The rates of payments were always lower than those for work injuries but the policy and development of the general DI were the same as of workmen's compensation (q.v.). At the present time the insurance rates are governed by the legislation of July 14, 1956. Partial invalidity pays 45 per cent of wages, a minimum of 160 rubles and a maximum of 400 rubles. Total invalidity pays a minimum of 230 rubles a month or 65 per cent of 450 rubles plus 10 per cent of higher wages. Total invalidity with the need of constant attendance pays a minimum of 300 rubles or 85 per

cent of 500 rubles plus 10 per cent of higher earnings, a maximum of 900 rubles. There are supplements for dependents unable to earn. Workers who performed difficult or underground work receive higher benefits.

Survivors Insurance. Survivors insurance in the USSR is an auxiliary of the health and disability and workmen's compensation insurances (q.v.).

Under the Labor Code of 1922 surviving husband, wife, parents, and children were all eligible to claim premiums only if the survivors were unable to work. In 1928 claims of parents or husband and wife were not made conditional upon evidence of the beneficiary's inability to work after reaching age 60 for men and 55 for women. According to the regulations of 1932, benefit rates were at least 75 per cent of the insured last earnings.

Now, under the new regulations of July 14, 1956 eligible survivors receive different percentages according to the number of eligible survivors and the earnings and eligibility of the insured. The rates range from a minimum of 160 rubles for one survivor and a maximum of 1,200 rubles for three orphans. For unhealthy and underground work of the insured the survivors receive higher benefits.

Eligible are widows over 55 or invalid or caring for children under 8, or brothers or sisters and parents invalid or caring for children under 8. Full percentage of rate is paid if insured had worked from 2 to 20 years (for men) or 1 to 15 years (for women). Otherwise, if years of work are insufficient, the pension is reduced proportionally.

Unemployment Insurance. During the first years of the Soviet government complicated provisions not exactly favoring unemployment were by and large acceptable. Then under the decree of Feb. 14, 1930 labor exchanges were authorized to deal severely with persons refusing an offer for a job or even vocational training. Another decree of Oct. 9, 1930 stopped all benefit payments to the unemployed and the labor exchanges were ordered to put all the unemployed back to work. The decree states that "applicants refusing work will be stricken from the rolls of labor exchanges," which practically meant that they would be deprived of any opportunity to work. This brought an end to the unemployment insurance in the Soviet Union.

Maternity Insurance. According to the Labor Code of 1922 working women had a right to stay away from six to eight weeks before and after birth, depending on the type of work performed. During that period women were entitled to full wages, one layette payment and a nine months' nursing benefit at the rate of 25 per cent of an average wage. From 1927 on nursing benefits were paid only if the insured had worked during six months in the year preceding the pregnancy and layette payments were made only if the earnings did not exceed 180 rubles a month.

Since 1931 only those union members who were employed for at least three years, with two of these years at the present place of work, are eligible for maternity benefits. Payments of layette and nursing benefits were made upon proof of consecutive employment as well. In 1936 nursing benefits for eligible mothers amounted to 10 rubles a month and layette payments, 45 rubles. In 1938 maternity leave could be granted for only five weeks before and after birth. In 1944, in connection with a special drive to promote an increase in population, maternity leaves were again extended to eight weeks before and after birth and payments for layette and nursing benefits somewhat increased.

At the present time the paid maternity leave is eight weeks before and after confinement but payment depends on the length of employment. If employed three years or more, the mother receives 100 per cent of her earnings; if less, she might receive a minimum of two-thirds of her wages. There is a small nursing benefit and a layette allowance. But the maternity benefits are not payable if the applicant has changed her place of work during the last six months before the pregnancy without the consent of the employer. Medical care for pregnant women is free.

BIBLIOGRAPHY: *Report on Social Security Programs in the Soviet Union.* Prepared by the U.S. team that visited the USSR, under the East-West Exchange Program in August-September 1958. Washington, 1960.

H. P.

SOCIAL STRATIFICATION.

Prior to the February revolution, S in Russia was of a mixed character. There was, on the one hand, the "estate" system, which had been formally established in the 18th century. Membership in an estate was determined principally by family of birth and carried with it various privileges and disabilities. Although many of the legal distinctions among the estates were revoked between 1861 and 1917, membership continued to be of some significance both in law and in custom.

With the spread of industrialism, a second and informal system of S was emerging which rested basically on economic factors: wealth, fertility of land, occupation and education, trade turnover, capital ownership, and control (in fact if not in law) over peasants as factory workers. Status in this hierarchy cut across estate membership and rendered the latter unimportant for many purposes, the more so as estate membership itself was more and more fluid. Membership in the nobility, for example, came to be conferred automatically upon attainment of a specified rank in the civil service; entrance into the civil service was open to any holder of a university diploma; and access to the universities was gradually broadened in the late 19th century, though it was still influenced by wealth and social origin right up to the revolution.

Neither of these social hierarchies had given rise to clearly defined interest groups, or "social classes," such as those which played so great a part in W. European history: groups occupying similar statuses and seeking economic and political objectives which they felt to be to their own advantage. Partly, this was because the existence of the economic hierarchy in the presence of the lingering effects of the estate system split each stratum into mutually hostile segments—well-to-do nobles against impoverished nobles, merchant capitalists against merchant peasants, and many others. Partly, it was because the tsar never wholly abandoned his power to alter status by imperial fiat. Faithful service to the tsar remained one method of social advancement down to the end of the empire.

In any case, there was no doubt that status differences did exist, in terms of money, land, prestige, education, and style of life. There was also widespread agreement that they were unjust in kind and degree, and that they had their harshest impact on the peasant. The at least tacit acceptance of such beliefs was one of the forces leading to the February revolution. Lenin then urged that the next step in the Marxist program —a proletarian revolution—be undertaken. Undeterred by the virtual absence of an industrial proletariat (which composed no more than 3 per cent of the population on the eve of World War I), he instead skillfully exploited the congruence between the conditions of R. society and the Marxist demand for social equality to convert the revolution of February into that of October. Resentment of the old ways, especially on the part of the peasant, was one of the factors which accounted for the victory of the Bolsheviks in the "proletarian" revolution and in the civil war which followed it.

Under the pressures of war and scarcity, Russia did take long strides toward material equality during War Communism. Moreover, Russia's new leaders were selfconsciously egalitarian; they eschewed the mannerisms of rank and formally abolished many of its prerequisites. When, however, groups of workers took Marxist doctrine literally and seized control of the factories in which they worked, expelling the managerial and technical staffs, the regime reacted in a way which hinted at a fundamental and far-reaching attitude and presaged what was to come: Lenin denounced such actions as a "vulgarization" of Marxism and pointed out that the revolution had been fought on behalf of the working class "as a whole," not for the narrowly selfish benefit of its separate segments. The brief period of "workers' control" yielded to nationalization of the factories under the direction of the CP, the self-styled vanguard of the proletariat.

During the years of the New Economic Policy, many of the conventional forms of social differentiation reappeared. The restoration of free trade in agriculture led to the return of the kulak, or wealthy peasant; in the factories and commercial enterprises, and even in the political administration, the regime found itself permitting, if not encouraging, inequalities of income and authority as necessary to the rehabilitation of the economy. Not only was the general pattern of S a familiar one, except for the lack of aristocratic titles, but in a dismaying number of cases, the individuals in positions of high status were the same ones who had occupied them before the revolution. Efforts were made to mitigate these tendencies through favoritism for workers and peasants in admission to the CP and to higher education, but with only limited effectiveness. In the last analysis, the regime was unwilling to risk destroying the society for the sake of achieving what it then regarded as a premature form of egalitarianism.

Yet, with the launching of rapid industrialization under the First Five Year Plan, there was a brief renascence of the original revolutionary spirit. Once again, wage and salary inequalities dwindled, this time the result of deliberate policy as much as of shortages of goods; important moves were made against the power and influence of the kulaks; the claims of the technical specialists were ridiculed, and many of the specialists themselves were brought to public trial and convicted of all manner of crimes. Although there was nothing approaching a revival of "workers' control," the consequences of these and other measures were similarly disruptive to economic and political functioning. In his famous "Six-Points" speech delivered on June 23, 1931, Stalin called a halt.

In this speech, Stalin explicitly denounced what he called "equality-mongering" (*uravnilovka*) and demanded that differences in skill and effort be recognized by material rewards, which would serve as incentives for the more laggard workers. Furthermore, he asserted, "No ruling class has managed without its own intelligentsia. There are no grounds for believing that the working class of the USSR can manage without its own industrial and technical intelligentsia." The special skills and responsibilities of these experts, he said, should also be appropriately rewarded. The result was the emergence of a system of S in the Soviet Union which bears strong resemblances to that of industrial nations everywhere, modified in important ways, however, by factors peculiar to Soviet society.

Although it is as hard in the Soviet Union as in other industrial societies to distinguish strata precisely, a fairly clear occupational hierarchy can be discerned, which has remained in effect since the middle 1930's. At the top is the ruling elite: the members of the Presidium of the CP and of the Supreme Soviet, the heads of the major ministries and governmental committees, and the leaders of the important territorial units of the party. Close to them are the managers of the biggest factories, top military officers, and the editors of the major newspapers and magazines. This group shades off into the "intelligentsia," which in Soviet usage includes scientists, writers, and artists (some of whom enjoy elite status), professionals, and the rank and file of CP and state officials and of managers and technicians. Their status is shared in many respects by a small number of manual workers whose skill, brawn, or good standing in the party has enabled them to rise above the masses, and by a smaller number of peasants on the more fortunately located kolkhozy. All of these people, together with their families, have never made up more than 20 per cent of the population. Below them stand most white-collar employees and the rest of the manual workers and peasants. None of these last groups are uniformly higher than any of the others; they spread over parallel and roughly comparable ranges of status rather than forming invidiously ranked strata. Party membership per se does not confer high status, though it is usually essential for high position in any occupation and, hence, is more common at the upper than at the lower levels.

Material income is closely associated with one's position in this hierarchy. The average Soviet industrial worker or employee earned, in the middle 1950's, about 850–900 rubles a month. Workers in higher-skill categories, in high-priority industries, or in remote parts of the country receive more. Further differentiation arises on account of the piece-work system under which most work has been performed: so much for each item produced, with deductions for failure to reach the "norm" or quota for the job, and progressively greater additions for exceeding it. The ordinary Soviet worker lives on a monotonous diet made up heavily of the cheaper food staples; he wears shabby clothes, and he and his family are likely to live in a one- or two-room apartment, sharing kitchen and lavatory facilities with several other families. The prices of many consumers' goods (half or more of which consist of the "turnover tax," an essentially regressive form of sales tax) often put them beyond his reach. Although it is quite impossible to express the peasant's earnings in monetary terms, since they are largely made up of payments in kind, there is little doubt that his average standard of living has been even lower than that of the industrial worker. Many villages seem unchanged since the revolution.

Among the intelligentsia, by contrast, salaries together with ample bonuses and other forms of extra income often amount to 50,000 rubles or more a year, sufficient to provide them with a way of life that, at least by Soviet standards, is almost luxurious. For the members of this group, the concern has been with obtaining not the necessities but the niceties of life—a better quality suit of clothes, a villa for the summer, a refrigerator or automobile. (Exceptions, however, are some poorly paid categories of professionals, particularly physicians and schoolteachers. These occupations, on the other hand, have evidently remained very high in the prestige accorded by the population.) At the peak of the apex, known incomes run into the hundreds of thousands of rubles annually. The salaries of the highest political officials are not known, and perhaps are not fixed at all, but in any case these men are provided by the state with whatever goods and services they want, often without accountability; indeed, for all practical purposes, they *are* the state.

Accompanying these monetary differences—which are only slightly diminished by income or inheritance taxes—have been many formal and informal privileges. Following Stalin's 1931 speech, the regime made it a point of deliberate policy to pay official honor to the intelligentsia. They were awarded prizes and medals; they were "invited" to join the CP and became the dominant element in its membership and among the delegates to the party congresses and the Supreme Soviet; many of them were given elaborate titles and were authorized to wear special uniforms and insignia. Their executive authority in factory and office was strengthened, at the expense particularly of the trade unions; in 1940, workers were forbidden to leave their jobs without the manager's permission. By virtue of their position and the support of the regime, members of the intelligentsia and higher officials in the bureaucracy had the kinds of connections and "pull" which gave them easier access to scarce and coveted goods and services, ranging from theater tickets to admission for their children to higher educational institutions.

In other respects, however, Soviet S has been characterized by a kind of egalitarianism which is a necessary attribute of the totalitarian society. The intelligentsia have been honored, but they have not been given a significantly greater share of political power. Outside the very highest circles of party leadership, there is a near-equality of political impotence, in which the intelligentsia are joined by white-collar employees, workers, and peasants at every status level. Not only the political machinery, but education, the media of communication, and all other social and technological resources are also subject to the ultimate control of the ruling elite, which has effectively prevented them from becoming instruments for the realization or even the expression of "class interests." Indeed, for the same reasons, it is probable that sharply delineated or well-organized social classes have not appeared at all; available evidence shows that public opinion in Soviet society is significantly more homogeneous than in other industrial societies. The Communist regime has been more successful even than its tsarist predecessor in allowing status differentiation while avoiding the rise of corresponding interest groups.

By the same token, status in Soviet society is essentially a conditional reward for outstanding service to the currently powerful political leader. This has meant that when an individual falls into disfavor with whoever is controlling the party at the moment, his previous status, his riches, privileges, and reputation are of no avail; in fact, he would not be permitted to keep any of them. But it has also meant that opportunities for advancement have always remained open to the humblest citizen. Unquestioning and conspicuous loyalty or unusual skill in an important area has opened the door to a career for many a worker and peasant.

These underlying truths were clearly demonstrated in the policy changes which followed the death of Stalin. The favored position of the intelligentsia in Stalin's last years had become so extreme as to raise the possibility that they might eventually be able to become more powerful than the central authorities. They were self-assured and arrogant; they felt their jobs were safe no matter what they did; they ignored or evaded directives from above; and their children regarded themselves as exempt from the duties imposed upon others. Khrushchev sensed the threat, and moved decisively to end it. Income inequalities were contracted, by both raising the lowest incomes and reducing the highest; civilian titles and uniforms were abolished; criticism from below was re-invigorated, and officials were warned not to neglect it; workers were given back the right to quit their jobs without managerial approval; the party once again turned its attention to recruiting ordinary workers and peasants to its membership; the educational structure and the procedures for admission to higher education were revised to improve the chances of the children of workers and peasants; even the modest tuition fees which, in 1940, had been levied upon most education from the eighth grade up were dropped. While these and other measures were being enacted, to the detriment of those in high status, no word of protest was heard from them; much less did they undertake any countervailing action.

This restoration of the honor and privilege of the low-status members of society is, however, only a relative matter. The hierarchical ranking of positions remains essentially the same. Material inequalities have been reduced, but not eliminated, and there is no hint of anything resembling "workers' control." "Equality-mongering," Khrushchev has said, is still inadmissible, and so is any "belittling of the significance of leadership and leaders." Nor is there any guarantee that workers and peasants will be able to maintain their newly won position should the regime find it desirable to move in the opposite direction once again.

The nearest approach in Soviet society to a "social class," as distinct from S, has been the ruling elite. Yet even here, political power has been attained and exercised not on behalf of a class but of an individual. In Soviet society, power, wealth, and privilege have been matters of personal manipulation rather than of class differentiation. The totalitarian leader represents not a class, but only himself.

BIBLIOGRAPHY: Cyril E. Black, ed., *The Transformation of Russian Society*, Cambridge, 1960; Robert A. Feldmesser, "Equality and Inequality under Khrushchev," *Problems of Communism*, IX (March-April, 1960); Michael T. Florinsky, *Russia: A History and an Interpretation*, 2 vols., New York, 1953; Alex Inkeles, "Social Stratification and Mobility in the Soviet Union: 1940–1950," *American Sociological Review*, XV (Aug., 1950); Alex Inkeles, and Raymond A. Bauer, *The Soviet Citizen*, Cambridge, 1959; Barrington Moore, Jr., *Soviet Politics—The Dilemma of Power*, Cambridge, 1950.

R. A. F.

SOCIALISM IN ONE COUNTRY. A term contributed to the doctrines of Marxism-Leninism (q.v.) by J. V. Stalin. It symbolizes the dogma that the proletariat of a single major country which has succeeded in seizing power will be able to construct a socialist society in that country even though no successful proletarian revolution has taken place in other parts of the world.

In 1917 the Bolsheviks seized power in the firm expectation that the Russian Revolution would lead to a chain reaction of proletarian revolutions in the entire civilized world. In their eyes, their own revolution would have made no sense as an isolated event, because Communist rule in a relatively backward country like Russia could not, in their opinion, lead to the emergence of socialism. On the contrary, it could only serve to embarrass the cause of Marxism. When despite their expectations the revolutionary chain reaction did not come forth, they had to make political as well as doctrinal adjustments. As usual, the actual solution of the problem was preceded by sharp disputes. In this case the adjustment was made in two stages, and as a result of two controversies.

The first of these erupted a few weeks after the Bolshevik seizure of power, during the Soviet-German peace negotiations at Brest-Litovsk. At that time, against bitter opposition on the part of many leading Bolsheviks, who objected to peace negotiations with an imperialist government and who would have preferred to sacrifice the newly created Soviet state in a heroic and suicidal revolutionary war, Lenin established the principle that the Soviet state was not expendable, and that its preservation was one of the major interests of the revolutionary world proletariat. To be sure, this doctrine was hedged in by the proviso that this applied only for a short period during which the world revolution should be able to catch its breath. During this short breathing space, there was no thought that Soviet Russia might attain socialism, even though she might take the first steps in that direction.

After Lenin's death, the controversy over the meaningfulness of the existence of an isolated Bolshevik regime broke out anew when it became apparent that the world revolution would be slow in coming. At that time the Trotsky opposition (q.v.) demanded renewed concentration on efforts to break out of the isolation confining the Soviet state, while the Stalin-Bukharin faction insisted that world capitalism had entered a period of stabilization; and the world revolution, a transition period during which the Soviet regime would have to hold on by itself. While socialism, constructed in such an isolated country, would never be secure against outside enemies, it could and should nonetheless be constructed; and the assertion that under such conditions socialism could not be created was branded as a defeatist heresy.

This doctrine of socialism in a single country not only conflicts with older Marxist notions about the preconditions for the growth of socialism; it also led to the incorporation of a Soviet national interest into Marxism-Leninism. It also led to the recognition of coexistence as an inescapable necessity for the duration of the transition period. Finally, through the concept of capitalist encirclement, it served to explain to the faithful why a strong dictatorship was required even after socialism had allegedly been achieved. (*See also* MARXISM, MARXISM-LENINISM, TROTSKYISM)

BIBLIOGRAPHY: Barrington Moore, Jr., *Soviet Politics: The Dilemma of Power*, Cambridge, Mass., 1950; E. H. Carr, *The Bolshevik Revolution*, Vol. III, New York, 1953; Isaac Deutscher, *Stalin: A Political Biography*, London and New York, 1949; Isaac Deutscher, *The Prophet Armed: Trotsky, 1879–1921*, London and New York, 1954.   A. G. M.

SOCIALIST REALISM: *see* LITERATURE, PAINTING.

SOCIALIST REVOLUTIONARIES. The party of the SR was formed through the unification of a number of populist groups which sprang up in Russia and among the R. *émigrés* abroad in the 1890's. The SR leaders of that period were Ye. Breshko-Breshkovskaya, A. Argunov, Ch. Zhytlovsky, L. Shishko, G. Gershuni, and M. A. Natanson-Bobrov. Among the younger revolutionaries who joined the party were V. M. Chernov, Mikhail Gots, N. S. Russanov. S. An-sky, I. Rubanovich, O. S. Minor, and others. In the years 1901–05, an important role was played by the Terroristic Organization of the SR party which committed a number of terrorist acts against high officials of the tsarist government. In 1901, P. Karpovich assassinated the minister of education, Bogolepov; in 1902, S. Balmashov killed the minister of the interior, Sipyagin; in 1903, the governors Obolensky and Bogdanovich were killed; in 1904, Ye. Sozonov killed the minister of the interior, Plehve; in 1905, I. Kalyayev killed the Grand Duke Sergey Aleksandrovich. The leaders of the Terroristic Organization were G. Gershuni, at first, then Azef (later exposed as an agent provocateur) and B. V. Savinkov.

The first congress of the SR party which took place in Finland from Dec. 29, 1905 to Jan. 4, 1906, adopted the draft of the party program submitted by its chief theorist, V. M. Chernov. The road to socialism via a democratic republic based on general franchise and the converting of Russia into a federative state were the basic principles of the program. The SR party tried to incorporate into its ranks peasants, urban laborers, and toiling members of the intelligentsia. In its agrarian program the party asked for the "socialization of the land" under the ownership and control of the "democratically organized communities on the basis of the equalization of holdings." Because of ideological differences, the party was soon split. The right wing under the leadership of V. A. Myakotin and A. V. Peshekhonov (later known as "People's Socialists") was hostile to political terror and insisted upon the use of only legal means in the political activities of the party. The left wing (known later as the "Maximalists") advocated the idea of socialization of the factories and plants, as well as of the land, and the establishment of a "Toilers' Republic." During the revolution of 1905, the SR took an active part in the first Soviet of the Workers' Deputies in St. Petersburg and in the Peasants' Union, as well as in the Moscow uprising in Dec. 1905. The SR party did not participate in the elections of the first State Duma in 1905, but the labor faction (*Trudoviki*) of the Duma (104 deputies) adopted the agrarian program of the SR.

The second congress of the SR party was convened in Tammerfors (Finland) in Feb. 1907, and a subsequent conference of the party took place in London in Aug. 1908. On Dec. 26, 1908, the central committee of the party denounced Azef as an agent of the security police. This disclosure, besides putting an end to the political terror in Russia, paralyzed the activities of the party for many years. During World War I, the party was split into two factions: the *Oborontsy* (supporters of a defensive war) under the leadership of Avksentyev, and the internationalists under the leadership of V. Chernov and M. Natanson who participated in the peace conference of the left socialists in Zimmerwald.

In the February revolution of 1917, the SR rose to the highest positions of government. Abram Gots was one of the leaders of the political bloc of the SR and the Mensheviks in the Petrograd Soviet. V. M. Chernov, Ye. Breshko-Breshkovskaya, N. D. Avksentyev, V. M. Zenzinov, and V. I. Lebedev led the Soviet of Peasants' Deputies. Through A. F. Kerensky, minister of justice and afterwards prime minister, the SR party acquired an enormous influence upon the Provisional Government where it held the ministerial offices of the interior (N. D. Avksentyev), defense (V. Savinkov), navy (V. Lebedev), agriculture (V. Chernov). The SR Shreyder and Rudnev served respectively as mayors in Petrograd and Moscow. O. S. Minor was chairman of the municipal council in Moscow. However, the fourth party congress (Nov. 25 to Dec. 5, 1917) was split by the left SR headed by M. A. Natanson and Maria Spiridonova. The majority of the party members took part in the various attempts to organize the democratic forces of the country around the Provisional Government in the struggle against the Bolsheviks. In the election of the All-Russian Constituent Assembly, in Nov. 1917, over

17 million out of the counted 41,700,000 votes went to the candidates of the SR party. V. M. Chernov was elected chairman and M. V. Vishniak secretary of the Constituent Assembly.

After the October revolution many SR fought in the civil war against the Bolsheviks. Their leaders were instrumental in organizing the committee of the members of the Constituent Assembly (Comuch). D. Avksentyev and V. Zenzinov were members of the Directory in Ufa. An SR member, Dora (Fanny) Kaplan, shot and wounded Lenin. As a result of these activities the SR were persecuted. In 1922 the Bolsheviks staged a public trial in which twelve members of the central committee of the SR party (A. Gots, A. Timofeyev, D. Donskoy, Ya. Gendelman and others) were sentenced to death. However, the sentence was not carried out. Long afterwards it was discovered that A. Gots was executed in 1937.

The left SR who broke away from the party in Dec. 1917 were at the beginning in full accord with the Bolsheviks. Their representatives (V. Karelin, A. Kolegayev, M. Proshyan, A. Shreyder, and I. Z. Shteynberg) participated in the Bolshevik government. They took an active part in the dispersal of the Constituent Assembly. However, after the signing of the peace Treaty of Brest-Litovsk, to which they were opposed, the left SR withdrew from the Soviet government. In July 1918, they organized the abortive Moscow uprising. A left SR, Blumkin, killed the German ambassador, Count Mirbach. As a result, numerous left SR, including one of the Cheka chiefs, Aleksandrovich, were shot by the Bolsheviks. Others (Spiridonova, Kamkov) were imprisoned. In July 1918, at the 5th Congress of the Soviets, the Bolshevik majority expelled the left SR from its ranks.

BIBLIOGRAPHY: V. M. Chernov, *The Great Russian Revolution*, trans. and abridged by Philip E. Mosely, New Haven, 1936; Oliver H. Radkey, *The Agrarian Foes of Bolshevism: Promise and Default of the Russian Socialist Revolutionaries*, New York, 1958.   G. A.

SOCIETY OF CIRCULATING EXHIBITIONS: *see* PAINTING.

SOILS. There is a great diversity of soils in the USSR. The distribution of zonal soils corresponds to the *geographic zones* (q.v.). Intrazonal S formed under conditions of very poor drainage occasionally are found in many regions; azonal S in mountains.

The zone of arctic and tundra soils lies along the coasts and on the islands of the Arctic Ocean, the total area exceeding 420 mill. acres (around 8% of the USSR). S of the tundra are affected by the presence of the permanently frozen layer lying at a shallow depth, by low summer temperature, and by extensive moisture; and they are noteworthy in having a thin peat-humus horizon underlain by the moist gley horizon. *Arctic soils* lie in the N. part of the zone; there is no vegetation in places, and there are peculiar systems of polygonal cracks in the ground. The *peat-bog soils* are characteristic of the S. part of the zone. Some areas in the S. are suitable for agriculture, particularly to vegetable production.

The zone of podzol and bog soil occupies some 1,800 mill. acres (around 33% of the USSR); yet by inclusion of the adjoining Siberian region of mountain-

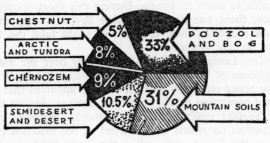

USSR SOIL ZONES

ous-forest podzol S, the total area covered with such S equals some 3,000 mill. acres, or more than 50% of the total area of the USSR. In the N. this zone adjoins the zone of tundra S; its S. border coincides with the S. border of mixed forests. The podzol soil formation takes place under the forests. With sufficient moisture the upper horizons of the soil become leached. In cross section, the striking feature of the podzol S is their three-colored profile: the top layer is grayish, colored by the humus; the middle layer is white, eluvial, sandy; while the bottom layer is of a yellow-brown color, illuvial and clayey. It is from the presence of the white layer that these S have been given the popular name of podzols ("the color of ash"). Leaching as it occurs in the middle horizon is given the name "podzolization." Some soil is podzolized slightly, some moderately, and some strongly. Simultaneously with podzolization, most of the podzolic S undergo the process of the formation of the humus horizon. This process is affected by the development of herbaceous cover and is more intensive in the S. of the forest zone. The *podzol-bog soils* are formed in swampy areas under coniferous forests, where there is excessive moisture and plant decay is greatly retarded. The partly decomposed plants accumulate into an upper layer. Below this is a horizon of sticky structureless clay known as the gley horizon, which is of characteristic gray-blue color. The podzol and bog soil types are interrelated through many transitional formations. The occurrence of the podzol, podzol-bog, or bog S depends on the elevation, paternal rocks, and the natural history of the area. There are several podzol soil provinces in the USSR. The distribution of areas under cultivation is extremely uneven within the zone of podzol soils. On the average 7% of the land is under cultivation. The most intensive utilization of podzol S for agriculture is in the Leningrad Oblast, the Lithuanian SSR, the Estonian SSR, in Polesye and Meshchera, on the Valday upland, and in the central forest province, where in places some 30%–40% of the soil is cleared and cultivated. The gley-podzol S found in the Dvina-Pechora area and occasionally in Siberia are practically not used for agriculture.

The zone of gray forest soils forms a narrow strip along the S. boundary of the zone of podzol S and in places encroaches into the chernozem soil belt—the total area being some 178 mill. acres, (around 3.5% of the USSR). The gray forest S form under the mixed forests having a herbaceous cover. Their profile has characteristics of both the podzol and the chernozem

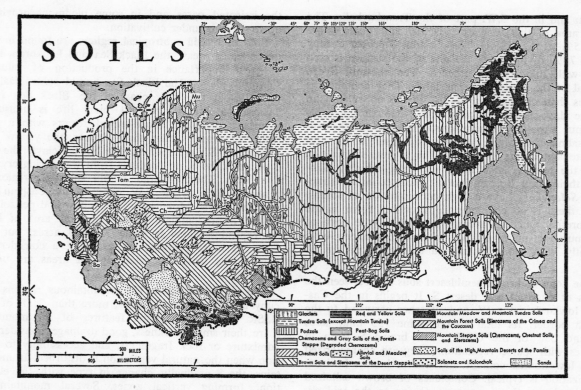

S, but their humus horizon is much thicker than that in the podzol S. Some 40–50% of the area that is covered with gray forest S is cleared and farmed.

The zone of chernozem soils extends continuously from the W. border of the USSR to the Altay foothills. These S can ensure very high crop yields. In the W. the zone attains a width of some 185 mi., and extends to the Black Sea, the Sea of Azov, and the Caucasus foothills. In the E., beyond the boundaries of the zone, the chernozem S (together with the gray forest S) are found in the intermontane depressions of Central Siberia and Transbaykalia. The total area of the zone exceeds 470 mill. acres (about 9% of the USSR). The chernozem is representative of the steppe type of soil formation. The main characteristics of its profile are: (1) the presence of the dark humus horizon which is generally thick and rich in organic matter; (2) the presence of the horizon of carbonate accumulation; (3) the saturation of the colloid complex with bases (usually with calcium and magnesium). There are several categories of chernozem and their geographic distribution is influenced by the climatic changes from N. to S. *The podzolized chernozems* appear in forest-steppe regions; *the leached chernozems* in the N. steppe (of the meadow type). These two varieties cover the N. part of this zone and include large massifs of the gray forest soils. They occur in the N. Ukraine, in Central Russia, and in areas adjoining the slopes of the Urals, as well as in the Altay foothills and in Central Siberia. *Typical deep chernozems* have the characteristic profile of the chernozem S, the humus content in the upper horizon exceeding 9%. They dominate in the forest-steppes of European Russia and are encountered in the Kuban region. *Chernozems of the prairie* contain 7–9% of humus in the upper horizon with a thickness smaller than that in the deep chernozems. They occupy the N. part of the steppe, i.e., most of the Ukraine, also an area on the Volga-Don watershed, an irregular strip extending from the Volga eastward over N. Kazakhstan to the Irtysh River, and an area in the Altay foothills. *The S. chernozems* have a lower content of humus (4–6%) and the smallest thickness of all types. They form an almost continuous belt encircling, from the S., the chernozems of the prairie. *The carbonaceous chernozems* which contain carbonates in the upper horizon are found mostly in the Caucasus foothills. *The salinized chernozems* which are characterized by the presence of sodium in their absorbed colloidal complex are found in places in the S. part of the zone and in the Ural foothills. *The meadow-chernozem soils* are formed mostly in river valleys where the ground water table is close to the surface. The zone of chernozem S is used for agriculture more intensively than all others: over 80% of the Ukraine is cultivated; and in 1953, an average of about 50% of the entire zone. The chernozem areas of Kazakhstan were least cultivated, but in recent years many efforts have been made to introduce farming on the Kazakhstan virgin soils.

The zone of chestnut soils lies S. of the zone of chernozems and extends as a continuous belt almost latitudinally from the Caucasus foothills over the Stavropol Kray, Stalingrad, West-Kazakhstan, Aktyubinsk, Kustanay, Karaganda, and Semipalatinsk oblasts up to the Altay foothills. In the Ukraine these S occupy the narrow strip along the coasts of the Black Sea and the Sea of Azov. They are also found in Siberia in the intermontane depressions of the Altay-Sayan mountain region and in the S.W. part of the Transbaykalia. The total area of this zone exceeds 300 mill. acres (more than 5% of the USSR). The chestnut S proper occupy some 70% of the zone, the rest of the surface is covered with *solonets* and other S. The chestnut S are typical of the semiarid steppe lands. They contain less humus than chernozems: 4–5% in the upper horizon of the dark-chestnut variety and 2–3% in the light-chestnut variety. A characteristic feature of chestnut S is salinization which develops as a result of the arid climate and differs in degree. The highest salinization is in the *solonets soils* which are usually highly alkaline; their lower horizon has a typical columnar structure. *Solonchaks* have a high concentration of soluble salts; there is no characteristic structural form in the soil profile. Only an average of 11% of the zone of chestnut S is under cultivation now, but efforts have recently been made to expand cultivation in the N. part.

The zone of brown semidesert soils lies between the zones of chestnut and desert S. It begins in the Caspian lowland in the W. and stretches eastward to the China border. Its total area is some 155 mill. acres (around 3% of the USSR). The brown S form in steppes with sparse vegetation. They are characterized by a low humus content and a thin humus horizon. Salinization is typical. Complexes of brown salinized S and solonets S are common. Owing to the arid climate, only some 4% of the zone is under cultivation.

The zone of desert soils is the southernmost soil zone of the USSR in Central Asia. Some patches of these S occur in the Kura-Araks and Caspian lowlands. The total area of this zone is around 395 mill. acres (some 7.5% of the USSR), of which some 138 mill. acres are covered with sand. As a result of recent investigations, the desert soils are divided into several varieties. *Gray-brown soils* form under the sparse polyn-halophytic vegetation on the products from weathering hard rocks. They contain less than 1% of humus and are characterized by salinization and accumulation of calcium carbonate and gypsum. *Takyr soils* (takyr-like serozems) form in takyrs which are flat clayey spaces occupying gentle depressions and generally covered with vegetation. *Serozems* are associated with the vegetation of the desert-ephemeric type and develop on lossial deposits of alluvial plains and piedmont areas; they are characterized by a high content of calcium carbonate. Serozems are divided into light, typical, and dark. The dark contain 3–4% of humus and occur in the mountainous regions; the other two varieties contain 1–2% of humus. *Solonchaks* develop in depressions where ground water comes close to the surface. In wide river valleys and in deltas there occur meadow-serozem, meadow, and meadow-bog S. The zone is divided into two subzones: one of gray-brown desert S, sands and takyr S; and the other of foothill serozems ringing the mountain systems of Central Asia. Within this zone plant breeding is possible only with irrigation. Under natural conditions, the land is widely used as pasture. An average of only about 3.5% of the zone is plowed, but in the irrigated oases and in some piedmont provinces up to 40% is under cultivation.

Soils of humid subtropical regions are found in two unconnected areas: the Black Sea and Lenkoran, both of great importance in the production of valuable subtropic plants. The Black Sea humid subtropical region lies at the N.E. coast of the Black Sea from Tuapse to Batumi. Natural plant life is unusually luxuriant; there are broad-leaved forests with a profusion of vines. Under these forests, the yellow and podzolized S developed in the N. on clays; the red S occur in the S. on products from weathering crystalline rocks. The Lenkoran humid subtropic region is a narrow strip at the S.W. coast of the Caspian Sea near the Talysh Mountains. The yellow and podzolized yellow S predominate here. The total area of both subtropical sections is some 750,000 acres, but the dissected relief prevents the usage of a considerable part of the land. All relatively flat areas are under cultivation.

The mountain soils. The mountainous regions occupy about 1,680 mill. acres, more than 31% of the USSR. The characteristic features of all mountain S are their small thickness, good drainage, considerable admixture or rock fragments, and accessibility to erosion when the natural vegetation is disturbed. In mountains, the S gradually change in type with the elevation, forming vertical zones. Several mountain-soil provinces are to be distinguished. Diversities in S are caused by differences in altitude of mountain regions, as well as in climate. For example, the *mountain-tayga-tundra provinces* include the North Urals, the mountains of N. Siberia and N.E. Asia; the *mountain-desert-steppe* provinces, the Tien Shan and Kopet Dagh. An average of about 1% of the area of mountain regions is under cultivation; in the S. regions some 6%.

BIBLIOGRAPHY: Lev S. Berg, *Natural Regions of the USSR*, John A. Morrison and C. C. Nikiforoff, Eds. New York, 1950.

L. D.

SOKÓLNIKOV (Brilliant), **Grigóry Yákovlevich** (1888–194?), Soviet leader and diplomat, born in the Ukraine, the son of a physician, and educated in Moscow. S joined the Bolshiveks in 1905, was arrested in 1907 and banished to Yenisey region, Siberia, for life. He escaped two years later and went abroad to meet Lenin in Paris. There he took a doctoral degree in law and economics. In 1910 he opposed Lenin's tactics and policy, and drew nearer to Trotsky. In 1917, S returned with Lenin to Russia by way of Germany and Sweden. At the 6th Party Congress (Aug. 1917), he was elected to the Central Committee. Following the October revolution, he carried through the nationalization of all private banks. He was a member, and later chairman, of the Soviet delegation to Brest-Litovsk and signed the peace treaty with the Germans.

During the civil war, S was a commissar to the Soviet armies on the Don. He went to Turkestan in Aug. 1920 to fight the anti-Soviet Basmach rebellion in Bukhara. In 1922–26, as people's commissar of finance, S carried through the monetary reform and introduced the *chervonets* based on gold. In the summer of 1926 he was sent to the United States to conduct financial negotiations, but was refused an entry permit. In 1925–26, S joined the "new opposition" of Kamenev and Zinoviev for a short time. In 1929–33 he was Soviet ambassador to London and then deputy commissar for foreign affairs. Expelled from the party and arrested in 1936, he was charged with Trotskyite treason and conspiracy and, the following year, was sentenced to ten years' imprisonment. Since then he has not been heard of.

SOKOLÓV-SKALYÁ, Pável Petróvich (1899–), painter. Member, Ac. of Fine Arts. People's Artist of USSR. Produced romantic pictures of the revolution and civil war (*Taman Campaign*, 1928; *Brothers*, 1932; *Workers Detachment*, 1937). During World War II painted historical pictures: *Ivan IV in Livonia* (1942). His more important postwar pictures are *Liberation of Kaluga* (1948) and *People of Krasnodon* (1948). Stalin prizes (1942, 1949).

SOKOLOVSKY, Vasíly Danílovich (1897–), Soviet marshal. Born in Grodno Province, in a peasant family.

After participating in the civil war, S underwent training at the Frunze Military Academy in the late 1920's and early 1930's, and then at the Voroshilov Higher General Staff Academy. During World War II he distinguished himself on several fronts and rose to the rank of general of the army. In 1947 he was promoted to marshal of the Soviet Union as well as commander of Soviet forces in Germany. After the failure of the Berlin blockade, he was recalled to Moscow and made deputy minister of defense. A party member since 1930, S was elected to the Central Committee of the CPSU in 1952 and has been a member since.

SOKOLÓVSKY, Vadím Vasílyevich (1912–), mechanical engineer. Corresponding member, Ac. of S., USSR (1946). Graduate of the Moscow Institute of Civil Engineering (1933). Affiliated with the Mathematical Institute (1936–39) and the Institute of Mechanical Engineering (1939). Research on shells, statics of free-flowing media, and the theory of plasticity. Solved numerous problems of the two-dimensional state of stress. Suggested several methods for the solution of problems on two-dimensional ultimate equilibrium of free-flowing and connecting media. Author of *Statics of Free-Flowing Media* (1942), *The Theory of Plasticity* (1950, 2nd ed.). Stalin prizes (1942, 1952).

SOLIKÁMSK, city in Perm Oblast, RSFSR; pop. 45,000 (1959). R.R. station, port on the Kama. Center of extensive potash, salt, and magnesium salt mining based on rich local deposits. Other ind. include paper and pulp milling and shipbuilding. Founded 1430.

SOL-ILÉTSK, town on Ilek River in Orenburg Oblast, RSFSR; pop. 20,200 (1959). Products include salt, gypsum, and bricks. Mud baths.

SOLOGÚB (Teternikov), **Fyódor Kuzmích** (1863–1927), a leading symbolist writer. His first volumes of prose and verse were published in 1896. Son of a cobbler and a domestic servant, he became a teacher and inspector of schools. The success of his novel *The Little Demon* (1907) gave him an opportunity to retire from teaching which he hated. He found a world of beauty

in Satanism and expressed in his decadent poetry the lure of night and death and sex. He wrote a collection of verse, *The Circle of Flames*; novels: *Bad Dreams* (1896), *The Sorcery of Death* (1908–12), *The Snake Charmer* (1921); plays: *The Victory of Death* (1907), *Love over Abyss* (1914).

SOLOVÉTSKY ISLANDS, in the White Sea, part of the Archangel Oblast, RSFSR; area 140 sq. mi. The site of a famous monastery and former concentration camp.

SOLOVTSÓV (Fyodorov), **Nikoláy Nikoláyevich** (1857–1902), actor and producer. Associated with the stage from 1875, first in provincial theaters and later in the Aleksandrinsky Theater in St. Petersburg. Appeared in dramatic and comedy parts in plays by Gogol and Ostrovsky. S was the first to produce L. Tolstoy's *The Fruit of Enlightenment* and A. K. Tolstoy's trilogy *Tsar Boris*.

SOLOVYÓV, Sergéy Mikháylovich (1820–1879), historian. Son of a priest, he studied at the University of Moscow where he was much influenced by T. N. Granovsky. His early studies of Novgorod and of the Ryurik dynasty were Slavophile in orientation; but he soon moved toward the position of the Westerners, reading widely and traveling in Europe. In 1844, he joined the faculty of the University of Moscow. Thereafter he wrote numerous articles and monographs and *A History of Russia from Earliest Times* (1851–79) in 29 volumes. In keeping with the "institutional" view of R. history, he saw the nation's growth largely determined by the development of a central state system. Peter the Great's introduction of western ideas he considered a key contribution in the transformation of Russia from oriental backwardness into a modern polity. His *History* is a vast compendium of facts and quotations on a scale far beyond anything attempted previously, rather than a neatly conceived work of interpretation.

SOLOVYÓV, Vladímir Sergéyevich (1853–1900), poet and philosopher, son of the distinguished historian and Moscow University professor. S developed his philosophy in apposition to the metaphysics, materialism, and empiricism of western philosophies and evolved his own system of universal "free theocracy." He advocated an organic "unity of the whole" for society, based on three main principles: (1) God's incarnation in Christ provided a guide to human life, implying the possibility of the gradual elevation of man to godliness; (2) social unity must be based on justice; and (3) individual liberty. He saw all three principles as essential to the mission of "Holy Russia," which he believed should provide a synthesis of eastern and western spiritual and social values. He argued for a unique universal church, to accommodate even Judaism, and came to regard Eastern Orthodoxy as a schism of primarily political origin. It has sometimes been said that his inclination toward the western Catholic church led to his actual conversion to Roman Catholicism in 1892.

S lectured at both Moscow (1873–77) and St. Petersburg (until 1881) universities, but the independence of his views, criticism of the official Russian Church, and tolerant attitude toward the non-Russian nationalities of the empire brought an early end to his academic career. Most of his writings on religion were published outside Russia. He nonetheless had a great following among the R. intelligentsia. S's major works are *Three Meetings* (a poem), *Three Conversations,* and *The History of the Antichrist.*

SÓMOV, Konstantín Andréyevich (1869–1909), painter and illustrator. Studied at the St. Petersburg Academy of Arts under Repin (1888–96). Member of *Mir Iskusstva.* S's early impressionist landscapes, followed by a series of brilliantly executed water colors depicting intimate scenes of old R. life with the delicate grace and charm of 18th-century painters, established his reputation as a vigorous colorist and a master designer. His work was exhibited in Russia (from 1894), Munich (1898), Berlin (1900–02), Dresden (1905), Vienna (International Exhibition, 1907), Rome (1909), Brussels (1928), Copenhagen (1929). A prolific illustrator (*Daphnis and Chloe, Manon Lescot,* the *Italian Voyage* by Goethe), S is known also as a portrait painter.

SOPHIE (Sófya Alekséyevna) (1657–1704), regent, daughter of Tsar Alexis and Maria Miloslavsky. After the death of her brother, Tsar Fedor (1682), the successors to the throne, according to tradition, were S's mentally deficient brother, Ivan (14 years old), or her half-brother, Peter (10 years old), son of Alexis' second wife Natalie Naryshkin. Three days after the proclamation of Peter as tsar, S instigated a rebellion of the *streltsy* (q.v.) and crushed the clan of the Naryshkins. S ruled the country with the assistance of Prince Golitsin, who became foreign minister and conducted two unsuccessful Crimean campaigns. In 1689, relations between Peter and S became strained, and S plotted to depose Peter. However, Peter was warned, fled to the Troitsky Monastery, and called in the chiefs of the Moscow troops to inform them of the betrayal. Peter was supported by the Moscow Patriarch, by many powerful nobles, and part of the *streltsy.* Golitsin was deported and S locked up in a convent. Ivan died in 1696. In 1698, while Peter was abroad, supporters of S organized a new rebellion. S was suspected of having been informed of the plot; she was compelled to take the veil and imprisoned in Novodevichy convent where she died.

SÓRIN, Savély Abrámovich (1887–1953), portrait painter. Studied under Repin at the St. Petersburg Academy of Art, where he won the *Prix de Rome.* At the *Salon d'Automne* in Paris (1922–23) and the International Exhibit in Pittsburgh (1923–24) S's canvases enjoyed considerable success. His sensitive interpretations and subtle use of color brought him wide recognition, both in Europe and in the United States, where he resided during the later part of his life. His portraits are exhibited at the Tretyakov Gallery in Moscow, the Russian Art Museum in Leningrad, and the Luxembourg Museum (portrait of Anna Pavlova).

SORÓKINO: *see* KRASNODON.

SÓRSKY, Nil: *see* NIL SORSKY.

SÓRTAVALA (f. Sérdobol), city in Karelian ASSR, on N. shore of Lake Ladoga; pop. 17,000 (1959). Metal- and leather-products, furniture and footwear mfg. Marble and granite quarried nearby are handled by the city plants.

SÓSVA RIVER, flows from E. Urals through Khanty-Mansi National Okrug to become left tributary of the Ob; 450 mi. long; navigable.

SÓSVA RIVER, flows from N. Urals through Sverdlovsk Oblast to become source of Tavda River; 420 mi. long; navigable.

SOUTH-KAZAKHSTÁN OBLAST, Kazakh SSR; area 58,000 sq. mi.; pop. 921,000 (1959). Cities: Chimkent (adm. center), Lenger, Turkestan. Major cotton- and fruit-growing region extending through a desert zone along the middle course of the Syr Darya, with the Kyzyl-Kum desert in the W., the foothills of Tien Shan in the E., and the Kara-Tau range crossing the central part; the Muyun-Kum and Bet-Pak-Dala deserts lie in its N. part. In recent years a large arid area known as Golodnaya Step (Hunger Steppe) was converted into an irrigated farmland. Coal and polymetallic deposits provided the base to rapidly developing non-ferrous metallurgy. Sheep are reared, mainly for meat, in the desert region. The Turksib and Trans-Caspian railroads were of major importance in the development of the oblast. Est. 1932.

SOUTH OSSETIAN AUTONOMOUS OBLAST, part of Georgian SSR; bounded on N. by North Ossetian ASSR, and on other three sides by Georgian SSR; area 1,500 sq. mi.; pop. 97,000 (1959): Ossetians 69 per cent, Georgians 27 per cent. Adm. center: Staliniri. High plateau region on S. slopes of Caucasus. Inhabitants engage mostly in raising sheep and goats. Orchards; lumber and lumber-sawing ind.; marble and talc processing. Est. 1922.

SOVÉTSK (f. Tilsit, East Prussia), city in Kaliningrad Oblast, RSFSR; pop. 31,200 (1959). Mfg. town and shipping point, on the Neman; R.R. junction. Its ind. include machine building, iron works, paper and pulp mills, lumbering, and woodworking plants; leather factories; creameries and cheese dairies; breweries and distilleries. Dates back to early 15th century. Ceded to USSR in 1945.

SOVÉTSKAYA GÁVAN, city in Khabarovsk Kray, RSFSR; pop. 12,000 (1939), 50,000 (1959). Recently built naval base and fishing port on the Tatar Strait, with a deep harbor and 5,000-ton floating dock; connected by rail to Komsomolsk city; fish processing and lumbering.

SOVIET LAW: *see* LAW.

SOVIET OF NATIONALITIES: *see* SOVIETS, CONSTITUTIONS.

SOVIET OF THE UNION: *see* SOVIETS, CONSTITUTIONS.

SOVIET UNION: *see* UNION OF SOVIET SOCIALIST REPUBLICS.

SOVIETS are the hierarchy of elected government bodies in Soviet Russia. Their title is derived from the word *sovety,* which means councils. Precursors of the present S appeared in Russia during the 1905 revolution as councils elected by strike committees to coordinate their work and direct the revolutionary movement. Trotsky, then close to the Mensheviks, ably led the St. Petersburg Soviet in which members of the various socialist parties predominated. S reappeared during the revolution of February 1917, first as S of

Workers' Deputies, soon becoming S of Workers' and Soldiers' Deputies. The creation of the Petrograd Soviet on March 12 and of the Provisional Government on March 16 ushered in the period of "dual power," of uneasy coexistence between the S and the Provisional Government, during which the S undermined the latter's authority, especially in the army. Bolsheviks were still a minority in the First All-Russian Congress of Soviets, June 1917.

Lenin had returned to Russia demanding "all power to the Soviets," by which he meant all power to the Bolsheviks working through the S. By Sept., the Bolsheviks had a majority in the Petrograd and some other S. over their Right Socialist Revolutionary and Menshevik opponents. They used the Military Revolutionary Committee of the Petrograd Soviet as coordinating center for the successful October Revolution (Nov. 7–8, Oct. 25–26 O.S.) in alliance with the Left Socialist Revolutionaries. The victors controlled the Second Congress of Soviets which met on Nov. 7, in time to confirm the beginning of a new order. Peasant S organized in March 1917 were soon merged with the other S under the rather cumbersome title of S of "Workers', Soldiers', Peasants' and Landless Peasants' Deputies." Power of decision gravitated to the executive committees of the S, and, within them, to the Bolsheviks.

By the early NEP period (1922), the former strike and revolutionary organs had evolved into one-party bodies of Bolsheviks or their supporters, with some exceptions in the provinces. By the later 1930's, the S were obedient transmitters of party policy, their initiative almost nil at the center, and reduced in the local S to the solution of community problems in line with plan directives, ministerial decrees and orders from the party, whose local committees paralleled the S at each level.

The Tenth All-Russian Congress of Soviets and Congresses of Soviets of the Ukrainian, Byelorussian and Transcaucasian Republics merged into the First USSR Congress of Soviets when the USSR was formed by the treaty of Dec. 30, 1922, which paved the way for the first USSR constitution, approved by the second USSR Congress of Soviets on Jan. 31, 1924. Until the late 1920's, there was lively debate in the Central Executive Committee elected by the Congress of Soviets. Legislative functions were shared by the bicameral Central Executive Committee; the Congress of Soviets which it overshadowed and which was too large and too inactive to have much to say; the government, called the Council of People's Commissars; and also, in fact, by the Central Committee of the Communist Party.

Rules of suffrage under the 1918 constitution of the RSFSR and the 1924 constitution of the USSR reversed the pattern of class discrimination which had existed in elections to the State Duma of tsarist Russia. The franchise was barred to persons hiring labor for profit or living on unearned income, to capitalists and middlemen, monks and priests, former police employees and members of the royal family, in all a few per cent of the population. Those who did vote had no secret ballot. Representation in the higher S was weighted against the peasantry, and indirect for all, whether peasants or urban dwellers.

The present system of S is based on the USSR constitution of 1936, which was confirmed by the Eighth USSR Congress of Soviets on Dec. 5, 1936. Class disabilities in voting were removed, and voting is universal, secret, direct, and equal. All citizens 18 years of age and older except the insane may vote for deputies to the USSR Supreme Soviet and the supreme S of the union republics, which replaced the congresses of S existing under the 1924 constitution; and to the local S of the oblasts and krays, autonomous republics, autonomous oblasts, national okrugs, cities, city districts, towns, rayons, and villages. Deputies to the USSR Supreme Soviet must be at least 23, and to the republic supreme S, at least 21 years old. Voting is in residential electoral precincts. It used to be primarily at places of work.

Every effort is made to get out the vote during the elections, which are not occasions when leaders are chosen out of competing candidates, but, rather, holiday demonstrations of loyalty to the regime involving participation by millions of agitators and workers in the electoral commissions at all levels, and affirmative voting by over 99 per cent of eligible voters. Candidates are nominated under party control by such public organizations as party committees, and in meetings of trade unions, schools, and collective farms. Only one candidate for deputy is registered in each electoral district, and only in elections to the local S are a few hundred of the 1,800,000 deputies rejected because they fail to get a majority vote. No registered candidate for deputy to the supreme soviet who was still in the running at election time has failed to be elected. In sum, as political controls became more complete, electoral provisions could be liberalized and made highly democratic in form. There were elections to the USSR Supreme Soviet in 1937, 1946, 1950, 1954, and 1958; to the republic supreme S in 1938, 1947, 1951, 1955, and 1959; and to the local S in 1939, 1947–48, 1950–51, 1953, 1955, 1957, and 1959.

The simplified two-tiered structure of the USSR Supreme Soviet and its Presidium replaced after 1936 the three-tiered Congress of Soviets, Central Executive Committee, and Presidium of the Central Executive Committee. Its two chambers, the Council of the Union and the Council of Nationalities, are larger and more equal descendants of the two chambers similarly named which made up the old Central Executive Committee. Deputies to the Council of the Union are elected on the basis of population, one from each constituency, averaging roughly 300,000 people. In 1958, 738 were chosen. Deputies to the Council of Nationalities are elected on the following basis: 25 from each union republic, 11 from each autonomous republic, 5 from each autonomous oblast, and 1 from each national okrug. In 1958, 640 were sent to the Council of Nationalities. About three-fourths of the deputies are members of the Communist party, and one half are party or state officials.

As the "highest organ of state power," the USSR Supreme Soviet is legally the sole legislator. In fact, many normative acts are passed by other state bodies such as the Presidium and the USSR Council of Ministers, and by the party Central Committee. Some measures which originate in the party or the government, especially the yearly budget and yearly economic plan, or new legislative basis in some field of the legal codification which is now proceeding in the USSR, are submitted to the Supreme Soviet through the Presidium and standing commissions, where deputies or invited specialists and jurists may be able to introduce changes, as long as they do not mean a major departure in policy and as long as they receive the approval of the party. The Supreme Soviet elects the USSR Supreme Court, USSR Procurator General, and its own Presidium and approves government appointments. It hears declarations on foreign policy and passes resolutions in that and other fields. Deputies have a chance to air local problems and criticize administrators. But policy originates outside the Supreme Soviet, whose discretion is limited by party controls, short sessions, and the custom of unanimous voting in all the matters mentioned above. The Supreme Soviet is largely but not entirely a decorative rubber stamp and ceremonial sounding board for official declarations. It does not feature spontaneous debates, but then neither do the party congresses—provided they do not infringe on the rule of unanimity.

The Presidium of the USSR Supreme Soviet, "collective president of the USSR," acts for the Supreme Soviet between sessions; issues edicts, some of which are never submitted to its parent body for approval; may grant pardons; fulfills ceremonial and diplomatic functions such as awarding orders and medals and ratifying treaties. Its chairman acts as head of state, receiving diplomatic credentials. The Presidium consists of a chairman, successively Kalinin, Shvernik, Voroshilov, and Brezhnev; 15 deputy chairmen (chairmen of the republic supreme soviets); a secretary and 16 members, none of whom should be in the government.

Supreme S of the union republics fulfill similar, limited functions at the republic level.

Local S form a strict chain of command, their executive committees, the true governing bodies, being subordinated not only to the S, but also, more important, to the executive committees of the next higher S. The S meet relatively infrequently in plenary sessions, and actually decide little. Their deputies participate in standing commissions which check on the state of schools, public catering and services, and other facilities. Their executive committees rule through departments for such community problems as education, the militia, public health, local industry, public catering, communal economy, and agriculture.

The full title of the S has been simplified to "Soviets of Toilers' Deputies." (*See also* CENTRAL GOVERNMENT, CONSTITUTIONS, GOVERNMENT LOCAL, GOVERNMENT MUNICIPAL, ELECTORAL SYSTEM.)

BIBLIOGRAPHY: John N. Hazard, *The Soviet System of Government*, Chicago, 1960; Herbert McClosky and John E. Turner, *The Soviet Dictatorship*, New York, 1960; Julian Towster, *Political Power in the U.S.S.R., 1917–1947*, New York, 1948; Derek J. R. Scott, *Russian Political Institutions*, London, 1958; A. Denisov and M. Kirichenko, *Soviet State Law*, Moscow, 1960.   P. H. J.

SOVKHOZ—abbreviated form of *sovetskoye khozyaystvo* (state farm)—is a state-owned and state-operated agricultural enterprise. In contrast to the *kolkhozes* the workers and employees of the S are wage-earners, but as in the *kolkhozes* these wage-earners are permitted to cultivate their own private plots.

In the early stage of the Soviet regime when the breaking up of large estates was taking place, a relatively small number of more efficient and better equipped estates were preserved as S. Operated at great loss, the S were at this time of little importance.

A great expansion of the S system started in the years of the collectivization of agriculture. Parallel to the organization of collective farms the existing S were enlarged and great numbers of new large-scale S were built. By 1938 the S had an area of 68 mill. hectares of which only 12.4 mill. were under cultivation, which amounted to not more than 8 per cent of the total sown area. Despite the fact that the Soviet authorities supplied the S with a greater amount of agricultural machinery than they did the *kolkhozes,* that the productivity of labor in the S was higher than in the collective farms, and that there existed a relatively higher degree of specialization in the S, the operation of the S showed a great deficit and many had to be supported through subsidies from the state budget.

With the development of virgin lands in 1953–55 the S system was expanded considerably. Between 1953 and 1959 the sown area of land belonging to the S increased more than threefold, from 45 mill. acres to 145.26 mill.; consequently the share of S in the total land under cultivation increased from 11.6 per cent in 1953 to 29.1 per cent in 1958 with a corresponding relative decline of sown land belonging to the *kolkhozes,* from 84.0 per cent to 67.2 per cent.

In addition to the new S organized in the virgin land regions, especially in Kazakhstan, a certain number of backward and inefficient collective farms were reorganized and transformed into S. As a result over a hundred mill. hectares of land previously belonging to the collective farms were transferred to the S.

Starting with 1954, state subsidies to the S were abrogated and, as in other state-operated enterprises, profitability became obligatory for the operation of the S. Prices paid to the S for their deliveries to the state procurement organizations were increased considerably, the S were allowed to sell some of their output produced in excess of the prescribed plan quotas at state retail prices. In addition, 20 per cent of profits made by the S are retained by the S management for productive and social investment. As a cumulative effect of these measures the financial situation of the S has improved in recent years. As a corollary the wage system applied in the S was also reorganized and, as in

NUMBER OF STATE FARMS

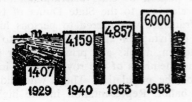

1929 1940 1953 1958
1,407 4,159 4,857 6,000

industry, piece work was introduced, together with a system of rewards for production above plan quotas.

With the abolition of the machine tractor stations and the introduction of fixed money wages on the collective farms, the differences in the administrative and operational set-up of collective and state farms became less distinct and it may be that at some future stage of development all *kolkhozes* will be turned into S.

The table below shows the development of the S in 1940–59:

	1940	1953	1959
Number of S (at end of year)	4,159	4,857	6,496
Average annual number of workers and employees, in thousands	1,373	1,844	4,177
Sown area, thous. hectares	11,559	15,155	53,894
Tractors, in terms of 15 HP units (at end of year), thousands	100	165	597
Cattle in thousands	2,462	3,404	10,501
of which			
Cows, thousands	952	1,128	3,557
Hogs, thousands	1,910	3,502	9,840
Sheep and goats, thousands	5,908	10,124	29,344

(*Narodnoye khozyaystvo SSSR v 1959 godu*, p. 443.)

(*See also* AGRICULTURE)

A. K.

SOVNARKHOZY: see INDUSTRY, INDUSTRIAL MANAGEMENT AND ORGANIZATION.

SOVNARKOM: see HISTORY, COMMUNIST PARTY.

SOVZNAKI: see MONETARY SYSTEM.

SOZH RIVER, flows from south of Smolensk via Byelorussia to form left tributary of Dnieper; 400 mi. long; navigable in lower course.

SOZÓNOV, Yegór Sergéyevich (1879–1910), Socialist Revolutionary. Joined the revolutionary movement in his student days. Was expelled from the university for participation in student riots. An active member of the terroristic organization of the Socialist Revolutionary party, S in 1904 assassinated the reactionary minister of the interior, V. K. Plehve. Was condemned to hard labor for life. In 1910, protesting against the practice of corporal punishment for political prisoners, S committed suicide.

SPACE SCIENCE. On Oct. 4, 1957, a R. man-made moon escorted mankind into the space age. And the world learned a new word: Sputnik—literally: fellow traveler, but here it is in the meaning of a fellow traveler to the planet Earth.

First of eight spectacular R. space explorations (up to July 1960), Sputnik I rose—as did its followers—from a secret base deep inside the Soviet Union. The rocket was secret, too, but believed to have been a modified three-stage military weapon.

Sputnik I also marked the beginning of the international race for space. Vying with each other to be first and best, the United States and the Soviet Union poured billions of dollars and rubles into giant rockets and scientific instruments.

Soviet scientists followed Sputnik I with heavy earth satellites, an interplanetary vehicle, a payload that struck the moon, a shot that passed the moon to take the first pictures of its back, and a satellite to test manned orbital flight and finally a race around the earth by Yury Gagarin. That last spectacular took Maj. Gagarin around the world in 89 minutes in one orbital sweep in a five ton spaceship. It was the sixth such spaceship that the Soviet Union had launched in its

man-in-space program, a program it denied having for many months. The flight, taking off at 1:07 A.M. EST April 12, 1961, marked the start of man's roaming through space. The Soviets called Gagarin a cosmonaut. Soon thereafter, on May 5, 1961, the United States sent Commander Alan B. Shepard into a high arching flight less than 302 miles down range. It was the symbol of the American-Soviet space game. The Soviet's first; the U.S. second with the spectacular achievements. (See chart)

Although the United States was bested repeatedly in the matter of weight lifted into orbit (some R. moons weighed five tons) and in doing something first, it launched more satellites and won more scientific prizes in space.

Up to May 1961, USSR launched eleven earth satellites and three space probes (one in solar orbit and one impacting the moon); the U.S. rocketed thirty-eight earth satellites and five space probes (two in solar orbit and three in near space).

As for scientific strides, it was an American earth satellite that discovered the ocean of electrically charged particles surrounding the earth and it is named for an American: the Van Allen belt.

In a document prepared in Dec. 1959 by Dr. Homer E. Newell, Jr., assistant director for space sciences for the U.S. National Aeronautics and Space Administration, U.S. and USSR space achievements are compared. Dr. Newell credits the Russians with the following firsts: first artificial earth satellite (Oct. 4, 1957); first lunar near miss (Lunik: Jan. 2, 1959); first lunar impact (Lunik II: Sept. 13, 1959); first pictures of the backside of the moon (Lunik III: Oct. 4, 1959) and first high capacity, maneuverable, and heavily instrumented space craft (Lunik III). Since then, the Russians were first to send into orbit a cabin capable of carrying a man (Sputnik IV: May 15, 1960) and a manned cabin (Vostok: April 12, 1961).

For the Russians, space science started with Konstantin Tsiolkovsky (1857–1935), a school teacher. As early as 1883, he developed principles of rocketry, and in 1903 he published a treatise: *Investigating Space with Rocket Devices*. It is reported that by 1908 R. engineers designed and constructed liquid fuel rockets. Under the direction of F. A. Tsander, an engineer, Soviet engineers had constructed a low thrust vehicle by the early 1930's.

More powerful rockets (for use in gliders) were designed by V. P. Glushko and L. S. Dushkin during World War II. Even though the Soviets had carried out this original development, there is no question they borrowed heavily from the technology of captured German V-2 rockets. By 1947, Yu. V. Kondratyuk had written a serious work on *The Conquest of Interplanetary Space*. During the early 1950's there were increasing numbers of stories in the Soviet press concerning outer space. At the same time there were intimations that the Soviet military establishment had undertaken development of large rockets.

Information is lacking on the official actions taken by the Soviet Academy of Sciences during the years preceding the first Sputnik. The Academy directs all space *science* work. However, soon after President Eisenhower announced in 1956 that the United States would launch an earth satellite as part of its contribution to the International Geophysical Year (I.G.Y.), the Soviet Union also announced such plans. But the statement was not taken at full value.

In the week preceding Oct. 4, 1957, the Panel on Space Sciences of the special international committee for I.G.Y. (CSAGI) met in Washington. Dr. Anatoly A. Blagonravov, a leading Soviet space scientist, said a Soviet satellite launching was "imminent." However, the Russian Embassy translator gave the delegates: "in the near future." Again little attention was paid to this statement. At the end of that week—it was a Friday—the Soviet delegation to the conference gave a cocktail party at the Soviet Embassy. Half way through the evening, Lloyd Berkner, American and chairman of the I.G.Y. space panel, interrupted the hubbub to declare that the Soviet News Agency Tass reported a Soviet earth satellite in orbit. And the space race was on.

That first earth satellite carried a scientific payload of 184 pounds, nine times the weight of the yet-to-be-fired Vanguard. The R. three-stage rocket also lifted the last stage into orbit, an unofficially estimated weight of four tons. The orbit inclined to the Equator by 65° and the sphere made one complete revolution about the earth (period) every 96.17 minutes with a speed at lowest point (perigee) of 18,000 miles an hour. The peak altitude was 558 miles.

Concerning the instruments, the official announcement stated that there were a thermometer, two radios, and chemical batteries.

The radios broadcast on 20.005 megacycles and 40.002 megacycles. Some Western scientists considered the Russians had reneged on an internationally agreed upon frequency of 108 mc. This made radio tracking difficult because the ionosphere (a charged layer of air forty miles up) bends the lower frequency signals out of line. However, it was believed that the Russians chose the reduced frequencies to study the effect of ionosphere on such signals. Also R. ham radio operators would be able to pick up the 20.005 and the 40.002 frequencies. In this way the Russians could establish a rough track across their own country. Instructions to this effect had been published in R. amateur radio journals several weeks before launching.

About the actual scientific results: again Dr. Newell's 5,000-word document presents the best comparative summary. He suggested that the U.S. and USSR scientists are at "about equal stages of advancement in the problems they are attacking or are about to attack in space research." However, the U.S. had the edge in scientific instrumentation (which accounted for the greater *scientific* achievements), Dr. Newell said. He added that USSR scientists often copy U.S. equipment directly. He predicted that the country which had the greater rocket capability would in time turn that engineering advantage to a scientific one, because, he said, such a nation could put instruments into remote unexplored regions of space.

Although Dr. Newell did not say it, this analysis predicts a future lead for the Soviet Union. It is conceded their rockets have greater load-lifting capability and it will not be until 1964 (perhaps 1963) that the United States has rockets able to put the same total weight in orbit that the USSR had in July 1960.

During the spring and summer of 1960, the USSR undertook a series of rocket test flights in the far Pacific. Although essentially military in character, the trials apparently were testing some very large rocket engines. Soviet information agencies touted them as "multi-stage carrier rockets for space exploration." Presumably, these rockets would be used in the exploration of Mars and Venus and for manned flight. There was some expectation that the Soviets would try to fire a rocket to the vicinity of Mars in Oct. 1960 because the time was astronomically propitious for such a flight.

In specific scientific fields, the Soviets have tried to lead in biological space science. They have sent up large numbers (undisclosed) of non-orbital rockets with dogs and rabbits which were studied in flight. The single orbital experiment with the dog, Layka, apparently provided much information on the reaction of a mammal to prolonged gravity-free conditions. Heart rate and respiration measurements reportedly showed little fluctuation once weightlessness was achieved. The dog died in three to four days from lack of oxygen.

Soviet scientists reportedly also made space-physiological measurements on human beings, presumably under the direction of Dr. Andrey G. Kuznetsov, a leading Soviet physiologist.

All this sounds like a prelude to manned space flight. Although Dr. Blagonravov had stated in 1959 that "we have no manned flight program," the Soviets threw a space cabin into orbit on May 15, 1960. They even attempted a re-entry experiment, i.e., to bring back the cabin through the dense atmosphere. But apparently the retro-rockets misfired and only ejected the capsule into a higher orbit. Again translation may have been a difficulty. Dr. Blagonravov may have been saying that his particular institute had no manned space program, implying that the project was in somebody else's hands.

In early 1960, it was the consensus of many informed American space scientists that the Soviets had the rocket and instrument capability to raise a man-carrying satellite into orbit and to bring it back safely either in late 1960 or in early 1961. And in early 1961 a man did go into orbit, ending all the speculation.

In lunar research, the Soviets again made three important strides. Lunik II, which hit the moon, found a lunar ionosphere. The lunar magnetic field was also determined and found to be absent, at least to the sensitivity of the instruments employed. The point is not yet settled.

One of the most spectacular scientific achievements was the photography of the hitherto unseen side of the moon. While the photographs were of low resolution, there was sufficient detail to permit Soviet scientists to name prominent features—with R. names.

However, because of their secretiveness, the Soviet scientists missed an opportunity to make one of the most important discoveries of I.G.Y., namely, the Van Allen radiation belts surrounding the earth. Although Sputnik II preceded Explorer I and had cosmic ray counters aboard which showed high counts at high latitudes, the R. scientists did not interpret this correctly. Having kept their telemetering code secret, the rest of the scientific world had no way of sending the data to them from other latitudes.

On August 6, 1961, another Soviet cosmonaut, Major G. S. Titov, was sent into orbit for 25 hours maintaining the Soviet leadership in the space race.

BIBLIOGRAPHY: F. J. Krieger, *Behind the Sputniks, A Survey of Soviet Space Science*, Washington, 1958; Albert Parry, *Russia's Rockets and Missiles*, New York, 1960; Alfred J. Zaehringer, *Soviet Space Technology*, New York, 1961.   E. U.

COMPARATIVE DATA ON THE FOUR SPACE FLIGHTS

Following is a comparison of the four space flights made so far, by Maj. German S. Titov, of the Soviet Union, Capt. Virgil I. Grissom and Cmdr. Alan B. Shepard, Jr. of the United States, and Maj. Yury A. Gagarin of the Soviet Union:

	TITOV	GRISSOM	SHEPARD	GAGARIN
Date	Aug. 6, 1961	July 21, 1961	May 5, 1961	April 12, 1961
Nature of flight	Earth orbit	Suborbital	Suborbital	Earth orbit
Altitude (miles)	111 to 158	118	116.5	187.75
Distance (miles)	435,000	303	302	About 25,000
Top Speed (m.p.h.)	17,750	5,280	5,100	17,400
Flight time	25 hrs. 18 min.	16 minutes	15 minutes	108 minutes
Weight of craft (lbs.)	10,430	4,040	4,040	10,460
Craft name	Vostok II	Liberty Bell 7	Freedom 7	Vostok I
Rocket thrust (lbs.)	800,000	78,000	78,000	800,000

SOVIET SPACE FLIGHT TABLE
PART I

Name	Lifetime	Orbit/Course	Perigee/Apogee	Payload Dimensions
Sputnik I (Satellite)	Oct. 4, 1957 to Jan. 4, 1958	65° incl. to equator Period: 96.17 min.	142 mi. 588 mi.	Weight: 184 lbs. Total in orbit: 4 tons Sphere: 22.8″ diameter
Sputnik II (Satellite)	Nov. 3, 1957 to April 14, 1958	65° incl. to earth equator Period: 103.7 min.	140 mi. 1,038 mi.	Weight: 1,120 lbs. Total in orbit: 4 tons Outside dimensions not given
Sputnik III	May 15, 1958 plus 15 months	65° incl. to earth equator Period: 106 min.	135 mi. 1,167 mi.	Weight: 2,925 lbs. Total in orbit: 7,000 pounds Cone shape; 11′9″ long; 5′8″ at base
Lunik I or Mechta (Space Probe)	Jan. 2, 1959. Extremely long life —thousands of years	15-month solar orbit around sun after passing moon at 5,000 mi. 15° incl. to earth	915 mill. mi. 123 mill. mi.	Weight: 796 lbs. Total: 3,425 lbs. Outside dimensions not given
Lunik II (Moon Impacter)	Sept. 12, 1959. Struck moon: 5:02:24 EDT, Sept. 12, 1959	Earth to moon Distance: 236,875 mi. Flight time: 35 hrs.	—	Weight: 858 lbs. 56 lb. Probe impacted moon
Lunik III (Earth Satellite + Space Probe)	Oct. 4, 1959. Very long life— thousands of years	Passed moon first orbit	30,000 mi. 291,000 mi.	Weight: 614 lbs.
Sputnik IV (Spacecraft I) (Earth Satellite)	May 15, 1960. Lifetime: ?	65° incl. to earth Varied period	Original: 188 mi.; 229 mi. After return attempt: 181 mi.; 409 mi.	Weight: 5 tons Equipment: 1½ tons Dimensions not given
Sputnik V (Spacecraft II) (Earth Satellite)	Aug. 19, 1960 to recovery on 18th orbit Aug. 20, 1960	65° incl. to equator Period: 90.7 min.	190 mi. 210 mi.	Weight: 5 tons Dimensions not disclosed
Sputnik VI (Spacecraft III) (Earth Satellite)	Dec. 1, 1960 to burnup on re- entry Dec. 2, 1960	65° incl. to equator Period: 88.6 min.	112 mi. 155 mi.	Weight: 5 tons Dimensions not disclosed
Sputnik VII (Earth Satellite)	Feb. 4, 1961 to Feb. 26, 1961	64° incl. to equator Period: 89.8 min.	138 mi. 204 mi.	Weight: 7.1 tons Dimensions not disclosed
Sputnik VIII plus Venus probe.	Launched: Feb. 12, 1961. Sput- nik down Feb. 25, 1961. Venus Probe going toward planet	Probe: .3° incl. to ecliptic Period: 300 days	66.7 mill. mi. from sun 9.46 mill. mi. from sun	Probe weight: 1,419 lbs. Dimensions: 80 in. long; 41 in. diam. Sputnik data not given
Sputnik IX (Spacecraft IV)	Mar. 9, 1961. Cabin recovered same day	Inclination and period not disclosed	115 mi. 155 mi.	Weight: 10,340 lbs. Dimensions not given
Sputnik X (Spacecraft V)	Mar. 25, 1961. Cabin recovered same day	65° incl. to equator Period: 88.4 min.	111 mi. 150 mi. (approx.)	Weight: 10,330 lbs. Dimensions not disclosed
Vostok (I) (Spacecraft VI)	April 12, 1961 — 1:07 a.m.; EST. Ship and man recovered same day 2:25 a.m. EST.*	65° incl. to equator Period: 89.1 min.	109 mi. 203 mi.	Weight: 10,418 lbs. Dimensions not disclosed
Vostok (II) (Spacecraft VII)	August 6, 1961 — 9:00 a.m.; Landing Aug. 7 — 10:18 a.m.	88 min.	111 mi. 158 mi.	Weight: 10,430 lbs.

* Subsequently the Soviets reported to the International Aeronautical Federation that the flight took 108 minutes.

SOVIET SPACE FLIGHT TABLE
PART II

Name	*Instruments and experiments.*
Sputnik I	Thermometers for internal temperature; two radio transmitters.
Sputnik II	Test dog Layka; cosmic ray, ultra-violet and X-ray counters, two radio transmitters.
Sputnik III	Air pressure, composition; magnetic field measurements; solar particle radiation; cosmic rays, earth's electric field, micro-meteorites, heavy cosmic particles, two radio transmitters.
Lunik I or Mechta	Internal temperature and pressure; interplanetary gas, solar particle radiation, earth and moon magnetism; three radio transmitters.
Lunik II	Internal temperature and pressure; earth and moon magnetism; space meteor particles, cosmic ray counters, five radio transmitters.
Lunik III	Lunar photography capable of taking several dozen pictures and transmitting them back. Cosmic ray counters.
Sputnik IV	Dummy spacement with equipment for manned flight. Cabin return rocket mechanism failed to operate properly sending vehicle into another orbit in two parts.
Sputnik V (Spacecraft II)	Recovery system for capsule containing two dogs, a number of rats, mice, flies, pants, fungi, microscopic water plants and seeds. Television cameras for pictures of animals, radio transmitter and life support system.
Sputnik VI (Spacecraft III)	Same as Sputnik V.
Sputnik VII	Radio and telemetry equipment.
Sputnik VIII + Venus Probe	Cosmic ray and micrometeorite counters. Temperature control system.
Sputnik IX (Spacecraft IV)	Same as Sputnik V, plus guinea pigs and other insects. However, only one dog.
Sputnik X (Spacecraft V)	Same as Sputnik IX.
Vostok I (Spacecraft VI)	Same as Sputnik IX except that the dogs and animals were replaced by Maj. Yury Gagarin. Launched at cosmodrome at Baykonur, Western Siberia, near Lake Aral, Lat. 47° N., Long. 65° E. Landed near Smelovka, Ternov District, Saratov Oblast.
Vostok II (Spacecraft VII)	Recovery system for capsule, automatic and manual control, two-way radio communication, TV camera, automatic tape recorder. Emphasis on study of weightlessness and its effects on human organism. Pressure kept constantly at one atmosphere (14.7 pounds a square inch), the temperature between 50° and 71.6° F. regulated by the pilot. Humidity 55 to 75 per cent. Oxygen content 25 to 27 per cent.

SPENDIÁROV (Spendiaryan), **Aleksándr Afanásyevich** (1871–1928), composer, the founder of the Armenian school of music. He wrote *Minuet* (1895), *Berceuse* (1897), *The Three Palms* (after a poem by Lermontov), and *Crimean Sketches* (1903, 1912). S began the opera *Almast* shortly before his death; it was completed by M. Shteynberg and was posthumously performed in 1930.

SPERÁNSKY, Alekséy Dmítrievich (1888–), pathologist and physiologist. Fellow, Ac. of S. (1939), Ac. of Medical S., USSR (1944). Worked under I. P. Pavlov (1923). Director, Institute of Normal and Pathological Physiology (1954). Research concerns trophic functions of the nervous system. Suggested a theory of nervous dystrophy and an original diagnosis of inflammatory processes, infections, and tumors. Author of *The Structural Elements of Medicine* (1937), I. P. Pavlov prize (1937); Stalin prize (1943).

SPERÁNSKY, Count Mikhaíl Mikháylovich (1772–1839), statesman. Son of a priest, he made a brilliant career, and accompanied Alexander I to the Erfurt conference, where he impressed favorably Napoleon who spoke of him as the "only clear head in Russia." S was responsible for sweeping projects of reform; though largely still-born they dominated R. constitutional thought in the 19th and 20th centuries. In 1809–12 S's power was seemingly unlimited. Alexander I consulted him on every issue.

In March 1812 he was summoned to the palace and after a long audience with Alexander was dismissed from office and sent into exile. In 1816 S was appointed governor of Penza, in 1819 governor general of Siberia, and in 1821 he was permitted to return to St. Petersburg. After the accession of Nicholas I (1825) S returned to active service. He was a member of the special court which tried the Decembrists and was the driving spirit of the codification of R. law in the 1830's. Created a count in Dec. 1838, two months before his death.

SPÉSHNEV, Nikoláy Aleksándrovich (1821–1882), leading member of the Petrashevsky Circle (q.v.). S lived abroad from 1842 to 1846 and became acquainted with socialist and communist theories. He advocated revolution, nationalization of the land and of the main industries. S was arrested for participating in Petrashevsky's meetings and was sentenced to death. His sentence was commuted to 10 years at hard labor.

SPIRIDÓNOVA, Maria Aleksándrovna (1889–?), a leading Socialist Revolutionary. As a girl of seventeen S joined the Socialist Revolutionary party and was chosen to kill Luzhenovsky, the tyrannical vice-governor of the Tambov Province. Luzhenovsky, a former radical, participated in mass flogging of the discontented peasantry. S killed him during one of his punitive expeditions and was condemned to hard labor in Siberia. Released in 1917, she became the leader of the left-wing Socialist Revolutionaries and led them into cooperation with Lenin. In 1918 S was chairman of the All-Russian Congress of Peasants' Deputies. In July 1918 she was one of the leaders of the abortive rebellion of the left-wing Socialist Revolutionaries in Moscow. S remained in the Soviet Union; was repeatedly jailed and exiled by the Bolsheviks. She died in prison.

SPÍTSYN, Viktor Ivánovich (1902–), chemist. Fellow, Ac. of S., USSR (1958). Graduate (1922) and professor of Moscow University (1942) and the Liebknecht Pedagogical Institute (1932). Head of the Laboratory of Radiochemistry at the Institute of Physical Chemistry, Ac. of S. (1949) and its director (1953). S's research deals with the chemistry and technology of rare elements and radiochemistry.

SPORT. Since the revolution, S in the Soviet Union has continuously expanded and has become an integral part of the social fabric of Soviet society. In 1917 only 50,000 participated in sports, but by 1960 there were over 24 million who are members of approximately 200,000 S groups; these are organized at factories, offices, collective farms, schools, labor reserve units, the armed forces, and the security police.

Spectator sports have increased proportionately and are a major divertissement for the peoples of the Soviet Union. Throughout the year a highly diversified S schedule is in operation, drawing huge crowds to S arenas which are to be found in all large centers of the country. Soccer is Russia's favorite S, and league play and cup play extending from April to November are avidly followed by millions. Other sports of great popularity and in which millions participate are track and field, basketball, volleyball, skiing, and skating. In all there are 46 recognized, official sports, including some which are para-military in nature (gliding and parachute jumping, for example) in which national championships, league play and cup play are held.

The party, the Komsomol, and trade unions exert constant pressure on individuals to join S societies and to engage in physical exercise. Facilities are made available to those citizens who join S groups paying a nominal membership fee of a few rubles a year. Since the revolution the Soviet government has built many S structures and there are at present approximately 25,000 soccer fields, 200,000 basketball and volleyball courts, 7,000 gymnasiums, 2,200 ski centers, and over fifty indoor pools. These facilities, not adequate to meet growing demands, range from modern stadia to poorly maintained playing fields.

Participation in physical activity is not limited to members of S groups. Throughout the year morning exercises are a daily radio feature and in plants and in factories *production calisthenics* is slowly winning acceptance. This unique program, typical of the party's utilitarian attitude, is a device to improve labor productivity. In 1960 six million workers engaged in periodic calisthenics during working hours in an effort to stimulate tired muscles.

The gigantic S program in effect in the Soviet Union at the present time is not the result of popular demand for sports, but the determined result of party planning, which regards the spiritual as well as the physical molding of Soviet citizens as a vital prerogative. In accordance with the Marxian imperative physical culture and S are to play an important part in forming the "new Soviet man." Soviet writers claim that S participation (as everything else) should nurture positive character traits, a spirit of collectivism, courage, will power, the determination to win, patience, endurance, and discipline. S viewed through the red lenses of Soviet socialism has attained new qualities, nonexistent in other historical periods. All evil features of bourgeois S (diverting the worker from the class struggle, arousing base instincts, developing undesirable traits: egoism, individualism, chauvinism, and others) have been negated. Nevertheless, the facts reveal a variety of abuses which are endemic to the system and which contradict the ideological halo with which it is adorned.

The party by its overemphasis on winning has created a caste system of athletes. The star athlete receives all the attention, money, glory, and the best facilities. Most successful athletes congregate in Moscow and Leningrad and other large centers and are directly or indirectly subsidized by the state. The record mania and the allocation of huge sums to support it have fostered undesirable practices such as the wooing of athletes to "jump" one S society for another, the hiring of personnel in factories, offices, and collective farms for their athletic ability and not for their productive capabilities,

a general lowering of S mores which includes fixing of games and habitual and malicious roughness on the playing field.

From the early years of the revolution the S program has been developed and conducted under party initiative and control. The Central Committee of the CP has issued four important resolutions on S, in 1925, 1929, 1948, and 1959, which have decisively determined the character and orientation of the S program. The broad nature of S was already clearly stated in the 1925 resolution: "Physical culture must be considered not only from the point of view of physical training and health but should be utilized as a means to rally the broad laboring masses around various party, government, and trade union organizations through which the masses of workers and peasants are drawn into social and political life."

The S administration dates its organizational beginnings to the early years of war communism when it was part of the pre-military training program. In 1923, the Supreme Council for Physical Culture for the RSFSR was established to coordinate the S program. Reorganized and strengthened according to the party resolution of 1929 as a federal agency (the All-Union Council of Physical Culture) it had since 1936 been called the All-Union Committee for Physical Culture and Sport. The committee was attached to the USSR Council of Ministers, exercising control over counterpart committees at republic and lower administrative levels, and was in fact a complex ministry responsible for the overall direction, planning, and financing of S.

In 1959 the committee was dissolved on party orders only to be renamed the Union of Sport Societies and Organizations USSR, ostensibly with a democratically elected sports leadership. The change has in no way affected party control over S, nor has it significantly altered the mode of administration, but was an outcome of Khrushchev's statement made at the 21st Party Congress in Jan. 1959 that in certain areas the state might begin to wither away as some state agencies (S was a leading example) would be replaced by public organizations.

The development of physical culture and S figures prominently in two major concerns of the party: heightening labor productivity and military preparedness. These two basic aims have been combined since 1931 in a mass physical fitness program appropriately called "Ready for Labor and Defense" (*Gotov k Trudu i Oborone,* or GTO).

Since its inception, more than fifty million persons have successfully mastered the GTO requirements. In addition to providing a mass physical culture base, the primary purpose of the GTO system is to attract those who are physically able to participate in a program which is designed to provide the Soviet leadership with soldier-workers, militarily trained and in glowing health. In addition to conventional sporting events, the system of GTO contains such test categories (for each of its divisions and for both sexes) as grenade-throwing for distance, rifle-shooting for accuracy, cross-country skiing, and the scaling of physical obstacles. Gliding and parachute jumping and other "sports" having military value are greatly encouraged.

Complementing GTO is the single all-union sport classification system. Having achieved a mass S base, the Soviet leadership was persistent and largely successful in raising the quality of S performances. The all-union sport classification system established in 1949 set up levels of excellence to be attained in seven categories, rated as: Master of Sport; first, second, and third categories; and first, second, and third categories, junior level. These steps are maintained for the 46 official sports practiced in the Soviet Union, and the classification system is revised and upgraded every four years in order to spur athletes to higher performances.

The basis of all physical culture activity is the primary S group, which is set up according to specific rules as belonging to one of the two types of S societies in the USSR, those sponsored by trade unions, and non-trade union organizations. S societies in their present form were organized on party direction in 1935–36 (with the exception of Dinamo, sponsored by the security police, which was founded in 1923). Spontaneous organization of S groups is impossible. S societies and their groups are formed according to prescribed model statutes, and may be restructured or abolished to serve party purposes. Until 1957 trade-union S societies were organized along industrial lines of trade unions. However, with the reorganization of industry, most trade-union S societies were re-formed to coincide with the territorial principle which was now in effect, merging their local teams, equipment, and structure for the combined use of the membership. Traditionally, the strongest S societies in the Soviet Union have been Dinamo, The Central House of the Red Army, and Spartak (sponsored by the producers' cooperatives), all three of which are non-trade union.

In the early 1950's in accordance with the recommendation of the party resolution of Dec. 1948, each union republic formed a S society for collective and state farmers. This was an effort to stimulate the rural areas to engage in S activities since in 1949 they had less than one million persons participating in S groups. By 1960 the totals had reached 5½ million, but despite the efforts of the last ten years, the rural districts still lag seriously behind the urban centers, both in the quantity and in the quality of S performances.

S has been subjected to detailed planning. The present Seven Year Plan calls for 50 million sportsmen by 1965 (with a target goal of 30 million by Jan. 1961), 30,000 Masters of Sport (there were over 12,000 in 1960) and 17 million athletes who will have achieved one of the six categories below the master level. Republic, kray, oblast, rayon, and cities are required to reach specific membership, proficiency, and GTO goals. These are further broken down for individual S societies and their groups. Championships in diverse S and *Spartakiades* (sport festivals) are regularly scheduled for S societies, trade unions, schools, and collective farms. Every four years an all-union *Spartakiade* is held which endeavors to impress everyone physically able into sports activity.

Party slogans since the 1930's have demanded of athletes that they beat bourgeois records. It was a Central Committee resolution of 1948, however, which launched the R. sports offensive of the 1950's, by vigorously demanding world records. Before World War II Soviet athletes rarely engaged in international S competition except against workers' teams. Following the war, the Soviets began to participate cautiously in foreign S competitions. By the time of the Olympic games of 1952 the S machine, after many years of preparation, was considered ready to challenge the world's top athletes; its entry marked the first Olympic appearance by a R. team since 1912.

The Soviet squad was highly successful in this initial Olympic appearance at Helsinki, winning 22 gold, 30 silver, and 15 bronze medals, and placing second to the United States in the unofficial score. In 1956 Soviet athletes were entered for the first time in the Winter Olympic games held at Cortina, Italy, winning seven gold, three silver, and six bronze medals, and scoring important victories in skiing, speed skating, and ice hockey. In the regular Olympic games held in Melbourne, Australia, in 1956, the Soviet Union scored significant triumphs in a variety of sports, winning 37 gold, 29 silver, and 32 bronze medals, and beating the

SPORT RECORDS SET BY SOVIET ATHLETES

OLYMPIC RECORDS			
MEN			
Holder	*Event*	*Record*	*Year*
Vladimir Kuts	5,000 meter run	13 m. 39.6 s.	1956
Pyotr Bolotnikov	10,000 meter run	28 m. 32.2 s.	1960
Robert Shavlakadze	high jump	7 ft. 1 in.	1960
Vasily Rudenkov	16 lb. hammer throw	220 ft. 2 in.	1960
WOMEN			
Lyudmila Shevtsova	800 meter run	2 m. 4.3 s.	1960
Vera Krepinka	broad jump	20 ft. 10⅞ in.	1960
Nina Ponomareva	discus throw	180 ft. 8¼ in.	1960
Elvira Ozolina	javelin throw	183 ft. 8 in.	1960
Tamara Press	shot put	56 ft. 9⅞ in.	1960
SPEED SKATING			
Yevgeny Grishin	500 meters	40.2 s.	1960
Yevgeny Grishin ⎫ Yury Mikhaylov ⎭	1,500 meters	2 m. 08.6 s.	1956
Boris Shilkov	5,000 meters	7 m. 51.3 s.	1956
WORLD RECORDS (AS OF OCT. 1, 1960)			
MEN			
Vladimir Kuts	5,000 meters	13 m. 35 s.	1957
Vladimir Kuts	10,000 meters	28 m. 30.4 s.	1956
A. Ivanov	30,000 meters	1 hr. 35 m. 1 s.	1957
WOMEN			
Maria Itkina	440 yards	53.7 s.	1959
Nina Otkalenko	880 yards	2 m. 06.6 s.	1956
Maria Itkina	400 meters	53.4 s.	1959
Nina Otkalenko	800 meters	2 m. 05.0 s.	1955
Galina Bystrova	80 m. hurdles	10.6 s.	1958
N. Dumbadze	discus	187 ft. 1½ in.	1952
E. Ozolina	javelin	195 ft. 2½ in.	1960
Irina Press	pentathlon	4,880 points	1959
WEIGHTLIFTING RECORDS SET IN THE 1960 OLYMPICS			
Yevgeny Minayev	featherweight class	821 lbs.	Equals world record
Victor Bushuyev	lightweight class	876 lbs.	World record
Aleksandr Kurynov	middleweight class	964½ lbs.	World record
Arkady Vorobyov	middle-heavyweight	1,039½ lbs.	World record
Yury Vlasov	heavyweight class	1,182½ lbs.	World record

United States in the unofficial score. Vladimir Kuts, the outstanding performer, won the acclaim of the crowds and the world with his brilliant victories in the 5,000 meter and 10,000 meter runs.

In 1960 the Soviet Union repeated its team triumphs at the winter and summer Olympic games. At Squaw Valley Soviet athletes captured seven gold, five silver, and nine bronze medals. Outstanding performances were given in speed skating by Yevgeny Grishin and Viktor Kosichkin for the men, and by Lidia Skoblikova, who won two speed skating events, for the women. At Rome the Soviet Union secured 43 gold, 33 silver, and 30 bronze medals. The outstanding performer was Boris Shakhlin, who won four gold medals in gymnastics. Other outstanding winners were Robert Shavlakadze in the high jump, Vasily Rudenkov in the hammer throw, Viktor Zdanovich in the foils, and Yury Vlasov in weight-lifting for the men; and Irena and Tamara Press, Nina Ponomareva and Ludmila Shevkova in track and field, and Larisa Latynina in gymnastics for the women.

In the decade of the 1950's the Soviet Union became the leading world sports power, engaging in most world and European championships. Between 1949 and 1959, 1,300 foreign S delegations and more than 18,000 athletes visited the USSR, while more than 20,000 Soviet athletes traveled abroad to various countries. In all, the Soviet Union maintains contact with S organizations in 64 countries, and is a member of 33 international S federations.

Soviet S triumphs have given the USSR much favorable publicity and have inflated Soviet prestige abroad.

H. W. M.

SPUTNIK: *see* SPACE SCIENCE, ROCKETRY.

SRÉTENSK, town in Chita Oblast, RSFSR, on Shilka River; pop. 15,100 (1959). R.R. terminus; food processing, felt-boots mfg.

SRÉTENSKY, Leoníd Nikoláyevich (1902–), mechanical engineer and mathematician. Corresponding member, Ac. of S., USSR (1939). Graduate (1923) and professor (1934) of Moscow University. Associated with the Central Institute of Aerodynamics (1934–41) and the Naval Hydrophysical Institute (1951). Research on wave motion of fluids, wave resistance, mathematical physics, integral equations, differential geometry, etc. His works are applied to the theory of ship building, geophysics, and naval sciences.

STAKHÁNOV, Alekséy Grigóryevich (1905–), miner, famous as symbol of Soviet speed-up system. He worked in the Donbas mines from 1927 to 1935, when he came to fame as a "coal industry innovator." He reportedly reorganized his work as a coal cutter so that he exceeded the established output quota 16-fold  (102 t. in 5¾ hrs., the quota being 7 t.). The party Central Committee publicly hailed his achievement and "Stakhanovism" became the focus of the official drive to raise labor productivity, formally launched by the First All-Union Conference of Stakhanovites in Nov. 1935. The "Stakhanovite movement" stressed overfulfillment of quotas, whether by rational innovation or sheer effort. It accompanied a government policy of giving exceptional rewards in wages and acclaim for high output, and provided the basis for several major norm increases throughout Soviet industry during the late 1930's.

S received the order of Lenin, the Red Labor Banner, and was made a full member of the Communist party without serving the usual candidacy, in June 1936. During 1936–41, he was assigned to the Industrial Academy, Moscow, also elected deputy to the USSR Supreme Soviet (1937). In 1941–42 he managed a mine in Karaganda, and since 1943 he has reportedly been with the Ministry of the Coal Industry, on the editorial board of the journal *Master Uglya* (Coal Master). Since the war, and especially after Stalin's death, the emphasis on Stakhanovism has declined to the point where S's name has disappeared from the news.

STÁLIN, Joseph (Iósif Vissariónovich Dzhugashvíli) (1879–1953), for many years leader of the Soviet Union and of the world communist movement. Of Georgian origin, born in the village of Gori, near Tiflis, son of a cobbler, S was educated in the Orthodox Theological Seminary in Tiflis, but, in 1899, was expelled before graduation. He joined the R. Social Democratic party in 1898, while working as a clerk in the Tiflis observatory. Several times arrested and banished, he always succeeded in escaping with extraordinary ease. During that period, S took part in the party congresses in Finland (Dec. 1905), in Stockholm (April 1906), and in London (May 1907). At the same time, S with the Caucasian terrorist Kamo organized the "expropriations" of banks (June 26, 1907, in Tiflis) for the benefit of the Bolshevik party. After the Prague conference (Jan. 1912), S was coopted into the Bolshevik Central Committee and for some time edited *Pravda* in St. Petersburg. In Nov. 1912, he went to see Lenin in Cracow, and spent several months in Vienna writing (with the assistance of Bukharin) *Marxism and the National Question*. On his return to St. Petersburg, on Feb. 23, 1913, S was once more arrested and banished to E. Siberia. Liberated by the February revolution in 1917, he went to Petrograd and until Lenin's arrival endorsed Kamenev's policy of support of the Provisional Government and collaboration with the Mensheviks and Socialist Revolutionaries. However, he turned to Lenin's line of seizure of power when the latter arrived in Russia in April 1917. In July-August 1917, at the 6th Congress of the Bolshevik party, when Lenin was hiding in Finland, S submitted the main report on the political situation. After the October revolution, S was people's commissar for Nationalities (1917–23) and for State Control (1919–23). In the Brest-Litovsk crisis, S supported Lenin's policy. During the civil war, S was a senior political commissar in the Red Army and in this capacity had frequent conflicts with Trotsky. In 1918, he organized the defense of Tsaritsyn (later Stalingrad). S was a member of the Politburo from its foundation. In 1922, he was appointed general secretary of the party. S's activity in the Caucasus, his "reorganization" of the party apparatus there, and his coarse way of dealing with people displeased Lenin. On Jan. 3, 1923, in his "Testament" he suggested S's removal from the post of general secretary. In March 1923, a few days before Lenin's third stroke and consequent loss of speech, he sent a letter to S threatening to break off all personal relations with him. However, at Lenin's funeral on Jan. 21, 1924, S gave his oath of fidelity to the leader's principles. After Lenin's death, the Politburo, with the approval of the "Elders" of the 13th Party Congress, decided to keep S in his post and not to publish Lenin's Testament. S jointly with Kamenev and Zinoviev formed the "triumvirate" which led the party and the state after the death of Lenin. In April 1924, at the Sverdlov Party University in Moscow, S started to formulate the principles of "Leninism." These lectures were later published under the title *The Foundations of Leninism*. In the following years, S first defeated Trotsky, using the slogan of "building socialism in one country" as against Trotsky's "permanent revolution"; he then, together with Bukharin and Rykov, defeated the "new opposition" of Kamenev and Zinoviev and the "combined opposition" of these two with Trotsky; finally, he defeated the "right" opposition of Bukharin and Rykov with the help of Molotov, Voroshilov, Kaganovich, Ordzhonikidze, and Kirov, whom he gradually promoted to the Politburo. Ruling as undisputed leader, in 1929–34, S launched industrialization through the Five Year Plans and the collectivization of agriculture, at a great cost of human life and with a severe debasing of the standard of living of the masses. In the political and cultural fields, this was the time of the first show trials (Shakhty, Prompartia) of the old intelligentsia and of the drive to replace it with a new one, hastily trained under the conditions of growing totalitarian control. On Dec. 1, 1934, after the murder of Kirov (q.v.) S started the "great purge" aimed at the extermination of all potential and imaginary opponents who were proclaimed "enemies of the people." On Dec. 6, 1936, the new "Stalin" constitution was promulgated, allegedly democratic and liberal, but, in fact, establishing S's unlimited dictatorship. During the great purge the oldest and closest associates of Lenin had perished, as well as the cream of the Soviet Army, and a new doctrine of "Stalinism" had replaced the former "Marxism-Leninism." A quasi-divine "cult" of S followed.

After a long and bitter "cold" propaganda war with the Nazis, on Aug. 23, 1939 S concluded a treaty of nonaggression with Hitler and thereby gave the green light to German aggression which unleashed World War II. On Sept. 28, 1939, after the joint German-Russian conquest of Poland, a second treaty "of friendship" followed. In May 1941 S formally became the head of the Soviet government, then chairman of the State Defense Committee, people's commissar (later minister) of defense, and supreme commander in chief of all the Soviet armed forces. He personally interfered with the work of the military commanders, assuming the rank of Generalissimo. In 1943–45, at the conferences of Teheran, Yalta, and Potsdam, S secured considerable advantages for the USSR. After a period of comparative relaxation during the war years, "Stalinism" was restored, in theory and practice, and imposed on the "satellite" countries of E. Europe. In 1950, S published *Marxism and the Questions of Linguistics*, and, in 1952, *Economic Problems of Socialism in the USSR*.

The last years of S's rule were characterized by extreme chauvinism, xenophobia, and anti-Semitism. The alleged discovery, in Jan. 1953, of the "Doctors' plot" foretold a new wave of purges. The unexpected death of S, on March 5, 1953, put an end to this rule of terror. In Feb. 1956, in his "secret" speech to the 20th Party Congress, Khrushchev admitted and condemned some of S's crimes as well as the "personality cult" which he had imposed. But S's great merits as communist theorist and statesman are still officially recognized in the USSR, and his embalmed body was placed with Lenin's body in the mausoleum in the Red Square in Moscow.

S was twice married—in 1904 to Catherine Svanidze who died of tuberculosis (her only son disappeared during World War II), and in 1919 to Nadezhda Alliluyeva, who died in Nov. 1932 in somewhat suspicious circumstances, leaving a son, Vasily, a general in the Air Force, who disappeared after S's death, and a daughter, Svetlana. There have been unconfirmed rumors about S's third marriage to L. M. Kaganovich's sister, Rosa.

S's *Works* have been published in several languages in 13 volumes (unfinished).

BIBLIOGRAPHY: L. Trotsky, *Stalin*, New York, 1941; I. Deutscher, *Stalin: A Political Biography*, London and New York, 1949; Bertram D. Wolfe, *Three Who Made a Revolution*, Boston, 1945; L. Schapiro, *The Communist Party of the Soviet Union*, New York, 1960; E. M. Carr, *A History of Soviet Russia*, London and New York, 1950–1958. V. Su.

STALIN PRIZES: *see* LENIN PRIZES.

STALINABÁD (f. Dyushambe), capital of Tadzhik SSR; pop. 83,000 (1939), 224,000 (1959). An old settlement on Dyushambinka River, it has developed into a major ind. community in the Gissar Valley and a cultural center of the republic. In addition to cotton and silk processing, the city produces building materials, farm machinery, and hardware; meat packing, leather tanning, woodworking, and distilleries are the other important ind. Besides being the site of Tadzhik Ac. of S., it has a number of higher technical schools and educational institutions.

STALINGRÁD (f. Tsarítsyn), city, adm. center of Stalingrad Oblast; site of the famous World War II battle; pop. 592,000 (1959). Important r. port on Volga waterway; R.R. center; E. terminus of the Volga–Don Canal; its ind. include giant tractor plant, the noted Red October metallurgical works, chemical, lumber, oil refineries. Has a number of higher educational and research institutions. Hydroelectric plant north of city has capacity of 2,500,000 kilowatts.

STALINGRÁD OBLAST, RSFSR; area 44,000 sq. mi.; pop. 1,854,000 (1959). Cities: Stalingrad (adm. center), Kamyshin, Frolovo, Dubovka. In lower Volga region, crossed also by Don River. Predominantly level, drought-ridden steppe; black earth and chestnut soils, with occasional sand and salt flats. Wheat, sunflowers, mustard plants cultivated extensively W. of Volga; cotton and dairy farming in the S.W.; vegetables, fruit, melons, and pumpkins grown in fertile flood valley of N. Volga; sheep reared for meat and wool in the dry Caspian lowlands E. of the r. Heavy ind. are centered in Stalingrad city. Hydroelectric plant at Stalingrad and Volga–Don Canal are highly essential for irrigation purposes and regional navigation. Est. 1936.

STALINÍRI (f. Tskhinvali), city, adm. center of S. Ossetian Autonomous Oblast, Georgian SSR; pop. 22,000 (1959). Situated at the foot of Great Caucasus Range, in the valley of Bolshaya Lyakhvi River, its principal ind. are sawmills, dairies, fruit canneries.

STÁLINO (f. Yuzovka), city, adm. center of Stalino Oblast; pop. 700,000 (1959), the largest town of Donbas region, on Kalmius R. Its ind. include a huge metallurgical plant, coal mining, machine-building works, coking installations.

STÁLINO OBLAST, Ukrainian SSR; area 10,250 sq. mi.; pop. 4,262,000 (1959). Cities: Stalino (adm. center), Kramatorsk, Makeyevka, Gorlovka. Is a highly industrialized coal-mining region of Donbas extending from N. Donets River to Sea of Azov; well watered by numerous rivers forming part of the Donets and Dnieper basins; dry climate. Agr. secondary, its main ind. are coal mining (Stalino, Zhdanov, Makeyevka), heavy machine building (Kramatorsk); also has nonferrous metallurgy; important salt mines and soda works based on local reserves, largest in USSR; mineral fertilizers and building materials are produced on a large scale. Est. 1938.

STALINOGÓRSK (f. Bobriki), city in Tula Oblast, RSFSR; pop. 107,000 (1959). Ind. city in Moscow lignite basin. Its chemical plants produce fertilizer, explosives, and sulfuric acid; has large power plant supplying Moscow ind. area. Has a number of highly specialized technical schools.

STÁLINSK (f. Kuznetsk; prior to 1932, Novo-Kuznetsk), city in Kemerovo Oblast, RSFSR, in Kuzbas, on Tom River; pop. 166,000 (1939), 377,000 (1959). One of major metallurgical centers in USSR; site of Kuznetsk metallurgical combine, aluminum and ferroalloy plants; West Siberian metallurgical mill; also coal, chemical, and machine-building ind. Founded 1617.

STANISLÁV, city, adm. center of Stanislav Oblast; pop. 66,000 (1959). R.R. junction; R.R. and machine shops, textile mills, and tanneries; lumber ind., ceramics, asphalt; food-processing plants.

STANISLÁV OBLAST, Ukrainian SSR; formerly a province of Poland; area 5,350 sq. mi.; pop. 1,095,000 (1959). Cities: Stanislav (adm. center), Bolekhov, Kolomiya. The S.W. section lies upon the foothills of Carpathian Mountains, covered with mixed oak, beech, and coniferous forests; the N.E. part occupies the S. wing of the Volyn-Podolian upland; drained by Dniester and Prut rivers; has warm, moderately continental climate. Grains, sugar beets, and tobacco are cultivated in agr. area on right bank of Dniester; orchards and vineyards predominate in the foothills; livestock breeding and lumbering in the mountains. Main ind. are based on rich local deposits of petroleum, salt, natural gas, potash, and ozocerite. Est. 1939.

STANISLÁVSKY (Alekséyev), **Konstantín Sergéyevich** (1863–1938), actor and director. People's Artist of the USSR. Born into a well-to-do Moscow family of the merchant class. From early youth he was fascinated by the theater and regularly participated in semi-professional performances (as an actor from 1877 on; as a  director from 1882). His extraordinary theatrical talent was nourished by systematic study of the technique of the great artists of the imperial theater (Yermolova, Fedotova, Lensky, the Sadovsky family, and others), and he took as his model of theatrical excellence the German troupe of the Duke of Meiningen. In 1898 S accepted Nemirovich-Danchenko's proposal to organize a private Moscow Art Theater (MKhT), which waged a difficult but successful battle against theatrical routine and the habitual use of the actor's stock in trade ("clichés"), and in behalf of a repertory of a high artistic order. In his creative gropings, S passed through the phases of naturalism, then symbolism, and finally became convinced of the validity of psychological realism. Under Nemirovich-Danchenko's influence, S became interested in the plays of Anton Chekhov. In staging them he created a "theater of moods" capable of projecting the most subtle psychological nuances, and inaugurated thereby a new era in theater art. Having made a painstaking study of the great European and R. theoreticians and practitioners of theater (Diderot, Riccoboni, Goethe, Shchepkin, and many others), S in 1907 decided to work out a "method" of theater art. The project lasted 30 years and in 1938 was published under the title *An Actor Prepares*. S is, first of all, opposed to what he considered a dilettante art in which emotions are manifested by purely external techniques, i.e., the "art of make-believe": at the moment of creativity, the experience of the actor must be sincere. In this he is aided by developing his emotional (affective) memory, i.e., his ability to evoke the memory of an emotion which he has previously experienced; the cultivation of such a degree of skill and nervous sensitivity is achieved only through complex and prolonged training, since acting is a psychophysical process. While studying his role, the actor must be aware of its ruling idea (in the words of S, its "supra-objective"), the attempt to reveal which becomes, on the stage, "through-action." Thus, the Stanislavsky method had as its aim the working out of a technique for intellectual as well as emotional re-creation of a role. The influence of S was significant also in the West. Even opponents of the Stanislavsky method (Yevreinov, Meyerhold, Tairov) acknowledge the fruitfulness of his directorial genius, just as powerful in the production of classics as of new works. An actor of many character parts, S created memorable roles (especially in the plays of Griboyedov, Ostrovsky, Chekhov, and Gorky). During the 1930's S directed the opera theater that bears his name. He is the author of an interesting autobiography *My Life in Art.*

P. E. YE.

STANITSA: *see* COSSACKS.

STANKÉVICH, Nikoláy Vladímirovich (1813–1840),

idealist philosopher and head of the so-called "Stankevich Circle" to which V. G. Belinsky, T. Granovsky, K. Aksakov, and others belonged. S was born in Voronezh of a noble family. He tried to group together the liberal-thinking intellectuals of his day. The great debate between the Slavophiles and the Westerners really began in S's circle. S did not create any original works but his personal influence was extremely strong especially upon Belinsky.

STANOVÓY MOUNTAIN RANGE, in Soviet Asia, extending from Yakut ASSR to Khabarovsk Kray, between the Olekma and upper Zeya rivers; greatest altitude 8,200 ft.

STANYUKÓVICH, Konstantín Mikháylovich (1843–1903), writer, best known for his collection of sea stories very popular with the young people. Many of them deal with the exploits of Russia's naval heroes and are entertaining stories of adventure at sea. S's radical political tendencies were reflected in novels and plays written in the 1870's, during the rise of the populist movement.

STÁRAYA RÚSSA, city in Novgorod Oblast, RSFSR; pop. 24,300 (1959). Old R. town on the Polist River, dating back to the 11th century; manufactures agr. machinery and wood products; is also a health resort known for its salt springs and mud baths.

STÁROV, Iván Yegórovich (1744/45–1808), architect, representative of the classical school. Studied architecture in Moscow, St. Petersburg, Paris, and Rome. S was a member (from 1769) and professor (from 1785) of the Academy of Fine Arts in St. Petersburg. Directed the reconstruction of the Aleksandro-Nevsky Monastery, St. Petersburg. Was the architect of the Taurida Palace, St. Petersburg (1783–88), and of the palace in Pelle, near St. Petersburg (1785–89). S designed many large residences. He made plans for the reconstruction of the city of Yekaterinoslav, in the Ukraine, and was the architect of the Monastery of the Virgin cathedral in Kazan.

STÁRY KRYM, Crimean town, site of tobacco farms and resort, 15 mi. from Feodosia; pop. 6,800.

STÁRY OSKÓL, city in Belgorod Oblast, RSFSR; pop. 26,400 (1959). Agr. center, with food ind. based on local produce and some mfg. plants; iron-ore deposits worked in the vicinity of the city.

STÁSOV, Vladímir Vasílyevich (1824–1906), music and art critic, art historian, archaeologist. From 1850 he headed the art division of the St. Petersburg Public Library. At the beginning of his career S supported classicism in art. In the 1860's promoted ideological naturalism. Participated in the activities of "The Five" and The Society of Circulating Exhibitions. Opposed academism and stressed national originality in art. Produced a number of monographs on R. art. His main works are *Twenty-Five Years of Russian Art* (1882–83) and *Art in the Nineteenth Century* (1901).

STÁSOVA, Yeléna Dmitrievna (1873–), old Bolshevik, born in St. Petersburg in a wealthy family. In 1898, she joined the social democratic movement and for several years, before and after the 1917 revolution, worked in the Bolshevik party's secretariat. In 1918–19, S was a member of the presidium of the Petrograd Cheka; in 1921–25, she was a Comintern agent in Germany; in 1927–38, chairman of the central committee of MOPR (International Red Aid). At the 16th Party Congress in 1930, S was elected to the Central Control Commission. In 1938–46, she was editor of the periodical *International Literature*.

STASYULÉVICH, Mikhaíl Matvéyevich (1826–1911), historian and journalist. S was prof. of history in St. Petersburg until 1861. He was a prominent representative of moderate liberalism which was striving for constitutional monarchy of the British type. From 1866 to 1908, S was editor and publisher of the journal *Vestnik Yevropy* (Messenger of Europe). He was one of the founders of the Party for Democratic Reforms which was to the right of the Constitutional Democratic party.

STATE BANK: *see* BANKING AND CREDIT.

STATE COUNCIL. An important advisory body created in 1810 to which the tsars submitted many legislative projects for consideration. The members were appointed by the tsar. In 1906 its status was revised and the SC became an upper chamber of distinctly conservative character; half of the members were appointed by the tsar, half were elected by the church, the nobility, the zemstvos, and other conservative groups. Through its composition and its power to veto any Duma bill, it weakened the legislative power of the lower chamber.

STATE CONFERENCE (*Gosudarstvennoye Soveshchanye*), a deliberative and consultative body convoked in Moscow on August 25–28, 1917 (N.S.) by the Provisional Government of Kerensky—which had been reconstructed after the July riots (q.v.)—seeking a generally recognized national assembly on which he could depend. The composition of the SC was carefully balanced between the Right and the Left by distributing the 2,414 seats among the members of the four Dumas (488 delegates), cooperatives (313), trade unions (176), commercial and industrial unions and banks (150), municipalities (147), army and navy (117), Soviets (329), and others. As a result, the SC was conspicuously split into two equal parts: one acclaimed the commander in chief, General Kornilov; the second, the prime minister, Kerensky. The Bolsheviks, who did not take part in the conference, denounced it as a counter-revolutionary gathering and on the day of its opening organized a rather successful general strike of protest. Thus, the SC, which was conceived as a rallying point of national unity, was in this respect a failure.

STATE DUMA—the representative assembly established by Tsar Nicholas II in 1905 under the pressure of revolutionary agitation. As originally announced in Feb. 1905, the SD was to be a weak consultative body participating in the preliminary discussion and elaboration of legislative bills. The law of Aug. 1905, governing elections to the SD, was framed so as to ensure a large representation of the peasantry, on the assumption that the peasants were devoted to the Crown, and effectively to disenfranchise the bulk of the urban population, especially the intellectuals and the workers.

By the October Manifesto (q.v.), extension of the suffrage was promised and the rule was laid down that no law should be promulgated without the approval of the SD. To weaken the effect of the representative nature of the SD, the passage of legislation was made conditional on the approval of the conservative upper chamber, the State Council, and the tsar, who had an absolute veto.

The *First Duma* convened in May 1906. Contrary to the expectations of the government, its composition was quite liberal. There were 179 Kadets; 44 Rightists (including 12 Octobrists); 94 Trudoviki (Laborites); 101 nonpartisans, most of them sympathetic to the radical groups; 18 Social Democrats; and 44 representatives of national groups, 486 members in all. If given the opportunity, the assembly might have initiated progressive legislation on agrarian reform and civil and political rights. After trying to ignore the SD and its attacks on the cabinet, the government finally dissolved the SD on July 8 (21), 1906 in order to prevent consideration of a draft bill providing for radical agrarian reform.

With Stolypin at the head of the government, steps were taken to ensure the election of a new SD dominated by representatives of the conservative political parties. Although all measures except fraud or outright use of force were used, the *Second Duma,* which opened in March 1907, again comprised an overwhelming majority in opposition to the government. The opposition deputies had held more than two-thirds of the seats in the First Duma; in the Second their number was only slightly less. On the Left were 65 Social Democrats, 37 Socialist Revolutionaries, 16 People's Socialists, and 104 Laborites. Kadet strength fell to 98. There were 42 Octobrists and other moderate conservatives, while the extreme Right commanded 10 seats. The remaining 144 deputies consisted of representatives from national or local groups. As the opposition majority was resolved to press for consideration of reform legislation, the conservative elements agitated for dissolution. The dissolution was decreed by the tsar in a manifesto of June 3 (16), 1907, which also promulgated a new electoral law.

The *Third Duma* was convened the following November, after elections in September, and was the only one to complete the full term of five years. The new electoral law, by violating the canons of democratic elections, had succeeded in disenfranchising those who might vote for opposition candidates. With the support of the parties of the Right and the Octobrists, the government under Stolypin commanded a majority. However, since the government was not responsible to the SD, but only to the tsar, this majority did not have the same significance as it would have had under a truly parliamentary system. The conservative character of the Third Duma was by no means representative of the opinion in the country. Yet it did reflect to some extent the cooling off of revolutionary ardor, the desire for order and more "normal" conditions which had brought a swing to the right. The Octobrists and parties of the Right numbered roughly 150 members

each. There were 53 Kadets and 28 Progressists, and 14 each from the Social Democratic and Labor groups. The remaining deputies represented national minorities or were nonpartisan. Subsequent by-elections brought nationalist strength to 80.

The elections to the *Fourth Duma* in 1912 again returned a conservative body in which the government remained dependent upon the Octobrists for a majority. The Right wing numbered 185 deputies, including 88 nationalists. There were 97 Octobrists, 58 Kadets, 47 Progressists, 14 Social Democrats, and 10 Laborites. Although the government was usually able to muster a majority, the opposition used every opportunity to attack its policies.

None of the four Dumas was able to achieve much that was of value. The power of the SD in the determination of government policy remained negligible throughout, and its role in legislation slight. The SD did record at least one positive achievement, however: it provided both a forum for criticism of the government and the first electoral and legislative experience of any consequence for the R. people.   c. j. f.

STATE FARM: *see* Sovkhoz, Agriculture.

STATE PEASANTS originally lived on land owned by the state. They were organized into agricultural communities whose members were jointly responsible for the payment of taxes and the performance of various obligations toward the state. The state was directly concerned with preventing such communities from losing their members, since every desertion reduced the paying capacity of the community as a whole.

During the administrative reforms in the beginning of the 18th century the SP retained their self-government, under a close supervision of state officials. SP were represented at the Legislative Commission of 1766, which was to prepare a code.

Gradually the tax burden of the SP who paid *obrok* (q.v.) grew heavier. Their general status, however, was more favorable than that of the serfs. SP could not be removed from the land. A decree of Dec. 12, 1801 extended to them the right to own agricultural land.

Administrative regulations of April 30, 1838 were aimed at creating from the large and growing group of SP a class of free farmers. The organs of village self-government, which they created, were subordinated to appointed officials. A cadastral survey permitted in 1855 a reassessment of the tax and recruitment obligations on a more equitable basis. There was also an attempt to improve the economic conditions of the SP by equalizing the size of their allotments. A comprehensive welfare and educational program was introduced and the number of schools for SP increased from 60 in the 1830's to over 2,500 in the early 1850's.

The number of male SP in 1859, on the eve of the emancipation, was 12.8 mill. or somewhat larger than that of the serfs.

The settlement of SP, in connection with the emancipation of 1861, was provided by a statute issued in 1866. Their average land allotments were about 20 acres per male person and were substantially larger than those of the serfs. Originally the financial obligations of the SP were relatively light but were nearly doubled by a law of June 12, 1886 which endeavored to make good the losses suffered by the treasury as a consequence of the repeal of poll tax (q.v.). The increased payments were to continue for 44 years but were written off by the manifesto of Nov. 3, 1905 which abolished all redemption payments (q.v.).

STATISTICS in the Soviet Union is seen primarily as one of the ancillary disciplines providing instruments for central planning and control. Its conceptual and methodological framework is derived from Marxist classics. The accepted doctrine—and its interpretation —has severely circumscribed, over decades, its possibilities and depressed its levels. Until recently the dominant school of thought rejected the view that mass phenomena with varying characteristics, in any field of natural or social life, were a proper subject of S; it emphatically repudiated the theory of probability; it considered any but the most primitive mathematical tools as anti-Marxist. The later years of the 1950's witnessed the beginning of a trend toward a revision of these attitudes, a trend connected with a search for advanced mathematical methods and devices in planning. The new school whose main protagonists are Nemchinov, Konyus, Lukomsky, Livshits—and, to a point, the dean of Soviet statisticians and economists, Strumilin—has lent a new formal refinement to Soviet statistical thought. This has paved the road for a resumption of intellectual links with past Russian, and with current western, statistical thinking.

The original post-revolutionary frame for statistical work was shaped by a June 1918 decree which called into existence a central authority placed in the hierarchy on a par with People's Commissariats. This frame, consolidated by a reform of 1926, did not survive the formative years of the planning era, when the statistical board was deprived of what operational independence it possessed (a thorough simultaneous change in its personnel was to make sure that its work would conform with the spirit of the times). By a Jan. 1931 decree it was incorporated—as a Division of Economic Records, subsequently renamed as Central Bureau of Economic Accounting—into the State Planning Commission, as a subsidiary agency. It was not till 1948 that it regained its old status of a ministerial office, as the Central Statistical Administration (Russian abbreviation TsSU).

The prime operational task of statistical agencies has been defined as the compiling of material for and the construction of an interrelated system of indexes. The area of statistical investigation has been delimited as follows: labor resources, their distribution and utilization; national wealth; generation, distribution, utilization, and circulation of the social product; standards of living; culture; public health; activities of governmental bodies and public organization.

In spite of potentialities opened to a collectivist, highly centralized, system the collection of basic materials—let alone their uses—has been inadequate. Only since the late 1950's has considerable effort been made to secure comprehensive and up-to-date information on the state of national resources. A population census with a more extensive questionnaire than previously practiced was held in 1959, for the first time in two

decades; after an interval of many decades a compilation of an inventory of fixed assets was carried out; housing resources were recorded; land is being catalogued and assessed.

The work on Soviet statistical index series has suffered from various inhibitive and distorting elements. Value indexes have been affected of necessity by the deficences of pricing, arbitrary and failing to mirror scarcities. Much warranted criticism has been leveled in particular against the main series measuring the physical volume of industrial production. This has been a gross-output Laspeyres-type series, derived from the enterprises' returns in constant prices of a given base year; until 1950 it was based on 1926–27; the time-remoteness of the base and the arbitrariness in supplementing of the price structure with inflated current prices (for the ever widening range of new commodities, during the period of dynamic development) robbed the series of much of its meaningfulness; the time-base was subsequently shifted to later dates, but the new series have been arbitrarily chained to the old ones. Another flaw stems from the fact that in the gross-output figures values of intermediate commodities are repeatedly included in the totals at each consecutive stage of production; hence an increase (or decrease) in the number of recorded stages tends to inflate (or deflate) the index. A relevant factor is that swelling the index corresponds to the managers' inclination because their success is gauged, in principle, by gross values produced. All in all it is safe to say that the series has been showing a very considerable upward bias. Authoritative but unofficial Soviet recalculations based on net-value outputs (broadly akin to the western concept of value-added) published at the end of the 1950's confirmed the high degree of exaggeration (*see* INDUSTRY). Irrationality of prices and the concentration of virtually the whole tax burden and profits on consumer goods has affected the significance of national income S; comparability with western data is also affected by the definitional differences, i.a. because—in compliance with the prevailing doctrine—Soviet practice excludes nonmaterial services considered to be non-productive (*see* NATIONAL INCOME AND PRODUCT). Statistics on agricultural performance were distorted over long periods in the past by recording crops on an estimated "biological" rather than actual "barn" basis (on the effects *see* AGRICULTURE).

A major shortcoming of the Soviet statistical machinery—as the supplier of material for planning agencies—has been its inability to provide the planners with adequate insight into the sectoral interdependence in the economy; no full-input coefficients (e.g., a coefficient showing the direct and indirect input of coal into a machine via all stages of production from iron-ore mining through pig-iron and steel making and rolling, and so on, to the manufacturing of a machine) have been placed at the disposal of the planner. It was only at the threshold of the 1960's, when attitudes toward the role of mathematics in S were revised, that the statistical administration embarked upon work on comprehensive *ex post* "chessboard" input-output tables, based in essence on the Leontief methodology—as a starting point for plan construction. The use of mathematical devices has also spread to other fields, e.g. to the statistical investigation of final demand.

The scope and quantity of the released statistical material have varied considerably in the USSR over time. The output of this material was substantial in the early 1920's; it shrank in the two following decades until—by the time of the fullest statistical blackout in the 1950's—it became confined to a mere trickle of indexes, with little light shed on their meaning. This tendency was reversed around the mid-fifties and ever since the range and quantity of published material have been continually growing. In particular the publication of statistical yearbooks (in Russia its tradition looks back to the early 1880's), discontinued in 1936, was resumed with the reappearance of the 1956 volume. Around the beginning of the 1960's there was already an abundance of material published by both all-Union and republican statistical agencies—however, with some striking gaps. These gaps concern in particular the absolute magnitudes of national income (a round total, the first after decades, was disclosed for 1959); the absolute figures of wages; the size of gold output and stocks; monetary circulation; certain items in foreign trade; non-commodity items of the balance of payments.

On the whole it is safe to believe that published Soviet statistical material is reliable as far as data of physical terms are concerned. A sufficient dose of caution, on the other hand, is justified in respect of index numbers, especially where international comparison is attempted with those obtained on different conventions, definitions, and methods.

BIBLIOGRAPHY: Abram Bergson, "Reliability and Usability of Soviet Statistics," *The American Statistician*, June-July 1953; Colin Clark, *A Critique of Russian Statistics*, London, 1939; Naum Jasny, "Some Thoughts on Soviet Statistics, An Evaluation," *International Affairs*, January 1959; Harry Schwartz, "The Renaissance of Soviet Statistics," *The Review of Economics and Statistics*, May 1958; Gregory Grossman, *Soviet Statistics of Physical Output of Industrial Commodities*, Princeton, 1960. A. Z.

STÁVROPOL, city in Stavropol Kray, RSFSR; pop. 140,000 (1959). Mfg. town, center of a major grain-producing area. In addition to food processing (creameries, canning, meat-packing plants) it produces leather, woolens, chemical equipment and farm implements. Has a number of higher educational institutes and technical schools. Founded 1777.

STÁVROPOL KRAY, RSFSR; includes the Karachai-Cherkess Autonomous Oblast; area 31,000 sq. mi.; pop. 1,885,000 (1959). Cities: Stavropol (adm. center), Cherkessk, Pyatigorsk, Kislovodsk, Georgievsk, Mineralniye Vody. Lies in the central part of N. Caucasus. Rivers: Kuban, Kuma, Kalaus, Yegorlyk. It is one of the major grain-producing areas of the Soviet Union, with wheat, sunflower, fodder, and essential oil crops grown on black-earth and chestnut soils. Truck and garden farming, melon and vine growing are widespread. Equally important is the breeding of livestock, chiefly fine-fleeced sheep. The recently completed Nevinnomyssk Canal will improve the irrigation of the drier areas. Has numerous mineral springs famous for their curative properties. Extensive heavy industries developed in recent decades include the machine tool plant at Stavropol, construction steel works at Georgievsk, the "Sel-

electro" (Pyatigorsk), and others. Food processing and light mfg. ind. are represented throughout the region. Health resorts at Pyatigorsk, Yessentuki, Zheleznovodsk, and Kislovodsk are of national importance. Est. 1924. During World War II the Karachai natives, of Turkic origin, were accused of collaborating with the Germans and deported. The major portion of the territory was incorporated in the adjacent regions; restored in 1957.

STÉCHKIN, Borís Sergéyevich (1891–), combustion engineer. Fellow, Ac. of S., USSR (1953). Graduate of the Moscow School of Technology (1918). Associated with the Moscow Institute of Aviation (1933–47); chief, Engine Laboratory, Ac. of S. (1954). With N. Ye. Zhukovsky S founded the Central Aerodynamic Institute; a founder and professor of the Academy of Military Aircraft Engineering. Research and development of calculation methods for aircraft engines. Formulated theory of ram-jet engines including formulas for the calculation of air consumption, determination of the filling factor, and indicator efficiency of aircraft engines. Developed methods for the analysis of ground and air characteristics of aircraft engines. Author of *A Course of the Theory of Aircraft Turbocompressors* (1944). Stalin prize (1946) and other decorations.

STEEL INDUSTRY: *see* IRON AND STEEL INDUSTRY.

STEINBERG: *see* SHTEYNBERG.

STEKLÓV, Vladímir Andréyevich (1863–1926), mathematician. Fellow (1912), vice president (1919–26), Ac. of S., USSR. Graduate (1887) and professor (1896), Kharkov University; joined St. Petersburg University (1906). Cofounder of the Institute of Physics and Mathematics (1921), Ac. of S., which was named after him. Research on mathematical physics with the application of Fourier series to boundary value problems, mathematical analysis; studied the theory of mechanical quadratures, elasticity, and hydromechanics.

STEKLÓV (Nakhámkes), **Yúry Mikháylovich** (1873–193?), active in the revolutionary movement from the 1890's. Member of the Bolshevik party from 1903. Arrested and exiled on several occasions, escaped from banishment. After the February revolution, S was a member of the Executive Committee of the Soviet of Workers' Deputies and editor of *Izvestia* of the St. Petersburg Soviet. After the October Revolution, a member of the Central Executive Committee of the Soviets. Author of many books including a four-volume biography of Mikhail Bakunin. In the thirties, apparently suspected of opposition to Stalin, S disappeared.

STEPANAKÉRT (f. Khankendy), city, adm. center of Nagorno-Karabakh Autonomous Oblast, Azerbaijan SSR; pop. 20,000 (1959). Situated at the foot of E. slope of the Karabakh range, is center of silk-milling and food-processing ind.

STEPÁNOV, Pável Ivánovich (1880–1947), geologist. Fellow, Ac. of S., USSR (1939). Graduate of St. Petersburg Mining Institute (1907); professor, Leningrad Mining Institute (1919–26). Cofounder and director of the F. N. Chernyshev Geological Museum (1926). S's geological investigation of the Donets Basin conducted under L. I. Lutugin led to the discovery of new coal-bearing deposits. S suggested a thesis of "zones and junctions for the accumulation of coal" which became a point of departure for the study of coal accumulation in different periods.

STEPNÓY: *see* ELISTA.

STEPNYÁK: *see* KRAVCHINSKY.

STEPPE: *see* PLANT LIFE, GEOGRAPHICAL ZONES.

STERLITAMÁK, city in Bashkir SSR, formerly capital of the republic; pop. 39,000 (1939), 111,000 (1959). On the left bank of Belaya River, in the vicinity of Ishimbay oil fields. Machine building, chemical, leather, woodworking ind.

STERN: *see* SHTERN.

STOGLÁV, a 100-chapter compendium of the decisions on church hierarchy and other ecclesiastic matters, adopted by the Church Council summoned by Ivan IV (Ivan the Terrible) in 1551. Numerous chapters deal with criminal, civil, and court regulations and procedures based on church law. Published for the first time in 1862.

STOLÉTOV, Aleksándr Grigóryevich (1839–1896), physicist. Graduate (1860) and professor (1873), Moscow University. Studied under G. Kirchhoff (Heidelberg) and W. Weber (Göttingen) as well as at the University of Paris. His research on the ferromagnetism of bodies has become the cornerstone of further investigations and his theories of the photoelectric effect won him world-wide recognition. Upon his initiative the ohm was officially adopted to designate the unit of electrical resistance at the International Congress of Electrical Engineers (1881).

STOLÝPIN, Pyótr Arkádyevich (1862–1911), statesman. After studying the natural sciences at the University of St. Petersburg, S joined the staff of the Ministry of Agriculture. He was governor of Grodno (1902), and of Saratov (1903). In April 1906 he was appointed minister of the interior in the Goremykin (q.v.) cabinet. After the elections to the first Duma he became president of the Council of Ministers in July 1906, while retaining the portfolio of the interior. An attempt was made on his life in Aug. 1906; he escaped unscathed. He was zealous in repressing the revolution and introduced a regime of courts-martial and punitive expeditions. Thousands were executed and exiled. At the same time he was aware that repression was not enough and that systematic reforms were inevitable.

After the dissolution of the second Duma (June 1907), a new electoral law restricted franchise and reduced the representation of the nationalities. Aggressive nationalism was a leading characteristic of S's rule. The right of enacting emergency legislation (Art. 87 of the Fundamental Laws) was considerably abused under S.

The agrarian reform associated with S (ukase of Nov. 1906) and laws of June 1910 and June 1911 were aimed at counteracting revolutionary influences among the peasantry, by introducing them to private property and by granting them the right to leave the village commune and to acquire their own plots of land. A class of well-to-do peasants was supposed to be created that would have a stabilizing influence in the countryside. The reform revolved around the goal of transforming the mass of peasants into a class of small and medium farmers. The resulting expanded domestic market was ultimately to be integrated by the industrialization of the country. The reform was opposed by the leftists, who favored expropriation of the big landowners. S was assassinated in the presence of the emperor at the opera house in Kiev by Dimitry Bogrov, a revolutionary and agent of the security police. (*See* AGRARIAN REFORMS.)

ST. PETERSBURG: *see* LENINGRAD.

STRÁKHOV, Nikoláy Mikháylovich (1900–), geologist. Fellow, Ac. of S., USSR (1953). Graduate (1928) and professor of Moscow University and of the Institute of Geological Prospecting (1930). Associated with the Geological Institute, Ac. of S. (1934). Research on sediment formation and the origin of iron ores, calcareous dolomites, bituminous shales, halogen sediments as well as on geochemistry of iron, manganese, phosphorus and other elements. Author of over 80 publications including *Iron Ore Facies and Their Analogue in the History of the Earth* (1947); *Principles of Historical Geology* (3rd ed., 1948). Stalin prize (1948).

STRÁKHOV, Nikoláy Nikoláyevich (1828–1896), critic and philosopher, defender of everything Russian against incursions from the West. With Dostoyevsky, he was editor of the journal *Time* from 1861 to 1863. S's major literary work is *The Struggle With the West in Russian Literature* (1882).

STRAVÍNSKY, Ígor Fyódorovich (1882–), a master of modern music. Son of a noted singer, S studied composition with Kalafati and later with Rimsky-Korsakov. His first symphony which was performed in St. Petersburg in 1908, as well as the cycle of songs *Le Faune et la bergère*, an orchestral fantasy *Feu d'artifice*, and *Scherzo fantastique*, revealed technical mastery and distinctive style. Commissioned by Serge Diaghilev to write a work on a R. subject, S produced his first ballet masterpiece, *The Firebird* (1910), a score of striking originality and brilliance, alive with provocative rhythms and lusty orchestral color. S's second ballet, *Petrushka*, produced by Diaghilev with outstanding success a year later (1911), marks a turning point in 20th-century modernism. The now famous "Petrushka chord" (in two different keys sounded simultaneously) started a trend toward atonality which influenced most of the contemporary composers. The earthy exuberance and poignant pathos of the music made *Petrushka* a perennial favorite on both the ballet stage and the concert platform. S frequently visited Paris, and made his permanent home there from 1911. In his next ballet score, *Le Sacre du printemps*, S emerges even more clearly as a composer who speaks in a musical idiom all his own. *The Wedding* (1923), a secular ballet-oratorio scored for a chorus, 4 pianos, and 17 percussion instruments, the stage play *The Soldier's Tale*, the comic opera *Mavra*, and *Renard* were S's last works based on R. musical folklore. *The Nightingale*, inspired by Hans Christian Andersen's fairy tale (1914), and *Pulcinella*, on themes attributed to Pergolesi, were both written for Diaghilev's ballet company. S's piano concerto (1924), now rarely heard, piano sonata (1925), and the orchestral pantomine *Apollon Musagète* present a sudden shift from the bold substantiality and pagan vigor of his earlier compositions to neoclassicist experimentation with baroque forms translated into the modern musical medium. His other notable works include the oratorio *Oedipus Rex* (1927), the *Symphony of Psalms* and violin concerto, both written in 1930, an opera-ballet *Persiphone* (1934), the *Card Party* ballet (1938), Symphony in C (1940), *The Mass* (1948), and *The Rake's Progress* (1951). U.S. citizen (1945).

BIBLIOGRAPHY: Merle Armitage, *Stravinsky*, New York, 1936; Roman Vlad, *Stravinsky*, New York, 1960.

STRELÉTSKY, Nikoláy Stanislávovich (1885–), construction and bridge engineer. Corresponding member, Ac. of S., USSR (1931); fellow, Academy of Building and Architecture, USSR (1956). Honored Scientist and Technologist, RSFSR (1944). Graduate of St. Petersburg Institute of Railway Engineering (1911); professor, School of Technology (1918) and Institute of Civil Engineering in Moscow (1933). Developed static theory on the safety factor in constructions.

STRELTSÝ (sharpshooters), the first R. troops (infantrymen) carrying firearms, formed by Ivan IV (Ivan the Terrible) in 1550. Recruited from all classes of commoners, they lived in separate settlements, practicing auxiliary crafts and trades. In 1698 these troops, numbering 50,000 men, were disbanded by Peter the Great, following a series of mutinies.

STRIGÓLNIKI, followers of a heresy which originated in late 14th century among the artisans and craftsmen of Great Novgorod and later spread to Pskov. They objected to paying for divine services, insisting on the right of lay believers to worship without the benefit of clergy. The heretical cult remained in existence up to the middle of the 15th century.

STRUMÍLIN (Strumillo-Petrashkevich), **Stanisláv Gustavovich** (1877–), economist and statistician. S was a convinced revolutionary socialist by the age of twenty and his activities in the social-democratic movement led to his arrest several times, and exile, from which he escaped twice. He nonetheless graduated from the  economics department of the St. Petersburg Polytechnic. Before the revolution, he worked as a professional statistician for the government flax committee (1911–14) and the wartime fuel distribution committee (1916–17). After 1917, S began his long career in Soviet statistical and planning organs, heading statistical offices for the Labor Commissariat and the All-Russian Council of Trade Unions (1918–23). His association with the State Planning Commission (Gosplan) began in 1921, as a presidium member. He subsequently became chief of the Central Statistical Administration and deputy chairman in Gosplan and was influential in evolving the "materials balances" techniques basic in Soviet planning; he was largely responsible for the earlier drafts of the First Five Year Plan. S left Gosplan in 1937, but returned during World War II (1943–51) as head of the Economic Accounting Department and a

member of the Council of Scientific Technical Experts. S also taught at various Moscow institutions. S has been a Communist party member since 1923, and a fellow of the USSR Ac. of S. since 1931. He is also head of the Institute of Economics in the Academy's Department of Economics, Philosophy and Law.

His writings comprise almost 200 books and articles including *Wealth and Labor* (1905), *Problems of Industrial Control in Russia* (1925), *Problems of Soviet Economics* (1928), *The Time Factor in Capital Investment Planning* (1945), *History of Ferrous Metallurgy* (1954), and *Outline of the Socialist Economy of the USSR* (1959). His honors include two orders of Lenin and the Red Labor Banner.

STRÚVE, Pyótr Berngárdovich (1870–1944), political leader, economist, and writer. In the 1890's S was a theorist of "legal" Marxism and was active in the social-democratic movement. Author of the manifesto of the Social Democratic party, he later joined the Constitutional Democratic (Kadet) party. From 1902 to 1905 he was editor of *Osvobozhdenie (Liberation)*, a journal of liberal orientation. In 1906 he was elected deputy to the second Duma. Evolving toward conservatism, S participated in 1909 in the publication *Vekhi* (Landmarks), (q.v.). In 1911 he published a series of articles under the title *Patriotica*. From 1907 to 1917 S was prof. at the St. Petersburg Polytechnic Institute. In 1917 he was elected fellow of the R. Ac. of S. After the October revolution S was a member of the anti-Bolshevik government in the South. In the emigration he was close to the monarchist circles. S edited a number of publications and wrote a score of books. The best known are *Critical Notes on the Economic Development of Russia* (1894), *Economics and Prices* (1913–16), *Social and Economic History of Russia* (1952).

STRÚVE, Vasíly Yákovlevich (Friedrich Georg Wilhelm von, born in Altona, Germany) (1793–1864), astronomer and geodesist. Fellow, Ac. of S. (1832). Graduate (1810) and professor (1813), Dorpat (Tartu) University. Founder of Pulkovo Observatory (1833). Research concerned stellar formations. Compiled a catalogue of the location of 2,874 stars. Designed astronomical instruments and established the phenomenon of light absorption in interstellar space. Honorary member of R. universities and many foreign academies and learned societies.

STRY, city in Drogobych Oblast, Ukrainian SSR; pop. 36,100 (1959). R.R. junction, on Stry River; produces oil-drilling equipment, textiles, lumber, furniture and matches. Natural gas in vicinity.

STÚCHKA (pseud. Veteran), **Pyótr Ivánovich** (1865–1932), one of the founders of the Communist party in Latvia, Soviet jurist. S comes from a Latvian peasant family. He graduated from the faculty of law of the University of St. Petersburg in 1888. In 1903 S joined the Bolshevik party and was the chairman of the central committee of the Latvian Social Democrats. After the October revolution S became people's commissar of justice (1917–18). In 1918–19 he was chairman of the Soviet government of Latvia. From 1921 on he was deputy people's commissar for justice of RSFSR and from 1923 to 1932 chairman of the Supreme Court of the RSFSR.

STURMER, Borís Vladímirovich (1848–1917), reactionary bureaucrat. S, a large landowner, graduated from the St. Petersburg University and served after 1877 in the Senate, the Ministry of Justice, and the Ministry of Interior. From 1894 to 1902 he was governor of Novgorod and Yaroslavl. In 1904 he was appointed member of the State Council. During his long bureaucratic career S opposed every liberal reform. He was a staunch reactionary and a servile supporter of the autocracy. In July 1916, at the suggestion of Rasputin and Empress Alexandra, he was appointed chairman of the Council of Ministers; simultaneously he was holding the post of minister of the interior and of foreign affairs. He was accused of pro-German leanings and was dismissed on Nov. 10, 1916. After the February revolution, he was imprisoned in the Peter and Paul Fortress, where he died in Sept. 1917.

STYR RIVER, flows N. from Lvov Oblast through N.W. Ukraine and Byelorussia to become right tributary of Pripyat River; navigable; 300 mi. long.

STYRIKÓVICH, Mikhaíl Adolfovich (1902–), heat power engineer. Corresponding member, Ac. of S., USSR (1946). Graduated from Leningrad Institute of Technology (1927). Associated with the Leningrad Regional Research Scientific Institute of Heat Power Engineering, renamed Central Boiler and Turbine Institute (1928–45). Simultaneously, associated with the Power Engineering Institute, Ac. of S. (1938), and the Moscow Power Engineering Institute (1939). Research concerns heat power systems and working processes of steam boilers; relationships governing the motion of heat-and-power mixture through pipes and heat transfer to boiling liquid at high pressure; the separation of steam and the solubility of salts in high-pressure steam. Established standards of heat and aerodynamic calculations of boiler units. Author of *Working Processes of Uniflow Super-High Pressure Boilers* (1956).

SUCHÁN, city in Maritime Kray, Far E., RSFSR; pop. 47,600 (1956). Center of important coal-mining region.

SUDÉYKIN, Sergéy Yúryevich (1882–1946), painter. Graduated from the St. Petersburg Academy of Fine Arts and joined the *Mir Iskusstva* (World of Art) group. Settled in the United States and became a United States citizen (1942). Designed settings for the Diaghilev ballet, the Metropolitan Opera, and Radio City in New York.

SUGAR BEETS CULTIVATION. Gross output of SB amounted, in mill. tons, to 11.3 in 1913 (within present Soviet boundaries), 10.1 in 1928, 18.0 in 1940, and 43.9 in 1959. A further steep rise is envisioned under the current Seven Year Plan, to some 80 mill. tons by 1965, so as to provide the base for increased sugar production of which SB are the only source in the USSR.

The main producer is Ukraine (61%), followed by the central chernozem areas in Russia (19%), and Kuban (5%). The Soviets have been successful in expanding fourfold above the 1913 level the area planted to SB, pushing it to regions such as Central Asia where

no SB were previously cultivated and improving the sugar contents of the beet. SB have been one of the priority crops throughout the Five Year Plans, one of the few receiving large allotments of mineral fertilizers. Delivery terms were somewhat more favorable than for most other crops; premiums in kind and tax rebates were granted at one time to SB growers. Harvesting was partly mechanized, 28,500 SB combines were in operation in 1957.

SUGAR-REFINING INDUSTRY. In 1960 6.4 mill. tons of sugar were produced (in 1959 the United States produced 2.6 mill. tons; Cuba, 6 mill. tons; Brazil, 3.1 mill. tons).

In the prerevolutionary period the beet-sugar industry consisted (in 1913) of 236 small refineries, most of which were built before 1870. It was one of the first industries to become highly cartelized.

During the 1930's the existing plants were modernized, particularly in the Ukraine, and 20 new plants were constructed. Of these, 11 were located in regions that did not possess any sugar-refining enterprises before, including Siberia, Kirgizia, Kazakhstan and Georgia, the Volga region, and the Far East. As a result of these measures the annual rate of sugar production reached 2.2 mill. tons in 1940, or twice the volume of 1913.

The production of sugar was considerably reduced during World War II, when 43 sugar-refining plants were entirely destroyed and 190 others affected. It increased rapidly during the postwar period, however, especially after 1950, following the implementation of an intensive program of technological modernization. In 1955 3.4 mill. tons of sugar were produced.

The objectives of the Seven Year Plan (1959–65) provide for increasing the production of sugar to 9.2–10.0 mill. tons.

SUGAR PRODUCTION IN THE USSR
(mill. tons)

1913	1.3
1928	1.3
1932	.8
1937	2.4
1940	2.2
1945	.5
1950	2.5
1955	3.4
1958	5.4
1959	6.0
1960	6.4
1965 (plan)	9.2–10.0 P. I. M.

SUKACHÓV, Vladímir Nikoláyevich (1880–), botanist, silviculturist, and geographer. Fellow, Ac. of S., USSR (1943). Graduate of the Institute of Forestry (1902) in St. Petersburg. Professor, Leningrad Academy of Forestry (1919–41); the Geographical Institute (1918–25); Moscow State University (1948–51). Director, Institute of Forestry, Ac. of S. (1946); president, All-Union Botanical Society (1946) and the Moscow Society of Naturalists (1955). Initiated a new branch of science—biogeocoenology. Led expeditions in various parts of the country and conducted extensive research of swamps and their formation. Developed methods of pollen analysis and methods applied in the study of pleistocene formations in the USSR. Prizes from the Geographical Society and Ac. of S.

SUKHÁNOV (Gimmer), **Nikoláy Nikoláyevich** (1882–?), revolutionary, economist, and journalist. In 1903–04 was a member of the Socialist Revolutionary party, but in 1909 joined the Mensheviks. Editor of the review *Sovremennik* (The Contemporary) (1914) and, with Maksim Gorky, editor of *Novaya Zhizn* (New Life) (1917). After the February revolution, a member of the Executive Committee of the Petrograd Soviet. In the early 1920's, he broke with the Mensheviks; from then on he remained unaffiliated with any party and worked in the Soviet economics apparatus. In 1931 was a defendant at the Menshevik trial and was given a 10-year sentence. S is the author of *Notes on the Russian Revolution*, an abridged version of which is available in English.

SUKHOMLÍNOV, Vladímir Aleksándrovich (1848–1926), general and minister of war. After service in the Russo-Turkish war, he headed the Cavalry School, St. Petersburg (1886–97), and in 1908 became chief of the general staff. Three years later he was appointed minister of war. As such he is held mainly responsible for the unpreparedness of R. arms at the outbreak of war in 1914. His conduct of the war ministry after 1914 aroused a storm of criticism culminating in his dismissal, June 1916. Convicted of malfeasance in office he escaped during the Bolshevik Revolution and went to Germany where he wrote his highly untruthful memoirs.

SÚKHONA RIVER, in Vologda Oblast, flows E. from Lake Kubena meeting Yug River near Veliky Ustyug to form N. Dvina River; 350 mi. long. Icebound five months; otherwise navigable.

SÚKHOVO-KOBÝLIN, Aleksándr Vasílyevich (1817–1903), playwright who wrote his first plays in prison while awaiting trial for the murder of his French mistress. He was acquitted and some of his later plays reflect his hatred for the bureaucratic red tape of criminal procedures. S's most successful plays form a trilogy; they are three comedies, of which *The Marriage of Krechinsky*, first staged in 1855, is still in the repertory of the Soviet theaters. The other two are *The Affair* (1869) and *Tarelkin's Death* (1869).

SUKHÚMI (f. Sukhum), capital of Abkhaz ASSR; pop. 64,000 (1959). Port on the Black Sea, on the W. slope of the Caucasus. The center of important tobacco growing area; it also has fruit canneries, tobacco factories, metalworking plants. An outstanding health resort, with subtropical vegetation and climatic conditions; is the site of the famed botanical garden and experimental horticultural station.

SULÍN: *see* KRASNY SULIN.

SUMGAÍT, city in Azerbaijan SSR; pop. 52,000 (1958). Newly developed ind. center, at the intersection of Sumgait River and Caspian coastal R.R., site of large pipe-rolling mills, aluminum and chemical plants. Founded 1949.

SUMARÓKOV, Aleksándr Petróvich (1717–1777), writer of the pseudo-classical school. Instrumental in the development of the R. literary language and a versatile writer of lyrical songs, fables, odes, epigrams, historical dramas, and comedies. His dramatic works *Khorev* (1747), *Sináv and Truvór* (1748), and *The*

False Dimitry (1771) stress civic duty, patriotism, and service to society. In his comedies *The Guardian* (1765) and *Extortionist* (1768) he satirized ignorance and provincialism.

SÚMY, city, adm. center of Sumy Oblast; pop. 97,000 (1959). Center of sugar-refining ind.; manufactures agr. machinery and equipment, chemical fertilizers; woolens; has light ind. and food-processing plants.

SÚMY OBLAST, Ukrainian SSR; area 9,300 sq. mi.; pop. 1,514,000 (1959). Cities: Sumy (adm. center), Shostka, Konotop. Wooded steppe in the black-earth belt, with mixed forests in the N. tip; is drained by the Desna-Seym and left tributaries of Dnieper: Vorskla, Sula, and Psel. Minerals: peat, oil, lignite, phosphorite. Sugar refining, flour milling, hemp retting are main ind., based on local crops; tobacco and mint are cultivated in the S.; hog rearing and dairy farming. Est. 1939.

SUPREME PRIVY COUNCIL. A body formed in 1726 after the death of Peter the Great as a compromise between the main contestants for power: the Petrine court advisers led by Menshikov and backing the Empress Catherine I, and the higher nobility backing the young Peter, the future Emperor Peter II. The SPC assumed the right to advise the empress, examine the principal affairs of state, and issue decrees, and became in fact, if not in law, the actual ruler of the country. When Peter II died in 1730, three years after Catherine I, the SPC agreed that Anna, the daughter of Ivan V, should be named empress. The SPC was dissolved by Anna by a manifesto of March 4, 1730 when the lower nobility and the guards regiments supported her assumption of absolute power.

SURAKHANÝ, town 11 mi. from Baku, Azerbaijan SSR; oil area; pop. 19,300 (1956).

SÚRIKOV, Vasíly Ivánovich (1848–1916), historical painter of the realistic school; born in a Cossack family  in Krasnoyarsk. Graduated from the Academy of Fine Arts in 1875. Member of the Society of Circulating Exhibitions (*Peredvizhniki*). Executed murals in the Cathedral of Christ the Saviour. In 1877 settled in Moscow. His best-known works are *Morning of the Streltsy Execution* (1881), *Menshikov in Beryozovo* (1883), *Boyarynya Morozova* (1887), *Conquest of Siberia by Yermak* (1895), *Crossing of the Alps by Suvorov's Troops* (1899), *Stepan Razin* (1901–07), *Tsar's Daughter Visiting a Convent* (1912). In 1888, S visited Siberia and painted *Seizure of the Snow Town* (1889–90). His pictures are in Tretyakov Gallery, Moscow, and the Russian Museum, Leningrad.

SURKHÁN-DARYÁ OBLAST, Uzbek SSR; area 17,500 sq. mi.; pop. 919,000 (1960). Cities: Termez (adm. center), and Denau. Its flatlands are watered by the Surkhan Darya and Amu Darya rivers; is bounded by Baysun-Tau and Kugitang-Tau ranges in the W., and by Amu Darya in the S. (state boundary with Afghanistan). Irrigation farming is essential, with largest acreage under cotton; wheat and barley are the chief products of dry farming; sheep, goats, some cattle and horses are bred in dry lowlands; sericulture widespread. There are oilfields at Khaudag, Kokayty, and Uch-Kzyl. Est. 1941. In 1960 absorbed Kashka-Darya Oblast.

SURKÓV, Alekséy Aleksándrovich (1899–), poet. S comes from a peasant family, and was a volunteer in the Red Army during the civil war. His first published work appeared in 1930. During World War II he wrote the poems *Behind Us Is Moscow, A Soldier's Heart, Song of the Defenders of Moscow,* and collections of verse from the front, published in 1942 and 1943. As a leader of the Union of Soviet Writers, S was Soviet representative in numerous pro-Communist international organizations and "peace movements." Deputy to the Supreme Soviet and recipient of several awards.

SUSÁNIN, Iván Ósipovich (died in 1613), peasant, native of the Kostroma region near Moscow who became a national hero. Captured by Polish invaders and forced to serve as guide, he led his captors into a dense forest where he was murdered after his treachery was discovered. His heroism inspired the well-known opera by Glinka, *Life for the Tsar* (renamed after the revolution *Ivan Susanin*).

SÚSLIN, Mikhaíl Yákovlevich (1894–1919), mathematician. A founder of the theory of *A*-sets not included in the Borel sets. His theory is expounded in a short paper (1917); a more detailed account is given by F. Hausdorf in *Principles of the Theory of Sets* (2nd edition, 1927) and by N. N. Luzin in *Lectures on Analytic Sets antd Their Application* (1930).

SÚSLOV, Mikhaíl Andréyevich (1902–), member of the party Presidium and a secretary of the Central Committee of the CPSU, primarily in charge of relations with foreign parties. S was born in Saratov Province, in a peasant family. Joined the party in 1921 and studied in a worker's faculty in Moscow. 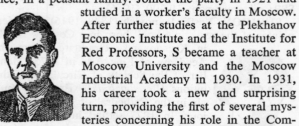 After further studies at the Plekhanov Economic Institute and the Institute for Red Professors, S became a teacher at Moscow University and the Moscow Industrial Academy in 1930. In 1931, his career took a new and surprising turn, providing the first of several mysteries concerning his role in the Communist party. According to his official biography, he was entrusted with "responsible work" in the Central Control Commission of the party and also in the Committee for State Control (the "Workers' and Peasants' Inspection"). The nature of this work has not been further disclosed, but for S it was the beginning of active participation in internal party affairs. In 1933–34, S conducted purges of party organizations in the Urals and Chernigov. In 1941, he became a member of the CPSU Central Committee and in 1944 he took charge of the Central Committee bureau for Lithuania, regained from the Germans, where he directed a purge. In 1946, S was made member of the Orgburo of the Central Committee, in Sept. 1947 secretary of the Central Committee in charge of the agitation and propaganda department, and in 1948 candidate member of the Politburo. From 1948 S was the Soviet representative in the Cominform. In this capacity he attended all the Cominform conferences and formulated the accusations against Tito. This rapid ascent indicates

that S enjoyed Stalin's favor and confidence, yet in 1949 he had an apparent setback when the directorship of the Agitprop department was transferred to Shepilov. However, S was given an important post as editor of *Pravda* later the same year and, though he held it only briefly, he had another promotion in 1952, after the 19th Party Congress, when he became member of the Presidium.

Recently, S has been widely regarded as a leading figure in the "Stalinist" opposition to Khrushchev, even as Khrushchev's principal and most dangerous rival. There is, however, little evidence for this. S was the first to denounce the "personality cult" at the 20th Party Congress and faithfully followed Khrushchev's line. In June 1957 he was reportedly one of three Presidium members who supported Khrushchev against the majority attack led by Molotov. More recently, in 1960, S's speeches have often repeated Khrushchev's statements and S has led in the praise of Khrushchev. S nonetheless is more theoretical and dogmatic than Khrushchev.

SUVÓRIN, Alekséy Sergéyevich (1834–1912), newspaper owner and editor. He began his career as a moderately liberal journalist in the 1850's. Is best known as publisher of the leading R. daily newspaper *Nóvoye Vrémya* (New Times) founded in 1876. He was a minor playwright, a friend of Chekhov and publisher of the latter's works.

SUVÓROV, Aleksándr Vasílyevich (1730–1800), one of Russia's most gifted generals, originator of the R. 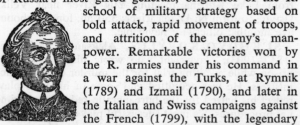 school of military strategy based on bold attack, rapid movement of troops, and attrition of the enemy's manpower. Remarkable victories won by the R. armies under his command in a war against the Turks, at Rymnik (1789) and Izmail (1790), and later in the Italian and Swiss campaigns against the French (1799), with the legendary crossing of the Alps, brought him world fame, as well as recognition of R. military valor. He is the author of a treatise *Science of Victory.* In 1942 a decoration named after Suvorov was established.
BIBLIOGRAPHY: W. L. Blease, *Suvorof*, London, 1920.

SURVIVORS INSURANCE: *see* SOCIAL INSURANCE.

SVANÉTIA, district in N.W. Georgia, inhabited by an old Caucasian race, the Svans, who farm and raise cattle.

SVERDLÓV, Yákov Mikháylovich (1885–1919), Bolshevik leader. S was born in Nizhny Novgorod (now Gorky) and as a youth was attracted to the revolutionary movement. In 1905 he went to the Ural mountain area and led revolutionary agitation there. He was eventually exiled to Siberia where he spent a  considerable time with Stalin who was also in exile. Yet the two men do not seem to have formed a strong friendship despite their close contact. After the overthrow of the tsarist regime, S returned to Petrograd and became one of the leading Bolsheviks, acting as virtually a one-man secretariat for the party during the year 1917. After the

Bolshevik Revolution he also held the post of chairman of the Central Executive Committee of the Congress of Soviets as well as secretary of the Central Committee of the Bolshevik party. With these two posts S virtually controlled the state apparatus in Soviet Russia. For a while, in cooperation with Lenin and Trotsky, S actually ran Soviet Russia and was able to bypass the party apparatus when he saw fit. S died suddenly in 1919. In later years the city of Yekaterinburg was renamed Sverdlovsk.

SVERDLÓVSK (f. Yekaterinburg), city, adm. center of Sverdlovsk Oblast; pop. 779,000 (1959). One of the Soviet Union's most important industrial centers, called Soviet Pittsburgh, it manufactures steel, metallurgical products, aircraft and armaments; site of Uralmash, the largest machine-building plant in the USSR. Has a number of higher educational institutions, including the Ural University and the Ural Div. of the Ac. of S. USSR. Place of execution of the last tsar and his family.

SVERDLÓVSK OBLAST, RSFSR; area 74,500 sq. mi.; pop. 4,044,000 (1959). Cities: Sverdlovsk (adm. center), Alapayevsk, Nizhny Tagil, and others. Situated upon the E. slopes of the Urals, it has long been a thriving agr. area, with grain farming and cattle breeding supported by rich podsol soils. In recent decades it has become the scene of remarkably rapid ind. development based on vast and varied mineral resources. Gold and platinum, iron, copper, magnesium, marble, and asbestos are of particular importance. Heavy machine building, ferrous and nonferrous metallurgy centered in Sverdlovsk and Nizhny Tagil. Est. 1934.

SVIR RIVER, in N.E. Leningrad area, flows from Lake Onega into Lake Ladoga; 140 mi. long; source of hydroelectric power.

SVOBÓDNY (f. Alekseyevsk), city in Amur Oblast, RSFSR; pop. 57,000 (1959). R.R. station, landing on Zeya River. Center of river shipping on the Amur, repair and servicing shops.

SVYATOPÓLK-MÍRSKY, Prince Pyótr Danílovich (1857–1914). Participated in the Russo-Turkish war of 1878. After demobilization, S-M studied at the university and upon graduation became governor of a province in the Ukraine. In 1900, he was appointed assistant minister of the interior. After the assassination of V. Plehve in August of 1904, S-M became minister of the interior. Owing to his liberal reputation, this appointment was hailed as the beginning of a new era which would lead to the liberalization of the R. political regime. However, Prince S-M did not succeed in this task. He was responsible for the suppression of the workers' demonstration in Jan. 1905 ("Bloody Sunday," q.v.) and was dismissed soon thereafter.

SWAMPS occupy some 750,000 sq. mi. or somewhat less than 10% of the territory of the USSR. Many are of economic importance as a source of peat. Their distribution is influenced by climatic conditions and the relief. They are widespread in the tundra zone because of the excessive moisture, high level of ground water, flatness of the country, and the presence of permanently frozen soils, up to 50% of the area being swampy in some places. The prevailing type is the lowland or sedge bog. In the tayga S constitute about 80% of all the peat bogs of the USSR. These usually belong to the upland sphagnum bogs and have a peat thickness of 25–33 ft. In the subzone of mixed forests, there occur both the upland and lowland (sedge) bogs which are fed mostly by ground waters. Vast S are found in the Polesye, Meshchera and other lowlands of European Russia, as well as in the lowlands of the Far East; but S. from the forest zone, S are infrequent in the flood plains of rivers and in small depressions. In the steppe zone, there are S in the flood plains of the large rivers, the Dniester, the Dnieper, the Don, the Kuban, and others; and in semideserts and deserts, there are depressions containing salty muds. S are found only in the deltas of large rivers, the Amu Darya, the Syr Darya, and the Ili.

SYKTYVKÁR (f. Ust-Sysolsk), capital of Komi ASSR; pop. 24,000 (1939), 64,000 (1959). River town, at the confluence of Sysola and Vychegda. Its recently developed ind. include shipbuilding and drydocks, leather and shoe factories, food-processing plants. Has a number of higher educ. and techn. schools; is the site of the regional branch of Ac. of S., USSR.

SYMBOLISM, the leading movement in R. literature from 1894 to 1910. Its beginning was marked by the publication of the almanac, *Russian Symbolists*, and the formation of the movement was influenced by French Parnassian and symbolist poets, older R. writers as Lermontov, Dostoyevsky, Fet, and Tyutchev, and, most of all, by the philosopher-poet V. Solovyov with his mystical adoration of Sophia, the incarnation of Divine Wisdom. The philosophical belief that the world is a system of symbols, which expresses abstract metaphysical realities, makes R. symbolism different from the French. The movement is characterized by mysticism, eroticism, belief in "art for art's sake," and the high musicality of verses, enriched by new rhythms and forms. The first generation of R. symbolists were Merezhkovsky, Hippius, Balmont, Bryusov, and Sologub. To the younger generation belong Blok, Bely, and V. Ivanov. Merezhkovsky and V. Ivanov sought the unification of classical Greek ideas with Christianity. Bryusov was more interested in aesthetics; F. Sologub expressed in his symbols the cult of Manicheism and Satanism. Blok was undoubtedly the most inspired among them. Bely's works were too overburdened with linguistic extravagances to be really enjoyable. The symbolists achieved higher levels in poetry than in prose, which was too morbid and erotic.

BIBLIOGRAPHY: Oleg Maslenikov, *The Frenzied Poets: Andrey Bely and the Russian Symbolists*, Berkeley, 1952.

SYR DÁRYA RIVER (ancient *Jaxartes*, Arab. *Si-hun*), second largest in central Asia, formed by junction of Naryn and Kara Darya R., flows from Tien Shan Mts., Kazakh SSR, W. and N.W. into N.E. Aral Sea. Its course includes Fergana Valley and along E. side of Kyzyl-Kum desert. Length 1,775 mi.; navigable and used for irrigation.

SYROMYÁTNIKOV, Sergéy Petróvich (1891–1951), locomotive designer and combustion engineer.

Fellow, Ac. of S., USSR (1943). Honored Scientist and Technologist, RSFSR (1943). Graduate of the Moscow School of Technology (1917); professor, Institute of Railway Engineering (1925–31), Electro-Mechanical Institute of Railway Transportation (1931). Designed and modernized locomotives. Developed a theory of thermal processes of locomotive boilers and steam superheaters. Author of *The Thermal Process of Locomotives* (1947); *Thermal Operation of Locomotive Combustion Chambers* (1953). Stalin prize (1943).

SYRTSÓV, Sergéy Ivánovich (1893–193?), member of the Bolshevik party from 1913. Repeatedly arrested. In 1917, was chairman of the Military Revolutionary Committee of the Rostov Soviet. During the civil war, was commander in the Red Army. From 1927, member of the Central Committee and from 1930, candidate member of the Politburo. Suspected of opposition to Stalin, S was arrested and disappeared in the 1930's.

SÝZRAN, city in Kuybyshev Oblast, RSFSR; pop. 83,000 (1939), 149,000 (1959). R.R. junction on the Volga. Since World War II it has grown into the second major industrial community of the oblast; produces hydroturbines and automotive harvesters, prefabricated houses, building materials, glass, leather, furniture, and processed foods; oil and oil-shale ind. Has a number of highly specialized technical schools. Founded 1683.

T

TABÝN-BOGDÓ-OLÁ, mountainous region with glaciers on Soviet-Mongolian-Chinese border; altitude 14,300 ft.

TABASARANS: *see* POPULATION.

TADZHIK SOVIET SOCIALIST REPUBLIC (TADZHIKISTAN) is located in Soviet Central Asia and borders on Afghanistan in the S., on China in the E., on the Uzbek SSR in the W., and on the Uzbek and Kirghiz republics in the N. In 1929 a section of the fer-

tile Fergana valley was attached to T, creating an extremely irregular frontier between T, Uzbekistan, and Kirghizia. Area, 55,150 sq. mi.; T includes Leninabad Oblast and the Gorno-Badakhshan Autonomous Oblast separated by a narrow wedge of Afghan territory from India and Pakistan. Capital, Stalinabad (224,000); city, Leninabad (77,000).

Population is 1,980,000 (1959); this includes 1,051,000 Tadzhiks (53.1%), 454,000 Uzbeks (23%), 26,000 Kirghiz (1.3%), 13,000 Kazakhs (0.6%), 57,000 Tatars (2.9%), as well as 263,000 Russians (13.3%), 27,000 Ukrainians (1.4%), and 94,000 or 4.6% other groups (Germans and other non-natives). The proportion of Tadzhiks in T dropped from 74.3% in 1926 to about 60% in 1939 and 53.1% in 1959. People of European origin (Russians, Ukrainians, Volga Germans, etc.) account for one-fifth of the present-day population while in 1926 they accounted for less than 1%. Although few Russians live in rural areas, urban life is dominated by R. settlers.

Nature and Climate. T is a high mountain country. Its S.E. part is occupied by the Pamir plateau (called "the roof of the world"). The Pamir-Altay chains cover the central section; lowlands are located on the fringes —the T part of the Fergana valley in the N., the Gissar valley in the S.W. The highest mountains in the USSR (Stalin Peak, 24,584 ft., and Lenin Peak, 24,400 ft.) are located in T. The climate varies depending on elevation: over 88° F in July and 39° F in Jan., with average yearly rainfall of 10 in. in the dry lowlands; 59°–70° F in the summer and 14° to 25° F in the winter, with rainfall of 20 in. in the foothills and lower mountain ranges. Snow and glaciers continually cover all areas over 10,000 ft. The average yearly temperature in Pamir is below freezing, rainfall 3 in. Among the natural resources are polymetallic and rare metal ores as well as fluorspar, coal, oil, gold, salt, sulfur, phosphorites, tin, and radioactive ores.

National Economy. Industry developed only recently. Mining is concentrated in the T part of the Fergana valley and adjacent ranges. The largest deposits of fluorspar in the USSR are located north of Stalinabad, gold mines in the Gorno-Badakhshan, oil wells in Kim and Nefteabad, coal mines in Shurab, hydroelectric stations along the rivers. Factories producing spare parts

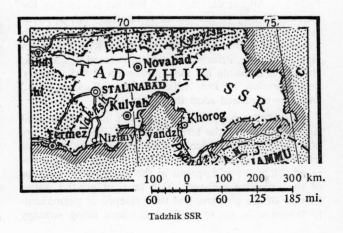

Tadzhik SSR

for motor vehicles and agricultural machinery, repair shops, and building-material plants are located in Stalinabad and Leninabad. The cotton-cleaning industry is second in the USSR. T also has silk, leather, and food-processing plants, wine distilleries, and other industries. In agriculture, cotton is the most important crop, followed by grains, fruit, wines, oil-producing plants. Irrigation is essential and is being constantly developed. Cattle breeding (main occupation in the uplands) suffered heavy losses during collectivization, but regained its former vigor in the 1950's. (For history and culture, *see* TURKESTAN.)   M. R.

TAGANRÓG, city in Rostov Oblast, RSFSR; pop. 202,000 (1959). Is a major coal- and grain-shipping port on Sea of Azov; the second largest ind. community of the oblast. Besides the great boiler works, it has machine-building, pipe-rolling, and metallurgical plants, builds airplanes and ships, and produces farm implements and precision instruments, leather, shoes, and processed foods. The fishing industry is also important. It is the birthplace of A. P. Chekhov; has a number of higher educational and technical schools. Founded 1698.

TAÍROV (Kornblit), **Aleksándr Yákovlevich** (1885–1950), actor and director. After graduating from the university, he worked from 1905 on in private metropolitan and provincial theaters. In 1914 he organized the avant-garde Moscow Kamerny Theater. An opponent of both the "theater of re-lived experience" as practiced in the Moscow Art Theater and the "conditional theater" of Meyerhold, T strove to create exquisite spectacles in which the dazzling beauty of "theater of make-believe" would be achieved by elegance, by exalted chanted or declaimed speech, graceful gesture and music. Experimenting with various genres (e.g., in the works of E. T. A. Hoffman, Lothar, Schnitzler, and LeCoque) and exploiting the splendid talent of the actress A. Koonen, T successfully produced such diverse plays as the works of Eugene O'Neill and Racine's *Phaedra*, as well as R. classics and new Soviet dramas. By 1936, however, after infuriating the party with his production of the opera *Bogatyri*, a malicious satire on ancient folklore, T was repeatedly attacked by party critics, and in 1949 his theater was closed because of "alien ideology and formalism."

TALÁS ALATÁU, mountain range in Kirghiz SSR, Central Asia, between Syr Darya basin and Talas River; greatest altitude 14,750 ft.

TALDÝ-KURGÁN, city in Alma-Ata Oblast, Kazakh SSR; pop. 41,000 (1959). Center of sugar-beet growing region; has sugar milling, rice polishing, and other ind. based on local products.

TALDÝ-KURGÁN OBLAST, Kazakh SSR, abolished June 1959, incorporated into Alma-Ata Oblast.

TÁLLIN or **TÁLLINN** (f. Revel or Reval), capital of Estonian SSR; pop. 282,000 (1959). It is an important port on the Gulf of Finland, in the Baltic Sea. Founded by the Danes in the early 13th century, it was seized by Peter the Great in 1710. Is a major ind. and cultural center with shipbuilding, machine-building (electrical equipment), paper and pulp milling most essential; a center of cotton and woolen fabrics, plywood and

furniture mfg.; clothing, leather, and footwear factories; dairy products; fish-processing plants. Has a number of higher schools.

TALÝSH, range on Iranian-Azerbaijan border, E. Transcaucasia, N.W. extension of Elbrus Mountains; altitude 8,200 ft.

TAMÁN PENINSULA, extreme N.W. Caucasus, with Kerch Strait on W., Black Sea on S., and Sea of Azov on N.; low land, many lakes; area 770 sq. mi.; oil, gas and iron deposits.

TAMANYÁN, Aleksándr Ivánovich (1878–1936), architect. Studied at the Academy of Fine Arts in St. Petersburg (1888–1904). Became vice-president of the Academy of Fine Arts in 1917. In 1923, moved to Yerevan, in Armenia, where he designed the hydroelectric power station, the theater, and the government house. Stalin prize (1942).

TAMBÓV, city, adm. center of Tambov Oblast, on Tsna River; pop. 172,000 (1959). Important rail center on Moscow–Saratov R.R., its ind. include synthetic rubber, aircraft, explosives, railroad accessories, lighting equipment, electric motors, machine building. Founded 1636.

TAMBÓV OBLAST, central RSFSR; area 13,250 sq. mi.; pop. 1,549,000 (1959). Cities: Tambov (adm. center), Kotovsk, Morshansk, Kirsanov. Is part of Oka–Don lowlands, between Central R. plateau and Volga heights; drained by the Tsna and Vorona rivers; hilly wooded steppe in the N., level plain in the S. Important agr. area, with rye, millet, sugar beets, hemp the dominant crops; meat cattle, horses, hogs bred extensively; main ind. are based on farm products; machine building centered in the principal cities. Important experimental work is carried on at the famed horticultural station at Michurinsk. Est. 1937.

TAMM, Ígor Yevgényevich (1895–), leading physicist. Fellow, Ac. of S., USSR (1953). Hero of Socialist Labor. Graduated from Moscow University (1918) and lectured at a number of colleges including Moscow University (1924–41 and since 1954). Since 1934, T has also been associated with the Lebedev Institute of

 Physics. T's research concerns quantum mechanics and its application, the theory of radiation and cosmic rays, and nuclear physics. He suggested the quantum theory of light dispersion in solid bodies and the theory of light dispersion by electrons on the basis of relativistic quantum mechanics (1930). With S. P. Shubin, T developed the theory of the photoelectric effect on metals (1931). Established the "Tamm levels" (1932), and with I. M. Frank advanced the theory of high-speed movement of radiation in an electron medium (1937), giving an explanation of the Cherenkov-Vavilov effect. His "Tamm-Dancoff" method is a technique for approximating to the wave-function of a system of nucleons and mesons (1945). He suggested the application of electric discharges in plasma placed within a magnetic field to achieve a controlled nuclear reaction (with A. D. Sakharov, 1950). Stalin prizes; Nobel prize (1958).

TANANÁYEV, Iván Vladímirovich (1904–), chemist. Fellow, Ac. of S. (1958). Graduate of Kiev Polytechnic Institute (1925). Head of department at the Institute of General and Inorganic Chemistry (1949). Research concerns fluorides and ferrocyanides of metals and compounds of rare elements. T. widely uses physicochemical analysis for the solution of problems of analytical chemistry.

TANÉYEV, Sergéy Ivánovich (1856–1915), composer, and teacher (at the Moscow Conservatoire) of a generation of R. composers: Rachmaninoff, Skryabin, Metner, and others. T had excellent knowledge of counterpoint and harmony and wrote books on the theory of music. His opera *Orestea* was too heavy and complex for the average listener. Better known is his chamber music: a quintet and a quartet for piano and strings, and his numerous romances. T composed 4 symphonies, *Overture on Russian Themes,* a suite for violin and orchestra, *Solemn Overture* and several choral pieces.

TANNÚ-OLÁ, mountain range running E. and W. between Tuva Autonomous Oblast and N.W. Outer Mongolia; altitude up to 10,000 ft.

TARAKÁNOVA (died in 1775), known as "Princess Tarakanova" (real name unknown), political adventuress pretending to be a daughter of Empress Elizabeth Petrovna. She sought support abroad for her claims to the R. throne; she died in the Peter and Paul Fortress soon after having been arrested in Italy.

TARASÉVICH, Lev Aleksándrovich (1868–1927), microbiologist and pathologist. Graduate, Novorossiysk University in Odessa (1891); professor, Moscow University (1908–24). Studied at the Pasteur Institute in Paris (1900–2). Research concerned immunology and hemolysics. Introduced large-scale anti-TB vaccination in the USSR. Founded and edited *Zhurnal Mikrobiologii, Epidemiologii i Immunologii* (Journal of Epidemiology, Microbiology, and Immunology) (1924).

TARÁSOV, Álla Konstantínovna (1898–), actress. People's Artist of the USSR. Began her work in the theater in 1916 with the 2nd Studio of the Moscow Art Theater and later continued with the Moscow Academic Art Theater. Interpreted the leading parts in plays by Ostrovsky, L. Tolstoy, and Chekhov. Has appeared in moving pictures, in the films *The Storm* and *Guilty Though Guiltless* (based on Ostrovsky's plays).

TARBAGATÁY, mountain range on Chinese-Kazakh border; altitude up to 9,800 ft.; many mineral resources (copper, silver-lead, sulfur, coal).

TARIFFS: see FOREIGN TRADE AND AID.

TÁRLE, Yevgény Víktorovich (1875–1955), historian. Author of monographs on the history of France,  international relations, and the foreign policies of prerevolutionary Russia. His best-known works are *The French Working Class During the Revolution,* 2 vols. (1909–11); *The Continental Blockade* (1913–16); *Europe in the Period of Imperialism 1871–1919* (1927); *Napoleon* (1936–39); *The Crimean War,* 2 vols (1941–43), and *The Russian Fleet and the Foreign Policy of Peter I* (1949). In the 1930's T was in disgrace, but shortly before World War II he became one of the most praised official historians and was awarded the Stalin prize three times.

TARNOPOL: see TERNOPOL.

TÁRTU (f. Yuryev, Ger. *Dorpat*), city in Estonian SSR; pop. 74,000 (1959). An old university town, on Emayig River; dates back to the early 11th century; is important producer of agr. machinery, linen fabrics, and lumber.

TASHAÚZ, city, adm. center of Tashauz Oblast, in lower Amu Darya region; pop. 37,000 (1959). Cotton ginning, oil-seed, jute mills, rug-making.

TASHAÚZ OBLAST, Turkmen SSR; area 29,000 sq. mi.; pop. 295,000 (1959). Adm. center, Tashauz city. The N. section lies in the Khiva oasis watered by numerous arms of the Amu Darya (navigable). Grains, short-staple cotton, jute, lucerne, sesame, melons cultivated on irrigated farmlands along the river valley; caracul and fat-tail sheep, goats, camels bred in the Karakum desert occupying the S. sector; limited saltpeter deposits, building-materials reserves worked. The Amu Darya waterway and the recently built Chardzhou–Kungrad R.R. are the main shipping routes. Est. 1939.

TASHKÉNT, capital of Uzbek SSR and adm. center of Tashkent Oblast, in the valley of Chirchik River; pop. 911,000 (1959). Ind. include agr. machinery, chemical combine, cotton and paper mills, clothing and footwear; meat-packing, fruit and vegetable canning, other food-processing plants. Important cultural center; Ac. of S. Uzbek SSR, university, research institutes. Subject to earthquakes. Founded probably 7th century B.C., mentioned in Chinese sources as Yuni in 2nd century B.C.; Arabic *Shash,* Persian *Binkent,* received in 12th century its Turkic name (Stone City); captured by R. 1865.

TASHKÉNT OBLAST, Uzbek SSR; area 7,750 sq. mi.; pop. 2,261,000 (1959). Cities: Tashkent (adm. center), Chirchik, Almalyk, Mirzachul, Yangi-Abad. Important agr. and ind. region, bounded by the spurs of Chatkal and Kurama ranges in the E. and N.E.; drained by the Syr Darya and tributaries, Chirchik and Angren; has semidesert vegetation growing on gray soils in the lowlands; dark gray and chestnut soils in mountainous country. Extensive irrigation cultures include cotton, lucerne, rice, jute; some wheat produced by dry farming; orchards, vineyards, and sericulture essential. Major ind. based on local reserves include copper (Almalyk), chemicals (Chirchik city), metallurgical (Begovat), coal (Angren), cement (Khilkovo), cotton ginning (Mirzachul, Yangi-Yul). Est. 1938.

TATAR ASSR (TATARIA), Volga region, RSFSR; area 26,250 sq. mi.; pop. 2,850,000 (1959). Cities: Kazan (capital), Bugulma, Chistopol, Leninogorsk. The region was colonized by Bulgars in the 5th century B.C.; was overrun by Mongols in the 13th century; was a Tatar khanate after the 15th century; and conquered by Russia in 1552. Today the Russians are the second largest population group (41 per cent) next to the Tatars (50.4 per cent), a Mongol people of the Tatar-Turkic strain. Geographically, the territory extends along the middle course of the Volga and lower Kama, through a transition area between the forest zone and wooded steppe, in the black-earth belt. Mixed coniferous and deciduous groves on grey podsolic soils in the N. change to broad-leaved woods in the S.W. The right bank of the Volga forms part of the Volga upland; the left bank is an open hilly plain. Mineral resources include deposits of oil, gypsum, fuller's earth, bituminous sandstone, peat, lignite, oil shale, and phosphorites. In the agrarian areas basic grain cultures, technical crops (hemp, flax, sunflower, mustard), potato and truck farming are emphasized, with some fruit growing W. of the Volga. Livestock breeding, poultry, and fur farming (silver fox and raccoon) and bee-keeping are essential. Heavy industry includes oil extraction and refining, metalworking and machine building (diesel engines, agr. machinery, railway equipment), chemical processes, lumbering and woodworking, fur and hide processing, food ind., and light mfg. A network of railways and numerous cross-country highways suffice to handle ind. transportation. The region has a number of educational institutions, including a branch of the Ac. of S., USSR. Est. 1920.

TATES: *see* POPULATION.

TATÍSCHEV, Vasíly Nikítich (1686–1750), historian, administrator, and a veteran of Peter the Great's military campaigns. Encouraged by Peter, he became interested in R. history, discovered the ancient code known as *Russkaya Pravda* and other documents, and, in 1739, completed his *Russian History from Earliest Times.* He contradicted the emphasis by German scholars on the role of Norman element in the early development of Russia and insisted that autocracy has made an important contribution to Russia's greatness. His work inaugurated modern R. historiography.

TAVDÁ RIVER, flows from E. Urals through Sverdlovsk and Tyumen oblasts, left tributary of Tobol River; 435 mi. long; navigable. Timber and saw mills in area.

TAWGI: *see* NGANASANS.

TAXES: *see* BUDGET.

TAYGA: *see* GEOGRAPHICAL ZONES, PLANT LIFE.

TAYMÝR (DOLGANO-NENETS) NATIONAL OKRUG, in Krasnoyarsk Kray, N.E. Siberia, RSFSR; area 332,000 sq. mi.; pop. 34,000 (1959). Cities: Dudinka (adm. center), Norilsk, Nordvik, Dickson. Rivers: Lower Yenisey, Pyasina, Taymyra, Khatanga. Formerly it was the Dolgano-Nenets National Okrug (so named for the two Siberian tribes inhabiting the region). Geographically, lying beyond the Arctic Circle, it is largely coextensive with the Taymyr Peninsula washed by the Kara and Laptev seas. The hilly plains, walled off by the Byrranga range in the N., support a scant tundra vegetation. The mixed population includes Russians, Dolgans (of the Tungus family), Nenets (Samoyeds), Evenkis (Tungus), Yakuts and lesser native tribes. In recent years important mining centers have been developed (the Norilsk mines, and others) based on rich deposits of nickel, copper, platinum, coal, and petroleum (mainly in the Nordvik area). Agriculture is limited to truck farming, because of the severe climate. Reindeer herds, more recently dairy cattle, are raised, with hunting and fishing still the basic source of livelihood for the majority of natives. The Great Northern Sea Route runs along the Taymyr Peninsula coastal line, with Dick-

son and Nordvik the main shipping ports and points of supply. Severnaya Zemlya and a few small islands scattered in the Kara Sea are incorporated in the Okrug. Est. 1930.

TAYMÝR PENINSULA, extreme N. of Asia in Arctic Ocean, culminating in Chelyuskin Cape; includes Byrrana Mountains and Lake Taymyr; area 150,000 sq. mi.

TAZ RIVER, in Tyumen Oblast, N.W. Siberia, RSFSR; empties into Taz Gulf, Kara Sea; 600 mi. long.

TBILÍSI (f. Tiflis), capital of Georgian SSR; pop. 695,000 (1959). Ancient trading town on the historic route from Europe to Asia, dating from the 4th century B.C.; came permanently under R. domination in 1799. Today it is the second largest ind. and cultural center of Transcaucasia; situated astride the Kura River, at the intersection of Georgian Military Road and the Trans-Caucasian R.R. Is important producer of building materials, oil-drilling equipment, and road-construction machinery; manufactures silk fabrics, knitted goods, leather, clothing, and footwear; food-processing based on local products (tobacco and tea factories, distilleries). Known also as a resort, with warm sulfur springs in the vicinity of the city, is seat of the Georgian branch of Ac. of S., USSR; has a number of higher educational and specialized technical schools.

TCHAIKÓVSKY, Pyótr Ilyích (1840–1893), famous composer, born in Votkinsk, son of a mining engineer. T graduated from the aristocratic Law School, St. Petersburg, and joined the staff of the Ministry of Justice. At the age of 21, he entered the musical institute of Anton Rubinstein and became professor of harmony

at the Moscow Conservatoire in 1866. He met Balakirev, Stasov, and other leading musicians and obtained the support of Nadezhda von Meck, who, though never condescending to meet T, provided for him financially and otherwise for some 13 years. His marriage in 1877 to Antonina Milyukov was a failure, intensifying his inclination toward melancholy and introspection. In 1878 he retired from the conservatoire to devote himself entirely to composition. He also traveled abroad extensively. His work at first had greater success in foreign countries than in Russia. T visited the United States in 1891 and was given an enthusiastic reception.

Of T's six symphonies, the Sixth (or *Pathétique*) (1893) enjoys great popularity. Among his compositions for piano and orchestra, the concerto in B flat minor is frequently performed as is the concerto for violin and orchestra. T wrote several well-known ballets —*Swan Lake* (1876), *The Sleeping Beauty* (1890), and *Nutcracker* (1892). He composed eight operas, including *Eugene Onegin* (1877–78) and *Pique Dame* (1890); also chamber music, *Cappricio Italien,* and the overture *1812.*

T's popularity has remained high, particularly outside Russia. His great gift of melody is largely responsible for his success, although among critics the verdict has been much less favorable. It is perhaps in his orchestral works, especially in the Fifth and Sixth symphonies, that he attained the highest expression of his genius.

BIBLIOGRAPHY: P. I. Tchaikovsky, *Diaries*, New York, 1945; H. Weinstock, *Tchaikovsky*, New York, 1934; D. Brook, *Six Great Russian Composers*, London, 1946.

TCHEBYSHEFF: *see* CHEBYSHOV.

TEACHERS' TRAINING. Teacher seminars trained teachers of elementary schools in prerevolutionary Russia. They were inaugurated in 1784. In 1917 there were 170 teachers' seminars with 20,000 students.

Pedagogical schools are schools on the secondary level which train teachers for kindergartens and elementary schools, physical education instructors, leaders of *pioneers* (communist children's organization) and others. Graduation from an ordinary secondary school is the condition for admission.

Pedagogical institutes train teachers for the 5- and 7-year schools. They offer a two-year course. Graduation from ordinary secondary school or pedagogical school is the condition for admission. In recent years, pedagogical schools have virtually disappeared, and teachers are trained almost exclusively in the institutes or in universities. In 1956 there were 222 pedagogical institutes with over 700,000 students (including correspondence students); pedagogical schools had over 200,000 students in 1956.

The number of teachers has increased from 280,000 in 1917 to 1,800,000 in 1959–60 (in U.S., elementary and secondary school teachers, as of fall 1959: 2,607,-000).

TEBERDÁ RIVER, tributary of Kuban River, Caucasus, 37 mi. long.

TECHNICAL CROPS. Here belong crops used by industry as raw materials for production of food, textiles, rubber, and so on. A wide variety of such crops is grown in the USSR including cotton, sugar beets (the country's only source of sugar supply), oil-bearing crops, tobacco, hemp, flax, rubber-yielding crops such as kok-sagyz, medicinal crops used in pharmaceutical industry, and others. In view of the great variety of climate and soil conditions in the Soviet Union, the production of each of these crops is usually concentrated in a few areas in which it finds most favorable natural conditions; for example, cotton is grown mainly in Central Asia, the sugar beet in the Ukraine, flax in Central Russia. Soviet planners have, however, pursued the policy of extending TC beyond the traditional areas of cultivation. Some of these efforts were successful, for example, introduction of sugar beets into Central Asiatic republics. Others, like the attempts to grow cotton on non-irrigated lands, to cultivate sunflowers in areas with unsuitable climate and soil, to grow sugar beets on a large scale in the Altay region, have been costly and less successful. Some—such as cotton on non-irrigated lands—had to be abandoned.

Expansion of TC was one of the main goals of the early Five Year Plans in agriculture. Collectivization of agriculture enabled the government to compel the farmers to increase their plantings of TC quite drastically. Thus, the total area sown to TC, which amounted (in mill. acres) to 12.1 in 1913 (within present Soviet boundaries) and to 21.2 in 1928, rose to

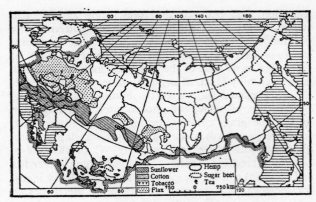

Areas under technical crops

as much as 36.8, or by 73 per cent, by 1932, reaching an acreage never again attained in the USSR. Yields were, however, very low and, as this was disappointing, the area sown to TC shrank somewhat in the late 1930's and then remained fairly stable: 29.1 mill. acres in 1940, 30.1 mill. in 1950, 31.1 mill. in 1959. (*See:* COTTON CROPS, FIBER CROPS, OIL-BEARING CROPS, SUGAR BEETS, TOBACCO.)

TECHNICAL SCIENCES. The remarkable expansion of Soviet technology and engineering had a sound foundation in its prerevolutionary progress represented by such names as B. S. Yakobi (1801–74), A. S. Popov (1859–1905), S. V. Lebedev (1874–1934) and many others active in the fields of electricity, mathematics, chemistry, physics, radio and communications, metallurgy, and mechanics. However, World War I followed by the revolution and civil war depleted the ranks of technologists, resulting in an acute shortage of trained engineers which noticeably affected progress in postrevolutionary years. The far-reaching educational reform of 1934 produced a new generation of scientists and technologists, and on the eve of World War II the level was back to normal. During the war over 600 research institutions were destroyed but postwar rehabilitation proceeded at a rapid pace. By 1960 Soviet science had reached an unprecedented height and great though uneven progress was made in various fields.

ELECTRICAL ENGINEERING. The advance of electrical engineering has been brought about by such distinguished scientists as I. Ye. Tamm, Ya. I. Frenkel, K. A. Krug, A. F. Ioffe, and V. K. Arkadyev. Electric power plant design was studied by R. E. Klasson and A. V. Winter. A. A. Gorev and A. M. Zalessky initiated the study of high-voltage technology at the High-Voltage Laboratory of the Ministry of Power Plants, the Moscow Institute of Energetics (MEI), the All-Union and the Leningrad Institutes of Electrical Engineering (under L. I. Sirotinsky and A. A. Smurov, respectively) and the Institute of Physical Technology and Physics, Ac. of S., USSR. In the 1930's K. A. Andrianov introduced insulating material made of polymer silicon compounds with a high molecular weight.

The calculation of short-circuit currents was carried out by N. N. Shchedrin and S. A. Ulyanov. The marked trend toward automation of electrical systems (A. M. Fedoseyev, I. I. Solovyov, R. A. Lyuter, A. Ye. Alekseyev) led to the large-scale introduction of automated electric drives in various branches of industry. Another achievement was the building of the Kuybyshev-Moscow alternate current line that transmits 1 million kw. at 400,000 volts over a distance of 560 mi. Much attention is given to the protection of power systems against lightning. At the present time, Soviet industry produces switching devices with a maximum of 400,000 volts.

HEAT-POWER ENGINEERING. Research in heat-power engineering is primarily concentrated at the All-Union Heat Engineering Institute (VTI), the Central Research Institute for Boilers and Turbines

(TsKTI), the Moscow Institute of Aviation (MAI), and at various universities and industrial laboratories. Problems concerned with heat transfer, high- and superhigh-pressure boilers, steam quality, and gradual vaporization are investigated (M. A. Mikheyev, E. I. Romm, G. Ye. Kholodovsky, L. K. Ramzin). The Soviet Union currently produces steam boilers with a productivity of 420 tons per hour (at the Taganrog Boiler Plant) and 300 tons per hour (at the Podolsk Plant); steam turbines made at the Leningrad Metallurgical Plant have a capacity of 200,000 kw. at 3,000 revolutions per minute.

HYDRO-ENGINEERING, HYDROLOGY, WATER RESOURCES

By combining the results of theoretical and practical experience, reconstruction projects of the Volga, Dnieper, Angara and Yenisey rivers have been completed for an efficient utilization of water resources. Spillway dams were built on the clayey and sandy grounds of Gorky, Kuybyshev, and Kakhovka. Research is conducted on soil mechanics. Modern methods of investigating the state of stress in concrete and other structures have gained wide applications (B. G. Galyorkin, N. M. Gersevanov and V. A. Florin). Various aspects of filtration have been extensively studied by N. N. Pavlovsky, O. Ya. Kochina, and L. S. Leybenzon. In the past decade, the efforts of Soviet experts have been directed toward the study of laws governing the variations in river flow, waterways formation, and regional hydrology. Control and utilization of river flows proved to be a major factor in the building of large reservoirs and powerful hydro-electric plants. The scope of work carried out in 1956 is reflected in the following figures: 5,258 million cubic ft. of earth were subjected to excavation; 320,000 tons of metal and 250,000 tons of assembled reinforced concrete were used as well as 388 million cubic ft. of gravel and sand. The trend toward the building of high dams is shown in Bratsk (443 ft.) and Krasnoyarsk (over 330 ft.).

MACHINE CONSTRUCTION.

The research of the 1930's was centered upon the theory of structure and kinematics of mechanisms, the theory of gear and cam mechanisms (V. A. Gavrilenko, A. N. Kaluzhnikov), computing machines and precision instruments (N. G. Bruyevich, S. A. Gershgorin).

The theory of friction was developed by N. I. Mertsalov, B. V. Deryagin, I. V. Kragelsky, and P. A. Rebinder. Examination of microhardness and microroughness was introduced by M. M. Khrushchov and V. P. Linnik. Investigations of the resistance to brittle and fatigue fractures proved effective in determining the load capacity of machine parts. Increase of strength in areas of stress concentration was achieved by I. V. Kudryavtsev with the help of work hardening and heat treatment. A. A. Blagonravov and A. I. Petrusevich were engaged in developing improved methods of calculation of machine parts with respect to strength, rigidity, and vibration. Extensive research evolves around such subjects as the theory and design of internal combustion engines, jets, steam and hydraulic turbines, farming, mining, metallurgical, road building, textile, and other machinery.

MECHANICS.

The general theory of the stability of motion in mechanical systems was applied to airplane construction and ballistics in the 1920's (A. M. Lyapunov). The theory of nonlinear, forced, and self-induced vibrations of systems with elastic joints in fluid and gas flow (A. N. Krylov, M. V. Keldysh) and the applied theory of gyroscopes (Ye. L. Nikolai, B. V. Bulgakov, A. Yu. Ishlinsky) were investigated. The basis for the development of jet engine design was laid before the revolution by K. E. Tsiolkovsky and I. V. Meshchersky. N. Ye Zhukovsky and S. A. Chaplygin, founders of the science of aerohydrodynamics in the Soviet Union, developed the design and calculation of the airplane propeller in cooperation with V. P. Vetchinkin (1926). The development of gas dynamics has greatly influenced high-speed aviation and rocketry (S. A. Chaplygin, L. S. Leybenzon, N. A. Slezkin). The theory of flow at subsonic and supersonic speeds was advanced by F. I. Frenkel and A. A. Nikolsky. L. I. Sedov proposed the theory of explosion in gas medium. A. I. Nekrasov's generalized theory of the motion of bodies in fluid led to the development of the theory of a boundary layer (N. Ye. Kochin, I. A. Kibel, A. A. Dorodnitsyn). In the past decade a new branch of hydrodynamics concerned with problems of take-off and landing of hydroplanes and increase of speed has been given particular attention. The outstanding work of A. N. Tupolev, A. I. Mikoyan, S. V. Ilyushin, and A. S. Yakovlev has greatly advanced aviation and rocketry. Research is conducted at the Central Aerohydrodynamic Institute (TsAGI) founded upon the initiative of S. A. Chaplygin.

POWER-ENGINEERING.

The incorporation of regional power plants operating on local fuel and water resources into over-all high-power systems was initiated by G. M. Krzhizhanovsky in the prerevolutionary period. His ideas, reflected in the State Plan of Electrification (GOELRO), were elaborated by the Institute of Power Engineering, Ac. of S., USSR. In the 1930's a systematic study of theoretical and applied power engineering was launched (V. I. Veyts, S. A. Kukel-Krayevsky, B. V. Vedeyev, V. V. Bolotov). After World War II research was directed toward the creation of a sole Soviet power system. Investigations are conducted at the All-Union State Institute for the Design and Planning of Power Plants and other scientific

organizations. The Soviet Union is second in the world production of electric power (265,112 mill. kw-hrs in 1959). Over 40 hydro-electric power plants producing 65 per cent of the total power are operated by remote control. (*See also:* AUTOMATION, CHEMICAL INDUSTRY, CHEMISTRY, ELECTRIC POWER STATIONS, ELECTRONICS, MACHINE MAKING INDUSTRY, METALLURGY, PHYSICS, ROCKETRY, SCIENCE, TECHNOLOGY).

S. S.; T. D.

TECHNIKUM: *see* EDUCATION.

TECHNOLOGY. The Soviets consistently emphasize the importance of T in building the socialist state; they follow the R. tradition of state support of scientific development and the 19th-century western tradition which links social and technical progress. But because of their limited resources, in funds and in trained personnel, they have concentrated their efforts in those few fields which are essential to the build-up of their industrial base and of military and economic power. This gives their technological progress spectrum a characteristically uneven appearance. Technological policy decisions generally consist of selecting for development the phenomena which promise the greatest improvement in the operation of society. Such choices require a knowledge of science and a set of standards to make social value judgments. The groups which make these decisions in the USSR include scientists and engineers and also party and government officials; because of the ideological motivation of Soviet society, the major goals are set by the party leadership.

The responsibility for technical decisions rests on three institutions. (1) The Ac. of S. of the USSR and, incidentally, the other academies (of Medical Sciences, of Architecture and Construction, of the constituent republics, and so on) plan and carry out basic research and make recommendations for long-range technical development; they also participate in the development of certain key fields of great complexity (rocketry, automatic controls for guidance and for automation, and others). (2) The Gosplan of the USSR and the Gosplans of the constituent republics allocate technical development funds to industries and other institutions. The Gosplan of the USSR administers several large development laboratories in fields important to the entire economy: production methods (machine tools, heavy machinery); power generation (turbines, electric power stations) and major industrial components (automotive and tractor power plants; electric conductors and insulators). The republic Gosplans and the local economic councils administer laboratories which develop lower-priority and consumer goods (construction materials, textiles, processed foods). (3) In certain key fields, ministries and ministry-level councils control research, development, and design. By far the most important of these is weapon design, which is assigned to the Defense and Defense Production ministries, the Council for Aircraft Production, and several others. The chemical industry, communications, transport, shipping, and public health are administered in a similar way.

Formal decisions on major investments are made by the Council of Ministers and the Presidium of the Central Committee of the CP (the memberships of these two bodies largely overlap). To help them reach a decision, the Council of Ministers has the advice, not only of the institutions just discussed, but of a State Committee on New Technology composed partly of scientists and engineers and partly of party leaders and administrators. Often the formal decision merely gives the highest sanction (especially needed in a dictatorship) to a decision reached at a lower level. But some important technical issues are decided at the top; and technical factors have carried greater weight with Soviet leaders than with those of the West. This reflected the earlier stage of Soviet development and the stress laid on power by Soviet leaders; power depends on the availability and performance of hardware more than on the efficiency of its production. As the economy matures, greater emphasis is placed on economic factors.

To appreciate the method of operation of the Soviet technical leadership, one must remember two important administrative practices. *Sovmestitelstvo* is multiple jobholding. Although persistently criticized in the Soviet press and legislated against, it is an indispensable channel of communication and an informal method of concentrating authority in the hands of relatively few able people. For example, over a third of the members of the Division of Technical Sciences of the Ac. of S. of the USSR also hold flag commissions in the engineering and technical services of the armed forces, and several are simultaneously senior designers and professors in engineering schools. *Yedino-nachalstvo* is single responsibility for a given task. Major technical problems are generally assigned to task forces assembled for that purpose; often the personnel is drawn from several sources and sometimes parts of the job are subcontracted to various laboratories. A pattern of successive dashes to fairly short-range specific goals results. The assignment of responsibility for specific tasks helps identify the ablest people; it also induces a conservative design policy calculated to minimize the probability of failure; for example, the development of a high-speed fighter aircraft from 1948 to 1957 proceeded in four small steps (MIG–15, MIG–17, MIG–19, and "Super Farmer"), while the United States made a similar advance in a single large step which took almost as long to carry out (from the F-86 to the "Century" series).

Development of advanced components is done directly in institutes and laboratories of the academies (for example, in automatic controls). Development of prototypes is done in large industrial research institutes administered either by Gosplan or by a specific industry; most of these consist of laboratories and of a pilot plant where prototypes are built and tested (tractors, turbines, machine tools, steel processing). For very complex hardware such as aircraft, the development work is assigned to large laboratories similar to those of the National Aeronautics and Space Administration (TsAGI, TsIAM, and others). The prototypes are designed by teams led by a chief designer (Tupolev, Yakovlev, Mikoyan) who also directs a pilot plant for their construction. A similar pattern applies to advanced communications equipment. Large-scale production of any approved prototype (car, tractor, aircraft, radio) is then assigned to factories responsible to local economic councils. Compare the United States wartime production of the Consolidated B-24 bomber at the Douglas Tulsa plant and the Ford Willow Run plant.

The scope and distribution of the Soviet development program are illustrated in the three attached tables. The first gives the distribution of engineers and scientists in the United States and the USSR according to the nature of their work. It shows that in the USSR the engineering personnel is more heavily engaged in keeping the industrial machine running than in the United States (63 per cent of the total force against 53 per cent, and a total of 820,000 engineers compared to 560,000 in the United States). This is because the Soviet labor force has not reached the sophistication of labor in the United States and needs closer professional supervision, and because many administrative tasks best handled by non-engineers in American society are entrusted to engineers in the USSR. On the other hand, the USSR and the United States have invested essentially equal pools of professional manpower (500,000 engineers and scientists) into new technology in rather different ways. The Soviets have made a large commitment to education and basic research (double the United States; 40 per cent of the total) in the hope of maintaining a large flow of new ideas and people to maintain a rapid rate of technical improvement. The United States has made a large commitment to product development to bring a wide, attractive assortment of products to the market.

TABLE A
TECHNICAL PROFESSIONAL PERSONNEL EMPLOYED
IN VARIOUS ACTIVITIES, 1959
UNITED STATES AND THE SOVIET UNION

	U.S.		USSR	
	Total	%	Total	%
Teaching of Science and Engineering	40,000	3.8	70,000	5.4
Research (Basic and Applied)	60,000	5.7	140,000	10.8
Development	300,000	28.3	100,000	7.7
Design	100,000	9.4	170,000	13.1
Production	200,000	18.9	260,000	20.0
Distribution, Service and Operation	180,000	17.0	200,000	15.4
Administration	80,000	7.5	180,000	13.8
Military Service	100,000	9.4	180,000	13.8
TOTAL	1,060,000	100.0	1,300,000	100.0

TABLE B
DEVELOPMENT BUDGET
SOVIET UNION AND UNITED STATES

	SOVIET UNION		UNITED STATES			
	1959		1956		1959 (est.)	
	Billion Rubles	Per Cent	Million Dollars	Per Cent	Million Dollars	Per Cent
Machinery	2.06	9	800	10	1,870	11
Food	.54	2	76	1	135	1
Public Health	.69	3	350	4	600	3
Chemical, Rubber, and Petroleum	1.54	7	884	11	1,710	10
Construction and Transportation	1.15	5	325	4	545	3
Power & Communications	1.35	6	750	9	1,500	8
Aircraft and Weapons	14.72	62	3,880	49	10,300	57
Precision & Computational Machinery	.72	3	273	4	540	3
Other	.69	3	600	8	800	4
Development Total	23.46	100	7,938	100	18,000	100
Basic Research	5.12				865	
TOTAL R & D	28.58				18,865	

TABLE C
SOVIET RESEARCH AND DEVELOPMENT (1959)

		TOTAL OUTLAY Bill. Rubles	Number of Institutes	Scientists & Engineers (Thousands)	Scientists & Engineers per Institute	Cost per Scientist Thous. R.
BASIC RESEARCH	Academy of Sciences, USSR	2.69	195	17.6	90	153
	Other USSR Academies: Archit. & Const.; Med. Sc.; Agric.; Arts	.92	218	7.2	33	128
	Republican Ac. of Sc.; Pedag. Sc.; Comm. Econ.; UkSSR Constr.	1.02	325	12.4	38	82
	Institutions of Higher Education (VUZY)	.49		7.9		62
	TOTAL, BASIC RESEARCH	**5.12**	**738**	**45.1**	**51**	**114**
MAJOR CIVILIAN APPLIED RESEARCH AND DEVELOPMENT — USSR	Gosplan, USSR	2.40	30	12.0	400	200
	Major Industries (Chemical, Transportation, Communic.)	1.40	35	7.0	200	200
	Food Production and Processing	.18	20	1.5	75	120
	Public Health	.38	18	2.4	133	160
	Standards, Weather, Natural Resources	.20	12	1.0	83	200
	Cultural Activities (Museums, etc.)	.05	15	1.0	67	50
	Institutions of Higher Education (VUZY)	.70		12.0		58
Republics	Gosplan	.68	30	4.5	150	150
	Major Industry	.12	10	1.0	100	120
	Sovnarkhoz	.12	50	2.0	40	60
	Public Health and Social Security	.24	32	2.0	63	120
	Institutions of Higher Education, Ukrainian SSR	.07		1.3		54
	TOTAL, CIVILIAN APPLIED RESEARCH	**6.54**	**252***	**47.7**	**136**	**137**
MILITARY R&D (including OKB)	Ministry of Aircraft Production	} 13.82	16	4.0	} 250	425
	General Machine Construction (Atomic Laboratories)		4	1.0		
	Defense and Defense Production		90	22.5		
	Radio Technology		10	2.5		
	Naval Construction		10	2.5		
	Institutions of Higher Education (VUZY)	.80		5.0		160
	TOTAL, MILITARY R&D	**14.62**	**130@**	**37.5**	**250**	**390**
OTHER R&D	Testing and Minor Research: Construction, Agriculture, Prospecting, Design of Consumer Goods, Research at Plants	2.30	2000	28.0	14	82
	TOTAL: (1) RESEARCH INSTITUTES	**26.52**	**3120**	**132.1******	**42**	**201**
	(2) INSTITUTIONS OF HIGHER EDUCATION	**2.06**		**26.2**		**79**
	GRAND TOTAL	**28.58**		**158.3**		**180**

* 108 Institutes in this category (identified in *Aspirantura*) are located in Moscow.
** Of this number approximately 10,000 are in industry.
@ Estimated at twice the number of institutes listed in *Vysshaya shkola*.

An estimated breakdown of the development budget in the USSR for 1959 and the United States for 1956 and 1959 is shown in Table B. The total expenditures are difficult to compare because of the uncertainty in the dollar value of the ruble and because of the distorted Soviet price pattern. For the purchase of consumer goods, the 1959 ruble may be worth ten cents; but, for the purchase of professional time and laboratory equipment by the state, it may be worth a quarter; on that basis, the Soviet research and development investment represents a fraction of gross national product comparable to that of the United States, between 3.5 and 4 per cent. The distribution of investment among various fields is strikingly similar in the two societies; well over half is devoted to the development of new weapons. There are a few minor differences: greater effort in communications in the United States and in power and construction in the USSR; and, in the category "machinery," more Soviet attention to machine tools and United States attention to automotive equipment. But Table B reflects the needs of a modern industrial society in the cold war, which are independent of social system.

Table C analyzes the Soviet 1959 research and development budget, showing both sponsors and performers. The Soviet federal budget consists of an "open" or itemized section which is devoted to basic (academy) research and of a "closed" applied research section for which only totals are published and breakdown is inferred. In addition, the Ministry of Higher Education has a research budget for programs at institutions of higher learning. The budgets of the constituent republics have itemized allocations for basic and applied research. Finally, some 15 per cent of the research and development budget consists of programs contracted to engineering schools and research institutes by industrial enterprises. In general, the cost of basic research is roughly twice the total payroll; development work costs four times the total payroll, and military development and testing cost seven times the total payroll. These cost ratios are very similar in the United States and the USSR, thus reflecting again the uniform nature of the technology required by a modern industrial state.

The picture of Soviet technology which emerges from this discussion displays many features characteristic of modern industrial society, and some which reflect Soviet conditions and values. The scale of the Soviet technological effort, measured by professional personnel and by fraction of gross national product allotted, is comparable to that of the United States. The distribution of effort reflects the technical nature of the various segments of the economy more than the social system. But the USSR has only recently become a major industrial power; a sizable fraction of its labor force is relatively new; Soviet youth is less exposed to machinery than American youth and less familiar with its quirks; and, at present, there is a need for more formally trained production supervisory personnel. The Soviets have made an unusually heavy investment in technical professional education and in the area between basic research and product development which allows rapid exploitation of break-throughs. That is the extension to research of the policy of stressing producers' goods which is characteristic of the Soviets' economic planning; it maximizes the probability of high forward momentum, and places state power ahead of satisfying consumer wants. As a result, there has been a chronic shortage of design talent and resources for product development; and, because the consumer could not make his wants heard, a strict priority system has favored military and industrial products. The performance, reliability, and sophistication of important hardware (aircraft, tanks, rockets, machine tools, control equipment, power generation equipment) are up to contemporary standards. But there is no effort to seek alternatives to compete in the consumer market, where a barely adequate product is good enough. As the Soviet economy matures, as consumer demand becomes more articulate, and as the supply of designers increases, it may become easier for Soviet technology to diversify its activities and make original design contributions in all areas without appreciable decrease in priority commitments. Possibly this increased freedom in choosing directions of technological development is one of the differences between the Stalin era and the present era.

BIBLIOGRAPHY: *Expenses on Social-Cultural Activities in the State Budget of the USSR*, Moscow, 1958; *The National Economy of the USSR*, Moscow, 1956; N. deWitt, *Soviet Professional Manpower*, National Science Foundation, Washington, D.C., 1955; A. G. Korol, *Soviet Education for Science and Technology*, New York, 1957; L. Trilling, *Research and Development in the USSR*, Massachusetts Institute of Technology, Cambridge, Mass., 1960.   L. T.

TEFFI (Nadézhda Aleksándrovna Lokhvítskaya) (1875–1952), writer. Popular in prerevolutionary Russia as a humorist, journalist, and lyrical poetess. After the revolution settled in Paris where she published short stories and humorous articles including *The Quiet Star* (1921), *Little Town* (1927), *The Witch* (1936).

TEHERAN CONFERENCE (Nov. 28 — Dec. 1, 1943). Stalin, Roosevelt, and Churchill met to strengthen Allied cooperation in the war against Germany. Stalin persuaded his allies to forego Churchill's idea of an Anglo-American invasion of the Balkans in favor of an assault on France. The Curzon Line was made the basis of a new Soviet-Polish frontier, a substantial territorial gain for the USSR. All powers joined in guaranteeing Iran's national rights, but plans for post-war Germany were barely touched on. The conference adjourned amid pledges of friendship and determination to press the war effort to a victorious conclusion.

TELEMECHANICS: *see* AUTOMATION.

TELEPHONE AND TELEGRAPH. The number of intercity telephone conversations in the USSR rose from 15 to 92 mill. between 1928 and 1940, a more than sixfold rise, according to Soviet records. By 1959, the total had risen to 172 mill. In 1959 there were almost 2.51 mill. telephones available, of which 380,000 were in rural areas. Five-sixths of the collective farms had a telephone, as did almost all state farms and rural government units. The 2,130,000 phones in cities were available for just under 100 mill. urban residents. Telephone directories could be consulted at main post offices, and phone numbers for properly identified individuals could be obtained from "Information."

Telegraph service, already available before the First World War, expanded substantially during the interwar period, to handle over 141 mill. telegrams in 1940. By 1959 the level had reached 230 mill. telegrams per year, or more than one per person for the total Soviet pop. of 209 mill.

The first long-distance telephone line (Moscow-Leningrad) was installed in 1922. The use of frequency converters (M. V. Shuleykin), telephone and telegraph transmission (V. V. Kovalenkov, M. Yu. Yuryev) combined with extensive research (P. V. Shmakov, P. A. Azbukin) contributed to the development of Soviet industry which has been manufacturing high-frequency communication equipment since 1925–26.

TÉLESHOV, Nikoláy Dmítrievich (1867–1945), radical writer, author of *Beyond the Urals* (1897), a volume which deals with Siberian settlers. T wrote other stories in a realistic vein. With Gorky, Chekhov, and others, he was one of the founders of the literary circle "Sredá" in the early 1900's. In 1943, T published his literary memoirs, *Notes of a Writer*.

TELÉTSKOYE LAKE, tourist center in Altay, fed by 70 rivers, source of Biya River; altitude 1,400 ft.

TELEVISION RECEIVERS: *see* ELECTRONICS.

TEMÍR-TÁU (f. Samarkandsky), town in Karaganda Oblast, Kazakh SSR; pop. increased more than tenfold, from 5,000 (1939) to 54,000 (1959). Foundry, synthetic rubber.

TÉREK RIVER, flows from Greater Caucasus Mountains, through Daryal Gorge and steppe into N.W. Caspian Sea; 370 mi. long.

TERÉNIN, Aleksándr Nikoláyevich (1896–), physical chemist. Fellow, Ac. of S., USSR (1939). Graduate (1921) and professor (1932) of Leningrad University. Research concerns the nature of physical and chemical processes as stimulated by light, spectroscopy and photometry of luminescent compounds, methods to bring about the emission of spectral lines in metallic atoms in the gaseous state, energy distribution in electron shells, splitting of gaseous salt molecules under the action of light, methods of splitting molecules to multiatom molecules under ultraviolet radiation. Expounded the nature of the phosphorescence of molecules of complex organic compounds and dyes. Author of *Photochemistry of Salt Vapors* (1934) and *Photochemical Processes in Aromatic Compounds* (1944). Stalin prize (1946); S. I. Vavilov medal of the Ac. of S. (1953).

TERÉSCHENKO, Mikhaíl Ivánovich (1884–1956), born into a rich family of sugar manufacturers. A man of liberal views, T was president of the Kiev regional War Industries Committee during World War I. After the February revolution was appointed minister of finance. Later, when P. N. Milyukov was forced to resign, he became minister of foreign affairs. After the October revolution, T emigrated.

TÉRIOKI: *see* ZELENOGORSK.

TERMÉZ, city, adm. center of Surkhan-Darya Oblast; pop. 22,000 (1959). Cotton-ginning, metalworking, food-processing center, on Amu Darya River and Kagan–Stalinabad R.R.; ancient city, with historical monuments.

TERNÓPOL (TARNOPOL), city, adm. center of Ternopol Oblast, on Seret River; pop. 52,000 (1959). Manufactures farm implements, clothing, lumber, cement; R.R. junction.

TERNÓPOL OBLAST, Ukrainian SSR, W. sector; formerly Tarnopol province of Poland; area 5,530 sq. mi.; pop. 1,086,000 (1959). Cities: Ternopol (adm. center), Zborov, Kremenets. Undulating plains on Volyn-Podolian upland, dissected by left affluents of Dniester, in the black-earth belt and subzone of broad-leaved forests; has moderate continental climate. Predominantly agr., with winter wheat, sunflowers, sugar beets, hemp, and tobacco as the principal crops; dairy and meat cattle raised; peat works, chalk, building-stone quarries; flour-milling equipment, cement and ceramics produced at Kremenets city. Annexed by R. and est. 1939.

TER-PETROSYAN: *see* KAMO.

TÉTEREV RIVER, in Zhitomir and Kiev oblasts, right tributary of Dnieper; about 240 mi. long. Navigable in its lower course, with Korostyshev and Zhitomir cities on its banks.

TETYÁYEV, Mikhaíl Mikháylovich (1882–1956), geologist. Graduate, Liège University (1912); professor, Leningrad University and the Institute of Mines (1930). Explored Transbaykalia, the Irkutsk basin, and other regions. Developed the theory on the forms of tectonic movements, the effects of oscillations on the formation of the structure of the earth, lamination, and geosynclines. One of the first to outline a geotectonic zoning of the USSR. Author of *Geotectonics of the USSR* (1938).

TEVOSYÁN, Iván Fyódorovich (1902–1958), Soviet state and party official. Graduate of a mining academy. Member of the CP after 1918. During the revolution, T fought for the establishment of a Bolshevik regime in Azerbaijan. In 1939–40, he was people's commissar of shipbuilding industry; 1940–48, minister of metallurgical industry. From 1949, deputy chairman of the Council of Ministers USSR and simultaneously minister of ferrous metallurgy. T was a member of the Central Committee of the CPSU. Recipient of various awards.

TEXTILE INDUSTRY: 6,455 mill. running meters of cotton fabrics, 340 mill. meters of woolen fabrics, 558 mill. meters of linen fabrics, and 1,515 mill. meters of silk fabrics were produced in 1960. (The United States in 1959: 8,770 mill. meters of cotton fabrics, and 284 mill. meters of woolen fabrics; the United Kingdom: 1,223 mill. sq. meters of cotton fabrics, and 305 mill. sq. meters of woolen fabrics.)

The first enterprises producing textiles were established in the 17th century. During the 18th century the production of linen cloth and of wool cloth increased rapidly in connection with a large naval and military

demand. It was not until the social reforms of 1861, however, that the production of cotton cloth and the employment of steam-powered machinery became important. In 1913, nevertheless, hand labor generally continued to prevail, while the necessary equipment, the dyes, and about half of the raw materials continued to be imported from other countries.

Although the further development of the TI was appreciable during the First Five Year Plan (1928–32) and especially during the Second (1933–37), it was subordinated, throughout the entire period that preceded World War II, to a policy that gave the highest priorities to investments in the sphere of industrial and military equipment. According to official data, the production of cotton cloth increased by only one third (to 3,954 mill. meters), from 1928 to 1940; that of wool cloth by one fourth (to 120 mill. meters); and that of linen cloth by one third (to 286 mill. meters).

This level of production was approximately the same ten years later, at the time of the completion of the postwar program of reconstruction. It began to increase substantially, however, after the adoption in 1953 of a general policy directed at increasing the production of consumers' goods.

The objectives of the Seven Year Plan provide for the production of 7.7–8.0 bill. meters of cotton fabrics, 500 mill. meters of woolen fabrics, 635 mill. meters of linen fabrics, and 1.5 bill. meters of silk fabrics. It is expected that the construction of a large number of new plants and the modernization of existing ones (at a rate of 925,000 new spindles and 21,500 looms each year) will increase the productive capacity of the TI during this period by more than 50 per cent, or by approximately as much as in the preceding 20 years.

PRODUCTION OF TEXTILES IN USSR
(bill. running meters)

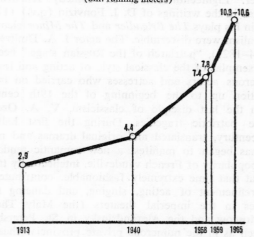

Year	Cotton yarn (th. tons)	Cotton cloth (mill. m.)	Wool cloth (mill. m.)	Linen cloth (mill. m.)	Silk cloth (mill. m.)
1913	223	2,582	103.0	120.0	42.6
1928	208	2,678	86.8	174.4	9.6
1940	849	3,954	119.7	285.5	76.6
1950	953	3,899	155.2	282.2	129.7
1958	1,480	5,800	303	481	845
1959	—	6,148	327	526	800
1960	—	6,455	340	558	1,515
1965 (pl.)		7.7–8.0 bill. m.	500	635	1,485 P.I.M.

THEATER. Several centuries before its actual appearance, the theater in Russia was foreshadowed by ancient folk traditions including dramatized games, songs and dances connected with pagan religious rites, work patterns, and folkways.

Historical data are available from the 11th century concerning the traveling mummers or *skomorokhi*, against whom the Eastern Orthodox Church waged unceasing warfare up to the 17th century. At about that time expanding W. influences brought about the first experiment in organizing a Court theater and also led to the establishment of student theatricals in the theological seminaries. These productions were similar in nature and repertory to the mystery, miracle, and morality plays of W. Europe.

As a result of the radical reforms of Peter I, itinerant bands of foreign actors with secular repertories appeared in Russia at the beginning of the 18th century, and by mid-century, in the reigns of Elizabeth and Catherine II, professional opera-ballet-drama theaters had sprung up side by side with amateur groups. Endowed with remarkable natural talents, the merchant Fyodor Volkov (1728–63) is considered the "father of the Russian theater": his provincial troupe achieved official Court status, performing not only translated works but also original tragedies and comedies; the most notable playwright was the theater director, A. P. Sumarokov (1717–77), "the Russian Racine" to his contemporaries. Sumarokov strengthened the influence of French classicism in the Russian theater. The manner of acting was declamatory and rhetorical. Toward the end of the century a number of dramatists appeared, the trend toward satire was intensified, comic operas for the first time touched on the peasantry as subject matter. Eighteenth-century R. comedy reached its apogee in the writings of D. I. Fonvizin (q.v.) (1745–92); in his plays *The Brigadier* and *The Minor* elements of realism were discernible. The actor I. A. Dmitrevsky (1734–1821), "patriarch of the Russian stage," became an exemplar of the classical style of acting and trained numerous actors and actresses who carried on in his tradition up to the beginning of the 19th century, when the last disciple of classicism, V. A. Ozerov, wrote patriotic tragedies. During the first half of the century, translated and original dramas and melodramas began to manifest a new romantic tendency; the popularity of French vaudeville, intellectually trivial but at that time extremely fashionable, contributed to the refinement of acting, singing, and dancing techniques in the imperial theaters (the Maly Theater in Moscow and the Alexandrinsky in St. Petersburg) as well as in the numerous private provincial theaters, some of which were owned by aristocratic patrons who created entire troupes of serf actors. During the second third of the century, dramatic troupes were definitively separated from opera-ballet groups.

The innovations of the great writers A. S. Griboyedov (1795–1829), whose comedy *The Misfortune of Being Wise* (also known as *Woe from Wit*) was completed in 1824, A. S. Pushkin (1799–1837), whose tragedy *Boris Godunov* was written in 1825, and M. V. Lermontov, whose tragedy *Masquerade* was completed in 1835, further added to the national repertory.

The greatest realistic playwright at mid-century was N. V. Gogol (1809–52). His brilliant and powerful satires directed at the bureaucratic regime of Nicholas I, the comedies *The Inspector-General* (1836) and *The Wedding* (1842), were a turning point in the evolution of the R. stage, demanding of their performers a technical mastery, naturalness, and depth that were realized in the Maly Theater under the direction of the great actor and former serf M. S. Shchepkin (1788–1863). It is from Shchepkin that the main line of R. psychological realism should be traced, the inner identification of actor with character which reached its highest degree of theoretical development and practical expression in the Moscow Art Theater at the turn of the 20th century. Worthy of note also are Shchepkin's contemporaries, the actors P. Mochalov and V. Karatygin.

The next important period in the evolution of the T is exemplified in the work of A. N. Ostrovsky (1823–36), who wrote more than fifty plays and was known as the "Columbus of the Muscovite Merchant," i.e., who revealed the world of the provincial merchant class—for example in his plays *Birds of a Feather* (1850) and *Storm* (1859). He also portrayed the lives of civil servants, aristocrats, actors; notable are his historical dramas containing elements of R. folklore. His vivid language, masterful dialogue, and complex characterizations stimulated the development of acting technique, to which the remarkable realistic actor of the Maly Theater, P. M. Sadovsky, and his company also made a notable contribution.

Toward the last quarter of the 19th century, the monopoly of the imperial theaters was broken by several progressive private theatrical enterprises which successfully combated a tendency to routinism. As a by-product of reactionary trends of government during the 80's and 90's, the Maly and Alexandrinsky theaters had markedly lowered their intellectual and artistic standards; such brilliant actors and actresses as V. Davydov, G. Fedotova, A. Lensky, K. Rybakov, M. Savina, the Sadovsky family, P. Strepetova, K. Varlamov, M. Yermolova, and A. Yuzhin-Sumbatov had frequently had to take part in mediocre plays, poorly directed and staged.

Fresh trends appeared in the private theatrical enterprises of Brenko, Korsh, Sinelnikov, Sobolshchikov-Samarin, and Solovtsov and in the operatic T of Mamontov. The plays of Leo Tolstoy and Anton Chekhov in the latter part of the century demanded the greatest subtlety of interpretation, which was realized in the Moscow Art Theater (MKhT), founded in 1898 by K. S. Stanislavsky and Vl. I. Nemirovich-Danchenko. This world-famous group became an exemplar of theatrical achievement in foreign countries as well as in Russia.

The MKhT went through several phases in its quest for style and repertory: from naturalism through impressionism and symbolism (e.g., in the plays of Leonid Andreyev) to psychological realism; its excellent company, including A. Artyom, V. Kachalov, O. Knipper, L. Leonidov, M. Lilina, V. Luzhsky, I. Moskvin, and many others, was particularly successful in the "mood plays" of Chekhov, Gorky, Ibsen, Turgenev, and Dostoyevsky. Their prolonged experimentation led to the crystallization (in the Soviet period) of the highly prized "Stanislavsky method" and its principle of psychological identification by which the actor strives to *become* the character whose part he is playing; elements of this method had first been developed by Shchepkin and his successors. From 1913 on, studios began to form within the MKhT, some of which later became independent theaters. In some cases identifying themselves with MKhT, in others contending against its methods, several outstanding directors moved to the fore at the beginning of the 20th century: V. E. Meyerhold, who later followed a complex and self-contradictory road from "conditional" T (in collaboration with the noted actress V. Komissarzhevskaya) to constructivism in the early Soviet period; Ye. B. Vakhtangov, creator of so-called "fantastic realism," close in spirit to the *commedia dell'arte;* N. N. Yevreinov, who from 1909 on was a passionate advocate of sheer spectacle ("theater of make-believe") and opponent of psychological realism (T in which the actor "relives" the experiences of the character portrayed by him). In 1914, the director A. Ya. Tairov opened the Kamerny Theater, whose aesthetic gropings also took the direction of "theater of make-believe," in which the actors were subjected to the dictatorial ideas of an overfastidious director in love with music and the melody of speech. The natural development of the various competing tendencies within the T gave promise of even greater achievements, but was abruptly halted by the revolutionary events of 1917.

Soviet Period. At the very outset of the Soviet regime the T, recognized as a powerful instrument of mass agitation and propaganda, attracted the close attention of the Communist party and the government: a series of party decisions, beginning in Feb. 1918, nationalized all theaters throughout the country and placed them under the control of TEO (Theater Dept.) of the Narkompros (People's Commissariat of Education) and, in the 30's, under the supervision of the Dept. of the Arts. Even during the period of civil war (1918–21) and the years of general collapse, theaters actually increased in number. All the old imperial theaters, as well as the MKhT and the Kamerny, were preserved and designated model academic theaters. Side by side with them arose new ones, not always long-lived—some under the aegis of local Soviet organs, others supported by the trade unions. Later, specialized theaters made their appearance: for children, for youth, for the Red Army, the peasants, and so forth.

In the early years an ideological resistance grew up within the academic theaters, which had held their repertories to the classics of R. and foreign drama. Meyerhold, who had become a CP member and who at first headed TEO, proclaimed a "Theatrical October" —a movement striving to tear down old conventions and to experiment in new forms (synthesis of T, circus, and music hall) and the new biomechanistic system of

acting (the earliest experiment in which was his convention-shattering production of Mayakovsky's *Mystery-Bouffe* in 1918). The staging of mass revolutionary pantomimes involving thousands of participants; a crude, slogan-infested music hall program for Red Army men at the front and in the rear; a host of amateur groups (the "Blue Blouses") using rudimentary scripts—these were the typical categories of Soviet T up to the 20's. In the NEP period, during the mid- and late 20's, the plays of Gorky and of new Soviet playwrights—A. Lunacharsky, V. Bill-Belotserkovsky, B. Romashov, V. Ivanov, K. Trenev—based on historical, revolutionary, and contemporary themes, were given with great frequency. Of the many new theaters, the following deserve mention: the Vakhtangov Theater (1922); the Leningrad Great State Drama Theater (BGDT), founded by a group including Maksim Gorky, Aleksandr Blok, and the actors N. Monakhov and Y. Yuryev in 1918; the Second Moscow Art Theater (MKhAT), directed by the actor M. A. Chekhov, who later emigrated to the United States; and the Meyerhold Theater (1920). In these, for a period of ten years, full-blooded creative activity was going on: the search for new forms, at times too eccentric (up to the point of eliminating the stage entirely as the acting area); the reworking of classical texts and their presentation in modern dress; the enthusiasm for W. expressionism.

Although these expressions often showed originality and talent, they found no response or support among party critics and leaders, and even the liberal Commissar of Education Lunacharsky in 1923 called the theaters "back to Ostrovsky," i.e., back to prerevolutionary realism, which in the opinion of Lenin and other leaders was more vital for the laboring masses. A series of resolutions by party congresses (particularly the 10th, 14th, and 15th in 1921, 1925, 1927) demanded thematic utilitarianism in the arts, a break with W. European "bourgeois-aesthetic, decadent" influences, and subordination to the current party line.

Despite their sharply curtailed freedom of expression, certain theaters and playwrights attempted to put on the so-called "free thought" productions, e.g. M. Bulgakov's *Days of the Turbins* (1926, MKhAT), Yu. Olesha's *Conspiracy of Feelings* (1929, Vakhtangov Theater), D. Bedny's *The Bogatyrs* (1936, Kamerny Theater). Many of the works of the new Soviet writers of the 30's—A. Afinogenov, A. Bezymensky, V. Kirshon, A. Korneychuk, I. Mikitenko, N. Pogodin, V. Vishnevsky, and others—were effectively staged, but were characterized by monotony of theme and by deliberate contrast between the "negative" characters (spies, secret enemies of Soviet power) and the idealized, hackneyed "positive" images of Communist heroes. The old and new plays of Gorky, whose name had been given to the MKhAT in 1932 "as a reward," remained the basis of the repertory. The comedies of this period (of which Finn, Gusev, Shkvarkin, and others were popular writers) did not rise above the level of comedies of manners, and the cautious satiric theaters (of which the oldest was the Moscow Theater of 1924) found themselves constantly at the crossroads of indecision.

The 30's as a whole, when the catch phrase "socialist realism" came to the fore, represented an oppressive period in the life of the Soviet T: the Central Committee of the CP resolved to liquidate "aesthetic" directorial experimentation; in 1936 the 2nd MKhAT was closed as "not corresponding to Soviet ideology"; the "formalistic" Meyerhold Theater closed down in 1938, its director arrested in 1939 and thereafter disappeared; Stanislavsky died in 1938; the MKhAT under the leadership of the aged Nemirovich-Danchenko became a citadel of realism with a tendency toward old-style naturalism. The provincial theaters, which had formerly followed in the footsteps of the experimental theaters, now strove assiduously to assimilate the new line.

With certain local modifications, a similar evolutionary process took place within the constituent republics also. During the 30's the playwrights N. Erdman, V. Kirshon, the director L. Kurbas, an innovator in the Ukrainian theater, I. Mikitenko, and many others were repressed. At the same time the system of rewards and honorary titles was instituted for whole theaters as well as individual participants. The productions of this period were significant only by virtue of the extraordinary skill of their actors, trained in the numerous schools of theater, on both secondary and higher levels, located throughout the country.

During the period of World War II (1941–45) the theaters again fulfilled a propagandistic function, performing highly patriotic plays on historical and contemporary themes. In the opera-ballet theaters, along with a small number of mediocre Soviet ballets and operas, the classical style and repertory are cultivated to the present day by an outstandingly excellent performing ensemble. After the war, anti-Western and anti-American themes were intensified in the dramatic repertory (the plays of K. Simonov, N. Virta, B. Lavrenev, and others).

A slight relaxation of censorship during wartime occasioned some revival of theatrical initiative, but this was sharply suppressed by the 1946 resolution of the Central Committee of the CP against "nationalistic deviations" in the republics, "malicious" caricature of the Soviet way of life, the displacement of Soviet plays by the classics, and "indifference to politics." During this period, which lasted till 1950, the "cosmopolitan, aesthetic" Kamerny Theater was liquidated, and its director, Tairov, died soon afterward. A degree of revitalization was observable during the 50's after the death of Stalin (the so-called "thaw"). However, nothing completely original was created: the theater arts submissively follow the party line up to the present day.

As of Jan. 1, 1960 the number of urban theaters in the USSR was 503, with approximately 500 on the collective farms, 105 children's theaters including the remarkable Obraztsov puppet theater and several Red Army theaters; up to 300,000 performances take place annually, attended by about 140 mill. spectators—theater-lovers after the fashion of old Russia. In the Soviet period, many talented directors and performers have appeared, of whom only a few can be mentioned because of space limitations: the directors I. Aksenov, I. Bersenev, N. Gorchakov, N. Okhlopkov, N. Petrov, A. Popov, S. Radlov, Yu. Zavadsky; the actresses M. Babanova, S. Birman, A. Koonen, A. Tarasova; and the actors N. Batalov, I. Ilinsky, the Yiddish actor S. Mikhoels, and B. Shchukin. At the present time the "Stanislavsky method" prevails, based on the theoretical principles of "affective memory" (memory of emotion stemming from the actor's own past experience, analogous to the emotion he wishes to portray), and psychological realism based on inner identification of the actor with the character portrayed—principles not always correctly understood by their advocates.

From the first decade of the 20th century on, many actors of the legitimate T began to specialize in motion pictures, which grew into an independent art. (*See also* MOVING PICTURES.)

BIBLIOGRAPHY: B. V. Varneke, *History of the Russian Theatre*, New York, 1951; N. A. Gorchakov, *The Theater in Soviet Russia*, New York, 1957; Peter Yershov, *Comedy in the Soviet Theater*, New York, 1956.   P. E. YE.

THIRD INTERNATIONAL: *see* COMINTERN.

TIEN SHAN, mountains extending W. to E. in the USSR and Sinkiang, China; highest peak Pobeda, 24,400 ft.; numerous glaciers.

TIFLÍS: *see* TBILISI.

TIKHOMÍROV, Lev Aleksándrovich (1859–1923), leading member of the populist "People's Will," which carried out the assassination of Alexander II. T submitted to Alexander III, the new tsar, a letter in which he promised that his party would shun terrorist activities if a constitutional regime were introduced in Russia.

TÍKHONOV, Andréy Nikoláyevich (1906–), mathematician and geophysicist. Corresponding member, Ac. of S., USSR (1939). Graduate (1927) and professor (1936) of Moscow University. Research concerns theoretical and multiple topology. Introduced the concept of the product of topological spaces (the "Tikhonov product"). T also studied various problems concerning mathematical physics, geophysics, the propagation of electromagnetic fields applied to prospecting, the theory of electromagnetic probing, etc. Author of *Equations of Mathematical Physics* (2nd edition, 1953, in cooperation with A. A. Samarsky).

TÍKHONOV, Nikoláy Semyónovich (1896–), writer and poet. A participant of the civil war, T extolled the revolutionary romanticism of the civil war and individual instances of bravery. This is the theme of his collections of poems, *The Horde* (1922) and *Braga* (1922.) His

Ballad About a Blue Package and *Ballad About Nails* acquired wide popularity. T's subsequent works bear the influence of his wide and frequent travels in the Caucasus and in Central Asia, as well as in W. Europe. The poems entitled *Yurga* (1926–30), the collection of essays *The Nomads*, the collection of short stories *Eternal Transit*, and the *Poems of Kakhetia* (1949–50) are concerned with contemporary life in Turkmenia and in Georgia. The collection of poems *The Shadow of a*

Friend (1936), on the other hand, contains impressionistic perspectives of the upheavals wrought in W. Europe by World War I, as well as premonitions of the coming of new battles. During World War II T published many patriotic poems and essays, including *Leningrad Tales* (1943) which describe the defense of Leningrad during the siege. Stalin prizes (1942, 1949, 1952).

TÍKHVIN WATERWAY, connecting Volga and Baltic Sea; of little use at present.

TILSIT: *see* SOVETSK.

TILSIT PEACE TREATY, signed by Napoleon and Alexander I on July 7, 1807 (N.S.). The agreement provided for an alliance between France and Russia, which was to join the Continental Blockade. Prussia ceded territories west of the Elbe, where France was to enjoy a hegemony, and a large portion of her possessions in Poland where a duchy of Warsaw under the aegis of the King of Saxony was created. Russia annexed the district of Belostok. The treaty remained in effect until Napoleon's invasion of Russia in 1812.

TÍMAN RIDGE, in Archangel Oblast, extends 500 mi. from Barents Sea to W. of upper Pechora River.

TIMBER INDUSTRY: Production of roundwood in 1959 was 397 mill. cu. m. (in the United States, 319.4 mill. cu. m.; Canada, 86.2 mill. cu. m.). It centers largely (70 per cent) on the wooded N. and E. regions of the USSR. In the prerevolutionary period it was carried out primarily by peasants during the winter months; and in the Soviet period, by the *lespromkhozy,* to which particular wooded areas as well as permanent personnel, equipment, and facilities (e.g., roads, shops) are assigned. In 1958, according to official data, 75–95 per cent of all basic operations in the production of timber were mechanized. Approximately 50 per cent of the timber is moved by water.

PRODUCTION OF TIMBER
IN THE USSR
(mill. cu. m.)

1948	249.7
1954	328.9
1955	333.9
1956	342.3
1957	361.4
1958	375.0
1959	397.0

P. I. M.

TIME OF TROUBLES (*Smútnoye vrémya*), period in Russian history full of inner strife, foreign intervention, and anarchy dating from 1605 to 1613. It began with the appearance of a pretender, the False Dmitry, who claimed to be the murdered son of Ivan the Terrible. Dmitry found support among the Poles and Cossacks. Boris Godunov's death at this time initiated a period of anarchy. Boyar families struggled for supremacy. At the same time the Cossacks, Poles, and Swedes tried to take advantage of the situation. In 1605, Fedor, son of Boris Godunov, became tsar. However, he was soon murdered by the followers of Dmitry who took Moscow in June 1605. In May 1606 Dimitry was assassinated and Vasily Shuysky became tsar. Meanwhile, a Cossack and peasant revolt was in progress in the south. A second pretender who also used the name of Dmitry challenged the authority of Tsar Vasily and established himself in Tushino, near Moscow. Vasily asked the Swedes for help and, in re-

turn, ceded to them sections of Russian-held Finland. Several months later the Polish king, Sigismund, took Smolensk and advanced toward Moscow. A boyar faction deposed Shuysky and elected Wladyslaw, Sigismund's son, to the throne. Sigismund, however, was anxious to secure the throne for himself and the war continued. In 1611 a powerful reaction against the Poles started in the N.E. Russian provinces. A national militia formed under Prince Pozharsky and the Nizhny-Novgorod butcher Minin relieved Moscow and drove out the Poles. In Feb. 1613, a *zemsky sobor* (q.v.) was summoned and it elected Michael Romanov to the throne, the first representative of a dynasty that ruled Russia for 300 years.

TIMIRYÁZEV, Kliment Arkadyevich (1843–1920), noted botanist and physiologist. Corr. member, St.  Petersburg Ac. of S. (1890). Graduate, St. Petersburg University (1865); professor, Academy of Agriculture and Forestry (1875), which has been named after him, and of Moscow University (1877). Worked abroad under the most outstanding physicists and physiologists of the time (1867–70). T's lifelong research concerned the photosynthesis of plants. Builder of the first hothouse in Russia for the growing of seeds in pots. An ardent Darwinist, T's ideas are reflected in his book *A Brief Course on the Darwinist Theory* (1865). His *Complete Works* in 10 volumes were published in 1940, and *Selected Works* in 2 volumes, in 1957. Member of numerous R. and foreign learned societies including the Royal Society of London; honorary degrees from the universities of Cambridge, Glasgow, and Geneva.

TIMOSHÉNKO, Semyón Konstantínovich (1895–), marshal of the Soviet Union. T was born in a peasant  family and drafted in the army in 1915; became a Bolshevik during the civil war and, despite his youth, held several important commands. After a specialized military training in the 1920's he was appointed commander of the Kiev military district. T led Soviet troops into Poland after the Nazi-Soviet pact of 1939. In 1940 he was appointed people's commissar of defense and was made a marshal. During World War II he was commander of the southwestern front. He has held many party posts, has been a member of the Central Committee of the CPSU since 1939, and served in the Byelorussian government.

TIRÁSPOL, city in Moldavian SSR; pop. 62,000 (1959). Formerly capital of the autonomous republic; is agr. town, on the Dniester; in addition to fruit and vegetable ind. of national importance, has large winemaking and oil-extracting plants.

TÍSZA RIVER, flows from Carpathian Mountains through Soviet, Hungarian, and Yugoslav territory; largest left tributary of the Danube; 600 mi. long.

TITÓV, Gérman (pron. Gherman) **Stepánovich** (1935–), second Soviet cosmonaut. Born in Verkhneye

Zhilino, a village of Kosikha Rayon, in the Altay Kray (S. Siberia). His father, a school teacher, was drafted in the Red Army during the war, and the boy moved with his mother to the May Morning Collective Farm where  he started his schooling in 1943 at the village grade school. After the war the family moved to Polkovnikovo where the father taught German and Russian. The young boy excelled in gymnastics and bicycle riding. In 1953 he was admitted to the Elementary Military Flying School, and in 1955 to the Stalingrad Flying Academy, from which he was graduated in 1957. He was assigned to serve in the Leningrad Military District where he applied for special training as an astronaut. He joined the Komsomol in 1949, and later became a candidate CP member. On August 6, 1961, he was launched in the Spaceship Vostok II, as the second Soviet spaceman. Orbiting at 17,-750 m.p.h., he made 17 circuits around the earth, one every 88 minutes, nearly 435,000 miles in all, whirling on an orbit that ranged from 111 miles to 158 miles above the earth. Then he landed by parachute in a plowed field some 460 miles from Moscow. While orbiting he was promoted from captain to major, and from candidate to full CP member.

TKACHÓV, Pyótr Nikítich (1844–1885), populist who advocated that the revolution should be carried out by a small body of professionals, acting in the name of the people. Born in Pskov Province of an impoverished noble family. In 1861, as a student at the St. Petersburg University, T was arrested and expelled from the University. Some years later he graduated in law as an external student. An able journalist, T contributed to *Russkoye Slovo* (Russian World), in which Pisarev published his articles. In 1868, T made the acquaintance of Nechayev and jointly with him led the St. Petersburg students' movement. T was arrested, tried and sentenced to 16 months in prison. Released in 1873, T went to Switzerland where, for a short time, he collaborated with P. Lavrov. After the break with Lavrov, in 1874, T joined a group of Russian-Polish "Jacobins" who were under the influence of Blanqui. In 1875–78, T edited *Nabat* (The Tocsin) in which he developed his revolutionary theories. According to T, the revolutionaries must first seize political power, with "direct or indirect" support of the people and then transform society, acting "from above." In tsarist Russia, where the state power had, according to T, no support of any social class and "hung in the air," this was especially easy. A small but well-organized group of revolutionists could overthrow the tsarist regime by a carefully prepared "stroke into the center." In spite of its limited circulation, the influence of *Nabat* was great. Engels engaged in open polemics with T's theories. In Russia T inspired the populist revolutionists (*Narodnaya Volya*), who, in 1881, assassinated Alexander II. T spent the last years of his life in Paris where he contributed to Blanqui's paper *Ni dieu, ni maitre.* He died insane, in a public hospital.

TKVARCHÉLI, city in Abkhaz ASSR; pop. 28,700 (1959). Since the thirties, a major coal-mining center, on the N. slope of the Greater Caucasus range.

TOBACCO CULTIVATION. Tobacco was introduced in Russia by Peter the Great who, in 1697, abolished the prohibition of its use. Most of Soviet T is grown in areas with relatively mild climate such as Ukraine (which accounts for 22% of all area under that crop), Caucasian regions (27%), and Central Asia (17%). About one-half of the area under T is accounted for by *makhorka* (*Nicotiana rustica*), a coarse variety with high nicotine content used mainly in home-made cigarettes. Sown area, in thousand acres, rose from 155.7 (1910–14 average) to 222.4 in 1928, 519 in 1940, and 469.5 in 1956. Collective farms cultivated 95% of the area sown. Moreover, 33 large state farms specializing in tobacco crops were in operation as of 1955. The entire crop is contracted for in advance by the Chief Tobacco Administration, a government agency, which purchases it at fixed prices. Marketings of T amounted (in thousand tons) to 28 in 1913, 39 in 1928, 102 in 1957. The government maintains a network of 39 plants in which the purchased T is stored and subjected to fermentation. The USSR was the world's fourth largest T producer in the late 1950's. A considerable part of the crop was of inferior quality: thus *makhorka* is used in most countries as an insecticide rather than for human consumption.

TOBÁDZE, Titián Yustínovich (1895–1937), Georgian poet, son of a village priest. He graduated from the gymnasium in Kutaisi and entered the philological faculty of Moscow University in 1913. While T was still a student, Georgian newspapers published his poems and translations of the works of Blok, Bryusov, Sologub, Annensky, and French poets, as well as of Dostoyevsky's *Legend of the Grand Inquisitor.* In 1920, T brought out his long poem, *Horse with Angel,* which was much admired by the Georgian intelligentsia. Some of his writings have been translated into Russian by B. Pasternak. In 1937, T was arrested and shot as a "bourgeois nationalist" but was rehabilitated after Stalin's death.

TOBOL RIVER, flows from S. Urals, Orenburg Oblast, through Kustanay, Kurgan, and Tyumen oblasts, forming left tributary of Irtysh River; 1,000 mi. long; lower course navigable.

TOBÓLSK, city in Tyumen Oblast, W. Siberia, RSFSR; pop. 39,000 (1959). Birthplace of the famous R. chemist, D. I. Mendeleyev. In the past, was an important fish and fur-trading town, at the confluence of the Irtysh and Tobol rivers; shipbuilding, lumbering, metal, and woodworking ind.

TOFALARS: *see* POPULATION.

TÓKAREV, Fyódor Vasílyevich (1871–), expert in the design of automatic machine guns. Hero of Socialist Labor (1940). Member of the Supreme Soviet (1937, 1946). Doctor of technical sciences (1940). The son of a Don Cossack, he graduated from a military school in Novocherkassk (1891) and entered an officers' school in Oranienbaum (1907). Designed his first automatic rifle in 1908. Subsequently, T worked at the Sestroretsk ammunition plant where he improved the design of automatic guns. His MT submachine gun, TT automatic pistol, and a self-loading rifle designed from 1924 to 1939 were used during World War II. Stalin prize (1940).

TOKHTAMÝSH (died ca. 1407), Khan of the Golden Horde. After the defeat of Mamay by the Russians in the battle of Kulikovo (1380) he became ruler of the Horde with the aid of Timur (Tamerlane). Two years later his troops stormed Moscow and laid waste the city. He was removed by Timur in 1395.

TOLBÚKHIN, Fyódor Ivánovich (1894–1949), Soviet marshal. Graduate of the Frunze Military Academy

(1934). T fought in the civil war and was a member of the CP since 1938. In World War II, he took part in the defense of Stalingrad. In 1942, he commanded the troops in Ukraine, and led the Soviet army which occupied Yugoslavia, Hungary, Austria, and Bulgaria. After the war T was in command of the Transcausian military district.

TOLSTÓY, Count Alekséy Konstantínovich (1817–1875), one of the most versatile of the mid-19th century writers. T's talents ranged from lyric poetry to historical ballads, dramatic plays, historical novels and pure nonsense poetry, epigrams, and proverbs, the latter constituting his contributions to the writings of the fictitious Kozma Prutkov (q.v.), invented jointly by T and his cousins, the brothers Zhemchuzhnikov. T was a distant cousin of Leo Tolstoy. Much of his work has been set to music by Rimsky-Korsakov and Tchaikovsky. Outstanding among his ballads are *Prince Kúrbsky, Vasíly Shibánov,* and *Prince Mikháylo Repnín,* and the poem *Saint John Damascene.* Many of T's ballads are based on the R. epics. Among these are *Sadkó, Ilyá Múromets,* and *Alyósha Popóvich.* He also wrote satirical poems, such as *The Dream of Popov,* and a parody in verse of the history of Russia in which he satirized the lack of order in the R. government. He wrote a dramatic *Fyodor Ioannovich,* and *Tsar Boris,* and the popular historical novel, *Prince Serébryanny,* which deals with the times of Ivan the Terrible and is an absorbing story of intrigue and adventure. **A. B. T.**

TOLSTÓY, Alekséy Nikoláyevich (1883–1945), outstanding writer, dramatist, and poet. T grew up on the family's estate "Sosnóvka" near Samara (now Kuybyshev). His novel *Childhood of Nikita* (1920) reflects his boyhood experiences and impressions. T attended the Samara secondary school at the St.

Petersburg Technological Institute. While he did not become an engineer, training in science served him well as the technical background for his science-fiction novels, *The Seven Days in Which the World Was Plundered, Aelita, The Hyperboloid of Engineer Garin* (translated into English as *The Death Box*), and others.

T began as a poet. The year 1907 saw the publication of his early verse *Lyrics.* Thereafter he turned to prose. From 1908 to the start of the World War I, he wrote several novels, including the outstanding *Eccentrics* (1911) and *The Lame Master* (1912). The principal theme of T's writings during this period was the degeneration and doom of the nobility and the forebodings of the coming catastrophe.

During World War I, T served as war correspondent of the daily *Russkie Vedomosti.* He was opposed to the Bolshevik Revolution and joined the White armies. Following the victory of the Reds, T emigrated and wrote several anti-communist pamphlets, but returned to Russia in 1923. During his relatively short stay abroad as an *émigré,* T wrote the first part of his trilogy *Way Through Hell* (English title, *Road to Calvary*). Part one, *The Sisters,* was published in 1920. It was followed by part two, *The Year Eighteen* (1927–28), and by part three, *Gloomy Morning* (1940–41). The leading characters of the three novels are representatives of the R. intelligentsia, who are tormented by loneliness and lack of contact with revolutionary realities and the tide of human emotions around them. The novels received the Stalin prize in 1943. T was previously awarded the Stalin prize in 1941 for parts one and two of the historical novel *Peter the First,* published respectively in 1929–30 and 1933–34. Part three (unfinished) was published in 1944–45, its completion being prevented by the author's death. The atmosphere and characteristic trends of the Petrine era are presented with realism and artistry, although the excesses and cruelties of the tsar and his courtiers are viewed by T as a historical necessity. Many literary critics have tended to regard T's portrayal of Peter as a prototype of Stalin. This work is possibly the most outstanding postrevolutionary historical novel.

Other works of T, written and published during the period between his return to Russia in 1923 and World War II—*The Adventures of Nevzorov, or Ibikus* (1925), *Black Gold* (1931), and the novel *Bread* (1937), among others—are of lesser importance. In many of them, notably in *Bread,* T displayed a servile attitude toward the Soviet regime. During World War II, T wrote a series of patriotic articles and short novels: *The Motherland* (1941), *Not A Step Backward* (1942), and the short novel *The Tales of Ivan Sudarev* (1942).

As a dramatist T was less successful. His drama *Ivan the Terrible,* in two parts—*The Eagle and Its Mate* (1942) and *Difficult Years* (1943)—earned him the last Stalin prize, awarded posthumously in 1946. Among his other dramatic works are *The Cuckoo's Tears, Love Is A Golden Book,* and *The Demented,* which is the story of Rasputin.

T was a distant relative of his famous namesake, Leo Tolstoy, and, as the latter, had the title of count. Although during the most creative period of his life he lived in the land of the Soviets and owed allegiance to Stalin and his henchmen in the Kremlin, T succeeded in living the life of a nobleman. He was often attacked by other Soviet writers because of his aristocratic origins, but was successful in leading an unmolested life, probably owing to a combination of the servility he exhibited in many of his writings, his illustrious name and his talents as a writer. While T never displayed much intellectual depth, his writings are distinguished for their clarity and purity of style. They are widely read in the Soviet Union. **V. Z.**

TOLSTÓY, Count Leo (Lev) Nikoláyevich (1828–1910), novelist, dramatist, social and religious thinker, one of the giants of world literature. The Tolstoys were an old and prominent family. Orphaned of both parents at an early age, T was brought up by relatives. After two years at the University of Kazan, he left the university and for two or three years led a life of dissipation in Moscow and St. Petersburg. His passions were as strong as his capacity for remorse and moral revolt against them. In 1851 he decided to leave the capital and traveled to the Caucasus where he joined the army as a subaltern and later as a commissioned officer in the artillery. His experience of a frontier war in the Caucasus, reading and meditation led him to writing: *Childhood* (part one of the trilogy *Childhood, Adolescence, Youth*) and several army life stories, *The Raid, The Cutting of the Forest.* The appearence of the first chapters of *Childhood* in a St. Petersburg magazine (1852) attracted wide attention. They revealed a new talent of unusual freshness, originality, and insight. The older and already established writer Turgenev hailed his younger colleague. Henceforth, T's literary career was to be a progression from one success to another. In 1853–56 T participated in the Danube campaign and, later, in the defense of Sevastopol, besieged by the allied armies. His *Sevastopol Sketches* made T's fame national. They foreshadow the wider perspective of *War and Peace.*

After the war, T resigned his commission and returned to St. Petersburg where he was much sought in literary circles, both right and left. In 1857 T undertook his first voyage to W. Europe and made a study of primary schools in Germany, France, and Switzerland. During this period he wrote such stories as *Polikushka* which, as well as the previously written *Morning of a Landlord*, was moderate in tone, but nevertheless an effective satirical exposure of the evils of serfdom. He also wrote *Kholstomer* (The Pacer), a notable realistic animal story.

With the approach of the emancipation of the serfs, T established a school for peasant children on his estate Yasnaya Polyana. Dissatisfied with the school routine of his time, T wrote a series of pedagogical essays demanding a creative, interesting, and flexible approach to teaching, and advocating the abolition of all punishments, which was a revolutionary innovation. He composed a reader (*Stories for Children*) which became a classic in Russian pedagogical literature. The small novel *The Cossacks*, begun earlier in the Caucasus, was finished at this time. The note of dissatisfaction with the artificialities of civilization was clearly sounded.

In 1862 T married Sophia Behrs and for the next 20 years he lived the life of a successful writer, well-to-do landowner, and happy husband and father on his estate Yasnaya Polyana. He worked on his epic novel *War and Peace*, a story of Russia in the wars of 1805, 1807, and 1812, considered by many the greatest novel ever written. Every layer of Russian and European society, from court circles to peasants, from field marshals to privates, is represented by hundreds of characters and scenes with authority, precision, and depth of vision. The problems of society—individual, moral, social, political, and religious—are examined and analyzed through the experiences of Andrey Bolkonsky,

Pierre Bezukhov, Platon Karatayev, Natasha and many others. T's philosophy of life became crystallized: war is brutal and cruel, only war in defense of one's country from invasion is justified. Napoleon and Alexander I, kings, statesmen, and generals are actors, vain and ineffective puppets, frequently heartless and hypocritical. The true hero is the "unknown soldier," the people, the pathetic, simple and wise peasant Platon Karatayev: he carries the burdens, he wins wars and battles. Society should be based on simple men, on children and family life.

In the 1870's T wrote *Anna Karenina*, a rival to *War and Peace.* He was disturbed by the sight of social injustice, by poverty and growing militarism: the uncompromising social and puritanic moralist comes to the fore. Personal happiness, even love, are not enough: illegitimate love is condemned. Anna commits suicide. Life is senseless without a deeper faith and purpose. For the last 30 years of his life T was a religious social thinker, Christian and partly Buddhist, a nonviolent anarchist. Christ's whole message was to him contained in the words "that ye resist not evil" (Matt. 5, 39). Non-resistance to evil became the foundation of Tolstoyism (*tolstovstvo*). He condemned all states and governments, all churches, imperialism and militarism, capitalism, domination of man over man—in short, the evils of modern civilization. He preached simple communal life. While opposing violence his teaching, nevertheless, was thoroughly revolutionary. He was excommunicated by the Orthodox church in 1901.

T explained his radicalism by his prevision, as early as 1880–82, of coming world wars, revolutions, and general disaster (*So What Should Be Done*, 1882–86). His "conversion" is explained in *My Confession* (1879), in *My Faith*, and in many other tracts and articles. Though rejecting most of his contemporary literature (including his own previous works) as artificial and corrupt, T nevertheless did not give up his art. In the 1880's and 1890's he wrote the stories *Death of Ivan Ilyich, Master and Servant, The Kreutzer Sonata*, the novel *The Resurrection*, and numerous stories "for the people." These, with the later tales—*Hadji-Murat, Father Sergius, The Devil*—are on a high literary level. T's plays are *The Power of Darkness, Fruits of Enlightenment*, and *The Living Corpse.* T published many moral tracts, including *I Cannot Keep Silent* (1908) which was a protest against the use of martial law against revolutionaries.

In the fall of 1910, at the age of 82, T, dissatisfied with life on his comfortable estate as too "luxurious," secretly escaped in search for a "simpler life." He contracted pneumonia and died a few days later at the R.R. station Astapovo.

BIBLIOGRAPHY: Janko Lavrin, *Tolstoy: An Approach*, New York, 1946; Alexandra Tolstoy, *My Father*, New York, 1955.

I. L. T.

TOM RIVER, flows from W. Abakan Mountains via Kemerovo and Tomsk oblasts to form right tributary of the Ob; 520 mi. long; navigable. Irrigation, with industrial towns of Tomsk, Stalinsk, and Kemerovo on its banks.

TOMSK, city, adm. center of Tomsk Oblast, rail center and river port on Tom, part of Ob waterway;

pop. 249,000 (1959). Important rail-river reloading point. Major cultural center, has a number of higher educational institutions, including the first Siberian university and the noted Institute of Technology. Manufactures electrical motors, lighting equipment, rubber and plastic goods; has metalworking, food-processing plants, canneries, sawmills. Founded 1604.

TOMSK OBLAST, W. Siberia, RSFSR; area 122,300 sq. mi.; pop. 741,000 (1959). Cities: Tomsk (adm. center), Kolpashevo, Asino. Marshy lowlands extending along the middle course of Ob River and tributaries, Vasyugan, Tom, Ket, Chulym; lake country, with podsol soils, in tayga subzone. Timbering and lumber the main ind., with lumber-milling center at Kolpashevo; wheat, barley, oats, flax grown in the S.; dairy and truck farming being developed; fishing and hunting important auxiliary occupations. Est. 1944.

TÓMSKY, Mikhaíl Pávlovich (1880–1936), Communist and trade-union leader, born in St. Petersburg into a worker's family. In 1904, joined the social-democratic movement. In 1905, moved to Revel (now Tallin) where he organized the local Soviet of Workers' Deputies. Arrested in 1906 but soon escaped. Participated in the party congress in London in 1907 and in Bolshevik conferences in Finland and Paris. In 1909 was arrested and sentenced to five years at hard labor. After the October revolution, was chairman of the Moscow congress of trade unions; from 1922 to 1929, chairman of the central committee of the trade unions. From 1919, member of the Central Committee of the CPSU and of the Politburo. Implicated in the "Rightist Opposition" (*see* OPPOSITION), T committed suicide.

TÓPCHIEV, Aleksándr Vasílyevich (1907–), organic chemist. Vice-President, Ac. of S., USSR (1958). Graduate of the Moscow Institute of Chemical Technology (1930); professor at the Institute of Technology of the Food Industry (1938–41) and at the Petroleum Institute (1940) in Moscow. Deputy Minister of Higher Education (1947–49). Research on processes of nitration, halogenation, polymerization, and alcylation of various hydrocarbons, the synthesis of physicochemical processes of new types of organosilicon compounds. He investigated thermal, photochemical and catalytic chlorination of lower paraffin hydrocarbons and new methods of catalytic conversion of chlorine derivatives of hydrocarbons. Author of *Nitration of Hydrocarbons and Other Organic Compounds* (1949), *Compounds of Boron Fluoride as Catalysts in Alcylation, Polymerization, and Condensation Reactions* (1949), and others. Stalin prize (1949).

TOPÓZERO, lake in Karelian ASSR; 430 sq. mi.; abundance of fish, log floating.

TOURISM: *see* TRAVELING AND TOURISM.

TOYOHARA: *see* YUZHNO-SAKHALINSK.

TRACTOR AND AGRICULTURAL MACHINERY INDUSTRY. In 1960, 238,500 tractors, 148,000 tractor ploughs, and 58,600 grain-harvester combines were produced (in the United States in 1954: 670,000 tractors, 244,000 tractor ploughs, and 82,000 combines). Although there were only 4.2 mill. metal

ploughs in use in Russia in 1910, the production of horse-drawn agricultural equipment had become substantial by 1913 (60.5 mill. rubles) and exceeded imports. A shift to mechanized agricultural equipment was begun in the 1920's, and in the 1930's the very large tractor factories at Stalingrad, Kharkov, and Chelyabinsk were constructed. From 1928 to 1937 the production of tractors increased from 1,300 to 51,000; that of tractor ploughs from 500 to 96,400; and that of grain harvester combines from 0 to 44,000.

During World War II factories producing agricultural machinery generally shifted to military production. Additional facilities which were built in the eastern areas included a tractor plant in the Altay region, a grain-harvester combine plant at Krasnoyarsk, and agricultural equipment plants in the Altay region, in Uzbekistan, and in Kazakhstan. The continued growth of the tractor and agricultural machinery industry after the war became particularly rapid in the 1950's, following the modernization of existing facilities and the further construction of new plants. In 1955, 163,000 tractors were produced. This represented a threefold increase over 1937. There were twice as many tractors and other major types of agricultural equipment in use in the fields in 1955 as in 1940. The Seven Year Plan calls for the production of about 1 mill. tractors and 400,000 grain-harvester combines during the period 1959–65.

PRODUCTION OF TRACTORS AND OF AGRICULTURAL
EQUIPMENT IN THE USSR
(in thousands)

Year	Tractors	Tractor ploughs	Grain-harvester combines
1928	1.3	.5	—
1932	48.9	61.1	10.0
1937	51.0	96.4	43.9
1940	31.6	38.4	12.8
1945	7.7	—	—
1950	108.8	121.9	46.3
1955	163.4	103.2	48.0
1958	219.7	164.0	65.0
1959	214.0	155.0	53.6
1960	238.5	148.0	58.6

P. I. M.

TRADE UNIONS. I. Trade unions were formed in Russia in the stormy year 1905 and immediately won wide support among workers. The reaction which rapidly ensued, however, prevented the healthy development of the trade-union movement. Any combination by local unions was forbidden and the local unions themselves were often suppressed and were barely able to survive, so that by the time of the revolution in 1917, the total trade-union membership in all of Russia numbered only a few tens of thousands.

In 1917, from the very beginning of the revolution, the TU expanded rapidly. At the All-Russian Conference of Trade Unions in the second half of June, a million and a half union-organized workers and employees were already represented. Within the union movement at this time, a bitter struggle was waged between those who thought the unions should be an autonomous branch of the workers movement, like the so-called free or socialist unions of Germany, and those who believed that the unions should be entirely dedicated to the task of preparing the overthrow of the government and the transfer of power to the proletariat.

After October, the former were called proponents of trade-union independence. The Mensheviks played a leading role among them and were supported by a majority of the union-organized workers and employees during the spring and summer of 1917 and at the June Conference. The president of the first All-Russian Central Council of Trade Unions, elected by the All-Russian Conference of Trade Unions, was the Menshevik Mikhail G. Grinevich who had also played a leading role in the trade-union movement during the 1905–06 revolution. Bolshevik influence in the unions had, however, been rising even before October. After October, sometimes by free "conquest" of unions, sometimes by using forceful measures, the Bolsheviks rapidly achieved a dominant position, which they expanded into complete control in 1919–20. From early 1918, it is possible to speak of the TU in Russia as a special, Soviet type. The leader of the movement, elected by the first All-Russian Congress of Trade Unions in Jan. 1918, was the Bolshevik Mikhail P. Tomsky, who became the outstanding figure of the trade-union movement for the next decade.

The distinguishing characteristic of the Soviet TU is the complete subordination of their control and management to the CP. The forms of the party's control have varied. In the early years of the revolution it was somewhat disguised, while now, as for many years, it is openly recognized. Extreme centralism is the second characteristic feature of the Soviet TU. Higher organs have exclusive and extensive powers over lower organs and the All-Union Central Council of Trade Unions, (ACCTU), though formally elected by the Trade Union Congress, is actually an authoritarian ruling body. Without the consent of the unions, it has often merged them, or split them into two or more. The ACCTU has also neglected to call congresses, changed its own composition without authorization from the Congress, and failed to account to the Congress for a period of more than a quarter of a century.

The Soviet trade-union organization did not immediately arrive at the theoretical concepts which are now typical of it. After the early years of change and experiment, once the country had made the transition to the NEP, the Soviet unions operated on the theories expressed in the general resolution of the Central Committee of the CP of Jan. 12, 1922. This resolution was drafted by Lenin, was entitled "On the Role and Tasks of the Trade Unions Under the Conditions of the New Economic Policy," and was later upheld by the 11th Party Congress (March-April 1922). It declared that, with state enterprises now operating on an "economic accounting" basis, "in connection with the urgent need to raise labor productivity and achieve solvency and profitability in each enterprise, and in connection with the inevitable bureaucratic interests and exaggerations of departmental effort, certain conflicts of interest on questions of labor inevitably arise between the working masses and the directors managing the state enterprises or departments to which they belong. Therefore the TU, in relation to socialized enterprises, have an unconditional obligation to defend the workers' interests and to facilitate all possible improvements in their material welfare, constantly correcting the errors and ex-

cesses of economic organs in so far as they arise from bureaucratic perversions of the state apparatus." Thus the Soviet state gave cognizance to an "economic struggle of the proletariat" in state enterprises, but this struggle was to be essentially different from the "class struggle" of workers against private capital. Disputes in this "economic struggle" were to be resolved through mutual agreement or by the decisions of "higher state authorities." Tolerating "the application of the strike weapon," as an exception, "in a state where the proletariat has power, can be justified only by bureaucratic perversions of the proletarian state and by the various remnants of the capitalistic past in its institutions on the one hand, and by the political immaturity and cultural backwardness of the masses on the other."

This view, which was subsequently termed the "protective theory of trade unions," became the official credo of the Soviet TU until near the end of the 1920's. In 1929, however, it was officially denounced by the CP as "opportunistic" and "trade-unionistic." The old central trade-union leadership headed by Mikhail P. Tomsky, which had just been re-elected by the 8th All-Union Congress of Trade Unions in Dec. 1928, was removed by an order of the Central Committee of the CP and replaced by new people who had not been elected by the Congress. Throughout the country and at all levels of the trade-union organization, there was an energetic "clean-up" of the members of the old school and they were, for the most part, replaced by party people, often by the local party secretaries at the various levels, while Nikolay Shvernik became the head of the ACCTU. A new "production theory of the trade unions" was formulated in the renovated ACCTU's appeal "To All Trade Union Organizations, All Union Members, All Workers," issued early in Sept. 1929.

The basic slogan proclaimed by this address was, "Production first." The primary duty of the unions now was to increase production, especially by raising output per worker (through "socialist competition," and such) and strengthening labor discipline. This was to supersede all other considerations, especially those of protecting labor's interests. Workers who complained about wages and working conditions were denounced in the ACCTU appeal as "consciously or unconsciously" acting as an "internal enemy within the ranks of the proletariat," as "destructive elements" which should be "done away with."

Similar ideas were expressed in the resolution of the CPSU's 16th Congress (June-July 1930) "On the Tasks of the Trade Unions in the Period of Reconstruction." The job of the TU was to see that economic plans were carried out. To be able to comply with this task, the unions were to be purged of the last remnants of "trade unionism" ("this struggle cannot be considered finished"), and they must be led and strictly controlled by the party.

Emphasis on production as the unions' chief concern had its most drastic effects in wage policies. The aim of union wage policies was no longer to maintain and raise the workers' living standards, but to contribute to increases in output and reductions of production costs. In an extreme expression of this trend, the trade-union leadership formally withdrew from defending workers' wage interests and even opposed wage concessions when the initiative came from the managements of enterprises. At a conference called by the ACCTU to discuss wage policies in Jan. 1933, the secretary of the ACCTU, Gavriil Veynberg, formulated this with great clarity: "You sometimes hear whispering in union ranks like this: 'Does it behoove the unions to oppose concessions which industrial executives grant in wage questions? If we do that, how can we face the workers?' This is the most shameful misconception of union tasks. It is 'trade unionism' pure and simple. . . . We must actively combat this kind of 'defense' of labor interests."

These seemingly inconceivable statements by an authoritative representative of the ACCTU on the trade-union movement's most basic issue provided a clear indication of the depths to which the Soviet TU fell in the 1930's. The unions were deprived of any influence on wages, or hiring and firing. Collective agreements became dead letters (*see* COLLECTIVE AGREEMENTS). The life went out of the union organizations and even the All-Union Congresses of Trade Unions ceased to be called after the 9th Congress in the spring of 1932 had approved the removal of the former leadership and denounced the old "trade-unionist" policies. The 10th Congress did not take place until 1949. Although the unions were given some functions as organs of the state, even this could not save them, and the press began, cautiously, to raise the question, "Do we need trade unions?"

The war saved the unions from destruction. Under wartime conditions, problems of helping workers in their everyday life arose in acute form. Food and housing, employment of women with families, care for soldiers' dependents, war orphans and returning disabled veterans, and innumerable other questions of workaday life—all required tremendous efforts in the communities and even more in the plants. The unions, with some pre-war experience in a number of these fields, were automatically drawn into war work. This gave them a new lease on life. The reorientation by no means implied abandoning the paramount importance of "production," on which trade-union policy thrived in the 1930's. "Care for the material and cultural needs and everyday existence of wage and salary earners," which was proclaimed the central task of the TU, was derived from the exigencies of production and justified by the need to expand and improve output. The struggle for higher output remained on the agenda and was thoroughly emphasized, though there was an obvious shift in the application of energy, attention, and personnel to the various tasks.

The combination of some welfare functions with emphasis on production remained characteristic of the Soviet TU throughout the 1940's. At the end of the decade, without dropping their basic "productive" aims, the TU began gradually to expand their influence on matters connected not only with workers' and employees' living conditions, but also with their working conditions. In the second half of the 1950's, the TU were once again drawn into enterprise decisions on questions of wages and output quotas, and, if not on questions of hiring, then on dismissals of workers and employees, and the like. In Dec. 1957, something basically new was added by the decree of the Central Committee of the CPSU plenum "On the Work of the Trade Unions of the USSR." This gave the unions certain rights to participate in the management of enterprises. Thus some elements of what is called "economic democracy" in the West were, at least in principle, introduced into the industrial management system. The formal significance of this innovation is beyond doubt and it is possible that it may acquire practical meaning in the future development of the TU.

II. TU in the Soviet Union are regarded to some degree as organs of state power. In 1933, the People's Commissariat of Labor, which had the functions of a ministry or, in America, department of labor, was abolished and its duties of supervising labor protection and directing social insurance were transferred to the TU. The TU also played an important role in labor disputes as arbitrators, rather than as labor's representatives. By the same token, they were deprived of the capacity to represent the interests of workers and employees. It is not accidental that these features took shape in the 1930's, just when the Soviet trade-union movement had reached its lowest point. In the second half of the 1950's, with a general reorientation of the TU beginning to take shape, there has also been a noteworthy change in the procedure for handling labor disputes, and the TU now function as the representative of labor's side.

The All-Union Central Council of Trade Unions has also moved, without any explicit indication in Soviet law, into legislative activity. A series of important basic laws on labor questions has been issued as joint resolutions of the USSR Council of Ministers, the Central Committee of the CPSU, and the ACCTU. The real significance of the ACCTU's participation in legislation, in the sense of effecting legislative expression of interests of workers and employees, remains, however, debatable.

III. As a result of industrialization and due to the fact that TU membership is practically compulsory in the USSR, the numerical growth of the Soviet TU has been impressive. From a membership of 2 million in October 1917 it reached 8.5 mill. in 1921, 10 mill. in 1929, 16.5 mill. in 1932, 19.5 mill. in 1935, 25 mill. in 1939, 47 mill. in 1957. In March 1959, (twelfth Congress of TU), the membership was 52,780,000. On Jan. 1, 1961 there were 22 central unions organized on the industrial principle and uniting practically all the wage-earners in the USSR employed in industry and agriculture (Sovkhoz workers are eligible for membership; members of the collective farms are not). ACCTU publishes its own daily newspaper *Trud*.

BIBLIOGRAPHY: I. Deutscher, *Soviet Trade Unions*, London, 1950; Solomon M. Schwarz, *Labor in the Soviet Union*, New York, 1952; *The Trade Union Situation in the USSR*, Report of a mission from the International Labour Office, Geneva, 1960; Thomas T. Hammond, *Lenin on Trade Unions and Revolution, 1893–1917*, New York, 1957; Solomon M. Schwarz, "Trade Unions in the Soviet State," *Current History*, August, 1959; International Labor Office, *Trade Union Rights in the USSR*, Geneva, 1959.   S. SCH.

TRANS-ALAY RANGE, mountain range in N. Pamir, on the border of Kirghiz SSR and Tadzhik SSR; elevation of Lenin peak 24,400 ft.

TRANSCARPATHIAN OBLAST, Ukrainian SSR; borders on Poland, Hungary, Rumania, and Czechoslovakia; area 4,950 sq. mi.; pop. 920,000 (1959), mostly Ukrainians. Cities: Uzhgorod (adm. center), Mukachevo, Beregovo, Vinogradov, and Khust. Situated on S. Carpathian slopes, forests cover almost half of area. Agr.: wheat, rye, oats, corn, tobacco, vineyards. Ind.: ceramics, food, woodworking. Has university (Uzhgorod), pedag. inst., theaters, philharmonic orchestra. Annexed in 1945; est. 1946.

TRANSCAUCASIA, area S. of Caucasus Mountain Range, comprising Azerbaijan SSR, Georgian SSR, and Armenian SSR.

TRANS-ILÍ ALA-TÁU, mountain range in Tien Shan system, on the border of Kazakh SSR and Kirghiz SSR; elevations reach 16,250 ft.

TRANSPORTATION AND COMMUNICATIONS. The importance of T and C in Russia reflects the large absolute area of the R. land mass. Natural resources, arable land, and established population centers are widely scattered, requiring T and C for their effective unification.

Until a century ago, rivers and overland trade routes were the major interregional arteries. The Dnieper and Volga rivers loom large in R. history, together with many others. As Muscovy expanded out to the edges of the N. Eurasian land mass, the great rivers were followed to their mouths. Some historians (e.g., Robert Kerner) have seen this as an "urge to the sea," while others (e.g., John Morrison) have seen it as a land-acquiring process. In any case, Russia's access to ocean communications is unfavorable, either because her far northern location means long freezing periods each year, or because her seas are peripheral and isolated.

Most freight T in the USSR is now handled by railroads. In 1958, they carried 85.2 per cent of all intercity freight ton-mi., with 7.0 per cent being handled by maritime ships, 5.6 per cent by river vessels, and 2.2 per cent by pipelines. The volume of intercity highway traffic is still negligible, as is air freight. Long-distance passenger carriage is also predominantly by railroad, though recently aircraft have entered the picture vigorously. Urban passenger service is efficiently provided by buses and trolley-buses, suburban rail lines, and by subway (in Moscow and Leningrad, with Kiev soon to be added).

Since 1928, the Soviet economy has expanded rapidly with a far less than proportionate expansion of T and C facilities. This deliberate policy of using transport very intensively has so far enabled the Soviet regime to concentrate on building heavy industry. Although at least one-fourth of Soviet C capacity was damaged in World War II, evacuation, prompt repairs, and improvisations enabled the Soviet Army to conduct military operations successfully. Since the war, T has met demands while being held to short rations. The current Seven Year Plan does not call for any reversal of the policy, though outside observers have long predicted that very large investments in T would soon be necessary. New T capacity has been built only where new production facilities required it, and the

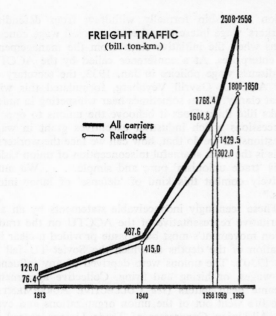

FREIGHT TRAFFIC
(bill. ton-km.)

2508-2558
1800-1850
1768.4
1604.8
1429.5
1302.0
487.6
415.0
126.0
76.4

— All carriers
○— Railroads

1913   1940   1958 1959 .1965

number of locations has not been large. Passenger travel by private automobile has not been allowed to draw resources into an extensive highway-building program.

Hence, although the Soviet economy calls for T and C on a large scale, the regime has found ways to keep these demands within bounds. Yet rising living standards and enlarged production capacities are likely to loosen these restraints in the coming years.

FREIGHT TRAFFIC, BY CARRIER
In billions of ton-kilometers

Year		Railroad	Sea	River	Road	Pipeline	Total
1913		76.4	20.3	28.9	0.1	0.3	126.0
1928		93.4	9.3	15.9	0.2	0.7	119.5
1940		415.0	23.8	36.1	8.9	3.8	487.6
1950		602.3	39.7	46.2	20.1	4.9	713.2
1959		1429.5	115.7	93.6	87.6	41.7	1768.1
1965	(plan)	1850.0	235.0	140.0	146.0	185.0	2556.0

PASSENGER TRAFFIC, BY CARRIER
In billions of passenger-kilometers

Year		Railroad	Bus	Air	River	Sea	Total
1913		30.3	—	—	1.4	1.0	32.7
1928		24.5	—	—	2.1	0.3	26.9
1940		98.0	3.4	0.2	3.8	0.9	106.3
1950		88.0	5.2	1.2	2.7	1.2	98.3
1959		164.4	50.7	7.8	4.1	1.4	228.4
1965	(plan)	192.0	125.0	30.0	5.0	2.0	354.0

(*See also* BUS TRANSPORTATION, CANALS, AVIATION, PIPELINES, POST AND MAIL, RAILROADS, RIVER TRANSPORTATION, ROADS, SEA-BORNE TRANSPORTATION, TELEPHONE AND TELEGRAPH.)

BIBLIOGRAPHY: Holland Hunter, *Soviet Transportation Policy,* Cambridge, 1957; Ernest W. Williams, Jr., *Freight Transportation in the Soviet Union,* New York, 1959; U.S. Congress, Joint Economic Committee, *Comparisons of the United States and Soviet Economies,* Washington, 1959, Part I, pp. 177–99; James H. Blackman, *Transport Development and Locomotive Technology in the Soviet Union,* Columbia, South Carolina; George Kish, *Economic Atlas of the Soviet Union,* Ann Arbor, 1960.   H. H.

TRANS-SIBERIAN RAILROAD. This line, built in 1891–1904, provided a reliable connection with the Pacific coast, stimulated the settling of W. Siberian wheat lands, and aided exploitation of Siberian minerals. Its eastern end first crossed Manchuria, but a connection wholly within R. borders was completed by

1916. From Leningrad to Vladivostok by rail is 6,117 mi.; from Moscow, 5,776 mi. Since 1955 a branch south from Ulan Ude has cut the Moscow-Peking distance to 4,911 mi.

TRAPÉZNIKOV, Vadím Aleksándrovich (1905–), electrical engineer and expert in automation. Fellow, Ac. of S., USSR (1960). Graduated from the Moscow School of Technology (1928). Associated with the All-Union Institute of Electrical Engineering (1928–33) and professor of the Moscow Institute of Power Engineering (1939–41). Director of the Institute of Automation and Telemechanics (1951). T developed new calculation methods for the design of electrical equipment including methods for technical and economical analysis of transformers; he has also studied problems of automatic dimensional control, high-speed automatic devices and units of automatic control and guidance. T directed the development of simulation systems for automatic control and the design construction of electronic modeling systems. Author of *Automatic Control of Linear Dimensions of Products* (1947). Stalin prize (1951).

TRAVELING AND TOURISM. The 1914—and final—edition of the excellent series of guides to Russia issued by Karl Baedeker of Leipzig contained a number of warnings to the would-be voyager to the great empire of the tsars.

He was told that it was absolutely impossible to enter Russia without a passport bearing a valid visa issued by the Russian consul (at a time when it was possible to travel from one end of Europe to the other without passport or visa). He was warned that he should keep his passport with him at all times; that it would often be demanded by the police; that it would have to be surrendered to the hotels; that, if he proposed to stay in Russia for any considerable time, the passport would be taken up and the Interior Ministry would issue him a *vid na zhitelstvo* or residence permit, good for one year. The traveler was warned that customs examination was likely to be severe (although the rigors might be eased by judicious tipping) and that if you were bringing in many books the censors surely would have a look at them. "One may not bring in books treating of political, social and historical questions and others of the same genre," Baedeker remarked succinctly.

While the R. postal service was described as generally good the visitor was warned that letters which, in some way, attracted the attention of authorities were apt to be opened. Persons who proposed to take snapshots in Russia were advised to join the Russian Photographic Society. The cost was 5 rubles and it would avoid trouble with local authorities. Even so Baedeker warned that regions designated by the emperor as having strategic importance could not be photographed. Should the traveler contemplate a visit to Central Asia he was cautioned that Turkestan could be visited only with special permission of the War Department which might well require several months, that some of the most interesting cities, such as Khiva and Merv, were completely off limits and that "the formalities concerning passports are severely observed by the military administration." Baedeker gave one final word of advice. Always take your own pillow, bed linen, and insecticide.

And in rural or remote areas never drink the water without first boiling it.

Nearly half a century has passed since Baedeker drew up his precise and thoughtful instructions for travel in Russia. We live in a new age. The jet airplane is rapidly replacing the comfortable R. railroad trains. The tsars have long since given way to the commissars and the commissars have themselves been transformed into the more conventional ministers of the present-day Soviet regime. And yet most of Baedeker's thoughtful admonitions with regard to travel in Russia still hold good to one extent or another.

Probably the outstanding single observation which can be made about travel in Russia—either before or since the Bolshevik Revolution—is that it has always rated as a very special experience in which the restrictions, suspicions, and red tape of the government vie with the natural hospitality and warmth of the people. It is necessary to emphasize these historical connotations of travel to Russia lest it be supposed (as is often the case) that it was the Communists who introduced difficulty into journeys to Russia. They have made their contribution, but they are working in a well-founded Russian state tradition.

In the earliest days of the Russian Revolution, from the February events of 1917 to the Bolshevik *coup d'état* on Nov. 7, 1917 there were no special impedimenta upon travel to the provisional Russian state other than those naturally imposed by the fact that Russia was engaged under increasingly difficult conditions in the great war against Germany and Austria-Hungary. There were few visitors except those upon official missions and few others who desired to visit the country.

With the seizure of power by the Bolsheviks a considerable change took place. The normal workings of authorities—customs, border officials and the like—were taken over by revolutionary agents. Passage to and fro across the frontier became increasingly dangerous, not so much because of any general orders but because of spreading anarchy. Travel within the country became even more hazardous as the civil war enveloped region after region and fighting spread between the Red Army on the one hand and various White Russian commanders and Allied detachments on the other.

But in this period, also, few travelers except some of the more mettlesome journalists, daring businessmen who sought to make profits out of the turbulent situation within the country, and Communist agents and sympathizers had any desire to go to Russia. The country was in such a state of general chaos that travelers who did manage to make their way to Petrograd or Moscow found that there was little they could accomplish without the personal intervention of high officials of the Soviet government. But, such was the informality of the time that they frequently managed to see such individuals as Lenin, Trotsky or Foreign Commissar Chicherin, Leonid Krassin who handled early trade relations, or other important Communists who often provided them with the necessary passes, authorizations, and chits for accomplishing their purposes in revolutionary Russia.

Once the civil war was over and Soviet power more

or less securely established, almost immediate efforts were made to encourage tourist travel to Russia although facilities for handling foreigners were woefully inadequate. Nonetheless, the effort was made for two reasons—the very serious need of the country for foreign currency and a hope that by giving visitors a favorable impression of the Soviet Union the weak position of the Communist regime in international relations (the Soviets were still generally unrecognized diplomatically in W. Europe until late in the decade of the 1920's) might be strengthened. Thus, even though Soviet Russia had no diplomatic connections with the United States until the Roosevelt-Litvinov agreement of Nov. 16, 1933, American visitors, particularly businessmen, technical specialists, and sympathizers with communism were welcomed from the start.

They were free to travel where they wished. They could stay where they liked. They were free to live in R. homes if they so desired. They exchanged their currency in the unrestricted black markets of the period. They were permitted to buy and sell freely with R. citizens. Special stores were set up in which foreigners were able to purchase rare objects of art, jewels, oriental rugs, and other precious items at fractions of their real value, paying for them only with *valyuta* (gold or foreign exchange). In this period if a foreigner wanted to travel to the heart of Siberia all he had to do was to go to the railroad station and buy a ticket. His real problem was getting or keeping a seat on the horribly overcrowded, filthy, slow-moving trains which sometimes would be sidetracked a day or two at a time to let priority military trains or badly needed freight shipments move ahead on the jammed, dilapidated lines.

It was not until 1929 that "Intourist," the State Tourist Co., was organized with offices in the Hotel Metropol in Moscow for the purpose of handling arrangements for the rapidly expanding flow of tourist travel to the Soviet Union. By this time a trip to Russia to observe the wonders of the communist experiment at first hand had become a fairly popular vacation expedient in W. Europe and the United States. Intourist established offices in Berlin, Paris, London, New York, Stockholm and other cities. It entered into contractual arrangements with western travel agencies and began the vigorous promotion of what would now be called "package tours" to the Soviet Union.

Because hotel facilities were scanty in Russia arrangements were made for cruise steamers to dock in Leningrad. Visitors lived on the boats—sometimes, however, going by rail to Moscow for a hurried two- or three-day visit there. Rates were low. Most of the tourists were in groups of 50 to 300. They were put up in dormitories on the upper floors of the Metropol and Novo-Moskovskaya hotels. De luxe tourists were accommodated in the Grand-Hotel, the Savoy, or later the National. Foreign Communist dignitaries invariably were housed in the Hotel Lux. During this period travel became more restricted in the USSR, largely because it began to be handled more and more by the Intourist organization which directed it to those cities and areas (largely Moscow, Leningrad, Kiev, Kharkov, Odessa, and the Black Sea resorts of the Crimea and the Caucasus) where it had hotel, restaurant and guide facilities.

Moreover, by the mid-1930's a new factor began to affect tourism. This was the Soviet security phobia set in motion by the great CP purge trials. There had been some stirrings of xenophobia earlier with the trial of several groups of foreigners, accused of espionage or wrecking (notably the trial of Metropolitan-Vickers engineers in March 1933). But the savage purges of the mid-1930's transformed the internal atmosphere of the Soviet Union. Not only did ordinary Russians begin to become fearful of contact with foreigners; foreigners more and more often began to encounter incidents of hostility: arrests for taking snapshots; arrests for going into "forbidden zones"; confiscation of books and papers at the frontiers; refusals of visas to enter the country; expulsions for one cause or another. Foreign consulates once located in most of the principal Russian cities systematically were closed down. Less and less was it possible for a foreigner to move freely about the country or reside outside a few specified hotels in a few large cities.

World War II brought an end to all tourist travel in the Soviet Union. A little-noticed decree of 1941 placed all foreigners in the Soviet Union under special restrictions so far as travel was concerned. Actually, all travel from 1941 through 1945 was diplomatic; most of it in the interests of the war effort; and almost all of it by the special order of the Soviet government. In the postwar years normal tourist travel was not resumed. Increasingly stringent restrictions were placed upon travel by diplomats and journalists stationed in the country. Outside of a handful of businessmen (almost exclusively traders in furs, tobacco, and cotton) visas were given to no one to come to the USSR except groups and delegations brought in for special propaganda or diplomatic purposes. Most of the groups were brought in under the auspices of various Soviet organizations, the most active being VOKS, the All Union Society for Cultural Relations with Foreign Countries.

With the death of Stalin, March 5, 1953, an almost immediate turnabout occurred in travel to Russia. In June 1953 about two-thirds of the Soviet Union was formally reopened to travel. Areas which remained sealed were the border regions, the Baltic states, and a number of industrial cities in the Urals and Siberia. Since that time the Baltic states have been opened in part to tourist travel. A good many areas in the interior to which access had been banned or only intermittently granted may now be visited. Most of the industrial Urals and Siberian cities, however, are still closed except by special permission usually granted only to a visitor upon whom the Soviet wishes to make a special impression. Travel procedures, however, have been streamlined. Whereas visas used to require six months or a year and were often refused in the Stalinist period, they are now issued to ordinary tourists in a week or so and almost invariably in less than a month.

Arrangements are handled by foreign travel agents, working with Intourist. An elaborate selection of trips and facilities is available from de luxe accommodations at $30 a day down to group student tourist rates of $5 or less a day. The motorist may drive his car into the Soviet Union, utilizing various highway approaches, via Helsinki and Leningrad, Warsaw and the western highway to Moscow through Minsk, or through Bucharest, Chernovtsy, Kiev, and Moscow. The motorist may go out by any of these routes. Within Russia he may travel to Crimea or the Caucasus resorts by car. Formerly he had to have an Intourist guide with him at all times. That no longer is required. Most of the world's airlines now fly to Moscow. By 1961 all of the principal airlines had entered into reciprocal flight schedules with Aeroflot, the Soviet government air monopoly. Tourist hotel facilities have been sharply expanded, particularly in Moscow where the skyscraper Hotels Ukraina and Leningradskaya and the luxurious Hotel Sovietskaya have placed more than 3,000 additional rooms at the disposal of visitors. New hotels are being built in Leningrad and are already in service in most of the principal tourist cities.

Tourism in the Soviet Union has grown by leaps and bounds since the death of Stalin. In 1953 only 42 ordinary tourists visited the country, as distinguished from members of groups and delegations. In 1956—the first full year of active encouragement of ordinary tourism—1,500 Americans visited the Soviet Union. In 1957 the number was 2,500; in 1958, 4,500; in 1959, 12,000. In 1960, despite cooling of Soviet-American relations produced by the failure of the summit conference, the number of American visitors was estimated at more than 15,000. The over-all number of visitors including delegations showed similar growth. In 1958 the figure was reported as 530,000; in 1959, "in excess of 600,000." The estimate for 1960 was 795,000.

What do the present-day visitors see? If they have no special interests their itinerary will be conventional: a visit to the Winter Palace, the Hermitage and Peterhof at Leningrad and a tour of the Kremlin, the All-Union Exhibition of Industry and Agriculture, the Tretyakov and Pushkin Art Museums, the Lenin-Stalin Mausoleum and the GUM department store in Moscow. If the tourist expresses sufficient interest he will be taken to Zagorsk to see the St. Sergius Monastery or he may visit a collective farm or a factory, possibly a chocolate works. Almost certainly he will be shown the subway systems of both Leningrad and Moscow and will see the ballet at the Bolshoy Opera House and possibly at the Mariinsky Theater in Leningrad, as well.

For the visitor with special interests the story is a little more uncertain. Much depends on his own ability to make contacts on his own. If he is, for example, a scientist or a scholar or a technical specialist and if he has been far-sighted enough to put himself in touch with some of his Soviet colleagues, he may, through them, find the path open to visit facilities in his special field of interest and to meetings with fellow workers. He may find it possible to travel to places not permitted the ordinary visitor and to meet with persons inaccessible to usual travelers. Sometimes, the specialist is aided by or even invited to the Soviet Union by one of two organizations—the State Committee for Cultural Relations with Foreign Countries or the Union of Soviet Societies for Friendship and Cultural Relations with Foreign Countries. Many persons visit the Soviet Union as part of formal exchange programs worked out between Soviet-American authorities. In many of these cases the visitors have elaborately worked out itineraries taking them to remote and normally closed areas of the country and including visits to facilities which are strictly classified.

Despite these major changes in travel conditions to the Soviet Union it still remains a comparatively difficult country for the foreigner. Taking snapshots is no longer an almost automatic invitation to the militia to arrest the tourist, but it is still a frequent cause of difficulty with the police and with officious citizens. The Soviet government, particularly beginning in 1960, carried on an intensive propaganda campaign, warning its citizens to beware of spies in the disguise of tourists. The advice automatically increased the number of unpleasant incidents to which tourists were subjected—including some arrests and expulsions. Physical facilities for the tourist are still often below the standard of W. Europe. Intourist guides and staffs are often inefficient, partly because so many employees are new and inexperienced in looking after foreigners. Language is a greater barrier than elsewhere in Europe. So are the many differences in Soviet custom and practice. Whereas a traveler may comfortably visit almost any W. European country with no special advance preparation, he is advised to familiarize himself at least generally with the specific conditions he is apt to encounter in the Soviet Union if he is to hold difficulties and hardships to a minimum. Even so, he will still find the country an adventure and an experience and quite probably a frustration—as have many generations of travelers before him.

BIBLIOGRAPHY: Karl Baedeker, *Russia: Guide for the Traveller*, Leipzig, 1914; Irving R. Levine, *Travel Guide to Russia*, Garden City, 1960; *Moscow: Short Travel Guide*, Moscow, 1960; Frederick C. Barghoorn, *The Soviet Cultural Offensive*, Princeton, 1960; Harrison E. Salisbury, *To Moscow—And Beyond*, New York, 1960.

H. E. S.

TRAVELING LIBRARIES supplement the work of stationary libraries. They carry books to factories, collective farms, experimental stations, and the less accessible parts of the Soviet Union. (There are approximately 1,200 bookmobiles in the U. S.).

TREDIAKÓVSKY, Vasíly Kiríllovich (1703–1769), poet, philologist, and literary theoretician. T did much to promote the syllabotonic system of modern verse, setting forth his views in *New and Brief Method for the Composition of Russian Verses* (1735). One of the earlier representatives of R. pseudo-classicism, T, in 1766, translated Fénelon's *Télémaque*, preserving its hexameter—the first use of that meter in R. poetry.

TRENYÓV, Konstantín Andréyevich (1876–1945), novelist and playwright. He is chiefly remembered for his play *Lyubov Yarovaya* (1926) which has been shown on the Soviet stage for many years. His plays *The Wife* (1928) and *Anna Luchinina* (1941) were rejected as "ideologically wrong" by the regime. However, the plays *On the Banks of the Neva* (1938) and the *Military Leader* (1944) are marked by propaganda. Stalin prize (1941).

TRÉPOVS—a family that rose to power in the R. police.

1. Fyódor Fyódorovich T (1803–1889) became chief of police of St. Petersburg in 1860. In 1878 he was shot and wounded by the populist, Vera Zasulich, for having ordered the flogging of the revolutionary Bogolyubov. Zasulich, a young girl, who later became one of the leaders of the Social Democratic party, was acquitted after a trial by jury and T retired.

2. Dmítry Fyódorovich T, his older son (1855–1906), was chief of police of Moscow from 1896 to 1905, and governor-general of St. Petersburg in 1905. He was one of those responsible for the massacre of Jan. 9, 1905 (*see* BLOODY SUNDAY) and was known for his ruthless suppression of the revolutionary movement (known for his "spare no cartridges" order to the troops and police). In 1906 he negotiated unsuccessfully with P. N. Milyukov regarding the formation of a government with the participation of Constitutional Democrats and other liberals.

3. Aleksándr Fyódorovich T, the younger son (1862–1928), became minister of transportation in 1915, and chairman of the Council of Ministers in 1916. He was dismissed in 1917 and died in exile.

TRETYAKOV GALLERY: *see* MUSEUMS.

TRETYAKÓV, Pável Mikháylovich (1832–1898), Moscow merchant. A dedicated patron of the arts, he was founder of the world renowned Tretyakov gallery in Moscow and enthusiastic sponsor of the Society of Circulating Exhibitions (*Peredvizhniki*).

TRIUMVIRATE: *see* OPPOSITION, CPSU.

TROFIMÚK, Andréy Alekséyevich (1911–), geologist and petroleum engineer. Fellow, Ac. of S., USSR (1958). Hero of Socialist Labor (1944). Graduated from Kazan University (1933). Director (1955–57) of the All-Union Scientific Research Institute of Petroleum and Gas and of the Institute of Geology and Geophysics, Siberian Branch, Ac. of S. (1957). Research concerns the tectonics of the Volga-Ural oil-bearing areas where T has directed an extensive prospecting project. The results are expounded in his publication *Conditions of Petroleum Deposit Formations in the Volga-Ural Oil-Bearing Region* (1955). Stalin prizes (1946, 1950).

TRÓITSK, city in Chelyabinsk Oblast, RSFSR, on Uy River; pop. 76,000 (1959). R.R. junction; electromechanical, Diesel-engine, machine-tool, food-processing, clothing and footwear ind. Numerous institutes of specialized training.

TROTSK: *see* CHAPAYEVSK.

TROITSKOSAVSK: *see* KYAKHTA.

TROPÍNIN, Vasíly Andréyevich (1776–1857), portrait painter of talent. First a serf, he later was sent to the Academy of Art and studied with Shchukin. He painted over three thousand portraits characterized by naturalness, simplicity, and pleasant ease of execution. Best known are his portraits of Pushkin and Karamzin.

TRÓTSKY, Leon (Lev Davidovich Bronstein) (1879–1940), revolutionary leader, born in the Ukraine (Kherson region) of a middle-class family. Studied at a college in Odessa. Became a revolutionary in 1898, was arrested and exiled to Siberia, but escaped abroad. In 1902, T first met Lenin in London and, despite Plekhanov's

objections, was invited by him to collaborate in *Iskra* (q.v.). When the party split in 1903, T strongly denounced Lenin's organizational principles believing them to lead to a one-man dictatorship. He became a friend of the cosmopolitan revolutionary Parvus (Helfand) (q.v.) and together with him worked out a theory of "permanent revolution."

T became prominent during the 1905 revolution as chairman of the St. Peterbsurg Soviet (second, after the arrest of Khrustalev-Nosar), was publicly tried and sentenced to life banishment to Siberia. However, he again escaped and settled in Vienna where he edited a R. paper, *Pravda*, continued to struggle against Lenin's dictatorial tactics, and tried to reunite all R. Social Democratic factions. During World War I, T directed revolutionary antiwar propaganda in France (*Nashe Slovo*) and later in New York (*Novy Mir*). After the February revolution, he embarked for Russia, but was detained by Britain at Halifax, Nova Scotia, and eventually released on the insistence of the new R. foreign minister, Milyukov. In Russia T formally joined the Bolshevik party in July 1917, and was elected to its Central Committee. He was arrested after the July riots (q.v.) but soon released. When, in Sept. 1917, the Bolsheviks won a majority in the Petrograd Soviet, T became its chairman. He was also chairman of the Military Revolutionary Committee which carried out the seizure of power in the capital. After the October revolution, T's popularity was second only to Lenin's.

In the first Soviet government, T was people's commissar for foreign affairs and conducted the negotiations with Germany at Brest-Litovsk, but, being against the signing of the peace treaty (his policy was "neither war nor peace"), he resigned. From 1918 to 1925, T was commissar for war, the chief organizer and leader of the Red Army. From 1919 to 1926, he was an eminent Politburo member, often in opposition to Lenin who (in his *Testament*) spoke highly of him, and who, in the last years of his life, took steps to join forces with him. After Lenin's death, T led the political opposition against the ruling "triumvirate" consisting of Kamenev, Stalin, and Zinoviev and, in Nov. 1924, attacked Kamenev and Zinoviev (in the book *Lessons of October*) for their "defeatist" attitude in 1917. Later on he worked with them in the "combined opposition" against Stalin's policy of "building socialism in one country" (T's policy was one of "permanent" and world revolution). After the defeat of the "combined opposition," in Dec. 1927, T was expelled from the party and exiled to Alma-Ata, in Kazakhstan. There he carried on his political activities by corresponding with his followers, most of them also in exile or in prison. In 1928, when Stalin began to attack the "right opposition," he adopted many ideas which had originally been advanced by T. As a result, several former oppositionists and Trotskyites became reconciled with Stalin, but T himself remained inexorably opposed to him. In Feb. 1929, the Collegium of GPU sentenced him, *in abstentia*, to life banishment from the USSR. Because of the difficulty of obtaining permanent visas, T went first to Turkey, then to France and Norway, and finally settled in Mexico. When abroad, T continued his political anti-Stalin activities, organizing his followers (who called themselves "Bolsheviks-Leninists") in the IV International, and writing anti-Stalinist books and articles. Consequently, the name of "Judas-Trotsky" acquired the most odious connotation in Soviet world propaganda. During the great purge, at the big show trials, T was accused of conducting espionage and subversive activities in the USSR on behalf of foreign (Nazi) intelligence services. All the members of T's family (two married daughters and one married son, Sergey) in Russia have been exterminated; his second son, Lev Sedov, was murdered in France in Feb. 1938, and, on Aug. 20, 1940, after several attempts on his life, T himself was murdered in his fortified villa in Mexico City by a certain "Jacques Mornard," an alleged friend of T's secretary and apparently a secret agent of Stalin's police. Followers of T still exist in several countries as communist splinter groups, and in Ceylon they form an important political party. Main T's works in English: *My Life*, New York, 1930; *The Permanent Revolution*, New York, 1931; *The History of the Russian Revolution*, 3 vols., New York, 1933; *The Revolution Betrayed*, New York, 1937; *The Stalin School of Falsification*, New York, 1937; *Stalin*, New York, 1941.

BIBLIOGRAPHY: I. Deutscher, *The Prophet Armed*, London and New York, 1954; I. Deutscher, *The Prophet Unarmed*, London and New York, 1959; Bertram D. Wolfe, *Three Who Made a Revolution*, Boston, 1955.

V. Su.

TROTSKYISM. Strictly speaking, "Trotskyism" is a term of opprobrium, coined by the Stalinists in 1924, but we may consider it more broadly to denote Trotsky's particular views and the tendency within the communist movement which supported them.

Trotsky's most distinctive contribution to communist theory is the idea of "permanent revolution," which he worked out in association with the German Social Democrat A. L. Parvus in 1905 and published in his book, *Our Revolution* (Geneva, 1906; abridged English translation, New York, 1918). To get around the problem of Russia's unripeness from the Marxist point of view, Trotsky suggested that the country was developing unevenly under the influence of the capitalist West, so that forces of both bourgeois and proletarian revolution were present simultaneously. Once revolution broke out, Trotsky predicted, the revolutionary situation would remain in effect continuously or permanently, and the *bourgeoisie* would be displaced by the small but politically active proletarian minority. A workers' government would thus come to power easily, but it would be condemned to quick overthrow by the petty-bourgeois majority of the country unless it received aid from foreign revolutionaries. This, Trotsky held, was guaranteed by the second aspect of the revolution's permanence—a permanent state of revolution as the Russian proletariat inspired the working class of W. Europe to rise up likewise and offer the aid of majority proletarian regimes to the outnumbered socialists in Russia.

Trotsky's position in 1905 was not substantially different from that of Lenin and the Bolsheviks, who also argued for working-class leadership in the anticipated revolution. Lenin made some closely parallel statements

about the "growing-over" of the bourgeois revolution into the socialist revolution. However, Lenin refused to accept Trotsky's terminology or his apprehension about the peasants, and "permanent revolution'" remained one of the points of issue between the two men before Trotsky finally joined the Bolsheviks in 1917.

The events of 1917 appeared to substantiate "permanent revolution" in its internal aspect. The moderate Provisional Government which succeeded the tsar was overthrown by the Bolsheviks and the urban workers. At this time many Bolsheviks—Bukharin, for instance—explicitly acknowledged the correctness of Trotsky's theory.

In its international aspect Trotsky's theory failed to be borne out. Proletarian revolution failed to materialize in the West, and the Bolsheviks were in a quandary of how to justify their continued tenure of power in Russia, in the absence of the widely developed industry which Marxism held to be the prerequisite for socialism. During the controversy over the peace with Germany early in 1918, the Utopian Left Communists, led by Bukharin, insisted that the new Soviet regime declare a "revolutionary war" to arouse western proletarian support. They were quite prepared to risk the future of Communist power in Russia because from the standpoint of "permanent revolution" such power isolated in Russia was doomed to defeat. Trotsky, as commissar of foreign affairs, at first endorsed the Left Communist position, but under the pressure of the German advance in February 1918 he abstained from voting in the Central Committee of the party, and Lenin's position of making peace and buying time—i.e. to hold power no matter what—became the permanent Communist policy.

During the Russian civil war of 1918–20 Trotsky began to formulate a second major body of thought which was closely associated with his name during the 1920's. He proposed to deal with the newly faced problems of an underdeveloped country such as Russia through the central power of the revolutionary state to plan industrial development and coerce the population into carrying it out. This involved: (1) Centralized and bureaucratic authority in army and industry, which Trotsky successfully defended in 1918–20 against the proponents of a guerrilla militia, decentralized soviet administration, and trade-union control of the factories. (2) Coercion, exemplified by Trotsky's proposal to militarize labor and industry in 1920, and his harsh suppression of the Kronstadt revolt in 1921. Coercive governmental violence was relaxed during the NEP, but returned under Stalin in 1928–29. (3) Central governmental planning of the economy, stressed by Trotsky from 1920 on, but poorly understood by most of the party, and resisted until the end of the NEP. (4) Intensive industrialization financed by the governmental exploitation of the population—especially the peasants—through fixed prices and taxes. This approach to industrial development was worked out in detail by Trotsky's supporter, the economist Yevgeny Preobrazhensky. Like planning, it was resisted by the party leadership during the NEP, only to become the basis of Stalin's economic policy during the five year plans.

A third body of Trotskyist thought took shape between 1923 and 1927, when Trotsky had gone into opposition against the party leadership of Stalin and Bukharin and was being openly attacked as an anti-Leninist and pro-Menshevik deviator. To protect themselves, Trotsky and his supporters undertook to defend the principle of "workers' democracy" in the party and to charge that the government under the NEP was violating the interests of the proletariat. "Permanent revolution" returned as a point of controversy because of its proposition that a socialist government could not keep power in Russia alone, and the implicit corollary that the Stalin-Bukharin regime was easing the circumstances of its rule by appeasing the peasants and middle class and becoming un-socialist. Stalin, to justify himself, contrived the theory of "socialism in one country," based on one 1915 quotation from Lenin taken out of context and misinterpreted. At the same time—1924—he and his supporters also contrived the term "Trotskyism" to counterpose Trotsky's presumed heresy to the official doctrine of "Leninism."

In 1926 and 1927, violent controversy raged between Trotsky—now joined by Zinoviev and Kamenev—and the Stalin-Bukharin leadership over party democracy, economic planning, "socialism in one country," and the fortunes of the Communist International. This has been erroneously interpreted to mean that Trotsky urged immediate world revolution and that Stalin opposed it. Actually the issue was only theoretical hair-splitting as to whether the security of the socialist regime in Russia depended on the spread of revolution abroad. Both Stalin and Trotsky favored the revolution in theory and were reluctant to take risks in practice, and the point of Trotsky's argument was to embarrass Stalin with the assertion that un-socialist influences threatened to penetrate the Soviet government as long as it lacked socialist allies.

In 1927, thanks to his control of the party organization, Stalin easily defeated the opposition of Trotsky and Zinoviev and expelled them from the party. When Stalin broke with the Communist right wing led by Bukharin and commenced the First Five Year Plan, many of Trotsky's supporters saw their own economic principles being put into effect, and "capitulated" to Stalin. Others remained adamantly opposed to Stalin, and one exiled Trotskyist, Christian Rakovsky, formerly prime minister of the Ukraine and ambassador to Great Britain, developed the Trotskyist critique of Stalinism into a general theory of the bureaucratic degeneration of the revolution. This theme was elaborated by Trotsky himself in his book, *The Revolution Betrayed* (1937); he also finally rejected the cardinal precept of Leninism, one-party rule. Inside Russia, however, Trotskyist influence—including the "capitulators"—was completely liquidated in the purges of 1936–1938.

The theme of bureaucratic degeneration has inspired a considerable neo-Trotskyist literature, represented by James Burnham's *Managerial Revolution* (1941) and Milovan Djilas' *New Class* (1957). These authors revise Marxism by suggesting that the anti-capitalist revolution has ushered in the rule not of the proletariat but of yet another exploiting minority, in this case the managers or bureaucratic office-holders.

The rejection of Stalinism as a bureaucratic betrayal of the workers was the guiding belief of the factions of Trotskyists who split off from most of the Communist parties around the world after 1927 and who formed the Fourth International in 1934. However, they rarely attracted any mass support, except in Southeast Asia and in Ceylon, where they are at present the largest left-wing movement.

Trotskyism in the Soviet Union was doomed by its lack of good leadership and organization as a political faction. The activity of the Trotskyists was hamstrung by their acceptance of the principles of Leninist unity in the Communist party. Furthermore, the whole vision of democratic proletarian socialism in Russia was based on dubious premises. Industry and the working class were too weak in Russia at the time of the revolution, and the socialistic industrialization of the country which Trotsky himself stressed involved methods and institutions which were the antithesis of democracy. Finally, there is reason to doubt that industrial development necessarily promotes democracy anywhere if liberal government is not strong already. The viable aspects of Trotsky's views were his stress on a governmentally planned industrialization drive plus the tactics of militarization and centralization which he stressed during the civil war. These points, in exaggerated form, are the basis of Stalinism and the present Soviet economy. Nonetheless, Trotsky and Trotskyism are still regarded as heretical in the communist movement today, and there are no signs of any easing of this condemnation.

BIBLIOGRAPHY: Robert V. Daniels, *The Conscience of the Revolution: Communist Opposition in Soviet Russia*, Cambridge, Mass., 1960; Isaac Deutscher, *The Prophet Armed: Trotsky, 1879–1921*, London and New York, 1954, and *The Prophet Unarmed: Trotsky, 1921–1929*, London and New York, 1959; Leon Trotsky, *The Real Situation in Russia*, New York, 1928; Bertram D. Wolfe, *Three Who Made a Revolution*, New York, 1948; *The Case of Leon Trotsky: Report of Hearings on the Charges Made against him in the Moscow Trials*, by the Preliminary Commission of Inquiry, John Dewey, Chairman, New York, 1938.   R. V. D.

TRUBETSKÓY, Prince Sergéy Nikoláyevich (1862–1905), philosopher, first elected rector of the Moscow University. At the head of a deputation of the zemstvo leaders to Nicholas II, T delivered a speech in which he pleaded, in accordance with the liberal program, for a representative assembly, freedom of press, and civil liberties. In philosophy, T was a disciple of Vladimir Solovyov (q.v.). He is the author of several books on philosophy.

TRUBETSKÓY, Prince Sergéy Petróvich (1790–1860), member of the Northern Society of Decembrists, but on the day of the uprising, Dec. 14, 1825, he failed to join the rebels. He was charged with high treason, but his death sentence was commuted to hard labor.

TRUCK FARMING: *see* VEGETABLE GARDENING.

TSAKHURS: *see* POPULATION.

TSAR, title of Russian and some other monarchs. In Russia the title of T was officially introduced by Ivan IV in 1547. From 1721 on the Russians tsars were also emperors.

TSAREVOKOKSHÁYSK: *see* YOSHKAR-OLA.

TSARÍTSYN: *see* STALINGRAD.

TSÁRSKOYE SELÓ: *see* PUSHKIN.

TSENTROSOYUZ: *see* COOPERATIVES.

TSELIKOV, Aleksándr Ivánovich (1904–), metallurgical engineer. Corresponding member, Ac. of S., USSR (1953). Graduate of the Moscow School of Technology (1928). Associated with the Central Design Bureau of Metallurgical Machinery (1945). Research on the design of steel rolling mills and the theory of rolling. Directed the design and construction of various types of high-productivity rolling mills. Author of *Problems of Metallurgy* (1953); *Advanced Technology of Machine Building* (1955). Stalin prizes (1947, 1948, 1951).

TSELINOGRÁD (f. Akmolinsk), city, adm. center of Virgin Lands Kray, Kazakh SSR; pop. 32,000 (1939), 101,000 (1959). On Ishim River. Ind.: farm machinery, railway-car repairs, chemical and vegetable-oil plants, tanneries.

TSERETÉLI, Irákly Geórgievich (1882–1960), Georgian and Russian Menshevik leader. In 1907 he was elected deputy to the second Duma where he became one of the most articulate spokesmen of the opposition. After the arrest of the Social Democratic deputies, T was condemned to hard labor and exile. After the February revolution T, a gifted orator, became one of the leaders of the Executive Committee of the Soviets. A partisan of a coalition government with the moderate parties, T participated in the Provisional Government as minister of communications (May-Aug.) and of the interior (July-Aug.). After the October revolution, T—an irreconcilable adversary of the Bolsheviks —went to his native Georgia where he became a member of the government of the Georgian Republic. Later he emigrated to France and in 1940 to New York where he worked on a history of the revolution.

TSIMLYANSK RESERVOIR, formed as a result of the construction of the hydroelectric station and dam, is the largest reservoir on the Don River. It is used for irrigation of the dry areas of Rostov and Stalingrad oblasts.

TSIOLKÓVSKY, Konstantín Eduárdovich (1857–1935), aeronautical inventor. Made major discoveries in aerodynamics, rocketry, and the theory of interplanetary flights. Owing to an almost complete loss of hearing in early childhood T was unable to attend regular school; was self-educated in mathematics and physics and received a diploma for teaching arithmetic, geometry, and physics. Being unaware of the discoveries of that time, he developed the principles of kinetic theories of gases (1881). His paper on *Mechanics of a Live Organism* brought him the membership of the Russian Physical and Chemical Society. Solved the following problems, in part: the scientific substantiation of the design of an all-metal dirigible (1885–92), of a streamlined airplane (1894), and of interplanetary rocket ships (1896). T built an aerodynamic wind tunnel (1897) and developed aerodynamic test methods. In his treatise *Investigating Space with Rocket Devices* (1903), he presented the theory of rocket flights with the consideration of mass variation in the process of motion and substantiated the use of reaction planes for interplanetary flights. After the 1917 revolution, T continued research on rocket ships and suggested two types of multistage rockets (1929). He is claimed to be the first to solve the problem of rocket flight in a uniform field of gravitation and calculate the amount of fuel required to overcome earth gravitation, and to originate the idea of interplanetary stations. Investigated the possibility of life and work in a manned space-capsule and at interplanetary stations. T suggested gyroscopic stabilization of rocket flights in space and a method for cooling the combustion chamber with fuel ingredients which is widely used in modern jet engine designs. His *Selected Works* (2 vols.) were published in 1934; *Works on Rocketry* in 1947; and *Collection of Works* (2 vols.) in 1951–54.

TSKHINVALI: *see* STALINIRI.

TSNA RIVER: (1) Left tributary of Pripyat River, Byelorussia; length 70 mi. **(2)** Flows via Tambov and Ryazan oblasts to form left tributary of Moksha River in European RSFSR; length 290 mi. **(3)** Flows into Lake Mstino, Kalinin Oblast; length 100 mi.

TSVETÁYEVA, Marína Ivánovna (1892–1941), poet. Born in Moscow, she emigrated to W. Europe in 1922 and returned to the USSR in 1939 where she committed suicide two years later. The larger part of her works, which consist mainly of poems, but also of plays and essays, was written either before her emigration or during her first years abroad.

T's works, which are in many ways similar to those of B. Pasternak and of O. Mandelshtam, have not received wide recognition because of their introvertedness and also because of the extreme individuality of her style. Among their leading themes are her philosophy of life and of art, and human passions. In presenting them T made abundant use of materials from R. folklore, as well as of heroic figures from the broader literary heritage of the West. In expressing her essentially romantic interpretation of these and other subjects she frequently relied on uneven rhythms and on complicated rhyming patterns. In her prose works, which consist of interpretive essays concerning contemporary poets, a similar effect is achieved through the use of the "stream of consciousness" technique. Her plays— *The End of Casanova, Theseus,* and *Phoedra*—were never presented on the stage.

T's first collection of poems, *Evening Album,* was published in 1910. It was followed by others: *The Magic Lantern, From Two Books,* and *Milestones,* which were published in Moscow; *The Parting* and *A Craft,* published both in Moscow and in Berlin; *Psyche, Poems to Blok,* and *After Russia,* published abroad; and by the poems published in *A Day of Poetry* (Moscow, 1956). T also wrote a number of long poems, including *Molodéts, A Poem of a Mountain, A Poem of the Barricade,* and *Tsar-Devitsa* (Maiden-Tsar).

TSYURÚPA, Aleksándr Dmítrievich (1870–1928), Bolshevik of the old guard and Soviet official. T carried out revolutionary propaganda among workers and intellectuals from the time he joined the Social Democratic Workers' party in 1898. Frequently arrested and exiled. After the October revolution he was appointed people's commissar for food supply. In 1922–23, he was commissar of workers and peasants inspection, and, in 1923–25, chairman of the Gosplan, USSR. In 1925–26,

T was people's commissar for domestic and foreign trade. From 1923 on T was a member of the Central Committee of the CPSU.

TUAPSÉ, city in Krasnodar Kray, RSFSR; pop. 37,000 (1959). Major petroleum shipping port on the Black Sea; center of shipbuilding and oil-refining ind.; terminal of pipeline from Grozny oil fields; large producer of machinery for petroleum ind.; health resort, in a fruit- and vine-growing district.

TUGÁN-BARANÓVSKY, Mikhaíl Ivánovich (1865–1919), economist and historian. First gained prominence for his study of industrial crisis in England (1894). In *The Russian Factory, Past and Present* (1898), he contradicted the populist belief that industrial capitalism was alien to Russia, contending that, since the reign of Peter I, capitalism had become essential to the nation's progress. A "Legal" (moderate) Marxist, T-B became steadily more conservative. During the civil war he served as minister of finance in the Ukrainian Central Rada.

TUKHACHÉVSKY, Mikhaíl Nikoláyevich (1893–1937), military leader, marshal of the Soviet Union. T  was a tsarist officer who fought valiantly in World War I until his capture by the Germans. Joined the Bolsheviks in 1918 and became one of their military commanders. During the civil war T had several important commands in the Volga region, in Siberia, and finally in the war against Poland in 1920. In 1921 T suppressed the Kronstadt revolt and later the Antonov peasant revolt. In 1924 he was appointed deputy chief of staff and head of the Military Academy. In 1931 he was promoted to deputy people's commissar of military and naval affairs and was elected a candidate member of the Central Committee of the CPSU. T was credited with the creation of the first parachute division. In 1935 he became one of the first five marshals of the Soviet Union. In 1936 he was sent abroad on several missions as the Soviet military representative. Then in 1937 T was relieved of his command and charged with Trotskyism as well as conspiracy with foreign powers. He was tried in secret, found guilty, and executed. A sweeping purge of the Red Army followed his execution. In 1956 T was posthumously exonerated and the charge against him refuted.

TÚLA, city, adm. center of Tula Oblast; pop. 345,-000 (1959; according to other sources, 316,000). A five-way rail junction, on the Upa (right tributary of the Oka); dates from the 12th century. The site of large metallurgical works; in the past, was famous for the skill of its gunsmiths and toolmakers; center of samovar and ironware mfg.

TÚLA OBLAST, Central RSFSR; area 9,900 sq. mi.; pop. 1,920,000 (1959). Cities: Tula (adm. center), Stalinogorsk, Yefremov, Bolokhovo, Plavsk, Chekalin. Situated in the N.W. section of the Central R. plateau; drained by the Oka and upper Don; dense deciduous forests on gray, weakly podsolized soils merge into wooded steppe, with leached black-earth soils, toward S.E. Important lignite deposits are mined at Kagano-

vich, Bogoroditsk, and other centers; iron reserves, construction materials (marble, gypsum, refractory clays); hardy grains, ind. crops (rubber-bearing plants, sugar beets, flax) emphasized; hog rearing based on extensive potato farming. Est. 1937.

TUNDRA: *see* GEOGRAPHICAL ZONES, PLANT LIFE.

TUNGUS: *see* EVENKI.

TUNGÚSKA PODKÁMENNAYA RIVER, flows through Krasnoyarsk Kray to form right tributary of Yenisey River; 960 mi. long.

TUNGÚSKA COAL BASIN, one of world's richest coal basins, area 400,000 sq. mi., resources 1,745 bill. t., in Krasnoyarsk Kray, Central Siberia, RSFSR. Main settlements: Tura, Norilsk, Igarka, Yeniseysk.

TÚPOLEV, Andréy Nikoláyevich (1888–), leading aeronautical engineer. Fellow, Ac. of S., USSR (1953). Lieutenant General, Air Force Engineering and Technical Service. Honored scientist and technologist RSFSR (1933). Hero of Socialist Labor (1945). Member of the Supreme Soviet USSR (1950, 1954, 1958). A student  of N. Ye. Zhukovsky, T graduated from the Moscow School of Technology (1918). Cofounder and assist. director of the Central Institute of Aerodynamics (1918–35), director of its Experimental Aircraft Construction Plant No. 46, and assist. director, Central Administration of the Aircraft Industry of the USSR. His early research concerned wind tunnels and training gliders and later work dealt with basic aerodynamic calculations of aircrafts, the use of duraluminum in aircraft and aerosleighs. A pioneer in the field of all-metal aircraft construction. In 1934, T designed the 40-ton, eight-engine aircraft "Maksim Gorky" with a radio station, printing press, photo laboratory, telephone switchboard, telegraph office, and motion-picture projectors. The plane, designed for propaganda purposes, collided with another plane in mid-air and killed 35 people (1935). T was accused of sabotage and espionage during a visit to the U.S. and Germany (1936). Arrested in 1938, T was sentenced to five-year imprisonment. While serving his term T designed the TU-2 dive bomber which was mass produced in 1939 and brought T rehabilitation. Designed over 100 types of aircraft, including TU-4 (a copy of the US B-29); TU-70, a superheavy four-engine bomber; TU-104, a 50-passenger jet aircraft; TU-106, a 170-passenger jet; TU-114, double-deck turboprop airliner and others. T also designed several types of torpedo launches. Stalin and Lenin prizes (1957), other awards.

TURÁ, town, adm. center of Evenki National Okrug, Krasnoyarsk Kray, RSFSR; pop. 2,000 (1959). River port on the Lower Tunguska, tributary of the Yenisey; trading town, ind. and cultural center of a rich coal region.

TURÁN LOWLAND, central Asia; area 580,000 sq. mi. Contains Karakum and Kyzylkum deserts, Amu Darya and Syr Darya rivers and an area below sea level.

TURGÉNEV, Iván Sergéyevich (1818–1883), novelist, born in the province of Orel in a family of provincial gentry. T was educated by private tutors and then at the universities of Moscow and St. Petersburg. His early outlook was influenced by a group of young R. intellectuals whom he met in Berlin in 1839–40, especially N. V. Stankevich and M. A. Bakunin, and also by Herzen and later by the critic Belinsky.

T's early works were poems. They include *Parasha* (1843), *Conversation* (1845), *Pomeshchik* (1846), and *Andrey* (1846). Subsequently, a poetic approach to literary themes and a general sensitivity to aesthetic elements continued to characterize his works. T's first notable success came with the publication in the journal *Sovremennik* (The Contemporary) of short stories entitled *A Sportsman's Sketches* (1847–52) which contained realistic descriptions of the plight of the serfs. Because this work was generally interpreted as a protest against serfdom, it led, together with a laudatory obituary of Gogol, to T's temporary exile to his estate in 1852. It is in the course of the following ten years that T's great novels were written. They reflected the critical issues of the time—conflict of the liberal nobility with the revolutionary democratic elements, and the impact of western scientific thought upon R. society. T's novels include *Rudin* (1856), in which he portrayed an enthusiastic liberal and a man of high ideals who lacks the will to put his principles into action; *A Nest of Gentlefolk* (1859); *On the Eve* (1860); and *Fathers and Sons* (1862), which centers on the conflict of its agnostic and nihilistic hero, Bazarov, with representatives of traditional attitudes. T's portrayal of Bazarov was widely interpreted as a deliberate attempt to condemn radical intellectuals, and led to bitter attacks on T by influential literary critics. T's subsequent writings were of lesser significance. Toward the end of his life he wrote a series of literary miniatures, *Poems in Prose* (1878–82), dealing with death, fate, and the futility of human endeavor. He died in 1883 in Bougival, near Paris, and was buried in St. Petersburg. T was a poet among the R. novelists of the realist school. His style is marked by simplicity and good taste. He was at his best describing nature.

T had a long liaison with the French singer Pauline Viardot-Garcia and spent much of his life abroad, in France and in Germany. He was the first R. author to gain recognition in W. Europe, and was close to many outstanding men of letters, among them Flaubert, Zola, and Henry James.

BIBLIOGRAPHY: David Magarshack, *Turgenev, A Life*, New York, 1954.   I. M.

TURGÉNEV, Nikoláy Ivánovich (1789–1871), cousin of the novelist, T was an ideologue of the Decembrist movement (1825). Though he fled Russia before the uprising, he was nevertheless sentenced *in absentia* to hard labor in Siberia. A gifted economist, his works included *Russia and Russians* (1849), and *An Essay on the Theory of Taxes* in which he advocated the emancipation of the peasantry.

TURKESTAN. History. The history of T prior to the R. conquest was a succession of invasions. The Persians, Scythians, Chinese, Turks, Arabs, and Mongols, successively invaded and occupied the country.

In the 7th century B.C. the area was inhabited by Aryan tribes and parts of it were known as Sogdiana, Margiana, and Bactriana. Under Persian domination from the 7th to the 8th century B.C., T, after the siege of Maracanda (contemporary Samarkand), fell into the hands of Alexander the Great. Greco-Bactrian states which developed in the 3rd century B.C. were subjected to Chinese rule from the 2nd century B.C. to the 2nd century A.D. and to a new Persian rule between the 3rd and 4th century. At that time the Zoroaster religion was introduced. The first Turkic invasion took place in the 5th century and already in the 7th century the Turkic elements became racially predominant. Then, once more, the Chinese conquered that region and the disintegration of Turkic state-units began. During the 8th century the Chinese were driven back by the Arabs, and the Moslem religion penetrated the area. In 999 Turkic rule was reestablished south of Amu Darya. A new Turkic invasion led by Sultan Sendjar took place in 1130, but a century later (1220) Genghiz Khan entered Samarkand and soon established Mongol rule over the entire region. However, 150 years later, Turkic elements prevailed once more; their leader Tamerlane (Timur) rose to power and pushed the Mongols into the steppes of today's Kazakhstan. At the same time a process of rapid Islamization and Turkification took place among the Mongols themselves. In the middle of the 15th century, the Turkic-Mongol horde of Kazakhstan broke into two groups: Kirghiz-Kazakh and Uzbek (the latter named after its Khan). Around 1500, the Uzbeks invaded T; Baber, the last of Timur's successors was deposed. The conquerors mixed with the indigenous Turkic population and formed the future Uzbek nation.

The 17th century saw the rise of Uzbek dynasties of Sheibanides and Astrakhanides in Bukhara. In 1740 Persian rule was temporarily established by Nadir Shah. In the meantime three state-units developed in T: Bukhara, Khiva, and Kokand. Soon they had to face a new danger: that of R. conquest.

As early as 1717 Prince A. Bekovich-Cherkassky led a Cossack troop of 6,000 men against Khiva, but failed. During the first half of the century, however, the Kirghiz-Kazakhs of the Lesser Horde (N. Kazakhstan) and of the Middle Horde (central Kazakhstan) were forced to recognize the nominal suzerainty of the R. tsar and R. started a slow but constant penetration into Kazakh steppes. By 1847 the Russians reached the northern shore of Syr Darya and constructed Fort Aralsk. By 1855 all Kazakh lands north of Syr Darya and of Lake Issyk-Kul were in R. hands. The conquest of T proper began; the weak and backward T states proved unable to defend their independence. In 1865 R. troops under General Chernyayev struck against the Khanate of Kokand and took Tashkent, the largest city of T. A military administration under a R. governor-general was established in the conquered territories. The Emir of Bukhara and the Khan of Khiva were compelled to give up large parts of their domains and to accept R. protectorate. In 1876 the state of Kokand was liquidated. In 1881 the last native resistance, that of nomad Turkmen, was broken at the battle of Gök-Tepe. A treaty was signed between Russia and Great

Britain, establishing southern limits of R. penetration (1885). A possibility of an Anglo-Russian conflict was thus averted and R. colonial conquest received formal recognition. R. conquest of T ended local feudal wars and slavery, weakened the power of local feudal-tribal aristocracy and opened the way for economic development. On the other hand R. administration was harsh and quite corrupt demanding absolute obedience, suppressing nationalist agitation and generally treating the natives with contempt. Native revolts against R. colonialism were suppressed by armed force (Andizhan uprising in 1898, general revolt against conscription in 1916, and so forth).

The 1917 revolution resulted in the establishment of a Moslem Central Council in Kokand (Mustapha Chokay, chairman) and of an all-Kazakh Congress in Orenburg, dominated by the nationalist Alash-Orda party (A. Bukheyhan, A. Baitursunov and others). The Russian Tashkent Soviet (Kolesov, chairman), using military force, soon got rid of its nationalistic competitor (Jan. 1918) and proclaimed the Turkestan Autonomous SSR. In Kazakhstan in 1918, the commander of the 4th Soviet Red Army, Mikhail Frunze appointed a Russian-dominated Kirrevkom (Kirghiz-Kazakh revolutionary committee) which soon eliminated all Kazakh nationalists.

Soviet policy provoked discontent among the native Moslem population and gave rise to the so-called Basmachi movement—a T Moslem movement of national liberation. In Jan. 1919 the discredited Tashkent Soviet was replaced by a five-man Moscow-appointed commission for T's affairs (including Eliava, Frunze, and Kuybyshev). The commission pursued a more restrained policy—granting the natives equal treatment and inviting them to participate in local Soviet institutions. In 1920 the Russian-dominated First Kirghiz-Kazakh Congress of Soviets established the Kirghiz-Kazakh Autonomous Republic within the framework of the RSFSR. Meanwhile, in T, Soviet troops seized Bukhara and Khiva and transformed them into "People's Republics." In 1921, however, the Basmachi revolt led by Ibrahim Bek and other nationalist leaders flared up with renewed strength. The Soviet emissary in T, a Turkish leftist, Enver Pasha, deserted to the Basmachi, followed by Osman Khodzha, the head of the government of the "People's Republic" of Bukhara, and several of his ministers. The Soviets intensified the struggle against the Basmachis and succeeded in breaking the backbone of the movement by 1923, although some Basmachi groups resisted until the end of the 1920's. In 1924 Moscow abolished the old administrative set-up, including the "People's Republics" and created instead two Union republics (Uzbekistan and Turkmenistan) and three autonomous republics (Tadzhikistan within Uzbekistan, and Kazakhstan and Kirghizia within the RSFSR).

The collectivization of agriculture carried on in 1929–31 met with strong resistance and resulted in the decimation of the animal stock of T. The 1930's were marked by constant purges of "bourgeois nationalist elements," culminated by the "great purge" of 1937–38. Noteworthy among the liquidated were N. Maksum

(1933) and Shotemar (1937), presidents of Tadzhikistan; Khodzhayev (1933) and Rakhimbayev (1937), premiers of Tadzhikistan; U. Kulambetov (1935) and U. Isayev (1938), premiers of Kazakhstan; Y. Abdrakhmanov, premier of Kirghizia; Faizulla Khodzhayev and Akmal Ikramov (1937), premier and first secretary of the CP of Uzbekistan; T. Ryskulov, vice-premier of RSFSR, former premier of Turkestan SSR; several other political figures of similar stature, scores of lesser officials and intellectuals and thousands of ordinary citizens. As a result of a constant influx of Slavic and other nonnative settlers and deportees, nonnatives constitute one-fourth of the population of T proper and two-thirds of the population of Kazakhstan (1959).

Prestige positions in T are usually given to the natives, but the armed forces, the political police, and the key positions in the party and government apparatus always remain in more reliable R. hands. During World War II, natives of T were most often drafted to the so-called "labor front" instead of the armed forces, and among those in active service many deserted to the Germans. After the fall of Beria new purges were carried on in the area. An Uzbek, Nuritdin A. Mukhitdinov, is a member of the Presidium of the Central Committee of the CPSU.

Culture. Old T literature is part of the general literary heritage of all Turkic peoples. Best known T folkloric epics are *Manas* and *Alpamysh;* both describe the struggle against foreign invaders, Chinese in the former, Kalmuks in the latter. Starting with the 11th century, religious subjects prevail in literature. Ahmed Yasavi (12th century) and Suleiman Bakirgami are the best known authors of that period. Secular literature is well represented in the 14th and 15th centuries. Yusuf Balagasun wrote *Yusuf and Zuleika,* Durbek and Liuft, poetry; and the foremost T poet and writer, Ali Shir Nevai (1440–1500), wrote his famous love story *Ferhad and Shirin.* With Nevai starts the "Golden Century of T literature," which produced the writers Sultan Babur, author of his famous *Autobiography* and Prince Muhammed Salikh, author of the historic epic poem *Sheibani-Name.* Beginning with the 16th century "Chagatai," the common literary language of almost all Turkic speaking peoples became the language of classical T literature. The classical T authors, Sekkali, Fuzuli, Mir Khaider, and Khelali, wrote in this language. Outstanding in the 18th century is the poet Mahtum Kuli; in the 19th century, poet Emir (pseudonym of the Khan Omar of Kokand) and Kazakh scientist-educator Ch. Valikhanov. Best-known 19th century writers are: Muhammed Mukimi and Zakirdzhan Firkat in T; Abay Kunanbay and Toltogul Satylgan in the Kirghiz-Kazakh steppes. Among 20th-century writers are Khamza, Aibek, A. Kakhar, G. Gulyam, A. Tokombay, T. Sydykbek, B. Kerbabay, S. Mukan, Mukhtar Auez, Kul-Muhammed, "reactionary" Batu, and Stalin's court poet Dzhambul. The famous T writers Fitrat, Cholpan, Elbek, Kadyri, M. Dzhumabay and K. Tynystan disappeared in the purges of the late 1930's.

Tadzhik literature, because of its close connections with that of Persia, stands apart. These roots go back to classical Persian literature: Ferdawsi, Omar Khayam,

Saadi, and Hafiz. The first local Tadzhik poets appeared in the 16th and 17th centuries: Mushkifi and Nasafi, respectively. The most prominent modern writer was S. Aini (beginning of the 20th century).

In the 1920's the Arabic alphabet, used by all the peoples of T, was replaced by the Latin alphabet, and by the end of the 1930's the latter was, in its turn, replaced by the Cyrillic (Russian) script.

Some architectural monuments in T date back to the 3rd and 2nd millennium B.C. The cities like Samarkand (ancient Maracanda), Termez, Khorezm, Merv, and Nisa existed already in the 1st millennium B.C. Oldest building materials were adobe and clay. The 6th and 8th century feudal castles were built on high platforms and had embossed walls and vaulted ceilings (Varakhsha Palace). Among the 9th and 10th century monuments are: mausoleum Ismail Samani in Bukhara and Afrisiabs palace in Samarkand. Between the 11th and the 13th century brick began to replace adobe; wood carvings appeared and portals became common in public buildings. Mosques and mausoleums were built in Bukhara, Urgench, Babkent, Uzgen, Dzhar-Kurgan. The Talhatan-Baba mosque in Merv, the mosque-mausoleum Muhammed Bashkara, the Yasavi mausoleum in the city of Turkestan and many other famous monuments were constructed in T. After a period of decline, architecture flourished again during the 15th-17th centuries—several beautiful structures were built in Samarkand: the mosque Bibi Khanum, the mausoleum Gur Emir, a group of buildings in the Registan Square, the madrasah (Moslem college) Shahi Zinda, the observatory Ulugbeg. During the same period were built the famous madrasahs Miri-Arab in Bukhara, the Kok-Humbez mosque in Ura Tiube, and the Anau mosque. T architecture declines from the middle of the 17th century on. A slight revival in the 18th-19th century was interrupted by R. conquest.

BIBLIOGRAPHY: A. G. Park, *Bolshevism in Turkestan, 1917–1927*, New York, 1957; S. Wurm, *Turkic Peoples of the USSR*, London, 1954; S. Zenkovsky, *Pan-Turkism and Islam in Russia*, Cambridge, 1960.   M. R.

TURKMANCHÁY TREATY between Persia and Russia, concluded on Feb. 22, 1828, terminating the war of 1826–28. By the treaty, the Yerevan and Nakhichevan khanates were ceded to Russia; Russia received preferential trade terms, together with the exclusive right to sail her warships on the Caspian Sea; and a 20-million ruble indemnity from Persia.

TURKMEN SOVIET SOCIALIST REPUBLIC (TURKMENISTAN) is located in Soviet Central Asia (formerly known as Turkestan, the land of the Turks). It borders on Kazakhstan in the N., on Uzbekistan in the N. and E., on Iran and Afghanistan in the S., and on the Caspian Sea on the W. It includes 3 oblasts: Mary, Chardzhou, and Tashauz. Area, 188,175 sq. mi.; capital, Ashkhabad (170,000).

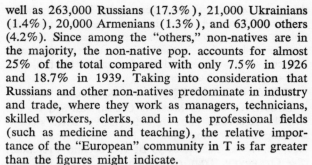

Population of T is 1,516,000 (1959); this includes 924,000 Turkmen (60.9%), 125,000 Uzbeks (8.3%), 70,000 Kazakhs (4.6%), 30,000 Tatars (2%), as well as 263,000 Russians (17.3%), 21,000 Ukrainians (1.4%), 20,000 Armenians (1.3%), and 63,000 others (4.2%). Since among the "others," non-natives are in the majority, the non-native pop. accounts for almost 25% of the total compared with only 7.5% in 1926 and 18.7% in 1939. Taking into consideration that Russians and other non-natives predominate in industry and trade, where they work as managers, technicians, skilled workers, clerks, and in the professional fields (such as medicine and teaching), the relative importance of the "European" community in T is far greater than the figures might indicate.

Nature and Climate. About 90 per cent of the territory is occupied by the Kara-Kum desert. Oases are located at the edges of the desert, at the foothills of Kopet Dagh and along the Amu Darya, Murgab, and Tedzhen rivers. The climate is continental, very dry and hot. The rainfall is poor—4 to 8 in. per year (16 in. in the mountains). The average temperature is between 25° F and 35° F in Jan., between 82° and 89° F in July. The soil is arid, the vegetation poor; farming is limited to a few areas and is heavily dependent on irrigation.

National Economy. The economy is based on oil and oil products, cotton, silk, and astrakhan. The oil industry, located near the Caspian Sea harbor of Krasnovodsk (Cheleken Peninsula, Nebit Dag, and Kum Dag areas) is the third largest in the USSR, after the RSFSR and Azerbaijan. Mirabilite, ozocerite, iodine, and bromine are processed in the same area and along the Kara-Bogaz-Gol Bay, and sulfur in Serny Zavod and at Gaurdak. Building materials (glass, bricks, calx) and manufacturing (machine and locomotive repair shops, agricultural tools, and others) are concentrated in Ashkhabad; textile (cotton and silk) and leather industries are in all the larger cities. Only slightly over 2 per cent of the land is arable of which 90 per cent is irrigated. Cotton, silk and grapes are produced in

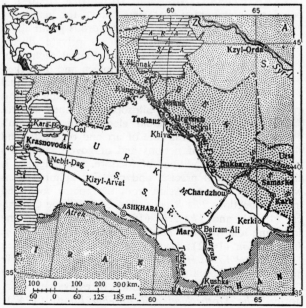

Turkmen SSR

the oases. Sheep breeding (especially karakul), horse and camel breeding are of importance. The transportation system is based on the Central Asian R.R. The Krasnovodsk harbor is the main transit freight center between Central Asia and the Caucasus. (For history and culture, *see* TURKESTAN.)   M. R.

TURYINSKIE RUDNIKI: *see* KRASNOTURYINSK.

TÚSHINO, city in Moscow Oblast, RSFSR, on the Khimki reservoir; pop. 90,000 (1959). R.R. station; weaving and knitting ind. In 1608–10 T, then a village, served as headquarters of the Second Pretender. (*See* OTREPYEV, TIME OF TROUBLES)

TUVÁ or **TUVINIAN AUTONOMOUS OBLAST,** S. Siberia, RSFSR; area 65,800 sq. mi.; pop. 172,000 (1959). Cities: Kyzyl (adm. center), Turan, Chadan, Shagonar. Formerly it was the Uryankhay region of Outer Mongolia. It won nominal independence in 1911; became R. protectorate 1914–17; Tannu-Tuva People's Republic, in the Soviet orbit, since 1921. It is populated largely by Tuvinians (Mongol natives related to the Kirghiz ethnic branch). It is drained by the headstreams of the Yenisey River; dry continental climate is predominant. The W. part lies in a mountain basin walled off by the Sayan and Tannu Ola ranges rising to 10,000 ft. The E. portion is taken up by a high wooded plateau. Reindeer herdsmen and huntsmen inhabit the forests and marshland of this part of the country, while sturdier crops are cultivated on irrigated farmlands, and cattle are raised for meat and wool, in the mountain bowl of the W. In recent years, timbering has become important, as well as the processing ind. based on local produce (sheepskin coats, leather and hides, flour milling, and so on). Coal is mined at Irbek, salt N. of Lake Ubsu Nur, gold placers, iron, copper, and asbestos near Chadan. The main transportation route is the highway linking Kyzyl to the railway town, Abakan. Est. 1944.

TUYMAZÝ, town in Bashkir ASSR; pop. 23,300 (1959). Center of oil region; pipeline to Omsk.

TVARDÓVSKY, Aleksándr Trífonovich (1910–), a popular contemporary poet, best known for his *Vasily*  *Tyórkin,* a long, humorous poem about the adventures of a private during World War II. The central themes of T's poems are patriotism and the development of new ethics based on mutual self-respect. Some of his later poems center on philosophical themes, such as the individual element in a person's fate, the role of art and of artists, and the historical fate of nations and of governments. T's style reflects the traditions of folklore. His language is simple, vivid, and precise, and contains aphorisms, as well as folk sayings. Aside from the poems contained in the collections *The Road* (1934–35), *Village Chronicle* (1939), and *The Hill* (1941), T has written the following long poems: *The Road to Socialism* (1931); *Introduction* (1932); *Muravia* (1936); *Vasily Tyorkin* (1946); and *From Horizon to Horizon* (1953–56). He has also published a novel, *Diary of a Collective Farm Chairman* (1932), and a collection of essays and short stories, *The Motherland and Foreign Lands* (1947). Stalin prizes (1941, 1946, 1957).

TVER: *see* KALININ.

TVER, GRAND DUCHY OF, one of the larger principalities of N.E. Russia in the 13th–15th centuries, formed by secession from the Suzdal principality. After two centuries of stubborn resistance to Moscow's policies of unification, it was annexed to Muscovy by Ivan III.

TYAN-SHAN OBLAST, Kirghiz SSR; area 19,500 sq. mi.; pop. 137,000 (1959). Adm. center Naryn city. Is an important stock-raising region (horses, sheep, and goat herds) lying in the Tien-Shan Mountain range; its principal river is the Naryn. Has a moderately cold climate; large lakes, Sonkyol and Chatyrkyol; chestnut and brown-forest soils; semidesert and steppe vegetation in the valleys; conifer growths in higher altitudes, with sub-alpine and alpine meadows above them. Irrigation farming in the valleys produces oats, barley, truck crops; hunting and fishing are essential occupations. Tungsten and molybdenum deposits are worked in Kashka-Su and Kum-Bel area. The Frunze–Naryn highway is the main transportation route. Est. 1939.

TYNYÁNOV, Yúry Nikoláyevich (1894–1943), critic and literary historian. Graduated in 1918 from the history and philology faculty of St. Petersburg University. From 1921 to 1930, he was a lecturer in the history of R. poetry in the Leningrad Historical Art Institute. He wrote three historical novels *Kyukhlya* (1925), *Death of Vazir Mukhtar* (1927–28), and *Pushkin,* an unfinished novel (1936–43). He also wrote two short novels, *Lieutenant Kishe* (1928) and *The Young Vitushishnikov* (1930).

TYUMÉN, city, adm. center of Tyumen Oblast, RSFSR, on Tura River; pop. 150,000 (1959). R.R. station; machine building, woodworking, plywood, shipbuilding and ship-repair works, plastics, fur-processing, footwear.

TYUMÉN OBLAST, in the Arctic region of RSFSR; includes Yamal-Nenets and Khanty-Mansi national okrugs; area 554,000 sq. mi.; pop. 1,192,000. A flat plain with tundra in the N., tayga in the middle and steppe in the S. Cities: Tyumen (adm. center), Ishim, Tobolsk, Salekhard. Through it flow the Ob and Irtysh rivers with their tributaries; contains over one thousand lakes. Hunting, fishing, reindeer raising, fur trapping. In the steppe there is some agriculture. Ind.: machine construction, lumber. Est. 1944.

TYÚRIN, Iván Vladímirovich (1892–), soil scientist. Fellow, Ac. of S., USSR (1953). Graduate of the Timiryazev Agricultural Academy in Moscow (1919). Associated with Kazan University and the Institute of Agriculture and Forestry (1919–30). Professor, Leningrad Academy of Forestry and Engineering (1930–41 and 1944–51) and Leningrad University (1944–52). Since 1930, director of the Soil Institute, Ac. of S. Research concerns fertility and organic compounds of soil and humus; established a relationship between geographical factors and the humus formation in the soil and advanced new methods of chemical soil analysis. Author of the textbook *A Course in Soil Science for Forestry Engineering Schools* (1933). Chief editor of the periodical *Pochvovedenie* (Soil Science) (1953).

TYUTCHEV, Fyódor Ivánovich (1803–1873), poet. Born into a noble family, he studied at the University  of Moscow and entered the diplomatic service in 1822. For many years his poetical works were unpublished and unknown. He returned to Russia in 1844 and became a censor, a position he kept until his death. His work was first discovered by Nekrasov in 1850. Four years later a collection of his poems was published by Turgenev. T's poetry is deeply lyrical; love and nature are his main themes. Influenced by the German romantic idealism, he considered nature the contradiction of two worlds, Cosmos and Chaos. This dualistic idea manifested itself in his themes of night and day—*A Vision* (1829), *Holy Night* (1849); shade and light—*Twilight* (1830). Nothingness is for him the only reality, and man is alone. T's language is musical and archaic. He wrote about three hundred poems of which *Silentium* (1833) is one of the better known. Symbolists found in him a kindred spirit, and admired his poetry.

U

UDMÚRT ASSR, the Urals, RSFSR; area 16,300 sq. mi.; pop. 1,337,000 (1959). Cities: Izhevsk (capital), Votkinsk, Glasov, Sarapul, Mozhga. An important section of the Ural ind. area, the region lies between the Kama and Vyatka river valleys, its N.E. portion hugging the Vyatka Uval, an outlier of the Ural range. Coniferous and mixed forests cover nearly half of the territory, changing into a wooded steppe in the S. Moderate continental climate and podsolized loamy and sandy soils permitted a recent expansion of agr., which now emphasizes potato and truck farming, basic grains and technical crops, mainly flax. Cattle are bred extensively for milk and meat. Mineral resources include oil shale, limestone, peat, and quartzite. Heavy ind. is based on iron ore shipped from the Urals; high-grade steel is produced by the Izhevsk plant, one of the oldest in Russia. Votkinsk and Sarapul are the two other metallurgical and machine-building centers. There are large glass works at Sergievsky and Valamaz, and numerous lumber mills operating at Mozhga and Izhevsk. The Russians are the second largest population group, next to the Udmurts, formerly known as Votyaks, a people of the Finno-Ugric strain. Est. 1934.

UFÁ, capital of Bashkir ASSR, Southern Urals; pop. 258,000 (1939), 546,000 (1959). River port at the confluence of Belaya and Ufa rivers, with rail connections to Ishimbay and Sterlitamak oil fields. It recently developed into an important industrial center, including ship and machine building, railway engine and car repair, cellulose and lumber milling, distilleries and food-processing plants and oil refining.

UFA DIRECTORATE: *see* COMUCH.

UGLÁNOV, Nikoláy Aleksándrovich (1886–193?). Bolshevik, born into a peasant family. Joined the Bolshevik party in 1907; was repeatedly arrested. Was active in the Petrograd Soviet after the February revolution; after the Bolshevik revolution, U was a commissar in the Red Army which fought against Yudenich near Petrograd. He took an active part in the suppression of the Kronstadt revolt in 1921. In 1922, U was a secretary of the Petrograd Bolshevik organization; from 1924 one of the secretaries of the Central Committee, secretary of the Moscow organization, and a candidate member of the Politburo. In the 1930's U was implicated in the "Rightist Opposition"; was arrested and disappeared.

ÚGLICH, city in Yaroslavl Oblast, RSFSR; pop. 28,000 (1959). Major port on the Volga; paper-milling and lumbering center; site of important hydroelectric power plant and water reservoir. Founded in 1148, was part of Muscovy from the late 14th century; is noted for many architectural monuments of historical significance.

UKRAINIAN SOVIET SOCIALIST REPUBLIC (UKRAINE, Little Russia) is the second largest Soviet republic in population and economic potentialities.

Population is 40,469,000 (1939), 41,869,000 (1959); out of this total: Ukrainians, 31,852,000 (76.1%); Russians, 7,400,000 (17.6%); Jews, 840,000 (2%); there is a small minority of Byelorussians, Moldavians, Poles, Bulgarians, Greeks, Hungarians, Albanians, and others. It is bounded by Byelorussia (on the N.), the RSFSR (on the N. and E.), the Sea of Azov and the Black Sea (on the S.), Moldavian SSR (on the S.W.), Czechoslovakia, Hungary, and Poland (on the W.), and Rumania (on the S.W.). In 1939 the Eastern territories of Poland were reunited with U (Western Ukraine). In 1940 N. Bukovina was ceded by Rumania, and the  Carpatho-Ukraine by Czechoslovakia in 1945; the Crimea was incorporated into the Ukraine in 1954. In 1934 the capital was transferred from Kharkov to Kiev (pop. 1,102,000); other major cities are Kharkov (934,-000), Stalino (700,000), Odessa (667,000), Dnepropetrovsk (660,-000), Zaporozhye (435,000), Lvov (411,000), Krivoy Rog (388,000), Makeyevka (358,000), Zhdanov (284,000), Lugansk (275,000), Nikolayev (226,000). The Ukrainian SSR is divided into 25 oblasts: Cherkassy, Chernigov, Chernovtsy, Crimea, Dnepropetrovsk, Kharkov, Kherson, Khmelnitsky, Kiev, Kirovograd, Lugansk, Lvov, Nikolayev, Odessa, Poltava, Rovno, Stalino, Stanislav, Sumy, Ternopol, Transcarpathian, Vinnitsa, Volyn, Zaporozhye, Zhitomir. Its area is 231,750 sq. mi. Density of population is 180 per sq. mi.

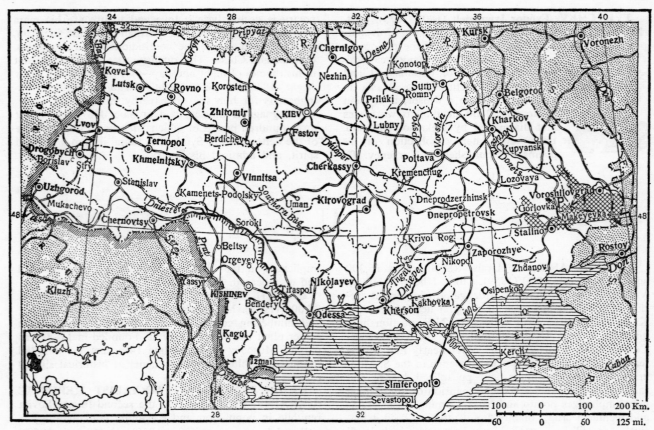

Ukrainian and Moldavian SSR

Nature and Climate. Its relief consists largely of a steppe lowland which rises to the Donets ridge (in the S.W.), the Volynian-Podolian upland (in the W.), the Crimean mountains (on the S.), and reaches the Carpathians in the extreme W. It is drained by the Dnieper and its affluents, the Pripyat, Desna, Sula, Psel, the S. Bug and the Donets; in the S.W. it borders on the Dniester. The climate is milder than in other parts of the Soviet Union, although winters are cold and droughts are not infrequent in S. areas. The Ukraine falls into three vegetation zones: mixed forests of the Polesye lowland in the N.W., including podsols and marshes, wooded steppes in the center of the country, with a fertile black-earth belt (*chernozem*) which merges in the E. with chestnut soils. Extensive irrigation systems are under construction to reclaim the less arable land in the S. (Ingulets, Krasnoznamensk, the Crimean Canal).

National Economy. The Ukraine is the largest wheat and sugar-beet producing area of the USSR and it is also of major importance in livestock breeding, including poultry, sheep, hogs, and dairy cattle. Other export items comprise vegetable oils, tobacco, horticultural products. Vineyards are found in the Crimea, around Odessa and Kherson. The Ukraine is the largest Soviet coal and metallurgical base with an important storage of high-grade coal, iron, and other metals. Its contribution to the total Soviet production amounts to the following: 30 per cent coal (from Donbas and Lvov-Volyn basins), 50 per cent pig iron, 48 per cent steel (produced at the "Azovstal" plant in Zhdanov, at the "Zaporozhstal" Iron and Steel Works and in other plants at Krivoy Rog, Kramatorsk, Kharkov), 35 per cent manganese (the ore from Nikopol field contains 35–48 per cent manganese) and over 25 per cent machinery (locomotives, railroad equipment, bearings, tractors, automobiles, machine tools). The chemical industry is leading in the production of acids, soda, fertilizers, aniline dyes. Rich mineral resources include mercury (Nikitovka), lignite (Kirovograd Oblast), peat (in the N. and N.W.), high grade (60–62 per cent Fe) iron ore (Krivoy Rog). All these deposits are favorably located, in close proximity to each other and in the lower Dnieper area which is the source of hydro-energy. A combination of these factors determined the leading economic part played by the Ukraine in Russia both before and after the revolution. The importance of the mining and metallurgical industries dates back to the late 19th century. Electric power comes next in importance; power plants operate on water (Dneproges, Kakhovka, Kremenchug, Dneprodzerzhinsk Hydroelectric plants) and coal dust (Shtergres, Zugres). There is also an extensive woodworking industry (Kiev, Zhitomir, Cherkassy) and a light industry which includes the manufacturing of footwear, leather, knitwear, jersey, cotton, and wood. Good transportation facilities are provided by such main railroad lines as Moscow-Donets basin, Kiev-Odessa, Kiev-Lvov. Rivers are navigable and the following cities serve as ports: Kiev, Dnepro-petrovsk, V. I. Lenin port, Kherson which is both a river and seaport. Odessa, Nikolayev, Kerch, and Zhdanov are used for marine traffic. Airlines link the republic to all key points in the Soviet Union.

History. Traces of the paleolithic man were found in the Ukraine. From the 8th to the 4th centuries B.C. it was inhabited by Scythians who were engaged in trade with the flourishing Greek colonies along the Black Sea coast. Successive westward migrations passed the S. steppes, including Goths, Huns, and Pechenegs. The appearance of the Slavs in the Dnieper area is a controversial issue and some scholars believe them to be the original inhabitants. The N.W. wooded portion of the Ukraine formed part of Kievan Russia in the 9th to 11th centuries. The geographical position of Kiev on the main trade route from the Baltic to the Black Sea and Byzantium and its importance as a bulwark against the invasion of southern and eastern nomads explains the leading part it played in the first three centuries of Russian history.

The W. part of the Ukraine (Galicia and Volynia), partly spared by the 13th-century Tatar invasion, was conquered by Poland in the 14th century and Volynia was annexed by Lithuania. The khanate of Crimean Tatars controlled the S. central steppes. In an attempt to escape Polish rule Ukrainian peasants settled in the unpopulated E. steppes along the Dnieper River; these free settlers called themselves Cossacks. The end of the 16th century and the early 17th century are marked by continuous peasant revolts against Polish rule. Led by Bogdan Khmelnitsky (q.v.) the Cossacks formed a Cossack state which became part of the Muscovite state in 1654. In 1667 the Ukraine was divided with the right bank of the Dnieper taken over by Poland and the left bank by Russia. During the Northern War (q.v.) Hetman Mazepa made an abortive attempt at allying himself with Sweden against Peter the Great. The partition of Poland (in 1793 and 1795) left the Ukraine once more divided: the left bank of the Dnieper River, Zaporozhye, the shores of the Black Sea and of the Sea of Azov came under Russia while W. Ukraine was occupied by Austria.

The middle of the 19th century saw the emergence of U nationalistic circles striving toward national autonomy. The best-known secret society was the Kiev Brotherhood of Cyril and Methodius organized by the poet and painter Taras Shevchenko and N. I. Kostomarov, professor of history at Kiev University. The program of the brotherhood which was founded in 1846 called for the emancipation of the serfs and the creation of a federated Slavic republic based on broad national autonomy. While Kostomarov and other leaders relied on peaceful methods of propaganda, Shevchenko advocated revolutionary means. In 1847 most of the members of the brotherhood were arrested by the police of Nicholas I.

Because of the hostility of the tsarist government toward the U nationalist movement, schools were taught in Russian before the revolution of 1917. However, the government tolerated U periodicals, books, plays.

After the February revolution there was a revival of the nationalist movement. This time, the nationalists led by the historian M. Hrushevsky, the novelist M. Vinnichenko, and S. Petlyura demanded independence within or outside a Russian federation, the introduction of the U language in Ukrainian schools, courts and administrative organs. A U Central Rada (council) which assumed the powers of a parliament was set up in Kiev. The Rada elected a general secretariat which functioned as a government and started the organization of a U army. On Nov. 7, 1917, the Rada proclaimed the establishment of the U People's Republic. However, in Jan. 1918 the Bolsheviks overthrew the Rada and Red troops overran the Ukraine. During the civil war the Ukraine was the scene of fierce struggle. The pro-German Hetman Skoropadsky, the Whites, and the Bolsheviks alternately ruled in Kiev. The Ukraine was finally incorporated into the USSR in 1922. In 1941 it was overrun by Germans and gradually rewon from Sept. 1943 to final victory in the spring of 1944 (see GERMAN OCCUPATION). The Ukraine is one of the co-founders of the United Nations.

Art and Literature. There are numerous vestiges of Byzantine art (St. Sophia Cathedral in Kiev, built in 1037) and 12th and 13th century architecture (Vladimir-Volynsky, Galich, Chernigov). Famous gospel miniatures date back to 1057. In the 14th and 15th centuries Gothic elements penetrated into the Ukraine. Musical tradition was at its height in the 12th century and is based on Greek and Bulgarian themes. Bandore and flute have been popular instruments since the 16th century. Ukrainian folklore is colorful and abounds in fairy tales, sayings, legends, ballads, riddles. The founder of the U literary language is I. Kotlyarovsky (1769–1838). Taras Shevchenko (1814–61), great U national poet, was the founder of the new U literature. Noted writers were Ivan Franko (1856–1916) and Lesya Ukrainka (1872–1913). Among contemporary poets there are P. G. Tychina, M. F. Rylsky, and M. P. Bazhan as well as the novelists Yu. I. Yanovsky (1902–54), A. T. Gonchar, and the playwright A. Ye. Korneychuk.

The Ukraine has museums, universities, colleges, branches of the Ac. of S. at Lvov and the Crimea, scientific institutions, laboratories, an observatory, national parks, theaters, TV stations, and motion picture studios at Kiev and Odessa. There is also a well-developed resort area.   T. D.

Ukrainian SSR: Administrative-Territorial Division

UKRAÍNKA, Lésya (Larisa Petrovna Kosach-Kvit-ka), (1871–1913), leading Ukrainian writer. First poem published in 1884. Among her better-known poems are: *On the Wings of Songs* (1893), *Fiat Nox!* (1896), *Thoughts and Dreams;* plays, *The Blue Rose* (1896), *Cassandra* (1908); novels, *The Forest Song* (1912). Wrote essays on art and theater. The Theater of Russian Drama in Kiev and numerous libraries, schools, and collective farms are named after her.

ULÁNOVA, Galína Sergéyevna (1910–), prima ballerina of the Moscow Bolshoy Ballet and, in fact, of the Soviet Union. Born in St. Petersburg, she is the daughter of Sergey Ulanov and Maria Romanova, both dancers of the St. Petersburg Mariinsky Theater. She came under the influence of the ballet teacher Agrippina Vaganova (who died in 1951), whose "classes of perfection" she had attended since 1925. U is a great dancer, and her elegance, style of dance, and restrained use of technique are clearly a result of her St. Petersburg training and performing experiences. U made her debut in *Chopiniana* by Fokine (q.v.) and her roles include *Swan Lake, Sleeping Beauty, Giselle, The Fountain of Bakhchisaray, Romeo and Juliet, La Bayadère* (all at the Kirov Theater) and *Cinderella* at the Bolshoy. London, Paris, New York, where Ulanova danced on the visits of the Bolshoy Ballet, share the Muscovites' admiration for her. She is a People's Artist of the USSR and has been awarded four Stalin prizes and the order of Lenin.

ULALA: *see* GORNO-ALTAYSK.

ULÁN-UDÉ (f. Verkhneudinsk), capital of Buryat ASSR, E. Siberia; pop. 175,000 (1959). Important rail center on the Trans-Siberian R.R., at the confluence of the Selenga and Uda rivers; since the thirties, a center of essential ind., producing railway engines and cars, lumber, glass, textiles. Has a number of higher educational institutions.

ULCHI: *see* POPULATION.

ULTIMATISTS: *see* OPPOSITION.

ULYÁNOV, Aleksándr Ilyích (1866–1887), Lenin's older brother, member of the "People's Will" revolutionary party. An active revolutionary since his student years, he became involved with a terrorist group planning an attempt upon the life of Emperor Alexander III. Sentenced to death, he was hanged in the Schlüsselburg Fortress on May 8, 1887, at the age of 21.

ULYÁNOVSK (f. Simbirsk), city, adm. center, Ulyanovsk Oblast, RSFSR; pop. 98,000 (1939), 205,000 (1959). Birthplace of V. I. Lenin (Ulyanov); situated on right bank of the Volga; an important rail-river transfer point. Has an automobile plant, large lumber and textile mills, metallurgical, electrical, and food-processing ind.

ULYÁNOVSK OBLAST, RSFSR, E. sector; area 14,400 sq. mi.; pop. 1,118,000 (1959). Cities: Ulyanovsk (adm. center), Melekess, Inza, Sengiley, Barysh. Situated in the middle Volga region; its important timber and lumbering ind. are based on broad-leaved and pine forests extending along the right bank of the r., part of Volga upland. Extensive farming emphasizes basic grains, fodder crops, potatoes in the N.W. section; flax, hemp, and sunflowers are cultivated in the lowlands E. of the Volga and in the S.; dairy and meat cattle and hogs are reared throughout the region; large oil shale, peat and phosphorite deposits worked. Heavy ind. are centered in Ulyanovsk city. Est. 1943.

UNEMPLOYMENT INSURANCE: *see* SOCIAL SECURITY.

UNESCO: *see* INTERNATIONAL ORGANIZATION.

UNION OF LIBERATION, a political movement initiated in 1903 in Geneva, Switzerland by ten members of the zemstvo Constitutionalists and ten representatives of the intelligentsia. At a constitutent conference that took place Jan. 3–5, 1904 under the guise of a conference on technical education, a program supporting universal suffrage and a variety of social and agrarian reforms was adopted. Among those selected to the Union's Central Council were I. I. Petrunkevich, Prince P. D. Dolgorukov, and N. N. Lvov, representing the zemstvo, and N. F. Annensky, V. Y. Bogucharsky, A. V. Peshekhonov, and S. N. Prokopovich, representing the intelligentsia (the so-called "third element"). A particularly active role within the Union was played by the "St. Petersburg Group" led by Ye. D. Kuskova. In Oct. 1905, it was decided to organize the Constitutional Democratic party (q.v.). At that time the Union of Liberation ceased to exist, even though some of its members refused to join the Constitutional Democratic party. The UL published the journal *Osvobozhdenie* (Liberation), edited by P. B. Struve, first in Stuttgart and then in Paris.

UNION OF OCTOBER 17: *see* OCTOBRISTS.

UNION OF SOVIET ARTISTS (*Soyuz Khudozhnikov SSR*), was created at the All-Union Congress of Soviet Painters which met in 1957. Various regional, district, and other groupings of Soviet artists which were established since 1932, in response to a party edict on "Reorganization of literary and artistic organizations," were incorporated into the single Union. As of Jan. 1, 1960 it had 96 locals with 8,664 members. It purports to help the painters to "create, on the basis of Socialist realism, highly ideological and artistically perfect works educating the Soviet people in the spirit of Communist ideas and Soviet patriotism." S. V. Gerasimov is first secretary.

UNION OF SOVIET SOCIALIST REPUBLICS (USSR, SOVIET UNION) occupies a territory of c. 8,640,000 sq. mi. and is located on two continents, Europe and Asia. It is the largest country in the world, almost three times the size of the United States, seven

times that of India, more than twice that of China. Its northernmost point is the N. tip of Rudolf Island of the Franz Josef Land archipelago (81° 51′ N.), and the southernmost is near Kushka in Turkmenistan (35° 08′ N.). From N. to S. the USSR measures 46° 43′ latitude

or 3,100 mi., i.e. over half the distance from the equator to the North Pole. The westernmost point is on a sandy spit in the Baltic Sea close to Kaliningrad (19° 38′ E.), and the easternmost on Ratmanov Island in the Bering Straits (169° 02′ W.). From W. to E. the USSR measures 171° 20′ longitude or 6,200 mi., i.e. approximately one-quarter of the length of the equator. The USSR is located in eleven time zones. When the time is 5 A.M. in Chukchi Peninsula it is only 7 P.M. of the night before in Moscow. Each of the eleven time zones welcomes the New Year at a different time.

The Soviet land frontier stretches for over 37,000 mi., nine times that of the U.S. The USSR's neighbors in Europe are: Norway, Finland, Poland, Czechoslovakia, Hungary, and Rumania; in Asia: Turkey, Iran, Afghanistan, China, Mongolia, and Korea.

The USSR is composed of 15 constituent republics: Russian Soviet Federated Socialist Republic (RSFSR), Ukrainian SSR, Byelorussian SSR, Uzbek SSR, Kazakh SSR, Georgian SSR, Azerbaijan SSR, Lithuanian SSR, Moldavian SSR, Latvian SSR, Kirghiz SSR, Tadzhik SSR, Armenian SSR, Turkmen SSR, and Estonian SSR; 19 autonomous republics (ASSR's); 9 autonomous oblasts; 10 national okrugs; 7 krays; 107 oblasts. It has 1,679 cities and 2,940 urban-type settlements. Its population is 208.8 mill. Capital city: Moscow.

UNION OF STRUGGLE FOR THE LIBERATION OF THE WORKING CLASS, an illegal Marxist organization formed in St. Petersburg late in 1895 on the initiative of Martov and Lenin with the aim of theoretical and political training of the workers, so as to prepare them for their role as a nucleus of the future political party. The Union played an important part in the great wave of strikes among the St. Petersburg workers which began in Dec. 1895, but its leaders were arrested by the police almost immediately. The Union survived the arrests and, under the leadership of S. I. Radchenko and I. V. Babushkin, became much more active in mid-1896 and in 1897, when it organized several strikes, putting the emphasis on economic rather than on political demands. This attitude of the Union was criticized by Lenin from his Siberian exile. From 1898, an illegal workers' paper *Rabochaya Mysl* (The Workers' Thought) became the organ of the Union. When similar unions were organized in Moscow, Kiev, and some other provincial towns, in March 1898, a small illegal congress met in Minsk and proclaimed the creation of the Russian Social Democratic Workers' Party. However, the arrests impeded the actual organization of the party; in fact, it was organized by *Iskra* (q.v.) in 1903.

UNION OF THE RUSSIAN PEOPLE, an ultranationalistic, anti-Semitic organization founded in 1905, in St. Petersburg, by extreme reactionaries influential in monarchist circles: Dr. A. I. Dubrovin, V. M. Purishkevich, and N. Ye. Markov II. With branches in major centers and a membership recruited among the more obscurantist, declassed or backward elements of the population, the URP, whose activities were sponsored by the government, was able to carry on its works with cooperation of the police. It published its own papers *Russkoe Znamya* (The Russian Banner) and others, organized pogroms, conducted a systematic campaign of slander and baiting against its political opponents, including physical mayhem and assassinations (Hertsenstein and Iollos, of the first Duma; Karavayev). In 1907 Purishkevich, dissatisfied with Dr. Dubrovin's policies, withdrew from the URP and founded a rival Union of Michael the Archangel. The February revolution of 1917 put an end to the existence of both organizations.

UNION OF UNIONS, a federation of radical intellectual groups active in 1905. It arose in 1904 at the initiative of the Union of Liberation (q.v.) and included unions of writers, professors, teachers of secondary schools and of elementary schools, engineers, lawyers, and veterinaries. The Peasant Union also joined this federation as did (in July 1905) the zemstvo Constitutionalists. Its first action in the political field took place on Jan. 8, 1905, when a delegation was sent to Prince Svyatopolk-Mirsky and Count Witte with the aim of persuading them not to employ firearms in dispersing the demonstration of St. Petersburg workers led by the priest Gapon (q.v.) that was scheduled for the next day. This attempt was ineffective and the delegation was arrested. The first convention of the U of U was held in Moscow on May 8–9, 1905. There were 60 delegates representing 14 organizations. A second ("constituent") convention on May 24–26, 1905 elected P. N. Milyukov as chairman of the central bureau and adopted a program that called for a national constituent assembly elected by universal suffrage. With the ebbing of the revolutionary tide and the convocation of the State Duma in 1906 the U of U elements faded away.

UNION REPUBLICS: *see* ADMINISTRATIVE AND TERRITORIAL DIVISIONS.

UNITED FRONT: *see* COMMUNIST INTERNATIONAL.

UNITED NATIONS: *see* INTERNATIONAL ORGANIZATION.

UNIVERSITY OF MOSCOW: *see* MOSCOW LOMONOSOV STATE UNIVERSITY.

UNKIAR–ISKELESSI treaty of mutual assistance between Russia and Turkey, signed in a village near Istanbul July 1833. In the event of war Turkey was obligated to close the Dardanelles Strait to foreign ships, thus making the Black Sea inaccessible to European navies.

UNSHLICHT, Iósif Stanislávovich (1879–193?), Bolshevik, born in Poland where he joined the Social Democrats. In 1912 he led the Bolshevik opposition in the Polish Social Democratic party. From 1914 was in exile. Was an active organizer of the October revolution after which he became F. Dzerzhinsky's chief aide in the Cheka (*see* SECURITY POLICE). From 1925 U held high positions in the Red Army, including that of deputy commissar of defense of the USSR. From 1933 U was chief of the Ossoaviakhim (q.v.) and a high official in the economic apparatus. Suspected of opposition to Stalin, he disappeared in 1937.

ÚNZHA RIVER, flows from Vologda Oblast, through Kostroma and Ivanov oblasts to form left tributary of Volga; 340 mi. long; navigable.

URÁLSK, city, adm. center of W.-Kazakhstan Oblast; pop. 67,000 (1939), 105,000 (1959). Railroad town on the Volga River; trading center of a cattle-raising and grain-producing district; food processing, leather mfg.

URALS, THE, one of the main Soviet industrial centers in the central and southern parts of the Ural Mountains. Area ca. 300,000 sq. mi. (including the Sverdlovsk, Perm, Chelyabinsk, Orenburg oblasts, Bashkir and Udmurt ASSR); pop. 16.5 mill. (1959): Russians, Bashkirs, Tatars, Udmurts. Rich mineral resources: iron ore, copper, chromium, nickel, bauxite, potassium, coal and lignite, asbestos, building materials, platinum, gold, precious stones. On this basis a heavy mining, metallurgical engineering and chemical industry developed. Principal cities: Sverdlovsk, Chelyabinsk, Perm, Ufa, Nizhny Tagil, Izhvesk, Orenburg. Metallurgy dates from early 18th century. Around 1800 the Urals was the largest pig-iron producer in the world.

URÁL MOUNTAINS, range stretching N.–S. for 1,300 mi. and dividing Europe from Asia. Continental climate. Highest peak is Mt. Narodnaya (6,212 ft.). Rich mineral deposits.

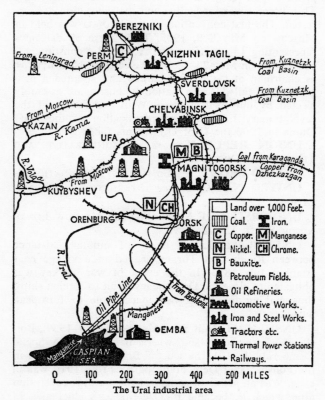

The Ural industrial area

URBAN HOUSING. Until the late 1950's the Soviet government assigned relatively low priority to UH construction and maintenance. Relatively small allocations of investment were planned for the housing sector

and these were frequently trimmed when it was found that additional resources were required to meet priority targets in other sectors of the economy. This policy, together with the sharp growth of urban population, stimulated by rapid industrialization, resulted in a marked deterioration in already inadequate UH facilities. Per capita urban living space declined from 64.5 sq. ft. in 1926 to 48.4 sq. ft. in 1938. Some 750 million sq. ft. of housing space were destroyed during World War II and it was not until 1953 that the 1938 level of per capita urban living space was restored. (In the mid 1950's per capita urban dwelling space in the United States amounted to about 365 sq. ft. or nearly 8 times the level prevailing in the USSR.)

In 1957 there was a shift in Soviet policy toward the housing economy. The government decided to step up investment allocations to the housing sector even though this implied, in the short run, some downward revision in output targets in the heavy industrial sector. The party leadership may have felt that in the long run it had more to gain in terms of increased productivity by providing Soviet citizens with more adequate housing facilities than it had to lose from diverting some resources from the industrial sector. The policy shift may also have been made with an eye to its external political and propoganda effect, particularly in the underdeveloped countries of the world. In any case, under a decree in July of 1957 the annual amount of UH space to be opened to tenancy in 1957 was to more than double by 1960. Official Soviet statistics through 1959 indicate that the provisions of the decree are in fact being fulfilled or overfulfilled.

The Seven Year Plan inaugurated in 1959 calls for continued high levels of housing construction through 1965. Even in 1965, however, per capita UH space is not expected to reach the minimum sanitary standard of 97 sq. ft. prescribed by the Soviet government. Moreover, there is no guarantee that the government will not revert to its former policy of trimming housing goals if it feels they are jeopardizing attainment of higher priority targets in other sectors of the economy. In addition, it should be stressed that emphasis in the new, expanded housing program is on quantity rather than quality. In order to save costs, corners are often cut, to the inconvenience of occupants. In order to economize on metal, for example, water is distributed to both the washbasin and the nearby bathtub in the bathrooms of some of the new apartments through a single faucet which rotates horizontally.

The organization of the Soviet housing economy has undergone numerous changes since 1917. The USSR has experimented with rent-free housing, small apartment houses managed by concessionaires, and housing built and managed by cooperatives. Since 1937, however, most urban dwellings have been state-owned and managed, either by municipal governments or by economic enterprises or institutions. In the latter group, housing is reserved for employees of a particular enterprise or institution and must be surrendered when a worker leaves. In addition, there are privately owned dwellings and dwellings owned by a small number of cooperative housing groups. By giving enterprise direc-

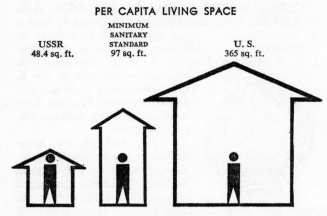

PER CAPITA LIVING SPACE

USSR 48.4 sq. ft.	MINIMUM SANITARY STANDARD 97 sq. ft.	U. S. 365 sq. ft.

tors control over a large portion of scarce housing facilities and making occupancy conditional upon continued employment in a given place of work, the government gives enterprise officials a potent weapon against labor turnover.

The scarcity of UH facilities has made rationing of housing space a feature of Soviet life for many years. In the allocation of housing space, preference is shown to workers with outstanding production records, to intellectuals with outstanding achievements in the arts and sciences, and, of course, to those who are politically well-connected. The government is besieged with complaints about inequities in the allocation of housing space.

Rent in the USSR is generally based on the income of the principal wage-earner and, together with heat, electricity and other utilities, accounts on the average for no more than 4 or 5 per cent of the family budget. The Soviet government, which is the landlord in most cases, makes no net income on housing. The rent charged is designed simply to cover the upkeep of the state's property and, judging by reports on the general state of disrepair of much Soviet housing, rent collections are probably inadequate even for this purpose. (*See also* HOUSING REGULATIONS)

BIBLIOGRAPHY: Harry Schwartz, *Russia's Soviet Economy*, Englewood Cliffs, N.J., 1954; Timothy Sosnovy, *The Housing Problem in the Soviet Union*, New York, 1954; Lynn Turgeon, *Levels of Living and Incentives in the Soviet and the United States Economies*, Paper Submitted to Joint Economic Committee, 86th Congress, 1st Session, Washington, 1959.   D. L.

URGÉNCH, city, adm. center of Khorezm Oblast, Uzbek SSR; pop. 43,000 (1959). Town industries based primarily on agr. produce include cotton-ginning and silk mills, clothing factories, food processing; distribution and trading center for an essentially agr. area. Has several higher educational institutions.

URÍTSKY, Moiséy Solomónovich (1873–1918), Bolshevik. Joined the revolutionary movement in the  1890's. In 1897 was arrested and exiled to Siberia for five years. In the revolution of 1905, U was chairman of the Soviet in Krasnoyarsk. Between the two revolutions (1905 and 1917) he was a member of the "Mezhrayontsy" (q.v.) and a friend of Trotsky. Joined the Bolshevik party in July 1917. As a member of the Military Revolutionary Committee he was one of the organizers of the October revolution, after which he was appointed head of the Cheka (*see* SECURITY POLICE) in Petrograd. On Aug. 13, 1918, he was killed by the Socialist Revolutionary L. Kanegiser.

URYSÓN, Pável Samuílovich (1898–1924), mathematician. Graduate, Moscow University (1919); professor, Second Moscow University (1921). Originated a new trend in topology, i.e. the theory of dimensionality proving several classical theorems. Research also concerned geometry, the theory of functions, and other branches of mathematics. His *Works on Topology and Other Mathematical Fields* in 2 volumes were published in 1951.

USHAKÓV, Dmítry Nikoláyevich (1873–1942), philologist, authority on the R. language, dialectology, and literary accent. Corresponding member, Ac. of S., USSR. Author of books on linguistics and editor of the widely used *Explanatory Dictionary of the Russian Language* (4 vols., 1935–40).

USHAKÓV, Fyódor Fyódorovich (1744–1817), admiral, one of the founders of the Russian Navy. U was the originator of new offensive naval tactics. Under his command the fleet won important victories against the French in the Adriatic and Mediterranean Sea. U was at the head of the Russian naval expedition in 1798. He organized descents which liberated Naples, Rome, and other Italian cities from French occupation. In his honor a Ushakov Order has been created by the Supreme Soviet of the USSR.

USHAKÓV, Símon (1626–1686), father of realism in R. icon painting. For sixteen years he headed the official agency responsible for art production. U painted frescoes and sentimental icons. An admirer of western art, he illustrated the Scriptures in a naturalistic manner; this was the first instance of R. copper engraving. U's highly eclectic art was a mixture of Byzantine, western, and R. characteristics, but it served as a widely imitated model until the middle of the nineteenth century.

USHÍNSKY, Konstantín Dmítrievich (1824–1870), educator. U was the first to propose the creation of pedagogical faculties in R. universities and of seminaries for the training of teachers. In his educational theories, stressed the importance of the national language. He is the author of several books on education and schools.

USÓLYE-SIBÍRSKOYE, city in Irkutsk Oblast, RSFSR; pop. 48,500 (1959). River port on the Angara, in a salt-mining and oil-extracting district; ind. include a chromium steel plant, salt works, matches, plywood factory.

ÚSOV, Mikhaíl Antónovich (1883–1939), geologist. Fellow, Ac. of S., USSR (1939). Graduate (1908) and professor (1913), the Institute of Technology in Tomsk. Participated in expeditions led by V. A. Obruchev; head, Siberian branch of the Geological Committee (1921–30), and scientific director, Trust of Geological Prospecting in W. Siberia until 1938. Research concerned the geology and mineral deposits of Siberia and of the adjoining regions of China and Mongolia.

USPÉNSKY, Gleb Ivánovich (1843–1902), a leading R. writer. U began his literary career as a journalist,

contributing articles to the *Sovremennik* (The Contemporary), *Russkoye Slovo* (The Russian Word), and *Otechestvennya Zapiski* (Notes of the Fatherland). He became known as a writer with the appearance of his books, *The Ways of Rasteryayeva Street* (1866) and *Ruin* (1869), in which he dealt with the life of peasants and slum dwellers. His later books, *Excerpts from a Village Diary* (1877), *The Peasant and Peasant Labor* (1880), and *Power of the Soil* (1882), realistically portray the position of the farmers.

USSR: *see* UNION OF SOVIET SOCIALIST REPUBLICS.

USSURÍYSK (f. Voroshilov), city in Maritime Kray, RSFSR; pop. 104,000 (1959). Food ind., including vegetable oil, sugar, distilleries; sawmills.

UST-KAMENOGÓRSK, city in E.-Kazakhstan Oblast; pop. has grown from 20,000 (1939) to 149,500 (1959). A recently developed ind. town, on Irtysh River, in the lead-zinc mining district; center of nonferrous metallurgy, with woodworking plants, tanneries, vegetable-oil presses, building-materials, all powered by a huge hydroelectric plant. Has several institutions of higher technical education.

UST-ORDÁ BURYAT NATIONAL OKRUG, in S.E. Irkutsk Oblast, E. Siberia, RSFSR; area 8,250 sq. mi.; pop. 133,000 (1959). Principal settlements: Ust-Ordynsky (adm. center), Kutulik, Bokhan. Formerly part of the Buryat-Mongolian ASSR, it is situated in the S. portion of mid-Siberian upland, W. of Lake Baykal. Is a fertile, wheat-producing region, drained by the Angara River. Meat and dairy cattle are raised extensively. Large creameries and other food-processing ind. are based on local produce; also coal-mining. The population includes 50,000 Buryats as a distinct ethnic group. Est. 1937.

UST-ORDÝNSKY, town, adm. center of Ust-Orda Buryat National Okrug; pop. 7,300 (1956). Creameries, brickyards, furniture factories.

UST-SYSÓLSK: *see* SYKTYVKAR.

ÚTIN, Nikoláy Isáakovich (1845–1883), revolutionary. Son of a banker, he was a member of the Central Committee of the secret populist society, Land and Freedom. In 1863, he emigrated, was a member of the first International and secretary of its Russian section in Geneva. He was one of the editors of the journal *Narodnoye Delo* (People's Cause), and later opposed Bakunin in the International.

UVÁROV, Count Sergéy Semyónovich (1786–1855), minister of education (1833–49) and president of the Ac. of S. U was an apologist of autocracy and of the existing order. He devised the formula "orthodoxy, autocracy and nationalism" as the expression of the leading principles of Russian educational policy. U is also known for his advocacy of rigorous censorship and his persecution of Pushkin.

UYEZD: *see* LOCAL GOVERNMENT, ADMINISTRATIVE AND TERRITORIAL DIVISIONS.

UYGURS: *see* KAZAKH SSR, KIRGHIZ SSR, POPULATION.

UZBEK SOVIET SOCIALIST REPUBLIC (UZBEKISTAN) is located in Central Asia (formerly known as Turkestan, the land of the Turks). It borders on Afghanistan and Tadzhikistan in the S., on Turkmenistan in the W., on Kazakhstan and the Aral Sea in the N., and on Kirgizia in the E. It is divided into 7 oblasts: Andizhan, Bukhara, Fergana, Khorezm, Samarkand, Surkhan-Darya, Tashkent.

It also includes the Kara-Kalpak Autonomous Republic. Area, 157,670 sq. mil. Capital, Tashkent (911,000), the largest city in Soviet Central Asia; the other most important cities are Samarkand (196,000), Andizhan (129,000), Namangan (122,000), Kokand (105,000), Fergana (80,000), Bukhara (69,000).

Population is 8,106,000 (1959); this includes 5,026,000 Uzbeks (62%), 445,000 Tatars (5.5%), 335,000 Kazakhs (4.1%), 312,000 Tadzhiks (3.8%), 168,000 Karakalpaks (2.1%), 92,000 Kirghiz (1.0%), 57,000 Turkmen (0.7%), 139,000 Koreans (1.7%), 94,000 Jews (1.2%), as well as 1,101,000 Russians (13.6%), 88,000 Ukrainians (1.1%), and 249,000 others (3.1%). Jews include both native Bukhara Jews who came to the area over 2,000 years ago and newly arrived R. Jews. Tatars include old arrivals as well as Crimean Tatars deported to U in 1944. Koreans were deported from the Soviet Far East to U in the second half of the 1930's. The unknown "others" are most probably comprised of various ethnic groups displaced by the regime, such as Volga Germans, Baltic nationalities, Chechen, and others. There are also Armenians in U. The total percentage of Europeans grew from 5.6 in 1926 to 17.8 in 1939 and 18.4 in 1959. The majority are in the largest urban centers, including the capital city of Tashkent and the ancient town of Samarkand. By contrast, there are few Russians in rural areas. Cities are generally divided into "new" (Russian) and "old" (native) districts. The large majority of technicians, white-collar workers, and skilled workers are Europeans, while almost all *kolkhozniks* and unskilled laborers are natives. In local government, party, and

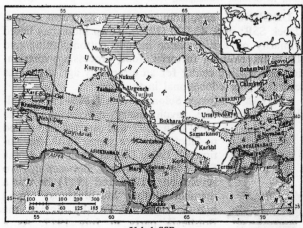

Uzbek SSR

management, natives are usually given prestige positions while power positions are in the hands of Russians.

Nature and Climate. U is located between the high ranges of the Tien Shan, with most of its territory a waterless desert plain although dotted by many oases, the largest of which are: the cotton rich Fergana valley, the Zeravshan oasis (where the cities of Bukhara and Samarkand are located), the Tashkent oasis, and the Khiva-Khorezm oasis. The climate is sharply continental and dry, making irrigation a necessity. The average temperature is 28.4° F in Jan. and 77°–86° F in July. The rainfall varies from 3 in. in the driest lowlands to 24 in. in the foothills. U has limited mineral resources: oil and salt in the Fergana valley, coal in the Angren valley, also copper, gold, marble, tungsten-molybdenum, and polymetallic ores.

National Economy. Prior to the Bolshevik Revolution of 1917, U was an essentially agrarian region with some cotton-ginning and silk-spinning mills. It is now the largest industrial region of Soviet Central Asia. Heavy industry (agricultural machinery works, chemical factories, steel mills) as well as large cotton mills are concentrated around Tashkent. U is third among the republics of the USSR as producer of chemical fertilizers and fifth in electroenergy. Coal, nonferrous metallurgy, and building-material industries are being developed. The percentages of all Soviet cotton, silk and karakul sheep grown or raised in U are (respectively) 67, 50, and 20. U is the largest producer of dried fruit in the USSR and also furnishes one-fifth of the entire vegetable oil produced. Rice, sesame, alfalfa, kenaf, tobacco, and flax as well as wheat are grown in U, but the Soviet government is consistent in reducing areas under wheat and rice cultivation while increasing those under cotton. The livestock (which suffered heavy losses during the collectivization) has again reached the 1929 level. (For history and culture, *see* TURKESTAN.)   M. R.

ÚZHGOROD, city, adm. center of Transcarpathian Oblast, Ukrainian SSR; pop. 47,000 (1959). Old university town, dating from the 9th century, on the Uzh River; center of machine-building, lumbering and food-processing ind.

UZLOVÁYA, city in Moscow Oblast, RSFSR; pop. tripled, from 18,000 (1939) to 54,900 (1959). Major rail and mining town in Moscow lignite basin; has large railway-servicing and repair shops.

V

VÁGA RIVER, in Vologda and Archangel oblasts, RSFSR, left tributary of N. Dvina; length 350 mi.; navigable for 150 mi.

VAGNER: *see* WAGNER.

VAKH RIVER, in Tyumen Oblast, RSFSR, right tributary of the Ob; length 700 mi.

VAKHÁN RANGE, in S. Tadzhik SSR and in Afghanistan; length about 150 mi.; highest peak (Karl Marx) 23,000 ft.; many glaciers.

VAKHSH RANGE, in W. Tadzhik SSR, dividing Vakhsh and Kyzylsu rivers; height over 10,000 ft.

VAKHSH RIVER, in Tadzhik SSR, right tributary (largest) of the Amu Darya; length about 435 mi., navigable in its lower course, where great irrigation system has been built lately for cotton and subtropical plantations.

VAKHTÁNGOV, **Yevgény Bagratiónovich** (1883–1922), outstanding avant-garde director who attempted  to reconcile two opposing schools of theater. He accepted the basic principles of the Stanislavsky method while aiming to synthesize them with the philosophy of the theater as brilliant spectacle. V called his method "fantastic realism"; he sought to evoke the "inner truth of acted emotion" against a background of unrealistic stage settings; i.e., "a theater of make-believe" but utilizing a psychological technique of acting taken from the "theater of re-lived experience." (*See* THEATER.) In the short period from 1913 to 1922 V introduced many controversial innovations into the various studies and theaters of Moscow.

It should suffice to mention only his productions of Berger's *The Flood*, Ibsen's *Rosmersholm*, Maeterlinck's *The Miracle of St. Anthony* and Ansky's *The Dybbuk*. The greater part of V's work was done in Studio Three of the Moscow Art Theater, renamed the Vakhtangov Theater in 1926. There, on the eve of his death, he reached the zenith of his career with his high-spirited production of Gozzi's *Princess Turandot*, presented in the manner of *Commedia del' Arte*.

VAKHÚSHTI (1696–1772), Georgian historian, geographer and lexicographer, son of Vakhtang VI, grandfather of P. I. Bagration, general. His work is historico-geographical description of Georgia, illustrated by original maps.

VALAÁM ISLANDS, group on Lake Ladoga; area 16 sq. mi.; pine woods; famous monastery.

VALDÁY UPLAND, in N.W. part of R. plain; elevations 1,000 ft.; is watershed of Volga, W. Dvina, and rivers belonging to Lake Ilmen basin.

VALÚYEV, **Count Pyótr Aleksándrovich** (1814–1890), Minister of the Interior (1861–68), and president of the Council of Ministers (1877–81). He actively participated in the preparation of peasant and other reforms. Wrote a political diary (1847–84).

VANCH RANGE, mountains in Pamir, Gorno-Badakhshan Autonomous Oblast; length about 50 mi.; elevations reach 18,400 ft.

VANKARÉM, cape in N. part of Chukchi Peninsula; flights were made from here to camp of the Chelyuskin Expedition in 1934.

VARANGIANS (*Varyági*), old R. name for Scandinavians. In the 9th century the V appeared in E. Europe as pirates and traders, invaded R. cities, and levied taxes from the population. In the 10th–11th century they served as soldiers of Slavic princes, adopting the culture of the country. According to tradition, Varangian leaders were the first princes of Kievan Russia.

VÁRGA, Yevgény Samóylovich (1879–), economist, specialist on international topics, born in Hungary. He joined the Hungarian Social Democratic party in 1906 and was economic editor and writer for its major publication, *Nepsava*. V taught at Budapest University in 1918. In 1919, under Bela Kun's communist government in Hungary, V was commissar of finance, then chairman of the Supreme Economic Council. On the collapse of Kun's regime, V fled to Austria, then to the USSR in 1920, where he joined the CPSU. V worked in the Comintern and was a member of the Communist Academy. In 1927, he became director of the Institute of World Economy and World Politics of the USSR Ac. of S. until its merger with the Institute of Economics in 1947. V was also editor of the journal *World Economy and World Politics*, and was elected a full member of the USSR Ac. of S. in 1939.

V was the author of many books on capitalist and colonial countries, contending the superiority of the communist system. These include *The Crisis of the Capitalist World Economic System* (1920), *New Phenomena in the World Economic Crisis* (1934), and *Twenty Years of Capitalism and Socialism* (1938). After the war, however, his *Changes in the Capitalist Economic System as a Result of World War II* (1946) was severely criticized in the Soviet press. It predicted a future "crisisless" development of both systems and was held to contain "serious mistakes of a bourgeois-reformist character." V partially regained favor by admitting to error in 1949 and resumed work in comparative obscurity, reportedly on Hungarian economic problems. His honors include the Stalin prize, and the order of Lenin (1954).

VARLÁMOV, Aleksándr Yegórovich (1801–1848), composer. Wrote popular songs including *The Red Sarafan* and romances of lyrics by M. Lermontov. Composed music for plays, vocal ensembles, and piano.

VARLÁMOV, Konstantín Aleksándrovich (1848–1915), actor. Associated with the Aleksandrinsky Theater which he joined in 1875 and where he remained until his death. V was one of the leading character actors and acted more than 1,000 roles.

VASILÉVSKY, Aleksándr Mikháylovich (1895–), marshal of the Soviet Union, born in Ivanovo Oblast.  He studied at a St. Petersburg higher technical school and at a military training school. He fought in World War I; joined the Red Army in 1918, and fought in the civil war; commanded an infantry regiment till 1931, and graduated from the Frunze Military Academy during this time. From 1931 to 1936 he held important posts in the Commissariat of Defense and graduated from the General Staff Academy in 1937. In 1942 he was appointed first deputy people's commissar of defense, chief of staff, and second deputy commander in chief of armed forces;

during World War II carried out coordination of front operations. In 1946 he was appointed first deputy minister of defense; in 1950 he was named USSR war minister. After Stalin's death in 1953, he was named first deputy minister of defense and headed the combined Ministries of Army and Navy in the Ministry of Defense. Several times he was deputy, USSR Supreme Soviet; in 1952 he was elected a member of the Central Committee, CPSU.

VASÍLY I, Dmitrievich (1371–1425), from 1389 Grand Duke of Moscow, oldest son of Dmitry Donskoy. He annexed the land of Súzdal, Nizhny-Novgorod, Murom, and Tarussa. His reign was filled with wars against Tatars and Lithuanians.

VASÍLY II, THE BLIND (Vasílyevich) (1415–1462), from 1425 Grand Duke of Moscow. Was blinded during a feudal civil war (1446) by Dmitry Shemyaka, but was victorious in the end. He united the principalities surrounding Moscow, subordinated Vologda, Novgorod, and Pskov to Moscow's influence. The R. church proclaimed its independence from the Patriarch of Constantinople during the reign of Vasily II.

VASNETSÓV, Víktor Mikháylovich (1848–1926), painter. Began as realistic genre painter, but later turned to fairy tales, epic, and historical subjects (*Alenushka, Epic Heroes, After the Battle with the Polovtsy, Ivan the Terrible* in Tretyakov Gallery, Moscow; *Hero at the Crossroads*, Russian Museum, Leningrad). V revived and modernized Byzantine religious painting in the murals which he executed for the Vladimir Cathedral in Kiev.

VATÁGIN, Vasíly Alekséyevich (1883–), animal painter and sculptor, graphic artist and lithographer. Excelled in representation of animals on the move. V illustrated the Zoological-Geographic Atlas and auto-lithographic album *India*. A number of his animal sculptures are in the Tretyakov Gallery, Moscow (*Lioness, Wild Boar, Condor*, and others).

VATÚTIN, Nikoláy Fyódorovich (1901–1944), Soviet general. Graduate of the Frunze Military Academy (1929) and of the Academy of the General Staff (1937). V was a member of the CP from 1921. During World War II, he commanded the armies on the southwestern, Voronezh and Ukrainian fronts. V took part in the battle for Stalingrad and contributed to the liberation of Kiev and the Ukraine. He was fatally wounded at the end of the war. Recipient of Lenin order, order of the Red Banner, and other awards.

VAVÍLOV, Nikoláy Ivánovich (1887–1943), plant geneticist. Fellow, Ac. of S., Ukrainian SSR (1929). Graduate, Moscow University (1911); professor, Saratov University (1917–21). Director, All-Union Institute for Plant Culture (1924–40); the Genetics Institute, Ac. of S. (1930–40). Participated in numerous expeditions throughout the world and founded a rich collection of plants. Research devoted to the origins of cultured plants and plant immunity. Lenin prize (1926). Was exiled for opposing the theories of Lysenko (q.v.) and died in a concentration camp.

VAVÍLOV, Sergéy Ivánovich (1891–1951), physicist. Fellow, Ac. of S., USSR (1932), its president (1945–51), and chairman of its editorial council (1945). Member,

Supreme Soviet RSFSR (1938), USSR (1946, 1950). Graduate (1914) and professor (1929) of Moscow University. Director, Institute of Physics (1932) and State  Optical Institute (1932–45) which was named after him. V's early work dealt with research on radio engineering. Most of his scientific activity was devoted to physical optics, photoluminescence of solutions ("Vavilov's law," generalizing and correcting the well-known Stoke's law; "Vavilov-Cherenkov effect"). During World War II supervised design of new devices for Soviet military forces. Author of *The Microstructure of Light* (1950) and editor of periodicals *Uspekhi fizicheskikh nauk* (Progress of Physical Sciences); *Zhurnal eksperimentalnoy i teoreticheskoy fiziki* (Journal of Theoretical and Experimental Physics); *Priroda* (Nature), and others. Chief editor of the second edition of the *Bolshaya Sovetskaya Entsiklopedia* (Large Soviet Encyclopedia) (1949). Stalin prizes (1943, 1946, 1951). The Institute of Physical Problems in Leningrad and a gold medal awarded annually by the Ac. of S. for the most outstanding work in physics bear his name.

VÁYGACH ISLAND, S. of Novaya Zemlya, part of Archangel Oblast, RSFSR; area 1,300 sq. mi.; reindeer breeding.

VÉCHE, people's assembly in ancient Russia which was the sovereign organ of power in certain cities from the 10th to the 15th century (in Novgorod, Pskov, Vladimir). It elected military leaders, bishops, and administrators, controlled their activity, decided questions of peace and war, confirmed laws, the distribution of lands, feudal privileges, and so on. The V lost its importance and disappeared in the 16th century, because of Tatar domination and the growing power of Moscow.

VEGETABLE GARDENING (TRUCK FARMING). Gross output of vegetables (other than potatoes), in mill. tons, was 5.5 in 1913 (within present Soviet boundaries), 10.5 in 1928, 13.7 in 1940, 14.3 in 1959. Marketings amounted to some 7 mill. tons in 1958. The RSFSR produced about one-half and Ukraine one-third of the total output.

Cabbage was the most popular crop, accounting for 29% of all the area under vegetables, cucumbers accounted for 17%, tomatoes for 16%, and root crops—onions, carrots and beets—for 9% each. In the 1950's, over 60% of the sown area was in collective farms, some 20% in farmers' household plots, and the remainder in urban dwellers' "victory gardens," the number of which rose from 5 mill. in 1942 to about 18 mill. in 1953, supplementing meager supplies of vegetables available in the market. The sown area expanded from .6 mill. hectares in 1913 to 1.5 mill. in 1958. Yields are low (4 tons per acre in 1958, as against 5.3 tons in 1928), partly as the result of the extreme fragmentation of plots, a rather paradoxical situation in the land of large-scale farming. Greenhouses were greatly expanded, their area amounting to 8.6 mill. sq. ft. in 1939, but they play a relatively minor role.

VÉKHI (Landmarks), a collection of articles directed against the revolutionary movement, written by prominent political and philosophical writers of liberal and Constitutional Democratic orientation (N. Berdyayev, S. Bulgakov, M. Gershenzon, A. Izgoyev, B. Kistyakovsky, P. Struve, and S. Frank). It was published in 1909, during the period of the Stolypin reforms. Most of its authors had at one time adhered to Marxist views. The articles were critical not only of revolutionary parties and of mass revolutionary movements, but of the general course of development of Russia's intellectuals as well. They describe the revolution of 1905 as a movement created by R. anarchists who succeeded in gaining the support of ignorant masses. An appeal was made to R. intellectuals to give up materialism and also their opposition to the government and to support a strong government based on the rule of law and R. nationalism.

VÉKUA, Ilyá Néstorovich (1907–), mathematician. Fellow, Ac. of S., USSR (1958) and Georgian SSR (1946). Graduate of Georgian State University (1930). V's work deals with the theory of analytic functions of a complex variable as applied to the solution of differential and integral equations in physics and mechanics, i.e. equations of oscillations of elastic cylinders, and nuclear shells. Author of *New Methods of Solving Elliptical Equations* (1948) which was awarded the Stalin prize (1950).

VELICHKÓ, Konstantín Ivánovich (1856–1927), military engineer. A tsarist general, V was one of the first who joined the Red Army. During World War I and the civil war, he directed the construction of fortifications.

VELÍKAYA RIVER, in Pskov Oblast, RSFSR, flows into Lake Pskov; length 265 mi.; navigable in its lower course; used for timber floating.

VELÍKIE LÚKI, city in Pskov Oblast, RSFSR; pop. 35,000 (1939), 59,000 (1959). Engine and car-repair shops, foundry and mechanical plant. Founded 1166.

VELÍKY ÚSTYUG, city in Vologda Oblast, RSFSR, landing on Sukhona River; pop. 35,800 (1956). Has shipyards, foundry and mechanical plant, bristle and brush factory, food production; ancient silver craftsmanship; had considerable economic importance in 16th-17th centuries.

VENETSIÁNOV, Alekséy Gavrílovich (1780–1847), founder of the realistic school of R. painting. Was influenced by the Dutch masters and the French artist Granet. Son of a Greek, V came to St. Petersburg in 1807, and studied art with Borovikovsky. He painted peasants in the fields, always neat and contented, e.g. *In the Barn* and *Sleeping Shepherd*.

VENEVÍTINOV, Dmítry Vladímirovich (1805–1827), poet, Pushkin's friend. Together with prince V. F. Odoyevsky he organized the first R philosophical society *Lyubomudry* ("Lovers of Wisdom"). By his premature death Russia lost a promising poet.

VÉNTA RIVER, in Latvian and Lithuanian SSR's, flows into the Baltic Sea; length about 240 mi., of which the lower 50 mi. are navigable. At its mouth is situated Ventspils, an ice-free port.

VÉNTSPILS (f. Vindava), city in Latvian SSR, a never freezing port on Baltic Sea; pop. 26,200 (1956). Has sawmills, fish industry.

VEPS: *see* POPULATION.

VERBÍTSKAYA, Anastásia Alekséyevna (1861–1928), chiefly known for her novel *The Keys to Happiness* (1909–13) which was popular with low-brow readers because of its emphasis on sex.

VERESÁYEV (Smidóvich), **Vikénty Vikéntyevich** (1867–1945), M.D., writer. In the novels, *Without Road* (1895) and *At the Turning Point* (1902), he continued the traditions of R. critical realism and described the rise of populism. In the *Notebook of a Doctor* (1901) he discussed the problem of the social calling of a doctor. During the Soviet period V wrote the novel *In Blind Alley* (1922) realistically depicting the struggle between Reds and Whites, and *The Sisters* (1933). He is the author of monographs on Dostoyevsky, Tolstoy and *Pushkin and His Life* (1926–27). He translated Homer's *Iliad* and other classics.

VERESHCHÁGIN, Vasíly Vasílyevich (1842–1904), painter-batalist. Painted historical war scenes, strongly opposed to war. A painter whose philosophical inhibitions killed his art, he portrayed the horrors of the Turkestan conquest (1874), was expelled from the Academy, travelled and exhibited in Europe and the United States (the Brooklyn Museum has several of his pictures).

Between 1888 and 1902 V produced large canvases representing the Napoleonic invasion of Russia in 1812. In 1904 he went, as an artist, to the Far East to obtain first-hand impressions of the Russo-Japanese war and was drowned in the sinking of the *Petropavlovsk*, the R. flagship.

VERÉYSKY, Geórgy Semyónovich (1886–), graphic artist, member of the Academy of Fine Arts of USSR. Studied in Kharkov. Lived in Italy and Germany; in 1907 returned to Russia. V was head of the drawing and printing section of the Hermitage in Leningrad (1918–1930). From 1936 he devoted himself to etching.

VÉRKHNE-CHUSOVSKÍYE GORODKÍ, settlement in Perm Oblast, RSFSR, on Chusovaya River. In 1929, the first Ural oil was discovered here.

VERKHNEÚDINSK: *see* ULAN-UDE.

VÉRKHNY UFALÉY, city in Chelyabinsk Oblast, RSFSR; pop. 32,700 (1956). Metallurgical industry, nickel.

VÉRKHNYAYA PYSHMÁ, town in Sverdlovsk Oblast, RSFSR, 7 mi. from Sverdlovsk; pop. 26,200 (1956). Copper mines, ore dressing.

VÉRKHNYAYA SALDÁ, town in Sverdlovsk Oblast, RSFSR; pop. 30,600 (1956). Metallurgical and metalworking ind.

VÉRKHNYAYA TURÁ, town in Sverdlovsk Oblast, RSFSR; pop. 17,000 (1956). Sawmill and plants processing agricultural products. Founded 1598.

VERNÁDSKY, Vladímir Ivánovich (1863–1945), naturalist, mineralogist and crystallographer. Founder of geochemistry and biogeochemistry. Fellow, St. Petersburg Ac. of S. (1912); first president of the Ac. of S. Ukrainian SSR (1919); member of the Czech and French Ac. of S. Graduated from St. Petersburg University (1865), professor of mineralogy and crystallography at Moscow University (1898). Director of the Mineralogical Museum (1914); founder of the State Radium Institute (1922) of which he was also director until 1939. Initiated the formation of the Committee for the Study of Permafrost (1929–30) and the International Committee for the Determination of the Absolute Age of Geological Deposits by Radioactive Methods (1937). Known for his extensive research of the chemical composition of the crust of the earth, the ocean and the atmosphere and the role of radioactive elements in the evolution of the earth. Pioneer in locating radium and uranium deposits in Russia (1910). Author of *Essays and Speeches* (1922); *Soil Silicates, Alumosilicates and Their Analogies* (1937); *Selected Works*, 2 vol. (1955). Stalin prize (1943).

VERNY: *see* ALMA-ATA.

VERSHÍGORA, Pyótr Petróvich (1905–), writer, actor, and producer. Author of *People with a Clear Conscience* (1946) about the struggle of Soviet partisans during World War II. Although he was awarded the Stalin prize for that novel, official criticism accused him of underestimating the role of the party organs in the partisan movement. The second edition of the book (1950) was revised accordingly. *The Carpathian Raid* (1950) describes the struggle against the German occupation in the Carpathian Mountains.

VERSHÍNIN, Konstantín Andréyevich (1900–), marshal of the air forces. Member of the CP since 1919. V first distinguished himself in the civil war. During the 1920's and 1930's he underwent intensive training in military aviation, specializing in fighter tactics. During World War II, he commanded the Soviet Air Force on the Ukrainian front. At the end of the war V was promoted to commander in chief of the Air Force and to deputy USSR war minister, as well as to the rank of marshal. In 1949, V was temporarily downgraded and relegated to supervising anti-aircraft detachments. In 1957 he regained his post as commander in chief of the Air Force. In the past several years he has also been appointed to high posts in the CP.

VERSTÓVSKY, Alekséy Nikoláyevich (1799–1862), composer and musical director of Moscow theaters, wrote vaudeville scores, ballads, romances. His opera *Tomb of Askold* (1835) was once very popular.

VESNÍN BROTHERS, architects: 1) Aleksandr Aleksandrovich (1883–), fellow, Academy of Architecture, USSR. Professor of architectural design at the Moscow Institute of Architecture (1926–35). In collaboration with his brothers Leonid and Viktor designed the Palace of Culture for the Stalin Automobile works in Moscow (1930–34). 2) Leonid Aleksandrovich (1880–1933), contributed to the development of city planning by laying out Tuapse and Kuznetsk. 3) Viktor Aleksandrovich (1882–1950), fellow, Ac. of S.; first president, Academy of Architecture (1938–49). Specialized in industrial architecture, and was one of the architects of the Dnepropetrovsk Hydroelectric Station (1927–30). Known also as stage designer.

VESYÓLY, Artyóm (Nikoláy Ivánovich Kochkuróv) (1899–1939), novelist. A former anarchist who later joined the Bolsheviks. During the civil war, was a political commissar in the Red Army. He was arrested in 1939 by the security police and has never been heard of again. His more important works draw a romantic parallel between the Pugachov and Razin uprisings and the October revolution. These are *The Fiery Rivers* (1924), *Land of My Birth* (1926), and *Russia Washed with Blood* (1929–31). In 1930 he brought out the historical novel *The Sporting Volga* depicting Yermak's conquest of Siberia which, along with Aleksey Tolstoy's *Peter the First* and Aleksey Chapygin's *Stepan Razin*, is one of the best historical novels in postrevolutionary literature.

VETERINARY SCIENCE. Veterinary medicine was well enough developed in tsarist Russia, mainly owing to the efforts of *zemstvos* which maintained a network of rural V clinics and stations throughout the country. Some 8,300 V surgeons were graduated prior to World War I. As of 1912, 4,000 were practicing. The *zemstvos* alone employed 1,400 and, in addition, about 2,000 junior veterinarians. Approximately 6 mill. animals were treated annually. Some successful research was done in V institutes, especially on anthrax.

In 1923, the V Law (amended in 1936) was promulgated dealing with the organization of the state V network, slaughter regulation, prophylactics, and so on. During the period 1917–50, 35,400 V surgeons were graduated from the V Academy in Kuzminki near Moscow and from 35 other V faculties and institutes, most of which were set up after the revolution. As of 1950, some 560 V ambulatories and polyclinics were in operation, 6,300 zoo-veterinary stations and 15,800 substations staffed with junior veterinarians. The output of vaccines, serums, and V preparations amounted to .9 mill. liters, produced in 24 factories, as against 5,000 liters produced in 1912 and 33,000 in 1926.

VETLÚGA RIVER, flows mainly in Gorky Oblast, RSFSR, left tributary of the Volga; length 530 mi.; navigable for 430 mi.; used for timber floating.

VETLÚGA, town in Gorky Oblast, RSFSR; pop. 9,500 (1956). Landing on Vetluga River; sawmills, woodworking, food production.

VEYTS, Veniamín Isáakovich (1905–), power engineer. Corresponding member, Ac. of S., USSR (1933). Graduate, Moscow University (1924), School of Technology (1925); associated with the Institute of Power Engineering (1932). Research concerns power resources and their utilization, power engineering statistics. Author of *Basic Problems of an Over-all Scheme of a Soviet Power Engineering System* (1956). Stalin prize (1942).

VÍCHUGA, city in Ivanovo Oblast, RSFSR; pop. 51,000 (1959). Textile and metal factories.

VIKZHÉL, All-Russian Executive Committee of the Railwaymen's Union, formed after the February revolution in 1917. It played an important role during the Kornilov "mutiny" (q.v.) when the railwaymen successfully sabotaged the movements of Kornilov's forces. The majority of the V's members were moderate socialists opposed to the October revolution, and they threatened to call a general railroad strike if fighting were not stopped by the night of Nov. 11, 1917. On the initiative of V a conference of representatives of all the socialist parties and trade unions opened on Nov. 11, with a view to discussing means for the formation of a new government which would include representatives of non-Bolsheviks. These negotiations dragged on for some time, but led to no positive results. The collapse of Kerensky's drive against Petrograd and the successes of the Reds in Moscow played into the hands of Lenin. On Nov. 14, his resolution was adopted by the Bolshevik Central Committee to the effect that the negotiations should be carried on "only for the purpose of finally exposing the impracticability of this policy and of finally stopping further negotiations for a coalition government." Shortly after the final break of the negotiations the V was dissolved by the Soviet government.   V. SU.

VILÉYKA, town in Byelorussian SSR; pop. 7,000 (1956). Building materials; food ind.

VÍLIA RIVER, flows mainly in Byelorussian SSR and Lithuanian SSR, right tributary of the Neman; length, 300 mi.

VILLAGE COMMUNE: see AGRICULTURE, EMANCIPATION OF THE SERFS, PEASANTS, POPULISM.

VILKÍTSKY STRAIT, between Severnaya Zemlya and Taymyr Peninsula, uniting the Kara Sea with the Laptev Sea in the Arctic Ocean; length 80 mi., width about 30 mi.

VÍLNIUS (Russian *Vilna*, Polish *Wilno*), capital of Lithuanian SSR; pop. 236,000 (1959). Ind.: machine building, paper, woodworking, leather, sewing and food plants. Has numerous colleges including a university (founded in 1579); several theaters, museums; is seat of Ac. of S. of Lithuanian SSR. Ancient city, mentioned in the 12th century; was the capital of Lithuanian Prince Gedimin in the 14th century; from the middle of the 16th century was under Poland; in 1795 was annexed by Russia; 1920–39, Polish.

VILYÚY RIVER, in Yakut ASSR, left tributary of the Lena; length 1,500 mi.; navigable for 750 mi.

VILYÚYSK, town in Yakut ASSR; pop. 4,000 (1956). Landing on Vilyuy River; center of cattle breeding and fur trading.

VINÁVER, Maksím Moiséyevich (1863–1926), one of the founders of the Constitutional Democratic party and a member of the first State Duma. After its dissolution, V was convicted for signing the Vyborg appeal. An adversary of Bolshevik rule, V was appointed minister of foreign affairs in 1918, in an anti-Bolshevik Crimean government. From 1919 he was abroad where he published the periodical *Zveno* (The Link). V was also active in Jewish affairs.

VINDÁVA: *see* VENTSPILS.

VINNICHÉNKO, Vladímir Kísilovich (1880–1951), Ukrainian nationalist revolutionary leader, novelist and playwright. In 1905, V took part in the revolution in Ukraine and spent the years 1907–14 abroad. In 1917, V participated in the formation of the Central Ukrainian Rada and became the secretary of its general secretariat. He was in charge of negotiations with the Provisional Government of Kerensky concerning the autonomy of Ukraine. After the October revolution, V advocated the independence of Ukraine and, in 1918, was at the head of the directorate which organized an uprising against the German occupation. For a short time, V headed the Ukrainian People's Republic. After the Soviets took over, he held various offices but, eventually, emigrated and died in France in 1951.

VÍNNITSA, city, adm. center of Vinnitsa Oblast, Ukrainian SSR; on the Southern Bug; pop. 121,000 (1959). Light ind.; food, meat and superphosphate fertilizer production, sewing factory.

VÍNNITSA OBLAST, in S.W. Ukrainian SSR, along upper course of the S. Bug; area 10,300 sq. mi.; pop. 2,142,000 (1959): Ukrainians (90 per cent), Russians, Jews. Cities: Vinnitsa (adm. center), Mogilev-Podolsky, Zhmerinka, Tulchin, Kazatin, Bar, Gaysin. A rolling plain with black earth, moderately warm and humid climate, is one of the major areas for sugar-beet production; other crops are wheat, rye, grapes. Ind.: sugar, food, building materials, agr. machinery. Several schools of higher education. Est. 1932.

VINOGRÁDOFF, Paul (Pável Gavrílovich) (1854–1925), Anglo-Russian jurist and historian. Born in Kostroma, Russia, V studied at the University of Moscow, then in Berlin under Mommsen and Brunner, and later in Bonn. A lover of music, he played the piano well and was an enthusiastic and expert chess player. In 1877 V began to teach history in the University of Moscow, traveled extensively in continental Europe, and in 1883 came to England for the first time. It was his influence that was responsible for F. W. Maitland's "conversion to the study of legal history" which "made his name immortal" (H. A. L. Fisher). In 1887 V became full professor at the University of Moscow. Simultaneously, he was deeply concerned with the reform of primary and secondary education, and was the author of manuals on ancient, medieval, and modern history which were used in practically every secondary school in Russia from the 1890's to 1917. In 1902, because of a conflict with the authorities, V resigned his professorship and went abroad. His departure from Moscow assumed the character of a national event. In 1903 he was elected Corpus Professor of Jurisprudence at Oxford, a chair formerly held by Sir Frederick Pollock and Sir Henry Maine. The seminar method of teaching introduced by V in Oxford was a revolutionary innovation and met with resistance but proved lasting and fruitful and produced nine volumes of *Oxford Studies in Social and Legal History* (1909–1927). From 1908 to 1911 V divided his time between the University of Oxford and the University of Moscow. He traveled widely, visited India, and in 1907 and 1923 taught in the United States. He was knighted in 1917, was a fellow of the British Academy, and member of several foreign academies and learned societies. In Dec. 1925 he was awarded an honorary doctorate by the University of Paris, caught a cold at a reception at the Sorbonne which developed into pneumonia and died in Paris. His body was cremated at Père Lachaise and his ashes buried at Oxford. His tomb bears the inscription of his own choice: *Hospitiae Britanniae Gratus Advena.*

V's principal books were *Villainage in England* (1892), *Growth of the Manor* (1905), *English Society in the Eleventh Century* (1908), *Roman Law in Medieval Europe* (1909), *Common Sense in Law* (1914), and *Outlines of Historical Jurisprudence*, 2 vols. (1920–1922). *The Collected Papers of Paul Vinogradoff*, 2 vols. (1928), contain an admirable biographical Memoir by H. A. L. Fisher and a bibliography of V's writings which lists 266 items.

VINOGRÁDOV, Aleksándr Pavlovich (1895–), chemist. Fellow, Ac. of S., USSR (1953). Hero of Socialist Labor (1949). Graduate of Military Medical Academy and Leningrad University (1924). Research in geochemistry, biochemistry, and analytical chemistry. Described more than 40 rare and dispersed chemical elements for various soil zones and their effects on processes of soil formation. In analytical chemistry, found methods of identifying traces of most elements by means of polarography, spectrometry, and radiometry. Author of *Geochemistry of Dispersed Elements of Sea Water* (1944); *Bio-geochemical Regions* (1949); *Geochemistry of Rare and Dispersed Chemical Elements in Soils* (1957). Stalin prizes (1949, 1951) and other decorations.

VINOGRÁDOV, Iván Matvéyevich (1891–), mathematician. Fellow, Ac. of S., USSR (1929). Hero of Socialist Labor (1945). Graduate of St. Petersburg University (1914). Professor, Perm University (1918–20), Leningrad Polytechnic Institute (1920–34), Leningrad University (1925–34), Moscow University (1934); director, Institute of Mathematics, Ac. of S., USSR (1932). Research on analytic number theory and important contributions to its development. Stalin prize (1941).

VINTER: *see* WINTER.

VIRGIN LANDS KRAY (R. *Tselinny Kray*), in N. Kazakh SSR; area 230,000 sq. mi.; pop. 2,743,000 (1959). Adm. center, Tselinograd (f. Akmolinsk). Includes Kokchetav, Kustanay, North Kazakhstan, Pavlodar oblasts and the territory of former Akmolinsk Oblast under its jurisdiction. Est. 1961.

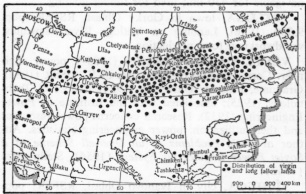

Virgin lands brought under cultivation

VIRTÁ, Nikoláy Yevgenyevich (1906–), novelist and playwright. His first novel *Solitude* (1935) was dramatized under the title *The Land* (1937). V's play *Our Daily Bread* (1947) pictures collective farm life in postwar years; *The Conspiracy of the Condemned* (1948) is an anti-American play. V was involved in a controversy over Soviet drama (1952); he favored a drama without conflicts which would avoid rejection on the part of theatrical censors, the only permissible conflict being between "good" and "better." At the time, his article, a courageous attack on the bureaucratic world of theater officials, was severely criticized. Stalin prizes (1941, 1948, 1949, 1950).

VÍSHERA RIVER, in Perm Oblast, RSFSR, left tributary of the Kama; length 280 mi.; navigable for 220 mi.

VISHNÉVSKY, Aleksándr Vasílyevich (1874–1948), surgeon. Fellow, Academy of Medical Sciences (1947). Graduate (1889), professor (1912), Kazan University. Director, Institute of Surgery, Academy of Medical Sciences (1946–48). Introduced the treatment of wounds and infections by oleo-balsamic and novocaine applications widely used in World War II. Stalin prize (1942). The Institute of Surgery of the Academy of Medical Sciences was named after V.

VISHNÉVSKY, Vsévolod Vitályevich (1900–1951), novelist and playwright. Took part in the civil war. Worked as a propagandist. He wrote the plays *Trial of the Kronstadt Mutineers* (1921), *The First Cavalry Division*, and his best play, *The Optimistic Tragedy* (1932). He wrote the screenplays *We from Kronstadt* (1933) and *The Unforgettable Year*. Stalin prize (1950).

VISHNIÁK, Mark Veniamínovich (1883–), prof. of public law, publicist, and editor. Since 1905, a member of the Socialist Revolutionary party; secretary of the Russian Constituent Assembly, 1918. Since 1919, an *émigré*, first in Paris and from 1940 in the United States. Formerly on the editorial staff of *Sovremennye Zapiski* (Contemporary Notes). V wrote (in Russian) *The All-Russian Constituent Assembly* (1932); biographies of Lenin, Leon Blum and Dr. Weizmann (1939). Since 1946 is consultant on R. affairs of *Time* magazine.

VÍSHNYA, Ostáp (Pável Mikháylovich Gubénko) (1889–1956), Ukrainian writer, born on a farm near Poltava, of a poor peasant family. He was educated at the village school, then at the University of Kiev, 1917. V began writing satirical sketches for newspapers. His best-known books are *Leningrad and Leningraders, Zaporozhians,* and *Anti-aircraft Gun.*

VÍTEBSK, city, adm. center of Vitebsk Oblast, Byelorussian SSR; 167,000 (1939), 148,000 (1959). Important R.R. junction, landing on W. Dvina. Ind.: knitted fabrics, sewing, carpets, woodworking, prefabricated houses, machine tools. Has pedag., medical and veterinarian inst. First mentioned in 1021.

VÍTEBSK OBLAST, in Byelorussian SSR; area 15,-100 sq. mi.; pop. 1,247,000 (1959). Cities: Vitebsk (adm. center), Orsha, Gorodok, Polotsk, Dubrovno, Lepel, Senno. A plain irrigated by the W. Dvina and Dnieper (in its upper course); has mixed forests (mostly needle), podsol soil; moderately continental climate. Agr.: flax, rye, oats, barley, wheat, buckwheat. Ind.: primary flax processing, peat, machine tools. Several schools of higher education. Est. 1938. Increased in 1960 by part of Molodechno Oblast.

VITICULTURE. Commercial V developed in the Ukraine, Crimea, Georgia, and Azerbaijan in the 19th century, as construction of railroads opened easy access to markets for grapes and wines. Still, prior to World War I consumption in kind by farmers accounted for one-half of gross output. The area of vineyards (in thousand acres) declined from about 642 in 1914 to 536 in 1928, but was then reported to have risen to 1,050 by 1940 and to 1,920 by 1958. The output of grapes amounted (in thousand tons) to 930 in 1913 and 450 in 1926. For later years, only the amount of grapes processed by industry is known: 239,000 tons in 1940, 597,000 in 1956. The output of grape wine, in mill. decaliters rose from 20 in 1940 to 61 in 1958.

VLADIKAVKÁZ: *see* ORDZHONIKIDZE.

VLADÍMIR, city, adm. center of Vladimir Oblast, on Klyazma River, RSFSR; pop. 67,000 (1939), 154,000 (1959). Ind.: tractor, auto parts, chemical, tool-construction plants. One of most ancient R. towns; in the 12th century it became the political center of Vladimir-Suzdal principality; historical monuments are Golden Gate (Zolotye Vorota), Uspensky, Dmitrievsky Cathedrals.

VLADÍMIR, GRAND DUCHY OF, a political association of small feudal principalities under the authority of the Grand Duke of Vladimir. In the first half of the 13th century the lands of Vladimir, Rostov, Suzdal, and Nizhny-Novgorod were incorporated into it.

VLADÍMIR OBLAST, in central RSFSR; in interfluvial space between the Oka and Klyazma rivers; area 11,150 sq. mi.; pop. 1,402,000 (1959). Cities: Vladimir (adm. center), Aleksandrov, Gus-Khrustalny, Kovrov, Kolchugino, Murom, Suzdal. A plain with mixed forests and podzol soil, its minerals are phosphorites, iron ore, peat, gypsum. Agr.: flax, potatoes, orchards. Ind.: chemical, textile, tractors, machine tools. Est. 1944.

VLADÍMIR-SÚZDAL, GRAND DUCHY OF, one of the principalities in N.W. Russia, known from the 10th to the 12th century as Rostov-Suzdal. The capital Vladimir-on-Klyazma was an important center in the 12th and 13th centuries. During the reigns of Andrey Bogolyubsky (1157–74) and Vsevolod Yuryevich (1176–1212) the principality reached its greatest influence. In the 13th century its component elements —the principalities of Rostov, Suzdal, Tver, and others —asserted increasingly their independence while Moscow began to develop as the center of the future national unification of R.

VLADÍMIR SVYATOSLÁVOVICH (978–1015), Grand Duke of Kiev, and virtually founder of Kievan Russia. He fought many local wars; fortified Kiev and adorned it with stone buildings. V introduced Christianity as Russia's official faith and was canonized by the Russian Church.

VLADÍMIR-VOLÝNSK, GRAND DUCHY OF, one of the S.W. principalities; its capital, the town of Vladimir-Volynsky. At the time of Prince Roman Mstislavovich (1172–1205) it achieved great importance. In 1199, it was united with Galicia.

VLADÍMIR VSÉVOLODOVICH MONOMÁKH (1053–1125), Grand Duke of Kiev. He was called to power by the boyars during an insurrection in 1113; united the principalities surrounding Kiev; fought successfully against invading Polovtsy (Cumans). He is the author of the first R. literary works, *Instructions to My Children* and messages to Oleg Svyatoslavovich.

VLADIVOSTÓK, city, adm. center of Maritime (Primorsky) Kray, RSFSR; pop. 291,000 (1959). Largest Soviet port on Pacific Ocean, terminus of Trans-Siberian R.R. Ind.: shipbuilding, ship repair, canned fish. Branch of Ac. of S., USSR; numerous colleges, trade high schools. Founded 1860; in 1918–20 was occupied by Japan.

THE VLASOV MOVEMENT takes its name from Lieutenant-General Andrey Andreyevich Vlasov, who in June 1942 surrendered to the Germans after commanding the Soviet Second Assault Army against them in the Volkhov area. Born of peasant parents in 1900, Vlasov was a professional army officer who had joined the CP in 1930. He had apparently escaped the Great Purges unharmed and was considered a trusted and promising Soviet commander. In 1938 he was a Soviet military adviser to Chiang Kai-shek and gained rapid promotions thereafter.

Since his surrender, Soviet propaganda has labeled him a traitor. His recapture by Soviet forces near Prague in May 1945 led to a summary trial, conviction, and execution of Vlasov and a number of associates, annonced in Moscow on Aug. 2, 1946. Vlasov did indeed symbolize the anti-Soviet struggle on the German side in World War II.

However, it is erroneous to equate (as is commonly done) all Soviet military and political collaborators in the German camp with the VM. Vlasov had no military authority or command until 1945. Even though collaborator units were used by German military on an *ad hoc* basis, it was not until the final months of the war that Vlasov was given nominal control over parts of two divisions and other miscellaneous units, most of which saw no combat and some of which during the final days of the war turned against the Germans in Prague.

On the political side, German anti-Soviet leaflets were issued over Vlasov's signature from Sept. 1942 on. The "Smolensk Committee" which was launched in Dec. 1942 as a substitute for a R. government-in-exile was a propaganda fiction. An attempt of German army commanders, early in 1943, to "launch" Vlasov as the head of a political movement in the German-held areas of Russia and among former Soviet citizens working with the Reich boomeranged and in June 1943 produced a ban on his use by Hitler. Only in Oct. 1944 was a new permission secured, this time from SS chief Heinrich Himmler, for Vlasov and his associates to operate as a political movement. A handpicked "Committee for the Liberation of the Peoples of Russia" (known by its R. initials as KONR) was formalized, with a corresponding fourteen-point manifesto, in Prague on Nov. 15, 1944. By then, Germany had in effect lost the war.

Vlasov never had any authority in the German-occupied territory of the USSR, where the Germans worked with collaborators as individuals on the local level and with a few self-styled R. warlords. Vlasov never got along with the separatist spokesmen for the non-Russian areas of the Soviet Union. And, as friends and foes agreed, Vlasov was not a puppet of the Nazis. Nonetheless, he was the best available symbol for those Soviet citizens in Germany who—as prisoners of war, collaborators, and *Ostarbeiter*—looked for a political cause and hoped for an indigenous anti-Stalinist movement to be identified with, and to give them a modicum of dignity and the promise of status and success.

Vlasov's own politics and philosophy remain obscure. Reflecting some residual elements of communist values and attitudes to the end, Vlasov accepted a strong central government, the notion of a welfare state with considerable controls and planning, and a strong anti-colonialism (presumably nurtured by his experience in China). But he vigorously protested against terror as a tool of government and insisted on civil rights. He considered himself a R. patriot and was generally tolerant of other nationalities. But, politically and personally not very sophisticated, he was apparently impressed by arguments of authoritarian advisers; time and again he let himself be maneuvered by the Germans into a corner where he had no choice but to yield—or ultimately turn against them. He knew that, once having taken a stand on the Nazi side, his road back into the Soviet fold was barred. What his real expectations were for the future remains unknown.

His aides and associates included some pro-Nazi elements, some Western-oriented anti-Communists, some R. "solidarists," some Right-wing anti-Stalinist Communists, some Soviet agents—and many who were too confused by the complexities of the situation to keep to a clear political line. Most of them had apparently thrown in their lot with the Axis because they had hoped for a better Russia, or because there was nowhere else for them to go. By 1944–45 many had become bitterly disillusioned. The payoff came with Soviet retribution after the war.

Though individual collaborator units performed important services for the Germans, the VM proper was of no significance as a military force. As a political focus, it was doomed in advance. German totalitarianism could afford no indigenous appeal to or from the rank and file against the other totalitarianism, in the Soviet Union, which it was fighting. The amalgam of R. nationalism, anti-communism, Marxism, Nazism, meliorism, and authoritarianism, moreover, could produce no viable political creed or movement, once the specifics of the Nazi struggle against the Soviet Union were removed. (*See also* WORLD WAR II, PARTISAN MOVEMENT, GERMAN OCCUPATION, RUSSIANS ABROAD)

BIBLIOGRAPHY: George Fischer, *Soviet Opposition to Stalin,* Cambridge, Mass., 1952; Alexander Dallin, *German Rule in Russia, 1941–1945,* New York, 1957.   A. D.

VLÁSOV, Vasíly Zakhárovich (1906–1958), mechanical and structural engineer. Corresponding member, Ac. of S., USSR (1953). Graduate, Moscow School of Engineering (1930); professor, Civil Engineering Institute of Moscow (1935). Joined the Institute of Mechanics, Ac. of S. (1946). Author of *Thin-Walled Elastic Rods* (1941); *Structural Mechanics of Thin-Walled Three-Dimensional Systems* (1950). Stalin prizes (1941, 1950).

VÓITINSKY, Vladímir Savélyevich (1877–1960), well-known economist; was a member of the Bolshevik faction of the Social Democratic party in 1905–06. He was sentenced to hard labor and spent ten years in prison and in Siberia. V returned to Petrograd after the revolution and was appointed army commissar of the northern front by the Provisional Government. By that time he had become an opponent of Bolshevik rule. After the October revolution, he was a member of the Menshevik Georgian government. As an *émigré,* V worked as an economist in Germany and then in the U.S. He is the author of several authoritative books on economic subjects in English and German.

VOKS (All-Union Society for Cultural Relations With Foreign Countries): *see* CULTURAL EXCHANGE.

VÓLGA–BALTIC WATERWAY (Mariinsk Water System), man-made waterway connecting the Volga with Baltic Sea; goes through Rybinsk water reservoir, Sheksna River, Beloozersky Canal, Kovzha River, Mariinsky Canal, Vytegra River, Onega Canal, Svir River, Ladoga Canal, Neva River; length from Rybinsk to Leningrad 680 mi. Cargoes: timber and minerals. Since the construction of the N. Dvina and the White Sea–Baltic Canal, the Volga is connected with the White Sea.

VOLGA–DON WATERWAY connecting the Volga with the Don, and the White, Baltic, and Caspian seas with the Sea of Azov and the Black Sea. Length of the waterway is 335 mi., of which the V. I. Lenin Canal is 63 mi. Completed in 1952.

VÓLGA RIVER, (ancient *Rha,* medieval *Itil, Atala*), the largest river in Europe, 2,290 mi. long, rises in Valday upland in Kalinin Oblast, flows with great winding course E. and S.E. to Kazan in Tatar ASSR, then in a sweep S. at Kuybyshev, S.W. to Stalingrad and S.E. to Caspian Sea near Astrakhan. Its basin is estimated at 533,000 sq. mi. Is navigable along almost its entire length, but in some sections too shallow for large vessels; subject to great floods. Fed by many tributaries including the Oka, Sura, Sviyaga (right), Sheksna, Mologa, Kostroma, Unzha, Vetluga, Kama, and Samara (left). Chief cities on its banks: Kalinin, Yaroslavl, Kostroma, Ivanovo, Gorky, Rybinsk, Kazan, Kuybyshev, Saratov, Stalingrad, Astrakhan. Fishing is important in its lower course; linked by canals with Baltic, Caspian, and Black seas and with the Sea of Azov, and in the lower course near Stalingrad with the Don. Government projects are concerned with the construction of hydroelectric power plants, irrigation, and flood control. Uglich Hydroelectric Power Plant was built in 1940 followed by Rybinsk Plant; others include Gorky, Kuybyshev, and Stalingrad power plants. Transportation facilities were greatly improved by the building of the Moscow Canal System. It carries about 30 per cent of total river freight of USSR. Has played an outstanding role in the life of R. people and is known as "Mother Volga" in R. folklore.

VOLGA–URAL OIL REGION ("Second Baku"), large oil producing region in USSR, situated between Volga and the Urals; bordering Emba oil region in the S., Ukhta-Pechora oil region in the N., includes the areas of Bashkir, Tatar, Udmurt ASSRs, Perm, Kuybyshev, Stalingrad, and other oblasts. Oil discovered first in 1929 in Verkhne-Chusovskiye Gorodki.

VÓLKHOV, city in Leningrad Oblast, RSFSR, on Volkhov River; pop. 33,700 (1956). Electric power plant; aluminum plant.

VÓLKOV, Fyódor Grigóryevich (1729–1763), actor and "the father of the Russian theater" according to Belinsky. In 1750 V organized an amateur company in Yaroslavl which in 1756 was transferred to St. Petersburg and was given official recognition.

VOLODÁRSKY, V. (Moiséy Márkovich Goldstein) (1890–1918), communist, son of a poor Jewish artisan from Poland. V was active first in the "Bund" and later in the Ukrainian Socialist Democratic party. He was frequently arrested, imprisoned, and exiled. In 1913, he emigrated to America, joined the American Socialist party, and carried out anti-war propaganda. V returned to Russia in 1917 and joined the Bolsheviks. In 1918, he became commissar for press, propaganda and agitation. In the same year, he was assassinated by a Socialist Revolutionary in Petrograd.

VÓLOGDA, city, adm. center, of Vologda Oblast RSFSR, landing on Vologda River; pop. 95,000 (1939), 138,000 (1959). Center of important butter-making area; machine-making, flax-processing, woodworking, food and lace ind. Founded in the 12th century, has monuments of 16th-18th centuries (cathedrals, churches, monastery walls, and towers).

VÓLOGDA OBLAST, in N. European RSFSR; area 56,000 sq. mi.; pop. 1,308,000 (1959). Cities: Vologda (adm. center), Veliky Ustyug, Sokol, Cherepovets. Rolling country in the region of needle forests, has podzol soil and many lakes. Agr.: dairy, animal breeding, flax, rye, oats, barley. Ind.: lumber, wood pulp, shipbuilding, chemical, mechanized butter plants. Several scientific research institutes. Est. 1937.

VOLOGDÍN, Valentín Petróvich (1881–1953), electrical engineer. Corresponding member, Ac. of S., USSR (1939). Honored Scientist and Technologist, RSFSR (1942). Graduate (1907), professor (1921), St. Petersburg Institute of Technology, Leningrad Institute of Electrical Engineering. Director, Scientific Research Institute of High-Frequency Currents, Laboratory of High-Frequency Thermal Technology, (1947). Designed high-frequency electrical machinery; high-voltage mercury rectifier; suggested metal surface hardening, welding, and soldering by high-frequency current. Supervised construction of radio station which established direct communication with the U.S. (1925). A. S. Popov Gold Medal (1948); Stalin prizes (1943, 1952).

VOLÓSHIN, Maksimilián Aleksándrovich (1877–1931), a symbolist poet and translator from the French. He was a colorful personality, a man of great erudition, and a mystic. His poems are loaded with gloomy prophecies and reflect deep love for Russia. His mystic interpretation of revolution is expressed in the collection of poems *Mute Demons* (1919) and *Poems of the Terror* (1924). He hated the revolution, but loved Russia. V remained in the Soviet Union, but was practically unheard of as a poet after 1925.

VOLOST: *see* GOVERNMENT LOCAL, ADMINISTRATIVE AND TERRITORIAL DIVISIONS.

VÓLSK, city in Saratov Oblast, RSFSR, landing on Volga; pop. 62,000 (1959). Important center of cement industry; leather production.

VÓLSKY, Antón Nikoláyevich (1897–), metallurgist. Fellow, Ac. of S., USSR (1960). Graduate of Moscow Institute of National Economy (1924). Associated with the State Scientific Research Institute of Nonferrous Metals (1928–48); professor, Moscow Institute of Nonferrous Metals and Gold. Research in physical metallurgy, with emphasis on the chemical equilibrium in melts during the smelting of nonferrous metals.

VOLUNTEER ARMY: *see* CIVIL WAR, HISTORY.

VOLÝN OBLAST, in N.W. Ukrainian SSR; area 7,700 sq. mi.; pop. 890,000 (1959), mostly Ukrainians (90 per cent). Cities: Lutsk (adm. center), Vladimir-Volynsky, Kovel, Berestechko, Gorokhov, Kamen-Kashirsky, Lyuboml, Ustilug, Kivertsy. Navigable rivers: Pripyat and Styr. In the N. has sandy lowlands of Polesye, forests, marshes, in the S. a plateau with black earth; mildly continental climate. Agr.: rye, wheat, barley, corn, flax, animal breeding and dairies. Ind.: agric. machinery, primarily processing of flax, hemp and hops. Est. 1939.

VOLZHSK (f. Lopatino), city in Mari ASSR, on Volga; pop. 27,400 (1956). Ind.: sawmills, paper-cellulose and woodworking plants.

VÓLZHSKY, city in Stalingrad Oblast, RSFSR, on Volga River; pop. 67,000 (1959). Was founded in 1951 in connection with the construction of the Stalingrad power station.

VORKUTÁ, city in Komi ASSR, terminal of the new Northern–Pechora R.R.; pop. 55,000 (1959). Center of Pechora coal mines.

VOROBYÓV HILLS: *see* LENIN HILLS.

VORÓNA RIVER, in Penza, Tambov, and Voronezh oblasts, RSFSR, right tributary of the Khoper; length 280 mi.; used for floating.

VORÓNEZH, city, adm. center of Voronezh Oblast, RSFSR, landing on the Voronezh River; pop. 344,000 (1939), 448,000 (1959). The center of machine-building, chemical, food and other ind.; has numerous colleges and technical schools. Founded in 1586, Peter the Great built here the fleet which sailed on the Voronezh and Don rivers and fought against the Turks who held Azov. The front line passed through it during World War II.

VORÓNEZH OBLAST, in Central European RSFSR, on the Don and its tributaries; area 20,200 sq. mi.; pop.

2,369,000 (1959). Cities: Voronezh (adm. center), Borisoglebsk, and others. A plain with black soil and mildly continental climate. Agr.: wheat, rye, sunflowers, tobacco, essential oils. Mineral resources: iron ore, phosphorites. Ind.: metalworking and machine-building plants, cars, locomotive repair shops. Agricultural Institute, several schools of higher education. Est. 1934.

VORÓNEZH RIVER, in Tambov, Lipetsk and Voronezh oblasts, RSFSR, left tributary of the Don; length 291 mi.; used for floating; navigable in its lower course.

VORONÍKHIN, Andréy Nikíforovich (1759–1814), architect and painter of the classical school. Serf of Count Stroganov; was given freedom in 1786. Studied in Moscow with Bazhenov and later in Paris. Was architect of the Institute of Mining and the Kazan Cathedral, both in St. Petersburg.

VÓRONOV, Nikoláy Nikoláyevich (1899–), marshal of artillery, born in St. Petersburg. He studied in an agricultural school; drafted in 1917; joined the Red Army and served till 1919 in artillery. He studied at a Leningrad military artillery training school; graduated from the Frunze Military Academy, 1930, then commanded artillery units in the Moscow area; in 1935 he was named head of the Leningrad Artillery Training School. He was appointed chief of the main artillery administration of the Red Army in 1937. In 1939–40 took part in the war against Finland. During World War II he was appointed commander in chief of artillery and commanded the artillery operations on the Leningrad front. He was a member of the Supreme Command staff till the end of the war and remained commander in chief of artillery till 1950, when he was elected president of the Artillery Academy formed after World War II. Member of the CP since 1919.

VORÓNSKY, Aleksándr Konstantínovich (1884–1943), literary critic, editor, and writer, an "old Bolshevik." In 1921 he founded in Moscow the monthly journal *Krasnaya Nov* (Virgin Red Land) and the illustrated weekly *Prozhektor* (The Searchlight). He sided with Trotsky in 1927, was expelled from the party and exiled, but returned to Moscow in the early 1930's. Later he was arrested and died in prison. In 1911 he wrote *Literary Notes* under the pseudonym of Nurmin. His chief publications are: *Art and Life* (1924), *On Art* (1925), *The Art of Viewing Life* (1928), the novel *Eye of the Hurricane* (1928) and a biography of the revolutionary Zhelyabov.

VORONTSÓV, Count Mikhaíl Illariónovich (1714–1767), statesman, chancellor, 1758–63. Participated in the palace revolution which led to the accession of Empress Elizabeth in 1741.

VORONTSÓV, Prince Mikhaíl Semyónovich (1782–1856), general, field marshal. He participated in wars with Napoleonic France, with Turkey (1806–12, 1828–29), was Governor General of Novorossia and Bessarabia (1823–44); from 1844, was commander in chief of R. troops and viceroy of the Caucasus. He was in favor of moderate reforms.

VORONTSÓV, Vasíly Pávlovich (1847–1917), populist economist and theorist. Wrote under the pseudonym V. V. In his numerous articles and books he expressed, in accordance with the populist belief, the view that a development of capitalism in Russia was undesirable. V ardently defended this position in debates with the early Marxists Struve, Plekhanov, and Lenin.

VORONTSÓV-DÁSHKOV, Count Illarión Ivánovich (1837–1917), tsarist minister. V-D served in the army and took part in the annexation of Central Asia. He was one of the leaders of the secret counterrevolutionary society Holy Host, 1881–82. From 1881 to 1897, he was minister of the imperial household and after 1897 member of the State Council. In 1905, V-D was appointed Viceroy of the Caucasus.

VOROSHÍLOV, Klimént Yefrémovich (1881–), marshal of the Soviet Union, party and government official. As a youth, V was active in organizing the revolutionary movement in Lugansk. Was repeatedly arrested. Was a delegate to the Social Democratic party congresses in Stockholm and London in 1906 and 1907.

In 1917, V was elected as a Bolshevik member to the short-lived Constituent Assembly. During the civil war he distinguished himself on many fronts, especially in the battle for Tsaritsyn (now Stalingrad). As a supporter of Stalin, V rose rapidly in military ranks and became people's commissar of military and naval affairs from 1925 to 1940. In this post he played a major role in the purge of the Red Army in 1937 and 1938. He also held correspondingly high party posts, having been a member of the Politburo since 1926. In 1935 he was promoted to marshal of the Soviet Union. At the beginning of the Soviet war against Nazi Germany, V commanded northwestern armies defending Leningrad. However, after his failure to prevent the German blockade of Leningrad, he was removed and transferred to the State Defense Committee. In 1943 he accompanied Stalin to the Teheran Conference. After the war, V was appointed head of the Allied Control Commission in Hungary and aided the sovietization of that country. From 1946 to 1953, was deputy chairman of the Council of Ministers. In 1953, after Stalin's death, he became chairman of the Presidium of the Supreme Soviet, i.e. the official head of the Soviet state. Visited China and other Asiatic countries. In 1960 he resigned his major posts because of age and ill health. V is the author of several books in which he extolled Stalin's role in the Red Army.

VOROSHÍLOV: *see* USSURIYSK.

VOROSHILOVGRÁD: *see* LUGANSK.

VOROSHÍLOVSK (f. Alchevsk), city in Lugansk Oblast, RSFSR; pop. 98,000 (1959). R.R. station; one of major metallurgical centers of Donbas; coke-chemical, building-materials ind.; coal mining.

VORÓVSKY, Vátslav Vátslavovich (literary and party pseudonyms Yu. Adamovich, P. Orlovsky, Favn, M. Shvarts) (1871–1923), Soviet diplomat and Marxist literary critic. V joined the Bolshevik party in 1903; in 1905, became one of the editors of the Bolshevik publication *Vpered* (Forward). Was repeatedly arrested and exiled. In 1915 he left for Stockholm and, after the February revolution, became a member of the bureau of the Central Committee abroad. In 1917–19, V was ambas-

sador to the Scandinavian countries; 1920–21, administrator of *Gosizdat* (State Publishing House); 1921–23, ambassador to Italy. He also participated in the Genoa and Lausanne conferences. In May 1923, V was assassinated by an *émigré* Konradi in Lausanne. V published many essays and articles on literary and political topics. He translated the *Communist Manifesto* into Russian. Among his more important writings are *History of Marxism in Russia* and *Literary Essays.*

VÓTKINSK, city in Udmurt ASSR; pop. 60,000 (1959). R.R. station; machine-building, sawmilling, peat-briquetting ind.

VOTYAK: *see* UDMURT.

VOYEVODA: *see* LOCAL GOVERNMENT.

VÓYKOV, Pyotr Lázarevich (1880–1927), Communist and Soviet diplomat. V was born in Kerch and was active in the revolutionary movement from his youth on. He lived in Switzerland from 1907 to 1917. After his return, he joined the Bolsheviks and fought in the Urals. In 1918, he was commissar for food supply in the Urals. In 1924, he was sent to Poland as Soviet envoy and was killed in Warsaw by a White Russian, Koverda.

VOZNESÉNSKY, Nikoláy Alekséyevich (1903–1950), Communist economist, state and party official, academician (1943). V became a Bolshevik in 1919 and underwent intensive training in economics. After a rapid rise in government service, he became chairman of the Gosplan in 1938. His rise in party ranks was correspondingly rapid—he was elected member of the Central Committee of the CPSU in 1939 and in 1947 promoted to the Politburo. During World War II, he was made member of the State Council of Defense where he was the chief economic planner. After the war, as a protégé of Zhdanov, V's prominence continued. He published *The Economy of the USSR during the Great Patriotic War.* Shortly after Zhdanov's sudden death in 1948, V disappeared. Later, it was learned that he had been executed as one of the participants of the so-called "Leningrad Case" of 1949.

VRÚBEL, Mikhaíl Aleksándrovich (1856–1910), tragic genius of R. art, painter of passionate religious murals at Kiev's St. Cyril (1884) and of impressionistic canvasses *Princess Swan, Pan, Fortune-Teller, Demon* (1901). Like Van Gogh he fell ill and was sent to a mental clinic. In 1903 V painted *The Pearl* which looked iridescent and, in 1905, the portrait of the poet Bryusov. Then final madness overtook him. V died five years later, blind and destitute. The lyricism and beauty of his paintings, his bold brushwork, and unusual colors made him the lonely giant of modern R. art.

VUCHÉTICH, Yevgény Víktorovich (1908–), sculptor, member of the Academy of Fine Arts. Awarded five Stalin prizes and order of Lenin. Designed and molded the following monuments: Stalin, at the terminal of the Volga-Don Canal; M. G. Yefremov, in Vyazma; General Vatutin, in Kiev; Warriors of the Soviet Army, in Berlin. Was awarded the Grand Prix at the International Exhibition, Brussels, in 1958.

VUL, Bentsion Moiséyevich (1903–), physicist. Corresponding member, Ac. of S., USSR (1939). Graduated from Kiev Polytechnic Institute (1928); associated with the Institute of Physics, Ac. of S., USSR (1932). Research concerns physics of dielectrics; discovered barium titanate endowed with high dielectrical permeability and determined fields of application (1944). Stalin prize (1946).

VULF, Yevgény Vladímirovich (1885–1941), botanist. Professor, University of Crimea (1921–26). Research concerned with geobotany, plant systematics, flora, and the history of botany. Author of *A Historical Geography of Plants* (1936).

VÚOKSA RIVER, in Finland and Leningrad Oblast, RSFSR; flows from Lake Saimaa into Lake Ladoga; length 63 mi.

VVEDÉNSKY, Borís Alekséyevich (1893–), radiophysicist. Fellow (1943) and member of the Executive Board (1946–53), academical secretary, Division of Technical Sciences (1946–51) and chairman, Division of Research on Radio Engineering (1944–53), Ac. of S., USSR. Chairman of the All-Union Scientific Council on Radiophysics and Radio Engineering. Acting chairman, Stalin Prize Award Committee. Graduate (1915) and professor (1929) of Moscow University. Research on propagation of ultrashort waves and magnetism, and laws governing them above the earth between transmitting and receiving stations. Calculations of eddy currents in ferromagnetism and substantiation of data on the effects of troposphere on propagation of ultrashort waves. Investigated physical phenomena in electronic tubes. Author of *Problems of Radio Wave Propagation* (1948); *Long-Distance Tropospheric Propagation of Ultrashort Waves* (1957). Chief editor, *Bolshaya Sovetskaya Entsiklopedia* (Large Soviet Encyclopedia) (1951), and of the periodical *Izvestia Akad. nauk SSSR* (News of the Ac. of S., USSR). A. S. Popov Gold Medal (1949), Stalin prize (1952).

VVEDÉNSKY, Nikoláy Yevgényevich (1852–1922), physiologist. In his youth, V was active in revolutionary populist circles; with Zhelyabov and 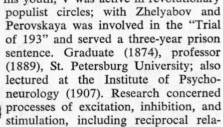 Perovskaya was involved in the "Trial of 193" and served a three-year prison sentence. Graduate (1874), professor (1889), St. Petersburg University; also lectured at the Institute of Psychoneurology (1907). Research concerned processes of excitation, inhibition, and stimulation, including reciprocal relationships between antagonist centers during the stimulation of the cortex, effects of electric shock on the nervous system, and so forth. Suggested the rhythmic nature of nervous excitation and the ability of the nervous system to reproduce rhythmical impulses for many hours without symptoms of fatigue (1884); introduced the concept of *parabiosis* (stationary excitation); established the correlation between excitation and inhibition. Advanced the theory of general laws governing the reaction of excitatory systems and advocated materialistic ideas in natural science. First Russian member of the Permanent International Committee on the Convention of Physiological Congresses, eventually succeeded by I. P. Pavlov.

VYÁTKA: *see* Kirov.

VYÁTKA RIVER, in Kirov Oblast, RSFSR and Tatar ASSR, right tributary of the Kama; length 530 mi.; navigable for 370 mi.

VYÁTSKAYA ZEMLYÁ (Khlynóvskaya Zemlyá), an ancient territory of Novgorod. In 1489 it was annexed by Ivan III to the Moscow principality.

VYÁZEMSKY, Prince Pyotr Andréyevich (1792–1878), poet, critic, journalist. In the 1820's he was close to Pushkin's group. V's poetry (epistles, epigrams) is caustic and witty. Nature is the subject of many of his poems (*The First Snow, Steppe*). At the end of his life he was an important bureaucrat. His memoirs *The Old Notebook* (1872–77) are interesting.

VYÁZMA, town in Smolensk Oblast, on Vyazma River, RSFSR; pop. 26,700 (1956). Processing of agr. raw materials, metalworking.

VYÁZNIKI, city in Vladimir Oblast, RSFSR, landing on Klyazma River; pop. 34,100 (1956). Ancient center of linen industry.

VYBORG APPEAL, a protest against the dissolution of the first State Duma signed in July 1906 in Vyborg, Finland, by 180 deputies, chiefly members of the Constitutional Democratic party (q.v.) and of the Labor Group (q.v.). The VA urged the population not to pay taxes or comply with army drafts until the Duma was summoned again. The signatories of the VA were tried and sentenced to brief prison terms, which, however, involved temporary disfranchisement and prevented them from being candidates for election to the second State Duma.

VÝBORG (Fin. *Viipuri*), city in Leningrad Oblast, RSFSR, port on Gulf of Finland, at Saimaa canal; pop. 51,000 (1959). Has food and metalworking industries; many historical monuments.

VÝCHEGDA RIVER, in Komi ASSR and Archangel Oblast, RSFSR; right tributary of the N. Dvina; length 430 mi.; navigable for 265 mi.

VYG RIVER, in Karelian ASSR; the upper Vyg (80 mi. long) flows into Vygozero, the lower Vyg (60 mi. long) flows from Vygozero into the White Sea. Is part of the White Sea–Baltic Canal.

VÝGOZERO, lake in Karelian SSR; area 386 sq. mi.; part of White Sea–Baltic Canal; has considerable fisheries.

VÝKSA, city in Gorky Oblast, RSFSR; pop. 35,900 (1956). Early center of metallurgy, dating back to 18th century.

VYSHESLÁVTSEV, Borís Petróvich (1877–1954), philosopher, born in Moscow, son of a lawyer. Following the publication of his *The Ethics of Fichte* (1914), he was appointed to the faculty at Moscow University. In 1922 he left for W. Europe because his philosophy was incompatible with official Marxist views. He settled in Paris, and later in Geneva. He wrote, in Russian, *The Ethics of Transformed Eros* (1929); *The Heart in Christian and in Hindu Mysticism* (1931); *God and Man*, and *Two Paths to Salvation* (1937); *The Philosophical Poverty of Marxism* (1952); *The Crisis of Industrial Culture* (1953). His last study, *The Eternal in Russian Philosophy*, was published in 1955.

VYSHÍNSKY, Andréy Yanuáryevich (1883–1954), soviet official, lawyer, and diplomat. V joined the Rus-

sian Social Democratic party in 1902 but supported the Menshevik faction for many years. In 1920, he changed allegiances and became a Bolshevik. During the 1920's he developed a considerable reputation as a Bolshevik legal theorist and became professor of law at Moscow University. In 1933 he was appointed deputy public prosecutor and in 1935 moved up to the post of public prosecutor. In this latter post he achieved international notoriety as the prosecuting attorney of the show trials of the 1930's. He also set forth, at this time, the official tenets of Soviet law, defining it as the expression of the will of the ruling classes, i.e., the working class. In the 1940's V moved into diplomatic affairs, becoming deputy minister of foreign affairs. He reached the high point of his career as foreign minister from 1949 to 1953. After Stalin's death, V was downgraded to Soviet delegate to the UN, a post he held until his death. V is the author of several books on Soviet law and international law. His theory, according to which a Soviet court can condemn a defendant on the basis of the latter's confession only, is considered erroneous now.

VYSHNEGRÁDSKY, Iván Alekséyevich (1831–1895), minister of finance. A former university professor, V was minister of finance (1882–92). V found R. public finances in utter confusion: depreciated currency, unbalanced budget, and large public debt. His policy was to arrest the increase of state indebtedness by increasing taxes, raising tariffs, and encouraging exports. He succeeded in balancing the budget, accumulated gold reserves, and stopped the excessive printing of paper money.

VÝSHNY VOLOCHÓK, city in Kalinin Oblast, RSFSR, on Vyshnevolotskaya water system; pop. 66,000 (1959). Ind.: textile, mirrors, tanning extracts, mechanical and tile plants.

VYSÓKAYA, mountain in E. part of central Urals in the area of Nizhny Tagil; 978 ft. high; rich iron ores.

W

WÁGNER, Yegor Yegorovich (1849–1903), organic chemist. Graduate of Kazan University (1874); professor of several institutes. Research on synthesis of secondary alcohols and their oxidation; development of general methods for oxidation of ethylene bonds with permanganate (Wagner oxidation) and their application for the investigation of terpenes and their structures. Discoverer of the Wagner-Meerwein rearrangement.

WAGES AND SALARIES. In Soviet planned economy the wages and salaries are regulated by central government agencies. Nonindustrial labor and the majority of salaried workers, including technicians and engineers, are paid on the basis of fixed monthly rates. The pay of industrial workers is based on a relatively complicated *differential wage system* (wage scales).

The *wage scale* establishes a series of coefficients (ratios) relating the rate of pay for various groups of workers in the same general category, graded according to skill level and the nature of work performed, to the lowest, or "first class," rate, which is taken as the basis. The more recent wage scales, as a rule, comprise eight graduated wage classes, with coefficient averaging as high as 2.0 (2:1) for the top wage rate.

The worker's earnings, based on the wage scale and output quota, are usually supplemented by a premium (bonus). The bonus systems, widely used in Soviet Russia today, are designed to provide a material incentive by rewarding wage-earners and salaried workers for achieving or exceeding the established quantitative and qualitative work indices. Bonuses are given to both timeworkers and pieceworkers, and are calculated in percentual relation to the wage scale, piece rates, or the amount of money saved through efficiency. The piece-and-premium patterns of work remuneration predominate, which are generally based on rewarding the individual, although collective reward techniques are also practiced. To illustrate the individual reward system: In the coal mines of the Donets basin a man working underground, on a piecework basis, who had fulfilled the weekly production quota, received a bonus in the amount of 20 per cent of the weekly rate plus 2 per cent for each per cent in excess of the quota. A typical example of the collective reward system: For the fulfilment of the monthly plan, in the mining of coking coals, or in preliminary drifting, the section teams received a bonus amounting to 30 per cent of the wage scale rate plus 1.5 per cent for each per cent in excess of the plan.

In the Soviet Union, which now has the second largest industry in the world, the wage level is still extremely low. This is one of the most serious inner contradictions of Soviet economic life which makes the building of a modern industrial society enormously difficult. During the first years of the revolution, a time of civil war and utter economic collapse, the workers' pay dropped far below the modest level achieved in Russia before World War I. The NEP period marked a steady increase of industrial wages. By 1928 the average wages, for industry as a whole, had reached and even slightly exceeded the prewar level. In 1928 the policy of rapid industrialization was inaugurated, which was accompanied by strong inflation. Increases in money wages lagged far behind the rising prices of consumers' goods. Real wages decreased steadily over the years, dropping lowest in the mid-thirties—for the entire industry, to about 50 per cent of the 1928–29 level. This was followed by a new rise of real wages, which came to an end in 1938 before the 1928–29 level was reached. The tense period preceding World War II marked another fall of real wages, rather slow at first, but far more rapid after the Soviet Union entered the war in 1941. The postwar increase started from a very low level. It was not until the currency reform of 1948, followed by a vigorous policy of lowering commodity prices without reducing the workers' pay, that real wages began to rise once more to the prewar level, and then to the level which existed before the era of rapid industrialization. Whether the latter level has actually been reached is not quite clear, since figures relating to the increase of money wages are still treated by Soviet statistics as a state secret. For some branches of Soviet economy, however, the relevant data, previously never reported, have been widely publicized since 1956.

The men who in recent years have been shaping Soviet policies realize that the exceedingly low wage level set for the vast majority of wage-earners and salaried workers seriously impedes the economic growth of the country. To eliminate the worst anomalies in work remuneration and raise the general wage level, various steps have been taken which include two groups of measures:

a) In September 1956, a general wage increase effective Jan. 1, 1957 was decreed for all low-paid wage-earners and salaried workers employed in industry, construction, transport, and communication. The minimum wage was set at 300 rubles per month for city workers and at 270 rubles for rural areas. An additional 8 billion rubles was appropriated in 1957 to cover an average 33 per cent increase for all categories of workers and salaried personnel. From the above figures it can be readily calculated that this increase had affected a total of 8½ million men whose earnings prior to the reform averaged 233 rubles per month.

This marked a break with extreme differentiation which for several decades had been the underlying principle of Soviet wage policy. So long as the general wage level remained extremely low, the men in charge of wage administration were concerned primarily with securing adequate pay for a relatively small number of highly skilled "leading" workers, whose labor was particularly important for the carrying out of the economic plan. The same was true in regard to higher personnel, with particular emphasis on technicians and engineers. The policy of drastic wage differentiation had been, in fact, proclaimed a true socialist policy, as distinct from the capitalist policy of wage equalization. The reform of 1956 marks a decided turn in this policy, abandoning the principle of extreme wage differentiation. The September directives of 1956 were carried further in the Seven Year Plan (1959–65) adopted by the 21st Party Congress, which provided for an increase of the minimum wage from 270–350 to 400–500 rubles per month in 1959–62, and to 500–600 rubles in 1963–65.

b) The second group of measures modifying the Soviet wage structure involved the so-called "adjustment of wages" put into effect since 1956, following the introduction of a shorter working day (q.v.). The new wage scale rates corresponding to reduced working hours must be calculated to raise, rather than depress, the general level of weekly or monthly earnings, both for workers and for white-collar personnel. Apparently this has been achieved in a large measure thanks to better organization of work and technological improvements introduced simultaneously with the "wage adjustment." The process, which apparently will be completed by 1961, tends inevitably to bring down the earnings of the highest-paid workers.

What is the present wage level in the Soviet Union? The *Monthly Labor Review* of April 1960 cites ample comparative figures, for the month of August 1959, on prices and commodities in relation to average earnings of industrial workers in the Moscow area. The latter are taken hypothetically to equal 800 rubles per month, which is probably close to the actual figure. The contrasting picture of wages and prices in Moscow and in New York (in rubles and kopecks vs. dollars and cents) acquires a graphic clarity if we recalculated the Soviet data in terms of the new currency in circulation after Jan. 1, 1961, i.e., reduce each figure to one-tenth of its value. The hourly rate in Moscow is found to be five times lower than in New York, while the prices of staple commodities—with the sole exception of bread, sold at a relatively low "politic" price—are in fact higher than New York prices. In other words, the purchasing power of the worker's wage with respect to consumers' goods, in terms of working hours and minutes, is at least five times lower than in New York. The contrast in purchasing power reaches fantastic proportions if we turn to such items as clothing.

The situation is somewhat alleviated by the various benefits which in the Soviet Union are referred to as the "socialized" or social welfare component of the worker's wage. These include social security pensions, with no payments contributed by wage-earners or salaried workers; free medical aid; numerous agencies for child care; free schooling, and so on. This type of care, partly covered by "fringe benefits" in the United States, has a far greater importance in the Soviet Union, where the vast majority of the working population is poor. Such measures, however, in no way eliminate the problem of raising the real wage level, which will remain urgent for some years to come.   S. SCH.

BIBLIOGRAPHY: Abram Bergson, *The Structure of Soviet Wages. A Study in Socialist Economics*, Cambridge, 1944; Solomon M. Schwarz, *Labor in the Soviet Union*, New York, 1952; Naum Jasny, *Soviet Industrialization, 1928–1952*, Chicago, 1961; Harry Schwartz, *The Red Phoenix. Russia Since World War II*, New York, 1952.

WAR COMMUNISM. This period of Soviet economic history lasted from the middle of 1918 to March 1921. WC represented an attempt at direct state control and operation of the entire nonagricultural production and distribution apparatus. These policies were partly inspired by the specific interpretation of the Marxist doctrine, but mainly represented *ad hoc* measures designed to cope with emergency situations.

Nationalization of all large industries was decreed on June 28, 1918, and was extended to small-scale plants and shops in Dec. 1920. All trade was nationalized on Nov. 21, 1918. The Supreme Economic Council (VSNKh) which was created in Dec. 1917 as a central coordinating and planning agency was gradually placed in charge of the actual day-by-day operation of the nationalized enterprises. Market relationships were superseded by state-organized requisitions, barter, and rationing. Huge amounts of paper money were issued, resulting in a runaway inflation and flight from money. In the final stages of WC a virtually moneyless economy came into being. After Oct. 1920 payments for rationed goods and for government services such as railroad transport were abolished and abolition of money taxes was to follow. As a food shortage and policies of an extreme wage equalization deprived industrial workers of an incentive to work, some categories of skilled personnel were mobilized in Jan. 1919, followed in Jan. 1920 by conscription of all labor. Workers were organized into "labor armies," subjected to military discipline and attached to their places of work, with disastrous effect upon productivity.

Perhaps the most violent manifestations of WC took place in agriculture. As money depreciated and peasants refused to sell grain to the government at fixed prices, armed workers' detachments were sent into villages to requisition grain (May 1918), and the organization of Village Poor Committees was decreed (June 1918). These Committees, composed of poor and landless peasants, assisted in confiscation of land and food belonging to their richer neighbors.

By spring 1921 the economy was threatened with a complete breakdown. The ruthless policies of WC were effective in redistributing the existing wealth and stocks but failed to provide incentives for the production of new goods. The highly centralized administration of nationalized plants and shops by the inexperienced personnel of the Supreme Economic Council, in a bottleneck-ridden economy, was a failure. By 1920, the output of large-scale industry declined to 11 per cent of its 1916 level. While grain requisitions were at first effective and yielded 3 mill. tons in 1919–20, peasants soon reduced their production to the subsistence minimum: the sown area declined from 238.5 to 170 mill. acres between 1917 and 1922–3. The 1921 gross agricultural output amounted to only 56 per cent of the 1917 level. Indiscriminate confiscation of grain reserves in the drought areas contributed to the great famine in the Volga regions. By 1921, peasant revolts spread to numerous areas. Industrial labor productivity declined catastrophically, as a result of poor living conditions, wage equalization, and military compulsion. The Kronstadt revolt in March 1921 provided the final impulse for a reversal of policy. Lenin decided that "a strategic retreat" was in order. The New Economic Policy (NEP) was proclaimed on March 15, 1921, aiming at a revival of markets and a rapid increase in the national product, at the cost of concessions to private enterprise and the relaxation of the state controls.

BIBLIOGRAPHY: A. Baykov, *The Development of the Soviet Economic System*, New York, 1947; M. Dobb, *Soviet Economic Development Since 1917*, New York, 1948; S. N. Prokopovicz, *Histoire Economique de l'URSS*, Paris, 1952.   L. S.

WAR INDUSTRIES COMMITTEES were created during World War I (in May 1915) under the influence of military defeats. The founders of the WIC sought to bring together prominent members of industry and commerce "so that following the example of our allies, everything that the Army needs be supplied to it." The WIC carried out the mobilization of industries supply-

ing the army and producing for contracts of the defense agency (970 enterprises) in close association with the special councils on food, fuel, transport, and other army supplies that had been created earlier and which consisted of representatives of the government, of the State Duma, and of various public organizations. In the presence of continuing political conflicts between the government and public opinion, the WIC, together with the *Zemgor* (q.v.), began to assume an increasingly active role in political affairs. In addition to the central WIC, the chairman of which was A. I. Guchkov and the vice-chairman A. I. Konovalov, WIC's were established at the local level, in industrial centers and in large cities. Already in the spring of 1916 they numbered 239. On Feb. 26–29, 1916 the second All-Russian Conference of WIC took place. The third (and last) met in May 1917.

A special role in the activities of the WIC was played by Workers' Groups. The chairman of the Workers' Group in the central WIC was K. Gvozdev, who subsequently became minister of labor in the Provisional Government. Its secretary was B. O. Bogdanov. Both were Mensheviks favoring support of the war effort. This issue was the source of sharp conflicts in the election of workers' representatives between the Mensheviks and the Bolsheviks, who called for a boycott of the WIC. In spite of this, a representation of workers was achieved in 70 of the committees. In 1916 a conference of the Workers' Groups of the WIC took place that had a considerable political significance. In Jan. 1917 the Workers' Group of the Central WIC was arrested by the imperial government. After its release during the February revolution it was among the early members of the Petrograd Soviet of Workers' Deputies.   G. A.

WARSAW PACT: *see* FOREIGN POLICY.

WAVERERS: *see* OPPOSITION.

WEIGHTS AND MEASURES. The metric system of weights and measures was introduced in Russia facultatively by the law of June 4, 1899 and obligatorily by the decree of the Soviet government on Sept. 14, 1918. For temperature, the Celsius (centigrade) scale is used.

OLD RUSSIAN MEASURES AND WEIGHTS

LINEAR MEASURE:
1 versta = 500 sazhens = .66 mile = 1.0668 km.
1 sazhen = 3 arshins = 7 feet = 2.13 m.
1 arshin = 16 vershoks = 28 dyuims (inches) = 71.12 cm.
1 fut = 12 dyuims = 1 foot = 30.48 cm.
1 vershok = 1.75 inches = 4.445 cm.
1 dyuim = 1 inch = 2.54 cm.

SQUARE MEASURE:
Desyatina = 2,400 square sazhens = 2.7 acres = 1.0925 hectare.

LIQUID MEASURE:
Vedro = 12.3 liters
Chetvert = 3.075 liters

METRIC SYSTEM:
1 mm. = 0.03937 in.
1 cm. = 0.3937 in.
1 m. = 3,28 ft. = 39.37 in.
1 km. = .621 mi.
1 sq. km. = .386 sq. mi.
1 kg. = 2.205 lb.
1 hectare = 2.471 acres
1 mile = 1.609 km.
1 sq. mile = 2.59 sq. km.

WEIGHTS:
1 pud (pood) = 40 funts = 36.11 lb.
1 funt = 96 zolotniks = 0.903 lb.

Conversion formula for temperature:

$$\frac{F° - 32}{9} = \frac{C°}{5}$$

Centigrade	Fahrenheit
— 40	— 40
— 17.8	0
— 12.2	+ 10
— 6.7	+ 20
— 1.1	+ 30
0	+ 32
+ 5	+ 41
+ 10	+ 50
+ 20	+ 68
+ 30	+ 86
+100	+212

WELDING: *see* METALLURGY.

WEST-KAZAKHSTÁN OBLAST, in Kazakh SSR; area 58,700 sq. mi.; pop. 383,000 (1959): Kazakhs, Russians, Ukrainians. One town, Uralsk (adm. center); main river: Ural. Situated in N. part of Caspian depression, is arid; has sharply continental climate; brown earth, partly black earth soils, sand deserts, many pastures. Agr.: wheat, rye, millet, barley, sunflower, mustard in the N., cattle breeding in the S. Ind.: processing of agr. products. Pedag. inst., theater. Est. 1932.

WESTERNERS: *see* PHILOSOPHY.

WILLIAMS, Pyótr Vladímirovich (1902–1947), stage designer. Born in Moscow; studied at an art school in Moscow. From 1925 to 1931 W was leader of the Association of Easel Painters. In 1929 he turned to theatrical painting; was stage designer of the Moscow Art Theater 1941–47. Staged the ballets *Romeo and Juliet, Ivan Susanin,* and others.

WINTER, Aleksándr Vasílyevich (1878–1958), power plant engineer. Fellow, Ac. of S., USSR (1932). Graduate of St. Petersburg Polytechnic Institute (1912). Director of the first peat-fed power plant; director of Dneprostroy (1927–32). From 1943, a leading figure in the technical council of the Ministry of Electric Power Plants, USSR. Modernized power plants by introducing steam turbines and 20,000 volt transmissions. Participated in designing the Kuybyshev and Stalingrad hydroelectric plants. Three Lenin orders, Order of the Red Banner of Labor, and other decorations.

WHITE ARMY: *see* CIVIL WAR, HISTORY.

WHITE LAKE (R. *Beloye Ozero*), lake in W. Vologda Oblast, RSFSR; 434 sq. mi.; has considerable fisheries. Town of Beloozersk is located on its shores.

WHITE RUSSIA: *see* BYELORUSSIA.

WHITE SEA (R. *Beloye More*), in N. part of European USSR; area 36,700 sq. mi.; maximum depth, 1,100 ft. Has four large gulfs, Mezen, Dvina, Onega, Kandalaksha, which freeze in winter. Ports: Archangel, Belomorsk, Kandalaksha, Mezen, Severodvinsk, Onega. Has fisheries (herring, salmon, cod); also used for floating timber. There are many islands: Solovetsky, Morzhovets, and others. White Sea–Baltic Canal connects it with Baltic Sea.

WHITE SEA–BALTIC CANAL connects White Sea with Lake Onega; crosses Karelian ASSR, rich in woods and building materials. Length 140 mi. Built in 1933 mostly by forced labor, is of great economic importance, it shortens the way from White Sea to Leningrad by 2,500 miles. Cities: Medvezhyegorsk, Belomorsk, Segezha. Was partly destroyed in World War II but rebuilt.

WILNO: *see* VILNIUS.

WITTE, Count Sergéy Yúlyevich (1849–1915), statesman, born in Tiflis (now Tbilisi). Studied at the Odessa university; entered the service of the Odessa Southwestern Railway 1886–88; minister of communications, Feb. 1892; in August of the same year succeeded Vyshnegradsky as minister of finance. Under W's leadership R. economy made substantial progress. His policies comprised the reorganization of the protective tariff, encouragement to foreign investments, broadening of the taxation system which was made to include the spirits monopoly, and the introduction of the gold standard which stabilized the exchange value of the ruble (1897–99). Advancement of industry, however, fostered the growth of the proletariat while the rapid rise in the amount of the foreign debt and the necessity to protect the gold standard led to massive exports of grain which, in years of poor harvest, affected the population adversely. Other important policies sponsored by W were the building of the Trans-Siberian R.R., the establishment of the Russo-Chinese Bank, and encouragement to the movement of settlers to Siberia. In Aug. 1903 W was dismissed as minister of finance and was relegated to the honorary position of president of the committee of ministers.

After the debacle of the Japanese war he headed the R. delegation to the peace conference at Portsmouth, New Hampshire, and negotiated a peace treaty which, while involving the loss of Port Arthur and some other territories, was on the whole far less severe than might have been expected in view of Russia's undistinguished war record. W was rewarded with the title of count. On his return to Russia in the midst of the revolution of 1905 he was again recalled from semi-retirement and was the author of the Manifesto of Oct. 17, 1905 (O.S.) which contained the elements of representative government and introduced in Russia a constitutional regime. W was appointed president of the council of ministers but his tenure of that office was brief. The emperor and the empress disliked him intensely and Nicholas II was not reconciled to the limitation of autocracy: early in May 1906, five days before the convocation of the new R. parliament, W tendered his resignation which was eagerly accepted. He is the author of a valuable and highly indiscreet memoir, an abridged version of which is available in English.

WORKING HOURS. A general restriction on WH in industrial enterprises was legally established in R. in the summer of 1897, under the influence of the mass strikes of St. Petersburg workers in 1896 and early 1897. The working day in industry was then limited to 11½ hours on weekdays and 10 hours on Saturdays. Actual practices at the beginning of the 20th century went beyond this legislation, and by 1905, when Russia's first extensive workers' agitation for an 8-hour day developed, the majority of industrial establishments had already gone over to a 10-hour day, and some to 9 hours. After a temporary success in shortening WH in 1905, the practice of 10- and 9-hour days was again enforced and maintained until the revolutions of 1917.

In the spring of 1917, an agreement between the St. Petersburg Soviet of Workers' Deputies and the St. Petersburg Association of Manufacturers and Factory Owners established an 8-hour day for St. Petersburg industry, with two hours less on Saturdays, which was tantamount to introducing a 46-hour week. Within a few weeks this standard for WH spread without legislative action throughout the country, not only in industry, but to all branches of work. After the formation of the Soviet government, the 8-hour day and 46-hour week were reaffirmed by legislation, in a decree of the Council of People's Commissars of Nov. 11 (Oct. 29, O.S.), 1917. Thereafter the 8-hour day and 46-hour week, though widely violated by improper practices of over-time work, were the rule for the next decade.

At the end of the 1920's, however, the entire system of regulating working time underwent a radical reorganization. On Oct. 15, 1927, a resolution was issued calling for industry's gradual transition to a 7-hour day with a 42-hour week. Shortening the work day was linked with a comprehensive change to operating enterprises on three shifts to make maximum possible use of the available equipment. The change to three shifts, however, encountered many obstacles and proved unrealizable. As a result, the interest in a 7-hour day among Soviet leaders dropped appreciably by the mid-1930's, and on June 26, 1940, in the context of the prewar effort, the 7-hour day was revoked and replaced by an 8-hour day.

Connected with the change to the 7-hour day in the late 1920's there was another measure which profoundly affected the whole system of regulating WH. In 1929, again in the interest of the maximum utilization of available equipment, the so-called continuous work week was introduced. General days off were abolished and a complicated system was established which varied both among different enterprises and in different parts of the same enterprise. It called for alternating hours and days of work and rest, and assigning days off to workers and employees in rotation. At the same time, almost all holidays were abolished (there were a great many in the R. tradition) and for general holidays only 5 days a year (6 in leap year) were established. To avoid an increase in the total number of WH per year, the usual 7-day week was changed to a 5-day "week" of four work days and one day off (which was also to compensate for the denial of shorter hours on the eve of the day off). This system—especially in Soviet conditions where two or more members of almost every family work and people live in very cramped quarters, often two or more families to one apartment—brought great disorder into the lives of workers and aroused great dissatisfaction. In June 1940, when the 7-hour day was abolished and replaced by 8 hours, the continuous work week was also revoked. It was replaced by a normal 7-day week with 6 working days and one, in principle general, day off. This was done, however, without reinstituting shorter hours on the day before the free day; i.e. it introduced a 48-hour week.

From 1940 until 1956, the country ran on the basis of an 8-hour day and a 48-hour week. In Feb. 1956, one of the 20th Party Congress decisions on the Sixth Five Year Plan (1956–60) was a directive to change workers and employees gradually over to a 7-hour day, and underground workers in coal and mining industries to a 6-hour day. Thereupon, immediately after the congress, a general shortening of hours on the eves of days off from 8 to 6 hours was ordered, which constituted a general shift to a 46-hour week.

The decision to change to a 7-hour day has been energetically implemented since the end of 1956 both in industry and in other branches of work. By Oct. 1, 1960, according to official data, 40 million workers and employees had been shifted to "shortened" (7- and 6-hour) work days—i.e. about two-thirds of the total

working force in the USSR. With the change, workers normally working 7 hours work 6 hours on Saturdays, so that the work week is 41 hours.

At the same time, both in the 20th Party Congress directives and in a series of subsequent government instructions on introducing shorter work days, it was projected that "where it is feasible, depending on production conditions," a 5-day week with an 8-hour day and 2 days off might be introduced, which would bring a 40-hour week. It remains unclear whether this meant that a number of enterprises in the Soviet Union would introduce a 5-day week of the American type, with an expanded week end, or that there might be two non-consecutive days off per week.

Considerable significance attaches to another decision taken by the 20th Party Congress that shorter WH should be introduced without lowering weekly labor productivity and without lowering the total level of workers' and employees' earnings. Both requirements are basically being fulfilled and this has, specifically, required an extensive reorganization of the whole wage system simultaneously with the transition to the shortened work day. (*See* WAGES.)

The 21st Party Congress (Feb. 1959) directives on the Seven Year Plan (1959–65) outlined a plan for a further decrease in WH. They projected another reduction of one hour on Saturdays for workers on a 7-hour day after 1962, introducing a 40-hour week, and after 1964 a general shift of workers and employees from 7- to 6-hour days, with a 35-hour week, and from 6- to 5-hour days, with a 30-hour week. The application of a 5-day work week (with 7-hour days and 6 for underground work) was also foreseen; it was no longer said that its introduction would be motivated "by feasibility, depending on production conditions," but that it would depend on whether, "for the majority of the workers and employees it is more convenient to have not a 5–6 hour day with a 5-day week, but a 6–7 hour day with two days off per week." Thus the system of extended week ends is perhaps contemplated.

BIBLIOGRAPHY: Solomon M. Schwarz, *Labor in the Soviet Union*, New York, 1952.   S. SCH.

WORKERS' AND PEASANTS' INSPECTION: *see* ADMINISTRATIVE CONTROL.

WORKERS' OPPOSITION: *see* OPPOSITION.

WORKMEN'S COMPENSATION: *see* SOCIAL INSURANCE.

WORLD PEACE COUNCIL: *see* PROPAGANDA.

WORLD WAR I. With the outbreak of the war, Russia planned to concentrate on the less formidable Austria, leaving Germany till she was better prepared. However, in response to a French appeal, Russia was persuaded to undertake a simultaneous offensive against East Prussia. Despite a 2–1 manpower superiority, this offensive was crushed by German forces under Hindenburg (Aug. 1914) in the Masurian swamps, and the commanding Russian general Samsonov committed suicide. Though Russia suffered enormous losses (300,-000 men and 650 guns), this attack did divert two German army corps from the W., thus helping to make possible France's "comeback" in the Battle of the Marne (Sept. 1914).

Russia fared much better against Austria in Galicia. Aided by a weak Austrian army, from whose ranks large numbers of Slavs defected en masse, the Russian army dealt Austria a staggering blow. Within three weeks, Austria lost some 350,000 men and part of Galicia. In late Sept., however, the German counteroffensive in Silesia pushed the Russians, after three months of seesaw fighting, back past Lodz, near Warsaw.

Though militarily not faring too badly during the first four months, there were already indications that Russia was incapable of conducting a prolonged war. During these two campaigns alone, the use of rifles and munitions far exceeded both domestic production and overseas deliveries. By mid-1915, about 30% of Russia's troops were unarmed and forced to snatch rifles from those already killed or wounded to continue fighting. More important, Russia's economy as a whole, though growing rapidly, was still backward in 1914. Largely isolated from her allies, neither the industrial nor the transportation system could meet the needs of the army of 12 mill. men that was mobilized between 1914 and 1917.

The W. front bogged down in trench warfare; Germany transferred 13 divisions to the E. in 1915 and unleashed an offensive which cost Russia not only all of Galicia but also R. Poland, Lithuania, and large parts of the Ukraine and Byelorussia. By mid-Aug. 750,000 R. troops had been taken prisoner. In Oct., the R. retreat came to a halt along a line running roughly from Riga to Chernovtsy. To ward off criticism and to bolster sagging morale tsar Nicholas himself took over from Grand Duke Nikolày Nikolàyevich as commander in chief.

Following the setbacks of 1915, the situation temporarily improved. Reversing the passive economic policy of the government, a new effort was made to mobilize industry. On the initiative of the Duma and of business circles, special councils and committees were established to facilitate the war effort. There was also an improvement in domestic production which resulted in increased munition supplies.

From Oct. 1915 to March 1916 the E. front remained relatively quiet as Germany focused on the campaign in the W. In March, refreshed after this badly needed respite, Russia launched a frontal attack on the German forces to relieve the pressure on France. For her pains, she lost over 100,000 men. However, that June Russia launched her greatest offensive of the war. Though this was originally planned as a diversionary maneuver, R. forces under Brusilov began an attack which smashed the Austrian army, capturing over 400,000 prisoners (200,000 in three days). Relieving the W. front during the battles of Verdun and the Somme, Brusilov's offensive also helped bring Rumania into the war. (This proved to be a blessing in disguise for Germany, as Rumania's quick collapse extended the length of Russia's front by 250 miles.)

Brusilov's offensive continued for three months, but with the transfer of 15 German divisions from the W., Russia gained little ground. Her losses, however, were enormous—during 1916, casualties approached one million—completely undermining Russia's material endurance and the morale of her troops. The whole operation left the army demoralized and discontented.

Faithful to Russia's treaties of alliance with her W. allies, the Provisional Government (q.v.) which came to power after the February revolution (q.v.) was determined to continue the war. In July 1917, Brusilov began a great offensive on the Galician front. After some initial successes, the R. forces crumbled before the German counterattack. Grievously weakened by a reorganization setting up a system of committee control, the R. army began to disintegrate. Whole regiments refused to carry out orders and even left the front when they grew weary of fighting. At the insistence of General Kornilov, Brusilov's successor, the death penalty for desertion was restored.

Though order was established at the fighting front, it did not carry over to the rear, for in Nov. the Bolsheviks seized power. In pursuance of Lenin's policy of immediate peace, the new government sought and procured an armistice (Dec. 1917). After arduous negotiations, both with the Germans and within the Bolshevik leadership, the Treaty of Brest-Litovsk (q.v.) was signed in March 1918. As a result of this treaty ending the war, Russia surrendered control of Poland, the Ukraine, much of Byelorussia, the Baltic region, and part of Transcaucasia.

BIBLIOGRAPHY: Sidney B. Fay, *The Origins of the World War*, New York, 1929; Winston S. Churchill, *The Unknown War: The Eastern Front*, New York, 1931; Michael T. Florinsky, *The End of the Russian Empire*, New Haven, 1931; N. N. Golovine, *The Russian Army in the World War*, New Haven, 1931; B. E. Nolde, *Russia in the Economic War*, New Haven, 1928.   M. S.

WORLD WAR II. Despite numerous warnings from the W., the German invasion, on June 22, 1941, caught the Soviet Union by surprise and a German army of about three million men advanced rapidly into R. territory. By Nov., almost all of S. Russia, including Kiev, had fallen and the German forces were ca. 20 miles from Moscow. Leningrad was virtually surrounded—the beginning of a siege which was not ended until Jan. 1944. As a result of this offensive, more than two million men were taken prisoner and a vast amount of war material was captured. Great though this victory was, Hitler's plan to crush Russia quickly had failed.

With the arrival of winter, the German offensive stalled. Ill-equipped and poorly clothed for a winter campaign, the Axis troops were exposed to brutal hardships. Hitler, fearing a repetition of Napoleon's flight from Moscow, had forbidden a general retreat. A large-scale R. offensive under General (later Marshal) Zhukov was launched, with some successes, but the main lines of the German front held until the spring thaws.

During the summer of 1942, Hitler launched another great offensive, this time aiming at the rich oil fields of the Caucasus. German armies swept the Russians out of the Crimea, across the Don to the Volga. Though they captured Rostov, Sevastopol, the Maykop oil fields, and the agricultural lands north of the Caucasus, the Germans were overly cautious. Overestimating Russia's ability to hold the lower Don, they diverted troops to the Rostov area, where no such help was needed, thus delaying the attack on Stalingrad.

The dotted line shows the farthest German advance in World War II.

When the postponed thrust on Stalingrad began in mid-August, the retreating Red Army had gathered sufficient strength to check the advance. It was not until Paulus' Sixth Army crossed the Don that the Soviet resistance was broken and the final assault could begin.

Seemingly forgetting his original objective, Caucasian oil, Hitler hurled all available forces against "the city of Stalin," draining reserves from other areas. He siphoned off a large part of the forces that might have been used to give a decisive impetus to the Caucasian offensive under General Kleist and by Nov. this front was stabilized. The German armies kept pounding away at Stalingrad for over two months, slowly smashing their way into the heart of the city. In mid-Oct., the situation seemed desperate as the Soviet forces were being forced with their backs up to the Volga. However, on Nov. 19, a Soviet counterattack was launched and, after only four days, 200,000 German troops were cut off. Another attack west of the Don prevented any reinforcements from reaching Paulus' stranded forces. On Jan. 31, 1943, as his troops were again without winter clothes and short of food and ammunition, the entrapped Paulus surrendered. Kleist's forces in the S. narrowly escaped a similar fate.

Though the resistance of the Soviet army and people was heroic, one must not ignore the fact that by Nov. 1942 there were ca. 800,000 Soviet citizens serving in the German army, the most prominent of them being Lieut. General Andrey Vlasov, one of the two commanders responsible for the defense of Moscow in 1941. Despite Soviet anti-fascist propaganda, the Germans were often welcomed as liberators, especially in non-R. areas such as the Ukraine. However, German ruthless treatment and brutal exploitation of both resources and population destroyed any support which they may have had in these regions.

After a minor German counteroffensive bogged down in the spring thaws, Hitler, in July 1943, launched what was to be his last major offensive. However, this attack, in which he committed most of his remaining armor, was quickly repulsed and the Soviet armies went over to the offensive, advancing rapidly on all fronts. In early Nov., the Red Army was back in Smolensk and Kiev.

By 1943, the Soviet army was much improved. The flow of new equipment had greatly increased both from the growing production of the factories which had been evacuated to the east and from the huge amounts of Allied aid which were now pouring in. More important, the Soviet military leadership had been overhauled. After the failure of the early campaigns, the Bolshevik "Old Guard" generals K. Ye. Voroshilov, S. M. Budyonny, and S. K. Timoshenko were replaced by such younger men as marshals G. K. Zhukov, I. S. Konev, R. Ya. Malinovsky, K. K. Rokossovsky, F. I. Tolbukhin. In 1943, when illness overtook him, the former tsarist officer, B. M. Shaposhnikov, Chief of the General Staff from 1929 to 1931 and again since 1937 (succeeding Tukhachevsky), was replaced by A. M. Vasilevsky.

During the winter 1943–44 the Soviet troops pushed steadily forward. Aided by a growing partisan movement behind the German lines, the Soviet offensive in March 1944 crossed the Dniester and reached the Rumanian-Bessarabian border. In early summer 1944, the Soviet Army reached or crossed the 1939 borders on virtually all fronts. Faced with enormous Soviet manpower and equipment superiority, in June the exhausted German forces were confronted with yet another problem—the Normandy invasion. Now incapable of reinforcing the E. front, the Germans surrendered Vyborg, Vitebsk, and Minsk during June and July and continued to retreat all along the line. By Aug., the Red Army had reached the borders of E. Prussia and were invading Poland and Rumania.

Reaching the Vistula in August, the Red Army made no effort to cross it. The Polish Home Army under General Bor-Komorowski, expecting the Soviet forces to continue into Warsaw, started a rising against the Germans in the city. With Soviet forces across the river, the insurgents continued their struggle without aid—Stalin even refusing Allied planes attempting to drop supplies into Warsaw permission to use Soviet airfields—until Oct. 5 when the Nazis crushed the uprising and systematically demolished Warsaw.

Aiming their next blow at Rumania, the Red Army crashed ahead and captured the mouth of the Danube. On Aug. 24 the Rumanian government surrendered, trapping large units of the German Navy in the Black Sea. Control of the Danube now gave Russia domination of the Black Sea and opened up an important supply route. By the end of Aug., the Ploesti oil center and Bucharest had been occupied. In late Aug.-early Sept. the Soviet Union declared war on Bulgaria and occupied Sofia.

With the aid of Tito's partisans, the Red Army advanced into Yugoslavia, entering Belgrade on Oct. 20. Two weeks later R. troops were at the gates of Budapest but a German last-ditch stand here managed to hold on until Feb. 1945. Simultaneously, Soviet forces advanced victoriously in the Baltic area, capturing Tallin and Riga by Oct. 1944.

In Jan. 1945 the campaign in Poland was reopened

as the final offensive against Germany was begun. Sweeping through Warsaw and Cracow by mid-Jan., the Red Army cracked through the German defense line along the Vistula. Coinciding with drives launched by the W. Allies, this new Soviet offensive pushed ahead rapidly, despite the German counterattack in W. Hungary in mid-March. By April 15 the Red Army had won virtually all of Central and E. Europe. With the W. Allies now in control of the Ruhr, Germany's industrial heartland, it was decided to allow Soviet troops to take Prague and Berlin. Beginning the final push on April 17, within three days the Red Army was in Berlin and on April 25 advance units of the American and R. armies met on the Elbe, at Torgau. With Berlin under continuous R. bombardment Hitler committed suicide on April 30 in his bunker beneath the Reich Chancellery and, on May 8, with virtually all of her territory in enemy hands, Nazi Germany signed the unconditional surrender.

Thus ended, for Russia, a war which inflicted staggering losses. According to official Soviet figures, the areas overrun by the Germans contained about 40% of Russia's pop., 66% of her heavy industry, 38% of her grain and 30% of her cattle. Fuel output between 1940 and 1942 fell from 38 to 18 mill. tons. For a time, Russia lost more than half of her coal and steel production, virtually all her ball-bearing plants, and almost half her railways. According to these same figures, by the end of the war the number of workers in the occupied areas was reduced by over 80%, and the number of industrial plants by 87%. Productive resources destroyed included 31,850 factories, 13,000 railway bridges, 137,000 tractors, 49,000 combines. In all, about two-thirds of the entire capital of the occupied regions, including the homes of ca. 25 mill. people, were destroyed.

However, much of the impact of these losses was offset by the order of the State Defense Committee (the supreme governing body of the USSR during the war) relocating industry. The Soviets claimed to have moved more than a thousand war plants to the Urals and Siberia from the Ukraine alone from Sept. to Dec. 1941. As the war progressed, the industrial and agricultural output of these regions, plus Central Asia and the Volga area, rose sharply—the coal production of the Kuzbas and Karaganda making up for the loss of the Donbas. Supplemented by increasing Allied shipments (total value of $11 bill.), total supplies proved more than adequate. (*See also* ARMED FORCES, VLASOV MOVEMENT, PARTISAN MOVEMENT, GERMAN OCCUPATION)

BIBLIOGRAPHY: Alexander Dallin, *German Rule in Russia, 1941–1945*, London, 1957; Herbert Feis, *Churchill-Roosevelt-Stalin*, Princeton, 1957; George Fischer, *Soviet Opposition to Stalin*, Cambridge, 1952; J. F. C. Fuller, *The Second World War, 1939–1945* New York, 1949; B. H. Liddell Hart, ed., *The Soviet Army*, London, 1946.
M. S.

WRÁNGEL ISLAND, in Arctic Ocean between E. Siberian and Chukchi seas; area about 2,800 sq. mi. Named after F. P. Wrangel, explorer.

WRÁNGEL, Ferdinánd Petróvich (1796–1870), explorer. He mapped the shores of N.E. Siberia from the Indigirka River to Kolyuchin Bay, and determined the location of an island, later named after him.

WRÁNGEL, Baron Pyótr Nikoláyevich (1878–1928), general, leader of the anti-Bolshevik forces during the civil war. In April 1920 he succeeded General Denikin as commander in chief of the "White" army in the S. of Russia. In October of that year, following a successful advance of the Bolsheviks in the Crimea, W and the remnants of his troops were evacuated to Turkey. His recollections, *The Memoirs of General Wrangel*, were published in English in 1930.

Y

YÁBLOCHKOV, Pável Nikoláyevich (1847–1894), electrical engineer. Graduate, Nikolayev School of Engineering (1866) and St. Petersburg School of Galvanization (1869). Inventor of the electrical candle, i.e. the first electric source of light based on the arc principle which as *procédé Jablochkoff* was patented in France (1876) along with numerous other inventions. Although he attracted attention after an exposition of his inventions in Paris (1878) he died in poverty. *Légion d'Honneur* (1881).

YABLONÓVY RANGE, extends N.E. to S.W. between Buryat ASSR and Chita Oblast; greatest altitude 5,150 ft.

YAGÓDA, Génrikh Grigórievich (1891–1938), security police chief. The son of an artisan, Ya joined the

Bolsheviks in 1907, was deported in 1911, and was mobilized into the army in 1915. During the civil war Ya worked in the army inspection at the southern front, and in 1919 at the Commissariat of Foreign Trade. In 1920 he was appointed member of the presidium of the Cheka, in 1924 deputy chief of the OGPU, and in 1934 chief of the NKVD. Under Ya the system of forced labor was greatly expanded. He organized the first two major trials of leading communist "oppositionists." At the 16th Party Congress in 1930 Ya was elected candidate member of the party Central Committee. He was removed from the NKVD in Sept. 1936, probably as a result of his earlier contacts with the "rightist opposition" in the party, was appointed people's commissar of communications, but was arrested in April 1937. He was accused of assassination of party leaders, of having admitted foreign spies into the NKVD, and so forth, was tried in March 1938 along with Bukharin, Rykov and others, sentenced to death, and executed.

YAGUZHÍNSKY, Pável Ivánovich (1683–1736), an army commander who rose to prominence in Peter the Great's state administration. He was appointed Procurator-General of the Senate in 1722; was banished to the Ukraine by Peter II; was Russia's Ambassador to Berlin 1732–35.

YAÍK RIVER, ancient name of the Ural River, prior to 1775.

YÁKIR, Yona Emanuílovich (1896–1937), general, active in radical student circles in Odessa before the revolution. He joined the Bolshevik party in April 1917, and became an organizer of the Red Guards. Held high positions during the civil war. In 1921 was commander of the Kiev military district and in 1925 of the Ukrainian military district. A member of the Central Committee and the Politburo in the CP of the Ukraine. Together with Tukhachevsky, Ya was instrumental in modernizing the Red Army. In 1937 he was arrested and executed.

YAKÓBI, Borís Semyónovich (Moritz Herman) (1801–1874), physicist and electrical engineer. Fellow, St. Petersburg Ac. of S. (1839). Born in Germany. Graduate of Göttingen University. Moved to Königsberg (1834) and Dorpat where he became professor at the university (1835). Accepted Russian citizenship and settled in St. Petersburg (1837). Research concerned electromagnetism and its practical application. Invented ten different types of telegraphic equipment and supervised the first R. electric motor (1834); also invented galvanoplastics, galvanic battery, electromagnetic generator, current distributor, mine fuses, voltmeters. Greatly contributed to the advancement of electrical engineering in Russia.

YÁKOVLEV, Aleksándr Sergéyevich (1906–), aeronautical engineer. Colonel general in the engineering and technical corps. Corresponding member, Ac. of S., USSR (1943). Hero of Socialist Labor. Member of the Supreme Soviet, USSR (1937, 1958). Graduated from Military Air Force Academy of Engineering (1931).  Chief designer, Experimental Bureau of Design (1934). Deputy people's commissar (1940); deputy minister of the aviation industry (1948). Ya's research concerns the design of military piston-type aircraft and jets, particularly fighters and fighter-interceptors. By 1941 he had designed model airplanes including training-plane UT-1, UT-2, and YAK-1; communication plane YAK-12; single-seat, high-speed fighter YAK-1 (1939) which was mass produced until the end of World War II; fighters YAK-3, YAK-7, and YAK-9 (1943–47) (the last was replaced by MIG-15 and YAK-11, an improved version of YAK-9). Ya was in charge of the design of the first jet fighters YAK-15 (1945), YAK-17, YAK-23, and several supersonic fight-

ers (1952–55). Designed the twin-engine helicopter YAK-24 ("the flying car") which has beaten several world records in regard to lifting capacity. Author of memoirs, *Tales of an Aeronautical Engineer* (1957). Stalin prizes (1941, 1942, 1943, 1946, 1947, 1948).

YÁKOVLEV, Vasíly Nikoláyevich (1893–1953), painter, fellow of the Academy of Fine Arts, from 1922. Awarded two Stalin prizes and the order of Lenin. Ya taught at the Academy of Fine Arts (1935–38); was chief artist of the All-Union Fair, 1939. He painted over one thousand pictures, among them *A Newspaper at the Battle Front* (1923), *Battle in Streletsk* (1942), *The Kolkhoz Herd* (1948), portrait of M. Gorky and others.

YAKUBÓVICH, Pyotr Filíppovich (pen name L. Melshin) (1860–1911), popular poet of radical leanings, condemned to death for participation in the society "People's Will." The sentence was commuted to 18 years of hard labor of which he served 8, from 1887 to 1895. His two-volume *Poetry*, written and published in 1898–1901, was popular in radical circles. He also wrote prose sketches of prison life *The World of The Outcasts*, two volumes, 1896–99.

YAKÚT ASSR (YAKUTIA), E. Siberia, RSFSR; area 1,198,000 sq. mi.; pop. 489,000 (1959). Cities: Yakutsk (capital), Aldan, Verkhoyansk, Vilyuysk, Sredne-Kolymsk, Tommot. The largest territorial unit in the USSR, it encompasses the vast Lena basin, the Aldan plateau, and the Verkhoyansk and Chersky mountain ranges, bordering on the Laptev and E. Siberian seas in the N. The entire region lies in the tundra and forest-tundra zones. Its climate is of the dry continental type, with extremely severe winters ("cold pole" at Oymyakon), but the short summers are sufficiently warm for the ripening of crops. The population, predominantly Yakut (*Sakha*), includes other groups of Tatar-Turkic strain (Evenki, Eveny, Chukchi, Oduly) and Russians (many of them descendants of political exiles deported in tsarist times). The mineral resources, not yet fully explored or exploited, are very considerable. The gold mines of the Aldan district alone yield one-fourth of the total gold extracted in the Soviet Union. Coal is now mined at Sangar, Bulun, Zyryanka, and in other areas. Important, also, are the known deposits of salt, iron, lead-zinc, tin, and platinum, as well as oil fields along the Tolba, tributary of the Lena. Lumbering and light mfg. are growing ind., but the Yakut population must still depend on hunting, fur trapping, and fishing as the chief source of livelihood. Truck and potato farming, and some grain cultivation, are on the increase, together with livestock breeding (cattle, horses, and reindeer). River navigation and the Northern Sea Route are the chief means of communication, but air and motor transport are gaining in importance. Est. 1922.

YAKÚTSK, capital of Yakut ASSR; pop. 74,000 (1959). Is the major trading and processing city of the Lena valley, with sawmills, woodworking plants, leather and food industries based on local produce; site of the Yakut branch of Ac. of S., USSR.

YÁLTA, city in Crimean Oblast, Ukrainian SSR; pop. 34,100 (1956). Famous year-round seaside resort on the subtropical N. coast of the Black Sea, near the Sevastopol naval base; site of the historic conference (Roosevelt, Churchill, Stalin) in 1945, shortly before the end of World War II.

YAMÁL-NENÉTS NATIONAL OKRUG, part of Tyumen Oblast, W. Siberia, RSFSR; area 290,600 sq. mi.; pop. 63,000 (1959), predominantly Nenets (Samoyed ethnic group). Principal cities and settlements: Salekhard (adm. center), Shuryshkary, Aksarka, Nyda, Novy Port. The region, extending through the forested tundra zone, with vast marshlands, in the northernmost part of W. Siberia, on both sides of the lower Ob River, includes the large Yamal Peninsula washed by the Kara Sea. Because of severe climate and frozen ground, essential occupations are limited to the raising of reindeer, hunting, and fishing. Fish canneries have been built at the larger settlements. Lumbering plants centered in Salekhard. Truck and potato farming is being developed, with some acreage under experimental hemp and flax crops.

YAMÁL PENINSULA, N.W. Siberia, between Kara Sea and Ob Bay; tundra; hunting and fishing by native Nenets.

YÁNA RIVER, in Yakut ASSR, flows from Verkhoyansk Mountains to delta on Arctic Ocean; length 547 mi.; partly navigable.

YANÓVSKY, Yúry Ivánovich (1902–1954), writer of Ukrainian origin, author of several short novels dealing with the civil war: *Tusks of the Mammoth* (1925), *Earth's Blood* (1927) and *Four Sabers* (1927). Ya also wrote plays about the civil war in the Ukraine, and a volume of stories, *Tales from Kiev* (1948). Stalin prize (1949).

YÁNSHIN, Aleksándr Leonídovich (1911–), geologist. Fellow, Ac. of S., USSR (1958). Graduate of the Moscow Institute of Geological Prospecting (1932). Joined the Department of Mining and Geology at the Scientific Institute of Fertilizers (1929) and the Geological Institute (1936), Ac. of S., where he was appointed director of the Department of Regional Tectonics (1956). Research concerns tectonics, stratigraphy, lithology, and hydrogeology of the western regions of Kazakh SSR and the S. Urals. Participated in compiling tectonic maps of the USSR. Author of *The Geology of the Northern Territory of the Aral Sea* (1953). A. P. Karpinsky prize (1953).

YANUSHKÉVICH, Nikoláy Nikoláyevich (1868–1918), tsarist general. In 1914, Ya was appointed Chief of the General Staff. He was an ardent supporter of the war against Germany, but not a distinguished strategist himself. H put General Danilov in charge of the actual planning of military operations. In 1915, he went with Grand Duke Nicholas Nikolayevich (q.v.) to the Caucasus where he was killed in 1918 under circumstances which remain unclear.

YAROSLÁV THE WISE (978–1054), Grand Duke, son of Vladimir Svyatoslavovich. Ruler of Kiev principality, and shrewd statesman, he was largely responsible for the consolidation of the power and prestige of the Kievan state. He was allegedly the compiler of *Russkaya Pravda* (Russian Truth), Russian first collection of laws.

YAROSLÁVL, city, adm. center of Yaroslavl Oblast, RSFSR; pop. 407,000 (1959). It is an important river-rail transfer point at the intersection of the Volga and the Moscow–Archangel R.R.; produces trailer trucks and trolley buses, synthetic rubber and asphalt, lacquers and paints, electrical motors; has shipyards and railway repair shops, linen and cotton mills, footwear factories, tobacco processing plants and sawmills. A number of higher educational institutions. Founded in 1024, it has remarkable monuments of 16th- and 17th-century architecture.

YAROSLÁVL OBLAST, RSFSR; area 14,000 sq. mi.; pop. 1,395,000 (1958). An upper Volga region, with predominantly level plains extending from N. to S. through the coniferous and mixed forest zones; podsol soils alternating with marshlands; moderate continental climate. Flax growing and dairy farming are emphasized in the N.W. sector, basic grains and potatoes in the E.; peat and building materials are mined in the forested area. The major regional industries include heavy machine building, chemical, textile, and food-processing plants. Navigation on the Volga is greatly improved since the construction of the vast Rybinsk reservoir. Est. 1936.

YAROSLÁVL UPRISING, anti-Bolshevik uprising (July 6–21, 1918) organized by the Union for the Defense of Fatherland and Freedom under the leadership of B. Savinkov in Yaroslavl. The uprising was timed to coincide with a landing of Allied troops in the north of Russia and was to touch off a general rebellion and a march on Moscow. At first successful, the insurgents set up a civil administration. However, the uprising was quickly suppressed by the Red Army.

YAROSLÁVSKY, Yemelyán Mikháylovich (1878–1943), an early Bolshevik. Ya joined the revolutionary  movement in 1898 and for a decade was active in socialist organizations in Chita, St. Petersburg, Odessa, and elsewhere. Participated in party congresses in 1906 and 1907. In 1908 was arrested and remained in prison and in Siberia for nine years. Was active in the October revolution in Moscow. For a while joined the Left Communists but was soon reconciled with Lenin. Ya then became active in the League for Militant Atheists and in the Party Control Commission. After siding with Stalin in the intra-party struggle, Ya was rewarded with promotion to the Central Committee of the CPSU (in 1934) and became the semiofficial historian of the party. His works were required reading for all party members as the "correct" interpretations of party history.

YASÉNSKY (Jasienski), **Brúno-Víktor Yákovlevich** (1901–1941), poet and novelist, born in Poland, son of a village physician. He studied at a gymnasium in Warsaw and entered Krakow University in 1918. His first poems were written in 1918–20 in Polish. He published the poem *Song of Hunger* in 1922, and in 1923 became literary editor of the communist newspaper *Workers' Tribune* in Lvov. Two books of his verses, *Land to the Left* and *A Word About Jacob Shela*, dealing with peasant uprisings, were published in 1924–25. He wrote his first novel, *I Burn Paris*, in Paris. As a member of the Communist party in France, he organized a workers' theater for Polish emigrants in Paris. He was expelled from France in 1929 and went to the USSR where he began to write in Russian. He published a satirical play, *Mannequin's Ball*, a novel, *Man Changes Skins* (about construction in Tadzhikistan), and several short stories: *Courage, Nose*, and *The Chief Culprit*. His last novel, *The Conspiracy of the Indifferent*, remained unfinished. He was arrested as a spy in 1937 and died in a concentration camp in 1941.

YASHIN, Aleksándr Yákovlevich (1913–), poet, short story writer. He graduated from a pedagogical institute in Vologda. His first publications appeared in 1928. He studied at Moscow's Gorky Literary Institute, 1935. During World War II he was a war correspondent. Ya was awarded the order of the Red Star, and was a recipient of the Stalin prize in 1950. His story *Levers* (1956) is widely known. It is sharply critical of the bureaucratic *kolkhoz* leadership, and depicts the *kolkhozniks'* lack of rights, and their fear of the authorities. The author was attacked by the official critics and communist leaders, including Khrushchev.

YÁSNAYA POLYÁNA, settlement in Tula Oblast; birthplace and residence of Leo Tolstoy; also Tolstoy's burial grounds. Tolstoy Museum, national shrine, destroyed by Germans in World War II, restored in 1946.

YASNÓV, Mikhaíl Alekséyevich (1906–), state and party official. Ya has been a member of the CPSU since 1925. He occupied high economic posts in the thirties. Since 1950 he has been chairman of the Executive Committee of the Moscow City Soviet. In 1957, he became deputy chairman of the Council of Ministers RSFSR. Ya has been deputy to the Supreme Soviet USSR and member of the Presidium of the Supreme Soviet RSFSR. He was elected member of the Central Committee of the CPSU in 1952 and 1956.

YAVÓRSKY, Stefán (1658–1722), theological writer prominent in the early history of the Russian Church. After 1700 he was acting Patriarch; later president of the Holy Synod created by Peter the Great. He was the author of the *Rock of Faith*, a theological treatise expounding the fundamental tenets of Russian orthodoxy.

YAZÝKOV, Nikoláy Mikháylovich (1803–1846), lyrical poet, admirer, friend, and follower of Pushkin. Much of his poetry has been set to music, popular with Soviet singers today.

YEDÍNSTVO (Unity), a Russian social democratic organization started in 1914 by Plekhanov with the aim of achieving unity between those Bolsheviks who were in opposition to Lenin, and the Mensheviks. From the very beginning, Ye had not much success; the left-wing Mensheviks (so-called *Mezhrayontsy*) separated from it, and, at the beginning of World War I, when Ye took a patriotic stand, some of the Bolsheviks seceded. In 1917, Ye became a right-wing social democratic group in revolutionary Russia. Its political platform stated the impossibility of the socialist revolution in Russia because of her low level of economic and social development, and voiced full support for the Provisional Government and for the continuation of war in close unity with the Allies. In June 1917, Ye had about 1,500

registered members recruited mostly from the intelligentsia. Its leaders were Plekhanov, Deutsch, Zasulich, Aleksinsky and some other veterans of the social democratic movement. They edited a daily paper in Petrograd under the name *Yedinstvo*, participated in patriotic demonstrations and opposed the Bolsheviks, both before and after the October revolution. The paper was closed by the Soviet government in the first days of 1918, and the whole organization was liquidated by the middle of the year.   V. Su.

YEFRÉMOV, Filípp Sergéyevich (1750–1811), traveler. He was captured in 1774 at Orenburg by nomads and sold into slavery to Bokhara; he escaped and reached Calcutta through Kashgara and W. Tibet. He published the description of his wanderings.

YEFRÉMOV, town in Tula Oblast, RSFSR; pop. 27,500 (1956). Synthetic rubber, alcohol, meat.

YEGÓROV, Aleksándr Ilyích (1885–193?), Soviet marshal, son of a peasant, little known prior to World War I. During the war he was wounded five times. After the fall of the monarchy Ye at first rejected the Bolsheviks and became a Socialist Revolutionary. However, his imprisonment by Petlyura and subsequent liberation by the Bolsheviks changed his allegiance. Ye led the Bolshevik 9th army through the civil war and the Russo-Polish war of 1920. In 1931, Ye became a member of the general staff and its head (1935). Ye was close to Marshal Tukachevsky. This association probably cost Ye his life—he disappeared after Tukachevsky's execution.

YÉGOROV, Alekséy Yegórovich (1776–1851), painter. Son of a Kalmyk, who was taken prisoner by the Cossacks. He was sent to an orphanage in Moscow, and later to the Academy of Fine Arts. In 1803, Ye went to Italy where he became a friend of Canova and Pammuccini in Rome, and was greatly influenced by Raphael. Later he was made prof. of historical painting at St. Petersburg. Ye's best-known picture is *The Scourging of Jesus*.

YÉGOROV, Dmítry Fyódorovich (1869–1931), mathematician. Honorary member, Ac. of S., USSR (1929). Professor, Moscow University (1903). President, Moscow Mathematical Society (1922–31). Research concerned differential geometry, theory and application of integral equations, variation calculus and the theory of functions of a real variable.

YEGÓRYEVSK, city in Moscow Oblast, RSFSR; pop. 59,000 (1959). Textile center.

YEKATERÍNA: *see* CATHERINE.

YEKATERINBÚRG: *see* SVERDLOVSK.

YEKATERINODÁR: *see* KRASNODAR.

YEKATERINOSLÁV: *see* DNEPROPETROVSK.

YELÉNKIN, Aleksándr Aleksándrovich (1873–1942), botanist. Official of St. Petersburg Botanical Garden (1898). Research concerned the study and classification of lichens. Author of *Blue-Green Algae of the USSR* (2nd ed., 1949).

YELÉTS, city in Lipetsk Oblast, RSFSR; pop. 78,000 (1959). Machine building, food production, sewing, building materials, lace handicrafts. Dates back to 12th century.

YÉLGAVA (f. Mitava, Latv. *Jelgava*), town in Latvian SSR on Lielupe River; pop. 31,700 (1956). Butter-making, sugar, canned fruits, linen. Founded 1226.

YELISAVETPÓL: *see* KIROVABAD.

YELIZAVETGRÁD: *see* KIROVOGRAD.

YEMANZHELÍNSK, city in Chelyabinsk Oblast, RSFSR; pop. 34,000 (1958). Coal mining.

YENÁKIEVO, city in Stalino Oblast, Ukrainian SSR; pop. 92,000 (1959). Industrial center of Donbas, coal mining, metallurgical, coke-chemical, cement plants.

YENISEY RIVER (Evenki: *Ioanesi*=Big River), one of the largest in USSR; length 2,565 mi. Begins in Tuva Autonomous Oblast, RSFSR, flows mainly through Krasnoyarsk Kray, empties into Yenisey Bay of Kara Sea. Its right tributaries are Tuba, Mana, Kan, Upper Tunguska (Angara), Podkamennaya Tunguska and Lower Tunguska, Kureyka; left tributaries are Abakan, Yeloguy, Turukhan, Sym. Shipping timber, grain, coal, oil, minerals. Landings at Minusinsk, Krasnoyarsk, Yenisey, Turukhansk; ports for sea ships at Igarka and Dudinka. Has fisheries; two hydroelectric power stations.

YENISÉY RIDGE, highland along the right bank of Yenisey R.; 559 mi. long; maximum elevations 3,680 ft. Gold, graphite mining.

YENISÉYSK, town in Krasnoyarsk Kray, RSFSR, landing on Yenisey River; pop 16,000 (1959). Boat building, pedag inst. Founded 1618.

YENUKÍDZE, Avel Sofrónovich (1877–193?), Bolshevik, joined the revolutionary movement in the Caucasus in the 1890's. Repeatedly arrested and exiled. After the October revolution, he became the secretary of the All-Russian Central Executive Committee of the Soviets. Concurrently, Ye was a member of the Central Committee of the party. He disappeared during the purges of the 1930's.

YEREVÁN (f. Erivan), capital of Armenian SSR, important economic and cultural center; pop. 509,000 (1959). Dates back to 7th century. Metallurgy, machine building, chemical, textiles, woodworking, food; wine, brandy, and canned-fruit production; many vineyards and gardens. Has numerous schools of higher education, research institutes, a university, opera, ballet, and theaters; is the seat of the Armenian Ac. of S.

YERMÁK TIMOFÉYEVICH (died in 1584), Cossack chieftain, conqueror of Siberia. His Cossacks, armed by the industrialists Stroganov, invaded W. Siberia in 1581 and fought against Khan Kuchum. In 1583, W. Siberia was annexed by Russia.

YERMÓLOVA, María Nikoláyevna (1853–1928), actress, the first to have been awarded the honorary title of the People's Artist of the Republic (1920). Acted at the Moscow Maly Theater, taking the leading parts in heroic and romantic plays, such as Gutzkov's *Uriel Acosta* and Schiller's *Maid of Orleans*. Her interpretations of Ostrovsky's comedies were also highly successful.

YERMÓLOV, Alekséy Petróvich (1772–1861), general. He took part in wars against Napoleon; was governor of Georgia and commander of the Caucasian corps, 1816–27.

YERSHÓV, Iván Vasílyevich (1867–1943), dramatic tenor, after 1895 soloist of the St. Petersburg Opera House (formerly The Mariinsky Theater).

YESÉNIN, Sergéy Aleksándrovich (1895–1925), one of the leading R. poets of the early 20th century. He

was born in a peasant family in the Ryazan Province, and began to write poems at the age of fourteen. His first collection of poems, *Radunitsa*, was published in 1916. Early in his creative life he became associated with a group of imaginist poets, and under their influence he came to attribute to images a central position in his works. Ye's early poems express a combination of a good-humored irreverence and daring with a religious acceptance of the traditional peasant culture within which he grew, as well as a deep sensitivity to the beauty of the rural landscape. They contain idyllic images of old village Russia, melodiously conveyed and colored by a simple pantheism as well as by religious themes of pilgrimage and of wandering. The leading theme of the second period in his work is the flying of an awakened and aroused Russia to an exciting destiny that is sometimes associated with images of paradise on earth (in *Grad Inonia*). At the same time, however, Ye was alarmed by the breaking up of traditional society as well as by the horrors of the revolutionary years, industrialization and urbanization. This came to be reflected in a mood of somber pathos and of sadness, and, later, of bitterness and of irritation. His short and unhappy marriage with Isadora Duncan (1922) lasted only a year. His subsequent discord with himself and with his surroundings, and the dissolute life that he led during this period, as well as his yearning for the simple life of his early years, are recorded in the long poems *Tavern Moscow* (1924) and *Confession of a Hooligan* (1924). His last poems were *Rus Sovetskaya* (1924), and *Anna Snegina* (1925), which contain sketches of the new village life. In 1925, disillusioned and embittered, Ye committed suicide. Among the outstanding features of Ye's art are the directness and simplicity of his style, the melodiousness of his verse, and the sincerity and intensity of the feelings that are expressed.   C. P. K.

YÉSIPOVA, Anna Nikoláyevna (1851–1914), pianist and teacher. Graduate of St. Petersburg Conservatoire (1871). Lived abroad, 1871–92. Professor at St. Petersburg Conservatoire, 1893–1914. Many outstanding musicians, including Sergey Prokofiev, studied under her. Internationally known, Ye frequently toured Europe and the United States.

YESSENTUKÍ, resort in Stavropol Kray, RSFSR, 9 mi. from Pyatigorsk; pop. 41,800 (1956). Alkali-salts mineral water, sulfur-carbonate bathing water, mud; treatment of stomach, liver, gynecological and other diseases.

YEVDOKÍMOV, Grigóry Yereméyevich (1884–

1936), in the revolutionary movement from 1903. Repeatedly arrested and exiled. After the February revolution, was active in the Petrograd Bolshevik Committee. He participated in the civil war as a political commissar with the army. Member of the Central Committee of the CP from 1919; in 1925, appointed secretary of the Leningrad party organization. With Zinoviev and Kamenev, Ye was tried at the first big "show trial" in Aug. 1936, was condemned to death, and executed.

YEVPATÓRIA, city in Crimean Oblast, RSFSR, resort on Black Sea; pop. 57,000 (1959).

YEVRÉINOV, Nikoláy Nikoláyevich (1879–1953), director and playwright. After studying law and music, he devoted himself to theater (1905). An opponent of the Moscow Art Theater method, his views were close to the aesthetics of Oscar Wilde. Convinced of the inborn "instinct for the theater" inherent in man as the foundation of a universal "creative evolution," Ye derived from it the theory of "the theater for its own sake" and the quest for a special form of "monodrama," in which the spectator would participate in the action. A master of stylized and brilliant spectacle, Ye staged a number of effective productions. He was fascinated by the parodies and satires which he produced in 1907–15 at the Theater *Krivoye Zerkalo* (Distorted Mirror), in St. Petersburg. An aesthete and subjectivist, Ye left the USSR in the 1920's and as an *émigré* wrote plays and articles and was a theatrical producer in W. Europe and America.

YEYSK, city in Krasnodar Kray, RSFSR, port on Sea of Azov; pop. 55,500 (1959). Machine-building, fish and other industries; balneological sea and mud-baths resort.

YEZHÓV, Nikoláy Ivánovich (1894–1939?), party and security police official, born in Leningrad. Ye joined  the Bolshevik party in 1917, and during the civil war was political commissar in the Red Army. From 1922 on he held party positions, except in 1929–30 when he was deputy people's commissar of agriculture. Ye then returned to the staff of the party Central Committee, and was appointed chief of the division of party cadres. At the 17th Party Congress in 1934 Ye was elected member of the Central Committee, of its Orgburo, and of the Control Commission; enjoying Stalin's confidence, he became the liaison man between the Politburo and the security police. In 1935 he was a secretary of the Central Committee and was elected member of the executive committee of the Komintern. In 1936 Ye was appointed chief of the NKVD and for two years, known as *Yezhovshchina*, administered Stalin's terror, directed the great purge, staged political trials, and so on. In 1938, Ye was dismissed as head of NKVD, and was appointed commissar of water transport. In 1939 he was released from that post and disappeared.

YEZHOVSHCHINA: *see* PURGES.

YOSHKÁR-OLÁ (prior to 1919, Tsarevokokshaysk; 1919–27, Krasnokokshaysk), city, capital of Mari ASSR; pop. 27,000 (1939), 88,000 (1959). Food pro-

duction, agricultural machine-building plants, sawmills; pedag. and technical forestry institutes. Founded 1578.

YOUNG COMMUNIST LEAGUE: *see* KOMSOMOL.

YUDÉNICH, Nikoláy Nikoláyevich (1862–1933), White commander. Yu emerged from the Russo-Japanese war a general and became chief of staff in 1913. He commanded all Russian forces in the Caucasus, 1914–15, and again in 1917. After the Bolshevik Revolution, he assumed command of the White army in the Baltic area. In Oct. 1919 he led the abortive offensive against Petrograd; Ye retreated to Estonia and died an exile in France.

YÚDIN, Pável Fyódorovich (1899–), communist philosopher and diplomat. Fellow, Ac. of S., USSR. Yu joined the Bolsheviks in 1918 but remained in relative obscurity for many years. In 1952 he was promoted to the Central Committee of the CPSU and began a career as a diplomat. After a brief mission to East Germany in Dec. 1953, Yu was appointed ambassador to the Chinese People's Republic. There he negotiated several treaties involving trade and the withdrawal of Soviet military forces. He appears to have been responsible, in part, for establishing closer ties between Moscow and Peiping. Yu is also a communist philosopher. In 1952 he was editor of the Cominform paper *For Lasting Peace, For People's Democracy,* and staff member of the *Bolshaya Sovetskaya Entsiklopedia.*

YUG RIVER, flows from Vologda Oblast, joining with Sukhoma River to form N. Dvina; 290 mi. long.

YUGÓRSKY SHAR, strait, separates Vaygach Island from mainland, and links Barents and Kara seas; length 28 mi., width 2 to 6 mi.

YUKAGHIRS: *see* POPULATION.

YUÓN, Konstantín Fyódorovich (1875–1958), painter and stage designer. Member of the Academy of Fine Arts. Awarded order of Lenin and Stalin prize. Yu painted landscapes (*March Sunshine,* for example) as well as genre and historical pictures (as *The Village Feast*). He designed the productions of *The Inspector General* by Gogol (1921); *Yegor Bulychov* by Gorky (1934); and *The Wolves and the Sheep* by Ostrovsky (1944).

YURÉNEV, Konstantín Konstantínovich (1889–1938), joined the revolutionary movement in 1905. In 1917 Yu was a member of the Executive Committee of the Soviets in Petrograd and the chairman of the general staff of the Red Guards. A leading commissar in the Red Armies, Yu turned to diplomacy in 1921. He was envoy to Latvia, Czechoslovakia, Italy, and Iran. In 1938 Yu, as an oppositionist to Stalin, was arrested and executed.

YÚRY DOLGORÚKY (about 1090–1157), Prince of Rostov-Suzdal, son of Vladimir Monomakh. In alliance with the Polovtsy (Cumans), YD fought for the possession of the grand duchy of Kiev and was engaged in numerous wars in the other R. principalities.

YÚRYEV: *see* TARTU.

YÚRYEV, Borís Nikoláyevich (1889–1957), aeronautical engineer. Fellow, Ac. of S., USSR (1943). Lieutenant general, engineering and technical corps. In cooperation with G. Kh. Sabinin, Yu formulated the theory of propellers, relating the propeller flow to the geometry of the blade; in the study of screw propellers he presented formulas for the calculation of relative velocities of the propeller blades and gave an accurate definition of Zhukovsky's vortical theorem. Devoted many years to the design of helicopters and participated in the creation of the EA-1 helicopter and the two-rotor "Omega" helicopter. Was instrumental in establishing standard designations in areodynamics. Author of *The Vortical Theory of Propellers* (1947); *The Aerodynamic Calculation of Helicopters* (1956). Stalin prize (1943).

YÚRYEV, Yúry Mikháylovich (1872–1948), actor. People's Artist of the USSR. Made his debut in 1892 at the Moscow Maly Theater and later joined the company of the Leningrad Theater of the Drama. Yu was noted as an interpretor of the classical repertory which included plays by Sophocles, Schiller, Griboyedov, and Lermontov.

YUSHKÉVICH, Semyón Solomónovich (1868–1927), writer. Born in Odessa, he described the everyday life of urban Jews. Started with the short story *The Tailor* (1887), steady contributor to the *Znanie* collections, 6 vols. of his collected works were published in 1911. His play *Miserere* was successfully produced by the Moscow Artistic Theater. Emigrated after the revolution and wrote his last novel, *Episodes,* abroad.

YÚZHNO-SAKHALÍNSK (f. Toyohara), city in Sakhalin Oblast, RSFSR, at S. end of Sakhalin Island; pop. 86,000 (1959). Center of paper, food-processing and metalworking industries.

YÚZOVKA: *see* STALINO.

YYKHVI (Est. *Jõhvi*), town in Estonian SSR; pop. 8,800 (1956). Center of shale deposits; mining equipment and building materials.

Z

ZÁBOLOTNY, Daniíl Kiríllovich (1866–1929), microbiologist and epidemiologist. Fellow, Ac. of S., USSR (1929) and Ukrainian SSR (1922). Studied under I. I. Mechnikov. Proposed the use of cholera serum. Participated in R. anti-plague campaigns in India (1897), Arabia, China, E. Mongolia, Iran, Mesopotamia, and Manchuria. Investigated the reasons for the propagation of the plague and developed vaccines against it. Founded a number of anti-plague stations. Also studied typhus, malaria, and other epidemic diseases.

ZABOLÓTSKY, Nikoláy Alekséyevich (1903–1958), poet. Z graduated from the Herzen Pedagogical Institute in Leningrad in 1925. His principal works are *Columns* (1929), *A Star* (1933), and *The Second Book* (1937). He also translated Georgian poets. Z's prewar work was distinguished by style, and in form had much in common with modern Western poetry. Z was arrested in the 1920's, but was eventually released. In one of the poems written during the "thaw," he warned—symbolically—that the "thaw" would be of short duration, and that the writers who took it seriously would have "to lose their voices."

ZAGÓRSK (f. Sergiev), city in Moscow Oblast, RSFSR; pop. 74,000 (1959). Founded in 1337 around Troitse-Sergievskaya Lavra (monastery), is a center of ancient R. crafts, such as carving and painting on wood, toy industry; has museum of toys. Ind.: farm machinery, school supplies, tire-repair, brick, knitting plants. Many historical monuments.

ZAGÓSKIN, Lavrénty Alekséyevich (1807–1890), explorer of Alaska's Norton and Kotzebue bays and basins of the Yukon and Kuskokvim rivers (1842–44).

ZAGÓSKIN, Mikhaíl Nikoláyevich (1789–1852), writer, known for his historical novel *Yúry Miloslávsky* (1829), crude historical idealization, and patriotic ideology. His novels, *Roslávlev* (1831), *Kúzma Róshchin* (1836), and others are written in a similar vein.

ZAICHNÉVSKY, Pyótr Grigóryevich (1842–1896), revolutionary. Z entered Moscow University and organized a student group for the distribution of illegal literature. In 1861, he was arrested for revolutionary propaganda among the peasants. In prison, Z wrote the proclamation *Young Russia* calling for the overthrow of autocracy. He was sentenced to hard labor and exile in Siberia. On his return to European Russia he resumed his revolutionary work and was again exiled.

ZAILIYSKY ALA-TAU: *see* TRANS-ILI ALA-TAU.

ZAKARPÁTSKAYA: *see* TRANSCARPATHIAN.

ZAKAVKÁZYE: *see* TRANSCAUCASIA.

ZAKHÁROV, Andréyan Dmítrievich (1761–1811), architect of the classical school. Born in St. Petersburg; graduated from the Academy of Fine Arts in 1782; was sent abroad, returned in 1787. Z was the architect of the Admiralty building (1823).

ZAKHÁRYIN, Grigóry Antónovich (1829–1897), physician. Fellow, St. Petersburg Ac. of S. (1885). Graduate (1852), professor (1869–96), Moscow University; director, Faculty Therapeutic Clinic. Worked under R. Virchow and C. Bernard (1854–59). Z emphasized the relations between man and his environment which led to the introduction of new methods of diagnosis and therapy based on the principle of treating the patient as a whole rather than an individual diseased organ. Suggested the use of mineral waters and calomel.

ZAMYÁTIN, Yevgény Ivánovich (1884–1937), novelist. Member of the Social Democratic party in his youth, arrested and exiled, but later pardoned. As a professional naval engineer he was sent to England during World War I. Returned to Russia after the revolution to become leading writer. One of the founders of the Serapion Brothers group. The publication of *The Islanders* (1922), a satire on English life, was followed by his significant novel *We* (1924) in which he advocates eternal nonconformism, criticizes totalitarianism and regimentation, and favors "infinite" revolution. Z was flayed by the Soviet Writers' Union and press after the appearance of his novel abroad. It is assumed that *We* influenced George Orwell (*1984*) and Aldous Huxley (*Brave New World*). Z is also the author of *A Tale about What Is Most Important* (1923), *X* (1927), *The Fires of St. Dominic.* Z's fiction is distinguished by fantasy and a great variety of stylistic effects. Z left Russia in 1931 and setled in Paris. *The Whip of God* was written there.

ZÁNGA RIVER: *see* RAZDAN RIVER.

ZANGEZÚR RANGE, mountains in Transcaucasia, on the border of Armenian SSR; highest mountain Kaputdzhukh (12,800 ft.), covered with perennial snow; copper mines.

ZAPORÓZHYE (f. Aleksandrovsk), city, adm. center of Zaporozhye Oblast, Ukrainian SSR, landing on the Dnieper; pop. 282,000 (1939), 435,000 (1959). Important industrial center: Dneproges power station, metallurgical plants "Zaporozhstal," "Dneprospetsstal"; produces ferroalloys, aluminum, tractors, refractories, transformers, food; has numerous technical schools. Founded in 1770.

ZAPORÓZHYE OBLAST, Ukrainian SSR, on Sea of Azov, crossed by Dnieper; area 10,400 sq. mi.; pop. 1,464,000 (1959): Ukrainians and Russians. Cities: Zaporozhye (adm. center), Melitopol, Berdyansk. A plain with fertile black earth and continental climate. Agr.: wheat, barley, corn, orchards and vineyards; cattle breeding, dairies. Ind.: one of the best-known hydroelectric power stations, Dneproges, partly destroyed during World War II and rebuilt after the war; steel mills, machine-building plants. Has numerous schools of higher education. Est. 1939.

ZAPORÓZHYE SÉCH, an autonomous Cossack military community which existed in the 16th-18th centuries on the island of Khortitsa, beyond the Dnieper rapids, in Ukraine. It was formed chiefly by peasants and serfs who escaped to Zaporozhye from Muscovy, and Poland-Lithuania. ZS fought against Turkey, Crimean Tatars, Poland, and Russia. After Ukraine was incorporated in R. in 1654, the military and political importance of ZS rapidly declined, and in 1775 the community was disbanded. (*See also* COSSACKS)

ZARÚTSKY, Iván Martýnovich (died in 1614), Cossack leader. During the Time of Troubles supported pseudo-Dimitry II and his infant son. In 1614 he was captured and executed. (*See also* OTREPYEV, MNISZEK, TIME OF TROUBLES)

ZASLÁVSKY, Davíd Iósifovich (1879–), Soviet journalist and literary critic, born in Yelizavetgrad (now Kirovograd). Joined the Bund in 1903. From 1904 to 1909 he contributed to the daily *Kievskaya Mysl* (Kievan Thought) and to other newspapers. He also wrote in Socialist publications. In 1924 he joined the Bolsheviks. Became one of the best-known political writers of *Izvestia* (1926) and *Pravda* (1928). Specializing in international questions, he was often quoted in the western press. In 1956, he wrote a critical biography of Dostoyevsky, wherein he set forth the party's new position on this author. In 1958, he led the campaign against Boris Pasternak and his novel *Dr. Zhivago.*

ZASÚLICH, Véra Ivánovna (1849–1919), revolutionary, born in Smolensk Province of a family of the gentry. Z was a teacher. In 1869, she made the acquaintance of Nechayev; later she was arrested in connection with his case and spent two years in prison. On Jan. 24, 1878, Z fired at and wounded the chief of the St. Petersburg police, Trepov who had ordered the flogging of a political prisoner, Bogolyubov. The jury acquitted her on April 1, 1878, and the crowd protected her from the gendarmes, who wished to rearrest her as she was leaving the courtroom. Z went underground and joined the "Black Repartition" (q.v.). In 1880, she fled to Switzerland and, with Lavrov (q.v.), led the "Red Cross of the People's Will," an organization helping the political prisoners in Russia. From 1883, Z was one of the leaders of "Liberation of Labor" (q.v.). She translated works of Marx and Engels into Russian and in 1888 published a *History of the First International.* From 1900, Z was a member of the editorial board of *Iskra* (q.v.). In 1903, she participated in the Russian Social Democratic Party congress in Brussels and London, supporting the Mensheviks. In 1905, Z returned to Russia and stayed there until her death. In 1917, she joined Plekhanov's *Yedinstvo* and was in opposition to the Bolsheviks.

ZAVÁDSKY, Yúry Aléksandrovich (1894–), producer and actor. People's Artist of the USSR. Began his theatrical career in 1916 in the studio directed by Vakhtangov. Z won acclaim for interpretation of the part of Anthony in Maeterlinck's *The Miracle of Saint Anthony* and that of Kalaf in Gozzi's *Princess Turandot.* In 1940 Z became the art director and producer of the "Mossoviet" Theater. His productions include plays from the classical western repertory as well as those by contemporary Soviet playwrights.

ZAYSÁN, lake in the upper part of Irtysh River in E. Kazakh SSR; area about 700 sq. mi.; fisheries.

ZÁYTSEV, Aleksándr Mikháylovich (1841–1910), organic chemist. Corresponding member, St. Petersburg Ac. of S. (1885). Disciple of A. M. Butlerov. Graduate (1862) and prof. (1871), Kazan University, President, Russian Physical and Chemical Society (1905). Research on saturated alcohols and development of methods for their manufacture. Most of his works dealt with polyatomic alcohols and oxides.

ZÁYTSEV, Borís Konstantínovich (1881–), writer and dramatist. Studied at Moscow Technical Institute and Moscow University. As a student was close to the revolutionary movement. By 1917, he had become president of the All-Russian Writers' Union. After the revolution, emigrated to France. His first volume of stories was published in 1903. This and the collections that followed gained Z the reputation as one of the best of R. "impressionist" writers, after Chekhov and Bunin. The Russian Orthodox religion left its indelible imprint on Z's work, which includes *The Golden Pattern* (1925–26), *Gleb's Journey* (1935), *Anna* (1929), *Moscow* (1939), and *The Tree of Life* (1953). Lately, Z has written biographies of Zhukovsky, Turgenev, and Chekhov and has worked on his memoirs and critical essays.

ZELDÓVICH, Yákov Borísovich (1914–), physicist. Fellow, Ac. of S., USSR (1958). Institute of Physical Chemistry (1931). Substantiated the mechanism of nitrogen oxidation under conditions of explosion. Proposed methods for the calculation of chain reaction in uranium decomposition. Developed the theory of flame propagation and suggested calculation method for velocity and pressure of detonation. Author of *Concerning Chain Decomposition of Uranium Isotope* (1939); *Theory of Combustion and Detonation of Gas* (1944); *Gas Flow Under the Action of Impact Pressure* (1956). Stalin prize (1943).

ZELENODÓLSK, city in Tatar ASSR, landing on the Volga; pop. 30,000 (1939), 60,000 (1959). Important timber industry (plywood and R.R. tie manufacturing).

ZELENOGÓRSK (f. Terioki), sea resort in Leningrad Oblast, RSFSR, on the left shore of Gulf of Finland, 30 mi. from Leningrad; pop. 11,400 (1957).

ZELÍNSKY, Nikoláy Dmítrievich (1861–1953), organic chemist. Fellow, Ac. of S., USSR (1929). Honored  Scientist (1926) and Hero of Socialist Labor (1945). Graduated from Novorossiysk University in Odessa (1884), studied in Göttingen where he was the first one to separate imprite. Professor of Moscow University (1893–1911, 1917–53). Founder of the Laboratory of Ultra-High Pressures at the Institute of Organic Chemistry which bears his name. Research concerned the catalysis of organic compounds and their properties at ultra-high pressures. During World War I suggested active carbon as poison-gas protection. Many prominent Soviet chemists including A. N. Nesmeyanov (q.v.) studied under Z. Author of *Selected Works*, 2 vol (1941); *Scientific Papers*, 3 vol. (1955). Stalin prizes (1942, 1946, 1948).

ZELYÓNY MYS, resort in Adzhar ASSR on the Black Sea, 5.5 mi. N. of Batumi; famous Batumi botanical garden located here.

ZEMGOR (*Zemsko-Gorodskoy Soyuz*), was founded on July 10, 1915, by the federation of the Union of Cities and of the Zemstvo Union. The chief representative of the Zemtsvo Union was Prince G. Ye. Lvov, and of the Union of Cities, M. V. Chelnokov. Z's tasks included assisting in the care of the sick and the wounded and in supplying the army, and the mobilizing of small-scale industries and of crafts working for national defense. In carrying out this program the Z established a large number of small-scale shops for the production of leather, textile, chemical, metallurgical, and other products. Military defeats and the growing disorganization of the economy after 1915–16 led Z to play an increasingly active part in the political life of the country, in close association with the State Duma and the Central War Industries Committee (q.v.). This led to conflicts between Z and the government. A conference of Z that had adopted a resolution urging the government be made responsible to the Duma was suppressed by the authorities. Although the Union of Cities was dissolved after the October revolution, a conference of representatives of Z met in Simferopol (Crimea) toward

the end of 1918, when that city was temporarily freed from Bolshevik control. In the 1920's Z renewed its activities abroad, in Czechoslovakia, Yugoslavia, and France, primarily in providing assistance to refugees.

ZEMLYÁCHKA, Rozália Samóylovna (1876–1947), Communist party and state official. Z was in the revolutionary movement from the 1890's; she became a member of the CP in 1903. In 1905, she was secretary of the Moscow committee. Repeatedly arrested and exiled. In 1917–18, Z was secretary of the Moscow Committee of Bolsheviks. From 1924 to 1934, member of the Central Control Commission of the CPSU; in 1934 she became member, and later chairman, of the Soviet Control Commission; 1939–43, deputy chairman of the Council of Peoples' Commissars USSR. Z was a member of the Central Committee of the CPSU from 1939 on. She was twice decorated with the order of Lenin.

"ZEMLYA I VOLYA": *see* POPULISM.

ZEMSKY SOBOR. A consultative body created by Ivan IV. It contained representatives of the princes, boyars, government officials, church, and merchants and met only at the tsar's pleasure. The ZS had no collective authority, could discuss only what the tsar wished it to discuss, and could give advice only when it was sought. After Ivan IV the ZS was neglected until revived by Boris Godunov in 1598. In 1613 the ZS elected the first Romanov tsar and occupied a position of influence until 1622 when it again fell into neglect.

ZEMSTVO. Institutions first introduced by Ivan IV as a means of collecting taxes through the transference of certain financial responsibilities from appointed to elected officials. After falling into disuse for a considerable period of time, Alexander II revived the Z's in 1864 as organs of rural self-government.

Each county (*uyezd*) was to elect an assembly with the population voting in three separate electoral colleges: the landowners, the wealthier urban population, and the village communes. Representation was weighted so that the nobility would predominate. The county Z assemblies chose the members of the provincial (*gubernia*) Z assemblies. Both bodies were elected for three years and met once a year. Each elected an executive board which carried on the business of local government when the assemblies were not in session. The functions and powers of the Z's were restricted primarily to local economic and social services (e.g., road and school construction and maintenance, public health, and poor relief).

Since the Z's lacked executive powers, they had to depend on the cooperation of the police and other Crown officials over whom they had no control. Their only sources of revenue were limited taxes on real estate and business enterprises, and were inadequate for the work of the Z's. An act of June 1890, during the period of reaction under Alexander III, altered the franchise so as to strengthen the representation of the landed nobility and increase the severity of bureaucratic controls.

Despite the limitations, the Z's were able to achieve

a great deal. Although the suffrage was very unequal, enabling the nobility to control the Z's, almost all classes of the population were able to participate in local government in the rural areas. The Z's were particularly active in the development of primary education, the improvement of public health, and in the improvement of agricultural technique, and employed an increasing number of teachers, doctors, agronomists, veterinarians, and other specialists. The Z's gradually became the leaders of the developing liberal movement within Russia in the late 1800's.

Almost as soon as they had been created, the Z's were subjected to administrative controls by restrictive legislation. Until the 1880's the Z's struggled for local autonomy against this central government interference; after this period the struggle of the liberal Z leaders was for constitutional reform. This reform tradition manifested itself in the 1890's in demands for some form of popular representation in the central government and for the creation of a central Z organization. In 1904 one of an increasing number of periodic illegal Z conferences founded an underground political organization called the Union of Liberation (q.v.), the first organized liberal political group. With the appearance of political parties and the creation of the State Duma in 1905, the Z's ceased to be the main spokesmen of liberal opinion, and in the conservative reaction after the revolution of 1905 many of the Z's passed under conservative control. By 1914 the Z's were functioning in over half of the provinces of European Russia. The Z's were reorganized after the revolution of February 1917 so as to make them more representative, and then were abolished after the Bolsheviks seized power. (*See also* GOVERNMENT LOCAL)

BIBLIOGRAPHY: Michael T. Florinsky, *Russia: A History and an Interpretation*, New York, 1953.

ZENZÍNOV, Vladímir Mikháylovich (1880–1953), political leader. Joined the Socialist Revolutionary party while studying philosophy, law, and history in Berlin, Halle, and Heidelberg (1900). Upon his return to Russia (1904) was arrested (1905) and escaped abroad. After the October Manifesto (1905) returned to Russia where he was once more arrested (1906) and again escaped, this time from Siberia to Japan. However, political interests brought Z back to Russia where he was arrested and exiled to the Arctic region (1910). In 1917 Z was elected to the Constituent Assembly. Left Russia in 1919 and settled in Paris (1919–39) and finally in New York (1940–53). Contributed to socialist and democratic publications. Author of *Ancient Peoples on the Shores of the Cold Ocean* (1914), *The Road to Oblivion* (New York, 1931), *Deserted: The Story of Children in Soviet Russia* (London, 1931), *Memoirs* (New York, 1953).

ZERAVSHÁN, range in Uzbek SSR and Tadzhik SSR, covered with perennial snow; highest peak Chimtarga (16,000 ft.).

ZERAVSHÁN RIVER, in Central Asia, right tributary of Amu Darya; length 484 mi. The lower part of its valley is an important agricultural area, densely populated (Samarkand, Bukhara); the Katta-Kurgan water reservoir is located on it; used for irrigation.

ZESTAFÓNI (f. Kvirily), town in Georgian SSR; pop. 16,300 (1959). Ferroalloys, champagne production, knitting.

ZÉYA RIVER, in Amur Oblast, RSFSR, left tributary of the Amur; length 764 mi.; partly navigable. Coal, gold, graphite, antimony are mined in its basin.

ZÉYA–BURÉYA PLAIN, between Zeya River and Bureya mountain range in Amur Oblast, RSFSR; elevations 1,000 ft.; granary of the Soviet Far East; coal deposits.

ZHÁROV, Aleksándr Alekséyevich (1904–), poet, born in a village near Moscow, son of a worker. He was a leading young communist poet, with A. Bezymensky and I. Utkin, in the 1920's and 1930's, and is known for his *Pioneer March* and the poems *Accordion* (1926), *Varya Odyntsova* (1938). During the war, Z served in the political administration of the navy. His verse is in the colloquial, popular-song, lyrical genre.

ZHDÁNOV, Andréy Aleksándrovich (1896–1948), communist leader and Soviet official, born in Mariupol (now Zhdanov) into a teacher's family. Z joined the Bolsheviks in 1913. He was active in the October revolution in the Urals. From 1924 to 1939 was party secretary in Gorky Oblast. In 1925, was elected a candidate  member of the Central Committee of the CPSU; in 1930 was promoted to full membership in the Central Committee. In 1935, he was given command of the Leningrad party organization, replacing the murdered S. Kirov. Here Z played a prominent role in the purges of the 1930's. In 1939 his position was further enhanced by promotion to the Politburo. During World War II, Z appears to have been engaged in a personal struggle with Malenkov for second-in-command status and to have emerged victorious. From 1945 to 1948, Z was at the zenith of his career. He became the virtual dictator of literary and artistic policies in the Soviet Union, establishing strict political standards for all writers and artists, directing the struggle against the so-called "cosmopolitans" (*see* LITERATURE). He was also the leading figure of the Cominform. Here Z forced the other communist parties to adhere to strict discipline from Moscow and to adopt a militantly anti-western stand. In 1948, at the height of power, Z suddenly died under suspicious circumstances.

ZHDÁNOV (prior to 1948 Mariupol), city in Stalino Oblast, Ukrainian SSR; pop. 284,000 (1959). Port on Sea or Azov; has large metallurgical plant "Azovstal"; pipe-drawing, machine-building, chemical-coke plants; metallurgical institute, metallurgical technical school. Founded 1779. Birthplace of A. A. Zhdanov.

ZHDÁNOV, Pyótr Sergéyevich (1903–1949), electrical engineer. Graduate (1933), professor (1941), Power Engineering Institute of Moscow. Associated with the All-Union Institute of Electrical Engineering (1927–42). With S. A. Lebedev, Z was the first to publish a monograph on the statistical stability of electric systems (1933). Research concerned long-distance transmission of electric power, e.g. Moscow-Kuybyshev (1938–39). Stalin prize (1947).

ZHELEZNOVÓDSK, resort in Stavropol Kray, 10.5 mi. from Pyatigorsk; pop. 10,000 (1956). Has sulfur-carbonic and alkali-glauber salt-lime springs (cold and warm) with considerable radioactivity.

ZHELYÁBOV, Andréy Ivánovich (1850–1881), outstanding revolutionary, leader of "People's Will." Son of a peasant serf, he spread propaganda among peasants and workers of S. Russia. In 1879 he started preparation for an attempt on the life of Alexander II; he was arrested two days before the assassination but volunteered a confession of his complicity and was hanged on April 3, 1881.

ZHEMCHÚZHNIKOV, Alekséy Mikháylovich (1821–1908), poet, mostly known for his satirical poetry. He, his two brothers, and a cousin, A. K. Tolstoy, published their works under the pen name "Kozma Prutkov," mostly aphorisms full of subtle humor.

ZHIGULÍ, highlands on the right bank of Volga in Kuybyshev Oblast, RSFSR; its elevations reach 1200 ft. Kuybyshev hydroelectric plant is located in this area; oil, asphalt.

ZHITÓMIR, city, adm. center of Zhitomir Oblast, Ukrainian SSR; pop. 105,000 (1959). Has woodworking, food, distilleries, metalworking and light industries; agricultural and pedag. institutes, technical schools. Dates back to 13th century.

ZHITÓMIR OBLAST, in Ukrainian SSR, on Dnieper's right bank; area 11,580 sq. mi.; pop. 1,603,000 (1959): Ukrainians, Russians, Jews. Cities: Zhitomir (adm. center), Berdichev, Novograd-Volynsky, Korosten. Has warm climate; podzol and partly black-earth soils. Agr.: rye, oats, barley, buckwheat, millet, flax, sugar beets, hops. Ind.: food processing, ceramics, machine building. Est. 1937.

ZHORDÁNIA, Noy Nikoláyevich (1870–1953), Menshevik leader. Graduated from the Tiflis Seminary and then attended the veterinary institute in Warsaw. In the revolutionary movement from 1894. Was repeatedly arrested and exiled. Participated in the 2nd Congress of the Social Democratic party in 1903 under the name of Kostrov. Was elected deputy to the First Duma, where he led the Social Democratic group. After the October revolution Z was head of the government of the independent Georgian Republic. In 1921, after the Bolsheviks had occupied Georgia, Z emigrated to Paris.

ZHUK, Sergéy Yákovlevich (1892–1957), hydraulic engineer. Fellow, Ac. of S., USSR (1953). Hero of Socialist Labor (1952). Assistant chief engineer in charge of the White Sea–Baltic Sea Canal project (1933–37); chief engineer for the construction of the Moscow Canal (1933–37), the Kuybyshev Hydroelectric Station and the Volga–Baltic Sea Waterway System (1937–42). Stalin prizes (1950, 1951).

ZHÚKOV, Geórgy Konstantínovich (1896–), prominent military leader, marshal of the Soviet Union. Born in Kaluga Province of a peasant family, he became a noncommissioned officer during World War I. In Oct. 1918, he joined the Red Army and distinguished himself in the civil war. In 1919 Z joined the CP. He

graduated from the Frunze Military Academy (1931) and was placed in command of the Soviet forces engaged in border skirmishes with Japanese troops on the Manchurian border (1939). In 1940 he served as chief of staff of the army in the Soviet-Finnish War; was then appointed commander of the Kiev military district. In Jan. 1941, Z was appointed chief of the General Staff; and when the Nazis invaded Russia, he was commander in chief, first in Leningrad and then of the western front, where he successfully defended Moscow. In Jan. 1943, was promoted to marshal. In April 1945, he directed the attack on Berlin and signed the document of German surrender; was appointed commander in chief of the Soviet occupation forces. His exploits having made him a national hero, at the end of the war he was second only to Stalin in popularity. After the war Z was relegated to relative obscurity. Following Stalin's death, Z returned to prominence and became minister of defense in 1955, and alternate Presidium member. In 1957 (June-October) was a member of the Presidium of the CPSU. Z was allied with Khrushchev in demoting the "antiparty group" of Malenkov, Molotov, and others. Then, in Oct. 1957, while on a state visit to Yugoslavia and Albania, he was removed from his post and retired into obscurity. The official charge was "violation of the principles of Lenin in the army."

ZHUKÓVSKY, Nikoláy Yegorovich (1847–1921), aeronautical engineer, referred to by Lenin as "The Father of Russian Aviation." Graduated from Moscow University. Professor of the Moscow School of Technology (1886). President of the Moscow Society of Naturalists (1905). Founder of the Institute of Aerodynamics (1904). Director of the Central Institute of Aerodynamics (1918). In addition to teaching, conducted extensive research on calculations of lifting capacity, wing contours, propellers, hydraulics, hydrodynamics, astronomy, mathematics (differential equations with partial derivatives and approximate integration of equations). During World War I studied bombing techniques, ballistics, and problems of theoretical mathematics. Applied the theory of functions of a complex variable to hydro- and aerodynamics. Developed simple methods for the determination of planet orbits. Medals awarded for outstanding achievements in aircraft technology by the Academy of Military Aircraft Engineering bear his name.

ZHUKÓVSKY, Vasíly Andréyevich (1783–1852), prominent romantic poet. His poetry is filled with melancholic and sentimental meditations and yearnings for the celestial (*Village Cemetery* (1802), *Theon and Eschyn* (1815). Best known are his ballads *Ludmila* (1808), *Svetlana* (1811), *Twelve Sleeping Maidens* (1817). He also is the author of patriotic poems writen during the Napoleonic war, such as *The Singer in the Camp of Russian*

Warriors (1812) and the Russian national anthem *God Save the Tsar*. As a poet he is the precursor of Pushkin. His translations of ancient classics are of very high quality, especially *Odyssey* (1849), and a portion of the *Iliad*. He also translated oriental epics, *Rustem and Sohrab* (1847), as well as works of W. European poets. He was the tutor of the future Alexander II.

ZINÓVIEV (Radomyslsky) **Grigóry Yevséyevich** (1883–1936), Bolshevik leader, born in Yelizavetgrad (now Kirovograd) of a middle-class family. Joined the Social Democratic party in 1901 and, after the split in 1903, became one of the closest associates of Lenin. Was active in the revolution of 1905. From 1909 to  1917, Z was, with Kamenev, in the leadership of the Bolshevik group abroad. Participated as Bolshevik representative at the Zimmerwald conference. In April 1917 returned with Lenin in the sealed train through Germany to Russia. On the eve of the October revolution, Z opposed, with Kamenev, Lenin's policy of seizure of power. However, immediately after the revolution Z became one of the most popular Bolshevik orators. Thereafter he was chairman of the Leningrad Soviet and leader of the Leningrad party organization (until 1926). In 1919 he became a member of the Politburo and, from 1919 to 1926, was chairman of the executive committee of the Comintern. In 1924, a letter, allegedly written by Z inciting rebellions, published in the London press, contributed to the defeat of the first Labor Government in Great Britain. During Lenin's illness and after his death in 1924, Z, Kamenev, and Stalin formed a triumvirate which led the party and the state. In Nov. 1924, Trotsky attacked Z and Kamenev in his pamphlet *The Lessons of October* for their stand in 1917. In Dec. 1925, at the 14th Party Congress, Z was leader of the "Leningrad" anti-Stalin opposition and was defeated. In 1926 he joined forces with Trotsky, and was expelled with him from the party in Nov. 1927. Readmitted in 1928 on recantation of his heretical views, Z was again expelled in 1932, and readmitted in 1933. After the assassination of Kirov (q.v.), Z was in 1935 sentenced to 10 years' imprisonment for "moral complicity" in the murder; was retried in 1936 at the first of the big public trials of the great purge, condemned to death and executed. Z published *The War and the Crisis of Socialism* (1920), articles in the collection *Against the Current* (1923), *For a Third International* (1924), and a *History of the Communist Party*.

ZINÓVIEVSK: *see* KIROVOGRAD.

ZIONISM: *see* JEWS, DOCTORS' PLOT.

ZLATOÚST, city in Chelyabinsk Oblast, RSFSR; pop. 99,000 (1939), 161,000 (1959). One of the oldest industrial centers in the Urals; high grade metallurgy, precision-tool production, machine building.

ZLATOÚST MASSACRE, the shooting by troops of striking workers in one of the military plants in the town of Zlatoust. On March 13, 1903, the troops shot three volleys against assembled workers. Sixty-nine were killed, 250 wounded, and 197 workers were sent to forced labor in Siberia.

ZLATOVRÁTSKY, Nikoláy Nikoláyevich (1845–1911), populist writer. In *Peasant-Jurors* (1874–75), *The Pillars* and *The History of One Village* (1878–83) he described the hard village life, at the same time idealizing the peasant commune.

ZÓSHCHENKO, Mikhaíl Mikháylovich (1895–1958), an outstanding satirical writer, born in Poltava in the  family of a painter. Studied law in the University of St. Petersburg. Following the revolution Z worked successively as a carpenter, a criminal investigator, a journalist and was at one time a card player and gambler. In the early 1920's he joined *The Serapion Brothers*. The exceptional popularity of his writings is based on his ability to reproduce in his stories the peculiar and typical combination of crudeness and exaggerated correctness in the speech of the ordinary "new" Soviet man. His first collections include *Stories* (1923) and *Esteemed Citizens* (1926). Starting with the collection *Nervous People* (1927), his stories reflect a waning of his own optimistic attitude. This decreasing trust in the real gains of the revolution, this change from optimism to pessimism, is typical of his second group of stories as exemplified by his collection *Private Life* (1933) and such stories as *Before Sunrise* (1943), and *Adventures of a Monkey* (1946). The latter story especially was the main reason for Z's expulsion from the Union of Soviet Writers in late 1946, following an all-out attack on him by Zhdanov. Among Z's major works, the cycle of stories, *Sentimental Stories* (1929) and *The Story of Michel Sinyagin* (1933–34), deserve mention, as they uncover the tragic side of this exceptionally gifted satirist. Z's talents were many-sided. Thus, he tried his hand successfully at a popularization of scientific ideas, as in *Restored Youth* (1933), in a stylized version of one of Pushkin's classics, *The New Tales of Belkin*, and in tales of adventure as *The Black Prince*.

ZUBÁTOV, Sergéy Vasílyevich (1863–1917), chief of the Moscow security police (1890–1903). Himself a former revolutionary, Z initiated a new policy of dealing with the rising revolutionary workers' movement. He created police-controlled "legal" workers' organizations to convince the workers of the good intentions of the government, and encouraged them to press their economic demands through these channels. In 1900 such organizations existed in many cities and extended their activity to the cultural field. However, in 1903 they got out of hand and proceeded to organize strikes. The government withdrew its protection, Z was dismissed and exiled. After the October revolution, he committed suicide.

ZÚBOV, Prince Platón Aleksándrovich (1767–1822), favorite of Catherine II, brother of V. A. Zubov. He was governor general of Novorossiysk and commander of the Black Sea fleet; also co-conspirator in plot against Paul I.

ZÚBOV, Valerián Aleksándrovich (1771–1804), general, one of the favorites of Catherine II. He took part in the attack on Izmail and in the suppression of the Polish uprising in 1794; also was commander in chief during the Persian Campaign of 1796. He participated in the assassination of Emperor Paul I (1801).

ZUGDÍDI, city in Georgian SSR; pop. 28,200 (1956). Wood-pulp and paper combine, tea and food packing industries.

ZUGRÉS, town in Stalino Oblast, Ukrainian SSR; founded in 1930 during the erection of the Zúyevka power plant; pop. 13,500 (1956). Mechanical foundry and building materials; Power-Technical Institute.

ZVENÍGOROD, town in Moscow Oblast, RSFSR; pop. 8,800 (1956). Picturesque surroundings; rest homes and sanatoriums; architectural monuments, Uspensky Cathedral (1398).

ZVÉREV, Mitrofán Stepánovich (1903–), astronomer. Corresponding member, Ac. of S., USSR (1953). Graduate (1931), professor (1948), Moscow University. Joined the State Astronomical Institute (1931–51); deputy director, Main Astronomical Observatory at Pulkovo (1951). Research concerns meridian astrometry, gravimetry, and variable star systems. Compiled star catalogues.

ZYRYAN: *see* KOMI.

ZYRYÁNOVSK, town in E.-Kazakhstan Oblast, Kazakh SSR, in Altay Mountains; pop. 16,000 (1939), 54,000 (1959). Lead, asphalt, concrete. Founded 1794.